di strada verge; *di autostrada* hard shoulder; **~ *spartitraffico*** central reservation, *US* median strip

banchisa *f* ice floe

banco *m* ⟨*pl* -chi⟩ **1.** FIN bank **2.** *di magistrati, di lavoro* bench; *di scuola* desk; *di bar* bar; *di chiesa* pew; *di negozio* counter; **~ *del check-in*** check-in desk; **~ *degli imputati*** dock; **~ *del lotto*** *place that sells State lottery tickets*; **~ *dei pegni*** pawnshop; ***farmaco** m* ***da ~*** over-the-counter medicine; ***vendere qc sotto ~*** sell sth under the counter **3.** **~ *corallino*** coral reef; **~ *di nebbia*** fog bank; **~ *di sabbia*** sandbank

bancogiro *m* giro

bancomat® *m* ⟨*pl* bancomat⟩ (*distributore*) cashpoint, *US* ATM; (*carta*) cash card

bancone *m* (work)bench

banconota *f* banknote, *US* bill

banda[1] *f di delinquenti* gang

banda[2] *f* MUS band

banda[3] *f* COMPUT: **~ *perforata*** punched tape; **~ *passante*** COMPUT pass band

banda[4] *f*: **~ *larga*** broadband

banderuola *f* weathercock (*a. fig*)

bandiera *f* flag; ***battere ~ britannica*** fly the Union Jack

bandire *v/t* ⟨4d⟩ proclaim; *concorso* announce; (*esiliare*) banish; *fig* (*abolire*) dispense with

banditismo *m* banditry

bandito *m* bandit

banditore *m*, **-trice** *f all'asta* auctioneer

bando *m* proclamation; (*esilio*) banishment; **~ *di concorso*** announcement of a competitive exam; ***mettere qc al ~*** ban sth; **~ *agli scherzi!*** stop the joking around

bandolo *m* end; *fig* ***cercare il ~*** (***della matassa***) look for the solution (to the problem); *fig* ***perdere il ~*** lose the thread

bang *m* ⟨*pl* bang⟩ bang; **~ *sonico*** AVIAT sonic boom

banner *m* ⟨*pl* banner⟩ COMPUT banner

baobab *m* ⟨*pl* baobab⟩ baobab

bar *m* ⟨*pl* bar⟩ bar

bara *f* coffin

baracca *f* ⟨*pl* -cche⟩ hut; *pej* hovel; ***mandare avanti la ~*** *infml* keep one's head above water

to differentiate senses

Definitions appear in *italics*

American lexical variants

Homonyms differentiated by superscript numbers

Part of speech and gender labels given in *italics*

The feminine form of nouns is always indicated

Examples and other phrases in ***bold italics***

The swung dash replaces the entire headword

Register labels given

Berlitz®

Italian

Easy Read Dictionary

Italian – English • Inglese – Italiano

Berlitz Publishing
New York · Munich · Singapore

Original edition edited by the Langenscheidt editorial staff

Project management: Heike Richini

Lexicographical work: Silvia Bonafede, Pat Bulhosen,
Dr. Helen Galloway, Anna Stella Giusto Franetzki,
Dr. Birgit Klausmann, Francesca Logi, Liz Potter,
Kate Singleton, Valentina Turri, Donald Watt, Ailsa Wood

Maps: Geographic Publishers GmbH & Co. KG, Munich

Book in cover photo: © Punchstock/Medioimages

Neither the presence nor the absence of a designation
indicating that any entered word constitutes a trademark
should be regarded as affecting the legal status thereof.

© 2009 Berlitz Publishing/APA Publications GmbH & Co. Verlag KG
Singapore Branch, Singapore

All rights reserved

Trademark Reg. U.S. Patent Office and other countries.
Marca Registrada.
Used under license from Berlitz Investment Corporation.

Berlitz Publishing
193 Morris Avenue
Springfield, NJ 07081
USA

Printed in Germany
ISBN 978-981-268-525-4

1. 2. 3. 4. 5. 13 12 11 10 09

Contents

Preface

This is a brand new dictionary of English and Italian based on completely new and up-to-date data.

With its 100,000 references and 130,000 translations focusing on modern usage, it is a tool that not only covers general present-day language, but also a wide range of important terminology from fields as diverse as information technology, politics and society, culture, genetics and many more. It is therefore particularly suitable for those people working with the Italian language at an advanced level.

Often the meaning of a word only becomes clear when it appears in context. This is why particular attention has been paid to idiomatic and colloquial expressions as they are the elements that bring a language to life. You will also find many geographical names and important abbreviations.

This dictionary has been specifically tailored to your needs as an English native speaker. For example, labelling has been provided in English on the English-Italian side of the dictionary, and all information regarding grammar, register, subject areas etc. is in English throughout the book.

Vocabulary needs to be backed up by grammar, so the dictionary also offers detailed guidance on English and Italian irregular verb and plural forms as well as Italian feminine endings.

The editorial team has aimed above all to create a clearly structured and extremely user-friendly dictionary. The blue headwords guide the user directly to the translation options which correspond to specific senses. Does the *fly* on your trousers, for example, have the same Italian translation as the *fly* you don't want in your soup? And is *high* referring to a person on drugs the same in Italian as *high* referring to a building? This dictionary will help you understand and use the headwords more accurately and distinguish between the translations in a reliable way.

This dictionary is packed with information. We hope it will become an indispensable and enjoyable part of your language toolkit.

How to use this dictionary

Where do I find what I am looking for?

This dictionary contains about 100,000 references listed in alphabetical order. This applies to both languages and includes irregular forms. The only exceptions to this strict rule are phrasal verbs which appear directly under the simple verb form. This means, for example, that **keep at**, **keep away**, **keep back**, **keep down**, **keep from**, **keep in**, **keep in with**, **keep off**, **keep on** etc. are all listed in an alphabetical block after **keep**. The entry for the word **keeper** follows the phrasal verbs, although strictly speaking it ought to come alphabetically between **keep down** and **keep from**.

Terms made up of two or more separate words, for example **fine settimana**, or hyphenated words, for example **off-road**, are treated in terms of their position in the alphabetical order as though they were a single word.

English **phrasal verbs** are preceded by a blue diamond:

◆**do away with** *v/t* (*abolish*) abolire

Feminine forms of Italian nouns can be found next to the corresponding masculine headword. They are shown as follows:

ammiratore *m*, **-trice** *f* admirer

Here **-trice** stands for **ammiratrice**.

On the English-Italian side of the dictionary, American spelling variants follow the British spelling of the headword and are labelled *US*:

colour-blind, *US* **color-blind** *adj* daltonico

On the Italian-English side of the dictionary, in cases where the American spelling of a word differs from the British spelling by the omission of just a single letter, the omitted letter appears in round brackets:

enciclopedia *f* encyclop(a)edia

For the pronunciation of Italian words, see the notes on pages 16–17.

How do I find what I am looking for?

Each headword entry is divided up in the following way:

I Roman numerals are used to differentiate parts of speech (transitive, intransitive or reflexive verb, noun, adjective, adverb etc.).

2. Arabic numerals are used to differentiate between the different senses of a word.

; semicolons are used to differentiate nuances of meaning and also appear before a phrase.

, commas are used to differentiate between the various translations of a word which are synonymous and interchangeable.

Tilde and long dashes

The tilde or swung dash (~) is used to replace the entire headword within an entry:

neck I *n* collo *m*; ***be ~ and ~*** essere testa a testa [...]

Here ***be ~ and ~*** means ***be neck and neck.***

foresta *f* forest; ***~ pluviale*** rain forest

Here ***~ pluviale*** stands for ***foresta pluviale.***

When the form of a headword is modified within an entry, e.g. put in the plural or past tense, then the appropriate ending follows the tilde. The tilde still replaces only that part of the word which directly corresponds with the headword:

slug³ I *v/t* tracannare; ***he ~ged the man on the jaw*** ha colpito l'uomo sulla mascella [...]

pelt¹ I *v/t*: ***~ s.o. with sth*** tirare qc a qn **II** *v/i*: ***they ~ed along the road*** *infml* sono sfrecciati per strada [...]

However, the tilde cannot be used in cases where the inflected form of a headword is very different to the uninflected form. In these cases, the required form of the headword is written out in full:

ride I *v/t* [...] **II** *v/i* [...] ***he rode home*** è andato a casa in bicicletta [...]

memory *n* [...] ***he had happy memories of his father*** aveva ricordi felici di suo padre [...]

In addition, headwords made up of two or more separate words are replaced by a single tilde:

pub-crawl *n*: ***go on a ~*** fare il giro dei pub

spending spree *n* spese *fpl* folli; ***go on a ~*** fare spese folli

On the Italian-English side of the dictionary, the altered form of a headword is represented by a long dash when it is used in a phrase or compound:

incrociato *adj* crossed; ***parole*** *fpl* ***-e*** crossword [...]

Here ***parole -e*** means ***parole incrociate***.

What do the different typefaces mean?

Bold print is used for all the English and Italian headwords as well as the Roman numerals that differentiate between parts of speech:

manifesto I *adj* obvious **II** *m* poster

◆ **breathe in I** *v/i* inspirare **II** *v/t sep* respirare

Grammatical information such as *adj*, *adv*, *v/i*, *v/t*, *m*, *f*, *mpl* etc. appears in *italics*. Similarly, indicators which are used to guide the user to the correct translation are also *italicised*. Indicators can be synonyms (words with a similar meaning) which appear in round brackets, but can also be possible subjects or objects in order to illustrate the range of usage of a particular translation:

condurre *v/t* ⟨3e⟩ lead; (*accompagnare*) take; *veicolo* drive; *azienda* run; *acque, gas* carry, take

◆ **draw back I** *v/i* (*recoil*) tirarsi indietro **II** *v/t sep hand* ritirare; *curtains* aprire

Italics are also used to clarify the meaning and use of a word for which there is no direct translation:

abbagliamento *m state of being dazzled*

L-plate *n cartello per conducenti con foglio rosa*

Examples, idioms and other phrases are given in ***secondary bold italics***:

assalto *m* attack; *fig* ***prendere d'~*** storm

Net *n* COMPUT Internet *m*; ***surf the ~*** navigare in Internet

Why are some headwords followed by superscript numbers?

Words which are spelled the same but which have totally different meanings are known as **homonyms**. In this dictionary, homonyms are treated as separate headwords and distinguished from one another by the use of superscript numbers. Headwords of this type directly follow one another in the headword list:

vite[1] *f* TECH screw; *fig* ***giro*** *m* ***di ~*** turn of the screw
vite[2] *f* AGR vine

pool[1] *n (swimming pool)* piscina *f*; *of water, blood* pozza *f*
pool[2] *n game* biliardo *m*
pool[3] **I** *n common fund* cassa *f* comune; ***car ~*** *gruppo di persone che per recarsi in un certo luogo fa uso di un'unica macchina* **II** *v/t resources* mettere insieme

rocket[1] **I** *n* razzo *m*; ***give s.o. a ~*** *infml* fare una parte a qn **II** *v/i of prices etc* salire alle stelle
rocket[2] *n* BOT, COOK ruchetta *f*

What are cross-references?

The cross-reference arrow (→) has several different functions. One of these is to refer the user from one headword to another which is identical in meaning but has a different spelling. The headword which the user is cross-referred to is dealt with in greater detail and includes the translation(s) and other information. Sometimes on the English-Italian side of the dictionary the arrow cross-refers the user from headwords given in American English to the British English variant:

anaemia, *US* **anemia** *n* anemia *f*

How does the dictionary distinguish between the different registers of a word?

If the register of the headword is neutral, no register label is used. Otherwise the level of register is indicated accordingly by using labels such as *infml* = informal; *sl* = slang; *vulg* = vulgar; *form* = formal; *liter* = literary. Additional information is given if the word is used in a negative (= *neg*), pejorative (= *pej*), ironic (= *iron*), euphemistic (= *euph*) or humorous (= *hum*) sense. The labels refer to headwords and phrases in the source language and also to the corresponding translations. If a register label appears at the beginning of an entry this means that it refers to the whole entry. Otherwise, a label only applies to the sense (Arabic numerals) or subsense in which it appears. As far as possible, translations are selected which match the register of the headword or phrase in the source language.

What type of grammatical information can I find in this dictionary?

All English and Italian headwords are followed by a label indicating their part of speech:

moreish *adj* *infml* invitante
foodie *n* *infml* buongustaio *m*, -a *f*
scrounge *v/t* scroccare
diretta *f* RADIO, TV live broadcast
bellimbusto *m* dandy
giocosamente *adv* playfully
però *cj* but
pomiciare *v/i* ⟨11 & f⟩ *infml* canoodle

The gender labels *m* and *f* stand for Italian masculine or feminine nouns.

Some English nouns appear to be plural, but are in fact singular. On the English-Italian side of the dictionary, these are labelled *nsg*, and on the Italian-English side *sg*:

cybernetics *nsg* cibernetica *f*

bioetica *f* ⟨*pl* -che⟩ bioethics *sg*

Irregular plural forms are given for both English and Italian headwords:

manioca *f* ⟨*pl* -che⟩ cassava plant
batticuore *m* ⟨*no pl*⟩ palpitations *pl*
synopsis *n* ⟨*pl* ***synopses***⟩ sinossi *f*

If an English verb is irregular or semi-irregular, its verb forms are supplied as well:

eat *v/t & v/i* ⟨*pret* ***ate***, *past part* ***eaten***⟩ mangiare [...]

drink **I** *v/t & v/i* ⟨*pret* ***drank***, *past part* ***drunk***⟩ bere [...]

qualify ⟨*pret & past part* ***-ied***⟩ **I** *v/t of degree, course etc* abilitare; *remark etc* precisare **II** *v/i* [...]

Italian verbs are followed by numbers and letters which illustrate which conjugation they take:

saltellare *v/i* ⟨1b⟩ hop

Here it can be inferred from ⟨1b⟩ that **saltellare** follows the same conjugation pattern as **celare**, the corresponding example verb given in the Italian conjugation table on pages 1127–1144 of the appendix.

Sometimes English translations of Italian adjectives can only be used in front of a noun, not after it. These translations are labelled *attr* (*attributive usage*):

latteo *adj* milk *attr*; ***Via** f* ***Lattea*** Milky Way

What can I find under each entry?

Look at the following entry:

manovrare ⟨1c⟩ **I** *v/t* TECH operate; RAIL shunt; *fig* manipulate; ***~ le masse*** manipulate the masses **II** *v/i* manoeuvre, *US* maneuver

These examples will serve to illustrate some of the main elements which are itemised and explained below:

manovrare	The **headword** is written out in full and appears in **blue bold type**.
⟨1c⟩	means that the verb follows conjugation pattern 1c. The inflectional forms of **manovrare** correspond with those of **lodare**, the verb that represents pattern 1c in the Italian conjugation table.
I	Roman numerals in bold type are used to define different parts of speech or verb forms.
v/t	The transitive verb is treated first. Transitive verbs are verbs which are followed by a direct object in the accusative case.
TECH operate;	'operate' is the appropriate translation when **manovrare** is used in a technological context.
RAIL shunt;	referring to railways, the English equivalent of **manovrare** is 'shunt'.
fig manipulate;	figuratively, **manovrare** can be translated as 'manipulate'.
~ le masse	is a common phrase which is translated as a whole. The tilde ~ replaces the headword **manovrare**.
manipulate the masses	is the translation of the previous phrase ***manovrare le masse***.
II	Roman numerals in bold type are used to define different parts of speech or verb forms.
v/i	This is where the intransitive verb is dealt with. Intransitive verbs are verbs that do not take a direct object.
manoeuvre,	is the translation.
US	indicates that the American spelling of the translation differs from the British one.
maneuver	gives the orthography of the American English variant.

riga *f* ⟨*pl* **-ghe**⟩ line; (*fila*) row; (*regolo*) rule; *in stoffa* stripe; *nei capelli* parting, *US* part; ***stoffa** f **a -ghe*** striped fabric

riga	The **headword** is written out in full and appears in **blue bold type**.
f	means that this is a feminine noun.
⟨*pl* -ghe⟩	indicates that the plural form of **riga** is irregular and takes the ending -ghe (= *righe*)
line	**riga** is generally translated as 'line'.
(*fila*) row	if **riga** is used in the sense of *fila*, 'row' is the appropriate translation. As *fila* is a synonym of riga used for semantic differentiation, it appears in round brackets.
(*regolo*) rule	if **riga** is used in the sense of *regolo*, 'rule' is the appropriate English equivalent. Just like *fila*, *regolo* is a synonym of riga, so it appears in round brackets as well.
in stoffa stripe	**riga** is translated as 'stripe' when it is used to describe the pattern of a fabric, which is indicated by *in stoffa*. Since *in stoffa* is an explanatory note and not a synonym, it does not appear in round brackets.
nei capelli parting,	**riga** can also refer to hairstyle. To differentiate this meaning from the previous ones, the note *nei capelli* is given and followed by the English equivalent 'parting'.
US	indicates that there is an American variant to the British translation.
part;	gives the American English variant to the British equivalent.
stoffa** f **a -ghe	is a common phrase which is translated as a whole. ***-ghe*** points out that the plural of the headword **riga** is irregular, so the full form used in this phrase is *righe*. The *f* following ***stoffa*** indicates that the Italian word ***stoffa*** is a feminine noun.
striped fabric	is the English translation of the phrase ***stoffa a righe***.

Abbreviations and symbols

also	*a.*	anche
abbreviation	*abbr*	abbreviazione
adjective	*adj*	aggettivo
administration	ADMIN	amministrazione
adverb	*adv*	avverbio
agriculture	AGR	agraria
anatomy	ANAT	anatomia
architecture	ARCH	architettura
article	*art*	articolo
art	ART	arte
astronomy	ASTR	astronomia
astrology	ASTROL	astrologia
attributive usage	*attr*	uso attributivo
Australian English	*AUS*	inglese australiano
motoring	AUTO	automobilismo
aviation	AVIAT	aeronautica
biology	BIOL	biologia
botany	BOT	botanica
British English	*Br*	inglese britannico
building and construction	BUILD	costruzioni
Canadian English	*Can*	inglese canadese
chemistry	CHEM	chimica
conjunction	*cj*	congiunzione
commerce	COMM	commercio
comparative	*comp*	comparativo
computers, IT	COMPUT	informatica, computer
cooking	COOK	gastronomia
and	*e*	e
economics	ECON	economia
education	EDU	educazione
electrical engineering	ELEC	elettronica, elettricità
especially	*esp*	specialmente
et cetera	*etc*	eccetera
European Union	EU	Unione Europea
euphemistic	*euph*	eufemismo
feminine	*f*	femminile
figurative	*fig*	senso figurato
film	FILM	cinema
finance	FIN	finanze
formal usage	*form*	uso formale
feminine plural	*fpl*	femminile plurale
feminine singular	*fsg*	femminile singolare
Great Britain	GB	Gran Bretagna
geography	GEOG	geografia
geology	GEOL	geologia
geometry	GEOM	geometria
grammar	GRAM	grammatica
historical	*hist*	storico
history	HIST	storia
humorous	*hum*	scherzoso

informal	*infml*	uso familiare
inseparable	*insep*	inseparabile
interjection	*int*	interiezione
invariable	*inv*	invariabile
ironic usage	*iron*	uso ironico
law	JUR	diritto, termine giuridico
linguistics	LING	linguistica
literature	LIT	letteratura
literary	*liter*	letterario
masculine	*m*	maschile
masculine and feminine	*m/f*	maschile e femminile
mathematics	MATH	matematica
mechanics	MECH	meccanica
medicine	MED	medicina
metallurgy	METAL	metallurgia
meteorology	METEO	meteorologia
military	MIL	scienza militare
mineralogy	MINER	mineralogia
masculine plural	*mpl*	maschile plurale
masculine singular	*msg*	maschile singolare
music	MUS	musica
mythology	MYTH	mitologia
noun	*n*	sostantivo
nautical	NAUT	marineria
negative	*neg*	in senso negativo
plural noun	*npl*	sostantivo plurale
singular noun	*nsg*	sostantivo singolare
number	*num*	numero
or	*o*	o
optics	OPT	ottica
oneself	o.s.	sé, se stesso
painting	PAINT	pittura
pejorative	*pej*	spregiativo
pharmacy	PHARM	farmacia
philosophy	PHIL	filosofia
photography	PHOT	fotografia
physics	PHYS	fisica
physiology	PHYSIOL	fisiologia
plural	*pl*	plurale
politics	POL	politica
past participle	*pp*	participio passato
prefix	*pref*	prefisso
preposition	*prep*	preposizione
press, journalism	*press*	giornalismo
preterite	*pret*	preterito
pronoun	*pron*	pronome
proverb, proverbial	*prov*	proverbio, proverbiale
psychology	PSYCH	psicologia
something	qc	qualcosa
someone	qn	qualcuno
registered trademark	®	marchio registrato
radio	RADIO	radio
railways	RAIL	ferrovie
regional	REG	regionale

religion	REL	religione
Scotland, Scottish	SCOT	Scozia, scozese
separable	*sep*	separabile
sewing, tailoring	SEW	sartoria
singular	*sg*	singolare
slang	*sl*	uso popolare
someone	s.o.	qualcuno
sports	SPORTS	sport
something	sth	qualcosa
suffix	suf	suffisso
superlative	sup	superlativo
technology	TECH	tecnologia
telephone	TEL	telefonia
textiles	TEX	industria tessile
theatre	THEAT	teatro
television	TV	televisione
typography, typesetting	TYPO	tipografia
university	UNIV	università
American English	*US*	inglese americano
usually	*usu*	generalmente
auxiliary verb	*v/aux*	verbo ausiliare
intransitive verb	*v/i*	verbo intransitivo
impersonal verb	*v/impers*	verbo impersonale
modal verb	*v/mod*	verbo modale
reflexive verb	*v/r*	verbo riflessivo
transitive verb	*v/t*	verbo transitivo
vulgar	*vulg*	volgare
zoology	ZOOL	zoologia
see	→	vedi

Italian spelling and pronunciation

The following table describes the Italian alphabet with its 21 letters (in **bold**). To make pronunciation easier, English equivalents have been chosen to illustrate the approximate sound. Letters that can only be found in borrowings from other languages have been included as well. These appear in normal type.

Letter	Name	Pronunciation	Example
a	a	like *a* in *star*, *father*	**pane**
b	bi	like *b* in *bed*, *abbey*	**bene**
c	ci	when directly followed by e or i: like *c* in *cheers*	**centro**, **ciabatta**
		when directly followed by a, o, u, h or a consonant: like *c* in *candy*	**cane**, **cosa**, **cultura**, **chilo**, **cristallo**
d	di	like *d* in *daddy*	**diamante**
e	e	like *e* in *yellow*	**bello**
		like *a* in *make*	**cena**
f	effe	like *f* in *fantasy*	**famiglia**
g	gi	when directly followed by e or i: like *g* in *genius*, *ginger*	**gelateria**, **gioco**
		when directly followed by a, o, u, h or a consonant: like *g* in *good*	**gatto**, **gondola**, **gusto**, **ghetto**, **grana**
h	acca	always silent; see also under c and g	**hanno**
i	i	when stressed: like *i* in *routine*	**vino**
		when unstressed and followed by a consonant: like *i* in *fish*	**sistema**
		when unstressed and followed by a vowel: like *y* in *backyard*	**fiamma**, **dietro**, **più**
		when unstressed, preceded by c, g or s and followed by a vowel: the sound of the i itself is not heard (see also under **c**, **g** and **s**)	**ciao**, **giusto**, **bacio**, **sciarpa**
j	i lunga	as in the original language from which the word is borrowed	**jazz**
k	cappa	like *k* in *keep*	**kiwi**
l	elle	like *l* in *lake*	**lago**
m	emme	like *m* in *mail*	**macchina**

Letter	Name	Pronunciation	Example
n	enne	like *n* in *nose*	**naso**
o	o	like *o* in *stop*	**nonna**
		like *o* in *door*	**amore**
p	pi	like *p* in *pepper*	**panna**
q	cu	always followed by u; like *qu* in *question*	**quando**
r	erre	like *r* in *rice*, but with a slight trill	**riso**
s	esse	when initial and preceding a vowel; between consonant and vowel; preceding c [k], f, p, q, t: like *s* in *sun*	**sole**, **persona**, **scarpa**
		between two vowels; when preceding b, d, g [g], l, m, n, r, v: like *z* in *zoom*	**chiesa**, **sblocco**, **svizzero**
		in a compound: when a component starts with s, its pronunciation remains that of initial s even if it now stands between two vowels	**mezzoservizio**
		sc followed by e or I: like *sh* in *shoe* (if the i that follows is unstressed and precedes another vowel, it is silent)	**scelta**, **sci**, **scioccato**
		sch is pronounced like *sc* in *scan*	**scheda**, **schizzare**
t	ti	like *t* in *tuna*	**tonno**
u	u	like *u* in *ruler*	**uva**
		when followed by a vowel: like *w* in *water*	**uomo**
v	vu	like *v* in *vanity*	**via**
w	vu doppia	like *w* in *water*	**wellness**
x	ics	like *x* in *exit*	**xenofobia**
y	ìpsilon	like *y* in *yacht*	**yogurtiera**
z	zeta	like *ts* in *itsy-bitsy*	**grazie**
		like *dz* in *adze*	**zaino**

Italian – English

A

a, A *m/f* ⟨*pl* a, A⟩ a, A; ***dalla a alla zeta*** from A to Z; ***vitamina*** *f* ***A*** vitamin A

a[1] *prep* **1.** *stato in luogo*: ***a casa*** at home; ***a destra*** on the right; ***a Roma*** in Rome; ***alla finestra*** at the window; ***lavorare alla FIAT*** work at FIAT **2.** *moto a luogo*: ***andare a casa*** go home; ***andare a Roma*** go to Rome; ***andare a sciare*** go skiing; ***andare al cinema*** go to the cinema; ***andare al mare*** go to the seaside **3.** *tempo*: ***a domani!*** see you tomorrow!; ***a giorni*** any day now; ***a maggio*** in May; ***a Natale*** at Christmas; ***alle quattro*** at four o'clock; ***a vent'anni*** at the age of twenty **4.** *modo*: COOK ***al burro*** in butter; ***a fatica*** *conoscere* hardly; *arrivare* with difficulty; ***alla moda*** in fashion; ***a piedi*** on foot; ***ad alta voce*** out loud **5.** *mezzo*: ***fatto a macchina*** machine-made; ***ricamato a mano*** embroidered by hand, hand-embroidered **6.** *con valore distributivo*: ***a due a due*** two at a time; ***a poco a poco*** little by little; ***due volte al giorno*** twice a day **7.** *prezzo, misura*: ***al metro*** by the metre; ***a che prezzo*** at what price; ***2 euro al chilo*** 2 euros a kilo; ***100 km all'ora*** 100 km an hour; ***a 5 km da qui*** 5 kms from here **8.** *complemento di termine*: ***dare qc a qn*** give sth to s.o., give s.o. sth **9.** *con inf* ***andare a prendere*** go and get

a[2] *abbr* (= **anno**) yr (year)

A *abbr* (= **autostrada**) M (motorway)

AAS *abbr* (= **Azienda Autonoma di Soggiorno**) *tourist board*

AAST *abbr* (= **Azienda Autonoma di Soggiorno e Turismo**) *tourist board*

ab. *abbr* (= **abitanti**) inhabitants

abate *m* abbot

abat-jour *m* ⟨*pl* abat-jour⟩ lampshade

abbacchiato *adj* downhearted

abbacchio *m* ⟨*pl* -cchi⟩ COOK young lamb

abbagliamento *m state of being dazzled*

abbagliante I *adj* dazzling **II** *m usu* ***-i*** *pl* AUTO full beam

abbagliare *v/t* ⟨1g⟩ dazzle

abbagliato *adj* dazzled; ***restare ~*** be dazzled

abbaglio *m* ⟨*pl* -gli⟩: ***prendere un ~*** make a blunder

abbaiare *v/i* ⟨1i⟩ bark

abbaino *m* dormer window; (*soffitta*) loft

abbaio *m* ⟨*pl* -ai⟩ bark

abbandonare *v/t* ⟨1a⟩ abandon; ***~ gli studi*** give up studying; *fig* ***~ il campo*** retreat

abbandonarsi *v/r* ⟨1a⟩ *sulla poltrona* flop; *alla corrente* let oneself go

abbandonato *adj casa* derelict; *bambino* abandoned; ***~ a se stesso*** left to one's own devices

abbandono *m* abandon; (*rinuncia*) abandonment; ***~ del tetto coniugale*** desertion; ***stato di ~*** state of disrepair

abbassamento *m* lowering; ***~ dei prezzi*** reduction in prices

abbassare *v/t* ⟨1a⟩ **1.** *prezzo* lower **2.** *radio* turn down **3.** ***~ lo sguardo*** look down; ***~ la testa*** lower one's head; ***~ la voce*** lower one's voice; ***~ i fari*** dip one's headlights

abbassarsi *v/r* (*chinarsi*) bend down; *prezzo* come down; *fig* ***~ a*** stoop to

abbasso *int*: ***~ la scuola!*** down with school!

abbastanza *adv* enough; (*alquanto*) quite; ***ho mangiato ~*** I've had enough to eat; ***sono ~ soddisfatto*** I'm quite satisfied; *fig* ***averne ~ di qc*** be fed up with sth; **~** that's enough

abbattere *v/t* ⟨3a⟩ knock down; *casa* demolish; *albero* cut down; *aereo* shoot down; *costi* slash; *fig* dishearten

abbattersi *v/r* **1.** fall; ***~ al suolo*** *aereo* crash-land **2.** *fig* become disheartened; ***dai, non ti abbattere!*** come on, don't lose heart!

abbattibile *adj sedile* fold-down; *tavolo* collapsible; *propeller blade* folding; ***capi*** *mpl* ***abbattibili*** *animals that can be hunted*

abbattimento *m* knocking down; *casa* demolition; *albero* cutting down; *aereo* shooting down; *fig* despondency

abbattitore *m*, **-trice** *f* lumberjack
abbattuto *adj* disheartened; ***alberi*** *mpl* ***-i*** felled trees
abbazia *f* abbey
abbaziale *adj*: ***chiesa*** *f* **~** abbey church
abbecedario *m* ⟨*pl* -ri⟩ alphabet book
abbellimento *m* embellishment; MUS ornament
abbellire *v/t* ⟨4d⟩ embellish
abbeveraggio *m* ⟨*pl* -ggi⟩ watering
abbeverare *v/t* ⟨1m⟩ water
abbeverarsi *v/r* ⟨1m⟩ drink
abbeverata *f atto* watering; *luogo* watering place **abbeveratoio** *m* ⟨*pl* -oi⟩ (drinking) trough
abbi, abbia → ***avere***
abbiccì *m* ⟨*no pl*⟩ abc; *fig* basics *pl*
abbiente *adj* well-off
abbigliamento *m* clothing; ***industria*** *f* ***dell'~*** clothing industry; ***capo*** *m* ***d'~*** article of clothing; **~ *femminile*** womenswear; **~ *maschile*** menswear; **~ *sportivo*** sportswear
abbinamento *m* matching; (*combinazione*) combination
abbinare *v/t* ⟨1a⟩ match; (*combinare*) combine; ***stivali da ~ alla gonna*** boots to go with the skirt
abbindolare *v/t* ⟨1a⟩ trick; ***farsi ~*** (***da qn***) be fooled (by s.o.)
abbiocco *m* ⟨*pl* -cchi⟩ *reg* sleepiness (after eating)
abboccamento *m* meeting
abboccare *v/i* ⟨1d⟩ *di pesce* bite; TECH join; *fig* swallow the bait
abboccato *adj vino* medium sweet
abbonamento *m a giornale* subscription; *a treno*, *bus*, THEAT season ticket; **~ *annuale*** yearly subscription; yearly ticket; **~ *mensile*** monthly subscription; monthly ticket; ***fare l'~*** *giornale* take out a subscription; THEAT, *treno*, *bus* have a season ticket
abbonare *v/t* ⟨1c & o⟩ take out a subscription for; (*condonare*) deduct
abbonarsi *v/r* ⟨1c & o⟩ subscribe; **~ *alla televisione*** subscribe to satellite / cable television
abbonato *m*, **-a** *f* subscriber; TEL ***elenco*** *m* ***degli -i*** telephone directory
abbondante *adj* abundant; *porzione* generous; *vestito* loose; *nevicata* heavy
abbondanza *f* abundance; ***ce n'è in ~*** there's plenty
abbondare *v/i* ⟨1a⟩ be plentiful; *fig* **~ *in / di qc*** be full of sth
abbordabile *adj persona* approachable; *prezzo* reasonable
abbordaggio *m* ⟨*pl* -ggi⟩ *di persona* approach; *fig di argomento* tackling; NAUT boarding; ***tentare l'~ di qn*** *infml* hit on s.o. *infml*
abbordare *v/t* ⟨1a⟩ **1.** *persona* approach; *infml persona dell'altro sesso* chat up *infml*; *argomento* tackle **2.** NAUT board
abborracciato *adj* botched
abbottonare *v/t* ⟨1a⟩ button up
abbottonato *adj* buttoned (up) **abbottonatura** *f* buttons
abbozzare *v/t* ⟨1c⟩ sketch; **~ *un sorriso*** smile faintly
abbozzato *adj* sketchy
abbozzo *m* sketch
abbracciare *v/t* ⟨1f⟩ embrace, hug; *fig* take up
abbracciarsi *v/r* ⟨1f⟩ embrace, hug
abbraccio *m* ⟨*pl* -cci⟩ embrace, hug; ***un ~*** *a fine lettera* love
abbreviare *v/t* ⟨1k & b⟩ abbreviate
abbreviato *adj* shortened; ***giudizio*** *m* **~** summary trial
abbreviazione *f* abbreviation
abbronzante *m* sun-tan lotion; ***lettino*** *m* **~** sunbed
abbronzare *v/t* ⟨1a⟩ *pelle* tan
abbronzarsi *v/r* ⟨1a⟩ get a tan
abbronzato *adj* tanned
abbronzatura *f* tan
abbrunato *adj* draped in black
abbrustolire *v/t* ⟨4d⟩ roast
abbrustolirsi *v/r* ⟨4d⟩: *fig* **~ *al sole*** *hum* soak up the sun
abbrutimento *m* degradation
abbuffarsi *v/r* ⟨1a⟩ stuff o.s. (***di*** with)
abbuffata *f* blow-out; ***farsi un'~ di qc*** have a bellyful of sth
abbuono *m* FIN discount
abdicare *v/i* ⟨1l & d⟩ abdicate
abdicazione *f* abdication
abduzione *f* abduction
aberrante *adj* abnormal; ***comportamento*** *m* **~** abnormal behaviour
aberrazione *f* abnormality; **~ *cromatica*** PHYS chromatic aberration; **~ *mentale*** MED mental abnormality
abete *m* fir; **~ *bianco*** silver fir
abetina *f* pinewood
abietto *adj persona*, *azione* despica-

ble; *stato* abject **abiezione** *f* abjectness

abigeato *m* JUR rustling

abile *adj* good (***in*** at); fit (***a*** for); ***~ a fare qc*** good at doing sth; ***diversamente ~*** differently abled; ***~ e arruolato*** fighting fit

abilità *f* ⟨*pl* abilità⟩ ability; ***~ manuale*** manual dexterity

abilitante *adj* qualifying; ***corso*** *m* ***~*** qualifying course

abilitare *v/t* ⟨11⟩ qualify; (*autorizzare*) certify; ***~ qn alla professione medica*** qualify s.o. to practise medicine **abilitarsi** *v/r* ⟨11⟩ qualify

abilitativo *adj* qualifying

abilitato *adj* qualified

abilitazione *f* qualification; ***corso*** *m* ***di ~*** qualifying course; ***esame*** *m* ***di ~*** qualifying exam

abilmente *adv* skilfully

abissale *adj* abyssal; *fig* profound; ***fauna*** *f* ***~*** abyssal fauna; ***essere di un'ignoranza ~*** be totally ignorant

abisso *m* abyss; ***sull'orlo dell'~*** on the brink of the abyss

abitabile *adj* habitable; ***cucina*** *f* ***~*** dining kitchen

abitabilità *f* ⟨*pl* abitabilità⟩ habitability

abitacolo *m* AUTO passenger compartment

abitante *m/f* inhabitant; ***~ a*** resident of

abitare ⟨11⟩ **I** *v/t* live in **II** *v/i* live; ***abito a Roma*** I live in Rome; ***abitano in campagna*** they live in the country

abitativo *adj* residential; ***edilizia*** *f* ***-a*** housebuilding

abitato **I** *adj* inhabited; ***centro*** *m* ***~*** built-up area **II** *m* built-up area

abitatore *m*, **-trice** *f* inhabitant

abitazione *f* house; ***~ principale*** main residence; ***casa*** *f* ***di ~*** house where one lives; ***diritto*** *m* ***di ~*** JUR right of occupancy

abiti *mpl* clothes *pl*

abitino *m* minidress

abito *m* dress; *da uomo* suit; ***~ da sera*** evening dress; ***~ da sposa*** wedding dress

abituale *adj* usual; ***delinquente*** *m* ***~*** habitual criminal

abitualità *f* ⟨*pl* abitualità⟩ *state of being habitual* **abitualmente** *adv* habitually

abituare *v/t* ⟨11⟩ accustom (***a*** to)

abituarsi *v/r*: ***~ a*** get used to; ***~ a fare qc*** get used to doing sth

abituato *adj*: ***essere ~ a fare qc*** be used to doing sth

abitudinario ⟨*mpl* -ri⟩ **I** *adj* of fixed habits **II** *m*, **-a** *f* creature of habit

abitudine *f* habit; ***avere la brutta ~ di fare qc*** have a nasty habit of doing sth; ***prendere l'~ di fare qc*** get into the habit of doing sth; ***d'~*** usually; ***per ~*** out of habit

abituro *m* hovel

abiura *f* abjuration *form* **abiurare** *v/t* ⟨11⟩ abjure *form*; ***~ la propria fede*** renounce one's faith

ablativo *m* ablative; ***~ assoluto*** ablative absolute

ablazione *f* removal

abluzione *f* ablution

abnegazione *f* self-denial; ***spirito*** *m* ***di ~*** spirit of self-sacrifice

abnorme *adj* abnormal

abolire *v/t* ⟨4d⟩ abolish; ***~ la pena di morte*** abolish the death penalty

abolizione *f* abolition

abolizionismo *m* abolitionism **abolizionista** *m/f* ⟨*mpl* -i⟩ abolitionist

abominevole *adj* abominable

abominio *m* ⟨*pl* -ni⟩ (*cosa abominevole*) abomination

aborigeno **I** *adj* aboriginal **II** *m*, **-a** *f* aboriginal

aborrire *v/t* ⟨4d & c⟩ abhor **aborrito** *adj* abhorred

abortire *v/i* ⟨4d⟩ MED miscarry; *volontariamente* have an abortion; *fig* fail

abortista *m/f* ⟨*mpl* -i⟩ pro-choice campaigner

aborto *m* MED miscarriage; *provocato* abortion; ***~ farmacologico*** chemical abortion

abracadabra *m* ⟨*pl* abracadabra⟩ abracadabra

abrasione *f* graze

abrasivo **I** *adj* abrasive; ***materiali*** *mpl* ***-i*** abrasives **II** *n*: ***abrasivo*** *m* abrasive

abrogare *v/t* ⟨1e & c or 11⟩ repeal

abrogativo *adj* abrogative; ***referendum*** *m* ***~*** *referendum to repeal a law*

abrogazione *f* repeal

abruzzese **I** *adj* of Abruzzo; *persona* from Abruzzo **II** *m/f* person from Abruzzo

Abruzzo *m* Abruzzo

ABS®, abs® *m abbr* ABS®
absidale *adj* apsidal
abside *f* apse
abstract *m* ⟨*pl* abstract⟩ abstract
abulia *f* lethargy; MED abulia **abulico** *adj* ⟨*mpl* -ci⟩ lethargic
abusare *v/i* ⟨1a⟩: **~ di** abuse; (*approfittare*) take advantage of; **~ nel bere** drink to excess
abusato *adj parola, espressione* hackneyed
abusivamente *adv* illegally **abusivismo** *m flouting of regulations*; **~ edilizio** illegal construction
abusivo *adj* illegal; **costruzioni** *fpl* **-e** illegal buildings; **tassista ~** unauthorized taxi-driver; **venditore ~** illicit trader
abuso *m* abuse; **~ di alcol** alcohol abuse; **~ di potere / d'ufficio** abuse of power / authority; **~ sessuale** sexual abuse
a.C. *abbr* (= **avanti Cristo**) BC (before Christ)
acacia *f* ⟨*pl* -cie⟩ acacia
acaricida *m* ⟨*pl* -i⟩ mite killer
acaro *m* mite
acattolico ⟨*mpl* -ci⟩ **I** *adj* non-Catholic **II** *m*, **-a** *f* non-Catholic
acca *f*: **non capire un'~** not understand a thing
accademia *f* academy; **~ di belle arti** academy of art; **~ militare** military academy
accademicamente *adv* academically
accademico *adj* ⟨*mpl* -ci⟩ academic
accademismo *m* academicism
accadere *v/i* ⟨2c⟩ happen
accaduto *m*: **raccontami l'~** tell me what happened
accalappiacani *m* ⟨*pl* accalappiacani⟩ dog-catcher
accalcarsi *v/r* ⟨1c⟩ crowd
accaldarsi *v/r* ⟨1a⟩ get overheated
accaldato *adj* overheated
accalorarsi *v/r* ⟨1a⟩ *fig* get excited
accampamento *m* camp
accampare ⟨1a⟩ **I** *v/t*: **~ scuse** come up with excuses **II** *v/i* camp
accamparsi *v/r* ⟨1a⟩ camp
accanimento *m* (*tenacia*) tenacity; (*furia*) rage
accanirsi *v/r* ⟨4d⟩ (*ostinarsi*) persist; **~ contro qn** rage against s.o.
accanito *adj odio* fierce; *tifoso* dedicated; *fumatore* inveterate; **lavoratore** *m* **~** hard worker
accanto I *prep*: **~ a** next to; **~ alla stazione** next to the station; **siediti ~ a me** sit beside me; **uno ~ all'altro** one next to the other **II** *adv* near, nearby; *abitare* next door; **è qui ~** it's just round the corner **III** *adj inv* next-door; **la stanza ~** the next room
accantonamento *m* setting aside (*a.* ECON); (*somma accantonata*) fund; MIL quartering
accantonare *v/t* ⟨1a⟩ put aside
accaparramento *m* hoarding; **~ di provviste** hoarding of supplies **accaparrare** *v/t* ⟨1a⟩ hoard **accaparrarsi** *v/r* ⟨1a⟩ obtain
accapigliarsi *v/r* ⟨1g⟩ fight
accapo *adv*: **andare ~** start a new line
accappatoio *m* ⟨*pl* -oi⟩ bathrobe; *da mare* beachrobe
accapponare *v/t* ⟨1a⟩ castrate; **far ~ la pelle a qn** make s.o.'s flesh creep
accapponarsi *v/r* ⟨1a⟩: **mi si è accapponata la pelle** it made my flesh creep
accarezzare *v/t* ⟨1a⟩ caress; *speranza* cherish; *animale* stroke
accartocciato *adj* crumpled up
accasarsi *v/r* ⟨1a⟩ get married; (*mettere su casa*) set up home
accasato *adj* married
accasciarsi *v/r* ⟨1f⟩ flop down
accasciato *adj fig* disheartened
accatastamento *m* heap
accatastare *v/t* ⟨1a⟩ pile up
accattivante *adj* engaging; **sorriso** *m* **~** winning smile **accattivarsi** *v/r* ⟨1a⟩ gain; **~ le simpatie di qn** get s.o. to like you
accatto *m* begging; **d'~** second-hand
accattonaggio *m* begging
accattone *m*, **-a** *f* beggar
accavallamento *m* overlap
accavallare *v/t* ⟨1a⟩ cross; **~ le gambe** cross one's legs
accavallarsi *v/r* ⟨1a⟩ *fig* overlap
accecamento *m* blinding (*a. fig*) **accecante** *adj* blinding
accecare ⟨1b & d⟩ **I** *v/t* blind **II** *v/i* be blinding
accecato *adj fig* blind; **~ dall'odio** blinded by hatred
accedere *v/i* ⟨3a⟩: **~ a** enter
accelerare *v/t* ⟨1b & m⟩ speed up;

AUTO accelerate
accelerato **I** *adj* fast; *treno* slow **II** *m* slow train
acceleratore *m* AUTO accelerator
accelerazione *f* acceleration; **~ *di gravità*** acceleration of gravity; **~ *di particelle*** PHYS particle acceleration
accelerometro *m* accelerometer
accendere *v/t* ⟨3c⟩ light; RADIO, TV turn on; **~ *una candela*** light a candle; **~ *una sigaretta*** light a cigarette; ***hai da ~?*** have you got a light?; **~ *il motore*** switch on the engine; **~ *la stufa*** light the fire; **~ *un conto*** open an account; **~ *un'ipoteca / un mutuo*** take out a mortgage / a loan
accendersi *v/r* ⟨3c⟩ light up; *apparecchio* come on
accendigas *m* ⟨*pl* accendigas⟩ gas lighter
accendino *m*, **accendisigari** *m* ⟨*pl* accendisigari⟩ lighter; **~ *usa e getta*** disposable lighter
accennare *v/t* ⟨1a⟩ indicate; *con parole* mention; **~ *a fare qc*** show signs of doing sth; **~ *un sorriso*** give a hint of a smile
accenno *m* (*cenno*) gesture; (*indizio*) sign; (*allusione*) hint; ***fare ~ a qn / qc*** mention s.o. / sth; ***si nota un ~ di ripresa economica*** there are signs of an economic recovery; ***sono i primi -i della vecchiaia*** they are the first signs of old age
accensione *f* ignition; **~ *difettosa*** AUTO faulty ignition; **~ *elettronica*** electronic ignition; ***temperatura*** *f* ***d'~*** ignition temperature; **~ *di un'ipoteca*** taking out of a mortgage
accentare *v/t* ⟨1b⟩ *nello scrivere*, *nel parlare* stress
accentato *adj nello scrivere*, *nel parlare* stressed
accento *m grafico* accent; *su sillaba* stress; *straniero* accent; **~ *grave / acuto*** grave / acute accent; ***avere un forte ~*** have a strong accent; ***su che sillaba cade l'~?*** which syllable is stressed?; ***parla con ~ napoletano*** he has a Neapolitan accent; *fig* ***porre l'~ su qc*** put the focus on sth
accentramento *m* centralization
accentrare *v/t* ⟨1b⟩ (*centralizzare*) centralize; (*concentrare*) concentrate; (*attirare*) attract; **~ *le funzioni nelle mani di qn*** concentrate power in s.o.'s hands **accentrarsi** *v/r* ⟨1b⟩ focus (***su*** on)
accentratore **I** *adj* centralizing **II** *m*, **-trice** *f* centralizer
accentuare *v/t* ⟨1b & m⟩ accentuate
accentuarsi *v/r* ⟨1b & m⟩ get worse
accentuato *adj* marked **accentuazione** *f* accentuation
accerchiamento *m* encirclement (*a.* MIL) **accerchiare** *v/t* ⟨1k⟩ encircle
accertabile *adj* verifiable **accertabilità** *f* ⟨*pl* accertabilità⟩ verifiability
accertamento *m* check; (*indagine*) investigation; **~ *di generalità*** identity check; **~ *dei fatti*** fact checking; **~ *dei danni*** damage assessment; **~ *fiscale*** tax assessment; **~ *con adesione*** JUR *procedure for agreeing on how much tax s.o. has to pay*; MED ***fare degli -i*** carry out investigations; ***fare -i su qn / qc*** carry out checks on s.o. / sth
accertare *v/t* ⟨1b⟩ check; **~ *l'identità di qn*** establish s.o.'s identity
accertarsi *v/r*: **~ *di qc*** check sth
acceso *adj colore* bright; *motore* running; *TV*, *luce* on; ***la luce è -a*** the light is on; ***essere ~ in volto*** be flushed; *fig* **~ *sostenitore*** *m* passionate supporter
accessibile *adj* accessible; *prezzo* reasonable; ***le sue teorie non sono -i a tutti*** not everyone can understand his / her theories
accessibilità *f* ⟨*pl* accessibilità⟩ accessibility
accesso *m* **1.** access; ***divieto d'~*** no entry; **~ *a Internet*** Internet access; ***avere ~ a un file*** be able to access a file; **~ *diretto / indiretto*** COMPUT direct / indirect access **2.** *fig and* MED fit; **~ *di collera*** fit of anger
accessori *mpl* accessories *pl*; **~ *da bagno*** bathroom accessories
accessoriato *adj* AUTO complete with accessories
accessorio *adj* secondary; ***causa*** *f* ***-a*** subsidiary case; ***spese*** *fpl* ***-e*** incidental expenses
accetta *f* ax(e) *fig* ***fatto*** *or* ***tagliato con l'~*** roughly done; *di persona* uncouth; *fisicamente* craggy
accettabile *adj* acceptable
accettabilità *f* ⟨*pl* accettabilità⟩ ac-

ceptability
accettare *v/t* ⟨1b⟩ accept; ***~ la realtà*** accept reality; ***~ di fare qc*** agree to do sth; ***~ un consiglio*** take advice; ***~ qn come socio*** accept s.o. as a member
accettarsi *v/r* ⟨1b⟩ accept oneself; ***bisogna imparare ad ~*** you have to learn to accept yourself
accettazione *f* acceptance; (*di albergo*) reception; ***~ bagagli*** check-in; ***~ bancaria*** bank *or* banker's acceptance; ***~ dell'eredità*** acceptance of inheritance (by an heir)
accetto *adj*: ***bene / male ~*** welcome / not welcome
accezione *f* meaning; ***questa parola ha più -i*** this word has several meanings
acchiappafarfalle *m* ⟨*pl* acchiappafarfalle⟩ butterfly net; *fig* woolgatherer
acchiappare *v/t* ⟨1a⟩ catch
acchiapparsi *v/r* ⟨1a⟩: play tag
acchiappino *m* (*gioco*) tag
acchito *m*: ***d'~*** at first
acciaccato *adj* (*indolenzito*) aching; *infml* below par
acciacco *m* ⟨*pl* -cchi⟩ ache; ***essere pieno di -cchi*** be full of aches and pains
acciaieria *f* steelworks *sg or pl*
acciaio *m* ⟨*pl* -ai⟩ steel; ***~ fuso*** ingot iron; ***~ grezzo*** raw steel; ***~ inossidabile*** stainless steel; ***costruzione*** *f* ***in ~*** manufacturing in steel; *fig* ***avere nervi d'~*** have nerves of steel
acciambellare *v/t* ⟨1b⟩ coil **acciambellarsi** *v/r* ⟨1b⟩ curl up
acciarino *m* steel
accidentale *adj* accidental
accidentalità *f* ⟨*pl* accidentalità⟩ (*casualità*) accidental nature; *di terreno*: roughness
accidentato *adj terreno* rough
accidente *m*: ***che gli venga un ~*** damn him / her; ***non fare un ~ tutto il giorno*** not do a stroke of work all day; ***non ci capisco un ~!*** I don't understand a bloody thing!
accidenti! *int infml* damn! *infml*; *di sorpresa* wow!; ***~ alla pioggia!*** bugger the rain *infml*
acciderba *int* → ***accidenti***
accidia *f* (*apatia*) idleness; REL sloth
accidioso **I** *adj* idle; REL slothful **II** *m*, **-a** *f* lazybones
accigliarsi *v/r* ⟨1g⟩ frown
accigliato *adj* frowning; ***avere lo sguardo ~*** have a frown on one's face
accingersi *v/r* ⟨3d⟩: ***~ a fare qc*** be about to do sth
acciottolato *m* cobbles *pl*
accipicchia! *int infml* bother! *infml*, *di sorpresa* wow!
acciuffare *v/t* ⟨1a⟩ grab; ***~ un ladro*** collar a thief *infml*
acciuga *f* ⟨*pl* -ghe⟩ anchovy; ***-ghe sott'olio*** anchovies in oil; ***pasta*** *f* ***di -ghe*** anchovy paste; ***essere (magro come) un'~*** be as skinny as a rake
acclamare *v/t* ⟨1a⟩ applaud; ***~ a qc*** applaud sth; ***~ qn presidente*** acclaim s.o. president
acclamazione *f per entusiasmo* applause; *per consenso* acclamation; ***eleggere qn per ~*** elect s.o. by acclamation
acclimatarsi *v/r* ⟨1m⟩ get acclimatized
acclimatazione *f* acclimatization
accludere *v/t* ⟨3q⟩ enclose
accluso *adj* enclosed; ***qui ~*** enclosed
accoccolarsi *v/r* ⟨1m & c⟩ squat
accoccolato *adj* squatting; ***stare ~*** squat
accodarsi *v/r* ⟨1a⟩ (*mettersi in coda*) queue up; *di traffico*: queue; ***~ a qn / qc*** (*aggregarsi*) follow s.o. / sth
accogliente *adj* welcoming
accoglienza *f* reception; ***centro di ~*** reception centre
accogliere *v/t* ⟨3ss⟩ welcome; *richiesta* grant
accollare *v/t* ⟨1c⟩ shoulder
accollarsi *v/r* ⟨1c⟩ take on; ***~ la responsabilità di qc*** take on responsibility for sth; ***~ tutte le spese*** bear all the expenses
accollato *adj abito* high-necked; ***scarpa*** *f* ***-a*** ankle-high shoe
accollo *m* JUR *agreement to take on another person's debt*
accoltellamento *m* stabbing
accoltellare *v/t* ⟨1b⟩ stab
accoltellarsi *v/r* ⟨1b⟩ stab each other
accoltellatore *m*, **-trice** *f* knifeman; *donna* knifewoman
accolto *past part* → ***accogliere***
accomandante **I** *adj* COMM limited;

socio *m* **~** limited partner **II** *m/f* limited partner **accomandatario** ⟨*mpl* -ri⟩ **I** *adj*: ***socio*** *m* **~** COMM active partner **II** *m*, **-a** *f* active partner
accomandita *f*: ***società*** *f* ***in* ~** limited partnership
accomiatare *v/t* ⟨1a⟩: **~ *qn*** say goodbye to s.o. (*who is leaving*)
accomiatarsi *v/r* ⟨1a⟩: **~ *da qn*** say goodbye to s.o. (*when one is leaving*)
accomodabile *adj* repairable
accomodamento *m* arrangement; (*accordo*) agreement; ***giungere a un* ~** reach an agreement
accomodante *adj* accommodating
accomodare *v/t* ⟨1c & m⟩ (*riparare*) mend; *lite* resolve; (*sistemare*) arrange
accomodarsi *v/r* ⟨1c & m⟩ make o.s. at home; ***si accomodi!*** come in!; (*sedersi*) have a seat!; ***accomodati pure sul divano*** have a seat on the sofa
accompagnamento *m* accompaniment; **~ *musicale*** (musical) accompaniment; ***indennità*** *f* ***di* ~** attendance allowance; ***lettera*** *f* ***di* ~** covering letter
accompagnare *v/t* ⟨1a⟩ accompany; **~ *qn a casa*** see s.o. home; *a piedi* walk s.o. home; **~ *qn alla porta*** show s.o. out; ***mi hanno accompagnato in macchina*** they gave me a lift; *fig* **~ *qn con lo sguardo*** gaze after s.o.
accompagnarsi *v/r* ⟨1a⟩ go (well) together; **~ *a*** *or* ***con qn*** associate with s.o.
accompagnato *adj* accompanied; ***meglio soli che male -i*** it's better to be alone than in bad company
accompagnatore *m*, **-trice** *f* escort; MUS accompanist
accomunare *v/t* ⟨1n⟩ (*mettere in comune*) share; (*unire*) join; **~ *i beni*** share one's resources; ***ci accomuna l'amore per la musica*** we have a love of music in common
acconciare *v/t* ⟨1f⟩ (*abbigliare*) dress; *capelli* style; **~ *una sposa*** dress a bride
acconciarsi *v/r* ⟨1f⟩: **~ *i capelli*** do one's hair
acconciatura *f* hairdo
accondiscendente *adj* accommodating; *pej* compliant; ***essere* ~ *con qn*** go along with s.o. **accondiscendere** *v/i* ⟨3c⟩: **~ *a qc*** go along with sth
acconsentire *v/i* ⟨4b⟩ consent (***a*** to); ***chi tace acconsente*** silence means consent
accontentare *v/t* ⟨1b⟩ satisfy
accontentarsi *v/r* ⟨1b⟩ be happy (***di*** with); **~ *di qc*** content oneself with sth
acconto *m* deposit; ***ritenuta*** *f* ***d'*~** *tax paid in advance*
accoppare *v/t* ⟨1a⟩ *infml* do in **accopparsi** *v/r* ⟨1a⟩ *infml* snuff it
accoppiamento *m* pairing off; *animali* mating; MECH coupling
accoppiare *v/t* ⟨1k & c⟩ couple; *animali* mate; ***Dio li fa e poi li accoppia*** *prov* they're two of a kind
accoppiarsi *v/r* ⟨1k & c⟩ pair off
accoppiatore *m* coupler; **~ *telefonico*** TEL phone adaptor
accoramento *m* distress
accorarsi *v/r* ⟨1c⟩: **~ *per qc*** be distressed about sth **accorato** *adj* distressed
accorciamento *m* shortening; LING short form
accorciare *v/t* ⟨1f⟩ shorten
accorciarsi *v/r* ⟨1f⟩ get shorter
accorciativo *m* short form
accordabile *adj* *permesso* grantable; *strumento* tunable
accordare *v/t* ⟨1c⟩ grant; MUS tune; (*armonizzare*) harmonize
accordarsi *v/r* ⟨1c⟩ agree; *di colori* match; **~ *con qn su qc*** agree with s.o. about sth
accordatore *m*, **-trice** *f* piano tuner
accordatura *f* tuning
accordo *m* agreement; (*armonia*) harmony; MUS chord; **~ *europeo*** European agreement; ***essere d'*~** agree; ***mettersi d'*~** reach an agreement; ***d'*~!** OK!
accorgersi *v/r* ⟨3d⟩: **~ *di*** notice
accorgimento *m* (*espediente*) trick
accorpamento *m* unification **accorpare** *v/t* ⟨1a⟩ unify
accorrere *v/i* ⟨3o⟩ hurry; **~ *in aiuto di qn*** rush to help s.o.
accortezza *f* forethought
accorto I *past part* → ***accorgersi*** **II** *adj* shrewd; ***stare* ~** be on one's guard
accostabile *adj* approachable **accostamento** *m di colori*: combination
accostare *v/t* ⟨1c⟩ approach; *porta* leave ajar; **~ *i colori*** combine colours; **~ *la tazzina alla bocca*** raise the cup

to one's lips
accostarsi *v/r* ⟨1c⟩ get close; ***non ti accostare troppo al fuoco*** don't get too close to the fire; *fig* **~ *alla musica*** start learning about music; *fig* **~ *ai sacramenti*** receive the sacraments
account executive *m/f* ⟨*pl* account executive⟩ account executive
accovacciarsi *v/r* ⟨1f⟩ crouch (down)
accovacciato *adj* crouching; ***stare* ~** crouch
accozzaglia *f* ⟨*pl* -glie⟩ *pej di persone*: odd assortment; *di cose*: jumble
accreditamento *m* COMM, FIN credit; ADMIN accreditation
accreditare *v/t* ⟨1b & m⟩ confirm; FIN credit
accreditato I *adj* confirmed; (*attendibile*) reliable; ***giornalista*** ***m*** **~** accredited journalist; ***da fonti -i*** from reliable sources **II** *m*, **-a** *f* accredited person
accredito *m* credit
accrescere *v/i* ⟨3n⟩ increase; ***l'alcol accresce il pericolo d'infarto*** alcohol increases the risk of heart disease
accrescersi *v/r* ⟨3n⟩ grow bigger
accrescimento *m* increase **accrescitivo I** *adj* augmentative **II** *n*: ***accrescitivo*** *m* augmentative
accucciarsi *v/r* ⟨1f⟩ *di animali*: lie down; *di persone*: huddle
accudire ⟨4d⟩ **I** *v/t* look after; **~ *i bambini*** look after the children **II** *v/i*: **~ *a qc*** attend to sth; **~ *alla casa*** take care of the house
accumulare *v/t* ⟨1m⟩ accumulate; **~ *errori su errori*** make one mistake after another; **~ *esperienze*** gain experience
accumularsi *v/r* ⟨1m⟩ accumulate
accumulatore *m* battery; **~ *idraulico*** hydraulic accumulator; **~ *termico*** thermal accumulator
accumulazione *f* accumulation
accumulo *m* accumulation; ***un* ~ *di debiti*** a build-up of debts
accuratezza *f* care
accurato *adj* careful
accusa *f* accusation; JUR charge; ***atto*** *m* **d'~** indictment; ***Pubblica Accusa*** public prosecutor; ***muovere un'~ di*** *or* ***per qc contro qn*** accuse s.o. of (doing) sth
accusare *v/t* ⟨1a⟩ **1.** accuse; JUR charge; **~ *qn di aver fatto qc*** accuse s.o. of doing sth; **~ *qn di corruzione*** accuse s.o. of corruption **2.** JUR **~ *ricevuta*** acknowledge receipt **3.** **~ *la stanchezza*** feel tired; **~ *un forte mal di testa*** have a bad headache
accusarsi *v/r* ⟨1a⟩ confess (***di*** to); *a vicenda*: accuse each other
accusativo *m* accusative
accusato *m*, **-a** *f* accused
accusatore *m*, **-trice** *f* prosecutor; ***sguardo*** *m* **~** accusing look
accusatorio *adj* ⟨*mpl* -ri⟩ accusatory
acefalo *adj* acephalous; ***statua*** *f* ***-a*** headless statue
acerbità *f* ⟨*pl* acerbità⟩ unripeness; *fig* immaturity
acerbo *adj* unripe; ***bellezza*** *f* ***-a*** youthful beauty
acero *m* maple
acerrimo *adj* bitter; ***essere* ~ *nemico di qn*** be s.o.'s bitter enemy
acetato *m* acetate
acetico *adj* ⟨*mpl* -ci⟩ acetic; ***acido*** *m* **~** acetic acid
acetilene *m* acetylene
aceto *m* vinegar; **~ *balsamico*** balsamic vinegar; ***mettere sott'~*** pickle
acetone *m* nail varnish remover
acetosa *f* sorrel **acetosella** *f* wood sorrel
Achei *mpl* Achaeans
Achille *m* Achilles; ***tallone*** *m* **d'~** Achilles heel; ***tendine*** *m* **d'~** Achilles tendon
achillea *f* achillea
ACI *abbr* (= **Automobile Club d'Italia**) *Automobile Club of Italy*
aciclico *adj* ⟨*mpl* -ci⟩ acyclic
acidificante *adj* acidifying **acidificare** *v/t* ⟨1d & n⟩ acidify **acidificazione** *f* acidification
acidità *f* acidity; **~ *di stomaco*** heartburn
acido I *adj* acid; *fig* sour; ***panna*** *f* ***-a*** sour cream; ***piogge*** *fpl* ***acide*** acid rain; ***battuta*** *f* ***-a*** acid comment; ***sorriso*** *m* **~** bitter smile *sg* **II** *m* acid
acidosi *f* MED acidosis
acidulo *adj* acidulous
acino *m* grape
ACLI *abbr* (= **Associazione Cristiana dei Lavoratori Italiani**) *Italian trade union association*
acme *f* ⟨*pl* acmi⟩ MED crisis

acne *f* acne
aconfessionale *adj* nondenominational **aconfessionalità** *f* ⟨*pl* aconfessionalità⟩ nondenominationalism
aconito *m* BOT aconite
acqua *f* **1.** water; **~ *alta*** high tide; *a Venezia* high water; **~ *corrente*** running water; **~ *dolce*** fresh water; **~ *fresca*** cold water; **~ *minerale*** mineral water; **~ *ossigenata*** hydrogen peroxide; **~ *piovana*** rainwater; **~ *potabile*** drinking water; **~ *di rubinetto*** tap water; **~ *tonica*** tonic water; **~ *di Colonia*** cologne **2. *-e*** *pl* waters; ***-e*** *pl* ***nere*** *or* ***luride*** sewage; ***-e*** *pl* ***reflue*** waste water; ***-e*** *pl* ***territoriali*** territorial waters; ***rottura*** *f* ***delle -e*** MED breaking of the waters **3.** *fig* ***calmare le -e*** pour oil on troubled waters; ***in cattive -e*** in deep water; **~ *in bocca!*** keep it under your hat!; ***ha l'~ alla gola*** (*non ha tempo*) he's pushed for time; ***ragazza*** *f* **~ *e sapone*** natural-looking girl; ***una teoria che fa ~*** a theory that doesn't hold water
acquaforte *f* etching
acquaio *m* ⟨*pl* -ai⟩ sink
acquaiolo *adj* water; ***merlo*** *m* **~** dipper
acquamarina **I** *f* aquamarine **II** *adj inv* aquamarine
acquaplano *m* aquaplane
acquaragia *f* turpentine
acquario *m* ⟨*pl* -ri⟩ **1.** aquarium **2.** ASTROL ***Acquario*** Aquarius; ***sono dell'Acquario*** I'm (an) Aquarius
acquasanta *f* holy water; ***essere come il diavolo e l'~*** be like oil and water **acquasantiera** *f* stoup
acquascooter *m* jet-ski
acquatico *adj* ⟨*mpl* -ci⟩ aquatic; ***sci*** *m* **~** water skiing; *oggetto* waterski; ***uccello*** *m* **~** waterfowl
acquattarsi *v/r* ⟨1a⟩ crouch (down)
acquavite *f* brandy
acquazzone *m* downpour
acquedotto *m* aqueduct
acqueo *adj*: ***vapore*** *m* **~** water vapo(u)r
acquerello *m* water-colo(u)r
acquerugiola *f* drizzle
acquicoltura *f* aquaculture
acquifero *adj* water-bearing; ***falda*** *f* ***-a*** aquifer
acquirente *m/f* purchaser; ***paese*** *m* **~** buyer country
acquisire *v/t* ⟨4d⟩ *cittadinanza* be granted; *proprietà* acquire; *capacità* gain
acquisito *adj* acquired; *parente* relative by marriage
acquisizione *f* acquisition
acquistabile *adj* purchasable
acquistare ⟨1a⟩ **I** *v/t* buy; *fig* gain *fig* **~ *fama*** become famous; **~ *tempo*** gain time **II** *v/i* improve (***in*** in); **~ *in sicurezza*** become safer
acquisto *m* purchase; ***potere*** *m* ***d'~*** purchasing power; ***prezzo*** *m* ***di ~*** purchase price; **~ *a rate*** hire purchase, *US* installment plan; ***fare -i*** go shopping
acquitrino *m* bog
acquitrinoso *adj* boggy
acquolina *f*: ***mi viene l'~ in bocca*** my mouth's watering
acquoso *adj* watery; (*allungato con acqua*) watered-down; ***minestra*** *f* ***-a*** watery soup
acre *adj* sour; *voce* harsh
acredine *f* bitterness (*a. fig*)
acribia *f* academic rigo(u)r; ***con ~*** with rigoro(u)s accuracy
acrilico *adj* ⟨*mpl* -ci⟩ acrylic; ***colori*** *mpl* ***-i*** acrylic paints; ***vetro*** *m* **~** Perspex®
acrimonia *f* acrimony
acritico *adj* ⟨*mpl* -ci⟩ uncritical
acrobata *m/f* ⟨*mpl* -i⟩ acrobat
acrobatica *f* ⟨*pl* -che⟩ acrobatics **acrobaticamente** *adv* acrobatically
acrobatico *adj* ⟨*mpl* -ci⟩ acrobatic; ***sci*** *m* **~** freestyle skiing; ***volo*** *m* **~** aerobatics
acrobatismo *m* acrobatics (*a.fig*)
acromatico *adj* ⟨*mpl* -ci⟩ achromatic
acronimo *m* acronym
acropoli *f* ⟨*pl* acropoli⟩ acropolis
acuire *v/t* ⟨4d⟩ *esp fig* (*aguzzare*) sharpen; (*inasprire*) worsen; **~ *l'ingegno*** hone intelligence; **~ *i contrasti*** exacerbate conflicts
acuirsi *v/r* ⟨4d⟩ increase; *dolore*, *malattia* get worse
acuità *f* ⟨*pl* acuità⟩ acuity; **~ *visiva*** visual acuity
aculeo *m di istrice* spine; *vespa* sting; *pianta* prickle
acume *m* perspicacity
acustica *f* acoustics *sg*; *di ambiente*

acoustics *pl*
acustico *adj* ⟨*mpl* -ci⟩ acoustic; ***apparecchio ~*** hearing aid; ***inquinamento** m **~*** noise pollution; ***isolamento** m **~*** soundproofing; ***nervo** m **~*** acoustic nerve
acuto I *adj* intense; *nota*, *dolore* sharp; *suono*, *voce* shrill; MED acute **II** *m* MUS high note
ad *prep* → ***a*** (*before vowels*)
adagiare *v/t* ⟨1f⟩ *persona* lay down
adagiarsi *v/r* ⟨1f⟩ lie down; ***~ nel lusso*** be in the lap of luxury
adagio I *adv* slowly; *con cautela* cautiously **II** *m* ⟨*pl* -gi⟩ MUS adagio
adamantino *adj* unbreakable; *fig* incorruptible; *fig* (*saldo*) firm; ***coscienza** f **-a*** unimpeachable integrity
adamitico *adj* ⟨*mpl* -ci⟩: ***in costume ~*** *hum* in one's birthday suit
Adamo *m* Adam; ***pomo** m **d'~*** Adam's apple; ***da ~ in qua*** since the beginning of time
adattabile *adj* adaptable **adattabilità** *f* ⟨*pl* adattabilità⟩ adaptability
adattamento *m* adaptation; (*rielaborazione*) reworking; ***~ all'ambiente*** adaptation to the environment; ***~ cinematografico*** film adaptation; ***spirito** m **di ~*** adaptability
adattare *v/t* ⟨1a⟩ adapt
adattarsi *v/r* (*adeguarsi*) adapt (***a*** to); (*addirsi*) be suitable (***a*** for); ***questo colore non ti si adatta*** the colour doesn't suit you
adattatore *m* adaptor
adatto *adj* right (***a*** for); ***~ allo scopo*** fit for purpose; ***un libro ~ ai bambini*** a children's book; ***al momento** m **~*** at the right moment; ***sei proprio la persona -a*** you're just the right person
addebitamento *m* debit
addebitare *v/t* ⟨1m⟩: FIN ***~ qc a qn*** debit s.o. with sth; *fig* ascribe sth to s.o.
addebito *m* FIN debit; ***nota** f **di ~*** debit note
addendo *m* MATH addend
addensamento *m* thickening; *di nuvole*: build-up of clouds **addensante I** *adj* thickening **II** *m* thickener **addensare** *v/t* ⟨1b⟩ thicken
addensarsi *v/r* ⟨1b⟩ thicken
addentare *v/t* ⟨1b⟩ bite into; ***~ un panino*** bite into a roll
addentrarsi *v/r* ⟨1a⟩ go into (*a.fig*); ***~ nella foresta*** go deep into the forest; ***~ nei particolari*** go into detail
addestramento *m* training
addestrare *v/t* ⟨1b⟩ train
addestratore *m*, **-trice** *f* trainer
addetto I *m*, **-a** *f* person responsible; ***~ culturale*** cultural attaché; *fig* ***~ ai lavori*** expert; ***~ alle pubbliche relazioni*** public relations officer; ***~ stampa*** press officer; ***vietato l'ingresso ai non -i*** authorized personnel only **II** *adj* assigned (***a*** to)
addiaccio *m*: ***all'~*** in the open air
addietro *adv*: ***tempo** m **~*** some time ago
addio I *int* goodbye; ***dire ~ a qn*** say goodbye to s.o.; ***~ vacanze!*** that's the end of the holidays! **II** *m* goodbye, farewell; ***dare l'~ a qn / qc*** s.o. / sth; ***~ al celibato / nubilato*** stag party / hen party
addirittura *adv* (*assolutamente*) absolutely; (*perfino*) even; ***è ~ incredibile*** it's absolutely incredible
addirsi *v/r* ⟨3t⟩ suit; ***questo non mi si addice*** this doesn't suit me
additare *v/t* ⟨1a⟩ point at / to; ***~ qn / qc*** point at s.o. / sth; *fig* expose
additivo *m* additive
addizionale *f*: ***~ Irpef*** FIN *type of income tax*
addizionare *v/t* ⟨1a⟩ add
addizione *f* addition
addobbare *v/t* ⟨1c⟩ decorate; ***~ l'albero di Natale*** decorate the Christmas tree
addobbarsi *v/r* ⟨1c⟩ *hum* get dolled up
addobbo *m* decoration
addolcire *v/t* ⟨4d⟩ sweeten; *fig* soften
addolcirsi *v/r* ⟨4d⟩ *clima*, *tempo* become milder; *fig* soften
addolorare *v/t* ⟨1a⟩ grieve
addolorarsi *v/r* ⟨1a⟩ grieve (***per*** for)
addolorato *adj* sad; ***essere ~ per qc*** be sad about sth
addome *m* abdomen
addomesticare *v/t* ⟨1b, d & n⟩ tame; ***~ un bilancio*** fiddle a balance sheet
addomesticato *adj* tame; *fig* fiddled
addominale *adj* abdominal
addormentare *v/t* ⟨1b⟩ get (off) to sleep
addormentarsi *v/r* ⟨1b⟩ fall asleep; ~

su un lavoro fall asleep on the job; ***mi si è addormentato un braccio*** my arm's gone to sleep *infml*
addormentato *adj* asleep; (*assonnato*) sleepy; ***cadere ~*** fall asleep; ***la Bella Addormentata*** Sleeping Beauty; *fig* ***uno scolaro ~*** a dozy student
addossare *v/t* ⟨1c⟩ (*appoggiare*) lean (***a*** on); *fig colpa* put, lay (***a*** on); ***~ le sedie al muro*** put the chairs against the wall
addossarsi *v/r* ⟨1c⟩ lean (***a*** on); *fig* shoulder; ***si è addossato tutte le responsabilità*** he shouldered all the responsibility
addosso I *prep* on; *vicino* next to; ***andare ~ a qn / qc*** crash into s.o. / sth; *fig* ***dare ~ a qn*** attack s.o.; *fig* ***mettere gli occhi ~ a qn / qc*** take a fancy to s.o. / sth; *fig* ***stare ~ a qn*** be on s.o.'s back **II** *adv*: ***avere ~*** *vestiti* have on; ***avere ~ qn*** have s.o. breathing down one's neck; ***avere ~ grandi responsabilità*** have a lot of responsibilities; ***avere molti anni ~*** be old; ***farsela ~*** wet o.s. *infml*; ***non mi mettere le mani ~!*** don't you dare touch me!
addurre *v/t* ⟨3e⟩ produce; ***~ una prova per qc*** produce evidence of sth
adduttore *m* TECH duct; ANAT adductor
adeguare *v/t* ⟨1a⟩ adjust
adeguarsi *v/r* ⟨1a⟩ conform; ***~ alle circostanze*** adjust to circumstances
adeguato *adj* adequate
adempiere *v/i* ⟨4d & g⟩: ***~ a*** *dovere* carry out, do
adempiersi *v/r* ⟨4d & g⟩ come true; ***la profezia si è adempiuta*** the prophecy came true **adempimento** *m* fulfilment
adenoidi *fpl* adenoids *pl*
adenoma *m* ⟨*pl* -i⟩ adenoma
aderente I *adj vestito* tight; ***~ alla realtà*** true to life **II** *m/f* follower; ***quel partito ha pochi -i*** that party doesn't have many supporters
aderire *v/i* ⟨4d⟩: ***~ a*** adhere to; *partito* support; *richiesta* agree to
adescamento *m* flattery; JUR soliciting
adescatore I *adj* enticing **II** *m*, **-trice** *f* seducer *woman* seductress
adesione *f* adhesion; (*consenso*) agreement; ***forza f di ~*** PHYS adhesion
adesività *f* ⟨*pl* adesività⟩ adhesiveness
adesivo I *adj* adhesive; ***nastro*** *m* ***~*** sticky tape **II** *m* sticker
adesso *adv* now; ***~ basta!*** that's enough!; ***~ che ...*** now that; ***da ~ in poi*** from now on; ***fino ~*** up to now; ***per ~*** for the moment; ***solo ~*** only now
ad hoc *adv* ad hoc; ***soluzione*** *f* ***~*** ad hoc solution
adiacente *adj* adjacent; ***~ a*** next to, adjacent to; ***essere ~ a qc*** be adjacent to sth
adiacenze *fpl* vicinity; ***nelle ~*** in the vicinity
adibire *v/t* ⟨4d⟩ use; ***~ qc a qc*** equip sth as sth
Adige *m* Adige; ***Alto ~*** Alto Adige
adipe *m* fat **adiposità** *f* ⟨*pl* adiposità⟩ adiposity **adiposo** *adj* adipose; ***tessuto*** *m* ***~*** adipose tissue
adirarsi *v/r* ⟨1a⟩ get angry; ***~ per qc*** get angry about sth
adirato *adj* angry; ***essere ~ con qn*** be angry with s.o.
adire *v/t* ⟨4d⟩: ***~ le vie legali*** commence legal proceedings
adito *m*: ***dare ~ a qc*** lead to sth
adocchiare *v/t* ⟨1k⟩ (*scorgere*) catch sight of; (*guardare con desiderio*) have one's eye on
adolescente *m/f* adolescent, teenager
adolescenza *f* adolescence, teens *pl infml*
adolescenziale *adj* adolescent; ***è in piena crisi ~*** he / she's having a teenage crisis
adone *m* Adonis; ***crede di essere un ~*** he thinks he's so hot *infml*
adoperabile *adj* usable
adoperare *v/t* ⟨1m & c⟩ use; ***adopera il cervello!*** use your head!
adoperarsi *v/r* ⟨1m & c⟩ go to a lot of bother (***per qc*** for sth)
adorabile *adj* adorable
adorare *v/t* ⟨1a⟩ adore
adorazione *f* adoration
adornare *v/t* ⟨1a⟩ adorn; ***~ di*** *or* ***con qc*** adorn with sth
adornarsi *v/r* ⟨1a⟩ adorn oneself
adorno *adj* adorned (***di*** with)
adottabile *adj* adoptable **adottabilità** *f* ⟨*pl* adottabilità⟩ adoptability
adottare *v/t* ⟨1c⟩ adopt *fig* ***~ un albero*** adopt a tree, *scheme whereby people living in cities 'adopt' a fruit tree and*

receive the fruit it produces; ~ ***misure contro qn / qc*** take steps against s.o. / sth
adottivo *adj genitori* adoptive; *figlio* adopted
adozione *f* adoption; ~ ***a distanza*** child sponsorship; ***patria*** *f* ***di*** ~ country of adoption
adrenalina *f* adrenalin
adriatico ⟨*mpl* -ci⟩ **I** *adj* Adriatic; ***mare*** *m* ***Adriatico*** Adriatic Sea **II** *m*: ***Adriatico*** Adriatic
ADSL *f abbr* (= **Asymmetric Digital Subscriber Line**) TEL ADSL
adulare *v/t* ⟨1a⟩ flatter
adulatore *m*, **-trice** *f* **I** *adj* flattering **II** *m*, **-trice** *f* flatterer
adulazione *f* flattery
adulterare *v/t* ⟨1m⟩ adulterate
adulterato *adj* adulterated **adulterazione** *f* adulteration
adulterino *adj relazione* adulterous; ***figlio*** ~ child of an adulterous relationship
adulterio *m* ⟨*pl* -ri⟩ adultery
adulto **I** *adj* adult; ***è una persona -a*** he's / she's a grown-up **II** *m*, **-a** *f* adult
adunare *v/t* ⟨1a⟩ assemble **adunarsi** *v/r* ⟨1a⟩ gather (together) **adunata** *f* MIL muster; (*convegno*) rally; ***luogo*** *m* ***di*** ~ meeting place
adunco *adj*: ***naso*** *m* ~ hooked nose
advisor *m* ⟨*pl* advisor⟩ ECON advisor
AEM *f abbr* (= **Azienda Energetica Municipale**) *municipal energy company*
aerare *v/t* ⟨1l⟩ air
aerato *adj* ventilated
aeratore *m* ventilator
aerazione *f* airing; ***impianto*** *m* ***di*** ~ ventilator
aereo **I** *m* plane; ~ ***da turismo*** light aircraft; ~ ***di linea*** airliner; ***ci vado in*** ~ I'm flying **II** *adj* air *attr*; *fotografia*, *radici* aerial; ***base*** *f* ***-a*** air base; ***compagnia*** *f* ***-a*** airline; ***ponte*** *m* ~ airlift; ***posta*** *f* ***-a*** airmail; ***spazio*** *m* ~ airspace
aerobica *f* aerobics *sg*
aerobico *adj* ⟨*mpl* -ci⟩ aerobic; ***ginnastica*** *f* ***-a*** aerobics *sg*
aerobus *m* ⟨*pl* aerobus⟩ *plane that makes short-haul flights*
aeroclub *m* ⟨*pl* aeroclub⟩ flying club
aerodinamica *f* ⟨*pl* -che⟩ aerodynamics *sg* **aerodinamicità** *f* ⟨*pl* aerodinamicità⟩ aerodynamic properties
aerodinamico *adj* aerodynamic; ***galleria*** *f* ***-a*** wind tunnel
aerodromo *m* aerodrome
aerofagia *f* MED aerophagia
aerofotografia *f* aerial photography
aerografo *m* airbrush
aerolinea *f* airline
aeromobile *m* aircraft
aeromodellismo *m* model-aircraft making
aeromodello *m* model aircraft
aeronautica *f* aeronautics *sg*; ~ ***militare*** Air Force
aeroplano *m* plane, aeroplane, *US* airplane
aeroporto *m* airport; ~ ***civile / militare*** civil / military airport
aeroportuale **I** *adj* airport *attr* **II** *n*: ***-i*** *mpl* airport workers
aeroscalo *m* airstrip
aerosol *m* ⟨*no pl*⟩ *contenitore* aerosol
aerospaziale *adj* aerospace *attr*; ***centro*** *m* ~ space centre
aerostatica *f* ⟨*pl* -che⟩ aerostatics
aerostatico *adj* ⟨*mpl* -ci⟩ aerostatic; ***pallone*** *m* ~ (hot air) balloon
aerostato *m* aerostat, lighter-than-air aircraft
aerostazione *f* air terminal
aerotaxi *m* ⟨*pl* aerotaxi⟩ air taxi
afa *f* closeness, mugginess; ***c'è*** ~ ***oggi*** it's muggy today
afasia *f* MED aphasia **afasico** *adj* ⟨*mpl* -ci⟩ aphasic
affabile *adj* affable
affabilità *f* ⟨*pl* affabilità⟩ affability; *di modi*: pleasantness
affabulatore *m*, **-trice** *f* storyteller
affaccendarsi *v/r* ⟨1b⟩ busy o.s. (***in*** with)
affaccendato *adj* busy
affacciarsi *v/r* ⟨1f⟩ appear; ***affacciati alla finestra!*** lean out of the window!; ~ ***sul giardino*** overlook the garden
affamato *adj* starving
affannare *v/t* ⟨1a⟩ leave breathless; *fig* (*turbare*) worry
affannarsi *v/r* ⟨1a⟩ worry (***per*** about); ***non affannarti per noi!*** don't worry about us!
affannato *adj* breathless; ***arrivò tutto*** ~ he arrived all out of breath

affanno *m* breathlessness; *fig* anxiety; ***essere in ~ per qn/qc*** be worried about s.o./sth
affannoso *adj fig* painful; ***ricerca*** *f* ***-a*** frantic search
affare *m* matter, business; FIN transaction; ***giro*** *m* ***d'-i*** turnover; ***ministro*** *m* ***degli Affari Esteri*** *Foreign Secretary*; ***uomo*** *m* ***d'-i*** businessman; ***concludere/sbrigare/trattare un ~*** conclude/strike/make a deal; ***-i*** *pl* business *sg*; ***come vanno gli -i?*** how's business?; ***entrare in -i con qn*** do business with s.o.; ***fare loschi -i*** be involved in dirty business; ***gli -i sono -i!*** business is business!; ***non sono -i tuoi*** it's none of your business; ***l'~ Dreyfus*** the Dreyfus affair; ***~ fatto!*** it's a deal!; ***bell'~ hai combinato!*** now look what you've done!; ***brutto ~!*** it's a nasty business!; ***cos'è quell'~ lì?*** *infml* what's that contraption?; ***sono -i miei!*** that's my business!
affarista *m/f* ⟨*mpl* -i⟩ wheeler-dealer
affarone *m infml* ***fare un ~*** get a great deal
affascinante *adj* fascinating
affascinare *v/t* ⟨1m⟩ fascinate
affastellare *v/t* ⟨1b⟩ (*legare*) bundle (up); (*ammassare*) pile up (*a. fig*)
affaticamento *m* tiredness
affaticare *v/t* ⟨1d⟩ tire; ***~ gli occhi*** strain one's eyes
affaticarsi *v/r* ⟨1d⟩ tire o.s. out
affaticato *adj* tired
affatto *adv* completely; ***non è ~ vero!*** there's not the slightest bit of truth in it!; ***non è ~ male*** it's not bad at all
affermare *v/t* ⟨1a⟩ state; ***~ il falso*** tell a lie; JUR perjure o.s.
affermarsi *v/r* ⟨1a⟩ become established; ***~ in una gara*** be successful in a competition
affermativo I *adj* affirmative **II** *adv*: ***~!*** RADIO roger!
affermato *adj* successful
affermazione *f* assertion; (*successo*) achievement
afferrabile *adj* (*comprensibile*) comprehensible
afferrare *v/t* ⟨1b⟩ seize, grab *infml*; (*comprendere*) grasp; ***~ qn per il braccio*** grab s.o. by the arm
afferrarsi *v/r* ⟨1b⟩ cling (***a*** to), hold on (***a*** to)
affettare[1] *v/t* ⟨1a⟩ (*tagliare*) slice
affettare[2] *v/t* ⟨1b⟩ *ammirazione etc* affect
affettato[1] *m* sliced meat
affettato[2] *adj* affected
affettatrice *f* slicer
affettazione *f* affectation
affettività *f* ⟨*pl* affettività⟩ PSYCH affect **affettivo** *adj* emotional; ***carenza*** *f* ***-a*** lack of affection
affetto I *m* affection; ***con ~*** affectionately; *nelle lettere*: love from **II** *adj*: ***~ da qc*** suffering from sth; ***essere ~ da anemia*** be anaemic
affettuosamente *adv* affectionately
affettuoso *adj* affectionate
affezionarsi *v/r* ⟨1a⟩: ***~ a qn*** become fond of s.o.
affezionato *adj*: ***~ a qn*** fond of s.o.; ***cliente*** *m* ***~*** regular customer
affezione *f* (*attaccamento*) affection; (*malattia*) disorder
affiancare *v/t* ⟨1d⟩ place side by side; *fig* support
affiancarsi *v/r* ⟨1d⟩ stand beside; ***~ a qn*** stand beside s.o.
affiancato *adj* side by side; ***~ a qn/qc*** next to s.o./sth
affiatamento *m* (*intesa*) understanding; *nel gioco*: team spirit **affiatare** *v/t* ⟨1a⟩ help to mesh **affiatarsi** *v/r* ⟨1a⟩ start to mesh
affiatato *adj*: ***sono molto -i*** they work well together; ***una coppia*** *f* ***-a*** a couple who are very close
affibbiare *v/t* ⟨1k⟩: ***~ qc a qn*** saddle s.o. with sth; ***~ uno schiaffo a qn*** give s.o. a slap
affidabile *adj* reliable
affidabilità *f* dependability
affidamento *m* trust; ***fare ~ su*** rely on; ***non dare nessun ~*** inspire no confidence; ***avere un bambino in ~*** foster a child
affidare *v/t* ⟨1a⟩ entrust; ***~ qc a qn*** *incarico* entrust sth to s.o.; *cane* leave sth in s.o.'s care; ***~ alla sorte*** leave to chance
affidarsi *v/r*: ***~ a*** rely on
affievolimento *m* weakening **affievolire** *v/t* ⟨4d⟩ weaken **affievolirsi** *v/r* ⟨4d⟩ get weaker (*a. fig*); *suono, speranza* fade
affiggere *v/t* ⟨3mm⟩ *avviso* put up
affilare *v/t* ⟨1a⟩ sharpen; *fig* make

thinner; ~ ***un coltello*** sharpen a knife
affilato *adj* sharp; *naso* thin; ~ ***come un rasoio*** razor-sharp (*a. fig*)
affilatrice *f* sharpener
affiliare *v/t* ⟨1g⟩ *a una società* affiliate
affiliato **I** *m*, **-a** *f* member **II** *adj*: ***società*** *f* ***-a*** affiliate
affiliazione *f* affiliation
affinare *v/t* ⟨1a⟩ sharpen: *stile* refine
affinarsi *v/r* ⟨1a⟩ *fig* become refined
affinché *cj* so that
affine *adj* similar; ***casi*** *pl* ***-i*** similar cases; ***lingue*** *fpl* ***-i*** cognate languages
affinità *f* ⟨*pl* affinità⟩ affinity
affiorare *v/i* ⟨1a⟩ *dall'acqua* emerge; *fig* (*mostrarsi*) appear; ~ ***dal mare*** emerge from the sea; ***un sorriso affiorò sul suo volto*** a smile appeared on his / her face
affissione *f* bill-posting; ***divieto*** *m* ***d'~*** stick no bills
affisso **I** *past part* → ***affiggere*** **II** *m* bill
affittabile *adj* rentable
affittacamere *m/f* ⟨*pl* affittacamere⟩ landlord; *donna* landlady
affittare *v/t* ⟨1a⟩ **1.** *locali, terre* let; ***affittasi*** to let **2.** (*prendere in affitto*) rent
affitto *m* rent; ***casa in*** ~ rented house; ***dare in*** ~ let; ***essere in*** ~ be rented; ***prendere in*** ~ rent; ~ ***d'azienda*** leasing of a business
affittuario *m*, **-a** *f* ⟨*mpl* -ri⟩ tenant; *di terreno*: tenant farmer
affliggere *v/t* ⟨3cc⟩ distress; *di malattia* trouble, plague
affliggersi *v/r* ⟨3cc⟩ grieve; ~ ***per qc*** worry about sth
afflitto *adj* distressed; ***essere*** ~ ***da una malattia*** suffer from an illness
afflizione *f* distress
afflosciare *v/t* ⟨1f⟩ make limp; *fig* weaken **afflosciarsi** *v/r* ⟨1f⟩ (*sgonfiarsi*) go down; *fig* (*accasciarsi*) go limp
affluente *m* tributary
affluenza *f fig* influx; ~ ***alle urne*** turnout
affluire *v/i* ⟨4d⟩ flow; *di persone* pour in
afflusso *m* influx
affogare *v/t & v/i* ⟨1c & e⟩ drown; ~ ***in un bicchier d'acqua*** make a mountain out of a molehill
affogarsi *v/r* ⟨1c & e⟩ drown
affollamento *m* crowd
affollare *v/t* ⟨1c⟩ crowd; ~ ***la sala*** fill the hall
affollarsi *v/r* ⟨1c⟩ crowd; ***la sala si affollò*** the hall filled up; ***i pensieri si affollano nella sua mente*** thoughts crowd his / her mind
affollato *adj* crowded
affondamento *m* sinking
affondare *v/t & v/i* ⟨1a⟩ sink; ~ ***le mani nelle tasche*** thrust one's hands into one's pockets; *fig* ~ ***il coltello nella piaga*** turn the knife in the wound
affossare *v/t* ⟨1c⟩ *fig* (*far fallire*) ditch; (*incavare*) rut
affrancare *v/t* ⟨1d⟩ free; *posta* frank
affrancarsi *v/r* ⟨1d⟩ free o.s. (*a. fig*) **affrancato** *adj* freed; *lettera* franked **affrancatrice** *f* franking machine
affrancatura *f* franking; *tassa di spedizione* postage
affranto *adj* overcome (***da*** with)
affrescare *v/t* ⟨1d⟩ paint with frescos
affresco *m* ⟨*pl* -chi⟩ fresco
affrettare *v/i* ⟨1a⟩ speed up
affrettarsi *v/r* ⟨1a⟩ hurry
affrontare *v/t* ⟨1a⟩ face, confront; *spese* meet
affrontarsi *v/r* ⟨1a⟩ face each other (*a.* SPORTS)
affronto *m* insult; ***fare un*** ~ ***a qn*** insult s.o.
affumicare *v/t* ⟨1d & m⟩ *stanza* fill with smoke; *alimenti* smoke
affumicato *adj* smoked; ***lenti*** *fpl* ***-e*** tinted lenses
affusolato *adj* tapering
Afghanistan *m* Afghanistan
afg(h)ano **I** *adj* Afghan **II** *m*, **-a** *f* Afghan
afonia *f* aphonia **afono** *adj* voiceless
aforisma *m* ⟨*pl* -i⟩ aphorism
afoso *adj* sultry
Africa *f* Africa
africano **I** *adj* African **II** *m*, **-a** *f* African
afroamericano **I** *adj* African-american **II** *m*, **-a** *f* African-american
afrocubano **I** *adj* Afro-Cuban **II** *m*, **-a** *f* Afro-Cuban
afrodisiaco *m/adj* aphrodisiac
AG *abbr* (= **Agrigento**) Agrigento
agave *f* agave
agenda *f* diary; ~ ***elettronica*** electronic organizer

agendina *f* pocket diary
agente *m/f* agent; ***~ di cambio*** stockbroker; ***~ immobiliare*** estate agent, *US* realtor; ***~ inquinante*** pollutant; ***~ di pubblica sicurezza*** police officer; ***~ di vendita*** sales representative; ***~ di viaggio*** travel agent; ***~ segreto*** secret agent; ***gli -i*** *pl* ***atmosferici*** atmospheric agents
agenzia *f* agency; ***~ di cambio*** bureau de change; ***~ immobiliare*** estate agency, *US* real estate office; ***~ pubblicitaria*** advertising agency; ***~ di stampa*** press agency; ***~ di viaggi*** travel agency; ***~ matrimoniale*** marriage bureau; ***Agenzia delle Entrate*** Inland Revenue
agevolare *v/t* ⟨1m⟩ make easier
agevolato *adj* FIN on easy terms
agevolazione *f* FIN special term; ***-i*** *pl* ***fiscali*** tax relief *sg*
agevole *adj* easy
agevolezza *f* ease **agevolmente** *adv* easily
agganciare *v/t* ⟨1f⟩ hook; *cintura, collana* fasten
agganciarsi *v/r* ⟨1f⟩ fasten **aggancio** *m* ⟨*pl* -ci⟩ MECH coupling; *fig* (*appiglio*) contact
aggeggio *m* ⟨*pl* -ggi⟩ gadget
aggettivo *m* adjective
agghiacciante *adj* spine-chilling
agghiacciare *v/t* ⟨1f⟩ *fig* chill
agghindare *v/t* ⟨1a⟩ dress up (*a. fig*) **agghindarsi** *v/r* ⟨1a⟩ dress up
aggio *m* ⟨*pl* aggi⟩ premium
aggiogare *v/t* ⟨1e⟩ yoke; *fig* subjugate
aggiornamento *m* updating; (*rinvio*) postponement; ***corso*** *m* ***d'~*** refresher course
aggiornare *v/t* ⟨1a⟩ (*mettere al corrente*) update; (*rinviare*) postpone
aggiornarsi *v/r* ⟨1a⟩ keep up to date
aggiornato *adj* updated; (*bene informato*) up-to-date; ***edizione*** *f* ***-a*** TYPO revised edition; ***tenere qn ~ su qc*** keep s.o. up to date about sth
aggiotaggio *m* ⟨*pl* -ggi⟩ rigging (of the market); ***~ su strumenti finanziari*** JUR (fraudulent manipulation of financial instruments
aggiramento *m* bypassing (*a. fig*); MIL outflanking
aggirare *v/t* ⟨1a⟩ surround; *fig ostacolo* get round
aggirarsi *v/r* ⟨1a⟩ hang about; FIN be in the region of; ***~ per casa*** wander around the house
aggiudicare *v/t* ⟨1d & m⟩ award; *all'asta* knock down
aggiudicarsi *v/r* ⟨1d & m⟩ win; ***~ un premio*** win a prize **aggiudicazione** *f* award
aggiungere *v/t* ⟨3d⟩ add
aggiungersi *v/r* ⟨3d⟩ join; (*annettersi*) annex; ***si aggiunse alla comitiva*** he / she joined the group
aggiunta *f* addition
aggiunto *adj* added; ***valore*** *m* ***~*** added value
aggiustare *v/t* ⟨1a⟩ (*riparare*) repair; (*sistemare*) settle; *vestiti* mend; ***ora ti aggiusto io!*** you asked for it!
aggiustarsi *v/r* ⟨1a⟩ (*mettersi a posto*) settle; (*adattarsi*) make do; (*mettersi d'accordo*) *infml* agree; ***~ i capelli*** tidy one's hair
agglomerato *m*: ***~ urbano*** built-up area
aggradare *v/i* ⟨1a⟩: ***fa' come meglio ti aggrada*** do as you wish
aggrapparsi *v/r* ⟨1a⟩ cling, hold on (***a*** to); ***~ al braccio di qn / a una speranza*** cling on to s.o.'s arm / a hope
aggravante **I** *adj* aggravating **II** *f* aggravating circumstance
aggravare *v/t* ⟨1a⟩ *punizione* increase; (*peggiorare*) make worse
aggravarsi *v/r* ⟨1a⟩ worsen, deteriorate
aggravio *m* ⟨*pl* -vi⟩: ***~ fiscale*** tax increase
aggraziato *adj* graceful
aggredire *v/t* ⟨4d⟩ attack
aggregare *v/t* ⟨1b & e⟩ bring together; ***~ qn a un gruppo*** let s.o. join a group
aggregarsi *v/r* ⟨1b & e⟩ tag along; ***~ a qn / qc*** join in with s.o. / sth
aggregazione *f di cose, persone* bringing together; CHEM aggregation; ***chiedere l'~ a qc*** apply to join sth; ***centro*** *m* ***di ~*** club (where people can meet)
aggressione *f* aggression; (*attacco*) attack; POL ***patto*** *m* ***di non ~*** non-aggression pact; ***~ a mano armata*** armed assault
aggressività *f* aggressiveness
aggressivo *adj* aggressive
aggressore *m* attacker; POL aggressor
aggrottare *v/t* ⟨1c⟩: ***~ la fronte*** wrinkle

one's brow; **~ *le sopracciglia*** frown
aggrovigliare *v/t* ⟨1g⟩ entangle **aggrovigliarsi** *v/r* ⟨1g⟩ get tangled (up) (*a. fig*); **aggrovigliato** *adj* tangled (*a. fig*)
aggrumarsi *v/r* ⟨1a⟩ clot
agguantare *v/t* ⟨1a⟩ seize
agguato *m* ambush; ***cadere in un ~*** be caught in an ambush; ***stare in ~*** lie in ambush; ***tendere un ~ a qn*** ambush s.o., set an ambush for s.o.
agguerrirsi *v/r* ⟨4d⟩ become hardened; **~ *contro qn*** harden one's heart against s.o.
agguerrito *adj* hardened
aghifoglia *f* ⟨*pl* -glie⟩ conifer **aghiforme** *adj* needle-shaped
agiatezza *f* comfort
agiato *adj* comfortable, well-off; (*comodo*) comfortable
agibile *adj* fit for human habitation
agibilità *f* ⟨*pl* agibilità⟩ *di impianto, edificio*: conformity with safety standards; *di strada*: passability; *a piedi*: passability on foot
agile *adj* agile
agilità *f* agility; *fig* liveliness
agio *m* ⟨*pl* -gi⟩ ease; ***vivere negli agi*** live in comfort; ***sentirsi a proprio ~*** feel at ease; ***mettere qn a proprio ~*** put s.o. at their ease
agire *v/i* ⟨4d⟩ act; *comportarsi* behave, act; *di medicina* take effect; JUR take action (***contro*** against); ***capacità/incapacità f di ~*** ability/inability to act; ***modo m di ~*** way of behaving
agitare *v/t* ⟨1l⟩ shake; *fazzoletto* wave; *fig* (*turbare*) upset, agitate; ***~ prima dell'uso*** shake before use
agitarsi *v/r* ⟨1l⟩ *mare* get rough; (*preoccuparsi*) worry (***per*** about); ***~ nel letto*** toss and turn (in one's sleep)
agitato *adj* agitated; *mare* rough
agitatore *m*, **-trice** *f* POL agitator
agitazione *f* agitation
agli = *prep* ***a*** *and art* ***gli***
aglianico *m* ⟨*pl* -ci⟩ COOK *dry red wine from the south of Italy*
aglio *m* ⟨*pl* -gli⟩ garlic; ***spicchio m d'~*** clove of garlic; ***testa f d'~*** bulb of garlic
agnello *m* lamb; ***costine fpl di ~*** COOK lamb chops
agnolotti *mpl type of ravioli*
agnostico ⟨*mpl* -ci⟩ **I** *adj* agnostic **II** *m*, **-a** *f* agnostic
ago *m* ⟨*pl* -ghi⟩ needle; ***~ magnetico*** magnetic needle; ***infilare un ~*** thread a needle; *fig* ***cercare un ~ in un pagliaio*** search for a needle in a haystack
agognare *v/t and v/i* ⟨1a⟩ yearn for
agone *m* ZOOL shad
agonia *f* agony
agonismo *m* competitiveness
agonistico *adj* ⟨*mpl* -ci⟩ competitive; ***spirito m ~*** competitive spirit; ***sport m ~*** competitive sport
agonizzante *adj* dying **agonizzare** *v/i* ⟨1a⟩ be dying; *fig* be in decline
agopuntura *f* acupuncture
agorafobia *f* agoraphobia
Agostino *m*: ***Sant'~*** Saint Augustine
agosto *m* August; ***in ~*** in August
agraria *f* agriculture
agrario *adj* ⟨*mpl* -ri⟩ agricultural; *riforma* agrarian
agreste *adj* rural
agrezza *f* sourness
agricolo *adj* agricultural
agricoltore *m*, **-trice** *f* farmer
agricoltura *f* agriculture
agrifoglio *m* holly
agrigentino I *adj* of Agrigento *persona* from Agrigento **II** *m*, **-a** *f* person from Agrigento
agrimensore *m* surveyor **agrimensura** *f* surveying
agriturismo *m* farm holidays *pl*; (*edificio*) dude ranch
agro *adj* sour; ***verdure fpl all'~*** vegetables with lemon or vinegar
agrodolce *adj* bittersweet; COOK sweet and sour
agronomo *m*, **-a** *f* agronomist
agrumeto *m* citrus grove
agrumi *mpl* citrus fruit *sg*
aguzzare *v/t* ⟨1a⟩ sharpen; *fig* ***~ l'ingegno*** sharpen one's wits; *fig* ***~ le orecchie*** prick up one's ears; ***~ la vista*** keep one's eyes peeled
aguzzo *adj* pointed; ***vista f -a*** sharp sight
ah! *int* oh!
ahi! *int* ouch!
ai = *prep* ***a*** *and art* ***i***
aia *f* farmyard
Aids *m or f* Aids
AIG *abbr* (= **Associazione Italiana alberghi per la Gioventù**) *Youth*

Hostel Association
airbag *m* ⟨*pl* airbag⟩ airbag
aire *m*: ***dare l'~ a qc*** set sth off
A.I.R.E. *abbr* (= **Anagrafe degli Italiani Residenti all'Estero**) *register of Italian citizens resident overseas*
airone *m* heron
aitante *adj* robust
aiuola *f* flower bed
aiutante *m/f* assistant
aiutare *v/t* ⟨1a⟩ help; ***~ qn a fare qc*** help s.o. (to) do sth
aiutarsi *v/r* ⟨1a⟩ help o.s.; ***aiutatevi a vicenda*** help each other
aiuto *m* help, assistance; *persona* assistant; ***~ cuoco*** assistant cook; ***~ allo sviluppo*** development aid *or* assistance; ***chiedere ~ a qn*** ask s.o. for help; ***essere di ~ a qn*** be of assistance to s.o.; ***gridare ~*** call for help
aizzare *v/t* ⟨1a⟩ incite; ***~ i cani contro qn*** set the dogs on s.o.
al = *prep* ***a*** *and art* ***il***
ala *f* ⟨*pl* -i⟩ wing; ***~ destra*** right wing
alabarda *f* halberd
alabastro *m* alabaster
alacre *adj* eager; *fig* (*vivace*) lively **alacrità** *f* ⟨*pl* alacrità⟩ eagerness; *fig* (*vivacità*) liveliness
alambicco *m* ⟨*pl* -cchi⟩ still
alano *m* Great Dane
alare *adj* wing *attr*; ***apertura*** *f* ***~*** wingspan
Alaska *f* Alaska
alato *adj* winged; *fig* sublime; ***parole*** *fpl* ***-e*** sublime words
alba *f* dawn; ***all'~*** at dawn
albanese *m/f & adj* Albanian
Albania *f* Albania
albeggiare *v/i* ⟨1f⟩ dawn
alberato *adj* tree-lined
albergare *v/t* ⟨1b & e⟩ put up
albergatore *m*, **-trice** *f* hotel keeper
alberghiero *adj* hotel *attr*
albergo *m* ⟨*pl* -ghi⟩ hotel; ***guida*** *f* ***degli -ghi*** hotel guide; ***~ della gioventù*** youth hostel; ***~ a quattro stelle*** four-star hotel
albero *m* **1.** tree; ***~ genealogico*** family tree; ***~ di Natale*** Christmas tree **2.** NAUT mast; AVIAT, AUTO shaft; NAUT ***~ maestro*** mainmast; ***~ motore*** drive shaft
albicocca *f* ⟨*pl* -cche⟩ apricot
albicocco *m* ⟨*pl* -cchi⟩ apricot (tree)
albinismo *m* albinism **albino I** *adj* albino **II** *m*, **-a** *f* albino
albo *m* notice board; (*registro*) register; ***radiare dall'~*** strike off
albori *mpl*: dawn *sg*; ***gli ~ della civiltà*** the dawn of civilization
album *m* ⟨*pl* album⟩ album; ***~ da disegno*** sketch pad; ***~ di fotografie*** photo album
albume *m* albumen
albumina *f* albumin
alcalino *adj* alkaline
alcaloide *m* alkaloid
alce *m* moose
alchimia *f* alchemy **alchimista** *m/f* ⟨*mpl* -i⟩ alchemist **alchimistico** *adj* ⟨*mpl* -ci⟩ alchemistic
alcol *m* ⟨*no pl*⟩ alcohol; ***darsi all'~*** take to drink; ***~ denaturato*** meths *infml*
alcolemia *f* level of alcohol in the blood **alcolicità** *f* ⟨*pl* alcolicità⟩ alcohol content
alcolico ⟨*mpl* -ci⟩ **I** *adj* alcoholic; ***poco ~*** low-alcohol; ***gradazione*** *f* ***-a*** alcohol content **II** *m* alcoholic drink
alcolismo *m* alcoholism
alcolista *m/f* ⟨*mpl* -i⟩: ***Alcolisti Anonimi*** Alcoholics Anonymous
alcolizzato *m*, **-a** *f* alcoholic
alcoltest *m* ⟨*pl* alcoltest⟩ Breathalyzer®
alcova *f* alcove
alcuno I *adj*: ***non c'è alcun pericolo*** there's no danger; ***-i giorni fa*** a few days ago; ***-e persone*** a few people **II** *pron* any; ***-i*** *pl* some, a few; ***non ce n'era ~*** there was no one there; ***-i sono miei*** some of them are mine; ***-i di noi*** some of us
aldilà *m*: ***l'~*** the next world, the hereafter
aleatorio *adj* ⟨*mpl* -ri⟩ uncertain
aleggiare *v/i* ⟨1f⟩ flutter; *fig* be in the air
alessandrino I *adj* of Alexandria; *persona* from Alexandria **II** *m*, **-a** *f* person from Alexandria
aletta *f* fin; AVIAT flap; *di uccelli*: winglet; ***-e*** *pl* ***di raffreddamento*** cooling fin **alettone** *m* AVIAT aileron; AUTO spoiler
alfa I *m/f* ⟨*pl* alfa⟩ alpha; ***dall'~ all'omega*** from A to Z **II** *adj inv* alpha; ***raggi*** *mpl* ***~*** alpha rays

alfabetico *adj* ⟨*mpl* -ci⟩ alphabetical
alfabeto *m* alphabet
alfanumerico *adj* ⟨*mpl* -ci⟩ COMPUT alphanumeric
alfiere *m scacchi* bishop
alfine *adv* eventually
alga *f* ⟨*pl* -ghe⟩ seaweed
algebra *f* algebra
algebrico *adj* ⟨*mpl* -ci⟩ algebraic
Algeri *f* Algiers
Algeria *f* Algeria
algerino I *adj* Algerian **II** *m*, **-a** *f* Algerian
algol *m* COMPUT ALGOL
algoritmo *m* MATH algorithm
aliante *m* glider
alias *adv* alias
alibi *m* ⟨*pl* alibi⟩ alibi
alice *f* anchovy
alienabile *adj* JUR alienable
alienare *v/t* ⟨1b⟩ JUR transfer; *persone* alienate
alienarsi *v/r* ⟨1b⟩ become alienated; **~ *le simpatie della gente*** alienate people
alienato I *adj* alienated **II** *m*, **-a** *f* madman; *donna* madwoman
alienazione *f* alienation; **~ *mentale*** madness
alimentare ⟨1a⟩ **I** *v/t* feed; **~ *l'odio di qn*** fuel s.o.'s hatred **II** *adj* food *attr*; ***catena*** *f* **~** food chain; ***generi*** *mpl* **-*i*** foodstuffs; ***regime*** *m* **~** diet
alimentarsi *v/r* ⟨1a⟩ eat
alimentatore *m* ELEC power pack
alimentazione *f* feeding; **~ *artificiale*** artificial feeding; **~ *forzata*** force-feeding; ***scienza*** *f* ***dell'*~** dietetics
alimento *m* food; **~ *base*** basic food (-stuff); **-*i*** *pl* JUR alimony *sg*
aliquota *f* share; MATH aliquot; **~ *d'imposta*** rate of taxation
aliscafo *m* hydrofoil
aliseo *m*: ***venti*** *mpl* **-*i*** trade winds
ALITALIA *f* Italian air line
alitare *v/i* ⟨1l⟩ breathe; LIT blow (softly)
alito *m* breath; **~ *di vento*** breath of wind
all. *abbr* (= **allegato**) enc(l) (enclosed)
all', alla = *prep* ***a*** *and art* ***l', la***
allacciamento *m* TECH connection; **~ *dell'acqua*** water connection; **~ *alla rete elettrica*** connection to the mains
allacciare *v/t* ⟨1f⟩ fasten; TECH connect; **~ *le cinture di sicurezza*** fasten one's seatbelts; **~ *la corrente*** connect the electricity; *fig* **~ *relazioni*** establish a relationship
allacciarsi *v/r* ⟨1f⟩ fasten
allagamento *m* flooding
allagare *v/t* ⟨1e⟩ flood
allagarsi *v/r* ⟨1e⟩ flood
allampanato *adj* lanky
allargamento *m* widening; *fig* enlargement
allargare *v/t* ⟨1e⟩ widen; *vestito* let out; *braccia* open
allargarsi *v/r* ⟨1e⟩ widen; *fig* ***mi si allarga il cuore!*** I'm so happy!; *fig* ***non ti allargare troppo!*** *infml* don't push it!
allarmante *adj* frightening; ***notizie*** *fpl* **-*i*** worrying news
allarmare *v/t* ⟨1a⟩ alarm
allarmarsi *v/r* ⟨1a⟩ become alarmed
allarme *m* alarm; **~ *antincendio*** fire alarm; ***falso*** **~** false alarm; **~ *smog*** smog alert; ***dare l'*~** raise the alarm; ***essere in stato d'*~** be in a state of alarm; ***mettere qn in*** **~** alarm s.o.
allarmismo *m* alarmism
allattamento *m* breastfeeding; *di animali*: suckling; **~ *artificiale*** bottle-feeding
allattare *v/t* ⟨1a⟩ *bambino* feed
alle = *prep* ***a*** *and art* ***le***
alleanza *f* alliance; **~ *con*** (*or* ***a***) ***qn*** / ***contro qn*** alliance with s.o. / against s.o.; ***stringere un'*~** form an alliance
allearsi *v/r* ⟨1b⟩ ally o.s.
alleato I *adj* allied **II** *m*, **-a** *f* ally
allegare *v/t* ⟨1e⟩ *documento* enclose, inclose
allegato *m* enclosure; COMPUT attachment; ***qui*** **~** enclosed
alleggerimento *m* lightening (*a. fig*)
alleggerire *v/t* ⟨4d⟩ lighten; *fig dolore* ease; **~ *qn del portafoglio*** *hum* pinch s.o.'s wallet
alleggerirsi *v/r* ⟨4d⟩ get lighter; **~ *la coscienza*** ease one's conscience
allegorico *adj* ⟨*mpl* -ci⟩ allegorical
allegria *f* cheerfulness
allegro I *adj* cheerful; *colore* bright **II** *m* MUS allegro
allenamento *m* training; ***essere fuori*** **~** be out of shape
allenare *v/t* ⟨1b⟩ train

allenarsi *v/r* ⟨1b⟩ train (***per*** for; ***a*** in)
allenatore *m*, **-trice** *f* trainer
allentamento *m* loosening; *fig* slackening; ***l'~ della tensione*** easing of tension
allentare ⟨1b⟩ **I** *v/t* loosen; *fig disciplina, sorveglianza* relax **II** *v/i* loosen
allentarsi *v/r* ⟨1b⟩ loosen
allentato *adj* loose; ***bottone*** *m* **~** undone button
allergenico *adj* ⟨*mpl* -ci⟩ allergenic
allergia *f* allergy
allergico *adj* ⟨*mpl* -ci⟩ allergic (***a*** to); ***~ alla polvere*** allergic to dust
allerta, all'erta *int*: ***stare ~*** be on the alert
allestimento *m* preparation; NAUT fitting out; THEAT ***~ scenico*** sets *pl*, scenery; ***in ~*** in preparation
allestire *v/t* ⟨4d⟩ prepare; NAUT fit out; THEAT stage; ***~ una vetrina*** dress a window
allettante *adj* attractive
allettare *v/t* ⟨1b⟩ attract; ***~ l'idea mi alletta*** the idea appeals to me
allevamento *m* BOT, ZOOL breeding; ***~ di bestiame*** stock breeding; ***pollo d'~*** battery hen
allevare *v/t* ⟨1b⟩ BOT, ZOOL breed; *bambini* bring up, raise
allevatore *m*, **-trice** *f* breeder
alleviamento *m* alleviation
alleviare *v/t* ⟨1b & k⟩ alleviate
allibire *v/i* ⟨4d⟩ be astounded
allibito *adj* astounded; ***rimanere ~*** be flabbergasted
allibratore *m*, **-trice** *f* bookmaker
allietare *v/t* ⟨1b⟩ delight
allievo *m*, **-a** *f* pupil, student
alligatore *m* alligator
allineamento *m* alignment
allineare *v/t* ⟨1m⟩ line up; FIN adjust; TYPO align
allinearsi *v/r* ⟨1m⟩ line up; *fig* ***~ con qn*** align o.s. with s.o.
allineato *adj* POL aligned (***a*** with)
allitterazione *f* alliteration
allo = *prep* ***a*** *and art* ***lo***
allocco ⟨*pl* -cchi⟩ **I** *m* ZOOL tawny owl **II** *m*, **-a** *f fig* fool
allodola *f* skylark
alloggiare ⟨1f & c⟩ **I** *v/t* put up; MIL billet **II** *v/i* stay, put up
alloggio *m* ⟨*pl* -ggi⟩ accommodation; ***dare ~ a qn*** put s.o. up; ***vitto e ~*** bed and board
allontanamento *m* removal; *fig* estrangement
allontanare *v/t* ⟨1a⟩ take away; *fig pericolo, sospetto* avert
allontanarsi *v/r* ⟨1a⟩ go away; *fig* grow apart; ***~ da casa*** leave home; ***non ti allontanare troppo!*** don't go too far!
allora **I** *adv* then; ***da ~*** since then; ***~? qual è il problema?*** so? what's the problem?; ***e ~?*** *e con ciò?* so what? **II** *cj* then; ***d'~ in poi*** from then on; ***fin d'~*** since then
allorché *cj* when
alloro *m* laurel; COOK bay; ***dormire sugli -i*** rest on one's laurels
alluce *m* big toe
allucinante *adj infml* incredible, mind-blowing *infml*
allucinato **I** *adj* shell-shocked **II** *m*, **-a** *f* person suffering from hallucinations
allucinazione *f* hallucination; ***avere -i*** hallucinate
allucinogeno **I** *adj* hallucinogenic **II** *n*: ***allucinogeno*** *m* hallucinogen
alludere *v/i* ⟨3q⟩ allude (***a*** to); ***~ a qn/qc*** allude to s.o./sth
alluminio *m* aluminium, *US* aluminum
allunaggio *m* ⟨*pl* -ggi⟩ moon landing
allunare *v/i* ⟨1a⟩ land on the moon
allungabile *adj* extendable; ***tavolo*** *m* **~** extendable table
allungamento *m* lengthening
allungare *v/t* ⟨1e⟩ **1.** lengthen **2.** (*diluire*) dilute **3.** *mano* stretch out, put out; *fig* ***~ le mani su qc*** get/lay one's hands on sth; ***~ le mani su qn*** (*con intenzioni violente*): raise one's hand to s.o.; *fig* ***~ le orecchie*** prick up one's ears **4.** ***~ il passo*** quicken one's step; ***~ la strada*** go the long way round **5.** ***allungami il pane*** pass me the bread, please; ***mi allunghi il telecomando?*** *infml* can you pass me the remote?; ***~ una sberla a qn*** *infml* slap s.o.
allungarsi *v/r* ⟨1e⟩ *di giorni* get longer; *di persona* stretch out, lie down
allupato *adj infml affamato* ravenous; *bramoso* randy
allusione *f* allusion; ***parlare per -i*** talk in riddles
allusivo *adj* allusive

alluvionale *adj* alluvial; ***terreno*** *m* **~** alluvial land **alluvionato I** *adj* flooded **II** *m*, **-a** *f* flood victim
alluvione *f* flood
almanaccare *v/i* ⟨1d⟩ rack one's brains
almanacco *m* ⟨*pl* -cchi⟩ almanac
almeno *adv* at least; **(*se*) ~** if only
alogena *f* halogen
alone *m* ASTR halo; *su tessuto* circle; ***è rimasto l'~*** it's left a mark
alpaca *m* ⟨*pl* alpaca⟩ alpaca
alpestre *adj delle Alpi* alpine; *delle montagne* mountainous
Alpi *fpl* Alps *pl*
alpinismo *m* mountaineering
alpinista *m/f* ⟨*mpl* -i⟩ mountain climber
alpino *adj* Alpine
alquanto I *adj* some **II** *adv* a little, somewhat
alt *int* stop; ***intimare l'~*** (***a qn***) order (s.o.) to stop
altalena *f* swing; ***l'~ della vita*** the ups and downs of life
altalenante *adj fig* up and down
altamente *adv* highly
altana *f* rooftop loggia
altare *m* altar
altarino *m* small altar; ***scoprire gli -i di qn*** *hum* discover s.o.'s guilty secrets
altea *f pianta* marshmallow
alterabile *adj* (*deteriorabile*) unstable; *fig* irritable
alterare *v/t* ⟨1l⟩ alter; **~ *la voce*** disguise one's voice; **~ *i fatti*** distort the facts
alterarsi *v/r* (*guastarsi*) go bad *or* off; (*irritarsi*) get angry
alterato *adj* altered; (*guastato*) spoiled; *persona* irritated
alterazione *f* alteration
alterco *m* ⟨*pl* -chi⟩ altercation
alterigia *f* hauteur
alternanza *f* alternation; ***l'~ del giorno e della notte*** the alternation of day and night
alternare *v/t* ⟨1b⟩ alternate
alternarsi *v/r* ⟨1b⟩ alternate
alternativa *f* alternative
alternativo *adj* alternative; ***medicina*** *f* ***-a*** alternative medicine; ***soluzione*** *f* ***-a*** alternative solution
alternato *adj*: ***corrente*** *f* ***-a*** alternating current
alternatore *m* alternator
alterno *adj*: ***a giorni*** *pl* ***-i*** on alternate days
altezza *f* **1.** height; ***a 900 metri d'~*** at an altitude of 900 metres; ***all'~ del bar giri a destra*** when you get to the bar turn right; ***essere all'~ di qc*** *situazione*, *compito* be up to sth **2.** *titolo* Highness
altezzosità *f* ⟨*pl* altezzosità⟩ arrogance **altezzoso** *adj* arrogant
alticcio *adj* ⟨*mpl* -cci⟩ tipsy
altimetria *f* altimetry **altimetro** *m* altimeter
altisonante *adj* sonorous; *fig* (*pomposo*) pompous
altitudine *f* GEOG altitude
alto I *adj* **1.** high; *persona* tall; ***-a moda*** haute couture; ***-a società*** *f* high society; ***-a stagione*** *f* high season; ***il palazzo è ~ 30 metri*** the building is 30 metres tall; ***sono -a un metro e settanta*** I'm one metre seventy; ***in ~*** at the top; *moto* up **2. *a voce -a*** in a loud voice; *leggere* aloud **3. *a notte -a*** in the middle of the night; ***in ~ mare*** on the high seas **II** *m* top; ***dall'~*** from above; ***mani in ~!*** hands up!
altoatesino I *adj* South Tyrolean **II** *m*, **-a** *f* person from South Tyrol
altoforno *m* blast furnace
altolocato *adj* highly placed
altoparlante *m* loudspeaker
altopiano *m* ⟨*pl* altipiani⟩ plateau
altrettanto I *adj / pron* as much; ***-i*** *pl* as many **II** *adv*: ***grazie, ~*** thank you and the same to you
altrimenti *adv* (*in modo diverso*) differently; (*in caso contrario*) otherwise; ***non possiamo fare ~*** we can't do anything else; ***sbrigati, ~ perdi il treno*** hurry up or you'll miss the train
altro I *adj* other; ***un ~*** another; ***l'altr'anno*** last year; ***l'~ giorno*** the other day; ***l'~ ieri*** the day before yesterday; ***vuoi ~ pane?*** do you want any more bread?; ***-e due birre*** another two beers **II** *pron* other; ***l'un l'~*** one another; ***gli altri*** other people; ***lo farà un ~*** someone else will do it; ***tra l'~*** what's more, moreover; ***desidera ~?*** anything else?; ***tutt'~ che*** anything but; ***pensare ad ~*** be thinking about something else; ***se non ~*** at least

altroché *adv* certainly; ***sei contento? – ~!*** are you happy? – you bet!

altronde *adv*: ***d'~*** on the other hand

altrove *adv* elsewhere

altrui *adj* other people's; ***senza l'aiuto ~*** without anyone's help

altruismo *m* altruism

altruista *m/f* ⟨*mpl* -i⟩ altruist

altruisticamente *adv* altruistically

altura *f* hill; ***pesca*** *f* ***d'~*** deep-sea fishing

alunno *m*, **-a** *f* pupil, student

alveare *m* hive

alveo *m* river bed

alveolo *m* ANAT alveolus

alzabandiera *m* ⟨*pl* alzabandiera⟩ flag-raising ceremony

alzacristallo *m* ⟨*pl* alzacristallo⟩ AUTO window winder; ***~ elettrico*** electric windows

alzare *v/t* ⟨1a⟩ raise, lift; *prezzi* increase, raise; (*costruire*) build, erect; ***~ una carta*** pick up a card; ***~ la voce*** raise one's voice; ***~ il volume*** turn up the volume; ***le spalle*** shrug (one's shoulders); ***~ il tiro*** raise the bar

alzarsi *v/r* ⟨1a⟩ stand up, rise; *da letto* get up; *di sole* come up, rise; ***~ in piedi*** stand up

alzata *f*: ***~ di spalle*** shrug; *iron* ***~ d'ingegno*** stroke of genius

alzato *adj*: ***essere ~*** be up; ***restare ~*** stay up

amabile *adj* lovable; (*gentile*) pleasant, kind; *vino* sweet

amabilità *f* pleasantness

amaca *f* ⟨*pl* -che⟩ hammock

amalfitano **I** *adj* of Amalfi; *persona* from Amalfi **II** *m*, **-a** *f* person from Amalfi

amalgama *m* ⟨*pl* -i⟩ amalgam (*a. fig*)

amalgamare *v/t* ⟨1m⟩ amalgamate

amalgamarsi *v/r* ⟨1m⟩ amalgamate

amanita *f*: ***~ falloide*** death cap

amante *m/f* lover; ***~ della musica*** music lover; ***~ dell'ordine*** lover of order

amanuense *m* amenuensis

amaranto *m* love-lies-bleeding

amare *v/t* ⟨1a⟩ love; *amico* be fond of; ***~ fare qc*** love doing sth; ***~ la buona tavola*** love good food; ***si ameranno per sempre*** they'll always love each other

amareggiare *v/t* ⟨1f⟩ embitter

amareggiato *adj* embittered; ***essere ~ per qc*** be bitter about sth

amarena *f* sour black cherry

amaretto *m biscotto* macaroon

amarezza *f* bitterness

amarico ⟨*mpl* -ci⟩ **I** *adj* Amharic **II** *m*, **-a** *f* Amhara

amaro **I** *adj* bitter; ***boccone*** *m* ***~*** bitter pill **II** *m liquore* bitters *pl*

amarognolo *adj* slightly bitter **amarone** *m* COOK *red wine from the Verona area*

amato *adj* beloved **amatore** *m*, **-trice** *f* (*appassionato*) lover; (*dilettante*) amateur **amatoriale** *adj* amateur

amatriciano **I** *adj* from Amatrice; ***bucatini*** *mpl* ***all'-a*** *pasta with sauce made of bacon, onion and tomatoes* **II** *m*, **-a** *f* person from Amatrice

amazzone *f* horsewoman; MYTH Amazon

amazzonico ⟨*mpl* -ci⟩ *adj* Amazonian; ***foresta -a*** Amazon rain forest

ambasciata *f* embassy

ambasciatore *m*, **-trice** *f* ambassador

ambedue *adj* both; ***~ i ragazzi*** both boys

ambidestro *adj* ambidextrous

ambientale *adj* environmental

ambientalista **I** *adj* environmental **II** *m/f* ⟨*mpl* -i⟩ environmentalist

ambientare *v/t* ⟨1b⟩ adapt; ***il film è ambientato in Italia*** the film is set in Italy

ambientarsi *v/r* ⟨1b⟩ become acclimatized; ***non mi sono ancora ambientata*** I haven't settled in yet

ambiente *m* BIOL environment; ***~ di lavoro*** work environment; ***protezione*** *f* ***dell'~*** environmental protection

ambiguità *f* ⟨*pl* ambiguità⟩ ambiguity

ambiguo *adj* ambiguous

ambire *v/i* ⟨4d⟩: ***~ a qc*** aspire to sth; ***~ a fare qc*** aspire to do sth

ambito[1] *m* sphere

ambito[2] *adj* sought-after

ambizione *f* ambition

ambizioso *adj* ambitious

ambo **I** *adj* both; ***in -i casi*** in both cases **II** *m* (*lotteria*) double

ambosessi *adj inv* of either sex

ambra *f* amber

ambrosiano **I** *adj* Milanese **II** *m*, **-a** *f* Milanese

ambulacro *m* ambulatory

ambulante I *adj* travel(l)ing; *fig* ***cadavere*** *m* **~** zombie **II** *m/f* pedlar
ambulanza *f* ambulance
ambulatoriale *adj* outpatients *attr*; ***visita*** *f* **~** outpatients appointment
ambulatorio *m* ⟨*pl* -ri⟩ MED outpatients; ***orario*** *m* ***di*** **~** clinic opening hours
amburghese I *adj* of Hamburg; *persona* from Hamburg **II** *m/f* person from Hamburg
Amburgo *m* Hamburg
ameba *f* amoeba
amen I *int* amen **II** *m* ⟨*pl* amen⟩ amen
amenità *f* ⟨*pl* amenità⟩ pleasantness; *iron* pleasantry **ameno** *adj* (*grazioso*) pleasant; (*divertente*) entertaining; ***lettura*** *f* ***-a*** light reading
America *f* America; **~ *Centrale*** Central America; **~ *latina*** Latin America; **~ *del Nord*** North America; **~ *del Sud*** South America
americano I *adj* American **II** *m*, **-a** *f* American **III** *m* American English
ametista *f* amethyst
amianto *m* asbestos
amichevole *adj* friendly; ***accordo*** *m* **~** amicable agreement
amichevolmente *adv* in a friendly way
amicizia *f* friendship; ***fare*** **~** make friends; ***fare*** **~ *con qn*** make friends with s.o.
amico ⟨*mpl* -ci⟩ **I** *m*, **-a** *f* friend; ***un mio*** **~** a friend of mine; **~ *intimo*** close friend; **~ *del cuore*** best friend; ***l'~ del giaguaro*** *hum* fake friend; ***essere -i per la pelle*** be bosom buddies; ***chi trova un ~ trova un tesoro*** *prov* a good friend is a treasure beyond price **II** *adj* friendly; ***essere ~ di qn*** be friends with s.o.
amido *m* starch
ammaccare *v/t* ⟨1d⟩ dent; *frutta* bruise
ammaccatura *f* dent; *su frutta* bruise
ammaestramento *m* teaching; *di animali*: training
ammaestrare *v/t* ⟨1b⟩ teach; *animali* train
ammaestrato *adj* performing **ammaestratore** *m*, **-trice** *f* trainer
ammainabandiera *m* ⟨*pl* ammainabandiera⟩ lowering of the flag **ammainare** *v/t* ⟨1a⟩ lower; **~ *le vele*** lower the sails; *fig* throw in the towel
ammalarsi *v/r* ⟨1a⟩ fall ill; **~ *di qc*** be taken ill with sth
ammalato I *adj* ill **II** *m*, **-a** *f* ill person
ammaliante *adj* captivating **ammaliare** *v/t* ⟨1g⟩ bewitch; *fig* captivate
ammanco *m* ⟨*pl* -chi⟩ deficit
ammanettare *v/t* ⟨1a⟩ handcuff, put handcuffs on
ammaraggio *m* ⟨*pl* -ggi⟩ splashdown
ammarare *v/i* ⟨1a⟩ *di aereo* put down in the water; *di navetta spaziale* splash down
ammassare *v/t* ⟨1a⟩ mass
ammassarsi *v/r* ⟨1a⟩ mass
ammasso *m* pile; GEOL mass; **~ *di rovine*** heap of rubble
ammattire *v/i* ⟨4d⟩ go mad; ***far ~ qn*** drive s.o. mad
ammazzacaffè *m* ⟨*pl* ammazzacaffè⟩ liqueur
ammazzare *v/t* ⟨1a⟩ kill; *animali* slaughter
ammazzarsi *v/r* (*suicidarsi*) kill o.s.; **~ *di lavoro*** work o.s. to death
ammenda *f* (*multa*) fine; ***fare ~ di*** make amends for
ammesso *past part* → ***ammettere***
ammettere *v/t* ⟨3ee⟩ admit; (*supporre*) suppose; (*riconoscere*) acknowledge; ***mi hanno ammesso al corso / all'esame*** they let me take the course / exam; ***ammette di aver sbagliato*** he admits he made a mistake; ***ammesso che …*** supposing (that) …
amministrare *v/t* ⟨1a⟩ administer; *azienda* manage, run
amministrarsi *v/r* ⟨1a⟩ organize oneself
amministrativo *adj* administrative
amministratore *m*, **-trice** *f* administrator; *di azienda* manager; **~ *delegato*** managing director
amministrazione *f* administration; **~ *comunale*** local council; **~ *controllata*** receivership; ***pubblica ~*** public administration; **~ *straordinaria*** *control of a public body by a government-appointed official*; ***spese*** *fpl* ***d'~*** administrative costs
amminoacido *m* amino acid
ammiraglia *f* flagship
ammiraglio *m* ⟨*pl* -gli⟩ admiral
ammirare *v/t* ⟨1a⟩ admire; **~ *qn per qc*** admire s.o. for sth

ammiratore *m*, **-trice** *f* admirer
ammirazione *f* admiration
ammirevole *adj* admirable
ammissibile *adj* admissible
ammissibilità *f* ⟨*pl* ammissibilità⟩ admissibility
ammissione *f* admission; ***esame*** *m* ***d'~*** entrance exam
ammobiliare *v/t* ⟨1g⟩ furnish
ammobiliato *adj* furnished; ***camera*** *f* ***-a*** furnished room
ammodo **I** *adj inv* respectable **II** *adv* properly
ammogliarsi *v/r* ⟨1g⟩ marry
ammollo *m*: ***in ~*** soaking
ammoniaca *f* ammonia
ammonimento *m* reprimand, admonishment; (*consiglio*) warning
ammonire *v/t* ⟨4d⟩ reprimand, admonish; (*avvertire*) warn; JUR caution
ammonizione *f* reprimand, admonishment; SPORTS warning; JUR caution
ammontare **I** *v/i* ⟨1a⟩: ***~ a*** amount to **II** *m* amount; ***per un ~ di …*** in the amount of …
ammonticchiare *v/t* ⟨1g⟩ pile up (*a. fig*)
ammorbare *v/t* ⟨1c⟩ infect
ammorbidente *m* fabric conditioner
ammorbidire *v/t* ⟨4d⟩ soften
ammortamento *m* FIN amortization; ***~ ordinario*** standard amortization
ammortizzabile *adj* repayable
ammortizzare *v/t* ⟨1a⟩ FIN amortize
ammortizzatore *m* AUTO shock absorber
ammosciato *adj infml* floppy; *fig* (*depresso*) depressed
ammucchiare *v/t* ⟨1g⟩ pile up
ammucchiarsi *v/r* ⟨1g⟩ pile up, accumulate
ammuffire *v/i* ⟨4d⟩ go mo(u)ldy; *fig* mo(u)lder away
ammuffito *adj* mo(u)ldy; *fig* mo(u)ldering
ammutinamento *m* mutiny
ammutinarsi *v/r* ⟨1m⟩ mutiny **ammutinato** *m*, **-a** *f* mutineer
ammutolire *v/i* ⟨4d⟩ be struck dumb
amnesia *f* amnesia
amniocentesi *f* ⟨*pl* amniocentesi⟩ amniocentesis
amnistia *f* amnesty
amnistiare *v/t* ⟨1h⟩ grant an amnesty to
amo *m* hook; *fig* bait
amorale *adj* amoral
amore *m* **1.** love; ***~ a prima vista*** love at first sight; ***~ del prossimo*** love of one's neighbour; ***amor proprio*** self-respect; ***storia*** *f* ***d'~*** love story; ***per l'~ di qn*** for love of s.o.; ***per l'amor di Dio*** for goodness' sake, for the love of God; ***fare l'~ con qn*** make love to s.o. **2.** *persona* ***è un ~!*** he/she/it's lovely!; ***ciao, ~!*** hello, darling!
amoreggiare *v/i* ⟨1f⟩ flirt
amorevole *adj* loving
amorevolezza *f* fondness
amorfo *adj* amorphous; *fig* colo(u)rless
amorino *m* cupid
amoroso *adj* loving, affectionate; *sguardo* amorous; *lettera*, *poesia* love *attr*
amperaggio *m* ⟨*pl* -ggi⟩ amperage
ampiezza *f di stanza* spaciousness; *di gonna* fullness; *fig di cultura* breadth; *fig* ***~ di vedute*** broadmindedness
ampio *adj* ⟨*mpl* -pi⟩ *stanza* spacious, large; *abito* roomy; *gonna* full; ***un'-a scelta*** a wide choice; ***di ~ respiro*** wide-ranging
ampliamento *m* broadening, widening; *di edificio* extension; ***lavori*** *mpl* ***di ~*** building of an extension
ampliare *v/t* ⟨1l⟩ broaden, widen; *edificio* extend
amplificare *v/t* ⟨1m & d⟩ TECH *suono* amplify
amplificatore *m* amplifier
amplificazione *f di suono*: amplification
ampolla *f* cruet
ampolloso *adj* pompous
amputare *v/t* ⟨1l⟩ amputate
amputazione *f* amputation
amuleto *m* amulet
AN *abbr* **1.** (= **Ancona**) Ancona **2.** (= **Alleanza Nazionale**) POL *National Alliance*
anabbagliante *adj* dipped
anabolizzante *m* anabolic steroid
anacronismo *m* anachronism
anacronistico *adj* ⟨*mpl* -ci⟩ anachronistic
anagrafe *f ufficio* registry office; ***~ tributaria*** ADMIN tax record office
anagrafico *adj* ⟨*mpl* -ci⟩: ***dati*** *mpl* ***-ci*** personal data

anagramma *m* ⟨*pl* -i⟩ anagram
analcolico ⟨*mpl* -ci⟩ **I** *adj* non-alcoholic **II** *m* non-alcoholic drink
anale *adj* anal
analfabeta *m/f* ⟨*mpl* -i⟩ illiterate person, person who cannot read or write
analfabetismo *m* illiteracy
analgesico *m/adj* ⟨*mpl* -ci⟩ analgesic
analisi *f* ⟨*pl* analisi⟩ analysis; **~ del sangue** blood test; **in ultima ~** in the final analysis; **fare le ~** MED have tests
analista *m/f* ⟨*mpl* -i⟩ analyst; **~ programmatore** systems analyst
analitico *adj* ⟨*mpl* -ci⟩ analytical; **indice** *m* **~** index
analizzare *v/t* ⟨1a⟩ analyse, *US* analyze
analogia *f* analogy
analogo *adj* ⟨*mpl* -ghi⟩ analogous
anamnesi *f* ⟨*pl* anamnesi⟩ medical history
ananas *m* ⟨*pl* ananas⟩ pineapple
anarchia *f* anarchy
anarchico ⟨*mpl* -ci⟩ **I** *adj* anarchic **II** *m*, **-a** *f* anarchist
anarchismo *m* anarchism
ANAS *abbr* (= **Azienda Nazionale Autonoma della Strada**) *Italian Roads Department*
anatema *m* anathema
anatolico ⟨*mpl* -ci⟩ **I** *adj* Anatolian **II** *m*, **-a** *f* Anatolian
anatomia *f* anatomy
anatomico *adj* ⟨*mpl* -ci⟩ anatomical
anatomopatologo *m*, **-a** *f* ⟨*mpl* -gi⟩ pathologist
anatra *f* duck
anca *f* ⟨*pl* -che⟩ hip
ancestrale *adj* ancestral
anche *cj* too, also, as well; (*perfino*) even; **~ se** even if; **vengo anch'io** I'm coming too; **~ volendo** even if we / he / she *etc* wanted to; **ci mancava ~ questa!** that's all we need!; **l'ho aspettato ~ troppo** I've waited too long for this already
ancheggiare *v/i* ⟨1f⟩ wiggle one's hips
anchilosato *adj* stiff
anconetano I *adj* of Ancona; *persona* from Ancona **II** *m*, **-a** *f* person from Ancona
ancora[1] *adv* still; *di nuovo* again; *di più* (some) more; **dorme ~** he's / she's still asleep; **non ~** not yet; **~ una volta** once more, one more time; **dammene ~ un po'** give me a bit more; **prima ~ che** even before
ancora[2] *f* anchor; **gettare l'~** drop anchor; **~ di salvezza** sheet anchor
ancoraggio *m* ⟨*pl* -ggi⟩ anchoring; *luogo* anchorage
ancorare *v/t* ⟨1l⟩ anchor
ancorarsi *v/r* ⟨1l⟩ anchor; *fig* **~ a** cling to
Andalusia *f* Andalusia **andaluso I** *adj* Andalusian **II** *m*, **-a** *f* Andalusian
andamento *m di vendite* performance; **~ del mercato** market trend
andante I *adj* (*scadente*) shabby **II** *m* MUS andante
andare ⟨1p⟩ **I** *v/i* **1.** go; **~ in bicicletta** cycle; **~ a cavallo** ride; **~ a passeggio** walk; **~ a piedi** walk; **~ a male** go off; **~ a fare qc** go and do sth; **~ a finire** turn out; **andiamo a mangiare** let's go and eat; **~ via** (*partire*) leave; *di macchia* come out **2.** (*funzionare*) work; **l'orologio non va più** the clock has stopped **3. ~ bene** suit; *taglia* fit **4. come va?** how are you?, how are things?; **non mi va** *di vestito* it doesn't fit me; **non mi va di venire** I don't feel like coming; **ti va un caffè?** do you fancy a coffee? **5. la camicia va lavata** the shirt has to be washed **II** *m*: **coll'~ del tempo** with the passage of time; **a lungo ~** in the long run
andarsene *v/r* go away
andata *f* outward journey; **c'era più traffico all'~** there was more traffic on the way there; **biglietto** *m* **di ~** single (ticket), *US* oneway ticket; **biglietto** *m* **di ~ e ritorno** return (ticket), *US* roundtrip ticket
andatura *f* walk; SPORTS pace
andazzo *m*: **prendere un brutto ~** go badly
Ande *fpl* Andes **andino I** *adj* Andean **II** *m*, **-a** *f* person from the Andes
andirivieni *m* ⟨*pl* andirivieni⟩ toing and froing
andito *m* (narrow) passage
Andrea *m*: **Sant'~** Saint Andrew; **croce** *f* **di Sant'~** Saint Andrew's cross
androgino I *adj* androgynous **II** *n*: **androgino** *m* androgyne; *fig* androgynous person

androne *m* hallway
aneddoto *m* anecdote
anelare *v/i* ⟨1b⟩: *fig* **~ a qc** long for sth
anello *m* ring; **~ di fidanzamento** engagement ring
anemia *f* an(a)emia
anemico *adj* ⟨*mpl* -ci⟩ an(a)emic
anemometro *m* wind gauge
anemone *m* anemone
anestesia *f* an(a)esthesia; *sostanza* an(a)esthetic; **~ locale / generale** local / general anaesthetic; **sotto ~** under anaesthetic
anestesista *m/f* ⟨*mpl* -i⟩ an(a)esthetist
anestetico *m* ⟨*pl* -ci⟩ an(a)esthetic
anestetizzare *v/t* ⟨1a⟩ an(a)esthetize
anfetamina *f* amphetamine
anfibio ⟨*mpl* -bi⟩ **I** *adj* amphibious **II** *m* ZOOL amphibian; MIL amphibious vehicle
anfiteatro *m* amphitheatre, *US* -theater
anfitrione *m* host
anfora *f* amphora
anfratto *m* cleft
angelico *adj* ⟨*mpl* -ci⟩ angelic
angelo *m* angel; **~ custode** guardian angel
angelus *m* ⟨*pl* angelus⟩ angelus
angheria *f* (act of) oppression
angina *f* tonsillitis
angioletto *m* cherub; *iron* little angel
anglicano I *adj* Anglican **II** *m*, **-a** *f* Anglican
anglicismo *m* Anglicism
anglista *m/f* ⟨*mpl* -i⟩ student of English
anglosassone *adj* Anglo-Saxon
Angola *f* Angola **angolano I** *adj* Angolan **II** *m*, **-a** *f* Angolan
angolare *adj* angular
angolazione *f fig* angle
angolo *m* corner; MATH angle; SPORTS **calcio** *m* **d'~** corner kick; **~ cottura** kitchenette; **~ acuto** MATH acute angle; **~ ottuso** obtuse angle; **~ retto** right angle; **essere all'~ tra** be on the corner of; **fare ~ con qc** come out in sth; **all'~** on the corner; **dietro l'~** round the corner; **ai quattro -i della terra** all over the world
angoloso *adj* angular
angora *f* angora
angoscia *f* ⟨*pl* -sce⟩ anguish
angosciante *adj* worrying
angosciare *v/i* ⟨1f⟩ worry; **non mi ~** don't get me worried
angosciarsi *v/r* ⟨1f⟩ get worried (**per** about)
angosciato *adj* worried
angoscioso *adj pieno d'angoscia* anguished; *che da angoscia* distressing, heart-rending
anguilla *f* eel
anguria *f* water melon
angustiare *v/t* ⟨1k⟩ worry **angustiarsi** *v/r* ⟨1k⟩ worry
angusto *adj* narrow
anice *m* COOK aniseed
anidride *f*: **~ carbonica** carbon dioxide
anima *f* soul; **non c'è ~ viva** there isn't a soul to be seen; **~ gemella** soul mate; **rompere l'~ a qn** *infml* get on s.o.'s nerves *infml*
animale I *m* animal; **~ domestico** pet **II** *adj* animal *attr*
animalesco *adj* ⟨*mpl* -chi⟩ animal-like
animalista *m/f* ⟨*mpl* -i⟩ animal rights activist
animare *v/t* ⟨1l⟩ give life to; *conversazione* liven up; (*promuovere*) promote
animarsi *v/r* ⟨1l⟩ (*ravvivarsi*) come to life; (*infervorarsi*) become animated
animato *adj strada* busy; *conversazione*, *persona* animated; **esseri** *mpl* **-i** living beings; **cartoni** *mpl* **-i** cartoons
animatore *m*, **-trice** *f di gruppo* leader; *in vacanza* entertainment organizer
animazione *f* animation; COMPUT **~ al computer** computer animation
animelle *fpl* sweetbreads *pl*
animista ⟨*mpl* -i⟩ **I** *adj* animist **II** *m/f* animist
animo *m* nature; (*coraggio*) heart; **farsi ~** be brave; **perdersi d'~** lose heart; **stato** *m* **d'~** state of mind
animosità *f* ⟨*pl* animosità⟩ animosity
anisetta *f aniseed-flavoured liqueur*
anitra *f* duck
Anna *f*: **Sant'~** Saint Anne
annacquare *v/t* ⟨1a⟩ water down
annaffiare *v/t* ⟨1k⟩ water
annaffiatoio *m* ⟨*pl* -oi⟩ watering can
annali *mpl* annals *pl*
annaspare *v/i* ⟨1a⟩ (*in acqua*) flounder

annata *f* vintage; (*anno*) year; *importo* annual amount
annebbiare *v/t* ⟨1k⟩ cloud **annebbiarsi** *v/r* ⟨1k⟩ get foggy; (*offuscarsi*) become confused
annebbiato *adj*: ***vista*** *f* ***-a*** blurred vision; ***mente*** *f* ***-a*** confusion
annegamento *m* drowning
annegare *v/t* & *v/i* ⟨1e⟩ drown
annegarsi *v/r* ⟨1e⟩ drown
annegato *m*, **-a** *f* drowned person
annerire ⟨4d⟩ **I** *v/t* blacken **II** *v/i* turn black, blacken
annerirsi *v/r* ⟨4d⟩ turn black, blacken
annerito *adj* blackened; ***~ dal fumo*** smoke-blackened
annessione *f* POL annexation
annesso I *past part* → ***annettere*** **II** *adj* annexed; (*allegato*) enclosed, attached **III** *m edificio* annex(e)
annettere *v/t* ⟨3m⟩ POL annex; ARCH add; (*allegare*) enclose, attach
annichilire *v/t* ⟨4d⟩ destroy **annichilito** *adj* devastated
annidarsi *v/r* ⟨1a⟩ nest
annientamento *m* destruction (*a. fig*)
annientare *v/t* ⟨1b⟩ destroy
anniversario *m* ⟨*pl* -ri⟩ anniversary
anno *m* year; ***buon ~!*** Happy New Year!; ***~ finanziario*** financial year; ***~ scolastico*** school year; ***faccio il primo ~ d'università*** I'm in the first year of university; ***~ luce*** light year; ***quanti -i hai?*** how old are you?; ***ho 33 -i*** I'm 33 (years old); ***quando compi gli -i?*** when's your birthday?; ***ieri ha compiuto 16 -i*** he / she was 16 yesterday; ***gli -i sessanta*** the sixties; ***abito qui da -i*** I've lived here for years
annodare *v/t* ⟨1c⟩ tie (together); *cravatta* tie, knot
annodarsi *v/r* ⟨1c⟩ become knotted
annodato *adj* knotted; ***~ a mano*** hand-knotted
annoiare *v/t* ⟨1i⟩ bore
annoiarsi *v/r* ⟨1i⟩ get bored; ***~ a morte*** be bored out of one's skull
annoiato *adj* bored
annotare *v/t* ⟨1c⟩ make a note of; *testo* annotate
annotazione *f* note; *in testo* annotation
annoverare *v/t* ⟨1c & m⟩ number; ***~ qn tra i propri amici*** count s.o. among one's friends
annuale *adj* annual, yearly; *di un anno* year-long; ***abbonamento*** *m* ***~*** annual season ticket
annualmente *adv* annually
annuario *m* ⟨*pl* -ri⟩ yearbook
annuire *v/i* ⟨4d⟩ (*assentire*) assent (***a*** to)
annullamento *m* cancellation; *di matrimonio* annulment
annullare *v/t* ⟨1a⟩ cancel; *matrimonio* annul; *gol* disallow; (*vanificare*) cancel out
annunciare *v/t* ⟨1f⟩ announce
annunciatore *m*, **-trice** *f* RADIO, TV announcer
Annunciazione *f* REL Annunciation
annuncio *m* ⟨*pl* -ci⟩ announcement; *in giornale* advertisement; ***-i*** *pl* ***economici*** classified ads, classifieds; ***piccoli -i*** *pl* small ads; ***~ pubblicitario*** ad(-vert), advertisement; ***mettere un ~ sul giornale*** put an ad(vert) in the paper
annunziare *v/t* ⟨1a⟩ → ***annunciare***
annuo *adj* annual, yearly
annusare *v/t* ⟨1a⟩ sniff; *fig* smell
annuvolarsi *v/r* ⟨1a⟩ cloud over
ano *m* anus
anodico *adj* ⟨*mpl* -ci⟩ anodic **anodizzare** *v/t* ⟨1a⟩ anodize **anodo** *m* anode
anomalia *f* anomaly
anomalo *adj* anomalous
anonimato *m* anonymity; ***agire nell'~*** do sth anonymously; ***mantenere l'~*** remain anonymous
anonimo *adj* anonymous; ***società*** *f* ***-a*** limited company; ***condurre un'esistenza*** *f* ***-a*** lead a life of obscurity
anoressia *f* anorexia
anoressico *adj* anorexic
anormale *adj* abnormal
anormalità *f* ⟨*pl* anormalità⟩ abnormality
ansa *f* handle; *di un fiume* bend
ANSA *abbr* (= **Agenzia Nazionale Stampa Associata**) *Italian Press Agency*
ansia *f* anxiety; ***con ~*** anxiously; ***stare in ~ per qn / qc*** be worried about s.o. / sth
ansimante *adj* wheezing
ansimare *v/i* ⟨1l⟩ wheeze
ansioso *adj* anxious; ***~ di fare qc*** eager to do sth; ***stato*** *m* ***~*** state of anxiety

anta *f* door
antagonismo *m* antagonism
antagonista *m/f* ⟨*mpl* -i⟩ antagonist
antagonistico *adj* ⟨*mpl* -ci⟩ antagonistic
antartico *adj* ⟨*mpl* -ci⟩ Antarctic *attr*; ***circolo*** *m* ***polare*** ~ Antarctic circle
Antartide *f* Antarctic
antecedente **I** *adj* preceding **II** *m* precedent
antefatto *m* prior event
anteguerra *m* pre-war years *pl*
antenato *m*, **-a** *f* ancestor
antenna *f* RADIO, TV aerial; ZOOL antenna; ~ ***parabolica*** satellite dish
anteporre *v/t* ⟨3ll⟩ put before; ~ ***il lavoro alla famiglia*** put one's job before one's family
anteposto *past part* → ***anteporre***
anteprima *f* preview; ~ ***di stampa*** COMPUT print preview; ***sapere qc in*** ~ know sth in advance
anteriore *adj* front; *precedente* previous; ***zampe*** *fpl* ***-i*** front legs
antesignano *m*, **-a** *f* standard-bearer
anti... *pref* anti...
antiabbagliante *adj* anti-dazzle
antiabortista ⟨*mpl* -i⟩ **I** *adj* anti-abortion **II** *m/f* anti-abortionist
antiaderente *adj* non-stick
antiaerea *f* anti-aircraft defences *pl*
antiaereo *adj* anti-aircraft; ***rifugio*** *m* ~ air raid shelter
antiatomico *adj* ⟨*mpl* -ci⟩ anti-nuclear; ***rifugio*** *m* ~ fallout shelter
antiautoritario *adj* ⟨*mpl* -ri⟩ anti-authoritarian
antibiotico *m/adj* ⟨*mpl* -ci⟩ antibiotic
antibloccaggio *adj inv* anti-lock; ***sistema*** *m* ~ anti-lock braking system
anticaglia *f* ⟨*pl* -glie⟩ (*antichità*) antique; *pej* piece of (old) junk
anticalcare *adj inv* anti-limescale
anticamente *adv* in ancient times
anticamera *f* anteroom; ***fare*** ~ be kept waiting; ***non mi passerebbe neanche per l'~ del cervello*** it wouldn't even cross my mind
anticanceroso *adj* anti-cancer
anticarro *adj inv* anti-tank; ***cannone*** *m* ~ anti-tank gun
antichità *f* ⟨*pl* antichità⟩ antiquity; ***negozio*** *m* ***d'~*** antique shop
anticiclone *m* anticyclone
anticipare *v/t* ⟨1m⟩ anticipate; *denaro* pay in advance; *partenza, riunione etc* bring forward
anticipato *adj* early; ***pagamento*** ~ payment in advance; ***pensionamento*** ~ early retirement
anticipo *m* advance; (*caparra*) deposit; ***versare un*** ~ put down a deposit; ***in*** ~ ahead of time, early; ***arrivare con un'ora d'~*** arrive an hour early; ***giocare d'~*** play on the rise
anticlericale *adj* anticlerical
antico ⟨*mpl* -chi⟩ **I** *adj* ancient; *mobile* antique **II** *m*: ***gli antichi*** *pl* the ancients
anticoagulante *adj* anticoagulant
anticomunista **I** *adj* anti-Communist **II** *m/f* ⟨*mpl* -i⟩ anti-Communist
anticoncezionale *m/adj* contraceptive
anticonformismo *m* nonconformity
anticonformista *m/f* ⟨*mpl* -i⟩ nonconformist
anticongelante *m* anti-freeze
anticorpo *m* antibody
anticostituzionale *adj* unconstitutional
anticrimine *adj inv* crime-fighting; ***squadra*** *f* ~ crime squad
anticristo *m* Antichrist
anticrittogamico *m* ⟨*pl* -ci⟩ fungicidal
antidemocratico *adj* ⟨*mpl* -ci⟩ undemocratic
antidiluviano *adj* ancient (*a. hum*)
antidolorifico ⟨*mpl* -ci⟩ **I** *adj* pain-relieving **II** *n*: ***antidolorifico*** *m* painkiller
antidoping **I** *adj inv* drugs *attr* **II** *m* ⟨*pl* antidoping⟩ drugs test
antidoto *m* antidote
antidroga *adj inv squadra* drug *attr*; ***cane*** *m* ~ sniffer dog
antiemorragico ⟨*mpl* -ci⟩ **I** *adj* h(a)emostatic **II** *n*: ***antiemorragico*** *m* h(a)emostatic
antifascista ⟨*mpl* -i⟩ **I** *adj* antifascist **II** *m/f* antifascist
antifebbrile *m* antipyretic
antifona *f* MUS antiphon; *fig* hint; ***capire l'~*** take the hint
antifurto **I** *adj* antitheft **II** *m* anti-theft device
antigas *adj inv* gas *attr*
antigelo *m* antifreeze
Antille *fpl* Antilles *pl*
antilope *f* antilope

antimafia *adj inv* anti-Mafia *attr*
antimeridiano *adj* morning *attr*; ***le 5 -e*** 5 in the morning
antimilitarista ⟨*mpl* -i⟩ **I** *adj* pacifist **II** *m/f* pacifist
antincendio *adj inv* fire *attr*; ***allarme** m* **~** fire alarm
antinebbia *m* ⟨*pl* antinebbia⟩ foglamp
antineve *adj inv* snow *attr*; ***pneumatici** mpl* **~** snow tyres, *US* tires
antinfortunistico *adj* ⟨*mpl* -ci⟩ safety *attr*; ***misure** fpl* ***-che*** health and safety measures
antinquinamento *adj inv* anti-pollution; ***norme** fpl* **~** anti-pollution laws
antinucleare *adj* POL antinuclear; ***movimento** m* **~** antinuclear movement
antiorario *adj*: ***in senso ~*** anticlockwise, *US* counterclockwise
antiparassitario ⟨*mpl* -ri⟩ **I** *adj* antiparasitic **II** *n*: ***antiparassitario** m* antiparasitic
antipasto *m* starter
antipatia *f* antipathy; ***prendere in ~ qn*** take a dislike to s.o.
antipatico *adj* ⟨*mpl* -ci⟩ disagreeable
antipiega *adj inv* crease-resistant
antipodi *mpl*: GEOG ***essere agli ~*** to be on the opposite side of the world; *fig* to be diametrically opposed
antipolio **I** *adj inv* polio *attr* **II** *f* ⟨*pl* antipolio⟩ polio vaccine
antiproibizionista *m/f* ⟨*mpl* -i⟩ *person who supports the decriminalization or legalization of illegal drugs*
antiproiettili *adj inv* bulletproof
antiquariato *m* antique business, antiques *pl*; ***negozio** m* ***di ~*** antique shop
antiquario *m*, **-a** *f* ⟨*mpl* -ri⟩ antique dealer
antiquato *adj* antiquated
antiriflesso *adj inv* anti-glare
antiruggine *m* rust inhibitor
antirughe *adj inv* antiwrinkle *attr*
antirumore *adj*: ***protezione** f* **~** soundproofing
antiscivolo *adj inv* non-slip
antisemita ⟨*mpl* -i⟩ **I** *adj* anti-Semitic **II** *m/f* anti-Semite
antisemitismo *m* anti Semitism
antisettico *m/adj* ⟨*mpl* -ci⟩ antiseptic
antisismico *adj* ⟨*mpl* -ci⟩ earthquake--proof
antisommossa *adj inv*: ***squadra** f* **~** riot squad
antispastico *adj* ⟨*mpl* -ci⟩ antispasmodic
antistante *adj* opposite
antistatico *adj* ⟨*mpl* -ci⟩ antistatic
antiterrorismo **I** *m* ⟨*no pl*⟩ antiterrorism **II** *adj inv* antiterrorist *attr*
antitesi *f* PHIL antithesis
antitetanica *f* (anti)tetanus injection
antitetico *adj* ⟨*mpl* -ci⟩ antithetical
antitrust *adj inv* antitrust
antiurto *adj* shockproof
antivirus *m* ⟨*pl* antivirus⟩ antivirus
antologia *f* anthology
antologico *adj* ⟨*mpl* -ci⟩ anthological
Antonio *m*: ***Sant'~*** Saint Anthony; ***fuoco** m* ***di Sant'~*** MED shingles *sg*
antonomasia *f*: ***per ~*** par excellence
antracite *f* anthracite
antro *m* cave
antropizzato *adj* shaped by man; ***ambiente** m* **~** environment shaped by man
antropofago ⟨*mpl* -gi⟩ **I** *adj* cannibalistic **II** *m*, **-a** *f* cannibal
antropologia *f* anthropology
anulare *m* ring finger; ***raccordo** m* **~** ring road
Anversa *f* Antwerp
anzi *adv* in fact; (*o meglio*) (or) better still; ***è antipatica? – no, ~!*** is she unpleasant? – no, quite the opposite!; ***è andato tutto bene, ~ benissimo*** it all went well, or rather very well
anzianità *f* ⟨*pl* anzianità⟩ old age; ***~ di servizio*** seniority
anziano **I** *adj* elderly; *per servizio* (most) senior **II** *m*, **-a** *f* old man; *donna* old woman; ***gli -i*** the elderly
anziché *cj* rather than; ***preferisco andare in pizzeria ~ cucinare*** I prefer to go for a pizza rather than cook
anzitutto *adv* first of all
AO *abbr* (= **Aosta**) Aosta
aorta *f* aorta
aostano **I** *adj* of Aosta; *persona* from Aosta **II** *m*, **-a** *f* person from Aosta
AP *abbr* (= **Ascoli Piceno**) Ascoli Piceno
apache ⟨*pl* apache⟩ **I** *adj* Apache **II** *m/f* Apache
apartheid *m* apartheid
apatia *f* apathy
apatico *adj* ⟨*mpl* -ci⟩ apathetic
ape *f* bee; ***~ operaia*** worker bee; ***~ regina*** queen bee

aperitivo *m* aperitif
apertamente *adv* openly; ***dire qc ~ (a qn)*** say sth straight out (to s.o.)
aperto **I** *past part* → ***aprire*** **II** *adj* open; ***a braccia -e*** with open arms; ***partita*** *f* ***-a*** open match; ***questione*** *f* ***-a*** open question; ***di mentalità -a*** broad-minded; ***parlare a cuore ~*** speak from the heart; ***all' ~*** *piscina* open-air; ***mangiare all'~*** eat outside *or* in the open air
apertura *f* opening; PHOT aperture; ***~ di credito*** credit opening; ***~ alare*** wingspan
apice *m* apex; *fig* height; ***essere all'~ della carriera*** be at the peak of one's career
apicoltore *m*, **-trice** *f* bee-keeper
apicoltura *f* bee-keeping
apnea *f* SPORTS apn(o)ea; ***immersione in ~*** free diving; ***andare in ~*** free-dive
apocalisse *f* apocalypse (*a. fig*) **apocalittico** *adj* ⟨*mpl* -ci⟩ apocalyptic (*a. fig*)
apocrifo **I** *adj* apocryphal **II** *n*: ***apocrifo*** *m* apocryphal text
apodittico *adj* ⟨*mpl* -ci⟩ apodeictic
apogeo *m* ASTR, *fig* apogee
apolide **I** *adj* stateless **II** *m* stateless person
apolitico *adj* ⟨*mpl* -ci⟩ apolitical
apologia *f* ⟨*pl* -gie⟩ HIST (*discorso*) apologia; (*elogio*) panegyric
apoplessia *f* apoplexy
apoplettico *adj* ⟨*mpl* -ci⟩ apoplectic
apostolato *m* apostolate
apostolico *adj* ⟨*mpl* -ci⟩ apostolic; ***nunzio*** *m* ***~*** papal nuncio
apostolo *m* apostle; ***i dodici -i*** the twelve apostles; ***~ della pace*** peace envoy
apostrofare *v/t* ⟨1m & c⟩ reprimand; GRAM add an apostrophe to
apostrofo *m* apostrophe
apoteosi *f* ⟨*pl* apoteosi⟩ apotheosis; *fig* (*esaltazione*) glorification
appagamento *m* satisfaction **appagante** *adj* satisfying
appagare *v/t* ⟨1e⟩ satisfy; ***~ un desiderio*** fulfil a wish
appagato *adj* satisfied; ***sentirsi ~ (di qc)*** be satisfied (with sth)
appaiare *v/t* ⟨1i⟩ match
appallottolare *v/t* ⟨1c & n⟩ roll up into a ball
appallottolarsi *v/r* ⟨1c & n⟩ roll up into a ball
appaltante *m/f* contractor
appaltare *v/t* ⟨1a⟩: ***~ qc (a qn)*** put sth out to contract (to s.o.); ***~ qc (da qn)*** undertake sth on contract (for s.o.)
appaltatore **I** *adj* contracting *attr* **II** *m* contractor
appalto *m* (*contratto*) contract; ***~ pubblico*** public tender; ***dare in ~*** contract out; ***prendere in ~*** win the contract for; ***gara*** *f* ***di ~*** call for tenders
appannaggio *m* ⟨*pl* -ggi⟩ annuity; *fig* prerogative
appannamento *m* misting up; *fig* clouding; ***~ della vista*** blurring of vision
appannare *v/t* ⟨1a⟩ mist up
appannarsi *v/r* ⟨1a⟩ *di vetro* mist up; *di vista* grow dim
appannato *adj* misted up; ***vetro*** *m* ***~*** misted up glass; ***vedere tutto ~*** have blurred vision
apparato *m* TECH, *fig* apparatus; ***~ digerente*** digestive system; ***~ di partito*** party machine; ***~ scenico*** set
apparecchiare *v/t* ⟨1g⟩ *tavola* set, lay; (*preparare*) prepare; ***~ la tavola*** lay *or* set the table
apparecchiatura *f* equipment
apparecchio *m* ⟨*pl* -cchi⟩ TECH device; AVIAT *infml* plane; *per denti* brace; ***~ fotografico*** camera; ***portare l'~*** *infml* wear a hearing aid
apparente *adj* apparent
apparentemente *adv* apparently
apparenza *f* appearance; ***salvare le -e*** save face; ***l'~ inganna*** appearances can be deceptive *or US* deceiving
apparire *v/i* ⟨4e⟩ appear
appariscente *adj* striking, eyecatching
apparizione *f* apparition; ***l'~ della Madonna*** the apparition of the Madonna
apparso *past part* → ***apparire***
appartamento *m* flat, *US* apartment
appartarsi *v/r* ⟨1a⟩ withdraw
appartato *adj* secluded
appartenente **I** *adj*: ***~ a*** belonging to **II** *m/f* member **appartenenza** *f* membership (***a*** of)
appartenere *v/i* ⟨2q⟩: ***~ a qn / qc*** belong to s.o. / sth
appassionante *adj* thrilling; (*commuovente*) moving
appassionare *v/t* ⟨1a⟩ excite; (*com-

muovere) move
appassionarsi *v/r* ⟨1a⟩ become excited (***a*** by)
appassionato **I** *adj* passionate; ***essere ~ di qc*** be keen on sth **II** *m*, **-a** *f* fan; ***un ~ di qc*** a fan of sth; ***un ~ di calcio*** a football *or* soccer fan; ***un' a di cinema*** a film *or* movie fan
appassire *v/i* ⟨4d⟩ wither
appellante *m/f* appellant
appellarsi *v/r* ⟨1b⟩ appeal (***a*** to; ***contro*** against)
appellativo *m* (*epiteto*) name
appello *m* appeal; ***fare ~ a qn*** appeal to s.o.; JUR ***ricorrere in ~*** lodge an appeal; ***fare l'~*** take the register *or US* roll
appena **I** *adv* just; ***è ~ andato via*** he's just gone; ***~ in tempo*** just in time; ***sono ~ 2 km*** it's no more than 2 km; ***lo conosco ~*** I hardly know him **II** *cj* as soon as; ***~ possibile*** as soon as possible; ***ti chiamo ~ arrivo*** I'll call you as soon as I get there
appendere *v/t* ⟨3c⟩: ***~ qc*** (***a qc***) hang sth (on sth); ***~ un quadro al muro*** hang a picture on the wall
appendersi *v/r* ⟨3c⟩ hang; ***~ al braccio di qn*** hang on s.o.'s arm
appendiabiti *m* hatstand
appendice *f* appendix
appendicectomia *f* MED appendectomy
appendicite *f* appendicitis
Appennini *mpl* Apennines *pl*
appenninico *adj* ⟨*mpl* -ci⟩ Apennine
appesantire *v/t* ⟨4d⟩ make heavier
appesantirsi *v/r* ⟨4d⟩ get heavier; (*ingrassare*) put on weight
appesi, appeso *past part* → ***appendere***
appestare *v/t* ⟨1b⟩ infect; *stanza* stink out; *fig* infest **appestato** *m*, **-a** *f* plague victim
appetibile *adj* appetizing; ***offerta*** *f* ***~*** attractive offer
appetito *m* appetite; ***avere / non avere ~*** have an / have no appetite; ***stuzzicare l'~*** whet one's appetite; ***perdere l'~*** lose one's appetite; ***buon ~!*** enjoy your meal!
appetitoso *adj* appetizing
appezzamento *m* plot (of land)
appianamento *m* levelling; *fig* smoothing over
appianare *v/t* ⟨1a⟩ level; *lite* smooth over
appiattimento *m* flattening (*a. fig*)
appiattire *v/t* ⟨4d⟩ flatten
appiattirsi *v/r* ⟨4d⟩ (*schiacciarsi*) get flatter; (*livellarsi*) *fig* flatten out; (*uniformarsi*) *fig* get dull
appiccare *v/t* ⟨1m & d⟩: ***~ il fuoco a qc*** set fire to sth
appiccicare *v/t* ⟨1m & d⟩ stick
appiccicarsi *v/r* ⟨1m & d⟩ stick
appiccicato *adj* stuck; ***restare ~ a qc*** get stuck to sth; *fig* get stuck on sth
appiccicoso *adj* sticky; *fig* clingy
appieno *adv* fully
appigliarsi *v/r* ⟨1g⟩ grab hold (***a*** of); ***~ a qc*** seize hold of sth
appiglio *m* ⟨*pl* -gli⟩ *per mani* fingerhold; *per piedi* toehold; *fig* excuse
appioppare *v/t* ⟨1c⟩ *infml*: ***~ qc a qn*** give s.o. sth; ***~ un ceffone a qn*** thump s.o.; ***~ un lavoro a qn*** land s.o. with a job; ***~ una multa a qn*** slap a fine on s.o.
appisolarsi *v/r* ⟨1m⟩ doze off
applaudire *v/t & v/i* ⟨4a or d⟩ applaud
applauso *m* applause; ***un ~*** a round of applause; ***fare un ~*** (***a qc***) applaud (sth)
applicabile *adj* applicable (***a*** to) **applicabilità** *f* ⟨*pl* applicabilità⟩ applicability
applicare *v/t* ⟨1l & d⟩ *etichetta* attach; *regolamento* apply; ***se vuoi essere promosso, ti devi ~ di più*** if you want to pass your exams, you'll have to work harder
applicarsi *v/r*: ***~ a qc*** apply o.s. to sth
applicativo *adj* applicable; ***norme*** *fpl* ***-e*** applicable rules; ***programma*** *m* ***~*** application
applicato *adj*: ***arti*** *fpl* ***-e*** applied arts
applicazione *f* application; ***campo*** *m* ***di ~*** area of application
applique *f* ⟨*pl* applique⟩ wall light
appoggiare *v/t* ⟨1f & c⟩ lean (***a*** against); (*posare*) put; *fig* support, back
appoggiarsi *v/r*: ***~ a*** lean on; *fig* rely on, lean on
appoggiatesta *m* ⟨*pl* appoggiatesta⟩ headrest
appoggio *m* ⟨*pl* -ggi⟩ support; ***punto*** *m* ***d'~*** source of support; ***avere degli -ggi*** have friends in high places

appollaiarsi *v/r* ⟨1i⟩ perch

apporre *v/t* ⟨3ll⟩ put; ***~ la firma su qc*** put one's signature to sth

apportare *v/t* ⟨1c⟩ bring; *fig* (*causare*) cause; ***~ danni*** damage; ***~ modifiche a qc*** change sth

apportatore *m*, **-trice** *f* bringer; ***il cibo è ~ di energia*** food provides energy

apporto *m* contribution; ECON stake; ***~ di sangue*** blood supply; ***~ di capitale*** injection of capital

appositamente *adv* expressly

apposito *adj* appropriate

apposta *adv* deliberately, on purpose; *specialmente* specifically; ***scusa, non l'ho fatto ~*** sorry, I didn't do it on purpose; ***l'ho cucinato ~ per te*** I made it specially for you; ***neanche a farlo ~*** as luck would have it

appostarsi *v/r* ⟨1a & c⟩ lie in wait

apprendere *v/t* ⟨3c⟩ learn; *notizia* hear

apprendimento *m* learning

apprendista *m/f* ⟨*mpl* -i⟩ apprentice

apprendistato *m* apprenticeship

apprensione *f* apprehension

apprensivo *adj* apprehensive

appreso *past part* → ***apprendere***

appresso I *prep* close, near; (*dietro*) behind; ***~ a qn*** near s.o., close to s.o. **II** *adv* near, close by; ***portarsi qc ~*** bring sth (with one)

apprestarsi *v/r* ⟨1b⟩: ***~ a fare qc*** get ready to do sth; ***~ a uscire*** get ready to go out

apprettare *v/t* ⟨1b⟩ starch **appretto** *m* starch

apprezzabile *adj* admirable; (*rilevante*) significant **apprezzamento** *m* approval; (*valutazione*) assessment; ECON (*aumento di valore*) appreciation; ***esprimere -i*** give one's opinion

apprezzare *v/t* ⟨1b⟩ appreciate

approccio *m* ⟨*pl* -cci⟩ approach; ***~ matematico*** mathematical approach; ***il mio ~ con quell'ambiente è stato difficile*** my first encounters with that environment weren't easy

approdare *v/i* ⟨1c⟩ land; *di barca* moor, tie up; *fig* ***non ~ a nulla*** come to nothing

approdo *m* landing; *luogo* landing stage

approfittare *v/i* ⟨1a⟩: ***~ di qc*** take advantage of sth; ***~ di qn*** take advantage of s.o.

approfittarsi *v/r* ⟨1a⟩ take advantage; ***si è approfittato della sua ingenuità*** he took advantage of his / her innocence

approfondimento *m* deepening; *fig* closer study

approfondire *v/t* ⟨4d⟩ deepen; *fig* study in depth

approfondito *adj* thorough; ***analisi f -a*** detailed analysis

approntare *v/t* ⟨1a⟩ get ready

appropriarsi *v/r* ⟨1m & c⟩: ***~ di qc*** appropriate sth

appropriato *adj* appropriate

approssimare *v/t* ⟨1m⟩ bring nearer **approssimarsi** *v/r* ⟨1m⟩ get *or* grow nearer; ***si approssima la primavera*** spring is coming

approssimativamente *adv* approximately

approssimazione *f* approximation; ***per ~*** approximately

approvare *v/t* ⟨1c⟩ approve of; *legge* approve

approvazione *f* approval; ***riscuotere l'~ del pubblico*** gain public approval

approvvigionamento *m* supply

approvvigionare *v/t* ⟨1a⟩ supply

approvvigionarsi *v/r* ⟨1n⟩ stock up (***di*** with)

appuntamento *m* appointment; ***dare ~ a qn*** give s.o. an appointment; ***mi ha dato ~ per domani*** she gave me an appointment for tomorrow; ***darsi ~*** arrange to meet; ***prendere un ~*** (***con / da qn***) make an appointment with s.o. / at s.o.'s; ***visite*** *fpl* ***su ~*** consultations by appointment; ***luogo*** *m* ***dell'~*** meeting place

appuntare *v/t* ⟨1a⟩ pin; *avviso* pin up

appuntato *m* (*carabiniere*) corporal

appuntito *adj* pointed; *matita* sharp

appunto I *m* note; ***prendere -i*** take notes; ***fare*** *or* ***muovere un ~ a qn*** find fault with s.o. **II** *adv*: (***per l'***)***~*** exactly

appurare *v/t* ⟨1a⟩ check

apribile *adj* that can be opened; ***tettuccio*** *m* ***~*** AUTO sunroof

apribottiglie *m* ⟨*pl* apribottiglie⟩ bottle opener

aprile *m* April; ***pesce*** *m* ***d'~*** April fool

apripista *m* ⟨*pl* apripista⟩ trailmaker; *fig* trailblazer

aprire *v/t* ⟨4f⟩ open; *rubinetto* turn on;

i negozi aprono alle nove the shops open at nine
aprirsi *v/r* ⟨4f⟩ open; ***~ con qn*** confide in s.o., open up to s.o.
apriscatole *m* ⟨*pl* apriscatole⟩ can opener, *Br* tin opener
apuano *adj*: ***Alpi Apuane*** Apuan Alps
apulo... *pref* Apulian
AQ *abbr* (= **L'Aquila**) Aquila
aquila *f* eagle; ***~ reale*** golden eagle
aquilano **I** *adj* of L'Aquila; *persona* from L'Aquila **II** *m*, **-a** *f* person from L'Aquila
aquilino *adj*: ***naso*** *m* ***~*** aquiline nose
aquilone *m* kite
aquilotto *m* eaglet
AR *abbr* (= **Arezzo**) Arezzo
ara *f misura* are (*equal to 100 sq m*); ZOOL macaw; (*altare*) altar
arabesco *m* ⟨*pl* -chi⟩ arabesque; *hum* scrawl, scribble
Arabia Saudita *f* Saudi Arabia
arabico *adj* ⟨*mpl* -ci⟩ Arabian; ***gomma*** *f* ***-a*** gum arabic
arabo **I** *adj* Arab **II** *m*, **-a** *f* Arab **III** *m* Arabic
arachide *f* peanut
Aragona *f* Aragon **aragonese** **I** *adj* Aragonese **II** *m/f* Aragonese
aragosta *f* lobster
araldica *f* ⟨*pl* -che⟩ heraldry **araldico** *adj* ⟨*mpl* -ci⟩ heraldic
aramaico ⟨*no pl*⟩ *m lingua*: Aramaic
aranceto *m* orange grove
arancia *f* ⟨*pl* -ce⟩ orange; ***succo d'~*** orange juice
aranciata *f* orangeade
arancio **I** *adj inv* orange **II** *m* ⟨*pl* -ci⟩ *albero* orange tree; *colore* orange
arancione **I** *adj* orange **II** *m colore* orange **III** *m/f* Hari Krishna follower
arare *v/t* ⟨1a⟩ plough, *US* plow
aratro *m* plough, *US* plow
aratura *f* ploughing, *US* plowing
arazzo *m* tapestry
arbitraggio *m* ⟨*pl* -ggi⟩ arbitration; SPORTS refereeing; ECON arbitrage
arbitrare *v/t* ⟨1l⟩ arbitrate in; SPORTS referee
arbitrariamente *adv* arbitrarily **arbitrarietà** *f* ⟨*pl* arbitrarietà⟩ arbitrary nature
arbitrario *adj* ⟨*mpl* -ri⟩ arbitrary
arbitrio *m* ⟨*pl* -tri⟩ (*discrezione*) will; (*dispotismo*) arbitrary power; ***libero ~*** free will
arbitro *m* arbiter; SPORTS referee
arboreo *adj* woody; ***vegetazione*** *f* ***-a*** trees *pl*
arbusto *m* shrub
arca *f* ⟨*pl* -che⟩ (*cassa*) chest; REL ***l'~ di Noè*** Noah's Ark
arcadico *adj* ⟨*mpl* -ci⟩ Arcadian
arcaicità *f* ⟨*pl* arcaicità⟩ antiquity
arcaico *adj* ⟨*mpl* -ci⟩ archaic
arcangelo *m* archangel
arcano **I** *adj* arcane **II** *n*: ***arcano*** *m* mystery; ***svelare l'~*** unravel the mystery
arcata *f* ANAT, ARCH arch; ***~ dentaria*** dental arch
archeologia *f* arch(a)eology
archeologico *adj* ⟨*mpl* -ci⟩ arch(a)eological; ***museo*** *m* ***~*** arch(a)eological museum
archeologo *m*, **-a** *f* ⟨*mpl* -gi⟩ arch(a)eologist
archetipo *m* archetype
archetto *m* MUS bow
archibugio *m* ⟨*pl* -gi⟩ HIST arquebus
architettare *v/t* ⟨1a⟩ devise; *macchinare* plot; ***che stai architettando?*** *hum* what are you plotting?
architetto *m* architect
architettonico *adj* ⟨*mpl* -ci⟩ architectural
architettura *f* architecture
architrave *f* architrave
archiviare *v/t* ⟨1k⟩ file; ***~ una pratica*** put away a file; ***~ un procedimento*** dismiss a case
archiviazione *f* filing; JUR *di processo*: dismissal
archivio *m* ⟨*pl* -vi⟩ archives *pl*, records *pl*
archivista *m/f* ⟨*pl* -i⟩ archivist
archivolto *m* archivolt
ARCI *abbr* (= **Associazione Ricreativa Culturale Italiana**) *Italian Recreational and Cultural Association*
arcicontento *adj hum* happy as Larry
arcidiocesi *f* ⟨*pl* arcidiocesi⟩ archdiocese
arciduca *m*, **-duchessa** *f* ⟨*mpl* -chi⟩ archduke; *donna* archduchess **arciducato** *m* archduchy
arciere *m*, **-a** *f* HIST archer
Arcigay *abbr* (= **Associazione lesbica e gay italiana**) *Italian gay and lesbian association*

arcigno *adj* forbidding

arcinoto *adj* extremely well-known

arcione *m* pommel

arcipelago *m* ⟨*pl* -ghi⟩ archipelago

arciprete *m* archpriest

arcistufo *adj* sick to death; ***essere ~ di qc*** *infml* be sick to death of sth

arcivescovado *m* archbishopric

arcivescovo *m* archbishop

arco *m* ⟨*pl* -chi⟩ bow; ARCH arch; ***~ di tempo*** space of time; ***orchestra*** *f* ***d'-chi*** string orchestra

arcobaleno *m* rainbow

arcolaio *m* ⟨*pl* -ai⟩ wool winder

arcuare *v/t* ⟨1l⟩ arch

arcuarsi *v/r* ⟨1l⟩ *asta* bend; *pannello di legno* warp

ardeatino **I** *adj* of Ardea; *persona* from Ardea; ***Fosse Ardeatine*** Ardeatine Caves (*scene of a massacre in 1944*) **II** *m*, **-a** *f* person from Ardea

ardente *adj fig* ardent

ardentemente *adv* ardently

ardere **I** *v/t & v/i* ⟨3uu⟩ burn; ***legna*** *f* ***da ~*** firewood **II** *v/i* burn (*a. fig*); ***~ d'amore*** burn with love

ardesia *f* slate

ardimento *m* daring

ardire **I** *v/i* ⟨4d⟩ *liter* dare **II** *m* daring

ardito *adj* (*coraggioso*) daring; (*audace*) bold; *fig* impudent; ***pensiero*** *m* ***~*** bold idea

ardore *m fig* (*passione*) ardo(u)r; (*zelo*) eagerness

arduo *adj* difficult; ***impresa*** *f* ***-a*** difficult task

area *f* surface; *zona* area; ***~ ciclonica / anticiclonica*** METEO cyclonic / anticyclonic area; *fig* ***~ culturale*** culture area; ***~ fabbricabile*** site that may be built on; ***~ di memoria*** COMPUT memory area; ***~ metropolitana*** metropolitan area; SPORTS ***~ di rigore*** penalty area; ***~ di servizio*** service area

areale **I** *adj* regional **II** *m* region

area manager *m* ⟨*pl* area manager⟩ regional manager

arena *f* arena

arenaria *f* GEOL sandstone

arenarsi *v/r* ⟨1a⟩ run aground; *fig* come to a halt

arenile *m* sandy shore

areo... *pref* → ***aereo...***

argano *m* winch

argentare *v/t* ⟨1b⟩ silver-plate

argentato *adj* silver-plated

argentatura *f* silver plating **argenteo** *adj* silver

argenteria *f* silver(ware)

Argentina *f* Argentina

argentino **I** *adj* Argentinian **II** *m*, **-a** *f* Argentinian

argento *m* silver; ***d'~*** silver; ***~ vivo*** quicksilver; *fig* ***avere l'~ vivo addosso*** be fidgety; RAIL ***carta*** *f* ***d'~*** *travel pass for people over a certain age*; ***nozze*** *fpl* ***d'~*** silver wedding *sg*

argilla *f* clay

argilloso *adj* clayey

arginare *v/t* ⟨1l⟩ embank

argine *m* embankment; ***rottura*** *f* ***degli -i*** bursting of the banks; *fig* ***mettere*** *or* ***porre un ~ a qc*** hold sth in check

argomentazione *f* argument

argomento *m* argument; (*contenuto*) subject; ***cambiare ~*** change the subject; ***entrare nel vivo dell'~*** get to the heart of the matter

arguire *v/t* ⟨4d⟩ deduce; ***da che cosa lo arguisce?*** what makes you / her / him think that?

arguto *adj* witty; (*perspicace*) shrewd

arguzia *f* wit; *espressione* witticism, witty remark; (*perspicacia*) shrewdness

aria *f* **1.** air; ***all'~ aperta*** outside, in the fresh air; ***~ condizionata*** air conditioning; ***corrente*** *f* ***d'~*** draught; ***cambiare ~*** get a change of air; ***cambiare l'~ in una stanza*** air a room; ***mandare all'~ qc*** ruin sth **2.** (*aspetto*) appearance; (*espressione*) air; ***aver l'~ stanca*** look tired; ***ha l'~ di non capire*** he looks as if he doesn't understand; ***darsi delle -e*** give o.s. airs **3.** MUS tune; *di opera* aria

ariano **I** *adj* Aryan **II** *m*, **-a** *f* Aryan

aridità *f* dryness

arido *adj* dry, arid

arieggiare *v/t* ⟨1f⟩ *stanza* air

ariete *m* ZOOL ram; ASTROL ***Ariete*** Aries; ***sono dell'Ariete*** I'm (an) Aries

aringa *f* ⟨*pl* -ghe⟩ herring; ***~ affumicata*** smoked herring, kipper

arioso *adj* airy; ***ambiente*** *m* ***~*** airy space

arista *f* COOK chine of pork

aristocratico ⟨*mpl* -ci⟩ **I** *adj* aristocratic; ***modi*** *mpl* ***-ci*** aristocratic manners **II** *m*, **-a** *f* aristocrat

aristocrazia *f* aristocracy
Aristotele *m* Aristotle **aristotelico** *adj* ⟨*mpl* -ci⟩ Aristotelian
aritmetica *f* arithmetic
aritmetico *adj* ⟨*mpl* -ci⟩ arithmetical
aritmia *f* MED arrhythmia
Arlecchino *m* Harlequin; *fig* clown
arma *f* ⟨*pl* -i⟩ weapon; ***-i** pl* ***atomiche, biologiche e chimiche*** atomic, biological and chemical weapons; ***-i** pl* ***convenzionali*** conventional weapons; *fig* ***~ a doppio taglio*** double-edged sword; ***~ da fuoco*** firearm; ***-i** pl* ***nucleari*** nuclear weapons; ***chiamare alle -i*** call up; *fig* ***andarsene con -i e bagagli*** leave with bag and baggage; *fig* ***essere alle prime -i*** be a beginner, be just starting out
armadietto *m* locker; ***~ dei medicinali*** medicine cabinet
armadio *m* ⟨*pl* -di⟩ wardrobe; ***~ a muro*** built-in wardrobe
armaiolo *m*, **-a** *f* gunsmith
armamentario *m* ⟨*pl* -ri⟩ *usu hum* paraphernalia
armamento *m* armament; ***industria** f* ***degli -i*** armaments industry
armare *v/t* ⟨1a⟩ arm; ARCH reinforce; NAUT commission
armarsi *v/r* ⟨1a⟩ arm o.s. (***di*** with)
armata *f* army; NAUT fleet; ***~ rossa*** *hist* Red Army; ***~ Brancaleone*** *hum* raggle-taggle army
armato *adj* armed; ***~ fino ai denti*** armed to the teeth; ***carro** m* ***~*** tank; ***cemento** m* ***~*** reinforced concrete; ***forze** fpl* ***-e*** armed forces
armatore *m*, **-trice** *f* shipowner
armatoriale *adj* shipping *attr*; ***società** f* ***~*** shipping company
armatura *f* armo(u)r; (*struttura*) framework
armeggiare *v/i* ⟨1f⟩ faff about *infml*
Armenia *f* Armenia
armeno **I** *adj* Armenian **II** *m*, **-a** *f persona* Armenian **III** *m lingua* Armenian
armento *m* herd
armeria *f* (*arsenale*) armo(u)ry; (*negozio*) gun shop
armistizio *m* ⟨*pl* -zi⟩ armistice
armonia *f* harmony; ***vivere in buona ~*** live in harmony
armonica *f* ⟨*pl* -che⟩ glass harmonica; ***~ a bocca*** mouth organ
armonico *adj* ⟨*mpl* -ci⟩ harmonic
armonioso *adj* harmonious
armonium *m* ⟨*pl* armonium⟩ harmonium
armonizzare *v/t* & *v/i* ⟨1a⟩ harmonize
armonizzazione *f* harmonization
arnese *m* tool; ***essere bene / male in ~*** be in good / poor shape
arnia *f* beehive
arnica *f* ⟨*pl* -che⟩ BOT arnica
aroma *m* ⟨*pl* -i⟩ aroma
aromaterapia *f* aromatherapy
aromatico *adj* ⟨*mpl* -ci⟩ aromatic
aromatizzante **I** *adj* flavo(u)r-enhancing **II** *m* flavo(u)ring
aromatizzare *v/t* ⟨1a⟩ flavo(u)r
arpa *f* harp
arpeggio *m* ⟨*pl* -ggi⟩ arpeggio
arpione *m pesca* harpoon
arpista *m/f* ⟨*mpl* -i⟩ harpist
arrabattarsi *v/r* ⟨1a⟩ do everything one can
arrabbiare *v/t* ⟨1k⟩: ***far ~ qn*** make s.o. angry
arrabbiarsi *v/r*: ***~ (con qn / per qc)*** get angry (with s.o. / at sth)
arrabbiato *adj* angry; (*idrofobo*) rabid; COOK ***all'-a*** in a spicy sauce
arrabbiatura *f* fit of rage; ***prendersi un'~*** fly into a rage
arraffare *v/t* ⟨1a⟩ *infml* snatch **arraffone** *m*, **-a** *f* freeloader
arrampicarsi *v/r* ⟨1m & d⟩ climb; *fig* ***~ sugli specchi*** clutch at straws
arrampicata *f* climb; ***~ libera*** free climbing
arrampicatore *m*, **-trice** *f* climber; ***~ sociale*** social climber
arrancare *v/i* ⟨1d⟩ limp; (*procedere con fatica*) struggle along
arrangiamento *m* arrangement
arrangiare *v/t* ⟨1f⟩ arrange
arrangiarsi *v/r* (*accordarsi*) agree (***su*** on); (*destreggiarsi*) manage; ***se non vuoi che ti aiuti, arrangiati!*** if you don't want me to help you, you can sort it out yourself!
arrangiatore *m*, **-trice** *f* arranger
arrapare *v/t* ⟨1m⟩ *infml* make randy **arraparsi** *v/r* ⟨1m⟩ *infml* get randy
arrecare *v/t* ⟨1b & d⟩ bring; *fig* cause; ***~ danni*** cause damage *sg*
arredamento *m* décor; *mobili* furniture; *arte* interior design
arredare *v/t* ⟨1b⟩ furnish

arredatore *m*, **-trice** *f* interior designer

arredo *m* piece of furniture; (*arredamento*) furniture; ***-i** pl* fixtures; ***-i** pl **sacri*** sacred vessels and vestments

arrembaggio *m* ⟨*pl* -ggi⟩ boarding; *fig* ***buttarsi all'~ di qc*** make a mad dash for sth

arrendersi *v/r* ⟨3c⟩ surrender; *fig* give up

arrendevole *adj* soft, yielding

arrendevolezza *f* compliance

arrestare *v/t* ⟨1b⟩ stop, halt; JUR arrest; ***~ l'emorragia*** stop the bleeding

arrestarsi *v/r* ⟨1b⟩ stop

arresto *m* **1.** coming to a stop; ***~ cardiaco*** cardiac arrest **2.** JUR arrest; ***-i domiciliari*** house arrest; ***dichiarare qn in ~*** put s.o. under arrest; ***essere in stato di ~*** be under arrest

arretramento *m* drawing back **arretrare** *v/i* ⟨1b⟩ draw back (*a. fig*); ***~ per la paura*** shrink back in fear **arretratezza** *f* backwardness

arretrato **I** *adj* in arrears; *paese* underdeveloped; ***numero** m **~** di giornale* back issue; ***avere del lavoro ~*** have a backlog of work **II** *m*: ***arretrati** pl* arrears *pl*; ***devo riscuotere gli -i*** I'm due my back pay

arricchimento *m* enrichment

arricchire *v/t* ⟨4d⟩ *fig* enrich

arricchirsi *v/r* ⟨4d⟩ get rich

arricchito **I** *m*, **-a** *f pej* nouveau riche **II** *adj* enriched; ***uranio** m **~*** enriched uranium

arricciare *v/t* ⟨1f⟩ *capelli* curl; ***~ il naso*** turn up one's nose

arricciarsi *v/r* ⟨1f⟩ curl; ***i suoi capelli si arricciano facilmente*** her hair curls easily **arricciato** *adj* curly **arricciatura** *f* curling

arridere *v/i* ⟨3b⟩ smile on; ***oggi la fortuna mi arride*** luck is on my side today

arringa *f* ⟨*pl* -ghe⟩ JUR closing speech for the defence; *fig **~ un giudizio*** hazard a judgment

arrivare *v/i* ⟨1a⟩ arrive; ***~ a*** (*raggiungere*) reach; ***~ a Roma*** arrive in Rome; ***~ a casa*** get home ***arriviamo in città/all'aeroporto alle sei*** we get to town/get into the airport at six; ***~ primo*** arrive first; ***~ primo/ultimo*** SPORTS come first/last; ***~ puntuale*** arrive on time; ***~ a fare qc*** manage to do sth; ***non ci arriva*** *infml* he doesn't get it *infml*, he doesn't understand; ***arrivo subito!*** I'm just coming!; ***~ a novant'anni*** turn ninety; ***~ a proposito*** turn up at the right time; ***~ al traguardo*** reach the finishing line; *fig* reach one's goal; ***dove vuoi ~?*** what are you getting at?; ***non credevo che sarebbe arrivato a tanto!*** I never thought he'd go that far!; ***possibile che non ci arrivi?*** how can you not understand?

arrivato *adj* (*affermato*) successful

arrivederci *int*, **arrivederLa** *int* goodbye

arrivista *m/f* ⟨*mpl* -i⟩ social climber

arrivo *m* arrival; SPORTS finishing line; ***essere in ~*** be arriving; ***il treno è in ~ al binario 3*** the train is coming in at platform 3; ***-i internazionali*** international arrivals

arroccarsi *v/r* ⟨1c e d⟩ MIL fall back (to a defensive position) (*a. fig*)

arrocco *m* ⟨*pl* -cchi⟩ *scacchi*: castling

arrochito *adj* hoarse

arrogante *adj* arrogant

arroganza *f* arrogance

arrogarsi *v/r* ⟨1c e g⟩: ***~ qc*** assume sth

arrossamento *m* reddening **arrossare** *v/t* ⟨1a⟩ redden; ***il freddo arrossa le guance*** the cold makes your cheeks red **arrossarsi** *v/r* ⟨1a⟩ blush **arrossato** *adj* red; ***avere gli occhi -i*** have red eyes

arrossire *v/i* ⟨4d⟩ blush

arrostire *v/t* ⟨4d⟩ *carne* roast; *ai ferri* grill

arrostirsi *v/r* ⟨4d⟩: *fig* ***~ al sole*** soak up the sun

arrosto *m* roast; ***~ d'agnello*** roast lamb; ***~ di maiale*** roast pork; ***patate** fpl **~*** roast potatoes

arrotare *v/t* ⟨1c⟩ (*affilare*) sharpen; (*molare*) grind; (*investire*) *infml* knock down **arrotatrice** *f* grinder **arrotino** *m*, **-a** *f* knife grinder

arrotolare *v/t* ⟨1m & c⟩ roll up

arrotondamento *m* rounding off

arrotondare *v/t* ⟨1a⟩ round off; *stipendio* supplement

arrovellarsi *v/r* ⟨1b⟩ (*tormentarsi*) fret; (*darsi da fare*) strive; ***~ il cervello*** rack one's brains

arroventato *adj* red-hot

arruffare *v/t* ⟨1a⟩ *capelli* ruffle
arruffarsi *v/r* ⟨1a⟩ get tousled
arruffato *adj* ruffled
arrugginire ⟨4d⟩ **I** *v/t* rust **II** *v/i* rust; *fig* become rusty
arrugginirsi *v/r* ⟨4d⟩ rust; *fig* become rusty
arruolamento *m* enlistment
arruolare *v/t* ⟨1o⟩ enlist
arruolarsi *v/r* ⟨1o⟩ enlist, join up
arsella *f* clam; ***spaghetti*** *mpl* ***alle -e*** spaghetti *sg* with clams
arsenale *m* arsenal; NAUT dockyard
arsenico I *adj* ⟨*mpl* -ci⟩ arsenic; ***acido*** *m* **~** arsenic acid **II** *m* ⟨*no pl*⟩ arsenic
arso I *past part* → ***ardere*** **II** *adj* burnt; (*secco*) dried-up; ***avere la gola -a*** be parched
arsura *f* blazing heat
arte *f* art; (*abilità*) gift; ***le -i*** *pl* ***figurative*** the figurative arts; ***-i*** *pl* ***grafiche*** graphic arts; **~ *sacra*** sacred art; ***storia*** *f* ***dell'~*** history of art; ***un discorso fatto ad ~*** a masterly speech; ***essere figlio*** *m* ***d'~*** come from a theatrical family; ***impara l'~ e mettila da parte*** *prov* learn a skill for a rainy day
artefatto *adj voce* disguised
artefice *m/f fig* author, architect
artemisia *f* mugwort
arteria *f* artery; **~ *stradale*** arterial road
arteriosclerosi *f* hardening of the arteries
arteriosclerotico *adj* ⟨*mpl* -ci⟩ arteriosclerotic; *fig* senile
arterioso *adj* arterial; ***pressione*** *f* ***-a*** arterial pressure
artico *adj* ⟨*mpl* -ci⟩ Arctic *attr*; ***circolo*** *m* ***polare*** **~** Arctic circle
articolare I *adj* articular **II** *v/t* ⟨1m⟩ articulate; (*suddividere*) divide
articolarsi *v/r* ⟨1m⟩ **~ *in*** be divided into
articolato *adj camion* articulated; *discorso* structured; ***preposizione*** *f* ***-a*** *preposition combined with the definite article*
articolazione *f* ANAT articulation; ***l'~ del polso*** the wrist joint
articolo *m* **1.** item, article; ***-i*** *pl* ***di consumo*** consumer goods; **~ *di prima necessità*** basic; ***-i*** *pl* ***da regalo*** gifts; ***-i*** *pl* ***sportivi*** sports *or US* sporting goods **2.** GRAM **~ *determinativo*** definite article; GRAM **~ *indeterminativo*** indefinite article **3.** **~ *di fondo*** leading article
Artide *m* Arctic
artificiale *adj* artificial; ***allattamento*** *m* **~** bottle-feeding
artificialmente *adv* artificially
artificiere *m* bomb disposal expert
artificio *m* ⟨*pl* -ci⟩ artifice; ***fuochi*** *mpl* ***d'~*** fireworks *pl*
artificioso *adj maniere* artificial
artigianale *adj* handmade, handcrafted
artigianalmente *adv*: ***prodotto ~*** craftsman-made
artigianato *m* craftsmanship; ***mostra*** *f* ***dell'~*** craft show
artigiano *m*, ***-a*** *f* craftsman; *donna* craftswoman
artigliere *m* artilleryman
artiglieria *f* artillery
artiglio *m* ⟨*pl* -gli⟩ talon
artista *m/f* ⟨*mpl* -i⟩ artist
artisticamente *adv* artistically
artistico *adj* ⟨*mpl* -ci⟩ artistic
arto *m* limb; ***-i*** *pl* ***inferiori / superiori*** upper / lower limbs
artrite *f* arthritis
artritico *adj* ⟨*mpl* -ci⟩ arthritic
artrosi *f* osteoarthritis; **~ *cervicale*** cervical spondylosis
arzigogolare *v/i* ⟨1n e c⟩: **~ *su qc*** ramble on about sth **arzigogolato** *adj* rambling **arzigogolo** *m* (*discorso cervellotico*) ramblings *pl*; (*trovata bizzarra*) weird idea
arzillo *adj* lively
asburgico *adj* ⟨*mpl* -ci⟩ Hapsburg; ***monarchia*** *f* ***-a*** Hapsburg monarchy
Asburgo *mpl* Hapsburgs
ascella *f* armpit
ascendente I *adj* ascending; *strada* sloping upwards; *movimento* upwards **II** *m* ASTROL ascendant; *fig* influence
ascensionale *adj* upward; ***spinta*** *f* **~** PHYS upward thrust
ascensione *f di montagna* ascent; REL Ascension
ascensore *m* lift, *US* elevator
ascesa *f* ascent; **~ *al trono*** accession
ascesi *f* ⟨*pl* ascesi⟩ asceticism
ascesso *m* abscess
asceta *m* ⟨*pl* -i⟩ ascetic
ascia *f* ⟨*pl* -sce⟩ adze
asciugabiancheria *m* ⟨*pl* asciuga-

biancheria⟩ (tumble) dryer
asciugacapelli *m* hairdryer
asciugamano *m* towel; ***~ da bagno*** bath towel
asciugare *v/t* ⟨1e⟩ dry
asciugarsi *v/r* ⟨1e⟩ dry o.s.; ***~ i capelli*** dry one's hair; ***~ le mani*** dry one's hands
asciugatrice *f* tumble dryer
asciuttezza *f* dryness
asciutto I *adj* dry; ***rimanere a bocca -a*** end up with nothing **II** *m*: *fig* ***trovarsi all'~*** be stony broke
ascolano I *adj* of Ascoli; *persona* from Ascoli **II** *m*, **-a** *f* person from Ascoli
ascoltare *v/t* ⟨1a⟩ listen to; ***~ qc/qn*** listen to sth/s.o.; ***ascoltami!*** listen (to me)!; ***mi ascolti, per favore!*** please listen to me!
ascoltatore *m*, **-trice** *f* listener
ascolto *m* listening; ***dare*** *or* ***prestare ~*** listen (***a*** to); ***indice*** *m* ***di ~*** ratings *pl*
ASCOM *abbr* (= **Associazione Commercianti**) *f association of shopkeepers*
ascorbico *adj* ⟨*mpl* -ci⟩ ascorbic; ***acido*** *m* ***~*** ascorbic acid
ascrivere *v/t* ⟨3tt⟩ (*attribuire*) ascribe; ***~ il merito di qc a qn*** give s.o. the credit for sth
asessuato *adj* asexual
asettico *adj* ⟨*mpl* -ci⟩ aseptic
asfaltare *v/t* ⟨1a⟩ asphalt
asfaltato *adj* asphalted; ***strada*** *f* ***-a*** asphalt road
asfalto *m* asphalt
asfissia *f* asphyxia
asfissiare *v/t* ⟨1k⟩ asphyxiate
as(h)kenazita ⟨*mpl* -i⟩ **I** *adj* Ashkenazi **II** *m/f* Ashkenazi
Asia *f* Asia; ***~ Minore*** Asia Minor
asiatico ⟨*mpl* -ci⟩ **I** *adj* Asian **II** *m*, **-a** *f* Asian
asilo *m* **1.** shelter; ***richiesta*** *f* ***di ~ politico*** request for political asylum **2.** ***~ infantile*** nursery school; ***~ nido*** day nursery
asimmetria *f* asymmetry
asimmetrico *adj* ⟨*mpl* -ci⟩ asymmetrical
asina *f* she-ass
asincrono *adj* asynchronous; ***modalità*** *f* ***-a*** COMPUT asynchronous modality
asino *m* ass (*a. fig*); ***fare come l'~ di Buridano*** *be unable to choose between two things and end up with neither*; ***lavar la testa all'~*** *waste one's time doing something useless*; ***qui casca l'~*** there's the rub
asintomatico *adj* ⟨*mpl* -ci⟩ asymptomatic
ASL *abbr* (= **Azienda Sanitaria Locale**) *local health authority*
asma *f* asthma
asmatico *adj* ⟨*mpl* -ci⟩ asthmatic
asociale *adj* antisocial
asola *f* buttonhole
asparago *m* ⟨*pl* -gi⟩ spear of asparagus; ***-gi*** asparagus *sg*; ***~ selvatico*** wild asparagus; ***punte*** *fpl* ***di -i*** asparagus tips
aspergere *v/t* ⟨3uu⟩ sprinkle (holy water); ***~ qn/qc d'acqua benedetta*** sprinkle holy water on s.o./sth
asperità *f* ⟨*pl* asperità⟩ roughness; *fig* harshness
aspersione *f* sprinkling (of holy water)
aspettare *v/t* ⟨1b⟩ wait for; ***aspettami!*** wait for me!; ***aspetta un attimo!*** wait a minute!; ***~ un bambino*** be expecting a baby; ***farsi ~*** keep people waiting; ***è un mese che aspettiamo*** we've been waiting a month
aspettarsi *v/r* ⟨1b⟩ expect; ***dovevo aspettarmelo*** I should have expected it; ***che ti aspettavi da lui?*** what did you expect from him?
aspettativa *f* expectation; *da lavoro* unpaid leave; ***deludere le -e di qn*** fall short of s.o.'s expectations; ***chiedere un anno di ~*** ask for a year's sabbatical
aspetto[1] *m* look, appearance; *di problema* aspect; ***sotto quest'~*** from that point of view
aspetto[2] *m*: ***sala*** *f* ***d'~*** waiting room
aspide *m* asp; ***~ di Cleopatra*** Egyptian cobra
aspirante I *m/f* applicant **II** *adj* TECH suction *attr*
aspirapolvere *m* vacuum cleaner; ***passare l'~*** vacuum
aspirare ⟨1a⟩ **I** *v/t* inhale; TECH suck up **II** *v/i*: ***~ a qc*** aspire to sth; ***~ a fare qc*** aspire to do sth
aspiratore *m* extractor (fan)
aspirazione *f* suction; (*ambizione*) aspiration
aspirina® *f* aspirin®

asportabile *adj* removable
asportare *v/t* ⟨1c⟩ take away
asporto *m*: ***da ~*** takeaway, *US* takeout
aspramente *adv* (*bruscamente*) harshly; (*violentemente*) roughly; ***rimproverare ~ qn*** give s.o. a good telling off; ***combattere ~*** fight fiercely
asprezza *f* (*sapore acre*) sourness; *di superficie*: roughness; *di clima*: harshness; *fig* (*severità*) severity **asprigno** *adj* rather sour
aspro *adj* sour; (*duro*) harsh; *litigio* bitter
assaggiare *v/t* ⟨1f⟩ taste, sample
assaggio *m* ⟨*pl* -ggi⟩ taste, sample
assai I *adj* a lot of **II** *adv con verbo* a lot; *con aggettivo* very; (*abbastanza*) enough; ***m'importa ~*** what do I care
assalire *v/t* ⟨4m⟩ attack
assalitore *m*, **-trice** *f* attacker
assaltare *v/t* ⟨1a⟩ → ***assalire***
assalto *m* attack; *fig* ***prendere d'~*** storm
assaporare *v/t* ⟨1a⟩ savo(u)r
assassinare *v/t* ⟨1a⟩ murder; POL assassinate
assassinio *m* murder; POL assassination
assassino I *m*, **-a** *f* murderer; POL assassin **II** *adj* murderous
assatanato *adj* possessed; *fig* randy
asse[1] *f* board; ***~ da stiro*** ironing board
asse[2] *m* TECH axle; MATH axis; ***~ terrestre*** earth's axis; ***~ ereditario*** JUR estate
assecondare *v/t* ⟨1a⟩ support; (*esaudire*) satisfy
assediante I *adj* besieging **II** *m/f* besieger
assediare *v/t* ⟨1k⟩ besiege
assedio *m* ⟨*pl* -di⟩ siege
assegnamento *m* hope; ***fare ~ su qn / qc*** rely on s.o. / sth
assegnare *v/t* ⟨1a⟩ *premio* award; (*destinare*) assign
assegnatario *m*, **-a** *f* ⟨*mpl* -ri⟩ assignee
assegno *m* **1.** cheque, *US* check; ***~ in bianco*** blank cheque (*US* check); ***~ sbarrato*** crossed cheque (*US* check); ***~ turistico*** traveller's cheque, *US* traveler's check; ***~ a vuoto*** bad cheque (*US* check); ***emettere un ~*** issue *or* write a cheque (*US* check) **2.** ***contro ~*** cash on delivery **3.** ***-i familiari*** child benefit
assemblaggio *m* ⟨*pl* -ggi⟩ assembly
assemblare *v/t* ⟨1a⟩ assemble
assemblea *f* meeting; ***~ generale*** annual general meeting
assembramento *m* gathering
assennato *adj* sensible
assenso *m* assent
assentarsi *v/r* ⟨1b⟩ go away, leave
assente *adj* absent, away; *fig* absent-minded
assenteismo *m* absenteeism **assenteista** *m/f* ⟨*mpl* -i⟩ absentee
assentire *v/i* ⟨4b⟩ agree; ***~ a una richiesta*** agree to a request
assenza *f* absence; ***~ di qc*** lack of sth; ***in sua ~*** in his / her absence
assenzio *m* ⟨*pl* -zi⟩ BOT wormwood; (*liquore*) absinthe; ***amaro come l'~*** (as) bitter as gall
asserire *v/t* ⟨4d⟩ maintain
asserragliarsi *v/r* ⟨1g⟩ barricade oneself; ***~ in casa*** shut oneself up at home
assertore *m*, **-trice** *f* supporter
asservimento *m* enslavement (*a. fig*)
asserzione *f* assertion
assessorato *m* office of council(l)or; ***~ alla cultura*** culture department
assessore *m* council(l)or; ***~ comunale*** local councillor
assestamento *m di terreno*: settlement; *fig* settling down; ***scosse*** *fpl* ***di ~*** aftershocks
assestare *v/t* ⟨1b⟩ (*sistemare*) organize; (*regolare*) adjust; (*affibbiare*) do up; ***~ la mira*** adjust one's aim; ***~ un colpo a qn*** land a blow on s.o.
assestarsi *v/r* ⟨1b⟩ *terreno* settle
assetato *adj* thirsty; ***~ di sangue*** bloodthirsty
assetto *m* order; NAUT trim
asseverare *v/t* ⟨1m & b⟩ certify **asseverazione** *f* certification
assiale *adj* axial; ***carico*** *m* ***~*** axial load
assicella *f* lath
assicurabile *adj* insurable
assicurare *v/t* ⟨1a⟩ **1.** insure; ***~ qc contro qc*** insure sth against sth **2.** (*legare*) secure **3.** *lettera*, *pacco* register **4.** ***~ a qn che*** assure s.o. that; ***te lo assicuro!*** I can assure you!
assicurarsi *v/r* **1.** make sure, ensure **2.** ***~ contro gli infortuni*** insure o.s. against accident

assicurata *f* registered letter
assicurativo *adj* insurance *attr*; ***agente*** *m* ~ insurance agent
assicurato I *adj* insured; *lettera, pacco* registered **II** *m*, **-a** *f* person with insurance
assicuratore I *adj* insurance *attr*; ***compagnia*** *f* ***-trice*** insurance company **II** *m*, **-trice** *f* insurance agent
assicurazione *f* insurance; ~ ***dei bagagli*** luggage insurance; ~ ***di responsabilità civile*** liability insurance; ~ ***sulla vita*** life insurance; ~ ***casco*** comprehensive insurance
assideramento *m* exposure; ***morte*** *f* ***per*** ~ death from exposure
assiduamente *adv* diligently; (*frequentare*) regularly **assiduità** *f* ⟨*pl* assiduità⟩ (*costanza*) diligence; (*frequentazione*) regularity
assiduo *adj* (*diligente*) assiduous; (*regolare*) regular
assieme *adv* together; ~ ***a qn / qc*** with s.o. / sth
assillante *adj* nagging
assillare *v/t* ⟨1a⟩ pester
assillo *m fig persona* pest, nuisance; (*preoccupazione*) nagging thought
assimilabile *adj* digestible **assimilabilità** *f* ⟨*pl* assimilabilità⟩ digestibility
assimilare *v/t* ⟨1m⟩ assimilate
assimilazione *f* assimilation
assioma *m* ⟨*pl* -i⟩ axiom
assiro I *adj* Assyrian **II** *m*, **-a** *f* Assyrian; ***gli Assiri*** the Assyrians **assiro-babilonese** *adj* Assyro-Babylonian
assise *fpl*: ***Corte*** *f* ***d'***~ *Crown Court*
assistente *m/f* assistant; ~ ***geriatrico*** care worker for the elderly; ~ ***sociale*** social worker; ~ ***di volo*** flight attendant
assistenza *f* assistance; ~ ***medica*** medical care; ~ ***sociale*** social work; ~ ***tecnica*** after-sales service
assistenziale *adj*: ***ente*** *m* ~ welfare organization
assistere ⟨3f⟩ **I** *v/t* assist, help; (*curare*) nurse **II** *v/i* (*essere presente*) be present (***a*** at), attend (***a*** sth)
assistito I *adj*: ~ ***dal servizio sanitario*** cared for by the NHS *or US* by Medicaid and Medicare; ~ ***da assicurazione sanitaria*** covered by health insurance; COMPUT ~ ***da computer*** computer-aided **II** *m*, **-a** *f*: ~ ***dal servizio sanitario*** NHS patient, *US* Medicaid *or* Medicare patient; ~ ***da assicurazione sanitaria*** person with health insurance
asso *m* ace; ~ ***del ciclismo*** cycling ace; ***essere un*** ~ ***in latino*** be brilliant at Latin; *fig* ***piantare in*** ~ leave in the lurch
associabile *adj*: ~ ***con*** that can be associated with
associare *v/t* ⟨1f⟩ take into partnership; *fig* ~ ***qn a qc*** associate s.o. with sth
associarsi *v/r* ⟨1f⟩ enter into partnership (***a*** with); (*unirsi*) join forces; (*iscriversi*) subscribe (***a*** to); (*prendere parte*) join (***a*** sth)
associato I *adj* associate; ***professore*** *m* ~ senior lecturer, *US* associate professor **II** *m*, **-a** *f* associate
associazione *f* association; ~ ***benefica*** charity; ~ ***per la difesa dei consumatori*** consumer association
assodare *v/t* ⟨1c⟩ (*accertare*) ascertain
assoggettamento *m* subjection
assoggettare *v/t* ⟨1b⟩ subject
assoggettarsi *v/r* ⟨1b⟩ subject oneself
assolato *adj* sunny
assoldare *v/t* ⟨1c⟩ hire
assolo *m* ⟨*pl* assolo⟩ MUS solo
assolto *past part* → ***assolvere***
assolutamente *adv* absolutely; ***devi*** ~ ***venire!*** you really must come!; ~ ***no!*** certainly not!
assolutezza *f* absoluteness **assolutismo** *m* absolutism **assolutista** *adj* ⟨*mpl* -i⟩ absolutist
assoluto *adj* absolute; ***potere*** *m* ~ absolute power; ***è il migliore in*** ~ he / she / it is the best by far
assoluzione *f* JUR acquittal; REL absolution
assolvere *v/t* ⟨3g⟩ JUR acquit; *da un obbligo* release; *compito* carry out, perform; REL absolve, give absolution to
assomigliare *v/i* ⟨1g⟩: ~ ***a qn*** be like s.o., resemble s.o.
assomigliarsi *v/r* ⟨1g⟩be like *or* resemble each other
assommare *v/t* ⟨1a⟩ combine; ~ ***qc in sé*** be the epitome of sth **assommarsi** *v/r* ⟨1b⟩ combine
assonnato *adj* sleepy
assopirsi *v/r* ⟨4d⟩ doze off; *fig* sub-

side
assorbente I *adj* absorbent II *m*: **~ igienico** sanitary towel; **~ interno** tampon
assorbimento *m* absorption; (*inglobamento*) incorporation
assorbire *v/t* ⟨4c or 4d⟩ absorb
assordamento *m* making deaf, (*peggioramento dell'udito*) becoming deaf
assordante *adj* deafening
assordare ⟨1a⟩ I *v/t* deafen II *v/i* go deaf
assortimento *m* assortment
assortire *v/t* ⟨4d⟩ (*mettere insieme*) combine; (*abbinare*) match
assortito *adj* assorted; **essere ben ~ con** go well with
assorto *adj* engrossed
assottigliamento *m* slimming down
assuefare *v/t* ⟨3aa⟩ accustom (**a** to)
assuefarsi *v/r* ⟨3aa⟩ become accustomed (**a** to)
assuefatto *past part* → **assuefare**
assuefazione *f* resistance, tolerance; *agli alcolici, alla droga* addiction; **dare ~** be habit-forming
assumere *v/t* ⟨3h⟩ **1.** *impiegato* take on, hire **2.** *incarico* take on **3. assume medicinali?** are you taking any medication? **4. ~ importanza** become important; **~ un atteggiamento** strike an attitude
assumersi *v/r* ⟨3h⟩: **~ l'incarico di qc** take on the job of (doing) sth; **~ la responsabilità di qn / qc** take responsibility for s.o. / sth
Assunta *f*: **l'~** Our Lady of the Assumption
assunto I *adj* employed II *m*, **-a** *f* recruit; **i nuovi -i** the new recruits III **assunto** *past part* → **assumere**
assunzione *f di impiegato* employment, hiring; REL **Assunzione** Assumption
assurdamente *adv* absurdly
assurdità *f* ⟨*pl* assurdità⟩ absurdity
assurdo *adj* absurd
asta *f* **1.** pole; **a mezz'~** at half mast **2.** FIN auction; **mettere all'~** sell at auction, put up for auction
astante *m/f* bystander
astemio ⟨*mpl* -mi⟩ I *adj* abstemious II *m*, **-a** *f* abstemious person
astenersi *v/r* ⟨2q⟩: **~ da** abstain from
astensione *f* abstention; **~ dal voto** abstention
asterisco *m* ⟨*pl* -chi⟩ asterisk
asteroide *m* asteroid
astice *m* ⟨*pl* -ci⟩ lobster
astigiano I *adj* of Asti; *persona* from Asti II *m*, **-a** *f* person from Asti
astigmatico *adj* ⟨*mpl* -ci⟩ astigmatic
astigmatismo *m* astigmatism
astinente *adj* abstinent
astinenza *f* abstinence; **essere in crisi d'~** have withdrawal symptoms
astio *m* ⟨*pl* -ti⟩ ranco(u)r
astioso *adj* resentful
astragalo *m* ANAT talus; BOT milk-vetch; *hist gioco* jacks
astrakan *m* ⟨*pl* astrakan⟩ astrakhan
astrale *adj*: **corpo** *m* **~** astral body
astrattamente *adv* in abstract **astrattezza** *f* abstract nature **astrattismo** *m* abstract art **astrattista** *m/f* ⟨*mpl* -i⟩ abstract artist
astratto *adj* abstract
astrazione *f* abstraction
astringente *m/adj* MED astringent
astro *m* star; **~ nascente** rising star
astrofisica *f* astrophysics *sg* **astrofisico** ⟨*mpl* -ci⟩ I *adj* astrophysical II *m*, **-a** *f* astrophysicist
astrolabio *m* ⟨*pl* -bi⟩ *hist* astrolabe
astrologia *f* astrology
astrologico *adj* ⟨*mpl* -ci⟩ astrological
astrologo *m*, **-a** *f* ⟨*mpl* -gi⟩ astrologer
astronauta *m/f* ⟨*mpl* -i⟩ astronaut
astronautica *f* astronautics
astronave *f* spaceship
astronomia *f* astronomy
astronomico *adj* ⟨*mpl* -ci⟩ astronomical; **prezzi** *mpl* **-ci** astronomical prices
astronomo *m*, **-a** *f* astronomer
astrusamente *adv* obscurely **astrusità** *f* ⟨*pl* astrusità⟩ (*stranezza*) oddness; (*incomprensibilità*) obscurity; (*ragionamento astruso*) gobbledegook
astruso *adj* odd; (*incomprensibile*) obscure
astuccio *m* ⟨*pl* -cci⟩ case
asturiano I *adj* Asturian II *m*, **-a** *f* Asturian
astutamente *adv* astutely
astuto *adj* astute
astuzia *f* astuteness; (*trovata*) trick; **ricorrere a un'~** resort to a trick
AT *abbr* (= **Asti**) Asti
atavico *adj* ⟨*mpl* -ci⟩ atavistic **atavis-**

mo *m* atavism
ateismo *m* atheism
Atene *f* Athens
ateneo *m* university
ateniese **I** *adj* Athenian **II** *m/f* Athenian
ateo *m*, **-a** *f* atheist
atesino **I** *adj* of Alto Adige; *persona* from Alto Adige **II** *m*, **-a** *f* person from Alto Adige
atipicità *f* ⟨*pl* atipicità⟩ atypicality **atipico** *adj* ⟨*mpl* -ci⟩ atypical
atlante *m* atlas
atlantico *adj* ⟨*mpl* -ci⟩ Atlantic; ***Oceano*** *m* ***Atlantico*** Atlantic Ocean
Atlantide *f* Atlantis
atleta *m/f* ⟨*mpl* -i⟩ athlete
atletica *f* athletics *sg*; ~ ***leggera*** track and field (events)
atletico *adj* ⟨*mpl* -ci⟩ athletic
atmosfera *f* atmosphere
atmosferico *adj* ⟨*mpl* -ci⟩ atmospheric; ***agenti*** *mpl* ***-ci*** atmospheric agents; ***condizioni*** *fpl* ***-che*** weather conditions
atollo *m* atoll
atomico *adj* ⟨*mpl* -ci⟩ atomic
atomo *m* atom
atonia *f* MED, LING atony **atonicità** *f* ⟨*pl* atonicità⟩ absence of stress **atonico** *adj* ⟨*mpl* -ci⟩ atonic **atono** *adj* unstressed
atossico *adj* ⟨*mpl* -ci⟩ non-toxic
atriale *adj* ANAT atrial
atrio *m* ⟨*pl* -ri⟩ foyer; ~ ***della stazione*** station concourse
atrioventricolare *adj* ANAT atrioventricular
atroce *adj* appalling; *fig* ***dubbi*** *mpl* ***-i*** *infml* terrible doubts
atrocemente *adv* terribly
atrocità *f* ⟨*pl* atrocità⟩ atrocity
atrofia *f* atrophy **atrofico** *adj* ⟨*mpl* -ci⟩ atrophic
attaccabrighe *m/f* ⟨*pl* attaccabrighe⟩ *infml* troublemaker
attaccamento *m* attachment
attaccante *m* SPORTS forward, striker
attaccapanni *m* ⟨*pl* attaccapanni⟩ clothes hook; *a stelo* clothes hanger
attaccare ⟨1d⟩ **I** *v/t* **1.** attach; (*incollare*) stick; (*appendere*) hang; ~ ***le figurine*** stick in stickers; ~ ***un quadro alla parete*** hang a picture on the wall; ~ ***un bottone alla camicia*** sew a button on a shirt; *fig* ~ ***bottone con qn*** bend s.o.'s ear **2.** (*assalire*) attack **3.** (*iniziare*) begin, start; ~ ***briga*** pick a fight; ~ ***discorso*** start a conversation **4.** ~ ***qc a qn*** *malattia* give s.o. sth **5.** ~ ***la corrente*** *infml* turn on the electricity; ~ ***il telefono*** hang up **II** *v/i* stick; ~ ***a fare qc*** *infml* start doing sth; ***smettila, con me non attacca!*** *hum* stop that, it won't work with me!
attaccarsi *v/r* stick; (*aggrapparsi*) hold on (***a*** to); ***attaccati al tram!*** *hum* you can whistle for it!
attaccaticcio *adj* ⟨*mpl* -cci⟩ sticky; *fig persona* clingy
attaccato *adj* (*affezionato*) fond; ***essere*** ~ ***a qn / qc*** be fond of s.o. / sth; ***è sempre stato*** ~ ***al denaro*** he's always been mean with money; (*molto vicino*) close (***a*** to)
attaccatura *f* join
attacchinaggio *m* ⟨*pl* -ggi⟩ bill posting **attacchino** *m*, **-a** *f* bill poster
attacco *m* ⟨*pl* -cchi⟩ attack; (*punto di unione*) junction; ELEC socket; *sci* binding; MED fit; (*inizio*) beginning; ~ ***cardiaco*** heart attack
attaché *m/f* ⟨*pl* attaché⟩ attaché
attanagliare *v/t* ⟨1g⟩ *fig* gnaw
attardarsi *v/r* ⟨1a⟩ linger; ***mi sono attardato in ufficio*** I stayed late at the office
attecchire *v/t* ⟨4d⟩ *pianta* take root; *moda* catch on
atteggiamento *m* attitude
atteggiare *v/t* ⟨1f⟩ put on; ~ ***il viso a sorpresa*** put on a surprised expression
atteggiarsi *v/r* ⟨1f⟩: ~ ***a*** pose as
attempato *adj* elderly
attendere ⟨3c⟩ **I** *v/t* wait for; ***attenda in linea, per cortesia*** hold the line, please **II** *v/i*: ~ ***a*** attend to
attendersi *v/r* ⟨3c⟩: ~ ***qc*** expect sth
attendibile *adj* reliable
attendibilità *f* ⟨*pl* attendibilità⟩ reliability; ***verificare l'***~ ***di una notizia*** check out whether a piece of news is true
attenersi *v/r* ⟨2q⟩ stick (***a*** to); ~ ***ai fatti*** stick to the facts
attentare *v/i* ⟨1b⟩: ~ ***a*** attack; ~ ***a la vita di qn*** make an attempt on s.o.'s life
attentato *m* attempted assassination; ~

alla libertà attack on civil liberties; ***compiere un ~ (contro qn)*** carry out an attack (on s.o.)
attentatore *m*, **-trice** *f* attacker
attenti *int* MIL attention!; ***mettersi sull'~*** come to attention
attento I *adj* attentive; ***stare ~ a*** be careful of; ***stai ~ a non cadere*** be careful you don't fall; ***stare ~ a qn*** *badare* pay attention to sth **II** *int*: ***~!*** look out!, (be) careful!; ***-i alle macchine!*** watch out for the cars!; ***~ allo scalino*** mind the step
attenuante *f* extenuating circumstance
attenuare *v/t* ⟨1m & b⟩ reduce; *colpo* cushion
attenuarsi *v/r* lessen, decrease
attenuazione *f* reduction
attenzione *f* attention; ***~!*** look out!, (be) careful!; ***far ~ a qc*** mind *or* watch sth; ***fai bene ~ alle istruzioni*** listen carefully to the instructions; ***coprire qn di -i*** *pl* lavish attention on s.o.; ***è sempre pieno di -i*** he's always very attentive
atterraggio *m* ⟨*pl* -ggi⟩ landing; ***~ di fortuna*** emergency landing; ***~ strumentale*** instrument landing
atterrare ⟨1b⟩ **I** *v/t avversario* knock down, knock to the ground; *edificio* demolish, knock down **II** *v/i* land
atterrire ⟨4d⟩ **I** *v/t* terrify; ***l'idea di rivederlo mi atterisce*** the thought of seeing him again terrifies me **II** *v/i* become terrified; ***~ alla vista di qn*** be terrified by the sight of s.o.
atterrito *adj* terrified; ***essere ~ da qc*** be terrified of sth
attesa *f* waiting; (*tempo d'attesa*) wait; (*aspettativa*) expectation; ***essere in ~ di qc*** be waiting for sth; ***essere in ~ di fare qc*** be waiting to do sth; ***restiamo in ~ di Vostre ulteriori notizie*** looking forward to hearing from you
atteso *past part* → ***attendere***
attestare *v/t* ⟨1b⟩ certify
attestato *m* certificate; ***~ di frequenza*** good attendance certificate; ***rilasciare un ~ a qn*** give s.o. a certificate
attestazione *f* (*dimostrazione*) demonstration; (*certificato*) certificate; *scolastica* student card; *medica* medical certificate
attico[1] *m* ⟨*pl* -ci⟩ penthouse
attico[2] *adj* Attic
attiguo *adj* adjacent (***a*** to)
attillato *adj* close-fitting
attimo *m* moment
attinente *adj* relevant (***a*** to)
attinenza *f* connection; ***non ci vedo nessuna ~*** I can't see what that has to do with it
attingere *v/t* ⟨3d⟩ draw; *fig* (*trarre*) draw on; *fig* (*prendere*) obtain; ***~ acqua alla fonte*** draw water from the spring; ***~ informazioni*** obtain information; ***~ ai propri risparmi*** dip into one's savings
attinto *past part* → ***attingere***
attirare *v/t* ⟨1a⟩ attract; ***~ l'attenzione di qn*** attract s.o.'s attention; ***l'idea mi attira*** the idea appeals to me
attirarsi *v/r* ⟨1a⟩ incur; ***attirarsi l'antipatia di qn*** incur s.o.'s dislike; ***~ le simpatie del pubblico*** win public support
attitudinale *adj* aptitude *attr*; ***test*** *m* ***~*** aptitude test
attitudine *f* skill; ***avere ~ per qc*** have an aptitude for sth
attivamente *adv* actively
attivare *v/t* ⟨1a⟩ activate; ***~ il sistema d'allarme*** trip the alarm; ***~ la modalità di standby*** COMPUT put the computer on standby; ***~ la segreteria telefonica*** TEL turn on the answering machine; ***è stato attivato un numero verde*** TEL a Freephone (*US* toll-free) number has been set up
attivazione *f* activation **attivismo** *m* activism **attivista** *m/f* ⟨*mpl* -i⟩ activist
attività *f* ⟨*pl* attività⟩ activity; ***~*** *pl* FIN assets *pl*; ***che ~ svolgi?*** what do you do (for a living)?; ***avere un'~ in proprio*** have one's own business; ***essere in piena ~*** be fully operational
attivo I *adj* active; FIN ***bilancio*** *m* ***~*** credit balance; ***condurre una vita -a*** lead an active life; ***il Vesuvio non è ~*** Vesuvius is not active **II** *m* FIN assets *pl*; GRAM active voice; ***in ~*** in credit
attizzare *v/t* ⟨1a⟩ poke; *fig* stir up **attizzatoio** *m* ⟨*pl* -oi⟩ poker
atto[1] *m* **1.** act; (*gesto*) gesture; ***~ di fede*** act of faith; ***-i*** *pl* ***osceni*** indecent acts; ***all'~ pratico*** when it comes to the crunch; ***dare ~ di qc a qn*** give s.o. credit for sth; ***essere in ~*** be in progress; ***lo sciopero è già in ~*** the

strike is already underway; ***fare (l')* ~ *di fare qc*** make as if to do sth; ***mettere in* ~** carry out; ***prendere* ~ *di*** note; ***recitare l'~ di dolore*** REL make an act of contrition; ***gli Atti degli Apostoli*** the Acts of the Apostles **2.** *documento* deed; ~ ***di vendita*** bill of sale; JUR ***mettere agli -i*** enter in the court records **3.** THEAT ~ ***unico*** one-act play
atto[2] *adj*: ~ ***a qc*** suitable for sth; ~ ***alla navigazione*** seaworthy; ~ ***a deliberare*** able to debate
attonito *adj* amazed
attorcigliare *v/t* ⟨1g⟩ twist
attorcigliarsi *v/r* ⟨1g⟩ twist
attore *m*, **-trice** *f* actor; *donna* actress; ~ ***cinematografico*** film (*US* movie) actor; ~ ***protagonista*** lead; ~ ***non protagonista*** supporting actor
attorniare *v/t* ⟨1g⟩ surround **attorniarsi** *v/r* ⟨1g⟩ surround oneself; ~ ***di amici*** surround oneself with friends
attorno *adv*: ~ ***a qc*** round sth; ***qui* ~** around here; ***girare* ~ *a un problema*** get round a problem; ***guardarsi* ~** look around (*a. fig*)
attraccare *v/t* ⟨1d⟩ NAUT berth, dock
attracco *m* ⟨*pl* -cchi⟩ NAUT berth
attraente *adj* attractive; ***donna*** *f* ~ attractive woman; ***idea*** *f* ~ appealing idea
attrarre *v/t* ⟨3xx⟩ attract
attrattiva *f* attraction
attratto *past part* → ***attrarre***
attraversamento *m* crossing; ~ ***pedonale*** pedestrian crossing, *US* crosswalk
attraversare *v/t* ⟨1b⟩ *strada*, *confine* cross; ***vietato* ~ *i binari*** do not cross the tracks; ~ ***un momento difficile*** be going through a bad time
attraverso *prep* across
attrazione *f* attraction; ~ ***fisica*** physical attraction; ~ ***magnetica*** magnetic attraction; ~ ***principale*** main attraction; ***forza*** *f* ***di*** ~ force of attraction; ***esercitare una forte*** ~ exert a strong pull; ***provare* ~ *per qn*** be attracted to s.o.; ***la città offre molte -i*** the city has a lot to offer
attrezzare *v/t* ⟨1a⟩ equip
attrezzarsi *v/r* get o.s. kitted out
attrezzato *adj* equipped
attrezzatura *f* equipment, gear *infml*
attrezzista *m/f* ⟨*mpl* -i⟩ THEAT property master
attrezzistica *f* ⟨*pl* -che⟩ artistic gymnastics *sg*
attrezzo *m* piece of equipment; ***-i*** *pl* ***da ginnastica*** apparatus
attribuibile *adj* attributable
attribuire *v/t* ⟨4d⟩ attribute; ~ ***qc a qn*** attribute sth to s.o.; ***l'affresco viene attribuito a Michelangelo*** the fresco is attributed to Michelangelo; ~ ***un premio a qn*** award a prize to s.o.
attribuirsi *v/r* ⟨4d⟩ assume; ~ ***un merito*** take credit
attributivo *adj* GRAM attributive
attributo *m* attribute; ***gli -i*** *infml hum* bits; ***l'~ del dipinto è incerta*** the painting's attribution is uncertain
attrice *f* → ***attore***
attricetta *f pej* bit-part actress
attrito *m* friction
attuale *adj* current
attualità *f* ⟨*pl* attualità⟩ news *sg*; ***d'~*** topical; ***di grande* ~** very topical, *infml* hot; ***rubrica*** *f* ***di*** ~ news section ***tornare d'~*** come to the fore again
attualizzare *v/t* ⟨1a⟩ update
attualizzazione *f* modernization
attualmente *adv* at present
attuare *v/t* ⟨1l⟩ put into effect
attuazione *f* putting into effect
attutire *v/t* ⟨4d⟩ *colpo* soften; *rumore* muffle; *dolore* dull
attutirsi *v/r* ⟨4d⟩ ease
audace *adj* bold
audacemente *adv* boldly
audacia *f* boldness
audio **I** *adj inv* audio *attr*; ***impianto*** *m* ~ sound system; ***scheda*** *f* ~ sound card **II** *m* sound; ~ ***posizionale*** positional audio
audiocassetta *f* cassette
audioleso **I** *adj* hearing-impaired **II** *m*, **-a** *f* person with hearing difficulties, person who is hearing-impaired
audiolibro *m* audio book, talking book
audiovisivo *adj* audiovisual
audit *m* ⟨*pl* audit⟩ ECON audit
auditel® *m organization that measures TV ratings*
auditing *m* ⟨*pl* auditing⟩ ECON auditing **auditor** *m* ⟨*pl* auditor⟩ auditor
audizione *f* audition
auge *f*: ***in* ~** at the top; ***essere in* ~** be at the top; ***venire in* ~** rise to the top

augurabile *adj* desirable
augurale *adj discorso* expressing good wishes
augurare *v/t* ⟨1l⟩ wish; **~ *a qn buon viaggio*** wish s.o. a good trip; ***me lo auguro!*** I hope so!; ***augurarsi di fare qc*** hope to do sth
augurio *m* ⟨*pl* -ri⟩ wish; ***fare gli -ri di Buon Natale a qn*** wish s.o. a Merry Christmas; ***tanti -ri!*** all the best!
aula *f di scuola* classroom; *di università* lecture theatre *or* room; **~ *magna*** Great Hall
aulico *adj* ⟨*mpl* -ci⟩ refined; ***poeta*** *m* **~** *poet who uses elevated language*
aumentare ⟨1a⟩ **I** *v/t* increase; *prezzi* increase, raise, put up **II** *v/i* increase; *di prezzi* increase, rise, go up; **~ *del 50 %*** increase (by) 50 %
aumento *m* increase, rise; **~ *salariale*** pay rise; ***chiedere / avere un ~*** ask for / get a rise; ***dare un ~ a qn*** give s.o. a rise; **~ *dei prezzi*** increase *or* rise in prices; ***essere in ~*** be going up
aura *f* aura
aureo *adj* golden
aureola *f* halo
auricolare *m* earphone
aurifero *adj* gold-bearing; ***giacimento*** *m* **~** gold deposit
aurora *f* dawn; **~ *boreale*** Northern Lights *pl*
auscultare *v/t* ⟨1a⟩ auscultate **auscultazione** *f* auscultation
ausiliare I *adj* auxiliary **II** *m* GRAM auxiliary
ausiliario *adj* ⟨*mpl* -ri⟩ auxiliary; ***personale*** *m* **~** auxiliary staff
ausilio *m* ⟨*pl* -li⟩ aid
auspicabile *adj*: ***è ~ che*** hopefully **auspicare** *v/t* ⟨1d⟩: **~ *qc*** hope for sth
auspicio *m* ⟨*pl* -ci⟩ omen; *esp pl* (*patrocinio*) auspices *pl*; ***essere di buon / cattivo ~*** be a good / bad omen; ***sotto gli -i del presidente*** under the auspices of the president
austerità *f* austerity
austero *adj* (*severo*) strict; (*solenne*) austere; (*sobrio*) severe
australe *adj* southern
Australia *f* Australia
australiano I *adj* Australian **II** *m*, **-a** *f* Australian
Austria *f* Austria
austriaco ⟨*mpl* -ci⟩ **I** *adj* Austrian **II** *m*, **-a** *f* Austrian
austro-ungarico *adj* ⟨*mpl* -ci⟩ Austro-Hungarian; ***impero*** *m* **~** Austro-Hungarian empire
autarchia *f* ECON autarky; JUR autonomy **autarchico** *adj* ⟨*mpl* -ci⟩ ECON autarkic; JUR autonomous; ***regime*** *m* **~** autonomy
aut aut *m* ⟨*pl* aut aut⟩ ultimatum; ***porre l'~ a qn*** give s. o. an ultimatum
autenticare *v/t* ⟨1m, d & b⟩ authenticate; **~ *la firma*** authenticate a signature
autenticazione *f* ADMIN authentication
autenticità *f* authenticity
autentico *adj* ⟨*mpl* -ci⟩ authentic
authority *f* ⟨*pl* authority⟩ POL authority
autismo *m* autism
autista *m/f* ⟨*mpl* -i⟩ driver
autistico *adj* ⟨*mpl* -ci⟩ autistic
auto *f* ⟨*pl* auto⟩ → ***automobile***
auto... *pref* (*di se stesso*) self-...; (*di veicolo*) auto...
autoabbronzante *adj* self-tanning
autoaccensione *f* TECH auto-ignition
autoadesivo I *adj* self-adhesive **II** *m* sticker
auto aiuto *m* self-help; ***gruppo*** *m* ***di ~*** self-help group
autoambulanza *f* ambulance
autoanalisi *f* ⟨*pl* autoanalisi⟩ self-analysis
autoarticolato *m* semi-trailer
autobiografia *f* autobiography
autobiografico *adj* ⟨*mpl* -ci⟩ autobiographical
autoblindo *m* ⟨*pl* autoblindo⟩ armo(u)red car
autobloccante *adj* self-locking
autobomba *f* car bomb
autobotte *f* tanker
autobus *m* bus; **~ *di linea*** city bus
autocaravan *f* camper van
autocarro *m* truck, *Br* lorry
autocensura *f* self-criticism
autocertificazione *f* self-certification
autocingolato *m* Caterpillar®
autocisterna *f* tanker
autoclave *f* autoclave
autocombustione *f* spontaneous combustion
autocontrollo *m* self-control
autocritica *f* self-criticism
autodafé *m* ⟨*pl* autodafé⟩ HIST auto da fé
autodenuncia *f* ⟨*pl* -ce⟩ confession
autodenunciarsi *v/r* ⟨1f⟩ confess

autodeterminazione *f* self-determination; ***diritto** m **all'~*** right to self-determination
autodidatta *m/f* ⟨*mpl* -i⟩ self-taught person
autodidattico *adj* ⟨*mpl* -ci⟩ teach yourself
autodifesa *f* self-defence, *US* -defense
autodisciplina *f* self-discipline
autodistruttivo *adj* self-destructive
autodistruzione *f* self-destruction
autodromo *m* motor racing circuit
autoerotismo *m* autoeroticism
autoferrotranvieri *mpl* transport workers
autofficina *f* garage
autofinanziamento *m* self-financing
autogeno *adj* autogenous; ***training** m **~*** autogenic training
autogestione *f* self-management
autogol *m* ⟨*pl* autogol⟩ own goal
autografo *m* autograph
autogrill *m* ⟨*pl* autogrill⟩ motorway café
autogrù *f* ⟨*pl* autogrù⟩ breakdown lorry; *US* tow truck
autoinganno *m* self-deception
autolavaggio *m* ⟨*pl* -ggi⟩ car-wash
autolesionista ⟨*mpl* -i⟩ **I** *adj* self-harming **II** *m/f* self-harmer
autolinea *f* bus service
automa *m* ⟨*pl* -i⟩ robot
automaticamente *adv* automatically
automatico ⟨*mpl* -ci⟩ **I** *adj* automatic **II** *m bottone* press stud fastener
automatismo *m* automation **automatizzare** *v/t* ⟨1a⟩ automize **automatizzazione** *f* automation **automazione** *f* automation
automezzo *m* motor vehicle
automobile *f* car; ***~ da corsa*** racing car; ***~ da noleggio*** hire car; ***andare in ~*** go by car
automobilismo *m* driving; SPORTS motor racing
automobilista *m/f* ⟨*mpl* -i⟩ driver
automobilistico *adj* ⟨*mpl* -ci⟩ car *attr*
automotrice *f* railcar
autonoleggio *m* ⟨*pl* -ggi⟩ car rental; (*azienda*) car rental firm
autonomamente *adv* autonomously
autonomia *f* autonomy; TECH battery life
autonomo *adj* autonomous
autopsia *f* autopsy
autoradio *f* ⟨*pl* autoradio⟩ car radio
autore *m*, **-trice** *f* author; JUR perpetrator; ***diritti** mpl **d'~*** royalties; (*compenso*) royalties
autorealizzazione *f* fulfilment
autoreferenziale *adj* self-referential
autoreggente *adj*: ***calze** fpl **-i*** hold ups
autoregolazione *f* self-regulation
autorespiratore *m* aqualung
autorete *f* → ***autogol***
autorevole *adj* authoritative
autorimessa *f* garage
autorità *f* ⟨*pl* autorità⟩ authority; ***~ portuale*** port authorities *pl*
autoritario *adj* ⟨*mpl* -ri⟩ authoritarian
autoritratto *m* self-portrait
autorizzare *v/t* ⟨1a⟩ authorize
autorizzato *adj*: ***officina** f **-a*** authorized garage
autorizzazione *f* authorization
autoscatto *m* automatic shutter release
autoscontro *m* bumper cars *pl*, dodgems *pl*
autoscuola *f* driving school
autosilo *m* ⟨*pl* autosilo⟩ multistorey car park, *US* parking garage
autosoccorso *m* self-help
autostima *f* self-esteem
autostop *m*: ***fare l'~*** hitchhike
autostoppista *m/f* ⟨*mpl* -i⟩ hitchhiker
autostrada *f* motorway, *US* highway; ***~ informatica*** information highway
autostradale *adj* motorway *attr*; *US* highway *attr*; ***raccordo** m **~*** slip road
autosufficiente *adj* self-sufficient; ***anziano** m **non ~*** elderly person in need of care
autosufficienza *f* self-sufficiency
autosuggestione *f* autosuggestion
autotreno *m* articulated lorry, *US* semi
autoveicolo *m* (motor) vehicle
autovelox *m* ⟨*pl* autovelox⟩ speed camera, *US* speed enforcement camera
autovettura *f* motor vehicle
autrice *f* → ***autore***
autunnale *adj* autumn *attr*, *US* fall *attr*
autunno *m* autumn, *US* fall
AV *abbr* (= **Avellino**) Avellino
avallare *v/t* ⟨1a⟩ guarantee; *fig* back
avallo *m* guarantee
avambraccio *m* ⟨*pl* -cci⟩ forearm
avamposto *m* outpost
avance *f* ⟨*pl* avance⟩ advances *pl*; ***fare***

delle ~ a qn hit on s.o.

avanguardia *f* avant-garde; ***all'~*** avant-garde *attr*; *azienda* leading-edge; ***essere all'~*** be in the forefront; ***essere all'~ in*** lead the way in

avanguardismo *m* avant-gardism

avanguardista *m/f* ⟨*mpl* -i⟩ avant-gardist **avanguardistico** *adj* ⟨*mpl* -ci⟩ avant-garde

avanscoperta *f* MIL reconnaissance; ***andare in ~*** reconnoitre

avanspettacolo *m* curtain raiser

avanti I *adv* in front, ahead; ***d'ora in ~*** from now on; ***andare ~*** *di orologio* be fast; ***mandare ~*** be the head of; ***essere ~ nel programma*** be ahead of schedule; ***fare ~ e indietro*** go back and forth; ***farsi ~*** come forward; ***più ~*** *nel tempo* later on; *nello spazio* farther on **II** *int*: ***~!*** come in! **III** *m* SPORTS forward

avanzamento *m* progress; *di carriera*: promotion

avanzare ⟨1a⟩ **I** *v/i* advance; *fig* make progress; (*rimanere*) be left over; ***è avanzato del pane*** there's some bread left over **II** *v/t* put forward

avanzata *f* advance

avanzato *adj* (*in avanti*) advance; (*inoltrato*) late; (*innovatore*) advanced; ***in età*** *f* ***-a*** elderly; ***a notte*** *f* ***-a*** late at night; ***idee*** *fpl* ***-e*** progressive ideas

avanzo *m* remainder; FIN surplus; ***gli -i*** *pl* the leftovers; ***mangiare gli -i*** eat leftovers; *fig* ***~ di galera*** *pej* jailbird

avaria *f* failure; ***un'~ al motore*** engine failure

avariarsi *v/r* ⟨1k⟩ spoil

avariato *adj* damaged; *cibi* spoiled

avarizia *f* avarice

avaro I *adj* miserly; ***~ di parole*** taciturn **II** *m*, **-a** *f* miser

avellinese I *adj* of Avellino; *persona* from Avellino **II** *m/f* person from Avellino

avemaria *f* (*preghiera*) Ave Maria, Hail Mary; (*suono delle campane*) Angelus; (*pastina*) *short tube-shaped pasta*; ***recitare l'~*** say a Hail Mary

avena *f* oats *pl*

avere ⟨2b⟩ **I** *v/t* **1.** have; ***~ 20 anni*** be 20 (years old); ***~ caldo / freddo*** be hot / cold; ***~ fame / sonno*** be hungry / sleepy; ***~ soldi*** be wealthy; ***~ ragione / torto*** be right / wrong; ***che hai?*** what's up with you?; ***aveva una maglietta rossa / gli occhiali*** she had a red T-shirt / glasses on; ***non aver niente a che vedere*** *or* ***fare con qn / qc*** have nothing to do with s.o. / sth; ***hai avuto l'assegno?*** did you get the cheque? **2.** ***avercela con qn*** have it in for s.o.; ***~ a che dire con qn*** quarrel with s.o.; ***averla vinta*** get one's own way; ***averle tutte vinte*** have it all one's own way; ***aversela a male*** take sth amiss **3.** ***~ qualcosa da fare*** have something to do; ***scusa, oggi ho da fare*** sorry, I've got things to do today; ***avrei da parlarti*** I've got to talk to you; ***non hai che da chiederlo*** you only have to ask **4.** ***ne hai per molto?*** are you going to be much longer?; ***oggi ne abbiamo 15*** it's the 15th today **II** *v/aux* have; ***hai visto Tony?*** have you seen Tony?; ***hai visto Tony ieri?*** did you see Tony yesterday? **III** *m* FIN credit; ***dare e ~*** debits and credits; ***-i*** *mpl* wealth *sg*

avi *mpl* ancestors *pl*

aviario ⟨*mpl* -ri⟩ **I** *adj* avian; ***influenza*** *f* ***-a*** avian *or* bird flu **II** *n*: ***aviaria*** *f* aviary

aviatore *m*, **-trice** *f* flyer

aviazione *f* aviation; MIL Air Force

avicolo *adj* poultry *attr*; ***azienda*** *f* ***-a*** poultry farm **avicoltura** *f* poultry farming

avidamente *adv* avidly

avidità *f* avidness

avido *adj* avid

avignonese I *adj* of Avignon; *persona* from Avignon; ***cattività*** *f* ***~*** *period when the papacy was based in Avignon* **II** *m/f* person from Avignon

aviogetto *m* jet

AVIS *abbr* (= **Associazione Volontari Italiani del Sangue**) *Italian blood donors' association*

avocado *m* avocado

avorio *m* ivory

avulso *adj* cut off; ***~ dal proprio ambiente*** out of one's usual environment; ***~ dalla realtà*** cut off from reality

avvalersi *v/r* ⟨2r⟩: ***~ di qc*** avail o.s. of sth

avvallamento *m* depression

avvalorare *v/t* ⟨1a⟩ confirm **avvalorarsi** *v/r* ⟨1a⟩ get stronger

avvampare *v/i* ⟨1a⟩ blaze (up); *fig* (*arrossire*) blush; *fig sentimento* flare (up)

avvantaggiare *v/t* ⟨1f⟩ favo(u)r

avvantaggiarsi *v/r*: ***~ di qc*** take advantage of sth

avvedersi *v/r* ⟨2s⟩: ***~ di qc*** notice sth

avvedutezza *f* astuteness

avveduto *adj* astute

avvelenamento *m* poisoning

avvelenare *v/t* ⟨1a⟩ poison

avvelenarsi *v/r* poison o.s.

avvenente *adj* attractive

avvenenza *f* attractiveness

avvenimento *m* event

avvenire ⟨4p⟩ **I** *v/i* (*accadere*) happen **II** *m* future

avveniristico *adj* ⟨*mpl* -ci⟩ futuristic

avventarsi *v/r* ⟨1b⟩: ***~ su*** *or* ***contro qn / qc*** fly at s.o. / sth

avventato *adj* rash

avventizio ⟨*mpl* -zi⟩ **I** *adj* (*provvisorio*) temporary; *personale* casual **II** *m*, **-a** *f* temp

avvento *m* advent; ***l'~ di una nuova era*** the dawn of a new era

Avvento *m* Advent

avventore *m*, **-trice** *f* regular customer

avventura *f* adventure; ***andare in cerca di -e*** go looking for adventure; ***imbarcarsi in un'~*** embark on an adventure

avventurarsi *v/r* ⟨1a⟩ venture

avventuriero *m*, **-a** *f* adventurer; *donna* adventuress

avventuroso *adj* adventurous

avvenuto *past part* → ***avvenire***

avveramento *m* realization

avverarsi *v/r* ⟨1a⟩ come true

avverbiale *adj* adverbial

avverbio *m* ⟨*pl* -bi⟩ adverb

avversare *v/t* ⟨1b⟩ (*combattere*) oppose; (*ostacolare*) thwart

avversario ⟨*mpl* -ri⟩ **I** *adj* opposing **II** *m*, **-a** *f* opponent

avversione *f* aversion (***per*** to)

avversità *f* ⟨*pl* avversità⟩ *di clima*: harshness; *di destino*: unkindness; *esp pl* adversity; ***le ~ della vita*** the hardships of life **avverso** *adj* adverse

avvertenza *f* (*ammonimento*) warning; (*premessa*) foreword; ***avere l'~ di*** be careful to; ***-e*** *pl* (*istruzioni per l'uso*) instructions; ***leggere attentamente le -e*** read the instructions carefully

avvertimento *m* warning

avvertire *v/t* ⟨4b⟩ warn; (*percepire*) catch; ***~ qn di qc*** warn s.o. about sth; (*informare*) inform s.o. of sth

avvezzo *adj* accustomed (***a*** to)

avviamento *m* introduction; TECH, AUTO start-up

avviare *v/t* ⟨1h⟩ start; ***~ il motore*** start the engine

avviarsi *v/r* set out, head off; ***avviatevi pure, vi raggiungo più tardi*** you go on, I'll catch you up later

avviato *adj* established; ***azienda*** *f* ***ben -a*** thriving business

avvicendamento *m* (*alternanza*) alternation; (*sostituzione*) replacement

avvicendare *v/t* ⟨1b⟩ alternate

avvicendarsi *v/r* alternate

avvicinabile *adj* approachable

avvicinamento *m* approach

avvicinare *v/t* ⟨1a⟩ approach; ***~ qc a qc*** move sth closer to sth

avvicinarsi *v/r* approach, near (***a*** sth); ***avvicinati, per favore*** come closer, please

avvilente *adj* depressing

avvilimento *m* depression; *mortificazione* humiliation

avvilire *v/t* ⟨4d⟩ depress; *mortificare* humiliate

avvilirsi *v/r* demean o.s.; *scoraggiarsi* become depressed

avvilito *adj scoraggiato* depressed

avviluppare *v/t* ⟨1a⟩ wrap (up) **avviluppàrsi** *v/r* ⟨1a⟩ wrap oneself (up)

avvincente *adj* fascinating

avvinghiare *v/t* ⟨1g⟩ clasp **avvinghiarsi** *v/r* ⟨1g⟩ cling; ***~ a qn / qc*** cling to s.o. / sth

avvio *m*: ***dare l'~ a qc*** get sth under way

avvisare *v/t* ⟨1a⟩: ***~*** (***qn di qc***) (*informare*) inform (s.o. of sth), advise (s.o. of sth); (*mettere in guardia*) warn (s.o. of sth); ***hai avvisato i tuoi che sei in ritardo?*** have you told your parents you're going to be late?

avvisatore *m* alarm; ***~ acustico*** horn

avviso *m* **1.** notice; ***~ di pagamento*** payment advice; ***~ bonario*** JUR payment notification; ***~ di addebito*** TEL bill; ***~ di garanzia*** JUR notification of investigation; ***fino a nuovo ~*** until further notice **2.** ***a mio ~*** in my opinion **3.** ***mettere qn sull'~*** warn s.o.

avvistamento *m* sighting

avvistare *v/t* ⟨1a⟩ sight

avvitare *v/t* ⟨1a⟩ screw in; *fissare* screw
avvitato *adj* SEW nipped in at the waist
avvizzire *v/i* ⟨4d⟩ wither **avvizzito** *adj* withered
avvocato *m*, **-essa** *f* lawyer; **~ *difensore*** defence *or US* defense counsel; **~ *di parte civile*** prosecutor; ***rivolgersi a un* ~** consult a lawyer
avvocatura *f* advocacy; *professione*: legal profession; **~ *dello Stato*** *government lawyers*
avvolgente *adj indumento* figure-hugging; *fig* (*avvincente*) fascinating
avvolgere *v/t* ⟨3d⟩ wrap
avvolgersi *v/r* ⟨3d⟩ (*arrotolarsi*) curl up; (*avvilupparsi*) wrap oneself (up)
avvolgibile *m* roller blind
avvolgimento *m* wrapping (up); ELEC winding
avvolto *past part* → ***avvolgere***
avvoltoio *m* ⟨*pl* -oi⟩ vulture
azalea *f* azalea
Azerbaigian *m* Azerbaijan **azerbaigiano I** *adj* of Azerbaijan; *persona* from Azerbaijan **II** *m*, **-a** *f* Azerbaijani
azienda *f* business; **~ *a conduzione familiare*** family business; **~ *autonoma di soggiorno*** tourist information office; **~ *agricola*** farm
aziendale *adj* company *attr*; ***gestione*** *f* **~** business management
azionamento *m* activation
azionare *v/t* ⟨1a⟩ activate; *allarme* set off
azionario *adj* share; ***capitale*** *m* **~** share capital; ***mercato*** *m* **~** stock market
azionato *adj*: **~ *a distanza*** remotely operated; **~ *a mano*** manually operated
azione *f* **1.** action; ***film*** *m* ***d'*~** action film *or* movie; ***entrare in* ~** come into operation; ***passare all'*~** take action **2.** (*effetto*) influence **3.** FIN share; FIN **~ *ordinaria*** ordinary share; ***emettere -i*** issue shares **4.** **~ *legale*** lawsuit
azionista *m/f* ⟨*mpl* -i⟩ shareholder; ***maggiore* ~** majority shareholder
azoto *m* nitrogen
azteco ⟨*mpl* -chi⟩ **I** *adj* Aztec **II** *m*, **-a** *f* Aztec
azzannare *v/t* ⟨1a⟩ bite into
azzardare *v/t* ⟨1a⟩ risk
azzardarsi *v/r* ⟨1a⟩: **~ (*a fare qc*)** dare (to do sth)
azzardato *adj* foolhardy
azzardo *m* hazard; ***gioco*** *m* ***d'*~** game of chance
azzeccagarbugli *m* ⟨*pl* azzeccagarbugli⟩ *pej* nitpicking lawyer
azzeccare *v/t* ⟨1d & b⟩ guess; ***non ne azzecca mai una!*** he never gets anything right!
azzeccato *adj* well-chosen; (*efficace*) effective
azzeramento *m* resetting
azzerare *v/t* ⟨1b⟩ TECH reset
azzimato *adj* dressed up
azzimo *adj*: ***pane*** *m* **~** unleavened bread
azzittire ⟨4d⟩ **I** *v/t* silence **II** *v/i* fall silent **azzittirsi** *v/r* ⟨4d⟩ fall silent
azzoppare *v/t* ⟨1c⟩ lame
Azzorre *fpl* Azores *pl*
azzuffarsi *v/r* ⟨1a⟩ come to blows
azzurrino *adj* light-blue; SPORTS ***gli -i*** *pl the Italian national youth team*
azzurro I *adj* blue **II** *m colore* blue; SPORTS ***gli -i*** *pl* the Italians, the Italian national team

B

b, B *m/f* ⟨*pl* b, B⟩ b, B; ***giocare in serie B*** play in the Championship
BA *abbr* (= **Bari**) Bari
babà *m* ⟨*pl* babà⟩ rum baba
babau *m* ⟨*pl* babau⟩ *infml* bogeyman
babbeo I *adj* foolish **II** *m*, **-a** *f* fool
babbo *m infml* dad *infml*, *US* pop *infml*; ***Babbo Natale*** Father Christmas, Santa (Claus)
babbuccia *f* ⟨*pl* -cce⟩ slipper; *per neonati* bootee
babbuino *m* baboon
babele *f* confusion
Babele *f* Babel; ***torre*** *f* ***di* ~** tower of Babel
babilonese I *adj* Babylonian **II** *m/f*

Babylonian
Babilonia *f* Babylon
babordo *m* NAUT port (side)
baby I *m/f* ⟨*pl* baby⟩ baby **II** *adj inv* baby; **~ *pensionato*** *m person who retires young* **baby boom** *m* ⟨*pl* baby boom⟩ baby boom **baby doll** *m* ⟨*pl* baby doll⟩ baby doll pyjamas
baby-sitter *m/f* ⟨*pl* baby-sitter⟩ baby-sitter
bacarsi *v/r* ⟨1d⟩ become wormeaten
bacato *adj* wormeaten; *fig* ***avere il cervello*** *m* **~** be soft in the head
bacca *f* ⟨*pl* -cche⟩ berry
baccalà *m* ⟨*pl* baccalà⟩ dried salt cod
baccalaureato *m* baccalaureate
baccano *m* din
baccante *f* HIST bacchante
baccarà *m* ⟨*pl* baccarà⟩ baccarat
bacchetta *f* rod; MUS *del direttore d'orchestra* baton; *per suonare il tamburo* (drum) stick; **~ *magica*** magic wand; ***comandare qn a*** **~** rule s.o. with a rod of iron
bacchettare *v/t* ⟨1a⟩ *fig* (*rimproverare*) tell off **bacchettata** *f* telling-off **bacchettone** *m*, **-a** *f infml* God-botherer
Bacco *m* Bacchus; ***per ~!*** goodness!
bacheca *f* ⟨*pl* -che⟩ notice board; *di museo* showcase
bachelite® *f* Bakelite®
bachicoltore *m*, **-trice** *f* sericulturist **bachicoltura** *f* sericulture
baciamano *m* kiss of the hand; ***fare il*** **~** kiss s.o.'s hand
baciapile *m/f* ⟨*pl* baciapile⟩ *infml* God-botherer
baciare *v/t* ⟨1f⟩ kiss
baciarsi *v/r* kiss (each other)
bacillo *m* bacillus
bacinella *f* basin; PHOT tray
bacino *m* basin; ANAT pelvis; NAUT port; **~ *del Mediterraneo*** Mediterranean; **~ *di carenaggio*** dry dock; *fig* **~ *di utenza*** territory
bacio *m* ⟨*pl* -ci⟩ kiss; ***dare un ~ a qn*** give s.o. a kiss; ***dare il ~ della buonanotte a qn*** kiss s.o. good night; ***-ci*** *saluto* love; **~ *di dama*** COOK *hazelnut and chocolate biscuit*
backgammon *m* ⟨*pl* backgammon⟩ backgammon
background *m* ⟨*pl* background⟩ background
backstage *m* ⟨*pl* backstage⟩ FILM behind-the-scenes activity
backup *m* COMPUT backup
baco *m* ⟨*pl* -chi⟩ worm; **~ *da seta*** silkworm
bacucco *adj* ⟨*mpl* -cchi⟩ senile
bada *f*: ***tenere a ~ qn*** keep s.o. at bay
badare *v/i* ⟨1a⟩: **~ *a*** look after; (*fare attenzione a*) look out for, mind; **~ *ai fatti propri*** mind one's own business; ***non ~ a spese*** spare no expense; ***bada di essere puntuale!*** make sure you're on time!
badessa *f* abbess
badia *f* abbey
badile *m* shovel
badminton *m* ⟨*pl* badminton⟩ badminton
baffo *m*: ***-i*** *pl* m(o)ustache; *di animali* whiskers; ***farsene un ~*** (***di qc***) give a damn (about sth); ***ridere sotto i -i*** laugh up one's sleeve
baffuto *adj* m(o)ustached
bagagliaio *m* ⟨*pl* -ai⟩ RAIL luggage van, *US* baggage car; AUTO boot, *US* trunk; AVIAT cargo hold
bagaglio *m* ⟨*pl* -gli⟩ luggage, *US* baggage; ***deposito*** *m* ***-i*** left luggage (office), *US* baggage checkroom; ***fare i -i*** pack; ***spedire come ~ appresso*** send as accompanied luggage; **~ *a mano*** hand baggage; **~ *in eccesso*** excess baggage; **~ *culturale*** education
bagascia *f* ⟨*pl* -sce⟩ *vulg* whore
baggianata *f* nonsense
bagliore *m* glare; *di speranza* glimmer
bagnacauda *f* COOK *Piedmontese dip made from oil, anchovies and garlic*
bagnante *m/f* bather
bagnare *v/t* ⟨1a⟩ wet; (*immergere*) dip; (*inzuppare*) soak; (*annaffiare*) water; *di fiume* flow through
bagnarola *f fig hum* (*macchina*) heap; (*battello*) tub
bagnarsi *v/r* get wet; *in mare etc* swim, bathe; **~ *i piedi/gli abiti*** get one's feet/clothes wet
bagnasciuga *m* ⟨*pl* bagnasciuga⟩ (*battigia*) foreshore; *di scafo*: waterline
bagnato *adj* wet; **~ *di sudore*** dripping with sweat; **~ *fradicio*** soaked, wet through
bagnino *m*, **-a** *f* lifeguard
bagno *m* **1.** bath; **~ *di fango*** mud bath;

~ di sangue bloodbath; **~ turco** Turkish bath; **costume** *m* **da ~** *da donna* swimsuit; *da uomo* (swimming) trunks; **essere in un ~ di sudore** be dripping with sweat; **fare il ~** have a bath; **mettere a ~** soak; *nel mare etc* (have a) swim; **mettere a ~ qc** put sth in soak **2.** *stanza* bathroom; *gabinetto* toilet; **~ per donne** ladies' (room); **~ degli uomini** gents, *US* men's room; **andare al ~** go to the toilet *or US* bathroom
bagnomaria *m* ⟨*no pl*⟩ double boiler, bain marie; **cuocere a ~** cook in a double boiler *or* bain marie
bagnoschiuma *m* ⟨*pl* bagnoschiuma⟩ bubble bath
bagordo *m* binge; **fare -i** paint the town red
Bahama *fpl* Bahamas
baia *f* bay
bailamme *m* hubbub
baio *m* ⟨*pl* bai⟩: **cavallo** *m* **~** bay
baionetta *f* bayonet
baita *f* (mountain) chalet
Balaton *m* lake Balaton
balaustra *f* balustrade
balbettare *v/i* ⟨1a⟩ stammer; *bambino* babble, prattle; **~ una scusa** mutter an excuse; **~ un po' di italiano** speak a bit of Italian
balbettio *m* stammering; *di bambino* babble, prattle
balbuzie *f* stutter
balbuziente *m/f* stutterer
Balcani *mpl* Balkans *pl*
balcanico *adj* ⟨*mpl* -ci⟩ Balkan; **paesi** *mpl* **-ci** Balkans
balconata *f* THEAT dress circle, *US* balcony
balcone *m* balcony
baldacchino *m* canopy; **letto** *m* **a ~** four-poster bed
baldanza *f* boldness **baldanzoso** *adj* bold
baldoria *f* revelry; **fare ~** have a riotous time
baldracca *f* ⟨*pl* -cche⟩ *vulg* whore
Baleari *fpl* Balearics *pl*
balena *f* whale
balenare *v/i* ⟨1a⟩: *fig* **gli è balenata un'idea** an idea flashed through his mind
baleniera *f* whaler
balenio *m* ⟨*pl* -ii⟩ *di lampi*: flash; *lontano* glimmer
baleno *m* lightning; **in un ~** in a flash
balenotto *m* (whale) calf
balestra *f* AUTO leaf spring
balia[1] *f*: **in ~ di** at the mercy of
balia[2] *f*: **~ asciutta** nanny; **spilla** *f* **da ~** nappy pin; *fig* **far(e) da ~ a qn** wet-nurse s.o.
balinese I *adj* Balinese **II** *m/f* Balinese
balistica *f* ⟨*pl* -che⟩ ballistics *sg*
balla[1] *f* bale; **~ di fieno** bale of hay
balla[2] *f infml* (*frottola*) fib *infml*
ballabile I *adj*: **musica** *f* **~** music you can dance to **II** *m* dance tune
ballare *v/t & v/i* ⟨1a⟩ dance; **~ un valzer** (dance the) waltz; **quando si è in ballo, bisogna ~** in for a penny, in for a pound
ballata *f* MUS ballad
ballatoio *m* ⟨*pl* -oi⟩ (*pianerottolo*) walkway; (*balcone*) running balcony
ballerina *f* dancer; *di balletto* ballet dancer; *di rivista* chorus girl; (*scarpa*) ballet shoe; ZOOL wagtail
ballerino *m* dancer; *di balletto* ballet dancer
balletto *m* ballet
ballo *m* **1.** dance; (*il ballare*) dancing; **corpo** *m* **di ~** corps de ballet **2.** (*festa*) ball **3.** *fig* **essere in ~** *persona* be involved; *essere in gioco* be at stake; **abbiamo in ~ un lavoro importante** we've got a big job on at the moment; **tirare in ~ qc** bring sth up
ballonzolare *v/i* ⟨1m⟩ (*ballare*) bop; (*saltare*) jump around
ballottaggio *m* POL second ballot, *US* runoff election; SPORTS playoff, decider
balneabile *adj* safe for swimming; **spiaggia** *f* **(non) ~** beach that is (un)-safe for swimming
balneare *adj località, centro* seaside *attr*; **stagione** *f* **~** swimming season; **stabilimento** *m* **~** lido; **stazione** *f* **~** seaside resort
balneazione *f* bathing; **divieto di ~** no bathing
baloccarsi *v/r* ⟨1c u d⟩ (*trastullarsi*) amuse oneself; (*perdere tempo*) fritter one's time away
balocco *m* ⟨*pl* -cchi⟩ toy; **il paese** *m* **dei -cchi** never-never land
balordaggine *f di ragionamento* shakiness; *di idea* stupidity; *di tempo, con-*

siglio unreliability
balordo I *adj ragionamento* shaky; *idea* stupid; *tempo*, *consiglio* unreliable **II** *m* (*teppista*) lout
balsamico *adj* ⟨*mpl* -ci⟩ *aceto* balsamic; *aria* balmy
balsamo *m per i capelli* hair conditioner; *fig* balm, solace
baltico *adj* ⟨*mpl* -ci⟩ Baltic; ***Mar Baltico*** Baltic Sea
baluardo *m* bulwark (*a. fig*)
balza *f* (*dirupo*) crag; SEW frill; ***a -e*** frilly
balzare *v/i* ⟨1a⟩ jump, leap; ***~ in piedi*** jump *or* leap to one's feet; *fig* ***un errore che balza subito agli occhi*** a mistake that suddenly jumps out at you
balzellare *v/i* ⟨1b⟩ hop
balzo *m* jump, leap; *fig* ***cogliere la palla al ~*** jump at the chance
bambagia *f* cotton wool, *US* absorbent cotton
bambinaia *f* nanny
bambinata *f* childish thing **bambinesco** *adj* ⟨*mpl* -chi⟩ childish
bambino *m*, **-a** *f* child; *in fasce* baby; ***~ in provetta*** test-tube baby; ***i -i*** *pl* the children; ***fin da ~*** from childhood; ***Gesù Bambino*** baby Jesus
bambola *f* doll
bambolotto *m* baby boy doll
bambù *m* bamboo; ***canna*** *f* ***di ~*** bamboo cane
banale *adj* banal
banalità *f* ⟨*pl* banalità⟩ banality
banana *f* banana
banano *m* banana tree
banca *f* ⟨*pl* -che⟩ bank; COMPUT ***~ dati*** data bank; ***~ degli organi*** organ bank; ***Banca Centrale Europea*** Central European Bank; ***andare in ~*** go to the bank
bancale *m* (*basamento*) bench; (*pallet*) pallet
bancarella *f* stall
bancario ⟨*mpl* -ri⟩ **I** *adj istituto*, *segreto* banking *attr*; *deposito*, *estratto conto* bank *attr* **II** *m*, **-a** *f* bank employee
bancarotta *f* bankruptcy; ***fare ~*** go bankrupt; ***dichiarare ~*** declare bankruptcy
banchetto *m* banquet
banchiere *m* banker
banchina *f* RAIL platform; NAUT quay; *di strada* verge; *di autostrada* hard shoulder; ***~ spartitraffico*** central reservation, *US* median strip
banchisa *f* ice floe
banco *m* ⟨*pl* -chi⟩ **1.** FIN bank **2.** *di magistrati*, *di lavoro* bench; *di scuola* desk; *di bar* bar; *di chiesa* pew; *di negozio* counter; ***~ del check-in*** check-in desk; ***~ degli imputati*** dock; ***~ del lotto*** *place that sells State lottery tickets*; ***~ dei pegni*** pawnshop; ***farmaco*** *m* ***da ~*** over-the-counter medicine; ***vendere qc sotto ~*** sell sth under the counter **3.** ***~ corallino*** coral reef; ***~ di nebbia*** fog bank; ***~ di sabbia*** sandbank
bancogiro *m* giro
bancomat® *m* ⟨*pl* bancomat⟩ (*distributore*) cashpoint, *US* ATM; (*carta*) cash card
bancone *m* (work)bench
banconota *f* banknote, *US* bill
banda[1] *f di delinquenti* gang
banda[2] *f* MUS band
banda[3] *f* COMPUT: ***~ perforata*** punched tape; ***~ passante*** COMPUT pass band
banda[4] *f*: ***~ larga*** broadband
banderuola *f* weathercock (*a. fig*)
bandiera *f* flag; ***battere ~ britannica*** fly the Union Jack
bandire *v/t* ⟨4d⟩ proclaim; *concorso* announce; (*esiliare*) banish; *fig* (*abolire*) dispense with
banditismo *m* banditry
bandito *m* bandit
banditore *m*, **-trice** *f all'asta* auctioneer
bando *m* proclamation; (*esilio*) banishment; ***~ di concorso*** announcement of a competitive exam; ***mettere qc al ~*** ban sth; ***~ agli scherzi!*** stop the joking around
bandolo *m* end; *fig* ***cercare il ~*** (***della matassa***) look for the solution (to the problem); *fig* ***perdere il ~*** lose the thread
bang *m* ⟨*pl* bang⟩ bang; ***~ sonico*** AVIAT sonic boom
banner *m* ⟨*pl* banner⟩ COMPUT banner
baobab *m* ⟨*pl* baobab⟩ baobab
bar *m* ⟨*pl* bar⟩ bar
bara *f* coffin
baracca *f* ⟨*pl* -cche⟩ hut; *pej* hovel; ***mandare avanti la ~*** *infml* keep one's head above water

baraccone *m* booth; ***fenomeno*** *m* ***da ~*** circus freak
baraccopoli *f* ⟨*pl* baraccopoli⟩ shanty town
baraonda *f* hubbub; (*di cose*) chaos
barare *v/i* ⟨1a⟩ cheat
baratro *m* abyss
barattare *v/t* ⟨1a⟩ barter
baratto *m* barter
barattolo *m* tin, *US* can; *di vetro* jar
barba *f* beard; ***farsi la ~*** shave; *fig* ***che ~!*** what a nuisance!, what a pain! *infml*
barbabietola *f* beetroot, *US* red beet; ***~ da zucchero*** sugar beet
barbagianni *m* ⟨*pl* barbagianni⟩ barn owl; *fig* twit
Barbara *f*: ***Santa ~*** Saint Barbara
barbaresco *m* COOK *dry red wine from Piedmont*
barbaricino I *adj* of Barbagia; *persona* from Barbagia **II** *m*, **-a** *f* person from Barbagia
barbarico *adj* ⟨*mpl* -ci⟩ barbaric
barbarie *f* barbarity
barbaro I *adj* barbarous **II** *m*, **-a** *f* barbarian
barbecue *m* ⟨*pl* barbecue⟩ barbecue
barbera *m* COOK *dry red wine from Piedmont*
barbiere *m* barber
barbino *adj*: ***che figura -a !*** *infml* how pathetic!
barbiturico *m* ⟨*pl* -ci⟩ barbiturate
barbo *m*, **barbio** *m* barbel
barbogio *adj* ⟨*mpl* -gi⟩: ***vecchio*** *m* ***~*** grumpy old man
barboncino *m* (miniature) poodle
barbone[1] *m* (*cane*) poodle
barbone[2] *m*, **-a** *f* (*vagabondo*) tramp
barbuto *adj* bearded
barca[1] *f* ⟨*pl* -che⟩ boat; ***~ a remi*** rowing boat, *US* rowboat; ***~ a vela*** sailing boat, *US* sailboat; ***andare in ~*** *mezzo di trasporto* go by boat; *a vela* go sailing; *a remi* go rowing; *fig* ***essere sulla stessa ~*** be in the same boat
barca[2] *f* ⟨*pl* -che⟩ *fig* load; ***avere una ~ di soldi*** have loads of money
barcaccia *f* ⟨*pl* -cce⟩ THEAT terrace
barcaiolo *m* boatman
barcarizzo *m* NAUT accommodation ladder
Barcellona *f* Barcelona **barcellonese I** *adj* of Barcelona; *persona* from Barcelona **II** *m/f* person from Barcelona
barcollare *v/i* ⟨1c⟩ stagger
barcone *m* barge
bardare *v/t* ⟨1a⟩ *cavallo* caparison; *con i finimenti* harness; *fig* dress up
bardarsi *v/r* ⟨1a⟩ *hum* get dolled up
bardolino *m* COOK *dry red wine from the Veneto*
barella *f* stretcher
barelliere *m*, **-a** *f* stretcher bearer
barese I *adj* of Bari; *persona* from Bari **II** *m/f* person from Bari
baricentro *m* centre of gravity
barile *m* barrel
barista *m/f* ⟨*mpl* -i⟩ barman, *US* bartender; *donna* barmaid; *proprietario* bar owner
baritono *m* baritone
barlume *m*: ***un ~ di speranza*** a glimmer of hope
baro *m* cardsharp
barocco *m/adj* ⟨*mpl* -cchi⟩ baroque
barolo *m* COOK *prized dry red wine from Piedmont*
barometro *m* barometer
barone *m*, **-essa** *f* baron; *donna* baroness; *fig* ***~ dell'industria*** tycoon
barra *f* bar; NAUT tiller; ***~ delle applicazioni*** COMPUT taskbar; ***~ dei menu*** COMPUT menu bar; ***~ spaziatrice*** space bar; ***~ di scorrimento*** COMPUT scroll bar; ***~ di stato*** COMPUT status bar; ***~ degli strumenti*** toolbar
barrare *v/t* ⟨1a⟩ bar **barrato** *adj*: ***assegno*** *m* ***~*** crossed cheque, *US* check
barricare *v/t* ⟨1l & d⟩ barricade
barricata *f* barricade; ***fare le -e*** rise up (against sth)
barriera *f* barrier (*a. fig*); ***~ doganale*** tariff barrier; ***~ corallina*** coral reef; ***-e*** *pl* ***architettoniche*** *physical obstacles impeding disabled access to buildings*
barrire *v/i* ⟨4d⟩ trumpet **barrito** *m* trumpeting
barroccio *m* ⟨*pl* -cci⟩ cart
baruffa *f* (*litigio*) squabble; (*zuffa*) brawl; ***far ~*** squabble; (*venire alle mani*) brawl
barzelletta *f* joke; ***raccontare una ~*** tell a joke
basalto *m* basalt
basamento *m* ARCH base; TECH bedplate
basare *v/t* ⟨1a⟩ base

basarsi *v/r* be based (***su*** on)
basco ⟨*mpl* -chi⟩ **I** *adj* Basque; ***i Paesi Baschi*** the Basque Country **II** *m*, **-a** *f* Basque **III** *m* (*berretto*) beret
bascula *f* weighbridge
base[1] *f* base; *fig* basis; ***~ aerea / navale*** air / naval base; ***~ militare*** military base; ***~ organica*** physical basis; ***~ spaziale*** spaceport; ***~ di lancio*** launch site; ***~ di partenza*** starting point; ***ricerca** f **di ~*** basic research; ***in ~ a*** on the basis of; ***a ~ di frutta*** fruit-based; ***gettare le -i*** lay the basis; ***rientrare alla ~*** return to base
base[2] *adj inv*: ***campo** m **~*** base camp; ***modello** m **~*** basic model; ***salario** m **~*** basic salary
baseball *m* ⟨*no pl*⟩ baseball
basette *fpl* sideburns *pl*
basico *adj* ⟨*mpl* -ci⟩ CHEM basic
basilare *adj* basic
Basilea *f* Basle
basilica *f* ⟨*pl* -che⟩ basilica
Basilicata *f* Basilicata
basilico *m* basil
basilisco *m* ⟨*pl* -chi⟩ basilisk
basista *m/f* ⟨*mpl* -i⟩ *person who supplies the information necessary to commit a crime but does not take part in it*
basito *adj* astounded
basket *m* ⟨*pl* basket⟩ basketball
bassezza *f* lowness; *fig* (*viltà, azione meschina*) vileness
bassifondi *mpl* slum areas *pl*
basso I *adj* **1.** low; *di statura* short; ***-a marea** f* low tide; ***-a stagione** f* low season; ***a capo ~*** with bowed head; ***a occhi -i*** looking downwards, with lowered eyes; *fig* ***fare man -a di qc*** steal sth **2.** MUS bass **3.** *fig* despicable; *fig* ***colpo** m **~*** low blow **4.** ***a -a voce*** in a low voice, quietly **II** *adv*: ***in ~** stato* down below; ***più in ~*** further down; ***da ~** in una casa* downstairs; ***volare ~*** fly low **III** *m* MUS bass; *fig* ***cadere in ~*** come down in the world
bassopiano *m* ⟨*pl* bassipiani⟩ GEOG lowland
bassorilievo *m* ⟨*pl* bassorilievi⟩ bas-relief
bassotto *m* dachshund
bassoventre *m* lower abdomen
basta → ***bastare***
bastardaggine *f* bastardy; *fig* meanness
bastardo *m*, **-a** *f cane* mongrel; *fig* bastard; ***è stato un gran ~!*** *infml pej* he was a real bastard!
bastare *v/i* ⟨1a⟩ be enough; (*durare*) last; ***basta!*** that's enough!; ***adesso basta!*** enough is enough!; ***basta che*** (*purché*) as long as; ***basta chiedere a qualcuno*** you only need to ask someone; ***ti bastano i soldi?*** do you have enough money?
bastian contrario *m* ⟨*pl* bastian contrari⟩ awkward customer
bastimento *m* ship
bastione *m* bastion
bastonare *v/t* ⟨1a⟩ beat
bastonata *f* blow; ***prendere qn a -e*** give s.o. a beating
bastonatura *f* beating
bastoncino *m* small stick; (*racchetta*) ski pole; ***-i** pl **di pesce*** fish fingers *or US* sticks
bastone *m* stick; *di pane* baguette, French stick; *fig* ***il ~ e la carota*** the carrot and stick (approach); ***~ da passeggio*** walking stick; ***mettere i -i tra le ruote a qn*** put a spoke in s.o.'s wheel; *fig* ***il ~ della vecchiaia di qn*** prop of s.o.'s old age
batacchio *m* ⟨*pl* -cchi⟩ *di campana*: clapper; *di porta*: knocker
batik *m* ⟨*pl* batik⟩ batik
batista *f* lawn
batosta *f* blow
battaglia *f* battle (*a. fig*); ***~ navale*** naval battle; ***campo** m **di ~*** battlefield
battagliero *adj* combative
battaglione *m* batallion
battello *m* boat
battente *m di porta* wing; *di finestra* shutter
battere ⟨3a⟩ **I** *v/i* (*bussare, dare colpi*) knock **II** *v/t* beat; *record* break; ***senza ~ ciglio*** without batting an eyelid; ***~ le mani*** clap (one's hands); ***~ i piedi*** stamp one's feet; ***batteva i denti dal freddo*** his teeth were chattering with cold; ***~ a macchina*** type; ***~ bandiera*** fly a flag; ***~ un rigore*** take a penalty; ***in un ~ d'occhio*** in the twinkling of an eye
batteri *mpl* bacteria *pl*
batteria *f* battery; MUS drums *pl*; ***~ da cucina*** pots and pans *pl*; ***~ solare*** solar battery

batterico *adj* ⟨*mpl* -ci⟩ bacterial; ***coltura*** *f* ***-a*** bacterial culture

batteriologico *adj* ⟨*mpl* -ci⟩ bacteriological; ***guerra*** *f* ***-a*** biological warfare

batteriologo *m*, **-a** *f* ⟨*mpl* -gi⟩ bacteriologist

batterista *m/f* ⟨*mpl* -i⟩ drummer

battersela *v/r* run off

battersi *v/r* fight; ***~ per qc*** fight for sth; ***~ contro qn / qc*** fight against s.o. / sth

battesimale *adj* baptismal; ***fonte*** *m* ***~*** font

battesimo *m* christening, baptism; ***~ del fuoco*** baptism of fire; ***tenere qn a ~*** be godfather *or* godmother to s.o.; ***tenere qc a ~*** be godfather *or* godmother to sth

battezzando *m*, **-a** *f* candidate for baptism

battezzare *v/t* ⟨1a⟩ christen, baptize

battibaleno *m*: ***in un ~*** in a flash

battibecco *m* ⟨*pl* -cchi⟩ argument; ***avere un ~ con qn*** have an argument with s.o.

batticarne *m* ⟨*pl* batticarne⟩ meat hammer

batticuore *m* ⟨*no pl*⟩ palpitations *pl*; *fig* ***con un gran ~*** with great anxiety; ***mi è venuto il ~ per l'agitazione*** I was so anxious I got palpitations

battigia *f* foreshore

battimano *m* applause

battipanni *m* ⟨*pl* battipanni⟩ carpet beater

battiscopa *m* ⟨*pl* battiscopa⟩ skirting board, baseboard *US*

battista ⟨*mpl* -i⟩ **I** *m/f* Baptist **II** *adj* Baptist; ***Giovanni Battista*** John the Baptist

battistero *m* baptistry

battistrada *m* ⟨*pl* battistrada⟩ AUTO tread

battito *m del polso* pulse; *delle ali* flap (of its wings); *della pioggia* beating; ***~ cardiaco*** heartbeat

battitore *m*, **-trice** *f nel cricket* batsman; *donna* batswoman; *nel baseball* batter

battitura *f a macchina*: typing; *del grano*: threshing; ***errore*** *m* ***di ~*** typo *infml*

battuta *f* **1.** beat; *in dattilografia* keystroke; MUS bar; THEAT cue; *nel tennis* service **2.** ***fare una ~ di caccia*** go hunting **3.** ***~ di spirito*** wisecrack **4.** ***in poche -e*** very quickly; ***non perdere una ~*** not miss a word; ***avere sempre la ~ pronta*** always have a ready answer; *fig* ***subire una ~ d'arresto*** suffer a setback

battuto **I** *adj* beaten; (*frequentato*) well-trodden; ***ferro*** *m* ***~*** wrought iron; ***sentiero*** *m* ***~*** beaten track **II** *n*: ***battuto*** *m* COOK *mixture of chopped vegetables used as base for sauces*; (*pavimento*) concrete floor

batuffolo *m*: ***un ~ di cotone*** a cotton wool ball

bau *int* woof, bow-wow; ***fare ~, ~*** bark

baule *m* trunk; AUTO boot, *US* trunk

bava *f di persona* dribble; *di cane* slaver; *fig* ***avere la ~ alla bocca*** be foaming at the mouth

bavaglino *m* bib

bavaglio *m* ⟨*pl* -gli⟩ gag; *fig* ***mettere il ~ a qn*** gag s.o.

bavero *m* collar

bavoso *adj* dribbling

bazar *m* ⟨*pl* bazar⟩ bazaar

bazzecola *f* trifle

bazzicare ⟨1l & d⟩ **I** *v/t un posto* haunt; *persone* associate with **II** *v/i* hang about

Bce *abbr* (= **Banca centrale europea**) Central European Bank

bearnese **I** *adj* of Béarn; *persona* from Béarn; ***salsa*** *f* ***~*** Béarnaise sauce **II** *m/f* person from Béarn

bearsi *v/r* ⟨1b⟩: ***~ di qc*** delight in sth

beatamente *adv* blissfully

beatificare *v/t* ⟨1n & d⟩ beatify

beatitudine *f* bliss

beato *adj* happy; REL blessed; ***~ te!*** lucky you!

beauty-case *m* ⟨*pl* beauty-case⟩ toilet bag

bebè *m* ⟨*pl* bebè⟩ baby

beccaccia *f* ⟨*pl* -cce⟩ woodcock

beccafico *m* ⟨*pl* -chi⟩ beccafico

beccamorto *m infml pej* gravedigger

beccare *v/t* ⟨1d⟩ peck; *infml fig* (*cogliere sul fatto*) nab *infml*; *infml fig malattia* catch, pick up *infml*

beccarsi *v/r fig bisticciare* squabble; *infml malattia* catch, pick up *infml*; ***mi sono beccata il raffreddore*** I've caught the cold

beccata *f* peck

beccheggiare *v/i* ⟨1f⟩ NAUT pitch

beccheggio *m* ⟨*pl* -ggi⟩ pitch

becchime *m* birdseed
becchino *m* grave digger
becco[1] *m* ⟨*pl* -cchi⟩ beak; *di teiera etc* spout; CHEM **~ *Bunsen*** Bunsen burner; **~ *d'oca*** hair clip; ***chiudi il ~!*** *infml* shut up! *infml*, shut it! *infml*; ***mettere (il) ~ in qc*** poke one's nose into sth; ***non avere il ~ di un quattrino*** be broke; ***restare a ~ asciutto*** be left empty-handed
becco[2] *m* ⟨*pl* -cchi⟩ *infml* cuckold
beccuccio *m* ⟨*pl* -cci⟩ *di recipiente*: spout
becero *adj* loutish
bed and breakfast *m* ⟨*pl* bed and breakfast⟩ bed and breakfast
beduino I *adj* Bedouin **II** *m*, **-a** *f* Bedouin
befana *f kind old witch who brings presents to children on Twelfth Night*; REL Twelfth Night; *fig* old witch
beffa *f* hoax; ***farsi -e di qn*** make a fool of s.o.
beffardamente *adv* mockingly
beffardo *adj* scornful; ***risata*** *f* ***-a*** mocking laugh
beffare *v/t* ⟨1b⟩ mock **beffarsi** *v/r*: **~ *di*** mock
beffeggiare *v/t* ⟨1f⟩ mock
bega *f* ⟨*pl* -ghe⟩ (*litigio*) fight, argument; (*problema*) can of worms
beghina *f pej* God-botherer
begli → ***bello***
begonia *f* begonia
bei → ***bello***
Bei *abbr* (= **Banca europea per gli investimenti**) EIB (European Investment Bank)
beige *adj inv* beige
belare *v/i* ⟨1b⟩ bleat
belato *m* bleating
belcanto *m* bel canto
belga *m/f & adj* ⟨*mpl* -gi⟩ Belgian
Belgio *m* Belgium
belgradese I *adj* of Belgrade; *persona* from Belgrade **II** *m/f* person from Belgrade
Belgrado *f* Belgrade
bella *f* fair copy; ***copiare in ~*** make a fair copy of
belladonna *f* BOT deadly nightshade
bellamente *adv* (*gentilmente*) nicely; (*comodamente*) comfortably; (*abilmente*) well and truly
belletto *m* blusher
bellezza *f* beauty; ***istituto*** *m* ***di ~*** beauty salon; ***prodotti*** *mpl* ***di ~*** cosmetics; ***concorso*** *m* ***di ~*** beauty contest; ***che ~!*** fantastic!; ***chiudere*** *or* ***finire in ~*** end on a high
bellicismo *m* warmongering
bellico *adj* ⟨*mpl* -ci⟩ (*di guerra*) war *attr*; (*del tempo di guerra*) wartime *attr*; ***industria*** *f* ***-a*** arms industry
bellicoso *adj* bellicose
belligerante *adj* belligerant **belligeranza** *f* belligerence
bellimbusto *m* dandy
bello I *adj* **1.** beautiful; *uomo* handsome; *tempo* fine, nice, beautiful; ***le -e arti*** *fpl* the fine arts; ***farsi ~*** get dressed up; ***domani farà ~*** it's going to be nice tomorrow; ***bell'e fatto*** done and dusted; ***hai un bel dire*** in spite of what you say; ***questa è -a !*** that's a good one!; ***a -a posta*** on purpose; ***alla bell'e meglio*** any old how; ***dirne delle -e*** tell whoppers; ***scamparla ~*** have a narrow escape; ***tante -e cose!*** best wishes! **2.** ***nel bel mezzo*** right in the middle; ***una bugia ~ e buona*** an outright lie **II** *m* beauty; ***sul più ~*** at the worst possible moment; ***cosa fai di ~?*** what are you up to?; ***il ~ deve ancora venire*** the best is yet to come; *hum* now for the best bit; ***pare che il tempo si metta al ~*** the weather seems to be turning fine
bellunese I *adj* of Belluno; *persona* from Belluno **II** *m/f* person from Belluno
belva *f* wild beast
belvedere *m* ⟨*pl* belvedere⟩ viewpoint
bemolle *m* ⟨*pl* bemolle⟩ MUS flat
benarrivato *adj* welcome
benché *cj* though, although; **~ *piova faccio un giro*** although it's raining, I'm going for a walk; ***non ha il ~ minimo sospetto*** she hasn't got the slightest suspicion
benchmark *m* ⟨*pl* benchmark⟩ benchmark
benda *f* bandage; *per occhi* blindfold
bendaggio *m* ⟨*pl* -ggi⟩ bandaging
bendare *v/t* ⟨1b⟩ MED bandage
bendisposto *adj*: ***essere ~*** (***nei confronti di qn***) be well-disposed (towards s.o.)
bene I *adv* well; **~!** good!; ***per ~*** prop-

erly; ***non ho capito ~*** I didn't understand; ***stare ~*** *di salute* be well; *di vestito* suit; ***ben ti sta!*** serves you right!; ***va ~!*** OK!; ***andare ~ a qn*** *di abito* fit s.o.; *di orario, appuntamento* suit s.o.; ***gli è andata ~!*** he got away with it!; ***di ~ in meglio*** better and better; ***sentirsi ~*** feel well; ***guadagnare ~*** earn a lot; ***fare ~ a fare qc*** do well to do sth; ***un uomo per ~*** a respectable man **II** *m* **1.** good; ***~ comune*** common good; ***il ~ e il male*** good and evil; ***fare del ~*** do good; ***fare ~ alla salute*** be good for you; ***per il tuo ~*** for your own good **2.** ***voler ~ a qn*** love s.o.; (*amare*) love s.o. **3.** ***-i*** *pl* assets, property *sg*; ***-i*** *pl* ***di consumo*** consumer goods; ***-i*** *pl* ***culturali*** cultural heritage *sg*; ***-i*** *pl* ***immobili*** real estate *sg*; ***-i*** *pl* ***di lusso*** luxury goods; ***-i*** *pl* ***mobili*** JUR personal property; ***-i*** *pl* ***pubblici*** public property *sg* **III** *adj inv* upper-class; ***la gente ~*** the upper classes

benedettino I *adj* Benedictine; ***regola*** *f* ***-a*** Benedictine rule **II** *n*: ***benedettino*** *m* Benedictine (*a. liquore*)

benedetto I *past part* → ***benedire*** **II** *adj* blessed; REL ***acqua*** *f* ***-a*** holy water

Benedetto *m*: ***San ~*** Saint Benedict

benedire *v/t* ⟨3t⟩ bless; ***Dio ti benedica!*** (God) bless you!; ***andare a farsi ~*** *infml* go to hell; ***mandare qn a farsi ~*** *infml* tell s.o. to go to hell

benedizione *f* blessing; ***impartire la ~*** bless

beneducato *adj* well-mannered

benefattore *m*, **-trice** *f* benefactor

beneficenza *f* charity; ***spettacolo*** *m* ***di ~*** benefit (performance); ***fare qc per ~*** do sth for charity; ***dare qc in ~*** give sth to charity

beneficiare *v/i* ⟨1f⟩: ***~ di qc*** benefit from sth

beneficiario ⟨*mpl* -ri⟩ **I** *adj* beneficiary; ***erede*** *m* ***~*** beneficiary **II** *m*, **-a** *f* FIN payee; ***~ di un credito*** recipient of a credit

beneficio *m* ⟨*pl* -ci⟩ benefit; ***a ~ di*** for the benefit of

benefico *adj* ⟨*mpl* -ci⟩ beneficial; *organizzazione, istituto* charitable; *spettacolo* charity *attr*

benefit *m* ⟨*pl* benefit⟩ fringe benefit

benemerenza *f* merit; ***attestato*** *m* ***di ~*** certificate of merit

benemerito *adj* worthy; ***rendersi ~ di qc*** become worthy of sth

beneplacito *m* approval; ***ottenere il ~*** obtain approval

benessere *m* well-being; (*agiatezza*) affluence; ***senso*** *m* ***di ~*** sense of well-being

benestante I *adj* well-off **II** *m/f* person with money

benestare *m* consent

beneventano I *adj* of Benevento; *persona* from Benevento **II** *m*, **-a** *f* person from Benevento

benevolenza *f* benevolence

benevolmente *adv* kindly

benevolo *adj* benevolent

benfatto *adj corpo* well-made; *lavoro* well-done

bengala *m* ⟨*pl* bengala⟩ (*fuoco*) flare; (*razzo*) Bengal light

bengalese I *adj* Bengali **II** *m/f* Bengali

beniamino *m*, **-a** *f* favo(u)rite; ***la -a del professore*** the teacher's pet; ***~ del pubblico*** public favo(u)rite

benignamente *adv* kindly **benignità** *f* ⟨*pl* benignità⟩ (*benevolenza*) kindness; MED benign nature

benigno *adj* MED benign

benino *adv* well; ***fare le cose per ~*** do things properly

benintenzionato *adj* well-meaning; ***quando l'ha detto era ~*** when he said it, he meant well

beninteso *adv* of course; ***~ che*** provided that

benone *adj* splendid

benpensante *m/f* moderate; *pej* conformist

benservito *m*: ***dare il ~ a qn*** thank s.o. for their services

bensì *cj* but rather

bentornato *adj* welcome back

benvenuto I *adj* welcome **II** *m* welcome; ***dare il ~ a qn*** welcome s.o.; ***-i a Firenze!*** welcome to Florence!

benvisto *adj* well thought of; ***essere ~ da qn*** be well thought of by s.o.

benvolere *v/t*: ***farsi ~ da qn*** win s.o. over

benvoluto *adj* well-liked; ***essere ~ da tutti*** be loved by all

benzina *f* petrol, *US* gas; ***serbatoio*** *m* ***della ~*** petrol (*US* gas) tank; ***~ normale*** 4-star, *US* premium; ***~ senza***

piombo unleaded petrol (*US* gas); ***fare ~*** get petrol (*US* gas)
benzinaio *m*, **-a** *f* ⟨*mpl* -ai⟩ petrol *or US* gas station attendant
benzolo *m* benzol(e)
beone *m*, **-a** *f pej* boozer
beota ⟨*mpl* -i⟩ **I** *adj* Boeotian; *fig* uncouth **II** *m/f* Boeotian; *fig* peasant
berbero I *adj* Berber **II** *m*, **-a** *f* Berber
bere I *v/t* ⟨3i⟩ drink; *fig* swallow; ***~ alla salute di qn / qc*** drink to s.o.'s / sth's health; ***offrire da ~ a qn*** buy s.o. a drink; ***vuoi qualcosa da ~?*** would you like a drink?; ***bersi una birra*** have a beer; *fig* ***darla a ~ a qn*** take s.o. in **II** *m bevanda* drink; *atto* drinking
bergamasco ⟨*mpl* -chi⟩ **I** *adj* of Bergamo; *persona* from Bergamo **II** *m*, **-a** *f* person from Bergamo
bergamotto *m* bergamot
berillio *m* ⟨*pl* -lli⟩ beryllium
berillo *m* beryl
berlina *f* AUTO saloon; ***mettere qn alla ~*** hold s.o. up to ridicule (*a. fig*)
Berlino *m* Berlin
bermuda I *mpl* Bermuda shorts *pl* **II** *fpl*: ***le Bermuda*** Bermuda
bernese I *adj* of Bern; *persona* from Bern **II** *m/f* person from Bern
bernoccolo *m* bump; *fig* flair; ***aver il ~ di qc*** have a flair for sth
berretto *m* cap
berrò → ***bere***
bersagliare *v/t* ⟨1g⟩: ***~ qn di colpi*** rain blows on s.o.; ***~ qn di domande*** bombard s.o. with questions
bersagliere *m*, **-a** *f Italian infantry soldier*; ***spaghetti*** *mpl* ***alla -a*** COOK *spaghetti with spicy tomato sauce*
bersaglio *m* ⟨*pl* -gli⟩ target; *fig di scherzi* butt; ***colpire il ~*** hit the target; *fig* achieve one's aim
besciamella *f* béchamel
bestemmia *f* swear-word; ***dire una ~*** swear
bestemmiare ⟨1k⟩ **I** *v/i* swear (***contro*** at) **II** *v/t* curse
bestemmiatore *m*, **-trice** *f* foul-mouthed person; REL blasphemer
bestia *f* animal; *persona brutale* beast; *persona sciocca* blockhead; *fig* ***andare in ~*** fly into a rage; ***~ rara*** rarity; ***lavorare come una ~*** work like a dog; *fig* ***la matematica è la sua ~ nera*** maths is his bête noire
bestiale *adj* bestial; *infml* (*molto intenso*) terrible; ***istinto*** *m* ***~*** animal instinct
bestialità *f* ⟨*pl* bestialità⟩ bestiality; (*sproposito*) blunder; ***dire una ~*** say sth stupid **bestialmente** *adv* bestially
bestiame *m* livestock; ***capo*** *m* ***di ~*** head of cattle
bestiola *f* beastie **bestione** *m* brute
betabloccante *m* beta blocker
betoniera *f* cement mixer
bettola *f pej* dive
betulla *f* birch
bevanda *f* drink
beve → ***bere***
bevibile *adj* drinkable
bevitore *m*, **-trice** *f* drinker; ***un forte ~*** a heavy drinker
bevuta *f* drink; *azione* drinking; ***fare una ~*** booze
BG *abbr* (= **Bergamo**) Bergamo
BI *abbr* (= **Biella**) Biella
biada *f* fodder
Biagio *m*: ***San ~*** Saint Blaise
Biancaneve *f* Snow White
biancastro *adj* whitish
biancheria *f* linen; ***~ intima*** underwear
bianchetto *m per correzioni* correction fluid; *per scarpe* whitener
bianco ⟨*mpl* -chi⟩ **I** *adj* **1.** white; ***settimana*** *f* ***-a*** winter-sports holiday *or US* vacation **2.** *foglio* blank **3.** *fig* ***dare carta -a a qn*** give s.o. a free hand, give s.o. carte blanche; ***notte*** *f* ***-a*** sleepless night; ***sciopero*** *m* ***~*** work-to-rule **II** *m* **1.** white; ***~ d'uovo*** egg white; ***lasciare in ~*** leave blank; ***in ~ e nero*** *film* black and white **2.** *fig* ***di punto in ~*** point-blank; ***mangiare in ~*** avoid rich food **3.** COOK ***riso*** *m* ***in ~*** rice with butter and cheese **4.** ***in ~*** *assegno* blank
biancore *m* whiteness
biancospino *m* hawthorn
biascicare *v/t* ⟨1l e d⟩ chomp; *fig* mumble
biasimare *v/t* ⟨1l⟩ blame
biasimevole *adj* blameworthy
biasimo *m* blame
bibbia *f* bible
biberon *m* ⟨*pl* biberon⟩ baby's bottle
bibita *f* drink; ***~ analcolica*** soft drink
biblico *adj* ⟨*mpl* -ci⟩ biblical

bibliofilia *f* love of books **bibliofilo** *m*, **-a** *f* book lover
bibliografia *f* bibliography
bibliografico *adj* ⟨*mpl* -ci⟩ bibliographical
bibliografo *m*, **-a** *f* bibliographer
biblioteca *f* ⟨*pl* -che⟩ library; *mobile* book-case
bibliotecario *m*, **-a** *f* ⟨*mpl* -ri⟩ librarian
biblista *m/f* ⟨*mpl* -i⟩ biblical scholar **biblistica** *f* Bible studies
bicamerale *adj* POL bicameral
bicameralismo *m* bicameral system; **~ *perfetto*** *bicameral system where both houses have equal power*
bicamere *m* ⟨*pl* bicamere⟩ two-room flat (*US* apartment)
bicarbonato *m*: **~ (*di sodio*)** bicarbonate of soda
bicchiere *m* glass; ***un ~ di birra*** a glass of beer; ***~ da birra*** beer glass; ***~ di carta*** paper cup; ***facile come bere un bicchier d'acqua*** as easy as ABC; ***affogare in un bicchier d'acqua*** make a mountain out of a molehill
bicentenario *m* bicentenary
bici *f* ⟨*pl* bici⟩ *infml* bike *infml*
bicicletta *f* bike, bicycle; ***andare in ~*** cycle, ride a bicycle; ***~ pieghevole*** folding bike; ***~ da corsa*** racing bike; ***gita** f **in ~*** bike ride
bicipite *m* biceps
bicocca *f* ⟨*pl* -cche⟩ hovel
bicolore *adj* two-tone
bidè *m* ⟨*pl* bidè⟩ bidet
bidello *m*, **-a** *f* *scuola* caretaker, *US* janitor; *università* porter
bidimensionale *adj* two-dimensional
bidirezionale *adj* COMPUT bidirectional; ***trasmissione** f **dati ~*** bidirectional data transmission
bidonare *v/t* ⟨1a⟩ cheat
bidoncino *m per rifiuti* small waste bin; *per liquidi* small churn
bidone *m* **1.** drum; *della spazzatura* (dust)bin, *US* garbage can **2.** *infml* (*imbroglio*) swindle *infml* **3.** ***tirare un ~ a qn*** *ad appuntamento* stand s.o. up
bidonville *f* ⟨*pl* bidonville⟩ shanty town
bieco *adj* ⟨*mpl* -chi⟩ *sguardo* dark
biella *f* TECH connecting rod
Bielorussia *f* Belarus
bielorusso I *adj* Belarusian **II** *m*, **-a** *f* Belarusian
biennale I *adj che si fa ogni due anni* biennial; *che dura due anni* two-year; ***fiera** f **~*** biennial fair **II** *f*: ***Biennale*** (***di Venezia***) Venice Arts Festival
biennio *m* ⟨*pl* -nni⟩ period of two years
bietola *f* beet
bifamiliare *adj* semi-detached; ***villetta** f **~*** semi-detached house
bifase *adj* two-phase
bifocale *adj* bifocal; ***lenti** fpl **-i*** bifocals
bifolco *m*, **-a** *f* ⟨*mpl* -chi⟩ *fig pej* yokel
bifora *f* ARCH mullioned window
biforcarsi *v/r* ⟨1d⟩ fork
biforcazione *f* fork
biforcuto *adj* forked; ***lingua** f **-a*** forked tongue (*a. fig*)
big *m/f* ⟨*pl* big⟩ *di musica*, *cinema* star; *di finanza*, *industria* big shot
bigamia *f* bigamy
bigamo *m*, **-a** *f* bigamist
big bang *m* ⟨*pl* big bang⟩ big bang
bighellonare *v/i* ⟨1a⟩ loaf about **bighellone** *m*, **-a** *f* loafer
bigio *adj* ⟨*mpl* -gi⟩ ash grey, *US* ash gray
bigiotteria *f* costume jewellery, *US* costume jewelry; (*negozio*) jewel(l)er's
bigliettaio *m*, **-a** *f* ⟨*mpl* -ai⟩ booking office clerk; *sul treno*, *tram* conductor
biglietteria *f* ticket office, booking office; *cinema*, *teatro* box office; *aeroporto* ticket counter; ***~ automatica*** ticket machine
biglietto *m* ticket; ***~ aereo*** airline *or* plane ticket; ***~ d'andata e ritorno*** return ticket, *US* roundtrip ticket; ***un ~ di sola andata per Pisa*** a single *or US* one-way ticket to Pisa; ***~ aperto*** open ticket; ***~ intero/ridotto***; full-price/cheap ticket ***~ d'auguri*** (greetings) card; ***~ da visita*** business card; ***~ di banca*** banknote, *US* bill; ***~ della lotteria*** lottery ticket; ***un ~ da 10 dollari*** a ten-dollar bill; ***fare il ~*** buy the ticket
bignè *m* ⟨*pl* bignè⟩ cream puff; ***~ al cioccolato*** chocolate cream puff
bigodino *m* roller
bigotto I *adj* bigoted **II** *m*, **-a** *f* bigot
bikini *m* ⟨*pl* bikini⟩ bikini

bilancia *f* ⟨*pl* -ce⟩ **1.** scales *pl* **2.** ASTROL ***Bilancia*** Libra; ***sono della Bilancia*** I'm (a) Libra **3.** FIN balance; ***~ commerciale*** balance of trade; ***~ dei pagamenti*** balance of payments

bilanciare *v/t* ⟨1f⟩ balance; (*pareggiare*) equal, be equal to; *fig* weigh up; FIN ***~ un conto*** balance an account

bilanciarsi *v/r* balance

bilanciere *m* MECH compensator; *di orologio*: balance wheel; SPORTS bar

bilancio *m* ⟨*pl* -ci⟩ balance; (*rendiconto*) balance sheet; ***~ annuale*** annual accounts *pl*; ***~ consuntivo*** closing balance; ***~ dello Stato*** national budget; ***~ di esercizio*** FIN financial statements; ***~ preventivo*** budget; ***fare il ~*** draw up a balance sheet; *fig* take stock; ***relazione** f **annuale di ~*** annual report

bilaterale *adj* bilateral

bilateralità *f* ⟨*pl* bilateralità⟩ bilateral nature

bilateralmente *adv* bilaterally

bile *f* bile; *fig* rage; ***verde dalla ~*** white with rage; ***rodersi dalla ~*** be consumed with rage

biliardino *m* mini billiards *sg*; (*flipper*) pinball

biliardo *m* billiards *sg*; ***giocare a ~*** play billiards

biliare *adj* bile *attr*; ***vie** fpl **-i*** bile ducts

bilico *m*: ***essere in ~*** be precariously balanced; *fig* be undecided

bilingue *adj* bilingual

bilinguismo *m* bilingualism

bilione *m* (*mille miliardi*) million million, *US* trillion; (*miliardo*) billion

bilioso *adj* bad-tempered

bilirubina *f* bilirubin

bilocale *m* two-room flat (*US* apartment)

bimbo *m*, **-a** *f* child

bimensile *adj* every two weeks, *Br* fortnightly

bimestrale *adj ogni due mesi* bimonthly; *che dura due mesi* two-month (long)

bimotore I *adj* twin-engine **II** *m* twin-engine plane

binario[1] *m* ⟨*pl* -ri⟩ track; (*marciapiede*) platform; ***il treno in arrivo sul** or **al ~ cinque*** the train arriving at platform five; ***il treno parte dal primo ~*** the train leaves from platform one

binario[2] *adj* ⟨*mpl* -ri⟩ binary; ***codice** m **~*** binary code

bingo *m* ⟨*pl* bingo⟩ bingo; ***sala** f **~*** bingo hall; ***fare ~*** get a line; ***giocare a ~*** play bingo

binocolo *m* binoculars *pl*

bioagricoltura *f* organic farming

bioarchitettura *f* environmentally-friendly architecture

biocarburante *m* biofuel

biochimica *f* biochemistry

biochimico ⟨*mpl* -ci⟩ **I** *adj* biochemical **II** *m*, **-a** *f* biochemist

biodegradabile *adj* biodegradable

biodinamica *f* biodynamics *sg*

biodinamico *adj* ⟨*mpl* -ci⟩ (*attività*) biodynamic; (*alimentazione*) organic

bioenergetica *f* ⟨*pl* -che⟩ bioenergetics *sg*

bioenergetico *adj* ⟨*mpl* -ci⟩ bioenergetic

bioetica *f* ⟨*pl* -che⟩ bioethics *sg*

bioetico *adj* ⟨*mpl* -ci⟩ bioethical; ***comitato** m **~*** bioethics committee

biofisica *f* biophysics *sg*

biofisico ⟨*mpl* -ci⟩ **I** *adj* biophysic **II** *m*, **-a** *f* biophysicist

biogenetica *f* biogenetics *sg*

biogenetico *adj* ⟨*mpl* -ci⟩ biogenetic

biografia *f* biography

biografico *adj* ⟨*mpl* -ci⟩ biographical

biografo *m*, **-a** *f* biographer

bioingegneria *f* bioengineering

biologia *f* biology

biologicamente *adv* biologically

biologico *adj* ⟨*mpl* -ci⟩ biological; (*verde*) organic; ***da culture -che*** organic

biologo *m*, **-a** *f* ⟨*mpl* -gi⟩ biologist

biomedicina *f* biomedicine

biomedico *adj* ⟨*mpl* -ci⟩ biomedical; ***laboratorio** m **~*** biomedical laboratory

biometria *f* biometrics *sg*

biondastro *adj* blondish

biondo *adj* blonde

bionica *f* bionics *sg* **bionico** *adj* ⟨*mpl* -ci⟩ bionic

biopsia *f* biopsy

bioritmo *m* biorhythm

biosfera *f* biosphere

biossido *m* dioxide

bioterrorismo *m* bioterrorism

biotopo *m* biotope
bipartisan *adj inv* POL bipartisan
bipartitico *adj* ⟨*mpl* -ci⟩ two-party **bipartitismo** *m* two-party system
bipede *adj* biped
biplano *m* biplane
bipolare *adj* bipolar
bipolarismo *m system in which the political parties in a country form two opposing blocks* **bipolarità** *f* ⟨*pl* bipolarità⟩ bipolarity
biposto *m/adj* two-seater
birba *f* rascal
birbante *m* rascal
birbone **I** *adj* naughty; ***tiro** m* **~** dirty trick **II** *m*, **-a** *f* rascal
bireattore **I** *adj* twin-engined **II** *m* twin-engined jet
birichinata *f* prank
birichino **I** *adj* naughty **II** *m*, **-a** *f* little devil
birillo *m* skittle; ***giocare a -i*** play skittles
Birmania *f* Burma **birmano** **I** *adj* Burmese; ***gatto** m* **~** Burmese (cat) **II** *m*, **-a** *f* Burmese
biro® *f* ⟨*pl* biro⟩ biro®, ballpoint (pen)
birra *f* beer; **~ *chiara*** lager; **~ *scura*** brown ale; **~ *in lattina*** canned beer; **~ *alla spina*** draught (beer); **~ *in bottiglia*** bottled beer; ***lievito** m **di*** **~** brewer's yeast; ***farsi una*** **~** have a beer; ***a tutta*** **~** flat out
birreria *f pub that sells only beer*; *fabbrica* brewery
bis *m/int* ⟨*pl* bis⟩ encore; ***concedere il*** **~** play *or* give an encore
bisaccia *f* ⟨*pl* -cce⟩ saddlebag
Bisanzio *f* Byzantium
bisarca *f* ⟨*pl* -che⟩ transporter
bisavolo *m*, **-a** *f* great-grandfather; *donna* great-grandmother
bisbetico *adj* ⟨*mpl* -ci⟩ bad-tempered
bisbigliare *v/t & v/i* ⟨1g⟩ whisper
bisbiglio *m* whisper
bisboccia *f* ⟨*pl* -cce⟩ binge; ***fare*** **~** go on a binge
bisca *f* ⟨*pl* -che⟩ gambling house; *clandestina* gambling den
Biscaglia *f*: ***golfo di*** **~** Bay of Biscay
biscazziere *m*, **-a** *f* gamblinghouse keeper
bischero *m*, **-a** *f reg hum* dickhead *vulg*
biscia *f* ⟨*pl* -sce⟩ grass snake
biscottato *adj*: ***fette** fpl **-e*** rusks
biscottiera *f* biscuit tin **biscottificio** *m* ⟨*pl* -ci⟩ biscuit factory
biscotto *m* biscuit, *US* cookie
biscugino *m*, **-a** *f* second cousin
bisdrucciolo *adj with the stress on the fourth-last syllable*
bisessuale *adj* bisexual
bisestile *adj*: ***anno** m* **~** leap year
bisettimanale *adj* every two weeks, *Br* fortnightly
bislacco *adj* ⟨*mpl* -cchi⟩ odd
bislungo *adj* ⟨*mpl* -ghi⟩ oblong
bismuto *m* bismuth
bisnipote *m/f di nonni*: great-grandchild; *maschio* great-grandson; *femmina* great-granddaughter; *di zii*: *maschio* great-nephew; *femmina* great--niece
bisnonno *m*, **-a** *f* great-grandfather; *donna* great-grandmother
bisognare *v/i* ⟨1a⟩: ***bisogna farlo*** it must be done, it needs to be done; ***non bisogna farlo*** it doesn't have to be done, there's no need to do it; ***bisogna che tu vada di persona*** you have to go in person; ***bisognerebbe telefonargli*** you should phone him
bisognevole *adj* needy
bisognino *m*: ***fare un*** **~** *infml* go to the loo
bisogno *m* need; (*mancanza*) lack; (*fabbisogno*) requirements; ***in caso di*** **~** if necessary, if need be; ***avere*** **~ *di qc*** need sth; ***di quanto tempo hai*** **~*?*** how much time do you need?; ***non ce n'è bisogno*** there is no need; ***fare i propri -i*** go to the toilet
bisognoso *adj* needy
bisonte *m* ZOOL bison
bisso *m* SEW fine linen
bistecca *f* ⟨*pl* -cche⟩ steak; **~ *di maiale*** pork steak; **~ *ai ferri*** grilled *or US* broiled steak; **~ *alla fiorentina*** charcoal grilled steak
bistecchiera *f* gridiron
bisticciare *v/i* ⟨1f⟩ quarrel; **~ *con qn per qc*** quarrel with s.o. about sth
bisticcio *m* ⟨*pl* -cci⟩ quarrel
bistrattare *v/t* ⟨1a⟩ mistreat
bistrò, bistrot *m* ⟨*pl* bistrò, bistrot⟩ bistro
bisturi *m* ⟨*pl* bisturi⟩ MED scalpel
bisunto *adj* very greasy; ***unto e*** **~** filthy

with grease
bit *m* ⟨*pl* bit⟩ COMPUT bit; **~ *di dati*** COMPUT data bit; **~ *di stop*** COMPUT stop bit
bitorzoluto *adj* warty
bitter *m* ⟨*pl* bitter⟩ aperitif
bitumatrice *f* bitumen sprayer **bitume** *m* bitumen
bivaccare *v/i* ⟨1d⟩ bivouac
bivacco *m* ⟨*pl* -cchi⟩ bivouac
bivalente *adj* bivalent
bivio *m* ⟨*pl* -vi⟩ junction; *fig* crossroads *sg*; *fig* ***essere giunto a un ~*** be at a crossroads
bizantino *adj* Byzantine
bizza *f* tantrum; ***fare le -e*** throw a tantrum
bizzarramente *adv* oddly **bizzarria** *f* strangeness
bizzarro *adj* bizarre
bizzeffe *adv*: ***a ~*** galore
bizzoso *adj* capricious; *cavallo* frisky
BL *abbr* (= **Belluno**) Belluno
bla bla *m* ⟨*pl* bla bla⟩ blah blah
black out *m* ⟨*pl* black out⟩ power cut *or* failure
blandamente *adv* mildly
blando *adj* mild, gentle
blasfemo I *adj* blasphemous **II** *m*, **-a** *f* blasphemer
blasonato *adj* emblazoned **blasone** *m* (*stemma*) coat of arms; (*nobiltà*) nobility
blastoma *m* ⟨*pl* -i⟩ MED blastoma
blaterare *v/i* ⟨1b⟩ *pej* blether
blatta *f* cockroach
bleffare *v/i* ⟨1a⟩ bluff
blesità *f* ⟨*pl* blesità⟩ lisp **bleso** *adj* lisping
blindare *v/t* ⟨1a⟩ armo(u)r-plate
blindato *adj* armo(u)red; ***camera*** *f* ***-a*** strongroom; ***vetro ~*** bulletproof glass; ***la città è -a*** the city is under tight security
blitz *m* ⟨*pl* blitz⟩ blitz
blob *m* ⟨*pl* blob⟩ TV *montage consisting of short pieces of TV programmes spliced together for comic or satirical effect*
bloccaggio *m* ⟨*pl* -ggi⟩ locking
bloccare *v/t* ⟨1c & d⟩ block; MIL blockade; (*isolare*) cut off; *prezzi, conto* freeze; **~ *il traffico*** hold up the traffic
bloccarsi *v/r di ascensore, persona* get stuck; *di freni, porta* jam; ***si è bloccata la ruota anteriore*** the front wheel has locked
bloccaruota *m* AUTO wheel clamp, *US* Denver boot; ***mettere il ~ a*** clamp
bloccasterzo *m* AUTO steering lock
bloccato *adj* blocked (*a.* PSYCH); ECON frozen; ***conto*** *m* **~** frozen bank account
blocchetto *m per appunti* notebook
blocco *m* ⟨*pl* -cchi⟩ **1.** block; *di carta* pad; **~ *da disegno*** sketchpad; **~ *di granito*** block of granite; **~ *motore*** engine block; ***comprare in ~*** buy in bulk **2.** MIL blockade; **~ *delle assunzioni*** recruitment freeze; **~ *delle esportazioni*** export ban, embargo; **~ *dei fitti*** rent freeze; **~ *dei prezzi*** price-freeze; **~ *renale*** MED kidney failure; **~ *stradale*** road block; **~ *dei salari*** wage freeze; **~ *tastiera*** TEL keyboard lock; ***posto*** *m* ***di ~*** checkpoint
bloc-notes *m* ⟨*pl* bloc-notes⟩ writing pad
blog *m* ⟨*pl* blog⟩ COMPUT blog; ***creare un ~*** start a blog **bloggare** *v/i* ⟨1c & d⟩ COMPUT blog
blu *adj inv* blue; ***auto*** *fpl* **~** *government or ministerial car*; ***caschi*** *mpl* **~** blue berets
bluff *m* ⟨*pl* bluff⟩ bluff
bluffare *v/i* ⟨1a⟩ bluff
blusa *f* blouse
BN *abbr* (= **Benevento**) Benevento
BNL *abbr* (= **Banca Nazionale del Lavoro**) *Italian bank*
BO *abbr* (= **Bologna**) Bologna
boa[1] *m* ⟨*pl* boa⟩ ZOOL boa constrictor
boa[2] *f* NAUT buoy; **~ *luminosa*** illuminated buoy; ***giro*** *m* ***di ~*** rounding of the buoy
boato *m* rumble
bob *m* ⟨*pl* bob⟩ SPORTS bobsleigh, bobsled; **~ *a quattro*** four-men bob
bobbista *m/f* ⟨*mpl* -i⟩ bobsledder
bobina *f* spool; *di film* reel; AUTO **~ *d'accensione*** ignition coil
bobtail *m* ⟨*pl* bobtail⟩ old English sheepdog
bocca *f* ⟨*pl* -cche⟩ **1.** mouth; ***igiene*** *f* ***della ~*** oral hygiene; ***correre di ~ in ~*** be on everyone's lips; ***essere di ~ buona*** eat anything; *fig* be easygoing; ***in ~ al lupo!*** good luck!; ***vuoi essere sulla ~ di tutti?*** do you want to be the talk of the town?; ***lasciare la ~ amara***

leave a bad taste; ***rimanere a ~ aperta*** be dumbfounded; *fig* ***rimanere a ~ asciutta*** come away empty-handed; ***togliere le parole di ~ a qn*** take the words right out of s.o.'s mouth **2.** (*apertura*) opening; ***~ del fucile*** muzzle of a gun **3.** ***Bocca della Verità*** *Roman sculpture of a human face believed to be able to detect lies*; ***Bocche*** *fpl* ***di Bonifacio*** *area of sea between Sardinia and Corsica*

boccaccesco *adj* ⟨*mpl* -chi⟩ (*licenzioso*) bawdy

boccaccia *f* ⟨*pl* -cce⟩ (*smorfia*) grimace; ***fare le -cce*** pull faces

boccaglio *m* ⟨*pl* -gli⟩ *di maschera per il nuoto* mouthpiece

boccale *m* jug; *da birra* tankard, mug

boccaporto *m* hatch

boccata *f*: ***prendere una ~ d'aria*** get a breath of fresh air

boccetta *f* small bottle

boccheggiare *v/i* ⟨1f⟩ gasp

bocchettone *m di tubo, serbatoio* opening

bocchino *m per sigarette* cigarette holder; MUS, *di pipa* mouthpiece

boccia *f* ⟨*pl* -cce⟩ (*palla*) bowl; ***gioco*** *m* ***delle -cce*** bowls *sg*

bocciare *v/t* ⟨1c & f⟩ (*respingere*) reject, vote down; EDU fail; *boccia* hit, strike

bocciatura *f* failure

bocciofilo **I** *adj* bowls *attr* **II** *m*, **-a** *f* bowls player **III** *n*: ***bocciofila*** *f* bowls club

bocciolo *m* bud

boccola *f* MECH bush

boccolo *m* ringlet

bocconcino *m* morsel

boccone *m* mouthful; ***~ amaro*** bitter pill

bocconi *adv* face down

body *m* ⟨*pl* body⟩ body

body art *f* ART body art

body-building *m* body building

boemo **I** *adj* Bohemian **II** *m*, **-a** *f* Bohemian

boero **I** *adj* Boer **II** *m*, **-a** *f* Boer **III** *n*: ***boero*** *m* cherry liqueur chocolate

bofonchiare *v/i* ⟨1g⟩ grumble

boh *int* who knows?; ***dov'è Paolo? – boh, non lo so*** where's Paolo? – couldn't say

bohème *f* bohemiam lifestyle **bohémien** ⟨*pl* bohémien⟩ *m* bohemian

boia *m* ⟨*pl* boia⟩ executioner; ***fa un freddo ~*** *infml* it's bloody freezing *infml*

boiata *f infml* crap *sl*; ***non dire -e!*** don't talk crap! *sl*

boicottaggio *m* boycott

boicottare *v/t* ⟨1c⟩ boycott

boiler *m* ⟨*pl* boiler⟩ boiler

boleto *m* cep

bolgia *f fig* bedlam

bolide *m* ASTR meteor; ***come un ~*** like greased lightning

bolina *f* bowline; ***navigare di ~*** sail close-hauled

Bolivia *f* Bolivia

boliviano **I** *adj* Bolivian **II** *m*, **-a** *f* Bolivian

bolla[1] *f* bubble; MED blister; ***~ di sapone*** soap bubble

bolla[2] *f documento* note, docket; ***~ di consegna*** delivery note ***~ papale*** *or* ***pontificia*** papal bull

bollare *v/t* ⟨1a⟩ stamp; *fig* brand; ***~ qn come traditore*** brand s.o. a traitor

bollato *adj* stamped; ***carta*** *f* ***-a*** stamped paper *for official documents*; *fig* ***essere ~ per sempre*** be branded for life

bollente *adj* boiling hot

bolletta *f* bill; ***~ della luce*** electricity bill; ***~ di consegna*** delivery note; ***essere in ~*** *infml* be hard up *infml*

bollettino *m*: ***~ meteorologico*** weather forecast

bollicina *f* bubble

bollino *m* stamp; *autoadesivo* sticker; ***~ di garanzia*** guarantee

bollire *v/t & v/i* ⟨4c⟩ boil; ***far ~ qc*** *patate* boil sth; *acqua* bring sth to the boil; ***~ dal caldo*** be boiling hot

bollito **I** *adj* boiled; ***patate*** *fpl* ***-e*** boiled potatoes **II** *m* boiled meat

bollitore *m* kettle

bollo *m* stamp; ***~*** (***di circolazione***) road tax (disk); ***marca*** *f* ***da ~*** revenue stamp

bollore *m* boil; (*calura*) stifling heat; *pl*: ***-i*** (*smanie*) over-excitement; ***portare a ~*** bring to the boil

bolognese **I** *adj* Bolognese; ***ragù alla ~*** bolognese sauce **II** *m/f* Bolognese

bolscevico ⟨*mpl* -chi⟩ **I** *adj hist* Bolshevik **II** *m*, **-a** *f* Bolshevik **bolscevismo** *m* HIST Bolshevism

bolso *adj* broken-winded; *fig* weak
bolzanino I *adj* of Bolzano; *persona* from Bolzano **II** *m*, **-a** *f* person from Bolzano
bomba *f* bomb; **~ *atomica*** atomic bomb; **~ *a mano*** hand grenade; **~ *a orologeria*** time bomb; ***a prova di* ~** bombproof
bombarda *f* HIST (*arma*) bombard; (*strumento*) bombarde
bombardamento *m* shelling, bombardment; (*attacco aereo*) air raid; *fig* bombardment
bombardare *v/t* ⟨1a⟩ bomb; *fig* bombard
bombardiere *m* bomber
bombarolo *m infml* bomber
bombato *adj* rounded
bomber ⟨*pl* bomber⟩ *m* (*cannoniere*) goal scorer; (*giubbotto*) bomber jacket
bombetta *f* bowler (hat), *US* derby
bombo *m* bumblebee
bombola *f* cylinder; **~ (*di gas*)** gas bottle, gas cylinder
bomboletta *f*: **~ (*spray*)** spray (can)
bombolone *m* COOK doughnut
bomboniera *f* wedding keep-sake
bompresso *m* NAUT bowsprit
bonaccia *f* NAUT calm
bonaccione *m*, **-a** *f* kind-hearted person
bonario *adj* ⟨*mpl* -ri⟩ kind-hearted
bond *m* ⟨*pl* bond⟩ FIN bond
bonifica *f* ⟨*pl* -che⟩ reclamation
bonificare *v/t* ⟨1m & d⟩ FIN (*scontare*) allow, discount; (*accreditare*) credit; AGR reclaim; (*prosciugare*) drain
bonifico *m* FIN (*sconto*) allowance, rebate; (*trasferimento*) (money) transfer
bonomia *f* affability
bonsai *m* ⟨*pl* bonsai⟩ bonsai
bontà *f* ⟨*pl* bontà⟩ goodness; (*gentilezza*) kindness; **~ *sua*** graciously
bonus-malus *m* ⟨*pl* bonus-malus⟩ *assicurazione* no-claims bonus system
bookmark *m* ⟨*pl* bookmark⟩ bookmark
boom *m* ⟨*pl* boom⟩ *economico* boom; (*moda*) craze; **~ *demografico*** baby boom
boomerang *m* ⟨*pl* boomerang⟩ boomerang (*a. fig*)
bora *f* bora (*a cold north wind*)
borace *m* borax **boracifero** *adj* borax-bearing
Borboni *mpl* Bourbons **borbonico** *adj* ⟨*mpl* -ci⟩ Bourbon
borbottare *v/i* ⟨1a⟩ mumble; (*brontolare*) grumble
borbottio *m* ⟨*pl* -ii⟩ mumbling; *il brontolare* grumbling **borbottone** *m*, **-a** *f* mumbler; (*brontolone*) grumbler
borchia *f per abbigliamento* stud; *per tappezzeria* upholstery nail
bordare *v/t* ⟨1a⟩ (*orlare*) edge; (*delimitare*) border
bordata *f fig* (*raffica*) volley
bordatura *f* edge
bordeaux *adj inv* (*colore*) burgundy
bordeggiare *v/i* ⟨1f⟩ hug the coast
bordello *m* brothel; *fig infml* bedlam *infml*; (*disordine*) mess
bordino *m* edging
bordo *m* (*orlo*) edge; NAUT, AVIAT, AUTO ***a* ~** on board; ***salire a* ~** board, go on board
bordolese I *adj* of Bordeaux; *persona* from Bordeaux ***poltiglia*** *f* **~** CHEM Bordeaux mixture **II** *m/f* person from Bordeaux
boreale *adj* northern; ***aurora*** *f* **~** northern lights *pl*
borgata *f* village; (*rione popolare*) suburb
borgataro *m*, **-a** *f infml person from the poor areas on the outskirts of Rome*
borghese I *adj* middle-class; ***in* ~** in civilian clothes; ***poliziotto*** *m* ***in* ~** plain-clothes policeman **II** *m/f* middle-class person; ***piccolo*** **~** petty bourgeois, lower middle-class person
borghesia *f* middle classes *pl*
borgo *m* ⟨*pl* -ghi⟩ village
borgogna *m* ⟨*pl* borgogna⟩ burgundy
Borgogna *f* Burgundy **borgognone I** *adj* Burgundian **II** *m*, **-a** *f* Burgundian
borgomastro *m* burgomaster
boria *f* conceit
borico *adj* ⟨*mpl* -ci⟩: ***acido*** *m* **~** boric acid
boriosità *f* ⟨*pl* boriosità⟩ conceit
borioso *adj* conceited
borlotto *m* (*fagiolo*) borlotti bean
borotalco *m* talcum powder, talc
borraccia *f* ⟨*pl* -cce⟩ flask
borragine *f* borage

borsa *f* **1.** bag; (*borsetta*) handbag, *US* purse; *per documenti* briefcase; **~ dell'acqua calda** hot-water bottle; **~ del ghiaccio** ice pack; **~ della spesa** shopping bag; **~ termica** cool bag; **metter mano alla ~** put one's hand in one's pocket **2.** FIN Stock Exchange; **~ merci** Commodities Exchange; **~ nera** black market; **~ valori** Stock Exchange; **bollettino** *m* (o **listino** *m*) **di ~** share index; **giocare in ~** gamble on the Stock Exchange **3. ~ di studio** scholarship
borsaiolo *m*, **-a** *f* pickpocket
borseggiatore *m*, **-trice** *f* pickpocket
borseggio *m* ⟨*pl* -ggi⟩ pickpocketing
borsellino *m* purse, *US* coin purse
borsetta *f* handbag, *US* purse
borsista *m/f* ⟨*mpl* -i⟩ *speculatore* speculator; *studente* scholarship holder
borsistico *adj* ⟨*mpl* -ci⟩ stock market *attr*; **mercato** *m* **~** stock market
boscaglia *f* brush, scrub
boscaiolo *m* woodcutter
boschetto *m* copse **boschivo** *adj* wooded; **terreno** *m* **~** wooded country
boscimano I *adj* Bushman *attr* **II** *m*, **-a** *f* Bushman
bosco *m* ⟨*pl* -schi⟩ wood
boscoso *adj* wooded
bosniaco ⟨*mpl* -ci⟩ **I** *adj* Bosnian **II** *m*, **-a** *f* Bosnian
Bosnia-Erzegovina *f* Bosnia-Herzegovina
bossolo *m di proiettili* (shell) case
bostoniano I *adj* Bostonian **II** *m*, **-a** *f* Bostonian
BOT, bot *abbr* (= **Buono Ordinario del Tesoro**) treasury bond
botanica *f* botany
botanico ⟨*mpl* -ci⟩ **I** *adj* botanical **II** *m*, **-a** *f* botanist
botola *f* trapdoor
botta *f* blow; (*rumore*) bang; **fare a -e** come to blows
botte *f* barrel; ARCH **volta** *f* **a ~** barrel vault; **volere la ~ piena e la moglie ubriaca** want to have one's cake and eat it
bottega *f* ⟨*pl* -ghe⟩ shop; (*laboratorio*) workshop; *fig* **chiudere ~** *infml* throw in the towel
bottegaio *m*, **-a** *f* ⟨*mpl* -ai⟩ shopkeeper
botteghino *m* box office; (*del lotto*) *sales outlet for lottery tickets*
bottiglia *f* **1.** bottle; **una ~ da mezzo litro** a half-litre *or US* half-liter bottle; **bere alla ~** drink straight from the bottle **2. ~ Molotov** Molotov cocktail
bottiglieria *f* wine merchant's
bottiglione *m* big bottle
bottino *m* loot
botto *m* (*rumore*) bang; **di ~** all of a sudden; **i -i di Capodanno** the New Year fireworks
bottone *m* button; **~ automatico** press-stud, *US* snap fastener; **attaccare un ~ a qn** sew a button on for s.o.; *fig* buttonhole s.o.
botulino *m* botulinus
bouquet *m* ⟨*pl* bouquet⟩ bouquet; **il ~ della sposa** the bride's bouquet
boutique *f* ⟨*pl* boutique⟩ boutique
bovaro *m* cattleman *m*; *pej* yokel
bovino I *adj* bovine **II** *m*: **bovini** *pl* cattle
bowling *m* ⟨*pl* bowling⟩ bowling; **giocare a ~** go bowling
box *m* ⟨*pl* box⟩ *per auto* lock-up garage; *per bambini* playpen; *per cavalli* loose box
boxe *f* boxing
boxer *mpl* (*mutande*) boxers *pl*, boxer shorts *pl*
boxeur *m* ⟨*pl* boxeur⟩ boxer
boy scout *m* ⟨*pl* boy scout⟩ scout
bozza *f* draft; TYPO proof; **~ di contratto** draft contract; **-e** *pl* **di stampa** proofs; **correggere le -e** correct proofs
bozzettista *m/f* ⟨*mpl* -i⟩ sketch writer; *di pubblicità* commercial artist
bozzetto *m* sketch; *scultura* model
bozzolo *m* cocoon; *fig* **chiudersi nel proprio ~** withdraw into one's shell; **uscire dal ~** emerge from the cocoon; *fig* come out of one's shell
bps *abbr* (= **bit al secondo**) COMPUT bps
Bps *abbr* (= **byte al secondo**) COMPUT BPS
BR *abbr* **1.** (= **Brindisi**) Brindisi **2.** (= **Brigate Rosse**) Red Brigades
Brabante *m* Brabant **brabantino I** *adj* of Brabant; *persona* from Brabant **II** *m*, **-a** *f* person from Brabant
braccare *v/t* ⟨1d⟩ hunt (*a. fig*)

braccetto *m*: ***a ~*** arm in arm
bracciale *m* bracelet; (*fascia*) armband; *di orologio* watch strap
braccialetto *m* bracelet
bracciante *m/f* farm labo(u)rer
bracciata *f nel nuoto* stroke
braccio *m* ⟨*pl* le braccia *and* i bracci⟩ arm; ***~ di ferro*** trial of strength; ***Braccio di Ferro*** *m* Popeye; ***~ di mare*** sound; *fig* ***essere il ~ destro di qn*** be s.o.'s right-hand man; ***incrociare le -a*** fold one's arms; *fig* go on strike; ***portare in ~ qn*** carry s.o.; ***prendere qn sotto ~*** take s.o.'s arm; ***a -a aperte*** with open arms; ***tenere un discorso a ~*** speak impromptu
bracciolo *m* arm(rest)
bracco *m* ⟨*pl* -cchi⟩ hound
bracconaggio *m* ⟨*pl* -ggi⟩ poaching
bracconiere *m* poacher
brace *f* embers *pl*; ***alla ~*** char-grilled, *US* -broiled; ***carne*** *f* ***alla ~*** char-grilled meat; ***cadere dalla padella nella ~*** go from the frying pan into the fire
braciola *f* COOK chop; ***~ di maiale*** pork chop
bradisismo *m* bradyseism
brado *adj* wild; ***vivere allo stato ~*** live in the wild state
Braille® **I** *m* braille **II** *adj inv* braille; ***alfabeto*** *m* ***~*** braille alphabet
brama *f* longing; ***~ di potere*** lust for power **bramare** *v/t* ⟨1a⟩ *liter* yearn for
bramire *v/i* ⟨4d⟩ *cervo* bell; *orso* growl **bramito** *m di cervo*: bell; *di orso*: growl
bramosia *f* longing (*a. fig*) **bramoso** *adj liter* yearning; ***essere ~ di qc*** long for sth
branca *f* ⟨*pl* -che⟩ branch (*a. fig*)
branchia *f* gill
branco *m* ⟨*pl* -chi⟩ ZOOL *di cani, lupi* pack; *di pecore, uccelli* flock; *fig pej* gang
brancolare *v/i* ⟨1l⟩ grope; *fig* ***~ nel buio*** grope in the dark
branda *f* camp-bed
brandeburghese **I** *adj* Brandenburg **II** *m/f* person from Brandenburg
brandello *m* shred, scrap; ***a -i*** in shreds *or* tatters; ***fare qc a -i*** tear sth to shreds
brandina *f* camp bed, *US* cot; ***~ pieghevole*** folding bed
brandire *v/t* ⟨4d⟩ brandish
brandy *m* ⟨*pl* brandy⟩ brandy
brano *m di testo, musica* passage
brasato *m* COOK *di manzo* braised beef
Brasile *m* Brazil
brasiliano **I** *adj* Brazilian **II** *m*, **-a** *f* Brazilian
bravata *f* boasting; *azione* bravado
bravo *adj* good; (*abile*) clever, good; ***~!*** well done!; ***-a persona*** *f* good person; ***essere ~ a (fare) qc*** be good at (doing) sth; ***fare il ~*** be good; ***notte*** *f* ***-a*** *hum* wild night
bravura *f* skill
break *m* ⟨*pl* break⟩ break
break dance *f* ⟨*pl* break dance⟩ breakdancing
breccia *f* ⟨*pl* -cce⟩ breach
brefotrofio *m* ⟨*pl* -fi⟩ orphanage (for abandoned children)
bresaola *f dried salted beef*
bresciano **I** *adj* of Brescia; *persona* from Brescia **II** *m*, **-a** *f* person from Brescia
bretella *f* (*raccordo*) slip road, *US* ramp; **-e** *pl* braces *pl*, *US* suspenders *pl*
bretone **I** *adj* Breton **II** *m/f* Breton
breve *adj* short; ***in ~*** briefly, in short; ***tra ~*** shortly
brevemente *adv* briefly
brevettabile *adj* patentable
brevettare *v/t* ⟨1a⟩ patent
brevetto *m* patent; *di pilota* licence, *US* license; ***ufficio*** *m* ***dei -i*** patent office; ***~ comunitario*** EU patent; ***rilasciare/depositare/ottenere un ~*** issue/deposit/obtain a patent
breviario *m* ⟨*pl* -ri⟩ breviary
brevi manu *adv* by hand
brevità *f* shortness
brezza *f* breeze
brianteo *adj* of Brianza **brianzolo** **I** *adj* of Brianza; *persona* from Brianza **II** *m*, **-a** *f* person from Brianza
bricco *m* ⟨*pl* -cchi⟩ jug, *US* pitcher
bricconata *f* dirty trick; *hum* prank **bricconcello** *m*, **-a** *f* little rascal **briccone** *m*, **-a** *f persona disonesta* crook; *persona malvagia* jerk; *hum* rogue
briciola *f* crumb
briciolo *m fig* grain, scrap; ***un ~ di verità*** a shred of truth; *fig* ***non avere un ~ di qc*** not have a scrap of sth; ***abbi un ~ di pazienza!*** wait just a second!

bricolage *m* ⟨*no pl*⟩ do-it-yourself
briga *f* ⟨*pl* -ghe⟩: ***darsi la ~ di fare qc*** take the trouble to do sth; ***attaccar ~ con qn*** pick a quarrel with s.o.
brigadiere *m* MIL sergeant
brigantaggio *m* ⟨*pl* -ggi⟩ banditry
brigante *m* bandit
brigantesco *adj* ⟨*pl* -chi⟩ bandit-like
brigantino *m* brig
brigare *v/i* ⟨1e⟩ plot
brigata *f* party, group; MIL brigade; ***le Brigate Rosse*** the Red Brigades
brigatista *m/f* ⟨*mpl* -i⟩ *member of the Red Brigades*
briglia *f* rein; *fig* ***a ~ sciolta*** at breakneck speed
brillantante *m* dishwasher detergent (*that makes dishes shine*)
brillante **I** *adj* sparkling; *colore* bright; *fig* brilliant; ***attore*** *m* **~** FILM comedy actor; ***carriera*** *f* **~** brilliant career; ***acqua*** *f* **~** tonic water **II** *m* diamond; ***anello*** *m* ***con -i*** diamond ring
brillantemente *adv* brilliantly; ***superare ~ una prova*** come through a test with flying colours **brillantezza** *f* brilliance
brillantina *f* brilliantine
brillare ⟨1a⟩ **I** *v/i* shine; ***~ di luce propria*** shine; ***gli brillavano gli occhi*** his eyes were shining; ***non brilla certo per intelligenza*** (s)he's not the brightest bulb on the tree **II** *v/t mina* blow up
brillo *adj* tipsy
brina *f* hoar-frost
brinata *f* frost
brindare *v/i* ⟨1a⟩ drink a toast (***a*** to), toast (***a*** sth); ***~ alla salute di qn*** drink to *or* toast s.o.
brindisi *m* ⟨*pl* brindisi⟩ toast; ***fare un ~ (a qn / qc)*** drink a toast (to s.o. / sth)
brindisino **I** *adj* of Brindisi; *persona* from Brindisi **II** *m*, **-a** *f* person from Brindisi
brio *m* liveliness; MUS brio; ***con ~*** MUS con brio
brioche *f* ⟨*pl* brioche⟩ brioche
briosità *f* ⟨*pl* briosità⟩ liveliness
brioso *adj* lively
briscola *f card game*
britannico ⟨*mpl* -ci⟩ **I** *adj* British; ***le Isole Britanniche*** the British Isles **II** *m*, **-a** *f* Briton; ***i Britannici*** the British
brivido *m di freddo*, *spavento* shiver; *di emozione* thrill; ***avere i -i*** *di freddo*, *spavento* shiver; ***far venire i -i a qn*** send a shiver down s.o.'s spine; ***da ~*** *scena* frightening
brizzolato *adj capelli* greying, *US* graying
brocca *f* ⟨*pl* -cche⟩ jug, *US* pitcher
broccato *m* brocade
brocco *m* ⟨*pl* -cchi⟩ (*cavallo*) nag; ***essere un ~*** *infml persona* be hopeless
broccoli *mpl* broccoli *sg*
brodaglia *f* ⟨*pl* -glie⟩ *pej* dishwater
brodetto *m* broth; ***~ di pesce*** *sort of bouillabaisse*
brodo *m* (clear) soup; *di pollo*, *di manzo*, *di verdura* stock; ***~ di dado*** stock made from stock cubes; ***minestra*** *f* ***in ~*** soup; ***~ ristretto*** consommé; ***tutto fa ~*** every little helps; ***andare in ~ di giuggiole*** go into ecstasies; ***~ di coltura*** BIOL growing medium
brodoso *adj* watery, thin
broglio *m* ⟨*pl* -gli⟩ fraud; ***~ elettorale*** vote-rigging
broker *m/f* ⟨*pl* broker⟩ FIN broker; ***~ di assicurazioni*** insurance broker
brokeraggio ⟨*pl* -ggi⟩ *m* brokerage
bromuro *m* bromide
bronchiale *adj* bronchial
bronchite *f* bronchitis
broncio *m*: ***avere*** (*or* ***tenere***) ***il ~*** sulk; ***mi ha tenuto il ~ per tre giorni*** he sulked for three days
bronco *m* ⟨*pl* -chi⟩ ANAT bronchus
broncopolmonite *f* bronchopneumonia
brontolare *v/i* ⟨1l⟩ grumble (***per*** about); *di stomaco* rumble
brontolio *m* grumble; *di stomaco* rumble
brontolone **I** *adj* grumbling **II** *m*, **-a** *f* grumbler
brontosauro *m* brontosaurus
bronzeo *adj* bronze; ***statua*** *f* ***-a*** bronze
bronzetto *m* small bronze
bronzo *m* bronze; ***età*** *f* ***del ~*** Bronze Age; *fig* ***faccia*** *f* ***di ~*** brazen cheek; ***i -i di Riace*** the Riace bronzes (*two Greek bronze statues of warriors found of the coast of Calabria in 1972*)
brossura *f*: ***in ~*** paperback
browser *m* ⟨*pl* browser⟩ browser
brucare *v/t* ⟨1d⟩ nibble at

brucellosi *f* brucellosis
bruciacchiare *v/t* ⟨1g⟩ scorch
bruciacchiarsi *v/r* ⟨1g⟩ get scorched; ***~ i capelli*** singe one's hair; ***la carne si è bruciacchiata*** the meat is burnt
bruciacchiatura *f* scorching; *segno* scorch (mark)
bruciante *adj fig* crushing
bruciapelo *adv*: ***a ~*** point-blank
bruciare ⟨1f⟩ **I** *v/t* burn; (*incendiare*) set fire to; ***~ energia*** use energy; *fig* ***~ gli anni migliori*** waste one's best years; ***~ le tappe*** forge ahead **II** *v/i* burn; *fig di occhi* sting; ***mi brucia la gola*** my throat's burning; ***mi bruciano gli occhi*** my eyes are stinging; *fig* ***la sconfitta gli brucia ancora*** he's still smarting from his defeat
bruciarsi *v/r* burn o.s.; ***si è bruciata la lampadina*** the bulb's gone; *fig* ***~ le ali*** get one's fingers burned
bruciato *adj* burnt; *dal sole* scorched, parched
bruciatore *m* burner
bruciatura *f* burn
bruciore *m* burning sensation; ***~ di stomaco*** heartburn
bruco *m* ⟨*pl* -chi⟩ grub; (*verme*) worm
brufolo *m* spot
brufoloso *adj* spotty
brughiera *f* heath, moor
brulicare *v/i* ⟨1l & d⟩ swarm
brulichio *m* swarming
brullo *adj* bare
bruma *f* mist
brumeggio *m* ⟨*pl* -ggi⟩ fishmeal (for feeding fish)
brumoso *adj* misty
brunastro *adj* brownish
brunello *m* COOK *red wine from Tuscany*
brunire *v/t* ⟨4d⟩ METAL polish **brunito** *adj* polished; ***pelle f -a*** tanned skin **brunitura** *f* polishing
bruno *adj* brown; *capelli* dark
bruscamente *adv rispondere* brusquely; *girarsi* suddenly
bruschetta *f* bruschetta (*toasted bread topped with olive oil, tomatoes etc.*)
brusco *adj* ⟨*mpl* -schi⟩ sharp; *persona, modi* brusque, abrupt; (*improvviso*) sudden
bruscolo *m* speck (of dust); ***ho un ~ nell'occhio*** I've got something in my eye
brusio *m* ⟨*pl* -ii⟩ *di insetto* buzzing; *di gente* murmuring
brutale *adj* brutal; ***istinti** mpl **-i*** animal instincts
brutalità *f* ⟨*pl* brutalità⟩ brutality
brutalizzare *v/t* ⟨1a⟩ maltreat; (*violentare*) rape **brutalmente** *adv* brutally
bruto I *adj*: ***forza** f **-a*** brute force **II** *m* brute
brutta *f*: ***~*** (***copia*** *f*) rough copy
bruttezza *f* ugliness
brutto I *adj* ugly; (*cattivo*) bad; *tempo, tipo, situazione, affare* nasty; ***una -a faccenda*** a nasty business; ***~ segno!*** bad sign!; ***~ stupido!*** stupid idiot!; ***una -a notizia*** bad news; ***qui fa ~*** (***tempo***) the weather's bad here; ***navigare in -e acque*** be sailing in rough waters; ***non farmi fare -a figura!*** don't make me look bad!; ***vedersela -a*** have a narrow escape **II** *m*: ***è questo il ~!*** that's the problem!; ***si sta mettendo al ~*** the weather is turning bad; ***alle -e*** if the worst comes to the worst
Bruxelles *f* Brussels
bruxellese I *adj* of Brussels; *persona* from Brussels **II** *m/f* person from Brussels
BS *abbr* (= **Brescia**) Brescia
BSE *abbr* (= **bovine spongiform encephalopathy**) BSE
bua *f infml* pain; ***avere la ~*** have a pain; ***ho la ~*** it hurts
bubbola *f infml* fib
bubbone *m* MED swelling; *fig* plague **bubbonico** *adj* ⟨*mpl* -ci⟩ bubonic; ***peste** f **-a*** bubonic plague
buca *f* ⟨*pl* -che⟩ hole; (*avvallamento*) hollow; *del biliardo* pocket; ***~ delle lettere*** letter-box, *US* mailbox
bucaneve *m* ⟨*pl* bucaneve⟩ snowdrop
bucaniere *m hist* buccaneer
bucare *v/t* ⟨1d⟩ make a hole in; (*pungere*) prick; *biglietto* punch; ***~ una gomma*** have a puncture, *US* have a flat (tire); *fig* ***avere le mani bucate*** be a spendthrift; *fig* ***~ il video*** TV light up the screen
Bucarest *f* Bucharest
bucarsi *v/r* prick o.s.; *con droga* shoot up
bucato *m* washing, laundry; ***fare il ~*** do the washing; ***~ a mano*** hand wash; ***fresco di ~*** freshly washed

bucchero *m* bucchero (*type of Etruscan black pottery*)
buccia *f* ⟨*pl* -cce⟩ peel; ***pelle f a ~ d'arancia*** cellulitis
bucherellare *v/t* ⟨1b⟩ make holes in; ***bucherellato dai tarli*** riddled with woodworm
buco *m* ⟨*pl* -chi⟩ hole; ***~ dell'ozono*** hole in the ozone layer; ***~ nero*** black hole; *fig* ***fare un ~ nell'acqua*** fail; *fig* ***tappare un ~*** pay a debt; ***vivere in un ~*** *infml* live in a dump
bucolico *adj* ⟨*pl* -ci⟩ bucolic; ***paesaggio*** *m* ***~*** pastoral landscape; ***poeta*** *m* ***~*** pastoral poet
Budapest *f* Budapest
buddismo *m* Buddhism
budello *m* ⟨*pl* le budella⟩ gut; (*vicolo*) alley; ***mi sento torcere le -a*** I've got butterflies (in my stomach)
budget *m* ⟨*pl* budget⟩ budget
budino *m* pudding
bue *m* ⟨*pl* buoi⟩ ox, *pl* oxen; *carne* beef; ***~ marino*** dugong
bufalo *m* buffalo; ***mozzarella*** *f* ***di -a*** COOK buffalo milk mozzarella
bufera *f* storm; ***~ di neve*** snowstorm
buffet *m* ⟨*pl* buffet⟩ buffet; *mobile* sideboard
buffetto *m* pat on the cheek
buffo *adj* funny
buffonaggine *f*, **buffonata** *f* clowning
buffone *m*, **-a** *f* buffoon, fool; *hist*: *di corte* fool, jester; ***fare il ~*** clown around
buganvillea *f* bougainvillea
buggerare *v/t* ⟨1l⟩ swindle
bugia[1] *f* candle holder
bugia[2] *f* (*menzogna*) lie; ***dire -e*** tell lies, lie
bugiardo I *adj* lying **II** *m*, **-a** *f* liar
bugigattolo *m* cubby-hole
bugnato *m* ARCH ashlar; ***~ liscio*** smooth ashlar; ***~ rustico*** rough ashlar
bugno *m* hive
buio I *adj* dark **II** *m* darkness; ***fare ~*** get dark; ***al ~*** in the dark; ***~ pesto*** pitch dark; ***salto*** *m* ***nel ~*** leap in the dark
bulbo *m* BOT bulb; ***~ oculare*** eyeball
Bulgaria *f* Bulgaria
bulgaro I *adj* Bulgarian **II** *m*, **-a** *f* Bulgarian
bulimia *f* bulimia
bulimico *adj* ⟨*mpl* -ci⟩ bulimic
bulldog *m* ⟨*pl* bulldog⟩ bulldog
bulldozer *m* ⟨*pl* bulldozer⟩ bulldozer
bulletta *f* tack
bullo *m* bully; ***fare il ~*** be a bully
bullone *m* bolt
bungalow *m* ⟨*pl* bungalow⟩ bungalow
bunjee jumping *m* ⟨*no pl*⟩ bungee jumping
bunker I *adj*: ***aula ~*** high-security court **II** *m* ⟨*pl* bunker⟩ bunker
buoi → ***bue***
buon → ***buono***
buonafede *f*: ***in ~*** in good faith; ***approfittare della ~ di qn*** take advantage of s.o.'s good faith
buonanotte *f / int* good night; ***dare la ~*** say good night
buonasera *f / int* good evening; ***dare la ~*** say good evening
buoncostume *f* vice squad
buongiorno *m/int* good morning, hello; ***dare il ~*** say good morning *or* hello
buongustaio *m*, **-a** *f* ⟨*mpl* -ai⟩ gourmet
buongusto *m* good taste; ***di ~*** in good taste
buonismo *m* do-goodery
buono I *adj* good; (*valido*) good, valid; *momento, occasione* right; ***alla -a*** informal, casual; ***-a fortuna*** good luck; ***buon viaggio!*** have a good trip!; ***a buon mercato*** cheap; ***di buon'ora*** early; ***di buon grado*** willingly; ***avere buon naso*** have a good sense of smell; ***~ a nulla*** good-for-nothing; ***~ a sapersi!*** that's good to know! **II** *m* **1.** good; ***con le -e o con le cattive*** one way or another **2.** FIN bond; (*tagliando*) coupon, voucher; ***~ pasto*** *or* ***mensa*** luncheon voucher; ***~ regalo*** gift voucher; ***~ sconto*** money-off coupon; ***~ del tesoro*** Treasury bond
buonora *f*: ***di ~*** early; ***alla ~!*** at last!
buonsenso *m* common sense
buontempone *m*, **-a** *f* fun-loving person
buonumore *m* good humo(u)r; ***essere di ~*** be in a good mood
buonuscita *f* (*liquidazione*) golden handshake
burattino *m* puppet
burbero *adj* gruff, surly
burla *f* practical joke, trick
burlarsi *v/r* ⟨1a⟩: ***~ di qn*** make fun of s.o.

burlesco *adj* ⟨*mpl* -chi⟩ joking; LIT burlesque **burletta** *f* joke; ***mettere in ~*** ridicule
burlone *m*, **-a** *f* joker
burocrate *m* bureaucrat
burocratico *adj* ⟨*mpl* -ci⟩ bureaucratic
burocrazia *f* bureaucracy
burrasca *f* ⟨*pl* -sche⟩ storm; *fig* ***c'è aria di ~*** there's trouble brewing
burrascoso *adj* stormy
burro *m* butter; COOK ***al ~*** in butter; ***tenero come il ~*** soft as butter; ***~ di cacao*** cocoa butter
burrone *m* ravine
bus *m* ⟨*pl* bus⟩ bus; ***prendere il / andare in ~*** get the bus / go by bus
buscare *v/t* ⟨1d⟩ *infml* get; ***buscarle*** *or* ***buscarne*** get a good hiding; ***mi sono buscata l'influenza*** I've got (the) flu
bussare *v/i* ⟨1a⟩ knock; ***~ alla porta*** knock at the door
bussola *f* compass; ***~ magnetica*** magnetic compass; ***perdere la ~*** lose one's bearings
bussolotto *m* dice box
busta *f per lettera* envelope; *per documenti* folder; (*astuccio*) case; ***~ a finestra*** window envelope; ***~ paga*** pay packet
bustarella *f* bribe
bustier *m* ⟨*pl* bustier⟩ bustier
bustina *f*: ***~ di tè*** tea bag
busto *m* ANAT torso; *scultura* bust; (*corsetto*) girdle; ***~ ortopedico*** surgical corset
buttafuori *m* ⟨*pl* buttafuori⟩ THEAT call-boy; *di locale notturno* bouncer
buttare ⟨1a⟩ **I** *v/i* BOT shoot, sprout **II** *v/t* throw; ***~ via*** throw away; *fig* waste; ***~ giù*** knock down; *lettera* scribble down; *boccone* gulp down; ***~ la pasta*** *infml* put the pasta on; ***~ fuori qn*** (***da qc***) throw s.o. out (of sth)
buttarsi *v/r* throw o.s.; *fig* have a go (***in*** at); ***~ giù*** (*saltare*) jump; *fig* lose heart, get discouraged; ***~ da qc*** *finestra* throw o.s. out sth; *trampolino* jump off sth; ***~ nel lavoro*** throw o.s. into one's work
butterato *adj* pock-marked
buttero *m* (*mandriano*) *mounted herdsman of the Maremma region*
button down *adj inv*: **colletto** *m* **~** button-down collar
buvette *f* ⟨*pl* buvette⟩ *temporary stall selling refreshments*
buzzo *m*: ***di ~ buono*** with a will
buzzurro *m*, **-a** *f* oaf
by-pass *m* ⟨*pl* by-pass⟩ bypass
bypassare *v/t* ⟨1a⟩ bypass; ***~ una difficoltà*** circumvent a problem
byte *m* ⟨*pl* byte⟩ COMPUT byte
BZ *abbr* (= **Bolzano**) Bolzano

C

c, C *m/f* ⟨*pl* c, C⟩ c, C
ca. *abbr* (= **circa**) ca (circa)
c.a. *abbr* (= **corrente alternata**) AC (alternating current)
CA *abbr* (= **Cagliari**) Cagliari
CAAF *abbr* (= **Centro Autorizzato di Assistenza Fiscale**) *authorized centre giving help with tax matters*
cabaret *m* ⟨*pl* cabaret⟩ cabaret
cabarettista *m/f* ⟨*mpl* -i⟩ cabaret artist **cabarettistico** *adj* ⟨*mpl* -ci⟩ cabaret *attr*
cabernet *m* ⟨*pl* cabernet⟩ COOK cabernet
cabina *f di nave*, *aereo* cabin; *di ascensore*, *funivia* cage; ***~ elettorale*** polling booth; ***~ balneare*** beach hut; ***~ di guida*** driver's cab; ***~ di pilotaggio*** cockpit; ***~ telefonica*** phone box, *US* pay phone
cabinato *m* cabin cruiser
cabinovia *f* cable car
cablaggio *m* ⟨*pl* -ggi⟩ ELEC wiring
cabotaggio *m* NAUT coastal navigation
cabriolet *m* ⟨*pl* cabriolet⟩ convertible
cacao *m* cocoa
cacare *v/i* ⟨1d⟩ *vulg* shit *vulg*; *fig* ***mandare a ~ qn*** *vulg* tell s.o. to piss off;

fig ***va' a ~!*** *vulg* piss off!
cacarella *f infml* runs; *fig* (*paura*) ***avere la ~*** be scared shitless *vulg* **cacasenno** *m* ⟨*pl* cacasenno⟩ *infml* pompous ass **cacasotto** *m* ⟨*pl* cacasotto⟩ *infml* wuss **cacata** *f vulg* shit; *cosa malfatta* (piece of) crap
cacatua *m* ⟨*pl* cacatua⟩ cockatoo
cacca *f infml* shit *vulg*; *linguaggio infantile* pooh *infml*; ***fare la ~*** *infml* do a poo, *vulg* shit
cacchiata *f infml* piece of crap; ***fare*** / ***dire -e*** talk crap
caccia **I** *f* ⟨*pl* -cce⟩ hunting; ***~ grossa*** big game hunting; ***andare a ~*** go hunting (***di*** sth); ***dare la ~ a qn*** chase after s.o.; ***~ al tesoro*** treasure hunt **II** *m* ⟨*pl* caccia⟩ MIL *aereo* fighter; *nave* destroyer
cacciabombardiere *m* fighter-bomber
cacciagione *f* COOK game
cacciare *v/t* ⟨1f⟩ hunt; (*scacciare*) drive out; (*ficcare*) shove; ***~*** (***via***) chase away; ***~ fuori qn*** throw s.o. out; ***~ un urlo*** let out a yell
cacciarsi *v/r*: ***dove ti eri cacciato?*** where did you get to?; ***~ nei guai*** get into trouble
cacciata *f* expulsion
cacciatora *f*: COOK ***alla ~*** stewed
cacciatore *m*, **-trice** *f* hunter; ***~ di frodo*** poacher; ***~ di teste*** head-hunter
cacciatorpediniere *m* destroyer
cacciavite *m* ⟨*pl* cacciavite⟩ screwdriver; ***~ a stella*** Phillips® screwdriver
caccola *f infml* bogey
cache *f* ⟨*pl* cache⟩ COMPUT cache
cachemire *m* ⟨*no pl*⟩ cashmere
cachet *m* ⟨*pl* cachet⟩ MED capsule
cachi **I** *adj* khaki **II** *m* ⟨*pl* cachi⟩ (*frutto*) persimmon
cacio *m* cheese; ***essere*** (***alto come***) ***un soldo di ~*** *infml* be kneehigh to a grasshopper
caciocavallo *m* ⟨*pl* caciocavalli⟩ *hard pear-shaped cheese from southern Italy* **caciotta** *f soft cheese from central Italy*
cacofonia *f* cacophony
cactus *m* ⟨*pl* cactus⟩ cactus
cadauno *adj and pron* each
cadavere *m* corpse
cadaverico *adj*: ***rigidità*** *f* ***-a*** rigor mortis
cadente *adj*: ***stella*** *f* ***~*** shooting star
cadenza *f di voce*: cadence; *di passo*: rhythm; MUS cadenza; ***a*** *or* ***con ~ bimestrale*** every two months **cadenzare** *v/t* ⟨1a⟩ give a rhythm to; ***~ il passo*** set the pace **cadenzato** *adj* rhythmical; ***passo*** *m* ***~*** measured pace
cadere *v/i* ⟨2c⟩ fall; *di edificio* fall down; *di capelli, denti* fall out; *di aereo* crash; ***far ~ qn*** / ***qc*** knock s.o. / sth over; ***lasciar ~*** drop; ***lasciarsi ~ su una poltrona*** collapse into an armchair; ***~ dalle nuvole*** be thunderstruck; ***~ per terra*** fall down; *fig* ***far ~ le braccia*** astonish; ***è caduta la linea*** we've *etc* been cut off; ***quest'anno Natale cade di martedì*** Christmas falls on a Tuesday this year
cadetto *m* MIL cadet
Cadice *f* Cadiz
cadmio *m* ⟨*pl* -mi⟩ cadmium
cadorino **I** *adj* of Cadore; *persona* from Cadore **II** *m*, **-a** *f* person from Cadore
caduta *f* fall; ***~ libera*** free fall; ***~ massi*** falling rocks; ***~ di tensione*** drop in voltage
caduto *m* fallen soldier; ***monumento*** *m* ***ai -i*** war memorial
caffè *m* ⟨*pl* caffè⟩ **1.** coffee; ***~ corretto*** *espresso with a shot of alcohol*; ***~ decaffeinato*** decaffeinated coffee; ***~ macchiato*** *espresso with a splash of milk*; ***~ macinato*** ground coffee; ***~ d'orzo*** barley coffee **2.** *locale* café
caffeina *f* caffeine; ***senza ~*** caffeine free
caffel(l)atte *m* ⟨*pl* caffel(l)atte⟩ *hot milk with a small amount of coffee*
caffettiera *f* (*bricco*) coffee pot; (*macchinetta*) coffee maker
cafonaggine *f* boorishness
cafone *m* boor
cagionare *v/t* ⟨1a⟩ cause
cagionevole *adj* delicate, sickly
cagliare *v/i* ⟨1g⟩ curdle
cagliaritano **I** *adj* of Cagliari; *persona* from Cagliari **II** *m*, **-a** *f* person from Cagliari
caglio *m* ⟨*pl* -gli⟩ rennet
cagna *f* bitch
cagnaccio *m* ⟨*pl* -cci⟩ *pej* horrible dog
cagnara *f infml* racket **cagnesco** *adj*

⟨*mpl* -chi⟩ hostile; ***guardare in ~*** scowl **cagnetta** *f* little (female) dog **cagnolino** *m* little dog
CAI *abbr* (= **Club Alpino Italiano**) *Italian Alpine Club*
caicco *m* ⟨*pl* -cchi⟩ NAUT caique
Cairo *m* Cairo
cajun ⟨*pl* cajun⟩ **I** *adj* Cajun **II** *m/f* Cajun
cala *f* inlet
calabrese *m/f & adj* Calabrian
Calabria *f* Calabria
calabro *adj* Calabrian
calabrone *m* hornet
calafatare *v/t* ⟨1n⟩ caulk
calamaio *m* ⟨*pl* -ai⟩ inkwell
calamari *mpl* squid *sg*; ***~ ripieni*** COOK stuffed squid
calamita *f* magnet
calamità *f* ⟨*pl* calamità⟩ calamity; ***~ naturale*** natural disaster
calamitare *v/t* ⟨1a⟩ magnetize; *fig* attract; ***~ l'attenzione di qn*** attract s.o.'s attention
calamitoso *adj* disastrous
calante *adj*: ***luna** f **~*** waning moon
calare ⟨1a⟩ **I** *v/t* lower; *prezzi* reduce, lower; ***~ una carta*** put down a card **II** *v/i di vento* drop; *di prezzi* fall, come down; *di sipario* fall; *di sole* set, go down; ***~ di peso*** lose weight; ***è calato del 20%*** it's down 20%; ***il livello dell'acqua continua a ~*** the water level is continuing to fall; ***al calar del sole*** at sunset; ***la febbre sta calando*** his/her temperature is going down
calarsi *v/r* ⟨1a⟩ lower o.s.
calata *f* (*invasione*) invasion; ***la ~ dei barbari*** the barbarian invasion
calca *f* throng
calcagno *m* ⟨*pl* i calcagni *or* le calcagna⟩ heel; ANAT calcaneum; ***avere qn alle -a*** have s.o. hot on one's heels
calcare[1] *v/t* ⟨1d⟩ (*pigiare*) press down; *con i piedi* tread; *parole* emphasize; ***~ la mano*** exaggerate; ***~ le scene*** become an actor, take up acting
calcare[2] *m* limestone
calcareo *adj* chalky
calce[1] *f* lime
calce[2] *m fig*: ***in ~*** below
calcestruzzo *m* concrete
calcetto *m* (*calcio*) five-a-side football *or* soccer; (*calcio-balilla*) table football, *US* foosball
calciare *v/t* ⟨1f⟩ kick
calciatore *m*, **-trice** *f* footballer, soccer player
calcina *f* (*malta*) mortar
calcinaccio *m* ⟨*pl* -cci⟩ (*intonaco*) bit of plaster; *di muro* bit of rubble
calcio[1] *m* ⟨*pl* -ci⟩ **1.** kick; ***prendere qn/qc a -ci*** kick s.o./sth; ***~ d'angolo*** corner (kick); ***~ di punizione*** free kick; ***~ di rigore*** penalty kick **2.** SPORTS football, soccer; ***campionato** m **di ~*** football *or* soccer championship; ***giocare a ~*** play football *or* soccer
calcio[2] *m* ⟨*pl* -ci⟩ CHEM calcium
calcio[3] *m* ⟨*pl* -ci⟩ MIL butt
calciobalilla *m* ⟨*pl* calciobalilla⟩ table football **calciomercato** *m* transfer market
calco *m* ⟨*pl* -chi⟩ cast
calcografia *f* copper engraving
calcolabile *adj* calculable
calcolare *v/t* ⟨1l⟩ calculate; (*valutare*) weigh up; ***~ a occhio e croce*** work out roughly
calcolatore *m* calculator; *fig* calculating person; *elettronico* computer; ***un freddo ~*** a cold and calculating person
calcolatrice *f* calculator; ***~ tascabile*** pocket calculator; ***~ da tavolo*** desktop calculator
calcolo[1] *m* calculation; ***~ preventivo*** estimate; ***fare il ~ di qc*** calculate; ***fare qc per ~*** do sth out of self-interest
calcolo[2] *m* MED stone; ***~ biliare*** gallstone
Calcutta *f* Kolkata
caldaia *f* boiler
caldana *f* hot flush; ***avere le -e*** have hot flushes
caldarrosta *f* roast chestnut
caldeggiare *v/t* ⟨1f⟩ support warmly
caldeo I *adj* Chaldean **II** *m*, **-a** *f* Chaldean
calderone *m* cauldron; *fig* hotchpotch; *fig* ***mettere tutto nello stesso ~*** lump everything together
caldo I *adj* warm; (*molto caldo*) hot; ***mangiare qualcosa di ~*** eat something hot **II** *m* warmth; *molto caldo* heat; ***ho ~*** I'm warm; I'm hot; ***fa ~*** it's warm; it's hot; ***un maglione che mi tiene ~*** a sweater that keeps me warm; ***soffrire il ~*** suffer from

the heat; ***tenere in ~ qc*** keep sth warm; ***non mi fa né ~ né freddo*** it's all the same to me
calduccio *m*: ***starsene / rimanere al ~*** stay in the warm
caleidoscopio *m* ⟨*pl* -pi⟩ kaleidoscope; *fig* ***un ~ di colori*** a rainbow of colours
calendario *m* ⟨*pl* -ri⟩ calendar; ***~ delle manifestazioni*** calendar of events
calende *fpl* HIST kalends (*first day of the month in the Roman calendar*); *fig* ***rimandare qc alle ~ greche*** put sth off indefinitely
calesse *m* gig
calibrare *v/t* ⟨11⟩ calibrate
calibrato *adj* calibrated; *fig* balanced
calibrazione *f* calibration
calibro *m* calibre, *US* caliber; TECH callipers *pl*; *fig* ***di grosso ~*** prominent
calice *m* goblet; REL chalice; BOT calyx
califfo *m* caliph
California *f* California
californiano I *adj* Californian **II** *m*, **-a** *f* Californian
caligine *f* smog **caliginoso** *adj* smoggy; *fig* foggy
call center *m* ⟨*pl* call center⟩ call centre, *US* center
calle *f a Venezia* lane
call-girl ⟨*pl* call-girl⟩ call girl
callifugo ⟨*pl* -ghi⟩ **I** *adj* corn *attr* **II** *n*: ***callifugo*** corn plaster
calligrafia *f* calligraphy; ***ha una pessima ~*** he / she has terrible handwriting
calligrafico *adj* ⟨*mpl* -ci⟩ calligraphic; (*di scrittura*) handwriting *attr* **calligrafo** *m*, **-a** *f* calligrapher; ***perito*** *m* ***~*** graphologist
callista *m/f* ⟨*mpl* -i⟩ chiropodist
callo *m* corn; ***fare il ~ a qc*** become hardened to sth
callosità *f* ⟨*pl* callosità⟩ callus **calloso** *adj* calloused
calma *f* calm; ***prendersela con ~*** take it easy; ***mantenere la ~*** keep calm; ***perdere la ~*** lose one's cool
calmante *m* sedative
calmare *v/t* ⟨1a⟩ calm; *dolore* soothe
calmarsi *v/r di dolore* ease (off); ***calmati!*** calm down!
calmata *f*: ***darsi una ~*** *infml* calm down
calmierare *v/t* ⟨1b⟩: ***~ qc*** control the price of sth **calmiere** *m* price control
calmo *adj* calm; ***stare ~*** stay calm
calo *m di peso* loss; *dei prezzi* drop, fall; ***essere in ~*** be falling
calore *m* warmth; *intenso* heat; ***cagna f in ~*** bitch on heat
caloria *f* calorie
calorico *adj* ⟨*mpl* -ci⟩ PHYS, MED calorific; ***a basso / alto contenuto ~*** with a low / high calorie content
calorifero *m* radiator
calorifico *adj* ⟨*pl* -ci⟩ calorific; ***potere m ~*** calorific value
calorosamente *adj* warmly
caloroso *adj fig* warm
calotta *f* GEOM segment; ARCH calotte; ANAT vault; MECH cap; GEOG ice cap; ***~ cranica*** cranial vault; ***~ polare*** polar ice cap
calpestare *v/t* ⟨1a⟩ walk on; *fig* trample over
calunnia *f* slander
calunniare *v/t* ⟨1k⟩ slander
calunniatore *m*, **-trice** *f* slanderer
calura *f* heat
calvario *m* REL Calvary; *fig* ordeal
calvinismo *m* Calvinism **calvinista** *m/f* ⟨*mpl* -i⟩ Calvinist
calvizie *f* baldness
calvo *adj* bald
calza *f da donna* stocking; *da uomo* sock; ***~ elastica*** support stocking; ***fare la ~*** knit
calzamaglia *f* tights *pl*, *US* pantyhose; *da ginnastica* leotard
calzante I *adj fig* appropriate **II** *m* shoehorn
calzare ⟨1a⟩ **I** *v/t scarpe* put on; (*indossare*) wear **II** *v/i fig* fit; ***~ a pennello a qn*** fit s.o. like a glove
calzascarpe *m* shoehorn
calzatoio *m* ⟨*pl* -oi⟩ shoehorn
calzature *fpl* footwear *sg*
calzaturiero *adj* footwear *attr*; ***industria f -a*** footwear industry
calzaturificio *m* ⟨*pl* -ci⟩ shoe factory
calzetta *f* ankle sock; *fig* ***essere una mezza ~*** be a nobody
calzettone *m* knee sock
calzino *m* sock
calzolaio *m*, **-a** *f* ⟨*mpl* -ai⟩ shoemaker
calzoleria *f* shoe shop
calzoncini *mpl* shorts *pl*; ***~ da bagno*** (swimming) trunks *pl*
calzone *m* COOK *folded-over pizza*

calzoni *mpl* trousers *pl*, *US* pants *pl*
camaleonte *m* chameleon
camaleontico *adj* ⟨*mpl* -ci⟩ opportunist **camaleontismo** *m* opportunism
camallo *m* docker, *US* longshoreman
cambiale *f* bill (of exchange); **~ *in bianco*** blank bill; **~ *a scadenza fissa*** fixed-term bill; **~ *a vista*** sight bill; ***girare una* ~** endorse a bill; ***pagare una* ~** hono(u)r a bill
cambiamento *m* change; **~ *climatico*** climate change; **~ *di programma*** change of plan
cambiare ⟨1k⟩ **I** *v/t* change; (*scambiare*) exchange; **~ *casa*** move (house); **~ *idea*** change one's mind; **~ *le lenzuola*** change the sheets; AUTO **~ *la marcia*** change gear; **~ *la macchina*** trade in one's car; **~ *vita*** change one's way of life; ***a Bologna devo* ~ *treno*** I have to change trains at Bologna; *fig* **~ *le carte in tavola*** move the goalposts **II** *v/i* change; ***non sei cambiato affatto!*** you haven't changed at all!
cambiario *adj* ⟨*mpl* -ri⟩ exchange *attr*; ***vaglia*** *m* **~** promissory note; ***legge*** *f* **-*a*** exchange law
cambiarsi *v/r* ⟨1k⟩ change; **~ *le scarpe*** change one's shoes
cambiavalute *m/f* ⟨*pl* cambiavalute⟩ currency dealer, money-broker
cambio *m* ⟨*pl* -bi⟩ **1.** change; FIN, (*scambio*) exchange; **~ *d'indirizzo*** change of address; **~ *dell'olio*** oil change; ***in* ~** in exchange (***di*** for); ***dare il* ~ *a qn*** relieve s.o.; ***fare* ~ *con qn*** swap *or* exchange with s.o. **2.** AUTO, TECH gear; **~ *automatico*** automatic gearshift
Cambogia *f* Cambodia
cambogiano I *adj* Cambodian **II** *m*, **-a** *f* Cambodian
cambusa *f* galley **cambusiere** *m* storekeeper
camcorder *m* ⟨*pl* camcorder⟩ camcorder
camelia *f* camellia
camera *f* **1.** room; **~ *in affitto*** rented room; **~ *d'albergo*** hotel room; ***una* ~ *ammobiliata*** a furnished room; **~ *ardente*** funeral parlo(u)r; **~ *d'aria*** inner tube; **~ *blindata*** strong room; **~ *a gas*** gas chamber; **~ *dell'industria e del commercio*** chamber of commerce; **~ *da letto*** bedroom; **~ *a due letti*** twin room; **~ *matrimoniale*** double room; PHOT **~ *oscura*** darkroom; **~ *singola*** single room; ***musica*** *f* ***da* ~** chamber music; ***prenotare una* ~** book a room **2.** POL chamber; ***Camera dei Deputati*** *House of Commons*
cameraman *m* ⟨*pl* cameraman⟩ cameraman
camerata[1] *f stanza* dormitory; *in ospedale* ward
camerata[2] *m/f* comrade **cameratesco** *adj* ⟨*mpl* -chi⟩ comradely **cameratismo** *m* comradeship
cameriera *f* waitress; (*domestica*) maid
cameriere *m* waiter; (*domestico*) manservant
camerino *m* dressing room
Camerun *m* Cameroon **camerunese I** *adj* Cameroonian **II** *m/f* Cameroonian
camice *m di medico* white coat; *di chirurgo* gown
camicetta *f* blouse
camicia *f* ⟨*pl* -cie⟩ shirt; **~ *da notte*** nightdress; **~ *sportiva*** sports shirt
camiciotto *m* casual shirt; *da lavoro*: work shirt
caminetto *m* fireplace
camino *m* chimney; (*focolare*) fireplace
camion *m* ⟨*pl* camion⟩ truck, *Br* lorry
camioncino *m* van
camionista *m* ⟨*pl* -i⟩ truck driver, *Br* lorry driver
camma *f* cam; ***albero*** *m* ***a* -*e*** camshaft
cammelliere *m* camel driver
cammello *m* camel; *stoffa* camel hair
cammeo *m* cameo
camminare *v/i* ⟨1a⟩ walk; (*funzionare*) work, go
camminata *f* walk; ***fare una* ~** go for a walk
camminatore *m*, **-trice** *f* walker; ***essere un buon* ~** be a good walker; ***essere un cattivo* ~** not be a great walker
cammino *m*: ***un'ora di* ~** an hour's walk; ***mettersi in* ~** set out
camomilla *f* camomile; (*infuso*) camomile tea
camorra *f* Camorra (*Neapolitan mafia*)
camorrista *m* ⟨*pl* -i⟩ *member of the*

Camorra
camorristico *adj* ⟨*mpl* -ci⟩ Camorra *attr*; ***organizzazione*** *f* **-a** Camorra--type organization
camoscio *m* ⟨*pl* -sci⟩ chamois; ***scarpe*** *fpl* ***di*** **~** suede shoes
campagna *f* **1.** country; ***vivere in*** **~** live in the country **2.** *fig*, POL campaign; **~** ***elettorale*** election campaign; **~** ***promozionale*** promotional campaign; **~** ***pubblicitaria*** advertising campaign
campagnolo **I** *adj* country *attr* **II** *m*, **-a** *f* countryman; *donna* country woman
campana *f* bell; (*gioco*) hopscotch; ***sordo come una*** **~** deaf as a post; ***sentire tutte le*** **-e** hear all sides of the story
campanaccio *m* ⟨*pl* -cci⟩ cow bell
campanario *adj* ⟨*mpl* -ri⟩ bell *attr*; ***torre*** *f* **-a** bell tower **campanaro** *m* bell-ringer **campanella** *f* bell; **~** ***della scuola*** school bell; BOT campanula
campanello *m* bell; *della porta* doorbell; **~** ***d'allarme*** alarm bell; ***suonare il*** **~** ring the bell
Campania *f* Campania
campanile *m* bell tower
campanilismo *m* local patriotism **campanilista** *m/f* ⟨*mpl* -i⟩ *s.o. who is excessively attached to their home town* **campanilistico** *adj* ⟨*mpl* -ci⟩ parochial
campano **I** *adj* of Campania; *persona* from Campania, **II** *m*, **-a** *f* person from Campania
campanula *f* BOT bell flower
campare *v/i* ⟨1a⟩ live; **~** ***alla giornata*** live for the moment
campata *f* BUILD span
campato *adj*: **~** ***in aria*** unfounded
campeggiare *v/i* ⟨1f⟩ camp
campeggiatore *m*, **-trice** *f* camper
campeggio *m* camping; *posto* campsite; ***fare*** **~** ***libero*** camp on land with no facilities
camper *m* ⟨*pl* camper⟩ camper van
campestre *adj* rural; ***corsa*** **~** cross--country race
Campidoglio *m* Capitol(ine) (*one of the seven hills of Rome*)
camping *m* camp site
campionamento *m* sampling **campionare** *v/t* ⟨1a⟩: **~** ***qc*** sample sth
campionario ⟨*mpl* -ri⟩ **I** *adj*: ***fiera*** *f* **-a** trade fair **II** *m* samples *pl*
campionato *m* championship; **~** ***mondiale*** world championship
campioncino *m* (small) sample
campione *m* sample; (*esemplare*) specimen; *di stoffa* swatch; SPORTS champion; **~** ***nazionale/olimpico*** national/Olympic champion; **~** ***gratuito*** *or* ***omaggio*** free sample; **~** ***senza valore*** sample only; ***prelevare un*** **~** take a sample
campionessa *f* champion
campo *m* **1.** field; **~** ***magnetico*** magnetic field; **~** ***minato*** minefield **2.** **~** ***da calcio*** football *or* soccer pitch; **~** ***giochi*** playground; **~** ***da golf*** golf course; **~** ***sportivo*** sports ground; **~** ***da tennis*** tennis court **3.** **~** ***di concentramento*** concentration camp; **~** ***profughi*** refugee camp **4.** **~** ***di ricerche*** area of research; ***ricerche sul*** **~** field research
campobassano **I** *adj* of Campobasso; *persona* from Campobasso **II** *m*, **-a** *f* person from Campobasso
camposanto *m* ⟨*pl* camposanti⟩ cemetery
camuffare *v/t* ⟨1a⟩ disguise
camuffarsi *v/r*: **~** ***da qc*** disguise o.s. as sth
camuno **I** *adj* of Val Camonica; *persona* from Val Camonica **II** *m*, **-a** *f* person from Val Camonica
camuso *adj*: ***naso*** *m* **~** snub nose
Canada *m* Canada
canadese **I** *adj* Canadian **II** *m/f* Canadian **III** *f half-litre* (*US -liter*) *bottle of beer*
canaglia *f* ⟨*pl* -glie⟩ rogue
canale *m* channel; *artificiale* canal; ***su che*** **~** ***è il film?*** which channel is the film on?; ***il Canale della Manica*** the English Channel; ***il Canal Grande*** the Grand Canal
canalizzare *v/t* ⟨1a⟩ channel (*a. fig*)
canalizzazione *f* channelling; (*conduttura*) pipe
cananeo **I** *adj* Canaanite **II** *m*, **-a** *f* Canaanite
canapa *f* hemp
Canarie *fpl* Canaries *pl*
canarino *m* canary
cancellabile *adj* erasable
cancellare *v/t* ⟨1b⟩ cross out; *con gomma* rub out, erase; COMPUT de-

lete; *debito* write off, cancel; *appuntamento* cancel; ***hanno cancellato tutti i voli*** all flights have been cancelled
cancellata *f* railings *pl*
cancellatura *f con gomma*: rubbing out; *con tratto di penna*: crossing out **cancellazione** *f* erasure; *di volo*: cancellation; (*estinzione*) disappearance
cancelleria *f*: ***articoli*** *mpl* ***di ~*** stationery
cancelletto *m* hash, *US* pound sign
cancelliere *m* chancellor; JUR clerk of the court
cancellino *m* rubber, *US* eraser
cancello *m* gate
cancerogeno *adj* carcinogenic
cancrena *f* gangrene
cancro *m* **1.** MED cancer; ***~ al fegato / della pelle / ai polmoni*** liver / skin / lung cancer; ***malato di ~*** cancer patient **2.** ASTROL, GEOG ***Cancro*** Cancer; ***sono del Cancro*** I'm (a) Cancer
candeggiante *m* stain remover
candeggiare *v/t* ⟨1f⟩ bleach
candeggina *f* bleach
candela *f* candle; ***a lume di ~*** by candlelight; ***~ d'accensione*** spark plug
candelabro *m* candelabra
candeliere *m* candlestick
candelina *f* candle; ***spegnere le -e*** blow out the candles
Candelora *f* Candlemas
candelotto *m* candle; ***~ di dinamite*** stick of dynamite
candidamente *adv* (*sinceramente*) frankly; (*innocentemente*) innocently; (*ingenuamente*) naively
candidare *v/t* ⟨1l⟩: ***~ qn a qc*** put s.o. up for sth
candidarsi *v/r* ⟨1l⟩ stand (for election)
candidato *m*, **-a** *f* candidate
candidatura *f* candidacy, candidature
candido *adj* pure white; (*sincero*) frank; (*innocente*) innocent, pure; (*ingenuo*) naive
canditi *mpl* candied fruit *sg*
cane *m* **1.** dog; ***~ antidroga*** sniffer dog; ***~ da guardia*** guard dog; ***non c'era un ~*** there wasn't a soul about; ***da -i*** awful; ***fatto da -i*** *infml* botched *infml*; ***attenti al ~*** beware of the dog; ***sto da -i*** I feel awful; ***essere come ~ e gatto*** fight like cat and dog; ***menare il can per l'aia*** beat about the bush; ***porco ~!*** *sl* bloody hell! *vulg* **2.** *di arma da fuoco* hammer, cock **3.** ***freddo ~*** freezing cold
canestraio *m*, **-a** *f* ⟨*mpl* -ai⟩ basket maker; *venditore* basket seller **canestrello** *m reg ring-shaped biscuit*
canestro *m* basket; ***fare ~*** make *or* shoot a basket
canfora *f* camphor
cangiante *adj* iridescent
canguro *m* kangaroo
canicola *f* midsummer heat
canile *m* (*casotto*) kennel; *luogo* kennels *pl*
canino I *adj* dog *attr* **II** *m* (*dente*) canine (tooth)
canna *f* **1.** reed; ***~ da zucchero*** sugar cane **2.** (*bastone*) stick; ***~ da pesca*** fishing rod **3.** *sl* joint *sl* **4.** ***~ fumaria*** flue
cannella *f* COOK cinnamon
cannelloni *mpl* cannelloni *sg*
canneto *m* reedbed
cannibale *m* cannibal
cannibalismo *m* cannibalism
canniccio *m* ⟨*pl* -cci⟩ rush mat
cannocchiale *m* telescope
cannonata *f fig*: ***è una ~*** it's terrific
cannonau *m* ⟨*pl* cannonau⟩ COOK *dry red wine from Sardinia*
cannone *m* MIL gun, cannon; (*asso*) ace
cannoniere *m* SPORTS goal scorer
cannuccia *f* ⟨*pl* -cce⟩ straw
canoa *f* canoe; ***fare ~*** go canoeing
canoista *m/f* ⟨*mpl* -i⟩ canoeist
canone *m* FIN rental (fee); RADIO, TV licence (fee); (*norma*) standard
canonica *f* ⟨*pl* -che⟩ presbytery
canonico ⟨*mpl* -ci⟩ **I** *adj* REL canonical; (*convenzionale*) standard **II** *n*: ***canonico*** *m* REL canon **canonizzare** *v/t* ⟨1a⟩ canonize **canonizzazione** *f* canonization
canoro *adj* song *attr*; ***manifestazione*** *f* ***-a*** festival of song
canottaggio *m a pagaie* canoeing; *a remi* rowing; ***circolo*** *m* ***di ~*** rowing club
canottiera *f* vest
canotto *m* rowing boat, *US* rowboat; ***~ pneumatico*** rubber dinghy; ***~ di salvataggio*** lifeboat
canovaccio *m* ⟨*pl* -cci⟩ dishcloth;

THEAT plot
cantabile *adj* singable; MUS cantabile
cantante *m/f* singer; **~ *lirico*** opera singer; **~ *di musica leggera*** pop singer
cantare *v/t & v/i* ⟨1a⟩ sing; **~ *vittoria*** crow; ***cantarlo chiaro a qn*** speak one's mind to s.o.
cantastorie ⟨*pl* cantastorie⟩ *m/f* storyteller
cantautore *m*, **-trice** *f* singer-songwriter
canterano *m* chest of drawers
canterino **I** *adj* singing; ***uccello m ~*** songbird **II** *m*, **-a** *f persona* person who loves to sing **canticchiare** ⟨1g⟩ **I** *v/i* sing to oneself; *a bocca chiusa* hum **II** *v/t*: **~ *un motivetto*** hum a tune **cantico** *m* ⟨*pl* -ci⟩ canticle; **~ *di lode*** hymn of praise
cantiere *m* building *or* construction site; NAUT shipyard
cantilena *f* (*filastrocca*) lullaby; (*lagna*) whining; *fig* ***sempre la stessa* ~** always the same old song
cantina *f* cellar; *locale* wineshop
canto[1] *m* (*canzone*) song; (*il cantare*) singing; **~ *popolare*** folk song; **~ *del cigno*** swan song
canto[2] *m*: ***dal ~ mio*** for my part; ***d'altro* ~** on the other hand
Canton *f* Canton
cantonale *adj* cantonal
cantonata *f* (*grosso sbaglio*) blunder; ***prendere una* ~** make a blunder
cantone *m* POL canton; ***Canton Ticino*** canton of Ticino; ***Lago** m **dei Quattro Cantoni*** Lake Lucerne
cantonese **I** *adj* Cantonese **II** *m/f* Cantonese
cantoniera *adj*: ***casa** f* **~** roadman's house; RAIL signalman's house
cantuccio *m* ⟨*pl* -cci⟩ corner; (***re***)***stare in un* ~** stay in a corner
canuto *adj* white-haired
canzonare *v/t* ⟨1a⟩ tease
canzonatorio *adj* ⟨*mpl* -ri⟩ teasing; ***sorriso** m* **~** mocking smile
canzone *f* song; ***la solita* ~** the same old story
canzonetta *f* popular song
canzoniere *m* songbook
caos *m* chaos
caotico *adj* ⟨*mpl* -ci⟩ chaotic
CAP *abbr* (= **Codice di Avviamento Postale**) postcode, *US* zip code
capace *adj* (*abile*) capable; (*ampio*) large, capacious; **~ *di fare qc*** capable of doing sth; **~ *di intendere e di volere*** JUR of sound mind
capacità *f* ⟨*pl* capacità⟩ ability; (*capienza*) capacity; FIN **~ *di acquisto*** purchasing power; **~ *giuridica*** JUR legal existence; **~ *di agire*** JUR legal capacity; **~ *di dati*** COMPUT data capacity; COMPUT **~ *di memoria*** memory
capacitarsi *v/r* ⟨1m⟩ understand; ***non ~ dell'accaduto*** not be able to take sth in
capanna *f* hut; ***pancia mia, fatti ~!*** *hum* let's get stuck in!
capannello *m* little group (of people); **~ *di curiosi*** little group of curious onlookers **capanno** *m* hut
capannone *m* shed; AVIAT hangar
caparbiamente *adv* stubbornly **caparbietà** *f* ⟨*pl* caparbietà⟩ stubbornness
caparbio *adj* ⟨*mpl* -bi⟩ stubborn
caparra *f* FIN deposit
capatina *f infml* brief visit; ***se posso farò una* ~** I'll pop in if I can
capeggiare *v/t* ⟨1b⟩ lead
capello *m* hair; ***-i** pl* hair *sg*; COOK ***-i d'angelo*** *very thin noodles*; ***ha i -i lunghi*** she has long hair; ***mettersi le mani nei -i*** tear one's hair out; ***ne ho fin sopra i -i!*** I've had it up to here! *fig* ***non torcere un ~ a qn*** not harm a hair of s.o.'s head; ***per un* ~** by the skin of one's teeth
capellone *m* hippy
capelluto *adj* bushy haired; ***cuoio** m* **~** scalp
capelvenere *m* BOT maidenhair
capestro *m* noose; *per animali* halter
capezzale *m* bedside; ***vegliare al ~ di qn*** stay at s.o.'s bedside
capezzolo *m* nipple
capiente *adj* large, capacious
capienza *f* capacity
capigliatura *f* hair
capillare *adj* MED capillary
capire *v/t* ⟨4d⟩ understand; ***capisco*** I see; ***non capisco una parola*** I don't understand a word; ***far ~ qc a qn*** make s.o. understand sth, get s.o. to see sth; ***farsi* ~** make o.s. understood
capirsi *v/r* ⟨4d⟩ understand each other
capitale **I** *f città* capital **II** *m* FIN capital; **~ *azionario*** share capital; **~**

disponibile available capital; **~** ***d'esercizio*** working capital; **~** ***fisso*** fixed capital; **~** ***iniziale*** start-up capital; **~** ***proprio*** equity capital; **~** ***sociale*** share capital; ***fuga*** *f* ***di -i*** flight of capital **III** *adj* capital; *fig* major
capitalismo *m* capitalism
capitalista *m/f & adj* ⟨*mpl* -i⟩ capitalist
capitalistico *adj* ⟨*mpl* -ci⟩ capitalist
capitalizzare *v/t* ⟨1a⟩ capitalize
capitanare *v/t* ⟨1a⟩ captain
capitaneria *f*: **~** ***di porto*** port authorities *pl*
capitano *m* captain
capitare *v/i* ⟨1l⟩ *di avvenimento* happen; *di persona* find o.s.; ***se mi capita l'occasione di venire*** if I get a chance to come; ***mi è capitata una buona occasione*** I got a good bargain; **~** ***in cattive mani*** fall into the wrong hands; ***mangio dove capita*** I don't always eat in the same place; **~** ***a proposito*** come along at the right time; ***sono cose che capitano*** these things happen
capitello *m* ARCH capital
capitolare *v/i* ⟨1m⟩ capitulate
capitolare *v/i* ⟨1m⟩ surrender (*a. fig*); **~** ***di fronte a qc*** give in to sth
capitolato *m* JUR specifications *pl*
capitolazione *f* surrender
capitolo *m* chapter; ***avere voce in*** **~** have a say in the matter
capitombolo *m* tumble, fall; ***fare un*** **~** take a tumble
capo *m* **1.** ANAT head; ***da*** **~** ***a piedi*** from head to toe; ***questa storia non ha né*** **~** ***né coda*** this story just doesn't make sense **2.** *persona* head, chief, boss *infml*; **~** ***del governo*** head of government; **~** ***dello Stato*** head of state **3.** GEOG cape **4.** **~** ***d'accusa*** charge; **~** ***di bestiame*** head of cattle; **~** ***di vestiario*** item of clothing **5.** *fig* ***da*** **~** from the beginning; ***da un*** **~** ***all'altro*** from one end to the other; ***ti seguirò in*** **~** ***al mondo*** I'll follow you to the ends of the earth; ***per sommi -i*** briefly; ***andare a*** **~** start a new paragraph; ***non venire a*** **~** ***di nulla*** be unable to come to any kind of conclusion
capobanda *m/f* ⟨*mpl* capibanda, *fpl* capobanda⟩ *di delinquenti* ringleader
capocantiere *m/f* ⟨*mpl* capicantiere, *fpl* capocantiere⟩ (site) foreman; *donna* (site) forewoman
capocchia *f* head; **~** ***di spillo*** pinhead
capoccia *m* ⟨*pl* capoccia⟩ *hum* boss
capocciata *f infml* bang on the head; ***prendere una*** **~** bang one's head
capoclasse *m/f* ⟨*pl* capiclasse⟩ form captain
capodanno *m* New Year's Day
capodoglio *m* ⟨*pl* -gli⟩ sperm whale
capofamiglia *m/f* ⟨*mpl* capifamiglia, *fpl* capofamiglia⟩ head of the family
capofitto *adv*: ***a*** **~** headlong; *fig* ***buttarsi a*** **~** ***in qc*** throw o.s. into sth
capogiro *m* dizzy spell; ***una cifra da*** **~** a staggering figure
capogruppo *m/f* ⟨*mpl* capigruppo, *fpl* capogruppo⟩ group leader; POL leader
capolavoro *m* masterpiece
capolinea *m* terminus
capolino *m*: ***fare*** **~** peep out
capolista *f* SPORTS leaders *pl*
capoluogo *m* ⟨*pl* capoluoghi⟩ principal town
capomafia *m* ⟨*pl* capimafia⟩ Mafia boss
capomastro *m* ⟨*pl* capomastri⟩ master builder
caporeparto *m/f* ⟨*mpl* capireparto, *fpl* caporeparto⟩ *di fabbrica* foreman; *donna* forewoman; *di ufficio* superintendent
caposala *m/f* ⟨*mpl* capisala, *fpl* caposala⟩ *in ospedale* ward sister; *uomo* charge nurse
caposaldo *m* ⟨*pl* capisaldi⟩ stronghold
caposezione *m/f* ⟨*mpl* capisezione, *fpl* caposezione⟩ section chief
caposquadra *m/f* ⟨*mpl* capisquadra, *fpl* caposquadra⟩ *di operai* foreman; *donna* forewoman; *di atleti* team captain
capostazione *m/f* ⟨*mpl* capistazione, *fpl* capostazione⟩ station master
capostipite *m/f* founder
capotavola *m*: ***a*** **~** at the head of the table
capote *f* ⟨*pl* capote⟩ AUTO hood, (soft) top
capotreno *m/f* ⟨*mpl* capitreno, *fpl* capotreno⟩ guard
capotribù *m/f* ⟨*pl* capitribù⟩ tribal chief

capoufficio *m/f* ⟨ ⟨*mpl* capiufficio, *fpl* capoufficio⟩ supervisor

Capo Verde *m* Cape Verde **capoverdiano I** *adj* Cape Verdean **II** *m*, **-a** *f* Cape Verdean

capoverso *m* ⟨*pl* capoversi⟩ paragraph; TYPO indent(ation)

capovolgere *v/t* ⟨3d⟩ turn upside down; *piani* upset; *situazione* reverse

capovolgersi *v/r* turn upside down; *di barca* capsize

capovolgimento *m* complete change

capovolto *past part* → ***capovolgere***

cappa *f* (*mantello*) cloak; *di cucina* hood; ***~ del camino*** cowl

Cappadocia *f* Cappadocia

cappella *f* chapel

cappellano *m* chaplain

cappelletti *mpl pasta, shaped like little hats, with meat, cheese and egg filling*

cappelliera *f* hatbox **cappellificio** *m* ⟨*pl* -ci⟩ hat factory

cappello *m* hat; ***~ di paglia*** straw hat; ***senza ~*** hatless; ***mettersi il ~*** put one's hat on; ***tanto di ~!*** congratulations!

cappero *m* caper

cappio *m* noose

cappone *m* capon; ***far venire la pelle di ~ a qn*** give s.o. the creeps

cappottare *v/t* ⟨1c⟩ overturn

cappotto *m* coat

cappuccino *m bevanda* cappuccino

cappuccio *m* ⟨*pl* -cci⟩ hood; *di penna* top, cap

capra *f* (nanny)goat; (*cavalletto*) trestle; ***salvare ~ e cavoli*** have your cake and eat it

caprese *f* COOK mozzarella, tomato and basil salad

capretto *m* kid

Capri *f* Capri

capriata *f* BUILD truss

capriccio *m* ⟨*pl* -cci⟩ whim; *di bambini* tantrum; MUS capriccio; ***fare i -i*** have tantrums

capriccioso *adj* capricious; *bambino* naughty; *tempo* changeable; ***insalata*** *f* ***-a*** COOK *type of mixed salad*; ***pizza*** *f* ***-a*** COOK *pizza with many different toppings*

Capricorno *m* ASTROL, GEOG Capricorn; ***sono del ~*** I'm (a) Capricorn

caprifoglio *m* ⟨*pl* -gli⟩ BOT honeysuckle

capriola *f* somersault; ***fare una ~*** turn a somersault

capriolo *m* roe deer; COOK venison

capro *m* billy goat; ***~ espiatorio*** scapegoat

caprone *m* he-goat, billy goat

capsula *f* capsule; *di dente* crown; ***~ spaziale*** space capsule

captare *v/t* ⟨1a⟩ RADIO pick up

capzioso *adj* specious; ***domanda*** *f* ***-a*** trick question

carabattole *fpl* odds and ends

carabina *f* carbine

carabiniere *m* police officer

caraffa *f* carafe

Caraibi *mpl* Caribbean; ***Mar dei ~*** Caribbean Sea

caraibico ⟨*mpl* -ci⟩ **I** *adj* Caribbean **II** *m*, **-a** *f* person from the Caribbean

carambola *f* cannon

caramella *f* sweet

caramellato *adj*: ***zucchero*** *m* ***~*** caramelized sugar

caramello *m* caramel

caramelloso *adj* sugary

caramente *adv* affectionately; ***ti saluto ~*** love from

carampana *f reg pej* crone

carapace *m* carapace

carato *m* carat; ***oro*** *m* ***a 18 -i*** 18-carat gold

carattere *m* **1.** character; (*caratteristica*) characteristic; ***una domanda di ~ tecnico / confidenziale*** a question of a technical / confidential nature **2.** (*lettera*) character, letter; TYPO type; ***-i*** *pl* TYPO typeface; COMPUT font

caratteriale *adj* character *attr*; PSYCH emotional

caratterista *m/f* ⟨*mpl* -i⟩ character actor; *donna* character actress

caratteristica *f* characteristic

caratteristico *adj* ⟨*mpl* -ci⟩ characteristic

caratterizzare *v/t* ⟨1a⟩ characterize

caratterizzazione *f* characterization

caratura *f* weighing in carats; *fig* value

caravan *m* ⟨*pl* caravan⟩ caravan

caravanning *m* ⟨*pl* caravanning⟩ caravanning

caravanserraglio *m* ⟨*pl* -gli⟩ caravanscrai

caravella *f* caravel

carboidrato *m* carbohydrate

carbonaia *f* charcoal kiln; (*locale*) coal

cellar **carbonaio** *m*, **-a** *f* ⟨*mpl* -ai⟩ charcoal-burner; *venditore* coalman

carbonara *f*: COOK ***alla ~*** in a bacon, egg, and cheese sauce

carbonato *m* carbonate; ***~ di sodio*** sodium carbonate

carbonchio *m* ⟨*pl* -chi⟩ MED anthrax

carboncino *m* charcoal (***disegno*** *m* ***a***) ~ charcoal drawing

carbone *m* coal; ***carbon fossile*** (fossil) coal

carbonella *f* charcoal

carbonico *adj* ⟨*mpl* -ci⟩ carbonic; ***acido*** *m* ***~*** carbonic acid; ***anidride*** *f* ***-a*** carbon dioxide

carbonifero *adj* coal bearing; ***bacino*** *m* ***~*** coalfield

carbonio *m* CHEM carbon

carbonizzato *adj resti* charred; *auto* burnt-out; *carne* burnt; ***morire ~*** be burnt to death

carburante *m* fuel

carburare *v/t* ⟨1a⟩ tune

carburatore *m* carburet(t)or

carburazione *f* carburation; ***motore*** *m* ***a ~*** internal combustion engine

carcadè *m* ⟨*pl* carcadè⟩ karkade

carcassa *f di animale* carcass; TECH (*intelaiatura*) frame; NAUT, *infml* wreck

carcerato *m*, **-a** *f* prisoner

carcerazione *f* imprisonment; ***~ preventiva*** preventive detention

carcere *m* ⟨*pl* le -ri⟩ jail, prison; ***~ di massima sicurezza*** maximum-security prison

carceriere *m*, **-a** *f* jailer, gaoler

carcinoma *m* ⟨*pl* -i⟩ carcinoma

carciofo *m* artichoke

cardanico *adj* ⟨*mpl* -ci⟩ cardan **cardano** *m* universal *or* cardan joint

cardare *v/t* ⟨1a⟩ *lana* card **cardatrice** *f* carder **cardatura** *f* carding

cardellino *m* goldfinch

cardiaco *adj* ⟨*mpl* -ci⟩ cardiac, heart *attr*; ***insufficienza*** *f* ***-a*** cardiac insufficiency

cardigan *m* ⟨*pl* cardigan⟩ cardigan

cardinale **I** *adj* cardinal; ***punto*** *m* ***~*** cardinal point; ***numeri*** *mpl* ***-i*** cardinal numbers **II** *m* REL cardinal

cardine *m* hinge

cardiochirurgia *f* heart surgery **cardiochirurgo** *m* ⟨*pl* -ghi⟩ heart surgeon

cardiocircolatorio *adj* ⟨*mpl* -ri⟩ cardiovascular; ***collasso*** *m* ***~*** cardiovascular collapse

cardiogramma *m* ⟨*pl* -i⟩ cardiogram

cardiologia *f* cardiology

cardiologo *m*, **-a** *f* ⟨*mpl* -gi⟩ heart specialist, cardiologist

cardiopalmo *m* palpitation; ***al ~*** thrilling

cardiopatico *m*, **-a** *f* ⟨*mpl* -ci⟩ heart patient

cardiotonico *m* ⟨*mpl* -ci⟩ heart stimulant

cardiovascolare *adj* cardiovascular

cardo *m* thistle; *verdura* cardoon

carema *m* ⟨*pl* carema⟩ COOK *dry red wine from Piedmont*

carena *f* NAUT bottom

carenaggio *m* ⟨*pl* -ggi⟩ graving; ***bacino*** *m* ***di ~*** dry dock

carente *adj* lacking (***di*** in)

carenza *f* lack (***di*** of)

carestia *f* shortage

caretta *f* loggerhead (turtle)

carezza *f* caress; ***fare una ~ a qn*** caress s.o.

carezzare *v/t* ⟨1a⟩ caress

carezzevole *adj* loving

cargo *m aereo* air freighter; *nave* cargo ship

cariare *v/t* ⟨1k⟩: ***~ i denti*** decay teeth **cariarsi** *v/r* ⟨1k⟩ decay

cariatide *f* ARCH caryatid; *fig* stick-in-the-mud

cariato *adj*: ***dente*** *m* ***~*** decayed tooth

caribico *adj* ⟨*mpl* -ci⟩ Caribbean

carica *f* ⟨*pl* -che⟩ (*incarico*) office; *fig* (*slancio*, *energia*) drive; TECH load; MIL (*attacco*) charge; SPORTS tackle; ***~ onorifica*** honorary post; ***in ~*** in office; ***durata*** *f* ***della ~*** term of office; ***tornare alla ~*** insist; ***~ di mantenimento*** TEL trickle charge; ***~ rapida*** TEL quick charge

caricabatteria *m* ⟨*pl* caricabatteria⟩ battery charger

caricamento *m* loading; ***piano*** *m* ***di ~*** loading platform; ***~ di un programma*** COMPUT loading of a program

caricare *v/t* ⟨1d & l⟩ load; MIL charge; *orologio* wind up; COMPUT ***~ un programma*** load a program; ***~ qn di lavoro / responsabilità*** overburden s.o. with work / responsibilities

caricarsi *v/r* overload o.s. (***di*** with); PSYCH psych o.s. up; ***~ di debiti*** get

heavily into debt
caricato *adj* (*affettato*) affected **caricatore** *m di armi da fuoco*: magazine; PHOT can; *di diapositive* carousel
caricatura *f* caricature
caricaturale *adj* grotesque
caricaturista *m/f* ⟨*mpl* -i⟩ caricaturist
carico ⟨*mpl* -chi⟩ **I** *m* load; FIN charge, expense; NAUT cargo; JUR ***a ~ di*** (*contro*) against; ***essere a ~ di qn*** be dependent on s.o.; ***~ utile*** payload; ***lettera*** *f* (o ***polizza*** *f*) ***di ~*** bill of lading; ***~ di lavoro*** workload; ***farsi ~ di qc*** take sth on **II** *adj* loaded; ELEC charged; *caffè* strong; *colore* deep; *orologio* wound up
carie *f* ⟨*pl* carie⟩ tooth decay
carino *adj* (*grazioso*) pretty; (*gentile*) nice
carinziano I *adj* Carinthian **II** *m*, **-a** *f* Carinthian
carisma *m* charisma
carismatico *adj* ⟨*mpl* -ci⟩ charismatic
carità *f* ⟨*no pl*⟩ charity; ***fare la ~ a qn*** give s.o. charity; ***per ~!*** for goodness sake!, for pity's sake!
caritatevole *adj* charitable **caritativo** *adj* charitable; ***associazione*** *f* ***-a*** charity
Carlo *m*: ***San ~*** Saint Charles
carlona: ***alla ~*** *infml* carelessly
carmelitano I *adj* Carmelite; ***ordine*** *m* ***~*** Carmelite order **II** *m*, **-a** *f* Carmelite *m*; ***-i*** *pl* ***scalzi*** discalced Carmelites
carminio I *m* ⟨*pl* -i⟩ carmine **II** *adj inv* carmine; ***rosso*** *m* ***~*** carmine (red)
carnagione *f* complexion
carnaio *m* ⟨*pl* -ai⟩: ***la spiaggia era un ~*** *pej* the beach was mobbed
carnale *adj* carnal; ***fratello*** *m* ***~*** blood brother
carnalità *f* ⟨*pl* carnalità⟩ carnality
carne *f* flesh; COOK meat; ***~ bianca / rossa*** white / red meat; ***~ di maiale / manzo*** pork / beef; ***~ tritata*** mince; ***in ~ e ossa*** in the flesh; ***essere bene in ~*** be plump; ***non essere né ~ né pesce*** be neither fish nor fowl; *fig* ***~ da macello*** cannon fodder; *fig* ***~ della propria ~*** one's own flesh and blood
carnefice *m* executioner; *fig* tormentor
carneficina *f* slaughter
carnet *m* ⟨*pl* carnet⟩ book; ***~ di assegni*** chequebook ***~ di ballo*** dance card
carnevalata *f pej* buffoonery
carnevale *m* carnival; ***a ~ ogni scherzo vale*** *prov* anything goes at carnival time
carnevalesco *adj* ⟨*pl* -chi⟩ carnival *attr*
carnico *adj* ⟨*mpl* -ci⟩ Carniolan; ***Alpi -che*** Carniolan Alps
carniere *m* game bag; (*selvaggina*) game
carnivoro I *m* carnivore **II** *adj* carnivorous; ***animali*** *mpl* ***-i*** carnivorous animals
carnoso *adj* fleshy
caro I *adj* dear; (*costoso*) dear, expensive; ***mi è molto ~*** I am very fond of him / it; ***a ~ prezzo*** dearly **II** *adv* a lot; ***costare ~*** be very expensive; *fig* have a high price; *fig* ***pagarla cara*** pay a high price **III** *m* dear; ***-i*** *pl* loved ones, family
carogna *f* carrion; *infml* swine
carognata *f infml* rotten trick
carosello *m* merry-go-round; ***~ storico*** historical pageant
carota *f* carrot
carotaggio *m* ⟨*pl* -ggi⟩ core sample
carotene *m* carotene
carotide *f* carotid artery
carovana *f* caravan; *fig* ***in ~*** in convoy
carovita *m* ⟨*no pl*⟩ high cost of living; ***indennità*** *f* ***di ~*** cost of living allowance
carpa *f* carp
carpaccio *m* COOK *thinly sliced raw meat with an olive oil, lemon, and Parmesan dressing*
carpale *adj* ANAT carpal; ***osso*** *m* ***~*** carpal bone
carpatico *adj* ⟨*mpl* -ci⟩ Carpathian
Carpazi *mpl* Carpathian mountains
carpentiere *m* carpenter
carpire *v/t* ⟨4d⟩: ***~ qc a qn*** get sth out of s.o.
carpo *m* carpus
carponi *adv* on all fours
carrabile *adj* → ***carraio***
carraio *adj*: ***passo*** *m* ***~*** driveway; ***porta*** *f* ***-a*** vehicle entrance
carrareccia *f* ⟨*pl* -cce⟩ cart track
carrarese I *adj* of Carrara; *persona* from Carrara **II** *m/f* person from Carrara

carreggiata *f* roadway; *fig* ***rimettersi in ~*** catch up

carrellata *f* FILM, TV tracking shot; *fig* round-up; ***una ~ di notizie*** a round-up of the news

carrello *m* trolley; AVIAT undercarriage; ***~ elevatore*** fork-lift truck; ***~ portabagagli*** baggage trolley, *US* baggage cart

carrettiere *m*, **-a** *f* carter

carretto *m* cart; ***~ siciliano*** painted handcart

carriera *f* career; ***fare ~*** come a long way; ***di gran ~*** at top speed; ***ufficiale*** *m* ***di ~*** regular officer

carrierismo *m* careerism **carrierista** *m/f* ⟨*mpl* -i⟩ careerist

carriola *f* wheelbarrow

carro *m* cart; ASTR Bear; ***~ allegorico*** carnival float; ***~ armato*** tank; ***~ attrezzi*** breakdown van, tow truck, *US* wrecker; RAIL ***~ bestiame*** cattle truck; ***~ funebre*** hearse; RAIL ***~ merci*** goods wagon, *US* freight car

carroccio *m* ⟨*pl* -cci⟩ HIST *medieval war chariot pulled by oxen*; POL (*simbolo della Lega Nord*) *symbol of the Northern League*

carroponte *m* ⟨*pl* carriponte⟩ gantry crane

carrozza *f* RAIL carriage; ***~ con cuccette*** sleeper; ***~ ristorante*** restaurant car

carrozzella *f per bambini* pram; *per invalidi* wheelchair

carrozzeria *f* bodywork, coachwork

carrozziere *m* AUTO (*progettista*) (car) designer; (*costruttore*) coachbuilder; *chi fa riparazioni* panel beater

carrozzina *f* pram

carrozzone *m* caravan, *US* trailer

carruba *f* carob **carrubo** *m* carob (tree)

carrucola *f* pulley

carsico *adj* ⟨*mpl* -ci⟩ karst; ***paesaggio*** *m* ***~*** karst landscape

Carso *m* Kras

carta *f* **1.** paper; ***~ assorbente*** blotting paper; ***~ bollata*** official stamped paper; ***~ da bollo*** official stamped paper; ***~ carbone*** carbon paper; ***~ igienica*** toilet paper; ***~ da lettere*** note paper; ***~ da macero*** waste paper (for pulping); ***~ da musica*** manuscript paper; ***~ oleata*** waxed paper; ***~ da parati*** wallpaper; ***~ stagnola*** silver paper; COOK tinfoil; ***~ velina*** tissue paper; ***~ vetrata*** sandpaper **2.** COOK (*menù*) menu; ***la ~ dei vini*** the wine list **3.** GEOG ***~ geografica*** map; ***~ stradale*** road map **4.** ***~ d'argento*** *card that entitles people over a certain age to reduced fares*; ***~ assegni*** cheque (guarantee) card; ***~ di credito*** credit card; ***~ d'identità*** identity card; AVIAT ***~ d'imbarco*** boarding pass; ***~ telefonica*** phone card; AUTO ***~ verde*** green card **5.** ***~ da gioco*** (playing) card; ***avere le -e in regola*** have all the necessary documentation; *fig* have what it takes; *fig* ***fare -e false*** go to great lengths; (***farsi***) ***fare*** *or* ***leggere le -e*** have one's fortune told (*using cards*); ***giocare a -e*** play cards; *fig* ***giocare a -e scoperte*** play fair **6.** ***Carta dei diritti fondamentali*** Charter of Human Rights; ***Carta Sociale Europea*** European Social Charter

cartacarbone *f* carbon paper

cartaccia *f* ⟨*pl* -cce⟩ waste paper

cartaceo *adj* paper; ***moneta*** *f* ***-a*** paper money

Cartagine *f* Carthage **cartaginese I** *adj* Carthaginian **II** *m/f* Carthaginian

cartamodello *m* ⟨*pl* cartamodelli⟩ paper pattern

cartamoneta *f* ⟨*no pl*⟩ paper money

cartapecora *f* parchment, vellum

cartapesta *f* papier-mâché

cartastraccia *f* waste paper

carteggio *m* ⟨*pl* -ggi⟩ correspondence

cartella *f* (*borsa*) briefcase; *di alunno* schoolbag, satchel; *copertina per documenti* folder, file; *foglio dattiloscritto* page; COMPUT folder; ***~ clinica*** medical record; ***~ esattoriale*** ADMIN penalty notice

cartellino *m* (*etichetta*) label; *con prezzo* price tag; (*scheda*) card; SPORTS ***~ giallo / rosso*** yellow / red card; ***~ orario*** clocking-in card

cartello *m* **1.** sign; ***~ pubblicitario*** poster; ***~ stradale*** road sign **2.** *nelle dimostrazioni* placard **3.** FIN cartel

cartellone *m pubblicitario* hoarding, *US* billboard; THEAT bill; ***~ pubblicitario*** poster; ***mettere in ~*** put on

cartellonista *m/f* ⟨*mpl* -i⟩ poster artist

Cartesio *m* Descartes

cartiera *f* paper mill

cartilagine *f* cartilage
cartina *f* GEOG map; (*bustina*) packet; *per sigarette* cigarette paper
cartoccio *m* ⟨*pl* -cci⟩ paper bag; *a cono* paper cone; COOK ***al ~*** baked in tinfoil, en papillote
cartografia *f* cartography
cartografico *adj* ⟨*mpl* -ci⟩ cartographic **cartografo** *m*, **-a** *f* cartographer
cartolaio *m*, **-a** *f* ⟨*mpl* -ai⟩ stationer
cartolarizzazione *f* securitization; ***~ di crediti*** credit securitization
cartoleria *f* stationer's
cartolina *f* postcard; ***~ illustrata*** picture postcard; ***~ postale*** postcard; ***~ precetto*** call-up papers *pl*, *US* draft card
cartomante *m/f* fortune-teller (*who uses cards*) **cartomanzia** *f* fortune-telling (*using cards*)
cartoncino *m* (thin) cardboard; (*biglietto*) card
cartone *m* cardboard; ***-i pl animati*** cartoons; ***~ ondulato*** corrugated paper; ***di ~*** cardboard *attr*
cartongesso *m* plasterboard
cartuccia *f* ⟨*pl* -cce⟩ cartridge
cartucciera *f* cartridge belt
casa *f edificio* house; (*abitazione*) home; FIN company; ***la Casa Bianca*** the White House; ***~ di cura*** nursing home; ***~ editrice*** publishing house; ***case popolari*** council houses; ***~ di riposo*** care home; ***~ a schiera*** terraced house; ***seconda ~*** second home; ***~ dello studente*** hall of residence; ***~ unifamiliare*** single-family dwelling; ***~ per le vacanze*** holiday home; ***andare a ~*** go home; ***cambiar ~*** move (house); ***essere a ~*** be at home; ***essere di ~*** be like one of the family; ***essere ~ e chiesa*** be homeloving and a churchgoer; SPORTS ***giocare in/fuori ~*** play at home/away; ***mettere su ~*** set up house *or* home; ***dove stai di ~?*** where do you live?; ***fai come se fossi a ~ tua*** make yourself at home; ***fatto in ~*** home-made
casacca *f* ⟨*pl* -cche⟩ tunic
casaccio *m*: ***a ~*** randomly
casale *m* hamlet
casalinga *f* ⟨*pl* -ghe⟩ housewife
casalingo *adj* ⟨*mpl* -ghi⟩ domestic; (*fatto in casa*) home-made; *persona* home-loving; ***cucina*** *f* ***-a*** home cooking; ***-ghi*** *mpl* household goods
casamatta *f* ⟨*pl* casematte⟩ pillbox
casato *m* family
cascame *m* waste; ***-i*** *pl* ***di cotone*** cotton waste *sg*
cascamorto *m* lovesick boy; ***fare il ~*** moon over a girl
cascare *v/i* ⟨1d⟩ fall (down); *fig* ***cascarci*** fall for it; *fig* ***~ bene/male*** be lucky/unlucky
cascata *f* waterfall
cascatore *m*, **-trice** *f* stunt man; *donna* stunt woman
caschetto *m* bob
cascina *f* (*casa colonica*) farmhouse; (*caseificio*) dairy farm
cascinale *m* farmhouse
casco[1] **I** *m* ⟨*pl* -chi⟩ helmet; *dal parrucchiere* hair dryer; ***-chi*** *pl* ***blu*** UN forces *pl*, blue berets *pl infml* **II** *adj inv*: ***polizza*** *f* ***~*** comprehensive insurance policy
casco[2] *m*: ***un ~ di banane*** a bunch of bananas
caseggiato *m* (*edificio*) block of flats, *US* apartment block; (*gruppo di case*) built-up area
caseificio *m* ⟨*pl* -ci⟩ dairy
caseina *f* casein
casella *f di schedario* pigeon hole; (*quadratino*) square; ***~ postale*** post office box
casellante *m/f* crossing keeper; *in autostrada*: toll collector
casellario *m* ⟨*pl* -ri⟩ pigeon holes; ***~ giudiziario*** criminal records (office)
casello *m autostradale* tollbooth
casentinese I *adj* of the Casentino; *persona* from the Casentino **II** *m/f* person from the Casentino
casereccio *adj* ⟨*mpl* -cci⟩ homemade
caserma *f* barracks *pl*
casermone *m* barracks *pl*
casertano I *adj* of Caserta; *persona* from Caserta **II** *m*, **-a** *f* person from Caserta
casinista *m/f* ⟨*mpl* -i⟩ *infml* bungler
casino *m sl* brothel; (*rumore*) din, racket; (*disordine*) mess; ***~ di caccia*** hunting lodge; ***un ~ di gente/libri*** a load of people/books
casinò *m* ⟨*pl* casinò⟩ casino
casistica *f* ⟨*pl* -che⟩ case study
caso *m* **1.** case; ***~ d'emergenza*** emer-

gency; ***un ~ limite*** an extreme case; (***in***) ***~ che*** in case; ***in ~ contrario*** should that not be the case; ***in nessun ~*** under no circumstances; ***in ogni ~*** in any case, anyway; ***nel peggiore dei -i*** if the worst comes to the worst **2.** (*destino*) chance; ***a ~*** at random; ***per ~*** by chance **3.** (*occasione*) opportunity **4.** ***fare ~ a qc*** pay attention to sth; ***non farci ~!*** don't pay any attention!

casolare *m* farmhouse

casomai I *cj* if **II** *adv* possibly

Caspio *m*: ***Mar ~*** Caspian Sea

caspita! *int* goodness (gracious)!, good heavens!

cassa *f* **1.** case; *di legno* crate; ***~ da morto*** coffin **2.** *di negozio* till; *sportello* cash desk, cashpoint; (*banca*) bank; ***~ automatica prelievi*** cash machine, ATM; ***~ comune*** kitty; ***~ continua*** night safe; ***Cassa per il Mezzogiorno*** *formerly, development fund for the South of Italy*; ***~ di risparmio*** savings bank; ***orario*** *m* ***di ~*** opening hours *pl* **3.** ***~ acustica*** speaker **4.** ***~ integrazione*** *form of income support*; ***~ malattia*** *department administering health insurance scheme* **5.** ***~ toracica*** ribcage

cassaforte *f* ⟨*pl* casseforti⟩ safe

cassapanca *f* ⟨*pl* cassapanche⟩ chest

cassare *v/t* ⟨1a⟩ delete; JUR overturn; ***~ una sentenza*** overturn a verdict

cassata *f*: ***~ siciliana*** tutti frutti

cassazione *f* JUR annulment; ***ricorso*** *m* ***in*** *or* ***per ~*** appeal; ***Corte*** *f* ***di Cassazione*** *the highest Appeal Court in Italy*

cassero *m* NAUT quarterdeck

casseruola *f* (sauce)pan

cassetta *f* **1.** box; *per frutta, verdura* crate; ***~ degli attrezzi*** toolbox; ***~ delle lettere*** (*buca*) post box, *US* mailbox; (*casella*) letterbox, *US* mailbox; ***~ del pronto soccorso*** first-aid kit; ***~ di sicurezza*** strong box **2.** ***successo*** *m* ***di ~*** box office hit **3.** ***pane*** *m* ***in ~*** sliced loafe **4.** (*musicassetta*) cassette; ***~ pirata*** pirate tape

cassettiera *f* chest of drawers

cassetto *m* drawer; AUTO ***~ portaoggetti*** glove compartment

cassettone *m* chest of drawers; ***soffitto*** *m* ***a -i*** panelled ceiling

cassiere *m*, **-a** *f* cashier; *di banca* teller; *di supermercato* checkout assistant

cassintegrato I *adj* laid-off **II** *m*, **-a** *f* laid-off worker

cassone *m* chest

cassonetto *m* dustbin

cast *m* ⟨*pl* cast⟩ THEAT cast

casta *f* caste

castagna *f* chestnut; ***prendere qn in ~*** catch s.o. in the act

castagnaccio *m* ⟨*pl* -cci⟩ COOK *cake made of chestnuts, pine nuts etc.* **castagneto** *m* chestnut wood

castagno *m* chestnut (tree)

castamente *adv* chastely

castano *adj capelli* chestnut; *occhi* brown

castellano *m*, **-a** *f* lord of the manor; *donna* lady of the manor

castello *m* castle; TECH (*impalcatura*) scaffolding; ***letti*** *mpl* ***a ~*** bunk beds *pl*; *fig* ***crollare come un ~ di carte*** (*or* ***di sabbia***) collapse like a house of cards; ***fare -i in aria*** build castles in the air

castigamatti *m* ⟨*pl* castigamatti⟩ *hum* enforcer

castigare *v/t* ⟨1e⟩ punish

castigato *adj costumi* sober

Castiglia *f* Castile **castigliano I** *adj* **II** *m*, **-a** *f* Castilian **III** *n*: ***castigliano*** *m* Castilian

castigo *m* ⟨*pl* -ghi⟩ punishment; ***mettere qn in ~*** punish s.o.

casting *m* ⟨*pl* casting⟩ casting

castità *f* chastity; ***cintura*** *f* ***di ~*** chastity belt

casto *adj* chaste; (*innocente*) pure

castorino *m* ZOOL coypu

castoro *m* beaver

castrare *v/t* ⟨1a⟩ castrate; *gatto* neuter; *femmina di animale* spay

castrato *m* (*cantante evirato*) castrato; (*agnello*) wether; (*cavallo*) gelding; ***arrosto*** *m* ***di ~*** roast mutton **castrazione** *f* castration

castroneria *f infml* rubbish

casual I *adj* casual **II** *m* casual clothes *pl*, casual wear

casuale *adj* chance, casual

casualità *f* chance nature

casualmente *adv* casually

casupola *f* simple little house

cataclisma *m* ⟨*pl* -i⟩ disaster

catacomba *f* catacomb
catafalco *m* ⟨*pl* -chi⟩ catafalque
catafascio *m*: ***mandare a ~*** wreck; ***tutto va a ~*** everything's going to rack and ruin
catalano I *adj* **II** *m*, **-a** *f* Catalan **III** *n*: ***catalano*** *m* Catalan
catalessi *f* catalepsy; ***cadere in ~*** go into a trance
catalisi *f* ⟨*pl* catalisi⟩ catalysis **catalitico** *adj* ⟨*mpl* -ci⟩ catalytic **catalizzare** *v/t* ⟨1a⟩ catalyse; *fig* act as a catalyst for
catalizzatore *m* catalyst; AUTO catalytic converter; ***~ a tre vie*** three-way catalytic converter
catalogabile *adj* classifiable
catalogare *v/t* ⟨1m & e⟩ catalog(ue)
Catalogna *f* Catalonia
catalogo *m* ⟨*pl* -ghi⟩ catalog(ue); ***~ di vendita per corrispondenza*** mail order catalog(ue)
catamarano *m* catamaran
catanese I *adj* of Catania; *persona* from Catania **II** *m/f* person from Catania
catanzarese I *adj* of Catanzaro; *persona* from Catanzaro **II** *m/f* person from Catanzaro
catapecchia *f* shack
cataplasma *m* ⟨*pl* -i⟩ MED poultice; *fig* bore
catapulta *f* catapult
catapultare *v/t* ⟨1a⟩ catapult
cataratta *f* MED cataract
catarifrangente *m* reflector; *lungo la strada* reflector, *Br* cat's eye
catarro *m* catarrh
catarsi *f* ⟨*pl* catarsi⟩ catharsis **catartico** *adj* ⟨*mpl* -ci⟩ cathartic
catasta *f* pile, heap
catastale *adj* land registry *attr*; ***partita f ~*** *property registration number*
catasto *m* land register; ***ufficio*** *m* ***del ~*** land registry office
catastrofe *f* catastrophe
catastrofico *adj* ⟨*mpl* -ci⟩ catastrophic
catastrofismo *m teoria* catastrophy theory; *tendenza* doom mongering; **catastrofista I** *adj inv* doomy **II** *m/f* ⟨*mpl* -i⟩ doomster
catechesi *f* catechesis
catechismo *m insegnamento* catechism; ***andare al ~*** go to catechism class
catechista *m/f* ⟨*mpl* -i⟩ catechist **catecumeno** *m*, **-a** *f* catechumen
categoria *f* category; *di albergo* class; ***~ a rischio*** at risk category
categoricamente *adv* categorically
categorico *adj* ⟨*mpl* -ci⟩ categoric(al)
catena *f* chain; ***-e*** *pl* ***da neve*** snow chains; ***reazione*** *f* ***a ~*** chain reaction; ***~ di montaggio*** assembly line; ***~ montuosa*** mountain range, chain of mountains; ***~ di Sant'Antonio*** chain letter
catenaccio *m* ⟨*pl* -cci⟩ bolt; SPORTS defensive tactics *pl*
catenina *f* chain
cateratta *f* (*chiusa*) sluice(gate); (*cascata*) falls *pl*; MED cataract
Caterina *f*: ***Santa ~*** Saint Catherine
catering *m*: ***servizio*** *m* ***~*** catering service
caterva *f di persone* horde; *di cose* heap
catetere *m* catheter
cateto *m* side (*of a triangle*)
catinella *f* basin; ***piove a -e*** it's bucketing down
catino *m* basin
catodico *m* ⟨*pl* -ci⟩: ***tubo*** *m* ***~*** cathode-ray tube
catodo *m* cathode
catorcio *m* ⟨*pl* -ci⟩ *hum* AUTO wreck
catramare *v/t* ⟨1a⟩ tar **catramato** *adj* tarred
catrame *m* tar
cattedra *f scrivania* desk; *incarico di insegnamento* teaching post; ***~ papale*** papal throne; ***~ universitaria*** university chair; *fig* ***salire in ~*** pontificate
cattedrale *f* cathedral
cattedratico I *adj* ⟨*mpl* -ci⟩ *fig pej* pedantic; ***tono*** *m* ***~*** pedantic tone **II** *n*: ***cattedratico*** *m* professor
cattiveria *f* wickedness; *di bambini* naughtiness; *azione* nasty thing to do; *parole crudeli* nasty thing to say
cattività *f* captivity; ***vivere in ~*** live in captivity
cattivo *adj* bad; *bambino* naughty, bad; ***di ~ augurio*** ill-omened; ***essere di ~ umore*** be in a bad mood; ***con le buone o con le -e*** by hook or by crook; ***essere sulla -a strada*** be on the wrong track
cattolicesimo *m* (Roman) Catholi-

cism

cattolico ⟨*mpl* -ci⟩ **I** *adj* (Roman) Catholic **II** *m*, **-a** *f* (Roman) Catholic

cattura *f* capture; (*arresto*) arrest; ***ordine*** *m* ***di ~*** arrest warrant

catturare *v/t* ⟨1a⟩ capture; (*arrestare*) arrest; ***~ l'attenzione di qn*** capture s.o.'s attention

caucasico I *adj* ⟨*mpl* -ci⟩ Caucasian **II** *m*, **-a** *f* Caucasian

Caucaso *m* Caucasus

caucciù *m* rubber

caudato *adj* caudate

causa *f* cause; (*motivo*) reason; JUR lawsuit; ***abbracciare la ~ di qn*** take up s.o.'s cause; ***chiamare in ~*** summon; ***fare ~*** sue (***a qn*** s.o.); ***giusta ~*** just cause; ***~ civile / penale*** civil / criminal case; ***a ~ di*** because of; ***per ~ tua*** because of you

causale *f* cause, reason; ***~ di pagamento*** reason for payment

causare *v/t* ⟨1a⟩ cause

caustico *adj* ⟨*mpl* -ci⟩ caustic; ***soda*** *f* ***-a*** caustic soda; *fig* ***battuta*** *f* ***-a*** caustic remark

cautamente *adv* cautiously

cautela *f* caution; (*precauzione*) precaution

cautelare *adj*: ***custodia*** *f* ***~*** JUR remand; ***provvedimenti*** *mpl* ***-i*** precautions

cautelarsi *v/r* ⟨1b⟩: ***~ contro le malattie*** take precautions against illness

cauterizzare *v/t* ⟨1n⟩ cauterize

cauto *adj* cautious

cauzione *f* (*deposito*) security; *per la libertà provvisoria* bail; ***dietro ~*** on bail

Cav. *abbr* (= **Cavaliere**) *Italian title awarded for services to the country*

cava *f* quarry; ***~ di marmo*** marble quarry

cavalcare *v/t* ⟨1d⟩ ride

cavalcata *f* ride

cavalcavia *m* ⟨*pl* cavalcavia⟩ flyover

cavalcioni *adv*: ***a ~*** astride

cavaliere *m* rider; *accompagnatore* escort; *al ballo* partner; ***~ del lavoro*** *s.o. who has received a knighthood for services to industry*; ***fare da ~ a una signora*** escort a lady

cavalla *f* mare

cavalleresco *adj* ⟨*mpl* -chi⟩ chivalrous (*a. fig*)

cavalleria *f* MIL cavalry; *galanteria* chivalry; ***~ rusticana*** *hist* rustic chivalry

cavallerizzo *m*, **-a** *f* horseman; *donna* horsewoman

cavalletta *f* grasshopper

cavalletto *m* trestle; PHOT tripod; *da pittore* easel

cavallina *f* (*gioco*) leapfrog; ***salto*** *m* ***della ~*** vault; *fig* ***correre la ~*** sow one's wild oats

cavallo *m* **1.** horse; *fig* ***~ di battaglia*** hobby horse; ***~ da corsa*** race horse; ***~ a dondolo*** rocking horse; ***~ di Frisia*** cheval de Frise; ***~ di Troia*** Trojan horse; AUTO ***~ vapore*** horsepower; ***andare a ~*** go riding; ***a caval donato non si guarda in bocca*** *prov* don't look a gift horse in the mouth; ***campa ~ che l'erba cresce!*** *prov* that'll be the day!; *fig* ***vivere a ~ di due secoli*** straddle two centuries **2.** *scacchi* knight **3.** *dei pantaloni* crotch

cavallone *m* breaker

cavalluccio *m* ⟨*pl* -cci⟩: ***~ marino*** sea horse; ***portare qn a ~*** give s.o. a piggy back

cavare *v/t* ⟨1a⟩ take out; *dente* take out, extract; ***cavarsela*** manage, get by; *fig* ***~ le parole di bocca a qn*** take the words out of s.o.'s mouth

cavarsi *v/r*: ***~ da un impiccio*** get out of trouble

cavatappi *m* ⟨*pl* cavatappi⟩ corkscrew

caveau *m* ⟨*pl* caveau⟩ vault

caverna *f* cave; ***uomo*** *m* ***delle -e*** caveman

cavernicolo I *adj* cave *attr* **II** *m*, **-a** *f* cave dweller; *fig* caveman

cavernoso *adj*: ***una voce -a*** a deep voice

cavezza *f* halter

cavia *f* guinea pig (*a. fig*); ***fare da ~*** be a guinea-pig

caviale *m* caviar

cavicchio *m* ⟨*pl* -cchi⟩ dibber

caviglia *f* ⟨*pl* -glie⟩ ANAT ankle

cavillare *v/i* ⟨1a⟩ quibble; ***~ su qc*** quibble about sth

cavillo *m* quibble

cavilloso *adj* hair-splitting; ***discorso*** *m* ***~*** hair-splitting speech

cavità *f* ⟨*pl* cavità⟩ cavity

cavo I *m* cable; ***~ d'accensione*** plug lead; ***~ di avviamento*** jump leads;

~ ***coassiale*** TV coaxial cable; ~ ***cross-over*** COMPUT crossover cable; ~ ***in fibra ottica*** optic fibre cable; ~ ***di ormeggio*** mooring rope; ~ ***da rimorchio*** tow rope; ~ ***seriale*** COMPUT serial cable; ***televisione*** *f* ***via*** ~ cable TV **II** *adj* hollow
cavolata *f infml* stupid thing; ***dire/fare una*** ~ say/do a stupid thing
cavolfiore *m* cauliflower
cavolo *m* cabbage; ~ ***di Bruxelles*** Brussels sprout; ~ ***rapa*** kohlrabi; ~ ***verzotto*** savoy (cabbage); ***non fare un*** ~ not do a damn thing; ***non me ne importa un*** ~ I couldn't give a damn; ***non ne capisce un*** ~ he doesn't understand a damn thing (about it); **(*non*) *sono -i miei*** (none of) my business
cazzata *f vulg* piece of crap *m* **cazzeggiare** *v/i* ⟨1f⟩ *vulg* talk crap; (*perdere tempo*) piss around
cazzo *m vulg* dick *vulg*, prick *vulg*
cazzotto *m sl* punch; ***dare un*** ~ ***a qn*** give s.o. a punch; ***fare a -i*** have a punch-up
cazzuola *f* trowel
CB *abbr* (= **Campobasso**) Campobasso
cc *abbr* (= **centimetri cubici**) cc (cubic centimetres)
c.c. *abbr* (= **corrente continua**) DC (direct current)
c/c *abbr* (= **conto corrente**) current account, *US* checking account
CC *abbr* (= **Carabinieri**) *Italian police force*
CCD *abbr* (= **Centro Cristiano Democratico**) *Christian Democratic Centre*
CD *m* ⟨*pl* CD⟩ CD; ***lettore*** *m* ~ CD player
C.d.A *abbr* (= **Consiglio d'Amministrazione**) board
CD-Rom *m* ⟨*pl* CD-Rom⟩ CD-Rom; ***drive*** *m* ***per*** ~ CD-Rom drive
ce → ***ci*** (before ***lo, la, li, le, ne***)
C.E. *abbr* (= **Consiglio d'Europa**) Council of Europe
c'è there is
cecchino *m* sniper
cece *m* chickpea; ***pasta*** *f* ***e -i*** pasta with chickpeas
Cecenia *f* Chechnya **ceceno I** *adj* Chechen **II** *m*, **-a** *f* Chechen
Cecilia *f*: ***Santa*** ~ Saint Cecilia
cecità *f* blindness
ceco I *adj* Czech **II** *m*, **-a** *f* Czech
cecoslovacco ⟨*mpl* -cchi⟩ *hist* **I** *adj* Czechoslovakian **II** *m*, **-a** *f* Czechoslovakian
cedere ⟨3a⟩ **I** *v/t* (*dare*) hand over, give up; (*vendere*) sell, dispose of; ~ ***qc a qn*** give sth to s.o.; ~ ***la parola*** (***a qn***) hand over (to s.o.); ~ ***il posto*** give up one's seat **II** *v/i* give in, surrender (***a*** to); *muro*, *terreno* collapse, give way; ***non*** ~***!*** don't give in!
cedevole *adj* soft
cedevolezza *f* pliability (*a. fig*)
cedibile *adj* transferable, assignable
cedimento *m* breakdown (*a. fig*); *di terreno*, *struttura* subsidence; ECON slide
cedola *f* coupon; ~ ***di consegna*** delivery note
cedrata *f* citron juice
cedrina *f* BOT lemon balm
cedro *m del Libano* cedar; (*frutto*) citron
cedrone *m*: ***gallo*** *m* ~ capercaillie **cedronella** *f* (*farfalla*) brimstone; *infml* BOT (*melissa*) lemon balm
CEE, Cee *abbr* (= **Comunità Economica Europea**) *hist* EEC (European Economic Community)
CEEA *abbr* (= **Comunità Europea dell'Energia Atomica**) *hist* Euratom (European Atomic Energy Community)
cefalea *f* headache
cefalo *m* ZOOL mullet
ceffo *m* (*faccia*) mug; ***brutto*** ~ *infml* ugly mug
ceffone *m* slap
celare *v/t* ⟨1b⟩ conceal
celarsi *v/r* ⟨1b⟩ hide
celebrante *m* celebrant
celebrare *v/t* ⟨1l & b⟩ celebrate; ~ ***una messa*** celebrate mass; ~ ***un processo*** hold a trial
celebrazione *f* celebration
celebre *adj* famous
celebrità *f* ⟨*pl* celebrità⟩ fame; (*persona*) celebrity
celere *adj* fast, speedy, swift; ***posta*** *f* ~ swiftair®, *US* Fedex®
celerità *f* speed
celermente *adv* swiftly
celeste *adj* sky blue; (*divino*) heavenly

(*a. fig*); ***corpo*** *m* ~ celestial body; ***volta*** *f* ~ sky
celestiale *adj* celestial (*a. fig*) **celestino** *adj* pale blue
celia *f liter* jest
celiachia *f* MED c(o)eliac disease **celiaco** *adj* 〈*mpl* -ci〉 c(o)eliac
celiare *v/i* 〈1b & k〉 *liter* jest
celibato *m* celibacy; ***addio al*** ~ stag night
celibe I *adj* single, unmarried **II** *m* bachelor
cella *f* cell; ~ ***frigorifera*** cold store; ***essere in*** ~ ***d'isolamento*** be in solitary confinement
Cellophane® *m* cellophane®
cellula *f* cell; ~ ***fotoelettrica*** photoelectric cell; ~ ***solare*** solar cell; ~ ***staminale*** stem cell
cellulare I *adj* cell *attr*; ***telefono*** *m* ~ mobile phone, *US* cell(ular) phone **II** *m* prison van; (*telefono*) mobile
cellulite *f* cellulite
celluloide *f* celluloid; *fig* ***il mondo della*** ~ the movies
cellulosa *f* cellulose
celta *m* 〈*pl* -i〉 Celt **celtibero** *adj* Celtiberian
celtico *adj* 〈*mpl* -ci〉 Celtic
cembalo *m* harpsichord
cementare *v/t* 〈1a〉 BUILD cement (*a. fig*); ~ ***un'amicizia*** seal a friendship **cementarsi** *v/r* 〈1a〉 be cemented (*a. fig*) **cementazione** *f* BUILD cementation; *fig* consolidation
cementificare *v/t* 〈1m & d〉 concrete over **cementificazione** *f* concreting over; ***la*** ~ ***delle coste*** *uncontrolled building in coastal areas* **cementificio** *m* 〈*pl* -ci〉 cement works *sg*
cemento *m* cement; ~ ***armato*** reinforced concrete
cena *f* supper, evening meal; *importante, con ospiti* dinner; ~ ***in piedi*** buffet; ***andare a*** ~ ***fuori*** go out to dinner; ***l'Ultima Cena*** REL the Last Supper
cenacolo *m* PAINT Last Supper
cenare *v/i* 〈1a〉 have supper; *formalmente* dine
cencio *m* 〈*pl* -ci〉 rag, piece of cloth; (*per spolverare*) duster; ***bianco come un*** ~ white as a sheet
cencioso *adj persona* dressed in rags; *vestiti* tattered
cenere *f* ash; ***biondo*** ~ ash blonde; ***le Ceneri*** *fpl* Ash Wednesday; ***ridurre in*** ~ burn to a cinder; *fig* destroy completely
Cenerentola *f* Cinderella
cenno *m* sign; *della mano* wave; *del capo* nod; *con gli occhi* wink; (*breve notizia*) mention; (*allusione*) hint; ***far*** ~ ***a qn*** *con la mano* wave to s.o.; *con il capo* nod to s.o.; *con gli occhi* wink at s.o.; ***mi ha fatto*** ~ ***di tacere*** she made a sign to me to be quiet; ***far*** ~ ***di voler andare*** signal that one wants to leave; ***far*** ~ ***di sì*** nod (one's head); ***far*** ~ ***di no*** shake one's head
cenobio *m* 〈*pl* -bi〉 BIOL coenobium; REL monastery
cenone *m* feast, banquet; ~ ***di San Silvestro*** *special celebratory meal on New Year's Eve*
censimento *m* census
censire *v/t* 〈4d〉 *popolazione* take a census of
CENSIS *abbr* (= **Centro Studi Investimenti Sociali**) *social research institute*
censore *m* censor (*a.* HIST); *fig* (*a.* **-a** *f*) critic
censura *f* censorship
censurare *v/t* 〈1a〉 censor
centauro *m* MYTH centaur; (*motociclista*) biker
centellinare *v/t* 〈1a〉 (*assaporare*) savo(u)r; (*dosare*) sip
centenario 〈*mpl* -ri〉 **I** *adj* hundred-year-old **II** *m* (*persona*) centenarian; (*anniversario*) centenary
centerbe *m* 〈*pl* centerbe〉 *herb liqueur from Abruzzo*
centesimo I *adj* hundredth **II** *m moneta* cent; ~ ***di dollaro*** cent; ***badare al*** ~ count every penny
centigrado *m* centigrade; ***15 gradi -i*** 15 degrees centigrade
centilitro *m* centilitre, *US* -liter
centimetro *m* centimetre, *US* -meter; ~ ***cubo*** cubic centimetre (*US* -meter); ~ ***quadrato*** square centimetre (*US* -meter)
centinaio *m* 〈*pl* le centinaia〉 hundred; ***a -a*** by the hundred; ***un*** ~ ***di*** about a hundred, a hundred or so
cento *num* hundred; ***per*** ~ per cent; ~ ***per*** ~ one hundred per cent; ~ ***di questi giorni*** many happy returns

centodieci *num* (*voto*) first-class honours, *US* summa cum laude; ***laurearsi con ~*** (***e lode***) get a first-class honours degree, *US* graduate summa cum laude
centometrista *m/f* ⟨*mpl* -i⟩ 100 meter runner *or* swimmer
centrafricano **I** *adj* of the Central African Republic; *persona* from the Central African Republic **II** *m*, **-a** *f* person from the Central African Republic
centrale **I** *adj* central; (*principale*) main; ***l'Italia ~*** central Italy; ***la sede ~*** the head office **II** *f* station, plant; ***~ atomica*** *or* ***nucleare*** nuclear power station; ***~ elettrica*** power station, *US* power plant
centralina *f* junction box
centralinista *m/f* ⟨*mpl* -i⟩ switchboard operator
centralino *m* switchboard
centralismo *m* POL centralism
centralizzare *v/t* ⟨1a⟩ centralize
centralizzazione *f* centralization
centrare *v/t* ⟨1b⟩ TECH centre, *US* center; ***~ il bersaglio*** hit a bull's eye; ***~ un obiettivo*** be right on target (*a. fig*); ***~ un problema*** hit the nail on the head
centrattacco *m* ⟨*pl* -cchi⟩ → ***centravanti***
centratura *f* MECH centreing, *US* centering
centravanti *m/f* ⟨*pl* centravanti⟩ SPORTS centre *or* *US* center forward
centrifuga **I** *adj* centrifugal **II** *f* spin-dryer; TECH centrifuge
centrifugare *v/t* ⟨1e & m⟩ spin-dry; TECH centrifuge
centrifugo *adj* ⟨*mpl* -ghi⟩ centrifugal; ***forza*** *f* ***-a*** centrifugal force
centrino *m* doily
centripeto *adj* centripetal; ***movimento*** *m* ***~*** centripetal movement
centro *m* centre, *US* center; *di bersaglio* bull's eye; ***~ abitato*** built-up area; ***~ della città*** town *or* city centre, *US* downtown; ***~ commerciale*** shopping centre; ***~ residenziale*** residential area; ***~ sociale*** community centre; ***~ storico*** old (part of) town; ***abitare in ~*** live in the city centre; ***essere al ~ dell'attenzione*** be the centre *or* *US* center of attention; ***fare ~*** hit the bull's eye; *fig* hit the nail on the head
centro- *pref* centre-, *US* center-; ***~nord*** centre-north; ***~sud*** centre-south; ***~occidentale*** centre-west; ***~orientale*** centre-east
centrocampista *m/f* ⟨*mpl* -i⟩ midfielder **centrocampo** *m* midfield
centrodestra *m* ⟨*pl* centrodestra⟩ centre right; ***deputato*** *m* ***del ~*** centre right MP
centroeuropeo *adj* central European
centropagina *m* ⟨*pl* centropagina⟩ *article or headline in the centre of a page*
centrosinistra *m* ⟨*pl* centrosinistra⟩ centre left; ***governo*** *m* ***di ~*** left-of-centre government
centrotavola *m* ⟨*pl* centrotavola⟩ centrepiece
centuplicare *v/t* ⟨1m & d⟩ multiply by a hundred; *fig* increase a hundredfold; ***~ gli sforzi*** redouble one's efforts **centuplo** *m* a hundred times as much
centurione *m hist* centurion
ceppo *m*: ***~ bloccarruota*** wheel clamp; ***mettere il ~ a*** clamp
cera[1] *f* wax; *per lucidare* polish; ***~ d'api*** beeswax; ***~ da scarpe*** shoe polish; ***di ~*** wax
cera[2] *f* look; ***avere una brutta ~*** look awful
ceralacca *f* sealing wax
ceramica *f* ⟨*pl* -che⟩ *arte* ceramics *sg*; *oggetto* piece of pottery
ceramista *m/f* ⟨*mpl* -i⟩ potter
cerata *f* oilskins *pl*
cerato *adj* waxed; ***tela*** *f* ***-a*** waxed cloth
cerbero *m* MYTH Cerberus; *infml persona* curmudgeon
cerbiatto *m* fawn
cerbottana *f arma* blowpipe; *giocattolo* peashooter
cerca *f*: ***in ~ di ...*** in search of ...
cercamine *m* ⟨*pl* cercamine⟩ mine detector
cercapersone *m* ⟨*pl* cercapersone⟩ pager, beeper, bleeper
cercare ⟨1d⟩ **I** *v/t* look for; ***~ fortuna*** seek one's fortune; ***~ lavoro*** look for work; ***~ qc col lanternino*** search high and low for sth; ***chi cerca trova*** *prov* seek and you shall find; ***mi ha cercato qualcuno?*** has anyone called?; ***se l'è proprio cercata*** s/he was asking

for it **II** *v/i*: ~ ***di fare*** try to do; ***cerca di sbrigarti*** try to hurry up
cercatore *m*, **-trice** *f* searcher; ~ ***d'oro*** gold prospector
cerchia *f* circle; ~ ***di mura*** city walls; ~ ***familiare*** family circle
cerchiato *adj* ringed; ~ ***di ferro*** iron-hooped; ***avere gli occhi*** *mpl* ***-i*** have circles round one's eyes
cerchietto *m* band; *per capelli* hairband
cerchio *m* ⟨*pl* -chi⟩ circle; ***avere un ~ alla testa*** have a headache; ***mettersi in ~*** form a circle; *fig* ***cercare la quadratura del ~*** try to square a circle; *fig* ***dare un colpo al ~ e uno alla botte*** run with the hare and hunt with the hounds
cerchione *m* TECH wheel cover
cereale I *adj* grain *attr* **II** *m*: ***cereali*** *pl* grain *sg*, cereals *pl*
cerealicoltura *f* grain farming
cerebrale *adj*: ***commozione*** *f* ~ concussion
cerebroleso I *adj* brain-damaged **II** *m*, **-a** *f* person with brain damage
cereo *adj* waxen; ***volto*** *m* ~ waxen face
cerfoglio *m* ⟨*pl* -gli⟩ chervil
cerimonia *f* ceremony; REL service; ***-e*** *pl* (*convenevoli*) pleasantries; ~ ***nuziale*** wedding ceremony; ***fare -e*** stand on ceremony; ***senza tante ~*** (*bruscamente*) unceremoniously
cerimoniale *m/adj* ceremonial
cerimonioso *adj* ceremonious
cerino *m* (wax) match
cernia *f* grouper
cerniera *f* hinge; ~ ***lampo*** zip (fastener), *US* zipper
cernita *f* selection, choice; ***fare una ~*** make a selection
cero *m* (large) candle; ***accendere un ~ alla Madonna*** *infml* thank one's lucky stars
cerone *m* greasepaint
cerotto *m* (sticking) plaster
certamente *adv* certainly
certezza *f* certainty; ***averne la ~*** be certain
certificare *v/t* ⟨1m & d⟩ certify
certificato *m* certificate; ~ ***internazionale di vaccinazione*** international vaccination certificate; ~ ***medico*** medical certificate; ~ ***di garanzia*** guarantee; ~ ***di morte*** death certificate; ~ ***di nascita*** birth certificate; ~ ***di sana e robusta costituzione*** certificate of good health
certificazione *f* certification; ~ ***di qualità*** quality certification; ***delle ritenute*** FIN *certificate of tax paid*
certo I *adj* (*sicuro*) certain, sure (***di*** of; ***che*** that); ***sono ~ di farcela*** I'm certain of succeeding; ***sapere qc per ~*** know sth for certain; ***un ~ signor Federici*** a (certain) Mr Federici; ***ci vuole un ~ coraggio*** it takes (some) courage; ***di una -a età*** of a certain age; ***-i*** some; ***in un ~ senso*** in a way; ***-e cose non si dicono*** there are some things you just don't say; ***un ~ non so che*** a certain something, a certain je ne sais quoi **II** *adv* (*certamente*) certainly; (*naturalmente*) of course; ~ ***che ...*** surely ... **III** *pron*: ***-i, -e*** some, some people
certosa *f* Carthusian monastery
certosino I *adj* Carthusian **II** *n*: ***certosino*** *m* Carthusian monk; ***lavoro*** *m* ***da ~*** painstaking work; ***pazienza*** *f* ***da ~*** patience of Job
certuni *pron* some people
cerume *m* (ear)wax
cervelletto *m* cerebellum
cervello *m* ⟨*pl* i cervelli, le cervella⟩ brain; COOK brains *pl*; ***farsi saltare le -a*** blow one's brains out; ***lambiccarsi il ~*** rack one's brains; ***uscire di ~*** go mad; ***è il ~ della banda*** he's the brains of the gang
cervellotico *adj* ⟨*mpl* -ci⟩ bizarre; ***ragionamento*** *m* ~ bizarre reasoning
cervicale *f* *infml* cervical osteoarthritis
cervice *f* ANAT cervix
Cervino *m* Matterhorn
cervo *m* deer; *carne* venison; ~ ***volante*** stag beetle
cesanese *m* COOK *sweet or dry wine from Lazio region*
Cesare *m* Caesar; ***dare a ~ quel che è di ~*** render unto Caesar that which is Caesar's
cesareo *adj*: ***taglio*** *m* ~ C(a)esarean (section), C section
cesellare *v/t* ⟨1b⟩ chisel
cesellatura *f* chiselling; ART engraving
cesello *m* chisel
cesio *m* c(a)esium
cesoie *fpl* shears *pl*

cespite *m* source of income
cespo *m* tuft; ***un ~ d'insalata*** a head of lettuce
cespuglio *m* ⟨*pl* -gli⟩ bush, shrub
cespuglioso *adj* shrubby; *hum capelli* bushy
cessare *v/t* ⟨1b⟩ stop, cease
cessate il fuoco *m* ceasefire
cessazione *f di contratto* termination; ***~ di esercizio*** closure, going out of business
cessione *f* transfer, handover
cesso *m sl* bog *sl*; ***quel film è un ~!*** that film's crap!
cesta *f* basket
cestello *m* crate; *nelle lavatrici*: drum
cestinare *v/t* ⟨1a⟩ throw away, bin *infml*
cestino *m* little basket; *per la carta* wastepaper basket; COMPUT recycle bin; ***~ da lavoro*** work *or* sewing basket; ***~ da viaggio*** packed *or US* bag lunch
cesto *m* basket
cesura *f* LIT, MUS caesura; *fig* pause
cetaceo *m* cetacean
ceto *m* (social) class; ***~ medio*** middle class
cetra *f* zither
cetriolino *m* gherkin
cetriolo *m* cucumber
cf., cfr. *abbr* (= **confronta**) cf (compare)
cg *abbr* (= **centigrammo**) cg (centigram)
CGIL *abbr* (= **Confederazione Generale Italiana del Lavoro**) *Italian trade union organization*
CH *abbr* (= **Chieti**) Chieti
chalet *m* ⟨*pl* chalet⟩ chalet
champagne *m* ⟨*pl* champagne⟩ champagne
chance *f* ⟨*pl* chance⟩ chance
chardonnay *m* ⟨*pl* chardonnay⟩ COOK chardonnay
charter *m* ⟨*pl* charter⟩ charter
chassis *m* chassis
chattare *v/i* ⟨1a⟩ chat
che I *adj* what; ***~ ore sono?*** what time is it?; ***~ tipo di film preferisci?*** what kind of films do you like?; ***a ~ cosa serve?*** what is that for?; ***~ brutta giornata!*** what a filthy day! **II** *pron persona*: soggetto who; *persona oggetto* who, that, *form* whom; *cosa* that, which; ***il ragazzo ~ ha telefonato*** the boy who phoned; ***l'attrice ~ hai visto*** the actress who you saw; ***il libro ~ è sul tavolo*** the book that's on the table; ***l'autobus ~ devi prendere*** the bus that you have to get; ***~?*** what?; ***ciò ~*** what; ***non c'è di ~*** don't mention it, you're welcome **III** *cj dopo il comparativo* than; ***sono tre anni ~ non la vedo*** I haven't seen her for three years; ***sia Luca ~ Daniela lavorano a Palermo*** both Luca and Daniela work in Palermo; ***spero ~ non piova*** I hope that it doesn't rain; ***io vado, ~ tu venga o no*** I'm going, whether you come or not
checca *f* ⟨*pl* -cche⟩ *pej* queer
check-in *m* ⟨*pl* check-in⟩ AVIAT check-in; ***fare il ~*** check in
check-up *m* ⟨*pl* check-up⟩ MED, TECH check-up; ***fare un ~*** have a check-up
chef *m* ⟨*pl* chef⟩ chef
chela *f di crostacei*: pincer
chemioterapia *f* chemotherapy, chemo *infml*
cherosene *m* paraffin, *US* kerosene
cherubino *m* cherub
chetichella *f*: ***alla ~*** stealthily
cheto *adj* quiet; ***l'acqua -a rompe i ponti*** *prov* still waters run deep
chewing gum *m* ⟨*pl* chewing gum⟩ chewing gum
chi *pron* who; ***~ è?*** who is it?; ***~ hai visto?*** who *or form* whom did you see?; ***di ~ è il libro?*** whose book is this?; ***a ~ ha venduto la casa?*** who did he sell the house to?; ***c'è ~ dice che*** some people say that; ***~ ... ~*** some ... others; ***senti ~ parla!*** look who's talking!
chiacchiera *f* chat; (*maldicenza*) gossip; (*notizia infondata*) rumo(u)r; ***far due -e con qn*** have a chat with s.o.
chiacchierare *v/i* ⟨1l⟩ chat, chatter; *pej* gossip
chiacchierata *f* chat; ***fare una ~*** have a chat
chiacchierone I *adj* talkative, chatty; (*pettegolo*) gossipy **II** *m*, **-a** *f* chatterbox; (*pettegolo*) gossip
chiamare *v/t* ⟨1a⟩ call; TEL (tele)phone, ring; ***~ alle armi*** call up, *US* draft; TEL ***~ in teleselezione*** call direct, dial direct; ***andare a ~ qn*** go and get s.o., fetch s.o.; ***mandare a ~***

qn send for s.o.; (*convocare*) call in
chiamarsi *v/r* be called; ***come ti chiami?*** what's your name?; ***mi chiamo ...*** my name is ...; ***~ fuori*** withdraw
chiamata *f* call; TEL (tele)phone call; ***~ in attesa*** call on hold; ***~ a carico del destinatario*** reverse charge call, *US* collect call; ***~ d'emergenza*** emergency call; ***~ interurbana*** long-distance call
chianti *m* COOK Chianti **chiantigiano I** *adj* of Chianti; *persona* from Chianti **II** *m*, **-a** *f* person from Chianti
chiappa *f infml* (bum) cheek
chiara *f* egg white
Chiara *f*: ***Santa ~*** Saint Cla(i)re
chiaramente *adv* clearly; (*apertamente*) openly; ***parlare ~ a qn*** speak to s.o. frankly
chiarezza *f* clarity; ***con ~*** clearly; ***fare ~*** clarify things *or* matters
chiarificare *v/t* ⟨1m & d⟩ clarify
chiarificatore *adj* explanatory; ***parole*** *fpl* ***-trici*** explanation *sg* **chiarificazione** *f di acqua* purification; *di burro, vino* clarification (*a. fig*); ***impianto*** *m* ***di ~*** purifier
chiarimento *m* clarification
chiarire *v/t* ⟨4d⟩ clarify
chiarirsi *v/r* become clear; ***~ le idee*** get things clear in one's mind; ***ci siamo chiariti*** we set things straight
chiarissimo *adj form* illustrious; ***~ professore*** Professor
chiaro I *adj* clear; *colore* light, pale; (*luminoso*) bright; ***~ e tondo*** definite; ***è ~ che ...*** it is clear that ...; ***sono stato ~?*** is what I said clear?; ***verde ~*** light *or* pale green **II** *m* light; ***~ di luna*** moonlight; ***mettere in ~*** (*appurare*) throw light on; (*spiegare*) clarify **III** *adv* plainly; (*con franchezza*) frankly; ***parlare ~*** speak frankly; ***vorrei vederci ~*** I'd like to get to the bottom of this
chiarore *m* brightness
chiaroscuro *m* PAINT chiaroscuro
chiaroveggente *m/f* clairvoyant
chiaroveggenza *f* clairvoyance; *fig* far-sightedness
chiassata *f* din; *fig* row
chiasso *m* din, racket; ***fare ~*** make a din *or* racket; *fig* cause a sensation
chiassoso *adj* noisy
chiatta *f* barge; ***ponte*** *m* ***di -e*** pontoon bridge
chiavare *v/t* ⟨1a⟩ *vulg* screw *vulg*
chiave I *adj inv* key; ***personaggio*** *m* ***~*** key figure **II** *f* key; MUS clef; ***~ d'accensione*** ignition key; ***~ inglese*** spanner, *US* monkey wrench; ***~ della macchina*** car key; ***chiudere a ~*** lock; ***prezzo -i*** *pl* ***in mano*** on-the-road price, *US* sticker price; ***sotto ~*** under lock and key; *fig* ***la ~ del mistero*** the key to the mystery; *fig* ***in ~ ideologica*** from an ideological point of view
chiavetta *f* MECH key
chiavica *f* ⟨*pl* -che⟩ sewer; *fig pej* hog
chiavistello *m* bolt
chiazza *f* (*macchia*) stain; *sulla pelle, di colore* patch; ***a -e*** in patches
chiazzare *v/t* ⟨1a⟩ stain; *con colore*: splash **chiazzarsi** *v/r* ⟨1a⟩ get stained
chic *adj inv* chic, stylish, elegant
chicca *f* ⟨*pl* -cche⟩ *fig* jewel
chicchessia *pron m/f* anyone, anybody; *in frasi negative*: not...anyone, not...anybody
chicco *m* ⟨*pl* -chi⟩ grain; ***~ di caffè*** coffee bean; ***~ di grandine*** hailstone; ***~ di riso*** grain of rice; ***~ d'uva*** grape
chiedere *v/t* ⟨3k⟩ *per sapere* ask (***di*** about); *per avere* ask for; (*esigere*) demand, require; ***~ qc a qn*** ask s.o. sth; ***~ a qn di fare qc*** ask s.o. to do sth; ***~ di qn*** (*chiedere notizie di*) ask about s.o.; *per parlargli* ask for s.o.; ***~ la mano di qn*** ask for s.o.'s hand in marriage; ***~ un piacere a qn*** ask s.o. a favo(u)r, ask a favo(u)r of s.o.; ***~ scusa a qn*** apologize to s.o.
chiedersi *v/r* wonder (***se*** whether)
chierica *f* ⟨*pl* -che⟩ REL tonsure; *hum* bald patch
chierichetto *m* altar boy **chierico** *m* ⟨*pl* -ci⟩ clergyman; (*seminarista*) seminarist
chiesa *f* church; ***andare in ~*** go to church
chiesto *past part* → ***chiedere***
chietino I *adj* of Chieti; *persona* from Chieti **II** *m*, **-a** *f* person from Chieti
chiglia *f* NAUT keel
chilo *m* kilo; ***mezzo ~*** half a kilo
chilogrammo *m* kilogram
chilometraggio *m* AUTO *mileage*; ***~ illimitato*** *unlimited mileage*
chilometrico *adj*: ***indennità*** *f* ***-a*** mileage allowance

chilometro *m* kilometre, *US* -meter; ***abito a 10 -i da Roma*** I live 10 kilometres (*US* -meters) from Rome; ***-i** pl **all'ora*** kilometres (*US* -meters) per hour
chilowatt *m* ⟨*pl* chilowatt⟩ kilowatt
chilowattora *m* ⟨*pl* chilowattora⟩ kilowatt-hour
chimera *f* MYTH chimera; *fig* illusion
chimica *f* chemistry
chimico ⟨*mpl* -ci⟩ **I** *adj* chemical; ***sostanze** fpl **-che*** chemicals **II** *m*, **-a** *f* chemist
chimono *m* ⟨*pl* chimono⟩ → ***kimono***
china[1] *f* (*inchiostro*) Indian *or US* India ink
china[2] *f* (*pendenza*) slope; *fig* ***risalire la ~*** be on the road to recovery
chinare *v/t* ⟨1a⟩ *testa* bend; *occhi* lower
chinarsi *v/r* stoop, bend down
chincaglierie *fpl* knick-knacks *pl*, ornaments *pl*
chinino *m* quinine
chinotto *m* (*bibita*) *fizzy bitter orange drink*
chioccia *f* ⟨*pl* -cce⟩ *fig* mother hen
chiocciola *f* snail; ***scala** f **a ~*** spiral staircase
chiodato *adj*: SPORTS ***scarpe** fpl **-e*** spikes
chiodino *m* (*fungo*) honey fungus; (*chiodo piccolo*) tack
chiodo *m* nail; ***~ di garofano*** clove; *fig* ***~ fisso*** obsession, idée fixe; ***~ scaccia ~*** *prov* one problem drives out another; ***roba da -i!*** it's unbelievable!
chioma *f* mane; *di cometa* tail
chiosa *f* gloss **chiosare** *v/t* ⟨1c⟩ gloss
chiosco *m* ⟨*pl* -chi⟩ kiosk
chiostro *m* cloister
chip *m* ⟨*pl* chip⟩ chip
chirghiso I *adj* Kyrgyz **II** *m*, **-a** *f* Kyrgyz
chiromante *m/f* palmist
chiropratico *m*, **-a** *f* chiropractor
chirurgia *f* surgery; ***~ estetica*** cosmetic surgery
chirurgicamente *adv* surgically
chirurgico *adj* ⟨*mpl* -ci⟩ surgical
chirurgo *m* ⟨*pl* -ghi⟩ surgeon
chissà *adv* who knows; (*forse*) maybe; ***~ come*** goodness know how; ***~ quando*** goodness knows when; ***si crede ~ chi*** s/he thinks s/he's so special
chitarra *f* guitar; ***~ classica*** classical guitar; ***~ elettrica*** electric guitar; ***tagliatelle** fpl **alla ~*** *type of pasta that is a speciality of Abruzzo*
chitarrista *m/f* ⟨*mpl* -i⟩ guitarist
chitina *f* chitin
chiudere *v/t* ⟨3b⟩ close, shut; *a chiave* lock; *strada* close off; *gas*, *luce* turn off; *fabbrica*, *negozio per sempre* close down, shut down; *fig* ***~ un occhio*** turn a blind eye; FIN ***~ in pareggio*** break even; ***~ in perdita / in attivo*** show a loss / a profit; ***con te ho chiuso!*** I've finished with you!
chiudersi *v/r di porta*, *ombrello* close, shut; *di ferita* heal up; ***~ in casa*** shut o.s. away; ***~ fuori*** lock o.s. out; ***~ in se stesso*** withdraw into o.s.
chiunque *pron* anyone; *relativo* whoever
chiusa *f di fiume* lock; *di discorso* conclusion
chiuso I *past part* → ***chiudere*** **II** *adj* closed, shut; *a chiave* locked; (*nuvoloso*) cloudy, overcast; *persona* reserved; ***avere il naso ~*** have a blocked nose; ***numero** m **~*** restricted entry (to a school or university)
chiusura *f* closing, shutting; AUTO ***~ centralizzata*** central locking; ***~ lampo*** zip (fastener), *US* zipper; ***ora** f **di ~*** closing time
choc *m* ⟨*pl* choc⟩ shock
ci I *pron* us; ***non ~ ha parlato*** he didn't speak to us; ***ce lo ha detto Marina*** Marina told us; ***~ siamo divertiti molto*** we had a great time; ***~ vogliamo bene*** we love each other; ***~ penso*** I'm thinking about it; ***~ puoi contare!*** you can bet on it! **II** *adv* here; (*lì*) there; ***~ sei?*** are you there?; ***c'è ...*** there is ...; ***~ sono ...*** there are ...; ***c'era una volta ...*** once upon a time there was ...; ***~ vuole tempo*** it takes time; ***~ vado spesso*** I often go there; ***ce l'hai una penna?*** do you have a pen?; ***io non c'entro*** it's got nothing to do with me
C.ia *abbr* (= **compagnia**) Co. (company)
ciabatta *f* slipper
ciabattare *v/i* ⟨1a⟩ shuffle about in slippers **ciabattino** *m* cobbler
ciac *m* ⟨*pl* ciac⟩ FILM (*ripresa*) clapperboard; ***~, si gira!*** action!

Ciad *m* Chad
cialda *f* wafer
cialtrone *m*, **-a** *f persona spregevole* rogue; *persona sciatta* slob **cialtroneria** *f* shabby behavio(u)r; *sciatteria* slovenliness
ciambella *f* COOK ring-shaped cake; (*salvagente*) lifebelt; ***non tutte le -e riescono col buco*** *prov* you can't win them all
ciambellano *m* chamberlain
ciancia *f* ⟨*pl* -ce⟩ tittle-tattle **cianciare** *v/i* ⟨1f⟩ prattle
cianfrusaglia *f* knick-knack
cianidrico *adj* ⟨*mpl* -ci⟩ hydrocyanic; ***acido*** *m* **~** hydrogen cyanide
cianotico *adj* ⟨*mpl* -ci⟩ cyanotic
cianuro *m* cyanide
ciao! *int nell'incontrarsi* hi!; *nel congedarsi* 'bye!, cheerio!
ciarla *f* piece of gossip; (*ciancia*) chat
ciarlataneria *f* charlatanism; *di falso medico*: quackery
ciarlatano *m*, **-a** *f* charlatan
ciarliero *adj* chatty
ciarpame *m* junk
ciascuno I *adj* each; (*ogni*) every; ***~ di voi*** each of you **II** *pron* everyone; ***due*** (***per***) **~** two each
cibarie *fpl* provisions
cibarsi *v/r* ⟨1a⟩ feed on, eat (***di*** sth)
cibernetica *f* cybernetics *sg*
cibernetico *adj* ⟨*mpl* -ci⟩ cybernetic
cibo *m* food; ***-i*** *pl* foodstuffs, foods; ***~ pronto*** fast food
cicala *f* (*insetto*) cicada
cicaleccio *m* ⟨*pl* -cci⟩ *fig* chatter
cicalino *m* buzzer, bleeper
CICAP *abbr* (= **Comitato Italiano per il Controllo delle Affermazioni sul Paranormale**) *Italian committee for the investigation of paranormal activity*
cicatrice *f* scar
cicatrizzante *adj* healing; ***pomata*** *f* **~** healing ointment
cicatrizzare *v/i* ⟨1a⟩ heal
cicatrizzarsi *v/r* ⟨1a⟩ heal
cicca *f* ⟨*pl* -che⟩ (*mozzicone*) stub, butt; (*gomma da masticare*) (chewing) gum; ***non valere una ~*** *infml* not be worth tuppence, *US* a dime
cicchetto *m infml* (*bicchierino*) drop; (*ramanzina*) telling-off
ciccia *f* (*grasso*) flab; ***mettere su ~*** put on weight
ciccione *m*, **-a** *f* fatty
cicciottello *adj* chubby
cicerone *m* guide
ciclabile *adj*: ***pista*** *f* **~** bike *or* cycle path
Cicladi *fpl* Cyclades
ciclamino *m* cyclamen
ciclicamente *adv* cyclically
ciclico cyclical
ciclismo *m* cycling, bike riding
ciclista *m/f* ⟨*mpl* -i⟩ cyclist
ciclistico *adj* bike *attr*, cycle *attr*; ***gara*** *f* ***-a*** cycle race
ciclo *m* cycle; ***~ economico*** economic cycle; ***~ di lavaggio*** washing cycle; ***~ di studi*** period of study
ciclomotore *m* moped
ciclone *m* cyclone; ***essere nell'occhio del ~*** be in the eye of the storm
ciclonico *adj* ⟨*mpl* -ci⟩ cyclonic; ***area*** *f* ***-a*** cyclonic area
ciclope *m* Cyclops **ciclopico** *adj* ⟨*mpl* -ci⟩ *fig* (*colossale*) huge, enormous
ciclostilare *v/t* ⟨1a⟩ cyclostyle, *US* mimeograph
cicloturismo *m* cycling holidays *pl*
cicloturista *m/f* ⟨*mpl* -i⟩ *person on a cycling holiday*
cicogna *f* stork
cicoria *f* chicory
cicuta *f* BOT hemlock
cieco ⟨*mpl* -chi⟩ **I** *adj* blind; ***diventare ~*** go blind; ***vicolo*** *m* **~** dead end, blind alley; ***alla -a*** blindly **II** *m*, **-a** *f* blind man; *donna* blind woman
ciellino *m*, **-a** *f member of Catholic youth movement Comunione e Liberazione*
cielo *m* sky; REL heaven; ***grazie al ~*** thank heaven(s); ***essere al settimo ~*** be in seventh heaven; ***non stare né in ~ né in terra*** have neither rhyme nor reason; ***per amor del ~!*** for the love of God!
cifra *f* figure; (*monogramma*) monogram; (*somma*) amount, sum; (*codice*) cipher, code; ***~ d'affari*** turnover; ***numero*** *m* ***di sei -e*** six digit number; ***fare ~ tonda*** make it a round figure
cifrare *v/t* ⟨1a⟩ (*ricamare*) monogram; (*codificare*) encode **cifrario** *m* ⟨*pl* -ri⟩ code book
cifrato *adj* (*messaggio*) in cipher, in code

ciglio *m* ⟨*pl* le ciglia⟩ ANAT eyelash; ⟨*pl* i cigli⟩ (*bordo*) edge; ***non battere ~*** not bat an eyelid

cigno *m* swan

cigolare *v/i* ⟨1l⟩ squeak

cigolio *m* squeak

Cile *m* Chile

cilecca *f*: ***far ~*** *di arma da fuoco* misfire

cileno I *adj* Chilean **II** *m*, **-a** *f* Chilean

cilicio *m* ⟨*pl* -ci⟩ hair shirt

ciliegia *f* ⟨*pl* -ge⟩ cherry

ciliegina *f* glacé cherry; ***questa è la ~ sulla torta*** this is the cherry on the cake

ciliegio *m* ⟨*pl* -gi⟩ cherry (tree)

cilindrata *f* TECH cubic capacity; ***automobile*** *f* ***di media ~*** middle of the range car

cilindrico *adj* ⟨*mpl* -ci⟩ cylindrical

cilindro *m* cylinder; *cappello* top hat

cima *f* top; ***in ~*** at the top; ***in ~ a*** at the top of; ***in ~ all'armadio*** on top of the wardrobe; ***da ~ a fondo*** from top to bottom; *fig* from beginning to end; ***non è una ~*** he's no Einstein

cimbro I *adj* Cimbrian **II** *m*, **-a** *f* Cimbrian

cimentarsi *v/r* ⟨1l⟩: ***~ in*** embark on

cimice *f* bug; *dei letti* bed bug; (*puntina da disegno*) drawing-pin

cimiero *m* crest

ciminiera *f* smokestack; ***fumare come una ~*** smoke like a chimney

cimitero *m* cemetery

cimosa *f* blackboard duster *or US* eraser

cimurro *m* distemper

Cina *f* China

cinciallegra *f* great tit

cincilla, cincillà *f* chinchilla

cin cin! *int infml* cheers

cincischiare ⟨1g⟩ **I** *v/t* (*sgualcire*) crumple; *fig* ***~ le parole*** mumble **II** *v/i infml* mess about

cineamatore *m* video enthusiast

cineasta *m/f* ⟨*mpl* -i⟩ film-maker, *US* movie-maker **cinefilo** *m*, **-a** *f* film buff, *US* movie buff

cineforum *m* ⟨*pl* cineforum⟩ *film followed by a discussion*; *club* film club

cinema *m* ⟨*pl* cinema⟩ cinema, *US luogo* movie theater; ***~ all'aperto*** open-air cinema *or US* movie theater; ***~ d'essai*** experimental cinema; *luogo* art cinema, art house; ***~ muto*** silent films *or US* movies; ***andare al ~*** go to the cinema *or US* movies

cinemascope *m* ⟨*pl* cinemascope⟩ cinemascope

cinematografare *v/t* ⟨1n & c⟩ film

cinematografia *f* cinematography; *industria* film *or* movie industry

cinematografico *adj* ⟨*mpl* -ci⟩ film *attr*, movie *attr*

cinematografo *m* cinema, *US* movie theater

cineoperatore *m*, **-trice** *f* cameraman, *donna* camerawoman

cinepresa *f* cine camera

cineraria *f* BOT cineraria

cinerario *adj* ⟨*mpl* -ri⟩ funerary; ***urna*** *f* ***-a*** funerary urn

cinese *m/f & adj* Chinese

cineteca *f* film library

cinetica *f* ⟨*pl* -che⟩ kinetics *sg*

cinetico *adj* ⟨*mpl* -ci⟩ kinetic; ***energia*** *f* ***-a*** kinetic energy

cingalese I *adj* Sinhalese **II** *m/f* Sinhalese

cingere *v/t* ⟨3d⟩ (*circondare*) surround; ***~ d'assedio*** besiege

cinghia *f* strap; (*cintura*) belt; ***stringere*** *or* ***tirare la ~*** tighten one's belt

cinghiale *m* wild boar; ***pelle*** *f* ***di ~*** pigskin

cingolato I *adj* tracked **II** *n*: ***cingolato*** *m* tracked vehicle

cinguettare *v/i* ⟨1a⟩ twitter

cinguettio *m* twittering

cinico ⟨*mpl* -ci⟩ **I** *adj* cynical **II** *m*, **-a** *f* cynic

ciniglia *f* chenille

cinismo *m* cynicism

cinodromo *m* dogtrack **cinofilo I** *adj* dog-loving; ***pattuglia*** *f* ***-a*** canine unit **II** *m* dog lover

cinquanta *num* fifty; ***gli anni Cinquanta*** the Fifties

cinquantenario *m* fiftieth anniversary

cinquantenne *m/f* 50-year-old

cinquantesimo *m/adj* fiftieth

cinquantina *f*: ***una ~ di*** about 50; ***essere sulla ~*** be about 50 (years old)

cinque *num* five; ***alle ~*** at five (o'clock); ***siamo in ~*** there are five of us; ***ha ~ anni*** she's five (years old); ***il ~ dicembre*** the fifth of December

cinquecentesco *adj* ⟨*mpl* -schi⟩

sixteenth-century
cinquecento I *num* five hundred **II** *m*: ***il Cinquecento*** the sixteenth century
cinquemila *num* five thousand
cinquina *f lotto* set of five winning numbers; *tombola* row of five
cinta *f*: ***~ muraria*** city walls *pl*; ***muro di ~*** perimeter wall
cintare *v/t* ⟨1a⟩ enclose
cinto *past part* → ***cingere***
cintura *f* belt; (*vita*) waist; *fig* ***~ industriale*** industrial belt; ***~ nera*** SPORTS black belt; ***~ di salvataggio*** lifebelt; ***~ di sicurezza*** seat belt
cinturino *m* strap
ciò *pron* (*questo*) this; (*quello*) that; ***~ che*** what; ***con tutto ~*** even so, in spite of all that; ***~ nonostante*** nevertheless
ciocca *f* ⟨*pl* -cche⟩ *di capelli* lock
cioccolata *f* chocolate; ***~ calda*** hot chocolate
cioccolatino *m* chocolate
cioccolato *m* chocolate; ***~ al latte / fondente*** milk / dark *or* plain chocolate
ciociaro I *adj* of Ciociaria; *persona* from Ciociaria **II** *m*, **-a** *f* person from Ciociaria
cioè *cj* that is, i. e.
ciondolare *v/i* ⟨1l⟩ dangle; *fig* hang about
ciondolo *m* pendant
ciondoloni *adv* dangling; ***con le gambe*** *fpl* ***~*** with legs dangling
ciononostante *adv* → ***ciò***
ciotola *f* bowl
ciottolato *m* cobbled
ciottolo *m* pebble
cipiglio *m* ⟨*pl* -gli⟩ frown
cipolla *f* onion; *di pianta* bulb
cipollina *f* small onion; ***erba*** *f* ***~*** chives *pl*
cippo *m* stone monument; ***~ funerario*** headstone
cipputi *m* ⟨*pl* cipputi⟩ *cartoon figure of a typical engineering worker*
cipresso *m* cypress (tree)
cipria *f* (face) powder; ***darsi la ~*** powder one's face
cipriota I *adj inv* Cypriot **II** *m/f* ⟨*mpl* -i⟩ Cypriot
Cipro *m* Cyprus
circa I *adv* (round) about; ***eravamo ~ dieci*** there were about ten of us; ***le tre e mezzo ~*** about half past three **II** *prep* about
circense *adj relating to the Roman circus*
circo *m* ⟨*pl* -chi⟩ circus
circolare I *v/i* ⟨1l⟩ circulate; *di persone* move along; ***le auto non possono ~*** it's impossible to drive; ***l'autobus non circola di notte*** the bus doesn't run at night **II** *adj* circular **III** *f lettera* circular
circolatorio *adj* ⟨*mpl* -ri⟩ circulatory; ***disturbi*** *mpl* ***-i*** circulatory problems
circolazione *f* traffic; MED circulation; ***divieto*** *m* ***di ~*** no vehicle access; JUR ***libera ~*** freedom of movement; ***~ del sangue*** blood circulation; ***mettere in ~*** *voci* spread; ***ritirare dalla ~*** withdraw from circulation; ***sparire dalla ~*** drop out of circulation
circolo *m* circle; (*club*) club; ***~ polare*** polar circle; ***~ vizioso*** vicious circle
circoncisione *f* circumcision
circonciso *adj* circumcized
circondare *v/t* ⟨1a⟩ surround
circondarsi *v/r* ⟨1a⟩ surround oneself; ***~ di amici*** surround oneself with friends
circonferenza *f* circumference
circonflesso *adj* circumflex; ***accento*** *m* ***~*** circumflex
circonvallazione *f* ring road
circonvenzione *f* circumvention; ***~ di incapace*** JUR *offence of inducing a minor or legally incapacitated person to act against their own interests*
circoscritto *adj* (*limitato*) circumscribed
circoscrivere *v/t* ⟨3tt⟩ circumscribe
circoscrizione *f* area, district; ***~ elettorale*** constituency
circospetto *adj* circumspect
circospezione *f* circumspection
circostante *adj* surrounding
circostanza *f* circumstance; (*occasione*) occasion; ***frasi*** *fpl* ***di ~*** conventional phrases
circuire *v/t* ⟨4d⟩ *fig* take in
circuito *m* SPORTS (*percorso*) track; ELEC circuit; ***~ chiuso*** closed circuit; ELEC ***corto ~*** short circuit
cirillico ⟨*mpl* -ci⟩ **I** *adj* Cyrillic **II** *m* (*alfabeto*) Cyrillic
cirro *m* METEO cirrus
cirrosi *f* cirrhosis; ***~ epatica*** cirrhosis

(of the liver)

Cisgiordania *f* West Bank

CISL *abbr* (= **Confederazione Italiana Sindacati Lavoratori**) *Italian trade union organization*

cispa *f* sleepy **cisposo** *adj*: ***occhio*** *m* ~ eye with sleep in it

cisterc(i)ense *m* Cistercian

cisterna *f* cistern; (*serbatoio*) tank; ***nave*** *f* ~ tanker

cisti *f* ANAT cyst

cistifellea *f* gall bladder

cistite *f* cystitis

CIT *abbr* (= **Compagnia Italiana del Turismo**) *Italian Tourist Board*

citare *v/t* ⟨1a⟩ quote; *come esempio* cite, quote; JUR *testimone* summons; *in giudizio* sue

citazione *f* quotation, quote; JUR summons *sg*

citofono *m* Entryphone®; *in uffici* intercom

citologia *f* cytology **citoplasma** *m* ⟨*pl* -i⟩ cytoplasm

citrato *m* citrate **citrico** *adj* ⟨*mpl* -ci⟩: ***acido*** *m* ~ citric acid **citronella** *f* citronella

citrullo *m*, **-a** *f* idiot

città *f* ⟨*pl* città⟩ **1.** town; *grande* city; ~ ***d'arte*** town of artistic interest; ~ ***dormitorio*** dormitory town; ***la ~ eterna*** the Eternal City; ~ ***giardino*** garden city; ~ ***universitaria*** university town (*in the provinces*); ***la ~ vecchia*** the old (part of) town **2.** ***Città del Capo*** Cape Town; ***Città del Messico*** Mexico City; ***Città del Vaticano*** Vatican City

cittadina *f* (small) town

cittadinanza *f* citizenship; (*popolazione*) citizens *pl*; ~ ***onoraria*** freedom of the city

cittadino I *m*, **-a** *f* citizen; (*abitante di città*) city dweller **II** *adj* town *attr*, city *attr*

ciucciare *v/t and v/i* ⟨1f⟩ *infml* suck; *neonato* suckle **ciucciarsi** *v/r* ⟨1f⟩ suck; ~ ***il dito*** suck one's thumb

ciuccio *m infml* (*succhiotto*) dummy, *US* pacifier

ciuco *m* ⟨*pl* -chi⟩ ass

ciuffo *m* tuft

civetta *f* ZOOL (little) owl; *fig* ***far la*** ~ flirt; ***auto*** *f* ~ unmarked police car

civettare *v/i* ⟨1a⟩ flirt **civetteria** *f* flirtatiousness **civettuolo** *adj* flirtatious

civico *adj* ⟨*mpl* -ci⟩ (*della città*) municipal, town *attr*; *delle persone* civic; ***educazione*** *f* **-a** civics *sg*; ***numero*** *m* ~ (street) number

civile I *adj* civil; *civilizzato* civilized; (*non militare*) civilian; ***autorità*** *fpl* **-i** civil authorities; ***diritti*** *mpl* **-i** civil liberties; ***guerra*** *f* ~ civil war; ***matrimonio*** *m* ~ civil marriage; ***persona*** *f* ~ civilised person; ***servizio*** *m* ~ community service; ***società*** *f* ~ civil society; ***stato*** *m* ~ marital status; ***tribunale*** *m* ~ civil court **II** *m* civilian

civilista *m/f* ⟨*mpl* -i⟩ civil lawyer **civilistico** *adj* ⟨*mpl* -ci⟩ civil law *attr*

civilizzare *v/t* ⟨1a⟩ civilize

civilizzazione *f* civilization

civilmente *adv* civilly

civiltà *f* ⟨*pl* civiltà⟩ civilization; (*cortesia*) civility

CL *abbr* **1.** (= **Caltanissetta**) Caltanissetta **2.** (= **Comunione e Liberazione**) *Roman Catholic lay movement*

clacson *m* ⟨*pl* clacson⟩ horn; ***suonare il*** ~ sound one's horn

clamore *m* (*scalpore*) uproar; (*rumore*) din; ***suscitare*** ~ cause a sensation

clamoroso *adj fig* sensational

clan *m* ⟨*pl* clan⟩ clan; (*cricca*) clique; ~ ***mafioso*** Mafia clan

clandestinità *f* secrecy; ***vivere nella*** ~ be in hiding

clandestino I *adj* clandestine; (*illegale*) illegal; ***organizzazione*** *f* **-a** secret organization **II** *m*, **-a** *f* stowaway

clarinettista *m/f* ⟨*mpl* -i⟩ clarinettist

clarinetto *m* clarinet

classe *f* class; (*aula*) classroom; ~ ***operaia*** working class; ~ ***turistica*** tourist class; ***viaggiare in prima*** ~ travel first class; ***che ~ fai?*** what class are you in?; ***eravamo in ~ insieme*** we were in the same class at school; ***di*** ~ classy

classicismo *m* classicism

classico ⟨*mpl* -ci⟩ **I** *adj* classical; (*tipico*) classic **II** *m* classic

classifica *f* classification; (*elenco*) list; *sportiva* league standings, league table; *musicale* charts *pl*

classificare *v/t* ⟨1m & d⟩ classify

classificarsi *v/r* be placed; ***si sono classificati secondi*** they came second; ***non si è classificato per i mondiali*** he didn't qualify for the world

championships
classificatore *m* (*cartella*) folder; *mobile* filing cabinet, *US* file cabinet
classificazione *f di animali* classification; *di studenti* marking, *US* grading; *~ **delle spese*** classification of expenses
classismo *m* class consciousness
classista *adj inv* class-conscious; ***società** f* ~ class-based society
claudicante *adj* limping
clausola *f* clause; (*riserva*) proviso; ***-e** pl **d'uso*** JUR conditions of use
claustrofobia *f* claustrophobia
claustrofobico *adj* ⟨*mpl* -ci⟩ claustrophobic
clausura *f* seclusion; ***monaca** f **di*** ~ nun belonging to an enclosed order
clava *f* club
clavicembalista *m/f* ⟨*mpl* -i⟩ harpsichordist
clavicembalo *m* harpsichord
clavicola *f* collar-bone, clavicle
clemente *adj* merciful; *tempo* mild
clemenza *f* clemency; *di tempo* mildness
cleptomane *m/f* kleptomaniac
cleptomania *f* kleptomania
clericale *adj* clerical
clero *m* clergy
clessidra *f* hourglass
clic *m* ⟨*pl* clic⟩ click; ***mediante*** ~ by clicking; ***fare doppio*** ~ **(*su qc*)** double-click (on sth)
cliccare *v/i* ⟨1d⟩ COMPUT click (***su*** on)
cliché *m* ⟨*pl* cliché⟩ *fig* cliché
cliente *m/f* customer; *di professionista* client; *di albergo* guest; MED patient; *~ **abituale*** regular; ***assistenza -i*** customer service
clientela *f* customers *pl*, clientele; *di professionista* clients *pl*; *di medico* patients *pl*; *~ **abituale*** patrons *pl*, regular customers *pl*
clientelare *adj* patronage-based **clientelismo** *m practice of giving jobs etc. in return for favours*
clima *m* ⟨*pl* -i⟩ climate
climaterio *m* ⟨*pl* -ri⟩ menopause
climatico *adj* ⟨*mpl* -ci⟩ climate *attr*, climatic; ***stazione** f **climatica*** health resort
climatizzatore *m* air-conditioning unit
climatizzazione *f* air conditioning
clinica *f* ⟨*pl* -che⟩ (*ospedale*) clinic; (*casa di cura*) nursing home; *~ **medica*** clinical medicine
clinicamente *adv* clinically; *~ **morto*** clinically dead
clinico ⟨*mpl* -ci⟩ **I** *adj* clinical; ***quadro** m* ~ case history; *fig **avere l'occhio*** ~ have an expert eye **II** *m* clinician
clip *m* ⟨*pl* clip⟩ clip
clistere *m* enema
clitoride *m or f* clitoris
cloaca *f* ⟨*pl* -che⟩ sewer; *fig* cesspit
cloche *f* ⟨*pl* cloche⟩ AVIAT joystick; AUTO gear stick, *US* shift stick
clonare *v/t* ⟨1a⟩ BIOL clone
clonazione *f* cloning
clone *m* clone
cloridrico *adj* ⟨*mpl* -ci⟩: ***acido** m* ~ hydrochloric acid
cloro *m* chlorine
clorofilla *f* chlorophyl(l)
clorofluorocarburo *m* chlorofluorocarbon
cloroformio *m* chloroform
cloruro *m* chloride
club *m* ⟨*pl* club⟩ club
cm *abbr* (= **centimetro**) cm (centimetre)
c.m. *abbr* (= **corrente mese**) of this month, inst. (instant)
CN *abbr* (= **Cuneo**) Cuneo
CNR *abbr* (= **Consiglio Nazionale delle Ricerche**) *Italian National Research Council*
CO *abbr* (= **Como**) Como
coabitare *v/i* ⟨1m⟩ share a flat (*US* an apartment), be flatmates (*US* roommates)
coabitazione *f* flat sharing, *US* apartment sharing
coadiuvare *v/t* ⟨1m⟩: *~ **qn*** cooperate with s.o.
coagulante I *adj* coagulative **II** *m* coagulant
coagularsi *v/r* ⟨1m⟩ *di sangue* coagulate, clot; *di latte* curdle
coalizione *f* coalition; ***governo** m **di*** ~ coalition government
coalizzare *v/t* ⟨1a⟩ unite in a coalition
coalizzarsi *v/r* ⟨1a⟩ join forces; POL form a coalition
coassiale *adj* coaxial; ***cavo** m* ~ coaxial cable
coatto *adj* forced
coautore *m*, **-trice** *f* co-author
cobalto *m* CHEM cobalt

CoBas *abbr* (= **Comitato di Base**) *trade union organizations*
cobra *m* ⟨*pl* cobra⟩ cobra
coca *f* ⟨*pl* -che⟩ *infml* **1.** *bevanda* Coke® **2.** *cocaina* coke
cocaina *f* cocaine
cocainomane I *adj* addicted to cocaine **II** *m/f* cocaine addict
coccarda *f* cockade
cocchiere *m*, **-a** *f* coachman **cocchio** *m* ⟨*pl* -cchi⟩ coach
coccige *m* ANAT coccyx
coccinella *f* ladybird, *US* ladybug
coccio *m* ⟨*pl* -cci⟩ earthenware; *frammento* fragment (of pottery), shard
cocciutaggine *f* stubbornness
cocciutamente *adv* stubbornly
cocciuto *adj* stubborn, obstinate
cocco[1] *m* ⟨*pl* -cchi⟩ (*albero*) coconut palm *or* tree; ***noce** f **di** ~* coconut
cocco[2] *m*, **-a** *f* ⟨*mpl* -cchi⟩ (*persona prediletta*) darling; *~ **di mamma*** *hum* mummy's boy *or* girl
coccodè *int*: ***fare** ~* cluck
coccodrillo *m* crocodile; *giornale* pre-obit; ***versare lacrime** fpl **di** ~* shed crocodile tears
coccola *f infml* cuddle; ***fare le -e a qn*** cuddle s.o.
coccolare *v/t* ⟨1l & c⟩ *infml* cuddle; (*viziare*) spoil
coccolone *m*, **-a** *f* cuddly person
coccoloni *adv*: ***stare** ~* squat on one's heels
cocente *adj* scorching; *fig* scathing
cocker *m* ⟨*pl* cocker⟩ cocker spaniel
cocktail *m* ⟨*pl* cocktail⟩ *bevanda* cocktail; *festa* cocktail party
cocomero *m* watermelon
cocorita *f* tame parrot
cocuzzolo *m di montagna*: peak
coda *f* **1.** tail; *~ (**di cavallo**)* *pettinatura* ponytail; ***pianoforte** m **a** ~* grand piano **2.** (*fila*) queue, *US* line; ***fare la** ~* queue (up), *US* stand in line; *~ **di stampa*** COMPUT print queue **3.** *di veicolo, treno* rear **4.** MUS coda **5.** *fig ~ **di paglia*** guilty conscience; ***con la** ~ **dell'occhio*** out of the corner of one's eye
codardia *f* cowardice; (*atto*) act of cowardice
codardo I *adj* cowardly **II** *m*, **-a** *f* coward
codazzo *m* swarm
codeina *f* codeine
codesto I *adj* that **II** *pron* that one
codice *m* code; (*libro*) codex; *~ **alfanumerico*** alphanumeric code; *~ **di avviamento postale*** post code, *US* zip code; *~ **a barre*** bar code; *~ **civile*** civil code; *~ **fiscale*** tax code; *~ **penale*** penal code; *~ **di procedura civile*** code of civil procedure; *~ **di procedura penale*** code of criminal procedure; *~ **della strada*** Highway Code; ***in** ~* in code
codicillo *m* codicil
codificare *v/t* ⟨1m & d⟩ *dati* encode; JUR codify
codificatore I *m*, **-trice** *f* coder **II** *m* coder **codificazione** *f* codification
codino *m* pigtail, plait
coefficiente *m* coefficient
coercitivo *adj* coercive; ***misure** fpl **-e*** coercive measures
coerede *m/f* joint heir
coerente *adj* coherent; *fig* consistent
coerentemente *adv* coherently; *fig* consistently
coerenza *f* coherence; *fig* consistency
coesione *f* cohesion
coesistenza *f* coexistence
coetaneo I *adj* the same age (***di*** as) **II** *m*, **-a** *f* contemporary, person of the same age
cofanetto *m* casket
cofano *m* AUTO bonnet, *US* hood
cogestione *f* joint management; *~ **aziendale*** worker participation
cogliere *v/t* ⟨3ss⟩ pick; (*raccogliere*) gather; (*afferrare*) seize; *occasione* take, seize, jump at; (*capire*) grasp; *~ **il senso di qc*** grasp the meaning of sth; *~ **di sorpresa*** catch unawares, take by surprise; *~ **sul fatto*** catch in the act, catch red-handed
coglione *m vulg* ***-i*** balls; (*persona*) dickhead; *fig **rompere i -i a qn*** *vulg* get on s.o.'s tits
cognac® *m* ⟨*pl* cognac®⟩ cognac®
cognato *m*, **-a** *f* brother-in-law; *donna* sister-in-law
cognizione *f* knowledge; PHIL cognition; ***parla con** ~ **di causa*** he knows what he's talking about
cognome *m* surname; ***nome** m **e** ~* full name; *~ **da ragazza*** maiden name
coi = *prep* **con** *and art* **i**
coibentazione *f* insulation

coincidenza *f* coincidence; RAIL connection; **~ *di opinioni*** agreement; ***perdere la ~*** miss one's connection; ***per pura ~*** by pure coincidence
coincidere *v/i* ⟨3q⟩ coincide
coinquilino *m*, **-a** *f in condominio* fellow tenant; *in appartamento* flatmate, *US* roommate
coinvolgente *adj* absorbing
coinvolgere *v/t* ⟨3d⟩ involve (***in*** in)
coinvolgimento *m* involvement
coinvolto *past part* → ***coinvolgere***
coito *m* coitus
coke *m* ⟨*pl* coke⟩ coke
col = *prep* ***con*** *and art* ***il***
colabrodo *m* ⟨*pl* colabrodo⟩ strainer
colapasta *m* ⟨*pl* colapasta⟩ colander
colare ⟨1a⟩ **I** *v/t* strain; *pasta* drain **II** *v/i* drip; (*perdere*) leak; *di naso* run; *di cera* melt; **~ *a fondo*** *or* ***a picco*** sink, go down
colata *f di metallo* casting; *di lava* flow
colazione *f prima* breakfast; *di mezzogiorno* lunch; **~ *al sacco*** picnic; **~ *di lavoro*** working lunch; ***fare ~*** have breakfast, breakfast
colbacco *m* ⟨*pl* -cchi⟩ cossack hat
colecisti → ***cistifellea***
colei *pron f* the one; **~ *che*** the one that
coleottero *m* coleopteran
colera *m* cholera
colesterolo *m* cholesterol; ***avere il ~ alto*** have a high level of cholesterol
colf *f* ⟨*pl* colf⟩ home help
colibrì *m* ⟨*pl* colibrì⟩ hummingbird
colica *f* ⟨*pl* -che⟩ colic
colino *m* strainer
colla *f* glue; *di farina* paste; **~ *di pesce*** isinglass
collaborare *v/i* ⟨1m⟩ co-operate, collaborate; *con giornale* contribute
collaboratore *m*, **-trice** *f* collaborator; *di giornale* contributor; ***collaboratore*** *m* ***esterno*** freelance(r); **-trice** *f*: ***domestica*** home help
collaborazione *f* co-operation, collaboration
collaborazionismo *m* collaboration
collaborazionista *m/f* ⟨*mpl* -i⟩ collaborator
collage *m* ⟨*pl* collage⟩ collage
collagene *m* collagen
collana *f* necklace; *di libri* series *sg*
collant *m* ⟨*pl* collant⟩ tights *pl*, *US* pantyhose
collante **I** *adj* adhesive **II** *m* glue
collare *m* collar
collassare *v/i* ⟨1a⟩ collapse (*a.* ASTR, *fig*)
collasso *m* collapse; **~ *cardiaco*** heart failure
collaterale *adj* collateral; ***danni*** *pl* ***-i*** collateral damage *sg*; ***effetti*** *mpl* ***-i*** side effects
collaudare *v/t* ⟨1a⟩ test; *fig* put to the test
collaudato *adj* tested **collaudatore** *m*, **-trice** *f* tester; **~ *di aerei*** test pilot
collaudo *m* test
colle *m* hill; (*valico*) pass
collega *m/f* ⟨*mpl* -ghi⟩ colleague, co-worker
collegamento *m* connection; MIL liaison; RADIO, TV link; **~ *aereo* / *ferroviario*** connecting flight / train; **~ *ipertestuale*** hyperlink
collegare *v/t* ⟨1a⟩ connect, link
collegarsi *v/r* RADIO, TV link up; **~ *ad Internet*** connect to the Internet
collegiale **I** *adj* collective **II** *m/f* boarder
collegialità *f* ⟨*pl* collegialità⟩ collective nature
collegio *m* ⟨*pl* -gi⟩ boarding school; **~ *elettorale*** constituency
collera *f* anger; ***andare in ~*** get angry; ***essere in ~ con qn*** be angry with s.o.
collerico *adj* ⟨*mpl* -ci⟩ irascible
colletta *f* collection; ***fare una ~*** have a collection
collettame *m* packages
collettivamente *adj* collectively **collettivismo** *m* collectivism
collettività *f* ⟨*pl* collettività⟩ community
collettivo *m/adj* collective
colletto *m* collar; ***-i*** *pl* ***bianchi*** white-collar workers; ***-i*** *pl* ***blu*** blue-collar workers
collettore *m* MECH, ELEC manifold; **~ *solare*** solar collector
collezionare *v/t* ⟨1a⟩ collect
collezione *f* collection; ***fare ~ di qc*** collect sth, make a collection of sth
collezionista *m/f* ⟨*mpl* -i⟩ collector; **~ *di francobolli*** stamp collector
collidere *v/i* ⟨3q⟩ collide
collier *m* ⟨*pl* collier⟩ necklace; **~ *di diamanti*** diamond necklace
collimare *v/i* ⟨1a⟩ correspond; *idee*

agree
collina *f* hill
collinare *adj* hilly; ***paesaggio*** *m* **~** hilly landscape
collinoso *adj* hilly
collirio *m* eyewash
collisione *f* collision; ***entrare in* ~** collide
collo *m* neck; (*bagaglio*) piece *or* item of luggage; (*pacco*) package; ***a* ~ *alto*** high-necked; **~ *del piede*** instep; *fig* ***arrivare tra capo e* ~** happen unexpectedly; ***fino al* ~** up to one's neck; *fig* ***essere nei guai fino al* ~** be in deep trouble; ***gettare le braccia al* ~ *a qn*** throw one's arms around s.o.'s neck; ***rompersi l'osso del* ~** break one's neck; ***a rotta di* ~** at breakneck speed
collocamento *m* placing; (*impiego*) employment; ***agenzia*** *f* ***di* ~** employment agency; ***ufficio*** *m* ***di* ~** Jobcentre
collocare *v/t* ⟨1l & d⟩ place, put; **~ *a riposo*** retire
collocarsi *v/r* ⟨1l & d⟩ be placed
collocazione *f* place, job
colloquiale *adj* colloquial; ***linguaggio*** *m* **~** colloquial language
colloquio *m* ⟨*pl* -qui⟩ talk, conversation; *ufficiale* interview; (*esame*) oral (exam); **~ *di lavoro*** job interview
collottola *f* nape of the neck
collusione *f* collusion; **~ *con la concorrenza*** price fixing; ***reato*** *m* ***di* ~** JUR collusion
colluso *adj guilty of collusion*; **~ *con la mafia*** *guilty of collusion with the Mafia*
colluttazione *f* scuffle
colmare *v/t* ⟨1a⟩ fill (***di*** with); **~ *di attenzioni*** overwhelm with kindness; **~ *una lacuna*** *or* ***un vuoto*** fill a gap
colmo I *adj* full (***di*** of) **II** *m* summit, top; *fig* (*culmine*) height; ***è il* ~!** that's the last straw!
colomba *f* ZOOL, *fig* dove; ***la* ~ *della pace*** the dove of peace
Colombia *f* Colombia
colombo *m* pigeon
colon *m* colon
colonia *f* colony; *per bambini* holiday camp; **~ *marina*** seaside holiday camp
Colonia *f*: ***acqua*** *f* ***di* ~** eau de Cologne
coloniale *adj* colonial
colonialismo *m* colonialism **colonialistico** *adj* ⟨*mpl* -ci⟩ colonialist
colonico *adj* ⟨*mpl* -ci⟩: ***casa*** *f* ***-a*** farmhouse
colonizzare *v/t* ⟨1a⟩ colonize
colonizzatore *m*, **-trice** *f* colonizer
colonizzazione *f* colonization
colonna *f* column; *di veicoli* line; *fig* mainstay; **~ *sonora*** sound track; **~ *vertebrale*** spinal column; ***-e*** *pl* ***d'Ercole*** pillars of Hercules; ***a due*/*tre -e*** in two/three columns; ***mettere in* ~** put into columns
colonnato *m* colonnade
colonnello *m* colonel
colonnina *f della benzina* petrol (*US* gas) pump
colono *m*, **-a** *f liter* farmer; *hist* colonist
colonscopia *f* colonoscopy
colorante *m* dye; ***senza -i*** with no artificial colo(u)rings
colorare *v/t* ⟨1a⟩ colo(u)r; *disegno* colo(u)r in
colorarsi *v/r* ⟨1a⟩ **~ *di rosso*** turn red
colorato *adj* colo(u)red
colorazione *f* colo(u)ring
colore *m* colo(u)r; *carte* suit; *poker* flush; **~ *primario*** primary colo(u)r; ***di che* ~ *è?*** what colo(u)r is it?; *fig* **~ *politico*** political hue; ***gente*** *f* ***di* ~** people of colo(u)r; ***scatola*** *f* ***dei -i*** paint box; **~ *a olio*** oil (paint); ***a -i*** *film*, *televisione* colo(u)r *attr*; ***farne di tutti i -i*** get up to all sorts of mischief
colorire *v/t* ⟨4d⟩ colo(u)r (*a. fig*)
colorito I *adj volto* rosy-cheeked; *fig* (*vivace*) colo(u)rful **II** *m* complexion
coloro *pron pl* the ones; **~ *che*** those who
colossale *adj* colossal
Colosseo *m* Coliseum
colosso *m* colossus
colostomia *f* MED colostomy
colpa *f* fault; REL sin; ***dare a qn la* ~ *di qc*** blame s.o. for sth; ***non è* ~ *sua*** it's not her fault; ***per* ~ *tua*** because of you; ***senso*** *m* ***di* ~** sense of guilt; ***sentirsi in* ~** feel guilty
colpevole I *adj* guilty; ***essere* ~ *di qc*** be guilty of sth **II** *m/f* culprit, guilty party
colpevolezza *f* guilt **colpevolizzare** *v/t* ⟨1a⟩; **~ *qn di qc*** make s.o. feel

guilty for sth **colpevolizzarsi** *v/r* ⟨1a⟩ feel guilty

colpire *v/t* ⟨4d⟩ **1.** hit, strike; **~ qn / qc in pieno** hit s.o. / sth right in the middle; **~ nel segno** hit the nail on the head; **~ qn / qc di striscio** graze s.o. / sth **2.** *fig* impress, leave an impression on; ***rimanere colpito da qn / qc*** be struck with s.o. / sth

colpo *m* **1.** blow; **~ basso** blow below the belt; **~ di fortuna** stroke of luck; **~ di fulmine** coup de foudre; **~ di scena** sudden turn of events; **~ di stato** coup d'état; **~ di testa** whim; ***al primo ~*** at the first attempt; ***andare a ~ sicuro*** be sure of success; ***fare ~*** make an impact; ***fare ~ su qn*** *infml* be a hit with s.o.; ***subire un duro ~*** suffer a heavy blow; ***sul ~, di ~*** suddenly; ***(tutto) di (un) ~*** suddenly **2.** *fig* blow, shock **3.** *di pistola* shot; **~ di grazia** coup de grâce **4.** MED stroke; **~ apoplettico** apoplectic fit; **~ di calore** heat stroke; **~ di sole** sunstroke; **~ della strega** *infml* back strain; ***gli è preso*** *or* ***venuto un ~*** *infml* he had a fit **5.** **~ di telefono** phone call **6.** **~ in banca** bank raid

coltellata *f ferita* stab wound

coltellino *m* small knife; *da portarsi al campeggio* penknife

coltello *m* knife; **~ a serramanico** jackknife; ***avere il ~ dalla parte del manico*** have the whip hand

coltivare *v/t* ⟨1a⟩ AGR, *fig* cultivate; **~ le amicizie** nurture one's friendships

coltivatore *m*, **-trice** *f* farmer

coltivazione *f* cultivation; *di prodotti agricoli e piante* growing; *campi coltivati* crops *pl*

colto[1] *adj* cultured, learned

colto[2] *past part* → **cogliere**

coltre *f* blanket; *fig* **~ di neve** blanket of snow

coltura *f* growing; *piante* crop; **~ batterica** bacterial culture; **~ intensiva** intensive farming

colui *pron m* the one; **~ che** the one that

colza *f* rape; ***olio*** *m* ***di ~*** rapeseed oil

coma *m* coma; ***essere in ~*** be in a coma; **~ farmaceutico** sedation; **~ irreversibile** irreversible coma; **~ profondo** deep coma; **~ vigile** persistent vegetative state

comandamento *m* commandment

comandante *m* commander; AVIAT, NAUT captain; **~ in capo** commander in chief

comandare ⟨1a⟩ **I** *v/t* (*ordinare*) order, command; *esercito* command; *nave* captain, be captain of; FIN *merci* order; TECH control; **~ a distanza** operate by remote control **II** *v/i* be in charge

comando *m* order, command; TECH control; **~ a distanza** remote control; **~ vocale** TEL voice-operated remote control

comasco **I** *adj* ⟨*mpl* -chi⟩ of Como; *persona* from Como **II** *m*, **-a** *f* person from Como

comatoso *adj* comatose; ***stato*** *m* **~** comatose state

combaciare *v/i* ⟨1f⟩ fit together; *fig* correspond

combattente *m* soldier, serviceman

combattere *v/t & v/i* ⟨3a⟩ fight

combattimento *m* fight; SPORTS match, fight; ***mettere qn fuori ~*** put s.o. out of action

combattività *f* ⟨*pl* combattività⟩ fighting spirit **combattivo** *adj* combative; SPORTS aggressive

combattuto *adj* SPORTS hard-fought; *fig* torn; ***essere ~ fra due alternative*** be torn between two alternatives

combinare *v/t* ⟨1a⟩ combine; (*organizzare*) arrange; **~ un guaio** make a mess; ***oggi ho combinato poco*** I got very little done today

combinarsi *v/r* go well together

combinata *f* SPORTS combined; **~ nordica** Nordic combined

combinato *adj* combined; (*organizzato*) arranged; ***partita*** *f* **-a** rigged match

combinazione *f* combination; (*coincidenza*) coincidence; ***per ~*** by chance

combriccola *f* gang

combustibile **I** *adj* combustible **II** *m* fuel

combustione *f* combustion

combutta *f*: ***essere in ~ con qn*** be in league with s.o.

come **I** *adv* as; (*in modo simile o uguale*) like; *interrogativo, esclamativo* how; (*prego?*) pardon?; ***fa' ~ ti ho detto*** do as I told you; ***fate ~ volete*** do what you like; ***lavora ~ inseg-***

nante he works as a teacher; ***~ me*** like me; ***un cappello ~ il mio*** a hat like mine; ***è alto ~ te*** he's as tall as you; ***bianco ~ la neve*** as white as snow; ***~ sta?*** how are you?, how are things?; ***~, scusi?*** sorry, what?; ***~ ti chiami?*** what's your name?; ***com'è bello!*** how nice it is!; ***~ mai?*** how come?, why?; ***ora ~ faccio?*** now what do I do?; ***oggi ~ oggi*** nowadays; ***~ al solito*** *or* ***sempre*** as usual; ***~ no!*** of course!; ***~ d'accordo*** as agreed; ***~ non detto*** never mind **II** *cj* (*come se*) as if, as though; (*appena*, *quando*) as (soon as); ***~ se niente fosse*** as if nothing had happened

comedone *m* blackhead

cometa *f* comet

comfort *m* ⟨*pl* comfort⟩ comfort; ***dotato di tutti i ~ moderni*** with all mod cons

comica *f* ⟨*pl* -che⟩ comic silent film

comicità *f* funniness

comico ⟨*mpl* -ci⟩ **I** *adj* funny, comical; *genere* comic **II** *m*, **-a** *f* comedian; *donna* comedienne

comignolo *m* chimney pot

cominciare *v/i* ⟨1f⟩ start, begin; ***~ a fare qc*** start doing sth / start to do sth; ***a ~ da oggi*** (starting) from today; ***tanto per ~*** to begin *or* start with

comitato *m* committee; ***~ direttivo*** steering committee; ***~ organizzatore*** organizing committee; ***Comitato delle regioni*** Committee of the Regions (in the EU)

comitiva *f* group, party; ***viaggiare in ~*** travel in a group; ***viaggio*** *m* ***in ~*** group travel

comizio *m* meeting; ***~ elettorale*** electoral meeting; ***fare un ~*** hold a rally

Comm. *abbr* (= **Commendatore**) *Italian title awarded for services to the country*

commando *m* commando

commedia *f* comedy; *fig* play-acting; ***~ musicale*** musical; ***era tutta una ~!*** it was all a sham!

commediante *m/f* (second-rate) actor

commediografo *m*, **-a** *f* playwright

commemorare *v/t* ⟨1m & b⟩ commemorate

commemorativo *adj* commemorative; ***monumento*** *m* ***~*** memorial

commemorazione *f* commemoration

commensale *m/f* fellow diner

commentare *v/t* ⟨1a⟩ comment on

commentatore *m*, **-trice** *f* commentator

commento *m* comment

commerciabile *adj* saleable

commerciale *adj* commercial; *relazioni*, *trattative* trade *attr*; *lettera* business *attr*

commercialista *m/f* ⟨*mpl* -i⟩ accountant

commercializzare *v/t* ⟨1a⟩ market

commercializzazione *f* marketing

commerciante *m/f* merchant; (*negoziante*) shopkeeper; ***~ al dettaglio*** retailer; ***~ all'ingrosso*** wholesaler

commerciare *v/i* ⟨1b & f⟩ deal (***in*** in)

commercio *m* ⟨*pl* -ci⟩ trade, business; *internazionale* trade; *di droga* traffic; ***~ all'ingrosso*** wholesale trade; ***~ al minuto*** retail trade; ***camera*** *f* ***di ~*** chamber of commerce; ***agente*** *m/f* ***di ~*** sales representative; ***essere in ~*** be available; *libro* be in print; ***mettere in ~ qc*** put sth on the market; ***fuori ~*** not for sale; *libro* out of print

commessa *f* (*ordinazione*) order

commesso *m*, **-a** *f* shop assistant, *US* sales clerk; (*impiegato*) clerk; ***~ viaggiatore*** travel(l)ing salesman

commestibile I *adj* edible **II** *m*: ***commestibili*** *pl* foodstuffs *pl*

commestibilità *f* ⟨*pl* commestibilità⟩ edibility

commettere *v/t* ⟨3ee⟩ commit; ***~ un delitto*** commit a crime; ***~ un errore*** make a mistake

commiato *m* leavetaking; ***prendere ~ da qn*** take one's leave of s.o.

commilitone *m* comrade in arms

comminare *v/t* ⟨1a⟩ JUR impose

commiserare *v/t* ⟨1m⟩ feel sorry for

commiserazione *f* commiseration

commissariamento *m* compulsory administration

commissariato *m*: ***~*** (***di pubblica sicurezza***) police station

commissario *m*, **-a** *f* ⟨*mpl* -ri⟩ *di polizia* (police) superintendent; *membro di commissione* commissioner; ***~ di bordo*** purser; ***~ straordinario*** *official who temporarily replaces the mayor*; ***~ tecnico*** team manager

commissionare *v/t* ⟨1a⟩ FIN commission

commissione *f* commission; (*incarico*) errand; **~ *esaminatrice*** EDU examining board; ***Commissione europea*** European Commission; **~ *d'inchiesta*** POL board of inquiry; **~ *parlamentare*** POL parliamentary commission; ***-i*** *pl* shopping *sg*; ***fare delle -i*** do some shopping; ***fatto su ~*** made to order

commisurare *v/t* ⟨1a⟩ adapt **commisurato** *adj* proportionate; (*corrispondente*) comparable

committente *m/f* commissioner

commodoro *m* NAUT commodore

commosso I *past part* → ***commuovere*** **II** *adj fig* moved, touched

commovente *adj* moving, touching

commozione *f* emotion; **~ *cerebrale*** concussion

commuovere *v/t* ⟨3ff⟩ move, touch

commuoversi *v/r* be moved *or* touched

commutare *v/t* ⟨1a⟩ commute; ELEC commutate **commutatore** *m* commutator

commutazione *f* commutation; **~ *della pena*** JUR commutation of the sentence; ***circuito*** *m* ***di ~*** ELEC commutation circuit

comò *m* ⟨*pl* comò⟩ chest of drawers

comodamente *adv* comfortably; (*facilmente*) easily

comodato *m* JUR *assignment to another person of the free use of a good for a certain period*

comodino *m* bedside table

comodità *f* ⟨*pl* comodità⟩ comfort; (*vantaggio*) convenience

comodo I *adj* comfortable; *vestito* loose, comfortable; (*facilmente raggiungibile*) easy to get to; (*utile*) useful, handy; *infml persona* laid back *infml*; ***stia ~!*** don't get up! **II** *m* comfort; ***con ~*** at one's convenience; ***far ~*** *di denaro* come in useful, be handy; ***le fa ~ così*** she finds it easier that way; ***fare il proprio ~*** do as one pleases; ***prendersela -a*** take one's time

Comore *fpl* Comoros (islands)

compact disk *m* ⟨*pl* compact disk⟩ compact disc

compaesano *m*, **-a** *f della stessa nazione* fellow countryman; *della stessa città* person from the same town

compagnia *f* company; (*gruppo*) group; REL order; **~ *aerea*** airline; **~ *di assicurazioni*** insurance company; ***far ~ a qn*** keep s.o. company

compagno *m*, **-a** *f* companion; (*convivente*), FIN partner; POL comrade; **~ *di scuola*** schoolfriend, schoolmate; **~ *di banco*** *person sitting next to you*; **~ *di stanza*** room mate; **~ *di squadra*** team mate; **~ *di viaggio*** travelling companion

companatico *m* ⟨*pl* -ci⟩ *food that can be eaten with bread*

comparabile *adj* comparable

comparativo *m/adj* comparative

comparire *v/i* ⟨4e⟩ appear; (*essere pubblicato*) come out, appear; (*far figura*) stand out

comparizione *f*: JUR ***mandato*** *m* ***di ~*** summons

comparsa *f* appearance; THEAT walk-on; *in film* extra

comparso *past part* → ***comparire***

compartecipazione *f* sharing **compartecipe** *m/f* ECON partner

compartimento *m* compartment

comparto *m* (*scomparto*) compartment; (*settore*) sector

compassato *adj* composed; (*misurato*) measured; ***modi*** *mpl* ***-i*** calm manner

compassione *f* compassion, pity; ***provare ~ per qn*** feel sorry for s.o.; ***fare ~ a qn*** move s.o. to pity

compassionevole *adj* compassionate; (*che fa compassione*) pitiful

compasso *m* (pair of) compasses *pl*

compatibile *adj* compatible

compatibilità *f* ⟨*pl* compatibilità⟩ compatibility **compatibilmente** *adv* compatibly

compatimento *m* condescension

compatire *v/t* ⟨4d⟩: **~ *qn*** feel sorry for s.o.

compatirsi *v/r* ⟨4d⟩ ***non possono ~*** they can't bear each other

compatriota *m/f* ⟨*mpl* -i⟩ compatriot

compattare *v/t* ⟨1a⟩ compact; *fig* unite; COMPUT compress **compattezza** *f* compactness; *fig* unity

compatto *adj* compact; *folla* dense; *fig* united

compendio *m* ⟨*pl* -di⟩ handbook

compenetrare *v/t* ⟨1m & b⟩ permeate (*a. fig*) **compenetrarsi** *v/r* ⟨1m & b⟩

be filled (***di*** with) **compenetrazione** *f* permeation
compensare *v/t* ⟨1b⟩ (*controbilanciare*) compensate for, make up for; (*ricompensare*) reward; (*risarcire*) pay compensation to
compensarsi *v/r* ⟨1b⟩ balance out
compensato *m* plywood
compensazione *f* compensation; FIN, ECON clearing
compenso *m* (*ricompensa, risarcimento*) compensation; (*retribuzione*) fee; ***in ~*** (*d'altra parte*) on the other hand; ***dietro ~*** for a fee
compera *f* purchase; ***fare le -e*** go shopping
competente *adj* competent; (*responsabile*) appropriate
competenza *f* (*esperienza*) competence; ***essere di ~ di qn*** be s.o.'s responsibility
competere *v/i* ⟨3a⟩ (*gareggiare*) compete; ***~ a qn / qc*** (*spettare*) be up to s.o. / sth
competitivamente *adv* competitively
competitività *f* competitiveness
competitivo *adj* competitive
competizione *f* competition; ***spirito*** *m* ***di ~*** competitiveness
compiacente *adj* too eager to please
compiacenza *f* overeagerness to please; ***fare qc per ~*** do sth as a courtesy
compiacere *v/t* ⟨2k⟩ please
compiacersi *v/r* (*provare piacere*) be pleased (***di*** with); ***mi compiaccio con te*** congratulations
compiacimento *m* satisfaction
compiaciuto *past part* → ***compiacere***
compiangere *v/t* ⟨3d⟩ pity; *per lutto* mourn
compiangersi *v/r* ⟨3d⟩ feel sorry for oneself
compianto *past part* → ***compiangere***
compiere *v/t* ⟨4g⟩ (*finire*) complete, finish; (*eseguire*) carry out; ***~ gli anni*** have one's birthday; ***~ il proprio dovere*** do one's duty
compiersi *v/r* (*avverarsi*) happen
compieta *f* REL compline
compilare *v/t* ⟨1a⟩ compile; *modulo* complete, fill in; ***~ un bilancio*** draw up a blance sheet; ***~ un elenco*** make a list
compilation *f* ⟨*pl* compilation⟩ compilation
compilatore *m* COMPUT compiler
compilazione *f* compilation
compimento *m* completion; ***portare qc a ~*** see sth through
compitare *v/t* ⟨1l⟩ spell out
compito[1] *adj* polite
compito[2] *m* task; EDU ***i -i*** *pl* homework *sg*; ***fare i -i*** do one's homework; ***~ in classe*** schoolwork
compiutamente *adv* completely **compiutezza** *f* completeness; (*perfezione*) perfection
compiuto *adj lavoro, opera* completed, finished; ***ha 10 anni -i*** he's 10
compleanno *m* birthday; ***buon ~!*** happy birthday!
complementare *adj* complementary; ***beni*** *mpl* ***-i*** ECON complementary goods
complemento *m* complement; GRAM object; ***~ oggetto*** direct object; ***ufficiale*** *m* ***di ~*** reserve officer
complessato *adj* full of complexes
complessità *f* ⟨*pl* complessità⟩ complexity
complessivamente *adv* (*nel complesso*) on the whole; (*in totale*) altogether
complessivo *adj* all-in
complesso I *adj* complex, complicated **II** *m* complex; MUS group, band; *di circostanze* set, combination; ***~ di colpa*** guilt compplex; ***~ di Edipo*** Oedipus complex; ***~ industriale*** industrial complex; ***~ d'inferiorità*** inferiority complex; ***~ ospedaliero*** hospital complex; ***in*** *or* ***nel ~*** on the whole
completabile *adj* completable
completamente *adv* completely
completamento *m* completion
completare *v/t* ⟨1b⟩ complete
completarsi *v/r* ⟨1b⟩ ***~ a vicenda*** complete one another
completo I *adj* complete; (*pieno*) full; THEAT sold out; ***artista*** *m* ***~*** complete artist; ***raccolta*** *f* ***-a*** complete works **II** *m* set; (*vestito*) suit; ***al ~*** (*pieno*) full (up); THEAT sold out; ***oggi siamo al (gran) ~*** we're fully booked today; ***~ da sci*** ski suit
complicanza *f* complication
complicare *v/t* ⟨1l & d⟩ complicate
complicarsi *v/r* get complicated
complicato *adj* complicated, complex

complicazione *f* complication; ***salvo -i*** all being well

complice I *adj*: ***sguardo*** *m* ~ knowing look **II** *m/f* JUR accomplice

complicità *f* ⟨*pl* complicità⟩ (*intesa*) understanding; *neg* complicity; JUR aiding and abetting

complimentarsi *v/r* ⟨1d⟩: ~ ***con qn*** congratulate s.o. (***per*** on)

complimento *m* compliment; ***fare un ~ a qn*** pay s.o. a compliment; ***-i!*** congratulations!; ***non fare -i!*** help yourself!

complottare ⟨1c⟩ **I** *v/i* plot; *hum* scheme; ~ ***contro lo Stato*** conspire against the state **II** *v/t infml* hatch; ***che state complottando?*** what are you up to?

complotto *m*: ***ordire un ~*** hatch a plot

componente I *m* component; ***i -i di un motore*** the parts of an engine **II** *m/f* (*persona*) member **III** *f* element; ***una ~ della cultura italiana*** an element of Italian culture

componentistica *f* ⟨*pl* -che⟩ TECH parts; (*industria*) components industry

componibile *adj* modular; *cucina* fitted

componimento *m* composition; JUR settlement; LIT work

comporre *v/t* ⟨3ll⟩ (*mettere in ordine*) arrange; MUS compose; ~ ***una lite*** JUR settle a dispute; TEL ~ ***un numero*** dial a number; ***essere composto di*** (*or* ***da***) consist of

comporsi *v/r*: ~ ***di*** consist of, be made up of; ***la mia famiglia si compone di 3 persone*** there are three people in my family

comportamentale *adj* behavio(u)ral; ***terapia*** *f* ~ behavio(u)r(al) therapy

comportamento *m* behavio(u)r; ***assumere un ~*** behave in a certain way

comportare *v/t* ⟨1c⟩ involve

comportarsi *v/r* behave; ~ ***da idiota*** behave like an idiot

composito *adj* composite; ***materiale*** *m* ~ composite material

compositore *m*, **-trice** *f* composer

composizione *f* composition; *di fiori* arrangement; JUR settlement; ~ ***rapida*** TEL speed dial

composta *f* stewed fruit; (*terricciato*) compost

compostamente *adv* composedly

compostezza *f* composure; *fig* decorum

composto I *past part* → ***comporre*** **II** *adj* compound; *abiti*, *capelli* tidy, neat; ~ ***da*** made up of; ***stai ~*** keep still; *seduto* sit properly **III** *m* compound

comprare *v/t* ⟨1a⟩ buy, purchase; (*corrompere*) bribe, buy off

compratore *m*, **-trice** *f* buyer, purchaser

compravendita *f* buying and selling

comprendere *v/t* ⟨3c⟩ (*includere*) comprise, include; (*capire*) understand; ***compresi che aveva mentito*** I realized that s / he had lied; ***il cofanetto comprende tre volumi*** the gift box contains three volumes; ***il prezzo comprende la colazione?*** does the price include breakfast?

comprendonio *m* ⟨*pl* -i⟩ *infml* brains *pl*; ***essere duro di ~*** be a bit slow on the uptake

comprensibile *adj* understandable

comprensibilità *f* ⟨*pl* comprensibilità⟩ comprehensibility

comprensibilmente *adv* understandably

comprensione *f* understanding

comprensivo *adj* (*tollerante*) understanding; ~ ***di*** inclusive of; ~ ***delle tasse*** including taxes; ***persona*** *f* ***-a*** understanding person

comprensorio *m* ⟨*pl* -ri⟩ district

compreso I *past part* → ***comprendere*** **II** *adj* inclusive; (*capito*) understood; ***tutto ~*** all in; ~ ***te*** including you; ~ ***nel prezzo*** included in the price; ***non mi sento -a*** I feel misunderstood

compressa *f* (*pastiglia*) tablet; *di garza* compress; ***farmaco*** *m* ***in -e*** drug in tablet form

compressione *f* compression

compresso *past part* → ***comprimere***; ***aria*** *f* ***-a*** compressed air

compressore *m* MECH compressor; *stradale* steamroller

comprimere *v/t* ⟨3r⟩ press; (*reprimere*) repress; PHYS compress; ~ ***un gas*** compress a gas

compromesso I *past part* → ***compromettere*** **II** *m* compromise; JUR ~ ***di vendita*** agreement to sell; ~ ***storico*** POL *the policy of cooperation between the Catholic and left-wing parties in*

Italy in the 1970s; ***giungere a un ~*** reach a compromise; ***vivere di -i*** make compromise after compromise
compromettente *adj* compromising; ***foto*** *fpl* ***-i*** compromising photos
compromettere *v/t* ⟨3ee⟩ compromise
compromettersi *v/r* compromise o.s.
comproprietà *f* joint ownership
comproprietario *m*, **-a** *f* ⟨*mpl* -ri⟩ JUR joint owner
comprova *f* proof **comprovabile** *adj* provable **comprovare** *v/t* ⟨1c⟩ prove
compulsione *f* PSYCH compulsion
compulsivo *adj* PSYCH compulsive; ***disturbo*** *m* ***ossessivo ~*** obsessive compulsive disorder
compunto *adj* contrite
computabile *adj* calculable **computare** *v/t* ⟨1l⟩ calculate
computer *m* ⟨*pl* computer⟩ computer; ***~ portatile*** portable (computer), laptop; ***assistito dal ~*** computer-assisted
computer grafica *f* computer graphics
computerizzare *v/t* ⟨1a⟩ computerize
computerizzato *adj* computerized
computerizzazione *f* computerization
computisteria *f* book-keeping, accountancy
comunale *adj del comune* municipal, town *attr*; ***consiglio*** *m* ***~*** town council; ***palazzo*** *m* ***~*** town hall
comunanza *f* community; ***~ di idee*** shared ideas
comune I *adj* common; *amico* mutual; (*ordinario*) ordinary, common; ***è una pianta molto ~*** it's a very common plant; ***luogo*** *m* ***~*** commonplace; ***non ~*** unusual, uncommon; ***opinione*** *f* ***~*** common opinion; ***di ~ accordo*** by mutual consent **II** *m* municipality; ***Camera dei Comuni*** House of Commons; ***palazzo*** *m* ***del ~*** town hall; ***avere qc in ~ (con qn)*** have sth in common (with s.o.); ***essere in ~ (con qn)*** be shared (with s.o.); ***mettere qc in ~ (con qn)*** pool sth (with s.o.); ***sposarsi in ~*** get married in a registry office; ***fuori del ~*** out of the ordinary
comunella *f*: ***fare ~ (con qn)*** *infml* band together (with s.o.)
comunemente *adv* commonly
comunicabile *adj* communicable **comunicabilità** *f* ⟨*pl* comunicabilità⟩ communicability
comunicando *m*, **-a** *f* REL communicant
comunicante *adj* communicating: ***stanze*** *fpl* ***-i*** communicating rooms
comunicare ⟨1m & d⟩ **I** *v/t notizia* pass on, communicate; *contagio* pass on; REL give Communion to **II** *v/i* (*esprimersi*) communicate; *di persone* keep in touch, communicate; ***~ a voce / per iscritto*** communicate orally / in writing; ***~ via e-mail*** communicate by email; ***è difficile ~ con lui*** it's hard to communicate with him; ***la cucina comunica con il soggiorno*** the kitchen opens into the living room
comunicarsi *v/r* ⟨1m & d⟩ (*diffondersi*) spread; REL take communion
comunicativa *f* communication skills
comunicativo *adj* communicative; ***carattere*** *m* ***~*** open character; ***risata*** *f* ***-a*** infectious laugh; ***è un tipo poco ~*** he's not very communicative
comunicato *m* announcement, communiqué; ***~ commerciale*** (TV / radio) ad; ***~ stampa*** press release
comunicatore *m*, **-trice** *f* communicator; ***~ tecnico*** technical author; ***~ telefonico*** TEL wireless communicator; ***quel politico è un gran ~*** that politician is a great communicator
comunicazione *f* communication; (*annuncio*) announcement; TEL (*collegamento*) connection; ***dare ~ di qc a qn*** tell s.o. about sth; ***interrompere la ~*** break off the connection; TEL ***la ~ si è interrotta*** I've been cut off; TEL ***~ internazionale*** international call; ***-i*** *pl* ***marittime*** maritime communications; ***~ di servizio*** service message; ***vie*** *fpl* ***di ~*** communications; ***mezzi*** *mpl* ***di ~*** means of communication; ***scienza*** *f* ***delle -i*** communication science
comunione *f* REL communion; *di idee* sharing; JUR ***~ dei beni*** community of goods; ***fare la ~*** take communion
comunismo *m* Communism
comunista *m/f* ⟨*mpl* -i⟩ Communist
comunità *f* ⟨*pl* comunità⟩ community; ***Comunità europea*** European Community; ***~ montana*** *legally recognized territory consisting of a group of mountain communities*; ***~ religiosa*** religious community; ***~ virtuale***

COMPUT virtual community; ***vivere in ~*** live in a commune

comunitario *adj* community *attr*; *dell'UE* Community *attr*; ***acquis** m* **~** acquired rights (in the EU); ***diritto** m* **~** EU law; ***spirito** m* **~** community spirit

comunque I *cj* however, no matter how; ***~ vadano le cose*** whatever happens **II** *adv* (*in ogni modo*) in any case, anyhow; (*in qualche modo*) somehow; (*tuttavia*) however; ***ti faccio sapere ~*** but I'll let you know; ***io ~ non sono d'accordo*** but I don't agree

con *prep* **1.** with; ***avere ~ sé*** have with *or* on one; ***andare ~ il treno / la macchina*** go by train / car; ***essere carino ~ qn*** be nice with s.o.; ***la ragazza ~ gli occhi azzurri*** the girl with blue eyes; ***vuoi venire ~ noi?*** do you want to come with us?; ***e ~ questo?*** so what?; ***~ piacere!*** with pleasure!; ***sta ~ Daniele da Natale*** she's been engaged to Daniele since Christmas **2.** (*mezzo*) by **3.** ***~ questo tempo*** in this weather; ***~ tutto ciò*** for all that

conato *m*: ***~ di vomito*** retching

conca *f* ⟨*pl* -che⟩ (*recipiente*) bowl; (*bacino*) valley; ***~ d'acqua*** pool

concatenare *v/t* ⟨1a⟩ connect **concatenazione** *f* connection

concausa *f* contributory factor

concavo *adj* concave

concedere *v/t* ⟨3l⟩ grant; *premio* award; ***~ un'intervista*** give an interview; ***~ la mano di qn*** give s.o.'s hand (in marriage); ***~ un permesso a qn*** give s.o. permission; ***ammesso e non concesso che ...*** even supposing...; ***concedimi due minuti*** give me a couple of minutes; ***non mi hanno concesso di parlargli*** they wouldn't let me speak to him; ***ti concedo che*** I admit that

concedersi *v/r*: ***~ qc*** treat o.s. to sth; ***mi sono concessa una vacanza*** I treated myself to a holiday, *US* vacation

concentramento *m* concentration

concentrare *v/t* ⟨1b⟩ concentrate; ***~ le proprie energie*** concentrate one's energies

concentrarsi *v/r* ⟨1b⟩ concentrate; ***non riuscire a ~*** be unable to concentrate

concentrato I *adj* absorbed (***in*** in); *brodo*, *succo* concentrated **II** *m*: ***~ di pomodoro*** tomato purée

concentrazione *f* concentration; ***~ di ozono*** ozone level; ***perdere la ~*** lose one's concentration

concentrico *adj* ⟨*mpl* -ci⟩ concentric; ***cerchio** m* **~** concentric circle

concepibile *adj* conceivable

concepimento *m* conception

concepire *v/t* ⟨4d⟩ conceive; (*ideare*) devise, conceive

conceria *f* tannery

concernente *adj* concerning, regarding

concernere *v/t* ⟨3a⟩ concern; ***per quanto mi concerne*** as far as I'm concerned

concertare *v/t* ⟨1b⟩ MUS harmonize; *fig* (*ordire*) hatch **concertato** *adj* concerted; ***azione** f* ***-a*** concerted action

concertino *m* concertino

concertista *m/f* ⟨*mpl* -i⟩ MUS concert artist **concertistico** *adj* ⟨*mpl* -ci⟩ concert *attr*; ***attività** f* ***-a*** concert giving

concerto *m* concert; *composizione* concerto; ***~ grosso*** concerto grosso; ***~ di pianoforte*** piano concerto

concessionario *m* ⟨*pl* -ri⟩ agent; ***~ esclusivo*** sole agent

concessione *f* concession; ***~ edilizia*** building permit; ***~ governativa*** government concession; ***fare -i a qn*** make concessions to s.o.

concesso *past part* → ***concedere***

concetto *m* concept; (*giudizio*) opinion; ***~ del dovere*** concept of duty; ***~ di libertà*** concept of freedom; ***farsi un ~ di qn / qc*** form an opinion of s.o. / sth; ***che ~ hai di lui?*** what do you think of him?

concettuale *adj* conceptual

concezione *f* conception; *fig* idea (***di*** for); ***~ del mondo*** view of the world; ***Immacolata Concezione*** Immaculate Conception

conchiglia *f* shell

concia *f* ⟨*pl* -ce⟩ *di pelli*: tanning; *di tabacco*, *sementi*: curing

conciare *v/t* ⟨1f⟩ *pelle* tan; (*sistemare*) arrange; ***~ qn per le feste*** tan s.o.'s hide, give s.o. a good hiding

conciarsi *v/r* ⟨1f⟩ get into a mess; ***come ti sei conciato!*** look what a state you're in! **conciatore** *m*, **-trice** *f* tanner

conciliabile *adj* compatible

conciliabolo *m* secret meeting

conciliante *adj* conciliatory; ***mostrarsi ~ con qn*** be conciliatory toward(s) s.o.

conciliare[1] *v/t* ⟨1k⟩ reconcile; *multa* pay, settle; ***~ qc con qc*** square sth with sth; ***~ il sonno*** be conducive to sleep

conciliare[2] *adj* council *attr*; ***sessione** f* **~** council session; ***padri** mpl* ***-i*** council elders

conciliarsi *v/r* ⟨1k⟩ go together; *trovare accordo* be reconciled **conciliatore I** *adj* peacemaking **II** *m*, **-trice** *f* peacemaker

conciliazione *f* reconciliation; JUR settlement

concilio *m* council; ***~ ecumenico*** ecumenical council; ***riunirsi in ~*** meet

concimare *v/t* ⟨1a⟩ *pianta* feed

concimazione *f* manuring, fertilizing

concime *m* manure, fertilizer; ***~ chimico*** chemical fertilizer; ***~ organico*** organic fertilizer

concio *m* ⟨*pl* -ci⟩ ARCH ashlar

concisamente *adv* concisely; ***esprimersi ~*** express oneself concisely

concisione *f* conciseness

conciso *adj* concise; ***stile** m* **~** concise style

concistoro *m* consistory

concitatamente *adv* excitedly

concitato *adj* excited

concitazione *f* excitement

concittadino *m*, **-a** *f* fellow citizen

conclamato *adj* clear; *malattia* full-blown

conclave *m* conclave

concludente *adj* conclusive; ***essere poco ~*** not be good at getting things done

concludere *v/t* ⟨3q⟩ conclude; (*portare a termine*) achieve, carry off; ***~ un affare*** clinch a deal; ***non ho concluso nulla*** I got nowhere

concludersi *v/r* end, close

conclusionale *adj* JUR concluding; ***comparsa** f* **~** summing up

conclusione *f* conclusion; ***in ~*** in short; ***arrivare alla ~ che*** come to the conclusion that; ***precisare le -i*** sum up the conclusions; ***trarre le proprie -i*** draw one's own conclusions

conclusivo *adj* conclusive

concluso *past part* → ***concludere***

concomitante *adj* concomitant; ***fenomeno** m* **~** accompanying phenomenon **concomitanza** *f* combination; ***in ~ con qc*** in combination with sth

concordabile *adj* negotiable; ***prezzo** m* **~** negotiable price

concordanza *f* agreement

concordare ⟨1c⟩ **I** *v/t* agree (on); GRAM make agree **II** *v/i* (*essere d'accordo*) agree; (*coincidere*) tally

concordatario *adj* ⟨*mpl* -ri⟩ according to an agreement; ***matrimonio** m* **~** religious marriage (that has civil validity)

concordato I *adj* agreed on **II** *m* agreement; REL concordat; JUR settlement; ***~ fallimentare*** bankruptcy settlement

concorde *adj* in agreement; (*unanime*) unanimous; (*simultaneo*) simultaneous

concordia *f* harmony

concorrente I *adj* (*rivale*) competing, rival **II** *m/f in una gara*, *gioco* competitor, contestant; FIN competitor

concorrenza *f* competition; ***fare ~ a qn / qc*** compete with s.o. / sth; ***~ sleale*** unfair competition

concorrenziale *adj* competitive

concorrere *v/i* ⟨3o⟩ (*contribuire*) concur; (*competere*) compete (***a*** for); *di strade* converge; ***~ per un posto*** compete for a position

concorso I *past part* → ***concorrere*** **II** *m* (*competizione*) competition, contest; ***~ di bellezza*** beauty contest; ***~ a cattedre*** *public competition for teaching posts*; ***~ ippico*** showjumping competition; ***~ a premi*** competition; ***bandire un ~*** announce a competition; ***fuori ~*** out of competition; ***~ in truffa*** JUR complicity in fraud; ***~ di pubblico*** public gathering; ***~ alle spese*** sharing of expenses

concretamente *adv* concretely **concretezza** *f* concreteness **concretizzare** *v/t* ⟨1a⟩ put into practice **concretizzarsi** *v/r* ⟨1a⟩ be realized **concretizzazione** *f* realization

concreto *adj* concrete; (*pratico*) practical

concubina *f* concubine

concupire *v/t* ⟨4d⟩ lust after **concupiscenza** *f* lust
concussione *f* JUR extortion
condanna *f* JUR sentence; *~ a morte* death sentence; *emettere or pronunciare una ~* pass sentence; *fig firmare la propria ~* sign one's own death warrant
condannabile *adj* blameworthy
condannare *v/t* ⟨1a⟩ condemn (*a* to); JUR sentence (*a* to); *le sue bugie lo hanno condannato* he was condemned by his own lies; *~ gli atti di terrorismo* condemn acts of terrorism
condannato *m*, **-a** *f* convicted person
condensa *f* condensation **condensante** *m* condenser
condensare *v/t* ⟨1b⟩ condense
condensarsi *v/r* ⟨1b⟩ condense
condensato I *adj* condensed; *latte m ~* condensed milk **II** *n*: *condensato m* PHYS condensate
condensatore *m* TECH condenser
condensazione *f* condensation
condiloma *m* ⟨*pl* -i⟩ condyloma
condimento *m* seasoning; *di insalata* dressing
condire *v/t* ⟨4d⟩ season; *insalata* dress; *fig* spice up
condirettore *m*, **-trice** *f* co-director
condiscendente *adj* (*arrendevole*) compliant; (*indulgente*) indulgent; *essere ~ verso qn* indulge s.o. **condiscendenza** *f* indulgence
condiscepolo *m*, **-a** *f* fellow disciple
condito *adj* seasoned
condividere *v/t* ⟨3q⟩ share
condivisibile *adj* that can be shared **condivisione** *f* sharing (out)
condiviso *past part* → *condividere*
condizionale I *m/adj* conditional **II** *f* suspended sentence
condizionamento *m* PSYCH conditioning; *~ dell'aria* air conditioning
condizionare *v/t* ⟨1a⟩ PSYCH condition; *non farti ~ da nessuno!* don't let anyone influence you!
condizionato *adj*: *con aria -a* with air conditioning, air-conditioned; *riflesso m ~* conditioned reflex
condizionatore *m* air conditioner
condizione *f* condition; *-i pl economiche* financial position; *-i pl favorevoli* favourable terms; *-i pl generali di contratto* general terms of a contract; *-i pl di lavoro* working conditions; *di ~ elevata* high-ranking; *di umili -i* low-ranking; *essere in buone/cattive -i* be in a good/bad state of repair; *imporre una ~* set a condition; *mettere qn in ~ di fare qc* make it possible for s.o. to do sth; *non essere in ~ di fare qc* be in no fit state to do sth; *a ~ che* provided that
condoglianze *fpl* condolences *pl*; *fare le ~ a qn* express one's condolences to s.o.
condominiale *adj riunione* flat owners'; *giardino* shared; *amministratore m ~* building administrator; *regolamento m ~* building rules; *spese fpl -i* maintenance charges
condominio *m* (*comproprietà*) joint ownership; *edificio* block of flats, *US* condo
condomino *m*, **-a** *f* owner-occupier, *US* condo owner
condonare *v/t* ⟨1a⟩ remit
condono *m* remission; *~ edilizio amnesty for infringement of building regulations*; *~ fiscale* conditional amnesty for tax evaders
condor *m* ⟨*pl* condor⟩ condor
condotta *f* (*comportamento*) behavio(u)r, conduct; (*canale*) piping; *~ forzata* TECH pressure pipeline; *buona ~* good behavio(u)r; *essere rilasciato per buona ~* be released early for good behavio(u)r; *che voto hai in ~?* EDU what mark did you get for conduct?
condottiero *m* HIST condottiere
condotto I *past part* → *condurre* **II** *m* pipe; ANAT duct; *~ biliare* bile duct
conducente *m/f* driver; *~ di autobus* bus driver
conducibilità *f* ⟨*pl* conducibilità⟩ PHYS conductivity
condurre *v/t* ⟨3e⟩ lead; (*accompagnare*) take; *veicolo* drive; *azienda* run; *acque, gas* carry, take
conduttore *m*, **-trice** *f* RADIO, TV presenter; RAIL (*controllore*) conductor; *~ elettrico* conductor of electricity; *essere un buon/cattivo ~* be a good/bad conductor; *filo m ~* thread
conduttura *f* (*condotto*) pipe
conduzione *f* management; TV host-

ing; PHYS conduction; ***azienda** f **a ~ familiare*** family-run business; ***~ termica*** heat conduction
confabulare *v/i* ⟨1m⟩ chat
confacente *adj* suitable
confarsi *v/r* ⟨3aa⟩ be suitable (***a qn/qc*** for s.o./sth); (*giovare*) suit; ***l'aria di mare non mi si confà*** sea air doesn't suit me
confederarsi *v/r* ⟨1m & b⟩ form a confederation
confederazione *f* confederation; ***~ sindacale*** trade union confederation; ***Confederazione Elvetica*** Switzerland
conferenza *f* conference; ***~ episcopale*** bishops' conference; ***~ stampa*** press conference; ***~ telefonica*** TEL conference call; ***~ al vertice*** summit (conference); ***tenere una ~*** hold a conference
conferenziere *m*, **-a** *f* speaker
conferimento *m* conferring; ***~ di capitale*** capital contribution; ***-i** pl **in natura*** contributions in kind
conferire ⟨4d⟩ **I** *v/t* (*dare*) confer; *premio* award **II** *v/i*: ***~ con qn*** confer with s.o.
conferma *f* confirmation***~ d'ordine*** order confirmation
confermare *v/t* ⟨1a⟩ confirm; ***~ qn in una carica*** confirm s.o. in a post; ***~ una deposizione*** confirm a deposition; ***i fatti lo hanno confermato*** the facts bore it out
confessare *v/t* ⟨1b⟩ confess
confessarsi *v/r* ⟨1b⟩ confess
confessionale *m* confessional
confessione *f* confession; ***le Confessioni di S. Agostino*** the Confessions of Saint Augustine; ***essere di ~ cattolica/evangelica*** be a Catholic/an evangelical
confessore *m* confessor
confetto *m* COOK sugared almond; MED pill
confettura *f* jam
confezionamento *m* packaging; ***data** f **di ~*** date of packaging
confezionare *v/t* ⟨1a⟩ *merce* wrap, package; *abiti* make
confezionatrice *f* (*macchina*) packaging machine
confezione *f* wrapping, packaging; *di abiti* making; ***~ regalo*** gift wrap; ***~ famiglia*** family pack; ***-i** pl* (*abiti*) garments
conficcare *v/t* ⟨1d⟩ hammer, drive
conficcarsi *v/r*: ***~ in qc*** go into sth
confidare ⟨1a⟩ **I** *v/t* confide **II** *v/i*: ***~ in*** trust in, rely on
confidarsi *v/r*: ***~ con*** confide in; ***~ con qn*** confide in s.o.
confidente *m/f* confidant(e); (*informatore*) informer
confidenza *f* (*familiarità*) familiarity; (*fiducia*) confidence, trust; ***avere ~*** (*or **essere in***) ***~ con qn*** be close to s.o.; ***detto in ~*** in confidence; ***fare una ~ a qn*** tell s.o. a secret; ***in tutta ~*** in strict confidence; ***prendere ~ con qc*** familiarize o.s. with sth; ***prendersi delle -e con qn*** be too familiar with s.o.
confidenziale *adj* (*riservato*) confidential; ***strettamente ~*** strictly confidential
confidenzialmente *adv* confidentially
configurare *v/t* ⟨1a⟩ configure
configurazione *f* configuration; ***~ del terreno*** lie (*US* lay) of the land
confinante *adj* neighbo(u)ring
confinare *v/i* ⟨1a⟩ border (***con*** sth); *fig* confine
confinarsi *v/r* ⟨1a⟩: ***~ in casa*** shut oneself up indoors
confine *m* border; *fra terreni*, *fig* boundary; ***al ~ con l'Italia*** at the Italian border; ***senza -i*** boundless; *fig **ai -i del mondo*** to the ends of the earth
confino *m* internal exile; ***mandare al ~*** send into internal exile
confisca *f* ⟨*pl* -che⟩ seizure
confiscare *v/t* ⟨1d⟩ confiscate
confiteor *m* ⟨*pl* confiteor⟩ Confiteor; ***recitare il ~*** say the Confiteor
conflagrazione *f fig* sudden outbreak of hostilities; PHIL *end of the world in Stoic philosophy*
conflitto *m* conflict; ***~ a fuoco*** gun fight; ***~ di interessi*** a conflict of interests
conflittuale *adj* troubled; ***rapporto** m **~*** troubled relationship **conflittualità** *f* ⟨*pl* conflittualità⟩ unrest
confluente *adj* ANAT, MED confluent
confluenza *f* confluence (*a. fig*)
confluire *v/i* ⟨4d⟩ merge
confondere *v/t* ⟨3bb⟩ confuse, mix up; (*imbarazzare*) embarrass; ***~ le idee***

confuse
confondersi *v/r* get mixed up; **~ fra la folla** mingle with the crowd; **il cielo si confonde con il mare** the sky and sea merge
confondibile *adj* easily confused
conformabile *adj* conformable
conformare *v/t* ⟨1a⟩ (*rendere adatto*) adapt
conformarsi *v/r*: **~ a** conform to; (*adattarsi*) adapt to; **~ alle regole** obey the rules
conformazione *f* shape; **~ del terreno** lie (*US* lay) of the land
conforme *adj* (*simile*) similar; **~ a** in accordance with; **~ alla legge** in accordance with the law; **~ all'originale** identical to the original; **~ al vero** true; **copia** *f* **~** (certified) true copy
conformismo *m* conformity
conformista *m/f* ⟨*mpl* -i⟩ conformist
conformità *f* conformity; **in ~ a** in accordance with
confortante *adj* comforting; **notizie** *fpl* **-i** reassuring news
confortare *v/t* ⟨1c⟩ comfort; **~ gli afflitti** comfort the afflicted; *fig* **~ la tesi di qn** support s.o.'s theory
confortevole *adj* comfortable
confortevolmente *adv* comfortably
conforto *m* comfort; **i -i della religione** the comforts of religion; **dare / trovare ~** give / get comfort; **essere di gran ~** be very comforting
confratello *m* brother **confraternita** *f* brotherhood
confrontabile *adj* comparable
confrontare *v/t* ⟨1a⟩ compare
confronto *m* confrontation; (*comparazione*) comparison; **a ~ di, in ~ a** compared with; **~ all'americana** identity parade, *US* lineup; **mettere qc a ~ con qc** compare sth with sth; **maleducato nei -i di qn** rude to s.o.
confusionale *adj*: **stato** *m* **~** confused state
confusionario ⟨*mpl* -ri⟩ **I** *adj* muddle-headed **II** *m*, **-a** *f* muddle-headed person
confusione *f* confusion; (*disordine*) muddle, mess; (*baccano*) noise, racket; (*imbarazzo*) embarrassment; **~ mentale** MED confused state; **creare ~** create confusion; **fare ~** *disordine* make a mess; *baccano* make a noise; **mi raccomando, non fate ~!** don't make a mess!; **faccio sempre ~** *con nomi, date* I always get mixed up
confuso I *past part* → **confondere II** *adj* (*non chiaro*) confused, muddled; (*imbarazzato*) embarrassed; **suono** *m* **~** confused noise; **avere le idee -e** be confused
confutabile *adj* refutable **confutare** *v/t* ⟨1l⟩ refute **confutazione** *f* refutation
congedare *v/t* ⟨1b⟩ dismiss; MIL discharge
congedarsi *v/r* take leave (**da** of)
congedo *m* (*permesso*) leave; MIL *assoluto* discharge; **~ matrimoniale** wedding leave; **prendere ~ da qn** say goodbye to s.o.; **ufficiale** *m* **in ~** reserve officer
congegno *m* (*dispositivo*) device
congelamento *m* freezing; ECON freeze; MED frostbite; **punto** *m* **di ~** freezing point; **~ dei salari** wage freeze
congelare *v/t & v/i* ⟨1b⟩ freeze; **~ un credito** freeze a credit
congelarsi *v/r* ⟨1b⟩ freeze
congelato *adj* frozen; **carne** *f* **-a** frozen meat
congelatore *m* freezer
congeniale *adj* congenial; **questo ruolo non mi è ~** this role doesn't suit me **congenialità** *f* ⟨*pl* congenialità⟩ congeniality
congenito *adj* congenital; **malattia** *f* **-a** congenital disease
congestionare *v/t* ⟨1a⟩ congest
congestionato *adj* congested; *volto* flushed
congestione *f* congestion; **~ polmonare** pulmonary (o)edema
congettura *f* conjecture; **fare -e** conjecture
congetturale *adj* conjectural **congetturare** *v/t* ⟨1a⟩ conjecture
congiungere *v/t* ⟨3d⟩ join; **~ in matrimonio** join in marriage
congiungersi *v/r* join (up)
congiungimento *m* joining
congiuntamente *adv* jointly
congiuntiva *f* conjunctiva
congiuntivite *f* conjunctivitis
congiuntivo *m* GRAM subjunctive; **~ presente / passato** present / past subjunctive

congiunto I *past part* → ***congiungere*** II *m*, **-a** *f* relative, relation

congiuntura *f* ANAT joint; ~ ***economica*** economic situation

congiunturale *adj* economic; ***crisi*** *f* ~ economic crisis

congiunzione *f* GRAM conjunction

congiura *f* conspiracy, plot; ***ordire una*** ~ hatch a conspiracy; ***ma questa è una*** **~!** *hum* this is a conspiracy!

congiurare *v/i* ⟨1a⟩ conspire; ~ ***contro qn*** conspire against s.o. **congiurato** *m*, **-a** *f* conspirator

conglobamento *m* merging; ADMIN consolidation **conglobare** *v/t* ⟨1l & c⟩ merge; ADMIN consolidate

conglomerato *m* conglomerate (*a.* GEOL); BUILD concrete

congolese I *adj* Congolese II *m/f* Congolese

congratularsi *v/r* ⟨1m⟩: ~ ***con qn*** congratulate s.o. (***per*** on)

congratulazioni *fpl*: ***fare le proprie*** ~ ***a qn*** congratulate s.o.; **~!** congratulations!

congrega *f* ⟨*pl* -ghe⟩ group; *pej* band **congregazione** *f* REL congregation

congressista *m/f* ⟨*mpl* -i⟩ convention participant

congresso *m* convention

congruente *adj* congruent (*a.* GEOM) **congruenza** *f* congruence (*a.* GEOM) **congruo** *adj* adequate

conguagliare *v/t* ⟨1g⟩ balance

conguaglio *m* ⟨*pl* -gli⟩ balance

CONI *abbr* (= **Comitato Olimpico Nazionale Italiano**) *Italian Olympic Committee*

coniare *v/t* ⟨1k & c⟩ mint; *fig* coin

coniazione *f* coining (*a. fig*)

conico *adj* ⟨*mpl* -ci⟩ conical

conifere *fpl* conifers *pl*

conigliera *f* rabbit hutch; *più grande* rabbit run

coniglio *m* ⟨*pl* -gli⟩ rabbit

conio *m* ⟨*pl* -i, -ii⟩ coining (*a. fig*); (*stampo*) die

coniugale *adj* conjugal; ***vita*** *f* ~ married life; ***doveri*** *mpl* **-i** conjugal duties

coniugare *v/t* ⟨1l, c & e⟩ conjugate

coniugato *adj* married

coniugazione *f* conjugation

coniuge *m/f* spouse; **-i** *pl* husband and wife; ***i -i Rossi*** Mr and Mrs Rossi

connaturale *adj* natural

connazionale *m/f* compatriot; ***i miei -i*** my compatriots

connessione *f* connection

connesso I *adj* connected; ***cause*** *fpl* **-e** JUR linked cases; ***strettamente*** ~ ***con qc*** closely connected to sth II ***connesso*** *past part* → ***connettere***

connettere *v/t* ⟨3m⟩ ELEC connect; ***non connetto*** I can't think straight

connettivo I *adj* connective; ***tessuto*** *m* ~ BIOL connective tissue II *n*: ***connettivo*** *m* connective; ~ ***logico*** logical connective

connivente *m/f* conniver **connivenza** *f* connivance

connotati *mpl* features *pl*; ***cambiare i*** ~ ***a qn*** *hum* rearrange s.o.'s features

connotazione *f* connotation

cono *m* cone; ~ ***gelato*** ice-cream cone; ***a*** (***forma di***) ~ conical

conoscente *m/f* acquaintance

conoscenza *f* **1.** knowledge; ***essere a*** ~ ***di qc*** know of sth; ***venire a*** ~ ***di qc*** find out about sth; ***per*** ~ cc **2.** ***fare la*** ~ ***di qn*** make s.o.'s acquaintance, meet s.o. **3.** *persona* acquaintance **4.** (*sensi*) consciousness; ***perdere*** ~ lose consciousness, faint

conoscere *v/t* ⟨3n⟩ know; (*fare la conoscenza di*) meet; ~ ***qn di vista*** know s.o. by sight; ***far*** ~ ***qn / qc a qn*** introduce s.o. to s.o. / sth; ***si conoscono da anni*** they've known each other for years

conoscitivo *adj* cognitive; ***atto*** *m* ~ cognitive act

conoscitore *m*, **-trice** *f* connoisseur

conosciuto *adj* well-known, famous

conquista *f* conquest

conquistare *v/t* ⟨1a⟩ conquer; *fig* win; ~ ***la fama*** become famous

conquistarsi *v/r* ⟨1a⟩ gain; ~ ***la stima di qn*** gain s.o.'s respect

conquistatore *m*, **-trice** *f* conqueror; *fig* seducer

consacrare *v/t* ⟨1a⟩ consecrate; *sacerdote* ordain; (*dedicare*) dedicate

consacrarsi *v/r* devote o.s. (***a*** to)

consacrato *adj* consecrated

consacrazione *f* consecration; *di sacerdote* ordination

consanguineità *f* ⟨*pl* consanguineità⟩ blood relationship

consanguineo *m*, **-a** *f* blood relative

consapevole *adj*: ~ ***di*** conscious of,

aware of

consapevolezza *f* consciousness, awareness

consapevolizzare *v/t* ⟨1a⟩ make aware; ***~ qn di qc*** make s.o. aware of sth **consapevolizzarsi** *v/r* ⟨1a⟩ become aware **consapevolmente** *adv* knowingly

consciamente *adv* consciously

conscio **I** *adj* conscious, aware; ***essere ~ di qc*** be conscious *or* aware of sth **II** *m*: ***il ~ e l'inconscio*** the conscious and the unconscious

consecutio temporum *f* ⟨*pl* consecutio temporum⟩ GRAM sequence of tenses

consecutivamente *adv* consecutively

consecutivo *adj* (*di seguito*) consecutive; ***proposizione*** *f* ***-a*** GRAM consecutive proposition; ***traduzione*** *f* ***-a*** consecutive translation; ***tre giorni -i*** three consecutive days, three days in a row

consegna *f di lavoro, documento* handing in; *di prigionero, ostaggio* handover; ***lasciare qc in ~ a qn*** leave sth with s.o.; ***prendere qc in ~*** take delivery of sth; ***~ a domicilio*** home delivery; ***~ bagagli*** left luggage, *US* baggage checkroom; ***~ in caserma*** confinement to barracks; ***pagamento*** *m* ***alla ~*** cash on delivery

consegnare *v/t* ⟨1a⟩ *lavoro, documento* hand in (***a*** to); *prigionero, ostaggio* hand over (***a*** to); *merci, posta* deliver (***a*** to)

consegnarsi *v/r* ⟨1a⟩ give oneself up; ***~ alla polizia*** give oneself up to the police **consegnatario** *m*, **-a** *f* ⟨*mpl* -ri⟩ consignee

conseguente *adj* consequent

conseguenza *f* consequence; ***di ~*** consequently; ***in ~ di qc*** as a result of sth

conseguibile *adj* achievable **conseguimento** *m* achievement

conseguire ⟨4a⟩ **I** *v/t* achieve; *laurea* obtain **II** *v/i* follow; ***ne consegue che ...*** it follows that ...

consenso *m* (*permesso*) consent, permission; ***chiedere/dare il ~*** ask for/give consent; ***negare il proprio ~ a qn*** refuse s.o. one's consent; ***riscuotere molti -i*** gain widespread approval

consensuale *adj* by mutual consent; ***separazione*** *f* ***~*** separation by mutual consent **consensualità** *f* ⟨*pl* consensualità⟩ consent **consensualmente** *adv* by mutual consent

consentire ⟨4b⟩ **I** *v/i* (*accondiscendere*) consent **II** *v/t* allow

consentito *adj* allowed, permitted; ***velocità*** *f* ***massima -a*** maximum speed allowed

consenziente *adj* consenting; ***essere ~ a qc*** consent to sth

consequenziale *adj* consequential

conserto *adj*: (***a***) ***braccia*** *fpl* ***-e*** with one's arms folded

conserva *f* preserve; ***~ di pomodoro*** tomato purée; ***~ di frutta*** jam

conservabile *adj* preservable **conservabilità** *f* ⟨*pl* conservabilità⟩ ability to be preserved

conservante *m* preservative

conservare *v/t* ⟨1b⟩ keep; COOK preserve

conservarsi *v/r* keep; *in salute* keep well

conservativo *adj* preservative; ***intervento*** *m* ***~*** MED conservative treatment; ***sequestro*** *m* ***~*** preventive confiscation of assets

conservato *adj alimento* preserved; (*in buono stato*) well-preserved; ***carne*** *f* ***-a*** preserved meat; ***ben ~*** well-preserved

conservatore *m*, **-trice** *f* conservative

conservatoria *f* ADMIN registry; ***~ dei registri immobiliari*** land registry

conservatorio *m* ⟨*pl* -ri⟩ music school, conservatoire; ***studiare al ~*** study at the conservatoire

conservazione *f* preservation

consesso *m* assembly; ***~ di popoli*** meeting of nations

considerare *v/t* ⟨1m⟩ consider; ***considerato che ...*** given that ...; ***lo considero un amico*** I think of him as a friend; ***lo considero un cretino*** I think he's an idiot

considerazione *f* consideration; (*osservazione*) remark, comment; ***dopo attente -i*** after careful consideration; ***fare -i su qc*** make some observations about sth; ***prendere in ~*** take into consideration; ***tenere qn in grande ~*** have a high regard for s.o.

considerevole *adj* considerable

considerevolmente *adv* considerably
consigliabile *adj* advisable
consigliare *v/t* ⟨1g⟩ advise; (*raccomandare*) recommend; ***~ a qn di fare qc*** advise s.o. to do sth; ***cosa mi consigli di fare?*** what do you think I should do?; ***cosa mi consiglia?*** *a ristorante* what do you recommend?
consigliarsi *v/r* ask for advice
consigliere *m*, **-a** *f* adviser; ***~ municipale*** town council(l)or
consiglio *m* ⟨*pl* -gli⟩ piece of advice; (*organo amministrativo*) council; ***~ d'amministrazione*** board (of directors); ***Consiglio d'Europa*** Council of Europe; ***~ dei ministri*** Cabinet; ***Consiglio dell'Unione Europea*** Council of Ministers; ***su ~ del medico*** on medical advice
consiliare *adj* council *attr*; ***sala*** *f* ***~*** council chamber
consistente *adj* substantial; (*denso*) thick
consistentemente *adv* substantially
consistenza *f* (*densità*) consistency, thickness; *di materiale* texture; *di argomento* basis; ***il progetto comincia a prendere ~*** the project is beginning to take shape
consistere *v/i* ⟨3f⟩ consist (***in, di*** of); ***in che cosa consiste la tua attività?*** what does your job consist of?
CONSOB *f abbr* (= **Commissione Nazionale per le Società e la Borsa**) *regulatory body for the Italian Stock Exchange*
consociata *f* sister company **consociativismo** *m* power-sharing **consociativo** *adj* power-sharing **consociato I** *adj* associated; *reciprocamente* sister *attr* **II** *m*, **-a** *f* associate
consocio *m*, **-a** *f* ⟨*mpl* -ci⟩ associate
consolante *adj* consoling
consolare[1] *v/t* ⟨1c⟩ console, comfort
consolare[2] *adj* consular
consolarsi *v/r* console o.s.
consolato *m* consulate; ***~ generale*** consulate general
consolatore I *adj* consoling; ***parole*** *fpl* ***-trici*** consoling words **II** *m*, **-trice** *f* comforter
consolazione *f* consolation; ***essere di ~ per qn*** be a consolation to s.o.; ***premio*** *m* ***di ~*** consolation prize
console[1] *m diplomatico* consul; ***~ generale*** consul general; ***~ onorario*** honorary consul
console[2] *f* ⟨*pl* console⟩ (*mobile*) console table; ELEC console
consolidamento *m* consolidation (*a. fig*, ECON)
consolidare *v/t* ⟨1m & c⟩ consolidate
consolidarsi *v/r* stabilize
consommé *m* ⟨*pl* consommé⟩ consommé; ***~ di pollo*** chicken consommé
consonante *f* consonant
consono *adj*: ***~ a qc*** consistent with sth
consorte *m/f* spouse; ***principe*** *m* ***~*** prince consort
consorteria *f* HIST *in medieval times, an association of a group of families*; *pej* faction
consorziale *adj* consortium *attr* **consorziato I** *adj* associated in a consortium; ***ditte*** *fpl* ***-e*** companies that have formed a consortium **II** *m*, **-a** *f* member of a consortium
consorzio *m* ⟨*pl* -zi⟩ *di imprese* consortium; ***~ agrario*** farmers' consortium
constatabile *adj* verifiable
constatare *v/t* ⟨1l⟩ ascertain, determine; (*notare*) note
constatazione *f* statement
consueto *adj* usual
consuetudine *f* habit, custom; (*usanza*) custom, tradition
consulente *m/f* consultant; ***~ legale*** legal adviser; ***~ tributario*** tax consultant
consulenza *f* consultancy; ***~ aziendale*** management consultancy
consulta *f* meeting
consultabile *adj* able to be consulted
consultare *v/t* ⟨1a⟩ consult
consultarsi *v/r*: ***~ con qn*** consult s.o.
consultazione *f* consultation; ***opera*** *f* ***di ~*** reference book; ***~ popolare*** consultation of the people
consultivo *adj* advisory; ***organo*** *m* ***~*** advisory body
consultorio *m*: ***~ familiare*** family planning clinic
consumabile *adj* edible
consumare *v/t* ⟨1a⟩ *acqua, gas* use, consume; (*logorare*) wear out; (*mangiare*) eat, consume; (*bere*) drink; ***~ il matrimonio*** consummate a marriage; ***~ le scarpe*** wear out one's shoes; ***da***

consumarsi preferibilmente entro il … use by …
consumarsi *v/r* wear out
consumato *adj fig* consummate; ***attore*** *m* ~ consummate actor
consumatore *m*, **-trice** *f* consumer
consumazione *f* food; (*bevanda*) drink; ***pagare la ~ alla cassa*** pay for food and drink beforehand
consumer benefit *m* ⟨*pl* consumer benefit⟩ consumer benefit
consumerismo *m* consumerism
consumismo *m* consumerism
consumistico *adj* ⟨*mpl* -ci⟩ consumer *attr*
consumo *m* consumption; (*usura*) wear; ***-i*** *pl* ***indotti*** unnecessary consumption *sg*; ***beni*** *mpl* ***di ~*** consumer goods
consuntivo **I** *m* FIN closing balance; ***fare un ~ della situazione*** take stock of the situation **II** *adj* final; ***relazione*** *f* ***-a*** final report; ***bilancio*** *m* ~ closing balance
consuocero *m*, **-a** *f* father / mother of son-in-law / daughter-in-law
conta *f* count; ***fare la ~*** see who is 'it'
contaballe *m/f* ⟨*pl* contaballe⟩ *infml* bullshitter *vulg*
contabile *m/f* bookkeeper
contabilità *f* ⟨*pl* contabilità⟩ FIN *disciplina* accounting; *ufficio* accounts department; ***tenere la ~*** keep the books
contabilizzare *v/t* ⟨1a⟩ record **contabilizzazione** *f* recording
contachilometri *m* ⟨*pl* contachilometri⟩ mileometer, clock *infml*
contadino **I** *m*, **-a** *f* peasant **II** *adj* rural, country *attr*
contado *m* HIST *area of countryside around a town*
contagiare *v/t* ⟨1f⟩ infect
contagio *m* ⟨*pl* -gi⟩ infection; *per contatto diretto* contagion; (*epidemia*) outbreak
contagioso *adj* infectious; ***malattia*** *f* ***-a*** infectious disease
contagiri *m* ⟨*pl* contagiri⟩ rev(olution) counter
contagocce *m* ⟨*pl* contagocce⟩ dropper
container *m* ⟨*pl* container⟩ container; ***~ marittimo*** shipping container
containerizzare *v/t* ⟨1a⟩ containerize
contaminante **I** *adj* contaminating **II** *m* contaminant; ***~ radioattivo*** radioactive substance
contaminare *v/t* ⟨1m⟩ contaminate, pollute
contaminato *adj* contaminated; ***zona*** *f* ***-a*** contaminated area
contaminazione *f* contamination, pollution
contaminuti *m* ⟨*pl* contaminuti⟩ timer
contante *m* cash; ***in -i*** cash; ***pagare in -i*** pay (in) cash
contapassi *m* ⟨*pl* contapassi⟩ pedometer
contare ⟨1a⟩ **I** *v/t* count; ***~ i giorni*** count the days; ***senza ~ che …*** not to mention …; ***contarle grosse*** *infml* tell porkies; ***gli spettatori si contavano sulle dita*** you could count the number of spectators on the fingers of one hand **II** *v/i* count; ***~ di fare qc*** plan on doing sth; ***~ su qn / qc*** rely on s.o. / sth; ***imparare a ~*** learn to count; ***~ come il due di picche*** not matter at all; ***è gente che conta*** they're important people; ***peccato, ci contavo molto!*** what a shame, I was counting on it; ***vedrai che verrà, contaci!*** s / he'll come, you'll see!; ***cosa conti di fare adesso?*** what do you think you'll do now?
contascatti *m* ⟨*pl* contascatti⟩ *time meter on phone*
contastorie *m/f* ⟨*pl* contastorie⟩ fibber
contatore *m* meter; ***~ dell'acqua*** water meter; ***~ del gas*** gas meter; ***~ Geiger*** Geiger counter; ***lettura*** *f* ***del ~*** meter reading
contattare *v/t* ⟨1a⟩ contact; ***~ qn*** contact s.o.
contatto *m* **1.** contact; ***avere un ~ all'estero*** have a contact abroad; ***avere molti -i*** have a lot of contacts; ***mettersi in ~ con qn / qc*** get in touch with s.o. / sth; ***restare in ~ con qn*** keep in touch with s.o.; ***venire a ~ con qn / qc*** come into contact with s.o. / sth **2.** ELEC, RADIO; ***~ radio*** radio contact; ***fare ~*** make contact
conte *m* count
contea *f* county
conteggiare *v/t* ⟨1f⟩ work out; ***~ le spese*** work out expenses **conteggio** *m* ⟨*pl* -ggi⟩ calculation; *nel pugilato*: count

contegno *m* behavio(u)r; (*atteggiamento*) restraint; ***darsi un ~*** try to appear calm and collected

contemplare *v/t* ⟨1b⟩ contemplate; JUR provide for

contemplativo *adj* contemplative; ***vita*** *f* ***-a*** contemplative life

contemplazione *f* contemplation; ***darsi alla ~*** be lost in contemplation; ***essere*** *or* ***stare in ~ di qc*** contemplate sth

contempo *m*: ***nel ~*** at the same time

contemporaneamente *adv* at the same time

contemporaneità *f* ⟨*pl* contemporaneità⟩ contemporaneity

contemporaneo **I** *adj* contemporary (***di*** with); *movimenti* simultaneous; ***in -a*** at the same time; ***pittori*** *mpl* ***-i*** modern painters **II** *m*, ***-a*** *f* contemporary

contendere ⟨3c⟩ **I** *v/t*: ***~ qc a qn*** compete with s.o. for sth **II** *v/i* (*competere*) contend

contendersi *v/r* contend for, compete for

contenente *adj* containing

contenere *v/t* ⟨2q⟩ contain, hold; (*reprimere*) repress; (*limitare*) limit; ***~ le spese*** control expenses

contenersi *v/r* contain o.s.

contenimento *m*: ***~ dei costi*** cost control

contenitore *m* container

contentare *v/t* ⟨1b⟩ please

contentarsi *v/r* be content (***di*** with)

contentezza *f* happiness

contentino *m* sop

contento *adj* pleased (***di*** with); (*lieto*) glad, happy; ***essere ~ di fare qc*** be pleased that one is doing sth; ***sono -a che tu sia venuta*** I'm glad you came

contenutistico *adj* ⟨*mpl* -ci⟩ with the emphasis on content

contenuto[1] *adj* (*represso*) restrained; (*ridotto*) contained; ***prezzi*** *mpl* ***-i*** reasonable prices

contenuto[2] *m* contents *pl*

contenzioso **I** *adj* contentious **II** *n*: ***contenzioso*** *m* JUR legal cases; ***~ amministrativo*** administrative cases

contesa *f* dispute

conteso *past part* → ***contendere***

contessa *f* countess

contestabile *adj* questionable

contestare *v/t* ⟨1b⟩ protest; JUR serve; ***~ la violazione della legge*** charge s.o. with breaking the law

contestatore *m*, ***-trice*** *f* protestor

contestazione *f* protest; ***~ studentesca*** student protests *pl*; ***~ giovanile*** youth protests *pl*

contesto *m* context

contestuale *adj* (*relativo al contesto*) contextual; ADMIN (*contemporaneo*) contemporaneous; ***certificato*** *m* ***~*** *official document stating the place of residence, nationality etc. of a person*

contestualizzare *v/t* ⟨1a⟩ contextualize **contestualmente** *adv* at the same time

contiene → ***contenere***

contiguità *f* ⟨*pl* contiguità⟩ proximity

contiguo *adj* adjacent (***a*** to)

continentale *adj* continental

continente *m* continent

contingentamento *m* ECON imposition of quotas **contingentare** *v/t* ⟨1b⟩ impose quotas (on) **contingente** **I** *m* contingent (*a.* MIL) **II** *adj* contingent **contingenza** *f* (*circostanza*) circumstance; PHIL contingency; ***indennità*** *f* ***di ~*** ECON cost-of-living allowance

continuamente *adv* *senza interruzione* constantly, continuously; *spessissimo* continually, time and again; ***mi domanda ~ di te*** he / she keeps asking about you

continuare ⟨1m⟩ **I** *v/t* continue **II** *v/i* continue, carry on (***a fare*** doing); ***continua*** to be continued; ***continuate a mangiare*** don't stop eating; ***se continua a nevicare partiamo*** if it keeps on snowing, we're leaving

continuativo *adj* continuing

continuato *adj* continuous; ***orario*** *m* ***~*** open all day

continuazione *f* continuation; *di film* sequel; ***in ~*** over and over again; (*ininterrottamente*) non stop

continuità *f* continuity; ***con ~*** continuously; ***gruppo*** *m* ***di ~*** ELEC UPS

continuo *adj* (*ininterrotto*) continuous; (*molto frequente*) continual; ***di ~*** (*ininterrottamente*) continuously; (*molto spesso*) continually; ELEC ***corrente*** *f* ***-a*** direct current

contitolare *m/f* joint owner

conto *m* **1.** (*calcolo*) calculation **2.** FIN account; *in ristorante* bill, *US* check; ***~ corrente*** current account, *US* checking account; ***~ corrente postale*** Post Office account; ***~ profitti e perdite*** profit and loss account; ***~ vincolato*** term deposit; ***il ~, per favore!*** can I have the bill (*US* check) please!; ***fare i propri -i*** do one's sums; *fig* ***fare i -i senza l'oste*** forget the most important thing **3.** *fig* ***avere un ~ aperto con qn*** have a score to settle with s.o.; *fig* ***dopo facciamo i -i!*** I'll deal with you later!; ***fare ~ su qn*** count on s.o.; ***rendere ~ di qc*** account for sth; ***rendersi ~ di qc*** realize sth; ***sapere qc sul ~ di qn*** know sth about s.o.; ***tenere ~ di qc*** take sth into account; ***in fin dei -i*** when all's said and done, after all; ***a -i fatti*** all things considered; ***per ~ di*** on behalf of; ***per ~ mio*** (*secondo me*) in my opinion; (*da solo*) on my own; ***tenere da ~ qc*** bear sth in mind **4.** ***~ alla rovescia*** countdown

contorcere *v/t* ⟨3d⟩ twist

contorcersi *v/r*: ***~ dal dolore / dalle risate*** roll about in pain / laughing

contorcimento *m* contortion

contornare *v/t* ⟨1a⟩ surround (*a. fig*) **contornarsi** *v/r* ⟨1a⟩ surround oneself (***di*** with)

contorno *m* outline, contour; COOK side dish; ***cosa c'è di ~?*** what side dishes are there?

contorsione *f* contortion (*a. fig*) **contorsionista** *m/f* ⟨*mpl* -i⟩ contortionist

contorto *adj* twisted

contrabbandare *v/t* ⟨1a⟩ smuggle

contrabbandiere *m* smuggler

contrabbando *m* contraband; ***merce** f **di ~*** smuggled goods *pl*

contrabbasso *m* MUS double bass

contraccambiare *v/t* ⟨1k⟩ return

contraccambio *m* ⟨*pl* -bi⟩ return

contraccettivo *m* contraceptive

contraccezione *f* contraception

contraccolpo *m* rebound; *di arma da fuoco* recoil

contrada *f* district

contraddire *v/t* ⟨3t⟩ contradict

contraddirsi **I** *v/i* contradict o.s. **II** *v/r* contradict each other

contraddistinguere *v/t* ⟨3d⟩ mark

contraddittorietà *f* ⟨*pl* contraddittorietà⟩ contradictory nature **contraddittorio** ⟨*mpl* -ri⟩ **I** *adj* contradictory **II** *n*: ***contraddittorio*** *m* debate

contraddizione *f* contradiction; ***cadere in ~*** get tied up in knots; ***spirito** m **di ~*** contrariness

contraente **I** *adj* contracting **II** *m/f* contracting party

contraerea *f* anti-aircraft artillery **contraereo** *adj* anti-aircraft

contraffare *v/t* ⟨3aa⟩ (*falsificare*) forge; (*imitare*) imitate; ***~ la voce*** disguise one's voice

contraffatto *adj* forged; *voce* imitated

contraffattore *m*, **-trice** *f* forger

contraffazione *f* (*imitazione*) imitation; (*falsificazione*) forgery

contrafforte *m* ARCH buttress; GEOG spur

contralto *m* MUS (contr)alto

contrappeso *m* counterbalance

contrapporre *v/t* ⟨3ll⟩ set against

contrapporsi *v/r* (*contrastare*) clash; ***~ a*** oppose

contrapposizione *f* opposition; ***mettere in ~*** contrast

contrapposto *past part* → ***contrapporre***

contrappunto *m* counterpoint

contrariamente *adv*: ***~ a*** contrary to

contrariare *v/t* ⟨1k⟩ *piani* thwart, oppose; *persona* irritate, annoy

contrariato *adj* irritated, annoyed

contrarietà *fpl* difficulties *pl*, problems *pl*

contrario ⟨*mpl* -ri⟩ **I** *adj* contrary; *direzione* opposite; *vento* adverse; ***essere ~*** be against (***a*** sth); ***in caso ~*** failing that **II** *m* contrary, opposite; ***al ~*** on the contrary; ***hai qualcosa in ~?*** have you any objection?; ***non ho niente in ~*** I've got nothing against it

contrarre *v/t* ⟨3xx⟩ contract; ***~ i muscoli*** contract one's muscles; ***~ matrimonio*** marry

contrarsi *v/r* contract

contrassegnare *v/t* ⟨1a⟩ mark

contrassegno *m* mark; FIN ***(in) ~*** cash on delivery

contrastante *adj* contrasting; ***colori** mpl **-i*** clashing colo(u)rs; ***sentimenti** mpl **-i*** mixed feelings

contrastare ⟨1a⟩ **I** *v/t* contrast; (*ostacolare*) hinder **II** *v/i* contrast (***con***

with)

contrastato *adj* hindered; ***amore** m* **~** *love that has to overcome a lot of obstacles*

contrasto *m* contrast; (*litigio*, *discordia*) disagreement, dispute; ***mezzo** m* **di ~** MED contrast medium

contrattaccare *v/t* ⟨1d⟩ counterattack

contrattacco *m* ⟨*pl* -cchi⟩ counter-attack; ***passare al ~*** make a counter-attack

contrattare *v/t* ⟨1a⟩ negotiate; *persona* hire; ***~ sul prezzo*** haggle over the price

contrattazione *f* bargaining

contrattempo *m* hitch; ***ho avuto un ~*** I had a bit of a mishap

contrattile *adj* contractile; ***muscoli** mpl* **-i** contractile muscles

contratto[1] *past part* → ***contrarre***

contratto[2] *m* contract; ***~ d'affitto*** lease; ***~ d'opera*** contract; ***~ a tempo indeterminato / determinato*** fixed term / permanent contract

contrattuale *adj* contractual; ***diritto** m* **~** contract law; ***condizioni** fpl* **-i** conditions of contract

contravvenire *v/i* ⟨4p⟩: ***~ a*** contravene; ***~ a una norma*** contravene a regulation

contravventore *m*, **-trice** *f* offender; ***~ abituale*** habitual offender

contravvenzione *f* contravention; (*multa*) fine

contrazione *f* contraction; (*riduzione*) reduction; ***~ delle vendite*** drop in sales; ***~ di un debito*** reduction of a debt

contribuente *m/f* taxpayer

contribuire *v/i* ⟨4d⟩ contribute; ***~ a fare qc*** play a part in doing sth

contributivo *adj* contributory; ***fascia** f* **-a** contributory band

contributo *m* contribution; **-i** *pl* ***sociali*** social security (*US* welfare) contributions

contrito *adj* contrite **contrizione** *f* contrition

contro *prep* against; ***appoggiare qc ~ il muro*** lean sth against the wall; ***~ di me / lui*** against me / him; ***rimedio** m* **~ *il raffreddore*** cold remedy; ***erano cinque ~ due*** it was five against two; ***l'Italia ~ la Scozia*** Italy versus Scotland; ***assicurarsi ~ il furto*** take out insurance against theft; ***puntare la pistola ~ qn*** point the gun at s.o.; ***votare ~ (qn / qc)*** vote against s.o. / sth; ***sbattere ~ qn / qc*** bang into s.o. / sth

controbattere *v/t* ⟨3a⟩ (*replicare*) answer back; (*confutare*) rebut

controbilanciare *v/t* ⟨1f⟩ counterbalance (*a. fig*)

controcorrente I *adj* non-conformist **II** *adv* against the current; *in fiume* upstream

controcultura *f* counterculture

controesame *m* cross-examination

controffensiva *f* counter-offensive

controfigura *f in film* stand-in

controfinestra *f* storm window

controfirmare *v/t* ⟨1a⟩ countersign

controindicazione *f* MED contraindication

controllabile *adj* controllable

controllare *v/t* ⟨1c⟩ control; (*verificare*) check

controllarsi *v/r* control o.s.; ***controllati!*** get a grip!

controller *m* ⟨*pl* controller⟩ COMPUT controller

controllo *m* control; (*verifica*) check; MED check-up; ***~ dei biglietti*** ticket inspection; ***~ alla frontiera*** customs inspection; ***~ delle nascite*** birth control; COMPUT ***~ dell'ortografia*** spell checker; ***~ (dei) passaporti*** passport control; ***~ della qualità*** quality control; ***unità** f* ***di ~*** COMPUT control unit; ***avere il ~ di una società*** ECON have a controlling interest in a company; ***essere fuori ~*** be out of control; ***perdere il ~*** lose control; ***è tutto sotto ~!*** everything's under control!

controllore *m* controller; *di bus*, *treno* ticket inspector; ***~ di volo*** air traffic controller

controluce *f*: ***in ~*** against the light

contromanifestazione *f* counter demonstration

contromano *adv*: ***andare a ~*** be going the wrong way

contromarca *f* ⟨*pl* -che⟩ token

contromisura *f* countermeasure

contromossa *f* counter-move (*a. fig*)

controparte *f* JUR opposing party

contropartita *f fig* quid pro quo; ***chiedere qc in** or **come ~*** ask for sth in return

contropelo **I** *adv*: ***spazzolare ~*** brush against the pile **II** *m*: *fig* ***fare il pelo e il ~ a qn*** tear s.o. to pieces
controperizia *f expert report for the opposing side*
contropiede *m* SPORTS counter-attack; *fig* ***prendere qn in ~*** catch s.o. off guard
controproducente *adj* counterproductive
controproposta *f* counter-proposal
controrrdine *m* counterorder
controriforma *f* HIST Counter-Reformation
controrivoluzione *f* counter-revolution
controsenso *m* contradiction in terms; (*assurdità*) nonsense
controsoffitto *m* false ceiling
controspionaggio *m* ⟨*pl* -ggi⟩ counterespionage
controvalore *m* equivalent (value)
controversia *f* controversy, dispute; JUR litigation
controverso *adj* controversial
controvoglia *adv* unwillingly
contumace *adj* JUR defaulting **contumacia** *f* JUR default; ***condannare qn in ~*** sentence s.o. in their absence **contumaciale** *adj*: ***sentenza*** *f* ~ JUR sentenced passed in s.o.'s absence
contundente *adj*: ***corpo*** *m* ~ blunt instrument
conturbante *adj* provocative
contusione *f* bruise
contuso **I** *adj* bruised; ***ferita*** *f* ***lacero-contusa*** bruising and cuts **II** *m*, **-a** *f person who has suffered bruising*; ***nell'incidente ci sono stati tre -i*** three people were slightly injured in the accident
convalescente **I** *adj* convalescent **II** *m/f* person who is convalescent
convalescenza *f* convalescence; ***essere in ~*** be convalescing
convalida *f di firma, biglietto, gol* validation
convalidare *v/t* ⟨1m⟩ validate
convegno *m* convention; *luogo* meeting place; ***darsi ~*** arrange to meet; (*riunirsi*) meet
convenevoli *mpl* pleasantries *pl*
conveniente *adj* (*vantaggioso*) good; (*opportuno*) appropriate
convenienza *f di prezzo, offerta* good value; *di gesto* appropriateness; ***fare qc per ~*** do sth out of self-interest; ***matrimonio*** *m* ***di ~*** marriage of convenience; ***visita*** *f* ***di ~*** courtesy call
convenire ⟨4p⟩ **I** *v/i* gather, meet; (*concordare*) agree; (*essere opportuno*) be advisable, be better; ***ti conviene aspettare*** you'd be better off waiting **II** *v/t* (*stabilire*) stipulate
convento *m di monache* convent; *di monaci* monastery
convenuto **I** *past part* → ***convenire*** **II** *adj* agreed; ***come ~*** as agreed **III** *m*, **-a** *f* JUR defendant
convenzionale *adj* conventional
convenzionato *adj tariffa* agreed; *negozio* that has an agreement; *medico* national health service; ***officina*** *f* ***-a*** authorized garage
convenzione *f* convention; (*accordo*) agreement, convention; ***Convenzione Europea*** European Convention
convergente *adj* converging
convergenza *f* (*di opinioni, strade*) convergence; AUTO wheel alignment
convergere *v/i* ⟨3uu⟩ converge
conversare *v/i* ⟨1b⟩ talk, make conversation
conversazione *f* conversation; ***fare ~*** chat
conversione *f* conversion; AUTO U-turn
convertibile *adj* convertible
convertibilità *f* convertibility
convertire *v/t* ⟨4b or d⟩ convert
convertirsi *v/r* be converted; ***~ all'Islam*** convert to Islam
convertito *m*, **-a** *f* convert **convertitore** *m* converter; ***~ di frequenza*** frequency converter
convessità *f* ⟨*pl* convessità⟩ convexity
convesso *adj* convex
convettore *m* convector
convincente *adj* convincing; ***prova*** *f* ~ convincing proof
convincere *v/t* ⟨3d⟩ convince (***di*** of); ***~ qn a fare qc*** persuade s.o. to do sth
convincimento *m* conviction; ***fare opera di ~*** persuade
convinto *past part* → ***convincere***
convinzione *f* conviction
convitato *m*, **-a** *f* guest **convito** *m* banquet
convitto *m* boarding school **convit-**

tore *m*, **-trice** *f* boarder
convivente *m/f* common-law husband; *donna* common-law wife
convivenza *f* living together, cohabitation; **~ *pacifica*** peaceful coexistence
convivere *v/i* ⟨3zz⟩ live together
conviviale *adj* convivial; ***atmosfera*** *f* **~** convivial atmosphere
convocare *v/t* ⟨1l, c & d⟩ call, convene; **~ *un testimone*** call a witness
convocazione *f* calling, convening
convogliare *v/t* ⟨1g & c⟩ channel
convogliatore *m* conveyor
convoglio *m* ⟨*pl* -gli⟩ MIL, NAUT convoy; RAIL train
convolare *v/i* ⟨1a⟩: **~ *a nozze*** tie the knot
convolvolo *m* BOT convulvulus
convulsamente *adv* convulsively
convulsioni *fpl* MED convulsions *pl*, fits *pl*; ***soffrire di*** **~** suffer from convulsions *or* fits
convulso *adj* convulsive; *fig* feverish; ***pianto*** *m* **~** violent weeping; ***vita*** *f* ***-a*** busy life
cookie *m* ⟨*pl* cookie⟩ COMPUT cookie
cooperare *v/i* ⟨1m & c⟩ co-operate (***a*** in); (*contribuire*) contribute (***a*** to)
cooperativa *f*: (***società*** *f*) **~** co-operative; **~ *di consumo*** cooperative (store)
cooperativo *adj* cooperative
cooperazione *f* cooperation
coordinamento *m* co-ordination
coordinare *v/t* ⟨1m⟩ co-ordinate
coordinata *f* MATH co-ordinate; ***-e*** *pl* ***bancarie*** bank details
coordinatore *m*, **-trice** *f* co-ordinator
coordinazione *f* co-ordination
coorte *f* HIST cohort
copeco *m* ⟨*pl* -chi⟩ kopeck
Copenaghen *f* Copenhagen
coperchio *m* ⟨*pl* -chi⟩ lid, top
copernicano *adj* Copernican; ***sistema*** *m* **~** Copernican system
Copernico *m* Copernicus
coperta *f* blanket; NAUT deck; **~ *imbottita*** quilt; **~ *termica*** electric blanket; ***sotto*** **~** below deck
copertina *f* cover
coperto I *past part* → ***coprire*** **II** *adj* covered (***di*** with); *cielo* overcast, cloudy; ***sei ben ~?*** are you warm enough? **III** *m* cover, shelter; *piatti e posate* place; *prezzo* cover charge; ***essere al*** **~** be under cover, be sheltered
copertone *m* AUTO tyre, *US* tire
copertura *f* cover; **~ *delle spese*** covering one's costs, ***attività*** *f* ***di*** **~** cover-up
copia *f* copy; PHOT print, copy; **~ *autenticata*** authenticated copy; ***bella*** / ***brutta*** **~** fair / rough copy; COMPUT **~ *di cortesia*** copy to; ***in duplice*** **~** in duplicate
copiacommissione *f* order book
copiare *v/t* ⟨1k & c⟩ copy
copiatura *f* copying
copilota *m/f* ⟨*mpl* -i⟩ co-pilot
copione *m per attore* script; *fig* ***come da*** **~** according to plan
copiosamente *adv* copiously
copioso *adj* copious, abundant
copisteria *f* copy centre (*US* center)
coppa *f* cup; (*calice*) glass; **~ *Davis*** Davis Cup; **~ (*di*) *gelato*** dish of ice-cream; AUTO **~ *dell'olio*** oil sump
coppetta *f di gelato* tub
coppia *f* couple, pair; ***gara*** *f* ***a -e*** doubles *pl*; ***a -e*** in twos; ***fare*** **~ *fissa*** go steady
coprente *adj* that covers well; ***vernice*** *f* paint that gives a good covering
copricapo *m* ⟨*pl* copricapo⟩ head covering
copricostume *m* ⟨*pl* copricostume⟩ beachrobe
coprifasce *m* ⟨*pl* coprifasce⟩ matinee jacket
coprifuoco *m* curfew
copriletto *m* ⟨*pl* copriletto⟩ bedspread, coverlet
coprimaterasso *m* mattress cover
coprire *v/t* ⟨4f & c⟩ cover; *errore*, *suono* cover up; **~ *qn di baci* / *insulti*** shower s.o. with kisses / insults; **~ *una distanza*** cover a distance; **~ *tutto il territorio*** cover the whole area
coprirsi *v/r* (*vestirsi*) put something on; (*rannuvolarsi*) become overcast; ***copritevi bene, fa freddo*** wrap up well, it's cold; **~ *di qc*** *muffa*, *ruggine* be covered with sth; *fig* **~ *di gloria*** cover oneself with glory
coprocessore *m* COMPUT coprocessor
coproduzione *f* co-production, joint production
coprofagia *f* coprophagy **coprologia** *f*

scatology
copto I *adj* Coptic II *m*, **-a** *f* Copt
copyright *m* ⟨*pl* copyright⟩ copyright
coque *f*: ***uovo*** *m* ***alla ~*** soft-boiled egg
coraggio *m* courage; (*sfacciataggine*) nerve; ***farsi ~*** be brave; ***~, andiamo!*** come on, let's go!
coraggiosamente *adv* courageously
coraggioso *adj* brave, courageous
corale I *adj* choral; *fig* unanimous; ***canto*** *m* ***~*** choral singing; ***protesta*** *f* ***~*** unanimous protest II *m* MUS chorale III *f* choir
corallifero *adj* coral *attr*; ***banco*** *m* ***~*** coral bank **corallino** *adj* coral *attr*; ***barriera*** *f* ***~*** coral reef
corallo *m* coral
Corano *m* Koran
corata, coratella *f* COOK offal
corazza *f* MIL armo(u)r; ZOOL shell
corazzata *f* battleship
corazzato *adj* MIL armo(u)red; *fig* hardened (***contro*** to)
corbeille *f* ⟨*pl* corbeille⟩ basket of flowers; FIN trading floor
corbelleria *f* stupid thing
corbello *m* basket
corbezzolo *m* BOT arbutus; ***corbezzoli!*** *int* blimey!
corda *f* **1.** cord; (*fune*) rope; (*cordicella*) string; MUS string **2.** ***~ vocale*** vocal cord **3.** *fig* ***dare ~ a qn*** *infml* give s.o. their head; ***essere giù di ~*** feel down *or* depressed; *fig* ***mettere qn alle -e*** make things difficult for s.o.; ***tagliare la ~*** cut and run; ***tenere qn sulla ~*** keep s.o. in suspense *or* on tenterhooks; *fig* ***tirare troppo la ~*** push one's luck
cordame *m* NAUT rigging; ***-i*** *pl* ropes
cordata *f* rope, roped party
cordiale I *adj* cordial; ***-i saluti*** *mpl* kind regards II *m* cordial
cordialità *f* cordiality
cordialmente *adv* cordially
cordless *m* cordless phone
cordoglio *m* (*dolore*) grief, sorrow; (*condoglianze*) condolences *pl*
cordolo *m* BUILD stringcourse
cordone *m* cord; *di marciapiedi* kerb, *US* curb; (*sbarramento*) cordon; ***~ ombelicale*** umbilical cord
Corea *f*: ***~ del Nord*** North Korea; ***~ del Sud*** South Korea
coreano I *adj* Korean II *m*, **-a** *f* Korean
coreografia *f* choreography
coreografico *adj* ⟨*mpl* -ci⟩ choreographic; *fig* (*spettacolare*) spectacular
coreografo *m*, **-a** *f* choreographer
coriaceo *adj* leathery; *fig* tough; ***pelle*** *f* ***-a*** leathery skin
coriandolo *m* BOT coriander; ***-i*** *mpl* confetti
coricare *v/t* ⟨1l, c & d⟩ (*adagiare*) lay down; (*mettere a letto*) put to bed
coricarsi *v/r* lie down
Corinto *f* Corinth **corinzio** *adj* ⟨*mpl* -zi⟩ Corinthian
corista *m/f* ⟨*mpl* -i⟩ *di chiesa* choral singer; *di gruppo pop* singer
cormorano *m* cormorant
corna → ***corno***
cornacchia *f* carrion crow
cornamusa *f* bagpipes *pl*
cornea *f* cornea
corner *m* ⟨*pl* corner⟩ corner
cornetta *f* MUS cornet; ***~ del telefono*** receiver
cornetto *m* (*brioche*) croissant; (*gelato*) cone, cornet
cornice *f* frame; ARCH cornice; ***fare da ~ a qc*** frame sth
cornicione *m* ARCH cornice
cornico ⟨*mpl* -ci⟩ I *adj* Cornish II *m*, **-a** *f* Cornishman, Cornishwoman
cornificare *v/t* ⟨1m⟩ *infml* cheat on
corniola *f* BOT cornelian cherry dogwood; MINER carnelian
cornista *m/f* ⟨*mpl* -i⟩ horn player
corno *m* ⟨*pl usu* le corna⟩ horn; *ramificate* antlers *pl*; ***~ da scarpe*** shoehorn; ***pettine*** *m* ***di ~*** horn comb; *fig* ***fare le -a a qn*** *infml* cheat on s.o. *infml*; ***facciamo le -a!*** touch wood!; ***non m'importa un ~*** *infml* I don't give a damn *infml*
Cornovaglia *f* Cornwall
cornucopia *f* cornucopia
cornuto *adj infml* cheated, betrayed
coro *m* chorus; *cantori* choir; ***in ~*** (*insieme*) all together
corolla *f* BOT corolla
corollario *m* ⟨*mpl* -ri⟩ MATH, PHYS corollary; (*aggiunta*) appendix
corona *f* crown; (*rosario*) rosary; ***~ d'alloro*** laurel crown; ***~ dentaria*** crown; ***~ di fiori*** wreath; ***~ di spine*** crown of thorns
coronamento *m* coronation; *fig* crowning achievement

coronare *v/t* ⟨1a⟩ *sogno* achieve
coronaria *f* ANAT coronary artery
coronarico *adj* ⟨*mpl* -ci⟩ coronary; ***unità*** *f* ***-a*** coronary care unit
coronario *adj*: ***vasi*** *mpl* ***-i*** coronary arteries
corpetto *m da donna* bodice
corpo *m* **1.** body; ***~ celeste*** heavenly body; ***~ dell'edificio*** main part of the building; ***~ estraneo*** foreign body; ***andare di ~*** *infml* have a bowel movement; ***buttarsi a ~ morto*** throw o.s. down heavily; ***buttarsi a ~ morto nel lavoro*** fling o.s. into one's work; (***a***) ***~ a ~*** hand-to-hand **2.** MIL corps *sg*; ***~ degli alpini*** Alpine corps *sg*; ***~ diplomatico*** diplomatic corps *sg*; ***~ di guardia*** guard **3.** ***~ di ballo*** corps de ballet **4.** JUR ***~ del reato*** corpus delicti **5.** ***~ di Cristo*** REL body of Christ
corporale *adj* bodily
corporativo *adj* corporate
corporatura *f* build
corporazione *f* corporation
corporeo *adj* body *attr*; ***temperatura*** *f* ***-a*** body temperature
corposità *f* ⟨*pl* corposità⟩ body **corposo** *adj* dense; *vino* full-bodied; ***tinte*** *fpl* ***-e*** saturated colo(u)rs
corpulento *adj* stout, corpulent
corpuscolo *m* particle; PHYS corpuscle
Corpus Domini *m* Corpus Christi
corredare *v/t* ⟨1b⟩ supply; ***~ di libri una biblioteca*** supply a library with books **corredato** *adj* supplied (***di*** with); ***testo*** *m* ***~ di note*** annotated text
corredino *m* layette
corredo *m* equipment; *da sposa* trousseau; *da neonato* layette
correggere *v/t* ⟨3cc⟩ correct
correggersi *v/r* correct o.s.
correità *f* ⟨*pl* correità⟩ complicity (in a crime); ***chiamata*** *f* ***in ~*** JUR accusation of complicity (in a crime)
correlare *v/t* ⟨1a⟩ correlate **correlativo** *adj* correlative
correlato *adj* correlated
correlatore *m*, **-trice** *f* assistant examiner (of a thesis)
correlazione *f* correlation
corrente[1] *f* **1.** current; *elettrica* power; ***~ continua*** direct current; ***~ del Golfo*** Gulf Stream; ***essere trascinato dalla ~*** be dragged along by the current; ***è andata via la ~*** the power's gone off; ***staccare la ~*** turn off the power **2.** *fig di opinione* trend; ***~ di destra*** POL right-wing trend **3.** ***~ d'aria*** draught; ***c'è ~, puoi chiudere la porta?*** there's a draught, could you close the door?
corrente[2] **I** *adj* current; *acqua* running; *lingua* fluent; ***di uso ~*** in common use; ***il 5 del mese ~*** the 5th of this month **II** *m*: ***essere al ~*** know (***di*** sth); ***mettere qn al ~*** fill s.o. in; ***tenere qn al ~*** keep s.o. up to date, keep s.o. informed
correntemente *adv* **1.** (*fluentemente*) fluently; ***parla ~ l'inglese*** he / she's fluent in English **2.** (*abitualmente*) usually
correntista *m/f* ⟨*mpl* -i⟩ current (*US* checking) account holder
correo *m*, **-a** *f* accomplice
correre ⟨3o⟩ **I** *v/t* run; ***~ i cento metri*** run the hundred meters; ***~ il pericolo*** run the risk; ***~ un rischio*** run a risk **II** *v/i* run; (*affrettarsi*) hurry; *di veicolo* speed; *di tempo* fly; ***~ a fare qc*** run and do sth; ***~ in aiuto di qn*** rush to help s.o.; ***ci corre una bella differenza*** there's a big difference; ***correva l'anno …*** it was the year …; ***~ dietro a qn*** run after s.o.; ***~ ai ripari*** take remedial action; ***corre voce*** it is rumo(u)red; ***lascia ~!*** let it go!, leave it!; ***piano, non ~!*** don't drive so fast!
corresponsabile *adj* jointly responsible; ***essere ~ di qc*** be jointly responsible for sth **corresponsabilità** *f* ⟨*pl* corresponsabilità⟩ joint responsibility
corresponsione *f* payment; *di affetti* reciprocation
correttamente *adv* correctly; ***comportarsi ~*** behave properly; ***eseguire ~ qc*** do sth properly
correttezza *f* correctness; (*onestà*) honesty
correttivo **I** *adj* corrective **II** *n*: ***correttivo*** *m* corrective
corretto **I** *past part* → ***correggere*** **II** *adj* correct; ***caffè*** *m* ***~*** coffee laced with alcohol
correttore **I** *m* (*liquido*) correcting fluid; *nel trucco* concealer; COMPUT ***~ ortografico*** spell checker **II** *m*, **-trice** *f*:

~ di bozze proofreader

correzione *f* TYPO correction; COMPUT ***~ ortografica*** spell checking; ***~ di bozze*** proofreading; ***~ d'errore*** COMPUT, TEL error correction

corrida *f* bullfight

corridoio *m* ⟨*pl* -oi⟩ corridor; *in aereo, teatro* aisle

corridore *m in auto* racing driver; *a piedi* runner

corriera *f* coach, bus

corriere *m* courier; ***~ diplomatico*** courier; ***~ della droga*** drugs courier, mule *sl*

corrimano *m* handrail

corrispettivo *m* (*compenso*) compensation; (*equivalente*) equivalent

corrispondente I *adj* corresponding **II** *m/f* correspondent; ***~ commerciale*** agent; ***~ estero*** foreign correspondent

corrispondenza *f* correspondence; (*posta*) post; ***in ~ di*** next to; ***vendita*** *f* ***per ~*** mail order (shopping); ***corso*** *m* ***per ~*** correspondence course

corrispondere ⟨3hh⟩ **I** *v/t* (*pagare*) pay; (*ricambiare*) reciprocate **II** *v/i* correspond; (*coincidere*) coincide; (*equivalere*) be equivalent

corrisposto I *past part* → ***corrispondere*** **II** *adj* reciprocated; ***amore*** *m* ***~*** mutual love

corroborante I *adj* invigorating **II** *m* pick-me-up **corroborare** *v/t* ⟨1m & c⟩ (*rinvigorire*) invigorate; (*avvalorare*) bear out

corrodere *v/t* ⟨3b⟩ corrode, rust

corrodersi *v/r* ⟨3b⟩ corrode, rust

corrompere *v/t* ⟨3rr⟩ corrupt; *con denaro* bribe

corrompibile *adj* corruptible

corrosione *f* corrosion

corrosivo *adj* corrosive

corroso *past part* → ***corrodere***

corrotto I *past part* → ***corrompere*** **II** *adj* corrupt

corrucciato *adj* worried

corrugare *v/t* ⟨1e⟩ wrinkle; ***~ la fronte*** frown

corrugato *adj* furrowed; ***fronte*** *f* ***-a*** furrowed brow

corruttibile *adj* (*deteriorabile*) perishable; (*corrompibile*) corruptible **corruttibilità** *f* ⟨*pl* corruttibilità⟩ (*alterabilità*) perishability **corruttore** *m*, **-trice** *f* corrupter; ***~ di minorenni*** child molester

corruzione *f* corruption; *con denaro* bribery; ***~ dei costumi*** moral corruption; ***~ di pubblico ufficiale*** bribery of a public official

corsa *f* run; *attività* running; *di autobus* trip, journey; (*gara*) race; ***~ agli armamenti*** arms race; ***~ contro il tempo*** race against time; ***~ a ostacoli*** *ippica* steeplechase; *atletica* hurdles; ***di ~*** at a run; *in fretta* in a rush; ***vettura*** *f* ***da ~*** racing car; ***fare una ~*** rush, dash; ***-e*** *pl* races

corsaro *m* corsair

corsetto *m* corset; MED surgical corset

corsia *f* **1.** aisle; AUTO lane; ***~ di emergenza*** emergency lane; AUTO ***~ preferenziale*** bus lane; *fig* fast track; ***~ di sorpasso*** overtaking lane; ***a tre -e*** three-lane **2.** *di ospedale* ward

Corsica *f* Corsica

corsista *m/f* ⟨*mpl* -i⟩ course participant

corsivo *m* italics *pl*

corso[1] **I** *adj* Corsican **II** *m*, **-a** *f* Corsican

corso[2] **I** *past part* → ***correre*** **II** *m* **1.** course; ***~ d'acqua*** watercourse; ***~ della vita*** course of life **2.** (*lezioni*) course; ***~ d'aggiornamento*** refresher course; ***~ di lingue*** language course; ***~ serale*** evening class; ***studente fuori ~*** *a student who has failed to complete the required courses in the time allowed* **3.** (*strada*) main street **4.** FIN *di moneta* circulation; *di titoli* rate; ***~ dei cambi*** exchange rate, rate of exchange; ***~ di chiusura*** closing rate; FIN ***fuori ~*** out of circulation **5.** TYPO ***in ~ di stampa*** being printed; ***lavori*** *mpl* ***in ~*** work in progress; ***si sposeranno nel ~ dell'anno*** they'll get married this year

corte *f* court; ***~ d'appello*** court of appeal; ***~ di giustizia*** law court; ***Corte di giustizia europea*** European Court of Justice; ***~ marziale*** court-martial; ***Corte Suprema*** Supreme Court; ***fare la ~ a qn*** court s.o.

corteccia *f* ⟨*pl* -cce⟩ bark

corteggiamento *m* courtship (*a.* ZOOL)

corteggiare *v/t* ⟨1f⟩ court

corteggiatore *m*, **-trice** *f* suitor

corteo *m* procession; **~ *funebre*** funeral cortège
cortese *adj* polite, courteous
cortesemente *adv* politely, courteously
cortesia *f* politeness, courtesy; ***per ~!*** please!; ***fare una ~ a qn*** do s.o. a favour; ***visita*** *f* ***di ~*** courtesy call
cortigiana *f fig* courtesan
cortigiano **I** *adj* courtly **II** *m*, **-a** *f* courtier; *pej* sycophant
cortile *m* courtyard; ***~ interno*** internal courtyard; ***~ della scuola*** playground
cortina *f* curtain; ***~ di nebbia / fumo*** curtain of mist / smoke; ***~ di ferro*** *hist* Iron Curtain
cortisolo *m* cortisone
cortisone *m* cortisone
corto *adj* short; ***tagliar ~*** cut it short; ***essere a ~ di quattrini*** be short of money
cortocircuito *m* short (circuit)
cortometraggio *m* short
corvé *f* ⟨*pl* corvé⟩ (*sfacchinata*) chore
corvetta *f* NAUT corvette
corvino *adj* jet-black
corvo *m* rook; ***~ imperiale*** raven
cosa *f* thing; (***che***) ***~*** what; ***~ c'è?*** what's the matter?; ***di ~ si tratta?*** what's it about?; ***qualche ~*** something; ***dimmi una ~*** tell me something; ***qualunque ~*** anything; ***una ~ da nulla*** a trifle; ***una ~ del genere*** something / anything like that; ***un'altra ~*** another thing; ***-e*** *pl* ***da vedere*** sights; ***da ~ nasce ~*** one thing leads to another; ***fra le altre -e*** among other things; ***tante belle -e!*** all the best!; ***per prima ~*** first of all; ***Cosa nostra*** the Mafia; ***le proprie -e*** one's things
cosacco ⟨*mpl* -cchi⟩ **I** *adj* Cossack **II** *m*, **-a** *f* Cossack
coscia *f* ⟨*pl* -sce⟩ thigh; COOK leg
cosciente *adj* conscious
coscientemente *adv* consciously
coscienza *f* conscience; (*consapevolezza*) consciousness; ***agire secondo ~*** listen to one's conscience; ***senza coscienza*** unscrupulous; ***avere qc sulla ~*** have sth on one's conscience; ***avere la ~ sporca*** have a guilty conscience; ***gli rimorde la ~*** his conscience is pricking him
coscienziosamente *adv* conscientiously
coscienzioso *adj* conscientious
cosciotto *m* leg; ***~ di agnello al forno*** roast leg of lamb
coscritto *m* conscript **coscrizione** *f* conscription
coseno *m* cosine
cosentino **I** *adj* of Cosenza; *persona* from Cosenza **II** *m*, **-a** *f* person from Cosenza
cosetta *f* little something
così *adv* so; (*in questo modo*) like this; ***~ alto / bello*** so tall / beautiful; ***~ ~*** so-so; ***e ~ via*** and so on; ***per ~ dire*** so to speak; ***proprio ~!*** exactly!; ***basta ~!*** that's enough!; ***meglio ~!*** it's for the best; ***~ … come*** as … as; ***ero ~ stanco che sono andato a letto*** I was so tired that I went to bed; ***non ho detto ~!*** that's not what I said!; ***voglio una macchina ~*** I want a car like that; ***non ho mai visto un film ~ stupido*** I've never seen such a stupid film
cosicché *cj* and so
cosiddetto *adj* so called
cosiffatto *adj* such
cosmesi *f* cosmetics *pl*
cosmetico ⟨*mpl* -ci⟩ **I** *adj* cosmetic **II** *m* cosmetic
cosmico *adj* ⟨*mpl* -ci⟩ cosmic
cosmo *m* cosmos
cosmografia *f* cosmography
cosmologia *f* cosmology
cosmonauta *m/f* ⟨*mpl* -i, *fpl* -e⟩ cosmonaut
cosmonave *f* spaceship
cosmopolita *adj* cosmopolitan
coso *m infml* what-d'you-call-it *infml*
cospargere *v/t* ⟨3uu⟩ sprinkle; (*coprire*) cover (***di*** with); ***~ di qc*** sprinkle with sth
cosparso *past part* → ***cospargere***
cospetto *m*: ***al ~ di qn / qc*** in the presence of s.o. / sth
cospicuo *adj* notable; *ingente* substantial
cospirare *v/i* ⟨1a⟩ conspire
cospiratore *m*, **-trice** *f* conspirator
cospirazione *f* conspiracy
costa *f* coast, coastline; (*pendio*) hillside; ANAT rib; *di libro* spine; ***Costa Azzurra*** Côte d'Azur; ***Costa Smeralda*** *up-market holiday area in Sardinia*; ***lungo la ~*** along the coast; ***velluto*** *m* ***a -e*** cord

Costa d'Avorio *f* Ivory Coast
costante I *adj* constant, steady; MATH constant **II** *f* MATH constant
costanza *f* perseverance
Costanza *f* Constance; ***lago*** *m* ***di*** **~** Lake Constance
costare *v/i* ⟨1c⟩ cost; **~ *caro*** be expensive, cost a lot; *fig* cost dearly; ***quanto costa?*** how much is it?; ***costi quel che costi*** whatever it costs
costaricano I *adj* Costa Rican **II** *m*, **-a** *f* Costa Rican
costata *f* rib steak; **~ *di agnello*** lamb chop; **~ *di maiale*** pork chop; **~ *di manzo*** rib of beef
costato *m* ribs *pl*
costeggiare *v/t* ⟨1f⟩ skirt, hug; ***la strada costeggia il fiume*** the road runs alongside the river
costei *pron* she; her
costellare *v/t* ⟨1o & b⟩ stud (***di*** with) **costellato** *adj* studded; ***cielo*** *m* **~ *di stelle*** sky full of stars
costellazione *f* constellation; **~ *familiare*** PSYCH family constellation
costernato *adj* dismayed **costernazione** *f* dismay
costiera *f* coast; **~ *amalfitana*** the Amalfi coast
costiero *adj* coastal
costipato *adj*: ***essere*** **~** *con stipsi* be constipated; *con raffreddore* be stuffed up *infml*
costituente I *adj* constituent **II** *m* constituent **III** *f* (*assemblea*) constituent assembly
costituire *v/t* ⟨4d⟩ constitute; *società* form, create
costituirsi *v/r* give o.s. up
costitutivo *adj* constituent
costituzionale *adj* constitutional
costituzionalità *f* ⟨*pl* cosituzionalità⟩ constitutionality **costituzionalmente** *adv* constitutionally
costituzione *f* constitution; **~ *europea*** European Constitution; ***certificato*** *m* ***di sana e robusta*** **~** certificate of good health
costo *m* **1.** cost; ***prezzo*** *m* ***di*** **~** cost price; ***-i*** *pl* ***di produzione*** production costs; **~ *della vita*** cost of living **2. *a*** **~ *di perdere*** even if it means losing; ***ad ogni*** **~** at all costs
costola *f* rib; *di libro* spine; ***avere qn alle -e*** have s.o. on one's tail; ***stare alle -e di qn*** stick to s.o.'s side
costoletta *f* COOK cutlet
costoro *pron pl* they; *complemento* them
costoso *adj* expensive, costly
costretto *past part* → ***costringere***
costringere *v/t* ⟨3d⟩ force, compel; **~ *qn a fare qc*** force s.o. to do sth
costrittivo *adj* coercive **costrizione** *f* coercion; **~ *morale*** moral pressure
costrizione *f* constraint
costruire *v/t* ⟨4d⟩ build, construct
costruttivismo *m* constructivism
costruttivo *adj fig* constructive
costruttore *m*, **-trice** *f* builder; (*fabbricante*) manufacturer
costruzione *f* building, construction; GRAM construction; ***in*** **~** under construction
costui *pron m* he; *complemento* him
costume *m* (*usanza*) custom; (*condotta*) morals *pl*; (*indumento*) costume; **~ *da bagno*** swimming costume, swimsuit; *da uomo* (swimming) trunks *pl*; **~ *nazionale*** national costume; ***di facili -i*** of loose morals; ***festa*** *f* ***in*** **~** fancy dress party
costumista *m/f* ⟨*mpl* -i⟩ costume designer
costura *f* seam
cotechino *m kind of pork sausage*
cotenna *f* pigskin; *della pancetta* rind
cotica *f* ⟨*pl* -che⟩ pork rind; ***fagioli con le -che*** beans with pork rinds
cotillon *m* ⟨*pl* cotillon⟩ favo(u)r
cotogna *f* quince
cotognata *f* quince jelly **cotogno** *m* quince tree
cotoletta *f* cutlet; **~ *alla milanese*** *breaded cutlet fried in butter*
cotonare *v/t* ⟨1a⟩ backcomb **cotonarsi** *v/r* ⟨1a⟩: **~ *i capelli*** backcomb one's hair
cotone *m* cotton; MED **~ *idrofilo*** cotton wool, *US* absorbent cotton; ***di*** **~** cotton
cotonificio *m* ⟨*pl* -ci⟩ cotton mill **cotonina** *f* calico
cotta[1] *f infml* crush; ***avere / prendersi una*** **~ *per qn*** have / get a crush on s.o.; *fig* ***furbo*** *m* ***di tre -e*** crafty devil
cotta[2] *f* (*tunica*) surcoat
cottimo *m*: ***lavorare a*** **~** do piecework
cotto I *past part* → ***cuocere*** **II** *adj* **1.** done, cooked; **~ *al forno*** oven-baked;

ben ~ well-done; ***vederne/sentirne di -e e di crude*** see/hear all kinds of things **2.** *infml fig* head over heels in love (***di*** with) **III** *m* terracotta; ***pavimento*** *m* ***in ~*** terracotta floor

cottolengo *m* ⟨*pl* -ghi⟩ *home for physically and mentally disabled people*

Cotton fioc® *m* ⟨*pl* Cotton fioc⟩ cotton bud

cottura *f* cooking; ***~ a vapore*** steaming

coupon *m* ⟨*pl* coupon⟩ coupon

covare ⟨1a⟩ **I** *v/t* sit on, hatch; *fig malattia* sicken for, come down with; *rancore* harbo(u)r **II** *v/i* sit on eggs

covata *f* brood

covo *m* den; (*nido*) nest; *fig* hideout; ***~ di briganti*** den of thieves

covone *m* sheaf

cozza *f* mussel; ***-e*** *pl* ***alla marinara*** COOK *mussels cooked with garlic, parsley and wine*

cozzare *v/i* ⟨1c⟩: ***~ contro*** crash into; *fig* clash with

C.P. *abbr* (= **Casella Postale**) PO Box (Post Office Box)

c.p.c. *m abbr* (= **codice di procedura civile**) civil code

c.p.p. *m abbr* (= **codice di procedura penale**) criminal code

CPT *abbr* (= **Centro di Permanenza Temporanea**) *immigrant detention centre*

CR *abbr* (= **Cremona**) Cremona

crac *m* ⟨*pl* crac⟩ *fig* crash

Cracovia *f* Cracow

crampo *m* cramp

cranico *adj* ⟨*mpl* -ci⟩ cranial; ***base*** *f* ***-a*** base of the skull; ***frattura*** *f* ***-a*** fracture of the skull

cranio *m* ⟨*pl* -ni⟩ skull; ***a ~*** *infml* a *or* per head

crapa *f infml hum* bonce

crash *m* COMPUT: ***andare in ~*** crash

crash-test *m* ⟨*pl* crash-test⟩ AUTO crash test

crasso *adj*: ***intestino*** *m* ***~*** large intestine

cratere *m* crater

cravatta *f* tie; ***~ a farfalla*** bow-tie

crawl *m* SPORTS crawl, freestyle

creanza *f* manners *pl*; ***mala ~*** bad manners *pl*

creare *v/t* ⟨1b⟩ create; *fig* (*causare*) cause

creativamente *adv* creatively

creatività *f* creativity

creativo I *adj* creative **II** *m*, **-a** *f* copywriter

creato I *past part* → ***creare*** **II** *m* creation

creatore I *adj* creative **II** *m* Creator **III** *m*, **-trice** *f* creator; ***~ di moda*** (fashion) designer

creatura *f* creature

creazione *f* creation

credente *m/f* believer

credenza[1] *f* belief

credenza[2] *f mobile* dresser

credenziali *fpl* credentials *pl*

credere ⟨3a⟩ **I** *v/t* believe; (*pensare*) believe, think; ***lo credo bene!*** I should think so too!; ***credo di sì*** I think so; ***credo di no*** I don't think so; ***credevo arrivassero oggi*** I thought they'd come today; ***ti credevo più forte*** I thought you were stronger than that **II** *v/i* believe; ***~ a qn*** believe s.o.; ***~ in qn*** believe in s.o.; ***credo in Dio*** I believe in God; ***non ci credo*** I don't believe it; ***non credevo ai miei occhi*** I couldn't believe my eyes

credersi *v/r* ⟨3a⟩ believe *or* think o.s. to be

credibile *adj* credible

credibilità *f* credibility

credibilmente *adv* credibly

creditizio *adj* ⟨*mpl* -zi⟩ credit *attr*

credito *m* **1.** credit; ***comprare a ~*** buy on credit; ***fare ~ a qn*** give s.o. credit **2.** *fig* trust; (*attendibilità*) reliability; ***dare ~ a qc*** believe sth

creditore *m*, **-trice** *f* creditor

credo *m* ⟨*pl* credo⟩ credo

credulità *f* ⟨*pl* credulità⟩ credulity, gullibility **credulone I** *adj* credulous, gullible **II** *m*, **-a** *f* dupe

crema *f* cream; *di latte e uova* custard; ***~ da barba*** shaving foam; ***~ idratante*** moisturizer, moisturizing cream; ***~ solare*** suntan lotion; ***torta*** *f* ***alla ~*** cream cake

cremagliera *f* TECH rack; ***ferrovia*** *f* ***a ~*** rack railway

cremare *v/t* ⟨1b⟩ cremate

crematorio *m* ⟨*pl* -ri⟩ crematorium

cremazione *f* cremation

crème caramel *m* ⟨*pl* crème caramel⟩ crème caramel

cremino *m chocolate with a creamy*

centre
cremisi **I** *adj inv* crimson **II** *m* ⟨*pl* cremisi⟩ crimson
Cremlino *m* Kremlin
cremonese **I** *adj* Cremonese **II** *m/f* Cremonese
cremoso *adj* creamy
cren *m* horseradish
creolo **I** *adj* Creole **II** *m*, **-a** *f* Creole **III** *n*: ***creolo*** *m* (*lingua*) creole
crepa *f* crack
crepaccio *m* ⟨*pl* -cci⟩ cleft; *di ghiacciaio* crevasse
crepacuore *m* heartbreak; ***morire di ~*** die of a broken heart
crepapelle *m*: ***ridere a ~*** scream with laughter
crepare *v/i* ⟨1b⟩ (*spaccarsi*) crack; *infml* (*morire*) kick the bucket *infml*; ***~ d'invidia*** be eaten up with envy; ***~ dalle risa*** split one's sides laughing; ***crepi il lupo!*** good luck!
crepato *adj* cracked
crêpe *f* ⟨*pl* crêpe⟩ pancake
crepitare *v/i* ⟨11 & b⟩ crackle
crepitio *m* ⟨*pl* -ii⟩ *di fuoco*: crackling; *di pioggia*: pattering
crepuscolare *adj* twilight (*a.* MED, PSYCH); LIT crepuscular; ***poeta*** *m* **~** *poet who wrote in the early 20th century style of crepuscolarismo*; ***stato*** *m* **~** twilight state
crepuscolo *m* twilight; ***~ degli dei*** twilight of the gods; ***~ della sera*** dusk; ***al ~*** at dusk
crescendo *m* MUS crescendo
crescente *adj* growing; *luna* waxing
crescere ⟨3n⟩ **I** *v/t* bring up, raise **II** *v/i* grow; (*aumentare*) grow, increase; ***farsi ~ i capelli*** grow one's hair
crescione *m* watercress
crescita *f* growth; (*aumento*) growth, increase; ***~ economica*** economic growth
cresima *f* confirmation
cresimando *m*, **-a** *f* confirmation candidate
cresimare *v/t* ⟨11 & b⟩ confirm
crespa *f* wrinkle
crespella *f* savoury pancake
crespo *adj capelli* frizzy; ***carta*** *f* ***-a*** crepe paper
cresta *f* crest; *di montagna* peak; *fig* ***abbassare la ~*** be brought down a peg or two; *fig* ***essere sulla ~ dell'onda*** be on the crest of the wave; *fig* ***fare la ~ sulla spesa*** *keep some of the shopping money for oneself by inflating the prices*
creta *f* clay
cretese **I** *adj* Cretan **II** *m/f* Cretan
cretinata *f* stupid thing; ***dire / fare una ~*** say / do something stupid
cretinetti *m/f* ⟨*pl* cretinetti⟩ idiot **cretinismo** *m* idiocy
cretino **I** *adj* stupid, idiotic **II** *m*, **-a** *f* idiot
CRI *abbr* (= **Croce Rossa Italiana**) *Italian Red Cross*
cribbio *int* crikey
cric *m* ⟨*pl* cric⟩ AUTO jack
cricca *f* ⟨*pl* -cche⟩ clique
criceto *m* hamster
criminale **I** *adj* criminal **II** *m/f* criminal; ***~ di guerra*** war criminal
criminalità *f* crime
criminalizzare *v/t* ⟨1a⟩ criminalize
Criminalpol *f* crime squad
crimine *m* crime; ***~ di guerra*** war crime; ***~ contro l'umanità*** crime against humanity
criminologia *f* criminology **criminologo** *m*, **-a** *f* ⟨*mpl* -gi⟩ criminologist
crinale *m* ridge
crine *m* horsehair
criniera *f* mane
crinolina *f* crinoline
criochirurgia *f* cryosurgery
cripta *f* crypt
criptare *v/t* ⟨1a⟩ encrypt
criptato *adj* TV encrypted
criptico *adj* ⟨*mpl* -ci⟩ (*enigmatico*) cryptic
crisalide *f* ZOOL chrysalis; ***trasformarsi in ~*** change into a chrysalis
crisantemo *m* chrysanthemum
crisi *f* crisis; MED fit; ***~ degli alloggi*** housing shortage; ***~ di astinenza*** withdrawal symptoms; ***~ energetica*** energy crisis; ***~ epilettica*** epileptic fit; ***~ di governo*** government crisis; ***avere una ~ di nervi*** have hysterics; ***essere in ~*** *persona* be having a breakdown; *settore* be in crisis
crisma *m* ⟨*pl* -i⟩ REL chrism; *fig* blessing; ***con tutti i -i*** in accordance with the rules
cristalleria *f* glassware; (*negozio*) glassware shop **cristalliera** *f* display cabinet

cristallino[1] *adj* crystalline; *fig* crystal clear; ***zucchero*** *m* **~** granulated sugar; ***acqua*** *f* ***-a*** crystal clear water
cristallino[2] *m* lens
cristallizzare *v/t* ⟨1a⟩ crystallize
cristallizzarsi *v/r* ⟨1a⟩ crystallize
cristallizzazione *f* crystallization (*a. fig*)
cristallo *m* crystal; ***bicchiere*** *m* ***di*** **~** crystal glass; ***-i*** *pl* ***liquidi*** liquid crystal; **~** ***di rocca*** rock crystal
cristianamente *adv* in a Christian way
cristianesimo *m* Christianity
cristianità *f* (*i cristiani*) Christendom
cristianizzazione *f* conversion to Christianity
cristiano **I** *adj* Christian **II** *m*, **-a** *f* Christian
Cristo *m* Christ; ***avanti*** **~** before Christ; ***dopo*** **~** Anno Domini
criterio *m* ⟨*pl* -ri⟩ criterion; (*buon senso*) common sense; ***-i*** *pl* ***di adesione*** EU rules for EU membership; ***-i*** *pl* ***di convergenza*** EU convergence criteria
critica *f* ⟨*pl* -che⟩ criticism; ***stroncato dalla*** **~** slaughtered by the critics
criticabile *adj* open to criticism **criticamente** *adv* critically
criticare *v/t* ⟨1l & d⟩ criticize
critico ⟨*mpl* -ci⟩ **I** *adj* critical **II** *m*, **-a** *f* critic
criticone *m*, **-a** *f* *infml* fault-finder
crittografia *f* COMPUT cryptography
crivellare *v/t* ⟨1b⟩: **~** ***qn*** **/** ***qc di colpi*** riddle s.o. / sth with bullets
crivello *m* sieve
croato **I** *adj* Croatian **II** *m*, **-a** *f* Croat, Croatian
Croazia *f* Croatia
croccante **I** *adj* crisp, crunchy **II** *m* COOK nut brittle
crocchetta *f* COOK potato croquette
crocchia *f* bun; ***farsi la*** **~** do one's hair in a bun
crocchio *m* ⟨*pl* -cchi⟩ group
croce *f* cross; ***Croce Rossa*** Red Cross; ***farsi il segno della*** **~** cross o.s.; ***a occhio e*** **~** at a rough guess; **~** ***e delizia*** *hum* source of joy and pain
crocerista *m/f* ⟨*mpl* -i⟩ cruise passenger
crocerossina *f* Red Cross nurse
crocetta *f* small cross; ***fare una*** **~** ***su qc*** make a cross on sth
crocevia *m* crossroads *sg*
crochet *m* ⟨*pl* crochet⟩ (*uncinetto*) crochet hook; (*lavoro*) crochet
crociata *f* crusade
crocicchio *m* ⟨*pl* -cchi⟩ crossroads *sg*; RAIL crossing
crociera[1] *f* cruise; ARCH crossing; ***velocità*** *f* ***di*** **~** cruising speed; ***andare in*** **~** to go on a cruise
crociera[2] *f*: ***volta*** *f* ***a*** **~** ARCH cross vault
crocifiggere *v/t* ⟨3mm⟩ crucify
crocifissione *f* crucifixion
crocifisso **I** *past part* → ***crocifiggere*** **II** *m* crucifix
croco *m* BOT crocus
crogiolarsi *v/r* ⟨1l & c⟩: **~** ***al sole*** bask in the sun; *fig* **~** ***nei ricordi*** wallow in one's memories
crogiolo *m* crucible; *fig* melting pot
crollare *v/i* ⟨1c⟩ collapse
crollo *m* collapse; **~** ***dei prezzi*** slump in prices
cromare *v/t* ⟨1c⟩ chrome, chromium-plate
cromaticità *f* ⟨*pl* cromaticità⟩ colo(u)r range
cromatico *adj* ⟨*mpl* -ci⟩ MUS chromatic
cromato *adj* chromium-plated
cromatura *f* chromium plating
cromo *m* chrome
cromosoma *m* ⟨*pl* -i⟩ chromosome
cronaca *f* ⟨*pl* -che⟩ chronicle; *di partita* commentary; ***fatto di*** **~** news item; **~** ***nera*** crime news *sg*; **~** ***rosa*** gossip column; ***essere al centro della*** **~** be front-page news
cronicamente *adv* chronically
cronicità *f* ⟨*pl* cronicità⟩ chronicity
cronicizzarsi *v/r* ⟨1a⟩ become chronic
cronico *adj* ⟨*mpl* -ci⟩ chronic
cronista *m/f* ⟨*mpl* -i⟩ reporter; *di partita* commentator
cronografo *m* stopwatch
cronologia *f* chronology
cronologicamente *adv* chronologically
cronologico *adj* ⟨*mpl* -ci⟩ chronological
cronometraggio *m* ⟨*pl* -ggi⟩ time-keeping
cronometrare *v/t* ⟨1a⟩ time
cronometrico *adj*: *fig* ***precisione*** *f* ***-a*** absolute precision

cronometro *m* chronometer; SPORTS stopwatch
cross *m* ⟨*pl* cross⟩ SPORTS cross; ***fare un ~*** cross the ball
crosta *f* crust; MED scab; *di formaggio* rind; ***~ terrestre*** earth's crust
crostacei *mpl* shellfish
crostata *f* COOK tart
crostino *m* COOK crouton
crotonese I *adj* from Crotone **II** *m/f* person from Crotone
croupier ⟨*pl* croupier⟩ croupier
crucciarsi *v/r* ⟨1f⟩ fret
crucciato *adj* worried
cruccio *m* ⟨*pl* -cci⟩ worry
crucco *m*, **-a** *f* ⟨*mpl* -cchi⟩ *pej* Kraut
cruciale *adj* crucial
cruciverba *m* ⟨*pl* cruciverba⟩ crossword (puzzle)
crudamente *adv* harshly
crudele *adj* cruel
crudelmente *adv* cruelly
crudeltà *f* ⟨*pl* crudeltà⟩ cruelty
crudezza *f del clima*: harshness; *fig* coarseness
crudo *adj* raw
cruento *adj battaglia* bloody; *film* bloodthirsty
cruiser *m* ⟨*pl* cruiser⟩ cabin cruiser
crumiro *m*, **-a** *f* scab
cruna *f* eye
crusca *f* bran; ***Accademia** f **della Crusca*** *institute set up in the 16th century in Florence to protect the Italian language*
cruscotto *m* dashboard; *scomparto* glove compartment
c.s. *abbr* (= **come sopra**) as above
CS *abbr* (= **Cosenza**) Cosenza
CSI *abbr* (= **Comunità di Stati Indipendenti**) CIS (Commonwealth of Independent States)
CSM *abbr* (= **Consiglio Superiore della Magistratura**) *in Italy, the upper council of judges*
CT *abbr* (= **Catania**) Catania
c.to *abbr* (= **conto**) acct (account)
Cuba *f* Cuba
cubano I *adj* Cuban **II** *m*, **-a** *f* Cuban
cubetto *m* (small) cube; ***~ di ghiaccio*** ice cube
cubico *adj* ⟨*mpl* -ci⟩ cubic
cubismo *m* cubism
cubista[1] I *adj* PAINT cubist **II** *m/f* ⟨*mpl* -i⟩ PAINT cubist
cubista[2] *m/f* ⟨*mpl* -i⟩ *someone who dances on a podium in a night club*
cubitale *adj*: ***a caratteri -i*** in block capitals
cubo I *adj* cubic; ***metro / centimetro ~*** cubic metre / centimetre **II** *m* cube; ***elevare al ~*** *numero* cube
cuccagna *f*: (***paese*** *m* ***della***) ~ land of plenty
cuccare *v/t* ⟨1d⟩ *infml* catch
cuccarsi *v/r* ⟨1d⟩ *infml* catch
cuccetta *f* RAIL couchette; NAUT berth
cuccettista *m/f* ⟨*mpl* -i⟩ sleeping carriage attendant
cucchiaiata *f* spoonful
cucchiaino *m* teaspoon
cucchiaio *m* ⟨*pl* -ai⟩ spoon; ***~ da tavola*** tablespoon
cuccia *f* ⟨*pl* -cce⟩ dog's basket; *esterna* kennel; (***a***) ***~!*** Down!
cucciolata *f* litter
cucciolo *m* cub; *di cane* puppy
cuccuma *f* coffee pot
cucina *f* **1.** kitchen; ***~ abitabile*** kitchen-diner **2.** *cibi* food; ***~ casalinga*** home cooking; ***libro di ~*** cook book **3.** ***~ a gas*** gas cooker *or* stove
cucinare *v/t* ⟨1a⟩ cook
cucinino *m* kitchenette
cucire *v/t* ⟨4a⟩ sew; ***macchina** f **da ~*** sewing-machine; *fig* ***~ la bocca a qn*** shut s.o. up
cucirsi *v/r* ⟨4a⟩: ***~ la bocca*** keep one's mouth shut
cucito I *adj* sewn **II** *m* sewing
cucitrice *f* needlewoman
cucitura *f* seam
cucù *m* ⟨*pl* cucù⟩: ***orologio** m **a ~*** cuckoo clock
cuculo *m* cuckoo
cuffia *f da piscina* swimming cap; RADIO, TV headphones *pl*; ***~ da bagno*** shower cap
cugino *m*, **-a** *f* cousin
cui *pron persona* who, whom *form*; *cose* which; ***l'amico con ~ gioco a tennis*** the friend I play tennis with; ***la donna i ~ figli sono scomparsi*** the woman whose children are missing; ***il medico di ~ non ricordo il nome*** the doctor whose name I can't remember; ***le persone a ~ accennavi*** the people you were beckoning to; ***la casa in ~ abitano*** the house they live in, the house in which they live, the

house where they live; ***i libri di ~ ho bisogno*** the books I need; ***il giorno in ~ ti ho incontrato*** the day I met you; ***per ~*** so

culatello *m* COOK type of pork salami from Emilia

culinaria *f* cooking, cookery

culinario *adj* cookery *attr*, culinary; ***arte*** *f* ***-a*** culinary art, cookery

culla *f* cradle

cullare *v/t* ⟨1a⟩ rock

cullarsi *v/r* ⟨1a⟩ rock oneself; *fig* delude oneself

culminante *adj*: ***punto*** *m* ***~*** climax

culminare *v/i* ⟨1l⟩ culminate

culmine *m* peak

culo *m vulg* arse *vulg*, *US* ass *vulg*; ***in ~ alla balena!*** *vulg* break a leg!; ***avere ~*** *vulg* be lucky

cult *adj inv* cult; ***libro*** *m* ***~*** cult book

culto *m* cult; *religione* religion; ***~ della personalità*** cult of personality; ***luogo*** *m* ***di ~*** place of worship

cultore *m*, **-trice** *f* lover; ***~ dell'arte*** connoisseur of art

cultura *f* culture; ***~ di massa*** mass culture; ***~ generale*** general knowledge

culturale *adj* cultural

culturalmente *adv* culturally

culturismo *m* body-building

culturista *m/f* ⟨*mpl* -i⟩ body-builder

cumino *m* cumin

cumulabile *adj that can be held at the same time*

cumulativo *adj* cumulative; ***biglietto*** *m* ***~*** group ticket

cumulo *m* heap, pile

cuneese I *adj* from Cuneo **II** *m/f* person from Cuneo

cuneiforme *adj* wedge-shaped; ***scrittura*** *f* ***~*** cuneiform script

cuneo *m* wedge

cunetta *f fondo stradale* bump

cunicolo *m* (*traforo*) tunnel; *di coniglio* burrow

cuocere *v/t* ⟨3p⟩ cook; *pane* bake; ***~ al forno*** *carne, patate* roast; ***~ in padella*** fry; ***~ in umido*** stew; ***~ a vapore*** steam; *fig* ***lasciar ~ nel proprio brodo*** leave s.o. to stew in his / her own juices

cuoco *m*, **-a** *f* ⟨*mpl* -chi⟩ cook

cuoio *m* leather; ***di vero ~*** real leather; ***~ capelluto*** scalp; ***tirare le -a*** *infml* kick the bucket *infml*

cuore *m* **1.** heart; ***avere un ~ d'oro*** have a heart of gold; ***col ~ in gola*** with one's heart in one's mouth; ***essere malato di ~*** have heart trouble, have a bad heart; ***parlare a ~ aperto*** have a heart-to-heart; ***prendersi qc a ~*** take sth to heart; ***stare a ~ a qn*** be very important to s.o.; ***a cuor leggero*** light-heartedly; ***di ~*** wholeheartedly; ***senza ~*** heartless **2.** *carte* ***-i*** *pl* hearts; ***donna*** *f* ***di -i*** queen of hearts **3.** *fig* ***nel ~ di*** in the heart of; ***nel ~ della notte*** in the middle of the night

cupamente *adv* darkly

cupezza *f* gloominess (*a. fig*)

cupidigia, cupidità *f* ⟨*pl* cupidità⟩ greed

Cupido *m* Cupid

cupo *adj* gloomy; *suono* deep

cupola *f* dome

cura *f* care; MED treatment; ***~ dimagrante*** diet; ***-e*** *pl* ***termali*** spa treatment; ***casa*** *f* ***di ~*** nursing home; ***avere ~ di qc*** take care of sth; ***fare una ~*** have treatment; ***a ~ di*** TYPO edited by

curabile *adj* curable

curante *adj*: ***medico ~*** general practitioner

curare *v/t* ⟨1a⟩ take care of; MED treat

curaro *m* curare

curarsi *v/r* look after o.s.; ***non curarti di loro*** don't care about them

curatela *f* guardianship; *di fallimento* receivership

curativo *adj* curative; ***potere*** *m* ***~*** healing powers

curato *m* parish priest

curatore *m*, **-trice** *f fiduciario* trustee; *di testo* editor; ***~ fallimentare*** official receiver

curdo I *m/adj* Kurdish **II** *m*, **-a** *f* Kurd

curia *f* curia

curiosaggine *f* curiosity

curiosamente *adv* curiously

curiosare *v/i* ⟨1a⟩ have a look around; *pej* pry (***in*** into)

curiosità *f* ⟨*pl* curiosità⟩ curiosity

curioso *adj* curious; ***sarei ~ di sapere se …*** I'd be intrigued to know whether …

curiosone *m*, **-a** *f* rubber-neck, nosy-parker

curling *m* curling

curriculum vitae *m* ⟨*pl* curriculum vitae⟩ CV

cursore *m* COMPUT cursor

curva *f* curve

curvare *v/t* ⟨1a⟩ curve; *schiena* bend; ***~ il capo*** obey; ***~ la schiena*** arch one's back

curvarsi *v/r* bend

curvatura *f* curve

curvilineo *adj* curvilinear

curvo *adj* curved; *persona* bent

cuscinetto *m* TECH bearing; ***~ a sfere*** ball bearing; POL ***stato*** *m* **~** buffer state

cuscino *m* cushion; (*guanciale*) pillow

cuspide *f* peak; ARCH spire; ANAT cusp

custode *m/f* caretaker; ***angelo*** *m* **~** guardian angel

custodia *f* care; JUR custody; (*astuccio*) case; ***dare qc in ~ a qn*** give sth to s.o. for safekeeping

custodire *v/t* ⟨4d⟩ (*conservare*) keep

custodito *adj* (*parcheggio*) supervised

customizzare *v/t* ⟨1a⟩ customize

cutaneo *adj* skin; ***eruzione*** *f* **-*a*** rash

cute *f* skin

cuticola *f* cuticle

CV *abbr* **1.** (= **Cavallo Vapore**) HP (horsepower) **2.** (= **curriculum vitae**) CV (curriculum vitae)

Cybercafé *m* ⟨*pl* Cybercafé⟩ Internet café

cyberspazio *m* ⟨*pl* -i⟩ COMPUT cyberspace

cyclette *f* exercise bike

CZ *abbr* (= **Catanzaro**) Catanzaro

D

d, D *m/f* ⟨*pl* d, D⟩ d, D

da *prep* **1.** *stato in luogo* at; ***sono ~ mio fratello*** I'm at my brother's (place); ***ero ~ loro*** I was at their place; ***sono passati dalla finestra*** they got in / out through the window **2.** *moto da luogo* from; ***~ lontano / vicino*** from far away / nearby; ***entrare dal cortile*** come in from the yard; ***scendere dal treno*** get off the train; ***viene ~ Roma*** he comes from Rome **3.** *moto a luogo* to; ***vado dal medico*** I'm going to the doctor's **4.** *tempo* since; ***~ bambino*** as a child; ***~ ieri*** since yesterday; ***è dalle tre che aspetto*** I've been waiting since three o'clock ***lo conosco ~ anni*** I've known him for years; ***~ oggi in poi*** from now on, starting from today **5.** *con verbo passivo* by; ***essere investito ~ un'auto*** be run over by a car; ***dipinto ~ un grande artista*** painted by a great artist **6.** ***passo ~ Firenze*** I'm going via Florence **7.** ***una cosa ~ poco*** nothing much, a little thing; ***una macchina ~ corsa*** a racing car; ***macchina ~ scrivere*** typewriter; ***l'ho fatto ~ me*** I did it myself; ***non è ~ lui*** it's not like him; ***te lo dico ~ amico*** I'm telling you as a friend **8.** ***avere ~ fare*** have things to do; ***qualcosa ~ mangiare*** something to eat; ***mi piace ~ morire*** I love it **9.** ***francobollo ~ 1 euro*** 1 euro stamp; ***la donna dai capelli grigi*** the woman with grey hair, the grey-haired woman **10.** ***tremare dal freddo*** shiver with the cold; ***è sordo ~ un orecchio*** he's deaf in one ear

dà → ***dare***

dabbasso *adv* downstairs; ***scendere ~*** *venire giù*: come downstairs; *andare giù*: go downstairs

dabbenaggine *f* gullibility; (*azione sciocca*) silly thing to do

dabbene *adj inv* decent

Dacca *f* Dacca

daccapo *adv* → ***capo***

dacia *f* dacha

dadaismo *m* Dadaism

dadaista ⟨*mpl* -i⟩ **I** *m/f* Dadaist **II** *adj* Dadaist

dadino *m* dice *pl*; ***tagliare a -i*** dice

dado *m* dice *pl*; COOK stock cube; TECH nut; ***il ~ è tratto*** the die is cast

daffare *m* ⟨*pl* daffare⟩ work; ***avere il proprio (bel) ~ con qn / qc*** have one's work cut out with s.o. / sth; ***darsi un gran ~*** get cracking

dagherrotipia *f* daguerreotypy
dagherrotipo *m* (*immagine*) daguerreotype
dagli = *prep* **da** *and art* **gli**
dai[1] = *prep* **da** *and art* **i**
dai[2] → ***dare***
daino *m* deer; (*pelle*) buckskin
dal = *prep* **da** *and art* **il**
dalia *f* dahlia
dall', dalla, dalle, dallo = *prep* **da** *and art* **l', la, le, lo**
dalmata I *adj costa* Dalmatian **II** *m cane* Dalmatian
Dalmazia *f* Dalmatia
daltonico *adj* ⟨*mpl* -ci⟩ colo(u)r-blind
daltonismo *m* colo(u)r-blindness
dama *f* lady; *gioco* draughts *sg*, *US* checkers *sg*
damascato *adj* damask
damasco *m* ⟨*pl* -chi⟩ damask
damerino *m* dandy
damigella *f*: ~ ***d'onore*** bridesmaid
damigiana *f* demijohn
dammuso *m small stone house typical of Pantelleria*
DAMS *abbr* (= **Disciplina delle Arti, della Musica, dello Spettacolo**) *in Italy, the faculty of arts, music and the performing arts*
danaro *m* → ***denaro***
danaroso *adj* wealthy
dancing *m* ⟨*pl* dancing⟩ dance-hall
dandy *m* ⟨*pl* dandy⟩ dandy
danese I *m/adj* Danish **II** *m/f* Dane
Danimarca *f* Denmark
dannare *v/t* ⟨1a⟩: ***far*** ~ ***qn*** *infml* drive s.o. mad
dannarsi *v/r* ⟨1a⟩ (*andare all'inferno*) be damned; *fig* (*arrovellarsi*) strive; ***mi sono dannata l'anima per trovarlo*** *infml* I ran myself ragged looking for it / him
dannatamente *adv* devilishly; ~ ***difficile*** damn hard
dannato I *adj* damned; ***dov'è finito quel*** ~ ***ombrello?*** where's that flaming umbrella? **II** *m*, **-a** *f* damned soul; *infml* wicked person; ***i -i*** the damned; ***lavorare come un*** ~ work like a man possessed
dannazione *f* REL damnation; *infml* curse; ~***!*** damn!
danneggiamento *m* (*danno*) damage; (*danneggiare*) damaging
danneggiare *v/t* ⟨1f⟩ (*rovinare*) damage; (*nuocere*) harm
danneggiarsi *v/r* be damaged
danneggiato I *adj* damaged **II** *m*, **-a** *f* injured party
danno *m* damage; (*a persona*) harm; ~ ***morale*** moral damage; ~ ***alla salute*** detriment to health; ***-i*** *pl* ***all'ambiente*** environmental damage, damage to the environment; ~ ***biologico*** biological damage; ***chiedere i -i a qn*** claim for damages from s.o.; ***risarcire i -i a qn*** compensate s.o. for the damage
dannoso *adj* harmful
d'antan *adj inv* of old; ***la Roma*** ~ Ancient Rome
dantesco *adj* ⟨*mpl* -schi⟩ Dantesque; ***versi*** *mpl* ***-schi*** Dante's verses
danubiano *adj* Danubian
Danubio *m* Danube
danza *f* dance; ~ ***classica*** ballet; ~ ***del ventre*** belly dance; ***aprire le -e*** lead the dancing
danzante *adj* dance; ***serata*** *f* ~ dance
danzare *v/t & v/i* ⟨1a⟩ dance
danzatore *m*, **-trice** *f* dancer
dappertutto *adv* everywhere
dappoco *adj inv* (*inetto*) worthless; (*irrilevante*) minor, unimportant
dapprima *adv* at first
dardo *m* dart
dare ⟨1r⟩ **I** *v/t* **1.** give; ~ ***qc a qn*** give s.o. sth, give sth to s.o.; ~ ***uno sguardo a qc*** have a look at sth; ***quanti anni mi dai?*** how old do you think I am?; ***quanto ti danno al mese?*** how much do you earn a month?; ***ci danno molti compiti*** we get a lot of homework; SPORTS ~ ***il via*** give the off; *fig* ~ ***il via a qc*** get sth under way **2.** ~ ***del tu*** call each other 'tu'; ***dammi del tu*** call me 'tu'; ***mi dia del Lei*** address me as 'lei' **3.** ~ ***peso a qc*** give weight to sth; ~ ***alla luce un bambino*** have a child; ~ ***aria alle stanze*** air the rooms; ~ ***atto di qc*** acknowledge sth; ~ ***buca a qn*** *infml* stand s.o. up; ***questa non me la dai a bere!*** you won't make me believe that!; ~ ***il via*** give the starting signal; ~ ***i numeri*** *infml* lose one's marbles; ~ ***man forte a qn*** come to s.o.'s aid; ~ ***noia a qn*** bother s.o.; ~ ***addosso a qn*** get at s.o.; ~ ***alla testa*** go to s.o.'s head; ~ ***a vedere*** show; ***dar***

da fare a qn give s.o. sth to do; ***darci dentro con qc*** to get cracking on sth **4.** ***~ qn per morto*** give s.o. up for dead; ***~ qc per scontato*** take sth as read **5.** ***dai, sbrigati!*** come on, hurry up! **II** *v/i* **1.** *di finestra* overlook (***su*** sth); *di porta* lead into (***su*** sth); ***la camera dà sul giardino*** the bedroom looks out onto the garden **2.** *fig* ***~ nell'occhio*** attract attention, be noticed **III** *m* FIN debit; ***~ e avere*** debit and credit

darsena *f* dock

darsi *v/r* **1.** give each other; ***~ un bacio*** kiss each other **2.** (*dedicarsi*) devote o.s. (***a*** to); ***~ al commercio*** go into business; ***~ da fare*** keep busy **3.** ***darsela a gambe*** take to one's heels; ***darsele di santa ragione*** give s.o. a good thrashing **4.** ***può ~*** perhaps; ***può ~ che …*** it might be that …

darwinismo *m* Darwinism

data *f* date; ***~ di nascita*** date of birth; ***~ di scadenza*** expiry date; ***senza indicazione di ~*** undated

database *m* database; ***~ relazionale*** COMPUT relational database

databile *adj* datable

data glove *m* ⟨*pl* data glove⟩ COMPUT data glove

datare ⟨1a⟩ **I** *v/t* date; *lettera* date, put the date on **II** *v/i*: ***a ~ da oggi*** from today

datario *m* ⟨*pl* -ri⟩ (*timbro*) date stamp; *in orologio* COMPUT: calendar

datato *adj* dated (*a. fig*)

datazione *f* dating; (*data*) date

dativo *m* dative

dato I *past part* → **dare II** *adj* **1.** (*certo*) given, particular; ***in -i casi*** in certain cases **2.** (*dedito*) addicted (***a*** to) **3.** ***-e le circostanze*** under / in the circumstances **4.** ***~ che*** given that **III** *m* piece of data; ***-i*** *pl* data; COMPUT ***elaborazione*** *f* ***dei ~*** data processing; ***supporto*** *m* ***~*** data medium

datore *m*, **-trice** *f*: ***~ di lavoro*** employer

dattero *m* date; (*albero*) date palm

dattilografare *v/t* ⟨1n⟩ type

dattilografia *f* typing

dattilografo *m*, **-a** *f* typist

dattiloscopia *f* fingerprinting

dattiloscopico *adj* ⟨*mpl* -ci⟩: ***esame*** *m* ***~*** fingerprinting

dattiloscritto *m* typescript

daunio *adj* ⟨*mpl* -ni⟩ Daunian

davanti I *prep*: ***~ a*** in front of; ***siediti ~ a me*** (*di fronte*) sit opposite me; (*dando le spalle*) sit in front of me; ***ti aspetto ~ al cinema*** I'll wait for you outside the cinema; ***passo sempre ~ a casa tua*** I'm always going past your house; ***abito ~ alla scuola*** I live opposite the school **II** *adv* in front; (*dirimpetto*) opposite; ***se mi stai ~*** if you stand in front of me; ***vuoi stare ~ o dietro?*** do you want to sit in the front or in the back?; ***mettersi una maglia ~ didietro*** put a sweater on back to front **III** *adj inv* front; ***i posti / le ruote ~*** the front seats / wheels **IV** *m* front; ***lo zaino ha una tasca sul ~*** the rucksack has a pocket on the front

davanzale *m* windowsill

davanzo *adv* more than enough

davvero *adv* really; ***dici ~?*** really?; ***fare qc per ~*** really do sth

day hospital *m* outpatients' clinic

dazio *m* ⟨*pl* -zi⟩ duty; (*posto*) customs *pl*; ***~ d'importazione*** import duty; ***~ d'esportazione*** export duty; ***esente da ~*** duty-free

d.C. *abbr* (= **dopo Cristo**) AD (anno domini)

dea *f* goddess

debellare *v/t* ⟨1b⟩ eradicate, wipe out

debilitante *adj* debilitating

debilitare *v/t* ⟨1m⟩ weaken

debilitarsi *v/r* ⟨1m⟩ grow weak

debitamente *adv* duly

debito[1] *m* debt; (*dovere*) duty; FIN ***~ pubblico*** national debt; ***avere un ~ con qn*** be in debt to s.o.; ***essere in ~ di qc*** (***con qn***) be under an obligation (to s.o.) for sth; *fig* ***sentirsi in ~ verso qn*** feel indebted to s.o.

debito[2] *adj* proper; (*necessario*) due; ***a tempo*** *m* ***~*** in due course

debitore *m*, **-trice** *f* debtor; ***essere ~ di qc a qn*** owe s.o. sth, owe sth to s.o.

debole I *adj* weak; (*voce*) weak, faint; (*luce*) dim; ***punto*** *m* ***~*** weak spot; ***essere ~ di cuore*** have a weak heart **II** *m* weakness; ***avere un ~ per qn*** have a soft spot for s.o.

debolezza *f* weakness

debolmente *adv* feebly; ***protestare ~*** protest weakly

debordare *v/i* ⟨1a⟩ overflow
debosciato **I** *adj* debauched **II** *m*, **-a** *f* debauched person
debuttante *m/f* beginner; *artista* performer at the start of his / her career; ***ballo** m **delle -i*** debutantes' ball
debuttare *v/i* ⟨1a⟩ make one's début
debutto *m* début
decade *f* ten days
decadente *adj* decadent
decadenza *f* decadence
decadere *v/i* ⟨2c⟩ decay, decline; JUR lapse; ***~ da un diritto*** forfeit a right
decadimento *m* decay, decline; ***~ di costumi*** losing of traditions
decaduto *adj* decayed; ***nobili** mpl **-i*** impoverished aristocrats
decaedro *m* decahedron
decaffeinato *adj* decaffeinated, decaff *infml*
decagono *m* decagon
decagrammo *m* decagram
decalcificare *v/t* ⟨1m & d⟩ decalcify
decalcificazione *f* decalcification
decalcomania *f* transfer, *US* decal
decalitro *m* decalitre
decalogo *m* ⟨*pl* -ghi⟩ Decalogue; (*norme*) set of rules; ***il ~ del turista*** guidebook
decametro *m* decametre
decanato *m* deanship
decano *m* dean
decantare[1] *v/t* ⟨1a⟩ (*elogiare*) extol; ***~ qc a qn*** sing sth's praise to s.o.
decantare[2] *v/t* ⟨1a⟩ CHEM purify; *fig* decant
decantazione *f* decantation
decapaggio *m* ⟨*pl* -ggi⟩ pickling
decapitare *v/t* ⟨1m⟩ decapitate
decapitazione *f* decapitation
decappottabile *f/adj* AUTO convertible
decasillabo **I** *adj* decasyllabic **II** *m* decasyllable
decathlon *m* decathlon
decatleta *m/f* ⟨*mpl* -i⟩ decathlete
decedere *v/i* ⟨3l⟩: ***è deceduto ieri*** he died yesterday
deceduto *adj* dead, deceased
decelerare *v/t & v/i* ⟨1b & m⟩ slow down
decennale **I** *adj* (*di dieci anni*) ten-year; (*ogni dieci anni*) ten-yearly **II** *m* decennial
decenne *adj bambino* ten-year-old *attr*, ten years old; *contratto* ten-year
decennio *m* ⟨*pl* -ni⟩ decade
decente *adj* decent
decentemente *adv* decently
decentramento *m* decentralization
decentrare *v/t* ⟨1b⟩ decentralize
decenza *f* decency; ***offendere la ~*** be offensive
decesso *m* death
decibel *m* ⟨*pl* decibel⟩ decibel
decidere ⟨3q⟩ **I** *v/t questione* settle; *data* decide on, settle on; ***~ di fare qc*** decide to do sth **II** *v/i* decide; ***~ di qc*** decide sth
decidersi *v/r* decide (***a*** to), make up one's mind (***a*** to); ***non riesce a ~*** he can't make his mind up
decifrabile *adj* decipherable
decifrare *v/t* ⟨1a⟩ decipher
decifratore *m*, **-trice** *f* decipherer
decifrazione *f* deciphering
decigrado *m* decigrade
decigrammo *m* decigram
decilitro *m* decilitre, *US* -liter
decimale *m/adj* decimal
decimare *v/t* ⟨1l & b⟩ decimate
decimazione *f* decimation (*a. fig*)
decimetro *m* decimetre, *US* -meter
decimo *m/adj* tenth
decina *f* MATH ten; ***una ~*** about ten
decisamente *adv* (*indubbiamente*) certainly; (*con risolutezza*) resolutely
decisione *f* decision; (*risolutezza*) decisiveness; ***prendere una ~*** make a decision; ***~ della maggioranza*** majority decision
decisivo *adj* decisive
deciso **I** *past part* → ***decidere*** **II** *adj* (*definito*) definite; (*risoluto*) determined; (*netto*) clear; (*spiccato*) marked; ***essere ~ a fare qc*** be determined to do sth
declamare *v/t* ⟨1a⟩ declaim
declamazione *f* declamation
declassamento *m di un'oggetto* downgrading; *di una persona* demoting
declassare *v/t* ⟨1a⟩ *oggetto* downgrade; *persona* demote
declinabile *adj* GRAM declinable
declinare ⟨1a⟩ **I** *v/t* decline; ***~ ogni responsabilità*** disclaim all responsibility **II** *v/i* (*tramontare*) set; (*diminuire*) decline
declinazione *f* GRAM declension; ASTR declination

declino *m fig* decline
declivio *m* ⟨*pl* -vi⟩ downward slope
decoder *m* ⟨*pl* decoder⟩ decoder
decodificabile *adj* decodable
decodificare *v/t* ⟨1m & d⟩ decode
decodificatore *m* decoder
decodificazione *f* decoding
decollare *v/i* ⟨1c⟩ take off
décolleté *m* ⟨*pl* décolleté⟩ decolletage
decollo *m* take-off
decolorante *m* bleach
decolorare *v/t* ⟨1a⟩ *tessuto* discolour; *capelli* bleach
decomponibile *adj* decomposable; ***sostanze*** *fpl* ***-i*** degradable substances
decomporre ⟨3ll⟩ **I** *v/i* (*putrefarsi*) decompose **II** *v/t* CHEM break down
decomporsi *v/r* decompose
decomposizione *f* decomposition; CHEM breaking down
decompressione *f* decompression
deconcentrarsi *v/r* ⟨1b⟩ lose one's concentration
deconcentrato *adj* distracted
deconcentrazione *f* lack of concentration; ECON redistribution
decongestionamento *m* MED decongestion; *fig* relief; ***il ~ del traffico*** easing of traffic
decongestionare *v/t* ⟨1a⟩ *strada*, MED relieve congestion in; ***~ il traffico*** relieve traffic congestion
decontaminare *v/t* ⟨1m⟩ decontaminate
decontaminazione *f* decontamination
decorare *v/t* ⟨1b⟩ decorate; ***~ al valor civile*** decorate for civil valour
decorativo *adj* decorative, ornamental
decorato I *adj* (*ornato*, *insignito*) decorated; ***~ a mano*** hand-painted **II** *m*, **-a** *f person decorated for his / her service*
decoratore *m*, **-trice** *f* decorator
decorazione *f* decoration
decoro *m* decorum
decorosamente *adv* decorously; ***vivere ~*** live a respectable life
decoroso *adj* decorous
decorrenza *f*: ***con immediata ~*** with immediate effect
decorrere *v/i* ⟨3o⟩ pass; ***a ~ da oggi*** with effect from today
decorso I *past part* → ***decorrere*** **II** *m di malattia* course
decotto *m* decoction
decremento *m* decrease; ***~ demografico*** drop in population
decrepito *adj* decrepit
decrescenza *f* decline
decrescere *v/i* ⟨3n⟩ decrease, fall
decretare *v/t* ⟨1a⟩ decree; ***è stato decretato lo stato di emergenza*** a state of emergency has been declared
decreto *m* decree; ***~-legge*** *m decree passed in exceptional circumstances that has the force of law*; ***~ ingiuntivo*** injunction; ***~ legislativo*** legislative decree; ***~ ministeriale*** ministerial decree
decubito *m* decubitus; ***piaga*** *f* ***da ~*** bedsore
de cuius *m* ⟨*pl* de cuius⟩ (deceased) testator
decuplicare *v/t* ⟨1m & d⟩ multiply tenfold
decuplo I *adj* tenfold **II** *m* ten times as much
decurtare *v/t* ⟨1a⟩ reduce, cut down; ***~ lo stipendio a qn*** cut / dock s.o.'s salary
decurtazione *f* reduction, cut
dedalo *m* maze, labyrinth
dedica *f* ⟨*pl* -che⟩ dedication
dedicare *v/t* ⟨1b & d⟩ dedicate; ***~ qc a qn*** *poesia*, *canzone* dedicate sth to s.o.; *via* name sth after s.o.
dedicarsi *v/r* dedicate o.s.; ***~ alla famiglia*** devote oneself to one's family
dedito *adj* dedicated (***a*** to); *a un vizio* addicted (***a*** to)
dedizione *f* dedication
dedotto *past part* → ***dedurre***
deducibile *adj* deducible; ECON deductible; ***spese*** *fpl* ***-i*** allowable expenses
dedurre *v/t* ⟨3e⟩ deduce; FIN deduct; (*derivare*) derive
deduttivo *adj* deductive
deduzione *f* deduction; ***~ dei mezzi di prova*** JUR deduction of evidence
deejay *m/f* ⟨*pl* deejay⟩ DJ
de facto *adv* de facto, as a matter of fact
défaillance *f* ⟨*pl* défaillance⟩ collapse
defalcare *v/t* ⟨1d⟩ deduct
defalcazione *f* deduction
defalco *m* ⟨*pl* -chi⟩ deduction
defecare *v/i* ⟨1b & d⟩ defecate

defecazione *f* defecation
defenestrare *v/t* ⟨1m⟩ *fig* oust
deferente *adj* (*ossequioso*) deferential
deferenza *f* deference
deferire *v/t* ⟨4d⟩ (*rimettere*) refer; JUR submit; **~ *una pratica a una commissione*** submit a file to a commission; **~ *qn all'autorità giudiziaria*** prefer charges against s.o.
defezione *f* defection
defibrillatore *m* defibrillator
deficiente I *adj* (*mancante*) deficient, lacking (***di*** in) **II** *m/f* backward person; *insulto* idiot, moron
deficienza *f* (*scarsezza*) deficiency, lack (***di*** of)
deficit *m* ⟨*pl* deficit⟩ deficit; **~ *del bilancio pubblico*** budget deficit, public spending deficit; **~ *democratico*** EU democratic deficit
deficitario *adj* ⟨*mpl* -ri⟩ showing a deficit; *fig* inadequate
defilarsi *v/r* ⟨1a⟩ shirk
défilé *m* ⟨*pl* défilé⟩ fashion show
definibile *adj* definable; ***facilmente/difficilmente*** **~** easy/hard to define
definire *v/t* ⟨4d⟩ define; (*risolvere*) settle; **~ *un concetto*** define a concept; ***non è facile*** **~ *quella persona*** he/she isn't an easy person to sum up; **~ *una controversia*** settle a dispute
definitivamente *adv chiudere* permanently; *decidere* once and for all
definitivo *adj* definitive; ***risposta*** *f* ***-a*** final answer; ***sentenza*** *f* ***-a*** JUR final judgement; *di divorzio* decree absolute; ***in -a*** ultimately
definito *adj* well-defined; ***nulla di*** **~** nothing definite
definizione *f* definition; JUR settlement
deflagrazione *f* explosion
deflazione *f* ECON deflation
deflettore *m* AUTO quarterlight
deflorare *v/t* ⟨1c⟩ deflower
deflorazione *f* deflowering
defluire *v/i* ⟨4d⟩ *acqua* drain (away); *folla* spill (out)
deflusso *m* ebb
defo(g)liante *m* defoliant
deforestazione *f* deforestation
deformabile *adj* deformable
deformante *adj* deforming; ***artrite*** *f* **~** rheumatoid arthritis; ***specchio*** *m* **~** distorting mirror
deformare *v/t* ⟨1a⟩ deform; *legno* warp; *metallo* buckle; *fig* distort
deformarsi *v/r di legno* warp; *di metallo* buckle; *di scarpe* lose their shape
deformazione *f* deformation; *di legno* warping; *di metallo* buckling; *fisica* deformity; *fig* distortion; **~ *professionale*** professional bias
deforme *adj* deformed
deformità *f* ⟨*pl* deformità⟩ deformity
deframmentazione *f* COMPUT: ***eseguire la*** **~** defrag
defraudare *v/t* ⟨1a⟩: **~ *qn di un diritto*** deprive s.o. of a right
defunto I *adj* dead; *fig* defunct **II** *m*, ***-a*** *f* JUR: ***il*** **~** the deceased
degenerare *v/i* ⟨1m & b⟩ degenerate (***in*** into)
degenerativo *adj* degenerative
degenerato *adj* degenerate
degenerazione *f* degeneracy; BIOL, MATH degeneration
degenere *adj* degenerate; ***figlio*** *m* **~** profligate son
degente *m/f* patient
degenza *f* stay (in bed/hospital)
degli = *prep* ***di*** *and art* ***gli***
deglutire *v/t* ⟨4d⟩ swallow
deglutizione *f* swallowing
degnamente *adv* properly
degnare ⟨1a⟩ **I** *v/t*: **~ *qn di una parola*** deign to speak to s.o. **II** *v/i*: **~ *di*** deign to, condescend to
degnarsi *v/r* ⟨1a⟩: **~ *di*** deign to, condescend to
degno *adj* worthy; **~ *di nota*** noteworthy; **~ *di un re*** fit for a king; ***non siete -i di vostro padre*** you can't hold a candle to your father
degradante *adj* degrading, demeaning
degradare *v/t* ⟨1a⟩ degrade; *da un rango* demote
degradarsi *v/r* demean o.s., lower o.s.; CHEM degrade; *di ambiente, edifici* deteriorate
degradazione *f* degradation
degrado *m* deterioration; **~ *ambientale*** damage to the environment; ***edificio*** *m* ***in stato di*** **~** building in disrepair; **~ *urbano*** urban decay
degustare *v/t* ⟨1a⟩ taste
degustazione *f* tasting; **~ *del vino*** wine tasting
dei[1] = *prep* ***di*** *and art* ***i***
dei[2] (*pl di* ***dio***): ***gli*** **~** *mpl* the Gods

deificare *v/t* ⟨1m & d⟩ deify
deindicizzare *v/t* ⟨1a⟩ ECON de-index
deindicizzazione *f* ECON de-indexation
de iure *adv* by right
déjà vu *m* ⟨*pl* déjà vu⟩ déjà vu
del = *prep* ***di*** *and art* ***il***
delatore *m*, **-trice** *f* informer
delazione *f* informing
delega *f* ⟨*pl* -ghe⟩ delegation; (*procura*) proxy; ***fare una ~ a qn*** delegate s.o.; ***per ~*** on s.o.'s authority
delegare *v/t* ⟨1l & b & e⟩ delegate
delegato I *adj*: ***amministratore*** *m* ***~*** managing director **II** *m*, **-a** *f* delegate; ***~ sindacale*** (trade) union delegate
delegazione *f* delegation
delegittimare *v/t* ⟨1a⟩ delegitimize
delegittimazione *f* delegitimization
deleterio *adj* ⟨*mpl* -ri⟩ *fumo*, *gas* toxic; *influenza* dangerous, bad
delfinario *m* ⟨*pl* -ri⟩ dolphinarium
delfinista *m/f* ⟨*mpl* -i⟩ dolphin stroke swimmer
delfino[1] *m* dolphin; ***nuotare a ~*** swim dolphin stroke
delfino[2] *m hist* (*erede al trono*) dauphin; POL (*successore*) heir apparent
delibera *f* ADMIN resolution; ***votare una ~*** pass a resolution
deliberante *adj* deliberative; ***organo*** *m* ***~*** deliberating body; ***potere*** *m* ***~*** deciding power
deliberare ⟨1m⟩ **I** *v/t* decide **II** *v/i* JUR deliberate (***su*** on)
deliberatamente *adv* deliberately
deliberato *adj* (*risoluto*) determined; (*intenzionale*) deliberate; ***con ~ proposito*** deliberately; ***azione*** *f* ***-a*** wilful act
deliberazione *f* resolution; ***~ del parlamento*** parliamentary decree
delicatamente *adv* gently, softly
delicatezza *f* delicacy; (*discrezione*) tact, delicacy; (*debolezza*) frailty, delicacy; ***trattare qc con ~*** handle sth carefully; ***ha avuto la ~ di non parlarne*** he / she was tactful enough not to mention it
delicato *adj* delicate; (*persona*) frail, delicate; (*colore*) soft; ***pelle*** *f* ***-a*** sensitive skin; ***lineamenti*** *mpl* ***-i*** fine features; ***tinte*** *fpl* ***-e*** subtle colours; ***animo*** *m* ***~*** sensitive soul; ***strumento*** *m* ***~*** delicate instrument; ***indumenti*** *mpl* ***-i*** delicates; ***è una situazione molto -a*** it's a very tricky situation
delimitare *v/t* ⟨1m⟩ define
delimitazione *f* boundary; ***~ delle competenze*** demarcation of authority
delineare *v/t* ⟨1m⟩ outline
delinearsi *v/r* ⟨1m⟩ come into sight; *fig* promise to be; ***il castello si delineava in lontananza*** the castle loomed up in the distance
delineato *adj* clear-cut; ***personaggio*** *m* ***ben ~*** well-drawn character
delinquente *m/f* criminal; *fig* scoundrel; ***~ minorile*** juvenile delinquent
delinquenza *f* crime; ***~ minorile*** juvenile delinquency; ***~ organizzata*** organized crime
delinquenziale *adj* delinquent; ***comportamento*** *m* ***~*** delinquency
delinquere *v/i* ⟨3a⟩: ***associazione*** *f* ***a ~*** criminal conspiracy
deliquio *m* ⟨*pl* -i⟩ swoon; ***cadere in ~*** swoon
delirante *adj* delirious; *fig* outlandish; (*frenetico*) feverish
delirare *v/i* ⟨1a⟩ be in raptures, rave; MED be delirious; ***stai delirando?*** *hum* are you crazy?
delirio *m* ⟨*pl* -ri⟩ delirium; *fig* frenzy; ***in ~*** going mad
delirium tremens *m* ⟨*pl* delirium tremens⟩ MED delirium tremens
delitto *m* crime; ***corpo*** *m* ***del ~*** corpus delicti; ***commettere un ~*** commit a crime; ***autore*** *m* ***del ~*** perpetrator of a crime; ***~ d'onore*** honour killing; ***~ passionale*** crime of passion; ***~ a sfondo sessuale*** sex-linked crime; ***~ perfetto*** perfect crime; ***~ preterintenzionale*** unintentional crime; *fig* ***buttarlo via sarebbe un ~!*** it would be a crime to throw it away!
delittuoso *adj* criminal; ***intenzione*** *f* ***-a*** loitering
delizia *f* delight; ***~ del palato*** tidbit; ***la mia nipotina è una ~!*** my granddaughter is an absolute joy!; ***questo dessert è una vera ~!*** this dessert is sheer heaven!
delizioso *adj* delightful; *cibo* delicious
dell', della, delle, dello = *prep* ***di*** *and art* ***l', la, le, lo***
delta *m* delta
deltaplanista *m/f* ⟨*mpl* -i⟩ hang-glider

deltaplano *m* hang-glider; *attività* hang-gliding

delucidazione *f* elucidation

deludente *adj* disappointing

deludere *v/t* ⟨3q⟩ disappoint

delusione *f* disappointment

deluso *adj* disappointed

demagogia *f* demagogy

demagogo I *adj* ⟨*mpl* -ghi⟩ demagogic **II** *m*, **-a** *f* demagog(ue)

demaniale *adj* state-owned; ***beni*** *mpl* ***-i*** state property

demanio *m* State property; (*ufficio*) *government department which looks after state-owned property and land*

demarcazione *f*: ***linea*** *f* ***di ~*** boundary

demente *m/f* MED person with dementia; *infml* lunatic *infml*

demenza *f* MED dementia; *infml* lunacy *infml*, madness *infml*; ***~ senile*** senile dementia; ***~ precoce*** premature dementia

demenziale *adj* crazy; ***atti*** *mpl* ***-i*** insane acts; ***musica*** *f* ***~*** manic music

demerito *m* (*colpa*) fault; (*biasimo*) blame; ***nota*** *f* ***di ~*** black mark

demi-sec *adj inv* medium-dry

demistificare *v/t* ⟨1m & d⟩ demystify

demistificazione *f* demystification

demitizzare *v/t* ⟨1a⟩ demythologize

demiurgo *m* ⟨*mpl* -gi *or* -ghi⟩ demiurge

democraticamente *adv* democratically

democratico ⟨*mpl* -ci⟩ **I** *adj* democratic **II** *m*, **-a** *f* democrat

democratizzare *v/t* ⟨1a⟩ democratize

democratizzazione *f* democratization

democrazia *f* democracy; ***~ costituzionale*** constitutional democracy

Democrazia Cristiana *f* Christian Democrat Party

democristiano *m/adj* Christian Democrat

démodé *adj inv* old-fashioned

demografia *f* demography

demografico *adj* demographic

demolire *v/t* ⟨4d⟩ demolish (*a. fig*); *macchine* crush; *navi* scrap

demolitore I *adj* demolition; *fig* destructive **II** *n*: ***demolitore*** *m di veicoli* wrecker

demolizione *f* demolition; *di macchine* crushing; ***edificio*** *m* ***in ~*** building being demolished

demone *m* spirit

demoniaco *adj* ⟨*mpl* -ci⟩ demonic; (*diabolico*) satanic

demonio *m* ⟨*pl* -ni⟩ devil

demonizzare *v/t* ⟨1a⟩ demonize

demoralizzante *adj* demoralizing

demoralizzare *v/t* ⟨1a⟩ demoralize

demoralizzarsi *v/r* ⟨1a⟩ become demoralized, lose heart

demoralizzazione *f* demoralization

demordere *v/i* ⟨3uu⟩ give up; ***non demordo (da qc)*** I won't give (sth) up

demoscopia *f* opinion survey

demoscopico *adj* ⟨*mpl* -ci⟩: ***indagine*** *f* ***-a*** opinion poll

demotivare *v/t* ⟨1a⟩ demotivate

demotivato *adj* demotivated

denaro *m* money; ***~ contante*** cash

denatalità *f* decline in the birth rate

denaturato *adj* CHEM: ***alcol*** *m* ***~*** methylated spirits *pl*

dendrite *f* MINER, BIOL dendrite

denigrare *v/t* ⟨1a⟩ run down

denigratore *m*, **-trice** *f* denigrator

denigratorio *adj* ⟨*mpl* -ri⟩ disparaging

denigrazione *f* denigration

denominare *v/t* ⟨1m & c⟩ name, call

denominarsi *v/r* be called

denominatore *m* MATH denominator; *fig* ***trovare un ~ comune*** find a common denominator

denominazione *f* name; ***~ di origine controllata*** *term signifying that a wine is of a certain origin and quality*; ***~ di origine controllata e garantita*** *term signifying that a wine is of a superior origin and quality*; ***~ sociale*** company name

denotare *v/t* ⟨1l & b or c⟩ denote, be indicative of

densamente *adv* thickly; ***~ popolato*** densely populated

densimetro *m* hydrometer

densità *f* ⟨*pl* densità⟩ density; *della nebbia* thickness, density; ***~ della popolazione*** population density

denso *adj* dense; *fumo*, *nebbia* thick, dense; ***crema*** *f* ***-a*** thick cream; ***nubi*** *fpl* ***-e di pioggia*** heavy rain clouds; ***un ~ programma*** a packed programme; *fig* ***~ di qc*** packed with sth; ***~ di significato*** full of meaning

dentale *adj* dental (*a.* LING); ***consonante*** *f* ***~*** dental consonant

dentario *adj* ⟨*mpl* -ri⟩ dental

dentata *f* bite; *segno* toothmark

dentato *adj* toothed; ***ruota f -a*** cogwheel

dentatura *f* set of teeth; TECH toothing

dente *m* tooth; ***~ cariato*** decayed tooth; ***~ del giudizio*** wisdom tooth; ***~ di latte*** milk tooth; ***~ di leone*** dandelion; ***-i*** *pl* ***canini*** canine teeth; ***-i*** *pl* ***inferiori / superiori*** lower / upper teeth; ***mal*** *m* ***di -i*** toothache; *fig* ***togliersi un ~*** have a tooth out; ***batteva i -i*** his teeth were chattering; ***lavarsi i -i*** clean / brush one's teeth; ***mettere i -i*** cut one's teeth; *fig* ***stringere i -i*** grit one's teeth; ***parlare fra i -i*** mumble; ***a -i stretti*** tight-lipped; ***i -i del pettine*** the teeth of a comb; COOK ***al ~*** al dente, *still slightly firm*

dentellatura *f* perforation

dentello *m* tooth; *di francobollo* perforation

dentice *m fish native to the Mediterranean*

dentiera *f* dentures *pl*

dentifricio *m* ⟨*pl* -ci⟩ toothpaste

dentista *m/f* ⟨*mpl* -i⟩ dentist; ***andare dal ~*** go to the dentist's

dentistico *adj* ⟨*mpl* -ci⟩: ***studio*** *m* ***~*** dentist's (surgery)

dentizione *f* dentition

dentro I *prep*: ***~ (a) qc*** in, inside sth; ***il vestito è ~ l'armadio*** the dress is in the wardrobe; ***~ alla scatola*** in the box; ***~ di sé*** inwardly; ***dire ~ di sé*** say to oneself **II** *adv* in, inside; (*nell'intimo*) inwardly; ***qui / lì ~*** in here / there; ***vieni ~*** come in; ***mangiamo ~ o fuori?*** shall we eat inside or out?; ***ti aspetto ~*** I'll wait for you inside; ***ripiegare in ~*** fold over; ***da ~*** from inside; ***metter ~*** *infml in carcere* put inside *or* away *infml*; ***tenersi tutto ~*** bottle things up; ***qui ~ non c'è nessuno*** there's nobody in here; ***fa freddo, andiamo ~*** it's cold, let's go inside

denuclearizzato *adj* nuclear-free, denuclearized; ***zona f -a*** nuclear-free zone

denudare *v/t* ⟨1a⟩ strip (*a. fig*)

denudarsi *v/r* ⟨1a⟩ strip off

denuncia *f* ⟨*pl* -ce⟩ denunciation; *alla polizia, alla società di assicurazione* complaint, report; *di nascita, morte* registration; ***sporgere ~ contro qn / qc*** lodge a complaint against s.o. / sth; ***~ dei redditi*** income tax return

denunciante *m/f* accuser

denunciare *v/t* ⟨1f⟩ denounce; *alla polizia, alla società di assicurazione* report; *nascita* register

denunzia *f* → ***denuncia***

denutrito *adj* undernourished

denutrizione *f* undernourishment

deodorante *m* deodorant

deontologico *adj* ⟨*mpl* -ci⟩ ethical; ***codice*** *m* ***~*** code of ethics

depenalizzare *v/t* ⟨1a⟩ decriminalize

depenalizzazione *f* decriminalization

dépendance *f* ⟨*pl* dépendance⟩ annex(e)

depennare *v/t* ⟨1a⟩ cross out; ***~ un nome dalla lista*** cross a name off the list

deperibile *adj* perishable; ***merce f ~*** perishable goods

deperibilità *f* ⟨*pl* deperibilità⟩ perishability

deperimento *m* wasting away; *di piante* decay

deperire *v/i* ⟨4d⟩ waste away; *piante* wither

depilare *v/t* ⟨1a⟩ *con pinzette* pluck; *con rasoio* shave; *con ceretta* wax

depilatorio ⟨*mpl* -ri⟩ **I** *adj* depilatory; ***crema f -a*** hair-remover **II** *m* hair-remover, depilatory

depistaggio *m* ⟨*pl* -ggi⟩ diversion

depistare *v/t* ⟨1a⟩ sidetrack; ***~ le indagini*** mislead the investigations

dépliant *m* ⟨*pl* dépliant⟩ leaflet; (*opuscolo*) brochure

deplorare *v/t* ⟨1c⟩ deplore

deplorevole *adj* deplorable

deporre ⟨3ll⟩ **I** *v/t* put down; *uova* lay; *re, presidente* depose; ***~ il falso*** commit perjury; ***~ il mandato*** resign from office; ***~ le armi*** lay down one's arms, surrender (*a. fig*); ***~ la corona*** refuse the crown **II** *v/i* JUR testify, give evidence (***a favore di*** for, ***a carico di*** against); ***~ a favore di qn*** give evidence for s.o.

deportare *v/t* ⟨1c⟩ deport

deportato *m*, **-a** *f* deportee

deportazione *f* deportation

depositante *m/f* depositor

depositare *v/t* ⟨1m & c⟩ deposit; (*posare*) put down, deposit; (*registrare*) register; ***~ un brevetto*** register a patent; ***~ un atto*** JUR lodge; ***~ la firma***

give a specimen signature
depositario ⟨*mpl* -ri⟩ **I** *adj* depositary **II** *m*, **-a** *f* trustee; *fig* repository
depositarsi *v/r* ⟨1m & c⟩ settle
depositato *adj*: ***marchio*** *m* **~** registered trademark
deposito *m* deposit; (*magazzino*) warehouse; MIL, *rimessa* depot; RAIL **~ *bagagli*** left-luggage office, *US* baggage checkroom; **~ *di armi*** arms dump; **~ *degli autobus*** bus depot; **~ *di grasso*** ANAT fatty deposits; **~ *di munizioni*** ammunition dump; **~ *bancario*** deposit; FIN **~ *vincolato*** term deposit
deposizione *f* deposition; *da un'alta carica* removal; *di regnante*; overthrow
deposto *past part* → ***deporre***
depravato I *adj* depraved **II** *m*, **-a** *f* depraved person
depravazione *f* depravation
deprecabile *adj* deplorable
deprecare *v/t* ⟨1l e b⟩ disapprove of
depredare *v/t* ⟨1b⟩ *soldati* plunder; *persone* loot
depressione *f* depression; **~ *atmosferica*** atmospheric depression; **~ *economica*** (economic) depression; ***zona*** *f* ***di*** **~ *atmosferica*** area of low pressure, low
depressivo *adj* depressive; ***crisi*** *f* ***-a*** fit of depression
depresso I *past part* → ***deprimere*** **II** *adj* depressed
depressurizzare *v/t* ⟨1a⟩ depressurize
depressurizzazione *f* depressurization
deprezzamento *m* depreciation
deprezzare *v/t* ⟨1b⟩ lower the value of
deprezzarsi *v/r* depreciate
deprimente *adj* depressing
deprimere *v/t* ⟨3r⟩ depress
deprimersi *v/r* get depressed
depurare *v/t* ⟨1a⟩ purify
depurativo I *adj* purifying **II** *n*: ***depurativo*** *m* depurant
depuratore I *m* purifier **II** *adj*: ***filtro*** *m* **~** cleaning filter; ***tecnico*** *m* **~** purifying technique
depurazione *f* purification; ***impianto*** *m* ***di*** **~** purification plant; **~ *dell'aria*** air purification
deputare *v/t* ⟨1l & b⟩ delegate
deputato *m*, **-a** *f* Member of Parliament, *US* Representative
deragliamento *m* derailment
deragliare *v/i* ⟨1g⟩ RAIL go off *or* leave the rails; ***far*** **~** derail
derattizzazione *f* pest control
dorby *m* ⟨*pl* derby⟩ *nel calcio*: derby
deregulation *f* ⟨*pl* deregulation⟩ ECON deregulation
derelitto *adj* derelict
deretano *m* backside
deridere *v/t* ⟨3g⟩ deride
derisione *f* derision
deriso *past part* → ***deridere***
derisorio *adj* ⟨*mpl* -ri⟩ derisive
deriva *f* NAUT drift; AVIAT fin; ***andare alla*** **~** drift; **~ *dei continenti*** continental drift
derivare ⟨1a⟩ **I** *v/t* derive **II** *v/i*: **~ *da*** come from, derive from
derivato *m* LING derivative; CHEM by-product, derivative; ***-i*** *pl* ***del petrolio*** oil by-products
derivazione *f* derivation; (*discendenza*) origin; ELEC shunt; TEL extension
dermatite *f* dermatitis
dermatologia *f* dermatology
dermatologo *m*, **-a** *f* ⟨*mpl* -gi⟩ dermatologist
dermatosi *f* ⟨*pl* dermatosi⟩ dermatosis
deroga *f* (*abrogazione*) departure; ***a*** **~ *qc*** contrary to sth; ***in*** **~ *a …*** departing from
derogabile *adj that can be derogated*
derogare *v/i* ⟨1l & b⟩: **~ *a qc*** *legge* infringe sth; *tradizione* break with sth
derogatorio *adj* ⟨*mpl* -ri⟩ derogatory; ***clausola*** *f* ***-a*** overriding clause
derrate *fpl* food *sg*
derubare *v/t* ⟨1a⟩ rob
derviscio *m* ⟨*pl* -sci⟩ dervish; ***la danza dei -sci*** whirling of the dervishes
descrittivo *adj* descriptive
descritto *past part* → ***descrivere***
descrivere *v/t* ⟨3tt⟩ describe
descrizione *f* description
desensibilizzare *v/t* ⟨1n⟩ desensitize; **~ *un dente*** desensitize a tooth
desertico *adj* ⟨*mpl* -ci⟩ desert; ***clima*** *m* **~** desert climate
deserto I *adj* deserted; ***isola*** *f* ***-a*** desert island **II** *m* desert
desiderabile *adj persona* desirable; (*auspicabile*) advisable
desiderare *v/t* ⟨1m⟩ (*volere*) want,

wish; *intensamente* long for, crave; *sessualmente* desire; ***desidera?*** can I help you?; ***desidera altro?*** would you like anything else?; ***La desiderano al telefono, signora*** you're wanted on the telephone, madam; ***farsi ~*** play hard to get; (*tardare*) keep people waiting; ***lascia a ~*** it leaves a lot to be desired

desiderio *m* ⟨*pl* -ri⟩ wish (***di*** for); *intenso* longing (***di*** for); *sessuale* desire (***di*** for)

desideroso *adj* eager

design *m* ⟨*pl* design⟩ design

designare *v/t* ⟨1a⟩ (*nominare*) appoint, name; (*fissare*) fix, set

designazione *f* appointment, nomination

designer *m/f* ⟨*pl* designer⟩ designer

desinenza *f* GRAM ending

desistere *v/i* ⟨3f⟩: ***~ da*** desist from; ***~ da un proposito*** give up a plan

desktop *m* ⟨*pl* desktop⟩ desktop

desolante *adj* distressing

desolatamente *adv* desolately

desolato *adj* desolate; ***sono ~!*** I am so sorry

desolazione *f* desolation; (*dolore*) distress

despota *m/f* ⟨*mpl* -i⟩ despot (*a. fig*)

dessert *m* ⟨*pl* dessert⟩ dessert

destabilizzare *v/t* ⟨1n⟩ destabilize

destabilizzarsi *v/r* ⟨1n⟩ become unstable

destabilizzazione *f* destabilization

destagionalizzato *adj* seasonally adjusted; ***dati*** *mpl* ***-i*** seasonally adjusted figures

destare *v/t* ⟨1a⟩ *fig* (a)rouse, awaken; ***~ scalpore*** cause raised eyebrows

destarsi *v/r fig* be aroused, be awakened

destinare *v/t* ⟨1a⟩ destine; (*assegnare*) assign; *con il pensiero* mean, intend; *data* fix, set; (*indirizzare*) address (***a*** to); ***essere destinato a qc*** be intended for sth; ***essere destinato a fare qc*** be doomed to do sth

destinatario *m*, **-a** *f* ⟨*mpl* -ri⟩ *di lettera* addressee

destinato *adj* destined, intended; ***essere ~ alla rovina*** doomed to failure

destinazione *f*: (***luogo*** *m* ***di***) ~ destination; ***~ d'uso*** designation of use

destino *m* destiny; ***era ~!*** it was fate!

destituire *v/t* ⟨4d⟩ dismiss; ***~ qn da una carica*** remove s.o. from office

destituzione *f* dismissal

desto *adj* alert (*a. fig*); ***sogno o son ~?*** am I dreaming?

destra *f* right; (*mano*) right hand; ***a ~*** *stato* on the right, to the right; *moto* to the right; ***a ~ e a manca*** left, right and centre; ***sulla ~*** on the right, to the right; ***essere di ~*** be right-wing; ***girare a ~*** turn right; ***tenere la ~*** keep right

destreggiarsi *v/r* ⟨1f⟩ manœuvre, *US* maneuver

destrezza *f* skill, dexterity; ***giochi*** *mpl* ***di ~*** juggling

destrimano I *adj* right-handed **II** *m*, **-a** *f* right-hander

destro *adj* right; (*abile*) skil(l)ful, dexterous; ***sul lato ~*** (***di qc***) on the right-hand side (of sth)

destrorso I *adj persona* right-handed; TECH clockwise **II** *m*, **-a** *f* right-hander, right-handed person

desueto *adj* obsolete

desumere *v/t* ⟨3h⟩ deduce, gather; (*trarre*) gather

desumibile *adj* deducible; ***~ da qc*** deducible from sth

desunto *past part* → ***desumere***

detassare *v/t* ⟨1a⟩ abolish the tax on

detassazione *f* tax exemption

detective *m/f* ⟨*pl* detective⟩ detective; ***~ privato*** private detective

detenere *v/t* ⟨2q⟩ hold; *in prigione* detain, hold; ***~ il monopolio*** hold the monopoly; ***~ un primato*** hold a record

detentivo *adj* custodial; ***pena*** *f* ***-a*** prison sentence

detentore *m*, **-trice** *f* holder; ***~ di una carica*** post holder; ***~ di un titolo*** defending champion

detenuto *m*, **-a** *f* prisoner

detenzione *f imprigionamento* detention; ***~ abusiva di armi*** possession of illegal weapons

detergente I *adj*: ***latte / crema ~*** cleansing milk / cream **II** *m* detergent; *per cosmesi* cleanser

detergere *v/t* ⟨3uu⟩ cleanse

deteriorabile *adj* perishable

deterioramento *m* deterioration

deteriorare *v/t* ⟨1a⟩ damage; *fig* ruin

deteriorarsi *v/r* ⟨1a⟩ deteriorate

determinabile *adj* determinable
determinante *adj* decisive
determinare *v/t* ⟨1m & b⟩ determine, establish; (*causare*) cause, lead to
determinativo *adj* determinative; ***articolo*** *m* **~** definite article
determinato *adj* certain; (*specifico*) particular, specific; (*risoluto*) determined
determinazione *f* determination
deterrente *m fig* deterrent
detersivo *m* detergent; *per piatti* washing-up liquid, *US* dishwashing liquid; *per biancheria* detergent, *Br* washing powder
detestabile *adj* awful
detestare *v/t* ⟨1b⟩ hate, detest
detonante I *adj* detonating **II** *m* explosive
detonare *v/i* ⟨1c⟩ detonate
detonatore *m* detonator
detonazione *f* detonation
detraibile *adj* deductible
detrarre *v/t* ⟨3xx⟩ deduct (***da*** from)
detratto *past part* → ***detrarre***
detrazione *f* deduction
detrimento *m*: ***a ~ di qn / qc*** to the detriment of s.o. / sth
detrito *m* debris; GEOL detritus
detronizzare *v/t* ⟨1a⟩ dethrone, depose (*a. fig*)
detta *f*: ***a ~ di*** according to
dettagliante *m/f* retailer
dettagliatamente *adv* in detail
dettagliato *adj* detailed
dettaglio *m* ⟨*pl* -gli⟩ detail; FIN ***commercio*** *m* ***al ~*** retail trade
dettame *m* dictate
dettare *v/t* ⟨1a⟩ dictate; ***~ legge*** lay down the law
dettato *m* dictation
dettatura *f* dictation; ***scrivere sotto ~*** take dictation
detto I *past part* → ***dire***; ***~ fatto*** no sooner said than done; ***come non ~*** let's forget it **II** *adj* said; (*soprannominato*) known as **III** *m* saying
deturpare *v/t* ⟨1a⟩ disfigure; ***~ il paesaggio*** deface the countryside
deturpato *adj* scarred, disfigured
deturpazione *f* disfigurement
deumidificatore *m* dehumidifier
deus ex machina *m* ⟨*pl* deus ex machina⟩ deus ex machina
devastante *adj* devastating
devastare *v/t* ⟨1a⟩ devastate
devastatore *adj* devastating
devastazione *f* devastation
deve, devi → ***dovere***
devianza *f* deviance
deviare ⟨1h⟩ **I** *v/t traffico, sospetti* divert; ***~ la palla*** deflect the ball; ***~ il discorso*** (***su qc***) change the subject (to sth) **II** *v/i* deviate; ***~ a destra*** turn right; ***~ da qc*** turn off sth
deviazione *f* deviation; *di traffico* diversion
devo → ***dovere***
devoluto *past part* → ***devolvere***
devoluzione *f* POL devolution
devolvere *v/t* ⟨3g⟩ POL devolve; ***~ qc in beneficenza*** give sth to charity
devotamente *adv* devotedly; REL devoutly
devoto I *adj* devoted; REL devout **II** *m*, **-a** *f* devotee; REL ***i -i*** the devout
devozionale *adj* devotional; ***oggetti*** *mpl* ***-i*** devotional objects; ***percorso*** *m* **~** devotional route
devozione *f* devotion; REL devoutness
di I *prep* **1.** of; ***~ ferro*** (made of) iron; ***l'abito ~ seta*** the silk dress; ***un anello d'oro*** a gold ring; ***~ dove sei?*** where are you from?; ***io sono ~ Roma*** I'm from Rome; ***uscire ~ casa*** leave home; ***l'auto ~ mio padre*** my father's car; ***la ragazza ~ mio fratello*** my brother's girlfriend; ***una commedia ~ Goldoni*** a play by Goldoni; ***~ chi è questo libro?*** whose is this book?, who does this book belong to?; ***le foto delle vacanze*** the holiday photos; ***il duomo ~ Milano*** Milan cathedral; ***parlare ~ politica*** talk about politics; ***un libro ~ storia*** a history book **2.** *con il comparativo* than; ***più bello ~*** prettier than **3.** ***d'estate*** in the summer; ***~ giorno*** by day; ***~ luglio*** in July; ***~ lunedì*** on Mondays **4.** ***~ questo passo*** at this rate **5.** ***~ meno*** *traffico, latte* less; *ragazzi, libri* fewer **6.** ***ricco ~ vitamine*** rich in vitamins; ***una bimba ~ tre anni*** a three-year-old girl; ***un pezzo ~ pane*** a piece of bread; ***una tazza ~ caffè*** a cup of coffee; ***una trota ~ un chilo*** a two-pound trout; ***un uomo ~ grande coraggio*** a very brave man; ***un vaso ~ valore*** a valuable vase; ***spalmare ~ burro*** spread with butter **II** *art* some; *interrogativo*

any, some; *neg* any; ***del vino*** some wine; ***delle caramelle*** some sweets
di' → ***dire***
dì *m* ⟨*pl* dì⟩ *liter* day; ***notte*** *f* ***e*** **~** night and day
dia → ***dare***
diabete *m* diabetes *sg*
diabetico ⟨*mpl* -ci⟩ **I** *adj* diabetic **II** *m*, **-a** *f* diabetic
diabetologo *m*, **-a** *f* ⟨*mpl* -gi⟩ diabetes specialist
diabolico *adj* ⟨*mpl* -ci⟩ diabolic; LIT infernal
diacono *m*, **-nessa** *f* deacon *m*, deaconess *f*
diadema *m* diadem
diafano *adj* diaphanous
diaforetico *adj* ⟨*mpl* -ci⟩ diaphoretic
diaframma *m* ⟨*pl* -i⟩ diaphragm
diagnosi *f* ⟨*pl* diagnosi⟩ diagnosis
diagnostica *f* ⟨*pl* -che⟩ diagnostics *sg*
diagnosticare *v/t* ⟨1n, c & d⟩ diagnose
diagnostico *adj* ⟨*mpl* -ci⟩ diagnostic; ***centro*** *m* **~** diagnostic centre
diagonale **I** *adj* diagonal **II** *f* diagonal (line)
diagonalmente *adv* diagonally
diagramma *m* ⟨*pl* -i⟩ diagram
dialettale *adj parola* dialect; *scrittore* in dialect
dialettica *f* ⟨*pl* -che⟩ dialectics *sg*
dialettico *adj* ⟨*mpl* -ci⟩ dialectical
dialetto *m* dialect; ***parlare in*** **~** speak dialect
dialisi *f* ⟨*pl* dialisi⟩ dialysis
dialogare *v/i* ⟨1l & e⟩ hold talks; **~** ***con qn di qc*** talk to s.o. about sth
dialogo *m* ⟨*pl* -ghi⟩ dialog(ue); **~** ***sociale*** POL social dialogue
diamante *m* diamond
diametralmente *adv*: **~** ***opposto*** diametrically
diametro *m* diameter
diamine *int* damn
diapason *m* ⟨*pl* diapason⟩ tuning fork
diapositiva *f* PHOT slide
diaria *f* travel allowance
diario *m* ⟨*pl* -ri⟩ diary; **~** ***di bordo*** log (-book); **~** ***segreto*** secret diary
diarrea *f* diarrh(o)ea
diaspora *f* HIST diaspora
diastolico *adj* ⟨*mpl* -ci⟩ diastolic
diavola *f*: ***alla*** **~** spatchcock
diavoleria *f* devilment
diavoletto *m* imp
diavolo *m* devil; ***un buon*** **~** a good fellow; ***mandare qn al*** **~** tell s.o. to get lost; ***fare il*** **~** ***a quattro*** kick up a fuss; ***essere come il*** **~** ***e l'acqua santa*** be like cat and dog
dibattere *v/i* ⟨3a⟩ debate, discuss
dibattersi *v/r* struggle; *fig* struggle (***in*** with)
dibattimentale *adj* of a trial; ***udienza*** *f* **~** hearing
dibattimento *m* JUR trial, hearing
dibattito *m* debate
dibattuto *adj* controversial
dicastero *m* ministry
dicembre *m* December
diceria *f* rumo(u)r
dichiarare *v/t* ⟨1a⟩ state; *ufficialmente* declare; *nei giochi di carte* bid; ***ha qualcosa da*** **~*?*** anything to declare?; **~** ***guerra*** declare war
dichiararsi *v/r* declare o.s.; **~** ***innocente*** plead not guilty
dichiarazione *f* declaration; **~** ***d'amore*** declaration of love; **~** ***doganale*** customs declaration; **~** ***dei redditi*** income tax statement; ***rilasciare una*** **~** release a statement; **~** ***di fallimento*** declaration of bankruptcy
diciannove *num* nineteen
diciannovenne **I** *adj* nineteen-year-old *attr*, nineteen years old **II** *m/f* nineteen-year-old
diciannovesimo *m/adj* nineteenth
diciassette *num* seventeen
diciassettenne **I** *adj* seventeen-year-old *attr*, seventeen years old **II** *m/f* seventeen-year-old
diciassettesimo *m/adj* seventeenth
diciottenne **I** *adj* eighteen-year-old *attr*, eighteen years old **II** *m/f* eighteen-year-old
diciottesimo *m/adj* eighteenth
diciotto *num* eighteen
dicitura *f* caption
didascalia *f di foto* caption; (*sottotitolo*) subtitle
didascalico *adj* ⟨*mpl* -ci⟩ didactic
didattica *f* didactics *sg*
didietro **I** *adj zampa* hind, back; *ruota, sedile* rear, back **II** *m* (*retro*) back; *infml* (*sedere*) behind, backside
dieci *num* ten; ***alle*** / ***verso le*** **~** at / about ten (o'clock)
diecimila *adj inv* ten thousand

diedi → ***dare***[1]
dieresi *f* ⟨*pl* dieresi⟩ (*segno*) diaeresis
diesel *m* diesel
diessino *m*, **-a** *f* POL *member of the Italian DS* (*Democratici di Sinistra*) *Party*
dieta[1] *f* diet; ***essere a ~*** be on a diet; ***~ mediterranea*** Mediterranean diet
dieta[2] *f* (*assemblea*) diet; HIST *imperiale* Diet; *regionale* diet
dietetica *f* dietetics *sg*
dietetico *adj* ⟨*mpl* -ci⟩ diet *attr*
dietista *m/f* ⟨*mpl* -i⟩ dietitian, dietician
dietro **I** *prep* **1.** behind; ***~ l'angolo*** round the corner; ***~ di me*** behind me; ***uno ~ l'altro*** *nello spazio* one behind the other; *nel tempo* one after the other; ***chi c'è ~ tutto ciò?*** who's behind all this?; ***stare ~ a qn*** (*badare, aiutare*) look after s.o.; (*corteggiare*) be after s.o **2.** ***~ compenso*** for a consideration; ***~ ricevuta*** on receipt **II** *adv* behind; *in auto* in the back; ***qua / là ~*** over here / there; *nella parte posteriore* behind here / there; ***di ~*** *stanza, porta* back; *zampe* hind; *ruota* rear; ***portarsi ~ qc / qn*** bring sth / s.o. along **III** *m* ⟨*pl* dietro⟩ back
dietro-front **I** *int* about turn **II** *m*: ***fare ~*** do a U-turn
difatti *cj* in fact
difendere *v/t* ⟨3c⟩ defend; (*proteggere*) protect
difendersi *v/r* defend o.s.; ***~ da qc*** *freddo* protect o.s. from sth; *accuse* stand up for onself against sth
difendibile *adj* defensible
difensiva *f* defensive; ***stare sulla ~*** be on the defensive
difensivo *adj* defensive
difensore *m* defender; ***~ d'ufficio*** legal aid lawyer, *US* public defender
difesa *f* defence, *US* defense; ***~ dell'ambiente*** protection of the environment; ***~ dei consumatori*** consumer protection; ***legittima ~*** self-defence (*US* -defense); ***prendere le -e di qn*** stick up for s.o.; ***~ personale*** self-defence (*US* -defense); ***-e*** *pl* ***immunitarie*** defence mechanisms (*US* defense)
difeso *past part* → ***difendere***
difettare *v/i* ⟨1b⟩ be lacking; ***a qn difetta qc*** *or* ***qn difetta di qc*** s.o. lacks sth
difetto *m* (*imperfezione*) defect; *morale* fault, flaw; (*mancanza*) lack; ***far ~*** be lacking; ***~ di fabbricazione*** manufacturing fault
difettoso *adj* defective; ***apparecchio*** *m* ***~*** faulty equipment; ***vista*** *f* ***-a*** impaired vision
diffamare *v/t* ⟨1a⟩ slander; *scrivendo* libel
diffamatore *m*, **-trice** *f* libeller
diffamatorio *adj* ⟨*mpl* -ri⟩ libellous
diffamazione *f* defamation of character
differente *adj* different (***da*** from, *US* than)
differenza *f* difference; ***~ di prezzo*** difference in price; ***a ~ di*** unlike; ***non fare -e*** (***tra qn / qc e qn / qc***) treat s.o. / sth and s.o. / sth the same; ***non fa ~*** it makes no difference
differenziale **I** *adj* differential (*a.* MED, MATH); ***calcolo*** *m* ***~*** differential calculus **II** *m* MECH, MATH differential
differenziare *v/t* ⟨1f⟩ differentiate
differenziarsi *v/r* differ (***da*** from); ***~ per qc*** differ in sth
differibile *adj* postponable
differimento *m* postponement
differire *v/t* ⟨4d⟩ postpone
differito **I** *adj* deferred; ***pagamento*** *m* ***~*** deferred payment **II** *n*: ***differita*** *f* recording; ***trasmettere in ~*** broadcast a recording of
difficile *adj* difficult; (*improbabile*) unlikely; ***fare il ~*** be fussy
difficilmente *adv* with difficulty; ***Paolo è ~ rintracciabile*** it's hard to contact Paolo; ***~ arriverà in orario*** he'll struggle to get here on time
difficoltà *f* ⟨*pl* difficoltà⟩ difficulty; ***senza ~*** easily, without any difficulty; ***essere*** *or* ***trovarsi in ~*** be in trouble; ***avere ~ a fare qc*** find it difficult to do sth; ***fare ~*** cause problems
difficoltoso *adj* difficult, hard
diffida *f* JUR injunction; SPORTS caution
diffidare ⟨1a⟩ **I** *v/t* JUR issue an injunction against; ***~ qn dal fare qc*** warn s.o. not to do sth **II** *v/i*: ***~ di qn*** distrust s.o., mistrust s.o.
diffidente *adj* distrustful, mistrustful
diffidenza *f* distrust, mistrust
diffondere *v/t* ⟨3bb⟩ diffuse; *fig* spread
diffondersi *v/r fig* spread; (*dilungarsi*)

enlarge

difforme *adj* unconformable; (*differente*) different

difformità *f* ⟨*pl* difformità⟩ unconformableness; (*differenza*) difference

diffusione *f di luce*, *calore* diffusion; *di giornale* circulation

diffuso I *past part* → ***diffondere*** **II** *adj* widespread; (*luce*) diffuse

difterico *adj* ⟨*mpl* -ci⟩ diphtherial

difterite *f* diphtheria

diga *f* ⟨*pl* -ghe⟩ *fluviale* dam; *litoranea* dyke; *portuale* breakwater

digerente *adj* digestive

digeribile *adj* digestible (*a. fig*)

digeribilità *f* ⟨*pl* digeribilità⟩ digestibility

digerire *v/t* ⟨4d⟩ digest; *infml* (*tollerare*) stomach *infml*

digestione *f* digestion

digestivo I *adj* digestive **II** *m after-dinner drink*, digestif

digitale[1] *adj* digital; ***impronta*** *f* ~ fingerprint

digitale[2] *f*: ~ (***purpurea***) foxglove

digitalina *f* digitalis

digitalizzare *v/t* ⟨1a⟩ digitize

digitare *v/t* ⟨1l⟩ COMPUT key

digiunare *v/i* ⟨1a⟩ fast

digiuno I *adj* fasting; *fig privo* lacking (***di*** in); ***essere ~ di notizie*** have no news, not have any news **II** *m* fast; ***a ~*** on an empty stomach

dignità *f* dignity

dignitario *m*, **-a** *f* ⟨*mpl* -ri⟩ dignitary

dignitosamente *adv* decorously

dignitoso *adj* dignified

digradante *adj* sloping; ***~ verso il mare*** sloping down to the sea

digradare *v/i* ⟨1a⟩ slope

digressione *f* digression

digressivo *adj* excursive

digrignare *v/t* ⟨1a⟩ gnash

dilagante *adj* widespread

dilagare *v/i* ⟨1e⟩ flood; *fig* spread rapidly

dilaniare *v/t* ⟨1k⟩ tear apart

dilapidare *v/t* ⟨1m⟩ squander

dilatabile *adj* dilatable

dilatare *v/t* ⟨1a⟩ PHYS expand; *occhi* open wide

dilatarsi *v/r di materiali*, *metalli* expand; *di pupilla* dilate

dilatazione *f* expansion; *di pupilla* dilation

dilavamento *m* GEOL scour

dilavare *v/t* ⟨1a⟩ GEOL scour

dilazionare *v/t* ⟨1a⟩ defer, delay

dilazione *f* extension; ***~ di pagamento*** deferral of payment

dileguarsi *v/r* ⟨1a⟩ vanish, disappear

dilemma *m* ⟨*pl* -i⟩ dilemma

dilettante *m/f* amateur; *pej* dilettante

dilettare *v/t* ⟨1b⟩ delight

dilettarsi *v/r*: ***~ di qc*** dabble in sth, do sth as a hobby; ***~ a fare qc*** take delight in doing sth

dilettevole *adj* LIT delightful; ***unire l'utile al ~*** mix business with pleasure

diletto[1] **I** *adj* beloved **II** *m*, **-a** *f* beloved

diletto[2] *m* (*piacere*) delight; ***fare qc per ~*** do sth for pleasure

diligente *adj* diligent; (*accurato*) accurate

diligentemente *adv* diligently; (*accuratamente*) accurately

diligenza[1] *f* diligence

diligenza[2] *f* (*carrozza*) coach

diliscare *v/t* ⟨1d⟩ bone

diluente I *adj* diluting **II** *m* diluter

diluire *v/t* ⟨4d⟩ dilute

diluizione *f* dilution

dilungarsi *v/r* ⟨1e⟩ *fig* dwell (***su*** on)

diluviare *v/impers* ⟨1k⟩ pour down

diluvio *m* downpour; *fig* deluge; ***~ universale*** Flood

dimagrante *adj*: ***cura*** *f* ~ diet

dimagrire *v/i* ⟨4d⟩ lose weight; ***sono dimagrito di 5 chili*** I've lost 5 kilos

dimenare *v/t* ⟨1a⟩ wave; *coda* wag

dimenarsi *v/r* throw o.s. about

dimensione *f* dimension; (*grandezza*) size; (*misure*) dimensions *pl*

dimenticanza *f* forgetfulness, absent-mindedness; (*svista*) oversight

dimenticare *v/t* ⟨1m & d⟩ forget

dimenticarsi *v/r* forget (***di*** sth; ***di fare qc*** to do sth)

dimenticatoio *m*: ***cadere*** *or* ***finire nel ~*** fall out of favour

dimestichezza *f* familiarity; ***prendere ~ con qc*** make oneself familiar with sth

dimettere *v/t* ⟨3ee⟩ dismiss (***da*** from); *da ospedali* discharge, release (***da*** from); *da carceri* release (***da*** from)

dimettersi *v/r* resign (***da*** from)

dimezzamento *m* halving

dimezzare *v/t* ⟨1b⟩ halve; (*dividere*) halve, divide in two

diminuire ⟨4d⟩ **I** *v/t* reduce, diminish; *prezzi* reduce, lower **II** *v/i* decrease, diminish; *di prezzi, valore* fall, go down; *di vento, rumore* die down; **~ di valore** go down in value

diminutivo *m* diminutive

diminuzione *f* decrease; *di prezzi, valore* fall, drop (***di*** in)

dimissionario *adj* ⟨*mpl* -ri⟩ resigning

dimissioni *fpl* resignation *sg*; ***dare le ~*** resign, hand in one's resignation

dimora *f* residence; ***senza fissa ~*** of no fixed abode

dimostrabile *adj* demonstrable

dimostrante **I** *adj* protesting **II** *m/f* protester, demonstrator

dimostrare *v/t* ⟨1a⟩ demonstrate; (*interesse*) show; (*provare*) prove, show; ***dimostra meno della sua età*** he / she looks younger than he / she is

dimostrarsi *v/r* prove to be

dimostrazione *f* demonstration; (*prova*) proof

dinamica *f* dynamics *sg*

dinamico *adj* ⟨*mpl* -ci⟩ dynamic

dinamismo *m* dynamism

dinamitardo **I** *adj* bomb; ***attentato*** *m* **~** bombing **II** *m*, **-a** *f* bomber

dinamite *f* dynamite

dinamo *f* ⟨*pl* dinamo⟩ dynamo

dinanzi *prep*: **~ a** *al cospetto di* before

dinastia *f* dynasty

dingo *m* ⟨*pl* dingo⟩ dingo

diniego *m* ⟨*pl* -ghi⟩ denial, refusal

dinoccolato *adj* loose-limbed

dinosauro *m* dinosaur

dintorno **I** *adv* around **II** *m*: ***dintorni*** *pl* neighbo(u)rhood; ***nei -i di Siena*** somewhere around Siena

dio *m* ⟨*pl* gli dei⟩ *idolo* god; ***Dio*** God; ***grazie a Dio!*** thank God!, thank goodness!; ***per l'amor di Dio*** for God's *or* goodness sake

diocesano *adj* diocesan

diocesi *f* ⟨*pl* diocesi⟩ diocese

diodo *m* diode; **~ *luminoso*** light-emitting diode, LED

diossido *m* dioxide

diossina *f* dioxin

diottria *f* diopter

dipanare *v/t* ⟨1a⟩ unravel; *fig* sort out

dipartimentale *adj* departmental

dipartimento *m* department; ***Dipartimento della Funzione Pubblica*** Civil Service; ***Dipartimento per le Politiche Fiscali*** Department for Fiscal Policy

dipendente **I** *adj* dependent **II** *m/f* employee

dipendenza *f* dependence; (*edificio*) annex(e); ***essere alle ~ di*** work for

dipendere *v/i* ⟨3c⟩: **~ *da*** (*essere subordinato a*) depend on; (*essere mantenuto da*) be dependent on; (*essere causato da*) derive from, be due to; ***dipende*** it depends; ***questo dipende da te*** it's up to you

dipeso *past part* → ***dipendere***

dipingere *v/t* ⟨3d⟩ paint; *fig* describe, depict

dipinto **I** *past part* → ***dipingere*** **II** *m* painting, picture

diploma *m* ⟨*pl* -i⟩ diploma, certificate; **~ *di laurea*** degree (certificate); **~ *di maturità*** high school leaving certificate

diplomando *m*, **-a** *f student in final year of secundary school*

diplomarsi *v/r* ⟨1c⟩ obtain a diploma

diplomatico ⟨*mpl* -ci⟩ **I** *adj* diplomatic; ***corpo*** *m* **~** diplomatic corps *sg* **II** *m* diplomat

diplomato **I** *adj* qualified **II** *m*, **-a** *f* holder of a diploma

diplomazia *f* diplomacy

diporto *m*: ***imbarcazione*** *f* ***da ~*** pleasure boat

diradamento *m* thinning (out)

diradare *v/t* ⟨1a⟩ thin out

diradarsi *v/r* thin out; *di nebbia* clear, lift

diramare *v/t* ⟨1a⟩ *notizia* broadcast; *ordine* send out

diramarsi *v/r fiume* branch off; *notizia* spread

diramazione *f* offshoot; *di strada, fiume*: branch

dire ⟨3t⟩ **I** *v/t* **1.** say; (*raccontare*) tell; **~ *qc a qn*** tell s.o. sth **~ *a qn di fare qc*** tell s.o. to do sth; ***ha detto che sarebbe venuto*** he said he would come; ***dicono che sia vero*** people say it's true; ***vale a ~*** that is, in other words; ***come si dice … in inglese?*** what's the English for …?; ***voler ~*** mean; ***dico sul serio*** I'm serious; ***dica*** (*in negozio*) can I help you?; ***si potrebbe cominciare, diciamo, alle due*** we could start, say, at two o'clock ***che ne dici di uscire?*** how about going out?; ***te l'avevo detto!*** I told you so!; ***me ne ha dette di tutti i colori!*** he called me all sorts! **2.** ***~ una bugia*** tell a lie; ***~ la messa*** say mass; ***~ le parolacce*** swear; ***a ~ il vero*** to tell the truth **II** *v/i*: ***~ bene di qn*** speak highly of s.o.; ***~ male di qn / qc*** speak ill of s.o. / sth; ***avere a che ~ di qc*** argue about sth **III** *m*: ***per sentito ~*** by hearsay; ***hai un bel ~*** say what you like; ***tra il ~ e il fare c'è di mezzo il mare*** *prov* there's many a slip 'twixt cup and lip

directory *f* ⟨*pl* directory⟩ COMPUT directory

diretta *f* RADIO, TV live broadcast; ***in ~*** live

direttamente *adv* directly

direttissima *f* shortest *or* most direct route; RAIL direct line; JUR ***processo** m **per ~*** summary proceedings *pl*

direttiva *f* directive; ***~ comunitaria*** EU directive

direttivo I *adj di direzione di società* managerial; *comitato*, *consiglio*, POL executive *attr* **II** *m di società* board (of directors); POL leadership

diretto I *past part* → ***dirigere*** **II** *adj* (*immediato*) direct; ***~ a*** aimed at; *lettera* addressed to; ***essere ~ a casa*** be heading for home; RADIO, TV ***in*** (***ripresa***) ***-a*** live **III** *m* direct train; SPORTS straight

direttore *m*, **-trice** *f* manager; *più in alto nella gerarchia* director; MUS conductor; EDU headmaster, headmistress *f*, *US* principal; *di giornale*, *rivista* editor (in chief); ***~ generale*** chief executive officer; ***~ delle vendite*** sales manager; ***~ d'orchestra*** conductor; ***~ tecnico*** technical manager; SPORTS coach and team manager; ***~ sanitario*** health director; ***~ didattico*** director of studies; ***~ artistico*** artistic director; ***~ di banca*** bank manager

direzionale *adj* executive; ***centro** m **~*** office district; ***freccia** f **~*** signpost, AUTO indicator

direzione *f* direction; *di società* management; *di partito* leadership; *ufficio* office; *sede generale* head office; ***in ~ di Roma*** in the direction of Rome

dirigente I *adj classe*, *partito* ruling; *personale* managerial **II** *m/f* executive; POL leader

dirigenza *f* management; ***assumere la ~*** take over as manager

dirigere *v/t* ⟨3u⟩ direct; *azienda* run, manage; *orchestra* conduct; ***~ il traffico*** direct the traffic; ***~ lo sguardo verso qc*** turn one's eyes towards sth, look at sth

dirigersi *v/r* head (***a, verso*** for, towards)

dirigibile *m* airship, dirigible

dirigismo *m* state control

dirimpettaio *m*, **-a** *f* ⟨*mpl* -ai⟩ *person living opposite*

dirimpetto *adv* opposite, across the way; ***~ a*** facing, in front of

diritto[1] *m* **1.** right; JUR law; ***-i d'autore*** copyright; ***~ commerciale*** commercial law; ***~ costituzionale*** constitutional law; ***~ internazionale*** international law; ***~ di precedenza*** right of way; ***-i** pl **umani*** human rights; ***~ di voto*** right to vote; ***parità** f **di -i*** equal rights *pl*; ***aver ~ a*** be entitled to; ***di ~*** by rights; ***dare ~ a qc*** entitle s.o. to sth; ***~ naturale*** natural law; ***~ pubblico / privato*** public / private law; ***~ societario*** company law **2.** ***-i** pl* (*il compenso*) fees

diritto[2] **I** *adj* straight; ***stare ~*** stand up straight **II** *adv* straight; ***andare ~ a casa*** go straight home; ***vai sempre ~*** go straight ahead; ***tirare ~*** continue

diritto-dovere *m* ⟨*pl* diritti-doveri⟩ right and duty; ***il ~ all'istruzione*** right and duty to education

dirittura *f* straight line; SPORTS straight; *fig* rectitude; ***in ~ d'arrivo*** in the home straight

diroccato *adj* ramshackle

dirompente *adj* disruptive; *fig* shattering; ***bomba** f **~*** fragmentation bomb; *fig* ***forza** f **~*** devastating power

dirottamento *m* hijack(ing)

dirottare *v/t* ⟨1c⟩ *traffico* divert; *aereo* reroute; *con intenzioni criminali* hijack

dirottatore *m*, **-trice** *f* hijacker

dirotto *adj*: ***piove a ~*** it's pouring; ***pianto** m **~*** flood of tears

dirozzare *v/t* ⟨1a⟩ *fig* refine

dirozzarsi *v/r* ⟨1a⟩ become more refined

dirupo *m* precipice

disabile I *adj* disabled **II** *m/f* disabled

person
disabilità *f* ⟨*pl* disabilità⟩ disability
disabilitare *v/t* ⟨1l⟩ disable
disabilitato *adj* disabled
disabituare *v/t* ⟨1n⟩: **~ *qn a qc*** get s.o. out of the habit of sth
disabituarsi *v/r* ⟨1n⟩ get out of the habit; **~ *a qc*** wean oneself off sth
disaccordo *m* disagreement; ***essere in ~ su qc*** disagree about sth
disadattamento *m* maladjustment
disadattato **I** *adj* maladjusted **II** *m/f* (social) misfit
disadatto *adj* unsuitable (***a*** for); *persona* unsuited (***a un lavoro*** to a job)
disadorno *adj* bare, unadorned
disaffezione *f* disaffection
disagevole *adj* uncomfortable
disaggio *m* ⟨*pl* -ggi⟩ ECON disagio
disagiato *adj* uncomfortable; *vita* hard
disagio *m* ⟨*pl* -gi⟩ (*difficoltà*) hardship; (*scomodità*) discomfort; (*imbarazzo*) embarrassment; ***essere a ~*** be ill at ease
disambientato *adj* out of place
disamorarsi *v/r* ⟨1a⟩ fall out of love; **~ *di qn*** fall out of love with s.o.
disappetenza *f* loss of appetite; ***soffrire di ~*** have lost one's appetite
disapprovare *v/t* ⟨1c⟩ disapprove of
disapprovazione *f* disapproval
disappunto *m* disappointment
disarcionare *v/t* ⟨1m⟩ toss; ***essere disarcionato*** be unseated
disarmante *adj* disarming
disarmare *v/t* ⟨1a⟩ disarm
disarmato *adj* unarmed; *fig* defenceless
disarmo *m* POL disarmament; NAUT put out of commision
disarmonia *f* disharmony (*a. fig*)
disarmonico *adj* ⟨*mpl* -ci⟩ disharmonious; (*sproporzionato*) inconsonant; ***voce*** *f* ***-a*** discordant voice
disarticolato *adj* disjointed; ***suoni*** *mpl* ***-i*** disconnected sounds
disassuefare *v/t* ⟨3aa⟩ disaccustom; **~ *qn da qc*** wean / get s.o. off sth
disassuefarsi *v/r* ⟨3aa⟩ wean oneself off sth
disastrato *adj zone* disaster; *famiglie* stricken
disastro *m* disaster
disastroso *adj* disastrous
disattendere *v/t* ⟨3a⟩ disregard; **~ *le aspettative*** not come up to expectations
disattento *adj* inattentive
disattenzione *f* inattention, lack of attention; *errore* careless mistake
disattivare *v/t* ⟨1a⟩ *antifurto*, *semaforo* disconnect; *bomba* defuse; *computer*, *antivirus* disable
disavanzo *m* deficit; **~ *della bilancia commerciale*** trade deficit; **~ *commerciale con l'estero*** foreign trade deficit
disavventura *f* misadventure
disboscamento *m* deforestation
disboscare *v/t* ⟨1d⟩ deforest
disbrigo *m* ⟨*pl* -ghi⟩ dispatch
discapito *m*: ***a ~ di qn*** to the detriment *or* disadvantage of s.o.
discarica *f* ⟨*pl* -che⟩ dumping; (*luogo*) dump; **~ *abusiva*** unauthorized dumping
discarico *m*: ***a mio ~*** in my defence (*US* defense); ***testimone a ~*** witness for the defence (*US* defense)
discendente **I** *adj inv* descending **II** *m/f* descendant
discendenza *f* descent; (*discendenti*) descendants *pl*
discendere *v/i* ⟨3c⟩ descend; (*trarre origine*) be a descendant (***da*** of), be descended (***da*** from); *da veicoli*, *da cavallo* alight (***da*** from)
discepolo *m*, **-a** *f* disciple
discernere *v/t* ⟨3a⟩ discern, perceive
discernimento *m* discernment
discesa *f* descent; (*pendio*) slope; *di bus* exit; *sci* **~ *libera*** downhill (race); ***strada*** *f* ***in ~*** street that slopes downwards
discesista *m/f* ⟨*mpl* -i⟩ downhill skier
dischetto *m* COMPUT diskette, floppy *infml*
dischiudere *v/t* ⟨3b⟩ unclose
dischiudersi *v/r* ⟨3b⟩ open; *fiori*, *gemme* come into flower
discinto *adj* scantily clad
disciogliere *v/t* ⟨3ss⟩ dissolve; *neve* melt
disciogliersi *v/r* ⟨3ss⟩ dissolve; *neve* melt
disciolto *past part* → ***disciogliere***
disciplina *f* discipline
disciplinare **I** *adj* disciplinary **II** *v/t* ⟨1a⟩ discipline

disciplinato *adj* disciplined
disc-jockey *m/f* ⟨*pl* disc-jockey⟩ disc jockey
disco *m* ⟨*pl* -chi⟩ **1.** disc, *US* disk; AUTO **~ *orario*** parking disc; **~ *volante*** flying saucer **2.** SPORTS discus **3.** MUS record; **~ *33 giri*** LP **4.** COMPUT disk; **~ *rigido*** hard disk
discobolo *m* discus thrower
discografia *f elenco* recordings *pl*, discography; *attività* record industry
discografico *adj* ⟨*mpl* -ci⟩ record; ***casa f -a*** record label
discolo **I** *adj* wild, unruly **II** *m* troublemaker
discolpa *f* exoneration (*a.* JUR); ***a propria ~*** in one's own defence (*US* defense)
discolpare *v/t* ⟨1a⟩ clear
discolparsi *v/r* ⟨1m⟩ vindicate oneself
disconoscere *v/t* ⟨3n⟩ disown, disclaim
disconoscimento *m* disownment; **~ *della paternità*** disclaimer of paternity
discontinuità *f* ⟨*pl* discontinuità⟩ discontinuity; *fig* irregularity
discontinuo *adj* intermittent; (*disuguale*) erratic
discopatia *f* MED discopathy
discopub *m* ⟨*pl* discopub⟩ *pub with dancing*
discordanza *f* disagreement, dissonance; PSYCH dissonance; GEOL unconformity; **~ *angolare*** angular discordance
discorde *adj* not in agreement, clashing
discordia *f* discord; (*differenza di opinioni*) disagreement; (*litigio*) argument
discorrere *v/i* ⟨3o⟩ talk (***di*** about); **~ *del più e del meno*** talk about this and that; ***e via discorrendo*** and so on
discorsivo *adj* fluent; ***tono m ~*** conversational tone
discorso **I** *past part* → ***discorrere*** **II** *m pubblico*, *ufficiale* speech; (*conversazione*) conversation, talk; **~ *diretto/indiretto*** direct/indirect speech; ***cambiare ~*** change the subject; ***che -i!*** what rubbish!; ***fare un ~*** make a speech
discostare *v/t* ⟨1c⟩ draw back
discostarsi *v/r* ⟨1c⟩ wander; **~ *dalla verità*** diverge from the truth
discosto **I** *adj* far **II** *adv* at some distance; ***starsene ~ dal gruppo*** keep apart from the group
discoteca *f* ⟨*pl* -che⟩ *locale* disco; *raccolta* record library
discount *m* ⟨*pl* discount⟩ discount
discreditare *v/t* ⟨1m⟩ discredit
discredito *m* discredit, disrepute; ***gettare ~ su qn/qc*** throw discredit on s.o./sth
discrepante *adj* contradictory
discrepanza *f* discrepancy
discretamente *adv* (*con discrezione*) discreetly; (*abbastanza*) rather; ***stare ~*** be not too bad
discreto *adj* (*riservato*) discreet; (*abbastanza buono*) fairly good; (*moderato*) moderate, fair
discrezionale *adj*: ***questione f ~*** matter of discretion
discrezionalità *f* ⟨*pl* discrezionalità⟩ discretionary power
discrezione *f* discretion; ***a ~ di*** at the discretion of
discriminante *adj* discriminating; ***circostanza ~*** extenuating circumstance
discriminare ⟨1m⟩ **I** *v/i* discriminate **II** *v/t stranieri*, *donne* discriminate against
discriminazione *f* discrimination
discussione *f* discussion; (*litigio*) argument; ***mettere in ~ qc*** call sth into question; ***essere fuori ~*** be out of the question
discusso **I** *adj* (*controverso*) controversial **II** *past part* → ***discutere***
discutere ⟨3v⟩ **I** *v/t proposta*, *caso* discuss, talk about; *questione* debate; (*mettere in dubbio*) question; (*contestare*) dispute **II** *v/i* talk; (*litigare*) argue; (*negoziare*) negotiate
discutibile *adj* debatable
discutibilità *f* ⟨*pl* discutibilità⟩ dubiousness
discutibilmente *adv* questionably
disdegnare *v/t* ⟨1a⟩ disdain
disdetta *f* JUR notice; *fig* bad luck; ***che ~!*** hard lines!
disdetto *past part* → ***disdire***
disdicevole *adj* disgraceful
disdire *v/t* ⟨3t⟩ *impegno* cancel; *contratto* terminate
diseducativo *adj* harmful; ***trasmis-***

sione *f* **-a** morally harmful programme
disegnare *v/t* ⟨1a⟩ draw; (*progettare*) design
disegnatore *m*, **-trice** *f* draughtsman, *US* draftsman; *donna* draughtswoman, *US* draftswoman; (*progettista*) designer
disegno *m* drawing; (*progetto*) design; ***~ di legge*** bill
diserbante *m* weed-killer, herbicide
diserbare *v/t* ⟨1a⟩ weed
diseredare *v/t* ⟨1b⟩ disinherit
diseredato *adj* underprivileged, disadvantaged
disertare ⟨1b⟩ **I** *v/t* desert; ***~ una riunione*** not attend a meeting **II** *v/i* desert
disertore *m* deserter
diserzione *f* desertion
disfacimento *m* decay; *fig* break-up
disfare *v/t* ⟨3aa⟩ undo; *letto* strip; (*distruggere*) destroy; ***~ la valigia*** unpack
disfarsi *v/r di neve*, *ghiaccio* melt; ***~ di*** get rid of
disfasia *f* MED dysphasia
disfatta *f* defeat
disfattismo *m* defeatism
disfattista ⟨*mpl* -i⟩ **I** *adj* defeatist **II** *m/f* defeatist; (*scettico*) disbeliever
disfatto *past part* → ***disfare***
disfunzione *f* MED disorder
disgelo *m* thaw
disgiungere *v/t* ⟨3d⟩ disjoint
disgiungersi *v/r* ⟨3d⟩ disjoin
disgiuntamente *adv* separately
disgrazia *f* misfortune; (*incidente*) accident; (*sfavore*) disgrace; ***per ~*** unfortunately
disgraziatamente *adv* unluckily
disgraziato **I** *adj* (*sfortunato*) unlucky, unfortunate **II** *m*, **-a** *f* poor soul; *infml* (*farabutto*) bastard *infml*
disgregare *v/t* ⟨1b⟩ break up
disgregarsi *v/r* break up, disintegrate
disgregazione *f* disintegration; *fig* disintegration, break-up
disguido *m* hiccup, hitch
disgustare *v/t* ⟨1a⟩ disgust
disgustarsi *v/r* be disgusted (***di*** by)
disgustato *adj* in disgust
disgusto *m* disgust
disgustosamente *adv* disgustingly
disgustoso *adj* disgusting
disidratare *v/t* ⟨1a⟩ dehydrate
disidratarsi *v/r* ⟨1a⟩ become dehydrated
disidratato *adj* dehydrated
disilludere *v/t* ⟨3b⟩ disillusion
disillusione *f* disillusionment
disilluso *adj* disillusioned
disimparare *v/t* ⟨1a⟩ forget
disimpegno *m* disengagement
disincagliare *v/t* ⟨1g⟩ NAUT refloat; *fig* unblock
disincagliarsi *v/r* ⟨1g⟩ *fig* get free
disincantare *v/t* ⟨1a⟩ disenchant
disincantato *adj* disenchanted
disincentivare *v/t* ⟨1a⟩ discourage, deter
disincentivo *m* disincentive
disinfestante *m* exterminator
disinfestare *v/t* ⟨1a⟩ get rid of
disinfettante *m* disinfectant
disinfettare *v/t* ⟨1b⟩ disinfect
disinfezione *f* disinfection
disinformazione *f* disinformation
disingannare *v/t* ⟨1a⟩ disillusion
disinganno *m* disillusionment
disinibire *v/t* ⟨4d⟩ free from inhibitions
disinibirsi *v/r* ⟨4d⟩ get rid of one's inhibitions
disinibito *adj* uninhibited
disinnescare *v/t* ⟨1d⟩ *bomba* defuse
disinnestare *v/t* ⟨1a⟩ AUTO *marcia* disengage
disinnesto *m* declutching
disinquinare *v/t* ⟨1a⟩ clean up
disinserire *v/t* ⟨4d⟩ disconnect
disintegrare *v/t* ⟨1m⟩ disintegrate
disintegrarsi *v/r* disintegrate
disinteressarsi *v/r* take no interest (***di*** in)
disinteressatamente *adv* unselfishly; ***agire ~*** be unselfish
disinteressato *adj* disinterested
disinteresse *m* lack of interest; (*generosità*) unselfishness
disintossicante *adj*: ***cura*** *f* ***~*** detox
disintossicare *v/t* ⟨1m, c & d⟩ detoxify
disintossicarsi *v/r* ⟨1m, c & d⟩ detox; ***~ dalla droga / dall'alcol*** come off drugs / alcohol
disintossicazione *f* treatment for drug / alcohol addiction, detox *infml*
disinvoltamente *adv* confidently
disinvolto *adj* confident
disinvoltura *f* confidence

disistima *f* contempt, low opinion
dislessia *f* dyslexia
dislessico *adj* dyslexic
dislivello *m* difference in height; *fig* difference
dislocamento *m* MIL deployment; NAUT displacement
dislocare *v/t* ⟨1d⟩ MIL deploy; NAUT displace
dislocazione *f* (*collocazione*) transfer
dismenorrea *f* dysmenorrhea
dismisura *f* excess; ***a ~*** out of all proportion; ***crescere a ~*** grow enormously
disobbedire *v/i* → ***disubbidire***
disoccupato I *adj* unemployed, jobless; ***rimanere ~*** be out of work **II** *m*, **-a** *f* person who is unemployed, person without a job; ***i -i*** the unemployed, the jobless
disoccupazione *f* unemployment; ***~ giovanile*** unemployment among the young, youth unemployment
disonestà *f* dishonesty
disonesto *adj* dishonest
disonorare *v/t* ⟨1a⟩ bring dishono(u)r on
disonorarsi *v/r* ⟨1a⟩ disgrace oneself
disonore *m* dishono(u)r
disonorevole *adj* dishono(u)rable
disopra I *adv* above; ***al ~ di*** above **II** *adj* upper **III** *m* top
disordinatamente *adv* untidily
disordinato *adj* untidy, messy
disordine *m* untidiness, mess; ***in ~*** untidy, in a mess; ***-i*** *pl* riots, public disorder *sg*
disorganizzato *adj* disorganized
disorganizzazione *f* disorganization, lack of organization
disorientamento *m* disorientation
disorientare *v/t* ⟨1b⟩ disorient(ate)
disorientato *adj* disorient(at)ed
disossare *v/t* ⟨1c⟩ bone
disotto I *adv* below; ***al ~ di*** beneath **II** *adj* lower **III** *m* underside
dispaccio *m* ⟨*pl* -cci⟩ dispatch
disparato *adj* disparate
dispari *adj inv* odd
disparità *f* ⟨*pl* disparità⟩ disparity
disparte *adv*: ***in ~*** aside, to one side
dispendio *m* waste
dispendioso *adj* expensive
dispensa *f stanza* larder; *mobile* cupboard; *pubblicazione* instal(l)ment; JUR exemption; ***~ universitaria*** duplicated lecture notes
dispensare *v/t* ⟨1b⟩ dispense; (*esonerare*) exonerate
dispenser *m* ⟨*pl* dispenser⟩ dispenser
disperare *v/i* ⟨1b⟩ despair (***di*** of); ***far ~ qn*** drive s.o. to despair
disperarsi *v/r* despair
disperatamente *adv* desperately
disperato *adj* desperate
disperazione *f* despair, desperation
disperdere *v/t* ⟨3uu⟩ disperse; *energie, sostanze* squander; ***non ~ nell'ambiente*** please dispose of carefully
disperdersi *v/r* disperse
dispersione *f* dispersal; CHEM, PHYS dispersion; *fig di energie* waste
disperso I *past part* → ***disperdere*** **II** *adj* scattered; (*sperduto*) lost, missing
dispetto *m* spite; ***per ~*** out of spite; ***a ~ di qc*** in spite of sth; ***fare -i a qn*** annoy *or* tease s.o.
dispettoso *adj* mischievous
dispiacere[1] *v/i* ⟨2k⟩ **1.** (*causare dolore*) upset (***a*** s.o.); ***mi dispiace*** I'm sorry **2.** (*non piacere*) displease (***a*** s.o.); ***ti dispiace di non essere andato?*** are you sorry you didn't go?; ***le dispiace se apro la finestra?*** do you mind if I open the window?; ***questo vino non mi dispiace*** this wine's not bad
dispiacere[2] *m* (*rammarico*) regret, sorrow; (*dolore*) grief, sadness; (*delusione*) disappointment; ***-i*** (*preoccupazioni*) worries, troubles; ***con mio grande ~*** much to my displeasure
dispiaciuto *adj*: ***essere*** (***molto***) ***~ di*** *or* ***per qc*** be (very) sorry about sth
dispiegamento *m* deployment; ***~ di forze*** troop deployment
display *m* display; PHOT control panel
disponibile *adj* available; (*cortese*) helpful, obliging; ***essere ~*** be helpful; ***posti*** *mpl* ***-i*** situations vacant; ***merce*** *f* ***non ~*** goods out of stock; ***~ al dialogo*** willing to talk
disponibilità *f* ⟨*pl* disponibilità⟩ availability; (*cortesia*) helpfulness; ***cospicue ~*** *pl* sizeable liquid assets
disporre ⟨3ll⟩ **I** *v/t* arrange; (*stabilire*) order **II** *v/i* (*decidere*) make arrangements; ***abbiamo già disposto diversamente*** we've made other arrangements; ***~ di qc*** have sth (at one's dis-

posal)
disporsi *v/r*: **~ *in cerchio* / *in due file*** form a circle / two rows
dispositivo *m* TECH device; **~ *antifurto*** anti-theft device; *in casa* burglar alarm; *in macchina* car alarm; **~ *di chiusura*** locking device; **~ *della sentenza*** JUR purview of the verdict
disposizione *f* arrangement; (*norma*) provision; (*attitudine*) aptitude (***a*** for); ***avere qc a ~*** have sth at one's disposal; ***stare* / *mettere a ~ di qn*** be / put at s.o.'s disposal; ***-i** pl **di legge*** terms of the law
disposto I *past part* → ***disporre*** **II** *adj*: **~ *a*** ready to, willing to; ***essere ben ~ verso qn*** be well disposed to s.o.
dispoticamente *adv* high-handedly
dispotico *adj* ⟨*mpl* -ci⟩ despotic
dispotismo *m* despotism; *fig* high-handedness
dispregiativo *adj* derogatory
disprezzabile *adj* despicable
disprezzare *v/t* ⟨1b⟩ despise
disprezzo *m* contempt
disputa *f* dispute, argument
disputare ⟨1l⟩ **I** *v/i* argue **II** *v/t* SPORTS take part in
disputarsi *v/r* ⟨1l⟩ compete for; **~ *un premio*** compete for a prize
disquisizione *f* disquisition
dissacrante *adj* desecrating
dissalare *v/t* ⟨1a⟩ desalinate; **~ *il baccalà*** get the salt out of the stockfish
dissalatore *m* desalinator
dissalazione *f* desalination
dissanguamento *m* bleeding; *fig* bleeding dry
dissanguare *v/t* ⟨1a⟩ *fig* bleed dry, bleed white; ***morire dissanguato*** bleed to death
dissanguarsi *v/r* ⟨1m⟩ bleed to death; *fig* go bankrupt
dissapore *m* misunderstanding
disseccare *v/t* ⟨1d⟩ *erba* scorch; *pianta* shrivel
disseminare *v/t* ⟨1m⟩ scatter, disseminate; *fig* spread
dissenso *m* dissent; (*dissapore*) argument, disagreement
dissenteria *f* dysentery
dissentire *v/i* ⟨4b⟩ disagree (***da*** with)
disseppellire *v/t* ⟨4d⟩ exhume
dissequestrare *v/t* ⟨1b⟩ lift a ban on
dissequestro *m* lifting of a ban
dissertare *v/i* ⟨1b⟩: **~ *di** or **su qc*** expatiate on sth
dissertazione *f* dissertation
disservizio *m* ⟨*pl* -zi⟩ poor service; (*inefficienza*) inefficiency; (*cattiva gestione*) mismanagement
dissestare *v/t* ⟨1b⟩ FIN destabilize
dissestato *adj strada* uneven; *finanze* precarious
dissesto *m* ruin, failure; **~ *ecologico*** environmental meltdown
dissetante *adj* thirst-quenching
dissetare *v/t* ⟨1a⟩: **~ *qn*** quench s.o.'s thirst
dissetarsi *v/r* quench one's thirst
dissidente *m/f* dissident
dissidio *m* ⟨*pl* -i, -ii⟩ quarrel
dissimile *adj* dissimilar
dissimulare *v/t* ⟨1m⟩ conceal, hide
dissimulazione *f* concealment
dissipare *v/t* ⟨1l⟩ dissolve; (*sperperare*) squander; **~ *i dubbi di qn*** dispel s.o.'s doubts
dissiparsi *v/r nebbia* lift; *fig* dissipate
dissipazione *f*: **~ *termica*** heat dissipation
dissociare *v/t* ⟨1f⟩ dissociate
dissociarsi *v/r* dissociate o.s. (***da*** from)
dissociazione *f* dissociation (*a.* CHEM); PSYCH withdrawal
dissodare *v/t* ⟨1c⟩ till
dissolutezza *f* debauchery; **~ *dei costumi*** laxness of morals
dissoluto *adj* dissolute
dissolvenza *f* fading
dissolvere *v/t* ⟨3g⟩ dissolve; *dubbi*, *nebbia* dispel
dissolversi *v/r* dissolve; (*svanire*) vanish
dissonante *adj* dissonant; *fig* discordant
dissonanza *f* MUS dissonance; *fig* clash
dissuadere *v/t* ⟨2i⟩: **~ *qn da fare qc*** dissuade s.o. from doing sth
dissuasione *f* dissuasion
dissuaso *past part* → ***dissuadere***
distaccamento *m* MIL detachment
distaccare *v/t* ⟨1d⟩ detach; SPORTS leave behind
distaccarsi *v/r da persone* detach o.s. (***da*** from)
distaccato *adj fig* detached; ***atteggiamento** m* **~** aloofness

distacco *m* ⟨*pl* -cchi⟩ detachment (*a. fig*); (*separazione*) separation; SPORTS lead
distante *adj* distant, remote, far-off; ~ *da* far from
distanza *f* distance (*a. fig*); ***comando*** *m* ***a*** ~ remote control; ***a*** ~ ***di due giorni*** two days apart; ~ ***di sicurezza*** safety distance; ***tenere le -e*** know one's place
distanziare *v/t* ⟨1g⟩ space out; SPORTS leave behind; (*superare*) overtake
distanziarsi *v/r* ⟨1g⟩ distance oneself
distare *v/i* ⟨1a⟩: ***l'albergo dista 100 metri dalla stazione*** the hotel is 100 metres from the station; ***quanto dista da qui?*** how far is it from here?
distendere *v/t* ⟨3c⟩ (*adagiare*) lay; *gambe, braccia* stretch out; *muscoli* relax; *bucato* hang out; *nervi* calm; ~ ***qn sul letto*** lay s.o. on the bed
distendersi *v/r* lie down; (*rilassarsi*) relax
distensione *f* relaxation; POL détente
distensivo *adj* relaxing
distesa *f* expanse; ~ ***di cemento*** area of cement; ~ ***di sabbia*** stretch of sand
disteso I *past part* → ***distendere*** **II** *adj* stretched out; (*rilassato*) relaxed; ***cadere lungo*** ~ ***per terra*** fall flat on one's face
distillare *v/t* ⟨1a⟩ distil, *US* distill
distillato I *adj* distilled **II** *n*: ***distillato*** *m* distillate; ~ ***di vinacce*** distillate of herbs
distillazione *f* distillation
distilleria *f* distillery
distinguere *v/t* ⟨3d⟩ distinguish
distinguersi *v/r*: ~ ***per qc*** stand out because of sth; *coraggio, onestà* distinguish o.s. for sth
distinta *f* list, slip
distintamente *adv* (*chiaramente*) clearly; (*separatamente*) separately; *nelle lettere*: ***La salutiamo*** ~ Yours faithfully; ***comportarsi*** ~ have refined manners
distintivo I *adj* distinctive **II** *m* badge
distinto I *past part* → ***distinguere*** **II** *adj* (*diverso*) different, distinct; (*chiaro*) distinct; *fig* distinguished; ***-i saluti*** yours faithfully
distinzione *f* distinction; ***senza -i*** without making any distinctions
distogliere *v/t* ⟨3ss⟩: ~ ***qc da qn / qc*** divert sth from s.o. / sth; ~ ***lo sguardo da qn / qc*** take one's eyes off s.o. / sth
distolto *past part* → ***distogliere***
distorcere *v/t* ⟨3d⟩ *braccio* twist; *significato, suono* distort
distorcersi *v/r*: ~ ***un braccio*** twist / sprain one's arm
distorsione *f* distortion; MED sprain
distorto *adj* sprained; *significato, suono* distorted
distrarre *v/t* ⟨3xx⟩ distract; (*divertire*) entertain; ~ ***qn dallo studio*** take s.o.'s mind off their studies
distrarsi *v/r* (*non essere attento*) get distracted; (*svagarsi*) take one's mind off things; ***non ti distrarre*** don't get distracted
distrattamente *adv* absent-mindedly
distratto I *past part* → ***distrarre*** **II** *adj* absent-minded
distrazione *f* absent-mindedness; (*errore*) inattention; (*svago*) amusement; *che distrae da un'attività* distraction; ***errore di*** ~ careless mistake
distretto *m* district; ~ ***di polizia*** police district
distribuire *v/t* ⟨4d⟩ distribute; *premi* award, present
distribuirsi *v/r* ⟨4d⟩ be distributed
distributivo *adj* distributive
distributore *m* distributor; ~ (***di benzina***) (petrol, *US* gas) pump; ~ ***automatico*** vending machine; ~ ***automatico di biglietti*** ticket machine
distribuzione *f* distribution; *posta* delivery; ~ ***dei doni*** giving out gifts; ***dell'energia elettrica*** electricity supply; ~ ***cinematografica*** film distribution; ***grande*** ~ big retailers; ***rete*** *f* ***di*** ~ distribution system; ~ ***del reddito*** income distribution
districare *v/t* ⟨1d⟩ untangle; *fig* unravel
districarsi *v/r*: ~ ***da qc*** disentangle o.s. from sth
distrofia *f*: ~ ***muscolare*** muscular dystrophy
distrofico *adj* ⟨*mpl* -ci⟩ dystrophic
distruggere *v/t* ⟨3cc⟩ destroy
distruggersi *v/r* ⟨3cc⟩: ~ ***la schiena / le gambe*** wreck one's back / legs
distruttivo *adj* destructive
distrutto *past part* → ***distruggere***
distruttore I *adj* destructive **II** *m*, **-trice** *f* destroyer; ~ ***di documenti***

shredder
distruzione *f* destruction
disturbare *v/t* ⟨1a⟩ disturb; (*dare fastidio a*) bother; (*sconvolgere*) upset; ***disturbo?*** am I disturbing you?
disturbarsi *v/r*: ***non si disturbi*** please don't bother
disturbatore *m*, **-trice** *f* troublemaker
disturbo *m* trouble, bother; ***-i*** RADIO interference *sg*; MED ***-i*** *pl* ***di circolazione*** circulation problems; ***-i di stomaco*** stomach trouble; ***togliere il ~*** be on one's way; ***prendersi il ~ di fare qc*** go to the bother of doing sth
disubbdienza *f* disobedience
disubbidiente *adj* disobedient
disubbidienza *f* disobedience
disubbidire *v/i* ⟨4d⟩: ***~ a*** disobey
disuguaglianza *f* disparity, difference
disuguale *adj* different; *terreno* uneven; *fig* inconsistent, erratic
disumanità *f* ⟨*pl* disumanità⟩ inhumanity
disumano *adj* inhuman
disuso *m*: ***in ~*** in disuse, disused
ditale *m* thimble
dito *m* ⟨*pl* le dita⟩ **1.** finger; ***mettersi le -a nel naso*** pick one's nose; ***mettere il ~ sulla piaga*** touch on a sore point; ***non muovere un ~*** not lift a finger **2.** *del piede* toe **3.** (*misura*) ***un ~ di polvere*** dust an inch thick; ***un ~ di vino*** a drop of wine
ditta *f* company, firm; ***~ fornitrice*** supplier; ***~ di vendite per corrispondenza*** mail-order company
dittafono® *m* dictaphone®
dittatore *m* dictator
dittatoriale *adj* dictatorial (*a. fig*); ***regime*** *m* ***~*** dictatorship
dittatura *f* dictatorship
dittongo *m* diphthong
diuretico *adj* ⟨*mpl* -ci⟩ diuretic
diurno *adj* daytime *attr*; ***albergo*** *m* ***~*** *place where travellers can have a shower / shave*
diva *f* diva
divagare *v/i* ⟨1e⟩ digress
divagazione *f* digression
divampare *v/i* ⟨1a⟩ *di rivolta, incendio* break out; *di passione* blaze
divano *m* sofa; ***~ letto*** sofa bed
divaricare *v/t* ⟨1m & d⟩ open (wide)
divario *m* ⟨*pl* -ri⟩ difference
divellere *v/t* ⟨2e⟩ uproot
divelto *past part* → ***divellere***
divenire *v/i* ⟨4p⟩ become
diventare *v/i* ⟨1b⟩ become; *rosso, bianco* turn, go; ***~ grande*** grow up; ***ora che sei diventato papà ...*** now that you're a father; ***far ~ matto qn*** drive s.o. crazy
diverbio *m* ⟨*pl* -bi⟩ argument
divergente *adj* diverging, divergent
divergenza *f* divergence; *di opinioni* difference
divergere *v/i* ⟨3uu & 3a⟩ diverge
diversamente *adv* differently; (*altrimenti*) otherwise; ***~ abile*** differently able
diversificare ⟨1n & d⟩ **I** *v/t* diversify **II** *v/i* differ
diversificarsi *v/r* ⟨1n & d⟩ differ
diversificazione *f* diversification
diversità *f* ⟨*pl* diversità⟩ difference; (*varietà*) diversity
diversivo I *adj*: ***azione*** *f* ***-a*** diversionary action **II** *m* diversion, distraction
diverso I *adj* (*differente*) different (***da*** from, *US* than); ***-i*** *pl* several; ***da -i giorni*** for the past few days; ***la mia giacca è -a dalla tua*** my jacket's different from yours **II** *pron*: ***diversi*** *pl* several people
divertente *adj* amusing
diverticolo *m* subterfuge
divertimento *m* amusement; ***buon ~!*** have a good time!, enjoy yourself / yourselves!
divertire *v/t* ⟨4b⟩ amuse
divertirsi *v/r* enjoy o.s., have a good time; ***~ a fare qc*** enjoy doing sth; ***divertiti!*** have a good time!, enjoy yourself!
dividendo *m* dividend
dividere *v/t* ⟨3q⟩ divide; (*condividere*) share; ***~ 16 per 4*** divide 16 by 4; ***~ qc in 3 parti*** divide sth into 3; ***~ qc a metà*** divide / split sth in half; ***~ qc con qn*** share sth with s.o.
dividersi *v/r* **1.** *di coppia* separate; ***~ dal marito / dalla moglie*** separate from one's husband / wife **2.** (*scindersi*) be split, be divided (***in*** into); ***~ in gruppi*** divide up into groups; ***~ tra casa e ufficio*** split o.s. between home and office **3.** (*distribuirsi*) ***~ le spese*** split the costs
divieto *m* ban; ***~ d'importazione*** import ban; AUTO ***~ di segnalazioni***

acustiche please do not use your horn; **~ *di sosta*** no parking
divinamente *adv* divinely
divinatorio *adj* ⟨*mpl* -ri⟩ divinatory; ***facoltà*** *f* ***-a*** divining powers
divinazione *f* divination
divincolarsi *v/r* ⟨1m⟩ twist, wriggle
divinità *f* ⟨*pl* divinità⟩ divinity
divinizzare *v/t* ⟨1a⟩ deify
divinizzazione *f* deification
divino *adj* divine
divisa *f* uniform; FIN currency
divisibile *adj* divisible (*a.* MATH)
divisibilità *f* ⟨*pl* divisibilità⟩ divisibility
divisione *f* division; **~ *del lavoro*** division of labo(u)r
divismo *m pej* hero worship
divisore *m* divider; MATH divisor
divisorio ⟨*mpl* -ri⟩ **I** *adj* dividing; ***parete*** *f* ***-a*** partition wall, stud wall **II** *m* partition
divo *m* star
divorare *v/t* ⟨1c⟩ devour; **~ *qn con gli occhi*** devour s.o. with one's eyes
divoratore *m*, **-trice** *f* devourer; **~ *di libri*** voracious reader
divorziare *v/i* ⟨1c & g⟩ get a divorce
divorziato *adj* divorced
divorzio *m* ⟨*pl* -zi⟩ divorce; ***chiedere il* ~** ask for a divorce; ***ottenere il* ~** get a divorce; **~ *consensuale*** no-fault divorce
divorzista *m/f* ⟨*mpl* -i⟩ (*avvocato*) divorce lawyer
divulgare *v/t* ⟨1e⟩ divulge, reveal; (*rendere accessibile*) popularize
divulgativo *adj* popular
divulgatore **I** *adj* popularizing **II** *m*, **-trice** *f* popularizer
divulgazione *f* divulging; *scientifica etc* popularization
dizigotico *adj* ⟨*mpl* -ci⟩: ***fratelli -i*** fraternal twins
dizionario *m* ⟨*pl* -ri⟩ dictionary; **~ *bilingue*** bilingual dictionary; **~ *monolingue*** monolingual dictionary; **~ *tascabile*** pocket dictionary; **~ *tecnico*** technical dictionary
dizione *f* diction; THEAT elocution
D.L. *m abbr* (= **Decreto Legge**) Legislative Decree
D.M. *m abbr* (= **Decreto Ministeriale**) Ministerial Decree
DNA *abbr* (= **acido deossiribonucleico**) DNA (deoxyribonucleic acid)
do[1] → ***dare***
do[2] *m* ⟨*pl* do⟩ MUS C; *nel solfeggio della scala* doh
dobbiamo → ***dovere***
D.O.C., doc *abbr* (= **Denominazione d'Origine Controllata**) *term signifying that a wine is of a certain origin and quality*
doccia *f* ⟨*pl* -cce⟩ shower; ***fare la* ~** take a shower
docciaschiuma *m* ⟨*pl* docciaschiuma⟩ shower gel
docente **I** *adj* teaching; ***personale*** *m* **~** teaching staff **II** *m/f* teacher
docenza *f* teaching
docile *adj* docile
docilità *f* ⟨*pl* docilità⟩ docility
docilmente *adv* meekly
documentabile *adj* documentable
documentale *adj* documentary; ***prova*** *f* **~** primary evidence
documentare *v/t* ⟨1a⟩ document
documentario *m* documentary
documentarsi *v/r* collect information
documentazione *f* documentation
documento *m* document; **~ *d'identità*** identification, ID; ***-i*** *pl* papers *pl*; ***-i dell'autoveicolo*** car documents; ***chiedere i -i*** ask to see s.o.'s documents
dodecaedro *m* dodecahedron
dodicenne **I** *adj* twelve-year-old *attr*, twelve years old **II** *m/f* twelve-year-old
dodici *num* twelve
doga *f* ⟨*pl* -ghe⟩ *di letto*: slat; *di botte*: stave
dogana *f* customs *pl*; (*dazio*) (customs) duty; AVIAT customs control; NAUT customs house
doganale *adj* customs *attr*; ***barriera*** *f* **~** tariff barrier; ***controllo*** *m* **~** customs check; ***dichiarazione*** *f* **~** customs declaration; ***formalità*** *fpl* ***-i*** customs formalities; ***unione*** *f* **~** customs union
doganiere *m* customs officer
doge *m* doge
doglie *fpl*: ***avere le* ~** be in labo(u)r
dogma *m* ⟨*pl* -i⟩ dogma
dogmatico ⟨*mpl* -ci⟩ **I** *adj* dogmatic **II** *m* dogmatist
dogmatismo *m* dogmatism
dogmatizzare *v/t* ⟨1n⟩ dogmatize

dolce **I** *adj* sweet; *carattere*, *voce*, *pendio* gentle; *acqua* fresh; *clima* mild; *ricordo* pleasant; *suono* soft; ***la ~ vita*** the dolce vita, living it up; ***~ far niente*** sweet idleness; ***-i ricordi*** *mpl* happy memories; ***ci*** *f* **~** LING soft c; ***cosa c'è di ~?*** what's for dessert? **II** *m* (*portata*) dessert, sweet; *di sapore* sweetness; (*torta*) cake; ***-i*** *pl* sweet things

dolcemente *adv* (*sorridere*, *parlare*) sweetly; (*salire*, *scendere*) gently

dolcetto *m* COOK (*vino*) *dry, slightly bitter red wine from Piedmont*

dolcevita *m* ⟨*pl* dolcevita⟩ polo neck (sweater)

dolcezza *f* sweetness; *di carattere*, *voce* gentleness; *di clima* mildness; *di ricordo* pleasantness; *di suono* softness

dolciario *adj* ⟨*mpl* -ri⟩ confectionery; ***industria*** *f* ***-a*** confectionery industry

dolciastro *adj* sweetish; *fig* syrupy, sugary

dolcificante *m* sweetener

dolciumi *mpl* sweets *pl*, *US* candy *sg*

dolente *adj* painful, sore; ***sono ~ di comunicarle ...*** I regret to inform you ...

dolere *v/i* ⟨2e⟩ hurt, be painful; ***mi duole la schiena*** my back hurts, I have a sore back

dolersi *v/r* be sorry (***di*** for); (*lagnarsi*) complain (***di*** about)

dollaro *m* dollar

dolmen *m* ⟨*pl* dolmen⟩ dolmen

dolo *m* malice

Dolomiti *fpl* Dolomites *pl*

dolomitico *adj* ⟨*mpl* -ci⟩ of the Dolomites

dolorante *adj* sore, painful

dolore *m* pain; ***ha ancora ~?*** does it still hurt?; ***~ alla spalla*** backache; ***-i di pancia*** stomachache

dolorosamente *adv* painfully

doloroso *adj* painful

dolosamente *adv* maliciously

doloso *adj* malicious

domabile *adj* tameable

domanda *f* **1.** question; ***fare una ~ a qn*** ask s.o. a question; ***rispondere a una ~*** answer a question **2.** (*richiesta*) request; ***~ di assunzione*** letter of application; ***fare ~ per qc*** apply for sth **3.** FIN demand; ***~ e offerta*** supply and demand

domandare ⟨1a⟩ **I** *v/t*: ***~ qc*** (***a qn***) *per sapere nome*, *ora etc* ask (s.o.) sth; *per ottenere informazioni*, *aiuto etc* ask (s.o) for sth; ***domanda quanto costa*** ask how much it is; ***~ un favore a qn*** ask s.o. a favour; ***~ scusa*** apologize **II** *v/i*: ***~ a qn*** ask s.o.; ***~ di qn*** *per sapere come sta* ask after s.o.; *per parlargli* ask for s.o.

domandarsi *v/r* wonder, ask o.s.; ***mi domando perché*** I wonder why

domani **I** *adv* tomorrow; ***~ l'altro*** the day after tomorrow; ***~ mattina*** tomorrow morning; ***~ pomeriggio*** tomorrow afternoon; ***~ sera*** tomorrow evening; ***a ~!*** see you tomorrow!; ***dall'oggi al ~*** from one day to the next; ***sì, ~!*** *hum* pigs might fly! **II** *m*: ***il ~*** future; ***un ~*** one day, in future

domare *v/t* ⟨1a⟩ tame; *fig* control

domatore *m*, **-trice** *f*: ***~ di leoni*** lion tamer

domattina *adv* tomorrow morning

domenica *f* ⟨*pl* -che⟩ Sunday; ***la ~, di ~*** on Sundays; ***Domenica delle Palme*** Palm Sunday

domenicale *adj* Sunday *attr*

domenicano **I** *adj* Dominican **II** *m*, **-a** *f* Dominican

Domenico *m*: ***San ~*** Saint Dominic

domestico ⟨*mpl* -ci⟩ **I** *adj* domestic; ***lavori*** *mpl* ***-ci*** housework; ***animale*** *m* **~** pet **II** *m*, **-a** *f* servant; *donna* maid

domiciliare[1] *adj* house *attr*, at home ***arresti*** *mpl* ***-i*** house arrest

domiciliare[2] *v/t* ⟨1k⟩ domicile; ***~ la bolletta della luce*** FIN pay the electricity bill by direct debit

domiciliatario *m*, **-a** *f* ⟨*mpl* -ri⟩ JUR addressee

domiciliato *adj*: ***~ a*** domiciled at

domiciliazione *f* FIN direct debit

domicilio *m* domicile; (*casa*) home; ***lavoro*** *m* ***a ~*** working from home; ***servizio*** *m* ***a ~*** home delivery; ***violazione*** *f* ***di ~*** breaking and entering; ***eleggere ~*** elect residence; ***~ fiscale*** fiscal domicile

dominante *adj* dominant; *idee* prevailing; *classe* ruling

dominare ⟨1l & c⟩ **I** *v/t* dominate; *materia* master; *passioni* master, overcome **II** *v/i* rule (***su*** over), be master (***su*** of); *fig di confusione* reign

dominarsi *v/r* ⟨1l & c⟩ control oneself

dominatore I *adj* domineering II *m*, **-trice** *f* dominator

dominazione *f* domination; ***sotto la ~ aragonese*** under the rule of Aragon

dominicano I *adj* Dominican II *m*, **-a** *f* Dominican

dominio *m* ⟨*pl* -ni⟩ (*controllo*) control, power; *fig* (*campo*) domain, field; ***essere di ~ pubblico*** be common knowledge

domino *m* mask, domino; (*gioco*) dominoes *pl*

domotica *f* ⟨*pl* -che⟩ domotics *sg*

don *m*: ***~ Silvano*** Father Silvano

donante *m/f* JUR donor

donare *v/t* ⟨1a⟩ donate, give; *sangue* give; ***~ qc a qn/qc*** give sth to s.o./sth, give s.o./sth sth

donatario *m*, **-a** *f* ⟨*mpl* -ri⟩ JUR donee

donatore *m*, **-trice** *f* donor; ***~ di organi*** organ donor; ***~ di sangue*** blood donor

donazione *f* donation

donchisciotte *m* ⟨*pl* donchisciotte⟩ Don Quixote; ***essere un ~*** be quixotic

dondolare ⟨1l⟩ I *v/t culla* rock; *testa* nod II *v/i* sway; (*oscillare*) swing

dondolarsi *v/r su altalena* swing; *su sedia* rock; *fig* hang around

dondolio *m* (gentle) rocking

dondolo *m*: ***cavallo*** *m* ***a ~*** rocking horse; ***sedia*** *f* ***a ~*** rocking chair

dongiovanni *m* ⟨*pl* dongiovanni⟩ Don Juan; ***fare il ~*** be a Casanova

donna *f* woman; *carte da gioco* queen; ***~ di servizio*** home help; ***scarpe*** *fpl* ***da ~*** women's *or* ladies' shoes; ***bicicletta*** *f* ***da ~*** woman's bike

donnaccia *f* ⟨*pl* -cce⟩ *pej* slut

donnaiolo *m* womanizer

donnicciola *f pej* (*uomo pauroso*) wuss

donnola *f* weasel

dono *m* gift; ***~ di natura*** natural talent

dopare *v/t* ⟨1a⟩ dope

doping *m* doping

dopo I *prep* after; ***~ di te*** after you; ***~ mangiato*** after eating, after meals; ***subito ~ il bar*** just past the bar; ***~ pranzo/cena*** after lunch/dinner; ***~ Cristo*** Anno Domini; ***uno ~ l'altro*** one after the other; ***poco ~ le due*** just after two o'clock II *adv* (*in seguito*) afterward(s), after; (*poi*) then; (*più tardi*) later; ***lo faccio ~*** I'll do it later; ***ci vediamo ~!*** see you later!; ***~ mezzora/un anno*** half an hour/a year later; ***a ~!*** (see you) later! III *cj*: ***~ che*** after; ***mi ha chiamato ~ aver letto l'avviso*** he called me after he read the notice IV *adj inv*: ***il giorno ~*** the day after, the next day; ***la fermata ~*** the next stop

dopobarba *m* ⟨*pl* dopobarba⟩ after-shave

dopodiché *adv* and then

dopodomani *adv* the day after tomorrow

dopoguerra *m* ⟨*pl* dopoguerra⟩ post-war period

dopopranzo *m* afternoon

doposci *m* ⟨*pl* doposci⟩ après-ski; ***~*** *pl stivali* après-ski boots

doposcuola *m* ⟨*pl* doposcuola⟩ after-school club

doposole *adj inv* aftersun

dopotutto *adv* after all

doppiaggio *m di film* dubbing

doppiamente *adv* doubly

doppiare *v/t* ⟨1k⟩ *film* dub; SPORTS lap; NAUT round

doppiatore *m*, **-trice** *f* dubber

doppietta *f* double-barrelled gun

doppiezza *f* double-dealing

doppine *m* duplicate

doppino *m* cable; ***~ telefonico*** TEL telephone wire

doppio ⟨*mpl* -pi⟩ I *adj* double; ***-pi servizi*** *mpl* two bathrooms; ***-pi vetri*** *mpl* double glazing; ***frase a ~ senso*** sentence with a double meaning; ***strada a -a corsia*** dual carriageway; ***chiudere a -a mandata*** double-lock; ***posteggiare in -a fila*** double-park II *m* **1.** double; ***lungo il ~ (di qc)*** twice as long (as sth) **2.** SPORTS doubles *pl*; ***~ misto*** mixed doubles *pl* III *adv*: ***vederci ~*** see double

doppiofondo *m* false bottom; NAUT double bottom; ***valigia*** *f* ***a ~*** suitcase with a false bottom

doppione *m* spare, duplicate

doppiopetto *m* double-breasted jacket

dorare *v/t* ⟨1c⟩ gild; COOK brown

dorato I *past part* → ***dorare*** II *adj* gilded; *sabbia, riflessi* golden; COOK browned

dorico *adj* ⟨*mpl* -ci⟩ ARCH Doric

dormicchiare *v/i* ⟨1k⟩ doze
dormiglione *m*, **-a** *f* late riser
dormire *v/i* ⟨4c⟩ sleep; ***andare a ~*** go to bed; ***non sono riuscito a ~*** I couldn't sleep; ***~ come un ghiro*** sleep like a log; ***dormirci sopra*** sleep on it; ***chi dorme non piglia pesci*** *prov* the early bird catches the worm
dormita *f* (good) night's sleep; ***farsi una bella ~*** have a good sleep
dormitina *f* nap; ***farsi una ~*** have a nap
dormitorio *m* ⟨*pl* -ri⟩ dormitory
dormiveglia *m*: ***essere nel ~*** be only half awake
dorsale *adj spina*, *muscolo* back; *pinna* dorsal
dorsista *m/f* ⟨*mpl* -i⟩ backstroke swimmer
dorso *m* back; (*di libro*) spine; SPORTS backstroke; ***~ della mano*** back of one's hand; ***~ del coltello*** blunt edge of the knife; ***a ~ di cammello*** on the back of a camel
dosaggio *m* ⟨*pl* -ggi⟩ proportion; *di medicina* dosage
dosare *v/t* ⟨1c⟩ measure out; *fig* be sparing with; *parole* weigh
dosatore *m* measuring jug, scoop
dose *f* quantity, amount; MED dose; ***una buona ~ di coraggio*** a lot of courage
dossier *m* ⟨*pl* dossier⟩ dossier
dosso *m di strada* hump; ***togliersi gli abiti di ~*** get undressed, take one's clothes off
dotare *v/t* ⟨1c⟩ provide, supply (***di*** with); *fig* provide, endow (***di*** with)
dotato *adj* gifted; ***~ di*** equipped with
dotazione *f* equipment; *finanziaria* endowment; ***dato in ~ a qn*** issued to s.o.
dote *f* dowry; *fig* gift
dott. *abbr* (= **dottore**) Dr (doctor)
dotto I *adj* learned **II** *m* scholar
dottorando *m*, **-a** *f* doctoral student
dottorato *m* doctorate; ***~ di ricerca*** doctorate in scientific research
dottore *m* doctor (***in*** of)
dottoressa *f* (woman) doctor
dottrina *f* doctrine
dott.ssa *abbr* (= **dottoressa**) Dr (doctor)
double face *adj inv* reversible; ***soprabito*** *m* ***~*** reversible coat
dove *adv* where; ***~ sei?*** where are you?; ***di ~ sei?*** where are you from?; ***fin ~?*** how far?; ***per ~ si passa?*** which way do you go?; ***mettilo ~ vuoi*** put it wherever you like; ***la città ~ abito*** the town I live in, the town where I live
dovere ⟨2f⟩ **I** *v/i* have to, must; ***devo averlo*** I must have it, I have to have it; ***non devo dimenticare*** I mustn't forget; ***deve arrivare oggi*** she is supposed to arrive today; ***come si deve*** (*bene*) properly; *persona* very decent; ***doveva succedere*** it was bound to happen; ***dovresti avvertirlo*** you ought to *or* should let him know; ***deve essere stato difficile*** it must have been difficult **II** *v/t* owe; ***~ qc a qn*** owe s.o. sth; ***gli devo 5 euro*** I owe him 5 euros; ***essere dovuto a qc*** be due to sth **III** *m* duty; ***per ~*** out of duty; ***avere il ~ di fare qc*** have a duty to do sth; ***sentirsi in ~ di fare qc*** feel duty bound to do sth; ***rivolgersi a chi di ~*** contact the person concerned
doverosamente *adv* duly
doveroso *adj* rightful
dovizia *f* abundance
dovunque I *adv* (*dappertutto*) everywhere; (*in qualsiasi luogo*) anywhere **II** *cj* wherever; ***lo incontro ~ vada*** I meet him everywhere / wherever I go
dovuto I *past part* → ***dovere*** **II** *adj* due; ***~ a*** because of, due to
dozzina *f* dozen; ***una ~ di uova*** a dozen eggs; ***se ne vendono a ~*** they are sold by the dozen
dozzinale *adj* run-of-the-mill
DPR *abbr* (= **Decreto del Presidente della Repubblica**) Presidential Decree
draconiano *adj* draconian
draga *f* ⟨*pl* -ghe⟩ dredge
dragaggio *m* ⟨*pl* -ggi⟩ dredging
dragamine *m* ⟨*pl* dragamine⟩ minesweeper
dragare *v/t* ⟨1e⟩ dredge
drago *m* ⟨*pl* -ghi⟩ dragon
dragoncello *m* tarragon
dramma *m* ⟨*pl* -i⟩ drama
drammaticamente *adv* dramatically
drammaticità *f* ⟨*pl* drammaticità⟩ drama
drammatico *adj* ⟨*mpl* -ci⟩ dramatic

drammatizzare *v/t* ⟨1a⟩ dramatize
drammaturgia *f* theatre, *US* theater
drammaturgo *m*, **-a** *f* ⟨*mpl* -ghi⟩ playwright
drappeggiare *v/t* ⟨1f⟩ drape
drappeggio *m* ⟨*pl* -ggi⟩ drape
drappello *m di soldati*: squad; *di persone*: group
drappo *m* cloth
drasticamente *adv* drastically
drastico *adj* ⟨*mpl* -ci⟩ drastic
drenaggio *m* drainage
drenare *v/t* ⟨1a⟩ drain
dribblare *v/t* ⟨1a⟩ SPORTS dribble
dritta *f* NAUT starboard; *infml* tip; ***mi puoi dare una ~?*** *infml* can you give me a tip?; ***a ~ e a manca*** to port and starboard; *fig* left, right and centre
dritto I *adj* straight **II** *adv* straight (ahead); ***vada sempre ~*** go straight on **III** *m di indumento*, *tessuto* right side **IV** *m*, **-a** *f infml* crafty devil *infml*
drive *m* ⟨*pl* drive⟩ COMPUT drive
drive-in *m* ⟨*pl* drive-in⟩ drive-in
drizzare *v/t* ⟨1a⟩ (*raddrizzare*) straighten; (*erigere*) put up, erect; ***~ le orecchie*** prick up one's ears
drizzarsi *v/r*: ***~ in piedi*** rise to one's feet
droga *f* ⟨*pl* -ghe⟩ drug; ***-ghe*** *pl* ***pesanti/leggere*** hard/soft drugs; ***fare uso di ~*** be on drugs, take drugs
drogare *v/t* ⟨1c & e⟩ drug
drogarsi *v/r* take drugs
drogato *m*, **-a** *f* drug addict
drogheria *f* grocer's
droghiere *m*, **-a** *f* grocer
dromedario *m* dromedary
druido *m* druid
druso *m*, **-a** REL Druze
DS *abbr* POL (= **Democratici di Sinistra**) *left-wing democrats, an Italian political party*
dualismo *m* dualism; *fig* rivalry
dualistico *adj* ⟨*mpl* -ci⟩ dualistic
dubbio ⟨*mpl* -bbi⟩ **I** *m* doubt; ***essere in ~ fra*** hesitate between; ***mettere qc in ~*** doubt sth; ***senza ~*** undoubtedly, without a doubt; ***mi viene il ~ che ...*** I started to suspect that ...; ***nutrire -bbi su qc*** have one's doubts about sth **II** *adj* doubtful; (*equivoco*) dubious
dubbiosamente *adv* dubiously, doubtfully
dubbioso *adj* doubtful
dubitare *v/i* ⟨11⟩ doubt (***di*** sth); ***dubito che venga*** I doubt whether he'll come; ***non ne dubito*** I don't doubt it
dublinese I *adj* from Dublin **II** *m/f* person from Dublin
Dublino *f* Dublin
duca *m* ⟨*pl* -chi⟩ duke
ducale *adj* ducal; ***palazzo*** *m* **~** the Doge's palace
ducato *m* (*territorio*) duchy
duce *m* LIT chief; HIST il Duce
duchessa *f* duchess
due *num* two; ***a ~ a ~*** in twos, two by two; ***tutt'e ~*** both of them; ***vorrei dire ~ parole*** I'd like to say a word or two; ***~ volte*** twice; ***noi/voi ~*** the two of us/you; ***su ~ piedi*** off the top of one's head; ***un corso di ~ anni*** a two-year course; ***spaccarsi in ~*** break in two; ***a ~ passi da qui*** just around the corner; ***non c'è ~ senza tre*** bad things always come in threes
duecento I *num* two hundred **II** *m*: ***il Duecento*** the thirteenth century
duellante *m* duellist
duellare *v/i* ⟨1b⟩: ***~ con qn*** fight a duel with s.o.
duello *m* duel; ***sfidare qn a ~*** challenge s.o. to a duel
duemila *num* two thousand; ***nel Duemila*** in the 21st century
duepezzi *m* ⟨*pl* duepezzi⟩ bikini; (*vestito*) two-piece (suit)
duetto *m* duet; (*persone*) duo, couple
dumping *m* ⟨*pl* dumping⟩ dumping
duna *f* (sand) dune
dunque I *cj* so; (*allora*) well (then); ***~, dove eravamo rimasti?*** so, where were we? **II** *m*: ***venire al ~*** come to the crunch
duo *m* ⟨*pl* duo⟩ duo
duodenale *adj* duodenal
duodeno *m* duodenum
duomo *m* cathedral
duopolio *m* duopoly
duplex *m* ⟨*pl* duplex⟩ party line
duplicare *v/t* ⟨11 & d⟩ duplicate; ***~ una chiave*** copy a key; ***~ un file*** copy a file
duplicato *m* duplicate
duplicazione *f* duplication; *di chiave*, *file* copying
duplice *adj* double; ***in ~ copia*** in duplicate

duramente *adv* harshly; ***lavorare ~*** work hard; ***trattare ~ qn*** be harsh with s.o.
durante *prep* during; ***~ le vacanze/la notte*** during the holidays/the night; ***vita natural ~*** for ever and ever
durare *v/i* ⟨1a⟩ last; (*conservarsi*) keep, last; ***~ fatica*** struggle; ***~ un'eternità*** go on forever
durata *f* duration, length; *di prodotto* life; ***per tutta la ~ di*** throughout; ***~ di volo*** flight time; ***~ media della vita*** average life span; ***essere di breve/lunga ~*** not last long/last for a long time
duraturo *adj* lasting; ***beni*** *mpl* ***-i*** durable goods
durevole *adj* lasting
durezza *f* hardness; *di carne* toughness; (*asprezza*) harshness
duro **I** *adj* hard; *carne, persona* tough; *inverno, voce* harsh; *congegno, meccanismo* stiff; *pane* stale; (*ostinato*) stubborn; *infml* (*stupido*) thick *infml*; ***~ d'orecchi*** hard of hearing; ***tieni ~!*** don't give up!, hang in there! **II** *m* tough guy; ***fare il ~*** be a bully
durone *m* callous
duttile *adj* ductile; *fig* malleable
duttilità *f* ⟨*pl* duttilità⟩ malleability
DVD *m* DVD

E

e, E *m/f* ⟨*pl* e, E⟩ e, E
e *cj* and; ***io ~ te*** you and me; ***le sette ~ dieci*** ten past seven; ***~ allora?*** well, then?; ***~ smettila!*** stop it!
E *abbr* (= **est**) E (east)
è → ***essere***
ebanista *m/f* ⟨*mpl* -i⟩ cabinet maker
ebanisteria *f* cabinet making
ebanite *f* vulcanite
ebano *m* ebony
ebbe, ebbi → ***avere***
ebbene *cj* well
ebbrezza *f* drunkenness; *fig* thrill; ***guida*** *f* ***in stato di ~*** drunk driving; ***l'~ della velocità*** the thrill of speed
ebbro *adj* intoxicated (*a. fig*); ***~ di gioia*** beside oneself with joy
ebdomadario ⟨*mpl* -ri⟩ **I** *adj* weekly **II** *n*: ***ebdomadario*** *m* weekly magazine
ebete **I** *adj* stupid **II** *m/f* idiot
ebetismo *m* idiocy
ebollizione *f* boiling; ***portare qc a ~*** bring sth to the boil
ebraico ⟨*mpl* -ci⟩ **I** *adj* Hebrew; *religione* Jewish **II** *m* Hebrew
ebraismo *m* Judaism
ebreo **I** *m*, **-a** *f* Jew; ***gli -i*** the Jews; ***l'~ errante*** the wandering Jew **II** *adj* Jewish
Ebridi *f* Hebrides
eburneo *adj liter* ivory
ecatombe *f* hecatomb
ecc. *abbr* (= **eccetera**) etc (et cetera)
eccedente *adj* excess
eccedenza *f* excess; (*il di più*) surplus; ***in ~*** in excess; ***peso*** *m* ***in ~*** excess weight
eccedere ⟨3a⟩ **I** *v/t* exceed, go beyond **II** *v/i* go too far; ***~ nel bere*** drink too much
eccellente *adj* excellent
eccellenza *f* excellence; *titolo* Excellency; ***per ~*** par excellence; ***Sua Eccellenza*** His Excellency
eccellere *v/i* ⟨3o⟩ excel; ***~ nello studio*** excel at school/university
eccelso *adj* sublime; (*ottimo*) excellent
eccentricamente *adv* eccentrically
eccentricità *f* ⟨*pl* eccentricità⟩ eccentricity (*a.* MATH)
eccentrico *adj* ⟨*mpl* -ci⟩ eccentric
eccepibile *adj* objectionable
eccepire *v/t* ⟨4d⟩ object; ***non ho nulla da ~*** I have no objection
eccessivamente *adv* excessively
eccessività *f* ⟨*pl* eccessività⟩ excessiveness
eccessivo *adj* excessive; ***prezzi*** *mpl* ***-i*** exorbitant prices
eccesso *m* excess; ***~ di personale*** overmanning; ***~ di velocità*** speeding;

~ ***di zelo*** excess of zeal; ***arrotondare per ~*** round up; ***spingere qc all'~*** make s.o. go to extremes

eccetera *adv* et cetera

eccetto *prep* except; ~ ***la domenica*** Sundays excepted, except Sunday; ***tutti ~ lei*** everyone except her; ~ ***che l'Italia*** except Italy

eccettuare *v/t* ⟨1m & b⟩ except

eccezionale *adj* exceptional; ***in via ~*** as an exception; ***persona*** *f* ~ extraordinary person

eccezionalmente *adv* exceptionally

eccezione *f* exception; ***ad ~ di*** with the exception of; ***fare un'~*** make an exception; ***senza -i*** without exception; ***l'~ conferma la regola*** the exception that proves the rule

ecchimosi *f* ⟨*pl* ecchimosi⟩ bruise

eccidio *m* ⟨*pl* -i⟩ slaughter

eccipiente **I** *adj* excipient **II** *m* excipient

eccitabile *adj* excitable

eccitabilità *f* ⟨*pl* eccitabilità⟩ excitability

eccitante **I** *adj* exciting **II** *m* stimulant

eccitare *v/t* ⟨11 & b⟩ excite

eccitarsi *v/r* get excited

eccitazione *f* excitement

ecclesiastico ⟨*mpl* -ci⟩ **I** *adj* ecclesiastical **II** *m* priest

ecco *adv* (*qui*) here; (*là*) there; ~ ***come*** this is how; ~ ***fatto*** that's that; ~ ***tutto*** that's all; ***~mi*** here I am; ***~li*** here they are; ***~ti il libro*** here is your book; ~ ***perché*** that's why; ***~, te l'avevo detto!*** you see, I told you!; ~ ***che arrivano*** here they are

eccome *adv* of course

echeggiare *v/i* ⟨1f⟩ echo; (*risuonare*) resonate

eclatante *adj* resounding

ecletticità *f* ⟨*pl* ecletticità⟩ eclecticism

eclettico ⟨*mpl* -ci⟩ **I** *adj* versatile; PHIL eclectic **II** *m*, **-a** *f* eclectic

eclettismo *m* electicism

eclissare *v/t* ⟨1a⟩ eclipse

eclissarsi *v/r fig* slip away

eclisse *f*, **eclissi** *f* ⟨*pl* eclissi⟩ eclipse; ~ ***solare*** solar eclipse; ~ ***lunare*** lunar eclipse

eco *m/f* ⟨*pl* gli echi⟩ echo

ecografia *f* scan

ecologia *f* ecology

ecologico *adj* ⟨*mpl* -ci⟩ ecological

ecologista ⟨*mpl* -i⟩ **I** *m/f* ecologist **II** *adj* ecological

ecologo *m*, **-a** *f* ⟨*mpl* -gi⟩ ecologist

ecomafia *f* ecomafia

ecometro *m* echo sounder

e-commerce *m* ⟨*pl* e-commerce⟩ e-commerce

ecomostro *m* eyesore; ***finalmente hanno demolito un ~*** they've finally demolished an eyesore

economato *m* stewardship

economia *f* **1.** economy; ~ ***aziendale*** business economics *sg*; ~ ***di mercato*** market economy; ~ ***sommersa*** black economy **2.** *scienza* economics *sg*; ***Economia e Commercio*** business school **3.** ***fare ~*** economize (***di*** on); ***-e*** *pl* savings

economicamente *adv* economically

economicità *f* ⟨*pl* economicità⟩ inexpensiveness

economico *adj* ⟨*mpl* -ci⟩ economic; (*poco costoso*) economical; ***classe*** *f* ***-a*** economy class; ***edizione*** *f* ***-a*** paperback

economista *m/f* ⟨*mpl* -i⟩ economist

economizzare ⟨1a⟩ **I** *v/t* save **II** *v/i* economize (***su*** on)

economo **I** *adj* thrifty **II** *m*, **-a** *f* bursar

ecosistema *m* ecosystem

ecosostenibile*adj* environmentally sustainable

ecstasy *f* Ecstasy

ecuadoriano **I** *adj* Ecuadorian **II** *m*, **-a** *f* Ecuadorian

ecumenico *adj* ⟨*mpl* -ci⟩ ecumenical

eczema *m* ⟨*pl* -i⟩ eczema

ed *cj* and

edema *m* ⟨*pl* -i⟩ oedema

eden *m* ⟨*pl* eden⟩ Eden (*a. fig*)

edera *f* ivy

edicola *f* newspaper kiosk

edicolante *m/f* bookstall keeper

edificabile *adj* (suitable for) building; ***area*** *f* ~ building area

edificabilità *f* ⟨*pl* edificabilità⟩ suitability for building

edificante *adj* edifying; ***letture*** *fpl* ***-i*** uplifting texts

edificare *v/t* ⟨1m & d⟩ build; *fig* edify

edificio *m* ⟨*pl* -ci⟩ building; *fig* structure

edile *adj* construction *attr*, building *attr*; ***impresa*** *f* ~ firm of builders

edilizia *f* construction, building; (*ur-*

banistica) town planning
edilizio *adj* ⟨*mpl* -i⟩ building; ***concessione*** *f* ***-a*** building permit
Edimburgo *f* Edinburgh
Edipo *m* Oedipus; ***complesso*** *m* ***di*** ~ Oedipus complex
editare *v/t* ⟨1a⟩ COMPUT edit
editing *m* ⟨*pl* editing⟩ editing
editor *m* ⟨*pl* editor⟩ COMPUT editor
editore I *adj* publishing **II** *m*, **-trice** *f* publisher; (*curatore*) editor
editoria *f* publishing
editoriale I *adj* publishing **II** *m* editorial
editto *m* edict
edizione *f* edition; ~ ***straordinaria*** *di telegiornale* special news bulletin; *di giornale* extra (edition); ***la quarta*** ~ ***del congresso XY*** the fourth XY conference; ~ ***integrale*** unabridged edition
edonismo *m* hedonism
educanda *f* convent schoolgirl; *fig hum shy girl*
educare *v/t* ⟨1l, b & d⟩ educate; (*allevare*) bring up; *gusto*, *orecchio*, *mente* train
educativo *adj* education *attr*; (*istruttivo*) educational; ***metodo*** *m* ~ teaching method
educato *adj*: (***ben***) ~ well brought-up, polite
educazione *f* education; *dei figli* upbringing; (*buone maniere*) (good) manners *pl*; ~ ***civica*** civics *sg*; ~ ***fisica*** physical education; ~ ***stradale*** road safety
edulcorante I *adj* sweetening **II** *m* sweetener
edulcorare *v/t* ⟨1l⟩ sweeten; *fig* soften
edulcorato *adj fig* softened
efelidi *fpl* freckles
Efeso *f* Ephesus
effeminato *adj* effeminate; *pej* camp; ***modi*** *mpl* ***-i*** effeminacy
efferatezza *f* cruelty
efferato *adj* heinous
effervescente *adj bibita* fizzy, effervescent; *aspirina* soluble; *personalità* bubbly, effervescent
effervescenza *f* effervescence; *fig* bubbliness; ~ ***naturale*** natural effervescence
effettivamente *adv* (*in effetti*) in fact; *per rafforzare un'affermazione* really, actually
effettivo I *adj* (*reale*) real, actual; (*efficace*) effective; *personale* permanent; MIL regular **II** *m* FIN sum total
effetto *m* **1.** (*conseguenza*) effect; (*impressione*) impression; ***-i*** *pl* ***collaterali*** side effects; ***-i*** *pl* ***personali*** personal effects *or* belongings; ~ ***serra*** greenhouse effect; ***fare*** ~ (*funzionare*) work; (*impressionare*) make an impression; ***fare l'~ di essere ...*** give the impression of being ...; ***a tutti gli -i*** to all intents and purposes; ***in -i*** in fact **2.** FIN (*cambiale*) bill (of exchange)
effettuabile *adj* practicable
effettuabilità *f* ⟨*pl* effettuabilità⟩ practicability
effettuare *v/t* ⟨1m & b⟩ carry out; *pagamento* make
effettuarsi *v/r* take place; ***il servizio non si effettua la domenica*** there is no Sunday service
efficace *adj* effective
efficacemente *adv* effectively
efficacia *f* effectiveness
efficiente *adj* efficient; (*funzionante*) in working order
efficienza *f* efficiency
effigie *f* ⟨*pl* -gi⟩ effigy
effimero *adj* ephemeral; (*che dura poco*) short-lived
effluvio *m* ⟨*pl* -i⟩ *di odori*: effluvium; *piacevole* fragrance; ~ ***di luce*** beam of light
effondere *v/t* ⟨3bb⟩ outpour; *luce* give out
effondersi *v/r* ⟨3bb⟩ spread
effrazione *f* (*scasso*) JUR burglary; (*violazione*) breaking the rules
effusioni *fpl* outpourings; ***scambiarsi*** (***tenere***) ~ have a kiss and a cuddle
Egadi *fpl* Egadi islands *pl*
egemonia *f* hegemony
Egeo I *adj* Aegean; ***costa*** *f* ***-a*** Aegean coast; ***Mar*** *m* ***Egeo*** Aegean (Sea) **II** *m* Aegean
Egitto *m* Egypt
egittologia *f* egyptology
egiziano I *adj* Egyptian **II** *m*, **-a** *f* Egyptian
egizio *adj* ancient Egyptian
egli *pron m* he; ~ ***stesso*** he himself
ego *m* ⟨*pl* ego⟩ PSYCH ego
egocentrico *adj* egocentric

egocentrismo *m* egocentrism
egoismo *m* selfishness, egoism
egoista ⟨*mpl* -i⟩ **I** *adj* selfish **II** *m/f* selfish person, egoist
egoisticamente *adv* selfishly
egoistico *adj* ⟨*mpl* -ci⟩ selfish
egr. *abbr* (= **egregio**) *form of address used in correspondence*
egregio *adj* ⟨*mpl* -gi⟩ distinguished; ***Egregio signore*** *nelle lettere* Dear Sir
eguagliare *v/t* → ***uguagliare***
eguale *adj* → ***uguale***
eh! *int* oh!
eh? *int* eh?, what?
ehi! *int* oi!
E.I. *abbr* (= **Esercito Italiano**) *Italian army*
eiaculare *v/i* ⟨1l & b⟩ ejaculate
eiaculazione *f* ejaculation
elaborare *v/t* ⟨1m⟩ elaborate; *dati* process; *piano* draw up, work out; ***~ un lutto*** come to terms with a bereavement
elaborato *adj* elaborate
elaboratore *m*: ***~ elettronico*** computer
elaborazione *f* elaboration; ***~ elettronica dei dati*** electronic data processing; ***~ dei testi*** word processing
elargire *v/t* ⟨4d⟩ lavish
elargizione *f* donation
elasticità *f* elasticity; (*agilità*) agility, suppleness; *fig* flexibility; *della mente* quickness
elasticizzato *adj* elasticated; ***tessuto*** *m* **~** stretch fabric
elastico ⟨*mpl* -ci⟩ **I** *adj* elastic; *norme, orari* flexible **II** *m* rubber band
elastina *f* elastin
Elba *f*: ***isola d'~*** (island of) Elba
elefante *m* elephant; ***~ marino*** sea elephant; ***essere un ~ in un negozio di porcellane*** be like a bull in a china shop
elegante *adj* elegant
elegantemente *adv* elegantly
eleganza *f* elegance
eleggere *v/t* ⟨3cc⟩ elect; ***~ domicilio*** elect domicile
eleggibile *adj* electable
elegia *f* ⟨*pl* -gie⟩ elegy
elegiaco *adj* ⟨*mpl* -ci⟩ elegiac
elementare *adj* elementary; ***scuola*** *f* **~** primary school, *US* elementary school
elemento *m* element; (*componente*) component; ***-i*** *pl* (*rudimenti*) rudiments; (*fatti*) data
elemosina *f* charity; ***chiedere l'~*** beg; ***fare l'~ a qn*** give (a donation) to s.o.
elemosinare *v/t & v/i* ⟨1n & c⟩ beg
elencare *v/t* ⟨1b & d⟩ list
elenco *m* ⟨*pl* -chi⟩ list; ***~ telefonico*** phone book *infml*, telephone directory
elettivo *adj* elective; ***domicilio*** *m* **~** elected domicile; ***affinità*** *fpl* ***-e*** elective affinities
eletto **I** *past part* → ***eleggere*** **II** *adj* chosen; ***il popolo ~*** the Chosen People
elettorale *adj* electoral; ***campagna*** *f* **~** election campaign
elettorato *m* electorate
elettore *m*, **-trice** *f* voter
elettrauto *m* ⟨*pl* elettrauto⟩ *auto electrics garage*; *persona* car electrician
elettricista *m/f* ⟨*mpl* -i⟩ electrician
elettricità *f* electricity
elettrico *adj* ⟨*mpl* -ci⟩ electric, electrical; ***centrale*** *f* ***-a*** power station
elettrificare *v/t* ⟨1n & d⟩ electrify
elettrificazione *f* electrification
elettrizzante *adj* electrifying
elettrizzare *v/t* ⟨1a⟩ electrify (*a. fig*)
elettrocardiogramma *m* ⟨*pl* -i⟩ electrocardiogram
elettrodo *m* electrode
elettrodomestico *m* ⟨*pl* -ci⟩ domestic appliance
elettrodotto *m* power line
elettrogeno *adj generating electricity*; ***gruppo*** *m* **~** generator
elettrolisi *f* electrolysis
elettrolitico *adj* ⟨*mpl* -ci⟩ electrolytic
elettromagnetico *adj* electromagnetic
elettromotore *m* electric motor
elettromotrice *f* RAIL electric locomotive
elettrone *m* electron
elettronica *f* electronics *sg*
elettronico *adj* electronic
elettroshock *m* electroshock
elettrotecnica *f* electrical engineering
elettrotecnico ⟨*mpl* -ci⟩ **I** *adj* electrical **II** *m*, **-a** *f* electrical engineer
elevare *v/t* ⟨1b⟩ raise; *costruzioni* erect; (*promuovere*) promote; *fig migliorare* better
elevato *adj* high; *fig* elevated, lofty

elevazione *f* elevation
elezione *f* election; **-i** *pl* **politiche** general election; **~ di domicilio** choice of domicile
elfo *m* MYTH elf
eliambulanza *f* air ambulance
eliapprodo *m* emergency helipad
elica *f* ⟨*pl* -che⟩ NAUT propeller, screw; AVIAT propeller
elicoidale *adj* helicoidal
elicotterista *m/f* ⟨*mpl* -i⟩ helicopter pilot
elicottero *m* helicopter
elicriso *m* BOT curry plant
eliminare *v/t* ⟨1m⟩ eliminate
eliminatoria *f* SPORTS heat
eliminazione *f* elimination
elio *m* helium
eliporto *m* heliport
elisione *f* GRAM elision
elisir *m* ⟨*pl* elisir⟩ elixir; **~ di lunga vita** elixir of life
elisoccorso *m* helicopter rescue
elitario *adj* ⟨*mpl* -ri⟩ elite, élite
elitaxi *m* ⟨*pl* elitaxi⟩ helibus
élite *f* elite, élite
ella *pron f* she
ellenico *adj* ⟨*mpl* -ci⟩ Hellenic
ellenismo *m* Hellenism
ellepì *m* ⟨*pl* ellepì⟩ LP
ellisse *f* GEOM ellipse
elmetto *m* helmet
elmo *m* helmet
elogiare *v/t* ⟨1f & c⟩ praise
elogio *m* ⟨*pl* -gi⟩ praise; **fare l'~ di qn** praise s.o.; **~ funebre** eulogy
eloquente *adj* eloquent
eloquenza *f* eloquence
elucubrare *v/t* ⟨1m⟩ dream up
elucubrazione *f* lucubration
eludere *v/t* ⟨3q⟩ elude; *sorveglianza, domanda* evade
elusivamente *adv* elusively
elusivo *adj* elusive
elvetico *adj* ⟨*mpl* -ci⟩ Swiss
emaciato *adj* emaciated
e-mail *f* ⟨*pl* e-mail⟩ e-mail; **indirizzo** *m* **~** e-mail address; **hai l'~?** are you on e-mail?; **inviare qc per ~** e-mail sth; **non ho ricevuto nessun ~ da Stefano** Stefano hasn't e-mailed me
emanare ⟨1a⟩ **I** *v/t* give off; *legge* pass **II** *v/i* emanate, come (**da** from)
emanazione *f di calore, raggi* emanation; *di legge* passing
emancipare *v/t* ⟨1m⟩ emancipate
emanciparsi *v/r* become emancipated
emancipato *adj* emancipated
emancipazione *f* emancipation
emarginare *v/t* ⟨1m⟩ marginalize
emarginarsi *v/r* ⟨1m⟩ become marginalized
emarginato *m*, **-a** *f* person on the fringes of society
emarginazione *f* marginalization (*a. fig*)
ematico *adj* ⟨*mpl* -ci⟩ h(a)ematic; **cellule** *fpl* **-che** blood cells
ematologico *adj* ⟨*mpl* -ci⟩ h(a)ematological; **quadro** *m* **~** blood panel
ematoma *m* ⟨*pl* -i⟩ h(a)ematoma
embargo *m* ⟨*pl* -ghi⟩ embargo
emblema *m* ⟨*pl* -i⟩ emblem
emblematico *adj* ⟨*mpl* -ci⟩ emblematic (*a. fig*)
embolia *f* embolism
embolo *m* embolus
embrionale *adj* embryonic (*a. fig*); **fase** *f* **~** embryonic stages
embrione *m* embryo
emendamento *m* amendment; JUR, POL amendment
emendare *v/t* ⟨1b⟩ revise; JUR, POL amend
emergente *adj* budding; *tendenza* emerging; **cantante ~** up-and-coming singer; **paesi** *mpl* **-i** emerging countries
emergenza *f* emergency; **freno** *m* **d'~** emergency brake; **in caso di ~** in an emergency; **uscita** *f* **di ~** emergency exit
emergere *v/i* ⟨3uu⟩ emerge; (*distinguersi*) stand out
emerito *adj* distinguished; **professore** *m* **~** emeritus professor; **un ~ cretino** *hum* an idiot of the first order
emeroteca *f* ⟨*pl* -che⟩ newspaper library
emersione *f* emersion
emerso *past part* → **emergere**
emesso *past part* → **emettere**
emettere *v/t* ⟨3ee⟩ *luce* give out, emit; *grido, verdetto* give; *calore* give off; FIN issue; TECH emit; **~ un assegno** draw a cheque, check *US*
emiciclo *m* semicircle
emicrania *f* migraine; **soffrire di ~** suffer from migraine

emigrante *m/f* emigrant
emigrare *v/i* ⟨1a⟩ emigrate
emigrato *m*, **-a** *f* person who has emigrated
emigrazione *f* emigration
emiliano I *adj* Emilian; ***la cucina -a*** Emilian cookery II *m*, **-a** *f* Emilian
eminente *adj* eminent; ***personaggi*** *mpl* ***-i*** distinguished people
eminenza *f* (*elevatezza*) eminence; *titolo* Eminence; ***~ grigia*** éminence grise
Emirati *mpl*: ***~ Arabi Uniti*** United Arab Emirates
emiro *m* emir
emisfero *m* hemisphere; ***~ boreale/australe*** northern/southern hemisphere
emissario *m* ⟨*pl* -ri⟩ GEOG outlet; (*agente segreto*) emissary
emissione *f* emission; *di denaro, francobolli* issue; RADIO broadcast; ***banca*** *f* ***di ~*** bank of issue, issuing bank; ***data*** *f* ***di ~*** date of issue; ***-i*** *pl* ***inquinanti*** toxic emissions; ***~ di obbligazioni*** bond issue
emittente I *adj* issuing; (*trasmittente*) broadcasting II *f* RADIO transmitter; TV channel; ***~ privata*** commercial channel
emittenza *f* broadcasting; ***~ privata/pubblica*** private/public broadcasting stations
emodialisi *f* ⟨*pl* emodialisi⟩ kidney dialysis
emofilia *f* h(a)emophilia
emofiliaco *m*, **-a** *f* ⟨*mpl* -ci⟩ h(a)emophiliac
emoglobina *f* h(a)emoglobin
emolumenti *mpl* emoluments
emorragia *f* h(a)emorrhage
emorroidi *fpl* h(a)emorroids *pl*, *infml* piles *pl*
emostatico *m* h(a)emostat; ***laccio*** *m* ***~*** tourniquet
emoteca *f* ⟨*pl* -che⟩ blood bank
emotivamente *adv* emotionally; ***coinvolgere ~ qn*** emotionally involve s.o.; ***essere ~ fragile*** be emotionally fragile
emotività *f* ⟨*pl* emotività⟩ emotionality
emotivo *adj* emotional; (*sensibile*) sensitive; ***impatto*** *m* ***~*** emotional impact
emozionabile *adj* emotional; ***essere facilmente ~*** be easily moved
emozionale *adj* emotional; ***stato*** *m* ***~*** emotional state
emozionante *adj* exciting, thrilling; ***esperienza*** *f* ***~*** moving experience; ***spettacolo*** *m* ***~*** thrilling show
emozionare *v/t* ⟨1a⟩ (*appassionare*) excite; (*commuovere*) move; (*turbare*) upset
emozionarsi *v/r* get excited; (*commuoversi*) be moved
emozionato *adj* excited; (*agitato*) nervous; (*commosso*) moved; (*turbato*) upset
emozione *f* emotion; (*agitazione*) excitement; ***essere in preda all'~*** be overcome by emotion; ***suscitare -i*** cause excitement
empatia *f* empathy
empietà *f* ⟨*pl* empietà⟩ wickedness
empiricamente *adv* empirically
empirico *adj* ⟨*mpl* -ci⟩ empirical
emporio *m* ⟨*pl* -ri⟩ *negozio* department store
emù *m* ⟨*pl* emù⟩ emu
emulare *v/t* ⟨1l⟩ emulate; ***~ qn*** copy s.o.
emulatore *m*: ***~ di terminale*** COMPUT emulator
emulazione *f* emulation; ***~ di terminale*** COMPUT terminal emulation
emulsionante I *adj* emulsifying II *m* emulsifier
emulsionare *v/t* ⟨1a⟩ emulsify
emulsione *f* emulsion
EN *abbr* (= **Enna**) Enna
encefalite *f* encephalitis
encefalo *m* encephalon
encefalogramma *m* ⟨*pl* -i⟩ encephalogram
enciclica *f* ⟨*pl* -che⟩ encyclical
enciclopedia *f* encyclop(a)edia
enciclopedico *adj* ⟨*mpl* -ci⟩ encyclop(a)edic
enclave *f* ⟨*pl* enclave⟩ enclave
encomiabile *adj* commendable
encomio *m* ⟨*pl* -i⟩ praise; (*discorso*) tribute; ***degno di ~*** praiseworthy
endecasillabo *m* hendecasyllable
endemico *adj* ⟨*mpl* -ci⟩ MED, BIOL endemic (*a. fig*)
endocrino *adj* endocrine; ***ghiandole*** *fpl* ***-e*** endocrine glands
endocrinologia *f* endocrinology
endocrinologo *m*, **-a** *f* ⟨*mpl* -gi⟩ en-

docrinologist
endogeno *adj* endogenous (*a.* GEOL); ***malattia*** *f* ***-a*** endogenous diseases
endoscopia *f* endoscopy
endoscopio *m* ⟨*pl* -i⟩ endoscope
endovena *f* intravenous injection; ***per ~*** intravenously
endovenoso *adj* intravenous
ENEL *abbr* (= **Ente Nazionale per l'Energia Elettrica**) *Italian electricity board*
energetico *adj fabbisogno, consumo etc* energy *attr*; *alimento* energy-giving
energia *f* energy; ***~ eolica*** wind power; ***~ nucleare*** nuclear energy; ***~ solare*** solar power; ***~ alternativa*** alternative energy; ***pieno di -e*** full of energy; ***~ rinnovabile*** renewable energy
energicamente *adv* energetically
energico *adj* ⟨*mpl* -ci⟩ strong, energetic
energumeno *m fig* maniac
enfasi *f* emphasis; ***dare ~ a qc*** emphasize sth
enfatico *adj* ⟨*mpl* -ci⟩ emphatic
enfatizzare *v/t* ⟨1a⟩ emphasize
enfisema *m* ⟨*pl* -i⟩ emphysema; ***~ polmonare*** pulmonary emphysema
enfiteusi *f* ⟨*pl* enfiteusi⟩ JUR emphyteusis
ENI *abbr* (= **Ente Nazionale Idrocarburi**) *state-owned oil company*
enigma *m* ⟨*pl* -i⟩ enigma
enigmatico *adj* ⟨*mpl* -ci⟩ enigmatic
enigmista *m/f* ⟨*mpl* -i⟩ (*solutore*) puzzle solver; (*scrittore*) puzzle setter
enigmistica *f* puzzle-solving
enigmistico *adj* ⟨*mpl* -ci⟩ puzzle *attr*; ***rivista*** *f* ***-a*** puzzle magazine
ENIT *abbr* (= **Ente Nazionale Italiano per il Turismo**) *Italian tourist board*
ennese I *adj* from Enna **II** *m/f* person from Enna
ennesimo *adj* MATH nth; ***per l'-a volta*** *infml* for the hundredth time *infml*
enologia *f* (o)enology
enologico *adj* ⟨*mpl* -ci⟩ (o)enological
enologo *m*, **-a** *f* ⟨*mpl* -gi⟩ (o)enologist
enorme *adj* enormous
enormemente *adv* tremendously
enoteca *f* ⟨*pl* -che⟩ (*negozio*) wine merchant's (*specializing in fine wines*)
ente *m* organization; PHIL being; ***~ per il turismo*** tourist board; ***gli enti locali*** the local authorities; ***~ assistenziale*** aid agency
entità *f* ⟨*pl* entità⟩ entity; (*importanza*) extent, degree; ***di notevole / scarsa ~*** substantial / slight; ***~ del danno*** extent of the damage
entomologia *f* entomology
entomologo *m*, **-a** *f* ⟨*mpl* -gi⟩ entomologist
entourage *m* ⟨*pl* entourage⟩ entourage
entraîneuse *f* ⟨*pl* entraîneuse⟩ hostess
entrambi *adj / pron* both; ***~ i genitori*** both parents
entrare *v/i* ⟨1a⟩ (*andare dentro*) go in, enter; (*venire dentro*) come in, enter; ***la chiave non entra*** the key won't go in, the key doesn't fit; ***entri!*** come in!; ***vietato ~*** no entry; ***entrò (in casa) correndo*** he ran in(to the house); *fig* ***questo non c'entra*** that has nothing to do with it; ***~ in una stanza*** enter a room, go into / come into a room; ***~ in carica*** take up one's duties; ***non entro più nei pantaloni*** I can't get into my trousers any more; ***~ a far parte di qc*** join sth
entrata *f* **1.** entrance; *in parcheggio* entrance, way in; *in un paese* entry; ***~ libera*** admission free; ***~ di servizio*** service entrance **2.** COMPUT input **3.** FIN ***-e*** *pl* (*reddito*) income; (*guadagno*) earnings *pl*; ***-e e uscite*** income and expenditure
entro *prep* within; ***lo vuole ~ due ore*** he wants it in two hours; ***~ domani*** by tomorrow; ***~ e non oltre il 31 maggio*** by not later than 31st May
entroterra *m* ⟨*pl* entroterra⟩ hinterland
entusiasmante *adj* exciting
entusiasmare *v/t* ⟨1a⟩ arouse enthusiasm in
entusiasmo *m* enthusiasm
entusiasta *adj* enthusiastic; ***essere ~ di qc*** be enthusiastic about sth
entusiastico *adj* ⟨*mpl* -ci⟩ enthusiastic
enumerare *v/t* ⟨1m⟩ enumerate
enumerazione *f* enumeration
enunciazione *f* enunciation
enzima *m* ⟨*pl* -i⟩ enzyme
eolico *adj* ⟨*mpl* -ci⟩ aeolian; ***energia*** *f* ***-a*** wind power

Eolie *fpl* the Aeolian Islands *pl*
epatico *adj* ⟨*mpl* -ci⟩ liver *attr*; ***cirrosi f -a*** cirrhosis of the liver
epatite *f* hepatitis; ***~ virale*** viral hepatitis
epica *f* epic
epicentro *m* epicentre, *US* -center; *fig* centre
epico *adj* ⟨*mpl* -ci⟩ epic (*a. fig*)
epicureo I *adj* epicurean **II** *m*, **-a** *f* epicure
epidemia *f* epidemic; ***~ di influenza*** flu epidemic
epidemico *adj* ⟨*mpl* -ci⟩ epidemic
epidermico *adj* ⟨*mpl* -ci⟩ epidermic; *fig* skin-deep
epidermide *f* skin; MED epidermis
epidurale *adj*: epidural; ***anestesia f ~*** epidural
Epifania *f* Epiphany
epigastrio *m* ⟨*pl* -i⟩ epigastrium
epilessia *f* epilepsy
epilettico ⟨*mpl* -ci⟩ **I** *adj* epileptic; ***attacco m ~*** epileptic fit **II** *m*, **-a** *f* epileptic
epilogo *m* ⟨*mpl* -ghi⟩ LIT, THEAT, *fig* epilogue
Epiro *m* Epirus
episcopale *adj* episcopal; ***carica f ~*** bishopric
episcopato *m* episcopate
episodico *adj* ⟨*mpl* -ci⟩ episodic
episodio *m* ⟨*pl* -di⟩ episode
epistassi *f* MED epistaxis, nosebleed
epistola *f* LIT epistle
epistolare *adj*: ***stile m ~*** style of letter-writing
epitaffio *m* ⟨*pl* -ffi⟩ epitaph
epiteto *m* (*insulto*) insult; ***coprire qn di -i*** call s.o. names
epizootico *adj* ⟨*mpl* -ci⟩: ***afta f -a*** foot and mouth (disease)
epoca *f* ⟨*pl* -che⟩ age; (*periodo*) period, time; ***auto f d'~*** vintage car; ***mobili mpl d'~*** period furniture; ***all'~ di qn / qc*** at the time of; ***a quell'~*** in those days, then; ***fare ~*** mark an era
epocale *adj* of a time; ***svolta f ~*** major turning-point
epopea *f* epic; (*genere*) epic (poetry)
eppure *cj* (and) yet
E.P.T. *abbr* (= **Ente Provinciale per il Turismo**) *provincial tourist board*
epurare *v/t* ⟨1a⟩ *fig* purge
equadoregno I *adj* Ecuadorian **II** *m*, **-a** *f* Ecuadorian
equamente *adv* fairly
equanime *adj* fair; (*senza pregiudizi*) impartial
equanimità *f* ⟨*pl* equanimità⟩ equanimity; (*mancanza di pregiudizi*) impartiality
equatore *m* equator
equatoriale *adj* equatorial
equazione *f* equation
equestre *adj* equestrian; ***monumento m ~*** equestrian monument
equidistante *adj* equidistant
equidistanza *f* equidistance
equilatero *adj* equilateral
equilibrare *v/t* ⟨1a⟩ balance
equilibrarsi *v/r* ⟨1a⟩ counterbalance, balance (out)
equilibrato *adj* balanced; *fig* well-balanced
equilibrio *m* ⟨*pl* -ri⟩ balance; *fig* common sense; ***perdere l'~*** lose one's balance; ***stare in ~ su qc*** balance on sth; ***~ economico*** economic stability
equilibrismo *m* tightrope walking; *fig* balancing act
equilibrista *m/f* ⟨*mpl* -i⟩ tightrope walker (*a. fig*)
equino *adj* horse *attr*; ***carne f -a*** horsemeat
equinozio *m* ⟨*pl* -zi⟩ equinox; ***~ d'autunno / di primavera*** autumnal / vernal equinox
equipaggiamento *m* equipment; ***~ di sicurezza*** safety gear
equipaggiare *v/t* ⟨1f⟩ equip; NAUT, AVIAT *con personale* man, crew
equipaggiarsi *v/r* equip o.s.
equipaggio *m* ⟨*pl* -ggi⟩ crew
equiparare *v/t* ⟨1m⟩ make equal
equiparato *adj* equivalent
equiparazione *f* equalization; ***~ dei diritti*** equal rights *pl*
équipe *f* ⟨*pl* équipe⟩ team; ***lavoro m di ~*** team work
equipollente *adj* ADMIN equivalent
equipollenza *f* ADMIN equivalency
equità *f* ⟨*pl* equità⟩ fairness
equitazione *f* horse riding; ***fare ~*** go riding
equivalente *m/adj* equivalent
equivalenza *f* equivalence
equivalere *v/i* ⟨2r⟩: ***~ a qc*** be equivalent to sth; ***equivale a dire ...*** it's tantamount to saying …

equivalersi *v/r* be much the same
equivocare *v/i* ⟨1m *and* d⟩: ***~ su qc*** misunderstand sth
equivoco ⟨*mpl* -ci⟩ **I** *adj* ambiguous; (*sospetto*) suspicious; *infml* (*losco*) shady *infml* **II** *m* misunderstanding; ***a scanso di -ci*** to avoid any misunderstandings
equo *adj* fair, just
era *f* (*epoca*) age, era; GEOL era; ***~ atomica*** atomic age; ***~ glaciale*** Ice Age
era, erano → ***essere***
erariale *adj* fiscal; ***imposta f ~*** revenue tax
erario *m* ⟨*pl* -ri⟩ treasury; (*finanze*) revenue
ERASMUS *m* Erasmus; ***con ~ ho studiato un anno in Inghilterra*** I studied for a year in England through the Erasmus scheme
erba *f* **1.** grass; *fig* ***fare d'ogni ~ un fascio*** tar everyone with the same brush; ***l'~ cattiva non muore mai*** a bad penny always turns up again **2.** COOK ***-e*** *pl* herbs; ***-e aromatiche*** herbs; ***-e*** *pl* ***medicinali*** medicinal herbs **3.** ***~ cipollina*** chives; ***alle -e*** with herbs **4.** *fig* ***in ~*** budding
erbaccia *f* ⟨*pl* -cce⟩ weed; ***estirpare le -cce*** weed
erbaggi *mpl* vegetables
erbario *m* ⟨*pl* -ri⟩ (*libro*) herbal; (*raccolta di piante*) herbarium
erbicida *m* ⟨*pl* -i⟩ herbicide
erbivoro **I** *adj* herbivorous **II** *m* herbivore
erborista *m/f* ⟨*mpl* -i⟩ herbalist
erboristeria *f* herbalist's
erboso *adj* grassy; ***spiazzo m ~*** patch of grass
Ercole *m* Hercules; ***le colonne d'~*** the pillars of Hercules
erculeo *adj* Herculean; ***forza f -a*** Herculean strength
erede *m/f* heir; *donna* heiress; ***~ unico*** only heir; ***~ universale*** sole heir
eredità *f* ⟨*pl* eredità⟩ inheritance; BIOL heredity; ***lasciare qc in ~ a qn*** leave sth to s.o. in one's will, bequeath sth to s.o.; ***avere qc in ~ (da qn)*** inherit sth (from s.o.)
ereditabilità *f* ⟨*pl* ereditabilità⟩ inheritability
ereditare *v/t* ⟨1m & b⟩ inherit
ereditarietà *f* heredity
ereditario *adj* ⟨*mpl* -ri⟩ hereditary; ***malattia f -a*** hereditary diseases; ***per via -a*** through inheritance
ereditiera *f* heiress
eremita *m* ⟨*pl* -i⟩ hermit; ***fare una vita da ~*** live the life of a recluse
eremitaggio *m* ⟨*pl* -ggi⟩ hermitage
eremo *m* hermitage
eresia *f* heresy
eretico ⟨*mpl* -ci⟩ **I** *adj* heretical **II** *m*, **-a** *f* heretic
eretto **I** *past part* → ***erigere*** **II** *adj* erect
erezione *f* building; PHYSIOL erection
ergastolano *m*, **-a** *f* person serving a life sentence, lifer *infml*
ergastolo *m* life sentence; ***scontare l'~*** serve life
ergersi *v/r* ⟨3d⟩ stand, rise (up)
ergonomia *f* ergonomics *sg* **ergonomico** *adj* ⟨*mpl* -ci⟩ ergonomic
erica *f* heather
erigere *v/t* ⟨3u⟩ erect; *fig* (*fondare*) establish, found
erigersi *v/r* *fig* set o.s. up (***a*** as)
eritema *m* ⟨*pl* -i⟩ *cutaneo* rash; ***~ solare*** sunburn
Eritrea *f* Eritrea
eritreo **I** *adj* Eritrean **II** *m*, **-a** *f* Eritrean
ermafrodito *m* hermaphrodite
ermellino *m* ermine
ermeticamente *adv* hermetically
ermeticità *f* ⟨*pl* ermeticità⟩ airtight sealing; *fig* obscurity
ermetico *adj* ⟨*mpl* -ci⟩ (*a tenuta d'aria*) airtight; *fig* obscure; ***a chiusura -a*** with an airtight seal; ***poesia f -a*** LIT *poetry belonging to Ermetismo*
ermetismo *m* LIT *a modern Italian school of obscure poetry*
ernia *f* MED hernia; ***~ del disco*** slipped disc; ***~ inguinale*** inguinal hernia
ero → ***essere***
erodere *v/t* ⟨3b⟩ GEOL *terreno* erode; *spiaggia* wash away; *fig* wear away
eroe *m* hero; ***da ~*** *vita, comportamento* of a hero; ***morire da ~*** die a hero; ***fare l'~*** be a hero
erogare *v/t* ⟨1l, b & e⟩ *denaro* allocate; *gas, acqua* supply; ***~ una somma*** pay out a sum
erogatore *adj* distributing *attr*; ***ente m ~*** supplier, distributor

erogazione *f di denaro* allocation; *di gas etc* supply

erogeno *adj*: ***zone** fpl* ***-e*** erogenous zones

eroicamente *adv* heroically

eroico *adj* ⟨*mpl* -ci⟩ heroic

eroina *f droga* heroin; *donna eroica* heroine

eroinomane *m/f* heroin addict

eroismo *m* heroism; ***atto** m* ***di ~*** heroic act

erosione *f* GEOL erosion

erotico *adj* ⟨*mpl* -ci⟩ erotic

erotismo *m* eroticism

errante *adj* wandering; ***cavaliere** m* **~** knight errant

errare *v/i* ⟨1b⟩ wander, roam; (*sbagliare*) be mistaken; ***se non erro*** if I'm not mistaken

errata corrige *m* ⟨*pl* errata corrige⟩ correction

erroneamente *adv* mistakenly

erroneità *f* ⟨*pl* erroneità⟩ erroneousness

erroneo *adj* erroneous; ***interpretazione** f* ***-a*** misinterpretation

errore *m* mistake, error; ***commettere -i*** make mistakes; ***~ di battitura*** typographical error, typo *infml*; ***~ di calcolo*** mistake in the addition, miscalculation; ***~ giudiziario*** miscarriage of justice; ***~ di gioventù*** *hum* youthful mistake; ***~ di grammatica*** grammatical error; ***~ di ortografia*** spelling mistake; ***~ di stampa*** misprint; ***per ~*** by mistake; ***salvo -i e omissioni*** errors and omissions excepted

erta *f*: ***stare all'~*** be on the alert

erudire *v/t* ⟨4d⟩ teach

erudirsi *v/r* ⟨4d⟩ educate oneself

erudito I *adj* erudite, learned **II** *m*, **-a** *f* erudite person

erudizione *f* erudition, learning

eruttare *v/i* ⟨1a⟩ *di vulcano* erupt

eruzione *f* eruption; MED rash

es. *abbr* (= **esempio**) eg (for example)

esacerbare *v/t* ⟨1b⟩ exacerbate; *malattia* aggravate

esacerbato *adj* exacerbated

esadecimale *adj* hexadecimal

esaedro *m* hexahedron

esagerare ⟨1m⟩ **I** *v/t* exaggerate **II** *v/i* exaggerate; (*eccedere*) go too far (***in*** in); ***hai esagerato con il sale*** you've used too much salt; ***~ nel bere*** drink too much

esageratamente *adv* excessively, too much

esagerato I *adj* exaggerated; *zelo* excessive; *prezzo* exorbitant **II** *m*, **-a** *f*: ***sei il solito ~!*** you're exaggerating as usual!

esagerazione *f* exaggeration

esagonale *adj* hexagonal, six-sided

esagono *m* hexagon

esalare ⟨1a⟩ **I** *v/t odori* give off; ***~ il respiro*** exhale **II** *v/i* come, emanate (***da*** from)

esalazione *f* exhalation; ***-i di gas*** gas emitted

esaltare *v/t* ⟨1a⟩ exalt; (*entusiasmare*) elate

esaltarsi *v/r* become elated

esaltato I *adj* elated; (*fanatico*) fanatical **II** *m*, **-a** *f* fanatic

esaltazione *f* exaltation; (*eccitazione*) elation

esame *m* **1.** exam(ination); ***~ di guida*** driving test; ***~ d'idoneità*** aptitude test; ***~ del sangue*** blood test; ***~ della vista*** eye test; ***dare un ~*** take / sit an exam; ***passare un ~*** pass an exam; ***prendere qc in ~*** examine sth **2.** MED (*test*) test; (*visita*) examination

esametro *m* hexameter

esaminabile *adj* examinable

esaminando *m*, **-a** *f* candidate

esaminare *v/t* ⟨1m⟩ examine (*a.* MED)

esaminatore I *adj*: ***commissione** f* ***-trice*** board of examiners **II** *m*, **-trice** *f* examiner

esangue *adj* (deathly) pale (*a. fig*)

esanime *adj* lifeless

esantema *m* ⟨*pl* -i⟩ exanthem

esasperante *adj* exasperating

esasperare *v/t* ⟨1m⟩ (*inasprire*) exacerbate; (*irritare*) exasperate

esasperarsi *v/r* become exasperated

esasperato *adj* exasperated

esasperazione *f* exasperation

esattamente *adv* exactly; ***ha ~ la tua età*** he's exactly the same age as you

esattezza *f* accuracy; ***con ~*** exactly; ***per l'~*** to be precise

esatto I *past part* → ***esigere*** **II** *adj* exact; *risposta* correct, right; *in punto* exactly; ***alle tre -e*** at three o'clock sharp; ***~!*** that's right!

esattore *m*, **-trice** *f* collector; ***~ domiciliare*** debt collector

esattoria *f* tax office
esaudire *v/t* ⟨4d⟩ grant; *speranze* fulfil; **~ un desiderio** fulfil a wish; **le mie preghiere sono state esaudite** my prayers have been answered
esauribile *adj* exhaustible; **risorse** *fpl* **-i** non-renewable resources
esauriente *adj* exhaustive
esaurientemente *adv* exhaustively
esaurimento *m* exhaustion; FIN **svendita** *f* **fino a ~ della merce** clearance sale; MED **~ nervoso** nervous breakdown
esaurire *v/t* ⟨4d⟩ exhaust; *merci* run out of
esaurito *adj* (*esausto*) exhausted; FIN sold out; *pubblicazioni* out of print; THEAT **fa il tutto ~** it is playing to a full house
esausto *adj* exhausted
esautorare *v/t* ⟨1m⟩ divest of authority
esautorazione *f* divestiture of authority
esazione *f* FIN (tax) collection
esborso *m* ADMIN disbursement
esca *f* ⟨*pl* -che⟩ bait (*a. fig*)
escavatore *m*, **escavatrice** *f* digger
escavatorista *m/f* ⟨*mpl* -i⟩ digger driver
escavazione *f* excavation
esce → ***uscire***
Eschilo *m* Aeschylus
eschimese *m/f* & *adj* Inuit, Eskimo
esclamare *v/t* ⟨1a⟩ exclaim
esclamativo *adj* exclamatory; **punto** *m* **~** exclamation mark
esclamazione *f* exclamation
escludere *v/t* ⟨3q⟩ exclude; *possibilità, ipotesi* rule out
esclusione *f* exclusion; **per ~** by (a process of) elimination
esclusiva *f* exclusive right, sole right; FIN **~ di vendita** sole agency; **concedere qc in ~** be sole distributor for sth
esclusivamente *adv* exclusively
esclusività *f* ⟨*pl* esclusività⟩ exclusiveness
esclusivo *adj* exclusive; **rappresentanza** *f* **-a** sole agency
escluso I *past part* → ***escludere*** **II** *adj* excluded; (*impossibile*) out of the question, impossible **III** *m*, **-a** *f* person on the fringes of society
esco → ***uscire***
escogitare *v/t* ⟨1m & c⟩ contrive
escoriarsi *v/r* ⟨1l⟩ be grazed
escoriazione *f* graze
escrementi *mpl* excrement *sg*
escrescenza *f* excrescence
escursione *f* trip, excursion; *a piedi* hike; **fare un'~** go on an excursion; *a piedi* go hiking; **~ di un giorno** day trip; **~ termica** METEO temperature range
escursionismo *m* touring; *a piedi* hiking, walking
escursionista *m/f* ⟨*mpl* -i⟩ tourist; *a piedi* hiker, walker
escussione *f* examination; **~ dei testimoni** examination of the witnesses
escutere *v/t* ⟨3v⟩ JUR *testimone* examine
esecrabile *adj* awful
esecutivo *m/adj* executive; **potere** *m* **~** executive power
esecutore *m*, **-trice** *f* JUR executor; MUS performer; **~ testamentario** executor
esecutorietà *f* ⟨*pl* esecutorietà⟩ enforceability
esecutorio *adj* ⟨*mpl* -ri⟩ JUR enforceable
esecuzione *f* (*realizzazione*) carrying out; MUS performance; JUR execution; **~ capitale** execution
esegesi *f* ⟨*pl* esegesi⟩ exegisis
esegeta *m/f* ⟨*mpl* -i⟩ exegete
eseguibile *adj* practicable; MUS performable
eseguire *v/t* ⟨4b or 4d⟩ carry out; MUS perform
esempio *m* ⟨*pl* -pi⟩ example; **per ~, ad ~** for example; **dare il buon ~** (**a qn**) set a good example (to s.o.); **fare un ~** give an example; **prendere ~ da qn** follow s.o.'s example
esemplare I *adj* exemplary **II** *m* specimen; (*copia*) copy
esemplarità *f* ⟨*pl* esemplarità⟩ exemplariness
esemplificare *v/t* ⟨1n & d⟩ exemplify
esemplificazione *f* exemplification
esentare *v/t* ⟨1b⟩ exempt (**da** from)
esente *adj* exempt; **~ da tasse** tax free
esenzione *f* exemption; **~ fiscale** tax exemption
esequie *fpl* funeral (service) *sg*; **celebrare le ~** perform the funeral rites

esercente *m/f* shopkeeper
esercitare *v/t* ⟨1m & b⟩ exercise; (*addestrare*) train; *professione* practise
esercitarsi *v/r* practise; ***~ a scrivere*** practise writing
esercitazione *f* exercise
esercito *m* army; ***~ della salvezza*** Salvation Army
esercizio *m* ⟨*pl* -zi⟩ **1.** exercise; ***nell'~ delle proprie funzioni*** while carrying out his / her duties **2.** (*pratica*) practice; ***essere fuori ~*** be out of practice; ***tenersi in ~*** keep in practice; ***è solo questione di ~*** it's just a matter of practice **3.** *di impianti* operation, use; ***spese d'~*** operating expenses **4.** (*anno finanziario*) financial year, *US* fiscal year **5.** FIN *azienda* business; *negozio* shop; ***~ pubblico*** commercial premises; ***cessazione*** *f* ***d'~*** closing down of business
esfoliante I *adj* exfoliating; ***crema*** *f* ***~*** exfoliating cream **II** *m* exfoliant
esibire *v/t* ⟨4d⟩ *documenti* produce; *mettere in mostra* display
esibirsi *v/r in uno spettacolo* perform; *fig* show off
esibizione *f* exhibition; (*ostentazione*) showing off; (*spettacolo*) performance
esibizionista *m/f* ⟨*mpl* -i⟩ show-off; PSYCH exhibitionist
esigente *adj* exacting, demanding
esigenza *f* demand; (*bisogno*) need
esigere *v/t* ⟨3w⟩ demand; (*riscuotere*) exact
esigibile *adj* due; ***credito*** *m* ***~*** outstanding debt
esigibilità *f* ⟨*pl* esigibilità⟩ collectability
esiguità *f* ⟨*pl* esiguità⟩ slenderness
esiguo *adj margine* slender; *reddito* meagre
esilarante *adj* hilarious; ***gas*** *m* ***~*** laughing gas
esile *adj* slender; (*voce*) faint
esiliare *v/t* ⟨1k⟩ exile
esilio *m* ⟨*pl* -li⟩ exile
esilità *f* ⟨*pl* esilità⟩ slenderness; (*voce*) faintness
esimere *v/t* ⟨3x⟩ excuse; ***~ qn da un incarico*** free s.o. from a load
esimersi *v/r* ⟨3x⟩: ***~ da qc*** get out of sth
esimio *adj* ⟨*mpl* -i⟩ illustrious
esistente *adj* existing
esistenza *f* existence
esistenziale *adj* existential; ***crisi*** *f* ***~*** existential crisis
esistenzialismo *m* existentialism
esistenzialista I *m/f* ⟨*mpl* -i⟩ existentialist **II** *adj* existentialist
esistere *v/i* ⟨3f⟩ exist; ***non esiste!*** no way!
esitare *v/i* ⟨1l & b⟩ hesitate
esitazione *f* hesitation
esito *m* result, outcome; FIN sales *pl*, turnover; ***avere ~ positivo / negativo*** turn out well / badly
eskimo *m* ⟨*pl* eskimo⟩ *giacca* parka
esodo *m* exodus; *di capitali* flight; ***l'~ degli Ebrei dall'Egitto*** the Flight from Egypt; ***~ estivo*** *the summer departure for the holidays*
esofago *m* ⟨*pl* -ghi⟩ œsophagus, *US* esophagus
esondare *v/i* ⟨1a⟩ break its banks
esondazione *f* flooding
esonerare *v/t* ⟨1m & c⟩ exempt (***da*** from)
esonero *m* exemption
esorbitante *adj* exorbitant
esorcismo *m* exorcism
esorcista *m/f* ⟨*mpl* -i⟩ exorcist
esorcizzare *v/t* ⟨1a⟩ exorcise (*a. fig*)
esordiente *m/f* beginner
esordio *m* ⟨*pl* -di⟩ introduction, preamble; (*inizio*) beginning; THEAT début
esordire *v/i* ⟨4d⟩ begin; THEAT make one's début
esortare *v/t* ⟨1c⟩ (*incitare*) urge; (*pregare*) beg; ***~ alla prudenza*** urge caution
esortazione *f* urging
esosità *f* ⟨*pl* esosità⟩ exorbitance
esoso *adj* excessive; ***prezzo*** *m* ***~*** exorbitant price
esoterico *adj* ⟨*mpl* -ci⟩ esoteric
esoterismo *m* esotericism
esotico *adj* ⟨*mpl* -ci⟩ exotic
esotismo *m* exoticism
espandere *v/t* ⟨3uu⟩ expand
espandersi *v/r* expand; (*diffondersi*) spread
espansione *f* expansion; ***in ~*** expanding
espansionismo *m* POL expansionism
espansionista ⟨*mpl* -i⟩ **I** *adj* expansionist **II** *m/f* expansionist

espansionistico *adj* ⟨*mpl* -ci⟩ expansionist; ***mire*** *fpl* ***-che*** goals to expand
espansività *f fig* warmth, friendliness
espansivo *adj* PHYS, TECH expansive; *fig* warm, friendly
espanso *past part*;→ ***espandere***
espatriare *v/i* ⟨1m & k⟩ leave one's country
espatrio *m* ⟨*pl* -i⟩ expatriation
espediente *m* expedient; ***vivere di -i*** live by one's wits
espellere *v/t* ⟨3y⟩ expel; *nel calcio* send off; ***è stato espulso dalla scuola*** he was expelled from school
esperanto *m* Esperanto
esperienza *f* experience; ***per ~*** from experience; ***avere ~ (con / di qn / qc)*** have experience (with s.o. / sth); ***avere ~ in qc*** have experience in sth; ***fare ~*** get some experience
esperimento *m* experiment; ***fare un ~ (con qc)*** carry out an experiment (with sth); ***-i*** *pl* ***sugli animali*** animal experimentation
esperto *m/adj* expert; ***~ di / in qc*** expert on sth
espettorante I *adj* expectorant **II** *m* expectorant
espettorare *v/t* ⟨1m e b⟩ expectorate
espiare *v/t* ⟨1h⟩ atone for; ***~ i propri errori*** make up for one's mistakes
espiatorio *adj* ⟨*mpl* -ri⟩ expiatory; ***sacrificio*** *m* ***~*** expiatory sacrifice; *fig* ***capro*** *m* ***~*** scapegoat
espiazione *f* atonement
espirare *v/i* ⟨1a⟩ breathe out, exhale
espirazione *f* exhalation
espletamento *m* ADMIN accomplishment
espletare *v/t* ⟨1b⟩ ADMIN accomplish
esplicativo *adj* explanatory
esplicitamente *adv* explicitly
esplicito *adj* explicit
esplodere ⟨3q⟩ **I** *v/t colpo* fire **II** *v/i* explode
esplorare *v/t* ⟨1c⟩ explore
esplorativo *adj* exploratory; ***missione*** *f* ***-a*** exploratory mission
esploratore *m*, **-trice** *f* explorer; ***giovane*** *m* ***~*** boy scout
esplorazione *f* exploration
esplosione *f* explosion; *fig* ***~ demografica*** population explosion
esplosività *f* ⟨*pl* esplosività⟩ explosiveness (*a. fig*)
esplosivo *m/adj* explosive; ***ordigno*** *m* ***~*** explosive device; *fig* ***rivelazioni*** *fpl* ***-e*** bombshell; *fig* ***situazione*** *f* ***-a*** volatile situation
esploso *past part* → ***esplodere***
esponente *m/f* exponent
esponenziale *adj* exponential; *fig* ***in modo*** *m* ***~*** exponentially; ***salire in modo ~*** rocket
esporre *v/t* ⟨3ll⟩ expose (*a.* PHOT); *avviso* put up; *in una mostra* exhibit, show; (*riferire*) present; *ragioni*, *caso* state; *teoria* explain; ***~ qn a un pericolo*** expose s.o. to danger
esporsi *v/r* expose o.s. (***a*** to); (*compromettersi*) compromise o.s.
esportare *v/t* ⟨1c⟩ export
esportatore I *adj* exporting; ***paese*** *m* ***~*** exporting country, exporter **II** *m*, **-trice** *f* exporter
esportazione *f* export
esposimetro *m* PHOT exposure meter
espositivo *adj* exhibition; ***area*** *f* ***-a*** show floor
espositore *m*, **-trice** *f* exhibitor
esposizione *f* (*mostra*) exhibition; (*narrazione*) presentation; PHOT exposure
esposto I *past part* → ***esporre*** **II** *adj in mostra* on show; ***~ a*** exposed to; *critiche* open to; ***~ a sud*** south facing **III** *m* statement; (*petizione*) petition
espressione *f* expression; ***privo di ~*** inexpressive
espressionismo *m* expressionism
espressionista ⟨*mpl* -i⟩ **I** *adj* expressionist **II** *m/f* expressionist
espressivamente *adv* expressively
espressività *f* ⟨*pl* espressività⟩ expressiveness
espressivo *adj* expressive
espresso I *past part* → ***esprimere*** **II** *adj* express; ***per suo ~ desiderio*** by his / her express wish; ***piatto*** *m* ***~*** dish made to order **III** *m posta* express letter; RAIL express; ***(caffè*** *m****)*** ***~*** espresso; ***macchina*** *f* ***~*** espresso machine; ***per ~*** express
esprimere *v/t* ⟨3r⟩ express; ***~ un desiderio*** make a wish; ***~ la propria opinione*** express one's opinion; ***~ gioia / dolore*** convey joy / pain
esprimersi *v/r* express o.s.; ***~ a gesti*** use sign language
espropriare *v/t* ⟨1m & c⟩ expropriate

espropriazione *f* expropriation
esproprio *m* expropriation; **~ *proletario*** expropriation by the people
espugnare *v/t* ⟨1a⟩ take (over)
espugnazione *f* capture
espulsione *f* expulsion; ***~ di un giocatore*** sending off of a player; ***~ delle feci*** bowel movement
espulso *past part* → ***espellere***
esquimese **I** *adj* Eskimo **II** *m/f* Eskimo
essa *pron f persona* she; *cosa*, *animale* it
essenza *f* essence; ***~ di arancio*** orange oil; *fig* ***l'~ del discorso*** the heart of the matter
essenziale **I** *adj* essential; ***la cosa ~*** the main thing **II** *m*: ***l'~ è*** the main thing is
essere ⟨3z⟩ **I** *v/i* be; ***~ di*** (*provenire di*) be *or* come from; ***~ di qn*** (*appartenere a*) belong to s.o.; ***lei è di Roma*** she is *or* comes from Rome; ***è di mio padre*** it is my father's, it belongs to my father; ***c'è*** there is; ***c'è Marta?*** is Marta here?; ***c'è nessuno?*** is anyone in?; ***c'è molto da fare*** there's a lot to do; ***cosa c'è?*** what's the matter?, what's wrong?; ***non c'è problema!*** no problem!; ***non c'è di che!*** don't mention it!; ***ci sono*** there are; ***c'erano molti libri*** there were a lot of books; ***ci siamo!*** here we are!; ***chi è?*** who is it?; ***sono io*** it's me; ***sono le tre*** it's three o'clock; ***siamo in quattro*** there are four of us; ***se fossi in te*** if I were you; ***sarà!*** if you say so!; ***sarebbe meglio / peggio*** it would be better / worse; ***sei stato bravo*** you've been good; ***era disteso sul letto*** he was lying on the bed; ***è di plastica*** it's plastic; ***porre in ~ qc*** carry sth out, realize sth **II** *v/aux*: ***siamo arrivati alle due*** we arrived at two o'clock; ***non siamo ancora arrivati*** we haven't arrived yet; ***è andata a casa*** she has gone home; ***la casa fu costruita nel 1820*** the house was built in 1820; ***è stato investito*** he has been run over **III** *m* being; ***~ umano*** human being; ***sei un ~ spregevole!*** you're a despicable creature!
esserino *m* little thing
essiccare *v/t* ⟨1d⟩ dry
essiccatoio *m* ⟨*pl* -i⟩ (*macchina*) dryer; (*locale*) drying room
essiccazione *f* drying (process)
esso *pron m persona* he; *cosa, animale* it
est *m* east; ***a ~ di*** east of; ***andare a ~*** go east / eastwards; ***Europa / Paesi dell'Est*** Eastern Europe / the countries of Eastern Europe
estasi *f* ecstasy; ***andare in ~*** go into ecstasies
estasiare *v/t* ⟨1k⟩ entrance
estasiarsi *v/r* ⟨1k⟩ go into ecstasies; ***~ alla vista di qc*** be enraptured by (the sight of) sth
estasiato *adj* rapt
estate *f* summer; ***~ di San Martino*** Indian summer; ***in ~, d'~*** in (the) summer; ***in piena ~*** at the height of summer
estatico *adj* ⟨*mpl* -ci⟩ ecstatic
estemporaneo *adj* off the cuff; ***discorso** m* **~** impromptu speech
estendere *v/t* ⟨3c⟩ extend
estendersi *v/r di territorio* extend; (*allungarsi*) stretch; *fig* (*diffondersi*) spread
Estensi *mpl* the House of Este
estensibile *adj* extendable
estensibilità *f* ⟨*pl* estensibilità⟩ *f* extendability
estensione *f* extension; (*vastità*) expanse; MUS range; ***una vasta ~ di terreno*** a vast expanse of land
estensore **I** *adj*: ***muscolo** m* **~** extensor **II** *m* (*compilatore*) ADMIN drafter; (*attrezzo ginnico*) chest-expander; ***~ della sentenza*** appeal assessor
estenuante *adj* exhausting
estenuare *v/t* ⟨1m & b⟩ *v/t* wear out; *fig* drain
estenuarsi *v/r* ⟨1m & b⟩ tire oneself out
esteriore *m/adj* exterior, outside
esteriorità *f* appearance
esteriorizzare *v/t* ⟨1b⟩ externalize, show
esteriormente *adv* outwardly
esternalizzare *v/t* ⟨1a⟩ ECON outsource
esternalizzazione *f di produzione* outsourcing
esternare ⟨1b⟩ *v/t* express, show
esternazione *f* manifestation
esterno **I** *adj* external; ***per uso ~*** for external use only; ***collaboratore** m*

~ freelancer **II** *m* outside; *in film* location shot; ***all'~*** on the outside; ***girare gli -i*** FILM go on location
estero I *adj* foreign; ***ministro*** *m* ***degli Affari -i*** Foreign Secretary, *US* Secretary of State **II** *m* foreign countries *pl*; ***all'~*** abroad
esterofilia *f* xenophilia
esterofilo *adj* xenophile
esterrefatto *adj* flabbergasted
esteso I *past part* → ***estendere*** **II** *adj* extensive; (*diffuso*) widespread; ***per ~*** in full
esteta *m/f* ⟨*mpl* -i⟩ (a)esthete
estetica *f* (a)esthetics *sg*
esteticamente *adv* (a)esthetically
estetista *f* beautician
estimatore *m*, **-trice** *f* surveyor
estimo *m* ⟨*pl* -i⟩ ADMIN estimate, valuation; ***~ catastale*** land survey
estinguere *v/t* ⟨3d⟩ extinguish, put out; *debito* pay off; *sete* quench; ***~ un'ipoteca*** pay off a mortgage
estinguersi *v/r* die out
estinto I *past part* → ***estinguere*** **II** *adj* extinct; *debito* paid off **III** *m*, **-a** *f* deceased
estintore *m* fire extinguisher
estinzione *f* extinction; FIN redemption, paying off; ***in ~*** endangered; ***~ di un debito*** paying off of a debt
estirpare *v/t* ⟨1a⟩ uproot; *dente* extract; *fig* eradicate
estivo *adj* summer *attr*; ***abito*** *m* ***~*** summer dress; ***temperature*** *fpl* ***-e*** summer temperatures
Estonia *f* Estonia
estorcere *v/t* ⟨3d⟩ *denaro* extort; ***~ qc a qn*** *confessione* wring sth out of s.o.; ***~ denaro a qn*** extort money from s.o.; ***~ una promessa*** extract a promise
estorsione *f* extortion
estorto *past part* → ***estorcere***
estradare *v/t* ⟨1a⟩ extradite
estradizione *f* extradition; ***chiedere l'~ di qn*** request the extradition of s.o.; ***domanda*** *f* ***di ~*** request for extradition
estraibile *adj* extractable; ***antenna*** *f* ***~*** TEL pull-out aerial
estraneità *f* ⟨*pl* estraneità⟩ extraneousness; ***senso*** *m* ***di ~*** sense of dislocation
estraneo I *adj* outside (***a*** sth); ***corpo*** *m* ***~*** foreign body **II** *m*, **-a** *f* stranger; *persona non autorizzata* unauthorized person
estraniarsi *v/r* ⟨1k⟩ cut oneself off; ***~ dal mondo*** withdraw from the world
estrapolare *v/t* ⟨1m⟩ (*estrarre da un contesto*) extrapolate; MATH extrapolate
estrarre *v/t* ⟨3xx⟩ extract; *pistola* draw out; ***~ a sorte*** draw
estrattivo *adj* MINER mining; ***industria*** *f* ***-a*** mining industry
estratto I *past part* → ***estrarre*** **II** *m* extract; *documento* abstract; FIN ***~ conto*** statement (of account)
estrazione *f* extraction; ***~ a sorte*** draw
estremista I *m/f* ⟨*mpl* -i⟩ extremist **II** *adj*: ***atteggiamento*** *m* ***~*** extremist stance; ***idee*** *fpl* ***-e*** extreme views
estremità *f* ⟨*pl* estremità⟩ extremity; *di corda* end; (*punta*) tip; (*punto superiore*) top; ***all'~ di*** at the end of
estremizzare *v/t* ⟨1n⟩ take to extremes
estremo I *adj* **1.** extreme; ***l'-a sinistra*** the far *or* extreme left; ***sport*** *mpl* ***-i*** extreme sports **2.** (*più lontano*) farthest; ***l'Estremo Oriente*** the Far East **3.** (*ultimo nel tempo*) last, final **II** *m* **1.** (*estremità*) extreme **2.** ***gli -i*** *di un documento* the main points **3.** ***passare da un ~ all'altro*** go from one extreme to the other
estrinseco *adj* ⟨*mpl* -ci⟩ extrinsic
estro *m* (*ispirazione artistica*) inspiration
estrogeno *m* (o)estrogen
estromesso *past part* → ***estromettere***
estromettere *v/t* ⟨3ee⟩ expel, *US* expell
estromettersi *v/r* ⟨3ee⟩ exclude oneself
estromissione *f* expulsion
estrosamente *adv* imaginatively
estrosità *f* ⟨*pl* estrosità⟩ creativity
estroso *adj* (*originale*) creative; (*bizzarro*) quaint
estroversione *f* extroversion
estroverso *adj* extrovert(ed)
estrusione *f* METAL extrusion
estuario *m* ⟨*pl* -ri⟩ estuary
esuberante *adj* (*vivace*) exuberant
esuberanza *f* exuberance
esubero *m* excess; ***~ di personale*** overstaffing

esulare *v/i* ⟨11 & b⟩: **~ *da qc*** lie outside sth
esule *m/f* exile
esultante *adj* exultant; ***folla*** *f* **~** jubilant crowd
esultanza *f* jubilation
esultare *v/i* ⟨1a⟩ rejoice
esumare *v/t* ⟨1a⟩ exhume
esumazione *f* exhumation
età *f* ⟨*pl* età⟩ **1.** age; ***la terza*** **~** the third age; ***limiti*** *mpl* ***d'~*** age limit; ***un signore di una certa*** **~** an elderly man; ***avere la stessa*** **~** be the same age; ***raggiungere la maggiore*** **~** come of age; ***all'~ di*** at the age of; **~ *critica*** menopause; ***in*** **~** ***avanzata*** late in life **2.** (*era*) **~ *della pietra*** Stone Age
etanolo *m* ethanol
etere *m* ether
etereo *adj* ethereal
eternamente *adv* eternally, forever
eternità *f* eternity
eterno *adj* eternal; (*interminabile*) endless, never-ending; *questione, problema* age-old; ***in*** **~** for ever and ever; ***la città -a*** the Eternal City, Rome
eterogeneità *f* ⟨*pl* etereogeneità⟩ heterogeneity
eterogeneo *adj* heterogen(e)ous
eterosessuale *adj* heterosexual
eterosessualità *f* ⟨*pl* eterosessualità⟩ heterosexuality
etica *f* ethics *sg*; **~ *professionale*** professional etiquette
etichetta *f* label; *cerimoniale* etiquette
etichettare *v/t* ⟨1a⟩ label (*a. fig*)
etichettatrice *f* labelling machine
etico *adj* ethical
etile *m* ethyl
etilene *m* ethene
etilico *adj* ⟨*mpl* -ci⟩ ethylic; ***alcol*** *m* **~** ethyl alcohol
etilismo *m* MED alcoholism
etilista *m/f* ⟨*mpl* -i⟩ alcoholic
etilometro *m* Breathalyzer®
etimologia *f* etymology
etimologico *adj* ⟨*mpl* -ci⟩ etymological
etiope *m/f* & *adj* Ethiopian
Etiopia *f* Ethiopia
etiopico *m/adj* Ethiopian
Etna *m* Etna
etneo *adj* of Etna
etnia *f* ethnic group
etnico *adj* ⟨*mpl* -ci⟩ ethnic; ***musica*** *f* ***-a*** world music; ***ristorante*** *m* **~** ethnic restaurant
etnologia *f* ethnology
etnologico *adj* ⟨*mpl* -ci⟩ ethnological
etnologo *m*, **-a** *f* ⟨*mpl* -gi⟩ ethnologist
Etruria *f* Etruria
etrusco ⟨*mpl* -chi⟩ **I** *adj* Etruscan **II** *m*, **-a** *f* Etruscan
ettagonale *adj* heptagonal
ettaro *m* hectare
etto *m* hundred grams
ettogrammo *m* ⟨*pl* -i⟩ hundred grams *pl*, hectogram
ettolitro *m* hectolitre, *US* -liter
eucalipto *m* eucalyptus
eucaristia *f* REL Eucharist
eucaristico *adj* ⟨*mpl* -ci⟩ Eucharistical
eufemismo *m* euphemism
euforbia *f* BOT euphorbia
euforia *f* euphoria
euforico *adj* ⟨*mpl* -ci⟩ euphoric
Eufrate *m* Euphrates
euganeo *adj* Euganean; ***Colli Euganei*** Euganean Hills
eugubino **I** *adj* from Gubbio **II** *m*, **-a** *f* person from Gubbio
eunuco *m* ⟨*pl* -chi⟩ eunuch (*a.* HIST)
euristica *f* heuristics *sg*
euristico *adj* heuristic
euro *m* ⟨*pl* euro⟩ euro
eur(o)asiatico ⟨*mpl* -ci⟩ **I** *adj* Eurasian **II** *m*, **-a** *f* Eurasian
eurocheque *m* ⟨*pl* eurocheque⟩ Eurocheque
eurocrate *m* Eurocrat
eurodeputato *m*, **-a** *f* Euro MP
eurodollaro *m* Eurodollar
Eurolandia *f* Euroland
euromercato *m* euromarket
Europa *f* Europe
europarlamentare *m/f* Euro-MP, MEP
europarlamento *m* European Parliament, Europarliament
europeo **I** *adj* European; ***campionato*** *m* **~** European championship **II** *m*, **-a** *f* European
eurovisione *f* Eurovision
eutanasia *m* euthanasia; **~ *attiva / passiva*** active / passive euthanasia; ***praticare l'~*** practise euthanasia
evacuare *v/t* ⟨1m⟩ evacuate

evacuazione *f* evacuation
evadere ⟨3q⟩ **I** *v/t* evade; (*sbrigare*) deal with; **~ le tasse** evade taxes **II** *v/i* escape (**da** from); **~ dal carcere** escape from prison
evanescente *adj immagine* evanescent; *suono* faint; **ricordo** *m* **~** vague recollection
evanescenza *f di immagini* evanescence; *di suoni* faintness
evangelico *adj* ⟨*mpl* -ci⟩ (*del Vangelo*) Gospel; *confessione* Evangelical; **Chiesa** *f* **-a** Evangelical Church
evangelista *m* ⟨*pl* -i⟩ Evangelist
evangelizzare *v/t* ⟨1a⟩ evangelize
evangelizzazione *f* evangelization
evaporare *v/i* ⟨1m⟩ evaporate
evaporazione *f* evaporation
evasione *f* escape; *fig* escapism; **film** *m* **d'~** feel-good film; **~ fiscale** *f* tax evasion
evasivamente *adv* evasively; **rispondere ~** be evasive (in one's answer)
evasivo *adj* evasive
evaso I *past part* → **evadere II** *m*, **-a** *f* fugitive
evasore *m*: **~ fiscale** tax evader
evenienza *f* eventuality; **per ogni ~** for any eventuality
evento *m* event
eventuale *adj* possible
eventualità *f* ⟨*pl* eventualità⟩ eventuality; **nell'~ che** in the event that; **per ogni ~** for every eventuality
eventualmente *adv* if necessary
eversione *f* POL subversion
eversivo *adj* subversive
evidente *adj* evident; **è ~ che ...** it's clear that ...
evidentemente *adv* clearly, obviously
evidenza *f* evidence; **mettere in ~** emphasize, highlight; **mettersi in ~** draw attention to oneself; **negare l'~** swear black is white
evidenziare *v/t* ⟨1b⟩ stress; (*marcare*) highlight
evidenziatore *m* highlighter
evincere *v/t* ⟨3d⟩: **~ qc da qc** deduce sth from sth
evirare *v/t* ⟨1a⟩ emasculate
evirazione *f* emasculation
evitabile *adj* avoidable
evitare *v/t* ⟨1l & b⟩ avoid; **~ di fare qc** avoid doing sth; **~ il fastidio a qn** spare s.o. the trouble
evocare *v/t* ⟨1b & d⟩ evoke (*a. fig*)
evocazione *f* evocation (*a. fig*)
evolutivo *adj* evolutionary; **stadio** *m* **~** development stage
evoluto I *past part* → **evolvere II** *adj* developed; (*progredito*) progressive, advanced; *senza pregiudizi* open minded, broad-minded
evoluzione *f* evolution; **in ~** evolving, developing
evolvere ⟨3s⟩ **I** *v/t* develop **II** *v/i* evolve, develop
evolversi *v/r* ⟨3s⟩ evolve, develop
evviva *int* hurray
ex ... (*nelle parole composte*) ex-, former; **~ marito** ex-husband
ex aequo *adv* joint, equal
excursus *m* ⟨*pl* excursus⟩ digression; **fare un ~** digress
exit poll *m* ⟨*pl* exit poll⟩ exit poll
ex novo *adv* from the beginning
expertise *f* ⟨*pl* expertise⟩ expertise
extra I *adj inv* extra; **di qualità ~** top quality **II** *m* ⟨*pl* extra⟩ extra; **gli ~ si pagano a parte** extras are paid for on top
extracomunitario I *adj* non-EU **II** *m*, **-a** *f* non-EU citizen
extraconiugale *adj* extramarital; **relazione** *f* **~** affair
extracontrattuale *adj* beyond the terms of the contract
extraeuropeo *adj* non-European
extrascolastico *adj* ⟨*mpl* -ci⟩ extra-curricular; **attività** *fpl* **-e** extra-curricular activities, after-school activities
extrasensoriale *adj* extra-sensory; **percezione** *f* **~** extra-sensory perception, ESP
extrasistole *f* MED extra-systole
extraterrestre *m/f & adj* extra-terrestrial
extraterritoriale *adj* extra-territorial
extraurbano *adj* suburban; **linea** *f* **-a** suburban line
extrauterino *adj* MED extra-uterine; **gravidanza** *f* **-a** ectopic pregnancy
extravergine *adj olio* extra-virgin
ex voto *m* ⟨*pl* ex voto⟩ ex voto (offering)

F

f, F *m/f* ⟨*pl* f, F⟩ f, F
fa[1] → ***fare***
fa[2] *adv*: ***5 anni ~*** 5 years ago
fa[3] *m* MUS F; *nel solfeggio della scala* fa(h)
fabbisogno *m* needs *pl*, requirements *pl*
fabbrica *f* ⟨*pl* -che⟩ factory, *US* plant
fabbricabile *adj* manufacturable; ***area*** *f* **~** building land
fabbricante *m/f* manufacturer
fabbricare *v/t* ⟨1l & d⟩ manufacture; ARCH build; *fig* fabricate; ***~ scarpe*** make shoes
fabbricato *m* building
fabbricazione *f* manufacturing; ARCH building
fabbro *m*: **~** (***ferraio***) blacksmith
faccenda *f* matter
faccende *fpl* housework *sg*; ***fare le ~*** do the housework
faccendiere *m*, **-a** *f pej* wheeler-dealer
facchino *m* porter
faccia *f* ⟨*pl* -cce⟩ **1.** face; ***~ tosta*** cheek; ***~ a ~*** face to face; ***di ~ a*** opposite, in front of; ***in ~*** in the face; ***avere una ~ stanca*** look tired; ***chiudere la porta in ~ a qn*** close the door in s.o.'s face; ***gliel'ha detto in ~*** he told him to his face; ***mettersi a ~ in giù*** lie face down; ***perché fai quella ~?*** why are you looking like that?; ***perdere la ~*** lose face; ***organizzare un ~ a ~*** organize a one-to-one discussion; ***non guardare in ~ nessuno*** go ahead regardless; ***alla ~ sua!*** good for you!; ***con che ~ ti presenti a quest'ora?*** how dare you turn up at this time of night?; ***salvare la ~*** save face; ***sulla ~ della Terra*** on the face of the Earth **2.** (*risvolto*, *aspetto*) facet **3.** (*lato*) side
facciale *adj* facial; ***paralisi*** *f* **~** paralysis of the face
facciata *f* ARCH front, façade; *di foglio* side; *fig* (*esteriorità*) appearance
faccio → ***fare***
faceto *adj* facetious; ***tra il serio e il ~*** half-jokingly
fachiro *m* fakir
facile *adj* easy; *di carattere* easy-going; (*incline*) prone (***a*** to); ***~ da usare*** user-friendly; ***è ~ a dirsi!*** easier said than done!; ***è ~ che venga*** he is likely to come; ***non è mica una cosa ~*** it isn't that easy; ***avere il grilletto ~*** be trigger-happy; ***essere ~ alle lacrime*** be easily moved to tears
facilità *f* ease; (*attitudine*) aptitude, facility; ***con ~*** easily; ***con molta ~*** very easily; COMPUT ***~ d'uso*** user-friendliness
facilitare *v/t* ⟨1m⟩ facilitate
facilitazione *f* facility; **-i** *pl* ***di prezzo*** easy terms; **-i** *pl* ***di pagamento*** easy (payment) terms
facilmente *adv* easily
facilone *m*, **-a** *f* careless person
faciloneria *f* carelessness
facinoroso **I** *adj* violent **II** *m*, **-a** *f* rough, rioter
facoltà *f* ⟨*pl* facoltà⟩ faculty; (*potere*) power; ***avere la ~ di scelta*** have a choice, be able to choose
facoltativo *adj* optional; ***materie*** *fpl* **-e** optional subjects
facoltoso *adj* wealthy
facsimile *m* facsimile
factoring *m* ⟨*pl* factoring⟩ factoring
factotum *m* ⟨*pl* factotum⟩ jack of all trades; ***è il ~ della ditta*** he's the company's Mr Fixit
faggeta *f*, **faggeto** *m* beech wood
faggio *m* ⟨*pl* -ggi⟩ beech (tree)
fagiano *m* pheasant
fagiolini *mpl* green beans *pl*
fagiolo *m* bean; **-i** *pl* ***secchi*** dried beans; **-i** *pl* ***in scatola*** tinned/canned beans; ***andare a ~ a qn*** *infml* suit s.o. down to the ground; ***capita proprio a ~*** it's happened at just the right moment
fagocitare *v/t* ⟨1a⟩ *fig* absorb
fagocito *m* BIOL phagocyte
fagotto[1] *m* bundle; *fig* ***far ~*** pack up and leave
fagotto[2] *m* MUS bassoon
fai → ***fare***
fai da te *m* ⟨*pl* fai da te⟩ do-it-yourself, DIY

faina *f* beech marten
falange *f* ANAT phalanx
falangista *m/f* ⟨*mpl* -i⟩ POL Falangist
falcata *f* SPORTS leg action, stride; (*salto del cavallo*) falcade
falce *f* scythe; *fig* ***~ di luna*** crescent moon; ***~ e martello*** hammer and sickle
falciare *v/t* ⟨1f⟩ cut (with a scythe); *fig* mow down; ***la peste falciava molte vite umane*** the plague wiped out many people
falciatrice *f* lawn-mower
falciatura *f* mowing
falco *m* ⟨*pl* -chi⟩ hawk; ***~ pellegrino*** peregrine (falcon)
falcone *m* falcon; ***caccia*** *f* ***col ~*** falconry
falconiere *m* falconer, hawker
falda *f* layer; GEOL stratum; *di cappello* brim; (*pendio*) slope; (*piede di monte*) foot; ***~ acquifera*** water table
faldone *m* file
falegname *m* carpenter
falegnameria *f* carpentry
falena *f* moth
falla *f* NAUT leak; ***tappare una ~*** stop *or* plug a leak (*a. fig*)
fallace *adj* fallacious
fallico *adj* ⟨*mpl* -ci⟩ phallic; ***simbolo*** *m* ***~*** phallic symbol
fallimentare *adj* bankruptcy; ***procedura*** *f* ***~*** bankruptcy proceedings; *fig* ***politica*** *f* ***~*** disastrous policy
fallimento *m* failure; FIN bankruptcy; ***mandare in ~ qn*** bankrupt s.o.
fallire ⟨4d⟩ **I** *v/t* miss; ***~ il bersaglio*** be wide of the mark **II** *v/i* fail; FIN go bankrupt; ***~ in qc*** fail in sth
fallito I *adj* unsuccessful, failed; FIN bankrupt **II** *m* failure; FIN bankruptcy
fallo *m* fault; (*errore*) error, mistake; SPORTS foul; ***~ di mano*** hand ball; ***cogliere in ~ qn*** catch s.o. out; (*in flagrante*) catch s.o red-handed; ***fare un ~ di mano*** handle the ball; ***mettere il piede in ~*** lose one's footing
fallout *m* ⟨*pl* fallout⟩ fall-out; *fig* spin-off
falò *m* ⟨*pl* falò⟩ bonfire
falsamente *adv* falsely
falsare *v/t* ⟨1a⟩ *verità, fatti* distort; ***~ un risultato*** alter a result
falsariga *f* ⟨*pl* -ghe⟩ *ruled sheet used as a guide for writing*; *fig* model; ***sulla ~ di qn*** following s.o.'s example; ***sulla ~ di qc*** along the lines of sth
falsario *m*, **-a** *f* ⟨*mpl* -ri⟩ forger
falsificabile *adj* forgeable; ***facilmente ~*** easy to forge
falsificare *v/t* ⟨1m & d⟩ forge; ***~ una firma*** forge a signature
falsificazione *f* forgery; ***~ di documenti*** forgery of documents
falsità *f* ⟨*pl* falsità⟩ falsity, falseness; (*menzogna*) lie; (*ipocrisia*) insincerity
falso I *adj* false; (*sbagliato*) incorrect, wrong; *oro, gioielli* imitation, fake *infml*; (*falsificato*) forged, fake *infml*; ***~ allarme*** false alarm; ***-a testimonianza*** perjured evidence; ***mettere sotto -a luce*** show under a false light; ***-a partenza*** *f* false start; ***banconota*** *f* ***-a*** fake note **II** *m* (*falsità*) falsehood; *oggetto falsificato* forgery, fake *infml*; JUR forgery; ***giurare il ~*** commit perjury; ***~ ideologico*** fraudulent misrepresentation
falsopiano *m* ⟨*pl* falsipiani⟩ *apparently flat ground*
fama *f* fame; (*reputazione*) reputation; ***di ~ mondiale*** world-famous; ***farsi una brutta ~*** get a bad reputation; ***godere di ottima ~*** enjoy an excellent reputation; ***conoscere qn di ~*** know s.o. by reputation
fame *f* hunger; ***un salario da ~*** starvation wages; ***aver ~*** be hungry; ***fare la ~*** be very badly off; ***sto morendo di ~!*** I'm starving!
famelico *adj* ⟨*mpl* -ci⟩ ravenous
famigerato *adj* infamous
famiglia *f* family; ***alloggio in ~*** *per studenti* boarding with a family; ***~ numerosa*** large family; ***essere di ~*** be one of the family; ***essere di buona ~*** come from a good family; ***fare Natale in ~*** spend Christmas with one's family; ***metter su ~*** start a family; ***nella mia ~ siamo in quattro*** there are four of us in my family; ***la Sacra Famiglia*** the Holy Family
familiare I *adj* family *attr*; (*conosciuto*) familiar; (*semplice*) informal; ***per motivi -i*** for family reasons **II** *m/f* relative, relation
familiarità *f* familiarity; ***avere ~ con qc*** be familiar with sth
familiarizzare *v/t* ⟨1a⟩ familiarize

familiarizzarsi *v/r* familiarize o.s.
familiarmente *adv* familiarly; **~ *detto* or *chiamato* ...** informally known as
famoso *adj* famous
fan *m/f* ⟨*pl* fan⟩ fan; **~ *club*** fan club
fanale *m* AUTO, NAUT, AVIAT, RAIL light; (*lampione*) street lamp
fanalino *m* AUTO: **~ *di coda*** tail-light; *fig* ***essere il ~ di coda*** bring up the rear
fanaticamente *adv* fanatically
fanatico ⟨*mpl* -ci⟩ **I** *adj* fanatical **II** *m*, **-a** *f* fanatic; ***essere un ~ di qc*** *rugby, cinema* fan; *Internet, videogiochi* addict; *puntualità, pulizia* fanatic; *fitness* freak
fanatismo *m* fanaticism
fanciullo *m*, **-a** *f lit* (young) boy; *ragazza* (young) girl
fandonia *f* lie
fanfaronata *f* bluster, boasting
fanghiglia *f* slime, ooze
fango *m* ⟨*pl* -ghi⟩ mud; MED ***-ghi*** *pl* mud-baths; *fig* ***gettare ~ addosso a qn*** throw mud at s.o.
fangoso *adj* muddy
fangoterapia *f* mud therapy
fannullone *m*, **-a** *f* lazy good-for-nothing
fantapolitica *f* political fantasy
fantascientifico *adj* ⟨*mpl* -ci⟩ science-fiction *attr*
fantascienza *f* science fiction
fantasia *f* **I** *m* fantasy; (*immaginazione*) imagination; (*capriccio*) fancy; MUS fantasia **II** *adj*: ***tessuto ~*** patterned
fantasioso *adj* imaginative
fantasma *m* ⟨*pl* -i⟩ ghost; ***credi ai -i?*** do you believe in ghosts; ***i -i del passato*** the ghosts of the past
fantasmagoria *f* phantasmagoria; **~ *di colori*** phantasmagoria of colours
fantasticare *v/i* ⟨1m & d⟩ day-dream (***di*** about)
fantasticheria *f* day-dream, fantasy
fantastico *adj* ⟨*mpl* -ci⟩ fantastic
fante *m carte da gioco* jack
fanteria *f* MIL infantry
fantino *m* jockey
fantoccio *m* ⟨*pl* -cci⟩ puppet (*a. fig*)
fantomatico *adj* ⟨*mpl* -ci⟩ mysterious; ***un ~ personaggio*** an elusive character
farabutto *m*, **-a** *f* nasty piece of work
faraglione *m* stack
faraona *f*: (***gallina*** *f*) **~** guinea fowl
faraone *m* pharoah
faraonico *adj* ⟨*mpl* -ci⟩ magnificent; ***una villa -a*** a sumptuous villa
farcire *v/t* ⟨4d⟩ COOK stuff; *torta* fill
farcito *adj* stuffed; *dolce* filled; **~ *di cioccolato*** with a chocolate centre, filled with chocolate
fard *m* ⟨*pl* fard⟩ blusher
fardello *m* bundle; *fig* burden; *fig* ***portare il proprio ~*** carry one's own burden
fare ⟨3aa⟩ **I** *v/t* **1.** do; *vestito, dolce, errore* make; ***che classe fai?*** which class/year are you in?; **~ *inglese*** do English; ***che ora fa il tuo orologio?*** what time do you make it?; **~ (*dello*) *sport*** play sport; ***non fa niente*** it doesn't matter; ***far ~ qc a qn*** get s.o. to do sth; **~ *150 all'ora*** do 150 kms an hour; ***abbiamo fatto 10 km*** we travelled 10 kms; ***non aver niente da ~*** have nothing to do; ***cosa hai fatto ieri sera?*** what did you do last night?; ***per farla breve*** to cut a long story short; ***farla franca*** get off scot-free; ***ma chi te lo fa ~ ?*** *infml* nobody's forcing you!; ***facciamola finita!*** let's get it over with!; ***è uno che ci sa ~*** he's the type who can get things done; ***chi la fa, l'aspetti*** *prov* two can play at that game; ***chi fa da sé, fa per tre*** *prov* if you want a job done right, do it yourself **2.** *biglietto, benzina* buy, get; **~ *il pieno*** fill up **3. ~ *un bagno*** have a bath; **~ *un bambino*** have a baby; **~ *il conto*** *al ristorante* prepare the bill; ***che lavoro fa?*** what's his/her job?, where does he/she work?; **~ *qn sindaco*** make s.o. mayor **4. ~ *il furbo/bullo*** be a wise guy/bully; **~ *il medico/l'insegnante*** be a doctor/teacher; **~ (*la parte di*) *Cesare*** play (the role of) Caesar **5. *far cadere qc*** drop sth; **~ *vedere qc a qn*** show sth to s.o. **6. *farcela*** manage; ***ce l'abbiamo fatta!*** we've done it!; ***non ce la faccio più*** I can't take any more; ***ce la faranno ad arrivare?*** will they manage to get here/there? **7. *2 più 2 fa 4*** 2 and 2 make(s) 4; ***quanto fa?*** how much is it? **II** *v/i* **1. *faccia pure!*** go ahead!, carry on!; ***fai tu!*** it's up to you! **2.** (*essere adatto*)

questo non fa per me this isn't for me **3.** ***qui fa bello / brutto*** the weather here is nice / awful; ***fa freddo / caldo*** it's cold / warm **4.** ***~ da padre a qn*** be like a father to s.o.; ***vi faccio io da interprete*** I'll interpret for you **5.** ***come fa la canzone?*** how does the song go?

faretra *f* quiver

faretto *m* spot(light)

farfalla *f* butterfly; SPORTS butterfly stroke

farfallone *m*, **-a** *f* lech

farfugliare *v/i* ⟨1g⟩ splutter

farina *f* flour; ***~ gialla*** cornmeal; ***~ integrale*** wholewheat flour; ***~ di pesce*** fish meal; ***non è ~ del suo sacco*** it isn't his own work

farinaceo I *adj* starchy **II** *m*: ***farinacei*** *pl* starchy foodstuffs *pl*

farinata *f* COOK *flatbread from Liguria made of chickpea flour*

faringe *f* pharynx

faringite *f* pharyngitis

farinoso *adj* floury; ***neve*** *f* ***-a*** powder snow

fariseo *m* Pharisee (*a. fig pej*)

farmaceutico *adj* ⟨*mpl* -ci⟩ pharmaceutical

farmacia *f* pharmacy; *negozio* chemist's, *US* drugstore; ***-e di turno*** chemist's open in the evening or on Sundays; ***studiare ~*** study pharmacy

farmacista *m/f* ⟨*mpl* -i⟩ chemist, *US* pharmacist

farmaco *m* ⟨*pl* -ci⟩ drug; ***~ generico*** generic drug

farmacodipendenza *f* drug dependency

farmacologia *f* pharmacology

farmacopea *f* pharmacopoeia

farneticare *v/i* ⟨1m, b & d⟩ *fig* talk rubbish

farneticazione *f* raving

faro *m* NAUT lighthouse; AVIAT beacon; AUTO headlight; ***-i*** *pl* ***fendinebbia*** fog lamps *or* lights

farraginoso *adj* muddled; ***discorso*** *m* ***~*** woolly speech

farro *m* spelt; ***zuppa*** *f* ***di ~*** spelt soup

farsa *f* farce; ***era tutta una ~*** it was farcical

farsi *v/r* **1.** (*diventare*) grow; ***~ grande*** grow tall; ***~ suora / buddista*** become a nun / Buddhist; ***si sta facendo tardi*** it's getting late **2.** *infml* (*drogarsi*) shoot up *infml* **3.** ***~ avanti*** step forward **4.** ***~ la barba*** shave; ***~ male*** hurt o.s. **5.** ***~ aiutare*** get help; ***~ animo*** take heart; ***~ furbo*** wise up; ***non si è più fatto vivo*** we didn't hear from him again

fascia *f* ⟨*pl* -sce⟩ band; MED bandage; ***~ elastica*** crepe bandage; ***~ oraria*** (time) slot; ***~ di ascolto*** TV prime time, peak viewing time; ***~ laterale*** SPORTS wing

fasciame *m di legno* planking; *di metallo* plating

fasciare *v/t* ⟨1f⟩ MED bandage

fasciarsi *v/r* ⟨1f⟩: *fig* ***~ il capo prima di rompierselo*** cross one's bridges before one comes to them

fasciatoio *m* ⟨*pl* -i⟩ (baby) changing table

fasciatura *f* (*fascia*) bandage; *azione* bandaging

fascicolo *m* (*opuscolo*) booklet, brochure; (*incartamento*) file, dossier; ***la procura ha aperto un ~*** the prosecutor has drawn up a file

fascina *f*: ***~ di sterpi*** bunch of twigs

fascino *m* fascination, charm

fascinoso *adj* charming

fascio *m* ⟨*pl* -sci⟩ bundle; *di fiori* bunch; *di luce* beam; ***essere un ~ di nervi*** be a bundle of nerves

fascismo *m* Fascism

fascista *m/f & adj* ⟨*mpl* -i⟩ Fascist

fase *f* phase; AUTO stroke; *fig* ***essere fuori ~*** be out of sorts; ***~ di lavorazione*** production stage; ***-i*** *pl* ***lunari*** phases of the moon

fastello *m* bundle, bunch

fast food *m* fast food restaurant

fastidio *m* ⟨*pl* -di⟩ bother, trouble; ***dare ~ a qn*** bother s.o.; ***le dà ~ se …?*** do you mind if …?; ***un sacco di -i*** a lot of bother

fastidioso *adj* (*irritante*) irritating, annoying

fasto *m* pomp

fastosamente *adv* sumptuously

fastoso *adj* sumptuous

fasullo *adj* fake, sham; ***promesse*** *fpl* ***-e*** vain promises

fata *f* fairy

fatale *adj* fatal; ***era ~ che non si sarebbero mai più rivisti*** they were fated never to meet again

fatalistico *adj* ⟨*mpl* -ci⟩ fatalistic
fatalità *f* ⟨*pl* fatalità⟩ (*il fato*) fate; (*disavventura*) misfortune
fatalmente *adv* fatally
fatato *adj* magic, enchanted
fatica *f* ⟨*pl* -che⟩ (*sforzo*) effort; (*stanchezza*) fatigue; ***a ~*** with a great deal of effort; ***faccio ~ a crederci*** I find it hard to believe; ***uomo*** *m* ***di ~*** drudge; ***le -che di Ercole*** the labours of Hercules
faticare *v/i* ⟨1d⟩ toil; ***~ a*** find it difficult to
faticata *f* slog *infml*, grind
faticosamente *adv* with difficulty
faticoso *adj* tiring; (*difficile*) laborious
fatidico *adj* fateful
fatiscente *adj* crumbling; ***palazzo*** *m* ***~*** dilapidated building
fato *m* fate
fatt. *abbr* (= **fattura**) inv (invoice)
fattaccio *m* ⟨*pl* -cci⟩ evil deed, crime
fatterello *m* anecdote
fattezze *fpl* features
fattibile *adj* feasible
fattispecie *f* ⟨*pl* fattispecie⟩ JUR case in point; ***nella ~*** in this case
fatto I *past part* → ***fare*** **II** *adj* done; AGR ripe; ***~ a mano*** hand-made; ***~ di legno*** made of wood; ***~ in casa*** home-made; ***~ per qn / qc*** (tailor-)made for s.o. / sth; ***(non) essere ~ per qc*** (not) be cut out for sth; ***essere -i l'uno per l'altra*** be made for each other; ***è -a !*** we did it!; ***a conti -i*** all in all; ***detto ~*** no sooner said than done **III** *m* fact; (*avvenimento*) event; (*faccenda*) affair, business; ***il ~ è che …*** the fact is that …; ***cogliere sul ~*** catch red-handed; ***di ~*** *adj* real; *adv* in fact, actually; ***passare a vie di ~*** come to blows; ***in ~ di*** as regards; ***farsi i -i propri*** mind one's own business; ***dato*** *m* ***di ~*** fact; ***di nome*** *m* ***e di ~*** in word and deed; ***unione*** *f* ***di ~*** common-law marriage; ***in ~ di*** as regards
fattore[1] *m* (*elemento*) factor; ***~ di protezione antisolare*** sun protection factor
fattore[2] *m* AGR farm manager
fattoria *f* farm; (*casa*) farmhouse; (*insieme di edifici*) farmstead
fattorino *m* messenger; *per consegne* delivery man; *posta* postman, *US* mailman
fattrice *f* ZOOL brood mare
fattucchiera *f* sorceress
fattura *f* (*lavorazione*) workmanship; *di abiti* cut; FIN invoice; ***rilasciare una ~ a qn*** invoice s.o.; ***~ pro forma*** pro-forma (invoice); *fig* ***fare la*** *or* ***una ~ a qn*** put the evil eye on s.o.
fatturare *v/t* ⟨1a⟩ FIN invoice
fatturato *m* FIN (*giro d'affari*) turnover
fatturazione *f* invoicing
fatuità *f* ⟨*pl* fatuità⟩ fatuousness
fatuo *adj* fatuous; ***fuoco*** *m* ***~*** will-o'-the-wisp; *fig* illusion
fatwa *f* fatwa
fauci *fpl* jaws *pl*
fauna *f* fauna
faunistico *adj* ⟨*mpl* -ci⟩ faunal; ***oasi*** *f* ***-a*** wildlife sanctuary
fauno *m* MYTH faun
fausto *adj liter* auspicious; ***giorni*** *mpl* ***-i*** prosperous times; ***~ evento*** happy event
fautore *m*, **-trice** *f* supporter
fava *f* broad bean; ***prendere due piccioni con una ~*** kill two birds with one stone
favilla *f* spark (*a. fig*); ***far -e*** sparkle; ***manda -e dagli occhi*** his / her eyes are sparkling
favo *m* honeycomb
favola *f* (*fiaba*) fairy tale; (*storia*) story; *morale* fable; (*meraviglia*) dream; ***una vacanza da ~*** a dream holiday; ***da ~*** fairy-tale, dream; ***essere la ~ del paese*** be the talk of the town
favolosamente *adv* fabulously
favoloso *adj* fabulous
favore *m* favo(u)r; ***prezzo*** *m* ***di ~*** special deal; ***a ~ di qn*** in favo(u)r of s.o.; ***per ~!*** please!; ***fare un ~ a qn*** do s.o. a favo(u)r
favoreggiamento *m* JUR aiding and abetting
favorevole *adj* favo(u)rable; ***essere ~ a qn / qc*** be in favour of s.o. / sth
favorire ⟨4d⟩ **I** *v/t* favo(u)r; (*promuovere*) promote **II** *v/i*: ***vuol ~?*** would you care to join me / us?; ***favorisca i documenti!*** your papers, please!; ***favorisca nello studio*** would you go into the study please
favoritismo *m* favo(u)ritism; ***fare (dei) -i*** have favo(u)rites
favorito *m/adj* favo(u)rite
fax *m* ⟨*pl* fax⟩ fax; ***mandare un ~ a qc***

send s.o. a fax, fax s.o.
faxare *v/t* ⟨1a⟩ fax
fazione *f* faction
faziosità *f* ⟨*pl* faziosità⟩ factiousness
fazioso I *adj* (*parziale*) sectarian; (*sovversivo*) factious **II** *m* (*di parte*) sectarian; (*sovversivo*) factious
fazzolettino *m*: **~ *di carta*** tissue
fazzoletto *m* handkerchief; *per la testa* headscarf
f.co *abbr* (= **franco**) free
FE *abbr* (= **Ferrara**) Ferrara
febbraio *m* February
febbre *f* fever; ***ha la ~*** he has a *or* is running a temperature; **~ *da fieno*** hay fever; ***misurare la ~ a qn*** take s.o.'s temperature; **~ *da cavallo*** raging temperature; **~ *dell'oro*** gold fever
febbricitante *adj*: ***essere ~*** be feverish
febbrifugo *m* ⟨*pl* -ghi⟩ MED *drug that reduces the temperature*
febbrile *adj* feverish
febbrilmente *adv* feverishly
fecale *adj* faecal
feccia *f fig* dregs
feci[1] *fpl* faeces *pl*
feci[2] → ***fare***
fecola *f*: **~ *di patate*** potato starch
fecondare *v/t* ⟨1a⟩ fertilize
fecondazione *f* fertilization; **~ *artificiale*** artificial insemination; **~ *assistita*** assisted fertilization; **~ *in vitro*** in vitro fertilization
fecondità *f* fertility
fecondo *adj* fertile
fedayin *m* ⟨*pl* fedayin⟩ fedayee (*pl* fedayeen)
fede *f* faith; (*fedeltà*) loyalty; *anello* wedding ring; ***aver ~ in qc*** have faith in s.o.; ***tener ~ a una promessa*** keep a promise; ***essere in buona ~*** be genuine; ***prestar ~ a qn/qc*** give credence to s.o./sth; ***degno di ~*** trustworthy; ***in ~*** yours sincerely, yours faithfully
fedele I *adj* faithful; (*esatto, conforme all'originale*) true **II** *m/f* REL believer; ***i -i*** *pl* the faithful
fedelmente *adv* faithfully
fedeltà *f* ⟨*pl* fedeltà⟩ faithfulness; MUS ***alta ~*** hi-fi, high fidelity
federa *f* pillowcase
federale *adj* federal; ***repubblica*** *f* **~** federal republic
federalismo *m* federalism
federalista *m/f* ⟨*mpl* -i⟩ federalist
federativo *adj* federal, federative
federazione *f* federation
fedifrago *adj* ⟨*mpl* -ghi⟩ unfaithful
fedina *f*: **~ *penale*** criminal record; ***avere la ~ penale sporca/pulita*** have a/no criminal record
feedback *m* ⟨*pl* feedback⟩ feedback
feeling *m* ⟨*pl* feeling⟩ rapport; (*intesa*) chemistry; (*atmosfera*) sense
fegatelli *mpl* COOK pieces of pig's liver
fegatini *mpl* COOK (chicken) livers; **~ *di pollo/tacchino*** chicken/turkey livers; ***crostini mpl ai ~*** crostini with chicken liver pâté
fegato *m* liver; *fig* courage, guts *pl infml*; **~ *di vitello/maiale*** calf's/pig's liver; **~ *d'oca*** goose liver; **~ *alla veneziana*** COOK *liver cooked with onions*; ***avere ~*** to have guts; ***rodersi il ~*** (***per la rabbia***) be eaten up (with anger); ***ci vuole un bel ~!*** you've got to have guts!
felce *f* fern
felice *adj* happy; (*fortunato*) lucky; **~ *anno nuovo!*** Happy New Year!; ***essere ~ per qn*** be happy for s.o.; ***essere ~ di fare qc*** be happy to do sth; ***sono ~ di vederti!*** it's lovely to see you; **~ *come una Pasqua*** be happy as a sandboy; ***non è stata un'idea ~*** it wasn't a good idea
felicemente *adv* happily; **~ *sposato*** happily married
felicità *f* ⟨*pl* felicità⟩ happiness
felicitarsi *v/r* ⟨1m⟩: **~ *con qn per qc*** congratulate s.o. on sth
felicitazioni *fpl* congratulations *pl*
felino *adj* feline
felpa *f* sweatshirt
felpato *adj* TEX fleece, plush; *fig* ***con passo m ~*** (treading) softly
feltro *m* felt
feluca *f* ⟨*pl* -che⟩ (*cappello*) cocked hat
femmina *f* (*figlia*) girl, daughter; ZOOL, TECH female
femmineo *adj* effeminate
femminile I *adj* feminine; (*da donna*) women's **II** *m* GRAM feminine
femminilità *f* feminity
femminismo *m* feminism
femminista *m/f* ⟨*mpl* -i⟩ feminist
femorale *adj* femoral; ***arteria f ~*** femoral artery

femore *m* femur
fendente *m* downward stroke; SPORTS *infml* hack
fendere *v/t* ⟨3l⟩ *liter* cleave; **~ *le onde*** cut through the waves; **~ *l'aria*** fly through the air
fendinebbia *m* ⟨*pl* fendinebbia⟩ fog lamp *or* light
fenditura *f* cracking; (*crepa*) crack
fenice *f* phoenix
fenicio ⟨*mpl* -ci⟩ **I** *adj* Phoenician **II** *m*, **-a** *f* Phoenician; ***i Fenici*** the Phoenicians
fenico *adj* ⟨*mpl* -ci⟩: ***acido*** *m* **~** carbolic acid
fenicottero *m* flamingo
fenolo *m* carbolic acid
fenomenale *adj* phenomenal
fenomeno *m* phenomenon
feriale *adj*: ***giorno*** *m* **~** weekday
ferie *fpl* holiday *sg*, *US* vacation *sg*; ***andare in ~*** go on holiday (*US* vacation); ***chiuso per ~*** closed for holidays; ***quando vai in ~ ?*** when are you going on holiday?
ferimento *m* wounding
ferire *v/t* ⟨4d⟩ wound; *in incidente* injure; *fig* hurt
ferirsi *v/r* injure o.s.; **~ *a una gamba*** hurt one's leg
ferita *f* wound; *in incidente* injury; **~ *da arma da fuoco*** gunshot wound; ***leccarsi le -e*** lick one's wounds
ferito I *adj* wounded; *in incidente* injured; *fig sentimenti* hurt; *orgoglio* injured **II** *m* casualty
feritoia *f* loophole; *per monete* slot
fermacalzoni *m* ⟨*pl* fermacalzoni⟩ bicycle clips
fermacapelli *m* ⟨*pl* fermacapelli⟩ (hair)slide
fermacarte *m* ⟨*pl* fermacarte⟩ paperweight
fermacravatta *m* ⟨*pl* fermacravatta⟩ tiepin
fermaglio *m* ⟨*pl* -gli⟩ clasp; *per capelli* hair slide; (*gioiello*) brooch
fermamente *adv* firmly; **~ *deciso*** (absolutely) determined
fermare *v/t* ⟨1a⟩ stop; JUR detain; ***essere fermato dalla polizia*** be arrested
fermarsi *v/r* stop; (*restare*) stay, remain; ***fermati!*** stop!; ***mi si è fermato l'orologio*** my watch has stopped; **~ *a parlare con qn*** stop to talk to s.o.; ***quanto ti fermi a Roma?*** how long are you staying in Rome?
fermata *f* stop; **~ *dell' autobus*** bus stop; **~ *facoltativa*** *or* **~ *a richiesta*** request stop; ***qual è la ~ per il duomo?*** which stop is it for the cathedral?, where do I get off for the cathedral?
fermentare *v/i* ⟨1a⟩ ferment
fermentazione *f* fermentation
fermento *m* yeast; *fig* ferment
fermezza *f* firmness
fermo I *adj* still, motionless; *veicolo* stationary; (*saldo*) firm; *mano* steady; ***star ~*** (*non muoversi*) keep still; ***l'orologio è ~*** the watch has stopped **II** *int*: **~!** (*alt!*) stop!; (*immobile!*) keep still! **III** *m* JUR detention
fermoposta *m* poste restante
fernet *m* ⟨*pl* fernet⟩ Fernet
feroce *adj* fierce, ferocious; *animale* wild; (*insopportabile*) dreadful
ferocemente *adv* fiercely
ferocia *f* ferocity
ferodo *m* lining
ferraglia *f* ⟨*pl* -glie⟩ scrap iron
ferragosto *m August 15 public holiday*; *periodo* August holidays *pl*
ferramenta *f* hardware; *negozio* hardware store, ironmonger's *Br*
ferrare *v/t* ⟨1b⟩ *cavallo* shoe
ferrarese I *adj* from Ferrara **II** *m/f* person from Ferrara
ferrato *adj* RAIL: ***strada*** *f* ***-a*** railway line, *US* railroad; *fig* ***essere ~ in qc*** be well up in sth
ferreo *adj* iron (*a. fig*); *fig* rigid; ***una logica -a*** strict logic
ferriera *f* ironworks
ferrista *m/f* ⟨*mpl* -i⟩ theatre nurse
ferrite *f* ferrite
ferro *m* **1.** iron; **~ *battuto*** wrought iron; **~ *di cavallo*** horseshoe; ***toccare ~*** touch wood; *fig* ***di ~*** *memoria, salute* excellent; *stomaco* cast-iron; COOK ***ai -i*** grilled, *US* broiled; ***venire ai -i corti con qn*** cross swords with s.o.; ***i -i del mestiere*** the tools of the trade; ***salute*** *f* ***di ~*** iron constitution; ***alibi*** *m* ***di ~*** cast-iron alibi; ***battere il ~ finché è caldo*** strike while the iron's hot **2.** (*arnese*) tool **3.** **~ *da calza*** knitting needle **4.** **~ *da stiro a vapore*** steam iron
ferroso *adj* ferrous

ferrovecchio *m* ⟨*pl* -cchi⟩ scrap merchant
ferrovia *f* railway, *US* railroad; **~ *metropolitana*** *or* ***sotterranea*** underground, *US* subway
ferroviario *adj* ⟨*mpl* -ri⟩ rail(way) *attr*, *US* railroad *attr*
ferroviere *m*, **-a** *f* rail (*US* railroad) worker
ferruginoso *adj* ferruginous
ferry-boat *m* ⟨*pl* ferry-boat⟩ ferry boat
fertile *adj* fertile
fertilità *f* fertility
fertilizzante *m* fertilizer
ferula *f* BOT ferula
fervente *adj* fervent; *fig* raging; *preghiera* ardent; ***cattolico m*** **~** devout Catholic
fervere *v/i* ⟨3a⟩ *liter* burn; *fig* rage; ***fervono i preparativi*** feverish preparations are being made
fervido *adj* fervent; *fig* ardent; ***con i più -i auguri*** with my most earnest wishes; ***-a immaginazione*** *f* lively imagination
fesa *f*: **~ *di vitello*** veal rump
fesseria *f* rubbish; ***dire*** / ***fare una*** **~** say / do something stupid
fesso *m* *infml* idiot *infml*; ***far*** **~ *qn*** con s.o *infml*
fessura *f* (*spaccatura*) crack; (*fenditura*) slit, slot
festa *f* feast; *di santo* feast day; (*ricevimento*) party; (*compleanno*) birthday; (*onomastico*) name day; **~ *di compleanno*** birthday party; **~ *della mamma*** / ***del papà*** Mother's / Father's Day; **~ *nazionale*** national holiday; ***buone -e!*** *a Natale* Merry Christmas and a happy New Year!; ***fare una*** **~** have a party; ***vestito a*** **~** dressed up to the nines; ***far*** **~ *a qn*** give s.o. a warm welcome; ***fare la*** **~ *a qn*** *infml* bump s.o. off
festante *adj* joyful
festeggiamenti *mpl* celebrations *pl*
festeggiare *v/t* ⟨1f⟩ celebrate; *persona* have a celebration for
festival *m* ⟨*pl* festival⟩ festival; **~ *del cinema*** film festival
festività *f* ⟨*pl* festività⟩ festival; **~** *pl* celebrations *pl*, festivities *pl*
festivo *adj* festive; ***giorno m*** **~** holiday
festosamente *adv* happily
festoso *adj* happy, cheerful
fetale *adj* f(o)etal; ***in posizione f*** **~** in a f(o)etal position
feticcio *m* ⟨*pl* -cci⟩ fetish
feticismo *m* fetishism
feticista *m/f* ⟨*mpl* -i⟩ fetishist
fetido *adj* fetid; *fig* contemptible
feto *m* f(o)etus
fetore *m* stench
fetta *f* slice; ***a -e*** sliced; ***fare a -e qc*** slice sth
fettina *f* thin steak; **~ *di vitello*** veal steak
fettuccine *fpl* noodles *pl*, fettuccine *pl*
feudale *adj* feudal
feudalesimo *m* feudalism
feudatario *m* ⟨*pl* -ri⟩ HIST landowner
feudo *m* HIST fief; *fig* stronghold
f.f. *abbr* (= **facente funzioni**) acting
FG *abbr* (= **Foggia**) Foggia
FI *abbr* (= **Firenze**) Florence
fiaba *f* fairy tale
fiabesco *adj* ⟨*mpl* -chi⟩ fairytale *attr*
fiacca *f* weariness; (*svogliatezza*) laziness; ***battere la*** **~** slack, be a shirker
fiaccamente *adv* sluggishly
fiacchezza *f* sluggishness; *fig* dullness
fiacco *adj* ⟨*mpl* -cchi⟩ (*debole*) weak; (*svogliato*) lazy; FIN *mercato* sluggish
fiaccola *f* torch
fiaccolata *f* torchlight procession
fiala *f* phial
fiamma *f* flame; NAUT pennant; COOK ***alla*** **~** flambé; ***andare in -e*** go up in flames; ***dare qc alle -e*** set fire to sth; *fig* ***una vecchia*** **~** an old flame; **~ *ossidrica*** oxyhydrogen flame; ***le Fiamme Gialle*** the Guardia di Finanza, *the body dealing with crimes involving customs and excise or taxes*
fiammante *adj*: ***rosso m*** **~** fiery red; ***nuovo*** **~** brand new
fiammata *f* blaze; *fig* flare-up
fiammeggiante *adj* flaming
fiammeggiare ⟨1f⟩ **I** *v/i fig occhi* flash; *cielo* glow **II** *v/t* COOK flambé
fiammella *f* small flame
fiammifero *m* match
fiammingo I *adj* ⟨*mpl* -ghi⟩ Flemish **II** *m lingua* Flemish
fiancata *f di auto* side; *di nave* broadside
fiancheggiare *v/t* ⟨1f⟩ border; *fig* support

fianco *m* ⟨*pl* -chi⟩ side; ANAT hip; ***~ a ~*** side by side; ***di ~ a qn*** beside s.o.; ***al tuo ~*** by your side; ***rimanere al ~ di qn*** be at s.o.'s side
fiandra *f*: ***tela di ~*** Flanders linen
fiano *m* COOK *a medium-bodied white wine from Campania*
fiaschetta *f* hip flask
fiasco *m* ⟨*pl* -chi⟩ flask; *fig* fiasco; ***fare ~*** fall flat, bomb
FIAT *abbr* (= **Fabbrica Italiana Automobili Torino**) *Italian car company*
fiatare *v/i* ⟨1a⟩ breathe; ***non ~!*** don't say a word! ***senza ~*** without a murmur
fiato *m* breath; ***senza ~*** breathless; MUS ***strumento*** *m* ***a ~*** wind instrument; ***tutto d'un ~*** in one go; ***avere il ~ grosso*** be out of breath; ***riprendere ~*** catch one's breath; ***è ~ sprecato!*** it's like water off a duck's back!; ***tirare il ~*** breathe, draw breath
fiatone *m*: ***avere il ~*** be out of breath, pant
fibbia *f* buckle
fibra *f* fibre, *US* fiber; ***di forte ~*** robust, sturdy; ***~ morale*** moral fibre (*US* fiber); ***~ ottica*** optical fibre; ***~ sintetica*** synthetic; ***~ di vetro*** fibreglass, *US* fiberglass; ***ricco di -e*** high in fibre (*US* fiber)
fibrillazione *f* fibrillation; *fig* fluttering; *fig* ***essere in ~*** be all of a flutter
fibroma *m* ⟨*pl* -i⟩ fibroma
fibroso *adj* fibrous
fica *f* ⟨*pl* -che⟩ *vulg* (*vagina*) cunt *vulg*; (*ragazza*) babe
ficcanaso *m/f* ⟨*pl* ficcanaso⟩ *infml* nosy parker *infml*
ficcare *v/t* ⟨1d⟩ thrust; *infml* (*mettere*) shove *infml*
ficcarsi *v/r* get; ***~ nei guai*** get into hot water; ***~ qc in testa*** get sth into one's head; ***dove s'è ficcato?*** where can it / he have got to?
fiche *f* ⟨*pl* fiche⟩ chip
fico[1] *m* ⟨*pl* -chi⟩ *frutto* fig; *albero* fig (tree); ***~ d'India*** prickly pear; ***~ secco*** dried fig; ***non me ne importa un ~ secco*** I couldn't care less
fico[2] *adj infml* cool
fiction *f* ⟨*pl* fiction⟩ TV drama
ficus *m* ⟨*pl* ficus⟩ ficus
fidanzamento *m* engagement
fidanzarsi *v/r* ⟨1a⟩ get engaged
fidanzata *f* fiancée
fidanzato *m* fiancé; ***i -i*** *pl* the engaged couple
fidarsi *v/r*: ***~ di qn / qc*** trust s.o. / sth, rely on s.o. / sth; ***non mi fido di chiederlo a mio padre*** I don't dare ask my father
fidato *adj* trustworthy
fideiussione *f* JUR guarantee
fideiussore *m* guarantor
fideiussorio *adj* ⟨*mpl* -ri⟩ surety
fido I *adj* trusted, trusty **II** *m* FIN credit; ***~ bancario*** bank overdraft; ***concedere / ottenere un ~*** grant / take out an overdraft
fiducia *f* confidence; ***avere ~ in qn*** have faith in s.o.; ***~ in se stessi*** self confidence; ***di ~*** *persona* reliable, trustworthy; *incarico* responsible
fiduciaria *f* (*a.* ***società*** *f* ***~***) FIN trust company
fiduciario ⟨*mpl* -ri⟩ **I** *adj* JUR *atto, società* trust *attr* **II** *m* trustee
fiducioso *adj* trusting
fiele *m* gall; *fig* gall, venom
fienile *m* hayloft
fieno *m* hay
fiera[1] *f animale* wild beast
fiera[2] *f mostra* fair; ***~ del libro*** book fair
fieramente *adv* proudly
fierezza *f* pride
fiero *adj* proud; ***essere ~ di qn / qc*** be proud of s.o. / sth
fievole *adj* feeble, weak
fievolmente *adv* weakly, dimly
fifa *f infml* nerves *pl*, jitters *pl infml*; ***aver ~*** have the jitters, be jittery
FIFA *abbr* (= **Fédération International Football Association**) FIFA
fifone *m*, **-a** *f infml* chicken
figata *f infml*: ***è una ~*** *or* ***che ~!*** it / that's really cool!
Figi *fpl* Fiji
figlia *f* daughter
figliare *v/t* ⟨1g⟩ *cani* have puppies; *gatti* have kittens; *bovini* calve; *cavalli* foal
figliastra *f* stepdaughter
figliastro *m* stepson
figlio *m* ⟨*pl* -gli⟩ son; ***avere -gli*** *pl* have children; ***essere ~ unico*** be an only child; ***~ di papà*** *rich, spoiled young man*; ***~ naturale*** natural child; ***~ di buona donna / di un cane / di putta-***

na *vulg* son of a bitch
figlioccia *f* ⟨*pl* -cce⟩ goddaughter
figlioccio *m* ⟨*pl* -cci⟩ godson
figliolo *m*, **-a** *f*: ***il figliol prodigo*** the prodigal son
figura *f* figure; (*illustrazione*) illustration; (*apparenza*) appearance; ***far brutta ~*** make a bad impression; ***fare ~*** look beautiful
figuraccia *f* ⟨*pl* -cce⟩ sorry sight; ***fare una ~*** put up a poor show
figurante *m/f* FILM, THEAT extra
figurare ⟨1a⟩ **I** *v/t fig* imagine; ***figurati!*** just imagine!, just think!; ***si figuri!*** not at all!, of course not! **II** *v/i* (*apparire*) appear; (*far figura*) make a good impression; ***il tuo nome non figura nell'elenco*** your name isn't on the list
figurato *adj* (*illustrato*) illustrated; *linguaggio*, *espressione* figurative; ***in senso ~*** figuratively
figurina *f da raccolta* collector card, trading card; ***le -e del presepio*** *the statuettes in the nativity scene*
figurinista *m/f* ⟨*mpl* -i⟩ fashion designer
figurino *m* fashion sketch; ***sembri un ~!*** you look like a supermodel!
figuro *m*: ***un losco ~*** a shady character
fila *f* line, row; (*coda*) queue, *US* line; ***di ~*** in succession; ***tre giorni di ~*** three days running, three days in succession; ***in ~ indiana*** in single file; ***fare la ~*** queue, *US* wait in line; ***mettersi in ~*** queue up; THEAT ***in prima / ultima ~*** in the front / back row; ***militare nelle -e di un partito*** be an active member of a party
filaccioso *adj* stringy
Filadelfia *f* Philadelphia
filamento *m* filament
filanca® *f* stretch nylon
filanda *f* spinning mill
filantropia *f* philanthropy
filantropico *adj* ⟨*mpl* -ci⟩ philanthropic
filantropo *m*, **-a** *f* philanthropist
filare[1] ⟨1a⟩ **I** *v/t* spin **II** *v/i* **1.** *di ragno* spin **2.** *di ragionamento* make sense **3.** *di formaggio* go stringy **4.** *di veicolo* travel **5.** *infml* (*andarsene*) take off *infml*; ***fila!*** go away!, shoo! **6.** ***~ diritto*** (*comportarsi bene*) behave (o.s.)
filare[2] *m di alberi*: row; ***~ di viti*** row of vines
filarino *m infml* boyfriend, girlfriend
filarmonica *f* ⟨*pl* -che⟩ philharmonic
filarmonico ⟨*pl* -ci⟩ philharmonic
filastrocca *f* ⟨*pl* -cche⟩ nursery rhyme
filatelia *f* philately
filatelista *m/f* ⟨*mpl* -i⟩ stamp-collector
filato I *adj* (*logico*) logical; ***andare di ~ a casa*** go straight home; ***per 10 ore filate*** for ten hours straight **II** *m* yarn; *per cucire* thread
file *m* ⟨*pl* file⟩ COMPUT file
filettato *adj* threaded
filetto *m* COOK fillet; TECH thread; ***~ di sogliola*** fillet of sole
filiale *f* branch; (*società affiliata*) affiliate
filibustiere *m*, **-a** *f fig* pirate
filiforme *adj* wiry
filigrana *f su carta* watermark; *in oreficeria* filigree
filigranato *adj carta* watermarked; *oro* filigreed
filippica *f* ⟨*pl* -che⟩ *hum* tirade
Filippine *fpl* Philippines *pl*
filippino I *adj* Filipino **II** *m*, **-a** *f* Filipino
filisteo I *adj* philistine **II** *m* HIST philistine (*a. fig*)
fillossera *f* vine pest
film *m* ⟨*pl* film⟩ film, movie; ***~ giallo*** thriller; ***~ in bianco e nero*** black and white film
filmare *v/t* ⟨1a⟩ film
filmato *m* short (film)
filo *m* ⟨*pl a.* le **-a**⟩ **1.** thread; ***~ interdentale*** (dental) floss; *fig* ***un ~ di vergogna / rispetto*** an ounce of shame / respect; ***~ di voce*** whisper; ***per ~ e per segno*** in detail; ***dare del ~ da torcere a qn*** make things difficult for s.o.; ***perdere il ~ del discorso*** lose the thread of the conversation; ***fare il ~ a qn*** chat s.o. up; ***essere sul ~ del rasoio*** be on a knife edge; ***reggere le -a*** pull the strings **2.** *metallico* wire; *fig* ***~ conduttore*** lead; ***fil di ferro*** wire; ***~ spinato*** barbed wire **3.** *di lama* edge **4.** *d'erba* blade
filoamericano *adj* pro-american
filobus *m* ⟨*pl* filobus⟩ trolley(bus)
filodendro *m* philodendron
filodiffusione *f* cable radio
filodrammatica *f* amateur dramatic society
filologia *f* philology

filologo *m*, **-a** *f* ⟨*mpl* -gi⟩ philologist
filoncino *m* small French loaf, flute
filone *m* MINER vein; *pane* French stick; *fig* tradition
filosofare *v/i* ⟨1m & c⟩ philosophize
filosofia *f* philosophy
filosofico *adj* ⟨*mpl* -ci⟩ philosophic(al)
filosofo *m*, **-a** *f* philosopher
filovia *f* trolley(bus)
filtrante *adj* filtering
filtrare ⟨1a⟩ **I** *v/t* strain, filter **II** *v/i fig* filter out
filtro[1] *m* filter; **~ *di carta*** filter paper; **~ *dell'olio*** oil filter; ***sigarette*** *fpl* ***col / senza ~*** filter-tipped / untipped cigarettes
filtro[2] *m* philtre; **~ *magico*** magic potion
filza *f* string; *fig* series *sg*; (*imbastitura*) running-stitch; ***una ~ di perline di vetro*** a string of glass beads
fin → ***fine, fino*[2], *fino*[3]**
finale I *adj* final **II** *m* end; **~ *a sorpresa*** surprise ending **III** *f* SPORTS final; ***quarti*** *mpl* ***di ~*** quarter finals; ***ottavi*** *mpl* ***di ~*** qualifying heats
finalista *m/f* ⟨*mpl* -i⟩ finalist
finalità *f* ⟨*pl* finalità⟩ aim, purpose
finalizzare *v/t* ⟨1a⟩: **~ *qc a qc*** direct sth to sth
finalizzato *adj* aimed
finalmente *adv* (*alla fine*) at last; (*per ultimo*) finally
finanza *f* finance; ***-e*** *pl* finances; ***ministro*** *m* ***delle -e*** Minister of Finance; **~ *aziendale*** ECON corporate finances; **~ *pubblica / privata*** public / private finance; ***alta ~*** high finance; ***Guardia di Finanza*** *body of police who deal with crimes involving Customs and Excise or Tax*; ***Ministero delle Finanze*** Ministry of Finance; ***le mie -e non me lo consentono*** I can't afford it
finanziabile *adj* financeable
finanziamento *m* funding
finanziare *v/t* ⟨1g⟩ fund, finance
finanziaria *f* (*società*) finance house; (*legge*) finance bill
finanziariamente *adv* financially
finanziario *adj* ⟨*mpl* -ri⟩ financial; ***situazione*** *f* ***-a*** financial situation; ***problemi*** *mpl* ***-i*** financial problems
finanziatore *m*, **-trice** *f* sponsor, financial backer
finanziera *f* COOK *a typical sauce from Piedmont made from chicken livers, giblets and mushrooms cooked in Marsala*
finanziere *m* financier; (*guardia di finanza*) *Customs and Excise officer*; *lungo le coste* coastguard
finché *cj* until; (*per tutto il tempo che*) as long as; ***rimango ~ posso*** I'll stay as long as I can; **~ *vivo*** for as long as I live
fine I *adj* fine; (*sottile*) thin; *udito, vista* sharp, keen; (*raffinato*) refined; ***è una persona molto ~*** he / she's very refined; ***avere il palato ~*** have an educated palate **II** *m* aim; ***al ~ di ...*** in order to ...; ***secondo ~*** ulterior motive; ***il ~ giustifica i mezzi*** the end justifies the means; ***a fin di bene*** well-meant **III** *f* end; ***alla ~*** in the end; ***alla ~ di maggio / della settimana*** at the end of May / of the week; ***alla fin ~, in fin dei conti*** after all, when all's said and done; ***senza ~*** endless; ***che ~ ha fatto il giornale?*** what happened to the paper?; ***fare una brutta ~*** come to a sticky end; ***in fin dei conti*** when all is said and done; ***è in fin di vita*** he / she's dying; ***mettere ~ a qc*** put a stop to sth
finemente *adv* finely; **~ *lavorato*** delicately worked
fine settimana *m* ⟨*pl* fine settimana⟩ weekend
finestra *f* window; ***affacciarsi alla ~*** look out of the window; **~ *panoramica*** *window with a beautiful view*
finestrino *m* window; AUTO **~ *posteriore*** rear window
finezza *f* fineness; (*sottigliezza*) thinness; (*raffinatezza*) refinement
fingere ⟨3d⟩ **I** *v/t*: **~ *sorpresa / dolore*** pretend to be surprised / to be in pain **II** *v/i*: **~ *di*** pretend to
fingersi *v/r* pretend to be
finimenti *mpl* harness
finimondo *m* big fuss; ***è successo il ~*** there was uproar
finire ⟨4d⟩ **I** *v/t* finish, end; **~ *di fare qc*** finish doing sth; ***finiscila!*** stop it!; ***finitela di lamentarvi!*** stop complaining!; ***abbiamo finito la benzina / i soldi*** we've run out of petrol / money **II** *v/i* end, finish (***in*** in); ***com'è andata a ~?*** how did it pan out?; ***andrà***

a ~ male *cosa* this will all end in tears; *persona* he / she will come to no good; ***~ con*** *or* ***per fare qc*** end up doing sth; ***~ a botte*** end in a fight; ***~ in prigione*** end up in prison; ***è finito il pane*** there's no bread left; ***dov'è finito il mio ombrello?*** where's my umbrella gone? **III** *m* end; ***sul ~ dell'estate*** towards the end of the summer
finissaggio *m* ⟨*pl* -ggi⟩ TEX finishing
finito *adj* finished; (*venduto*) sold out; ***è finita*** it's over; ***farla finita con qc*** put an end to sth; *fig* ***è un uomo ~*** he's done for; ***prodotto*** *m* ***~*** end product
finlandese I *m/adj* Finnish **II** *m/f* Finn
Finlandia *f* Finland
finnico *adj* ⟨*mpl* -ci⟩ Finnic
fino[1] *adj* fine; (*acuto*) sharp; *oro* pure
fino[2] *prep tempo* till, until; *luogo* as far as; ***~ a domani*** until tomorrow; ***~ a che*** (*per tutto il tempo che*) as long as; (*fino al momento in cui*) until; ***fin da ieri*** since yesterday; ***fin da piccolo*** since I / he / she *etc* was little; ***~ a prova contraria*** until proved otherwise; ***~ a quando?*** how long?; ***fin d'ora*** here and now
fino[3] *adv* even; ***fin troppo*** more than enough
finocchio *m* ⟨*pl* -cchi⟩ fennel
finocchiona *f Tuscan salami flavoured with fennel seeds*
finora *adv* so far
finta *f* pretence, *US* pretense, sham; SPORTS feint; ***far ~ di*** pretend to
fintantoché *cj* until
finto I *past part* → ***fingere*** **II** *adj* false; (*artificiale*) artificial; (*simulato*) feigned; ***baffi*** *mpl* ***-i*** false moustache; ***fiori*** *mpl* ***-i*** artificial flowers; ***perle*** *fpl* ***-e*** fake / simulated pearls
finzione *f* pretence, *US* pretense, sham
fio *m*: ***pagare il ~*** pay the penalty
fioccare *v/i* ⟨1c & d⟩ fall in flakes; *fig* shower; ***la neve fiocca*** it's snowing; ***fioccano ceffoni*** slaps are being thrown
fiocco *m* ⟨*pl* -cchi⟩ **1.** bow; *fig* ***coi -cchi*** first-rate **2.** ***~ di neve*** snowflake; ***-cchi*** *pl* ***d'avena*** oat flakes, rolled oats
fiocina *f* harpoon
fiocinare *v/t* ⟨1m & c⟩ harpoon
fioco *adj* ⟨*mpl* -chi⟩ weak; *luce* dim; ***voce*** *f* ***-a*** hoarse voice
fionda *f Br* catapult, *US* slingshot
fioraio *m*, **-a** *f* ⟨*mpl* -ai⟩ florist
fiordaliso *m* cornflower
fiordo *m* fiord
fiore *m* **1.** flower; ***disegno*** *m* ***a -i*** floral design; ***essere in ~*** be in flower; ***-i*** *pl* ***di campo*** wild flowers; ***-i*** *pl* ***di Bach*** Bach flowers; ***-i*** *pl* ***d'arancio*** orange blossom **2.** *fig* ***il*** (***fior***) ***~*** the cream; ***il fior ~ dell'aristocrazia*** the cream of the aristocracy; ***essere il ~ all'occhiello*** (***di qc***) be the pride (of sth); ***nel ~ degli anni*** in the prime of life **3.** *nelle carte* ***-i*** *pl* clubs **4.** ***a fior d'acqua*** on the surface of the water
fiorellino *m* little flower
fiorente *adj* flourishing
fiorentino I *adj* Florentine **II** *m*, **-a** *f* Florentine; COOK ***alla -a*** with spinach; *bistecca* charcoal grilled **III** *f* COOK T-bone steak
fiorettista *m/f* ⟨*mpl* -i⟩ foilist
fioretto *m* SPORTS foil; ***fare un ~*** make a sacrifice; ***i -i di San Francesco*** LIT *passages from the work of St Francis*
fioriera *f* planter
fiorino *m* florin
fiorire *v/i* ⟨4d⟩ flower; *fig* flourish
fiorista *m/f* ⟨*mpl* -i⟩ florist
fiorito *adj* (*coperto di fiori*) flowered; (*a fiori*) in bloom; ***ramo*** *f* ***~*** flowering branch; ***prato*** *m* ***~*** wildflower meadow; ***aiuola*** *f* ***-a*** bed of flowers; *fig* ***linguaggio*** *m* ***~*** flowery language
fioritura *f* flowering (*a. fig*); ***periodo*** *m* ***della ~*** time of flowering (*a. fig*)
fiotto *m*: ***sgorgare a -i*** spurt; ***~ di sangue*** spurt of blood
Firenze *f* Florence
firma *f* signature; (*il firmare*) signing; FIN ***avere la ~*** be an authorized signatory; ***~ digitale*** COMPUT digital signature; ***mettere la ~ su qc*** put one's signature to sth; ***raccogliere le -e*** collect signatures (on a petition); ***le grandi -e della moda*** the big designer labels
firmamento *m* firmament
firmare *v/t* ⟨1a⟩ sign
firmatario *m*, **-a** *f* ⟨*mpl* -ri⟩ signatory
firmato *adj abito*, *borsa* designer *attr*
fisarmonica *f* ⟨*pl* -che⟩ accordion; ***a ~*** folding; ***suonare la ~*** play the accordion

fisarmonicista *m/f* ⟨*mpl* -i⟩ accordionist
fiscal drag *m* ⟨*pl* fiscal drag⟩ FIN fiscal drag
fiscale *adj* tax, fiscal; *fig pej* rigid, unbending; ***pressione*** *f* **~** unyielding pressure
fiscalista *m/f* ⟨*mpl* -i⟩ tax accountant
fiscalità *f* taxation; (*pignoleria*) rigidity, lack of flexibility
fiscalizzare *v/t* ⟨1n⟩ exempt
fiscalizzazione *f* exemption; **~ *degli oneri sociali*** exemption from social security charges
fischiare ⟨1k⟩ **I** *v/t* whistle; **~ *qn*** boo s.o. **II** *v/i di vento* whistle; ***mi fischiavano le orecchie*** my ears were burning
fischiettare *v/t & v/i* ⟨1k⟩ whistle
fischietto *m* whistle
fischio *m* ⟨*pl* -chi⟩ whistle; SPORTS **~ *finale*** final whistle; ***prendere -i per fiaschi*** get hold of the wrong end of the stick
fisco *m* tax authorities *pl*, Inland Revenue, *US* Internal Revenue; ***il*** **~** the taxman
fisiatra *m/f* ⟨*mpl* -i⟩ physiatrics *sg*
fisica *f* physics *sg*; **~ *nucleare*** nuclear physics *sg*
fisicamente *adv* physically
fisico ⟨*mpl* -ci⟩ **I** *adj* physical **II** *m*, **-a** *f* physicist **III** *m* ANAT physique; ***avere un bel*** **~** have a good figure
fisima *f* foible
fisiologia *f* physiology
fisiologicamente *adv* physiologically
fisionomia *f* face; *fig di popolo, città* appearance; (*carattere*) character
fisionomista *m/f* ⟨*mpl* -i⟩ *person with a good memory for faces*
fisioterapia *f* physiotherapy
fisioterapista *m/f* ⟨*mpl* -i⟩ physiotherapist
fissaggio *m* ⟨*pl* -ggi⟩ fastening; PHOT, TEX fixing
fissamente *adv* fixedly
fissare *v/t* ⟨1a⟩ (*fermare*) fix; (*guardare intensamente*) stare at; (*stabilire*) arrange; (*prenotare*) book; **~ *un appuntamento*** arrange an appointment; **~ *una regola*** set a rule; ***hai già fissato la data?*** have you fixed the date?; ***ho fissato un tavolo per le otto*** I've booked a table for eight o'clock
fissarsi *v/r* (*stabilirsi*) settle; (*ostinarsi*) set one's mind (***di*** on); (*avere un'idea fissa*) become obsessed (***di*** with); **~ *in mente*** memorize
fissato I *adj*: ***essere*** **~ *con qn*** / ***qc*** be dead keen on s.o. / sth **II** *m*, **-a** *f* real fan
fissatore *m* (*per capelli*) hair-spray; PHOT fixer
fissazione *f* (*mania*) fixation (***di*** about)
fissione *f* fission; **~ *nucleare*** nuclear fission
fisso I *adj* fixed; *stipendio, cliente* regular; *lavoro* permanent; ***disco*** *m* **~** hard disk; ***avere un posto*** **~** have a permanent job; ***senza -a dimora*** with no fixed address; *fig* ***avere un chiodo*** *m* **~** have a one-track mind **II** *adv* fixedly; ***guardare*** **~ *qn*** / ***qc*** stare at s.o. / sth
fistola *f* MED fistula
fitness *f* ⟨*pl* fitness⟩ fitness; ***centro*** (***di***) **~** *or* **~ *club*** fitness club
fitofarmaco *m* ⟨*pl* -ci⟩ plant protection product
fitoterapia *f* phytotherapy
fitta *f* sharp pain; *fig* ***una*** **~ *al cuore*** a pang in one's heart
fittamente *adv* densely, thickly
fittavolo *m*, **-a** *f* tenant farmer
fittile *adj* fictile; ***vasi*** *mpl* ***-i*** clay pots
fittizio *adj* ⟨*mpl* -zi⟩ fictional; ***ditta*** *f* ***-a*** dummy company; ***nome*** *m* **~** fictitious name
fitto[1] **I** *adj* (*denso*) thick; **~ *di*** full of **II** *adv nevicare, piovere* hard
fitto[2] *m* rent
fiumana *f* deluge (*a. fig*); ***una*** **~ *di persone*** a flood of people; ***una*** **~ *di parole*** a torrent of words
fiume *m* river; *fig* flood, torrent; ***letto*** *m* ***del*** **~** river bed; ***Fiume Azzurro*** Yangtze River; ***Fiume Giallo*** Yellow River
fiutare *v/t* ⟨1a⟩ smell; *cocaina* snort; **~ *un imbroglio*** smell a rat; **~ *un buon affare*** sniff out a bargain
fiuto *m* sense of smell; *fig* nose; ***avere un ottimo*** **~ *per gli affari*** have a nose for a bargain
flaccido *adj* flabby, limp
flacone *m* bottle
flagellante *m* HIST flagellant

flagellare *v/t* ⟨1b⟩ flagellate (*a. fig*)
flagellazione *f* flagellation (*a. fig*)
flagello *m* scourge (*a. fig*)
flagrante *adj* flagrant; ***cogliere qn in ~*** catch s.o. red-handed
flagranza *f* flagrancy; ***in ~ di reato*** in flagrante (delicto)
flambé *adj inv* COOK flambé
flamenco *m* ⟨*pl* -chi⟩ flamenco
flan *m* ⟨*pl* flan⟩ COOK flan
flanella *f* flannel; ***pigiama*** *m* ***di ~*** flannelette pyjamas
flangia *f* ⟨*pl* -ge⟩ flange
flash *m* ⟨*pl* flash⟩ PHOT flash; *stampa* newsflash
flashback *m* ⟨*pl* flashback⟩ flashback
flatulenza *f* flatulence
flautista *m/f* ⟨*mpl* -i⟩ flautist
flauto *m* flute; ***~ dolce*** recorder; ***~ barocco*** Baroque flute; ***~ traverso*** transverse flute
flebile *adj* tremulous
flebilmente *adv* tremulously
flebite *f* phlebitis
flebo *f* → ***fleboclisi***
fleboclisi *f* ⟨*pl* fleboclisi⟩ drip
flegreo *adj* Phlegraean; ***Campi Flegrei*** Phlegraean Fields
flemma *f* calm
flemmatico *adj* ⟨*mpl* -ci⟩ phlegmatic
flessibile *adj* flexible
flessibilità *f* ⟨*pl* flessibilità⟩ flexibility (*a. fig*)
flessione *f* bending; GRAM inflection; (*diminuzione*) dip, (slight) drop; ***fare una ~ in avanti*** bend down; ***~ sulle braccia*** press-up; ***~ dei prezzi*** dip in prices
flessore *adj* flexor; ***muscolo*** *m* ***~*** flexor
flessuosità *f* ⟨*pl* flessuosità⟩ suppleness
flessuoso *adj* supple
flettere *v/t* ⟨3qq⟩ bend; GRAM inflect
flettersi *v/r* bend
flipper *m* ⟨*pl* flipper⟩ pinball machine; ***giocare a ~*** play pinball
flirt *m* ⟨*pl* flirt⟩ flirtation
flirtare *v/i* ⟨1a⟩ flirt
F.lli *abbr* (= **fratelli**) Bros (brothers)
floppy disk *m* ⟨*pl* floppy disk⟩ floppy (disk)
flora *f* flora; ***~ alpina*** alpine flowers; ***~ intestinale*** intestinal flora
floreale *adj* floral; ***omaggio*** *m* ***~*** floral tribute
floricoltore *m*, **-trice** *f* flower grower
floricultura *f* flower-growing industry
floridezza *f* robustness; *dell'aspetto* floridity
florido *adj* flourishing
floscio *adj* ⟨*mpl* -sci⟩ limp; *muscoli* flabby; ***cappello*** *m* ***~*** floppy hat
flotta *f* fleet; ***~ aerea*** air fleet
fluente *adj* flowing; *fig* fluid; ***chioma*** *f* ***~*** flowing locks
fluidità *f* ⟨*pl* fluidità⟩ fluidity (*a. fig*); ***la ~ di uno stile*** the fluency of a style
fluido *m/adj* fluid; ***~ magnetico*** magnetism
fluire *v/i* ⟨4d⟩ *liquidi, gas* flow (*a. fig*); *fig capelli* stream
fluorescente *adj* fluorescent
fluorescenza *f* fluorescence
fluoridrico *adj* ⟨*mpl* -ci⟩: ***acido*** *m* ***~*** hydrofluoric acid
fluorite *f* fluorspar
fluoro *m* fluorine
flusso *m* flow; ***~ e riflusso*** ebb and flow; ***~ del traffico*** traffic flow; ***~ economico*** financial flow; ***~ mestruale*** menstrual flow
flutto *m* LIT surge; *pl*: ***-i*** (*mare*) waves
fluttuante *adj* swirling; FIN floating (*a. fig*)
fluttuare *v/i* ⟨1l⟩ FIN, *fig* fluctuate
fluttuazione *f* fluctuation; ***~ dei prezzi*** price fluctuation
fluviale *adj* river *attr*
f.m. *abbr* (= **fine mese**) end of the month
FMI *abbr* (= **Fondo Monetario Internazionale**) IMF (International Monetary Fund)
FO *abbr* (= **Forlì-Cesena**) Forlì-Cesena
fobia *f* hang-up; PSYCH phobia
fobico *adj* ⟨*mpl* -ci⟩ phobic
foca *f* ⟨*pl* -che⟩ seal; ***~ monaca*** monk seal
focaccia *f* ⟨*pl* -cce⟩ focaccia; (*dolce*) *sweet type of bread*; ***rendere pan per ~*** give tit for tat
focaia *adj*: ***pietra*** *f* ***~*** flint
focale *adj* GEOM, OPT focal; ***punto*** *m* ***~*** focal point (*a. fig*)
focalizzare *v/t* ⟨1a⟩ focus on
focalizzarsi *v/r*: ***~ su qc*** focus on sth
focalizzazione *f* focusing
foce *f* mouth

focolaio *m* ⟨*pl* -ai⟩ *fig* hotbed
focolare *m* hearth; TECH furnace; **~ *domestico*** home life
focomelico I *adj* ⟨*mpl* -ci⟩ phocomelic **II** *m*, **-a** *f* phocomelic person
focosamente *adv* fierily
focoso *adj* fiery
fodera *f interna* lining; *esterna* cover
foderare *v/t* ⟨1l & c⟩ *all'interno* line; *all'esterno* cover
foderato *adj* quilted; (*rivestito*) lined; ***avere gli occhi -i di prosciutto*** go around with one's eyes closed
fodero *m* sheath
foga *f* ⟨*pl* ghe⟩ heat
foggia *f* ⟨*pl* -gge⟩ *di abito, acconciatura* style
foggiano I *adj* from Foggia **II** *m*, **-a** *f* person from Foggia
foggiare *v/t* ⟨1f⟩ mould (*a. fig*)
foglia *f* leaf; ***mangiare la ~*** smell a rat; ***tremare come una ~*** shake like a leaf; **~ *d'oro*** gold leaf
fogliame *m* foliage
foglietto *m* piece of paper; **~ *per appunti*** note paper
foglio *m* ⟨*pl* -gli⟩ sheet; COMPUT **~ *elettronico*** spreadsheet; **~ *rosa*** *provisional driving licence*; **~ *di via obbligatorio*** expulsion order; **~ *di giornale*** newsprint
fogna *f* sewer
fognatura *f* sewers *pl*, sewage pipes *pl*
folaga *f* ⟨*pl* -ghe⟩ ZOOL coot
folata *f* gust
folclore *m* folklore
folcloristico *adj* ⟨*mpl* -ci⟩ folk *attr*; ***balli*** *mpl* ***-ci*** folk dances, country dances
folgorante *adj* dazzling; *fig* striking; ***idea*** *f* **~** brilliant idea; ***bellezza*** *f* **~** dazzling beauty
folgorare *v/t* ⟨1l⟩ *di fulmine, idea* strike; *di corrente elettrica* electrocute; **~ *qn con lo sguardo*** glare at s.o.
folgorato *adj* struck
folgorazione *f* MED electrocution; *fig* brainwave
folgore *f liter* lightning *m*
folklore *m* → ***folclore***
folla *f* crowd; *fig* host
folle[1] *adj* mad
folle[2] *f* AUTO: ***in ~*** in neutral; ***mettere in ~*** AUTO put into neutral
folleggiare *v/i* ⟨1f⟩ live it up
follemente *adv* madly
folletto *m* goblin
follia *f* madness; ***fare una ~*** do something crazy; ***amare alla ~*** be madly in love with; ***fare -e per qn*** be mad about s.o.; ***essere in preda alla ~*** be taken over by madness; **~ *omicida*** homicidal mania
follicolo *m* follicle
follow-up *m* ⟨*pl* follow-up⟩ (*assistenza*) follow-up service; COMM follow-up
foltezza *f* thickness
folto *adj* thick; ***un ~ pubblico*** a wide audience
fomentare *v/t* ⟨1a⟩ fuel; **~ *una rivolta*** stir up a revolt
fon *m* ⟨*pl* fon⟩ hairdryer; ***asciugare i capelli col ~*** dry one's hair (with a hairdryer)
fondaco *m* ⟨*pl* -chi⟩ HIST warehouse
fondale *m* NAUT sea bed; THEAT backcloth, backdrop
fondamentale *adj* fundamental
fondamentalismo *m* fundamentalism
fondamentalista ⟨*mpl* -i⟩ **I** *adj* fundamentalist **II** *m/f* fundamentalist
fondamentalmente *adv* (*nei principi*) fundamentally; (*soprattutto*) basically
fondamento *m* foundation; ***le -a*** *fpl* the foundations; ***senza ~*** unfounded; ***gettare le -a*** lay the foundations
fondare *v/t* ⟨1a⟩ found; **~ *qc su qc*** base sth on sth
fondarsi *v/r* be based (***su*** on)
fondatezza *f* validity
fondato *adj* founded
fondatore *m*, **-trice** *f* founder
fondazione *f* foundation
fondelli *mpl*: ***prendere qn per i ~*** *infml* make fun of s.o., pull s.o.'s leg
fondente *adj*: ***cioccolata ~*** plain / dark chocolate
fondere ⟨3bb⟩ **I** *v/t* (*liquefare*) melt; METAL smelt; *colori* blend; **~ *due società*** merge two companies **II** *v/i* melt
fonderia *f* foundry
fondersi *v/r* melt; FIN merge
fondiario *adj* ⟨*mpl* -ri⟩ land *attr*
fondina *f* holster
fondista *m/f* ⟨*mpl* -i⟩ *nello sci*: cross-country skier; *in atletica*: long-distance runner

fondo I *m* **1.** bottom; **-*i*** *pl* ***di magazzino*** old *or* unsold stock *sg*; **~ *del mare*** seabed; **~ *stradale*** road (bed); ***a* ~** (*profondamente*) in depth; *fig* ***in* ~** basically; ***in* ~ *alla strada* / *al corridoio*** at the end *or* bottom of the road / of the corridor; ***in* ~ *all'armadio*** at the bottom of the cupboard; ***in* ~ *alla pagina*** at the foot of the page; ***andare a* ~** (*affondare*) sink; (*approfondire*) get to the bottom (***di*** of); ***andare fino in* ~** get to the bottom (of sth); ***dare* ~ *a qc*** *soldi* blow sth *infml*; ***essere in* ~ *al treno*** be at the rear of the train; NAUT ***toccare il* ~** touch ground / bottom; *fig* hit rock bottom; **-*i*** *pl* ***di caffè*** coffee grounds **2.** (*sfondo*) background **3.** *terreno* property **4.** FIN fund; **-*i*** *pl* *denaro* funds; FIN **~ *d'ammortamento*** depreciation fund; **~ *comune d'investimento*** FIN investment fund; **~ *pensione*** FIN contributory pension scheme; **-*i*** *pl* ***strutturali*** FIN structural funds; ***a* ~ *perduto*** without security; **-*i*** *pl* ***neri*** FIN slush fund; ***Fondo Monetario Internazionale*** FIN International Monetary Fund **5.** SPORTS long-distance; *sci* cross-country, langlauf **II** *adj* deep

fondoschiena *m* ⟨*pl* fondoschiena⟩ *infml* bottom

fondotinta *m* ⟨*pl* fondotinta⟩ foundation

fondovalle *m* ⟨*pl* fondivalle⟩ valley bottom; ***a*** *or* ***nel* ~** in the bottom of the valley

fonduta *f* cheese fondue

fonema *m* ⟨*pl* -i⟩ phoneme

fonetica *f* phonetics *sg*

fonetico *adj* ⟨*mpl* -ci⟩ phonetic

fonico I *adj* ⟨*mpl* -ci⟩ phonic **II** *n*: ***fonico*** *m* sound engineer

fonoassorbente *adj* acoustic

fonografo *m* phonograph

fonoisolante *adj* soundproof

fonometria *f* phonometry

fontana *f* fountain

fontanella *f* drinking fountain; ANAT fontanelle

fontaniere *m*, **-a** *f* fountain attendant

fonte *m/f* spring; *fig* source; **~ *energetica*** source of energy; ***da* ~ *attendibile*** from a reliable source; **~ *battesimale*** font; **-*i*** *pl* ***del diritto*** source of law

fontina *f* COOK *soft cheese from Valle d'Aosta*

footing *m* ⟨*no pl*⟩ jogging

foraggiare *v/t* ⟨1f⟩ forage; *con bustarelle* bankroll

foraggio *m* ⟨*pl* -ggi⟩ forage

forare *v/t* ⟨1a⟩ *di proiettile* pierce; *con il trapano* drill; *biglietto* punch; *pneumatico* puncture; ***ho forato*** I've got a puncture

foratura *f di pneumatico* puncture

forbici *fpl* scissors *pl*; ***un paio di* ~** a pair of scissors

forbiciata *f* snip

forbicine *fpl*: **~ *da unghie*** nail scissors *pl*

forbito *adj* refined; ***linguaggio*** *m* **~** elegant language

forca *f* (*forcone*) pitchfork; **-*che*** *pl* ***caudine*** *hist* Caudine Forks, *a place between two mountain passes where the Romans suffered a humiliating defeat*; *fig* ***fare* ~** *infml* play truant

forcaiolo *m*, **-a** *f pej* reactionary; *infml* (*scolaro*) truant

forcella *f* TECH fork

forchetta *f* fork; ***essere una buona* ~** have a big appetite; ***in punta di* ~** affectedly

forchettata *f* forkful

forchettone *m* carving fork

forcina *f* hairpin

forcipe *m* forceps *pl*

forcone *m* pitchfork

forellino *m* small hole

forense *adj* forensic; ***pratica*** *f* **~** forensics *sg*

foresta *f* forest; **~ *pluviale*** rain forest

forestale *adj* forest *attr*

foresteria *f* guest accommodation

forestiero I *adj* foreign **II** *m*, **-a** *f* foreigner

forfait *m* ⟨*pl* forfait⟩ lump sum; SPORTS withdrawal; ***a* ~** on a lump-sum basis; ***dichiarare* ~** default; ***vincere per* ~** win by default

forfettario *adj* flat-rate, all in; ***prezzo*** *m* **~** lump sum

forfora *f* dandruff

forgia *f* ⟨*pl* -ge⟩ forge, furnace

forgiare *v/t* ⟨1f⟩ forge; *fig* shape

foriero *adj* foreboding; **~ *di sventura*** ominous

forlivese I *adj* from Forlì **II** *m/f* person from Forlì

forma *f* form; (*sagoma*) shape; TECH (*stampo*) mo(u)ld; ***una ~ di formaggio*** a round of cheese; ***di ~ ovale*** oval-shaped; ***a ~ di cuore/stella*** in the shape of a heart/star, heart-shaped/star-shaped; ***in ~ ufficiale/privata*** officially/privately; ***essere in ~*** be in good form; ***tenersi in ~*** keep fit; ***sotto ~ di*** in the shape of; ***(non) badare alla ~*** disregard convention; ***prendere ~*** take shape
formaggiera *f dish for grated cheese*
formaggino *m* processed cheese
formaggio *m* ⟨*pl* -ggi⟩ cheese; ***~ grattugiato*** grated cheese
formaldeide *f* formaldehyde
formale *adj* formal
formalina *f* formalin
formalismo *m* formalism
formalità *f* ⟨*pl* formalità⟩ formality; ***è una semplice ~*** it's just a formality
formalizzare *v/t* ⟨1a⟩ formalize
formalizzarsi *v/r* take offence
formalmente *adv* formally
formare *v/t* ⟨1a⟩ shape; TEL ***~ il numero*** dial the number; ***essere formato da qn/qc*** *squadra*, *famiglia* be made up of s.o./sth; ***~ una squadra*** make up a team
formarsi *v/r* form; (*svilupparsi*) develop; *di un'idea* take shape
format *m* ⟨*pl* format⟩ TV format
formativo *adj* formative, instructive; ***percorso*** *m* ***~*** educational career
formato *m* size; *di libro* format; ***~ famiglia*** family-size; ***~ tessera*** passport-size; PHOT ***~ verticale/orizzontale*** portrait/landscape
formattare *v/t* ⟨1a⟩ COMPUT format
formattazione *f* COMPUT formatting
formazione *f* formation; *fig addestramento* training; SPORTS line-up; ***~ professionale*** vocational training; ***in (via di) ~*** being trained; ***volo*** *m* ***in ~*** flight in formation
formella *f* ARCH caisson; (*mattonella*) tile; ***soffitto*** *m* ***a -e*** coffered ceiling; ***~ di bronzo*** bronze panel
formica[1] *f* ⟨*pl* -che⟩ ZOOL ant
formica[2]® *f* Formica®
formicaio *m* ⟨*pl* -ai⟩ anthill
formichiere *m* anteater
formicolante *adj* swarming
formicolare *v/i* ⟨1m⟩ *di mano*, *gamba* tingle; *fig* ***~ di*** teem with
formicolio *m sensazione* pins and needles *pl*
formidabile *adj* (*straordinario*) incredible; (*poderoso*) powerful
formina *f* shape (for making sand castles, etc)
formoso *adj* buxom
formula *f* formula; ***~ magica*** (magic) spell; ***Formula Uno*** Formula One
formulare *v/t* ⟨1l⟩ *teoria* formulate; (*esprimere*) express; ***~ una domanda*** phrase a question; ***~ un'ipotesi*** advance/put forward a hypothesis
formulario *m* ⟨*pl* -ri⟩ *modulo* form; ***compilare un ~*** fill in/out a form; ***~ farmaceutico*** drug formulary
formulazione *f* wording, phrasing
fornace *f* furnace; *per ceramiche* kiln
fornaio ⟨*mpl* -ai⟩ **I** *m*, **-a** *f* baker **II** *m negozio* bakery
fornelletto *m* stove; ***~ da campeggio*** camping stove
fornello *m* stove; ***~ elettrico*** electric ring
fornicare *v/i* ⟨1l & d⟩ fornicate
fornicazione *f* fornication
fornire *v/t* ⟨4d⟩ supply (***qc a qn*** s.o. with sth); ***~ informazioni*** give information
fornirsi *v/r* get (***di*** sth), get hold (***di*** of)
fornito *adj*: ***ben ~*** well-stocked
fornitore *m*, **-trice** *f* supplier
fornitura *f* supply
forno *m* **1.** oven; ***~ a legna*** wood-burning oven; ***~ a microonde*** microwave (oven); COOK ***al ~*** *carne*, *patate* roast; *mele*, *pasta* baked **2.** (*panetteria*) bakery
foro[1] *m* (*buco*) hole
foro[2] *m* **1.** *romano* forum **2.** JUR (*tribunale*) (law) court
forse *adv* perhaps, maybe; ***mettere in ~*** cast doubt on
forsennato I *adj* mad **II** *m*, **-a** *f* madman, madwoman (*a. fig*); ***gridare come un ~*** yell like a lunatic
forsythia *f* BOT forsythia
forte I *adj* strong; *suono* loud; *pioggia* heavy; *taglia* large; *somma* considerable, substantial; *dolore* severe; ***la tentazione fu più ~ di me*** temptation got the better of me; *fig* ***pezzo*** *m* ***~*** pièce de résistance; ***piatto*** *m* ***~*** main course; *fig* main item; ***taglie*** *fpl* ***-i*** big sizes **II** *adv* (*con forza*) hard; (*ad alta*

voce) loudly; (*velocemente*) fast **III** *m* (*fortezza*) fort; ***questo è il suo ~*** it's his strong point

fortezza *f* MIL fortress; ***~ d'animo*** strength of character

fortificare *v/t* ⟨1m & d⟩ *rendere più forte* strengthen; MIL fortify

fortificazione *f* fortification

fortilizio *m* ⟨*pl* -zi⟩ fortalice

fortino *m* MIL blockhouse

fortuitamente *adv* by chance

fortuito *adj* chance; ***per un caso ~*** by chance

fortuna *f* fortune; ***atterraggio*** *m* ***di ~*** emergency landing; ***avere ~*** be successful; (*essere fortunato*) be lucky; ***fare ~*** make a fortune; ***perdere una ~ al gioco*** lose a fortune gambling; ***portare ~*** (***a qn***) bring (s.o.) luck; ***buona ~!*** good luck!; ***per ~*** luckily; ***mezzi*** *mpl* ***di ~*** makeshift; ***colpo*** *m* ***di ~*** stroke of luck; ***con alterne -e*** with mixed luck

fortunale *m* tempest

fortunatamente *adv* fortunately

fortunato *adj* lucky, fortunate; ***essere ~ a fare qc*** be lucky to do sth

forum *m* ⟨*pl* forum⟩ forum

foruncolo *m* pimple

forza *f* **1.** strength; (*potenza*) power; *muscolare* force; ***~ di gravità*** force of gravity; ***-e della natura*** forces of nature; ***~ pubblica*** police force; ***~ di volontà*** willpower; ***un vento ~ 8*** a force 8 gale; ***a tutta ~*** at full speed; ***a viva ~*** by force; ***bella ~!*** of course!; ***con tutte le proprie -e*** with all one's might; ***~ e coraggio!*** come on!; ***prova*** *f* ***di ~*** test of strength; ***per cause di ~ maggiore*** because of circumstances beyond my / our control; ***per ~*** against my / our will; ***per ~!*** (*naturalmente*) of course!; ***~!*** come on!; ***farsi ~*** screw up one's courage; ***Forza Italia*** POL *an Italian political party of the centre right* **2.** MIL ***-e*** *pl* (***armate***) armed forces *pl* **3.** ***a ~ di ...*** by dint of ...

forzare *v/t* ⟨1c⟩ force; ***~ qn a fare qc*** force s.o. to do sth; ***~ la mano a qn*** force s.o.'s hand; ***~ la serratura*** force the lock

forzarsi *v/r* ⟨1c⟩: ***~ a fare qc*** force oneself to do sth

forzatamente *adv* unnaturally

forzato I *adj* forced; ***sorriso*** *m* ***~*** unnatural smile; ***alimentazione*** *f* ***-a*** force-feeding; ***lavori*** *mpl* ***-i*** forced labour **II** *n*: ***forzato*** *m* convict; *fig* ***i -i delle vacanze*** *hum* the herds of holidaymakers

forzatura *f fig* cracking

forziere *m* safe

forzista ⟨*mpl* -i⟩ **I** *adj of Forza Italia, the political party* **II** *m/f someone who follows Forza Italia*

forzuto *adj hum* brawny

foschia *f* haze

fosco *adj* ⟨*mpl* -schi⟩ dark; ***dipingere qc a tinte -che*** *fig* paint a bleak picture of sth

fosfato *m* phosphate

fosforeo *adj* phosphorescent

fosforescente *adj* phosphorescent

fosforescenza *f* phosphorescence

fosforo *m* phosphorus

fossa *f* pit, hole; (*tomba*) grave; ***~ comune*** mass grave; ***~ biologica*** septic tank; ***~ oceanica*** deep-sea trench; ***avere un piede nella ~*** have one foot in the grave

fossato *m* ditch; *di fortezza* moat

fossetta *f* dimple

fossile I *adj* fossil *attr* **II** *m* fossil

fossilizzarsi *v/r* fossilize; *fig* stagnate; ***~ su qc*** get stuck in a rut on sth

fossilizzazione *f* fossilization; *fig* ossification

fosso *m* ditch; *fig* ***saltare il ~*** take the plunge

foto *f* ⟨*pl* foto⟩ photo, snap; ***~ ricordo*** souvenir photo; ***~ di gruppo*** group photo; ***scattare una ~*** take a photo

fotoamatore *m*, **-trice** *f* amateur photographer

fotocamera *f* camera; ***~ digitale*** digital camera

fotocellula *f* photocell

fotocopia *f* photocopy

fotocopiare *v/t* ⟨1k & c⟩ photocopy

fotocopiatrice *f* photocopier

fotoelettrico *adj* ⟨*mpl* -ci⟩ photoelectric; *cellula* solar; ***effetto*** *m* ***~*** photoelectric effect

fotoforesi *f* ⟨*pl* fotoforesi⟩ photophoresis

fotogenico *adj* ⟨*mpl* -ci⟩ photogenic

fotografare *v/t* ⟨1m & c⟩ photograph

fotografia *f arte* photography; (*foto*) photograph; ***~ aerea*** aerial photograph; ***~ a colori*** colo(u)r photo-

graph; ~ ***formato tessera*** passport-size photograph; ***fare una*** ~ (***a qn***) take a photograph (of s.o.)
fotografico *adj* ⟨*mpl* -ci⟩ photographic; ***macchina*** *f* ***-a*** camera; ***articoli*** *mpl* ***-ci*** photographic equipment
fotografo *m*, **-a** *f* photographer
fotogramma *m* ⟨*pl* -i⟩ frame
fotolisi *f* ⟨*pl* fotolisi⟩ photolysis
fotolitico ⟨*mpl* -ci⟩ photolytic
fotometria *f* photometry
fotometro *m* photometer
fotomodello *m*, **-a** *f* model
fotomontaggio *m* ⟨*pl* -ggi⟩ photomontage
fotoreporter *m/f* ⟨*pl* fotoreporter⟩ photojournalist
fotoromanzo *m* story told in pictures
fotosafari *f* ⟨*pl* fotosafari⟩ photographic safari
fotosintesi *f* photosynthesis
fototessera *f* passport photo
fottere *v/t* ⟨3a⟩ *vulg* fuck *vulg*, screw *vulg*; (*rovinare*, *imbrogliare*) fuck up, screw up; (*rubare*) rip off; ***fottersene di qn/qc*** *sl* give a fuck/shit about s.o./sth; ***va' a farti ~!*** *vulg* fuck off!, screw you!
fottuto *adj*: ***essere*** ~ *vulg* be screwed; ***fa un freddo*** ~ it's brass monkey weather; ***avere una paura -a*** be scared shitless
foulard *m* ⟨*pl* foulard⟩ scarf
foyer *m* ⟨*pl* foyer⟩ foyer
FR *abbr* (= **Frosinone**) Frosinone
fra[1] *prep* **1.** *tra due*: between; ~ ***di noi*** between you and me; ~ ***Roma e Londra*** between Rome and London; ~ ***sé e sé*** to himself/herself **2.** *tra più di due*: among; ~ ***questi ragazzi*** out of all these boys; ~ ***l'altro*** what's more **3.** (*entro*) in; ~ ***breve*** in a very short time, soon; ~ ***tre giorni*** in three days
fra[2], **frà**, **fra'** *m* brother; ~ ***Giovanni*** Brother John
frac *m* ⟨*pl* frac⟩ tails *pl*
fracassare *v/t* ⟨1a⟩ smash
fracassarsi *v/r* shatter; ~ ***una gamba*** break a leg
fracasso *m di persone* din; *di oggetti che cadono* crash
fracco *m*: ***un ~ di botte*** *infml* a walloping, a good hiding
fradicio *adj* ⟨*mpl* -ci⟩ rotten; (*bagnato*) soaked, soaking wet; ***sudato*** ~ running with sweat; ***ubriaco*** ~ blind drunk *infml*, blotto *infml*
fragile *adj* fragile; *persona* frail, delicate
fragilità *f* ⟨*pl* fragilità⟩ fragility; TECH brittleness; *fig* frailty
fragola *f* strawberry; ***-e*** *pl* ***di bosco*** wild strawberries; ***uva*** *f* ~ strawberry vine
fragolino *m wine made from strawberry vines*
fragore *m* roar; *di tuono* rumble
fragorosamente *adv* loudly
fragoroso *adj* loud; ***risata*** *f* ***-a*** uproarious laughter
fragrante *adj* fragrant
fragranza *f* fragrance
fraintendere *v/t* ⟨3c⟩ misunderstand; ***sono stata fraintesa*** he/she/they misunderstood me
frainteso *past part* → ***fraintendere***
frammentare *v/t* ⟨1a⟩ break up
frammentarietà *f* ⟨*pl* frammentarietà⟩ fragmentariness
frammentario *adj* ⟨*mpl* -ri⟩ fragmentary
frammentarsi *v/r* ⟨1a⟩ split up
frammentazione *f* fragmentation
frammento *m* fragment
frammezzare *v/t* ⟨1b⟩ interpose
frammisto *adj* mixed; ***pioggia*** *f* ***-a a neve*** rain mixed with snow, sleet
frana *f* landslide; ***sei proprio una*** ~ you're really useless
franare *v/i* ⟨1a⟩ collapse
francamente *adv* frankly
francescano **I** *adj* Franciscan **II** *m*, **-a** *f* Franciscan
Francesco *m*: ***San*** ~ St Francis
francese **I** *m/adj* French **II** *m/f* Frenchman; *donna* Frenchwoman; ***i -i*** *pl* the French
franchezza *f* frankness
Franchi *mpl*: ***i*** ~ *hist* the Franks
franchigia *f* FIN exemption; *posta* freepost; ~ ***doganale*** exemption from customs duties
franchising *m* franchising; ***negozio in*** ~ franchised shop
franchisor *m/f* ⟨*pl* franchisor⟩ franchisor
Francia *f* France
franco ⟨*mpl* -chi⟩ **I** *adj* frank; FIN free; ***farla -a*** get away with it; ~ ***domicilio*** free delivery, carriage paid; ~ ***fabbr-***

ica ex-factory; **~ *tiratore*** *politician who votes against his party* **II** *m* FIN franc
francobollo *m* stamp; ***due -i da … euro*** two … euros stamps
francofono *adj* francophone
Francoforte *f* Frankfurt
francone I *adj* Franconian **II** *m/f* Franconian
Franconia *f* Franconia
frangente *m* (*onda*) breaker; (*situazione*) (difficult) situation
frangetta *f* fringe
frangia *f* ⟨*pl* -ge⟩ fringe
frangiflutti *m* ⟨*pl* frangiflutti⟩ breakwater
frangionde *m* ⟨*pl* frangionde⟩ breakwater
frangisole *m* ⟨*pl* frangisole⟩ brise soleil
frangivento *m* ⟨*pl* frangivento⟩ windbreak
franoso *adj* loose; ***terreno*** *m* **~** soft ground
frantoio *m* mill, press
frantumare *v/t* ⟨1a⟩ shatter
frantumarsi *v/r* shatter
frantumazione *f* shattering
frantumi *mpl* splinters *pl*; ***in* ~** in smithereens; ***mandare in* ~** smash to smithereens; ***andare in* ~** smash to smithereens
frappé *m* ⟨*pl* frappé⟩ milkshake
frapporre *v/t* ⟨3ll⟩ put; (*inserire*) interpose; *fig* **~ *ostacoli*** make things difficult
frapporsi *v/r* ⟨3ll⟩ intervene; *fig* arise
frapposizione *f* interposition
frasario *m* ⟨*pl* -ri⟩ language
frasca *f* ⟨*pl* -che⟩ spray; ***saltare di palo in* ~** jump from one subject to another
frase *f* phrase; **~ *fatta*** cliché; **~ *di circostanza*** formality
fraseologia *f* phraseology
fraseologico *adj* ⟨*mpl* -ci⟩ phraseological; ***dizionario*** *m* **~** dictionary of idioms
frassino *m* ash (tree)
frastagliato *adj*: ***costa*** *f* ***-a*** jagged coastline
frastornato *adj* befuddled
frastuono *m* racket
frate *m* REL friar, monk; **~ *cappuccino*** Capuchin; **~ *domenicano*** Dominican
fratellanza *f* brotherhood
fratellastro *m* step-brother; *con legami di consanguineità* half-brother
fratellino *m* little brother
fratello *m* brother; ***-i*** *pl fratello e sorella* brother and sister; ***mio* ~ *gemello*** my twin brother
fraternamente *adv* fraternally
fraternità *f* ⟨*pl* fraternità⟩ fraternity
fraternizzare *v/i* ⟨1a⟩ fraternize; **~ *con qn*** fraternize with s.o.
fraternizzazione *f* fraternization
fraterno *adj* brotherly, fraternal; ***amico*** *m* **~** close friend
fratricida I *adj* fratricidal; ***guerra*** *f* **~** fratricidal war **II** *m/f* ⟨*mpl* -i⟩ fratricide
fratricidio *m* ⟨*pl* -i⟩ fratricide
frattaglie *fpl* COOK offal *sg*; *di pollo* giblets *pl*
frattanto *adv* meanwhile, in the meantime
frattempo *m*: ***nel* ~** meanwhile, in the meantime
frattura *f* fracture
fratturare *v/t* ⟨1a⟩ fracture
fratturarsi *v/r*: **~ *una gamba*** break one's leg
fraudolento *adj* fraudulent
frazionabile *adj* divisible
frazionamento *m* division; POL split; CHEM fractionation
frazionare *v/t* ⟨1a⟩ (*dividere in parti*) break up, split up
frazionarsi *v/r* split (***in*** into)
frazione *f* **1.** fraction; **~ *decimale*** decimal fraction; ***una* ~ *di secondo*** a split second **2.** POL small group **3.** (*borgata*) hamlet
freatico *adj* ⟨*mpl* -ci⟩ phreatic; ***falda*** *f* ***-a*** water table
freccetta *f* dart; (*segno grafico*) small arrow; ***giocare a -e*** play darts
freccia *f* ⟨*pl* -cce⟩ **1.** arrow; ***correre come una* ~** run like the wind **2.** AUTO **~ (*di direzione*)** indicator; ***mettere la* ~** indicate
frecciata *f* (arrow-)shot; *fig* dig, barb
freddamente *adv* coldly; ***accogliere* ~ *qn*** give s.o. a frosty reception
freddare *v/t* ⟨1a⟩ cool; (*uccidere*) mow down; *con occhiata* chill; **~ *l'entusiasmo*** dampen enthusiasm; ***lasciare*** *or* ***far* ~** cool, chill
freddarsi *v/r* get cold

freddezza *f* coldness
freddo **I** *adj* cold; *fig* ***a sangue ~*** in cold blood; ***a mente*** *f* ***-a*** in the light of day; *fig* ***doccia*** *f* ***-a*** bucket of cold water; ***guerra*** *f* ***-a*** cold war **II** *m* cold; ***ho ~*** I'm cold; ***fa ~*** it's cold
freddoloso *adj*: ***essere ~*** feel the cold
freddura *f* pun, play on words
freelance *adj inv* freelance; ***giornalista*** *m* ***~*** freelance journalist
freestyle *m* ⟨*pl* freestyle⟩ freestyle
freezer *m* ⟨*pl* freezer⟩ freezer
fregare *v/t* ⟨1e⟩ rub; *infml* (*imbrogliare*) swindle *infml*; *infml* (*battere*) beat, wipe the floor with *infml*; *infml a un esame* fail; *infml* (*rubare*) pinch *infml*, lift *infml*; ***ti ho fregato!*** I tricked you!
fregarsi *v/r sl*: ***fregarsene di*** give a damn about; ***me ne frego di quello che pensano*** I don't give a damn what they think *infml*
fregata *f* NAUT frigate
fregatura *f infml* (*imbroglio*) rip-off *infml*; (*ostacolo, contrarietà*) pain *infml*; ***prendere una ~*** be swindled
fregiare *v/t* ⟨1f⟩ decorate
fregiarsi *v/r* ⟨1f⟩ adorn oneself; ***~ di qc*** adorn oneself with sth; ***~ di un titolo*** be titled
fregio *m* ARCH frieze
fregola *f fig* (*smania*) *infml* urge
fremere *v/i* ⟨3a⟩ (*tremare*) tremble, quiver; ***~ per l'impazienza*** seethe with impatience; ***~ di rabbia*** shake with anger
frenare *v/t* ⟨1a⟩ AUTO brake; *folla, lacrime, risate* hold back; *entusiasmo, impulso* restrain; ***frena la lingua!*** curb your tongue!
frenarsi *v/r* (*dominarsi*) restrain o.s.
frenata *f* braking; ***fare una ~*** brake; ***segni*** *mpl* ***di ~*** tyre marks; ***brusca ~*** violent braking
frenesia *f* frenzy; ***~ del gioco*** craze for gambling; ***~ degli acquisti*** shopping spree
freneticamente *adv* frantically
frenetico *adj* frantic; ***applausi*** *mpl* ***-ci*** rapturous applause; ***pazzo*** *m* ***~*** frenzied madman; ***attività*** *f* ***-a*** hectic activity
freno *m* AUTO brake; *del cavallo* bit; ***~ d'allarme*** emergency brake; ***~ a mano*** handbrake, *US* parking brake; ***~ a disco*** disc brake; ***~ d'emergenza*** communication cord; ***~ a pedale*** foot-brake; *fig* ***mettere un ~ a qc*** put a check on sth; ***porre ~ a qc*** curb sth; ***tenere a ~ la lingua*** curb one's tongue; *fig* ***senza ~*** without restraint
frenulo *m* fraenum
frequentare *v/t* ⟨1b⟩ *luoghi* frequent; *scuola, corso* attend; *persona* associate with; ***~ cattive compagnie*** get in with a bad crowd
frequentato *adj* popular; *strada* busy
frequentatore *m*, **-trice** *f* frequenter; ***~ abituale*** (***di un locale***) regular
frequente *adj* frequent; ***di ~*** frequently
frequentemente *adv* frequently
frequenza *f* frequency; *scolastica* attendance; ***un'alta ~ di spettatori*** a large audience; ***con ~*** frequently
fresa *f* cutter
fresare *v/t* ⟨1b⟩ mill
fresatore *m*, **-trice** *f* **I** miller **II** *n*: ***fresatrice*** *f* milling machine
fresatura *f* milling
freschezza *f* freshness; *di temperatura* coolness
fresco ⟨*mpl* -chi⟩ **I** *adj* fresh; *temperatura* cool; ***vernice*** *f* ***-a*** wet paint; *fig* ***stai ~ !*** *infml* you're for it! *infml*, you've had it! *infml*; ***essere ~ di studi*** be fresh out of school / university **II** *m* coolness; ***fa ~*** it's cool; ***mettere in ~*** put in a cool place; ***prendere il ~*** take the air; *fig* ***al ~*** *infml* inside *infml*
frescolana *m* ⟨*pl* frescolana⟩ light wool; ***pantaloni*** *mpl* ***in ~*** light wool trousers
frescura *f* cool(ness)
fresia *f* freesia
fretta *f* hurry; ***aver ~*** be in a hurry; ***non c'è ~*** there's no hurry, there's no rush; ***essere*** *or* ***andare di ~*** be in a hurry; ***mettere ~ a qn*** hurry s.o. up; ***fai in ~!*** hurry up!; ***in tutta ~, in ~ e furia*** in great haste
frettolosamente *adv* hastily
frettoloso *adj saluto, sorriso* hurried; *lavoro* rushed; *persona* in a hurry
friabile *adj* crumbly
friabilità *f* ⟨*pl* friabilità⟩ *di biscotto*: crispness; *di roccia* crumbliness
fricassea *f* COOK fricassee
fricchettone *m*, **-a** *f* freak
friggere ⟨3cc⟩ **I** *v/t* fry **II** *v/i* sizzle; ***mandare qn a farsi ~*** tell s.o. to push

off
friggitoria *f shop that sells deep fried fish etc*
friggitrice *f* deep fryer
Frigia *f* Phrygia
frigidità *f* ⟨*pl* frigidità⟩ MED frigidity
frigido *adj* MED frigid
frigio ⟨*mpl* -gi⟩ **I** *adj* Phrygian **II** *m*, **-a** *f* Phrygian
frignare *v/i* ⟨1a⟩ *infml* whimper
frignone *m*, **-a** *f* whiner
frigo *m* fridge
frigobar *m* ⟨*pl* frigobar⟩ mini-bar
frigorifero I *m* refrigerator **II** *adj* cold *attr*; *camion*, *nave*, *vagone* refrigerated; ***cella** f **-a*** freezer compartment
fringe benefit *m* ⟨*pl* fringe benefit⟩ fringe benefit
fringuello *m* chaffinch
frinire *v/i* ⟨4d⟩ chirp
frisbee *m* ⟨*pl* fresbee⟩ frisbee; ***giocare a ~*** play frisbee
Frisia *f* Friesland; ***cavallo** m **di ~*** cheval-de-frise
frittata *f* COOK omelette, *US* omelet; *fig* ***ormai la ~ è fatta*** the damage is done; *fig* ***rivoltare la ~*** *infml* twist an argument
frittella *f* fritter; *fig* (*macchia*) grease stain
fritto I *past part* → ***friggere*** **II** *adj* fried; ***patate** fpl **-e*** chips; ***se ci scoprono siamo -i*** if they catch us, we've had it; *fig* ***aria** f **-a*** hot air; *fig* ***~ e rifritto*** old-hat, clichéed **III** *m* fried food; ***~ misto*** assortment of deep-fried food
frittura *f metodo* frying; ***~ di pesce*** fried fish
friulano I *adj* Friulian **II** *m*, **-a** *f* Friulian
Friuli *m* Friuli
frivolezza *f* frivolity
frivolo *adj* frivolous
frizionare *v/t* ⟨1a⟩ rub
frizionarsi *v/r* ⟨1a⟩ rub oneself down
frizione *f* friction; AUTO clutch
frizzante *adj bevanda* fizzy, sparkling; *aria* crisp; *fig parola*, *motto* biting, sharp; ***vino** m **~*** sparkling wine
frizzantino *m* sparkling white wine
frizzare *v/i* ⟨1a⟩ fizz, sparkle
frocio *m* ⟨*pl* -ci⟩ *pej* fairy, queen
frodare *v/t* ⟨1c⟩ defraud (***di*** of); ***~ il fisco*** evade *or* dodge *infml* tax
frode *f* fraud; ***~ alimentare*** food adulteration
frodo *m*: ***pesca** f / **caccia** f **di ~*** poaching; ***pescare / cacciare di ~*** poach; ***pescatore** m / **cacciatore** m **di ~*** poacher; ***merce** f **di ~*** smuggled goods *pl*
frogia *f* ⟨*pl* -ge⟩ nostril
frollare *v/t* ⟨1c⟩ hang
frollino *m* shortbread
fronda[1] *f* frond
fronda[2] *f* HIST Fronde; POL revolt
frondoso *adj* leafy
frontale *adj* frontal; ***scontro** m **~*** head-on collision
frontalmente *adv* head on; ***si sono scontrati ~*** they met head on
fronte I *f* forehead; ***a ~ alta*** with a high forehead; ***di ~ a*** (*dirimpetto*) opposite, facing; *in presenza di* before; *a confronto di* compared to *or* with; ***la casa, vista dal di ~*** the house, seen from the front; ***ti si legge in ~*** it's written all over your face **II** *m* front; ***~ caldo*** warm front; ***far ~ agli impegni*** face up to one's responsibilities; ***far ~ alle spese*** make ends meet
fronteggiare *v/t* ⟨1f⟩ (*stare di fronte a*) face; (*far fronte a*) face, confront
frontespizio *m* ⟨*pl* -zi⟩ title page; ARCH frontispiece
frontiera *f* border, frontier; ***alla ~*** at the border; ***guardia** f **di ~*** border guard; ***valico** m **di ~*** border crossing
frontone *m* ARCH pediment
fronzolo *m* frill
frotta *f* swarm; ***a -e*** in droves
frottola *f infml* fib *infml*
frugale *adj* frugal
frugalità *f* ⟨*pl* frugalità⟩ frugality
frugare ⟨1e⟩ **I** *v/i* (*rovistare*) rummage **II** *v/t* (*cercare con cura*) search, rummage through
frugoletto *m*, **-a** *f* kid
fruibile *adj* usable
fruire *v/i* ⟨4d⟩: ***~ di qc*** benefit from sth
fruitore *m*, **-trice** *f* ADMIN beneficiary; *di un prodotto altrui* consumer, user
fruizione *f* ADMIN enjoyment; (*uso*) use
frullare *v/t* ⟨1a⟩ COOK blend, liquidize; *uova* whisk; ***ma che ti frulla in testa?*** what on earth are you thinking of?
frullato *m* milk-shake
frullatore *m* liquidizer, blender
frullino *m* whisk

frumento *m* wheat
frusciare *v/i* ⟨1f⟩ rustle
fruscio *m* rustle
frusinate **I** *adj* from Frosinone **II** *m/f* person from Frosinone
frusta *f* whip; COOK whisk
frustare *v/t* ⟨1a⟩ whip
frustata *f* lash (*a. fig*)
frustino *m* riding crop
frusto *adj* worn-out; *fig* tired; ***argomento*** *m* **~** hackneyed argument
frustrante *adj* frustrating
frustrare *v/t* ⟨1a⟩ frustrate
frustrato *adj* frustrated
frustrazione *f* frustration
frutta *f* fruit; **~ *candita*** candied fruit; **~ *fresca*** fresh fruit; **~ *secca*** nuts *pl*; *fig* ***ormai siamo alla* ~** we've reached the end
fruttare ⟨1a⟩ **I** *v/t* yield **II** *v/i* fruit; ***far* ~ *il capitale*** make one's capital grow; **~ *bene*** be very productive
fruttato *adj vino* flowery, fruity
frutteto *m* orchard
frutticoltore *m*, **-trice** *f* fruit grower
frutticoltura *f* fruit farming
fruttiera *f* fruit bowl
fruttifero *adj* fruitful; FIN interest-bearing
fruttivendolo *m*, **-a** *f* greengrocer
frutto *m* fruit; ***-i*** *pl* ***di bosco*** soft fruit; ***-i*** *pl* ***di mare*** seafood *sg*; ***è* ~ *della tua immaginazione*** it's a figment of your imagination; ***i -i del proprio lavoro*** the fruits of one's labours; ***mettere a* ~** put to good use; ***cogliere il* ~ *quando è maturo*** wait until the right moment
fruttosio *m* ⟨*pl* -si⟩ fructose
fruttuoso *adj* profitable
FS *abbr* (= **Ferrovie dello Stato**) *Italian State railways*
f.to *abbr* (= **firmato**) sgd (signed)
fu → ***essere***
fucilare *v/t* ⟨1a⟩ shoot
fucilata *f* shot
fucilazione *f* fusillade
fucile *m* rifle; **~ *subacqueo*** speargun; **~ *da caccia*** shotgun
fucina *f* forge; breeding ground (*a. fig*)
fuco *m* ⟨*pl* -chi⟩ ZOOL drone; BOT kelp
fucsia *m/adj inv* fuchsia
fuga *f* ⟨*pl* -ghe⟩ **1.** escape; FIN **~ *di capitali*** flight of capital; **~ *di gas*** gas leak; **~ *di notizie*** leak; **~ *di cervelli*** brain drain; ***darsi alla* ~** take flight; ***mettere in* ~ *qn*** put s.o. to flight **2.** MUS fugue
fugace *adj* fleeting
fugacemente *adv* fleetingly
fugacità *f* ⟨*pl* fugacità⟩ transience
fugare *v/t* ⟨1e⟩ drive away; **~ *i dubbi*** dispel any doubts
fuggente *adj* elusive; ***l'attimo*** *m* **~** a fleeting minute
fuggevole *adj* fleeting
fuggevolezza *f* transience
fuggiasco *m*, **-a** *f* ⟨*mpl* -schi⟩ fugitive
fuggifuggi *m* ⟨*pl* fuggifuggi⟩ stampede
fuggire *v/i* ⟨4a⟩ flee; **~ *di casa*** run away from home
fuggitivo *m*, **-a** *f* fugitive
fulcro *m* fulcrum; ***il* ~ *della questione*** the nub of the matter
fulgido *adj* brilliant (*a. fig*)
fulgore *m* brilliance (*a. fig*)
fuliggine *f* soot
fuligginoso *adj* sooty
fulminante *adj sguardo* withering; *malattia* which strikes suddenly
fulminare *v/t* ⟨1l⟩ *di sguardo* look daggers at, glare at; ***rimanere fulminato*** *da fulmine* be struck by lightning; *da elettricità* be electrocuted; *fig* be thunderstruck
fulminarsi *v/r di lampadina* blow
fulminato *adj* ELEC *lampadina* burnt out
fulmine *m* lightning; ***come un* ~ *a ciel sereno*** like a bolt out of the blue; *fig* ***colpo*** *m* ***di* ~** love at first sight
fulmineo *adj* fast, rapid
fulvo *adj* tawny
fumaiolo *m* NAUT funnel; RAIL chimney; *di casa* chimney pot
fumante *adj* smoking; ***rovine*** *fpl* ***-i*** smoking ruins
fumare *v/i* ⟨1a⟩ smoke; ***vietato* ~** no smoking
fumario *adj*: ***canna*** *f* ***-a*** flue
fumarola *f* GEOL fumarole
fumata *f*: ***farsi una* ~** have a smoke; **~ *bianca / nera*** *a white / black smoke signal that indicates whether a new Pope has been elected*
fumatore *m*, **-trice** *f* smoker; RAIL ***scompartimento*** *m* ***per -i / non -i*** smoking / non-smoking compartment
fumettista *m/f* ⟨*mpl* -i⟩ cartoonist

fumetto *m* comic strip; **-i** *pl per ragazzi* comics
fumo *m* smoke; (*vapore*) steam; **~ passivo** passive smoking; *fig* **andare in ~** (*fallire*) go up in smoke; (*svanire*) come to nothing; **mandare in ~** shatter; **tanto ~ e poco arrosto** it's all just hot air; **essere come il ~ negli occhi (per qn)** be like a red rag to a bull; **vendere ~** be a phoney
fumogeno *adj* smoke; **candelotto** *m* **~** smoke candle
fumoso *adj* smoky; *fig* (*oscuro*) muddled
funambolismo *m* tightrope walking (*a. fig*)
funambolo *m*, **-a** *f* tightrope walker (*a. fig*)
fune *f* rope; (*cavo*) cable; **tiro** *m* **alla ~** tug-of-war
funebre *adj* funeral *attr*; *fig* gloomy, funereal; **carro** *m* **~** hearse
funerale *m* funeral
funerario *adj* ⟨*mpl* -ri⟩ funerary, funeral; **iscrizione** *f* **-a** *inscription on a tomb*
funereo *adj* funereal
funesto *adj* fatal; **conseguenze** *fpl* **-e** dire consequences
fungere *v/i* ⟨3d⟩ act (**da** as)
funghicoltura *f* mushroom growing
fungicida *m* ⟨*pl* -i⟩ fungicide
fungo *m* ⟨*pl* -ghi⟩ mushroom; MED fungus; **~ velenoso** poisonous mushroom; **~ prataiolo** field mushroom; **andare a cercar -ghi** go mushroom picking
funicella *f* string
funicolare *f* funicular railway
funivia *f* cableway
funzionale *adj* functional (*a.* MED)
funzionalità *f* ⟨*pl* funzionalità⟩ functionality (*a.* MED)
funzionamento *m* operation, functioning
funzionante *adj* in working order
funzionare *v/i* ⟨1a⟩ operate, function; **non ~** be out of order; *di orologio* have stopped
funzionario *m*, **-a** *f* ⟨*mpl* -ri⟩ official, civil servant
funzione *f* function; (*carica*) office; REL service, ceremony; **mettere in ~** put into operation; **in ~ di …** depending on; **variare in ~ di …** vary with …; **vivere in ~ dei figli** live for one's children
fuoco *m* ⟨*pl* -chi⟩ **1.** fire; **-chi d'artificio** fireworks *pl*; **dar ~ a qc** set fire to sth; MIL **aprire / cessare il ~** open / cease fire; MIL **far ~** (open) fire; **~ amico** MIL friendly fire; **prendere ~** catch fire; **fare ~ e fiamme** breathe fire; **mettere a ferro e ~** put to fire and sword; **mettere la mano sul ~ per qn / qc** bet on s.o. / sth **2.** PHYS, PHOT focus; **mettere a ~** focus
fuorché *cj* except
fuori **I** *prep stato* outside, out of; *moto* out of, away from; **~ di casa** outside the house; **~ città** out of town; **~ luogo** out of place; **~ mano** out of the way; **~ di sé** beside o.s.; **~ uso** out of use; **al di ~ di** except for; **~ commercio** not for sale; *libro* out of print; **~ concorso** ineligible to compete; **fuor di misura** beyond measure; **~ servizio** *persona* off duty; *apparecchio* out of order **II** *adv* **1.** outside; *all'aperto* out of doors; **di ~** outside; **~!** out!; **~ dai piedi!** *infml* out of my way! **2.** SPORTS out **3. fare ~ qn** do s.o. in
fuoribordo *m* ⟨*pl* fuoribordo⟩ motorboat; *motore* outboard motor
fuoriclasse *m/f & adj* ⟨*pl* fuoriclasse⟩ champion
fuorigioco *m* ⟨*pl* fuorigioco⟩ offside; **essere nel ~** be offside
fuoriserie **I** *adj* made to order, custom made **II** *f* ⟨*pl* fuoriserie⟩ AUTO custom-built model
fuoristrada *m* ⟨*pl* fuoristrada⟩ off--road vehicle
fuoriuscita *f di gas* leakage, escape
fuoruscito *m*, **-a** *f* exile
fuorviare ⟨1h⟩ **I** *v/i* go astray **II** *v/t* lead astray
furbacchione **I** *adj* sly **II** *m*, **-a** *f* rogue
furbastro **I** *adj* sly **II** *m*, **-a** *f* weasel
furbizia *f* cunning
furbo *adj* cunning, crafty; **fare il ~** be clever
furente *adj*: **~ d'ira** furiously angry
furetto *m* ZOOL ferret; *fig curious person*
furfante *m* rascal, rogue
furfantello *m*, **-a** *f* urchin
furfanteria *f* roguery
furgoncino *m* (small) van
furgone *m* van

furia *f* fury, rage; ***a ~ di …*** by dint of …; ***a ~ d'insistere mi ha convinto*** he insisted so much that he convinced me; ***andare*** *or* ***montare su tutte le -e*** hit the roof; ***si comporta come una ~*** she behaves like a madwoman
furibondo *adj* furious, livid
furiere *m* MIL quartermaster
furiosamente *adv* furiously
furioso *adj* furious; *vento, lotta* violent; ***essere ~ con*** *or* ***contro qn*** be furious with s.o.; ***un ~ temporale*** a violent storm
furore *m* fury, rage; ***far ~*** be all the rage
furoreggiare *v/i* ⟨1f⟩ be all the rage
furtivamente *adv* furtively
furtivo *adj* furtive
furto *m* theft; ***~ con scasso*** burglary; ***~ con destrezza*** pickpocketing; ***commettere un ~*** do a burglary / robbery
fusa *fpl*: ***fare le ~*** purr
fuscello *m* twig; *fig* ***essere un ~*** be stick thin
fusciacca *f* ⟨*pl* -cche⟩ sash
fuseaux *mpl* leggings *pl*
fusibile *m* ELEC fuse
fusione *f* fusion; FIN merger; ***~ nucleare*** nuclear fusion; ***punto*** *m* ***di ~*** melting point
fuso[1] *past part* → ***fondere***; METAL molten; *burro* melted
fuso[2] *m* spindle; ***~ orario*** time zone; ***dritto come un ~*** straight as an arrow
fusoliera *f* fuselage
fustagno *m* fustian
fustella *f* punch
fustellare *v/t* ⟨1b⟩ punch out
fustellatrice *f* punch
fustigare *v/t* ⟨1l & e⟩ flog; *fig* lambast
fustigatore *m*, **-trice** *f* flogger
fustigazione *f* flogging; *fig* lambasting
fustino *m* drum
fusto *m* (*tronco*) trunk; (*stelo*) stem, stalk; *di metallo* drum; *di legno* barrel
futile *adj* futile
futilità *f* futility
futurismo *m* futurism
futurista ⟨*mpl* -i⟩ **I** *m/f* futurist **II** *adj* futurist
futuristico *adj* futuristic
futuro *m/adj* future; ***in ~*** in future; ***in un lontano / prossimo ~*** in the distant / near future

G

g, G *m/f* ⟨*pl* g, G⟩ g, G
g *abbr* (= **grammo**) g (gram)
gabardine *f* ⟨*pl* gabardine⟩ gaberdine
gabbana *f* overcoat; ***voltare ~*** be a turncoat
gabbare *v/t* ⟨1a⟩ cheat
gabbia *f* cage; *fig* ***~ di matti*** madhouse; ***~ toracica*** rib cage; ***sentirsi in ~*** feel hemmed in; ***vivere in una ~ dorata*** live in a gilded cage; ***è una ~ di matti!*** it's a madhouse!; ***~ degli imputati*** dock; ***~ dell'ascensore*** lift car; ***finire in ~*** *infml* end up in prison
gabbiano *m* (sea)gull
gabinetto *m* toilet; POL cabinet; ***~ medico / dentistico*** doctor's / dentist's surgery; POL ***~ ombra*** shadow cabinet; ***~ alla turca*** Turkish toilet
Gabon *m* Gabon
gabonese **I** *adj* Gabonese **II** *m/f* Gabonese
Gabriele *m*: ***San ~*** St Gabriel
gaditano **I** *adj* from Cadiz **II** *m*, **-a** *f* person from Cadiz
gaelico *m* Gaelic
gaffe *f* blunder, gaffe
gagà *m* ⟨*pl* gagà⟩ *infml* dandy
gagliardetto *m* pennant
gagliardo *adj* strong; *fig* lively
gaglioffo *m*, **-a** *f* (*cialtrone*) slob; (*furfante*) scoundrel
gaiamente *adv* gaily
gaiezza *f* gaiety
gala *f* (*ricevimento*) gala; ***serata*** *f* ***di ~*** gala evening
galante *adj* gallant; ***avventura*** *f* ***~*** love affair; ***fare il ~*** play the ladies' man
galanteria *f* gallantry
galantina *f* COOK galantine; ***~ di pollo***

chicken galantine
galantuomo *m* ⟨*pl* -uomini⟩ gentleman
galassia *f* galaxy
galateo *m libro* book of etiquette; *comportamento* etiquette, (good) manners *pl*
galattico *adj* ⟨*mpl* -ci⟩ galactic
galea *f hist* galley
galeone *m hist* galleon
galeotto *m*, **-a** *f* convict; HIST galley slave
galera *f* (*prigione*) jail, prison
Galilea *f* Galilee
Galizia *f* Galicia
galiziano **I** *adj* Galician **II** *m*, **-a** *f* Galician
galla *f* BOT gall; ***a ~*** afloat; ***venire a ~*** (come to the) surface; *fig* come to light; ***tenersi a ~*** stay *or* keep afloat
galleggiamento *m* floating; ***linea*** *f* ***di ~*** water line
galleggiante **I** *adj* floating **II** *m* (*boa*) buoy
galleggiare *v/i* ⟨1f⟩ float
gallego **I** *adj* Galician **II** *n* Galician; ***gallego*** *m* (*lingua*) Galician
galleria *f* gallery; *passaggio con negozi* (shopping) arcade; RAIL, MINER tunnel; THEAT circle
gallerista *m/f* ⟨*mpl* -i⟩ art gallery owner
Galles *m* Wales
gallese **I** *m/adj* Welsh **II** *m/f* Welshman; *donna* Welshwoman
galletta *f* NAUT ship's biscuit
galletto *m* cockerel; *fig* ladies' man; ***fare il ~*** flirt with everybody
gallico *adj* ⟨*mpl* -ci⟩ Gallic, Gaulish
gallina *f* hen; ***zampe*** *fpl* ***di ~*** crows' feet; ***~ vecchia fa buon brodo*** *prov* good broth can be made in an old pot; ***~ dalle uova d'oro*** golden goose
gallinaccio *m* ⟨*pl* -cci⟩ (*fungo*) chanterelle
gallo[1] *m* cock; SPORTS ***peso*** *m* ***~*** bantam weight; ***~ cedrone*** capercaillie
gallo[2] **I** *adj* Gaulish **II** *m*, **-a** *f* Gaul; ***i Galli*** the Gauls
gallone *m* MIL stripe; *unità di misura* gallon
gallurese **I** *adj* from Gallura **II** *m/f* person from Gallura
galoppare *v/i* ⟨1c⟩ gallop
galoppata *f* gallop; *in gara* sprint; *fig* race against time
galoppatoio *m* ⟨*pl* -oi⟩ gallop
galoppino *m*, **-a** *f infml* gofer; ***~ elettorale*** canvasser
galoppo *m* gallop; ***al ~*** at a gallop
galvanico *adj* ⟨*mpl* -ci⟩ galvanic
galvanizzare *v/t* ⟨1a⟩ MED, TECH galvanize (*a. fig*)
galvanizzazione *f* MED, TECH galvanization
galvanometro *m* galvanometer
gamba *f* leg; *fig* ***in ~*** (*capace*) smart, bright; (*in buona salute*) healthy, (fighting) fit; *persona anziana* spry, sprightly; ***darsela a -e*** take to one's heels; ***è un tipo in ~*** he's on the ball; ***-e in spalla!*** run!; ***a mezza ~*** SEW half-length; ***finire a -e all'aria*** be sent flying; ***prendere qc sotto ~*** underestimate sth; ***scappare a -e levate*** make a run for it
gambale *m* legging
gambaletto *m* pop sock
gamberetto *m* shrimp
gambero *m* prawn; ***rosso come un ~*** as red as a lobster; *fig* ***fare come i -i*** go backwards
gambizzare *v/t* ⟨1a⟩ *infml*: ***~ qn*** kneecap s.o.
gambo *m di fiore, bicchiere* stem; *di pianta, fungo* stalk
gamma[1] *f* range; MUS scale; ***una vasta ~ di prodotti*** a huge range of products
gamma[2] **I** *m/f* ⟨*pl* gamma⟩ gamma **II** *adj inv* gamma; ***raggi ~*** gamma rays
ganascia *f* ⟨*pl* -sce⟩ jaw; MECH clamp
gancio *m* ⟨*pl* -ci⟩ hook; ***~ di traino*** tow-hook
Gange *m* Ganges
ganghero *m* pivot; ***uscire dai -i*** blow one's top
ganglio *m* ⟨*pl* -i⟩ ANAT ganglion
gangsterismo *m* gangsterism
ganzo **I** *adj infml* cool; ***un tipo ~*** a cool dude **II** *m*, **-a** *f infml* cool customer
gap *m* ⟨*pl* gap⟩ gap
gara *f* competition; *di velocità* race; ***~ automobilistica*** car race; ***~ eliminatoria*** heat; ***fare a ~*** compete
garage *m* ⟨*pl* garage⟩ garage; ***~ sotterraneo*** underground car park (*US* parking garage)
garagista *m* ⟨*pl* -i⟩ (*custode*) garage attendant; (*meccanico*) mechanic

garante *m* guarantor
garantire ⟨4d⟩ **I** *v/t* guarantee; (*assicurare*) ensure **II** *v/i* (*farsi garante*) stand guarantor (***per*** for); ***garantisco io per lui*** I'll stand surety for him
garantito *adj* guaranteed
garanzia *f* guarantee; ***essere in ~*** be under guarantee; ***periodo*** *m* ***di ~*** guarantee period; JUR notification period; ***avviso*** *m* ***di ~*** JUR notification
garbare *v/i* ⟨1a⟩ *reg*: ***qc garba a qn*** s.o. likes sth
garbato *adj* courteous, polite
garbo *m* courtesy, politeness; (*modi gentili*) good manners *pl*; (*tatto*) tact
Garda: ***Lago*** *m* ***di ~*** Lake Garda
gardenese I *adj* from the Val Gardena **II** *m/f* person from the Val Gardena
gardenia *f* gardenia
gardesano I *adj* from Lake Garda **II** *m*, **-a** *f* person from Lake Garda
gareggiare *v/i* ⟨1f⟩ compete
garganella *f*: ***bere a ~*** *drink from a bottle without touching it with one's lips*
gargarismo *m* gargle; (*collutorio*) mouthwash; ***fare i -i*** gargle
gargarozzo *m infml* gullet
garitta *f* sentry-box
garofano *m* carnation; COOK ***chiodi*** *mpl* ***di ~*** cloves
garrese *m* ZOOL withers *pl*
garretto *m* ZOOL hock; *infml umano* (back of the) heel
garrire *v/i* ⟨4d⟩ shriek
garrito *m* shriek
garrulo *adj liter* garrulous
garza *f* gauze
garzone *m* boy
gas *m* ⟨*pl* gas⟩ gas; ***~ asfissiante*** poison gas; ***~ lacrimogeno*** tear gas; ***~ naturale*** natural gas; ***~ di scarico*** exhaust (fumes *pl*); ***a ~*** gas *attr*; AUTO ***dare ~*** accelerate; ***a tutto ~*** with one's foot down, at full speed
gasare *v/t* ⟨1a⟩ → ***gassare***; *fig infml* hype up
gasarsi *v/r* ⟨1a⟩ *infml* get hyped up
gasato I *adj bibita* fizzy; (*eccitato*) excited **II** *m*, **-a** *f* bighead
gasolio *m per riscaldamento* oil; AUTO diesel fuel
gassare *v/t* ⟨1a⟩ *bibita* carbonate; *persona* gas
gassato *adj bibita* carbonated; *persona* gassed; ***acqua*** *f* ***-a*** sparkling water
gassosa *f* → ***gazzosa***
gassoso *adj* gaseous
gastrico *adj* ⟨*mpl* -ci⟩ gastric; ***succhi*** *mpl* ***-ci*** digestive juices
gastrite *f* gastritis
gastronomia *f* gastronomy
gastronomico *adj* ⟨*mpl* -ci⟩ gastronomic; ***specialità*** *fpl* ***-che*** gastronomic specialities
gastronomo *m*, **-a** *f* gastronome
gastropatia *f* gastropathy
gastroscopia *f* gastroscopy
gatta *f* (female) cat; ***qui ~ ci cova*** there's something going on here; ***avere una bella ~ da pelare*** have a hard job to do
gattabuia *f hum* clink, slammer
gattamorta *f*: ***fare la ~*** *infml* act dumb
gattino *m* kitten
gatto *m* cat; *maschio* (tom) cat; ***~ d'angora*** Angora cat; ***~ randagio*** stray cat; ***~ siamese*** Siamese cat; ***~ soriano*** tabby (cat); ***c'erano quattro -i*** there was hardly anybody there; ***~ delle nevi*** snowcat
gattonare *v/i* ⟨1a⟩ crawl
gattoni *adv*: ***andare ~*** crawl
gattopardo *m* serval
gaudente I *adj* pleasure-seeking **II** *m* pleasure-seeker
gaudio *m* ⟨*pl* -i⟩ joy; ***mal comune mezzo ~*** a trouble shared is a trouble halved
gavetta *f* MIL mess tin; ***fare la ~*** come up through the ranks
gay *m/adj* gay
gazza *f*: ***~*** (***ladra***) magpie
gazzarra *f* racket
gazzella *f* gazelle
gazzetta *f* gazette; ***~ ufficiale*** official journal, gazette
gazzosa *f* lemonade
GB *abbr* (= **Gran Bretagna**) GB (Great Britain)
G.d.F. *abbr* (= **Guardia di Finanza**) *Customs and Excise*
GE *abbr* (= **Genova**) Genoa
geiger *m* ⟨*pl* geiger⟩: ***contatore*** *m* ***~*** Geiger counter
gel *m* ⟨*pl* gel⟩ gel
gelare *v/t & v/i* ⟨1b⟩ freeze
gelarsi *v/r* ⟨1b⟩ freeze; ***qui si gela*** it's freezing in here; ***mi si è gelato il sangue*** my blood ran cold

gelata *f* frost
gelataio *m*, **-a** *f* ice-cream seller
gelateria *f* ice-cream parlo(u)r
gelatina *f* gelatine; **~ *di frutta*** fruit jelly
gelatinoso *adj* gelatinous
gelato I *m* ice cream; **~ *alla fragola*** strawberry ice cream; **~ *sfuso*** loose ice cream; **~ *alla vaniglia*** vanilla ice cream **II** *adj* frozen
gelidamente *adv* frostily
gelido *adj* freezing
gelo *m* (*brina*) frost; *fig* chill; ***di* ~** chilly
gelone *m* chilblain
gelosamente *adv* jealously; ***custodire* ~ *qc*** guard sth closely
gelosia *f* jealousy
geloso *adj* jealous (***di*** of)
gelso *m* mulberry (tree)
gelsomino *m* jasmine
gemellaggio *m* twinning
gemellato *adj* twinned
gemello I *adj* twin; ***mia sorella*** *f* **-a** my twin sister; ***letti*** *mpl* **-i** twin beds *pl* **II** *m di camicia* cuff link **III** *m*, **-a** *f* **1.** twin; ***ha avuto tre*/*quattro* -i** she had triplets/quads **2.** ASTROL ***Gemelli*** *pl* Gemini; ***sono dei Gemelli*** I'm (a) Gemini
gemere *v/i* ⟨3a⟩ groan
gemito *m* groan
gemma *f* (*pietra preziosa*) gem, jewel; BOT bud; *fig* gem
gendarme *m* policeman; *fig* (*donna energica*) battle-axe
gendarmeria *f* police force
gene *m* BIOL gene
genealogia *f* genealogy
genealogico *adj* ⟨*mpl* -ci⟩ genealogical; ***albero*** *m* **~** family tree
generale I *adj* general; ***in* ~** in general; THEAT ***prova*** *f* **~** dress rehearsal **II** *m* MIL general
generalità *f* ⟨*pl* generalità⟩ general nature; ***le* ~** *pl* personal details
generalizzare *v/t* ⟨1a⟩ generalize
generalizzazione *f* generalization
generalmente *adv* generally
generare *v/t* ⟨1l & b⟩ (*dar vita a*) give birth to; (*causare*) generate, create; *sospetti* arouse; *elettricità*, *calore* generate
generatore *m* ELEC generator
generazionale *adj* generational; ***conflitto*** *m* **~** conflict between the generations
generazione *f* generation; ***di* ~ *in* ~** from generation to generation
genere *m* **1.** (*tipo*, *specie*) kind; BIOL genus; **~ *umano*** mankind, humanity; ***in* ~** generally; ***unico nel suo* ~** unique; ***di cattivo* ~** bad; ***non è il mio* ~** he's not my type **2.** GRAM gender **3.** LIT, FILM genre **4. -i** *pl* ***alimentari*** foodstuffs; **-i** *pl* ***di consumo*** consumer goods; **-i** *pl* ***di lusso*** luxury goods
genericamente *adv* generically
generico *adj* ⟨*mpl* -ci⟩ generic; ***medico*** *m* **~** GP, general practitioner; ***rimanere sul* ~** stick to generalities
genero *m* son-in-law
generosamente *adv* generously
generosità *f* generosity
generoso *adj* generous (***con*** to)
genesi *f* genesis
Genesi *f* Genesis
genetica *f* genetics *sg*
geneticamente *adv*: **~ *modificato*** genetically modified
genetico *adj* ⟨*mpl* -ci⟩ genetic; ***ingegneria*** *f* **-a** genetic engineering
genetliaco *m* ⟨*pl* -ci⟩ *form* birthday; ***celebrare il* ~ *di qn*** celebrate s.o.'s birthday
gengiva *f* gum
gengivite *f* gingevitis
geniale *adj* ingenious; *idea* brilliant
genialità *f* genius; (*ingegnosità*) ingeniousness
genialmente *adv* brilliantly
genico *adj* ⟨*mpl* -ci⟩ gene *attr*; ***mutazione*** *f* **-a** gene mutation
geniere *m* sapper
genio[1] *m* ⟨*pl* -ni⟩ genius; (*inclinazione*) talent; ***andare a* ~** be to one's liking; ***lampo*** *m* ***di* ~** brainwave; ***il* ~ *della lampada*** the genie of the lamp; **~ *militare*/*civile*** Engineers/civil engineers *pl*; ***sei un* ~!** you're a genius!; **~ *incompreso*** misunderstood genius
genio[2] *m*: **~ *civile*** civil engineers *pl*
genitali *mpl* genitals *pl*
genitivo *m* genitive; **~ *sassone*** possessive (case)
genitori *mpl* parents *pl*
genitoriale *adj* parental; ***responsabilità*** *f* **~** parental responsibility
gennaio *m* January

genocidio *m* genocide
genoma *m* BIOL genome
Genova *f* Genoa
genovese *m/adj* Genoese
gentaglia *f* scum
gente *f* people *pl*; ***quanta ~ !*** what a crowd!; ***~ bene*** *iron* upper-crust; ***domani ho ~ a cena*** I've got people coming to dinner tomorrow; ***la ~ comune*** common people; ***c'è troppa ~*** it's too crowded
gentildonna *f* gentlewoman
gentile *adj* kind; *nelle lettere* ***~ signora*** Dear Madam; ***è stato davvero ~ ad accompagnarmi*** it was really kind of you to come with me
gentilezza *f* kindness; ***fare una ~ a qn*** do s.o. a favo(u)r; ***per ~*** please
gentilissimo *adj*: *nelle lettere* Dear
gentilizio *adj* ⟨*mpl* -i⟩ noble; ***stemma*** *m* ***~*** coat of arms
gentilmente *adv* kindly
gentiluomo *m* ⟨*pl* -uomini⟩ gentleman
genuflessione *f* genuflection
genuflettersi *v/r* ⟨3qq⟩ genuflect
genuinità *f* ⟨*pl* genuinità⟩ genuineness
genuino *adj* genuine; *prodotto alimentare* traditionally made; *risata* spontaneous
genziana *f* gentian
geodesia *f* geodesy
geofisica *f* ⟨*pl* -che⟩ geophysics *sg*
geografia *f* geography; ***~ economica*** economic geography
geograficamente *adv* geographically
geografico *adj* ⟨*mpl* -ci⟩ geographic; ***carta*** *f* ***-a*** map
geografo *m*, **-a** *f* geographer
geologia *f* geology
geologicamente *adv* geologically
geologico *adj* ⟨*mpl* -ci⟩ geological
geologo *m*, **-a** *f* ⟨*mpl* -gi⟩ geologist
geometra *m/f* ⟨*mpl* -i⟩ surveyor
geometria *f* geometry; ***~ piana / solida*** plane / solid geometry
geometrico *adj* ⟨*mpl* -ci⟩ geometric(al)
Georgia *f* Georgia
georgiano I *adj* Georgian **II** *m*, **-a** *f* Georgian
geranio *m* ⟨*pl* -ni⟩ geranium
gerarca *m* ⟨*pl* -chi⟩ HIST *a key person in the National Fascist Party during the Fascist period*
gerarchia *f* hierarchy
gerarchico *adj* ⟨*mpl* -ci⟩ hierarchical; ***per via -a*** through the proper channels
gerente *m/f* manager
gerenza *f* management
gergale *adj* slang
gergo *m* ⟨*pl* -ghi⟩ slang; *di una professione* jargon
geriatra *m/f* ⟨*mpl* -i⟩ geriatrician
geriatria *f* geriatrics *sg*
geriatrico *adj* ⟨*mpl* -ci⟩ geriatric; ***istituto*** *m* ***~*** old people's home
germanesimo *m* Germanism
Germani *mpl* Germans
Germania *f* Germany
germanico *adj* ⟨*mpl* -ci⟩ Germanic
germano[1] *adj* (*carnale*) german; ***fratello*** *m* ***~*** full brother
germano[2] *m* ZOOL: ***~ reale*** wild duck
germanofilo *adj* Germanophile
germe *m* germ; *fig* (*principio*) seeds *pl*; ***in ~*** in embryo
germicida I *adj inv* germicidal **II** *m* ⟨*pl* -i⟩ germicide
germinale *adj* embryonic; ***cellula*** *f* ***~*** germ cell
germinare *v/i* ⟨1l & b⟩ germinate
germinazione *f* germination
germogliare *v/i* ⟨1g & c⟩ sprout
germoglio *m* ⟨*pl* -gli⟩ shoot
geroglifico *m* ⟨*pl* -ci⟩ hieroglyph
gerontologia *f* gerontology
gerontologo *m*, **-a** *f* ⟨*mpl* -gi⟩ gerontologist
gerosolimitano I *adj* from Jerusalem **II** *m*, **-a** *f* person from Jerusalem
gerundio *m* ⟨*pl* -di⟩ gerund
Gerusalemme *f* Jerusalem
gessato *adj* pinstripe
gesso *m* MINER gypsum; MED, *scultura* plaster; *per scrivere* chalk
gessoso *adj* chalky
gesta *fpl* LIT deeds
gestante *f* pregnant woman
gestazione *f* pregnancy; *fig* gestation
gesticolare *v/i* ⟨1m⟩ gesticulate
gesticolio *m* ⟨*pl* -ii⟩ gesticulations *pl*
gestionale *adj* management; ***politica*** *f* ***~*** management policy
gestione *f* management; ***~ aziendale*** business management; ***avere qc in ~*** manage sth
gestire *v/t* ⟨4d⟩ manage; ***~ una situa-***

zione handle a situation; **~ *le proprie forze*** husband one's forces

gesto *m con il braccio, la mano* gesture; *con la testa* nod; ***esprimersi a -i*** use gestures to express oneself

gestore *m*, **-trice** *f* manager

gestuale *adj* gestural; ***linguaggio*** *m* **~** sign language

gestualità *f* ⟨*pl* gestualità⟩ *expressiveness with gestures*

Gesù *m* Jesus; **~ *bambino*** baby Jesus

gesuita **I** *adj* Jesuit **II** *m* ⟨*pl* -i⟩ Jesuit

gettare *v/t* ⟨1b⟩ throw; *fondamenta* lay; *grido* give, let out; **~ *fuori*** throw out; **~ *via*** throw away; **~ *l'ancora*** drop anchor; **~ *le fondamenta*** lay the foundations; **~ *per terra*** throw on the ground; **~ *un ponte*** build a bridge; **~ *un urlo*** utter a scream; **~ *la spugna*** throw in the towel

gettarsi *v/r* throw o.s.; *di fiume* flow, empty (***in*** into); **~ *nella mischia*** join the fray

gettata *f* casting (*a.* BUILD)

gettito *m*: **~ *fiscale*** internal revenue

getto *m* jet; ***di*** **~** in one go; ***a*** **~ *continuo*** continuously

gettonato *adj* popular

gettone *m* token; *per giochi* counter; *per giochi d'azzardo* chip; **~ (*telefonico*)** (telephone) token; **~ *di presenza*** (*indennità*) attendance fee; ***telefono*** *m* ***a*** **~** *telephone that takes tokens*

geyser *m* ⟨*pl* geyser⟩ geyser

gg. *abbr* (= **giorni**) days

ghenga *f* ⟨*pl* -ghe⟩ *hum* mob, crowd

ghepardo *m* cheetah

gheriglio *m* ⟨*pl* -i⟩ (walnut) kernel

ghermire *v/t* ⟨4d⟩ grip

ghetta *f* spat

ghetto *m* ghetto

ghiacciaia *f* icebox

ghiacciaio *m* ⟨*pl* -ai⟩ glacier

ghiacciare ⟨1f⟩ **I** *v/i* freeze; ***stanotte è ghiacciato*** there was a frost last night **II** *v/t* freeze (*a. fig*)

ghiacciato *adj lago, stagno* frozen; *bibita* ice-cold; ***tè*** *m* **~** iced tea

ghiaccio *m* ⟨*pl* -cci⟩ ice; *sulla strada* black ice; ***banco*** *m* ***di*** **~** ice floe; ***rimanere di*** **~** be stunned; *fig* ***rompere il*** **~** break the ice

ghiacciolo *m* icicle; (*gelato*) ice lolly

ghiaia *f* gravel

ghianda *f* acorn

ghiandaia *f* jay

ghiandola *f* gland

ghibellino **I** *adj* Ghibelline **II** *m*, **-a** *f* Ghibelline; ***i Ghibellini*** the Ghibellines

ghiera *f* ferrule; MECH (*anello metallico*) ring nut

ghigliottina *f* guillotine

ghigliottinare *v/t* ⟨1n⟩ guillotine

ghignare *v/i* ⟨1a⟩ sneer

ghigno *m* sneer

ghingheri *mpl*: ***in*** **~** in one's glad rags; ***mettersi in*** **~** get dressed up, *infml* get dressed up to the nines

ghiotto *adj persona* greedy; *fig*: *di notizie etc* avid (***di*** for); (*appetitoso*) appetizing; ***essere*** **~ *di dolci*** love cakes

ghiottone *m* glutton

ghiottoneria *f difetto* gluttony; *cibo* delicacy

ghiribizzo *m* whim

ghirigoro *m* doodle

ghirlanda *f* garland

ghiro *m* dormouse; ***dormire come un*** **~** sleep like a log

ghisa *f* cast iron; ***di*** **~** cast-iron

ghostwriter *m/f* ⟨*pl* ghostwriter⟩ ghostwriter

già *adv* already; (*ex*) formerly; **~*!*** of course!; ***ci siamo*** **~ *incontrati*** we've already met; ***è*** **~ *una settimana che è partito*** he left over a week ago; **~ *che ci sei …*** since you're here …

Giacarta *f* Jakarta

giacca *f* ⟨*pl* -cche⟩ jacket; **~ *di pelle*** leather jacket; **~ *a vento*** windproof jacket, windcheater; **~ *a doppio petto*** double-breasted jacket; **~ *da camera*** smoking jacket; ***mettersi / togliersi la*** **~** put on / take off one's jacket

giacché *cj* since

giacchetta *f* jacket

giaccone *m* car coat

giacenza *f* ⟨*pl* -ze⟩ (*merce per la vendita*) stock; (*merce invenduta*) unsold goods *pl*; *periodo* stock time; **~ *di cassa*** cash in *or* on hand; ***-e*** *pl* ***di magazzino*** stock in hand

giacere *v/i* ⟨2k⟩ lie

giaciglio *m* ⟨*pl* -i⟩ bed

giacimento *m* MINER deposit; **~ *petrolifero*** oilfield

giacinto *m* hyacinth

giacobino **I** *adj* Jacobin **II** *m*, **-a** *f* Jacobin; ***i Giacobini*** the Jacobins

giaculatoria *f* REL short prayer; *hum* catalogue
giada *f* jade; ***di ~*** jade *attr*
giaggiolo *m* iris
giaguaro *m* jaguar
giallista *m/f* ⟨*mpl* -i⟩ crime writer
giallo I *adj* **1.** yellow; ***pagine*** *fpl* ***-e*** Yellow Pages **2.** ***libro*** *m* ***~***, ***film*** *m* ***~*** thriller **II** *m* **1.** yellow; ***~ limone*** lemon yellow **2.** (*libro*, *film*) thriller
giallognolo *adj* sallow
Giamaica *f* Jamaica
giamaicano *m/f & adj* Jamaican
gianduia *m type of hazelnut chocolate*
gianduiotto *m small hazelnut chocolate*
giannizzero *m* HIST janissary; *fig* henchman
Giano *m* Janus; ***~ bifronte*** *two-faced person*
giansenismo *m* Jansenism
giansenista ⟨*mpl* -i⟩ **I** *adj* Jansenist **II** *m/f* Jansenist
Giappone *m* Japan
giapponese *m/f & adj* Japanese
giara *f* jug
giardinaggio *m* gardening; ***dedicarsi al ~*** take up gardening
giardinetta *f estate car*
giardinetto *m* park; ***portare i bambini ai -i*** take the children to the playground
giardiniera *f donna* gardener; *mobile* plant stand; COOK (mixed) pickles *pl*
giardiniere *m* gardener
giardino *m* garden; ***~ botanico*** botanical gardens *pl*; ***~ d'infanzia*** kindergarten; ***~ d'inverno*** conservatory; ***~ pubblico*** park; ***~ zoologico*** zoological gardens
giarrettiera *f* garter
Giava *f* Java
giavanese I *adj* Javanese **II** *m/f* Javanese
giavellottista *m/f* javelin thrower **giavellotto** *m* javelin
gibbosità *f* ⟨*pl* gibbosità⟩ hump, lump
gibboso *adj* bumpy
giberna *f* ammunition box
Gibilterra *f* Gibraltar; ***stretto*** *m* ***di ~*** Strait of Gibraltar
Gibuti *m* Djibouti
gigabyte *m* ⟨*pl* gigabyte⟩ gigabyte
gigante I *adj* gigantic, giant *attr* **II** *m* giant; ***fare passi da ~*** make huge strides
gigantesco *adj* ⟨*mpl* -chi⟩ gigantic
gigantografia *f* giant poster
giglio *m* ⟨*pl* -gli⟩ lily; ***puro come un ~*** as pure as the driven snow; ***~ selvatico*** wild lily
gilè *m* ⟨*pl* gilè⟩ waistcoat, *US* vest
gimcana *f*, **gincana** *f* gymkhana; *fig* ***fare la ~*** weave in and out
gin *m* ⟨*pl* gin⟩ gin
ginecologo *m*, **-a** *f* ⟨*mpl* -gi⟩ gyn(a)ecologist
ginepraio *m* ⟨*pl* -ai⟩ juniper bushes; *fig* hot water; ***cacciarsi in un ~*** get into a fix
ginepro *m* juniper
ginestra *f* broom
Ginevra *f* Geneva; ***Lago*** *m* ***di ~*** Lake Geneva
ginevrino I *adj* Genevan **II** *m*, **-a** *f* Genevan
gin fizz *m* ⟨*pl* gin fizz⟩ gin fizz
ginger *m* ⟨*pl* ginger⟩ ginger ale
gingillarsi *v/r* ⟨1a⟩ fiddle; (*perder tempo*) fool around
gingillo *m* plaything; (*ninnolo*) knick-knack
ginnasiale I *adj* of a ginnasio; ***licenza*** *f* ***~*** ginnasio exam **II** *m/f student in a ginnasio*
ginnasio *m* ⟨*pl* -i⟩ *in the Italian secondary-school system, the first two years of the liceo classico*
ginnasta *m/f* ⟨*mpl* -i⟩ gymnast
ginnastica *f* exercises *pl*; *disciplina sportiva* gymnastics *sg*; *in palestra* P.E., physical education; ***fare ~*** exercise; ***~ presciistica*** warm-up exercises (for skiers); ***una ~ mentale*** a mental exercise
ginnico *adj* ⟨*mpl* -ci⟩ gymnastic; ***esercizi*** *mpl* ***-i*** gymnastics *sg*
ginocchiata *f blow with the knee*
ginocchiera *f* knee-pad
ginocchio *m* ⟨*pl* -cchi *and* le -cchia⟩ knee; ***stare in ~*** be on one's knees, be kneeling; ***mettersi in ~*** kneel (down); ***sulle -a*** on one's knee
ginocchioni *adv*: ***in ~*** on one's knees
ginseng *m* ⟨*pl* ginseng⟩ ginseng
gin tonic *m* ⟨*pl* gin tonic⟩ gin and tonic
giocare ⟨1o⟩ **I** *v/i* play; *d'azzardo*, *in Borsa* gamble; (*scommettere*) bet; ***~ a*** *tennis*, *flipper* play; ***~ d'astuzia***

use cunning; ***~ in casa / fuori casa*** play at home / away; ***~ in borsa*** gamble on the stock exchange; ***~ d'azzardo*** gamble **II** *v/t* play; (*ingannare*) trick; ***~ una carta*** play a card; ***~ un numero*** bet on a number; ***~ un brutto scherzo a qn*** play a dirty trick on s.o.; ***ci giocherei la camicia*** I'd put my shirt on it

giocarsi *v/r* (*perdere al gioco*) gamble away; (*beffarsi*) make fun; *carriera* destroy, throw away

giocata *f* (*partita*) game; (*puntata*) bet; ***una ~ forte*** a heavy bet

giocatore *m*, **-trice** *f* player; *d'azzardo* gambler

giocattolo *m* toy

giocherellare *v/i* ⟨1b⟩ fiddle with

giocherellone *m*, **-a** *f*: ***essere un ~*** be a joker

giochetto *m infml* game; *fig* piece of cake; ***basta con i -i!*** that's enough of your tricks!

gioco *m* ⟨*pl* -chi⟩ game; ***il ~*** gambling; ***~ d'azzardo*** game of chance; ***~ elettronico*** computer game; ***~ di parole*** pun; ***~ a premi*** prize competition; (*telequiz*) quiz show; ***~ di prestigio*** conjuring trick; ***~ da ragazzi*** child's play; ***~ da tavolo*** board game; ***Giochi Olimpici*** Olympic Games; ***avere buon ~*** have a good hand; ***entrare in ~*** come into play; ***fare il ~ di qn*** play into s.o.'s hands; ***stare al ~*** play along; ***il ~ non vale la candela*** the game isn't worth the candle; ***prendersi ~ di qn*** make fun of s.o., laugh at s.o.; ***un bel ~ dura poco*** *prov* the shortest jokes are the best; ***l'ho detto per ~ !*** I was joking!; ***in ~*** *a rischio* at stake; ***fare il doppio ~ con qn*** double-cross s.o.; ***prendersi ~ di qn*** make a fool of s.o.

giocoforza *m*: ***essere ~*** be necessary

giocoliere *m*, **-a** *f* juggler

giocondità *f* ⟨*pl* giocondità⟩ gaiety

giocondo *adj* jolly

giocosamente *adv* playfully

giocosità *f* ⟨*pl* giocosità⟩ playfulness

giocoso *adj* playful; (*scherzoso*) funny

giogo *m* ⟨*mpl* -ghi⟩ yoke (*a. fig*); GEOL col

gioia *f* joy; (*gioiello*) jewel; *fig* ***darsi alla pazza ~*** go wild (with excitement)

gioielleria *f* jeweller's (shop), *US* jewelry store

gioielliere *m*, **-a** *f* jeweller, *US* jeweler

gioiello *m* jewel; ***i -i*** *pl* jewellery, *US* jewelry

gioiosamente *adv* joyfully

gioioso *adj* joyful

gioire *v/i* ⟨4d⟩ rejoice (***di*** in); ***~ per*** *or* ***di qc*** rejoice at *or* over sth

Giordania *f* Jordan

giordano I *adj* Jordanian **II** *m*, **-a** *f* Jordanian

Giorgio *m*: ***San ~*** St George

giornalaio *m*, **-a** *f* ⟨*mpl* -ai⟩ newsagent

giornale *m* (news)paper; (*rivista*) magazine; (*registro*) journal; ***~ radio*** news (bulletin); ***~ scandalistico*** *testata* tabloid; *stampa in genere* gutter press

giornaliero I *adj* daily; ***abbonamento*** *m* ***~*** day pass; ***spese*** *fpl* ***-e*** day-to-day expenses **II** *m* day labo(u)rer

giornalino *m per ragazzi* comic; ***~ aziendale*** inhouse newspaper, staff magazine

giornalismo *m* journalism

giornalista *m/f* ⟨*mpl* -i⟩ journalist, reporter

giornalistico *adj* ⟨*mpl* -ci⟩ *attività, esperienza* journalistic; *agenzia, servizio* news *attr*

giornalmente *adv* daily

giornata *f* day; ***~ (lavorativa) di 8 ore*** 8-hour day; ***~ nera*** bad day; ***oggi non è ~!*** now isn't the time!; ***lo finiremo in ~*** we'll finish it today *or* by the end of the day; ***vivere alla ~*** live from day to day

giornataccia *f* ⟨*pl* -cce⟩ bad day, off day

giorno *m* day; ***~ di arrivo / partenza*** arrival / departure date; ***~ feriale*** weekday, working day; ***~ festivo*** (public) holiday; ***~ libero*** *di riposo* day off; ***~ di paga*** payday; ***illuminato a ~*** floodlit; ***l'altro ~*** the other day; ***un ~ o l'altro*** one of these days; ***ogni ~*** every day; ***a -i*** (*fra pochi giorni*) in a few days (time); ***al ~*** a day; ***al ~ d'oggi*** nowadays; ***in pieno ~*** in broad daylight; ***di ~*** by day; ***di ~ in ~*** from day to day; ***che ~ è oggi?*** what day is it today?; ***due -i fa*** two days ago; ***~ e notte*** day and night; ***~ del giudizio*** Judgement Day

giostra *f* roundabout, *US* carousel
giostraio *m*, **-a** *f* ⟨*mpl* -ai⟩ roundabout attendant
giostrarsi *v/r* ⟨1c⟩ navigate
giovamento *m* benefit; ***trarre ~ da qc*** draw benefit from sth
giovane **I** *adj* young; (*giovanile*) youthful **II** *m/f* young man, youth; *ragazza* young woman, girl; ***i -i*** pl young people; ***da ~*** when I *etc* was young
giovanile *adj* youthful
Giovanni *m*: ***San ~*** St John; ***~ Battista*** John the Baptist; ***l'evangelista ~*** John the Evangelist
giovanotto *m* young man, youth
giovare *v/i* ⟨1a⟩ (*essere utile*) be useful (***a*** to); (*far bene*) be good (***a*** for)
giovarsi *v/r*: ***~ di*** make use of; *consigli* take
Giove *m* Jupiter; ***per ~!*** by Jove
giovedì *m* ⟨*pl* giovedì⟩ Thursday; ***di ~*** on Thursdays; ***~ grasso*** Thursday before Lent; ***Giovedì Santo*** Maundy Thursday
giovenca *f* ⟨*pl* -che⟩ heifer
gioventù *f* youth; (*i giovani*) young people *pl*
gioviale *adj* jovial, jolly
giovialità *f* ⟨*pl* giovialità⟩ joviality
giovinastro *m* lout, yob
giovincello *m* lad
giovinezza *f* youth
giradischi *m* record player
giraffa *f* giraffe; FILM, TV boom
giramento *m*: ***~ di testa*** dizzy spell; ***avere il ~ di scatole*** *infml* be hacked off *infml*
giramondo *m/f* ⟨*pl* giramondo⟩ rolling stone, wanderer
girandola *f* (*fuoco d'artificio*) Catherine wheel; (*giocattolo*) windmill; (*banderuola*) weather vane
girante *m* FIN endorser
girare ⟨1a⟩ **I** *v/t* **1.** turn; *ostacolo* get round; *posto*, *città*, *negozi* go round; *mondo*, *paese* travel round; ***~ per la città*** go round the town; ***~ l'Italia*** travel around Italy **2.** *film* shoot **3.** (*mescolare*) mix **4.** FIN endorse **II** *v/i* **1.** turn; *rapidamente* spin; ***~ a sinistra / destra*** turn left / right; ***gira e rigira*** at the end of the day; ***mi gira la testa*** I feel dizzy, my head is spinning; ***mi girano le scatole*** *infml* I'm hacked off *infml*; ***se mi gira*** *infml* if I feel like it; ***~ a vuoto*** race; ***~ intorno a un argomento*** keep skirting a subject; ***cosa ti gira?*** what's got into you?; ***in quel bar gira la droga*** they deal drugs in that bar; ***~ al largo*** steer clear **2.** (*andare in giro*) wander *or* roam around; *con un veicolo* drive around
girarrosto *m* COOK spit
girarsi *v/r* ⟨1a⟩ turn round; ***~ su un fianco*** turn on one side
girasole *m* sunflower
girata *f* turn; (*passeggiata a piedi*) walk, stroll; *in macchina* drive; FIN endorsement; ***~ in bianco*** blank endorsement; ***fare una ~*** *infml* go for a walk
giratario *m*, **-a** *f* ⟨*mpl* -ri⟩ endorsee *m*
giravolta *f* turn; AUTO spin; *fig* U-turn
girello *m* baby walker; COOK silverside
girevole *adj* revolving
girino *m* tadpole
giro *m* **1.** turn; *di motore* rev(olution); (*circolo*) circle; ***~ d'affari*** turnover; ***~ di capitali*** circulation of capital; ***~ di prova*** test drive; ***essere su di -i*** be all fired up; ***lasciare in ~ qc*** leave sth lying around; ***mettere in ~*** spread; *fig* ***prendere in ~ qn*** pull s.o.'s leg; ***a ~ di posta*** by return of post; ***senza tanti -i di parole*** without beating about the bush so much **2.** (*percorso abituale*) round; (*deviazione*) detour; (*passeggiata a piedi*) walk, stroll; *in macchina* drive; *in bicicletta* ride; (*viaggio*) tour; ***~ turistico della città*** city sightseeing tour; ***andare in ~*** go around; ***essere in ~*** (*da qualche parte*) be around (somewhere); (*fuori*) be out; ***fare il ~ dei negozi*** go round the shops; ***portare qn in ~ per qc*** take s.o. around sth; ***è sempre in ~!*** he / she's always around! **3.** *di pista* lap; ***~ d'onore*** SPORTS lap of honour **4.** ***nel ~ di una settimana*** within a week **5.** ***il Giro di Francia*** the Tour de France; ***il Giro d'Italia*** the Giro d'Italia
girocollo *m* ⟨*pl* girocollo⟩: ***maglione m ~*** crew-neck, crew-neck sweater
giroconto *m* giro
girone *m* SPORTS group; ***~ di andata / ritorno*** first / second round
gironzolare *v/i* ⟨1m⟩ hang around; ***~ per negozi*** wander about the shops;

~ per la città hang around the streets
girotondo *m* ring-a-ring-o' roses
girovagare *v/i* ⟨1m, c & e⟩ wander about
girovago ⟨*mpl* -ghi⟩ **I** *adj* ***gente*** nomadic **II** *m*, **-a** *f* wanderer; (*ambulante*) itinerant
girovita *m* ⟨*pl* girovita⟩ waist size
gita *f* trip, excursion; ***~ in bicicletta*** bike ride; ***~ domenicale*** Sunday outing; ***~ scolastica*** school trip; ***andare in ~*** go on a trip *or* excursion
gitano *m*, **-a** *f* gypsy
gitante *m/f* (day) tripper
gittata *f* range; ***missile*** *m* ***a media ~*** medium-range missile
giù *adv* down; (*sotto*) below; (*da basso*) downstairs; ***andar ~*** go down; *fig* ***non mi va ~*** it sticks in my throat; *fig* ***essere ~*** be down *or* depressed; *di salute* be run down; ***mandar ~*** swallow (*a. fig*); ***un po' più in ~*** a bit lower down; ***su e ~*** up and down; ***da Roma in ~*** south of Rome; ***dai 15 anni in ~*** aged 15 and under; ***vieni ~!*** come down!, get down!
giubba *f* jacket (*a.* MIL)
giubbetto *m*, **giubbino** *m* jacket
giubbotto *m* sports jacket; ***~ antiproiettile*** bulletproof vest; ***~ di salvataggio*** life jacket
giubilante *adj* jubilant
giubilare[1] *v/i* ⟨1l⟩ jubilate
giubilare[2] *adj*: ***anno*** *m* ***~*** jubilee year
giubilo *m* jubilation
Giuda *m* Judas; ***bacio*** *m* ***di ~*** Judas kiss
giudaico *adj* ⟨*mpl* -ci⟩ Judaic
giudaismo *m* Judaism
giudicare ⟨1l & d⟩ **I** *v/t* judge; (*considerare*) consider, judge; ***~ male qn*** misjudge s.o.; ***lo hanno giudicato colpevole*** he has been found guilty. **II** *v/i* judge
giudicato *m*: ***passare in ~*** finalize; ***sentenza*** *f* ***passata in ~*** decree absolute
giudice *m* judge; ***~ di gara*** referee; ***~ istruttore*** examining magistrate; ***~ per le indagini preliminari*** examining magistrate
giudiziale *adj* judicial; ***casellario*** *m* ***~*** (*ufficio*) Criminal Records Office; (*registro*) police records
giudiziario *adj* ⟨*mpl* -ri⟩ judicial; ***procedimento*** *m* ***~*** legal procedure; ***ufficiale*** *m* ***~*** bailiff; ***spese*** *fpl* ***-e*** legal costs; ***per via -a*** through legal channels; ***vendita*** *f* ***-a*** sale by order of the court
giudizio *m* ⟨*pl* -zi⟩ **1.** judg(e)ment; (*senno*) wisdom; ***a mio ~*** in my opinion; ***mettere ~*** turn over a new leaf; ***farsi*** *or* ***formarsi un ~ su qn / qc*** form an opinion about s.o. / sth; ***dente*** *m* ***del ~*** wisdom tooth; ***Giudizio Universale*** Last Judgement **2.** JUR (*causa*) trial; (*sentenza*) verdict; ***~ civile*** civil action, lawsuit
giudiziosamente *adv* wisely
giudizioso *adj* sensible
giuggiola *f* trifle; ***andare in brodo*** *m* ***di -e*** be tickled pink
giuggiolone *m*, **-a** *f* simpleton
giugno *m* June
giugulare *adj* jugular; ***vena*** *f* ***~*** jugular (vein)
Giulia *f*: ***Santa ~*** St Julia
giuliano I *adj* from Venezia Giulia **II** *m*, **-a** *f* person from Venezia Giulia
giulivo *adj* happy
giullare *m* clown
giumenta *f* mare
giunco *m* ⟨*pl* -chi⟩ reed
giungere ⟨3d⟩ **I** *v/t*: ***~ le mani*** clasp one's hands **II** *v/i* arrive (***a*** in, at), reach (***a*** sth); ***~ a Roma / alla stazione*** arrive in Rome / at the station, reach Rome / the station; *fig* ***~ in porto*** reach one's goal; ***questa mi giunge nuova*** it's news to me
giungla *f* jungle
Giunone *f* Juno
giunonico *adj* ⟨*mpl* -ci⟩ Junoesque; ***bellezza*** *f* ***-a*** Junoesque beauty
giunta *f* addition; POL junta; ***~ comunale*** town council; ***per ~*** in addition, moreover
giunto *past part* → ***giungere***
giuntura *f* ANAT joint
giuramento *m* oath; ***falso ~*** perjury; ***fare un ~*** swear an oath; ***prestare ~*** take the oath; ***sotto ~*** under oath
giurare *v/t* ⟨1a⟩ swear; ***ti giuro che è vero*** I swear to you it's true; ***~ su qc*** swear on sth; ***~ di fare qc*** swear to do sth; ***non ci giurerei*** I wouldn't swear to it
giurassico *adj* ⟨*mpl* -ci⟩ Jurassic
giurato I *adj* sworn **II** *m*, **-a** *f* member

of the jury
giuria *f* jury
giuridicamente *adv* legally
giuridico *adj* ⟨*mpl* -ci⟩ legal
giurisdizionale *adj* jurisdictional
giurisdizione *f* jurisdiction
giurisprudenza *f* jurisprudence
giurista *m/f* ⟨*mpl* -i⟩ jurist
Giuseppe *m*: ***San ~*** St Joseph
giustamente *adv* rightly
giustezza *f* accuracy; *di argomentazione* soundness; TYPO justification
giustificabile *adj* justifiable
giustificare *v/t* ⟨1m & d⟩ justify; ***il fine giustifica i mezzi*** the end justifies the means
giustificarsi *v/r* justify o.s.
giustificativo *adj*: ***pezza*** *f* ***-a*** ADMIN documentary evidence
giustificazione *f* justification
giustizia *f* justice; ***fare ~ sommaria*** administer summary justice; ***farsi ~ da sé*** take the law into one's own hands
giustiziare *v/t* ⟨1g⟩ execute
giustiziere *m*, **-a** *f* executioner
giusto I *adj* just, fair; (*adatto*) right, appropriate; (*esatto*) correct, right, exact; ***è ~ di sale?*** is there enough salt in it? **II** *adv* correctly; *mirare* accurately; (*proprio, per l'appunto*) just; ***~!*** that's right!; ***cercavo ~ te*** you're the very person I was looking for **III** *m* (*uomo giusto*) just man; ***essere nel ~*** be in the right; ***pretendo solo il ~*** I just want what is rightfully mine
glabro *adj* hairless; BOT glabrous
glaciale *adj* glacial, icy; ***era*** *f* ***~*** Ice Age; ***Mar Glaciale Artico*** *m* Arctic Ocean
glaciazione *f* glaciation
gladiatore *m*, **-trice** *f* gladiator
gladio *m* ⟨*pl* -i⟩ sword
gladiolo *m* gladiolus
glassa *f* COOK icing
glassare *v/t* ⟨1a⟩ ice
glauco *adj* ⟨*mpl* -chi⟩ glaucous
glaucoma *m* ⟨*pl* -i⟩ glaucoma
gleba *f*: ***servo*** *m* ***della ~*** serf
gli I *art mpl* the; ***avere gli occhi azzurri*** have blue eyes **II** *pron* (*a lui*) (to) him; (*a esso*) (to) it; (*a loro*) (to) them; ***non ~ hai detto nulla?*** didn't you say anything to him?; ***dagli i libri*** give him/them the books, give the books to him/them; ***gliel'ho dato*** I gave it to him/her/them; ***gliene ho parlato*** I spoke to him/her/them about it
glicemia *f* glyc(a)emia
glicemico *adj* ⟨*mpl* -ci⟩ glyc(a)emic; ***indice*** *m* ***~*** glyc(a)emic index
glicerina *f* glycerine
glicine *m* wisteria
glicogeno *m* glycogen
glie: ***~la, ~lo, ~li, ~le, ~ne*** = *pron* **gli** *or* **le** *with pron* **la, lo, li, le, ne**
glissare *v/i* ⟨1a⟩ *fig* skate over
globale *adj* global
globalità *f* ⟨*pl* globalità⟩ totality
globalizzare *v/t* ⟨1a⟩ globalize
globalizzazione *f* ECON globalization
globalmente *adv* globally, as a whole
globo *m* globe; ***~ oculare*** eyeball; ***~ terrestre*** globe
globulina *f* globulin
globulo *m* globule; MED corpuscle; ***~ rosso/bianco*** red/white blood cell
gloria *f* glory; ***lavorare per la ~*** *hum* work for peanuts
gloriarsi *v/r* ⟨1k & c⟩ boast; ***~ di qc*** boast about sth
glorificare *v/t* ⟨1m & d⟩ glorify
glorificazione *f* glorification (*a.* REL)
gloriosamente *adv* gloriously
glorioso *adj* glorious
glossa *f* gloss
glossario *m* ⟨*pl* -ri⟩ glossary
glottide *f* glottis
glottologia *f* linguistics *sg*
glottologo *m*, **-a** *f* ⟨*mpl* -gi⟩ glottologist
glucosio *m* glucose
gluteo *m* buttock
glutinato *adj* gluten; ***pasta*** *f* ***-a*** pasta with gluten
glutine *m* gluten
gnocchi *mpl* (*di patate*) gnocchi *pl* (*small potato dumplings*); ***~ alla romana*** *small semolina dumplings topped with butter and Parmesan and baked in the oven*
gnomo *m* gnome
gnorri *m infml*: ***fare lo ~*** act dumb *infml*
gnosi *f* ⟨*pl* gnosi⟩ gnosis
gnostico ⟨*mpl* -ci⟩ **I** *adj* gnostic **II** *m*, **-a** *f* gnostic
gnu *m* ⟨*pl* gnu⟩ gnu

GO *abbr* (= **Gorizia**) Gorizia
goal *m* ⟨*pl* goal⟩ SPORTS goal; ***fare** or **segnare ~*** score a goal
gobba *f* hump
gobbo **I** *adj* hunchbacked **II** *m* hunchback; ***~ elettronico*** autocue
gobelin *m* ⟨*pl* gobelin⟩ Gobelin
goccetto *m* drop; ***beviamoci un ~!*** let's have a drop!
goccia *f* ⟨*pl* -cce⟩ drop; ***a ~ a ~*** little by little; ***essere una ~ nel mare*** be a drop in the ocean; ***la ~ che fa traboccare il vaso*** the last straw; ***somigliarsi come due -cce d'acqua*** be like two peas in a pod
goccio *m* drop; ***un ~ di vino*** a drop of wine
gocciolare *v/i* ⟨1l⟩ drip
gocciolatoio *m* ⟨*pl* -oi⟩ weather mo(u)lding
gocciolio *m* ⟨*pl* -ii⟩ drip
godere ⟨2a⟩ **I** *v/t* enjoy **II** *v/i* (*rallegrarsi*) be delighted (***di*** at)
godereccio *adj* ⟨*mpl* -cci⟩ pleasure-seeking *attr*
godersi *v/r* ⟨2a⟩: ***godersela*** enjoy o.s.; ***~ le ferie / l'estate*** enjoy the holidays *or US* vacation / the summer
godimento *m* enjoyment
goffaggine *f* clumsiness
goffamente *adv* clumsily
goffo *adj* awkward, clumsy
gogna *f* stocks (*a. fig*); ***mettere alla ~*** pillory
go-kart *m* ⟨*pl* go-kart⟩ go-kart
gol *m* ⟨*pl* gol⟩ goal
gola *f* throat; (*ingordigia*) greed(iness), gluttony; GEOG gorge; *fig* ***~ profonda*** deep throat; ***mal*** *m* ***di ~*** sore throat; ***far ~ a*** tempt
golden share *f* ⟨*pl* golden share⟩ golden share
golena *f* flood plain
goletta *f* NAUT schooner
golf *m* ⟨*pl* golf⟩ golf; (*cardigan*) cardigan; (*maglione*) sweater; ***giocatore*** *m* ***di ~*** golf player, golfer
golfista *m/f* ⟨*mpl* -i⟩ golfer
golfo *m* gulf; ***il ~ di Napoli*** Bay of Naples; ***Golfo Persico*** Persian Gulf; ***la guerra del ~*** the Gulf War
goliardia *f* university students *pl*
goliardico *adj* ⟨*mpl* -ci⟩ student; ***canto*** *m* ***~*** students' song; ***berretto*** *m* ***~*** *traditional hat worn by students on formal occasions*
gollista *adj* ⟨*mpl* -i⟩ POL Gaulist
golosamente *adv* greedily
golosità *f* (*ghiottoneria*) greed(iness), gluttony; (*leccornia*) delicacy
goloso *adj* greedy; ***essere ~ di dolci*** have a sweet tooth
golpe *m* ⟨*pl* golpe⟩ coup
golpista ⟨*mpl* -i⟩ **I** *adj taking part in a coup* **II** *m/f person taking part in a coup*
gomena *f* hawser
gomitata *f*: ***dare una ~ a qn*** elbow s.o.; *fig* ***fare a -e*** do sth by elbowing one's way
gomito *m* elbow; ***curva*** *f* ***a ~*** sharp bend; ***olio*** *m* ***di ~*** *infml* elbow grease; *fig* ***alzare il ~*** hit the bottle
gomitolo *m* ball (of wool)
gomma *f* **1.** rubber; *per cancellare* eraser; ***~ da masticare*** (chewing) gum **2.** (*pneumatico*) tyre, *US* tire; AUTO ***~ di scorta*** spare tyre (*US* tire); ***trasporto*** *m* ***su ~*** truckage; ***avere una ~ a terra*** have a flat tyre (*US* tire)
gommapiuma *f* foam rubber
gommato *adj carta* gummed; *tessuto* rubberized
gommino *m* rubber top *o* cover
gommista *m* ⟨*pl* -i⟩ tyre (*US* tire) specialist
gommone *m* rubber dinghy
gondola *f* gondola
gondoliere *m* gondolier
gonfalone *m* banner
gonfaloniere *m* HIST Gonfalonier
gonfiabile *adj* inflatable; ***canotto*** *m* ***~*** rubber dinghy; ***materassino*** *m* ***~*** lilo
gonfiare ⟨1k⟩ **I** *v/t con aria* inflate; *le guance* puff out; *fig* (*esagerare*) exaggerate, magnify **II** *v/i* swell up; *fig* puff up
gonfiarsi *v/r* ⟨1k⟩ swell up; *fig* puff up
gonfio *adj* ⟨*mpl* -fi⟩ swollen; *pneumatico* inflated; *stomaco* bloated; *fig* puffed up (***di*** with); *fig* ***a -e vele*** splendidly
gonfiore *m* swelling
gong *m* ⟨*pl* gong⟩ gong
gongolare *v/i* ⟨1l⟩: ***~ di gioia*** be overjoyed
goniometro *m* goniometer
gonna *f* skirt; ***~ a pieghe*** pleated skirt; ***~ pantalone*** culottes *pl*
gonnella *f* skirt; *fig* ***stare attaccato al-***

la ~ della mamma cling to one's mother's apron strings; ***poliziotto in ~*** *hum* policewoman
gonnellino *m* short skirt; ***~ scozzese*** kilt
gonorrea *f* gonorrh(o)ea
gora *f* (*canale*) mill race
gordiano *adj*: ***nodo*** *m* ***~*** Gordian knot
gorgheggiare *v/t and v/i* ⟨1f⟩ warble
gorgheggio *m* ⟨*pl* -ggi⟩ warble
gorgiera *f di armatura*: throat-piece; ZOOL ruff
gorgo *m* ⟨*pl* -ghi⟩ whirlpool
gorgogliare *v/i* ⟨1g⟩ *di stomaco* rumble; *dell'acqua* gurgle
gorgoglio *m* ⟨*pl* -ii⟩ gurgle; *di stomaco*: rumble
gorgonzola *m* Gorgonzola
gorilla *m* ⟨*pl* gorilla⟩ gorilla; *infml* (*guardia del corpo*) bodyguard, gorilla *infml*
goriziano I *adj* from Gorizia **II** *m*, **-a** *f* person from Gorizia
gospel *m* ⟨*pl* gospel⟩ gospel music
gossip *m* ⟨*pl* gossip⟩ gossip
gotha *m* ⟨*pl* gotha⟩ élite; ***il ~ della finanza*** the financial élite
gotico *m*/*adj* ⟨*mpl* -ci⟩ Gothic
goto *m*, **-a** *f* Goth
gotta *f* MED gout; ***attacco*** *m* ***di ~*** attack of gout
gottoso I *adj* gouty **II** *m*, **-a** *f person with gout*
gourmet *m*/*f* ⟨*pl* gourmet⟩ gourmet
governabile *adj* POL governable; (*manovrabile*) manoeuvrable
governabilità *f* ⟨*pl* governabilità⟩ POL governability; (*manovrabilità*) manoeuvrability
governance *f* governance
governante I *f* housekeeper **II** *m*/*f* ruler
governare *v/t* ⟨1b⟩ POL govern, rule; NAUT steer
governativo *adj* government *attr*; *scuola* state *attr*
governatore *m*, **-trice** *f* governor
governo *m* government; NAUT steering; ***~ di coalizione*** coalition government; ***~ di minoranza*** minority government
gozzo *m* MED goitre, *US* goiter
gozzovigliare *v/t* ⟨1g⟩ make merry
GPS *m abbr* (= **Global Position System**) GPS; ***navigatore*** *m* ***~*** GPS navigator
GR *abbr* (= **Grosseto**) Grosseto
gracchiare *v/i* ⟨1k⟩ *di corvo* caw; *di rane* croak; *di persona* squawk
gracidare *v/i* ⟨1l⟩ croak
gracile *adj* (*debole*) delicate
gracilità *f* ⟨*pl* gracilità⟩ frailty
gradasso *m* boaster; ***non fare il ~!*** don't brag!
gradatamente *adv* gradually
gradazione *f* gradation; (*sfumatura*) shade; ***~ alcolica*** alcohol(ic) content
gradevole *adj* pleasant, agreeable
gradevolmente *adv* pleasantly
gradimento *m* liking; ***indice*** *m* ***di ~*** viewing figures
gradinata *f* flight of steps; *stadio* stand; *a teatro* gallery, balcony
gradino *m* step
gradire *v/t* ⟨4d⟩ like; (*desiderare*) wish; ***gradirei sapere*** I would like to know; ***gradisce un po' di vino?*** would you like some wine?
gradito *adj* pleasant; (*bene accetto*) welcome
grado[1] *m* **1.** degree; ***30 -i all'ombra*** 30 degrees in the shade; ***per -i*** by degrees; ***fare il terzo ~ a qn*** give s.o. the third degree **2.** *in una gerarchia*, MIL rank; ***cugino di primo / secondo ~*** first / second cousin **3.** ***essere in ~ di*** be in a position to; ***in ~ di lavorare*** capable of working, fit for work
grado[2] *m*: ***di buon ~*** willingly
graduabile *adj* graduatable
graduale *adj* gradual
gradualmente *adv* gradually
graduare *v/t* ⟨1l⟩ graduate
graduato *adj* graduated; ***recipiente*** *m* ***~*** measuring jug
graduatoria *f* list
graduazione *f* graduation
graffa *f* TYPO brace
graffetta *f* (*fermaglio*) paper clip; (*di pinzatrice*) staple
graffiare *v/t* ⟨1k⟩ scratch
graffiarsi *v/r* ⟨1k⟩ get scratched
graffiata *f* scratch; ***dare una ~*** scratch
graffiatura *f* scratch
graffio *m* ⟨*pl* -ffi⟩ scratch
graffiti *mpl* graffiti *pl*
graffitista *m*/*f* ⟨*mpl* -i⟩ graffiti artist
grafia *f* (hand)writing
grafica *f* graphics *pl*
grafico ⟨*mpl* -ci⟩ **I** *adj* graphic **II** *m*

(*diagramma*) graph **III** *m*, **-a** *f* (*disegnatore*) graphic artist
grafite *f* graphite
grafologia *f* handwriting analysis
gramaglie *fpl*: ***in ~*** in mourning
gramigna *f* dogtooth violet; *fig* weed; ***crescere come la ~*** grow like weeds
graminacea *f* grass
grammatica *f* grammar
grammaticale *adj* grammatical
grammaticalmente *adv* grammatically
grammelot *m* ⟨*pl* grammelot⟩ THEAT *form of theatre using invented words and sounds*
grammo *m* gram(me)
grammofono *m* gramophone
gramo *adj* LIT wretched; ***fare una vita -a*** lead a life of misery
gran → ***grande***
grana I *f* grain; *infml* (*seccatura*) trouble; *infml soldi* dough *infml*, cash; ***di ~ fine / grossa*** fine- / coarse-grained; ***piantare una ~*** *o* ***piantare -e*** *infml* stir up trouble; ***pieni di ~*** *infml* rolling in money *infml*; ***non voglio avere -e!*** I don't want any trouble! **II** *m* ⟨*pl* grana⟩: ***~ padano*** *cheese similar to Parmesan*
granaglie *fpl* grain, corn
granaio *m* ⟨*pl* -ai⟩ barn
granata *f* MIL grenade; BOT pomegranate
granatiere *m* grenadier
granatina *f* grenadine
Gran Bretagna *f* Great Britain
grancassa *f* bass drum
granché *pron* not much; ***non capire ~ di qc*** not understand much of sth; ***questo film non è un ~*** this film isn't up to much
granchio *m* ⟨*pl* -chi⟩ crab; *fig* blunder; *fig* ***prendere un ~*** make a blunder
grandangolare *m* PHOT wide-angle lens
grande *adj* big, large; (*alto*) big, tall; (*largo*) wide; *fig* (*intenso*, *notevole*) great; (*adulto*) grown-up, big; (*vecchio*) old; ***il fratello / figlio più ~*** the eldest brother / son; ***i -i magazzini*** the department stores; RAIL ***~ velocità*** high speed; ***non è un gran che*** it's nothing special; ***cosa vuoi fare da ~?*** what do you want to be when you grow up?; ***sei stato ~!*** *infml* you've been great!; ***alla ~*** in style; ***fare le cose in ~*** do things in a big way; ***in gran parte*** by and large
grandezza *f* (*dimensione*) size; (*larghezza*) width; (*ampiezza*) breadth; (*altezza*) height; *fig* (*eccellenza*) greatness; (*grandiosità*) grandeur; ***a ~ naturale*** life-size
grandicello *adj* growing up
grandinare *v/impers* ⟨1l⟩ hail
grandinata *f* hailstorm
grandine *f* hail
grandiosamente *adv* grandly
grandiosità *f* ⟨*pl* grandiosità⟩ grandeur
grandioso *adj* grand
granduca *m* ⟨*pl* -chi⟩ grand duke
granducato *m* grand duchy
granduchessa *f* grand duchess
granello *m* grain; ***~ di pepe*** peppercorn; ***~ di polvere*** speck of dust; ***~ di sabbia*** grain of sand
granita *f type of ice made of frozen crystals of coffee or fruit syrup*
granitico *adj* ⟨*mpl* -ci⟩ granite; *fig* like granite; ***volontà*** *f* ***-a*** will of iron
granito *m* granite
grano *m* (*chicco*) grain; (*frumento*) wheat; *fig* grain, ounce
granturco *m* maize, corn
granulato *m* granulated coffee
granulo *m* granule; ***in -i*** in granules
granuloso *adj* granular
grappa *f* grappa, *brandy made from the remains of the grapes used in wine-making*
grappino *m infml* small glass of grappa
grappolo *m* bunch; ***a -i*** in clusters
grassetto *m* TYPO bold (type)
grasso I *adj* fat; (*unto*) greasy; *cibo* fatty **II** *m* fat; *di bue*, *pecora* suet; ***-i*** *pl* ***animali / vegetali*** animal / vegetable fats; ***macchia*** *f* ***di ~*** grease stain; ***~ lubrificante*** grease; ***privo di -i*** fat-free
grassoccio *adj* ⟨*mpl* -cci⟩ plump
grassone I *adj* fatty **II** *m*, **-a** *f pej* fatty
grassottello I *adj* chubby **II** *m*, **-a** *f* chubby person
grata *f* grating
gratella *f*, **graticola** *f* COOK grill
graticcio *m* ⟨*pl* -cci⟩ hurdle
gratifica *f* bonus
gratificante *adj* rewarding

gratin *m*: ***al ~*** au gratin
gratinato *adj* → ***al gratin***
gratis *adv* free (of charge); ***entrare ~*** get in free
gratitudine *f* gratitude
grato *adj* grateful; (*gradito*) welcome; ***vi sarei grato se …*** I would be grateful if …, I would appreciate it if …; ***essere ~ a qn per*** *or* ***di qc*** be grateful to s.o. for sth
grattacapo *m* problem, headache *infml*
grattacielo *m* skyscraper
gratta e vinci *m* ⟨*pl* gratta e vinci⟩ scratch card
grattare *v/t* ⟨1a⟩ scratch; (*raschiare*) scrape; (*grattugiare*) grate; *infml* swipe *infml*, pinch *infml*
grattarsi *v/r* scratch o.s.; *fig* ***~ la pancia*** *infml* laze about; ***~ la schiena*** scratch one's back
grattugia *f* ⟨*pl* -ge⟩ grater
grattugiare *v/t* ⟨1f⟩ grate; ***pane*** *m* ***grattugiato*** breadcrumbs *pl*
gratuità *f* ⟨*pl* gratuità⟩ gratuitousness (*a. fig*)
gratuitamente *adv* free
gratuito *adj* free (of charge); (*infondato*) gratuitous
gravabile *adj*: ***~ d'imposta*** subject to tax
gravame *m* burden
gravare ⟨1a⟩ **I** *v/t* burden; ***~ qn di qc*** heap sth on s.o. **II** *v/i* weigh (***su*** on); ***gravava tutto su di me*** everything was hanging over me
grave *adj* (*pesante*) heavy; (*serio*) serious; (*difficile*) hard; MUS grave; ***malattia*** *f* ***~*** serious illness; ***una ~ responsabilità*** a heavy responsibility
gravemente *adv* seriously; ***~ malato / ferito*** seriously ill / injured
gravidanza *f* pregnancy
gravido *adj* pregnant (*a. fig*); *animale* gravid; ***~ di conseguenze*** be fraught with consequences
gravità *f* seriousness, gravity; PHYS (***forza*** *f* ***di***) ***~*** (force of) gravity
gravitare *v/i* ⟨1l⟩gravitate; ***~ intorno al sole*** orbit around the sun; *fig* ***~ intorno a qn / qc*** gravitate towards s.o. / sth
gravitazionale *adj* gravitational
gravitazione *f* gravitation
gravosamente *adv* heavily
gravoso *adj* onerous
grazia *f* grace; (*gentilezza*) favo(u)r; REL grace; JUR pardon; ***in ~ di*** thanks to; ***con ~*** gracefully; ***colpo*** *m* ***di ~*** coup de grâce; ***concedere la ~ a qn*** grant mercy to s.o.; ***chiedere una ~ alla Madonna*** pray to the Virgin Mary for mercy; ***le tre Grazie*** the three Graces; ***troppa ~!*** *hum* thanks so much!
graziare *v/t* ⟨1g⟩ pardon
grazie *int* thank you, thanks; ***tante ~*** thank you so much; ***~ a*** thanks to; ***~ a Dio!*** thank goodness!; ***sì, ~!*** yes please!; ***no, ~!*** no thank you!
graziosamente *adv* gracefully
grazioso *adj* charming; (*carino*) pretty
grecale *m* northeast wind
Grecia *f* Greece
greco ⟨*mpl* -ci⟩ **I** *adj* Greek **II** *m*, **-a** *f* Greek
greco-romano *adj* Gr(a)eco-Roman; ***lotta*** *f* ***-a*** Gr(a)eco-Roman wrestling
gregario *m* ⟨*pl* -ri⟩ (*ciclista*) domestique; *fig* follower
gregge *m* ⟨*pl* le -ggi⟩ flock
greggio ⟨*mpl* -ggi⟩ **I** *adj* (*non lavorato*) raw, crude **II** *m* crude (petroleum)
gregoriano *adj* Gregorian; ***canto*** *m* ***~*** Gregorian chant; ***calendario*** *m* ***~*** Gregorian calendar
grembiule *m* apron
grembiulino *m* smock
grembo *m* lap; (*materno*) womb; *fig* bosom; ***sedersi in ~ a qn*** sit on s.o.'s lap; ***~ materno*** mother's womb
gremire *v/t* ⟨4d⟩ crowd
gremito *adj* crowded; ***~ di persone*** crammed with people
greppia *f* crib; *hum* cushy little number
gres *m* ⟨*pl* gres⟩ stoneware
greto *m* shore; ***il ~ del torrente*** the bank of the stream
grettamente *adv* stingily
grettezza *f* (*avarizia*) stinginess; (*meschinità*) meanness
gretto *adj* (*avaro*) mean; (*di mente ristretta*) narrow-minded
greve *adj* heavy; *fig* crude; ***aria*** *f* ***~*** stuffiness
grezzo *adj* raw; TEX coarse; *persona* crude; ***materiale*** *m* ***~*** raw material; ***tela*** *f* ***-a*** raw canvas
grida *fpl* → ***grido***

gridare ⟨1a⟩ **I** *v/t* shout, yell; **~ *aiuto*** shout for help **II** *v/i* shout, yell; (*strillare*) scream; **~ *a squarciagola*** shout one's head off

grido *m* ⟨*pl usu* le -da⟩ shout, cry; ***di* ~** famous; ***all'ultimo* ~** the latest

griffato *adj infml* designer; ***abito m* ~** designer dress

griffe *f* ⟨*pl* griffe⟩ designer label

grifone *m* griffin (*a.* MYTH)

grigiastro *adj* greyish, *US* grayish

grigio *adj* ⟨*mpl* -gi⟩ grey, *US* gray; *fig* (*triste*) sad; (*scialbo*) dull, dreary

grigiore *m* greyness, *US* grayness; *fig* (*monotonia*) dullness, dreariness

grigioverde *adj inv* greenish-grey, *US* -gray

griglia *f* (*grata*) grating; COOK grill; ***alla* ~** grilled

grigliata *f* grill; **~ *mista*** mixed grill

grignolino *m red wine from Piedmont*

grilletto *m* trigger; ***premere il* ~** press the trigger

grillo *m* cricket; *fig* (*capriccio*) fancy, whim; ***avere -i per la testa*** be full of strange ideas; ***fare il* ~ *parlante*** be a know-all; ***indovinala* ~!** your guess is as good as mine!

grillotalpa *m/f* ⟨*pl* grillotalpe⟩ mole-cricket

grill-room *m* ⟨*pl* grill-room⟩ grill

grimaldello *m device for picking locks*

grinfie *fpl fig* clutches *pl*; *fig* ***cadere nelle* ~ *di qn*** fall into s.o.'s clutches

grinta *f* grit; *fig* determination; ***avere* ~** have drive

grintoso *adj infml* gritty; SPORTS determined

grinza *f di stoffa* crease

grinzoso *adj viso* wrinkled; (*spiegazzato*) creased

grisaglia *f* ⟨*pl* -glie⟩ (*tessuto*) grisaille

grisou *m*, **grisù** *m* ⟨*pl* grisou, grisù⟩ MINER firedamp

grissino *m* breadstick

groenlandese I *adj* Greenlandic **II** *m/f* Greenlander

Groenlandia *f* Greenland

grondaia *f* gutter

grondante *adj* streaming; **~ *di sudore*** running with sweat

grondare ⟨1a⟩ **I** *v/i* (*colare*) pour; (*gocciolare*) drip; **~ *di sudore*** be dripping with sweat **II** *v/t* drip with; **~ *sangue*** pour with blood

groppa *f* back; ***in* ~ *al cavallo*** on horseback

groppo *m*: ***avere un* ~ *alla gola*** have a lump in one's throat

groppone *m hum* back; ***avere molti anni sul* ~** be getting on (in years)

grossetano I *adj* from Grosseto **II** *m*, **-a** *f* person from Grosseto

grossezza *f* (*dimensione*) size; (*spessore*) thickness; (*l'essere grosso*) largeness

grossista *m/f* ⟨*mpl* -i⟩ wholesaler

grosso I *adj* big, large; (*spesso*) thick; *mare* rough; *sale*, *ghiaia* coarse; ***pezzo m* ~** *infml* big shot *infml*; ***questa è -a !*** this is too much!; ***sbagliarsi di* ~** make a big mistake; ***farla -a*** make a fine mess; *fig* ***spararle -e*** talk big **II** *m* bulk

grossolanamente *adv* roughly

grossolanità *f* ⟨*pl* grossolanità⟩ coarse word; (*cafonaggine*) coarseness

grossolano *adj* coarse; *errore* serious

grossomodo *adv* roughly

grotta *f* cave; *artificiale* grotto; ***la Grotta Azzurra*** the Blue Grotto (*on the island of Capri*)

grottesco *adj* ⟨*mpl* -chi⟩ grotesque

groviera *m* Gruyère

groviglio *m* ⟨*pl* -gli⟩ tangle; *fig* muddle

gru *f* ⟨*pl* gru⟩ crane

gruccia *f* ⟨*pl* -cce⟩ crutch; *per vestiti* hanger

grufolare *v/i* ⟨1l⟩ root around

grugnire *v/i* ⟨4d⟩ grunt

grugno *m fig pej* snout; ***spaccare il* ~ *a qn*** *infml* smash s.o.'s face in

gruista *m/f* ⟨*mpl* -i⟩ crane driver

grullo *reg* **I** *adj* silly **II** *m*, **-a** *f* fool

grumo *m* clot; *di farina* lump; **~ *di sangue*** blood clot

gruppo *m* group; **~ *di lavoro*** working group; **~ *sanguigno*** blood group; ***a -i*** in groups; ***terapia f di* ~** group therapy

gruppuscolo *m* POL fringe group

gruzzolo *m* nest egg

G.U. *abbr* (= **Gazzetta Ufficiale**) *official gazette*

guadagnare *v/t* ⟨1a⟩ earn; (*ottenere*) gain; **~ *tempo*** save time; ***cosa ci guadagni a farlo?*** what do you gain by doing it?

guadagnarsi *v/r* ⟨1a⟩ earn; *~* ***da vivere*** earn one's living
guadagno *m* gain; (*profitto*) profit; (*entrate*) earnings *pl*; ***margine*** *m* ***di*** *~* profit margin
guadare *v/t* ⟨1a⟩ ford, wade across
guado *m* ford
guaglione *m reg* boy
guaina *f* sheath; (*busto*) corset, girdle
guaio *m* ⟨*pl* -ai⟩ trouble; (*danno*) damage; ***-ai a te se lo fai!*** woe betide you if you do!; ***essere nei -ai*** be in trouble
guaire *v/i* ⟨4d⟩ whine
guaito *m* whine (*a. fig*)
gualcire *v/t* ⟨4d⟩ crease
gualdrappa *f* saddlecloth
guancia *f* ⟨*pl* -ce⟩ cheek; ***porgere l'altra*** *~* turn the other cheek
guanciale *m* pillow
guano *m* guano
guantaio *m*, **-a** *f* ⟨*mpl* -ai⟩ glove-maker
guantiera *f* glovebox
guanto *m* glove; ***trattare qn con i -i*** handle s.o. with kid gloves; ***calzare come un*** *~* fit like a glove
guantone *m*: *~* ***da boxe*** boxing glove
guappo *m reg member of the Camorra*
guaranì **I** *adj inv* Guarani **II** *m/f* ⟨*pl* guaranì⟩ Guarani
guardaboschi *m* ⟨*pl* guardaboschi⟩ forest ranger
guardacaccia *m* ⟨*pl* guardacaccia⟩ gamekeeper
guardacoste *m* ⟨*pl* guardacoste⟩ NAUT coastguard
guardalinee *m* ⟨*pl* guardalinee⟩ SPORTS assistant referee, linesman
guardamacchine *m* car park (*US* parking lot) attendant
guardare ⟨1a⟩ **I** *v/t* look at; (*osservare, stare a vedere*) watch; (*custodire*) watch, look after; (*esaminare*) check; *~* ***la tivù*** watch TV; *~* ***le vetrine*** go window-shopping; ***guarda dove metti i piedi!*** watch where you're walking!; ***guarda (qui / laggiù / lassù)!*** look (here / down there / up there)!; ***ma guarda un po'!*** fancy that!; ***guarda caso!*** as luck would have it; ***non*** *~**!*** don't look! **II** *v/i* **1.** look **2.** (*controllare*) check **3.** *di finestra* overlook (***su*** sth); *di porta* lead (***su*** to); *~* ***a sud*** face south **4.** ***guarda di non far tardi*** see you're not late
guardaroba *m* ⟨*pl* guardaroba⟩ cloakroom, *US* checkroom; *armadio* wardrobe
guardarobiere *m*, **-a** *f* cloakroom attendant
guardarsi *v/r* look at o.s.; *~* ***da*** beware of; (*astenersi*) refrain from
guardasigilli *m* ⟨*pl* guardasigilli⟩ *justice minister*
guardata *f infml* look, glance; ***dare una*** *~* ***al giornale*** have a quick look at the newspaper
guardia *f* guard; *~* ***carceraria*** prison officer; *~* ***costiera*** coastguard; *~* ***del corpo*** bodyguard; *~* ***di finanza*** *Customs and Excise office*; *~* ***forestale*** forest ranger; *~* ***giurata*** security guard; *~* ***di pubblica sicurezza*** policeman; ***Guardie svizzere*** Swiss Guard; ***cane*** *m* ***da*** *~* guard dog; *~* ***medica, medico*** *m* ***di*** *~* doctor on duty; ***fare la*** *~* keep guard *or* watch; ***giocare a -e e ladri*** play cops and robbers; ***stare in*** *~* be on one's guard; ***mettere qn in*** *~* ***contro qn / qc*** warn s.o. about s.o. / sth
guardiano *m* **-a** *f* (*custode*) warden; (*portiere*) caretaker; (*guardia*) guard; *di parco* keeper; *~* ***di museo*** custodian; *~* ***notturno*** night watchman
guardina *f* lock-up; ***finire in*** *~* end up in jail
guardiola *f* porter's lodge
guardone *m* voyeur
guardrail *m* ⟨*pl* guardrail⟩ guardrail
guaribile *adj* curable
guarigione *f* recovery; ***in via di*** *~* on the mend
guarire ⟨4d⟩ **I** *v/t* cure **II** *v/i* recover; *di ferita* heal; ***guarisci presto!*** get well soon!
guarnigione *f* garrison
guarnire *v/t* ⟨4d⟩ decorate; *abiti* trim; COOK garnish
guarnizione *f* (*abbellimento*) trimming; COOK garnish; *di rubinetto* washer; AUTO *~* ***del freno*** brake lining
Guascogna *f* Gascony
guascone **I** *adj* Gascon **II** *m/f* Gascon
guastafeste *m/f* ⟨*pl* guastafeste⟩ spoilsport; ***fare il*** *~* be a spoilsport
guastare *v/t* ⟨1a⟩ spoil, ruin; *meccanismo* break; ***un po' d'ironia non guasta mai*** a little irony never does

any harm

guastarsi *v/r* break down; *di tempo* change for the worse; *di cibi* go bad, spoil

guasto I *adj* broken; *telefono*, *ascensore* out of order; AUTO broken down; *cibi* bad, off *infml*; *dente* rotten, decayed **II** *m* fault, failure; AUTO breakdown; ***un ~ al motore*** engine failure; ***avere un ~ alla macchina*** break down

guatemalteco ⟨*mpl* -chi⟩ **I** *adj* Guatemalan **II** *m*, **-a** *f* Guatemalan

guazza *f* (heavy) dew

guazzabuglio *m* ⟨*pl* -gli⟩ jumble (*a. fig*)

guêpière *f* ⟨*pl* guêpière⟩ guêpière

guercio ⟨*mpl* -ci⟩ **I** *adj infml* cross-eyed; (*cieco da un occhio*) one-eyed **II** *m*, **-a** *f* squinter; (*cieco da un occhio*) one-eyed man / woman

guerra *f* war; ***~ civile*** civil war; ***~ fredda*** Cold War; ***~ lampo*** blitz; ***~ santa*** holy war; ***in tempo di ~*** in wartime; ***la prima / seconda ~ mondiale*** the First / Second World War; ***dichiarare ~ a qn / qc*** declare war on s.o. / sth

guerrafondaio *m*, **-a** *f* ⟨*mpl* -ai⟩ war-monger

guerreggiare *v/i* ⟨1f⟩: ***~ con*** *or* ***contro qn*** wage war with *or* against s.o.

guerriero *m* warrior

guerriglia *f* guerrilla warfare

guerrigliero *m*, **-a** *f* guerrilla

gufo *m* owl

guida *f* **1.** guidance; ***sotto la ~ di qn*** under s.o.'s guidance **2.** (*persona*, *libro*) guide; ***~ alpina*** mountain guide; ***~ telefonica*** phone book; ***~ turistica*** tourist guide; ***fare da ~ a qn*** act as s.o.'s guide; ***vorrei una ~ della Gran Bretagna*** I'd like a guide to Great Britain **3.** AUTO driving; ***~ a destra / a sinistra*** right-hand / left-hand drive; ***posto*** *m* ***di ~*** driving seat; ***prendere lezioni di ~*** take driving lessons

guidare *v/t* ⟨1a⟩ guide; AUTO drive; ***~ la classifica*** SPORTS be top of the league

guidatore *m*, **-trice** *f* driver

Guinea *f* Guinea; ***~ Bissau*** Guinea-Bissau; ***~ Equatoriale*** Equatorial Guinea

guineano I *adj* from Guinea **II** *m*, **-a** *f* person from Guinea

guinzaglio *m* ⟨*pl* -gli⟩ lead, *US* leash; ***tenere il cane al ~*** have the dog on a lead *or US* leash

guisa *f liter* guise; ***a ~ di*** like; ***in tal ~*** in that way

guitto *m* THEAT strolling player

guizzare *v/i* ⟨1a⟩ dart

guizzo *m* spurt

gulasch *m* ⟨*pl* gulasch⟩ goulash

guscio *m* ⟨*pl* -sci⟩ shell; ***chiudersi nel proprio ~*** go back into one's shell; ***~ di noce*** nutshell (*a. fig*)

gustare *v/t* ⟨1a⟩ taste; *fig* enjoy

gustativo *adj* taste; ***papille*** *fpl* ***-e*** taste buds

gusto *m* taste; (*sapore*) flavo(u)r; *fig* (*piacere*) pleasure; ***al ~ di fragola*** strawberry-flavo(u)red; ***buon / cattivo ~*** good / bad taste; ***senza ~*** tasteless; ***prenderci ~*** get a taste for it; ***mangiare di ~*** eat with gusto; ***ridere di ~*** laugh heartily; ***persona*** *f* ***di buon ~*** person with taste; ***scherzo*** *m* ***di pessimo ~*** joke in very poor taste; ***togliersi il ~ di*** (***fare***) ***qc*** get out of the habit of (doing) sth; ***non è di mio ~*** it isn't to my taste; ***che ~ ci provi?*** what does it taste like?

gustosamente *adv* with relish

gustoso *adj* tasty; *fig* delightful

gutturale *adj* guttural; ***suoni*** *mpl* ***-i*** guttural sounds

H

h, H *m/f* ⟨*pl* h, H⟩ h, H; ***bomba*** *f* ***H*** h bomb
h *abbr* (= **ora**) h (hour)
ha[1] *abbr* (= **ettaro**) ha (hectare)
ha[2], **hai, hanno** → ***avere***
habitat *m* ⟨*pl* habitat⟩ BIOL habitat
habitué *m/f* ⟨*pl* habitué⟩ regular customer
habitus *m* ⟨*pl* habitus⟩ BIOL habitus; *fig* habit; **~ *mentale*** attitude
hacker *m/f* ⟨*pl* hacker⟩ COMPUT hacker
haitiano I *adj* Haitian **II** *m*, **-a** *f* Haitian
hall *f* ⟨*pl* hall⟩ foyer
hamburger *m* ⟨*pl* hamburger⟩ hamburger
handicap *m* ⟨*pl* handicap⟩ handicap; **~ *psichico / fisico*** mental / physical handicap; ***portatore*** *m* ***di* ~** disabled *or* handicapped person
handicappato I *adj* disabled, handicapped **II** *m*, **-a** *f* disabled *or* handicapped person
hangar *m* ⟨*pl* hangar⟩ hangar
happy end *m* ⟨*pl* happy end⟩ happy ending
happy hour *f* ⟨*pl* happy hour⟩ happy hour
hard-core *adj inv* hard-core; ***film* ~** hard-core film
hard-cover *m* ⟨*pl* hard-cover⟩ hard cover
hard discount *m* ⟨*pl* hard discount⟩ hard discount
hard disk *m* ⟨*pl* hard disk⟩ COMPUT hard disk
hard rock *m* ⟨*pl* hard rock⟩ hard rock
hardware *m* ⟨*pl* hardware⟩ COMPUT hardware
harem *m* ⟨*pl* harem⟩ harem
hashish *m* hashish
hawaiano I *adj* Hawaiian **II** *m*, **-a** *f* Hawaiian
heavy metal *m* heavy metal
henné *m* ⟨*pl* henné⟩ henna
herpes *m* ⟨*pl* herpes⟩ herpes
hertz *m* ⟨*pl* hertz⟩ hertz
hg *abbr* (= **ettogrammo**) hg (hectogram)
hi-fi *m* hi-fi
Himalaya *m* Himalayas *pl*
himalayano *adj* Himalayan
hinterland *m* ⟨*pl* hinterland⟩ hinterland
hip-hop *m* ⟨*pl* hip-hop⟩ hip hop
hippy ⟨*pl* hippy⟩ **I** *adj* hippy **II** *m/f* hippy
hit *m* ⟨*pl* hit⟩ hit
hit parade *f* ⟨*pl* hit parade⟩ hit parade
hl *abbr* (= **ettolitro**) hl (hectolitre)
hm *abbr* (= **ettometro**) hm (hectometre)
ho → ***avere***
hobby *m* ⟨*pl* hobby⟩ hobby; ***fare qc per* ~** do sth as a hobby; ***avere l'~ del giardinaggio*** have gardening as a hobby
hockeista *m/f* ⟨*mpl* -i⟩ hockey player
hockey *m* ⟨*pl* hockey⟩ hockey; **~ *su ghiaccio*** ice hockey
holding *f* ⟨*pl* holding⟩ holding
hollywoodiano *adj* Hollywood *attr*
honduregno I *adj* Honduran **II** *m*, **-a** *f* Honduran
honoris causa *adv*: ***ricevere la laurea* ~** get an honorary degree
hooligan *m* ⟨*pl* hooligan⟩ hooligan
horror *adj inv* horror; ***film*** *m* **~** horror film
hostess *f* ⟨*pl* hostess⟩ hostess; **~ *di terra*** (*guida*) member of ground staff
hosting *m* ⟨*pl* hosting⟩ COMPUT hosting
hot dog *m* ⟨*pl* hot dog⟩ hot dog
hotel *m* ⟨*pl* hotel⟩ hotel
hot line *f* ⟨*pl* hot line⟩ hot line
hovercraft *m* ⟨*pl* hovercraft⟩ NAUT hovercraft
hub *m* ⟨*pl* hub⟩ hub
hula-hoop *m* ⟨*pl* hula-hoop⟩ Hula Hoop®
humour *m* ⟨*pl* humour⟩ humour; **~ *nero*** black mood; ***avere* ~ / *il senso dello* ~** have a sense of humour
humus *m* ⟨*pl* humus⟩ humus; *fig* breeding ground; ***terreno*** *m* ***ricco di* ~** soil rich in humus
husky *m* ⟨*pl* husky⟩ husky; SEW husky jacket
hutu ⟨*pl* hutu⟩ **I** *adj* Hutu **II** *m/f* Hutu

I

i, I *m/f* ⟨*pl* i, I⟩ i, I; **~ greca** y; **~ lunga** j; *fig* **mettere i puntini sulle ~** dot the i's and cross the t's
i *art mpl* the
iatale *adj* hiatal; **ernia** *f* **~** hiatus hernia
iato *m* hiatus (*a. fig*)
iattura *f infml* calamity
iberico *adj* ⟨*mpl* -ci⟩ Iberian
ibernare ⟨1a⟩ **I** *v/t* freeze **II** *v/i* hibernate
ibernazione *f* hibernation
ibid. *abbr* (= **ibidem**) ibid. (ibidem)
ibis *m* ⟨*pl* ibis⟩ ibis
ibisco *m* ⟨*pl* -schi⟩ hibiscus
ibridare *v/t* ⟨1l⟩ cross-breed
ibrido I *adj* hybrid (*a. fig*) **II** *m* hybrid (*a. fig*)
Icaro *m* Icarus; *fig* **volo** *m* **di ~** flight of Icarus
ICE *abbr* (= **Istituto Nazionale per il Commercio Estero**) *National Institute for Foreign Trade*
iceberg *m* ⟨*pl* iceberg⟩ iceberg
ICI *abbr* (= **Imposta Comunale sugli Immobili**) council tax
icona *f* icon; **~ di collegamento** COMPUT link
iconoclasta *m/f* ⟨*mpl* -i⟩ HIST *fig* iconoclast
iconografia *f* iconography
ictus *m* ⟨*pl* ictus⟩ MED stroke
Iddio *m* God
idea *f* idea; (*opinione*) opinion; **~ balorda** mad idea; **~ geniale** brainwave; **~ fissa** obsession, idée fixe; **~ luminosa** brilliant idea; **scambio** *m* **di -e** exchange of views; **cambiare ~** change one's mind; **avere le -e chiare** have clear ideas; **non avere la minima ~ di qc** not have the slightest idea about sth; **neanche per ~!** of course not!
ideale *m/adj* ideal; **sarebbe l'~** that would be the best thing
idealismo *m* idealism
idealista *m* ⟨*mpl* -i⟩ idealist
idealistico *adj* ⟨*mpl* -ci⟩ idealistic
idealizzare *v/t* ⟨1a⟩ idealize
idealizzazione *f* idealization
idealmente *adv* ideally
ideare *v/t* ⟨1b⟩ *scherzo, scusa* think up; *metodo, oggetto nuovo* invent; *piano, progetto* devise
ideatore *m*, **-trice** *f* originator; *di metodo, oggetto nuovo* inventor
ideazione *f* devising
idem *adv* ditto
identicità *f* ⟨*pl* identicità⟩ identity
identico *adj* ⟨*mpl* -ci⟩ identical
identificabile *adj* identifiable
identificare *v/t* ⟨1n & d⟩ identify
identificarsi *v/r*: **~ con qn / qc** identify with s.o. / sth
identificazione *f* identification; **~ di un cadavere** identifying a body; **~ di una chiamata** TEL caller display
identikit® *m* ⟨*pl* identikit⟩ Identikit®
identità *f* ⟨*pl* identità⟩ identity; **carta** *f* **d'~** identity card, ID; **crisi** *f* **d'~** identity crisis
ideogramma *m* ⟨*pl* -i⟩ ideogram
ideologia *f* ideology
ideologicamente *adv* ideologically
ideologico *adj* ⟨*mpl* -ci⟩ ideological
ideologizzare *v/t* ⟨1n⟩ ideologize
idilliaco *adj* ⟨*mpl* -ci⟩ idyllic
idillio *m* ⟨*pl* -i⟩ idyll
idioma *m* ⟨*pl* -i⟩ idiom
idiomatico *adj* ⟨*mpl* -ci⟩ idiomatic
idiota I *adj* idiotic, stupid **II** *m/f* ⟨*mpl* -i⟩ idiot, fool
idiozia *f* stupidity, idiocy; (*assurdità*) nonsense; **un'~** a stupid *or* idiotic thing to do / say
idolatrare *v/t* ⟨1a⟩ idolize (*a. fig*)
idolatria *f* idolatry (*a. fig*)
idolo *m* idol
idoneità *f* ⟨*pl* idoneità⟩ suitability; *qualifica* qualification; **esame** *m* **di ~** aptitude test
idoneo *adj* suitable (**a** for); **~ all'insegnamento** suitable for teaching
Idra *f* Hydra
idrante *m* hydrant
idratante *adj della pelle* moisturizing; **crema** *f* **~** moisturizer
idratare *v/t* ⟨1a⟩ *la pelle* moisturize
idrato *m* hydrate; **-i** *pl* **di carbonio** carbon hydrates
idraulica *f* hydraulics *sg*

idraulicamente *adv* hydraulically; ***azionato ~*** hydraulic

idraulico I *adj* hydraulic; ***impianto*** *m* ~ plumbing **II** *m* ⟨*pl* -ci⟩ plumber

idrico *adj* water *attr*; ***riserva*** *f* ***-a*** water reserves; ***fabbisogno*** *m* ~ water requirements

idrocarburo *m* hydrocarbon

idrocefalia *f* hydrocephalus

idrocefalico *adj* ⟨*mpl* -ci⟩ hydrocephalic

idrocefalo *m* hydrocephalus

idrocoltura *f* hydroponics *sg*

idrodinamica *f* hydrodynamics *sg*

idroelettrico *adj* hydroelectric; ***centrale*** *f* ***-a*** hydroelectric power station

idrofilo *adj*: ***cotone*** *m* ~ cotton wool, *US* absorbent cotton

idrofobia *f* rabies *sg* **idrofobo** *adj* ZOOL rabid; (*furioso*) foaming at the mouth

idrogeno *m* hydrogen

idrogeologico *adj* ⟨*mpl* -ci⟩ hydrogeological; ***rischio*** *m* ~ hydrogeological risk; ***vincolo*** *m* ~ hydrogeological constriction

idrografia *f* hydrography

idrolisi *f* ⟨*pl* idrolisi⟩ hydrolysis

idrologia *f* hydrology

idrologico *adj* ⟨*mpl* -ci⟩ hydrological

idromassaggio *m* Jacuzzi®, whirlpool bath

idrometro *m* hydrometer

idroplano *m* hydroplane

idrorepellente *adj* waterproof

idroscalo *m* seaplane base

idroscopio *m* ⟨*pl* -i⟩ hydroscope

idrosolubile *adj* water-soluble

idrossido *m* hydroxide

idrostatica *f* hydrostatics *sg*

idroterapia *f* hydrotherapy, hydrotherapeutics *sg*

idrovolante *m* seaplane

idrovora *f* draining pump

idrovoro *adj* draining; ***impianto*** *m* ~ drainage system

idruro *m* CHEM hydride; ***~ di nickel*** TEL nickel hydride

iella *f* *infml* bad luck; ***portare ~*** bring bad luck

iellato *adj* *infml* unlucky

iena *f* hyena

ieratico *adj* ⟨*mpl* -ci⟩ hieratic

ieri *adv* yesterday; ***~ l'altro, l'altro ~*** the day before yesterday; ***~ mattina*** yesterday morning; ***~ sera*** yesterday evening; ***~ notte*** last night; ***il giornale di ~*** yesterday's paper; ***non sono mica nato ~*** I wasn't born yesterday

iettatura *f* bad luck, jinx

igiene *f* hygiene; ***~ orale*** oral hygiene; ***~ del corpo*** personal hygiene; ***centro*** *m* ***d'~ mentale*** mental health centre; ***ufficio*** *m* ***d'~*** public health office

igienicamente *adv* hygienically

igienico *adj* ⟨*mpl* -ci⟩ hygienic; ***carta*** *f* ***-a*** toilet paper; ***condizioni*** *fpl* ***-che*** sanitary conditions; ***impianti*** *mpl* ***~-sanitari*** sanitation

igienista *m/f* ⟨*pl* -i⟩: ***~ dentale*** dental hygienist

igloo *m* ⟨*pl* igloo⟩ igloo

ignaro *adj* unaware (***di*** of)

ignobile *adj* vile

ignominia *f* ignominy

ignorante *adj* (*non informato*) ignorant; (*incolto*) uneducated; (*maleducato*) rude

ignoranza *f* ignorance

ignorare *v/t* ⟨1a⟩ (*non considerare*) ignore; (*non sapere*) not know; ***lo ignoro*** I don't know; ***~ i consigli di qn*** disregard s.o.'s advice

ignoto *adj* unknown; ***denuncia*** *f* ***contro -i*** action against a person or persons unknown; ***il Milite Ignoto*** the Unknown Soldier

igrometro *m* hygrometer

igroscopico *adj* ⟨*mpl* -ci⟩ hygroscopic

ikebana *m* ⟨*pl* ikebana⟩ ikebana, *Japanese flower-arranging*

il *art msg* the; ***~ signor Conte*** Mr Conte; ***~ martedì*** on Tuesdays; ***~ Tevere*** the Tiber; ***2 euro ~ chilo*** 2 euros a kilo; ***mi piace il caffè*** I like coffee; ***fa ~ postino*** he's a postman; ***lavati ~ viso*** wash your face; ***vive con ~ padre*** she lives with her father; ***tutto ~ pomeriggio*** all afternoon; ***~ mio ombrello*** my umbrella; ***l'ho pagato ~ triplo*** I paid three times as much for it; ***~ 6 luglio*** the 6th of July; ***~ 2006*** 2006; ***lo conosci ~ Piemonte?*** do you know Piedmont?

ilare *adj* cheerful

ilarità *f* ⟨*pl* ilarità⟩ hilarity; ***suscitare l'~ generale*** cause great hilarity

ileo *m* ANAT ileum; (*osso*) ilium

Iliade *f* Iliad

illanguidire ⟨4d⟩ **I** *v/t* weaken **II** *v/i* become weaken

illanguidirsi *v/r* ⟨4d⟩ flag; *fig* fade
illazione *f* conjecture; (*giudizio*) conclusion; ***fare delle -i*** infer
illecito *adj* illicit; ***~ penale*** criminal offence
illegale *adj* illegal
illegalità *f* ⟨*pl* illegalità⟩ illegality
illegalmente *adv* illegally
illeggibile *adj* illegible
illegittimità *f* ⟨*pl* illeggittimità⟩ illegitimacy; ***~ costituzionale*** constitutional illegitimacy
illegittimo *adj* illegitimate
illibatezza *f* chastity
illibato *adj* chaste
illiberale *adj* POL illiberal
illeso *adj* unhurt
illimitatamente *adv* limitlessly
illimitato *adj* unlimited
Illiria *f* Illyria
illirico ⟨*mpl* -ci⟩ **I** *adj* Illyrian **II** *m*, **-a** *f* Illyrian
illividire *v/i* ⟨4d⟩ go blue
ill.mo *abbr* (= **illustrissimo**) *formal style of address in correspondence*
illogico *adj* ⟨*mpl* -ci⟩ illogical
illudere *v/t* ⟨3q⟩ deceive
illudersi *v/r* delude o.s.; ***si era illuso di farcela da solo*** he had deluded himself that he could do it alone
illuminante *adj* illuminating; *fig* inspiring; ***razzo** m* **~** flare
illuminare *v/t* ⟨1m⟩ light up; *fig* enlighten
illuminarsi *v/r* ⟨1m⟩ light up
illuminato *adj* lit up; ***~ a giorno*** floodlit; ***mente** f* ***-a*** enlightened mind; ***spirito** m* **~** enlightened mind
illuminazione *f* lighting; *fig* flash of inspiration; ***~ stradale*** street lighting
Illuminismo *m* Enlightenment
illuminista I *adj* Enlightenment **II** *m/f* ⟨*mpl* -i⟩ Enlightenment philosopher
illusione *f* illusion; ***non farsi -i*** not delude o.s.
illusionismo *m* conjuring
illusionista *m/f* ⟨*mpl* -i⟩ conjuror
illuso I *past part* → ***illudere*** **II** *m*, **-a** *f* (*sognatore*) dreamer; ***sei un povero ~ !*** you're such a mug!
illusorio *adj* ⟨*mpl* -ri⟩ illusory
illustrare *v/t* ⟨1a⟩ illustrate
illustrativo *adj* illustrative; ***foglio** m* **~** explanatory sheet; ***materiale** m* **~** illustrative material
illustrato *adj* illustrated; ***libro** m* **~** illustrated book
illustratore *m*, **-trice** *f* illustrator
illustrazione *f* illustration
illustre *adj* illustrious; ***Illustre professore*** *nelle lettere* Dear Professor
IM *abbr* (= **Imperia**) Imperia
imbacuccarsi *v/r* wrap up
imbacuccato *adj* wrapped up
imbaldanzirsi *v/r* ⟨4d⟩ grow bolder
imballaggio *m* ⟨*pl* -ggi⟩ *operazione* packing; (*involucro*) package; ***~ a rendere*** packaging to be returned; ***~ a perdere*** disposable packaging; ***spese** fpl* ***d'~*** packing charges
imballare[1] *v/t* ⟨1a⟩ pack
imballare[2] *v/t* ⟨1a⟩: ***~ il motore*** race the engine
imballo *m* → ***imballaggio***
imbalsamare *v/t* ⟨1a⟩ embalm; *animale* stuff
imbalsamatore *m*, **-trice** *f* embalmer; *animale* taxidermist
imbalsamazione *f* embalming; *di animali*: taxidermy
imbambolarsi *v/r* ⟨1m⟩ be stunned
imbambolato *adj occhi, sguardo* blank; *dal sonno* bleary-eyed; ***non star lí fermo ~!*** don't stand there gawping!
imbandierare *v/t* ⟨1b⟩ decorate with flags
imbandire *v/t* ⟨4d⟩: ***~ la tavola*** set the table
imbarazzante *adj* embarrassing
imbarazzare *v/t* ⟨1a⟩ embarrass
imbarazzato *adj* embarrassed; ***avere lo stomaco ~*** have an upset stomach
imbarazzo *m* embarassment; (*disturbo*) trouble; ***~ di stomaco*** upset stomach; ***non avere che l'~ della scelta*** be spoilt for choice; ***mettere in ~ qn*** embarrass s.o.
imbarbarimento *m* barbarization; ***~ dei costumi*** decline of morals
imbarbarire *v/t* ⟨4d⟩ barbarize
imbarbarirsi *v/r* ⟨4d⟩ become barbarous
imbarcadero *m* landing stage
imbarcare *v/t* ⟨1d⟩ embark; *carico* load; ***~ acqua*** ship water
imbarcarsi *v/r* go on board, embark; ***~ in un'impresa*** embark on an undertaking
imbarcazione *f* boat; ***~ da diporto***

pleasure boat
imbarco *m* ⟨*pl* -chi⟩ *di passeggeri* boarding, embarkation; *di carico* loading; (*banchina*) landing stage
imbastardire *v/t* ⟨4d⟩ bastardize; *fig* corrupt
imbastardirsi *v/r* ⟨4d⟩ become corrupted
imbastire *v/t* ⟨4d⟩ baste, tack; *fig* outline
imbastitura *f* basting, tacking; *fig* outline
imbattersi *v/r* ⟨3a⟩: ***~ in qn*** bump into s.o.
imbattibile *adj* unbeatable
imbavagliare *v/t* ⟨1g⟩ gag
imbeccata *f* cue; ***dare l'~ a qn*** prompt s.o.
imbecille I *adj* idiotic, stupid **II** *m/f* imbecile, fool
imbecillità *f* ⟨*pl* imbecillità⟩ stupidity; MED imbecility
imbellettarsi *v/r* ⟨1a⟩ put on make up
imbellire ⟨4d⟩ **I** *v/t* make attractive **II** *v/i* become attractive
imberbe *adj* smooth-cheeked; *fig* callow
imbestialire *v/i* ⟨4d⟩ enrage; ***la sua arroganza mi fa ~*** his arrogance makes me so angry
imbestialirsi *v/r* ⟨4d⟩ fly into a rage
imbevibile *adj* undrinkable
imbevuto *adj*: ***~ di qc*** soaked in sth
imbiancare ⟨1d⟩ **I** *v/t* whiten; *con pitture* paint; *tessuti* bleach; ***~ le pareti*** whitewash to walls **II** *v/i* go white
imbiancarsi *v/r* ⟨1d⟩ go white
imbianchino *m* (house) painter
imbiondire *v/t* ⟨4d⟩ turn blond; COOK lightly brown
imbizzarrire *v/i* ⟨4d⟩ become frisky
imboccare *v/t* ⟨1d⟩ *persona* feed; *fig* prompt; ***~ una strada*** turn into a road
imboccatura *f* (*apertura*) opening; (*ingresso*) entrance; MUS mouthpiece
imbocco *m* entrance
imbonire *v/t* ⟨4d⟩ spiel
imbonitore *m*, **-trice** *f* huckster
imborghesire *v/t* ⟨4d⟩ *pej* make bourgeois
imborghesirsi *v/r* *pej* become bourgeois
imboscarsi *v/r* ⟨1d⟩ MIL evade military service, *US* dodge the draft
imboscata *f* ambush; ***tendere un'~ a qn*** lay an ambush for s.o.; ***cadere in un'~*** be ambushed
imbottigliamento *m* bottling; AUTO traffic jam
imbottigliare *v/t* ⟨1g⟩ bottle; *di veicoli* hold up; ***sono rimasto imbottigliato nel traffico*** I was stuck in a traffic jam
imbottire *v/t* ⟨4d⟩ stuff; *giacca* pad; *fig* (*riempire*) cram, stuff
imbottirsi *v/r*: ***~ di qc*** stuff o.s. with sth
imbottito *adj* stuffed; *panino* filled
imbottitura *f* stuffing; *di giacca* padding
imbracare *v/t* ⟨1d⟩ sling
imbracatura *f* sling
imbracciare *v/t* ⟨1f⟩: ***~ il fucile*** take aim (with a gun)
imbranataggine *f* *infml* clumsiness
imbranato *adj* clumsy
imbrattare *v/t* ⟨1a⟩ soil; (*macchiare*) stain
imbrattarsi *v/r* get o.s. dirty; ***~ le mani / i pantaloni*** get one's hands / trousers *or US* pants dirty
imbrattatele *m/f* ⟨*pl* imbrattatele⟩ dauber
imbrigliare *v/t* ⟨1g⟩ *cavallo* bridle; *fig* curb
imbroccare *v/t* ⟨1c & d⟩ *fig* hit; ***non imbroccarne una*** not get any right
imbrogliare ⟨1g & c⟩ **I** *v/t* (*raggirare*) take in; (*truffare*) cheat, swindle; *fig* confuse; ***~ le carte*** confuse the issue; *fig* ***~ la matassa*** create confusion **II** *v/i* cheat
imbrogliarsi *v/r* *matassa* become tangled; *fig* *persona* become confused
imbroglio *m* ⟨*pl* -gli⟩ (*truffa*) trick; *fig* (*pasticcio*) mess
imbroglione *m*, **-a** *f* cheat, swindler
imbronciarsi *v/r* ⟨1f⟩ sulk
imbronciato *adj* sulky
imbrunire *v/impers* ⟨4d⟩ get dark; ***all'~*** at dusk
imbruttire ⟨4d⟩ **I** *v/t* make ugly **II** *v/i* become ugly
imbucare *v/t* ⟨1d⟩ *posta* post, *US* mail
imburrare *v/t* ⟨1a⟩ butter
imbustare *v/t* ⟨1a⟩ put into an envelope
imbuto *m* funnel
imene *m* ANAT hymen
imitabile *adj* imitable

imitare *v/t* ⟨1a or 1l⟩ imitate
imitatore *m*, **-trice** *f* impressionist
imitazione *f* imitation; ***fare l'~ di qn*** do an impression of s.o.
Immacolata *f* Immaculate Conception
immacolato *adj* (*puro*) immaculate; (*candido*) spotless; ***l'Immacolata Concezione*** the Immaculate Conception
immagazzinamento *m* storage
immagazzinare *v/t* ⟨1a⟩ store
immaginabile *adj* imaginable
immaginare *v/t* ⟨1m⟩ imagine; (*supporre*) suppose; ***s'immagini!*** not at all!; ***immagina di essere ricco*** imagine being rich; ***avrei dovuto immaginarlo!*** I must have imagined it!; ***è più facile / difficile di quanto immaginassi*** it's easier / harder than you might think
immaginario *adj* ⟨*mpl* -ri⟩ imaginary; ***~ collettivo*** collective imagination
immaginarsi *v/r* ⟨1m⟩ imagine; ***~ qc*** picture sth
immaginazione *f* imagination; ***privo di ~*** with no imagination; ***è solo una sua ~*** it's just something he / she imagined
immagine *f* image
immaginetta *f* holy picture
immalinconire *v/t* ⟨4d⟩ sadden
immalinconirsi *v/r* ⟨4d⟩ grow sad
immancabile *adj cortesia*, *sorriso* unfailing; *persona* ever present; *macchina fotografica* inevitable
immancabilmente *adv* without fail, unfailingly
immane *adj* awful
immanente *adj* immanent
immanenza *f* immanence
immangiabile *adj* inedible
immateriale *adj* intangible (*a.* JUR)
immatricolare *v/t* ⟨1n⟩ register
immatricolarsi *v/r* enrol, *US* enroll; *all'università* matriculate, enrol
immatricolazione *f* registration; *all'università* matriculation, enrol(l)ment
immaturità *f* immaturity
immaturo *adj persona* immature; (*precoce*) premature; *frutto* unripe
immedesimarsi *v/r* ⟨1n⟩ identify (***in*** with)
immedesimazione *f* identification; ***capacità f di ~*** ability to identify
immediatamente *adv* immediately
immediatezza *f* directness; (*rapidità*) immediacy
immediato *adj* immediate; (*pronto*) prompt; ***nelle -e vicinanze*** in the immediate vicinity; ***con effetto m ~*** with immediate effect; ***consegna f -a*** spot delivery
immemorabile *adj* immemorial; ***da tempo m ~*** from time immemorial
immensamente *adv* immensely
immensità *f* ⟨*pl* immensità⟩ immensity
immenso *adj* immense
immensurabile *adj* immeasurable
immergere *v/t* ⟨3uu⟩ immerse, dip; (*lasciare immerso*) soak
immergersi *v/r* plunge; *di subacqueo*, *sottomarino* dive; *fig* immerse o.s. (***in*** in)
immeritato *adj* undeserved
immeritevole *adj* unworthy
immersione *f* immersion; *di subacqueo*, *sottomarino* dive; ***fare -i*** go diving
immerso **I** *past part* → ***immergere*** **II** *adj* immersed
immettere *v/t* ⟨3ee⟩ introduce (***in*** into); COMPUT *dati* enter; (*portare*) lead (***in*** into)
immettersi *v/r*: ***~ in*** get into
immigrante *m/f* immigrant
immigrare *v/i* ⟨1a⟩ immigrate
immigrato *m*, **-a** *f* immigrant
immigratorio *adj* ⟨*mpl* -ri⟩ immigratory; ***flusso m ~*** flow of immigrants
immigrazione *f* immigration; (*immigrati*) immigrants *pl*; FIN inflow
imminente *adj* imminent; *pericolo* impending; *pubblicazione* forthcoming
imminenza *f* imminence
immischiare *v/t* ⟨1k⟩ involve
immischiarsi *v/r* meddle (***in*** with), interfere (***in*** in)
immiserimento *m* impoverishment
immiserire *v/t* ⟨4d⟩ impoverish
immiserirsi *v/r* ⟨4d⟩ become impoverished
immissione *f* introduction; *di manodopera* intake; COMPUT *di dati* entry
immobile **I** *adj* motionless, still; ***beni mpl -i*** real estate **II** *m*: ***immobili*** *pl* real estate *sg*
immobiliare *adj*: ***agente m/f ~*** estate agent, *US* realtor; ***società f ~*** *di compravendita* property company; *di*

costruzione construction company
immobiliarista *m/f* ⟨*mpl* -i⟩ estate agent
immobilismo *m* inactivity; POL opposition to progress
immobilità *f* immobility; POL, FIN inactivity
immobilizzare *v/t* ⟨1a⟩ immobilize; FIN *capitali* tie up
immobilizzarsi *v/r* ⟨1a⟩ freeze
immobilizzazione *f* immobilization; ECON locking up (of capital)
immodestia *f* immodesty
immodesto *adj* immodest
immolare *v/t* ⟨1m⟩ sacrifice
immolarsi *v/r* ⟨1m⟩ sacrifice oneself; ***~ per la libertà*** sacrifice oneself for freedom
immondezzaio *m* ⟨*pl* -ai⟩ rubbish dump; *fig* pig sty
immondizia *f* (*usu pl*) rubbish, refuse, *US* trash
immondo *adj* filthy; REL unclean
immorale *adj* immoral
immoralità *f* immorality
immortalare *v/t* ⟨1a⟩ immortalize
immortale *adj* immortal
immortalità *f* immortality
immotivato *adj* unmotivated
immune *adj* MED immune (***a*** to); (*esente*) free (***da*** from); ***~ da difetti*** without any defects
immunità *f* ⟨*pl* immunità⟩ immunity; ***~ parlamentare / diplomatica*** parliamentary / diplomatic immunity
immunitario *adj*: ***sistema*** *m* ***~*** immune system
immunizzante *adj* immunizing
immunizzare *v/t* ⟨1a⟩ immunize
immunizzarsi *v/r* ⟨1a⟩ become immune (*a. fig*)
immunizzazione *f* immunization
immunodeficienza *f* immunodeficiency; ***sindrome*** *f* ***da ~ acquisita*** acquired immune deficiency syndrome
immunosoppressore *m* MED immunosuppressant
immusonirsi *v/r* ⟨4d⟩ sulk
immusonito *adj* sulky
immutabile *adj* *decisione*, *legge* unchangeable; *principi*, *tradizioni* unchanging
immutabilità *f* ⟨*pl* immutabilità⟩ changelessness
immutato *adj* unchanged
impacchettare *v/t* ⟨1a⟩ (*confezionare*) wrap (up); (*mettere in pacchetti*) package
impacciare *v/t* ⟨1f⟩ *movimenti* hamper; *persona* hinder
impacciato *adj* (*imbarazzato*) embarrassed; (*goffo*) awkward, clumsy
impaccio *m* ⟨*pl* -cci⟩ (*ostacolo*) hindrance; (*situazione difficile*) awkward situation; (*imbarazzo*) awkwardness; ***essere d'~ a qn*** be a hindrance to s.o.; ***trarsi d'~*** get o.s. out of an awkward situation
impacco *m* ⟨*pl* -cchi⟩ MED compress
impadronirsi *v/r* ⟨4d⟩: ***~ di qc*** take possession of sth, seize sth; *fig* master sth
impagabile *adj* priceless
impaginare *v/t* ⟨1m⟩ TYPO paginate
impaginazione *f* page make-up
impagliare *v/t* ⟨1g⟩ *sedia* bottom with straw; *animale* stuff with straw
impagliatore *m*, **-trice** *f* *di sedie* chair-mender; *di animali* taxidermist
impalato *adj* *infml* bolt upright; ***non stare lì ~!*** don't just stand there!
impalcatura *f* *temporanea* scaffolding; *fig* framework, structure
impallidire *v/i* ⟨4d⟩ *di persona* turn pale
impallinare *v/t* ⟨1a⟩ riddle
impalmare *v/t* ⟨1a⟩ NAUT splice; *hum* (*sposare*) get spliced
impalpabile *adj* very fine
impalpabilità *f* ⟨*pl* impalbabilità⟩ intangibility
impaludare *v/t* ⟨1a⟩ swamp
impaludarsi *v/r* ⟨1a⟩ get stuck; *fig* get bogged down; ***~ in una discussione*** get bogged down in an argument
impanare *v/t* ⟨1a⟩ COOK coat with breadcrumbs
impanato *adj* in breadcrumbs, breaded
impantanarsi *v/r* ⟨1a⟩ get bogged down
impaperarsi *v/r* ⟨1m⟩ falter
impappinarsi *v/r* ⟨1a⟩ become flustered
imparare *v/t* ⟨1a⟩ learn (***a*** to); ***~ a nuotare*** learn to swim; ***~ qc a memoria*** learn sth by heart; ***avere molto da ~*** have a lot to learn; ***bene, così impari!*** well, that'll teach you!; ***impara l'arte e mettila da parte*** *prov* learn

a trade for a rainy day; ***sbagliando s'impara*** *prov* you learn from your mistakes
impareggiabile *adj* incomparable
imparentarsi *v/r* ⟨1b⟩: ***~ con qn*** become related to s.o.
impari *adj inv* unequal; MATH odd
imparruccato *adj* bewigged
impartire *v/t* ⟨4d⟩ give; ***~ qc a qn*** give sth to s.o.; ***~ la benedizione*** bless
imparziale *adj* impartial
imparzialità *f* impartiality
impasse *f* ⟨*pl* impasse⟩ impass
impassibile *adj* impassive
impassibilità *f* ⟨*pl* impassibilità⟩ emotionlessness
impastare *v/t* ⟨1a⟩ mix; *pane* knead
impastato *adj*: ***lingua f -a*** furred tongue
impastatrice *f* mixer
impasticcarsi *v/r* ⟨1d⟩ *infml* pop pills
impasto *m* COOK dough; (*mescolanza*) mixture
impataccare *v/t* ⟨1d⟩ *infml* spatter
impataccarsi *v/r* ⟨1d⟩ *infml* dirty oneself
impatto *m* impact; ***~ ambientale*** environmental impact
impaurire *v/t* ⟨4d⟩ frighten
impaurirsi *v/r* become frightened
impaurito *adj* frightened
impavido *adj* fearless
impaziente *adj* impatient; ***essere ~ di fare qc*** be eager to do sth
impazientemente *adv* impatiently
impazientirsi *v/r* ⟨4d⟩ grow impatient
impazienza *f* impatience
impazzare *v/i* ⟨1a⟩ revel
impazzata *adv*: ***all'~*** *correre* at breakneck speed; *colpire* wildly
impazzire *v/i* ⟨4d⟩ go mad *or* crazy; ***far ~ qn*** drive s.o. mad *or* crazy; ***quel cappello mi piace da ~*** I just love that hat
impeccabile *adj* impeccable
impeccabilità *f* ⟨*pl* impeccabilità⟩ flawlessness
impeccabilmente *adv* impeccably
impedenza *f* PHYS impedance
impedimento *m* hindrance; (*ostacolo*) obstacle; JUR impediment; ***essere d'~*** be a hindrance; ***salvo -i*** unless something comes up
impedire *v/t* ⟨4d⟩ prevent; (*ostruire*) block, obstruct; (*impacciare*) hinder; ***~ a qn di fare qc*** prevent s.o. *or* keep s.o. from doing sth; ***~ che qc accada*** stop sth happening; ***niente glielo impedisce*** there's nothing stopping him; ***~ il passaggio a qn*** bar s.o.'s way
impedito *adj* disabled; ***avere un braccio ~*** have lost the use of one arm
impegnare *v/t* ⟨1a⟩ (*dare come pegno*) pawn; (*riservare*) reserve, book; *spazio, corsia* occupy, take up; SPORTS *avversario* keep under pressure; (*costringere*) oblige; ***~ qn*** *di lavoro* keep s.o. busy *or* occupied; ***~ qn per contratto*** bind s.o. by contract
impegnarsi *v/r* (*prendersi l'impegno*) commit o.s., undertake (***a*** to); (*concentrarsi*) apply o.s. (***in*** to); ***mi sono impegnata a farlo*** I've committed myself to doing it, I've undertaken to do it
impegnativa *f document issued by the National Health Service authorising treatment*
impegnativo *adj* (*che richiede impegno*) demanding; *pranzo, serata, abito* formal; (*vincolante*) binding
impegnato *adj* (*occupato*) busy; *fig* (politically) committed; ***sono già ~*** I've made other arrangements, I'm doing something else; ***~ nella lotta alla droga*** involved in the war on drugs
impegno *m* **1.** commitment; ***-i di lavoro*** work commitments; COMM ***senza ~*** with no commitment **2.** (*appuntamento*) engagement; ***stasera no, ho un ~*** not tonight: I've got something on **3.** (*zelo*) zeal, care; ***mettersi d'~ a fare qc*** make an effort to do sth; ***studiare con ~*** study hard
impegolarsi *v/r* ⟨1m⟩: ***~ in qc*** get mixed up in sth
impelagarsi *v/r* ⟨1m & b⟩ *infml* get entangled
impellente *adj* urgent
impellenza *f* urgency
impellicciato *adj* fur-clad *attr*, wearing furs
impenetrabile *adj* impenetrable; ***mistero m ~*** unsolvable mystery
impenetrabilità *f* ⟨*pl* impenetrabilità⟩ impenetrability
impenitente *adj scapolo* confirmed; *donnaiolo* incorrigible; *fumatore* chain *attr*; *peccatore* unrepentant

impennarsi *v/r* ⟨1a⟩ *di cavallo* rear; *di moto* do a wheelie
impennata *f di cavallo* rearing; *di moto* wheelie; ***i prezzi hanno avuto un'~*** prices have soared
impensabile *adj* unthinkable
impensato *adj* unexpected
impensierire *v/t* ⟨4d⟩ worry
impensierirsi *v/r* ⟨4d⟩ become worried
impepata *f*: ***~ di cozze*** *Campanian dish of mussels cooked with garlic and black pepper*
imperante *adj* (*dominante*) prevailing
imperare *v/i* ⟨1b⟩ rule (***su*** over)
imperativo *m/adj* imperative; ***norme*** *fpl* ***-e*** binding regulations
imperatore *m*, **-trice** *f* emperor; *donna* empress
impercettibile *adj* imperceptible
impercettibilmente *adv* imperceptibly
imperdonabile *adj* unforgivable
imperfetto *m/adj* imperfect
imperfezione *f* imperfection
imperiale *adj* imperial
imperialismo *m* imperialism
imperialista *m/f* ⟨*mpl* -i⟩ imperialist
imperiese I *adj* from Imperia **II** *m/f* person from Imperia
imperioso *adj* imperious; *bisogno* urgent
imperituro *adj form* eternal
imperizia *f* inexperience
imperlare *v/t* ⟨1b⟩ bead; ***il sudore gli imperlava la fronte*** beads of sweat covered his brow
imperlarsi *v/r* ⟨1b⟩: ***~ di rugiada*** be beaded with dew
impermalirsi *v/r* ⟨4d⟩ take offence *or US* offense; ***~ per qc*** take offence at sth, *US* offense
impermeabile I *adj* waterproof **II** *m* raincoat
impermeabilità *f* impermeability
impermeabilizzare *v/t* ⟨1a⟩ waterproof
impermeabilizzato *adj* waterproof
impermeabilizzazione *f* waterproofing
imperniare *v/t* ⟨1b & k⟩ TECH hinge; *fig* focus
imperniarsi *v/r* ⟨1b & k⟩ TECH hinge; *fig* depend
impero *m* empire; (*potere*) rule; ***il Sacro Romano Impero*** the Holy Roman Empire; ***l'~ austro-ungarico*** the Austro-Hungarian Empire; ***stile*** *m* ***~*** Empire style
imperscrutabile *adj* inscrutable
imperscrutabilità *f* ⟨*pl* imperscrutabilità⟩ inscrutability
impersonale *adj* impersonal
impersonare *v/t* ⟨1a⟩ personify; (*interpretare*) play (the part of)
imperterrito *adj*: ***continuare ~ a fare qc*** carry on doing sth undaunted
impertinente *adj* impertinent
impertinenza *f* impertinence
imperturbabile *adj* imperturbable
imperturbabilità *f* imperturbability
imperversare *v/i* ⟨1b⟩ rage; *fig di moda* be all the rage
impervio *adj* impassable
impeto *m* impetus, force; (*accesso*) outburst; (*slancio*) passion, heat; ***parlare con ~*** speak forcefully; ***in un ~ d'ira*** in a fit of rage
impettito *adj* with one's chest out
impetuosamente *adv* impetuously
impetuoso *adj* impetuous
impiallacciato *adj* veneered
impiallacciatura *f* veneer
impiantare *v/t* ⟨1a⟩ *azienda*, *ufficio* set up; *congegno*, *apparecchiatura* install; MED implant
impiantistica *f* plant engineering
impiantito *m* floor, flooring
impianto *m operazione* installation; (*apparecchiature*) plant; (*sistema*) system; MED implant; ***~ elettrico*** wiring; ***~ di risalita*** ski lift; ***~ di riscaldamento*** heating system; ***-i*** *pl* ***sanitari*** bathroom fixtures and fittings; ***~ sportivo*** sports complex; ***~ stereo*** stereo (system)
impiastrare *v/r* ⟨1a⟩ smear
impiastricciare *v/t* ⟨1f⟩ smear
impiastricciarsi *v/r* ⟨1f⟩ become smeared
impiastro *m* poultice; *fig* pain in the neck
impiccagione *f* hanging
impiccare *v/t* ⟨1d⟩ hang
impiccarsi *v/r* hang o.s.
impiccato *m*, **-a** *f* hanged man, hanged woman
impicciare *v/t* ⟨1f⟩ be in the way
impicciarsi *v/r*: ***~ di*** *or* ***in qc*** interfere *or* meddle in sth

impiccio *m* ⟨*pl* -cci⟩ (*ostacolo*) hindrance; (*seccatura*) bother; ***essere d'~*** be in the way; ***essere in un ~*** be in trouble
impiccione *m*, **-a** *f* nosy parker *infml*
impiegabile *adj* employable; (*utilizzabile*) usable
impiegare *v/t* ⟨1b & e⟩ (*usare*) use; *tempo*, *soldi* spend; (*metterci*) take; (*assumere*) employ; ***ho impiegato un'ora*** it took me an hour
impiegatizio *adj* ⟨*mpl* -zi⟩ white-collar
impiegato *m*, **-a** *f* employee; ***~ di banca*** bank clerk; ***~ di ruolo*** permanent employee; ***~ statale*** civil servant
impiego *m* ⟨*pl* -ghi⟩ (*uso*) use; (*occupazione*) employment; (*posto*) job; FIN investment; ***domanda*** *f* ***d'~*** job application; ***offerta*** *f* ***d'~*** job offer; ***pubblico*** *m* ***~*** public sector employment
impietosire *v/i* ⟨4d⟩ move to pity
impietosirsi *v/r* be moved to pity
impietrire *v/i* ⟨4d⟩ *fig* petrify, stun
impietrito *adj* petrified; ***~ dal dolore*** transfixed by pain
impigliare *v/t* ⟨1g⟩ entangle
impigliarsi *v/r* get entangled
impignorabile *adj* undistrainable
impigrire ⟨4d⟩ **I** *v/t* make lazy **II** *v/i* get lazy
impigrirsi *v/r* ⟨4d⟩ get lazy
impilare *v/t* ⟨1a⟩ pile up
impinguare *v/t* ⟨1a⟩ fatten
impinguarsi *v/r* ⟨1a⟩ grow fat; *fig* get rich
implacabile *adj* implacable
implacabilmente *adv* implacably
implementare *v/t* ⟨1a⟩ COMPUT implement
implementazione *f* COMPUT layout
implicare *v/t* ⟨1l & d⟩ (*coinvolgere*) implicate; (*comportare*) imply; ***~ qn in qc*** implicate s.o. in sth
implicazione *f* implication
implicitamente *adv* implicitly
implicito *adj* implicit
implodere *v/i* ⟨3q⟩ implode
implorante *adj* pleading
implorare *v/t* ⟨1c⟩ implore
implorazione *f* entreaty
implosione *f* implosion
implume *adj* featherless
impollinare *v/t* ⟨1m⟩ pollinate
impollinazione *f* pollination
impoltronire ⟨4d⟩ **I** *v/t* make lazy **II** *v/i* become lazy
impoltronirsi *v/r* ⟨4d⟩ become lazy
impolverare *v/t* ⟨1m⟩ dust
impolverarsi *v/r* ⟨1m⟩ get dusty
impolverato *adj* dusty, covered with *or* in dust
impomatare *v/t* ⟨1a⟩ rub ointment on
imponderabile I *adj* imponderable **II** *m* imponderable
imponderabilità *f* ⟨*pl* imponderabilità⟩ imponderability
imponente *adj* imposing, impressive
imponenza *f* impressiveness
imponibile I *adj* taxable **II** *m* taxable income
impopolare *adj* unpopular
impopolarità *f* unpopularity
imporre *v/t* ⟨3ll⟩ impose; *prezzo* fix; ***~ il silenzio*** call for silence; ***~ le mani su*** lay hands on; ***~ a qn di fare qc*** force s.o. to do sth
imporsi *v/r* (*farsi valere*) assert o.s.; (*avere successo*) be successful, become established; (*essere necessario*) be necessary; ***~ di fare qc*** force o.s. to do sth; ***~ sul mercato*** dominate the market; ***~ all'attenzione*** attract attention; ***s'impone una pausa*** they called for a break
importante *adj* important
importanza *f* importance; ***darsi ~*** give o.s. airs; ***senza ~*** not important, unimportant; (***non***) ***dare ~ a qc*** attach (no) importance to sth
importare ⟨1c⟩ **I** *v/t* FIN, COMPUT import **II** *v/i* matter, be important; (*essere necessario*) be necessary; ***e a te che te ne importa?*** what's it to you?; ***non importa*** it doesn't matter; ***non gliene importa niente*** he couldn't care less
importatore *m*, **-trice** *f* importer
importazione *f* import; ***~ clandestina*** smuggling; ***permesso*** *m* ***d'~*** import permit; ***prodotti*** *mpl* ***d'~*** imported goods
importo *m* amount
importunare *v/t* ⟨1a⟩ (*assillare*) pester; (*disturbare*) bother
importuno *adj* troublesome; *domanda*, *osservazione* ill-timed
imposizione *f* imposition; (*tassazione*) taxation; (*tassa*) tax; ***~ fiscale*** FIN tax

impossessarsi *v/r* ⟨1b⟩: **~ *di*** seize
impossibile *adj* impossible; ***fare l'~*** do one's utmost
impossibilità *f* impossibility; ***essere nell'~ di fare qc*** be unable to do sth
imposta[1] *f* tax; ***~ di consumo*** excise duty; ***~ diretta / indiretta*** direct / indirect tax; ***~ sul reddito*** income tax; ***~ sul valore aggiunto*** value added tax; ***~ sul fatturato*** sales tax; ***ufficio*** *m* ***delle -e*** tax office
imposta[2] *f di finestra* shutter
impostare *v/t* ⟨1c⟩ *lavoro* plan; *problema* set out; *lettera* post, *US* mail
impostazione *f di lavoro* organization; *di tema* structure; *di domanda* formulation; COMPUT setup
imposto *past part* → ***imporre***
impostore *m*, **-a** *f* impostor
impostura *f* deception
impotente *adj* powerless; (*inefficace*) ineffectual; MED impotent
impotenza *f* powerlessness; MED impotence
impoverimento *m* impoverishment
impoverire ⟨4d⟩ **I** *v/t* impoverish; AGR overcrop **II** *v/i* become poor
impoverirsi *v/r* ⟨4d⟩ become poor
impraticabile *adj strada* impassable; *campo* unplayable
impraticabilità *f* ⟨*pl* impraticabilità⟩ impracticability; *con veicoli* impassability; SPORTS unplayability; ***l'~ di un progetto*** the unfeasibility of a plan
impratichirsi *v/r* ⟨4d⟩ get practice (***in*** in); ***~ a fare qc*** practise *or US* practice doing sth
imprecare *v/i* ⟨1d & b⟩ curse, swear (***contro*** at)
imprecazione *f* curse
imprecisato *adj numero*, *quantità* indeterminate; *motivi*, *circostanze* not clear
imprecisione *f* inaccuracy
impreciso *adj* inaccurate
impregnare *v/t* ⟨1a⟩ impregnate; (*imbevere*) soak
impregnarsi *v/r* become impregnated (***di*** with)
impregnato *adj*: ***~ di qc*** *sudore* soaked with sth; *fumo* filled with sth
imprenditore *m*, **-trice** *f* entrepreneur
imprenditoriale *adj* entrepreneurial
impreparato *adj* unprepared
impreparazione *f* unpreparedness
impresa *f* (*iniziativa*) enterprise, undertaking; (*azienda*) business, firm; ***~ familiare*** family business; ***piccola ~*** small business; ***~ di pompe funebri*** undertaker's; ***~ di servizi pubblici*** utility company; ***convincerlo sarà un'~!*** we'll have a job to convince him!
impresario *m*, **-a** *f* ⟨*mpl* -ri⟩ contractor; THEAT impresario
imprescindibile *adj* unavoidable
imprescrittibile *adj* imprescriptible
impressionabile *adj* impressionable; PHOT sensitive
impressionabilità *f* ⟨*pl* impressionabilità⟩ impressionability; PHOT sensitivity
impressionante *adj* impressive; (*spaventoso*) frightening; (*sconvolgente*) upsetting, shocking
impressionare *v/t* ⟨1a⟩ (*turbare*) upset, shock; (*spaventare*) frighten; (*colpire*) impress; PHOT expose
impressionarsi *v/r* (*spaventarsi*) get frightened
impressionato *adj* PHOT exposed; ***~ favorevolmente*** (favourably) impressed
impressione *f* impression; (*turbamento*) shock; (*paura*) fright; TYPO printing; ***fare una buona ~*** (***a qn***) make a good impression (on s.o.); ***ho l'~ che ...*** I get the impression that ...; ***il sangue mi fa ~*** I can't stand the sight of blood
impressionismo *m* Impressionism
impressionista **I** *adj* Impressionist **II** *m/f* ⟨*mpl* -i⟩ Impressionist
impresso *past part* → ***imprimere***
imprestare *v/t* ⟨1b⟩ lend
imprevedibile *adj* unforeseeable; *persona* unpredictable
imprevidente *adj* unforeseeing
imprevidenza *f* lack of foresight
imprevisto **I** *adj* unexpected **II** *m* unforeseen event; ***salvo imprevisti*** all being well, barring accidents
impreziosire *v/t* ⟨4d⟩ embellish (*a. fig*)
imprigionare *v/t* ⟨1a⟩ imprison
imprimatur *m* ⟨*pl* imprimatur⟩ imprimatur
imprimere *v/t* ⟨3r⟩ impress; *fig nella mente* fix firmly, imprint; *movimento*

impart; TYPO print

imprimersi *v/r* ⟨3r⟩ be engraved; **~ *nella mente*** be fixed in one's mind

imprinting *m* ⟨*pl* imprinting⟩ imprinting

improbabile *adj* unlikely, improbable

improbabilità *f* unlikelihood, improbability

improcrastinabile *adj that can't be put off*

improduttività *f* ⟨*pl* improduttività⟩ unproductiveness

improduttivo *adj* unproductive

improferibile *adj* unutterable

impronta *f* impression, mark; (*orma*) footprint; (*traccia*) track; *fig* mark; ***-e*** *pl* ***digitali*** fingerprints; ***lasciare un'~*** leave a mark; ***rilevare le -e*** take s.o.'s fingerprints

improntare *v/t* ⟨1a⟩ imprint; *fig* characterize

improntarsi *v/r* ⟨1a⟩ take on

impronunciabile *adj* unpronouncable; (*irrispettoso*) unrepeatable

improperio *m* ⟨*pl* -ri⟩ curse

impropriamente *adv* improperly

improprio *adj* ⟨*mpl* -ri⟩ improper

improrogabile *adj that can't be postponed*

improrogabilità *f* ⟨*pl* improrogabilità⟩ unpostponability

improvvisamente *adv* suddenly

improvvisare *v/t* ⟨1a⟩ improvize

improvvisarsi *v/r* take on the role of

improvvisata *f* surprise; ***fare un'~ a qn*** give s.o. a surprise

improvvisato *adj* improvized, impromptu

improvviso *adj* sudden; (*inaspettato*) unexpected; ***all'~*** suddenly; (*inaspettatamente*) unexpectedly

imprudente *adj* careless; (*non saggio*) imprudent, rash

imprudentemente *adv* imprudently

imprudenza *f* carelessness; (*mancanza di saggezza*) imprudence, rashness; ***è stata un'~*** it was a rash thing to do

impudente *adj* impudent

impudentemente *adv* impudently

impudenza *f* impudence

impudicamente *adv* shamelessly

impudicizia *f* lewdness

impudico *adj* ⟨*mpl* -ci⟩ shameless

impugnabile *adj* JUR contestable

impugnabilità *f* ⟨*pl* impugnabilità⟩ JUR contestability

impugnare *v/t* ⟨1a⟩ grasp; JUR contest

impugnatura *f* grip; (*manico*) handle

impulsivamente *adv* impulsively

impulsività *f* ⟨*pl* impulsività⟩ impulsiveness

impulsivo *adj* impulsive

impulso *m* impulse; ***d'~*** on impulse; ***dare ~ alla ricerca*** stimulate research

impunemente *adv* with impunity

impunità *f* impunity

impunito *adj* unpunished

impuntarsi *v/r* (*ostinarsi*) dig one's heels in; ***~ a fare qc*** dig one's heels in about doing sth

impuntura *f* (*punto*) stitch; (*cucitura*) stitching

impunturare *v/t* ⟨1a⟩ stitch

impurità *f* ⟨*pl* impurità⟩ impurity

imputabile *adj* chargeable; ***essere ~ a qn / qc*** be attributable to s.o. / sth; ***essere ~ di qc*** be responsible for sth

imputabilità *f* ⟨*pl* imputabilità⟩ chargeability

imputare *v/t* ⟨1a⟩ attribute; COMM charge; ***~ la colpa a qn*** ascribe the blame to s.o.; ***~ qn di un delitto*** charge s.o. with a crime

imputato *m*, **-a** *f* accused

imputazione *f* charge

imputridimento *m* putrefaction

imputridire *v/i* ⟨4d⟩ rot

in *prep* **1.** in; *moto a luogo* to; ***~ casa*** at home; ***va ~ Inghilterra*** he is going to England; ***è ~ Scozia*** he is in Scotland; ***~ italiano*** in Italian; ***vivono ~ campagna*** they live in the country; ***siamo andati ~ campagna*** we went to the country; ***essere ~ viaggio*** be travelling; ***viaggiare ~ macchina*** travel by car; ***nel 2006*** in 2006; ***mettilo ~ valigia*** put it in the suitcase; ***una giacca ~ pelle*** a leather jacket; ***~ vacanza*** on holiday; ***cambiare gli euro ~ dollari*** change the euros into dollars; ***lo faccio ~ un paio di giorni*** I'll do it in a couple of days; ***mettersi ~ costume*** put on fancy dress; ***un giro ~ città*** a trip around town; ***~ estate / agosto*** in summer / August; ***la signora Rossi ~ Bianchi*** Mrs Rossi, née Bianchi; ***~ alto*** high up; ***~ effetti*** in fact; ***~ pratica*** in practice; ***~ verità*** actually; (*veramente*) really; ***tradurre***

~ inglese translate into English **2.** ***erano ~ due*** there were two of them **3.** ***se fossi ~ te*** if I were you, if I were in your place

inabbordabile *adj prezzi* prohibitive; *fig persona* unapproachable

inabile *adj* unfit (***a*** for); (*disabile*) disabled; ***~ al lavoro*** unfit for work; ***~ al servizio militare*** unfit for military service

inabilità *f* ⟨*pl* inabilità⟩ unfitness; (*disabilità*) disability

inabilitato *m*, **-a** *f* JUR incapacitated

inabissare *v/t* ⟨1a⟩ sink

inabissarsi *v/r* ⟨1a⟩ sink (*a. fig*)

inabitabile *adj* uninhabitable

inabitabilità *f* ⟨*pl* inabitabilità⟩ uninhabitability

inabitato *adj* uninhabited

inaccessibile *adj* inaccessible, out of reach; *fig persona* unapproachable; *prezzi* exorbitant

inaccessibilità *f* ⟨*pl* inaccessibilità⟩ inaccessibility

inaccettabile *adj* unacceptable

inaccettabilità *f* ⟨*pl* inaccettabilità⟩ unacceptability

inacidimento *m* souring

inacidire *v/t* ⟨4d⟩ turn sour

inacidirsi *v/r* ⟨4d⟩ turn sour

inacidito *adj* sour; *fig* embittered; ***latte*** *m* **~** sour milk

inadattabilità *f* ⟨*pl* inadattabilità⟩ unsuitableness

inadatto *adj* unsuitable (***a*** for), unsuited (***a*** to)

inadeguatezza *f* inadequacy

inadeguato *adj* inadequate

inadempiente *adj* COMM in default; JUR defaulting

inadempienza *f* non-fulfilment; COMM default

inafferrabile *adj* elusive; (*incomprensibile*) incomprehensible

inafferrabilità *f* ⟨*pl* inafferrabilità⟩ elusiveness

inaffidabile *adj* unreliable

inaffidabilità *f* ⟨*pl* inaffidabilità⟩ unreliability

inagibile *adj edificio* unsafe; *strada* impassable

inagibilità *f* ⟨*pl* inagibilità⟩ unfitness

INAIL *abbr* (= **Istituto Nazionale per l'Assicurazione contro gli Infortuni sul Lavoro**) *National Institute for Insurance against Injuries at Work*

inalare *v/t* ⟨1a⟩ inhale

inalatore *m* inhaler, puffer *infml*

inalazione *f* inhalation

inalberarsi *v/r* ⟨1m⟩ rear; *fig* get angry

inalienabile *adj* inalienable; ***diritto*** *m* **~** inalienable right

inalienabilità *f* ⟨*pl* inalienabilità⟩ inalienability

inalterabile *adj sentimento* unchangeable; *colore* fast; *metallo* non-tarnish

inalterabilità *f* ⟨*pl* inalterabilità⟩ unchangeability (*a. fig*); *di colore* fastness

inalterato *adj* unchanged

inamidare *v/t* ⟨1m⟩ starch

inamidato *adj* starched; *fig* stiff; ***colletto*** *m* **~** stiff collar

inammissibile *adj* inadmissible

inammissibilità *f* ⟨*pl* inammissibilità⟩ JUR inadmissibility

inanellato *adj covered with rings*; (*arricciato*) curly

inanimato *adj* inanimate; (*senza vita*) lifeless; ***corpo*** *m* **~** lifeless body

inappagabile *adj* unsatisfiable

inappagato *adj* unfulfilled

inappellabile *adj* final, irrevocable

inappellabilità *f* ⟨*pl* inappellabilità⟩ finality; JUR irrevocability

inappetenza *f* lack of appetite

inapplicabile *adj* inapplicable

inappropriato *adj* inappropriate

inappuntabile *adj* impeccable

inappuntabilità *f* ⟨*pl* inappuntabilità⟩ faultlessness

inarcare *v/t* ⟨1d⟩ *schiena* arch; *sopracciglia* raise

inarcarsi *v/r* ⟨1d⟩ *muro* bulge; *persona* arch one's back

inargentare *v/t* ⟨1b⟩ silver

inaridire ⟨4d⟩ **I** *v/t* parch **II** *v/i* dry up

inaridirsi *v/r di terreno* dry up

inaridito *adj* dried up; *fig* barren

inarrestabile *adj* unstoppable

inarrivabile *adj* inaccessible; *persona* unapproachable

inarticolato *adj* inarticulate

inascoltato *adj* unheard

inaspettatamente *adv* unexpectedly

inaspettato *adj* unexpected

inasprimento *m* (*intensificazione*) worsening; *di carattere* embitterment

inasprire *v/t* ⟨4d⟩ exacerbate, make

worse; *carattere* embitter
inasprirsi *v/r* get worse; *di persona* become embittered
inattaccabile *adj* unassailable
inattaccabilità *f* ⟨*pl* inattaccabilità⟩ impregnability; *fig* unassailability
inattendibile *adj* unreliable
inattendibilità *f* ⟨*pl* inattendibilità⟩ untrustworthiness
inatteso *adj* unexpected
inattività *f* inactivity
inattivo *adj persona*, *capitale* idle; *vulcano* dormant
inattuabile *adj* (*non fattibile*) impracticable; (*non realistico*) unrealistic
inattuabilità *f* ⟨*pl* inattuabilità⟩ impracticality
inaudito *adj* unheard of
inaugurale *adj* inaugural; ***discorso*** *m* **~** inaugural speech
inaugurare *v/t* ⟨1m⟩ *mostra* (officially) open, inaugurate; *lapide*, *monumento* unveil; *infml oggetto nuovo* christen *infml*
inaugurazione *f di mostra* (official) opening, inauguration; *di lapide* unveiling; *infml di oggetto nuovo* christening *infml*
inavvertenza *f* inadvertence
inavvertitamente *adv* inadvertently
inavvertito *adj* unnoticed
inavvicinabile *adj* unapproachable
inazione *f* inaction; ***costretto*** *m* ***all'~*** forced to remain inactive
incacchiarsi *v/r* ⟨1d⟩ *infml* get one's knickers in a twist
incagliarsi *v/r* ⟨1g⟩ NAUT run aground
incaico *adj* ⟨*mpl* -ci⟩ Incan
incalcolabile *adj* incalculable
incalcolabilità *f* ⟨*pl* incalcolabilità⟩ incalculability
incallimento *m* hardening (*a. fig*)
incallito *adj giocatore* inveterate; *fumatore* heavy; *bugiardo* incorrigible; *scapolo* confirmed
incalzante *adj pericolo* imminent; *richieste* pressing
incalzare *v/t* ⟨1a⟩ pursue; *fig con richieste* ply
incamerare *v/t* ⟨1m⟩: **~ *qc*** confiscate sth
incamminarsi *v/r* ⟨1m⟩ set out
incanalare *v/t* ⟨1a⟩ channel
incanalatura *f* channelling; (*canale*) canal
incancellabile *adj* indelible
incancrenire *v/i* ⟨4d⟩ become gangrenous
incancrenirsi *v/r* ⟨4d⟩ become gangrenous
incandescente *adj* incandescent; *fig* heated
incandescenza *f* incandescence; ***lampada*** *f* ***a*** **~** incandescent lamp
incantare *v/t* ⟨1a⟩ enchant; **~ *i serpenti*** charm snakes; ***farsi*** **~ *da qn* / *qc*** fall under s.o.'s spell
incantarsi *v/r* (*restare affascinato*) be spellbound; (*sognare a occhi aperti*) be in a daze; TECH jam
incantato *adj per effetto di magia* enchanted; (*trasognato*) in a daze; (*affascinato*) spellbound; ***castello*** *m* **~** magic castle; ***muoviti, non stare lì ~!*** get a move on! Don't just stand there
incantatore *m*, **-trice** *f*: **~ *di serpenti*** snake charmer
incantesimo *m* spell; ***fare un*** **~** cast a spell; ***liberare da un*** **~** break a spell
incantevole *adj* delightful, charming
incanto[1] *m* (*incantesimo*) spell; ***come per*** **~** as if by magic; ***al sole si sta d'~*** it's lovely in the sun
incanto[2] *m* COMM auction; ***mettere all'~*** sell at auction, put up for auction
incanutire *v/i* ⟨4d⟩ turn grey, *US* gray
incapace I *adj* incapable (***di*** of); (*incompetente*) incompetent; ***essere*** **~ *di fare qc*** be incapable of doing sth; **~ *d'intendere e di volere*** mentally incompetent **II** *m/f* incompetent person
incapacità *f* ⟨*pl* incapacità⟩ (*inabilità*) inability; (*incompetenza*) incompetence; **~ *di agire*** inability to act; **~ *naturale*** natural ineptitude
incaponirsi *v/r* ⟨4d⟩: **~ *a fare qc*** insist on doing sth
incappare *v/i* ⟨1a⟩: **~ *in*** *nebbia*, *difficoltà* run into; **~ *in un'insidia*** fall into a trap; **~ *in un truffatore*** run into a swindler
incappucciarsi *v/r* ⟨1f⟩ put a hood on
incappucciato *adj* hooded
incaprettare *v/t* ⟨1n⟩ *kill a victim by tying him up, so that when he moves he strangles himself* (*used by the Mafia*)
incapricciarsi *v/r* ⟨1f⟩: **~ *di qn*** take a

liking to s.o.

incapsulare *v/t* ⟨1m⟩ encapsulate; ***~ un dente*** cap *or* crown a tooth

incarcerare *v/t* ⟨1m⟩ imprison

incaricare *v/t* ⟨1m & d⟩ (*dare istruzioni a*) instruct; ***~ qn di fare qc*** tell *or* instruct s.o. to do sth

incaricarsi *v/r*: ***~ di qc*** (*occuparsi di*) see to sth, deal with sth

incaricato *m*, **-a** *f* (*responsabile*) person in charge; (*funzionario*) official, representative; ***docente*** *m* ***~*** *teacher on a temporary contract*

incarico *m* ⟨*pl* -chi⟩ (*compito*) task, assignment; (*nomina*) appointment; ***per ~ di*** on behalf of

incarnare *v/t* ⟨1a⟩ embody

incarnazione *f* incarnation

incarnirsi *v/r* ⟨4d⟩ become ingrowing *or US* ingrown

incarognire *v/i* ⟨4d⟩ turn nasty

incarognirsi *v/r* ⟨4d⟩ turn nasty

incartamento *m* file, dossier

incartapecorito *adj* wizened

incartare *v/r* ⟨1a⟩ wrap (up) (in paper)

incarto *m* wrapping; (*incartamento*) file, dossier

Inca(s) *mpl* Incas

incasellare *v/t* ⟨1f & c⟩ pigeonhole; ***~ la posta*** deliver the post

incasinare *v/t* ⟨1b⟩ *infml* mess up

incasinarsi *v/r* ⟨1b⟩ *infml* foul up

incasinato *adj infml faccenda*, *settimana* chaotic; *persona* all over the place

incassabile *adj assegno* cashable; *mobile*, *elettrodomestico* built-in

incassare *v/t* ⟨1a⟩ COMM (*riscuotere*) cash; *fig colpi*, *insulti etc* take; ***~ un assegno*** cash a cheque; ***~ il colpo*** take a blow

incassato *adj water* hidden; *tv* built-in; *vasca da bagno* sunken; *tubi* recessed

incasso *m* (*riscossione*) collection; (*somma incassata*) takings *pl*

incastellatura *f* scaffolding

incastonare *v/t* ⟨1a⟩ set

incastonatura *f* setting

incastrare *v/t* ⟨1a⟩ fit in; *infml fig* (*far apparire colpevole*) frame *infml*; (*mettere in una posizione difficile*) corner *infml*; ***ti sei fatto ~*** you've been framed

incastrarsi *v/r* (*bloccarsi*) get stuck; (*inserirsi*) fit

incastro *m* joint; ***a ~*** interlocking

incatenare *v/t* ⟨1a⟩ chain

incatenarsi *v/r* ⟨1a⟩ chain oneself

incatramare *v/t* ⟨1a⟩ tar

incattivire *v/t* ⟨4d⟩ make nasty

incattivirsi *v/r* ⟨4d⟩ turn nasty

incautamente *adv* imprudently

incauto *adj* rash

incavato *adj* hollow; *occhi* deep-set

incavo *m* hollow

incavolarsi *v/r* ⟨1a⟩ *infml* lose one's rag *infml*; ***~ con qn*** lose one's temper with s.o. *infml*

incazzarsi *v/r* ⟨1a⟩ *vulg* get pissed off *vulg*; ***~ con qn*** get pissed off with s.o. *vulg*

incedere I *v/i* ⟨2a⟩ walk solemnly **II** *m* gait

incendiare *v/t* ⟨1b & k⟩ set fire to

incendiario I *m*, **-a** *f* ⟨*mpl* -ri⟩ arsonist, firebug *infml* **II** *adj*: ***bomba*** *f* ***-a*** incendiary bomb

incendiarsi *v/r* catch fire

incendio *m* ⟨*pl* -di⟩ fire; ***~ doloso*** arson

incenerimento *m* incineration

incenerire *v/t* ⟨4d⟩ reduce to ashes; *fig* ***~ qn con un'occhiata*** look daggers at s.o.

inceneritore *m* incinerator

incensare *v/t* ⟨1b⟩ incense; *fig* flatter

incenso *m* incense

incensurabile *adj* irreproachable

incensurabilità *f* ⟨*pl* incensurabilità⟩ irreproachability

incensurato *adj* irreproachable; JUR ***essere ~*** have a clean record

incentivare *v/t* ⟨1a⟩ (*incrementare*) boost; ***~ le vendite*** boost sales

incentivo *m* incentive; ***essere d'~*** be an incentive; ***-i*** *pl* ***finanziari*** financial incentives

incentrare *v/t* ⟨1b⟩ centre

incentrarsi *v/r* ⟨1b⟩ *fig* ***~ su qc*** focus on sth

incepparsi *v/r* ⟨1a⟩ jam; ***il fucile si è inceppato*** the gun misfired

incerata *f* oilcloth

incerottare *v/t* ⟨1a⟩ *infml* put a plaster on

incertezza *f* uncertainty

incerto I *adj* uncertain; ***sono ~ sul da farsi*** I'm uncertain what to do; ***~ nella guida*** not confident about one's

driving **II** *m* uncertainty; ***gli -i del mestiere*** occupational hazards
incespicare *v/i* ⟨1m & d⟩: ***~ in qc*** trip over sth; ***~ nel parlare*** stumble in one's speech
incessante *adj* incessant
incessantemente *adv* incessantly
incesto *m* incest
incestuoso *adj* incestuous
incetta *f*: ***fare ~ di qc*** stockpile sth
inchiesta *f* investigation; *giornale* report; FIN ***~ di mercato*** market survey; ***commissione*** *f* ***d'~*** committee *or* board of inquiry; ***~ parlamentare*** government inquiry; ***~ sul terrorismo*** inquiry into terrorism
inchinare *v/t* ⟨1a⟩ bow
inchinarsi *v/r* bow
inchino *m* bow; *di donna* curtsy; ***fare un ~*** bow; *di donna* curtsy
inchiodare ⟨1c⟩ **I** *v/t* nail; *coperchio* nail down; *fig* ***essere inchiodato in un luogo*** be stuck in a place **II** *v/i* AUTO jam on the brakes
inchiostro *m* ink; ***~ di china*** Indian ink
inciampare *v/i* ⟨1a⟩ trip (***in*** over); ***~ in qn*** run into s.o.
incidentale *adj* (*casuale*) accidental; (*secondario*) incidental
incidentalmente *adv* (*casualmente*) accidentally; (*secondariamente*) incidentally
incidente *m* (*episodio*) incident; ***~ aereo*** plane crash; ***~ diplomatico*** diplomatic incident; ***~ stradale*** road accident; ***~ di percorso*** snag; ***~ probatorio*** JUR collateral proceeding; ***fare un ~*** *in auto, moto* have an accident
incidenza *f*: ***avere ~ su qc*** influence sth
incidere[1] *v/i* ⟨3q⟩ affect (***su*** sth)
incidere[2] *v/t* ⟨3q⟩ engrave; (*tagliare*) cut; (*registrare*) record; ***~ un disco*** cut a disc
incidersi *v/r fig* (*restare impresso*) be engraved (***in*** on)
incinta *adj* pregnant; ***essere ~ di tre mesi*** be three months pregnant; ***rimanere ~*** get pregnant
incipiente *adj* incipient
incipriare *v/t* ⟨1m⟩ powder
incipriarsi *v/r* ⟨1m⟩ powder one's face
incirca *adv*: ***all'~*** more or less
incisione *f* engraving; (*acquaforte*) etching; (*taglio*) cut; MED incision; (*registrazione*) recording
incisivamente *adv* incisively
incisività *f* ⟨*pl* incisività⟩ incisiveness
incisivo **I** *adj* incisive; ***stile*** *m* ***~*** trenchant style **II** *m* (*dente*) incisor
inciso **I** *past part* → ***incidere*** **II** *m*: ***per ~*** incidentally
incisore *m*, **-a** *f* engraver; ***~ a mano*** hand engraver
incitamento *m* incitement
incitare *v/t* ⟨1l⟩ incite; ***~ qn a fare qc*** stir s.o. into doing sth
inciuccarsi *v/r* ⟨1d⟩ *infml* get pissed
inciucio *m* ⟨*pl* -ci⟩ *infml* POL *agreement between opposing political parties*
incivile *adj* uncivilized; (*villano*) rude, impolite
incivilire *v/t* ⟨4d⟩ civilize
incivilirsi *v/r* ⟨4d⟩ become civilized
incivilmente *adv* impolitely
inciviltà *f* ⟨*pl* inciviltà⟩ incivility
inclassificabile *adj* unclassifiable; *a scuola*: unclassified; *fig* ***comportamento*** *m* ***~*** unspeakable behaviour
inclemente *adj* harsh; ***tempo*** *m* ***~*** inclement weather
inclemenza *f* harshness; *di clima*: inclemency
inclinabile *adj* reclining
inclinare ⟨1a⟩ **I** *v/t* tilt **II** *v/i*: ***~ a*** (*tendere a*) be inclined to
inclinato *adj* tilted; ***piano*** *m* ***~*** inclined plane
inclinazione *f* inclination; ***seguire le proprie -i*** follow one's own inclinations
incline *adj* inclined (***a*** to); ***essere ~ a*** (***fare***) ***qc*** be inclined to (do) sth
includere *v/t* ⟨3q⟩ include; (*allegare*) enclose, inclose; ***incluso il servizio*** service included
inclusione *f* inclusion
inclusivo *adj* inclusive
incluso **I** *past part* → ***includere*** **II** *adj* included; (*compreso*) inclusive; (*allegato*) enclosed
incocciare *v/t* ⟨1f⟩ *infml* bump into
incoerente *adj* (*incongruente*) inconsistent
incoerentemente *adv* inconsistently
incoerenza *f* inconsistency
incognita *f* unknown quantity
incognito *m*: ***in ~*** incognito

incollare *v/t* ⟨1c⟩ stick; *con colla liquida* glue; ***incollato alla tivù*** glued to the TV

incollarsi *v/r* stick (***a*** to)

incollerirsi *v/r* ⟨4d⟩ get angry

incolmabilità *f* ⟨*pl* incolmabilità⟩ unassailability

incolonnamento *m di veicoli* tailback; *di numeri* putting into columns

incolonnare *v/t* ⟨1a⟩ *numeri etc* put in a column; *persone* line up; ***~ le cifre*** arrange the figures in columns

incolonnarsi *v/r* ⟨1n⟩ line up

incolore *adj* colo(u)rless

incolpare *v/t* ⟨1a⟩ blame; ***~ qn di qc*** blame s.o. for sth

incolparsi *v/r*: ***~ a vicenda*** blame each other

incolto *adj* uneducated; (*trascurato*) unkempt; AGR uncultivated

incolume *adj* unharmed

incolumità *f* safety

incombente *adj pericolo* impending

incombenza *f* task

incombere *v/i* ⟨3a⟩ loom

incominciare *v/t* ⟨1f⟩ start, begin (***a*** to)

incommensurabile *adj* immeasurable (*a. fig*)

incommensurabilità *f* ⟨*pl* incommensurabilità⟩ immeasurability (*a. fig*)

incomodare *v/t* ⟨1m & c⟩ inconvenience

incomodarsi *v/r* put o.s. out; ***non si incomodi!*** don't put yourself out!, please don't go to any trouble!

incomodo **I** *adj* (*inopportuno*) inconvenient; (*scomodo*) uncomfortable **II** *m* inconvenience

incomparabile *adj* incomparable

incomparabilità *f* ⟨*pl* incomparabilità⟩ incomparability

incomparabilmente *adv* incomparably

incompatibile *adj* incompatible; (*intollerabile*) unacceptable

incompatibilità *f* ⟨*pl* incompatibilità⟩ incompatibility; ***~ di carattere*** mutual incompatibility

incompetente *adj* incompetent; ***sono ~ in materia*** I'm no expert

incompetenza *f* incompetence

incompiutezza *f* incompleteness

incompiuto *adj* unfinished

incompletezza *f* incompleteness

incompleto *adj* incomplete

incomprensibile *adj* incomprehensible, impossible to understand

incomprensibilità *f* incomprehensibility

incomprensibilmente *adv* incomprehensibly

incomprensione *f* lack of understanding; (*malinteso*) misunderstanding

incompreso *adj* misunderstood; ***sentirsi ~*** feel misunderstood

incomunicabile *adj* inexpressible

incomunicabilità *f* ⟨*pl* incomunicabilità⟩ inexpressibility

inconcepibile *adj* inconceivable

inconciliabile *adj* irreconcilable

inconciliabilità *f* ⟨*pl* inconciliabilità⟩ irreconcilability

inconcludente *adj* inconclusive; *persona* ineffectual

inconcludenza *f* inconclusiveness

incondizionato *adj* unconditional

inconfessabile *adj* unmentionable; (*vergognoso*) shameful

inconfondibile *adj* unmistakable

inconfutabile *adj* indisputable

inconfutabilità *f* ⟨*pl* inconfutabilità⟩ indisputability

inconfutabilmente *adv* indisputably

incongruenza *f* incongruity

inconsapevole *adj* (*ignaro*) unaware

inconsapevolezza *f* lack of awareness

inconsapevolmente *adv* unwittingly

inconsciamente *adv* unconsciously

inconscio *m/adj* unconscious

inconsistente *adj* insubstantial; *fig* (*infondato*) unfounded; (*vago*) vague

inconsistenza *f* flimsiness

inconsolabile *adj* inconsolable

inconsolabilità *f* ⟨*pl* inconsolabilità⟩ inconsolability

inconsueto *adj* unusual

incontaminato *adj* uncontaminated; ***natura*** *f* ***-a*** unpolluted nature

incontenibile *adj* uncontainable

incontentabile *adj* hard to please, very demanding; (*perfezionista*) perfectionist

incontentabilità *f* ⟨*pl* incontentabilità⟩ perfectionism

incontestabilmente *adv* indisputably

incontestato *adj* undisputed

incontinente *adj* MED incontinent

incontinenza *f* incontinence

incontrare ⟨1a⟩ **I** *v/t* meet; *difficoltà* come up against, encounter; ***~ il favore di qn*** find favo(u)r with s.o. **II** *v/i* meet (***con*** s.o.)
incontrario *adv*: ***all'~*** the other way round; (*nel modo sbagliato*) the wrong way round
incontrarsi *v/r* ⟨1a⟩ meet (***con*** s.o.)
incontrastabile *adj* unstoppable; (*incontestabile*) indisputable
incontrastato *adj* undisputed
incontro I *m* meeting; ***~ di calcio*** football match; POL ***~ al vertice*** summit (meeting) **II** *prep*: ***~ a*** towards; ***andare ~ a qn*** go and meet s.o.; *fig* meet s.o. halfway
incontrollabile *adj* uncontrollable
incontrollabilità *f* ⟨*pl* incontrollabilità⟩ uncontrollableness
incontrollato *adj* unchecked; ***voci*** *fpl* ***-e*** unverified rumours
inconveniente *m* (*svantaggio*) drawback; (*ostacolo*) hitch
inconvertibile *adj* unconvertible
incoraggiamento *m* encouragement; ***parole*** *fpl* ***d'~*** words of encouragement; ***premio*** *m* ***d'~*** incentive bonus
incoraggiante *adj* encouraging
incoraggiare *v/t* ⟨1f⟩ encourage; ***~ qn a fare qc*** encourage s.o. to do sth
incornare *v/t* ⟨1c⟩ gore
incorniciare *v/t* ⟨1f⟩ frame
incoronare *v/t* ⟨1a⟩ crown
incoronazione *f* coronation
incorporare *v/t* ⟨1m & c⟩ incorporate; ***~ qc in qc*** incorporate sth into sth
incorporazione *f* incorporation
incorporeo *adj* incorporeal
incorreggibile *adj* incorrigible
incorreggibilità *f* ⟨*pl* incorreggibilità⟩ incorrigibility
incorrere *v/i* ⟨3o⟩: ***~ in*** *sanzioni* incur; *errore* make
incorruttibile *adj* incorruptible
incorruttibilità *f* ⟨*pl* incorruttibilità⟩ incorruptibility
incosciente *adj* unconscious; (*irresponsabile*) reckless
incoscienza *f* unconsciousness; (*insensatezza*) recklessness
incostante *adj* changeable; *negli affetti* fickle
incostantemente *adv* inconsistently
incostanza *f* changeableness; *negli affetti* fickleness
incostituzionale *adj* unconstitutional
incostituzionalità *f* unconstitutionality
incredibile *adj* incredible
incredibilmente *adv* incredibly
incredulità *f* ⟨*pl* incredulità⟩ incredulity
incredulo *adj* incredulous, disbelieving
incrementare *v/t* ⟨1a⟩ increase
incremento *m* increase, growth; ***~ demografico*** population growth
increscioso *adj* regrettable
increspare *v/t* ⟨1a⟩ *acque* ripple; *capelli* frizz; *tessuto* gather
incresparsi *v/r* ⟨1m⟩ *fronte* wrinkle; *capelli* go frizzy
increspatura *f della pelle* wrinkle; *di tessuto* gather
incretinire *v/t* ⟨4d⟩ drive mad
incriminabile *adj* indictable
incriminare *v/t* ⟨1m⟩ indict; ***~ qn di*** *or* ***per qc*** charge s.o. with sth
incriminazione *f* accusation
incrinarsi *v/r* ⟨1a⟩ *tazza*, *vetro* crack; *rapporti*, *amicizia* suffer
incrinatura *f* crack
incrociare ⟨1f⟩ **I** *v/t* cross; ***~ le dita*** cross one's fingers **II** *v/i* NAUT, AVIAT cruise; ***~ con qc*** meet s.o.
incrociato *adj* crossed; ***parole*** *fpl* ***-e*** crossword; ***fuoco*** *m* ***~*** crossfire; ***razza*** *f* ***-a*** crossbreed
incrociatore *m* cruiser
incrocio *m* ⟨*pl* -ci⟩ (*intersezione*) crossing; (*crocevia*) crossroads *sg*; *di razze animali* cross(-breed); ***all'~*** at the crossroads
incrollabile *adj* indestructible; *fig* unshakeable
incrostare *v/t* ⟨1a⟩ *fango* cake; *calcare* scale up
incrostarsi *v/r* ⟨1a⟩ *di fango* cake; *tube* fur up
incrostazione *f* deposit, sediment
incrudelire *v/i* ⟨4d⟩ behave cruelly
incrudelirsi *v/r* ⟨4d⟩ become cruel
incruento *adj* bloodless
incubatrice *f* incubator
incubazione *f* incubation
incubo *m* nightmare; ***avere un ~*** have a nightmare
incudine *f* anvil; ANAT incus; ***essere tra l'~ e il martello*** be caught between a rock and a hard place

inculcare *v/t* ⟨1d⟩: **~ qc a qn** inculcate sth into s.o.
incunabolo *m* incunabulum, *early printed book*
incupire *v/t* ⟨4d⟩ darken
incurabile *adj* incurable
incurabilità *f* ⟨*pl* incurabilità⟩ incurability
incurante *adj* heedless (**di** of); **~ del pericolo** mindless of the danger
incuria *f* negligence
incuriosire *v/t* ⟨4d⟩: **~ qn** make s.o. curious, arouse s.o.'s curiosity
incuriosirsi *v/r* become curious
incursione *f* raid; **~ aerea** air raid
incurvare *v/t* ⟨1a⟩ bend
incurvarsi *v/r di ramo* bend; *di schiena* become bent
incurvatura *f* bend
incustodito *adj* unattended, unguarded; *passaggio a livello* unmanned; **parcheggio** *m* **~** unattended parking; **lasciare qc ~** leave sth unattended
incutere *v/t* ⟨3v⟩: **~ qc** (**a qn**) inspire sth (in s.o.)
indaco *m/adj* indigo
indaffarato *adj* busy
indagare ⟨1e⟩ **I** *v/t cause, fenomeni* investigate **II** *v/i* investigate (**su, intorno a** sth); **~ su un delitto** investigate a crime
indagatore *adj* inquiring; **occhiata** *f* **-trice** inquisitive look
indagine *f* (*ricerca, studio*) research; *della polizia* investigation; **~ di mercato** market survey; **~ demoscopica** (public) opinion poll; **depistare le -i** mislead the investigation; **~ preliminare** preliminary inquiry
indebitamente *adv* unduly
indebitamento *m* debt, borrowing
indebitare *v/t* ⟨1m⟩ plunge into debt
indebitarsi *v/r* get into debt; **~ fino al collo** get up to one's neck in debt
indebitato *adj* in debt
indebito *adj* wrongful; **appropriazione** *f* **-a** embezzlement
indebolimento *m* weakening
indebolire *v/t* & *v/i* ⟨4d⟩ weaken
indebolirsi *v/r* become weaker
indecente *adj* indecent
indecentemente *adv* indecently
indecenza *f* (*vergogna*) disgrace, outrage; (*mancanza di pudore*) indecency; **è un'~!** it's a disgrace!
indecifrabile *adj* indecipherable
indecifrabilità *f* ⟨*pl* indecifrabilità⟩ indecipherability
indecisione *f* indecision; *abituale* indecisiveness
indeciso *adj* undecided; *abitualmente* indecisive; **sono ~ se andare o no** I can't decide whether to go or not
indecoroso *adj* indecorous
indefesso *adj* untiring
indefinibile *adj* indefinable
indefinibilità *f* ⟨*pl* indefinibilità⟩ indefinability
indefinito *adj* indefinite; **pronome** *m* **~** indefinite pronoun
indeformabile *adj cartone* crush-proof; *tessuto* non-shrink
indeformabilità *f* ⟨*pl* indeformabilità⟩ unalterability
indegnamente *adv* unworthily
indegnità *f* ⟨*pl* indegnità⟩ worthlessness; (*azione*) despicable act
indegno *adj* unworthy
indelebile *adj* indelible; *colore* fast; **inchiostro** *m* **~** indelible ink; **ricordo** *m* **~** abiding memory
indelicatezza *f* tactlessness
indelicato *adj* tactless
indemoniato *adj* possessed; (*scalmanato*) wild
indenne *adj persona* uninjured; *cosa* undamaged
indennità *f* ⟨*pl* indennità⟩ (*gratifica*) allowance, benefit; (*risarcimento*) compensation; **~ di disoccupazione** unemployment benefit; **~ di accompagnamento** attendance allowance; **~ di trasferta** travel allowance; **~ parlamentare** MP's allowance
indennizzare *v/t* ⟨1a⟩ compensate (**per** for)
indennizzo *m* (*compenso*) compensation
inderogabile *adj* mandatory
inderogabilità *f* ⟨*pl* inderogabilità⟩ mandatoriness
indescrivibile *adj* indescribable
indesiderabile *adj* undesirable
indesiderato *adj* unwanted
indeterminabile *adj* indeterminable
indeterminatezza *f* indeterminacy; (*indecisione*) indecision
indeterminato *adj tempo* unspecified, indefinite; *quantità* indeterminate
indetto *past part* → **indire**

India *f* India; ***-ie occidentali*** West Indies
indiano I *adj* Indian; ***in fila -a*** in single file; ***Oceano Indiano*** Indian Ocean **II** *m*, **-a** *f* Indian
indicare *v/t* ⟨1l & d⟩ show, indicate; *col dito* point at *or* to; (*consigliare*) suggest, recommend; (*significare*) mean
indicativo *m* GRAM indicative
indicato *adj* (*consigliabile*) advisable; (*adatto*) suitable
indicatore I *adj* indicative; ***cartello*** *m* **~** road sign **II** *m* indicator; (*strumento*) gauge, indicator; ***~ biologico*** biological indicator; ***~ del livello di carburante*** fuel gauge; AUTO ***~ di direzione*** indicator; ***~ di chiamata*** TEL call indicator
indicazione *f* indication; (*direttiva*) direction; (*informazione*) piece of information; MED ***-i*** *pl* directions (for use); ***-i*** *pl* ***stradali*** road signs
indice *m* **1.** index; TV ***~ di ascolto*** ratings *pl*; ***~ azionario*** share index; ***~ analitico*** index; ***~ di gradimento*** viewing figures; ***essere ~ di qc*** be indicative of sth; ***mettere all'~*** blacklist **2.** ANAT index finger, forefinger
indicibile *adj* indescribable, inexpressible
indicizzare *v/t* ⟨1a⟩ index, index-link
indicizzazione *f* indexation
indietreggiare *v/i* ⟨1f⟩ draw back; *camminando all'indietro* step back; MIL retreat
indietro *adv* behind; *tornare, girarsi* back; ***essere ~*** *con il lavoro* be behind; *mentalmente* be backward; *nei pagamenti* be in arrears; *di orologio* be slow; ***dare ~*** (*restituire*) give back; AUTO ***fare marcia ~*** reverse; *fig* back-pedal; ***tirarsi ~*** draw back; *fig* back out; ***all'~*** backwards; ***andare avanti e ~*** go backwards and forwards; ***tornare ~*** come *o* go back; ***rimanere ~ con un lavoro*** fall behind with a job; ***l'orologio va ~*** the clock's slow; ***mettere ~ l'orologio*** put the clock back
indifendibile *adj* indefensible (*a. fig*)
indifeso *adj* undefended; (*inerme*) defenceless, helpless
indifferente *adj* indifferent; ***lasciare qn ~*** leave s.o. cold, cut no ice with s.o.; ***non ~*** appreciable, considerable; ***per me è ~*** it's all the same to me; ***fare l'~*** pretend that nothing has happened
indifferentemente *adv* indifferently, equally
indifferenza *f* indifference
indifferibile *adj that can't be put off*
indifferibilità *f* ⟨*pl* indifferibilità⟩ unpostponability
indigeno I *adj* native, indigenous **II** *m*, **-a** *f* native
indigenza *f* destitution
indigeribile *adj* indigestible (*a. fig*)
indigestione *f* indigestion; ***fare ~ di qc*** get indigestion from eating sth
indigesto *adj* indigestible
indignare *v/t* ⟨1a⟩: ***~ qn*** make s.o. indignant, arouse s.o.'s indignation
indignarsi *v/r* get indignant (***per*** about)
indignato *adj* indignant; ***essere ~ per qc*** be indignant about sth
indignazione *f* indignation
indilazionabile *adj that can't be put off*
indimenticabile *adj* unforgettable
indimostrabile *adj* undemonstrable
indimostrabilità *f* ⟨*pl* indimostrabilità⟩ undemonstrability
indio ⟨*mpl* indi *or* indios⟩ **I** *adj of the native people of Central and South America* **II** *m*, **-a** *f a member of the native people of Central and South America*
indipendente *adj* independent (***da*** of); ***~ dalla mia volontà*** outside my control
indipendentemente *adv* independently; ***~ dall'età*** regardless of age, whatever the age
indipendentismo *m support for the political independence of an area or state*
indipendentista ⟨*mpl* -i⟩ **I** *adj* independence **II** *m/f supporter of the political independence of an area or state*
indipendenza *f* independence
indire *v/t* ⟨3t⟩ *conferenza, elezioni, sciopero* call; *concorso* announce; ***~ un referendum*** hold a referendum
indirettamente *adv* indirectly
indiretto *adj* indirect; ***imposte*** *fpl* ***-e*** indirect taxes; ***discorso*** *m* **~** reported speech

indirizzare *v/t* ⟨1a⟩ direct; *lettera* address; (*spedire*) send
indirizzario *m* address book; *per spedizione* mailing list
indirizzarsi *v/r* ⟨1a⟩ (*dirigersi*) set out for; (*rivolgersi*) address oneself
indirizzo *m* address; (*direzione*) direction; ***~ di posta elettronica*** e-mail address
indisciplina *f* lack of discipline, indiscipline
indisciplinatamente *adv* rowdily; ***comportarsi ~*** behave disruptively
indisciplinatezza *f* indiscipline
indisciplinato *adj* undisciplined; ***scolaro*** *m* **~** disruptive student; ***traffico*** *m* **~** chaotic traffic
indiscreto *adj* indiscreet; ***non vorrei sembrare ~*** I don't want to be nosy
indiscrezione *f* indiscretion
indiscriminatamente *adv* indiscriminately
indiscriminato *adj* indiscriminate; ***fare un uso ~ di qc*** make wholesale use of sth
indiscusso *adj* unquestioned
indiscutibile *adj* unquestionable
indiscutibilmente *adv* unquestionably
indispensabile **I** *adj* indispensable, essential; ***ritenersi ~*** think oneself irreplaceable; ***rendersi ~*** make oneself indispensable **II** *m* essentials *pl*
indispettire *v/t* ⟨4d⟩ irritate
indispettirsi *v/r* get irritated
indispettito *adj* irritated
indisponente *adj* irritating
indisporre *v/t* ⟨3ll⟩ irritate
indisposizione *f* indisposition
indisposto *adj* (*ammalato*) indisposed
indissolubile *adj* indissoluble
indissolubilità *f* ⟨*pl* indissolubilità⟩ indissolubility; ***l'~ del matrimonio*** the indissolubility of marriage
indissolubilmente *adv* indissolubly
indistintamente *adv senza distinzioni* without distinction; *in modo confuso* indistinctly, faintly
indistinto *adj* indistinct, faint
indistruttibile *adj* indestructible
indistruttibilità *f* ⟨*pl* indistruttibilità⟩ indestructibility
indisturbato *adj* undisturbed; (*senza rumore*) peaceful
indivia *f* endive
individuabile *adj* identifiable
individuale *adj* individual
individualismo *m* individualism
individualista *m/f* ⟨*mpl* -i⟩ individualist
individualità *f* ⟨*pl* individualità⟩ individuality
individualizzare *v/t* ⟨1a⟩ personalize
individualizzazione *f* individualization
individualmente *adv* individually
individuare *v/t* ⟨1n⟩ (*localizzare*) pinpoint; (*scoprire*) spot; ***la polizia ha individuato i colpevoli*** the police have identified the culprits
individuazione *f* detection
individuo *m* individual; ***~ sospetto*** a shady-looking character
indivisibile *adj* indivisible
indivisibilità *f* ⟨*pl* indivisibilità⟩ indivisibility
indiviso *adj* undivided
indiziare *v/t* ⟨1g⟩: ***~ qn di qc*** identify s.o. as a suspect in sth
indizio *m* ⟨*pl* -zi⟩ clue; (*segno*) sign; (*sintomo*) symptom; JUR ***-i*** *pl* circumstantial evidence *sg*
Indo *m* Indus
indocilità *f* ⟨*pl* indocilità⟩ intractability
Indocina *f* Indochina
indocinese **I** *adj* Indochinese **II** *m/f* Indochinese
indole *f* nature
indolente *adj* indolent
indolenza *f* indolence
indolenzimento *m* soreness, ache
indolenzire *v/t* ⟨4d⟩ make sore
indolenzirsi *v/r* ⟨4d⟩ become sore
indolenzito *adj* aching; ***essere ~*** be sore
indolore *adj* painless
indomabile *adj* indomitable
indomani *m*: ***l'~*** the next day
indomito *adj* unsubduable; *fig* unconquerable
Indonesia *f* Indonesia
indoor *adj inv* indoor; ***torneo*** *m* **~** indoor tournament
indorare *v/t* ⟨1c⟩ gild (*a. fig*); ***~ la pillola*** sugar the pill
indossare *v/t* ⟨1c⟩ (*mettersi*) put on; (*portare*) wear
indossatore *m*, **-trice** *f* model
indotto **I** *past part* → ***indurre*** **II** *adj*:

corrente *f* ***-a*** induction current **III** *m*: ***aziende*** *fpl* ***dell'~*** satellite companies
indottrinamento *m* POL indoctrination
indottrinare *v/t* ⟨1d⟩ POL indoctrinate
indovinare *v/t* ⟨1a⟩ guess; *futuro* predict; ***tirare a ~*** have a guess
indovinato *adj* (*ben riuscito*) successful; (*ben scelto*) well chosen
indovinello *m* riddle
indovino *m*, **-a** *f* fortune-teller
indù I *adj* Hindu **II** *m/f* ⟨*pl* indù⟩ Hindu
indubbiamente *adv* undoubtedly
indubitabile *adj* indubitable
indugiare ⟨1f⟩ **I** *v/t partenza* delay **II** *v/i* (*tardare*) delay; (*esitare*) hesitate; (*attardarsi*) linger
indugiarsi *v/r* linger
indugio *m* ⟨*pl* -gi⟩ delay; ***senza ~*** without delay
induismo *m* Hinduism
induista ⟨*mpl* -i⟩ **I** *adj* Hindu **II** *m/f* Hindu
indulgente *adj* indulgent; *giudice*, *sentenza* lenient
indulgenza *f* indulgence; *di giudice*, *sentenza* leniency
indulgere *v/i* ⟨3d⟩ comply with; (*abbandonarsi*) overindulge
indulto *m* pardon
indumento *m* garment, item of clothing; ***gli -i*** *pl* clothes
indurimento *m* hardening
indurire ⟨4d⟩ **I** *v/t* harden; *fig cuore* harden; *corpo* toughen (up) **II** *v/i* go hard, harden
indurirsi *v/r* ⟨4d⟩ go hard, harden
indurito *adj* hardened
indurre *v/t* ⟨3e⟩ induce; ***~ qn in tentazione*** / ***errore*** tempt / mislead s.o.; ***~ qn a fare qc*** induce s.o. to do sth
industria *f* industry; (*operosità*) industriousness; ***~ automobilistica*** car industry; ***~ dei servizi*** service industry, services; ***~ pesante*** heavy industry
industriale I *adj* industrial; ***su scala ~*** on an industrial scale; *fig* in huge amounts **II** *m/f* industrialist
industrializzare *v/t* ⟨1a⟩ industrialize
industrializzato *adj* industrialized; ***paesi*** *mpl* ***-i*** industrialized countries
industrializzazione *f* industrialization
industrioso *adj* industrious
induttivo *adj* inductive
induttore *m* ELEC inductor
induzione *f* induction
inebetire *v/t* ⟨4d⟩ stun
inebetirsi *v/r* ⟨4d⟩ become stupid
inebetito *adj* woozy
inebriare *v/t* ⟨1m & b⟩ intoxicate (*a. fig*)
inebriarsi *v/r* ⟨1m & b⟩ get drunk; ***~ di qc*** become intoxicated with sth
ineccepibile *adj* irreproachable; *ragionamento* faultless
ineccepibilità *f* ⟨*pl* ineccepibiltà⟩ irreproachability
inedia *f* starvation; *fig* ***morire d'~*** starve to death
inedito *adj* unpublished; *fig* novel; ***notizia*** *f* ***-a*** hot news
ineffabile *adj* inexpressible
ineffabilità *f* ⟨*pl* ineffabilità⟩ ineffability
inefficace *adj* ineffective
inefficacia *f* ineffectiveness
inefficiente *adj* inefficient
inefficienza *f* inefficiency
ineguagliabile *adj* (*senza rivali*) unrivalled; (*senza confronto*) incomparable, beyond compare
ineguaglianza *f* inequality
ineguale *adj* (*non uguale*) unequal; (*discontinuo*) uneven
ineluttabile *adj* inescapable
ineluttabilità *f* ⟨*pl* ineluttabilità⟩ inevitability
inequivocabile *adj* unequivocal
inequivocabilmente *adv* unequivocally
inerente *adj*: ***~ a qc*** inherent in sth
inerenza *f* inherence
inerpicarsi *v/r* ⟨1m & d⟩: ***~ su qc*** clamber up sth
inerte *adj* (*inoperoso*) idle; (*immobile*) inert, motionless; (*senza vita*) lifeless; PHYS inert
inerzia *f* inertia; (*inattività*) inactivity; ***forza*** *f* ***d'~*** force of inertia
inesattezza *f* inaccuracy
inesatto *adj* inaccurate
inesaudibile *adj* ungrantable
inesaudito *adj* unfulfilled
inesauribile *adj* inexhaustible
inesigibile *adj* irrecoverable
inesistente *adj* non-existent
inesistenza *f* non-existence
inesorabile *adj* inexorable
inesorabilità *f* ⟨*pl* inesorabilità⟩ inex-

orability
inesorabilmente *adv* inexorably
inesperienza *f* inexperience, lack of experience
inesperto *adj* inexperienced
inesplicabile *adj* inexplicable
inesplicabilità *f* ⟨*pl* inesplicabilità⟩ inexplicability
inesplorato *adj* unexplored
inesploso *adj* unexploded
inespressività *f* ⟨*pl* inespressività⟩ inexpressiveness
inespressivo *adj* unexpressive
inesprimibile *adj* (*indicibile*) indescribable
inespugnabile *adj* impregnable
inestimabile *adj* inestimable; *bene* invaluable; ***di valore ~*** priceless
inestinguibile *adj* unextinguishable; *fig sete* unquenchable; *odio* undying; *debito* undischargeable
inestirpabile *adj* ineradicable
inestricabile *adj* inextricable
inettitudine *f* ineptitude
inetto *adj* inept
inevaso *adj* pending
inevitabile *adj* inevitable
inevitabilità *f* ⟨*pl* inevitabilità⟩ inevitability
inevitabilmente *adv* inevitably
inezia *f* trifle
infallibile *adj* infallible
infallibilità *f* ⟨*pl* infallibilità⟩ infallibility
infamante *adj* defamatory, slanderous; ***accuse*** *fpl* ***-i*** slander
infamare *v/t* ⟨1a⟩ disgrace
infame **I** *adj* (*turpe*) infamous, foul; *hum* horrible, terrible; ***~ calunnia*** *f* disgraceful slander **II** *m/f sl* (*delatore*) grass *sl*
infangare *v/t* ⟨1e⟩ cover with mud; *buon nome* tarnish; ***~ il ricordo di qn*** besmirch s.o.'s memory
infangarsi *v/r* ⟨1e⟩ get muddy
infante *m*, **-a** *f reale* infante
infanticida *m/f* ⟨*mpl* -i⟩ infanticide
infanticidlo *m* ⟨*pl* -i⟩ infanticide
infantile *adj letteratura*, *giochi* children's; *malattie* childhood; (*immaturo*) childish, infantile; ***malattie*** *fpl* ***-i*** childhood diseases
infantilismo *m* PSYCH infantilism; (*puerilità*) babyishness
infanzia *f* childhood; (*primi mesi*) infancy (*a. fig*); (*bambini*) children
infarcire *v/t* ⟨4d⟩ COOK stuff; *fig* cram
infarinare *v/t* ⟨1a⟩ (dust with) flour
infarinatura *f fig* smattering
infarto *m cardiaco* heart attack; *fig* ***finale*** *f* ***da ~*** heart-stopping final
infartuato *m*, **-a** *f* heart-attack patient
infastidire *v/t* ⟨4d⟩ annoy, irritate
infastidirsi *v/r* ⟨4d⟩ get annoyed; ***~ per qc*** get annoyed about sth
infastidito *adj* annoyed
infaticabile *adj* tireless
infatti *cj* in fact
infatuarsi *v/r* ⟨1m⟩: ***~ di qn*** become infatuated with s.o.
infatuazione *f* infatuation
infausto *adj* ill-fated
infedele **I** *adj* unfaithful; *traduzione* inaccurate **II** *m/f* REL infidel
infedeltà *f* ⟨*pl* infedeltà⟩ unfaithfulness
infelice *adj* unhappy; (*inopportuno*) unfortunate; (*malriuscito*) bad
infelicemente *adv* unhappily; (*senza fortuna*) unsuccessfully
infelicità *f* unhappiness
infeltrirsi *v/r* ⟨4d⟩ become matted
inferiore **I** *adj* lower; *fig* inferior (***a*** to); ***di qualità ~*** of inferior quality; ***essere ~ a qn*** be inferior to s.o., be s.o.'s inferior; ***~ alla media*** below average **II** *m/f* inferior; (*subalterno*) subordinate
inferiorità *f* inferiority; ***complesso*** *m* ***d'~*** inferiority complex
inferiormente *adv* inferiorly
inferire *v/t* ⟨4d⟩: ***~ qc a qn*** deal s.o. sth; *fig* inflict
infermeria *f* infirmary
infermiere *m*, **-a** *f* nurse; ***~ aziendale*** agency nurse
infermieristico *adj* ⟨*mpl* -ci⟩ nursing *attr*; ***assistenza*** *f* ***-a*** nursing
infermità *f* ⟨*pl* infermità⟩ illness; ***~ mentale*** insanity
infermo **I** *adj* (*ammalato*) ill; (*invalido*) invalid **II** *m*, **-a** *f* invalid
infernale *adj* infernal
inferno *m* hell; ***fare una vita d'~*** live a life of sheer hell; ***va all'~!*** go to hell!
inferocito *adj* enraged
inferriata *f* grating; (*cancellata*) railings *pl*
infertilità *f* infertility
infervorare *v/t* ⟨1m & b⟩ stir up

infervorato *adj* fired up
infestante *adj* infesting; ***pianta*** *f* **~** weed; ***insetti*** *mpl* **-i** pests
infestare *v/t* ⟨1b⟩ infest
infestazione *f* infestation
infettare *v/t* ⟨1b⟩ infect
infettarsi *v/r* become infected
infettivo *adj* infectious; ***malattia*** *f* **-a** infectious disease
infetto *adj* infected
infezione *f* infection; ***fare*** **~** become infected
infiacchire *v/t* ⟨4d⟩ weaken
infiacchirsi *v/r* ⟨4d⟩ grow weaker
infiammabile *adj* flammable
infiammabilità *f* ⟨*pl* infiammabilità⟩ inflammability
infiammare *v/t* ⟨1a⟩ *fig*, MED inflame; *fig* **~ *gli animi*** set hearts alight
infiammarsi *v/r* become inflamed
infiammato *adj* MED inflamed; *fig* angry; (*rosso*) flaming
infiammatorio *adj* ⟨*mpl* -ri⟩ inflammatory; ***processo*** *m* **~** inflammatory process
infiammazione *f* inflammation; **~ *alla gola*** inflammation of the throat
infiascare *v/t* ⟨1d⟩ *put into flasks*
inficiare *v/t* ⟨1f⟩ invalidate
infido *adj* treacherous
infierire *v/i* ⟨4d⟩ *di maltempo*, *malattie* rage; **~ *su*** o ***contro*** savagely attack
infiggere *v/t* ⟨3cc⟩ drive; *nel suolo*: sink; *fig* engrave
infilare *v/t* ⟨1a⟩ *fili*, *corde*, *ago* thread; (*inserire*) insert, put in; (*indossare*) put on; *strada* take; **~ *l'ago*** thread a needle; **~ *le mani in tasca*** put one's hands in one's pockets; **~ *la porta*** *uscendo / entrando* slip out / in
infilarsi *v/r indumento* slip on; (*conficcarsi*) stick; (*introdursi*) slip (***in*** into); (*stiparsi*) squeeze (***in*** into); **~ *sotto le coperte*** slip under the covers; **~ *il cappotto*** slip on one's coat
infiltrare *v/t* ⟨1a⟩ infiltrate
infiltrarsi *v/r* seep; *fig* infiltrate
infiltrazione *f* infiltration; *di liquidi* seepage
infilzare *v/t* ⟨1a⟩ pierce; *perle* thread; *fig* string together; **~ *qn con la spada*** run s.o. through with a sword
infimo *adj* lowest
infine *adv* (*alla fine*) finally, eventually; (*insomma*) in short
infingardaggine *f* sloth
infingardo **I** *adj* lazy **II** *m*, **-a** *f* idler
infinità *f* infinity; ***ho un'~ di cose da fare*** I've got no end of things to do
infinitamente *adv* infinitely
infinitesimale *adj* infinitesimal
infinitesimo *m* infinitesimal part
infinito **I** *adj* infinite **II** *m* infinity; GRAM infinitive; ***ripetere all'~*** say over and over again
infioccare *v/t* ⟨1c & d⟩ decorate with ribbons
infiorare *v/t* ⟨1a⟩ decorate with flowers
infiorescenza *f* inflorescence
infischiarsi *v/r* ⟨1k⟩ *infml*: **~ *di*** not give a hoot about *infml*; ***me ne infischio*** I couldn't care less *infml*
infisso *m* frame; **-i** shutters and frames
infittire *v/t* & *v/i* ⟨4d⟩ thicken; *fig* **~ *le visite*** visit more frequently
inflaccidire *v/i* ⟨4d⟩ make flabby
inflaccidirsi *v/r* ⟨4d⟩ get flabby
inflazionato *adj fig* hackneyed
inflazione *f* inflation; ***tasso*** *m* ***d'~*** (rate of) inflation
inflazionistico *adj* ⟨*mpl* -ci⟩ inflationary
inflessibile *adj* inflexible
inflessibilità *f* inflexibility
inflessione *f* inflection
infliggere *v/t* ⟨3cc⟩ inflict; **~ *una punizione*** dole out a punishment
inflitto *past part* → ***infliggere***
influente *adj* influential
influenza *f* influence; MED flu, influenza; ***avere / prendere l'~*** have / get the flu; **~ *aviaria*** avian flu; ***avere molta / poca ~ su qn*** have a lot / little influence over s.o.
influenzabile *adj* easily influenced, impressionable
influenzale *adj* influenzal; ***virus*** *m* **~** flu virus
influenzare *v/t* ⟨1b⟩ influence; ***lasciarsi ~ da qn / qc*** let s.o. / sth influence one
influenzarsi *v/r* ⟨1b⟩ influence each other; (*ammalarsi d'influenza*) catch flu
influire *v/i* ⟨4d⟩: **~ *su*** influence, have an effect on
influsso *m* influence
infognarsi *v/r* ⟨1a⟩ *infml* get mixed up
infoltire *v/t* ⟨4d⟩ thicken

infondatezza *f* groundlessness

infondato *adj* unfounded, without foundation

infondere *v/t* ⟨3bb⟩ *fig* instil

inforcare *v/t* ⟨1d⟩ *occhiali* put on; *bicicletta* get on, mount

informale *adj* informal; ***incontro*** *m* **~** informal meeting; ***abbigliamento*** *m* **~** casual clothes

informare *v/t* ⟨1a⟩ inform (***di*** of)

informarsi *v/r* find out (***di, su*** about)

informatica *f scienza* information technology, computer science

informatico ⟨*mpl* -ci⟩ **I** *m*, **-a** *f* computer scientist **II** *adj* computer *attr*

informativa *f* ADMIN information report

informativo *adj* informative; ***a titolo*** *m* **~** for information

informatizzare *v/t* ⟨1a⟩ computerize

informatizzazione *f* computerization

informato *adj* informed; ***tenersi ~*** keep up to date

informatore *m*, **-trice** *f* informant; *della polizia* informer

informazione *f* piece of information; ***ufficio*** *m* ***-i*** information office; ***chiedere -i*** (***a qn***) ask (s.o.) for information; ***assumere -i su qn*** make inquiries about s.o.; ***libertà*** *f* ***d'~*** freedom of information; ***~ di garanzia*** JUR guarantee information; ***~ genetica*** genetic information

informe *adj* shapeless

informicolirsi *v/r* ⟨4d⟩ have pins and needles

infornare *v/t* ⟨1a⟩ put in the oven

infortunarsi *v/r* ⟨1a⟩ injure oneself

infortunio *m* ⟨*pl* -ni⟩ accident; ***~ sul lavoro*** accident at work, industrial accident; ***assicurazione*** *f* ***contro gli -i*** accident insurance

infortunistica *f* research into industrial accidents

infossare *v/t* ⟨1c⟩ store in a pit

infossarsi *v/r* ⟨1c⟩ subside; (*incavarsi*) sink

infossato *adj* sunken; ***guance*** *fpl* ***-e*** hollow cheeks; ***occhi*** *mpl* ***-i*** deep-set eyes

infradiciare *v/t* ⟨1m⟩ soak

infradiciarsi *v/r* ⟨1m⟩ get soaked

infradito *m or f* flip-flop, *US* thong

infrangere *v/t* ⟨3d⟩ break; ***~ la legge*** break the law

infrangibile *adj* unbreakable; ***vetro*** *m* **~** shatterproof glass

infrangibilità *f* ⟨*pl* infrangibilità⟩ unbreakableness

infranto I *past part* → infrangere **II** *adj fig* ***cuore*** *m* **~** broken heart

infrarosso *adj* infrared

infrasettimanale *adj* midweek

infrastruttura *f* infrastructure

infrastrutturale *adj* infrastructural

infrasuono *m* infrasound

infrazione *f* offence, *US* offense; ***~ al codice stradale*** traffic offence (*US* offense); ***commettere un'~*** commit an offence (*US* offense)

infreddatura *f* cold

infreddolito *adj* cold

infruttuoso *adj* fruitless; ***investimento*** *m* **~** unproductive investment; ***tentativi*** *mpl* ***-i*** vain attempts

infuocare *v/t fig* inflame

infuocarsi *v/r* ⟨1d⟩ become hot; *fig* grow heated

infuocato *adj* (*caldissimo*) scorching, blistering; *discorso*, *tramonto* fiery

infuori *adv*: ***all'~*** outwards; ***all'~ di*** except

infuriare ⟨1k⟩ **I** *v/t* infuriate, enrage **II** *v/i* rage

infuriarsi *v/r* fly into a rage

infuriato *adj* furious

infusione *f*, **infuso** *m* infusion; (*tisana*) herbal tea; ***~ di camomilla*** camomile tea; ***~ di tiglio*** lime-blossom tea

infusore *m* infusor

ing. *abbr* (= **ingegnere**) engineer

ingaggiare *v/t* ⟨1f⟩ (*reclutare*) recruit; *attore, cantante lirico* engage; SPORTS sign (up); (*iniziare*) start, begin; ***~ battaglia*** do battle

ingaggio *m* ⟨*pl* -ggi⟩ (*reclutamento*) recruitment; SPORTS signing; (*somma*) fee

ingannare *v/t* ⟨1a⟩ deceive; ***~ il tempo*** kill time; ***l'apparenza inganna*** appearances can be deceptive

ingannarsi *v/r* deceive o.s.; ***~ sul conto di qn*** be deceived by s.o.

ingannatore I *adj* deceptive **II** *m*, **-trice** *f* swindler

ingannevole *adj* deceptive

inganno *m* deception, deceit; ***ottenere qc con l'~*** obtain sth by deceipt; ***trarre qn in ~*** deceive s.o.

ingarbugliare *v/t* ⟨1g⟩ tangle; *fig* con-

fuse, muddle
ingarbugliarsi *v/r* get entangled; *fig* get confused
ingarbugliato *adj* *matassa*, *fili* tangled; *discorso* confused
ingegnarsi *v/r* ⟨1a⟩ do one's utmost (***a, per*** to)
ingegnere *m* engineer
ingegneria *f* engineering; ***~ genetica*** genetic engineering; ***~ meccanica*** mechanical engineering; ***~ navale*** marine engineering; ***studiare ~*** study engineering
ingegneristico *adj* ⟨*mpl* -ci⟩ engineering; ***studio m ~*** engineers' office
ingegno *m* (*mente*) mind; (*intelligenza*) brains *pl*; (*genio*) genius; (*inventiva*) ingenuity
ingegnosamente *adv* ingeniously
ingegnoso *adj* ingenious
ingelosire ⟨4d⟩ **I** *v/t* make jealous **II** *v/i* be jealous
ingelosirsi *v/r* ⟨4d⟩ become jealous; ***~ per qc*** get jealous about sth
ingemmare *v/t* ⟨1a⟩ adorn
ingenerosità *f* ⟨*pl* ingenerosità⟩ lack of generosity
ingeneroso *adj* ungenerous
ingente *adj* enormous
ingentilire *v/t* ⟨4d⟩ (*abbellire*) prettify; (*affinare*) refine
ingentilirsi *v/r* ⟨4d⟩ (*affinarsi*) become refined
ingenuità *f* ingenuousness
ingenuo *adj* ingenuous
ingerenza *f* interference
ingerire *v/t* ⟨4d⟩ swallow
ingerirsi *v/r* interfere
ingessare *v/t* ⟨1b⟩ put in plaster
ingessatura *f* plaster
ingestione *f* ingestion; ***~ di sostanze nocive*** ingestion of harmful substances
Inghilterra *f* England
inghiottire *v/t* ⟨4d⟩ swallow
inghippo *m* *infml* (*trucco*) trick; (*intoppo*) snag
inghirlandare *v/t* ⟨1a⟩ garland
ingiallire *v/t* & *v/i* ⟨4d⟩ turn yellow
ingiallito *adj* yellowed
ingigantire *v/t* ⟨4d⟩ *immagine*, *suono* magnify; *problema* exaggerate
ingigantirsi *v/r* ⟨4d⟩ become enormous
inginocchiarsi *v/r* ⟨1k⟩ kneel (down); ***~ davanti a qn*** kowtow to s.o.
inginocchiatoio *m* ⟨*pl* -oi⟩ prie-dieu
ingioiellare *v/t* ⟨1b⟩ bejewel
ingioiellarsi *v/r* ⟨1b⟩ put on one's jewellery, *US* jewelry
ingiù *adv*: ***all'~*** down(wards)
ingiungere *v/t* ⟨3d⟩: ***~ a qn di fare qc*** order s.o. to do sth
ingiuntivo *adj* injunctive; ***decreto m ~*** injunction
ingiunzione *f* injunction; ***~ di pagamento*** final demand
ingiuria *f* insult
ingiuriare *v/t* ⟨1k⟩ insult
ingiurioso *adj* insulting
ingiustamente *adv* unjustly, unfairly
ingiustificabile *adj* unjustifiable
ingiustificato *adj* unjustified
ingiustizia *f* injustice
ingiusto *adj* unjust, unfair
inglese **I** *m/adj* English **II** *m/f* Englishman; *donna* Englishwoman *f*; ***gli Inglesi*** the English
inglobamento *m* incorporation
inglobare *v/t* ⟨1c⟩ absorb
inglorioso *adj* shameful
ingobbire *v/t and v/i* ⟨4d⟩ curve
ingobbirsi *v/r* ⟨4d⟩ develop a stoop
ingobbito *adj* stooped
ingoiare *v/t* ⟨1i⟩ swallow; *fig* ***~ il rospo*** bite the bullet
ingolfare *v/t* ⟨1a⟩ flood
ingolfarsi *v/r* ⟨1a⟩ flood
ingombrante *adj* cumbersome, bulky
ingombrare *v/t* ⟨1a⟩ *passaggio* block (up); *stanza*, *mente* clutter (up)
ingombro **I** *adj* *passaggio* blocked; *stanza*, *mente* cluttered (up) **II** *m* hindrance, obstacle; ***essere d'~*** be in the way
ingordigia *f* greed (*a. fig*)
ingordo *adj* greedy
ingorgare *v/t* ⟨1e⟩ block
ingorgarsi *v/r* get blocked
ingorgo *m* ⟨*pl* -ghi⟩ blockage; ***~ stradale*** traffic jam
ingovernabile *adj* ungovernable
ingovernabilità *f* ⟨*pl* ingovernabilità⟩ ungovernability
ingozzare *v/t* ⟨1a⟩ *cibo* devour, gobble up; *persona* stuff (***di*** with)
ingozzarsi *v/r* stuff o.s (***di*** with)
ingranaggio *m* ⟨*pl* -ggi⟩ gear; *fig* machine; *fig* ***gli -i della politica*** the workings of politics

ingranare *v/t* ⟨1a⟩ engage; *fig* ***le cose cominciano a ~*** *infml* things are beginning to work out
ingrandimento *m* enlargement; *di azienda, città* expansion, growth; ***lente*** *f* ***d'~*** magnifying glass
ingrandire *v/t* ⟨4d⟩ enlarge; *azienda, città* expand, develop; (*esagerare*) exaggerate
ingrandirsi *v/r* grow
ingrassaggio *m* ⟨*pl* -ggi⟩ (*lubrificazione*) lubrication, greasing
ingrassamento *m* MED fattening
ingrassare ⟨1a⟩ **I** *v/t animali* fatten (up); (*lubrificare*) grease **II** *v/i* get fat, put on weight; *di birra, burro etc* be fattening; ***far ~*** be fattening; ***sono ingrassata di 2 chili*** I've put on 2 kilos
ingrasso *m* fattening; ***bestiame*** *m* ***da ~*** fattening stock
ingratitudine *f* ingratitude
ingrato *adj* ungrateful; *lavoro, compito* thankless
ingravidare *v/t* ⟨1m⟩ make pregnant
ingraziarsi *v/r* ⟨1g⟩ ingratiate o.s.
ingrediente *m* ingredient
ingresso *m* entrance; (*atrio*) hall; (*accesso*) admittance; COMPUT input; ***~ libero*** admission free; ***~ principale*** main entrance; ***~ di servizio*** service entrance; ***porta*** *f* ***d'~*** front door; ***vietato l'~*** no entry, no admittance; ***la primavera ha fatto il suo ~*** spring has sprung
ingrossamento *m* enlargement; MED swelling
ingrossare ⟨1c⟩ **I** *v/t* make bigger; (*gonfiare, accrescere*) swell **II** *v/i* get bigger; (*gonfiarsi*) swell
ingrossarsi *v/r* ⟨1c⟩ get bigger; (*gonfiarsi*) swell; ***il fiume si è ingrossato*** the river is high
ingrossato *adj* swollen
ingrosso *m*: ***all'~*** (*all'incirca*) roughly, about; COMM wholesale; ***commercio*** *m* ***all'~*** wholesale (trade)
inguaiare *v/t* ⟨1i⟩ *infml* get into trouble
inguaiarsi *v/r* ⟨1i⟩ get into trouble
inguaiato *adj infml*: ***essere ~*** be in a mess
inguainare *v/t* ⟨1a⟩ sheathe
ingualcibile *adj* crease-resistant
inguaribile *adj* incurable
inguinale *adj* groin *attr*; ***ernia*** *f* ***~*** hernia
inguine *m* ANAT groin
ingurgitare *v/t* ⟨1m⟩ gulp down
inibire *v/t* ⟨4d⟩ prohibit, forbid; PSYCH inhibit
inibito *adj* inhibited
inibitore, -trice I *adj* inhibiting; ***freni*** *mpl* ***-i*** inhibitors **II** *n* ***inibitore*** *m* MED inhibitor
inibizione *f* PSYCH inhibition
inidoneo *adj* unfit, unsuitable
iniettare *v/t* ⟨1b⟩ inject; ***~ qc a qn*** inject s.o. with sth
iniettarsi *v/r*: ***~ qc*** inject o.s. with sth
iniettato *adj*: *fig* ***occhi*** *mpl* ***-i di sangue*** bloodshot eyes
iniezione *f* injection; ***fare un'~ a qn*** give s.o. an injection; ***motore*** *m* ***a ~*** fuel-injection engine
inimicarsi *v/r* ⟨1d⟩: ***~ qn*** fall out with s.o.
inimicizia *f* enmity
inimitabile *adj* inimitable
inimmaginabile *adj* unimaginable
inintelligibile *adj* unintelligible
inintelligibilità *f* ⟨*pl* inintelligibilità⟩ incomprehensibility
ininterrottamente *adv* continuously
ininterrotto *adj* continuous
iniquamente *adv* inequitably
iniquità *f* ⟨*pl* iniquità⟩ iniquity
iniquo *adj* (*ingiusto*) unfair; (*maligno*) wicked
iniziale I *adj* initial; ***stipendio*** *m* ***~*** starting salary **II** *f* initial
inizializzare *v/t* ⟨1a⟩ COMPUT initialize, boot up
inizializzazione *f* booting up
inizialmente *adv* initially
iniziare ⟨1g⟩ **I** *v/t* begin, start; *ostilità, dibattito* open; *fig* initiate; ***~ qn a una religione*** initiate s.o. into a religion **II** *v/i* begin, start; *di ostilità, dibattito* open; ***~ a fare qc*** begin *or* start doing sth, begin *or* start to do sth
iniziatico *adj* ⟨*mpl* -ci⟩ initiatory; ***rito*** *m* ***~*** initiation rites
iniziativa *f* initiative; ***~ privata*** private enterprise; ***di mia ~*** on my own initiative; ***prendere l'~*** take the initiative; ***spirito*** *m* ***d'~*** initiative; ***per*** *or* ***su ~ di qn*** on s.o.'s initiative; ***di propria ~*** on one's own initiative
iniziato I *adj*: ***essere ~ a qc*** be initiat-

ed into sth **II** *m*, **-a** *f* initiate
iniziatore *m*, **-trice** *f* initiator
iniziazione *m* initiation; *fig* introduction; ***cerimonia*** *f* ***d'~*** initiation ceremony
inizio *m* ⟨*pl* -zi⟩ start, beginning; ***avere ~*** start, begin; ***dare ~ a qc*** start sth; ***dall'~ alla fine*** from start to finish; ***all'~*** at the start *or* beginning; ***all'~ di agosto*** at the beginning of August; ***agli -zi del Settecento*** at the start *or* beginning of the eighteenth century; ***essere agli -zi*** be just starting *or* beginning
in loco *adj inv* / *adv* on the premises
innaffiare *v/t* ⟨1k⟩ water
innaffiatoio *m* ⟨*pl* -oi⟩ watering can
innalzare *v/t* ⟨1a⟩ raise; (*erigere*) erect
innalzarsi *v/r* rise
innamoramento *m* falling in love
innamorarsi *v/r* ⟨1a⟩ fall in love (***di*** with); ***si innamorarono subito*** they fell in love at first sight
innamorato I *adj* in love (***di*** with); ***~ cotto*** *infml* head over heels in love **II** *m*, **-a** *f* boyfriend; *donna* girlfriend
innanzi I *prep* before; ***~ a*** in front of; ***~ tutto*** first of all; (*soprattutto*) above all **II** *adv stato in luogo* in front; (*avanti*) forward; (*prima*) before; ***d'ora ~*** from now on
innato *adj* innate, inborn
innaturale *adj* unnatural
innegabile *adj* undeniable; ***è ~ che …*** it is undeniable that …
inneggiare *v/i* ⟨1f⟩ sing hymns; ***~ alla vittoria*** sing the praises of victory
innervare *v/t* ⟨1a⟩ innervate
innervarsi *v/r* ⟨1a⟩ steel oneself
innervosire *v/t* ⟨4d⟩: ***~ qn*** make s.o. nervous; (*irritare*) get on s.o.'s nerves
innervosirsi *v/r* get nervous; (*irritarsi*) get irritated
innescare *v/t* ⟨1d⟩ *ordigno* prime; *reazione* trigger; ***~ una reazione a catena*** trigger a chain reaction
innesco *m* ⟨*pl* -chi⟩ primer; *fig* trigger
innestare *v/t* ⟨1b⟩ BOT, MED graft; ELEC *spina* insert; AUTO *marcia* engage
innesto *m* BOT, MED graft; AUTO clutch; ELEC connection
innevamento *m* snowfall, snow cover; ***~ artificiale*** artificial snow
innevare *v/t* ⟨1b⟩: ***~ una pista*** cover a ski run with snow
innevarsi *v/r* ⟨1b⟩ get covered with snow
inno *m* hymn; ***~ nazionale*** national anthem
innocente *adj* innocent; ***aria*** *f* ***~*** air of innocence; ***dichiararsi ~*** plead not guilty
innocentemente *adv* innocently
innocentino *m*, **-a** *f*: ***fare l'~*** play the innocent
innocenza *f* innocence
innocuità *f* ⟨*pl* innocuità⟩ innocuousness
innocuo *adj* innocuous, harmless
innovare *v/t* ⟨1c⟩ reform
innovativo *adj* innovative
innovazione *f* innovation
innumerevole *adj* innumerable
inoculare *v/t* ⟨1m & c⟩ inoculate
inoculazione *f* inoculation
inodore *adj* odo(u)rless
inoffensivo *adj* harmless, inoffensive
inoltrare *v/t* ⟨1a⟩ forward
inoltrarsi *v/r* advance, penetrate (***in*** into); ***~ nel bosco*** go further into the woods
inoltrato *adj* late; ***a notte / primavera -a*** late at night / in late spring
inoltre *adv* besides
inoltro *m* forwarding
inondare *v/t* ⟨1a⟩ flood
inondazione *f* flood
inoperabile *adj* inoperable
inoperoso *adj* idle
inopinabile *adj* unforeseeable
inopinato *adj* unforeseen
inopportunamente *adv* inappropriately
inopportuno *adj* (*inadatto*) inappropriate; (*intempestivo*) untimely; *persona* tactless
inoppugnabile *adj* indisputable
inoppugnabilità *f* ⟨*pl* inoppugnabilità⟩ indisputability
inorganico *adj* ⟨*mpl* -ci⟩ CHEM inorganic; (*disorganico*) disjointed
inorgoglire *v/t* ⟨4d⟩ make proud
inorgoglirsi *v/r* ⟨4d⟩ pride oneself
inorridire ⟨4d⟩ **I** *v/t* horrify **II** *v/i* be horrified
inorridito *adj* horrified
inospitale *adj* inhospitable, unwelcoming
inosservanza *f* noncompliance; ***~ delle norme*** failure to comply with

the regulations

inosservato *adj* unobserved, unnoticed; (*non rispettato*) disregarded; ***passare ~*** go unnoticed

inossidabile *adj* stainless; ***acciaio*** *m* **~** stainless steel

INPS *abbr* (= **Istituto Nazionale Previdenza Sociale**) *national insurance agency*

input *m* ⟨*pl* input⟩ COMPUT input; *fig* ***dare l'~ a qc*** input sth

inquadramento *m* (*assegnazione*) posting; *fig* setting

inquadrare *v/t* ⟨1a⟩ *dipinto, fotografia* frame; *fig* put into context

inquadrarsi *v/r* be part of

inquadratura *f* frame; FILM shot

inqualificabile *adj fig* unspeakable

inquietante *adj che preoccupa* worrying; *che turba* disturbing

inquietare *v/t* ⟨1b⟩ (*preoccupare*) worry; (*turbare*) disturb; ***fare ~ qn*** make s.o. cross

inquietarsi *v/r* (*preoccuparsi*) get worried; (*impazientirsi*) get cross

inquieto *adj* restless; (*preoccupato*) worried, anxious; (*adirato*) angry

inquietudine *f* anxiety

inquilino *m*, **-a** *f* tenant

inquinamento *m* pollution; *da sostanze radioattive* contamination; ***~ acustico*** noise pollution; ***~ atmosferico*** air pollution; ***~ dell'ambiente*** pollution; ***~ luminoso*** light pollution

inquinante I *adj* polluting; ***non ~*** environmentally friendly; ***sostanza*** *f* **~** pollutant **II** *m* pollutant

inquinare *v/t* ⟨1a⟩ pollute; *fig* (*corrompere*) corrupt; JUR *prove* tamper with; ***~ le prove*** JUR tamper with evidence

inquinatore *m*, **-trice** *f* polluter

inquirente *adj* JUR examining *attr*; ***commissione*** *f* **~** commission of inquiry

inquisire *v/t* ⟨4d⟩ JUR investigate; ***~ su qc*** inquire into sth; ***~ su qn*** inquire after s.o.

inquisitore, -trice I *adj fig* probing; JUR inquisitorial; ***sguardo*** *m* **~** searching look **II** *m*, **-trice** *f* HIST Inquisitor

inquisitorio *adj* ⟨*mpl* -ri⟩ inquisitory; *fig* ***tono*** *m* **~** questioning tone

insabbiamento *m di porto* silting up; *fig* shelving

insabbiare *v/t* ⟨1k⟩ *fig* shelve

insabbiarsi *v/r di porto* get silted up; *fig* grind to a halt

insaccare *v/t* ⟨1d⟩ put in bags; *salumi* make

insaccati *mpl* sausages *pl*

insalata *f* salad; ***~ mista*** mixed salad; ***~ di cetrioli*** cucumber salad; ***~ di pomodori*** tomato salad; ***~ di riso*** rice salad; ***~ russa*** Russian salad; ***~ verde*** green salad; ***fagiolini*** *mpl* ***in ~*** salad of green beans

insalatiera *f* salad bowl

insalivare *v/t* ⟨1a⟩ insalivate

insalivazione *f* insalivation

insalubre *adj* unhealthy

insanabile *adj* (*incurabile*) incurable; *fig* (*irrimediabile*) irreparable

insanabilità *f* ⟨*pl* insanabilità⟩ incurability

insanguinare *v/t* ⟨1m⟩ bloody

insanguinarsi *v/r* ⟨1m⟩ become bloodstained; ***~ le mani*** dirty one's hands

insanguinato *adj* bloodstained

insano *adj* insane

insaponare *v/t* ⟨1a⟩ soap

insaponarsi *v/r* soap o.s.; ***~ le mani*** soap one's hands

insapore *adj* tasteless

insaporire *v/t* ⟨4d⟩ flavo(u)r

insaporirsi *v/r* ⟨4d⟩ become tasty

insaputa *adv*: ***all'~ di qn*** unknown to s.o.; ***a mia / tua ~*** without my / your knowledge

insaturo *adj* CHEM unsaturated

insaziabile *adj* insatiable

insaziabilità *f* ⟨*pl* insaziabilità⟩ insatiability

inscatolare *v/t* ⟨1m⟩ tin, can

inscenare *v/t* ⟨1a⟩ stage

inscindibile *adj* inseparable

insecchire *v/t* ⟨4d⟩ dry up

insecchirsi *v/r* ⟨4d⟩ get dry

insediamento *m* settlement; *in carica* installation; ***-i*** *pl* ***romani / preistorici*** Roman / prehistoric settlements

insediare *v/t* ⟨1b & k⟩ install

insediarsi *v/r* ⟨1b & k⟩ settle; *in carica* take up office

insegna *f* sign; (*bandiera*) flag; (*stemma*) symbol; (*decorazione*) decoration; ***~ luminosa*** neon sign; ***~ pubblicitaria*** hoarding, billboard *US*; ***all'~***

di qc under the banner of sth

insegnamento *m* teaching; ***trarre ~ da qc*** learn (a lesson) from sth

insegnante I *m/f* teacher; ***~ di matematica*** maths teacher; ***~ di sostegno*** learning support teacher **II** *adj* teaching; ***corpo*** *m* **~** staff

insegnare *v/t* ⟨1a⟩ teach; ***~ qc a qn*** teach s.o. sth; ***~ a qn a fare qc*** teach s.o. to do sth

inseguimento *m* chase, pursuit

inseguire *v/t* ⟨4b⟩ chase, pursue

inseguitore *m*, **-trice** *f* pursuer

inselvatichirsi *v/r* ⟨4d⟩ grow wild; *fig* become unsociable

inseminazione *f* insemination; ***~ artificiale*** artificial insemination

insenatura *f* inlet

insensatezza *f* (*avventatezza*) recklessness; (*sciocchezza*) senselessness

insensato I *adj* senseless, idiotic **II** *m*, **-a** *f* fool, idiot

insensibile *adj* insensitive (***a*** to); *parte del corpo* numb

insensibilità *f* insensitivity; *di parte del corpo* numbness

inseparabile *adj* inseparable

insequestrabile *adj* immune from seizure

inserimento *m* (*ambientazione*) integration

inserire *v/t* ⟨4d⟩ insert; (*collegare in elettrotecnica*) connect; *annuncio* put in, place; ***~ la marcia*** engage the gear; ***~ dati nel computer*** enter data into a computer; ***~ un nominativo in un elenco*** enter a name on a list

inserirsi *v/r* fit in; *in una conversazione* join in

inserto *m* (*pubblicazione*) supplement; (*insieme di documenti*) file

inservibile *adj* unusable

inserviente *m/f* attendant

inserzione *f* insertion; *sul giornale* ad(-vert), advertisement; ***mettere un'~ sul giornale*** put an ad in the paper

inserzionista *m/f* ⟨*mpl* -i⟩ advertiser

insetticida *m* ⟨*pl* -i⟩ insecticide

insettifugo *m* ⟨*pl* -ghi⟩ insect repellant

insettivoro I *adj* insectivorous **II** *n*: ***Insettivori*** *mpl* Insectivora

insetto *m* insect

insicurezza *f* insecurity, lack of security

insicuro *adj* insecure

insider *m/f* ⟨*pl* insider⟩ insider

insidia *f* (*tranello*) snare; (*inganno*) trick; ***tendere un'~ a qn*** set a trap for s.o.

insidiare *v/t* ⟨1k⟩ set traps; ***~ una donna*** force one's attentions on a woman

insidioso *adj* insidious; ***domanda*** *f* **-a** loaded question; ***malattia*** *f* **-a** insidious disease

insieme I *adv* together; (*contemporaneamente*) at the same time; ***siamo andati tutti ~*** we all went together; ***i due treni sono partiti ~*** the two trains left at the same time; ***sono ~ da un anno*** they've been together for a year now; ***abbiamo messo ~ i soldi*** we pooled our money; ***mettere ~ un po' di amici*** get some friends together; ***mettersi ~*** pair off; ***stare bene ~*** (***a***) *colori* go well together; *persone* get on well together **II** *prep*: ***~ a, ~ con*** together with **III** *m* whole; *di abiti* outfit; ***nell'~*** on the whole

insigne *adj* illustrious

insignificante *adj* insignificant; ***persona*** *f* **~** nondescript person

insignire *v/t* ⟨4d⟩ invest; ***~ qn di un titolo*** bestow a title on s.o.

insincero *adj* insincere

insindacabile *adj* indisputable

insinuante *adj* insinuating

insinuare *v/t* ⟨1m⟩ insert; *fig dubbio, sospetto* sow the seeds of; ***~ che*** insinuate that; ***~ un dubbio*** instil a doubt; ***cosa stai insinuando?*** what are you insinuating?

insinuarsi *v/r* penetrate; *fig* ***~ in*** creep into

insinuazione *f* insinuation

insipido *adj* insipid

insipiente *adj* foolish

insipienza *f* foolishness

insistente *adj* insistent

insistenza *f* insistence; ***cedere alle -e di qn*** give in to s.o.'s persistent requests

insistere *v/i* ⟨3f⟩ insist; (*perseverare*) persevere; ***~ a fare qc*** insist on doing sth; ***non ~, tanto non vengo!*** don't keep going on about it: there's no way I'm coming!

insito *adj* (*innato*) innate; (*implicito*) implicit

insoddisfacente *adj* unsatisfactory

insoddisfatto *adj* unsatisfied; (*scontento*) dissatisfied

insoddisfazione *f* dissatisfaction

insofferente *adj* intolerant

insofferenza *f* intolerance

insolazione *f* sunstroke; ***si è preso un'~*** he got sunstroke

insolente *adj* insolent

insolenza *f* insolence; *espressione* insolent remark

insolito *adj* unusual

insolubile *adj* insoluble

insoluto *adj* unsolved; *debito* unpaid, outstanding

insolvente *adj* insolvent

insolvenza *f* insolvency

insolvibile *adj* insolvent

insomma **I** *adv* (*in breve*) briefly, in short **II** *int*: ***~!*** well, really!

insondabile *adj* unfathomable

insonne *adj* sleepless; ***trascorrere notti -i*** spend sleepless nights

insonnia *f* insomnia; ***soffrire d'~*** suffer from insomnia

insonnolito *adj* sleepy

insonorizzare *v/t* ⟨1n⟩ soundproof

insonorizzazione *f* soundproofing

insopportabile *adj* unbearable, intolerable

insopprimibile *adj* insuppressible; ***impulso*** *m* ***~*** irrepressible impulse

insorgenza *f*: ***~ di una malattia*** onset of an illness

insorgere *v/i* ⟨3d⟩ rise (up) (***contro*** against); *di difficoltà* come up, crop up

insormontabile *adj* insurmountable

insorto **I** *past part* → ***insorgere*** **II** *m*, **-a** *f* rebel

insospettabile *adj* above suspicion; (*impensato*) unsuspected

insospettato *adj* unsuspected

insospettire ⟨4d⟩ **I** *v/t*: ***~ qn*** make s.o. suspicious, arouse s.o.'s suspicion **II** *v/i* become suspicious

insospettirsi *v/r* ⟨4d⟩ become suspicious

insostenibile *adj* untenable; (*insopportabile*) unbearable

insostenibilità *f* ⟨*pl* insostenibilità⟩ untenability

insostituibile *adj* irreplaceable

insozzare *v/t* ⟨1a⟩ dirty

insozzarsi *v/r* ⟨1a⟩ get dirty

insperato *adj* unhoped for; (*inatteso*) unexpected

inspiegabile *adj* inexplicable

inspiegabilmente *adv* inexplicably

inspirare *v/t* ⟨1a⟩ breathe in, inhale

inspirazione *f* inhalation

instabile *adj* unstable; *tempo* changeable; ***equilibrio*** *m* ***~*** unstable equilibrium; ***carattere*** *m* ***~*** unstable character

instabilità *f* instability; *del tempo* changeability

installare *v/t* ⟨1a⟩ install

installarsi *v/r* settle in

installatore *m*, **-trice** *f* fitter

installazione *f* installation

instancabile *adj* tireless, untiring

instancabilmente *adv* untiringly

instaurare *v/t* ⟨1a⟩ *regime*, *clima* establish; *riforma* introduce; *rapporto* develop; ***~ una dittatura*** establish a dictatorship

instaurarsi *v/r di regime*, *clima* be established; *rapporto* develop

instaurazione *f* establishment

institore *m* agent

instradare *v/t* ⟨1a⟩ *fig* set up

insù *adv*: ***all'~*** upwards; ***naso*** *m* ***all'~*** turned-up nose

insubordinato *adj* insubordinate

insubordinazione *f* insubordination

insuccesso *m* failure

insudiciare *v/t* ⟨1m & f⟩ dirty

insudiciarsi *v/r* get dirty; ***~ le mani / i pantaloni*** get one's hands / trousers *or US* pants dirty

insufficiente *adj* insufficient; (*inadeguato*) inadequate

insufficienza *f* (*scarsità*) insufficiency; (*inadeguatezza*) inadequacy; ***~ cardiaca*** cardiac insufficiency; ***~ di prove*** lack of evidence; ***ho un'~ in latino*** I failed Latin

insufflare *v/t* ⟨1a⟩ instil

insulare *adj popolazione*, *flora etc* island *attr*; ***Italia*** *f* ***~*** the Italian islands

insulina *f* insulin

insulsaggine *f di cose* banality; *di persone* vapidity

insulso *adj fig* (*privo di vivacità*) dull; (*vacuo*) inane; (*sciocco*) silly

insultare *v/t* ⟨1a⟩ insult

insulto *m* insult

insuperabile *adj* insuperable; (*ineguagliabile*) incomparable

insuperato *adj* unsurpassed
insuperbire *v/t* ⟨4d⟩ make proud
insuperbirsi *v/r* ⟨4d⟩ boast
insurrezione *f* insurrection
insussistente *adj* non-existent; (*infondato*) unfounded
insussistenza *f* non-existence; (*infondatezza*) groundlessness
intabarrato *adj* well wrapped up
intaccare *v/t* ⟨1d⟩ (*corrodere*) corrode; *fig* (*danneggiare*) damage; *scorte*, *capitale* make inroads into; **~ il patrimonio** eat into one's capital
intagliare *v/t* ⟨1g⟩ carve
intagliatore *m*, **-trice** *f di metallo* engraver; *di legno* carver
intaglio *m* carving
intangibile *adj* intangible; *fig* inviolable
intangibilità *f* ⟨*pl* intangibilità⟩ intangibility; *fig* inviolability
intanto *adv* (*nel frattempo*) meanwhile; (*per ora*) for the time being; (*invece*) yet; **~ che** while
intarsiato *adj* inlaid
intarsiatore *m*, **-trice** *f* inlayer
intarsio *m* ⟨*pl* -si⟩ inlay
intasamento *m* blockage; **~ del traffico** traffic jam
intasare *v/t* ⟨1a⟩ block
intasarsi *v/r* get blocked; ***si è intasato il lavandino*** the washbasin's blocked up
intasato *adj* blocked
intascare *v/t* ⟨1d⟩ pocket; **~ una bella somma** pocket a tidy sum
intatto *adj* intact
intavolare *v/t* ⟨1m⟩: **~ una discussione** start a discussion
integerrimo *adj* very honest
integrabile *adj* integrable
integrale I *adj* whole; MATH integral; *edizione* unabridged; ***pane*** *m* **~** wholemeal bread; ***versione*** *f* **~** *di film* uncut version **II** *m* MATH integral
integralismo *m* fundamentalism
integralista ⟨*mpl* -i⟩ **I** *adj* fundamentalist **II** *m/f* fundamentalist
integrante *adj* integral *attr*
integrare *v/t* ⟨1l⟩ integrate; (*aumentare*) supplement
integrarsi *v/r* integrate
integratore *m* supplement; **~ alimentare** food supplement
integrazione *f* integration; ***cassa*** *f* **~** *form of income support*
integrazionismo *m* integrationism
integrazionista ⟨*mpl* -i⟩ **I** *adj* integrationist **II** *m/f* integrationist
integrità *f* integrity
intelaiatura *f* framework
intellettivo *adj* intellectual; ***facoltà*** *fpl* **-e** intellectual faculties
intelletto *m* intellect
intellettuale *m/f & adj* intellectual; ***attività*** *f* **~** mental activity
intelligence *f* ⟨*pl* intelligence⟩ intelligence
intelligente *adj* intelligent
intelligentemente *adv* intelligently
intelligenza *f* intelligence; **~ artificiale** artifical intelligence, AI
intellighenzia *f* intelligentsia
intelligibile *adj* intelligible
intelligibilità *f* ⟨*pl* intelligibilità⟩ intelligibility
intemerato *adj* irreproachable
intemperante *adj* immoderate
intemperanza *f* intemperance
intemperie *fpl* elements *pl*
intempestività *f* ⟨*pl* intempestività⟩ untimeliness
intempestivo *adj* untimely
intendente *m/f* MIL quartermaster; ADMIN superintendent
intendenza *f* MIL quartermastering; **~ di finanza** inland revenue office
intendere *v/t* ⟨3c⟩ **1.** (*comprendere*) understand; ***dare a ~ a qn che …*** give s.o. to understand that …; ***s'intende!*** naturally!, of course! **2.** (*udire*) hear **3.** (*voler dire*) mean; ***cosa intendi dire?*** what are you trying to say? **4.** (*avere intenzione*) intend; ***cosa intendi fare?*** what do you intend to do?; ***non intendo cedere*** I have no intention of giving up; ***non intende ragione*** he / she doesn't listen to reason; ***chi ha orecchie per ~ intenda*** a word to the wise **5.** (*pretendere*) want
intendersi *v/r* **1.** (*capirsi*) understand each other; ***intendiamoci bene!*** let's get this clear!; ***s'intende che …*** it means that …; ***tanto per intenderci*** just to make things clear … **2.** (*accordarsi*) agree **3. ~ *di qc*** know a lot about sth; ***non me ne intendo molto*** I don't know much about it **4. *intendersela*** have an affair (***con*** with)
intendimento *m* (*intenzione*) inten-

tion

intenditore *m*, **-trice** *f* connoisseur, expert

intenerimento *m* tenderness

intenerire *v/t* ⟨4d⟩ *fig* move

intenerirsi *v/r* ⟨4d⟩ *fig* be moved

intensamente *adv* intensely

intensificare *v/t* ⟨1n & d⟩ intensify

intensificarsi *v/r* intensify

intensificazione *f* intensification

intensità *f* ⟨*pl* intensità⟩ intensity; ELEC strength

intensivo *adj* intensive

intenso *adj* intense; ***freddo*** *m* **~** intense cold; ***vivere una vita -a*** live a full life; ***colore*** *m* **~** deep colour

intentare *v/t* ⟨1b⟩: **~ *causa*** (***contro qn***) start proceedings (against s.o.)

intentato *adj*: ***non lasciare nulla di ~*** try absolutely everything

intento I *adj* engrossed (***a*** in), intent (***a*** on); ***essere ~ a fare qc*** be busy doing sth **II** *m* aim, purpose; ***riuscire nel proprio ~*** succeed in one's aim

intenzionale *adj* intentional, deliberate

intenzionalità *f* ⟨*pl* intenzionalità⟩ intent; JUR premeditation

intenzionato *adj*: ***essere bene / male ~*** be well- / ill-intentioned; ***essere ~ a fare qc*** intend to do sth

intenzione *f* intention; ***avere l'~ di fare qc*** intend to do sth; ***con ~*** intentionally; ***senza ~*** unintentionally; ***che -i hai?*** what are your intentions?

interagire *v/i* ⟨4d⟩ interact

interamente *adv* entirely, wholly

interattività *f* ⟨*pl* interattività⟩ interactivity

interattivo *adj* interactive

interazione *f* interaction; **~ *elettromagnetica*** PHYS electromagnetic interaction

interbancario *adj* ⟨*mpl* -ri⟩ interbank; ***rapporto*** *m* **~** interbank report

intercalare I *v/t* ⟨1a⟩ insert **II** *m* stock phrase **III** *adj*: ***colture*** *fpl* **-i** catch crops

intercambiabile *adj* interchangeable

intercambiabilità *f* ⟨*pl* intercambiabilità⟩ interchangeability

intercapedine *f* cavity; ARCH hollow space

intercedere *v/i* ⟨3a⟩ intercede (***presso*** with; ***per*** on behalf of)

intercessione *f* intercession; ***per ~ di qn*** through the mediation of s.o.

intercessore *m*, **-ditrice** *f* mediator

intercettare *v/t* ⟨1b⟩ intercept; **~ *un aereo nemico*** intercept an enemy aircraft

intercettatore I *adj* interceptive **II** *n*: ***intercettatore*** *m* MIL interceptor

intercettazione *f* interception; **-i** *pl* ***telefoniche*** phone tapping *sg*

intercity *m* ⟨*pl* intercity⟩ intercity

interclassismo *m movement promoting solidarity between social classes*

intercomunicante *adj* intercommunicating

interconnessione *f* interconnection; ***elemento*** *m* ***d'~*** interconnection

interconnettere *v/t* ⟨3m⟩ interconnect

interconnettersi *v/r* ⟨3a⟩ TEL connect

intercontinentale *adj* intercontinental; ***volo*** *m* **~** intercontinental flight

intercorrere *v/i* ⟨3o⟩ *di tempo* elapse; (*esserci*) exist, be; ***tra noi intercorrono buoni rapporti*** we get on well

interculturale *adj*: ***scambio*** *m* **~** cross-cultural exchange

interdentale *adj*: ***filo*** *m* **~** (dental) floss

interdetto I *past part* → ***interdire*** **II** *adj* (*sbalordito*) astonished; (*sconcertato*) puzzled; ***rimanere ~*** be flabbergasted **III** *m*, **-a** *f infml* idiot *infml*

interdipendente *adj* interdependent

interdipendenza *f* interdependence

interdire *v/t* ⟨3t⟩ forbid; **~ *a qn di fare qc*** forbid s.o. to do sth; JUR **~ *qn*** deprive s.o. of his / her civil rights

interdisciplinare *adj* interdisciplinary

interdizione *f* ban; **~ *dai pubblici uffici*** ban from public office; **~ *da una professione*** ban from a profession

interessamento *m* interest; (*intervento*) intervention

interessante *adj* interesting; ***in stato ~*** pregnant

interessare ⟨1b⟩ **I** *v/t* interest; (*riguardare*) concern **II** *v/i* matter; ***a me non interessa*** it doesn't appeal to me

interessarsi *v/r* be interested, take an interest (***a, di*** in); (*occuparsi*) take care (***di*** of)

interessato I *adj* interested (***a*** in); (*implicato*) involved (***a*** in); *pej parere, opinione* biased; *persona* self-interested **II** *m*, **-a** *f* person concerned

interesse *m* **1.** interest; ***tasso*** *m* ***d'~***

interest rate; ***~ composto*** compound interest; ***per ~*** out of self-interest; ***senza ~*** of no interest; FIN ***senza -i*** interest-free; ***-i*** *pl* ***passivi*** interest allowed; ***-i*** *pl* ***usurari*** usurious interest **2.** (*tornaconto*) benefit; ***~ legale*** legal interest; ***matrimonio*** *m* ***d'~*** marriage for money; ***te lo dico nel tuo ~*** I'm telling you for your own good

intereuropeo *adj* inter-European

interezza *f* entirety; ***nella sua ~*** as a whole

interfaccia *f* ⟨*pl* -cce⟩ COMPUT interface; ***~ utente*** COMPUT user interface

interferenza *f* interference

interferire *v/i* ⟨4d⟩ interfere

interfono *m* intercom

intergovernativo *adj* intergovernmental; ***conferenza*** *f* ***-a*** intergovernmental conference

interiezione *f* interjection

interim *m* ⟨*pl* interim⟩ interim; ***governo*** *m* ***ad ~*** interim government

interinale *adj*: ***lavoro*** *m* ***~*** temping job

interiora *fpl* entrails *pl*

interiore *m/adj* interior; ***vita*** *f* ***~*** inner life

interiorità *f* ⟨*pl* interiorità⟩ interiority

interiorizzare *v/t* ⟨1a⟩ internalize

interiormente *adv* inwardly; ***cambiare ~*** change inside

interlacciamento *m* COMPUT, TV interconnection

interlacciare *v/t* ⟨1a⟩ COMPUT, TV interconnect

interlinea *f* spacing; ***~ semplice / doppia*** single / double spacing

interlineare[1] *adj* interlinear; ***versione*** *f* ***~*** interlinear version

interlineare[2] *v/t* ⟨1a⟩ space

interlocutore *m*, **-trice** *f*: ***la sua -trice*** the woman he was in conversation with

interlocutorio *adj* ⟨*mpl* -ri⟩ interlocutory

interloquire *v/i* ⟨4d⟩ interject

interludio *m* interlude

intermediario *m*, **-a** *f* ⟨*mpl* -ri⟩ intermediary; ***fare da ~ tra*** act as an intermediary between

intermediazione *f* intermediation

intermedio *adj* ⟨*mpl* -di⟩ intermediate; *bilancio*, *relazione* interim; ***stadio*** *m* ***~*** halfway stage

intermezzo *m* intermezzo

interminabile *adj* interminable

interministeriale *adj* interdepartmental

intermittente *adj* intermittent

intermittenza *f* intermittence; ***a ~*** on and off, off and on

intermodale *adj* intermodal; ***trasporto*** *m* ***~*** intermodal transport

internamento *m* internment; *in manicomio* committal

internare *v/t* ⟨1b⟩ intern; *in manicomio* commit; ***~ qn in una clinica psichiatrica*** commit s.o. to a psychiatric clinic

internato *m*, **-a** *f* inmate

internauta *m/f* ⟨*mpl* -i⟩ Internet user

internazionale *adj* international; ***commercio*** *m* ***~*** international trade

internazionalità *f* ⟨*pl* internazionalità⟩ internationality

internazionalizzazione *f* internationalization

internazionalmente *adv* internationally

Internet *m* Internet; ***navigare in ~*** surf the Net ***l'ho trovato su ~*** I found it on the Internet

Internet Café *m* ⟨*pl* Internet Café⟩ Internet café

internista *m/f* ⟨*mpl* -i⟩ internist

interno I *adj* **1.** internal, inside *attr*; ***alunno*** *m* ***~*** boarder; ***verso l'~*** inwards **2.** GEOG inland **3.** POL, FIN domestic; ***mercato*** *m* ***~*** domestic market **4.** *fig* inner **II** *m* **1.** (*parte interna*) inside, interior; ***ministero*** *m* ***dell'Interno*** *or* ***degli Interni*** Home Office, *US* Department of the Interior; ***all'~*** inside; ***all'~ dell'edificio*** inside the building; SPORTS ***~ destro / sinistro*** inside right / left **2.** GEOG interior **3.** TEL extension **4.** FILM interior shooting **5.** ***via Dante n. 6 ~ 9*** 6 via Dante, Flat 9

intero *adj* whole, entire; (*completo*) complete; ***un anno ~*** a whole *or* full year; ***biglietto*** *m* ***~*** full-price ticket; ***latte*** *m* ***~*** whole milk; MATH ***numero*** *m* ***~*** integer; ***per ~*** in full; ***l'-a somma*** the full amount

interparlamentare *adj* interparliamentary

interpellanza *f* question; ***~ parlamentare*** parliamentary inquiry

interpellare *v/t* ⟨1b⟩ consult

interpersonale *adj* interpersonal; ***rapporti*** *mpl* ***-i*** interpersonal relations
interplanetario *adj* ⟨*mpl* -ri⟩ interplanetary
interpolare *v/t* ⟨1m⟩ interpolate
interpolazione *f* interpolation
interporre *v/t* ⟨3ll⟩ *autorità*, *influenza* bring to bear
interporsi *v/r* intervene
interporto *m* freight village
interposizione *f* interposal
interposto *adj* interposed; ***per -a persona*** vicariously
interpretare *v/t* ⟨1m & b⟩ interpret; *personnagio* play; MUS play, perform; ***~ il pensiero di qn*** read s.o.'s thoughts; ***non so come ~ il suo atteggiamento*** I don't know how to interpret his behaviour
interpretariato *m* interpretership
interpretativo *adj* interpretative
interpretazione *f* interpretation; THEAT, MUS, *film* performance; ***~ dei sogni*** dream interpretation
interprete *m/f* interpreter; *attore*, *musicista* performer; ***~ simultaneo/-a*** interpreter; ***fare da ~*** interpret, act as interpreter
interpunzione *f* punctuation; ***segni*** *mpl* ***di ~*** punctuation marks
inter-rail *m* ⟨*pl* inter-rail⟩ inter-rail
interramento *m* burying
interrare *v/t* ⟨1b⟩ (*sotterrare*) bury; (*coprire di terra*) fill in
interrato I *adj* buried; ***cavo*** *m* ***~*** underground cable **II** *n*: ***interrato*** *m* basement
interregionale *adj* inter-regional; ***treno*** *m* ***~*** inter-regional train
interregno *m* interregnum
interrimento *m* GEOL silting up
interrogare *v/t* ⟨1m, b & e⟩ question; EDU test
interrogarsi *v/r* ⟨1m, b & e⟩ wonder
interrogativo I *adj* GRAM interrogative; *occhiata* questioning; ***punto*** *m* ***~*** question mark **II** *m* (*domanda*) question; (*dubbio*) doubt; ***porsi degli -i*** raise questions
interrogatorio *m* ⟨*pl* -ri⟩ questioning
interrogazione *f* questioning; *domanda* question; EDU oral test
interrompere *v/t* ⟨3rr⟩ interrupt; (*sospendere*) break off, stop; *comunicazioni*, *forniture* cut off
interrotto *past part* → ***interrompere***
interruttore *m* ELEC switch
interruzione *f* interruption; ***~ della corrente*** *per guasto* blackout; *per lavori* powercut; ***~ di gravidanza*** termination (of pregnancy)
interscambio *m* exchange
intersecare *v/t* ⟨1m, b & d⟩ intersect
intersezione *f* intersection
interstiziale *adj* interstitial
interstizio *m* ⟨*pl* -i⟩ interstice
intertesto *m* intertext
interurbana *f* long-distance (phone) call
interurbano *adj* intercity; ***comunicazione*** *f* ***-a*** long-distance (phone) call; ***trasporto*** *m* ***~*** long-distance transport
intervallare *v/t* ⟨1a⟩ (*distanziare*) stagger; (*alternare*) break up
intervallo *m* interval; *di scuola*, *lavoro* break
intervenire *v/i* ⟨4p⟩ intervene; (*partecipare*) take part, participate (***a*** in); MED operate
interventismo *m* interventionism
interventista ⟨*mpl* -i⟩ **I** *adj* interventionist; ***politica*** *f* ***~*** interventionist policy **II** *m/f* interventionist
intervento *m* intervention; (*partecipazione*) participation; MED operation; ***~ chirurgico*** surgery; ***pronto ~*** emergency services
intervertebrale *adj* spinal; ***disco*** *m* ***~*** spinal disc
intervista *f* interview; ***rilasciare un'~*** give an interview; ***fare un' ~ a qn*** interview s.o.
intervistare *v/t* ⟨1a⟩ interview
intervistato I *adj* interviewed **II** *m*, **-a** *f* interviewee
intervistatore *m*, **-trice** *f* interviewer
intesa *f* (*accordo*) understanding; (*patto*) agreement; SPORTS team work; ***agire d'~*** act in agreement; ***l'Intesa*** HIST the Entente
inteso I *past part* → ***intendere*** **II** *adj* (*capito*) understood; (*destinato*) intended, meant (***a*** to); ***siamo -i?*** agreed?; ***ben ~*** needless to say, of course
intessere *v/t* ⟨3a⟩ interweave
intessuto I *adj* woven (*a. fig*) **II** *past part* → ***intessere***
intestardirsi *v/r* ⟨4d⟩: ***~ su qc*** dig

one's heels in about sth

intestare *v/t* ⟨1b⟩ *assegno* make out (***a*** to); *proprietà* register (***a*** in the name of); ***carta*** *f* ***intestata*** letterhead, letterheaded notepaper; ***~ la casa ai figli*** put the house in one's children's names; ***~ un assegno a qn*** make out a cheque to s.o.

intestatario *m*, **-a** *f* ⟨*mpl* -ri⟩ *di assegno* payee; *di proprietà* registered owner

intestato *adj* JUR intestate; ***carta*** *f* ***-a*** headed paper

intestazione *f* heading; *su carta da lettere* letterhead

intestinale *adj* intestinal; ***disturbi*** *mpl* ***-i*** intestinal problems

intestino[1] *m* intestine, gut

intestino[2] *adj* internal; ***lotte*** *fpl* ***-e*** internecine battles

intiepidire *v/t* ⟨4d⟩ (*raffreddare*) cool; (*riscaldare*) warm; *fig* (*affievolire*) dampen

intiepidirsi *v/r* ⟨4d⟩ (*perdere calore*) cool down; (*acquistare calore*) warm up; *fig* (*affievolirsi*) cool down

intifada *f* intifada

intimamente *adv* intimately; ***essere ~ persuaso*** *m* be quietly persuaded; ***conoscere qn ~*** know s.o. intimately

intimare *v/t* ⟨1l or 1a⟩ order; ***~ l'alt a qn*** order s.o. to stop; ***~ a qn di fare qc*** order s.o. to do sth

intimazione *f* order; ***~ di pagamento*** injunction to pay; ***~ di sfratto*** eviction notice

intimidatorio *adj* intimidating; ***azioni*** *fpl* ***-e*** intimidation

intimidazione *f* intimidation

intimidire *v/t* ⟨4d⟩ intimidate

intimidirsi *v/r* ⟨4d⟩ become frightened

intimità *f* privacy; *di un rapporto* intimacy

intimo I *adj* intimate; (*segreto*) private; (*accogliente*) cosy, *US* cozy; *amico* close, intimate; ***biancheria*** *f* ***-a*** underwear; ***cerimonia*** *f* ***-a*** private ceremony; ***avere rapporti -i con qn*** be intimate with s.o. **II** *m* **1.** *persona* close friend, intimate **2.** (*abbigliamento*) underwear; ***nel mio ~*** in my heart of hearts

intimorire *v/t* ⟨4d⟩ frighten

intingere *v/t* ⟨3d⟩: ***~ qc in qc*** dip sth in sth; ***~ i biscotti nel latte*** dip the biscuits in the milk

intingolo *m* sauce

intirizzire *v/t* ⟨4d⟩ numb

intirizzirsi *v/r* ⟨4d⟩ become numb

intitolare *v/t* ⟨1m⟩ (*dare il titolo a*) call, entitle; (*dedicare*) dedicate (***a*** to)

intitolarsi *v/r* be called; ***come si intitola il film / libro?*** what's the title of the film / book?

intoccabile I *adj* untouchable **II** *m/f* untouchable (*a. fig*)

intollerabile *adj* intolerable

intollerabilità *f* ⟨*pl* intollerabilità⟩ intolerability

intollerante *adj* intolerant; ***~ verso un farmaco*** allergic to a drug

intolleranza *f* intolerance

intonacare *v/t* ⟨1m, c & d⟩ plaster

intonaco *m* ⟨*pl* -chi⟩ plaster

intonare *v/t* ⟨1c⟩ *strumento* tune; *colori* co-ordinate; ***~ una canzone*** strike up a tune

intonarsi *v/r* (*armonizzare*) go well (***a, con*** with)

intonato *adj* MUS in tune; ***colori*** *pl* ***-i*** colours that go well together

intonazione *f* (*strumento*) tuning; (*canto*) pitch

intonso *adj libro* uncut

intontire *v/t* ⟨4d⟩ daze

intontirsi *v/r* ⟨4d⟩ be dazed

intontito *adj* dazed

intoppare *v/i* ⟨1c⟩ *infml*: ***~ in qc*** trip over sth; *fig* come up against sth

intoppo *m* (*ostacolo*) hindrance; (*contrattempo*) snag

intorbidamento *m* muddiness

intorbidire *v/t* ⟨4d⟩ muddy; *fig* confuse; ***~ le acque*** muddy the waters

intorbidirsi *v/r* ⟨4d⟩ cloud; *fig* become confused

intorno I *prep*: ***~ a*** around; (*circa*) (round) about, around; (*riguardo a*) about; ***~ ai 100 euro*** about 100 euros; ***~ al 1850*** around 1850; ***il giardino ~ alla casa*** the garden around the house **II** *adv* around; ***tutt'~*** all around; ***guardarsi ~*** look around; ***qui ~ non ci sono negozi*** there aren't any shops around here

intorpidimento *m* numbness; *fig* dullness

intorpidire *v/t* ⟨4d⟩ numb; *fig* dull

intorpidirsi *v/r* ⟨4d⟩ stiffen; *fig* become lethargic

intorpidito *adj* numb; ***sentirsi ~*** feel lethargic
intossicare *v/t* ⟨1m, c & d⟩ poison
intossicazione *f* poisoning; ***~ alimentare*** food poisoning
intracomunitario *adj* ⟨*mpl* -i⟩ intra-Community; ***acquisto*** *m* ***~*** COMM intra-Community purchase
intraducibile *adj* untranslatable
intraducibilità *f* ⟨*pl* intraducibilità⟩ untranslatability
intralciare *v/t* ⟨1f⟩ hinder, hamper
intralcio *m* ⟨*pl* -ci⟩ hindrance
intrallazzare *v/i* ⟨1a⟩ scheme
intramontabile *adj* everlasting
intramuscolare *adj* MED intramuscular
Intranet *f* COMPUT intranet
intransigente *adj* intransigent
intransigenza *f* intransigence
intransitabile *adj* impracticable
intransitabilità *f* ⟨*pl* intransitabilità⟩ impracticability
intransitivo *adj* intransitive
intrappolare *v/t* ⟨1m⟩ trap; ***rimanere intrappolato in qc*** get caught up in sth
intraprendente *adj* enterprising
intraprendenza *f* enterprise
intraprendere *v/t* ⟨3c⟩ undertake; ***~ una carriera*** take up a career
intrapreso *past part* → ***intraprendere***
intrasferibile *adj* FIN non-transferable
intrattabile *adj* intractable; *prezzo* fixed, non-negotiable
intrattabilità *f* ⟨*pl* intrattabilità⟩ intractability
intrattenere *v/t* ⟨2q⟩ entertain; ***~ buoni rapporti con qn*** be on good terms with s.o.
intrattenersi *v/r* dwell (***su*** on); ***~ con qn*** have a consultation with s.o.
intrattenimento *m* entertainment
intrattenitore *m*, **-trice** *f* entertainer
intrauterino *adj* intrauterine
intravedere *v/t* ⟨2s⟩ glimpse, catch a glimpse of; *fig* (*presagire*) anticipate, see
intravisto *past part* → ***intravedere***
intrecciare *v/t* ⟨1f⟩ plait, braid; (*intessere*) weave; *fig* ***~ rapporti di amicizia*** build a friendship
intrecciarsi *v/r* intertwine
intreccio *m* ⟨*pl* -cci⟩ *fig* (*trama*) plot
intrepido *adj* intrepid
intricare *v/t* ⟨1d⟩ tangle; *fig* complicate
intricarsi *v/r* ⟨1d⟩ get tangled up; *fig* get more complicated
intricato *adj* tangled; *disegno* intricate; *fig* complicated
intrico *m* ⟨*mpl* -chi⟩ muddle (*a. fig*)
intridere *v/t* ⟨3q⟩ soak
intrigante *adj* scheming; (*affascinante*) intriguing
intrigare ⟨1e⟩ **I** *v/i* plot **II** *v/t* intrigue
intrigo *m* ⟨*pl* -ghi⟩ plot
intrinseco *adj* ⟨*mpl* -ci⟩ intrinsic
intriso *adj*: ***~ di qc*** soaked in sth; ***~ di sudore*** drenched in sweat
intristire *v/t* ⟨4d⟩ pine
intristirsi *v/r* become sad
introdotto **I** *adj* well-known; ***essere ~ in qc*** be knowledgeable about sth **II** *past part* → ***introdurre***
introdurre *v/t* ⟨3e⟩ introduce; (*inserire*) insert; ***~ un argomento*** bring up a topic; ***~ qn in società*** introduce s.o. into society
introdursi *v/r* get in
introduttivo *adj* introductory
introduzione *f* introduction
introito *m* income; (*incasso*) takings *pl*
intromesso *past part* → ***intromettersi***
intromettersi *v/r* ⟨3ee⟩ interfere; (*interporsi*) intervene
intromissione *f* interference; (*intervento*) intervention
intronare *v/t* ⟨1c⟩ *infml* daze
introspettivo *adj* introspective
introspezione *f* introspection
introvabile *adj* impossible to find
introversione *f* introversion
introverso **I** *adj* introverted **II** *m*, **-a** *f* introvert
intrufolarsi *v/r* ⟨1m⟩ sneak in
intruglio *m* ⟨*pl* -gli⟩ concoction
intrusione *f* intrusion
intruso *m*, **-a** *f* intruder
intubare *v/t* ⟨1a⟩ MED intubate
intubazione *f* MED intubation; TECH tubage
intuibile *adj* intuitable; (*prevedibile*) easy to guess
intuire *v/t* ⟨4d⟩ know instinctively
intuitivamente *adv* by intuition
intuitivo *adj* intuitive
intuito *m* intuition; ***avere ~ per qc*** have a gut feeling about sth
intuizione *f* intuition

inturgidimento *m* swelling
inturgidirsi *v/r* ⟨4d⟩ swell
inumano *adj* inhuman
inumare *v/t* ⟨1a⟩ bury
inumazione *f* burial
inumidire *v/t* ⟨4d⟩ dampen, moisten
inumidirsi *v/r* get damp
inurbamento *m* urban drift
inurbano *adj* impolite
inusitato *adj* uncommon
inusuale *adj* unusual
inutile *adj* useless; (*superfluo*) unnecessary, pointless; ***è ~ insistere / che tu insista*** there's no point persisting
inutilità *f* uselessness
inutilizzabile *adj* unusable
inutilizzato *adj* unused
inutilmente *adv* pointlessly, needlessly
invadente **I** *adj* nosy **II** *m/f* busybody
invadenza *f* nosiness
invadere *v/t* ⟨3q⟩ invade; (*occupare*) occupy; (*inondare*) flood; ***i tifosi hanno invaso il campo*** the fans invaded the pitch
invaghirsi *v/r* ⟨4d⟩: ***~ di*** take a fancy to
invalicabile *adj* impassable
invalidamento *m* invalidation
invalidante *adj* MED disabling; JUR invalidating; ***malattia** f **~*** crippling illness
invalidare *v/t* ⟨1m⟩ invalidate
invalidità *f* ⟨*pl* invalidità⟩ disability
invalido **I** *adj* disabled; JUR invalid; ***rimanere ~*** be disabled **II** *m*, **-a** *f* disabled person; ***~ di guerra*** disabled ex-serviceman; ***~ del lavoro*** victim of an industrial accident
invano *adv* in vain
invariabile *adj* invariable
invariabilità *f* unchanging nature
invariabilmente *adv* invariably
invariato *adj* unchanged
invasato **I** *adj* possessed **II** *m*, **-a** *f* madman, madwoman
invasatura *f* NAUT launching cradle
invasione *f* invasion (***di*** of); ***~ di campo*** pitch invasion; ***-i** pl **barbariche*** Barbarian invasions
invasivo *adj* MED invasive; ***intervento** m **~*** invasion
invaso *past part* → ***invadere***
invasore *m* invader
invecchiamento *m* ageing
invecchiare ⟨1k⟩ **I** *v/t* age; ***la barba ti invecchia*** the beard makes you look older **II** *v/i* age, get old(er); *di vini, cibi* mature; *fig* (*cadere in disuso*) date
invece *adv* instead; (*ma*) but; ***~ di fare*** instead of doing
inveire *v/i* ⟨4d⟩: ***~ contro*** inveigh against
invelenire *v/t* ⟨4d⟩ embitter
invelenirsi *v/r* ⟨4d⟩ become embittered
invelenito *adj* embittered
invendibile *adj* unmarketable
invenduto *adj* unsold
inventare *v/t* ⟨1b⟩ invent; ***inventarsi una scusa*** make up an excuse; ***inventarne di tutti i colori*** make up all sorts of stories; ***~ di sana pianta*** completely make things up
inventariare *v/t* ⟨1k⟩: ***~ qc*** draw up an inventory of sth
inventario *m* ⟨*pl* -ri⟩ inventory, stock-taking; ***fare l'~*** (***di qc***) give a detailed account (of sth)
inventiva *f* inventiveness
inventivo *adj* inventive
inventore *m*, **-trice** *f* inventor
invenzione *f* invention
inverdire ⟨4d⟩ **I** *v/t* make green **II** *v/i* go green
inverdirsi *v/r* ⟨4d⟩ go green
inverecondo *adj* shameless
invernale *adj* winter *attr*; ***sport** mpl **-i*** winter sports; ***nel periodo ~*** in wintertime
inverno *m* winter; ***d'~*** in winter
inverosimile *adj* improbable, unlikely
inversamente *adv*: ***~ proporzionale*** in inverse proportion
inversione *f* (*scambio*) reversal; ***fare ~*** AUTO turn around; ***~ a U*** AUTO U-turn; ***~ di marcia*** AUTO three-point turn; *fig* U-turn; *fig* ***~ di rotta*** U-turn
inverso **I** *adj* reverse **II** *m* opposite; ***all'~*** the wrong way
invertebrato *m/adj* invertebrate
invertire *v/t* ⟨4b or 4d⟩ reverse; (*capovolgere*) turn upside down; CHEM, ELEC invert; ***~ la marcia*** turn round; ***~ le parti*** exchange roles
invertirsi *v/r* be reversed
invertito **I** *adj* reversed **II** *n*:***invertito** m* homosexual
invertitore *m* inverter
investigare *v/t & v/i* ⟨1m, b & e⟩ in-

vestigate; ~ ***su qc*** investigate sth
investigativo *adj* investigative; ***attività*** *f* ***-a*** investigation; ***nucleo*** *m* ~ investigative group
investigatore *m*, **-trice** *f* investigator; ~ ***privato*** private detective
investigazione *f* investigation
investimento *m* investment; *di veicolo* crash; *di pedone* running over; ~ ***di capitali*** capital investment
investire *v/t* ⟨4d or 4b⟩ *pedone* run over; *veicolo* smash into, collide with; FIN, *fig* invest; ~ ***in azioni*** invest in shares; ~ ***molto tempo in qc*** invest a lot of time in sth; ~ ***qn di una carica*** give s.o. a post; ***è stato investito da una moto*** he was knocked down by a motorbike
investitore *m*, **-trice** *f* ECON investor
investitura *f* investiture
inveterato *adj* inveterate; (*incallito*) confirmed
invetriata *f* full-length window
invettiva *f* invective
inviare *v/t* ⟨1h⟩ send; ~ ***qc a qn / qc*** send sth to s.o. / sth
inviato *m*, **-a** *f* envoy; *di giornale* correspondent; ~ ***di guerra*** war correspondent; ~ ***speciale*** special correspondent
invidia *f* envy; ***essere roso dall'~*** be green with envy; ***crepare d'~*** *infml* be sick with envy
invidiabile *adj* enviable
invidiare *v/t* ⟨1k⟩ envy; ~ ***qc a qn*** envy s.o. sth
invidioso *adj* envious; ***essere ~ di qn / qc*** be envious of s.o. / sth
invigorimento *m* invigoration
invigorire *v/t* ⟨4d⟩ invigorate
invincibile *adj* invincible
invincibilità *f* ⟨*pl* invincibilità⟩ invincibility
invio *m* ⟨*pl* -vii⟩ dispatch; COMPUT ***tasto*** *m* ***d'~*** enter key
inviolabile *adj* inviolable
inviolabilità *f* ⟨*pl* inviolabilità⟩ inviolability
inviolato *adj* inviolate; ***segreti*** *mpl* ***-i*** absolute secrets; ***vette*** *fpl* ***-e*** virgin peaks
inviperirsi *v/r* ⟨4d⟩ fly off the handle
inviperito *adj* vicious
invischiare *v/t* ⟨1k⟩ inveigle
invischiarsi *v/r* ⟨1k⟩ become involved
invischiato *adj* entangled; ***essere ~ in uno scandalo*** be embroiled in a scandal
invisibile *adj* invisible
invitante *adj profumo* enticing; *offerta* tempting
invitare *v/t* ⟨1a⟩ invite; ~ ***qn a pranzo / cena*** ask s.o. to lunch / dinner; ~ ***qn a tacere*** ask s.o. to be quiet
invitato *m*, **-a** *f* guest
invito *m* invitation; ~ ***a presentarsi*** summons *sg*
invocare *v/t* ⟨1c & d⟩ invoke; (*implorare*) plead for, beg for
invocazione *f* invocation; (*richiesta*) plea
invogliare *v/t* ⟨1g & c⟩ induce
involgarimento *m* coarsening
involgarire *v/t* ⟨4d⟩ coarsen
involgarirsi *v/r* ⟨4d⟩ become coarser
involontariamente *adv* involuntarily
involontario *adj* ⟨*mpl* -ri⟩ involuntary
involtini *mpl* COOK *rolled stuffed slices of meat*
involto *m* bundle; (*pacco*) parcel
involucro *m* wrapping
involuzione *f* regression; MED involution
invulnerabilità *f* ⟨*pl* invulnerabilità⟩ invulnerability
inzaccherare *v/t* ⟨1m⟩ spatter with mud
inzuccherare *v/t* ⟨1m⟩ *caffè* sugar; *teglia, torta* sprinkle with sugar
inzuppare *v/t* ⟨1a⟩ soak; (*intingere*) dip
inzupparsi *v/r* ⟨1a⟩ get soaked
inzuppato *adj* soaked
io I *pron* I; ~ ***stesso*** myself; ***sono ~!*** it's me!; ***ci vado io*** I'll go; ***anch'~*** me too; ***ci penso ~*** I'll see to it; ***non sono stato ~*** it wasn't me **II** *m* ⟨*pl* io⟩ ego
iodato I *adj* iodized **II** *n*: ***iodato*** *m* iodate
iodio *m* iodine
ioduro *m* iodide
ione *m* ion; ~ ***positivo / negativo*** positive / negative ion; ***-i di litio*** TEL lithium ions
ionico *adj* ⟨*mpl* -ci⟩ ARCH Ionic
Ionio *m* Ionian
ionizzare *v/t* ⟨1a⟩ ionize
ionosfera *f* ionosphere
iosa *adv*: ***a ~*** in abundance, aplenty

iperacidità *f* ⟨*pl* iperacidità⟩ hyperacidity
iperalimentazione *f* overfeeding
iperattività *f* ⟨*pl* iperattività⟩ hyperactivity
iperattivo *adj* hyperactive
iperbole *f figura retorica* hyperbole; MATH hyperbola
iperbolico *adj* ⟨*mpl* -ci⟩ MATH hyperbolic (*a.* MATH)
iperfunzione *f* hyperfunction
ipermercato *m* hypermarket
iperproteico *adj* ⟨*mpl* -ci⟩ high-protein
iperprotettivo *adj* over-protective
ipersensibile *adj* hypersensitive
ipersensibilità *f* ⟨*pl* ipersensibilità⟩ hypersensitivity
ipertensione *f* high blood pressure
iperteso *adj* hypertensive
ipertrofia *f* overdevelopment
ipnosi *f* hypnosis; ***essere sotto ~*** be hypnotized
ipnotizzare *v/t* ⟨1a⟩ hypnotize
ipnotizzatore *m*, **-trice** *f* hypnotizer
ipocalorico *adj* ⟨*mpl* -ci⟩ low in calories
ipocondria *f* hypochondria
ipocondriaco I *adj* ⟨*mpl* -ci⟩ hypochondriacal **II** *m*, **-a** *f* hypochondriac
ipocrisia *f* hypocrisy
ipocrita I *adj* hypocritical **II** *m/f* ⟨*mpl* -i⟩ hypocrite
ipofisi *f* pituitary gland
ipogastrio *m* ⟨*pl* -i⟩ hypogastrium
ipoglicemia *f* hypoglyc(a)emia
ipoteca *f* ⟨*pl* -che⟩ mortgage; ***accendere un'~*** take out a mortgage
ipotecabile *adj* mortgageable
ipotecare *v/t* ⟨1b & d⟩ mortgage
ipotecario *adj* ⟨*mpl* -ri⟩ mortgage; ***mutuo*** *m* ***~*** mortgage loan
ipotenusa *f* hypotenuse
ipotesi *f* hypothesis; ***nella migliore/peggiore delle ~*** at best/at worst; ***formulare un'~*** put forward an hypothesis; ***per ~*** supposing
ipotetico *adj* ⟨*mpl* -ci⟩ hypothetical
ipotiroidismo *m* hypothyroidism
ipotizzabile *adj* presumable
ipotizzare *v/t* ⟨1a⟩ hypothesize
ippica *f* (horse) riding; ***datti all'~!*** why don't you take up knitting!
ippico *adj*: ***centro*** *m* ***~*** equestrian centre; ***concorso*** *m* ***~*** horseshow
ippocastano *m* horse chestnut
ippodromo *m* racecourse
ippopotamo *m* hippo(potamus)
ipsilon *m/f* ⟨*pl* ipsilon⟩ letter Y
ira *f* anger; ***avere uno scatto d'~*** fly into a rage
iracheno I *adj* Iraqi **II** *m*, **-a** *f* Iraqi
iracondo *adj* short-tempered, *form* irascible
irakeno → ***iracheno***
Iran *m* Iran
iraniano I *adj* Iranian **II** *m*, **-a** *f* Iranian
iranico *adj* ⟨*mpl* -ci⟩ ⟨Iranian
IRAP *abbr* (= **Imposta Regionale sulle Attività Produttive**) *regional tax on productive activities*
Iraq *m* Iraq
irascibile *adj* irritable, irascible
irascibilità *f* ⟨*pl* irascibilità⟩ short temper, *form* irascibility **irato** *adj* angry
iridato *adj* rainbow-striped; ***maglia*** *f* ***-a*** SPORTS rainbow-striped jersey
iride *f* **1.** (*arcobaleno*) rainbow **2.** ANAT, BOT iris
iridescente *adj* iridescent **iridologia** *f* iridology
Irlanda *f* Ireland; ***~ del Nord*** Northern Ireland
irlandese I *adj* Irish **II** *m* Irish (Gaelic) **III** *m/f* Irishman; *donna* Irishwoman; ***gli -i*** the Irish
ironia *f* irony; ***fare dell'~*** be ironic
ironicamente *adv* ironically
ironico *adj* ⟨*mpl* -ci⟩ ironic(al)
ironizzare *v/i* ⟨1a⟩ be ironic; ***~ su qc*** be ironic about sth
iroso *adj* short-tempered, (*irato*) angry
IRPEF *abbr* (= **Imposta sul Reddito delle Persone Fisiche**) income tax
IRPEG *abbr* (= **Imposta sul Reddito delle PErsone Giuridiche**) *Corporate Income Tax*
irpino I *adj* from Irpinia, Irpinian **II** *m*, **-a** *f* person from Irpinia
irradiamento *m* irradiance; PHYS irradiation
irradiare *v/t & v/i* ⟨1k⟩ radiate
irradiazione *f* radiation
irraggiungibile *adj* unattainable
irraggiungibilità *f* ⟨*pl* irraggiungibilità⟩ unattainableness
irragionevole *adj* unreasonable
irragionevolezza *f* irrationality, unreasonableness

irragionevolmente *adv* unreasonably, irrationally
irrancidire *v/i* ⟨4d⟩ go rancid
irrazionale *adj* irrational
irrazionalità *f* ⟨*pl* irrazionalità⟩ irrationality **irrazionalmente** *adv* irrationally
irreale *adj* unreal
irrealistico *adj* ⟨*mpl* -ci⟩ unrealistic
irrealizzabile *adj* unattainable; ***desiderio*** *m* ~ unattainable desire
irrealtà *f* ⟨*pl* irrealtà⟩ unreality
irrecuperabile *adj* unrecoverable; *persona* past redemption
irredimibile *adj* COMM, JUR irredeemable, unredeemable; ***debito*** *m* ~ unredeemable debt
irrefrenabile *adj* uncontrollable
irrefutabile *adj*irrefutable
irregolare *adj* irregular
irregolarità *f* ⟨*pl* irregolarità⟩ irregularity
irreligiosità *f* ⟨*pl* irreligiosità⟩ impiety **irreligioso** *adj* impious
irremovibilità *f* ⟨*pl* irremovibilità⟩ obstinacy
irreparabile *adj* irreparable
irreparabilità *f* ⟨*pl* irreparabilità⟩ irremediableness
irreperibile *adj* impossible to find
irreperibilità *f* ⟨*pl* irreperabilità⟩ untraceability
irreprensibile *adj* irreproachable
irreprensibilità *f* ⟨*pl* irreprensibilità⟩ blamelessness, *form* irreproachability
irreprimibile *adj* uncontrollable
irreprimibile *adj* irrepressible
irrequietezza *f* restlessness
irrequieto *adj* restless
irresistibile *adj* irresistible
irresolutezza *f* uncertainty **irresoluto** *adj* uncertain
irrespirabile *adj*: ***aria*** *f* ~ stuffy air; *fig* ***atmosfera*** *f* ~ stifling / oppressive atmosphere
irresponsabile *adj* irresponsible
irresponsabilità *f* irresponsibility
irrestringibile *adj* non-shrink; *parzialmente* shrink-resistant
irretire *v/t* ⟨4d⟩ trap; *a. fig*
irreversibile *adj* irreversible **irreversibilità** *f* ⟨*pl* irreversibilità⟩ irreversibility
irrevocabile *adj* irrevocable
irrevocabilità *f* ⟨*pl* irrevocabilità⟩ irrevocability **irrevocabilmente** *adv* irrevocably
irriconoscibile *adj* unrecognizable
irriducibile *adj fig* implacable MATH irreducibile
irriflessivo *adj* thoughtless
irrigare *v/t* ⟨1e⟩ irrigate
irrigatore I *adj* irrigatory, irrigation *attr.*; ***impianto*** *m* ~ irrigation system **II** *n*: ***irrigatore*** *m* sprinkler
irrigazione *f* irrigation
irrigidimento *m* stiffening (*a. fig*); *di muscoli* tightening; *di clima*: cooling
irrigidire *v/t* ⟨4d⟩ stiffen; *fig disciplina* tighten
irrigidirsi *v/r* stiffen
irrigidito *adj* stiff
irriguardoso *adj* disrespectful
irrilevante *adj* irrelevant
irrilevanza *f* irrelevance
irrimandabile *adj* unpostponable
irrimediabile *adj* irremediable
irrimediabilmente *adv* irremediably
irrintracciabile *adj* untraceable
irrinunciabile *adj diritto* inalienable
irripetibile *adj* unrepeatable
irripetibilità *f* ⟨*pl* irripetibilità⟩ unrepeatability
irriproducibile *adj* unreproducible
irrisolto *adj* unsolved
irrisorio *adj* ⟨*mpl* -ri⟩ derisive; *quantità, somma di denaro* derisory; *prezzo* ridiculously low
irritabile *adj* irritable
irritabilità *f* irritability
irritante *adj* irritating
irritare *v/t* ⟨1l or 1a⟩ irritate
irritarsi *v/r* become irritated
irritato *adj* irritated; (*infiammato*) sore (*a.* MED); ***pelle*** *f* ***-a*** irritated skin
irritazione *f* annoyance; ~ ***cutanea*** skin irritation
irriverente *adj* irreverent **irriverenza** *f* irreverence
irrobustimento *m* strengthening
irrobustire *v/t* ⟨4d⟩ strengthen, build up
irrompere *v/i* ⟨3rr⟩ burst (***in*** into)
irrorare *v/t* ⟨1c⟩ wet; (*innaffiare*) spray **irrorazione** *f* AGR spraying; ANAT ~ ***sanguigna*** blood supply
irruente *adj* violent; (*irrompente*) impetuous **irruenza** *f* violence; (*impeto*) impetuosity; ***agire con*** ~ act with vi-

olence
irruvidimento *m* roughening **irruvidire** ⟨4d⟩ **I** *v/t* roughen; *fig* roughen (up) **II** *v/i* get rough **irruvidirsi** *v/r* ⟨4d⟩ become rough; *fig* get rough
irruzione *f*: ***fare ~ in*** burst into; *di polizia* raid
irsuto *adj* hairy; (*barba*) shaggy
irto *adj* spiky; ***col pelo ~*** with fur standing on end; *fig* ***~ di*** bristling with; (*ostacoli*) fraught with
IS *abbr* (= **Isernia**) Isernia
ischeletrire *v/t* ⟨4d⟩ reduce to a skeleton **ischeletrirsi** *v/r* ⟨4d⟩ be reduced to a skeleton
ischemia *f* ischaemia
Ischia *f* Ischia; ***l'isola d'~*** the Island of Ischia **ischitano I** *adj* Ischian, from Ischia **II** *m*, **-a** *f* Ischian
iscritto I *past part* → ***iscrivere*** **II** *m*, **-a** *f* member; *a gare*, *concorsi* entrant; EDU pupil, student **III** *m*: ***per ~*** in writing
iscrivere *v/t* ⟨3tt⟩ register; *a gare*, *concorsi* enter (***a*** for, in); EDU enrol(l) (***a*** at); ***~ a ruolo*** JUR enter for trial
iscriversi *v/r in un elenco* register; ***~ a*** *partito*, *associazione* join; *gara* enter; EDU enrol(l) at
iscrizione *f* inscription
isernino I *adj* Isernian, from Isernia **II** *m*, **-a** *f* Isernian
Islam *m* Islam; ***convertirsi all'~*** convert to Islam
Islam *m* Islam
islamico *adj* ⟨*mpl* -ci⟩ Islamic
islamismo *m* Islamism
islamista *m/f* ⟨*mpl* -i⟩ Islamist **islamizzare** *v/t* ⟨1a⟩ Islamicize **islamizzazione** *f* Islamicization
Islanda *f* Iceland
islandese I *m/adj* Icelandic **II** *m/f* Icelander
islandico *adj* ⟨*mpl* -ci⟩ Icelandic
ISO *abbr* (**International Organization for Standardization**) International Standards Organization
isola *f* island; ***~ pedonale*** pedestrian precinct; ***~ spartitraffico*** traffic island; ***-e*** *pl* ***di Langerhans*** ANAT islets of Langerhans; ***vivere in un'~*** live on an island
isolabile *adj* isolable
isolamento *m* isolation; TECH insulation; ***~ acustico*** soundproofing; ***~ termico*** heat insulation; ***cella*** *f* ***d'~*** solitary confinement cell; ***reparto*** *m* ***di ~*** isolation ward; ***in completo ~*** in complete seclusion
isolano *m*, **-a** *f* islander
isolante I *adj* insulating **II** *m* insulator; ***nastro*** *m* ***~*** insulating tape
isolare *v/t* ⟨1l⟩ isolate; TECH insulate
isolarsi *v/r* isolate o.s., cut o.s. off
isolato I *adj* isolated; TECH insulated **II** *m* outsider; *di case* block
isolazionismo *m* isolationism **isolazionista** *adj* ⟨*mpl* -i⟩ isolationist; ***politica*** *f* ***~*** isolationist policy
isoletta *f* islet **isolotto** *m* islet
isomero *m* isomer
isoscele *adj*: ***triangolo*** *m* ***~*** isosceles triangle; ***trapezio*** *m* ***~*** isosceles trapezium
isotermico *adj* ⟨*mpl* -ci⟩ isothermic
isotopo *m* isotope
isotteri *mpl* Isoptera *pl.*
ispanico *adj* ⟨*mpl* -ci⟩ Hispanic **ispano-americano** *adj* Hispanic American
ispessimento *m* thickening **ispessire** *v/t* ⟨4d⟩ thicken; ***far ~ un sugo*** thicken a sauce **ispessirsi** *v/r* ⟨4d⟩ get thicker
ispettivo *adj* inspectional; ***visita*** *f* ***-a*** inspection **ispettorato** *m* inspectorate; ***~ del lavoro*** work inspectorate
ispettore *m*, **-trice** *f* inspector; ***~ di polizia*** Inspector
ispezionare *v/t* ⟨1a⟩ inspect
ispezione *f* inspection
ispido *adj* prickly (*a.fig*); BOT spiny; (*barba*) bristling
ispirare *v/t* ⟨1a⟩ inspire; ***~ fiducia*** inspire trust
ispirarsi *v/r di artista* get inspiration (***a*** from)
ispiratore I *adj* inspirational **II** *m*, **-trice** *f* inspirator
ispirazione *f* inspiration; (*impulso*) impulse; (*idea*) idea; ***trarre ~ da qc*** draw inspiration from sth
Israele *m* Israel
israeliano *m*, **-a** *f* Israeli
israelita *m/f* ⟨*mpl* -i⟩ Israelite **israelitico** *adj* ⟨*mpl* -ci⟩ Israelite
issa *int*: ***oh ~!*** Heave-ho!
issare *v/t* ⟨1a⟩ hoist
istallare *v/t* ⟨1a⟩ → ***installare***
istantanea *f* snap

istantaneamente *adv* instantly **istantaneità** *f* ⟨*pl* istantaneità⟩ instantaneousness
istantaneo *adj* instantaneous
istante *m* instant; ***all'~*** instantly
istanza *f* (*esigenza*) need; (*domanda*) application; JUR petition; ***in ultima ~*** as the last resort; ***su ~ di*** at s.o.'s instance; ***cedere alle -e di qn*** give in to s.o.'s needs
ISTAT *abbr* (= **Istituto Centrale di Statistica**) *central statistics office*
isteria *f* hysteria; MED hysterics **isericamente** *adv* hysterically
isterico *adj* ⟨*mpl* -ci⟩ hysterical; ***crisi*** *f* ***-a*** hysterics *pl*
isterismo *m* hysteria
istigare *v/t* ⟨1l & e⟩ instigate
istigatore **I** *adj* trouble-making; *form* instigating **II** *m*, **-trice** *f* trouble-maker; *form* instigator; JUR aider and abettor
istigazione *f* incitement; JUR ***~ a delinquere*** instigation
istintivamente *adv* instinctively
istintivo *adj* instinctive
istinto *m* instinct; ***agire d'~*** act instinctively; ***~ di conservazione*** (self-) preservation instinct; ***~ materno*** maternal instinct
istituire *v/t* ⟨4d⟩ establish
istitutivo *adj* institutive; ***norme*** *fpl* ***-e*** institutional regulations
istituto *m* institute; *assistenziale* institution, home; ***~ di bellezza*** beauty salon; ***~ di credito*** bank; ***~ tecnico*** *technical school for 14 to 19-year-olds*
istituzionale *adj* institutional; EDU basic; ***corso*** *m* ***~*** basic course **istituzionalizzare** *v/t* ⟨1a⟩ institutionalize
istituzione *f* institution
istmo *m* isthmus
istologia *f* histology **istologico** *adj* ⟨*mpl* -ci⟩ histologic(al)
Istria *f* Istria **istriano** **I** *adj* Istrian **II** *m*, **-a** *f* Istrian
istrice *m* porcupine
istrionico *adj* ⟨*mpl* -ci⟩ histrionic; *pej* melodramatic
istruire *v/t* ⟨4d⟩ educate, teach; (*dare istruzioni a, addestrare*) instruct; ***~ una pratica*** ADMIN open a file
istruirsi *v/r* educate o.s.
istruito *adj* educated
istruttivo *adj* instructive
istruttore *m*, **-trice** *f* instructor; ***~ di guida*** driving instructor
istruttorio *adj* ⟨*mpl* -ri⟩ instructional; ***fase*** *f* ***-a*** instructional phase
istruzione *f* education; (*direttiva*) instruction; ***~ civile*** JUR civil education; ***-i*** *pl* ***per l'uso*** instructions (for use); ***dare -i a qn*** give s.o. instructions
istupidimento *m* stupidity **istupidire** *v/t* ⟨4d⟩ stupefy; *fig* become stupid **istupidirsi** *v/r* ⟨4d⟩ become stupid
Italia *f* Italy; ***~ meridionale / centrale / settentrionale*** southern / central / northern Italy; ***andare in ~*** go to Italy
italianista *m/f* ⟨*mpl* -i⟩ Italianist **italianistica** *f* Italian studies
italiano **I** *m/adj* Italian; ***parla ~?*** do you speak Italian? **II** *m*, **-a** *f* Italian
italico ⟨*mpl* -ci⟩ **I** *adj hist* Italic **II** *m*, **-a** *f hist* Italic **italiota** *m/f* ⟨*mpl* -i⟩ Italiot
italoamericano **I** *adj* Italo-american **II** *m*, **-a** *f* Italo-american
iterativo *adj* iterative; GRAM frequentative
itinerario *m* ⟨*pl* -ri⟩ route, itinerary; ***seguire un ~*** follow a route
itterico *adj* ⟨*mpl* -ci⟩ jaundiced
ittico *adj* ⟨*mpl* -ci⟩ fish
ittita ⟨*mpl* -i⟩ **I** *adj* Hittite **II** *m/f* Hittite; ***gli Ittiti*** the Hittites
Iugoslavia *f hist* Yugoslavia
iugoslavo *hist* **I** *adj* Yugoslav(ian) **II** *m*, **-a** *f* Yugoslav(ian)
iuta *f* jute
IVA *abbr* (= **Imposta sul Valore Aggiunto**) VAT (value-added tax)
ivi *adv* there; therein; *nelle citazioni*: ibidem; ***~ compreso*** enclosed therein
ivoriano **I** *adj* Ivorian **II** *m*, **-a** *f* Ivorian

J

J, J *m/f* ⟨*pl* J, J⟩ J, J; ***J come Jolly*** J for Joker
jackpot *m* ⟨*pl* jackpot⟩ jackpot
jacquard I *adj inv* Jacquard; ***tessuto*** *m* **~** Jacquard fabric **II** *m* ⟨*pl* jacquard⟩ Jacquard
jazz *m* jazz
jazzista *m/f* ⟨*mpl* -i⟩ jazz musician
jazzistico *adj* ⟨*mpl* -ci⟩ jazz; ***stile*** *m* **~** jazz-style
jeans *mpl* jeans *pl*; ***gonna*** *f* / ***camicia*** *f* ***di*** **~** denim skirt / shirt
jeanseria *f* jeans shop
jeep® *f* ⟨*pl* jeep⟩ jeep®
jersey *m* ⟨*pl* jersey⟩ jersey
jet *m* ⟨*pl* jet⟩ jet
jet-lag *m* ⟨*no pl*⟩ jet lag
jet-set *m* ⟨*no pl*⟩ jet set
jihad *f* ⟨*pl* jihad⟩ Jihad **jihadista** *m/f* ⟨*mpl* -i⟩ Jihadist
jingle *m* ⟨*pl* jingle⟩ jingle
jockey *m* ⟨*pl* jockey⟩ jockey
jogging *m* ⟨*no pl*⟩ jogging; ***fare*** **~** jog, go for a jog
joint-venture *f* ⟨*pl* joint-venture⟩ joint venture
jolly *m* ⟨*pl* jolly⟩ joker; ***carattere*** *m* **~** COMPUT joker character
joule *m* ⟨*pl* joule⟩ joule
joy-stick *m* ⟨*pl* joy-stick⟩ joystick
judo *m* ⟨*no pl*⟩ judo
judoista *m/f* ⟨*mpl* -i⟩ Judoist
jugoslavo I *adj* Yugoslav(ian) **II** *m*, **-a** *f* Yugoslav(ian); → ***iugoslavo***
jujitsu *m* ⟨*pl* jujitsu⟩ ju-jitsu
juke-box *m* ⟨*pl* juke-box⟩ jukebox
jumbo *m* jumbo
junior *m/adj* ⟨*pl* juniores⟩ junior

K

k, K *m/f* ⟨*pl* k, K⟩ k, K; ***K come Kursaal*** K for kangaroo
kafkiano *adj* Kafkaesque
kamasutra *m* ⟨*pl* kamasutra⟩ Kama Sutra
karakiri *m* ⟨*pl* karakiri⟩ hara-kiri (*a. fig*); ***fare*** **~** commit hara-kiri
karaoke *m* karaoke; *locale* karaoke bar
karatè *m* ⟨*no pl*⟩ karate
kayak *m* ⟨*pl* kayak⟩ kayak
kazaco ⟨*mpl* -chi⟩ **I** *adj* Kazakh **II** *m*, **-a** *f* Kazakh
Kazakistan *m* Kazakhstan
keniano I *adj* Kenyan **II** *m*, **-a** *f* Kenyan **keniota I** *adj* Kenyan **II** *m/f* ⟨*mpl* -i⟩ Kenyan
Kenya *m* Kenya
kg *abbr* (= **chilogrammo**) kg (kilogram)
khmer ⟨*pl* khmer⟩ **I** *adj* Khmer **II** *m/f* Khmer
kibbutz *m* ⟨*pl* kibbutz⟩ kibbutz
Kilimangiaro *m* Kilimanjaro
killer *m* ⟨*pl* killer⟩ killer
kilobyte *m* ⟨*pl* kilobyte⟩ kilobyte
kimono *m* kimono
Kirghizistan *m* Kyrgyzstan
kit *m* ⟨*pl* kit⟩ kit; **~ *di pronto soccorso*** first-aid kit **~ *di montaggio*** assembly kit
kitsch *m/adj inv* ⟨*no pl*⟩ kitsch
kiwi *m* ⟨*pl* kiwi⟩ BOT kiwi (fruit)
kleenex® *m* ⟨*pl* kleenex⟩ tissue
km *abbr* (= **chilometro**) km (kilometre)
km / h *abbr* (= **chilometri all'ora**) km / h (kilometres per hour)
kmq *abbr* (= **chilometri quadrati**) km² (square kilometres)
knock-out *m* knock-out
know-how *m* ⟨*pl* know-how⟩ know-how
k.o. *adj*: ***mettere qn*** **~** knock s.o. out; *fig* trounce s.o.; ***vincere* / *perdere per*** **~** win or lose by knock-out; ***andare*** *or*

finire/essere ~ be/get knocked out
koala *m* koala
kolossal *m* ⟨*pl* kolossal⟩ epic
kos(s)ovaro I *adj* Kosovan **II** *m*, **-a** *f* Kosovar
Kossovo *m* Kosovo
KR *abbr* (= **Crotone**) Crotone
krapfen *m* ⟨*pl* krapfen⟩ COOK doughnut
kümmel *m* kümmel
kursaal *m* ⟨*pl* kursaal⟩ kursaal
kuwaitiano I *adj* Kuwaiti **II** *m*, **-a** *f* Kuwaiti
kV *abbr* (= **chilovolt**) kV (kilovolt)
kW *abbr* (= **chilowatt**) kW (kilowatt)
k-way *m or f* ⟨*pl* k-way⟩ cagoule
kWh *abbr* (= **chilowattora**) kWh (kilowatt hour)

L

l, L *m/f* ⟨*pl* l, L⟩ (the letter) L; ***L come Livorno*** L for Lima
l *abbr* (= **litro**) l (litre)
L *abbr* (= **lira**) *hist* L (lire)
l' = ***lo, la***; ***l'amico*** *m* the friend; ***l'attrice*** *f* the actress; ***l'ho incontrato*** I met him
la[1] *art fsg* the; ***~ signora Rossi*** Mrs Rossi; ***~ domenica*** on Sundays; ***mi piace la birra*** I like beer
la[2] *pron* **I** *sg* (*persona*) her; (*cosa, animale*) it; ***~ prenderò*** I'll take it **II** *a.* ***La*** *sg* you
la[3] *m* MUS A; *nel solfeggio della scala* la(h); ***~ bemolle*** A flat; ***~ maggiore/minore*** A major/minor; ***dare il ~*** set the tone (*a. fig*)
là *adv* there; ***di ~*** that way; (*in quel luogo*) in there; ***di ~ di*** on the other side of; ***più in ~*** further on; *nel tempo* later on; ***qua e ~*** here and there; ***fatti in ~!*** *infml* budge up!; MIL ***alto ~!***; halt!; ***essere in ~ con gli anni*** be getting on; *fig* ***essere più di ~ che di qua*** *infml* be pretty far gone
labbro *m* ⟨*pl* le -a⟩ lip; ***~ inferiore/superiore*** lower/upper lip; *fig* ***mordersi le -a*** bite one's lips; ***a fior di -a*** in a whisper; *fig* ***pendere dalle -a di qn*** hang on s.o.'s every word
labiale I *adj* labial **II** *f* labial
labile *adj* (*passeggero*) fleeting, short-lived
labilità *f* ⟨*pl* labilità⟩ faintness, *form* transience
labirintico *adj* ⟨*mpl* -ci⟩ labyrinthine
labirinto *m* labyrinth; ***~ di specchi*** mirror maze
laboratorio *m* ⟨*pl* -ri⟩ lab, laboratory; (*officina*) workshop; ***~ di analisi*** medical laboratory; ***~ linguistico*** language lab
laboriosamente *adv* laboriously
laboriosità *f* laboriousness; *di persona* industriousness
laborioso *adj* laborious; *persona* hard-working, industrious
labrador *m* ⟨*pl* labrador⟩ Labrador
labronico ⟨*mpl* -ci⟩ *liter* **I** *adj* Livornese **II** *m*, **-a** *f* person from Livorno
laburista ⟨*mpl* -i⟩ **I** *adj* Labo(u)r **II** *m/f* Labo(u)r Party member; *elettore* Labo(u)r supporter
lacca *f* ⟨*pl* -cche⟩ lacquer; *per capelli* hair spray, lacquer
laccare *v/t* ⟨1d⟩ lacquer
laccato *adj* lacquered
laccio *m* ⟨*pl* -cci⟩ tie, (draw)string; ***-cci*** *pl* ***delle scarpe*** shoe laces; ***~ emostatico*** tourniquet
lacerante *adj dolore, grido* piercing
lacerare *v/t* ⟨1a⟩ lacerate
lacerarsi *v/r* tear
lacerazione *f* tearing; ***~ cutanea*** skin laceration
lacero *adj* tattered, in tatters; ***ferita*** *f* ***~-contusa*** lacerated and contused wound
laconicamente *adv* laconically **laconicità** *f* ⟨*pl* laconicità⟩ laconicism
laconico *adj* ⟨*mpl* -ci⟩ laconic; (*persona*) reticent
lacrima *f* tear; *fig* ***-e*** *pl* ***di coccodrillo*** crocodile tears; ***-e*** *pl* ***di gioia/di dolore*** tears of joy/sorrow; ***scoppiare in -e*** burst into tears; ***con le -e agli***

occhi with tears in one's eyes; ***valle** f* ***di -e*** vale of tears
lacrimale *adj* lachrymal; ***sacco*** *m* **~** lachrymal sac
lacrimare *v/i* ⟨1l⟩ water; ***mi lacrimano gli occhi*** my eyes are watering
lacrimevole *adj* sad; heart-rending; *pej* tear-jerking; ***film*** *m* **~** tear-jerker
lacrimogeno *adj*: ***gas*** *m* **~** tear gas
lacuna *f* gap; ***una grave ~ nella memoria*** a serious gap in one's memory
lacunoso *adj* incomplete
lacustre *adj* lake; ***paesaggio ~*** lakeland landscape
laddove *cj form* whereas
ladino I *adj* South Tyrolean **II** *m*, **-a** *f* South Tyrolean
ladro *m*, **-a** *f* thief; ***al ~!*** stop, thief!; **~ *di galline*** petty crook
ladrone *m* robber **ladroneria** *f* (*qualità*) thievishness; (*azione*) theft **ladruncolo** *m*, **-a** *f* petty thief
lager *m* ⟨*pl* lager⟩ concentration camp
laggiù *adv* down there; *distante* over there
laghetto *m* pond
lagna *f* (*lamentela*) whining; *persona* whiner; (*cosa noiosa*) bore
lagnanza *f* complaint
lagnarsi *v/r* ⟨1a⟩ complain (***di*** about)
lagnoso *adj* (*che si lamenta*) whingeing; (*noioso*) tedious
lago *m* ⟨*pl* -ghi⟩ **1.** lake; **~ *artificiale*** reservoir; **~ *vulcanico*** volcanic lake; *fig* ***un ~ di sangue*** a pool of blood **2.** ***Lago di Garda*** Lake Garda; ***Lago di Lugano*** Lake Lugano; ***Lago Maggiore*** Lake Maggiore; ***Lago Trasimeno*** Lake Trasimeno; ***villa** f **sul ~*** lakeside villa
laguna *f* lagoon
lagunare *adj* lagoon; ***città*** *f* **~** lagoon city
L'Aia *f* The Hague
laicismo *m* secularism **laicista I** *adj* secularist **II** *m/f* ⟨*mpl* -i⟩ secularist **laicità** *f* ⟨*pl* laicità⟩ laity
laicizzare *v/t* ⟨1a⟩ secularize **laicizzarsi** *v/r* ⟨1a⟩ become secularized; **laicizzazione** *f* secularization; *di clero*: laicization
laico ⟨*mpl* -ci⟩ **I** *adj scuola* lay **II** *m*, **-a** *f* member of the laity; ***stato*** *m* **~** lay state; ***partito*** *m* **~** secular party
laido *adj liter* dirty
lallazione *f* lallation
lama[1] *f* blade; **~ *di coltello*** knife blade; *fig* **~ *a doppio taglio*** knife that cuts both ways
lama[2] *m* ⟨*pl* lama⟩ ZOOL llama
lama[3] *m* ⟨*pl* lama⟩ REL lama
lambiccarsi *v/r* ⟨1a⟩: **~ *il cervello*** rack one's brains
lambire *v/t* ⟨1a⟩ *fiamma* lick; *acqua* lap
lambrusco *m* ⟨*pl* -schi⟩ COOK Lambrusco
lamella *f* foil; BIOL lamella
lamentare *v/t* ⟨1a⟩ lament, deplore
lamentarsi *v/r* complain (***di*** about)
lamentela *f* complaint
lamentevole *adj* complaining; (*compassionevole*) pitiful
lamento *m* whimper; (*guaito*) whine
lamentosamente *adv* plaintively
lamentoso *adj* whining; ***in tono ~*** dolefully
lametta *f*: **~ (*da barba*)** razor blade
lamiera *f* metal sheet; **~ *ondulata*** corrugated iron
lamina *f* foil; **~ *d'oro*** gold leaf
laminato I *adj* laminated; (*fabric*) lamé; ***lamiera -a*** rolled sheet metal **II** *n*: ***laminato*** *m* laminate
laminatoio *m* ⟨*pl* -oi⟩ rolling mill
lampada *f* lamp; **~ *alogena*** halogen lamp; **~ *a stelo*** floor lamp, *Br* standard lamp; **~ *al neon*** neon light; **~ *abbronzante*** tanning lamp; **~ *da tavolo*** table-lamp; ***fare la ~*** have a tanning session
lampadario *m* ⟨*pl* -ri⟩ chandelier
lampadina *f* light bulb; **~ *tascabile*** torch, *US* flashlight; **~ *da 60 watt*** 60-watt bulb
lampante *adj* blindingly obvious
lampara *f* night-fishing boat
lampeggiamento *m* blinking; *di fari*: flashing **lampeggiante** *adj* flashing; ***luce** f* **~** flashing light
lampeggiare *v/i* ⟨1f⟩ flash
lampeggiatore *m* AUTO indicator; PHOT flashlight
lampioncino *m* Chinese lantern
lampione *m* streetlight
lampo *m* lightning; ***chiusura ~*** zip; ***in un ~*** in a flash; ***un ~ di genio*** a brainwave
lampone *m* raspberry
lana *f* wool; **~ *d'acciaio*** wire-wool; **~ *di***

vetro fibreglass; *~ **pettinata*** worsted; ***di*** ~ wool, woollen; ***pura ~ vergine*** pure new wool

lancetta *f* needle, indicator; *di orologio* hand

lancia *f* ⟨*pl* -ce⟩ **1.** spear **2.** NAUT launch; ~ ***di salvataggio*** lifeboat

lanciafiamme *m* ⟨*pl* lanciafiamme⟩ flame-thrower **lanciamissili I** *adj inv* missile-launching; ***rampa*** *f* ~ missile-launching pad **II** *m* ⟨*pl* lanciamissili⟩ missile launcher **lanciarazzi I** *adj* ⟨*pl* lanciarazzi⟩ rocket-launcher; ***pistola*** *f* ~ warning pistol **II** *m* rocket-launcher

lanciare *v/t* ⟨1f⟩ throw; *prodotto* launch; ~ ***un'occhiata*** glance, take a quick look; ~ ***un urlo*** give a shout, shout; ~ ***una bomba*** launch a bomb; ~ ***un cantante*** launch a singer; ~ ***un grido*** scream; ~ ***un prodotto*** launch a product

lanciarsi *v/r* rush; ~ ***contro*** throw o.s at, attack; ~ ***in un' impresa*** *infml* embark on a venture; ***mi lancio*** *infml* I'll go for it *infml*, I'll take the plunge *infml*; ~ ***all'inseguimento di qn*** set off in hot pursuit of s.o.

lanciatore *m*, **-trice** *f* thrower; *nel cricket* bowler

lancinante *adj dolore* piercing

lancio *m* ⟨*pl* -ci⟩ throwing; *di prodotto* launch; ~ ***del disco*** discus; ~ ***del giavellotto*** javelin; ~ ***del peso*** putting the shot

landa *f* moorland

langa *f reg* ⟨*pl* -ghe⟩ hilly area; ***le Langhe*** the Langhe area

langravio *m* ⟨*pl* -vi⟩ HIST landgrave

languidamente *adv* languidly

languido *adj sguardo* languid

languire *v/i* ⟨4a or 4d⟩ languish

languore *m* lang(u)or; ***ho un ~ allo stomaco*** I'm feeling peckish

laniero *adj* wool; ***industria*** *f* ***-a*** wool industry

lanificio *m* ⟨*pl* -ci⟩ wool mill

lanolina *f* lanolin

lanterna *f* lantern; (*faro*) lighthouse; ***la Lanterna di Genova*** Genoa's light-house

lanternino *m* small lantern; *fig* ***cercare qc con il*** ~ look high and low for s.o.

lanugine *f* down **lanuginoso** *adj* downy

lanzichenecco *m* ⟨*pl* -cchi⟩ lansquenet

Laos *m* Laos **laotiano I** *adj* Lao **II** *m*, **-a** *f* Laotian

lapalissiano *adj* axiomatic; ***verità*** *f* ***-a*** a self-evident truth

laparoscopia *f* MED laparoscopy **laparotomia** *f* MED laparotomy

lapidare *v/t* ⟨1l⟩ stone to death; *fig* lambaste

lapidario *adj* ⟨*mpl* -ri⟩ pithy; ***frase*** *f* ***-a*** a pithy comment

lapidazione *f* stoning to death

lapide *f* gravestone; *su monumento* plaque

lapillo *m* lapillus

lapis *m* ⟨*pl* lapis⟩ pencil

lapislazzuli *m* lapis lazuli

lappone I *adj* Lap **II** *m/f* Laplander, Lap

Lapponia *f* Lapland

lapsus *m* ⟨*pl* lapsus⟩ slip of the tongue; ***fare un*** ~ make a slip of the tongue

lardellare *v/t* ⟨1b⟩ COOK lard; *fig* pepper

lardo *m* lard

largamente *adv* widely; ~ ***diffuso*** widespread; ***ricompensare ~ qn*** reward s.o. generously

largheggiare *v/i* ⟨1f⟩ be generous

larghezza *f* width, breadth; ~ ***di idee*** breadth of interests; ~ ***di vedute*** broad-mindedness

largo ⟨*mpl* -ghi⟩ **I** *adj* wide, broad; *indumento* loose, big; (*abbondante*) large, generous; MUS largo; ~ ***di manica*** generous **II** *m* width; (*piazza*) square; ***andare al*** ~ head for the open sea; ***al ~ di*** off the coast of; ***farsi*** ~ elbow one's way through; ***stare alla -a da*** steer clear of, keep away from; ***stare -ghi*** be comfortable; ***essere più ~ che lungo*** be fat; ***in -a misura*** mainly; ***in lungo e in*** ~ far and wide; ***prendere alla -a*** approach in a roundabout way; ***su -a scala*** large scale; ***avere le spalle -ghe*** have broad shoulders; *fig* be able to cope; ***la corrente ci porta al*** ~ the current is sweeping us out to sea

larice *m* larch

laringe *f* larynx

laringite *f* laryngitis

larva *f* ZOOL larva; *fig* ***essere ridotto ad una ~*** be worn down to a wraith

lasagne *fpl* lasagne *sg*; ***~ al forno*** baked lasagna; ***~ al pesto*** lasagna with pesto sauce

lasciapassare *m* ⟨*pl* lasciapassare⟩ pass

lasciare *v/t* ⟨1f⟩ **1.** leave; ***lasciami stare!*** leave me alone!; ***~ a desiderare*** leave a lot to be desired; ***~ detto a qn*** leave a message for s.o. **2.** (*abbandonare*) give up **3.** (*concedere*) let; ***~ fare*** let **4.** (*smettere di tenere*) let go; ***lascia andare!, lascia perdere!*** forget it!; ***prendere o ~*** take it or leave it

lasciarsi *v/r* separate, leave each other; ***~ andare*** let o.s. go

lascito *m* legacy

lascivia *f* lasciviousness

lascivo *adj* lascivious

lasco *adj* ⟨*mpl* -chi⟩ loose

laser *m/adj inv* ⟨*pl* laser⟩ laser; ***stampante*** *f* ***~*** laser printer

laserchirurgia *f* laser surgery

lassativo *m/adj* laxative

lassismo *m* laxity

lasso *m*: ***~ di tempo*** period of time

lassù *adv* up there; ***guarda ~!*** look up there!; ***andiamo ~*** let's go up there; ***le cose di ~*** heavenly things

lastra *f di pietra* slab; *di metallo, ghiaccio, vetro* sheet; MED x-ray; ***~ di ghiaccio*** sheet of ice; ***farsi le -e*** *infml* have an X-ray

lastricare *v/t* ⟨1l & d⟩ pave

lastrico *m* ⟨*pl* -chi *or* -ci⟩: *fig* ***ridursi sul ~*** lose everything

latente *adj* latent

laterale *adj* lateral; ***entrata*** *f* ***~*** side entrance

laterizio *m* ⟨*pl* -zi⟩ brick

laterizio *m* ⟨*mpl* -zi⟩ bricks and tiles *pl*

latifoglia *f* ⟨*pl* -glie⟩ broad-leaf

latifondista *m/f* ⟨*mpl* -i⟩ big landowner

latifondo *m* landed estate

latinense I *adj* from Latina **II** *m/f* person from Latina

latinità *f* ⟨*pl* latinità⟩ Latinity; *letteratura latina* Latin literature

latin lover *m* ⟨*pl* latin lover⟩ Latin lover

latino I *adj* Latin; ***~-americano*** Latin-American **II** *m* Latin

latitante *m/f* fugitive

latitanza *f* evasion of responsibilities; ***darsi alla ~*** abscond

latitudinale *adj* latitudinal

latitudine *f* latitude

lato *m* side; (*punto di vista*) point of view; ***a ~ di, di ~ a*** beside; ***d'altro ~*** on the other hand; ***dal ~ mio*** on my side; ***sul ~ destro / sinistro*** on the right-hand / left-hand side; ***di ~ a*** sideways on to; ***dal ~ economico*** from a financial point of view

lato[2] *adj*: ***in senso ~*** in a broad sense

latore *m*, **-trice** *f* bearer

latrare *v/i* ⟨1a⟩ bark

latrato *m* barking

latrina *f* latrine

latrocinio *m* ⟨*pl* -i⟩ *Br.* theft; *Am.* larceny

latta *f* can, tin; ***~ di benzina*** petrol can, *US* gas can; ***di ~*** tin

lattaio *m*, **-a** *f* ⟨*mpl* -ai⟩ milkman; *donna* milkwoman

lattante *m* infant, small baby

latte *m* milk; ***~ a lunga conservazione*** long-life milk; ***~ detergente*** cleansing milk; ***~ intero*** whole milk; ***~ materno*** mother's milk; ***~ (parzialmente) scremato*** (semi-)skimmed milk; ***~ in polvere*** powdered milk; ***~ magro*** low-fat milk; ***~ di mandorle*** almond milk; ***maialino*** *m* ***da ~*** sucking pig; ***far venire il ~ alle ginocchia*** turn one's stomach

latteo *adj* milk *attr*; ***Via*** *f* ***Lattea*** Milky Way

latteria *f* dairy

lattice *m* latex

latticino *m* ⟨*pl* -ni⟩ dairy product

lattiginoso *adj* milky

lattina *f* can, tin; ***una ~ di birra*** a can of beer

lattosio *m* ⟨*pl* -i⟩ lactose

lattuga *f* ⟨*pl* -ghe⟩ lettuce; ***~ romana*** cos lettuce

laudano *m* laudanum

laurea *f* degree; ***~ breve*** *Italian degree similar to a Bachelor of Arts or Sciences*; ***~ ad honorem*** (*or* ***honoris causa***) honorary degree; ***esame*** *m* ***di ~*** degree examination

laureando *m*, **-a** *f* final year student

laurearsi *v/r* ⟨1l⟩ graduate; ***~ in legge*** take a degree in law

laureato *m*, **-a** *f* graduate

lauto *adj cosa* lavish; *persona* generous; ***-a mancia*** a generous tip; **~ *pranzo*** a lavish lunch
lava *f* lava
lavabile *adj* washable; **~ *in lavatrice*** machine-washable
lavabo *m* basin
lavacristallo *m* AUTO windscreen (*US* windshield) washer
lavaggio *m* ⟨*pl* -ggi⟩ washing; **~ *a secco*** dry-cleaning; **~ *del cervello*** brainwashing
lavagna *f* blackboard; GEOL slate; **~ *luminosa*** overhead projector
L'Avana *f* ⟨Havana⟩
lavanda *f* BOT lavender
lavanda[2] *f* washing (out); MED lavage; **~ *gastrica*** gastric lavage
lavandaia *f* washerwoman; *fig infml* fishwife
lavanderia *f* laundry; **~ *a gettone*** laundrette
lavandino *m* basin; *nella cucina* sink
lavapiatti *m/f* ⟨*pl* lavapiatti⟩ dishwasher
lavare *v/t* ⟨1a⟩ wash; **~ *i panni*** do the washing; *fig* **~ *il capo a qn*** give s.o. a slating
lavarsi *v/r* wash; **~ *le mani*** wash one's hands; *fig* ***lavarsene le mani*** wash one's hands of it; **~ *i denti*** brush *or* clean one's teth
lavasecco *m/f* ⟨*pl* lavasecco⟩ dry cleaner's
lavastoviglie *f* ⟨*pl* lavastoviglie⟩ dishwasher
lavata *f* wash; ***darsi una* ~ *veloce*** have a quick wash; *fig* ***dare una* ~ *di capo a qn*** give someone a telling-off
lavativo *m*, **-a** *f fig infml*skiver
lavatoio *m* ⟨*pl* -oi⟩ laundry; *di casa* laundry (room), utility room
lavatrice *f* washing machine
lavavetri *m/f* ⟨*pl* lavavetri⟩ window-cleaner
lavello *m* basin; *nella cucina* sink
lavico *adj* ⟨*mpl* -ci⟩ lavic; ***roccia*** *f* ***-a*** lavic rock
lavina *f* avalanche
lavoraccio *m* ⟨*pl* -cci⟩ *pej* (*faticoso*) chore; (*fatto male*) botch (job)
lavorante *m/f* worker
lavorare ⟨1a⟩ **I** *v/i* work; **~ *saltuariamente*** do occasional work; **~ *sodo*** work hard **II** *v/t materia prima* process; *legno* carve; *terra* work; **~ *a maglia*** *or* ***ai ferri*** knit; **~ *a tempo pieno*** work full-time; **~ *in nero*** work on the side; **~ *in proprio*** work for oneself; **~ *part-time*** work part-time; *fig* **~ *di fantasia*** daydream
lavorarsi *v/r* ⟨1a⟩: **~ *qn*** work on s.o.
lavorativo *adj*: ***giorno*** *m* **~** working day
lavorato *adj legno* carved
lavoratore *m*, **-trice** *f* worker; **~ *autonomo*** self-employed person; **~ *dipendente*** employee
lavorazione *f di materia prima* processing; *di legno* carving
lavoretto *m* small job **lavoricchiare** *v/i* ⟨1k⟩ potter about; *saltuariamente* do odd jobs **lavorio** *m* ⟨*pl* -ii⟩ bustle; *fig* scheming
lavoro *m* work; (*impiego*) job; ***-i*** *pl* ***domestici*** housework; **~ *fisso*** permanent job; ***-i*** *pl* ***forzati*** forced labour; **~ *di gruppo*** teamwork; **~ *interinale*** temporary job; **~ *malfatto*** botched job; **~ *manuale*** manual labour; **~ *minorile*** child labour; **~ *nero*** off-the--books work; ***-i*** *pl* ***occasionali*** *or* ***saltuari*** odd jobs; **~ *socialmente utile*** community service; **~ *straordinario*** overtime; ***per* ~** on business; ***condizioni*** *fpl* ***di* ~** working conditions; ***permesso*** *m* ***di* ~** work permit; ***posto*** *m* ***di* ~** place of work, workplace; ***-i in corso*** roadworks *pl*, work in progress; ***senza* ~** unemployed; ***mettersi al* ~** get to work
lay-out *m* lay-out
laziale **I** *adj* of Latium **II** *m/f* person from Latium
Lazio *m* Latium
lazzaretto *m* isolation hospital
lazzarone *m*, **-a** *f* shirker
lazzo *m* THEAT jest; *liter* jest
LC *abbr* (= **Lecco**) Lecco
le[1] *art fpl* the
le[2] *pron* **1.** *fsg* to her; **~ *ho telefonato stamattina*** I rang her this morning **2.** *fpl* them; **~ *ho incontrate ieri sera*** I met them last night **3.** *a.* ***Le*** you; ***Le dispiace se apro il finestrino?*** do you mind if I open the window?
leacril® *m* ⟨*pl* leacril⟩ leacril
leader *m/f* ⟨*pl* leader⟩ leader
leadership *f* ⟨*pl* leadership⟩ leadership

leale *adj* loyal

lealtà *f* loyalty

leasing *m* ⟨*pl* leasing⟩ lease; ***contratto*** *m* ***di ~*** leasing agreement; ***prendere in ~*** lease

lebbra *f* leprosy

lebbroso *m*, **-a** *f* leper

leccaculo *m/f* ⟨*pl* leccaculo⟩ *vulg Br.* arse-licker; *Am.* ass-licker)

lecca-lecca *m* ⟨*pl* lecca-lecca⟩ lollipop

leccapiedi *m/f* ⟨*pl* leccapiedi⟩ *pej* crawler

leccare *v/t* ⟨1d⟩ lick *infml*; ***~ un francobollo*** lick a stamp; ***~ un gelato*** lick an ice-cream; ***~ il culo a qn*** *vulg* lick s.o.'s arse; ***~ qn*** *infml* suck up to s.o. *infml*, lick s.o.'s boots

leccarsi *v/r* lick; *fig* ***~ i baffi*** lick one's chops; *fig* ***~ le dita*** lick one's fingers

leccata *f*: ***dare una ~*** lick

leccese I *adj* from Lecce **II** *m/f* person from Lecce

lecchese I *adj* from Lecco **II** *m/f* person from Lecco

lecchino *m*, **-a** *f* *pej*bootlicker

leccio *m* ⟨*pl* -cci⟩ holm oak

leccornia *f* appetizing dish, delicacy

lecitamente *adv* legitimately

lecitina *f* lectin

lecito *adj* legal, permissible; ***domanda*** *f* ***-a*** a legitimate question; ***nei limiti del ~*** within the boundaries of the law; ***se mi è ~*** if I may

led *m* ⟨*pl* led⟩ ELEC Light Emitting Diode, LED

ledere *v/t* ⟨3q⟩ harm (*a. fig*); ***~ i diritti di qn*** infringe s.o.'s rights

lega *f* ⟨*pl* -ghe⟩ **1.** league **2.** METAL alloy

legaccio *m* ⟨*pl* -cci⟩ string

legale I *adj* legal; ***studio ~*** firm of solicitors **II** *m/f* lawyer; ***assistenza*** *f* ***~*** legal aid; ***numero*** *m* ***~*** quorum; ***ora*** *f* ***~*** daylight saving time; ***rappresentante*** *m* ***~*** legal representative

legalità *f* legality

legalizzare *v/t* ⟨1a⟩ legalize

legalizzazione *f* decriminalization; *di droga* legalization **legalmente** *adv* lawfully; (*per vie legali*) legally

legame *m* tie, relationship; (*nesso*) link, connection; ***~ di amicizia*** a bond of friendship

legamento *m* ANAT ligament

Lega Nord *f* Northern League (*Italian regionalist political party*)

legare *v/t* ⟨1e⟩ tie; *persona* tie up; (*collegare*) link; *fig di lavoro* tie down; ***ho le mani legate*** my hands are tied; ***matto da ~*** as mad as a hatter

legarsi *v/r fig* tie o.s. down; *fig* ***legarsela al dito*** bear a grudge; ***~ i capelli*** tie one's hair back; ***~ a qn*** develop an attachment to s.o.

legatario *m*, **-a** *f* ⟨*mpl* -ri⟩ legatee

legato *m* REL legate

legato I *adj* (*unito*) tied; (*affezionato*) close; (*vincolato*) bound; (*impacciato*) awkward; *di libri*: bound; MUS slurred; ***essere ~ a qc*** be close to someone; ***portare i capelli -i*** wear one's hair tied back; ***~ alla tradizione*** linked to tradition; ***~ al contesto*** context-related **II** *n*: ***legato*** *m* JUR legacy; ***~ pontificio*** Pope's legate; ***~ apostolico*** Pope's legate

legatoria *f* book binding

legazione *f* legation; (*edificio*) embassy

legazione *f* legation

legenda *f* ⟨*pl* legenda⟩ legend

legge *f* law; ***~ delega*** JUR enabling act; ***~ finanziaria*** the Budget; ***~ ordinaria*** JUR common law; ***~ regionale*** JUR local law; ***studiare ~*** study *or* read law; ***a norma di ~*** up to standard; ***a norma di ~ …*** complies with …; ***fuori ~*** illegal, unlawful; ***per ~*** by law; ***uomo*** *m* ***di ~*** law-abiding man, lawyer; ***approvare / abrogare una*** JUR ***~*** pass / repeal a law; *fig* ***dettar ~*** lord it; ***la ~ del più forte*** the law of the jungle; ***fatta la ~, trovato l'inganno*** *prov* every law has a loophole

leggenda *f* legend; *di carta geografica etc* key

leggendario *adj* ⟨*mpl* -ri⟩ legendary

leggere *v/t* ⟨3cc⟩ read; ***~ le labbra*** lip-read; ***~ nel pensiero a qn*** read s.o.'s mind; ***~ la mano*** read s.o.'s palm; ***te lo leggo negli occhi*** I can read it in your eyes

leggerezza *f* lightness; *fig* casualness; ***con ~*** thoughtlessly, unthinkingly

leggermente *adv* (*con leggerezza*) lightly; (*lievemente*) slightly

leggero *adj* light; (*lieve, di poca importanza*) slight; (*superficiale*) thoughtless; *caffè* weak; ***~ come***

una piuma as light as a feather; ***un tè ~*** weak tea; ***alla -a*** lightly, lightheartedly; ***prendere qc alla -a*** make light of sth; ***tenersi ~*** eat sth light
leggiadria *f* grace **leggiadro** *adj* graceful, *di viso* pretty
leggibile *adj* legible
leggibilità *f* ⟨*pl* leggibilità⟩ legibility
leggio *m* ⟨*pl* -ii⟩ lectern; MUS music stand
leghista ⟨*mpl* -i⟩ **I** *adj* of the Northern League **II** *m/f* member of the Northern League
legiferare *v/i* ⟨1m⟩ make laws; (*dettar legge*) lay down the law
legionario ⟨*mpl* -ri⟩ **I** *adj* legionary; ***truppe*** *fpl* ***-rie*** legionary troops **II** *n*: ***legionario*** *m* legionnaire; HIST legionary
legione *f* legion; ***~ straniera*** Foreign Legion
legislativo *adj* legislative
legislatore *m*, **-trice** *f* legislator
legislatura *f periodo* term of parliament
legislazione *f* legislation
legittima *f* forced heirship
legittimare *v/t* ⟨1m⟩ approve
legittimazione *f* approval
legittimità *f* ⟨*pl* legittimità⟩ legitimacy; (*fondatezza*) justness
legittimo *adj* legitimate; ***-a difesa*** *f* self defence; ***figlio*** *m* ***~*** legitimate child
legna *f* (fire)wood; ***far ~*** collect firewood; ***~ da ardere*** firewood
legnaia *f* woodshed
legname *m* timber; ***~ da costruzione*** lumber
legnata *f infml* blow; ***prendere un sacco di -e*** get beaten up
legno *m* ⟨*pl* i -i⟩ wood; ***di ~*** wooden; ***~ di faggio*** beech wood; ***~ compensato*** plywood; ***pavimento*** *m* ***in ~*** wooden floor; *fig* ***testa di ~*** *pej* blockhead
legnoso *adj* (*pianta*) woody; *fig* wooden
lego® *m* ⟨*pl* lego⟩ Lego
leguleio *m pej* ⟨*pl* -ei⟩ pettyfogger
legumi *mpl* peas *pl* and beans *pl*; *secchi* pulses *pl*
lei *pron* **1.** *fsg soggetto* she; *oggetto, con preposizione* her; ***~ stessa*** herself; ***vai da ~ stasera?*** are you going round to her house this evening? **2.** *a.* ***Lei*** you; ***dare del ~ a qn*** address s.o. as 'lei'
lembo *m di gonna* hem, bottom; *di terra* stip; ***un ~ di cielo*** strip of sky
lemma *m* ⟨*pl* -i⟩ lemma; TYPO headword **lemmario** *m* ⟨*pl* -ri⟩ headwords
lemme lemme *adv* slowly; (*tranquillo*) calmly
lemure *m* ZOOL lemur
lena *f* staying-power; ***lavorare di buona ~*** work hard
lenire *v/t* ⟨4d⟩ alleviate
lenire *v/t* ⟨4d⟩ ease
lenitivo I *adj* easing **II** *m* alleviator
lentamente *adv* slowly
lente *f* lens; ***-i*** *pl* glasses *pl*, spectacles *pl*, specs *pl infml*; ***-i*** *pl* (***a contatto***) contact lenses *pl*, contacts *pl infml*; ***~ d'ingrandimento*** magnifying glass
lentezza *f* slowness
lenticchia *f* lentil
lenticolare *adj* lenticular
lentiggine *f* freckle
lentigginoso *adj* freckled
lentisco *m* ⟨*pl* -chi⟩ BOT mastic (tree)
lento I *adj* slow; (*allentato*) slack; *abito* loose **II** *m* MUS slow dance; (*movimento*) lento
lenza *f* fishing rod
lenzuolo *m* ⟨*pl* i -i *and* le **-a**⟩ sheet; ***cambiare le -a*** change the bed
leoncino *m* lion cub
leone *m* lion; ASTROL ***Leone*** Leo; ***essere del Leone*** be a Leo; ***~ marino*** sea-lion; ***fare la parte del ~*** get the lion's share
leonessa *f* lioness
leonino *adj* leonine; ***chioma*** *f* ***-a*** mane of thick hair
leopardo *m* leopard; *fig* ***a macchia di ~*** leopard-spotted
lepidotteri *mpl* Lepidoptera
leponzio ⟨*mpl* -zi⟩ **I** *adj* Lepontic **II** *m*, **-a** *f* Lepontic
leporino *adj*: harelike ***labbro*** *m* ***~*** harelip
lepre *f* hare; ***~ in salmì*** stewed hare; ***correre come una ~*** hare away
leprotto *m* leveret
lercio *adj* filthy
lerciume *m* dirt
lesbica *f* lesbian
lesbico *adj* ⟨*mpl* -ci⟩ lesbian; ***amore*** *m* ***~*** lesbian love
lesena *f* ARCH pilaster (strip)

lesinare ⟨1l⟩ *v/t and v/i*: **~ (su) qc** skimp on sth
lesionare *v/t* ⟨1a⟩ damage
lesione *f* MED injury; JUR **~ personale** personal injury
lesivo *adj* harmful **leso** *adj* damaged; MED, JUR injured; **-a maestà** lèse-majesté
lessare *v/t* ⟨1a⟩ boil
lessicale *adj* lexical
lessico *m* ⟨*pl* -ci⟩ vocabulary; (*dizionario*) glossary
lessicografia *f* lexicography **lessicografico** *adj* ⟨*mpl* -ci⟩ lexicographic(al) **lessicografo** *m*, **-a** *f* lexicographer
lessicologia *f* lexicology **lessicologico** *adj* ⟨*mpl* -ci⟩ lexicological
lesso I *adj* boiled **II** *m* boiled beef
lesto *adj* quick; **essere ~ di mano** be light-fingered
lestofante *m* (*impostore*) fraud; (*imbroglione*) con-man
letale *adj* lethal
letamaio *m* ⟨*pl* -ai⟩ muck-heap; *fig* pigsty
letame *m* manure, dung
letargia *f* lethargy **letargico** *adj* ⟨*mpl* -ci⟩ lethargic
letargo *m* ⟨*pl* -ghi⟩ lethargy; **andare in ~** go into hibernation
lettera *f* **1.** letter; **per ~** by letter; **~ di accompagnamento** covering letter; **~ assicurata** registered letter; FIN **~ di cambio** bill of exchange; **~ commerciale** business letter; **~ espresso** (letter sent) express delivery; **~ per l'estero** letter for abroad; **~ raccomandata** recorded delivery letter; ECON **~ di vettura** consignment note **2. alla ~** to the letter; **prendere qc alla ~** take sth literally; *fig* take sth at face value **3. laurearsi in -e** (*facoltà*) have an arts degree; **uomo** *m* **di -e** a man of letters
letterale *adj* literal
letteralmente *adv* literally
letterario *adj* ⟨*mpl* -ri⟩ literary; **critico** *m* **~** literary critic
letterato *m*, **-a** *f* man / woman of letters
letteratura *f* literature
lettiera *f* litter
lettiga *f* ⟨*pl* -ghe⟩ (*portantina*) litter; (*barella*) stretcher
lettino *m* cot; *dal medico* bed; *dallo psicologo* couch; **~ solare** sunbed
letto[1] *m* bed; **~ a una piazza** single bed; **~ matrimoniale** double bed; **~ a castello** bunk bed; **~ pieghevole** foldaway bed; **andare a ~** go to bed; **essere a ~** be in bed; **andare a ~ con le galline** go to bed early; **andare a ~ con qn** go to bed with s.o.; **figlio** *m* **di primo ~** child from one's first marriage; **rifare il ~** make the bed; **~ del fiume** river-bed
letto[2] *past part* → **leggere**
lettone I *adj* Latvian **II** *m/f* Latvian
Lettonia *f* Latvia
lettorato *m* HIST lectorate; lectureship
lettore *m* **I** *m*, **-trice** *f* reader; *all' università* lecturer in a foreign language **II** *m*: **lettore** COMPUT disk drive; **~ compact disc** CD player; **~ DVD** DVD player; **~ ottico** optical character reader
lettura *f* reading; **chiave** *f* **di ~** interpretive key; **libro** *m* **di ~** reader
leucemia *f* leuk(a)emia
leucocita *m* ⟨*pl* -i⟩ leucocyte, white blood cell
leva *f* **1.** lever; AUTO **~ del cambio** gear lever; *fig* **far ~ su qc** play on sth **2.** MIL call-up, *US* draft; MIL **servizio di ~** military service
levante *m* east
levantino I *adj* Levantine; *fig* unscrupulous **II** *m*, **-a** *f* Levantine; *fig* unscrupulous person
levare *v/t* ⟨1b⟩ (*alzare*) raise, lift; (*togliere*) take, (re)move; (*rimuovere*) take out, remove; *macchia* remove, get out; *dente* take out, extract; **~ l'ancora** weigh anchor; *fig* **~ le tende** decamp; **~ del sole** sunrise; **~ un dente** have a tooth out; **levare di mezzo** get sth / s.o. out of the way; *fig* **~ il pane di bocca** take the bread out of s.o.'s mouth; **~ gli occhi al cielo** lift one's eyes to heaven
levarsi *v/r* get up, rise; *di sole* rise, come up; *indumento* take off; **~ il vizio di fare qc** get out of the habit of doing sth; **levatelo dalla testa!** you can get that idea out of your head!; **~ di mezzo** *or* **dai piedi** get out of the way
levata *f di posta* collection
levataccia *f* ⟨*pl* -cce⟩ **fare una ~** get up at some ungodly hour
levatrice *f* midwife

leverage *m* ⟨*pl* leverage⟩ FIN leverage
levigare *v/t* ⟨1l, b & e⟩ smooth down
levigato *adj* smooth; ***pelle*** *f* ***-a*** smooth skin
levigatura *f* smoothing
levitare *v/i* ⟨1l⟩ levitate
levriero *m* greyhound
lezione *f* lesson; *all'università* lecture; ***~ privata*** private lesson; ***~ di lingua straniera*** language class; ***dare -i*** tutor; *fig* ***dare una ~ a qn*** teach s.o. a lesson; ***un'amara ~*** a hard lesson; ***fare ~*** teach; ***andare a ~*** go to class
leziosità *f* ⟨*pl* leziosità⟩ affectation **lezioso** *adj* affected; (*sdolcinato*) mawkish
lezzo *m* stink; (*sudiciume*) filth
li[1] *pron mpl* them
li[2] *art mpl* ADMIN: ***Roma, ~ 12 novembre*** Rome, 12th November
lì *adv* there; ***~ dentro*** in there; ***~ sopra*** up / on there; ***~ per ~*** there and then; ***fin ~*** up to that point; ***giù di ~*** thereabouts; ***di ~ a pochi giorni*** a few days later; ***siamo sempre ~*** we're still there; ***via di ~!*** get away from there!
liana *f* liana
libagione *f* libation; *hum* a heavy drinking session
libanese *m/f & adj* Lebanese
Libano *m* (the) Lebanon
libbra *f* pound
libecciata *f* south-westerly gale **libeccio** *m* south-west (wind)
libellula *f* dragon-fly
liberale I *adj* generous; POL liberal **II** *m/f* liberal
liberalismo *m* liberalism; ***~ economico*** economic liberalism
liberalità *f* ⟨*pl* liberalità⟩ generosity
liberalizzare *v/t* ⟨1a⟩ liberalize
liberalizzazione *f* liberalization
liberamente *adv* freely
liberare *v/t* ⟨1l⟩ release, free; (*sgomberare*) empty; *stanza* vacate; ***~ la camera*** vacate the room; ***~ gli ostaggi*** ⟨release the hostages⟩
liberarsi *v/r*: ***~ di*** get rid of; ***si è liberato un posto*** a place has become free; ***cerco di liberarmi per le otto*** I'll try to be free for eight; ***~ dai pregiudizi*** free oneself of prejudices
liberatore I *adj* liberating **II** *m*, **-trice** *f* liberator **liberatorio** *adj* ⟨*mpl* -ri⟩ liberating; ECON, JUR redeeming; ***risata*** *f* ***-a*** liberating laughter
liberazione *f* release; *di nazione* liberation; ***~ dalle ipoteche*** redemption of a mortgage
libercolo *m* worthless book
Liberia *f* Liberia **liberiano I** *adj* Liberian **II** *m*, **-a** *f* Liberian
liberismo *m* liberalism
libero *adj* free; *camera d'albergo* vacant, free; ***~ arbitrio*** free will; ECON ***~ scambio*** free trade; ***via -a!*** all clear!; ***~ / -a professionista*** *m/f* freelance, freelancer; ***a piede ~*** JUR free on bail; ***lasciare ~ il passaggio*** keep clear; ***tempo*** *m* ***~*** free time
libertà *f* ⟨*pl* libertà⟩ freedom, liberty; ***mettersi in ~*** change into more comfortable clothes; ***~ d'opinione*** freedom of thought; ***~ di stampa*** freedom of the press; ***prendersi la ~ di fare qc*** take the liberty of doing sth; ***prendersi delle ~ con qn*** take liberties with s.o.; ***~ provvisoria*** bail; JUR ***~ vigilata*** probation; ***rimettere in ~*** release; ***Statua della Libertà*** Statue of Liberty
libertinaggio *m* ⟨*pl* -ggi⟩ libertinism **libertino I** *adj* libertine; PHIL, POL freethinking **II** *n*: ***libertino*** *m* libertine; PHIL, POL freethinker
liberto *m* HIST freedman
liberty *m/adj* art nouveau
Libia *f* Libya
libico ⟨*mpl* -ci⟩ **I** *adj* Libyan **II** *m*, **-a** *f* Libyan
libidine *f* lust; ***atti*** *mpl* ***di ~*** lewd behaviour
libido *f* ⟨*pl* libido⟩ PSYCH libido
libidonoso *adj* lecherous
libraio *m*, **-a** *f* ⟨*mpl* -ai⟩ bookseller
librario *adj* ⟨*mpl* -ri⟩ book *attr*
librarsi *v/r* ⟨1a⟩be poised; ***~ in aria*** hover, fly
libreria *f* bookstore, *Br* -shop; (*biblioteca*) book collection, library; *mobile* bookcase; ***~ di oggetti*** COMPUT library
librettista *m/f* ⟨*mpl* -i⟩ librettist
libretto *m* booklet; MUS libretto; ***~ degli assegni*** cheque book, *US* check book; AUTO ***~ di circolazione*** registration document; ***~ di risparmio*** bank book; ***~ universitario*** university student's personal record book
libro *m* book; ***~ di testo*** textbook; ***~ illustrato*** picture book; ***~ tascabile*** pa-

perback; **~ *bianco*** ADMIN white paper; **~ *verde*** ADMIN green paper; ***essere nel*** *or* ***sul ~ nero*** be on the blacklist; ***essere un ~ aperto*** be an open book

licantropo *m*, **-a** *f* werewolf

liceale *m/f* high-school student

liceità *f* ⟨*pl* liceità⟩ legitimacy

licenza *f* **1.** FIN licence, *US* license, permit; **~ *di caccia / pesca*** hunting / fishing permit; **~ *di costruzione*** building *or* construction permit; **~ *di esercizio*** trading licence (*US* license) **2.** EDU school leaving certificate; **~ *media*** *leaving certificate from middle school* **3.** MIL leave

licenziamento *m* dismissal; *per motivi economici* dismissal, *Br* redundancy

licenziare *v/t* ⟨1g⟩ dismiss; *per motivi economici* dismiss, lay off, *Br* make redundant; **~ *alle stampe*** pass for press

licenziarsi *v/r* resign; **~ *il 15 aprile*** hand in one's notice on 15th April

licenziatario *m*, **-a** *f* ⟨*mpl* -ri⟩ licensee

licenzioso *adj* licentious

liceo *m* high school; **~ *classico*** (***scientifico***) *high school specializing in arts* (*science*) *subjects*; **~ *linguistico*** *high school specializing in languages*

lichene *m* lichen

licitazione *f* auction; **~ *privata*** private treaty

lido *m* beach

lietamente *adv* happily

lieto *adj* happy; **~ *di conoscerla*** nice *or* pleased to meet you; **~ *evento*** the birth of a baby; **~ *fine*** a happy ending

lieve *adj* light; (*di poca gravità*) slight, minor; *sorriso*, *rumore* faint

lievemente *adv* slightly

lievitare *v/i* ⟨1l & b⟩ rise; *fig* rise, be on the increase

lievitazione *f* rising; *fig* fermentation; ***pane a ~ naturale*** natural rising bread

lievito *m* yeast; **~ *in polvere*** baking powder; **~ *di birra*** brewer's yeast

liftare *v/t* ⟨1a⟩ *infml* undercut

lifting *m* face-lift; ***farsi il ~*** have a face-lift

ligio *adj* ⟨*mpl* -gi⟩ loyal; **~ *al dovere*** dutiful

lignaggio *m* ⟨*pl* -ggi⟩ lineage; ***di alto ~*** of aristocratic blood

ligure *adj* Ligurian; ***Mar Ligure*** *m* Ligurian Sea; ***Riviera Ligure*** *f* Ligurian Riviera

Liguria *f* Liguria

ligustro *m* BOT privet

LILA *abbr* (= **Lega Italiana Lotta all'Aids**) *Italian league fighting against AIDS*

lilla *m/adj* lilac

lillà *m* ⟨*pl* lillà⟩ lilac (tree)

lillipuziano I *adj* lilliputian; miniature (*a. fig*) **II** *m*, **-a** *f* Lilliputian

lima *f* file

limaccioso *adj* muddy; *fig* murky

limare *v/t* ⟨1a⟩ file

limarsi *v/r* ⟨1a⟩: **~ *le unghie*** file one's nails **limatura** *f* filing; (*residuo*) filings

limbo *m* limbo

limetta *f* emery board; *di metallo* nail file

limitabile *adj* limitable

limitare *v/t* ⟨1l⟩ limit, restrict (***a*** to); (*contenere*) limit, contain

limitarsi *v/r* limit o.s. (***a*** to)

limitatamente *adv* in a limited / specific way **limitatezza** *f* limitation; **~ *mentale*** limitation **limitativo** *adj* limiting

limitato *adj* limited; FIN ***società f a responsabilità -a*** limited company; ***è ~*** *di persona* he's got his limitations

limitazione *f* limitation; **~ *delle nascite*** birth control; ***senza -i*** without restriction

limite *m* limit; (*confine*) boundary; **~ *di carico*** AUTO load limit; **~ *di età*** age limit; **~ *di velocità*** speed limit; **~ *massimo*** cut-off; ***al ~*** at most, at the outside; ***nei -i del possibile*** to the best of one's ability; ***un caso ~*** a borderline case; ***porre un ~ a qc*** draw the line at sth

limitrofo *adj* bordering, neighbo(u)ring

limo *m* slime; GEOL silt

limonare *v/i* ⟨1a⟩ *infml* pet heavily

limonata *f* lemonade

limoncello *m* lime

limone *m* lemon; (*albero*) lemon tree; ***succo m di ~*** lemon juice; ***tè m al ~*** lemon tea; ***spremere come un ~*** squeeze s.o. dry

limoneto *m* lemon grove

limousine *f* ⟨*pl* limousine⟩ limousine, *infml* limo
limpidamente *adv* clearly
limpidezza *f* cleanness
limpido *adj* clear; *acqua* crystal-clear, limpid
lince *f* lynx
linciaggio *m* lynching
linciare *v/t* ⟨1f⟩ lynch
lindo *adj* neat (*a. fig*)
linea *f* **1.** line; **~ *aerea*** airline; **~ *d'arrivo / di partenza*** finishing / starting line; **~ *commutata*** TEL switchable line; **~ *dedicata*** COMPUT dedicated; **~ *dell'autobus*** bus route; ***aereo / nave di ~*** airliner / liner; ***in ~ d'aria*** as the crow flies; ***di ~ sportiva*** sports fashion; ***una ~ di prodotti per la casa*** a line of household products **2.** TEL **~ *occupata*** engaged line; TEL ***restare in ~*** stay on the line, not hang up; ***servizio*** *m* ***di ~*** liner service; ***è caduta la ~*** I / we *etc* have got cut off **3.** ***mantenere la ~*** keep one's figure **4.** ***a grandi -e*** broadly; ***in ~ di massima*** as a general rule; ***stare in prima ~*** be on the front line **5.** ***avere qualche ~ di febbre*** have a slight temperature; *fig* ***passare in seconda ~*** fade into the background
lineamenti *mpl* (*fisionomia*) features *pl*
lineare *adj* linear
linearità *f* ⟨*pl* linearità⟩ linearity; *fig* straightforwardness **linearmente** *adv* linearly
lineetta *f* dash
linfa *f* ANAT lymph; BOT sap; **~ *vitale*** life blood
linfatico *adj* ⟨*mpl* -ci⟩ lymphatic
linfocito *m* lymphocyte
linfonodo *m* lymph node
lingotto *m* ingot; **~ *d'oro*** gold ingot; ***oro*** *m* ***in -i*** gold bars
lingua *f* **1.** tongue; *fig* ***avere la ~ lunga*** have a loose tongue; ***non avere peli sulla ~*** not mince one's words; ***la ~ batte dove il dente duole*** *prov* the tongue goes to the sore tooth; *fig* ***mordersi la ~*** bite one's tongue; ***ce l'ho sulla punta della lingua*** it's on the tip of my tongue; ***tieni la ~ a posto!*** hold your tongue! **2.** (*linguaggio*) language; ***madre ~*** mother tongue; **~ *materna*** first language; **~ *nazionale*** official language; **~ *parlata*** spoken language; **~ *straniera*** foreign language; ***conoscenza*** *f* ***delle -e*** knowledge of languages
linguaccia *f* ⟨*pl* -cce⟩: ***fare le -cce*** put one's tongue out
linguacciuto *adj* back-biting
linguaggio *m* ⟨*pl* -ggi⟩ language; **~ *tecnico*** technical language, jargon; COMPUT **~ *di programmazione*** programming language; **~ *macchina*** COMPUT machine language; **~ *gestuale*** sign language
linguale *adj* lingual; ANAT lingual; ***consonante*** *f* **~** lingual consonant
linguetta *f* tab; *di scarpe*: tongue; *di buste*: tear-tape
linguista *m/f* ⟨*mpl* -i⟩ linguist
linguistica *f* linguistics *sg*
linguistico *adj* ⟨*mpl* -ci⟩ linguistic; *studi* language; ***liceo*** *m* **~** *language-focused Italian secondary school*
linimento *m* liniment
link *m* ⟨*pl* link⟩ COMPUT link
lino *m* BOT flax; *tessuto* linen
linoleum *m* ⟨*pl* linoleum⟩ lino
linotipia *f* linotyping; (*stabilimento*) linotype house **linotipista** *m/f* ⟨*mpl* -i⟩ linotypist
liocorno *m* unicorn
liofilizzare *v/t* ⟨1a⟩ freeze-dry
liofilizzato *adj* freeze-dried
Lione *f* Lyons **lionese I** *adj* from Lyons **II** *m/f* person from Lyons
lipide *m* lipid **lipidico** *adj* ⟨*mpl* -ci⟩ lipidic; ***strato*** *m* **~** fatty layer
lipizzano *m* Lipizaner
liposolubile *adj* fat-soluble
liposoma *m* BIOL liposome
LIPU *f abbr* (**Lega Italiana Protezione Uccelli**) *Italian league for the protection of birds*
liquame *m* sewage
liquefare *v/t* ⟨3aa⟩ melt
liquefarsi *v/r* melt
liquefazione *f* liquefaction
liquidabile *adj* that can be liquidated; *impresa* that can be wound up; *debito* that can be cleared; *fig problema* solvable
liquidare *v/t* ⟨11⟩ (*pagare*) pay; *merci* clear; *azienda* liquidate; *fig questione* settle; *problema* dispose of; *persona infml* liquidate *infml*, dispose of *infml*; *fig* **~ *qn con una scusa*** dismiss

s.o. with an excuse
liquidazione *f* liquidation; ~ ***totale*** clearance sale
liquidità *f* liquid assets *pl*, liquidity
liquido *m/adj* liquid; ~ ***amniotico*** amniotic fluid; ~ ***seminale*** seminal fluid; ***denaro*** *m* ~ ready money
liquigas *m* gas sold in cylinders
liquirizia *f* liquorice
liquor *m* ⟨*no pl*⟩ cerebrospinal fluid
liquore *m* liqueur
liquoroso *adj* similar to liqueur
lira *f hist* lira; ~ ***turca*** Turkish lira
lira² *f* MUS lyre; HIST lyric poetry
lirica *f* ⟨*pl* -che⟩ lyric poem; MUS ***la*** ~ opera
lirico *adj* ⟨*mpl* -ci⟩ lyric; ***cantante*** *m* ~ opera singer; ***musica*** *f* **-a** operatic music; ***teatro*** *m* ~ opera house
lirismo *m* lyricism
Lisbona *f* Lisbon
lisca *f* ⟨*pl* -che⟩ fishbone; ***a*** ~ ***di pesce*** herringbone
lisciare *v/t* ⟨1f⟩ smooth (down); (*accarezzare*) stroke; *capelli* straighten
lisciarsi *v/r* ⟨1g⟩ stroke; ~ ***i capelli*** straighten one's hair
liscio *adj* ⟨*mpl* -sci⟩ smooth; *bevanda* straight, neat; *fig* ***passarla -a*** get away with it; ***è andato tutto*** ~ it all went smoothly
liscivia *f* lye
liseuse *f* ⟨*pl* liseuse⟩ bedjacket
liso *adj* worn
lisoformio *m* ⟨*pl* -i⟩ lysoform
lista *f* (*elenco*) list; (*striscia*) strip; ~ ***d'attesa*** waiting list; ***in*** ~ ***d'attesa*** on the waiting list, wait-listed; AVIAT on standby; ~ ***elettorale*** electoral roll; ~ ***di nozze*** wedding list; ~ ***della spesa*** shopping list; ~ ***dei vini*** wine list
listare *v/t* ⟨1a⟩ edge; ***listato a lutto*** black-edged
listello *m* (wooden) strip; ARCH fillet
listino *m*: ~ ***di borsa*** share index; ~ ***prezzi*** price list
Lit. *abbr* (= **lire italiane**) *hist* L (lire)
litania *f* litany (*a. fig*)
litantrace *f* bituminous coal
lite *f* quarrel, argument; JUR lawsuit; ~ ***coniugale*** marital dispute; ***essere in*** ~ ***con qn*** be at odds with s.o.; ***attaccare*** ~ start a fight
litigante *m/f* quarreller; JUR litigant; ***fra due -i il terzo gode*** the onlooker gets the best of a fight
litigare *v/i* ⟨1l & e⟩ quarrel, argue
litigio *m* ⟨*pl* -gi⟩ quarrel, argument
litigiosità *f* ⟨*pl* litigiosità⟩ quarrelsomeness; JUR litigiousness
litigioso *adj* argumentative, quarrelsome
litispendenza *f* JUR lawsuit pendency
litografia *f* lithography
litografo *m* lithograph
litorale I *adj* coastal **II** *m* coast
litoranea *f* coast road
litoraneo *adj* coast *attr*, coastal
litro *m* litre, *US* liter
littorio *adj* ⟨*mpl* -ri⟩ HIST; ***fascio*** *m* ~ bundle of birch rods (symbol of Fascism)
Lituania *f* Lithuania
lituano I *adj* Lithuanian **II** *m*, **-a** *f* Lithuanian
liturgia *f* liturgy
liturgico *adj* ⟨*mpl* -ci⟩ liturgical
liutaio *m* ⟨*pl* -ai⟩ lute maker
liutista *m/f* ⟨*mpl* -i⟩ lutanist
liuto *m* lute
livella *f* level
livellamento *m* levelling
livellare *v/t* ⟨1b⟩ level
livellatrice *f* (road) grader
livello *m* level; ~ ***dell'acqua*** water-level; ~ ***dei prezzi*** price level; ~ ***di guardia*** danger point; AUTO ~ ***dell'olio*** oil level; *fig* ***ad altissimo*** ~ first-class, first-rate; ***sopra il*** ~ ***del mare*** above sea level; ~ ***di vita*** standard of living
lividezza *f* lividness
livido I *adj* livid; *braccio*, *viso* black and blue; *occhio* black; *per il freddo* blue; ***labbra*** *fpl* **-e** lips blue with cold; ***faccia -a di paura*** ashen-faced with fear **II** *m* bruise; ***farsi un*** ~ bruise o.s.
livore *m* resentment
livornese I *adj* from Livorno **II** *m/f* person from Livorno
livrea *f* livery; ZOOL plumage
lizza *f*: ***entrare*** / ***scendere in*** ~ enter the lists
lo I *art msg* the **II** *pron msg* him; *cosa*, *animale* it; ***non*** ~ ***so*** I don't know
lobbista *m/f* ⟨*mpl* -i⟩ lobbyist
lobby *f* ⟨*pl* lobby⟩ lobby
lobelia *f* BOT lobelia
lobo *m* lobe; ~ ***dell'orecchio*** ear-lobe; ~ ***polmonare*** lobe of lung

lobotomia *f* lobotomy
locale I *adj* local; MED ***anestesia*** *f* ~ local an(a)esthetic; ***stampa*** *f* ~ local press; ***ora*** *f* ~ local time; ***treno*** *m* ~ local train **II** *m* room; *luogo pubblico* place; RAIL local train; ~ ***notturno*** nightclub
località *f* ⟨*pl* località⟩ town; ~ ***balneare*** seaside resort; ~ ***turistica*** tourist resort
localizzabile *adj* locatable
localizzare *v/t* ⟨1a⟩ locate; (*delimitare*) localize; ~ ***un GSM*** TEL locate a GSM cellphone
localizzazione *f* location; COMPUT localization
localmente *adv* locally
locanda *f* inn
locandiere *m*, **-a** *f* innkeeper
locandina *f* THEAT playbill
locare *v/t* ⟨1d⟩ rent
locatario *m*, **-a** *f* ⟨*mpl* -ri⟩ tenant
locativo I *adj* JUR rent(al); ***valore*** *m* ~ rental value⟩ **II** *n*: ***locativo*** *m* GRAM locative
locatore *m*, **-trice** *f* landlord; *donna* landlady
locazione *f* rental; ***dare in*** ~ rent out, let out; ***contratto*** *m* ***di*** ~ lease; ***prendere in*** ~ lease
locco *adj* ⟨*mpl* -cchi⟩ *reg* tawny owl; *fig* twit
locomotiva *f* locomotive
locomotore *m*, **-trice** *f* locomotive
locomotorio *adj* ⟨*mpl* -ri⟩ locomotive
locomozione *f* locomotion; ***mezzo*** *m* ***di*** ~ means *sg* of transport
loculo *m* burial cell; ANAT loculus
locusta *f* locust
locuzione *f* fixed expression
lodare *v/t* ⟨1c⟩ praise
lode *f* praise; ***prendere trenta e*** ~ get full marks; ***tessere le -i di qn*** sing s.o.'s praises
loden *m* ⟨*pl* loden⟩ loden *m*
lodevole *adj* praiseworthy, laudable
lodevolmente *adv* commendably
lodge *m* ⟨*pl* lodge⟩ lodge
lodigiano I *adj* from Lodi **II** *m*, **-a** *f* person from Lodi
lodo *m*: ~ ***arbitrale*** arbitration ruling
loft *m* ⟨*pl* loft⟩ loft
logaritmico *adj* ⟨*mpl* -ci⟩ logarithmic; ***tavole*** *fpl* ***-e*** logarithm tables
logaritmo *m* logarithm
loggia *f* ⟨*pl* -gge⟩ loggia
loggione *m* THEAT gallery
logica *f* logic; ***a rigor di*** ~ logically speaking
logicamente *adv* logically
logico *adj* ⟨*mpl* -ci⟩ logical
login *m* log-in; COMPUT ***fare il*** ~ log in
logistica *f* ⟨*pl* -che⟩ logistics **logistico** *adj* ⟨*mpl* -ci⟩ logistic
loglio *m* ⟨*pl* -gli⟩ BOT ryegrass; *fig* ***separare il grano dal*** ~ separate the wheat from the chaff
logo *m* ⟨*pl* logo⟩ logo
logopedia *f* speech therapy
logopedista *m/f* ⟨*mpl* -i⟩ speech therapist
logoramento *m* deterioration; *fig* wear (and tear); *di nervi*: wear; ***segni*** *mpl* ***di*** ~ signs of wear and tear
logorante *adj* back-breaking; ***un'attesa*** ~ a nerve-racking wait
logorare *v/t* ⟨1l⟩ wear out; ~ ***i nervi*** wear one's nerves down
logorarsi *v/r* ⟨1l⟩ wear down / out; *fig* ~ ***per qc*** wear oneself out / down for sth
logorio *m* wear and tear
logoro *adj indumento* worn (out), threadbare; ***idee*** *fpl* / ***frasi*** *fpl* ***-e*** worn-out ideas / phrases
logorrea *f* longwindedness
logorroico *adj* ⟨*mpl* -ci⟩ longwinded
logotipo *m* logotype
logout *m* ⟨*pl* logout⟩ logout⟩
logudorese I *adj* from the region of Logudoro **II** *m/f* person from Logudoro
Loira *f* Loire
lolita *f* nymphet
lolla *f* chaff
lombaggine *f* lumbago
Lombardia *f* Lombardy
lombardo I *adj* of Lombardy **II** *m*, **-a** *f* native of Lombardy
lombare *adj* lumbar
lombata *f* loin
lombo *m* loin
lombrico *m* ⟨*pl* -chi⟩ earthworm
londinese I *adj persona* from London; *bus* London **II** *m/f* Londoner
Londra *f* London
longanimità *f* ⟨*pl* longanimità⟩ (*clemenza*) indulgence; (*pazienza*) tolerance
long drink *m* ⟨*pl* long drink⟩ long

drink
longevità *f* ⟨*pl* longevità⟩ longevita
longevo *adj* longlived
longherina *f* BUILD stringer; RAIL sleeper **longherone** *m* AVIAT stringer
longilineo *adj* long-limbed
longitudinale *adj* longitudinal
longitudine *f* GEOG longitude
longobardo I *adj* Longobard, Lombard **II** *m*, **-a** *f* ⟨Longobard, Lombard
long-playing, long play *m* ⟨*pl* long-playing, long play⟩ long-playing, LP⟩
lontanamente *adv* vaguely; ***non ci penso neanche ~*** I wouldn't dream of it
lontananza *f* distance; *tra persone* separation; ***in ~*** distant
lontano I *adj* far; *nel tempo* far-off; *passato*, *futuro*, *parente* distant; ***alla -a*** *concoscere* vaguely, slightly; ***siamo cugini alla -a*** we're distant cousins **II** *adv* far (away); ***da ~*** from a distance; ***abita molto ~?*** do you live very far away?; ***tenersi ~ da qn*** steer clear of s.o.; ***alla -a*** distant(ly); ***andare ~*** go far away; ⟨(*avere successo*) go far; ***~ dagli occhi, ~ dal cuore*** out of sight, out of mind
lontra *f* otter
lonza *f* COOK loin of pork
look *m* ⟨*pl* look⟩ look; ***cambiare ~*** have a new look
loop *m* ⟨*pl* loop⟩ COMPUT loop
looping *m* ⟨*pl* looping⟩ looping the loop
loquace *adj* talkative
loquacemente *adv* loquaciously **loquacità** *f* ⟨*pl* loquacità⟩ loquaciousness
lordare *v/t* ⟨1a⟩ dirty **lordarsi** *v/r* ⟨1a⟩: ***~ di qc*** dirty oneself with sth
lordo *adj* dirty; *peso*, *reddito etc* gross; ***incasso*** *m* ***~*** gross proceeds; ***stipendio*** *m* ***~*** gross wage
lordosi *f* ⟨*pl* lordosi⟩ lordosis
lordume *m* filth
Lorena *f* Lorraine
lorenese I *adj* from Lorraine **II** *m/f* person from Lorraine
Lorenzo *m*: ***San ~*** Saint Lawrence
loro I *pron soggetto* they; *oggetto* them; *forma di cortesia*, *a*. **Loro** you **II** *possessivo* their; *forma di cortesia*, *a*. **Loro** your; ***il ~ amico*** their/your friend; ***i ~ genitori*** their/your parents **III** *pron*: ***il ~*** theirs; *forma di cortesia*, *a*. **Loro** yours
losanga *f* ⟨*pl* -ghe⟩ lozenge
Losanna *f* Lausanne
losco *adj* ⟨*mpl* -chi⟩ suspicious; ***un affare ~*** a dirty business; ***un tipo ~*** a suspicious character
loto *m*: ***fior*** *m* ***di ~*** lotus flower
lotta *f* struggle; SPORTS wrestling; *fig* fight; ***~ biologica*** AGR biological struggle; ***~ contro la droga*** fight against drugs; ***~ di classe*** class struggle; ***~ greco-romana*** Graeco-Roman wrestling; ***~ integrata*** AGR integrated struggle; ***~ libera*** all-in wrestling; ***~ senza quartiere*** no-holds-barred fighting; ***fare la ~*** wrestle; ***~ sindacale*** union struggle
lottare *v/i* ⟨1c⟩ wrestle, struggle (***con*** with); *fig* fight (***contro*** against; ***per*** for); ***~ corpo a corpo*** hand-to-hand fighting
lottatore *m*, **-trice** *f* wrestler
lotteria *f* lottery; ***biglietto*** *m* ***della ~*** lottery ticket; ***vincere alla ~*** win the lottery
lottizzare *v/t* ⟨1a⟩ lot; ***~ un terreno*** divide a plot of land into lots; POL ***~ le reti televisive*** carve up the television channels
lottizzazione *f di terreno* parcelling out; POL carve-up
lotto *m* lottery; *di terreno* plot; ***estrazioni*** *fpl* ***del ~*** lottery draw; ***giocare al ~*** play the lottery
lozione *f* lotion; ***~ da barba*** shaving lotion; ***~ dopobarba*** aftershave; ***~ per capelli*** hair lotion
LP *m abbr* (= **Long Playing**) LP
LSD *m* LSD, *fam.* acid
L.st. *abbr* (= **lira sterlina**) £ (pound)
LT *abbr* (= **Latina**) Latina
LU *abbr* (= **Lucca**) Lucca
lubrico *adj* ⟨*mpl* -ci⟩ LIT *fig* slippery
lubrificante *m* lubricant; AUTO lubricating oil
lubrificare *v/t* ⟨1m & d⟩ lubricate
Luca *m*: ***San ~*** Saint Luke; ***l'evangelista ~*** St. Luke the Evangelist
Lucania *f* Basilicata
lucano I *adj* from Basilicata **II** *m*, **-a** *f* person from Basilicata
lucchese I *adj* from Lucca **II** *m/f* person from Lucca
lucchetto *m* padlock

luccicante *adj* sparkling
luccicare *v/i* ⟨11 & d⟩ sparkle; ***gli luccicano gli occhi*** his eyes are shining
luccichio *m* sparkle
luccicone *m* tear-drop
luccio *m* ⟨*pl* -cci⟩ pike
lucciola *f* glowworm; *fig* ***prendere -e per lanterne*** get (hold of) the wrong end of the stick
luce *f* light; ***~ al neon*** neon light; AUTO ***-i*** *pl* ***di posizione*** side lights; ***-i*** *pl* ***posteriori*** rear lights; ***cinema*** *m* ***a -i rosse*** porn cinema; ***dare alla ~ un figlio*** give birth to a son; *fig* ***far ~ su qc*** shed light on sth; *fig* ***fare tutto alla ~ del sole*** do things above board; ***mettere qc in buona / cattiva ~*** show sth in a good / bad light; ***è andata via la ~*** the electricity's gone off
lucente *adj* shining, gleaming
lucentezza *f* shininess
lucerna *f* oil-lamp
Lucerna *f* Lucerne
lucernario *m* ⟨*pl* -ri⟩ skylight
lucertola *f* lizard
Lucia *f*: ***Santa ~*** Saint Lucy
lucidalabbra *m* ⟨*pl* lucidalabbra⟩ lip-gloss
lucidamente *adv* clearly; ***ragionare ~*** reason clearly **lucidante** *m* polish
lucidare *v/t* ⟨11⟩ polish; *disegno* trace; ***~ l'argenteria*** polish the silver; ***~ i mobili*** polish the furniture; ***~ il pavimento*** polish the floor; ***~ le scarpe*** clean the shoes
lucidatrice *f* floor polisher
lucidatura *f di mobili*: polishing; *di metallo*: polishing
lucidità *f* (*acutezza*) clearheadedness; (*stato di coscienza*) lucidity
lucido I *adj superficie*, *scarpe* shiny; PHOT glossy; *persona* lucid **II** *m* polish; *disegno* transparency; ***~ da scarpe*** shoe polish; ***~ per mobili*** furniture polish
Lucifero *m* Lucifer, Satan
lucignolo *m* wick
lucioperca *m or f* ⟨*fpl* -che⟩ *f* pike-perch
lucrare *v/t* ⟨1a⟩ profit financially
lucrativo *adj* lucrative
lucro *m*: ***a scopo di ~*** profit-making; ***senza fini / scopo di ~*** non-profit-making
lucculliano *adj* lavish
ludico *adj*: ***attività*** *fpl* ***-che*** games
ludoteca *f* toy library
luganiga *f*, **luganega** *f* ⟨*pl* -ghe⟩ COOK long sausage
luglio *m* July; ***a metà ~*** in mid-July
lugubre *adj* sombre, *US* somber, lugubrious
lugubremente *adv* gloomily
lui *pron msg soggetto* he; *oggetto* him; ***a ~*** to him; ***~ stesso*** himself
Luigi *m*: ***San ~*** Saint Louis
LUISS *abbr* (= **Libera Università Internazionale degli Studi Sociali**) *private university in Rome*
lumaca *f* ⟨*pl* -che⟩ slug; ***a passo di ~*** at a snail's pace
lume *m* (*lampada*) lamp; *luce* light; ***cenare a ~ di candela*** have a candle-lit dinner; ***chiedere -i a qn*** pick s.o.'s brains; *fig* ***perdere il ~ della ragione*** lose one's mind; ***a ~ di naso*** by intuition
lumicino *m* small light; *fig* ***essere*** (***ridotto***) ***al ~*** be at death's door **luminare** *m fig* luminary **luminaria** *f* illuminations **luminescente** *adj* luminescent; ***sostanza ~*** luminescent substance **luminescenza** *f* luminescence
lumino *m* grave-light
luminosità *f* luminosity; PHOT speed
luminoso *adj* luminous; *stanza* bright, full of light; ***sorgente*** *f* ***-a*** light source; ***sorriso*** *m* ***~*** radiant smile; ***stanza*** *f* ***-a*** light-filled room; ***idea*** *f* ***-a*** a brilliant idea; ***insegna*** *f* ***-a*** neon sign
luna *f* **1.** moon; ***~ crescente / calante*** crescent / waning moon; ***~ di miele*** honeymoon; ***~ piena*** full moon; ***chiaro*** *m* ***di ~*** moonlight **2.** *fig* ***avere la ~ storta*** be in a mood
luna-park *m* ⟨*pl* luna-park⟩ amusement park, *Br* funfair
lunare *adj* lunar; ***paesaggio*** *m* ***~*** moonscape
lunario *m*: ***sbarcare il ~*** make ends meet
lunatico *adj* ⟨*mpl* -ci⟩ moody
lunedì *m* ⟨*pl* lunedì⟩ Monday; ***il*** *or* ***di ~*** on Mondays; ***~ dell'Angelo*** Easter Monday
lunetta *f* ARCH lunette
lungaggine *f* slowness; ***-i*** *pl* ***burocratiche*** bureaucratic hold-ups

lungamente *adv* for a long time
lunghezza *f* length; **~ *d'onda*** wavelength; ***10 metri di ~*** 10 metres long; ***vincere per una ~*** win by a length
lungi *adv liter* far; **~ *da me una simile idea!*** I wouldn't dream of it!
lungimirante *adj* far-sighted **lungimiranza** *f* far-sightedness
lungo ⟨*mpl* -ghi⟩ **I** *adj* long; *caffè* weak; ***non essere ~!*** don't be long!, don't take forever!; ***a ~*** at length, for a long time; *fig* ***alla -a*** in the long run; ***andare per le -ghe*** drag on; ***di gran -a*** by far; ***saperla -a su qc*** know all about sth; ***di -a data*** old, long-standing, long-established **II** *prep* along; (*durante*) throughout; **~ *la strada*** up the street; ***in ~ e in largo*** far and wide; ***a ~ termine*** long-term; ***più a ~*** longer; ***a ~ andare*** in the long run; ***questo la dice -a sul suo carattere*** that speaks volumes about his character; ***farla -a*** *infml* go on about sth
lungodegenza *f* long hospitalization
lungofiume *m* riverbank; ***sul ~*** on the riverside
lungolago *m* ⟨*pl* -ghi⟩ lakeside, lakeshore
lungomare *m* ⟨*pl* lungomare⟩ sea front
lungometraggio *m* ⟨*pl* -ggi⟩ feature-length film
lunotto *m* AUTO rear window; **~ *termico*** heated rear window
luogo *m* ⟨*pl* -ghi⟩ place; **~ *comune*** cliché; **~ *di culto*** cult venue; ***il ~ del delitto*** the scene of the crime; **~ *di nascita*** birthplace, place of birth; ***avere ~*** take place, be held; ***dare ~ a*** cause; ***essere del ~*** be a local; ***fuori ~*** out of place; ***in nessun ~*** nowhere; ***sul ~*** on the spot; ***il non ~ a procedere*** JUR non suit; ***in ~ di*** instead of; ***in primo ~*** in the first place; ***in qualche ~*** somewhere, someplace
luogotenente *m* MIL lieutenant
lupacchiotto *m*, **-a** *f* wolf cub
lupanare *m* brothel
lupara *f* sawn-off shotgun; **~ *bianca*** *used in newspapers to describe a mafia-type killing where no body is found*
lupetto *m* (*scout*) cub (scout)
lupino *m* lupino
lupo *m*, **-a** *f* wolf; **~ *mannaro*** *sl* werewolf; **~ *di mare*** sea dog; ***cane ~*** German shepherd (dog); ***in bocca al ~!*** break a leg!; ***Lupi grigi*** POL Grey Wolves; ***tempo*** *m* ***da -i*** brass-monkey weather; ***il ~ perde il pelo ma non il vizio*** *prov* a leopard cannot change its spots
luppolo *m* hops *pl*
lupus *m* ⟨*no pl*⟩ MED lupus
lupus in fabula *adv* talk of the devil
lurido *adj* filthy
luridume *m* filth
lurker *m/f* ⟨*pl* lurker⟩ COMPUT lurker
lusinga *f* ⟨*pl* -ghe⟩ flattery
lusingare *v/t* ⟨1e⟩ flatter
lusingato *adj*: ***sentirsi ~*** feel flattered
lusinghiero *adj* flattering
lusitano *hist* **I** *adj* Lusitanian, Portuguese **II** *m*, **-a** *f* person from Lusitania, Portugal
lussare *v/t* ⟨1a⟩ dislocate **lussarsi** *v/r* ⟨1a⟩ dislocate
lussazione *f* dislocation
lussemburghese **I** *adj* Luxembourgian **II** *m/f* Luxembourgian
Lussemburgo *m* Luxembourg
lusso *m* luxury; ***albergo*** *m* ***di ~*** luxury hotel; ***ci è andata di ~*** we had a narrow escape
lussuosamente *adv* luxuriously
lussuoso *adj* luxurious
lussureggiante *adj* lush; ***vegetazione*** *f* **~** lush vegetation; ***stile*** *m* **~** florid style
lussuria *f* lust **lussurioso** *adj* lustful
lustrare *v/t* ⟨1a⟩ polish; *fig* ***non essere degno di ~ le scarpe a qn*** be inferior to s.o.; *fig* ***lustrarsi gli occhi*** feast one's eyes (on)
lustrascarpe *m* ⟨*pl* lustrascarpe⟩ shoeshine boy; *fig* crawler
lustrata *f*: ***dare una ~ a qc*** tell s.o. off
lustrino *m* sequin
lustro *m* shine, lustre, *US* luster; *fig* prestige; (*periodo*) five-year period
lustro[2] **I** *adj argenteria* shiny; *capelli* glossy; ***occhi*** *mpl* ***-i*** shining eyes **II** *n*: ***lustro*** *m* shine; ***dare ~ a qc*** give sth a polish
luteranesimo *m* Lutheranism **luterano** **I** *adj* Lutheran **II** *m*, **-a** *f* Lutheran
Lutero *m* (Martin) Luther
lutto *m* mourning; ***essere in ~*** be in mourning; ***portare il ~*** wear mourn-

ing; ***chiuso per ~*** closed due to mourning; ***dichiarare il ~ nazionale*** announce a national day of mourning; ***parare a ~*** deck in mourning

luttuoso *adj* mournful; ***notizia*** *f* ***-a*** sad news

M

m, M *m/f* ⟨*pl* m, M⟩ m, M; ***M come Milano*** M for Mike

m *abbr* (= **metro**) m (metre)

ma *cj* but; (*eppure*) and yet; ***~ cosa dici?*** what are you talking about?; ***~ va!*** nonsense!; ***~ no!*** not at all!, of course not!

macabro *adj* macabre

macaco *m* ⟨*pl* -chi⟩ macaque; *pej* twit

macaone *m* swallowtail

macché *int* of course not

maccheroni *mpl* macaroni *sg*; ***come il cacio sui ~*** *hum* just the job

maccheronico *adj* ⟨*mpl* -ci⟩: ***parlare un inglese ~*** speak broken English

macchia *f* spot; *di sporco* stain; (*bosco*) scrub; ***~ mediterranea*** maquis; ***~ d'olio*** oil stain; ***allargarsi / diffondersi a ~ d'olio*** spread like wildfire; *fig* ***darsi alla ~*** go into hiding; (***non***) ***avere -e sulla coscienza*** have a troubled / clean conscience

macchiaiolo *m* PAINT *painter adhering to the movement begun in 19th century Florence*

macchiare *v/t* ⟨1k⟩ stain, mark

macchiarsi *v/r* stain; ***~ di una colpa / un delitto*** dirty one's hands with a sin / a crime

macchiato *adj* stained; ***caffè*** *m* ***~*** *espresso with a splash of milk*; ***~ di sugo*** stained with tomato sauce

macchietta *f* speck; THEAT character part; *fig* eccentric **macchiettista** *m/f* ⟨*mpl* -i⟩ character actor

macchina[1] *f* machine; *fig* machinery; ***~ da caffè*** coffee machine; ***~ da cucire*** sewing machine; ***~ fotografica*** camera; ***~ da presa*** cine camera; ***~ da scrivere*** typewriter; ***~ sportiva*** sports car; ***fatto a ~*** machine made

macchina[2] *f* (*auto*) car; ***~ a noleggio*** hire car, rental car; ***andare in ~*** drive, go by car

macchinare *v/t* ⟨1l⟩ scheme; ***~ qc contro qn*** brew up sth against s.o.

macchinario *m* ⟨*pl* -ri⟩ machinery

macchinazione *f* machination

macchinetta *f* machine; ***~ del caffè*** coffee-maker **macchinina** *f* small car

macchinista *m* ⟨*pl* -i⟩ RAIL train driver; FILM, THEAT stagehand

macchinoso *adj* over-complicated

macedone I *adj* Macedonian **II** *m/f* Macedonian

macedonia *f*: ***~*** (***di frutta***) fruit salad

macellaio *m*, **-a** *f* ⟨*mpl* -ai⟩ butcher

macellare *v/t* ⟨1b⟩ butcher

macellazione *f* slaughter

macelleria *f* butcher's

macello *m* slaughterhouse; (*carneficina*) carnage; *infml* (*finimondo*) disaster; *infml* (*confusione*) shambles *sg*; ***c'era un ~ di gente*** there were masses of people; ***bestie*** *fpl* ***da ~*** animals for slaughter; *fig* ***carne*** *f* ***da ~*** *pej* cannon fodder

macerare *v/t* ⟨1l⟩ marinade; BIOL, CHEM macerate; ***lasciar ~ nell'alcol*** steep in alcohol **macerarsi** *v/r* ⟨1l⟩ waste away; *fig* torture oneself

maceratese I *adj* from Macerata **II** *m/f* person from Macerata

macerazione *f* maceration

macerie *fpl* rubble *sg*

macero *m* steeping; ***mandare qc al ~*** pulp

machete *m* machete

machiavellico *adj* ⟨*mpl* -ci⟩ Machiavellian, scheming

macho I *adj inv* macho **II** *m* macho (man)

macigno *m* boulder

macilento *adj* gaunt

macina *f* grinder; (*mola*) grindstone

macinacaffè *m* ⟨*pl* macinacaffè⟩ coffee mill, coffee grinder

macinapepe *m* ⟨*pl* macinapepe⟩ pep-

per mill, pepper grinder
macinare *v/t* ⟨1l⟩ grind
macinato *adj* ground; ***pepe*** *m* **~** ground pepper; ***carne*** *f* ***-a*** minced meat
macinatura *f* grinding **macinazione** *f* grinding
macinino *m* mill; *hum* old banger
maciste *m*: ***essere un*** **~** be a hulk
maciullare *v/t* ⟨1a⟩ TEX scutch; (*stritolare*) mangle
macramè *m* ⟨*pl* macramè⟩ macramé
macrobiotica *f* health food; ***negozio*** *m* ***di*** **~** health food shop
macrobiotico *adj* ⟨*mpl* -ci⟩ macrobiotic; ***dieta*** *f* ***-a*** a macrobiotic diet
macrocefalo **I** *adj* macrocephalic **II** *m*, **-a** *f* a person with macrocephalia
macrocosmo *m* macrocosm
macroeconomia *f* macroeconomics *sg* **macroeconomico** *adj* ⟨*mpl* -ci⟩ macroeconomic
macroscopico *adj* ⟨*mpl* -ci⟩ *fig* huge, enormous; *errore* monumental, colossal
macrosistema *m* ⟨*pl* -i⟩ macrosystem
macrostruttura *f* macrostructure
maculato *adj* spotted **maculatura** *f* maculation
Madagascar *m* Madagascar
madama *f* madam; *sl* (*polizia*) fuzz
made in Italy *m* ⟨*no pl*⟩ made in Italy
madia *f* wooden bread-bin
madido *adj*: **~** ***di sudore*** soaked with sweat
Madonna *f* Madonna, Our Lady; PAINT **~** ***con bambino*** Madonna and Child
madonnaro *m*, **-a** *f pavement artist specializing in sacred images*
madornale *adj* massive; ***un errore*** **~** a blunder *infml*
madre *f* mother; ***ragazza*** **~** single mother; ***casa*** **~** parent company; ***fare da*** **~** ***a qn*** mother s.o.
madrelingua **I** *adj inv*: ***insegnante*** *m/f* **~** mother-tongue teacher **II** *f* mother tongue **III** *m/f* ⟨*pl* madrelingua⟩ native speaker; ***un*** **~** ***inglese*** a native speaker of English
madrepatria *f* native land, mother country
madreperla *f* mother-of-pearl
madrepora *f* madrepore
madrevite *f* nut
madrigale *m* madrigal
madrileno **I** *adj* from / of Madrid **II** *m*, **-a** *f* person from Madrid
madrina *f* godmother; **~** ***di battesimo*** godmother
MAE *abbr* (= **Ministero degli Affari Esteri**) Foreign Ministry
maestà *f* majesty; ***Sua Maestà*** Her Majesty
maestosamente *adv* majestically **maestosità** *f* ⟨*pl* maestosità⟩ majesty
maestoso *adj* majestic; MUS maestoso
maestrale *m* north-west wind
maestranze *fpl* workers *pl*
maestria *f* mastery
maestro **I** *m*, **-a** *f* teacher; **~** ***di nuoto*** swimming teacher *or* instructor; **~** ***di sci*** ski instructor **II** *m* master; MUS, PAINT maestro, master; ***colpo*** *m* ***da*** **~** masterstroke; **~** ***d'ascia*** shipwright; **~** ***di cerimonie*** master of ceremonies, MC **III** *adj* (*principale*) main; NAUT ***albero*** *m* **~** main mast; ***muro*** *m* **~** load-bearing wall; ***strada*** *f* ***-a*** main road
mafia *f* Mafia
mafioso **I** *adj* Mafia **II** *m*, **-a** *f* Mafioso
maga *f* witch
magagna *f* defect
magari **I** *adv* maybe, perhaps **II** *int*: **~!** if only! **III** *cj*: **~** ***venisse*** if only he would come
magazzinaggio *m* storage
magazziniere *m*, **-a** *f* warehouseman, storeman
magazzino *m* warehouse; *di negozio* stock room; (*emporio*) factory shop; ***grandi -i*** *pl* department stores
magenta *m* ⟨*pl* magenta⟩ magenta
maggese *m* fallow; ***tenere un campo a*** **~** keep a field fallow
maggio *m* May
maggiolino *m* June bug, May beetle
maggiorana *f* marjoram
maggioranza *f* majority; **~** ***assoluta*** absolute majority; **~** ***azionaria*** majority shareholding; ***a larga*** **~** by a large majority; ***voto di*** **~** majority vote; **~** ***qualificata*** POL qualified majority; **~** ***silenziosa*** silent majority
maggiorare *v/t* ⟨1a⟩ increase
maggiorazione *f* increase
maggiordomo *m* butler
maggiore **I** *adj* bigger; (*più vecchio*) older; MUS major; ***il*** **~** the biggest; *figlio* the oldest; *artista* the greatest;

azionista the major, the largest; ***la maggior parte del tempo / di noi*** most of the time / of us, the majority of the time / of us; ***andare per la ~*** be a crowd pleaser **II** *m* MIL major; ***do*** *m* ~ C major; ~ ***età*** age of consent; ***a maggior ragione*** (with) all the more reason); ***andare per la ~*** be popular

maggiorenne *adj* adult *attr*

maggiorente *m/f* worthy

maggioritario *adj* ⟨*mpl* -ri⟩ majority; ***sistema*** *m* ~ first-past-the-post system

maggiormente *adv* (*di più*) more; (*principalmente*) mainly

mag(h)rebino **I** *adj* Maghrebi **II** *m*, **-a** *f* Maghrebi

magia *f* magic; ~ ***nera*** black magic; ***come per ~*** as if by magic; ***fare una ~ a qn*** cast a spell on s.o.

magiaro **I** *adj* Magyar, Hungarian **II** *m*, **-a** *f* Hungarian

magico *adj* ⟨*mpl* -ci⟩ magic(al)

magistero *m* (*professione*) teaching; (*abilità*) skill; ***il ~ pontificio*** Papal teaching

magistrale *adj* (*eccellente*) masterful; ***istituto*** *m* ~ teacher training college

magistralmente *adv* skilfully

magistrato *m* JUR magistrate; ~ ***di sorveglianza*** surveillance magistrate

magistratura *f* magistrature; ~ ***inquirente*** investigating magistrature; ~ ***ordinaria*** court of law

maglia *f* **1.** top; (*maglione*) sweater; SPORTS shirt, jersey; SPORTS ~ ***gialla*** yellow jersey **2.** *ai ferri* stitch; ***lavorare a ~*** knit; ***lavorare a ~ rasata*** knit in stocking stitch

magliaro *m fig* swindler

maglieria *f* knitwear

maglierista *m/f* ⟨*mpl* -i⟩ knitter

maglietta *f* tee-shirt

maglificio *m* ⟨*pl* -ci⟩ knitwear factory

maglio *m* ⟨*mpl* -i⟩ mallet; *nell'hockey*: stick

maglione *m* sweater

magma *m* ⟨*pl* -i⟩ magma (*a. fig*)

magnaccia *m* ⟨*pl* magnaccia⟩ *sl* pimp

magnanimamente *adv* magnanimously

magnanimità *f* ⟨*pl* magnanimità⟩ magnanimity

magnanimo *adj* magnanimous

magnesia *f* magnesia

magnesio *m* magnesium

magnete *m* magnet

magnetico *adj* ⟨*mpl* -ci⟩ magnetic; *fig* ***sguardo*** *m* ~ magnetic eyes; ***ago*** *m* ~ magnetic needle ***sguardo*** *m* ~ hypnotic stare

magnetismo *m* magnetism; *fig* attraction **magnetizzare** *v/t* ⟨1a⟩ magnetize (*a. fig*) **magnetizzazione** *f* magnetization **magnetofono** *m* magnetophone *n*

magnetofono *m* video recorder

magnificamente *adv* magnificently **magnificare** *v/t* ⟨1m & d⟩ extol **magnificenza** *f* magnificence

magnifico *adj* ⟨*mpl* -ci⟩ magnificent; ***Lorenzo il Magnifico*** Lorenzo the Magnificent; ***Magnifico Rettore*** *m* UNIV Vice-Chancellor

magniloquente *adj oratore* grandiloquent; *stile* pompous **magniloquenza** *f* grandiloquence

magno *adj* great; ***aula*** *f* **-a** auditorium; ***Magna Grecia*** Magna Graecia

magnolia *f* magnolia

mago *m* ⟨*pl* -ghi⟩ wizard

magone *m*: ***avere il ~*** have the blues

magra *f* low water; ***tempi*** *mpl* ***di ~*** shortage; ***fare una ~*** make a poor impression

Magreb *m* Maghreb

magrezza *f* thinness

magro *adj* thin; *cibo* low in fat; *fig consolazione* small; *guadagno* meagre, *US* meager; *fig* ***una -a consolazione*** cold comfort; ***mangiare di ~*** not eat meat; ***carne*** *f* **-a** lean meat; ~ ***come un'acciuga*** as thin as a rail

magrolino *adj* skinny

mai *adv* never; (*qualche volta*) ever; ~ ***più*** never again; ***più che ~*** more than ever; ***non accetterò ~ e poi ~*** I will never agree, never; ***caso ~*** in case; ***chi l'avrebbe ~ detto?*** who ever would have thought it?; ***chi ha ~ detto che …*** who said that …; ***come ~?*** how come?; ***come non ~*** like never before; ***dove / perché ~?*** where / why on earth?; ***più che ~*** more than ever; ***se ~*** if ever; ***meglio tardi che ~*** better late than never; ***non è ~ contento*** he's never happy; ~ ***dire ~*** never say never

maialata *f infml* smutty behaviour

maiale *m* pig; (***carne*** *f* ***di***) **~** pork
maialino *m* piglet
mail *f* email
mailbox *f* ⟨*pl* mailbox⟩ COMPUT mailbox
maiolica *f* ⟨*pl* -che⟩ majolica
maionese *f* mayonnaise
mais *m* maize
maiuscola *f* capital (letter)
maiuscolo *adj* capital; ***scrivere*** (***in***) **~** write in (block) capitals
majorette *f* ⟨*pl* majorette⟩ majorette
mal → ***male***
malaccorto *adj* imprudent
malachite *f* malachite
malacreanza *f* ⟨*pl* malecreanze⟩ rudeness
malafede *f* bad faith; ***agire in* ~** act in bad faith
malaffare *m*: ***di* ~** shady; ***donna*** *f* ***di* ~** a disreputable woman; ***gente*** *f* ***di* ~** crooks
malagevole *adj* difficult
malagrazia *f* bad grace; ***rispondere di* ~** answer with bad grace
malalingua *f* ⟨*pl* malelingue⟩ scandalmonger
malamente *adv* badly; (*sgarbatamente*) rudely; ***lavoro*** *m* ***eseguito* ~** poorly executed work; ***sono caduto* ~** I had a bad fall
malandato *adj vestito*, *divano*, *macchina* dilapidated; *persona* poorly, not very well
malandrino I *adj* dishonest; *hum* mischievous **II** *m*, **-a** *f* crook; *hum* rascal
malanimo *m* ill will; ***con* ~** grudgingly
malanno *m* misfortune; (*malattia*) illness; ***prendersi un* ~** catch one's death (of cold)
malapena *f*: ***a* ~** hardly, barely
malaria *f* malaria
malarico *adj* ⟨*mpl* -ci⟩ malarial; ***febbre*** *f* ***-a*** malaria; ***zona*** *f* ***-a*** malarial zone
malasanità *f used by Italian journalists to describe evidence of how poorly the health service is functioning*
malasorte *f* bad luck
malaticcio *adj* ⟨*mpl* -cci⟩ sickly
malato I *adj* ill; ***essere* ~ *di cuore*** have heart problems; **~ *di mente*** mentally ill; **~ *immaginario*** hypochondriac; **~ *terminale*** terminal patient **II** *m*, **-a** *f* ill person
malattia *f* illness; **~ *infantile*** childhood illness; **~ *infettiva*** infectious disease; ***-e*** *pl* ***della pelle*** skin diseases; ***-e*** *pl* ***veneree*** sexually transmitted diseases; ***essere*** / ***mettersi in* ~** be / go on sick leave
malauguratamente *adv* unfortunately
malaugurato *adj* unfortunate; ***nella -a ipotesi che …*** in the unfortunate event that…
malaugurio *m*: ***uccello*** *m* ***di* ~** jinx
malavita *f* underworld
malavitoso *adj* underworld
malavoglia *f* unwillingness, reluctance; ***di* ~** unwillingly, grudgingly, reluctantly
malcapitato I *adj* unfortunate **II** *m*, **-a** *f* unfortunate individual
malconcio *adj* ⟨*mpl* -ci⟩ *vestito*, *divano*, *macchina* dilapidated, the worse for wear; *persona* poorly, not very well
malcontento I *adj* discontented, dissatisfied **II** *m* discontent
malcostume *m* immorality
maldestro *adj* awkward, clumsy
maldicente I *adj* slanderous **II** *m/f* scandalmonger **maldicenza** *f* scandalmongering
maldisposto *adj*: ***essere* ~ *nei confronti di*** *or* ***verso qn*** be prejudiced against s.o.
Maldive *fpl* Maldives *pl*
maldiviano I *adj* Maldivian **II** *m*, **-a** *f* Maldivian
male I *m* **1.** evil; ***che c'è di* ~?** where's the harm in it?; ***andare a* ~** go off, go bad; ***aversela*** *or* ***prendersela a* ~** take it the wrong way; ***il cioccolato mi fa* ~** chocolate doesn't agree with me; ***fare* ~ *alla salute*** be bad for you **2.** MED ***mal di gola*** sore throat; ***mal di mare*** seasickness; ***mal di testa*** / ***di denti*** headache / toothache; ***far* ~ *a qn*** hurt s.o.; ***mi fa* ~ *il braccio*** my arm hurts; ***farsi* ~** hurt o.s. **II** *adv* badly; ***capire* ~** misunderstand; ***dire* ~ *di qn*** speak ill of s.o.; ***rimanerci* ~** feel bad; ***sentirsi* ~** feel ill; ***stare* ~** (*essere malato*) be ill; (*essere giù*) be depressed; **~ *che vada*** at worst; ***il giallo mi sta* ~** yellow doesn't suit me, I don't suit yellow; ***il divano sta* ~ *qui*** the couch doesn't look right here;

sta ~ … it's not done to …; ***mi ha risposto ~*** he gave me a rude answer; ***di ~ in peggio*** from bad to worse; ***meno ~!*** thank goodness!; ***non farebbe ~ a una mosca*** he wouldn't hurt a fly; ***poco ~!*** It could have been worse! ***mal comune, mezzo gaudio*** *prov* a trouble shared is a trouble halved; ***non tutto il ~ viene per nuocere*** *prov* every cloud has a silver lining; ***non c'è ~*** not bad; ***voler ~ a qn*** wish s.o. harm; ***siamo proprio messi ~*** we're in big trouble; ***le cose si mettono ~*** things are looking bad; ***finire ~*** come to a sticky end; ***niente ~*** not bad; ***mi è andata ~*** it went wrong / badly; ***bene o ~*** one way or another

maledettamente *adv* dreadfully

maledetto I *past part* → ***maledire*** **II** *adj* dratted, damn(ed)

maledire *v/t* ⟨3t⟩ curse

maledizione *f* curse; ***~!*** damn!

maleducatamente *adv* rudely

maleducato *adj* bad-mannered, uncouth

maleducazione *f* rudeness

maleficio *m* ⟨*pl* -ci⟩ spell **malefico** *adj* ⟨*mpl* -ci⟩ harmful; evil

maleodorante *adj* foul-smelling

malerba *f* weed; ***la ~ non muore mai*** *prov* the bad outlive the good

malese I *adj* Malaysian **II** *m/f* Malaysian **Malesia** *f* Malaysia

malessere *m* indisposition; *fig* malaise

malevolenza *f* malevolence **malevolo** *adj* malevolent

malfamato *adj* disreputable

malfatto *adj cosa* badly made

malfattore *m*, **-trice** *f* criminal

malfermo *adj* unsteady; ***essere ~ sulle gambe*** be unsteady on one's legs; ***passo*** *m* ***~*** unsteady step

malfidato I *adj* diffident **II** *m*, **-a** *f* diffident person

malformazione *f* MED, BIOL malformation

malga *f* ⟨*pl* -ghe⟩ alpine grazing; (*baita*) alpine hut

malgarbo *m* rude act; (*sgarbo*) rudeness

malgascio ⟨*mpl* -sci⟩ **I** *adj* Madagascan **II** *m*, **-a** *f* Madagascan

malgoverno *m* POL misgovernment

malgrado I *prep* in spite of, despite **II** *adv*: ***mio / tuo ~*** against my / your will **III** *cj* although

malia *f* spell; *fig* charm **maliarda** *f* enchantress **maliardo** *adj* bewitching

malignamente *adv* wickedly **malignare** *v/i* ⟨1a⟩: ***~ su qn / qc*** gossip about s.o. / sth

malignità *f* ⟨*pl* malignità⟩ malicious remark

maligno *adj* malicious, spiteful; MED malignant; ***il Maligno*** the devil, Satan

malinconia *f* melancholy

malinconicamente *adv* gloomily

malinconico *adj* ⟨*mpl* -ci⟩ melancholic

malincuore *m*: ***a ~*** reluctantly, unwilling

malintenzionato I *adj* shady, suspicious **II** *m*, **-a** *f* shady character

malinteso *m* misunderstanding

malizia *f* (*cattiveria*) malice, spite; (*astuzia*) trick; ***con ~*** maliciously, spitefully; ***le -e del mestiere*** the tricks of the trade

malizioso *adj* malicious, spiteful; *sorriso* mischievous

malleabile *adj* malleable (*a. fig*) **malleabilità** *f* ⟨*pl* malleabilità⟩ malleability

malleolo *m* malleolus

mallevadore *m*, **-drice** *f* guarantor

malleveria *f* surety

mallo *m* husk

malloppo *m* (*refurtiva*) loot

malmenare *v/t* ⟨1a⟩ mistreat

malmesso *adj vestito*, *divano*, *macchina* the worse for wear; ***sono un po' ~*** I'm a bit hard up

malnato *adj* LIT wretched

malnutrito *adj* under-nourished

malnutrizione *f* malnutrition

malo *adj*: ***in ~ modo*** rudely, spitefully

malocchio *f* ⟨*no pl*⟩ evil eye; ***fare il ~*** give the evil eye; ***togliere il ~*** remove the evil eye

malora *f* ruin; ***alla ~!*** to hell with it!; ***andare in ~*** come to grief

malore *m*: ***è stato colto da un ~*** he was suddenly taken ill

malpagato *adj* badly paid

malpartito *m*: ***trovarsi a ~*** have one's back to the wall

malpensante *adj* mean-minded

malridotto *adj* in a sorry state

malriuscito *adj* unsuccessful

malsano *adj* unhealthy; ***clima** m* **~** unhealthy climate
malsicuro *adj* unsafe
malta *f* mortar
maltempo *m* bad weather
maltese I *adj* Maltese **II** *m/f* Maltese
malto *m* malt
maltolto *m* spoils; ***restituire il* ~** hand back the ill-gotten gains
maltosio *m* ⟨*mpl* -i⟩ maltose
maltrattamento *m* ill-treatment; ***subire -i*** be ill-treated
maltrattare *v/t* ⟨1a⟩ mistreat, ill-treat
malumore *m* bad mood; ***essere di* ~** be in a bad mood
malva *f* mallow
malvagiamente *adv* viciously
malvagio *adj* ⟨*mpl* -gi⟩ evil, wicked
malvagità *f* ⟨*pl* malvagità⟩ viciousness
malvasia *f type of dessert wine*
malversare *v/t* ⟨1a⟩ misappropriate; JUR embezzle **malversatore** *m*, **-trice** embezzler **malversazione** *f* misappropriation; JUR embezzlement
malvestito *adj* badly dressed
malvisto *adj* unpopular
malvivente *m* lout
malvolentieri *adv* unwillingly, reluctantly
malvolere *v/t* ⟨2t⟩ dislike; ***farsi* ~ *da qn*** make o.s. unpopular with s.o.
mamma *f* mother, mum; **~ *mia!*** goodness!; ***la festa della* ~** Mother's Day; ***cocco** m **di*** **~** mummy's boy
mammalucco *m* ⟨*pl* -cchi⟩ idiot
mammana *f infml* illegal abortionist; *reg* midwife
mammario *adj* ⟨*mpl* -ri⟩ mammary; ***ghiandole** fpl* **-e** mammary glands
mammella *f* breast
mammellone *m* GEOL mamelon
mammifero *m* mammal
mammismo *m exaggerated attachment to the mother*
mammografia *f* mammography
mammola *f* BOT violet
mammone *m iron* mummy's boy, *US* mama's boy
mammut *m* ⟨*pl* mammut⟩ mammoth
management *m* management
manager *m/f* ⟨*pl* manager⟩ manager
manageriale *adj* managerial, management *attr*; ***capacità** f* **~** managerial ability
manata *f* slap

manca *f* left; ***a destra e a* ~** right, left and centre
mancamento *m* faint
mancante *adj* missing; **~ *di qc*** missing sth
mancanza *f* lack (***di*** of), (*errore*) oversight; **~ *di abitazioni*** housing shortage; **~ *di corrente*** power failure; **~ *di personale*** lack of staff, staff shortage; **~ *di tatto*** tactlessness; ***per* ~ *di tempo*** for lack of time; ***sentire la* ~ *di qn / qc*** miss s.o. / sth; ***in* ~ *di meglio*** for want of anything better
mancare ⟨1d⟩ **I** *v/i* be missing; (*venire meno*) fail; (*morire*) pass away; **~ *di rispetto a qn*** lack of respect towards s.o.; **~ *di qc*** (*non avere*) lack sth, be lacking in sth; **~ *di fare qc*** fail *or* omit to do sth; **~ *di parola*** break one's promise; ***a qn manca qc*** s.o. lacks sth; ***mi mancano le forze*** I don't have the strength; ***mi manca la casa*** I miss home; ***mi manchi molto*** I really miss you; ***mi mancano 500 euro*** I'm 500 euros short; ***manca l'acqua*** there's no water; ***manca la benzina nella macchina*** the car needs filling up; ***manca un quarto alle tre*** it's a quarter to *or US* of three; ***mancano tre mesi a Natale*** it's three months to Christmas; ***quanto manca per arrivare?*** how long till we get there?; ***sentirsi* ~** feel faint; ***non mancherò*** I'll do that, I'll be sure to do it; ***c'è mancato poco che cadesse*** he almost fell; ***ci mancherebbe!*** don't worry about it!; ***ci mancherebbe altro!*** no way!, you must be joking!; ***mi manca il fiato*** I'm breathless; **~ *all'appello*** be missing; ***gli manca la parola*** *hum* he's speechless; ***è mancato poco che cadesse*** he nearly fell; ***non le ho mai fatto* ~ *nulla*** I've never deprived her of anything; ***non manca certo di fantasia*** he has a lively imagination **II** *v/t* miss
mancato *adj occasione* missed, lost; *tentativo* unsuccessful; ***è un poeta* ~** he should have been a poet; **~ *pagamento*** non-payment
mancese I *adj* Manchurian **II** *m/f* Manchu
manche *f* ⟨*pl* manche⟩ SPORTS leg
manchevole *adj* defective
manchevole *adj* faulty, defective

manchevolezza *f* (*scorrettezza*) fault
mancia *f* ⟨*pl* -ce⟩ tip
manciata *f* handful
mancino **I** *adj* left-handed; *fig* ***colpo*** *m* **~** blow beneath the belt, dirty trick **II** *m*, **-a** *f* left-hander
manciù **I** *adj inv* Manchu **II** *m/f* ⟨*pl* manciù⟩ Manchurian
Manciuria *f* Manchuria
manco *adv infml* not even; **~ *a dirlo*** it goes without saying; **~ *per idea!*** absolutely not!; **~ *a farlo apposta*** even if you tried
mandala *m* ⟨*pl* mandala⟩ mandala
mandamentale *adj* relative to a magistracy **mandamento** *m* magistracy
mandante *m/f* JUR client; *infml person who hires a contract killer*; ***il* ~ *dell'omicidio*** instigator of a murder
mandarancio *m* ⟨*pl* -ci⟩ clementine
mandare *v/t* ⟨1a⟩ send; **~ *qn a prendere qc*** send s.o. for sth; **~ *a monte*** ruin, send up in smoke *infml*; **~ *fuori*** send out; *fig* **~ *giù*** digest, take in; **~ *avanti la famiglia*** provide for one's family; **~ *avanti la casa*** run the household; **~ *via*** send away; **~ *a chiamare qn*** send for s.o.; **~ *a dire*** send word round; **~ *al diavolo* / *a quel paese*** tell s.o. to get lost; **~ *in onda*** RADIO, TV air; **~ *in visibilio*** send s.o. into raptures; ***che Dio ce la mandi buona!*** may God help you!
mandarino[1] *m* BOT mandarin (orange)
mandarino[2] *m* (*funzionario*) mandarin; (*lingua*) Mandarin
mandata *f di chiave*: turn of the key; ***chiudere a doppia* ~** double-lock a door
mandatario *m*, **-a** *f* ⟨*mpl* -ri⟩ JUR mandatary
mandato *m* POL mandate; JUR warrant; **~ *bancario*** banker's order; **~ *di cattura*** arrest warrant; **~ *di comparizione*** summons *sg*; **~ *di pagamento*** payment order; **~ *di perquisizione*** search warrant; **~ *d'arresto*** arrest warrant; **~ *parlamentare*** POL parliamentary term of office
mandibola *f* jaw; ANAT mandible
mandibolare *adj* mandibular
mandingo ⟨*pl* mandingo⟩ **I** *adj* Mande **II** *m/f* Mande
mandolino *m* mandolin
mandorla *f* almond; ***occhi*** *mpl* ***a* ~** almond eyes
mandorlato **I** *adj* with almonds; ***cioccolato*** *m* **~** chocolate with almonds **II** *n*: ***mandorlato*** *m* cake with almonds
mandorlo *m* almond tree
mandragola *f* mandrake
mandria *f* herd; ***una* ~ *di buoi*** a herd of oxen; ***una* ~ *di ignoranti*** *pej* a bunch of boors
mandriano *m* cattleman
mandrillo *m* ZOOL mandrill; *fig hum* lecher
mandrino *m* MECH mandrel
maneggevole *adj* easy to handle, manageable
maneggevolezza *f* manageability
maneggiare *v/t* ⟨1f⟩ handle (*a. fig*); **~ *con cura*** handle with care
maneggio *m* ⟨*pl* -ggi⟩ handling; *per cavalli* riding school
manesco *adj* ⟨*mpl* -chi⟩ a bit too ready with one's fists
manette *fpl* handcuffs *pl*; ***mettere le* ~ *a qn*** handcuff s.o.
manforte *f*: ***dare* ~ *a qn*** give s.o. assistance
manfrina *f* (*messinscena*) the same old story; (*lungaggine*) a song and dance about sth
manganellata *f* blow with a truncheon
manganello *m* truncheon
manganese *m* manganese
mangano *m* TEX mangle
mangereccio *adj* ⟨*mpl* -ci⟩ edible; ***funghi*** *mpl* ***-ci*** edible mushrooms
mangiabile *adj* edible
mangiacassette *m* ⟨*pl* mangiacassette⟩ cassette player
mangianastri *m* ⟨*pl* mangianastri⟩ cassette player
mangiapane *m/f*: **~ *a tradimento*** sponger
mangiapreti *m/f* ⟨*pl* mangiapreti⟩ *infml* rabid anticlerical
mangiare **I** *v/t* ⟨1f⟩ eat; *fig* squander; ***far da* ~** cook; ***che c'è di buono da* ~*?*** are we having something nice to eat?; **~ *in bianco*** eat plain food; *fig* **~ *la foglia*** smell a rat; **~ *qn con gli occhi*** devour s.o. with one's eyes; **~ *a ufo*** scrounge a meal **II** *m* food
mangiarino *m infml* titbit
mangiarsi *v/r* fritter away; **~ *le unghie*** bite one's nails; *fig* **~ *le mani*** kick o.s.; **~ *il fegato*** be furious; **~ *le parole***

mumble; ~ ***un'occasione*** throw away *or* waste an opportunity
mangiata *f* huge meal; ***farsi una bella ~*** have a huge meal
mangiatoia *f* trough
mangiatore *m*, **-trice** *f* eater; ***essere un buon ~*** be a big eater; ~ ***di spade*** sword-swallower; **-trice** *f*: ***di uomini*** maneater
mangime *m* fodder
mangiucchiare *v/t* ⟨1g⟩ snack, eat between meals
mango *m* ⟨*pl* -ghi⟩ mango
mangrovia *f* mangrove
mangusta *f* mongoose
mania *f* mania; ~ ***di persecuzione*** persecution complex; ***ha la ~ dell'ordine*** he is obsessively tidy
maniacale *adj* paranoid
maniaco ⟨*mpl* -ci⟩ **I** *adj* manic **II** *m*, **-a** *f* maniac; ~ ***sessuale*** sex maniac; ***~-depressivo*** manic depressive
manica *f* ⟨*pl* -che⟩ sleeve; ***senza -che*** sleeveless; ***a mezze -che*** short-sleeved; ***in -che di camicia*** in one's shirt sleeves; ***è un altro paio di -che!*** that's another kettle of fish; ***rimboccarsi le -che*** roll up one's sleeves; ***essere di ~ larga*** be easy-going; ***una ~ di delinquenti*** a pack of outlaws; ***~ a vento*** wind-sock
Manica *f* GEOG: ***La Manica*** the Channel
manicaretto *m* delicacy
manicheismo *m* Manichaeism **manicheo** **I** *adj* Manichaean **II** *m*, **-a** *f* Manichaean
manichino *m* dummy
manico *m* ⟨*pl* -chi *or* -ci⟩ handle; *di violino* neck; *fig* ***avere il coltello dalla parte del ~*** have the upper hand
manicomio *m* ⟨*pl* -mi⟩ mental home, asylum; ~ ***giudiziario*** *or* ***criminale*** criminal (lunatic) asylum
manicotto *m* TECH sleeve
manicure *f* ⟨*pl* manicure⟩ manicure; (*persona*) manicurist; ***farsi la ~*** have/give oneself a manicure
maniera *f* (*modo*) way, manner; (*stile*) manner; ***di ~ che*** so that; ***-e*** *pl* manners; ***buone/cattive -e*** *pl* good/bad manners; ***che -e!*** what a way to behave!; ***quadro*** *m* ***di ~*** a mannerist painting
manierismo *m* LIT, ART mannerism
manieristico *adj* ⟨*mpl* -ci⟩ manneristic
maniero *m* manor
manifattura *f* manufacture; (*stabilimento*) factory
manifatturiero *adj* manufacturing *attr*; ***industria*** *f* ***-a*** manufacturing industry
manifestamente *adv* openly
manifestante *m/f* demonstrator
manifestare ⟨1b⟩ **I** *v/t* (*esprimere*) express; (*mostrare*) show, demonstrate **II** *v/i* demonstrate
manifestarsi *v/r* appear, show up; *di malattia* manifest itself
manifestazione *f* expression; *il mostrare* show, demonstration; ~ ***di protesta*** demonstration, demo *infml*; ~ ***di affetto*** display of affection; ***la ~ di un fenomeno*** the outbreak of a phenomenon; ~ ***sportiva*** sporting event
manifestino *m* leaflet
manifesto **I** *adj* obvious **II** *m* poster
maniglia *f* handle; *di autobus*, *metro* strap; ***la ~ della finestra*** window handle; ***le -e dell'amore*** *hum* love-handles
manigoldo *m* scoundrel
manioca *f* ⟨*pl* -che⟩ cassava plant
manipolabile *adj* manipulable
manipolare *v/t* ⟨1m⟩ manipulate; *vino* adulterate
manipolato *adj* manipulated; *vino* adulterated; BIOL ~ ***geneticamente*** genetically modified
manipolatore *m*, **-trice** *f* swindler
manipolazione *f* manipulation; *di vino* adulteration; ~ ***genetica*** genetic modification
manipolo *m* HIST maniple; *liter* bundle
maniscalco *m* ⟨*pl* -chi⟩ farrier
manna *f* BOT manna; *fig* godsend; ***aspettare la ~ dal cielo*** wait for pennies from heaven
mannaggia *int* dammit!; ***~ la miseria!*** blast it! ***~ a te!*** blast you!
mannaia *f* axe
mannequin *f* ⟨*pl* mannequin⟩ mannequin
mannite *f* mannite
mano *f* ⟨*pl* -i⟩ **1.** hand; ***tenersi per ~*** hold hands; ***-i in alto!*** hands up! **2.** ***dare una ~ a qn*** give s.o. a hand; ***dare una ~ di vernice a qc*** give sth a coat of paint **3.** *fig* ***a portata di ~*** within

reach; ***di prima ~*** first hand; ***fuori ~*** out of the way, not easy to get at; ***giù le -i*** (***da qc***) hands off (sth); *fig* ***alla ~*** approachable; ***di seconda ~*** second-hand; ***mettere ~ a qc*** start sth; ***lavo le pentole che sporco a ~ a ~*** I wash the dirty pots as I go along; ***man ~ che*** as (and when); ***a quattro -i*** a duet; ***qua la ~!*** let's shake hands!; ***restare a -i vuote*** end up empty-handed; ***toccare con ~*** see for oneself; ***mettersi le -i nei capelli*** be at one's wits' end; ***stare con le -i in ~*** twiddle one's thumbs; ***prendere in ~ la situazione*** take the situation in hand; ***una ~ lava l'altra*** one hand washes the other; ***ha le -i bucate*** money just slips through his fingers; ***avere le -i in pasta*** have a finger in every pie; ***fare man bassa*** make a clean sweep; ***stringere la ~*** shake hands; ***venire alle -i*** come to blows; ***calcare troppo la ~*** be heavy-handed; ***chiedere la ~*** ask for a woman's hand (in marriage); ***mettere le -i avanti*** protect oneself; ***ho le -i legate*** my hands are tied

manodopera *f* labo(u)r; ***il costo della ~*** labo(u)r costs *pl*

manomesso *past part* → ***manomettere***

manometro *m* manometer

manomettere *v/t* ⟨3ee⟩ tamper with

manomissione *f* tampering; ***~ di una prova*** tampering with evidence; ***~ di un plico*** tampering with a parcel

manomorta *f* JUR mortmain; ***fare la ~*** *hum* grope s.o.

manopola *f* knob

manoscritto *m* manuscript

manovalanza *f* unskilled labour

manovale *m* hod carrier

manovella *f* starting handle; TECH crank

manovra *f* manoeuvre, *US* maneuver

manovrabile *adj* manoeuvrable; *fig persona* flexible **manovrabilità** *f* ⟨*pl* manovrabilità⟩ manoeuvrability (*a. fig*)

manovrare ⟨1c⟩ **I** *v/t* TECH operate; RAIL shunt; *fig* manipulate; ***~ le masse*** manipulate the masses **II** *v/i* manoeuvre, *US* maneuver

manovratore *m*, **-trice** *f* (*addetto alle manovre*) manoeuvrer (*a. fig*); RAIL shunter

manrovescio *m* ⟨*pl* -i⟩ backhander

mansarda *f* (*locale*) attic

mansardato *adj*; ***soffitta*** *f* ***-a*** mansarded attic

mansione *f* task; ***svolgere una ~*** carry out a task

mansueto *adj* docile

mansuetudine *f* meekness; *di animale* tameness

manta *f* ZOOL manta (ray)

mantecare *v/t* ⟨1d⟩ cream **mantecato I** *adj* creamed **II** *n*: ***mantecato*** *m* soft ice-cream

mantella *f* cape **mantellina** *f* shoulder cape; MIL mantelet

mantello *m* (*cappa*) cloak; *di animale* coat; (*strato*) covering, layer

mantenere *v/t* ⟨2q⟩ keep; *famiglia* keep, maintain; *in buono stato* maintain; ***~ un segreto*** keep a secret; ***~ le promesse*** keep one's promises; ***~ la parola data*** keep one's word; ***farsi ~ da qn*** live off s.o.

mantenersi *v/r* keep; ***~ in forma*** keep in shape; ***~ da solo*** provide for o.s.; ***~ giovane*** stay young

mantenimento *m* maintenance; *di famiglia* keep; ***assegno*** *m* ***di ~*** alimony cheque

mantenuto *m*, **-a** *f pej* kept man; *donna* kept woman

mantice *m* bellows *pl*

mantide *f* mantis; ***~ religiosa*** praying mantis

mantiglia *f* ⟨*pl* -glie⟩ mantilla

manto *m* cloak; *di animale* coat; ***~ stradale*** road surface; *fig* ***~ di neve*** mantle of snow

Mantova *f* Mantua

mantovana *f di tenda* pelmet

mantovano I *adj* Mantuan **II** *m*, **-a** *f* Mantuan

manuale I *adj* manual **II** *m* manual, handbook

manualistica *f* manuals

manualità *f* ⟨*pl* manualità⟩ manual skill **manualmente** *adv* manually

manubrio *m* ⟨*pl* -ri⟩ handlebars *pl*

manufatto I *adj* handmade **II** *m* artefact

manutenzione *f* maintenance

manzo *m* steer, bullock; *carne* beef

maomettano I *adj* Muslim **II** *m*, **-a** *f* Muslim

Maometto *m* Muhammad
maori ⟨*pl* maori⟩ **I** *adj* Maori **II** *m/f* Maori
mappa *f* map; **~ *catastale*** cadastral survey; **~ *cromosomica*** chromosome map; **~ *genetica*** genetic map
mappamondo *m* globe
mappare *v/t* ⟨1a⟩ map **mappatura** *f* mapping
maquillage *m* ⟨*pl* maquillage⟩ make-up
marachella *f* mischief
maracuja *f* ⟨*pl* maracuja⟩ passion-fruit
maragià *m* ⟨*pl* maragià⟩ maharajah
marameo *int* snook; ***fare ~ a qn*** thumb one's nose at s.o.
maraschino *m* maraschino
marasma *m* ⟨*pl* -i⟩ chaos
maratona *f* marathon
maratoneta *m/f* ⟨*mpl* -i⟩ marathon runner
marca *f* ⟨*pl* -che⟩ brand, make; (*etichetta*) label; **~ *da bollo*** revenue stamp
marcantonio *m* ⟨*pl* -i⟩ *hum* sturdy man
marcare *v/t* ⟨1d⟩ mark; *goal* score
marcato *adj accento, lineamenti* strong
marcatore I *m*, **-trice** *f* SPORTS marker **II** *m* goalscorer; **~ *biologico*** BIOL marker **marcatura** *f* marking; SPORTS defence
marcetta *f* MUS march
Marche *fpl* Marches *pl*
marchese *m*, **-a** *f* marquis; *donna* marchioness
marchetta *f infml* prostitute; ***fare -e*** *infml* hustle
marchiare *v/t* ⟨1k⟩ brand (*a. fig*)
marchiatura *f* branding; **~ *a fuoco*** fire-branding
marchigiano I *adj* of the Marches **II** *m*, **-a** *f* person from the Marches
marchingegno *m* gadget
marchio *m* ⟨*pl* -chi⟩ FIN brand; **~ *depositato*** *or* ***registrato*** registered trademark; **~ *di qualità*** certification mark; **~ *protetto*** registered trademark
marcia *f* ⟨*pl* -ce⟩ **1.** march; SPORTS walk; ***mettersi in ~*** set off; **~ *per la pace*** peace march; **~ *funebre*** funeral march **2.** TECH, AUTO gear; **~ *indietro*** reverse; ***cambiare ~*** change gear **3.** ***tabella di ~*** schedule; ***avere una ~ in più*** be particularly gifted
marciapiede *m* pavement, *US* sidewalk; RAIL platform; *fig* ***battere il ~*** be on the game
marciare *v/i* ⟨1f⟩ march; ***marciarci*** *infml* take advantage of
marciatore *m*, **-trice** *f* marcher
marcio *adj* ⟨*mpl* -ci⟩ bad, rotten; (*corrotto*) corrupt, rotten to the core; ***avere torto ~*** be totally wrong
marcire *v/i* ⟨4d⟩ go bad, rot; *fig* rot
marciume *m* rot; depravity (*a. fig*)
Marco *m*: ***San ~*** Saint Mark; ***piazza San ~*** Saint Mark's square; ***l'evangelista Marco*** Saint Mark the evangelist
marconista *m/f* ⟨*mpl* -i⟩ radio-operator
mare *m* **1.** sea; **~ *calmo / mosso / agitato*** calm / choppy / rough sea; ***in alto ~*** on the high seas; ***via ~*** by sea; ***sul livello del ~*** at sea level; ***andare al ~*** go to the seaside **2.** ***Mare Adriatico*** *m* Adriatic Sea; ***Mar Baltico*** *m* Baltic Sea; ***Mar Egeo*** *m* Aegean Sea; ***Mar Ionio*** *m* Ionian Sea; ***Mar Ligure*** *m* Ligurian Sea; ***Mare Mediterraneo*** *m* Mediterranean Sea; ***Mar Morto*** *m* Dead Sea; ***Mar Nero*** *m* Black Sea; ***Mare del Nord*** *m* North Sea; ***Mar Rosso*** *m* Red Sea; ***i -i*** *pl* ***del Sud*** the South Seas; ***Mar Tirreno*** *m* Tyrrhenian Sea; ***un ~ di gente*** a crowd of people
marea *f* tide; *fig* ***una ~ di*** loads of; ***alta ~*** high tide; ***bassa ~*** low tide; **~ *nera*** oil slick
mareggiata *f* storm
Maremma *f* GEOG Maremma
maremmano I *adj* of Maremma **II** *m*, **-a** *f* person from Maremma; ***pastore*** *m* **~** ZOOL Maremma sheepdog
maremoto *m* tidal wave
maresciallo *m* marshal; **~ *capo*** chief marshall
maretta *f* choppy sea; *fig* tension
marezzato *adj* marbled; ***legno*** *m* **~** marbled wood **marezzatura** *f* marbling; *di legno* veining
margarina *f* margarine
margherita *f* marguerite
margheritina *f* daisy
marginale *adj* marginal; ***note*** *fpl* ***-i*** marginal notes; ***questione*** *f* **~** peripheral question; ***costo*** *m* **~** marginal

cost

marginalità *f* ⟨*pl* marginalità⟩ marginality **marginalmente** *adv* marginally

margine *m* margin; (*orlo*) edge, brink; **~ *di guadagno*** profit margin; **~ *di sicurezza*** safety margin; **~ *di errore*** margin for error; ***vivere ai -i della società*** live on the fringes of society; ***a ~*** margin; ***vivere ai -i della società*** live on the fringes of society

margravio *m* ⟨*pl* -i⟩ margrave

Maria *f* Mary; ***Santa ~*** Saint Mary **mariano** *adj* Marian

marijuana *f* marijuana

marina *f* coast(line); NAUT navy; PAINT seascape; **~ *mercantile*** merchant navy

marinaio *m* ⟨*pl* -ai⟩ sailor; *fig* ***promessa f da ~*** sailor's oath

marinara *f*: ***alla ~*** sailor *attr.*; COOK marinara; ***vestire alla ~*** dress like a sailor

marinare *v/t* ⟨1a⟩ COOK marinate; **~ *la scuola*** *infml* play truant, *Br* bunk off school *infml*

marinaresco *adj* ⟨*mpl* -chi⟩ nautical

marinato *adj* COOK marinated

marino *adj* sea, marine

mariolo, mariuolo *m* villain; *hum* rascal

marionetta *f* puppet, marionette

marionettista *m/f* ⟨*mpl* -i⟩ puppet master

maritare *v/t* ⟨1a⟩ marry off; **~ *una figlia*** marry off one's daughter **maritarsi** *v/r* ⟨1a⟩ get married **maritato** *adj* married; ***donna f -a*** married woman

marito *m* husband; ***prendere ~*** get married; ***essere in età da ~*** be of a marriageable age

maritozzo *m* bun

marittimo *adj* maritime; ***navigazione f -a*** sailing; ***clima m ~*** maritime climate

marker *m* ⟨*pl* marker⟩ MED marker

marketing *m* marketing

marmaglia *f* rabble

marmellata *f* jam; **~ *di arance*** marmalade; **~ *di fragole* / *pesche*** strawberry / peach jam

marmista *m/f* ⟨*mpl* -i⟩ marble-worker

marmitta *f* AUTO silencer, *US* muffler; COOK stockpot; **~ *catalitica*** catalytic converter

marmo *m* marble; **~ *di Carrara*** Carrara marble; ***pavimento m di ~*** marble floor

marmocchio *m*, **-a** *f* ⟨*mpl* -cchi⟩ *infml* kid, *pej* brat

marmoreo *adj* marble

marmorizzato *adj* marbled

marmotta *f* marmot; ***dormire come una ~*** sleep like a log

marna *f* marl

marocchino I *adj* Moroccan **II** *m*, **-a** *f* Moroccan

Marocco *m* Morocco

maroso *m* breaker

marpione *m infml* slyboots

marrano *m liter* renegade

marroncino *adj* light brown

marrone I *adj* (chestnut) brown **II** *m colore* (chestnut) brown; (*castagno*) chestnut

marron glacé *m* ⟨*pl* marron glacé⟩ marron glacé

marsala *m* Marsala, *type of dessert wine*

marsicano *adj* marsicano; ***orso m ~*** ZOOL marsicano bear

Marsiglia *f* Marseilles

marsigliese *f*: ***la ~*** Marseillaise

marsina *f* tails (of a tailcoat)

marsina *f* tails *pl*

marsupio *m* **I** ZOOL marsupial **II** (*borsetta*) bum bag, *US* fanny pack; *per neonati* sling

Marte *m* Mars

martedì *m* ⟨*pl* martedì⟩ Tuesday; **~ *grasso*** Shrove Tuesday, *Br* Pancake Day *infml*

martellamento *m* hammering; **~ *dell'artiglieria*** pounding from the artillery **martellante** *adj* pounding; ***pubblicità f ~*** relentless adverts **martellare** *v/t and v/i* ⟨1b⟩ hammer; *fig* **~ *qn di domande*** keep firing questions at s.o. **martellata** *f* hammer-blow

martelletto *m* mallet; MED plessor

martello *m* hammer; ANAT malleus; **~ *da falegname*** carpenter's hammer; **~ *pneumatico*** pneumatic drill

Martino *m*: ***San ~*** Saint Martin; ***estate f di San ~*** Indian summer

martin pescatore *m* kingfisher

martire *m/f* martyr

martirio *m* ⟨*pl* -ri⟩ martyrdom

martora *f* marten

martoriare *v/t* ⟨1k & c⟩ torment; *fig* distress **martoriarsi** *v/r* ⟨1k & c⟩ *fig*

torture oneself
marxismo *m* Marxism
marxista *m/f* ⟨*mpl* -i⟩ Marxist
marzapane *m* marzipan
marziale *adj* (*passo*) martial bearing; (*aspetto*) military appearance; ***arti** fpl* ***-i*** martial arts; ***corte** f* **~** martial court
marziano *m*, **-a** *f* Martian
marzo *m* March
marzolino *adj* (of) March
mascalzonata *f* dirty trick
mascalzone *m*, **-a** *f* rogue, rascal
mascara *m* ⟨*pl* mascara⟩ mascara
mascarpone *m* mascarpone
mascella *f* jaw; ANAT maxilla
maschera *f* mask; *in cinema*, *teatro* usher; *donna* usherette; ***~ antigas*** gas mask; ***~ subacquea*** face mask; ***ballo** m* ***in ~*** masked ball; ***~ di bellezza*** face pack; ***gettare la ~*** show one's true colours
mascheramento *m fig* disguise MIL camouflage
mascherare *v/t* ⟨1l⟩ mask; *fig* camouflage, conceal
mascherarsi *v/r* put on a mask; (*travestirsi*) dress up (***da*** as)
mascherata *f* (*messa in scena*) masquerade
mascherato *adj* disguised; ***banditi** mpl* ***-i*** masked thieves
mascherina *f* (*mezza maschera*) half-mask; *di carnevale*: Carnival mask; *di scarpe*: toecap
maschiaccio *m* ⟨*pl* -cci⟩ *infml* tomboy **maschietto** *m* baby boy
maschile *adj spogliatoio*, *abito* men's; *caratteristica* male; GRAM masculine; ***sesso** m* **~** male sex
maschilismo *m* male chauvinism
maschilista ⟨*pl* -i⟩ **I** *m* male chauvinist, sexist **II** *adj* chauvinistic, sexist
maschio ⟨*pl* -chi⟩ **I** *adj* male; ***hanno tre figli -i*** they have three sons *or* boys **II** *m* (*ragazzo*) boy; (*uomo*) man; ZOOL male
mascolinità *f* ⟨*pl* mascolinità⟩ masculinity
mascolino *adj* masculine; ***voce** f* ***-a*** masculine voice
mascotte *f* ⟨*pl* mascotte⟩ mascot
masnada *f* gang **masnadiere** *m* LIT bandit
masochismo *m* masochism
masochista *m/f* ⟨*mpl* -i⟩ masochist
massa *f* mass; ELEC earth; ***una ~ di cosa da fare*** *infml* masses of things to do *infml*; ***turismo** m* ***di ~*** mass tourism
massacrante *adj* back-breaking
massacrare *v/t* ⟨1a⟩ massacre
massacrarsi *v/r* smash o.s. up; *fig* ***~ di lavoro*** work o.s. to death
massacro *m* massacre
massaggiare *v/t* ⟨1f⟩ massage
massaggiarsi *v/r* massage o.s.
massaggiatore *m*, **-trice** *f* masseur; *donna* masseuse
massaggio *m* ⟨*pl* -ggi⟩ massage; ***~ cardiaco*** heart massage
massaia *f* housewife
massello *m di legno* solid wood
masseria *f* farm **masserizie** *fpl* furniture; *hum* stock
massese **I** *adj* from Massa **II** *m/f* person from Massa
massicciata *f* roadbed
massiccio ⟨*pl* -cci⟩ **I** *adj* massive; *oro*, *noce etc* solid **II** *m* massif
massima *f* saying, maxim; (*temperatura*) maximum; ***di ~*** *progetto*, *accordo* preliminary; ***in linea di ~*** generally speaking, on the whole
massimale *m* maximum
massimalismo *m* POL maximalism
massimalista *m/f* ⟨*mpl* -i⟩ maximalist **massimamente** *adv* maximally
massimizzare *v/t* ⟨1a⟩ maximize
massimo **I** *adj* greatest, maximum; ***la -a velocità** f* ***consentita*** the maximum speed limit **II** *m* maximum; ***al ~*** at most; ***il ~ della pena*** the maximum sentence
mass media *mpl* mass media *pl*
massmediologo *m*, **-a** *f* ⟨*mpl* -gi⟩ media expert
masso *m* rock; ***caduta -i*** falling rocks *pl*
massone *m* (*affiliato alla massoneria*) (free)mason
massoneria *f* Freemasonry **massonico** *adj* ⟨*mpl* -ci⟩ Masonic; ***loggia** f* ***-a*** Masonic lodge
massoterapista *m/f* ⟨*mpl* -i⟩ massotherapist
mastectomia *f* mastectomy
mastello *m* washtub
master *m* ⟨*pl* master⟩ master
masterizzare ⟨1a⟩ *v/t* COMPUT burn

masterizzatore *m* COMPUT writer; ~ ***DVD*** DVD writer
masticare *v/t* ⟨1l & d⟩ chew; ~ ***un po' di inglese*** have a smattering of English
masticazione *f* chewing
mastice *m* mastic; (*stucco*) putty
mastino *m* mastiff
mastite *f* mastitis
mastodonte *m* mastodon; *fig* big, clumsy person
mastodontico *adj* ⟨*mpl* -ci⟩ gigantic, enormous
mastro I *adj*: ***libro*** *m* ~ ledger **II** *m* master; ~ ***falegname*** master-carpenter
masturbare *v/t* ⟨1a⟩ masturbate
masturbarsi *v/r* ⟨1a⟩ masturbate
masturbazione *f* masturbation
matassa *f* skein; ***trovare il bandolo della*** ~ find the solution to the problem
match *m* ⟨*pl* match⟩ match **match ball** *m* ⟨*pl* match ball⟩ match-ball **match point** *m* ⟨*pl* match point⟩ match point
matematica *f* mathematics *sg*, maths *sg infml*, *US* math *infml*; ***se la*** ~ ***non è un'opinione*** logically
matematicamente *adv* mathematically; ~ ***impossibile*** mathematically impossible
matematico ⟨*mpl* -ci⟩ **I** *adj* mathematical **II** *m*, **-a** *f* mathematician
materano I *adj* from Matera **II** *m*, **-a** *f* person from Matera
materassaio *m*, **-a** *f* ⟨*mpl* -ai⟩ mattress maker
materassino *m* airbed, Lilo®
materasso *m* mattress; ~ ***a molle*** sprung mattress; ~ ***ad acqua*** water-bed
materia *f* **1.** matter **2.** (*materiale*) material; ~ ***prima*** raw material; ~ ***sintetica*** synthetic (material); ~ ***grigia*** grey matter **3.** (*disciplina*) subject; ~ ***d'esame*** examination subject; ~ ***facoltativa*** optional subject; ~ ***obbligatoria*** compulsory subject; ***in*** ~ ***di*** on the subject of
materiale I *m* material; TECH equipment; ~ ***da costruzione*** building materials *pl* **II** *adj* material; (*rozzo*) coarse, rough
materialismo *m* materialism
materialista ⟨*mpl* -i⟩ **I** *adj* materialistic **II** *m/f* materialist
materialistico *adj* ⟨*mpl* -ci⟩ materialistic **materialità** *f* ⟨*pl* materialità⟩ materiality **materializzare** *v/t* ⟨1a⟩ materialize **materializzarsi** *v/r* ⟨1a⟩ materialize **materializzazione** *f* materialization
materialmente *adv*: *fig* ***è*** ~ ***impossibile*** it's practically impossible
maternamente *adv* maternally
maternità *f* ⟨*pl* maternità⟩ **1.** motherhood; ***tutela della*** ~ maternity rights *pl*; ***mettersi in*** ~ go on maternity leave; ~ ***sostitutiva*** surrogate motherhood **2.** *in ospedale* maternity; ***reparto*** *m* ~ maternity ward
materno *adj* maternal; ***scuola*** *f* **-a** nursery school; ***nonni*** *mpl* **-i** maternal grandparents
matinée *f* ⟨*pl* matinée⟩ matinée
matita *f* pencil; ~ ***colorata*** colo(u)red pencil; ~ ***per gli occhi*** eye pencil; ~ ***per sopracciglia*** eyebrow pencil
matriarcale *adj* matriarchal **matriarcato** *m* matriarchy
matrice *f* matrix; ~ ***attiva / passiva*** COMPUT active / passive matrix
matricida *m/f* ⟨*mpl* -i⟩ matricide **matricidio** *m* ⟨*pl* -i⟩ matricide
matricola *f* register; *all'università* first-year student; ***numero*** *m* ***di*** ~ matriculation number
matricolato *adj* registered; ***furfante*** *m* ~ downright crook
matrigna *f* stepmother
matrimoniale *adj* matrimonial; ***la vita*** ~ married life
matrimonio *m* ⟨*pl* -ni⟩ marriage; *rito* wedding; ~ ***civile / religioso*** civil / church wedding; ~ ***d'interesse*** marriage of convenience
matrona *f* matron **matronale** *adj* matronly, matronal **matroneo** *m* women's gallery
mattacchione *m*, **-a** *f* prankster
mattanza *f tuna fish slaughter*
mattatoio *m* ⟨*pl* -oi⟩ slaughterhouse
mattatore *m*, **-trice** *f* THEAT, FILM show-stealer (*a. fig*)
Matteo *m*: ***San*** ~ Saint Matthew; ***l'evangelista*** ~ Saint Matthew the evangelist
matterello *m* rolling-pin
mattina *f* morning; ***di*** ~ in the morn-

ing; ***questa ~*** this morning; ***domani ~*** tomorrow morning; ***alle sette di ~*** at seven in the morning
mattinata *f* morning; THEAT matinee; ***ci vediamo in ~*** see you in the morning
mattiniero *m/adj*: ***essere ~*** be an early bird
mattino *m* morning; ***di buon ~*** early in the morning; ***il ~ seguente*** the following morning
matto I *adj* mad, crazy, insane (***per*** about); ***andare ~ per qc*** be mad about sth; ***avere una voglia -a di qc*** be dying for sth; ***essere ~ da legare*** be insane, be mad as a hatter **II** *m*, **-a** *f* madman, lunatic; *donna* madwoman, lunatic; ***mi piace da -i andare al cinema*** I'm mad about the cinema
mattone *m* brick; *fig* ***che ~!*** what a turgid piece of writing!
mattonella *f* tile
mattutino *adj* morning *attr*; ***passeggiata*** *f* ***-a*** morning walk
maturare *v/t* ⟨1a⟩ *interessi* accrue; ***~ una decisione*** reach a decision
maturazione *f* ripening (*a. fig*); ECON interest accrual
maturità *f* ⟨*pl* maturità⟩ maturity; (*diploma*) *A level*
maturo *adj frutto* ripe; *persona* mature; ***i tempi sono -i*** the time is ripe
matusa *m/f* ⟨*pl* matusa⟩ *infml* old fogey
Matusalemme *m* decrepit old man; ***essere un ~*** be as old as the hills
Mauritania *f* Mauritania
Maurizio *fpl* Maurice
mausoleo *m* mausoleum
maxillofacciale *adj* maxillo-facial
maxiprocesso *m* major trial
maxischermo *m* big screen
maya *adj* Mayan; ***civiltà*** *f* ***~*** Mayan civilization
mazza *f* club; (*martello*) sledgehammer; *da baseball* bat; ***~ da golf*** golf club
mazzata *f* heavy blow (with a cudgel) (*a. fig*)
mazzetta *f* (*martello*) beetle; *di banconote* wad; *fig* bribe
mazzo *m* bunch, bundle; ***~ di fiori*** bunch of flowers, bouquet; ***~ di chiavi*** bunch of keys; ***~ di carte*** pack *or* deck of cards
mazzolino *m* posy
MB *abbr* (= **megabyte**) Mb
mc *abbr* (= **metro cubo**) m^3 (cubic metre)
me (– ***mi*** before ***lo, la, li, le, ne***) *pron* me; ***dammelo*** give me it, give it to me; ***come ~*** like me; ***fai come ~*** do what I do; ***per ~*** for me; ***secondo ~*** in my opinion
meandro *m* meander; ***-i*** *pl* maze (*a. fig*)
mecca *f fig* Mecca
Mecca *f*: ***La ~*** Mecca
meccanica *f* mechanics *sg*; *di orologio* mechanism; ***la ~ di un incidente*** how an accident happened; ***~ di precisione*** precision engineering
meccanicamente *adv* mechanically
meccanico ⟨*mpl* -ci⟩ **I** *adj* mechanical; ***ingegnere*** *m* ***~*** mechanical engineer; ***officina*** *f* ***-a*** garage **II** *m* mechanic
meccanismo *m* mechanism
meccanizzare *v/t* ⟨1a⟩ automate **meccanizzazione** *f* automation
meccanografia *f* automatic data processing **meccanografico** *adj* ⟨*mpl* -ci⟩ computerised, machine; ***centro*** *m* ***~*** data-processing centre
mecenate *m/f* sponsor
mecenatismo *m* patronage
mèche *f* ⟨*pl* mèche⟩ streak; ***farsi le ~*** get one's hair streaked
medaglia *f* medal; ***~ alla memoria*** posthumous honour / medal; *fig* ***il rovescio della ~*** the other side of the coin
medagliere *m* SPORTS medals table **medaglietta** *f* small medal; *per cani*: dog tag
medesimo *adj* (very) same; ***il ~*** the (very) same; ***la -a*** the (very) same
media *f* average; ***in ~*** on average; ***superiore*** (***inferiore***) ***alla ~*** above (below) average; ***~ oraria*** average speed
mediale *adj* medial **medialmente** *adv* medially
mediamente *adv* on average
mediana *f* GEOG median; *statistica*: median; SPORTS midfield
mediano I *adj* central, middle **II** *m* SPORTS half-back
mediante *prep* by (means of)

mediatico *adj* ⟨*mpl* -ci⟩ media *attr*; ***evento*** *m* ~ media event
mediatore *m*, **-trice** *f* mediator; ~ ***europeo*** EU European Ombudsman; ~ ***culturale*** cultural mediator: ~ ***familiare*** family mediator
mediazione *f* mediation
medicabile *adj* treatable
medicamento *m* medicine
medicare *v/t* ⟨1l, b & d⟩ *persona* treat; *ferita* clean, disinfect
medicarsi *v/r* dress one's wounds; ~ ***una ferita*** dress one's wound
medicastro *m pej* quack (doctor)
medicazione *f* treatment; (*bende*) dressing; ***fare una ~ a qn*** dress s.o.'s wound
medicina *f* medicine; ~ ***alternativa*** / ***tradizionale*** alternative / traditional medicine; ~ ***interna*** internal medicine; ~ ***legale*** forensic medicine; ~ ***sportiva*** sports medicine; ***prendere la*** ~ take one's medicine
medicinale **I** *adj* medicinal; ***erba*** *f* ~ medicinal herb **II** *m* medicine
medico ⟨*mpl* -ci⟩ **I** *m* doctor; ~ ***curante*** doctor in charge; ~ ***generico*** general practitioner, *Br* GP; ~ ***di famiglia*** family doctor; ~ ***di guardia*** doctor on duty; ~ ***legale*** police doctor; ***andare dal*** ~ go to the doctor **II** *adj* medical; ***visita*** *f* ***-a*** medical examination, physical *infml*; ***erba*** *f* ***-a*** lucerne
medievale *adj* medi(a)eval
medievalista *m/f* ⟨*mpl* -i⟩ medievalist
medio ⟨*mpl* -di⟩ **I** *adj età*, *classe etc* middle *attr*; *guadagno*, *statura*, *rendimento* average; ***il ceto*** ~ the middle class; ***taglia*** *f* ***-a*** medium size; ***a*** ~ ***termine*** in the medium term **II** *m* middle finger
mediocre *adj* mediocre
mediocrità *f* ⟨*pl* mediocrità⟩ mediocrity
medioevo *m* Middle Ages *pl*
mediorientale *adj* Middle Eastern
meditabondo *adj* meditative
meditare ⟨1l & b⟩ **I** *v/t* think about; (*progettare*) plan **II** *v/i* meditate; (*riflettere*) think; ~ ***su qc*** think about sth
meditazione *f* meditation; (*riflessione*) consideration, reflection
mediterraneo **I** *adj* Mediterranean; ***dieta*** *f* ***-a*** Mediterranean diet **II** *m*: ***Mediterraneo*** Mediterranean (Sea)
medium *m/f* ⟨*pl* medium⟩ medium
medusa *f* ZOOL jellyfish
meeting *m* ⟨*pl* meeting⟩ meeting
MEF *abbr* (= **Ministero dell'Economia e delle Finanze**) Ministry of Finance
megabyte *m* ⟨*pl* megabyte⟩ megabyte
megafono *m* megaphone
megagalattico *adj* ⟨*mpl* -ci⟩ *hum* gigantic
megalitico *adj* ⟨*mpl* -ci⟩ megalithic
megalomane *adj* megalomaniac
megalomania *m* megalomania
megera *f* hag
meglio **I** *adv* better; ***~!, tanto ~!*** so much the better!, good!; ~ ***di no!*** better not!; ***alla*** ~ to the best of one's ability; ***di bene in*** ~ better and better; ***al*** ~ as best one can; ~ ***tardi che mai*** better late than never **II** *adj* better; *superlativo* best **III** *m* best; ***fare del proprio*** ~ do one's best; ***dare il*** ~ ***di sé*** do one's best **IV** *f*: ***avere la*** ~ ***su*** get the better of
mela *f* apple; ~ ***cotogna*** quince
melagrana *f* pomegranate
Melanesia *f* Melanesia
melanina *f* melanin
melanoma *m* MED melanoma
melanzana *f* aubergine, *US* eggplant; ***-e*** *pl* ***alla parmigiana*** Parma-style aubergines
melassa *f* treacle
melenso *adj* backward, insipid; ***sorriso*** *m* ~ vapid smile
melissa *f* BOT (lemon) balm
mellifluo *adj fig* sugary, smarmy
melma *f* mud
melmoso *adj* slimy
melo *m* apple (tree)
melodia *f* melody
melodico *adj* ⟨*mpl* -ci⟩ melodic
melodiosamente *adv* melodiously
melodiosità *f* ⟨*pl* melodiosità⟩ *fig* tunefulness
melodioso *adj* melodious
melodramma *m* ⟨*pl* -i⟩ melodrama
melodrammatico *adj* melodramatic
melograno *m* pomegranate tree
melone *m* melon
membrana *f* membrane; ~ ***del timpano*** eardrum
membranoso *adj* membranous
membro *m* ⟨*pl* le membra⟩ ANAT limb; *persona* ⟨*pl* i -i⟩ member

memorabile *adj* memorable
memorandum *m* ⟨*pl* memorandum⟩ memo(randum); (*promemoria*) memo
memore *adj*: **~ di** mindful, *grato* grateful
memoria *f* **1.** memory; ***a ~*** by heart; ***in ~ di*** in memory of; ***in ~ di qn*** in memory of s.o.; ***vuoto** m **di ~*** (a memory) blank; ***questo nome non ti richiama alla ~ niente?*** doesn't that name remind you of anything?; ***~ di ferro*** an excellent memory; ***avere la ~ corta*** have a poor memory; ***a ~ d'uomo*** in living memory **2.** COMPUT storage capacity; ***~ centrale*** main memory; ***~ cache*** COMPUT cache memory; ***~ di massa** or **secondaria*** COMPUT secondary memory; ***~ di sistema*** COMPUT system memory; ***~ virtuale*** COMPUT virtual memory **3.** **-e** *pl* memoirs
memoriale *m* (*narrazione*) record; *di difesa*: memorandum; (*petizione*) petition
memorizzare *v/t* ⟨1a⟩ memorize; COMPUT save
memorizzazione *f* memorisation; COMPUT storage
menadito *m*: ***sapere qc a ~*** know sth back to front
menagramo *m/f* ⟨*pl* menagramo⟩ jinx
menarca *m* ⟨*pl* -chi⟩ menarche
menare *v/t* ⟨1a⟩ lead; *infml* (*picchiare*) hit; ***~ le mani*** hit out (at)
menarsi *v/r* ⟨1a⟩ *infml* come to blows
menata *f infml* rubbish; ***è sempre la stessa ~*** it's always the same old story; ***questo film è una ~*** this film is rubbish
mendace *adj* mendacious
mendicante *m/f* beggar
mendicare ⟨1l, d or 1d⟩ **I** *v/t* beg (for); *aiuto*, *lavoro etc* beg for, plead for **II** *v/i* beg
menefreghismo *m* couldn't-care-less attitude
menefreghista *m/f* ⟨*mpl* -i⟩ *person with a couldn't care less attitude*
menestrello *m* HIST minstrel
meninge *f*: ***spremersi le -i*** *infml* rack one's brains *infml*
meningite *f* meningitis
menisco *m* ⟨*pl* -chi⟩ meniscus
meno **I** *adv* less; *superlativo* least; MATH minus; ***devo mangiare ~*** I should eat less; ***il ~ possibile*** as little as possible; ***il ~*** the least; ***parlare del più e del ~*** talk about this and that; ***di ~*** at least; ***a ~ che*** unless; ***in men che non si dica*** in next to no time; ***~ male!*** thank goodness!; ***~ che mai*** let alone; ***niente di ~ che*** nothing less than; ***più o ~*** more or less; ***per lo ~*** at least; ***sono le sei ~ un quarto*** it's a quarter to six; ***sempre ~*** less and less; ***fare a ~ di qc*** do without sth; ***venir ~ a qn*** *forze* desert s.o.; ***venir ~ alla parola data*** not keep one's word **II** *prep* except; ***tutti ~ lui*** everyone but him
menomato *adj* damaged; (*handicappato*) disabled
menomazione *f* disability; **-i** *pl* damage *sg*
menopausa *f* MED menopause
menorah *m* ⟨*pl* menorah⟩ menorah
mensa *f di fabbrica* canteen; MIL mess; ***~ universitaria*** cafeteria
mensile **I** *adj* monthly; ***tessera** f **~*** *per treno*, *autobus* monthly season ticket **II** *m* (*periodico*) monthly
mensilità *f* ⟨*pl* mensilità⟩ salary
mensilmente *adv* monthly
mensola *f* bracket
menta *f* mint; ***~ piperita*** peppermint; ***sciroppo** m **di ~*** mint syrup
mentale *adj* mental; ***facoltà** fpl **-i*** mental faculties; ***calcolo** m **~*** mental arithmetic
mentalità *f* ⟨*pl* mentalità⟩ mentality
mentalmente *adv* mentally
mente *f* mind; ***malato di ~*** mentally ill; ***avere in ~ di fare qc*** be planning to do sth, be thinking about doing sth; ***tenere a ~ qc*** bear sth in mind; ***non mi viene in ~ il nome di ...*** I can't remember the name of ...; ***mi è uscito di ~*** it slipped my mind; ***a ~ fredda*** objectively; ***che ti salta in ~?*** what's got into you?; ***fare ~ locale*** reflect
mentecatto **I** *adj* mad **II** *m*, **-a** *f* madman, madwoman
mentina *f* peppermint
mentire *v/i* ⟨4d or b⟩ lie; ***~ a qn*** lie to s.o.; ***~ a sé stessi*** lie to oneself
mentitore *m*, **-trice** *f* liar
mento *m* chin
mentolo *m* menthol
mentore *m* LIT mentor
mentre *cj* while

mentuccia *f* ⟨*pl* -cce⟩ calamint
menù *m* ⟨*pl* menù⟩ menu *a.* COMPUT
menzionare *v/t* ⟨1a⟩ mention
menzione *f* mention; ADMIN citation; ***~ speciale*** special mention
menzogna *f* lie
menzognero *adj di persona* deceitful; *di cosa* false; (*illusorio*) phoney
meramente *adv* merely
Merano *m* Merano
meraviglia *f* wonder; ***a ~*** marvel(l)ously, wonderfully
meravigliare *v/t* ⟨1g⟩ astonish
meravigliarsi *v/r*: ***~ di*** be astonished by; ***mi meraviglio di te*** you astonish me
meravigliato *adj* astonished, amazed
meravigliosamente *adv* wonderfully
meraviglioso *adj* marvel(l)ous, wonderful
mercante *m* merchant; ***~ d'arte*** art dealer; ***fare orecchie da ~*** turn a deaf ear (to)
mercanteggiare *v/i* ⟨1f⟩ bargain, haggle
mercantile I *adj nave* cargo *attr*; *porto* commercial **II** *m* cargo ship
mercanzia *f* merchandise
mercatino *m* small market
mercato *m* **1.** market; ***~ coperto*** covered market, indoor market; ***~ estero*** foreign market; ***~ interno*** domestic market; ***~ mondiale*** world market; ***~ nero*** black market; ***~ delle pulci*** flea market; ***~ rionale*** local market; ***~ del lavoro*** ECON labour market; ***~ unico europeo*** single European market; ***analisi*** *f* ***di ~*** market analysis; ***prezzo*** *m* / ***valore*** *m* ***di ~*** going price / rate; ***andare al ~*** go to the market; ***introdurre*** (***immettere***) ***qc sul ~*** put sth on the market **2.** ***a buon ~*** cheap, inexpensive; *fig* ***cavarsela a buon ~*** get off lightly
merce *f* goods *pl*; ***~ di contrabbando*** contraband; ***libera circolazione*** *f* ***delle -i*** free movement of goods; ***treno / vagone -i*** goods train / wagon, *US* freight train / car
mercé *f liter*: ***essere alla ~ di qn*** be at the mercy of s.o.
mercenario ⟨*mpl* -ri⟩ **I** *adj* mercenary; *pej* hireling **II** *n*: ***mercenario*** *m* mercenary
merceologia *f* product analysis **merceologico** *adj* ⟨*mpl* -ci⟩ commodity
merceria *f* ⟨*pl* -ie⟩ haberdashery
mercerizzazione *f* TEX mercerization
merchandising *m* ⟨*pl* merchandising⟩ ECON merchandising; JUR merchandising
merciaio *m*, **-a** *f* ⟨*mpl* -ai⟩ haberdasher
mercoledì *m* ⟨*pl* mercoledì⟩ Wednesday; ***~ delle Ceneri*** Ash Wednesday
mercurio *m* mercury; ASTR **Mercurio** Mercury
mercurocromo *m* mercurochrome
merda *f sl* shit *sl*; ***fare una figura di ~*** *vulg* make a right fool of oneself; ***pezzo*** *m* ***di ~*** *vulg* shitbrain; ***tempo*** *m* ***di ~*** *vulg* shitty weather
merdoso *adj vulg* shitty
merenda *f* snack; ***fare ~*** have a snack
merendina *f* snack
meretrice *f liter* prostitute
merger *m* ⟨*pl* merger⟩ FIN merger
meridiana *f* sundial
meridiano I *adj* **1.** midday *attr* **2.** meridian **II** *m* meridian; ***il ~ di Greenwich*** the Greenwich meridian
meridionale I *adj* southern; ***Italia*** *f* ***~*** southern Italy **II** *m/f* southerner
meridione *m* south; ***il Meridione*** southern Italy
meringa *f* ⟨*pl* -ghe⟩ meringue
meritare ⟨1l & b⟩ **I** *v/t* deserve; ***non merita un prezzo così alto*** it's not worth that much **II** *v/i*: ***un libro che merita*** a worthwhile book; ***non ti arrabbiare, non merita*** don't get angry, it's / he's not worth it
meritarsi *v/r* deserve
meritatamente *adv* deservedly
meritevole *adj* worthy (***di*** of); ***~ di lode*** praiseworthy
merito *m* merit; ***in ~ a*** as regards; ***per ~ suo*** thanks to him; ***arrivare primo a pari ~*** come in joint first; ***entrare nel ~ della questione*** enter into the merits of a matter
meritocrazia *f* meritocracy
merlato *adj*: ***torre*** *f* ***-a*** crenellated tower
merlettaia *f* lacemaker
merletto *m* lace
merlo *m* ZOOL blackbird; ARCH ***-i*** *pl* battlements; ***~ indiano*** hill mynah or mynah bird
merluzzo *m* cod

mero *adj* mere; ***per -a curiosità*** merely out of curiosity
merovingio ⟨*mpl* -gi⟩ **I** *adj hist* Merovingian **II** *m*, **-a** *f* Merovingian
mesata *f infml* month's pay, month's rent
mescere *v/t* ⟨3dd⟩ pour; ***~ il vino*** decant wine
meschinamente *adv* (*infelicemente*) wretchedly; (*miseramente*) miserably; (*grettamente*) narrow-mindedly **meschinità** *f* ⟨*pl* meschinità⟩ (*grettezza*) narrow-mindedness; (*inadeguatezza*) meanness
meschino *adj* mean, petty; (*infelice*) wretched; ***fare una figura*** *f* ***-a*** cut a poor figure
mescolanza *f* mixture
mescolare *v/t* ⟨1l⟩ mix; *insalata* toss; *caffè* stir
mescolarsi *v/r* mix, blend
mese *m* month; ***una volta al ~*** once a month; ***ai primi del ~*** on the first of every month
Mesopotamia *f* HIST Mesopotamia
mesopotamico *adj* ⟨*mpl* -ci⟩ Mesopotamian
mesozoico *adj* ⟨*mpl* -ci⟩: ***era*** *f* ***-a*** Mesozoic Era
messa[1] *f*: PHOT ***~ a fuoco*** focussing; AUTO ***~ in marcia*** starting; ***~ in moto*** start-up; ***~ in piega*** set; ***~ a punto*** *di meccanismo* adjustment; *di motore* (fine-)tuning; *di testo* finalization; ***~ in scena*** production
messa[2] *f* REL mass; ***~ solenne*** high mass; ***andare a ~*** go to Mass ***~ solenne*** high Mass; ***~ di Natale*** Christmas Mass
messaggero *m*, **-a** *f* messenger
messaggino *m* TEL text (message)
messaggio *m* ⟨*pl* -ggi⟩ message; COMPUT ***~ di posta elettronica*** e-mail message; ***~ di benvenuto*** TEL welcome address; ***~ pubblicitario*** advert; ***il ~ del presidente*** Presidential address
messaggistica *f* ⟨*pl* -che⟩ TEL telephone messages
messale *m* missal
messapico *adj* ⟨*mpl* -ci⟩ Messapian
messe *f* (*raccolto*) harvest
messere *m* HIST Master
messia *m* ⟨*pl* messia⟩ REL Messiah; *fig* saviour **messianico** *adj* ⟨*mpl* -ci⟩ Messianic
messicano **I** *adj* Mexican **II** *m*, **-a** *f* Mexican
Messico *m* Mexico; ***Città del ~*** Mexico City
messinese **I** *adj* from, of Messina **II** *m/f* person from Messina
messinscena *f* production; *fig* act
messo **I** *past part* → ***mettere*** **II** *m*, messenger; ***~ comunale*** council messenger
mestamente *adv* sorrowfully
mestierante *m/f* money-grubber
mestiere *m* trade; (*professione*) profession; ***essere del ~*** be a professional *or* an expert; ***il ~ più vecchio del mondo*** the oldest profession in the world
mestizia *f* anguish **mesto** *adj* mournful
mestolino *m* small ladle
mestolo *m* ladle
mestruale *adj* menstrual
mestruazione *f* menstruation; ***avere le -i*** have one's period
meta *f* destination; SPORTS try; *fig* goal, aim; ***~ finale*** ultimate objective
metà *f* ⟨*pl* metà⟩ half; *punto centrale* middle, centre; ***siamo a ~ del viaggio*** we're half-way there; ***a ~ prezzo*** half price; ***a ~ strada*** halfway; ***fare a ~*** go halves (***di*** on); ***la mia dolce ~*** *infml* my better half; ***pieno*** *m* ***a ~*** half-full
metabolico *adj* metabolic
metabolismo *m* metabolism
metabolizzante *adj* metaboliser **metabolizzare** *v/t* ⟨1a⟩ metabolise (*a. fig*)
metacarpo *m* metacarpus
metadone *m* methadone
metafisica *f* metaphysics **metafisico** *adj* ⟨*mpl* -ci⟩ metaphysical; *fig* imaginary
metafora *f* metaphor; ***parlare per -e*** speak metaphorically
metaforico *adj* ⟨*mpl* -ci⟩ metaphorical
metal detector *m* ⟨*pl* metal detector⟩ metal detector
metalinguaggio *m* ⟨*pl* -ggi⟩ metalanguage
metallaro *m*, **-a** *f* heavy metal fan
metallico *adj* ⟨*mpl* -ci⟩ metallic
metallifero *adj* metalliferous; ***colline*** *fpl* ***-e*** metalliferous hills
metallizzato *adj* metallic

metallo *m* metal; ~ ***prezioso*** precious metal; ***di*** ~ metal
metallurgia *f* metallurgy
metallurgico *adj* ⟨*mpl* -ci⟩ metallurgical; ***industria*** *f* ***-a*** metallurgical industry
metalmeccanico *adj* ⟨*mpl* -ci⟩ engineering *attr*; ***operaio*** *m* ~ engineering worker
metamorfosi *f* ⟨*pl* metamorfosi⟩ metamorphosis
metano *m* methane
metanodotto *m* gas pipeline
metanolo *m* methanol
metastasi *f* MED ⟨*pl* metastasi⟩ metastasis
metatarso *m* metatarsus
metempsicosi *f* ⟨*pl* metempsicosi⟩ metempsychosis
meteora *f* meteor
meteorite *m or f* meteorite
meteorologia *f* meteorology
meteorologico *adj* ⟨*mpl* -ci⟩ meteorological, weather *attr*; ***bollettino*** *m* ~ weather forecast; ***servizio*** *m* ~ weather service; ***previsioni*** *fpl* ***-che*** weather forecast
meteorologo *m*, **-a** *f* ⟨*mpl* -gi⟩ meteorologist
meteoropatia *f* meteoropathy
meteoropatico *adj* ⟨*mpl* -ci⟩ affected by the weather
meticcio ⟨*mpl* -cci⟩ **I** *adj* mixed-race **II** *m*, **-a** *f* person of mixed race
meticolosamente *adv* meticulously **meticolosità** *f* ⟨*pl* meticolosità⟩ meticulousness
meticoloso *adj* meticulous
metilico *adj* ⟨*mpl* -ci⟩ methyl
metodica *f* ⟨*pl* -che⟩ methodology **metodicamente** *adv* methodically **metodicità** *f* ⟨*pl* metodicità⟩ methodicalness
metodico *adj* ⟨*mpl* -ci⟩ methodical
metodista *m/f* ⟨*mpl* -i⟩ Methodist
metodo *m* method; ~ ***scientifico*** scientific method
metodologia *f* methodology **metodologico** *adj* ⟨*mpl* -ci⟩ methodological
metraggio *m* ⟨*pl* -ggi⟩ length in metres, *film* footage
metrica *f* metrics *sg*
metrico *adj* ⟨*mpl* -ci⟩ metric; ***sistema*** *m* ~ ***decimale*** metric system
metro[1] *m* metre, *US* meter; ~ ***quadrato*** square metre (*US* meter); ~ ***cubo*** cubic metre (*US* meter); ***giudicare con lo stesso*** ~ use the same criterion
metro[2] *f infml*, **metrò** *m* ⟨*pl* metro, metrò⟩ (*metropolitana*) underground, *US* subway; *infml London*: tube
metronomo *m* metronome
metronotte *m* ⟨*pl* metronotte⟩ night watchman
metropoli *f* ⟨*pl* metropoli⟩ metropolis
metropolita *m* ⟨*pl* -i⟩ metropolitan
metropolitana *f* underground, *US* subway
metropolitano *adj* metropolitan; ***territorio*** *m* ~ metropolitan land; ***leggenda*** *f* ***-a*** urban legend
mettere *v/t* ⟨3ee⟩ **1.** put **2.** *vestito* put on **3.** ~ ***in conto*** put on the bill; *consider* take into account; ~ ***in luce*** highlight; ~ ***in moto*** start (up); ~ ***in ordine*** tidy up; ~ ***a punto*** *meccanismo* adjust; *motore* (fine-)tune; ~ ***al sicuro*** put away safely **4.** ~ ***allegria a qn*** cheer s.o. up; ~ ***fine a qc*** put an end to sth **5.** ~ ***su casa*** set up house **6.** ***mettiamo che*** let's assume that **7.** ***metterci*** take **8.** ***mettercela tutta*** do one's best; ~ ***da parte*** *soldi* put aside; *fig rancori* forgive and forget; *fig* ~ ***in piedi qc*** set s.o. up; ~ ***a posto*** mend; ~ ***in pratica*** practice
mettersi *v/r* **1.** *abito, cappello etc* put on; ~ ***un abito*** put on a dress; AVIAT, AUTO ~ ***la cintura*** fasten one's seat belt **2.** ~ ***a letto*** go to bed, take to one's bed **3.** ~ ***a fare qc*** start to do sth; ~ ***a piangere*** start to cry; ~ ***a sedere*** sit down; ~ ***a tavola*** sit at the table; ~ ***con qn*** *infml* go out with s.o. **4.** ~ ***in cammino*** set out, get going; ~ ***in coda / in fila*** queue up, *US* join a line; ~ ***in salvo*** reach safety
mezzacartuccia *f* ⟨*pl* mezzecartucce⟩ *fig* squirt
mezzadria *f* share-cropping **mezzadro** *m*, **-a** *f* share-cropper
mezzaluna *f* ⟨*pl* mezzelune⟩ half moon, crescent; COOK *two-handled chopper*
mezzanino *m* mezzanine
mezzanotte *f* midnight; GEOG north; ***a*** ~ at midnight
mezzo **I** *adj* half; ***uno e*** ~ one and a half; ***mezz'ora*** half-hour; ***le sei e*** ~

half-past six; **~ *chilo*** a half kilo; ***-a porzione*** *f* a half-portion; ***a -a strada*** halfway; ***di -a età*** middle-aged **II** *adv* half **III** *m* **1.** (*parte centrale*) middle; ***a ~*** half; ***in ~ a*** *due persone*, *due libri* between; ***in ~ a quei documenti*** in the middle of *or* among those papers; ***in ~ alla stanza*** in the middle of the room; ***nel ~ di*** in the middle of; ***togliersi di ~*** get out of the way **2.** (*metà*) half **3.** (*strumento*) means *sg*; (*veicolo*) means *sg* of transport; ***-i*** *pl* ***di comunicazione di massa*** mass media *pl*; ***-i*** *pl* ***di pagamento*** means of payment; ***~ di trasporto pubblico*** means *sg* of public transport; ***prendere un ~ pubblico*** use public transport; ***per ~ di*** by means of; ***a ~ posta*** by post **4.** ***giusto ~*** happy medium

mezzobusto *m* ⟨*pl* mezzibusti⟩ half-length photograph / portrait; TV *hum* talking head

mezzodì *m* → ***mezzogiorno***

mezzofondista *m/f* ⟨*mpl* -i⟩ middle-distance runner

mezzofondo *m* middle distance

mezzogiorno *m* midday; GEOG ***Mezzogiorno*** south (of Italy), southern Italy; ***a ~*** at midday

mezzoservizio *m*: ***lavorare a ~*** work part-time

mg *abbr* (= **milligrammo**) mg (milligram)

mi[1] *m* MUS E; *nel solfeggio della scala* me, mi

mi[2] *pron* me; *riflessivo* myself; ***eccomi*** here I am; ***~ dai la mano?*** can you give me a hand?; ***lasciami in pace*** leave me alone

miagolare *v/i* ⟨1l⟩ miaow, mew

miagolio *m* miaowing, mewing

MIBAC *abbr* (= **Ministero per i Beni e le Attività Culturali**) Ministry for Cultural Heritage

MIBTEL *abbr* (= **Milano Indice Borsa Telematico**) Milan Stock Exchange Index

mica *adv*: ***non ho ~ finito*** I'm nowhere near finished; ***non è ~ vero*** there's not the slightest bit of truth in it; ***~ male*** not bad at all

miccia *f* ⟨*pl* -cce⟩ fuse

Micene *f* Mycenae **miceneo I** *adj* Mycenaean **II** *m*, **-a** *f* Mycenaean

Michele *m*: ***San ~*** Saint Michael; ***l'arcangelo ~*** the archangel Michael

micidiale *adj veleno*, *clima* deadly; *fatica*, *sforza* exhausting, killing

micio *m*, **-a** *f* ⟨*mpl* -ci⟩ *infml* (pussy) cat

micosi *f* ⟨*pl* micosi⟩ mycosis

micro... *pref* micro...

microbiologia *f* microbiology

microbo *m* microbe

microcamera *f* miniature camera

microchip ⟨*pl* microchip⟩ COMPUT microchip

microchirurgia *f* microsurgery

microclima *m* microclimate

microcomputer *m* ⟨*pl* microcomputer⟩ PC, microcomputer

microcosmo *m* microcosm

microcriminalità, microdelinquenza *f* petty crime

microfilm *m* ⟨*pl* microfilm⟩ microfilm

microfono *m* microphone, mike *infml*

micron *m* ⟨*pl* micron⟩ micrometre

Micronesia *f* Micronesia

microonda *f* microwave; ***forno*** *m* ***a -e*** microwave (oven)

microprocessore *m* microprocessor

microrganismo *m* microorganism

microscopico *adj* ⟨*mpl* -ci⟩ microscopic

microscopio *m* ⟨*pl* -pi⟩ microscope

microsonda *f* microprobe

microspia *f* bug

midollare *adj* medullary

midollo *m* marrow; ***~ osseo*** bone marrow; ***~ spinale*** spinal cord; ***fino al ~*** to the core

miei *mpl* di ***mio*** my

mielato *adj fig* honeyed

miele *m* honey

mietere *v/t* ⟨3a⟩ harvest

mietitore *m*, **-trice** *f* harvester **mietitrebbiatrice** *f* combine harvester

mietitura *f* harvest; (*tempo*) harvesting; (*raccolto*) crop

migliaio *m* ⟨*pl* le -aia⟩ thousand; ***un ~*** a *or* one thousand; *fig* ***un ~ di persone*** thousands of people; ***a migliaia*** in their thousands

miglio[1] *m* ⟨*pl* le -glia⟩ *misura* mile; ***~ marino*** nautical mile

miglio[2] *m grano* millet

miglioramento *m* improvement

migliorare ⟨1a⟩ **I** *v/t* improve **II** *v/i* improve, get better

migliorarsi *v/r* ⟨1a⟩ improve, get better
migliore *adj* better; ***il ~*** the best; ***il mio ~ amico*** my best friend
miglioria *f* improvement
mignolo *m* (*or* **dito ~**) little finger; *del piede* little toe
mignotta *f vulg* bitch
migrare *v/i* ⟨1a⟩ migrate
migratore *adj* migratory; ***uccello*** *m* **~** migratory bird **migratorio** *adj* ⟨*mpl* -ri⟩ migratory
migrazione *f* migration
-mila *nei composti*: thousand; ***due~*** two thousand
milanese I *adj* of Milan **II** *m/f* inhabitant of Milan; ***risotto alla ~*** risotto with saffron; ***cotoletta*** *f* ***alla ~*** Milanese steak
Milano *f* Milan
miliardario *m*, **-a** *f* ⟨*mpl* -ri⟩ billionaire, multimillionaire
miliardo *m* billion
miliare *adj* milliary; ***pietra*** *f* **~** milestone (*a. fig*)
milionario *m*, **-a** *f* ⟨*mpl* -ri⟩ millionaire; *donna* millionairess
milione *m* million
milionesimo *adj* millionth
militante I *adj* militant **II** *m/f* activist **militanza** *f* militancy
militare[1] *v/i* ⟨1l⟩ fight, militate (***contro*** against; ***per*** for); ***~ in un partito*** be a member of a party
militare[2] **I** *adj* military **II** *m* soldier; ***fare il ~*** do one's military service
militarismo *m* militarism
militarista *m/f* ⟨*mpl* -i⟩ militarist
militarizzare *v/t* ⟨1a⟩ hand over to the military; *partito* structure like the army
militarizzazione *f* militarization
milite *m* soldier; ***il ~ ignoto*** the Unknown Soldier
militesente *adj* exempt from military service
milizia *f* militia
millantare *v/t* ⟨1a⟩: ***~ qc*** extol **millantarsi** *v/r* ⟨1a⟩: ***~ di qc*** boast about sth **millantato** *adj*: ***~ credito*** *m* JUR false pretences **millantatore** *m*, **-trice** *f* braggart
mille *num* ⟨*pl* mila⟩ a thousand; ***~ grazie!*** thank you very much!
millefoglie *m* ⟨*pl* millefoglie⟩ vanilla slice
millenario *adj* thousand-year-old
millennio *m* ⟨*pl* -nni⟩ millennium
millepiedi *m* ⟨*pl* millepiedi⟩ millipede
millesimo *m/adj* thousandth
milligrammo *m* milligram(me)
millimetro *m* millimetre, *US* -meter
milza *f* spleen
mimare *v/t* ⟨1a⟩ mime
mimetico *adj* ⟨*mpl* -ci⟩ camouflage *attr*; ***tuta*** *f* ***-a*** camouflage
mimetizzare *v/t* ⟨1a⟩ MIL camouflage
mimetizzarsi *v/r* camouflage o.s.; *fig* ***~ tra la folla*** get lost in the crowd
mimetizzato *adj* camouflaged **mimetizzazione** *f* camouflage; ZOOL mimicry
mimica *f* gesticulation
mimo *m* mime
mimosa *f* mimosa
min. *abbr* (= **minuto**) min (minute)
mina *f* mine; *di matita* lead; ***~ antiuomo*** antipersonnel mine
minaccia *f* ⟨*pl* -cce⟩ threat
minacciare *v/t* ⟨1f⟩ threaten
minaccioso *adj* threatening
minare *v/t* ⟨1a⟩ mine; *fig* undermine
minareto *m* minaret
minato *adj*: ***campo*** *m* **~** minefield
minatore *m* miner
minatorio *adj* ⟨*mpl* -ri⟩ threatening
minchia *f reg vulg* dick **minchiata** *f vulg* bullshit *m* **minchione** *m*, **-a** *f infml* dickhead
minerale *m/adj* mineral
mineralogia *f* mineralogy **mineralogico** *adj* ⟨*mpl* -ci⟩ mineralogical **minerario** *adj* ⟨*mpl* -ri⟩ mining-; *giacimento* mineral deposit; ***settore*** *m* **~** mining industry
minestra *f* soup; ***~ di fagioli*** bean soup; ***~ di verdura*** vegetable soup; ***o mangi la ~ o salti la finestra*** *prov* like it or lump it
minestrina *f* clear soup, broth
minestrone *m* minestrone, *thick vegetable soup*
mingherlino *adj* slight
miniatura *f* miniature
miniaturista *m/f* ⟨*mpl* -i⟩ miniaturist **miniaturistico** *adj* ⟨*mpl* -ci⟩ miniature; *fig* miniature **miniaturizzare** *v/t* ⟨1a⟩ miniaturize
minibar *m* ⟨*pl* minibar⟩ minibar
minibus *m* ⟨*pl* minibus⟩ minibus

minicomputer *m* ⟨*pl* minicomputer⟩ minicomputer
miniera *f* mine (*a. fig*); ***~ di carbone*** coalmine; ***~ d'oro*** goldmine; *fig* goldmine
minigolf *m* ⟨*pl* minigolf⟩ miniature golf
minigonna *f* mini(skirt)
minimale *adj* minimal; ***tariffa** f **~*** minimal fee **minimalista** *m/f* ⟨*mpl* -i⟩ minimalist **minimamente** *adv* minimally, in the least
minimarket *m* ⟨*pl* minimarket⟩ minimarket
minimizzare *v/t* ⟨1a⟩ minimize
minimo **I** *adj* least, slightest; *prezzo*, *offerta* lowest; *salario*, *temperatura* minimum; ***età** f **-a*** minimum age **II** *m* minimum; ***come ~, dovresti …*** you should at least …; ***come ~*** at the very least; ***il ~ indispensabile*** the bare minimum
ministeriale *adj* ministerial; ***crisi** f **~*** cabinet crisis; ***funzionario** m **~*** departmental officer
ministero *m* ministry; (*gabinetto*) government, ministry; ***~ dell'Economia e delle Finanze*** Treasury, *US* Treasury Department; ***~ della Giustizia*** Lord Chancellor's Department, *US* Department of Justice; ***Ministero dell'Interno*** Home Office; ***pubblico ~*** *state prosecutor*; ***Ministero dell'Economia e delle Finanze*** Ministry of Finance; ***Ministero della Giustizia*** Ministry of Justice; ***Ministero dell'Interno*** Home Office
ministro *m*, **-a** *f* minister; ***~ degli Esteri*** Foreign Secretary, *US* Secretary of State; ***~ degli Interni*** Home Secretary, *US* Secretary of the Interior; ***consiglio** m **dei -i*** Cabinet; ***Primo Ministro*** Prime Minister
minoranza *f* minority; ***essere in ~*** be in the minority
minorato **I** *adj* severely handicapped **II** *m*, **-a** *f* severely handicapped person
minorazione *f* MATH reduction; (*menomazione*) disability
minore **I** *adj* minor; *di età* younger; *distanza* shorter; *più piccolo* smaller **II** *m/f*: ***vietato ai -i di 18 anni*** no admittance to those under 18 years of age; *film* X-rated; ***~ emancipato*** JUR emancipated minor
minorenne **I** *adj* under-age **II** *m/f* minor
minorile *adj* juvenile *attr*; ***delinquenza** f **~*** juvenile delinquency
minorità *f* ⟨*pl* minorità⟩ infancy
minoritario *adj* minority *attr*
minuetto *m* minuet
minuscola *f* small letter, lower case letter
minuscolo *adj* tiny, miniscule
minusvalenza *f* ECON depreciation, capital loss
minuta *f* minute **minutaglia** *f* ⟨*pl* -glie⟩ odds and ends **minutamente** *adv* meticulously **minuteria** *f* knick-knacks
minuto **I** *adj persona* tiny; *oggetto* minute; *descrizione*, *indagine* detailed; ***commercio** m **al ~*** retail trade **II** *m* minute; ***60 pulsazioni al ~*** 60 beats a minute; ***ho i -i contati*** I don't have a minute to spare; ***spaccare il ~*** keep perfect time
minuziosamente *adv* meticulously
minuzioso *adj descrizione* detailed; *ricerca* meticulous
mio ⟨*pl* miei⟩ **I** *adj* my; ***un ~ amico*** a friend of mine, one of my friends; ***i miei amici*** my friends **II** *pron*: ***il ~*** mine; ***questo libro è ~*** this book is mine, this is my book; ***i miei*** my parents
miope *adj* short-sighted
miopia *f* short-sightedness, myopia
mira *f* aim; (*obiettivo*) target; ***prendere la ~*** take aim; ***prendere di ~*** aim at; *fig* ***prendere di ~ qn*** have it in for s.o.
mirabile *adj* admirable **mirabilmente** *adv* admirably
mirabolante *adj* astonishing
miracolato *adj* saved/healed miraculously
miracolo *m* miracle; ***per ~*** by a miracle, miraculously; *fig* ***fare -i*** work wonders
miracolosamente *adv* miraculously
miracoloso *adj* miraculous
miraggio *m* ⟨*pl* -ggi⟩ mirage
mirare *v/i* ⟨1a⟩ aim (***a*** at)
miriade *f* myriad
mirino *m* MIL sight; PHOT viewfinder; ***essere nel ~ di qn*** be in s.o.'s sights
mirra *f* myrrh

mirtillo *m* blueberry
mirto *m* myrtle
misantropo I *adj* misanthropic **II** *m*, **-a** *f* misanthropist
miscela *f* mixture; *di caffè, tabacco* blend
miscelare *v/t* ⟨1b⟩ blend
miscelatore *m* COOK mixer; *rubinetto* mixer tap
mischia *f* (*rissa*) scuffle; SPORTS, (*folla*) scrum; ***gettarsi nella ~*** join the fray
mischiare *v/t* ⟨1k⟩ mix; *carte* shuffle
mischiarsi *v/r* mix
misconoscere *v/t* ⟨3d⟩ disregard; (*sottovalutare*) underestimate
miscredente *m/f* unbeliever
miscuglio *m* ⟨*pl* -gli⟩ mixture
miserabile *adj* wretched, miserable
miseramente *adv* miserably (*in modo spregevole*) despicably
miserevole *adj* pitiful
miseria *f* (*povertà*) poverty; (*infelicità*) misery; ***costare una ~*** cost next to nothing; ***porca ~!*** *infml* damn and blast! *infml*
misericordia *f* mercy; ***avere ~ di qn*** have pity on s.o.
misericordiosamente *adv* mercifully
misericordioso *adj* merciful
misero *adj* wretched
misfatto *m* misdeed
misogino *m* misogynist
missaggio *m* ⟨*pl* -ggi⟩ mixing; ***impianto*** *m* ***di ~*** mixing console
missaggio *m* ⟨*pl* -ggi⟩ → ***mixaggio***
missare *v/t* → ***mixare***
missile *m* missile; ***~ a lunga gittata*** long-range missile; ***~ terra-aria*** ground-to-air missile
missilistica *f* ⟨*pl* -che⟩ missilry
missionario *m*, **-a** *f* ⟨*mpl* -ri⟩ missionary
missione *f* mission
Mississipi *m* Mississippi
misteriosamente *adv* mysteriously
misterioso *adj* mysterious
mistero *m* mystery; ***fare ~ di qc*** make a mystery out of sth
misticismo *m* mysticism
mistico *adj* ⟨*mpl* -ci⟩ mystic(al)
mistificare *v/t* ⟨1m & d⟩ (*falsificare*) misrepresent; (*ingannare*) mystify **mistificatore** *adj* fraud **mistificatorio** *adj* ⟨*mpl* -ri⟩ mystifying **mistificazione** *f* misrepresentation (*inganno*) trickery
misto I *adj* mixed **II** *m* mixture; ***~ lana*** wool mix
mistura *f* mixture (*a. fig*)
misura *f* measurement; (*taglia*) size; (*provvedimento*), *fig* measure; MUS bar; ***-e*** *pl* ***preventive*** preventive measures; ***a ~ d'uomo*** on a human scale; ***unità*** *f* ***di ~*** unit of measurement; ***con ~*** in moderation; ***su ~*** made to measure
misurabile *adj* measurable, which can be measured
misurare *v/t* ⟨1a⟩ measure; *vestito* try on; ***~ le spese*** limit one's spending
misurarsi *v/r in una gara* compete; ***~ con*** compete with
misurato *adj* restrained
misurazione *f* measurement
misurino *m* measuring cup
mite *adj persona, inverno* mild; *condanna* light
mitezza *f* meekness *di animale*: tameness; *fig* mildness
mitico *adj* ⟨*mpl* -ci⟩ *infml* fantastic; ***un concerto ~*** a fantastic concert
mitigare *v/t* ⟨1l & e⟩ lessen; *dolore* ease, lessen
mitigazione *f* mitigation
mitizzare *v/t* ⟨1a⟩ turn into myth (*a. fig*) **mitizzazione** *f* mythicization
mito *m* myth
mitologia *f* mythology
mitologico *adj* ⟨*mpl* -ci⟩ mythological
mitra[1] *m* ⟨*pl* mitra⟩ machine gun
mitra[2] *f* REL mitre, *US* miter
mitraglia *f* ⟨*pl* -glie⟩ *infml* machine-gun; ***parlare a ~*** talk fast **mitragliamento** *m* machine-gun fire; *fig* shooting
mitragliatrice *f* machine gun
mitt. *abbr* (= **mittente**) from
mitteleuropeo *adj* Central European
mittente *m/f* sender
mixaggio *m* mixing
mixare *v/t* ⟨1k⟩ mix
mixer *m* ⟨*pl* mixer⟩ (*frullatore*) (food) mixer; MUS mixer
ml *abbr* (= **millilitro**) ml (millilitre)
mm *abbr* (= **millimetro**) mm (millimetre)
M.M. *abbr* (= **Marina Militare**) *Italian navy*
MN *abbr* (= **Mantova**) Mantua

mnemonica *f* mnemonic **mnemonico** *adj* ⟨*mpl* -ci⟩ mnemonic **mnemotecnica** *f* ⟨*pl* -che⟩ mnemonics

mo' *m*; ***a ~ di esempio*** by way of an example

MO *abbr* (= **Modena**) Modena

mobbing *m* victimization; ***fare ~*** engage in victimization

mobile I *adj* mobile; *ripiano*, *pannello* removeable; ***beni*** *mpl* ***-i*** movable property *sg*; ***scala*** *f* **~** escalator; FIN sliding scale; ***squadra*** *f* **~** flying squad **II** *m* piece of furniture; ***-i*** *pl* furniture; ***~ bar*** cocktail cabinet

mobilia *f* furnishings *pl*

mobiliare *adj* ECON security; ***credito*** *m* **~** security credit; ***mercato*** *m* **~** property market

mobiliere *m*, **-a** *f* furniture maker; *commerciante* furniture dealer

mobilificio *m* furniture factory

mobilio *m* → ***mobilia***

mobilità *f* ⟨*pl* mobilità⟩ mobility

mobilitare *v/t* ⟨1m⟩ mobilize

mobilitarsi *v/r* ⟨1m⟩ rally round

mobilitazione *f* mobilization

mobilizzare *v/t* ⟨1a⟩ mobilize; ECON mobilize **mobilizzazione** *f* mobilization

moca *m* mocha

mocassino *m* moccasin

moccioso *m*, **-a** *f* snotty-nosed child

moccolo *m* candle-end; *infml* (*moccio*) snot; *sl* curse; ***reggere il ~*** play gooseberry; ***tirare -i*** utter oaths

moda *f* fashion; ***alla ~*** fashionable, in fashion; *vestirsi* fashionably; ***di ~*** fashionable, in fashion; ***fuori ~*** out of fashion, unfashionable

modaiolo I *adj* trendy **II** *m*, **-a** *f* dandy

modale *adj* modal

modalità *f* ⟨*pl* modalità⟩ method; ***~ di pagamento*** method of payment; ***~ d'uso*** directions *pl* for use

modanatura *f* ARCH moulding; *di mobili* beading

modella *f* model

modellabile *adj* malleable

modellare *v/t* ⟨1b⟩ model

modellatura *f* modelling

modellino *m* model; ***~ di aereo*** airplane model **modellismo** *m* model-making **modellista** *m/f* ⟨*mpl* -i⟩ pattern maker **modellistica** *f* ⟨*pl* -che⟩ model-making, pattern-making

modello I *m* model; (*indossatore*) male model; *di vestito* style; (*formulario*) form; ***~ unico*** FIN tax form; ***azienda*** *f* **~** standard company **II** *adj* model; ***l'ultimo ~*** latest model; ***il ~ di un edificio*** a model of a building; ***ispirarsi a un ~*** take inspiration from a model

modem *m* ⟨*pl* modem⟩ COMPUT modem

modenese I *adj* from Modena **II** *m/f* person from Modena

moderare *v/t* ⟨1l & c⟩ moderate; ***~ la velocità*** slow down; ***~ i termini*** weigh one's words

moderarsi *v/r* be moderate; ***~ nel bere*** restrict one's drinking

moderatamente *adv* moderately

moderatezza *f* moderation

moderato *adj* moderate; MUS moderato; ***partito*** *m* **~** moderate party

moderatore *m*, **-trice** *f* moderator

moderazione *f* moderation

modernamente *adv* in a modern manner **modernismo** *m* modernism **modernità** *f* ⟨*pl* modernità⟩ modernity

modernizzare *v/t* ⟨1a⟩ modernize

modernizzarsi *v/r* ⟨1a⟩ get up-to-date

moderno *adj* modern

modestamente *adv* simply (*con modestia*) modestly

modestia *f* modesty; ***~ a parte*** though I say so myself

modesto *adj* modest; *prezzo* very reasonable; ***essere di origini -e*** of humble birth

modicano I *adj* of, from Modica; ***cioccolata*** *f* ***-a*** Modica chocolate **II** *m*, **-a** *f* person from Modica

modico *adj* ⟨*mpl* -ci⟩ reasonable

modifica *f* ⟨*pl* -che⟩ modification; ***apportare una ~*** alter

modificabile *adv* modifiable

modificare *v/t* ⟨1m & d⟩ modify

modificato *adj* modified; ***~ geneticamente*** BIOL genetically modified

modificatore *m* COMPUT modifier

modificazione *f* modification

modista *f* milliner

modo *m* (*maniera*) way, manner; (*mezzo*) way; MUS mode; GRAM mood; ***~ di dire*** saying; ***~ di vedere*** way of looking at things; ***per ~ di dire*** so to speak; ***se hai ~ di passare da me*** if you could drop by; ***a ~ mio***

in my own way; ***ad ogni ~*** anyway, anyhow; ***di ~ che*** so that; ***in che ~?*** how?; ***in special ~*** especially; ***fare in ~ che*** arrange things so that; ***in malo ~*** unkindly; ***in un ~ o nell'altro*** one way or the other; ***nel ~ migliore*** in the best possible way; ***oltre ~*** beyond measure; ***in qualche ~*** somehow; ***in particolar ~*** particularly

modulabile *adj* able to be modulated

modulare[1] *v/t* ⟨1l & c⟩ modulate

modulare[2] *adj* modular; ***sistema*** *m* ***~*** modular system

modulazione *f* PHYS, MUS modulation; ELEC modulation

modulo *m* **1.** form; ***~ di domanda*** application form; ***~ d'iscrizione*** registration form; ***~ di versamento*** *banca* pay-in slip; ***compilare un ~*** fill in a form **2.** (*elemento*) module; ***libreria a -i*** modular bookcase **3.** ***~ lunare*** lunar module

modus operandi *m* ⟨*pl* modus operandi⟩ modus operandi **modus vivendi** *m* ⟨*pl* modus vivendi⟩ modus vivendi

moffetta *f* ZOOL skunk

mogano *m* mahogany; ***di ~*** mahogany

moghul ⟨*pl* moghul⟩ **I** *adj* mogul **II** *m/f* Mogul

mogio *adj* ⟨*mpl* -gi⟩ depressed; ***~ ~*** depressed

moglie *f* ⟨*pl* -gli⟩ wife

mogliettina *f iron* wifey

mohair *m* ⟨*pl* mohair⟩ mohair

moicano I *adj* Mohican **II** *m*, **-a** *f*⟩ Mohican; ***i Moicani*** the Mohicans

moina *f* coaxing; ***fare le -e a qn*** coax s.o.

mola *f* grindstone; *di mulino* millstone

molare I *v/t* ⟨1c⟩ grind **II** *m* molar

molatrice *f* grinding machine **molatura** *f* grinding; (*risultato*) grounds

Moldavia *f* Moldavia

moldavo I *adj* Moldavian **II** *m*, **-a** *f* Moldavian

mole *f* (*grandezza*) size; *fig* ***una ~ di lavoro*** loads *pl* of work

molecola *f* molecule

molecolare *adj* molecular

molestare *v/t* ⟨1b⟩ bother, trouble; *sessualmente* sexually harass

molestatore *m*, **-trice** *f* molester

molestia *f* bother, nuisance; ***~ sessuale*** sexual harassment

molesto *adj* annoying

molisano I *adj* of Molise **II** *m*, **-a** *f* person from Molise

molla *f* spring; *fig* spur; ***-e*** *pl* tongs; *fig* ***prendere con le -e*** treat with kid gloves

mollare *v/t* ⟨1c⟩ *corda* release, let go; *infml schiaffo*, *ceffone* give; *infml fidanzato* dump; ***~ la presa*** let go; NAUT ***~ gli ormeggi*** cast off; ***~ un ceffone a qn*** *infml* give s.o. a slap; *fig* ***~ l'osso*** let go; ***non ~!*** don't give up!

molle *adj* soft; (*bagnato*) wet

molleggiare *v/t* ⟨1f⟩ be springy

molleggiato *adj* springy

molleggio *m* springs *pl*

mollemente *adv* floppily, loosely

molletta *f* hairgrip; *da bucato* clothes peg *or* pin; ***~ per capelli*** hair-grip; ***~ da bucato*** clothes peg

mollettone *m* thick flannel

mollezza *f* softness, *debolezza* weakness; ***-e*** *pl* luxury; ***vivere nelle -e*** live in luxury

mollica *f* ⟨*pl* -che⟩ crumb

molliccio *adj* ⟨*mpl* -cci⟩ limp, *impregnato d'acqua* soggy **mollo** *m*: ***mettere qc a ~*** soak sth

mollusco *m* ⟨*pl* -chi⟩ mollusc, *US* mollusk

molo *m* pier

molotov *f* ⟨*pl* molotov⟩ Molotov cocktail

molteplice *adj* multifaceted

molteplicità *f* multiplicity

moltiplicabile *adj* multipliable **moltiplicando** *m* multiplicand

moltiplicare ⟨1m & d⟩ **I** *v/t* multiply (***per*** by) **II** *v/i* multiply

moltiplicarsi *v/r* ⟨1m & d⟩ multiply

moltiplicativo *adj* multiplicative **moltiplicatore** *m* MATH multiplier; MECH multiplier **moltiplicazione** *f* MATH multiplication; *fig* increase

moltitudine *f* multitude, host; ***una ~ di persone*** a crowd of people

molto I *adj* a lot of; *con nomi plurali* a lot of, many; ***-a gente*** *f* many people **II** *adv* a lot; *con aggettivi* very; ***~ meglio*** much better, a lot better; ***da ~*** for a long time; ***fra non ~*** before long

Molucche *fpl* (the) Molucca Islands

momentaccio *m* ⟨*pl* -cci⟩ a bad moment

momentaneamente *adv* temporarily

momentaneo *adj* momentary, temporary; ***è una situazione -a*** it's a temporary situation
momentino *m* a moment
momento *m* moment; ***dal ~ che*** from the moment that; *causale* since; ***a -i*** sometimes, at moments; ***al ~*** at present; ***al ~ di partire ha cambiato idea*** when it was time to leave he changed his mind; ***per il ~*** for the moment; ***del ~*** short-lived; ***sul ~*** at the time; ***al ~ giusto*** at the right time; ***-i** pl **difficili*** difficult times; ***in un primo ~*** at first; ***ti sembra questo il ~?*** this is hardly the right time; ***da un ~ all'altro*** from one moment to the next; ***all'ultimo ~*** at the very last minute; ***un ~!*** just a minute!; ***in ogni ~*** all the time; ***per un ~ mi sono illuso*** for a moment I was deceived
monaca *f* ⟨*pl* -che⟩ nun
monacale *adj* monastic; ***abito** m **~*** monk's / nun's habit; ***vita** f **~*** monastic life
monachella *f*, **monacella** *f* clip
monachesimo *m* monasticism
monaco *m* ⟨*pl* -ci⟩ monk; ***l'abito non fa il ~*** clothes don't make the man
monade *f* PHIL monad
monarca *m* ⟨*pl* -chi⟩ monarch
monarchia *f* monarchy
monarchico ⟨*mpl* -ci⟩ **I** *adj* monarchical **II** *m*, **-a** *f* monarchist
monastero *m* monastery; *di monache* convent
monastico *adj* ⟨*mpl* -ci⟩ monastic
monatto *m hist person who removed and buried those dead from the plague*
moncherino *m* stump **monco** *adj* ⟨*mpl* -chi⟩ amputated (*a. fig*); ***essere ~ di un braccio*** be one-armed **moncone** *m* stump
mondanità *f* ⟨*pl* mondanità⟩ worldliness; (*frivolezza*) frivolity; (*alta società*) high society
mondano *adj* society; (*terreno*) worldly; ***fare vita -a*** go out
mondare *v/t* ⟨1a⟩ *frutta* peel
mondatura *f* chaff; peelings; weeds; shellings; (*ulitura*) *legumi* shelling; *diserbare* weeding; *frutta e verdura* peeling; cleaning
mondezzaio *m* ⟨*pl* -ai⟩ rubbish *or US* garbage dump
mondiale I *adj* world *attr*; *economia* world *attr*, global; *fenomeno*, *scala* worldwide; ***di fama ~*** world-famous **II** *m*: ***i mondiali** pl di calcio* the World Cup
mondializzazione *f* globalization
mondina *f* rice weeder
mondo *m* world; ***l'altro ~*** the next world; ***il più bello del ~*** the most beautiful in the world; ***la fine del ~*** the end of the world; ***giro** m **del ~*** world tour, tour round the world; ***il terzo ~*** the Third World; ***andare all'altro ~*** pass away; ***divertirsi un ~*** enjoy o.s. enormously *or* a lot; ***venire al ~*** come into the world; ***per niente al ~*** (not) for anything in the world; ***essere fuori dal ~*** be out of this world; ***ci siamo divertiti un ~*** we had a whale of a time
mondovisione *f* worldwide broadcasting; ***trasmettere in ~*** to broadcast worldwide
monegasco ⟨*mpl* -chi⟩ **I** *adj* Monégasque, from Monaco **II** *m*, **-a** *f* Monégasque
monelleria *f* (*azione*) prank
monello *m*, **-a** *f* imp, little devil
moneta *f* coin; (*valuta*) currency; (*denaro*) money; (*spiccioli*) change; ***~ d'oro*** gold coin; ***~ unica*** single currency; ***svalutazione** f* (*or **deprezzamento** m*) ***della ~*** currency devaluation
monetario *adj* ⟨*mpl* -ri⟩ monetary; ***riforma** f **-a*** EU monetary reform; ***Fondo Monetario Internazionale** m* International Monetary Fund; ***Sistema Monetario Europeo** m* European Monetary System; ***unione** f **-a*** ECON monetary union
monetarismo *m* monetarism **monetina** *f* little coin **monetizzabile** *adj* convertible into cash **monetizzare** *v/t* ⟨1a⟩ monetize; (*realizzare*) convert into cash
monferrino I *adj* from Monferrato **II** *m*, **-a** *f* person from Monferrato
mongolfiera *m* hot-air balloon
Mongolia *f* Mongolia
mongolismo *m* Down's syndrome
mongolo I *adj* Mongolian **II** *m*, **-a** *f* Mongolian
mongoloide MED **I** *adj* mongol **II** *m/f* mongol

monile *m* necklace; (*gioiello*) jewel
monito *m* reprimand
monitor *m* ⟨*pl* monitor⟩ monitor
monitoraggio *m* ⟨*pl* -ggi⟩ monitoring
monitorare *v/t* ⟨1a⟩ monitor
monitorio *adj* ⟨*mpl* -ri⟩ monitory; ***lettera** f **-a*** monitory
monoasse *adj* BOT, ZOOL monoaxial; ***rimorchio** m* **~** single-axle tow
monoblocco *adj inv* single-block; ***motore** m* **~** engine block
monocamera *f* studio flat *or US* apartment
monocellulare *adj* single-cell
monocolo *m* (*lente*) monocle; (*cannocchiale*) telescope, spyglass
monocolore *adj inv* self-colo(u)red; POL one-party
monocoltura *f* monoculture
monodose *adj inv* single-dose; ***confezione** f* **~** single-dose pack
monofamiliare *adj inv* single-family; ***casa** f* **~** small flat
monofase *adj inv* single-phase; ***corrente** f* **~** single-phase electricity
monogamia *f* monogamy
monogamo **I** *adj* monogamous **II** *m*, **-a** *f* monogamist
monogenitore *adj inv*: ***famiglia** f* **~** single-parent family
monografia *f* monograph
monogramma *m* ⟨*pl* -i⟩ monogram
monokini *m* ⟨*pl* monokini⟩ one-piece swimming costume
monolingue *adj inv* monolingual
monolito *m* monolith
monolocale *m* bedsit
monologo *m* ⟨*pl* -ghi⟩ monolog(ue)
monomero *m* CHEM monomer
monopartitico *adj* ⟨*mpl* -ci⟩ one-party
monopattino *m* child's scooter
monopetto *adj* single-breasted
monoplano *m* monoplane
monopolio *m* ⟨*pl* -li⟩ monopoly
monopolistico *adj* ⟨*mpl* -ci⟩ monopoly
monopolizzare *v/t* ⟨1a⟩ monopolize
monopolizzazione *f* monopolization
monoposto *m* single-seater
monoreddito *adj inv* single-income; ***famiglia** f* **~** single-income family
monorotaia *adj*: ***ferrovia** f* **~** monorail
monosillabo *m* monosyllable; ***rispondere a -i*** answer in monosyllables
monossido *m* monoxide
monoteismo *m* monotheism **monoteista** ⟨*mpl* -i⟩ **I** *adj* monotheistic **II** *m/f* monotheist
monotonamente *adv* monotonously
monotonia *f* monotony
monotono *adj* monotonous
monouso *adj* disposable, throwaway
monovolume *adj inv* AUTO multi-purpose
monozigotico *adj* ⟨*mpl* -ci⟩ monozygotic; ***gemelli** mpl **-ci*** monozygotic twins
monsignore *m* monsignor
monsone *m* monsoon
monta *f* ZOOL stud
montacarichi *m* ⟨*pl* montacarichi⟩ goods lift
montaggio *m* ⟨*pl* -ggi⟩ TECH assembly; *di film* editing
montagna *f* mountain; *fig* masses; *fig* **-e** *pl* ***russe*** roller coaster *sg*; ***alta** ~* high mountain; ***strada** f **di** ~* mountain road; ***andare in** ~* go to the mountains
montagnoso *adj* mountainous
montanaro *m*, **-a** *f person who lives in the mountains*
montano *adj* mountain *attr*; ***flora** f **-a*** mountain flora; ***fauna** f **-a*** mountain fauna
montante **I** *adj* rising **II** *m* post; ECON amount
montare ⟨1a⟩ **I** *v/t* go up, climb; *cavallo* get onto, mount; TECH assemble; *film* edit; COOK whip; ***~ a neve*** whisk sth until stiff; ***~ la panna*** whip cream; ***~ la guardia*** mount guard; ***~ la tenda*** put up a tent **II** *v/i* go up; *venire* come up; ***~ in*** *macchina* get into; ***~ su*** *scala* climb; *pullman* get on; ***~ a cavallo / in bicicletta*** get on a horse / bicycle; *fig* ***~ in collera*** get angry
montarsi *v/r*: ***~ la testa*** get a swollen head, get bigheaded
montascale *m* ⟨*pl* montascale⟩ stair-lift
montatore *m*, **-trice** *f* TECH assembler; (*installatore*) fitter; FILM, TV editor
montatura *f di occhiali* frame; *di gioiello* mount; *fig* set-up *infml*, frame-up *infml*
montavivande *m* ⟨*pl* montavivande⟩ dumb waiter
monte *m* **1.** mountain; ***a** ~* upstream **2.**

fig mountain, pile; *fig* ***andare a ~*** come to nothing; ***mandare a ~*** ruin, mess up *infml* **3.** ***Monte Bianco*** Mont Blanc; ***Monte Cervino*** Matterhorn **4.** ***~ dei pegni*** pawnshop **5.** ***~ premi*** jackpot

montenegrino I *adj* from Montenegro, Montenegrin **II** *m*, **-a** *f* person from Montenegro

Montenegro *m* Montenegro

montepulciano *m* COOK Montepulciano wine

montgomery *m* ⟨*pl* montgomery⟩ duffel coat

montone *m* ram; *pelle*, *giacca* sheepskin

montuosità *f* ⟨*pl* montuosità⟩ hillock; (*qualità*) mountainous character

montuoso *adj* mountainous

monumentale *adj* monumental; *fig* enormous

monumento *m* monument

moon boot *m* ⟨*pl* moon boot⟩ moon boot

moquette *f* ⟨*pl* moquette⟩ fitted carpet

mora[1] *f* BOT *del gelso* mulberry; *del rovo* blackberry

mora[2] *f* JUR delay; ***essere in ~*** be in arrears

morale I *f* morals *pl*; *di favola etc* moral **II** *m* morale; ***essere giù di ~*** be feeling a bit down; ***tirare su il ~ a qn*** cheer s.o. up, lift s.o.'s spirits **III** *adj* moral; ***danno*** *m* ***~*** moral damage

moralismo *m* moralism

moralista *m/f* ⟨*mpl* -i⟩ moralist

moralità *f* ⟨*pl* moralità⟩ morality **moralmente** *adv* morally

moratoria *f* JUR moratorium; (*sospensione*) suspension **moratorio** *adj* ⟨*mpl* -ri⟩ delay; ***interessi*** *mpl* ***-ri*** delay interest

morbidamente *adv* softly

morbidezza *f* softness

morbido *adj* soft

morbillo *m* measles *sg*

morbo *m* disease; ***~ di Parkinson / Alzheimer*** Parkinson's / Alzheimer's disease

morbosamente *adv* morbidly **morbosità** *f* ⟨*pl* morbosità⟩ morbidness; MED morbidity

morboso *adj fig* unhealthy, unnatural; *curiosità* morbid

mordace *adj fig* biting, mordant

mordacità *f* ⟨*pl* mordacità⟩ *form* mordacity; bite (*a. fig*) **mordente I** *adj* cutting **II** *m* stain; *fig* bite

mordere *v/t* ⟨3uu⟩ bite; *fig* ***~ il freno*** be raring to go; ***turismo*** *m* ***mordi e fuggi*** weekend / short break tourism

mordersi *v/r* bite o.s.; ***~ le labbra*** bite one's lip; *fig* ***~ la lingua*** bite one's tongue; *fig* ***~ le mani*** kick o.s.

mordicchiare *v/t* ⟨1a⟩ nibble (at / on) **mordicchiarsi** *v/r* ⟨1a⟩ nibble fretfully; ***~ le labbra*** chew one's lips (fretfully)

morellino *m* COOK morellino wine

morello *m* blackish

morena *f* moraine

morente I *adj* dying **II** *m/f* dying person

moresco *adj* ⟨*mpl* -chi⟩ Moorish; ***stile*** *m* ***~*** Moorish style

moretto *adj di capelli*: dark-haired; *di pelle*: dark-skinned

morfina *f* morphine

morfinomane *m/f* morphine addict

morfologia *f* LING, BIOL morphology; ***~ di un territorio*** morphology of an area **morfologico** *adj* ⟨*mpl* -ci⟩ morphological

morganatico *adj* ⟨*mpl* -ci⟩: ***matrimonio*** *m* ***~*** *hist* morganatic marriage

moria *f* disease; ***~ di pesci*** fish kill

moribondo *adj* dying

morigeratezza *f* temperance **morigerato** *adj* (*sobrio*) temperate; (*giusto*) decent

morire *v/i* ⟨4k⟩ die; *fig* ***~ di paura*** be scared to death; ***~ dal ridere*** die laughing; *fig* ***~ dietro a qn*** be dying of love for s.o.; ***mi piace da ~!*** I absolutely love it; ***muoio dalla voglia di una birra*** *infml* I could murder a pint *infml*, I'm dying for a beer *infml*

mormone *m/f* Mormon

mormora *f* ZOOL striped seabream

mormorare *v/t* ⟨1l⟩ murmur; (*bisbigliare*, *lamentarsi*) mutter; ***si mormora che ...*** rumor has it that…

mormorio *m* murmuring; (*brontolio*) muttering

moro I *adj* dark **II** *m* ***i Mori*** *hist* the Moors; ***testa*** *f* ***di ~*** dark brown

morosità *f* ⟨*pl* morosità⟩ default **moroso** *adj* JUR delinquent payer; *infml* sweetheart

morra *f* mora

morsa *f* MECH clamp; (*stretta*, *presa*) grip; *fig* grip

morse *adj inv*: (***alfabeto***) ~ Morse code

morsetto *m* TECH clamp; ELEC terminal

morsicare *v/t* ⟨1l, c & d⟩ bite

morsicatura *f* bite; *di ape / vespa* sting

morso I *past part* → ***mordere*** **II** *m* bite; *di cibo* bit, mouthful; *per cavallo* bit; ***i -i*** *pl* ***della fame*** the pangs of hunger; *fig* ***allentare / stringere il ~*** loosen / tighten one's grip on sth

mortadella *f* Bologna sausage

mortaio *m* ⟨*pl* -ai⟩ mortar (*a.* MIL)

mortale *adj ferita*, *malattia* fatal; *offesa*, *nemico* deadly; *uomo* mortal

mortalità *f* mortality

mortalmente *adv* fatally

mortaretto *m* banger, firework

morte *f* death; ***~ bianca*** death by freezing; ***pericolo*** *m* ***di ~*** danger; ***in punto di ~*** at death's door; ***condannare a ~*** sentence to death; *fig* ***avercela a ~ con qn*** hate s.o.'s guts; ***avere la ~ nel cuore*** have a heavy heart

mortificare *v/t* ⟨1m & d⟩ mortify; ***~ la carne*** mortify the flesh

mortificazione *f* mortification

morto I *past part* → ***morire*** **II** *adj* dead; ***stanco ~*** dead tired; ***natura*** *f* ***-a*** still life **III** *m*, ***-a*** *f* dead man; *donna* dead woman; ***i -i*** *pl* the dead; ***giorno*** *m* ***dei -i*** All Souls' Day; ***essere un ~ di fame*** be a down-and-out; ***fare il ~*** float on one's back

mortorio *m*: ***essere un ~*** *infml* be deadly dull *or* boring

mortuario *adj* ⟨*mpl* -ri⟩ death; ***annuncio*** *m* ***~*** obituary; ***camera*** *f* ***-a*** morgue

mosaico *m* ⟨*pl* -ci⟩ mosaic

mosca *f* ⟨*pl* -che⟩ fly; ***peso*** *m* ***~*** flyweight; ***~ cieca*** blind man's buff; ***restare con un pugno di -che*** come away empty-handed; ***far saltare la ~ al naso a qn*** make s.o.'s hackles rise; ***non si sentiva volare una ~*** you could have heard a pin drop

moscardino *m* (*mollusco*) curled octopus

moscatello *m* muscatel

moscato I *adj* muscat; ***noce*** *f* ***-a*** nutmeg **II** *m* muscat (wine)

moscerino *m* gnat, midge

moschea *f* mosque

moschettiere *m* HIST musketeer **moschetto** *m* musket **moschettone** *m* snap-hook

moschicida *m/adj* ⟨*pl* -i⟩ fly spray; ***carta*** *f* ***~*** fly-paper

moscio *adj* ⟨*mpl* -sci⟩ thin, flimsy; *fig* limp, washed out

moscone *m* ZOOL bluebottle; (*imbarcazione*) pedalo

moscovita ⟨*mpl* -i⟩ **I** *adj* Muscovite **II** *m/f* Muscovite

mossa *f* movement; *fig e di judo*, *karate* move; *fig* ***darsi una ~*** get a move on

mosso I *past part* → ***muovere*** **II** *adj*; ***mare*** *m* ***~*** rough sea; ***capelli*** *mpl* ***-i*** wavy hair; ***foto*** *f* ***-a*** blurred photo

mostarda *f* mustard; ***~ di Cremona*** *sweet fruit pickles*

mosto *m* must, *unfermented grape juice*

mostra *f* show; (*esposizione*) exhibition; ***~ mercato*** fair; *fig* ***mettere in ~*** show off; ***mettersi in ~*** show off

mostrare *v/t* ⟨1a⟩ show; (*indicare*) point out; *fig* ***~ i denti*** bare one's teeth

mostrarsi *v/r* appear

mostriciattolo *m* little monster

mostrina *f* tab; MIL flash

mostro *m* monster; ***~ sacro*** guru

mostruosamente *adv* monstrously **mostruosità** *f* ⟨*pl* mostruosità⟩ monstrosity; *fig* horror

mostruoso *adj* monstrous

mota *f* mud

motel *m* ⟨*pl* motel⟩ motel

motivare *v/t* ⟨1a⟩ cause; *personale* motivate; (*spiegare*) explain, give reasons for

motivato *adj* motivated; ***essere ~*** be motivated

motivazione *f* (*spiegazione*) explanation; (*stimolo*) motivation

motivo *m* reason; MUS theme, motif; *su tessuto* pattern; ***per quale ~?*** for what reason?, why?

moto[1] *m* movement; ***fare ~*** get some exercise; ***~ dell'animo*** feeling; ***mettere in ~*** *motore* start (up); *fig* set in motion

moto[2] *f* (motor)bike; ***~ d'acqua*** Jet Ski®; ***andare in ~*** motor-bike

motobarca *f* ⟨*pl* -che⟩ motor-boat

motocarro *m* three-wheeled van

motocicletta *f* motorcycle
motociclismo *m* motorcycling
motociclista *m/f* ⟨*mpl* -i⟩ motorcyclist
motociclistico *adj*: ***gara** f* ***-a*** motor--bike race
motociclo *m* **1.** motorbike, (*50cc*) moped **2.** motorcycling
motocross *m* SPORTS motocross
motocrossista *m/f* ⟨*mpl* -i⟩ scramble rider
motodromo *m* motorbike race track
motonautica *f* ⟨*pl* -che⟩ motor-boating; SPORTS speedboat racing
motonave *f* motorship
motopeschereccio *m* ⟨*pl* -cci⟩ motor fishing-boat
motopompa *f* motor pump
motoraduno *m* motorbike rally
motore *m* engine; ***~ a combustione*** internal combustion engine; ***~ Diesel*** diesel engine; ***~ a iniezione*** fuel--injection engine; COMPUT ***~ di ricerca*** search engine; ***~ a due tempi*** two--stroke engine; ***~ a quattro tempi*** four-stroke engine; ***~ fuoribordo*** outboard (motor *or* engine); ***veicolo** m* ***a ~*** motor vehicle; ***accendere il ~*** start (up) the engine, turn the key in the ignition; ***fermare il ~*** turn off the engine
motorino *m* moped; ***~ d'avviamento*** starter
motorista *m/f* ⟨*mpl* -i⟩ motor mechanic; NAUT, AVIAT engineer
motorizzare *v/t* ⟨1a⟩ motorize **motorizzarsi** *v/r* ⟨1a⟩ get a car
motorizzato *adj* motorized; ***sei ~*** *infml* have you got wheels? *infml*
motorizzazione *f*: ***~ civile*** Driver and Vehicle Licensing Centre
motoscafo *m* motorboat
motoscooter *m* ⟨*pl* motoscooter⟩ (motor) scooter
motosega *f* ⟨*pl* -ghe⟩ chain-saw
motoslitta *f* snowcat
motovedetta *f* NAUT patrol boat
motozappa *f* Rotavator
motrice *f* RAIL railcar
motteggiare *v/i* ⟨1f⟩ joke; (*beffare*) make fun of
motteggio *m* ⟨*pl* -ggi⟩ joke
mottetto *m* motet
motto *m* motto
mountain bike *f* ⟨*pl* mountain bike⟩ mountain bike
mouse *m* ⟨*pl* mouse⟩ COMPUT mouse
movente *m* motive
movenza *f* bearing; MUS modulation
movida *f* night-life
movimentare *v/t* ⟨1a⟩ enliven **movimentarsi** *v/r* ⟨1a⟩ liven up **movimentato** *adj* lively
movimento *m* movement; (*vita*) life, bustle
moviola *f* FILM, TV movieola; ***alla ~*** in slow motion
Mozambico *m* Mozambique
mozione *m* motion; ***~ di fiducia*** vote of confidence
mozzafiato *adj inv* breathtaking
mozzare *v/t* ⟨1a⟩ cut off
mozzarella *f* mozzarella, *buffalo-milk cheese*
mozzicone *m* cigarette end, (cigarette) stub
mozzo *m* TECH hub
mozzo[2] *adj* cabin boy; ***parole** fpl* / ***frasi** fpl* ***-e*** unfinished words / sentences
mq *abbr* (= **metro quadrato**) sq m (square metre)
MS *abbr* (= **Massa-Carrara**) Massa--Carrara
MT *abbr* (= **Matera**) Matera
mucca *f* ⟨*pl* -cche⟩ cow
mucchio *m* ⟨*pl* -cchi⟩ pile, heap; ***un ~ di soldi*** a lot of money
mucillagine *f* mucilage
muco *m* ⟨*pl* -chi⟩ mucus
mucolitico ⟨*mpl* -ci⟩ **I** *adj* mucolytic **II** *n*: ***mucolitico** m* mucolytic
mucosa *f* mucous membrane
muezzin *m* ⟨*pl* muezzin⟩ muezzin
muffa *f* mo(u)ld; ***sapere di ~*** taste mo(u)ldy; ***fare la ~*** go mo(u)ldy
muffola *f* mitten; TECH muffle
muflone *m* mouflon
muggine *m* ZOOL grey mullet
muggire *v/i* ⟨4d⟩ moo
muggito *m* moo
mughetto *m* lily of the valley
mugnaio *m*, **-a** *f* ⟨*mpl* -ai⟩ miller
mugolare *v/i* ⟨1l⟩ *di cane* whine; (*gemere*) moan, whine
mugolio *m* whining
mugugnare *v/i* ⟨1a⟩ grumble
mula *f* she-mule
mulattiera *f* mule track
mulatto *m*, **-a** *f* mulatto
mulinare *v/t and v/i* ⟨1a⟩ spin; (*archi-*

tettare) contrive; *fig* daydream

mulinello *m su canna da pesca* reel; *vortice d'acqua* eddy

mulino *m* mill; ***~ a vento*** windmill; ***tirare l'acqua al proprio ~*** drive a hard bargain

mullah *m* ⟨*pl* mullah⟩ mullah

mulo *m*, **-a** *f* mule

multa *f* fine

multare *v/t* ⟨1a⟩ fine

multicolore *adj* multicolo(u)red

multiculturale *adj* multicultural

multiculturalismo *m* multiculturalism

multietnico *adj* ⟨*mpl* -ci⟩ multi-ethnic

multiforme *adj* varied

multifunzionale *adj* multifunctional

multilaterale *adj* multilateral

multimediale *adj* multimedia

multinazionale *f/adj* multinational

multiplo *adj* multiple

multiprocessore *m* COMPUT multiprocessor

multiproprietà *f* ⟨*pl* multiproprietà⟩ (*immobili*) timeshare

multirazziale *adj* multiracial

multisala *f* multiplex

multiuso *adj* multipurpose

mummia *f* mummy

mummificato *adj* mummified

mungere *v/t* ⟨3d⟩ milk

mungitura *f* milking

mungo *m* ⟨*pl* -ghi⟩ ZOOL Indian mongoose

municipale *adj* municipal; ***consiglio** m **~*** town council

municipalizzare *v/t* ⟨1a⟩ municipalize **municipalizzato** *adj*; ***azienda** f **-a*** municipalized company **municipalizzazione** *f* municipalization

municipio *m* ⟨*pl* -pi⟩ town council, municipality; *edificio* town hall

munificenza *f* munificence **munifico** *adj* ⟨*mpl* -ci⟩ bountiful

munire *v/t* ⟨4d⟩: ***~ di*** supply with, provide with

munirsi *v/r* ⟨4d⟩ equip / arm oneself (with) (*a. fig*); ***~ di coraggio*** arm oneself with courage

munizioni *fpl* ammunition *sg*

muovere ⟨3ff⟩ **I** *v/t* move **II** *v/i partire* move off (***da*** from); ***~ incontro a qn*** move towards s.o.; ***non ha mosso un dito per aiutarci*** he didn't lift a finger to help us

muoversi *v/r* move; *infml* (*sbrigarsi*) get a move on *infml*; ***muoviti!*** get a move on!; ***non mi sono mosso da casa*** I didn't leave the house

muraglia *f* wall; ***la ~ cinese*** the Great Wall of China

muraglione *m* wall

murale I *adj* wall *attr* **II** *m* PAINT mural

murales *m* ⟨*pl* murales⟩ murals

murare *v/t* ⟨1a⟩ (*chiudere*) wall up

muratore *m* bricklayer

muratura *f* brickwork

murena *f* moray (eel)

muriatico *adj*: ***acido** m **~*** muriatic acid

muricciolo *m* low wall

muro *m* ⟨*pl a.* le mura⟩ wall; ***le -a** fpl* (city) walls; ***~ a secco*** drystone wall; ***~ del suono*** sound barrier; *fig* ***mi ha messo con le spalle al ~*** he'd got my back against the wall; *fig* ***~ di gomma*** a wall of silence; ***~ del pianto*** the Wailing Wall; ***~ di Berlino*** HIST the Berlin Wall

musa *f* Muse

muschiato *adj* musky; ***bue** m **~*** musk-ox

muschio *m* ⟨*pl* -chi⟩ BOT moss

muscolare *adj* muscular; ***strappo** m **~*** strained muscle

muscolatura *f* muscles *pl*

muscolo *m* muscle

muscoloso *adj* muscular

museo *m* museum; ***~ archeologico*** archaeological museum; ***~ d'arte*** museum; ***~ etnologico*** folk museum; ***~ nazionale*** national museum; ***~ delle cere*** wax museum

museruola *f* muzzle

musetto *m di persona* pretty little face

musica *f* music; ***~ da camera*** chamber music; ***~ classica*** classical music; ***~ leggera*** light music, easy-listening music; *fig* ***cambiare ~*** change one's tune

musical *m* ⟨*pl* musical⟩ musical

musicale *adj* musical; ***strumento** m **~*** musical instrument

musicalità *f* ⟨*pl* musicalità⟩ musicality **musicante** *m/f* musician *pej* poor performer **musicare** *v/t* ⟨1l & d⟩ set to music

musicassetta *f* (music) tape

musicista *m/f* ⟨*mpl* -i⟩ musician

musicologo *m*, **-a** *f* ⟨*mpl* -gi⟩ musicologist

muso *m di animale* muzzle; *di aereo*

nose; ***tenere il ~ a qn*** be in a huff with s.o.; ***brutto ~*** *infml* ugly mug!
musone *m*, **-a** *f* sulker
mussare *v/i* ⟨1a⟩ foam
mussola *f* muslin
must *m* ⟨*pl* must⟩ must; ***essere un ~*** be a must
musulmano I *adj* Muslim, Moslem **II** *m*, **-a** *f* Muslim, Moslem
muta *f di cani* pack; SPORTS wetsuit
mutabile *adj* changeable
mutamento *m* change
mutande *fpl da donna* knickers *pl*; *da uomo* (under)pants *pl*; *fig* ***restare in ~*** *infml* be ruined
mutandine *fpl* knickers *pl*; ***~ (da bagno)*** (swimming) trunks *pl*
mutante *m/f* mutant
mutare *v/t & v/i* ⟨1a⟩ change
mutazione *f* change; (*sostituzione*) substitution; MED mutation; ***~ genetica*** genetic mutation
mutevole *adj* → ***mutabile***
mutilare *v/t* ⟨1l⟩ mutilate
mutilato *m* disabled ex-serviceman
mutilazione *f* mutilation
mutismo *m* mutism
muto I *adj* dumb; (*silenzioso*) silent, dumb; ***film m ~*** silent film; ***essere ~ dallo stupore*** be struck dumb with astonishment; ***fare scena -a*** not say a word; ***~ come un pesce*** mum's the word **II** *m*, **-a** *f* mute
mutua *f fund that pays out sickness benefit*; ***medico m della ~*** doctor recognized by the mutua
mutuabile *adj* ADMIN loanable; ***farmaco m ~*** medicine granted under the National Health Service **mutualistico** *adj* ⟨*mpl* -ci⟩ National Health Service **mutuatario** *m*, **-a** *f* ⟨*mpl* -ri⟩ borrower
mutuato *m*, **-a** *f person entitled to sickness benefit*
mutuo I *adj* mutual **II** *m* mortgage; ***~ soccorso*** mutual aid

N

n, N *m/f* ⟨*pl* n, N⟩ n, N; ***N come Napoli*** N for November
N *abbr* (= **nord**) N (north)
n. *abbr* (= **numero**) No. (number)
NA *abbr* (= **Napoli**) Naples
nababbo *m*: ***vita f da ~*** luxurious lifestyle
nacchere *fpl* castanets *pl*
nafta *f* naphtha
naftalina *f* mothballs; CHEM naphthalene
naia *f infml* military service
naif *adj inv di persona*: naïve; ***pittura f ~*** naïf painting
Namibia *f* Namibia **namibiano I** *adj* Namibian **II** *m*, **-a** *f* Namibian
nanerottolo *m*, **-a** *f* dwarf **nanismo** *m* dwarfism
nanna *f infml* (*child*) bye-byes; ***fare la ~*** go bye-byes (to sleep); ***andare a ~*** go to sleep
nano I *adj* dwarf **II** *m*, **-a** *f* dwarf
Napoleone *m* Napoleon **napoleonico** *adj* ⟨*mpl* -ci⟩ Napoleonic
napoletano I *adj* Neapolitan **II** *m*, **-a** *f* Neapolitan
Napoli *f* Naples
nappa *f* tassel; (*pelle*) nappa (*type of soft leather*)
Narbona *f* Narbonne
narcisismo *m* narcissism **narcisista** *m/f* ⟨*mpl* -i⟩ narcissist **narcisistico** *adj* ⟨*mpl* -ci⟩ narcissistic
narciso *m* BOT narcissus
Narciso *m* Narcissus
narcodollari *mpl* narcodollars
narcosi *f* ⟨*pl* narcosi⟩ narcosis
narcotico *m* ⟨*pl* -ci⟩ narcotic
narcotizzare *v/t* ⟨1a⟩ drug
narcotrafficante *m/f* drug dealer
narcotraffico *m* ⟨*pl* -ci⟩ drug dealing
narghilè *m* ⟨*pl* narghilè⟩ hookah
narice *f* nostril
narrare *v/t* ⟨1a⟩ tell, narrate
narrativa *f* fiction
narratore *m*, **-trice** *f* narrator
narrazione *f* narration
nasale *adj* nasal; ***voce f ~*** nasal voice;

setto *m* **~** nasal septum

nascente *adj giorno* dawning; *sole, astro* rising

nascere *v/i* ⟨3gg⟩ be born; BOT come up; *fig* develop, grow up; *di sole* rise, come up; ***sono nato a Roma*** I was born in Rome; ***le è nata una figlia*** she's had a little girl; ***da cosa nasce cosa*** one thing leads to another

nascita *f* birth; ***data*** *f* / ***luogo*** *m* ***di*** **~** date / place of birth; ***fin dalla*** **~** from birth

nascituro *m* unborn child

nasco *m* COOK Sardinian grape used to make sweet fortified wine

nascondere *v/t* ⟨3hh⟩ hide, conceal

nascondersi *v/r* hide

nascondiglio *m* ⟨*pl* -gli⟩ hiding place

nascondino *m*: ***giocare a*** **~** play hide-and-seek *or US* hide-and-go-seek

nascosto I *past part* → ***nascondere*** **II** *adv*: ***di*** **~** in secret; ***di*** **~** ***a qn*** unbeknownst to s.o.

nasello *m* (*pesce*) hake

nasino *m* pretty little nose

naso *m* nose; **~** ***aquilino*** Roman nose; **~** ***all'insù*** turned-up nose; ***andare a*** **~** follow one's nose; *fig* ***ficcare il*** **~** ***negli affari altrui*** stick one's nose into other people's business; ***menare qn per il*** **~** lead s.o. up the garden path; (***non***) ***mettere il*** **~** ***fuori dalla porta*** (not) put one's nose out of the door; ***soffiarsi il*** **~** blow one's nose

nastro *m* tape; *per capelli, di decorazione* ribbon; **~** ***adesivo*** adhesive tape, Sellotape®, *US* Scotch tape®; **~** ***isolante*** insulating tape, *US* friction tape; **~** ***magnetico*** magnetic tape; **~** ***trasportatore*** conveyor belt

nasturzio *m* ⟨*pl* -zi⟩ nasturtium

natale *adj* of one's birth; ***paese*** *m* **~** country of one's birth

Natale *m* Christmas; ***a*** **~** at Christmas; ***vigilia*** *f* ***di*** **~** Christmas Eve; ***buon*** **~*!*** Merry Christmas!

natalità *f* birth rate, number of births; ***tasso di*** **~** birthrate

natalizio *adj* ⟨*mpl* -zi⟩ Christmas; ***atmosfera*** *f* ***-a*** Christmassy atmosphere

natante I *adj* floating **II** *m* boat

natica *f* ANAT buttock

natività *f* ⟨*pl* natività⟩ nativity; ***la*** **~** ***di Cristo*** the birth of Christ (*a.* ART)

nativo I *adj* native **II** *m*, **-a** *f* native

nato → ***nascere***; ***appena*** **~** new-born; ***essere*** **~** ***con la camicia*** be born with a silver spoon in one's mouth

NATO *abbr* (= **Organizzazione del Trattato nord-atlantico**) NATO (North Atlantic Treaty Organization)

natura *f* nature; PAINT **~** ***morta*** still life; ***la*** **~** ***umana*** human nature; ***essere paziente per*** **~** be patient by nature, be naturally patient; ***contro*** **~** unnatural; ***secondo*** **~** in harmony with nature

naturale *adj* natural; ***scienze*** *fpl* ***-i*** natural sciences; ***al*** **~** COOK au naturel

naturalezza *f* naturalness; ***con*** **~** naturally

naturalismo *m* naturalism **naturalista I** *adj* naturalist **II** *m/f* ⟨*mpl* -i⟩ nature lover; LIT, ART naturalism **naturalistico** *adj* ⟨*mpl* -ci⟩ naturalist; PHIL, LIT naturalistic

naturalizzare *v/t* ⟨1a⟩: ***è naturalizzato americano*** he's a naturalized American

naturalizzarsi *v/r* ⟨1a⟩ naturalize; BIOL adapt

naturalmente *adv* naturally, of course; *comportarsi* naturally

naturismo *m* naturism, nudism

naturista *m/f* ⟨*mpl* -i⟩ naturist

naufragare *v/i* ⟨1l & e⟩ *di nave* be wrecked; *di persona* be shipwrecked; *fig* be ruined, come to grief

naufragio *m* ⟨*pl* -gi⟩ shipwreck; *fig* ruin; ***fare*** **~** *di nave* be wrecked; *di persona* be shipwrecked

naufrago *m*, **-a** *f* ⟨*mpl* -ghi⟩ survivor of a shipwreck

nausea *f* nausea; ***avere la*** **~** feel sick, *US* feel nauseous; ***dare la*** **~** ***a qn*** make s.o. feel sick, nauseate s.o. (*a. fig*); *fig* ***fino alla*** **~** ad nauseam

nauseante *adj* nauseating (*a. fig*) revolting

nauseare *v/t* ⟨1l⟩ nauseate (*a. fig*)

nautica *f* seamanship, boating; **~** ***da diporto*** pleasure boating

nautico *adj* ⟨*mpl* -ci⟩ nautical; ***sci*** *m* **~** water-skiing; ***patente*** *f* ***-a*** sailing licence *or US* license; ***salone*** *m* **~** boat show

navale *adj* naval; ***cantiere*** *m* **~** shipyard; ***battaglia*** *f* **~** naval battle; (*gioco*) battleship(s)

navata *f* ARCH: **~** ***centrale*** nave; **~** ***later-***

ale aisle
nave *f* ship; **~ *da carico*** cargo ship *or* vessel; **~ *passeggeri*** passenger ship; **~ *traghetto*** ferry
navetta I *adj inv*: ***bus*** *m* **~** shuttle bus **II** *f* shuttle; **~ *spaziale*** space shuttle
navicella *f di astronave* nose cone; **~ *spaziale*** spaceship
navigabile *adj* navigable
navigabilità *f* ⟨*pl* navigabilità⟩ NAUT seaworthiness AVIAT airworthiness
navigante *m* sailor
navigare *v/i* ⟨1l & e⟩ sail; COMPUT navigate
navigato *adj* expert
navigatore *m*, **-trice** *f* navigator; **~ *satellitare*** AUTO GPS
navigazione *f* navigation
nazareno *adj* Nazarene
nazionale I *adj* national **II** *f* national team; ***la ~ italiana*** the Italian team
nazionalismo *m* nationalism
nazionalista *m/f* ⟨*mpl* -i⟩ nationalist
nazionalistico *adj* ⟨*mpl* -ci⟩ nationalistic
nazionalità *f* ⟨*pl* nazionalità⟩ nationality
nazionalizzare *v/i* ⟨1a⟩ nationalize
nazionalsocialismo *m* National Socialism
nazione *f* nation; ***Nazioni Unite*** *fpl* POL United Nations
naziskin *m/f* ⟨*pl* naziskin⟩ skinhead
nazismo *m* Nazism
nazista ⟨*mpl* -i⟩ **I** *adj* Nazi **II** *m/f* Nazi
N. B. *abbr* (= **nota bene**) NB (nota bene)
N.d.A. *abbr* (= **nota dell'autore**) author's note
N.d.E. *abbr* (= **nota dell'editore**) publisher's note
N.d.R. *abbr* (= **Nota del Redattore**) editor's note
'ndrangheta *f Calabrian Mafia*
N.d.T. *abbr* (= **nota del traduttore**) translator's note
ne I *pron* (*di lui*) about him; (*di lei*) about her; (*di loro*) about them; (*di ciò*) about it; **~ *sono contento*** I'm happy about it; **~ *ho abbastanza*** I have enough; ***che ~ dici?*** what do you say?; **~ *voglio 1 chilo*** I want a kilo **II** *adv* from there; **~ *vengo adesso*** I've just come back from there
NE *abbr* (= **nord-est**) NE (northeast)
né *cj*: **~ ... ~** neither ... nor; ***non l'ho trovato ~ a casa ~ in ufficio*** I couldn't find him either at home or in the office
neanche *adv* neither; ***io non vado – neanch'io*** I'm not going – neither am I *or* me neither *infml*; ***non l'ho ~ visto*** I didn't even see him; **~ *per sogno!*** in your dreams!
nebbia *f* fog
nebbiolo *m* COOK Piedmontese black grape and wine
nebbione *m* thick fog
nebbioso *adj* foggy
nebulizzatore *m* atomiser; AGR sprayer (nozzle)
nebulosa *f* ASTR nebula
nebuloso *adj fig* vague, hazy
necessaire *m* ⟨*pl* necessaire⟩: **~ (*da viaggio*)** beauty case
necessariamente *adv* necessarily
necessario ⟨*mpl* -ri⟩ **I** *adj* necessary **II** *m*: ***il ~ per vivere*** the basic necessities *pl*; ***lo stretto ~*** the bare essentials *pl*
necessità *f* ⟨*pl* necessità⟩ need; ***ho ~ di parlarti*** I need to talk to you; ***articolo*** *m* ***di prima ~*** essential; ***in caso di ~*** if necessary, if need be; ***fare qc senza ~*** do sth needlessly; ***per ~*** out of necessity; ***fare di ~ virtù*** make (a) virtue of necessity
necessitare ⟨1m & b⟩ **I** *v/i*: **~ *di qc*** **II** *v/t* need sth
necrofilo I *adj* necrophilous **II** *m*, **-a** *f* necrophiliac
necrologio *m* ⟨*pl* -gi⟩ death notice
necropoli *f* ⟨*pl* necropoli⟩ burial ground; *antica* necropolis
necroscopico *adj* ⟨*mpl* -ci⟩: ***esame*** *m* **~** post-mortem
necrosi *f* ⟨*pl* necrosi⟩ MED necrosis
ne(d)erlandese I *adj* Dutch, Netherlandic **II** *m/f* Dutchman, Netherlander
nefandezza *f* (*qualità*) wickedness; (*azione*) atrocity
nefasto *adj* unlucky
nefrite *f* MED nephritis
negare *v/t* ⟨1e⟩ deny; (*rifiutare*) refuse; **~ *l'evidenza*** deny the facts
negarsi *v/r* ⟨1e⟩ refuse to do sth; **~ *a qn*** refuse to have sex with s.o.
negativa *f* negative
negativamente *adv* negatively **negatività** *f* ⟨*pl* negatività⟩ negativity

negativo *m/adj* negative
negato *adj*: ***essere ~ per qc*** be hopeless at sth
negazione *f* denial; GRAM negative
negletto *adj* (*trascurato*) neglected; (*sciatto*) unkempt
negli = *prep* ***in*** *and art* ***gli***
négligé *m* ⟨*pl* négligé⟩: ***essere in ~*** wear a negligée
negligente *adj* careless, negligent
negligenza *f* carelessness, negligence
negoziabile *adj* negotiable
negoziante *m/f* shopkeeper
negoziare ⟨1g & c⟩ **I** *v/t* negotiate **II** *v/i* negotiate, bargain; FIN ***~ in*** trade in, deal in
negoziato *m* negotiation; ***-i*** *pl* ***di pace*** peace negotiations; ***-i*** *pl* ***di adesione*** EU EU membership negotiations
negoziazione *f* negotiation
negozio *m* ⟨*pl* -zi⟩ shop; (*affare*) deal; ***~ di generi alimentari*** food shop; ***~ specializzato*** specialist shop
negriero *m fig* slave-driver
negro *pej* **I** *adj* black **II** *m*, **-a** *f* black (man / woman)
negromante *m/f* necromancer **negromanzia** *f* necromancy
nei, nel, nell', nella, nelle, nello = *prep* ***in*** *and art* ***i, il, l', la, le, lo***
nembo *m* rain-cloud
nemico ⟨*mpl* -ci⟩ **I** *m*, *fig* ***essere ~ di qc*** be opposed to sth; **-a** *f* enemy **II** *adj* enemy *attr*
nemmeno *adv* neither; ***~ io*** me neither; ***~ per idea!*** don't even think about it!
neo *m* mole; *fig* flaw
neoclassico ⟨*mpl* -ci⟩ **I** *adj* neoclassical **II** *n*: ***neoclassico*** *m* neoclassicism
neodiplomato **I** *adj* school-leaving; ***geometra*** *m* ***~*** newly qualified surveyor **II** *m*, **-a** *f* school-leaver
neoeletto *adj* newly-appointed
neofascismo *m* neofascism
neofascista ⟨*mpl* -i⟩ **I** *adj* neofascist **II** *m/f* neofascist
neofita *m* ⟨*mpl* -i⟩ REL neophyte; *fig* neophyte
neolaureato **I** *adj*: ***giovane*** *m* ***~*** a young recent graduate **II** *m*, **-a** *f* newly graduated person
neolitico ⟨*mpl* -ci⟩ **I** *adj* neolithic **II** *n*: ***neolitico*** *m* neolithic period
neon *m* neon; ***luce*** *f or* ***lampada*** *f* ***al ~*** neon light
neonato *m*, **-a** *f* infant, newborn baby
neonatologia *f* neonatology
neonazismo *m* neo-Nazism
neonazista *m/f* ⟨*mpl* -i⟩ neonazi
neorealismo *m* neorealism
neorealista ⟨*mpl* -i⟩ **I** *adj* neo-realist; ***il cinema ~*** neo-realist cinema **II** *m/f* neo-realist
neozelandese **I** *adj* New Zealand *attr* **II** *m/f* New Zealander
Nepal *m* Nepal **nepalese** **I** *adj* Nepalese **II** *m/f* Nepalese
nepotismo *m* nepotism
neppure *adv* not even; ***non ci vado – ~ io*** I'm not going – neither am I *or* me neither *infml*
nerastro *adj* blackish
nerbata *f* lash **nerbo** *m* whip; *fig* (*energia*) strength; (*anima*) nerve; ***senza ~*** weak **nerboruto** *adj* brawny; ***braccia*** *fpl* ***-e*** brawny arms
neretto *m* TYPO bold(face); ***in ~*** in bold (face)
nero **I** *adj* black; *umore* awful, filthy *infml*; ***occhio*** *m* ***~*** black eye; ***uva*** *f* ***-a*** black grapes; *fig* ***giornata*** *f* ***-a*** off-day; *fig* ***terrorismo*** *m* ***~*** right-wing terrorism; ***essere di umore ~*** be in a bad mood; ***fare ~ qn*** *hum* beat s.o. up **II** *m* black; *di seppia* ink; ***mettere ~ su bianco*** put down sth in writing **III** *m*, **-a** *f* black (man, woman)
nerofumo *m* lampblack
nervatura *f* BOT nerve; ARCH, MECH rib
nervino *adj*: ***gas*** *m* ***~*** nerve gas
nervo *m* nerve; ***dare sui*** (*or* ***ai***) ***-i a qn*** get on s.o.'s nerves; ***avere i -i a fior di pelle*** be on edge; ***avere i -i a pezzi*** be on edge; ***avere i -i saldi*** be calm; ***mi fai venire i -i*** you're getting on my nerves
nervosamente *adv* nervously **nervosetto** *adj hum* edgy
nervosismo *m* nervousness
nervoso **I** *adj* nervous; (*irritabile*) edgy; (*asciutto*) sinewy; ***esaurimento*** *m* ***~*** nervous breakdown **II** *m infml*: ***il ~*** irritation; ***mi viene il ~*** I'm beginning to get really irritated, this is getting on my nerves
nespola *f* medlar
nespolo *m* medlar (tree)

nesso *m* connection; **~ *logico*** logical connection
nessuno I *adj* no; ***non chiamare in nessun caso*** don't call in any circumstances; ***c'è -a notizia?*** is there any news?; ***da -a parte*** nowhere **II** *pron* nobody, no one; ***hai visto ~?*** did you see anyone *or* anybody?; ***c'è ~?*** is there anybody there?
netiquette *f* COMPUT netiquette
nettamente *adv* clearly; (*con decisione*) decisively
nettare[1] *m* nectar
nettare[2] *v/t* ⟨1a⟩ clean
nettezza *f* cleanliness; **~ *urbana*** cleansing department
netto *adj* clean; (*chiaro*) clear; *reddito, peso* net; ***di ~*** cleanly; ***peso m ~*** net weight; ***al ~ di*** net; ***al ~ delle imposte*** net of tax; ***interrompere qn di ~*** break in on s.o.
Nettuno *m* Neptune
netturbino *m*, **-a** *f* dustman
network *m* ⟨*pl* network⟩ network
neurochirurgia *f* brain surgery, neurosurgery **neurochirurgo** *m* ⟨*pl* -ghi⟩ neurosurgeon, brain surgeon
neurodermite *f* neurodermatitis
neurologia *f* neurology
neurologico *adj* neurological
neurologo *m*, **-a** *f* ⟨*mpl* -gi⟩ neurologist
neuropsichiatra *m/f* ⟨*mpl* -i⟩ neuropsychiatrist **neuropsichiatria** *f* neuropsychiatry **neurovegetativo** *adj* neurovegetative
neutrale *adj* neutral
neutralità *f* neutrality
neutralizzare *v/t* ⟨1a⟩ neutralize
neutralizzarsi *v/r* ⟨1a⟩ neutralize
neutro *adj* neutral; ***sapone m ~*** mild soap; GRAM neuter
neutrone *m* neutron
neve *f* snow; **~ *artificiale*** artificial snow; ***fiocco m di ~*** snowflake; **~ *fresca*** fresh snow
nevicare *v/impers* ⟨1l & d⟩ snow
nevicata *f* snowfall
nevischio *m* sleet
nevoso *adj* snowy
nevralgia *f* neuralgia
nevralgico *adj* ⟨*mpl* -ci⟩ neuralgic; ***punto m ~*** specially painful point; *fig* weak point
nevrastenico ⟨*mpl* -ci⟩ **I** *adj* MED neurasthenic; *infml* irritable **II** *m* neurasthenic; *infml* irritable person
nevrosi *f* neurosis
nevrotico ⟨*mpl* -ci⟩ **I** *adj* neurotic; *infml* short-tempered, quick to fly off the handle *infml* **II** *m*, **-a** *f* neurotic
new age I *f* ⟨*pl* new age⟩ new age **II** *adj inv*. ***musica f ~*** new age music
new economy *f* ⟨*pl* new economy⟩ new economy **new entry** *f* ⟨*pl* new entry⟩ new entry
newsgroup *m* ⟨*pl* newsgroup⟩ newsgroup **newsletter** *f* ⟨*pl* newsletter⟩ newsletter
newyorkese I *adj* from New York **II** *m/f* New Yorker
ni *infml* **I** *adv* yes and no **II** *m* ⟨*pl* ni⟩ yes and no
nibbio *m* ⟨*pl* -bbi⟩ kite; **~ *reale*** red kite
Nibelunghi *mpl*: ***i ~*** Nibelung
Nicaragua *m* Nicaragua **nicaraguense I** *adj* Nicaraguan **II** *m/f* Nicaraguan
nicchia *f* niche; **~ *di mercato*** ECON niche market
nicchiare *v/i* ⟨1k⟩ hedge, *infml* shilly-shally
niceno I *adj* Nicene **II** *m*, **-a** *f* Nicene
nichel *m* nickel
nichilismo *m* nihilism **nichilista** ⟨*mpl* -i⟩ **I** *adj* nihilist **II** *m/f* nihilist
Nicola *m*: ***San ~*** Saint Nicholas
nicotina *f* nicotine
nidiata *f* brood
nidificare *v/i* ⟨1m & d⟩ nest
nido *m* nest; ***asilo m ~*** day nursery; ***a ~ d'ape*** honeycomb
niente I *pron m* nothing **II** *adv* nothing; ***non ho ~*** I don't have anything, I have nothing; ***lo fai tu? – ~ affatto!*** are you going to do it? – no, I am not!; ***tu hai detto che … – ~ affatto!*** you said that … – no, I did not!; ***non ho per ~ fame*** I'm not at all hungry; ***non ho capito per ~*** I didn't understand a thing; **~ *da fare!*** nothing doing!; ***non fa ~!*** it doesn't matter!; ***grazie! – di ~!*** thank you! – you're welcome!; ***è una cosa da ~*** it's nothing; ***non c'entra ~*** it's got nothing to do with it; ***ti serve ~?*** do you need anything?; ***il dolce far ~*** sweet idleness; ***basta un ~*** a small thing is enough

niente(di)meno *adv* no less; **~!** that's incredible! you don't say!
Nigeria *f* Nigeria **nigeriano I** *adj* Nigerian **II** *m*, **-a** *f* Nigerian
nightclub *m* ⟨*pl* nightclub⟩ nightclub
Nilo *m* Nile
nimbo *m* nimbus
ninfa *f* MYTH nymph
ninfea *f* water-lily
ninfomane *f* nymphomaniac
Ninive *f* Nineveh
ninnananna *f* lullaby; ***cantare una ~*** sing a lullaby
ninnare *v/t* ⟨1a⟩ sing/rock to sleep
ninnoli *mpl* trivia
nipote *m/f di zio* nephew; *donna, ragazza* niece *f*; *di nonno* grandson; *donna, ragazza* granddaughter *f*
nipponico *adj* ⟨*mpl* -ci⟩ Japanese
nirvana *m* ⟨*pl* nirvana⟩ Nirvana
nisseno I *adj* from Caltanisetta **II** *m*, **-a** *f* person from Caltanisetta
nitidamente *adv* (*in ordine*) cleanly; (*distintamente*) clearly
nitidezza *f* clarity, clearness; PHOT sharpness
nitido *adj* clear; PHOT sharp; ***contorni*** *mpl* ***-i*** sharp outlines
nitrato *m* nitrate **nitrico** *adj* ⟨*mpl* -ci⟩ nitric; ***acido*** *m* **~** nitric acid
nitrire *v/i* ⟨4d⟩ neigh
nitrito *m* neigh
nitrito[1] *m* whinny
nitroglicerina *f* nitroglycerine
Nizza *f* Nice **nizzardo I** *adj* from Nice **II** *m*, **-a** *f* person from Nice
no *adv* no; ***~ e poi ~*** absolutely not!, no and that's final!; ***come ~!*** of course!, naturally!; ***se ~*** otherwise; ***dire di ~*** say no; ***credo di ~*** I don't think so
NO *abbr* (= **nord-ovest**) NW (northwest)
nobildonna *f* lady; HIST noblewoman
nobile I *adj* noble; ***piano*** *m* **~** first/main floor **II** *m/f* aristocrat
nobiliare *adj* noble
nobilitare *v/t* ⟨1m⟩ dignifying (*a. fig*); ***il lavoro nobilita l'uomo*** work ennobles man **nobilitazione** *f fig* ennoblement **nobilmente** *adv* nobly
nobiltà *f* nobility; ***~ d'animo*** noble-mindedness
nobiluomo *m* ⟨*pl* nobiluomini⟩ gentleman; HIST nobleman
nocca *f* ⟨*pl* -cche⟩ knuckle
nocchiere *m*, **-a** *f* MIL helmsman
nocciola *f* hazelnut; ***color*** *m* **~** hazel
nocciolina *f*: **~** (***americana***) peanut, ground-nut, monkey-nut
nocciolo[1] *m* (*albero*) hazel (tree)
nocciolo[2] *m di frutto* stone; *di questione* heart, kernel
noce I *m* walnut (tree); (*legno*) walnut **II** *f* walnut; ***~ di cocco*** coconut; ***~ moscata*** nutmeg; ***una ~ di burro*** a knob of butter
nocepesca *f* nectarine
nocino *m* walnut liqueur
nocivo *adj* harmful
NOCS *abbr* (= **Nucleo Operativo Centrale di Sicurezza**) *Italian police antiterrorist unit*
nodino *m*: ***~ di vitello*** COOK veal rib
nodo *m* knot; *fig* crux; RAIL junction; ***farsi il ~ alla cravatta*** tie one's tie; ***avere un ~ in gola*** have a lump in one's throat
nodoso *adj* knotty, gnarled **nodulo** *m* MED lump; (*linfatico*) node
Noè *m* Noah
no global I *adj inv* no global; ***movimento*** *m* **~** no global movement **II** *m/f* ⟨*pl* no global⟩ no global member
noi *pron soggetto* we; *con prep* us; ***a ~*** to us; ***con ~*** with us; ***senza di ~*** without us
noia *f* boredom; **-e** *pl* trouble *sg*; ***dar ~ a qn*** annoy s.o.; ***venire a ~ a qn*** start to bore s.o.; ***avere delle -e*** have problems
noioso *adj* boring; (*molesto*) annoying
noisette *adj inv* hazel
noleggiare *v/t* ⟨1f⟩ hire; ***~ una macchina*** rent a car; ***~ una nave/un aereo*** NAUT, AVIAT charter a ship/a plane; NAUT, AVIAT charter
noleggiatore *m*, **-trice** *f* charterer
noleggio *m* hire; NAUT, AVIAT charter; ***~ (di) biciclette*** bike hire
nolente *adj*: ***volente o ~*** willy-nilly
nolo *m* hire; ***prendere a ~*** hire; ***dare a ~*** hire out
nome *m* **1.** name; ***~ di battesimo*** Christian name; ***~ di famiglia*** surname; ***~ e cognome*** full name; ***conoscere qn di ~*** know s.o. by name; *fig* ***farsi un ~*** make a name for o.s; ***a ~ di qn*** on behalf of ***di ~ e di fatto*** by name and by nature; ***~ proprio*** proper noun; ***in ~ di*** in the name of **2.**

GRAM noun
nomea *f* reputation **nomenclatura** *f* nomenclature
nomignolo *m* nickname
nomina *f* appointment
nominale *adj* nominal; ECON ***valore*** *m* ~ nominal value
nominare *v/t* ⟨1l & c⟩ (*menzionare*) mention; *a un incarico* appoint (***a*** to)
nominativo **I** *adj* ECON nominative; ***titolo*** *m* ~ registered share; ***elenco*** *m* ~ nominal list **II** *n*: ***nominativo*** *m* GRAM nominative; ADMIN name
non *adv* not; ~ ***ho fratelli*** I don't have any brothers, I have no brothers; ~ ***ancora*** not yet; ~ ***appena*** as soon as; ~ ***che io non voglia*** not that I don't want to; ~ ***cedibile*** not transferable, non-transferable; ~ ***valido*** invalid
nonchalance *f* ⟨*pl* nonchalance⟩ nonchalance
nonché *cj* let alone; (*e a.*) as well as
non credente *m/f* non-believer
noncurante *adj* nonchalant, casual; ~ ***di*** mindless of, heedless of
noncuranza *f* nonchalance, casualness
nondimeno *cj* nevertheless
non fumatore **I** *m* non-smoker **II** *adj* non-smoking
nonnismo *m bullying of recruits by senior soldiers*
nonno *m*, **-a** *f* grandfather; *donna* grandmother; ***-i*** *pl* grandparents
nonnulla *m* ⟨*pl* nonnulla⟩ trifle
nono *m/adj* ninth
nonostante *prep* despite; ***ciò*** ~ however
nonsenso *m* nonsense
non stop *adj inv* nonstop
nontiscordardimé *m* ⟨*pl* nontiscordardimé⟩ forget-me-not
non vedente *m/f* blind person
non violenza *f* non-violence
nord *m* north; ***mare*** *m* ***del*** ~ North Sea; ***a(l)*** ~ ***di*** (to the) north of; ***a*** ~ ***di Roma*** north of Rome
nordafricano **I** *adj* North African **II** *m*, **-a** *f* North African **nordamericano** **I** *adj* North American **II** *m*, **-a** *f* North American
nord-est *m* north-east
nordeuropeo **I** *adj* ⟨*mpl* -ei⟩ Northern European **II** *m*, **-a** *f* Northern European
nordico *adj* ⟨*mpl* -ci⟩ northern; *lingue* Nordic
nordirlandese **I** *adj* Northern Irish **II** *m/f* Northern Irishman
nord-ovest *m* north west
norico *adj* ⟨*mpl* -ci⟩ Noric
Norimberga *f* Nuremberg; ***il processo di*** ~ the Nuremberg trials
norma *f* (*precetto*) rule, precept; TECH standard; ***-e per l'uso*** instructions (for use); ***a*** ~ ***di legge*** up to standard; ***a*** ~ ***di legge ...*** complies with ...; ***di*** ~ normally
normale *adj* normal
normalità *f* normality
normalizzare *v/t* ⟨1a⟩ normalize; (*uniformare*) standardize
normalizzarsi *v/r* return to normal
normalizzazione *f* normalization; TECH normalization **normalmente** *adv* normally
Normandia *f* Normandy
normanno **I** *adj* Norman **II** *m*, **-a** *f* Norman
normativa *f* regulations **normativo** *adj* regulative
normografo *m* stencil
norvegese *m/f & adj* Norwegian
Norvegia *f* Norway
nosocomio *m* ⟨*pl* -i⟩ hospital
nostalgia *f* nostalgia; ~ ***di casa*** homesickness; ***avere*** ~ ***di casa*** feel homesick; ***avere*** ~ ***di qn*** miss s.o.; ***avere*** ~ ***dell'Italia*** miss Italy
nostalgico **I** *adj* ⟨*mpl* -ci⟩ nostalgic **II** *m*, **-a** *f* nostalgic person
no-stop *adj inv* non-stop; ***trasmissione*** *f* ~ non-stop programme
nostrale *adj* local, home *attr*
nostrano *adj* local, home *attr*; ***vino*** *m* ~ local wine; ***formaggio*** *m* ~ locally-made cheese
nostro **I** *adj* our; ***i -i genitori*** *pl* our parents; ***un*** ~ ***amico*** a friend of ours **II** *pron*: ***il*** ~ ours
nostromo *m* boatswain, bosun
nota *f* **1.** note; ***degno di*** ~ noteworthy; ~ ***spese*** expense account; ***prendere*** ~ ***di qc*** make a note of sth; *situazione, comportamento* take note of sth; ~ ***a piè di pagina*** footnote; ~ ***della spesa*** shopping list; ~ ***di merito*** note of merit; ~ ***del traduttore*** translator's note **2.** FIN bill

notabile *m* personality, VIP; ***-i*** *pl* VIPs
notaio *m* ⟨*pl* -ai⟩ notary (public)
notare *v/t* ⟨1c⟩ (*osservare*) notice; ***~ qn / qc*** notice s.o. / sth; ***l'ho notata subito*** I noticed her straight away; (*annotare*) make a note of, note down; *con segni* mark; ***è da ~ che*** please note that; ***ti faccio ~ che*** I'll have you know that
notariato *m* notaryship
notarile *adj* notarial; ***studio ~*** notary's office
notebook *m* ⟨*pl* notebook⟩ COMPUT notebook
notevole *adj* *degno di nota* notable, noteworthy; *grande* considerable, substantial
notevolmente *adv* significantly
notifica *f* ⟨*pl* -che⟩ notice
notificare *v/t* ⟨1m & d⟩ serve (***a*** on)
notificazione *f* notice; JUR service
notizia *f* piece *or* bit *or* item of news; ***avere -e di qn*** have news of s.o., hear from s.o.; ***~ d'agenzia*** wire story; ***-e*** *pl* ***sportive*** sports news *sg*; ***le ultime -e*** *pl* the latest news
notiziario *m* ⟨*pl* -ri⟩ RADIO, TV news *sg*
noto *adj* well-known; ***rendere ~*** announce
notoriamente *adv* as everybody knows
notorietà *f* fame; *pej* notoriety
notorio *adj* ⟨*mpl* -ri⟩ well-known; *pej* notorious
nottambulismo *m* sleep-walking
nottambulo *m*, ***-a*** *f* night owl
nottata *f* night; ***fare la ~*** stay up all night
notte *f* night; ***di ~*** at night; ***buona ~!*** good night!; ***nel cuore della ~*** in the middle of the night; ***a ~ inoltrata*** in the dead of the night; ***la ~ porta consiglio*** sleep on a problem; ***passare la ~ in bianco*** have a sleepless night
nottetempo *adv* in the night
nottola *f* TECH latch
notturno *adj* night(-time) *attr*; *animale* nocturnal; ***ore*** *fpl* ***-e*** hours of darkness; ***vita*** *f* ***-a*** nightlife
novanta *num* ninety
novantenne *m/f* ninety-year-old
novantesimo *m/adj* ninetieth
novantina *f*: ***una ~*** about ninety
novarese I *adj* from Novara **II** *m/f* person from Novara
nove *num* nine
novecento I *num* nine hundred **II** *m*: ***il Novecento*** the twentieth century
novella *f* short story
novellino *m*, ***-a*** *f* novice
novello *adj* early; (*da poco tempo*) new; ***patate*** *fpl* ***-e*** early potatoes; ***sposi*** *mpl* ***-i*** newly-weds; ***pollo*** *m* ***~*** spring chicken
novembre *m* November
novilunio *m* ⟨*pl* -ni⟩ new moon
novità *f* ⟨*pl* novità⟩ novelty; (*notizia*) piece *or* item of news; ***essere una ~ sul mercato*** be new on the market; ***ci sono ~?*** Is there any news?; ***sai che ~!*** *hum* that's nothing new!
noviziato *m* REL novitiate; *ad un mestiere* apprenticeship
novizio ⟨*mpl* -zi⟩ **I** *adj* novice **II** *m*, ***-a*** *f* beginner, novice; REL novice
nozione *f* notion, idea; ***-i*** *pl* ***di base*** rudiments; *fig* ***perdere la ~ del tempo*** lose all sense of time
nozionistico *adj* ⟨*mpl* -ci⟩ superficial
nozze *fpl* wedding *sg*; ***~ d'argento*** silver wedding (anniversary); ***~ d'oro*** golden wedding (anniversary); ***sposarsi in seconde ~*** get married for the second time, remarry
ns. *abbr* (= **nostro**) our(s), *used in correspondence*
NU *abbr* **1.** (= **Nazioni Unite**) UN (United Nations) **2.** (= **nettezza urbana**) *cleansing department*
nube *f* cloud
Nubia *f* Nubia **nubiano I** *adj* Nubian **II** *m*, ***-a*** *f* Nubian
nubifragio *m* ⟨*pl* -gi⟩ cloudburst
nubile *adj* *donna* single, unmarried
nuca *f* ⟨*pl* -che⟩ nape of the neck
nucleare *adj* nuclear
nucleico *adj* ⟨*mpl* -ci⟩ nucleic; ***acido*** *m* ***~*** nucleic acid
nucleo *m* PHYS nucleus (*a. fig*); ***~ atomico*** PHYS atomic nucleus; ***~ familiare*** family unit; ***~ urbano*** urban centre
nudismo *m* naturism, nudism
nudista *m/f* ⟨*mpl* -i⟩ naturist, nudist
nudità *f* nudity, nakedness
nudo I *adj* nude, naked; (*spoglio*) bare; ***a occhio ~*** to the naked eye; ***a piedi*** *mpl* ***-i*** barefoot; ***~ e crudo*** unvarnished **II** *m* PAINT nude; *fig* ***mettere a ~*** lay bare
nugolo *m* *di insetti*: swarm; *di bambi-*

ni: crowd

nulla I *adv* nothing; ***è solo una cosa da ~*** it's nothing; ***per ~*** for nothing; ***non per ~*** not for nothing **II** *m* nothing; ***non ti ho portato un bel ~*** I haven't brought you anything at all; ***svanire nel ~*** vanish into thin air

nullaosta *m*: *fig* ***ottenere il ~*** get the green light *or* go-ahead

nullatenente I *adj* destitute **II** *m/f* pauper **nullità** *f* ⟨*pl* nullità⟩ JUR invalidity; *fig* insignificance; ***essere una ~*** be a nonentity

nullo *adj* invalid; *gol* disallowed; *voto* spoiled; ***dichiarare ~*** declare null and void

nume *m liter* deity; *fig* God; ***~ tutelare*** tutelary deities

numerabile *adj* countable

numerale *m* numeral

numerare *v/t* ⟨1l⟩ number

numerato *adj* numbered

numericamente *adv* numerically; ***~ inferiore*** fewer

numerico *adj* ⟨*mpl* -ci⟩ numerical; ***inferiorità** f **-a*** numerical inferiority

numero *m* **1.** number; *arabo*, *romano* numeral; ***~ di casa*** home (tele)phone number; ***~ pari / dispari*** even / odd number; ***~ di targa*** registration number, *US* license number; ***~ di telefono*** phone number; ***~ verde*** 0800 number, *US* toll-free number; ***~ di volo*** flight number; ***dare i -i*** *infml* talk nonsense; TEL ***sbagliare ~*** dial the wrong number **2.** *di scarpa* size **3.** TYPO ***~ unico*** special issue **4.** POL ***~ legale*** quorum **5.** EDU ***~ chiuso*** restricted enrol(l)ment **6.** ***sono venuti in gran ~*** lots of them came

numeroso *adj* numerous; *famiglia*, *classe* large

numida *m/f* ⟨*mpl* -i⟩ Numidian

numismatica *f* numismatics *sg*

numismatico I *adj* ⟨*mpl* -ci⟩ numismatic **II** *m*, **-a** *f* numismatist

nunzio *m* ⟨*pl* -zi⟩ REL nuncio; ***~ apostolico*** nuncio

nuocere *v/i* ⟨3ii⟩: ***~ a*** harm; ***il fumo nuoce alla salute*** smoking is bad for you

nuora *f* daughter-in-law

nuorese I *adj* from Nuoro **II** *m/f* person from Nuoro

nuotare *v/i* ⟨1c⟩ swim; ***ho nuotato*** I have swum; ***~ a rana*** do the breaststroke; ***~ sul dorso*** do the backstroke; *fig* ***~ nell'oro*** be rolling in it

nuotata *f* swim

nuotatore *m*, **-trice** *f* swimmer

nuoto *m* swimming; ***attraversare la Manica a ~*** swim across the Channel; ***~ sincronizzato*** synchronized swimming

Nuova Guinea *f* New Guinea

nuovamente *adv* again

Nuova Zelanda *f* New Zealand

nuovo I *adj* new; ***di ~*** again; ***essere ~ in una città*** be new to a town; ***~ fiammante*** brand new **II** *m*: ***che c'è di ~?*** what's new?

nuragico *adj* ⟨*mpl* -ci⟩ nuragic; ***civiltà** f **-a*** nuragic civilization

nursery *f* ⟨*pl* nursery⟩ nursery

nutria *f* coypu

nutrice *f* wet-nurse

nutriente *adj* nourishing

nutrimento *m* food

nutrire *v/t* ⟨4d or 4a⟩ feed

nutrirsi *v/r*: ***~ di*** live on

nutritivo *adj* nutritious; ***valore** m **~*** nutritional value

nutrizionale *adj* nutritional; ***valore** m **~*** nutritional value

nutrizione *f* nutrition

nutrizionista *m/f* ⟨*mpl* -i⟩ nutritionist

nuvola *f* cloud; *fig* ***cadere dalle -e*** be taken aback

nuvoloso *adj* cloudy

nuziale *adj* wedding *attr.*; ***torta** f **~*** wedding cake

nylon® *m* nylon®

O

o, O *m/f* ⟨*pl* o, O⟩ o, O; ***O come Otranto*** O for Oscar
o *cj* or; **~ ... ~** either ... or
O *abbr* (= **ovest**) W (west)
oasi *f* ⟨*pl* oasi⟩ oasis
obbedire *v/i* → ***ubbidire***
obbligare *v/t* ⟨1l, c & e⟩: ***~ qn a fare qc*** oblige *or* compel s.o. to do sth
obbligarsi *v/r* commit o.s. (***a fare*** to doing), undertake (***a fare*** to do)
obbligato *adj* obliged; (*grato*) thankful; ***sentirsi ~ verso qn*** feel obliged towards s.o.; ***percorso*** *m* **~** fixed course (*a. fig*)
obbligatorio *adj* ⟨*mpl* -ri⟩ obligatory, compulsory
obbligazionario *adj* ⟨*mpl* -ri⟩ bond; ***titolo*** *m* **~** bond
obbligazione *f* obligation; FIN bond
obbligazionista *m/f* ⟨*mpl* -i⟩ bondholder
obbligo *m* ⟨*pl* -ghi⟩ obligation; ***d'~*** obligatory; ***adempiere un ~*** fulfil(l) an obligation
obbrobrio *m* ⟨*pl* -ri⟩ disgrace; (*cosa brutta*) eyesore **obbrobrioso** *adj* disreputable; (*orrendo*) repulsive
obelisco *m* ⟨*pl* -chi⟩ obelisk
oberare *v/t* ⟨1l⟩ overload
oberato *adj*: ***~ di lavoro*** up to one's eyes in work; ***~ di debiti*** up to one's eyes in debt
obesità *f* obesity
obeso *adj* obese
obice *m* howitzer
obiettare *v/t* ⟨1b⟩ object, say (***a*** to)
obiettivamente *adv* objectively
obiettività *f* ⟨*pl* obiettività⟩ objectivity
obiettivo I *adj* objective **II** *m* aim, objective; PHOT lens
obiettore *m*: ***~ di coscienza*** conscientious objector
obiezione *f* objection; ***fare ~ di coscienza*** be a conscientious objector
obitorio *m* ⟨*pl* -ri⟩ mortuary
oblazione *f* donation
oblio *m* ⟨*pl* -ii⟩ oblivion *di persone una volta famose*: obscurity; ***cadere nell'~*** fall into oblivion
obliquo *adj* oblique
obliterare *v/t* ⟨1m⟩ *biglietto* punch
obliteratrice *f* ticket punch
oblò *m* ⟨*pl* oblò⟩ NAUT porthole
oblungo *adj* ⟨*mpl* -ghi⟩ oblong
oboe *m* oboe **oboista** *m/f* ⟨*mpl* -i⟩ oboe player
obolo *m* offering
obsoleto *adj* obsolete
obtorto collo *adv* reluctantly
oca *f* ⟨*pl* -che⟩ goose; *fig* silly woman; ***avere la pelle d'~*** have goose pimples; ***~ giuliva*** *infml* dumb blonde
ocarina *f* ocarina
occasionale *adj* casual; ***i rapporti*** *mpl* ***-i*** casual sex; ***prestazione*** *f* **~** casual work
occasionalmente *adv* occasionally
occasione *f* (*opportunità*) opportunity, chance; (*evento*) occasion; (*affare*) bargain; ***automobile*** *f* ***d'~*** second-hand *or* used car; ***cogliere l'~*** seize the opportunity, jump at the chance *infml*; ***all'~*** if necessary; ***in ~ di*** on the occasion of
occhiacci *mpl*: ***fare gli ~ a qn*** scowl at s.o.
occhiaie *fpl* bags *pl* under the eyes
occhiali *mpl* glasses *pl*, specs *pl Br infml*; ***~ da sole*** sunglasses *pl*; ***~ da vista*** glasses *pl*; ***un paio di ~*** a pair of glasses; ***mettersi / togliersi gli ~*** put one's glasses on / take one's glasses off
occhialuto *adj* spectacled
occhiata[1] *f* look, glance; ***dare un'~ a*** have a look at, glance at; (*sorvegliare*) keep an eye on
occhiata[2] *f* ZOOL blacktail
occhieggiare ⟨1f⟩ **I** *v/t*: ***~ qn*** eye up s.o. **II** *v/i* peep
occhiello *m* buttonhole; *giornale* subheading; *fig* ***il fiore all'~*** a feather in one's cap
occhio *m* ⟨*pl* -cchi⟩ eye; ***chiudere un ~*** turn a blind eye; ***costare un ~ della testa*** cost the earth; ***dare nell'~*** attract attention, be noticed; ***tenere d'~*** keep an eye on; ***vedere di buon ~*** look favo(u)rably on; ***a ~*** at a guess; *fig* ***a -i chiusi*** blindfold; ***con la coda***

dell'~ out of the corner of one's eye; ***a ~ nudo*** to the naked eye; ***a ~ e croce*** roughly; ***a perdita*** *f* ***d'~*** as far as the eye can see; ***a vista*** *f* ***d'~*** before one's very eyes; ***a quattr' -i*** in private; ***in un battor d'~*** in the twinkling of an eye; ***avere gli -i foderati di prosciutto*** have one's head in the sand; ***anche l'~ vuole la sua parte*** looks also count; ***~!*** careful!
occhiolino *m*: ***fare l'~*** wink
occidentale *adj* western; ***Europa*** *f* **~** Western Europe
occidente *m* west; ***a ~ di*** (to the) west of
occipite *m* occiput
occlusione *f* MED obstruction; METEO, ANAT occlusion
occorrente I *adj* necessary **II** *m* necessary materials *pl*
occorrenza *f*: ***all'~*** if necessary, if need be
occorrere *v/impers* ⟨3o⟩ be necessary; (*accadere*) occur; ***mi occorre*** I need; ***Le occorre altro?*** (do you need) anything else?; ***occorre programmare le cose*** we / you need to plan things; ***non occorre!*** there's no need!
occultamento *m* concealment; ***~ di cadavere*** JUR concealment of a corpse; ***~ di prove*** JUR suppression of evidence
occultare *v/t* ⟨1a⟩ conceal; *fig*, *di sentimenti*: mask; (*insabbiare*) hush up
occulto I *adj* occult; ***forze*** *fpl* ***-e*** occult powers; ***scienze*** *fpl* ***-e*** occult sciences **II** *n*: ***occulto*** *m* occult
occupante I *adj* occupying **II** *m/f di veicoli* occupant; (*abusivo*) squatter
occupare *v/t* ⟨1l & c⟩ *spazio* take up, occupy; ***~ molto / poco spazio*** take up a lot of space / little space; *tempo* occupy, fill; *posto* have, hold; *persona* keep busy; *di esercizio* occupy
occuparsi *v/r* take care (***di*** of), deal (***di*** with); ***occupati degli affari tuoi!*** mind your own business!; ***~ di qn*** look after s.o., take care of s.o.
occupato *adj* TEL engaged, *US* busy; *posto*, *appartamento* taken; *gabinetto* engaged; *persona* busy; *città*, *nazione* occupied
occupazionale *adj* occupational; ***crisi*** *f* **~** unemployment crisis
occupazione *f di città*, *paese* occupation; (*attività*) pastime; (*impiego*) job
Oceania *f* Oceania
oceanico *adj* ⟨*mpl* -ci⟩ ocean; *fig* ***folla -a*** enormous crowd
oceano *m* ocean; ***Oceano Atlantico*** Atlantic Ocean; ***Oceano Indiano*** Indian Ocean; ***Oceano Pacifico*** Pacific Ocean
oceanografia *f* oceanography **oceanografico** *adj* ⟨*mpl* -ci⟩ oceanographic **oceanografo** *m*, **-a** *f* oceanologist
ocra *f* ochre; ***color*** *m* **~** ochre
OCSE *abbr* (= **Organizzazione per la Cooperazione e lo Sviluppo Economico**) OECD (Organization for Economic Co-operation and Development)
oculare *adj* ocular-; ***globo*** *m* **~** eyeball; ***testimone*** *m* **~** eyewitness
oculatezza *f* discernment **oculato** *adj* discerning
oculista *m/f* ⟨*mpl* -i⟩ ophthalmologist
oculistico *adj* ⟨*mpl* -ci⟩ oculistic; ***visita*** *f* ***-a*** eye-test
od *cj* = **o** (*before a vowel*)
odalisca *f* ⟨*pl* -che⟩ odalisque
ode *f* ode
odiare *v/t* ⟨1k⟩ hate, detest
odiarsi *v/r* hate o.s.
odiato *adj* hated
odierno *adj* modern-day *attr*, of today, today's
odio *m* hatred
odioso *adj* hateful, odious
odissea *f* odyssey (*a. fig*)
odontoiatra *m/f* ⟨*mpl* -i⟩ dentist **odontoiatria** *f* dentistry **odontoiatrico** *adj* ⟨*mpl* -ci⟩ dental; ***studio*** *m* **~** dental surgery **odontotecnica** *f* ⟨*pl* -che⟩ prosthetic dentistry
odontotecnico *m*, **-a** *f* dental technician
odorare ⟨1a⟩ **I** *v/t* smell **II** *v/i* smell (***di*** of)
odorato *m* sense of smell
odore *m* smell, odo(u)r; ***-i*** *pl* COOK herbs; ***sentire ~ di qc*** smell sth; ***in ~ di santità*** in odour of sanctity
odorino *m* pleasant smell; *fig* stench
odoroso *adj* fragrant, sweet-smelling
offendere *v/t* ⟨3c⟩ offend; ***~ il pudore*** outrage decency
offendersi *v/r* take offence, *US* offense
offensiva *f* offensive

offensivo *adj* offensive
offerente *m* bidder; ***maggior ~*** highest bidder; ***al miglior ~*** to the highest bidder
offerta *f* offer; FIN supply; REL offering; (*dono*) donation; *in asta* bid; ***~ d'impiego*** job offer; ***~ di lavoro*** job vacancy; ***~ pubblica di acquisto*** takeover bid; ***~ speciale*** special offer; ***prodotto in ~*** product on special offer *or US* on sale
offerto → ***offrire***
offertorio *m* ⟨*pl* -ri⟩ REL offertory
offesa *f* offence, *US* offense
offeso *past part* → ***offendere***; ***fare l'~*** go into a huff
officiante **I** *adj* officiating **II** *m* ministrant **officiare** *v/t and v/i* ⟨1f⟩ officiate
officina *f* workshop; *per macchine* garage
officinale *adj* officinal; ***pianta f ~*** medicinal plant
off-limits *adj inv* off-limits **off-line** *adj inv* COMPUT off-line; ***navigazione f ~*** off-limits navigation
offrire *v/t* ⟨4f & c⟩ offer; ***ti offro da bere*** I'll buy *or* stand you a drink; ***posso offrirti qualcosa?*** can I get you anything?; ***offre la casa*** it's on the house; ***offro io*** it's on me
offshore *adj inv* offshore
offuscamento *m* darkening, blurring
offuscare *v/t* ⟨1a⟩ blur, darken (*a. fig*); ***~ la mente*** confuse
offuscarsi *v/r* ⟨1a⟩ darken; ***mi si è offuscata la vista*** my vision is blurred; ***il cielo si è offuscato*** it has clouded over
oftalmico *adj* ⟨*mpl* -ci⟩ ophthalmic **oftalmologia** *f* ophthalmology **oftalmologo** *m*, **-a** *f* ⟨*mpl* -gi⟩ ophthalmologist
oggettistica *f* gifts and fancy goods *pl*
oggettivamente *adv* objectively **oggettività** *f* ⟨*pl* oggettività⟩ objectivity
oggettivo *adj* objective
oggetto *m* object; ***-i*** *pl* ***di valore*** valuables; ***-i*** *pl* ***smarriti*** lost property *sg*, *US* lost-and-found *sg*; ***essere ~ di scherno*** be a laughing stock
oggi *adv* today; ***d'~*** of today, today's; ***da ~ a domani*** overnight; ***da ~ in poi*** from now on; ***~ stesso*** today, this very day; ***~ come ~*** as things are today; ***al giorno d'~*** nowadays; ***~ pomeriggio*** this afternoon
oggigiorno *adv* nowadays
ogiva *f* ARCH Gothic arch; MIL ogive; ***~ nucleare*** nuclear warhead
OGM *abbr* (= **organismo geneticamente modificato**) GMO (genetically modified organism)
ogni *adj* every; ***~ giorno*** very day; ***~ tanto*** every so often; ***~ sei giorni*** every six days; ***ad ~ modo*** anyway; ***in ~ caso*** in any case; ***~ volta che*** every time that; ***in ~ modo*** anyway; ***ti auguro ~ bene!*** I wish you all the best!
ogniqualvolta *cj* whenever
Ognissanti *m* ⟨*pl* Ognissanti⟩ All Saints Day
ognuno *pron* everyone, everybody
oh! *int* oh!
ohi! *int* ow!
ohibò! *int* tut-tut!
ohimè! *int* oh dear!
OLAF *abbr* (= **Ufficio europeo per la lotta antifrode**) OLAF (European Anti-Fraud Office)
Olanda *f* Holland
olandese **I** *adj* Dutch **II** *m lingua* Dutch **III** *m/f* Dutchman; *donna* Dutchwoman
oleandro *m* oleander
oleato *adj*: ***carta f -a*** greaseproof *or US* waxed paper
oleificio *m* oil mill
oleodotto *m* oil pipeline
oleoso *adj* oily
olezzo *m* fragrance; *hum* stench
olfattivo *adj* olfactory
olfatto *m* sense of smell
oliare *v/t* ⟨1k⟩ oil
oliera *f type of cruet for oil and vinegar bottles*
oligarchia *f* oligarchy
oligopolio *m* ⟨*pl* -i⟩ ECON oligopoly; ***~ bilaterale*** bilateral oligopoly
Olimpiadi *fpl* Olympic Games *pl*, Olympics *pl*; ***~ invernali*** Winter Olympics
olimpico *adj* ⟨*mpl* -ci⟩ Olympic (*a. fig*), Olympian; ***calma f -a*** Olympian calm; ***villaggio m ~*** Olympic village
olimpionico ⟨*mpl* -ci⟩ **I** *adj* Olympic *attr*; ***atleta m ~*** Olympic athlete; ***piscina f ~*** Olympic (size) swimming pool **II** *m*, **-a** *f* Olympic contestant
olimpo *m fig* top, peak

Olimpo *m* GEOG, MYTH Olympus

olio *m* ⟨*pl* -li⟩ oil; **~ *combustibile*** (fuel) oil; **~ *dei freni*** brake fluid; **~ *lubrificante*** lubricating oil, lube; **~ *per il cambio*** gearbox oil; **~ *d'oliva*** olive oil; **~ *extravergino d'oliva*** extra virgin olive oil; **~ *di ricino*** castor oil; **~ *di semi*** vegetable oil; **~ *solare*** suntan oil; ***funghi sott'~*** mushrooms in oil; ***dipinto a ~*** oil-painting; *fig* ***liscio come l'~*** smoothly; ***ci vuole ~ di gomito*** some elbow grease is needed

oliva *f* olive

olivastro I *adj* olive *o* olive-coloured; ***pelle*** *f* ***-a*** olive skin **II** *n*: ***olivastro*** *m* BOT oleaster

oliveto *m* olive grove

olivicoltore *m*, **-trice** *f* olive grower

olivicoltura *f* olive growing

olivo *m* olive (tree); ***ramoscello*** *m* ***d'~*** olive branch

olmo *m* elm (tree)

olocausto *m hist* holocaust

olografo *adj* holograph; ***testamento*** *m* **~** holographic will

OLP *abbr* (= **Organizzazione per la Liberazione della Palestina**) PLO (Palestine Liberation Organization)

oltraggiare *v/t* ⟨1f⟩ offend, outrage

oltraggio *m* ⟨*pl* -ggi⟩ offence, *US* offense, outrage; **~ *a pubblico ufficiale*** *insulting a public official*

oltraggioso *adj* offensive

oltralpe *adv* on the other side of the Alps; ***d'~*** on the other side of the Alps

oltranza *f*: ***a ~*** to the bitter end; ***sciopero*** *m* ***a ~*** indefinite strike

oltranzismo *m* extremism **oltranzista** *m/f* ⟨*mpl* -i⟩ extremist

oltre I *prep in spazio, tempo* after, past; (*più di*) over; **~ *il fiume*** beyond the river; **~ *misura*** beyond measure; **~ *la metà*** over half; ***vai ~ il semaforo*** go across *o* through the traffic lights; ***aspetto da ~ un'ora*** I've been waiting for over an hour; **~ *a*** as well as, not to mention **II** *adv nello spazio* further; *nel tempo* longer; ***non posso aspettare ~*** I can't wait any longer

oltrefrontiera *adv* across the border

oltremare *adv* overseas

oltremodo *adv* excessively

oltrepassare *v/t* ⟨1a⟩ go beyond; *fig* **~ *ogni limite*** go too far

oltretomba *m* ⟨*pl* oltretomba⟩ afterlife

oltretutto *adv* moreover

omaggio *m* ⟨*pl* -ggi⟩ homage; (*dono*) gift; ***copia*** (***in***) **~** free *or* complimentary copy; **~ *floreale*** floral tribute; **~ *pubblicitario*** (free) gift; ***essere in ~ con*** come free with; ***rendere ~ a qn*** pay homage to s.o.

ombelicale *adj* umbilical; ***cordone*** *m* **~** umbilical cord

ombelico *m* ⟨*pl* -chi⟩ navel; **~ *di Venere*** BOT pennywort

ombra *f* shadow; *zona non illuminata* shade; *fig* ***un'~ di tristezza*** a touch of sadness; ***all'~*** in the shade; ***restare nell'~*** stay in the shadows; ***fare ~ a qn / qc*** shade s.o. / sth; *fig* overshadow; ***senza ~ di dubbio*** without a shadow of a doubt; ***bandiera*** *f* **~** flag of convenience

ombreggiare *v/t* ⟨1f⟩ shade; ART shade (in)

ombreggiato *adj* shady

ombrellino *m* sunshade

ombrello *m* umbrella

ombrellone *m* parasol; *sulla spiagggia* beach umbrella

ombretto *m* eye shadow

ombrina *f* umbra

ombroso *adj* shady; *fig persona* touchy

omega *m or f* ⟨*pl* omega⟩: ***dall'alfa all'~*** from a to z

omelette *f* ⟨*pl* omelette⟩ omelette, *US* omelet

omelia *f* REL homily

omeopata *m/f* ⟨*mpl* -i⟩ homoeopathist

omeopatia *f* homeopathy

omeopatico ⟨*mpl* -ci⟩ **I** *adj* homeopathic **II** *m*, **-a** *f* homeopath

omero *m* humerus

Omero *m* Homer

omertà *f* conspiracy of silence

omesso *past part* → ***omettere***

omettere *v/t* ⟨3ee⟩ omit, leave out

omicida ⟨*mpl* -i⟩ **I** *adj* murderous **II** *m/f* murderer

omicidio *m* ⟨*pl* -di⟩ murder; **~ *colposo*** manslaughter; ***tentato ~*** attempted murder; ***squadra*** *f* ***-di*** murder squad

omissione *f* omission; ***salvo errori e -i*** apart from errors and omissions; **~ *di soccorso*** failure to offer assistance

omissis *m* ⟨*pl* omissis⟩ omission
omogeneità *f* ⟨*pl* omogeneità⟩ homogeneity
omogeneizzato *adj* homogenized
omogeneo *adj* homogenous
omologare *v/t* ⟨1m, c & e⟩ approve
omologato *adj* approved
omologazione *f* approval
omonimia *f* homonymy
omonimo I *adj* of the same name **II** *m* homonym **III** *m*, **-a** *f* namesake
omosessuale *m/f & adj* homosexual
omosessualità *f* homosexuality
OMS *abbr* (= **Organizzazione Mondiale della Sanità**) WHO (World Health Organization)
omuncolo *m* dwarf; PHYSIOL homunculus; *pej* nonentity
on. *abbr* (= **onorevole**) Hon (honourable)
onanismo *m* onanism
oncia *f* ⟨*pl* -ce⟩ ounce; *fig* scrap; ***non avere un'~ di giudizio*** not to have a scrap of common sense
oncologia *f* oncology
oncologico *adj* ⟨*mpl* -ci⟩ oncological
oncologo *m*, **-a** *f* ⟨*mpl* -gi⟩ oncologist
onda *f* wave; ***-e*** *pl* ***corte*** short wave; ***-e*** *pl* ***lunghe*** long wave; ***-e*** *pl* ***medie*** medium wave; ***~ anomala*** freak wave; ***lunghezza*** *f* ***d'~*** wavelength; RADIO ***andare in ~*** go on the air; ***essere sulla cresta dell'~*** be on the crest of a wave
ondata *f* wave; ***~ di caldo*** heat wave; ***~ di freddo*** cold spell
ondeggiamento *m* sway; (*oscillazione*) oscillation **ondeggiante** *adj* swaying; (*oscillante*) rocking; MECH oscillating
ondeggiare *v/i* ⟨1f⟩ *di barca* rock; *di bandiera* flutter
ondina *f* MYTH undine
ondoso *adj*: ***moto*** *m* ***~*** wave motion
ondulato *adj capelli* wavy; *superficie* uneven; *cartone*, *lamiera* corrugated
ondulatorio *adj* ⟨*mpl* -ri⟩ undulatory; ***movimento*** *m* ***~*** undulation; ***teoria*** *f* ***-a*** wave theory
onere *m* burden; ***~ deducibile/detraibile*** FIN deductable expense, tax deduction; ***-i*** *pl* ***sociali*** social security contributions; ECON ***-i*** *pl* ***fiscali*** taxes
onerosità *f* ⟨*pl* onerosità⟩ weightiness
oneroso *adj* onerous
onestà *f* honesty
onestamente *adv* honestly; ***~ penso che...*** frankly I think that...
onesto *adj* honest; *prezzo*, *critica* fair
ONG *abbr* (= **Organizzazione Non Governativa**) NGO (non-governmental organization)
onice *m* onyx
onirico *adj* ⟨*mpl* -ci⟩ oneiric; *fig* dreamlike
on-line *adv* COMPUT online
ONLUS *abbr* (= **Organizzazione non lucrativa di utilità sociale**) non-profit organization
onnipotente *adj* omnipotent
onnipotenza *f* omnipotence
onnipresente *adj* ubiquitous
onnisciente *adj* omniscient
onniscienza *f* omniscience
onnivoro I *adj* omnivorous **II** *m*, **-a** *f* omnivore
onomastico *m* ⟨*pl* -ci⟩ name day
onomatopeico *adj* ⟨*mpl* -ci⟩ onomatopoeic
onorabilità *f* ⟨*pl* onorabilità⟩ respectability
onoranze *fpl*: ***~ funebri*** funeral hono(u)rs
onorare *v/t* ⟨1a⟩ be a credit to; ***~ i propri impegni*** respect one's commitments; ***~ qn di qc*** hono(u)r s.o. with sth
onorario ⟨*mpl* -ri⟩ **I** *adj* honorary; ***socio*** *m* ***~*** honorary member **II** *m* fee
onorato *adj* respected, hono(u)red; ***l'-a società*** *f iron* the Mafia
onore *m* hono(u)r; ***in ~ di*** in hono(u)r of; ***farsi ~*** do o.s. proud; ***parola*** *f* ***d'~*** word of hono(u)r; ***uomo d'~*** *iron* man of hono(u)r; ***fare gli -i di casa*** do the honours
onorevole I *adj* hono(u)rable **II** ***Onorevole*** *m/f* Member of Parliament
onorevolmente *adv* honourably
onorificenza *f* hono(u)r
onorifico *adj* ⟨*mpl* -ci⟩ honorary; ***a titolo ~*** honorary title
onta *f* disgrace; (*offesa*) offence; ***a ~ di qc*** in defiance of
ontano *m* alder
ONU *abbr* (= **Organizzazione delle Nazioni Unite**) UN (United Nations)
OPA *abbr* (= **Offerta Pubblica d'acquisto (di azioni di società)**) takeover bid

opacità *f di vetro* opaqueness; *di colore, foto* darkness
opaco *adj* ⟨*mpl* -chi⟩ *vetro* opaque; *calze, rossetto* dark
opale *m* opal **opalescente** *adj* opal **opalescenza** *f* opalescence **opalina** *f* opal glass; TEX light cotton cloth
op.cit. *abbr* (= **opera citata**) op.cit. (opere citato)
open space *m* ⟨*pl* open space⟩ open space
opera *f* **1.** work; **~ *d'arte*** work of art; **~ *buona*** good deed; ***-e*** *pl* ***pubbliche*** public works; ***mettersi all'~*** set to work; ***chi ben comincia è a metà dell'~*** *prov* well begun is half done **2.** MUS opera
operabile *adj* operable
operaio ⟨*mpl* -ai⟩ **I** *m*, **-a** *f* worker; **~ *specializzato*** skilled worker **II** *adj* working
opera omnia *f* complete works
operare ⟨1l & c⟩ **I** *v/t cambiamento* make; *miracoli* work; MED operate on **II** *v/i* act
operarsi *v/r* have an operation; **~ *d'appendicite*** have one's appendix out
operativo *adj* operational; *ricerca* applied; *ordine* operative; ***piano*** *m* **~** plan of operations; ***sul piano ~*** on the operational front; ***unità*** *f* ***-a*** operational unit; COMPUT ***sistema*** *m* **~** operating system
operato *m* work; *azioni* actions; *comportamento* behavio(u)r
operatore *m*, **-trice** *f* operator; *televisivo, cinematografico* cameraman; **~ *di Borsa*** market trader; **~ *ecologico*** refuse *or US* garbage collector; **~ *sociale*** social worker; **~ *turistico*** tour operator
operatorio *adj* operating *attr*; ***sala*** *f* ***-a*** operating theatre *or US* room
operazione *f* operation; **~ *bancaria*** bank transaction; **~ *commerciale*** business deal; **~ *di Borsa*** stock-exchange transaction; **~ *finanziaria*** transaction; **~ *militare*** military operation; ***subire un'~*** have an operation
operetta *f* operetta
operistico *adj* ⟨*mpl* -ci⟩ operatic; ***stagione*** *f* ***-a*** opera season
operosità *f* ⟨*pl* operosità⟩ industriousness
operoso *adj* hard-working, industrious
opificio *m* ⟨*pl* -ci⟩ mill
opinabile *adj* debatable, open to question **opinabilità** *f* ⟨*pl* opinabilità⟩ dubiousness
opinione *f* opinion; ***secondo la tua ~*** in your opinion; **~ *pubblica*** public opinion
opinionista *m/f* ⟨*mpl* -i⟩ political columnist
oppio *m* opium
opponente **I** *adj* opposing **II** *m/f* opponent; JUR opponent
opporre *v/t* ⟨3ll⟩ put forward, offer; *scuse, resistenza* offer
opporsi *v/r* be opposed
opportunamente *adv* duly
opportunismo *m* opportunism
opportunista *m/f* ⟨*mpl* -i⟩ opportunist
opportunistico *adj* ⟨*mpl* -ci⟩ opportunistic (*a.* MED)
opportunità *f* ⟨*pl* opportunità⟩ opportunity; *di decisione* timeliness; ***pari ~*** *pl* equal opportunities
opportuno *adj* suitable, appropriate; ***al momento ~*** at a suitable time, at the opportune moment
oppositore *m*, **-trice** *f* opponent
opposizione *f* opposition; POL ***all'~*** in opposition; ***proporre ~*** JUR object
opposto **I** *past part* → ***opporre*** **II** *adj* opposite **III** *m* opposite
oppressione *f* oppression
oppressivo *adj* oppressive
oppressore *m* oppressor
opprimente *adj* oppressive
opprimere *v/t* ⟨3r⟩ oppress
oppure *cj* or (else)
optare *v/i* ⟨1c⟩: **~ *per*** choose, opt for
optional *m* ⟨*pl* optional⟩ (*accessorio*) optional; (*scelta*) option; ***con tutti gli ~*** extras included
opulento *adj* opulent; *fig* lavish; ***stile*** *m* **~** elaborate style **opulenza** *f* wealth; *fig* lavishness
opuscolo *m* brochure
OPV *abbr* (= **Offerta Pubblica di Vendita**) ECON public offer for sale
opzionale *adj* optional
opzione *f* option
OR *abbr* (= **Oristano**) Oristano
ora[1] *f* time; *unità di misura* hour; ***che ~ è?, che -e sono?*** what time is it?, what's the time?; **~ *legale*** daylight saving time; **~ *locale*** local time; ***-e***

pl ***straordinarie*** overtime *sg*; ~ ***di punta*** rush hour; TEL peak time; ***di buon'~*** early; ***non vedere l'~*** not be able to wait; ***all'~*** per hour; ***a 160 km all'~*** 100 miles / 160 kilometres per hour; ***a quest'~*** by now; ***essere a un'~ di macchina*** be an hour's drive away; ***era ~!*** *hum* about time too!; ***fare le -e piccole*** *infml* stay up till the small hours

ora [2] **I** *adv* now; ***sono rientrato or ~*** I've only just got back; ***per ~*** for the moment, for the time being; ***~ come ~*** at the moment; ***d'~ in poi*** from now on **II** *cj* now

oracolo *m* oracle (*a. fig*)

orafo *m*, **-a** *f* goldsmith

orale I *adj* oral; ***esame*** *m* ~ oral exam; ***per via ~*** orally **II** *m* oral (exam)

orango *m* ⟨*pl* -ghi⟩ orang-utan

orario ⟨*mpl* -ri⟩ **I** *m di treno, bus, aeroplano* timetable, *US* schedule; *di negozio* hours *pl* of business; *al lavoro* hours *pl* of work; ***~ di apertura / chiusura*** opening / closing time; ***~ di ricevimento*** office hours; ***~ di sportello*** banking hours *pl*; ***~ flessibile*** flexitime; ***in ~*** on time; ***~ continuato*** all-day opening; ***fuori ~*** out of hours; ***~ ferroviario*** train timetable **II** *adj tariffa*, hourly; *velocità* per hour; RADIO ***segnale ~*** time signal; ***in senso ~*** clockwise

orata *f* gilthead bream

oratore *m*, **-trice** *f* speaker

oratorio [1] **I** *adj* ⟨*mpl* -ri⟩ as an orator **II** *m* oratory

oratorio [2] *adj* ⟨*mpl* -ri⟩ rhetorical; ***abilità*** *f* ***-a*** oratorical skills

orazione *f* oratorical skills; (*discorso*) address; ***recitare le -i*** say prayers, pray

orbace *m* HIST black Fascist uniform; TEX hand-made coarse woollen fabric

orbettino *m* ZOOL slow-worm, blind-worm

orbita *f* ASTR orbit; ANAT eye-socket; ***in ~*** in orbit; ***~ terrestre*** orbit around the Earth; *fig* ***andare in ~*** get going

orbitare *v/i* ⟨11 & c⟩ orbit (*a. fig*); ***~ attorno a qn / qc*** gravitate around s.o. / sth

orbo I *adj* blind; ***~ da un occhio*** blind in one eye **II** *m*, **-a** *f*: ***botte*** *fpl* ***da -i*** hail *sg* of blows

orca *f* ZOOL killer whale

orchestra *f* orchestra; (*luogo*) (orchestra) pit

orchestrale I *adj* orchestral **II** *m/f* member of an orchestra

orchestrare *v/t* ⟨1b⟩ orchestrate (*a. fig*)

orchestrazione *f* orchestration

orchestrina *f* band

orchidea *f* orchid

orcio *m* ⟨*pl* -ci⟩ jar

orco *m* ⟨*pl* -chi⟩ ogre

orda *f* horde (*a. pej*)

ordigno *m* device; ***~ esplosivo*** explosive device

ordinale *m/adj* ordinal

ordinamento *m* rules and regulations; ***~ giuridico*** legal system; ***~ sociale*** rules governing society

ordinanza *f* order; ***divisa*** *f* ***d'~*** regimentals

ordinare *v/t* ⟨11⟩ order; *stanza* tidy up; MED prescribe; REL ordain; ***~ qn sacerdote*** ordain s.o. a priest

ordinarietà *f* ⟨*pl* ordinarietà⟩ ordinariness; (*volgarità*) vulgarity

ordinario *adj* ⟨*mpl* -ri⟩ ordinary; *mediocre* pretty average; ***professore*** *m* ~ professor; ***assemblea*** *f* ***-a*** ordinary meeting; ***cose*** *fpl* ***di -a amministrazione*** routine matters; ***professore*** *m* ~ (full) professor; ***fuori dell'~*** out of the ordinary

ordinarsi *v/r* ⟨11⟩ line up; ***~ in due file*** line up in two rows **ordinatamente** *adv* in an orderly way

ordinativo *adj*: ***principio*** *m* ~ ordering principle

ordinato *adj* tidy

ordinazione *f* order; REL ordination; ***su ~*** to order

ordine *m* **1.** order; ***~ alfabetico*** alphabetical order; ***Ordine al Merito del Lavoro*** Order of Merit for Work; ***~ del giorno*** agenda; ***~ d'arrivo*** order of arrival; ***d'infimo ~*** lowermost, worthless; ***in ~ a*** ADMIN as regards; ***per ~ di*** by order of; ***fino a nuovo ~*** until further notice; ***essere in ~*** be in order; ***mettere in ~*** tidy up; ***mettere in ~ una stanza*** tidy up a room; ***in ~ di altezza*** in order of height; ***in ~ sparso*** in open order; ***~ pubblico*** law and order; ***prendere gli -i*** take the vows; ***procedere con ~***

take one thing at a time; ***richiamare all'~*** call to order **2.** ***~ di pagamento*** payment order; FIN ***~ permanente*** standing order **3.** ***di prim'~*** first-rate, first-class **4.** ***l'~ dei medici*** *the medical association*
ordire *v/t* ⟨4d⟩ *fig* plot
ordito *m* TEX warp
orecchiabile *adj* catchy; ***motivetto*** *m* ***~*** catchy tune
orecchiette *fpl* COOK *Type of pasta from Puglia*
orecchino *m* earring
orecchio *m* ⟨*pl* -cchi *or* -cchie⟩ ear; MUS ***a ~*** by ear; ***-cchie a sventola*** sticking-out ears; ***avere ~ (musicale)*** have an ear for music; ***~ assoluto*** perfect pitch; ***drizzare le -cchie*** prick up one's ears; ***stare con l'~ teso*** keep one's ears open; *fig* ***tirare le -cchie a qn*** rap s.o.'s knuckles; ***essere duro d'-cchi*** be hard of hearing; ***essere tutt'-cchi*** be all ears
orecchioni *mpl* mumps *sg*
orefice *m/f* goldsmith
oreficeria *f* goldsmithing; (*gioielleria*) jewel(l)er's
oretta *f* about an hour
orfanello *m*, **-a** *f* little orphan
orfano **I** *adj* orphan **II** *m*, **-a** *f* orphan; ***~ di padre / madre*** fatherless / motherless
orfanotrofio *m* orphanage
organetto *m* (*organo meccanico*) barrel-organ; (*fisarmonica*) accordion; *da bocca* mouth-organ
organico ⟨*mpl* -ci⟩ **I** *adj* organic **II** *m* personnel
organigramma *m* ⟨*pl* -i⟩ organization chart
organismo *m* organism; *fig* body
organista *m/f* ⟨*mpl* -i⟩ organist
organizzare *v/t* ⟨1a⟩ organize
organizzarsi *v/r* organize o.s.
organizzativo *adj* organizational; ***avere spirito ~*** be a good organizer
organizzato *adj* organized; ***viaggio*** *m* ***~*** package tour
organizzatore **I** *adj* organizing; ***comitato*** *m* ***~*** organizing committee **II** *m*, **-trice** *f* organizer
organizzazione *f* organization
organo *m* organ; ***~ di vigilanza*** supervisory body
organolettico *adj* ⟨*mpl* -ci⟩ organoleptic; ***esame*** *m* ***~*** organoleptic analysis
organza *f* organza
orgasmo *m* orgasm
orgia *f* orgy
orgiastico *adj* ⟨*mpl* -ci⟩ orgiastic
orgoglio *m* pride
orgogliosamente *adv* proudly
orgoglioso *adj* proud; ***essere ~ di qn / qc*** be proud of s.o. / sth
orientabile *adj* adjustable, swivelling
orientale **I** *adj* eastern; (*dell'Oriente*) Oriental; ***Europa*** *f* ***~*** Eastern Europe **II** *m/f* Oriental
orientalista *m/f* ⟨*mpl* -i⟩ orientalist
orientamento *m*: ***senso*** *m* ***d'~*** sense of direction; ***~ professionale*** professional advice
orientare *v/t* ⟨1b⟩ *antenna*, *schermo* turn; ***~ qn verso una carriera*** guide *or* steer s.o. towards a career
orientarsi *v/r* get one's bearings
orientativo *adj* indicative; ***a livello*** *m* ***~*** as a (general) guide
orientato *adj* oriented (*a. fig*); ***~ a sinistra / a destra*** POL left / right-leaning; ***~ verso l'alto*** upward-turned; ***~ verso il basso*** downward-turned
oriente *m* east; ***l'Oriente*** the Orient; ***Medio Oriente*** Middle East; ***Estremo Oriente*** Far East; ***Vicino Oriente*** Near East; ***ad ~ di*** (to the) east of
orifizio *m* ⟨*pl* -i⟩ orifice (*a.* ANAT)
origami *m* ⟨*pl* origami⟩ origami
origano *m* oregano
originale *m/adj* original; ***conforme all'~*** faithful to the original; ***in lingua ~*** in the original language
originalità *f* ⟨*pl* originalità⟩ originality
originalmente *adv* originally
originariamente *adv* originally
originario *adj* ⟨*mpl* -ri⟩ original; ***essere ~ di*** come from, be a native of; *popolo* originate in
origine *f* origin; ***in ~*** originally; ***di ~ italiana*** of Italian origin; ***in ~*** in the beginning; ***risalire alle -i*** go back to one's origins
origliare *v/t* ⟨1g⟩ eavesdrop
orina *f* → ***urina*** **orinale** *m* chamber pot **orinare** ⟨1a⟩ **I** *v/i* urinate **II** *v/t* urinate **orinatoio** *m* ⟨*pl* -oi⟩ urinal
oristanese **I** *adj* from Oristano **II** *m/f* person from Oristano
oriundo *adj*: ***~ di Napoli*** of Neapolitan

extraction
orizzontale *adj* horizontal
orizzontalmente *adv* horizontally
orizzonte *m* horizon; ***all'~*** on the horizon
orlare *v/t* ⟨1a⟩ hem
orlatura *f* hem
orlo *m* edge; *di vestito* hem; ***~ a giorno*** SEW hemstitch work; ***pieno fino all'~*** full to the brim; ***sull'~ del precipizio*** on the brink of the abyss
orma *f* footprint; *fig* ***seguire le -e di qn*** follow in s.o.'s footsteps; ***calcare le -e di qn*** follow in s.o.'s footsteps
ormai *adv* by now
ormeggiare *v/t* ⟨1n⟩ NAUT moor
ormeggio *m* NAUT mooring
ormonale *adj* hormonal; ***terapia*** *f* ***~*** hormone therapy
ormone *m* hormone
ornamentale *adj* ornamental; ***piante*** *fpl* ***-i*** ornamental plants
ornamento *m* ornament
ornare *v/t* ⟨1a⟩ decorate
ornato I *adj* decorated; *fig* elaborate; ***prosa*** *f* ***-a*** flowery prose **II** *n*: ***ornato*** *m* ARCH ornamentation; ART decoration
ornitologia *f* ornithology
ornitologico *adj* ornithological
ornitologo *m*, **-a** *f* ornithologist
ornitorinco *m* ⟨*pl* -chi⟩ platypus
oro *m* gold; ***d'~*** (made of) gold; ***~ bianco*** white gold; ***affare d'~*** *infml* great bargain; ***per tutto l'~ del mondo*** for all the world; ***non è tutto ~ quello che luccica*** all that glitters is not gold; ***prendere qc per ~ colato*** take sth as gospel; ***vale tanto ~ quanto pesa*** be worth one's weight in gold
orografia *f* orography
orologeria *f* clock- and watch-making; *negozio* watchmaker's; ***bomba*** *f* ***a ~*** time bomb
orologiaio *m*, **-a** *f* ⟨*mpl* -ai⟩ (clock- and) watch-maker
orologio *m* ⟨*pl* -gi⟩ clock; *portatile* watch; ***~ a cucù*** cuckoo clock; ***~ da polso*** wristwatch; ***~ subacqueo*** waterproof watch; ***~ da tasca*** pocket watch
oroscopo *m* horoscope; ***fare l'~ a qn*** cast s.o.'s horoscope
orpello *m liter* pinchbeck; *fig* tinsel
orrendo *adj* horrendous
orribile *adj* horrible
orribilmente *adv* horribly
orrido I *adj* horrid **II** *n*: ***orrido*** *m* ravine; (*gola*) gorge **orripilante** *adj* horrifying
orrore *m* horror (***di*** of); ***avere qc in ~*** hate sth; ***film dell'~*** horror film *or* movie; ***avere ~ di qc*** be terrified by sth
orsa *f* she-bear; ***Orsa maggiore / minore*** Ursa Major / Minor, the Great / Little Bear
orsacchiotto *m* bear cub; (*giocattolo*) teddy (bear)
orsetto *m* young bear; ***~ lavatore*** raccoon
orso *m* bear; *fig* hermit; ***~ bianco*** polar bear
orsolina *f* Ursuline
orsù *int liter* come!
ortaggio *m* ⟨*pl* -ggi⟩ vegetable
ortensia *f* BOT hydrangea
ortica *f* ⟨*pl* -che⟩ nettle
orticaria *f* nettle rash
orticello *m* vegetable garden; *fig* ***coltivare il proprio ~*** mind one's own business
orticoltura *f* horticulture
orto *m* vegetable garden, kitchen garden; ***~ botanico*** botanical gardens *pl*
ortodontista *m/f* ⟨*mpl* -i⟩ MED orthodontist
ortodonzia *f* MED orthodontics *sg*
ortodossia *f* orthodoxy
ortodosso *adj* orthodox
ortofrutticolo *adj*: ***mercato*** *m* ***~*** fruit and vegetable market
ortogonale *adj* orthogonal
ortografia *f* spelling
ortografico *adj* ⟨*mpl* -ci⟩ orthographic, spelling; ***errore*** *m* ***~*** spelling mistake
ortolano *m*, **-a** *f* market gardener
ortomercato *m* fruit and vegetable market
ortopedia *f* orthop(a)edics *sg*
ortopedico ⟨*mpl* -ci⟩ **I** *adj* orthop(a)edic **II** *m*, **-a** *f* orthop(a)edist
orvieto *m* COOK Orvieto wine
orzaiolo *m* stye
orzata *f* orgeat syrup
orzo *m* barley; ***~ perlato*** pearl barley
osanna I *int* hosanna **osannare** ⟨1a⟩ **I** *v/i* praise **II** *v/t* hail; ***~ qn*** hail s.o.
osare *v/t* ⟨1c⟩ dare; ***come osa?*** how

dare he / she!; ***oserei dire che ...*** I'd venture to say that ...
OSCE *abbr* (= **Organizzazione per la Sicurezza e la Cooperazione Europea**) OSCE (Organization for Security and Cooperation in Europe)
oscenità *f* ⟨*pl* oscenità⟩ obscenity
osceno *adj* obscene
oscillante *adj* swinging; MECH, MATH oscillating; *fluttuante* fluctuating; *indeciso* wavering
oscillare *v/i* ⟨1a⟩ *di corda* sway, swing; *di barca* rock; PHYS oscillate; *fig di persona* waver, hesitate; *di prezzi* fluctuate
oscillatorio *adj* ⟨*mpl* -ri⟩ oscillatory
oscillazione *f di barca* rocking; ***~ dei prezzi*** price fluctuations *pl*
osco ⟨*mpl* -sci *or* -schi⟩ **I** *adj* Oscan **II** *m*, **-a** *f* Oscan
oscuramento *m* blackout
oscurare *v/t* ⟨1a⟩ obscure; *luce* block out; ***~ la fama di qn*** discredit s.o.
oscurarsi *v/r* ⟨1a⟩ darken; *cielo* cloud over
oscurità *f* darkness; *fig* obscurity; ***nell'~*** in the dark
oscuro **I** *adj* dark; ***camera*** *f* ***-a*** darkroom; (*sconosciuto*) obscure; ***un ~ passato*** a mysterious past **II** *m* dark; ***essere all'~ di qc*** be in the dark about sth
osé *adj inv* saucy
osmosi *f* ⟨*pl* osmosi⟩ osmosis; *fig* osmosis
ospedale *m* hospital
ospedaliero *adj* hospital *attr*
ospitale *adj* hospitable
ospitalità *f* hospitality
ospitante *adj* host; ***famiglia*** *f* ***~*** host family; ***squadra*** *f* ***~*** SPORTS home team
ospitare *v/t* ⟨1l & c⟩ put up; SPORTS be at home to
ospite *m/f* guest; *chi ospita* host; *donna* hostess
ospizio *m* ⟨*pl* -zi⟩ old folks' home
ossario *m* ⟨*pl* -ri⟩ ossuary
ossatura *f* bone structure; *fig*, ARCH structure
osseo *adj* bone *attr*
ossequiare *v/t* ⟨1m e b⟩: ***~ qn*** pay homage to s.o. **ossequio** *m* ⟨*pl* -ui⟩ deference; ***porga i miei -i alla signora*** give my best regards to your wife
ossequioso *adj* deferential; (*servile*) servile
osservabile *adj* visible
osservante *adj* practising, *US* practicing; ***cattolico*** *m* ***~*** practising *or US* practicing Catholic
osservanza *f* compliance; REL religious orthodoxy; ***~ dei regolamenti*** compliance with the rules; ***in ~ alle disposizioni*** in accordance with orders; ***con ~*** yours respectfully
osservare *v/t* ⟨1b⟩ (*guardare*) look at, observe; ***~ qc da vicino*** examine sth closely; (*notare*) see, notice, observe; (*far notare*) point out, remark; (*seguire*) abide by, obey; ***~ una dieta*** keep to a diet, follow a diet; ***le faccio ~ che*** I'll have you know that
osservatore *m*, **-trice** *f* observer, watcher
osservatorio *m* ⟨*pl* -ri⟩ ASTR observatory; ***~ astronomico*** astronomical observatory; ***~ meteorologico*** *f* weather station
osservazione *f* observation; (*affermazione*) remark, observation; ***fare un'~ a qn*** criticize s.o.
ossessionante *adj* obsessive **ossessionare** *v/t* ⟨1a⟩ obsess **ossessionato** *adj* obsessed (***da*** with)
ossessione *f* obsession (***di*** with); ***avere l'~ di*** be obsessed with
ossessivamente *adv* obsessively
ossessivo *adj* obsessive
ossesso *m*, **-a** *f* person possessed *fig* madman
osseta ⟨*mpl* -i⟩ **I** *adj* Ossete **II** *m/f* Ossete **Ossezia** *f* Ossetia
ossia *cj* or rather
ossicino *m* small bone; ANAT ossicle
ossidabile *adj* liable to tarnish
ossidare *v/t* ⟨1l & c⟩ tarnish
ossidazione *f* tarnish; CHEM oxidation
ossidrico *adj* ⟨*mpl* -ci⟩ oxy-hydrogen; ***fiamma*** *f* ***-a*** oxy-hydrogen flame
ossigenare *v/t* ⟨1m⟩: ***~ qc*** oxygenate sth **ossigenarsi** *v/r* ⟨1m⟩: ***~ i capelli*** bleach one's hair
ossigenato *adj* oxygenated; ***acqua*** *f* ***-a*** peroxide; ***bionda*** *f* ***-a*** peroxide blonde
ossigenazione *f* oxygenation
ossigeno *m* oxygen; ***bombola*** *f* ***di ~*** oxygen cylinder; ***tenda*** *f* ***~*** oxygen tent

ossimoro *m* oxymoron
osso *m* (ANAT *pl* le ossa) bone; ***di ~*** bone *attr*, made of bone; ***~ sacro*** sacrum; ***~ del collo*** neck bone; ***farsi le -a*** cut one's teeth; ***in carne e -a*** in the flesh; ***avere le -a rotte*** be tired out; ***essere pelle*** *f* ***e -a*** be nothing but skin and bones; ***essere un ~ duro*** be a hard nut; ***rompersi l'~ del collo*** break one's neck *fig* be ruined
ossobuco *m* ⟨*pl* ossibuchi⟩ marrowbone; COOK ossobuco, *stew made with knuckle of veal*
ossuto *adj* bony
ostacolare *v/t* ⟨1m⟩ hinder
ostacolarsi *v/r*: ~ (***a vicenda***) hinder each other
ostacolo *m* obstacle; *nell'atletica* hurdle; *nell'equitazione* fence, jump; *fig* stumbling block, obstacle; ***corsa*** *f* ***a -i*** hurdles; ***cento metri a -i*** one-hundred metres hurdles
ostaggio *m* ⟨*pl* -ggi⟩ hostage; ***prendere qn in ~*** take s.o. hostage
ostativo *adj* JUR impedimental
oste *m* innkeeper; ***fare i conti senza l'~*** forget the most important thing
osteggiare *v/t* ⟨1f⟩: ***~ qn / qc*** be against s.o. / sth
ostello *m*: ***~ della gioventù*** youth hostel
ostensorio *m* ⟨*pl* -ri⟩ REL ostensory
ostentare *v/t* ⟨1b⟩ (*esibire*) flaunt; (*fingere*) affect **ostentatamente** *adv* ostentatiously **ostentato** *adj* ostentatious; *falso* affected **ostentazione** *f* (*esibizione*) ostentation; (*finzione*) affectation
osteocito *m* osteocyte
osteoporosi *f* osteoporosis
osteria *f* inn
ostetrica *f* obstetrician; (*levatrice*) midwife
ostetricia *f* obstetrics *sg*
ostetrico ⟨*mpl* -ci⟩ **I** *adj* obstetric(al) **II** *m*, **-a** *f* obstetrician
ostia *f* Host
ostico *adj* ⟨*mpl* -ci⟩ difficult
ostile *adj* hostile
ostilità *f* ⟨*pl* ostilità⟩ hostility
ostinarsi *v/r* ⟨1a⟩ dig one's heels in; ***~ a fare qc*** persist in doing sth
ostinatamente *adv* doggedly
ostinato *adj* obstinate
ostinazione *f* obstinacy
ostracismo *m* HIST ostracism; (*esilio*) banishment; *fig* exclusion; ***subire l'~*** face ostracism; ***fare dell'~ nei confronti di qn / qc*** boycott s.o. / sth
ostrica *f* ⟨*pl* -che⟩ oyster
ostrogoto I *adj* Ostrogoth **II** *m*, **-a** *f* Ostrogoth; *hum* barbarian
ostruire *v/t* ⟨4d⟩ block, obstruct
ostruirsi *v/r* ⟨4d⟩ get clogged up
ostruito *adj* blocked
ostruzione *f* (*ostacolo*) obstruction, blockage
ostruzionismo *m* obstructionism
otite *f* ear infection
otorinolaringoiatra *m/f* ⟨*mpl* -i⟩ ear, nose and throat specialist, ENT specialist
otre *f* skin bag, leather bag; ***~ della zampogna*** windbag; ***~ di Klein*** MATH Klein bottle; *fig* ***~ di vento*** windbag; ***~ per l' acqua*** water-bag; *fig* ***pieno come un ~*** full to bursting
ottagonale *adj* octagonal
ottagono *m* octagon
ottano *m* octane; ***numero*** *m* ***di -i*** octane rating *or* number
ottanta *num* eighty; ***gli anni ~*** the Eighties
ottantenne *m/f* eighty-year-old
ottantesimo *m/adj* eightieth
ottantina *f*: ***un'~*** about eighty; ***essere sull'~*** be about eighty, be in one's eighties
ottava *f* MUS octave
ottavo *m/adj* eighth
ottemperanza *f* compliance; ***in ~ a*** in compliance with
ottenebrare *v/t* ⟨1m & b⟩ obscure; *fig* cloud
ottenere *v/t* ⟨2q⟩ get, obtain
ottengo → ***ottenere***
ottenibile *adj* attainable; (*conseguibile*) achievable
ottenibile *adj* obtainable
ottenimento *m* attainment
ottica *f* optics *sg*; *fig* viewpoint, point of view; ***visto in quest'~*** from this point of view
ottico ⟨*mpl* -ci⟩ **I** *adj* optical **II** *m*, **-a** *f* optician
ottimale *adj* optimum
ottimamente *adv* perfectly
ottimismo *m* optimism
ottimista *m/f* ⟨*mpl* -i⟩ optimist
ottimistico *adj* ⟨*mpl* -ci⟩ optimistic

ottimizzare *v/t* ⟨1a⟩ optimize
ottimizzazione *f* optimization
ottimo *adj* excellent, extremely good; ***in -a salute*** in excellent health
otto I *num* eight; ***oggi a ~*** a week today **II** *m* eight; ***~ volante*** big dipper
ottobre *m* October
ottocentesco *adj* ⟨*mpl* -chi⟩ nineteenth-century
ottocento I *num* eight hundred **II** *m*: ***il Ottocento*** the nineteenth century
ottomana *f* ottoman
ottomano I *adj* Ottoman; ***impero*** *m* ***~*** Ottoman empire **II** *m*, **-a** *f* Ottoman
ottomila I *adj* eight thousand **II** *m* ⟨*pl* ottomila⟩ the eight-thousanders
ottone *m* brass; MUS ***-i*** *pl* brass (instruments)
ottundimento *m* blunting
otturare *v/t* ⟨1a⟩ block; *dente* fill
otturatore *m* PHOT shutter
otturazione *f* blocking; *di dente* filling
ottusamente *adv* in a dull way **ottusità** *f* ⟨*pl* ottusità⟩ dullness (*stupidità*) thickness
ottuso *adj* obtuse
outdoor *adj inv* outdoor
outing *m* ⟨*no pl*⟩: ***fare ~*** come out
output *m* ⟨*pl* output⟩ output **outsider** *m/f* ⟨*pl* outsider⟩ outsider
outsorcing, outsourcing *m* outsourcing
ovaia *f* ANAT ovary
ovale *m/adj* oval
ovatta *f* cotton wool, *US* cotton
ovattato *adj fig* muffled
ovazione *f* ovation
overbooking *m* ⟨*pl* overbooking⟩ overbooking
overdose *f* ⟨*pl* overdose⟩ overdose; ***morire per ~*** die from an overdose
overflow *m* ⟨*pl* overflow⟩ COMPUT overflow
ovest *m* west
ovile *m* sheep-pen; *fig* fold; *fig* ***tornare all'~*** return to the fold
ovini *mpl* sheep *pl*
oviparo *adj* oviparous
ovocito *m* ANAT oocyte
ovolo *m* BOT agaric; ***~ buono*** royal agaric; ***~ malefico*** fly agaric
ovovia *f* cable car
ovulazione *f* ovulation
ovulo *m* BOT ovule; MED ovum, egg (cell); ***~ fecondato*** fertilized egg
ovunque *adv* everywhere
ovvero *cj* or rather; (*cioè*) that is
ovverosia *cj* or rather; (*cioè*) that is
ovviamente *adv* obviously
ovviare *v/i* ⟨1l⟩: ***~ a qc*** get around sth
ovvietà *f* ⟨*pl* ovvietà⟩ obviousness
ovvio *adj* ⟨*mpl* -vvi⟩ obvious
oziare *v/i* ⟨1g⟩ laze around, be idle
ozio *m* ⟨*pl* -zi⟩ laziness, idleness; ***~ forzato*** forced inactivity; ***stare in ~*** lounge about; ***l'~ è il padre dei vizi*** *prov* the devil finds work for idle hands
oziosamente *adv* lazily
ozioso *adj* lazy, idle
ozono *m* ozone; ***buco*** *m* ***nell'~*** hole in the ozone layer; ***strato*** *m* ***d'~*** ozone layer
ozonosfera *f* ozone layer

P

p, P *m/f* ⟨*pl* p, P⟩ p, P; ***P come Padova*** p for papa
p. *abbr* (= **pagina**) p (page)
PA *abbr* (= **Palermo**) Palermo
PAC *abbr* (= **Politica agricola comune**) EU CAP (Common Agricultural Policy)
pacatamente *adv* calmly **pacatezza** *f* calmness
pacato *adj* calm, unhurried
pacca *f* ⟨*pl* -cche⟩ slap; ***dare una ~ sulla spalla a qn*** give s.o. a slap on the back
pacchetto *m* package, small parcel; *di biscotti* packet; ***~ azionario*** block of shares; ***~ turistico*** package holiday; ***un ~ di sigarette*** a packet *or US* pack of cigarettes
pacchia *f infml* pleasure; ***che ~!*** What a pleasure! How delightful!

pacchiano *adj* vulgar, in bad taste

pacco *m* ⟨*pl* -cchi⟩ parcel, package; **~ *bomba*** parcel bomb; **~ *dono*** aid package; **~ *postale*** parcel

paccottiglia *f* junk

pace *f* peace; ***trattato*** *m* ***di* ~** peace treaty; ***lasciare in* ~ *qn*** leave s.o. alone *or* in peace; ***fare* ~** make peace; ***mettersi il cuore in* ~** set one's mind at rest; ***non dare* ~ *a qn*** give s.o. no peace; ***non darsi* ~** not resign o.s.; ***per amor di* ~** for the sake of peace and quiet

pace-maker *m* ⟨*pl* pace-maker⟩ pacemaker

pachiderma *m* pachyderm; (*persona*) *hum* elephant

pachistano I *adj* Pakistani **II** *m*, **-a** *f* Pakistani

paciere *m*, **-a** *f* peacemaker

pacificamente *adv* peacefully **pacificare** *v/t* ⟨1m & d⟩ reconcile **pacificarsi** *v/r* ⟨1m & d⟩ calm down

pacifico ⟨*mpl* -ci⟩ **I** *adj* peaceful **II** *m*: ***il Pacifico*** the Pacific; ***è* ~ *che …*** it's undeniable that…

pacifismo *m* pacifism

pacifista *m/f* ⟨*mpl* -i⟩ pacifist

pacioccone I *adj* (*bonario*) easy-going **II** *m*, **-a** *f* easy-going person **pacioso** *adj* placid

package *m* ⟨*pl* package⟩ COMM package **packaging** *m* ⟨*pl* packaging⟩ COMM packaging

PACS *abbr* (= **Patto Civile di Solidarietà**) *Civil Partnership / Union*

Padania *f* Po area

padano *adj* of the Po; ***pianura*** *f* ***-a*** Po Valley

padella *f di cucina* frying pan; ***cascare dalla* ~ *nella brace*** jump out of the frying pan into the fire

padiglione *m* pavilion; **~ *auricolare*** auricle

Padova *f* Padua

padovano I *adj* Paduan **II** *m*, **-a** *f* native of Padua

padre *m* father; **~ *spirituale*** spiritual director; ***da parte di* ~** on the father's side; ***il Santo Padre*** the Holy Father; ***tale* ~ *tale figlio*** like father, like son; ***tramandare di* ~ *in figlio*** hand down from father to son; ***fare da* ~ *a qn*** be a father to s.o.

Padrenostro *m* REL Lord's Prayer, Our Father; ***recitare il* ~** say the Lord's Prayer

padre-padrone *m* tyrannical father

padreterno *m* God; ***fare il* ~** play God

padrino *m* godfather; **~ *di battesimo*** godfather

padronale *adj* privately owned, owner's; ***casa* ~** owner's house

padronanza *f* (*controllo*) control; (*conoscenza*) mastery; **~ *di una lingua*** command of a language; **~ *di sé*** self-control

padronato *m* ownership **padroncino** *m* (*piccolo imprenditore*) owner of a small enterprise; (*giovane padrone*) young owner

padrone *m*, **-a** *f* boss; (*proprietario*) owner; *di cane* master; *donna* mistress; **~ *di casa*** man / lady of the house; *per inquilino* landlord; *donna* landlady; ***farla da* ~** boss (s.o.) about; (***non***) ***essere* ~ *della situazione*** not to be in control; ***sei* ~ *di andartene*** you're free to go; ***chi è il* ~ *di quel cane?*** who is the owner of that dog?

padroneggiare *v/t* ⟨1f⟩ dominate, (*sopprimere*) suppress

paesaggio *m* ⟨*pl* -ggi⟩ scenery; PAINT, GEOG landscape

paesaggista *m/f* ⟨*mpl* -i⟩ PAINT landscape painter *or* artist

paesaggistico *adj* ⟨*mpl* -ci⟩ landscape

paesano I *adj* country *attr* **II** *m*, **-a** *f* person from the country; *pej* country bumpkin

paese *m* **1.** country; **~ *della cuccagna*** land of plenty; **~ *esportatore*** exporting country, exporter; **~ *membro*** member state; **~ *natale*** country of one's birth; **~ *d'origine*** country of origin; **~ *produttore di petrolio*** oil-producing country; ***-i*** *pl* ***in via di sviluppo*** developing countries; ***mandare qn a quel* ~** tell s.o. to go to hell; **~ *che vai, usanza che trovi*** when in Rome(, do as the Romans do) **2.** (*villaggio*) village **3.** (*territorio*) region, area

Paesi Bassi *mpl*: ***i Paesi Bassi*** the Netherlands *pl*

paesino *m* hamlet; *infml* small village

paffuto *adj* chubby

paga *f* ⟨*pl* -ghe⟩ pay; ***busta*** *f* **~** pay packet, *US* paycheck

pagabile *adj* payable; **~ *alla consegna*** payable on delivery; **~ *a vista*** payable at sight
pagaia *f* paddle
pagamento *m* payment; ECON **-*i*** *pl* payments; **~ *anticipato*** payment in advance; **~ *alla consegna*** cash on delivery; **~ *in contanti*** payment in cash, cash payment; **~ *in contrassegno*** cash on delivery; **~ *in natura*** payment in kind; **~ *a rate*** payment in insta(l)l-ments; ***condizioni*** *fpl* ***di*** **~** payment terms; ***altre sono a*** **~** others you have to pay for; ***a*** **~** subject to a charge
paganesimo *m* paganism
pagano *adj* pagan
pagare ⟨1e⟩ **I** *v/t acquisto* pay for; *conto, fattura, debito* pay; ***ti pago qualcosa da bere*** I'll buy you *or* stand you a drink; ***gliela faccio*** **~** he'll pay for this; *fig* ***pagarla cara*** pay dearly **II** *v/i* pay; **~ *anticipatamente*** pay in advance; **~ *in contanti*** pay (in) cash; **~ *a rate*** pay in instal(l)-ments; **~ *di persona*** suffer the consequences
pagato *adj* paid; ***ben*** / ***mal*** **~** well / badly paid
pagella *f* report, *US* report card
pagello *m* ZOOL bream
paggio *m* ⟨*pl* -ggi⟩ page(-boy)
pagherò *m* ⟨*pl* pagherò⟩ promissory note; **~ *bancario*** banker's note
paghetta *f* pocket money
pagina *f* page; ***a*** **~ *10*** on page 10; ***-e gialle*** Yellow Pages; **~ *elettronica*** screen page; **~ *Web*** Web site; *fig* ***voltare*** **~** turn over a new leaf
paglia *f* straw; ***fuoco*** *m* ***di*** **~** flash in the pan; ***avere la coda di*** **~** have a guilty conscience
pagliaccetto *m* (*abbigliamento intimo*) teddy; (*per bambini*) romper-suit
pagliacciata *f* farce
pagliaccio *m* clown
pagliaio *m* ⟨*pl* -ai⟩ haystack; ***cercare un ago in un*** **~** look for a needle in a haystack
pagliericcio *m* ⟨*pl* -cci⟩ straw mattress, pallet
paglierino *adj*: ***giallo*** **~** straw-yellow
paglietta *f* (*cappello*) straw hat; (*lana d'acciaio*) scourer
pagliolo *m* NAUT floor
pagliuzza *f* straw; *d'oro*: speck
pagnotta *f* loaf; *fig* ***guadagnarsi la*** **~** earn one's living
pago *adj* ⟨*mpl* -ghi⟩ content; **~ *di qc*** satisfied with sth
pagoda *f* pagoda
paguro *m* hermit crab
paillard *f* ⟨*pl* paillard⟩ COOK minute steak
paillette *f* ⟨*pl* paillette⟩ paillette
paio *m* ⟨*pl* le paia⟩: ***un*** **~ *di*** *scarpe, guanti etc* a pair of; ***un*** **~ *di pantaloni*** / ***di forbici*** / ***di occhiali*** a pair of trousers *or US* pants / scissors / glasses; ***un*** **~ *di volte*** a couple of times
paiolo *m* cauldron
Pakistan *m* Pakistan **pakistano** → **pachistano**
pala *f* shovel; *di elica, turbina, remo* blade; **~ *d'altare*** altarpiece
paladino *m* paladin; *fig* champion
palafitta *f* pile-work; *abitazione* pile--dwelling
palafreniere *m* HIST groom
palaghiaccio *m* ⟨*pl* palaghiaccio⟩ ice rink
palamito *m* trawl (line); ***pescare col*** **~** to trawl
palanca *f* ⟨*pl* -che⟩ penny; ***-che*** *pl infml* cash
palandrana *f* long loose coat
palasport *m* ⟨*pl* palasport⟩ indoor sports arena
palata *f* shovelful; (*colpo*) blow with a shovel; ***a -e*** plentifully
palatale *adj* palatal
palatino *adj* Palatine; ***biblioteca*** *f* ***-a*** Palatine library
palato *m* palate; **~ *fine*** gourmet
palazzina *f* luxury home
palazzinaro *m* building speculator
palazzo *m* palace; (*edificio*) building; *con appartamenti* block of flats, *US* apartment block; **~ *comunale*** town hall; **~ *di giustizia*** courthouse; **~ *dello sport*** indoor stadium; ***Palazzo Chigi*** Chigi Palace; *fig* the Prime Minister; ***Palazzo Madama*** Madama Palace *fig* the Italian Senate; **~ *reale*** royal palace
palco *m* ⟨*pl* -chi⟩ dais; THEAT stage; (*balcone*) box; (*impalcatura*) scaffolding; **~ *delle autorità*** authorities stand
palcoscenico *m* ⟨*pl* -ci⟩ stage
paleocristiano *adj* early Christian **pa-**

leografia *f* palaeography **paleontologia** *f* palaeontology **paleontologo** *m*, **-a** *f* ⟨*mpl* -gi⟩ palaeontologist
palermitano **I** *adj* of Palermo **II** *m*, **-a** *f* person from Palermo
palesare *v/t* ⟨1a⟩ reveal **palesarsi** *v/r* ⟨1a⟩ show oneself
palese *adj* obvious
palesemente *adv* openly
Palestina *f* Palestine
palestinese *m/f & adj* Palestinian
palestra *f* gym; **~ di roccia** practice wall; ***fare un'ora di ~ al giorno*** train at the gym for an hour a day
paletta *f* shovel; *per la spiaggia* spade; RAIL signal(l)ing paddle
paletto *m* tent peg; *fig* ***mettere dei -i*** limit; *definire* define
palinsesto *m* TV schedule
palio *m* banner; ***mettere in ~*** offer as a prize; ***il Palio di Siena*** *the horse race in Siena*
palissandro *m* rosewood; ***di ~*** rosewood
palizzata *f* palisade
palla *f* **1.** ball; ***~ di neve*** snowball; ***~ prigioniera*** dodgeball; *fig* ***cogliere la ~ al balzo*** jump at the chance; ***essere una ~ al piede*** be a drag; ***giocare a ~*** play with a ball **2.** ***non mi rompere le -e!*** *vulg* don't be such a pain in the arse *vulg or US* ass *sl*; ***che -e!*** *vulg* what a drag! (*or* what a pain!)
pallacanestro *f* basketball
pallamano *f* handball
pallanotista *m/f* ⟨*mpl* -i⟩ water polo player
pallanuoto *f* water polo
pallavolista *m/f* ⟨*mpl* -i⟩ volleyball player
pallavolo *f* volleyball
palleggiare *v/i* ⟨1f⟩ dribble **palleggio** *m* ⟨*pl* -ggi⟩ dribbling; *fig* dribbling
pallet *m* ⟨*pl* pallet⟩ pallet
pallettone *m* buckshot
palliativo *m* palliative
pallido *adj* pale; ***azzurro ~*** pale blue; ***non avere la più -a idea di qc*** not have the faintest idea about sth
pallina *f* **1.** *di vetro* marble **2.** ***~ da golf*** golf ball; ***~ da tennis*** tennis ball
pallino *m nel biliardo* cue ball; *nelle bocce* jack; *munizione* pellet; *fig* ***avere il ~ della pesca*** be mad about fishing, be fishing mad; ***a -i*** *pl* with spots, spotted
pallonata *f* blow with a ball; ***ricevere una ~ in faccia*** get the ball in one's face
palloncino *m* balloon
pallone *m* ball; *calcio* football, soccer; AVIAT balloon; ***~ sonda*** weather balloon; *fig* ***un ~ gonfiato*** be full of o.s.; *fig* ***andare nel ~*** have a mental block
pallore *m* paleness, pallor
palloso *adj infml* boring
pallottola *f* pellet; *di pistola* bullet; ***~ vagante*** stray bullet
pallottoliere *m* abacus
palma *f* palm; *fig* ***meritare la ~*** deserve victory, carry off the palm (of victory); ***~ nana*** dwarf palm
palmare *m* COMPUT palmtop
palmarès *m* ⟨*pl* palmarès⟩ prize-list
palmato *adj*: ***piede m ~*** web-foot; ***foglia f -a*** palmate leaf
palmipede *m* web-footed bird
palmo *m* hand's breadth; ANAT palm; ***a ~ a ~*** gradually, bit by bit, inch by inch; ***rimanere con un ~ di naso*** be very disappointed; ***non cedere nemmeno di un ~*** not to budge an inch
palo *m* pole; *nel calcio* (goal)post; *fig* ***saltare di ~ in frasca*** jump from one subject to another; ***fare il ~*** keep watch
palombaro *m* diver
palombo *m* smooth hound
palpabile *adj fig* palpable
palpare *v/t* ⟨1a⟩ feel; MED palpate
palpazione *f* MED palpation
palpebra *f* eyelid
palpeggiare *v/t* ⟨1f⟩ feel; *a scopo erotico* grope
palpitante *adj cuore* throbbing; (*fremente*) trembling; ***~ di emozione*** trembling with emotion
palpitare *v/i* ⟨1l⟩ *del cuore* pound
palpitazione *f* palpitation; ***avere le -i*** have palpitations
palpito *m del cuore* beat; ***~ d'amore*** thrill of love
paltò *m* ⟨*pl* paltò⟩ overcoat, heavy coat
paludato *adj* dressed-up; *fig* formal, solemn
palude *f* marsh

paludoso *adj* marshy
palustre *adj* marshy; *pianta* marsh
pamphlet *m* ⟨*pl* pamphlet⟩ pamphlet
pampino *m* vine leaf
panacea *f* panacea
panama *m* ⟨*pl* panama⟩ panama (hat)
Panama *m* Panama; ***lo stretto di ~*** the Straits *pl* of Panama
panamense **I** *adj* from Panama **II** *m/f* person from Panama
panamericano *adj* pan-american
panca *f* ⟨*pl* -che⟩ bench; *in chiesa* pew
pancake *m* ⟨*pl* pancake⟩ pancake
pancarré *m* sliced loaf
pancetta *f* pancetta, *cured belly of pork*
panchetto *m* footstool
panchina *f* bench
pancia *f* ⟨*pl* -ce⟩ stomach, belly *infml*; *di animale* belly; ***mal*** *m* ***di ~*** stomach-ache, belly-ache *infml*; ***mettere su ~*** develop a paunch; ***sdraiarsi a ~ in su / in giù*** lie (down) on one's stomach / on one's back; *fig* ***stare a ~ all'aria*** not do a stroke; *fig* ***grattarsi la ~*** twiddle one's thumbs
panciera *f* girdle
pancino *m* little tummy **panciolle** *adv*: ***stare in ~*** loaf about / around
panciotto *m* waistcoat, *US* vest
panciuto *adj* big-bellied
pancotto *m* panada
pancreas *m* ⟨*pl* pancreas⟩ pancreas
pancreatite *f* pancreatitis
panda *m* ⟨*pl* panda⟩ panda
pandemia *f* pandemic
pandemonio *m* ⟨*pl* -i⟩ bedlam; ***si è scatenato il ~*** all hell broke loose
pandolce *m Genoese Christmas cake*
pandoro *m Italian Christmas cake*
pane *m* bread; ***~ azzimo*** unleavened bread; ***~ bianco*** white bread; ***~ integrale*** wholemeal bread; ***~ nero*** pumpernickel; ***pan di Spagna*** sponge cake; ***essere buono come il ~*** have a heart of gold; ***dire ~ al ~ e vino al vino*** call a spade a spade; ***rendere pan per focaccia*** give tit for tat
panegirico *m* ⟨*pl* -ci⟩ panegyric
panetteria *f* bakery
panettiere *m*, **-a** *f* baker
panetto *m*: ***~ di burro*** pat of butter
panettone *m* panettone, *cake made with candied fruit*
panfilo *m* yacht; ***~ a motore*** motor yacht
panforte *m round flat cake from Siena made with candied fruit and nuts*
pangrattato *m* breadcrumbs *pl*
panico *m* ⟨*pl* -ci⟩ panic; ***farsi prendere dal ~*** panic, lose one's head
paniere *m* basket
panificio *m* ⟨*pl* -ci⟩ bakery
panino *m* roll; ***~ imbottito*** filled roll
paninoteca *f* sandwich shop
panna *f* cream; ***~ da cucina*** cream; ***~ cotta*** *dessert made from cream and sugar*; ***~ montata*** whipped cream
panne *f*: ***essere in ~*** have broken down, have had a breakdown
panneggio *m* ⟨*pl* -ggi⟩ draping
pannello *m* panel; ***~ solare*** solar panel
panno *m pezzo di stoffa* cloth; ***-i*** *pl* clothes; ***mettersi nei -i di qn*** put o.s. in s.o.'s shoes; ***i -i sporchi si lavano in famiglia*** wash one's dirty linen at home; ***se fossi nei tuoi -i*** if I were in your shoes
pannocchia *f* cob
pannolino *m* nappy; *per donne* sanitary towel; ***~ mutandina*** disposable nappy *or US* diaper
pannolone *m* incontinence pad
Pannonia *f* Pannonia
panorama *m* ⟨*pl* -i⟩ panorama; *fig* overview
panoramica *f* PHOT panorama, panoramic view; *fig* overview; FILM pan shot
panoramico *adj* ⟨*mpl* -ci⟩ panoramic; ***schermo*** *m* ***~*** wide screen
panpepato *m* cake made with honey
pantagruelico *adj* ⟨*mpl* -ci⟩: ***pranzo*** *m* ***~*** gargantuan meal
pantaloncini *mpl* shorts *pl*
pantaloni *mpl* trousers *pl*, *US* pants *pl*; ***~ di velluto*** cords *pl*; ***~ a zampa d'elefante*** bell-bottoms
pantano *m* bog; *fig* ***cacciarsi in un ~*** get into trouble
pantegana *f* sewer rat
panteismo *m* pantheism **panteista** *m/f* ⟨*mpl* -i⟩ pantheist
pantera *f* ZOOL panther
pantheon *m* ⟨*pl* pantheon⟩ pantheon
pantofola *f* slipper
pantofolaio *m* ⟨*pl* -ai⟩ slipper maker; *casalingo* stay-at-home; *indolente* couch potato
pantografo *m* TECH pantograph; ELEC

pantograph
pantomima *f* pantomime
pantomimo *m*, **-a** *f* pantomimer
panzana *f* whopper; ***non raccontarmi -e*** don't give me some cock-and-bull story
panzanella *f* COOK Tuscan bread salad
panzerotto *m sweet or savoury filled pastry half-moons*
Paolo *m*: ***San ~*** Saint Paul
paonazzo *adj* purple; ***diventare ~ in viso*** go purple in the face
papa *m* Pope; ***a ogni morte di ~*** once in a blue moon; ***morto un ~ se ne fa un altro*** there are plenty more fish in the sea
papà *m* ⟨*pl* papà⟩ daddy, dad; ***figlio*** *m* ***di ~*** *pej* spoilt boy
papabile *adj* eligible for the papacy
papaia *f* papaya
papale *adj* papal
papalina *f* nightcap **papalino** *adj* papalist **papamobile** *f* Pope-mobile
paparazzo *m*: ***i -i*** *pl* the paparazzi
papato *m* pontificate; (*carica*) papacy; (*periodo*) pontificate
papavero *m* poppy
papera *f fig* (*errore*) slip of the tongue; ***fare una ~*** make a slip of the tongue
paperback *m* ⟨*pl* paperback⟩ paperback
Paperino *m* Donald Duck
papero *m*, **-a** *f* gosling
Paperone *m*: ***zio*** *m* ***~*** Uncle Scrooge
papessa *f* popess
papilla *f* ANAT, BOT papilla; ***-e*** *pl* ***gustative*** taste buds
papillon *m* ⟨*pl* papillon⟩ bow tie
papiro *m* papyrus
pappa *f* food; ***trovare la ~ pronta*** get everything handed to one on a plate
pappagallino *m* budgerigar *infml* budgie
pappagallo *m* parrot
pappagorgia *f* ⟨*pl* -ge⟩ double chin
pappamolle *m/f* ⟨*pl* pappamolle⟩ *infml hum* wet
pappardella *f* COOK *wide pasta strip*
pappina *f* linseed poultice
pappone *m*, **-a** *f infml* greedy eater
paprica *f* paprika
pap-test *m* ⟨*pl* pap-test⟩ smear test
Papua Nuova Guinea *f* Papua New Guinea
par. *abbr* (= **paragrafo**) para (paragraph)
para *f*: ***suola*** *f* ***di ~*** crêpe rubber sole
parà *m* ⟨*pl* parà⟩ MIL paratrooper
parabola *f* REL parable; MATH parabola
parabolico *adj* ⟨*mpl* -ci⟩ parabolic; ***antenna*** *f* ***-a*** satellite dish
parabordo *m* NAUT fender
parabrezza *m* ⟨*pl* parabrezza⟩ windscreen, *US* windshield
paracadutare *v/t* ⟨1a⟩ parachute in
paracadutarsi *v/r* parachute
paracadute *m* ⟨*pl* paracadute⟩ parachute
paracadutista *m/f* ⟨*mpl* -i⟩ parachutist
paracarro *m* post
paradigma *m* ⟨*pl* -i⟩ paradigm
paradisiaco *adj* ⟨*mpl* -ci⟩ heavenly; (*piacevole*) blissful; (*divino*) divine
paradiso *m* heaven, paradise; ECON ***~ fiscale*** tax haven; ***~ terrestre*** heaven on earth, Eden; ***andare in ~*** go to heaven
paradossale *adj* paradoxical
paradossalmente *adv* paradoxically
paradosso *m* paradox
parafango *m* ⟨*pl* -ghi⟩ mudguard, *US* fender
paraffina *f* paraffin
paraflying *m* ⟨*pl* paraflying⟩ paraflying
parafrasare *v/t* ⟨1m⟩ paraphrase **parafrasi** *f* ⟨*pl* parafrasi⟩ paraphrase
parafulmine *m* lightning rod
paraggi *mpl* neighbo(u)rhood *sg*; ***nei ~ di*** (somewhere) near
paragonabile *adj* comparable
paragonare *v/t* ⟨1a⟩ compare
paragonarsi *v/r* ⟨1a⟩: ***~ a qn*** compare oneself to s.o.
paragone *m* comparison; ***a ~ di*** compared with, in *or* by comparison with; ***senza ~*** incomparable
paragrafare *v/t* ⟨1m⟩ paragraph
paragrafo *m* paragraph
paraguaiano I *adj* Paraguayan **II** *m*, **-a** *f* Paraguayan **Paraguay** *m* Paraguay
paralisi *f* paralysis
paralitico *m*, **-a** *f* ⟨*mpl* -ci⟩ paralyzed person
paralizzare *v/t* ⟨1a⟩ paralyze
paralizzato *adj* paralyzed; ***avere un braccio ~*** have a paralyzed arm
parallela *f* parallel line; ***-e*** *pl* parallel bars

parallelamente *adv* in parallel (*contemporaneamente*) simultaneously
parallelepipedo *m* parallelepiped
parallelismo *m* parallelism (*a.* GEOM); (*somiglianza*) similarity
parallelo *m/adj* parallel
paraluce *m* ⟨*pl* paraluce⟩ PHOT lens hood
paralume *m* lampshade
paramedico ⟨*mpl* -ci⟩ **I** *adj* paramedical; ***personale*** *m* **~** paramedics *pl* **II** *m*: ***i paramedici*** *pl* the paramedics
parametro *m* parameter
paramilitare *adj* paramilitary
paranco *m* ⟨*pl* -chi⟩ tackle
paranoia *f* paranoia
paranoico ⟨*mpl* -ci⟩ **I** *adj* paranoid **II** *m*, **-a** *f* person with paranoia
paranormale **I** *adj* paranormal; ***facoltà*** *fpl* ***-i*** psychic powers **II** *m* paranormal
paranza *f* otter trawl
paraocchi *mpl* blinkers *pl* (*a. fig*)
paraolimpiadi *fpl* Paralympics
paraorecchi *m* ⟨*pl* paraorecchi⟩ (*di berretto*) ear-flap; (*a passante*) ear-muff
parapendio *m* SPORTS paragliding
parapetto *m* parapet; NAUT rail; ARCH battlement
parapiglia *m* ⟨*pl* parapiglia⟩ stampede; (*confusione*) mayhem; (*baruffa*) tussle
paraplegico **I** *adj* paraplegic **II** *m*, **-a** *f* paraplegic
parapsicologia *f* parapsychology
parare ⟨1a⟩ **I** *v/t* *ornare* decorate; *proteggere* shelter; *occhi* shield; *scansare* parry; **~ *il colpo*** stand up for oneself **II** *v/i* save; ***dove vuoi andare a ~?*** what are you getting at?
pararsi *v/r* ⟨1a⟩ appear; *fig* **~ *il culo*** *infml* save one's ass; **~ *davanti a qn*** appear before s.o.
parasole *m* parasol; PHOT lens hood
paraspigolo *m* edge protector
paraspruzzi *m* ⟨*pl* paraspruzzi⟩ splash guard
parassita *m/f* ⟨*mpl* -i⟩ parasite (*a. fig*)
parassitario *adj* ⟨*mpl* -ri⟩ parasitic
parastatale *adj* parastatal
parastinchi *m* ⟨*pl* parastinchi⟩ shin-pad
parata *f* parade
paratia *f* NAUT bulkhead
paraurti *m* ⟨*pl* paraurti⟩ bumper
paravento *m* screen
Parca *f* ⟨*pl* -che⟩ MYTH Parca; *pl* Parchae
parcella *f* fee; **~ *catastale*** parcel
parcellizzare *v/t* ⟨1a⟩ parcel out
parcheggiare *v/t* & *v/i* ⟨1f⟩ park
parcheggiatore *m*, **-trice** car park attendant
parcheggio *m* parking; *luogo* car park, *US* parking lot; **~ *sotterraneo*** underground car park; ***divieto di ~*** no parking; **~ *custodito* / *incustodito*** attended / unattended car park; **~ *a pagamento*** paying car park
parchimetro *m* parking meter
parco[1] *adj* ⟨*mpl* -chi⟩: ***essere ~ nel mangiare*** eat sparingly
parco[2] *m* ⟨*pl* -chi⟩ park; **~ *acquatico*** water park; **~ *dei divertimenti*** amusement park; **~ *giochi*** play ground; **~ *marino*** seaworld park; **~ *naturale*** nature reserve; **~ *nazionale*** national park; **~ *macchine*** fleet (of vehicles); **~ *tecnologico*** technology park
par condicio *f* ⟨*pl* par condicio⟩ par condicio
parecchio **I** *adj* a lot of **II** *pron*: ***parecchi*** *mpl*, ***parecchie*** *fpl* quite a few **III** *adv* quite a lot
pareggiare ⟨1f⟩ **I** *v/t* even up; (*uguagliare*) match, equal; *conto* balance **II** *v/i* SPORTS draw
pareggio *m* ⟨*pl* -ggi⟩ SPORTS draw
parenchima *m* ⟨*pl* -i⟩ ANAT parenchyma
parentado *m* *infml* relatives
parente *m/f* relative; **~ *acquisito*** in-law; ***-i*** *pl* ***stretti*** immediate relatives ***essere -i*** be related
parentela *f* relationship; *parenti* relatives *pl*, relations *pl*
parentesi *f* bracket; **~ *graffa*** curly bracket; **~ *quadra*** square bracket; **~ *tonda*** round bracket; **~ *uncinata*** angle bracket; (***detto***) ***fra ~*** by the by; *fig* ***aprire una ~*** digress slightly
pareo *m* pareu
parere **I** *v/i* ⟨2h⟩ seem, appear; ***pare che*** it seems that, it would appear that; ***che te ne pare?*** what do you think (of it)?; ***non ti pare?*** don't you think?; ***a quanto pare*** by all accounts; ***non mi pare vero!*** I can't be-

lieve it!; ***che te ne pare?*** what do you think (of it)?; ***fai come ti pare!*** do as you like; ***mi pareva*** (***bene***)***!*** I thought so!; ***ma Le pare!*** not at all! don't mention it! *infml* thanks! **II** *m* opinion; ***a mio ~*** in my opinion, to my way of thinking; ***~ di un esperto*** expert opinion

paresi *f* ⟨*pl* paresi⟩ partial paralysis; MED paresis

parete *f* wall; ***~ divisoria*** partition wall

pargolo *m liter* child

pari **I** *adj* equal; *numero* even; ***~ opportunità*** *fpl* equal opportunities; ***essere di ~ altezza*** be the same height; ***a ~ merito*** equal; ***primo a ~ merito*** first equal; ***finire a ~ merito*** draw; ***al ~ di*** like; ***alla ~*** the same; SPORTS ***finire alla ~*** end in a draw; ***senza ~*** unrivalled, unequalled; ***ora siamo ~!*** now we are quits *o* even! **II** *m* (social) equal, peer; ***da ~ a ~*** as an equal; ***ragazza*** *f* ***alla ~*** au pair (girl)

Paride *m* MYTH Paris

parietale *adj* ANAT parietal; ***osso*** *m* ***~*** parietal bone

parificare *v/t* ⟨1m & d⟩ make equal; *scuola* recognize officially **parificato** *adj*: ***scuola*** *f* ***-a*** officially recognized school **parificazione** *f* equalization; *di scuola* official recognition

Parigi *f* Paris

parigino *adj* (of) Paris, Parisian

pariglia *f* ⟨*pl* -glie⟩ pair; *fig* ***rendere la ~ a qn*** give s.o. tit for tat

parimenti *adv* similarly

parità *f* equality, parity; ***~ di diritti*** equal rights *pl*; ***a ~ di condizioni*** all things being equal

paritario *adj* ⟨*mpl* -ri⟩ equal **paritetico** *adj* ⟨*mpl* -ci⟩ equal; ***commissione -a*** joint committee

parka *m* ⟨*pl* parka⟩ parka

parlamentare **I** *adj* Parliamentary **II** *v/i* ⟨1a⟩ negotiate **III** *m/f* ⟨*mpl* -ri⟩ Member of Parliament, MP

parlamento *m* parliament; ***Parlamento europeo*** European Parliament

parlante *adj* speaking; *fig* eloquent; ***ritratto*** *m* ***~*** lifelike portrait **parlantina** *f* talkativeness; *infml* the gift of the gab; ***avere una bella ~*** have the gift of the gab

parlare *v/i* ⟨1a⟩ talk, speak (***a qn*** to s.o.; ***di qc*** about sth); ***~ del più e del meno*** make small talk; ***~ a vanvera*** talk off the top of one's head; ***parla inglese?*** do you speak English?; ***con chi parlo?*** who's speaking please?; ***i fatti parlano da soli*** the facts speak for themselves; ***non me ne parli !*** don't mention it!; ***non se ne parla proprio!*** there's no question about it!; ***per non ~ di*** not to mention; ***senti chi parla!*** hark who's talking!

parlarsi *v/r* talk, speak; ***~ addosso*** like the sound of one's voice (*a vanvera*) talk nonsense

parlata *f* speech; (*modo di esprimersi*) way of speaking; (*accento*) accent

parlatorio *m* ⟨*pl* -ri⟩ parlour, (*in conventi*) locutory **parlottare** *v/i* ⟨1c⟩ mutter **parlottio** *m* ⟨*pl* -ii⟩ murmur

parmense **I** *adj* from the Parma area **II** *m/f* person from the Parma area

parmigiana COOK: ***alla ~*** *mixed with tomato sauce and grated Parmesan cheese and baked in the oven*

parmigiano **I** *m* (*formaggio*) Parmesan **II** *adj* from Parma **III** *m*, -a *f* person from Parma

Parnaso *m* Parnassus; (*poesia*) poetry

parodia *f* parody

parodiare *v/t* ⟨1h⟩ parody **parodistico** *adj* ⟨*mpl* -ci⟩ mock

parola *f* word; (*facoltà*) speech; ***~ d'ordine*** password; ***-e*** *pl* ***crociate*** crossword (puzzle) *sg*; ***~ magica*** magic word; ***in altre -e*** in other words; ***nel vero senso della ~*** in the true sense of the word; ***giro*** *m* ***di -e*** circumlocution; ***essere di ~*** keep one's word; ***chiedere la ~*** ask for the floor; ***~ per ~*** word for word; ***essere di poche -e*** be a man / woman of few words; ***~ d'onore!*** on my word of honour!; ***rimangiarsi la ~ data*** go back on one's word

parolaccia *f* ⟨*pl* -cce⟩ swear word

parolaio *m*, **-a** *f* ⟨*mpl* -ai⟩ windbag

paroliere *m*, **-a** *f* lyricist

parolina *f* endearment; *alcune parole* a few words; ***dire due -e*** say a few words; ***~ dolce*** sweet nothings

parolona *f* high-sounding word

parossismo *m* MED, GEOL paroxysm; *fig* fit; ***portare qc al ~*** send s.o. into a fit

parotide *f* parotid

parotite *f* parotitis; **~ *epidemica*** infectious parotitis, mumps *sg*
parquet *m* parquet floor
parricida *m/f* ⟨*mpl* -i⟩ patricide; *fig* patricide **parricidio** *m* ⟨*pl* -i⟩ patricide
parrocchia *f* parish
parrocchiale *adj* parish; ***comunità f* ~** parish community
parrocchiano *m*, **-a** *f* parishioner
parrochiale *adj* parish *attr*
parroco *m* ⟨*pl* -ci⟩ parish priest
parrucca *f* ⟨*pl* -cche⟩ wig
parrucchiere *m*, **-a** *f* hairdresser; **~ *per signora*** ladies' hairdresser
parrucchino *m* toupee **parruccone** *m fig* fuddy-duddy
parsimonia *f* thriftiness; *fig* frugality **parsimonioso** *adj* thrifty
partaccia *f* ⟨*pl* -cce⟩: ***fare una ~ a qn*** *infml* give s.o. an earful
parte *f* **1.** part; (*porzione*) portion; ***far ~ di una società*** belong to a society, be a member of a society; ***prendere ~ a*** take part in; ***a ~*** separate; ***a ~ il fatto che ...*** apart from the fact that…; ***da un anno a questa ~*** since last year; ***scherzi a ~*** joking apart; ***in ~*** in part, partly; ***in gran ~*** largely **2.** (*lato*) side; ***mettere da ~ qc*** put sth aside; ***dall'altra ~ della strada*** on the other side of the street; ***da ~ mia*** for my part, as far as I'm concerned; *regalo etc* from me; ***da nessuna ~*** nowhere; ***da tutte le -i*** everywhere; ***fare le -i di qc*** play the part of; ***farsi da ~*** move aside; ***non so da che ~ cominciare*** I don't know where to start **3.** JUR party; **~ *civile*** plaintiff; **~ *lesa*** injured party; ***-i*** *pl* ***sociali*** social parts
partecipante *m/f* participant; **~ *ad una gara*** competitor in a race
partecipare ⟨1m⟩ **I** *v/t* announce **II** *v/i*: **~ *a*** *gara* take part in; *dolore*, *gioia* share
partecipazione *f* (*intervento*) participation; (*annunzio*) announcement; **~ *di matrimonio*** wedding invitation; (*cartolina*) wedding-card; FIN holding; **~ *agli utili*** profit-sharing
partecipe *adj* participating; (*interessato*) concerned; (*informato*) informed JUR privy; ***essere ~ di qc*** be informed about sth
parteggiare *v/i* ⟨1f⟩: **~ *per*** support
partenopeo *adj* Neapolitan
partenza *f* departure; SPORTS start; COMPUT **~ *a freddo*** cold start; ***essere di ~*** be just about to leave, be on the point of leaving; ***falsa ~*** false start; *fig* ***punto m di ~*** starting point, point of departure
parterre *m* ⟨*pl* parterre⟩ THEAT parterre
particella *f* PHYS particle
particina *f* bit part
participio *m* ⟨*pl* -pi⟩ participle
particola *f* REL particle
particolare I *adj* particular; *segretario* private; ***in ~*** in particular **II** *m* particular, detail
particolareggiato *adj* detailed
particolarismo *m* particularism; POL particularism
particolarità *f* ⟨*pl* particolarità⟩ special nature
particolarmente *adv* particularly
partigiano *m*, **-a** *f* partisan
partire *v/i* ⟨4a⟩ leave; AUTO, SPORTS start; **~ *per*** leave for; **~ *per l'estero*** go abroad; *fig* **~ *in quarta*** get off to a flying start
partita *f* **1.** SPORTS match; *di carte* game; **~ *amichevole*** friendly (match); **~ *di calcio*** football match; ***fare una ~ a scacchi*** play chess **2.** *di merce* shipment **3. ~ *IVA*** VAT registration number
partito *m* **1.** POL party; **~ *d'opposizione*** opposition (party) **2.** *fig* ***essere ridotto a mal ~*** be in a bad way; ***essere un buon ~*** be a good catch; ***prendere ~*** make up one's mind
partitocrazia *f* partitocracy
partitura *f* score
partizione *f* division; **~ *della memoria*** COMPUT memory allocation
partner *m/f* ⟨*pl* partner⟩ partner
partnership *f* ⟨*pl* partnership⟩ partnership
parto *m* birth; **~ *cesareo*** C(a)esarean (section); **~ *prematuro*** premature birth; ***sala f ~*** delivery room
partoriente *f* woman about to give birth
partorire *v/t* ⟨4d⟩ give birth to
part time I *adj* part-time; ***lavoro ~*** part-time work **II** *adv* part time
party *m* ⟨*pl* party⟩ party
parure *f* ⟨*pl* parure⟩ *di gioielli*: parure;

di biancheria: set

parvenza *f* guise; ***una ~ di libertà*** an illusion of freedom

parziale *adj* partial; *fig* biased

parzialità *f* ⟨*pl* parzialità⟩ partiality

parzialmente *adv* partially; (*in parte*) partly; ***~ scremato*** semi-skimmed

pascere ⟨3dd⟩ **I** *v/t* feed **II** *v/i* graze; *fig* ***~ di illusioni*** live in a dreamworld

pascià *m* ⟨*pl* pascià⟩ HIST pasha; ***vivere da*** *or* ***come un ~*** live like a lord

pasciuto *adj*: (***ben***) ***~*** plump

pascolare ⟨11⟩ **I** *v/t* pasture **II** *v/i* graze; ***condurre al ~*** pasture

pascolo *m* pasture

Pashtun *mpl* Pashtun

Pasqua *f* Easter; ***Buona ~!*** Happy Easter!; ***essere felice come una ~*** be as happy as a lark

pasquale *adj* Easter *attr*

Pasquetta *f* Easter Monday

passa *adv*; ***e ~*** plus; ***avrà trent'anni e ~*** he / she must be over thirty

passabile *adj* passable

passaggio *m* ⟨*pl* -ggi⟩ passage; *in macchina* lift, *US* ride; *atto* passing; SPORTS pass; ***~ a livello*** level crossing, *US* grade crossing; ***~ pedonale*** pedestrian crossing, *Br* zebra crossing; ***dare un ~ a qn*** give s.o. a lift (*US* ride); ***essere di ~*** be passing through

passamano *m* handing over; ***fare il ~*** hand over

passamontagna *m* ⟨*pl* passamontagna⟩ balaclava, ski-mask

passante *m/f* passer-by; ***~ ferroviario*** underground railway link

passaparola *m* ⟨*pl* passaparola⟩ order passed on by word of mouth; *fig* word-of-mouth information; ***fare il ~*** pass it on

passapatate *m* ⟨*pl* passapatate⟩ potato masher

passaporto *m* passport; ***controllo*** *m* ***dei -i*** passport control

passare ⟨1a⟩ **I** *v/i* **1.** (*trasferirsi*) go (***in*** into); SPORTS pass; ***~ attraverso delle difficoltà*** have a difficult time; ***~ da / per Milano*** go through Milan; ***~ dal panettiere*** drop by the baker's **2.** *di legge* be passed, pass **3.** *di tempo* go by *or* past, pass; ***con il passar del tempo*** as time goes by **4.** *fig*; ***mi è passata la voglia*** I don't feel like it any more; ***farsi ~ per qn*** pass oneself off as; ***mi è passato di mente*** it slipped my mind; ***~ di moda*** go out of fashion; ***~ inosservato*** go unnoticed; ***~ per imbecille*** be taken for a fool **II** *v/t* **1.** *confine* cross; (*sorpassare*) overstep; ***~ un esame*** pass an exam **2.** (*porgere*) pass **3.** (*trascorrere*) spend; ***come te la passi?*** how's it going? **4.** TEL ***ti passo Claudio*** here's Claudio

passata *f* quick wipe; ***dare una ~ con lo straccio*** give a quick wipe with a cloth *pavimento* mop the floor; COOK ***~*** (***di pomodoro***) passata, *sieved tomato pulp*

passatempo *m* pastime, hobby

passato **I** *past part* → ***passare*** **II** *adj* past; *alimento* pureed; ***l'anno ~*** last year; *fig* ***ormai è acqua*** *f* ***-a*** it's all water under the bridge now **III** *m* past; ***sono le due -e*** it's after two o'clock; COOK puree; ***~ di verdura*** vegetable puree

passatoia *f* (*guida*) runner; (*colatoio*) strainer; (*ferr*) crossing

passatoia *f* runner

passatore *m*, **-trice** *f* illegal immigrant smuggler

passatutto *m* ⟨*pl* passatutto⟩ masher

passaverdura *m* ⟨*pl* passaverdura⟩ food mill

passeggero **I** *adj* passing, short-lived **II** *m*, **-a** *f* passenger

passeggiare *v/i* ⟨1f⟩ stroll, walk

passeggiata *f* stroll, walk; (*percorso*) walk

passeggiatrice *f fig* streetwalker

passeggino *m* pushchair

passeggio *m* ⟨*pl* -ggi⟩: ***andare a ~*** go for a walk

passe-partout *m* ⟨*pl* passe-partout⟩ (*chiave*) master key

passerella *f* (foot)bridge; NAUT gangway; AVIAT ramp; *per sfilate* catwalk

passero *m* sparrow

passerotto *m* young sparrow

passettini *mpl*: ***camminare a ~*** tiptoe

passibile *adj*: ***~ di sanzione*** finable

passiflora *f* passionflower

passionale *adj* passionate; *delitto* of passion

passionalità *f* ⟨*pl* passionalità⟩ passionateness

passione *f* passion; ***~ giovanile*** *interesse* hobby of one's youth; *sentimen-*

tale love of one's youth; REL Passion

passito *m* (*vino*) wine made from raisins

passivamente *adv* passively **passività** *f* ⟨*pl* passività⟩ apathy; *pl* ECON liabilities

passivo I *adj* passive; ***fumo** m* **~** second-hand smoke **II** *m* GRAM passive; FIN liabilities *pl*

passo *m* **1.** step; (*impronta*) footprint; ***~ falso*** false move; ***a ogni ~*** every step of the way; ***a ~ di lumaca*** at a snail's pace; AUTO ***avanzare a ~ d'uomo*** craw; ***andare di pari ~*** keep pace with; ***fare due -i*** go for a walk *or* a stroll; ***fare il ~ più lungo della gamba*** bite off more than one can chew; *fig* ***fare il primo ~*** take the first step; ***e via di questo ~*** and so on and so forth; ***stare al ~ coi tempi*** move with the times **2.** *di libro* passage **3.** GEOG pass; ***Passo del San Gottardo*** St Gothard pass **4.** ***~ carrabile*** driveway

password *f* ⟨*pl* password⟩ COMPUT password

pasta *f* paste; (*pastasciutta*) pasta; (*impasto*) dough; (*dolce*) pastry; ***~ all'uovo*** egg pasta; ***~ dentifricia*** toothpaste; ***~ fresca*** fresh pasta; ***~ frolla*** shortcrust pastry; ***~ sfoglia*** puff pastry; *fig* ***è una ~ d'uomo*** a sweet *o* lovely man

pastaio *m*, **-a** *f* ⟨*mpl* -ai⟩ pasta maker

pastasciutta *f* pasta

pasteggiare *v/i* ⟨1f⟩ dine; ***~ a** or **con champagne*** have champagne with one's meal

pastella *f* batter

pastello *m* pastel

pasticca *f* ⟨*pl* -cche⟩ pastille

pasticceria *f* pastries *pl*, cakes *pl*; *negozio* cake shop

pasticciere *m*, **-a** *f* confectioner

pasticcino *m* tartlet

pasticcio *m* ⟨*pl* -cci⟩ COOK pie; *fig* mess; ***~ di fegato d'oca*** pâté de foie gras; ***essere nei -i*** be in a mess; ***ho combinato un bel ~*** I've made a right mess

pasticcione *m*, **-a** *f* blunderer

pastiera *f* COOK pastiera, *ricotta flan*

pastificio *m* pasta shop

pastiglia *f* MED tablet, pill; ***~ effervescente*** soluble tablet

pastina *f small pasta shapes for soup*

pasto *m* meal; *fig* ***dare in ~ al pubblico*** unveil sth (to the public)

pastoia *f* fetter; *fig* fetter

pastone *m per animali* swill; *fig* mush

pastorale I *m* bishop's staff, crozier **II** *f* REL pastoral letter; MUS pastorale

pastore I *m*, **-a** *f* shepherd **II** *m* REL: ***~ (evangelico)*** pastor

pastorello *m*, **-a** *f* young shepherd

pastore tedesco *m* ZOOL German shepherd (dog)

pastorizia *f* sheep-farming

pastorizzare *v/t* ⟨1a⟩ pasteurize

pastorizzato *adj* pasteurized

pastorizzazione *f* pasteurization

pastoso *adj* doughy

pastrano *m* greatcoat

pastrocchio *m* ⟨*pl* -cchi⟩ *infml* mix-up

patacca *f* ⟨*pl* -cche⟩ piece of junk; (*truffa*) fraud; *infml* (*macchia*) grease mark

Patagonia *f* Patagonia

patata *f* potato; ***-e** pl **fritte*** (French) fries, *Br* chips; ***-e** pl **lesse*** boiled potatoes; ***-e** pl **novelle*** early potatoes; ***-e** pl **arrosto*** roast potatoes

patatine *fpl* crisps *pl*, *US* chips *pl*; (*fritte*) French fries *pl*, *Br* chips *pl*

patatrac I *int* crash **II** *m* ⟨*pl* patatrac⟩ *infml* collapse; *fig* complete failure

patchwork *adj inv* patchwork

pâté *m* ⟨*pl* pâté⟩ pâté

patella *f* ZOOL limpet; ANAT kneecap

patema *m* ⟨*pl* -i⟩: ***~ d'animo*** anxiety

patentato *adj infml* licensed; ***bugiardo** m* **~** outright liar

patente *f*: ***~ (di guida)*** driving licence, *US* driver's license; ***ritiro** m **della ~*** loss of one's licence; ***la ~ a punti*** points system driving licence; ***~ di sanità*** NAUT bill of health; ***prendere la ~*** pass one's driving test

patentino *m* provisional licence; *per motorino etc* licence to drive a moped

paternale *f* scolding; ***fare la ~ a qn*** give s.o. a dressing-down

paternalismo *m* paternalism

paternalistico *adj* ⟨*mpl* -ci⟩ paternalist; *con aria di sufficienza* patronizing

paternamente *adv* paternally

paternità *f* paternity

paterno *adj* paternal, fatherly

patetico *adj* ⟨*mpl* -ci⟩ pathetic

pathos *m* ⟨*pl* pathos⟩ pathos

patibolo *m* gallows
patimento *m* suffering
patina *f* sheen; **~ *del tempo*** patina of age **patinato** *adj* glossed; *fig* glazed
patire ⟨4d⟩ **I** *v/i* suffer (***di*** from) **II** *v/t* suffer (from)
patito I *adj* of suffering **II** *m*, **-a** *f* fan; **~ *del jazz*** jazz fan
patogenesi *f* ⟨*pl* patogenesi⟩ pathogenesis **patogeno** *adj* pathogenic
patologia *f* pathology
patologico *adj* pathological
patologo *m*, **-a** *f* ⟨*mpl* -gi⟩ pathologist
patria *f* homeland
patriarca *m* ⟨*pl* -chi⟩ patriarch
patriarcale *adj* patriarchal **patriarcato** *m* patriarchy (*a.* REL)
patrigno *m* stepfather
patrimoniale I *adj* property **II** *f* property tax; ***imposta f* ~** property tax; ***stato m* ~** asset and liability statement
patrimonio *m* ⟨*pl* -ni⟩ estate; **~ *artistico*** artistic heritage; **~ *ereditario*** genetic inheritance; **~ *immobiliare*** property; **~ *dell'umanità*** world heritage centre; *fig* ***un* ~** a fortune
patriota *m/f* ⟨*mpl* -i⟩ patriot
patriottico *adj* patriotic
patriottismo *m* patriotism
patrizio ⟨*mpl* -zi⟩ **I** *adj* HIST patrician **II** *m*, **-a** *f* patrician
patrocinante *m/f* JUR barrister **patrocinare** *v/t* ⟨1a⟩ JUR plead (for) s.o.; *fig* defend
patrocinio *m* support, patronage; ***gratuito* ~** JUR legal aid; ***sotto il* ~ *di qn*** with s.o.'s backing
patronato *m* patronage, sponsorship; (*istituzione benefica*) charitable institution
patronessa *f* benefactress
patrono *m*, **-a** *f* REL patron saint
patta *f dei pantaloni*: flies *pl*
patteggiamento *m* JUR plea bargaining
patteggiare *v/t* ⟨1f⟩ negotiate; **~ *la pena*** JUR plea bargain
pattinaggio *m* ⟨*pl* -ggi⟩ skating; **~ *artistico*** figure skating; **~ *su ghiaccio*** ice skating; **~ *a rotelle*** roller skating
pattinare *v/i* ⟨1l⟩ skate; AUTO skid
pattinatore *m*, **-trice** *f* skater
pattino[1] *m* SPORTS skate; **~ *a rotelle*** roller skate; **~ *in linea*** roller blade
pattino[2] *m* sliding block; AVIAT skid
patto *m* pact; **~ *territoriale*** POL territorial treaty; ***a* ~ *che*** on condition that; ***stare ai -i*** keep to the agreement; ***venire a -i*** come to terms; ***-i chiari, amicizia lunga*** *prov* clear agreements make long friendships; *parola data* a bargain's a bargain
pattuglia *f* patrol; **~ *acrobatica*** AVIAT acrobatic squad; ***essere di* ~** be on patrol
pattugliamento *m squadra* patrol; *atto* patrolling **pattugliare** *v/i and v/t* ⟨1g⟩ patrol
pattuire *v/t* ⟨4d⟩ negotiate
pattumiera *f* dustbin
paturnie *fpl*: bad mood; ***avere le* ~** *infml* be on a short fuse
paura *f* fear; ***avere* ~ *di*** be frightened of; ***mettere*** (*or* ***fare***) **~ *a qn*** frighten s.o.; ***niente* ~!** never fear!; ***magro da far* ~** terribly thin; ***ho* ~ *di no*** I'm afraid not
paurosamente *adv* dreadfully; ***sbandare* ~** skid dreadfully
pauroso *adj* fearful; *che fa paura* frightening
pausa *f* pause; *durante il lavoro* break
pavé *m* ⟨*pl* pavé⟩ paved road / path
pavesare *v/t* ⟨1a⟩ dress (with flags)
pavese I *adj* Pavian; from Padania **II** *m/f* Pavian
pavido *adj* faint-hearted
pavimentare *v/t* ⟨1a⟩ pave
pavimentazione *f* flooring; road surface
pavimento *m* floor
pavoncella *f* peewit
pavone *m* peacock
pavoneggiarsi *v/r* ⟨1f⟩ show off
pay-TV *f* pay TV
pazientare *v/i* ⟨1b⟩ be patient
paziente *m/f & adj* patient
pazientemente *adv* patiently
pazienza *f* patience; **~!** never mind!; ***santa* ~!** *infml* for goodness sake!
pazzamente *adv* madly **pazzerello I** *adj* (*eccentrico*) eccentric; (*strano*) odd; (*imprevedibile*) capricious; ***tempo m* ~** strange weather **II** *m*, **-a** *f* loony
pazzesco *adj* ⟨*mpl* -chi⟩ crazy
pazzia *f* madness; ***è una* ~!** It's pure madness!
pazzo I *adj* mad, crazy; ***è* ~ *da legare***

he's off his head; ***andare ~ per*** be mad *or* crazy about; ***darsi alla -a gioia*** go really wild **II** *m*, **-a** *f* madman; *donna* madwoman; ***cose da -i!*** sheer madness!
pazzoide I *adj* mad **II** *m/f US* weirdo, *Br* nutter
p.c. *abbr* (= **per conoscenza**) cc (carbon copy)
PC *abbr* **1.** (= **personal computer**) PC (personal computer) **2.** (= **Piacenza**) Piacenza
p.c.c. *abbr* (= **per copia conforme**) certified copy
PD *abbr* (= **Padova**) Padua
pdf *abbr* (= **Portable Document Format**) COMPUT pdf
p.e. *abbr* (= **per esempio**) eg (for example)
PE *abbr* **1.** (= **Pescara**) Pescara **2.** (= **Parlamento Europeo**) European Parliament
pecca *f* ⟨*pl* -cche⟩ fault
peccaminoso *adj* sinful
peccare *v/i* ⟨1b & d⟩ sin; ***~ di*** be guilty of
peccato *m* sin; **(*che*) *~ !*** what a pity!; ***~ originale*** REL original sin; ***~ veniale*** venial sin
peccatore *m*, **-trice** *f* sinner
pece *f* pitch; ***nero come la ~*** pitch-black
pecetta *f* patch, sticking plaster; *per censura* censor bar
pechinese I *adj* Pekinese **II** *m/f* Pekinese **III** *m cane* Pekinese
Pechino *m* Beijing, Peking
pecora *f* sheep; ***~ nera*** black sheep
pecorella *f* young or small sheep; (*nuvola*) fleecy cloud; *fig* ***la ~ smarrita*** the lost sheep
pecorino *m/adj*: (***formaggio*** *m*) ***~*** pecorino (*ewe's milk cheese*)
pecorone *m fig* sheeplike
peculato *m* peculation
peculiare *adj* peculiar
peculiarità *f* ⟨*pl* peculiarità⟩ special feature, peculiarity
pecuniario *adj* ⟨*mpl* -ri⟩ monetary; ***sanzione*** *f* ***-a*** pecuniary sanction
pedaggio *m* ⟨*pl* -ggi⟩ toll
pedagogia *f* pedagogy, science of education
pedagogico *adj* ⟨*mpl* -ci⟩ teaching
pedagogo *m*, **-a** *f* ⟨*mpl* -ghi⟩ pedagogue
pedalare *v/i* ⟨1a⟩ pedal
pedale *m* pedal; ***~ dell'acceleratore*** accelerator
pedalino *m* sock
pedalò *m* ⟨*pl* pedalò⟩ pedalo
pedana *f* footrest; SPORTS springboard
pedante *adj* pedantic
pedanteria *f* pedantry, hair-splitting
pedata *f* kick; (*impronta*) footprint
pederasta *m* ⟨*pl* -i⟩ pederast
pedestre *adj*: ***statua*** *f* ***~*** pedestrian statue
pediatra *m/f* ⟨*mpl* -i⟩ p(a)ediatrician
pediatria *f* p(a)ediatrics *sg*
pediatrico *adj* ⟨*mpl* -ci⟩ paediatric
pedicure ⟨*pl* pedicure⟩ **I** *m/f* chiropodist, *US* podiatrist **II** *m* pedicure
pedigree *m* ⟨*pl* pedigree⟩ pedigree
pediluvio *m* footbath
pedina *f* draughtsman; *fig* cog in the wheel; *fig* ***essere una ~ nelle mani di qn*** be a pawn in s.o.'s hands
pedinamento *m* tailing
pedinare *v/t* ⟨1a⟩ shadow, follow
pedinatore *m*, **-trice** *f* tail
pedissequo *adj traduzione* slavish
pedofilia *f* p(a)edophilia
pedofilo *m*, **-a** *f* p(a)edophile
pedologo *m*, **-a** *f* ⟨*mpl* -gi⟩ pedologist
pedonale *adj* pedestrian; ***zona*** *f* ***~*** pedestrian precinct; ***strisce*** *fpl* ***-i*** pedestrian crossing *sg*
pedone *m* pedestrian; *scacchi* pawn
pedopornografia *f* child pornography
pedula *f* climbing shoe
peduncolo *m* stalk
peeling *m* ⟨*pl* peeling⟩ peeling
peggio I *adv* worse **II** *m*: ***c'è di ~*** worse things happen at sea; ***il ~*** the worst; ***il ~ è che*** the worst of it is that; ***avere la ~*** get the worst of it; ***di male in ~*** from bad to worse; ***tanto ~!*** so much the worse!; ***~ per te / lui / lei / voi / loro!*** tough (luck)!
peggioramento *m* deterioration, worsening
peggiorare ⟨1a⟩ **I** *v/t* make worse, worsen **II** *v/i* get worse, worsen
peggiorativo *adj* pejorative
peggiore *adj* worse; *superlativo* worst; ***il ~*** the worst; ***nel ~ dei casi*** if the worst comes to the worst
pegno *m d'amore, respetto etc* token; ***banco*** *m* ***dei -i*** pawn agency; ***~***

d'amore pledge of love; ***dare qc in ~*** pawn sth
pelame *m* fur
pelandrone *m*, **-a** *f infml* lazybones
pelapatate *m* ⟨*pl* pelapatate⟩ potato peeler
pelare *v/t* ⟨1a⟩ peel; *pollo* pluck; *fig infml* fleece *infml*
pelasgico *adj* ⟨*mpl* -ci⟩ Pelasgian
pelato *adj* shaved; (*calvo*) bald; ***pomodori*** *mpl* ***-i*** peeled tomatoes
pellagra *f* pellagra
pellame *m* skin, pelt
pelle *f* skin; ***~ di camoscio*** chamois; ***~ scamosciata*** suede; ***avere la ~ dura*** have a thick skin; ***avere la ~ d'oca*** have gooseflesh; *fig* ***essere ~ e ossa*** be nothing but skin and bones; ***essere amici per la ~*** be as thick as thieves; ***lasciarci la ~*** lose one's life; ***vendere cara la ~*** sell one's life dearly; ***non vorrei essere nella sua ~*** I wouldn't like to be in his / her shoes
pellegrinaggio *m* ⟨*pl* -ggi⟩ pilgrimage; ***andare in ~*** go on a pilgrimage
pellegrino *m*, **-a** *f* pilgrim
pellerossa *m/f* ⟨*pl* pellerossa *or* pellirosse⟩ *neg* redskin
pellet *m* ⟨*pl* pellet⟩ pellet
pelletteria *f* leatherwork; ***-e*** *pl* leather goods
pellicano *m* pelican
pellicceria *f* furrier's
pelliccia *f* ⟨*pl* -cce⟩ fur; *cappotto* fur coat; ***~ ecologica*** imitation fur
pellicciaio *m*, **-a** *f* ⟨*mpl* -ai⟩ furrier
pellicciotto *m* fur jacket
pellicina *f* cuticle
pellicola *f* film; ***~ a colori*** colo(u)r film; ***~ trasparente*** cling film
pellirossa → ***pellerossa***
pelo *m* **1.** hair, coat; (*pelliccia*) coat; ***contro ~*** against the nap; *fig* ***per un ~*** by the skin of one's teeth; ***non avere -i sulla lingua*** not mince one's words; ***avere il ~ sullo stomaco*** be ruthless; ***cercare il ~ nell'uovo*** nitpick **2.** ***a ~ dell'acqua*** on the surface of the water
Peloponneso *m* Peloponnese
peloso *adj* hairy; *fig* ***carità*** *f* ***-a*** interested charity
peltro *m* pewter
pelucco *m* ⟨*pl* -cchi⟩ *pl* bobbles
peluche *f* ⟨*pl* peluche⟩ cuddly toy; ***un cane*** *m* ***di ~*** a fluffy dog
peluria *f* down
pelvi *f* ⟨*pl* pelvi⟩ ANAT pelvis **pelvico** *adj* ⟨*mpl* -ci⟩ pelvic
pena *f* (*sofferenza*) pain, suffering; (*punizione*) punishment; ***~ di morte*** death penalty; ***stare in ~ per qn*** worry about s.o.; ***vale la ~ soffrire tanto?*** is it worth suffering so much?; ***non ne vale la ~*** it's not worth it; ***mi fa ~*** I feel sorry for him / her; ***a mala ~*** hardly
penale I *adj* criminal; *codice* penal **II** *f* penalty
penalista *m/f* ⟨*mpl* -i⟩ criminal lawyer
penalità *f* ⟨*pl* penalità⟩ penalty
penalizzare *v/t* ⟨1a⟩ penalize
penalizzazione *f* penalization; *fig* penalty
penare *v/i* ⟨1a⟩ (*patire*) suffer; (*faticare*) struggle
pendaglio *m* ⟨*pl* -gli⟩ pendant; *di catenina* fob; ***~ da forca*** gallows-bird
pendente *adj* hanging; JUR pending; ***una causa ~*** a pending lawsuit; ***crediti -i*** outstanding credits; ***orecchino*** *m* ***~*** ear-drop; ***la torre ~*** the leaning tower
pendenza *f* slope
pendere *v/i* ⟨3a⟩ hang; (*essere inclinato*) slope; *fig* ***~ dalle labbra di qn*** hang on s.o.'s every word
pendice *f* slope; *di collina* hillside
pendio *m* slope
pendolare *m/f* commuter
pendolo *m* pendulum; ***orologio*** *m* ***a ~*** grandfather clock; *alto* tall pendulum clock
pene *m* penis
penetrabile *adj* penetrable; *fig* understandable
penetrante *adj dolore*, *freddo* piercing; *fig sguardo* piercing, penetrating; *analisi* penetrating
penetrare ⟨11 & b⟩ **I** *v/t* penetrate **II** *v/i*: ***~ in*** enter
penetrazione *f nell'atto sessuale*: penetration
penicillina *f* penicillin
peninsulare *adj* peninsular
penisola *f* peninsula; ***~ iberica*** Iberian peninsula
penitente I *adj* repentant **II** *m/f* penitent
penitenza *f* REL penance; *in gioco* for-

feit; ***fare ~*** do penance
penitenziario *m* ⟨*pl* -ri⟩ prison
penna *f* **1.** pen; ***~ biro***® ballpoint (pen), biro®; ***~ a feltro*** felt-tip (pen); COMPUT ***~ ottica*** light pen; ***~ a sfera*** ballpoint pen, biro®; ***~ stilografica*** fountain pen **2.** *di uccello* feather; *fig* ***lasciarci le -e*** lose one's life
pennacchio *m* ⟨*pl* -cchi⟩ plume; ***~ di fumo*** plume of smoke
pennarello *m* felt-tip (pen)
pennellata *f* brush stroke
pennello *m* brush; ***a ~*** to a tee; ***andare*** *or* ***stare a ~*** fit like a glove
pennichella *f* siesta; *infml* forty-winks
pennino *m* nib; *di strumenti* pen
pennone *m* flagstaff; NAUT yard; (*stendardo*) ensign; HIST pennon
pennuto I *adj* feathered **II** *n*: ***pennuto*** *m* bird
penombra *f* half-light
penosamente *adv* painfully
penoso *adj* painful
pensabile *adj* conceivable **pensante** *adj* thinking
pensare *v/i* ⟨1b⟩ think; ***~ a*** think about *or* of; ***~ a fare qc*** (*ricordarsi di*) remember to do sth; ***~ di fare qc*** think of doing sth; ***che ne pensa?*** what do you think?; ***cosa stai pensando?*** what are you thinking about?; ***ci penso io*** I'll take care of it; ***senza ~*** without thinking; ***e ~ che...*** to think that...; ***non la pensiamo allo stesso modo*** we don't see things the same way
pensata *f infml* brainwave; (*idea*) idea
pensatore *m*, **-trice** *f* thinker
pensierino *m* small gift; ***farci un ~*** think about it
pensiero *m* thought; (*preoccupazione*) worry; ***stare in ~*** be worried *or* anxious (***per*** about); ***un piccolo ~*** (*regalo*) a little something; ***togliersi il ~*** (***di qc***) stop worrying about sth; ***è il ~ che conta*** it's the thought that counts
pensieroso *adj* pensive
pensile *adj* hanging; ***armadietto*** *m* ***~*** wall cupboard
pensilina *f* shelter
pensionabile *adj quota*, *anni* pensionable earnings / years; *per gli statali* of a pensionable age; *persona* entitled to a pension, eligible for retirement; ***età*** *f* ***~*** pensionable age
pensionamento *m* retirement
pensionante *m/f* boarder, lodger
pensionare *v/t* ⟨1a⟩ pension off
pensionato *m*, **-a** *f* pensioner, retired person; (*alloggio*) boarding house
pensione *f* **1.** pension; ***~ integrativa*** occupational pension scheme; ***~ di vecchiaia*** old-age pension; ***andare in ~*** retire **2.** (*albergo*) boarding house; ***~ completa*** full board; ***mezza ~*** half board
pensionistico *adj* ⟨*mpl* -ci⟩ pension; ***sistema*** *m* ***~*** pension plan
pensoso *adj* pensive, thoughtful
pentaedro *m* pentahedron
pentagonale *adj* pentagonal
pentagono *m* pentagon
pentagramma *m* ⟨*pl* -i⟩ stave
pentapartito *m* (*governo*) five-party government; (*coalizione*) five-party coalition
pentathlon *m* SPORTS pentathlon
pentatleta *m/f* ⟨*mpl* -i⟩ pentathlete
Pentecoste *f* Whitsun
pentimento *m* remorse
pentirsi *v/r* ⟨4b or 4d⟩ *di peccato* repent; ***~ di aver fatto qc*** be sorry for doing sth
pentito I *adj* repentant **II** *m*, **-a** *f* (*collaboratore di giustizia*) *criminal who has turned state's evidence*
pentola *f* pot, pan; ***~ a pressione*** pressure cooker; *fig* ***qualcosa bolle in ~*** something's brewing / going on
pentolaccia *f*: (***gioco*** *m* ***della***) ***~*** piñata **pentolino** *m* small pot; (*bollitore*) kettle
penultimo *adj* last but one, penultimate
penuria *f* shortage (***di*** of); ***~ di alloggi*** housing shortage
penzolare *v/i* ⟨1l⟩ dangle
penzolarsi *v/r* dangle
penzoloni *adv* dangling
peonia *f* peony
pepare *v/t* ⟨1a⟩ pepper
pepato *adj* peppered
pepe *m* pepper; ***una ragazza tutta ~*** a feisty girl
peperonata *f* COOK *dish of peppers, tomatoes and onions cooked in oil*
peperoncino *m* BOT pepper
peperone *m* pepper; ***-i*** *pl* ***ripieni*** stuffed peppers; ***rosso come un ~*** as red as a beetroot

pepita *f* nugget
peplo *m* HIST peplum
pepsina *f* pepsin
per I *prep* for; *mezzo* by; ~ ***qualche giorno*** for a few days; ~ ***questa ragione*** for that reason; ~ ***tutta la notte*** throughout the night; ~ ***iscritto*** in writing; ~ ***esempio*** for example; ***dieci ~ cento*** ten per cent; ***uno ~ uno*** one by one; ~ ***adesso*** (*or* ***ora***) (*provvisoriamente*) for the time being; (*momentaneamente*) for the moment; ~ ***caso*** by chance; ~ ***favore*** please; ~ ***il momento*** (*provvisoriamente*) for the time being; (*momentaneamente*) for the moment; ~ ***di qua*** this way; ***la strada ~ l'ospedale*** the way to the hospital; ~ ***tempo*** well in advance; ~ ***le sei sono da voi*** I'll be with you by six; ***stavo ~ uscire*** I was about to go out; ~ ***di più*** furthermore; ~ ***lo più*** generally; ~ ***carità!*** for God's sake!; ***condannare ~ omicidio*** convict for murder; ***lo faccio ~ te*** I'll do it / I'm doing it for you **II** *cj*: ~ ***fare qc*** (in order) to do sth; ***stare ~*** be about to; ***è troppo bello ~ essere vero*** it's too good to be true; ***lo hanno punito ~ aver disobbedito*** they punished him for being disobedient; ~ ***buono che sia...*** although it / he is good...
pera *f* pear; ***farsi una ~*** *infml* get a fix
peraltro *adv* however
perbacco *int* Good Lord
perbene I *adj* respectable **II** *adv* properly
perbenismo *m* conformism
perborato *m* perborate
perca *f* ⟨*pl* -che⟩ ZOOL perch
percento I *m* percentage **II** *adv* per cent
percentuale *f/adj* percentage
percepibile *adj* perceptible; COMM collectible
percepire *v/t* ⟨4d⟩ perceive; (*riscuotere*) cash
percezione *f* perception
perché *cj* because; (*affinché*) so that; ~***?*** why?; ~ ***no?*** why not?; ~ ***no!*** *reso con verbi modali al negativo* because you can't!, because I won't; ~ ***sì!*** because I say so!
perciò *cj* so, therefore
percorrenza *f* distance; ***tempo*** *m* ***di ~*** travelling time
percorrere *v/t* ⟨3o⟩ *distanza* cover; *strada, fiume* travel along; ~ ***l'autostrada*** drive on the motorway
percorribile *adj strada* open; (*libero*) clear **percorribilità** *f* ⟨*pl* percorribilità⟩ practicability
percorso I *past part* → ***percorrere*** **II** *m* (*tragitto*) route; COMPUT path
percossa *f* blow
percosso → ***percuotere***
percuotere *v/t* ⟨3ff⟩ strike
percussione *f* percussion; MUS ***-i*** *pl* percussion
percussionista *m/f* ⟨*mpl* -i⟩ percussionist **percussore** *m* striker
perdente I *adj* losing (*a. fig*), losing **II** *m/f* loser
perdere ⟨3b & 3uu⟩ **I** *v/t* lose; *treno, occasione* miss; *fig* ~ ***colpi*** be slipping; ~ ***conoscenza*** faint; *infml* black out; *fig* ~ ***le staffe*** lose one's temper; ~ ***tempo*** waste time; *fig* ~ ***la testa*** lose one's head, go crazy; ~ ***di vista*** lose sight of; *fig* lose touch with; ***lasciamo ~!*** forget it!; ***il lupo perde il pelo ma non il vizio*** *prov* a leopard cannot change its spots **II** *v/i* lose; *di rubinetto, tubo* leak; ***a ~*** disposable; ***vuoto a ~*** non-returnable bottle
perdersi *v/r* get lost; ~ ***d'animo*** lose heart; ~ ***in un bicchier d'acqua*** make a mountain out of a molehill; ***non ti sei perso niente*** you didn't miss much
perdiana, perdinci, perdindirindina *int* crumbs!; goodness gracious!; (my) goodness!
perdifiato *m*: ***urlare a ~*** shout at the top of one's voice
perdigiorno *m* ⟨*pl* perdigiorno⟩ loafer, idler
perdita *f* loss; *di gas, di acqua* leak; ***essere in ~*** be making a loss; ~ ***di tempo*** waste of time; ***si estendeva a ~ d'occhio*** it stretched as far as the eye could see
perditempo ⟨*pl* perditempo⟩ **I** *m/f* idler **II** *m* waste of time
perdonare *v/t* ⟨1a⟩ forgive
perdono *m* forgiveness; ***ti chiedo ~*** please forgive me
perdurare I *v/i* ⟨1a⟩ persist **II** *m* duration

perdutamente *adv* passionately
perduto *adj* lost; *fig* (*depravato*) fallen; ***andar ~*** go missing
peregrinare *v/i* ⟨1n⟩ wander
perenne *adj* eternal, never-ending; BOT perennial
perennemente *adv* perpetually
perentorio *adj* (*tassativo*) imperative; (*autoritario*) peremptory
perequazione *f* equalization; ***~ degli oneri*** tax equalization
peretta *f* (*clistere*) enema
perfettamente *adv* perfectly
perfetto I *adj* perfect **II** *m* GRAM perfect (tense)
perfezionamento *m* adjustment, further improvement; ***corso m di ~*** further training
perfezionare *v/t* ⟨1a⟩ perfect, further improve
perfezionarsi *v/r* improve; ***~ nella lingua italiana*** improve one's Italian
perfezione *f* perfection; ***a ~*** to perfection, perfectly
perfezionismo *m* perfectionism
perfezionista *m/f* ⟨*mpl* -i⟩ perfectionist
perfidamente *adv* treacherously **perfidia** *f* wickedness
perfido *adj* treacherous
perfino *adv* even
perforare *v/t* ⟨1c⟩ drill through
perforato *adj* perforated; ***timpano m ~*** MED perforated eardrum
perforazione *f* perforation
performance *f* ⟨*pl* performance⟩ performance; (*spettacolo*) performance, show
pergamena *f* parchment
Pergamo *f* Pergamon / Pergamum
pergola *f* pergola
pergolato *m* pergola
pericardio *m* ⟨*pl* -di⟩ ANAT pericardium
pericolante *adj* on the verge of collapse
pericolo *m* danger; (*rischio*) risk; ***~ di contagio*** risk of infection; ***~ di epidemie*** risk of epidemics; ***~ d'incendio*** fire hazard; ***~ di morte*** mortal danger; ***essere in ~*** be in danger; ***mettere in ~*** endanger, put at risk; ***a proprio rischio e ~*** at one's own risk; ***fuori ~*** out of danger
pericolosamente *adv* dangerously
pericolosità *f* ⟨*pl* pericolosità⟩ dangerousness
pericoloso *adj* dangerous
periferia *f* periphery; *di città* outskirts *pl*
periferica *f* COMPUT peripherals
periferico *adj* ⟨*mpl* -ci⟩ peripheral; *quartiere* outlying; COMPUT ***unità f -a*** peripheral
perifrasi *f* ⟨*pl* perifrasi⟩ circumlocution
perimetrale *adj* perimetric; ***muro m ~*** side-wall
perimetro *m* perimeter
perineale *adj* perineal **perineo** *m* ANAT perineum
periodicamente *adv* periodically
periodicità *f* ⟨*pl* periodicità⟩ periodicity; ***legge f di ~*** CHEM periodic law
periodico ⟨*mpl* -ci⟩ **I** *adj* periodic **II** *m* periodical; ***~ mensile*** monthly
periodo *m* period; ***~ di transizione*** transition period; ***andare a -i*** go in ups and downs
peripezia *f* misadventure
periplo *m* circumnavigation
perire *v/i* ⟨4d⟩ perish
periscopio *m* ⟨*pl* -i⟩ periscope
peristalsi *f* peristalsis
peristilio *m* ⟨*pl* -i⟩ peristyle
peritale *adj* expert; ***accertamento m ~*** surveyor assessment, expert's assessment, expert's report
perito I *adj* expert **II** *m*, **-a** *f* expert; ***~ agrario*** agronomist; ***~ commerciale*** business expert
peritoneo *m* peritoneum
peritonite *f* peritonitis
perizia *f* skill, expertise; *esame* examination (by an expert); ***~ balistica*** ballistic test; ***~ calligrafica*** handwriting analysis
perizoma *m* ⟨*pl* -i⟩ G-string; (*tanga*) thong
perla *f* pearl; ***~ coltivata*** cultured pearl; ***collana f di -e*** pearl necklace
perlaceo *adj* pearly; *simile a perla* pearl-like
perlina *f* bead
perlomeno *adv* at least
perlopiù *adv* usually
perlustrare *v/t* ⟨1a⟩ patrol
perlustrazione *f* patrol, search; ***andare in ~*** scout out, go on a reconnaissance

permaloso *adj* easily offended, touchy
permanente I *adj* permanent **II** *f* perm
permanenza *f* permanence; *in un luogo* stay; ***buona ~!*** have a nice stay!
permeabile *adj* permeable **permeabilità** *f* ⟨*pl* permeabilità⟩ permeability
permeare *v/t* ⟨1l & b⟩ permeate; *fig* pervade
permesso I *past part* → ***permettere*** **II** *m* permission; (*breve licenza*) permit; MIL leave; ***~ d'atterraggio*** permission to land; ***~ di lavoro*** work permit; ***~ di soggiorno*** residence permit; (***è***) ***~?*** may I?; ***con ~*** excuse me; ***con il tuo ~*** if you will allow me; ***è ~?*** may I / we come in?
permettere *v/t* ⟨3ee⟩ allow, permit
permettersi *v/r* afford
permissivo *adj* permissive
permuta *f* trade-in **permutare** *v/t* ⟨1a⟩ exchange
pernacchia *f infml* raspberry *infml*
pernice *f* partridge
pernicioso *adj* harmful; MED pernicious
perno *m* pivot
pernottamento *m* night, overnight stay
pernottare *v/i* ⟨1c⟩ spend the night, stay overnight
pero *m* pear (tree)
però *cj* but
perone *m* fibula
peronospora *f* downy mildew; ***~ della patata*** potato blight
perorare *v/t* ⟨1c⟩: ***~ la causa di qn*** plead in s.o.'s defence
perossido *m* peroxide
perpendicolare *f/adj* perpendicular
perpendicolarmente *adv* perpendicularly
perpetrare *v/t* ⟨1l⟩ perpetrate
perpetua *f* priest's housekeeper
perpetuare *v/t* ⟨1m & b⟩ perpetuate **perpetuarsi** *v/r* ⟨1m & b⟩ last
perpetuo *adj* perpetual; ***moto*** *m* ~ perpetual movement
perplessità *f* ⟨*pl* perplessità⟩ uncertainty; (*dubbio*) doubt; ***avere qualche ~ su qc*** have some doubt about sth
perplesso *adj* perplexed
perquisire *v/t* ⟨4d⟩ search
perquisizione *f* search; ***~ personale*** body search; ***mandato*** *m* ***di ~*** search warrant
persecutore I *adj* persecutory **II** *m*, **-trice** *f* persecutor **persecutorio** *adj* ⟨*mpl* -ri⟩ persecutory; *fig* ***campagna*** *f* ***-a*** persecutory campaign
persecuzione *f* persecution; ***mania*** *f* ***di ~*** persecution complex
perseguibile *adj* JUR actionable
perseguimento *m* pursuit
perseguire *v/t* ⟨4a⟩ pursue JUR prosecute
perseguitare *v/t* ⟨1m⟩ persecute
perseguitato *m*, **-a** *f*: ***~ politico*** person being persecuted for their political views
perseverante *adj* persevering
perseveranza *f* perseverance
perseverare *v/i* ⟨1m & b⟩ persevere
Persia *f hist* Persia
persiana *f* shutter
persiano *adj* Persian; ***gatto*** *m* ~ Persian cat
persico *adj* ⟨*mpl* -ci⟩: ***Golfo*** *m* ***Persico*** the Persian Gulf; ***pesce*** *m* ~ perch
persino *adv* → ***perfino***
persistente *adj* persistent
persistenza *f* persistence
persistere *v/i* ⟨3f⟩ persist
perso *past part* → ***perdere***
persona *f* person; ***a*** (*or* ***per***) ~ a head, each; ***in ~, di ~*** in person, personally; ***~ fisica / giuridica*** JUR legal person; ***-e*** people
personaggio *m* ⟨*pl* -ggi⟩ character; (*celebrità*) personality
personal computer *m* ⟨*pl* personal computer⟩ personal computer, PC
personale I *adj* personal; ***igiene*** *f* ~ personal hygiene **II** *m* staff, personnel; AVIAT ***~ di terra*** ground staff *or* crew; ***riduzione*** *f* ***del ~*** cuts in staff, personnel cutbacks; ***avere un bel ~*** look good
personalità *f* ⟨*pl* personalità⟩ personality; ***~ giuridica*** JUR personality
personalizzare *v/t* ⟨1a⟩ personalize; (*adattare alle proprie esigenze*) customize **personalizzato** *adj* customized; COMPUT customized **personalizzazione** *f* personalization; *adattamento* customization
personalmente *adv* personally
personificare *v/t* ⟨1n & d⟩ personify
personificazione *f* (*incarnazione*) embodiment; (*rappresentazione*) per-

sonification *fig* symbol
perspicace *adj* shrewd
perspicacia *f* shrewdness
persuadere *v/t* ⟨2i⟩ convince; **~ *qn a fare qc*** persuade s.o. to do sth
persuadersi *v/r* convince o.s.
persuasione *f* persuasion
persuasivo *adj* persuasive
persuaso *past part* → **persuadere**; ***essere ~ di qc*** be convinced of sth
pertanto *cj* and so, therefore
pertica *f* ⟨*pl* -che⟩ rod, pole; *hum* (*persona*) beanpole
pertinace *adj* persistent, persevering
pertinente *adj* relevant, pertinent
pertinenza *f* relevance, pertinence; ***di mia ~*** my concern / business
pertosse *f* MED whooping cough
pertugio *m* ⟨*pl* -gi⟩ hole, cavity
perturbare *v/t* ⟨1a⟩ perturb, alarm
perturbarsi *v/r* ⟨1a⟩ get upset; METEO break
perturbazione *f* disturbance; ***~ atmosferica*** atmospheric disturbance
Perù *m* Peru
perugino **I** *adj* from Perugia **II** *m*, **-a** *f* person from Perugia
peruviano **I** *adj* Peruvian **II** *m*, **-a** *f* Peruvian
pervadere *v/t* ⟨3q⟩ pervade **pervaso** **I** *adj* filled (with), pervaded (with) **II** *past part* → **pervadere**
pervenire *v/i* ⟨4p⟩ arrive; ***far ~*** send
perversione *f* perversion
perverso *adj* perverse
pervertito *m*, **-a** *f* pervert
pervicace *adj* headstrong, obstinate
pervicacia *f* obstinacy
pervinca *f* ⟨*pl* -che⟩ periwinkle
p.es. *abbr* (= **per esempio**) eg (for example)
pesa *f*: ***~ pubblica*** weigh-house
pesalettere *m* ⟨*pl* pesalettere⟩ letter scales *pl*
pesante *adj* heavy; *fig libro*, *film* boring; ***avere la mano ~*** be heavy-handed; ***battuta*** *f* **~** tasteless remark; ***droghe*** *fpl* **-i** heavy drugs; ***mezzo*** *m* **~** heavy vehicle; ***scherzo*** *m* **~** tasteless prank
pesantemente *adv*: ***cadere ~ a terra*** fall heavily to the ground
pesantezza *f* heaviness; ***~ di stomaco*** indigestion
pesapersone *f* ⟨*pl* pesapersone⟩ scales *pl*; *in negozio etc* weighing machine
pesare ⟨1a⟩ **I** *v/t* weigh; *ingredienti* weigh out **II** *v/i* weigh; ***~ le parole*** weigh one's words; ***~ sulla coscienza*** lie heavy on s.o.'s conscience; ***stirare non mi pesa*** ironing doesn't bother me
pesarese **I** *adj* from Pesaro **II** *m/f* person from Pesaro
pesarsi *v/r* weigh o.s.
pesatura *f* weighing
PESC *abbr* (= **Politica estera di sicurezza comune**) EU Common Foreign and Security Policy
pesca[1] *f* ⟨*pl* -che⟩ (*frutto*) peach; ***~ noce*** nectarine
pesca[2] *f* fishing; ***~ con la lenza*** angling; ***~ subacquea*** underwater fishing; ***~ di beneficienza*** raffle
pescaggio *m* ⟨*pl* -ggi⟩ NAUT draught; ***~ a nave carica / scarica*** load / light draught
pescare *v/t* ⟨1d⟩ fish for; (*prendere*) catch; *fig* dig up; *ladro*, *svaligiatore etc* catch (red-handed); *fig* ***~ nel torbido*** fish in troubled waters; ***~ qn a fare qc*** *infml* catch s.o. doing sth
pescarese **I** *adj* from Pescara **II** *m/f* person from Pescara
pescatora *f*: ***calzoni*** *mpl* ***alla ~*** bermuda shorts; ***risotto*** *m* ***alla ~*** seafood risotto
pescatore *m*, **-trice** *f* fisherman, *donna* fisherwoman
pesce *m* fish; ***~ azzurro*** bluefish, (*acciughe*) anchovies; ***~ rosso*** goldfish; ***~ spada*** swordfish; ***~ d'aprile*** April Fool; ***buttarsi a ~*** make a dive (for); ***prendere qn a -i in faccia*** treat s.o. like dirt; ***sentirsi un ~ fuor d'acqua*** feel like a square peg in a round hole / a fish out of water; *fig* ***non sapere che -i prendere*** be at a loss, be at one's wit's end; ASTROL ***Pesci*** *pl* Pisces *sg*
pescecane *m* ⟨*pl* pescicani⟩ shark
peschereccio *m* ⟨*pl* -cci⟩ fishing boat
pescheria *f* fishmonger's
peschiera *f* fish-pond, fish-tank
Pesci *mpl* ASTROL Pisces *sg*
pesciolino *m* small fish
pescivendolo *m*, **-a** *f* fishmonger
pesco *m* ⟨*pl* -chi⟩ peach (tree)
pescoso *adj* with abundant supplies

of fish

PESD *abbr* (= **Politica europea di sicurezza e di difesa**) European policy for security and defence

peso *m* weight; **~ *lordo*** gross weight; **~ *netto*** net weight; **~ *massimo consentito*** maximum load; ***aumento*** *m* ***di* ~** weight gain; ***perdita*** *f* ***di* ~** weight loss; ***a* ~** by weight; ***pagare qc a* ~ *d'oro*** pay through the nose for sth; *fig* ***di nessun* ~** of no importance, unimportant; *fig* ***avere un* ~ *sullo stomaco*** have a weight on one's mind; *fig* ***non voglio essere un* ~ *per te*** I don't want to be a burden to you; ***essere di* ~ *a qn*** be a burden to s.o.; ***essere un* ~ *morto*** be a deadweight; ***usare due -i e due misure*** have a double standard; ***si è tolto un* ~ *dal cuore*** get sth out of one's system / off one's chest

pessimismo *m* pessimism

pessimista ⟨*mpl* -i⟩ **I** *adj* pessimistic **II** *m/f* pessimist

pessimistico *adj* ⟨*mpl* -ci⟩ pessimistic

pessimo *adj* very bad, terrible

pesta *f esp pl*: ***trovarsi*** *or* ***essere nelle -e*** be in trouble / in a mess

pestaggio *m* ⟨*pl* -ggi⟩ *infml* going-over *infml*

pestare *v/t* ⟨1a⟩ *carne*, *prezzemolo* pound; *con piede* step on; (*picchiare*) beat up; **~ *i piedi a qn*** tread on s.o.'s toes (*a. fig*)

peste *f* plague; *persona* pest; **~ *bubbonica*** bubonic plague

pestello *m* pestle

pesticida *m* ⟨*pl* -i⟩ pesticide

pestifero *adj* (*pestilenziale*) pestilential; ***quel ragazzo è* ~** that boy's a pest

pestilenza *f* plague **pestilenziale** *adj* pestilential; (*puzzolente*) stinking

pesto *m* pesto, *paste of basil*, *olive oil and pine nuts*

pesto[2] *adj*: ***occhio*** *m* **~** black eye; ***buio*** *m* **~** pitch dark

petalo *m* petal

petardo *m* banger

petizione *f* petition; ***diritto*** *m* ***di* ~** JUR petition right

peto *m infml* fart *infml*

petrolchimica *f* petrochemistry

petrolchimico *adj* petrochemical; ***industria*** *f* **~** petrochemical industry

petroliera *f* (oil) tanker

petroliere *m*, **-a** *f* oil merchant; (*operaio*) oil worker

petrolifero *adj* oil *attr*

petrolio *m* oil, petroleum, **~ *greggio*** crude; ***lume*** *m* ***a* ~** paraffin lamp

pettegolare *v/i* ⟨1m⟩ gossip

pettegolezzo *m* piece *or* item of gossip

pettegolo I *adj* gossipy **II** *m*, **-a** *f* gossip

pettinare *v/t* ⟨1l & b⟩ comb

pettinarsi *v/r* comb one's hair

pettinata *f*: ***darsi una* ~** give one's hair a comb **pettinato I** *adj* TEX combed **II** *n*: ***pettinato*** *m* combed **pettinatrice** *f* hairdresser

pettinatura *f* hairstyle, hairdo

pettine *m* comb

pettinino *m* pocket comb

pettirosso *m* robin

petto *m* chest; (*seno*) breast; **~ *di pollo*** chicken breast; ***a doppio* ~** double-breasted; ***prendere qc di* ~** face up to sth

pettorale I *adj* pectoral; ***muscoli*** *mpl* ***-i*** pectoral muscles **II** *m* SPORTS number

petulante *adj* nagging

petulanza *f* petulance

petunia *f* petunia

pezza *f* cloth; (*toppa*) patch; *fig* ***trattare qn come una* ~ *da piedi*** treat s.o. like a doormat

pezzato I *adj* spotted **II** *n*: ***pezzato*** *m* piebald

pezzente *m/f* tramp

pezzetto *m* bit; *carta* scrap; *cibo* morsel; (*briciola*) crumb

pezzo *m* **1.** piece; *di motore* part; *scacchi* man; ***due -i*** bikini; *fig* **~ *grosso*** big shot; **~ *di ricambio*** spare (part); ***andare in -i*** break into pieces; ***in -i da cento euro*** in denominations of one hundred euros; **~ *di merda*** *vulg* shit, shithead; (*cretino*) twat; ***sono a -i!*** I'm shattered / exhausted **2. *da*** *or* ***per un* ~** for a long time

pezzuola *f* cloth; (*straccio*) rag

PG *abbr* (= **Perugia**) Perugia

ph *m* pH

pi *m* ⟨*pl* pi⟩: **~ *greco*** pi

PI *abbr* (= **Pisa**) Pisa

piacente *adj* attractive

piacentino I *adj* from Piacenza **II** *m*,

-a *f* person from Piacenza
piacere I *v/i* ⟨2k⟩: ***le piace il vino?*** do you like wine?; ***non mi piace il cioccolato*** I don't like chocolate; ***non mi piacciono i tuoi amici*** I don't like your friends; ***mi piacerebbe saperlo*** I'd really like to know; ***faccio come mi pare e piace*** I do as I please **II** *m* pleasure; (*favore*) favo(u)r; ***~!*** pleased to meet you!; ***~ di conoscerla*** pleased to meet you; ***viaggio** m **di ~*** pleasure trip; ***aver ~ di*** be delighted to; ***mi fa ~*** I'm happy to; ***che ~!*** what a pleasure!; ***con ~*** with pleasure; ***per ~*** please; ***serviti a ~*** take as much as you like
piacevole *adj* pleasant
piacevolmente *adv* pleasantly
piacimento *m*: ***a ~*** as much as you like
piadina *f* COOK *type of flat bread made in Romagna*
piaga *f* ⟨*pl* -ghe⟩ (*ferita*) wound; *fig* scourge; ***mettere il dito sulla ~*** touch on a sore point; ***agitare il coltello nella ~*** rub salt into the wound; *fig* ***essere una ~*** be a pain (in the neck)
piagato *adj* sore; *coperto* covered in sores
piaggeria *f* sycophancy
piagnisteo *m* whingeing **piagnone** *m*, **-a** *f* whinger, cry-baby **piagnucolare** *v/i* ⟨1m⟩ whine, whimper, grizzle **piagnucolio** *m* ⟨*pl* -ii⟩ whining, whingeing **piagnucoloso** *adj* whining, whingeing
pialla *f* plane
piallare *v/t* ⟨1a⟩ plane
piana *f* plain
pianale *m* level surface
pianeggiante *adj* flat
pianella *f pantofola* slipper; BUILD tile
pianerottolo *m* landing
pianeta *m* planet
piangente *adj* crying; ***salice ~*** weeping willow; ***voce** f **~*** tearful voice
piangere ⟨3d⟩ **I** *v/i* cry, weep **II** *v/t* mourn; ***~ miseria*** plead / cry poverty
piangersi *v/r*: ***~ addosso*** *infml* act the martyr
pianificare *v/t* ⟨1m & d⟩ plan
pianificazione *f* planning
pianista *m/f* ⟨*mpl* -i⟩ pianist
piano I *adj* flat **II** *adv* (*adagio*) slowly; (*a voce bassa*) quietly, in a low voice; ***~ ~*** in one's own good time; (*gradatamente*) gradually ***andarci ~ con qc*** take it / things easy; (*a voce bassa*) softly **III** *m* **1.** plan; ***~ di cottura*** cooking surface; ***~ di emergenza*** emergency plan; ***~ regolatore*** town-planning scheme **2.** (*pianura*) plane **3.** *di edificio* floor; ***~ rialzato*** mezzanine (floor) **4.** ***primo ~*** foreground; PHOT close-up **5.** MUS piano
piano bar *m* ⟨*pl* piano bar⟩ piano bar
pianoforte *m* piano; ***~ a coda*** grand piano
pianola *f* pianola
pianoro *m* plateau
pianoterra *m* ⟨*pl* pianoterra⟩ ground floor
pianta¹ *f* BOT plant; ***~ di appartamento*** house plant; ***~ medicinale** or **officinale*** medicinal plant; ***~ ornamentale*** ornamental plant; ***~ rampicante*** creeper, creeping plant, climbing plant; ***di sana ~*** from start to finish
pianta² *f di città* map; ***~ della città*** town plan
pianta³ *f*: ***~ del piede*** sole (of the foot)
piantagione *f* plantation; *il piantare* planting
piantagrane *m/f* ⟨*pl* piantagrane⟩ *infml* trouble-maker
piantana *f* upright; BUILD scaffold pole
piantare *v/t* ⟨1a⟩ plant; *chiodo* hammer in; ***piantala!*** *infml* cut that out! *infml*; ***~ qn*** *infml* dump s.o. *infml*; ***~ grane*** make difficulties; ***~ in asso qn*** let s.o. down, leave s.o. in the lurch; ***~ un chiodo nel muro*** drive a nail into the wall
piantarsi *v/r infml*: ***si sono piantati*** they've split up *infml*
piantato *adj*: ***ben ~*** sturdy, thickset
pianterreno *m* ground floor, *US* first floor; ***al ~*** on the ground floor
piantina *f* map; BOT small plant; *appena nata* seedling
pianto I *past part* → ***piangere*** **II** *m* crying, weeping; (*lacrime*) tears *pl*
piantonamento *m* surveillance
piantonare *v/t* ⟨1a⟩ guard; ***~ un edificio*** watch a building
piantone *m* guard
pianura *f* plain
piastra *f* plate; ***cuocere alla ~*** griddle
piastrella *f* tile
piastrellare *v/t* ⟨1b⟩ tile **piastrellista** *m/f* ⟨*mpl* -i⟩ tiler

piastrina *f* plaque; MIL identification tag
piattaforma *f* platform; **~ *di lancio*** launch pad
piattello *m*: ***tiro*** *m* ***al* ~** clay pigeon shooting
piattezza *f* flatness
piattino *m* saucer
piatto I *m* **1.** plate; **~ *fondo*** soup plate; **~ *piano*** dinner plate; **~ *di carta*** paper plate; ***lavare i -i*** *Br* wash up; wash the dishes **2.** COOK dish; **~ *forte*** main course; **~ *del giorno*** day's special; **~ *nazionale*** national dish; ***primo* ~** first course; **~ *unico*** main course **3.** MUS ***-i*** *pl* cymbals **II** *adj* flat
piattola *f* crab; *fig* pain in the neck, bore
piazza *f* square; COMM market (place); **~ *del mercato*** market square; *fig* ***fare* ~ *pulita*** make a clean sweep; ***letto*** *m* ***a una* ~** single bed
piazzale *m* large square; *in autostrada* toll-booth area; *in aeroporto* apron
piazzamento *m* placing; *elenco, graduatoria* position
piazzare *v/t* ⟨1a⟩ place, put; (*vendere*) sell
piazzarsi *v/r* (*collocarsi*) settle; (*classificarsi*) be placed
piazzata *f* loud vulgar scene, row; ***fare una* ~** make a scene **piazzista** *m/f* ⟨*mpl* -i⟩ (*intermediario*) middleman; (*commesso viaggiatore*) travelling salesman
piazzista *m/f* ⟨*mpl* -i⟩ salesman; *donna* saleswoman
piazzola *f* small square; **~ *di sosta*** lay-by
picaresco *adj* ⟨*mpl* -chi⟩: ***romanzo*** *m* **~** picaresque novel
piccante *adj* spicy, hot
Piccardia *f* Picardy
piccarsi *v/r* ⟨1d⟩: **~ *di qc*** claim sth
piccata *f* COOK *slice of veal fried in a pan with chopped parsley and lemon juice*
piccato *adj* piqued
picche *fpl* spades; ***asso*** *m* ***di* ~** ace of spades; *fig* ***contare come il due di* ~** be worth nothing; *fig* ***rispondere* ~** give s.o. a flat refusal
picchettaggio *m* ⟨*pl* -ggi⟩ picketing **picchettare** *v/t* ⟨1a⟩ picket **~ *una fabbrica*** picket a factory **picchetto** *m* (*piolo*) stake; *di militanti* picket; MIL guard; *di scioperanti*: picket; ***essere di* ~** be on picket duty
picchiare *v/t* ⟨1a⟩ beat
picchiarsi *v/r* ⟨1a⟩ fight; *violentemente* come to blows, hit each other
picchiata *f* AVIAT nosedive
picchiato *adj*: ***essere* ~** be off one's head **picchiatore** *m*, **-trice** *f* basher **picchiettare** ⟨1a⟩ **I** *v/i* pat, rap **II** *v/t* pat, rap **picchiettio** *m* ⟨*pl* -ii⟩ tapping, drumming, (*pioggia*) pattering
picchio *m* ⟨*pl* -cchi⟩; ZOOL woodpecker
piccino *adj* tiny
picciolo *m* stalk
piccionaia *f* THEAT gods *pl*
piccione *m* pigeon; **~ *viaggiatore*** carrier pigeon; ***prendere due -i con una fava*** kill two birds with one stone
picciotto *m young Sicilian lad, low-ranking in the Mafia*
picco *m* ⟨*pl* -cchi⟩ peak; NAUT ***colare a* ~** sink
piccolezza *f* smallness; (*inezia*) trifle; *fig* pettiness, small-mindedness
piccolo I *adj* small, little; *di statura* short; *meschino* petty **II** *m*, **-a** *f* child; ***la gatta con i suoi -i*** the cat and her young; ***da* ~** as a child; ***fin da* ~** since I/he was a child; ***nel proprio* ~** in one's own small way
picconata *f* blow with a pickaxe; *fig* criticism **piccone** *m* pickaxe
piccozza *f* ice ax(e)
picnic *m* ⟨*pl* picnic⟩ picnic; ***fare un* ~** have a picnic, picnic
pidocchio *m* ⟨*pl* -cchi⟩ louse
pidocchioso *adj* lousy
piè *m*: ***a* ~ (*di*) *pagina*** at the foot of the page; ***ad ogni* ~ *sospinto*** at every turn; ***saltare a* ~ *pari*** hop with both feet together; *fig* skip
pied-à-terre *m* ⟨*pl* pied-à-terre⟩ pied-à-terre **pied-de-poule** *adj inv* houndstooth
piede *m* foot; ***-i*** *pl* ***piatti*** flat feet; *sl* cops *sl*, flatfoots *sl*; ***a -i*** on foot; ***su due -i*** suddenly; ***cadere in -i*** fall on one's feet; ***prendere* ~** catch on; ***stare in -i*** stand; ***a* ~ *libero*** at large; ***a -i nudi*** barefoot, with bare feet; ***in punta di -i*** on tip-toe; ***togliti dai -i!*** get out of my way!; ***andarci coi -i di piombo*** tread carefully; **~ *di porco*** wrecking

bar; ***ragionare con i -i*** be a bit dense; *fig* ***tenere il ~ in due staffe*** have a foot in both camps

Piedi Neri *mpl* Black feet indians

piedino *m* footsie; ***fare ~ a qn*** *infml* play footsie with s.o.

piedipiatti *m* ⟨*pl* piedipiatti⟩ *infml* cop

piedistallo *m* pedestal

piega *f* ⟨*pl* -ghe⟩ wrinkle; *di pantaloni* crease; *di gonna* pleat; ***a -ghe*** *gonna* pleated; *fig* ***prendere una brutta ~*** take a turn for the worse; ***il tuo ragionamento non fa una ~*** this is airtight reasoning

piegamento *m* press-ups; ***~ sulle gambe*** knee-bends

piegare ⟨1b & e⟩ **I** *v/t* bend; (*ripiegare*) fold; ***~ il capo*** bow one's head **II** *v/i* bend

piegarsi *v/r* bend; *fig* ***~ a*** comply with

pieghettato *adj* TEX pleated

pieghevole *adj sedia* folding

Piemonte *m* Piedmont

piemontese *m/f & adj* Piedmontese

piena *f* flood; *a teatro* full house

pienezza *f* fullness

pieno I *adj* full (***di*** of); (*non cavo*) solid; ***~ di sé*** full of himself; ***~ zeppo*** (jam-)packed; ***a -i voti*** with full marks; ***in ~ giorno*** in broad daylight; ***in -a notte*** in the middle of the night; ***lavorare a tempo ~*** work full time **II** *m*: ***nel ~ dell'inverno*** in the depths of winter; AUTO ***fare il ~*** fill up; ***sbagliarsi in ~*** be totally wrong

pienone *m* full house

piercing *m* ⟨*pl* piercing⟩ piercing

pierre *m/f* ⟨*pl* pierre⟩ PR man, PR woman

pietà *f* pity (***di*** for); PAINT pietà; ***avere ~ di qn*** take pity on s.o.; ***per ~!*** for pity's sake!; ***senza ~*** pitiless, merciless

pietanza *f* dish

pietismo *m* HIST Pietism; *fig* sanctimoniousness

pietoso *adj* pitiful; (*compassionevole*) merciful

pietra *f* stone; ***~ focaia*** flint; ***~ miliare*** milestone (*a. fig*); ***~ preziosa*** precious stone; ***~ dello scandalo*** cause of all the trouble; *fig* ***mettiamoci una ~ sopra*** let's forget all about it

pietraia *f* GEOL quarry

pietrificato *adj* petrified; *fig* terrified

pietrina *f* flint

pietrisco *m* ⟨*pl* -chi⟩ rubble, gravel

Pietro *m*: ***San ~*** Saint Peter; ***basilica f di San ~*** Saint Peter's Basilica

pietroburghese I *adj* from St Petersburg **II** *m/f* person from St Petersburg

pietroso *adj* stony

pieve *f* HIST parish church

pifferaio *m*, **-a** *f* ⟨*mpl* -ai⟩ piper; ***il ~ magico*** the Pied Piper **piffero** *m* pipe; *infml* gullible person

pigiama *m* pyjamas *pl*, PJs *infml*

pigia pigia *m* ⟨*pl* pigia pigia⟩ crush, jam

pigiare *v/t* ⟨1f⟩ crush

pigiatura *f dell'uva*: pressing *o* crushing

pigionante *m/f* lodger

pigione *f* rent

pigliare *v/t* ⟨1g⟩ catch; ***~ fiato*** catch one's breath

piglio *m* ⟨*pl* -i⟩ (*espressione*) expression; (*tono*) *fig* tone *m*

Pigmei *mpl* Pygmies

pigmentazione *f* pigmentation **pigmento** *m* pigment

pigmeo *m*, **-a** *f* pygmy

pigna *f* pinecone

pignatta *f infml* cooking pot

pignoleria *f carattere* fussiness

pignolo *adj* pedantic, nit-picking *infml*

pignone *m* MECH pinion; BUILD gable

pignorabile *adj* seizable, distrainable; (*impegnabile*) pawnable

pignoramento *m* distraint

pignorare *v/t* ⟨1a⟩ distrain

pigolare *v/i* ⟨1l⟩ cheep

pigolio *m* ⟨*pl* -ii⟩ cheeping

pigrizia *f* laziness

pigro *adj* lazy

pigrone *m*, **-a** *f infml* loafer, lazybones

PIL *abbr* (= **prodotto interno lordo**) GDP (gross domestic product)

pila *f* ELEC battery; (*catasta*) pile, heap; ***~ dell'acquasanta*** holy water basin

pilastro *m* pillar

pile *m* ⟨*pl* pile⟩ TEX pile

pillola *f* pill; ***~ (anticoncezionale)*** pill; ***prendere la ~*** be on the pill; ***addolcire la ~ a qn*** sugar the pill; ***in -e*** in pill form; *fig* in small doses

pilone *m* pier; ELEC pylon

piloro *m* ANAT pylorus

pilota I *m/f* ⟨*mpl* -i⟩ AVIAT, NAUT pilot; AUTO driver; ***~ automatico*** automatic

pilot **II** *adj inv* pilot *attr*
pilotaggio *m* ⟨*pl* -ggi⟩ pilotage; ***scuola di ~*** flying school
pilotare *v/t* ⟨1c⟩ pilot; AUTO drive
piluccare *v/t* ⟨1d⟩ pick; ***~ qc a qn*** scrounge money from s.o.
pimpante *adj* gaudy
PIN *m* FIN PIN; ***codice*** *m* ~ PIN code
pinacoteca *f* ⟨*pl* -che⟩ art gallery
pince *f* ⟨*pl* pince⟩ tuck
pince-nez *m* ⟨*pl* pince-nez⟩ pince-nez
pinco pallino *m infml* John Doe; *fig infml* twit, *Br* prat
pineta *f* pine forest
ping-pong *m* table tennis, ping-pong
pingue *adj* fat; (*grassoccio*) plump; chubby **pinguedine** *f* corpulence, fatness
pinguino *m* ZOOL penguin
pinna *f di pesce* fin; SPORTS flipper; ***~ caudale*** tail fin
pinnacolo *m* ARCH pinnacle
pino *m* pine; ***~ marittimo*** maritime pine
pinolo *m* pine nut
pinot *m* ⟨*pl* pinot⟩ COOK Pinot; ***~ bianco / nero*** Pinot Blanc / Noir
pinza *f* pliers *pl*; MED forceps *pl*
pinzare *v/t* ⟨1a⟩ staple
pinzatrice *f* stapler
pinzette *fpl* tweezers *pl*
pinzillacchera *f hum* trifle
pinzimonio *m dip for vegetables made with olive oil, pepper and salt*
pio *adj* pious
pioggerella *f* drizzle
pioggia *f* ⟨*pl* -gge⟩ rain; ***~ acida*** acid rain; ***interventi*** *mpl* ***a ~*** across-the-board
piolo *m* (*paletto*) peg, stake; (*di scala*) rung; (*cricket*) stump; ***scala*** *f* ***a -i*** stepladder
piombare ⟨1a⟩ **I** *v/t dente* fill **II** *v/i* fall; *precipitarsi* rush (***su*** at); ***mi è piombato in casa*** he dropped in unexpectedly; *fig* ***~ nella disperazione*** sink into despair
piombatura *f di dente* filling
piombino *m* sinker
piombo *m* lead; ***a ~*** plumb; ***con / senza ~*** *benzina* leaded / unleaded; *fig* ***andare con i piedi di ~*** tread carefully
pioniere *m*, **-a** *f* pioneer
pionieristico *adj* ⟨*mpl* -ci⟩ pioneering (*a. fig*)
pioppo *m* poplar
piorrea *f* pyorrhoea; ***~ alveolare*** periodontitis
piovano *adj* rain; ***acqua*** *f* ***-a*** rainwater
piovasco *m* ⟨*pl* -chi⟩ squall
piovere *v/impers* ⟨3kk⟩ rain; ***piove a dirotto*** it's raining cats and dogs; *fig* ***non ci piove!*** that's flat!; ***piove sul bagnato*** it never rains but it pours
piovigginare *v/impers* ⟨1m⟩ drizzle
piovigginoso *adj* drizzly
piovoso *adj* rainy
piovra *f* octopus
pipa *f* pipe; ***fumare la ~*** smoke a pipe
pipetta *f* CHEM pipette; LING inverted circumflex
pipì *f infml* pee *infml*; ***fare la ~*** *infml* go for a pee *infml*
pipistrello *m* bat
pira *f* LIT pyre
piramidale *adj* pyramid (*a. fig*)
piramide *f* pyramid
piranha *m* ⟨*pl* piranha⟩ piranha
pirata *m* ⟨*pl* -i⟩ pirate; ***~ dell'aria*** hijacker; ***~ della strada*** hit-and-run driver; (*guidatore spericolato*) roadhog; ***copia*** *f* ~ pirate copy
pirateria *f* piracy (*a. fig*); ***~ informatica*** hacking **piratesco** *adj* ⟨*mpl* -chi⟩ pirate
Pirenei *mpl* Pyrenees *pl*
pirite *f* pyrite
pirla *vulg m* prick; ***fare la figura del ~*** look a real prick
piroetta *f* pirouette; ***fare una ~*** perform a pirouette
pirofila *f* oven-proof dish
piroga *f* ⟨*pl* -ghe⟩ pirogue
piromane *m/f* pyromaniac
piroscafo *m* steamer, steamship
pirosi *f* pyrosis
pirotecnica *f* fireworks *pl*
pirotecnico *adj* ⟨*mpl* -ci⟩ fireworks *attr*; ***spettacolo*** *m* ~ firework display
pisano I *adj* from Pisa **II** *m*, **-a** *f* person from Pisa
pisciare *v/i* ⟨1f⟩ *sl* piss *sl*; ***pisciarsi addosso*** *or* ***sotto dal ridere*** piss oneself laughing
pisciata *f vulg* piss, slash
piscina *f* (swimming) pool; ***~ coperta*** indoor pool; ***~ olimpionica*** Olympic-size swimming pool

pisello *m* pea
pisolino *m* nap
pisside *f* REL pyx
pista *f di atletica* track; *di equitazione* racecourse; *di circo* ring; (*traccia*) trail; *di autostrada* toll-lane; *di aeroporto* runway; **~ da ballo** dance floor; **~ da sci** ski slope; **~ da sci di fondo** cross country ski trail; **~ ciclabile** cycle path
pistacchio *m* ⟨*pl* -cchi⟩ pistachio
pistillo *m* pistil
pistoiese **I** *adj* from Pistoia **II** *m/f* person from Pistoia
pistola *f* pistol; **~ ad acqua** water pistol; **~ automatica** automatic (pistol); **~ a spruzzo** spray gun; **~ giocattolo** toy gun
pistolero *m* gunman **pistolettata** *f* pistol-shot
pistone *m* piston
Pitagora *m* Pythagoras **pitagorico** *adj* ⟨*mpl* -ci⟩ Pythagorean; **tavola** *f* **-a** *infml* (multiplication) table
pitale *m infml* chamber-pot
pitocco ⟨*mpl* -cchi⟩ **I** *adj* stingy **II** *m*, **-a** *f* miser
pitone *m* python
pittima *f* ZOOL godwit; *fig* pain (in the neck)
pittogramma *m* ⟨*pl* -i⟩ pictogram
pittore *m*, **-trice** *f* painter
pittoresco *adj* ⟨*mpl* -chi⟩ picturesque
pittura *f* painting
pitturare *v/t* ⟨1a⟩ paint
più **I** *adv* more (**di, che** than); *superlativo* most; MATH plus; **~ grande** bigger; **il ~ grande** the biggest; **di ~** more; **non ~** no more; *tempo* no longer; **~ o meno** more or less; **per di ~** what's more; **mai ~** never again; **al ~ presto** as soon as possible; **al ~ tardi** at the latest **II** *adj* more; *superlativo* most; **~ volte** several times **III** *m* most; MATH plus sign; **per lo ~** mainly; **i ~, le ~** the majority; **parlare del ~ e del meno** talk about this and that
piuccheperfetto *m* past perfect; *form* pluperfect
piuma *f* feather
piumaggio *m* ⟨*pl* -ggi⟩ plumage
piumaggio *m* plumage
piumino *m* down; *giacca* down jacket
piumone *m* Continental quilt, duvet
piuttosto *adv* rather
piva *f* bagpipe; **andarsene con le -e nel sacco** be crestfallen
P.IVA *abbr* (= **Partita IVA**) VAT registration number
pivello *m*, **-a** *f* novice; *infml* fledgeling; *pej* upstart
pixel *m* ⟨*pl* pixel⟩ COMPUT pixel
pizza *f* pizza
pizzaiolo *m*, **-a** *f* pizza maker; **alla -a** *cooked with tomato sauce, garlic, oregano and oil*
pizzeria *f* pizzeria, pizza parlo(u)r
pizzetto *m* goatee
pizzicare ⟨1l & d⟩ **I** *v/t braccio, persona* pinch; *infml ladro* catch (red-handed), nick *infml* **II** *v/i* pinch
pizzicarsi *v/r* ⟨1l & d⟩ *fig infml* tease each other
pizzicheria *f* grocer's (shop)
pizzico *m* ⟨*pl* -chi⟩ pinch
pizzicore *m* itch; *fig* whim
pizzicotto *m* pinch
pizzo *m* (*merletto*) lace
placare *v/t* ⟨1d⟩ placate; *dolore* ease
placarsi *v/r* ⟨1d⟩ calm down
placca *f* ⟨*pl* -cche⟩ plate; (*targhetta*) plaque; **~ dentaria** plaque
placcare *v/t* ⟨1d⟩ plate; *nel rugby* tackle; **placcato d'oro** gold-plated
placebo **I** *adj inv* placebo; **effetto** *m* **~** placebo effect **II** *m* ⟨*pl* placebo⟩ placebo
placenta *f* placenta
placidamente *adv* placidly
placido *adj* placid
plafoniera *f* ceiling light
plagiare *v/t* ⟨1f⟩ plagiarize; (*soggiogare*) subjugate
plagio *m* ⟨*pl* -gi⟩ plagiarism
plaid *m* ⟨*pl* plaid⟩ tartan rug
planare *v/i* ⟨1a⟩ glide
planata *f* glide; **fare una ~** glide
plancia *f* bridge; (*passerella*) gangway, gangplank
plancton *m* plankton
planetario ⟨*mpl* -ri⟩ **I** *adj* planetary **II** *m* planetarium
planimetria *f* plan; (*scienza*) planimetry
planisfero *m* planisphere; **~ (celeste)** planisphere; NAUT star chart
plantare *m* insole
plasma *m* plasma; **~ sanguigno** blood plasma
plasmabile *adj* malleable

plasmare *v/t* ⟨1a⟩ mo(u)ld
plastica *f* plastic; MED plastic surgery; ***posate** fpl* ***di ~*** plastic cutlery
plasticità *f* ⟨*pl* plasticità⟩ plasticity; ART plasticity; METAL plasticity
plastico ⟨*mpl* -ci⟩ **I** *adj* plastic; ***chirurgo** m* ***~*** plastic surgeon **II** *m* ARCH scale model; ***esplosivo** m* ***al ~*** plastic bomb
plastificare *v/t* ⟨1m & d⟩ cover with plastic
plastificato *adj ricoperto* plastic coated; *trasformato* plasticized
plastilina® *f* Plasticine®
platano *m* plane (tree)
platea *f* THEAT stalls *pl*
plateale *adj*: ***gesto** m* ***~*** theatrical gesture; ***errore** m* ***~*** blatant mistake
plateau *m* ⟨*pl* plateau⟩: ***~ per frutta*** crate
platinato *adj* platinized; *capelli* platinum blonde
platino *m* platinum
Platone *m* Plato
platonico *adj* ⟨*mpl* -ci⟩ platonic
plausibile *adj* plausible
plauso *m fig* approval
playback *m* lip-synching
playboy *m* ⟨*pl* playboy⟩ playboy
plebaglia *f* mob **plebe** *f* HIST plebs **plebeo** **I** *adj* HIST plebeian; *pej* vulgar **II** *n*: ***plebei** mpl* pleb
plebiscitario *adj* ⟨*mpl* -ri⟩ plebiscitary; (*unanime*) unanimous
plebiscito *m* POL general vote; plebiscite
plenilunio *m* ⟨*pl* -ni⟩ full moon
plenipotenziario ⟨*mpl* -ri⟩ **I** *adj* plenipotentiary **II** *m*, **-a** *f* plenipotentiary; ***ministro** m* ***~*** (minister) plenipotentiary; *diplomatico inferiore ad ambasciatore* envoy (extraordinary)
pleonasmo *m* pleonasm **pleonastico** *adj* ⟨*mpl* -ci⟩ pleonastic
plesso *m* (*complesso*) establishment; ANAT plexus; ***~ scolastico*** school complex; ***~ solare*** ANAT solar plexus
pletora *f* plethora, excess; MED plethora
pletora *f fig* plethora
plettro *m* plectrum
pleura *f* pleura
pleurite *f* pleurisy
plexiglas® *m* plexiglass®
plico *m* ⟨*pl* -chi⟩ envelope; ***in ~ separato*** under separate cover
plissettato *adj* pleated
plotone *m* MIL platoon; ***~ di esecuzione*** firing squad
plumbeo *adj* leaden, lead-coloured; *fig* gloomy
plurale *m/adj* plural
pluralismo *m* pluralism **pluralistico** *adj* ⟨*mpl* -ci⟩ pluralistic **pluralità** *f* ⟨*pl* pluralità⟩ plurality
pluricellulare *adj* multicellular
pluridecorato *adj* much-decorated
pluriennale *adj* several year's; ***corso di studi ~*** course lasting several years; ***esperienza ~*** several years' experience
plurifamiliare *adj* multi-family; ***casa ~*** multi-family residencel
plurigemellare *adj* multiparous; ***parto** m* ***~*** multiparous birth
plurilaterale *adj* multilateral
pluriomicida *m/f* ⟨*mpl* -i⟩ serial killer
pluripartitico *adj* ⟨*mpl* -ci⟩ multiparty
plusvalenza *f* ECON capital gain; (*apprezzamento*) appreciation
plusvalore *m* capital gains *pl*; ***tassa** f* ***sul ~*** capital gains tax
plutocrazia *f* plutocracy
Plutone *m* Pluto
plutonio *m* plutonium
pluviale **I** *adj* rain; ***foresta** f* ***~*** rain forest **II** *m* downsput
PN *abbr* (= **Pordenone**) Pordenone
pneumatico ⟨*mpl* -ci⟩ **I** *adj* pneumatic **II** *m* tyre, *US* tire; ***-i da neve** pl* snow tyres (*US* tires)
pneumologia *f* (*reparto*) pneumatology **pneumologo** *m*, **-a** *f* pneumologist ⟨*mpl* -gi⟩ pneumologists; **pneumotorace** *m* pneumothorax
PNL *abbr* (= **prodotto nazionale lordo**) GNP (gross national product)
po' *adv*: ***un ~*** a little (***di*** sth), a little bit (***di*** of); ***un bel ~*** quite a lot; ***vuoi un ~ di tè?*** do you want some tea?; → ***poco***
Po *m* GEOG Po
PO *abbr* (= **Prato**) Prato
pochezza *f* scarcity; insufficiency; *fig* meanness
pochino *adv infml*: (***un***) ***~*** a little
pocket **I** *adj inv*: ***edizione** f* ***~*** pocket edition **II** *m* ⟨*pl* pocket⟩ pocketbook
poco ⟨*mpl* -chi⟩ **I** *adj* little; *con nomi plurali* few; ***-a gente** f* not many peo-

ple **II** *adv* not much; *con aggettivi* not very, not greatly; ***~ prima*** just before; ***senti un po'!*** just listen!; ***a ~ a ~*** little by little, gradually; ***~ fa*** a little while ago; ***fra ~*** in a little while, soon; ***~ dopo*** a little while later, soon after; ***per ~*** cheap; (*quasi*) almost, nearly; ***essere in -chi*** be a small group of people; ***quel ~ che guadagno non basta*** the little I earn is not enough; ***è un ~ di buono*** he / she is a bad sort

podagra *f* MED gout

podcasting *m* ⟨*pl* podcasting⟩ COMPUT podcasting

podere *m* farm

poderoso *adj* forceful, powerful (*a. fig*)

podestà *m* ⟨*pl* podestà⟩ HIST podestà; *nel fascismo*: podestà

podio *m* ⟨*pl* -di⟩ podium, dais; MUS podium; ***salire sul ~*** SPORTS step up to the podium; *fig* qualify

podismo *m* walking

podista *m/f* ⟨*mpl* -i⟩ SPORTS walker

podologo *m*, **-a** *f* ⟨*mpl* -ghi⟩ chiropodist *Br*; podiatrist *US*

poema *m* ⟨*pl* -i⟩ poem **poemetto** *m* short poem

poesia *f* poetry; *componimento* poem

poeta *m* ⟨*pl* -i⟩ poet

poetastro *m*, **-a** *f pej* poetaster

poetessa *f* poet

poetico *adj* ⟨*mpl* -ci⟩ poetic

poggiare *v/t* ⟨1f & c⟩ lean; (*posare*) put, place

poggiarsi *v/r*: ***~ a*** lean on

poggiatesta *m* ⟨*pl* poggiatesta⟩ head rest

poggio *m* ⟨*pl* -ggi⟩ mound

poggiolo *m* balcony

pogrom *m* ⟨*pl* pogrom⟩ pogrom

poi *adv* then; ***d'ora in ~*** from now on; ***questa ~!*** well I'm blowed!; ***dalle 6 in ~*** from 6 o'clock on(wards); ***d'ora in ~*** from now on; ***da oggi in ~*** from today; ***prima o ~*** sooner or later; ***non è ~ così caro*** it's not that expensive after all

poiana *f* buzzard

poiché *cj* since

pointer *m* ⟨*pl* pointer⟩ pointer

pois *m* ⟨*pl* pois⟩: ***a ~*** spotted, spotty

poker *m* poker; (*combinazione*) four-of-a-kind

polacchina *f* ankle boot

polacco ⟨*mpl* -cchi⟩ **I** *m/adj* Polish **II** *m*, **-a** *f* Pole

polare *adj* Polar; ***circolo*** *m* ***~ artico / antartico*** Arctic / Antarctic Circle; ***freddo*** *m* ***~*** bitter cold

polarità *f* ⟨*pl* polarità⟩ polarity (*a. fig*)

polarizzare *v/t* ⟨1a⟩ polarize; *fig* ***~ su di sé l'attenzione*** monopolize s.o.'s attention

polarizzarsi *v/r* ⟨1a⟩ focus (on) **polarizzazione** *f* PHYS polarization, ELEC bias

polaroid *f* ⟨*pl* polaroid⟩ *materiale* polaroid; *macchina fotografica* Polaroid camera

polemica *f* ⟨*pl* -che⟩ argument; ***fare -che*** argue

polemico *adj* ⟨*mpl* -ci⟩ argumentative

polemizzare *v/i* ⟨1a⟩ argue

polena *f* figurehead

polenta *f* polenta, *cornmeal porridge*

polentone *m*, **-a** *f pej* slowcoach

pole position *f* ⟨*pl* pole position⟩ pole position

polesano I *adj* from Polesine **II** *m*, **-a** *f* person from Polesine

Polesine *m*: ***il ~*** the Polesine area

POLFER *abbr* (= **Polizia ferroviaria**) *Italian railway police*

poliambulatorio *m* ⟨*mpl* -ri⟩ *di ospedale* outpatients; *di medici* group practice

poliammide *f* polyamide **poliammidico** *adj* ⟨*mpl* -ci⟩ polyamide

policlinico *m* ⟨*pl* -ci⟩ general hospital

policromo *adj* multicoloured

poliedrico *adj* ⟨*mpl* -ci⟩ polyhedral; *fig artista* multitalented; *mente* eclectic

poliedro *m* polyhedron

poliestere *m* polyester **polietilene** *m* polythene

polifonia *f* poliphony **polifonico** *adj* ⟨*mpl* -ci⟩ poliphonic

polifunzionale *adj inv* multi-purpose; CHEM polyfunctional

poligamia *f* polygamy

poligamo I *adj* polygamous **II** *m*, **-a** *f* polygamist

poligenesi *f* ⟨*pl* poligenesi⟩ polygenesis

poliglotta ⟨*mpl* -i⟩ **I** *adj* multilingual **II** *m/f* polyglot

poligonale *adj* polygonal

poligono *m* MATH polygon; MIL ***~ di ti-***

ro firing range
poligrafico ⟨*mpl* -ci⟩ **I** *adj* polygraphic; ***stabilimento*** *m* ~ printing-house **II** *m*, **-a** *f* printer
polimero *m* polymer
polimorfo *adj* polymorphic
polinesiano I *adj* Polynesian **II** *m*, **-a** *f* Polynesian
polio *f infml* polio *infml*
poliomielite *f* poliomyelitis
poliomielitico ⟨*mpl* -ci⟩ **I** *adj* polio **II** *m*, **-a** *f* polio sufferer
polipo *m* polyp
polirematica *f* ⟨*pl* -che⟩ LING polyrhematic
polisemia *f* LING polysemy **polisemico** *adj* ⟨*mpl* -ci⟩ LING polysemic
polisillabo *m* LING polysyllable
polisportiva *f* sports club
polistirolo *m* polystyrene
politeama *m* ⟨*pl* -i⟩ multi-purpose theatre
politecnico *m* ⟨*pl* -ci⟩ polytechnic; *university institute of engineering and architecture*
politeismo *m* polytheism **politeista** ⟨*mpl* -i⟩ **I** *adj* polytheist **II** *m/f* polytheist **politeistico** *adj* ⟨*mpl* -ci⟩ polytheistic
politica *f* politics *sg*; (*strategia*) policy; ~ ***estera*** foreign policy; ~ ***interna*** domestic policy; ~ ***sanitaria*** health policy; ~ ***economica*** economic policy
politicamente *adv* politically; *punto di vista* from a political point of view; ~ ***corretto*** politically correct, pc; ~ ***scorretto*** politically incorrect
politico ⟨*mpl* -ci⟩ **I** *adj* political **II** *m*, **-a** *f* politician
politologo *m*, **-a** *f* ⟨*mpl* -gi⟩ political scientist
polittico *m* ⟨*pl* -ci⟩ ART polyptych
polivalente *adj* CHEM polyvalent; ***farmaco*** *m* ~ multi-purpose medicine **polivalenza** *f* CHEM polyvalence; *fig* versatility
polivinilcloruro *m* polyvinyl chloride
polizia *f* police *pl*; ~ ***ferroviaria*** transport police *pl*; ~ ***giudiziaria*** investigative police *pl*; ~ ***scientifica*** forensics; *dipartimento* forensic department; ~ ***segreta*** secret police; ~ ***stradale*** (o ***della strada***) traffic police *pl*, *US* highway patrol; ***agente*** *m* ***di*** ~ police officer
poliziesco *adj* ⟨*mpl* -chi⟩ police *attr*; ***romanzo*** *m* ~ detective story
poliziotto I *m* policeman; ~ ***in borghese*** plain clothes policeman **II** *adj*: ***donna*** *f* ***-a*** policewoman; ***cane*** *m* ~ police dog
polizza *f* policy; ~ ***di assicurazione*** insurance policy; ~ ***di carico*** bill of lading; *di navi* shipment bill of lading; ~ ***casco*** no-fault motor policy; ~ ***del Monte dei Pegni*** pawnbroker bill
polla *f* spring *fig* source
pollaio *m* ⟨*pl* -ai⟩ chicken run
pollame *m* poultry; *carne di volatile* fowl
pollastrello *m*, **-a** *f* spring chicken **pollastro** *m*, **-a** *f* chicken; *fig hum* sucker **polleria** *f* poultry shop
pollice *m* thumb; *unità di misura* inch; ***avere il*** ~ ***verde*** have green fingers; *fig* ~ ***verso*** thumbs-down
pollicoltore *m*, **-trice** *f* poultry farmer **pollicoltura** *f* poultry farming
polline *m* pollen
pollivendolo *m*, **-a** *f* poulterer
pollo *m* chicken; ~ ***arrosto*** roast chicken; ***petto*** *m* ***di*** ~ chicken breast; ***è roba da far ridere i -i*** it's enough to make a cat laugh!; ***conosco i miei -i*** I am nobody's fool
polmonare *adj* pulmonary
polmone *m* lung; ~ ***d'acciaio*** iron lung
polmonite *f* pneumonia
polo[1] *m* GEOG pole; ~ ***negativo*** / ***positivo*** negative / positive pole; ~ ***nord*** North Pole; ~ ***sud*** South Pole
polo[2] **I** *m* SPORTS polo **II** *f* ⟨*pl* polo⟩ polo shirt
Polonia *f* Poland
polpa *f* flesh; *di manzo*, *vitello* meat
polpaccio *m* ⟨*pl* -cci⟩ calf
polpastrello *m* fingertip
polpetta *f di carne* meatball
polpettone *m* meat loaf
polpo *m* octopus
polposo *adj* fleshy
polsino *m* cuff
polso *m* ANAT wrist; *di camicia* cuff; *pulsazione* pulse; *fig* ~ ***fermo*** *or* ***di ferro*** firm / heavy hand; ***tastare il*** ~ ***a qn*** take s.o.'s pulse; *fig* ***uomo*** *m* ***di*** ~ a firm man
POLSTRADA *abbr* (= **Polizia Stradale**) *traffic police*
poltiglia *f* mush

poltrire *v/i* ⟨4d⟩ laze around
poltrona *f* armchair; THEAT stall (seat)
poltroncina *f* small chair
poltrone *m*, **-a** *f* lazybones
poltroneria *f* laziness
poltronissima *f* front stall
polvere *f* dust; (*sostanza polverizzata*) powder; ***caffè** m **in** ~* instant coffee; ***latte** m **in** ~* powdered milk; ***~ da sparo*** gunpowder; ***in ~*** powdered; ***ridurre in ~*** powder; (*macinare*) grind (up); *fig* pulverize; annihilate
polveriera *f* powder-room; *fig* powder-keg
polverina *f* powder
polverizzare *v/t* ⟨1a⟩ crush, pulverize; *fig* pulverize
polverizzarsi *v/r* ⟨1a⟩ powder; *fig* crumble **polverizzazione** *f* pulverization
polverone *m* dustcloud; *fig* ***sollevare un ~*** make waves
polveroso *adj* dusty
pomata *f* cream
pomello *m* cheek; *di porta* knob
Pomerania *f* Pomerania
pomeridiano *adj* afternoon *attr*; ***alle tre -e*** at three in the afternoon, at three pm
pomeriggio *m* ⟨*pl* -ggi⟩ afternoon; ***di ~, nel ~*** in the afternoon; ***domani ~*** tomorrow afternoon
pomice *f/adj*: (***pietra*** *f*) ***~*** pumice (stone)
pomiciare *v/i* ⟨1l & f⟩ *infml* canoodle
pomo *m* knob; ***~ d'Adamo*** Adam's apple; ***~ della discordia*** bone of contention
pomodoro *m* tomato; ***al ~*** tomato; ***-i** pl **pelati*** peeled tomatoes
pompa[1] *f* pomp; ***impresa** f **di -e funebri*** undertaker's, *US* mortician; ***in ~ magna*** *hum* in all one's finery; ***~ antincendio*** fire pump; ***~ della benzina*** fuel pump; (*colonnina*) petrol pump
pompa[2] *f* TECH pump
pompare *v/t* ⟨1a⟩ pump
Pompei *f* Pompeii **pompeiano I** *adj* Pompeian **II** *m*, **-a** *f* Pompeian
pompelmo *m* grapefruit
pompetta *f* hand pump
pompiere *m* firefighter, *Br* fireman; ***-i** pl* firefighters, *Br* fire brigade
pompino *m vulg* blow-job
pompon *m* ⟨*pl* pompon⟩ pompom
pomposo *adj* pompous
poncho *m* ⟨*pl* poncho⟩ poncho
ponderare *v/t* ⟨1l & c⟩ ponder
ponderato *adj decisione*, *scelta* carefully considered; *persona* reflective
ponderazione *f* (*dibattito*) deliberation; (*riflessione*) meditation; (*cautela*) caution; ***~ dei voti*** POL weighting of the votes
pone → ***porre***
ponente *m* west; ***a ~*** west *verso* westward
pongo → ***porre***
pongo ® *m* Plasticine
ponte *m* bridge; ARCH scaffolding; NAUT deck; NAUT ***~ di comando*** bridge; ***~ girevole*** swing bridge; ***~ levatoio*** drawbridge; ***~ sospeso*** suspension bridge; ***~ radio*** radio link; ***~ aereo*** airlift; ***fare il ~*** have a four-day weekend; *fig* ***tagliare** or **rompere i -i con qn*** break off with s.o.
pontefice *m* pontiff
ponteggiatore *m*, **-trice** *f* scaffolder
ponteggio *m* scaffolding
ponticello *m* MUS bridge
pontico *adj* ⟨*mpl* -ci⟩ Pontine
pontificale *adj* pontifical **pontificare** *v/i* ⟨1m & d⟩ *fig hum* dogmatize **pontificato** *m* (*papato*) papacy; (*periodo*) pontificate
pontificio *adj* ⟨*mpl* -ci⟩ papal; ***Stato Pontificio*** *m* Papal States *pl*
pontile *m* jetty
pontino *adj* pontine
pontone *m* pontoon
pony *m* ⟨*pl* pony⟩ pony
pony express *m* ⟨*pl* pony express⟩ dispatch delivery service
pool *m* ⟨*pl* pool⟩ (*équipe*) équipe; ECON pool
pop *m*: ***musica** f **~*** pop (music)
popcorn *m* popcorn
popeline *f* ⟨*pl* popeline⟩ poplin
popò *f* ⟨*pl* popò⟩ *infml* poo; ***fare la ~*** (have a) poo
popolamento *m di città*, *Stato* population
popolano *m*, **-a** *f* commoner
popolare[1] **I** *adj* popular; *quartiere* working-class; ***ballo** m **~*** folk dance **II** *v/t* ⟨1l⟩ populate
popolare[2] *v/t* ⟨1l⟩ populate
popolarità *f* popularity
popolato *adj* populated; (*abitato*) in-

habited; (*pieno*) crowded
popolazione *f* population
popolino *m pej* riff-raff, hoi polloi
popolo *m* people; ***il ~ bue*** *pej* the herd
popoloso *adj* densely populated
popone *m reg* melon
poppa *f* NAUT stern; ***a ~*** astern
poppante *m/f* suckling; *hum* fledgeling **poppare** *v/t and v/i* ⟨1a⟩ breastfeed **poppata** *f* feed(ing)
poppiere *m* sternman
pop star *f* ⟨*pl* pop star⟩ pop star
populismo *m* populism **populista** ⟨*mpl* -i⟩ **I** *adj* populist **II** *m/f* populist
porcaro *m* swineherd **porcata** *f* dirty trick; (*porcheria*) obscenity; (*schifezza*) *fig* rubbish, crap
porcellana *f* porcelain, china
porcellino *m* piglet; ***~ d'India*** guinea-pig
porcello *m*, **-a** *f* piglet **porcellone** *m*, **-a** *f fig pej* dirty old man
porcheria *f* disgusting thing; *fig* ***una ~*** filth; ***mangiare -e*** eat junk food
porchetta *f suckling pig roasted whole in the oven*
porcile *m* pigsty, *US* pigpen
porcino *m* cep
porco ⟨*pl* -ci⟩ **I** *m*, **-a** *f* pig **II** *adj*: ***~ cane!*** *vulg* bloody hell!; ***~ diavolo!*** damn it!; ***-a miseria!*** *vulg* my goodness!; ***fare i propri -i comodi*** go one's own sweet way
porcospino *m* porcupine
pordenonese I *adj* from Pordenone **II** *m/f* person from Pordenone
porfido *m* porphyry
porgere *v/t* ⟨3d⟩ *mano*, *oggetto* hold out; *aiuto*, *saluto etc* proffer; *fig* ***~ la mano*** hold out one's hand; ***~ l'altra guancia*** turn the other cheek
porno *infml* **I** *adj* porn(o) *infml* **II** *m* porn *infml*; ***attrice*** *f* ***~*** porn actress; ***film*** *m* ***~*** porn film
pornocassetta *f* porn video
pornografia *f* pornography
pornografico *adj* ⟨*mpl* -ci⟩ pornographic; ***rivista*** *f* ***-a*** porn magazine
pornostar *f* ⟨*pl* pornostar⟩ porn star
poro *m* pore
porosità *f* ⟨*pl* porosità⟩ porosity
poroso *adj* porous
porpora *f* purple; (*colore*) purple; ***indossare la ~*** become a cardinal **porporato** *m fig* cardinal
porre *v/t* ⟨3ll⟩ place, put; ***~ una domanda*** ask a question; ***poniamo che ...*** let's suppose (that) ...***~ rimedio a qc*** remedy, repair
porro *m* leek; MED wart
porsi *v/r* ⟨3ll⟩ put oneself; ***~ un interrogativo*** ask oneself; ***~ un obiettivo*** set oneself a goal
porta *f* door; ***~ antincendio*** fire door; ***~ infrarossi*** TEL infrared port; ***~ a soffietto*** folding door; ***~ a vetri*** glass door; ***~ scorrevole*** sliding door; ***a -e chiuse*** behind closed doors; ***abitare ~ a ~*** live right next to; ***gita*** *f* ***fuori ~*** outing; *fig* ***mettere qn alla ~*** show s.o. the door; ***vendere ~ a ~*** sell door-to-door
portabagagli *m* ⟨*pl* portabagagli⟩ luggage rack; AUTO roof rack
portabandiera *m/f* ⟨*pl* portabandiera⟩ standard-bearer (*a. fig*)
portabiancheria *m* ⟨*pl* portabiancheria⟩ laundry bin
portabile *adj* (*abito*) wearable
portabilità *f* ⟨*pl* portabilità⟩ COMPUT portability
portaborse *m* ⟨*pl* portaborse⟩ *pej* flunkey
portabottiglie *m* ⟨*pl* portabottiglie⟩ wine rack
porta-cd *m* ⟨*pl* porta-cd⟩ CD rack
portacenere *m* ⟨*pl* portacenere⟩ ashtray
portachiavi *m* ⟨*pl* portachiavi⟩ keyring
portacipria *m* ⟨*pl* portacipria⟩ powder compact
portacravatte *m* ⟨*pl* portacravatte⟩ tie rack
portadocumenti *m* ⟨*pl* portadocumenti⟩ (*valigetta*) briefcase; (*faldone*) portfolio; *protetto* attaché case
portaerei *f* ⟨*pl* portaerei⟩ aircraft carrier
portafinestra *f* ⟨*pl* portefinestre⟩ French window
portafoglio *m* ⟨*pl* -gli⟩ wallet
portafortuna *m* ⟨*pl* portafortuna⟩ good luck charm, talisman
portafrutta *m* ⟨*pl* portafrutta⟩ fruit bowl
portagioie *m* ⟨*pl* portagioie⟩ jewel case
portalampada *m* ⟨*pl* portalampada⟩ bulb socket

portale *m* portal (*a.* COMPUT)
portalettere *m/f* ⟨*pl* portalettere⟩ → ***postino***
portamento *m* bearing
portamonete *m* ⟨*pl* portamonete⟩ purse
portante *adj* supporting; *fig* fundamental; (***struttura*** *f* **~** supporting structure; *fig* bedrock; (*fondamenta*) foundation; *insieme pl* fundamentals
portantina *f* sedan(-chair); (*lettiga*) stretcher
portaoggetti *adj inv*: ***vano*** *m* **~** glove compartment
portaombrelli *m* ⟨*pl* portaombrelli⟩ umbrella stand
portaordini *m* ⟨*pl* portaordini⟩ dispatch-rider
portapacchi *m* ⟨*pl* portapacchi⟩ *di macchina* roof rack; *di bicicletta* carrier
portapane *m* ⟨*pl* portapane⟩ bread tray
portapenne *m* ⟨*pl* portapenne⟩ pencil case
portare *v/t* ⟨1c⟩ **1.** (*trasportare*) carry; (*accompagnare*) take; (*avere adosso*) wear; (*condurre*) lead; ***~ avanti qc*** see sth through; ***~ fortuna*** be lucky; ***~ a termine*** accomplish, see through to the end; ***~ fuori il cane*** walk the dog; ***~ in trionfo*** carry s.o. shoulder-high; ***~ via*** take away; ***mi ha portato un regalo*** he brought me a present; ***portale un regalo*** take her a present; ***~ in tavola*** serve; ***porta bene i propri anni*** he doesn't look his age; ***dove porta questo sentiero?*** where does this path lead to? **2.** *fig* ***essere portato per qc / per fare qc*** have a gift for (doing) sth
portariviste *m* ⟨*pl* portariviste⟩ magazine rack
portarsi *v/r* (*recarsi*) go; (*spostarsi*) move; (*con sé*) take (along); ***~ il lavoro a casa*** take work home; ***~ avanti con il lavoro*** make progress / headway at work
portasapone *m* ⟨*pl* portasapone⟩ soap dish; *viaggio* soap case
portasci *m* ⟨*pl* portasci⟩ AUTO ski rack
portasciugamani *m* ⟨*pl* portasciugamani⟩ *barra* towel rail; *anello* towel ring
portasigarette *m* ⟨*pl* portasigarette⟩ cigarette case
portata *f* COOK course; *di danni* extent; TECH *di camion* load capacity; *di cannocchiale* range; ***alla ~ di*** *film, libro etc* suitable for; ***a ~ di mano*** within reach
portatessera *m* ⟨*pl* portatessera⟩ card-wallet
portatile *adj* portable; ***computer*** *m* **~** portable (computer); ***radio*** *f* **~** portable (radio); ***telefono*** *m* **~** mobile (phone), *US* cell(ular) phone; ***farmacia*** *f* **~** first-aid kit
portatore *m*, **-trice** *f* bearer; *di malattia* carrier; MED ***~ sano*** symptom-free carrier; ***~ di handicap*** handicapped person; ***libretto*** *m* ***al ~*** savings book
portatovagliolo *m* (*anello*) napkin-ring; (*busta*) napkin-holder
portattrezzi *adj* ⟨*pl* portattrezzi⟩: ***cassetta*** *f* **~** toolbox
portauovo *m* ⟨*pl* portauovo⟩ eggcup
portavalori ⟨*pl* portavalori⟩ **I** *adj* security **II** *m/f* security guard
portavasi *m* ⟨*pl* portavasi⟩ flowerpot stand
portavoce *m/f* ⟨*pl* portavoce⟩ spokesperson
porte-enfant *m* ⟨*pl* porte-enfant⟩ carrycot
portello *m* NAUT, AVIAT hatch **portellone** *m* NAUT, AVIAT hatch
portento *m* portent; (*prodigio*) prodigy; (*meraviglia*) wonder **portentoso** *adj* (*prodigioso*) prodigious; (*straordinario*) marvellous
porticciolo *m* small harbour
portico *m* ⟨*pl* -ci⟩ porch; **-i** *pl* arcades
portiera *f* door
portiere *m*, **-a** *f* doorman, *donna* doorwoman; (*portinaio*) caretaker; SPORTS goalkeeper, goalie *infml*
portinaio *m*, **-a** *f* ⟨*mpl* -ai⟩ caretaker
portineria *f* porter's lodge
porto[1] *past part* → ***porgere***
porto[2] *m posta* postage; ***~ d'armi*** gun licence (*US* license)
porto[3] *m* NAUT port; ***~ d'imbarco*** port of embarkation; ***~ mercantile*** merchant port; ***~ turistico*** marina; ***è un ~ di mare*** *hum* it's like Piccadilly Circus; *fig* ***andare in ~*** be successful; ***uscire dal ~*** leave the harbour
porto d'armi *m* gun licence
Portogallo *m* Portugal

portoghese *m/f & adj* Portuguese; ***fare il ~*** deadhead
portoncino *m* wicket
portone *m* main entrance
portoricano I *adj* Puerto Rican **II** *m*, **-a** *f* Puerto Rican
Portorico *m* Puerto Rico
portuale I *adj* harbour, port; ***città*** *f* / ***quartiere*** *m* / ***zona*** *f* **~** seaport / harbour district / harbour area **II** *m* dock worker; *infml* docker
porzione *f* share; COOK portion
POS *abbr* (= **Point of Sale**) POS
posa *f di cavi*, *tubi* laying; PHOT exposure; PHOT ***mettersi in ~*** pose; ***~ in opera*** laying (of sth); ***~ della prima pietra*** laying of the first stone
posacenere *m* ⟨*pl* posacenere⟩ ashtray
posare ⟨1c⟩ **I** *v/t* put, place **II** *v/i* (*stare in posa*) pose; ***~ su*** rest on; *fig* ***~ da intellettuale*** pose as an intellectual
posarsi *v/r* alight
posate *fpl* cutlery *sg*; ***~ da pesce*** fish cutlery
posatezza *f* composure
posato *adj* composed
posidonia *f* BOT Posidonia oceanica
positivamente *adv* positively **positivismo** *m* positivism **positivista** *m/f* ⟨*mpl* -i⟩ positivist; *fig* practical person, businesslike person
positivo *adj* positive
posizionamento *m* positioning **posizionare** *v/t* ⟨1n⟩ position **posizionarsi** *v/r* ⟨1n⟩ position oneself
posizione *f* position; ***~ chiave*** key position; ***~ comune*** EU common position; ***farsi una ~*** acquire an enviable position; ***presa*** *f* ***di ~*** stance
posologia *f* MED posology, dose
posporre *v/t* ⟨3ll⟩: ***~ qc a qc*** place sth after sth; *fig* (*subordinare*) subordinate; (*posticipare*) postpone
possedere *v/t* ⟨2o⟩ own, possess
possedimento *m* possession
posseduto *adj* possessed; *m* person possessed
possente *adj* mighty
possessione *f* possession
possessività *f* ⟨*pl* possessività⟩ possessiveness
possessivo *adj* possessive; ***amore*** *m* **~** possessive love
possesso *m* possession; ***in suo ~*** in his / her / its hands
possessore *m*, **-ditrice** *f* owner, possessor
possiamo → ***potere***
possibile I *adj* possible; ***il più presto ~*** as soon as possible **II** *m*: ***fare il ~*** do everything one can, do one's best; ***nei limiti del ~*** without leaving any stone unturned; ***per quanto ~*** as well / far as possible
possibilità *f* ⟨*pl* possibilità⟩ possibility; (*occasione*) opportunity, chance; ***~ di guadagno*** earning potential
possibilmente *adv* if possible, if I / you *etc* can
possidente *m/f* owner; *terreni* landowner; *immobili* landlord; ***un ricco ~*** a rich landowner
posso → ***potere***
posta *f* mail, *Br* post; (*ufficio postale*) post office; ***~ aerea*** airmail; ***per ~*** by post; ***a giro di ~*** by return of post; COMPUT ***~ elettronica*** e-mail; ***~ prioritaria*** first class post; ***fermo ~*** poste restante; *fig* ***~ in gioco*** stake(s); ***la ~ in gioco è alta*** there's a lot at stake; ***sta rischiando una posta molto alta*** he / she is playing for very high stakes
postale *adj* postal; ***servizio*** *m* **~** postal service; ***cartolina*** *f* **~** postcard
postazione *f* MIL battery
postbellico *adj* ⟨*mpl* -ci⟩ postwar
postdatare *v/t* ⟨1a⟩ postdate
posteggiare *v/t* ⟨1f⟩ park
posteggiatore *m*, **-trice** *f* car-park attendant; *a Napoli*: busker
posteggio *m* ⟨*pl* -ggi⟩ carpark; ***~ dei taxi*** taxi rank
poster *m* ⟨*pl* poster⟩ poster
posteri *mpl* posterity *sg*
posteriore *adj* back *attr*, rear *attr*; (*successivo*) later; ***sedile*** *m* **~** back seat; ***uscita*** *f* **~** rear exit
posticcio *adj* ⟨*mpl* -cci⟩ artificial
posticino *m* nice / pleasant spot; *locale pubblico* unpretentious place
posticipare *v/t* ⟨1m⟩ postpone
posticipato *adj*: ***pagamento*** *m* **~** payment in arrears
posticipazione *f* postponement
postilla *f* note; *fig* clarification
postino *m*, **-a** *f* postman, *US* mailman; *donna* postwoman, *US* mailwoman
post-it® *m* ⟨*pl* post-it⟩ post-it®
postmoderno I *adj* postmodern **II** *n*:

postmoderno *m* post-modernist
post mortem *adj inv* post-mortem; ***esperienza*** *f* **~** after-life experience
posto¹ *past part* → ***porre***; **~ *che*** supposing that
posto² *m* place; (*lavoro*) job, position; **~ *barca*** berth; **~ *di blocco*** checkpoint su strada roadblock; **~ *letto*** bed; ***al* ~ *tuo / suo*** in your / his / her / its place; ***mettere a* ~** *stanza* tidy (up); ***prendere* ~** (*occupare*) take up room; (*accomodarsi*) take a seat; ***la tua camera è a* ~*?*** is your room tidy?; **~ *macchina*** parking space; **~ *finestrino / corridoio*** window / aisle seat; ***ho trovato solo un* ~ *in piedi*** I had to stand; **~ *a sedere*** seat; **~ *di guardia*** guard post; COMPUT **~ *di lavoro*** workstation; **~ *di polizia*** police station; **~ *di pronto soccorso*** first aid post; **~ *di villeggiatura*** holiday resort; ***vado io al* ~ *tuo*** I'll go in your place, I'll go instead of you; ***fuori* ~** out of place; ***sul* ~** on the spot
postoperatorio *adj* ⟨*mpl* -ri⟩ postoperative
postprandiale *adj* postprandial
postribolo *m* brothel
post scriptum *m* ⟨*pl* post scriptum⟩ postscript
postulante *m/f* petitioning; REL postulant **postulato** *m* PHIL, MATH postulate; REL postulancy
postumo *adj* posthumous
postuniversitario *adj* ⟨*mpl* -ri⟩: ***corso*** *m* **~** postgraduate course; *master* Master's degree; *dottorato* PhD, doctorate
postura *f* posture
potabile *adj* fit to drink; ***acqua*** *f* **~** drinking water
potabilizzazione *f* purification
potare *v/t* ⟨1a⟩ prune
potassio *m* potassium
potatura *f* pruning
potentato *m* potentate
potente *adj* powerful; (*efficace*) potent
potentino I *adj* from Potenza **II** *m*, **-a** *f* person from Potenza
potenza *f* power; **~ *mondiale*** world power; **~ *del motore*** engine power
potenziale I *adj* potential **II** *m* potential
potenzialità *f* ⟨*pl* potenzialità⟩ potential; MECH power **potenzialmente** *adv* potentially **potenziamento** *m* strengthening
potenziare *v/t* ⟨1a⟩ strengthen
potere I *v/i* ⟨2l⟩ can, be able to; ***non posso andare*** I can't go; ***non ho potuto farlo*** I couldn't do it, I was unable to do it; ***posso fumare?*** do you mind if I smoke?; *formale* may I smoke?; ***può essere*** perhaps, maybe; ***può darsi*** perhaps, maybe; ***può darsi che…*** maybe…; ***si può fare*** *infml* (it) can be done / arranged; ***si può?*** May I / we come in?; ***volere è* ~** *prov* where there is a will there is a way **II** *m* power; **~ *d'acquisto*** purchasing power; **~ *legislativo / esecutivo*** legislative / executive power; **~ *giudiziario*** judiciary; ***essere al* ~** be in power; ***in mio* ~** in my power
potestà *f* ⟨*pl* potestà⟩ *generale* power (*controllo*) control (*autorità*) authority; **~ *dei genitori*** parental authority
pot-pourri *m* ⟨*pl* pot pourri⟩ MUS medley, pot-pourri
poveraccio *m*, **-a** *f* ⟨*mpl* -cci⟩ poor thing, poor creature
poveramente *adv* (*inadeguatamente*) inadequately (*insufficientemente*) poorly (*male*) badly
poveretto *m*, **-a** *f*, **poverino** *m*, **-a** *f* poor man, *donna* poor thing
povero I *adj* poor; ***essere* ~ *in canna*** be as poor as a church mouse; **~ *Cristo*** *infml* poor soul, poor devil **II** *m*, **-a** *f* poor man; *donna* poor woman; ***i -i*** *pl* the poor; **~ *di idee*** unimaginative; *infml* hard up for ideas; ***in parole*** *fpl* ***-e*** in a nutshell; ***per dirla in parole -e*** not to put too fine a point on it
povertà *f* ⟨*pl* povertà⟩ poverty
pozzanghera *f* puddle
pozzetto *m* NAUT cockpit; TECH catch basin / pit; *per acqua di scolo*: manhole
pozzo *m* well; **~ *petrolifero*** oil well; **~ *nero*** cesspit; *fig* **~ *di San Patrizio*** St Patrick's well; *fig* **~ *di scienza*** walking encyclopedia; *fig* **~ *senza fondo*** bottomless pit; *fig* **~ *di notizie*** mine of information
pp. *abbr* (= **pagine**) pp (pages)
p. p. *abbr* **1.** (= **per procura**) pp (for, on behalf of) **2.** (= **pacco postale**) small parcel
PPI *abbr* (= **Partito Popolare Ita-**

liano) *Italian political party based on Catholic principles*
PP.TT. *abbr* (= **Poste e Telecomunicazioni**) *Italian Post Office*
P.Q.M. *abbr* (= **per questi motivi**) for these reasons
PR *abbr* (= **Parma**) Parma
PRA *abbr* (= **Pubblico Registro Automobilistico**) *vehicle registration office*
Praga *f* Prague
praghese **I** *adj* Praguean **II** *m/f* Praguean
pragmatico ⟨*mpl* -ci⟩ **I** *adj* pragmatic **II** *m*, **-a** *f* pragmatist **pragmatismo** *m* pragmatism
prammatica *f*: LING pragmatics; ***di ~*** by default; ***essere di ~*** be customary; *comportamento* practical
pranoterapia *f* faith-healing **pranoterapista** *m/f* ⟨*mpl* -i⟩ faith-healer
pranzare *v/i* ⟨1a⟩ *a mezzogiorno* have lunch; *la sera* have dinner
pranzo *m* lunch; ***~ di lavoro*** business lunch; ***dopo ~*** after lunch; (*nel pomeriggio*) in the afternoon
prassi *f* ⟨*pl* prassi⟩ standard procedure; ***seguire la ~*** follow the procedure
prataiolo *m* field mushroom
prateria *f* grassland, (*pianura*) plain; *Nord America* prairie; *infml* range; *Sud America* pampas
pratese **I** *adj* from Prato **II** *m/f* person from Prato
pratica *f* ⟨*pl* -che⟩ **1.** practice; (*esperienza*) experience; ***avere ~ di qc*** have experience of sth; ***fare ~*** gain experience, become more experienced; ***mettere in ~*** put into practice; ***in ~*** in practice **2.** (*atto*) file; ***-che*** *pl* papers, documents; ***fare le -che necessarie per qc*** take the necessary steps for sth; ***fare le -che per*** *passaporto* gather together the necessary documentation for
praticabile *adj sport* which can be practised; *strada* passable
praticabilità *f* ⟨*pl* praticabilità⟩ feasibility; *con veicoli* practicability; *fig* viability **praticamente** *adv* practically; (*quasi*) nearly, virtually; *in sostanza* for all practical purposes, to all intents and purposes
praticantato *m* apprenticeship
praticante *m/f* (*tirocinante*) trainee
praticare *v/t* ⟨1l & d⟩ *virtù*, *pazienza* show; *professione*, *sport* practise; *locale* frequent; ***~ molto sport*** do a lot of sport
praticità *f* ⟨*pl* praticità⟩ practicalness; (*concretezza*) practicality
pratico *adj* ⟨*mpl* -ci⟩ practical; ***essere ~ di*** *conoscere bene* know a lot about; ***all'atto*** *m* ***~*** in practice; (*di fatto*) in (actual) fact
prato *m* meadow; ***~ all'inglese*** English-style lawn
pratolina *f* (common) daisy
preallarme *m stato* alert; *segnale* warning signal; ***dare il ~*** give the warning signal; ***in stato di ~*** on the alert
Prealpi *fpl* Prealps *pl*
prealpino *adj* prealpine
preambolo *m* preamble; *fig* ***senza -i*** without beating about the bush
preanestesia *f* pre-anaesthetic
preannunciare *v/t* ⟨1f⟩ forebode (*annunciare*) announce **preannunciarsi** *v/r* ⟨1f⟩ look / feel like
preavviso *m* notice; ***termine*** *m* ***di ~*** notice period
prebenda *f* living REL prebend; *fig* gain; (*profitto*) profit
precarietà *f* ⟨*pl* precarietà⟩ precariousness; *lavoro* temporary work
precario *adj* ⟨*mpl* -ri⟩ precarious; ***personale*** *m* ***~*** temporary staff
precauzionale *adj* precautionary
precauzione *f* caution; ***-i*** *pl* precautions; ***per ~*** as a precaution
precedente **I** *adj* preceding; COMPUT previous **II** *m* precedent; ***avere dei -i penali*** have a record; ***senza -i*** without precedent
precedenza *f* precedence; AUTO ***diritto*** *m* ***di ~*** right of way; ***avere la ~*** have precedence; AUTO have right of way; ***dare la ~*** give priority; AUTO give way
precedere *v/t* ⟨3a⟩ precede
precettare *v/t* ⟨1b⟩ MIL call up; *sciopero* order to resume work **precettazione** *f* MIL call-up; *nello sciopero*: order to resume work
precetto *m* precept; JUR writ; MIL call-up **precettore** *m*, **-trice** *f* tutor
precipitare ⟨1m⟩ **I** *v/t* throw; *fig* rush; ***non precipitiamo!*** let's not rush / act in haste **II** *v/i* fall, plunge; ***la situa-***

zione precipita events are coming to a head
precipitarsi *v/r* (*affrettarsi*) rush; ***mi precipitai a casa*** I rushed home
precipitazione *f* (*fretta*) haste, hurry; *atmosferica* precipitation
precipitosamente *adv* hurriedly
precipitoso *adj* hasty
precipizio *m* ⟨*pl* -zi⟩ precipice
precisamente *adv* precisely
precisare *v/t* ⟨1a⟩ specify
precisazione *f* specification; (*dichiarazione*) statement; (*chiarimento*) clarification **precisino I** *adj* meticulous **II** *m*, **-a** *f* fusspot
precisione *f* precision, accuracy; ***con*** ~ precisely; ***lavoro*** *m* ***di*** ~ precision work
preciso *adj* accurate; *persona* precise; ***alle tre -e*** at three o'clock exactly *or* precisely, at three o'clock sharp
precludere *v/t* ⟨3q⟩ preclude **precluso** *past part* → ***precludere***
precoce *adj* precocious; *pianta* early; ***morte*** *f* ~ premature / early death
precocemente *adv* precociously, early
precocità *f* ⟨*pl* precocità⟩ precociousness
precolombiano *adj*: pre-Columbian; ***civiltà*** *f* ***-a*** pre-Columbian civilization(s)
preconcetto I *adj* preconceived, prejudiced **II** *n*: ***preconcetto*** *m* prejudice
preconfezionato *adj* prepacked; ***calcestruzzo*** *m* ~ prestressed concrete
precontrattuale *adj* prior to a contract
precostituito *adj* pre-established
precotto *m* ready-made, pre-cooked
precursore I *adj* precursory **II** *m*, **precorritrice** *f* forerunner
preda *f* prey; ***in ~ alla disperazione*** in despair
predare *v/t* ⟨1a⟩ pillage **predatore I** *adj* predatory **II** *n*: ***predatore*** *m* predator; ZOOL predatory animal
predecessore *m*, **-a** *f* predecessor
predefinito *adj* predetermined
predella *f* predella; *di cattedra* raised platform; *di altare* altar-step **predellino** *m* footboard
predestinare *v/t* ⟨1a⟩ predestine
predestinato *adj* predestined
predeterminato *adj* set, *concordato* prearranged
predica *f* ⟨*pl* -che⟩ sermon
predicare *v/t* ⟨1l, b & d⟩ preach; ~ ***bene e razzolare male*** not to practise what one preaches
predicato *m* GRAM predicate
predicatore *m*, **-trice** *f* preacher **predicozzo** *m hum* reproof
prediletto I *past part* → ***prediligere*** **II** *adj* favo(u)rite
predilezione *f* predilection
prediligere *v/t* ⟨3u⟩ prefer
predire *v/t* ⟨3t⟩ predict
predisporre *v/t* ⟨3ll⟩ draw up in advance; ~ ***a*** encourage, promote
predisposizione *f* predisposition
predisposto *past part* → ***predisporre***
predizione *f* prediction; (*profezia*) prophecy; (*previsione*) forecasting
predominante *adj* predominant; *per intensità*: overriding **predominanza** *f* predominance
predominare *v/t* ⟨1m & c⟩ predominate
predominio *m* ⟨*pl* -ni⟩ predominance
predone *m* plunderer; *di strada* robber; ***-i del mare*** the raiders of the seas
preelettorale *adj* pre-election
preesistente *adj* pre-existing
prefabbricato I *adj* prefabricated **II** *m* prefabricated building
prefazione *f* preface
preferenza *f* preference
preferenziale *adj* preferential; ***corsia*** *f* ~ bus-lane; *fig* fast track
preferibile *adj* preferable
preferibilmente *adv* preferably
preferire *v/t* ⟨4d⟩ prefer
preferito *adj* favo(u)rite
prefestivo *adj*: ***giorno*** *m* ~ day before a holiday
prefettizio *adj* ⟨*mpl* -zi⟩ prefectoral
prefetto *m* prefect
prefettura *f* prefecture
prefica *f* ⟨*pl* -che⟩ weeper; *pagato* paid mourner; *fig hum* whiner
prefiggersi *v/r* ⟨3mm⟩ set o.s.
prefigurare *v/t* ⟨1a⟩ foreshadow **prefigurarsi** *v/r* ⟨1a⟩ appear
prefinanziamento *m fondi* pre-finance; *azione* pre-financing
prefisso I *past part* → ***prefiggersi*** **II** *m* TEL code; ~ ***internazionale*** TEL international (dialling / area) code
pregare *v/t* ⟨1b & e⟩ beg (***di fare*** to do); *divinità* pray to; ***ti prego di ascoltarmi*** please listen to me; ***farsi*** ~

be coaxed; ~ ***Dio*** pray to God; ***prego*** please; ***prego?*** I'm sorry (what did you say)?; ***grazie! – prego!*** thank you! – you're welcome! *or* not at all!

pregevole *adj* worthy; *estetica* exquisite

preghiera *f* request; REL prayer

pregiato *adj metallo*, *pietra* precious

pregio *m* (*qualità*) good point

pregiudicare *v/t* ⟨1m & d⟩ (*giudicare prima*) prejudge; (*compromettere*) compromise; (*danneggiare*) damage

pregiudicato *m*, **-a** *f* previous offender

pregiudizievole *adj* detrimental; (*dannoso*) harmful

pregiudizio *m* ⟨*pl* -zi⟩ prejudice

preg.mo *abbr* (= **pregiatissimo**) *formal style of address used in correspondence*

pregnanza *f* pregnancy; *fig* pregnance

pregno *adj* ZOOL pregnant; *cagna* in pup; *cavalla* in foal; ~ ***di qc*** saturated with sth

prego *int* you' re welcome; please, go ahead; *infml* cheers, *US* OK

pregustare *v/t* ⟨1a⟩ look forward to

preindustriale *adj* pre-industrial

preistoria *f* prehistory

preistorico *adj* ⟨*mpl* -ci⟩ prehistoric

prelato *m* REL prelate

prelavaggio *m* pre-wash

prelazione *f* pre-emption; ***diritto*** *m* ***di*** ~ right of pre-emption (over sth)

prelevamento *m* extraction; FIN withdrawal

prelevamento *m di sangue*, *campione* taking; FIN withdrawal; ~ ***in contanti*** cash withdrawal

prelevare *v/t* ⟨1b⟩ *sangue*, *campione* take; *denaro* withdraw

prelibatezza *f gusto* deliciousness *qualità* excellence *cibo* delicacy, titbit

prelibato *adj* exquisite

prelievo *m* (*prelevamento*) taking; FIN withdrawal; ~ ***del sangue*** blood sample; ~ ***fiscale*** levy

preliminare **I** *adj* preliminary; ***fase*** *f* ~ preparatory work **II** *n*: ***-i*** *mpl* preliminaries

preludere *v/i* ⟨3q⟩: ~ ***a qc*** foreshadow sth **preludio** *m* ⟨*pl* -di⟩ MUS prelude; *fig* run-in / run-up

pre-maman **I** *adj* maternity *attr* **II** *m* ⟨*pl* pre-maman⟩ maternity dress; ***abito*** *m* ~ maternity dress

prematrimoniale *adj* premarital

prematuro *adj* premature

premeditato *adj* premeditated; ***omicidio*** *m* ~ murder

premeditazione *f* premeditation

premere ⟨3a⟩ **I** *v/t* press **II** *v/i* press (***su*** on); ***mi preme che*** it is important to me that

premessa *f* introduction

premesso *past part* → ***premettere***; ~ ***che...*** considering that; *di prove* seeing that; JUR whereas...

premettere *v/t* ⟨3ee⟩ say first

premiare *v/t* ⟨1k & b⟩ give an award *or* prize to; *onestà*, *coraggio* reward

premiato *adj* prize-winning, award-winning

premiazione *f* award ceremony

premier *m* ⟨*pl* premier⟩ POL premier, prime minister

premierato *m* POL premiership

première *f* ⟨*pl* première⟩ première

preminente *adj* prominent **preminenza** *f* prominence

premio *m* ⟨*pl* -mi⟩ prize, award; FIN premium; ~ ***fedeltà*** loyalty bonus; ***Premio Nobel*** *m* ***per la pace*** Nobel peace prize; ***assegnare un*** ~ award a prize; ***avere qc in*** ~ receive sth as a prize

premolare *m* premolar

premonitore *adj* premonitory; ***segno*** *m* ~ warning sign **premonizione** *f* premonition

premunirsi *v/r* ⟨4d⟩: ~ ***contro qc*** guard oneself; ~ ***di pazienza*** arm oneself with patience

premura *f* (*fretta*) hurry, rush; ***essere pieno di -e nei confronti di qn*** be very attentive to s.o.; ***mettere*** ~ ***a qn*** hurry s.o. along; ***non c'è*** ~ there's no hurry *or* rush

premurarsi *v/r* ⟨1a⟩: ~ ***di fare qc*** take care to do sth; (*affrettarsi*) hurry

premurosamente *adv* thoughtfully

premuroso *adj* attentive

prenatale *adj* prenatal

prendere ⟨3c⟩ **I** *v/t* take; *malattia*, *treno* catch; ***cosa prendi?*** what will you have?; ~ ***qn per un italiano*** take *or* mistake s.o. for an Italian; ***andare / venire a*** ~ ***qn*** fetch s.o.; ~ ***corpo*** materialize; ~ ***fuoco*** catch fire; ~ ***il sole*** sunbathe; ~ ***paura*** take fright, get frightened; AVIAT ~ ***quota*** gain height;

~ ***in giro qn*** pull s.o.'s leg; ***prendersela*** get upset (***per*** about; ***con*** with); ***che ti prende?*** what's got into you?; ***l'ho preso per Franco*** I took him for Frank; ~ ***sul serio*** take seriously **II** *v/i*: ~ ***a destra*** turn right

prendersi *v/r* take; ~ ***un raffreddore*** catch a cold; ~ ***cura di qn*** look after s.o., take care of s.o.; ~ ***a cuore qc*** take sth to heart

prendisole *m* ⟨*pl* prendisole⟩ sundress

prenotare *v/t* ⟨1c⟩ book, reserve

prenotato *adj* booked, reserved

prenotazione *f* booking, reservation

prensile *adj* prehensile

preoccupante *adj* worrying

preoccupare *v/t* ⟨1m & c⟩ worry, preoccupy

preoccuparsi *v/r* worry

preoccupato *adj* worried, preoccupied

preoccupazione *f* worry

prepagato *adj* prepaid; ***carta*** *f* ***-a*** FIN prepaid card; ***scheda*** *f* ***-a*** TEL prepaid phone card

preparare *v/t* ⟨1a⟩ prepare

prepararsi *v/r* get ready (***a*** to), prepare (***a*** to)

preparativi *mpl* preparations *pl*

preparato I *adj* ready, prepared; ***essere*** ~ ***a qc*** be ready for sth; ***essere*** ~ ***in qc*** be competent in sth **II** *m* preparation

preparatorio *adj* ⟨*mpl* -ri⟩ preliminary

preparazione *f* preparation

prepensionamento *m* early retirement

preponderante *adj* predominant **preponderanza** *f numerica* predominance; (*predominio*) superiority

preporre *v/t* ⟨3ll⟩ prepose; ~ ***qn al comando*** appoint as chief

preposizione *f* preposition

preposto *past part* → ***preporre***

prepotente *adj* domineering; *bisogno* pressing

prepotenza *f di persona* domineering nature; *di bisogno* pressing nature

prepuzio *m* ⟨*pl* -zi⟩ ANAT foreskin

preriscaldare *v/t* ⟨1a⟩ preheat

prerogativa *f* prerogative; *fig* property

presa *f* grip, hold; ELEC ~ ***di corrente*** socket; ~ ***di coscienza*** awareness, consciousness raising; *fig* ~ ***di possesso*** conquest, capture; ***macchina*** *f* ***da*** ~ cinecamera; ***abbandonare la*** ~ let go; ***essere alle -e con qc*** be grappling with sth; ***fare una*** ~ *presso corriere* call a courier

presagio *m* ⟨*pl* -gi⟩ omen, sign

presagire *v/t* ⟨4d⟩ (*pronosticare*) predict; (*presentire*) have a premonition; (*cose sgradevoli*) forebode

presalario *m* scholarship

presbite *adj* far-sighted, long-sighted

presbiteriano I *adj* Presbyterian **II** *m* Presbyterian

presbiterio *m* ⟨*pl* -ri⟩ presbytery (*a.* ARCH)

prescegliere *v/t* choose

prescelto I *adj* chosen **II** *m*, **-a** *f* chosen person **III** *past part* → ***prescegliere***

presciistico *adj* ⟨*mpl* -ci⟩ pre-skiing; ***ginnastica*** *f* ***-a*** pre-skiing exercise

prescindere *v/i* ⟨3v⟩: ~ ***da*** have nothing to do with, not be connected with; ***a*** ~ ***da*** aside from

prescolare *adj*: ***età*** *f* ~ pre-school age

prescritto *past part* → ***prescrivere***

prescrivere *v/t* ⟨3tt⟩ prescribe

prescrizione *f* prescription; ***andare*** *or* ***cadere in*** ~ lapse

preselezionare *v/t* ⟨1a⟩ preselect; *traffico* route **preselezione** *f* preselection; *traffico* routing; TEL area code

presentabile *adj* presentable

presentare *v/t* ⟨1b⟩ *documenti, biglietto* show, present; *domanda* submit; *scuse* make; THEAT present; (*contenere*) contain; (*far conoscere*) introduce (***a*** to); ~ ***domanda*** apply; ~ ***le armi*** *azione* present; *comando* present arms

presentarsi *v/r* look; (*esporre*) show itself; *occasione* present itself, occur; ~ ***bene*** / ***male*** look good / bad; ***permetta che mi presenti*** allow me to introduce myself

presentatore *m*, **-trice** *f* presenter

presentazione *f* presentation; *di richiesta* submission; ***fare le -i*** make the introductions; ***la*** ~ ***di un nuovo prodotto*** launch of a new product

presente I *adj* present; ***hai*** ~ ***il negozio …?*** do you know the shop …? **II** *m* present; GRAM present (tense); ***i -i*** *pl* those present, those in attendance

presentimento *m* premonition
presentire *v/t* ⟨4b⟩ have a premonition (of / that)
presenza *f* **1.** presence; ~ ***di spirito*** presence of mind; ***alla*** (*or* ***in***) ~ ***di*** in the presence of **2.** ***di bella*** ~ fine-looking
presenzialismo *m* ubiquitousness **presenzialista** *m/f* ⟨*mpl* -i⟩ *person always present at events* **presenziare** *v/t and v/i* ⟨1g & b⟩: ~ ***a qc*** attend sth
presepe *m* crèche
presepio *m* ⟨*pl* -pi⟩ crib
preservare *v/t* ⟨1b⟩ protect, keep (***da*** from)
preservativo *m* condom
preservazione *f* conservation
preside *m/f* head teacher; ~ ***di facoltà*** dean
presidente *m/f* chairman; POL president; ***Presidente della Repubblica*** President of the Republic; ***Presidente dello Stato*** President; ***Presidente del Consiglio*** (***dei Ministri***) Prime Minister; ~ ***del Tribunale*** JUR presiding judge
presidentessa *f* chairwoman; *moglie del presidente US* first lady
presidenza *f* chairmanship; POL presidency; EDU headmaster's study; ~ ***dell'Unione Europea*** EU Presidency
presidenziale *adj* presidential
presidiare *v/t* ⟨1k⟩ MIL garrison *con molti uomini* man; (*sorvegliare*) protect
presidio *m* ⟨*pl* -di⟩ MIL garrison; ~ ***ospedaliero*** ADMIN hospital facilities; ~ ***terapeutico*** MED medications
presiedere ⟨3a⟩ **I** *v/t*: ~ ***qc*** preside over sth; *come presidente* chair sth **II** *v/i*: ~ ***a qc*** manage sth; *fig* govern sth
presina *f* kettle-holder
preso *past part* → ***prendere***
pressa *f* TECH press
press-agent *m/f* ⟨*pl* press-agent⟩ press agent
pressante *adj* (*urgente*) pressing; (*insistente*) insistent
pressappochismo *m* carelessness
pressappoco *adv* more or less
pressare *v/t* ⟨1b⟩ crush; TECH press
pressatura *f* pressing
pressing *m* ⟨*pl* pressing⟩ SPORTS pressing
pressione *f* pressure; ~ ***atmosferica*** atmospheric pressure; ~ ***massima*** / ***minima*** maximum / minimum blood pressure; ~ ***delle gomme*** tyre pressure; MED ~ ***del sangue*** blood pressure; ~ ***sanguigna*** blood pressure; ***pentola*** *f* ***a*** ~ pressure cooker; ***avere la*** ~ ***alta*** / ***bassa*** have high / low blood pressure; ***essere sotto*** ~ be under pressure; *fig* ***far*** ~ ***su*** put pressure on, pressure
presso I *prep* (*vicino a*) near; *nella sede di* on the premises of; *posta* care of; ***vive*** ~ ***i genitori*** he lives with his parents; ***lavoro*** ~ ***la FIAT*** I work for Fiat **II** *adv* nearby **III** *m*: ***nei -i di*** in the vicinity of, in the neighbo(u)rhood of
pressoché *adv* almost
pressurizzato *adj* pressurized **pressurizzazione** *f* pressurization
prestabilire *v/t* ⟨4d⟩ prearrange **prestabilito** *adj* prearranged
prestampato I *adj* preprinted **II** *n*: ***prestampato*** *m* preprint *modulo* preprinted form
prestanome *m/f* ⟨*pl* prestanome⟩ figurehead; ***fare da*** ~ be a figurehead
prestante *adj* good-looking, fit **prestanza** *f* good looks, fitness
prestare *v/t* ⟨1b⟩ lend; ~ ***ascolto*** / ***aiuto a qn*** listen to / help s.o.; ~ ***un servizio*** provide a service; ~ ***ascolto*** lend an ear (to); ~ ***aiuto*** lend a hand (to)
prestarsi *v/r* offer one's services; (*essere adatto*) lend itself (***a*** to)
prestatore *m*, **-trice** *f di servizio* provider
prestazione *f* service
prestigiatore *m*, **-trice** *f* conjurer
prestigio *m* prestige; ***giochi*** *mpl* ***di*** ~ conjuring tricks
prestigioso *adj* prestigious
prestito *m* loan; ***in*** ~ on loan; ***dare in*** ~ lend; ***prendere in*** ~ borrow
presto *adv* (*fra poco*) soon; (*in fretta*) quickly; (*di buon'ora*) early; MUS presto; ~ ***o tardi*** sooner or later; ***la mattina*** ~ early in the morning; ***a*** ~***!*** see you soon!; ***al più*** ~ as soon as possible *infml* asap; ***far*** ~ be quick; ***torna*** ~***!*** *invito* come back soon!; *orario* don't be late!
presule *m* REL prelate

presumere *v/t* ⟨3h⟩ presume
presumibile *adj* presumable; ***è ~ che...*** we can presume that... **presumibilmente** *adv* presumably
presunto *adj* presumed
presuntuoso *adj* presumptuous
presunzione *f* presumption; ***~ d'innocenza*** JUR presumption of innocence
presupporre *v/t* ⟨3ll⟩ (*comportare*) entail; (*presumere*) suppose
presupposto *m* assumption; ***partiamo dal ~ che...*** let's start from the premise that...
prêt-à-porter *m* ⟨*pl* prêt-à-porter⟩ prêt-à-porter; ***abiti*** *mpl* **~** ready-to-wear clothes
prete *m* priest; ***vuole farsi ~*** he wants to become a priest
pretendente *m/f* claimant
pretendere *v/t* ⟨3c⟩ claim
pretensioso *adj* pretentious
preterintenzionale *adj* JUR unintentional; ***omicidio*** *m* **~** manslaughter
pretesa *f* pretension; ***avanzare -e*** put forward claims; ***senza -e*** unpretentious
pretesto *m* pretext
pretestuoso *adj* alleged; ***un argomento ~*** a specious argument
pretore *m* magistrate
pretoriano *m* HIST praetorian
pretorio *adj* ⟨*pl* -i⟩: ***albo*** *m* **~** ADMIN municipal notice board; ***palazzo*** *m* **~** magistrate's court
prettamente *adv* purely
pretura *f* magistrates' court
prevalente *adj* prevailing (*preminente*) foremost **prevalentemente** *adv* mostly
prevalenza *f* prevalence; ***in ~*** prevalently
prevalere *v/i* ⟨2r⟩ prevail
prevaricare *v/i* ⟨1m & d⟩ prevaricate **prevaricatore** *m*, **-trice** *f* transgressor; **prevaricazione** *f* abuse of power
prevedere *v/t* ⟨2s⟩ foresee, predict; *tempo* forecast; *di legge* provide for
prevedibile *adj* predictable
prevendita *f* advance sale
prevenire *v/t* ⟨4p⟩ *domanda, desiderio* anticipate; (*evitare*) prevent
preventivare *v/t* ⟨1a⟩ COMM estimate; *bilancio* budget *fig* plan
preventivo I *adj* preventive **II** *m* estimate
prevenuto *adj* biased
prevenzione *f* prevention
previdente *adj* foresighted
previdenza *f* foresight; ***~ sociale*** social security, *US* welfare
previdenziale *adj* social security; ***assicurazione*** *f* **~** social security policy; ***contributi*** *mpl* **-i** social security contributions
previo *adj* ⟨*mpl* -vi⟩: ***~ accordo*** prior agreement
previsione *f* forecast; ***-i*** *pl* ***del tempo*** weather forecast *sg*
previsto *past part* → ***prevedere***; ***prima del ~*** sooner than expected
preziosamente *adv* preciously *affettato* affectedly **preziosità** *f* ⟨*pl* preziosità⟩ preciousness; *affettato* affectedness
prezioso *adj* precious; ***fare il ~*** *infml* play hard to get
prezzaccio *m infml* ⟨*pl* -cci⟩ giveaway price
prezzemolo *m* parsley
prezzo *m* price; ***~ complessivo*** total price; ***~ di fabbrica*** factory price; ***~ fisso*** set price; ***~ di listino*** recommended retail price; ***~ netto*** net price; ***~ promozionale*** special introductory price; ***~ scontato*** discounted price; ***aumento*** *m* ***del ~*** price increase; ***crollo*** *m* ***dei -i*** price slump; ***a buon ~*** cheap; *fig* ***a caro ~*** dearly; ***a metà ~*** half-price; ***a qualunque ~*** at any cost
prezzolato *adj* hired
PRI *abbr* (= **Partito Repubblicano Italiano**) *hist Italian Republican Party*
prigione *f* prison; ***mettere in ~*** jail, put into prison
prigionia *f* imprisonment
prigioniero *m*, **-a** *f* prisoner; ***fare ~*** take prisoner
prima[1] *adv* before; (*in primo luogo*) first; ***~ di*** before; ***~ di fare qc*** before doing sth; ***~ o poi*** sooner or later; ***~ che*** before; ***quanto ~*** as soon as possible; ***un mese ~*** *precedente* a month before *in anticipo* a month in advance
prima[2] *f* RAIL first class; AUTO first gear; THEAT first night
primadonna *f* prima-donna (*a. fig*)
primario *adj* ⟨*mpl* -ri⟩ prime
Primati *mpl* ZOOL primates

primatista *m/f* ⟨*mpl* -i⟩ *nuovo* record-breaker; *precedente* record-holder
primato *m* primacy; SPORTS record
primavera *f* spring; ***in ~*** in the spring; *periodo* in (the) springtime; ***avere 60 -e*** have 60 winters
primaverile *adj* spring *attr*
primeggiare *v/i* ⟨1f⟩: ***~ in qc*** shine / excel in sth
prime rate *m* ⟨*pl* prime rate⟩ prime rate
primigenio *adj* ⟨*mpl* -ni⟩ first-born
primipara *f pre-parto* nulliparous female; *post-parto* primipara
primitività *f* ⟨*pl* primitività⟩ primitiveness; (*rozzezza*) coarseness
primitivo *adj* primitive; (*iniziale*) original; ***uomo*** *m* **~** primitive man
primizia *f* early crop
primo I *adj* first; ***~ piano*** *m* first floor; FILM, PHOT close-up; ***di ~ mattino*** first in the morning; ***di prim'ordine*** first-rate; ***di ~ acchito*** at first; ***di ~ letto*** of one's first marriage; ***in ~ luogo*** first of all; ***in un ~ tempo*** at first; ***in -a visione*** *film* just out; ***arrivare ~*** win; *fig* come out on top; ***il ~ della classe*** *adj* top of the class **II** *m*, **-a** *f* first; ***ai -i del mese*** at the beginning of the month; ***sulle -e*** in the beginning, at first **III** *m* COOK first course, starter
primogenito I *adj* first-born **II** *m*, **-a** *f* first-born
primogenitura *f* birthright
primordiale *adj* primeval; *civiltà* primitive civilization
primula *f* primula
principale I *adj* main **II** *m* boss
principalmente *adv* above all, mainly; (*specialmente*) particularly; (*fondamentalmente*) basically
principato *m* principality
principe *m* prince; ***~ azzurro*** Prince Charming
principessa *f* princess
principessina *f giovane* young princess; *figlia* prince's daughter
principiante *m/f* beginner
principino *m giovane* young prince; *figlio* prince's son
principio *m* ⟨*pl* -pi⟩ **1.** (*inizio*) start, beginning; ***~ attivo*** active ingredient; ***al ~*** at the start, in the beginning; ***da ~*** from the start *or* beginning *or* outset **2.** (*norma*) principle; ***~ contabile*** accounting principle; ***~ di precauzione*** JUR precautionary principle; ***questione*** *f* ***di ~*** matter of principle; ***per ~*** as a matter of principle; ***in linea di ~*** in theory
prione *m* BIOL prion
priore *m* REL prior
priorità *f* ⟨*pl* priorità⟩ priority
prioritario *adj* ⟨*mpl* -ri⟩ priority
prisma *m* ⟨*pl* -i⟩ GEOM, OPT prism
privacy *f* ⟨*pl* privacy⟩ privacy
privare *v/t* ⟨1a⟩ deprive (***di*** of)
privarsi *v/r* deprive o.s. (***di*** of)
privatamente *adv* privately
privatista *m/f* ⟨*mpl* -i⟩ (*studente*) external / private student; JUR expert in private law
privatizzare *v/t* ⟨1a⟩ privatize
privatizzazione *f* privatization
privato I *adj* private; ***in ~*** in private **II** *m*, **-a** *f* private citizen
privazione *f* deprivation; (*sacrificio*) privation
privilegiare *v/t* ⟨1f⟩ favo(u)r, prefer
privilegiato *adj* privileged
privilegio *m* ⟨*pl* -gi⟩ privilege
privo *adj*: ***~ di*** lacking in, devoid of; ***~ di mezzi*** resourceless; ***~ di sensi*** unconscious
pro I *m* ⟨*pl* pro⟩: ***i ~ e i contro*** the pros and cons; ***a che ~?*** what's the point *or* use? **II** *prep* for; ***~ capite*** per capita, each
probabile *adj* probable
probabilità *f* ⟨*pl* probabilità⟩ probability
probabilmente *adv* probably
probatorio *adj* ⟨*mpl* -ri⟩ probative; ***elemento*** *m* **~** evidential proof; ***incidente*** *m* **~** JUR probative evidence
problema *m* ⟨*pl* -i⟩ problem; ***c'è qualche ~?*** *infml* is there a problem?; ***senza -i*** no problem
problematica *f* ⟨*pl* -che⟩ problems
problematico *adj* ⟨*mpl* -ci⟩ problematic
probo *adj* honest, upright
proboscide *f* trunk
procacciare *v/t* ⟨1f⟩ secure **procacciarsi** *v/r* ⟨1f⟩ gain **procacciatore** *m*, **-trice** *f*: ***~ d'affari*** runner
procace *adj* provocative; (*licenzioso*) lewd **procacità** *f* ⟨*pl* procacità⟩ provocativeness; (*licenziosità*) lewdness
pro capite I *adj inv* per head; ***reddito***

m ~ per capita income **II** *adv* per head
procedere *v/i* ⟨3a⟩ carry on; *fig* (*agire*) proceed; JUR ~ ***contro qn*** take legal proceedings against s.o.; ***tutto procede secondo le previsioni*** everything is going according to plan
procedimento *m* process; ~ ***civile*** / ***penale*** civil / criminal case
procedura *f* procedure; JUR proceedings *pl*; ~ ***di codecisione*** EU codecision procedure; ***osservare la*** ~ follow the procedure
procedurale *adj* procedural
procella *f liter* tempest **procellaria** *f* petrel
processare *v/t* ⟨1b⟩ try
processionaria *f* processionary moth
processione *f* procession
processo *m* **1.** process; ~ ***di fabbricazione*** manufacturing process **2.** JUR trial; ~ ***civile*** civil proceedings; ~ ***penale*** JUR criminal case; ~ ***verbale*** minutes *pl*; ***essere sotto*** ~ be on trial
processore *m* TECH, ELEC processor
processuale *adj* JUR trial *attr*
procinto *m*: ***essere in*** ~ ***di*** be about to, be on the point of
procione *m* rac(c)oon
proclama *m* ⟨*pl* -i⟩ proclamation
proclamare *v/t* ⟨1a⟩ proclaim
proclamazione *f* proclamation
proconsole *m* HIST proconsul
procreare *v/t* ⟨1b⟩ procreate **procreazione** *f* procreation; ~ ***assistita*** assisted procreation
procura *f* power of attorney; ***Procura di Stato*** public prosecutor's office; ***per*** ~ by proxy
procurare *v/t* ⟨1a⟩ (*causare*) cause; ~ ***qc a qn*** cause s.o. sth
procurarsi *v/r* get hold of, obtain
procuratore *m*, **-trice** *f* person with power of attorney; JUR lawyer for the prosecution; ~ ***generale*** Attorney General; ~ ***legale*** solicitor; ***sostituto*** ~ deputy prosecutor
prode *adj* LIT valiant **prodezza** *f liter* valour; (*bravata*) escapade (*a. iron*)
prodiere *m*, **-a** *f* NAUT bowman
prodigalità *f* ⟨*pl* prodigalità⟩ bounty
prodigare *v/t* ⟨1l⟩ (*elargire*) lavish; (*dilapidare*) squander
prodigarsi *v/r* ⟨1l⟩: ~ ***in complimenti*** lavish s.o. with compliments; ~ ***per qn*** go out of one's way for s.o.
prodigio *m* ⟨*pl* -gi⟩ prodigy; ***bambino m*** ~ child prodigy
prodigiosamente *adv* miraculously
prodigioso *adj* tremendous, prodigious
prodigo *adj* ⟨*mpl* -ghi⟩ (*scialacquatore*) spendthrift; (*generoso*) lavish; *fig* spendthrift; ***il figliol*** ~ the prodigal son; ***essere*** ~ ***di consigli*** generous in giving s.o. advice
prodotto I *past part* → ***produrre*** **II** *m* product; ***-i*** *pl* ***alimentari*** foodstuffs; ***-i*** *pl* ***di bellezza*** cosmetics; ***-i*** *pl* ***farmaceutici*** pharmaceuticals; ~ ***finito*** finished product; ~ ***interno*** / ***nazionale lordo*** gross domestic / national product
prodromo *m* signal; MED premonitory symptom
producibile *adj* producible
produco → ***produrre***
product manager *m/f* ⟨*pl* product manager⟩ product manager
produrre *v/t* ⟨3e⟩ produce; *danni* cause; ~ ***un film*** produce a film; ~ ***danni*** cause damage
prodursi *v/r* ⟨3e⟩ appear; (*esibirsi*) perform
produttività *f* productivity; ~ ***personale*** COMPUT personal productivity
produttivo *adj* productive
produttore *m*, **-trice** *f* producer
produzione *f* production; ~ ***giornaliera*** daily production *or* output; ~ ***di calore*** heat generation; ~ ***in serie*** mass production
prof. *abbr* (= **professore**) Prof. (Professor)
profanare *v/t* ⟨1a⟩ desecrate
profanatore I *adj* desecrating **II** *m*, **-trice** *f* desecrator; ~ ***di tombe*** grave robber **profanazione** *f* (*sacrilegio*) desecration; (*violazione*) violation (*a. fig*)
profano I *adj* profane **II** *m fig*: ***sono un*** ~ ***di*** I know nothing about
professionale *adj esperienza*, *impegno* professional; *scuola*, *corso* vocational
professionalità *f* ⟨*pl* professionalità⟩ professionalism **professionalmente** *adv* professionally
professione *f* profession; ~ ***di fede*** profession of faith; ***calciatore m di***

~ professional footballer
professionismo *m* SPORTS professionalism
professionista *m/f* ⟨*mpl* -i⟩ professional, pro *infml*; ***libero*** **~** self-employed person
professionistico *adj* ⟨*mpl* -ci⟩ professional
professore *m*, **-essa** *f* teacher; *d'università* professor
profeta *m* ⟨*pl* -i⟩ prophet
profetico *adj* ⟨*mpl* -ci⟩ prophetic **profetizzare** *v/t* ⟨1a⟩ prophesy
profezia *f* prophecy
proficuo *adj* profitable
profilare *v/t* ⟨1a⟩ profile; SEW trim; TECH streamline **profilarsi** *v/r* ⟨1a⟩ loom (up) (*a. fig*)
profilassi *f* ⟨*pl* profilassi⟩ prophylaxis
profilato *m* section; **~ *d'acciaio*** steel bar
profilattico *adj* ⟨*mpl* -ci⟩ prophylactic
profilo *m* profile; **~ *professionale*** career brief; ***di*** **~** in profile ***sotto il*** **~** ***della qualità*** from a qualitative viewpoint
profiterole *m* ⟨*pl* profiterole⟩ profiterole
profittatore *m*, **-trice** *f pej* exploiter
profitto *m* (*vantaggio*) advantage; ***mettere a*** **~** make the most (of); FIN ***conto -i e perdite*** profit and loss account
profondamente *adv* deeply
profondere *v/t* ⟨3bb⟩: **~ *denaro/parole/elogi*** squander money/waste words/heap praise
profondersi *v/r* ⟨3bb⟩: **~ *in ringraziamenti*** thank profusely; **~ *in scuse*** apologize profusely
profondità *f* ⟨*pl* profondità⟩ depth; PHOT **~ *di campo*** depth of field
profondo *adj* deep; ***dal*** **~** ***del cuore*** from the bottom of one's heart
pro forma *adj inv* pro forma
prof.ssa *abbr* (= **professoressa**) Prof. (Professor)
profugo *m*, **-a** *f* ⟨*mpl* -ghi⟩ refugee
profumare *v/t* ⟨1a⟩ perfume, scent
profumarsi *v/r* ⟨1a⟩ put on perfume
profumatamente *adv*: ***pagare*** **~** pay through the nose, pay a fortune
profumato *adj* perfumed, fragrant; ***una -a mancia*** a generous tip
profumeria *f* perfume shop
profumo *m* perfume, scent; **~ *di rose*** fragrance/smell of roses
profusione *f* (*sperpero*) squandering; (*abbondanza*) profuseness; ***a*** **~** profusely; ***narrare con*** **~** ***di particolari*** tell with abundance of detail
profuso *past part* → ***profondere***
progenie *f* ⟨*pl* progenie⟩ *liter* (*stirpe*) offspring; (*discendenza*) descendants **progenitori** *mpl* forefathers
progettare *v/t* ⟨1b⟩ plan; ARCH design
progettazione *f* design
progettista *m/f* ⟨*mpl* -i⟩ planner, designer
progetto *m* design; *di costruzione* project; **~ *pilota*** pilot project; **~ *di legge*** bill; ***fare -i*** make plans; ***-i*** *pl* ***per le vacanze*** plans for one's holidays
prognosi *f* ⟨*pl* prognosi⟩ prognosis; **~ *riservata*** uncertain prognosis
programma *m* ⟨*pl* -i⟩ programme, *US* program; COMPUT program; **~ *applicativo*** application; **~ *di scrittura*** word processor; **~ *televisivo*** TV program(me); ***fuori*** **~** unscheduled; ***avere in*** **~** ***qualcosa*** have something planned
programmabile *adj* programmable (*a.* COMPUT)
programmare *v/t* ⟨1a⟩ plan; COMPUT program
programmatico *adj* ⟨*mpl* -ci⟩ programmatic
programmato *adj* COMPUT programmed; (*pianificato*) planned; (*orario*) scheduled
programmatore *m*, **-trice** *f* programmer
programmazione *f* programming; FIN **~ *economica*** economic planning; COMPUT ***linguaggio*** *m* ***di*** **~** programming language
progredire *v/i* ⟨4d⟩ progress
progredito *adj* advanced
progressione *f* progression
progressista ⟨*mpl* -i⟩ **I** *adj* progressive; (*radicale*) radical; (*liberale*) liberal **II** *m/f* progressivist; (*radicale*) radical; (*liberale*) liberal
progressivamente *adv* progressively
progressivo *adj* progressive
progresso *m* progress; ***fare -i*** make progress
proibire *v/t* ⟨4d⟩ ban, prohibit; **~ *a qn di fare qc*** forbid s.o. to do sth

proibitivo *adj* prohibitive; ***prezzo*** *m* **~** prohibitive price **proibito I** *adj* forbidden; *fig* ***sogni*** *mpl* ***-i*** impossible dreams
proibizione *f* ban
proibizionismo *m* prohibition (*a.* HIST); ***periodo del ~*** prohibition
proiettare *v/t* ⟨1b⟩ throw; *film* screen, show; *fig* project
proiettile *m* projectile
proiettore *m* projector; ***~ per diapositive*** slide projector
proiezione *f* projection; *di film* screening, showing
project manager *m/f* ⟨*pl* project manager⟩ project manager
prolasso *m* MED prolapse
prole *f* children, offspring
proletariato *m* proletariat; *infml* working class
proletario ⟨*mpl* -ri⟩ **I** *adj* proletariat **II** *m*, **-a** *f* proletarian
proliferare *v/i* ⟨1m⟩ BIOL proliferate; *fig* spread **proliferazione** *f* BIOL proliferation; *fig* abundance
prolificare *v/i* ⟨1m & d⟩ BIOL proliferate; BOT proliferate; *fig* breed **prolificazione** *f* BIOL prolification; BOT prolification; *fig* reproduction **prolifico** *adj* ⟨*mpl* -ci⟩ prolific; *fig* prolific
prolisso *adj* verbose *infml* long-winded
pro loco *f* ⟨*pl* pro loco⟩ local tourist board
prologo *m* ⟨*pl* -ghi⟩ prolog(ue)
prolunga *f* ELEC extension cord
prolungabile *adj nel tempo* prolongable; *in lunghezza* extensible
prolungamento *m* extension
prolungare *v/t* ⟨1e⟩ *nel spazio* extend; *nel tempo* prolong, extend
prolungarsi *v/r di strada* extend; *di riunione* go on, continue
promemoria *m* ⟨*pl* promemoria⟩ memo
promessa *f* promise
promesso *past part* → ***promettere***
promettente *adj* promising
promettere *v/t* ⟨3ee⟩ promise; ***~ bene*** look promising
prominente *adj* (*rilevato*) protruding; (*eminente*) eminent **prominenza** *f* prominence; GEOL rise
promiscuità *f* ⟨*pl* promiscuità⟩ promiscuity **promiscuo** *adj* promiscuous
promo *m* ⟨*pl* promo⟩ promo
promo *n* promotional film
promontorio *m* ⟨*pl* -ri⟩ promontory, headland
promosso *past part* → ***promuovere***
promotore I *adj* promoting **II** *m*, **-trice** *f* promoter (*sostenitore*) supporter
promozionale *adj* promotional
promozione *f* promotion; EDU year; ***~ delle vendite*** sales promotion
promulgare *v/t* ⟨1e⟩ JUR promulgate **promulgazione** *f* JUR promulgation
promuovere *v/t* ⟨3ff⟩ promote; EDU move up
pronao *m* ARCH pronaos
pronipote *m/f di nonni* great-grandson; *donna, ragazza* great-granddaughter; *di zii* great-nephew; *donna, ragazza* great-niece
prono *adj* (*supino*) prone; (*chino*) bowed
pronome *m* pronoun
pronominale *adj* pronominal; ***verbi*** *mpl* ***-i*** pronominal verbs
pronosticare *v/t* ⟨1m⟩ prognosticate **pronostico** *m* ⟨*pl* -ci⟩ prediction
prontamente *adv* (*subito*) promptly; (*velocemente*) quickly
prontezza *f* readiness, promptness; (*rapidità*) speediness, promptness; ***~ di spirito*** quick thinking
pronto *adj* (*preparato*) ready (***a fare qc*** to do sth; ***per qc*** for sth); (*rapido*) speedy, prompt; TEL ***~!*** hello!; ***pagamento*** *m* ***-a cassa*** payment in cash, cash payment; ***~ soccorso*** first aid; *in ospedale* accident and emergency, A&E; ***~ per l'uso*** ready to use
prontuario *m* ⟨*pl* -ri⟩ handbook
pronuncia *f* pronunciation
pronunciabile *adj* pronounceable
pronunciare *v/t* ⟨1f⟩ pronounce; ***non ha pronunciato una parola*** he didn't say a word
pronunciarsi *v/r* give an opinion (***su*** on)
pronunciato *adj fig* definite, pronounced
propaganda *f* propaganda; POL ***~ elettorale*** electioneering
propagandare *v/t* ⟨1a⟩ advertise
propagandistico *adj* ⟨*mpl* -ci⟩ advertising; ***materiale*** *m* **~** advertising / promotional material
propagare *v/t* ⟨1e⟩ propagate; *fig*

spread
propagarsi *v/r* spread (*a. fig*)
propagazione *f* propagation; ~ ***del calore*** propagation of heat
propaggine *f* AGR layer; *fig* (*diramazione*) offshoot; ***le -i delle Alpi*** the offshoots of the Alps
propano *m* propane
propedeutica *f* ⟨*pl* -che⟩ propaedeutics **propedeutico** *adj* ⟨*mpl* -ci⟩ introductory; (*preliminare*) preparatory
propellente *m* propellant; (*carburante*) fuel
propendere *v/i* ⟨3a⟩: ~ ***per qc*** favour sth **propensione** *f* disposition (*predisposizione*) flair; (*simpatia*) liking; (*disponibilità*) willingness
propenso *adj* inclined (***a fare qc*** to do sth)
propinare *v/t* ⟨1a⟩ give sth to drink; (*servire*) treat; *hum* serve up
propiziarsi *v/r* ⟨1g⟩: ~ ***il favore di qn*** endear oneself to s.o. **propiziatorio** *adj* ⟨*mpl* -ri⟩ propitiating; ***rito*** *m* ~ propitiatory rite
propizio *adj* ⟨*mpl* -zi⟩ suitable
propoli *m/f* ⟨*pl* propoli⟩ propolis
proponente *m/f* proponent
propongo → ***proporre***
proponibile *adj* proposable
proponimento *m* resolution; ***fare*** ~ ***di fare qc*** decide *or* make up one's mind to do sth
proporre *v/t* ⟨3ll⟩ propose
proporsi *v/r* stand (***come*** as); ~ ***di fare qc*** intend to do sth
proporzionale *adj* proportional
proporzionato *adj* in proportion (***a*** to)
proporzione *f* proportion; ***in*** ~ in proportion (***a, con*** to)
proposito *m* intention; ***a che*** ~***?*** what about?; ***a*** ~ by the way; ***a*** ~ ***di*** about, with reference to; ***di*** ~ deliberately, on purpose; ***capitare a*** ~ turn up at just the right moment
proposizione *f* GRAM sentence; MATH proposition
proposta *f* proposal
proposto *past part* → ***proporre***
propriamente *adv* really
proprietà *f* ⟨*pl* proprietà⟩ property; *diritto* ownership; ~ ***privata*** private property; ***essere di*** ~ ***di qn*** belong to s.o., be s.o.'s property; ~ ***intellettuale*** JUR intellectual property; ***appartamento*** *m* ***di*** ~ private apartment
proprietario *m*, **-a** *f* ⟨*mpl* -ri⟩ owner
proprio ⟨*mpl* -ri⟩ **I** *adj* own; (*caratteristico*) typical; (*adatto*) proper; ***nome*** *m* ~ proper noun; ***amor*** *m* ~ pride; ***a -e spese*** at one's own expense **II** *adv* (*davvero*) really; ***è*** ~ ***lui che me l'ha chiesto*** he's the one who asked me!; ***è*** ~ ***impossibile*** that is quite impossible **III** *m* (*beni*) personal property; ***lavorare in*** ~ be self-employed
propugnare *v/t* ⟨1a⟩ *fig* defend **propugnatore** *m*, **-trice** *f fig* advocate
propulsione *f* propulsion
propulsore *m* propeller
prora *f* prow
proroga *f* ⟨*pl* -ghe⟩ postponement; (*prolungamento*) extension
prorogabile *adj* extendible
prorogare *v/t* ⟨1l, e & c⟩ (*rinviare*) postpone; (*prolungare*) extend
prorompente *adj* overwhelming **prorompere** *v/i* ⟨3rr⟩ (*fuoriuscire*) gush (out); (*sbottare*) *fig* burst (out / into)
prosa *f* prose; ***scrivere in*** ~ write in prose; ***teatro*** *m* ***di*** ~ playhouse
prosaicità *f* ⟨*pl* prosaicità⟩ prosaicness **prosaico** *adj* ⟨*mpl* -ci⟩ prosaic; (*ordinario*) dull; (*poco fantasioso*) uninspired
proscenio *m* ⟨*pl* -ni⟩ proscenium
prosciogliere *v/t* ⟨3ss⟩ release; JUR acquit
proscioglimento *m* JUR acquittal
prosciugamento *m* drainage; (*asciugare*) drying up; BUILD dewatering
prosciugare *v/t* ⟨1e⟩ drain; *di sole* dry up
prosciutto *m* ham, prosciutto; ~ ***cotto*** cooked ham; ~ ***crudo*** *salted air-dried ham*
proscritto I *adj* banished **II** *m*, **-a** *f* exile **proscrivere** *v/t* ⟨3tt⟩ ban; (*esiliare*) to exile **proscrizione** *f* proscription; (*esilio*) exile; (*divieto*) prohibition
prosecco *m* ⟨*pl* -cchi⟩ COOK (*dry white wine produced in the region of Veneto*) prosecco
proseguimento *m* continuation; ***buon*** ~***!*** good luck! *di viaggio*: enjoy the rest of your journey!
proseguire ⟨4a⟩ **I** *v/t* continue **II** *v/i* continue, carry on, go on
proselitismo *m* proselytization **pro-**

selito *m*, **-a** *f* REL proselyte; POL proselyte
prosopopea *f pej* pomposity; *arie* airs and graces
prosperare *v/i* ⟨1l & c⟩ prosper
prosperità *f* prosperity
prospero *adj* prosperous
prospero *adj* (*fiorente*) thriving; (*propizio*) favourable
prosperoso *adj* (*proficuo*) flourishing; (*formoso*) buxom
prospettare *v/t* ⟨1b⟩ set forth / out **prospettarsi** *v/r* ⟨1b⟩ seem
prospettico *adj* ⟨*mpl* -ci⟩ perspective; ***punto*** *m* **~** *fig* perspective point
prospettiva *f* perspective; (*panorama*) view; *fig* point of view; ***-e** pl **finanziarie*** EU economic prospects; ***senza -e*** without prospects
prospetto *m disegno* elevation; (*facciata*) facade; (*tabella*) table; ***~ pubblicitario*** brochure
prospiciente *adj*: ***~*** (***su***) ***qc*** looking (onto) sth
prossimamente *adv* shortly, soon
prossimità *f* ⟨*pl* prossimità⟩ proximity; ***in ~ di*** near, close to
prossimo **I** *adj* close; ***la -a volta*** the next time; ***il lavoro è ~ alla fine*** the work is nearly finished **II** *m* fellow human being, neighbo(u)r
prostata *f* prostate
prostituire *v/t* ⟨4d⟩: ***far ~*** force s.o. to become a prostitute **prostituirsi** *v/r* ⟨4d⟩ prostitute oneself (*a. fig*)
prostituta *f* prostitute
prostituzione *f* prostitution
prostrare *v/t* ⟨1c⟩ *malattia etc* debilitate; *fig* crush **prostrarsi** *v/r* ⟨1c⟩ kneel down; *fig* crawl **prostrato** *adj* prostrate; *fig* depressed **prostrazione** *f* prostration; (*sfinimento*) exhaustion; (*abbattimento*) depression
protagonismo *m* self-advertisement
protagonista *m/f* ⟨*mpl* -i⟩ protagonist
proteggere *v/t* ⟨3cc⟩ protect (***da*** from)
proteggersi *v/r* protect o.s. (***da*** from)
proteico *adj* protein *attr*
proteina *f* protein
protendere *v/t* ⟨3c⟩ stretch out **protendersi** *v/r* ⟨3c⟩ lean forward
protervia *f* arrogance **protervo** *adj* arrogant
protesi *f* ⟨*pl* protesi⟩ prosthesis; ***~ dentaria*** false teeth *pl*, dentures *pl*
proteso → ***protendere***
protesta *f* protest
protestante *m/f* & *adj* Protestant
protestantesimo *m* Protestantism
protestare *v/t* & *v/i* ⟨1b⟩ protest
protestatario ⟨*mpl* -ri⟩ **I** *adj* protesting **II** *m*, **-a** *f* remonstrant
protestato *adj* (*dichiarato*) declared; (*rifiutato*) rejected
protettivo *adj* protective
protetto *past part* → ***proteggere***
protettorato *m* protectorate
protettore **I** *m*, **-trice** *f* patron; *santo* patron saint **II** *m*: ***protettore** di prostituta* pimp
protezione *f* protection; ***~ delle acque*** prevention of water pollution; ***~ dell'ambiente*** environmental protection, protection of the environment; ***~ degli animali*** prevention of cruelty to animals; ***~ dei consumatori*** consumer protection; COMPUT ***~ dati*** data protection; ***~ del paesaggio*** nature conservation
Protezione civile *f* civil defence
protezionismo *m* protectionism **protezionista** ⟨*mpl* -i⟩ **I** *adj* protectionist **II** *m/f* protectionist **protezionistico** *adj* ⟨*mpl* -ci⟩ protectionist
protocollare **I** *adj* official **II** *v/t* ⟨1c⟩ register
protocollare[1] *adj* official
protocollare[2] *v/t* ⟨1c⟩ register
protocollo *m* protocol; (*registro*) register; TECH standard; ***foglio** m **~*** foolscap; ***mettere a ~*** register
protone *m* proton
prototipo *m* prototype
protozoico *adj* ⟨*mpl* -ci⟩ GEOL Proterozoic
protrarre *v/t* ⟨3xx⟩ prolong **protrarsi** *v/r* ⟨3xx⟩ protract **protrazione** *f* protraction
protuberante *adj* protruding **protuberanza** *f* protuberance; BOT knob; *infml sul naso*: bump
prova *f* **1.** (*esame*) test; ***~ di laboratorio*** lab test; ***banco** m **di ~*** test bench; ***a ~ di bomba*** bombproof; ***periodo** m **di ~*** trial period; ***mettere alla ~*** put to the test **2.** (*tentativo*) attempt **3.** (*testimonianza*) proof; ***salvo ~ contraria*** unless otherwise stated; ***per insufficienza di -e*** for lack of evidence **4.** *di abito* fitting **5.** SPORTS heat **6.** THEAT

-e** pl* rehearsal *sg*; THEAT ***-e** pl **generali dress rehearsal *sg*
provare *v/t* ⟨1c⟩ test, try out; *vestito* try (on); (*dimostrare*) prove; THEAT rehearse; ***~ a fare qc*** try to do sth; ***provarci gusto*** enjoy
provato *adj* proven; *fig* marked (***da*** by)
provengo → ***provenire***
provenienza *f* origin
provenire *v/i* ⟨4p⟩ come (***da*** from)
proventi *mpl* income *sg*
provenzale I *adj* Provençal **II** *m* (*lingua*) Provençal
proverbiale *adj* proverbial (*a. fig*)
proverbio *m* ⟨*pl* -i⟩ proverb
provetta *f* test-tube; ***bambino*** *m* ***in ~*** test-tube baby
provider *m* ⟨*pl* provider⟩ COMPUT service provider
provincia *f* ⟨*pl* -ce⟩ province
provinciale I *adj* provincial; ***strada*** *f* ***~*** *B road* **II** *m/f* provincial **III** *f B road*
provincialismo *m* provincialism
provino *m* screen-test; (*campione*) sample
provocante *adj* provocative
provocare *v/t* ⟨1l, c & d⟩ (*causare*) cause; (*sfidare*) provoke; *invidia* arouse
provocatore I *adj* provocative **II** *m*, **-trice** *f* troublemaker **provocatorio** *adj* ⟨*mpl* -ri⟩ provocative **provocazione** *f* provocation
provolone *m cheese sort*
provvedere ⟨2s⟩ **I** *v/t* provide (***di*** with) **II** *v/i*: ***~ a*** take care of
provvedimento *m* measure; ***~ d'urgenza*** emergency measure
provveditorato *m* local superintendency; ***~ agli studi*** Local Education Authority **provveditore** *m*, **-trice** *f* local superintendent; ***~ agli studi*** Education Superintendent
provvidenza *f* providence
provvidenziale *adj* providential; ***essere ~*** be heaven-sent **provvido** *adj* provident; (*utile*) fortunate
provvigione *f* commission
provvisoriamente *adv* provisionally **provvisorietà** *f* ⟨*pl* provvisorietà⟩ transitoriness
provvisorio *adj* ⟨*mpl* -ri⟩ provisional
provvista *f*: ***fare -e*** go (food) shopping; ***far ~ di qc*** stock up on sth
provvisto I *past part* → ***provvedere*** **II** *adj*: ***essere ~ di*** be provided with, have; ***essere ben ~ di qc*** have lots of sth
prozio *m*, **-a** *f* great-uncle; *donna* great-aunt
prua *f* bow
prudente *adj* careful, cautious
prudentemente *adv* carefully; *senno* sensibly
prudenza *f* care, caution
prudenziale *adj* sensible
prudere *v/i* ⟨3a⟩: ***mi prude la mano*** my hand itches
prugna *f* plum; ***~ secca*** prune
prurigine *f* itchiness **pruriginoso** *adj* itchy; *fig* titillating
prurito *m* itch
PS *abbr* (= **Pesaro**) Pesaro
P.S. *abbr* **1.** (= **Pubblica Sicurezza**) police *pl* **2.** (= **post scriptum**) PS (post scriptum)
pseudo... *pref* pseudo...
pseudonimo *m* pseudonym
psicanalisi *f* psychoanalysis
psicanalista *m/f* ⟨*mpl* -i⟩ psychoanalyst
psicanalizzare *v/t* ⟨1a⟩ psychoanalyse
psiche *f* psyche
psichedelico *adj* ⟨*mpl* -ci⟩ psychedelic
psichiatra *m/f* ⟨*mpl* -i⟩ psychiatrist
psichiatria *f* psychiatry
psichiatrico *adj* ⟨*mpl* -ci⟩ psychiatric
psichico *adj* ⟨*mpl* -ci⟩ psychic
psicoanalisi *f* psychoanalysis
psicoanalista *m/f* ⟨*mpl* -i⟩ psychoanalyst
psicoattitudinale *adj*: ***test*** *m* ***~*** aptitude test
psicodramma *m* ⟨*pl* -i⟩ psychodrama
psicofarmaco *m* ⟨*pl* -ci⟩ psychotropic (drug)
psicolabile I *adj* mentally unstable **II** *m/f* mentally unstable person
psicologia *f* psychology
psicologicamente *adv* psychologically
psicologico *adj* ⟨*mpl* -ci⟩ psychological
psicologo *m*, **-a** *f* ⟨*mpl* -gi⟩ psychologist
psicopatico I *adj* ⟨*mpl* -ci⟩ psychopathic **II** *m*, **-a** *f* psychopath
psicosi *f* ⟨*pl* psicosi⟩ psychosis

psicosomatico *adj* ⟨*mpl* -ci⟩ psychosomatic
psicoterapeuta *m/f* ⟨*mpl* -i⟩ psychotherapeutic
psicoterapia *f* psychotherapy
PT *abbr* (= **Pistoia**) Pistoia
P.T.P. *abbr* (= **Posto Telefonico Pubblico**) public telephone
pub *m* ⟨*pl* pub⟩ pub; ***fare il giro dei ~*** go on a pub crawl
pubblicamente *adv* in public
pubblicare *v/t* ⟨1l & d⟩ publish
pubblicazione *f* publication; ***-i** pl **matrimoniali*** banns
pubblicità *f* ⟨*pl* pubblicità⟩ publicity, advertising; *annuncio* ad(vert); ***~ televisiva*** TV ad, *Br* commercial; ***fare ~ a*** *evento* publicize; *prodotto* advertise
pubblicitario I *adj* advertising **II** *m*, **-a** *f* publicist
pubblicizzare *v/t* ⟨1a⟩: ***~ qc*** publicize sth; *commercio* advertise sth; *promozione* promote sth **pubblicizzazione** *f* promotion; *commercio* advertising
pubblico ⟨*mpl* -ci⟩ **I** *adj* public; ***Pubblico Ministero*** public prosecutor; ***aperto al ~*** open to the public **II** *m* public; (*spettatori*) audience; ***in ~*** in public
pube *m* pubis
pubertà *f* puberty
pudico *adj* ⟨*mpl* -ci⟩ modest; (*timido*) bashful
pudore *m* modesty; ***senza ~*** shameless, immodest
puericultore *m* baby doctor; (*pediatra*) paediatrician **puericultrice** *f* nursery nurse **puericultura** *f* paedology **puerile** *adj* childish; *pej* juvenile **puerilità** *f* ⟨*pl* puerilità⟩ childishness
puerpera *f* puerperant
puffo *m* debt; *fumetti* Smurf
pugilato *m* boxing; ***incontro** m **di ~*** boxing match
pugile *m* boxer
Puglia *f* Puglia, Apulia
pugliese I *adj* from Apulia **II** *m/f* Apulian
pugnalare *v/t* ⟨1a⟩ stab; *fig* ***~ qn alle spalle*** stab s.o. in the back
pugnale *m* dagger
pugno *m* **1.** fist; ***di proprio ~*** in one's own handwriting; ***avere in ~ qc*** have sth in one's grasp; ***ti ho in ~*** I've got you now; ***rimanere con un ~ di mosche*** come away empty-handed **2.** (*colpo*) punch; ***fare a -i*** fight, come to blows; *fig colori* clash; *fig* ***essere (come) un ~ in un occhio*** be an eyesore; *fig* ***~ di ferro in guanto di velluto*** iron hand / fist in the velvet glove **3.** *quantità* handful
puk *abbr* (= **Personal Unlock Key**) TEL PUK (number)
pulce *f* flea; *fig* ***mettere la ~ nell'orecchio*** arouse s.o.'s suspicions; *fig* ***fare le -i a qn*** *infml* find fault with s.o.; ***mercatino** m **delle -i*** flea market
Pulcinella *m* Pulcinella; ***segreto** m **di ~*** open secret
pulcino *m* chick; *fig* ***essere un ~ bagnato*** be as wet as a drowned rat
puledro *m*, **-a** *f* colt; (*femmina*) filly
puleggia *f* ⟨*pl* -gge⟩ sheave
pulire *v/t* ⟨4d⟩ clean
pulirsi *v/r* ⟨4d⟩ clean oneself; (*lavarsi*) (have a) wash
pulita *f*: ***dare una ~*** give sth a clean / wipe
pulito *adj* clean; *fig* cleaned-out; ***faccenda** f **poco -a*** dirty business
pulitura *f* cleaning; ***~ a secco*** dry cleaning
pulizia *f* cleanliness; *fig* ***~ etnica*** ethnic cleansing; ***donna** f **delle -e*** cleaner; ***fare le -e*** do the cleaning, clean; ***-e** pl **di primavera*** spring cleaning
pullman *m* ⟨*pl* pullman⟩ coach, bus
pullover *m* ⟨*pl* pullover⟩ pullover
pullulare *v/i* ⟨1l⟩: ***~ di*** be teeming or swarming with
pulmino *m* minibus
pulpito *m* pulpit
pulsante *m* button
pulsare *v/i* ⟨1a⟩ pulsate
pulsazione *f* pulsation
pulviscolo *m* dust
puma *m* ⟨*pl* puma⟩ cougar *o* puma
pungente *adj* *foglia* prickly; *freddo*, *parola* sharp, biting; *desiderio* sharp
pungere *v/t* ⟨3d⟩ prick; *di ape*, *vespa* sting; ***~ qn sul vivo*** cut s.o. to the quick
pungiglione *m* sting
pungitopo *m* ⟨*pl* pungitopo⟩ BOT ruscus; *infml* butcher's broom
pungolare *v/t* ⟨1l⟩ prod; *fig* spur (on)
pungolo *m* *fig* spur
punibile *adj* punishable (**con** by)

punico ⟨*mpl* -ci⟩ **I** *adj* Punic; ***guerre*** *fpl* ***-che*** Punic Wars **II** *m*, **-a** *f* Punic
punire *v/t* ⟨4d⟩ punish
punitivo *adj* punishing; ***spedizione*** *f* ***-a*** punitive expedition
punizione *f* punishment; SPORTS ***calcio*** *m* ***di ~*** free kick; ***per ~*** as a punishment
punk ⟨*pl* punk⟩ **I** *adj* punk **II** *m/f* punk
punkabbestia *f* hardcore punk
punta *f di spillo, coltello* point; *di dita, lingua* tip; GEOG peak; *fig* touch, trace; *fig* ***~ di diamante*** diamond-point; ***in ~ di piedi*** on tiptoes; ***cane*** *m* ***da ~*** pointer; *fig* ***una ~ d'ironia*** a touch of irony; ***ora*** *f* ***di ~*** peak hour; ***ce l'ho sulla ~ della lingua*** it's on the tip of my tongue; *fig* ***prendere qc di ~*** face sth head-on
puntale *m* ferrule
puntare ⟨1a⟩ **I** *v/t* pin (***su*** to); (*dirigere*) point (***verso*** at); (*scommettere*) bet (***su*** on); *fig* ***~ i piedi*** dig one's heels; *fig* ***~ i piedi*** dig one's heels in in **II** *v/i* (*dirigersi*) head (***verso*** for); ***~ a*** *successo, matrimonio* aspire to, set one's sights on; ***~ su*** *contare su* rely on; ***~ la pistola*** aim a gun
puntata *f* instal(l)ment; (*scommessa*) bet
puntatore *m* COMPUT pointer
punteggiatura *f* punctuation
punteggio *m* score
puntellare *v/t* ⟨1b⟩ shore up; *fig* prop up **puntellarsi** *v/r* ⟨1b⟩ brace oneself **puntellatura** *f* shoring *di muro* underpinning **puntello** *m* shore; *fig* prop
punteruolo *m* punch; ZOOL snout-beetle
puntiforme *adj* punctiform
puntiglio *m* obstinacy; ***per ~*** out of spite
puntiglioso *adj* punctilious
puntina *f di giradischi* stylus; ***~ (da disegno)*** drawing pin, *US* thumbtack
puntino *m* dot; ***a ~*** perfectly, to perfection
punto I *past part* → ***pungere*** **II** *m* **1.** point; ***~ cardinale*** cardinal point; ***~ culminante*** height; ***~ di fusione*** melting point; ***~ di partenza*** starting point; ***~ vendita*** point of sale; ***~ di vista*** point of view, viewpoint; ***-i*** *pl* ***neri*** black spots; ***a un certo ~*** somewhere along the line; ***a che ~ sei?*** how far have you got?; ***di ~ in bianco*** suddenly, without warning; ***arrivare al ~ di*** (*or* ***che***) ***…*** get to the bottom of…; ***essere sul ~ di fare qc*** be on the point of doing sth, be about to do sth; ***fare il ~ della situazione*** take stock of the situation; ***fino a un certo ~*** up to a point; ***mettere a ~ qc*** fine-tune; ***in ~ di morte*** on one's deathbed; ***vincere ai -i*** outpoint; ***fino a che ~ sei arrivato?*** how far have you got?; ***alle dieci in ~*** at ten o'clock exactly *or* on the dot **2.** *segno d'interpunzione*: ***~ fermo*** full stop, *US* period; ***due -i*** colon; ***~ e virgola*** semicolon; ***~ esclamativo*** exclamation mark; ***~ interrogativo*** question mark **3.** MED, (*maglia*) stitch
puntuale *adj* punctual
puntualità *f* punctuality
puntualizzare *v/t* ⟨1a⟩ make clear
puntualizzazione *f* qualification
puntualmente *adv* (*in orario*) on time; (*precisamente*) accurately; (*invariabilmente*) invariably
puntura *f di ape, vespa* sting; *di ago* prick; MED injection; ***~ d'insetto*** insect bite
punzecchiare *v/t* ⟨1k⟩ prick; *fig* (*provocare*) tease
punzecchiatura *f* jabbing; *fig* needling
punzonare *v/t* ⟨1a⟩ punch **punzonatrice** *f* puncher **punzone** *m* (*conio*) stamp; (*punteruolo*) punch
può, puoi → ***potere***
puparo *m infml* puppet-master
pupattola *f* doll; *infml* dolly (*a. fig*); *fig* chick
pupazzetto *m* stick-figure; (*caricatura*) caricature
pupazzo *m* puppet; ***~ di neve*** snowman
pupilla *f* pupil
pupillo *m* JUR ward; *fig* protégé
pupo *m*, **-a** *f infml* child; ***teatro*** *m* ***dei -i*** puppet theatre
pur → ***pure***
puramente *adv* purely
purché *cj* provided, on condition that
pure I *cj* even if; (*tuttavia*) (and) yet **II** *adv* too, as well; ***pur di*** in order to; ***venga ~ avanti!*** do come in!; ***dica ~!*** tell me! *servizio* can I help you?;

è pur vero che... it's also true that…; ***faccia ~ come se fosse a casa sua*** please make yourself at home; ***ci mancava ~ questa!*** this is the last straw!; ***parla ~*** do tell me
purè *m* puree
purezza *f* purity
purga *f* ⟨*pl* -ghe⟩ purge
purgante *m* laxative
purgare *v/t* ⟨1e⟩ MED give a laxative to; POL purge; ***~ qn*** give a laxative to s.o. **purgarsi** *v/r* ⟨1e⟩ MED take a laxative
purgativo *adj* laxative
purgatorio *m* purgatory
purificare *v/t* ⟨1m & d⟩ purify; (*raffinare*) refine; (*filtrare*) filter; *fig* clear **purificarsi** *v/r* ⟨1m & d⟩ purify oneself; *fig* clear oneself **purificatore** *adj* purifying; *fig* cleansing **purificazione** *f* purification; (*raffinazione*) refinement; *fig* clearing; REL purification
purismo *m* purism **purista** *m/f* ⟨*mpl* -i⟩ purist
puritanesimo *m* puritanism; *fig* prudishness **puritano** *adj* REL puritan; *fig* prudish
puro *adj* pure
purosangue ⟨*pl* purosangue⟩ **I** *adj* thoroughbred **II** *m/f* thoroughbred
purpureo *adj*: **(*rosso*) ~** deep red, burgundy
purtroppo *adv* unfortunately
purulento *adj* suppurating
pus *m* ⟨*no pl*⟩ pus
pusher *m/f* ⟨*pl* pusher⟩ pusher
pusillanime I *adj* cowardly **II** *m/f* coward; *infml* chicken **pusillanimità** *f* ⟨*pl* pusillanimità⟩ cowardice
Pusteria *f*: ***Val ~*** Pusteria valley
pustola *f* pimple
puszta *f* puszta
putacaso *adv* suppose / supposing…; ***se ~ non fosse vero...*** if by chance it wasn't true…
putativo *adj* supposed; JUR putative; ***padre*** *m* **~** putative father
putiferio *m* ⟨*pl* -ri⟩ pandemonium; ***fare un ~*** make a song and dance (about sth); ***si scatenò un ~*** all hell broke loose
putrefare *v/i* ⟨3aa⟩ rot, putrefy
putrefazione *f* putrefaction; *fig* corruption **putridume** *m* rot; *fig* corruption
putsch *m* ⟨*pl* putsch⟩ coup
puttana *f sl* whore *sl*
puttanata *f vulg* *dire* bullshit; *fare* dirty trick **puttanesco** *adj* ⟨*mpl* -schi⟩: ***spaghetti*** *mpl* ***alla -a*** *spaghetti with anchovies, olives, capers, tomatoes, garlic and chilli pepper* **puttaniere** *m vulg* womanizer
putto *m* putto
puzza *f* stink; ***c'è ~ di imbroglio*** *infml* something smells fishy
puzzare *v/i* ⟨1a⟩ stink (***di*** of)
puzzle *m* ⟨*pl* puzzle⟩ puzzle
puzzo *m* stink
puzzola *f* ZOOL polecat
puzzolente *adj* stinking, evil-smelling
p.v. *abbr* (= **prossimo venturo**) next
PV *abbr* (= **Pavia**) Pavia
PVC *abbr* (= **polivinilcloruro**) polyvinyl chloride
PZ *abbr* (= **Potenza**) Potenza

Q

q, Q *m/f* ⟨*pl* q, Q⟩ q, Q; ***Q come Quarto*** Q for Quebec
q *abbr* (= **quintale**) 100 kilograms
Qatar *m* Qatar
qua *adv* here; ***passa di ~*** come this way; ***al di ~ di*** on this side of
quacchero *m*, **-a** *f* Quaker
quaderno *m* exercise book; ***~ a righe / a quadretti*** ruled / squared exercise book
quadrangolare *adj* four-sided
quadrangolo *m* quadrangle
quadrante *m* quadrant; *di orologio* dial
quadrare ⟨1a⟩ **I** *v/t* MATH square; *conti* balance **II** *v/i di conti* balance, square *infml*; *fig* ***far ~ i conti*** balance the books; ***qc non mi quadra*** there's

sth I don't like; *fig* ***i conti non quadrano*** there's something fishy going on
quadrato I *adj* square; *fig persona* rational; ***un chilometro*** *m* **~** a square kilometre; ***due al*** **~** two squared; *fig* ***fare*** **~** ***attorno a qn*** close ranks **II** *m* square; *tabella etc* list
quadratura *f* GEOM, SPACE squaring; *fig* ***la*** **~** ***del cerchio*** the squaring of the circle
quadrettato *adj* squared; TEX chequered, checked **quadrettatura** *f* squaring off; *forma* chequered pattern; TEX chequer-work
quadrettino *m* small square; TEX small check; (*scena*) scene; (*quadro*) small painting
quadretto *m* (*casella*) small square; (*pezzetto quadrato*) small square; TEX small check ***a -i*** squared TEX checked / chequered, **~** ***familiare*** glimpse of family life
quadriennale *adj* quadrennial; *ogni quattro anni* every four years **quadriennio** *m* ⟨*pl* -nni⟩ four-year period
quadrifoglio *m* ⟨*pl* -gli⟩ four-leaf clover
quadriglia *f* ⟨*pl* -glie⟩ quadrille
quadrilatero *m* quadrilateral
quadrimestre *m* four-month period
quadrimotore I *adj* four-engine(d) **II** *m* four-engined plane
quadrivio *m* ⟨*pl* -vi⟩ four-way crossroads *sg*; HIST quadrivium; ***arti*** *fpl* ***del*** **~** quadrivials
quadro I *m* **1.** painting, picture; **~** ***a olio*** oil painting; ***collezione*** *f* ***di -i*** painting collection **2.** MATH square; ***il fante di -i*** the jack of diamonds; ***a -i*** check *attr* **3.** *fig* ***nel*** **~** ***di*** as part of **4.** **~** (***sinottico***) table; **~** ***di comando*** control panel **5.** ***-i*** *pl* ***direttivi*** senior executives, senior management *sg* **6.** ***legge*** *f* **~** draft law **II** *adj* square
quadrupede *m* quadruped
quadruplicare *v/t* ⟨1m & d⟩ quadruple **quadruplicarsi** *v/r* ⟨1m & d⟩ quadruple
quadruplice *adj* fourfold
quadruplo *m/adj* quadruple
quaggiù *adv* down here
quaglia *f* quail
qualche *adj* a few; (*un certo*) some; *interrogativo* any; ***rimango*** **~** ***giorno*** I'm staying for a few days; **~** ***giorno usciamo insieme*** we'll go out some day; **~** ***cosa*** something; **~** ***volta*** sometime; *alcune volte* a few times; *a volte* sometimes; ***in*** **~** ***luogo*** somewhere; **~** ***mese fa*** a few months ago; ***in*** **~** ***modo*** somehow
qualcheduno *pron* someone, somebody
qualcosa *pron* something; *interrogativo* anything, something; ***qualcos'altro*** something else; **~** ***da mangiare*** something to eat; **~** ***di bello*** something beautiful
qualcuno *pron* someone, somebody; *in interrogazioni a.* anyone, anybody; ***qualcun'altro*** someone *or* somebody else; ***c'è*** **~*****?*** (is) anybody *or* anyone home?
quale I *adj* what; **~** ***libro vuoi?*** which book do you want?; ***città*** **~** ***Roma*** cities like Rome **II** *pron*: ***prendi un libro – ~?*** take a book – which one?; ***il / la*** **~** *persona* who, that; *cosa* which, that; ***la persona della*** **~** ***stai parlando*** the person you're talking about **III** *adv* as; ***è tale e*** **~** ***suo padre*** he's just like his father
qualifica *f* ⟨*pl* -che⟩ qualification; **~** ***professionale*** profession
qualificabile *adj* qualifiable
qualificare *v/t* ⟨1m & d⟩ qualify; (*definire*) describe
qualificarsi *v/r* give one's name (***come*** as); *a esame, gara* qualify; SPORTS **~** ***per la finale*** get through to the final
qualificato *adj* qualified
qualificazione *f* qualification
qualità *f* ⟨*pl* qualità⟩ quality; ***merce*** *f* ***di prima*** **~** top quality goods *pl*; **~** ***della vita*** quality of life; ***in*** **~** ***di*** as; JUR in the capacity of
qualitativamente *adv* qualitatively
qualitativo *adj* qualitative
qualora *cj* in the event that
qualsiasi *adj* any; *non importa quale* whatever; **~** ***persona*** anyone; **~** ***cosa faccia*** whatever I do
qualunque *adj* any; ***uno*** **~** any one; **~** ***cosa*** anything; **~** ***cosa faccia*** whatever I do; ***in*** **~** ***stagione*** whatever the season; ***l'uomo*** **~** the man in the street
qualunquismo *m pej* indifferentism
qualunquista *m/f* ⟨*mpl* -i⟩ *someone who's indifferent to or sceptical about*

politics
qualvolta *cj*: ***ogni ~*** every time that
quando *adv* when; ***per ~?*** when?; ***da ~?*** how long?; ***fino a ~*** until; ***~ vengo*** when I come; *ogni volta che* whenever I come; ***di ~ in ~*** now and then, from time to time
quantificare *v/t* ⟨1d & n⟩ quantify
quantificazione *f* quantification
quantità *f* ⟨*pl* quantità⟩ quantity, amount
quantitativo *m* quantity, amount
quanto I *adj* how much; *con nomi plurali* how many; ***tutto ~ il libro*** the whole book; ***tutti -i*** *pl* every single one *sg*; ***-i ne abbiamo oggi?*** what is the date today?, what is today's date? **II** *adv*: ***~ dura ancora?*** how long will it go on for?; ***~ a me*** as for me; ***~ costa?*** how much is it?; ***~ prima*** as soon as possible; ***in ~*** since, because; ***per ~ ne sappia*** as far as I know; ***non tanto ... ~ ...*** not so much ..., as ...; ***rimani pure ~ vuoi*** please stay as long as you wish; ***~ mai*** more than ever before **III** *m*: ***teoria*** *f* ***dei -i*** quantum theory
quantomeno *adv* at least
quantunque *cj* although
quaranta *num* forty
quarantena *f* quarantine
quarantenne I *adj* forty or so **II** *m/f* person in his/her forties
quarantesimo *m/adj* fortieth
quarantina *f*: ***essere sulla ~*** be about forty
quarantotto *m*: ***successe un ~*** all hell broke loose
quaresima *f* Lent
quaresimale *adj* Lent
quarta *f* AUTO fourth (gear); *fig* ***partire in ~*** get off to a flying start
quartetto *m* MUS quartet
quartiere *m* district; MIL quarters *pl*; ***~ generale*** headquarters *pl*; ***~ residenziale*** residential area; ***-i*** *pl* ***alti*** higher districts; *fig* exclusive quarters
quartina *f* LIT quatrain; MUS quadruplet **quartino** *m* quarter; *infml* tipple
quarto I *adj* fourth **II** *m* fourth; (*quarta parte*) quarter; ***~ d'ora*** quarter of an hour; ***sono le due e un ~*** it's (a) quarter past two; ***un ~ di rosso*** a quarter-litre (*US* liter) of red; ***-i di finale*** quarter-finals; *fig* ***passare un brutto ~ d'ora*** have an unpleasant quarter of an hour
quarzo *m* quartz; ***orologio*** *m* ***al ~*** quartz watch
quasi *adv* almost; ***~ mai*** hardly ever
quassù *adv* up here
quaterna *f nel lotto*: set of four numbers
quaternario *adj* ⟨*mpl* -ri⟩ GEOL Quaternary
quatto *adj* squatting; ***~ ~*** on the quiet; ***avanzare ~ ~*** to prowl
quattordicenne *m/f* fourteen-year-old
quattordicesimo *m/adj* fourteenth
quattordici *num* fourteen
quattrini *mpl* money *sg*, cash *sg*; ***guadagnare fior di ~*** earn a bomb
quattro *num* four; ***il ~ (di) maggio*** (on) the fourth of May; ***al ~ per cento*** at four per cent; ***in ~ e quattr'otto*** in less than no time; ***a quattr'occhi*** in private; ***fare ~ chiacchiere con qn*** have a chat with s.o.; ***fare ~ passi*** go for a stroll; ***farsi in ~ per fare qc*** go to a lot of trouble to do sth; ***farsi in ~ per qn*** bend over backwards for s.o.
quattrocchi *m* ⟨*pl* quattrocchi⟩: ***a ~*** in private
quattrocento I *num* four hundred **II** *m*: ***il Quattrocento*** the fifteenth century
quattromila *num* four thousand
quegli, quei → ***quello***
quello I *adj* that, *pl* those **II** *pron* that (one), *pl* those (ones); ***~ che*** the one that; ***tutto ~*** all that; ***tutto ~ che*** all (that), everything (that); ***chi è ~?*** who's that?; ***per quel che ne so io*** as far as I know
querceto *m* oak-wood
quercia *f* ⟨*pl* -ce⟩ oak
querela *f* legal action; ***sporgere ~ contro qc*** take legal action against s.o., sue s.o.; ***~ per diffamazione*** action for slander
querelante I *adj* complaining **II** *m/f* JUR plaintiff
querelare *v/t* ⟨1a⟩ sue, take legal action against
quesito *m* question
questi → ***questo***
questionario *m* ⟨*pl* -ri⟩ questionnaire
questione *f* question; ***~ sociale*** social question; ***~ di fiducia*** question *or*

matter of trust; ***qui non è ~ di*** it is not a question *or* matter of; ***è ~ di fortuna*** it's a matter of luck; ***è fuori ~*** it is out of the question; ***mettere qc in ~*** cast doubt on sth; ***il caso in ~*** the case in point; ***questa è un'altra ~*** it's another / a different matter

questo I *adj* this, *pl* these; ***quest'oggi*** today **II** *pron* this (one), *pl* these (ones); ***~ qui*** this one here; ***con ~*** with that; ***per ~*** for that reason; ***quest'oggi*** today; ***-a poi!*** well I'm blowed!; ***ci mancherebbe anche -a !*** that's all we'd need!; ***-a non me l'aspettavo*** I wasn't expecting this; ***senti -a !*** (you) never!

questore *m chief of police*

questuante *adj* begging; ***frate m ~*** mendicant friar

questura *f offices of the chief of police*

questurino *m infml* cop

qui *adv* here; ***di ~*** from here; ***~ vicino*** near here; ***fin ~*** up to here; ***passa di ~!*** come this way!; ***vieni ~*** come here; ***voglio uscire di ~*** I want to get out of here; ***di ~ a un mese*** a month from now, in a month's time; ***fuori di ~!*** get out of here!; ***tutto ~?*** is that all?

quietanza *f* receipt; ***per ~*** paid

quietare *v/t* ⟨1b⟩ calm (down); (*rabbonire*) appease; (*appagare*) appease **quietarsi** *v/r* ⟨1b⟩ calm (down); (*zittirsi*) shut up; *vento* abate

quiete *f* peace and quiet; ***turbare la ~ pubblica*** disturb the peace

quieto *adj* quiet; ***per amore del ~ vivere*** for the sake of peace

quindecismo *m/adj* fifteenth

quindi I *adv* then **II** *cj* therefore

quindicenne *m/f* fifteen-year-old

quindici *num* fifteen; ***tra ~ giorni*** in two weeks (time), *Br* in a fortnight('s time)

quindicina *f*: ***una ~*** about fifteen; ***una ~ di giorni*** about two weeks, *Br* about a fortnight

quinquennale I *adj* five-year **II** *m* fifth anniversary

quinta *f* AUTO fifth (gear); THEAT ***le -e*** the wings; *fig* ***dietro le -e*** behind the scenes

quintale *m* hundred kilos; ***mezzo ~*** fifty kilos

quintessenza *f* quintessence (*a. fig*)

quintetto *m* quintet (*a. fig*); ***~ d'archi*** string quintet

quinto *m/adj* fifth

quintuplo I *adj* fivefold **II** *m* quintuple

qui pro quo *m* ⟨*pl* qui pro quo⟩ equal exchange

quiz *m* ⟨*pl* quiz⟩ quiz

quorum *m* ⟨*pl* quorum⟩ quorum

quota *f* **1.** (*parte*) share, quota **2.** (*altitudine*) altitude; ***perdere ~*** lose altitude; ***prendere ~*** gain altitude

quotare *v/t* ⟨1c⟩ (*valutare*) value; FIN ***azioni** pl **quotate in borsa*** shares listed *or* quoted on the Stock Exchange

quotato *adj* respected

quotazione *f di azioni* value, price; ***~ d'acquisto*** bid price; ***~ di vendita*** offer price

quotidianamente *adv* daily

quotidianità *f* ⟨*pl* quotidianità⟩ everyday life **quotidiano I** *adj* daily **II** *n*: ***quotidiano** m* daily (paper)

quotidiano I *adj* daily **II** *m* daily (newspaper)

quoziente *m*: ***~ d'intelligenza*** IQ

R

r, R *m/f* ⟨*pl* r, R⟩ r, R; ***R come Roma*** R for Romeo

R. *abbr* (= **raccomandata**) recorded delivery, *US* certified mail

RA *abbr* (= **Ravenna**) Ravenna

rabarbaro *m* rhubarb

rabberciare *v/t* ⟨1f⟩ patch up (*a. fig*)

rabbia *f* rage; (*stizza*) anger; MED rabies *sg*; ***accesso** m **di ~*** fit of rage; ***fare ~ a qn*** make s.o. cross; ***che ~!*** how irritating!

rabbino *m* rabbi

rabbiosamente *adv* angrily

rabbioso *adj gesto*, *sguardo* of rage;

cane rabid

rabbonire *v/t* ⟨4d⟩ calm down

rabbonirsi *v/r* ⟨4d⟩ calm down

rabbrividire *v/i* ⟨4d⟩ shudder; *per paura* shiver

rabbuffo *m* scolding

rabbuiarsi *v/r* ⟨1i⟩ get dark, darken; *fig* darken

rabdomante *m/f* dowser

racc. *abbr* (= **raccomandata**) recorded delivery, *US* certified mail

raccapezzarsi *v/r* ⟨1a⟩ figure out

raccapricciante *adj* appalling, sickening

raccapriccio *m* horror

raccattapalle *m/f pl* raccattapalle⟩ *m* ballboy; *f* ballgirl

raccattare *v/t* ⟨1a⟩ (*tirar su*) pick up

racchetta *f* racquet; ***~ da sci*** ski pole

racchia *f* hideously ugly woman

racchiudere *v/t* ⟨3b⟩ contain

racchiudersi *v/r* ⟨3b⟩ close up

raccogliere *v/t* ⟨3ss⟩ (*tirar su*) pick up; (*radunare*) gather, collect; AGR harvest; ***~ i frutti di qc*** reap the benefits of sth

raccogliersi *v/r* ⟨3ss⟩ (*riunirsi*) assemble; (*rannicchiarsi*) curl up; ***~ in preghiera*** collect oneself in prayer; ***~ i capelli*** put one's hair up

raccoglimento *m* contemplation

raccoglitore *m* ring binder; ***~ del vetro*** bottle bank

raccolgo → ***raccogliere***

raccolta *f* collection; AGR harvest; ***~ differenziata*** separate waste collection; ***~ dell'uva*** grape harvest; ***~ di frutta*** fruit picking; ***~ di poesie*** poetry anthology; ***~ vetro*** glass recycling bin; ***chiamare a ~*** summon (up); ***fare ~ di francobolli*** collect stamps

raccolto **I** *past part* → ***raccogliere*** **II** *m* harvest; (*fase*) harvesting

raccomandabile *adj*: ***un tipo poco ~*** a shady character

raccomandare ⟨1a⟩ **I** *v/t* recommend **II** *v/i*: ***~ a qn di fare qc*** tell s.o. to do sth; ***~ a qn la puntualità*** urge s.o. to be on time; ***~ l'anima a Dio*** commend one's soul to God

raccomandarsi *v/r* ⟨1a⟩ urge; ***~ a qn*** implore s.o.; ***mi raccomando!*** be careful!

raccomandata *f* recorded delivery (letter), *US* certified mail; ***~ con ricevuta di ritorno*** letter *or* parcel that has to be signed for

raccomandato *adj* recommended; *lettera* sent by recorded delivery

raccomandazione *f* recommendation

raccontare *v/t* ⟨1a⟩ tell; ***~ per filo e per segno*** tell in great detail; ***che mi racconti?*** what's up?

racconto *m* short story

raccorciare *v/t* ⟨1f⟩ shorten; (*tagliare*) cut **raccorciarsi** *v/r* ⟨1f⟩ grow / become shorter

raccordo *m* TECH connection; *strada* slip road; ***~ anulare*** ring road; ***~ autostradale*** junction

racemo *m* ART rinceau; BOT raceme

rachitico *adj* ⟨*mpl* -ci⟩ scrawny

rachitismo *m* rickets

racimolare *v/t* ⟨1l⟩ gather

racket *m* ⟨*pl* racket⟩ racket

rada *f* roads *pl*, roadstead

radar *m* ⟨*pl* radar⟩ radar; ***impianto*** *m* ~ radar installation; ***uomini*** *pl* ~ air traffic controllers

raddolcimento *m* sweetening; *fig* softening

raddolcire *v/t* ⟨4d⟩ sweeten; *fig* soften

raddolcirsi *v/r di aria* grow milder; *di carattere* mellow

raddoppiare *v/t* ⟨1k⟩ double; *sforzi* redouble

raddoppio *m* ⟨*pl* -ppi⟩ redoubling; MUS double

raddrizzamento *m* straightening; *fig* remedy

raddrizzare *v/t* ⟨1a⟩ straighten

raddrizzarsi *v/r* straighten up

radere *v/t* ⟨3b⟩ shave; *sfiorare* skim; ***~ al suolo*** raze (to the ground)

radersi *v/r* shave

radiale **I** *adj* MATH, PHYS radial **II** *f* radial **radialmente** *adv* radially

radiare *v/t* ⟨1k⟩ strike off; ***~ dall'albo professionale*** strike off (the professional register)

radiatore *m* radiator

radiazione *f* radiation

radica *f* ⟨*pl* -che⟩ *per le pipe* briar; ***~ di noce*** walnut root

radical chic *adj inv* radical chic

radicale *m/adj* radical; ***-i pl liberi*** free radicals

radicalismo *m* radicalism **radicalità** *f* ⟨*pl* radicalità⟩ radicality

radicalizzare *v/t* ⟨1a⟩ radicalize; *dive-*

nire become more radical **radicalizzarsi** *v/r* ⟨1a⟩ become (more) radical **radicalizzazione** *f* radicalization
radicalmente *adv* radically
radicamento *m* BOT radication; *radici* rooting **radicare** *v/i* ⟨1l & d⟩ take (root) **radicarsi** *v/r* ⟨1l & d⟩ take (root); *fig* catch on
radicato *adj* deep-rooted
radicchio *m* ⟨*pl* -cchi⟩ chicory
radice *f* root; *~ **quadrata*** square root; ***mettere -i*** put down roots
radio *f* ⟨*pl* radio⟩ radio; (*stazione*) radio station; ***alla ~*** on the radio; ***giornale*** *m* *~* (radio) news *sg*; ***via ~*** by radio; ***ascoltare la ~*** listen to the radio
radioamatore *m*, **-trice** *f* radio ham
radioascoltatore *m*, **-trice** *f* (radio) listener
radioattività *f* radioactivity
radioattivo *adj* radioactive
radiocomandato *adj* radio-controlled
radiocronaca *f* (radio) commentary
radiocronista *m/f* ⟨*mpl* -i⟩ (radio) commentator
radiodramma *m* ⟨*pl* -i⟩ (radio) play
radiofonico *adj* radio *attr*
radiogoniometro *m* radiogoniometer; *infml* direction-finder
radiografare *v/t* ⟨1a⟩ MED X-ray; *fig* analyse
radiografia *f* x-ray
radiografico *adj* ⟨*mpl* -ci⟩: ***esame*** *m* *~* x-ray
radiolina *f* (transistor) radio
radiologia *f* radiology (*a.* MED) *f*; (*reparto*) radiology ward **radiologico** *adj* ⟨*mpl* -ci⟩ radiological **radiologo** *m*, **-a** *f* ⟨*mpl* -gi⟩ radiologist
radiomobile *f* radio car
radioregistratore *m* radio cassette recorder
radioricevente *f* radio receiver
radioscopia *f* radioscopy **radioscopico** *adj* ⟨*mpl* -ci⟩ radioscopic
radioso *adj* radiant
radiosveglia *f* clock radio
radiotaxi *m* ⟨*pl* radiotaxi⟩ taxi, cab
radiotelefono *m* radio
radiotelegrafista *m/f* ⟨*mpl* -i⟩ radio operator
radioterapia *f* radiation treatment
radiotrasmittente *f* *apparecchio* radio transmitter; *stazione* radio station
rado *adj* *pettine* wide-toothed; *alberi*, *capelli* sparse; ***di ~*** seldom
radunare *v/t* ⟨1a⟩ collect, gather
radunarsi *v/r* collect, gather
raduno *m* rally
radura *f* glade; *spazio* clearing
rafano *m* horseradish
raffazzonato *adj* (*rozzo*) rough; (*negativo*) crude; (*vestito*) patched-up; (*con disinteresse*) slapdash
raffermo *adj* *pane* stale
raffica *f* ⟨*pl* -che⟩ gust; *di mitragliatrice* burst; *fig* ***una ~ di domande*** a stream of questions
raffigurare *v/t* ⟨1a⟩ represent
raffigurazione *f* (*prodotto*) portrayal; (*azione*) portraying
raffinare *v/t* ⟨1a⟩ refine
raffinarsi *v/r* ⟨1a⟩ refine / become refined (*a. fig*)
raffinatezza *f* refinement; ***gli piacciono le -e*** he likes the finer things in life
raffinato *adj* *fig* refined
raffinazione *f* refining
raffineria *f* refinery
rafforzamento *m* strengthening; (*consolidamento*) consolidation
rafforzare *v/t* ⟨1c⟩ strengthen
rafforzarsi *v/r* ⟨1c⟩ strengthen / get stronger
rafforzato *adj* strengthened; ***cooperazione*** *f* ***-a*** EU reinforced cooperation
raffreddamento *m* cooling; *~ **ad acqua*** water cooling
raffreddare *v/t* ⟨1a⟩ cool
raffreddarsi *v/r* cool down; MED catch cold
raffreddato *adj* *fig*: ***essere molto ~*** have a very bad cold
raffreddore *m* cold; *~ **da fieno*** hay fever
raffrontare *v/t* ⟨1a⟩ compare **raffronto** *m* comparison
rafting *m* SPORTS rafting
rag. *abbr* (= **ragioniere**) accountant
ragadi *fpl* MED rhagades
raganella *f* rattle
ragazza *f* girl; ***la mia ~*** my girlfriend; *~ **alla pari*** au pair; ***nome*** *m* ***da ~*** maiden name; *~ **madre*** young unmarried mother
ragazzaccio *m*, **-a** *f* ⟨*mpl* -cci⟩ naughty boy **ragazzata** *f* prank **ragazzino** *m*, **-a** *f* little boy
ragazzo *m* boy; ***il mio ~*** my boyfriend;

da ~ as a boy
raggelante *adj* chilling **raggelare** *v/t* ⟨1a⟩ freeze; *fig* chill **raggelarsi** *v/r* ⟨1a⟩ freeze; *fig* chill
raggiante *adj* radiant
raggiera *f* rays; ***a ~*** radial
raggio *m* ⟨*pl* -ggi⟩ **1.** ray; ***~ d'azione*** range; ***ad ampio ~*** wide-range / wide-ranging; ***nel ~ di cento metri*** within a hundred-metre radius; *fig* duties *pl*, responsibilities *pl*; ***~ di sole*** ray of sunshine; ***-i*** *pl* ***X*** x-rays; ***-i*** *pl* ***infrarossi / ultravioletti*** infrared / ultraviolet rays **2.** MATH radius
raggirare *v/t* ⟨1a⟩ fool, take in
raggiro *m* trick
raggiungere *v/t* ⟨3d⟩ *luogo* reach, get to; *persona* join; *scopo* achieve; ***~ la meta*** achieve one's aim; ***ti raggiungo subito*** I'll be right with you
raggiungibile *adj* accessible, (*obiettivo*) attainable; *fig* reachable **raggiungimento** *m* attainment
raggomitolare *v/t* ⟨1n⟩ wind *or* roll into a ball
raggomitolarsi *v/r* curl up
raggranellare *v/t* ⟨1a⟩ scrape together
raggrinzire ⟨4d⟩ **I** *v/t* wrinkle **II** *v/i* wrinkle
raggrinzito *adj* wrinkled
raggrumato *adj* curdled; (*rappreso*) clotted
raggruppamento *m* grouping; *gruppo* group
raggruppare *v/t* ⟨1a⟩ group (together)
raggrupparsi *v/r* combine
ragguagliare *v/t* ⟨1g⟩: ***~ qn su qc*** brief s.o. on sth; *infml* give s.o. a run-down on sth **ragguaglio** *m* ⟨*pl* -gli⟩ run-down
ragguardevole *adj* noteworthy
ragionamento *m* reasoning; ***errore*** *m* ***di ~*** error of logic
ragionare *v/i* ⟨1a⟩ reason; ***~ di*** talk about, discuss; ***che modo di ~ è questo?*** this is pure nonsense!; *fig* ***~ con i piedi*** reason like an idiot; ***cerca di ~!*** try and be reasonable
ragionato *adj* reasoned; (*logico*) logical; (*ponderato*) well-thought; (*razionale*) rational; (*sensato*) reasonable; ***bibliografia*** *f* ***-a*** annotated bibliography
ragione *f* **1.** reason; ***ragion per cui ...*** which is why; ***la ragion di Stato*** reason of State; ***a ragion veduta*** after due consideration; ***a maggior ~*** all the more so; ***in ~ di qc*** at a rate of; ***per -i di salute*** for health reasons; ***senza ~*** for no reason; ***darle / prenderle di santa ~*** give s.o. a good thrashing / get a sound thrashing; ***devi fartene una ~*** get over sth **2.** (*diritto*) right; ***aver ~*** be right; ***dare ~ a qn*** admit that s.o. is right; ***a ~, con ~*** rightly **3.** ***~ sociale*** company name
ragioneria *f* book-keeping; EDU *high school specializing in business studies*
ragionevole *adj* reasonable
ragionevolezza *f* reasonableness
ragionevolmente *adv* reasonably
ragioniere *m*, **-a** *f* accountant
ragliare *v/i* ⟨1g⟩ bray **raglio** *m* ⟨*pl* -gli⟩ bray
ragnatela *f* spider's web
ragno *m* spider; ***non cavare un ~ dal buco*** get nowhere; ***Uomo Ragno*** *m* Spiderman
ragù *m* ⟨*pl* ragù⟩ *meat sauce for pasta*
ragusano I *adj* Ragusan **II** *m*, **-a** *f* person from Ragusa
RAI, RAI-TV *abbr* (= **Radio Televisione Italiana**) *Italian state radio and television*
raid *m* ⟨*pl* raid⟩ MIL raid (*a. fig*)
rallegramenti *mpl* congratulations *pl*
rallegrare *v/t* ⟨1a⟩ cheer up, brighten up
rallegrarsi *v/r* cheer up, brighten up; ***~ con qn di qc*** congratulate s.o. on sth
rallentamento *m* slowdown
rallentare *v/t* ⟨1b⟩ slow down; *fig* ***~ il lavoro*** ease off in one's work
rallentatore *m*: ***al ~*** in slow motion
rally *m* ⟨*pl* rally⟩ rally
RAM *abbr* (**Rand Access Memory**) COMPUT RAM; ***disco*** *m* ***~*** RAM disk
ramaglia *f* brushwood
ramaio *m*, **-a** *f* ⟨*mpl* -ai⟩ coppersmith
ramaiolo *m* ladle
ramanzina *f* lecture, telling-off; ***fare una ~ a qn*** tell s.o. off
ramarro *m* ZOOL green lizard
ramato *adj colore* copper-colo(u)red; *filo* copper; *zolfo* copper sulphate
ramazza *f* broom
rame *m* copper; ***incisione*** *f* ***su ~*** copper-plate
ramengo *m*: ***andare a ~*** go to wrack and ruin, go to the dogs; ***mandare***

a ~ send to wrack and ruin
ramificarsi *v/r* ⟨1m & d⟩ *di fiume* branch
ramificazione *f* ramification
ramingo *adj* ⟨*mpl* -ghi⟩ wandering; ***andare ~ per il mondo*** go wandering around the world; ***vita*** *f* ***-a*** roving life
ramino *m* (*gioco*) rummy
rammaricare *v/t* ⟨1m & d⟩ disappoint
rammaricarsi *v/r* be disappointed (***di*** at)
rammarico *m* ⟨*pl* -chi⟩ regret
rammendare *v/t* ⟨1a⟩ darn
rammendo *m* darn
rammentare *v/t* ⟨1n⟩ recall
rammentarsi *v/r* remember
rammolito *adj pej* spineless
rammollimento *m* softening (*a.* MED); *fig* relaxing
rammollire *v/t & v/i* ⟨4d⟩ soften
rammollirsi *v/r* ⟨4d⟩ become soft
ramo *m* branch
ramoscello *m* twig
rampa *f* flight; ***~ di carico*** loading ramp; ***~ d'accesso*** slip road; ***~ di lancio*** launch(ing) pad
rampante *adj* climbing; *fig* high-flying
rampicante I *adj* climbing; ***pianta*** *f* ***~*** climber **II** *m* climber
rampino *m* hook
rampogna *f* reproach
rampollo *m* offshoot (*a. fig*)
rampone *m* crampon
rana *f* frog; *nuoto* breaststroke; ***uomo*** *m* ***~*** frogman; ***nuotare a ~*** do the breaststroke
ranch *m* ⟨*pl* ranch⟩ ranch
rancido *adj* rancid
rancio *m* ⟨*pl* -ci⟩ MIL (mess) rations
rancore *m* ranco(u)r; ***senza ~*** with no hard feelings
randa *f* NAUT mainsail
randagio *adj* ⟨*mpl* -gi⟩ stray; ***cane*** *m* ***~*** stray
randellata *f* blow with a cudgel
randello *m* club
random *adj inv*: ***accesso*** *m* ***~*** COMPUT random access
rango *m* ⟨*pl* -ghi⟩ rank; ***di alto ~*** high-ranking; ***rientrare nei -ghi*** fall in, fall into line
rannicchiarsi *v/r* ⟨1k⟩ huddle up
rannuvolamento *m* clouding over
rannuvolarsi *v/r* ⟨1m⟩ cloud over
ranocchio *m* ⟨*pl* -cchi⟩ frog
rantolante *adj* wheezy
rantolare *v/i* ⟨1l⟩ wheeze
rantolo *m* wheeze
ranuncolo *m* BOT buttercup
rap *m* rap; ***musica ~*** rap music
rapa *f* turnip; *hum* ***testa*** *f* ***di ~*** blockhead
rapace I *m* bird of prey **II** *adj fig* predatory; ***uccello*** *m* ***~*** bird of prey; ***animali*** *mpl* ***-i*** predators
rapacità *f* ⟨*pl* rapacità⟩ rapaciousness
rapare *v/t* ⟨1a⟩ shave
raparsi *v/r* ⟨1a⟩ shave one's head
raperonzolo *m* rampion
rapida *f* rapids *pl*
rapidamente *adv* quickly
rapidità *f* speed, rapidity
rapido I *adj* quick, fast; *crescita*, *aumento* rapid **II** *m* (***treno*** *m*) ***~*** intercity train
rapimento *m* abduction, kidnap(p)ing
rapina *f* robbery
rapinare *v/t* ⟨1a⟩ rob; ***~ una banca*** rob a bank
rapinatore *m*, **-trice** *f* robber
rapire *v/t* ⟨4d⟩ abduct, kidnap
rapitore *m*, **-trice** *f* abductor, kidnap(p)er
rappacificare *v/t* ⟨1n & d⟩ reconcile
rappacificarsi *v/r* make up
rappacificazione *f* reconciliation
rapper *m/f* ⟨*pl* rapper⟩ rapper
rappezzare *v/t* ⟨1b⟩ patch; *fig discorso*, *articolo* cobble together
rappezzo *m* patch
rapportare *v/t* ⟨1c⟩ compare, relate
rapportarsi *v/r* ⟨1c⟩: ***~ a qc*** refer to sth
rapporto *m* **1.** *resoconto* report **2.** *relazione* relationship; *nesso* connection, link; ***~ d'affari*** business relation; ***~ d'amicizia*** friendship; ***~ epistolare*** correspondence; ***~ giuridico*** JUR privity; ***-i*** *pl* ***interpersonali*** personal relationships; ***~ protetto*** safe sex; ***~ sessuale*** sexual relationship; ***aver -i con*** have sex with; ***avere -i*** *pl* ***di lavoro con qn*** be a colleague of s.o., work with s.o.; ***in ~ a*** in connection with; ***chiamare qn a ~*** debrief s.o.; ***essere in buoni -i con qn*** be on good terms with s.o.; ***le due cose sono in ~*** the two things are related *or* connected
rapprendersi *v/r* ⟨3d⟩ *salsa* thicken; *sangue* clot; *grasso* congeal
rappresaglia *f* ⟨*pl* -glie⟩ reprisal

rappresentabile *adj* THEAT performable
rappresentante *m/f* representative
rappresentanza *f* agency; **~ *esclusiva*** sole agency; ***spese*** *fpl* ***di ~*** expenses for entertainment
rappresentare *v/t* ⟨1b⟩ represent; THEAT perform
rappresentativo *adj* typical, representative
rappresentazione *f* representation; THEAT performance
rappreso I *adj salsa* thickened; *sangue* clotted; *grasso* congealed; ***latte*** *m* **~** curdled milk **II** *past part* → ***rapprendersi***
rapsodia *f* rhapsody
raptus *m* ⟨*pl* raptus⟩ raptus
raramente *adv* rarely
rarefarsi *v/r* ⟨3aa⟩ become thinner
rarefatto *adj* rarefied
rarefazione *f* rarefaction
rarità *f* ⟨*pl* rarità⟩ rarity
raro *adj* rare; *fig* ***bestia*** *f* ***-a*** queer fish
rasare *v/t* ⟨1a⟩ shave
rasarsi *v/r* shave; **~ *la testa a zero*** shave one's head
rasato *adj* shaved; TEX satin; ***maglia*** *f* ***-a*** stocking stitch
rasatura *f* shaving
raschiamento *m* MED curettage
raschiare *v/t* ⟨1k⟩ scrape; *ruggine*, *sporco* scrape off
raschiarsi *v/r*: **~ *la gola*** clear one's throat
raschietto *m* scraper
rasentare *v/t* ⟨1b⟩ (*sfiorare*) scrape; *fig* (*avvicinarsi*) verge on; **~ *il muro*** hug the wall; **~ *il ridicolo*** verge on the ridiculous
rasente *adj*: **~ *a*** very close to; ***camminare ~ il muro*** hug the wall
raso[1] **I** *adj* (*rasato*) shaven; (*liscio*) flat; ***cucchiaio*** *m* **~** level spoonful **II** *past part* → ***radere***
raso[2] *m* satin
rasoio *m* ⟨*pl* -oi⟩ razor; **~ *di sicurezza*** safety razor; **~ *elettrico*** electric razor
rasoterra I *adj inv* low **II** *m* ⟨*pl* rasoterra⟩ SPORTS low shot
raspa *f* rasp
raspare *v/t* ⟨1a⟩ scratch
raspo *m* cluster
rassegna *f* **1.** festival **2.** *di pittura etc* exhibition; **~ *di moda*** fashion show **3. ~ *stampa*** review of the papers **4.** ***passare in ~*** review
rassegnare *v/t* ⟨1a⟩: **~ *un mandato*** resign from a post; **~ *le dimissioni*** hand in one's resignation
rassegnarsi *v/r* ⟨1a⟩ resign o.s (***a*** to)
rassegnato *adj* resigned
rassegnazione *f* resignation
rasserenamento *m* brightening (*a. fig*)
rasserenante *adj* comforting
rasserenare *v/t* ⟨1a⟩ calm down
rasserenarsi *v/r di cielo*, *tempo* clear up
rassettare *v/t* ⟨1b⟩ (*riordinare*) tidy up; (*accomodare*) mend
rassettarsi *v/r* ⟨1b⟩ tidy oneself up
rassicurante *adj* reassuring
rassicurare *v/t* ⟨1a⟩ reassure
rassicurarsi *v/r* feel reassured
rassodamento *m* toning up; *fig* strengthening
rassodare *v/t* ⟨1c⟩ tone up; *fig* strengthen
rassodarsi *v/r* ⟨1c⟩ tone up; *fig* strengthen
rassomigliante *adj* similar
rassomiglianza *f* resemblance
rassomigliare *v/i* ⟨1g⟩: **~ *a*** look like, resemble
rassomigliarsi *v/r* look like *or* resemble each other
rastrellamento *m* MIL combing
rastrellare *v/t* ⟨1b⟩ rake; *fig* comb
rastrelliera *f* rack; PHOT print drying rack; **~ *per biciclette*** bike rack
rastrello *m* rake
rata *f* instal(l)ment; ***a -e*** in instal(l)ments; **~ *qc a rate*** buy sth on hire purchase *or US* the installment plan
ratatouille *f* ⟨*pl* ratatouille⟩ ratatouille
rateale *adj*: ***pagamento*** *m* **~** payment in insta(l)lments; ***vendita*** *f* **~** hire purchase, *US* installment plan
rateizzare *v/t* ⟨1a⟩ divide into instal(l)ments
rateizzazione *f* division into instal(l)ments
rateo *m*: **~ *d'interesse*** FIN accrued interest
ratifica *f* ⟨*pl* -che⟩ ratification
ratificare *v/t* ⟨1m & d⟩ ratify
ratto[1] *m* ZOOL rat
ratto[2] *m* (*rapimento*) JUR abduction; ***il ~ delle Sabine*** the rape of the Sabine

women
rattoppare *v/t* ⟨1c⟩ patch
rattoppo *m* patch
rattrappimento *m* contraction
rattrappire *v/i* ⟨4d⟩ go stiff
rattrappirsi *v/r* ⟨4d⟩ go stiff
rattrappito *adj* stiff
rattristare *v/t* ⟨1a⟩ sadden, make sad
rattristarsi *v/r* become sad
raucedine *f* hoarseness
rauco *adj* ⟨*mpl* -chi⟩ hoarse
ravanello *m* radish
raveggiolo *m* *Tuscan cream cheese made from goat's and sheep's milk*
ravennate **I** *adj* from Ravenna **II** *m/f* person from Ravenna
ravioli *mpl* ravioli *sg*
ravvedersi *v/r* ⟨2s⟩ mend one's ways
ravvedimento *m* reformation
ravviare *v/t* ⟨1h⟩ tidy up
ravviarsi *v/r* ⟨1h⟩ tidy oneself up; ***~ i capelli*** comb one's hair
ravvicinamento *m* approach; *fig* reconciliation
ravvicinare *v/t* ⟨1a⟩ move closer; *fig* (*confrontare*) compare; (*riappacificare*) reconcile
ravvicinarsi *v/r* draw near, draw nearer
ravvisabile *adj* recognizable
ravvisare *v/t* ⟨1a⟩ recognize
ravvivare *v/t* ⟨1a⟩ rekindle (*a. fig*); *colori* revive; ***~ il fuoco*** make up the fire
ravvivarsi *v/r* ⟨1a⟩ rekindle
rayon *m* ⟨*pl* rayon⟩ TEX rayon
raziocinante *adj* rational
raziocinio *m* ⟨*pl* -ni⟩ reasoning
razionale *adj* rational
razionalista ⟨*mpl* -i⟩ **I** *adj* rationalist **II** *m/f* rationalist
razionalistico *adj* ⟨*mpl* -ci⟩ rationalistic
razionalità *f* rationality
razionalizzare *v/t* ⟨1a⟩ rationalize
razionalizzazione *f* rationalization (*a.* PSYCH, MATH)
razionalmente *adv* rationally
razionamento *m* rationing
razionare *v/t* ⟨1a⟩ ration
razione *f* ration
razza *f* race; *fig* sort, kind; ZOOL breed; *fig* ***che ~ di …?*** *pej* what kind of …?; ***animale*** *m* ***di ~*** pedigree; (*cavallo*) thoroughbred
razzia *f* raid
razziale *adj* racial
razziare *v/t* ⟨1h⟩ steal
razzismo *m* racism
razzista *m/f & adj* ⟨*mpl* -i⟩ racist
razzo *m* rocket; ***come un ~*** like greased lightning, like a bat out of hell
razzolare *v/i* ⟨1l⟩ scratch around
RC *abbr* (= **Reggio Calabria**) Reggio Calabria
re *m* ⟨*pl* re⟩ **1.** king; ***i Re Magi*** the Three Wise Men, the Magi **2.** MUS D; ***~ maggiore / minore*** D major / minor
reagente *m* reagent
reagire *v/i* ⟨4d⟩ react (***a*** to)
reale *adj vero* real; *regale* royal
realismo *m* realism
realista *m/f* ⟨*mpl* -i⟩ realist
realistico *adj* ⟨*mpl* -ci⟩ realistic
reality *m* ⟨*pl* reality⟩ reality TV show
realizzabile *adj* feasible
realizzare *v/t* ⟨1a⟩ carry out
realizzarsi *v/r di sogno* come true; *di persona* find o.s., find fulfilment
realizzazione *f* fulfilment; (*cosa realizzata*) achievement
realizzo *m* ECON return
realmente *adv* really
realtà *f* ⟨*pl* realtà⟩ reality; ***in ~*** in fact, actually; ***~ virtuale*** virtual reality
reame *m* realm
reatino **I** *adj* from Rieti **II** *m*, **-a** *f* person from Rieti
reato *m* (criminal) offence (*US* offense); ***-i pl minori*** minor offences
reattività *f* ⟨*pl* reattività⟩ CHEM reactivity; PHYS, PSYCH responsiveness
reattivo *adj* responsive; CHEM reactive
reattore *m* AVIAT jet engine; *aereo* jet; ***~ nucleare*** nuclear reactor
reazionario ⟨*mpl* -ri⟩ **I** *adj* reactionary **II** *m*, **-a** *f* reactionary
reazione *f* reaction
rebbio *m* ⟨*pl* -bbi⟩ prong
rebus *m* ⟨*pl* rebus⟩ puzzle
recalcitrante *adj* reluctant
recalcitrare *v/i* ⟨1m⟩ ZOOL kick; *fig* balk
recapitare *v/t* ⟨1m⟩ deliver
recapito *m* delivery; (*indirizzo*) address; ***~ telefonico*** phone number
recare *v/t* ⟨1d⟩ *portare* bring; *arrecare* cause
recarsi *v/r* go

recedere *v/i* ⟨2a⟩ back out; **~ *da un contratto*** withdraw from a contract

recensione *f* review

recensire *v/t* ⟨4d⟩ review

recensore *m*, **-sitrice** *f* reviewer, critic

recente *adj* recent; ***di* ~** recently

recentemente *adv* recently

recepire *v/t* ⟨4d⟩ acknowledge; JUR absorb

reception *f* ⟨*pl* reception⟩ reception

receptionist *m/f* ⟨*pl* receptionist⟩ receptionist

recessione *f* ECON recession

recesso *m fig* depth; JUR withdrawal; MED recess

recidere *v/t* ⟨3q⟩ cut off

recidersi *v/r* ⟨3q⟩ be severed

recidiva *f* JUR second offence, *US* offense; MED relapse

recidività *f* ⟨*pl* recidività⟩ recidivism

recidivo I *adj* JUR habitual; MED recurring **II** *m*, **-a** *f* JUR recidivist; MED relapser

recintare *v/t* ⟨1a⟩ enclose

recinto *m* enclosure; *per animali* pen, enclosure; *steccato* fence

recinzione *f* enclosure

recioto *m* COOK *a sweet red wine from the Veneto*

recipiente *m* container

reciprocamente *adv* mutually, reciprocally

reciprocità *f* ⟨*pl* reciprocità⟩ mutuality, reciprocity

reciproco *adj* ⟨*mpl* -ci⟩ mutual, reciprocal

recita *f* performance

recitare ⟨1l & b⟩ **I** *v/t* recite; THEAT play (the part of); *preghiera* say **II** *v/i* act

recitativo *m* recitative

recitazione *f* recitation; (*arte*) drama; (*spettacolo*) acting

reclamare ⟨1a⟩ **I** *v/i* complain **II** *v/t* claim

réclame *f* ⟨*pl* réclame⟩ advert

reclamizzare *v/t* ⟨1a⟩ advertise

reclamizzazione *f* advertising

reclamo *m* complaint

reclinabile *adj* reclining

reclinare *v/t* ⟨1m⟩ *testa* bow; *sedile* recline

reclusione *f* seclusion

recluso *m*, **-a** *f* prisoner

recluta *f* recruit

reclutamento *m* recruitment

reclutare *v/t* ⟨1a⟩ recruit

recondito *adj* hidden, remote (*a. fig*)

record *m* ⟨*pl* record⟩ record; ***stabilire il* ~** set the record; ***a tempo di* ~** in record time

recriminare *v/i* ⟨1m⟩ recriminate; **~ *su qc*** drag up sth

recriminazione *f* recrimination

recrudescenza *f di malattia, violenza* fresh outbreak; *di conflitto* flare-up

recuperabile *adj* recoverable

recuperare *v/t* → ***ricuperare***

recupero *m* → ***ricupero***

redarguire *v/t* ⟨4d⟩ reprimand

redatto *past part* → ***redigere***

redattore *m*, **-trice** *f* editor; *di articolo* writer; **~ *capo*** editor-in-chief

redazione *f* editorial staff; *di articolo* writing

redditizio *adj* ⟨*mpl* -zi⟩ profitable

reddito *m* income; **~ *annuo*** annual income; ***dichiarazione*** *f* ***dei -i*** income tax return; ***imposta*** *f* ***sul* ~** income tax

redento *past part* → ***redimere***

Redentore *m* REL Redeemer

redenzione *f* REL redemption

redigere *v/t* ⟨3oo⟩ *testo, articolo* write; *lista* draw up

redimere *v/t* ⟨3pp⟩ REL redeem

redimersi *v/r* ⟨3pp⟩ redeem oneself; **~ *dal peccato*** redeem oneself from sin

redimibile *adj* redeemable (*a.* JUR)

redingote *f* ⟨*pl* redingote⟩ frock coat; *da donna* coat dress

redini *fpl* reins *pl*

redivivo *adj* restored to life

reduce *m/f* ex-serviceman

refe *m* twist; (*filo*) yarn

referendario ⟨*mpl* -ri⟩ **I** *adj* referendum *attr* **II** *m*, **-a** *f* JUR, ADMIN referendary

referendum *m* ⟨*pl* referendum⟩ referendum

referente I *adj* reporting **II** *m/f* point of reference; LING referent

referenza *f* reference

referenziale *adj* referential

referto *m* (official) report

refettorio *m* ⟨*pl* -ri⟩ refectory

refill *m* ⟨*pl* refill⟩ refill

reflex *f* ⟨*pl* reflex⟩ reflex

refluo *adj* refluent; ***acque*** *fpl* ***-e*** sewage

reflusso *m* MED reflux
refolo *m* gust of wind
refrattarietà *f* ⟨*pl* refrattarietà⟩ refractoriness (*a.* MED)
refrattario *adj materiale* refractory; *~ **al lavoro** iron* not cut out for work
refrigerante *adj* cooling
refrigerare *v/t* ⟨1m⟩ refrigerate
refrigeratore **I** *m* refrigerator; (*freezer*) freezer **II** *adj* refrigerating
refrigerio *m* ⟨*pl* -ri⟩ coolness
refurtiva *f* stolen property
refuso *m* misprint, typo
regalare *v/t* ⟨1a⟩ give; ***regalarsi qc*** treat o.s. to sth
regale *adj* regal
regalino *m* gift, present, little something *infml*
regalità *f* ⟨*pl* regalità⟩ regality
regalo *m* gift, present; ***articolo*** *m* ***da ~*** gift; ***~ di compleanno / di Natale*** birthday / Christmas present
regata *f* (boat) race
reggente **I** *adj* governing; (*sostituto*) regent **II** *m/f* regent
reggenza *f* regency
reggere ⟨3cc⟩ **I** *v/t* (*sostenere*) support; (*tenere in mano*) hold; (*sopportare*) bear; GRAM take; ***~ il confronto*** stand comparison; *fig* ***~ il moccolo*** play gooseberry; *fig* ***~ l'anima coi denti*** hang on for dear life; *fig* ***~ il sacco a qn*** aid and abet s.o. **II** *v/i di tempo* last; *di ragionamento* stand up; *fig* ***non reggo più*** I can't take any more; ***non ~ l'alcol*** not hold one's drink
reggersi *v/r* stand; ***non ~ in piedi*** not be able to stand up; ***reggiti forte!*** hold tight!
reggia *f* ⟨*pl* -gge⟩ palace
reggiano **I** *adj* from Reggio Emilia **II** *m*, **-a** *f* person from Reggio Emilia
reggicalze *m* ⟨*pl* reggicalze⟩ suspender belt
reggimento *m* regiment; *fig* crowd
reggino **I** *adj* from Reggio Calabria **II** *m*, **-a** *f* person from Reggio Calabria
reggipetto *m*, **reggiseno** *m* bra, *US* brassiere
regia *f* direction
regime *m* régime; MED diet; ***~ alimentare*** diet; ***~ patrimoniale*** property system; MED ***essere a ~*** be on a diet
regina *f* queen
reginetta *f*: ***~ di bellezza*** beauty queen
regio *adj* ⟨*mpl* -gi⟩ royal
regionale *adj* regional
regione *f* region; ***~ a statuto speciale*** *Italian region that has some autonomy under a special statute*
regista *m/f* ⟨*mpl* -i⟩ director
registrare *v/t* ⟨1a⟩ *in un registro* enter, record, register; *rilevare* show, register; *canzone*, *messaggio* record
registrato *adj* registered; (*inciso*) recorded; ***marchio*** *m* ***~*** registered trademark
registratore *m*: ***~*** (***a cassetta***) cassette recorder; ***~ a nastro*** tape recorder; ***~ di cassa*** cash register
registrazione *f* recording
registro *m* register; ECON ***~ delle imprese*** Companies House; *fig* ***cambiare ~*** change one's tune
regnante **I** *adj* reigning; *fig* dominant **II** *m/f* sovereign
regnare *v/i* ⟨1a⟩ reign
regno *m* kingdom; *periodo* reign; ***Regno Unito*** United Kingdom
regola *f* rule; ***in ~*** in order; ***di ~*** as a rule; ***fatto a ~ d'arte*** done expertly; ***le -e del gioco*** the rules of the game; ***avere le carte in ~ per qc*** *infml* meet the requirements for sth
regolabile *adj* adjustable
regolabilità *f* ⟨*pl* regolabilità⟩ adjustability
regolamentare[1] *adj* regulation *attr*
regolamentare[2] *v/t* ⟨1a⟩ regulate
regolamentazione *f* regulations *pl*
regolamento *m* regulation; ***~ comunitario*** JUR EEC regulations; ***~ dei conti*** settling of accounts
regolare **I** *v/t* ⟨1l & b⟩ regulate; *spese*, *consumo* cut down on; TECH adjust; *questione* sort out, settle; *conto*, *debito* settle **II** *adj* regular
regolarità *f* ⟨*pl* regolarità⟩ regularity
regolarizzare *v/t* ⟨1a⟩ *situazione* sort out, put in order
regolarizzazione *f* regularization
regolarmente *adv* regularly
regolarsi *v/r* act; ***~ secondo qc*** behave according to sth; ***non sapere come ~*** not know how to act; ***~ nel mangiare / nel bere*** watch what one eats / one drinks
regolata *f*: ***darsi una ~*** *infml* pull one's socks up
regolato *adj* regulated

regolatore I *adj* regulating; ***piano*** *m* **~** land use **II** *n*: ***regolatore*** *m* regulator
regolazione *f* adjustment (*a.* TECH)
regolo *m* ruler; BUILD rule; **~ *calcolatore*** slide rule, *US* slide ruler
regredire *v/i* ⟨4d⟩ regress
regressione *f* regression
regressivo *adj* regressive
regresso *m* regression; ***azione*** *f* ***di*** **~** JUR action of recourse
reietto *adj* rejected
reiezione *f* JUR rejection
reimpiego *m* ⟨*pl* -ghi⟩ *di capitali* re-investment; *di personale* re-employment
reimportazione *f* reimport
reincarnare *v/t* ⟨1a⟩: **~ *qn*** be just like s.o.
reincarnarsi *v/r* ⟨1a⟩ be reincarnated
reincarnazione *f* reincarnation
reinserimento *m* reintegration
reinserire *v/t* ⟨4d⟩ reintegrate
reinserirsi *v/r* ⟨4d⟩ become reintegrated
reintegrare *v/t* ⟨1m⟩: **~ *qn in una carica*** reinstate s.o. in a position
reintegrarsi *v/r* ⟨1m⟩ become reintegrated
reintegrazione *f* ECON restoration; ADMIN reinstatement
reinvestire *v/t* ⟨4d⟩ reinvest
reiterare *v/t* ⟨1m⟩ repeat
reiteratamente *adv* repeatedly
relata *f*: **~ *di notifica*** official notification certificate
relativamente *adv* relatively
relatività *f* relativity; ***teoria*** *f* ***della*** **~** theory of relativity
relativizzare *v/t* ⟨1a⟩ relativize
relativo *adj* relative (***a*** to); (*corrispondente*) relevant
relatore *m*, **-trice** *f* speaker
relax *m* relaxation
relazione *f* **1.** *legame* relationship; ***avere una*** **~ *con qn*** have an affair *or* a relationship with s.o.; ***in*** **~ *a*** with reference to; ***-i pubbliche*** public relations, PR **2.** *esposizione* report; ***presentare una*** **~** present a report
relegare *v/t* ⟨1e⟩ (*esiliare*) banish; *fig* relegate
religione *f* religion
religiosa *f* nun
religiosamente *adv* religiously
religiosità *f* religion
religioso I *adj* religious; ***comunità*** *f* ***-a*** religious community; ***festa*** *f* ***-a*** religious festival; ***funzione*** *f* ***-a*** religious service **II** *m* monk
reliquia *f* relic (*a. fig*)
reliquiario *m* ⟨*pl* -ri⟩ reliquary
relitto *m* wreck
remare *v/i* ⟨1b⟩ row
rematore *m*, **-trice** *f* rower
reminiscenza *f* reminiscence
remissione *f*: **~ *di un debito*** remittal of a debt; **~ *dei peccati*** remission of sins; **~ *della pena*** remission of sentence; **~ *di una malattia*** remission of an illness
remissività *f* ⟨*pl* remissività⟩ submissiveness
remissivo *adj* submissive
remo *m* oar
remora *f* scruple; ***non avere -e*** have no hesitation
remoto *adj* remote; ***passato*** *m* **~** GRAM past historic
remunerare *v/t* ⟨1m⟩ pay
remunerativo *adj* remunerative, well-paid; ***non*** **~** unpaid
remunerazione *f* payment, remuneration
rena *f* sand
renale *adj* kidney *attr*, renal; ***blocco*** *m* **~** kidney failure
Renania *f* Rhineland
renano I *adj* (*del Reno*) Rhine *attr*, Rhenish; (*della Renania*) Rhinelandish **II** *m*, **-a** *f* Rhinelander
rendere *v/t* ⟨3c⟩ *restituire* give back, return; *fruttare* yield; *senso*, *idea* render; **~ *un servizio a qn*** do s.o. a favo(u)r; **~ *conto a qn di qc*** account to s.o. for sth; **~ *felice*** make happy; ***a buon*** **~** my turn next; **~ *difficile / facile qc*** make sth difficult / easy; **~ *grazie (a Dio)*** say grace; **~ *merito a qn*** bless s.o.; **~ *onore a qn*** hono(u)r s.o.; **~ *un servizio a qn*** repay s.o.'s kindness; ***non rende molto*** it doesn't bring in a lot; ***rendo l'idea?*** have I got it across?; ***vuoto*** *m* ***a*** **~** returnable bottle
rendersi *v/r* ⟨3c⟩ make oneself; **~ *simpatico / utile*** be nice / make oneself useful; **~ *conto di qc*** appreciate sth, realize sth
rendiconto *m* report; COMM account
rendimento *m di macchina*, *impiegato*

performance; ~ ***giornaliero*** daily output *or* production

rendita *f* income; ~ ***catastale*** cadastral rent; ~ ***vitalizia*** annuity; ***vivere di*** ~ have private means

rene *m* kidney; ~ ***artificiale*** kidney machine

renetta *adj*: ***mela*** *f* ~ rennet

renitente *adj* reluctant

renitenza *f* reluctance

renna *f* ZOOL reindeer

Reno *m* Rhine; ***la valle del*** ~ the Rhine valley

reo *m*, **-a** *f* JUR offender; ~ ***confesso*** self-confessed criminal

reparto *m di impresa, grande magazzino* department; *di ospedale* ward; ~ ***d'isolamento*** isolation ward

repellente *adj* revolting; *fig* repulsive

repellenza *f* repellence

repentaglio *m*: ***mettere a*** ~ risk, endanger

repentino *adj* sudden

reperibile *adj* available; ***difficilmente*** ~ difficult to find

reperibilità *f* ⟨*pl* reperibilità⟩ *di persona, prodotto*: availability

reperimento *m* search

reperire *v/t* ⟨4d⟩ find

repertare *v/t* ⟨1a⟩ find; JUR exhibit

reperto *m* find; JUR exhibit

repertorio *m* ⟨*pl* -ri⟩ THEAT, MUS repertory

replay *m* ⟨*pl* replay⟩ replay

replica *f* ⟨*pl* -che⟩ (*copia*) replica; TV repeat; THEAT repeat performance; (*risposta*) answer, response; ***il suo tono non ammette -che*** his tone of voice leaves no room for discussion

replicante *m/f* android

replicare *v/t* ⟨1l, b & d⟩ *ripetere* repeat; *ribattere* reply, answer

reportage *m* ⟨*pl* reportage⟩ report

reporter *m/f* ⟨*pl* reporter⟩ reporter, journalist

repressione *f* repression

repressivo *adj* repressive

represso *past part* → ***reprimere***

reprimere *v/t* ⟨3r⟩ repress

reprimersi *v/r* restrain o.s.

reprobo *adj* reprobate

repubblica *f* ⟨*pl* -che⟩ republic

Repubblica Ceca *f* Czech Republic

Repubblica Centrafricana *f* Central African Republic

Repubblica Democratica del Congo *f* Democratic Republic of the Congo

Repubblica Dominicana *f* Dominican Republic

repubblicano *adj* republican

Repubblica Sudafricana *f* Republic of South Africa

repulisti *m*: ***far*** ~ clean everything out

repulsione *f* repulsion

repulsivo *adj* PHYS repulsive (*a. fig*)

reputare *v/t* ⟨1l & b⟩ consider, deem

reputarsi *v/r* consider o.s.

reputazione *f* reputation

requie *f* peace; ***non trovare*** ~ not find a moment's peace

requiem *m* ⟨*pl* requiem⟩ requiem (*a.* MUS)

requisire *v/t* ⟨4d⟩ requisition

requisito *m* requirement

requisitoria *f closing speech from public prosecutor*; *fig* lecture

requisizione *f* requisition

resa *f* surrender; *restituzione* return; ~ ***incondizionata*** unconditional surrender; ~ ***dei conti*** settling of accounts

rescindere *v/t* ⟨3mm⟩: ~ ***un contratto*** terminate a contract

rescissione *f* termination

rescisso *past part* → ***rescindere***

resezione *f* MED resection

residence *m* ⟨*pl* residence⟩ block of service flats (*US* apartments)

residente I *adj* resident **II** *m/f*: ***solo per -i*** residents only

residenza *f* (official) address; *sede* seat; *soggiorno* stay; ***cambiamento*** *m* ***di*** ~ change of address; ~ ***protetta*** sheltered housing

residenziale *adj* residential; ***zona*** *f* ~ residential area

residuato *m*: ~ ***bellico*** war surplus

residuo *m* remainder

resina *f* resin

resinoso *adj* resinous

resistente *adj* sturdy, strong; ~ ***al fuoco*** fire-resistant

resistenza *f* resistance; *instancabilità* stamina

Resistenza *f* Resistance

resistere *v/i* ⟨3f⟩ *al freddo etc* stand up to; *opporsi* resist; ***non resisto più*** I can't take any more

reso *past part* → ***rendere***

resoconto *m* report

respingente *m* buffer, *US* bumper
respingere *v/t* ⟨3d⟩ *richiesta*, *pretendente* reject, turn down; *nemico*, *attacco* repel
respinto *past part* → ***respingere***
respirabile *adj* breathable
respirare ⟨1a⟩ **I** *v/t* breathe (in) **II** *v/i* breathe; *fig* draw breath
respiratore *m* respirator; *per apnea* snorkel
respirazione *f* breathing; ~ ***artificiale*** artificial respiration; ~ ***bocca a bocca*** mouth-to-mouth resuscitation
respiro *m* breathing; ***di ampio*** ~ wide-ranging; ***trattenere il*** ~ hold one's breath; *fig* ***un attimo di*** ~ a moment's rest; ***fare un*** ~ ***di sollievo*** breathe a sigh of relief
responsabile *adj* responsible (***di*** for); JUR liable (***di*** for)
responsabilità *f* ⟨*pl* responsabilità⟩ responsibility; JUR liability; ~ ***civile*** civil liability; ~ ***limitata*** limited liability; ~ ***penale*** JUR criminal liability; ***assumersi la*** ~ ***di qc*** / ***per qn*** take on *o* accept responsibility for sth / s.o.
responsabilizzare *v/t* ⟨1a⟩: ~ ***qn*** give s.o. a sense of responsibility
responsabilizzarsi *v/r* ⟨1a⟩ take on responsibilities
responso *m*: ~ ***della giuria*** jury's verdict
ressa *f* crowd
restante **I** *adj* left over, remaining **II** *m* rest
restare *v/i* ⟨1b⟩ stay, remain; *avanzare* be left; ~ ***indietro*** stay behind; ~ ***perplesso*** / ***vedovo*** be puzzled / widowed; ***restarci male*** be hurt; ~ ***alzato fino a tardi*** stay up late; ***non mi resta altro da fare*** there's nothing more for me to do
restaurare *v/t* ⟨1a⟩ restore
restauratore *m*, **-trice** *f* restorer
restauro *m* restoration; ***chiuso per -i*** closed for restoration
restio *adj* ⟨*mpl* -ii⟩ reluctant
restituire *v/t* ⟨4d⟩ return; *saluto* restore
restituzione *f* return
resto *m* rest, remainder; (*soldi*) change; ***-i*** *pl* remains; ***del*** ~ anyway, besides
restringere *v/t* ⟨3d⟩ narrow; *vestito*, *giacca* take in
restringersi *v/r* *di strada* narrow; *di stoffa* shrink
restringimento *m* *di strada* narrowing; *di stoffa* shrinking; MED contraction
restrittivo *adj* restrictive
restrizione *f* restriction
resurrezione *f* → ***risurrezione***
resuscitare *v/t* → ***risuscitare***
retaggio *m* ⟨*pl* -ggi⟩ legacy
retata *f* netful; *fig* raid; ***fare una*** ~ carry out a raid
rete *f* *per pescare etc* net; SPORTS goal; COMPUT, TEL, RAIL network; ~ ***autostradale*** road network; ~ ***commerciale*** business network; ~ ***civica*** COMPUT civic network; ~ ***locale*** COMPUT local area network, LAN; TEL ~ ***fissa*** land-line network; ~ ***metallica*** wire netting; ~ ***telefonica*** telephone network; ***calze a*** ~ fishnet stockings; COMPUT ***collegarsi in*** ~ connect to the Internet
reticella *f* string bag
reticente *adj* reticent
reticenza *f* reticence; JUR omission
retico ⟨*mpl* -ci⟩ **I** *adj* Rhaetic **II** *m*, **-a** *f* Rhaetian
reticolare *adj* reticular
reticolato *m* wire netting
reticolo *m* network, lattice
retina *f* ANAT retina
retorica *f* rhetoric; *pej* talk
retorico ⟨*mpl* -ci⟩ **I** *adj* rhetorical **II** *n*: ***retorico*** *m* rhetorician
retoromanzo **I** *adj* Rhaeto-Romanic **II** *n*: ***retoromanzo*** *m* Rhaeto-Romance
retribuire *v/t* ⟨4d⟩ pay
retribuzione *f* payment
retrivo *adj* reactionary
retro *m* back
retroattivo *adj* retroactive
retrobottega *m* ⟨*pl* retrobottega⟩ back shop
retrocedere *v/i* ⟨3l⟩ retreat; *fig* lose ground; SPORTS ~ ***in serie B*** be relegated to the second division
retrodatare *v/t* ⟨1a⟩ backdate
retrogrado *adj* reactionary
retroguardia *f* MIL rearguard; SPORTS defence, *US* defense
retromarcia *f* ⟨*pl* -ce⟩ AUTO reverse (gear); ***fare*** ~ reverse
retroscena *mpl* *fig* background *sg*

retrospettiva *f* retrospective
retrospettivo *adj mostra* retrospective
retroterra *m* 〈*pl* retroterra〉 hinterland
retrovia *f* MIL rear
retrovisivo *adj*: ***specchietto*** *m* **~** rear-view mirror
retrovisore *adj*: AUTO ***specchietto*** *m* **~** rear-view mirror
retta[1] *f somma* fee
retta[2] *f* MATH straight line
retta[3] *f*: ***dare ~ a qn*** listen to s.o.
rettangolare *adj* rectangular
rettangolo *m* rectangle
rettifica *f* 〈*pl* -che〉 correction
rettificare *v/t* 〈1m & d〉 correct
rettifilo *m* straight stretch of road
rettile *m* reptile
rettilineo *adj* straight
rettitudine *f* uprightness
retto I *adj* straight; (*probo*) upright; ***angolo*** *m* **~** right angle; ***la -a via*** the straight and narrow **II** *n*: ***retto*** *m* ANAT rectum **III** *past part* → ***reggere***
rettorato *m* rectorship
rettore *m* rector
rettoscopia *f* rectoscopy
reumatico *adj* 〈*mpl* -ci〉 rheumatic; ***i dolori*** *mpl* ***-ci*** rheumatic pain *sg*
reumatismo *m* rheumatism
reumatologia *f* rheumatology
reumatologico *adj* 〈*mpl* -ci〉 rheumatological
reumatologo *m*, **-a** *f* 〈*mpl* -gi〉 rheumatologist
revanscismo *m* revanchism
revanscista *m/f* 〈*mpl* -i〉 revanchist
reverendo *adj* Reverend; ***Reverendo!*** Reverend!
reversibile *adj* reversible; JUR, ECON reversionary
reversibilità *f* 〈*pl* reversibilità〉 reversibility; JUR, ECON reversion; ***pensione*** *f* ***di ~*** reversionary pension
revisionare *v/t* 〈1a〉 *conti* audit; AUTO MOT, put through the MOT test; *testo* revise
revisione *f di conti* audit; AUTO MOT; *di testo* revision
revisore *m*, **-a** *f* editor; ***~ dei conti*** auditor
revival *m* 〈*pl* revival〉 revival
revoca *f* 〈*pl* -che〉 repeal
revocabile *adj* revocable
revocare *v/t* 〈1l, b & d〉 repeal, revoke
revolver *m* 〈*pl* revolver〉 revolver
revolverata *f* shot (from a revolver)
RG *abbr* (= **Ragusa**) Ragusa
Rhodesia *f* Rhodesia
ri- *pref* (*di nuovo*, *indietro*) re-
R.I. *abbr* (= **Repubblica Italiana**) Italian Republic
riabilitare *v/t* 〈1n〉 rehabilitate
riabilitazione *f* rehabilitation
riabituarsi *v/r* 〈1l〉: ***~ a qc*** get used to sth again
riaccendere *v/t* 〈3c〉 light again; ELEC switch on again; *fig sentimento* rekindle, revive
riaccendersi *v/r* 〈3c〉 rekindle (*a. fig*)
riacciuffare *v/t* 〈1a〉 *infml* catch again
riaccompagnare *v/t* 〈1a〉 take *o* bring back
riacquistare *v/t* 〈1a〉 get back, regain; *casa* buy back
riacutizzarsi *v/r* 〈1a〉 *fig* worsen
riacutizzazione *f fig* worsening; MED flare-up
riaddormentarsi *v/r* 〈1〉 go back to sleep
riaffiorare *v/i* 〈1a〉 reappear (*a. fig*)
riagganciare *v/t* 〈1f〉 TEL hang up
riallacciare *v/t* 〈1f〉 refasten; TEL reconnect
rialzare *v/t* 〈1a〉 *alzare di nuovo* pick up; *aumentare* raise, increase
rialzo *m* rise, increase; ***essere in ~*** be on the rise; ***speculare al ~*** speculate on a rise
riamare *v/t* 〈1a〉: ***~ qn*** return s.o.'s love; (*amare di nuovo*) love s.o. again
riambientarsi *v/r* 〈1b〉 readjust
rianimare *v/t* 〈1m〉 *speranze*, *entusiasmo* revive; (*rallegrare*) cheer up; MED resuscitate
rianimarsi *v/r* revive
rianimazione *f* resuscitation; ***centro*** *m* ***di ~*** intensive care unit, ICU; ***reparto*** *m* ***di ~*** intensive care ward
riapertura *f* reopening
riaprire *v/t* 〈4f〉 reopen
riarmare *v/t* 〈1a〉 rearm
riarmo *m* rearmament
riassettare *v/t* 〈1b〉 tidy up
riassetto *m* tidy-up
riassicurare *v/t* 〈1a〉 JUR reinsure
riassicuratore *m*, **-trice** *f* JUR reinsurer
riassicurazione *f* JUR reinsurance
riassorbimento *m* reabsorption; *fig di*

manodopera re-employment; MED resorption
riassorbire *v/t* ⟨4d⟩ reabsorb; *fig* re-employ; MED reduce
riassorbirsi *v/r* ⟨4d⟩ be reabsorbed
riassumere *v/t* ⟨3h⟩ re-employ; (*riepilogare*) summarize; ***riassumendo*** to sum up
riassuntivo *adj* summarizing
riassunto **I** *past part* → ***riassumere*** **II** *m* summary
riassunzione *f* re-engagement
riattaccare *v/t* ⟨1d⟩ (*riagganciare*) *infml* hang up
riattivare *v/t* ⟨1m⟩ reopen
riattivazione *f* reactivation; MED stimulation
riavere *v/t* ⟨2b⟩ get back, regain; ***ho riavuto il raffreddore*** I've got another cold
riaversi *v/r* recover (***da*** from), get over (***da*** sth)
riavviare *v/t* ⟨1h⟩ COMPUT reboot
riavvicinamento *m* reapproaching; *fig* rapprochement
riavvicinare *v/t* ⟨1a⟩: ***~ qn*** bring s.o. closer together
riavvicinarsi *v/r* ⟨1a⟩ make up, become reconciled
riavvolgere *v/t* ⟨2m⟩ wrap up again
ribadire *v/t* ⟨4d⟩ *fig* reassert
ribaldo *m* rascal
ribalta *f* (drop-)leaf; THEAT apron stage; *fig* limelight; ***a ~*** folding, foldaway; ***luci*** *fpl* ***della ~*** footlights
ribaltabile *adj* folding
ribaltamento *m* folding; *di automezzo*: overturning; *fig* reversal
ribaltare ⟨1a⟩ **I** *v/t* overturn **II** *v/i di macchina, barca* turn over
ribaltone *m fig* reversal
ribassare ⟨1a⟩ **I** *v/t* lower **II** *v/i* fall, drop
ribasso *m* fall, drop; *sconto* discount; ***essere in ~*** be falling *or* dropping
ribattere ⟨3a⟩ **I** *v/t argomento* refute **II** *v/i* (*replicare*) answer back; (*insistere*) insist; ***~ a un'accusa*** deny an accusation
ribattezzare *v/t* ⟨1a⟩ rename
ribattino *m* rivet
ribellarsi *v/r* ⟨1b⟩ rebel (***a*** against)
ribelle **I** *adj* rebellious **II** *m/f* rebel
ribellione *f* rebellion
ribes *m* ⟨*pl* ribes⟩ currant; ***~ nero*** blackcurrant; ***~ rosso*** redcurrant
ribollire ⟨4a⟩ **I** *v/i* boil; ***~ d'ira*** seethe **II** *v/t* boil again
ribollita *f* COOK *Tuscan soup of beans, cabbage and bread that is reheated and eaten the day after it's cooked*
ribrezzo *m* horror; ***fare ~ a*** disgust
ributtante *adj* disgusting
ricacciare *v/t* ⟨1f⟩ *nemico* force back; ***~ le lacrime*** blink back tears
ricadere *v/i* ⟨2c⟩ fall; *cadere di nuovo* fall back; *fig* relapse
ricaduta *f* relapse
ricalcare *v/t* ⟨1d⟩ *cappello* pull down; *disegno* trace ***~ le orme di qn*** follow in s.o.'s footsteps
ricamare *v/t* ⟨1a⟩ embroider
ricamatrice *f* embroiderer
ricambiare *v/t* ⟨1k⟩ change; *contraccambiare* return, reciprocate
ricambio *m* change; (*sostituzione*) replacement; *pezzo* (spare) part; ***pezzo*** *m* ***di ~*** spare part
ricamo *m* embroidery
ricandidarsi *v/r* ⟨1l⟩ put oneself forward as a candidate again
ricapitalizzare *v/t* ⟨1a⟩ recapitalize
ricapitolare *v/t* ⟨1n⟩ sum up, recapitulate
ricapitolazione *f* recap
ricarica *f* ⟨*pl* -che⟩ refill; ***~ per stampanti*** printer cartridge; ***~ del cellulare*** recharging a mobile phone; ***~ dell'accendino*** refilling a cigarette lighter
ricaricabile *adj* rechargeable
ricaricare *v/t* ⟨1m & d⟩ *batteria* recharge; ***~ il telefonino*** recharge a mobile phone
ricaricarsi *v/r* ⟨1c & l⟩ recharge; *fig* recharge one's batteries
ricattabile *adj* liable to be blackmailed
ricattare *v/t* ⟨1a⟩ blackmail
ricattatore *m*, **-trice** *f* blackmailer
ricatto *m* blackmail
ricavare *v/t* ⟨1a⟩ derive; *denaro* get
ricavato *m di vendita* proceeds
ricavo *m* takings *pl*
ricchezza *f* wealth
ricciarello *m almond biscuits from Siena*
riccio[1] *m* ⟨*pl* -cci⟩ ZOOL hedgehog; BOT *spiny outer casing of the chestnut*; ***~ di mare*** sea urchin; ***chiudersi a ~*** shut up like a clam

riccio[2] ⟨*mpl* -cci⟩ **I** *adj* curly; ***capelli*** *mpl* ***-cci*** curly hair *sg* **II** *m* curl

ricciolo *m* curl; ***~ di burro*** curl of butter

riccioluto, **ricciuto** *adj capelli* curly; *persona* curly-haired

ricco ⟨*mpl* -cchi⟩ **I** *adj* rich, wealthy; ***~ di*** rich in; ***~ sfondato*** loaded **II** *m*, **-a** *f* rich *or* wealthy man / woman; ***i -cchi*** *pl* the rich; ***nuovi -cchi*** *pl* nouveaux riches

riccone *m*, **-a** *f* fat cat

ricerca *f* ⟨*pl* -che⟩ **1.** research; ***~ di mercato*** market research; ***~ nucleare*** nuclear research **2.** *di persona scomparsa*, *informazione etc* search (***di*** for); COMPUT ***~ nel testo completo*** full-text search; ***alla ~ di*** in search of **3.** EDU project

ricercare *v/t* ⟨1d⟩ (*cercare di nuovo*) look again for; (*cercare con cura*) search *or* look for

ricercatezza *f* refinement

ricercato **I** *adj oggetto*, *artista* sought--after **II** *m* man wanted by the police

ricercatore *m*, **-trice** *f* researcher

ricetrasmittente *f* transceiver

ricetta *f* prescription; COOK recipe

ricettacolo *m* receptacle; ***~ di polvere*** dust collector

ricettare *v/t* ⟨1b⟩ JUR receive, handle

ricettario *m* ⟨*pl* -ri⟩ MED prescription book; COOK recipe book

ricettatore *m*, **-trice** *f* JUR receiver

ricettazione *f* JUR receiving

ricettività *f* ⟨*pl* ricettività⟩ receptiveness; *fig* susceptibility; RADIO, TV receptivity

ricettivo *adj*: ***essere ~ a qc*** be responsive to sth

ricevente **I** *adj* receiving **II** *m/f* ADMIN recipient **III** *f* RADIO, TV receiver

ricevere *v/t* ⟨3a⟩ receive; *di medico* see patients; ***~ gente*** have guests

ricevimento *m* receipt; *festa* reception; ***giorno*** *m* ***di ~*** delivery day

ricevitore *m* receiver

ricevitoria *f* office; ***~ del lotto / totocalcio*** lottery / pools office

ricevuta *f* receipt; ***~ fiscale*** tax receipt; ***~ di versamento*** receipt of payment; ***accusare ~*** acknowledge receipt

ricezione *f* receipt; RADIO, TV, (*-accoglienza*) reception

richiamabile *adj* COMPUT recallable

richiamare *v/t* ⟨1a⟩ (*chiamare di nuovo*) call again; (*chiamare indietro*) call back; *attirare* draw; *fig rimproverare* rebuke, reprimand; ***~ l'attenzione di qn*** draw s.o.'s attention (***su*** to); ***~ qn all'ordine*** call s.o. to order

richiamarsi *v/r*: ***~ a*** refer to

richiamo *m* call; ADMIN reference; *fig* (*attrazione*) allure; (*ammonimento*) admonition; *caccia* decoy; MED booster; ***accorrere ai -i di qn*** respond to s.o.'s cries for help; ***~ alle armi*** call to arms; ***fare da ~*** act as a decoy (*a. fig*)

richiedente *m/f* applicant

richiedere *v/t* ⟨3k⟩ ask for again; (*necessitare di*) take, require; *documento* apply for

richiesta *f* request (***di qc*** for sth); FIN demand; ***a*** (*or* ***su***) ***~ di*** at the request of; ***più informazioni saranno disponibili su ~*** further information on request

richiesto **I** *past part* → ***richiedere*** **II** *adj*: ***molto ~*** much in demand, much sought after

riciclabile *adj* recyclable

riciclaggio *m* ⟨*pl* -ggi⟩ recycling

riciclare *v/t* ⟨1a⟩ recycle

riciclato *adj* recycled; ***carta*** *f* ***-a*** recycled paper

ricino *m* castor-oil plant; ***olio*** *m* ***di ~*** castor oil

ricognitivo *adj* JUR of acknowledgement

ricognitore **I** *m*, **-trice** *f* MIL reconnaissance **II** *m* reconnoit(e)rer

ricognizione *f* MIL reconnaissance; JUR acknowledgement; ***andare in ~*** reconnoitre, *US* reconnoiter

ricollegare *v/t* ⟨1e⟩ TECH ***~ qc a*** *or* ***con qc*** reconnect sth to sth; *fig* connect sth with sth

ricollegarsi *v/r* ⟨1e⟩ be connected; *fig* ***~ a qc*** refer to sth

ricolmo *adj* brimful

ricominciare *v/i* ⟨1f⟩ start again; ***~ da zero*** go back to square one

ricompattare *v/t* ⟨1a⟩ reconsolidate

ricompattarsi *v/r* ⟨1a⟩ be reconsolidated

ricompensa *f* reward

ricompensare *v/t* ⟨1b⟩ reward (***qn di qc*** s.o. for sth)

ricomporre *v/t* ⟨3ll⟩ rewrite; TEL redial; *fig* **~ *una lite*** go over a quarrel
ricomporsi *v/r* ⟨3ll⟩ compose oneself
ricomprare *v/t* ⟨1a⟩ repurchase, buy back
riconciliare *v/t* ⟨1g⟩ reconcile
riconciliarsi *v/r* make up
riconciliazione *f* reconciliation
riconducibile *adj* ascribable (***a*** to)
ricondurre *v/t* ⟨3e⟩ (*riportare*) take back (***a*** to); (*imputare*) attribute (***a*** to)
riconfermare *v/t* ⟨1a⟩ reconfirm; **~ *qn in una carica*** reappoint s.o. to a position
riconfermarsi *v/r* ⟨1a⟩ confirm oneself again; **~ *campione*** successfully defend one's championship
ricongiungere *v/t* ⟨3d⟩ rejoin
ricongiungersi *v/r* ⟨3d⟩ rejoin; *strade* meet
ricongiungimento *m* rejoining
riconoscente *adj* grateful; ***mostrarsi* ~** show one's gratitude
riconoscenza *f* gratitude; ***per* ~** out of gratitude
riconoscere *v/t* ⟨3n⟩ **1.** recognise; ***non si riconosce più*** he's unrecognisable **2.** *ammettere* acknowledge; ***riconosco che*** I admit that
riconoscibile *adj* recognizable
riconoscimento *m* recognition; COMPUT **~ *vocale*** voice recognition; **~ *di maternità / paternità*** legal recognition of a child; ***un segno** m **di* ~** a distinguishing mark
riconquistare *v/t* ⟨1a⟩ reconquer
riconsegnare *v/t* ⟨1a⟩ hand in *o* over again; COMM deliver again
ricontare *v/t* ⟨1a⟩ (*rifare i conti*) re-count
ricontrollare *v/t* ⟨1c⟩ check again, double-check
riconvenzionale *adj*: ***azione** f* **~** JUR counterclaim
riconversione *f* ECON reorganization
riconvertire *v/t* ⟨4b or 4d⟩ restructure
ricoperto *adj*: **~ *di qc*** covered with sth; **~ *di cioccolato*** chocolate-coated; **~ *di fiori*** covered in flowers
ricopiare *v/t* ⟨1h⟩ copy
ricoprire *v/t* ⟨4f & c⟩ cover; **~ *le poltrone con un telo*** cover the armchairs with a dust sheet; **~ *una carica*** hold a post; **~ *i bulbi*** cover up the bulbs; *fig* **~ *d'oro qn*** shower s.o. with gifts
ricoprirsi *v/r* ⟨4f & c⟩ become covered with
ricordare *v/t* ⟨1c⟩ remember; (*menzionare*) mention; **~ *qc a qn*** remind s.o. of sth; ***facile da* ~** easy to remember; ***non ricordo niente*** I can't remember anything
ricordarsi *v/r* remember (***di qc*** sth; ***di fare qc*** to do sth); ***ti ricordi di Franco?*** can you remember Franco?; ***ricordatevi di annaffiare i fiori*** remember to water the flowers
ricordino *m* souvenir
ricordo *m* memory; *oggetto* memento; **~ *di viaggio*** souvenir
ricorrente *adj* recurrent, recurring
ricorrenza *f* recurrence; *di evento* anniversary
ricorrere *v/i* ⟨3o⟩ **1.** *di date*, *di festa* take place, happen; ***oggi ricorre l'aniversario del nostro matrimonio*** today is our wedding anniversary **2. ~ *a qn*** turn to s.o.; **~ *a qc*** have recourse to sth
ricorso I *past part* → ***ricorrere*** **II** *m* JUR appeal; **~ *in appello*** JUR appeal; **~ *in cassazione*** JUR appeal to the Supreme Court; ***avere* ~ *a*** *avvocato*, *medico* see; ***avere* ~ *all'aiuto di qn*** ask for s.o.'s help; ***fare* ~ *a qc*** have recourse to sth; ***fare* ~ *a qn*** turn to s.o.; ***presentare* ~** appeal
ricostituente I *adj* restorative; ***cura** f* **~** restorative treatment **II** *m* tonic
ricostituire *v/t* ⟨4d⟩ restore
ricostituirsi *v/r* ⟨4d⟩ recover
ricostituzione *f* re-establishment
ricostruibile *adj* reconstructable (*a. fig*)
ricostruire *v/t* ⟨4d⟩ rebuild; *fig* reconstruct
ricostruzione *f* rebuilding; *fig* reconstruction
ricotta *f* ricotta, *soft cheese made from ewe's milk*; ***avere le mani di* ~** *infml* be a butter fingers
ricoverare *v/t* ⟨1m & c⟩ admit
ricoverarsi *v/r* ⟨1m & c⟩ take shelter; **~ *in ospedale*** go into hospital
ricoverato I *adj* admitted **II** *m*, **-a** *f in ospedale* patient
ricovero *m in ospedale* admission; (*refugio*) shelter

ricreare *v/t* ⟨1b⟩ recreate; (*ritemprare*) restore
ricrearsi *v/r* ⟨1b⟩ amuse oneself
ricreativo *adj* entertaining; ***attività*** *fpl* ***-e*** leisure pursuits
ricreazione *f* recreation; *nelle scuole* break, recreation, *US* recess
ricredersi *v/r* ⟨3a⟩ change one's mind; ***mi sono ricreduto sul suo conto*** I've changed my mind about him
ricrescere *v/i* ⟨3n⟩ grow again, regrow
ricucire *v/t* ⟨4d⟩ sew up; ***~ uno strappo*** stitch up a tear; *fig* ***~ i rapporti con qn*** repair one's relationship with s.o.
ricuperare ⟨1m⟩ **I** *v/t* get back, recover; *libertà, fiducia* regain; *spazio* gain; *tempo* make up; ***~ il tempo perso*** make up for lost time **II** *v/i* catch up
ricupero *m* recovery; ***~ del centro storico*** development of the old part of town; ***~ di debiti*** debt collection; EDU ***corso*** *m* ***di ~*** remedial course; ***materiale*** *m* ***di ~*** scrap; SPORTS ***partita*** *f* ***di ~*** rescheduled match
ricurvo *adj* bent, crooked
ricusare *v/t* ⟨1a⟩ refuse; JUR challenge
ricusazione *f* JUR challenge; ***~ del giudice*** objection to a judge
ridacchiare *v/i* ⟨1k⟩ giggle
ridanciano *adj* funny
ridare *v/t* ⟨1r⟩ *restituire* give back, return; *fiducia, forze* restore; ***dai e ridai*** *infml* try and try again
ridarella *f infml* fit of giggles
ridda *f*: ***una ~ di pensieri*** jumbled thoughts
ridente *adj paesaggio* delightful
ridere *v/i* ⟨3b⟩ laugh (***di*** at); ***far ~ di sé*** make a fool of o.s.; ***~ di cuore*** laugh heartily; ***far ~ i polli*** make a cat laugh; ***~ sotto i baffi*** laugh up one's sleeve; ***ma non farmi ~!*** don't make me laugh!; ***non c'è niente da ~*** it's no laughing matter; ***ridersela di qc*** laugh at sth
ridersi *v/r*: ***~ di qn*** laugh at s.o.; ***se la ride del parere degli altri*** he couldn't care less what people think
ridicolaggine *f* (*qualità*) absurdity; (*cosa ridicola*) nonsense
ridicolizzare *v/t* ⟨1a⟩ ridicule
ridicolo **I** *adj* ridiculous; ***rendersi ~*** make a fool of oneself **II** *m* ridicule; ***mettere qn in ~, gettare il ~ su qn*** ridicule s.o.
ridimensionamento *m* reorganization; ***~ dell'organico*** reduction in staff
ridimensionare *v/t* ⟨1a⟩ downsize; *fig* get into perspective
ridire *v/t* ⟨3t⟩ repeat; ***ha sempre da ~*** he / she always finds fault
ridisegnare *v/t* ⟨1a⟩ redraw; *fig* restructure
ridistribuire *v/t* ⟨4d⟩ reallocate; ECON redistribute
ridistribuzione *f* reallocation; ECON redistribution
ridondante *adj* superfluous
ridondanza *f* redundancy (*a.* COMPUT)
ridosso *m*: ***a ~ del muro*** behind the wall
ridotto **I** *past part* → ***ridurre*** **II** *adj* small; (*scontato*) reduced; ***~ a uno scheletro*** skin and bone; ***a prezzi -i*** at reduced prices; ***edizione*** *f* ***-a*** abridged edition; ***formato*** *m* ***~*** pocket edition
riduco → ***ridurre***
ridurre *v/t* ⟨3e⟩ reduce (***a*** to); *prezzi, sprechi* reduce, cut; *personale* reduce, cut back; ***~ al silenzio*** reduce to silence
ridursi *v/r* decrease, diminish; ***~ a fare qc*** be reduced to doing sth; ***~ male*** be in a bad way; ***~ in miseria*** ruin o.s.
riduttivo *adj* reductive
riduttore *m* MECH adapter; ***~ di tensione*** transformer
riduzione *f* reduction, cut; ***~ del personale*** staff cutbacks
riecheggiare *v/i* ⟨1a⟩ resound; *fig* echo
riedizione *f* revival (*a. fig*); *di film*: reissue
rieducare *v/t* ⟨1l⟩ rehabilitate; MED *membra* restore to normal functioning
rieducazione *f* rehabilitation; MED physiotherapy
rielaborare *v/t* ⟨1m⟩ revise
rielaborazione *f* revision; THEAT revival
rieleggere *v/t* ⟨3cc⟩ re-elect
rielezione *f* re-election
riempimento *m* filling; *di modulo* filling-in, filling-out
riempire *v/t* ⟨4g⟩ fill (up); *formulario*

fill in

riempirsi *v/r* stuff o.s.

rientranza *f* recess

rientrare *v/i* ⟨1a⟩ come back; *a casa* come home; ***questo non rientrava nei miei piani*** that was not part of the plan; ***non rientra nei tuoi compiti*** it doesn't fall within your brief; ***l'emergenza è rientrata*** the problem has recurred

rientro *m* return; ***al tuo ~*** when you get back

riepilogare *v/t* ⟨1m⟩ summarize

riepilogo *m* ⟨*pl* -ghi⟩ summary

riesame *m* reconsideration

riesaminare *v/t* ⟨1m⟩ reconsider, reassess

riesumare *v/t* ⟨1a⟩ exhume; *fig* unearth, uncover

rievocare *v/t* ⟨1m⟩: ***~ qc*** bring back sth; ***~ qn*** commemorate s.o.

rievocazione *f*: ***~ di qc*** reminder of sth

rifacimento *m* rebuilding; FILM, TV remake

rifare *v/t* ⟨3aa⟩ do again; (*rinnovare*) do up; *stanza* tidy (up); ***~ il letto*** make the bed

rifarsi *v/r* **1.** *casa* renovate; *guardaroba* replace; ***~ il seno / il naso*** have a boob / nose job *infml*; ***~ una vita*** rebuild one's life **2.** ***~ di qc*** make up for sth; ***~ delle spese*** recoup one's costs **3.** ***~ vivo*** reappear

riferibile *adj* (*ripetibile*) repeatable; (*ascrivibile*) ascribable

riferimento *m* reference; ***punto** m **di ~*** point of reference; ***con ~ a*** with reference to; ***fare ~ a qn / qc*** refer to s.o. / sth

riferire *v/t* ⟨4d⟩ report

riferirsi *v/r*: ***~ a*** refer to

riffa *f sort of raffle*

rifilare *v/t* ⟨1m⟩ trim; ***~ qc a qn*** palm sth off on s.o.; ***mi hanno rifilato un falso*** they slipped me a fake

rifinire *v/t* ⟨4d⟩ finish off

rifinitura *f* finishing; (*guarnizione*) finish; ***dare l'ultima ~*** make the finishing touches

rifiorire *v/i* ⟨4d⟩ reblossom; *fig* flourish again; *macchia* reappear

rifiutare *v/i* ⟨1a⟩ refuse

rifiutarsi *v/r* ⟨1a⟩ refuse

rifiuto *m* **1.** refusal **2.** ***-i*** *pl* waste *sg*, refuse *sg*; (*spazzatura*) rubbish *sg*; ***-i tossici*** toxic waste

riflessione *f* thought, reflection; PHYS reflection

riflessivo *adj* thoughtful; GRAM reflexive

riflesso **I** *past part* → ***riflettere*** **II** *m* reflection; (*gesto istintivo*) reflex (movement); ***di ~*** automatically; ***ho agito di ~*** it was a reflex action, I did it automatically; ***avere i -i pronti*** have quick reflexes

riflessologia *f* reflexology; ***~ plantare*** foot reflexology

riflettente *adj* reflective

riflettere ⟨3qq⟩ **I** *v/t* reflect **II** *v/i* think; ***~ su qc*** think about sth, reflect on sth

riflettersi *v/r* be reflected

riflettore *m* floodlight; *fig* ***trovarsi sotto i -i*** be under the spotlights

rifluire *v/i* ⟨4d⟩ flow again; *indietro* flow back

riflusso *m* ebb

rifocillare ⟨1a⟩ *v/t* feed

rifondazione *f* refoundation; ***Rifondazione Comunista*** *Italian political party of hardline communists*

riforma *f* reform; REL Reformation; ***~ monetaria*** monetary reform

riformare *v/t* ⟨1a⟩ (*rifare*) re-shape, re-form; (*cambiare*) reform; MIL declare unfit

riformato *adj* REL Reformed; MIL declared unfit

riformatore **I** *adj* reforming **II** *m*, **-trice** *f* reformer **III** *m* HIST, REL Reformer, *in the Middle Ages, a town magistrate who had the job of introducing reforms or new regulations*

riformatorio *m* young offenders' institution, *US* reform school

riformismo *m* reformism

riformista ⟨*pl* -i⟩ **I** *adj* reformist **II** *m/f* reformist

riformulare *v/t* ⟨1m⟩ rephrase

rifornimento *m* AVIAT refuelling; ***-i*** *pl* supplies, provisions; ***fare ~ di cibo*** stock up on food; ***fare ~ di benzina*** fill up

rifornire *v/t* ⟨4d⟩ *macchina* fill (up); *frigo* restock, fill (***di*** with); ***~ il magazzino*** restock

rifornirsi *v/r* stock up (***di*** on)

rifornitore *m*, **-trice** *f* supplier

rifrangente *adj* refractive

rifrangere *v/t* ⟨3d⟩ refract (*a.* PHYS)

rifrangersi *v/r* ⟨3d⟩ be refracted (*a.* PHYS)
rifrazione *f* refraction
rifuggire *v/i* ⟨4a⟩ *fig*: ***~ da qc*** shy away from sth
rifugiarsi *v/r* ⟨1f⟩ take refuge
rifugiato *m*, **-a** *f* refugee; ***~ politico*** political refugee
rifugio *m* ⟨*pl* -gi⟩ shelter; ***~ alpino*** mountain hut; ***~ antiaereo*** air-raid shelter
rifusione *f* refund; ***~ di un danno*** reimbursement for damages
riga *f* ⟨*pl* -ghe⟩ line; (*fila*) row; (*regolo*) rule; *in stoffa* stripe; *nei capelli* parting, *US* part; ***stoffa*** *f* ***a -ghe*** striped fabric
rigagnolo *m* gutter
rigare *v/t* ⟨1e⟩ rule; ***~ dritto*** *infml* toe the line; ***mi hanno rigato la macchina*** my car's been scratched
rigassificatore *m* regasification system
rigatino *m striped cotton or linen cloth*
rigato *adj* TYPO ruled; *stoffa* striped; ***viso*** *m* ***~ di lacrime*** tear-stained face
rigatoni *mpl* rigatoni *sg*
rigattiere *m*, **-a** *f infml* secondhand dealer
rigenerante *adj* regenerating
rigenerare *v/t* ⟨1m & b⟩ regenerate
rigenerarsi *v/r* be regenerated
rigenerativo *adj* regenerative
rigenerazione *f* regeneration
rigettare *v/t* ⟨1b⟩ *fig* (*respingere*) reject; *infml* (*vomitare*) vomit
rigetto *m* MED rejection; *fig* mental block
righello *m* ruler, rule
rigidamente *adv* rigidly; *camminare* stiffly; *fig* strictly
rigidità *f* ⟨*pl* rigidità⟩ rigidity
rigido *adj* (*duro*) rigid; *muscolo, articolazione* stiff; *clima* harsh; *fig*: *severo* strict
rigirare ⟨1a⟩ **I** *v/i* walk around **II** *v/t* turn over and over; *denaro* launder; ***~ il discorso*** change the subject; *fig* ***~ qc*** twist sth round; *fig* ***~ la frittata*** twist an argument; ***gira e rigira ...*** all things considered
rigirarsi *v/r* turn round; *nel letto* toss and turn
rigo *m* ⟨*pl* -ghi⟩ line; ***~ musicale*** staff, stave
rigoglio *m* ⟨*pl* -ii⟩ BOT luxuriance; *fig* bloom
rigoglioso *adj* lush, luxuriant
rigogolo *m* golden oriole
rigonfiamento *m* MED swelling, lump
rigonfio *adj* ⟨*mpl* -fi⟩ swollen; *fig* puffed up
rigore *m di clima* harshness; (*severità*) strictness; SPORTS (*a.* ***calcio*** *m* ***di ~***) penalty (kick); ***area*** *f* ***di ~*** penalty area; ***di ~*** compulsory
rigorosamente *adv* strictly
rigoroso *adj* rigorous
rigovernare *v/t* ⟨1b⟩ *stoviglie* wash
riguardante *adj* about, regarding
riguardare *v/t* ⟨1a⟩ look at again; (*rivedere*) review, look at; (*riferirsi*) be about, concern; ***per quanto riguarda ...*** as far as ... is concerned; ***non ti riguarda*** it's none of your business, it doesn't concern you
riguardarsi *v/r* take care of o.s.
riguardo *m* (*attenzione*) care; (*rispetto*) respect; ***mancanza*** *f* ***di ~*** lack of respect; ***di ~*** important; ***~ a*** as regards, about; ***senza ~*** carelessly
riguardoso *adj* respectful
rigurgitare ⟨1m⟩ **I** *v/i* overflow; *fig* ***~ di*** be packed with **II** *v/t* regurgitate
rigurgito *m di fogna, canale* overflow; (*vomito*) regurgitation; *fig* revival
rilanciare *v/t* ⟨1f⟩ throw again; *offensive* relaunch ***~ la palla*** throw the ball back; ***~ un'offerta*** make a higher bid
rilancio *m* ⟨*pl* -ci⟩: ***~ di una moda*** revival of a fashion; ***~ di un'offerta*** higher bid
rilasciare *v/t* ⟨1f⟩ release; *documento* issue
rilascio *m* release; *di passaporto* issue
rilassamento *m* relaxation
rilassare *v/i* ⟨1a⟩ relax
rilassarsi *v/r* ⟨1a⟩ relax
rilassato *adj* relaxed
rilegare *v/t* ⟨1e⟩ *libro* bind
rilegatore *m*, **-trice** *f* bookbinder
rilegatura *f* binding
rileggere *v/t* ⟨3cc⟩ reread, go over
rilento *adv*: ***a ~*** slowly
rilettura *f* rereading; (*reinterpretazione*) new reading
rilevamento *m* survey; ECON takeover; GEOL mapping; ***~ topografico*** survey
rilevante *adj* (*importante*) important; (*grande*) considerable

rilevanza *f* (*importanza*) importance; (*grandezza*) large size

rilevare *v/t* ⟨1b⟩ (*ricavare*) find; (*osservare*) note, notice; *ditta* acquire, buy up; ***far ~ qc a qn*** point sth out to s.o.; ***da quanto è successo si rileva che ...*** from what has happened, we can gather that ...

rilievo *m* relief; *fig* ***dare ~ a qc, mettere qc in ~*** emphasize *or* highlight sth; ***di ~*** important; ***di nessun ~*** of no importance

riloga *f* curtain rail, *US* traverse rod

rilucente *adj* shining

riluttante *adj*: ***essere ~ a fare qc*** be reluctant to do sth

riluttanza *f* reluctance

rima *f* rhyme; ***far ~*** rhyme; *fig* ***rispondere per le -e*** answer in kind

rimandare *v/t* ⟨1a⟩ send again; (*restituire*) send back, return; *palla* return; (*rinviare*) postpone

rimando *m* SPORTS goal kick; (*riferimento*) cross-reference; ***di ~*** promptly

rimaneggiare *v/t* ⟨1f⟩ rework

rimanente **I** *adj* remaining **II** *m* rest, balance

rimanenza *f* remainder

rimanere *v/i* ⟨2m⟩ stay, remain; (*avanzare*) be left (over); ***rimanerci male*** be hurt; ***come siete rimasti per stasera?*** what arrangements did you make for this evening?; ***come siete rimasti?*** what did you decide on?

rimangiarsi *v/r* ⟨1f⟩ take back; ***~ la parola*** (***data***) eat one's words

rimango → ***rimanere***

rimarcare *v/t* ⟨1d⟩ point out

rimarchevole *adj* remarkable

rimare *v/i* ⟨1a⟩ write poetry; ***~ con qc*** rhyme with sth

rimarginare *v/t* ⟨1m⟩ heal

rimarginarsi *v/r* ⟨1m⟩ heal

rimasto *past part* → ***rimanere***

rimasuglio *m* ⟨*pl* -gli⟩ remnant

rimbalzare *v/i* ⟨1a⟩ bounce

rimbalzo *m* bounce

rimbambimento *m* *infml* confusion

rimbambire ⟨4d⟩ *pej* **I** *v/i* go senile **II** *v/t* befuddle

rimbambito *adj* senile

rimboccare *v/t* ⟨1d⟩ *coperte* tuck in; ***rimboccarsi le maniche*** roll up one's sleeves

rimbombante *adj* booming; *fig* bombastic

rimbombare *v/i* ⟨1a⟩ echo (*a. fig*), ring

rimbombo *m* rumble; *fig* boom

rimborsabile *adj* COMM refundable

rimborsare *v/t* ⟨1a⟩ reimburse, refund, pay back

rimborso *m* reimbursement, repayment; ***~ spese*** reimbursement of expenses; ***contro ~*** COD, cash on delivery

rimboschimento *m* reforestation

rimboschire *v/t* ⟨4d⟩ reforest

rimbrottare *v/t* ⟨1c⟩ tell off

rimbrotto *m* telling-off

rimediare ⟨1k & b⟩ **I** *v/i*: ***~ a*** make up for, remedy; ***come posso ~?*** how can I put things right? **II** *v/t* find, scrape together

rimedio *m* ⟨*pl* -di⟩ remedy; MED medicine; ***senza ~*** hopeless

rimescolamento *m* mixing again

rimescolare *v/t* ⟨1m⟩ mix again; *più volte* mix thoroughly; *caffè* stir again

rimessa *f* shed; *di auto* garage; *degli autobus* depot; FIN remittance; SPORTS ***~ laterale*** throw-in; ***~ in funzione*** reactivation

rimessaggio *m* ⟨*pl* -ggi⟩ garaging

rimestare *v/t* ⟨1a⟩ stir; *fig* rake up

rimettere *v/t* ⟨3ee⟩ **1.** put back, return; (*affidare*) refer; ***~ a nuovo*** renovate; ***~ a posto*** put back; ***~ in ordine*** tidy up; ***~ in libertà*** set free; ***~ mano a qc*** take sth up again; ***~ in sesto*** sort out **2.** *vomitare* bring up **3.** ***ci ho rimesso molti soldi*** I lost a lot of money

rimettersi *v/r* *di tempo* improve; ***~ da qc*** get over sth; ***~ a qn*** put o.s. in s.o.'s hands; *fig* ***~ in sella*** get back in the saddle

riminese **I** *adj* from Rimini **II** *m/f* person from Rimini

rimmel® *m* ⟨*pl* rimmel⟩ mascara

rimodernamento *m* modernizing

rimodernare *v/t* ⟨1b⟩ modernize

rimonta *f* SPORTS recovery

rimorchiare *v/t* ⟨1k & c⟩ AUTO tow (away)

rimorchiatore *m* tug

rimorchio *m* AUTO tow; *veicolo* trailer

rimordere *v/t* ⟨3uu⟩ *fig* bite again; ***gli rimorde la coscienza*** his conscience is pricking him

rimorso *m* remorse

rimosso *past part* → ***rimuovere***

rimostranza *f* complaint

rimovibile *adj* detachable

rimozione *f* removal

rimpasto *m fig* reshuffle

rimpatriare ⟨1k & m⟩ **I** *v/t* repatriate **II** *v/i* return *or* go home

rimpatriata *f* get-together; ***fare una ~*** have a get-together

rimpatrio *m* ⟨*pl* -ri⟩ repatriation

rimpiangere *v/t* ⟨3d⟩ regret (***di avere fatto qc*** doing sth); *tempi passati, giovinezza* miss

rimpianto I *past part* → ***rimpiangere*** **II** *m* regret

rimpiattino *m* hide and seek

rimpiazzare *v/t* ⟨1a⟩ replace

rimpicciolire ⟨4d⟩ **I** *v/t* make smaller **II** *v/i* become smaller, shrink

rimpinzare *v/t* ⟨1a⟩ fill up; *fig* ***~ qn di frottole*** fill s.o.'s head with lies

rimpinzarsi *v/r* ⟨1a⟩ stuff oneself

rimpolpare *v/t* ⟨1a⟩ fatten up

rimpolparsi *v/r* ⟨1a⟩ put on weight

rimpossessarsi *v/r* ⟨1a⟩: ***~ di qc*** retake possession of sth

rimproverare *v/t* ⟨1m & c⟩ scold; *impiegato* reprimand; ***~ qc a qn*** reproach s.o. for sth

rimproverarsi *v/r* ⟨1m & c⟩ blame oneself

rimprovero *m* scolding; *dal capo* reprimand; ***-i*** *pl* reproaches

rimuginare ⟨1m⟩ **I** *v/t* ruminate on; *infml* chew over **II** *v/i*: ***~ su qc*** brood over sth

rimuovere *v/t* ⟨3ff⟩ remove; *muovere di nuovo* move again

rinascere *v/i* ⟨3gg⟩ be born again; *di passione, speranza* be revived; *fig* ***sentirsi ~*** feel rejuvenated

rinascimentale *adj* Renaissance *attr*

Rinascimento *m* HIST Renaissance

rinascita *f* rebirth; *fig* revival

rincalzare *v/t* ⟨1a⟩: ***~ le coperte*** fold back the covers

rincantucciarsi *v/r* ⟨1f⟩ snuggle up

rincarare ⟨1a⟩ **I** *v/t* increase, put up; ***~ la dose*** make matters worse **II** *v/i* increase in price

rincaro *m* increase in price

rincasare *v/i* ⟨1a⟩ *venire* come home; *andare* go home

rinchiudere *v/t* ⟨3b⟩ shut up

rinchiudersi *v/r* shut o.s. up

rincitrullire I *v/t* ⟨4d⟩ drive round the bend **II** *v/i* go round the bend

rincoglionire ⟨4d⟩ *vulg* **I** *v/i* go senile **II** *v/t* fuck up, screw up

rincoglionito *adj* soft in the head

rincorrere *v/t* ⟨3o⟩ run *or* chase after

rincorrersi *v/r* ⟨3o⟩: run after each other; ***giocare a ~*** play tag

rincorsa *f* run-up; ***prendere la ~*** take a run

rincorso *past part* → ***rincorrere***

rincrescere *v/i* ⟨3n⟩: ***mi rincresce*** I'm sorry; ***se non ti rincresce*** if you don't mind

rincrescimento *m* regret

rincretinire ⟨4d⟩ **I** *v/t* make stupid **II** *v/i* become stupid

rinculo *m di fucile* recoil

rincuorare *v/t* ⟨1c⟩ hearten

rincuorarsi *v/r* ⟨1c⟩ cheer up

rinfacciare *v/t* ⟨1f⟩: ***~ qc a qn*** cast sth up to s.o.

rinforzare *v/t* ⟨1c⟩ strengthen

rinforzarsi *v/r* get stronger

rinforzo *m* reinforcement; MIL ***-i*** *pl* reinforcements

rinfrancare *v/t* ⟨1d⟩ reassure

rinfrancarsi *v/r* ⟨1d⟩ perk up

rinfrescante *adj* refreshing

rinfrescare ⟨1d⟩ **I** *v/t* cool down, make cooler; (*ristorare*) refresh; (*rinnovare*) freshen up; ***~ la memoria a qn*** refresh s.o.'s memory **II** *v/i* cool down

rinfrescarsi *v/r* freshen up

rinfrescata *f*: ***darsi una ~*** have a quick wash; ***dare una ~ alle pareti*** give the walls a fresh coat of paint

rinfresco *m* ⟨*pl* -chi⟩ buffet (party)

rinfusa *f*: ***alla ~*** any which way, all higgledy-piggledy

ring *m* ⟨*pl* ring⟩ boxing ring

ringalluzzire *v/t* ⟨4d⟩ *hum* make cocky

ringalluzzirsi *v/r* ⟨4d⟩ *hum* become cocky

ringhiare *v/i* ⟨1k⟩ growl

ringhiera *f* railing

ringhio *m* ⟨*pl* -ghi⟩ growl

ringiovanimento *m* rejuvenation

ringiovanire ⟨4d⟩ **I** *v/t* make feel younger; *di aspetto* make look younger **II** *v/i* feel younger; *di aspetto* look younger

ringraziamento *m*: ***un ~*** a word of thanks; ***lettera*** *f* ***di ~*** thank you letter, letter of thanks; ***i miei -i*** *pl* my

thanks; ***-i*** *in libro* acknowledgments
ringraziare *v/t* ⟨1g⟩ thank (***di*** for)
rinnegare *v/t* ⟨1e⟩ disown
rinnovabile *adj* renewable; ***energia*** *f* **~** renewable energy
rinnovamento *m* change; *di contratto, tessera* renewal
rinnovare *v/t* ⟨1c⟩ renovate; *guardaroba* replace; *abbonamento* renew; (*ripetere*) renew, repeat
rinnovarsi *v/r* renew itself; (*ripetersi*) be repeated, happen again
rinnovo *m* renovation; *di guardaroba* replacement; *di abbonamento* renewal; *di richiesta* repetition
rinoceronte *m* rhinoceros, rhino
rinomato *adj* famous
rinsaldare *v/t* ⟨1a⟩ cement
rinsaldarsi *v/r* ⟨1a⟩ consolidate
rinsavire ⟨4d⟩ **I** *v/t*: **~ *qn*** bring s.o. back to his/her senses **II** *v/i* come to one's senses
rinsecchire *v/i* ⟨4d⟩ wither
rintanarsi *v/r* ⟨1a⟩ hide, go to earth
rintocco *m* ⟨*pl* -cchi⟩ toll; **~ *di campana*** ring of a bell
rintontire *v/t* ⟨4d⟩ stun
rintontirsi *v/r* ⟨4d⟩ be dazed
rintontito *adj* stunned
rintracciabile *adj* traceable; *al telefono*: reachable
rintracciare *v/t* ⟨1f⟩ track down
rintronare ⟨1c⟩ **I** *v/t* deafen **II** *v/i* boom
rintronato *adj* deafened
rintuzzare *v/t* ⟨1a⟩ (*smussare*) blunt; (*reprimere*) repress; *accusa, rimprovero* counter
rinuncia *f* ⟨*pl* -ce⟩ renunciation (***a*** of)
rinunciare *v/i* ⟨1f⟩ give up (***a*** sth)
rinunciatario ⟨*mpl* -ri⟩ **I** *adj* renunciative **II** *m*, ***-a*** *f* renouncer
rinunzia *f* → ***rinuncia***
rinvenimento *m* recovery; *di resti* discovery; ***luogo*** *m* ***del*** **~** recovery site
rinvenire ⟨4p⟩ **I** *v/t* recover; *resti* discover **II** *v/i* regain consciousness, come round
rinverdire ⟨4d⟩ **I** *v/t* turn green again; *fig* refresh **II** *v/i* become green again
rinviare *v/t* ⟨1h⟩ (*mandare indietro*) return; (*posticipare*) postpone, put off; *a letteratura* refer
rinvigorire *v/t* ⟨4d⟩ reinvigorate (*a. fig*)
rinvigorirsi *v/r* ⟨4d⟩ revive
rinvio *m* ⟨*pl* -vii⟩ return; *di riunione* postponement; *in un testo* cross-reference
rio *m* ⟨*pl* rii⟩ *liter* stream; *a Venezia* canal
Rio delle Amazzoni *m* Amazon
rionale *adj* local
rione *m* district
riordinamento *m* reorganization
riordinare *v/t* ⟨1m⟩ tidy up; **~ *le idee*** set one's ideas in order
riorganizzare *v/t* ⟨1a⟩ reorganize
riorganizzazione *f* reorganization
riottoso *adj* rowdy; *carattere* quarrelsome
ripagare *v/t* ⟨1e⟩: **~ *qn di qc*** compensate s.o. for sth (*a. fig*); **~ *qn con la stessa moneta*** give s.o. a taste of their own medicine
riparare ⟨1a⟩ **I** *v/t* (*proteggere*) protect (***da*** from); (*aggiustare*) repair; *un torto* make up for **II** *v/i* escape
ripararsi *v/r dalla pioggia* shelter, take shelter (***da*** from)
riparato *adj* sheltered
riparatore **I** *adj* remedial; ***gesto*** *m* **~** reparative gesture **II** *m*, ***-trice*** *f* repairer
riparazione *f* repair; *fig di torta, ingiustizia* putting right, reparation; ***officina*** *f* ***-i*** garage
riparlare *v/i* ⟨1a⟩ talk again
riparlarsi *v/r* ⟨1a⟩ be on speaking terms again
riparo *m* shelter; ***mettersi al*** **~** take shelter
ripartire[1] *v/i* ⟨4a⟩ leave again
ripartire[2] *v/t* ⟨4d⟩ divide (up)
ripartizione *f* division
ripassare ⟨1a⟩ **I** *v/i* → ***passare*** **II** *v/t col ferro* iron; *lezione* revise, *US* review
ripassata *f*: ***dare una*** **~** ***a qc*** give sth a quick iron
ripasso *m* revision
ripensamento *m*: ***avere un*** **~** have second thoughts
ripensare *v/i* ⟨1b⟩ *riflettere* think; **~ *a qc*** think about sth again; ***ci ho ripensato*** I've changed my mind
ripercorrere *v/t* ⟨3o⟩ trace; *in senso inverso* track back; *con veicoli* retrace; *fig* trace back
ripercuotersi *v/r* reverberate

ripercussione *f* repercussion
ripescare *v/t* ⟨1d⟩ fish out; *fig* dig out
ripetente *m/f* student repeating a year at school, *US* repeater
ripetere *v/t* ⟨3a⟩ repeat; ***ti ho ripetuto mille volte la stessa cosa*** I've told you the same thing a thousand times
ripetitività *f* ⟨*pl* ripetitività⟩ repetitiveness
ripetitivo *adj* repetitive
ripetitore *m* TEL relay
ripetizione *f* repetition; ***dare -i a qn*** tutor s.o.
ripetuto *adj* repeated
ripiano *m* shelf
ripicca *f* ⟨*pl* -cche⟩: ***fare qc per ~ (verso qn)*** do sth out of spite (to s.o.)
ripidamente *adv* steeply
ripidezza *f* steepness; *accentuata* sheerness
ripido *adj* steep
ripiegamento *m* MIL retreat
ripiegare ⟨1b & e⟩ **I** *v/t* fold (up) again **II** *v/i* fall back
ripiego *m* ⟨*pl* -ghi⟩ makeshift (solution)
ripieno I *adj* full; COOK stuffed **II** *m* stuffing
ripopolamento *m* repopulation; *di animali*: restocking
ripopolare *v/t* ⟨1a⟩ repopulate; *animali* restock
ripopolarsi *v/r* ⟨1a⟩ be repopulated; *fig* come back to life
riporre *v/t* ⟨3ll⟩ put away; ***~ le speranze in qn / qc*** place one's hopes in s.o. / sth
riportare *v/t* ⟨1c⟩ take back; (*riferire*) report; *vittoria, successo* achieve; MATH carry over; *tasche* sew on; *danni, ferite* sustain
riporto *m* MATH, COMM number to be carried over; ECON, FIN brought forward; *di capelli* comb-over
riposante *adj* relaxing
riposare *v/t & v/i* ⟨1c⟩ rest
riposarsi *v/r* rest
riposato *adj*: ***a mente -a*** once I've / you've had some rest
riposino *m* rest
riposo *m* rest; ***buon ~ !*** sleep well!; ***casa*** *f* ***di ~*** rest home; ***giorno*** *m* ***di ~*** day off; ***collocare a ~*** retire; ***senza ~*** non-stop
ripostiglio *m* ⟨*pl* -gli⟩ boxroom, storeroom
riposto *past part* → ***riporre***
riprendere *v/t* ⟨3c⟩ take again; (*prendere indietro*) take back; *lavoro* go back to; PHOT record; ***~ coscienza*** regain consciousness; ***~ fiato*** get one's breath back; ***~ a fare qc*** start doing sth again
riprendersi *v/r*: ***~ da qc*** get over sth
ripresa *f* resumption; *di vestito* alteration; *film* shot; AUTO acceleration; RADIO, TV ***in ~ diretta*** (broadcast) live; ***a più -e*** several times, on several occasions
ripresentare *v/t* ⟨1b⟩ re-present; *ricorso* resubmit
ripresentarsi *v/r* ⟨1b⟩ re-enter; *occasione* arise again; ***~ alle elezioni*** stand for re-election
ripristinare *v/t* ⟨1m⟩ restore; ***~ una linea ferroviaria*** reopen a railway *or US* railroad line; ***~ l'ordine*** restore order; ***~ i contatti con qn*** re-establish contact with s.o.
ripristino *m* re-establishment; (*restauro*) restoration
riproduco → ***riprodurre***
riprodurre *v/t* ⟨3e⟩ reproduce
riprodursi *v/r di animali* breed, reproduce; *di situazione* happen again
riproduttivo *adj* reproductive
riproduzione *f* reproduction; ***~ vietata*** copyright
ripromettersi *v/r*: ***~ di fare qc*** intend to do sth
riproporre *v/t* ⟨3ll⟩ ask again; *problema, questione* pose again
riproporsi *v/r* ⟨3ll⟩ *problema, questione* arise again; ***~ di fare qc*** promise oneself to do sth
riprova *f*: ***a ~ di qc*** in confirmation of sth
riprovare ⟨1c⟩ **I** *v/t* feel again; *vestito* try on again **II** *v/i* try again
riprovevole *adj* reprehensible
ripudiare *v/t* ⟨1k⟩ repudiate; ***~ la propria fede*** renounce one's faith
ripugnante *adj* disgusting, repugnant
ripugnanza *f* disgust, repugnance
ripugnare *v/i* ⟨1a⟩: ***~ a qn*** disgust s.o.
ripulire *v/t* ⟨4d⟩ clean again; (*rimettere in ordine*) tidy (up); *hum* empty, clean out
riquadro *m* square (*a.* ARCH)
riqualificare *v/t* ⟨1m & d⟩ retrain;

ADMIN upgrade

riqualificarsi *v/r nel lavoro* become better qualified

riqualificazione *f di personale* acquisition of better qualifications; *di ambiente* improvement; ***misure di ~*** improvements

RIS *abbr* (= **Reparto Investigazioni Scientifiche**) *the Scientific Investigations Department of the carabinieri*

risa *fpl* laughter *sg*; ***sbellicarsi dalle ~*** split one's sides laughing

risacca *f* ⟨*pl* -cche⟩ undertow

risaia *f* rice field

risalire ⟨4m⟩ **I** *v/t scale* go back up; ***~ la china*** bounce back **II** *v/i* (*rincarare*) go up again; ***~ alle origini*** go back to source; ***la chiesa risale al Medioevo*** the church dates back to the Middle Ages

risalita *f* ascent; ***impianti*** *mpl* ***di ~*** ski lifts

risaltare *v/i* ⟨1a⟩ stand out

risalto *m*: ***fare ~*** stand out; ***mettere in ~, dare ~ a*** highlight

risanabile *adj* reclaimable; *situazione economica* able to be improved

risanamento *m* redevelopment; FIN improvement; ***~ del deficit pubblico*** reduction in the public deficit

risanare *v/t* ⟨1a⟩ redevelop; FIN improve

risaputo *adj* well-known

risarcimento *m* compensation

risarcire *v/t* ⟨4d⟩ *persona* compensate (***di*** for); *danno* compensate for

risata *f* laugh; ***farsi una bella ~*** have a good laugh

risatina *f* chuckle

riscaldamento *m* heating; ***~ autonomo*** central heating system (*for an individual flat*); ***~ centrale*** central heating system (*for a block of flats*); ***impianto*** *m* ***di ~*** heating system; ***~ dell'atmosfera*** global warming

riscaldare *v/t* ⟨1a⟩ heat *or* warm up

riscaldarsi *v/r* warm o.s.

riscattabile *adj* ECON, JUR callable; *pegno* redeemable

riscattare *v/t* ⟨1a⟩: ***~ un'ipoteca*** clear a mortgage; ***~ un pegno*** redeem a pledge

riscattarsi *v/r* ⟨1a⟩ redeem oneself

riscatto *m* ransom

rischiararsi *v/r* ⟨1a⟩ clear (up); *cielo* clear (up); ***~ la voce*** clear one's throat; ***~ in volto*** cheer up

rischiare ⟨1k⟩ **I** *v/t* risk **II** *v/i*: ***~ di sbagliare*** risk making a mistake

rischio *m* ⟨*pl* -chi⟩ risk; ***a ~ di*** at the risk of; ***a ~ della propria vita*** risking one's own life; ***mettere a ~*** put at risk; *persona, zona*: ***a ~*** at risk; ***correre dei -chi*** run risks; ***a proprio ~ e pericolo*** at one's own risk

rischiosamente *adv* imprudently

rischioso *adj* risky

risciacquare *v/t* ⟨1a⟩ rinse

risciacquarsi *v/r* ⟨1a⟩ rinse (out)

risciacquata *f* rinse

risciacquo *m* rinsing; *nelle lavatrici e lavastoviglie*: rinse

riscontrabile *adj* (*verificabile*) checkable; (*paragonabile*) comparable

riscontrare *v/t* ⟨1a⟩ (*confrontare*) compare; (*controllare*) check; (*incontrare*) come up against; *errori* come across

riscontro *m* comparison; check; ***in ~ alla Vostra*** in response to yours

riscoperta *f* rediscover

riscoprire *v/t* ⟨4f⟩ rediscover

riscossa *f* countercharge; ***alla ~!*** to the rescue!

riscossione *f* collection

riscrivere *v/t* ⟨3tt⟩ rewrite; (*rispondere per iscritto*) write back

riscuotere *v/t* ⟨3ff⟩ FIN *soldi* draw; *assegno* cash; *fig* earn

risentimento *m* resentment

risentire ⟨4b⟩ **I** *v/t* hear again **II** *v/i* feel the effects (***di*** of)

risentirsi *v/r* TEL talk again; (*offendersi*) take offence (*US* offense)

risentito *adj* (*offeso*) offended; (*indignato*) resentful

riserbo *m* reserve; ***senza ~*** openly; ***mantenere il massimo ~*** refuse to say anything at all

riserva *f* **1.** reserve; (*scorta*) stock, reserve; ***fondo*** *m* ***di ~*** reserve stock; AUTO ***essere in ~*** be running out of fuel; ***fare ~ di*** stock up on **2.** *fig* reservation; ***avere delle -e*** *pl* ***su qc*** have reservations about sth; ***con ~*** with reservations; ***senza -e*** without reservation, wholeheartedly **3. *~ indiana*** Native American reservation **4. *~ naturale*** nature reserve

riservare *v/t* ⟨1b⟩ keep; (*prenotare*)

book, reserve
riservarsi *v/r* reserve; ***mi riservo di non accettare*** I reserve the right not to accept
riservatezza *f* reserve
riservato *adj* reserved; (*confidenziale*) confidential
risicato *adj* scanty
risiedere ⟨3a⟩ be resident, reside
risma *f*: ***essere della stessa ~*** *pej* be birds of a feather
riso[1] **I** *past part* → ***ridere*** **II** *m* laughing
riso[2] *m* rice
risolino *m* titter
risollevare *v/t* ⟨1b⟩ raise again; *fig* ***~ il morale*** lift *o* raise morale
risollevarsi *v/r* ⟨1b⟩ get up again
risolto *past part* → ***risolvere***
risolutezza *f* determination, resolution; ***con ~*** with determination
risolutivo *adj* decisive
risoluto *adj* determined
risoluzione *f* resolution; (*soluzione*) solution; ***~ d'un contratto*** cancellation of a contract; ***prendere una ~*** make a decision
risolvere *v/t* ⟨3g⟩ solve; (*decidere*) resolve
risolversi *v/r* be solved; (*decidersi*) decide, resolve; ***~ in nulla*** come to nothing
risolvibile *adj* solvable; JUR determinable
risonanza *f* MUS resonance; *fig*: *di scandolo* reverberations *pl*; ***avere una vasta ~*** have major repercussions; ***~ magnetica*** MED magnetic resonance
risorgere *v/i* ⟨3d⟩ rise; *fig*: *di industria etc* experience a rebirth
Risorgimento *m hist* Risorgimento, *the reunification of Italy*
risorsa *f* resource; ***senza -e*** without resources; ***-e*** *pl* ***economiche*** financial resources; ***-e*** *pl* ***energetiche*** energy resources; ***è una persona piena di -e*** he's a very resourceful person
risorto I *adj* REL risen **II** *past part* → ***risorgere***
risotto *m* risotto; ***~ alla milanese*** *risotto made with onion and saffron*
risparmiare *v/t* ⟨1k⟩ save; *fig* spare
risparmiarsi *v/r* conserve one's energy
risparmiatore *m*, **-trice** *f* saver; FIN depositor
risparmio *m* ⟨*pl* -mi⟩ saving; ***-i*** *pl* savings; ***cassa*** *f* ***di ~*** savings bank; ***libretto*** *m* ***di ~*** bank book
rispecchiare *v/t* ⟨1k⟩ reflect
rispecchiarsi *v/r* ⟨1k⟩ be reflected (*a. fig*)
rispedire *v/t* ⟨4d⟩ redirect; *indietro* send back
rispettabile *adj* respectable
rispettabilità *f* ⟨*pl* rispettabilità⟩ respectability
rispettare *v/t* ⟨1b⟩ respect; *legge, contratto* abide by; ***farsi ~*** command respect
rispettarsi *v/r* ⟨1b⟩ have self-respect
rispettivamente *adv* respectively
rispettivo *adj* respective
rispetto I *m* respect **II** *prep*: ***~ a*** (*confronto a*) compared with; (*in relazione a*) as regards
rispettoso *adj* respectful
risplendere *v/i* ⟨3a⟩ shine, glitter
rispolverare *v/t* ⟨1l⟩ *fig* brush up
rispondente *adj*: ***~ a qc*** corresponding to sth
rispondenza *f* correspondence
rispondere *v/i* ⟨3hh⟩ answer (***a*** sth), reply (***a*** to); (*reagire*) respond; *saluto* acknowledge; ***~ alle speranze*** come up to expectations; ***~ di qc*** be accountable for sth (***a*** to); ***~ male*** answer back; TEL ***non risponde*** there's no answer
risposarsi *v/r* remarry
risposta *f* answer, reply; (*reazione*) response; ***~ pagata*** reply paid; ***in ~ a qc*** in answer to sth
rissa *f* brawl
rissoso *adj* quarrelsome
ristabilimento *m di ordine* restoration; *di regolamento* re-introduction; (*guarigione*) recovery
ristabilire *v/t* ⟨4d⟩ *ordine* restore; *regolamento* re-introduce; ***~ la verità*** set the record straight
ristabilirsi *v/r* recover
ristagnare *v/i* ⟨1a⟩ stagnate (*a. fig*)
ristagno *m* stagnation (*a. fig*, ECON); MED stasis
ristampa *f* reprint
ristampare *v/t* ⟨1a⟩ reprint
ristorante *m* restaurant
ristoratore,-trice I *adj* restorative **II** *n*: ***ristoratore*** *m* restaurateur
ristorazione *f* catering

ristoro *m* refreshment; RAIL ***servizio*** *m* ***di ~*** buffet car
ristrettezza *f di idee* narrowness; ***vivere nelle -e*** live in straitened circumstances
ristretto *adj*: ***caffè*** *m* **~** very strong coffee; ***mercato*** *m* **~** FIN thin market
ristrutturare *v/t* ⟨1a⟩ *azienda* restructure
ristrutturazione *f* restructuring
risucchiare *v/t* ⟨1k⟩ suck
risucchio *m* ⟨*pl* -cchi⟩ suction
risultare *v/i* ⟨1a⟩ (*derivare*) result; (*rivelarsi*) turn out; ***mi risulta che ...*** as far as I know ...
risultato *m* result; ***senza ~*** unsuccessfully
risuolare *v/t* ⟨1o⟩ resole
risuonare *v/i* ⟨1o⟩ *campanello* ring again; *suoni* resound; (*echeggiare*) echo
risurrezione *f* REL Resurrection
risuscitare *v/i* ⟨1m⟩ rise from the dead
risvegliare *v/i* ⟨1g⟩ *fig* reawaken
risvegliarsi *v/r* ⟨1g⟩ *fig* reawaken
risveglio *m* ⟨*pl* -gli⟩ awakening; *fig* reawakening; ***al mio ~*** when I woke
risvolto *m* SEW, TYPO flap; *fig* implication; ***~ di copertina*** flap; (*testo*) blurb
Rita *f*: ***Santa ~*** Saint Rita
ritagliare *v/t*⟨1g⟩ cut out
ritagliarsi *v/r*⟨1g⟩: ***~ uno spazio*** carve out a space for oneself
ritaglio *m* ⟨*pl* -gli⟩ scrap; ***nei -gli di tempo*** in one's spare time
ritardare ⟨1a⟩ **I** *v/t* delay **II** *v/i* be late; *orologio* be slow
ritardatario *m*, **-a** *f* ⟨*mpl* -ri⟩ latecomer
ritardato *adj* delayed; PSYCH, *fig* retarded
ritardo *m* delay; ***senza ~*** without delay; ***essere in ~*** be late
ritegno *m* restraint; ***senza ~*** to excess
ritemprare *v/t* ⟨1b⟩ *fig* restore
ritemprarsi *v/r* ⟨1b⟩ recover one's strength
ritenere *v/t* ⟨2q⟩ (*credere*) believe; ***~ opportuno fare qc*** consider it opportune to do sth
ritenersi *v/r*: ***si ritiene molto intelligente*** he thinks he is very intelligent
ritentare *v/t* ⟨1b⟩ try again
ritenuta *f* deduction (***su*** from); ***~ alla fonte*** deduction at source
ritenzione *f*: ***~ idrica*** MED water retention
ritirare *v/t* ⟨1a⟩ withdraw, pull back; (*tirare di nuovo*) throw again; *proposta* withdraw; (*prelevare*) collect, pick up; ***~ il passaporto a qn*** retain s.o.'s passport
ritirarsi *v/r* (*restringersi*) shrink; ***~ a vita privata*** retire into private life; ***~ da*** *gara, esame etc* withdraw from
ritirata *f* MIL withdrawal; (*toilette*) lavatory
ritiro *m* withdrawal; ***~ della patente*** suspension of s.o.'s driving licence; ***~ spirituale*** spiritual retreat
ritmico *adj*: ***ginnastica*** *f* ***-a*** eurhythmics *sg*
ritmo *m* rhythm
rito *m* ceremony; ***~ abbreviato*** JUR summary procedure; ***essere di ~*** be customary
ritoccare *v/t* ⟨1d⟩ touch up
ritocco *m* ⟨*pl* -cchi⟩ touch-up
ritorcersi *v/r* ⟨3d⟩ *fig*: ***~ contro qn / qc*** backfire on s.o. / sth
ritornare ⟨1a⟩ **I** *v/i venire* get back, come back, return; *andare* go back, return; *su argomento* go back (***su*** over); ***~ verde*** turn green again; ***~ in sé*** come to one's senses **II** *v/t* return
ritornello *m* refrain
ritorno *m* return; ***far ~*** come back, return; ***essere di ~*** be back; ***viaggio*** *m* ***di ~*** return trip; ***andata e ~*** return (ticket), *US* roundtrip ticket
ritorsione *f* retaliation (*a.* JUR)
ritorto *adj* (*contorto*) twisted (*a.* TEX)
ritrarre *v/t* ⟨3xx⟩ pull away; PAINT portray; (*rappresentare*) depict
ritrattare *v/t* ⟨1a⟩ retract
ritrattazione *f* retraction
ritrattista ⟨*mpl* -i⟩ **I** *adj* portrait *attr* **II** *m/f* portraitist
ritratto *m* portrait; *fig* ***il ~ di qn*** the spitting image of s.o.; ***fare il ~ della situazione*** paint a picture of the situation; ***è il ~ della salute*** he's the picture of health
ritrosia *f* reluctance
ritroso *adj*: ***andare a ~*** go backwards
ritrovamento *m* retrieval
ritrovare *v/t* ⟨1c⟩ find; (*riacquistare*) regain

ritrovarsi *v/r* meet again; (*capitare*) find o.s.; (*orientarsi*) get one's bearings
ritrovo *m* meeting; *luogo* meeting place; **~ notturno** nightclub
ritto *adj* straight
rituale I *adj* ritual **II** *m* ritual (*a. fig*)
riunificare *v/t* ⟨1m & d⟩ reunify
riunificarsi *v/r* ⟨1m & d⟩ reunify
riunificazione *f* reunification
riunione *f* meeting; *di amici, famiglia* reunion; **essere in ~** be in a meeting
riunire *v/t* ⟨4d⟩ gather
riunirsi *v/r* meet
riuscire *v/i* ⟨4o⟩ succeed; (*essere capace*) manage **riesco a fare** *or* **mi riesce di fare** I manage to do; **non riesco a capire** I can't understand; **~ bene/male** be a success/a failure; *di foto* come out well/badly; **~ in qc** be successful in sth; **mi riesce difficile/facile** it's hard/easy for me
riuscita *f* success
riuscito *adj* successful; **mal ~** unsuccessful
riutilizzabile *adj* re-usable
riutilizzare *v/t* ⟨1a⟩ re-use
riutilizzazione *f* re-use
riva *f* shore; **in ~ al mare/al lago** at the seashore/lakeside
rivale I *adj* rival *attr* **II** *m/f* rival
rivaleggiare *v/t* ⟨1f⟩ compete
rivalità *f* ⟨*pl* rivalità⟩ rivalry
rivalsa *f* revenge; **azione** *f* **di ~** JUR recourse
rivalutare *v/t* ⟨1a⟩ revalue; *persona* change one's mind about
rivalutazione *f* revaluation
rivangare *v/t* ⟨1e⟩ *fig* drag up
rivedere *v/t* ⟨2s⟩ see again; (*ripassare*) review, look at again; (*verificare*) check
rivelare *v/t* ⟨1a⟩ reveal
rivelatore I *adj* revelatory **II** *n*: **rivelatore** *m* detector
rivelazione *f* revelation
rivendere *v/t* ⟨3a⟩ resell
rivendicare *v/t* ⟨1m & d⟩ demand; **~ un attentato** claim responsibility for an attack
rivendicazione *f* demand; **-i** *pl* **salariali** wage demands
rivendita *f* resale; *negozio* retail outlet
rivenditore *m*, **-trice** *f* retailer; **~ specializzato** dealer
riverbero *m* reflection
riverente *adj* reverent
riverenza *f* respect; **fare una ~** *uomo* bow; *donna* curtsey
riverire *v/t* ⟨4d⟩ revere
riverito *adj* respected
riversare *v/t* ⟨1b⟩: **~ il proprio affetto su qn** lavish affection on s.o.; **~ la colpa su qn** lay the blame on s.o.
riversarsi *v/r* ⟨1b⟩ overflow; *fig* fall
rivestimento *m* covering
rivestire *v/t* ⟨4b⟩ (*foderare*) cover; *ruolo* play; *carica* fill
rivestirsi *v/r* get dressed again
rivestito *adj* covered; *di legno* paneled
rivetto *m* rivet
riviera *f* coast; **la Riviera Ligure** the Ligurian Riviera
rivierasco *adj* ⟨*mpl* -chi⟩ coast
rivincita *f* return match; **prendersi la ~** get one's revenge
rivista *f* magazine; THEAT revue; MIL review; **~ di moda** fashion magazine
rivitalizzare *v/t* ⟨1a⟩ revitalize; MED revive
rivitalizzarsi *v/r* ⟨1a⟩ be revitalized
rivivere ⟨3zz⟩ **I** *v/i fig* be revived **II** *v/t* relive; **far ~** bring back to life
rivolgere *v/t* ⟨3d⟩ turn; *domanda* address (**a qn** to s.o.); **non mi rivolge mai il saluto** he never acknowledges me; **~ la parola a qn** speak to s.o., address s.o.; **~ l'attenzione a qc** turn one's attention to sth
rivolgersi *v/r*: **~ a qn** apply to s.o. (**per** for)
rivolgimento *m fig* upheaval
rivolo *m* trickle
rivolta *f* revolt
rivoltante *adj* turning; *fig* revolting
rivoltare *v/t* ⟨1c⟩ turn; (*mettere sottosopra*) turn upside down; (*disgustare*) revolt
rivoltarsi *v/r* ⟨1c⟩ turn over; *fig* rebel
rivoltella *f* revolver
rivoltellata *f* (revolver) shot
rivoluzionare *v/t* ⟨1a⟩ revolutionize
rivoluzionario *adj* ⟨*mpl* -ri⟩ revolutionary
rivoluzione *f* revolution
rizzare *v/t* ⟨1a⟩ put up; *bandiera* raise; *orecchie* prick up
rizzarsi *v/r* straighten up; **mi si sono rizzati i capelli in testa** my hair stood on end

RM *abbr* (= **Roma**) Rome
RMN *abbr* (= **Risonanza magnetica nucleare**) MED NMR (nuclear magnetic resonance)
RN *abbr* (= **Rimini**) Rimini
RO *abbr* (= **Rovigo**) Rovigo
roaming *m* ⟨*pl* roaming⟩ TEL roaming; *~ **internazionale*** international roaming
roast beef *m* roast beef
roba *f* things *pl*, stuff; ***~ da mangiare*** food, things *or* stuff to eat; ***~ da matti!*** would you believe it!; ***è ~ mia!*** that's my stuff!; ***che ~ è?*** what's this?; ***non è ~ per me*** it's not my cup of tea
robaccia *f* junk
robetta *f* cheap stuff
robiola *f soft cheese from Piedmont and Lombardy*
robivecchi *m/f* ⟨*pl* robivecchi⟩ secondhand dealer
roboante *adj* resonant; *fig* bombastic
robot *m* ⟨*pl* robot⟩ robot; *da cucina* food processor
robotica *f* ⟨*pl* -che⟩ robotics *sg*
robotizzato *adj* automated
robustezza *f* sturdiness
robusto *adj* sturdy
rocambolesco *adj* ⟨*mpl* -chi⟩ incredible
rocca *f* ⟨*pl* -cche⟩ fortress
roccaforte *f* ⟨*pl* roccheforti⟩ stronghold (*a. fig*)
rocchetto *m* reel
roccia *f* ⟨*pl* -cce⟩ rock; ***fare ~*** go rock climbing
rocciatore *m*, **-trice** *f* rock climber
roccioso *adj* rocky
Rocco *m*: ***San ~*** Saint Rocco
rock *m* ⟨*pl* rock⟩ MUS rock; ***concerto** m **~*** rock concert
rockettaro *m*, **-a** *f* rocker
rockstar *f* ⟨*pl* rockstar⟩ rockstar
roco *adj* ⟨*mpl* -chi⟩ hoarse
rodaggio *m* running in; *fig* ***sono ancora in ~*** I'm still finding my feet; ***in ~*** running in
rodare *v/t* ⟨1c⟩ run in; *fig* bring up to scratch
rodeo *m* rodeo
rodere *v/t* ⟨3b⟩ gnaw at
rodersi *v/r*: ***~ dalla gelosia*** be eaten up with jealousy; ***~ il fegato*** eat one's heart out
Rodi *f* Rhodes
rodigino I *adj* from Rovigo **II** *m*, **-a** *f* person from Rovigo
rodimento *m* gnawing; *fig* anxiety
roditore *m* rodent
rododendro *m* BOT rhododendron
rogante *m/f* drafter
rogatoria *f* rogatory letter
rogito *m* notarial deed
rogna *f infml di cane* mange; *problema* hassle
rognone *m di animale* kidney
rognoso *adj* scabby; *fig* annoying
rogo *m* ⟨*pl* -ghi⟩ stake; (*incendio*) pyre
rollerblade *m* ⟨*pl* rollerblade⟩ rollerblade
rollio *m* ⟨*pl* -ii⟩ roll
rom *m/f* ⟨*pl* rom⟩ Rom
ROM *f* COMPUT ROM
Roma *f* Rome
romagnolo I *adj* Romagnole **II** *m*, **-a** *f* Romagnole
romando I *adj* French-speaking *attr*; ***Svizzera** f **-a*** French-speaking Switzerland **II** *n*: ***romando** m* Swiss French
romanesco *adj* ⟨*mpl* -chi⟩ Roman; ***dialetto** m **~*** Roman dialect
Romania *f* Romania
romanico *adj* ⟨*mpl* -ci⟩ Romanesque
romano I *adj* Roman; ***fare alla -a*** go Dutch **II** *m*, **-a** *f* Roman
romanticheria *f* sentimentality
romanticismo *m* Romanticism
romantico ⟨*mpl* -ci⟩ **I** *adj* romantic **II** *m*, **-a** *f* romantic
romanza *f* romance
romanzato *adj* romanticized
romanzesco *adj* ⟨*mpl* -chi⟩ fictional
romanziere *m*, **-a** *f* novelist
romanzo I *m* novel; ***~ giallo*** thriller; ***~ rosa*** romantic novel **II** *adj* Romance
rombare *v/i* ⟨1a⟩ rumble
rombo[1] *m* rumble
rombo[2] *m* ZOOL turbot
rombo[3] *m* MATH rhombus
romboidale *adj* rhomboid(al)
romeno → ***rumeno***
rompere ⟨3rr⟩ **I** *v/t* break; ***~ le scatole / l'anima a qn*** *infml* get on s.o.'s nerves *infml* **II** *v/i infml* be a pain *infml*; *fig* ***~ con qn*** break it off with s.o.; ***non ~!*** *infml* stop being a pain!
rompersi *v/r* break; ***~ un braccio*** break one's arm

rompiballe *m/f* ⟨*pl* rompiballe⟩ *vulg* pain in the arse *vulg or US* ass *infml*
rompicapo *m* ⟨*pl* rompicapo⟩ puzzle; (*problema*) headache
rompighiaccio *m* ⟨*pl* rompighiaccio⟩ icebreaker; (*attrezzo*) ice-pick
rompiscatole *m/f* ⟨*pl* rompiscatole⟩ *infml* pain in the neck *infml*
roncola *f* bill hook
ronda *f* patrol; ***fare la ~*** patrol
rondella *f* washer
rondine *f* swallow; ***una ~ non fa primavera*** *prov* one swallow doesn't make a summer
rondò *m* ⟨*pl* rondò⟩ MUS rondo
rondone *m* swift
ronfare *v/i* ⟨1k⟩ *infml* snore
ronzare *v/i* ⟨1a⟩ buzz
ronzino *m* nag
ronzio *m* buzzing
ROS *abbr* (= **Raggruppamento Operativo Speciale**) *special operations unit of the Carabinieri*
rosa I *f* rose; ***~ selvatica*** wild rose; ***~ dei venti*** wind rose **II** *m/adj inv* pink
rosaio *m* ⟨*pl* -ai⟩ *pianta* rosebush
rosario *m* ⟨*pl* -ri⟩ REL rosary
rosato *m* rosé
rosbif *m* ⟨*pl* rosbif⟩ roast beef
roseo *adj* pink; *avvenire* rosy
roseto *m* rose garden
rosetta *f* rosette (*a.* BOT); ARCH rose; COOK *bread roll shaped like a rose*
rosicare *v/t* ⟨1d & l⟩: ***~ qc*** gnaw sth; ***chi non risica non rosica*** nothing ventured, nothing gained
rosicchiare *v/t* ⟨1a⟩ gnaw
rosicchiarsi *v/r* ⟨1a⟩: ***~ le unghie*** bite one's finger nails
rosmarino *m* rosemary
rosolare *v/t* ⟨1l & c⟩ brown
rosolia *f* German measles *sg*
rosone *m* ARCH rose window
rospo *m* toad; *fig* ***ingoiare il ~*** *infml* lump it *infml*
rossastro *adj* reddish
rossetto *m* lipstick
rossiccio *adj* ⟨*mpl* -cci⟩ reddish
rosso I *adj* red; ***film a luci*** *fpl* ***-e*** blue film *or* movie **II** *m* red; ***~ d'uovo*** egg yolk; ***fermarsi al ~*** stop at a red light; ***passare col ~*** go through a red light; ***~ di sera, bel tempo si spera*** *prov* red sky at night, shepherd's delight
rossore *m* red patch
rosticceria *f* rotisserie (*shop selling roast meat*)
rosticciana *f* COOK *grilled pork chops*
rosticciere *m*, **-a** *f* roast meat seller
rostro *m* ZOOL bill; AUTO guard
rotabile *adj*: ***materiale*** *m* ***~*** rolling stock
rotaia *f* rail
rotante *adj* revolving
rotare *v/i* ⟨1o⟩ rotate
rotativa *f* rotary press
rotatoria *f* roundabout, *US* traffic circle
rotazione *f* rotation
roteare ⟨1l⟩ **I** *v/t* twirl; ***~ gli occhi*** roll one's eyes **II** *v/i* gyrate
rotella *f* castor
rotocalco *m* ⟨*pl* -chi⟩ magazine
rotolare *v/t & v/i* ⟨1l & c⟩ roll
rotolarsi *v/r* roll (around)
rotolino *m* PHOT film
rotolo *m* roll; PHOT film; ***andare a -i*** go to rack and ruin; ***mandare a -i*** ruin
rotonda *f* rotunda; *per il traffico* roundabout
rotondetto *adj* roundish
rotondità *f* ⟨*pl* rotondità⟩ roundness; *pl hum* curves
rotondo *adj* round; ***tavola*** *f* ***-a*** round table
rotore *m* MECH, AVIAT rotor
rotta[1] *f* NAUT, AVIAT course; *fig* (*giusta direzione*) straight and narrow; ***cambiare ~*** change course
rotta[2] *f*: ***a ~ di collo*** at breakneck speed
rottamare *v/t* ⟨1m⟩ AUTO scrap
rottamazione *f* AUTO scrapping
rottame *m* wreck
rotto I *past part* → ***rompere*** **II** *adj* broken
rottura *f* breaking; *infml tra innamorati* break-up; ***che ~!*** *infml* what a pain! *infml*
rotula *f* knee cap
roulette *f* ⟨*pl* roulette⟩ roulette
roulotte *f* ⟨*pl* roulotte⟩ caravan
round *m* ⟨*pl* round⟩ SPORTS round
routine *f* routine
rovente *adj* red-hot (*a. fig*)
rovere *m/f* durmast
rovescia *f*: ***alla ~*** (*davanti didietro*) back to front; (*con l'interno all'esterno*) inside out; (*con il sotto sopra*) upside down

rovesciamento *m di oggetti* overturning; *di liquidi* spilling; *fig* reversal; POL overthrowing
rovesciare *v/t* ⟨1f & b⟩ *liquidi* spill; *oggetto* knock over; (*capovolgere*) overturn, upset; *fig* turn upside down
rovesciarsi *v/r* overturn, capsize
rovesciata *f calcio* bicycle kick
rovescio *m* ⟨*pl* -sci⟩ **1.** reverse; *in tennis* backhand; ***~ di fortuna*** reversal of fortune; ***il ~ della medaglia*** the other side of the coin; ***mettersi una maglia al ~*** put a sweater on inside out **2.** *fig* ***~ d'acqua*** downpour, cloudburst
roveto *m* bramble bush
rovighese **I** *adj* from Rovigo **II** *m/f* person from Rovigo
rovina *f* ruin; ***andare in ~*** go to rack and ruin; ***mandare in ~*** ruin; ***-e*** *pl* ruins
rovinare *v/t* ⟨1a⟩ ruin
rovinarsi *v/r* ruin o.s.
rovinoso *adj* ruinous, disastrous
rovistare *v/t and v/i* ⟨1a⟩: ***~ (in) qc*** ransack sth, *infml* rummage through sth
rovo *m* bramble
royalties *fpl* royalties
rozzezza *f* roughness
rozzo *adj* rough and ready
RSM *abbr* (= **Repubblica di San Marino**) Republic of San Marino
R.U. *abbr* (= **Regno Unito**) UK (United Kingdom)
Ruanda *m* Rwanda
ruandese **I** *adj* Rwandan **II** *m/f* Rwandan
ruba *f*: ***andare a ~*** sell like hot cakes, walk out the door
rubacchiare *v/t* ⟨1k⟩ *infml* pilfer
rubacuori *m/f* ⟨*pl* rubacuori⟩ heartbreaker
rubare *v/t* ⟨1a⟩ steal
ruberia *f* robbery
rubicondo *adj* ruddy
rubinetteria *f* taps and bath fittings
rubinetto *m* tap; ***~ dell'acqua calda*** hot water tap
rubino *m* ruby
rubizzo *adj* sprightly
rublo *m* rouble
rubrica *f* ⟨*pl* -che⟩ *di libro* table of contents; *quaderno* address book; *di giornale* column; TV report
rucola *f* rocket
rude *adj* rough and ready
rudemente *adv* roughly
rudere *m* ruin; ***-i*** *pl* ruins
rudezza *f* roughness
rudimentale *adj* rudimentary, basic
rudimenti *mpl* basics *pl*, rudiments *pl*
ruffiano *m*, **-a** *f* creep
ruga *f* ⟨*pl* -ghe⟩ wrinkle, line
rugby *m* ⟨*pl* rugby⟩ rugby
ruggente *adj* roaring
ruggine *f* rust
rugginoso *adj* rusty
ruggire *v/i* ⟨4d⟩ roar
ruggito *m* roar
rugiada *f* dew
rugoso *adj* rough; *pelle* wrinkled; *albero* gnarled
rullaggio *m* ⟨*pl* -ggi⟩ taxiing; ***pista di ~*** taxiway
rullare *v/i* ⟨1a⟩ NAUT roll; AVIAT taxi
rullino *m* PHOT film
rullio *m* roll
rullo *m* roll; ***~ compressore*** steam roller
rum *m* rum
rumeno **I** *adj* Romanian **II** *m*, **-a** *f* Romanian **III** *m lingua* Romanian
ruminante *m* ruminant
ruminare *v/i* ⟨1a⟩ chew the cud; *fig* ruminate
rumore *m* noise; ***far ~*** make a noise, be noisy
rumoreggiare *v/i* ⟨1f⟩ be noisy; *di tuono* growl, rumble; *di folla* mutter
rumorosità *f* ⟨*pl* rumorosità⟩ noisiness
rumoroso *adj* noisy
ruolo *m* role; ***~ principale*** lead, leading role; ***personale m di ~*** (permanent) members of staff
ruota *f* wheel; ***~ anteriore*** front wheel; ***~ dentata*** cog; ***~ motrice*** drive wheel; ***~ posteriore*** back wheel; ***~ di scorta*** spare wheel; *fig* ***mettere i bastoni tra le -e a qn*** put a spoke in s.o.'s wheel; *fig* ***essere l'ultima ~ del carro*** count for nothing; ***seguire a ~*** follow hot on s.o.'s heels; *fig* ***parlare a ~ libera*** blabber on
ruotare ⟨1c⟩ **I** *v/i* rotate **II** *v/t* roll; ***~ gli occhi*** roll one's eyes
rupe *f* cliff
rupestre *adj* rock *attr*; ***arte f ~*** wall painting
rurale *adj* rural; ***cassa f ~*** *credit bank*

for farmers
ruscello *m* stream
ruspa *f* bulldozer
ruspante *adj pollo* free-range
russare *v/i* ⟨1a⟩ snore
Russia *f* Russia
russo I *adj* Russian **II** *m*, **-a** *f* Russian
rusticità *f* ⟨*pl* rusticità⟩ rusticity
rustico *adj* ⟨*mpl* -ci⟩ rural, rustic; *fig* unsophisticated
ruta *f* rue
ruttare *v/i* ⟨1a⟩ belch; *di bambino* burp
ruttino *m* burp
rutto *m* belch
ruvidezza *f* roughness
ruvido *adj* rough
ruzzolare *v/i* ⟨1l⟩ fall
ruzzolone *m* fall; ***fare un ~*** fall, have a fall

S

s, S *m/f* ⟨*pl* s, S⟩ s, S
s *abbr* (= **secondo**) s, sec (second)
S *abbr* (= **sud**) S (south)
S. *abbr* (= **santo**) St (Saint)
sa → ***sapere***
S.A. *abbr* (= **Società Anonima**) Ltd (Limited)
sabato *m* Saturday; ***di ~*** on Saturdays; ***è meglio uscire di ~*** it's better to go out on a Saturday
sabaudo I *adj* from (the House of) Savoy **II** *m*, **-a** *f* person from (the House of) Savoy
sabbatico *adj* ⟨*mpl* -ci⟩: ***anno*** *m* ***~*** sabbatical
sabbia *f* sand; ***-e*** *pl* ***mobili*** quicksands
sabbiatura *f* sand bath
sabbioso *adj* sandy
sabino I *adj* Sabine **II** *m*, **-a** *f* Sabine
sabotaggio *m* sabotage
sabotare *v/t* ⟨1a⟩ sabotage
sabotatore *m*, **-trice** *f* saboteur
sacca *f* ⟨*pl* -cche⟩ bag; ANAT, BIOL sac
saccarina *f* saccharin
saccarosio *m* ⟨*pl* -i⟩ sucrose
saccente *adj* presumptuous
saccheggiare *v/t* ⟨1f⟩ sack; *hum* raid
saccheggiatore *m*, **-trice** *f* looter
saccheggio *m* ⟨*pl* -ggi⟩ sack, sacking
sacchetto *m* bag
sacco *m* ⟨*pl* -cchi⟩ **1.** sack; ***~ da montagna*** backpack, rucksack; ***~ di patate*** sack of potatoes; ***~ a pelo*** sleeping bag; ***cogliere qn con le mani nel ~*** catch s.o. red-handed; ***mangiare al ~*** have a packed *or US* bag lunch; *fig* ***vuotare il ~*** spill the beans; *confidarsi* pour one's heart out **2.** *fig* ***un ~ di*** *infml* piles of *infml*; ***un ~ di soldi*** a packet; ***costa un ~*** it costs a fortune; ***divertirsi un ~*** have a great time; ***darsi un ~ di arie*** put on airs
saccoccia *f*: *fig* ***mettersi in ~*** pocket
saccopelista *m/f* ⟨*mpl* -i⟩ backpacker, hiker
sacerdotale *adj* priestly
sacerdote *m* priest
sacerdotessa *f* priestess
sacerdozio *m* ⟨*pl* -zi⟩ priesthood
Sacra Corona Unita *f Mafia organization based in Puglia*
sacrale *adj* sacred; ANAT sacral
sacralità *f* ⟨*pl* sacralità⟩ sacredness
sacramentare *v/i* ⟨1a⟩ *infml* swear
sacramento *m* sacrament
sacrario *m* ⟨*pl* -ri⟩ memorial; ***~ ai caduti*** war memorial
Sacra Rota *f* Rota
Sacra Scrittura *f* Holy Scripture
sacrestano *m*, **-a** *f* sacristan
sacrestia *f* sacristy
sacrificare *v/t* ⟨1m & d⟩ sacrifice
sacrificarsi *v/r* sacrifice o.s.
sacrificato *adj* (*vita*) of sacrifice; (*non valorizzato*) wasted
sacrificio *m* ⟨*pl* -ci⟩ sacrifice; ***a costo di -i*** through making sacrifices
sacrilegio *m* sacrilege
sacrilego *m*, **-a** *f* ⟨*mpl* -ghi⟩ sacrilegious person
sacro *adj* sacred; ***Sacra Famiglia*** *f* Holy Family; ***luogo*** *m* ***~*** holy place; ***osso*** *m* ***~*** sacrum
Sacro Cuore *m* Sacred Heart

sacrosanto *adj* sacrosanct; (*legittimo*) well-deserved; ***diritto*** *m* ~ inviolable right
sadicamente *adv* sadistically
sadico ⟨*mpl* -ci⟩ **I** *adj* sadistic **II** *m*, **-a** *f* sadist
sadismo *m* sadism
sadomasochismo *m* sadomasochism
sadomasochista ⟨*mpl* -i⟩ **I** *adj* sadomasochistic **II** *m/f* sadomasochist
saetta *f* thunderbolt
saettare *v/i* ⟨1a⟩ shoot arrows
safari *m* ⟨*pl* safari⟩ safari; ~ ***fotografico*** photo safari
Saffo *f* Sappho
saga *f* ⟨*pl* -ghe⟩ saga
sagace *adj* witty; (*intelligente*) astute
sagacia *f* shrewdness; (*intelligenza*) sagacity
saggezza *f* wisdom
saggiare *v/t* ⟨1f⟩ test
saggina *f* sorghum; ***scopa*** *f* ***di*** ~ sorghum brush
saggio[1] ⟨*mpl* -ggi⟩ **I** *adj* wise **II** *m* wise man, sage
saggio[2] *m* ⟨*pl* -ggi⟩ test; (*campione*) sample; *scritto* essay; *di danza, musica* end of term show; ~ ***d'interesse*** interest rate, rate of interest; ~ ***di sconto*** discount rate
saggista *m/f* ⟨*mpl* -i⟩ essayist
saggistica *f* non-fiction
Sagittario *m* ASTROL Sagittarius
sagoma *f* outline; (*modello*) template; (*bersaglio*) target; *fig* character
sagomare *v/t* ⟨1l⟩ mo(u)ld
sagra *f* festival; ~ ***delle castagne*** chestnut festival
sagrato *m* churchyard
sagrestano *m* → ***sacrestano***
sagrestia *f* → ***sacrestia***
Sahara *m* Sahara
sahariana *f* safari jacket
sahariano *adj* Saharan
saint-honoré *m and f* ⟨*pl* saint-honoré⟩ gâteau St Honoré, *pastry case filled with cream and topped with cream puffs*
saio *m* habit
sala *f* room; (*soggiorno*) living room; ~ ***d'aspetto*** waiting room; ~ ***da pranzo*** dining room; ~ ***di lettura*** reading room; ~ ***giochi*** amusement arcade; ~ ***operatoria*** (operating) theatre, *US* operating room; ~ ***parto*** delivery room
salace *adj* (*triviale*) lewd; (*mordace*) biting
salamandra *f* salamander
salame *m* salami
salamelecco *m* ⟨*pl* -cchi⟩ salaam; ***fare*** (***mille***) ***-chi*** bow and scrape
salamoia *f*: ***in*** ~ in brine
salare *v/t* ⟨1a⟩ salt
salariale *adj* pay *attr*
salariato *m*, **-a** *f* employee
salario *m* ⟨*pl* -ri⟩ salary, wages *pl*; ~ ***base*** basic salary *or* wage
salassare *v/t* ⟨1a⟩ bleed; *fig* fleece
salasso *m* bleeding; *fig* drain
salatino *m* savo(u)ry
salato *adj* savo(u)ry; *acqua* salt; *cibo* salted; *infml* (*caro*) steep *infml*; ***troppo*** ~ salty
saldamente *adv* firmly
saldare *v/t* ⟨1a⟩ weld; *ossa* set; *fattura* pay (off)
saldatore *m*, **-trice** *f* welder
saldatura *f* welding; ***una*** ~ a weld
saldezza *f* firmness; *fig* steadfastness
saldo I *adj* steady, secure; ***cuore*** *m* ~ steadfast heart; *fig* ***essere*** ~ ***nelle proprie convizioni*** be unshakeable in one's beliefs; ***tenersi*** ~ hold on tight; ***avere i nervi*** *mpl* ***-i*** have steady nerves **II** *m* payment; *in svendita* sale item; (*resto*) balance; ***-i*** *pl* ***di fine stagione*** end-of-season sales; ***articolo in*** ~ sale item; ~ ***attivo*** net assets *pl*; ~ ***passivo*** net liabilities *pl*
sale *m* salt; ~ ***da cucina*** cooking salt; ***-i da bagno*** bath salts; ***rimanere di*** ~ be dumbfounded; ***ha poco*** ~ ***in zucca*** he's not very bright
salentino I *adj* from Salento **II** *m*, **-a** *f* person from Salento
salernitano I *adj* from Salerno **II** *m*, **-a** *f* person from Salerno
salesiano I *adj* Salesian **II** *m*, **-a** *f* Salesian; ***i Salesiani*** the Salesians
sales manager *m/f* ⟨*pl* sales manager⟩ sales manager
salgemma *m* ⟨*pl* salgemma⟩ rock salt
salgo → ***salire***
salice *m* willow; ~ ***piangente*** weeping willow
saliente *adj* protruding; *fig* salient; ***il punto*** ~ the salient point
saliera *f* salt cellar
salina *f* salt works *sg or pl*

salino *adj* saline, salt
salire ⟨4m⟩ **I** *v/i* climb; *di livello*, *prezzi*, *temperatura*, rise; **~ su** *scala* climb; *treno*, *autobus* get on; **~ sulla montagna** climb the mountain; **aiutare qn a ~** help s.o. to get on; **~ sul treno** get on the train; **~ in macchina** get in the car; **~ a cavallo** get on a horse; *fig* **~ alla testa** go to one's head; **~ al trono** ascend the throne **II** *v/t*: **~ le scale** *andare* go up, climb; *venire* come up, climb
salisburghese I *adj* from Salzburg **II** *m/f* person from Salzburg
saliscendi *m* ⟨*pl* saliscendi⟩: **finestra** *f* **a ~** sash window
salita *f* climb; *strada* slope; **strada** *f* **in ~** steep street
saliva *f* saliva
salivare *adj* salivary; **ghiandole** *fpl* **-i** salivary glands
salivazione *f* salivation
salma *f* corpse, body
salmastro I *adj* briny **II** *m* salt
salmì *m* salmi; **lepre in ~** hare salmi
salmistrato *adj* corned; **lingua** *f* **-a** corned tongue
salmo *m* REL psalm
salmodiare *v/i* ⟨1k⟩ chant
salmone *m* salmon; **~ affumicato** smoked salmon
salmonella *f* salmonella (poisoning)
salnitro *m* saltpetre, *US* saltpeter
Salomone[1] *m* Solomon
Salomone[2] *fpl* the Solomon Islands
salomonico *adj* ⟨*mpl* -ci⟩ Solomonic; **giudizio** *m* **~** judgement of Solomon
salone *m* living room; (*esposizione*) show; **~ dell'automobile** motor show; **~ di bellezza** beauty salon
salopette *f* ⟨*pl* salopette⟩ dungarees *pl*
salotto *m* drawing room, lounge; **fare ~** gossip; **~ letterario** literary salon
salpare *v/i* ⟨1a⟩ leave port
salsa *f* sauce; **~ di pomodoro** tomato sauce
salsedine *f* saltiness
salsiccia *f* ⟨*pl* -cce⟩ sausage
salsicciotto *m* frankfurter
saltare ⟨1a⟩ **I** *v/t* **1.** jump **2.** (*omettere*) skip; **~ il pranzo** miss lunch **3. ~** (**in padella**) sauté **II** *v/i* **1.** jump; **~ in piedi** leap to one's feet; **~ (giù) dal letto** jump out of bed; **~ dalla gioia** jump for joy; **~ fuori** turn up; *fig* **cosa ti salta in mente?** what's the idea?; **~ addosso a qn** jump on s.o.; **~ agli occhi** leap at s.o.; **~ di palo in frasca** jump from one subject to another; **la riunione è saltata** the meeting's cancelled; **saltò fuori che ...** it came out that ...; **gli sono saltati i nervi** he went mad **2.** *di bottone* come off **3.** *di fusibile* blow; ELEC **è saltata la corrente** there's been a power cut; MIL **~ / far ~ in aria** blow up **4.** *infml di impegno* be cancelled
saltellante *adj* hopping
saltellare *v/i* ⟨1b⟩ hop
saltello *m* hop
saltimbanco *m* ⟨*pl* -chi⟩ acrobat
saltimbocca *m* ⟨*pl* saltimbocca⟩ *fried veal topped with prosciutto and a sage leaf*
salto *m* jump; (*dislivello*) change in level; **~ mortale** somersault; *fig* **fare i -i mortali** somersault; **~ in alto** high jump; **~ in lungo** long jump; *fig* **~ nel buio** leap in the dark; **a -i** by fits and starts; **fare un ~ di qualità** make a qualitative leap; **fare quattro -i** have a bit of a dance; **faccio un ~ da te** I'll drop by *or* in; **fare un ~ al supermercato** pop to the supermarket; **~ con l'asta** pole vault, pole vaulting
saltuariamente *adv* occasionally
saltuario *adj* ⟨*mpl* -ri⟩ occasional; **lavoro** *m* **~** casual work
salubre *adj* healthy
salubrità *f* ⟨*pl* salubrità⟩ wholesomeness
salumeria *f* shop that sells salumi
salumi *mpl* cold meat *sg*
salumiere *m*, **-a** *f person who owns a shop that sells cold meats*
salumificio *m place where different types of cold meat are produced*
salutare[1] *adj* healthy; *fig discussione* helpful
salutare[2] *v/t* ⟨1a⟩ say hello to, greet; **salutami la tua famiglia** say hello to the family for me
salutarsi *v/r* say hello / goodbye
salute *f* health; **~!** cheers!; **alla tua ~!** cheers!, here's to you!; **ministero** *m* **della Salute** Ministry of Health
salutista *m/f* ⟨*mpl* -i⟩ health fanatic
saluto *m* wave; **tanti -i** greetings; **distinti -i** best regards; **togliere il ~ a qn** snub s.o.

salvabile *adj*: ***salvare il ~*** save what one can
salvacondotto *m* pass
salvadanaio *m* moneybox
salvadoregno I *adj* Salvadorean **II** *m*, **-a** *f* Salvadorean
salvagente *m* ⟨*pl* salvagente⟩ lifebelt; *giubbotto* life jacket; *per bambini* ring; (*isola spartitraffico*) traffic island
salvaguardare *v/t* ⟨1a⟩ protect, safeguard
salvaguardia *f* protection; ***a ~ dell'ambiente*** to protect the environment
salvare *v/t* ⟨1a⟩ save, rescue; ***~ le apparenze*** keep up appearances; ***~ la faccia*** save face; ***~ la vita a qn*** save s.o.'s life; ***~ capra e cavoli*** have it both ways
salvarsi *v/r* escape; ***si salvi chi può!*** every man for himself!
salvaschermo *m* COMPUT screensaver
salvaslip *m* ⟨*pl* salvaslip⟩ panty-liner
salvataggio *m* ⟨*pl* -ggi⟩ salvage; ***azione*** *f* ***di ~*** rescue operation; ***barca*** *f* ***di ~*** lifeboat; ***giubbotto*** *m* ***di ~*** life jacket; ***scialuppa*** *f* ***di ~*** lifeboat
salvatore *m*, **-trice** *f* rescuer; ***il Salvatore*** the Saviour
salvavita *m* ⟨*pl* salvavita⟩ circuit-breaker
salve *fpl*: ***sparare a ~*** fire blanks
salve! *int* hello!
salvezza *f* salvation
salvia *f* sage
salvietta *f* napkin, *Br* serviette
salvo I *adj* safe **II** *prep* except; ***~ che*** unless; ***~ imprevisti*** barring accidents, all being well **III** *m*: ***mettersi in ~*** take shelter
Samaria *f* Samaria
samaritano I *adj* Samaritan **II** *m*, **-a** *f* Samaritan; ***il buon ~*** the good Samaritan
sambuca *f* Sambuca (*kind of aniseed alcoholic drink*)
sambuco *m* ⟨*pl* -chi⟩ elder
sammarinese I *adj* from San Marino **II** *m/f* person from San Marino
samoano I *adj* Samoan **II** *m*, **-a** *f* Samoan
Samoa Occidentali *fpl* Western Samoa
samoiedo I *adj* Samoyede **II** *m*, **-a** *f* Samoyede **III** *n*: ***samoiedo*** *m* (*cane*) Samoyede
sampietrino *m porphyry paving slab as originally used for Saint Peter's Square in Rome*
San *adj* = ***Santo***
sanabile *adj* amendable (*a.* JUR); ECON retrievable; *fig* remediable
sanare *v/t* ⟨1a⟩ heal; FIN, ARCH restore
sanarsi *v/r* ⟨1a⟩ heal
sanatoria *f* JUR act of amendment
sanatorio *m* ⟨*pl* -ri⟩ sanatorium, *US* sanitarium
sanbernardo *m* ZOOL Saint Bernard
sancire *v/t* ⟨4d⟩ (*stabilire*) sanction; (*approvare*) ratify; ***~ il diritto al lavoro*** sanction the right to work
sandalo *m* sandal; BOT sandalwood
sandolino *m* scull
sandwich *m* ⟨*pl* sandwich⟩ sandwich
sangallo *m* ⟨*pl* sangallo⟩ broderie anglaise
sangiovese *m* COOK *red wine typical of Tuscany and Romagna*
sangue *m* blood; ***a ~ freddo*** in cold blood; ***donare il ~*** give blood; COOK ***al ~*** rare; ***analisi*** *f* ***del ~*** blood test; ***donare il ~*** give blood; ***il ~ non è acqua*** blood's thicker than water; ***picchiare qn a ~*** beat s.o. black and blue; ***sudare ~*** sweat blood
sanguigno *adj*: ***gruppo*** *m* ***~*** blood group; ***vaso*** *m* ***~*** blood vessel
sanguinaccio *m* ⟨*pl* -cci⟩ black pudding, *US* blood sausage
sanguinante *adj* bleeding (*a. fig*); *bistecca* rare
sanguinare *v/i* ⟨1l⟩ bleed; ***mi sanguina il naso*** my nose is bleeding
sanguinario *adj* ⟨*mpl* -ri⟩ bloody
sanguinolento *adj* bleeding
sanguinoso *adj* bloody
sanguisuga *f* ⟨*pl* -ghe⟩ leech
sanità *f* health; *amministrazione* health care; ***~ pubblica*** public health; ***~ di mente*** mental health; ***ministro*** *m* ***della ~*** Minister of Health
sanitario *adj* ⟨*mpl* -ri⟩ health *attr*; ***assistenza*** *f* ***-a*** health care
San Marino *m* San Marino
sannita *m/f* ⟨*mpl* -i⟩ Samnite
sannitico *adj* ⟨*mpl* -ci⟩ Samnite
sanno → ***sapere***
sano *adj* healthy; ***~ e salvo*** safe and sound; ***essere ~ come un pesce*** be

as fit as a fiddle
San Pietroburgo *f* Saint Petersburg
sanscrito *m* Sanskrit
San Silvestro *m* New Year's Eve
Sansone *m* Samson
santabarbara *f* dynamite
santarellina *f* goody two shoes
santificare *v/t* ⟨1m & d⟩ sanctify; ***~ le feste*** observe the religious festivals
santificazione *f* sanctification
santino *m* card with a holy picture on it
santissimo I *adj* most holy **II** *m*: ***il Santissimo*** the Holy Sacrament
santità *f* saintliness; ***Sua Santità*** His / Your Holiness
santo I *adj* holy; ***acqua*** *f* ***-a*** holy water; ***parole -e!*** how right you are!; ***starsene in -a pace*** be in peace and quiet; ***la settimana -a*** Holy Week; ***tutto il ~ giorno*** the whole blessed day; ***~ cielo!*** Good Heavens! *fig* ***avere qualche ~ in paradiso*** have friends in high places; ***non è uno stinco di ~*** he's no angel **II** *m*, **-a** *f* saint; *davanti al nome* St; ***San Francesco*** Saint Francis; ***il Santo Padre*** the Holy Father; ***la Santa Sede*** the Holy See; ***lo Spirito Santo*** the Holy Spirit
santone *m pej* guru
santuario *m* ⟨*pl* -ri⟩ sanctuary
sanzionare *v/t* ⟨1a⟩ (*sancire*) sanction; (*punire*) punish
sanzione *f* sanction; ***~ disciplinare*** disciplinary measure
sapere ⟨2n⟩ **I** *v/t* **1.** know; (***venire a***) **~** hear; ***lo so*** I know; ***saperla lunga*** know all about it; ***~ il fatto proprio*** know what's what; ***far ~ qc a qn*** let s.o. know sth; ***la sai l'ultima?*** have you heard the latest?; ***non saprei*** I wouldn't know **2.** (*essere capace di*) be able to; ***sai nuotare?*** can you swim? **II** *v/i* **1.** ***non si sa mai*** you never know; ***per quel che ne so*** as far as I know; ***buono a sapersi*** that's worth knowing; ***sapersi al sicuro*** know one is safe; ***che io sappia*** as far as I know **2.** ***~ di*** (*avere sapore di*) taste of; ***non sa di nulla*** it doesn't taste of anything **3.** ***saperci fare con qn*** be good with s.o.; ***saperci fare con qc*** have a way with sth **III** *m* knowledge
sapido *adj* savo(u)ry; *fig* witty
sapiente I *adj* wise **II** *m/f* (*scienzato*) scientist
sapientemente *adv* wisely
sapientone *m*, **-a** *f* know-all
sapienza *f* wisdom
sapone *m* soap; ***~ neutro*** mild soap; ***~ liquido*** liquid soap; *fig* ***acqua e ~*** with no make-up on; ***bolla*** *f* ***di ~*** soap bubble; *fig* ***finire in una bolla di ~*** come to nothing
saponetta *f* toilet soap
saponificio *m* ⟨*pl* -ci⟩ soap factory
saponoso *adj* soapy
sapore *m* taste (***di*** of); ***-i*** *pl* aromatic herbs; ***~ strano*** strange taste; ***avere ~ di qc*** taste of sth; ***senza ~*** tasteless
saporitamente *adv fig* with gusto; ***dormire ~*** sleep soundly
saporito *adj* tasty
saputello *m*, **-a** *f* know-all, *US* know-it-all
saputo *past part* → ***sapere***
sarabanda *f* MUS sarabande; *fig* bedlam; (*rumore*) hullabaloo
saraceno I *adj* Saracen; ***grano*** *m* ***~*** buckwheat **II** *m*, **-a** *f* Saracen
saracinesca *f* ⟨*pl* -sche⟩ roller shutter
sarago *m* ⟨*pl* -ghi⟩ sargo
sarcasmo *m* sarcasm; ***fare del ~*** be sarcastic; ***non fare ~!*** don't be sarcastic!
sarcastico *adj* ⟨*mpl* -ci⟩ sarcastic
sarchiare *v/t* ⟨1f⟩ weed
sarcofago *m* ⟨*pl* -gi e -ghi⟩ sarcophagus
sarcoma *m* sarcoma
Sardegna *f* Sardinia
sardina *f* sardine
sardo I *adj* Sardinian **II** *m*, **-a** *f* Sardinian
sardonico *adj* ⟨*mpl* -ci⟩ sardonic
sarò → ***essere***
sartiame *m* NAUT rigging
sarto *m*, **-a** *f* tailor; *per donne*, THEAT dressmaker
sartoria *f* tailor's; *per donne* dressmaker's; *arte* tailoring, dressmaking
sartù *m* ⟨*pl* sartù⟩ COOK *a Neapolitan speciality of a rice mould with tomato sauce, meatballs, mushrooms, mozzarella and eggs*
SAS *abbr* (= **Società in accomandita semplice**) *limited partnership*
sassarese I *adj* from Sassari **II** *m/f* person from Sassari

sassata *f* blow (with a stone); ***prendere a -e qn*** stone s.o.
sassifraga *f* ⟨*pl* -ghe⟩ saxifrage
sasso *m* stone; ***restare di ~*** be thunderstruck
sassofonista *m/f* ⟨*mpl* -i⟩ saxophone player, saxophonist
sassofono *m* saxophone
sassolino *m* pebble; *fig* ***togliersi un ~ dalla scarpa*** get sth off one's chest
sassoso *adj* stony
satana *m* Satan
satanasso *m* devil; *fig* fiend
satanico *adj* ⟨*mpl* -ci⟩ satanic; ***setta f -a*** satanic sect
satanismo *m* satanism
satellitare *adj* satellite; ***navigatore m ~*** satellite navigator; ***telefono m ~*** satellite phone
satellite I *m* satellite; ***collegamento m via ~*** satellite link **II** *adj* satellite *attr*; ***città f ~*** satellite town
satin *m* ⟨*pl* satin⟩ satin
satinato *adj* satinized; ***carta f -a*** glazed paper; ***pelle f -a*** silky smooth skin
satira *f* satire
satirico *adj* ⟨*mpl* -ci⟩ satirical
satollo *adj* satiated
satrapo *m* satrap; *fig* moghul
saturare *v/t* ⟨1l⟩ saturate (***di*** with)
saturazione *f* saturation
Saturno *m* Saturn
saturo *adj* saturated
saudita ⟨*mpl* -i⟩ **I** *adj* Saudi (Arabian) **II** *m/f* Saudi (Arabian)
sauna *f* sauna; ***fare la ~*** have a sauna
savana *f* savannah
savio ⟨*mpl* -vi⟩ **I** *adj* wise **II** *m*, **-a** *f* wise person; ***i sette -i*** the Seven Sages
Savoia *f* Savoy
savoiardo I *adj* Savoyard **II** *m*, **-a** *f* Savoyard **III** *n*: ***savoiardo*** *m sponge finger*
savoir-faire *m* ⟨*pl* savoir faire⟩ savoir-faire
savoir-vivre *m* ⟨*pl* savoir vivre⟩ savoir-vivre
savonese I *adj* from Savona **II** *m/f* person from Savona
saziare *v/t* ⟨1g⟩ satiate
saziarsi *v/r* eat one's fill; ***non ~ mai di fare qc*** never get tired of doing sth
sazietà *f*: ***mangiare a ~*** eat one's fill
sazio *adj* ⟨*mpl* -zi⟩ full (up)
sbaciucchiare *v/t* ⟨1k⟩ smother with kisses
sbaciucchiarsi *v/r* ⟨1k⟩ smooch, snog
sbadataggine *f* absentmindedness
sbadatamente *adv* absentmindedly
sbadato *adj* absent-minded
sbadigliare *v/i* ⟨1g⟩ yawn
sbadiglio *m* ⟨*pl* -gli⟩ yawn; ***fare uno ~*** yawn
sbafare *v/t* ⟨1l⟩ *infml* polish off
sbafatore *m*, **-trice** *f* scrounger
sbafo *m*: ***a ~*** by scrounging
sbagliare ⟨1g⟩ **I** *v/i* make a mistake; ***~ a fare qc*** be wrong to do sth; ***hai sbagliato a dirle la verità*** you were wrong to tell her the truth; ***sbagliando s'impara*** *prov* you learn by your mistakes **II** *v/t* make a mistake in; ***~ direzione*** go the wrong way; ***~ mestiere*** miss one's vocation; ***~ numero*** dial / get the wrong number; ***~ persona*** have the wrong person; ***~ strada*** go the wrong way
sbagliarsi *v/r* ⟨1g⟩ make a mistake; ***~ sul conto di qn*** be wrong about s.o.; ***se non mi sbaglio*** if I'm not mistaken
sbagliato *adj* wrong
sbaglio *m* ⟨*pl* -gli⟩ mistake; ***per ~*** by mistake; ***senza -i*** flawless
sbalestrato *adj* confused
sballare ⟨1a⟩ **I** *v/t* unpack; *fig* get wrong **II** *v/i* miscalculate
sballato *adj discorso* absurd; *idea* scatterbrained; *infml persona* high
sballo *m* unpacking; *infml* high; ***da ~*** rip-roaring, fantastic
sballottamento *m*, **sballottio** *m* ⟨*pl* -ii⟩ tossing, jolting
sballottare *v/t* ⟨1m⟩ jolt, toss
sbalordimento *m* amazement, stupefaction
sbalordire *v/t* ⟨4d⟩ stun, amaze
sbalordirsi *v/r* amaze
sbalorditivo *adj* amazing, incredible
sbalordito *adj* amazed; ***restare ~*** be flabbergasted
sbalzare *v/t* ⟨1a⟩ throw; *temperatura* change
sbalzo *m* jump; ***~ di temperatura*** sudden change in temperature
sbancare *v/t* ⟨1d⟩ *banco* break; *persona* bankrupt
sbandamento *m* AUTO skid; *fig* disori-

entation; MIL *fig* disbandment; ***avere un attimo di ~*** be confused for a moment

sbandare *v/i* ⟨1a⟩ AUTO skid; RAIL, *fig* go off the rails

sbandarsi *v/r* ⟨1a⟩ disband, disperse

sbandata *f* AUTO skid; ***prendersi una ~ per qn*** *infml* develop a crush on s.o.

sbandato **I** *adj* disbanded; ***soldati*** *mpl* ***-i*** disbanded soldiers **II** *m*, **-a** *f fig* drifter, misfit

sbandierare *v/t* ⟨1a⟩ *bandiere* fly; *fig* ***~ qc ai quattro venti*** flaunt sth from the rooftops

sbandieratore *m* **-trice** *f* flag flyer

sbando *m* disorder; ***essere allo ~*** be running wild

sbaraccare *v/t* ⟨1d⟩ clear; *infml* clear out

sbaragliare *v/t* ⟨1g⟩ defeat; MIL rout

sbaraglio *m*: ***mandare qn allo ~*** send s.o. to certain defeat; ***andare allo ~*** risk one's life

sbarazzare *v/t* ⟨1a⟩ clear

sbarazzarsi *v/r*: ***~ di*** get rid of

sbarazzino *adj* jaunty

sbarbarsi *v/r* have a shave

sbarbatello *m hum* young pup

sbarcare ⟨1d⟩ **I** *v/t merci* unload; *persone* disembark; *fig* ***~ il lunario*** make ends meet **II** *v/i* disembark

sbarco *m* ⟨*pl* -chi⟩ *di merce* unloading; *di persone* disembarkation

sbarra *f* bar; ***essere alla ~*** be on trial; ***essere dietro le -e*** be behind bars; ***mettere alla ~*** put in the dock

sbarramento *m* fence; (*ostacolo*) barrier

sbarrare *v/t* ⟨1a⟩ bar; *assegno* cross; *occhi* open wide; ***~ il passo a qn*** block s.o.'s way

sbarrato *adj assegno* crossed; *occhi* wide open

sbatacchiare ⟨1k⟩ **I** *v/t porta* slam; *oggetti* hurl **II** *v/i* slam

sbattere ⟨3a⟩ **I** *v/t porta* slam, bang; (*urtare*) bang; COOK beat; ***~ per terra*** knock down; ***~ la porta in faccia a qn*** close the door in s.o.'s face; ***~ le ali*** flap one's wings; ***~ fuori*** throw out; ***non sapere dove ~ la testa*** be at one's wits' ends **II** *v/i* bang; ***andare a ~ contro un albero*** crash into a tree

sbattersene *v/r* ⟨3a⟩ *vulg*: ***me ne sbatto!*** *vulg* I don't give a fuck! *vulg*

sbattitore *m* hand mixer

sbavare *v/i* ⟨1a⟩ dribble; *fig* ***~ dietro a qn*** drool over s.o.

sbavarsi *v/r* ⟨1a⟩ *infml* dribble

sbavatura *f* dribble; *di vernice* smudge; METAL trimming

sbeccato *adj* chipped

sbeffeggiare *v/t* ⟨1n⟩ jeer

sbellicarsi *v/r*: ***~ dalle risa*** shake with laughter

sbendare *v/t* ⟨1b⟩ take the bandage(s) off

sbendarsi *v/r* ⟨1a⟩ take one's bandage(s) off

sberla *f infml* slap

sberleffo *m* grimace

sbiadire *v/i* ⟨4d⟩ fade

sbiadirsi *v/r* ⟨4d⟩ fade (*a. fig*)

sbiadito *adj* faded; *stile* colo(u)rless

sbiancante *m* whitener, bleach

sbiancare ⟨1d⟩ **I** *v/t* bleach **II** *v/i* turn pale

sbieco *adj*: ***di ~*** aslant, askew; *fig* ***guardare qn di ~*** cast sidelong glances at s.o.

sbigottimento *m* consternation

sbigottire *v/t* ⟨4d⟩ dismay

sbigottirsi *v/r* be dismayed

sbigottito *adj* dismayed

sbilanciare *v/t* ⟨1f⟩ unbalance, throw off balance

sbilanciarsi *v/r* lose one's balance; *fig* commit o.s.

sbilenco *adj* ⟨*mpl* -chi⟩ lopsided

sbirciare *v/t* ⟨1k⟩ peek

sbirciata *f* peek; ***dare una ~ a qc*** take a peek at sth

sbirro *m infml pej* cop

sbizzarrirsi *v/r* ⟨4d⟩ indulge o.s.

sbloccare *v/t* ⟨1c & d⟩ clear; *macchina* unblock; *prezzi* deregulate; *fig* ***~ la situazione*** end the deadlock; ***~ il traffico*** clear the traffic

sblocco *m* ⟨*pl* -cchi⟩ clearing; *di macchina* unblocking; *di prezzi* deregulation; ***~ degli affitti*** decontrol of rents

sbobinare *v/t* ⟨1m⟩ transcribe

sboccare *v/i* ⟨1d⟩: ***~ in*** *di fiume* flow into; *di strada* lead to

sboccato *adj* coarse, vulgar; foul-mouthed

sbocciare *v/t* ⟨1f & c⟩ open (out)

sbocco *m* ⟨*pl* -cchi⟩ FIN outlet; *di situazione* way out; ***strada*** *f* ***senza ~*** dead end, cul-de-sac; ***situazione*** *f*

senza -cchi dead-end situation
sbocconcellare *v/t* ⟨1b⟩: **~ *qc*** nibble at sth
sbollire *v/i* ⟨4d⟩ *fig* cool down
sbolognare *v/t* ⟨1a⟩ *infml*: **~ *qc a qn*** dump sth on s.o.
sbornia *f infml* hangover; ***prendersi una* ~** get drunk
sborsare *v/t* ⟨1a⟩ *infml* cough up *infml*
sbottare *v/i* ⟨1c⟩ burst out; **~ *a ridere*** burst out laughing
sbottonare *v/t* ⟨1a⟩ unbutton
sbottonarsi *v/r fig* open up (***con*** to); **~ *la giacca*** unbutton one's jacket; *fig* ***non si sbottona facilmente*** he / she doesn't show his / her feelings easily
sbozzare *v/t* ⟨1c⟩ ART rough-hew; TECH draft; (*schizzare*) sketch out, outline (*a. fig*)
sbracato *adj infml* sloppy; (*sguaiato*) vulgar
sbracciarsi *v/r* ⟨1f⟩ roll up one's sleeves
sbracciato *adj persona* with bare arms; *abito* sleeveless
sbraitare *v/i* ⟨1a⟩ shout, yell
sbranare *v/t* ⟨1a⟩ tear apart
sbrecciarsi *v/r* ⟨1f⟩ be chipped
sbriciolare *v/t* ⟨1l⟩ crumble
sbriciolarsi *v/r* crumble
sbrigare *v/t* ⟨1e⟩ attend to
sbrigarsi *v/r* hurry up; ***sbrigati!*** hurry (up)!; ***con lui me la sbrigo io*** I'll deal with him
sbrigativo *adj* (*rapido*) hurried, rushed; (*brusco*) brusque
sbrigliarsi *v/r* ⟨1g⟩ romp; *fig* let oneself go
sbrinamento *m* defrosting
sbrinare *v/t* ⟨1a⟩ *frigorifero* defrost
sbrinatore *m* defrost control
sbrindellato *adj* shabby
sbrodolare *v/t* ⟨1l & c⟩ dribble
sbrodolarsi *v/r* ⟨1l & c⟩ make a mess of oneself
sbrodolone *m*, **-a** *f infml* messy eater
sbrogliare *v/t* ⟨1g & c⟩ untangle, disentangle; ***sbrogliarsela*** sort things out
sbronza *f infml* hangover; ***prendersi una* ~** get drunk
sbronzarsi *v/r* ⟨1a⟩ *infml* get drunk
sbronzo *adj infml* tight *infml*, sloshed *infml*
sbruffonata *f* bluster
sbruffone *m*, **-a** *f* boaster
sbucare *v/i* ⟨1d⟩ emerge; ***da dove sei sbucato?*** where did you spring from?
sbucciare *v/t* ⟨1f⟩ *frutta, patate* peel
sbucciarsi *v/r* graze; **~ *le ginocchia*** skin one's knees
sbucciato *adj* peeled; *ginocchio* skinned
sbucciatura *f* graze
sbudellare *v/t* ⟨1b⟩ *animale* disembowel; *pesce* gut
sbudellarsi *v/r* ⟨1b⟩: **~ *dalle risa*** be in stitches
sbuffare *v/i* ⟨1a⟩ puff and pant
sbuffo *m di fumo*: puff; *di vento*: gust; ***manica f a* ~** puff(ed) sleeves
sbugiardare *v/t* ⟨1a⟩ give the lie to
s.c. *abbr* (= **sopra citato**) above-mentioned
scabbia *f* scabies
scabrosità *f* ⟨*pl* scabrosità⟩ (*crudezza*) roughness; (*asperità*) difficulty
scabroso *adj* rough, uneven; *fig* offensive
scacchiera *f* chessboard
scacchiere *m* MIL zone; *inglese* Exchequer
scacciacani *f* ⟨*pl* scacciacani⟩ dummy pistol
scacciapensieri *m* ⟨*pl* scacciapensieri⟩ Jew's harp
scacciare *v/t* ⟨1f⟩ chase away; **~ *una mosca*** whisk away a fly; **~ *di casa*** throw s.o. out of the house
scacco *m* ⟨*pl* -cchi⟩ (chess) piece; *fig* setback; **~ *matto*** checkmate; ***-cchi*** *pl* chess *sg*; ***giocare a -cchi*** play chess; ***a -cchi*** checked
scadente I → ***scadere*** **II** *adj* second-rate
scadenza *f* deadline; *su alimento* best before date; **~ *del termine*** deadline, last date; ***a breve* ~** short-term; ***a lunga* ~** long-term
scadere *v/i* ⟨2c⟩ *di passaporto* expire; *di cambiale* fall due; (*perdere valore*) decline (in quality)
scadimento *m* decline
scaduto *adj* expired; *alimento* past its sell-by date
scafandro *m* diving suit
scafato *adj* shrewd
scaffalatura *f* shelves *pl*

scaffale *m* shelf
scafista *m* ⟨*pl* -i⟩ *someone who transports illegal immigrants in boats, especially across the Adriatic*
scafo *m* hull
scagionare *v/t* ⟨1a⟩ clear
scagionarsi *v/r* ⟨1a⟩ clear oneself
scaglia *f* flake; *di legno* chip; *di pesce* scale; ***-e** pl* ***di sapone*** soapflakes
scagliare *v/t* ⟨1g⟩ hurl
scagliarsi *v/r*: ***~ contro*** attack
scaglionamento *m* staggering
scaglionare *v/t* ⟨1a⟩ space out, stagger
scaglione *m* MIL echelon; ADMIN, ECON bracket; ***a -i*** staggered
scala *f* **1.** staircase; ***~*** (***a pioli***) ladder; ***~ a chiocciola*** spiral staircase; ***~ antincendio*** fire escape; ***~ mobile*** escalator; ***fare le -e*** climb the stairs **2.** GEOG scale; FIN sliding scale; ***~ Richter*** Richter scale; ***disegno** m* ***in ~*** scale drawing; ***su larga ~*** on a large scale; ***su ~ nazionale*** country-wide; ***riprodurre in ~*** draw to scale **3.** MUS (musical) scale **4.** *carte* straight
scalabile *adj* COMPUT scalable
scalabilità *f* ⟨*pl* scalabilità⟩ COMPUT scalability
scalare[1] *v/t* ⟨1a⟩ climb
scalare[2] *adj* graded; (*graduale*) progressive; FIN graduated; MATH, PHYS scalar
scalata *f* climb; ***~ al successo*** rise to fame
scalato *adj* reduced; *capelli* layered
scalatore *m*, **-trice** *f* climber
scalcagnato *adj scarpe* worn-out; *fig* shabby
scalciare *v/i* ⟨1f⟩ kick one's legs; *cavallo* kick
scalcinato *adj* shabby
scaldabagno *m* water heater
scaldare *v/t* ⟨1a⟩ heat (up); *fig* ***~ la testa a qn*** get s.o. worked up
scaldarsi *v/r* warm up; *fig* get worked up, get excited
scaldavivande *m* ⟨*pl* scaldavivande⟩ food warmer
scaldino *m* bedwarmer
scaletta *f* small staircase; *a pioli*: small ladder; (*schema di testo*) outline; TV treatment
scalfire *v/t* ⟨4d⟩ scratch
scalfittura *f* scratch
scalfo *m* armhole
scaligero I *adj* from Verona; THEAT *referring to the Scala Theatre in Milan* **II** *m*, **-a** *f* person from Verona
scalinata *f* steps *pl*
scalino *m* step
scalmanarsi *v/r* ⟨1a⟩ bustle about; *fig* get worked up
scalmanato I *adj* (*sudato*) in a sweat; (*turbolento*) all worked up **II** *m*, **-a** *f* hothead
scalmo *m* NAUT rowlock
scalo *m* AVIAT stop; NAUT port of call; ***volo** m* ***senza ~*** nonstop flight; ***fare ~ a*** call at
scalogna *f* bad luck; ***portare ~*** be unlucky
scalognato *adj* unlucky
scalogno *m* shallot
scaloppina *f* escalope
scalpellino *m* stone mason
scalpello *m* chisel
scalpicciare *v/i* ⟨1f⟩ shuffle one's feet
scalpiccio *m* ⟨*pl* -ii⟩ shuffle
scalpitare *v/i* ⟨1l⟩ paw the ground; *fig* get restless
scalpitio *m*, ⟨*pl* -ii⟩ *m* stamping
scalpo *m* scalp
scalpore *m* noise, uproar; ***suscitare ~*** cause a sensation
scaltramente *adv* slyly
scaltrezza *f* slyness
scaltro *adj* shrewd
scalzare *v/t* ⟨1a⟩ *fig*: ***~ qn da una carica*** edge s.o. out of a job
scalzo *adj* barefoot
scambiare *v/t* ⟨1k⟩ (*confondere*) mistake (***per*** for); (*barattare*) exchange, swap *infml* (***con*** for)
scambiarsi *v/r* ⟨1k⟩ exchange; ***~ gli auguri*** exchange greetings
scambievolmente *adv* reciprocally
scambio *m* ⟨*pl* -bi⟩ exchange; *di persona* mistake; RAIL points *pl*; ***-i** pl* ***commerciali*** trade *sg*; ***~ di lettere*** exchange of letters; ***~ d'opinioni*** exchange of views; ***-i** pl* ***culturali*** cultural exchange *sg*; ***libero ~*** free trade
scambista *m/f* ⟨*mpl* -i⟩ RAIL pointsman; ECON stockbroker; *infml* swinger
scamiciato I *adj* in one's shirt sleeves **II** *n*: ***scamiciato*** *m* pinafore dress
scamorza *f type of pear-shaped cheese from Abruzzi or Campania, often*

smoked
scamosciato *adj* suede; ***scarpe*** *fpl* **-*e*** suede shoes
scampagnata *f* day out in the country; ***fare una ~*** go for a jaunt
scampanato *adj* flared; ***pantaloni*** *mpl* **-*i*** flares
scampanellare *v/i* ⟨1b⟩ ring
scampanellata *f* ring
scampanellio *m* ⟨*pl* -ii⟩ long ring
scampare *v/i* ⟨1a⟩ escape; ***~ alla morte*** escape death; ***l'hai scampata bella!*** You had a narrow escape; ***Dio ce ne scampi e liberi!*** God forbid!
scampi *mpl* ZOOL scampi *pl*
scampo *m* escape, way out; ***cercare / trovare ~*** find / seek refuge
scampolo *m* remnant
scanalatura *f* groove; ARCH flute
scandagliare *v/t* ⟨1g⟩ sound; *fig* sound out
scandalistico *adj* ⟨*mpl* -ci⟩ scandal-mongering
scandalizzare *v/t* ⟨1a⟩ scandalize, shock
scandalizzarsi *v/r* be scandalized *or* shocked (***di*** by)
scandalizzato *adj* scandalized
scandalo *m* scandal; ***suscitare ~*** cause a scandal; ***gridare allo ~*** make a scandal out of
scandalosamente *adv* outrageously
scandaloso *adj* scandalous
Scandinavia *f* Scandinavia
scandinavo I *adj* Scandinavian **II** *m*, **-a** *f* Scandinavian
scandire *v/t* ⟨4d⟩ pronounce clearly; TV scan; ***~ le parole*** articulate one's words; ***~ le ore*** mark the hours
scannare *v/t* ⟨1a⟩ scan
scannarsi *v/r* ⟨1a⟩ slaughter each other; *fig* be at each other's throats
scanner *m* ⟨*pl* scanner⟩ COMPUT scanner
scannerizzare *v/t* ⟨1a⟩ COMPUT scan
scanno *m* stool
scansafatiche *m/f* ⟨*pl* scansafatiche⟩ lazybones
scansare *v/t* ⟨1a⟩ (*allontanare*) move; (*evitare*) avoid
scansarsi *v/r* move out of the way
scansia *f* bookcase
scanso *m*: ***a ~ di equivoci*** to avoid any misunderstandings
scantinato *m* cellar
scantonare *v/i* ⟨1a⟩ turn round a corner; (*svignarsela*) slip away; *fig* change the subject
scanzonato *adj* free and easy
scapaccione *m* smack
scapestrato *adj* reckless
scapicollarsi *v/r* ⟨1a⟩ rush down
scapigliato *adj* (*spettinato*) tousled; *fig* reckless
scapitarci *v/i* ⟨1l⟩ lose out (on sth)
scapito *m*: ***a ~ di*** to the detriment of
scapola *f* shoulder blade, ANAT scapula
scapolo I *adj* single, unmarried **II** *m* bachelor
scappamento *m* TECH exhaust
scappare *v/i* ⟨1a⟩ (*fuggire*) run away; (*affrettarsi*) rush, run; ***lasciarsi ~ l'occasione*** let the opportunity slip; ***mi è scappata la pazienza*** I lost patience; ***mi è scappato detto*** it slipped out; ***mi scappa da ridere*** I can't help laughing; ***mi scappa la pipì*** I'm dying for a pee
scappata *f*: ***fare una ~*** pay a quick visit, pop; ***fare una ~ a casa*** pop home
scappatella *f* *di bambino* escapade; ***fare delle -lle*** get into mischief
scappatoia *f* way out
scappellotto *m* clip on the ear
scapricciarsi *v/r* ⟨1f⟩ satisfy one's fancies
scarabeo *m* beetle; (*gioco*) scrabble
scarabocchiare *v/t* ⟨1k & c⟩ scribble
scarabocchio *m* ⟨*pl* -cchi⟩ scribble
scarafaggio *m* ⟨*pl* -ggi⟩ cockroach
scaramantico ⟨*mpl* -ci⟩ good luck *attr*
scaramanzia *f*: ***per ~*** for good luck
scaramuccia *f* ⟨*pl* -cce⟩ MIL skirmish (*a. fig*)
scaraventare *v/t* ⟨1b⟩ throw, hurl
scaraventarsi *v/r* throw *or* hurl o.s. (***contro*** at)
scarcassato *adj* ramshackle
scarcerare *v/t* ⟨1l⟩ release
scarcerazione *f* release
scardinare *v/t* ⟨1l⟩ take off the hinges
scardinarsi *v/r* ⟨1l⟩ come off it's hinges; *fig* break up
scarica *f* ⟨*pl* -che⟩ discharge; ***~ elettrica*** electrical discharge; ***~ di pugni*** hail of blows; ***~ di invettive*** barrage of abuse; ***~ di mitra*** round of machine-gun fire

scaricabarile *m* ⟨*pl* scaricabarile⟩ buck-passing; *fig* ***fare a ~*** pass the buck

scaricare *v/t* ⟨1l & d⟩ unload; *batteria* run down; *rifiuti*, *sostanze nocive* dump; *responsabilità* offload, get rid of; ***~ qn*** *infml* get rid of s.o.; COMPUT ***~ dalla rete*** download; COMPUT ***~ su dischetto*** download to disk; ***~ dalle tasse*** deduct from tax; *fig* ***~ la colpa su qn*** off-load the blame on s.o.

scaricarsi *v/r* relax, unwind *infml*; *di batteria* run down; ***~ la coscienza*** ease one's conscience; ***il cellulare mi si è scaricato*** my mobile needs charging

scaricatore *m* unloader; MECH drainpipe; ELEC discharger; ***~ di porto*** docker

scarico ⟨*mpl* -chi⟩ **I** *adj camion* empty; *batteria* run-down; *fig* ***avere le batterie -che*** be run down; ***ho il cellulare ~*** my mobile needs charging; ***pistola*** *f* ***-a*** unloaded gun **II** *m* **1.** *di merce* unloading; *luogo* dump; ***divieto di ~*** no dumping **2.** *di responsabilità* offloading **3.** ***gas*** *m* ***di ~*** exhaust (fumes *pl*); ***tubo*** *m* ***di ~*** exhaust (pipe) **4.** ***-chi*** *pl* ***industriali*** industrial waste *sg*

scarlattina *f* scarlet fever

scarlatto I *adj* scarlet **II** *n*: ***scarlatto*** *m* scarlet

scarmigliato *adj* dishevel(l)ed

scarno *adj* bony; *fig* scanty

scarola *f* escarole

scarpa *f* shoe; ***-e*** *pl* ***da uomo / da donna*** men's / women's shoes; ***-e*** *pl* ***da ginnastica*** *Br* trainers, *US* sneakers; ***mettersi / togliersi le -e*** put on / take off one's shoes; *fig* ***fare le -e a qn*** stab s.o. in the back

scarpata *f* (*burrone*) escarpment

scarpetta *f* shoe; ***-e*** *pl* ***da ginnastica*** trainers; ***~ di Venere*** BOT lady's slipper; *fig* ***fare la ~*** *mop one's plate with a piece of bread*

scarpiera *f* shoerack

scarpinare *v/i* ⟨1a⟩ trek

scarpinata *f* trek

scarpone *m* (heavy) boot; ***~ da sci*** ski boot

scarrozzare *v/t* ⟨1m⟩ chauffeur around

scarsamente *adv* poorly

scarseggiare *v/i* ⟨1f⟩ become scarce; ***~ di qc*** not have much of sth, be short of sth

scarsezza *f*, **scarsità** *f* shortage, scarcity; ***~ di viveri*** food shortage

scarso *adj* scarce, in short supply; ***essere ~ di qc*** be lacking in sth; ***quattro chilometri -si*** barely four kilometres

scartabellare *v/t* ⟨1b⟩ leaf through

scartafaccio *m* ⟨*pl* -cci⟩ notepad

scartamento *m* RAIL gauge; ***~ ridotto*** small

scartare *v/t* ⟨1a⟩ (*svolgere*) unwrap; (*eliminare*) reject

scarto *m* rejection; (*cosa scartata*) reject; ***merce*** *f* ***di ~*** imperfect goods *pl*

scartocciare *v/t* ⟨1c⟩ unwrap

scartoffia *f* bumf

scassare *v/t* ⟨1a⟩ *infml* ruin, wreck

scassarsi *v/r infml* give up the ghost *infml*

scassato *adj infml* done for *infml*

scassinare *v/t* ⟨1a⟩ force open

scassinatore *m*, **-trice** *f* burglar

scasso *m* forced entry; ***furto*** *m* ***con ~*** breaking and entering, burglary; ***a prova di ~*** burglar-proof

scatarrare *v/i* ⟨1a⟩ *infml* hawk and spit

scatenare *v/t* ⟨1a⟩ *fig* unleash

scatenarsi *v/r fig*: *di tempesta* break; *di collera* break out; *di persona* let one's hair down

scatenato *adj* unrestrained

scatola *f* box; *di tonno*, *piselli* tin, can; ***~ cranica*** cranium; ***in ~*** *cibo* tinned, canned; ***~ da scarpe*** shoebox; AVIAT ***~ nera*** black box; *fig* ***comprare qc a ~ chiusa*** buy sth sight unseen; ***rompere le -e a qn*** *infml* be a pain in s.o.'s neck; ***averne piene le -e*** *infml* be sick and tired of; ***togliersi dalle -e*** *infml* get out of s.o.'s way; *fig* ***-e*** *pl* ***cinesi*** Chinese puzzle

scatolame *m* tinned food

scatoletta *f* tin, can; ***~ di tonno*** tin of tuna

scatolone *m* cardboard box

scattante *adj* quick, agile

scattare ⟨1a⟩ **I** *v/t* PHOT take **II** *v/i* go off; *di serratura* catch; (*arrabbiarsi*) lose one's temper; *di atleta* put on a spurt; ***~ in piedi*** jump up; ***far ~*** activate; ***~ sull'attenti*** MIL spring to attention

scattista *m/f* ⟨*mpl* -i⟩ sprinter
scatto *m* click; SPORTS spurt; PHOT exposure; *di foto* taking; TEL unit; PHOT **~ *automatico*** automatic timer; ***uno ~ di rabbia*** an angry gesture; ***~ di stipendio*** automatic raise; ***a -i*** jerkily; ***di ~*** brusquely; ***serratura** f **a ~*** spring lock; ***~ d'anzianità*** *increment for seniority*
scaturire *v/i* ⟨4d⟩ pour out
scavalcare *v/t* ⟨1d⟩ *muro* climb (over); ***~ il recinto*** climb over the fence
scavare *v/t* ⟨1a⟩ *con pala* dig; *con trivella* excavate
scavato *adj fig lineamenti* sunken
scavatrice *f* digger
scavezzacollo *m/f* ⟨*pl* scavezzacollo⟩ daredevil
scavi *mpl archeologici* dig *sg*
scavo *m* digging; (*luogo*) excavation; SEW hole
scazzottata *f* fist fight
scegliere *v/t* ⟨3ss⟩ choose, pick, select; ***c'è poco da ~*** there's not much to choose from
sceglíersi *v/r* ⟨3ss⟩ choose for oneself
sceicco *m* ⟨*pl* -cchi⟩ sheik
scelgo → ***scegliere***
scellino *m hist*, *austriaco* shilling
scelta *f* choice, selection; ***a ~*** of one's choice; ***~ di vita*** life choice; ***di prima ~*** first-rate; ***prendine uno a ~*** take your pick; ***fare la ~*** choose
scelto I *past part* → ***scegliere*** **II** *adj* handpicked; *merce*, *pubblico* (specially) selected
scemare *v/i* ⟨1a⟩ lessen
scemata *f*, **scemenza** *f* stupidity
scemo I *adj* stupid, idiotic **II** *m*, **-a** *f* idiot; ***fare lo ~*** act the fool
scempiaggine *f* stupidity
scempio[1] *adj* single
scempio[2] *m*: ***fare ~ di qc*** ruin sth
scena *f* theatre, *US* theater; (*scenata*) scene; ***~ madre*** big drama; *fig* ***colpo** m **di ~*** coup de théâtre; ***andare in ~*** be staged; ***è tutta ~!*** it's all an act!; ***mettere in ~*** produce; *fig* ***fare ~ muta*** be struck dumb; ***applauso** m **a ~ aperta*** applause in the middle of a scene; ***entrare in ~*** go on stage; *fig* make an entrance; ***uscire di ~*** go off
scenario *m* ⟨*pl* -ri⟩ screenplay; *fig* scenery
scenata *f* scene; ***fare una ~ (a qn)*** make a scene
scendere ⟨3c⟩ **I** *v/i andare* go down, descend; *venire* come down, descend; *da cavallo* get down, dismount; *dal treno*, *dall' autobus* get off; *dalla macchina* get out; *di temperatura*, *prezzi* go down, drop; ***~ le scale*** *andare* go downstairs; *venire* come downstairs; ***~ a terra*** come (back) down to earth; *fig* ***~ in piazza*** take to the streets; ***~ nei particolari*** go into details **II** *v/t*: ***~ le scale*** *andare* go down the stairs; *venire* come down the stairs
scendiletto *m* bedside rug
sceneggiata *f* scene
sceneggiato *m* TV serial
sceneggiatore *m*, **-trice** *f* scriptwriter, screenwriter
sceneggiatura *f* screenplay
scenetta *f* sketch
scenografia *f* sets *pl*
scenografico *adj* ⟨*mpl* -ci⟩ set *attr*
scenografo *m*, **-a** *f* set designer
sceriffo *m* sheriff
scervellarsi *v/r* rack one's brains
scervellato *adj* harebrained
scetticismo *m* scepticism, *US* skepticism
scettico I *adj* sceptical, *US* skeptical **II** *m*, **-a** *f* sceptic, *US* skeptic
scettro *m* sceptre, *US* scepter
scheda *f* **1.** card; (*formulario*) form; COMPUT ***~ audio*** sound card; COMPUT ***~ grafica*** graphics card; ***~ madre*** COMPUT motherboard; ***~ PC*** TEL PC card; ***~ video*** COMPUT video card; ***~ telefonica*** phone card **2.** POL ***~ elettorale*** ballot (paper); ***~ bianca*** blank vote
schedare *v/t* ⟨1b⟩ file
schedario *m* ⟨*pl* -ri⟩ file
schedato *m*, **-a** *f person with a police record*
schedina *f* pools coupon
scheggia *f* ⟨*pl* -gge⟩ sliver; *fig* ***~ impazzita*** loose cannon
scheggiato *adj* splintered
scheggiatura *f* (*azione*) splintering; (*danno*) chip
scheletrico *adj* ⟨*mpl* -ci⟩ skeletal
scheletrito *adj* skeletal; ***albero** m **~*** bare tree
scheletro *m* skeleton; *fig* ***avere uno ~ nell'armadio*** have a skeleton in one's cupboard

schema *m* ⟨*pl* -i⟩ diagram; (*abbozzo*) outline; **~ *elettrico*** wiring diagram
schematicamente *adv* schematically
schematico *adj* ⟨*mpl* -ci⟩ general; *disegno* schematic
schematizzare *v/t* ⟨1a⟩ outline
Schengen *f*: EU ***accordo*** *m* ***di* ~** Schengen Agreement
scherma *f* fencing; ***tirare di* ~** fence
schermaglia *f* ⟨*pl* -glie⟩ skirmish; *fig* cut-and-thrust
schermare *v/t* ⟨1a⟩ screen (*a.* RADIO, TV)
schermatura *f* screening
schermirsi *v/r* ⟨4d⟩ shield o.s.
schermitore *m*, **-trice** *f* fencer
schermo *m* screen; (*riparo*) shield; **~ *piatto*** flat screen
schermografia *f* X-rays *pl*
schernire *v/t* ⟨4d⟩ mock
scherno *m* scorn
scherzare *v/i* ⟨1a⟩ play; (*burlare*) joke; **~ *col fuoco*** play with fire
scherzo *m* joke; MUS scherzo; ***essere uno* ~** (*facile*) be child's play; ***-i a parte*** joking aside; ***per* ~** *fare*, *dire qc* as a joke; ***stare allo* ~** be a good sport; **~ *da prete*** *infml* silly prank
scherzosamente *adv* playfully
scherzoso *adj* playful
schiaccianoci *m* ⟨*pl* schiaccianoci⟩ pair of nutcrackers, nutcrackers *pl*
schiacciante *adj* overwhelming; *prova* damning
schiacciare ⟨1f⟩ **I** *v/t* crush; *noce* crack; **~ *un pulsante*** press a button; **~ *un piede a qn*** step on s.o.'s toes; **~ *un sonnellino*** *infml* have a snooze *infml*, have forty winks *infml* **II** *v/i* SPORTS smash
schiacciarsi *v/r* ⟨1f⟩ squash oneself
schiacciasassi *m* ⟨*pl* schiacciasassi⟩ steamroller (*a. fig*)
schiacciata *f* SPORTS smash; COOK *type of focaccia from Tuscany or Umbria*
schiacciato *adj* crushed, squashed
schiaffare *v/t* ⟨1a⟩ *infml* fling
schiaffarsi *v/r* ⟨1a⟩ *infml* fling oneself
schiaffeggiare *v/t* ⟨1f⟩ slap
schiaffo *m* slap; **~ *morale*** slap in the face; ***avere una faccia da -i*** look cheeky
schiamazzare *v/i* ⟨1a⟩ make a din
schiamazzo *m* yell, scream; JUR ***-i*** *pl* ***notturni*** breach of the peace
schiantare ⟨1a⟩ **I** *v/t* crash, smash **II** *v/i* crash
schiantarsi *v/r* ⟨1a⟩ crash
schianto *m* crash
schiappa *f infml* washout
schiarente I *adj* lightening **II** *m* lightener
schiarire *v/t* ⟨4d⟩ lighten
schiarirsi *v/r* brighten up; **~ *la voce*** clear one's throat; **~ *le idee*** buck one's ideas up
schiarita *f* bright spell
schiavismo *m* slavery
schiavista *m/f* ⟨*mpl* -i⟩ *fig* slave-driver
schiavitù *f* slavery
schiavizzare *v/t* ⟨1a⟩ enslave (*a. fig*)
schiavo I *adj*: ***essere* ~ *di*** be a slave to **II** *m*, **-a** *f* slave
schiena *f* back; ***mal*** *m* ***di* ~** back ache
schienale *m di sedile* back
schiera *f* group; ***a* ~** in ranks; ***villette*** *fpl* ***a* ~** terraced houses, *US* row houses
schieramento *m* formation; **~ *politico*** political alignment
schierare *v/t* ⟨1b⟩ line up
schierarsi *v/r*: **~ *in favore di qn*** come out in favo(u)r of s.o.; **~ *contro qc*** come out against sth
schiettamente *adv* bluntly
schiettezza *f* bluntness
schietto *adj* pure; *fig* frank
schifato *adj* disgusted
schifezza *f*: ***che* ~!** how disgusting!
schifiltoso *adj* fussy
schifo *m* disgust; ***fare* ~ *a qn*** disgust s.o.; ***che schifo!*** how disgusting!
schifoso *adj* disgusting; (*pessimo*) dreadful
schioccare ⟨1c & d⟩ **I** *v/t*: **~ *le dita*** click one's fingers; **~ *la lingua*** click one's tongue **II** *v/i* crack
schiocco *m* ⟨*pl* -cchi⟩ flick; *delle dita / della lingua* click
schiodare *v/t* ⟨1c⟩: **~ *qc*** take the nail out of sth
schiodarsi *v/r* ⟨1c⟩ come unnailed; *fig infml* get going
schioppettata *f* gunshot; ***prendere a -e*** shoot at
schioppo *m* shotgun; ***a un tiro di* ~** a stone's throw away
schiudere *v/t* ⟨3b⟩ open slightly
schiudersi *v/r* ⟨3b⟩ *uovo* hatch; *fiore*

bloom; *fig* open up
schiuma *f* foam; ~ ***da bagno*** bubble bath; ~ ***da barba*** shaving foam
schiumare ⟨1a⟩ **I** *v/t brodo, latte* skim **II** *v/i di birra* froth; *di cavallo* lather
schiumarola *f* slotted spoon
schiumogeno I *adj* foaming **II** *n*: ***schiumogeno*** *m* foam extinguisher
schiumoso *adj* foamy
schiuso *past part* → ***schiudere***
schivare *v/t* ⟨1a⟩ avoid, dodge *infml*
schivo *adj* shy
schizofrenia *f* schizophrenia
schizofrenico *adj* ⟨*mpl* -ci⟩ schizophrenic
schizoide I *adj* schizoid **II** *m/f* schizoid
schizzare ⟨1a⟩ **I** *v/t* (*spruzzare*) squirt; (*abbozzare*) sketch **II** *v/i* squirt; (*saltare*) jump
schizzarsi *v/r* get dirty
schizzinoso *adj* fussy
schizzo *m* squirt; (*abbozzo*) (lightning) sketch
sci *m* ⟨*pl* sci⟩ ski; *attività* skiing; ~ ***acquatico*** water ski / skiing; ~ ***di fondo*** cross-country ski / skiing; ~ ***nautico*** water skiing
scia *f* wake
scià *m* ⟨*pl* scià⟩ Shah
sciabola *f* sabre, *US* saber
sciabolata *f* sabre-cut, *US* saber-
sciabordio *m* ⟨*pl* -ii⟩ lapping
sciacallaggio *m* looting
sciacallo *m* ZOOL jackal; (*chi ruba*) vulture
sciacquare *v/t* ⟨1a⟩ rinse
sciacquarsi *v/r* ⟨1a⟩ rinse
sciacquatura *f* rinse
sciacquetta *f pej* airhead
sciacquio *m* ⟨*pl* -ii⟩ splashing
sciacquone *m* flush; ***tirare lo*** ~ flush the toilet
sciagura *f* disaster
sciaguratamente *adv* unfortunately
sciagurato *adj giorno, evento* unfortunate
scialacquare *v/t* ⟨1a⟩ squander
scialacquatore I *adj* spendthrift **II** *m*, **-trice** *f* spendthrift
scialare ⟨1a⟩ **I** *v/i* waste **II** *v/t* squander
scialbo *adj* pale; *fig* colo(u)rless
scialle *m* shawl
scialo *m* waste
scialuppa *f* dinghy; ~ ***di salvataggio*** lifeboat
sciamanismo *m* shamanism
sciamano *m* shaman
sciamare *v/i* ⟨1a⟩ swarm
sciame *m* swarm; ***uno ~ di zanzare*** a swarm of mosquitoes
sciancato *adj* injured
sciancrato *adj* fitted at the waist
sciarada *f* charade; *fig* enigma
sciare *v/i* ⟨1h⟩ ski
sciarpa *f* scarf; ~ ***tricolore*** tricolo(u)red (*sash worn by a mayor*)
sciatalgia *f* ischialgia
sciatica *f* sciatica
sciatico *adj* ⟨*mpl* -ci⟩ sciatic; ***nervo*** *m* ~ sciatic nerve
sciatore *m*, **-trice** *f* skier
sciatteria *f* untidiness, sloppiness *infml*
sciatto *adj* untidy, sloppy *infml*
sciattone *m*, **-a** *f* slob
scibile *m* knowledge
sciccheria *f infml* hot stuff
sciccoso *adj infml* swanky
science fiction *f* ⟨*pl* science fiction⟩ science fiction
scientemente *adv* consciously
scientifica *f* (*polizia*) police scientists; ***la ~ ha trovato molte tracce*** the police scientists found a lot of evidence
scientificamente *adv* scientifically
scientifico *adj* ⟨*mpl* -ci⟩ scientific
scienza *f* science; ~ ***delle comunicazioni*** communication science; **-e** *pl* ***naturali*** natural science; **-e** *pl* ***politiche*** political science
scienziato *m*, **-a** *f* scientist
sciistico *adj* ⟨*mpl* -ci⟩ skiing, ski *attr*
sciita ⟨*mpl* -i⟩ **I** *adj* Shiite, Shia **II** *m/f* Shiite, Shia
Scilla *f* MYTH Scylla; ~ ***e Cariddi*** Scylla and Charybdis
scimitarra *f* scimitar
scimmia *f* monkey
scimmiesco *adj* ⟨*mpl* -schi⟩ simian; *pej* monkeyish
scimmietta *f* little monkey
scimmione *m* gorilla
scimmiottare *v/t* ⟨1c⟩ ape
scimpanzé *m* ⟨*pl* scimpanzé⟩ chimpanzee, chimp *infml*
scimunito I *adj* foolish **II** *m*, **-a** *f* idiot
scindere *v/t* ⟨3v⟩ PHYS, CHEM split; *fig* split up

scindersi *v/r* ⟨3v⟩ split up
scindibile *adj* divisible
scintigrafia *f* scan
scintilla *f* spark; ***fare -e*** go great guns
scintillante *adj* sparkling
scintillare *v/i* ⟨1a⟩ sparkle
scintillio *m* sparkle
scintoismo *m* Shintoism
sciò *int infml* shoo
scioccante *adj* shocking
scioccare *v/t* ⟨1c⟩ shock
scioccato *adj*: ***rimanere ~ per qc*** be shocked by sth
sciocchezza *f* (*idiozia*) stupidity; ***è solo una ~*** it's nothing
sciocco ⟨*mpl* -cchi⟩ **I** *adj* silly **II** *m*, **-a** *f* silly thing
sciogliere *v/t* ⟨3ss⟩ untie; *capelli* undo, let down; *matrimonio* dissolve; *neve* melt; *dubbio*, *problema* clear up; ***~ la lingua a qn*** loosen s.o.'s tongue; ***~ la prognosi di qn*** take s.o. off the danger list; ***~ la riserva*** break down s.o.'s reserve; ***~ un dubbio*** resolve a doubt; ***una riunione*** close a meeting
sciogliersi *v/r di corda*, *nodo* come undone; *di burro*, *neve* melt; *di questione*, *problema* resolve itself; ***~ in bocca*** melt in the mouth
scioglilingua *m* ⟨*pl* scioglilingua⟩ tongue-twister
scioglimento *m di assemblea*, *governo* dissolution; *di burro*, *neve* melting; ***~ di un contratto*** termination of a contract
sciolina *f* ski wax
scioltezza *f* nimbleness; *fisica* agility
sciolto **I** *past part* → ***sciogliere*** **II** *adj neve*, *ghiaccio* melted; *matrimonio* dissolved; ***a briglia -a*** at breakneck speed
scioperante *m/f* striker
scioperare *v/i* ⟨1l & c⟩ strike
scioperato **I** *adj pej* lazy **II** *m*, **-a** *f pej* layabout
sciopero *m* strike; ***fare ~*** go on strike; ***~ bianco*** work-to-rule; ***~ generale*** general strike; ***~ della fame*** hunger strike
sciorinare *v/t* ⟨1a⟩ (*ostentare*) show off (*a. fig*)
sciovia *f* ski-lift
sciovinismo *m* chauvinism
sciovinista *m/f* ⟨*mpl* -i⟩ chauvinist
scipito *adj* bland
scippare *v/t* ⟨1a⟩: ***~ qn*** snatch s.o.'s bag
scippatore *m*, **-trice** *f* bag-snatcher
scippo *m* bag-snatching
scirocco *m* sirocco
sciroppato *adj* in syrup; ***pesche*** *fpl* ***-e*** peaches in syrup
sciroppo *m* syrup; ***~ per la tosse*** cough mixture
sciropposo *adj* syrupy (*a. fig*)
scisma *m* ⟨*pl* -i⟩ schism
scissione *f* splitting
scisso *past part* → ***scindere***
scissura *f* disagreement; ANAT fissure
scisto *m* GEOL schist
sciupafemmine *m* ⟨*pl* sciupafemmine⟩ seducer
sciupare *v/t* ⟨1a⟩ (*logorare*) wear out; *salute* ruin; *tempo*, *denaro* waste, fritter away
sciuparsi *v/r* (*rovinarsi*) get ruined; (*deperire*) get run down; (*sprecarsi*) strain o.s.
sciupato *adj persona* drawn; *cosa* worn out
sciuscià *m* ⟨*pl* sciuscià⟩ shoeshine boy
scivolare *v/i* ⟨1l⟩ slide; (*cadere*) slip
scivolata *f* slip
scivolino *m* slide
scivolo *m* slide; (*caduta*) slip; *gioco* chute; ***~ d'emergenza*** escape chute
scivolone *m* slip; *fig* slip-up
scivoloso *adj* slippery
sclerosi *f* ⟨*pl* sclerosi⟩ MED sclerosis; ***~ multipla*** multiple sclerosis, MS
sclerotico *adj* ⟨*mpl* -ci⟩ sclerotic; *fig* senile
sclerotizzarsi *v/r* ⟨1a⟩ harden; *fig* become fossilized
scocca *f* ⟨*pl* -cche⟩ bodywork
scoccare ⟨1c⟩ **I** *v/t freccia* fire; *bacio* smack; *sguardo* shoot **II** *v/i scintilla* shoot out; *ore* strike
scocciante *adj* annoying
scocciare *v/t* ⟨1f⟩ *infml* bother, annoy, hassle *infml*; ***~ qn*** bother s.o.
scocciarsi *v/r infml* be fed up
scocciatore *m*, **-trice** *f infml* pest *infml*, nuisance *infml*
scocciatura *f infml* nuisance *infml*
scodella *f* bowl
scodellare *v/t* ⟨1b⟩ dish up; *fig* dish out

scodinzolare *v/i* ⟨1m⟩ *cane* wag one's tail
scodinzolio *m* ⟨*pl* -ii⟩ wagging
scogliera *f* cliff
scoglio *m* ⟨*pl* -gli⟩ rock; *fig* stumbling block
scoiattolo *m* squirrel
scolapasta *m* ⟨*pl* scolapasta⟩ colander
scolapiatti *m* ⟨*pl* scolapiatti⟩ plate-rack
scolare[1] *v/t* ⟨1a⟩ drain; ***~ la pasta*** drain the pasta
scolare[2] *adj* school *attr*
scolaresca *f* ⟨*pl* -che⟩ class
scolaretto *m*, **-a** *f* schoolboy, schoolgirl
scolarità *f* ⟨*pl* scolarità⟩ schooling
scolarizzazione *f* education
scolaro *m*, **-a** *f* schoolboy; *ragazza* schoolgirl
scolarsi *v/r* knock back; *hum* ***~ una bottiglia di vino*** down a bottle of wine
scolastico *adj* ⟨*mpl* -ci⟩ school *attr*
scoliosi *f* ⟨*pl* scoliosi⟩ curvature of the spine
scollacciato *adj* low-cut; *fig* coarse
scollamento *m* peeling off; MED detachment; *fig* split
scollarsi *v/r* peel off; ***la suola si è scollata*** the sole's come unstuck
scollato *adj* low-necked; *donna* wearing a low neck; ***scarpe*** *fpl* ***-e*** court shoes
scollatura *f* neck(line)
scollegare *v/t* ⟨1e⟩ disconnect
scollegarsi *v/r* ⟨1e⟩ disconnect
scollinare *v/i* ⟨1a⟩ complete a stage
scollo *m* neck
scolo *m* drainage
scolorina *f* ink remover
scolorire *v/t* & *v/i* ⟨4d⟩ fade
scolorirsi *v/r* ⟨4d⟩ fade
scolorito *adj* faded
scolpire *v/t* ⟨4d⟩ *marmo*, *statua* sculpt; *legno* carve; *fig* engrave
scombinato *adj* confused
scombussolamento *m* upset
scombussolare *v/t* ⟨1m⟩ shake
scombussolarsi *v/r* ⟨1m⟩ get upset
scommessa *f* bet; ***fare una ~*** have / place a bet
scommesso *past part* → ***scommettere***
scommettere *v/i* ⟨3ee⟩ bet; ***~ su un cavallo*** bet on a horse
scomodare *v/t* ⟨1l & c⟩ disturb
scomodarsi *v/r* put o.s. out; ***non si scomodi*** please don't go to any bother
scomodo *adj* uncomfortable; (*non pratico*) inconvenient
scompaginare *v/t* ⟨1m⟩ muddle up
scompaginarsi *v/r* ⟨1m⟩ be disrupted
scompagnato *adj* disarranged
scomparire *v/i* ⟨4e⟩ disappear
scomparsa *f* disappearance; ***letto*** *m* ***a ~*** fold-away bed
scomparso *past part* → ***scomparire***
scompartimento *m* compartment; RAIL ***~ per (non) fumatori*** (non-) smoking compartment
scomparto *m* compartment
scompenso *m* imbalance; ***~ cardiaco*** cardiac insufficiency
scompigliare *v/t* ⟨1g⟩ *persona* ruffle the hair of; *capelli* ruffle
scompigliarsi *v/r* ⟨1g⟩ get messed up; *capelli* become tangled
scompiglio *m* ⟨*pl* -gli⟩ confusion; ***creare ~*** cause confusion
scomponibile *adj* flat pack *attr*, modular
scomporre *v/t* ⟨3ll⟩ break down
scomporsi *v/r*: ***senza ~*** without showing any emotion
scomposizione *f* breakdown; *di frasi*: breaking down
scompostezza *f* dishevelment
scomposto *adj* ruffled; ***stare ~ a tavola*** have bad table manners
scomunica *f* excommunication
scomunicare *v/t* ⟨1n⟩ excommunicate
sconcertante *adj* disconcerting
sconcertare *v/t* ⟨1b⟩ *fig* upset; ***la notizia ha sconcertato tutti*** they were staggered by the news
sconcerto *m* bewilderment
sconcezza *f* obscenity; (*oggetto*) disgusting thing; ***dire -e*** utter obscenities
sconcio *adj* ⟨*mpl* -ci⟩ indecent; *parola* disgusting, filthy
sconclusionatezza *f* incoherence
sconclusionato *adj* incoherent
scondito *adj* *insalata* undressed; *riso* plain
sconfessare *v/t* ⟨1b⟩ *opinione* disavow; *fede* renounce

sconfiggere *v/t* ⟨3cc⟩ defeat
sconfinamento *m* trespassing
sconfinare *v/i* ⟨1a⟩ trespass; MIL cross the border
sconfinato *adj* vast, boundless
sconfitta *f* defeat; ***infliggere / subire una ~*** inflict / suffer a defeat
sconfitto[1] *past part* → ***sconfiggere***
sconfitto[2] *adj* defeated; (SPORTS *fig*) beaten
sconfortante *adj* discouraging, disheartening
sconfortare *v/t* ⟨1c⟩ discourage, dishearten
sconfortarsi *v/r* lose heart
sconforto *m* discouragement
scongelare *v/t* ⟨1b⟩ thaw
scongiurare *v/t* ⟨1a⟩ beg; *pericolo* avert
scongiuro *m*: ***fare gli -i*** touch wood, keep one's fingers crossed
sconnesso *adj pavimento* bumpy; *discorso* disjointed
sconosciuto **I** *adj* unknown **II** *m*, **-a** *f* stranger
sconquassare *v/t* ⟨1a⟩ break up; *fig* ***~ qn*** tire s.o. out; *infml* shatter s.o.
sconquassarsi *v/r* ⟨1a⟩ break up
sconquasso *m* disaster; *fig* chaos
sconsacrato *adj* deconsecrated
sconsideratezza *f* recklessness
sconsiderato *adj* thoughtless
sconsigliabile *adj* inadvisable
sconsigliare *v/t* ⟨1g⟩ advise against; ***~ qc a qn*** advise s.o. against sth
sconsolato *adj* disconsolate
scontare *v/t* ⟨1a⟩ FIN deduct, discount; *pena* serve
scontato *adj* discounted; (*previsto*) expected; ***~ del 30 %*** 30 % discount *or* deduction; ***dare per ~*** take for granted
scontentare *v/t* ⟨1m⟩ dissatisfy
scontento **I** *adj* unhappy, not satisfied (***di*** with) **II** *m* unhappiness, dissatisfaction
sconto *m* discount; ***chiedere lo ~*** ask for a discount; ***fare lo ~*** discount; ***praticare uno ~*** give a discount
scontrarsi *v/r* ⟨1a⟩ collide (***con*** with); *fig* clash (***con*** with)
scontrino *m* receipt; ***fare lo ~ alla cassa*** please pay at the cash desk before ordering
scontro *m* AUTO collision; *fig* clash; ***~ a fuoco*** gunfight
scontrosità *f* ⟨*pl* scontrosità⟩ grumpiness
scontroso *adj* unpleasant, disagreeable
sconveniente *adj* inappropriate, unacceptable
sconvolgente *adj* upsetting, distressing; ***di un'intelligenza ~*** incredibly intelligent
sconvolgere *v/t* ⟨3d⟩ upset
sconvolgimento *m* disruption; *fig* upheaval
sconvolto **I** *past part* → ***sconvolgere*** **II** *adj paese* in upheaval
scoop *m* ⟨*pl* scoop⟩ scoop
scoordinato *adj* unco-ordinated; *fig* disjointed
scooter *m* ⟨*pl* scooter⟩ scooter
scopa *f* broom
scopare *v/t* ⟨1a⟩ sweep; *sl* shag *sl*
scopata *f* sweep; ***dare una ~ in cucina*** sweep the kitchen ***farsi una ~*** *vulg* get laid
scoperchiare *v/t* ⟨1k⟩ *pentola* take the lid off
scoperchiarsi *v/r* ⟨1k⟩ lose the roof
scoperta *f* discovery
scoperto **I** *past part* → ***scoprire*** **II** *adj pentola* uncovered; ***a capo ~*** bareheaded; ***assegno*** *m* ***~*** bad cheque, rubber cheque *infml* **III** *m* **1.** FIN overdraft **2.** ***allo ~*** in the open
scopiazzare *v/t* ⟨1a⟩ copy
scopino *m* brush
scopo *m* aim, purpose; ***allo ~ di fare qc*** in order to do sth; ***senza ~*** aimlessly; ***a che ~?*** what for?
scoppiare *v/i* ⟨1k & c⟩ *di bomba, petardo* explode; *di palloncino, pneumatico* burst; ***~ in lacrime*** burst into tears; ***~ a ridere*** burst out laughing; ***~ di caldo*** be boiling hot
scoppiato *adj infml* (*esausto*) worn-out; *infml* (*drogato*) stoned
scoppiettare *v/i* ⟨1a⟩ *motore* splutter; *fuoco* spit
scoppio *m* ⟨*pl* -ppi⟩ explosion; *di palloncino* bursting; *fig* outbreak
scoppola *f* thrashing
scoprire *v/t* ⟨4f⟩ *contenitore* take the lid off; (*denudare*) uncover; *piani, verità* discover, find out; ***~ l'acqua calda*** reinvent the wheel
scoprirsi *v/r* (*denudarsi*) strip off;

(*smascherarsi*) reveal o.s.
scopritore *m*, **-trice** *f* discoverer
scoraggiamento *m* despondency
scoraggiante *adj* disheartening
scoraggiare *v/t* ⟨1f⟩ discourage, dishearten
scoraggiarsi *v/r* become discouraged, lose heart
scoraggiato *adj* discouraged, disheartened
scorbutico *adj* ⟨*mpl* -ci⟩ surly
scorbuto *m* scurvy
scorciare *v/t* ⟨1f⟩ shorten
scorciatoia *f* short cut
scorcio *m* patch
scordare *v/t* ⟨1c⟩ forget; MUS untune
scordarsi *v/r* forget; ***~ di qc / di fare qc*** forget sth / to do sth
scordato *adj* MUS out of tune
scoreggia *f* ⟨*pl* -gge⟩ *infml* fart *infml*
scoreggiare *v/t* ⟨1f⟩ *infml* fart *infml*
scorfano *m* ZOOL rockfish; *fig pej* fright
scorgere *v/t* ⟨3d⟩ see, make out; ***farsi ~*** be spotted; ***non farsi ~*** not let o.s. be seen
scoria *f* waste
scorno *m* shame
scorpacciata *f*: ***fare** or **farsi una ~*** pig out
scorpione *m* scorpion; ASTROL ***Scorpione*** Scorpio
scorporare *v/t* ⟨1c e 1⟩ hive off
scorrazzare *v/i* ⟨1a⟩ run around; *con veicoli* drive around
scorrere ⟨3o⟩ **I** *v/i* flow, run; *di tempo* go past, pass **II** *v/t giornale* skim
scorreria *f* foray
scorrettezza *f* mistake
scorretto *adj* (*errato*) incorrect; (*non onesto*) unfair
scorrevole *adj porta* sliding; *stile* flowing
scorrevolezza *f* fluency
scorribanda *f* incursion; *fig* joyride
scorrimento *m di liquidi*: flow; MECH sliding; ***arteria** f **di grande ~*** road with heavy traffic
scorsa *f* glance; ***dare una ~ a qc*** browse through sth
scorso **I** *past part* → ***scorrere*** **II** *adj*: ***l'anno ~*** last year; ***la settimana -a*** last week; ***lunedì ~*** last Monday
scorsoio *adj* ⟨*pl* -oi⟩: ***nodo** m **~*** slipknot
scorta *f* escort; (*provvista*) supply, stock; ***di ~*** spare; ***sulla ~ di*** according to; ***mettere qn sotto ~*** put s.o. under guard
scortare *v/t* ⟨1c⟩ escort
scortecciare *v/t* ⟨1f⟩ strip
scortecciarsi *v/r* ⟨1f⟩ peel
scortese *adj* rude, discourteous
scortesemente *adv* rudely
scortesia *f* rudeness, lack of courtesy
scorticare *v/t* ⟨1l⟩ (*spellare*) skin; (*escoriare*) scrape
scorticarsi *v/r* ⟨1l⟩ graze oneself
scorticatura *f* skinning; (*abrasione*) graze
scorto *past part* → ***scorgere***
scorza *f* peel; *fig* exterior; *fig* ***avere la ~ dura*** be thickskinned
scosceso *adj* steep
scossa *f* shake; ***~ di terremoto*** (earth) tremor; ***~ elettrica*** electric shock; ***~ ondulatoria / sussultoria*** undulatory / sussultatory tremor; ***prendere la ~*** get an electric shock
scosso **I** *past part* → ***scuotere*** **II** *adj* (*turbato*) shaken
scossone *m* shake; *fig* jolt
scostamento *m* shift
scostante *adj* standoffish
scostare *v/t* ⟨1c⟩ move away (***da*** from)
scostarsi *v/r* move (aside); *fig* ***~ della retta via*** leave the straight and narrow
scostumato *adj* rude
scotch[1] *m* (*whisky*) Scotch
scotch®[2] *m* (*nastro adesivo*) Sellotape®
scotennare *v/t* ⟨1a⟩ *maiale* skin; *persona* scalp
scottante *adj* delicate; ***argomento** m **~*** burning question
scottare ⟨1c⟩ **I** *v/t* burn; COOK *verdure* blanch; ***mi sono scottato le dita*** I burned my fingers **II** *v/i* burn; ***scotta!*** it's hot!; ***la sabbia scotta*** the sand's burning hot; ***quella merce scotta*** those things have fallen off the back of a lorry; *fig* ***problemi** mpl **che scottano*** burning questions
scottato *adj verdure* blanched
scottatura *f* burn; ***ho già avuto troppe -e*** I've had my fingers burned once too often
scotto[1] *m*: ***pagare lo ~*** pay the penalty
scotto[2] *adj* overcooked, overdone

scout *m/f* ⟨*pl* scout⟩ scout

scovare *v/t* ⟨1l⟩ unearth, track down; ***ma dove l'hai scovato?*** where on earth did you find it?

Scozia *f* Scotland

scozzare *v/t* ⟨1c⟩ *carte* shuffle

scozzese I *adj* Scottish; ***doccia*** *f* **~** hot and cold shower; *fig* rollercoaster of good and bad events **II** *m/f* Scot

screanzato *adj* bad-mannered

screditare *v/t* ⟨1l⟩ discredit

screening *m* ⟨*pl* screening⟩ MED screening

scremare *v/t* ⟨1a⟩ skim

scremato *adj* skimmed; ***parzialmente* ~** semi-skimmed

screpolare *v/t* ⟨1l & b⟩ crack

screpolarsi *v/r* ⟨1l & b⟩ crack

screpolato *adj* cracked; *labbra, mani* chapped

screpolatura *f* crack

screziato *adj* streaked, speckled

screziatura *f* streak, fleck

screzio *m* ⟨*pl* -zi⟩ rift

scribacchiare *v/t* ⟨1k⟩ scribble

scribacchino *m pej* pen-pusher

scricchiolare *v/i* ⟨1l⟩ creak

scricchiolio *m* ⟨*pl* -ii⟩ creak

scricciolo *m* ZOOL wren

scrigno *m* casket

scriminatura *f* parting, *US* part

scriteriato *adj* wild

scritta *f* inscription

scritto I *past part* → **scrivere II** *adj*: ***esame*** *m* **~** written exam; **~ *a mano*** handwritten **III** *m* writing; ***per* ~** in writing

scrittoio *m* ⟨*pl* -oi⟩ writing desk

scrittore *m*, **-trice** *f* writer

scrittura *f* writing; REL scripture; THEAT engagement; **~ *gotica*** gothic script; **~ *privata*** JUR private deed

scritturare *v/t* ⟨1a⟩ engage, sign *infml*

scritturazione *f* THEAT, FILM, TV engagement, booking

scrivania *f* desk

scrivano *m*, **-a** *f* writer

scrivere *v/t* ⟨3tt⟩ write; (*annotare*) write down; ***come si scrive …?*** how do you spell …?

scroccare *v/t* ⟨1c & d⟩ *infml* scrounge *infml*

scroccone *m*, **-a** *f* scrounger

scrofa *f* sow

scrollare *v/t* ⟨1c⟩ shake; **~ *le spalle*** shrug (one's shoulders)

scrollarsi *v/r* shake o.s., wake up; *fig* **~ *qc di dosso*** shake sth off

scrollata *f* shake; ***dare una* ~** shake

scrollone *m* shake

scrosciante *adj* pouring; *fig* roaring; ***applausi*** *mpl* ***-i*** thunderous applause

scrosciare *v/i* ⟨1f & c⟩ *di pioggia* fall in torrents

scroscio *m* roar; **~ *di pioggia*** downpour

scrostarsi *v/r* flake

scrostato *adj* flaking, peeling

scrostatura *f* flaking

scroto *m* scrotum

scrupolo *m* scruple; ***senza -i*** unscrupulous; ***mancanza*** *f* ***di -i*** unscrupulousness

scrupolosamente *adv* scrupulously

scrupolosità *f* scrupulousness

scrupoloso *adj* scrupulous

scrutare *v/t* ⟨1a⟩ look at intently; *orrizonte* scan

scrutatore *m*, **-trice** *f* POL person counting votes

scrutinare *v/t* ⟨1a⟩: **~ *le schede / i voti*** count the votes

scrutinio *m* ⟨*pl* -ni⟩ POL counting; EDU *teachers' meeting to discuss pupils' performance*; EDU ***fare gli -ni*** do pupils' assessments

scucire *v/t* ⟨4a⟩ unpick; ***scuci i soldi!*** *infml* cough up! *infml*

scucirsi *v/r* come apart at the seams

scucito *adj* undone

scuderia *f* stable

scudetto *m* SPORTS championship

scudiero *m* HIST squire

scudiscio *m* ⟨*pl* -sci⟩ riding crop

scudo *m* shield

scugnizzo *m Neapolitan street urchin*

sculacciare *v/t* ⟨1f⟩ spank

sculacciata *f*: ***prendere a -e qn*** spank s.o., smack s.o.'s bottom

sculaccione *m* spank

sculettare *v/i* ⟨1a⟩ *infml* wiggle one's hips

scultore *m*, **-trice** *f* sculptor

scultoreo *adj* sculptural

scultura *f* sculpture

scuoiare *v/t* ⟨1h⟩ skin, flay

scuola *f* school; **~ *elementare*** primary school; **~ *guida*** driving school; **~ *di lingue*** language school; **~ *materna*** nursery school; **~ *media*** secondary

school; **~ *dell'obbligo*** compulsory education; **~ *parificata*** *private school officially recognized by the state*; **~ *serale*** evening classes *pl*; **~ *superiore*** high school; ***andare a ~*** go to school; *fig* ***fare ~*** gain a following
scuolabus *m* ⟨*pl* scuolabus⟩ school bus
scuotere *v/t* ⟨3ff⟩ shake; **~ *qc di dosso*** shake sth off (*a. fig*)
scuotersi *v/r* shake off
scure *f* ax(e)
scurire *v/t & v/i* ⟨4d⟩ darken
scurirsi *v/r* ⟨4d⟩ darken (*a. fig*)
scuro I *adj* dark **II** *m* darkness; ***essere allo ~ di qc*** be in the dark about sth
scurrile *adj* scurrilous
scurrilità *f* ⟨*pl* scurrilità⟩ foulness
scusa *f* excuse; ***chiedere ~*** apologize; ***aver sempre la ~ pronta*** always have a ready excuse
scusabile *adj* excusable
scusante *f* excuse
scusare *v/t* ⟨1a⟩ forgive; (*giustificare*) excuse; ***mi scusi*** I'm sorry; ***scusi, scusa*** excuse me; ***scusi il disturbo*** sorry to bother you; ***scusa! scusate!*** sorry!; **~ *per*** (*or* ***di***) ***qc con qn*** apologize to s.o. for sth
scusarsi *v/r* apologize
scuter *m* ⟨*pl* scuter⟩ scooter
S.C.V. *abbr* (= **Stato della Città del Vaticano**) Vatican City
s.d. *abbr* (= **senza data**) undated
sdebitarsi *v/r* ⟨1l⟩ pay one's debts
sdegnare *v/t* ⟨1a⟩ (*disprezzare*) despise; (*fare arrabbiarre*) incense
sdegnarsi *v/r* get angry (***con*** with)
sdegnato *adj* indignant
sdegno *m* moral indignation
sdegnoso *adj* (*sprezzante*) scornful; (*altero*) supercilious
sdentato *adj* toothless
SDI *abbr* (= **Socialisti Democratici Italiani**) *Italian Democratic Socialist party*
sdilinquimento *m* faint
sdoganamento *m* customs clearance
sdoganare *v/t* ⟨1a⟩ clear through customs
sdolcinato *adj* sloppy
sdoppiamento *m* splitting in two; **~ *della personalità*** split personality
sdoppiare *v/t* ⟨1k⟩ split in two
sdoppiarsi *v/r* ⟨1k⟩ split in two
sdraiare *v/t* ⟨1i⟩ lay
sdraiarsi *v/r* lie down
sdraiato *adj* lying down
sdraio *m*: (***sedia*** *f* ***a***) **~** deck chair
sdrammatizzare *v/t* ⟨1n⟩ play down
sdrucciolare *v/i* ⟨1l⟩ slip
sdrucciolevole *adj* slippery
sdrucciolo *adj*: ***parola*** *f* **-*a*** *word with the stress on the antepenultimate syllable*
sdrucire *v/t* ⟨4d⟩ unstitch
sdrucito *adj* unstitched
se[1] *cj* **1.** if, whether; **~ *mai*** if need be; **~ *mai arrivasse …*** should he arrive …; **~ *fossi in te*** if I were you; ***come ~*** as if; **~ *no*** if not; **~ *non altro*** if nothing else; **~ *Dio vuole*** God willing **2.** *seguito da frase dubitativa*: whether; ***mi chiedo ~ verrà*** I wonder whether he'll come
se[2] *pron* = ***si*** *in front of* ***lo, la, li, le, ne***
sé *pron* oneself; *lui* himself; *lei* herself; *loro* themselves; *esso*, *essa* itself; ***da ~*** (by) himself / herself / themselves; ***va da ~*** it goes without saying; ***chi fa da ~ fa per tre*** *prov* if you want something done right, do it yourself
sebaceo *adj* sebaceous
Sebastiano *m*: ***San ~*** St Sebastian
sebbene *cj* even though, although; **~ *abbia detto la verità*** even though he told the truth
sebo *m* sebum
seborrea *f* seborrhoea
secca *f* ⟨*pl* -cche⟩ shallows *pl*; ***incagliarsi in una ~*** run aground; ***fiume*** *m* ***in ~*** dried-up river
seccante *adj fig* annoying; ***non essere ~!*** don't be annoying!
seccare ⟨1d⟩ **I** *v/t* dry; *fig* annoy **II** *v/i* dry; *fig* get annoyed
seccarsi *v/r* ⟨1d⟩ dry; *fig* get annoyed
seccato *adj* annoyed
seccatore *m*, **-trice** *f* nuisance, pest
seccatura *f* nuisance
secchiello *m* (toy) bucket
secchio *m* ⟨*pl* -cchi⟩ bucket, pail; ***buonanotte al ~!*** and that's that!
secchione *m*, **-a** *f* swot
secco ⟨*mpl* -cchi⟩ **I** *adj* dry; *fiori*, *pomodori* dried; *risposta*, *tono* curt; ***frutta*** *f* **-*a*** dried fruit; (*noci*) nuts *pl*; ***vino*** *m* **~** dry wine **II** *m*: ***rimanere a ~*** run out of petrol; *fig* run out of money; ***lavare*** *or* ***pulire a ~*** dryclean

secentesco *adj* ⟨*mpl* -chi⟩ seventeenth century
secernere *v/t* ⟨3a⟩ secrete, excrete
secessione *f* secession
secolare *adj albero, tradizione* hundred-year old
secolarizzazione *f* secularization
secolo *m* century; ***ti ho aspettato un ~!*** I waited hours for you!
seconda *f* AUTO second (gear); RAIL second class; EDU second year
secondario *adj* ⟨*mpl* -ri⟩ secondary
secondino *m* prison officer
secondo[1] *m* second; ***hai un ~ di tempo?*** do you have a minute?
secondo[2] **I** *adj* second; ***di -a mano*** second-hand; ***~ fine*** ulterior motive, hidden agenda; ***-a casa*** *f* second home; ***in un ~ tempo*** another time **II** *prep* according to; ***~ me*** in my opinion; ***~ le istruzioni*** as per instructions; ***~!*** it depends; ***~ i casi*** as the case may be; ***~ le circostanze*** according to the circumstances **III** *m* COOK main course; ***hai già ordinato il ~?*** have you already ordered the main course?
secondogenito I *adj* second-born **II** *m*, **-a** *f* second-born
secrétaire *m* ⟨*pl* secrétaire⟩ *mobile* writing desk
secretato *adj* classified
secrezione *f* secretion
sedano *m* celery
sedare *v/t* ⟨1b⟩ calm (down)
sedativo *m* sedative
sede *f* headquarters *pl*; ***la Santa Sede*** the Holy See; ***lavorare fuori ~*** work out of the office; ***~ centrale*** head office; ***~ del Governo*** seat of government; ***~ di una ditta*** branch of a company; ***~ stradale*** roadway; ***in separata ~*** in private
sedentario *adj* ⟨*mpl* -ri⟩ sedentary
sedere I *m infml* rear end *infml* **II** *v/i* ⟨2o⟩ sit down; ***mettersi a ~*** sit down; *da sdraiato* sit up
sederino *m infml* bottom
sedersi *v/r* ⟨2o⟩ sit down; ***~ su una sedia*** sit on a chair; ***~ all'ombra*** sit in the shade; ***~ alla scrivania*** sit at the desk; ***~ per terra*** sit on the ground
sedia *f* chair; ***~ a sdraio*** deckchair; ***~ a dondolo*** rocking chair; ***~ a rotelle*** wheelchair; ***~ elettrica*** electric chair
sedicenne *m/f* sixteen-year-old
sedicente *adj* so-called, self-styled
sedicesimo *m/adj* sixteenth; ***Benedetto ~*** Benedict XVI
sedici *num* sixteen
sedile *m* seat; AUTO ***~ posteriore*** back seat
sedimentare *v/i* ⟨1a⟩ settle
sedimentazione *f* sedimentation
sedimento *m* sediment
sedizioso *adj* (*sovversivo*) seditious; (*rissoso*) belligerent
sedotto *past part* → ***sedurre***
seducente *adj* attractive
sedurre *v/t* ⟨3e⟩ seduce; (*attrarre*) attract
seduta *f* session; (*posa*) sitting; ***~ plenaria*** plenary session; ***~ spiritica*** seance
seduto *adj* seated
seduttore *m*, **-trice** *f* seducer; *donna* seductress
seduzione *f* seduction
S.E. e O. *abbr* (= **salvo errori e omissioni**) E & OE (errors and omissions excepted)
sefardita ⟨*mpl* -i⟩ **I** *adj* Sephardic **II** *m/f* Sephardi
seg. *abbr* (= **seguente**) foll. (following)
sega *f* ⟨*pl* -ghe⟩ saw; ***~ elettrica*** power saw; *fig* ***farsi una ~*** *vulg* wank
segaiolo *m vulg* wanker
segale *f* rye; ***pane*** *m* ***di ~*** rye bread
segaligno *adj fig* skinny
segare *v/t* ⟨1e⟩ saw
segatura *f* sawdust
seggio *m* ⟨*pl* -ggi⟩ seat; ***~*** (***elettorale***) polling station
seggiola *f* chair
seggiolino *m di macchina, bicicletta* child's seat
seggiolone *m* high chair
seggiovia *f* chair lift
seggo → ***sedere***
seghettato *adj* serrated; ***coltello*** *m* ***~*** serrated knife
seghetto *m* saw
segmentazione *f* GEOM, LING segmentation (*a. fig*)
segmento *m* segment; ***~ di rete*** COMPUT network segment
segnalare *v/t* ⟨1a⟩ signal; (*annunciare*) report
segnalazione *f* signalling, signs

segnale *m* signal; (*segno*) sign; **~ acustico** buzzer; *al telefono* beep; **~ d'allarme** alarm; **~ di divieto** sign prohibiting something, prohibition sign; **~ luminoso** light signal, flare; **~ orario** (*alla radio*) time signal; **~ stradale** road sign
segnaletica *f* signs *pl*; **~ stradale** road signs *pl*
segnalibro *m* bookmark
segnare *v/t* ⟨1a⟩ (*marcare*) mark; (*annotare*) note down; SPORTS score; **~ a dito qn** point s.o. out, point to s.o.; **sentirsi segnato a dita** feel the finger pointed at you; **ha segnato due gol** he scored two goals
segnarsi *v/r* cross o.s.
segnato *adj* marked
segno *m* sign; (*traccia*) mark, trace; (*cenno*) gesture, sign; **~ d'amicizia** mark of friendship; **-i** *pl* **caratteristici** distinguishing marks; **~ d'interpunzione** punctuation mark; **~ zodiacale** sign of the zodiac; **cogliere nel ~** hit the nail on the head; *fig* **non dar -i di vita** not get in touch; **farsi il ~ de la croce** cross o.s.; **lasciare il ~** leave a mark; **riferire per filo e per ~** relate in great detail
sego *m* ⟨*pl* -ghi⟩ tallow; COOK suet
segregare *v/t* ⟨1b & u⟩ segregate
segregarsi *v/r* ⟨1b & u⟩ shut oneself away
segregazione *f* segregation; **~ cellulare** solitary confinement; **~ razziale** racial segregation
segregazionismo *m* segregationism
segreta *f* dungeon
segretamente *adv* secretly
segretaria *f* secretary; **~ di direzione** executive secretary
segretariato *m* secretariat
segretario *m* ⟨*pl* -ri⟩ secretary; POL **~ di partito** party leader; **~ di Stato** minister, *negli Stati Uniti* Secretary of State
segreteria *f carica* secretaryship; *ufficio* administrative office; *attività* secretarial duties *pl*; **~ telefonica** answering machine, answerphone
segretezza *f* secrecy
segreto **I** *adj* secret **II** *m* secret; **~ professionale** confidentiality; **~ di Pulcinella** open secret; **~ bancario** bank confidentiality; **~ confessionale** seal of the confession; **~ istruttorio** *secrecy relating to a preliminary investigation*; **in gran ~** in strict secrecy; **confidare / mantenere / svelare un ~** confide / keep / disclose a secret
seguace *m/f* disciple, follower
seguente *adj* next, following
segugio *m* ⟨*pl* -gi⟩ bloodhound (*a. fig*)
seguire ⟨4a⟩ **I** *v/t* follow; *corso* take **II** *v/i* follow (**a qc** sth); **come segue** as follows
seguitare *v/i* ⟨1l⟩: **~ a fare qc** carry on doing sth
seguito *m persone* retinue; (*sostenitori*) followers *pl*; *di film* sequel; **di ~** one after the other, in succession; **in ~** after that; **in ~ a** following, in the wake of; **al ~ di** supporting
sei[1] → **essere**
sei[2] *num* six
Seicelle *fpl* the Seychelles
seicentesco *adj* ⟨*mpl* -schi⟩ seventeenth century
seicento **I** *num* six hundred **II** *m*: **il Seicento** the seventeenth century
selciato *m* paving
selettivo *adj* selective
selezionare *v/t* ⟨1a⟩ select
selezione *f* selection; **~ naturale** natural selection; **~ della lingua** COMPUT, TEL language selection; **~ vocale** TEL voice dialling
self-control *m* ⟨*pl* self-control⟩ self control
self-service *m* ⟨*pl* self-service⟩ self-service
sella *f* saddle; *fig* **restare in ~** stay in the saddle
sellaio *m* ⟨*pl* -ai⟩ saddler
sellare *v/t* ⟨1a⟩ saddle
sellino *m* saddle
seltz *m*: **acqua** *f* **di ~** soda (water)
selva *f* forest; *fig* swarm; **~ di capelli** mass of hair
selvaggiamente *adv* wildly, savagely
selvaggina *f* game
selvaggio ⟨*mpl* -ggi⟩ **I** *adj animale, fiori* wild; *tribù, omicidio* savage **II** *m*, **-a** *f* savage
selvatico *adj* ⟨*mpl* -ci⟩ wild
semaforo *m* traffic lights *pl*; **fermarsi al ~** stop at the lights
semantica *f* semantics *sg*
semantico *adj* ⟨*mpl* -ci⟩ semantic
sembrare *v/i & v/impers* ⟨1a⟩ seem;

(*assomigliare a*) resemble, look like; ***sembra facile!*** it looks easy!; ***sembra che ...*** it looks as if ...
seme *m* seed; ***-i*** *pl* ***di zucca*** pumpkin seeds; ***senza -i*** seedless
semenza *f* seeds
semestrale *adj* half-year, six-monthly
semestre *m* six months; EDU term
semianalfabeta *m/f* ⟨*mpl* -i⟩ semi-literate person
semiaperto *adj* ajar
semiautomatico *adj* ⟨*mpl* -ci⟩ semi-automatic
semicerchio *m* ⟨*pl* -chi⟩ semi-circle, half-moon
semicircolare *adj* semi-circular
semiconduttore *m* ELEC semi-conductor
semicrudo *adj* half-cooked
semifinale *f* semi-final
semifreddo *m soft ice cream*
semilavorato *m* semi-finished
semina *f* sowing
seminale *adj* seminal; ***liquido*** *m* ~ seminal fluid
seminare *v/t* ⟨1l⟩ sow; *fig* ~ ***qn*** shake s.o. off; ***il ladro ha seminato la polizia*** the thief gave the police the slip
seminario *m* ⟨*pl* -ri⟩ seminar; REL seminary
seminarista *m* ⟨*pl* -i⟩ REL seminarian
seminato I *adj* sown; *fig* riddled **II** *n*: ***seminato*** *m* sown field; ***uscire dal*** ~ go off the subject
seminatore *m*, **-trice** *f* sower
seminterrato *m* basement
seminudo *adj* half-naked
seminuovo *adj* practically new
semiologia *f* semiology
semiologo *m*, **-a** *f* ⟨*mpl* -gi⟩ semiologist
semioscurità *f* ⟨*pl* semioscurità⟩ semi-darkness
semiotica *f* semiotics *sg*
semirimorchio *m* ⟨*pl* -chi⟩ semitrailer
semisfera *f* hemisphere
semita *m/f* ⟨*mpl* -i⟩ Semite
semitico *adj* ⟨*mpl* -ci⟩ Semitic
semmai *adv* if; (*casomai*) if you happen; ~ ***vengo a piedi*** if necessary I'll walk
semola *f* semolina; ~ ***di grano duro*** durum wheat semolina
semolato *adj* refined; ***zucchero*** ~ caster sugar
semolino *m* semolina
semovente *adj* self-propelled
sempiterno *adj* sempiternal
semplice *adj* simple; (*non doppio*) single; (*spontaneo*) natural; ***ragazza*** *f* ~ simple girl
semplicemente *adv* simply
sempliciotto *m*, **-a** *f* simpleton
semplicistico *adj* ⟨*mpl* -ci⟩ simplistic
semplicità *f* simplicity
semplificare *v/t* ⟨1m & d⟩ simplify
semplificarsi *v/r* ⟨1m & d⟩ become simpler
semplificazione *f* simplification; ~ ***legislativa*** JUR legislative simplification
sempre *adv* always; ***ci conosciamo da*** ~ we've known each other practically for ever; ***è quello di*** ~ he's the same as always; ***per*** ~ for ever; ~ ***più*** more and more; ~ ***più vecchio*** older and older; ***piove*** ~ ***di più*** the rain's getting heavier and heavier; ~ ***che*** as long as, on condition that
sempreverde I *adj* evergreen **II** *m/f* evergreen
semprevivo *m* house-leek
sen. *abbr* (= **senatore**) Sen (senator)
senape *f* mustard
senato *m* senate
senatore *m*, **-trice** *f* senator
Senegal *m* Senegal
senegalese I *adj* Senegalese **II** *m/f* Senegalese
senese I *adj* Sienese **II** *m/f* Sienese
senile *adj* senile
senilità *f* senility
senior *m* ⟨*pl* seniores⟩ senior; ***consulente*** *m* ~ senior consultant; SPORTS ***seniores*** *mpl* seniors
Senna *f* Seine
senno *m* common sense; ***uscire di*** ~ lose one's mind; (*arrabbiarsi*) lose control; ***con il*** ~ ***di poi*** with hindsight
sennò *adv* / *cj* or else, otherwise
sennonché *cj* but, except
seno *m* breast; GEOG inlet; MATH sine; ***in*** ~ ***a*** in
sensale *m/f* broker
sensatamente *adv* sensibly
sensatezza *f* (good) sense
sensato *adj* sensible
sensazionale *adj* sensational
sensazionalismo *m* sensationalism
sensazione *f* sensation, feeling; (*im-*

pressione) feeling; ***fare ~*** cause a sensation; ***ho la ~ che*** I have a feeling that
sensibile *adj* sensitive; (*evidente*) significant, substantial
sensibilità *f* ⟨*pl* sensibilità⟩ sensitivity
sensibilizzare *v/t* ⟨1a⟩ make more aware (***a*** of)
sensibilmente *adv* noticeably
sensitivo I *adj* sensitive **II** *m*, **-a** *f* psychic
senso *m* **1.** sense; ***buon ~*** common sense; ***avere buon ~*** have common sense; ***~ civico*** public spirit; ***~ pratico*** practicality; ***sesto ~*** sixth sense; ***privo di -i*** unconscious; ***perdere i -i*** faint **2.** (*sensazione*) feeling; ***~ di colpa*** guilty feeling **3.** (*significato*) meaning; ***doppio ~*** double meaning **4.** (*direzione*) direction; ***~ unico*** one way; ***~ vietato*** no entry; ***in ~ orario*** clockwise **5.** ***fare ~*** disgust, repel
sensore *m* TECH sensor
sensuale *adj* sensual
sensualità *f* sensuality
sentenza *f* JUR verdict; ***~ di morte*** death sentence; *fig* ***sputar -e*** *infml* pontificate
sentenziare *v/i* ⟨1g⟩ *fig* pass judgment
sentiero *m* path
sentimentale *adj* sentimental
sentimentalismo *m* sentiment
sentimentalista *m/f* ⟨*mpl* -i⟩ sentimentalist
sentimento *m* feeling, sentiment
sentina *f* NAUT bilge
sentinella *f* sentry
sentire *v/t* ⟨4b⟩ **1.** feel; ***~ la mancanza di*** miss **2.** (*udire*) hear; (*ascoltare*) listen to; ***sentir dire*** hear (tell); ***sentirci bene / male*** hear well / not hear well; ***a ~ lei / lui*** to listen to her / him; ***non ~ ragioni*** not listen to reason; ***ci sentiamo domani*** I'll call you tomorrow; ***fatti ~!*** keep in touch!; ***per sentito dire*** by hearsay **3.** *odore* smell; *cibo* taste
sentirsi *v/r* **1.** feel; ***come ti senti?*** how do you feel? **2.** ***sentirsela di fare qc*** feel up to doing sth
sentitamente *adv* sincerely; ***ringraziare ~ qn*** thank s.o. from the bottom of one's heart
sentito *adj* overheard
sentore *m*: *fig* ***aver ~ di qc*** have an inkling of sth
senza *prep* without; ***senz'altro*** definitely; ***~ dubbio*** more than likely, probably; ***~ fine*** endless; ***~ fondo*** bottomless; ***~ impegno*** (with) no obligation *or* commitment; ***~ di me*** without me
senzatetto *m/f* ⟨*pl* senzatetto⟩ homeless person; ***i -i*** *pl* the homeless
separabile *adj* separable
separare *v/t* ⟨1a or 1l & b⟩ separate
separarsi *v/r* separate, split up *infml*
separatamente *adv* separately
separatismo *m* separatism
separatista I *adj* separatist **II** *m/f* ⟨*mpl* -i⟩ separatist
separato I *adj* separate; ***-i in casa*** *of a married couple, separated but still living in the same house* **II** *m*, **-a** *f* separated person
separazione *f* separation; ***~ dei beni*** division of property; ***~ di fatto*** de facto separation; ***~ consensuale*** separation by mutual consent; ***~ giudiziale*** legal separation
séparé *m* ⟨*pl* séparé⟩ private room
sepolcrale *adj* sepulchral
sepolcro *m* sepulchre; *fig* ***~ imbiancato*** whited sepulchre
sepolto *past part* → ***seppellire***
sepoltura *f* burial
seppellimento *m* burial
seppellire *v/t* ⟨4d⟩ bury
seppellirsi *v/r* ⟨4d⟩ *fig* bury oneself
seppia *f* cuttle fish
seppure *cj* even if
sequela *f* series *sg*, sequence
sequenza *f* series *sg*, sequence
sequenziale *adj* COMPUT sequential; ***accesso*** *m* ***~*** COMPUT sequential access
sequestrare *v/t* ⟨1b⟩ confiscate; JUR impound, seize; (*rapire*) kidnap
sequestratore *m*, **-trice** *f* kidnapper
sequestro *m* kidnap(ping); JUR impounding, seizure; ***~ di persona*** kidnap(ping)
sequoia *f* sequoia, redwood
sera *f* evening; ***di ~*** in the evenings; ***questa ~*** this evening; ***verso ~*** towards evening
serafico *adj* ⟨*mpl* -ci⟩ *fig* seraphic
serale *adj* evening *attr*
serata *f* evening; (*festa*) party; THEAT performance; ***~ danzante*** dance; ***~***

di gala gala (evening)
serbare *v/t* ⟨1b⟩ store up; *fig* **~ *rancore per qn*** bear a grudge against s.o.
serbatoio *m* ⟨*pl* -oi⟩ tank; **~ *di riserva*** reserve tank
Serbia *f* Serbia
serbo[1] **I** *adj* Serbian **II** *m*, **-a** *f* Serb
serbo[2] *m*: ***tenere in ~*** keep; ***avere qc in ~*** have sth in store
serbocroato I *adj* Serbo-Croatian **II** *m lingua* Serbo-Croatian
serenamente *adv* calmly
serenata *f* serenade
serenità *f* serenity
sereno *adj* serene; *fig* relaxed, calm
serial *m* ⟨*pl* serial⟩ serial
seriale *adj* COMPUT serial; ***porta*** *f* **~** serial port
serial killer *m* ⟨*pl* serial killer⟩ serial killer
seriamente *adv* seriously
serico *adj* ⟨*mpl* -ci⟩ silken, silk *attr*
sericoltura *f* silk-worm farming
serie *f* ⟨*pl* serie⟩ series *sg*; ***articolo*** *m* ***di* ~** mass produced item; ***produzione*** *f* ***in* ~** mass production; ***la* ~ *A*** SPORTS *top division in Italian football league, equivalent to English premiership*; ***squadra di* ~ *B*** *team in the second division of the Italian football league*; ***fuori* ~** custom-built; ***numero di* ~** serial number
serietà *f* seriousness
serigrafia *f* silk-screen printing
serio ⟨*mpl* -ri⟩ **I** *adj* serious; (*affidabile*) reliable; ***poco* ~** unreliable **II** *m*: ***sul* ~** seriously
sermone *m* sermon
serpaio *m* ⟨*pl* -ai⟩ snake catcher
serpe *f* grass snake
serpeggiare *v/i* ⟨1f⟩ wind
serpente *m* snake; **~ *a sonagli*** rattlesnake
serpentina *f linea* wavy line; *strada* winding street
serra *f* greenhouse; ***effetto*** *m* **~** greenhouse effect
serraglio *m* ⟨*pl* -gli⟩ menagerie
serramanico *m*: ***coltello*** *m* ***a* ~** flick knife
serranda *f* shutter
serrare *v/t* ⟨1b⟩ close; *denti, pugni* clench; **~ *il ritmo*** step up the pace
serrata *f* lock-out
serrato *adj*: ***a ritmo* ~** at a fast pace
serratura *f* lock; **~ *a combinazione*** combination lock
server *m* ⟨*pl* server⟩ COMPUT server
servigio *m* ⟨*pl* -gi⟩ service
servile *adj pej* servile; *pej* slavish
servilismo *m* servility
servire ⟨4b⟩ **I** *v/i* be useful; ***non mi serve*** I don't need it; ***a che serve questo?*** what's this for?; **~ *da bere a qn*** pour s.o. a drink; ***non serve a niente*** it's no use **II** *v/t* serve; ***mi serve aiuto*** I need help; **~ *la Messa*** serve mass
servirsi *v/r* (*usare*) use (***di*** sth); ***prego, si serva!*** *a tavola* please help yourself!
servitore *m*, **-a** *f* servant (*a. fig*)
servitù *f* slavery, servitude; (*personale*) servants *pl*
servizievole *adj* helpful
servizio *m* ⟨*pl* -zi⟩ **1.** service; **~ *civile*** *community service in lieu of military service*; **~ *militare*** military service; **~ *postale*** postal service; **~ *pubblico*** public service; **~ *d'emergenza*** emergency service; ***lavorare a mezzo* ~** work part-time; ***al* ~ *di qn*** in s.o.'s service; ***di* ~** on duty; ***fuori* ~** out of order; ***in* ~** on duty **2.** (*favore*) favo(u)r **3.** (*dipartimento*) department; **~ *assistenza tecnica*** after-sales service **4.** *in giornale* feature (story) **5.** *piatti, posate*: **~ *da caffè*** coffee set; **~ *da tavola*** dinner service **6.** *di cameriere*: service; **~ *in camera*** room service **7.** ***-zi*** *pl* services; ***-zi igienici*** toilet facilities; ***-zi segreti*** secret service; ***-zi sociali*** social services
servofreno *m* servo brake
servosterzo *m* power steering
sesamo *m* sesame
sessanta *num* sixty
sessantenne *m/f & adj* sixty-year-old
sessantesimo *m/adj* sixtieth
sessantina *f*: ***una* ~** about sixty (***di*** sth); ***sulla* ~** about sixty
sessantottino *m*, **-a** *f activist in the 1968 student protests*
sessione *f* session (*a.* COMPUT); **~ *d'esami*** examination session
sessismo *m* sexism
sessista I *adj* sexist **II** *m/f* ⟨*mpl* -i⟩ sexist
sesso *m* sex; *fig* ***il* ~ *debole/forte*** the

weaker / stronger sex; **~ *sicuro*** safe sex; ***fare* ~** have sex
sessuale *adj* sexual; ***organo*** *m* **~** sex organ
sessualità *f* sexuality
sessuologo *m*, **-a** *f* ⟨*mpl* -ghi⟩ sexologist
sestante *m* sextant
sesto[1] *m/adj* sixth
sesto[2] *m*: ***rimettersi in* ~** get back on one's feet; ***arco*** *m* ***a* ~ *acuto*** pointed arch
set *m* (*serie*) set; *cinema*: set; SPORTS set
seta *f* silk; **~ *artificiale*** artificial silk; ***di* ~** silk
setacciare *v/t* ⟨1a⟩ sift (*a. fig*); **~ *la zona*** comb the area
setaccio *m* sifter; (*colino*) sieve; ***passare al* ~** sieve
sete *f* thirst; ***aver* ~** be thirsty; **~ *di sapere* / *potere*** thirst *o* hunger for knowledge / power
setificio *m* ⟨*pl* -ci⟩ silk factory
setola *f* bristle
setoso *adj* silken, silky
setta *f* sect
settanta *num* seventy
settantenne *m/f & adj* seventy-year-old
settantesimo *m/adj* seventieth
settantina *f*: ***una* ~** about seventy (***di*** sth); ***sulla* ~** about seventy
settare *v/t* ⟨1a⟩ *macchina*, *computer* set up
settario *adj* ⟨*mpl* -ri⟩ sectarian
sette *num* seven
settecentesco *adj* ⟨*mpl* -schi⟩ eighteenth century
settecento **I** *num* seven hundred **II** *m*: ***il Settecento*** the eighteenth century
settembre *m* September
settemila *adj inv* seven thousand
settennato *m* POL septenate
settentrionale **I** *adj* northern **II** *m/f* northerner
settentrione *m* north
setticemia *f* septic(a)emia
settimana *f* week; **~ *corta*** five-day week; **~ *grassa*** Shrovetide; ***Settimana Santa*** *f* Easter week
settimanale *m/adj* weekly
settimo *m/adj* seventh; ***essere al* ~ *cielo*** be in seventh heaven
setto *m*: **~ *nasale*** nasal septum
settore *m* sector; ***pubblico* / *privato*** ECON public / private sector
settoriale *adj* sectorial; MATH sectoral
settuagenario *m*, **-a** *f* ⟨*mpl* -ri⟩ septuagenarian
setup *m* setup
severamente *adv* severely
severità *f* severity
severo *adj* severe
sevizia *f* torture
seviziare *v/t* ⟨1f⟩ torture
seviziatore *m*, **-trice** *f* torturer
sexy *adj inv* sexy
sezionare *v/t* ⟨1a⟩ dissect
sezione *f* section
sfaccendare *v/i* ⟨1a⟩ bustle about
sfaccendato *adj* idle
sfaccettato *adj* multi-faceted; *fig* many sided
sfaccettatura *f* faceting; *fig* facet
sfacchinare *v/i* ⟨1a⟩ slave away
sfacchinata *f* backbreaking job; ***fare una* ~** slog
sfacciataggine *f* cheek
sfacciatamente *adv* cheekily
sfacciato *adj* cheeky
sfacelo *m* ruin; ***andare in* ~** fall into decay
sfaldamento *m* flaking; *fig* break-up
sfaldarsi *v/r* ⟨1a⟩ flake; *fig* break up
sfalsare *v/t* ⟨1a⟩ stagger
sfamare *v/t* ⟨1a⟩ feed
sfamarsi *v/r* ⟨1a⟩ feed oneself
sfare *v/t* melt
sfarfallare *v/i* ⟨1a⟩ ZOOL come out of the cocoon; (*svolazzare*) flit about; FILM, OPT, TV flicker
sfarfallio *m* ⟨*pl* -ii⟩ flickering, flicker
sfarsi *v/r* melt
sfarzo *m* splendo(u)r
sfarzoso *adj* magnificent
sfasare *v/t* ⟨1a⟩ PHYS displace the phase of; *fig* bewilder
sfasato *adj* out of phase; *fig* out of synch
sfasciacarrozze *m* ⟨*pl* sfasciacarrozze⟩ breaker
sfasciare *v/t* ⟨1f⟩ smash; MED unbandage; **~ *tutto*** ruin everything
sfasciarsi *v/r* smash
sfascio *m* ⟨*pl* -sci⟩ wreck; *fig* breakdown; ***essere*** (***ridotto***) ***allo* ~** be ruined
sfatare *v/t* ⟨1a⟩: **~ *una leggenda*** debunk a legend
sfaticata *f* grind

sfaticato *m*, **-a** *f* idler
sfavillante *adj* sparkling; *fig* beaming
sfavillare *v/i* ⟨1a⟩ *di occhi* sparkle; *di fuoco* flicker
sfavillio *m di occhi* sparkle
sfavore *m* disadvantage; ***a ~ di qn*** against s.o.
sfavorevole *adj* unfavourable
sfavorito *adj* unlikely to succeed
sfebbrare *v/i* ⟨1b⟩ return to normal (temperature)
sfegatarsi *v/r* ⟨1l⟩: ***~ per qc*** sweat blood for sth
sfegatato *adj* fanatical
sfenoide *m* ANAT sphenoid
sfera *f* **1.** sphere; ***~ d'azione*** responsibilities *pl*, duties *pl*; ***~ di competenza*** area of expertise; ***le alte -e*** the higher echelons **2.** ***~ celeste*** celestial sphere; ***~ terrestre*** globe; ***~ di cristallo*** crystal ball
sferico *adj* ⟨*mpl* -ci⟩ spherical
sferragliare *v/i* ⟨1g⟩ clatter, rattle
sferrare *v/t* ⟨1b⟩: *fig* ***~ un calcio / pugno*** throw a kick / punch
sferruzzare *v/i* ⟨1a⟩ knit
sferza *f* scourge (*a. fig*)
sferzante *adj pioggia* lashing; *fig* cutting
sferzare *v/t* ⟨1a⟩ lash
sfiammare *v/t* ⟨1a⟩ reduce the inflammation
sfiammarsi *v/r* ⟨1a⟩ become less swollen
sfiancarsi *v/r* ⟨1d⟩ knock oneself out
sfiatare *v/i* ⟨1a⟩ leak
sfiatarsi *v/r* ⟨1a⟩ *infml* become hoarse
sfiato *m* vent
sfibrante *adj* exhausting
sfibrare *v/t* ⟨1a⟩ remove fibres from; *fig* wear out
sfibrarsi *v/r* ⟨1a⟩ *fig* wear oneself out
sfibrato *adj* worn out; ***~ dalla malattia*** exhausted by illness
sfida *f* challenge; ***lanciare / raccogliere una ~*** issue / accept a challenge
sfidante **I** *adj* challenging **II** *m/f* challenger
sfidare *v/t* ⟨1a⟩ challenge; ***~ il pericolo*** face danger; ***sfido io!*** I can well believe it!
sfidarsi *v/r* defy each other
sfiducia *f* distrust, mistrust; ***voto*** *m* ***di ~*** vote of no confidence
sfiduciare *v/t* ⟨1f⟩ discourage; POL pass a vote of no confidence (on the government)
sfiduciato *adj* discouraged, disheartened
sfiga *f infml* bad luck; ***portare ~*** be bad luck, be a jinx
sfigato *adj infml* (*sfortunato*) unlucky, jinxed
sfigurare ⟨1a⟩ **I** *v/t* disfigure **II** *v/i* look out of place
sfigurato *adj* disfigured
sfilacciarsi *v/r* ⟨1f⟩ unravel
sfilacciato *adj* frayed
sfilare ⟨1a⟩ **I** *v/t* unthread; (*togliere*) take off **II** *v/i* parade
sfilarsi *v/r* ⟨1a⟩ *collana* come unstrung; (*togliersi*) take off
sfilata *f*: ***~ di moda*** fashion show
sfilatino *m reg* French loaf
sfilza *f* stream; ***una ~ di errori*** a string of mistakes
sfinge *f* Sphinx
sfinimento *m* exhaustion
sfinire *v/t* ⟨4d⟩ wear out
sfinirsi *v/r* ⟨4d⟩ wear oneself out
sfinito *adj* exhausted
sfintere *m* sphincter
sfiorare *v/t* ⟨1a⟩ brush; *argomento* touch on; ***essere sfiorato da un dubbio*** have a twinge of doubt
sfiorarsi *v/r* brush against each other
sfiorire *v/i* ⟨4d⟩ fade, wither
sfiorito *adj* withered; *fig* faded
sfittire *v/t* ⟨4d⟩ thin out
sfittirsi *v/r* ⟨4d⟩ get thinner
sfitto *adj* empty, not let
sfizio *m* ⟨*pl* -zi⟩ whim; ***per ~*** on a whim
sfizioso *adj cibo* tasty
sfocato *adj foto* blurred
sfociare *v/i* ⟨1f⟩ flow
sfoderare *v/t* ⟨1l & c⟩ *spada* draw; *fig* produce; ***~ gli artigli*** show one's claws
sfoderato *adj* unlined
sfogare *v/t* ⟨1e⟩ *rabbia, frustrazione* vent, get rid of (***con, su*** on)
sfogarsi *v/r* vent one's feelings; ***non ti sfogare su di me*** don't take it out on me; ***~ con qn*** confide in s.o., pour one's heart out to s.o.
sfoggiare *v/t* ⟨1f⟩ flaunt
sfoggio *m* ⟨*pl* -ggi⟩ parade; ***fare ~ di qc*** make a display of sth
sfoglia *adj*: ***pasta*** *f* ***~*** puff pastry
sfogliare *v/t* ⟨1g & c⟩ *libro* leaf

through
sfogliarsi *v/r* ⟨1g & c⟩ shed leaves
sfogliata *f* COOK puff pastry; ***dare una ~ a un giornale*** have a look at a paper
sfogliatella *f* COOK *puff pastry filled with ricotta and candied fruit*
sfogo *m* ⟨*pl* -ghi⟩ outlet; MED rash; ***dare ~ alla fantasia*** give free rein to one's imagination
sfolgorante *adj* sparkling
sfolgorare *v/i* ⟨1l⟩ shine
sfolgorio *m* ⟨*pl* -ii⟩ shine
sfollagente *m* ⟨*pl* sfollagente⟩ baton
sfollato I *adj* evacuated **II** *m*, **-a** *f* evacuatee
sfoltire *v/t* ⟨4d⟩ thin
sfondamento *m* breaking; MIL breakthrough
sfondare *v/t* ⟨1a⟩ break; *porta* break down; *muro* knock down; *pavimento* break through; *fig* ***~ una porta aperta*** preach to the converted
sfondarsi *v/r muro* collapse; *tetto* cave in
sfondato *adj* broken; ***essere ricco ~*** *infml* be filthy rich, be loaded
sfondo *m* background; ***sullo ~*** in the background; ***a ~ romantico*** with a romantic background
sforacchiato *adj* riddled with holes
sforare *v/t and v/i* ⟨1a⟩ over-run
sforbiciata *f* snip; SPORTS *nella ginnastica* scissors jump; *nel calcio* scissors kick
sformare *v/t* ⟨1a⟩ stretch out of shape
sformarsi *v/r* ⟨1a⟩ lose one's shape
sformato[1] *m* COOK soufflé, mould
sformato[2] *adj* shapeless
sfornare *v/t* ⟨1a⟩ take out of the oven; *fig* churn out
sfornito *adj*: ***essere ~ di qc*** be out of sth
sfortuna *f* bad luck, misfortune; ***che ~!*** what bad luck!; ***portare ~*** bring bad luck
sfortunatamente *adv* unfortunately
sfortunato *adj* unlucky, unfortunate
sforzare *v/t* ⟨1c⟩ strain
sforzarsi *v/r* try very hard, make every effort
sforzo *m* effort; *fisico* strain; ***fare uno ~*** make an effort; *fisicamente* strain o.s.; ***senza ~*** effortlessly
sfottere *v/t* ⟨2a⟩ tease, *infml* take the mickey
sfottò *m* ⟨*pl* sfottò⟩ *infml* teasing, mickey-taking
sfracellare *v/t* ⟨1b⟩ smash
sfracellarsi *v/r* break into pieces, shatter
sfracello *m* destruction
sfrangiarsi *v/r* ⟨1f⟩ fray
sfrattare *v/t* ⟨1a⟩ evict
sfratto *m* eviction; *avviso* notice to quit
sfrecciare *v/i* ⟨1f⟩ speed, rocket
sfregamento *m* rubbing, chafing
sfregare *v/t* ⟨1e⟩ rub
sfregarsi *v/r* ⟨1e⟩ rub oneself; ***~ gli occhi*** rub one's eyes
sfregiare *v/t* ⟨1f⟩ scar; *fig* dishono(u)r
sfregiarsi *v/r* ⟨1f⟩ be scarred
sfregiato *adj* scarred
sfregio *m* ⟨*pl* -gi⟩ scar
sfrenatamente *adv* wildly
sfrenatezza *f* wildness
sfrenato *adj* unrestrained; ***attività*** *f* **-a** wild activity
sfrigolare *v/i* ⟨1l⟩ sizzle
sfrondato *adj* pruned; *fig* trimmed
sfrontatezza *f* insolence
sfrontato *adj* insolent
sfruttamento *m* exploitation; ***~ della prostituzione*** pimping
sfruttare *v/t* ⟨1a⟩ exploit
sfruttatore *m*, **-trice** *f* exploiter
sfuggente *adj sguardo*, *sorriso* evasive; *mento* receding
sfuggevole *adj* fleeting
sfuggire *v/i* ⟨4a⟩ (*scampare*) escape (***a*** from); ***lasciarsi ~ un'occasione*** miss out on an opportunity; ***~ di mano*** slip from one's grasp; ***~ di bocca*** let slip, slip out; ***~ le tentazioni*** avoid temptation; ***mi è sfuggito di mente*** it slipped my mind
sfuggita *f*: ***di ~*** in passing
sfumare ⟨1a⟩ **I** *v/i* fade away; *fig* fall through; *capelli* thin out; ***~ nel grigio*** shade into grey **II** *v/t* tone down; MUS lower
sfumato *adj fig* fallen through; *colore* shaded; (*vago*) hazy
sfumatura *f* nuance; *di colore* shade
sfuriata *f* (angry) tirade
sfuso *adj* loose; *burro* melted; *vino* in bulk
sgabello *m* stool
sgabuzzino *m* cubbyhole

sgambato *adj* high-cut

sgambettare *v/i* ⟨1f⟩ kick one's legs

sgambetto *m*: ***fare lo ~ a qn*** trip s.o. up

sganasciarsi *v/r* ⟨1f⟩: ***~ dalle risate*** laugh one's head off

sganascione *m infml* slap

sganciamento *m* unhooking; *di bomba* release

sganciare *v/t* ⟨1f⟩ unhook; RAIL uncouple; *infml soldi* fork out *infml*; ***~ una bomba*** drop a bomb

sganciarsi *v/r* become unhooked; *di persona* release o.s.; *fig* free o.s.

sgangherato *adj casa* ramshackle; *sedia* rickety; ***risata*** *f* ***-a*** wild laughter

sgarbatamente *adv* rudely

sgarbato *adj* rude

sgarbo *m* discourtesy; ***fare uno ~ a qn*** slight s.o.

sgargiante *adj* bright, flashy

sgarrare *v/i* ⟨1a⟩ *infml* slip up; ***il mio orologio non sgarra di un secondo*** my watch keeps perfect time

sgarro *m* slip (*a. fig*); *infml breach of the criminal code*

sgattaiolare *v/i* ⟨1m⟩ slip away

sgelare *v/i* ⟨1b⟩ thaw

sgelo *m* thaw

sghembo *adj* crooked; ***di ~*** crookedly, not in a straight line

sghignazzare *v/i* ⟨1m⟩ guffaw

sghignazzata *f* guffaw

sghimbescio *adj* ⟨*mpl* -sci⟩ crooked; ***a ~*** crookedly

sgobbare *v/i* ⟨1c⟩ slave

sgobbone *m*, **-a** *f infml* swot *infml*

sgocciolare *v/t & v/i* ⟨1l⟩ drip

sgoccioli *mpl*: ***agli ~*** almost over; ***le scorte sono agli ~*** supplies are running out; ***la mia pazienza è agli ~*** I'm running out of patience

sgolarsi *v/r* ⟨1a⟩ shout oneself hoarse

sgomberare *v/t* ⟨1l⟩ → ***sgombrare***

sgombero *m di strada* clearing; (*trasloco*) removal

sgombrare *v/t* ⟨1a⟩ *strada, stanza* clear; *ostacolo* remove; *appartamento* clear out, empty; ***far ~ l'aula*** clear the court

sgombro[1] *adj strada, stanza* empty; ***avere la mente -a*** have a clear mind

sgombro[2] *m* mackerel

sgomentare *v/t* ⟨1a⟩ frighten

sgomentarsi *v/r* be frightened

sgomento[1] *m* fear; ***essere in preda allo ~*** be filled with dismay

sgomento[2] *adj* dismayed

sgominare *v/t* ⟨1l⟩ break up; ***~ una banda di rapinatori*** break up a gang of kidnappers; *fig* ***~ gli avversari*** crush one's enemies

sgommare *v/i* ⟨1a⟩ make one's tyres squeal

sgonfiare ⟨1k⟩ **I** *v/t* let the air out of **II** *v/i* become deflated

sgonfiarsi *v/r* ⟨1k⟩ become deflated; ***il braccio si è sgonfiato*** the swelling in the arm has gone down

sgonfio *adj* ⟨*mpl* -fi⟩ flat; MED not swollen

sgorbio *m* scribble; ***la sua firma è uno ~*** his signature is a scrawl

sgorgare *v/i* ⟨1e⟩ spurt, pour; *lacrime* well up

sgozzare *v/t* ⟨1a⟩ slit s.o.'s throat

sgradevole *adj* unpleasant

sgradito *adj* unwelcome

sgraffignare *v/t* ⟨1a⟩ *infml* nick

sgrammaticato *adj* ungrammatical

sgranare *v/t* ⟨1a⟩ shell; ***~ il rosario*** say the rosary; ***~ gli occhi*** goggle

sgranchire *v/t* ⟨4d⟩ stretch

sgranchirsi *v/r* ⟨4d⟩: ***~ le gambe*** stretch one's legs

sgranocchiare *v/t* ⟨1k⟩ crunch, munch

sgrassare *v/t* ⟨1a⟩ skim the fat from

sgravare *v/t* ⟨1a⟩ relieve

sgravarsi *v/r* ⟨1a⟩: ***~ di qc*** unburden oneself of sth; ***~ la coscienza*** ease one's conscience

sgravio *m* ⟨*pl* -vi⟩ relief; ***~ fiscale*** tax allowance

sgraziato *adj* awkward

sgretolamento *m* crumbling

sgretolare *v/t* ⟨1l⟩ crumble

sgretolarsi *v/r* crumble

sgridare *v/t* ⟨1a⟩ scold, tell off *infml*

sgridata *f* scolding, telling off *infml*

sgrossare *v/t* ⟨1c⟩ outline; ***~ qn*** refine s.o.

sgrossarsi *v/r* ⟨1c⟩ become refined

sgrovigliare *v/t* ⟨1g⟩ unravel, disentangle (*a. fig*)

sguaiatamente *adv* raucously

sguaiato *adj* raucous

sguainare *v/t* ⟨1a⟩ *spada* draw

sgualcire *v/t* ⟨4d⟩ crumple, crease

sgualcirsi *v/r* ⟨4d⟩ crumple, crease

sgualcito *adj* creased
sgualdrina *f* tart
sguardo *m* look; (*occhiata*) glance; ***al primo ~*** at first glance; ***dare uno ~ a qn / qc*** glance at s.o. / sth; ***~ d'insieme*** overview
sguarnito *adj* SEW untrimmed
sguattero *m*, **-a** *f* skivvy
sguazzare *v/i* ⟨1a⟩ splash about; *fig* ***~ nei soldi*** *infml* be rolling (in it) *infml*; ***~ nell'oro*** wallow in luxury
sguinzagliare *v/t* ⟨1g⟩ set on (*a. fig*)
sgusciare ⟨1f⟩ **I** *v/t* shell; ***~ i piselli*** shell peas; ***~ le noci*** shell nuts **II** *v/i* slip away; *fig* ***~ via*** slip away; ***mi è sgusciato di mano*** it slipped out of my hand
shaker *m* ⟨*pl* shaker⟩ (cocktail) shaker
shakerato *adj* shaken; ***caffè*** *m* ***~*** iced espresso
shampista *m/f* ⟨*mpl* -i⟩ shampooer
shampoo *m* ⟨*pl* shampoo⟩ shampoo; ***~ secco*** dry shampoo; *fig* ***fare uno ~ a qn*** *infml* give s.o. a telling-off
shareware *m* ⟨*pl* shareware⟩ shareware
sherpa *m* ⟨*pl* sherpa⟩ Sherpa
sherry *m* ⟨*pl* sherry⟩ sherry
shiatsu *m* ⟨*pl* shiatsu⟩: ***massaggio*** *m* ***~*** shiatsu massage
shoah *f* ⟨*no pl*⟩ Shoah
shock *m* ⟨*pl* shock⟩ shock; ***~ culturale*** culture shock; ***essere sotto ~*** be in shock
shopping *m* ⟨*no pl*⟩ shopping
shorts *mpl* shorts *pl*
show *m* ⟨*pl* show⟩ show
showgirl *f* ⟨*pl* showgirl⟩ showgirl
showman *m* ⟨*pl* showman⟩ showman
showroom *m* ⟨*pl* showroom⟩ showroom
si[1] *pron* oneself; *lui* himself; *lei* herself; *esso*, *essa* itself; *loro* themselves; *reciproco* each other; ***spazzolarsi i capelli*** brush one's hair; ***~ è spazzolato i capelli*** he brushed his hair; ***~ dice*** they say; ***cosa ~ può dire?*** what can one say?, what can I say?; ***~ capisce da sé*** it's self-evident; ***che ~ dice in giro?*** what are people saying?; (***non***) ***~ può fare*** it can't be done; ***~ mette il cappello*** put your hat on; ***non ~ salutano*** they don't speak to each other
si[2] *m* MUS B; ***~ maggiore / minore*** B major / minor
sì *adv* yes; ***dire di ~*** say yes; ***~ e no*** yes and no; ***penso di ~*** I think so; ***certo che ~*** of course it is / he will etc.; ***questa ~ che è bella*** that's a good one!; ***uno ~ e uno no*** every other person / thing
sia *cj*: ***~ … ~ …*** both … and …; (*o l'uno o l'altro*) either … or …; ***~ che … ~ che …*** whether … or whether …
SIAE *abbr* (= **Società Italiana Autori ed Editori**) *Italian authors' and publishers' association*
Siam *m* Siam
siamese *adj* Siamese; ***gatto*** *m* ***~*** Siamese cat; ***gemelli*** *mpl* **-i** Siamese twins
siamo → ***essere***
siberiano *adj* Siberian
sibilare *v/i* ⟨1l⟩ hiss; *di vento* whistle
sibilla *f hum* Sibyl
sibillino *adj* Sibylline; *fig* cryptic
sibilo *m* hiss; *di vento* whistle; ***il ~ del vento*** the howling of the wind
sic *adv* sic
sicario *m* hired killer, hit man *infml*
sicché *cj* (and) so
siccità *f* drought
siccome *cj* since
Sicilia *f* Sicily
siciliano I *adj* Sicilian **II** *m*, **-a** *f* Sicilian
sicomoro *m* sycamore
siculo I *adj hist* Siculan **II** *n*: ***Siculi*** *m/fpl hist* the Siculans
sicumera *f* arrogance
sicura *f* safety catch; ***mettere / togliere la ~*** put on / take off the safety catch
sicuramente *adv* certainly; *guidare* safely
sicurezza *f* security; (*protezione*) safety; (*certezza*) certainty; ***~ alimentare*** food safety; ***pubblica ~*** police *pl*; ***cassetta*** *f* ***di ~*** safe-deposit box; ***distanza*** *f* ***di ~*** safe distance; ***cintura*** *f* ***di ~*** safety belt; ***misure*** *fpl* ***di ~*** safety measures; ***per maggior ~*** to be safer
sicuro I *adj luogo* safe; *investimento* sound, safe; (*certo*) sure; ***~ di sé*** self-confident, sure of o.s.; ***di ~*** definitely; ***andare a colpo ~*** be dead certain about sth **II** *m*: ***andare sul ~*** play it safe; ***essere al ~ da qc*** be safe from sth; ***mettere al ~*** put in a safe place
SID *abbr* (= **Servizio Informazioni**

Difesa) *m Italian Secret Service from 1965 to 1977*
sidecar *m* ⟨*pl* sidecar⟩ sidecar
siderale *adj* sidereal
siderurgia *f* iron and steel industry
siderurgico *adj* ⟨*mpl* -ci⟩ iron-and--steel *attr*
sidro *m* cider
siedo → ***sedere***
siepe *f* hedge
siero *m* MED serum; ***~ del latte*** whey
sieropositività *f* ⟨*pl* sieropositività⟩ *being HIV positive*
sieropositivo *adj* HIV positive
siesta *f* siesta
siete → ***essere***
siffatto *adj* such
sifilide *f* MED syphilis
sifone *m* syphon
sig. *abbr* (= **signore**) Mr (mister)
sigaretta *f* cigarette; ***~ col filtro*** filter tip
sigaro *m* cigar
sigg. *abbr* (= **signori**) Messrs
sigillare *v/t* ⟨1a⟩ seal
sigillo *m* seal
sigla *f* initials *pl*; *musicale* theme (tune)
siglare *v/t* ⟨1a⟩ initial; ADMIN pass; ***~ un accordo*** sign an agreement
sigma **I** *m or f* sigma **II** *m* ANAT sigmoid colon
sig.na *abbr* (= **signorina**) Miss, Ms
significare *v/t* ⟨1m & d⟩ mean; ***non significa niente*** it doesn't mean anything
significativo *adj* significant
significato *m* meaning
signora *f* lady; ***mi scusi, ~!*** excuse me!; ***la ~ Rossi*** Mrs Rossi; ***-e e signori*** ladies and gentlemen; ***fare la ~*** live like a lady; ***lei è una vera ~!*** she's a real lady!; ***Nostra Signora*** Our Lady
signore *m* **1.** gentleman; ***il signor Rossi*** Mr Rossi; ***i -i Rossi*** Mr and Mrs Rossi; ***mi scusi, ~!*** excuse me! **2.** REL ***il Signore*** the Lord
signoreggiare ⟨1f⟩ **I** *v/t* dominate, tower over (*a. fig*) **II** *v/i* domineer
signoria *f* lordship
signorile *adj appartamento* luxury; *modi* gentlemanly; ***palazzo*** *m* **~** luxury townhouse
signorilità *f* ⟨*pl* signorilità⟩ elegance
signorina *f* young lady; ***è ancora ~*** she's not married; ***la ~ Rossi*** Miss Rossi
signorino *m* master; *pej hum* lordship
signorotto *m* country gentleman
signorsì *adv* MIL yes sir
sig.ra *abbr* (= **signora**) Mrs, Ms
silenziatore *m* silencer, *US* muffler
silenzio *m* silence; ***fare ~*** be quiet; ***~!*** silence!, quiet!; ***~ stampa*** press blackout; ***cadere nel ~*** fall silent; ***rompere il ~*** break one's silence; ***suonare il ~*** MIL sound the last post; ***il ~ è d'oro*** silence is golden
silenzio assenso *m* tacit agreement
silenziosamente *adv* silently
silenzioso *adj* silent
silfide *f* MYTH sylph
silhouette *f* ⟨*pl* silhouette⟩ figure
silicio *m* silicon
siliconato *adj* silicone; ***seno*** *m* **~** silicone breast
silicone *m* silicone
silicosi *f* ⟨*pl* silicosi⟩ silicosis
sillaba *f* syllable; *fig* ***non capire una ~*** not understand a word
sillabare *v/t* ⟨1l⟩ split into syllables
sillabario *m* ⟨*pl* -ri⟩ spelling book
sillabico *adj* ⟨*mpl* -ci⟩ syllabic
sillogismo *m* syllogism
silo *m* silo
siluramento *m* torpedoing (*a. fig*); *fig* firing
silurare *v/t* ⟨1m⟩ torpedo; *fig* ***~ un progetto*** scupper a plan; ***~ il direttore*** fire the manager
siluro *m* NAUT torpedo
silvestre *adj* woodland
silvicoltura *f* forestry
SIM *abbr*: TEL ***carta*** *f* **~** SIM card
simbiosi *f* symbiosis; ***vivere in ~*** live in symbiosis
simboleggiare *v/t* ⟨1f⟩ symbolize
simbolico *adj* ⟨*mpl* -ci⟩ symbolic
simbolismo *m* symbolism
simbolo *m* symbol
simbologia *f* symbology
similare *adj* similar
similarità *f* ⟨*pl* similarità⟩ similarity
simile **I** *adj* similar **II** *m*: ***i propri -i*** one's fellow creatures
similitudine *f* similitude; MATH similarity
similpelle *f* ⟨*pl* similpelle⟩ imitation leather

simmetria *f* symmetry
simmetrico *adj* ⟨*mpl* -ci⟩ symmetric(al)
simonia *f* simony
simoniaco *adj* ⟨*mpl* -ci⟩ simoniac
simpatia *f* liking; (*affinità*) sympathy; ***avere ~ per qn*** like s.o.
simpatico *adj* ⟨*mpl* -ci⟩ likeable; ***sistema*** *m* ***nervoso ~*** sympathetic nervous system; ***inchiostro*** *m* ***~*** invisible ink
simpaticone *m*, **-a** *f* great person
simpatizzante *m/f* sympathizer
simpatizzare *v/i* ⟨1a⟩ become friends
simposio *m* ⟨*pl* -si⟩ symposium
simulacro *m* simulacrum (*a. fig*)
simulare *v/t* ⟨1l⟩ feign; TECH simulate
simulatore *m*, **-trice** *f* pretender; ***~ di guida*** driving simulator
simulazione *f* pretence, *US* pretense; TECH simulation; ***~ elettronica*** electronic simulation
simultaneamente *adv* simultaneously
simultaneista *m/f* ⟨*mpl* -i⟩ simultaneous translator
simultaneità *f* ⟨*pl* simultaneità⟩ simultaneousness
simultaneo *adj* simultaneous
sinagoga *f* ⟨*pl* -ghe⟩ synagogue
sinapsi *f* ⟨*pl* sinapsi⟩ synapsis
sinceramente *adv* sincerely; (*in verità*) honestly
sincerarsi *v/r* ⟨1b⟩ make sure
sincerità *f* sincerity
sincero *adj* sincere
sincopato *adj* MUS syncopated
sincope *f* MED fainting fit; MUS syncopation
sincretismo *m* syncretism
sincronia *f* synchrony; ***in ~*** synchronized
sincronizzare *v/t* ⟨1a⟩ synchronize
sincronizzato *adj* synchronized; ***nuoto*** *m* ***~*** synchronized swimming
sincronizzazione *f* synchronization *f*
sincrono *adj* synchronous; ***modalità*** *f* ***-a*** COMPUT synchronous mode
sindacale *adj* trade-union *attr*
sindacalista *m/f* ⟨*mpl* -i⟩ trade unionist
sindacare *v/t* ⟨1l & d⟩ inspect
sindacato *m* trade union
sindaco *m* ⟨*pl* -ci⟩ mayor
sindone *f* shroud; ***la Sacra Sindone*** the Turin shroud
sindrome *f* syndrome
sinedrio *m* ⟨*pl* -dri⟩ HIST synedrion
sinergia *f* synergy
sinergico *adj* ⟨*mpl* -ci⟩ synergetic
sinfonia *f* symphony
sinfonico *adj* ⟨*mpl* -ci⟩ symphonic
singalese **I** *adj* Singhalese **II** *m/f* Singhalese
Singapore *f* Singapore
singhiozzare *v/i* ⟨1a⟩ sob
singhiozzo *m*: ***avere il ~*** have hiccups; ***-zi*** *pl* sobs; ***a ~*** in fits and starts; ***scoppiare in -i*** burst into tears
single *m/f* ⟨*pl* single⟩ single
singolare **I** *adj* **1.** singular **2.** (*insolito*) unusual; (*strano*) strange **II** *m* singular; SPORTS singles *sg*
singolarità *f* ⟨*pl* singolarità⟩ singularity
singolarmente *adv* individually
singolo **I** *adj* individual; *camera*, *letto* single **II** *m* individual; SPORTS singles *sg*
singulto *m* → ***singhiozzo***
siniscalco *m* ⟨*pl* -chi⟩ HIST seneschal
sinistra *f* left; ***a ~*** on the left; *andare* to the left; ***essere di ~*** be left-wing; ***circolazione*** *f* ***a ~*** driving on the left; ***alla mia ~*** on / to my left; ***di estrema ~*** of the extreme left
sinistrato **I** *adj* damaged; ***zona*** *f* ***-a*** disaster area **II** *m*, **-a** *f* disaster victim
sinistro **I** *adj* left, left-hand; *fig* sinister **II** *m* accident; ***colpire di ~*** hit with one's left hand, kick with one's left foot
sinistrorso *adj* backwards, anticlockwise (*a.* CHEM, PHYS)
sino → ***fino***
sinodo *m* synod; ***il ~ dei vescovi*** the Synod of Bishops
sinologia *f* sinology
sinologo *m*, **-a** *f* ⟨*mpl* -gi⟩ sinologist
sinonimo **I** *adj* synonymous **II** *m* synonym
sinora *adv* so far
sinottico *adj* ⟨*mpl* -ci⟩ synoptic; ***tavola*** *f* ***-a*** synoptic table
sinovite *f* synovitis
sintagma *m* ⟨*pl* -i⟩ phrase
sintassi *f* syntax
sintattico *adj* ⟨*mpl* -ci⟩ syntactic
sintesi *f* ⟨*pl* sintesi⟩ synthesis; (*riassunto*) summary; ***in ~*** in short
sinteticamente *adv* briefly; CHEM syn-

thetically, by synthesis

sintetico *adj* ⟨*mpl* -ci⟩ synthetic; (*riassunto*) brief; ***materiale*** *m* **~** synthetic (material)

sintetizzare *v/t* ⟨1a⟩ synthesize; (*riassumere*) summarize, sum up; ***cerca di*** **~** try to be brief

sintetizzatore *m* synthesizer

sinti ⟨*pl* sinti⟩ **I** *adj* Sinto (gypsy) **II** *m/f* Sinto (gypsy)

sintomatico *adj* ⟨*mpl* -ci⟩ symptomatic

sintomatologia *f* symptomatology

sintomatologico *adj* ⟨*mpl* -ci⟩ symptomatological

sintomo *m* symptom

sintonia *f* RADIO tuning; *fig* ***essere in*** **~** be on the same wavelength (***con*** as)

sintonizzare *v/t* ⟨1a⟩ RADIO tune

sintonizzarsi *v/r* tune in (***su*** to)

sintropia *f* syntrope

sinuoso *adj* sinuous (*a. fig*)

sinusite *f* sinusitis

sionismo *m* Zionism

sionista *m/f* ⟨*mpl* -i⟩ Zionist

sipario *m* ⟨*pl* -ri⟩ curtain; *fig* ***cala il*** **~** draw a veil

Siracusa *f* Syracuse

siracusano I *adj* Syracusan **II** *m*, **-a** *f* Syracusan

sire *m* Sire

sirena *f* siren; *mitologica* mermaid; **~** ***d'allarme*** alarm; **~** ***dell'ambulanza*** ambulance siren

sirenetta *f fig* nymph

Siria *f* Syria

siriaco *adj* ⟨*mpl* -ci⟩ Syriac

siriano I *adj* Syrian **II** *m*, **-a** *f* Syrian

siringa *f* ⟨*pl* -ghe⟩ MED syringe; **~** ***monouso*** disposable syringe

sirtaki *m* ⟨*pl* sirtaki⟩ sirtaki

sisma *f* earthquake

sismico *adj* ⟨*mpl* -ci⟩ seismic; ***zona*** *f* ***-a*** earthquake zone

sismografo *m* seismograph

sismologia *f* seismology

sismologo *m*, **-a** *f* ⟨*mpl* -gi⟩ seismologist

sissignora *adv* yes madam!

sissignore *adv* yes sir!

sistema *m* ⟨*pl* -i⟩ system; **~** ***antibloccaggio*** anti-lock braking system; **~** ***elettorale proporzionale*** proportional representation; **~** ***immunitario*** immune system; **~** ***maggioritario*** majority system; **~** ***esperto*** COMPUT experts system; **~** ***monetario*** monetary system; COMPUT **~** ***operativo*** operating system; ***che -i sono questi?*** what sort of behaviour is that?

sistemare *v/t* ⟨1b⟩ put; (*mettere in ordine*) arrange; *casa* do up; **~** ***qn*** *infml* fix s.o. up

sistemarsi *v/r* tidy o.s. up; (*trovare casa, sposarsi*) settle down; **~** ***la cravatta*** do up one's tie

sistematicamente *adv* systematically

sistematico *adj* ⟨*mpl* -ci⟩ systematic

sistemazione *f* place; (*lavoro*) job; *in albergo* accommodation

sistemista *m/f* ⟨*pl* -i⟩ systems expert; COMPUT systems analyst

Sistina *adj*: ***Cappella*** *f* **~** Sistine Chapel

sistole *f* systole

sistolico *adj* ⟨*mpl* -ci⟩ systolic

sit in *m* ⟨*pl* sit in⟩ sit-in

sito *m* **1.** site; **~** ***Internet*** Internet site; **~** ***archeologico*** archaeological site **2.** ***in*** **~** on the premises

sitografia *f* COMPUT link list

situare *v/t* ⟨1l⟩ locate, find

situarsi *v/r* ⟨1l⟩ *fig* find one's place

situato *adj*: ***essere*** **~** be situated

situazione *f* situation; ***data la*** **~** given the situation

Siviglia *f* Seville

sivigliano I *adj* from Seville **II** *m*, **-a** *f* person from Seville

skateboard *m* ⟨*pl* skateboard⟩ skateboard

sketch *m* ⟨*pl* sketch⟩ sketch

skilift *m* ⟨*pl* ski-lift⟩ ski lift

skinhead *m/f* ⟨*pl* skinhead⟩ skinhead

skipass *m* ⟨*pl* skipass⟩ ski pass

skipper *m* ⟨*pl* skipper⟩ skipper

skyline *m* ⟨*pl* skyline⟩ skyline

slabbrarsi *v/r* ⟨1a⟩ open up; *ferita* gape

slacciare *v/t* ⟨1f⟩ undo

slacciarsi *v/r* come undone

slalom *m* slalom; **~** ***gigante*** giant slalom

slanciare *v/t* ⟨1f⟩ *abiti* lengthen; *braccia* stretch out

slanciarsi *v/r* ⟨1f⟩: **~** ***contro qn*** throw oneself upon s.o.

slanciato *adj* slender

slancio *m* ⟨*pl* -ci⟩ impulse; ***in uno*** **~** ***di generosità*** feeling generous; ***pieno***

m ***di ~*** full of pep
slargare *v/t* ⟨1e⟩ widen
slargarsi *v/r* ⟨1e⟩ widen
slavato *adj* washed out
slavina *f* snowslide
slavista *m/f* ⟨*pl* -i⟩ Slavonic scholar
slavistica *f* Slavic studies
slavo I *adj* Slav, Slavonic **II** *m*, **-a** *f* Slav
sleale *adj* disloyal
slealtà *f* disloyalty
slegare *v/t* ⟨1e⟩ untie
slegarsi *v/r* free o.s.
slegato *adj fig* incoherent, disjointed
slip *m* ⟨*pl* slip⟩ underpants *pl*; *da donna* knickers *pl*; ***~ da bagno*** bathing trunks *pl*
slitta *f* sledge; ***andare in ~*** go sledging
slittare *v/i* ⟨1a⟩ (*scivolare*) skid; (*essere rinviato*) be put off; ***~ di un'ora*** put off for an hour
slittino *m* sled; SPORTS luge
s.l.m. *abbr* (= **sul livello del mare**) above sea level
slogan *m* ⟨*pl* slogan⟩ slogan
slogare *v/t* ⟨1e⟩ dislocate
slogarsi *v/r*: ***~ una caviglia*** sprain one's ankle
slogato *adj* sprained; *fig* loose
slogatura *f* sprain
sloggiare *v/i* ⟨1f⟩ move out
slot-machine *f* ⟨*pl* slot-machine⟩ slot machine
Slovacchia *f* Slovakia
slovacco ⟨*mpl* -cchi⟩ **I** *adj* Slovak **II** *m*, **-a** *f* Slovak
Slovenia *f* Slovenia
sloveno I *adj* Slovenian **II** *m*, **-a** *f* Slovenian
slow food *m* ⟨*no pl*⟩ slow food
smacchiare *v/t* ⟨1k⟩ take the stains out of
smacchiatore *m* stain remover
smacco *m* ⟨*pl* -cchi⟩ comedown
smagliante *adj* dazzling
smagliarsi *v/r* ⟨1g⟩ ladder, *US* run; MED get stretch marks
smagliatura *f* ladder, *US* run; MED stretch mark
smagnetizzare *v/t* ⟨1a⟩ demagnatize
smagnetizzazione *f* demagnetization
smagrire ⟨4d⟩ **I** *v/t* make thinner **II** *v/i* lose weight
smaliziato *adj* crafty; (*esperto*) skilled
smaltare *v/t* ⟨1a⟩ enamel
smaltato *adj unghie* varnished, polished; *vetro* enamel(l)ed
smaltimento *m* FIN disposal of stock; *di rifiuti tossici* disposal; ***~ dei rifiuti*** waste disposal
smaltire *v/t* ⟨4d⟩ dispose of; ***~ un pranzo*** digest a meal; ***~ la sbornia*** sober up; ***~ le scorte*** sell off stock; ***~ i rifiuti*** dispose of waste
smalto *m* enamel; *per ceramiche* glaze; ***~ dentario*** dental enamel; ***~ per unghie*** nail varnish *or* polish; *fig* ***perdere lo ~*** lose one's edge
smammare *v/i* ⟨1a⟩ *infml* scram
smancerie *fpl* gushing remarks
smania *f* agitation; ***~ di potere*** lust for power
smaniare *v/i* ⟨1h⟩: ***~ per qc*** fret for sth; *fig* yearn for sth
smanioso *adj* restless; *fig* ***essere ~ di qc*** be eager for sth
smantellamento *m* dismantling
smantellare *v/t* ⟨1b⟩ dismantle
smarcare *v/t* ⟨1d⟩ SPORTS free from a marker
smarcarsi *v/r* ⟨1d⟩ lose one's marker
smargiassata *f* bragging
smargiasso *m* boaster
smarrimento *m* loss; ***in caso di ~*** in the event of a loss
smarrire *v/t* ⟨4d⟩ lose; ***~ la strada*** lose one's way
smarrirsi *v/r* get lost
smarrito I *past part* → ***smarrire*** **II** *adj* lost; ***ufficio*** *m* ***oggetti -i*** lost property office
smart card *f* ⟨*pl* smart card⟩ smart card
smascheramento *m* unmasking
smascherare *v/t* ⟨1l⟩ unmask
smascherarsi *v/r* ⟨1l⟩ give oneself away
smaterializzare *v/t* ⟨1n⟩ dematerialize
smaterializzazione *f* dematerialization
Sme *abbr* (= **Sistema monetario europeo**) EMS (European Monetary System)
smembramento *m* dismemberment
smembrare *v/t* ⟨1b⟩ dismember; *fig* disperse
smembrarsi *v/r* ⟨1b⟩ split up
smemoratezza *f* forgetfulness
smemorato *adj* forgetful
smentire *v/t* ⟨4d⟩ prove to be wrong; ***~ una voce*** deny a rumo(u)r; ***non si***

smentisce mai! he doesn't change!
smentita *f* denial
smeraldino *adj* emerald
smeraldo **I** *m* emerald **II** *adj* emerald (green); ***color** m* **~** emerald; ***verde* ~** emerald green
smerciabile *adj* saleable
smerciare *v/t* ⟨1f & b⟩ sell off
smercio *m* ⟨*pl* -ci⟩ sale
smerigliare *v/t* ⟨1g⟩ polish
smerigliato *adj* frosted; ***carta*** *f* ***-a*** emery paper; ***vetro*** *m* **~** frosted glass
smeriglio *m* MINER emery
smerlo *m* SEW scallop
smesso[1] *past part* → ***smettere***
smesso[2] *adj abito* cast-off
smettere ⟨3ee⟩ **I** *v/t & v/i* stop (***di fare qc*** doing sth); ***smettila!*** stop it!; ***smettetela di litigare*** stop arguing; ***vorrei* ~ *di fumare*** I want to give up smoking **II** *v/t abiti* stop wearing
smidollato **I** *adj fig* spineless **II** *m*, **-a** *f* spineless person
smilitarizzare *v/t* ⟨1a⟩ demilitarize
smilitarizzazione *f* demilitarization
smilzo *adj* thin; *fig* insubstantial
sminuire *v/t* ⟨4d⟩ *problema* downplay; *persona* belittle
sminuzzare *v/t* ⟨1a⟩ crumble
smistamento *m* RAIL shunting
smistare *v/t* ⟨1a⟩ RAIL shunt
smisuratamente *adv* immeasurably
smisurato *adj* boundless
smitizzare *v/t* ⟨1a⟩ deglamorize
smitizzazione *f* deglamorization
smobilitare *v/t* ⟨1m⟩ MIL demobilize
smobilitazione *f* MIL demobilization
smoccolare *v/i* ⟨1l & c⟩ *infml* swear
smodatezza *f* excess
smodato *adj* excessive
smoderatezza *f* immoderation
smoderato *adj* excessive
smog *m* ⟨*no pl*⟩ smog
smoking *m* ⟨*pl* smoking⟩ dinner jacket, *US* tuxedo
smontabile *adj* which can be taken apart, *US* knockdown
smontaggio *m* dismantling
smontare ⟨1a⟩ **I** *v/i* (*da cavallo*) dismount **II** *v/t* dismantle; *persona* deflate; **~ *una tesi*** demolish an argument; *fig* **~ *qn*** deflate s.o.
smontarsi *v/r* ⟨1a⟩ *fig* lose heart
smorfia *f* grimace; ***fare -e*** pull faces
smorfioso *adj* affected, simpering
smorto *adj persona* deathly pale; *colore* dull
smorzamento *m di tensione* reduction; *di entusiasmo* dampening; *di colori* toning down
smorzare *v/t* ⟨1c⟩ *colore* tone down; *luce* dim; *entusiasmo* dampen
smorzarsi *v/r* ⟨1c⟩ dim; *suono* die away
smorzato *adj colore* toned down; *luce* dimmed; *entusiasmo* dampened
smosso **I** *adj* displaced; ***terreno*** *m* **~** loose earth **II** *past part* → ***smuovere***
smottamento *m* landslide
smottare *v/i* ⟨1c⟩ slide down
sms *m* ⟨*pl* sms⟩ TEL text (message)
smunto *adj* haggard
smuovere *v/t* ⟨3ff⟩ shift, move
smuoversi *v/r* ⟨3ff⟩ move; *fig* get a move on
smussare *v/t* ⟨1a⟩ blunt; *fig* tone down
smussarsi *v/r* ⟨1a⟩ get blunt
snack *m* ⟨*pl* snack⟩ snack
snack bar *m* ⟨*pl* snack bar⟩ snack bar
snaturare *v/t* ⟨1a⟩ pervert; *fig senso* misrepresent
snaturarsi *v/r* ⟨1a⟩ be perverted
snaturato *adj* devestated; ***figlio*** *m* **~** degenerate son; ***madre*** *f* ***-a*** degenerate mother
snellezza *f* slenderness
snellimento *m* slimming; *fig* streamlining
snellire *v/t* ⟨4d⟩ slim down; *fig* pare down
snellirsi *v/r* ⟨4d⟩ slim down
snello *adj* slim, slender
snervante *adj* irritating, wearing on the nerves
snervare *v/t* ⟨1a⟩ exhaust
snidare *v/t* ⟨1a⟩ flush out
sniffare *v/t* ⟨1a⟩ sniff; **~ *cocaina*** snort cocaine
snob **I** *adj* snobbish **II** *m/f* ⟨*pl* snob⟩ snob
snobbare *v/t* ⟨1a⟩ snub
snobismo *m* snobbery
snobistico *adj* ⟨*mpl* -ci⟩ snobbish
snocciolare *v/t* ⟨1l & c⟩ stone; *fig* **~ *una sfilza di bugie*** reel off a tissue of lies
snodabile *adj* jointed
snodare *v/t* ⟨1c⟩ untie
snodarsi *v/r* ⟨1c⟩ come untied

snodato *adj* loose
snodo *m* MECH articulation; ~ ***autostradale*** motorway junction
snorkeling *m* ⟨*pl* snorkeling⟩ snorkelling; ***fare*** ~ go snorkelling
snowboard *m* ⟨*pl* snowboard⟩ snowboard
snowboardista *m/f* ⟨*mpl* -i⟩ snowboarder
so → ***sapere***
SO *abbr* (= **sud-ovest**) SW (southwest)
soap opera *f* ⟨*pl* soap opera⟩ soap opera
soave I *adj* sweet **II** *m* COOK *white wine from the northeast of Italy*
soavemente *adv* sweetly
soavità *f* ⟨*pl* soavità⟩ sweetness
sobbalzare *v/i* ⟨1a⟩ *veicoli* jerk; *persone* jump
sobbalzo *m di persona* start; *di veicolo* jolt
sobbarcarsi *v/r* ⟨1d⟩: ~ ***qc*** take sth upon oneself
sobborgo *m* ⟨*pl* -ghi⟩ suburb
sobillare *v/t* ⟨1a⟩ stir up
sobillatore I *adj* fomenting **II** *m*, **-trice** *f* instigator
sobriamente *adv* soberly
sobrietà *f* sobriety
sobrio *adj* ⟨*mpl* -ri⟩ sober
Soc. *abbr* (= **società**) Co (company); soc. (society)
socchiudere *v/t* ⟨3b⟩ half-close
socchiuso I *past part* → ***socchiudere*** **II** *adj* half-closed; *porta* ajar
soccombere *v/i* ⟨3a⟩ succumb
soccorrere *v/t* ⟨3o⟩ help
soccorritore *m*, **-trice** *f* rescue worker
soccorso I *past part* → ***soccorrere*** **II** *m* rescue; ***venire in*** ~ ***a qn*** come to s.o.'s rescue; ***pronto*** ~ first aid; ~ ***alpino*** mountain rescue; ~ ***marittimo*** sea rescue; ~ ***stradale*** breakdown service, *US* wrecking service; ***segnale*** *m* ***di*** ~ distress signal
socialdemocratico ⟨*mpl* -ci⟩ **I** *adj* social democratic **II** *m*, **-a** *f* social democrat
sociale I *adj* social **II** *m*: ***impegnarsi nel*** ~ do social work
socialismo *m* socialism
socialista *m/f* & *adj* ⟨*mpl* -i⟩ socialist
socialità *f* ⟨*pl* socialità⟩ social relations
socializzare *v/t* ⟨1a⟩ socialize
socialmente *adv*: ~ ***pericoloso*** dangerous to society; ~ ***utile*** useful to society
società *f* ⟨*pl* società⟩ **1.** *usu*, COMM company; ~ ***in accomandita*** limited partnership; ~ ***per azioni*** joint stock company; ~ ***in nome collettivo*** general partnership; ~ ***a responsabilità limitata*** limited liability company; ***mettersi in*** ~ ***con qn*** go into partnership with s.o.; ~ ***dell'informazione*** information society; ~ ***di capitali*** ECON joint-stock company; ~ ***di persone*** ECON partnership; ***l'onorata*** ~ the Mafia **2.** (*associazione*) society; ~ ***sportiva*** sports club **3.** POL society; ***alta*** ~ high society; ~ ***del benessere*** welfare society; ~ ***dei consumi*** consumer society; ~ ***multiculturale*** multicultural society
societario *adj* ⟨*mpl* -ri⟩ company *attr*
socievole *adj* sociable
socievolezza *f* sociability
socio *m*, **-a** *f* ⟨*mpl* -ci⟩ member; FIN partner; ~ ***fondatore*** founding member
socioassistenziale *adj* social security *attr*
socioculturale *adj* socio-cultural
sociologia *f* sociology
sociologo *m*, **-a** *f* ⟨*mpl* -gi⟩ sociologist
sociopolitico *adj* ⟨*mpl* -ci⟩ socio-political
Socrate *m* Socrates
socratico *adj* ⟨*mpl* -ci⟩ Socratic
soda *f* soda (*a.* CHEM)
sodalizio *m* ⟨*pl* -zi⟩ *fig* brotherhood
soddisfacente *adj* satisfying
soddisfare *v/t* ⟨3aa⟩ satisfy
soddisfarsi *v/r* ⟨3aa⟩ be satisfied
soddisfatto I *past part* → ***soddisfare*** **II** *adj* satisfied; ***essere*** ~ ***di qn*** be satisfied with s.o.
soddisfazione *f* satisfaction; ***dare -i a qn*** be rewarding for s.o.
sodio *m* sodium
sodo *adj uovo* hard-boiled; *fig* ***venire al*** ~ get down to brass tacks
sodomia *f* sodomy
sodomita *m* ⟨*pl* -i⟩ sodomite
sofà *m* ⟨*pl* sofà⟩ sofa
sofferente *adj* suffering
sofferenza *f* suffering
soffermare *v/t* ⟨1a⟩ *attenzione* turn

soffermarsi *v/r* dwell (***su*** on)
sofferto[1] *past part* → ***soffrire***
sofferto[2] *adj* anguished; ***scelta*** *f* ***-a*** difficult choice
soffiare *v/t* ⟨1k⟩ blow; *infml* swipe *infml*; ***soffiarsi il naso*** blow one's nose; *fig* ***~ sul fuoco*** fan the flames; *fig* ***~ qc a qn*** *infml* blurt sth out to s.o.
soffiata *f* *infml* tip-off
soffiato *adj*: ***vetro*** *m* ***~*** blown glass; ***riso*** *m* ***~*** puffed rice
soffice *adj* soft
soffietto *m* bellows
soffio *m* puff; ***in un ~*** in an instant; ***avere un ~ al cuore*** MED have a heart murmur
soffione *m* *di vapore* jet; BOT *infml* dandelion; ***~ boracifero*** fumarole
soffitta *f* attic
soffitto *m* ceiling
soffocamento *m* suffocation; *fig* suppression
soffocante *adj* suffocating
soffocare *v/t* ⟨1l, c & d⟩ suffocate
soffriggere *v/t* ⟨3cc⟩ fry gently
soffrire ⟨4f⟩ **I** *v/t* suffer; *persone* bear, stand; ***~ la fame / la sete*** suffer from hunger / thirst; ***non poter ~ qn*** not be able to stand s.o. **II** *v/i* suffer (***di*** from)
soffritto *m* (*base di cottura*) fried onion, bacon, and herb mixture
soffuso *adj* *luce* subdued
sofisma *m* ⟨*pl* -i⟩ sophism
sofista *m/f* ⟨*pl* -i⟩ sophist; *fig* casuist
sofisticato *adj* sophisticated
sofisticazione *f* adulteration; *di vino*: doctoring
software *m* ⟨*pl* software⟩ software
softwarista *m/f* ⟨*mpl* -i⟩ software engineer
soggettività *f* ⟨*pl* soggettività⟩ subjectivity
soggettivo *adj* subjective
soggetto **I** *adj* subject; ***~ a tassa*** subject to tax; ***andare ~ a qc*** suffer from sth **II** *m* GRAM subject; ***recitare a ~*** improvise
soggezione *f* subjection; ***incutere ~*** make feel uneasy
sogghignare *v/i* ⟨1a⟩ sneer
sogghigno *m* sneer
soggiacere *v/i* ⟨2k⟩: ***~ a qc*** be subject to sth
soggiogare *v/t* ⟨1e⟩ subdugate
soggiornare *v/i* ⟨1a⟩ stay
soggiorno *m* stay; (*stanza*) living room; ***permesso*** *m* ***di ~*** residence permit
soggiungere *v/t* ⟨3d⟩ add
soglia *f* threshold; ECON ***~ di povertà*** poverty threshold; ***~ del dolore*** pain threshold
soglio *m* ⟨*pl* -gli⟩: ***~ pontificio*** papal throne
sogliola *f* sole
sognare *v/t* ⟨1a⟩ dream (***di*** about, of); ***~ qn / qc*** dream about s.o. / sth; ***sognare a occhi aperti*** daydream; ***te lo sogni!*** in your dreams!
sognarsi *v/r* ⟨1a⟩ dream (***di*** about, of)
sognatore *m*, **-trice** *f* dreamer
sogno *m* dream; ***da ~*** dream *attr*; ***-i d'oro!*** sweet dreams!; ***neanche*** *or* ***neppure per ~!*** in your dreams!
soia *f* soya
sol *m* ⟨*pl* sol⟩ MUS G
solaio *m* ⟨*pl* -ai⟩ attic, loft
solamente *adv* only; ***~ ieri*** just yesterday
solare *adj* solar; ***pannello*** *m* ***~*** solar panel; *fig* ***persona*** *f* ***~*** sunny personality
solarium *m* ⟨*pl* solarium⟩ solarium
solcare *v/t* ⟨1d⟩ *fig* *rughe* line; ***~ l'aria*** sail through the air; ***~ le onde*** sail the waves
solco *m* ⟨*pl* -chi⟩ furrow
soldatesca *f* ⟨*pl* -sche⟩ troops; *pej* undisciplined troops
soldatino *m*; ***~ di piombo*** tin soldier
soldato *m*, **-essa** *f* soldier; ***~ di carriera*** regular soldier
soldi *mpl* money *sg*; ***un mucchio di ~*** a lot of money
soldo *m*: ***non avere un ~*** not have a penny; ***non valere un ~ bucato*** be completely worthless
sole *m* sun; ***c'è il ~*** it's sunny; ***colpo*** *m* ***di ~*** sunstroke; ***prendere il ~*** sunbathe; ***il Sol Levante*** the Rising Sun
soleggiare *v/t* ⟨1f⟩ dry in the sun
soleggiato *adj* sun-dried
solenne *adj* solemn
solennità *f* ⟨*pl* solennità⟩ solemnity
solere *v/i* ⟨2p⟩: ***~ fare*** be in the habit of doing; ***come si suol dire*** as people usually say
solerte *adj* hardworking
solerzia *f* diligence
soletta *f* insole

solfa *f*: ***la solita ~*** the same old story
solfatara *f* sulphur mine
solfato *m* sulphate, *US* sulfate
solfeggiare *v/t and v/i* ⟨1f⟩ sol-fa
solfeggio *m* ⟨*pl* -ggi⟩ sol-fa
solforico *adj* ⟨*mpl* -ci⟩ sulphur, *US* sulfur *attr*; ***acido** m* **~** sulphuric, *US* sulfuric acid
solforoso *adj*: ***anidride** f* **-a** sulphur, *US* sulfur dioxide
solidale *adj fig* in agreement
solidarietà *f* ⟨*pl* solidarietà⟩ solidarity
solidarizzare *v/i* ⟨1a⟩ agree, be in agreement
solidificarsi *v/r* ⟨1n⟩ solidify, set
solidità *f* solidity
solido *adj* solid; (*robusto*) sturdy
soliloquio *m* ⟨*pl* -qui⟩ soliloquy
solista *m/f* ⟨*mpl* -i⟩ soloist
solitario ⟨*mpl* -ri⟩ **I** *adj* solitary; *luogo* lonely; *navigatore* solo **II** *m* solitaire; *gioco* patience
solito *adj* usual, same; ***al*** *or* ***di ~*** usually; ***come al ~*** as usual; ***più del ~*** more than usual; ***essere ~ fare qc*** usually do sth; ***diverso dal ~*** different from usual
solitudine *f* solitude, being alone
sollazzare *v/t* ⟨1a⟩ entertain
sollazzarsi *v/r* ⟨1a⟩ entertain oneself
sollazzo *m* entertainment
sollecitare *v/t* ⟨1m⟩ (*stimolare*) urge; *risposta* ask (again) for
sollecitazione *f* urging; MECH stress; *fig* stimulus
sollecito I *adj persona* diligent; *risposta, reazione* prompt; ***lettera** f* ***di ~*** reminder **II** *m* reminder
sollecitudine *f di persona* diligence; *di risposta* promptness
solleone *m* dog days *pl*
solleticare *v/t* ⟨1m & d⟩ tickle; *appetito* whet
solletico *m* tickling; ***fare il ~ a qn*** tickle s.o.; ***soffrire il ~*** be ticklish
sollevamento *m* lifting; (*insurrezione*) rising; ***~ pesi*** weightlifting
sollevare *v/t* ⟨1b⟩ lift; *problema, obiezione* bring up; ***~ qn da un incarico*** dismiss s.o. from a job; ***~ una questione*** raise a question
sollevarsi *v/r di popolo* rise up; AVIAT climb, rise
sollievo *m* relief
sollucchero *m*: ***andare in ~*** go into raptures
solo I *adj* lonely; (*non accompagnato*) alone; (*unico*) only; MUS solo; ***da ~*** by myself/yourself etc, on my/your *etc* own; ***sentirsi ~*** feel lonely; ***~ soletto*** all alone **II** *adv* only; ***spero ~ che ...*** I only hope that ... **III** *m* MUS solo
solstizio *m* ⟨*pl* -zi⟩ solstice; ***~ d'estate*** summer solstice; ***~ d'inverno*** winter solstice
soltanto *adv* only; ***~ ieri*** only yesterday
solubile *adj* soluble
soluzione *f* solution; ***~ alcalina*** alkaline solution; ***~ di ripiego*** makeshift solution; ***~ provvisoria*** stopgap
solvente I *adj* FIN solvent **II** *m* CHEM solvent
solvibile *adj persona* solvent; *debito* payable
solvibilità *f* ⟨*pl* solvibilità⟩ solvency
soma *f* burden (*a. fig*); ***bestia** f* ***da ~*** beast of burden
Somalia *f* Somalia
somalo I *adj* Somali **II** *m*, **-a** *f* Somali
somaro *m* donkey (*a. pej*)
somatico *adj* ⟨*mpl* -ci⟩ somatic
somatizzare *v/t* ⟨1a⟩ have psychosomatic symptoms in reaction to
somigliante *adj* similar
somiglianza *f* resemblance
somigliare *v/i* ⟨1g⟩: ***~ a qn*** resemble s.o.
somigliarsi *v/r* resemble each other
somma *f* (*addizione*) addition; *risultato* sum; (*importo*) amount (of money), sum; ***fare la ~ di*** add (up); *fig* ***tirare le -e*** sum up
sommare *v/t* ⟨1a⟩ add; ***~ a*** total, come to
sommario ⟨*mpl* -ri⟩ **I** *adj* summary; ***giudizio** m* **~** rough justice **II** *m* summary; *di libro* table of contents
sommato *past part*: ***tutto ~*** all things considered, on the whole
sommelier *m/f* ⟨*pl* sommelier⟩ sommelier, wine waiter
sommergere *v/i* ⟨3uu⟩ submerge; *fig* overwhelm (***di*** with); *fig* ***essere sommerso dai debiti*** be up to one's ears in debt
sommergersi *v/r* submerge, dive
sommergibile *m* submarine
sommerso *adj città* submerged; *strade* inches deep in water; ***economia** f* **-a**

black economy; ***lavoro*** *m* **~** moonlighting
sommesso *adj voce* quiet
somministrare *v/t* ⟨1a⟩ MED administer; **~ *i sacramenti*** REL administer the sacrament
somministrazione *f* MED administration
sommità *f* ⟨*pl* sommità⟩ peak
sommo I *adj* supreme (*a. fig*); ***di -a importanza*** of supreme importance; ***per -i capi*** briefly; ***il Sommo Pontefice*** the Supreme Pontiff **II** *m* summit; *fig* height
sommossa *f* uprising
sommozzatore *m*, **-trice** *f* diver
sonaglio *m* ⟨*pl* -gli⟩ bell; ***serpente*** *m* ***a -gli*** rattlesnake
sonante *adj* ringing; ***moneta*** **~** ready cash
sonar *m* ⟨*pl* sonar⟩ sonar
sonata *f* MUS sonata
sonda *f* probe (*a.* MED, MINER); NAUT sounding lead; TECH drill
sondaggio *m* ⟨*pl* -ggi⟩: **~ (*d'opinione*)** (opinion) poll
sondare *v/t* ⟨1a⟩ sound; *fig* test
sondriese I *adj* from Sondrio **II** *m/f* person from Sondrio
sonetto *m* sonnet
sonnacchioso *adj* sleepy; *fig* sluggish
sonnambulismo *m* sleepwalking
sonnambulo *m*, **-a** *f* sleepwalker
sonnecchiare *v/t* ⟨1k⟩ doze
sonnellino *m* nap; ***fare un*** **~** have a nap
sonnifero *m* sleeping tablet
sonno *m* sleep; ***aver*** **~** be sleepy; ***prendere*** **~** fall asleep
sonnolento *adj* drowsy
sonnolenza *f* drowsiness
sono → ***essere***
sonorità *f* ⟨*pl* sonorità⟩ sonority
sonorizzare *v/t* ⟨1a⟩ FILM add the soundtrack
sonorizzazione *f* FILM adding the soundtrack
sonoro *adj* sound *attr*; *risa*, *applausi* loud; ***colonna*** *f* ***-a*** sound-track
sontuosamente *adv* sumptuously
sontuosità *f* magnificence
sontuoso *adj* sumptuous, magnificent
sopire *v/t* ⟨4d⟩ soothe
sopirsi *v/r* ⟨4d⟩ feel sleepy
soporifero *adj* soporific (*a. fig*)
soppalco *m* ⟨*pl* -cchi⟩ mezzanine
sopperire *v/i* ⟨4d⟩ compensate; **~ *a un bisogno*** meet a need
soppesare *v/t* ⟨1a⟩ weigh; *fig* weigh up
soppiantare *v/t* ⟨1a⟩ supplant
soppiatto *adj*: ***di*** **~** stealthily
sopportabile *adj* bearable, tolerable
sopportare *v/t* ⟨1c⟩ *peso* bear; *fig* bear, stand *infml*
sopportazione *f* tolerance
soppressione *f* deletion; *di regola* abolition
soppresso *past part* → ***sopprimere***
sopprimere *v/t* ⟨3r⟩ delete; *regola* abolish
sopra I *prep* **1.** on; **~ *il tavolo*** on the table; *fig* ***averne fin*** **~ *i capelli*** have had it up to the back teeth with sth **2.** (*più in alto di*) above; ***l'uno*** **~ *l'altro*** one on top of the other; ***al di*** **~ *di qc*** over sth; ***al di*** **~ *di ogni sospetto*** above suspicion **3.** (*riguardo a*) about, on **4.** *fig* ***i bambini*** **~ *cinque anni*** children over five; ***5 gradi*** **~ *zero*** 5 degrees above zero **II** *adv* **1.** on top; ***vedi*** **~** see above; ***la parte di*** **~** the top *or* upper part **2.** (*al piano superiore*) upstairs **3.** ***dormirci*** **~** sleep on it
soprabito *m* (over)coat
sopracciglio *m* ⟨*pl* le -a⟩ eyebrow
sopraccoperta *f di letto* bedspread; *di libro* dustjacket
sopraelevata *f* flyover, *US* overpass
sopraffare *v/t* ⟨3aa⟩ overwhelm
sopraffazione *f* bullying
sopraffilo *m* SEW whipstitch
sopraffino *adj* COOK delicious
sopraggiungere *v/i* ⟨3d⟩ *di persona* turn up, arrive on the scene; *di difficoltà* arise, come up *infml*
sopralluogo *m* ⟨*pl* -ghi⟩ inspection (of the site); ***fare un*** **~** inspect
soprammobile *m* ornament
soprannaturale *adj* supernatural
soprannome *m* nickname
soprannominare *v/t* ⟨1l & c⟩: **~ *qn/qc*** nickname s.o./sth
soprannumero *m*: ***in*** **~** overcrowded
soprano *m* soprano; ***mezzo*** **~** mezzo (-soprano)
soprappensiero *adv* → ***sovrappensiero***
soprassalto *m*: ***di*** **~** with a start

soprattassa *f* surcharge
soprattutto *adj* particularly, (e)specially, above all
sopravvalutare *v/t* ⟨1a⟩ overvalue; *fig* overestimate
sopravvalutazione *f* overestimation
sopravvenire *v/i* ⟨4p⟩ turn up, appear
sopravvento *m*: ***avere*** *or* ***prendere il ~*** have the upper hand
sopravvissuto I *adj* surviving **II** *m*, **-a** *f* survivor
sopravvivenza *f* survival; ***istinto*** *m* ***di ~*** survival instinct
sopravvivere *v/i* ⟨3zz⟩ survive, outlive (***a qn*** s.o.)
soprintendente *m/f* supervisor
sopruso *m* abuse of power
soqquadro *m*: ***mettere a ~*** turn upside down
sorbetto *m* sorbet
sorbire *v/t* ⟨4d⟩ sip
sorbirsi *v/r* put up with
sorbo *m* service (tree)
sorcio *m* ⟨*pl* -ci⟩ mouse; ***far vedere i -i verdi*** put s.o. through the mill
sordido *adj* dirty; *fig* sordid
sordina *f* mute; ***in ~*** in secret, on the quiet *infml*
sordità *f* deafness
sordo *adj* deaf; ***~ da un orecchio*** deaf in one ear
sordomuto *adj* deaf and dumb
sorella *f* sister
sorellastra *f* stepsister
sorgente[1] *f* spring; *fig* source
sorgente[2] *adj* COMPUT: ***codice*** *m* ***~*** source code
sorgere *v/i* ⟨3d⟩ **1.** *di sole* rise, come up; ***al ~ del sole*** at sunrise **2.** *fig* arise, come up
sorgivo *adj* spring *attr*
soriano *m* tabby
sormontare *v/t* ⟨1a⟩ *difficoltà* overcome, surmount
sornione *adj* sly
sorpassare *v/t* ⟨1a⟩ go past; AUTO pass, overtake; *fig* exceed
sorpassato *adj* out of date
sorpasso *m*: ***divieto di ~*** no passing, no overtaking; ***fare un ~*** pass, overtake
sorprendente *adj* surprising
sorprendere *v/t* ⟨3c⟩ surprise; (*cogliere sul fatto*) catch
sorprendersi *v/r* ⟨3c⟩ be surprised
sorpresa *f* surprise
sorpreso[1] *past part* → ***sorprendere***
sorpreso[2] *adj* surprised
sorreggere *v/t* ⟨3cc⟩ support (*a. fig*)
sorreggersi *v/r* ⟨3cc⟩ stand up
Sorrento *f* Sorrento
sorretto *past part* → ***sorreggere***
sorridente *adj* smiling
sorridere *v/i* ⟨3b⟩ smile
sorriso I *past part* → ***sorridere*** **II** *m* smile; ***fare un ~ a qn*** give s.o. a smile
sorseggiare *v/t* ⟨1f⟩ sip
sorso *m* mouthful; ***un ~ d'acqua*** a sip of water; ***in un ~*** in one gulp
sorta *f* sort, kind
sorte *f* fate; ***tirare a ~*** draw lots
sorteggiare *v/t* ⟨1f⟩ draw
sorteggio *m* ⟨*pl* -ggi⟩ draw
sortilegio *m* ⟨*pl* -gi⟩ witchcraft
sortire *v/t* ⟨4d⟩: ***~ un effetto*** achieve an effect
sortita *f* (*battuta*) quip
sorto *past part* → ***sorgere***
sorvegliante *m/f* (*guardiano*) guard; (*custode*) caretaker, *US* janitor; (*ai lavori*) supervisor
sorveglianza *f* supervision; *di edificio* security
sorvegliare *v/t* ⟨1g⟩ supervise; *edificio* provide security for; *bagagli etc* look after, take care of
sorvolare ⟨1a⟩ **I** *v/t* AVIAT fly over **II** *v/i fig*: ***~ su*** skim over, skip
sorvolo *m* flying over
SOS *m* SOS; ***lanciare / ricevere un ~*** send out / receive an SOS
sosia *m* ⟨*pl* sosia⟩ double
sospendere *v/t* ⟨3c⟩ suspend; (*appendere*) hang; ***~ un alunno*** EDU suspend a pupil
sospensione *f* suspension
sospeso I *past part* → ***sospendere*** **II** *adj* hanging; *fig questione* pending; ***tenere in ~*** *persona* keep in suspense
sospettabile *adj* suspect
sospettare *v/t* ⟨1b⟩ suspect; ***~ qn*** o ***di qn*** suspect s.o.
sospetto I *adj* suspicious **II** *m*, **-a** *f* suspect
sospettoso *adj* suspicious
sospingere *v/t* ⟨3d⟩ drive; *fig* urge
sospinto I *adj*: ***a ogni piè ~*** at every turn **II** *past part* → ***sospingere***
sospirare ⟨1a⟩ **I** *v/i* sigh **II** *v/t* long for
sospiro *m* sigh; ***tirare un ~ di sollievo***

heave a sigh of relief
sosta *f* stop; (*pausa*) break, pause; ***senza ~*** nonstop; ***divieto di ~*** no parking
sostantivo *m* noun
sostanza *f* substance; ***in ~*** in short, to sum up
sostanziale *adj* essential
sostanzialmente *adv* substantially
sostanzioso *adj* substantial
sostare *v/i* ⟨1c⟩ stop
sostegno *m* support; ***a ~ di*** in support of
sostenere *v/t* ⟨2q⟩ support; (*affermare*) maintain; ***~ un esame*** take an exam
sostenersi *v/r* ⟨1c⟩ stand up
sostengo → ***sostenere***
sostenibile *adj* tenable; ***sviluppo*** *m* ***~*** sustainable development
sostenitore *m*, **-trice** *f* supporter
sostentamento *m* support
sostenuto *adj stile* formal; *velocità* high; ***a velocità -a*** at high speed; ***a ritmo*** *m* ***~*** at a fast tempo
sostituibile *adj* which can be replaced, replaceable
sostituire *v/t* ⟨4d⟩: ***~ X con Y*** replace X with Y, substitute Y for X
sostituirsi *v/r* ⟨4d⟩: ***~ a qn*** take s.o.'s place
sostitutivo *adj* substitute
sostituto *m*, **-a** *f* substitute, replacement
sostituzione *f* substitution, replacement
sostrato *m* GEOL substratum; *fig* background; LING, PHIL foundation
sottaceti *mpl* pickles *pl*
sottana *f* slip, underskirt; (*gonna*) skirt; REL cassock
sottecchi *adv*: ***di ~*** covertly
sotterfugio *m* ⟨*pl* -gi⟩ subterfuge
sotterranea *f* underground
sotterraneo **I** *m* cellar **II** *adj* underground *attr*
sotterrare *v/t* ⟨1b⟩ bury
sottigliezza *f* thinness; (*arguzia*) subtlety; (*cavillo*) quibble
sottile *adj* fine; *fig* subtle; *udito* keen; ***non andare per il ~*** not mince one's words
sottiletta® *f* cheese slice
sottilizzare *v/i* ⟨1a⟩ quibble
sottintendere *v/t* ⟨3c⟩ imply
sottinteso **I** *past part* → ***sottintendere*** **II** *m* allusion
sotto **I** *prep* under; ***i bambini ~ cinque anni*** children under five; ***5 gradi ~ zero*** 5 degrees below (zero); ***~ la pioggia*** in the rain; ***al di ~ di qc*** under sth **II** *adv* below; (*più in basso*) lower down; (*al di sotto*) underneath; (*al piano di sotto*) downstairs
sottobanco *adv* under the counter
sottobicchiere *m* coaster
sottobosco *m* ⟨*pl* -schi⟩ undergrowth
sottobraccio *adv*: ***camminare ~*** walk arm-in-arm; ***prendere qn ~*** take s.o.'s arm
sottocchio *adv*: ***tenere ~ qc*** keep an eye on sth; ***avere ~ qc*** have sth in front of one
sottochiave *adv* under lock and key
sottocoperta **I** *adv* below deck **II** *f* below deck
sottocosto *adv* at less than cost price
sottocutaneo *adj* subcutaneous
sottoesposto *adj* PHOT underexposed
sottofondo *m* background
sottogamba *adv*: ***prendere qc ~*** make light of sth
sottogonna *f* underskirt
sottogruppo *m* subgroup
sottolineare *v/t* ⟨1n⟩ underline; *fig* emphasize, underline
sottomano *adv*: ***avere qc ~*** have sth to hand
sottomarino **I** *m* submarine **II** *adj* underwater *attr*
sottomenu *m* ⟨*pl* sottomenu⟩ COMPUT submenu
sottomesso **I** *past part* → ***sottomettere*** **II** *adj* submissive; *popolo* subject *attr*
sottomettere *v/t* ⟨3ee⟩ submit; *popolo* subdue
sottomettersi *v/r* ⟨3ee⟩ submit
sottomissione *f* submission
sottopancia *m* ⟨*pl* sottopancia⟩ girth
sottopassaggio *m* ⟨*pl* -ggi⟩ underpass
sottoporre *v/t* ⟨3ll⟩ submit
sottoporsi *v/r*: ***~ a*** undergo; ***~ a un esame*** undergo an examination
sottoscala *m* ⟨*pl* sottoscala⟩ cupboard *or* space under the stairs
sottoscritto **I** *past part* → ***sottoscrivere*** **II** *m* undersigned
sottoscrivere *v/t* ⟨3tt⟩ *documento*

sign; *teoria* subscribe to; *abbonamento* take out
sottoscrizione *f* signing; (*abbonamento*) subscription
sottosegretario *m* ⟨*pl* -ri⟩ undersecretary
sottosopra *adv fig* upside-down
sottostante *adj* below
sottostare *v/i* ⟨1q⟩ be subordinate to; ***~ a una regola*** abide by a rule
sottosuolo *m* subsoil; ***ricchezze*** *fpl* ***del ~*** mineral wealth; ***nel ~*** underground
sottosviluppato *adj* underdeveloped
sottotenente *m* second lieutenant
sottoterra *adv* underground
sottotetto *m* loft
sottotitolo *m* subtitle
sottovalutare *v/t* ⟨1a⟩ undervalue; *persona* underestimate
sottoveste *f* slip
sottovoce *adv* quietly, sotto voce
sottovuoto *adv*: ***conservare ~*** vacuum-pack
sottrarre *v/t* ⟨3xx⟩ MATH subtract; *denaro* embezzle
sottrarsi *v/r*: ***~ a qc*** avoid sth
sottratto *past part* → ***sottrarre***
sottrazione *f* MATH subtraction; *di denaro* embezzlement
sottufficiale *m* non-commissioned officer, NCO
soubrette *f* ⟨*pl* soubrette⟩ showgirl
soufflé *m* ⟨*pl* soufflé⟩ soufflé; ***~ di spinaci*** spinach soufflé
souvenir *m* ⟨*pl* souvenir⟩ souvenir
soverchiare *v/t* ⟨1k⟩ outdo
sovietico *adj* ⟨*mpl* -ci⟩ *hist* Soviet; ***Unione*** *f* ***Sovietica*** Soviet Union
sovrabbondante *adj* overabundant
sovrabbondanza *f* overabundance
sovrabbondare *v/i* ⟨1a⟩ be overabundant; ***~ di*** have an overabundance of
sovraccaricare *v/t* ⟨1c & l⟩ overload
sovraccarico I *adj* overloaded (***di*** with) **II** *m* overload
sovraffaticamento *m* overexertion, overwork
sovranità *f* ⟨*pl* sovranità⟩ JUR sovereignty; ***~ popolare*** sovereignty of the people
sovrano I *adj* sovereign **II** *m*, **-a** *f* sovereign
sovrappensiero *adv*: ***essere ~*** be lost in thought
sovrappeso I *adj* overweight **II** *m* excess weight; ***essere in ~*** be overweight
sovrappiù *m*: ***in ~*** in surplus
sovrappopolamento *m* overpopulation
sovrappopolato *adj* overpopulated
sovrapporre *v/t* ⟨3ll⟩ overlap
sovrapporsi *v/r* ⟨3ll⟩ be superimposed; *fig* overlap
sovrapposizione *f* overlapping
sovrapposto I *adj*: ***essere -i*** *in posizione orizzontale* overlap; *in posizione verticale* be superimposed **II** *past part* → ***sovrapporre***
sovrapprezzo *m* overcharge
sovrapproduzione *f* overproduction
sovrastante *adj*: ***l'appartamento ~*** the flat *or* apartment above
sovrastare *v/t* ⟨1a⟩ overlook, dominate
sovrastruttura *f* BUILD superstructure (*a.* NAUT); complication (*a.* PHIL)
sovrimpressione *f* superimposition; ***mostrare in ~*** superimpose
sovrintendente *m/f* → ***soprintendente***
sovrumano *adj* superhuman
sovvenzionare *v/t* ⟨1a⟩ give a grant to
sovvenzione *f* grant
sovversivo *adj* subversive
sovvertire *v/t* ⟨4b⟩ subvert
SP *abbr* (= **La Spezia**) La Spezia
S.P. *abbr* (= **Strada Provinciale**) B road
S.p.A. *abbr* (= **Società per Azioni**) joint stock company
spaccare *v/t* ⟨1d⟩ break in two; *legna* split, chop
spaccarsi *v/r* break in two
spaccatura *f* crevice
spacciare *v/t* ⟨1f⟩ *droga* deal in, push *infml*
spacciarsi *v/r*: ***~ per*** pass o.s. off as
spacciato *adj* done for; ***siamo -i!*** we've had it!; ***dare qn per ~*** give s.o. up for dead
spacciatore *m*, **-trice** *f di droga* dealer
spaccio *m* ⟨*pl* -cci⟩ *negozio* general store; ***~ di stupefacenti*** drug dealing
spacco *m* ⟨*pl* -cchi⟩ *in gonna* slit; *in giacca* vent
spaccone *m*, **-a** *f* braggart
spada *f* sword
spadaccino *m* swordsman

spadroneggiare *v/i* ⟨1f⟩ throw one's weight around
spaesato *adj* disorient(at)ed, confused
spaghettata *f*: ***fare una ~*** have some spaghetti
spaghetti *mpl* spaghetti *sg*
Spagna *f* Spain
spagnoletta *f* spool
spagnolo I *m/adj* Spanish **II** *m*, **-a** *f* Spaniard
spago *m* ⟨*pl* -ghi⟩ string; *fig* ***dare ~ a qn*** encourage s.o.
spaiato *adj* odd; ***calzini*** *mpl* ***-i*** odd socks
spalancare *v/t* ⟨1d⟩ open wide
spalancarsi *v/r* ⟨1d⟩ burst open
spalare *v/t* ⟨1a⟩ shovel
spalla *f* **1.** shoulder; ***era di -e*** he had his back to me; ***girare le -e a qn*** turn one's back on s.o.; ***stringersi nelle -e*** shrug; ***trasportare a ~*** carry on one's shoulders **2.** *fig* ***mettere qn con le -e al muro*** have s.o. over a barrel; ***ridere alle -e di qn*** laugh behind s.o.'s back; ***vivere alle -e di qn*** live off s.o. **3.** ***~ di prosciutto*** shoulder ham **4.** ARCH abutment
spallata *f* push with the shoulder; ***dare una ~ a qn*** give s.o. a push with one's shoulder
spalleggiare *v/t* ⟨1f⟩ support, back up
spalletta *f* parapet
spalliera *f* wallbars
spallina *f* shoulder pad
spallucce *fpl*: ***fare ~*** shrug one's shoulders
spalmare *v/t* ⟨1a⟩ spread
spalmarsi *v/r* rub on
spalti *mpl* terraces *pl*
spam *m* spam; ***fare ~*** *di e-mail* spam
spamming *m* spamming; ***fare ~*** *con e-mail* spam
spanciarsi *v/r* ⟨1f⟩: ***~ dalle risate*** split one's sides
spandere *v/t* ⟨3a⟩ spread
spandersi *v/r* spread
spanna *f* span; ***alto*** *m* ***una ~*** be knee-high to a grasshopper
spanto *past part* → ***spandere***
spaparanzarsi *v/r* ⟨1a⟩ *infml* slouch
spappolare *v/t* ⟨1l⟩ beat to a pulp
spappolarsi *v/r* ⟨1l⟩ become mushy
sparare ⟨1a⟩ **I** *v/i* shoot (***a*** at) **II** *v/t*: ***~ un colpo*** fire a shot
spararsi *v/r* shoot o.s.
sparatoria *f* gunfire, series *sg* of shots
sparecchiare *v/t* ⟨1k⟩ clear
spareggio *m* SPORTS play-off
spargere *v/t* ⟨3uu⟩ spread; *lagrime, sangue* shed
spargersi *v/r* ⟨3uu⟩ scatter
spargimento *m* shedding; ***senza ~ di sangue*** bloodshed
sparire *v/i* ⟨4d or 4e⟩ disappear
sparizione *f* disappearance
sparo *m* (gun)shot
sparpagliare *v/t* ⟨1g⟩ scatter
sparpagliarsi *v/r* scatter
sparso I *past part* → ***spargere*** **II** *adj* scattered
spartano *adj* Spartan
spartiacque *m* ⟨*pl* spartiacque⟩ watershed
spartire *v/t* ⟨4d⟩ divide (up), split *infml*
spartirsi *v/r* divide (up)
spartito *m* score
spartitraffico *m* ⟨*pl* -ci⟩ traffic island
spartizione *f* division
sparuto *adj* (*emaciato*) emaciated; (*esiguo*) scanty
sparviero *m* ZOOL sparrowhawk
spasimante *m/f* admirer
spasimare *v/i* ⟨1l⟩: ***~ per qn*** be in love with s.o.
spasimo *m* agony
spasmo *m* MED spasm
spasmodico *adj* ⟨*mpl* -ci⟩ MED spasmodic (*a. fig*); *fig* agonizing
spassarsi *v/r* ⟨1a⟩: ***spassarsela*** live it up
spassionato *adj* dispassionate
spasso *m* fun; ***andare a ~*** go for a walk; *fig* ***essere a ~*** be out of work, be unemployed; ***è uno ~*** he/it's a good laugh; ***per ~*** as a joke, for fun
spassoso *adj* very funny
spastico *adj* ⟨*mpl* -ci⟩ spastic
spatola *f* palette knife, spatula (*a.* MED)
spauracchio *m* ⟨*pl* -cchi⟩ scarecrow; *fig* bugbear
spaurito *adj* frightened
spavalderia *f* arrogance
spavaldo *adj* cocky, over-confident
spaventapasseri *m* ⟨*pl* spaventapasseri⟩ scarecrow
spaventare *v/t* ⟨1b⟩ frighten, scare
spaventarsi *v/r* be frightened, be scar-

ed
spavento *m* fright; ***mi sono preso uno*** **~** I got a fright
spaventoso *adj* frightening
spaziale *adj* space *attr*; ***volo*** *m* **~** space flight
spaziare *v/i* ⟨1g⟩ sweep; *fig sguardo* range over
spaziatura *f* TYPO spacing
spazientirsi *v/r* ⟨4d⟩ get impatient, lose one's patience
spazio *m* ⟨*pl* -zi⟩ space; **~ *aereo*** airspace; **~ *pubblicitario*** advertising space; **~ *pubblico*** JUR public space *o* area
spazioso *adj* spacious
spazzacamino *m* chimney sweep
spazzaneve *m* ⟨*pl* spazzaneve⟩ snowplough, *US* -plow
spazzare *v/t* ⟨1a⟩ sweep
spazzatura *f* rubbish, garbage
spazzino *m*, **-a** *f* street sweeper
spazzola *f* brush; ***capelli mpl a*** **~** crewcut
spazzolare *v/t* ⟨1l⟩ brush
spazzolarsi *v/r* ⟨1l⟩: **~ *i denti / i capelli*** brush one's teeth / hair
spazzolata *f*: ***dare una*** **~ *a qc*** give sth a brush
spazzolino *m* brush; **~ *da denti*** toothbrush
spazzolone *m* brush
speaker *m* ⟨*pl* speaker⟩ announcer
specchiarsi *v/r* ⟨1k⟩ look at o.s.; (*riflettersi*) be mirrored, be reflected
specchiato *adj fig* exemplary
specchiera *f* large mirror; (*mobile*) dresser
specchietto *m* mirror; (*prospetto*) table; **~ *retrovisore*** AUTO rear-view mirror; *fig* **~ *per le allodole*** bait
specchio *m* ⟨*pl* -cchi⟩ mirror; **~ *d'acqua*** sheet of water
speciale *adj* special; ***treno*** *m* **~** special (train)
specialista *m/f* ⟨*mpl* -i⟩ specialist
specialità *f* ⟨*pl* specialità⟩ special(i)ty
specializzarsi *v/r* ⟨1a⟩ specialize
specializzato *adj* skilled
specializzazione *f* specialization
specialmente *adv* especially, particularly
specie I *f* ⟨*pl* specie⟩ species *sg*; ***una*** **~ *di*** a sort *or* kind of **II** *adv* especially
specifica *f* ⟨*pl* -che⟩ specification
specificamente *adv* specifically
specificare *v/t* ⟨1m & d⟩ specify
specificazione *f* specification
specifico *adj* ⟨*mpl* -ci⟩ specific
speculare[1] *adj* specular; ***immagine*** *f* **~** mirror image
speculare[2] *v/i* ⟨1l & b⟩ speculate (***in*** in, ***su*** on)
speculativo *adj* speculative
speculatore *m*, **-trice** *f* speculator
speculazione *f* speculation
spedire *v/t* ⟨4d⟩ send; **~ *qn all'altro mondo*** knock s.o. to kingdom come
speditamente *adv* quickly
speditezza *f* velocity
spedito *adj* fast
speditore *m* sender
spedizione *f* **1.** dispatch, sending; *di merce* shipping; ***agenzia*** *f* ***di*** **~** shipping agency; ***spese*** *pl* ***di*** **~** shipping costs **2.** (*viaggio*) expedition
spedizioniere *m* courier
spegnere *v/t* ⟨3vv⟩ put out; *luce*, *motore*, *radio* turn off, switch off
spegnersi *v/r di fuoco* go out; *di motore* stop, die *infml*
spegnimento *m* putting out (*a. fig*); ELEC switching off; **~ *automatico*** COMPUT automatic shutdown
spelacchiato *adj* mangy, bald; *pelliccia* threadbare
spelare *v/t* ⟨1a⟩ remove hair from
spelarsi *v/r* ⟨1a⟩ go bald
speleologo *m*, **-a** *f* ⟨*mpl* -gi⟩ speleologist
spellare *v/t* ⟨1a⟩ skin
spellarsi *v/r* peel
spelling *m* ⟨*no pl*⟩ spelling; ***fare lo*** **~** spell
spelonca *f* ⟨*pl* -che⟩ cave
spendaccione *m*, **-a** *f* spendthrift
spendere *v/t* ⟨3c⟩ spend; *fig* invest
spennacchiato *adj* bald
spennare *v/t* ⟨1a⟩ *pollo* pluck; *fig* ***in quel negozio ti spennano*** they rip you off in that shop
spennellare *v/t* ⟨1b⟩ brush; paint (*a.* MED)
spensieratezza *f* lightheartedness
spensierato *adj* carefree
spento[1] *past part* → ***spegnere***
spento[2] *adj* out; *candela* unlit; ELEC, *motore* off; *colori* dull; *voce* lifeless; *sguardo* expressionless
sperabile *adj* desirable

speranza *f* hope; ***senza ~*** hopeless
speranzoso *adj* hopeful
sperare ⟨1b⟩ **I** *v/t* hope for; ***speriamo bene*** let's hope so **II** *v/i* trust (***in*** in)
sperduto *adj* lost; *luogo* remote, isolated
sperequazione *f* inequality
spergiurare *v/t* ⟨1a⟩ perjure o.s.; *rafforzativo* ***giurare e ~*** swear blind
spergiuro I *m* perjury **II** *m*, **-a** *f* perjurer
spericolatezza *f* recklessness
spericolato I *adj* reckless **II** *m*, **-a** *f* daredevil
sperimentale *adj* experimental
sperimentare *v/t* ⟨1a⟩ try; *in laboratorio* test; *fig*: *fatica, dolore* feel; *droga* experiment with; ***~ sulla propria pelle*** test on o.s.
sperimentazione *f* experimentation
sperma *m* sperm
spermatozoo *m* ⟨*pl* -oi⟩ spermatozoon
speronare *v/t* ⟨1a⟩ ram
sperone *m* spur
sperperare *v/t* ⟨1l & b⟩ fritter away, squander
sperpero *m* frittering away, squandering
sperso *adj* → ***sperduto***
spersonalizzare *v/t* ⟨1a⟩ depersonalize
spesa *f* expense; ***fare la ~*** do the shopping; ***fare -e*** go shopping; ***-e** pl* ***di produzione*** production costs; ***-e** pl* ***di pubblicità*** advertising costs; ***-e** pl* ***vive*** incidental expenses; ***a proprie -e*** at one's own expense; ***non badare a -e*** spare no expense; *fig* ***fare le -e di qc*** pay for sth
spesato *adj*: ***essere ~*** have all one's expenses paid
spesso I *adj* thick; ***-e volte*** many times, often **II** *adv* often, frequently
spessore *m* thickness
spett. *abbr* (= **spettabile**) Messrs; ***Spett. Ditta*** *in lettera* Dear Sirs
spettabile *adj* Messrs; ***Spettabile Ditta*** *nelle lettere* Dear Sirs
spettacolare *adj* spectacular
spettacolarizzare *v/t* ⟨1a⟩: ***~ qc*** turn sth into a show
spettacolo *m* show; (*panorama*) spectacle, sight; ***~ teatrale*** show; ***ultimo ~*** last performance
spettacoloso *adj* spectacular
spettanza *f* ADMIN remit
spettare *v/i* ⟨1b⟩: ***questo spetta a te*** this is yours; ***non spetta a te giudicare*** it's not up to you to judge; ***non spetta a me*** it's not my place
spettatore *m*, **-trice** *f* spectator; THEAT member of the audience
spettegolare *v/i* ⟨1m⟩ gossip
spettinare *v/t* ⟨1l & b⟩: ***~ qn*** ruffle s.o.'s hair
spettinarsi *v/r* mess up one's hair
spettinato *adj* messy
spettrale *adj* spectral
spettro *m* ghost; PHYS spectrum
spettrometro *m* spectrometer
spezie *fpl* spices *pl*
spezzare *v/t* ⟨1b⟩ break in two; ***~ il cuore a qn*** break s.o.'s heart; *fig* ***~ una lancia in favore di qn*** strike a blow for s.o.
spezzarsi *v/r* break
spezzatino *m* stew
spezzato I *adj* broken (in two) **II** *m* co-ordinated two-piece suit
spezzettare *v/t* ⟨1a⟩ break up
spezzino I *adj* from La Spezia **II** *m*, **-a** *f* person from La Spezia
spezzone *m* bomb; FILM clip; ***~ incendiario*** incendiary device
spia *f* spy; TECH pilot light; ***fare la ~*** tell, sneak; ***la ~ dell'olio*** oil warning light
spiaccicare *v/t* ⟨1l e d⟩ squash
spiaccicarsi *v/r* ⟨1l e d⟩ get squashed
spiacente *adj*: ***essere ~*** be sorry; ***sono molto ~*** I am very sorry
spiacere *v/i* ⟨2k⟩: ***mi spiace*** I am sorry; ***Le spiace se mi siedo?*** do you mind if I sit down?
spiacevole *adj* unpleasant
spiaggia *f* ⟨*pl* -gge⟩ beach; ***~ libera*** public beach; *fig* ***ultima ~*** last resort
spianare *v/t* ⟨1a⟩ roll; ***~ la pasta*** roll out the pasta; ***~ la strada** or **via*** pave the way; ***con il fucile** m **spianato*** with one's gun drawn
spianarsi *v/r* ⟨1a⟩ smooth
spianata *f* smoothing
spianatoia *f* pastry board
spiano *m*: ***a tutto ~*** flat out
spiantato I *adj* penniless **II** *m*, **-a** *f* penniless person
spiare *v/t* ⟨1h⟩ spy on
spiata *f* tip-off, whistle-blowing

spiattellare *v/t* ⟨1b⟩ blurt out
spiazzare *v/t* ⟨1a⟩ SPORTS wrongfoot; *fig* catch off guard
spiazzato *adj*: ***trovarsi ~*** be caught off guard
spiazzo *m* empty space; *in bosco* clearing
spiccare ⟨1a⟩ **I** *v/t*: ***~ un mandato di cattura*** issue an arrest warrant; ***~ un salto*** jump; ***~ il volo*** spread one's wings (*a. fig*) **II** *v/i* stand out
spiccato *adj* strong
spicchio *m* ⟨*pl* -cchi⟩ *di frutto* section; ***~ d'aglio*** clove of garlic
spicciarsi *v/r* ⟨1f⟩ hurry up
spiccicare *v/t* ⟨1d⟩ (*staccare*) peel off, unstick; (*separare*) split up (*a. fig*); *fig* ***non ~*** (***una***) ***parola*** not utter a word
spiccicarsi *v/r* ⟨1d⟩ (*staccarsi*) come unstuck; (*separarsi*) split up (*a. fig*); ***~ qn di torno*** *infml* get rid of s.o.
spiccicato *adj* identical; ***è suo padre ~*** he's the spitting image of his father
spiccio *adj* ⟨*mpl* -cci⟩ rough-and-ready; *fig* ***andare per le -ce*** get straight to the point
spicciolata *f*: ***alla ~*** in dribs and drabs
spiccioli *mpl* (small) change *sg*
spicciolo *adj* plain; ***moneta** f **-a*** change; ***in parole -e*** in plain words
spicco *m* ⟨*pl* -cchi⟩ prominence; ***di ~*** prominent
spidocchiare *v/t* ⟨1k⟩ delouse
spidocchiarsi *v/r* ⟨1k⟩ delouse oneself; *a vicenda* delouse each other
spiedino *m* skewer; ***-i** pl **di carne*** meat kebab *or US* kabob
spiedo *m* spit; ***allo ~*** spit-roasted
spiegabile *adj* possible to explain
spiegamento *m* MIL deployment; ***~ di forze*** deployment of forces
spiegare *v/t* ⟨1b & e⟩ (*stendere*) spread; (*chiarire*) explain; ***~ le vele*** unfurl the sails
spiegarsi *v/r* explain what one means; ***mi spiego?*** have I made myself clear?; ***non so se mi spiego*** I don't know if I make myself clear
spiegato *adj*: ***a vele -e*** in full sail; ***a voce -a*** full-throated
spiegazione *f* explanation
spiegazzare *v/t* ⟨1a⟩ crease
spiegazzarsi *v/r* ⟨1a⟩ crease
spietato *adj* merciless, pitiless; ***giudizio** m **~*** ruthless judgement
spifferare *v/t* ⟨1l⟩ blurt out
spiffero *m* draught, *US* draft
spiga *f* ⟨*pl* -ghe⟩ *di grano* ear
spigato *adj* herring-bone *attr*
spigliatezza *f* jauntiness
spigliato *adj* confident
spignattare *v/i* ⟨1m⟩ *infml* be busy cooking
spigo *m* ⟨*pl* -ghi⟩ BOT lavender
spigola *f* sea bass
spigolare *v/t* ⟨1l⟩: ***~ il grano*** glean corn
spigolo *m* corner
spigoloso *adj* angular
spilla *f gioiello* brooch; ***~ da balia*** safety pin
spillare[1] *v/t* ⟨1a⟩ tap; *fig* ***~ denaro a qn*** squeeze money out of s.o.
spillare[2] *v/t* ⟨1a⟩ (*unire*) staple *or* pin together
spillo *m* pin; ***~ di sicurezza*** safety pin; ***tacchi** mpl **a ~*** stiletto heels
spilluzzicare *v/t* ⟨1m & d⟩ nibble, peck at
spilorceria *f* stinginess
spilorcio *adj* stingy
spilungone *m*, **-a** *f* beanpole
spina *f* **1.** BOT thorn; ZOOL spine; *fig* ***stare sulle -e*** be on tenterhooks; *fig* ***una ~ nel fianco*** a thorn in one's side **2.** *di pesce* bone; ANAT ***~ dorsale*** spine; ***parcheggio** m **a ~ di pesce*** angle parking **3.** ELEC plug; *fig* ***staccare la ~*** unwind **4.** ***birra** f **alla ~*** draught beer, beer on tap
spinaci *mpl* spinach *sg*
spinale *adj* spinal
spinare *v/t* ⟨1a⟩ bone
spinato *adj* boned; ***filo** m **~*** barbed wire
spinello *m infml* joint *infml*
spinetta *f* spinet
spingere *v/t* ⟨3d⟩ push; *fig* drive; ***non spingete!*** don't push!; ***~ oltre*** push past; *fig* ***~ qn a fare qc*** drive s.o. to do sth
spingersi *v/r* go
spinnaker *m* ⟨*pl* spinnaker⟩ spinnaker
spino *m* thorn
spino[1] *adj*: ***uva** f **-a*** gooseberry
spino[2] *m* thorn; (*prugno selvatico*) thorn tree
spinone *m* hunting dog, griffon
spinosità *f* ⟨*pl* spinosità⟩ *di questione*: ticklishness; *di carattere*: prickliness

spinoso *adj* thorny
spinotto *m* pin; ELEC plug
spinta *f* push; ***dare una ~ a qn*** give s.o. a push
spintarella *f* leg-up; ***grazie a una ~*** thanks to some string-pulling
spinterogeno *m* AUTO distributor
spinto[1] *past part* → ***spingere***
spinto[2] *adj* risqué; ***sentirsi ~ a fare qc*** feel driven to do sth
spintonare *v/t* ⟨1a⟩ push
spintone *m* push; ***dare uno ~ a qn*** give s.o. a leg-up
spionaggio *m* ⟨*pl* -ggi⟩ espionage
spioncino *m* spy hole, *infml* peephole
spione *m*, **-a** *f* telltale
spiovente *adj* droopy; ***tetto*** *m* **~** pitched roof
spiovere *v/impers* ⟨3kk⟩ stop raining
spira *f* spiral; ELEC coil; ***le -e di una molla*** the coils of a spring
spiraglio *m* ⟨*pl* -gli⟩ crack; *di luce, speranza* gleam, glimmer
spirale *f* spiral; *contraccettivo* coil
spirare *v/i* ⟨1a⟩ blow; *fig* die
spiritato *adj* possessed; ***occhi*** *mpl* ***-i*** wild eyes
spiritico *adj* ⟨*mpl* -ci⟩ spiritualist; ***seduta*** *f* ***-a*** seance
spiritismo *m* spiritualism
spirito *m* **1.** spirit; (*disposizione*) mind; ***avere ~ d'osservazione*** be observant **2.** (*umorismo*) wit; ***fare dello ~*** be witty; ***battuta*** *f* ***di ~*** witticism **3.** REL ***Spirito Santo*** Holy Spirit
spiritosaggine *f* wittiness
spiritoso *adj* witty
spirituale *adj* spiritual
spiritualità *f* spirituality
spiritualizzare *v/t* ⟨1a⟩ spiritualize
spirografia *f* spirography
spiroidale *adj* spiroid
spirometria *f* spirometry
spirometro *m* spirometer
spiumarsi *v/r* ⟨1a⟩ lose one's feathers
spizzicare *v/t* ⟨1l & d⟩ peck at
spizzico *m* ⟨*pl* -chi⟩: ***a ~ / -chi*** bit by bit
spleen *m* ⟨*pl* spleen⟩ melancholy
splendente *adj* bright
splendere *v/i* ⟨3a⟩ shine
splendido *adj* wonderful, splendid
splendore *m* splendo(u)r
splitting *m* ⟨*pl* splitting⟩ FIN splitting
spocchia *f fig* conceit
spocchioso *adj* self-important
spodestare *v/t* ⟨1b⟩ depose, remove from office
spoglia *f* ⟨*pl* -glie⟩ *fig* ***le -e mortali*** mortal remains; *fig* ***sotto mentite -e*** in disguise
spogliare *v/t* ⟨1g⟩ undress; (*rubare*) rob
spogliarellista *m/f* ⟨*mpl* -i⟩ stripper
spogliarello *m* striptease
spogliarsi *v/r* undress, strip; ***~ di qc*** give sth up
spogliatoio *m* ⟨*pl* -oi⟩ dressing room, locker room
spoglio[1] *adj* ⟨*mpl* -gli⟩ bare
spoglio[2] *m*: ***~ delle schede*** counting of the votes
spoiler *m* ⟨*pl* spoiler⟩ spoiler
spola *f*: ***fare la ~ da un posto all'altro*** shuttle backwards and forwards between two places
spoletta *f* TEX spool; *di arma* fuse
spolmonarsi *v/r* ⟨1a⟩ shout one's head off
spolpare *v/t* ⟨1a⟩ remove the flesh from; *frutto* remove the pulp from; *fig* fleece
spolverare *v/t* ⟨1l⟩ dust
spolverata *f* dusting; COOK sprinkling; ***dare una ~ ai mobili*** polish the furniture
spolverino *m* dust coat, *US* duster
spolverizzare *v/t* ⟨1a⟩ dust (***di*** with)
spompato *adj infml* pooped
sponda *f di letto* edge, side; *di fiume* bank; *nel biliardo* cushion
spondilite *f* spondylitis
spondilosi *f* ⟨*pl* spondilosi⟩ spondylosis
sponsor *m* ⟨*pl* sponsor⟩ sponsor
sponsorizzare *v/t* ⟨1a⟩ sponsor
sponsorizzazione *f* sponsorship
spontaneamente *adv* spontaneously
spontaneità *f* spontaneity
spontaneo *adj* spontaneous; ***vegetazione*** *f* ***-a*** natural vegetation
spopolamento *m* depopulation; ***~ delle campagne*** depopulation of the countryside
spopolare ⟨1l & c⟩ **I** *v/t* depopulate; *infml* empty **II** *v/i fig* be all the rage
spopolarsi *v/r* ⟨1l & c⟩ become depopulated *or* deserted
spora *f* spore
sporadicamente *adv* sporadically

sporadico *adj* ⟨*mpl* -ci⟩ sporadic
sporcaccione *m*, **-a** *f* pig; ***un vecchio ~*** a dirty old man
sporcare *v/t* ⟨1c & d⟩ dirty
sporcarsi *v/r* get dirty; *fig* ***~ le mani*** dirty one's hands
sporchevole *adj* that shows the dirt
sporcizia *f* dirt
sporco ⟨*mpl* -chi⟩ **I** *adj* dirty **II** *m* dirt
sporgente *adj* projecting, protruding
sporgenza *f* projection
sporgere ⟨3d⟩ **I** *v/t* hold out; ***~ denuncia*** lodge a complaint; ***~ reclamo*** make a claim **II** *v/i* jut out
sporgersi *v/r* lean out
sport *m* ⟨*pl* sport⟩ sport; ***~ pl invernali*** winter sports; ***fare dello ~*** do sport; ***per ~*** for fun
sporta *f* shopping bag; *di vimini* shopping basket
sportello *m* door; ***~ automatico*** automatic teller machine, cash dispenser
sportivamente *adv*: ***accettare ~ una sconfitta*** be sporting in defeat, be a good loser
sportività *f* ⟨*pl* sportività⟩ sportsmanship; (*lealtà*) good sportsmanship
sportivo **I** *adj* sports *attr*; *persona* sporty; ***campo m ~*** playing field **II** *m*, **-a** *f* sportsman; *donna* sportswoman
sporto *past part* → ***sporgere***
sposa *f* bride; ***abito m da ~*** wedding dress
sposalizio *m* ⟨*pl* -zi⟩ wedding
sposare *v/t* ⟨1c⟩ marry
sposarsi *v/r* get married
sposato *adj* married
sposo *m* bridegroom; ***-i*** *pl* newlyweds
spossante *adj* exhausting
spossare *v/t* ⟨1e⟩ exhaust
spossatezza *f* exhaustion
spostamento *m* movement; ***~ d'aria*** blast; ***~ d'orario*** change in the timetable
spostare *v/t* ⟨1a⟩ (*trasferire*) move, shift; (*rimandare*) postpone
spostarsi *v/r* move
spot *m* ⟨*pl* spot⟩ advertisement
S.P.Q.R. *abbr* (= **Senatus Populusque Romanus**) the Senate and People of Rome
spranga *f* ⟨*pl* -ghe⟩ bar
sprangare *v/t* ⟨1e⟩ bar
spray *m* ⟨*pl* spray⟩ spray
sprazzo *m* flash; ***~ di sole*** burst of sunlight; ***~ d'ingegno*** spark of genius; ***~ di allegria*** hint of gaiety; ***a -i*** fitfully
sprecare *v/t* ⟨1b & d⟩ waste, squander; *fig* ***~ il fiato*** waste one's breath
sprecarsi *v/r* ⟨1b & d⟩: ***~ in qc*** waste one's time on sth; ***non ti sei certo sprecato!*** *hum* you certainly didn't waste your time!
sprecato *adj* wasted; ***fatica f -a*** a waste of effort; ***tempo m ~*** a waste of time
spreco *m* ⟨*pl* -chi⟩ waste
sprecone *m*, **-a** *f* spendthrift
spregevole *adj* contemptible, despicable
spregiare *v/t* ⟨1f & b⟩ be scornful of
spregiativo *adj* derogatory; LING pejorative
spregio *m* ⟨*pl* -gi⟩ contempt; ***in ~ a qn*** contemptuous of s.o.
spregiudicatezza *f* open-mindedness; (*mancanza di scrupoli*) unscrupulousness
spregiudicato *adj* unprejudiced, unbiased; *pej* unscrupulous
spremere *v/t* ⟨3a⟩ squeeze
spremersi *v/r* ⟨3a⟩ *fig*: ***~ le meningi*** rack one's brain
spremiagrumi *m* ⟨*pl* spremiagrumi⟩ lemon squeezer
spremilimoni *m* ⟨*pl* spremilimoni⟩ lemon squeezer
spremitura *f di olive* pressing; *di agrumi* squeezing
spremuta *f* squash; ***~ di limone*** lemon squash; ***~ d'arancia*** orange squash
spretarsi *v/r* ⟨2b⟩ leave the priesthood
spretato *m* defrocked priest
sprezzante *adj* scornful
sprezzo *m* defiance; ***~ del pericolo*** defiance of danger
sprigionare *v/t* ⟨1a⟩ release
sprigionarsi *v/r* ⟨1a⟩ be given off
sprimacciare *v/t* ⟨1f⟩ fluff up
sprint *m* ⟨*pl* sprint⟩ sprint; ***~ finale*** finish
sprinter *m/f* ⟨*pl* sprinter⟩ sprinter
sprizzare *v/t* ⟨1a⟩ spurt; *fig* exude
sprofondare *v/i* ⟨1a⟩ sink; *fig* ***~ dalla vergogna*** be overcome with embarrassment
sprofondarsi *v/r* flop (***in*** into)
sproloquio *m* ⟨*pl* -qui⟩ waffle

spronare *v/t* ⟨1a⟩ spur on
sprone *m* spur
sproporzionato *adj* disproportionate (***a*** to), out of proportion (***a*** to)
sproporzione *f* disproportion
spropositato *adj fig* enormous
sproposito *m* blunder; ***fare uno ~*** do something silly; ***costare uno ~*** cost a fortune; ***a ~*** out of turn
sprovvedutezza *f* inexperience; (*ingenuità*) naivety
sprovveduto *adj* inexperienced
sprovvisto *adj*: ***~ di*** lacking; ***sono ~ di …*** I don't have any …; ***alla -a*** unexpectedly; ***cogliere qn alla -a*** catch s.o. off guard
spruzzare *v/t* ⟨1a⟩ spray; ***~ di fango*** splash with mud
spruzzata *f* spray
spruzzatore *m* spray
spruzzo *m* spray; *fango* splatter; ***~ di pioggia*** sprinkling of rain; ***verniciare a ~*** spray paint
spudoratamente *adv* shamelessly
spudoratezza *f* shamelessness; (*sfrontatezza*) impudence
spudorato *adj* shameless
spugna *f* sponge; ***bere come una ~*** drink like a fish; *fig* ***gettare la ~*** throw in the towel
spugnoso *adj* spongy
spulciare *v/t* ⟨1f⟩ pick fleas off; *fig* comb through
spulciarsi *v/r* ⟨1f⟩ get rid of fleas
spuma *f* foam; (*bibita*) soda®; COOK mousse
spumante I *adj*: ***vino*** *m* ***~*** sparkling wine **II** *m* sparkling wine
spumeggiante *adj* frothy; *persona* bubbly
spumeggiare *v/i* ⟨1f⟩ foam; *vino* sparkle
spumone *m* COOK *fluffy dessert made from whipped cream and eggs*; (*semifreddo*) *soft ice-cream with whipped cream*
spumoso *adj bagnoschiuma* foaming *attr*
spuntare *v/i* ⟨1a⟩ stick out; BOT come up; *di sole* appear; *di giorno* break; ***gli è spuntato un dente*** he has cut a tooth; ***~ come funghi*** pop up like mushrooms; ***da dove spunti?*** where did you spring from?; ***~ i capelli*** sprout hair; ***~ un buon prezzo*** fetch a good price; ***con me non la spunti!*** you won't beat me!; ***allo spuntar del sole*** at sunrise
spuntarsi *v/r* ⟨1a⟩ die down
spuntino *m* snack
spunto *m* suggestion; ***~ di riflessione*** food for thought; ***dare lo ~ per qc*** give rise to; ***prendere ~ da*** be inspired by
spuntone *m di roccia*: projection of rock
spupazzare *v/t* ⟨1a⟩ *infml* cuddle
spurgare *v/t* ⟨1e⟩ *canali, fogne* dredge; MED clear
spurgo *m* ⟨*pl* -ghi⟩ emptying; MED discharge
spurio *adj* ⟨*mpl* -ri⟩ false
sputacchiare *v/i* ⟨1k⟩ spit
sputacchiera *f* spittoon
sputare ⟨1a⟩ **I** *v/i* spit; ***~ per terra*** spit on the ground; ***~ su*** *or* ***addosso a qn*** turn one's nose up at s.o.; *fig* ***~ nel piatto in cui si mangia*** bite the hand that feeds you **II** *v/t* spit out; *fig* ***~ l'anima*** go mad; ***~ il rospo*** spit sth out; ***sputa l'osso!*** spit it out!; ***~ veleno*** speak with great venom
sputasentenze *m/f* ⟨*pl* sputasentenze⟩ smart alec
sputato *adj infml* spat; ***è suo padre ~*** he's the spitting image of his father
sputo *m* spittle
sputtanare *v/t* ⟨1m⟩ *vulg* badmouth
sputtanarsi *v/r* ⟨1m⟩ *vulg* piss away *vulg*
squadra *f* **1.** *strumento* set square **2.** (*gruppo*) squad; SPORTS team; ***~ femminile*** women's team; ***~ mobile*** *or* ***volante*** flying squad; ***~ nazionale*** national team; ***a -e*** in teams
squadrare *v/t* ⟨1a⟩ square
squadrato *adj* squared
squadriglia *f* ⟨*pl* -glie⟩ NAUT, AVIAT squadron
squadrista *m* ⟨*pl* -i⟩ HIST *member of the Fascist paramilitary*
squadrone *m* squadron
squagliare *v/t* ⟨1g⟩ melt
squagliarsi *v/r* ⟨1g⟩ melt; ***il burro si è squagliato*** the butter's melted; ***squagliarsela*** *fig* clear off
squalifica *f* ⟨*pl* -che⟩ disqualification
squalificare *v/t* ⟨1m & d⟩ disqualify
squallido *adj* squallid
squallore *m* squalor

squalo *m* shark
squama *f* flake; *di pesce* scale
squamare *v/t* ⟨1a⟩ scale; ***~ un pesce*** scale a fish
squamarsi *v/r* flake off
squamoso *adj* scaly
squarciagola *f*: ***a ~*** at the top of one's voice
squarciare *v/t* ⟨1f⟩ tear up; *fig* shatter
squarciarsi *v/r* ⟨1f⟩ rip
squarcio *m* ⟨*pl* -ci⟩ *in stoffa* rip, tear; *in nuvole* break; ***uno ~ di azzurro*** a patch of blue sky
squartare *v/t* ⟨1a⟩ butcher, quarter
squartatore *m*, **-trice** *f* quarterer; ***Jack lo Squartatore*** Jack the Ripper
squash *m* ⟨*pl* squash⟩ squash
squassare *v/t* ⟨1a⟩ shake violently
squattrinato *adj* penniless
squilibrare *v/t* ⟨1a⟩ unbalance (*a.* PSYCH)
squilibrato I *adj* insane **II** *m*, **-a** *f* lunatic
squilibrio *m* ⟨*pl* -ri⟩ imbalance
squillante *adj suono*, *voce* shrill; *fig colore* harsh
squillare *v/i* ⟨1a⟩ ring
squillo *m* ring; ***ragazza*** *f* ***~*** callgirl
squinternato *adj libro* falling to pieces; *fig* rambling
squisitezza *f* tastiness; *di modi*: suaveness
squisito *adj cibo* delicious
squittio *m* ⟨*pl* -ii⟩ *uccelli* chirp; *topi* squeak; *fig hum* shriek
squittire *v/i* ⟨4d⟩ *uccelli* chirp; *topi* squeak; *fig hum* shriek
SR *abbr* (= **Siracusa**) Syracuse
sradicare *v/t* ⟨1l & d⟩ uproot; *fig* (*eliminare*) eradicate, uproot
sradicato *adj* uprooted; *fig* rootless
sragionare *v/i* ⟨1a⟩ rave
sregolatezza *f* loose living
sregolato *adj* wild
S.r.l. *abbr* (= **Società a responsabilità limitata**) Ltd (limited)
srotolare *v/t* ⟨1a⟩ unroll
srotolarsi *v/r* ⟨1a⟩ unwind
SS *abbr* (= **Sassari**) Sassari
SS. *abbr* (= **santi**) Saints
S.S. *abbr* **1.** (= **Sua Santità**) His Holiness (the Pope) **2.** (= **Strada Statale**) A road
stabbio *m* ⟨*pl* -bbi⟩ pen
stabile I *adj* steady; (*duraturo*) stable; *tempo* settled **II** *m* building
stabilimento *m* (*fabbrica*) plant, *Br* factory; ***~ balneare*** lido
stabilire *v/t* ⟨4d⟩ *data*, *obiettivi*, *record* set; (*decidere*) decide, settle
stabilirsi *v/r* settle
stabilità *f* steadiness; *di relazione*, *moneta* stability
stabilizzante *adj* stabilizing
stabilizzare *v/t* ⟨1a⟩ stabilize
stabilizzarsi *v/r* ⟨1a⟩ stabilize
stabilizzatore I *adj* stabilizing **II** *n*: ***stabilizzatore*** *m* stabilizer; AVIAT tailplane
stabilizzazione *f* stabilization
stacanovismo *m hum* Stakhanovism
stacanovista *m/f* ⟨*mpl* -i⟩ *hum* eager-beaver behaviour
staccare I *v/t* ⟨1d⟩ remove, detach; ELEC unplug; TEL ***~ il ricevitore*** lift the receiver; ***~ la corrente*** turn off the electricity; ***~ lo sguardo*** take one's eyes off; ***~ il telefono*** unplug the phone; ***~ un concorrente*** pull ahead of a competitor; ***~ i cavalli*** untie the horses **II** *v/i*: ***il rosa stacca sul nero*** the pink stands out against the black
staccarsi *v/r* ⟨1d⟩ come away (*a. fig*); ***~ da terra*** leave the ground
staccato *m* MUS staccato
staccionata *f* fence
stacco *m* ⟨*pl* -cchi⟩ detachment; *fig* contrast; ***~ pubblicitario*** advertising break
stadera *f* steelyard
stadio *m* ⟨*pl* -di⟩ stage; SPORTS stadium; ***~ olimpico*** Olympic stadium
staff *m* ⟨*pl* staff⟩ staff
staffa *f* stirrup; ANAT stirrup bone; ***perdere le -e*** blow one's top
staffetta *f* SPORTS relay; ***corsa*** *f* ***a ~*** relay race
staffettista *m/f* ⟨*mpl* -i⟩ relay runner
staffilata *f* lash; *fig* harsh remark
staffile *m* stirrup leather; (*frusta*) whip
stafilococco *m* ⟨*pl* -cchi⟩ staphylococcus
stage *m* ⟨*pl* stage⟩ training period
stagionale *adj* seasonal
stagionare *v/t* ⟨1a⟩ age, mature; *legno* season
stagionato *adj* aged, mature; *legno* seasoned
stagionatura *f formaggio* maturing;

legno seasoning
stagione *f* season; ***alta ~*** high season; ***bassa ~*** low season; ***mezza ~*** Spring and Autumn; ***~ morta*** off-season; ***frutta*** *f* ***di ~*** fruit in season, seasonal fruit; ***~ delle piogge*** rainy season
stagista *m/f* ⟨*mpl* -i⟩ person on work placement, *US* intern
stagnante *adj* stagnant; ***acqua*** *f* ***~*** stagnant water
stagnare *v/i* ⟨1a⟩ *dell'acqua* grow stagnant; FIN stagnate
stagnazione *f* stagnation
stagnino *m* tinsmith
stagno[1] *m laghetto* pond
stagno[2] *m metallo* tin
stagno[3] watertight; ***compartimento*** *m* ***~*** watertight compartment; *fig* ***ragionare a compartimenti -i*** consider problems completely separately
stagnola *f*: (***carta*** *f*) ***~*** tinfoil
staio *m* ⟨*pl* -ai⟩ bushel
stalagmite *f* stalagmite
stalattite *f* stalactite
stalinismo *m* Stalinism
stalla *f per bovini* cowshed; *per cavalli* stable; *fig* ***dalle stelle alle -e*** from riches to rags
stallatico *m* ⟨*pl* -ci⟩ dung
stalliere *m*, **-a** *f* stablehand
stallo *m* stall; *fig* stalemate
stallone *m* stallion
stamani, stamattina *adv* this morning
stambecco *m* ⟨*pl* -cchi⟩ ibex
stamberga *f* ⟨*pl* -ghe⟩ hovel
stambugio *m* ⟨*pl* -gi⟩ cubbyhole
stame *m* stamen
staminale *adj* staminal; ***cellule*** *fpl* ***-i*** stem cells
stampa *f* **1.** press; ***~ locale*** local press; ***~ scandalistica*** tabloids, gutter press; ***libertà*** *f* ***di ~*** freedom of the press **2.** *tecnica* printing; PHOT print; ***libro*** *m* ***in corso di ~*** book that has gone to press **3.** *posta* ***-e*** *pl* printed matter
stampante *f* COMPUT printer; ***~ a getto di inchiostro*** ink-jet printer; ***~ laser*** laser printer
stampare *v/t* ⟨1a⟩ print; COMPUT print out
stampatello *m* block letters *pl*
stampato **I** *adj* printed; ***tessuto*** *m* ***~*** printed fabric **II** *m* COMPUT printout, hard copy; ***-i*** *pl* printed matter *sg*
stampatore *m*, **-trice** *f* printer
stampatrice *f* TYPO printer
stampella *f* crutch; ***camminare con le -e*** walk with crutches
stampo *m* mo(u)ld; ***crimine*** *m* ***di ~ mafioso*** Mafia-style crime; *fig* ***essere di vecchio ~*** be old school
stanare *v/t* ⟨1a⟩ flush out (*a. fig*)
stancante *adj* tiring
stancare *v/t* ⟨1d⟩ tire (out)
stancarsi *v/r* get tired, tire; ***~ di qn / qc*** get tired of s.o. / sth
stanchezza *f* tiredness, fatigue
stanco *adj* ⟨*mpl* -chi⟩ tired; ***~ morto*** dead beat
stand *m* ⟨*pl* stand⟩ stand
standard *m/adj inv* standard
standardizzare *v/t* ⟨1a⟩ standardize
standardizzazione *f* standardization
stand-by *m* ⟨*pl* stand-by⟩ COMPUT, ELEC, AVIAT stand-by
standing ovation *f* ⟨*pl* standing ovation⟩ standing ovation
standista *m/f* ⟨*mpl* -i⟩ exhibitor
stanga *f* ⟨*pl* -ghe⟩ bar
stangare *v/t* ⟨1e⟩ beat with a bar; *fig* rip off; *agli esami*: flunk
stangata *f* (*batosta*) *fig* blow with a bar; ***~ fiscale*** tax hike
stanghetta *f* leg
Stanlio *m*: ***~ e Ollio*** Laurel and Hardy
stanotte *adv* tonight; (*la notte scorsa*) last night
stante *prep*: ***a sé ~*** separate; ***seduta*** *f* ***~*** on the spot
stantuffo *m* piston
stanza *f* room
stanziamento *m* allocation
stanziare *v/t* ⟨1g⟩ *somma di denaro* allocate, earmark
stanzino *m* boxroom
stappare *v/t* ⟨1a⟩ take the top off
star *f* ⟨*pl* star⟩ star
stare *v/i* ⟨1q⟩ **1.** be; (*restare*) stay; ***lascialo ~*** leave him alone, let him be; ***ci sto!*** here I am!; ***~ alla cassa*** be paying **2.** (*abitare*) live; ***è andato a ~ in città*** he's moved into town **3.** ***~ in piedi*** stand; ***~ fermo*** keep still; ***~ zitto*** keep quiet; ***~ allo scherzo*** take a joke **4.** ***~ bene*** be well; *di vestiti* suit; ***come sta?*** how are you?, how are things?; ***sta bene*** all right, ok; ***stia bene!*** take care!; ***stammi bene!*** take care!; (***non***) ***sta a te decidere*** it isn't up to you to

decide **5.** ~ ***per fare qc*** be about to do sth; ~ ***telefonando*** be on the phone, be making a phonecall **6.** ***stammi a sentire*** listen to me; ~ ***a vedere*** wait and see **7.** ***ben ti sta!*** serves you right!
starna *f* grey, *US* gray partridge
starnazzare *v/i* ⟨1m⟩ squawk
starnutire *v/i* ⟨4d⟩ sneeze
starnuto *m* sneeze
start *m* ⟨*pl* start⟩ off
starter *m* ⟨*pl* starter⟩ SPORTS starter; AUTO choke
stasare *v/t* ⟨1a⟩ unblock
stasera *adv* this evening, tonight
stasi *f* ⟨*pl* stasi⟩ MED stasis; *fig* stagnation
statale I *adj* state *attr* **II** *m/f* ⟨*usu pl* -i⟩ civil servant **III** *f* main road
statalizzare *v/t* ⟨1a⟩ bring under state control
statalizzazione *f* state control
statica *f* statics *sg*
statico *adj* ⟨*mpl* -ci⟩ static (*a. fig*)
statino *m* UNIV examination form
station wagon *f* ⟨*pl* station-wagon⟩ estate (car), *US* station wagon
statista *m/f* ⟨*mpl* -i⟩ statesman; (*donna*) stateswoman
statistica *f* ⟨*pl* -che⟩ statistics *sg*
statistico *adj* ⟨*mpl* -ci⟩ statistical
Stati Uniti d'America *mpl* United States of America *pl*, USA
stativo *m* stative verb
statizzare *v/t* ⟨1a⟩ nationalize
stato I *past part* → ***essere*** *and* ***stare*** **II** *m* **1.** (*condizione*) state; ~ ***d'animo*** state of mind; ~ ***civile*** marital status; ~ ***di emergenza*** state of emergency; ~ ***di famiglia*** *official document detailing one's family members*; ~ ***di salute*** state of health, condition; ~ ***sociale*** social status; ***essere in ~ di fare*** be in a position to do; ***essere in ~ interessante*** be pregnant **2.** POL state; ~ ***assistenziale*** Welfare State; ~ ***federale*** federal state; ***Stato pontificio*** *m* Papal States *pl* **3.** MIL ~ ***maggiore*** general staff
statua *f* statue
statuario *adj* ⟨*mpl* -ri⟩ sculptural; *fig* statuesque
statuina *f* statuette
statuire *v/t* ⟨4d⟩ ADMIN order
statuizione *f* order
statunitense I *adj* US *attr*, American **II** *m/f* US citizen, citizen of the United States
statura *f* height; *fig* stature
status quo *m* ⟨*pl* status quo⟩ status quo
status symbol *m* ⟨*pl* status symbol⟩ status symbol
statutario *adj* ⟨*mpl* -ri⟩ statutory
statuto *m* statute
stavolta *adv* this time
stazionamento *m* parking
stazionare *v/i* ⟨1a⟩ be parked
stazionario *adj* ⟨*mpl* -ri⟩ stationary
stazione *f* **1.** RAIL station; ~ ***centrale*** main station **2.** ~ ***di servizio*** service station **3.** ~ ***balneare*** seaside resort; ~ ***climatica*** health resort; ~ ***termale*** spa **4.** ~ ***trasmittente*** radio station
stazza *f* NAUT tonnage
stazzare ⟨1a⟩ **I** *v/t imbarcazioni* gauge the tonnage of **II** *v/i* have a tonnage of
stazzonato *adj* creased
stearina *f* stearine
stecca *f* ⟨*pl* -cche⟩ **1.** *di biliardo* cue; *di sigarette* carton; MED splint **2.** MUS wrong note; ***fare una ~*** strike a false note
steccare *v/t* ⟨1d⟩ MED splint; MUS *suonando* play the wrong note; *cantando* sing the wrong note; COOK stud
steccato *m* fence
stecchetto *m*: ***a ~*** on short rations; ***tenere qn a ~*** keep s.o. short of money
stecchino *m* toothpick
stecchito *adj*: ***morto*** *m* ~ stone dead
stecco *m* ⟨*pl* -cchi⟩ stick; *fig* ***essere*** (***magro come***) ***uno ~*** be as thin as a rake
Stefano *f*: ***Santo ~*** St Stephen; (*giorno*) Boxing Day
stele *f* stele; ~ ***funeraria*** tombstone
stella *f* star; ~ ***alpina*** edelweiss; ~ ***polare*** North Star, Pole Star; ~ ***cadente*** shooting star; ***-e*** *pl* ***filanti*** paper streamers; ~ ***di mare*** starfish; ~ ***di Natale*** poinsettia; ***-e*** *pl* ***e strisce*** *pl* Stars and Stripes *sg*; ***albergo*** *m* ***a tre -e*** three-star hotel; *fig* ***vedere le -e*** see stars
stellare *adj* star *attr*
stellato *adj* starry; (*a forma di stella*) starshaped; ***notte*** *f* ***-a*** starry night
stelo *m* stem, stalk

stemma *m* ⟨*pl* -i⟩ coat of arms
stemperare *v/t* ⟨1l & b⟩ dilute; TECH soften; *fig* dampen
stendardo *m* banner
stendere *v/t* ⟨3c⟩ spread; *braccio* stretch out; *biancheria* hang out, hang up; *verbale* draw up; **~ *la mano*** hold out one's hand; **~ *i panni*** hang out the washing; **~ *un verbale*** draw up the minutes
stendersi *v/r* stretch out; **~ *sul letto*** lie down on the bed
stendibiancheria *m* ⟨*pl* stendibiancheria⟩ clothes dryer
stenodattilografia *f* shorthand typing
stenodattilografo *m*, **-a** *f* shorthand typist
stenografare *v/t* ⟨1m & c⟩ take down in shorthand
stenografia *f* shorthand
stenografico *adj* ⟨*mpl* -ci⟩ stenographic, shorthand *attr*
stenografo *m*, **-a** *f* shorthand writer
stenogramma *m* ⟨*pl* -i⟩ shorthand symbol
stenotipia *f* shorthand typing
stenotipista *m/f* ⟨*mpl* -i⟩ shorthand typist
stentare *v/i* ⟨1b⟩: **~ *a fare qc*** find it hard to do sth, have difficulty doing sth
stentato *adj* hard; ***sorriso*** *m* **~** forced smile
stento *m*: ***a*** **~** with difficulty; ***-i*** *pl* hardship; ***una vita di -i*** a life of privation
stentoreo *adj* ⟨*mpl* -ei⟩ stentorian
step *m* ⟨*pl* step⟩ step
steppa *f* steppe
sterco *m* ⟨*pl* -chi⟩ dung
stereo *m* ⟨*pl* stereo⟩ stereo
stereofonico *adj* ⟨*mpl* -ci⟩ stereophonic
stereoscopico *adj* ⟨*mpl* -ci⟩ stereoscopic
stereoscopio *m* ⟨*pl* -pi⟩ stereoscope
stereotipato *adj* clichéd, stereotyped (*a. fig*); ***risposta*** *f* ***-a*** fixed reply
stereotipia *f* stereotypy
stereotipo I *adj* stereotypical **II** *m* stereotype
sterile *adj* sterile
sterilità *f* sterility
sterilizzare *v/t* ⟨1a⟩ sterilize
sterilizzazione *f* sterilization
sterlina *f* sterling
sterminare *v/t* ⟨1l & b⟩ exterminate
sterminato *adj* vast
sterminatore I *adj* destructive **II** *m*, **-trice** *f* exterminator
sterminio *m* ⟨*pl* -ni⟩ extermination
sterno *m* breastbone, ANAT sternum
sterpaglia *f* ⟨*pl* -glie⟩ brushwood
sterpi *mpl* brushwood *sg*
sterrato I *adj* dirt; ***strada*** *f* ***-a*** dirt road **II** *n*: ***sterrato*** *m* dirt road
sterratore *m*, **-trice** *f* digger
sterro *m* earthwork
sterzare *v/t* ⟨1b⟩ steer; **~ *a sinistra*** turn left
sterzata *f* swerve
sterzo *m* AUTO steering
steso *past part* → ***stendere***
stesso *adj* same; ***lo*** **~*, la stessa*** the same one; ***è lo*** **~** it's all the same; ***oggi*** **~** this very day; ***io*** **~** myself; ***se*** **~** himself; ***l'ho visto coi miei stessi occhi*** I saw it with my very own eyes
stesura *f* laying; *di verbale*: drawing up; *di romanzo* draft; **~ *del bilancio*** compilation of the budget
stetoscopio *m* ⟨*pl* -pi⟩ stethoscope
steward *m* ⟨*pl* steward⟩ steward
stia *f* hen coop
stick *m* ⟨*pl* stick⟩ stick; **~ *deodorante*** stick deodorant
stigmate *fpl* stigmata
stigmatizzare *v/t* ⟨1a⟩ stigmatize (*a. fig*)
stilare *v/t* ⟨1a⟩ write up
stile *m* style; SPORTS **~ *libero*** freestyle, crowl; ***in grande*** **~** in style; ***vecchio*** **~** old-school; ***mancanza*** *f* ***di*** **~** lack of style
stiletto *m* dagger
stilista *m/f* ⟨*mpl* -i⟩ fashion designer
stilizzato *adj* stylized
stillicidio *m* ⟨*pl* -di⟩ dripping; *fig* trickle
stilografica *f* fountain pen
stima *f* (*ammirazione*) esteem; (*valutazione*) estimate
stimare *v/t* ⟨1a⟩ *persona* esteem; *oggetto* value, estimate (the value of); (*ritenere*) think, consider
stimarsi *v/r* think *or* consider o.s.
stimato *adj* respected
stimatore *m*, **-trice** *f* valuer, appraiser
stimolante I *adj* stimulating **II** *m* stimulant
stimolare *v/t* ⟨1l⟩ stimulate

stimolo *m* stimulus

stinco *m* ⟨*pl* -chi⟩ shin; ***non è certo uno ~ di santo*** he's no angel

stingere *v/t & v/i* ⟨3d⟩ fade

stingersi *v/r* ⟨3d⟩ fade

stinto *past part* → ***stingere***

stipare *v/t* ⟨1a⟩ cram

stiparsi *v/r* ⟨1a⟩ cram

stipato *adj* crammed (***di*** with)

stipendiare *v/t* ⟨1b & k⟩ pay for

stipendiato *m*, **-a** *f* person on a salary

stipendio *m* ⟨*pl* -di⟩ salary

stipetto *m* cabinet

stipite *m* jamb

stipsi *f* ⟨*pl* stipsi⟩ constipation

stipulare *v/t* ⟨1l⟩ stipulate

stipulazione *f* stipulation

stiracchiato *adj* far-fetched; *voto* tight

stiramento *m* MED strain; ***~ muscolare*** pulled muscle

stirare *v/t* ⟨1a⟩ iron; ***non si stira*** it's non-iron

stirarsi *v/r* pull

stiratrice *f* ironing woman

stiratura *f* ironing

stiro *m*: ***ferro** m **da ~*** iron; ***non ~*** non-iron

stirpe *f* (*origine*) birth

stitichezza *f* constipation

stitico *adj* ⟨*mpl* -ci⟩ constipated

stiva *f* NAUT, AVIAT hold

stivaggio *m* ⟨*pl* -ggi⟩ stowage

stivale *m* boot; ***-i** pl **di gomma*** rubber boots, *Br* wellingtons

stivare *v/t* ⟨1a⟩ NAUT, AVIAT stow

stizza *f* irritation

stizzire *v/t* ⟨4d⟩ annoy

stizzirsi *v/r* ⟨4d⟩ get annoyed

stizzito *adj* irritated

stizzoso *adj* tetchy; (*facile a stizzirsi*) irritable

sto → ***stare***

stoccafisso *m* stockfish (*air-dried cod*)

stoccaggio *m* ⟨*pl* -ggi⟩ stocking

stoccare *v/t* ⟨1d⟩ stock

stoccata *f* shot; *fig* dig

Stoccolma *f* Stockholm

stock *m* ⟨*pl* stock⟩ inventory

stoffa *f* material; *fig* ***avere ~*** be talented

stoicismo *m* stoicism (*a. fig*)

stoico ⟨*mpl* -ci⟩ **I** *adj* stoic (*a. fig*); ***atteggiamento** m **~*** stoical attitude **II** *n*: ***stoico*** *m* stoic (*a. fig*)

stola *f* stole; ***~ di visone*** mink stole

stolido *adj* obtuse

stoltezza *f* stupidity

stolto *adj* stupid

stomacare *v/t* ⟨1l⟩ turn one's stomach

stomacarsi *v/r* ⟨1l⟩ be disgusted

stomachevole *adj* disgusting

stomaco *m* ⟨*pl* -chi⟩ stomach; ***dolori** mpl **di ~*** stomach pains; ***mi sono tolto un peso dallo ~*** I got it off my chest; ***dare di ~*** vomit; ***quel tipo mi sta sullo ~*** I can't stomach that bloke; ***~ di ferro** or **di struzzo*** cast-iron stomach

stonare *v/i* ⟨1c⟩ *di cantante* sing out of tune; *fig* be out of place; *di colori* clash

stonato *adj persona* tone deaf; *nota* false; *strumento* out of tune

stonatura *f* false note

stop *m* ⟨*pl* stop⟩ AUTO brake light; *cartello* stop sign

stoppa *f* tow

stoppare *v/t* ⟨1c⟩ stop

stoppia *f* stubble

stoppino *m* wick

stopposo *adj* towy; *fig carne* tough; ***capelli** mpl **-i*** stringy hair

storcere *v/t* ⟨3d⟩ twist; ***~ il naso*** make a face

storcersi *v/r* bend; ***~ un piede*** twist one's ankle

stordimento *m* dizziness

stordire *v/t* ⟨4d⟩ stun

stordirsi *v/r* ⟨4d⟩ become numb

stordito *adj* stunned

storia *f* history; (*narrazione*) story; ***~ dell'arte*** history of art; ***non far -e!*** don't make a fuss *or* scene!; ***avere una ~ con qn*** have an affair with s.o.; ***~ contemporanea*** contemporary history; ***passare alla ~*** go down in history; ***quante -e!*** what a fuss about nothing!

storico ⟨*mpl* -ci⟩ **I** *adj* historical; (*memorabile*) historic **II** *m*, **-a** *f* historian

storiella *f* anecdote; (*barzelletta*) joke

storiografia *f* historiography

storiografo *m*, **-a** *f* historigrapher

storione *m* sturgeon

stormire *v/i* ⟨4d⟩ rustle

stormo *m di uccelli* flock

stornare *v/t* ⟨1a⟩ *pericolo* avert

stornello *m* MUS *short popular Italian*

song
storno[1] *m uccello* starling
storno[2] *m* COMM writing-off*n*
storpiare *v/t* ⟨1k & c⟩ cripple; *fig parole, testi* misspell; *lingua* mispronounce
storpiatura *f* crippling; *fig* mangling
storpio ⟨*mpl* -pi⟩ **I** *adj* crippled **II** *m*, **-a** *f* cripple
storta *f*: ***prendere una ~ al piede*** twist one's ankle
storto *adj* crooked; ***andare ~*** go wrong
stoviglie *fpl* dishes *pl*
strabico *adj* ⟨*mpl* -ci⟩ cross-eyed
strabiliante *adj* stunning
strabiliare ⟨1k⟩ **I** *v/t* stun **II** *v/i* be astounded
strabiliato *adj* astonished
strabismo *m* strabismus; ***~ di Venere*** a slight cast in one's eye
strabuzzare *v/t* ⟨1a⟩: ***~ gli occhi*** roll one's eyes
stracarico *adj* ⟨*mpl* -chi⟩ overloaded
stracaro *adj* exceedingly expensive
straccetto *m* rag
stracchino *m soft cheese produced in Lombardy*
stracciare *v/t* ⟨1f⟩ tear up
stracciarsi *v/r* ⟨1f⟩ tear; *fig* ***~ le vesti*** cry shame
stracciatella *f* **1.** *type of soup* **2.** *gelato* chocolate chip
stracciato *adj* in shreds; ***prezzi*** *mpl* ***-i*** knockdown prices
straccio ⟨*mpl* -cci⟩ **I** *m per pulire* cloth; *per spolverare* duster; ***essere (ridotto a) uno ~*** be worn to a frazzle; ***passare lo ~ su qc*** wipe sth with a cloth; ***sentirsi uno ~*** *infml* feel like a wet rag; ***trattare come uno ~*** treat s.o. like dirt **II** *adj*: ***carta*** *f* ***-a*** waste paper
straccione **I** *adj* ragged **II** *m*, **-a** *f* tramp
straccivendolo *m*, **-a** *f* rag and bone man
stracco *adj* ⟨*mpl* -cchi⟩ *infml* worn out
stracolmo *adj* packed
stracotto **I** *adj* overdone, overcooked **II** *n*: ***stracotto*** *m* COOK *beef stewed in red wine*
strada *f* road; ***per ~*** down the road; ***sono (già) per ~*** I'm coming, I'm on my way; ***~ facendo, per la ~*** on the way; ***~ con diritto di precedenza*** road with the right of way; ***~ principale*** main road; ***~ provinciale*** B-road; ***~ a senso unico*** one-way street; ***~ statale*** A-road; ***farsi ~*** push one's way through; *nella vita* get on in life; ***a mezza ~*** half-way; ***sbagliare ~*** go the wrong way; ***portare qn sulla cattiva ~*** lead s.o. astray
stradale *adj* road *attr*; ***incidente*** *m* ***~*** road accident; ***polizia*** *f* ***~*** traffic police *pl*; ***regolamento*** *m* ***~*** rule of the road; ***rete*** *f* ***~*** road network
stradario *m* street-finder, street map
stradino *m* roadman
strafalcione *m* howler, blunder
strafare *v/t* ⟨3aa⟩ exaggerate
strafottente *adj* arrogant, insolent
strafottenza *f* arrogance, insolence
strage *f* slaughter; ***fare ~ di cuori*** be a heartbreaker
stragrande *adj*: ***la ~ maggioranza*** the vast majority
stralciare *v/t* ⟨1f⟩ (*depennare*) remove
stralcio *m* ⟨*pl* -ci⟩ removal; ***legge*** *f* ***~*** transitional law
stramaledire *v/t* ⟨3f⟩ curse
stramazzare *v/i* ⟨1a⟩ collapse; ***~ al suolo*** fall heavily to the ground
stramberia *f* strangeness
strambo *adj* strange
strame *m* bedding straw
strampalato *adj* strange
stranamente *adv* strangely
stranezza *f* strangeness
strangolamento *m* strangling
strangolare *v/t* ⟨1l⟩ strangle
straniarsi *v/r* ⟨1k⟩ cut oneself off
straniero **I** *adj* foreign; ***lingua*** *f* ***-a*** foreign language **II** *m*, **-a** *f* foreigner
stranito *adj* dizzy
strano *adj* strange
straordinariamente *adv* exceptionally
straordinarietà *f* ⟨*pl* straordinarietà⟩ extraordinariness
straordinario ⟨*mpl* -ri⟩ **I** *adj* special; *eccezionale* extraordinary **II** *m* overtime
strapagare *v/t* ⟨1e⟩ overpay
straparlare *v/i* ⟨1a⟩ rave, *infml* talk rubbish
strapazzare *v/t* ⟨1a⟩ treat badly; ***uova*** *fpl* ***strapazzate*** scrambled eggs
strapazzarsi *v/r* overdo it
strapazzo *m* strain; ***essere uno ~*** be exhausting; ***da ~*** third-rate

strapieno *adj* crowded
strapiombo *m*: ***a ~*** overhanging
strapotenza *f* excess of power
strappalacrime *adj inv*: ***film ~*** tear-jerker
strappare *v/t* ⟨1a⟩ tear, rip; (*staccare*) tear down; (*togliere*) grab, snatch (***a qn*** out of s.o.'s hands); *fig* ***~ il cuore*** break one's heart
strapparsi *v/r* ⟨1a⟩ tear; ***~ i capelli*** tear one's hair out
strappato *adj* torn, ripped
strappo *m* tear, rip; MED torn ligament; *fig* ***uno ~ alla regola*** an exception to the rule; ***dare uno ~ a qn*** *infml* give s.o. a lift
strapuntino *m* tip-up seat
straricco *adj* ⟨*mpl* -cchi⟩ extremely rich
straripamento *m* overflowing
straripante *adj* overflowing
straripare *v/i* ⟨1a⟩ flood, overflow its banks
Strasburgo *f* Strasbourg
strascicare *v/t* ⟨1a⟩ drag
strascico *m* ⟨*pl* -chi⟩ train; *fig* after-effects
stratagemma *m* ⟨*pl* -i⟩ stratagem
strategia *f* strategy
strategico *adj* ⟨*mpl* -ci⟩ strategic
stratificazione *f* stratification (*a. fig*)
stratiforme *adj* stratiform
strato *m* layer; ***~ d'ozono*** ozone layer; ***~ protettivo*** protective coating; ***~ sociale*** social stratum; ***a -i*** in layers
stratosfera *f* stratosphere
stratosferico *adj* ⟨*mpl* -ci⟩ *fig* astronomical
strattonare *v/t* ⟨1a⟩ pull; SPORTS barge
strattone *m* jerk
stravaccarsi *v/r* ⟨1d⟩ *infml* sprawl
stravagante *adj* extravagant
stravaganza *f* extravagance
stravecchio *adj* ⟨*mpl* -cchi⟩ ancient
stravedere *v/i* ⟨2s⟩: ***~ per qn*** worship s.o.
stravincere *v/t* ⟨3d⟩ win by a mile
stravizio *m* ⟨*pl* -zi⟩ *nel mangiare* overeating; *nel bere* overdrinking; ***darsi agli -zi*** give oneself over to a life of debauchery
stravolgere *v/t* ⟨3d⟩ change radically; (*travisare*) twist; (*stancare*) exhaust
stravolto **I** *past part* → ***stravolgere*** **II** *adj* (*stanco*) exhausted
straziante *adj* heartrending
straziare *v/t* ⟨1g⟩ tear apart; *fig* butcher; *fig* (*sciupare*) mangle
strazio *m* ⟨*pl* -zi⟩: ***era uno ~*** it was painful
strega *f* ⟨*pl* -ghe⟩ witch; ***colpo*** *m* ***della ~*** back strain
stregare *v/t* ⟨1e⟩ bewitch
stregato *adj* bewitched (*a. fig*)
stregone *m* wizard
stregoneria *f* witchcraft (*a. fig*); (*incantesimo*) spell
stregua *f*: ***alla ~ di*** like
strelitzia *f* BOT bird-of-paradise flower
stremare *v/t* ⟨1b⟩ exhaust
stremato *adj* exhausted
stremo *m*: ***allo ~*** at the end of one's tether
strenuamente *adv* bravely
strenuo *adj fig* brave
strepitare *v/i* ⟨1l & b⟩ make a noise; (*gridare*) roar
strepitio *m* ⟨*pl* -ii⟩ roar
strepito *m* roar
strepitoso *adj fig* extraordinary; ***applauso*** *m* ***~*** thunderous applause; ***successo*** *m* ***~*** resounding success
streptococco *m* ⟨*pl* -cchi⟩ streptococcus
streptomicina *f* streptomycin
stress *m* ⟨*pl* stress⟩ stress
stressante *adj* stressful
stressare *v/t* ⟨1b⟩ stress
stressarsi *v/r* ⟨1b⟩ get stressed
stressato *adj* stressed
stretch *m* ⟨*pl* stretch⟩ stretchy material
stretching *m* ⟨*no pl*⟩ stretching
stretta *f* hold; ***~ di mano*** handshake; ***allentare la ~*** release one's grip; ***mettere qn alle -e*** put s.o. in a tight corner
strettamente *adv* closely; ***~ confidenziale*** strictly confidential; ***~ necessario*** strictly necessary; ***tenere qc ~ (in mano)*** clutch sth (in one's hand)
strettezza *f* narrowness
stretto **I** *past part* → ***stringere*** **II** *adj* narrow; *vestito*, *scarpe* too tight; ***lo ~ necessario*** the bare minimum; ***-a sorveglianza*** *f* close surveillance; ***ridere a denti -i*** grin and bear it; ***a ~ giro di posta*** by return of post **III** *m* GEOG strait
strettoia *f* bottleneck

striato *adj* streaked
striatura *f* streak
stricnina *f* strychnine
stridente *adj* shrill; *contrasto* sharp; *colore* clashing
stridere *v/i* ⟨3a⟩ *di porta* squeak; *di colori* clash
stridore *m* squeal; ~ ***di denti*** gnashing of teeth
stridulo *adj* shrill
strigliare *v/t* ⟨1g⟩ groom
strigliata *f* grooming; *fig* telling-off
strillare *v/i* ⟨1a⟩ scream
strillo *m* scream
strillone *m someone who sells newspapers in the street, shouting out the main items of news*
striminzito *adj* skimpy
strimpellamento *m* strum, strumming
strimpellare *v/t* ⟨1b⟩ strum
stringa *f* ⟨*pl* -ghe⟩ lace; ~ ***di inizializzazione*** COMPUT booting string
stringato *adj* concise
stringente *adj* pressing
stringere ⟨3d⟩ **I** *v/t* make narrower; *abito* take in; *vite* tighten; ~ ***amicizia*** become friends; ~ ***la mano a qn*** squeeze s.o.'s hand; ~ ***qn tra le braccia*** hold s.o. in one's arms; ~ ***a sé qn*** hug s.o.; *fig* ~ ***i denti*** grit one's teeth; ~ ***la cinghia*** tighten one's belt; ~ ***i tempi*** conclude; ***stringi!*** squeeze up!; ***stringi stringi*** in the end **II** *v/i di tempo* press
stringersi *v/r intorno a tavolo* squeeze up; ~ ***nelle spalle*** be tight across the shoulders; ***mi si stringe il cuore*** my heart aches
striptease *m* ⟨*pl* striptease⟩ striptease
striscia *f* ⟨*pl* -sce⟩ strip; *dipinta* stripe; ***-sce*** *pl* ***pedonali*** pedestrian crossing *sg*, *Br* zebra crossing *sg*; ***a -sce*** striped
strisciante *adj pianta* creeping; *pej persona* grovel(l)ing; ***inflazione*** *f* ~ creeping inflation
strisciare ⟨1f⟩ **I** *v/t piedi* scrape; (*sfiorare*) brush, smear (***contro*** against) **II** *v/i* crawl
striscio *m* ⟨*pl* -i⟩ creeping; MED smear; ***colpire di*** ~ graze
striscione *m* banner
stritolare *v/t* ⟨1l⟩ crush
stritolarsi *v/r* ⟨1l⟩ be crushed
strizza *f infml* jitters *pl*
strizzare *v/t* ⟨1a⟩ wring; ~ ***l'occhio a qn*** wink at s.o.
stroboscopio *m* ⟨*pl* -i⟩ stroboscope
strofa *f* verse
strofinaccio *m* ⟨*pl* -cci⟩ dish towel
strofinamento *m* rubbing
strofinare *v/t* ⟨1a⟩ rub
strofinarsi *v/r* ⟨1a⟩: ~ ***contro qc*** rub against sth; *fig* toady
strombazzare ⟨1n⟩ **I** *v/i infml* honk **II** *v/t* trumpet
stroncare *v/t* ⟨1d⟩ *albero* knock down; *vita* snuff out; *infml idea* shoot down; ***essere stroncato da una malattia*** be struck down by illness
stroncatura *f* breaking off; *fig* panning
stronzaggine *f vulg* shittiness
stronzata *f vulg* crap, bullshit; ***fare una*** ~ fuck up
stronzo *m*, **-a** *f vulg Br* arsehole, *US* asshole, bastard
stropicciare *v/t* ⟨1f⟩ crush, wrinkle
stropicciarsi *v/r* ⟨1f⟩ wrinkle; ~ ***gli occhi / le mani*** rub one's eyes / hands
strozzapreti *m* ⟨*pl* strozzapreti⟩ COOK *gnocchi made from flour and potatoes, typical of Southern Italy*
strozzare *v/t* ⟨1c⟩ strangle
strozzatura *f* narrowing
strozzinaggio *m* ⟨*pl* -ggi⟩ loan sharking
strozzino *m*, **-a** *f* loan shark *infml*
struccarsi *v/r* ⟨1d⟩ take one's make-up off
strudel *m* ⟨*pl* strudel⟩ COOK strudel
struggente *adj* all-consuming
struggere *v/t* ⟨3cc⟩ melt; *fig* consume
struggersi *v/r* ⟨3cc⟩ be consumed; ~ ***per qc*** pine for sth; ~ ***per qn*** languish for s.o.
struggimento *m* torment
strullo *m*, **-a** *f reg* silly
struma *f* MED goitre, *US* goiter
strumentale *adj* instrumental (*a.* MUS); ***uso*** *m* ~ instrumental use; ***beni*** *mpl* ***-i*** ECON capital goods
strumentalizzare *v/t* ⟨1a⟩ make use of
strumentalizzazione *f* exploitation; MUS orchestration
strumentario *m* ⟨*pl* -ri⟩ instruments *pl*
strumentazione *f* MUS instrumentation
strumento *m* instrument; ***-i*** equip-

ment; **~ musicale** musical instrument; **~ ad arco / a fiato** string / wind instrument; **-i** *pl* **a corda** MUS string instruments
strusciare ⟨1f⟩ **I** *v/t* drag **II** *v/i* trail; **~ contro il muro** rub against the wall
strusciarsi *v/r* ⟨1f⟩ rub oneself
strusciata *f*: **dare una ~** rub
struscio *m* ⟨*pl* -scii⟩ stroll
strutto *m* lard
struttura *f* structure
strutturabile *adj* structurable
strutturale *adj* structural
strutturare *v/t* ⟨1a⟩ structure
strutturarsi *v/r* ⟨1a⟩ be structured
strutturato *adj* organized
strutturazione *f* organization
struzzo *m* ZOOL ostrich; *fig* **fare lo ~** bury one's head in the sand
stuccare *v/t* ⟨1d⟩ plaster
stuccatore *m*, **-trice** *f* plasterer
stucchevole *adj* *cibo* sickening; *fig* *parole* sugary
stucco *m* ⟨*pl* -cchi⟩ plaster; **rimanere di ~** be thunderstruck, *Br* be gobsmacked *infml*
studente *m*, **-essa** *f* student; **casa** *f* **dello ~** hall of residence
studentesco *adj* ⟨*mpl* -schi⟩ school *attr*; UNIV student *attr*
studiare *v/t* ⟨1k⟩ study; **~ le mosse di qn** examine s.o.'s movements; **studiarle tutte** *infml* try everything
studiarsi *v/r* ⟨1k⟩ study oneself; *reciprocamente* study each other
studio *m* ⟨*pl* -di⟩ study; *di artista*, RADIO, TV studio; *di professionista* office; *di medico* surgery; **~ legale** law firm; **borsa** *f* **di ~** bursary
studiolo *m* small study
studioso **I** *adj* studious **II** *m*, **-a** *f* scholar
stufa *f* stove; **~ elettrica / a gas** electric / gas fire; **~ a legna** wood-burning stove
stufare *v/t* ⟨1a⟩ COOK stew; *fig* bore
stufarsi *v/r* get bored (**di** with); **~ di qc / qn** get tired of sth / s.o.
stufato *m* stew
stufo *adj*: **essere ~ di qc** be bored with sth
stuntman *m* ⟨*pl* stuntman⟩ stuntman
stuoia *f* mat
stuoino *m* doormat
stuolo *m* host
stupefacente **I** *adj* amazing, stupefying **II** *m* narcotic
stupefatto *adj* amazed, stupefied
stupendo *adj* stupendous
stupidaggine *f* stupidity; **è una ~** (*cosa senza importanza*) it's nothing
stupidamente *adv* stupidly
stupidità *f* stupidity
stupido **I** *adj* stupid **II** *m*, **-a** *f* idiot
stupire ⟨4d⟩ **I** *v/t* amaze **II** *v/i* be amazed
stupirsi *v/r* ⟨4d⟩ be amazed; **~ di qn / qc** be surprised at s.o. / sth
stupito *adj* amazed
stupore *m* amazement
stuprare *v/t* ⟨1a⟩ rape
stupratore *m* rapist
stupro *m* rape
sturare *v/t* ⟨1a⟩ clear, unblock; **~ il lavandino** unblock the sink
stuzzicadenti *m* ⟨*pl* stuzzicadenti⟩ toothpick
stuzzicare *v/t* ⟨1l & d⟩ tease; **~ l'appetito** whet the appetite
stuzzicarsi *v/r* ⟨1l & d⟩: **~ i denti** pick one's teeth
stuzzichino *f* COOK appetizer, snack
su **I** *prep* **1.** on; **sul tavolo** on the table; **dormirci ~** sleep on it; **stare sul chi vive** be on the look out; **sul far del giorno** at daybreak **2.** *argomento* about **3.** (*circa*) (round) about; **sulle tremila euro** round about three thousand euros **4. sul mare** by the sea **5. ~ misura** made to measure **6. nove volte ~ dieci** nine times out of ten **II** *adv* **1.** up; **guardare in ~** look up **2.** (*al piano di sopra*) upstairs **3. ~!** come on!; **~ col morale!** keep your chin up!; **essere ~ di giri** be on a high; **salta ~!** chip in! **4. avere ~** *vestito* have on
sua **I** *adj* *di lui*: his; *di lei*: her **II** *pron* *di lui*: his; *di lei*: hers
suadente *adj* persuasive; (*accattivante*) mellow
sub *m/f* ⟨*pl* sub⟩ skin diver
subacqueo **I** *adj* underwater **II** *m*, **-a** *f* skin diver
subaffittare *v/t* ⟨1a⟩ sublet
subaffitto *m* sublet; **camera** *f* **in ~** sublet room
subaffittuario *m*, **-a** *f* ⟨*mpl* -ri⟩ subtenant
subaffluente *m* subtributary

subagente *m/f* subagent
subalpino *adj* subalpine
subalterno I *adj* subordinate **II** *m*, **-a** *f* subordinate
subappaltare *v/t* ⟨1a⟩ subcontract
subappaltatore *m*, **-trice** *f* subcontractor
subappalto *m* subcontract
subbuglio *m* ⟨*pl* -gli⟩ turmoil; ***essere in ~*** be in turmoil
subconscio *adj* subconscious
subcosciente *m* subconscious
subdirectory *m* ⟨*pl* subdirectory⟩ COMPUT subdirectory
subdolo *adj* underhand
subentrare *v/i* ⟨1a⟩: ***~ a qn*** replace s.o., take s.o.'s place
subfornitore *m*, **-trice** *f* sub-supplier
subire *v/t* ⟨4d⟩ *danni*, *perdita* suffer
subissare *v/t* ⟨1a⟩: ***~ qn di qc*** overwhelm s.o. with sth
subitaneità *f* ⟨*pl* subitaneità⟩ suddenness
subitaneo *adj* sudden
subito *adv* immediately
sublimare *v/t and v/i* ⟨1a⟩ CHEM, PSYCH sublimate (*a. fig*)
sublimazione *f* CHEM, PSYCH sublimation (*a. fig*)
sublime *adj* sublime
subliminale *adj* subliminal
sublimità *f* ⟨*pl* sublimità⟩ sublimity
sublocazione *f* sublet
subnormale I *adj* subnormal **II** *m/f* *person of subnormal intelligence*
subordinare *v/t* ⟨1m⟩ subordinate
subordinato I *adj* subordinate; ***~ a qn / qc*** subject to s.o. / sth **II** *m*, **-a** *f* subordinate
subordinazione *f* subordination
subordine *m*: ***in ~*** ADMIN subordinately
substrato *m* substratum (*a.* BIOL)
subtropicale *adj* subtropical
suburbano *adj* suburban
succedere *v/i* ⟨3a or 3l⟩ (*accadere*) happen; ***~ a*** *in carica* succeed; ***che succede?*** what's going on?; ***sono cose che succedono*** these things happen
succedersi *v/r* ⟨3a or 3l⟩ succeed
successione *f* succession; ***~ ereditaria*** hereditary succession; ***imposta*** *f* ***di ~*** death duty; ***~ al trono*** succession to the throne
successivamente *adv* subsequently
successivo *adj* successive; ***il giorno ~*** the following day
successo I *past part* → ***succedere*** **II** *m* success; ***di ~*** successful
successone *m infml* smash hit
successore *m*, **-a** *f* successor
successorio *adj* ⟨*mpl* -ri⟩ succession *attr*; ***patto*** *m* ***~*** succession agreement
succhiare *v/t* ⟨1k⟩ suck; ***~ una caramella*** suck a sweet; ***succhiarsi il pollice*** suck one's thumb; *fig* ***~ il sangue*** suck dry
succhiata *f*: ***dare una ~ a qc*** give sth a suck
succhiello *m* gimlet
succhiotto *m* dummy; *infml* (*livido*) love bite, *US* hickey
succintamente *adv* scantily
succinto *adj* scanty; *fig* succinct; ***in abiti*** *mpl* ***-i*** scantily clad
succlavio *adj* ⟨*mpl* -vi⟩ ANAT subclavian
succo *m* ⟨*pl* -cchi⟩ juice; ***~ d'arancia*** orange juice; ***~ gastrico*** gastric juice; ***il ~ della questione*** the nub of the argument
succoso *adj* juicy
succube *adj* dominated; ***essere ~ di qn / qc*** be entirely dominated by s.o. / sth
succulento *adj* succulent; (*gustoso*) tasty
succursale *f* branch
sud *m* south; ***~ ovest*** south-west; ***~ est*** south-east; ***al ~ di*** (to the) south of
Sudafrica *m* South Africa
sudafricano I *adj* South African **II** *m*, **-a** *f* South African
Sudamerica *m* South America
sudamericano I *adj* South American **II** *m*, **-a** *f* South American
Sudan *m* Sudan
sudanese I *adj* Sudanese **II** *m/f* Sudanese
sudare *v/i* ⟨1a⟩ perspire, sweat; *fig* ***~ sangue*** sweat blood; ***~ sette camicie*** sweat blood
sudario *m* ⟨*pl* -ri⟩ shroud
sudarsi *v/r* ⟨1a⟩: *fig* ***~ qc*** labour for sth
sudata *f* perspiration, sweat
sudaticcio *adj* ⟨*mpl* -cci⟩ sweaty
sudato *adj* sweaty
suddetto *adj* afore-said
sudditanza *f* subjection; *fig* submis-

sion
suddito *m*, **-a** *f* subject
suddividere *v/t* ⟨3q⟩ subdivide
suddividersi *v/r* ⟨3q⟩ divide; ***~ qc*** share sth
suddivisibile *adj* subdivisible
suddivisione *f* subdivision
sud-est *m* south-east
sudicio ⟨*mpl* -ci⟩ **I** *adj* dirty **II** *m* dirt
sudicione *m*, **-a** *f* dirty person
sudiciume *m* dirt
sudista ⟨*mpl* -i⟩ **I** *adj* HIST Confederate **II** *m/f* HIST Confederate
sudoccidentale *adj* south-west
sudorazione *f* perspiration
sudore *m* perspiration, sweat; ***~ freddo*** cold sweat; ***con il ~ della fronte*** with the sweat of one's brow
sudorientale *adj* south-east
sudoriparo *adj* ANAT sudoriferous; ***ghiandola*** *f* ***-a*** sweat gland
sud-ovest *m* south-west
sudtirolese *adj* South Tyrolean
Sud-Tirolo *m* South Tyrol
sue I *adj di lui*: his; *di lei*: her **II** *pron di lui*: his; *di lei*: hers
sufficiente *adj* sufficient
sufficienza *f* sufficiency; ***a ~*** enough; ***aria*** *f* ***di ~*** smugness; ***prendere la ~*** EDU pass
suffisso *m* suffix
suffragetta *f* HIST suffragette; *infml pej* women's libber
suffragio *m* ⟨*pl* -gi⟩ suffrage; ***~ universale*** universal suffrage; ***messa*** *f* ***in ~*** mass for the soul
sufismo *m* Sufism
suggellare *v/t* ⟨1b⟩ seal; *fig* set the seal on
suggello *m* seal (*a. fig*)
suggerimento *m* suggestion
suggerire *v/t* ⟨4d⟩ suggest; THEAT prompt
suggeritore *m*, **-trice** *f* THEAT prompter
suggestionabile *adj* suggestible
suggestionare *v/t* ⟨1a⟩ influence
suggestione *f* influence
suggestivo *adj* picturesque, evocative
sughereto *m* cork plantation
sughero *m* cork; ***tappo*** *m* ***di ~*** cork
sugli = *prep* ***su*** *and art* ***gli***
sugo *m* ⟨*pl* -ghi⟩ sauce; *di arrosto* juice; ***al ~*** with sauce
sugoso *adj pesca, carne* juicy; *pasta* with a lot of sauce
sui = *prep* ***su*** *and art* ***i***
suicida *m/f* ⟨*mpl* -i⟩ suicide (victim)
suicidarsi *v/r* ⟨1a⟩ commit suicide, kill o.s.
suicidio *m* ⟨*pl* -di⟩ suicide
suino *adj* pork *attr*
sul = *prep* ***su*** *and art* ***il***
sulfureo *adj* sulphureous, *US* sulfureous
sull', sulla, sulle, sullo = *prep* ***su*** *and art* ***l', la, le, lo***
sultanina *f* sultanas *pl*
sultano *m* sultan
sumerico *adj* ⟨*mpl* -ci⟩ Sumerian
sumero I *adj* Sumerian **II** *m*, **-a** *f* Sumerian
summit *m* ⟨*pl* summit⟩ summit
sunnita ⟨*mpl* -i⟩ **I** *adj* Sunni **II** *m/f* Sunni
suo I *adj* his; *di cosa* its; **-a** *f* her; *di cosa* its; ***il ~ maestro*** his teacher; ***i suoi amici*** his friends; ***questo libro è ~*** this is his book; ***Suo*** your **II** *pron*: ***il ~*** his; *di cosa* its; ***la -a*** *f* hers; *di cosa* its
suocera *f* mother-in-law
suocero *m* father-in-law; ***-i*** *pl* mother- and father-in-law, in-laws *infml*
suoi I *adj di lui*: his; *di lei*: her **II** *pron di lui*: his; *di lei*: hers; ***i ~*** *di lui*: his family; *di lei*: her family
suola *f* sole
suolare *v/t* ⟨1c⟩ sole
suolo *m* ground; (*terreno*) soil; ***cadere al ~*** fall to the ground
suonare ⟨1o⟩ **I** *v/t* play; *campanello* ring; ***~ il clacson*** sound the horn; ***suonarle a qn*** *infml* beat the living daylights out of s.o. **II** *v/i* play; *alla porta* ring
suonata *f* ring; (*bastonatura*) beating
suonato *adj infml* off one's head; ***avere trent'anni -i*** be well into one's thirties
suonatore *m*, **-trice** *f* player; ***~ ambulante*** busker
suoneria *f* ringing
suono *m* sound
suora *f* REL nun; ***farsi ~*** become a nun
super *f* ⟨*pl* super⟩ *infml* 4-star
superalcolico I *adj* ⟨*mpl* -ci⟩ strong **II** *n*: ***superalcolici*** *mpl* strong drink
superamento *m fig* overcoming
superare *v/t* ⟨1l⟩ go past; *fig* over-

come; *esame* pass; *~ **il peso*** exceed the weight
superato *adj* out of date
superattico *m* ⟨*mpl* -ci⟩ penthouse
superbia *f* haughtiness
superbo *adj* haughty
supercarcere *m infml* maximum security prison
superdotato *adj* gifted; *hum* well-hung
superficiale *adj* superficial
superficialità *f* ⟨*pl* superficialità⟩ superficiality (*a. fig*)
superficialmente *adv* superficially
superficie *f* surface; ***in ~*** on the surface; ***emergere in ~*** come to the surface
superfluo *adj* superfluous
superiora *f* Mother Superior
superiore I *adj* top; *qualità* superior; ***~ alla media*** better than average **II** *m* superior
superiorità *f* superiority
superlativo *m/adj* superlative
supermarket *m* ⟨*pl* supermarket⟩ supermarket
supermercato *m* supermarket
superpotenza *f* superpower
supersonico *adj* ⟨*mpl* -ci⟩ supersonic
superstite I *adj* surviving **II** *m/f* survivor
superstizione *f* superstition
superstizioso *adj* superstitious
superstrada *f* motorway, *US* highway (*with no tolls*)
superteste *m/f*, **supertestimone** *m/f* key witness
superuomo *m* ⟨*pl* -uomini⟩ superman
supervisione *f* supervision; FILM executive direction
supervisore *m* supervisor; FILM executive director
supino *adj* supine
suppellettile *f* furnishings and fittings; (*reperto archeologico*) remains
suppergiù *adv* about
supplementare *adj* additional, supplementary
supplemento *m* supplement; ***~ intercity*** intercity supplement; RAIL ***fare il ~*** pay a supplement
supplente *m/f* replacement; EDU supply teacher
supplenza *f* supply teaching
suppletivo *adj* supplementary
supplì *m* ⟨*pl* supplì⟩ *balls of rice stuffed with cheese or minced meat etc*
supplica *f* plea
supplicare *v/t* ⟨1l & d⟩ beg
supplichevole *adj* imploring
supplire ⟨4d⟩ **I** *v/i*: ***~ a qc con qc*** make up for sth with sth **II** *v/t* stand in for
supplizio *m* ⟨*pl* -zi⟩ torture
supponente *adj* haughty
supponenza *f* haughtiness
suppongo → ***supporre***
supporre *v/t* ⟨3ll⟩ suppose
supportare *v/t* ⟨1c⟩: ***~ qn*** / ***qc*** support s.o. / sth
supporto *m* TECH support; COMPUT ***~ dati*** data support
supposizione *f* supposition
supposta *f* MED suppository
supposto *past part* → ***supporre***
suppurare *v/i* ⟨1a⟩ MED suppurate
suppurazione *f* suppuration
supremazia *f* supremacy
supremo *adj* supreme
surclassare *v/t* ⟨1a⟩ outclass
surf *m* ⟨*pl* surf⟩ surfboard; ***fare ~*** surf, go surfing
surfista *m/f* ⟨*mpl* -i⟩ surfer
surgelare *v/t* ⟨1b⟩ freeze
surgelato I *adj* frozen **II** *m*: ***surgelati*** *pl* frozen food *sg*
surplus *m* ⟨*pl* surplus⟩ surplus
surreale *adj* surreal
surrealismo *m* surrealism
surrealista *m/f* ⟨*mpl* -i⟩ surrealist
surriscaldamento *m* overheating; PHYS, TECH superheating
surriscaldare *v/t* ⟨1a⟩ overheat
surrogato *m* substitute
suscettibile *adj* touchy; ***è ~ di miglioramento*** it's likely to improve
suscettibilità *f* touchiness
suscitare *v/t* ⟨1l⟩ arouse
susina *f* plum
susino *m* plum (tree)
susseguirsi *v/r* ⟨4b⟩ follow one another
sussidiarietà *f* ⟨*pl* sussidiarietà⟩ JUR subsidiarity
sussidiario ⟨*mpl* -ri⟩ **I** *adj* subsidiary **II** *n*: ***sussidiario*** *m textbook used in primary schools*
sussidio *m* ⟨*pl* -di⟩ grant, allowance; ***~ di disoccupazione*** unemployment benefit

sussiego *m* ⟨*pl* -ghi⟩ self-importance
sussistente *adj* subsisting
sussistenza *f* subsistence; ***mezzi*** *mpl* ***di ~*** means of support
sussistere *v/i* ⟨3f⟩ subsist
sussultare *v/i* ⟨1a⟩ start, jump
sussulto *m* start, jump
sussurrare *v/t & v/i* ⟨1a⟩ whisper
sussurro *m* whisper
sutura *f* MED stitches *pl*
SUV *abbr* (= **Sport Utility Vehicle**) SUV
suvvia *int* come on
SV *abbr* (= **Savona**) Savona
S.V. *abbr* (= **Signoria Vostra**) Your Lordship
svagarsi *v/r* ⟨1e⟩ take one's mind off things
svagatezza *f* absentmindedness
svagato *adj* absentminded
svago *m* ⟨*pl* -ghi⟩ distraction; ***per ~*** to take one's mind off things
svaligiare *v/t* ⟨1f⟩ burgle, *US* burglarize
svalutare *v/t* ⟨1a⟩ devalue
svalutarsi *v/r* ⟨1a⟩ devalue
svalutazione *f* devaluation
svampito *adj* flighty
svanire *v/i* ⟨4d⟩ vanish
svantaggiare *v/t* ⟨1f⟩ penalize
svantaggio *m* ⟨*pl* -ggi⟩ disadvantage; ***essere in ~*** SPORTS be behind
svantaggioso *adj* disadvantageous
svaporare *v/i* ⟨1a⟩ *di vino* lose flavour; *di profumo* lose scent
svariato *adj* varied
svarione *m* blunder
svasato *adj* SEW flared
svastica *f* ⟨*pl* -che⟩ swastika
svecchiare *v/t* ⟨1k⟩ update
svedese I *m/adj* Swedish **II** *m/f* Swede
sveglia *f* alarm clock; ***mettere la ~ alle sei*** set the alarm for six o'clock
svegliare *v/t* ⟨1g⟩ waken (up)
svegliarsi *v/r* waken up
sveglio *adj* awake; *fig* alert
svelare *v/t* ⟨1a⟩ *segreto* reveal; ***~ un mistero*** uncover a mystery
sveltezza *f* quickness
sveltina *f vulg* quickie; ***farsi una ~*** have a quickie
sveltire *v/t* ⟨4d⟩ speed up
sveltirsi *v/r* ⟨4d⟩ liven up
svelto *adj* quick; ***alla -a*** quickly
svenarsi *v/r* ⟨1a⟩ cut one's veins
svendere *v/t* ⟨3a⟩ sell at a reduced price
svendita *f* clearance
svenevole *adj* soppy
svenevolezza *f* soppiness
svenimento *m* fainting fit
svenire *v/i* ⟨4p⟩ faint
sventagliare *v/t* ⟨1g⟩: ***~ qc*** wave sth
sventagliarsi *v/r* ⟨1g⟩ fan oneself
sventare *v/t* ⟨1b⟩ *congiura* foil; *pericolo* thwart
sventatezza *f* thoughtlessness
sventato *adj* thoughtless
sventola *f infml* slap; ***orecchie*** *fpl* ***a ~*** sticking-out ears
sventolare *v/t & v/i* ⟨1l & b⟩ wave
sventolio *m* ⟨*pl* -ii⟩ waving
sventramento *m* disembowelment; BUILD gutting
sventrare *v/t* ⟨1b⟩ disembowel; BUILD gut
sventura *f* misfortune
sventurato *adj* unfortunate
svenuto *past part* → ***svenire***
sverginare *v/t* ⟨1l⟩ deflower
svergognare *v/t* ⟨1a⟩ shame
svergognato *adj* shameless
svernare *v/i* ⟨1b⟩ spend the winter in
svestire *v/t* ⟨4b⟩ undress
svestirsi *v/r* get undressed, undress
svettare *v/i* ⟨1a⟩ stand over
svevo I *adj* Swabian **II** *m*, **-a** *f* Swabian
Svezia *f* Sweden
svezzamento *m* weaning
svezzare *v/t* ⟨1a⟩ wean
svezzarsi *v/r* ⟨1a⟩: ***~ da qc*** wean oneself off sth
sviare *v/t* ⟨1h⟩ deflect; *fig* divert
svignarsela *v/i* ⟨1a⟩ slip away
svigorire *v/t* ⟨4d⟩ weaken
svigorirsi *v/r* ⟨4d⟩ grow feeble
svilimento *m* debasement
svilire *v/t* ⟨4d⟩ debase
sviluppare *v/t* ⟨1a⟩ develop
svilupparsi *v/r* develop
sviluppato *adj* developed
sviluppatore *m*, **-trice** *f* developer
sviluppo *m* development; ***~ rurale*** rural development; ***età*** *f* ***dello ~*** puberty
svincolare *v/t* ⟨1l⟩ ECON, JUR redeem
svincolarsi *v/r* ⟨1l⟩ free oneself
svincolo *m* motorway junction
sviolinare *v/t* ⟨1a⟩: ***~ qn*** *infml* sweet-talk s.o.; *pej* suck up to s.o.

sviolinata *f infml* sweet-talk; *pej* sucking-up
svisare *v/t* ⟨1a⟩ distort
sviscerare *v/t* ⟨1l⟩ *fig* examine in depth
sviscerarsi *v/r* ⟨1l⟩ *fig* be consumed
sviscerato *adj* passionate; *pej* extravagant
svista *f* oversight; ***per ~*** by some oversight
svitare *v/t* ⟨1a⟩ unscrew
svitarsi *v/r* ⟨1a⟩ unscrew
svitato *adj* unscrewed; *fig* ***essere ~*** have a screw loose
Svizzera *f* Switzerland
svizzero I *adj* Swiss **II** *m*, **-a** *f* Swiss
svogliatamente *adv* lazily
svogliatezza *f* laziness
svogliato *adj* lazy
svolazzare *v/i* ⟨1a⟩ flutter
svolazzo *m* fluttering; (*orpello*) embellishment
svolgere *v/t* ⟨3d⟩ *rotolo* unwrap; *tema* develop; *attività* carry out
svolgersi *v/r* happen; *di commedia, film* be set (***in*** in)
svolgimento *m* course; *di tema* development
svolta *f* (*curva*) turning; *fig* turning point
svoltare *v/i* ⟨1c⟩: ***~ a destra*** turn right
svolto *past part* → ***svolgere***
svuotamento *m* emptying
svuotare *v/t* ⟨1c⟩ empty
svuotarsi *v/r* ⟨1c⟩ empty

T

t, T *m/f* ⟨*pl* t, T⟩ t, T
t *abbr* (= **tonnellata**) t (tonne)
TA *abbr* (= **Taranto**) Taranto
tabaccaio *m*, **-a** *f* ⟨*mpl* -ai⟩ tobacconist
tabaccheria *f* tobacconist's
tabacco *m* ⟨*pl* -cchi⟩ tobacco
tabagismo *m* smoking
tabarro *m* tabard
tabella *f* table; ***~ dei prezzi*** price list; *fig* ***~ di marcia*** schedule
tabellina *f* multiplication table
tabellone *m* board; *per avvisi* notice board; ***~ pubblicitario*** billboard
tabernacolo *m* tabernacle
tabloid I *adj inv*: ***formato*** *m* ***~*** tabloid format **II** *m* ⟨*pl* tabloid⟩ tabloid
tabù *m/adj inv* taboo
tabuizzare *v/t* ⟨1n⟩ taboo
tabulato *m* printout
tabulatore *m* tabulator, tab
TAC *abbr* (= **Tomografia Assiale Computerizzata**) CAT (computerized axial tomography)
tacca *f* ⟨*pl* -cche⟩ flaw; *di lama*: nick; *fig* ***uomo*** *m* ***di mezza ~*** small-timer
taccagneria *f* stinginess
taccagno *adj* mean, stingy *infml*
taccheggiare ⟨1f⟩ **I** *v/i* shoplift **II** *v/t* shoplift
taccheggiatore *m*, **-trice** *f* shoplifter
taccheggio *m* shoplifting
tacchetto *m* thin heel
tacchino *m* turkey; ***carne*** *f* ***di ~*** turkey
tacciare *v/t* ⟨1f⟩: ***~ qn di qc*** tax s.o. with sth
tacco *m* ⟨*pl* -cchi⟩ heel; ***~ a spillo*** stiletto (heel); *fig* ***alzare i -chi*** show a clean pair of heels
taccola *f* ZOOL jackdaw
taccuino *m* notebook
tacere ⟨2k⟩ **I** *v/t* keep quiet about, say nothing about **II** *v/i* not say anything, be silent
tachicardia *f* tachycardia
tachimetro *m* speedometer
tacitare *v/t* ⟨1l⟩ *scandalo* hush up; COMM pay off
tacito *adj* tacit
taciturno *adj* taciturn
tafano *m* ZOOL horsefly
tafferuglio *m* ⟨*pl* -gli⟩ scuffle
taffe(t)tà *m* ⟨*pl* taffe(t)tà⟩ taffeta
tagico ⟨*mpl* -ci⟩ **I** *adj* Tajik **II** *m*, **-a** *f* Tajik
Tagikistan *m* Tajikistan
taglia *f* (*misura*) size; ***di ~ media*** medium; ***~ forte*** outsize; ***~ unica*** one

size

tagliacarte *m* ⟨*pl* tagliacarte⟩ paper-knife

tagliafuoco **I** *adj inv*: ***porta*** *f* ***~*** fire door **II** *m* ⟨*pl* tagliafuoco⟩ fire wall

taglialegna *m* ⟨*pl* taglialegna⟩ woodcutter

tagliando *m* coupon; AUTO service; ***fare il ~*** have the vehicle serviced

tagliare *v/t* ⟨1g⟩ cut; *albero* cut down; *legna* chop; ***~ i capelli*** have one's hair cut; *fig* ***~ la strada a qn*** cut in front of s.o.; *fig* ***~ la corda*** clear off; ***~ la testa al toro*** settle something once and for all; ***taglia corto!*** *infml* cut it short!; ***~ a metà*** cut in half; ***~ i fondi a qn*** cut off s.o.'s money; ***~ l'eroina*** cut heroin

tagliarsi *v/r* cut o.s.; ***mi sono tagliata un dito*** I've cut my finger

tagliatelle *fpl* tagliatelle *sg*

tagliato *adj vino*, *stupefacenti* cut; *fig* ***essere ~ per qc*** be cut out for sth

taglieggiare *v/t* ⟨1g⟩ extort

taglieggiatore *m*, **-trice** *f* extortionist

tagliente *adj* sharp

tagliere *m* chopping board

taglierina *f* guillotine

taglierini *mpl type of noodles*

taglio *m* ⟨*pl* -gli⟩ cut; ***~ cesareo*** C(a)esarean (section); ***~ di capelli*** haircut; ***arma*** *f* ***a doppio ~*** double-edged sword (*a. fig*); ***banconote*** *fpl* ***di grosso / piccolo ~*** high / low denomination banknote; ***pizza*** *f* ***al ~*** pizza by the slice; *fig* ***diamoci un ~!*** cut it out!

tagliola *f* trap

tagliuzzare *v/t* ⟨1a⟩ chop; *infml* score

tahitiano **I** *adj* Tahitian **II** *m*, **-a** *f* Tahitian

tailleur *m* ⟨*pl* tailleur⟩ suit

talare *adj*: ***abito*** *m* ***~*** cassock

talassemia *f* thalassemia

talassemico *adj* ⟨*mpl* -ci⟩ thalassemic

talassoterapia *f* thalassotherapy

talco *m* ⟨*pl* -chi⟩ talc, talcum powder

tale *adj / pron* such a; ***-i*** *pl* such; ***~ e quale*** just like; ***un ~*** someone; ***il signor tal dei -i*** Mr So-and-so; ***in tal caso*** in that event; ***come ~*** as such

talea *f* cutting

talebano *m* Taliban

talento *m* talent

talismano *m* talisman

talk show *m* ⟨*pl* talk show⟩ talk show

tallero *m* thaler

tallonamento *m* tailing

tallonare *v/t* ⟨1a⟩ *persona* follow close behind; *nel rugby* heel

talloncino *m* coupon

tallone *m* heel; ***il ~ di Achille*** Achilles' heel

talmente *adv* so

talora *adv* sometimes

talpa *f* mole

talvolta *adv* sometimes

tamarindo *m* tamarind; (*bibita*) tamarind drink

tamarisco *m* ⟨*pl* -schi⟩ tamarisk

tamburello *m* MUS tambourine; (*telaio*) embroidery frame

tamburino *m* drummer; *giornale* entertainments guide

tamburo *m* drum

Tamigi *m* Thames

tamil ⟨*pl* tamil⟩ **I** *adj* Tamil **II** *m/f* Tamil

tamponamento *m* AUTO collision; ***~ a catena*** multi-vehicle pile-up

tamponare *v/t* ⟨1a⟩ *falla* plug; AUTO collide with, crash into

tampone *m* MED swab; *per donne* tampon; *per timbri* (ink) pad; COMPUT buffer

tam tam *m* ⟨*pl* tam tam⟩ MUS tom tom; *fig* grapevine

tana *f* den

tandem *m* ⟨*pl* tandem⟩ tandem

tanga *m* ⟨*pl* tanga⟩ thong

Tanganica *m* Tanganyika

tangente *f* MATH tangent; *infml* (*percentuale illecita*) kickback *infml*; *infml* (*bustarella*) bribe; *infml* (*pizzo*) protection money

tangentopoli *f* ⟨*no pl*⟩ bribesville

tangenziale *f* ring road

tangere *v/t* ⟨3a⟩ concern

Tangeri *f* Tangier

tanghero *m* yokel; *infml* yob

tangibile *adj* tangible (*a. fig*)

tango *m* ⟨*pl* -ghi⟩ tango

tanica *f* container; NAUT *per fuoribordo* tank

tannino *m* tannin

tanto **I** *adj* so much; ***-i*** *pl* so many; ***-i saluti*** best wishes; ***-e grazie*** thank you so much, many thanks **II** *pron* much; ***-i*** *pl* many **III** *adv* (*così*) so; *con verbi* so much; ***di ~ in ~*** from time to time; ***~ quanto*** as much as; ***è da ~ (tempo) che non lo vedo*** I haven't

seen him for a long time; ***~ per cambiare*** for a change; ***un ~ per cento*** X percent; ***~ è lo stesso*** it makes no difference; ***~ per dire*** (*or* ***fare***) just to say (*or* do) sth; ***~ più che …*** all the more so because …; ***da ~*** for a long time; ***di ~ in ~*** from time to time
Tanzania *f* Tanzania
tanzaniano I *adj* Tanzanian **II** *m*, **-a** *f* Tanzanian
tapino I *adj* miserable **II** *m*, **-a** *f* wretch
tapioca *f* ⟨*pl* -che⟩ tapioca
tapiro *m* tapir
tapis roulant *m* ⟨*pl* tapis roulant⟩ moving walkway
tappa *f* stop; *di viaggio* stage
tappabuchi *m/f* ⟨*pl* tappabuchi⟩ *infml* stopgap
tappare *v/t* ⟨1a⟩ plug; *bottiglia* put the cork in; *fig* ***~ la bocca a qn*** shut s.o. up
tapparella *f* rolling shutter
tapparsi *v/r* get blocked (up); ***si è tappato il lavandino*** the washbasin's blocked up; ***~ il naso*** hold one's nose; ***~ in casa*** shut oneself up at home
tappetino *m* AUTO mat; *per mouse* mousemat
tappeto *m* carpet; ***bombardamento*** *m* ***a ~*** carpet bombing; ***indagine*** *f* ***a ~*** wholesale survey; ***mandare al ~*** SPORTS knock out; *fig* ***porre una questione sul ~*** lay a question on the table; ***~ verde*** baize
tappezzare *v/t* ⟨1a⟩ (wall)paper
tappezzeria *f di pareti* wallpaper; *di sedili* upholstery
tappezziere *m*, **-a** *f di pareti* decorator; *di sedili* upholsterer
tappo *m* cap, top; *di sughero* cork; *di lavandini, vasche* plug
tara *f* tare
taralluccio *m* ⟨*pl* -cci⟩ COOK *ring-shaped biscuit typical of Southern Italy*; ***finire a -i e vino*** *infml* end up in a friendly way
tarantella *f* tarantella
tarantino I *adj* from Taranto **II** *m*, **-a** *f* person from Taranto
Taranto *m* Taranto
tarantola *f* tarantula
tarare *v/t* ⟨1a⟩ TECH calibrate
tarassaco *m* ⟨*pl* -chi⟩ taraxacum
tarato *adj* MED affected by a hereditary condition; TECH calibrated
tarchiato *adj* stocky
tardare ⟨1a⟩ **I** *v/t* delay **II** *v/i* be late; ***~ a rispondere*** delay in replying
tardi *adv* late; ***più ~*** later (on); ***al più ~*** at the latest; ***a più ~!*** see you!; ***far ~*** (*arrivare in ritardo*) be late; (*stare alzato*) stay up late; *in ufficio* work late; ***meglio ~ che mai*** better late than never; ***chi ~ arriva male alloggia*** *prov* first come first served
tardivo *adj* late; *fig* retarded, slow
tardo *adj* late; ***~ Medioevo*** *m* late Middle Ages; ***a -a ora*** at a late hour
targa *f* ⟨*pl* -ghe⟩ nameplate; AUTO numberplate
targato *adj* with a numberplate; *fig* super-typical
target *m* ⟨*pl* target⟩ target
targhetta *f* tag; *su porta* nameplate
tariffa *f* rate; *nei trasporti* fare; *doganale* tariff
tariffario ⟨*mpl* -ri⟩ **I** *adj* price *attr* **II** *n*: ***tariffario*** *m* price list
tarlato *adj* worm-eaten
tarlo *m* woodworm
tarma *f* (clothes) moth
tarmarsi *v/r* ⟨1a⟩ become motheaten
tarmicida *m* ⟨*pl* -i⟩ moth killer
taroccato *adj* fake, false
tarocco *m* ⟨*pl* -cchi⟩ tarot
tarpare *v/t* ⟨1a⟩: ***~ le ali*** clip s.o.'s wings
tarso *m* ANAT tarsus
tartagliare *v/i* ⟨1g⟩ stammer
tartaglione *m*, **-a** *f* stammerer
tartaro[1] *m* tartar
tartaro[2] **I** *adj* Tartar **II** *m*, **-a** *f* Tartar
tartaruga *f* ⟨*pl* -ghe⟩ *terrestre* tortoise; *aquatica* turtle
tartassare *v/t* ⟨1a⟩ harrass
tartina *f* canapé
tartufo *m* truffle
tasca *f* ⟨*pl* -che⟩ pocket; ***ne ho piene le -che*** I'm fed up with this; ***conoscere come le proprie -sche*** know like the back of one's hands
tascabile I *adj* pocket *attr* **II** *m* paperback
tascapane *m* ⟨*pl* tascapane⟩ haversack
taschino *m* breast pocket
task force *f* ⟨*pl* task force⟩ task force
Tasmania *f* Tasmania
tassa *f* tax; ***~ aeroportuale*** airport tax; ***~ di circolazione*** road tax; ***~ d'iscri-***

zione entrance fee; **~ *di possesso*** AUTO car tax; ***-e*** *pl* ***universitarie*** university tuition fees ***ufficio*** *m* ***delle -e*** tax office; **~ *di soggiorno*** visitor tax; ***esente da ~*** tax free; ***soggetto a ~*** subject to tax
tassabile *adj* taxable
tassametro *m* meter, clock *infml*
tassare *v/t* ⟨1a⟩ tax
tassativo *adj* imperative
tassazione *f* taxation, tax
tassello *m nel muro* plug; *fig* ***il ~ mancante*** missing piece
tassista *m/f* ⟨*mpl* -i⟩ taxi driver
tasso[1] *m* FIN rate; **~ *d'inflazione*** inflation rate, rate of inflation; **~ *d'interesse*** interest rate; **~ *di sconto*** discount rate
tasso[2] *m* ZOOL badger
tasso[3] *m* BOT yew
tastare *v/t* ⟨1a⟩ feel; *fig* **~ *il terreno*** test the water, see how the land lies
tastiera *f* keyboard
tastierino *m* TEL keypad
tastierista *m/f* ⟨*mpl* -i⟩ keyboards player; TYPO, COMPUT keyboarder
tasto *m* key; COMPUT **~ *operativo*** function key; *fig* ***un ~ delicato*** a difficult subject
tastoni *adv*: ***a ~*** gropingly
tata *f infml* nanny
tattica *f* ⟨*pl* -che⟩ tactics *pl*
tattico *adj* ⟨*mpl* -ci⟩ tactical
tattile *adj* tactile
tatto *m* (*senso*) touch; *fig* tact; ***mancanza*** *f* ***di ~*** tactlessness, lack of tact; ***essere morbido / ruvido al ~*** be soft / rough to the touch
tatuaggio *m* ⟨*pl* -ggi⟩ tattoo
tatuare *v/t* ⟨1l⟩ tattoo
tatuarsi *v/r* get a tattoo
taumaturgico *adj* ⟨*mpl* -ci⟩ thaumaturgical
taumaturgo *m* ⟨*pl* -ghi⟩ miracle worker
taurino *adj*: ***collo*** *m* **~** bull neck
tautologia *f* tautology
tautologico *adj* ⟨*mpl* -ci⟩ tautological
TAV *abbr* (= **Treno ad Alta Velocità**) *high speed train*
taverna *f country-style restaurant*
tavola *f* **1.** (*tavolo*) table; **~ *rotonda*** round table; ***mettersi a ~*** sit down to eat; ***portare in ~*** bring to the table; ***a ~!*** lunch / dinner is ready!, come and get it! *infml*; ***apparecchiare / sparecchiare la ~*** set / clear the table; **~ *pitagorica*** *infml* multiplication table **2.** (*asse*) plank, board, SPORTS **~ *a vela*** sailboard **3.** *in libro* plate **4.** **~ *calda*** snackbar
tavolaccio *m* ⟨*pl* -cci⟩ plank bed
tavolata *f* table(ful)
tavoletta *f*: **~ *di cioccolata*** bar of chocolate
tavoliere *m* GEOG tableland; *biliardo* table
tavolino *m* table; ***risolvere qc a ~*** solve sth in theory
tavolo *m* table; **~ *allungabile / pieghevole*** extending / folding table
tavolozza *f* palette (*a. fig*)
taxi *m* ⟨*pl* taxi⟩ taxi
tazza *f* cup
tazzina *f* espresso cup
tbc, TBC *abbr* (= **tubercolosi**) TB (tuberculosis)
TCI *abbr* (= **Touring Club Italiano**) *Italian motoring organization*
te *pron* you; **~ *l'ho venduto*** I sold it to you; ***beato*** *m* **~** lucky you!
tè *m* tea; **~ *freddo*** iced tea; ***sala*** *f* ***da ~*** tearoom; ***tazza*** *f* ***da ~*** teacup
teatrale *adj* theatre, *US* theater; *fig* theatrical; ***rappresentazione*** *f* **~** play
teatralità *f* ⟨*pl* teatralità⟩ theatricalism
teatrante *m/f* actor; *fig* theatrical person
teatrino *m* small theatre; *di burattini*: puppet theatre; ***il ~ della politica*** *pej* the political farce
teatro *m* theatre, *US* theater; (*materia*) drama; *fig* (*luogo*) scene; **~ *all'aperto*** open-air theatre (*US* theater); **~ *lirico*** opera (house); ***andare a ~*** go to the theatre
Tebe *f* Thebes
teca *f* ⟨*pl* -che⟩ display case
technicolor *m*: ***film*** *m* ***in ~*** film in Technicolor®
tecnica *f* ⟨*pl* -che⟩ technique; (*tecnologia*) technology
tecnicizzare *v/t* ⟨1a⟩ technicalize
tecnico ⟨*mpl* -ci⟩ **I** *adj* technical; ***dizionario*** *m* **~** technical dictionary **II** *m* technician
tecnocrate *m/f* technocrat
tecnologia *f* technology; ***alta ~*** high technology, high tech *infml*
tecnologico *adj* ⟨*mpl* -ci⟩ technologi-

cal
tedesco ⟨*mpl* -chi⟩ **I** *m/adj* German **II** *m*, **-a** *f* German
tediare ⟨1k & b⟩ *v/t* bore
tedio *m* ⟨*pl* -i⟩ boredom
tedioso *adj* boring
teenager *m/f* ⟨*pl* teenager⟩ teenager
tegame *m* (sauce)pan
tegamino *m* small pan; ***uova*** *fpl* ***al ~*** fried eggs
teglia *f* baking tin
tegola *f* tile
teiera *f* teapot
teina *f* theine
tel. *abbr* (= **telefono**) tel (telephone)
tela *f* cloth; PAINT canvas; ***~ cerata*** oilcloth
telaio *m* ⟨*pl* -ai⟩ loom; *di automobile* chassis; *di bicicletta*, *finestra* frame
telare *v/i* ⟨1a⟩ *infml* make oneself scarce
telato *adj* like canvas; ***carta*** *f* ***-a*** linen paper
teleabbonato *m*, **-a** *f* television licence holder
telecamera *f* camera
telecomandato *adj* remote-controlled
telecomando *m* remote control
telecomunicazioni *fpl* telecommunications *pl*, telecomms *pl*
teleconferenza *f* conference call
telecronaca *f* television report
telecronista *m/f* ⟨*mpl* -i⟩ television commentator
telediffusione *f* broadcasting
teledipendente *adj* addicted to TV
telefax *m* ⟨*pl* telefax⟩ fax
teleferica *f* ⟨*pl* -che⟩ cableway
telefilm *m* ⟨*pl* telefilm⟩ film made for television
telefonare *v/i* ⟨1m & b⟩ (tele)phone, ring (***a qn*** s.o.)
telefonata *f* (tele)phone call; ***~ interurbana*** long-distance (phone) call; ***~ urbana*** local call; ***fare una ~ a qn*** ring *or* phone s.o.
telefonia *f* telephony
telefonico *adj* ⟨*mpl* -ci⟩ (tele)phone *attr*
telefonino *m* mobile (phone), *US* cell (-ular) phone
telefonista *m/f* ⟨*mpl* -i⟩ (switchboard) operator
telefono *m* **1.** (tele)phone; ***~ cellulare*** cellphone, cellular (tele)phone; ***~ fisso*** land line; ***~ a gettoni*** *telephone that takes tokens*; ***~ a scheda (magnetica)*** cardphone; ***~ a tastiera*** push-button (tele)phone; ***dare un colpo di ~ a qn*** give s.o. a ring **2.** ***~ azzurro*** ChildLine (*24-hour helpline for children*)
telegenico *adj* ⟨*mpl* -ci⟩ telegenic
telegiornale *m* news *sg*
telegrafare *v/t* ⟨1m & b⟩ telegraph
telegrafico *adj* ⟨*mpl* -ci⟩ *stile* telegraphic; *risposta* very brief
telegrafo *m* telegraph
telegramma *m* ⟨*pl* -i⟩ telegram
teleguidato *adj* remote controlled
telelavoro *m* teleworking
telematica *f* telematics *sg*
teleobiettivo *m* telephoto lens
telepass® *m* ⟨*pl* telepass⟩ *automatic toll payment system for motorways*
telepatia *f* telepathy
telepatico *adj* ⟨*mpl* -ci⟩ telepathic
telepromozione *f* TV advertising; *durante I programmi* product placement
telequiz *m* ⟨*pl* telequiz⟩ TV quiz
teleriscaldamento *m* district heating
teleromanzo *m* TV serial
teleschermo *m* TV screen
telescopico *adj* ⟨*mpl* -ci⟩ telescopic (*a.* TECH); ***antenna*** *f* ***-a*** telescopic aerial
telescopio *m* ⟨*pl* -pi⟩ telescope
teleselezione *f* STD
telespettatore *m*, **-trice** *f* TV viewer
televendita *f* telesales *sg or pl*
televideo® *m* ⟨*pl* televideo⟩ teletext
televisione *f* television, TV; ***~ via cavo*** cable television *or* TV; ***~ via satellite*** satellite television *or* TV; ***~ digitale*** digital television; ***guardare la ~*** watch television
televisivo *adj* television *attr*, TV *attr*
televisore *m* television (set), TV (set); ***~ a colori*** colo(u)r TV
telex *m* ⟨*pl* telex⟩ telex
tellina *f* cockle
tellurico *adj* ⟨*mpl* -ci⟩ telluric
tellurio *m* tellurium
telo *m* sheet; ***~ da spiaggia*** beach towel; ***~ di salvataggio*** jumping sheet
telone *m* tarpaulin; THEAT curtain
tema *m* theme, subject; ***andare fuori ~*** wander off the subject; (*sbagliare*) go off track
tematica *f* ⟨*pl* -che⟩ theme (*a.* MUS)

temerarietà *f* ⟨*pl* temerarietà⟩ recklessness
temerario *adj* ⟨*mpl* -ri⟩ reckless
temere *v/t* ⟨2a⟩ be afraid *or* frightened of
tempaccio *m*: ***che ~!*** what awful weather!
tempera *f* tempera *f*; ***colori*** *mpl* ***a ~*** poster paints
temperamatite *m* ⟨*pl* temperamatite⟩ pencil sharpener
temperamento *m* temperament
temperanza *f* temperance
temperare *v/t* ⟨1l & b⟩ *acciaio* temper; *matita* sharpen
temperato *adj acciaio* tempered; *matita* sharp; *clima* temperate
temperatura *f* temperature; ***~ ambiente*** room temperature
temperino *m coltellino* penknife; *temperamatite* pencil sharpener
tempesta *f* storm
tempestare *v/t* ⟨1b⟩: ***~ di pugni*** rain punches; ***~ di domande*** fire questions
tempestato *adj*: ***~ di diamanti*** diamond-studded
tempestivamente *adv* at the right time, promptly
tempestività *f* ⟨*pl* tempestività⟩ timeliness
tempestivo *adj* timely, prompt
tempestoso *adj* stormy
tempia *f* temple
tempio *m* ⟨*pl* -pli⟩ temple
tempismo *m* (sense of) timing
tempo *m* **1.** time; ***~ libero*** free time; ***a ~ parziale*** part-time; ***a ~ perso*** in one's spare time; ***a ~ pieno*** full-time; SPORTS ***-i*** *pl* ***supplementari*** extra time *sg*, *US* overtime *sg*; ***a ~, in ~*** in time; ***col ~*** in time, eventually; ***un ~*** once, long ago; ***per ~*** (*presto*) in good time; (*di buon'ora*) early; ***non ho ~*** I don't have (the) time; ***lavora da molto ~*** he has been working for a long time; ***~ di conversazione*** TEL length of call; ***a ~ debito*** in due course; ***a ~ determinato / indeterminato*** fixed term / permanent; ***~ fa*** some time ago; ***coi -i che corrono*** with things as they are; ***il miglior ~*** the best time; ***in un primo ~*** at first; ***ammazzare il ~*** kill time; ***stringere i -i*** quicken the tempo **2.** METEO weather; ***fa bel / brutto ~*** the weather is lovely / nasty; ***che ~ fa?*** what's the weather like?
temporale[1] *adj* temporal; ***potere*** *m* ***~*** secular power
temporale[2] *m* thunderstorm
temporalesco *adj* ⟨*mpl* -schi⟩ thundery
temporaneo *adj* temporary
temporeggiare *v/i* ⟨1f⟩ stall
temporeggiatore *m*, **-trice** *f* procrastinator
tempra *f* TECH tempering; *fig* character; ***(non) avere la ~ per qc*** (not) be cut out for sth
temprare *v/t* ⟨1b⟩ TECH temper; *fig* harden
temprarsi *v/r* ⟨1b⟩ *fig* toughen up
tenace *adj materiali*, *sostanze* strong; *fig* tenacious
tenacemente *adv* tenaciously
tenacia *f fig* tenacity
tenaglie *fpl* pincers *pl*
tenda *f* curtain; *da campeggio* tent; ***~ a ossigeno*** oxygen tent; *fig* ***levare le -e*** pack up and leave
tendaggio *m* ⟨*pl* -ggi⟩ hanging, curtain
tendenza *f* tendency; ***di ~*** by inclination; ***fare ~*** set a trend, be trendy
tendenzialmente *adv* tendentially
tendenzioso *adj* tendentious, biased
tendere ⟨3c⟩ **I** *v/t molla*, *elastico*, *muscoli* stretch; *corde del violino* tighten; *mano* hold out, stretch out; *fig trappola* lay; ***~ un braccio per fare qc*** reach out to do sth; ***~ le braccia a qn*** hold one's arms out to s.o.; ***~ la mano a qn*** give s.o. a helping hand; ***~ un tranello a qn*** set a trap for s.o. **II** *v/i*: ***~ a*** (*aspirare a*) aim at; (*essere portati a*) tend to; (*avvicinarsi a*) verge on
tendersi *v/r* ⟨3c⟩ tense up
tendina *f* net curtain
tendine *m* tendon
tendone *m* marquee; ***~ del circo*** big top
tendopoli *f* ⟨*pl* tendopoli⟩ tent city
tenebre *fpl* darkness *sg*
tenebroso *adj* dark (*a. fig*)
tenente *m* lieutenant
teneramente *adv* tenderly
tenere ⟨2q⟩ **I** *v/t* hold; (*conservare*, *mantenere*) keep; (*gestire*) run; *spazio* take up; *conferenza* give; ***~ d'occhio***

keep an eye on, watch; ~ ***in mano qc*** hold sth in one's hand; ~ ***banco*** be banker; ~ ***conto di qc*** take sth into account; ~ ***il broncio*** *or* ***il muso*** sulk, be in a sulk; ~ ***il mare*** NAUT be seaworthy **II** *v/i* hold (on); ~ ***a*** (*dare importanza a*) care about; SPORTS support; *fig* ~ ***duro*** hold one's own; ***la colla tiene*** the glue's sticking; ~ ***a bada*** hold at bay; ~ ***a freno*** keep in check; ~ ***qn in sospeso*** keep s.o. in suspense; ~ ***per una squadra*** support a team

tenerezza *f* tenderness

tenero *adj* tender; *pietra*, *legno* soft

tenersi *v/r* (*reggersi*) hold on (***a*** to); (*mantenersi*) keep o.s.; ~ ***in piedi*** stand (up); ~ ***a galla*** keep afloat; ~ ***lontano da qn*** keep away from s.o.

tengo → ***tenere***

tenia *f* tapeworm

tennis *m* tennis; ~ ***da tavolo*** table tennis

tennista *m/f* ⟨*mpl* -i⟩ tennis player

tenore *m* MUS tenor; ~ ***di vita*** standard of living

tensione *f* voltage; *fig* tension; ***alta*** ~ high voltage

tensore *adj*: ***muscolo*** *m* ~ tensor muscle

tentacolare *adj fig* sprawly

tentacolo *m* ZOOL tenticle (*a. fig*)

tentare *v/t* ⟨1b⟩ try, attempt; (*allettare*) tempt; ~ ***tutto il possibile*** do everything possible

tentativo *m* attempt

tentazione *f* temptation

tentennamento *m* vacillation (*a. fig*)

tentennare *v/i* ⟨1m⟩ (*traballare*) wobble; (*esitare*) vacillate

tentoni *adv* gropingly; *fig* blindly; ***procedere*** (***a***) ~ feel one's way (*a. fig*)

tenue *adj colore* pale; *luce*, *speranza* faint

tenuta *f* (*capacità*) capacity; (*resistenza*) stamina; (*divisa*) uniform; (*abbigliamento*) outfit; AGR estate; ***a ~ d'aria*** airtight; AUTO ~ ***di strada*** roadholding ability

tenutario *m*, **-a** *f* ⟨*mpl* -ri⟩ keeper

tenuto *adj*: ***non essere ~ a fare qc*** not be required to do sth

teocrazia *f* theocracy

teologia *f* theology

teologico *adj* ⟨*mpl* -ci⟩ theological

teologo *m*, **-a** *f* ⟨*mpl* -gi⟩ theologian

teorema *m* ⟨*pl* -i⟩ theorem

teoria *f* theory

teorico *adj* ⟨*mpl* -ci⟩ theoretical

teorizzare *v/t* ⟨1a⟩: ~ ***qc*** theorize

teosofia *f* theosophy

teosofo *m*, **-a** *f* theosopher

tepidario *m* ⟨*pl* -ri⟩ HIST tepidarium

tepore *m* warmth

teppa, teppaglia *f* riff-raff

teppismo *m* hooliganism

teppista *m/f* ⟨*pl* -i⟩ hooligan

teramano I *adj* from Teramo **II** *m*, **-a** *f* person from Teramo

terapeuta *m/f* ⟨*mpl* -i⟩ therapist

terapeutico *adj* ⟨*mpl* -ci⟩ therapeutic

terapia *f* therapy

terapista *m/f* ⟨*mpl* -i⟩ therapist

Teresa *f*: ***Santa*** ~ Saint Theresa

tergere *v/t* ⟨3uu⟩ LIT wipe

tergersi *v/r* ⟨3uu⟩ wipe oneself

tergicristallo *m* AUTO windscreen (*US* windshield) wiper

tergiversare *v/i* ⟨1b⟩ prevaricate

tergo *m*: ***a*** ~ overleaf

terital *m* ⟨*pl* terital⟩ Terylene®

termale *adj* thermal; ***stazione*** *f* ~ spa; ***stabilimento*** *m* ~ baths *pl*

terme *fpl* baths *pl*

termico *adj* ⟨*mpl* -ci⟩ thermal; ***borsa*** *f* ***-a*** cool bag; ***centrale*** *f* ***-a*** thermal power station; ***isolamento*** *m* ~ heat insulation; ***lunotto*** *m* ~ heated rear window

terminal *m* ⟨*pl* terminal⟩ AVIAT air terminal, terminal building

terminale I *adj* terminal; ***malato*** *m* ~ terminally ill (patient); ***stazione*** *f* ~ terminus **II** *m* COMPUT, ELEC terminal

terminalista *m/f* ⟨*mpl* -i⟩ computer terminal operator

terminare *v/t & v/i* ⟨1l & b⟩ end, finish, terminate

termine[1] *m* end; (*confine*) limit; FIN (*scadenza*) deadline; ***-i*** *pl* ***di consegna*** terms of delivery; ***a breve/lungo*** ~ in the short/long term; ***volgere al*** ~ come to an end; ***il ~ è scaduto*** we've passed the deadline; ***a medio termine*** medium-term

termine[2] *m* (*parola*) term; ~ ***tecnico*** technical term; ***in altri -i*** in other words; ***senza mezzi -i*** frankly

terminologia *f* terminology

terminologico *adj* ⟨*mpl* -ci⟩ termino-

logical
termitaio *m* ⟨*pl* -ai⟩ termitarium
termite *f* termite
termoautonomo *adj* with separate heating
termoconduttore *m* thermoconductor
termocoperta *f* electric blanket
termodinamica *f* ⟨*pl* -che⟩ thermodynamics *attr*
termoelettrico *adj* ⟨*mpl* -ci⟩ thermoelectrical; ***centrale*** *f* ***-a*** thermoelectric power station
termoforo *m* MED heat pad
termoisolante **I** *adj* heat-proof **II** *m* heat-proofer
termometro *m* thermometer
termonucleare *adj* thermonuclear
termoplastico *adj* ⟨*mpl* -ci⟩ thermoplastic
termoreattore *m* jet engine
termoregolatore **I** *adj* thermoregulatory **II** *n*: ***termoregolatore*** *m* thermoregulator
termoregolazione *f* thermoregulation
termos *m* ⟨*pl* termos⟩ thermos®
termosifone *m* radiator
termostato *m* thermostat
ternano **I** *adj* from Terni **II** *m*, **-a** *f* person from Terni
terno *m*: ***un ~ al lotto*** jackpot (*a. fig*)
terra *f* earth; (*regione*, *proprietà*, *terreno agricolo*) land; (*superficie del suolo*) ground; (*pavimento*) floor; ***-e*** *pl* earths; ***a ~*** on the ground; AVIAT, NAUT ***scendere a ~*** get off; TECH ***mettere a ~*** earth; ***cadere a*** *or* ***per ~*** fall (down); ***sentirsi a ~*** feel rundown; ***arare la ~*** plough the land; ***fare ~ bruciata*** make life impossible for oneself; ***la ~ promessa*** the Promised Land; ***non stare né in cielo né in ~*** be completely unheard of; ***sedersi per ~*** sit on the ground; ***sotto ~*** underground; *fig* ***~ terra*** (*semplice*) no-nonsense; (*pratico*) down-to-earth; (*mediocre*) ordinary; ***~ di Siena*** sienna
terracotta *f* ⟨*pl* terrecotte⟩ terracotta
terraferma *f* dry land, terra firma
terraglia *f* ⟨*pl* -glie⟩ earthenware
terranova *m* ⟨*pl* terranova⟩ Newfoundland
terrapieno *m* embankment
terrario *m* ⟨*pl* -ri⟩ terrarium
Terra Santa *f* Holy Land
terrazza *f*, **terrazzo** *m* balcony, terrace
terrazzare *v/t* ⟨1a⟩ terrace
terremotato **I** *adj* destroyed / affected by an earthquake **II** *m*, **-a** *f* earthquake victim
terremoto *m* earthquake; ***scossa*** *f* ***di ~*** earth tremor
terreno **I** *m* (*superficie*) ground; (*suolo*, *materiale*) soil; (*appezzamento*) plot of land; *fig* (*settore*, *tema*) field, area; ***perdere / guadagnare ~*** lose / gain ground; ***~ agricolo*** farmland; ***~ edificabile*** building land; ***~ fabbricabile*** land that may be built on; ***~ incolto*** wild countryside; *fig* ***trovare il ~ adatto*** find fertile ground **II** *adj* earthly; *piano* ground, *US* first
terreo,a- *adj fig* sallow; ***farsi ~ in volto*** turn ashen
terrestre *adj* land *attr*, terrestrial; *della Terra* of the Earth; ***globo*** *m* ***~*** globe
terribile *adj* terrible
terribilmente *adv* terribly
terriccio *m* ⟨*pl* -cci⟩ mo(u)ld
terrier *m* ⟨*pl* terrier⟩ terrier
terriero *adj* land *attr*; ***proprietario*** *m* ***~*** landowner
terrificante *adj* terrifying
terrina *f* bowl
territoriale *adj* territorial; ***acque*** *fpl* ***-i*** territorial waters
territorio *m* ⟨*pl* -ri⟩ territory; ***marcare il ~*** ZOOL mark out one's territory
terrone *m*, **-a** *f pej* peasant (*used to describe someone from southern Italy*)
terrore *m* terror; ***avere il ~ di qc*** be terrified of sth
terrorismo *m* terrorism
terrorista *m/f* ⟨*mpl* -i⟩ terrorist
terroristico *adj* ⟨*mpl* -ci⟩ terrorist
terrorizzare *v/t* ⟨1a⟩ terrorize
terrorizzato *adj* terror-stricken
terroso *adj* earthy
terso **I** *adj* clear **II** *past part* → ***tergere***
terza *f* AUTO third (gear)
terzetto *m* MUS trio; *hum* threesome
terziario *m* ⟨*pl* -ri⟩ tertiary sector, services *pl*; ***~ francescano*** REL Franciscan tertiary
terziarizzazione *f* expansion of the service sector; (*trasferimento ad esterni*) outsourcing
terzina *f* LIT tercet; MUS triplet
terzino *m* SPORTS back
terzo **I** *adj* third; ***il ~ mondo*** the Third

World; ***-a pagina*** *f* arts page; ***la -a età*** the third age; ***il ~ incomodo*** gooseberry; ***fare il ~ grado a qn*** give s.o. the third degree; ***per conto* (*di*) *-i*** on behalf of a third party; ***il Terzo Reich*** the Third Reich **II** *m* third
terzultimo *adj* antepenultimate
tesa *f* brim
tesaurizzare *v/t* ⟨1a⟩ hoard
tesaurizzazione *f* hoarding
teschio *m* ⟨*pl* -chi⟩ skull
tesi *f* ⟨*pl* tesi⟩: **~ (*di laurea*)** thesis
tesina *f* paper
teso I *past part* → ***tendere*** **II** *adj* taut; *fig* tense
tesoreria *f* treasury
tesoriere *m*, **-a** *f* treasurer
tesoro *m* treasure; (*tesoreria*) treasury; ***caccia f al ~*** treasure hunt; ***fare ~ di qc*** treasure sth
Tessaglia *f* Thessaly
tessera *f* card; ***~ d'abbonamento*** season ticket; ***~ magnetica*** magnetic card
tesseramento *m* membership; (*razionamento*) rationing
tesserato *m*, **-a** *f* cardholder; *atleta* member (of a sports club)
tessere *v/t* ⟨1a⟩ weave; *fig* ***~ le lodi di qn*** praise s.o. to the rafters; *fig* ***~ le fila di un complotto*** weave the strands of a plot
tesserino *m* *dell'autobus* travel card; *di club* membership card; *di riconoscimento* identity card; ***~ elettronico*** electronic card
tessile I *adj* textile **II** *m*: ***tessili*** *pl* textiles *pl*
tessitore *m*, **-trice** weaver
tessitura *f* weaving; *fig* plot
tessuto *m* fabric, material; ***~ di lana*** wool; ***-i*** *pl* fabrics, material *sg*; ***il ~ sociale*** social fabric
test *m* ⟨*pl* test⟩ test; ***~ attitudinale*** aptitude test
testa *f* **1.** head; ***~ d'aglio*** bulb of garlic; ***~ di rapa*** thickhead; ***a ~*** each, a head; ***essere una ~ calda*** be a hothead; ***montarsi la ~*** get bigheaded; ***perdere la ~*** go off one's head; ***a ~ alta / bassa*** with one's head held high / bowed; ***a ~ in giù*** headfirst; ***andare fuori di ~*** go off one's head; *fig* ***colpo*** *m* ***di ~*** impulse; ***fare a ~ o croce*** toss for it, call heads or tails; ***dalla ~ ai piedi*** from head to foot; ***~ in cassetta*** COOK *type of brawn made with pig's head in Central and Northern Italy*; ***-e*** *pl* ***di cuoio*** *special anti-terrorist police force* **2.** *fig* ***alla ~ di*** at the head of; ***essere in ~*** lead
testacoda *m* ⟨*pl* testacoda⟩: ***fare un ~*** spin around
testamentario *adj* ⟨*mpl* -ri⟩ testamentary; ***disposizioni -e*** last will and testament
testamento *m* will; ***Antico / Nuovo Testamento*** Old / New Testament; ***~ olografo*** hand-written will
testardaggine *f* stubbornness
testardo *adj* stubborn
testare *v/t* ⟨1b⟩ test
testata *f* *giornale* heading; *di letto* headboard; AUTO cylinder head; ***~ nucleare*** nuclear warhead; ***dare una ~ contro qc*** headbutt sth
testatore *m*, **-trice** testator
teste *m/f* witness
testicolo *m* testicle
testimone *m/f* witness; ***~ oculare*** eyewitness; ***Testimoni*** *pl* ***di Geova*** Jehovah's Witnesses
testimonial *m/f* ⟨*pl* testimonial⟩ spokesperson
testimoniale *adj* witness; ***prova*** *f* **~** evidence
testimonianza *f* testimony; (*prova*) proof; ***falsa ~*** perjury
testimoniare ⟨1k & c⟩ **I** *v/i* testify, give evidence **II** *v/t* *fig* testify to; JUR ***~ il falso*** commit perjury
testina *f* TECH head
testo *m* text; ***~ a fronte*** parallel text; ***-i*** *pl* ***sacri*** sacred books; ***~ unico*** unified code; (***non***) ***fare ~*** have (no) influence
testone *m*, **-a** *f* *fig* bighead
testosterone *m* testosterone
testuale *adj* verbatim
testualmente *adv* verbatim
testuggine *f* tortoise
tetano *m* tetanus
tête à tête *m* ⟨*pl* tête à tête⟩ tête-à--tête
tetraedro *m* tetrahedron
tetraggine *f* gloominess (*a. fig*)
tetragono *m* tetrahedron
tetrapak® *m* ⟨*pl* tetrapak⟩ Tetrapak® *m*
tetraplegico *adj* ⟨*mpl* -ci⟩ quadriple-

gic
tetro *adj* gloomy
tetta *f infml* tit, boob
tettarella *f Br* teat; *US* nipple
tetto *m* roof; **~ *piano*** flat roof, terrace; **~ *a due spioventi*** gable roof
tettoia *f* roof
tettonica *f* tectonics
tettonico *adj* ⟨*mpl* -ci⟩ tectonic
tettuccio *m* ⟨*pl* -cci⟩ AUTO roof; **~ *apribile*** sunroof
teutone *m* Teuton
teutonico *adj* ⟨*mpl* -ci⟩ Teutonic; ***Cavalieri Teutonici*** Teutonic Knights
Tevere *m* Tiber
texano I *adj* Texan **II** *m*, **-a** *f* Texan
TFR *m abbr* (= **Trattamento di fine rapporto**) severance pay
TG *abbr* (= **Telegiornale**) TV news *sg*
thailandese I *adj* Thai **II** *m/f* Thai
Thailandia *f* Thailand
thermos® → ***termos***
thesaurus *m* ⟨*pl* thesaurus⟩ thesaurus
thriller *m* ⟨*pl* thriller⟩ thriller
ti *pron* you; *riflessivo* yourself; ***che cosa ~ consiglia?*** what's his / her advice (to you)? ***fatti sentire!*** keep in touch!
tiara *f*: **~ *papale*** papal tiara
tiberino *adj* Tiberine
Tibet *m* Tibet
tibetano I *adj* Tibetan **II** *m*, **-a** *f* Tibetan
tibia *f* shinbone, tibia
tic *m* ⟨*pl* tic⟩ *di orologio* tick; MED tic; **~ *nervoso*** nervous habit
ticchettare *v/i* ⟨1a⟩ tick
ticchettio *m di orologio* ticking; *di pioggia* patter
ticchio *m* ⟨*pl* -cchi⟩ whim
ticinese I *adj* of or from Ticino **II** *m/f* person from Ticino
Ticino *m*: ***Canton ~*** canton of Ticino
ticket *m* ⟨*pl* ticket⟩ MED charge
tiene → ***tenere***
tiepido *adj* lukewarm, tepid; *fig* half-hearted, lukewarm
tifare *v/i* ⟨1a⟩: **~ *per*** support
tifo *m* MED typhus; *fig* ***fare il ~ per una squadra*** be a fan *or* supporter of a team
tifone *m* typhoon
tifoseria *f* supporters *pl*
tifoso *m*, **-a** *f* fan, supporter
tiglio *m* ⟨*pl* -gli⟩ lime tree
tigna *f* ringworm, *infml* nuisance
tignola *f* moth
tignoso *adj* mean
tigrato *adj* striped
tigre *f* tiger; *fig* **~ *di carta*** paper tiger
Tigri *m* Tigris
tigrotto *m* tiger cub
tilde *m/f* tilde
tilt *m*: ***andare in ~*** *persona* go into a tailspin; *congegno* go haywire
timballo *m* COOK timbale
timbrare *v/t* ⟨1a⟩ stamp
timbro *m* stamp; MUS timbre; **~ *postale*** postage stamp; **~ *di voce*** tone of voice
timer *m* ⟨*pl* timer⟩ timer
timidamente *adv* shyly
timidezza *f* shyness, timidity
timido *adj* shy, timid
timo *m* BOT thyme
timone *m* NAUT, AVIAT rudder; *fig* helm
timoniere *m*, **-a** *f* helmsman, *donna* helmswoman
timorato *adj* respectful; **~ *di Dio*** God-fearing
timore *m* fear
Timor Est *m* East Timor
timoroso *adj* timorous
timpano *m* MUS kettledrum; ANAT eardrum; ARCH tympanum
tinello *m* dinette
tingere *v/t* ⟨3d⟩ dye
tingersi *v/r* ⟨3d⟩ dye; *fig* make up
tino *m* vat
tinozza *f* tub; (*vasca*) bathtub
tinta *f* (*colorante*) dye; (*colore*) colo(u)r
tintarella *f* (sun)tan
tinteggiare *v/t* ⟨1f⟩ paint
tinteggiatura *f* painting, paintwork
tintinnare *v/i* ⟨1a⟩ tinkle, jingle
tintinnio *m* ⟨*pl* -ii⟩ tinkle, jingle
tinto *past part* → ***tingere***
tintoria *f* dry-cleaner's
tintura *f* dyeing; (*colorante*) dye; **~ *di iodio*** iodine
tipicamente *adv* typically
tipico *adj* ⟨*mpl* -ci⟩ typical
tipo *m* sort, kind, type; *infml fig* guy
tipografia *f* printing; *stabilimento* printer's
tipografico *adj* typographical
tipografo *m*, **-a** *f* printer
tipologia *f* typology
tip tap *m* ⟨*pl* tip tap⟩: ***ballare il ~*** tap-dance

tir *m* heavy goods vehicle, HGV
tiraggio *m* ⟨*pl* -ggi⟩ draught, *US* draft
tiralinee *m* ⟨*pl* tiralinee⟩ drawing pen
tiramisù *m* ⟨*pl* tiramisù⟩ tiramisù
tiranneggiare *v/t* ⟨1f⟩ tyrannize
tirannia *f* tyranny
tirannico *adj* ⟨*mpl* -ci⟩ tyrannical
tiranno **I** *adj* tyrannical **II** *m* tyrant
tirante *m* guy rope; BUILD tie beam
tirapiedi *m* ⟨*pl* tirapiedi⟩ *pej* stooge, minion
tirare ⟨1a⟩ **I** *v/t* **1.** pull; **~ *fuori*** take out; **~ *su*** *da terra* pick up; *bambino* bring up; **~ *giù*** take down; **~ *qc per le lunghe*** spin sth out; **~ *in ballo*** drag in **2.** (*tendere*) stretch **3.** (*lanciare*) throw **4.** (*sparare*) fire **5.** (*tracciare*) draw **II** *v/i* **1.** pull; **~ *a sorte*** draw lots **2.** *di abito* be too tight **3.** *di vento* blow **4.** (*sparare*) shoot **5.** **~ *avanti*** (*arrangiarsi*) get by, manage **6.** (*continuare*) keep going; **~ *dritto*** go straight on; **~ *via*** take off; **~ *a indovinare*** take a guess; ***con l'aria che tira …!*** the way things are going …!; **~ *sul prezzo*** haggle over the price
tirarsi *v/r*: **~ *indietro*** back off; *fig* back out; **~ *su*** cheer up, bounce back
tirata *f* pull, tug; *di sigaretta* drag; *fig* **~ *d'orecchie*** ear-bending
tiratardi *m/f* ⟨*pl* tiratardi⟩ night owl
tirato *adj* tight; *fig* haggard; **~ *per i capelli*** far-fetched; **~ *nello spendere*** tight-fisted
tiratore *m*, **-trice** *f* shot; **~ *scelto*** sharpshooter; ***franco* ~** sniper; POL *politician who secretly votes against his own party*
tiratura *f di libro* print run; *di giornale* circulation
tirchieria *f* stinginess
tirchio ⟨*mpl* -chi⟩ **I** *adj* mean, stingy *infml* **II** *m*, **-a** *f* miser, skinflint *infml*
tiremmolla *m* ⟨*pl* tiremmolla⟩ dithering
tiritera *f infml* rigmarole
tiro *m* **1.** (*lancio*) throw **2.** (*sparo*) shot; **~ *con l'arco*** archery; **~ *al piattello*** clay pigeon shooting; **~ *a segno*** target shooting; *luogo* rifle range; ***essere a* ~** be within range; ***essere a un* ~ *di schioppo*** be a stone's throw away; ***essere sotto* ~** be under fire (*a. fig*) **3.** *fig* ***un brutto* ~** a nasty trick
tirocinante *m/f* trainee
tirocinio *m* ⟨*pl* -ni⟩ training
tiroide *f* thyroid
tirolese *m/f & adj* Tyrolean, Tyrolese
Tirolo *m* Tyrol
tirrenico *adj* ⟨*mpl* -ci⟩ Tyrrhenian
tirreno *adj*: ***Mar Tirreno*** *m* Tyrrhenian Sea
tisana *f* herbal tea, tisane
tisi *f* ⟨*pl* tisi⟩ consumption
tisico *adj* ⟨*mpl* -ci⟩ MED consumptive
titanico *adj* ⟨*mpl* -ci⟩ titanic
titolare *m/f* owner
titolo *m* title; *dei giornali* headline; FIN security; **~ *a reddito fisso*** fixed income security; ***a* ~ *di*** as; **~ *di studio*** qualification; ***a* ~ *di cronaca*** (*or* ***d'informazione***) for information; ***-i*** *pl* ***di testa* / *coda*** FILM, TV opening / closing credits
titubante *adj* hesitant
titubanza *f* hesitancy, hesitation
titubare *v/i* ⟨1l⟩ hesitate
tivù *f* ⟨*pl* tivù⟩ *infml* telly
tizio *m*, **-a** *f*: ***un* ~** somebody, some man; ***una -a*** somebody, some woman
tizzone *m* firebrand
TMEC *abbr* (= **Tempo Medio dell'Europa Centrale**) Central European Time
TN *abbr* (= **Trento**) Trento
TO *abbr* (= **Torino**) Turin
toast *m* ⟨*pl* toast⟩ *toasted sandwich with ham and cheese*
toccante *adj* touching
toccare ⟨1d⟩ **I** *v/t* **1.** touch; **~ *ferro*** touch wood; **~ *il fondo*** touch the bottom **2.** (*riguardare*) concern, be about **II** *v/i* **1.** happen (***a*** to) **2.** ***gli tocca metà dell'eredità*** half the estate is going to him; ***tocca a me*** it's my turn **3.** ***mi tocca partire*** I must go, I have to go
toccarsi *v/r* ⟨1d⟩ feel oneself; *a vicenda* touch each other
toccasana *m* ⟨*pl* toccasana⟩ panacea
toccata *f* MUS toccata
tocco *m* ⟨*pl* -cchi⟩ touch (*a. fig*, MUS); PAINT stroke; *infml* piece; ***il* ~** one o'clock (in the afternoon)
toga *f* ⟨*pl* -ghe⟩ HIST toga; (*magistrato*) gown, robe
togato *adj* robed
togliere *v/t* ⟨3ss⟩ take (away), remove; (*eliminare*) take off; (*tirare fuori*) take out, remove; (*revocare*) lift, raise;

dente take out, extract; ***~ di mezzo*** get rid of; ***ciò non toglie che*** the fact remains that; ***tolgo il disturbo*** I'll get out of your way

togliersi *v/r giacca* take off, remove; (*spostarsi*) take o.s. off; ***~ dai piedi*** get out of the way; ***~ il cappello / gli occhiali*** take one's hat / glasses off; *fig* ***~ la maschera*** reveal oneself; ***~ qc dalla testa*** put an idea out of your mind; ***~ la vita*** take one's life; ***~ la voglia*** kick up one's heels; ***~ un dente*** have a tooth out; ***~ un peso dallo stomaco*** get sth out of one's system

Togo *m* Togo

togolese **I** *adj* Togolese **II** *m/f* Togolese

toh *int* (*tieni*) here!; (*beh*) well

toilette *f* ⟨*pl* toilette⟩ toilet; ***fare ~*** have a wash; ***andare alla ~*** go to the toilet

tolda *f* NAUT deck

tolgo → ***togliere***

tollerabile *adj* tolerable

tollerante *adj* tolerant

tolleranza *f* tolerance; ***casa*** *f* ***di ~*** (licensed) brothel

tollerare *v/t* ⟨1l & c⟩ tolerate

tolto *past part* → ***togliere***

tomaia *f di scarpa* upper

tomba *f* grave

tombarolo *m*, **-a** *f* graverobber

tombino *m* manhole

tombola *f* bingo; ***giocare a ~*** play bingo; ***fare ~*** win at bingo; *fig* hit the jackpot

tombolo *m* bolster; (*caduta*) tumble; ***lavorare al ~*** do lacemaking

tomino *m fresh cheese from Piedmont made with goat's or cow's milk*

tomo *m* tome

tomografia *f* MED tomography; ***~ assiale computerizzata*** computerized axial tomography

tonaca *f* ⟨*pl* -che⟩ habit

tonalità *f* ⟨*pl* tonalità⟩ tonality

tonante *adj* explosive

tondeggiante *adj* roundish

tondino *m* coaster

tondo *adj* round; (*grassoccio*) plump; ***chiaro e ~*** quite clearly

toner *m* ⟨*pl* toner⟩ toner

tonfo *m in acqua* splash; ***fare un ~*** take a tumble

tonico[1] *m* ⟨*pl* -ci⟩ tonic

tonico[2] *adj* ⟨*mpl* -ci⟩ (*in forma*) toned; *accento*: tonic

tonificante *adj aria, passeggiata* bracing; *per la pelle* toning

tonificare *v/t* ⟨1m & d⟩ tone up

tonificarsi *v/r* ⟨1m & d⟩ become toned

tonnara *f* tuna nets *pl*

tonnato *adj*: ***salsa*** *f* ***-a*** tuna mayonnaise

tonnellata *f* tonne

tonno *m* tuna

tono *m* tone; ***darsi un ~*** give oneself airs; ***rispondere a ~*** (*a proposito*) answer to the point; *per le rime* answer back

tonsille *fpl* ANAT tonsils *pl*

tonsillite *f* tonsillitis

tonsura *f* tonsure

tonto *adj* thickheaded; ***fare il finto ~*** act stupid

top *m* ⟨*pl* top⟩ SEW sleeveless top; *infml* top

topaia *f* rathole; *fig* dump

topazio *m* ⟨*pl* -zi⟩ topaz

topica *f* ⟨*pl* -che⟩ topic; (*gaffe*) faux-pas

topicida *m* ⟨*pl* -i⟩ rat poison

topico *adj* ⟨*mpl* -ci⟩ topical

topless *m* ⟨*pl* topless⟩ topless

top model *f* ⟨*pl* top model⟩ supermodel

topo *m* mouse; ***~ d'albergo*** someone who steals from luxury hotels; *fig* ***~ d'auto*** someone who steals from cars; ***~ di biblioteca*** bookworm

topografia *f* topography

topografico *adj* ⟨*mpl* -ci⟩ topographical

Topolino *m* Mickey Mouse

topologia *f* GEOG topology; GRAM word order; ***~ delle reti*** COMPUT network topology

toponimo *m* place name

toponomastica *f* ⟨*pl* -che⟩ toponymy

toporagno *m* ZOOL shrew

toppa *f* (*serratura*) keyhole; (*rattoppo*) patch

toppare *v/t* ⟨1a⟩ *infml* stop; (*arrestare*) arrest

top secret *adj inv* top secret

torace *m* chest

toracico *adj* ⟨*mpl* -ci⟩ thoracic; ***cavità*** *f* ***-a*** chest cavity

torba *f* peat
torbidezza *f*, **torbidità** *f* cloudiness; *fig* murkiness
torbido *adj liquid* cloudy; ***pescare nel ~*** fish in troubled waters
torbiera *f* peat bog
torcere *v/t* ⟨3d⟩ twist; *biancheria* wring; ***~ la bocca*** purse one's lips; ***~ il naso*** turn one's nose up; ***non ~ un capello a qn*** not harm a hair on s.o.'s head
torcersi *v/r*: ***~ dal dolore*** writhe in pain; ***~ dalle risa*** double up with laughter
torchiare *v/t* ⟨1k & c⟩ squeeze, press; *fig* give the third degree
torchio *m* ⟨*pl* -chi⟩ press; ***mettere sotto ~ qn*** put s.o. through the mill
torcia *f* ⟨*pl* -ce⟩ torch; ***~ elettrica*** *Br* torch, *US* flashlight
torcicollo *m* stiff neck
tordo *m* thrush
torello *m* ZOOL bullock
torero *m* bullfighter
torinese I *adj* of Turin, Turin *attr* **II** *m/f* person from Turin
Torino *f* Turin
tormalina *f* tourmaline
tormenta *f* snowstorm
tormentare *v/t* ⟨1a⟩ torment
tormentarsi *v/r* torment o.s.
tormentato *adj* anguished; ***scelta -a*** difficult choice
tormento *m* torment
tormentone *m* pest
tornaconto *m* benefit
tornado *m* tornado
tornante *m* hairpin bend
tornare *v/i* ⟨1a⟩ **1.** *venire* come back, return; *andare* go back, return; ***~ a fare / dire qc*** do / say sth again; ***ben tornato!*** welcome back!; ***~ in sé*** come to one's senses; ***~ in mente*** come back to mind; ***~ di moda*** come back into fashion; ***il conto non torna*** it doesn't add up (*a. fig*); ***vado e torno*** I'm going there and back **2.** (*quadrare*) balance **3.** ***~ utile*** prove useful
tornasole *m* ⟨*pl* tornasole⟩ litmus
torneo *m* tournament; ***Torneo delle Sei Nazioni*** Six Nations Cup
tornio *m* ⟨*pl* -ni⟩ lathe
tornire *v/t* ⟨4d⟩ turn (*a.* METAL); *fig* polish
tornito *adj* turned, shaped
toro *m* bull; ARCH torus; ASTROL ***Toro*** Taurus
torpedine *m* ZOOL electric ray
torpediniera *f* MIL torpedo boat
torpedone *m* coach
torpore *m* torpor
torre *f* tower; *scacchi* castle; ***~ di Babele*** Tower of Babel; ***~ di controllo*** control tower; ***la ~ di Pisa*** Tower of Pisa; ***le Torri Gemelle*** the Twin Towers; *fig* ***chiudersi in una ~ d'avorio*** shut oneself up in an ivory tower
torrefare *v/t* ⟨3aa⟩ roast
torrefazione *f* roasting
torreggiare *v/i* ⟨1f⟩ tower (***su*** over)
torrente *m* stream
torrenziale *adj* torrential; ***pioggia*** *f* ***~*** torrential rain
torretta *f* turret; NAUT, AVIAT, MIL gun turret
torrido *adj* torrid
torrione *m* keep; NAUT turret mast
torrone *m* nougat
torsione *f* twisting; TECH torsion
torso *m* torso; ***a ~ nudo*** naked to the waist
torsolo *m* core
torta *f* cake
tortellini *mpl* tortellini *sg*
tortiera *f* cake tin
tortino *m*: ***~ di pesce*** fishcake; *cotto in forno* (individual) pie
torto *m* wrong; ***aver ~*** be wrong; ***a ~*** wrongly
tortora *f* turtledove
tortuosità *f* ⟨*pl* tortuosità⟩ deviousness (*a. fig*)
tortuoso *adj* (*sinuoso*) winding; (*ambiguo*) devious
tortura *f* torture
torturare *v/t* ⟨1a⟩ torture
torturarsi *v/r* ⟨1a⟩ torture oneself
torturatore *m*, **-trice** *f* torturer
torvo *adj sguardo* dark, black
tosacani *m/f* ⟨*pl* tosacani⟩ dog clipper
tosaerba *f or m* lawnmower
tosare *v/t* ⟨1a⟩ *pecore* shear
tosatura *f* shearing
Toscana *f* Tuscany
toscano *adj* Tuscan
tosse *f* cough; ***~ canina*** whooping cough; ***avere la ~*** have a cough
tossicchiare *v/i* ⟨1k⟩ clear one's throat

tossicità *f* ⟨*pl* tossicità⟩ toxicity
tossico ⟨*mpl* -ci⟩ **I** *adj* toxic **II** *m*, **-a** *f infml* druggie *infml*
tossicodipendente *m/f* drug addict
tossicodipendenza *f* drug addiction
tossicologia *f* toxicology
tossicologo *m*, **-a** *f* ⟨*mpl* -gi⟩ toxicologist
tossicomane *m/f* drug addict
tossina *f* toxin
tossire *v/i* ⟨4a & d⟩ cough
tostapane *m* toaster
tostare *v/t* ⟨1c⟩ *pane* toast; *caffè* roast
tosto *adj infml* great; ***avere la faccia -a*** have the nerve
tot I *adj* so many **II** *pron* so much
totale *m/adj* total
totalità *f* (*interezza*) entirety, totality; ***nella ~ dei casi*** in all cases
totalitario *adj* ⟨*mpl* -ri⟩ totalitarian
totalitarismo *m* totalitarianism
totalizzare *v/t* ⟨1a⟩ total
totalizzatore *m* totalizator, tote
totano *m* squid
totem *m* ⟨*pl* totem⟩ totem
totip *m competition similar to football pools, based on horse racing*
totocalcio *m competition similar to football pools*
totonero *m illegal system of football pools*
toupet *m* ⟨*pl* toupet⟩ toupee
tour de force *m* tour de force
tournée *f* ⟨*pl* tournée⟩ tour
tour operator *m/f* ⟨*pl* tour operator⟩ tour operator
tovaglia *f* tablecloth
tovagliolo *m* napkin, serviette
tozzo I *adj* stocky **II** *m di pane* crust; ***per un ~ di pane*** for next to nothing
TP *abbr* (= **Trapani**) Trapani
TR *abbr* (= **Terni**) Terni
tra *prep* → ***fra***
traballante *adj* wobbly
traballare *v/i* ⟨1a⟩ stagger; *mobile* wobble
trabiccolo *m* broken-down old thing; (*auto*) boneshaker
traboccare *v/i* ⟨1d⟩ overflow (*a. fig*)
trabocchetto *m* trapdoor; ***domanda*** *f* **~** trick question; ***tendere un ~ a qn*** set s.o. a trap
tracagnotto *adj* stocky
tracannare *v/t* ⟨1a⟩ put away
traccia *f* ⟨*pl* -cce⟩ (*orma*) footprint; *di veicolo* track; (*indizio*) clue; (*segno*) trace; (*abbozzo*) sketch
tracciabilità *f* ⟨*pl* tracciabilità⟩: ***la ~ di un prodotto*** COMM a product's trackability
tracciante *adj* tracing; ***proiettile*** *m* **~** tracer bullet
tracciare *v/t* ⟨1f⟩ *linea* draw; (*delineare*) outline; (*abbozzare*) sketch
tracciato *m* layout
trachea *f* windpipe
tracheotomia *f* MED tracheotomy
Tracia *f* Thrace
tracimare *v/i* ⟨1a⟩ overflow
tracimazione *f* flooding
tracio *adj* ⟨*mpl* -ci⟩ Thracian
tracolla *f* (shoulder) strap; ***a ~*** slung over one's shoulder; ***borsa*** *f* ***a ~*** shoulder bag
tracollo *m* collapse
tracotante *adj* impertinent
tracotanza *f* impertinence
tradimento *m* betrayal; POL treason; ***a ~*** treacherously
tradire *v/t* ⟨4d⟩ betray; *coniuge* be unfaithful to; ***~ la fiducia di qn*** betray s.o.'s trust
tradirsi *v/r* give o.s. away
traditore I *adj* (*infedele*) unfaithful **II** *m*, **-trice** *f* traitor
tradizionale *adj* traditional
tradizionalista ⟨*mpl* -i⟩ **I** *adj* traditionalist **II** *m/f* traditionalist
tradizione *f* tradition
tradotta *f* MIL troop train
tradotto *past part* → ***tradurre***
traducibile *adj* translatable
tradurre *v/t* ⟨3e⟩ translate; ***~ in inglese*** translate into English; ***~ un detenuto*** transfer a prisoner
traduttore *m*, **-trice** *f* translator; ***~ giurato*** sworn translator
traduzione *f* translation
trafelato *adj* breathless
trafficante *m/f pej* dealer; ***~ di droga*** drug dealer
trafficare *v/i* ⟨1l & d⟩ deal, trade (***in*** in); *pej* traffic (***in*** in); (*armeggiare*) tinker; (*affaccendarsi*) bustle about
trafficato *adj strada* busy
traffico *m* ⟨*pl* -chi *and* -ci⟩ traffic; ***~ aereo*** air traffic; ***~ stradale*** road traffic; ***densità*** *f* ***del ~*** volume of traffic
trafficone *m*, **-a** *f pej* trafficker
trafiggere *v/t* ⟨3cc⟩ pierce (*a. fig*)

trafila *f* procedure; MECH die
trafilare *v/t* ⟨1a⟩ MECH draw out
trafiletto *m* paragraph
trafitto *past part* → ***trafiggere***
traforare *v/t* ⟨1a⟩: ***~ qc*** pierce sth
traforo *m* tunnel
trafugamento *m* theft, stealing
trafugare *v/t* ⟨1c⟩ steal
tragedia *f* tragedy
traghettamento *m* ferrying
traghettare *v/t* ⟨1a⟩ ferry
traghetto *m* ferry
tragicamente *adv* tragically
tragico *adj* ⟨*mpl* -ci⟩ tragic; ***il ~ è che ...*** *infml* the pity of it is that ...
tragicomico *adj* ⟨*mpl* -ci⟩ tragicomic
tragicommedia *f* tragicomedy (*a. fig*)
tragitto *m* journey
traguardo *m* finishing line; ***arrivare al ~*** reach the finishing post; *fig* reach one's goal
traiettoria *f* trajectory
trainante *adj* driving
trainare *v/t* ⟨1l⟩ (*rimorchiare*) tow; *di animali* pull, draw
trainer *m* ⟨*pl* trainer⟩ trainer
training *m* ⟨*pl* training⟩ training; ***~ autogeno*** self-generated training
traino *m* towing; *veicolo* vehicle on tow; ***a ~*** on tow; ***fare da ~*** be the driving force
tralasciare *v/t* ⟨1f⟩ (*omettere*) omit, leave out; (*interrompere*) interrupt
tralcio *m* ⟨*pl* -ci⟩ vine branch
traliccio *m* ⟨*pl* -cci⟩ ELEC pylon; TECH trellis
tralice *adj*: ***in*** *or* ***di ~*** sidelong
tram *m* ⟨*pl* tram⟩ tram; ***attaccati al ~!*** *infml* you can whistle for it!
trama *f fig* plot
tramaglio *m* ⟨*pl* -gli⟩ trammel
tramandare *v/t* ⟨1a⟩ hand down
tramandarsi *v/r* ⟨1a⟩ be passed down
tramare *v/t* ⟨1a⟩ *fig* plot
trambusto *m* (*confusione*) bustle; (*tumulto*) uproar, commotion
tramestio *m* ⟨*pl* -ii⟩ bustle
tramezzino *m* sandwich
tramezzo *m* partition
tramite **I** *m* (*collegamento*) link; (*intermediario*) go-between; ***fare da ~*** mediate **II** *prep* through
tramoggia *f* ⟨*pl* -gge⟩ hopper
tramontana *f* north wind
tramontare *v/t* ⟨1a⟩ set
tramonto *m* sunset; *fig* decline; ***al ~*** at sunset
tramortire *v/t* ⟨4d⟩ knock out
tramortito *adj* knocked out
trampoliere *m* wader
trampolino *m* diving board; *sci* ski jump
trampolo *m* stilt (*a. hum*); ***camminare sui -i*** walk on stilts
tramutare *v/t* ⟨1a⟩: ***~ qn / qc in qc*** transform s.o. / sth into sth
tramutarsi *v/r* ⟨1a⟩ turn into
trance *f* ⟨*pl* trance⟩ trance; ***andare in ~*** go into a trance
trancia *f* ⟨*pl* -ce⟩ COOK slice
tranciare *v/t* ⟨1f⟩ sever; METAL mill; COOK slice
tranello *m* trap
trangugiare *v/t* ⟨1f⟩ guzzle; *fig* swallow
tranne *prep* except
tranquillamente *adv* calmly, peacefully; (*senza pericolo*) safely; (*senza difficoltà*) easily
tranquillante *m* tranquil(l)izer
tranquillità *f* peacefulness, tranquillity; ***in tutta ~*** safely
tranquillizzante *adj* reassuring
tranquillizzare *v/t* ⟨1a⟩: ***~ qn*** set s.o.'s mind at rest
tranquillo *adj* calm, peaceful; ***avere la coscienza -a*** have a clear conscience
transalpino *adj* transalpine
transatlantico ⟨*mpl* -ci⟩ **I** *adj* transatlantic **II** *m* liner
transazione *f* JUR settlement; FIN transaction
transenna *f* barrier
transennare *v/t* ⟨1b⟩ cordon off
transessuale **I** *adj* transsexual **II** *m/f* transsexual
transetto *m* ARCH transept
transfer *m* ⟨*pl* transfer⟩ transfer
transfert *m* ⟨*pl* transfert⟩ PSYCH transference
transfuga *m/f* ⟨*mpl* -ghi⟩ *liter* defector
transgenico *adj* ⟨*mpl* -ci⟩ genetically modified
transiberiana *f* Trans-Siberian railway
transigere ⟨3w⟩ **I** *v/t* settle **II** *v/i* compromise
Transilvania *f* Transylvania
transilvano *adj* Transylvanian
transistor *m* ⟨*pl* transistor⟩ transistor
transitabile *adj strada* passable

transitabilità *f* ⟨*pl* transitabilità⟩ practicability

transitare *v/t* ⟨1l⟩ pass

transitivo *adj* GRAM transitive

transito *m* transit; ***divieto di ~*** no thoroughfare

transitorietà *f* ⟨*pl* transitorietà⟩ transience

transitorio *adj* ⟨*mpl* -ri⟩ transitory

transizione *f* transition

transoceanico *adj* ⟨*mpl* -ci⟩ ocean *attr*

transumanza *f* transhumance

transustanziazione *f* REL transubstantiation

trantran *m infml* routine

tranviario *adj* ⟨*mpl* -ri⟩ tram *attr*

tranviere *m*, **-a** *f* (*manovratore*) tram driver; (*controllore*) tram conductor

trapanare *v/t* ⟨1l⟩ drill

trapanazione *f* drilling

trapanese **I** *adj* from Trapani **II** *m/f* person from Trapani

trapano *m* drill; ***~ a percussione*** percussion drill

trapassare *v/t* ⟨1a⟩ penetrate (*a. fig*)

trapassato *m*: ***~ prossimo / remoto*** GRAM past perfect

trapasso *m* passage

trapelare *v/i* ⟨1a⟩ leak out (*a. fig*); *luce* filter through

trapezio *m* ⟨*pl* -zi⟩ trapeze; MATH trapezium; ANAT trapezius

trapezista *m/f* ⟨*mpl* -i⟩ trapeze artist

trapiantare *v/t* ⟨1a⟩ transplant

trapianto *m* transplant

trappola *f* trap

trapunta *f* quilt

trapuntato *adj* quilted; ***giacca f -a*** quilted jacket

trarre *v/t* ⟨3xx⟩ *conclusioni* draw; *vantaggio* derive; ***tratto da un libro di*** taken from a book by

trasalire *v/i* ⟨4m⟩ jump

trasandato *adj* scruffy; *lavoro* slipshod

trasbordare *v/t* ⟨1a⟩ transfer

trasbordo *m* transfer

trascendentale *adj* transcendental

trascendere ⟨3c⟩ **I** *v/t* go beyond; PHIL transcend **II** *v/i* go too far

trascinamento *m* dragging

trascinare *v/t* ⟨1a⟩ drag; (*travolgere*) sweep away; *fig* (*entusiasmare*) carry away

trascinarsi *v/r* ⟨1a⟩ crawl; *fig* drag on

trascorrere ⟨3o⟩ **I** *v/t* spend **II** *v/i* pass, go by

trascorso *past part* → ***trascorrere***

trascritto *past part* → ***trascrivere***

trascrivere *v/t* ⟨3tt⟩ transcribe

trascrizione *f* transcription

trascurabile *adj* unimportant

trascurare *v/t* ⟨1a⟩ neglect; (*tralasciare*) ignore; ***~ di fare qc*** fail to do sth

trascuratezza *f* negligence

trascurato *adj* careless, negligent; (*trasandato*) slovenly; (*ignorato*) neglected

trasduttore *m* ELEC transducer

trasecolare *v/i* ⟨1m & b⟩ be amazed

trasferibile *adj* transferable

trasferibilità *f* ⟨*pl* trasferibilità⟩ transferability; *di persona* flexibility; COMM, JUR negotiability

trasferimento *m* transfer; ***~ di chiamata*** TEL call diversion; ***~ di file*** COMPUT file transfer

trasferire *v/t* ⟨4d⟩ transfer

trasferirsi *v/r* move

trasferta *f* transfer; SPORTS away game

trasfigurarsi *v/r* ⟨1a⟩ become transfigured

trasfigurazione *f* Transfiguration; *fig* transformation

trasformare *v/t* ⟨1a⟩ transform; TECH process; *nel rugby* convert

trasformarsi *v/r* change, turn (***in*** into)

trasformatore **I** *adj* transforming **II** *n*: ***trasformatore*** *m* transformer

trasformazione *f* transformation

trasformista *m/f* ⟨*mpl* -i⟩ quick-change artist; *infml politician who changes allegiance*

trasfusione *f* transfusion

trasgredire *v/t* ⟨4d⟩ disobey

trasgressione *f* disobedience

trasgressività *f* ⟨*pl* trasgressività⟩ subversiveness

trasgressivo *adj* subversive

trasgressore *m*, **-ditrice** *f* transgressor

traslato *adj* figurative; ***in senso m ~*** metaphorically

traslazione *f* translation (*a.* REL); ECON, JUR transfer

traslocare *v/t & v/i* ⟨1c & d⟩ move

trasloco *m* ⟨*pl* -chi⟩ move

traslucido *adj* translucent

trasmettere *v/t* ⟨3ee⟩ pass on; RADIO, TV broadcast, transmit; JUR *diritti* transfer

trasmettitore *m* sender; RADIO, ELEC transmitter

trasmigrare *v/i* ⟨1a⟩ transmigrate

trasmigrazione *f* transmigration

trasmissibile *adj* transmissible

trasmissibilità *f* ⟨*pl* trasmissibilità⟩ transmissibility

trasmissione *f* transmission; RADIO, TV broadcast, transmission; (*programma*) programme, *US* program; RADIO, TV **~ *in diretta*** live broadcast; COMPUT **~ *dati*** data transmission

trasmittente *f* transmitter

trasognato *adj* dreamy

trasparente **I** *adj* transparent **II** *m* transparency

trasparenza *f* transparency

trasparire *v/i* ⟨4d⟩ show through; *fig* ***non lasciar ~ nulla*** not let anything show

traspirare ⟨1a⟩ **I** *v/i* perspire **II** *v/t* exude

traspirazione *f* perspiration

trasporre *v/t* ⟨3ll⟩ transpose

trasportabile *adj* transportable; *malato* movable

trasportare *v/t* ⟨1c⟩ transport

trasportatore **I** *adj* transporting; ***nastro*** *m* **~** conveyor belt **II** *n*: ***trasportatore*** *m* carrier; TECH conveyor

trasporto *m* transport; **~ *combinato rotaia-strada*** piggyback transport; ***-i*** *pl* ***pubblici*** public transport *sg*; ***fare qc con ~*** do sth with feeling

trasposizione *f* transposition

trastullare *v/t* ⟨1a⟩: **~ *qn*** amuse s.o.

trastullarsi *v/r* ⟨1a⟩ play

trastullo *m* pastime; (*giocattolo*) toy

trasudare ⟨1a⟩ **I** *v/i* ooze **II** *v/t* ooze with

trasversale **I** *adj* transverse **II** *f* MATH transversal

trasvolare *v/t* ⟨1a⟩ *oceano* fly across; *montagne* fly over

trasvolata *f* non-stop flight

tratta *f* trade; FIN draft; **~ *delle bianche*** white slave trade

trattabile *adj prezzo* negotiable; *persona* tractable

trattamento *m* treatment

trattare ⟨1a⟩ **I** *v/t* treat; TECH treat, process; FIN deal in; (*negoziare*) negotiate **II** *v/i* deal; **~ *di*** be about; FIN **~ *in*** deal in

trattarsi *v/r*: ***di che si tratta?*** what's it about?

trattative *fpl* negotiations *pl*, talks *pl*

trattato *m* treatise; JUR, POL treaty; **~ *di pace*** peace treaty

trattazione *f di un argomento* coverage

tratteggiare *v/t* ⟨1f⟩ sketch; (*ombreggiare*) shade; *fig* outline

tratteggio *m* ⟨*pl* -ggi⟩ dotted line; (*ombreggiatura*) shading

trattenere *v/t* ⟨2q⟩ (*far restare*) keep, hold; (*far perder tempo*) hold up; (*frenare*) restrain; *fiato, respiro* hold; *lacrime* hold back; *somma* withhold

trattenersi *v/r* (*rimanere*) stay; (*frenarsi*) restrain o.s.; **~ *dal fare qc*** refrain from doing sth

trattenimento *m* entertainment

trattenuta *f* deduction

trattino *m* dash; *in parole composte* hyphen

tratto **I** *past part* → ***trarre*** **II** *m di spazio, tempo* stretch; *di penna* stroke; (*linea*) line; ***a un ~*** all of a sudden; ***-i*** *pl* (*lineamenti*) features; ***a -i*** at intervals

trattore *m* tractor

trattoria *f* restaurant

trauma *m* ⟨*pl* -i⟩ trauma

traumatico *adj* ⟨*mpl* -ci⟩ traumatic

traumatizzare *v/t* ⟨1a⟩ traumatize (*a. fig*)

traumatologia *f* traumatology

traumatologico *adj* ⟨*mpl* -ci⟩ trauma *attr*; ***reparto*** *m* **~** trauma ward

traumatologo *m*, **-a** *f* ⟨*mpl* -gi⟩ traumatologist

travaglio *m*: MED **~ *di parto*** labo(u)r

travasare *v/t* ⟨1a⟩ decant

travaso *m* decanting; MED extravasation

travatura *f* BUILD beams *pl*

trave *f* beam

traveggole *fpl*: ***avere le ~*** be seeing things

traversa *f* side road

traversare *v/t* ⟨1b⟩ cross

traversata *f* crossing

traversie *fpl* hardships

traversina *f* sleeper

traverso *adj*: ***flauto*** *m* **~** flute; ***andare di ~*** *di cibi* go down the wrong way;

per vie -e by devious means
travestimento *m* disguise
travestire *v/t* ⟨4b⟩ disguise
travestirsi *v/r* disguise o.s., dress up (***da*** as)
travestito *m* transvestite
traviare *v/t* ⟨1h⟩ lead astray
travisamento *m* distortion
travisare *v/t* ⟨1a⟩ distort
travolgente *adj fig* overwhelming
travolgere *v/t* ⟨3d⟩ carry away (*a. fig*); *con un veicolo* run over
travolto *past part* → ***travolgere***
trazione *f* TECH traction; AUTO **~ *anteriore* / *posteriore*** front- / rear-wheel drive
tre *num* three
trebbia *f* threshing
trebbiano *m* COOK *dry white wine made in central and nothern Italy*
trebbiare *v/t* ⟨1k⟩ AGR thresh
trebbiatrice *f* threshing machine
treccia *f* ⟨*pl* -cce⟩ plait
trecento I *adj* three hundred **II** *m*: ***il Trecento*** the fourteenth century
tredicenne *m/f* thirteen-year-old
tredicesimo *m/adj* thirteenth
tredici *num* thirteen
tregua *f* truce; *fig* break, let-up; ***senza*** **~** ceaselessly
trekking *m* hiking
tremante *adj* trembling, shaking
tremare *v/i* ⟨1b⟩ tremble, shake (***di, per*** with)
tremarella *f* shivers *pl*; ***avere la*** **~** have the shakes, *infml* have the heebie-jeebies
tremebondo *adj* trembling; *fig* frightened
tremendo *adj* terrible
trementina *f* turpentine
tremila *num* three thousand
tremito *m* tremble; *fig* quiver
tremolante *adj* trembling; *luce* twinkling; *fiamma* flickering
tremolare *v/i* ⟨1l & b⟩ tremble; *luce* twinkle; *fiamma* flicker
tremolio *m* ⟨*pl* -ii⟩ trembling; *di luce* twinkling; *di fiamma* flickering
tremore *m* trembling; MED tremor
trench *m* ⟨*pl* trench⟩ trench coat
trend *m* ⟨*pl* trend⟩ trend
trenette *fpl*: **~ *al pesto*** *long thin pasta strips with pesto*
trenino *m* miniature train, toy train
treno *m* train; **~ *intercity*** intercity train; **~ *merci*** goods train; ***in*** **~** by train
trenta *num* thirty
trentenne *m/f & adj* thirty-year-old
trentennio *m* ⟨*pl* -nni⟩ thirty-year period
trentesimo *m/adj* thirtieth
trentina *f*: ***una*** **~** about thirty; ***essere sulla*** **~** be about thirty, be in one's thirties
Trentino-Alto Adige *m* Trentino-Alto Adige
Trento *f* Trento
trepidante *adj* anxious
trepidare *v/i* ⟨1l & b⟩ be anxious
treppiede ⟨*pl* treppiedi⟩ *m* trivet; PHOT tripod
trequarti *m* ⟨*pl* trequarti⟩ three-quarter length coat
treruote *m* ⟨*pl* treruote⟩ three-wheeler
tresca *f* ⟨*pl* -sche⟩ intrigue; *amorosa* affair
trespolo *m* stand
trevisano I *adj* from Treviso **II** *m*, **-a** *f* person from Treviso
triade *f* triad (*a.* CHEM, MUS)
triangolare *adj* triangular
triangolo *m* triangle; AUTO warning triangle
triat(h)lon *m* ⟨*pl* triat(h)lon⟩ triathlon
tribale *adj* tribal; ***usanze*** *fpl* ***-i*** tribal customs
tribolare *v/i* ⟨1l⟩ suffer; ***far*** **~ *qn*** cause s.o. pain
tribolato *adj* tormented
tribolazione *f* tribulation
tribordo *m* starboard
tribù *f* ⟨*pl* tribù⟩ tribe
tribuna *f* platform
tribunale *m* court; **~ *per i minorenni*** juvenile court
tribuno *m* tribune; *fig* demagogue
tributare *v/t* ⟨1a⟩ pay
tributaria *f tax and excise police*
tributario *adj* ⟨*mpl* -ri⟩ tax
tributarista *m/f* ⟨*mpl* -i⟩ tax expert
tributo *m* tax; *fig* tribute
tricheco *m* ⟨*pl* -chi⟩ walrus
triciclo *m* tricycle
tricolore I *adj* tricolo(u)r(ed) **II** *m* tricolo(u)r
tricorno *m* three-cornered hat
tridente *m* trident

tridentino *adj* Tridentine
tridimensionale *adj* three-dimensional
triennale *adj contratto, progetto* three-year; *mostra, festival* three-yearly
triennio *m* ⟨*pl* -nni⟩ three-year period
Trieste *f* Trieste
triestino *adj* of Trieste, Trieste *attr*
trifase *adj inv* ELEC three-phase; ***corrente** f* **~** three-phase current
trifoglio *m* ⟨*pl* -gli⟩ clover
trifolato *adj* cooked in oil, garlic, and parsley
trifora I *adj* mullioned with three lights **II** *f* triple lancet window
trigemino *adj*: ***parto*** *m* **~** triplet birth; ***nervo*** *m* **~** trigeminal nerve
triglia *f* red mullet
trigonometria *f* trigonometry
trilaterale *adj* trilateral
trillare *v/i* ⟨1a⟩ trill
trillo *m* trill (*a.* MUS)
trilogia *f* trilogy
trim. *abbr* (= **trimestre**) term
trimestrale *adj* quarterly
trimestre *m* quarter; EDU term
trina *f* lace
trincare *v/t* ⟨1d⟩ *infml* knock back
trincea *f* trench
trinceramento *m* entrenchment (*a. fig*)
trincerare *v/t* ⟨1b⟩ entrench
trincerarsi *v/r* entrench o.s.
trincetto *m* skiving knife
trinchetto *m* foremast
trinciare *v/t* ⟨1f⟩ cut up, chop
Trinità *f* Trinity
trio *m* trio
trionfale *adj* triumphal
trionfante *adj* triumphant
trionfare *v/i* ⟨1a⟩ triumph (***su*** over)
trionfatore I *adj* triumphing **II** *m*, **-trice** *f* winner
trionfo *m* triumph
tripartire *v/t* ⟨4d⟩ divide into three
tripartitico *adj* ⟨*mpl* -ci⟩ POL tripartite
tripletta *f* SPORTS hat trick
triplicare *v/t* ⟨1l & d⟩ triple
triplice *adj* triple; ***in ~ copia*** in triplicate
triplo I *adj* triple **II** *m*: ***il ~*** three times as much (***di*** as)
trippa *f* tripe
tripudio *m* ⟨*pl* -di⟩ jubilation
tris *m* ⟨*pl* tris⟩ *gioco delle carte* three-of-a-kind; ***un ~ d'assi*** three aces *pl*
triste *adj* sad
tristezza *f* sadness
tritacarne *m* ⟨*pl* tritacarne⟩ mincer
tritaghiaccio *m* ⟨*pl* tritaghiaccio⟩ ice crusher
tritare *v/t* ⟨1a⟩ mince
tritato I *adj aglio* chopped; *carne* minced **II** *m*: ***~ d'aglio*** chopped garlic
tritatutto *m* ⟨*pl* tritatutto⟩ mincer
trito *adj* minced; *fig* ***~ e ritrito*** rehashed
tritone *m* MYTH Triton; ZOOL newt
trittico *m* ⟨*pl* -ci⟩ triptych
triturare *v/t* ⟨1a⟩ grind
triturazione *f* grinding
triumvirato *m* triumvirate
trivella *f* drill
trivellare *v/t* ⟨1b⟩ drill
trivellazione *f* drilling
triviale *adj* trivial
trofeo *m* trophy
troglodita *m/f* ⟨*mpl* -i⟩ troglodyte (*a. fig*)
trogloditico *adj* ⟨*mpl* -ci⟩ troglodytic (*a. fig*)
trogolo *m* trough
troia *f sl* sow; *vulg* whore
Troia *f* Troy
troiano I *adj* Trojan **II** *m*, **-a** *f* Trojan
troika *f* troika
trolley *m* ⟨*pl* trolley⟩ trolley
tromba *f* MUS trumpet; AUTO horn; ***~ d'aria*** whirlwind; ***~ delle scale*** stairwell
trombettiere *m* trumpeter
trombettista *m/f* ⟨*mpl* -i⟩ trumpet player
trombo *m* MED thrombus
trombocita *m* ⟨*pl* -i⟩ ANAT thrombocyte
trombone *m* trombone; BOT wild daffodil
trombosi *f* thrombosis
troncamento *m* breaking off (*a. fig*)
troncare *v/t* ⟨1d⟩ cut off; *fig* break off
troncarsi *v/r* ⟨1d⟩ be broken off
tronchesina *f infml* nail clippers *pl*
tronco[1] *m* ⟨*pl* -chi⟩ ANAT, BOT trunk; RAIL section; ***licenziare in ~*** fire on the spot *or* there and then
tronco[2] *adj* ⟨*mpl* -chi⟩ cut-off; GEOM truncated; LING *fig* incomplete
troncone *m* stump
troneggiare *v/i* ⟨1f⟩ dominate; *fig*

hold court
tronfio *adj* ⟨*mpl* -fi⟩ pompous; *fig* over-blown
trono *m* throne; ***salire al ~*** come to the throne
tropicale *adj* tropical
tropici *mpl* tropics *pl*
tropico *m* ⟨*pl* -ci⟩ tropic; ***~ del Cancro*** Tropic of Cancer
troposfera *f* troposphere
troppo **I** *adj* too much; ***-i*** *pl* too many; ***c'era -a gente*** there were too many people; ***-e difficoltà*** *fpl* too many difficulties **II** *adv* too much; ***non ~*** not too much; ***è ~ tardi*** it's too late; ***costa ~*** it costs too much; ***è ~ bello per essere vero*** it's too good to be true **III** *pron* too much; ***siete in -i*** there are too many of you; ***sentirsi di ~*** feel in the way
trota *f* trout
trottare *v/i* ⟨1c⟩ trot; SPORTS harness racing
trotto *m* trot
trottola *f* (spinning) top
troupe *f* ⟨*pl* troupe⟩ troupe; THEAT, FILM crew
trousse *f* ⟨*pl* trousse⟩ make-up bag
trovare *v/t* ⟨1c⟩ find; (*inventare*) find, come up with; ***andare a ~ qn*** (go and) see s.o.; ***chi cerca trova*** *prov* seek and you shall find; ***paese che vai, usanze che trovi*** *prov* when in Rome, do as the Romans do
trovarsi *v/r* be; ***~ bene*** be happy
trovata *f* good idea
trovatello *m*, **-a** *f* foundling
trovatore *m* troubadour
truccare *v/t* ⟨1d⟩ make up; *motore* soup up; *partita*, *elezioni* fix
truccarsi *v/r* put on one's make-up
truccato *adj* made-up; ***carte*** *fpl* ***-e*** marked cards
truccatore *m*, **-trice** *f* make-up artist
trucco *m* ⟨*pl* -cchi⟩ make-up; (*inganno, astuzia*) trick
truce *adj* fierce; (*crudele*) cruel
trucidare *v/t* ⟨1l⟩ massacre
truciolare *adj* chipboard; ***pannello*** *m* ***~*** chipboard panel
truciolato *m* chipboard
truciolo *m* shaving
truculento *adj* truculent
truffa *f* fraud; ***~ aggravata*** aggravated fraud
truffaldino *adj* fraudulent
truffare *v/t* ⟨1a⟩ defraud (***di*** of)
truffatore *m*, **-trice** *f* trickster, con artist *infml*
trullo *m in Puglia, a small round house made of stone with a conical roof*
truppa *f* troops *pl*; *fig* horde
TS *abbr* (= **Trieste**) Trieste
T-shirt *f* ⟨*pl* T-shirt⟩ T-shirt
tsunami *m* ⟨*pl* tsunami⟩ tsunami
tu *pron* you; ***dammi del tu*** call me 'tu'; ***sei ~?*** is that you?
tua → ***tuo***
Tuareg *mpl* Tuareg
tuba *f* tuba
tubare *v/i* ⟨1a⟩ coo; *fig* bill and coo
tubatura *f*, **tubazione** *f* pipes *pl*, piping
tubercolo *m* tubercle
tubercolosi *f* tuberculosis
tubercolotico ⟨*mpl* -ci⟩ **I** *adj* tubercular **II** *m*, **-a** *f* person with tuberculosis
tubero *m* tuber
tubetto *m* tube
tubino *m* SEW sheath dress
tubista *m* ⟨*pl* -i⟩ pipe maker
tubo *m* pipe; *flessibile* hose; AUTO ***~ di scappamento*** exhaust (pipe); ***~ fluorescente*** fluorescent light; ***~ di scarico*** waste pipe; *fig* ***non capire un ~*** *infml* not understand a thing
tubolare **I** *adj* tubular **II** *m* tubular tyre, *US* tire
tue → ***tuo***
tufaceo *adj* tuffaceous
tuffare *v/t* ⟨1a⟩ dip
tuffarsi *v/r* (*immergersi*) dive; (*buttarsi dentro*) throw o.s. (*a. fig*)
tuffatore *m*, **-trice** *f* diver
tuffo *m* dip; SPORTS dive; ***-i*** SPORTS diving; ***~ di testa*** header
tufo *m* tuff
tugurio *m* ⟨*pl* -ri⟩ hovel
tulipano *m* tulip
tulle *m* net; ***velo*** *m* ***di ~*** tulle veil
tumefatto *adj* swollen
tumefazione *f* swelling
tumorale *adj* tumorous
tumore *m* tumo(u)r
tumulare *v/t* ⟨1l⟩ entomb
tumulazione *f* burial
tumulo *m* mound; *in archeologia* tumulus; (*tomba*) burial mound
tumulto *m* riot
tumultuoso *adj* tumultuous

alia settentrionale e centrale: cartina politica

Italia: cartina fisica

1 : 5 750 000
0 50 100 150 km
ITALIA
Roma
CITTÀ DEL VATICANO
Ostia
Sulmona
P. N. d'Abruzzo
Molise
Campobasso
Volturno
Gargano
P. N. del Gargano
Testa del Gargano
Tavoliere
Foggia
Golfo di Manfredonia
Puglia
Bari
Brindisi
Lecce
Otranto
Capo Sta. Maria di Leuca
Taranto
Golfo di Taranto
Matera
Basilicata
Potenza
Campania
Napoli
1277 Vesuvio
POMPEI
Salerno
PAESTUM
1131
Golfo di Salerno
Capri
G. di Napoli
Ischia
Ventotene
Ponza
Golfo di Gaeta
541 Circeo
Parco Nazionale del Pollino
2248 Mte. Pollino
Golfo di Policastro
Sila 1928
Cosenza
Calabria
1765
Catanzaro
Punta Alice
Capo Rizzuto
Golfo di Squillace
Punta Stilo
1955 Aspromonte
Reggio di Calabria
Capo Spartivento
Mar Ionio
Str. di Messina
Messina
Peloritani
Taormina
3350 Etna
Catania
Golfo di Catania
Siracusa
Capo Passero
896
Sicilia
1979 Madonie
Palermo
Punta Raisi
C. San Vito
SEGESTA
Marsala
Favignana
Marettimo
Isole Egadi
Agrigento
VALLE DEI TEMPLI
Salso
Sicilia
Ustica
Isole Eolie
Stromboli
Panarea
Capo Vaticano
Salina
Filicudi
Alicudi
Lipari
Vulcano
Mar Tirreno
Corsica
Ajaccio
(Fr.)
Bocche di Bonifacio
P. N. dell'Arcipelago de la Maddalena
Maddalena
Caprera
Asinara
Golfo dell'Asinara
Punta Falcone
Olbia
Mte. Limbara 1359
Sassari
Capo Comino
Nuoro
Golfo di Orosei
Sardegna
Gennargentu 1834
Oristano
Tirso
G. di Oristano
1236 Mte. Linas
S. Pietro
Sant'Antioco
Cagliari
C. Carbonara
Golfo di Cagliari
Capo Teulada
Sardegna
Mar Mediterraneo
Galite
K. de Fer
Cap Serrat
P. N. de l'Ichkeul
Cap Blanc
Zembra
Golfo di Tunisi
Cap Bon
CARTAGINE
Tunisi
TUNISIA
ALGERIA
Medjerda
Mellegue
1084
Meliane
1295
Pantelleria
836
MALTA
2806
162
2870
3600
750
3500
1700
164
152
70
505
1800
1233
64
13
53
58
40°
38°
8°
10°
12° Est
14°
16°
18°

Gran Bretagna e Irlanda: cartina fisica
Mar del Nord
OCEANO ATLANTICO
Isole Shetland
Mainland
Yell Sound
Fair
Isole Orcadi
Pentland Firth
Moray Firth
North West Highlands
Ben More
998
Wester Ross
The Minch
Little Minch
Rona
Isola di Lewis
Harris
Uist Sett.
Uist Merid.
Barra
Isole Ebridi
Isole Flannan
St. Kilda
Isola di Skye
Portree
1009
Rhum
Coll
Tiree
Isola di Mull
Firth of Lorne
Colonsay
Jura
Islay
Kintyre
Isola di Arran
Scozia
Mti. Grampiani
Ben Macdhui
1309
Ben Nevis
1343
Great Glen
Loch Ness
Inverness
Aberdeen
Dundee
Perth
Stirling
Kirkcaldy
Firth of Forth
Loch Lomond
Glasgow
Edimburgo
Tweed
816
269
117
140
238
1088
106
1 : 4 500 000
0 50 100 150 km

IRLANDA
Connaught
Leinster
Munster
Dublino
Belfast
Dundalk
Galway
Limerick
Cork
Waterford
Wexford
Kilkenny
Tullamore
Roscommon
Sligo
Bangor
Westport
Clifden
Tralee
Kerry
Connemara
Isole Aran
Baia di Sligo
Baia di Clew
Baia di Galway
Baia di Dingle
Baia di Bantry
Lough Erne
Upper Lough Erne
Lough Mask
Lough Corrib
Lough Ree
Lough Derg
Shannon
Suir
Barrow
Blackwater
Benbulben
Nephin
Monti Mourne
Wicklow
TARA
GLENDALOUGH
Mar d'Irlanda
Isola di Man
(Brit.)
Douglas
Canale di San Giorgio
Mare Celtico
Isole Scilly
Land's End
Inghilterra
Galles
Monti Cambrici
Snowdon
Anglesey
Holyhead
Caernarvon
Aberystwyth
Cardigan
Baia di Cardigan
Swansea
Cardiff
Canale di Bristol
Cumberland
Yorkshire and Humberside
York
Scarborough
Harrogate
Leeds
Bradford
Kingston-upon-Hull
Humber
Lancaster
Blackpool
Baia di Morecambe
Baia di Liverpool
North West
Liverpool
Manchester
Sheffield
Chester
Stoke-on-Trent
Derby
Nottingham
Trent
East Midlands
The Wash
The Fens
Norfolk
Norwich
Suffolk
Ipswich
East Anglia
Ouse
Cambridge
Colchester
Leicester
Walsall
Wolverhampton
Birmingham
Coventry
Northampton
West Midlands
Worcester
Severn
Cotswolds
Tamigi
Oxford
Watford
Londra
Reading
Windsor
Greenwich
Canterbury
North Downs
South East
Kent
South Downs
Dover
Stretto di Dover
Hastings
Eastbourne
Brighton
Portsmouth
Southampton
Bournemouth
Isola di Wight
Bristol
Bath
STONEHENGE
Avon
South West
Exmoor
Taunton
Devon
Exeter
Dartmoor
Cornovaglia
Plymouth
Baia di Lyme
Canale della Manica
Alderney
Guernsey
Isole del Canale
(Brit.)
Jersey
Golfo di St.-Malo
FRANCIA
Cherbourg
Le Havre
Baia della Senna
Caen
Alta Normandia
Rouen
Évreux
Dieppe
Piccardia
Amiens
Nord-Pas-de-Calais
Dunkerque
Calais
St.-Omer
Boulogne-sur-Mer
Ovest 0° Est
54°
52°
50°
10°
8°
6°
4°
2°

America Settentrionale e Centrale: cartina fisica
Mar Glaciale
Isole Regina Elisabeth
Borden
Ellef Ringnes
Mackenzie King
Prince Patrick
Isole Parry
Melville
Stretto di McClure
Melville Sound
Stefansson
Banks
Victoria
Golfo di Amundsen
Mar di Beaufort
Punta Barrow
Mount Michelson
2816
Catena di Brooks
2682
Stretto di Bering
Circolo Polare Artico
ASIA
Alaska
Fairbanks
Yukon
Catena d'Alaska
6194
Mount McKinley
Anchorage
Mount Logan
6050
Barren Grounds
Gran Lago degli Orsi
Mackenzie
Monti Mackenzie
2972
Keele Peak
Gran Lago degli Schiavi
Liard
Peace
Lago Athabasca
Lago delle Renne
Nunivak
Mar di Bering
Isole Aleutine e Penisola dell'Alaska
Kodiak
Golfo di Alaska
Juneau
Montagne Costiere
MONTAGNE ROCCIOSE
Arcipelago Alexander
Isole Regina Carlotta
3954
Mount Robson
Fossa delle Aleutine
Vancouver
Columbia
Grandi Pianure
Missouri
Mount Rainier
4392
Catena delle Cascate
Yellowstone
OCEANO
PACIFICO
Frattura di Mendocino
Capo Mendocino
Catene Costiere
Snake
Black Hills
2207
Gran Lago Salato
Monti Wasatch
4317
Mount Shasta
Gran Bacino
Mount Elbert
4399
Sierra Nevada
San Francisco
Valle della Morte
-86
Grand Canyon
Colorado
Altopiano del Colorado
Los Angeles
-72
San Diego
Penisola di California
Golfo di California
Altopiano Messicano
Sierra Madre Occidentale
Guadalupe
Capo San Lucas
Guadalajara
Nevado de Colima
4265
Isole Revillagigedo
Catena delle Hawaii
Isole Midway
Lisianski
Gardner
Laysan
Nihoa
Kauai
Oahu
Maui
Kaula
Mauna Kea
4205
Hawaii
Isole Hawaii
Tropico del Cancro
1 : 60 000 000
0 700 1400 2100 km

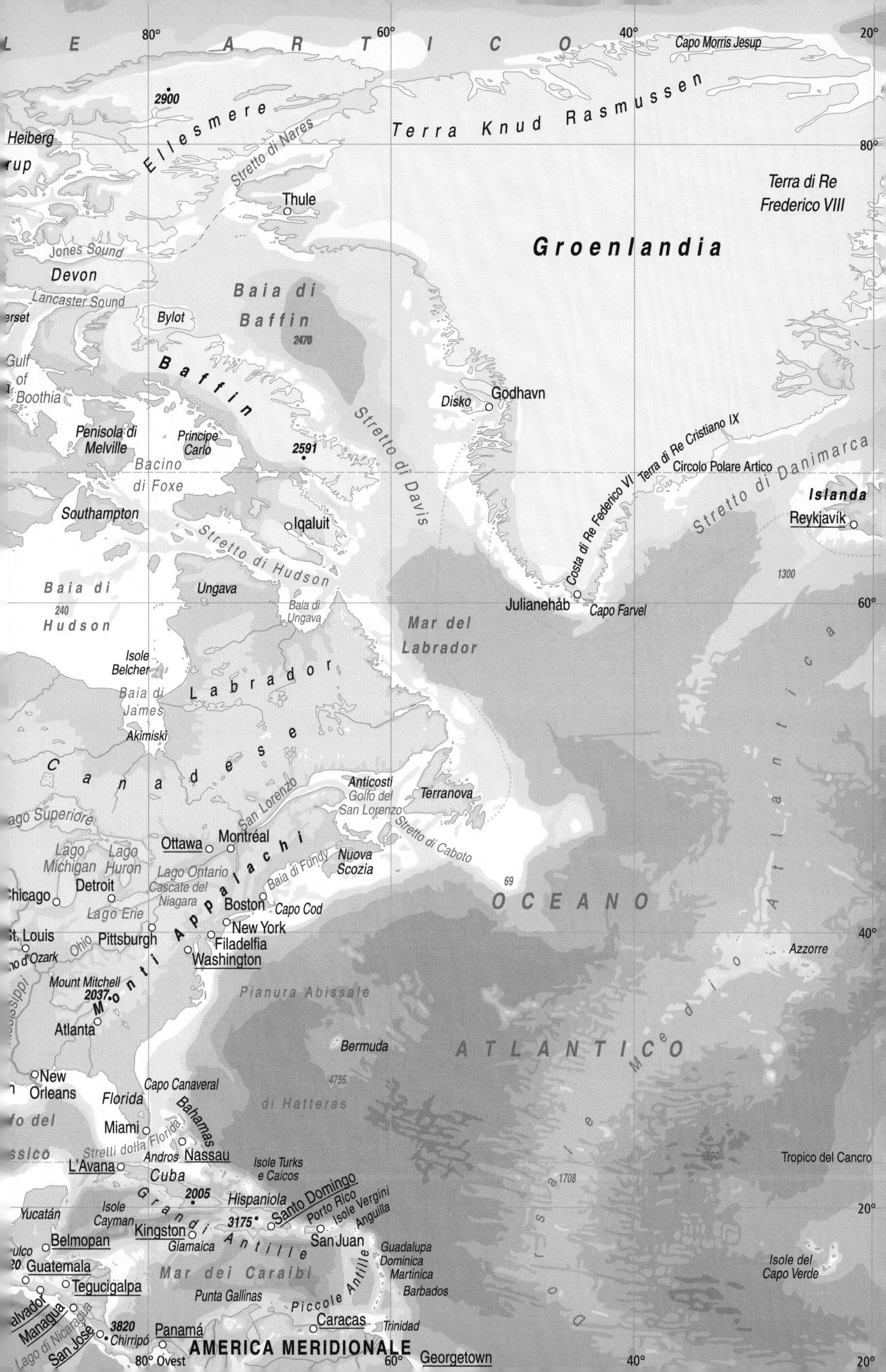

Capo Morris Jesup
Terra Knud Rasmussen
Ellesmere
Stretto di Nares
Heiberg
Thule
Terra di Re Frederico VIII
Groenlandia
Jones Sound
Devon
Lancaster Sound
Baia di Baffin
Bylot
Baffin
Gulf of Boothia
Disko
Godhavn
Stretto di Davis
Terra di Re Cristiano IX
Circolo Polare Artico
Stretto di Danimarca
Islanda
Reykjavík
Penisola di Melville
Principe Carlo
Bacino di Foxe
Southampton
Iqaluit
Stretto di Hudson
Costa di Re Frederico VI
Baia di Hudson
Ungava
Baia di Ungava
Julianehåb
Capo Farvel
Mar del Labrador
Isole Belcher
Baia di James
Labrador
Akimiski
Canadese
Anticosti
Golfo del San Lorenzo
Terranova
San Lorenzo
Lago Superiore
Ottawa
Montréal
Stretto di Caboto
Lago Michigan
Lago Huron
Lago Ontario
Nuova Scozia
Baia di Fundy
Detroit
Chicago
Cascate del Niagara
Boston
Capo Cod
Lago Erie
OCEANO
St. Louis
Pittsburgh
New York
Filadelfia
Washington
Monti Appalachi
Ohio
Azzorre
Mount Mitchell
2037
Pianura Abissale di Hatteras
Atlanta
Bermuda
ATLANTICO
Dorsale Medio Atlantica
New Orleans
Capo Canaveral
Florida
Bahamas
Miami
Stretti della Florida
Andros
Nassau
Isole Turks e Caicos
Tropico del Cancro
L'Avana
Cuba
2005
Grandi Antille
Hispaniola
Santo Domingo
Porto Rico
Isole Vergini
Anguilla
Yucatán
Isole Cayman
3175
Kingston
Giamaica
San Juan
Belmopan
Guadalupa
Dominica
Martinica
Isole del Capo Verde
Guatemala
Tegucigalpa
Mar dei Caraibi
Barbados
Punta Gallinas
Piccole Antille
Managua
Caracas
Trinidad
Lago di Nicaragua
3820
Chirripó
Panamá
San José
AMERICA MERIDIONALE
Georgetown
80° Ovest
60°
40°
20°
80°
2900
2470
2591
240
1300
69
4755
6690
1708

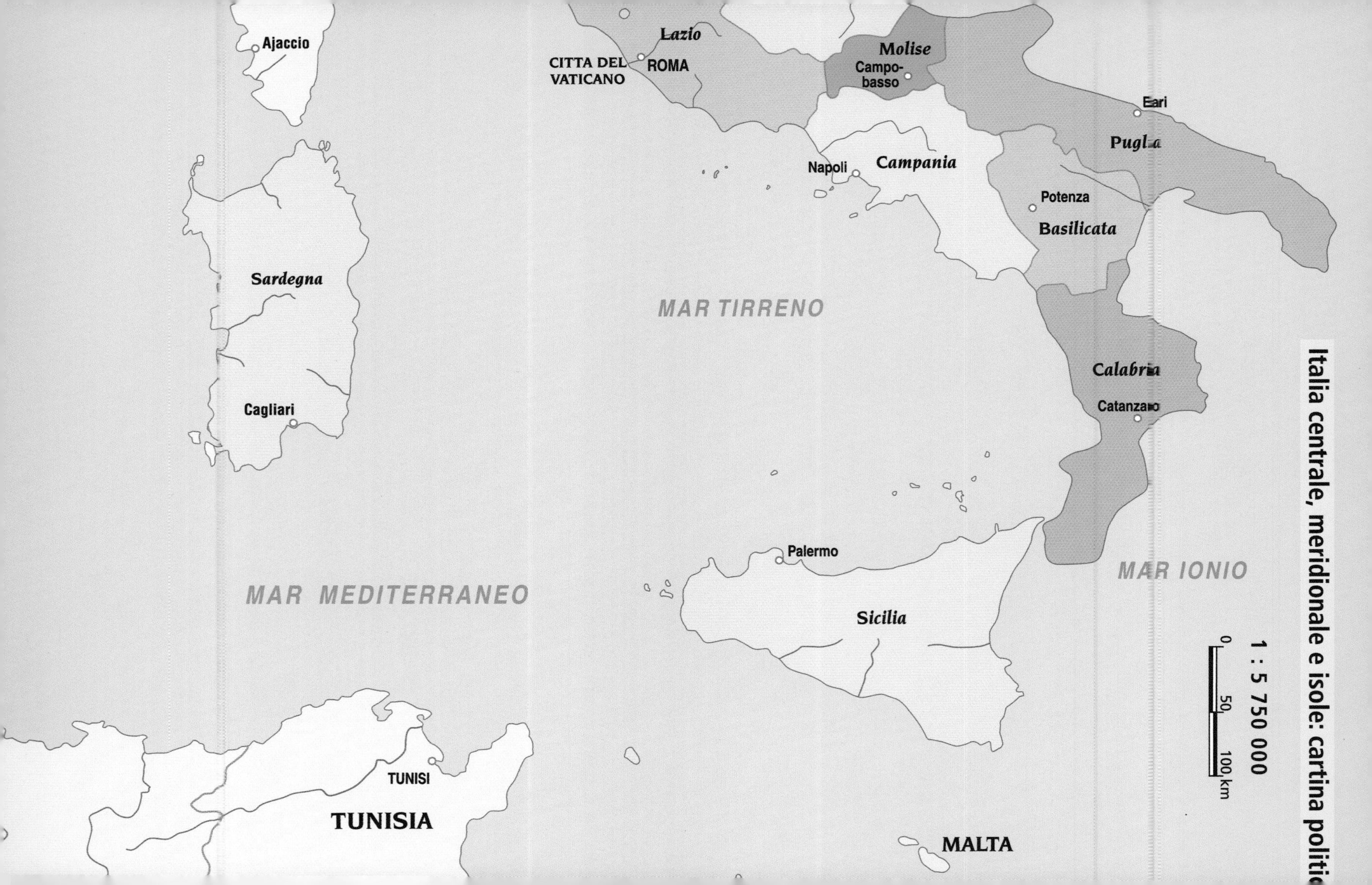
Italia centrale, meridionale e isole: cartina politic
1 : 5 750 000
0
50
100 km
Ajaccio
Lazio
CITTA DEL
VATICANO
ROMA
Molise
Campo-
basso
Campania
Napoli
Potenza
Basilicata
Sardegna
MAR TIRRENO
Catanzaro
Cagliari
Palermo
MAR IONIO
MAR MEDITERRANEO
Sicilia
TUNISI
TUNISIA
MALTA

tundra *f* tundra
tungsteno *m* CHEM tungsten
tunica *f* ⟨*pl* -che⟩ tunic
Tunisi *f* Tunis
Tunisia *f* Tunisia
tunisino **I** *adj* Tunisian **II** *m*, **-a** *f* Tunisian
tunnel *m* ⟨*pl* tunnel⟩ tunnel; *~ dell'orrore* ghost train
tuo ⟨*pl* tuoi⟩ **I** *adj* your; ***il ~ amico*** your friend; ***un ~ amico*** a friend of yours **II** *pron*: ***il ~*** yours
tuoi *pl* → ***tuo***; ***i ~*** your parents
tuonare *v/i* ⟨1c⟩ thunder
tuono *m* thunder
tuorlo *m* yolk
tupi ⟨*pl* tupi⟩ **I** *adj* Tupi **II** *m/f* Tupi
turacciolo *m* stopper
turare *v/t* ⟨1a⟩ stop; *bottiglia* put the top on
turarsi *v/r* ⟨1a⟩ clog; ***~ il naso*** hold one's nose
turba *f* MED disorder; ***-e*** *pl* ***psichiche / nervose*** mental / nervous disorders
turbamento *m* perturbation
turbante *m* turban
turbare *v/t* ⟨1a⟩ upset, disturb
turbina *f* turbine
turbinare *v/i* ⟨1l⟩ whirl (*a. fig*)
turbine *m* whirlwind
turbinio *m* ⟨*pl* -ii⟩ flurry
turbinoso *adj* swirling
turbo… *pref nelle parole composte* turbo…
turbolento *adj persona* unruly; *periodo* turbulent
turbolenza *f* turbulence
turboreattore *m* turbojet
turchese *m/adj* turquoise
Turchia *f* Turkey
turchino **I** *adj* bice **II** *n*: ***turchino*** *m* bice
turco ⟨*mpl* -chi⟩ **I** *m/adj* Turkish; ***bagno*** *m* ***~*** Turkish bath **II** *m*, **-a** *f* Turk; ***fumare come un ~*** smoke like a chimney
turgido *adj* turgid
turgore *m* turgor
turibolo *m* thurible
turismo *m* tourism; ***~ di massa*** mass tourism
turista *m/f* ⟨*mpl* -i⟩ tourist
turistico *adj* ⟨*mpl* -ci⟩ tourist; ***assegno*** *m* ***~*** traveller's cheque, *US* traveler's check
Turkmenistan *m* Turkmenistan
turkmeno **I** *adj* Turkmen **II** *m*, **-a** *f* Turkmen
turlupinare *v/t* ⟨1m⟩ bamboozle
turnista *m/f* ⟨*mpl* -i⟩ shift worker
turno *m* turn; *di lavoro* shift; ***a ~*** in turn; ***di ~*** on duty; ***è il mio ~*** it's my turn; ***~ di riposo*** rest day; ***darsi il ~*** take turns
turpe *adj* foul
turpiloquio *m* ⟨*pl* -qui⟩ filthy language
turpitudine *f* foulness
turrito *adj* turreted
tuta *f da lavoro* boiler suit, overalls *pl*; ***~ sportiva*** *or* ***da ginnastica*** track suit; ***~ da sci*** salopettes
tutela *f* protection; JUR guardianship; ***~ dell'ambiente*** environmental protection
tutelare *v/t* ⟨1b⟩ protect
tutelarsi *v/r* ⟨1b⟩ protect oneself
tutina *f* leotard; *per neonato* Babygro®
tutor *m/f* ⟨*pl* tutor⟩ tutor
tutore *m*, **-trice** *f* guardian
tutorial *m* ⟨*pl* tutorial⟩ COMPUT tutorial
tutorio *adj* ⟨*mpl* -ri⟩ tutelary
tutsi ⟨*pl* tutsi⟩ **I** *adj* Tutsi **II** *m/f* Tutsi
tuttalpiù, tutt'al più *adv* at the most
tuttavia *cj* still
tutto **I** *adj* **1.** whole; ***~ il libro*** the whole book; ***con ~ il cuore*** with all one's heart **2.** ***-i, -e*** *pl* all; ***-i i giorni*** every day; ***-i e tre*** all three; ***noi -i*** all of us **II** *adv* all; ***era ~ solo*** he was all alone; ***del ~*** quite; ***in ~*** altogether, in all **III** *pron* all; *gente* everybody, everyone; *cose* everything; ***lo ha mangiato ~*** he ate it all; ***~ bene?*** is everything all right?; ***~ compreso*** all-inclusive; ***nonostante ~*** in spite of everything
tuttofare **I** *adj domestico* general *attr* **II** *m/f* ⟨*pl* tuttofare⟩ general servant
tuttologo *m*, **-a** *f* ⟨*mpl* -gi⟩ *hum* know-all
tuttora *cj* still
tutù *m* ⟨*pl* tutù⟩ tutu
TV *abbr* (= **televisione**) TV (television); ***guardare la ~*** watch television

U

u, U *m/f* ⟨*pl* u, U⟩ u, U; ***inversione*** *f* ***a U*** U-turn
ubbidiente *adj* obedient
ubbidienza *f* obedience
ubbidire *v/i* ⟨4d⟩ obey; ***~ ai genitori*** obey one's parents
ubicato *adj* ADMIN located
ubicazione *f* location
ubiquità *f* ⟨*pl* ubiquità⟩ ubiquitousness
ubriacare *v/t* ⟨1d⟩: ***~ qn*** get s.o. drunk
ubriacarsi *v/r* get drunk
ubriachezza *f* drunkenness
ubriaco ⟨*mpl* -chi⟩ **I** *adj* drunk **II** *m*, **-a** *f* drunk
ubriacone *m*, **-a** *f* drunk
uccello *m* bird; ***~ notturno*** nocturnal *or* night bird; ***~ rapace*** bird of prey; ***non fare l'~ del malaugurio!*** don't be such a killjoy!
uccidere *v/t* ⟨3q⟩ kill
uccidersi *v/r* kill o.s.
uccisione *f* killing
ucciso *past part* → ***uccidere***
Ucraina *f* Ukraine
ucraino I *adj* Ukrainian **II** *m*, **-a** *f* Ukrainian
UD *abbr* (= **Udine**) Udine
UDC *abbr* (= **Unione Democratici Cristiani e Democratici del Centro**) *Union of Christian Democrats and Centre Democrats*
UDEUR *abbr* (= **Unione Democratici per l'Europa**) *Union of Democrats for Europe*
udibile *adj* audible
udienza *f* audience; JUR hearing; ***~ a porte chiuse*** closed hearing
udinese I *adj* from Udine **II** *m/f* person from Udine
udire *v/t* ⟨4n⟩ hear
uditivo *adj* aural; ***facoltà*** *f* ***-a*** hearing
udito *m* hearing
uditore *m*, **-trice** *f* (*di lezioni*) *student sitting in unofficially on classes or lectures*, *US* auditor; JUR auditor
uditorio *m* ⟨*pl* -ri⟩ audience
Ue *abbr* (= **Unione europea**) EU (European Union)
Uem *abbr* (= **Unione economica e monetaria europea**) EMU (Economic and Monetary Union)
uffa *int* oof
ufficiale I *adj* official; ***non ~*** unofficial; ***gazzetta*** *f* ***~*** official journal, gazette **II** *m* official; MIL officer; ***~ giudiziario*** bailiff; ***~ sanitario*** health officer; ***~ di stato civile*** registrar
ufficialità *f* ⟨*pl* ufficialità⟩ officers *pl*
ufficializzare *v/t* ⟨1a⟩ officialize
ufficialmente *adv* officially
ufficio *m* ⟨*pl* -ci⟩ office; ***~ cambi*** bureau de change; ***~ oggetti smarriti*** lost property; ***~ postale*** post office; ***~ stampa*** press office; ***~ di collocamento*** Jobcentre; ***~ turistico*** tourist information office; ***procedere d'~*** act officially
ufficioso *adj* unofficial
Uffizi *mpl* the Uffizi, *a major art gallery in Florence*
ufo[1] *m*: ***a ~*** at other people's expense, free (of charge)
ufo[2] *m* UFO
Uganda *f* Uganda
ugandese I *adj* Ugandan **II** *m/f* Ugandan
ugello *m* nozzle
uggia *f* ⟨*pl* ugge⟩ boredom; ***venire in ~*** get bored
uggioso *adj* dull; ***tempo*** *m* ***~*** dreary weather
ugola *f* uvula
Ugonotti *mpl* Huguenots
uguaglianza *f* equality
uguagliare *v/t* ⟨1g⟩ make equal; (*livellare*) level; (*essere pari a*) equal
uguale *adj* equal; *lo stesso* the same; *terreno* level
ugualmente *adv* equally; (*ciononostante*) all the same; ***riusciremo ~ a farcela*** we will do it anyway
UIC *abbr* (= **Ufficio Italiano Cambi**) *Italian Exchange Office*
UIL *abbr* (= **Unione Italiana del Lavoro**) *Italian trade union organization*
ulcera *f* ulcer; ***~ gastrica*** gastric ulcer
ulivo *m* → ***olivo***
ulna *f* ulna
ulteriore *adj* further

ultima *f* latest; ***la sai l'~?*** have you heard the latest?
ultimamente *adv* recently
ultimare *v/t* ⟨1l⟩ complete
ultimatum *m* ⟨*pl* ultimatum⟩ ultimatum
ultimazione *f* completion
ultimo I *adj* last; *più recente* latest; ***~ piano*** top floor; ***da ~*** finally; ***l'~ prezzo*** the closing price; ***l'-a moda*** the latest fashion; ***in -a analisi*** in the final analysis **II** *m*, **-a** *f* last; ***fino all'~*** till the end; ***l'~ del mese*** the last day of the month; ***l'~ dell'anno*** New Year's Eve
ultra- *pref* ultra-
ultrà *m* ⟨*pl* ultrà⟩ hooligan
ultracorto *adj*: ***onde*** *fpl* ***-e*** ultrashort waves
ultraleggero *adj* ultralight
ultramoderno *adj* ultramodern
ultrarapido *adj servizio* high-speed
ultrarosso *adj* infrared
ultrasuono *m* ultrasound
ultravioletto *adj* ultraviolet
ululare *v/i* ⟨1l⟩ howl
ululato *m* howl
umanamente *adv* humanely
umanesimo *m* humanism
umanista *m/f* ⟨*mpl* -i⟩ humanist
umanistico *adj* ⟨*mpl* -ci⟩ humanistic
umanità *f* humanity
umanitario *adj* ⟨*mpl* -ri⟩ humanitarian; ***aiuti*** *mpl* ***-i*** humanitarian aid *sg*
umanizzazione *f* humanization; REL incarnation
umano *adj* human; *trattamento etc* humane; ***natura*** *f* ***-a*** human nature; ***esseri*** *mpl* ***-i*** human beings
Umbria *f* Umbria
Ume *abbr* (= **unione monetaria (europea)**) EMU (European Monetary Union)
umettare *v/t* ⟨1a⟩ moisten
umidificare *v/t* ⟨1n⟩ humidify
umidificatore *m* humidifier
umidificazione *f* humidification
umidità *f* dampness
umido I *adj* damp; ***caldo*** *m* ***~*** sticky heat **II** *m* dampness; COOK ***in ~*** stewed
umile *adj* (*modesto*) humble; *mestiere* menial; ***essere di -i origini*** be of humble origins
umiliante *adj* humiliating
umiliare *v/t* ⟨1g⟩ humiliate
umiliarsi *v/r* humiliate o.s.
umiliazione *f* humiliation
umilmente *adv* humbly
umiltà *f* humility
umorale *adj* humoral (*a.* MED)
umore *m* mood; ***di buon ~*** in a good mood; ***di cattivo ~*** in a bad mood
umorismo *m* humo(u)r
umorista *m/f* ⟨*mpl* -i⟩ humorist
umoristico *adj* ⟨*mpl* -ci⟩ humorous; ***battuta*** *f* ***-a*** quip
un, una → ***uno***
unanime *adj* unanimous
unanimità *f* unanimity; ***all'~*** unanimously
una tantum I *adj inv* one-off **II** *adv* only once **III** *f* ⟨*no pl*⟩ (*tassa*) one--off payment
uncinato *adj* uneiform; ***croce*** *f* ***-a*** swastika
uncinetto *m* crochet hook; ***lavorare all'~*** crochet
uncino *m* hook
under *adj inv*: ***gli ~ ventuno*** SPORTS the under twenty-ones
undicenne *m/f* eleven-year-old
undicesimo *m/adj* eleventh
undici *num* eleven; ***sono le ~*** it's eleven (o'clock); ***l'~ di agosto*** the eleventh of August
ungere *v/t* ⟨3d⟩ grease
ungersi *v/r* get greasy
ungherese *m/f & adj* Hungarian
Ungheria *f* Hungary
unghia *f* nail; ZOOL claw; (*attrezzo*) firmer chisel; ***pagare sull'~*** pay on the nail; *fig* ***lottare con le -e e con i denti*** fight tooth and nail
unghiata *f* scratch; ***dare un'~ a qn*** scratch s.o.
unguento *m* ointment, cream
ungulati *mpl* ungulates
unicamente *adv* solely, only
unicamerale *adj* POL unicameral
unicità *f* ⟨*pl* unicità⟩ uniqueness
unico *adj* ⟨*mpl* -ci⟩ only; (*senza uguali*) unique; ***atto*** *m* ***~*** one-act play; ***moneta*** *f* ***-a*** single currency; ***figlio*** *m* ***~*** only child; ***pezzo*** *m* ***~*** unique item
unidirezionale *adj* one-way (*a. fig*)
unifamiliare *adj*: ***casa*** *f* ***~*** detached house
unificare *v/t* ⟨1m & d⟩ unify
unificazione *f* unification

uniformare *v/t* ⟨1a⟩ standardize
uniformarsi *v/r*: **~ *a*** conform to; *regole, direttive* comply with
uniforme *f/adj* uniform
uniformità *f* uniformity
unilaterale *adj* unilateral
unilateralità *f* ⟨*pl* unilateralità⟩ unilaterality; *fig* one-sidedness
uninominale *adj*: ***sistema*** *m* **~** one-vote system
unione *f* **1.** union; ***Unione economica e monetaria*** *hist* Economic and Monetary Union; ***Unione Europea*** European Union; ***Unione monetaria (europea)*** (European) Monetary Union; ***l'ex Unione Sovietica*** *hist* the former Soviet Union; **~ *di fatto*** common-law marriage; ***l'~ fa la forza*** *prov* united we stand, divided we fall **2.** *fig* unity
unipolare *adj* unipolar
unire *v/t* ⟨4d⟩ unite; *congiungere* join; **~ *l'utile al dilettevole*** mix business with pleasure
unirsi *v/r* unite; **~ *in matrimonio*** marry
unisex *adj inv* unisex
unisono *adj* concordant (*a. fig*); ***all'~*** in unison
unità *f* ⟨*pl* unità⟩ unit; **~ *cinofila*** canine corps *sg*; **~ *di controllo*** control unit; **~ *logica*** COMPUT logical unit; **~ *monetaria*** monetary unit; **~ *motorizzata*** MIL motorized unit; **~ *di misura*** unit of measurement; COMPUT **~ *a dischi flessibili*** disk drive; **~ *pl periferiche*** peripherals
unitamente *adv*: **~ *a qc*** together with sth
unitario *adj* ⟨*mpl* -ri⟩ (*omogeneo*) uniform; COMM unit
unito *adj* united; ***in tinta*** *f* **-a** self-colo(u)red
universale *adj* universal; ***erede*** *m* **~** sole heir
universalità *f* ⟨*pl* universalità⟩ universality
universiadi *fpl* world university games
università *f* ⟨*pl* università⟩ university; **~ *della terza età*** university of the third age
universitario ⟨*mpl* -ri⟩ **I** *adj* university *attr* **II** *m*, **-a** *f* university student; (*professore*) university lecturer
universo *m* universe
univoco *adj* ⟨*mpl* -ci⟩ unequivocal
unno I *adj* Hunnish **II** *m*, **-a** *f* Hun
uno I *art* a; *davanti a una vocale* an; ***un' uovo*** an egg **II** *adj* a, one **III** *m* one; **~ *e mezzo*** one and a half **IV** *pron* one; ***a ~ a ~*** one by one; ***l'~ dopo l'altro*** one after the other; ***l'un l'altro*** each other, one another; **~ *alla volta*** one at a time
unto I *past part* → ***ungere*** **II** *adj* greasy **III** *m* grease; REL ***l'Unto del Signore*** the Lord's Anointed
untuoso *adj* greasy; (*subdolo*) *fig* unctuous
unzione *f*: ***estrema ~*** last rites
uomo *m* ⟨*pl* uomini⟩ man; **~ *d'affari*** businessman; **~ *comune*** *or* ***qualunque*** man in the street; **~ *di fiducia*** right-hand man; **~ *di mondo*** man of the world; **~ *d'onore*** (*mafioso*) Mafia member; ***da ~*** *abbigliamento etc* for men, men's; ***da ~ a ~*** man to man
uovo *m* ⟨*pl* le -a⟩ egg; **~ *alla coque*** soft-boiled egg; **~ *di Pasqua*** Easter egg; **~ *sodo*** hard-boiled egg; **~ *al tegame*** fried egg; **-a** *pl*: ***strapazzate*** scrambled eggs; ***meglio un ~ oggi che una gallina domani*** *prov* a bird in the hand is worth two in the bush
upgrade *m* ⟨*pl* upgrade⟩ COMPUT upgrade
upupa *f* ZOOL hoopoe
uragano *m* hurricane
uranio *m* uranium
Urano *m* MYTH, SPACE Uranus
urbanesimo *m* urbanization
urbanista *m/f* ⟨*mpl* -i⟩ town planner
urbanistica *f* town planning
urbanistico *adj* ⟨*mpl* -ci⟩ planning
urbanizzare *v/t* ⟨1a⟩ urbanize
urbanizzarsi *v/r* ⟨1a⟩ become urbanized
urbanizzazione *f* urbanization
urbano *adj* urban; *fig* urbane
urbinate I *adj* from Urbino **II** *m/f* person from Urbino
urea *f* urea
uretra *f* urethra
urgente *adj* urgent
urgentemente *adv* urgently
urgenza *f* urgency; ***in caso d'~*** in an emergency
urgere *v/i* ⟨3yy⟩ be urgent
urina *f* urine
urinare *v/i* ⟨1m⟩ urinate

urlare *v/t* ⟨1a⟩ scream
urlio *m* ⟨*pl* -ii⟩ shouting
urlo *m* ⟨*pl a.* le -a⟩ scream
urna *f* urn; *elettorale* ballot box; ***~ funeraria*** funeral urn
urogallo *m* ZOOL capercaillie
urologia *f* urology
urologo *m*, **-a** *f* ⟨*mpl* -gi⟩ urologist
urrà! *int* hooray!
urtante *adj* irritating
urtare *v/t* ⟨1a⟩ bump into, collide with; *con un veicolo* hit; *fig* offend; ***~ qn/qc*** bump into s.o./sth; ***~ contro qc*** bump into sth; ***~ i nervi a qn*** get on s.o.'s nerves
urtarsi *v/r* collide; *fig* clash
urto *m* bump; (*scontro*) collision
uruguaiano I *adj* Uruguayan **II** *m*, **-a** *f* Uruguayan
Uruguay *m* Uruguay
uruguayano → ***uruguaiano***
u.s. *abbr* (= **ultimo scorso**) last, ult. (ultimo)
USA *abbr* (= **Stati uniti d'America**) USA (United States of America)
usa e getta *adj* disposable; ***articoli*** *mpl* **~** disposable items
usanza *f* custom, tradition; ***paese che vai, ~ che trovi*** *prov* when in Rome, do as the Romans do
usare ⟨1a⟩ **I** *v/t* use **II** *v/i* use; (*essere di moda*) be in fashion; ***in Italia si usa cenare tardi*** in Italy people usually eat late; ***quest'anno (si) usa molto il nero*** black is in this year
usato *adj* used; (*di seconda mano*) second-hand
usbergo *m* ⟨*pl* -ghi⟩ hauberk
uscente *adj* (*alla fine del mandato*) outgoing
usciere *m*, **-a** *f* bailiff; *in tribunale*: usher
uscire *v/i* ⟨4o⟩ come out; (*andare fuori*) go out; ***~ di casa*** go out; ***~ di corsa*** rush out; ***~ da scuola*** get out of school; ***~ dall'ufficio*** leave the office; ***mi è uscito di mente*** it slipped my mind; ***~ di strada*** go off the road
uscita *f* exit, way out; COMPUT output; ***buona ~*** golden handshake; ***~ di sicurezza*** emergency exit; ***via d'~*** way out
usignolo *m* nightingale
uso *m* **1.** use; ***~ indebito*** misuse; ***fuori ~*** out of use; ***pronto per l'~*** ready to use; ***con ~ di cucina*** with use of kitchen; ***per ~ esterno*** not to be taken internally; ***per ~ interno*** for internal use **2.** (*abitudine*) custom; ***gli -i e i costumi*** customs and traditions
ussaro *m* hussar
US(S)L, Us(s)l *abbr* (= **Unità (Socio-) sanitaria Locale**) *hist local health authority*
ustionare *v/t* ⟨1a⟩ burn; *con liquidi* scald
ustionarsi *v/r* ⟨1a⟩ burn o.s.
ustionato I *adj* burnt; *con liquidi* scalded **II** *m*, **-a** *f* person suffering from burns; ***centro*** *m* ***grandi -i*** burns unit
ustione *f* burn
usuale *adj* usual
usucapione *f* squatter's rights *pl*
usufruire *v/i* ⟨4d⟩: ***~ di qc*** have the use of sth
usufrutto *m* JUR usufruct
usufruttuario ⟨*mpl* -ri⟩ **I** *adj* usufructuary **II** *m*, **-a** *f* usufructuary
usura[1] *f di denaro* illegal money lending
usura[2] *f* (*strozzinaggio*) wear and tear
usuraio *m*, **-a** *f* ⟨*mpl* -i⟩ loan shark
usurare *v/t* ⟨1a⟩ wear
usurarsi *v/r* ⟨1a⟩ wear
usurpare *v/t* ⟨1a⟩: ***~ qc*** usurp sth
usurpatore *m*, **-trice** *f* usurper
usurpazione *f* usurpation
utensile I *adj*: ***macchina*** *f* **~** machine tool **II** *m* utensil; ***-i*** *pl* tools; ***-i*** *pl* ***domestici*** household goods, *US* housewares; ***-i*** *pl* ***di cucina*** kitchen utensils
utente *m/f* user; ***~ della strada*** road user
utenza *f* (*uso*) use, consumption; (*utenti*) users *pl*, consumers *pl*
uterino *adj* uterine
utero *m* womb
utile I *adj* useful; ***in tempo ~*** within the time limit; ***posso esserLe ~?*** can I help you? **II** *m* FIN profit; ***~ d'esercizio*** operating profit; ***~ netto*** net profit; ***unire l'~ al dilettevole*** combine business with pleasure
utilità *f* ⟨*pl* utilità⟩ usefulness
utilitaria *f* economy car
utilizzabile *adj* usable
utilizzare *v/t* ⟨1a⟩ use
utilizzatore *m*, **-trice** *f* user
utilizzazione *f* use
utilizzo *m* use

utopia *f* utopia
utopista *m/f* ⟨*mpl* -i⟩ dreamer
uva *f* grapes *pl*; **~ *passa*** raisins *pl*; **~ *spina*** gooseberry
uvetta *f* raisins *pl*
uxoricida *m/f* ⟨*mpl* -i⟩ uxoricide
uxoricidio *m* ⟨*pl* -i⟩ uxoricide
Uzbekistan *m* Uzbekistan
uzbeko **I** *adj* Uzbek **II** *m*, **-a** *f* Uzbek

V

v, V *m/f* ⟨*pl* v, V⟩ v, V
v. *abbr* (= **vedi**) see
V *abbr* (= **volt**) V (volt)
V. *abbr* (= **via**) St (street)
va → ***andare***
vacante *adj* vacant
vacanza *f* holiday; ***-e*** *pl* ***estive*** summer holiday(s); ***-e*** *pl* ***natalizie*** Christmas holidays; ***andare in ~*** go on holiday; ***buone -e!*** have a nice holiday!
vacanziere *m*, **-a** *f* holidaymaker
vacca *f* ⟨*pl* -cche⟩ cow
vaccinare *v/t* ⟨1a⟩ vaccinate
vaccinazione *f* vaccination; **~ *antitetanica*** tetanus injection *or* shot
vaccino *m* vaccine; **~ *antinfluenzale*** flu vaccine
vacillante *adj* shaky (*a. fig*)
vacillare *v/i* ⟨1a⟩ waver (*a. fig*); *teoria* totter; *mente* fail
vacuità *f* ⟨*pl* vacuità⟩ emptiness; *fig* vacuousness
vacuo *adj fig* vacuous
vademecum *m* ⟨*pl* vademecum⟩ handbook
vado → ***andare***
vaffanculo *int pej* fuck off! *vulg*
vagabondaggio *m* ⟨*pl* -ggi⟩ vagrancy
vagabondare *v/i* ⟨1a⟩ wander
vagabondo **I** *adj* (*girovago*) wandering; (*fannullone*) idle **II** *m*, **-a** *f* (*giramondo*) wanderer; (*fannullone*) idler, layabout *infml*; (*barbone*) tramp
vagamente *adv* vaguely
vagare *v/i* ⟨1e⟩ wander (aimlessly)
vagheggiare *v/t* ⟨1f⟩: **~ *qc*** contemplate sth
vaghezza *f* vagueness
vagina *f* ANAT vagina
vaginale *adj* ANAT vaginal
vagito *m* wail
vaglia *m* ⟨*pl* vaglia⟩: **~ (*postale*)** postal order; **~ *bancario*** bill of exchange, draft
vagliare *v/t* ⟨1a⟩ *fig* examine
vaglio *m* ⟨*pl* -gli⟩ sieve; *fig* sifting
vago *adj* ⟨*mpl* -ghi⟩ vague
vagoncino *m* MINER tram
vagone *m* carriage; **~ *letto*** sleeper; **~ *merci*** goods wagon; **~ *ristorante*** dining car
vai → ***andare***
vaiolo *m* smallpox
Valacchia *f* Walachia
valanga *f* ⟨*pl* -ghe⟩ avalanche
valchiria *f* Valkyrie; *fig* Amazon
valdese **I** *adj* Waldensian **II** *m/f* REL Waldensian
valdostano **I** *adj* of the Valle d'Aosta **II** *m*, **-a** *f* person from the Valle d'Aosta
valenciano **I** *adj* Valencian **II** *m*, **-a** *f* Valencian
valente *adj* skil(l)ful
Valentino *m*: ***San ~*** Saint Valentine; ***giorno*** *m* ***di San ~*** St Valentine's Day
valenza *f* CHEM valency; *fig* value
valere *v/t* ⟨2r⟩ **1.** be worth; ***non vale nulla*** it's worthless, it isn't worth anything; **~ *la pena*** be worth it **2.** (*essere valido*) be valid; ***far ~*** *diritti*, *autorità* assert; ***non vale!*** that's not fair!; ***vale a dire*** that is to say
valeriana *f* valerian
valersi *v/r*: **~ *di qc*** avail o.s. of sth; (*usare*) make use of
valevole *adj* valid
valgo[1] → ***valere***
valgo[2] *adj* ⟨*mpl* -ghi⟩ MED valgus; ***alluce*** *m* **~** hammer toe
valicare *v/t* ⟨1l⟩ cross
valico *m* ⟨*pl* -chi⟩ pass
validità *f* validity
valido *adj* valid; *persona* fit; ***non ~*** in-

valid
valigetta *f*: **~ *ventiquattrore*** overnight bag
valigia *f* ⟨*pl* -gie⟩ suitcase; ***fare le -e*** pack
vallata *f* valley
valle *f* valley; *fig* **~ *di lacrime*** vale of tears; ***scendere a ~*** go downhill; ***Val Pusteria*** Val Pusteria
Valle d'Aosta *f* Valle d'Aosta
Vallese *m* Valais
valligiano *m*, **-a** *f* valley dweller
vallone I *adj* Walloon **II** *m/f* Walloon
valore *m* **1.** value; **~ *aggiunto*** added value; **~ *commerciale*** market value; **~ *corrente*** current value; **~ *energetico*** energy value; ***di ~*** valuable; ***senza ~*** worthless **2.** COMM **-*i*** *pl* securities **3.** (*coraggio*) bravery, valo(u)r; **~ *civile*** civil valo(u)r
valorizzare *v/t* ⟨1a⟩ increase the value of; (*far risaltare*) show off
valorizzazione *f* increase in value; (*miglioramento*) improvement
valorosamente *adv* courageously
valoroso *adj* courageous
valsesiano I *adj* Valsesian **II** *m*, **-a** *f* Valsesian
Valsugana *f* Valsugana
Valtellina *f* Valtellina
valtellinese I *adj* from Valtellina **II** *m/f* person from Valtellina
valuta *f* currency; ***stabilità*** *f* ***della ~*** monetary stability
valutare *v/t* ⟨1a⟩ value
valutario *adj* monetary
valutazione *f* valuation
valva *f* ZOOL valve
valvola *f* valve; ELEC fuse; **~ *dell'aria*** air valve
valzer *m* ⟨*pl* valzer⟩ waltz
vamp *f* ⟨*pl* vamp⟩ vamp
vampa *f* flame
vampata *f* flame; *di calore*: burst
vampiro *m*, **-a** vampire
vanagloria *f* conceit
vanaglorioso I *adj* boastful **II** *m*, **-a** *f* braggart
vandalico *adj* ⟨*mpl* -ci⟩ vandalistic
vandalismo *m* vandalism
vandalo *m*, **-a** *f* vandal
Vandea *f* Vendée
vanesio ⟨*mpl* -si⟩ **I** *adj* vain **II** *m*, **-a** *f* vain person, *infml* fop
vanessa *f* ZOOL vanessa
vanga *f* ⟨*pl* -ghe⟩ spade
vangare *v/t* ⟨1e⟩ dig
vangelo *m* gospel
vanificare *v/t* ⟨1m & d⟩ thwart
vaniglia *f* vanilla
vanigliato *adj* vanilla-flavo(u)red
vanità *f* vanity
vanitoso *adj* vain
vanno → ***andare***
vano I *adj minacce*, *promesse* empty; (*inutile*) vain **II** *m* (*spazio vuoto*) hollow; (*stanza*) room; AUTO **~ *portaoggetti*** glove compartment
vantaggio *m* ⟨*pl* -ggi⟩ advantage; *in gara* lead
vantaggioso *adj* advantageous
vantare *v/t* ⟨1a⟩ speak highly of; *possedere* boast; **~ *diritti su qc*** lay claim to sth
vantarsi *v/r* boast (***di*** of)
vanto *m* boast; ***essere il ~ di qn*** be s.o.'s boast
vanvera *f*: ***parlare a ~*** talk nonsense
vapore *m* **1.** vapo(u)r; **~ (*d'acqua*)** steam; **~ *acqueo*** steam; ***cucinato al ~*** steamed **2.** NAUT steamer
vaporetto *m* water bus
vaporizzare *v/t* ⟨1a⟩ (*nebulizzare*) spray
vaporizzatore *m* atomizer
vaporizzazione *f* spraying; CHEM vaporization
vaporoso *adj* floaty; (*vago*) woolly
varare *v/t* ⟨1a⟩ launch
varcare *v/t* ⟨1d⟩ cross
varco *m* ⟨*pl* -chi⟩ passage; ***aprirsi un ~ tra la folla*** push one's way through the crowd; ***aspettare qn al ~*** head s.o. off at the pass
varechina *f* bleach
varesino I *adj* from Varese **II** *m*, **-a** *f* person from Varese
variabile I *adj* changeable **II** *f* MATH variable
variabilità *f* ⟨*pl* variabilità⟩ variability; **~ *d'umore*** fickleness of mood
variante *f* variation
variare *v/t* & *v/i* ⟨1k⟩ vary
variazione *f* variation
varice *f* varicose vein
varicella *f* chickenpox
varicoso *adj*: ***vena*** *f* ***-a*** varicose vein
variegato *adj* variegated
varietà I *f* ⟨*pl* varietà⟩ variety **II** *m* ⟨*pl* varietà⟩ variety, *US* vaudeville;

(***spettacolo*** *m* ***di***) ~ variety (*US* vaudeville) show
vario *adj* ⟨*mpl* -ri⟩ varied; ***-ri*** *pl* various
variopinto *adj* multicolo(u)red
varo *m* NAUT launching (*a. fig*)
Varsavia *f* Warsaw
vasaio *m*, **-a** *f* ⟨*mpl* -ai⟩ potter
vasca *f* ⟨*pl* -che⟩ (*serbatoio*, *cisterna*) tank; (*lunghezza di piscina*) length; *di fontana* basin; ~ (***da bagno***) bath, (bath)tub
vascello *m* vessel
vaschetta *f* tub
vascolare *adj* ANAT, BOT vascular
vasectomia *f* vasectomy
vaselina *f* vaseline
vasellame *m* dishes *pl*
vasistas *m* ⟨*pl* vasistas⟩: ***finestra*** *f* ***a*** ~ transom window
vaso *m* pot; ANAT vessel; ***il ~ di Pandora*** Pandora's box
vasocostrittore *adj* vasoconstrictive
vasodilatatore *adj* vasodilatory
vassallo *m* HIST vassal; (*suddito*) subject
vassoio *m* ⟨*pl* -oi⟩ tray
vastità *f* ⟨*pl* vastità⟩ vastness; *fig* extent
vasto *adj* vast
vaticanista *m/f* ⟨*mpl* -i⟩ Vatican correspondent
vaticano *adj* Vatican *attr*
Vaticano *m* Vatican
vaticinio *m* ⟨*pl* -ni⟩ prophecy
VB *abbr* (= **Verbano-Cusio-Ossola**) Verbano-Cusio-Ossola
VC *abbr* (= **Vercelli**) Vercelli
V.d.F. *abbr* (= **vigili del fuoco**) fire brigade, *US* fire department
ve = ***vi*** *before* ***lo, la, li, le, ne***
vecchiaia *f* old age
vecchietto *m*, **-a** *f* little old man, little old woman
vecchio ⟨*mpl* -cchi⟩ **I** *adj* old **II** *m*, **-a** *f* old man; *donna* old woman
vecchiotto *adj* oldish
veccia *f* ⟨*pl* -cce⟩ BOT vetch
vece *f*: ***in ~ di*** instead of; ***fare le -i di qn*** take s.o.'s place
vedente *m/f*: ***non ~*** visually handicapped
vedere *v/t* ⟨2s⟩ see; ***far ~*** show; ***stare a ~*** watch; ***vedremo!*** we'll see!; ***ci vediamo!*** see you!; ***vedersela brutta*** have a narrow escape; ***ti vedo bene!*** you look well!; ***non avere nulla a che ~ con qn / qc*** have nothing to do with s.o. / sth; ***non ~ l'ora di fare qc*** be looking forward to sth; ***vedersela con qn*** sort it out with s.o.
vedetta *f* look-out; NAUT patrol boat; ***stare di ~*** be on the look-out
vedova nera *f* ZOOL black widow spider
vedovanza *f* widowhood
vedovile *adj* widowed; *di vedova* widow's *attr*; *di vedovo* widower's *attr*
vedovo I *adj* widowed **II** *m*, **-a** *f* widower; *donna* widow
veduta *f* view (***su*** of); ***~ aerea*** aerial view; *fig* ***larghezza*** *f* ***di -e*** broad-mindedness
veemente *adj* vehement
veemenza *f* vehemence
vegetale I *adj* vegetable *attr*; *regno*, *vita* plant *attr* **II** *m* plant
vegetare *v/i* ⟨11 & b⟩ vegetate
vegetariano I *adj* vegetarian *attr* **II** *m*, **-a** *f* vegetarian
vegetativo *adj* vegetative
vegetazione *f* vegetation
vegeto *adj vecchio* spry; ***vivo e ~*** hale and hearty
vegetominerale *adj*: ***acqua*** *f* ~ vegeto-mineral water
veggente *m/f* (*chiaroveggente*) clairvoyant
veglia *f* (*l'essere svegli*) wakefulness; (*il vegliare*) vigil; ***essere tra la ~ e il sonno*** be half asleep; ***fare la ~ a un malato*** sit up with a sick person; ***~ funebre*** wake
vegliardo *m*, **-a** *f* venerable old man *o* woman
vegliare ⟨1g⟩ **I** *v/i* keep watch **II** *v/t*: ***~ qn*** watch over s.o.
veglione *m* party; ***~ di Capodanno*** New Year's Eve party
veicolare *v/t* ⟨11⟩ carry; *fig idee etc* spread
veicolo *m* vehicle; ***~ spaziale*** spaceship
vela *f* sail; *attività* sailing; ***fare ~*** set sail; ***andare a ~*** go sailing; ***issare / ammainare le -e*** hoist / lower the sails; ***tutto è andato a gonfie -e*** everything went swimmingly
velato *adj* hazy; ***calze*** *fpl* ***-e*** sheer stockings; *fig* ***minacce*** *fpl* ***-e*** veiled

threats
velcro® *m*: ***chiusura*** *f* ***a ~*** Velcro®
veleggiare *v/i* ⟨1l⟩ NAUT sail; AVIAT glide
veleggiatore *m* AVIAT glider
veleno *m* poison; *di animali* venom (*a. fig*)
velenoso *adj* poisonous; *fig* venomous
veletta *f* veil
velico *adj* ⟨*mpl* -ci⟩ sailing *attr*; ***regata*** *f* ***-a*** sailing regatta
veliero *m* sailing ship
velina *adj*: ***carta*** *f* ***~*** *per imballaggio* tissue paper
velismo *m* sailing
velista *m/f* ⟨*mpl* -i⟩ sailor
velivolo *m* aircraft
velleità *f* ⟨*pl* velleità⟩ vague desire
velleitario *adj* ⟨*mpl* -ri⟩ overambitious (*a. fig*), *pej* unrealistic
vello *m* fleece; ***il ~ d'oro*** the Golden Fleece
vellutato *adj* velvety
velluto *m* velvet; ***di ~*** velvet *attr*; ***~ a coste*** corduroy
velo *m* veil; ***un ~ d'ironia*** a layer of irony; ***prendere il ~*** take the veil
veloce *adj* fast, quick
velocemente *adv* quickly
velocipede *m hist* velocipede
velocista *m/f* ⟨*mpl* -i⟩ SPORTS sprinter
velocità *f* ⟨*pl* velocità⟩ speed; ***alta ~*** RAIL high-speed; ***~ di trasferimento*** COMPUT transfer speed; ***limite*** *m* ***di ~*** speed limit; ***eccesso*** *m* ***di ~*** speeding; ***~ della luce*** speed of light; ***~ di crociera*** cruising speed
velocizzare *v/t* ⟨1a⟩ speed up
velodromo *m* velodrome
velours *m* ⟨*pl* velours⟩ velours
vena *f* vein; ***essere in ~*** be in the mood
venale *adj* (*avido di denaro*) venal
venalità *f* ⟨*pl* venalità⟩ venality
venatorio *adj* hunting *attr*; ***stagione*** *f* ***-a*** hunting season
venatura *f* vein; *fig* streak
vendemmia *f* (grape) harvest
vendemmiare *v/t & v/i* ⟨1k⟩ harvest
vendere *v/t* ⟨3a⟩ sell; ***~ all'ingrosso*** sell wholesale; ***~ al minuto*** retail; *fig* ***da ~*** in spades
vendersi *v/r fig* sell o.s.
vendetta *f* revenge
vendeuse *f* ⟨*pl* vendeuse⟩ female shop assistant, *US* female sales clerk
vendibile *adj* sal(e)able
vendicare *v/t* ⟨1f & d⟩ avenge
vendicarsi *v/r* get one's revenge (***di qn*** on s.o.; ***di qc*** for sth)
vendicativo *adj* vindictive
vendita *f* sale; ***~ di fine stagione*** end-of-season sale; ***~ diretta*** direct selling; ***~ all'asta*** auction; ***mettere in ~*** put up for sale
venditore *m*, **-trice** *f* salesman; *donna* saleswoman; ***~ ambulante*** hawker; ***~ di fumo*** charlatan
venduto I *adj fig* corrupt **II** *n*: ***venduto*** *m* goods sold *pl*; ***salvo il ~*** subject to prior sale
venefico *adj* ⟨*mpl* -ci⟩ noxious
venerabile *adj* venerable
venerando *adj* venerable
venerare *v/t* ⟨1l & b⟩ revere
venerazione *f* veneration
venerdì *m* ⟨*pl* venerdì⟩ Friday; ***di ~*** on Fridays; ***Venerdì Santo*** Good Friday
Venere *f* Venus
venereo *adj* venereal; ***malattia*** *f* ***-a*** venereal disease, VD
veneto I *adj* of the Veneto **II** *m*, **-a** *f* person from the Veneto
Veneto *m* Veneto
Venezia *f* Venice
veneziana *f* Venetian blind
veneziano I *adj* of Venice, Venetian **II** *m*, **-a** *f* Venetian
venezolano → ***venezuelano***
Venezuela *m* Venezuela
venezuelano I *adj* Venezuelan **II** *m*, **-a** *f* Venezuelan
vengo → ***venire***
venia *f*: ***chiedere ~*** beg for forgiveness
veniale *adj*: ***peccato*** *m* ***~*** venial sin
venire *v/i* ⟨4p⟩ **1.** come; ***~ al dunque*** get to the point; ***mi sta venendo fame*** I'm getting hungry; ***~ in mente*** occur; ***~ a prendere*** come for; ***~ a proposito*** come just in time; ***mi viene da ridere*** it makes me laugh; ***vieni giù / su*** come down / up; ***~ a capo di qc*** thrash sth out; ***~ alla luce*** come to light; ***~ a noia*** get bored; ***~ meno*** (*svenire*) faint; (*mancare*) fail; *promessa* break **2.** (*riuscire*) turn out **3.** ***~ a costare*** total, work out at; ***~ a sapere qc*** learn sth, find sth out; ***~ a trovare*** come and see **4.** *come ausiliare* be; ***i suoi disegni vengono***

ammirati da tutti his drawings are admired by all
venoso *adj* venous
ventaglio *m* ⟨*pl* -gli⟩ fan
ventata *f* gust; *fig* ***portare una ~ di aria fresca*** bring a breath of fresh air
ventenne *m/f & adj* twenty-year-old
ventennio *m* ⟨*pl* -nni⟩ twenty-year period
ventesimo *m/adj* twentieth
venti *num* twenty; ***il ~ di maggio*** the twentieth of May
venticello *m* breeze
ventilato *adj* ventilated; ***stanza*** *f* ***-a*** airy room
ventilatore *m* fan
ventilazione *f* ventilation
ventina *f*: ***una ~*** about twenty
ventiquattrore *f* ⟨*pl* ventiquattrore⟩ (*valigetta*) overnight bag
vento *m* wind; ***c'è ~*** it's windy; ***farsi ~*** fan oneself; ***qual buon ~?*** to what do I owe the pleasure?; *fig* ***navigare col ~ in poppa*** have the wind in one's sails; ***parlare al ~*** waste one's breath
ventola *f* lampshade; TECH fan
ventosa *f* sucker (*a.* ZOOL); MED cupping glass
ventoso *adj* windy
ventre *m* stomach; ***basso ~*** lower abdomen
ventresca *f* ⟨*pl* -che⟩: ***~ di tonno*** *white tuna in oil*
ventricolare *adj*: ***cavità*** *f* ***~*** ventricular cavity
ventricolo *m* ANAT ventricle
ventriloquo *m*, **-a** *f* ventriloquist
ventura *f liter* fate; ***andare alla ~*** trust to luck; ***soldato*** *m* ***di ~*** soldier of fortune
venturo *adj* next
venusiano *adj* Venusian
venuta *f* arrival
venuto I *past part* → ***venire*** **II** *m*, **-a** *f*: ***il primo ~*** just anyone; ***non è certo il primo ~*** he's not just anyone
verace *adj fig* true
veramente *adv* really
veranda *f* veranda
verbale I *adj* verbal; ***processo*** *m* ***~*** trial record **II** *m* record; *di riunione* minutes *pl*; ***~ d'una seduta*** minutes *pl* of a session; ***mettere a ~*** minute
verbalizzare *v/t* ⟨1a⟩ record (in writing), take down; *riunione* take the minutes of; (*esprimere a parole*) verbalize
verbalizzazione *f* recording; (*espressione a parole*) verbalization
verbalmente *adv* verbally
verbena *f* BOT verbena
verbo *m* GRAM verb
vercellese I *adj* from Vercelli **II** *m/f* person from Vercelli
verde I *adj* green; *benzina* unleaded; ***numero ~*** freephone number; ***essere al ~*** be broke **II** *m* green; POL ***i -i*** *pl* the Greens
verdeggiante *adj* green
verderame *m* ⟨*pl* verderame⟩ verdigris
verdetto *m* verdict
verdicchio *m* COOK *medium white wine from central Italy*
verdognolo *adj* greenish
verdolino *adj* pale green
verdone *m* ZOOL greenfinch
verdura *f* vegetables *pl*
verduraio *m*, **-a** *f* ⟨*mpl* -ai⟩ greengrocer
verecondo *adj* prudish
verga *f* ⟨*pl* -ghe⟩ branch
vergine I *adj* virgin *attr* **II** *f* virgin; ASTROL ***Vergine*** Virgo
verginità *f* virginity
vergogna *f* shame; (*timidezza*) shyness; ***è una ~!*** it's a disgrace!
vergognarsi *v/r* ⟨1a⟩ be ashamed; (*essere timido*) be shy
vergognoso *adj* ashamed; (*timido*) shy; *azione* shameful
veridicità *f* ⟨*pl* veridicità⟩ truthfulness
verifica *f* ⟨*pl* -che⟩ check
verificabile *adj* verifiable
verificare *v/t* ⟨1m & d⟩ check
verificarsi *v/r* (*accadere*) occur, take place; (*avverarsi*) come true
verismo *m* realism (*a. fig*)
verista ⟨*mpl* -i⟩ **I** *adj* verist **II** *m/f* verist
verità *f* ⟨*pl* verità⟩ truth
veritiero *adj* ⟨*mpl* -ri⟩ truthful
verme *m* worm; ***~ solitario*** tapeworm; ***nudo come un ~*** stark naked; *fig* ***sentirsi un ~*** feel terrible
vermentino *m* COOK *dry white wine from Liguria, Tuscany and Sardinia*
vermicelli *mpl* COOK vermicelli *sg*
vermiglio *adj* ⟨*mpl* -gli⟩ vermilion
verminosi *f* ⟨*pl* verminosi⟩ verminosis
vermut *m* vermouth

vernaccia *f white wine from Liguria, Tuscany and Sardinia*
vernacolo *m* vernacular
vernice *f* paint; *trasparente* varnish; *pelle* patent leather; *fig* veneer; **~ antiruggine** rust-proofing paint; **~ fresca** wet paint; **~ protettiva** protective coating; **scarpe** *fpl* **di ~** patent leather shoes
verniciare *v/t* ⟨1f⟩ paint; *con vernice trasparente* varnish; **verniciato di fresco** wet paint
verniciatore *m*, **-trice** *f* varnisher
verniciatura *f* painting; *con vernice trasparente* varnishing; *fig* veneer
vernino *adj* winter *attr*
vernissage *m* ⟨*pl* vernissage⟩ private view
vero I *adj* (*rispondente a verità*) true; (*autentico*) real; **sei contento, ~?** you're happy, aren't you?; **ti piace il gelato, ~?** you like ice cream, don't you?; **fosse ~!** if only (it were true)!; **il ~ motivo** the real reason; **~ e proprio** real; **non mi par ~!** I can hardly believe it! **II** *m* truth; PAINT **dal ~** from life; **a dire il ~** to tell the truth
veronese I *adj* of Verona **II** *m/f* inhabitant of Verona
verosimiglianza *f* likelihood
verosimile *adj* likely
verricello *m* winch
verro *m* ZOOL boar
verruca *f* ⟨*pl* -che⟩ wart
versaccio *m* ⟨*pl* -cci⟩ raspberry
versamento *m* payment; **ricevuta** *f* **di ~** deposit receipt
versante *m* slope
versare ⟨1b⟩ **I** *v/t vino* pour; *denaro* pay; (*rovesciare*) spill **II** *v/i* (*trovarsi, essere*) be; **~ in gravi difficoltà** be in serious trouble; **~ in gravi condizioni** be in a bad state
versatile *adj* versatile
versatilità *f* ⟨*pl* versatilità⟩ versatility
versione *f* version; (*traduzione*) translation; **~ integrale** uncut version; **in ~ originale** original language version; **raccontare la propria ~ dei fatti** tell one's side of the story
verso[1] *prep* **1.** towards; **andare ~ casa** head for home **2.** *temporale*: **~ le otto** about eight o'clock
verso[2] *m* (*modo*) manner; **non c'è ~** there is no way; **prendere qn per il ~ giusto** handle s.o. the right way
verso[3] *m di poesie* verse; **fare il ~ a qn** take s.o. off
vertebra *f* vertebra
vertebrale *adj*: **colonna** *f* **~** spinal column
vertebrato I *adj* vertebrate **II** *m*: **i vertebrati** *pl* the vertebrates
vertenza *f*: **~ sindacale** industrial dispute
vertere *v/i* ⟨3a⟩: *fig* **~ su qc** revolve around sth
verticale I *adj* vertical **II** *f* vertical (line); *in ginnastica* handstand
vertice *m* summit; **incontro** *m* **al ~** summit (meeting); **essere al ~ della carriera** be at the peak of one's career
vertigine *f* vertigo, dizziness; **ho le -i** I feel dizzy
vertiginoso *adj altezza* dizzy; *prezzi* staggering, sky-high; *velocità* breakneck
verve *f* ⟨*pl* verve⟩ verve
verza *f* savoy (cabbage)
vescica *f* ⟨*pl* -che⟩ ANAT bladder
vescovado *m* episcopate; (*diocesi*) see
vescovile *adj* episcopal
vescovo *m* bishop
vespa *f* ZOOL wasp
vespaio *m* ⟨*pl* -ai⟩ wasps' nest; *fig* hornets' nest
vespasiano *m* public urinal
vespertino *adj* evening *attr*
vespro *m* REL vespers *pl*
vessatorio ⟨*mpl* -ri⟩ *adj* oppressive
vessillo *m* banner
vestaglia *f* dressing gown, *US* robe
vestale *f* HIST vestal virgin
veste *f fig* (*capacità, funzione*) capacity; **in ~ ufficiale** in an official capacity; **in ~ di** (in one's capacity) as
Vestfalia *f* Westphalia
vestiario *m* clothes, clothing
vestigia *fpl*: **le ~ del passato** the relics of the past
vestire *v/t* ⟨4b⟩ dress; (*portare*) wear
vestirsi *v/r* get dressed; *in un certo modo* dress; **~ da** (*travestirsi*) dress up as
vestitino *m* baby's dress
vestito[1] *m da uomo* suit; *da donna* dress; (*capo di vestiario*) item of clothing, garment; **-i** *pl* clothes; **-i** *pl*

da uomo men's wear
vestito[2] *adj* dressed; ***~ di bianco / di nero*** dressed in white / in black
vestizione *f* habit, clothing
Vesuvio *m* Vesuvius
veterano I *adj* MIL veteran (*a. fig*) **II** *n*: ***veterano*** *m* MIL veteran (*a. fig*)
veterinaria *f* veterinary medicine
veterinario *m*, **-a** *f* ⟨*mpl* -ri⟩ veterinary surgeon, vet *infml*
veto *m* veto; ***porre il ~ a*** veto
vetraio *m*, **-a** *f* ⟨*mpl* -i⟩ (*installatore*) glazier
vetrata *f finestra* large window; *porta* glass door; *di chiesa* stained-glass window
vetreria *f* (*fabbrica*) glass works *sg or pl*; (*negozio*) glazier's
vetrina *f* (shop) window; *mobile* display cabinet; *di museo*, *fig* showcase
vetrinista *m/f* ⟨*mpl* -i⟩ window dresser
vetrino *m* slide
vetriolo *m* vitriol; *fig* ***critica*** *f* ***al ~*** caustic criticism
vetro *m* glass; *di finestra*, *porta* pane; ***di ~*** glass *attr*; ***~ armato*** reinforced glass; ***~ blindato*** bulletproof glass; ***~ infrangibile*** shatterproof glass; ***~ isolante*** double glazing; ***~ smerigliato*** frosted glass; ***pittura*** *f* ***su ~*** painting on glass
vetroresina *f* fibreglass, *US* fiber-
vetta *f* top; *di montagna* peak; ***in ~ alla classifica*** at the top of the table
vettore I *adj* vector; MED carrier **II** *n*: ***vettore*** *m* MATH, PHYS vector; COMM, JUR, SPACE, BIOL carrier
vettoriale *adj* MATH vectorial; ***grafica*** *f* ***~*** COMPUT vector graphics
vettovaglie *fpl* provisions
vettura *f* AUTO car; RAIL carriage; ***~ da corsa*** racing car; ***in ~!*** all aboard!
vetturino *m* coach driver
vetusto *adj* ancient
vezzeggiativo *m* GRAM diminutive
vezzo *m* habit; ***-i*** *pl* quirks
vi I *pron* you; *riflessivo* yourselves; *reciproco* each other **II** *adv* → ***ci***
via[1] **I** *adv* away; ***andar ~*** go away, leave; ***~ ~*** (*gradualmente*) little by little, gradually; (*man mano*) as (and when); ***e così ~*** and so on; ***~!*** *per scacciare* go away!, scram! *infml*; (*suvvia*) come on! ***vattene ~!*** go away! **II** *prep* via, by way of; ***~ Brennero*** via the Brenner Pass; ***~ telefax*** by fax
via[2] *f* **1.** street, road; ***la Via Crucis*** the Way of the Cross; ***Via Lattea*** Milky Way; ***~ Marconi*** Marconi St; ***~ di fuga*** escape route; ***~ laterale*** side street; ***principale / secondaria*** main / secondary road; ***sulla ~ del ritorno*** on the way back; *fig* ***trovare una ~ d'uscita*** find a way out; ***-e*** *pl* ***respiratorie*** airway **2.** *fig* way; ***in ~ amichevole*** amicably; ***in ~ eccezionale*** as an exception; ***lettera*** *f* **(*per*)** ***~ aerea*** airmail letter; ***~ legale*** legal method; ***ricorrere alle -e legali*** take legal action; ***per ~ di*** by; (*a causa di*) because of
via[3] *m* off, starting signal; SPORTS ***dare il ~*** give the off; *fig* ***dare il ~ a qc*** get sth under way
viabilità *f* ⟨*pl* viabilità⟩ road conditions *pl*; (*rete stradale*) road network; (*traffico stradale*) road traffic
viacard® *f* ⟨*pl* viacard⟩ card for paying motorway tolls
viadotto *m* viaduct
viaggiante *adj* travel(l)ing; ***personale*** *m* ***~*** train crew
viaggiare *v/i* ⟨1f⟩ travel; ***~ per affari*** travel on business
viaggiatore *m*, **-trice** *f* travel(l)er
viaggio *m* ⟨*pl* -ggi⟩ journey; ***~ aereo*** flight; ***~ per mare*** voyage; ***~ di nozze*** honeymoon; ***~ in comitiva*** group travel; ***~ organizzato*** package tour; ***~ in treno*** train journey; ***~ d'affari*** business trip; ***~ di studio*** study trip; ***cestino*** *m* ***da~*** packed meal; ***mettersi in~*** set out; ***essere in ~*** be away, be travelling; ***buon~!*** Bon Voyage! Have a good trip!
viagra® *m* Viagra®
viale *m* avenue
via libera *m* ⟨*pl* via libera⟩: ***dare il ~*** give the all clear
viandante *m/f* wayfarer
viario *adj* ⟨*mpl* -ri⟩ road *attr*; ***rete*** *f* ***-a*** road network
viatico *m* ⟨*pl* -ci⟩ REL viaticum; *fig* comfort
viavai *m* ⟨*pl* viavai⟩ coming and going
vibonese I *adj* from Vibo Valentia **II** *m/f* person from Vibo Valentia
vibrafono *m* vibes
vibrante *adj* vibrating; *voce* vibrant
vibrare *v/i* ⟨1a⟩ vibrate
vibratore *m* vibrator

vibrazione *f* vibration
vicariato *m* vicariate
vicario *m* ⟨*pl* -ri⟩ substitute; REL vicar
vice *m/f* ⟨*pl* vice⟩ deputy
vice... *pref* vice-
viceconsole *m* vice-consul
vicedirettore *m*, **-trice** *f* assistant manager; *giornale* subeditor
vicenda *f* (*episodio*) event; (*storia*) story; ***alterne -e*** changing fortunes; ***a ~*** (*a turno*) in turn; (*scambievolmente*) each other, one another
vicendevole *adj* mutual
vicentino I *adj* of Vicenza **II** *m*, **-a** *f* person from Vicenza
vicepremier *m* ⟨*pl* vicepremier⟩ POL deputy prime minister
viceversa *adv* vice versa
vichingo *m*, **-a** *f* ⟨*mpl* -ghi⟩ Viking
vicinanza *f* nearness, proximity; ***-e*** *pl* neighbo(u)rhood *sg*, vicinity *sg*
vicinato *m* neighbo(u)rhood; (*persone*) neighbo(u)rs *pl*
vicino I *adj* near, close; ***~ a*** near, close to; (*accanto a*) next to; ***da ~*** *esaminare* closely; *visto* close up **II** *adv* nearby, close by; ***vieni più ~*** come closer **III** *m*, **-a** *f* neighbo(u)r; ***il ~ di casa*** the next-door neighbo(u)r
vicissitudini *fpl* vicissitudes; ***le ~ della vita*** life's ups and downs
vicolo *m* lane; ***~ cieco*** dead end
videata *f* COMPUT display
video *m* video; *infml* (*schermo*) screen
videocamera *f* videocamera
videocassetta *f* video (cassette)
videocellulare *m* video mobile phone, *US* video cell phone
videochiamare *v/t* ⟨1a⟩ TEL video-call
videochiamata *f* TEL video-call
videocitofono *m* video entryphone
videoclip *m* ⟨*pl* videoclip⟩ video
videoconferenza *f* videoconference
videocontrollo *m* video surveillance
videofonino *m*, **videotelefonino** *m* TEL video-phone
videogioco *m* video game
videopoker *m* ⟨*pl* videopoker⟩ COMPUT on-line poker
videoregistratore *m* video (recorder)
videoscrittura *f* COMPUT word processing
videoteca *f* video library; (*negozio*) video shop
videotel *m* ⟨*pl* videotel⟩ *Italian Videotex®*
videotelefono *m* videophone, viewphone
vidimare *v/t* ⟨1l⟩ certify
vidimazione *f* authentication
Vienna *f* Vienna
viennese I *adj* Viennese **II** *m/f* Viennese
vietare *v/t* ⟨1b⟩ forbid; ***~ a qn di fare qc*** forbid s.o. to do sth
vietato *adj*: ***~ fumare*** no smoking
Viet Nam *m* Vietnam
vietnamita ⟨*mpl* -i⟩ **I** *adj* Vietnamese **II** *m/f* Vietnamese
vigente *adj* in force
vigere *v/i* ⟨3yy⟩ be in force
vigilante *m* security guard
vigilanza *f* vigilance; ***sotto ~*** under surveillance; ***servizio*** *m* ***di ~*** monitoring service
vigilare *v/t & v/i* ⟨1l⟩ *persone* watch (over); (*pattugliare*) patrol
vigilatrice *f*: ***~ d'infanzia*** nursery nurse
vigile I *m/f*: ***~*** (***urbano***) traffic policeman; ***~ del fuoco*** firefighter **II** *adj* watchful
vigilia *f* night before, eve; ***~ di Natale*** Christmas Eve
vigliaccata *f* dirty trick
vigliaccheria *f* cowardice
vigliacco ⟨*mpl* -cchi⟩ **I** *adj* coward **II** *m*, **-a** *f* coward
vigna *f* (small) vineyard
vignaiolo *m*, **-a** *f* vine-dresser
vigneto *m* vineyard
vignetta *f* cartoon
vignettista *m/f* ⟨*mpl* -i⟩ cartoonist
vigogna *f* SEW vicuna
vigore *m* vigo(u)r; ***nel ~ degli anni*** in the prime of life; ***entrare in ~*** come into force
vigoroso *adj* vigorous
vile I *adj* vile; (*codardo*) coward **II** *m* coward
vilipendio *m* ⟨*pl* -di⟩ contempt
villa *f* villa
villaggio *m* ⟨*pl* -ggi⟩ village; ***~ olimpico*** Olympic village; ***~ turistico*** holiday camp
villania *f* boorishness
villano I *adj pej* boorish **II** *m pej* lout; ***~!*** how rude!
villeggiante *m/f* holidaymaker
villeggiatura *f* holiday

villetta *f* detached house; **~ *a schiera*** terraced *or US* row house
villino *m* house
villoso,a *adj* hairy
Viminale *m* Italian Ministry of the Interior
vimine *m* osier; ***cesto*** *m* ***di -i*** wicker basket
vinaccia *f* ⟨*pl* -cce⟩ marc; ***acquavite*** *f* ***di ~*** marc brandy
vincente I *adj* winning; ***biglietto*** *m* **~** winning ticket; ***mossa*** *f* **~** winning move (*a. fig*) **II** *m/f* winner
vincere ⟨3d⟩ **I** *v/t* win; *avversario, nemico* defeat, beat; *difficoltà* overcome; **~ *un premio / una medaglia*** win a prize / a medal; ***lasciarsi ~ dallo sconforto*** be overcome by depression **II** *v/i* win
vincersi *v/r* (*dominarsi*) control o.s.
vincita *f* win; **~ *al lotto*** lottery win
vincitore *m*, **-trice** *f* winner
vincolare *v/t* ⟨1l⟩ bind; *capitale* tie up
vincolato *adj* bound; FIN ***conto ~*** time deposit
vincolo *m* bond
vinicolo *adj* wine *attr*; ***azienda*** *f* ***-a*** wine company
vino *m* wine; **~ *amabile*** sweet wine; **~ *bianco*** white wine; ***vin brûlè*** mulled wine; **~ *rosso*** red wine; **~ *secco*** dry wine; **~ *da pasto*** *or* ***da tavola*** table wine; ***vin santo*** sweet white wine; **~ *da taglio*** blended wine
vinto *past part* → ***vincere***
viola *f* **1.** MUS viola **2.** BOT violet; **~ *del pensiero*** pansy
violacciocca *f* ⟨*pl* -cche⟩ stock
violaceo *adj* purplish-blue
violare *v/t* ⟨1l⟩ violate; **~ *la legge*** break the law; **~ *il segreto professionale*** violate professional confidentiality; **~ *un giuramento*** break an oath; **~ *un patto*** break an agreement
violazione *f* violation; *di leggi, patti, accordi* breach; **~ *di domicilio*** unlawful entry
violentare *v/t* ⟨1b⟩ rape
violentatore *m* rapist
violentemente *adv* violently
violento *adj* violent
violenza *f* violence; **~ *carnale*** sexual assault *o* abuse
violetta *f* violet
violetto I *adj* violet **II** *n*: ***violetto*** *m* violet
violinista *m/f* ⟨*mpl* -i⟩ violinist
violino *m* violin
violoncello *m* cello
viottolo *m* lane
VIP *m* ⟨*pl* vip⟩ VIP
vipera *f* viper
virale *adj* viral; ***infezione*** *f* **~** viral infection
virare *v/i* ⟨1a⟩ AVIAT, NAUT veer; *nel nuoto* turn
virata *f* AVIAT, NAUT veer; *nel nuoto* turn; POL swing
virgola *f* comma; MATH decimal point; **~ *mobile*** MATH floating point system; *fig* ***senza cambiare una ~*** not change anything at all
virgolette *fpl* inverted commas *pl*; ***tra ~*** in inverted commas
virile *adj* manly, virile
virilità *f* ⟨*pl* virilità⟩ masculinity; MED virility; *fig* manliness
virologia *f* virology
virologo *m*, **-a** *f* ⟨*mpl* -gi⟩ virologist
virtù *f* ⟨*pl* virtù⟩ virtue; **~ *cardinali / teologali*** cardinal / theological virtues; ***fare di necessità ~*** make a virtue of necessity; ***in ~ di qc*** by virtue of sth
virtuale *adj* virtual
virtuosismo *m* virtuosity
virtuoso I *adj* virtuous **II** *m*, **-a** *f* virtuoso
virulento *adj* virulent
virus *m* ⟨*pl* virus⟩ virus
visagista *m/f* ⟨*mpl* -i⟩ beautician
viscerale *adj* ANAT visceral (*a. fig*)
viscere *fpl* insides *pl*; *fig*: *della terra* bowels *pl*
vischio *m* ⟨*pl* -chi⟩ mistletoe
vischioso *adj* viscous
viscido *adj* slimy
visciola *f* BOT morello cherry
visconte *m*, **-essa** *f* viscount, viscountess
viscosa *f* viscose
viscosità *f* ⟨*pl* viscosità⟩ viscosity (*a.* PHYS)
viscoso *adj* viscous (*a.* PHYS)
visibile *adj* visible
visibilio *m*: ***andare in ~*** go into ecstasies
visibilità *f* visibility
visiera *f di berretto* peak; *di casco* visor

visigoto I *adj* Visigothic **II** *m*, **-a** *f* Visigoth
visionare *v/t* ⟨1m⟩ examine
visionario *adj* visionary
visione *f* sight, vision; ***avere una ~*** have a vision; ***prendere ~ di qc*** have a look at sth; ***in ~*** for examination
visita *f* visit; ***~ medica*** medical (examination); ***far ~ a qn*** visit s.o.; ***~ guidata*** guided tour; ***~ a domicilio*** house call
visitare *v/t* ⟨1l⟩ visit; MED examine
visitatore *m*, **-trice** *f* visitor
visivo *adj* visual; ***facoltà*** *f* ***-a*** vision
viso *m* face; ***a ~ aperto*** openly; ***fare buon ~ a cattivo gioco*** make the best of it
visone *m* mink
vispo *adj* lively
vissuto *past part* → ***vivere***
vista *f* (*senso*) sight; (*capacità visiva*) eyesight; (*veduta*) view; ***punto*** *m* ***di ~*** point of view; ***a prima ~*** at first sight; MUS at sight; ***in ~ di*** in sight of; *fig* in view of; ***conoscere qn di ~*** know s.o. by sight; *fig* ***perdere qn di ~*** lose touch with s.o.; ***a ~ d'occhio*** before one's very eyes; ***con ~ sul mare*** with a sea view
vistare *v/t* ⟨1a⟩ ADMIN stamp
visto I *past part* → ***vedere***; ***~ che*** seeing that **II** *m* visa; ***~ d'entrata*** entry visa; ***~ di transito*** transit visa; ***~ d'uscita*** exit visa
vistoso *adj* eye-catching
visuale I *adj* visual **II** *f* (*veduta*) view
visualizzare *v/t* ⟨1a⟩ visualize
vita[1] *f* life; (*durata della vita*) lifetime; ***a ~*** for life; ***costo*** *m* ***della ~*** cost of living; ***senza ~*** lifeless; ***fare una ~ da cani*** have a dog's life; ***avere una doppia ~*** lead a double life; ***~ media*** life expectancy; ***~ natural durante*** for one's natural life; ***come va la ~?*** how's life?; ***è una ~ che non ci vediamo!*** it's ages since I saw you!; ***essere in fin di ~*** be dying; ***la dolce ~*** the dolce vita
vita[2] *f* ANAT waist; ***giro*** *m* ***~*** waist measurement
vitaccia *f* ⟨*pl* -cce⟩ *infml* dog's life
vitale *adj* vital; *persona* lively, full of life
vitalità *f* ⟨*pl* vitalità⟩ vitality
vitamina *f* vitamin
vitaminico *adj* ⟨*mpl* -ci⟩ vitamin *attr*
vite[1] *f* TECH screw; *fig* ***giro*** *m* ***di ~*** turn of the screw
vite[2] *f* AGR vine
vitello *m* calf; COOK veal
vitellone *m* bullock; *fig infml* layabouts
viterbese I *adj* from Viterbo **II** *m/f* person from Viterbo
viticoltore *m*, **-trice** *f* vine-grower
viticoltura *f* vine-growing
vitigno *m* grape variety
vitreo *adj fig sguardo*, *occhio* glazed, glassy
vittima *f* victim; *fig* ***fare la ~*** be a martyr
vittimismo *m* making a martyr of oneself
vitto *m* diet food; ***~ e alloggio*** bed and board
vittoria *f* victory; ***cantare ~*** crow over a victory; ***avere la ~ in pugno*** have victory in one's grasp
Vittoria *m*: ***Lago ~*** Lake Victoria
vittorioso *adj* victorious
vituperare *v/t* ⟨1m⟩ vituperate
viuzza *f* alleyway
viva *int*: ***~ ...!*** long live ...!
vivacchiare *v/i* ⟨1k⟩ scrape by
vivace *adj* lively; *colore* bright; MUS vivace
vivacità *f* liveliness; *di colori* brightness
vivacizzare *v/t* ⟨1a⟩ brighten up
vivaio *m di pesci* tank; *di piante* nursery; *fig* breeding ground
vivamente *adv*: ***congratularsi ~ con qn*** warmly congratulate s.o.
vivanda *f* food
viva voce *m* ⟨*pl* viva voce⟩ speakerphone
vivente *adj* living
vivere ⟨3zz⟩ **I** *v/i* live (***di*** on); ***~ alla giornata*** live from hand to mouth; ***~ in città / in campagna*** live in the city / in the country; ***guadagnarsi da ~*** make a living **II** *v/t* (*passare*, *provare*) experience; ***~ una vita tranquilla*** live quietly, lead a quiet life; ***per amore del quieto ~*** for a quiet life
viveri *mpl* food (supplies *pl*); *fig* ***tagliare i ~ a qn*** cut off s.o.'s allowance
viveur *m* ⟨*pl* viveur⟩ pleasure-seeker
vivibile *adj* liveable
vivido *adj colore* bright; *ricordo* vivid
viviparo I *adj* ZOOL viviparous **II** *m*, **-a**

f ZOOL viviparous mammal
vivisezione *f* vivisection
vivo I *adj* (*in vita*) alive; (*vivente*) living; *colore* bright; ***farsi ~*** get in touch; (*arrivare*) turn up; ***~ e vegeto*** hale and hearty; ***non c'era anima -a*** there wasn't a soul there; ***~ e vegeto*** alive and kicking; ***è ancora ~?*** is he / she still alive? **II** *m*: ***dal ~*** *trasmissione, concerto* live; ***entrare nel ~ della questione*** get to the heart of the matter; ***nel ~ della discussione*** in the middle of the discussion; ***ritrarre dal ~*** paint from life; ***i -i*** *pl* the living; ***pungere qn sul ~*** cut s.o. to the quick
viziare *v/t* ⟨1g⟩ *persona* spoil
viziato *adj persona* spoiled; ***aria*** *f* ***-a*** stale air
vizio *m* ⟨*pl* -zi⟩ vice; (*cattiva abitudine*) (bad) habit; (*dipendenza*) addiction; ***~ cardiaco*** heart defect; ***è un ~ di famiglia*** it's a family defect; ***l'ozio è il padre dei -zi*** the devil makes work for idle hands
vizioso *adj persona* dissolute; ***circolo*** *m* ***~*** vicious circle
vizzo *adj* wrinkled
v.le *abbr* (= **viale**) St (street)
vocabolario *m* ⟨*pl* -ri⟩ (*lessico*) vocabulary; (*dizionario*) dictionary
vocabolo *m* word
vocale I *adj* vocal; ***corde*** *fpl* ***-i*** vocal cords **II** *f* vowel
vocazione *f* vocation
voce *f* voice; *fig* rumo(u)r; *in dizionario, elenco* entry; ***ad alta ~*** in a loud voice, loudly; ***a bassa ~*** in a low voice, quietly; ***spargere la ~*** spread rumo(u)rs; ***non avere ~ in capitolo*** have no say in the matter; ***~ bianca*** treble voice; ***a ~*** in person; ***a mezza ~*** in a whisper; ***corre ~ che ...*** there's a rumo(u)r that ...; ***spargere la ~*** spread a rumo(u)r; ***sotto ~*** in a whisper; ***~ di bilancio*** item in the budget
vociare *v/i* ⟨1f⟩ shout
vociferare *v/t* ⟨1m⟩ clamour
vocio *m* ⟨*pl* -cii⟩ shouting
vodka *f* vodka
voga *f*: ***essere in ~*** be in fashion
vogare *v/i* ⟨1e⟩ row
vogatore *m*, **-trice** *f* rower
voglia *f* (*desiderio*) wish, desire; (*volontà*) will; *sulla pelle* birthmark; ***avere ~ di fare qc*** feel like doing sth; ***morire dalla ~ di fare qc*** be dying to do sth; ***contro ~, di mala ~*** unwillingly, reluctantly
voglio → ***volere***
voglioso *adj* whimsical
voi *pron* you; *riflessivo* yourselves; *reciproco* each other; ***a ~*** to you; ***senza di ~*** without you
vol. *abbr* (= **volume**) vol (volume)
volano *m* shuttlecock; (*gioco*) badminton
volante I *adj* flying; ***otto*** *m* ***~*** roller coaster; ZOOL ***cervo*** *m* ***~*** stag beetle; ***squadra*** *f* ***~*** flying squad **II** *m* AUTO (steering) wheel **III** *f* flying squad
volantinaggio *m* ⟨*pl* -ggi⟩ leafleting
volantino *m* leaflet
volare *v/i* ⟨1a⟩ fly; ***il tempo vola*** time flies
volata *f* SPORTS final sprint; ***di ~*** in a rush
volatile I *adj* volatile **II** *m* bird
volatilizzarsi *v/r* ⟨1n⟩ volatilize; *fig* disappear into thin air
vol-au-vent *m* ⟨*pl* vol-au-vent⟩ vol-au--vent
volente *adj*: ***~ o nolente*** whether one likes it or not
volenteroso *adj* willing
volentieri *adv* willingly; ***~!*** with pleasure!
volere I *v/t & v/i* ⟨2t⟩ **1.** want; ***vorrei ...*** I would *or* I'd like ...; ***vorrei partire*** I'd like to leave; ***~ dire*** mean; ***~ bene a qn*** (*amare*) love s.o.; ***senza ~*** without meaning to; ***come vuole*** as you wish; ***non ne voglio più*** I don't want any more of it; ***ti vogliono al telefono*** you are wanted on the telephone; ***~ o no...*** whether one likes it or not; ***questa non ci voleva!*** that's just what we needed!; ***in grado d'intendere e di ~*** be of sound mind **2.** ***ci vogliono dieci mesi*** it takes ten months **II** *m* will; ***~ è potere*** *prov* where there's a will there's a way
Volga *m* Volga
volgare *adj* vulgar; ***nome*** *m* ***~*** common noun
volgarità *f* ⟨*pl* volgarità⟩ vulgarity
volgarmente *adv* vulgarly; ***parlare / comportarsi ~*** talk / behave vulgarly
volgere ⟨3d⟩ **I** *v/t*: ***~ le spalle*** turn one's back; ***~ lo sguardo verso qn / qc*** turn one's gaze towards s.o. / sth

II *v/i*: ~ ***al termine*** draw to a close; ***il tempo volge al brutto*** the weather is getting worse; ~ ***al peggio*** take a turn for the worse
voliera *f* aviary
volitivo *adj* volitional
volo *m* **1.** flight; ~ ***charter*** charter flight; ~ ***diretto*** direct flight; ~ ***internazionale*** international flight; ~ ***last minute*** last-minute flight; ~ ***di andata e ritorno*** return flight; ~ ***di linea*** scheduled flight; ~ ***low cost*** cheap *or* low-cost flight; ~ ***nazionale*** domestic flight; ~ ***a vela*** gliding; ~ ***senza scalo*** nonstop flight; *fig* ***afferrare qc al*** ~ be quick to grasp sth; ***prendere il*** ~ *di uccello* fly away; *di persona* run away; ***cogliere l'occasione al*** ~ jump at the opportunity **2.** (*caduta*) fall
volontà *f* ⟨*pl* volontà⟩ will; ***a*** ~ as much as you like; ***buona*** ~ goodwill; ***con tutta la buona*** ~ with the best will in the world
volontariato *m* voluntary work
volontario ⟨*mpl* -ri⟩ **I** *adj* voluntary **II** *m*, **-a** *f* volunteer
volpe *f* fox; *femmina* vixen
volpino I *adj* foxlike; *fig* foxy **II** *n*: ***volpino*** *m* Pomeranian
volpone *m*, **-a** *f fig* smooth operator
volt *m* ⟨*pl* volt⟩ volt
volta[1] *f* time; (*turno*) turn; ***una*** ~ once; ***due -e*** twice; ***qualche*** ~ sometimes; ***questa*** ~ this time; ***quante -e?*** how many times?; ***ogni*** ~ every time; ***rare -e*** rarely; ***una*** ~ ***tanto*** from time to time; ***una*** ~ ***o l'altra*** one time or another; ***una*** ~ ***per sempre*** (*or* ***tutte***) once and for all; ***poco per*** ~ little by little; ***un po' per*** *or* ***alla*** ~ little by little; ***un'altra*** ~ *ancora una volta* one more time; ***lo faremo un'altra*** ~ we'll do it some other time; ***molte -e*** many times, often; ***c'era una*** ~ once upon a time there was
volta[2] *f* ARCH vault; ***a*** ~ ARCH vaulted
voltafaccia *m* ⟨*pl* voltafaccia⟩ volte-face
voltagabbana *m/f* ⟨*pl* voltagabbana⟩ turncoat
voltaggio *m* ⟨*pl* -ggi⟩ voltage
voltare ⟨1c⟩ **I** *v/t* turn; *pagina* turn (over); ~ ***le spalle a qn*** *azione* turn one's back on s.o.; *posizione* have one's back to s.o. *fig* ~ ***pagina*** turn over a new leaf **II** *v/i* turn; ~ ***a destra*** turn right
voltarsi *v/r* turn (round)
voltastomaco *m* ⟨*no pl*⟩ nausea; ***mi viene il*** ~ I'm going to be sick; *fig* it makes me sick
volteggiare *v/i* ⟨1f⟩ circle; *nelle danze* spin; SPORTS vault; *ippica* jump
volteggio *m* ⟨*pl* -ggi⟩ SPORTS vaulting; *ippica* jumping
volto[1] *m* face
volto[2] *past part* → ***volgere***
voltura *f* JUR transfer; ADMIN assignment
volubile *adj* fickle
volubilità *f* ⟨*pl* volubilità⟩ fickleness
volume *m* volume; ***a tutto*** ~ at full volume
volumetria *f* volumetry
voluminoso *adj* bulky
volutamente *adv* deliberately
voluttà *f* voluptuousness
voluttuario *adj* ⟨*mpl* -ri⟩ unnecessary; ***bene*** *m* ~ luxury good
voluttuoso *adj* sensuous
vomere *m* plough share, *US* plow
vomitare *v/t* ⟨1l & c⟩ vomit, throw up *infml*; *fig* ***mi fa*** ~ it makes me sick
vomitevole *adj fig* disgusting
vomito *m* vomit; ***conato*** *m* ***di*** ~ retch
vongola *f* ZOOL, COOK clam
vorace *adj* voracious
voracità *f* voraciousness, voracity
voragine *f* chasm, abyss
vortice *m* whirl; *in acqua* whirlpool; *di vento* whirlwind
vorticoso *adj* whirling; *fig* dizzy
vostro I *adj* your; ***i -i amici*** your friends **II** *pron*: ***il*** ~ yours; ***questi libri sono -i*** these books are yours
votante I *adj* voting **II** *m/f* voter
votare *v/t* ⟨1a⟩ vote; ~ ***un candidato*** vote for a candidate; ~ ***una legge*** pass a law
votazione *f* vote
votivo *adj* votive; ***cappella*** *f* ***-a*** votive chapel; ***offerta*** *f* ***-a*** votive offering
voto *m* POL vote; EDU mark; REL, *fig* vow; ***mettere qc ai -i*** put sth to the vote, take a vote on sth; ***fare un*** ~ REL take a vow; ~ ***segreto*** secret ballot; ~ ***di castità*** vow of chastity
voucher *m* ⟨*pl* voucher⟩ voucher
v.r. *abbr* (= **vedi retro**) see over

VR *abbr* (= **Verona**) Verona
v.s. *abbr* (= **vedi sopra**) see above
Vs. *abbr* (= **vostro**) your
VT *abbr* (= **Viterbo**) Viterbo
V.U. *abbr* (= **Vigili Urbani**) police *pl*
vucumprà *m* ⟨*pl* vucumprà⟩ *infml* hawker (*usually of African origin*)
vulcanico *adj* ⟨*mpl* -ci⟩ volcanic
vulcanizzazione *f* vulcanization
vulcano *m* volcano; ***essere un ~ d'idee*** be a powerhouse of ideas
vulnerabile *adj* vulnerable
vulnerabilità *f* ⟨*pl* vulnerabilità⟩ vulnerability
vulva *f* vulva
vuole → ***volere***
vuotare *v/t* ⟨1c⟩ empty
vuotarsi *v/r* empty
vuoto I *adj* empty; (*non occupato*) vacant; (*privo*) devoid (**di** of); ***a stomaco ~*** on an empty stomach **II** *m* **1.** (*spazio*) empty space; ***~ d'aria*** air pocket **2.** (*recipiente*) empty; ***~ a perdere*** non-returnable container; ***~ a rendere*** returnable container **3.** PHYS vacuum; (***confezionato***) ***sotto ~*** vacuum-packed **4.** *fig* void; ***andare a ~*** fall through; ***~ di memoria*** memory lapse; ***farsi il ~ intorno*** isolate oneself
VV *abbr* (= **Vibo Valentia**) Vibo Valentia

W

w, W *m/f* ⟨*pl* w, W⟩ w, W
W *abbr* **1.** (= **watt**) W (watt) **2.** (= **viva**) long live
wafer *m* ⟨*pl* wafer⟩ wafer
walkie-talkie *m* ⟨*pl* walkie-talkie⟩ walkie-talkie
walkman® *m* ⟨*pl* walkman⟩ Walkman®
wap *m* ⟨*pl* wap⟩ COMPUT, TEL wap
water *m* ⟨*pl* water⟩ toilet
watt *m* ⟨*pl* watt⟩ watt
watusso I *adj* Watutsi **II** *m*, **-a** *f* Watutsi
WC *abbr* (= **gabinetto**) WC (water closet)
web *m* Web; ***sito*** *m* ***~*** website
weblog *m* ⟨*pl* weblog⟩ COMPUT weblog
week-end *m* ⟨*pl* week-end⟩ weekend
wellness *f* ⟨*pl* wellness⟩ wellness
western *m* ⟨*pl* western⟩ Western; ***~ all'italiana*** spaghetti Western
whisky *m* ⟨*pl* whisky⟩ whisky
windsurf *m* ⟨*pl* windsurf⟩ (*tavola*) sailboard; *attività* windsurfing; ***fare ~*** go windsurfing
W.L. *abbr* (= **vagone letto**) sleeping car
word processor *m* ⟨*pl* word processor⟩ word processor
workshop *m* ⟨*pl* workshop⟩ workshop
workstation *f* ⟨*pl* workstation⟩ workstation
würstel *m* ⟨*pl* würstel⟩ frankfurter

X

x, X *f* x, X; ***raggi*** *mpl* ***~*** X-rays
xenofobia *f* xenophobia
xenofobo I *adj* xenophobic **II** *m*, **-a** *f* xenophobe
xilofono *m* xylophone
xilografia *f* xylograph

Y

y, Y *m/f* ⟨*pl* y, Y⟩ y, Y
yacht *m* ⟨*pl* yacht⟩ yacht
Yemen *m* Yemen
yemenita ⟨*mpl* -i⟩ **I** *adj* Yemeni **II** *m/f* Yemeni
yeti *m* ⟨*pl* yeti⟩ yeti
yoga *m* ⟨*no pl*⟩ yoga
yogurt *m* ⟨*pl* yogurt⟩ yoghurt
yogurtiera *f* yoghurt-maker
yo-yo® *m* ⟨*pl* yo-yo⟩ yo-yo
yuppie *m* ⟨*pl* yuppie⟩ yuppy

Z

z, Z *m/f* ⟨*pl* z, Z⟩ z, Z
zabaione *m* zabaglione
zafferano *m* saffron
zaffiro *m* sapphire
Zagabria *f* Zagreb
zagara *f* orange blossom
zaino *m* rucksack
Zaire *m* Zaire
Zambesi *m* Zambesi
Zambia *m* Zambia
zambiano **I** *adj* Zambian **II** *m*, **-a** *f* Zambian
zampa *f* ZOOL (*piede*) paw; *di uccello* claw; (*zoccolo*) hoof; (*arto*) leg; COOK *di maiale* trotter; *fig* ***giù le -e!*** hands off!; ***a ~ di elefante*** flared; ***camminare a quattro -e*** get down on all fours; *fig* ***-e*** *pl* ***di gallina*** crow's feet
zampata *f* (*colpo*) blow with a paw; (*impronta*) track
zampettare *v/i* ⟨1a⟩ patter
zampillare *v/i* ⟨1a⟩ gush
zampillo *m* spurt
zampino *m*: ***metterci lo ~*** interfere
zampirone *m* mosquito coil
zampogna *f* (bag)pipes *pl*
zampognaro *m* (bag)piper
zampone *m* COOK stuffed pig's trotter
zanna *f* tusk
zanzara *f* mosquito
zanzariera *f* mosquito net; *su finestre* insect screen
zappa *f* hoe
zappare *v/t* ⟨1a⟩ hoe
zappatore *m*, **-trice** *f* hoer
zapping *m* ⟨*no pl*⟩: ***fare lo ~*** zap
zar *m* ⟨*pl* zar⟩ tsar
zarina *f* tsarina
zattera *f* raft
zatterone *m* raft; (*scarpa*) platform (shoe)
zavorra *f* ballast
zazzera *f* mop (of hair)
zebra *f* zebra
zecca[1] *f* ⟨*pl* -cche⟩ ZOOL tick
zecca[2] *f* ⟨*pl* -cche⟩ Mint; ***nuovo di ~*** brand-new
zecchino *m* sequin
zelante *adj* zealous
zelo *m* zeal
zen ⟨*pl* zen⟩ **I** *adj inv* Zen **II** *m* Zen
zenit *m* zenith
zenzero *m* ginger
zeppa *f* wedge; ***scarpe*** *fpl* ***con le -e*** platform shoes
zeppo *adj*: ***pieno ~*** crammed (***di*** with)
zerbino *m* doormat
zerbinotto *m* dandy
zero *m* zero; *nel tennis* love; *nel calcio* nil; *fig* ***partire da ~*** start from scratch; ***2 gradi sotto ~*** 2 degrees below zero; ***~ assoluto*** absolute zero; *fig* ***sparare a ~*** blast s.o. out of the water
zibaldone *m* notebook of thoughts, ideas, etc.; *pej* hotch-potch
zibellino *m* ZOOL zibelline; (*pelliccia*) sable
zibibbo *m white wine from the south of Italy*
zigano **I** *adj* gipsy **II** *m*, **-a** *f* gipsy
zigomo *m* cheekbone
zigote *m* BIOL zygote

zigrinato *adj* MECH milled
zigzag *m* ⟨*pl* zigzag⟩ zigzag
zigzagare *v/i* ⟨1e⟩ zigzag
Zimbabwe *m* Zimbabwe
zimbello *m* decoy; *fig* laughing stock
zincare *v/t* ⟨1d⟩ zinc
zinco *m* zinc
zingarata *f* prank
zingaresco *adj* ⟨*mpl* -schi⟩ gipsy
zingaro *m*, **-a** *f* gipsy
zinnia *f* BOT zinnia
zio *m*, **-a** *f* uncle; *donna* aunt
zip *f* ⟨*pl* zip⟩ zip, *US* zipper
ziqqurat *f* ⟨*pl* ziqqurat⟩ ziggurat
zitella *f pej* old maid *pej*
zittire *v/t* ⟨4d⟩ silence
zitto *adj* quiet; ***sta ~!*** be quiet!; *in tono minaccioso* keep your mouth shut! *infml*
zizzania *f fig* trouble; ***seminare ~*** sow discord
zoccola *f pej* slut *pej*
zoccolo *m* clog; ZOOL hoof; ARCH base
zodiacale *adj*: ***segni*** *mpl* ***-i*** signs of the Zodiac
zodiaco *m* Zodiac
zolfanello *m* match
zolfo *m* sulphur, *US* sulfur
zolla *f* clod; ***~ continentale*** continental plate
zolletta di zucchero *f* sugar cube
zombie *m* ⟨*pl* zombie⟩ zombie
zona *f* zone, area; ***~ blu*** *city centre area with no or limited parking or access for vehicles*; ***~ disco*** short-stay parking area; ***~ industriale*** industrial area; ***~ di libero scambio*** free trade area; ***~ pedonale*** pedestrian precinct; ***~ residenziale*** residential area; ***~ a traffico limitato*** *urban area with restricted access for vehicles*; ***~ verde*** green belt; ***essere in ~*** be in the neighbo(u)rhood
zonzo *m*: ***andare a ~*** wander around
zoo *m* ⟨*pl* zoo⟩ zoo
zoologia *f* zoology
zoologico *adj* ⟨*mpl* -ci⟩ zoological
zoom *m* ⟨*pl* zoom⟩ PHOT zoom lens; ***~ digitale*** COMPUT digital zoom
zoomare *v/t* ⟨1a⟩ PHOT zoom
zoomata *f* PHOT zoom
zoosafari *m* ⟨*pl* zoosafari⟩ safari park
zootecnica *f* ⟨*pl* -che⟩ zootechnics *sg*
zootecnico ⟨*mpl* -ci⟩ **I** *adj* zootechnical **II** *m*, **-a** *f* zootechnician
zoppicante *adj* lame (*a. fig*)
zoppicare *v/i* ⟨1l, c & d⟩ limp; *di mobile* wobble
zoppo *adj* lame; (*zoppicante*) limping; *mobile* wobbly; ***chi va con lo ~ impara a zoppicare*** *prov* bad company brings bad habits
zoticone *m*, **-a** *f* boor
zuavo *m* Zouave; ***pantaloni*** *mpl* ***alla -a*** knickerbockers
zucca *f* ⟨*pl* -cche⟩ pumpkin, marrow; *fig infml* (*testa*) bonce *infml*, nut *infml*; *fig* ***avere sale in ~*** have common sense
zuccherare *v/t* ⟨1l⟩ sugar
zuccherato *adj* sweetened; ***non ~*** unsweetened
zuccheriera *f* sugar bowl
zucchero *m* sugar; ***~ di canna*** cane sugar; ***~ filato*** candyfloss, *US* cotton candy; ***~ greggio*** brown sugar; ***~ vanigliato*** vanilla sugar; ***~ in zollette*** sugar cubes
zucchetto *m* skull cap
zucchina *f* courgette, *US* zucchini
zuccone *m*, **-a** *f* blockhead
zuccotto *m* COOK *dessert consisting of a dome-shaped sponge filled with cream, chocolate, and candied fruit*
zuffa *f* scuffle
zufolare *v/t and v/i* ⟨1l⟩ whistle
zufolo *m* whistle
zulù ⟨*pl* zulù⟩ **I** *adj* Zulu **II** *m/f* Zulu
zumare *v/t & v/i* zoom
zuppa *f* soup; ***~ di verdura*** vegetable soup; ***~ di pesce*** fish soup; ***~ inglese*** trifle; *fig* ***è sempre la solita ~!*** *infml* it's always the same old thing!; ***se non è ~ è pan bagnato*** it's six of one and half a dozen of the other
zuppiera *f* tureen
zuppo *adj* soaked, wet through
zurighese **I** *adj* from Zurich **II** *m/f* person from Zurich
Zurigo *f* Zurich
zuzzurellone *m*, **-a** *f* fun-lover

English – Italian

A

A, a *n* a, A *f inv*; MUS la *m inv*; EDU (*mark*) ottimo *m*; ***A sharp*** MUS la *m inv* diesis; ***A flat*** MUS la *m inv* bemolle

a *stressed art* **1.** un *m*, una *f*; *masculine before s + consonant, gn, ps, z* uno; *feminine before vowel* un'; **~ *cat*** un gatto; **~ *joke*** uno scherzo; **~ *girl*** una ragazza; ***an island*** un'isola; ***he's ~ doctor / Frenchman*** è medico / francese **2.** ***half an hour*** mezz'ora **3.** ***twice ~ week*** due volte alla settimana; ***£5 ~ ride*** 5 sterline a corsa; ***£2 ~ litre*** 2 sterline al litro; ***five flights ~ day*** cinque voli al giorno

A *abbr* (= **answer**) risposta *f*

AA *abbr* **1.** (= **Automobile Association**) *club automobilistico inglese* **2.** (= **Alcoholics Anonymous**) Alcolisti Anonimi

aback *adv*: ***taken ~*** preso alla sprovvista

abandon I *v/t* abbandonare; *hope, scheme* rinunciare a; **~ *ship*** abbandonare la nave **II** *n* (*surrender of inhibition*) trasporto *m*, slancio *m*; ***gay ~*** entusiasmo *m*

abandonment *n* (*forsaking, desertion*) abbandono *m* (*a.* JUR); (*giving-up*) rinuncia *f*

abase *v/r*: **~ *o.s.*** umiliarsi, degradarsi

abashed *adj* imbarazzato

abate *v/i of storm, flood waters* calmarsi

abattoir *n* mattatoio *m*

abbey *n* abbazia *f*

abbot *n* abate *m*

abbr., abbrev. *abbr* (= **abbreviation**) abbr. (abbreviazione)

abbreviate *v/t* abbreviare

abbreviation *n* abbreviazione *f*

ABC[1] *n, US* **ABC's** *npl* alfabeto *msg*

ABC[2] *abbr* **1.** (= **American Broadcasting Company**) *società americana di radiodiffusione* **2.** (= **Australian Broadcasting Commmission**) *ente radiotelevisivo australiano*

abdicate *v/i* abdicare

abdication *n* abdicazione *f*

abdomen *n* addome *m*

abdominal *adj* addominale

abduct *v/t* sequestrare, rapire

abduction *n* sequestro *m*, rapimento *m*

abet *v/i* → ***aid***

abeyance *n*: ***be in ~*** essere in disuso

abhor *v/t* ⟨*pret & past part* **-red**⟩ *form* aborrire

abhorrence *n form* orrore *m*

abhorrent *adj form* ripugnante; ***the very idea is ~ to me*** la sola idea mi fa ribrezzo

abide *v/t* sopportare; ***I can't ~ him*** non lo sopporto

◆**abide by** *v/t* attenersi a; ***I abide by what I said*** tengo fede a ciò che ho detto

ability *n* abilità *f inv*; **~ *to*** abilità di; ***to the best of my ~*** al meglio delle mie capacità

abject *adj poverty* estremo

ablaze *adj* in fiamme; ***set sth ~*** appiccare il fuoco a qc.; *fig* ***be ~*** essere infervorato; ***be ~ with light*** risplendere di luci

able *adj* (*skilful*) capace; ***be ~ to*** essere capace di; ***I wasn't ~ to see / hear*** non ero in grado di vedere / sentire

able-bodied *adj* robusto; MIL abile

ablution *n* abluzione *f*; ***perform one's ~s*** farsi le abluzioni

ABM *abbr* (= **anti-ballistic missile**) missile *m* antimissile

abnormal *adj* anormale

abnormally *adv* in modo anomalo

aboard I *prep* a bordo di; ***all ~!*** tutti a bordo! **II** *adv*: ***be ~*** essere a bordo; ***go ~*** salire a bordo

abode *n*: ***of no fixed ~*** *Br* senza fissa dimora

abolish *v/t* abolire

abolition *n* abolizione *f*

abominable *adj* abominevole

abomination *n* abominio *m*

aboriginal I *adj* aborigeno **II** *n* → ***Aborigine***

Aborigine *n* aborigeno *m*, -a *f*

abort *v/t mission, rocket launch* annullare; COMPUT: *program* interrompere

abortion *n* aborto *m*; ***have*** *or* ***get an ~***

abortire
abortion pill *n* pillola *f* abortiva
abortive *adj* fallito; ***the plan proved ~*** il piano si è rivelato un fallimento; ***~ attempt*** tentativo *m* abortito
abound *v/i* abbondare
◆**abound in, abound with** *v/t* abbondare di
about I *prep* (*concerning*) su; ***I'll tell you all ~ it*** ti dirò tutto al riguardo; ***talk ~ sth*** parlare di qc; ***be angry ~ sth*** essere arrabbiato per qc; ***there's nothing you can do ~ it*** non ci puoi fare niente; ***and be quick ~ it!*** e fallo velocemente!; ***he knows ~ it*** lo sa; ***how** or **what ~ me?*** e io?; ***how** or **what ~ it / going to the cinema?*** che ne pensi / diresti di andare al cinema?; ***what's it ~?*** *of book, film* di cosa parla?; *of complaint, problem* di cosa si tratta? **II** *adv* **1.** (*roughly*) intorno a, verso; (*nearly*) quasi; ***we arrived ~ noon*** siamo arrivati verso mezzogiorno; ***he's ~ 50*** è sulla cinquantina; ***it's ~ ready*** è quasi pronto; ***that's ~ it*** questo è quanto **2.** ***there are a lot of people ~*** c'è un sacco di gente qui; ***there's a thief ~*** c'è un ladro in giro; ***leave things (lying) ~*** lasciare le cose in giro; ***be up and ~ again*** essere di nuovo in piedi; ***be ~*** essere nei paraggi **3.** ***be ~ to …*** (*be going to*) essere sul punto di, stare per…
above I *prep* (*higher than*) sopra; (*more than*) sopra, oltre; ***he's ~ that sort of thing*** è superiore a queste cose; ***it's ~ my head** or **~ me*** è al di là delle mie possibilità; ***get ~ o.s.*** *infml* montarsi la testa; ***I couldn't hear ~ the din*** non riuscivo a sentire a causa del baccano; ***500 m ~ sea level*** 500 m sul livello del mare; ***~ all*** soprattutto **II** *adv* sopra; ***on the floor ~*** al piano di sopra **III** *adj*: ***the ~ persons*** i suddetti; ***the ~ paragraph*** il paragrafo precedente **IV** *n*: ***the ~*** quanto sopra
above-average *adj* superiore alla media
above board *adj* regolare; *fig* ***open and ~*** chiaro e pulito
above-mentioned *adj* suddetto
abrasion *n* abrasione *f*
abrasive *adj substance* ruvido; *personality* irritante
abreast *adv* fianco a fianco; ***march four ~*** marciare quattro a quattro; ***keep ~ of*** tenere / tenersi al corrente di
abridge *v/t* ridurre
abridgement *n* (*act*) abbreviazione *f*; (*abridged work*) edizione *f* ridotta
abroad *adv* all'estero; ***from ~*** dall'estero; ***there is a rumour** Br or **rumor** US **~ that …*** corre voce che…
abrupt *adj departure* improvviso; *manner* brusco
abruptly *adv leave* improvvisamente; *say* bruscamente
ABS *abbr* (= **antilock braking system**) ABS *m* (sistema *m* antibloccaggio); ***~ brakes*** freni *mpl* ABS
abscess *n* ascesso *m*
abscond *v/i* fuggire (col denaro)
abseil *v/i Br* calarsi in corda doppia
absence *n* assenza *f*; ***~ of mind*** distrazione *f*
absent I *adj* assente; ***be ~ from school** or **work*** essere assente da scuola *or* dal lavoro; ***~ parent*** genitore *m* assente; ***to ~ friends!*** (un brindisi) agli amici lontani! **II** *v/r*: ***~ o.s. (from)*** assentarsi (da)
absentee *n* assente *m/f*; ***~ vote*** voto *m* per corrispondenza; ***~ landlord*** proprietario *m* assenteista; ***there were a lot of ~s*** c'erano molti assenti
absenteeism *n* assenteismo *m*
absent-minded *adj* distratto
absent-mindedly *adv* distrattamente
absent-mindedness *n* distrazione *f*
absolute *adj power* assoluto; *idiot* totale
absolutely *adv* (*completely*) assolutamente; ***~ not!*** assolutamente no!; ***do you agree? – ~*** sei d'accordo? – assolutamente sì
absolute majority *n* maggioranza *f* assoluta **absolute zero** *n* zero *m* assoluto
absolution *n* REL assoluzione *f*
absolve *v/t* assolvere
absorb *v/t* assorbire; ***~ed in …*** assorto in …; ***be ~ed in a book*** essere immerso nella lettura di un libro
absorbency *n* assorbenza *f*
absorbent *adj* assorbente
absorbing *adj* avvincente
absorption *n* assorbimento *m*; ***shock ~*** ammortizzamento *m*; ***her total ~ in***

her studies la sua totale immersione nello studio
abstain *v/i from voting* astenersi; **~ *from alcohol*** astenersi dall'alcol
abstention *n in voting* astensione *f*
abstinence *n* astinenza *f*
abstract I *adj* astratto; **~ *noun*** sostantivo *m* astratto; **~ *art*** arte *f* astratta **II** *n* astratto *m*; (*summary*) abstract *m inv*; ***in the ~*** in astratto
abstraction *n* (*abstract term, notion*) astrazione *f*; (*extraction*) estrazione *f*
abstruse *adj* astruso
absurd I *adj* assurdo; ***don't be ~!*** non essere assurdo! **II** *n*: ***the Absurd*** ART l'assurdo; ***the theatre of the ~*** il teatro dell'assurdo
absurdity *n* assurdità *f inv*
absurdly *adv* in modo assurdo
abundance *n* abbondanza *f*; ***in ~*** in abbondanza
abundant *adj* abbondante
abundantly *adv* abbondantemente; ***make it ~ clear that …*** rendere chiaro che…
abuse[1] *n* (*ill treatment*) maltrattamento *m*; (*insults*) insulti *mpl*; (*misuse*) abuso *m*; ***a term of ~*** un termine offensivo; ***shout ~ at s.o.*** gridare insulti a qc; **~ *of authority*** abuso *m* di potere; ***the system is open to ~*** il sistema si presta ad essere usato in modo scorretto
abuse[2] *v/t* abusare di; (*treat badly*) maltrattare; (*insult*) insultare
abusive *adj language* offensivo; ***become ~*** diventare aggressivo; **~ *relationship*** relazione *f* violenta
abysmal *adj infml* (*very bad*) pessimo
abysmally *adv* pessimamente; ***perform ~*** recitare in modo pessimo
abyss *n* abisso *m*
a / c *abbr* (= **account**) c (conto *m*)
AC *abbr* (= **alternating current**) c.a. (corrente *f* alternata)
acacia *n* acacia *f*
academic I *n* docente *m/f* universitario, -a **II** *adj* accademico; *person* portato per lo studio; *question* speculativo; **~ *year*** anno *m* accademico
academically *adv* accademicamente; ***be ~ inclined*** essere incline allo studio; **~ *gifted*** che ha talento per lo studio; ***she is not doing well ~*** EDU non va bene a scuola
academy *n* accademia *f*
acc. *abbr* **1.** (= **account**) FIN conto *m* **2.** (= **accusative**) GRAM accusativo *m*
accede *v/i*: **~ *to*** *throne* accedere a
accelerate *v/t & v/i* accelerare
acceleration *n of car* accelerazione *f*
accelerator *n of car*, PHYS acceleratore *m*; ***step on the ~*** premere sull'acceleratore
accent I *n* accento *m*; ***speak with / without an ~*** parlare con un / senza accento **II** *v/t fig* accentuare, mettere l'accento su; LING accentare
accentuate *v/t* accentuare
accept *v/t* accettare; ***it is generally*** *or* ***widely ~ed that …*** è generalmente accettato che…; ***she has been ~ed at Oxford*** è stata ammessa a Oxford
acceptable *adj* accettabile
acceptance *n* accettazione *f*; ***gain ~*** *theory* essere riconosciuto
access I *n* accesso *m*; ***wheelchair ~*** accesso *m* per disabili; ***have ~ to*** COMPUT avere accesso a; *child* avere il permesso di vedere **II** *v/t* accedere a
access code *n* COMPUT codice *m* di accesso
accessible *adj* accessibile
accession *n* ascesa *f*
accessory *n for wearing* accessorio *m*; JUR complice *m/f*; ***accessories*** *pl* accessori *mpl*; ***toilet accessories*** accessori *mpl* per il bagno
access road *n* svincolo *m* **access time** *n* COMPUT tempo *m* di accesso
accident *n* incidente *m*; ***have an ~*** avere un incidente; ***by ~*** per caso; **~ *insurance*** assicurazione *f* contro gli infortuni; **~ *and emergency department*** *or* ***unit*** unità *f inv* di pronto soccorso
accidental I *adj* accidentale; **~ *damage*** danno *m* accidentale **II** *n* MUS (*sign*) alterazione *f*
accidentally *adv* accidentalmente
accident-prone *adj* incline agli incidenti
acclaim I *n* consenso *m* **II** *v/t* acclamare
acclamation *n* acclamazioni *fpl*
acclimate, acclimatize I *v/t* acclimatare; ***become ~d*** acclimatarsi **II** *v/i* acclimatarsi
acclimatization *n*, *US* **acclimation** *n*

acclimatazione *f*
accolade *n* (*award*) onorificenza *f*; (*praise*) elogio *m*
accommodate *v/t* ospitare; *special requirements* tenere conto di; (*have room for*) alloggiare; (*contain*) contenere; *form* venire incontro a; ***I think we might be able to ~ you*** penso che potremo venire incontro alla sua richiesta
accommodating *adj* accomodante
accommodation *n* (*lodging*) alloggio *m*, sistemazione *f*; (*room*) stanza *f*; (*flat*) appartamento *m*; posto *m*; ***seating ~*** posti *mpl* a sedere; ***sleeping ~ for six*** sei posti *mpl* letto
accommodations *n US* → ***accommodation***
accompaniment *n* MUS accompagnamento *m*
accompanist *n* MUS: ***with Gerald Moore as his ~*** con l'accompagnamento di Gerald Moore
accompany *v/t* ⟨*pret & past part* **-ied**⟩ accompagnare; ***~ing letter*** lettera *f* di accompagnamento
accomplice *n* complice *m/f*; ***be an ~ to a crime*** essere complice di un reato
accomplish *v/t task* compiere; *goal* conseguire; ***that didn't ~ anything*** non è servito a niente
accomplished *adj* dotato
accomplishment *n of a task* realizzazione *f*; (*talent*) talento *m*; (*achievement*) risultato *m*
accord **I** *n* accordo *m*; ***of his / my own ~*** di sua / mia spontanea volontà; ***with one ~*** di comune accordo **II** *v/t* accordare; *honorary title* concedere; ***he ~ed me his blessing*** mi ha dato la sua approvazione
accordance *n*: ***in ~ with*** conformemente a
according *adv*: ***~ to*** secondo; ***~ the map*** secondo la cartina; ***~ Peter*** a detta di Peter; ***we did it ~ to the rules*** abbiamo agito conformemente alle regole
accordingly *adv* di conseguenza
accordion *n* fisarmonica *f*
accordionist *n* fisarmonicista *m/f*
accost *v/t form* accostare
account *n* **1.** *financial* conto *m*; ***please charge it to my ~*** lo addebiti sul mio conto; *fig* ***settle*** *or* ***square ~s*** *or* ***one's ~ with s.o.*** regolare i conti con qn; *fig* ***she turned her talents to good ~*** ha fatto buon uso del proprio talento **2.** (*report*, *description*) resoconto *m*; ***by*** *or* ***from all ~s*** a detta di tutti; ***give an ~ of*** fare un resoconto di **3.** ***take … into ~*** *or* ***take ~ of …*** tenere conto di …; ***on no ~*** per nessuna ragione; ***on ~ of*** a causa di; ***that is of no ~*** non ha alcuna importanza; ***he's a man of some ~*** è un uomo di una certa importanza **4.** COMPUT codice *m* cliente; ***e-mail ~*** account *m inv* di posta elettronica
◆**account for** *v/t* (*explain*) giustificare; (*make up*, *constitute*) ammontare a; (*be the source of*) rappresentare; ***be called*** *or* ***held to account for sth*** essere chiamati a render conto di qc.; ***this area accounts for most of the country's mineral wealth*** quest'area contiene la maggior parte della ricchezza mineraria del paese
accountability *n* responsabilità *f inv*
accountable *adj* responsabile; ***be held ~*** essere considerato responsabile
accountancy *n* contabilità *f inv*
accountant *n* contabile *m/f*; *running own business* commercialista *m/f*
account book *n* libro *m* contabile **account holder** *n* titolare *m/f* di conto; *of current account* correntista *m/f* **account number** *n* numero *m* di conto
accounts *npl* contabilità *f inv*
accounts department *n* (*US* **accounting department**) ufficio *m* contabilità
accoutrements *npl*, *US a.* **accouterments** *npl* attrezzatura *f*
accrue *v/i* accumularsi; *interest* maturare
accumulate **I** *v/t* accumulare **II** *v/i* accumularsi
accumulation *n* accumulazione *f*
accumulative *adj* cumulativo
accuracy *n* precisione *f*
accurate *adj* preciso; ***my watch is ~*** il mio orologio è preciso
accurately *adv* con precisione
accusation *n* accusa *f*
accusative **I** *n* accusativo *m*; ***in the ~*** all'accusativo **II** *adj* accusativo; ***~ case*** caso *m* accusativo

accusatory *adj* accusatorio

accuse *v/t* accusare; ***he ~d me of lying*** mi ha accusato di mentire; ***be ~d of ...*** JUR essere accusato di ...

accus·ed *n* JUR accusato *m*, -a *f*; ***the ~*** l'imputato *m*, -a *f*; *pl* gli imputati *mpl*

accusing *adj* accusatorio; ***he had an ~ look on his face*** aveva uno sguardo accusatorio

accusingly *adv look, point* con aria accusatoria; *say* con tono accusatorio

accustom *v/t*: ***get*** *or* ***become ~ed to*** abituarsi a; ***be ~ed to*** essere abituato a

AC / DC *abbr* (= **alternating current / direct current**) c.a. / c.c. (corrente alternata / corrente continua); (*bisexual*) bisessuale

ace *n in cards* asso *m*; (*tennis shot*) ace *m inv*; (*champion*) asso *m*

acerbic *adj remark, style* aspro

acetate *n* acetato *m*

ache **I** *v/i* fare male; ***my head ~s*** mi fa male la testa; *fig* ***it makes my heart ~ to see him*** vederlo mi fa male al cuore; *fig* ***~ to do sth*** morire dalla voglia di fare qc **II** *n* dolore *m*

achieve *v/t* realizzare; *success, fame* ottenere; ***he will never ~ anything*** non otterrà mai niente

achievement *n of ambition* realizzazione *f*; (*thing achieved*) successo *m*

achiever *n* persona *f* di successo; ***be an ~*** riuscire a raggiungere i propri obiettivi; ***high ~*** EDU studente *m* prodigio

Achilles *n*: *fig* ***~ heel*** tallone *m* d'Achille

aching *adj* dolorante **achy** *adj*: ***I feel ~ all over*** *infml* mi fa male ovunque

acid **I** *n* acido *m*; ***he used to drop a lot of ~*** si faceva un sacco di acidi **II** *adj* acido; ***~ reflux*** riflusso *m* acido

acidic *adj* acido

acidity *n* acidità *f inv* (*a. fig*)

acid rain *n* pioggia *f* acida **acid test** *n fig* prova *f* della verità

acknowledge *v/t* riconoscere; *by smile, nod* far capire di aver notato; ***he ~d the applause with a smile*** ha risposto all'applauso con un sorriso; ***~ (receipt of) a letter*** accusare ricezione di una lettera

acknowledg(e)ment *n* riconoscimento *m*; (*smile, nod*) cenno *m*; (*letter*) lettera *f* di accusata ricezione; ***in ~ of*** *thanking* come pegno di riconoscenza di; ***~s*** *in book* ringraziamenti *mpl*

acne *n* MED acne *m*

acorn *n* BOT ghianda *f*

acoustic *adj* acustico

acoustic guitar *n* chitarra *f* acustica

acoustics *nsg or npl* acustica *f*

acquaint *v/t*: ***be ~ed with*** *form* conoscere; ***become*** *or* ***get ~ed with s.o.*** fare la conoscenza di qn; ***~ o.s.*** *or* ***make o.s. ~ed with sth*** familiarizzare con qc

acquaintance *n person* conoscenza *f*; ***make s.o.'s ~*** fare la conoscenza di qn

acquiesce *v/i form* acconsentire

acquiescence *n form* consentimento *m*

acquire *v/t* acquisire; ***caviar is an ~d taste*** quello del caviale è un gusto acquisito; ***where did you ~ that?*** dove te lo sei procurato?

acquisition *n* acquisizione *f*

acquisitive *adj* avido

acquit **I** *v/t* JUR assolvere; ***be ~ted of a crime*** essere assolto da un'accusa di reato **II** *v/r*: ***he ~ted himself well*** se l'è cavata bene

acquittal *n* JUR assoluzione *f*

acre *n* acro *m*

acreage *n* estensione *f* in acri

acrid *adj smell* acre

acrimonious *adj* aspro

acrimony *n* acrimonia *f*

acrobat *n* acrobata *m/f*

acrobatic *adj* acrobatico

acrobatics *npl* acrobazie *fpl*

acronym *n* acronimo*m*

across **I** *prep on other side of* dall'altro lato di; ***sail ~ the Atlantic*** attraversare l'Atlantico in barca a vela; ***walk ~ the street*** attraversare la strada; ***a bridge ~ the river*** un ponte sul fiume; ***~ Europe*** *all over* in tutta Europa; ***you could hear him (from) ~ the hall*** si sentiva dall'altro lato della sala; ***a tree lay ~ the path*** un albero caduto sbarrava la strada **II** *adv to other side* dall'altro lato; ***10 m ~*** largo 10 m; ***they came to the river and swam ~*** sono arrivati al fiume e l'hanno attraversato a nuoto; ***shall I go ~ first?*** attraverso io per primo?

across-the-board *adj* generale; *US horse* piazzato
acrylic *adj* acrilico
act I *v/i* agire; THEAT recitare; (*pretend*) fare finta; **~ as** fare le funzioni di; **she ~ed as if** *or* **as though she was surprised** da come si comportava, sembrava sorpresa **II** *n* **1.** (*deed*) atto *m*; **an ~ of mercy** un atto di pietà; **an ~ of madness** un atto di follia; **~ of God** causa *f* di forza maggiore **2.** *of play* atto *m*; *in variety show* numero; **one-~ play** atto *m* unico **3.** (*pretence*) finta *f* **4.** (*law*) atto *m* **5. catch s.o. in the ~ of doing sth** sorprendere qn nell'atto di fare qc; *fig* **get in on the ~** *infml* essere coinvolto in un'attività; **she'll be a hard** *or* **tough ~ to follow** sarà difficile da eguagliare; **he's really got his ~ together** *infml* si è proprio organizzato
◆ **act on** *v/i +obj* (*affect*) avere effetto su; *warning, advice* seguire; **acting on an impulse / hunch** agire in base a un impulso / un'intuizione
◆ **act out** *v/t sep* imitare; (*perform*) recitare, interpretare
◆ **act up** *v/i infml* funzionare male; **my back is acting up** mi fa male la schiena
acting I *n* recitazione *f*; **she went into ~** si è data alla recitazione; **he's done some ~** ha già recitato **II** *adj* (*temporary*) facente funzione; **the ~ president** il facente funzione di presidente
action *n* **1.** azione *f*; **a man of ~** un uomo d'azione; **take ~** agire; **put a plan into ~** mettere in atto un piano; **course of ~** linea *f* di azione **2. out of ~** (*not functioning*) fuori uso **3. bring an ~ against** JUR fare causa a **4.** MIL (*fighting*) azione *f*, combattimento *m*; **enemy ~** azione *f* nemica; **killed in ~** ucciso in combattimento; **the first time they went into ~** la prima volta che sono entrati in azione
action film *n* film *m inv* d'azione **action-packed** *adj* ricco di azione **action replay** *n* TV replay *m inv* **action shot** *n* PHOT istantanea *f* **action stations** *npl* posti *mpl* di combattimento; **~!** ai posti di combattimento!
activate *v/t* attivare
active *adj* attivo; GRAM attivo; **be politically / sexually ~** essere politicamente / sessualmente attivo; **~ ingredient** CHEM principio *m* attivo
actively *adv* attivamente
activist *n* POL attivista *m/f*
activity *n* attività *f inv*; **the church organizes many activities** la chiesa organizza molte attività; **criminal ~** attività *f inv* criminale
activity holiday *n Br* vacanza *f* sportiva
actor *n* attore *m*
actress *n* attrice *f*
actual *adj* reale; *cost* effettivo; **the ~ ceremony starts at 10** la cerimonia vera e propria comincia alle 10; **in ~ fact** in realtà
actually *adv* (*in fact, to tell the truth*) in realtà; *expressing surprise* veramente; **I haven't ~ started yet** a dire il vero non ho ancora cominciato; **~ I do know him** *stressing the converse* in effetti, lo conosco
actuary *n insurance* attuario *m*, -a *f*
acuity *n* acuità *f inv*; **visual ~** acuità *f inv* visiva
acumen *n* acume *m*; **business ~** fiuto *m* per gli affari
acupuncture *n* agopuntura *f*
acute *adj pain, sense* acuto; *shortage* estremo; MATH *angle* acuto; **~ accent** LING accento *m* acuto
acutely *adv* (*extremely*) estremamente
ad *n infml* → **advertisement**
AD *abbr* (= **anno domini**) d.C. (dopo Cristo)
adage *n* adagio *m*
Adam *n*: **~'s apple** pomo *m* d'Adamo; **I don't know him from ~** *infml* non lo conosco affatto
adamant *adj* categorico
adamantly *adv* categoricamente
Adam's apple *n* pomo *m* di Adamo
adapt I *v/t* adattare **II** *v/i of person* adattarsi; **~ to sth** adattarsi a qc; **~ed from the Spanish** adattato dallo spagnolo
adaptability *n* adattabilità *f inv*
adaptable *adj* adattabile
adaptation *n of play etc* adattamento *m*
adaptor, adapter *n electrical* adattatore *m*
add I *v/t* aggiungere; **they ~ 10% for service** aggiungono il 10% per il servizio; **~ed value** valore *m* aggiunto;

MATH addizionare **II** *v/i of person* fare le somme
◆**add on** *v/t sep 15 % etc* aggiungere
◆**add to** *v/t* accrescere
◆**add up I** *v/t sep* sommare **II** *v/i fig* quadrare
◆**add up to** *v/t* (*total*) ammontare a; (*constitute*) costituire nell'insieme
ADD *abbr* (= **attention deficit disorder**) DDA *m* (Disturbo *m* da Deficit di Attenzione)
adder *n* vipera *f* rossa
addict *n to football, chess* maniaco *m*, -a *f*; ***drug** ~* tossicomane *m/f*, tossicodipendente *m/f*; ***heroin** ~* eroinomane *m/f*; ***TV** ~* teledipendente *m/f*
addicted *adj* dipendente; ***be ~ to*** *drugs, alcohol* essere dedito a; *football, computer games etc* essere un maniaco di
addiction *n to drugs* dipendenza *f*, assuefazione *f*; *to TV, chocolate etc* dipendenza *f*
addictive *adj*: ***be ~*** *of drugs* provocare dipendenza *or* assuefazione; *of TV, chocolate etc* provocare dipendenza
addition *n* MATH addizione *f*; *to list, company etc* aggiunta *f*; ***in ~*** inoltre; ***in ~ to*** in aggiunta a
additional *adj* aggiuntivo
additive *n* additivo *m*
addle *v/t* confondere; *egg* andare a male; ***his brain is ~d by too much drink*** ha il cervello confuso dal troppo bere
add-on *n* complemento *m*
address I *n* indirizzo *m*; ***form of ~*** appellativo *m* **II** *v/t letter* indirizzare; *audience* tenere un discorso a; *person* rivolgersi a
address book *n* indirizzario *m*
addressee *n* destinatario *m*, -a *f*
adenoids *npl* adenoidi *fpl*
adept *adj* esperto; ***be ~ at*** essere esperto in
adequacy *n* adeguatezza *f*
adequate *adj* adeguato; (*sufficient*) sufficiente; (*good enough*) discreto; ***be ~*** essere adatto; ***more than ~*** più che soddisfacente
adequately *adv* adeguatamente
adhere *v/i* aderire
◆**adhere to** *v/t surface* aderire a; *rules* attenersi a
adherence *n* adesione *f*; *to belief* fedeltà *f inv*; *to rule* osservanza *f*
adherent *n* aderente; *to belief* fedele
adhesion *n particles* adesione *f*; *glue* presa *f*; (*loyalty*) attaccamento *m*
adhesive *n* adesivo *m*
adhesive plaster *n* cerotto *m* **adhesive tape** *n* nastro *m* adesivo
ad hoc *adj/adv* ad hoc
ad infinitum *adv* all'infinito
adipose I *adj* adiposo **II** *n* adipe *m*
adjacent *adj* adiacente; ***it's ~ to the station*** è adiacente alla stazione; ***the ~ room*** la camera *f* adiacente
adjectival *adj* aggettivale
adjectivally *adv* con funzione aggettivale
adjective *n* aggettivo *m*
adjoin *v/t* essere adiacente a
adjoining *adj* adiacente
adjourn *v/i* aggiornare; ***he ~ed the meeting for three hours*** ha sospeso la riunione per tre ore; ***~ for lunch / one hour*** rinviare per pranzo / di un'ora; ***shall we ~ to the living room?*** ci spostiamo in salotto?
adjournment *n* aggiornamento *m*
adjudicate I *v/t competition* giudicare **II** *v/i in competition* fare da giudice
adjudication *n* giudizio *m*
adjudicator *n* giudice *m*; *jury* membro *m* della giuria
adjust *v/t* regolare; ***~ o.s. to*** adattarsi a
adjustable *adj* regolabile
adjustment *n* regolazione *f*; *psychological* adattamento *m*; ***make ~s*** apportare modifiche; ***make ~s to one's plans*** modificare i propri piani
ad lib I *v/i* ⟨*pret & past part* **-bed**⟩ improvvisare **II** *adj/adv* a braccio *infml*
admin *abbr* (= **administration**) amm.ne (amministrazione *f*)
administer *v/t medicine* somministrare; *company* amministrare; *country* governare; ***~ justice*** amministrare la giustizia
administration *n* amministrazione *f*; (*government*) governo *m*; ***the Bush ~*** l'amministrazione Bush
administrative *adj* amministrativo
administrative body *n* organismo *m* amministrativo **administrative costs** *npl* spese *fpl* amministrative
administrator *n* amministratore *m*, -trice *f*

admirable *adj* ammirevole
admirably *adv* ammirevolmente
admiral *n* ammiraglio *m*
Admiralty *n Br* ammiragliato *m*
admiration *n* ammirazione *f*
admire *v/t* ammirare
admirer *n* ammiratore *m*, -trice *f*
admiring *adj* ammirativo
admiringly *adv* con ammirazione
admissible *adj* ammissibile
admission *n* (*confession*) ammissione *f*; *to university* iscrizione *f*; *to hospital* ricovero *m*; ***on*** *or* ***by his own ~*** per sua stessa ammissione; ***that would be an ~ of failure*** significherebbe ammettere di aver fallito; ***gain ~ to a club*** essere ammessi in un club; ***~ free*** entrata *f* libera
admission charge, admission fee *n* (prezzo d')ingresso *m*
admit *v/t* ⟨*pret & past part* ***-ted***⟩ **1.** (*acknowledge*) ammettere; ***~ that*** ammettere che; ***~ doing sth*** ammettere di aver fatto qc; ***I have to ~ a certain feeling of admiration*** devo ammettere che provo una certa ammirazione **2.** *to a place* lasciare entrare; *to school*, *club etc* ammettere; *to hospital* ricoverare; ***he was ~ted to hospital*** è stato ricoverato in ospedale; ***children not ~ted*** vietato l'ingresso ai bambini
admittance *n*: ***no ~*** vietato l'accesso
admittedly *adv* effettivamente; ***~ this is true*** bisogna ammettere che è vero
admonish *v/t form* ammonire
admonition *n form* (*rebuke*) ammonizione *f*, rimprovero *m*; (*warning*) ammonimento *m*
ad nauseam *adv* fino alla nausea
ado *n*: ***without further ~*** senza ulteriori indugi; ***much ~ about nothing*** tanto rumore per nulla
adolescence *n* adolescenza *f*
adolescent **I** *n* adolescente *m/f* **II** *adj* adolescenziale
adopt *v/t* adottare; *mannerisms*, *identity* assumere; *candidate* POL candidare
adopted *adj* adottivo; ***~ child*** figlio *m* adottivo; ***her ~ country*** la sua patria adottiva
adoption *n* adozione *f*
adoption agency *n* centro *m* adozioni
adoptive parents *npl* genitori *mpl* adottivi
adorable *adj* adorabile
adoration *n* adorazione *f*
adore *v/t* adorare
adoring *adj* in adorazione
adorn *v/t* ornare
adrenalin *n* adrenalina *f*
Adriatic *n* Adriatico *m*
adrift *adj* alla deriva; *fig* sbandato; *fig* ***come ~*** staccarsi
adroit *adj* destro, abile
adroitly *adv* abilmente
ADSL *abbr* (= **asymmetric digital subscriber line**) TEL ADSL *m*
adulation *n* adulazione *f*
adult **I** *n* adulto *m*, -a *f* **II** *adj* adulto; ***he spent his ~ life in New York*** da adulto ha vissuto a New York
adult education *n* corsi *mpl* per adulti
adulterate **I** *v/t wine*, *food* adulterare **II** *adj wine*, *food* adulterato
adulteration *n of wine*, *food* adulterazione *f*
adulterer *n* adultero *m*
adulteress *n* adultera *f*
adulterous *adj relationship* extraconiugale
adultery *n* adulterio *m*; ***commit ~*** commettere adulterio
adult film *n euph* film *m inv* per adulti
advance **I** *n* **1.** (*money*) anticipo *m* **2.** *in science etc* progresso *m*; ***make ~s*** (*progress*) fare progressi; *sexually* fare delle avance **3.** MIL avanzata *f* **4.** ***in ~*** in anticipo; ***£ 100 in ~*** 100 sterline di anticipo; ***be in ~ of*** essere più all'avanguardia di **II** *v/i* MIL avanzare; (*make progress*) fare progressi **III** *v/t theory* avanzare; *sum of money* anticipare; *human knowledge*, *a cause* fare progredire
advance booking *n* prenotazione *f*
advance booking office *n* THEAT box office *m* **advance copy** *n* copia *f* staffetta (*di un libro*, *presentata prima della messa in vendita*)
advanced *adj country*, *level* avanzato; *learner* di livello avanzato; ***he is very ~ for his age*** è molto avanti per la sua età; ***in the ~ stages of the disease*** negli stadi avanzati della malattia
advancement *n* (*furtherance*) avanzamento *m*; (*promotion in rank*) promozione *f*; ***he worked for the ~ of science*** ha lavorato per il progresso

della scienza
advance notice *n* preavviso *m* **advance payment** *n* pagamento *m* anticipato **advance warning** *n* → ***advance notice***
advantage I *n* vantaggio *m*; ***it's to your ~*** è a tuo vantaggio; ***have an ~*** (***over s.o.***) avere un vantaggio (su qn); ***he turned the situation to his own ~*** ha volto la situazione a proprio vantaggio; ***take ~ of*** *opportunity* approfittare di; ***take ~ of s.o.*** (*exploit*) sfruttare qn; *euph sexually* approfittarsi di qn **II** *v/t* avvantaggiare, favorire
advantageous *adj* vantaggioso
advent *n fig* avvento *m*
Advent calendar *n calendario dell'Avvento con finestrelle numerate che i bambini aprono giorno per giorno*
adventure *n* avventura *f*; ***love / spirit of ~*** passione *f* per l'avventura / spirito *m* di avventura
adventure playground *n parco giochi attrezzato con ponti, corde e altre strutture per arrampicarsi*
adventurous *adj* avventuroso
adverb *n* avverbio *m*
adverbial I *adj* avverbiale **II** *n* locuzione *f* avverbiale
adversary *n* avversario *m*, -a *f*
adverse *adj* avverso
adversely *adv* negativamente
adversity *n* avversità *f inv*; ***in ~*** nelle avversità
advert *n Br* → ***advertisement***
advertise I *v/t job* mettere un annuncio per; *product* reclamizzare; ***~ for s.o. / sth*** cercare qn / qc (pubblicando un annuncio) **II** *v/i for job* mettere un annuncio; *for product* fare pubblicità
advertisement *n* annuncio *m*, inserzione *f*; *for product* pubblicità *f inv*; ***put*** *or* ***place an ~ in the paper*** mettere *or* pubblicare un annuncio sul giornale
advertiser *n* acquirente *m/f* di uno spazio pubblicitario; *in magazine, newspaper* inserzionista *m/f*
advertising *n* pubblicità *f inv*
advertising agency *n* agenzia *f* pubblicitaria **advertising budget** *n* budget *m inv* per la pubblicità **advertising campaign** *n* campagna *f* pubblicitaria **advertising revenue** *n* proventi *mpl* della pubblicità
advice *n* consigli *mpl*; *legal, financial* consulenza *f*; ***a piece of ~*** un consiglio; ***take s.o.'s ~*** seguire il consiglio di qn; ***seek*** (***s.o.'s***) ***~*** chiedere il parere (di qn); ***take legal ~*** avere una consulenza legale; ***he gave me some ~*** mi ha dato qualche consiglio
advisability *n* opportunità *f inv*
advisable *adj* consigliabile
advise *v/t person* consigliare a; *caution etc* consigliare; ***~ s.o. to ...*** consigliare a qn di ...; ***~ s.o. against*** (***doing***) ***sth*** sconsigliare a qn (di fare) qc
advisedly *adv* deliberatamente; ***and I use the word ~*** e uso il termine con cognizione di causa
adviser, advisor *n* consulente *m/f*
advisory *adj* consultivo
advocacy *n of action, plan* sostegno *m*, appoggio *m*; JUR avvocatura *f*
advocate¹ *v/t* propugnare
advocate² *n* (*supporter*) sostenitore *m*, -trice *f*; (*lawyer*) avvocato *m*; *fig* ***the Devil's ~*** l'avvocato del diavolo
Aegean *adj*: ***the ~*** (***Sea***) l'Egeo *m*
aegis *n*: ***under the ~ of*** sotto l'egida di
Aeolian *adj* HIST eolio; ***~ harp*** MUS arpa *f* eolia; ***~ erosion*** *of wind* erosione *f* eolica
aeon *n*: *fig* ***~s ago*** milioni di anni fa
aerate *v/t soil* aerare; *blood* ossigenare; *liquid* gassare
aerial I *n* antenna *f* **II** *adj* aereo
aerial photograph *n* fotografia *f* aerea
aerobics *nsg* aerobica *f*
aerodynamic *adj* aerodinamico
aerodynamics *nsg* aerodinamica *f*
aeronautical *adj* aeronautico
aeroplane *n* aeroplano *m*
aerosol *n* spray *m inv*
aerospace industry *n* industria *f* aerospaziale
Aesop *n* Esopo; ***~'s fables*** le favole di Esopo
aesthete, *US* **esthete** *n* esteta *m/f*
aesthetic, *US* **esthetic** *adj* estetico
aesthetically, *US* **esthetically** *adv* esteticamente, dal punto di vista estetico; ***~ pleasing*** esteticamente piacevole
aesthetics, *US* **esthetics** *nsg* estetica *f*

afar *adv*: ***from ~*** da lontano
affable *adj* affabile
affair *n* **1.** (*matter*) affare *m*; ***that's my ~!*** sono affari miei!; ***this is a sorry state of ~s!*** è una situazione incresciosa; (*event*) caso *m*; (*business*) affare *m*; ***foreign ~s*** affari *mpl* esteri; ***the Watergate ~*** il caso Watergate **2.** (*love*) relazione *f*; ***have an ~ with*** avere una relazione con
affect *v/t* MED colpire; (*influence*) influire su; (*concern*) riguardare; (*cause feelings to*) colpire
affectation *n* (*mannerism*) affettazione *f*; (*attitude*) posa *f*; ***he speaks with a lisp, but it's really just an ~*** parla con un difetto di pronuncia, ma lo fa apposta
affected *adj* (*artificial*) affettato; (*disposed*) incline; (*moved*) commosso; MED affetto
affectedly *adv* affettatamente
affection *n* affetto *m*; ***I have*** *or* ***feel a great ~ for her*** provo un grande affetto per lei; ***he has a special place in her ~s*** occupa un posto speciale nel suo cuore
affectionate *adj* affettuoso
affectionately *adv* affettuosamente; ***yours ~, Wendy*** *letter-ending* con affetto, Wendy
affidavit *n* JUR affidavit *m*
affiliate I *v/t* affiliare (***to*** a); ***the two banks are ~d*** le due banche sono affiliate; ***~d company*** società *f inv* affiliata **II** *v/i* affiliarsi (***with*** a) **III** *n* filiale *f*
affiliation *n* affiliazione *f* (***to, with*** a); ***what are his political ~s?*** qual è la sua appartenenza politica?
affinity *n* affinità *f inv*
affirm *v/t form* confermare
affirmation *n* affermazione *f*
affirmative *adj* affermativo; ***answer in the ~*** rispondere affermativamente; ***~ action*** *US politica contro la discriminazione delle donne e delle minoranze nell'istruzione e nel mondo del lavoro nell'assegnazione di posti di lavoro o di studio*
affix *v/t form* applicare
afflict *v/t* tormentare; ***be ~ed with*** soffrire di
affliction *n* (*blindness etc*) disturbo *m*; (*suffering*) dolore *m*; (*grief*) afflizione *f*
affluence *n* benessere *m*
affluent *adj* benestante; ***~ society*** società *f inv* del benessere
afford *v/t*: ***be able to ~ sth*** *financially* potersi permettere qc; ***I can't ~ the time*** non ne ho il tempo; ***I can't ~ to go on holiday*** non posso permettermi di andare in vacanza; ***it's a risk we can't ~ to take*** è un rischio che non possiamo permetterci di correre
affordable *adj* abbordabile
afforestation *n* imboschimento *m*
affray *n esp* JUR rissa *f*; (*riot*) tafferuglio *m*
affront *n* affronto *m*
Afghan I *n* afgano *m*, -a *f*; (*language*) afgano *m*; ZOOL (*a.* **Afghan hound**) afgano *m* **II** *adj* afgano
Afghanistan *n* Afghanistan *m*
aficionado *n* aficionado *m*, -a *f*, appassionato *m*, a- *f*
afield *adv*: ***go further ~*** andare più lontano
afloat *adj boat* a galla; ***keep the company ~*** tenere a galla l'azienda
afoot *adv* in vista; ***there is something ~*** sta per succedere qualcosa
aforementioned *adj form* suddetto, summenzionato
aforesaid *adj form* suddetto
afraid *adj*: ***be ~*** avere paura; ***he's not ~ to say what he thinks*** non ha paura di dire quello che pensa; ***be ~ of*** avere paura di; ***be ~ to*** avere paura di; ***that's what I was ~ of*** *or* ***I was ~ that would happen*** è proprio quello che temevo; ***I'm ~*** *expressing regret* sono spiacente; ***I'm ~ I can't do it*** mi dispiace, ma non posso farlo; ***I'm ~ so*** temo che sia così; ***I'm ~ not*** purtroppo no; ***I'm ~ I've got to go*** purtroppo devo andare
afresh *adv* da capo
Africa *n* Africa *f*
African I *n* africano *m*, -a *f* **II** *adj* africano
African-American I *n* afroamericano *m*, -a *f* **II** *adj* afroamericano
Afrikaans *n* afrikaans *m/f*
Afrikaner *n* afrikander *m/f inv*
Afro-American I *adj* afroamericano **II** *n* afroamericano *m*, -a *f*
Afro-Caribbean I *adj* afrocaraibico **II** *n* afrocaraibico *m*, -a *f*

aft *adv* NAUT *sit* a poppa; *go* verso poppa

after I *prep* **1.** dopo; **~ *her/me/you*** dopo di lei/me/te; ***about a mile ~ the village*** a circa un miglio dal paese; **~ *El Greco*** alla maniera di El Greco; **~ *all I've done for you!*** dopo tutto quello che ho fatto per te!; **~ *all*** dopo tutto; **~ *all, he is your brother*** dopo tutto è tuo fratello; **~ *that*** dopo; ***the day ~ tomorrow*** dopodomani; ***it's ten ~ two*** *US* sono le due e dieci **2.** ***be ~ s.o./sth*** cercare qn/qc; ***he's just ~ a free meal*** sta solo cercando di mangiare a sbafo **3.** ***take ~ s.o.*** somigliare a qn; ***she takes ~ her mother*** è tutta sua madre **4.** ***ask ~*** chiedere notizie di; ***she asked ~ you*** mi ha chiesto come stavi **II** *adv* dopo; ***the day ~*** il giorno dopo **III** *cj* dopo (che); ***I found out ~ he had left*** l'ho scoperto dopo che era partito

afterbirth *n placenta e annessi fetali*

after-dinner *adj* dopo cena; **~ *speech*** *discorso al termine di un pranzo*

aftereffects *npl* postumi *mpl*

after-hours I *n* after hours *m inv* **II** *adj*: **~ *trading*** ECON *contrattazioni che si svolgono dopo la chiusura ufficiale delle borse*

afterlife *n* vita *f* dopo la morte, vita *f* ultraterrena

aftermath *n*: ***the ~ of war*** il dopoguerra; ***in the ~ of*** nel periodo immediatamente successivo a

afternoon I *n* pomeriggio *m*; ***in the ~*** nel pomeriggio; ***this ~*** oggi pomeriggio; ***good ~*** buongiorno **II** *adj*: **~ *performance*** matinée *m inv*

afternoon tea *n Br* tè *m inv* del pomeriggio

afters *npl Br*: ***what's for ~?*** cosa c'è per dessert?

after sales service *n* servizio *m* dopovendita **aftershave** *n* dopobarba *m inv* **aftershock** *n* GEOL scossa *f* di assestamento; *fig* conseguenze *fpl* **after sun cream** *n* crema *f* doposole

aftertaste *n* retrogusto *m*

afterthought *n* ripensamento *m*

afterwards *adv* dopo

again *adv* di nuovo; da capo; (*on the other hand*) d'altra parte; (*moreover*) inoltre; ***begin ~*** ricominciare; ***what's his name ~?*** come hai detto che si chiama?; ***I never saw him ~*** non l'ho mai più visto; **~ *and ~*** ripetutamente; ***all over ~*** tutto da capo; ***as much ~*** *in quantity* altrettanto; ***but then*** *or* ***there ~, it may not be true*** ma d'altra parte potrebbe non essere vero

against *prep lean* contro; ***push all the chairs right back ~ the wall*** metti tutte le sedie contro il muro; ***America ~ Brazil*** SPORTS America contro Brasile; ***I'm ~ the idea*** sono contrario all'idea; ***what do you have ~ her?*** cos'hai contro di lei?; **~ *the law*** contro la legge; (***as***) **~** (*compared with*) rispetto a; ***she had three prizes*** (***as***) **~ *his six*** lei ha vinto tre premi, lui sei; ***protection ~ the cold*** protezione *f* dal freddo

age I *n* (*a. era*) età *f inv*; ***at the ~ of*** all'età di; ***under ~*** minorenne; ***what ~ is he?*** quanti anni ha?; ***act your ~!*** non fare il bambino! ***she's five years of ~*** ha cinque anni; ***but he's twice your ~!*** ma ha il doppio dei tuoi anni!; ***the Edwardian ~*** l'epoca edoardiana (di Edoardo VII, 1901-1910); ***down the ~s*** attraverso i secoli; ***I've been waiting for ~s*** *infml* ho aspettato un secolo *infml* **II** *v/i* invecchiare **III** *v/t* invecchiare; ***he ~s his wine in barriques*** invecchia il vino nei barrique; ***the experience ~d him*** l'esperienza l'ha fatto invecchiare

aged[1] *adj*: ***a boy ~ 16*** un ragazzo di 16 anni; ***he was ~ 16*** aveva 16 anni

aged[2] **I** *adj*: ***her ~ parents*** i suoi anziani genitori **II** *n*: ***the ~*** gli anziani

age defying *n creme* antietà *inv*

age gap *n* differenza *f* di età **age group** *n* fascia *f* d'età

ag(e)ing I *adj person*, *population* che invecchia **II** *n* invecchiamento *m*; **~ *process*** processo *m* di invecchiamento; ***these bottles improve with ~*** il vino di queste bottiglie migliora con l'invecchiamento

ageism *n discriminazione contro gli anziani*

ageless *adj* senza età

age limit *n* limite *m* d'età

agency *n* agenzia *f*; ***aid ~*** ente *f* assistenziale

agenda *n* ordine *m* del giorno; ***on the***

~ all'ordine del giorno; ***they have their own ~*** hanno le loro priorità; ***it's her personal ~ that makes her act like that*** sono i suoi interessi personali che la spingono a comportarsi così

agent *n* agente *m/f*; ***business ~*** agente *m* di vendita, rappresentante *m*; ***cleansing ~*** CHEM agente *m* pulente; ***secret ~*** agente *m* segreto

age of consent *n* JUR *for marriage* età *f inv* minima per il matrimonio; *for sexual relationship* età *f inv* del consenso **age-old** *adj* antichissimo; *problem* annoso **age-related** *adj* correlato all'età; ***~ Macular Degeneration*** degenerazione maculare senile

aggravate *v/t* aggravare; (*annoy*) seccare

aggravating *adj infml* irritante; JUR aggravante

aggravation *n* (*worsening*) aggravamento *m*, peggioramento *m*; (*annoyance*) irritazione *f*; ***she was a constant ~ to him*** lo esasperava continuamente

aggregate *n* insieme *m*; ***in (the) ~*** nel complesso; ***win on ~*** SPORTS vincere ai punti

aggression *n* aggressione *f*

aggressive *adj* (*a. dynamic*) aggressivo

aggressively *adv* con aggressività

aggressiveness *n* aggressività *f inv*

aggressor *n* aggressore *m*, -ditrice *f*

aggrieved *adj* offeso (***at, by*** da); JUR leso; ***the ~ party*** la parte lesa

aggro *n sl* grane *fpl*; ***don't give me any ~*** non darmi delle grane

aghast *adj* inorridito

agile *adj* agile

agility *n* agilità *f inv*

agitate *v/i*: ***~ for / against*** mobilitarsi per / contro

agitated *adj* agitato

agitation *n* agitazione *f*

agitator *n* agitatore *m*, -trice *f*

aglow *adj* acceso; *face* raggiante

AGM *abbr* (= **annual general meeting**) assemblea *f* annuale

agnostic *n* agnostico *m*, -a *f*

agnosticism *n* agnosticismo *m*

ago *adv*: ***2 days ~*** due giorni fa; ***long ~*** molto tempo fa; ***how long ~?*** quanto tempo fa?

agog *adj* (*curious*) curioso; (*excited*) eccitato; (*eager*) impaziente; ***the whole village was ~ (with curiosity)*** tutto il paese non stava più nella pelle (per la curiosità)

agonize *v/i* angosciarsi; ***~ over*** angosciarsi per

agonizing *adj* angosciante

agonizingly *adv* atrocemente; ***~ slow*** lento in modo esasperante

agony *n* agonia *f*; *mental* angoscia *f*; ***he was in ~*** soffriva atrocemente

agony aunt *n Br responsabile di una rubrica di posta del cuore* **agony column** *n Br infml* posta *f* del cuore

agoraphobia *n* MED agorafobia *f*

agoraphobic MED **I** *adj* agorafobo **II** *n* agorafobo *m*, -a *f*

agrarian *adj* agrario, agricolo

agree I *v/i* essere d'accordo; *of figures, accounts* quadrare; (*reach agreement*) mettersi d'accordo; ***I ~*** sono d'accordo; ***we ~ to differ*** accettiamo di avere opinioni diverse; ***~ on*** mettersi d'accordo su; ***~ to*** accettare di; ***it doesn't ~ with me*** *of food* mi fa male; ***the subject doesn't ~ with the verb*** GRAM il soggetto non concorda con il verbo **II** *v/t price* concordare; ***~ that sth should be done*** concordare che si dovrebbe fare qc

agreeable *adj* (*pleasant*) piacevole; ***be ~*** (*in agreement*) essere d'accordo; ***is that ~ to you?*** sei d'accordo?

agreeably *adv* gradevolmente

agreed *adj* (*in agreement*) concordato; ***are we all ~?*** siamo tutti d'accordo?

agreement *n* (*consent, contract*) accordo *m*; ***fortunately we had a written ~*** per fortuna avevamo un accordo scritto; ***reach ~ on*** trovare un accordo su; ***be in ~*** essere d'accordo; ***by mutual ~*** di comune accordo

agribusiness *n* agribusiness *m*

agricultural *adj* agricolo

agricultural college *n* istituto *m* agrario

agriculture *n* agricoltura *f*

aground *adv*: ***go*** *or* ***run ~*** arenarsi

ahead *adv* **1.** davanti; (*in advance*) avanti; ***in the months ~*** nei mesi a venire; ***we've a busy time ~*** ci aspetta un periodo pieno; ***full speed ~*** NAUT, *fig* avanti tutta; ***200 m ~*** 200 m più avanti; ***be ~ of*** essere davanti a; ***arrive***

*~ **of the others*** arrivare prima degli altri **2.** ***plan*** *or* ***think ~*** programmare per tempo
ahem *int* ehm
ahoy *int*: ***ship ~!*** ehi, di bordo!
AI *abbr* **1.** (= **artificial intelligence**) IA (intelligenza *f* artificiale) **2.** (= **artificial insemination**) inseminazione *f* artificiale
aid I *n* aiuto *m*; (***foreign***) ~ aiuti *mpl* stranieri; ***what's all this in ~ of?*** *infml* a che serve tutto questo?; ***with the ~ of a screwdriver*** con l'aiuto di un cacciavite **II** *v/t* aiutare; ***~ s.o.'s recovery*** aiutare la guarigione di qn; ***~ and abet s.o.*** JUR essere colpevole di concorso in reato e favoreggiamento
aide *n* assistente *m/f*
aide-de-camp *n* ⟨*pl* ***aides-de-camp***⟩ MIL aiutante *m* di campo
aide-memoire *n* promemoria *m inv*
AIDS, Aids *abbr* (= **acquired immune deficiency syndrome**) AIDS *m* (sindrome da immunodeficienza acquisita)
AIDS-infected *adj* affetto da AIDS **AIDS-related** *adj* legato all'AIDS **AIDS test** *n* test *m* dell'HIV **AIDS victim** *n* vittima *f* dell'AIDS
ail *v/t* addolorare; ***what's ~ing you?*** cosa ti affligge?
ailing *adj economy* malato
ailment *n* disturbo *m*; ***minor ~s*** disturbi *mpl* minori
aim I *n in shooting* mira *f*; (*objective*) obiettivo *m*; ***what is your ~ in life?*** qual è il tuo scopo nella vita?; ***take ~*** prendere la mira **II** *v/i in shooting* mirare; ***~ at doing sth*** *or* ***~ to do sth*** aspirare a fare qc; ***we ~ to please*** il nostro scopo è la vostra soddisfazione **III** *v/t*: ***be ~ed at*** *of remark etc* essere rivolto a; ***this book is ~ed at the general public*** questo libro si rivolge a tutto il pubblico; ***be ~ed at*** *of guns* essere puntato contro
aimless *adj* senza obiettivi; *wandering* senza meta
ain't *sl* → ***am not***, ***is not***, ***are not***, ***has not***, ***have not***
air I *n* aria *f*; ***in the open ~*** all'aperto; ***a change of ~*** un cambiamento d'aria; *fig* ***it's still all up in the ~*** *infml* è ancora campato in aria; ***be walking*** *or* ***floating on ~*** essere al settimo cielo; ***by ~*** *travel* in aereo; *send mail* per via aerea; ***on the ~*** RADIO, TV in onda; ***with an ~ of bewilderment*** con aria sconcertata; ***she adopted a superior ~*** si dava delle arie di superiorità; ***~s and graces*** arie *fpl* di superiorità **II** *v/t room* arieggiare; *fig*: *views* rendere noto
airbag *n* airbag *m inv*
airbase *n* base *f* aerea
airbed *n* materassino *m* gonfiabile
airborne *adj*: ***be ~*** essere in volo; ***~ troops*** MIL truppe *fpl* aviotrasportate
air brake *n on truck* freno *m* ad aria compressa
airbrush *n* ART aerografo *m*
air cargo *n* aereo *m* da carico **air-conditioned** *adj* con aria condizionata **air conditioning** *n* aria *f* condizionata
aircraft *n* aereo *m*
aircraft carrier *n* portaerei *f inv*
airfare *n* tariffa *f* aerea
airfield *n* campo *m* d'aviazione
air force *n* aeronautica *f* militare **air freshener** *n* deodorante *m* per ambienti
airgun *n* pistola *f*, fucile *m* ad aria compressa
airhead *n pej infml* svampito
air hostess *n* hostess *f inv*
airily *adv say etc* con leggerezza
airing *n of linen etc* asciugatura *f*; ***give sth a good ~*** arieggiare bene qc; *fig* ***give an idea an ~*** *infml* diffondere un'idea
airing cupboard *n Br armadio riscaldato per l'asciugatura della biancheria*
air letter *n* aerogramma *m*
airlift I *n* ponte *m* aereo **II** *v/t* trasportare per via aerea
airline *n* compagnia *f* aerea
airliner *n* aereo *m* di linea
air lock *n in pipe* bolla *f* d'aria
airmail *n*: ***by ~*** per via aerea
Air Miles® *npl* miglia *fpl* aeree
airplane *n* aeroplano *m*
air pocket *n* vuoto *m* d'aria **air pollution** *n* inquinamento *m* atmosferico
airport *n* aeroporto *m*
air pressure *n* pressione *f* atmosferica **air pump** *n* pompa *f* pneumatica **air raid** *n* incursione *f* aerea **air rifle** *n* fu-

cile *m* ad aria compressa
airship *n* dirigibile *m*
airsick *adj*: ***get ~*** soffrire il mal d'aereo *or* l'aereo
airspace *n* spazio *m* aereo
airspeed *n* velocità *f inv* di volo
airstrip *n* pista *f*
air terminal *n* terminale *m*
airtight *adj container* ermetico
airtime *n* RADIO, TV tempo *m* di trasmissione; TEL tempo *m* di conversazione
air traffic *n* traffico *m* aereo **air-traffic control** *n* controllo *m* del traffico aereo **air-traffic controller** *n* controllore *m* di volo **air vent** *n* bocca *f* d'aerazione; (*shaft*) condotto *m* d'aerazione
airwaves *npl* onde *fpl* radio
airy *adj* (*+er*) *room* arieggiato; *attitude* noncurante
airy-fairy *adj Br infml* bislacco; *excuse* campato in aria
aisle *n* corridoio *m*; *in supermarket* corsia *f*; *in church* navata *f* laterale
aisle seat *n* posto *m* corridoio
ajar *adj*: ***be ~*** essere socchiuso
aka *abbr* (= **also known as**) alias
akin *adj*: ***~ to (doing) sth*** simile a (fare) qc
à la carte *adj/adv* alla carta
alacrity *n* alacrità *f inv*
à la mode *adj US* COOK con gelato
alarm I *n* allarme *m*; ***car ~*** allarme *m* antifurto (per auto); ***raise the ~*** dare l'allarme **II** *v/t* allarmare; ***don't be ~ed*** non stare in apprensione
alarm bell *n* campanello *m* d'allarme; *fig* ***set ~s ringing*** far scattare il campanello d'allarme **alarm clock** *n* sveglia *f*
alarming *adj* allarmante
alarmingly *adv* in modo allarmante
alas *int liter* ahimé
Alaska *n* Alaska *f*
Albania *n* Albania *f*
Albanian I *adj* albanese **II** *n person* albanese *m/f*; *language* albanese *m*
albatross *n* ZOOL albatro *m*
albeit *cj form* sebbene
albino I *n* albino *m*, -a *f* **II** *adj* albino
album *n for photographs*, (*record*) album *m inv*
alcohol *n* alcol *m*; ***~-free*** analcolico
alcoholic I *adj* alcolico **II** *n* alcolizzato *m*, -a *f*
alcoholism *n* alcolismo *m*
alcopop *n bibita alcolica dolce e gassata*
alcove *n* nicchia *f*
alder *n* BOT ontano *m*
alderman *n US membro del consiglio comunale*; *Br fino al 1974, importante membro del consiglio comunale*
ale *n* birra *f*
alert I *adj* all'erta *inv*; ***be ~ to sth*** essere consapevoli di qc **II** *v/t* mettere in guardia **III** *n* (*signal*) allarme *m*; ***be on the ~*** stare all'erta; *of troops, police* essere in stato di allerta
alertness *n* (stato *m* di) vigilanza *f*
A-level *n diploma di scuola media superiore in Gran Bretagna che permette di accedere all'università*
alfresco *adj/adv* all'aperto
algae *npl* alghe *fpl*
algebra *n* algebra *f*
Algeria *n* Algeria *f*
algorithm *n* algoritmo *m*
alias I *adv* alias **II** *n* falso nome *m*
alibi *n* alibi *m inv*
alien I *n* (*foreigner*) straniero *m*, -a *f*; *from space* alieno *m*, -a *f* **II** *adj* estraneo; ***be ~ to s.o.*** essere estraneo a qn
alienate *v/t* alienarsi; ***~ o.s. from s.o./sth*** alienarsi da qn/qc
alienation *n* alienazione *f* (**from** da)
alight[1] *adj*: ***be ~*** essere in fiamme; ***set sth ~*** dare fuoco a qc
alight[2] *v/i*: ***his eyes ~ed on the ring*** gli occhi gli si illuminarono alla vista dell'anello; ***she ~ed from the car*** scese dall'auto
align *v/t* allineare
alignment *n* allineamento *m*; ***be out of ~*** non essere allineato (**with** con)
alike I *adj* simile; ***be ~*** assomigliarsi; ***they look very much ~*** si assomigliano moltissimo **II** *adv*: ***it appeals to old and young ~*** attira vecchi e giovani allo stesso tempo; ***they always think ~*** la pensano sempre allo stesso modo
alimentary *adj*: ***~ canal*** ANAT tubo *m* digerente
alimony *n* alimenti *mpl*
alive *adj*: ***be ~*** essere vivo; ***~ and kicking*** *hum* vivo e vegeto; ***be ~ with tourists/insects*** brulicare di turisti/insetti; ***come ~*** animarsi

alkali *n* alcali *m inv*
alkaline *adj* alcalino
all I *adj* tutto; (*each*) ogni; (*any whatever*) qualsiasi; **~ *my books*** tutti i miei libri; **~ *kinds*** *or* ***sorts of people*** ogni sorta di persone; **~ *day*** (***long***) tutto il giorno; **~ *the time*** tutto il tempo; ***beyond* ~ *doubt*** oltre ogni dubbio **II** *pron* **1.** tutto, (tutto) quello che; ***he ate* ~ *of it*** lo ha mangiato tutto; ***he's seen / done it* ~** ha visto / fatto di tutto; **~ *of us / them*** tutti noi / loro; ***that's* ~, *thanks*** è tutto, grazie; **~ *but John agreed*** erano tutti d'accordo tranne John; **~ *of Paris / of the house*** tutta Parigi / la casa; **~ *are fine by me*** per me va tutto bene; **~ *or nothing*** tutto o niente; ***she gave her* ~** ha dato anima e corpo; ***for* ~ *I know*** per quello che ne so; ***for* ~ *I care*** per quello che me ne importa; **~ *and sundry*** tutti quanti; *pej* cani e porci; ***it was* ~ *I could do not to laugh*** ho fatto fatica a non ridere **2. *not at* ~!** niente affatto!; ***they're not at* ~ *alike*** non si assomigliano affatto; ***I don't like him at* ~** non mi piace per niente; ***it's not bad at* ~** non è niente male; ***most of* ~** soprattutto; **~ *in* ~** tutto sommato **III** *adv* **1.** tutto; **~ *excited*** *etc* tutto eccitato; ***all over*** dappertutto; ***it was red* ~ *over*** era tutto rosso; **~ *along the road*** lungo tutta la strada; **~ *at once*** tutto in una volta; (*suddenly*) tutt'a un tratto; ***he's not* ~ *there*** *infml* non ci sta con la testa **2. ~ *down the front of her dress*** su tutto il davanti del vestito; **~ *the funnier because …*** tanto più divertente perché…; **~ *the better*** molto meglio; **~ *but*** (*nearly*) quasi; ***he* ~ *but fainted*** è quasi svenuto; **~ *the same*** tuttavia; **~ *the same, it's a pity*** nonostante tutto è un peccato; ***it's* ~ *one*** *or* ***the same to me*** per me è lo stesso; ***two* ~** SPORTS due pari
Allah *n* Allah *m*
all-American *adj team composto solo dai migliori giocatori americani*; ***an* ~ *boy*** un americano purosangue
allay *v/t* attenuare
all clear *n* (segnale *m* di) cessato allarme *m*; ***give*** *or* ***sound the* ~** dare il via libera **all-day** *adj* che dura tutto il giorno; ***it was an* ~ *meeting*** l'incontro è durato tutta la giornata
allegation *n* accusa *f*
allege *v/t* dichiarare; ***he is* ~*d to have said that …*** si dice che abbia affermato che…
alleged *adj* presunto
allegedly *adv* a quanto si suppone
allegiance *n* fedeltà *f inv*; ***oath of* ~** giuramento *m* di fedeltà
allegoric(al) *adj* allegorico
allegorically *adv* allegoricamente
allegory *n* allegoria *f*
all-embracing *adj* onnicomprensivo
allergic *adj* allergico; ***be* ~ *to*** essere allergico a
allergy *n* allergia *f*
alleviate *v/t* alleviare
alleviation *n* alleviamento *m*
alley *n* vicolo *m*
alliance *n* alleanza *f*
allied *adj* MIL alleato; ***the Allied forces*** le forze alleate
Allies *npl*: ***the* ~** HIST gli alleati
alligator *n* alligatore *m*
all-important *adj* importantissimo; ***the* ~ *question*** la domanda cruciale **all-in** *adj* spossato, esausto **all in** *adj* (*inclusive*) comprensivo; **~ *price*** prezzo *m* tutto compreso **all-inclusive** *adj* tutto compreso **all-in-one** *adj sleepsuit* intero
alliteration *n* allitterazione *f*
all-night *adj café* aperto tutta la notte; *vigil* di notte; ***we had an* ~ *party*** la festa è durata tutta la notte; ***there is an* ~ *bus service*** c'è un servizio di autobus notturno
allocate *v/t* assegnare
allocation *n* assegnazione *f*; (*amount*) parte *f*
allot *v/t* ⟨*pret & past part* **-ted**⟩ assegnare
allotment *n Br* lotto *m* da coltivare
allow *v/t* **1.** (*permit*) permettere; ***be* ~*ed*** essere autorizzato; ***it's not* ~*ed*** è vietato; ***passengers are not* ~*ed to smoke*** ai passeggeri è vietato fumare; ***dogs not* ~*ed*** vietato l'ingresso ai cani; **~ *s.o. to …*** permettere a qn di …; **~ *me!*** mi consenta! **2.** (*calculate for*) calcolare; **~ (*yourself*) *an hour to cross the city*** calcola due ore per attraversare la città
◆**allow for** *v/t* tenere conto di; ***allowing for the fact that …*** tenendo conto

del fatto che…; ***after allowing for*** avendo tenuto conto di
allowance *n* **1.** (*money*) sussidio *m*; (*pocket money*) paghetta *f*; ***clothing ~*** indennità *f inv* di vestiario; ***he gave her an ~ of £500 a month*** le dava un assegno di 500 sterline al mese **2.** ***make ~s for sth*** tenere conto di qc; ***make ~s for s.o.*** essere indulgente con qn **3.** FIN (*tax allowance*) deduzione *f*
alloy *n* lega *f*
all-purpose *adj* multiuso *inv*
all right I *adj* discreto, abbastanza buono; ***it's ~*** (*not too bad*) non è male; (*working properly*) va bene; ***that's*** *or* ***it's ~*** *after thanks, apology* figurati; ***taste ~*** avere un sapore discreto; ***is it ~ for me to leave early?*** va bene se vado via presto?; ***it's ~ by me*** per me va bene; ***it's ~ for you to talk*** fai presto a parlare; ***he's ~*** *infml* (*is a good guy*) è simpatico; ***are you feeling ~?*** ti senti bene? **II** *adv* bene; (*certainly*) sicuramente; ***did I do it ~?*** l'ho fatto per bene?; ***did you find it ~?*** l'hai trovato a posto?; ***that's the boy ~*** quello è senza dubbio il ragazzo; ***oh yes, we heard you ~*** certo che ti abbiamo sentito **III** *int* va bene; ***may I leave early? — ~*** posso andare via presto? – va bene; ***~, ~! I'm coming*** va bene, va bene, arrivo!
all-round *adj improvement* generale; *person* eclettico **all-rounder** *n Br* persona *f* versatile; SPORTS atleta *m/f* completo,-a **All Saints' Day** *n* Ognissanti *m* **All Souls' Day** *n* giorno *m* dei morti
allspice *n* COOK pimento *m*
all-time *adj*: ***be at an ~ low*** *of inflation, unemployment* aver raggiunto il minimo storico; ***the ~ record*** il record di tutti i tempi; ***an ~ high/low*** livello *m* massimo/minimo mai raggiunto
◆**allude to** *v/t* alludere a
allure I *n* fascino *m*; ***she was a woman of considerable ~*** era una donna di grande fascino **II** *v/t* allettare; *sexually* sedurre
alluring *adj* attraente
alluringly *adv* in modo attraente
allusion *n* allusione *f*
all-weather *adj per tutte le condizioni atmosferiche*; ***~ pitch*** campo *m* sintetico
ally[1] *n* alleato *m*, -a *f*
ally[2] *v/t* ⟨*pret & past part* ***-ied***⟩: ***~ o.s. with s.o.*** allearsi con qn
almighty *adj* fortissimo; ***there was an ~ bang and …*** c'è stato un rumore tremendo e…
Almighty *n*: ***the ~*** l'Onnipotente *m*; ***~ God*** Dio *m* Onnipotente; ***Christ Almighty!*** *infml* Cristo!
almond *n* mandorla *f*
almost *adv* quasi; ***he ~ fell*** è quasi caduto
alms *npl* elemosina *f*
almshouse *n* albergo *m* dei poveri
aloe vera *n* aloe vera *f*
aloft *adv into the air* in aria; *in the air* in alto
alone I *adj* solo; ***Simon ~ knew the truth*** solo Simon conosceva la verità **II** *adv* da solo; *fig* ***stand ~*** essere indipendente; *building* essere isolato; ***go it ~*** *infml* essere indipendente
along I *prep* lungo; ***walk ~ the street*** camminare lungo la strada; ***move ~*** circolare **II** *adv*: ***~ with*** insieme con; ***all ~*** (*all the time*) per tutto il tempo; ***we're going, would you like to come ~?*** noi andiamo, vuoi venire con noi?
alongside *prep* di fianco a; *person* al fianco di; ***draw up ~*** accostare; ***draw up ~ s.o.*** accostare vicino a qn; ***~ him*** al suo fianco
aloof *adj* in disparte
aloud *adv* ad alta voce; *laugh, call* forte
alphabet *n* alfabeto *m*
alphabetical *adj* alfabetico
alpine *adj* alpino; ***~ scenery*** paesaggio *m* alpino
Alps *npl* Alpi *fpl*
already *adv* già
alright *adj* **1.** ***it's ~*** va bene; ***is it ~ with you if I …?*** ti va bene se …?; ***~, you can have one!*** va bene, puoi averne uno!; ***~, I heard you!*** sì, ti ho sentito!; ***everything is ~ now between them*** adesso va tutto bene tra di loro; ***that's ~*** (*don't mention it*) non c'è di che; (*I don't mind*) non fa niente; ***~, that's enough!*** basta così! **2.** ***are you ~?*** (*not hurt*) stai bene?; ***I'm ~*** (*not hurt*) sto bene; (*have got enough*)

va bene così; ***is the monitor ~?*** (*in working order*) funziona il monitor?
Alsace *n* Alsazia *f*
Alsatian *n Br* pastore *m* tedesco
also *adv* anche; (*besides*) inoltre; ***her cousin ~ came*** è venuto anche suo cugino; ***not only … but ~*** non solo… ma anche; ***~, I must explain that …*** inoltre, vorrei spiegare che…
altar *n* REL altare *m*
altar boy *n* chierichetto *m*
alter *v/t* modificare; *clothes* fare una modifica a; ***it does not ~ the fact that …*** non cambia il fatto che…
alteration *n* modifica *f*; ***make ~s to sth*** apportare delle modifiche a qc; ***closed for ~s*** chiuso per lavori
altercation *n* alterco *m*
alter ego *n* alter ego *m*
alternate I *v/i* alternare; ***~ one thing with another*** alternare una cosa all'altra **II** *adj* alternato; ***on ~ days*** a giorni alterni; ***on ~ Mondays*** un lunedì su due
alternately *adv* alternamente
alternating current *n* corrente *f* alternata
alternation *n* alternanza *f*
alternative I *n* alternativa *f*; ***have no ~*** non avere altra scelta **II** *adj* alternativo
alternatively *adv* alternativamente; ***or ~, he could come with us*** o altrimenti potrebbe venire con noi
alternative medicine *n* medicina *f* alternativa
alternator *n* ELEC, AUTO alternatore *m*
although *cj* benché, sebbene
altimeter *n* altimetro *m*
altitude *n* altitudine *f*
alt key *n* tasto *m* alt
alto I *n female* contralto *m*; *male* controtenore *m* **II** *adj instrument* contralto **III** *adv*: ***sing ~*** essere un contralto
altogether *adv* (*entirely*) completamente; (*on the whole*) complessivamente; ***he wasn't ~ surprised*** non era del tutto sorpreso; ***that is another matter ~*** è un problema totalmente diverso; ***~ it was very pleasant*** nel complesso è stato molto piacevole; ***~ 3000 people were present*** (*with all included*) c'erano in tutto 3000 persone
altruism *n* altruismo *m*
altruistic *adj* altruistico
aluminium *n*, *US* **aluminum** *n* alluminio *m*; ***~ foil*** foglio *m* d'alluminio
alumnus *n* ⟨*pl* ***alumni***⟩ *form* EDU ex alunno *m*; UNIV ex studente *m*, -essa *f*
always *adv* sempre; ***we could ~ go by train*** potremmo sempre andare in treno
alyssum *n* BOT alisso *m*
Alzheimer's disease *n* morbo *m* di Alzheimer
am → ***be***
a. m. *abbr* (= **ante meridiem**) di mattina; ***at 9 ~*** alle 9 (di mattina)
amalgam *n* amalgama *m* (*a. fig*)
amalgamate I *v/i of companies* fondersi **II** *v/t* amalgamare
amalgamation *n* (*merger*) fusione *f*; CHEM amalgamazione *f*
amass *v/t* accumulare
amateur I *n* (*unskilled*) dilettante *m/f*; SPORTS non professionista *m/f* **II** *adj* amatoriale; ***~ painter*** pittore *m*, -trice *f* dilettante; *pej* → ***amateurish***
amateurish *adj pej* dilettantesco
amaze *v/t* stupire; ***it ~s me that …*** mi stupisce che…
amazed *adj* stupito, meravigliato; ***I was ~ to learn that …*** mi sono stupito nell'apprendere che…
amazement *n* stupore *m*; ***much to my ~*** con mio grande stupore
amazing *adj* (*surprising*) sorprendente; *infml* (*very good*) incredibile
amazingly *adv* incredibilmente
Amazon *n* (*river*) Rio *m* delle Amazzoni; (*region*) Amazzonia *f*
ambassador *n* ambasciatore *m*, -trice *f*
amber *n* ambra *f*; ***at ~*** giallo
ambidextrous *adj* ambidestro
ambience *n* atmosfera *f*
ambiguity *n* ambiguità *f inv*
ambiguous *adj* ambiguo
ambiguously *adv* ambiguamente
ambition *n* ambizione *f*
ambitious *adj* ambizioso **ambitiously** *adv* ambiziosamente
ambivalence *n* ambivalenza *f*
ambivalent *adj* ambiguo
amble *v/i* camminare con calma; ***we were ambling along the riverbank*** stavamo passeggiando lungo il fiume
ambrosia *n liter* ambrosia *f*

ambulance *n* ambulanza *f*
ambulance driver *n* autista *m/f* di ambulanza **ambulance service** *n* servizio *m* di ambulanza
ambush I *n* agguato *m* **II** *v/t* tendere un agguato a; ***be ~ed by*** subire un agguato da parte di
amen *int* amen; *fig* ***~ to that!*** *infml* sono d'accordo!
amenable *adj* accondiscendente
amend *v/t* emendare
amendment *n* emendamento *m*
amends *npl*: ***make ~*** fare ammenda
amenity *n*: **(*public*) ~** struttura *f* pubblica; ***close to all amenities*** in prossimità dei servizi e delle strutture pubbliche
Amerasian *n* amerasiatico *m*, -a *f*, *persona con un genitore americano ed uno asiatico*
America *n* America *f*
American I *n* americano *m*, -a *f* **II** *adj* americano
Americanism *n* LING americanismo *m*
Americanization *n* americanizzazione *f*
Amerindian I *n* amerindio *m*, -a *f* **II** *adj* amerindio
amethyst *n* ametista *f*
Amex *abbr US* **1.** (= **American Stock Exchange**) *borsa valori in USA* **2.** (= **American Express**) American Express
amiable *adj* amichevole
amiably *adv* amabilmente
amicable *adj* amichevole; ***be on ~ terms*** essere in rapporti amichevoli
amicably *adv* amichevolmente
amid(st) *prep* tra
amino acid *n* amminoacido *m*
amiss I *adj*: ***there's something ~*** c'è qualcosa che non va **II** *adv*: ***take sth ~*** *Br* prendersela per qc; ***a drink would not go ~*** un drink non ci starebbe male
ammo *n infml* munizioni *fpl*
ammonia *n* ammoniaca *f*
ammunition *n* munizioni *fpl*; *fig* arma *f*
ammunition belt *n* cartucciera *f*
amnesia *n* amnesia *f*
amnesty *n* amnistia *f*
amniocentesis *n* MED amniocentesi *f*
amoeba, *US* **ameba** *n* ameba *f*
amok *adv*: *fig* ***run ~*** essere in preda ad una furia omicida
among(st) *prep* tra; ***he's ~ our best players*** è uno dei nostri giocatori migliori; ***this habit is widespread ~ the French*** è un costume diffuso tra i francesi; ***stand ~ the crowd*** essere in mezzo alla folla
amoral *adj* amorale
amorous *adj* amoroso
amount *n* quantità *f inv*; (*sum of money*) importo *m*; ***an enormous ~ of work*** un'enorme quantità di lavoro; ***total ~*** totale *m*; ***a small ~ of money*** una piccola somma di denaro; ***debts to*** *Br or* ***in US the ~ of £2000*** debiti per un totale di 2000 sterline
◆**amount to** *v/i of income*, *sum* ammontare a; (*be equal to*) equivalere a
ampere *n* ampere *m inv*
amphetamine *n* anfetamina *f*
amphibian *n* anfibio *m*
amphibious *adj animal* anfibio; *vehicle* anfibio
amphitheatre, *US* **amphitheater** *n* anfiteatro *m*
ample *adj* (*+er*) abbondante; (*more than enough*) in abbondanza
amplification *n* RADIO amplificazione *f*; (*explanation*) approfondimento *m*
amplifier *n* amplificatore *m*
amplify *v/t* ⟨*pret & past part* **-ied**⟩ *sound* amplificare
amputate *v/t* amputare
amputation *n* amputazione *f*
amputee *n* mutilato *m*, -a *f*
amuck *adv* → ***amok***
amuse *v/t* (*make laugh etc*) divertire; (*entertain*) intrattenere; ***~ o.s.*** distrarsi
amused *adj* divertito; ***she seemed ~ at my suggestion*** sembrava divertita dalla mia proposta; ***keep s.o. / o.s. ~*** divertire / divertirsi
amusement *n* (*merriment*) divertimento *m*; (*entertainment*) intrattenimento; ***do sth for one's own ~*** fare qc per divertimento; ***~s*** (*games*) divertimenti *mpl*; ***to our great ~*** con nostro grande divertimento
amusement arcade *n* sala *f* giochi
amusement park *n* parco *m* giochi
amusing *adj* divertente
an *art* → **a**
anabolic steroid *n* anabolizzante *m*
anachronism *n* anacronismo *m*

anachronistic *adj* anacronistico
anaemia, *US* **anemia** *n* anemia *f*
anaemic, *US* **anemic** *adj* anemico
anaesthetic, *US* **anesthetic** *n* anestetico *m*; ***general ~*** anestetico *m* generale; ***local ~*** anestetico *m* locale
anaesthetist, *US* **anesthetist** *n* anestesista *m/f*
anaesthetize, *US* **anesthetize** *v/t* anestetizzare
anagram *n* anagramma *m*
anal *adj* anale; *vulg person* ossessivo; ***~ intercourse*** rapporto *m* anale
analgesic *n* analgesico *m*
analog *adj* COMPUT analogico
analogy *n* analogia *f*
analyse, *US* **analyze** *v/t* analizzare; (*psychoanalyse*) psicanalizzare
analysis ⟨*pl* ***analyses***⟩ *n* analisi *f inv*; ***on*** (***closer***) ***~*** ad un'analisi più attenta
analyst *n* analista *m/f* (*a.* PSYCH); ***systems ~*** analista *m/f* di sistemi
analytical *adj* analitico
analyze *v/t US* → ***analyse***
anarchic(al) *adj* anarchico
anarchism *n* anarchismo *m*
anarchist *n* anarchico *m*, -a *f*
anarchy *n* anarchia *f*
anathema *n form*: ***my political views were ~ to them*** vedevano le mie idee politiche come fumo negli occhi
anatomical *adj* anatomico **anatomically** *adv* anatomicamente
anatomy *n* anatomia *f*
ANC *abbr* (= **African National Congress**) *partito politico sudafricano antirazzista guidato in passato da Nelson Mandela*
ancestor *n* antenato *m*, -a *f*
ancestral *adj* ancestrale; ***~ home*** dimora *f* avita
anchor I *n* NAUT ancora *f* **II** *v/i* NAUT gettare l'ancora
anchorman *n* TV presentatore *m*, anchorman *m inv* **anchorwoman** *n* TV presentatrice *f*
anchovy *n* acciuga *f*
ancient I *adj* antico; ***in ~ times*** nei tempi antichi; ***~ Rome*** Roma *f* antica; ***~ history*** storia *f* antica; *fig* ***that's ~ history*** sono cose vecchie **II** *n*: ***the ~s*** gli antichi
ancillary *adj staff* ausiliario
and *stressed cj* **1.** e; ***5 ~ 5 makes 10*** 5 più 5 fa 10; ***three hundred ~ sixty*** trecentosessanta; ***bread ~ butter*** pane e burro; ***I'll come ~ pick you up*** vengo a prenderti **2.** ***worse ~ worse*** sempre peggio; ***for miles ~ miles*** per moltissime miglia
Andes *npl* Ande *fpl*
anecdotal *adj* aneddotico; *evidence* non fondato
anecdote *n* aneddoto *m*
anemia *n US* → ***anaemia*** *etc*
anemic *adj US* → ***anaemic***
anemone *n* anemone *m*
anesthetic *etc US* → ***anaesthetic*** *etc*
anew *adv form* da capo
angel *n* REL, *fig* angelo *m*
angelfish *n* pesce *m* angelo
angel food cake *n* COOK *soffice dolce americano a base di albume e a forma di ciambella*
angelic *adj* angelico
angelica *n* BOT angelica *f*
anger I *n* rabbia *f*; ***speak in ~*** parlare con rabbia **II** *v/t* fare arrabbiare
angina *n* angina *f* (pectoris)
angle[1] **I** *n* angolo *m*; (*position, fig*) angolazione *f* **II** *v/t lamp etc* orientare; *shot* angolare
angle[2] *v/i esp Br fishing* pescare
◆**angle for** *v/t fig* andare a caccia di; ***angle for sth*** cercare di ottenere qc
angler *n* pescatore *m*, -trice *f* (con amo e lenza)
Anglican REL **I** *adj* anglicano **II** *n* anglicano *m*, -a *f*
anglicism *n* anglicismo *m*
anglicize *v/t* anglicizzare
angling *n esp Br* pescare con la lenza
Anglo-American I *n* angloamericano *m*, -a *f* **II** *adj* angloamericano **Anglo-Indian I** *n persona di origini britanniche e indiane* **II** *adj di origini miste britanniche e indiane* **Anglo-Irish I** *n* anglo-irlandese **II** *adj* anglo-irlandese
anglophile *n* anglofilo *m*, -a *f*
anglophobe *n* anglofobo *m*, -a *f*
Anglo-Saxon I *adj* anglosassone **II** *n person* anglosassone *m/f*
angora I *adj* d'angora; ***~ wool*** lana *f* d'angora **II** *n* angora *f*
angrily *adv* con rabbia
angry *adj* (+*er*) arrabbiato; ***be ~ with s.o.*** essere arrabbiato con qn; ***be ~ about sth*** essere arrabbiato per qc;

get ~ arrabbiarsi
anguish *n* angoscia *f*; ***the decision caused her great ~*** la decisione le diede un grande dolore
angular *adj face, shape* spigoloso
animal I *n* animale *m* **II** *adj* animale; ***~ magnetism*** magnetismo *m* animale; ***~ instincts*** istinti *mpl* primari
Animal Liberation Front *n Br organizzazione animalista fondata in Inghilterra* **animal lover** *n* amante *m*/*f* degli animali **animal rights** *npl* diritti *mpl* degli animali **animal welfare** *n* protezione *f* degli animali
animate I *v*/*t* animare **II** *adj* animato; *creatures* vivente
animated *adj* animato
animated cartoon *n* cartone *m* animato
animation *n* animazione *f*
animosity *n* animosità *f inv*
aniseed *n* (*flavouring*) anice *m*
ankle *n* caviglia *f*
anklebone *n* ANAT astragalo *m*
ankle-deep I *adj* che arriva alla caviglia **II** *adv*: ***he was ~ in water*** l'acqua gli arrivava alle caviglie **ankle sock** *n* calzino *m* corto
annals *npl* annali *mpl*
annex I *v*/*t state* annettere **II** *n* (*building*) annesso *m*
annexation *n* annessione *f*
annexe *n* (*building*) edificio *m* annesso; *to document* annesso *m*
annihilate *v*/*t* annientare
annihilation *n* annientamento *m*
anniversary *n* anniversario *m*; ***~ gift*** regalo *m* di anniversario; ***the ~ of his death*** l'anniversario della sua morte
annotate *v*/*t report* annotare
announce *v*/*t* annunciare
announcement *n* annuncio *m*
announcer *n* TV, *Radio* annunciatore *m*, -trice *f*
annoy *v*/*t* infastidire; ***be ~ed*** essere infastidito; ***get ~ed*** infastidirsi
annoyance *n* (*anger*) irritazione *f*; (*nuisance*) fastidio *m*
annoying *adj* irritante
annual *adj* annuale
annual general meeting *n* assemblea *f* annuale
annuity *n* rendita *f* annuale
annul *v*/*t* ⟨*pret & past part* **-led**⟩ *marriage* annullare
annulment *n* annullamento *m*
Annunciation *n* Annunciazione *f*
anodyne I *adj* anodino **II** *n* calmante *m*
anoint *v*/*t* ungere; ***~ s.o. king*** consacrare qn re
anomalous *adj* anomalo
anomaly *n* anomalia *f*
anon *adv liter* tra poco; ***see you ~*** *hum* a presto
anon. *abbr* (= **anonymous**) *Br* anonimo
anonymity *n* anonimato *m*
anonymous *adj* anonimo
anonymously *adv* anonimamente, in forma anonima
anorak *n Br* giacca *f* a vento
anorexia *n* anoressia *f*
anorexic *adj* anoressico
another I *adj* un altro *m*, un'altra *f*; ***~ ten years*** altri dieci anni; ***that's quite ~ matter*** è tutta un'altra faccenda; ***there is not ~ man like him*** non esiste un altro uomo come lui **II** *pron* un altro *m*, un'altra *f*; ***one ~*** l'un l'altro; ***do they know one ~?*** si conoscono?
ANSI *abbr* (= **American National Standards Institute**) *organizzazione statunitense che produce standard industriali*
answer I *n to letter, person, problem* risposta *f*; ***in ~ to*** in risposta a **II** *v*/*t letter, person* rispondere a; ***~ the door*** aprire la porta; ***~ the telephone*** rispondere al telefono
◆**answer back I** *v*/*t sep person* ribattere a **II** *v*/*i* ribattere
◆**answer for** *v*/*t* rispondere di
◆**answer to** *v*/*t*: ***answer to s.o. for sth*** rendere conto di qc a qn; ***answer to a description*** rispondere ad una descrizione; ***answer to the name of ...*** rispondere al nome di…
answerable *adj*: ***be ~ to s.o. for s.o.*** / ***sth*** rispondere a qn di qn / qc
answering machine *n* TEL segreteria *f* telefonica
answerphone *n* segreteria *f* telefonica
ant *n* formica *f*
antacid *n* antiacido *m*
antagonism *n* antagonismo *m*
antagonist *n* antagonista *m*/*f*
antagonistic *adj* ostile

antagonize *v/t* contrariare
Antarctic *n* Antartico *m*
anteater *n* formichiere *m*
antecedent **I** *adj* antecendente **II** *n* antecedente *m*; (*ancestor*) antenato *m*, -a *f*
antelope *n* antilope *f*
antenatal *adj* durante la gravidanza; ***~ classes*** corso *m* di preparazione al parto; ***~ clinic*** clinica *f* per gestanti; ***~ care*** cure *fpl* durante la gravidanza
antenna *n* antenna *f*
anterior *adj* anteriore
anteroom *n* anticamera *f*
anthem *n* inno *m*
anthill *n* formicaio *m*
anthology *n* antologia *f*
anthrax *n* antrace *m*
anthropocentric *adj* antropocentrico
anthropological *adj* antropologico
anthropologist *n* antropologo *m*, -a *f*
anthropology *n* antropologia *f*
anthropomorphic *adj* antropomorfico
anthropomorphism *n* antropomorfismo *m*
anthropophagy *n* antropofagia *f*
anthroposophy *n* antroposofia *f*
anti-abortionist *n* antiabortista *m/f*
anti-aircraft *adj* antiaereo **anti--American** *adj* antiamericano
antibiotic *n* antibiotico *m*
antibody *n* anticorpo *m*
anticipate *v/t* prevedere; ***as ~d*** come previsto
anticipation *n* previsione *f*; ***wait in ~*** attendere con trepidazione
anticlerical *adj* anticlericale
anticlimax *n* delusione *f*
anticlockwise *Br* **I** *adj* antiorario **II** *adv* in senso antiorario
antics *npl* buffonate *fpl*; ***he's up to his old ~ again*** è tornato ai suoi vecchi scherzi
anticyclone *n* anticiclone *m*
antidepressant *n* antidepressivo *m*
antidote *n* antidoto *m*
antifreeze *n* antigelo *m inv*
anti-globalization **I** *n* antiglobalizzazione *f* **II** *adj*: ***~ protester*** manifestante *m/f* no global
antihistamine *n* antistaminico *m*
antinuclear *adj*: ***~ protester*** manifestante *m/f* contro il nucleare
antipathy *n* antipatia *f*
antiperspirant *n* deodorante *m* antitraspirante
antipodean *adj Br che viene dall'Australia o dalla Nuova Zelanda*
Antipodes *npl*: ***the ~*** *Br* l'Australia e la Nuova Zelanda
antiquarian **I** *adj* antiquario; ***~ bookshop*** libreria *f* antiquaria **II** *n* antiquario *m*, -a *f*
antiquated *adj* antiquato
antique *n* pezzo *m* d'antiquariato
antique dealer *n* antiquario *m*, -a *f*
antique shop *n* negozio *m* d'antiquariato
antiquity *n* antichità *f inv*
antiriot *adj*: ***~ police*** polizia *f* antisommossa
anti-Semite *n* antisemita *m/f*
anti-Semitic *adj* antisemita, antisemitico
anti-Semitism *n* antisemitismo *m*
antiseptic **I** *n* antisettico *m* **II** *adj* antisettico
antisocial *adj* asociale; ***I work ~ hours*** lavoro in orari diversi da tutti gli altri
antiterrorist *adj* antiterroristico
antithesis *n* antitesi *f inv* (***to, of*** con, di)
antivirus program *n* COMPUT programma *m* antivirus
antivivisectionist *n* antivivisezionista *m/f*
antlers *npl* corna *fpl*
antonym *n* antonimo *m*
anus *n* ano *m*
anvil *n* incudine *f* (*a.* ANAT)
anxiety *n* ansia *f*
anxious *adj* ansioso; ***be ~ for …*** *for news etc* essere ansioso di avere …; ***be ~ to*** essere impaziente di
any **I** *adj* **1.** qualche; ***are there ~ diskettes / glasses?*** ci sono dei dischetti / bicchieri?; ***is there ~ bread?*** c'è del pane?; ***is there ~ improvement?*** c'è qualche miglioramento?; ***thank you — ~ time*** grazie – quando vuoi; ***there aren't ~ diskettes / glasses*** non ci sono dischetti / bicchieri; ***there isn't ~ bread*** non c'è pane; ***there isn't ~ improvement*** non c'è nessun miglioramento; ***have you ~ idea at all?*** hai qualche idea? **2.** (*no matter which*) ***take ~ one you like*** prendi quello che vuoi; ***take ~ book on that subject*** prendi qualsiasi libro sull'ar-

gomento **II** *pron*: ***do you have ~?*** ne hai?; ***there aren't ~ left*** non ce ne sono più; ***I want to meet a psychologist, do you know ~?*** vorrei andare da uno psicologo, ne conosci qualcuno?; ***there isn't ~ left*** non ce n'è più; ***~ of them could be guilty*** chiunque di loro potrebbe essere colpevole; ***few, if ~, will come*** saranno in pochi, se mai verranno; ***if ~ of you can sing*** se qualcuno di voi sa cantare **III** *adv* un po'; ***is that ~ better/easier?*** è un po' meglio / più facile?; ***I don't like it ~ more*** non mi piace più; ***do you want ~ more soup?*** vuoi dell'altra zuppa?

anybody *pron* **1.** qualcuno; ***is there ~ there?*** c'è qualcuno? **2.** *with negative* nessuno; ***there wasn't ~ there*** non c'era nessuno **3.** (*whoever*) chiunque; ***~ could do it*** lo potrebbe fare chiunque

anyhow *adv* comunque; ***if I can help you ~, let me know*** se ti posso aiutare in qualsiasi modo, fammi sapere

anyone *pron* → ***anybody***

anything **I** *pron* qualcosa; *with negatives* niente, nulla; ***I didn't hear ~*** non ho sentito niente *or* nulla; ***is there ~ I can do?*** posso fare qualcosa?; ***take ~ you like*** prendi quello che ti pare; ***~ but*** per niente; ***she was ~ but helpful*** non è stata per niente d'aiuto; ***~ else?*** qualcos'altro?; ***he's as smart as ~*** *infml* è intelligentissimo; ***~ but that!*** tutto fuorché quello! **II** *adv infml*: ***it isn't ~ like him*** non è da lui; ***it didn't cost ~ like £100*** costava molto meno di 100 sterline

anyway *adv* → ***anyhow***

anywhere *adv* da qualche parte; *with negative* da nessuna parte; (*wherever*) dovunque; ***the cottage was miles from ~*** il cottage era lontanissimo da tutto; ***I wasn't getting ~*** non stavo andando da nessuna parte; ***I can't find it ~*** non riesco a trovarlo da nessuna parte; ***there could be ~ between 50 and 100 people*** *any quantity or degree* ci saranno dalle 50 alle 100 persone

apart *adv in distance* distante; ***the two cities are 250 miles ~*** le due città distano 250 miglia l'una dall'altra; ***live ~*** *of people* vivere separati; ***~ from*** (*excepting*) a parte, tranne; (*in addition to*) oltre a; ***~ from that, the gearbox is also faulty*** oltre a quello, anche il cambio è rotto; ***come*** *or* ***fall ~*** rompersi *or* andare in pezzi; ***take sth ~*** fare a pezzi qc; ***I can't tell them ~*** non riesco a riconoscere l'uno dall'altro

apartheid *n* apartheid *m*

apartment *n* appartamento *m*; ***~ house*** *or* ***block*** *or* ***building*** *US* palazzo *m* (di appartamenti)

apathetic *adj* apatico

apathy *n* apatia *f*

ape **I** *n* scimmia *f* **II** *v/t* scimmiottare

aperitif *n* aperitivo *m*

aperture *n* PHOT apertura *f*

apex *n* ⟨*pl* ***apexes*** *or* ***apices***⟩ apice *m* (*a. fig*)

APEX *abbr* (= **advance purchase excursion fare**) RAIL, AVIAT **I** *adj* scontato (*di biglietto acquistato con certo anticipo*) **II** *n tariffa che dà diritto ad uno sconto per l'acquisto anticipato di un biglietto*

aphrodisiac *n* afrodisiaco *m*

apiece *adv* l'uno *m*, l'una *f*; ***you can have one ~*** potete averne uno a testa

aplomb *n* aplomb *m inv*; ***with ~*** con disinvoltura

Apocalypse *n* Apocalisse *f*

apocalyptic *adj* apocalittico

apocryphal *adj* apocrifo

apolitical *adj* apolitico

apologetic *adj letter, smile* di scuse; ***he was very ~ for being late*** si è scusato molto di essere in ritardo **apologetically** *adv* con tono di scusa

apologize *v/i* scusarsi; ***~ for*** scusarsi per *or* di; ***~ to s.o.*** scusarsi con qn

apology *n* scusa *f*; ***make an ~ to s.o.*** fare le proprie scuse a qn

apoplectic *adj infml* furibondo; ***~ fit*** MED colpo *m* apoplettico

apoplexy *n* apoplessia *f*

apostle *n* REL apostolo *m*

apostrophe *n* GRAM apostrofo *m*

appal, *US* **appall** *v/t* sconvolgere; ***be ~led at*** *or* ***by*** rimanere sconvolto da

appalling *adj* sconvolgente; *language* scioccante

apparatus *n* apparecchio *m*

apparel *n form*, COMM abbigliamento *m*

apparent *adj* evidente; (*seeming real*) apparente; ***become ~ that ...*** diventare evidente che ...

apparently *adv* apparentemente

apparition *n* (*ghost*) apparizione *f*

appeal **I** *n* (*charm*) attrattiva *f*; *for funds etc* raccolta *f*; *against decision* JUR appello *m*; ***his music has (a) wide ~*** la sua musica attira molte persone; ***sex ~*** sex appeal *m*; ***Court of Appeal*** Corte d'Appello *f* **II** *v/i* JUR fare appello

◆**appeal for** *v/t blood, help* fare un appello per ottenere; ***the President appealed for calm*** il Presidente ha fatto appello alla calma

◆**appeal to** *v/i* (*be attractive to*) attirare

appealing *adj idea, offer* allettante; *glance* supplichevole

appear *v/i* apparire, comparire; *in film etc* apparire; *of new product* comparire; *in court* comparire; (*look, seem*) apparire; ***~ as a witness*** comparire come teste; ***he ~ed (to be) drunk*** sembrava ubriaco; ***it ~s that ...*** sembra che ...

appearance *n* (*arrival*) apparizione *f*, comparsa *f*; *in film etc* apparizione *f*; *in court* comparizione *f*; (*look*) aspetto *m*; ***put in an ~*** fare un salto; ***judge by ~s*** giudicare dalle apparenze

appease *v/t gods, anger* placare; *tyrant* compiacere

appeasement *n* pacificazione *f*

append *v/t form* apporre

appendage *n fig* appendice *f*

appendectomy *n* appendicectomia *f*

appendicitis *n* appendicite *f*

appendix ⟨*pl* ***appendices*** *or* ***appendixes***⟩ *n* MED, *of book etc* appendice *f*; ***have one's ~ out*** venire operati di appendicite

appetite *n* appetito *m*; ***spoil one's ~*** rovinare l'appetito di qn; *fig* ***~ for sth*** sete *f* di qc

appetizer *n food* stuzzichino *m*; *drink* aperitivo *m*

appetizing *adj* appetitoso

applaud **I** *v/i* applaudire **II** *v/t* applaudire (*a. fig*)

applause *n* applauso *m*; (*praise*) approvazione *f*

apple *n* mela *f*; ***be the ~ of s.o.'s eye*** essere la pupilla degli occhi di qn

apple-green *adj* verde mela **apple pie** *n* torta *f* di mele **apple-pie bed** *n* (*joke*) sacco *m* **apple sauce** *n* composta *f* di mele

appliance *n* apparecchio *m*; *household* elettrodomestico *m*

applicable *adj* applicabile; ***that isn't ~ to you*** questo non è adatto a te

applicant *n* candidato *m*, -a *f*

application *n* candidatura *f*; *for job* domanda *f* di lavoro; *for passport, visa* domanda *f*, richiesta *f*; *for university* domanda *f* di iscrizione; (*software*) applicazione *f*; (*effort*) applicazione *f*; ***for external ~ only*** MED per uso esterno

application form *n* modulo *m* di richiesta; *for passport, visa* modulo *m* di richiesta; *for university* modulo *m* di iscrizione

applicator *n* applicatore *m*

applied *adj maths etc* applicato

appliqué SEW **I** *n* applicazione *f* **II** *adj*: ***~ work*** ricamo *m* applicato

apply ⟨*pret & past part* ***-ied***⟩ **I** *v/t* applicare (***to*** su); *paint* dare **II** *v/i of rule, law* applicarsi; ***that rule does not ~ in this country*** quella legge non è applicabile in questo paese

◆**apply for** *v/t job, passport* fare domanda per; *university* fare domanda di iscrizione a

◆**apply to** *v/t* (*contact*) rivolgersi a; (*affect*) applicarsi a; ***she has applied to college*** ha fatto domanda di ammissione all'università

appoint *v/t to position* nominare

appointee *n* incaricato *m*, -a *f*; *to a role* persona *f* designata

appointment *n to position* nomina *f*; (*meeting*) appuntamento *m*; ***make an ~*** prendere un appuntamento; ***by ~*** su appuntamento

appointments diary *n* agenda *f* degli appuntamenti

apportion *v/t* distribuire; *duties* ripartire; ***~ sth to s.o.*** ripartire qc tra qn

appraisal *n* valutazione *f*

appraise *v/t value, damage* stimare; *ability* valutare

appreciable *adj* notevole

appreciably *adv* notevolmente

appreciate **I** *v/t* apprezzare; (*acknowledge*) rendersi conto di; ***thanks, I ~ it*** grazie, te ne sono grato; ***I ~ that ...*** mi rendo conto che ... **II** *v/i* FIN rivalutarsi

appreciation *n of kindness etc* riconoscenza *f*; *of art, music etc* apprezzamento *m*; (*assessment*) valutazione *f*; (*increase in value*) rivalutazione *f*; ***he provided a fair ~ of the country's economy*** ha dato una giusta stima dell'economia del paese
appreciative *adj* (*showing gratitude*) riconoscente; (*showing pleasure*) soddisfatto
apprehend *v/t* (*take into custody, arrest*) arrestare; (*understand*) apprendere
apprehension *n* apprensione *f*
apprehensive *adj* apprensivo; ***he was ~ about the future*** era preoccupato per il futuro
apprentice **I** *n* apprendista *m/f*; ***~ electrician*** elettricista *m/f* apprendista **II** *v/t*: ***be ~d to s.o.*** fare pratica presso qn
apprenticeship *n* apprendistato *m*; ***serve one's ~*** fare un tirocinio
approach **I** *v/t* (*get near to*) avvicinarsi a; (*be nearly equivalent to*) essere quasi pari a; (*contact*) contattare; *problem* abbordare; ***the train is now ~ing platform 3*** il treno è in arrivo al binario 3 **II** *n* avvicinamento *m*; (*proposal*) contatto *m*; (*attitude*) approccio *m*
approachable *adj person* abbordabile
approach road *n to city etc* strada *f* di accesso; *to motorway* rampa *f* di accesso; (*slip road*) svincolo *m*
approbation *n* approvazione *f*; *from critics* elogio *m*
appropriate[1] *adj* (*fitting*) appropriato, adatto; (*relevant*) rilevante; ***delete as ~*** cancellare la voce che non interessa
appropriate[2] *v/t* appropriarsi di (*a. euph*)
appropriately *adv* appropriatamente; *dressed* in modo appropriato (**for, to** per, a)
appropriation *n of land, property* appropriazione *f*
approval *n* approvazione *f*; ***on ~*** salvo approvazione
approve *v/t & v/i* approvare
♦**approve of** *v/t* approvare; ***I don't approve of children smoking*** non approvo che i bambini fumino
approving *adj* di approvazione; (*consenting*) favorevole; ***she gave him an ~ smile*** gli ha fatto un sorriso di approvazione
approx. *abbr* (= **approximately**) ca. (circa)
approximate[1] *adj* approssimativo
approximate[2] *v/i*: ***~ to sth*** approssimarsi a qc
approximately *adv* approssimativamente
approximation *n* approssimazione *f*
appurtenance *n* (*accessory*) accessorio *m*; JUR pertinenza *f*
APR *abbr* (= **annual percentage rate**) tasso *m* di interesse annuale
après-ski **I** *n attività di svago dopo una giornata di sci* **II** *adj* dopo lo sci
apricot *n* albicocca *f*
April *n* aprile *m*
April fool *n* pesce *m* d'aprile **April Fools' Day** *n* primo *m* d'aprile
apron *n* grembiule *m*; AVIAT piazzale *m*
apron strings *npl*: ***be tied to s.o.'s ~*** essere attaccato alla sottana di qn
apropos *prep* (*a.* **apropos of**) a proposito di
apt *adj* (+er) *pupil* portato; *remark* appropriato; ***be ~ to ...*** avere tendenza a ...
Apt. *abbr* (= **apartment**) appartamento *m*
APT *abbr* (= **Advanced Packaging Tool**) COMPUT APT *m*
aptitude *n* attitudine *f*; ***~ for*** attitudine a
aptitude test *n* test *m inv* attitudinale
aqualung *n* autorespiratore *m*
aquamarine **I** *n* acquamarina *f*; (*colour*) color *m* acquamarina **II** *adj* acquamarina
aqua noodle *n* SPORTS cilindro *m* flessibile
aquaplane **I** *n* SPORTS acquaplano *m* **II** *v/i* SPORTS andare in acquaplano; *car etc* slittare per effetto dell'aquaplaning
aquarium *n* acquario *m*
Aquarius *n* ASTROL Acquario *m*
aquatic *adj* acquatico
aqueduct *n* acquedotto *m*
Arab **I** *n* arabo *m*, -a *f* **II** *adj* arabo; ***~ horse*** cavallo *m* arabo
arabesque *n* arabesco *m*; MUS, SPORTS arabesque *f*
Arabia *n* Arabia *f*
Arabian *adj* arabo; ***the ~ Sea*** il Mare

Arabico
Arabic I *n* arabo *m*, -a *f* II *adj* arabo
arable *adj* coltivabile; *~ farming* agricoltura *f*
arbitrarily *adv* arbirtariamente
arbitrary *adj* arbitrario
arbitrate *v/i* arbitrare
arbitration *n* arbitrato *m*
arbitrator *n* arbitro *m*
arc *n* arco *m*
arcade *n* (*games arcade*) sala *f* giochi
arcane *adj* arcano
arch[1] I *n* arco *m* II *v/t back* inarcare; *eyebrows* aggrottare; ***the cat ~ed its back*** il gatto ha inarcato il dorso
arch[2] *adj* malizioso; ***~ enemy*** nemico *m* temibile
archaeological, *US* **archeological** *adj* archeologico
archaeologist, *US* **archeologist** *n* archeologo *m*, -a *f*
archaeology, *US* **archeology** *n* archeologia *f*
archaic *adj* arcaico
archaism *n* arcaismo *m*
archangel *n* arcangelo *m*
archbishop *n* arcivescovo *m*
arched *adj* arcuato; ***~ window*** finestra *f* ad arco
archeology *etc US* → ***archaeology*** *etc*
archer *n* arciere *m*, -a *f*
archery *n* tiro *m* con l'arco
archetypal *adj* archetipico; (*typical*) tipico; ***he is the ~ millionaire*** è l'archetipo del milionario
archetype *n* archetipo *m*
archipelago *n* ⟨*pl* **-(e)s**⟩ arcipelago *m*
architect *n* architetto *m*
architectural *adj* architettonico
architecture *n* architettura *f*
archives *npl* archivi *mpl*
archivist *n* archivista *m/f*
archway *n* arco *m*
Arctic I *adj* artico II *n*: ***the ~*** l'Artico *m*
Arctic Circle *n* Circolo Polare Artico *m* **Arctic Ocean** *n* Oceano Artico *m*
ardent *adj* ardente
arduous *adj* arduo
are → ***be***
area *n* (*measure*) area *f*; (*region*) zona *f*; ***do you live in the ~?*** vivi in zona?; ***protected ~*** area *f* protetta; ***no smoking ~*** zona *f* non fumatori; ***penalty ~*** *esp Br football* area *f* di rigore
area code *n US* TEL prefisso *m* telefonico; *official name* indicativo *m* distrettuale **area office** *n* ufficio *m* di zona
arena *n* SPORTS arena *f*
aren't → ***are not***
Argentina *n* Argentina *f*
Argentinian I *adj* argentino II *n* argentino *m*, -a *f*
arguable *adj*: ***it is ~ that ...*** si può sostenere che...; ***it is ~ whether ...*** ci si può chiedere se...
arguably *adv* probabilmente; ***he's ~ the best*** si può dire che è il migliore
argue I *v/i* **1.** (*quarrel*) litigare; ***~ with*** litigare con; ***~ about*** litigare per **2.** (*reason*) sostenere **3.** ***~ for / against*** esprimersi a favore di / contro qc II *v/t*: ***~ that ...*** sostenere che ...
argument *n* (*quarrel*) litigio *m*; (*reasoning*) argomento *m*; ***have an ~*** litigare; ***Professor Ayer's ~ is that ...*** secondo l'argomentazione del professor Ayer...
argumentative *adj* polemico
aria *n* MUS aria *f*
arid *adj land* arido
Aries *n* ASTROL Ariete *m*
arise *v/i* ⟨*pret* ***arose***, *past part* ***arisen***⟩ *of situation*, *problem* emergere; (*get up*) alzarsi
arisen *past part* → ***arise***
aristocracy *n* aristocrazia *f*
aristocrat *n* aristocratico *m*, -a *f*
aristocratic *adj* aristocratico
arithmetic *n* aritmetica *f*
ark *n*: ***Noah's Ark*** arca *f* di Noè
arm[1] *n of person* braccio *m*; *of chair* bracciolo *m*; (*sleeve*) manica *f*; ***~ in ~*** a braccetto; ***within ~'s reach*** a portata di mano; ***it cost him an ~ and a leg*** *infml* gli è costato un occhio della testa
arm[2] I *v/t* armare; ***~ s.o. / sth with sth*** armare qn / qc di qc II *n* (*weapon*) arma *f*
armaments *npl* armamenti *mpl*
armband *n* fascia *f*
armchair *n* poltrona *f*
armed *adj* armato
armed forces *npl* forze *fpl* armate **armed robbery** *n* rapina *f* a mano armata
Armenia *n* Armenia *f*
Armenian I *adj* armeno II *n* (*person*) armeno *m*, -a *f*; (*language*) armeno *m*

armful *n* bracciata *f*
armistice *n* armistizio *m*
Armistice Day *n 11 novembre, anniversario dell'armistizio della Prima Guerra Mondiale*
armour, *US* **armor** *n* armatura *f*, corazza *f*; (*metal plates*) blindatura *f*; ***suit of ~*** armatura *f*
armoured vehicle, *US* **armored vehicle** *n* veicolo *m* blindato
armpit *n* ascella *f*
armrest *n* bracciolo *m* (*di poltrona*)
arms *npl* (*weapons*) armi *fpl*; ***take up ~*** (***against s.o. / sth***) prendere le armi (contro qn / qc); *fig* ***be up in ~*** (***about sth***) *infml* essere pronti a ribellarsi (per qc); ***coat of ~*** *heraldry* stemma *m*
arms race *n* corsa *f* agli armamenti
army *n* esercito *m*
A-road *n Br* strada *f* statale
aroma *n* aroma *m*
aromatherapy *n* aromaterapia *f*
aromatic *adj* aromatico
arose *pret* → ***arise***
around **I** *prep* (*in circle*, *roughly*) intorno a; *room*, *world* attraverso; ***it's ~ the corner*** è dietro l'angolo **II** *adv* **1.** (*in the area*) qui intorno; ***he lives ~ here*** abita da queste parti; ***he's still ~*** *infml* (*alive*) è ancora in circolazione **2.** (*encircling*) intorno **3.** (*roughly*) circa; ***it's ~ two o'clock*** sono circa le due; ***it costs ~ five pounds*** costa circa cinque sterline **4.** ***walk ~*** andare in giro; ***she has been ~*** (*has travelled*, *is experienced*) ha girato; ***see you ~!*** *infml* ci vediamo in giro!
arouse *v/t* suscitare; (*sexually*) eccitare
arrange *v/t* (*put in order*) sistemare; *music* arrangiare; *meeting*, *party etc* organizzare; *time and place* combinare; ***I've ~d to meet her*** ho combinato di incontrarla; ***shall I ~ the flowers?*** sistemo i fiori?; ***~d marriage*** matrimonio *m* combinato
◆**arrange for** *v/t* provvedere a; ***I've arranged for him to meet us*** ho provveduto affinché ci incontrasse
arrangement *n* (*agreement*) accordo *m*; *of party*, *meeting* organizzazione *f*; (*layout*: *of furniture etc*) disposizione *f*; *of music* arrangiamento *m*; ***~s*** *for party*, *meeting* preparativi *mpl*; ***make ~s*** prendere disposizioni; ***seating ~s*** disposizione *f* dei posti; ***flower ~*** composizione *f* floreale
array *n* gamma *f*
arrears *npl* arretrati *mpl*; ***be in ~*** *of person* essere in arretrato; ***be paid in ~*** *for job* essere pagato a lavoro effettuato
arrest **I** *n* arresto *m*; ***be under ~*** essere in arresto **II** *v/t* arrestare
arresting *adj* affascinante
arrest warrant *n* mandato *m* di cattura
arrival *n* arrivo *m*; ***~s*** *at airport* arrivi *mpl*; ***on ~*** al momento dell'arrivo
arrive *v/i* arrivare; ***~ home*** arrivare a casa; (*after journey etc*) tornare
◆**arrive at** *v/t place*, *decision* arrivare a; ***arrive at a town / the airport*** arrivare ad una città / all'aeroporto; ***the train will arrive at platform 10*** il treno arriverà al binario 10; ***arrive at a decision / result*** giungere ad una decisione / un risultato
arrogance *n* arroganza *f*
arrogant *adj* arrogante
arrogantly *adv* con arroganza
arrow *n* freccia *f*
arse *n* (*fool*) imbecille *m*; *vulg* culo *m vulg*; ***tell him to get his ~ into my office*** digli di venire subito nel mio ufficio
◆**arse about** *or* **around** *v/i Br infml* cazzeggiare
arsehole *n Br vulg* stronzo *m*, -a *f vulg*
arsenal *n* MIL arsenale *m* (*a. fig*)
arsenic *n* arsenico *m*
arson *n* incendio *m* doloso
arsonist *n* piromane *m/f*
art *n* arte *f*; ***the ~s*** l'arte; ***~s and crafts*** arti *fpl* e mestieri *mpl*; ***~s*** UNIV materie *fpl* umanistiche; ***there's an ~ to it*** per farlo ci vuole una capacità particolare
art college *n* scuola *f* di belle arti
artefact *n* → ***artifact***
arterial *adj*: ***~ road*** AUTO arteria *f* di traffico
artery *n* MED arteria *f*
artesian well *n* pozzo *m* artesiano
art gallery *n* galleria *f* d'arte **art-house** *adj*: ***~ film*** film *m inv* d'autore
arthritic *adj* artritico
arthritis *n* artrite *f*
arthropod *n* artropode *m*
artichoke *n* carciofo *m*

article **I** *n* articolo *m*; **~ *of faith*** articolo *m* di fede; **~ *of clothing*** capo *m* d'abbigliamento **II** *v/t* articolare; **~*d clerk*** tirocinante *m/f*
articulate *adj speech* chiaro; ***be ~*** *of person* esprimersi bene
articulated lorry / truck *n Br* autoarticolato *m*
articulation *n sound* articolazione *f*; (*expression*) espressione *f*
artifact *n* manufatto *m*
artificial *adj* artificiale; (*not sincere*) finto; (*synthetic*) sintetico; **~ *silk*** seta *f* sintetica; **~ *limb*** arto *m* artificiale
artificial intelligence *n* intelligenza *f* artificiale
artillery *n* artiglieria *f*
artisan *n* artigiano *m*, -a *f*
artist *n* artista *m/f*
artiste *n* artista *m/f*
artistic *adj* artistico
artistic director *n* direttore *m*, -trice *f* artistico, -a
artless *adj* naturale
Art Nouveau *n* liberty *m*, art nouveau *f*
arts degree *n* laurea *f* in discipline umanistiche **Arts Faculty, Faculty of Arts** *n* facoltà *f inv* di materie umanistiche
artwork *n in book* illustrazioni *fpl*; *for advert etc* grafica *f*; (*painting etc*) opere *fpl* d'arte
arty *adj* (*+er*) *infml* che ha pretese artistiche; *person* creativo; *film* pseudoartistico
arty-farty *adj hum* intellettualoide
Aryan **I** *n* ariano *m*, -a *f* **II** *adj* ariano
as **I** *prep* **1.** come; **~ *a child*** da bambino; **~ *a schoolgirl*** quando andava a scuola; ***I'm talking to you ~ a friend*** ti parlo come amico; ***dressed ~ a policeman*** vestito da poliziotto; ***work ~ a teacher / translator*** essere insegnante / traduttore; **~ *Hamlet*** nel ruolo di Amleto **2.** **~ *for*** quanto a **II** *adv*: **~ *high / pretty ~ …*** alto / carino come …; **~ *much ~ that?*** così tanto?; ***run ~ fast ~ you can*** corri più veloce che puoi **III** *cj* **1.** (*while, when*) mentre; **~ *he grew older, …*** diventando più vecchio, … **2.** (*because*) dato che **3.** (*like*) come; ***as it were*** per così dire; **~ *if*** come se; **~ *usual*** come al solito; **~ *it is*** così **4.** **~ *necessary*** in base alla necessità
asap *abbr* (= **as soon as possible**) quanto prima
asbestos *n* amianto *m*
ascend *form* **I** *v/t slope, stairs* salire; *ladder* salire su **II** *v/i* salire; ***in ~ing order*** in ordine ascendente
ascendancy, ascendency *n* ascendente *m*; ***gain (the) ~ over s.o.*** avere un ascendente su qn
Ascension *n* REL Ascensione *f*
ascent *n path* salita *f*; *of mountain* ascensione *f*; *fig* ascesa *f*
ascertain *v/t form* accertare, accertarsi di
ascetic **I** *adj* ascetico **II** *n* asceta *m/f*
ASCII *abbr* (= **American Standard Code for Information Interchange**): **~ *file*** file *m* ASCII
ascorbic acid *n* acido *m* ascorbico
ascribe *v/t*: **~ *sth to s.o. / sth*** attribuire qc a qn / qc
asexual *adj reproduction* asessuato
ash¹ *n* (*a.* **ash tree**) frassino *m*
ash² *n* cenere *f*; **~*es*** ceneri *fpl*
ashamed *adj*: ***be ~ of*** vergognarsi di; ***you should be ~ of yourself*** dovresti vergognarti
ash blonde *adj* biondo cenere
ashen-faced *adj* dal viso pallido
ashlar, ashler *n* concio *m*
ashore *adv* a terra; ***go ~*** sbarcare
ashram *n in India* ashram *f*, *comunità induista*
ashtray *n* posacenere *m*, portacenere *m*
Ash Wednesday *n* mercoledì *m inv* delle Ceneri
Asia *n* Asia *f*
Asia Minor *n* Asia Minore *f*
Asian **I** *n* asiatico *m*, -a *f*; (*Indian, Pakistani*) indiano *m*, -a *f* **II** *adj* asiatico; (*Indian, Pakistani*) indiano
Asian-American **I** *adj americano di origine asiatica* **II** *n americano di origine asiatica*
aside *adv* da parte; ***take s.o. ~*** prendere a parte qn; ***joking ~*** scherzi a parte; **~ *from*** a parte
asinine *adj* asinino
ask **I** *v/t* **1.** *person* chiedere a; ***can I ~ you something?*** posso chiederti una cosa?; **~ *s.o. about sth*** chiedere a qn di qc; **~ *s.o. for …*** chiedere a qn …; **~ *s.o. to …*** chiedere a qn di … **2.** (*in-

vite) invitare **3.** *question* fare **4.** *favour* chiedere **II** *v/i* chiedere
◆**ask after** *v/t person* chiedere di
◆**ask back** *v/t sep* (*invite*) ricambiare l'invito; ***they never asked me back again*** non hanno mai ricambiato il mio invito
◆**ask for** *v/t* chiedere; *person* chiedere di
◆**ask out** *v/t sep for a drink*, *night out* invitare fuori a
askance *adv*: ***look ~ at s.o. / sth*** guardare storto qn / qc
askew *adv* di traverso
asking price *n* prezzo *m* di domanda
asleep *adj*: ***he's (fast) ~*** sta dormendo (profondamente); ***fall ~*** addormentarsi
asocial *adj* asociale
asparagus *n* asparagi *mpl*
aspect *n* aspetto *m*; *of building*, *window* esposizione *f*; ***what about the security ~?*** e per quanto riguarda la sicurezza?; ***have a southerly ~*** essere esposto a sud
asperity *n* asprezza *f*
asphalt *n* asfalto *m*
asphyxiate *v/t* asfissiare
asphyxiation *n* asfissia *f*
aspic *n* COOK aspic *m inv*
aspirate *v/t* aspirare
aspiration *n* aspirazione *f*
aspire *v/i*: ***~ to sth / to do sth*** ambire a qc / a fare qc
aspirin® *n* aspirina® *f*
aspiring *adj* aspirante
ass *n infml* (*idiot*) cretino *m*, -a *f*; *US sl* (*backside*) culo *m sl*; *US vulg* (*woman*) figa *f vulg*; *US vulg* (*sexual intercourse*) scopata *f vulg*; ***kick ~*** fare il culo *vulg*; ***work one's ~ off*** spaccarsi il culo *vulg*
assail *v/t* assalire; ***be ~ed by doubts*** essere assalito dai dubbi
assailant *n* assalitore *m*, -trice *f*
assassin *n* assassino *m*, -a *f*
assassinate *v/t* assassinare
assassination *n* assassinio *m*
assault I *n* assalto *m*; JUR aggressione *f* **II** *v/t* aggredire
assault course *n* percorso *m* di guerra **assault troops** *npl* truppe *fpl* d'assalto
assemble I *v/t parts* assemblare, montare **II** *v/i of people* radunarsi
assembly *n* assemblea *f*; *of parts* assemblaggio *m*; ***the Welsh Assembly*** Assemblea Gallese *f*
assembly hall *n* EDU sala *f* riunioni **assembly line** *n* catena *f* di montaggio **assembly plant** *n* officina *f* di montaggio
assent I *v/i form* acconsentire **II** *n form* assenso *m*
assert *v/t*: ***~ o.s.*** farsi valere; ***~ one's rights*** affermare i propri diritti
assertion *n* asserzione *f*
assertive *adj person* sicuro di sé
assertiveness *n* assertività *f inv*
assess *v/t* valutare
assessment *n* valutazione *f*
assessor *n insurance* perito *m*, -a *f*; UNIV esaminatore *m*, -trice *f*
asset *n* FIN attivo *m*; *fig*: *thing* vantaggio *m*; *person* elemento *m* prezioso
asshole *n US sl* buco *m* del culo *vulg*; (*stupid person*) coglione *m vulg*
assiduous *adj* assiduo **assiduously** *adv* assiduamente
assign *v/t person* destinare; *thing* assegnare
assignment *n* (*task*, *study*) compito *m*
assimilate *v/t information* assimilare; *person into group* integrare
assimilation *n* assimilazione *f*
assist *v/t* assistere
assistance *n* assistenza *f*; ***can I be of any ~?*** posso esserLe d'aiuto?
assistant *n* assistente *m/f*; *in shop* commesso *m*, -a *f*
assistant director *n* vice-direttore *m*; *of film* aiuto-regista *m/f* **assistant manager** *n of business* vice-responsabile *m/f*; *of hotel*, *restaurant* vice-direttore *m*
associate I *v/t* associare **II** *v/i*: ***~ with*** frequentare **III** *n* socio *m*, -a *f*
associate director *n* direttore *m*, -trice *f* associato, -a, vicedirettore *m*, -trice *f* **associate member** *n* membro *m* associato **associate professor** *n* professore *m* associato, professoressa *f* associata
association *n* associazione *f*; ***in ~ with*** in associazione con
assorted *adj* assortito
assortment *n* assortimento *m*; ***there was a whole ~ of people*** c'era gente di tutti i tipi
assume *v/t* (*suppose*) supporre; (*take*

for granted) presumere; ***assuming that*** ammesso che; **~ *office*** assumere una carica
assumed *adj*: **~ *name*** falso nome *m*
assumption *n* supposizione *f*; ***The Assumption*** REL l'Assunzione *f*
assurance *n* assicurazione *f*, garanzia *f*; (*confidence*) sicurezza *f*; ***he gave me his personal ~ that …*** mi ha assicurato personalmente che …
assure *v/t* (*reassure*): **~ *s.o. of sth*** assicurare qc a qn; (***you can***) ***rest ~d that*** stia sicuro che
assured *adj* (*confident*) sicuro; ***rest ~ that …*** stai sicuro che…
assuredly *adv* sicuramente
asterisk *n* asterisco *m*
astern *adv* NAUT a poppa
asteroid *n* asteroide *m*
asthma *n* asma *f*
asthmatic *adj* asmatico
astonish *v/t* sbalordire; ***be ~ed*** essere sbalordito
astonishing *adj* sbalorditivo
astonishingly *adv* in modo sbalorditivo
astonishment *n* stupore *m*
astound *v/t* stupefare
astounding *adj* stupefacente
astoundingly *adv* in modo stupefacente
astray *adv*: ***go ~*** smarrirsi; *morally* uscire dalla retta via
astride I *adv* a cavalcioni **II** *prep* a cavalcioni di
astringent *adj* astringente; *remark, humour* duro
astrologer *n* astrologo *m*, -a *f*
astrological *adj* astrologico
astrology *n* astrologia *f*
astronaut *n* astronauta *m*/*f*
astronomer *n* astronomo *m*, -a *f*
astronomical *adj price etc* astronomico
astronomically *adv* astronomicamente
astronomy *n* astronomia *f*
astrophysics *nsg* astrofisica *f*
astute *adj* astuto **astutely** *adv* astutamente
asunder *adv liter* a pezzi
asylum *n mental* manicomio *m*; *political* asilo *m*
asylum seeker *n persona che fa richiesta di asilo*
asymmetric(al) *adj* asimmetrico
asymmetry *n* asimmetria *f*
at *stressed prep* **1.** *with places* a; ***he works ~ the hospital*** lavora in ospedale; **~ *the door*** alla porta; ***at the top*** in cima **2.** *with persons*: **~ *the baker's*** dal panettiere *or* in panetteria; **~ *Joe's*** da Joe **3.** *price, speed etc*: **~ *10 pounds*** a 10 sterline; **~ *150 km/h*** a 150 km/h **4.** *time*: **~ *the age of 18*** all'età di 18 anni; **~ *5 o'clock*** alle cinque; **~ *night*** di notte; **~ *the moment you called*** nel momento in cui hai chiamato **5.** *activity*: **~ *lunch*** a pranzo; **~ *work*** al lavoro; **~ *war*** in guerra **6.** ***be good/bad ~ sth*** essere/non essere bravo in qc **7.** (*as a result of, upon*) **~ *his request*** alla sua richiesta; **~ *an advantage*** in vantaggio; **~ *a profit*** con profitto
ate *pret of* **eat**
atelier *n* atelier *m*
atheism *n* ateismo *m*
atheist *n* ateo *m*, -a *f*
Athens *n* Atene *f*
athlete *n* atleta *m*/*f*
athlete's foot *n* MED piede *m* d'atleta
athletic *adj* atletico
athletics *nsg* atletica *f*
Atlantic *n* Atlantico *m*
atlas *n* atlante *m*
ATM *abbr* (= **automated teller machine**) Bancomat® *m inv*
atmosphere *n of earth, mood* atmosfera *f*
atmospheric pollution *n* inquinamento *m* atmosferico **atmospheric pressure** *n* pressione *f* atmosferica
atoll *n* atollo *m*
atom *n* atomo *m*
atom bomb *n* bomba *f* atomica
atomic *adj* atomico
atomic energy *n* energia *f* nucleare **Atomic E nergy Authority** *n Br*, **Atomic E nergy Commission** *n US* Commissione per l'energia atomica *f*
atomic waste *n* scorie *fpl* nucleari
atomizer *n* vaporizzatore *m*
atonal *adj* atonale
atone *v/i*: **~ *for*** scontare
atonement *n* espiazione *f*; ***in ~ for sth*** per il perdono di qc
A to Z® *n* stradario *m*
atrocious *adj* atroce **atrociously** *adv* atrocemente

atrocity *n* atrocità *f inv*
atrophy I *n* atrofia *f* **II** *v/i* atrofizzarsi
at sign *n* chiocciola *f* (*simbolo*)
attach *v/t* attaccare; *importance* attribuire; *document*, *file* allegare; ***be ~ed to*** (*fond of*) essere attaccato a
attachment *n* (*fondness*) attaccamento *m*; *to email* allegato *m*
attack I *n* aggressione *f*; MIL, MED attacco *m*; ***be under ~*** subire un attacco; ***go on to the ~*** sferrare un attacco; ***have an ~ of nerves*** avere un attacco di nervi **II** *v/t* aggredire; MIL attaccare
attain *v/t aim*, *rank* conseguire; *independence* ottenere; *happiness* raggiungere
attainable *adj power* ottenibile; *happiness* raggiungibile
attempt I *n* tentativo *m*; ***make an ~ on s.o.'s life*** attentare alla vita di qn **II** *v/t* tentare; ***~ to do sth*** provare a fare qc; ***~ed murder*** tentato omicidio *m*
attend *v/t wedding*, *funeral* partecipare a; *school*, *classes* frequentare
◆**attend to** *v/t* (*deal with*) sbrigare; *customer* servire; *patient* assistere; ***are you being attended to?*** La stanno servendo?; ***that's being attended to*** se ne stanno occupando
attendance *n* partecipazione *f*; *at school* frequenza *f*; ***be in ~ at sth*** essere presenti a qc
attendance record *n* EDU numero *m* di presenze; ***he doesn't have a very good ~*** EDU è stato spesso assente
attendant *n in museum etc* sorvegliante *m/f*
attention *n* attenzione *f*; ***bring sth to s.o.'s ~*** informare qn di qc; ***your ~ please*** attenzione; ***pay ~*** fare attenzione; ***for the ~ of*** *in faxes etc* alla cortese attenzione di; ***stand to ~*** MIL stare sull'attenti; ***~!*** MIL sull'attenti!
Attention Deficit Disorder *n* MED disturbo *m* da deficit dell'attenzione
attention span *n* capacità *f inv* di concentrazione
attentive *adj listener* attento
attenuate *v/t* attenuare; ***attenuating circumstances*** circostanze *fpl* attenuanti
attest *v/t* (*testify to*) attestare; *on oath* dichiarare (sotto giuramento)
◆**attest to** *v/t* testimoniare
attestation *n* (*document*) attestazione *f*
attic *n* soffitta *f*
attire I *v/t* vestire (***in*** in, di) **II** *n* abbigliamento *m*; ***ceremonial ~*** abito *m* da cerimonia
attitude *n* atteggiamento *m*; ***women with ~*** donne *fpl* di carattere
attn *abbr* (= **attention**) c.a. (alla cortese attenzione di)
attorney *n* avvocato *m*; ***power of ~*** delega *f*; ***letter of ~*** procura *f*
Attorney General *n* ⟨*pl* ***Attorneys General*** *or* ***Attorney Generals***⟩ *US procuratore generale e ministro della giustizia*; *Br magistrato di livello più alto e membro del governo*
attract *v/t* attirare; ***be ~ed to s.o.*** essere attirato da qn
attraction *n* attrazione *f*
attractive *adj* attrattivo; *person* attraente
attractively *adv dressed* in modo seducente; *furnished* in modo gradevole; ***~ priced*** con un prezzo interessante (***at*** di)
attributable *adj*: ***be ~ to s.o.*** / ***sth*** essere da attribuire a qn / qc
attribute[1] *v/t* attribuire; ***~ sth to …*** attribuire qc a …
attribute[2] *n* attributo *m*
attrition *n fig* attrito *m*
attune *v/t fig* accordare (***to*** a); ***be ~d to sth*** essere in sintonia con qc
atypical *adj* atipico
aubergine *n* melanzana *f*
auburn *adj hair* castano ramato
auction I *n* asta *f* **II** *v/t* vendere all'asta; ***put sth up for ~*** mettere qc all'asta
◆**auction off** *v/t* vendere all'asta
auctioneer *n* banditore *m*, -trice *f*
audacious *adj* audace
audacity *n* audacia *f*
audible *adj* udibile **audibly** *adv* distintamente
audience *n* pubblico *m*; TV telespettatori *mpl*; *with the Pope etc* udienza *f*
audio *adj* audio *inv*
audio book *n* audiolibro *m* **audio cassette** *n* audiocassetta *f* **audio equipment** *n in recording studio* attrezzatura *f* audio; (*hi-fi*) impianto *m* audio
audiotape *n* nastro *m* audio

audiotypist *n chi batte a macchina testi registrati*
audiovisual *adj* audiovisivo
audit I *n of accounts* revisione *f or* verifica *f* contabile; ***software ~*** inventario *m* dei software **II** *v/t* verificare
audition I *n* audizione *f* **II** *v/i* fare un'audizione
auditor *n* revisore *m* contabile
auditorium *n of theatre etc* sala *f*
au fait *adj*: ***be ~ with sth*** essere informato su qc
aught *pron*: ***for ~ I know*** per quanto ne so
augment *v/t form* aumentare
augmentation *n* aumento *m*; MUS aumentazione *f*
augur *v/i*: ***~ well / ill*** *form* essere di buon / cattivo auspicio
august *adj* augusto
August *n* agosto *m*
aunt *n* zia *f*
auntie, aunty *n infml* zia *f*
au pair (girl) *n* ragazza *f* alla pari
aura *n*: ***she has an ~ of confidence*** emana sicurezza
aureole *n* aureola *f*
auspices *npl*: ***under the ~ of*** sotto l'egida di
auspicious *adj* propizio **auspiciously** *adv* sotto buoni auspici
Aussie *n infml* australiano *m*, -a *f*
austere *adj* austero **austerely** *adv* austeramente
austerity *n economic* austerità *f inv*
Australasia *n Asia insulare e Oceania*
Australasian *adj dell'Asia insulare e dell'Oceania*
Australia *n* Australia *f*
Australian I *adj* australiano **II** *n* australiano *m*, -a *f*
Austria *n* Austria *f*
Austrian I *adj* austriaco **II** *n* austriaco *m*, -a *f*
autarchy *n* autarchia *f*
authentic *adj* autentico **authentically** *adv* sinceramente
authenticate *v/t* verificare (l'autenticità di); *document* autenticare
authenticity *n* autenticità *f inv*
author *n* autore *m*, autrice *f*
authoritarian *adj* autoritario
authoritarianism *n* autoritarismo *m*
authoritative *adj* autoritario; *information* autorevole **authoritatively** *adv* (*with authority*) in modo autoritario; (*reliably*) autorevolmente
authority *n* **1.** autorità *f inv*; ***be in ~*** avere l'autorità; ***be an ~ on*** essere un'autorità in materia di; ***the authorities*** le autorità **2.** (*permission*) autorizzazione *f*
authorization *n* autorizzazione *f*
authorize *v/t* autorizzare; ***be ~d to ...*** essere autorizzato a ...; ***~d personnel only*** solo personale autorizzato; ***~ signature*** firma *f* autorizzata
autism *n* autismo *m*
autistic *adj* autistico
auto *n US* auto *f inv*
autobiographical *adj* autobiografico
autobiography *n* autobiografia *f*
autocrat *n* autocrate *m/f*
autocratic *adj* autocratico
Autocue® *n Br* TV gobbo *m*
autoeroticism, autoerotism *n* autoerotismo *m*
autofocus *n* PHOT autofocus *m*
autograph *n* autografo *m*
automate *v/t* automatizzare
automated teller machine *n* sportello *m* bancario automatico
automatic I *adj* automatico **II** *n car* macchina *f* con il cambio automatico; *gun* pistola *f* automatica; *washing machine* lavatrice *f* automatica
automatically *adv* automaticamente
automation *n* automazione *f*
automaton *n* ⟨*pl* **-s** *or* **automata**⟩ automa *m*
automobile *n* automobile *f*
autonomous *adj* autonomo
autonomy *n* autonomia *f*
autopilot *n* pilota *m* automatico; ***do sth on ~*** fare qc meccanicamente
autopsy *n* autopsia *f*
autumn *n* autunno *m*
auxiliary I *adj* ausiliario; ***~ nurse*** infermiere *m*, -a *f* ausiliario, -a; ***~ verb*** verbo *m* ausiliario **II** *n* (*assistant*) ausiliare *m/f*
avail I *n*: ***to no ~*** invano **II** *v/t*: ***~ o.s. of*** avvalersi di
availability *n* disponibilità *f inv*; ***offer subject to ~*** offerta *f* soggetta a disponibilità
available *adj* disponibile; ***he caught the next ~ flight to Rome*** ha preso il primo volo disponibile per Roma; ***when will you be ~ to start in the***

new job? quando sarà disponibile per iniziare il nuovo lavoro?
avalanche *n* valanga *f*; ***an ~ of letters*** una valanga di lettere
avant-garde *adj* d'avanguardia
avarice *n* avarizia *f*
Ave. *abbr* (= **Avenue**) C.so (Corso *m*); V.le (Viale *m*); V. (Via *f*)
avenge *v/t* vendicare; ***~ o.s. on s.o.*** (***for sth***) vendicarsi su qn (per *or* di qc)
avenue *n* corso *m*; *fig* strada *f*
aver *v/t* affermare
average I *adj* medio; (*of mediocre quality*) mediocre; ***of ~ height*** di statura media **II** *n* media *f*; ***above / below ~*** sopra / sotto la media; ***on ~*** in media, mediamente; ***by the law of ~s*** secondo le probabilità **III** *v/t* raggiungere in media; ***we ~d 80 km / h*** abbiamo mantenuto una media di 80 km / h
◆ **average out** *v/t sep* fare la media di; ***if you average it out*** se calcoli la media; ***it'll average itself out*** si distribuirà in modo equo
◆ **average out at** *v/t* risultare in media a
averse *adj*: ***not be ~ to*** non avere niente contro; ***I am not ~ to a glass of wine*** non ho niente in contrario ad un bicchiere di vino
aversion *n* avversione *f*; ***have an ~ to*** avere un'avversione per
aversion therapy *n* terapia *f* di conversione (per omosessuali)
avert *v/t one's eyes* distogliere; *crisis* evitare
avian flu *n* influenza *f* aviaria
aviary *n* voliera *f*
aviation *n* aviazione *f*; ***~ industry*** industria *f* aeronautica
aviator *n* aviatore *m*, -trice *f*
aviculture *n* avicoltura *f*
avid *adj* avido
avitaminosis *n* avitaminosi *f*
avocado *n* avocado *m inv*
avoid *v/t* evitare; ***~ doing sth*** evitare di fare qc
avoidable *adj* evitabile
avoidance *n* l'evitare
avoirdupois *n* sistema *m* (di misura) anglosassone
await *v/t* attendere; ***the long ~ed day*** il giorno tanto atteso; ***he is ~ing trial*** è in attesa di giudizio
awake I *adj* sveglio; ***wide ~*** bello sveglio; ***it's keeping me ~*** mi impedisce di dormire; ***be / lie / stay ~*** essere sveglio / restare a letto sveglio / restare sveglio **II** *v/i* ⟨*pret* ***awoke***, *past part* ***awoken***⟩ svegliarsi
awaken *v/t & v/i* → ***awake***
awakening *n* risveglio *m*; ***a rude ~*** un brusco risveglio
award I *n* (*prize*) premio *m* **II** *v/t* assegnare; *damages* riconoscere; ***be ~ed damages*** ricevere il risarcimento dei danni; ***she was ~ed the Nobel Prize for ...*** le hanno assegnato il premio Nobel per…
award(s) ceremony *n* FILM, THEAT, TV cerimonia *f* di premiazione
award-winning *adj* premiato
aware *adj* conscio, consapevole; ***be ~ of sth*** essere conscio *or* consapevole di qc; ***become ~ of sth*** rendersi conto di qc; ***as far as I'm ~*** per quanto ne so
awareness *n* consapevolezza *f*
away *adv* **1.** via; ***be ~*** *travelling, sick etc* essere via; ***be ~ on business*** essere via per lavoro; ***go / run ~*** andare / correre via; ***look ~*** guardare da un'altra parte; ***it's 2 miles ~*** dista 2 miglia; ***Christmas is still six weeks ~*** mancano ancora sei settimane a Natale; ***take sth ~ from s.o.*** togliere qc a qn; ***put sth ~*** mettere via qc; ***right*** *or* ***straight ~*** subito **2.** SPORTS fuori casa
away match *n* SPORTS partita *f* fuori casa
awe *n* soggezione *f*; ***be in ~ of s.o.*** provare timore reverenziale per qn
awe-inspiring *adj* che incute timore reverenziale
awesome *adj infml* (*terrific*) fantastico
awe-stricken, **awe-struck** *adj* intimorito
awful *adj* tremendo, terribile; ***an ~ lot of ...*** un sacco di; ***I feel ~*** *infml* sto da cani *infml*
awfully *adv infml* (*very*) da matti *infml*
awhile *adv liter* un momento
awkward *adj* (*clumsy*) goffo; (*difficult*) difficile; (*embarrassing*) scomodo; ***~ customer*** cliente *m/f* difficile; ***feel ~*** sentirsi a disagio; ***feel ~ in s.o.'s company*** sentirsi a disagio con qn

awl *n for leather* lesina *f*; *for wood* punteruolo *m*
awning *n* tenda *f*
awoke *pret* → ***awake***
awoken *past part* → ***awake***
AWOL *abbr* (= **absent without leave**) MIL assente ingiustificato
awry *adj/adv*: ***go ~*** andare per il verso sbagliato
axe, *US* **ax I** *n* scure *f*, accetta *f*; ***get*** *or* ***be given the ~*** *employee* essere licenziato; *project* essere abbandonato **II** *v/t project, job* sopprimere
axial *adj* assiale
axiom *n* assioma *m*
axiomatic *adj* assiomatico
axis *n* ⟨*pl* ***axes***⟩ asse *m*
axle *n* asse *f*
azalea *n* azalea *f*
Azores *npl* Azzorre *fpl*
Aztec I *n* azteco *m*, -a *f* **II** *adj* azteco
azure *adj* azzurro

B

b *abbr* (= **born**) n. (nato)
B, b *n* b, B *f inv*; MUS si *m inv*; EDU (*mark*) buono *m*; ***B flat*** si *m inv* bemolle; ***B sharp*** si *m inv* diesis
BA *abbr* (= **Bachelor of Arts**) (*degree*) *laurea in lettere*; (*person*) *laureato in lettere*
baas *n SAfr* padrone *m*
babble I *v/i* parlottare **II** *n* parlottio *m*
babe *n infml* discretone *m*, -a *f*
babel *n* babele *f*
baboon *n* babbuino *m*, -a *f*
baby *n* bambino *m*, -a *f*; ***have a ~*** avere un bambino
baby blues *npl* baby blues *m*, *forma lieve di depressione post partum* **baby boom** *n* baby boom *m inv* **baby buggy** *n Br* passeggino *m*; *US* carrozzina *f* **baby carriage** *n US* carrozzina *f* **baby clothes** *npl* abbigliamento *m* per bambini **baby-faced** *adj* che ha il viso da bambino **baby food** *n* cibo *m* per neonati
babyish *adj* infantile
baby seat *n* AUTO seggiolino *m* per bambini
baby-sit *v/i* ⟨*pret & past part* ***-sat***⟩ fare il / la baby-sitter
baby-sitter *n* baby-sitter *m/f inv*
baby talk *n* linguaggio *m* infantile **baby tooth** *n* dente *m* da latte
bacchanal *n* baccanale *m*
bacchanalian *adj* da baccanale
bachelor *n* scapolo *m*
bachelor flat *n* garçonniere *f*, appartamento *m* da scapolo
Bachelor of Arts *n* (*degree*) *laurea in discipline umanistiche*; (*person*) *laureato in discipline umanistiche* **Bachelor of Science** *n* (*degree*) *laurea in discipline scientifiche*; (*person*) *laureato in discipline scientifiche*
bacillus *n* ⟨*pl* ***bacilli***⟩ bacillo *m*
back I *adv* **1.** *place*: ***please move / stand ~*** indietro, per favore; ***~ and forth*** avanti e indietro; ***2 metres ~ from the edge*** a 2 metri dal bordo; ***take sth ~ to the store*** *because unsatisfactory* riportare qc indietro al negozio **2.** ***my family ~ home in England*** la mia famiglia a casa in Inghilterra **3.** (*returning*) ***she'll be ~ tomorrow*** sarà di ritorno domani; ***when are you coming ~?*** quando torni? **4.** *time*: ***~ in 2001*** nel 2001; ***as far ~ as the 18th century*** già nel XVIII secolo **5.** *in return*: ***give sth ~ to s.o.*** restituire qc a qn; ***they wrote / phoned ~*** hanno risposto alla lettera / telefonata; ***he hit me ~*** mi ha restituito il colpo **II** *n* **1.** *of person* schiena *f*; *of animal, hand* dorso *m* **2.** *of car, bus* parte *f* posteriore; *of book, house* retro *m*; *of clothes* rovescio *m*; *of drawer* fondo *m*; *of chair* schienale *m*; ***in the ~*** (***of the car***) (nei sedili) di dietro; ***at the ~ of the bus*** in fondo all'autobus; ***right at the ~ of the cupboard*** proprio in fondo all'armadietto **3.** SPORTS terzino *m* **4.** *fig* ***~ to front*** al contrario; ***at the ~ of beyond*** in capo al mondo **III** *v/t* (*support*) appog-

giare; *car* guidare in retromarcia; *horse* puntare su; ~ ***the car into the garage*** mettere la macchina in garage in retromarcia **IV** *v/i of driver* fare retromarcia **V** *adj* **1.** *door, steps* di dietro; *wheels, legs* posteriore; *garden, room* sul retro; ~ ***road*** strada secondaria **2.** *payment, issue* arretrato

◆**back away** *v/i* indietreggiare

◆**back down** *v/i fig* fare marcia indietro

◆**back off** *v/i* spostarsi indietro; *from danger* tirarsi indietro

◆**back onto** *v/t* dare su

◆**back out** *v/i fig* tirarsi indietro

◆**back up I** *v/t sep* (*support*) confermare; *claim, argument* supportare; *file* fare un backup di; ***back s.o. up*** spalleggiare qn; ***be backed up*** *of traffic* essere congestionato **II** *v/i in car* fare retromarcia

backache *n* mal *m inv* di schiena

backbencher *n* parlamentare *m/f* ordinario, -a

backbiting *n* maldicenze *fpl*

backbone *n* spina *f* dorsale (*a. fig*)

back-breaking *adj* massacrante **back burner** *n*: ***put sth on the*** ~ accantonare qc

backchat *n infml* risposta *f* impertinente

back copy *n* arretrato *m* **back cover** *n* quarta *f* di copertina

backdate *v/t* retrodatare; ***salary increase ~d to May*** aumento *m* di stipendio con effetto retroattivo dal mese di a maggio

back door *n* porta *f* di dietro; *fig* ***through the*** ~ di straforo

backdrop *n* THEAT fondale *m*; *fig* sfondo *m*

backer *n* FIN finanziatore *m*, -trice *f*

backfire *v/i fig* avere effetto contrario; ~ ***on s.o.*** ritorcersi contro qn

backgammon *n* backgammon *m*

back garden *n* giardino *m* sul retro **background I** *n* sfondo *m*; *fig*: *of person* background *m inv*; *of story, event* retroscena *mpl* **II** *adj music* di sottofondo; ~ ***information*** *informazioni per inquadrare meglio una situazione o una persona*

backhand *n in tennis* rovescio *m* **backhander** *n infml* bustarella *f infml*

backing *n moral* appoggio *m*; *financial* finanziamento *m*; MUS accompagnamento *m*; ~ ***vocals*** coristi *mpl*, -e *fpl*

backing group *n* MUS gruppo *m* d'accompagnamento

backlash *n* reazione *f* violenta **backlog** *n*: ~ ***of work*** lavoro *m* arretrato; ~ ***of unanswered letters*** corrispondenza *f* arretrata **backpack I** *n* zaino *m* **II** *v/i viaggiare con zaino e sacco a pelo* **backpacker** *n* saccopelista *m/f* **backpacking** *n il viaggiare con zaino e sacco a pelo* **backpedal** *v/i fig* fare marcia indietro **back road** *n* strada *f* secondaria **back seat** *n of car* sedile *m* posteriore **back-seat driver** *n*: ***you're a terrible ~!*** smettila di dire come si deve guidare! **backside** *n infml* sedere *m* **backslash** *n* backslash *m inv* **backspace** (**key**) *n* (tasto di) ritorno *m* **backstage** *adj/adv* dietro le quinte **backstairs** *npl* scala *f* di servizio **backstreet** *adj* clandestino; ~ ***abortion*** aborto *m* clandestino **back streets** *npl* vicoli *mpl* **backstroke** *n* SPORTS dorso *m* **back to front** *adv* al contrario **back tooth** *n* molare *m* **backtrack** *v/i* tornare indietro **backup** *n* (*support*) rinforzi *mpl*; COMPUT backup *m inv* **backup disk** *n* COMPUT disco *m* di backup

backward *adj child* tardivo; *society* arretrato; *glance* all'indietro

backwardness *n mental* ritardo *m*; *of region* arretratezza *f*

backwards *adv* indietro; ***walk ~ and forwards*** camminare avanti e indietro; ***bend over ~ to do sth*** *infml* farsi in quattro per fare qc; ***I know it ~*** *Br or* ~ ***and forwards*** *US* lo conosco da cima a fondo

backwash *n water* risacca *f*; (*resulting condition*) ripercussione *f*

backwater *n water* acqua *f* stagnante; (*backward place*) luogo *m* sperduto

backyard *n* cortile *m*; *fig* ***not in my ~*** non in casa mia

bacon *n* pancetta *f*; ***bring home the ~*** *infml* portare il pane a casa

bacteria *n* → ***bacterium*** batteri *mpl*

bacterial *adj* batterico

bacterium *n* ⟨*pl* ***bacteria***⟩ batterio *m*

bad[1] *adj* ⟨*comp* ***worse***, *sup* ***worst***⟩ *news, manners* cattivo; *weather, cold,* *headache* brutto; ***I've had a really ~ day*** ho avuto proprio una brutta giornata; *mistake, accident* grave; *egg, food* guasto; ***go ~*** andare a male; ***smoking is ~ for you*** il fumo fa male; ***it's not ~*** non è male; ***that's too ~*** peccato!; ***feel ~ about sth*** sentirsi in colpa per qc; ***be ~ at*** essere negato per; ***he's ~ at French*** va male in francese; ***Friday's ~, how about Thursday?*** venerdì non posso, che ne dici di giovedì?; ***he's got it ~*** *infml* è preso di brutto

bad[2] *pret* → ***bid***

bad blood *n* cattivo sangue *m*; ***there is ~ between them*** tra loro non corre buon sangue **bad debt** *n* debito *m* insoluto

baddie *n infml* cattivo *m*, -a *f*

bade *pret* → ***bid***

badge *n* distintivo *m*

badger I *n* ZOOL tasso *m* **II** *v/t* tormentare

bad language *n* parolacce *fpl*

badly *adv* male; *wounded, mistaken* gravemente; (*very much*) molto; ***I did really ~ in the exam*** sono andato malissimo all'esame; ***think ~ of s.o.*** pensare male di qn; ***want sth ~*** avere molta voglia di qc; ***I need it ~*** ne ho un gran bisogno; ***he ~ needs a haircut/rest*** ha urgente bisogno di tagliarsi i capelli/riposare; ***he is ~ off*** (*poor*) è povero

bad-mannered *adj* maleducato

badminton *n* badminton *m inv*

bad-mouth *v/t* sparlare di

bad-tempered *adj* irascibile

baffle *v/t* sconcertare; ***it really ~s me how …*** mi lascia perplesso il modo in cui…; ***be ~d*** essere perplesso

baffling *adj* sconcertante

bag I *n* borsa *f*; *plastic, paper* busta *f*; *hunting* caccia *f*; ***ugly old ~*** *pej infml* vecchia strega *f*; ***~s under the eyes*** borse *fpl* sotto gli occhi; ***they had ~s of money*** avevano un sacco di soldi **II** *v/t* ⟨*pret & past part* **- ged**⟩ *hunting* catturare; (*put into a bag*) mettere in un sacco; (*reserve*) *infml* accaparrarsi

bagel *n panino a forma di ciambella*

baggage *n* bagagli *mpl*; *ideas* bagaglio *m*; *pej infml* ragazza *f* sfrontata

baggage allowance *n* bagaglio *m* consentito **baggage reclaim** *n* ritiro *m* bagagli **baggage trolley** *n* carrello *m*

baggy *adj* (+*er*) senza forma

bag lady *n* barbona *f* **bagpipes** *npl* cornamusa *fsg* **bag-snatcher** *n* scippatore *m*, -trice *f*

baguette *n* filoncino *m* alla francese

Bahamas *npl*: ***the ~*** le Bahamas

bail[1] *n* JUR cauzione *f*; ***on ~*** su cauzione

bail[2] *n cricket* traversina *f* (che unisce i picchetti)

◆**bail out I** *v/t sep* JUR scarcerare su cauzione; *fig* tirare fuori dai guai **II** *v/i of aeroplane* lanciarsi col paracadute; *of boat* aggottare; *fig* tirare fuori dai guai

bailiff *n ufficiale giudiziario*

bait I *n* esca *f* **II** *v/t hook* fornire di esca; (*torment*) tormentare

bake *v/t* cuocere al forno

baked beans *npl fagioli in salsa rossa*

baked potatoes *npl patate cotte al forno con la buccia*

baker *n* fornaio *m*, -a *f*

baker's *n* panetteria *f*; ***at the ~*** in panetteria

baker's dozen *n* tredici *m*

bakery *n* panetteria *f*

baking dish *n* teglia *f* da forno, casseruola *f* **baking pan** *n US* teglia *f* da forno; tortiera *f* **baking powder** *n* lievito *m* **baking tin** *n Br* teglia *f* da forno **baking tray** *n Br* teglia *f* da forno (in metallo)

baksheesh *n* (*alms*) elemosina *f*; (*tip*) mancia *f*; (*bribe*) bustarella *f*

balaclava *n* passamontagna *m inv*

balance I *n* equilibrio *m*; ***keep one's ~*** tenersi in equilibrio; ***lose one's ~*** perdere l'equilibrio; *fig* ***hang in the ~*** essere in bilico; (*remainder*) resto *m*; *of bank account* saldo *m*; ***~ carried forward*** riporto *m* **II** *v/t* tenere in equilibrio; ***the seal ~s a ball on its nose*** la foca tiene la palla in equilibrio sul naso; ***~ the books*** fare il bilancio **III** *v/i* stare in equilibrio; *of accounts* quadrare

balanced *adj* (*fair*) obiettivo; *diet, personality* equilibrato

balance of payments *n* bilancia *f* dei pagamenti **balance of power** *n* equilibrio *m* di potere **balance of trade** *n*

bilancia *f* commerciale **balance sheet** *n* bilancio *m* (di esercizio)
balancing act *n fig* equilibrismo *m*
balcony *n of house* balcone *m*; *in theatre* prima galleria *f*
bald *adj* (+*er*) *man* calvo; ***he's going ~*** sta perdendo i capelli
bald eagle *n* aquila *f* di mare dalla testa bianca (simbolo degli USA)
balderdash *n* sciocchezze *fpl*
bald-faced *adj US lie* sfacciato
balding *adj* stempiato
baldness *n* calvizie *f*
bale *n* balla *f*
◆**bale out** *Br* **I** *v/i from aircraft* lanciarsi col paracadute; *from unpleasant situation* tirare fuori dai guai **II** *v/t sep water* aggottare
Balearics *npl*: ***the ~*** le Baleari
baleful *adj* funesto
balk I *v/i* essere restio; *US baseball* interrompere un movimento di lancio **II** *v/t liter* ostacolare
Balkan *adj* balcanico
Balkans *npl*: ***the ~*** i Balcani *mpl*
ball[1] *n* palla *f*; *football* pallone *m*; *fig* ***be on the ~*** essere sveglio; *fig* ***play ~*** collaborare; *fig* ***the ~'s in his court*** la prossima mossa è sua; *fig* ***start the ~ rolling*** essere il primo a cominciare; ***~ of the foot*** ANAT avampiede *m*; ***~s*** *infml* (*courage*) palle *fpl*
ball[2] *n* (*dance*) ballo *m*; ***have a ~*** *infml* darsi alla pazza gioia
ballad *n* ballata *f*
ball-and-socket joint *n* TECH giunto *m* sferico
ballast *n* zavorra *f*
ball bearing *n* cuscinetto *m* a sfere
ball boy *n* raccattapalle *m inv*
ballerina *n* ballerina *f*
ballet *n art* danza *f* classica; *dance* balletto *m*
ballet dancer *n* ballerino *m* classico, ballerina *f* classica
ball game *n infml*: ***that's a different ~*** è un altro paio di maniche
ballistic *adj* balistico; ***go ~*** *infml* andare su tutte le furie
ballistic missile *n* missile *m* balistico
balloon I *n child's* palloncino *m*; *for flight* mongolfiera *f*; ***that went down like a lead ~*** *infml* è stato un fiasco **II** *v/i* (*swell out*) gonfiarsi
balloonist *n* aeronauta *m/f*
ballot I *n* votazione *f* **II** *v/t members* consultare tramite votazione
ballot box *n* urna *f* elettorale
ballot paper *n* scheda *f* elettorale
ballot rigging *n* brogli *mpl* elettorali
ball park *n infml*: ***be in the right ~*** essere nell'ordine corretto di cifre
ball-park figure *n infml* cifra *f* approssimativa
ballpoint (pen) *n* penna *f* a sfera
ballroom *n* sala *f* da ballo
ballroom dancing *n* ballo *m* da sala
balls *npl vulg* (*a. courage*) palle *fpl vulg*
balls-up *n*, *US* **ball up** *n infml* casino *m infml*; ***he made a complete ~ of the job*** ha fatto un casino totale con il lavoro
balm *n* balsamo *m*
balmy *adj* (+*er*) mite
baloney *n infml* balle *fpl*; *US* → ***bologna***
Baltic *n*: ***the ~*** il (Mar) Baltico
Baltics *npl* paesi *mpl* baltici
balustrade *n* balaustra *f*
bamboo *n* bambù *m inv*
bamboozle *v/t* (*trick*) ingannare; (*confuse*) confondere
ban I *n* divieto *m* (**on** di); ***a ~ on smoking*** divieto *m* di fumare **II** *v/t* ⟨*pret & past part* ***-ned***⟩ proibire; ***~ s.o. from doing sth*** proibire a qn di fare qc; ***she was ~ned from driving*** le è stato proibito di guidare
banal *adj* banale
banana *n* banana *f*
bananas *adj infml* (*crazy*) pazzo; ***go ~*** dare i numeri
banana skin *n* buccia *f* di banana; *fig* ***slip on a ~*** scivolare su una buccia di banana **banana split** *n* COOK banana split *f*
band *n* (*brass band*) banda *f*; *pop* gruppo *m*; *of material* nastro *m*; *of cloth*, *iron* fascia *f*; *on machine* cinghia *f*
◆**band together** *v/i* riunirsi
bandage I *n* benda *f* **II** *v/t* bendare
Band-Aid® *n* cerotto *m*
B&B *abbr* (= **bed and breakfast**) pensione *f* familiare, bed and breakfast *m inv*
bandit *n* brigante *m*
band leader *n* direttore *m* d'orchestra
bandmaster *n* MUS capobanda *m/f*

bandstand *n in a park* palco *m* dell'orchestra
bandwagon *n*: ***jump on the ~*** seguire la corrente
bandwidth *n* RADIO, COMPUT larghezza *f* di banda
bandy *adj legs* storto
◆**bandy about** *Br or* **around** *v/t sep s.o.'s name* mettere in giro; *ideas* far circolare
bane *n* disgrazia *f*; ***it's the ~ of my life*** è la rovina della mia vita
bang[1] **I** *n* colpo *m*; *vulg* botta *f sl*; ***there was a ~ outside*** ho sentito un forte rumore venire da fuori **II** *v/t door* chiudere violentemente; (*hit*) sbattere; ***I ~ed my knee on the table*** ho battuto il ginocchio contro il tavolo **III** *v/i* sbattere; ***the door ~ed shut*** la porta si è chiusa con un colpo **IV** *adv*: ***she arrived ~ on time*** è arrivata in perfetto orario
◆**bang on about** *v/i +obj Br infml* parlare continuamente
◆**bang out** *v/t sep*: ***bang out a tune on the piano*** strimpellare un motivo al pianoforte
◆**bang up** *v/t sep sl prisoner* sbattere dentro
bang[2] *n*: ***~s*** *pl US* frangia *f*
banger *n infml* (*sausage*) salamino *m*; ***an old ~*** (*car*) una vecchia carretta
bangle *n* braccialetto *m*
banish *v/t* esiliare
banishment *n* bando *m*
banister *n* ringhiera *f*
banjo *n* banjo *m inv*
bank[1] *n of river* riva *f*; *mound* terrapieno *m*
bank[2] **I** *n* FIN banca *f* **II** *v/i*: ***~ with*** avere un conto presso **III** *v/t money* mettere in banca
◆**bank on** *v/t* contare su; ***don't bank on it*** non ci contare; ***bank on s.o. doing sth*** dare per scontato che qn faccia qc
bank account *n* conto *m* bancario **bank balance** *n* saldo *m* **bank card** *n* carta *f* assegni **bank draft** *n* assegno *m* bancario **bank holiday** *n* giorno *m* festivo
banker *n* banchiere *m*
banker's card *n* carta *f* assegni **banker's order** *n* ordine *m* di pagamento
banking *n* professione *f* bancaria
bank loan *n* prestito *m* bancario **bank manager** *n* direttore *m* di banca **bank note** *n* banconota *f* **bank rate** *n* tasso *m* ufficiale di sconto **bank robbery** *n* rapina *f* in banca **bankroll** *v/t* finanziare
bankrupt I *adj* fallito; ***go ~*** fallire **II** *v/t* portare al fallimento
bankruptcy *n* bancarotta *f*
bank sort code *n* codice *m* bancario **bank statement** *n* estratto *m* conto **bank transfer** *n* bonifico *m* bancario
banner *n* striscione *m*
banner headlines *n* titolo *m* a tutta pagina
bannister *n* → ***banister***
banns *npl* pubblicazioni *mpl* (matrimoniali)
banquet *n* banchetto *m*
banter *n* scambio *m* di battute
bap (bun) *n Br* panino *m*
baptism *n* battesimo *m*
Baptist *n* battista *m/f*; ***the ~ Church*** la Chiesa Battista
baptize *v/t* battezzare
bar[1] *n of iron* spranga *f*; *of chocolate* tavoletta *f*; *for drinks* bar *m inv*; (*counter*) bancone *m*; MUS battuta *f*; ***a ~ of soap*** una saponetta; ***be behind ~s*** (*in prison*) essere dietro le sbarre; ***~ of gold*** lingotto *m* d'oro; ***the window has ~s*** la finestra è sprangata
bar[2] *v/t* ⟨*pret & past part* ***-red***⟩ vietare l'ingresso a; ***he's been ~red from the club*** gli hanno vietato l'ingresso al club
bar[3] *prep* (*except*) tranne
Bar *n*: JUR ***the ~*** l'avvocatura; ***be called*** *or US* ***admitted to the ~*** essere ammesso all'ordine degli avvocati
barb *n of hook* ardiglione *m*
Barbados *n* Barbados *fpl*
barbarian *n* barbaro *m*, -a *f*
barbaric *adj* barbaro
barbecue I *n* barbecue *m inv* **II** *v/t* cuocere al barbecue
barbed wire *n* filo *m* spinato
barber *n* barbiere *m*
barbershop I *n US* negozio *m* di barbiere **II** *adj*: ***~ quartet*** *quartetto maschile che canta solitamente a cappella*
barbiturate *n* barbiturico *m*
bar code *n* codice *m* a barre
bare I *adj* (*+er*) (*naked*) nudo; (*empty*:

room) spoglio; *mountainside* brullo; *facts* essenziale; ***in one's ~ feet*** a piedi nudi; ***the ~ necessities*** lo stretto necessario; ***the ~ minimum*** il minimo indispensabile **II** *v/t breast, leg* scoprirsi; *at doctor's* spogliarsi; *teeth* mostrare; ***~ one's soul*** aprire il proprio cuore
bareback *adj/adv ride* senza sella
barefaced *adj fig* sfacciato
barefoot *adj*: ***be ~*** essere scalzo
bare-headed *adj* senza cappello
barely *adv* appena
barf *US infml* **I** *n* vomito *m* **II** *v/i* vomitare
bargain I *n* (*deal*) patto *m*; ***keep one's side of the ~*** rispettare i patti; (*good buy*) affare *m*; ***it's a ~!*** (*deal*) è un affarone!; ***strike a ~*** concludere un affare; ***into the ~*** per giunta **II** *v/i* tirare sul prezzo
◆**bargain for** *v/t* (*expect*) aspettarsi; ***he got more than he bargained for*** non se l'aspettava
bargain basement *n* reparto *m* occasioni **bargain hunter** *n chi cerca accanitamente occasioni di acquisto vantaggiose*
bargaining *n* il mercanteggiare *m*; (*negotiating*) contrattazione *f*; ***~ power*** potere *m* contrattuale
bargain price *n* prezzo *m* conveniente
barge I *n* NAUT chiatta *f* **II** *v/t*: ***he ~d his way through the crowd*** si è fatto largo tra la folla a spintoni
◆**barge into** *v/t* piombare su; ***barge into a room*** irrompere in una stanza
bargepole *n*: ***I wouldn't touch him with a ~*** *Br infml* non voglio avere niente a che fare con lui
baritone *n* baritono *m*
bark[1] **I** *v/i* abbaiare; ***~ at*** abbaiare a **II** *n of dog* abbaiare *m*; *fig* ***be ~ing up the wrong tree*** *infml* essere fuori strada; ***his ~ is worse than his bite*** *prov* can che abbaia non morde
bark[2] *n of tree* corteccia *f*
barking (mad) *adj infml* fuori di testa
barley *n* orzo *m*
barley sugar *n* zucchero *m* d'orzo; (*sweet*) caramella *f* d'orzo **barley water** *n* (*soft drink*) *bibita preparata con farina d'orzo, simile all'orzata*; (*infusion*) (infuso *m* di) orzo *m*; ***lemon ~*** *orzata al limone*
barmaid *n* barista *f*
barman *n* barista *m*
barmy *adj* (+*er*) *infml* pazzoide *infml*
barn *n* granaio *m*
barn dance *n festa in cui si ballano danze tradizionali* **barn owl** *n* ZOOL barbagianni *m*
barnyard *n* aia *f*
barometer *n* barometro *m* (*a. fig*)
baron *n* (*noble*) barone *m*; ***press/steel ~*** magnate *m* della carta stampata/dell'acciaio
baroness *n* baronessa *f*
baroque *adj* barocco
barracks *npl* MIL caserma *fsg*
barrage *n* MIL sbarramento *m*; *fig* raffica *f*
barrel *n* (*container*) barile *m*; *of handgun* canna *f*; ***they've got us over a ~*** *infml* ci hanno messo con le spalle al muro; ***he's a ~ of laughs*** *infml* fa morire dalle risate
barrel organ *n* organo *m* a rullo
barren *adj land* arido
barricade *n* barricata *f*
barrier *n* barriera *f*; ***language ~*** l'ostacolo della lingua; ***trade ~s*** barriere *fpl* commerciali
barring *prep*: ***~ accidents*** salvo imprevisti
barrister *n* avvocato *m*
barrow *n* carriola *f*
bar stool *n* sgabello *m* da bar **bar tender** *n* barista *m/f*
barter I *n* baratto *m* **II** *v/i* barattare
base I *n* base *f*; ***return to ~*** rientrare alla base; ***at** or **on second ~*** SPORTS in seconda base; ***touch ~*** *US infml* prendere contatto (***with*** con) **II** *v/t* basare; ***~ sth on sth*** basare qc su qc; ***be ~d in*** *in city, country* essere di base a; ***be ~d on*** essere basato su
baseball *n* baseball *m inv*
baseball bat *n* mazza *f* da baseball
baseball cap *n* berretto *m* da baseball
Basel *n* Basilea *f*
baseless *adj* infondato
basement *n* seminterrato *m*; ***~ flat*** *Br* or ***apartment*** *US* (appartamento *m* al) seminterrato *m*
base rate *n* FIN tasso *m* base
bash I *n infml* colpo *m*; (*party*) festa *f*; ***I'll have a ~ (at it)*** *infml* ci provo **II** *v/t infml* sbattere; ***~ s.o. on** or **over the head with sth*** colpire qn alla testa

con qc
◆**bash up** *v/t sep esp Br infml person* pestare; *car* distruggere
bashful *adj* timido
basic I *adj knowledge, equipment* rudimentale; *salary* di base; *beliefs* fondamentale; **~ salary** salario *m* base; **~ vocabulary** vocabolario *m* di base II *npl*: **the ~s** i rudimenti *mpl*; **get down to (the) ~s** venire al sodo
BASIC *abbr* (= **beginner's all-purpose symbolic instruction code**) COMPUT basic *m inv*
basically *adv* essenzialmente
basic English *n* basic english *m* **basic rate** *n of tax* aliquota *f* base; **the ~ of income tax** l'aliquota dell'imposta sul reddito
basil *n* basilico *m*
basilica *n* basilica *f*
basin *n for washing* lavandino *m*
basis *n* ⟨*pl* **bases**⟩ base *f*; **on the ~ of** in base a; **on a regular ~** regolarmente
bask *v/i* crogiolarsi
basket *n* cestino *m*; *in basketball* cesto *m*
basketball *n* basket *m inv*, pallacanestro *f*
basket case *n* (*country*) paese *m* allo sfascio; *sl person* caso *m* disperato
Basle *n* → **Basel**
Basque I *n* (*person*) basco *m*, -a *f*; (*language*) basco II *adj* basco
bas-relief *n* bassorilievo *m*
bass I *n* (*part*) voce *f* di basso; (*singer*) basso *m*; (*double bass*) contrabbasso *m*; (*guitar*) basso *m* II *adj* di basso
bass clef *n* chiave *f* di basso **bass drum** *n* grancassa *f*
bassinet *n* culla *f* di vimini
bassoon *n* MUS fagotto *m*
bastard *n infml* bastardo *m*, -a *f*; **this question is a real ~** *infml* questa domanda è davvero bastarda
baste *v/t* COOK cospargere di burro *or* grasso; *sew* imbastire
bastion *n* bastione *m* (*a. fig*)
bat[1] I *n* mazza *f*; *for table tennis* racchetta *f* II *v/i* ⟨*pret & past part* **-ted**⟩ SPORTS battere
bat[2] *v/t* ⟨*pret & past part* **-ted**⟩: **he didn't ~ an eyelid** non ha battuto ciglio
bat[3] *n* (*animal*) pipistrello *m*; **he drove like a ~ out of hell** guidava come una scheggia; (**as**) **blind as a ~** cieco come una talpa
batch *n of students* gruppo *m*; *of goods* lotto *m*; *of bread* infornata *f*
batch file *n* COMPUT file *m* batch
bate *n* ammorbidente *m*
bated *adj*: **with ~ breath** col fiato sospeso
bath *n* bagno *m*; **have a ~, take a ~** farsi il bagno; **give s.o. a ~** fare il bagno a qn
bathe *v/i* (*swim, have bath*) fare il bagno; **~ one's eyes** lavare gli occhi; **~d in tears** inondato di lacrime; **be ~d in sweat** essere in un bagno di sudore
bathing cap *n* cuffia *f* da bagno
bathing costume, bathing suit *n* costume *m* da bagno
bath mat *n* tappetino *m* da bagno **bathrobe** *n* accappatoio *m* **bathroom** *n* (stanza *f* da) bagno *m*
baths *npl Br* bagni *mpl* pubblici
bath towel *n* asciugamano *m* da bagno
bathtub *n* vasca *f* da bagno
baton *n of conductor* bacchetta *f*
batsman *n* ⟨*pl* **-men**⟩ SPORTS battitore *m*
battalion *n* MIL battaglione *m*
batten *n roof* trave *f*; *floor* asse *f*; *door* traversa *f*
◆**batten down** *v/t sep*: **batten down the hatches** NAUT chiudere i boccaporti; *fig* prepararsi ad un'emergenza
batter I *v/t baby, wife* picchiare II *n* COOK pastella *f*; SPORTS battitore *m*, -trice *f*
battered *adj* maltrattato; *old hat, suitcase etc* malridotto
battering *n*: **he/it got** *or* **took a real ~** è stato ridotto veramente male
battery *n* pila *f*; AUTO batteria *f*
battery charger *n* caricabatterie *m inv* **battery farming** *n* AGR allevamento *m* in batteria **battery hen** *n* AGR pollo *m* d'allevamento
battery-operated *adj* a pile
battle I *n* battaglia *f* (*a. fig*); **~ of wits** gara *f* di cervelli; **getting an interview is only half the ~** ottenere un colloquio è solo il primo passo II *v/i against illness etc* lottare
battleaxe, *US* **battleax** *n* (*woman*) donna *f* autoritaria
battlefield, battleground *n* campo *m* di battaglia

battlements *npl* parapetto *m*
battleship *n* corazzata *f*
batty *adj* (+*er*) *Br infml* pazzo
bauble *n* (*jewellery*) gioiello *m* di poco conto; (*Christmas decoration*) palla *f* (per l'albero di Natale); ***~s*** bagatelle *fpl*
baulk *v/i* → **balk**
Bavaria *n* Baviera *f*
Bavarian **I** *n* (*person*) bavarese *m/f*; (*dialect*) bavarese *m* **II** *adj* bavarese
bawdy *adj* (+*er*) spinto
bawl *v/i* (*shout*) urlare; (*weep*) strillare
◆**bawl out** *v/t sep infml* fare una lavata di capo a
bay[1] *n* (*inlet*) baia *f*
bay[2] *n* (*loading bay*) zona *f* di carico; (*parking bay*) area *f* di parcheggio
bay[3] *n*: ***keep*** *or* ***hold s.o. / sth at ~*** tenere qn / qc a distanza
bay[4] **I** *adj horse* baio **II** *n* (*horse*) baio *m*
bay leaf *n* (foglia *f* d') alloro *m*
bayonet *n* baionetta *f*
bayonet fitting *adj* ELEC con attacco a baionetta
bay window *n* bovindo *m*
bazaar *n* bazar *m*
BBC *abbr* (= **British Broadcasting Corporation**) BBC *f inv*
BBQ *abbr* (= **barbecue**) barbecue *m*
BC *abbr* (= **before Christ**) a. C. (avanti Cristo)
be **I** *v/i* ⟨*pret* ***was / were***, *past part* ***been***⟩ **1.** essere; ***it's me*** sono io; ***was she there?*** era lì?; ***how much is / are ...?*** quant'è / quanto sono ...?; ***there is, there are*** c'è, ci sono; ***~ careful*** sta' attento; ***don't ~ sad*** non essere triste; ***how are you?*** come stai?; ***he's very well*** sta bene; ***I'm hot / cold*** ho freddo / caldo; ***it's hot / cold*** fa freddo / caldo; ***he's seven*** ha sette anni **2.** ***has the postman been?*** è passato il postino?; ***I've never been to Japan*** non sono mai stato in Giappone; ***I've been here for hours*** sono qui da tanto **3.** *tags*: ***that's right, isn't it?*** giusto, no?; ***she's American, isn't she?*** è americana, vero? **II** *v/aux* **1.** *progressive*: ***I am thinking*** sto pensando; ***he was running*** stava correndo; ***you're ~ing silly*** stai facendo lo sciocco; ***he's working in London*** lavora a Londra; ***I'll be waiting for an answer*** aspetterò una risposta **2.** *obligation*: ***you are to do what I tell you*** devi fare quello che ti dico; ***I was to tell you this*** dovevo dirtelo; ***you were not to tell anyone*** non dovevi dirlo a nessuno **3.** *passive* essere, venire (*not with past tenses*); ***he was killed*** è stato ucciso; ***they have been sold*** sono stati venduti; ***it will ~ sold for £ 100*** sarà *or* verrà venduto a 100 sterline
◆**be in for** *v/t* doversi aspettare; ***you're in for a disappointment*** resterai deluso
beach *n* spiaggia *f*; ***on the ~*** sulla spiaggia
beach ball *n* pallone *m* da spiaggia
beach buggy *n* AUTO dune buggy *m*
beach towel *n* telo *m* da spiaggia
beachwear *n* abbigliamento *m* da spiaggia
beacon *n* faro *m*; (*radio beacon*) radiofaro *m*
beading *n* decorazione *f* a perline; ARCH modanatura *f*
beads *npl* perline *fpl*
beady *adj*: ***I've got my ~ eye on you*** *infml* ti tengo d'occhio
beagle *n* ZOOL bracchetto *m*
beak *n* becco *m*
beaker *n* bicchiere *m*
be-all *n*: ***the ~ and end-all*** la cosa più importante
beam **I** *n in ceiling etc* trave *f*; *of light* raggio *m* **II** *v/i* (*smile*) fare un sorriso radioso **III** *v/t* (*transmit*) trasmettere
bean *n* (*vegetable*) fagiolo *m*; *of coffee* chicco *m*; ***he hasn't (got) a ~*** *Br infml* non ha il becco di un quattrino; ***be full of ~s*** *infml* essere particolarmente vivace
beanbag *n seat* poltrona *f* sacco
beanpole *n* spilungone *m*, -a *f*
beansprout *n* germoglio *m* di soia
bear[1] *n animal* orso *m*; FIN ribassista *m/f*; ***he is like a ~ with a sore head*** è di pessimo umore; ***the Great / Little Bear*** ASTR l'Orsa Maggiore / Minore
bear[2] ⟨*pret* ***bore***, *past part* ***borne***⟩ **I** *v/t weight* portare; *costs* sostenere; (*tolerate*) sopportare; *child* dare alla luce; ***~ fruit*** dare frutti; ***~ a resemblance to s.o.*** assomigliare a qn; ***~ in mind*** tenere presente; ***can't ~ sth*** non sopportare qc; ***he was borne***

along by the crowd venne trascinato dalla folla; ***it doesn't ~ thinking about*** meglio non pensarci **II** *v/i*: ***bring pressure to ~ on*** fare pressione su; ***~ left / north*** andare verso sinistra / nord

◆**bear away** *v/t sep* portare via; *victory etc* strappare

◆**bear down** *v/i* (*push on*) premere su; *threatening* piombare su

◆**bear out** *v/t sep* (*confirm*) confermare; ***bear s.o. out*** appoggiare qn

◆**bear up** *v/i* tener duro; ***she bore up well under the circumstances*** ha retto bene vista la situazione; ***how are you? — bearing up!*** come sta? – si tira avanti!

◆**bear with** *v/t* avere pazienza con; ***if you would bear with me for a moment*** se ha un attimo di pazienza

bearable *adj* sopportabile

beard *n* barba *f*

bearded *adj* con la barba

bearer *n* (*carrier*) portatore *m*, -trice *f*; *of news* latore *m*, -trice *m*, *cheque* portatore *m*, -trice *f*; *of name*, *passport* titolare *m/f*

bear hug *n* abbraccio *m* forte

bearing *n in machine* cuscinetto *m*; ***that has no ~ on the case*** ciò non ha alcuna attinenza col caso; ***get** or **find one's ~s*** orientarsi; ***lose one's ~s*** perdere l'orientamento

bear market *n* FIN mercato *m* cedente

beast *n* bestia *f*

beastly *adj infml* orribile

beat I *v/i* ⟨*pret* **beat**, *past part* **beaten**⟩ *of heart* battere; *of rain* picchiettare; ***~ about the bush*** menar il can per l'aia **II** *v/t* ⟨*pret* **beat**, *past part* **beaten**⟩ *in competition* battere; (*hit*) picchiare; MUS *drum* suonare; ***I'll ~ you down to the beach*** facciamo a chi arriva prima alla spiaggia; ***if you can't ~ them, join them*** *infml* se non puoi batterli, diventa loro alleato; ***~ the deadline*** finire prima della scadenza; ***~ on the door*** (***with one's fists***) picchiare sulla porta (con il pugno); ***~ time*** MUS battere il tempo; ***~ it!*** *infml* fila!; ***it ~s me*** non capisco **III** *n of heart* battito *m*; *of music* ritmo *m*; *of policeman* zona *f* di sorveglianza; ***be on the ~*** fare la ronda

◆**beat down I** *v/i rain* battere; *sun* picchiare **II** *v/t sep*: ***I managed to beat him down*** (***on the price***) l'ho convinto a scendere (sul prezzo)

◆**beat up** *v/t sep* picchiare

beaten I *adj*: ***off the ~ track*** fuori mano **II** *past part* → ***beat***

beater *n kitchen implement* sbattitore *m*; *hunting* battitore *m*, -trice *f*

beat generation *n* beat generation *f*

beating *n* (*physical*) botte *fpl*; *of heart*, *wings* battito *m*; (*defeat*) batosta *f*; ***give s.o. a ~*** picchiare qn; ***get a ~*** prenderle; ***take a ~*** (***at the hands of s.o.***) essere sconfitto (per mano di qn); ***take some ~*** essere difficile da superare

beatnik *n* beatnik *m/f inv*

beat-up *adj infml* malconcio

beaut *n US infml* bellezza *f infml*

beautician *n* estetista *m/f*

beautiful *adj* bello; ***thanks, that's just ~!*** grazie, così va bene

beautifully *adv* stupendamente

beauty *n of woman*, *sunset* bellezza *f*; ***the ~ of it is that …*** il bello è che…

beauty contest *n* concorso *m* di bellezza **beauty queen** *n* reginetta *f* (di bellezza) **beauty salon** *n* istituto *m* di bellezza **beauty sleep** *n hum sonno necessario a non perdere la bellezza* **beauty spot** *n* neo *m*; (*place*) luogo *m* incantevole

beaver *n* castoro *m*

◆**beaver away** *v/i infml* sgobbare *infml*

became *pret* → ***become***

because *cj* perché; ***~ of*** a causa di; ***I only did it ~ of you*** l'ho fatto solo per te

beck *n*: ***be at s.o.'s ~ and call*** essere sempre agli ordini di qn

beckon *v/i* fare cenno

become I *v/i* ⟨*pret* **became**, *past part* **become**⟩ diventare; ***he wants to ~ a doctor*** vuole fare il dottore; ***it became clear that*** divenne chiaro che; ***what's ~ of her?*** che ne è stato di lei? **II** *v/t be appropriate* addirsi a; *look good* stare bene a; ***it would not ~ him to interfere*** non è il caso che lui interferisca; ***that colour ~s your complexion*** quel colore ti dona

becoming *adj* grazioso

bed I *n* letto *m*; ***~ of flowers*** aiuola *f*; ***go to ~*** andare a letto; ***he's still in ~*** è ancora a letto; ***make the ~*** rifare il letto; ***go to ~ with*** andare a letto con **II** *v/t* piantare

◆**bed down** *v/i* mettersi a dormire; ***can I bed down here tonight?*** posso dormire da te stanotte?

◆**bed out** *v/t* trapiantare

B Ed *abbr* (= **Bachelor of Education**) (*degree*) *laurea in scienze dell'educazione*; (*person*) *laureato in scienze dell'educazione*

bed and board *n* pensione *f* completa **bed and breakfast** *n* pensione *f* familiare, bed and breakfast *m inv* **bedclothes** *npl* coperte e lenzuola *fpl* **bedcover** *n* (*bedspread*) copriletto *m*

bedding *n materasso e lenzuola*

bedding plant *n* pianta *f* da travasare

bedeck *v/t* decorare

bedevil *v/t* affliggere

bedhead *n* testata *f* del letto

bedlam *n infml* manicomio *m*

bed linen *n* biancheria *f* da letto

bedpan *n* padella *f*

bedraggled *adj* (*wet*) inzuppato; (*dirty*) inzaccherato; (*untidy*) in disordine

bedridden *adj* costretto a letto

bedroom *n* camera *f* da letto

bedside *n*: ***be at the ~ of*** essere al capezzale di

bedside lamp *n* lampada *f* da comodino **bedside manner** *n modo di parlare dei medici* **bedside table** *n* comodino *m*

bed-sit, bed-sitter *n* monolocale *m*

bedsore *n* piaga *f* da decubito; ***get ~s*** avere le piaghe da decubito

bedspread *n* copriletto *m*

bedtime *n* ora *f* di andare a letto; ***his ~ is 10 o'clock*** va a dormire alle 10

bedtime story *n* favola *f* della buonanotte

bed-wetting *n* MED enuresi *f*

bee *n* ape *f*; ***have a ~ in one's bonnet*** *infml* avere un'idea fissa

Beeb *n abbr* (= **British Broadcasting Corporation**) *Br infml* BBC *f*

beebread *n mistura di miele e polline*

beech *n* faggio *m*

beef I *n* manzo *m*; *infml* (*complaint*) problema *m* **II** *v/i infml* (*complain*) lagnarsi

◆**beef up** *v/t sep* rinforzare

beefburger *n* hamburger *m inv*

beefcake *n infml* uomini *mpl* muscolosi

beehive *n* alveare *m*

beeline *n*: ***make a ~ for*** andare diritto a

been *past part* → ***be***

beep I *n* bip *m inv*; ***leave your name and number after the ~*** lasciate il vostro nome e numero di telefono dopo il segnale acustico **II** *v/i* suonare **III** *v/t* (*call on pager*) chiamare sul cercapersone

beeper *n* (*pager*) cercapersone *m inv*

beer *n* birra *f*

beer belly *n infml* pancetta *f* (gonfia per la birra) **beer garden** *n Br* birreria *f* all'aperto **beer glass** *n* boccale *m* di birra

beermat *n* sottobicchiere *m*

bee sting *n* puntura *f* d'ape

beeswax *n* cera *f* d'api

beet *n* barbabietola *f*

beetle *n* coleottero *m*; (*VW car*) maggiolino *m*

beetroot *n* barbabietola *f*; ***as red as a ~*** rosso come un peperone

befit *v/t form* addirsi a; *occasion* convenire a

before I *prep* prima di; ***~ eight o'clock*** prima delle otto; ***~ long*** dopo poco tempo; ***the task ~ us*** il compito che abbiamo di fronte; ***~ tax*** al lordo **II** *adv* prima; ***have you been to England ~?*** sei già stato in Inghilterra?; ***I've seen this film ~*** questo film l'ho già visto; ***the week ~*** la settimana prima; ***life went on as ~*** la vita è continuata come prima **III** *cj* prima che; ***I saw him ~ he left*** l'ho visto prima che partisse; ***I saw him ~ I left*** l'ho visto prima di partire

beforehand *adv* prima; ***you must tell me ~*** devi dirmelo per tempo

befriend *v/t* fare amicizia con

beg ⟨*pret & past part* ***-ged***⟩ **I** *v/i* mendicare **II** *v/t* (*dog*) aspettare il cibo; ***~ s.o. to …*** pregare qn di …; ***I ~ to differ*** mi permetto di dissentire; ***~ the question*** dare per scontato

began *pret* → ***begin***

beget *v/t* ⟨*pret* ***-got***, *past part* ***-gotten***⟩ generare

beggar I *n* mendicante *m/f*; *Br infml* tizio *m*, -a *f*; ***poor ~!*** poveraccio!; ***a lucky ~*** un tipo fortunato **II** *v/t fig*:

~ ***belief*** essere da non credere
begin *v/t & v/i* 〈*pret* ***began***, *past part* ***begun***〉 cominciare; ~ ***on sth*** cominciare con qc; ~ ***doing*** *or* ***do sth*** cominciare a fare qc; ~***ning from Monday*** a cominciare da lunedì; ***to ~ with*** per cominciare
beginner *n* principiante *m/f*
beginning *n* inizio *m*; (*origin*) origine *f*; ***it was the ~ of the end for him*** per lui è stato l'inizio della fine; ***his humble ~s*** le sue umili origini
begonia *n* begonia *f*
begrudge *v/t* (*envy*) invidiare; (*give reluctantly*) dare malvolentieri; ~ ***s.o. sth*** invidiare qc a qn
begrudgingly *adv* malvolentieri
beguile *v/t* (*persuade*) ingannare; (*charm*) incantare
begun *past part* → ***begin***
behalf *n*: ***on ~ of*** a nome di; ***on my/his ~*** a nome mio/suo
behave *v/i* comportarsi; ~ (***o.s.***) comportarsi bene; ~ (***yourself***)***!*** comportati bene!
behaviour *n* comportamento *m*
behead *v/t* decapitare
behind **I** *prep in position* dietro; *in progress* indietro rispetto a; *fig* ***be ~ the times*** essere indietro rispetto ai tempi; *in order* dietro a; ***be ~*** (*responsible for*) essere dietro a; (*support*) appoggiare **II** *adv* (*at the back*) dietro; ***she had to stay ~*** è dovuta rimanere; ***be ~*** *in match* essere in svantaggio; ***be ~ with sth*** essere indietro con qc; ***he got ~ with his payments*** è indietro con i pagamenti **III** *n infml* didietro *m*
behold *v/t* 〈*pret & past part* ***beheld***〉 *liter* contemplare
beholden *adj* grato
behove *v/t*: ***it ~s s.o. to do sth*** è il caso che qn faccia qc
beige *adj* beige *inv*
being *n* (*existence*) esistenza *f*; (*creature*) essere *m*
bejewelled *adj* ingioiellato
belated *adj* in ritardo
belch **I** *v/i* ruttare **II** *n* rutto *m*
beleaguer *v/t* (*besiege*) assediare; (*tease*) assillare
belfry *n* campanile *m*
Belgian **I** *adj* belga **II** *n* belga *m/f*
Belgium *n* Belgio *m*
Belgrade *n* Belgrado *f*
belie *v/t* (*prove false*) smentire; (*give false impression of*) mascherare
belief *n* convinzione *f*; *in God* fede *f*; ***your ~ in me*** il fatto che tu creda in me; ***beyond ~*** incredibile; ***in the ~ that …*** nella convinzione che…; ***it is my ~ that …*** sono convinto che…
believe *v/t* credere; ~ ***it or not!*** strano ma vero; ***he is ~d to be ill*** lo credono malato; ~ ***you me!*** *infml* credimi!
◆**believe in** *v/t God*, *person* credere in; *ghost*, *person* credere a; ***I don't believe in compromises*** non credo ai compromessi
believer *n* REL credente *m/f*; ***I'm a great ~ in …*** credo fermamente in …
belittle *v/t* sminuire
bell *n in church*, *school* campana *f*; *on door* campanello *m*; ***as clear as a ~*** *voice* forte e chiaro
bellboy *n esp US* fattorino *m* d'albergo
bellhop *n US* → ***bellboy***
belligerence *n of nation* belligeranza *f*; *of person* aggressività *f inv*
belligerent *adj* bellicoso
bellow **I** *v/i* urlare; *of bull* muggire **II** *n* urlo *m*; *of bull* muggito *m*
bellows *npl* soffietto *m*; ***a pair of ~*** un mantice
belly *n* pancia *f*
bellyache *v/i infml* brontolare *infml*
belly button *n infml* ombelico *m* **belly dance** *n* danza *f* del ventre
bellyful *n*: ***I've had a ~ of writing these letters*** *infml* non ne posso più di scrivere lettere
belly laugh *n* grassa risata *f*; ***he gave a great ~*** è scoppiato in una grassa risata **belly up** *adv*: ***go ~*** *company* fallire
belong *v/i*: ***where does this ~?*** dove va questo?; ***I don't ~ here*** mi sento un estraneo; ***at last he found a place where he ~ed*** finalmente ha trovato un posto adatto a lui
◆**belong to** *v/t* appartenere a; ***belong to a club*** far parte di un club
belongings *npl* cose *fpl*; ***personal ~*** effetti *mpl* personali; ***all his ~*** armi e bagagli
Belorussia *n* Bielorussia *f*
beloved *adj* adorato
below **I** *prep* sotto **II** *adv* di sotto; *in*

text sotto; ***see ~*** vedi sotto; ***10 degrees ~*** 10 gradi sotto zero

belt I *n* cintura *f*; TECH cinghia *f*; (*conveyor belt*) nastro *m*; ***industrial ~*** cintura *f* industriale; *fig* ***tighten one's ~*** stringere la cinghia; *fig* ***that was below the ~*** è stato un colpo basso **II** *v/t infml* tirare; ***she ~ed him one in the eye*** gli ha tirato un colpo in un occhio

◆**belt out** *v/t sep infml tune* cantare a squarciagola; *on piano* suonare a tutto volume

◆**belt up** *v/i* (*fasten seat belt*) allacciare la cintura (di sicurezza); ***belt up!*** *infml* sta' zitto!

bemoan *v/t* lamentarsi di

bemused *adj* confuso; ***be ~ by sth*** rimanere sconcertato per qc

bench *n* (*seat*) panchina *f*; (*workbench*) banco *m*; ***on the ~*** SPORTS in panchina

benchmark *n* punto *m* di riferimento

bend I *v/t* ⟨*pret & past part* ***bent***⟩ piegare **II** *v/i* ⟨*pret & past part* ***bent***⟩ curvarsi; *of person* inchinarsi; ***this metal ~s easily*** *negative* questo metallo si piega facilmente; *positive* questo metallo è facile da piegare **III** *n* curva *f*; ***drive s.o. around the ~*** *infml* far ammattire qn

◆**bend down** *v/i* chinarsi

bender *n infml* sbronza *f infml*;*Br infml* (*male homosexual*) frocio *m*

bendy bus *n* autobus *m* articolato

beneath I *prep* sotto **II** *adv* di sotto; ***they think he's ~ her*** lo considerano inferiore a lei

benediction *n* benedizione *f*

benefactor *n* benefattore *m*, -trice *f*

benefice *n* REL beneficio *m*

beneficial *adj* vantaggioso; ***~ to*** benefico per

beneficiary *n* beneficiario *m*, -a *f*

benefit I *n* (*advantage*) vantaggio *m*; *payment* indennità *f inv*; ***for the ~ of the poor*** a beneficio dei poveri; ***be on ~(s)*** percepire un sussidio **II** *v/t* andare a vantaggio di **III** *v/i* trarre vantaggio (***from*** da); ***he would ~ from a week off*** gli farebbe bene una settimana di vacanza

benefit concert *n* concerto *m* di beneficenza

Benelux *n* Benelux *m*

benevolence *n* benevolenza *f*

benevolent *adj* benevolo

Bengali I *n language* bengali *m*; *person* bengalese *m/f* **II** *adj* bengalese

benign *adj* benevolo; MED benigno

bent I *adj* piegato; (*out of shape*) storto; *infml* corrotto; ***he ~ on sth / doing sth*** essere deciso su qc / a fare qc **II** *pret & past part* → ***bend*** **III** *n* inclinazione (***for*** per); ***people with*** *or* ***of a musical ~*** persone *fpl* portate per la musica

benzene *n* CHEM benzene *m*

benzine *n* CHEM etere *m* di petrolio

bequeath *v/t* lasciare in eredità (*a. fig*); ***~ sth to s.o.*** lasciare qc in eredità a qn

bequest *n* lascito *m*

berate *v/t form* rimproverare

bereaved I *adj* addolorato **II** *n*: ***the ~*** i familiari *mpl* del defunto

bereavement *n* lutto *m*

bereft *adj*: ***be ~ of sth*** essere privo di qc

beret *n* basco *m*

berk, burk *n Br infml* stupido *m*, -a *f*

Berlin *n* Berlino *f*; ***the ~ Wall*** il muro di Berlino

Bermuda shorts *npl* bermuda *mpl*

Berne *n* Berna *f*

berry *n* bacca *f*

berserk *adv*: ***go ~*** dare in escandescenze

berth *n on ship*, *train* cuccetta *f*; ***give s.o. a wide ~*** stare alla larga da qn

beseech *v/t*: ***~ s.o. to do sth*** implorare qn di fare qc

beset *v/t* ⟨*pret & past part* ***beset***⟩ *form* affliggere; ***a project ~ by problems*** un progetto irto di problemi

beside *prep* accanto a; ***be ~ o.s.*** essere fuori di sé; ***that's ~ the point*** questo non c'entra

besides I *adv* inoltre **II** *prep* (*apart from*) oltre a; ***others ~ ourselves*** altri a parte noi; ***~ which he was unwell*** in più non stava bene

besiege *v/t* assediare (*a. fig*)

besotted *adj* infatuato; ***be ~ with s.o.*** essere infatuato di qn

bespectacled *adj* con gli occhiali

bespoke *adj*: ***~ suit*** abito *m* su misura

best I *adj* migliore **II** *adv* meglio; ***it would be ~ if …*** sarebbe meglio se …; ***I like her ~*** lei è quella che mi piace di più; ***do as you think ~*** fa' come ritieni più opportuno; ***as ~ they could*** come meglio potevano; ***~ before*** da consumarsi preferibilmente entro **III** *n*: ***do one's ~*** fare del proprio meglio; ***the ~*** il meglio; (*outstanding thing or person*) il / la migliore; ***they've done the ~ they can*** hanno fatto tutto il possibile; ***make the ~ of*** cogliere il lato buono di; ***at ~*** nel migliore dei casi; ***all the ~!*** tanti auguri!

best before date *n* scadenza *f* **best-dressed** *adj*: ***~ woman in town*** la donna meglio vestita della città

bestial *adj* bestiale

bestiality *n sexual* bestialità *f inv*; *form* (*cruel behaviour*) brutalità *f inv*

bestiary *n* bestiario *m*

bestir *v/t* attivarsi

best man *n at wedding* testimone *m* dello sposo

bestow *v/t form*: ***~ sth on s.o.*** conferire qc a qn

best-seller *n* bestseller *m inv*

bet I *v/i* ⟨*pret & past part* **bet**⟩ scommettere; ***want to ~?*** vuoi scommettere?; ***~ on*** scommettere su; ***you ~!*** ci puoi scommettere!; ***I ~ him £5*** ho scommesso con lui 5 sterline; ***I ~ he'll come!*** scommetto che verrà! **II** *n* scommessa *f*

beta-blocker *n* betabloccante *m*

betray *v/t* tradire

betrayal *n* tradimento *m*; ***~ of trust*** tradimento *m* della fiducia

better I *adj* migliore; ***get ~*** migliorare **II** *adv* meglio; ***you'd ~ ask permission*** faresti meglio a chiedere il permesso; ***go one ~*** fare ancora meglio; ***you'd ~ do what he says*** è meglio che tu faccia come dice lui; ***I'd really ~ not*** sarebbe meglio di no; ***all the ~ for us*** tanto meglio per noi; ***I like her ~*** lei mi piace di più **III** *n*: ***get the ~ of s.o.*** *person* avere la meglio su qn; *problem etc* superare qc **IV** *v/t* migliorare; ***she ~ed her position*** ha migliorato la sua posizione

better off *adj*: ***be ~*** stare meglio finanziariamente; ***the ~*** la classe abbiente

betting shop *n* sala *f* corse

between I *prep* tra; ***~ you and me*** tra me e te; ***I was sitting ~ them*** ero seduto in mezzo a loro; ***that's just ~ ourselves*** che rimanga tra noi; ***we had ten pounds ~ the two of us*** tra tutti e due avevamo 10 sterline **II** *adv* in mezzo; ***in ~*** in mezzo

bevel *n* angolo *m* smussato

beverage *n form* bevanda *f*

bevy *n* (*group of people*) gruppo *m*

bewail *v/t* (*weep over*) piangere; (*regret*) lamentare

beware *v/t*: ***~ of ...!*** (stai) attento a ...!

bewilder *v/t* sconcertare

bewilderment *n* perplessità *f inv*

bewitch *v/t fig* stregare

bewitching *adj* seducente, affascinante

beyond I *prep* (*on the other side of*) oltre, al di là di; ***~ the Alps*** al di là delle Alpi; (*surpassing*) ***it's ~ me*** (*don't understand*) non capisco; (*can't do it*) va oltre le mie capacità; ***a task ~ her abilities*** un compito che supera le sue capacità; ***~ repair*** irreparabile; ***have you any money ~ what you have in the bank?*** hai altro denaro oltre a quello in banca? **II** *adv* più in là; ***India and the lands ~*** India e le terre lontane; ***... a river, and ~ is a small field*** ...un fiume, oltre al quale c'è un piccolo campo

bias *n against* pregiudizio *m*; *in favour of* preferenza *f*; ***have a ~ against sth*** *newspaper etc* essere parziali nei confronti di qc; *person* avere un pregiudizio contro qc; ***have a left- / right-wing ~*** avere una tendenza politica a sinistra / destra

bias binding *n* sbieco *m*

bias(s)ed *adj* parziale

bib *n for baby* bavaglino *m*

bib and tucker *n* vestito *m* della festa

bibber *n* bevitore *m*, -trice *f*

Bible *n* bibbia *f*

Bible-basher *n infml* predicatore *m* severo **Bible belt** *n stati meridionali degli USA in cui domina il fondamentalismo protestante*

biblical *adj* biblico

bibliography *n* bibliografia *f*

bibliophile *n* bibliofilo *m*, -a *f*

bibulous *adj* beone, ubriacone

bicarb *n abbr* (= **bicarbonate**) *infml* bicarbonato *m*

bicarbonate of soda *n* bicarbonato *m* di sodio

bicentenary *US* **bicentennial I** *n* bi-

centenario *m* **II** *adj* bicentenario
biceps *npl* bicipiti *mpl*
bicker *v/i* bisticciare; ***they are always ~ing*** bisticciano continuamente
bicycle *n* bicicletta *f*
bid I *n at auction* offerta *f*; (*attempt*) tentativo *m*; ***make a ~ for freedom*** fare un tentativo di raggiungere la libertà; ***in a ~ to stop smoking*** nel tentativo di smettere di fumare **II** *v/t & v/i* ⟨*pret & past part* **bid**⟩ *at auction* offrire; **~ on** *or* **for** fare un'offerta per; ***~ s.o. farewell*** dire addio a qn
bidder *n* offerente *m/f*
bide *v/t*: ***~ one's time*** aspettare il momento più opportuno
bidet *n* bidè *m*
biennial *adj* biennale
bifocals *npl* occhiali *mpl* bifocali
big I *adj* (+*er*) grande; ***the coat is too ~ for me*** il cappotto mi sta troppo grande; ***my ~ brother / sister*** mio fratello / mia sorella maggiore; ***~ name*** nome importante; ***our company is ~ on service*** *infml* la nostra società è forte nei servizi; ***be onto something ~*** *infml* stare per scoprire qualcosa di grosso **II** *adv*: ***talk ~*** spararle grosse
bigamist *n* bigamo *m*, -a *f*
bigamous *adj* bigamo
bigamy *n* bigamia *f*
Big Apple *n*: ***the ~*** *infml* la Grande Mela **big bang** *n* ASTR big bang *m*
big game *n* caccia *f* grossa
bighead *n infml* pallone *m* gonfiato *infml*
big-headed *adj infml* presuntuoso
bigmouth *n infml* pettegolo *m*, -a *f*; (*blabbermouth*) chiacchierone *m*, -a *f*
bigot *n* fanatico *m*, -a *f*
bigoted *adj* intollerante
bigotry *n* bigotteria *f*
big shot *n* pezzo *m* grosso **big time** *n infml*: ***make the ~*** sfondare **big-time** *adv*: ***they lost ~*** *infml* hanno perso di brutto **big toe** *n* alluce *m* **big wheel** *n Br* ruota *f* panoramica
bigwig *n infml* pezzo *m* grosso; ***the local ~s*** i pezzi grossi del posto
bike I *n infml* bici *f inv infml* **II** *v/i* andare in bici; ***I ~d here*** sono venuto in bici
biker *n* motociclista *m/f*; (*courier*) corriere *m*
bikini *n* bikini *m inv*
bikini line *n* inguine *m*, linea *f* bikini
bilateral *adj* bilaterale
bilberry *n* mirtillo *m* nero
bile *n* bile *f*
bilge *n*: **~s** *pl* NAUT sentina *f*
bilingual *adj* bilingue
bilious *adj* MED bilioso; (*irritable*) irritabile
bill[1] **I** *n in hotel, restaurant* conto *m*; (*gas, electricity bill*) bolletta *f*; (*invoice*) fattura *f*; *US money* banconota *f*; THEAT cartellone *m*; POL disegno *m* di legge; (*poster*) avviso *m*; (***could I have***) ***the ~, please?*** (mi porta) il conto, per favore; ***head*** *or* ***top the ~*** in cima al cartellone; ***give s.o. a clean ~ of health*** emettere un certificato di buona salute; *fig* ***fit the ~*** essere adatto ad un compito **II** *v/t* (*invoice*) mandare la fattura a
bill[2] *n of bird, turtle* becco *m*
billboard *n* cartellone *m* pubblicitario
billet *v/t* MIL alloggiare (***on s.o.*** presso)
billfold *n US* portafoglio *m*
billhook *n* roncola *f*
billiards *nsg* biliardo *m*
billion *num* (*1,000,000,000*) miliardo *m*
billionaire *n* miliardario *m*, -a *f*
billionth I *adj* miliardesimo **II** *n* miliardesimo *m*
bill of exchange *n* FIN cambiale *f* **bill of rights** *n* carta *f* dei diritti **bill of sale** *n* atto *m* di vendita
billow *v/i* (*sail*) solcare le onde; *dress* gonfiarsi; *smoke* fluttuare
billposter, billsticker *n* attacchino *m*, -a *f*
billy goat *n* caprone *m*
bimbo *n infml* oca *f*
bin *n* bidone *m*
binary *adj* binario
binary code *n* COMPUT codice *m* binario **binary number** *n* MATH numero *m* binario **binary system** *n* MATH sistema *m* binario
bind I *v/t* ⟨*pret & past part* **bound**⟩ legare (*a. fig*); JUR (*oblige*) obbligare; ***bound hand and foot*** legare mani e piedi; ***~ s.o. to sth*** vincolare qn a qc **II** *n infml* ***what a ~!*** che seccatura!
◆**bind together** *v/t sep* legare; *fig* unire
binder *n* raccoglitore *m*

binding I *adj agreement, promise* vincolante II *n of book* rilegatura *f*; *of ski* attacco *m*
binge *infml* I *n on food* abbuffata *f*; ***go on a drinking ~*** farsi delle gran bevute II *v/i* abbuffarsi; ***~ on*** abbuffarsi di
bingo *n* tombola *f*
bin liner *n Br* sacco *m* della spazzatura
binoculars *npl* binocolo *msg*
biochemical *adj* biochimico
biochemist *n* biochimico *m*, -a *f*
biochemistry *n* biochimica *f*
biodegradability *n* biodegradabilità *f inv*
biodegradable *adj* biodegradabile
biodiversity *n* biodiversità *f inv*
biodynamic *adj* biodinamico
biographer *n* biografo *m*, -a *f*
biographical *adj* biografico
biography *n* biografia *f*
biological *adj* biologico; ***~ detergent*** detersivo *m* biologico
biologist *n* biologo *m*, -a *f*
biology *n* biologia *f*
biomass *n* biomassa *f*
bionic *adj* bionico
biopsy *n* biopsia *f*
biosphere *n* biosfera *f*
biotechnology *n* biotecnologia *f*
bioterrorism *n* bioterrorismo *m*
birch *n* (*tree, wood*) betulla *f*
bird *n* uccello *m*; *Br infml* pollastrella *f*; ***tell s.o. about the ~s and the bees*** spiegare a qn come si fanno i bambini; ***she's an odd ~*** *infml* è una tipa divertente; ***give s.o. the ~*** *Br* fischiare qn; *US vulg* fare a qn il gesto del dito medio alzato
birdbath *n* vaschetta *f* per uccelli
bird-brain *n*: ***be a ~*** *infml* avere un cervello di gallina **birdcage** *n* gabbia *f* per uccelli **bird flu** *n* influenza *f* aviaria **bird of prey** *n* (uccello *m*) rapace *m* **bird sanctuary** *n* rifugio *m* per uccelli
birdseed *n* becchime *m*
bird's eye view *n* vista *f* a volo d'uccello
birdsong *n* canto *m* degli uccelli
bird table *n tavola sulla quale si sparge il becchime* **bird-watcher** *n* birdwatcher *m/f*
biro® *n* biro® *f*
birth *n* nascita *f* (*a. fig*); (*labour*) parto *m*; ***give ~ to*** *child* partorire; ***date of ~*** data di nascita; ***she's English by ~*** è inglese di nascita; ***the country of his ~*** il suo paese natale; ***of humble ~*** di umili origini; ***from*** *or* ***since ~*** dalla nascita; ***at ~*** alla nascita
birth certificate *n* certificato *m* di nascita **birth control** *n* controllo *m* delle nascite
birthdate *n* data *f* di nascita
birthday *n* compleanno *m*; ***happy ~!*** buon compleanno!
birthday cake *n* torta *f* di compleanno **birthday card** *n* biglietto *m* di auguri (per il compleanno) **birthday party** *n* festa *f* di compleanno **birthday present** *n* regalo *m* di compleanno **birthday suit** *n*: ***in his ~*** *hum* come mamma l'ha fatto
birthmark *n* voglia *f*
birthplace *n* luogo *m* di nascita
birthrate *n* tasso *m* di nascita
birthright *n* diritto *m* di nascita
biscuit *n* biscotto *m*; *US* pasticcino *m*; ***that takes the ~!*** *Br infml* è il colmo!
bisect *v/t* dividere in due parti uguali; MATH bisecare
bisexual I *adj* bisessuale II *n* bisessuale *m/f*
bishop *n* vescovo *m*
bishopric *n* (*diocese*) vescovato *m*
bison *n USerican* bufalo *m*, -a *f*; *European* bisonte *m*
bisque *n* COOK zuppa *f*; *ceramics* biscotto *m*
bissextile *adj* bisestile
bistro *n* bistrot *m*
bit[1] *n* **1.** (*piece*) pezzo *m*; (*part*) parte *f*; ***~ by ~*** poco a poco; ***do one's ~*** fare la propria parte; ***a few ~s of furniture*** alcuni elementi di arredamento; ***pull*** *or* ***tear sth to ~s*** *infml* fare a pezzi qc; ***a ~ of all right*** *infml* molto bene **2.** ***a ~*** (*a little*) un po'; ***you haven't changed a ~*** non sei cambiato per niente; ***he's a ~ of a rogue*** è piuttosto furbo; ***a ~ of*** (*a little*) un po' di; ***a ~ of advice*** qualche consiglio; ***a ~ on the side*** *infml* un/un'amante; ***a ~ of news/advice*** una notizia/un consiglio; ***I'll be there in a ~*** (*in a little while*) sarò lì tra poco; ***it cost quite a ~*** è costato un bel po' **3.** COMPUT bit *m inv*
bit[2] *n for a horse* morso *m*
bit[3] *pret* → ***bite***

bitch I *n dog* cagna *f*; *infml woman* bastarda *f infml*, stronza *f vulg*; ***that was a ~ of a situation*** *infml* era una situazione incasinatissima **II** *v/i infml* (*complain*) lamentarsi; ***~ about*** lamentarsi di
bitchiness *n* malignità *f inv*
bitchy *adj* (*+er*) *infml person, remark* velenoso
bite I *v/t* ⟨*pret* **bit**, *past part* **bitten**⟩ mordere; *one's nails* mangiarsi **II** *v/i* ⟨*pret* **bit**, *past part* **bitten**⟩ mordere; *of fish* abboccare **III** *n* morso *m*; ***let's have a ~*** (***to eat***) mangiamo un boccone; ***he didn't get a ~*** *of angler* non ha abboccato neanche un pesce
biting *adj* pungente; *wind* tagliente
bitmap *n* COMPUT (*a.* **bitmapped image**) immagine *f* bitmap
bitmapped *adj* COMPUT bitmap; ***~ graphics*** grafica *f* bitmap
bit part *n* particina *f*
bitten *past part* → ***bite***
bitter I *adj* (*+er*) *taste* amaro; *person* amareggiato; *weather* gelido; *argument* aspro; ***to the ~ end*** fino in fondo **II** *n beer* birra *f* amara
bitterly *adv resent* profondamente; ***~ cold*** gelido
bittern *n* ZOOL tarabuso *m*
bitterness *n* amarezza *f*; *of wind* inesorabilità *f inv*; *of struggle* asprezza *f*
bittersweet *adj* agrodolce
bitumen *n* bitume *m*
bizarre *adj* bizzarro
blab *v/i* ⟨*pret & past part* **-bed**⟩ *infml* spifferare *infml*
blabber *v/i* chiacchierare incessantemente
blabbermouth *n infml* spione *m*, -a *f*
black I *adj* (*+er*) nero (*a. fig*); *person* negro, nero; *tea* senza latte **II** *n* (*colour*) nero *m*; (*person*) nero *m*, -a *f*; ***dressed in ~*** vestito di nero; ***in the ~*** FIN in attivo; *fig* ***in ~ and white*** nero su bianco
◆**black out** *v/i* svenire
black and white *adj* TV, TYPO in bianco e nero
blackberry *n* mora *f* di rovo
BlackBerry® *n* BlackBerry® *m*
blackbird *n* merlo *m* **blackboard** *n* lavagna *f*; ***write sth on the ~*** scrivere qc alla lavagna **black book** *n*: ***be in s.o.'s ~s*** essere sul libro nero di qn
black box *n* scatola *f* nera **blackcurrant** *n* ribes *m inv* nero **black economy** *n* economia *f* sommersa
blacken *v/t* annerire; *fig*: *person's name* infangare
black eye *n* occhio *m* nero **blackhead** *n* punto *m* nero, comedone *m* **black hole** *n* ASTR, *fig* buco *m* nero **black humour**, *US* **black humor** *n* umorismo *m* nero **black ice** *n* ghiaccio *m* (sulla strada) **blacklist I** *n* lista *f* nera **II** *v/t* mettere sulla lista nera **black magic** *n* magia *f* nera **blackmail I** *n* ricatto *m* (*a. fig*) **II** *v/t* ricattare **blackmailer** *n* ricattatore *m*, -trice *f* **black market** *n* mercato *m* nero
blackness *n of night* oscurità *f inv*
blackout *n* ELEC black-out *m inv*; MED svenimento *m*
black pepper *n* pepe *m* nero **black pudding** *n sanguinaccio* **Black Sea** *n* Mar Nero *m* **black sheep** *n fig* pecora *f* nera **blacksmith** *n* fabbro *m* ferraio **black tie I** *n on invitation* abito *m* scuro **II** *adj* in abito scuro
bladder *n* vescica *f*
blade *n of knife*, *sword* lama *f*; *of helicopter* pala *f*; *of grass* filo *m*
blame I *v/t* biasimare; ***~ s.o. for sth*** ritenere qn responsabile di qc; ***I don't ~ you for being angry*** non ti biasimo per essere arrabbiato; ***be to ~ for*** essere responsabile di **II** *n* colpa *f*; (*responsibility*) responsabilità *f inv*; ***put the ~ for sth on s.o.*** dare la colpa di qc a qn
blameless *adj* innocente
blanch I *v/t* COOK *vegetables* scottare; *almonds* pelare **II** *v/i liter person* impallidire (***with*** di)
blancmange *n* COOK biancomangiare *m*
bland *adj* (*+er*) *smile*, *answer* insulso; *food* insipido
blandish *v/t* lusingare
blandishments *npl* lusinghe *fpl*
blank I *adj* (*+er*) (*not written on*) bianco; *tape* vergine; *look* vuoto; ***leave ~*** lasciare in bianco **II** *n* (*empty space*) spazio *m*; (*cartridge*) cartuccia *f* a salve; ***my mind's a ~*** ho la testa vuota; *fig* ***draw a ~*** fare un buco nell'acqua
◆**blank out** *v/t sep thought* cancellare dalla memoria
blank cheque, *US* **blank check** *n* as-

segno *m* in bianco
blanket *n a. fig* coperta *f*
blankly *adv* (*expressionlessly*) in modo assente; (*uncomprehendingly*) in modo sconcertato; ***she just looked at me ~*** mi guardò sconcertata
blare *v/i* suonare a tutto volume
◆**blare out** **I** *v/i* strepitare **II** *v/t sep* fare rimbombare
blaspheme *v/i* bestemmiare
blasphemous *adj* blasfemo
blasphemy *n* bestemmia *f*
blast **I** *n* (*explosion*) esplosione *f*; (*gust*) raffica *f*; ***an icy ~*** una folata di vento gelido; **(*at*) *full ~*** a tutto volume; ***with the heating on* (*at*) *full ~*** con il riscaldamento al massimo; ***a ~ from the past*** *infml* un tuffo nel passato **II** *v/t* far esplodere; ***~!*** accidenti! **III** *int*: ***~* (*it*)*!*** *infml* maledizione!; ***~ this car!*** maledetta macchina!
◆**blast off** *v/i of rocket* essere lanciato
blasted *adj infml* maledetto
blast furnace *n* altoforno *m*
blast-off *n* lancio *m*
blatant *adj* palese **blatantly** *adv* evidentemente; ***she ~ ignored it*** lo ha ignorato ostentatamente
blaze **I** *n* (*fire*) incendio *m*; ***six people died in the ~*** sei persone hanno perso la vita nell'incendio; ***a ~ of colour*** un'esplosione di colore **II** *v/i sun, fire* ardere; *guns* fare fuoco; ***~ with anger*** *liter eyes* essere iniettati di sangue (dalla rabbia); ***with all guns blazing*** ad armi spianate
◆**blaze away** *v/i with gun* sparare a raffica
blazer *n* blazer *m inv*
bleach **I** *n for clothes* varechina *f*; *for hair* acqua *f* ossigenata **II** *v/t hair* ossigenarsi
bleak *adj* (+*er*) *countryside* desolato; *weather* cupo; *future* deprimente
bleakness *n of landscape* tetraggine *f*; *fig* squallore *m*; *of prospects* desolazione *f*
bleary-eyed *adj*: ***be ~*** avere lo sguardo appannato
bleat *v/i of sheep* belare
bled *pret & past part* → ***bleed***
bleed ⟨*pret & past part* ***bled***⟩ **I** *v/i* sanguinare **II** *v/t fig* dissanguare
bleeding **I** *n* emorragia *f*; ***internal ~*** emorragia *f* interna **II** *adj* sanguinante; *Br infml* maledetto
bleep **I** *n* blip *m inv* **II** *v/i* suonare **III** *v/t* (*call on pager*) chiamare sul cercapersone
bleeper *n* (*pager*) cercapersone *m inv*
blemish **I** *n on skin* imperfezione *f*; *on fruit* ammaccatura *f* **II** *v/t reputation* infangare
blend **I** *n* miscela *f* **II** *v/t* miscelare
◆**blend in** **I** *v/i* inserirsi; (*look good*) armonizzare **II** *v/t sep in cooking* incorporare
blender *n machine* frullatore *m*
bless *v/t* benedire; **(*God*) *~ you!*** Dio ti benedica!; ***~ you!*** *in response to sneeze* salute!; ***~ me!, ~ my soul!*** santo cielo!; ***be ~ed with*** godere di
blessed *adj* REL benedetto; (*cursed*) santo; ***the Blessed X*** la Santa Croce
Blessed Virgin *n* Beata Vergine *f*
blessing *n a. fig* benedizione *f*; ***give s.o. / sth one's ~*** dare a qn / qc la propria benedizione; ***it was a ~ in disguise*** in fondo è stato un bene; ***it was a mixed ~*** è stata una mezza fortuna
blew *pret* → ***blow***
blight **I** *v/t* rovinare **II** *n* BOT ruggine *f*; *fig* flagello *m*
blind **I** *adj* (+*er*) cieco; AVIAT *fly* strumentale; *fig* ***be ~ to*** non vedere; ***turn a ~ eye to sth*** chiudere un occhio su qc; ***~ faith* (*in sth*)** fede *f* cieca (in qc); ***~ drunk*** *infml* ubriaco fradicio; ***bake sth ~*** COOK infornare qc senza farcitura **II** *n*: ***the ~*** i ciechi **III** *v/t* accecare
blind alley *n* vicolo *m* cieco **blind date** *n* appuntamento *m* al buio
blinder *n* (*patch*) paraocchi *m inv*; *Br infml* (*accomplishment*) cosa *f* eccezionale; *Br infml* (*alcohol*) sbronza *f*; ***go on a ~*** ubriacarsi
blindfold **I** *n* benda *f* **II** *v/t* bendare (gli occhi a) **III** *adj* con gli occhi bendati; ***I could do it ~*** *infml* potrei farlo ad occhi chiusi
blinding *adj* atroce; *light* accecante, abbagliante **blindingly** *adv*: ***it is ~ obvious*** è palese
blindly *adv feel, grope* a tastoni; *fig* ciecamente
blind man's buff *n game* moscacieca *f*
blindness *n* cecità *f inv*
blind spot *n in road* punto *m* cieco; (*ability that is lacking*) punto *m* debo-

le

blink *v/i of person* sbattere le palpebre; *of light* tremolare

blinkered *adj fig* ottuso

blinkers *npl Br* paraocchi *mpl*

blip *n on radar screen* segnale *m*; *fig* battuta *f* d'arresto

bliss *n* felicità *f inv*; ***this is ~!*** che gioia!

blissful *adj time, feeling* delizioso; *smile* beato; ***in ~ ignorance of the fact that ...*** *iron* ignorando beatamente che...

blissfully *adv peaceful* deliziosamente; ***~ happy*** assolutamente felice; ***he remained ~ ignorant of what was going on*** rimase beatamente ignaro di tutto quello che stava succedendo

blister **I** *n* vescichetta *f* **II** *v/i* formare una vescichetta; *of paint* formare delle bolle

blister pack *n* blister *m inv*

blithe *adj* (*happy*) gaio; (*reckless*) sconsiderato

blitz *n* MIL incursione *f* aerea; ***have a ~ on the cleaning*** fare un'operazione di pulizia

blizzard *n* bufera *f* di neve

bloated *adj* gonfio

blob *n of liquid* goccia *f*

bloc *n* POL blocco *m*

block **I** *n* blocco *m*; *in town* isolato *m*; *of shares* pacchetto *m*; (*blockage*) blocco *m*; (*executioner's block*) ceppo *m*; *in pipe,* MED ostruzione *f*; ***~ of flats*** palazzo *m* (d'appartamenti); ***~s*** (*toys*) costruzioni *fpl*; ***she lived in the next ~*** *esp US* viveva nell'isolato vicino; ***I've a mental ~ about it*** ho un blocco mentale; ***knock s.o.'s ~ off*** *infml* spaccare la testa a qn; *fig* ***put one's head on the ~*** rischiare **II** *v/t* bloccare

◆**block in** *v/t sep with vehicle* bloccare la macchina di; ***somebody's car was blocking me in*** qualcuno ha bloccato la mia macchina parcheggiando la sua

◆**block out** *v/t sep light* impedire; ***the trees are blocking out all the light*** gli alberi bloccano la luce

◆**block up** *v/t sep sink etc* otturare; *pipe* ostruire; ***my nose is*** *or* ***I'm all blocked up*** ho il naso chiuso *or* sono tutto intasato (dal raffreddore)

blockade **I** *n* blocco *m* **II** *v/t* bloccare

blockage *n* ingorgo *m*

blockbuster *n* successone *m*

block capitals, block letters *npl* maiuscole *fpl*

blockhead *n infml* citrullo *m*, -a *f*

bloke *n infml* tipo *m infml*

blond *adj* biondo

blonde *n* (*woman*) bionda *f*

blood *n* sangue *m*; ***in cold ~*** a sangue freddo; ***it makes my ~ boil*** mi fa ribollire il sangue

blood alcohol level *n* concentrazione *f* di alcol etilico nel sangue **blood bank** *n* banca *f* del sangue **blood bath** *n* bagno *m* di sangue **blood clot** *n* grumo *m* di sangue

bloodcurdling *adj* aggiacciante; ***they heard a ~ cry*** hanno sentito un urlo da far gelare il sangue

blood donor *n* donatore *m*, -trice *f* di sangue **blood group** *n* gruppo *m* sanguigno

bloodhound *n* segugio *m*

bloodless *adj coup* senza spargimento di sangue

blood poisoning *n* setticemia *f* **blood pressure** *n* pressione *f* del sangue **blood relation, blood relative** *n* consanguineo *m*, -a *f* **blood sample** *n* prelievo *m* di sangue **bloodshed** *n* spargimento *m* di sangue **bloodshot** *adj* iniettato di sangue **blood sports** *npl* sport *m inv* violento **bloodstain** *n* macchia *f* di sangue **bloodstained** *adj* macchiato di sangue **bloodstream** *n* circolazione *f* (del sangue) **blood sugar** *n* glicemia *f*; ***~ level*** livello *m* di glicemia **blood test** *n* analisi *f inv* del sangue **bloodthirsty** *adj* assetato di sangue **blood transfusion** *n* trasfusione *f* di sangue **blood type** *n* gruppo *m* sanguigno **blood vessel** *n* vaso *m* sanguigno

bloody **I** *adj* (+*er*) *hands etc* insanguinato; *battle* sanguinoso; *infml* maledetto; ***~ hell!*** porca miseria! *infml*; ***it's a ~ nuisance*** è una gran rottura *infml*; ***you're a ~ genius!*** sei un geniaccio! *infml* **II** *adv*: ***that's ~ difficult / easy!*** è facile / difficile da morire!; ***I'm ~ tired*** sono stanco morto; ***not ~ likely*** neanche per sogno; ***you'll ~ well do it!*** eccome se lo farai!

bloody-minded *adj infml* ostinato
bloom I *n* fiore *m*; ***in full ~*** in piena fioritura **II** *v/i a. fig* fiorire
bloomer *n infml* cantonata *f*
bloomers *n pantaloni sportivi da donna*
blooming *Br infml* **I** *adj* maledetto **II** *adv*: ***that's ~ marvellous!*** perfetto!
blooper *n US infml* papera *f*
blossom I *n* fiori *mpl*; ***in ~*** in fiore **II** *v/i a. fig* fiorire
blot I *n* macchia *f*; ***be a ~ on the landscape*** rovinare il paesaggio **II** *v/t* ⟨*pret & past part* **-ted**⟩ (*dry*) asciugare
◆**blot out** *v/t sep memory* cancellare; *view* nascondere
blotch *n* chiazza *f*
blotchy *adj* (+*er*) coperto di chiazze
blotting paper *n* carta *f* assorbente
blouse *n* camicetta *f*
blow I *v/t* ⟨*pret* **blew**, *past part* **blown**⟩ *of wind* spingere; *smoke* soffiare; *infml* (*spend*) sperperare; *infml opportunity* mandare all'aria; (*fuse*) saltare; ***~ a whistle*** fischiare; ***~ one's nose*** soffiarsi il naso; ***~ s.o. a kiss*** mandare un bacio a qc; ***he blew the money on drink*** ha sperperato tutti i soldi nel bere; *fig* ***~ one's own trumpet*** *Br or* ***horn*** *US* cantare le proprie lodi; *fig* ***when I told him he really blew a fuse*** quando gliel'ho detto è andato su tutte le furie; ***~!*** *Br infml* maledizione!; ***~ the expense!*** al diavolo le spese! **II** *v/i* ⟨*pret* **blew**, *past part* **blown**⟩ *of wind, person* soffiare; *of fuse* saltare; *of tyre* scoppiare; ***the whistle blew for half-time*** è stato fischiato l'intervallo; ***the door blew open / shut*** la porta si è chiusa / aperta per il vento **III** *n* colpo *m*; ***come to ~s*** venire alle mani; *fig* ***deal s.o. / sth a ~*** assestare un duro colpo a qn / qc
◆**blow in** *v/i sep person etc* arrivare improvvisamente; ***I've just blown in to say hello*** ho fatto un salto solo per salutarvi
◆**blow off I** *v/t sep* portar via **II** *v/i* volar via
◆**blow out I** *v/t sep candle* spegnere **II** *v/i of candle* spegnersi
◆**blow over I** *v/t sep* abbattere **II** *v/i* rovesciarsi; *of storm, argument* calmarsi
◆**blow up I** *v/t sep with explosives* far saltare; *balloon* gonfiare; *photograph* ingrandire **II** *v/i a. fig* esplodere
blow-by-blow *adj* dettagliato; ***a ~ account of the accident*** un resoconto dettagliato dell'incidente **blow-dry** *v/t* ⟨*pret & past part* **-ied**⟩ asciugare col phon **blow job** *n vulg* pompino *m vulg*
blowlamp *n Br* cannello *m* per saldatura
blown *past part* → **blow**
blow-out *n of tyre* scoppio *m*; *infml* (*big meal*) abbuffata *f*
blowtorch *n* cannello *m* per saldatura
blow-up *n of photo* ingrandimento *m*
blowy *adj* (+*er*) ventoso
blubber I *n of whale* grasso *m* **II** *v/i infml cry* frignare
bludgeon *v/t* percuotere; ***~ s.o. to death*** percuotere qn a morte
blue I *adj* (+*er*) blu; *infml film* porno; ***be feeling ~*** sentirsi giù; ***once in a ~ moon*** ogni morte di papa **II** *n* blu *m inv*; ***dressed in ~*** vestito di blu; ***out of the ~*** *infml* all'improvviso
bluebell *n* giacinto *m* di bosco
blueberry *n* mirtillo *m* **blue-blooded** *adj* di sangue blu **bluebottle** *n* mosca *f* azzurra della carne **blue cheese** *n formaggio simile al gorgonzola* **blue chip** *adj* sicuro; *company* di alto livello **blue-collar worker** *n* operaio *m*, -a *f* **blue-eyed** *adj* dagli occhi blu; *fig* ***s.o.'s ~ boy*** il pupillo di qn
blueprint *n* cianografia *f*; (*fig: plan*) programma *m*
blues *npl* MUS blues *m inv*; ***have the ~*** essere giù
blues singer *n* cantante *m/f* blues
bluestocking *n* donna *f* intellettualoide **bluetit** *n* ZOOL cinciarella *f*
bluff I *n* (*deception*) bluff *m inv*; ***call s.o.'s ~*** scoprire le carte di qn **II** *v/i* bluffare **III** *adj* schietto; ***his manner was a little ~*** aveva dei modi un po' bruschi
blunder I *n* errore *m* **II** *v/i* fare un errore
blunt I *adj* (+*er*) spuntato; *person* diretto; ***he was very ~ about it*** è stato molto esplicito sull'argomento **II** *v/t* smorzare
bluntly *adv speak* senza mezzi termini; ***he told us quite ~ what he thought***

ci ha detto cosa pensava senza mezzi termini

blur I *n* massa *f* indistinta **II** *v/t* 〈*pret & past part* **-red**〉 offuscare; ***have ~red vision*** avere la vista offuscata

blurb *n on book* note *fpl* di copertina

◆**blurt out** *v/t sep* spiattellare

blush I *v/i* arrossire **II** *n* rossore *m*

blusher *n cosmetic* fard *m inv*

bluster *v/i* protestare

blustery *adj* ventoso

Blu-Tack® *n pasta adesiva di colore blu*

Blvd. *abbr* (= **boulevard**) viale *m*

BMA *abbr* (= **British Medical Association**) *ordine dei medici in Gran Bretagna*

B-movie *n* film *m inv* di serie B

BO *abbr* (= **body odour**) odori *mpl* corporei

boa *n* boa *m*; ***~ constrictor*** boa *m*

boar *n* (*male pig*) verro *m*; *wild* cinghiale *m*

board I *n* **1.** asse *f*; *for game* scacchiera *f*; *for notices* tabellone *m* **2.** ~ (***of directors***) consiglio *m* (d'amministrazione); ***Board of Trade*** *Br* Ministero del Commercio *m* **3.** ***on ~*** (*plane, train, boat*) a bordo **4.** *fig* ***across the ~*** a tutti i livelli; ***take on ~*** *comments etc* prendere in esame; ***take on ~*** (*fully realize truth of*) accettare **5.** ***full/half ~*** pensione *f* completa / mezza pensione *f* **II** *v/t aeroplane etc* salire a bordo di; ***flight ZA173 now ~ing at gate 13*** imbarco immediato al gate 13 per il volo ZA173 **III** *v/i of passengers* salire a bordo

◆**board up** *v/t sep* chiudere con assi

◆**board with** *v/t* essere a pensione da

board and lodging *n* vitto e alloggio *m*

boarder *n* pensionante *m/f*; EDU convittore *m*, -trice *f*

board game *n* gioco *m* da tavolo

boarding card *n* carta *f* d'imbarco **boarding house** *n* pensione *f* **boarding pass** *n* carta *f* d'imbarco **boarding school** *n* collegio *m*

board meeting *n* riunione *f* di consiglio

board room *n* sala *f* del consiglio

boardwalk *n US* passerella *f* (in riva al mare)

boast I *v/i* vantarsi; ***~ of*** *or* ***about*** vantarsi di **II** *n* vanteria *f*

boastful *adj* vanaglorioso

boastfully *adv* in modo presuntuoso

boat *n* (*small, for leisure*) barca *f*; (*ship*) nave *f*; ***go by ~*** andare in nave; *fig* ***miss the ~*** *infml* perdere il treno; *fig* ***push the ~ out*** *infml* (*celebrate*) fare le cose in grande; *fig* ***we're all in the same ~*** *infml* siamo tutti sulla stessa barca

boathouse *n* rimessa *f* per le barche

boatload *n* carico *m* (di una barca)

boat train *n treno in coincidenza con l'arrivo e la partenza delle navi*

boatyard *n* cantiere *m* navale; (*as dry dock*) rimessa *f*

bob[1] *n* (*haircut*) caschetto *m*; *Br* scellino *m*; ***a few bits and ~s*** qualche cosuccia; ***that must have cost him a ~ or two*** *infml* gli deve essere costato un bel po' di soldi

bob[2] *v/i* 〈*pret & past part* **-bed**〉 *of boat etc* andare su e giù

◆**bob up** *v/i* spuntare

bobbin *n* bobina *f*; (*cotton reel*) spola *f*

bobble hat *n Br* berretto *m* con pompon

bobsleigh, bobsled *n* bob *m inv*

bode *adv form*: ***~ well/ill*** essere di buon / cattivo auspicio

bodge *v/t* → ***botch***

bodice *n* corpetto *m*

bodily I *adj* corporale; ***~ functions*** funzioni *fpl* fisiologiche **II** *adv eject* di peso

body *n* corpo *m*; *dead* cadavere *m*; *clothing* body *m*; ***~ of water*** massa *f* d'acqua; ~ (**suit**) (*undergarment*) body *m inv*; ***earn just enough to keep ~ and soul together*** guadagnare il minimo per vivere; ***the student ~*** il corpo studentesco; ***a large ~ of people*** una grande massa di gente; ***a ~ of evidence*** una quantità di prove

body armour, *US* **body armor** *n* giubbotto *m* antiproiettile **body blow** *n fig* colpo *m* allo stomaco (***to, for*** a, per) **body building** *n* body building *m* **body clock** *n* orologio *m* biologico

bodyguard *n* guardia *f* del corpo

body language *n* linguaggio *m* del corpo **body lotion** *n* crema *f* per il corpo **body odour**, *US* **body odor** *n* odori *mpl* corporei **body piercing** *n* piercing *m inv* **body shop** *n* AUTO carrozzeria *f* **body stocking** *n* body *m inv* **body warmer** *n* giacca *f* senza maniche **bodywork** *n* AUTO carrozzeria *f*

bog *n* palude *f*; *Br vulg* cesso *m sl*

bogey, bogy *n* ⟨*pl* ***bogeys, bogies***⟩ (*bugbear*) folletto *m*; *Br infml* caccola *f*

bogeyman *n* ⟨*pl* ***bogeymen***⟩ orco *m*

bogged down *adj* impantanato; ***get ~ in*** impantanarsi in

boggle *v/i*: ***the mind ~s!*** è incredibile!

bog paper *n Br vulg* carta *f* igienica

bog-standard *adj Br infml* comunissimo

bogus *adj* fasullo

Bohemia *n* Boemia *f*; *fig* bohème *f*

bohemian I *n* bohémien *m inv* **II** *adj lifestyle* da bohémien

boil[1] *n* (*swelling*) foruncolo *m*

boil[2] **I** *v/t* far bollire; ***~ed/hard ~ed egg*** uovo *m* bollito/sodo; ***bring sth to the*** *Br or* ***a*** *US* ***~*** portare qc a ebollizione **II** *v/i* bollire; ***~ing hot water*** acqua *f* bollente; ***it was ~ing*** (***hot***) ***in the office*** *infml* faceva un caldo tremendo in ufficio; ***I was ~ing*** (***hot***) *infml* stavo morendo di caldo

◆**boil down to** *v/t* ridursi a; ***what it boils down to is that …*** in parole povere…

◆**boil over** *v/i of milk etc* traboccare bollendo

boiler *n* caldaia *f*

boiler suit *n Br* tuta *f* da lavoro

boiling point *n of liquid* punto *m* d'ebollizione; *fig* ***reach ~*** perdere le staffe

boisterous *adj* turbolento

bold I *adj* (+*er*) (*brave*) audace **II** *n* (*print*) neretto *m*; ***in ~*** in neretto

bole *n liter* tronco *m*

Bolivia *n* Bolivia *f*

bollard *n* colonnina *f* spartitraffico; NAUT bitta *f*

bollocking *n Br sl* cazziatone *m sl*; ***give s.o. a ~*** fare un cazziatone a qn

bollocks *npl sl* cazzata *f vulg*; (***that's***) ***~!*** che cazzate! *vulg*

bologna *n* COOK *specie di salsiccia*

bolshie, bolshy *adj* intrattabile

bolster *v/t confidence* rafforzare

bolt I *n on door* catenaccio *m*; (*metal pin*) bullone *m*; *of lightning* fulmine *m*; ***like a ~ from the blue*** come un fulmine a ciel sereno; ***he made a ~ for the door*** si precipitò ad aprire la porta **II** *adv*: ***~ upright*** diritto come un fuso **III** *v/t* (*fix with bolts*) fissare con bulloni; (*close*) chiudere col catenaccio **IV** *v/i* (*run off*) scappare via

bolthole *n* rifugio *m*

bomb I *n* bomba *f*; ***the car goes like a ~*** *Br infml* la macchina va come una scheggia; ***the car cost a ~*** la macchina è costata una fortuna **II** *v/t* bombardare; (*blow up*) fare esplodere una bomba in, far saltare

bombard *v/t* (*attack*) bombardare; ***~ with questions*** bombardare di domande

bombardment *n* bombardamento *m*

bombast *n* ampollosità *f inv*

bombastic *adj* ampolloso

bomb attack *n* attacco *m* dinamitardo **bomb disposal** *n* disinnesco *m*

bomber *n* (*aeroplane*) bombardiere *m*; (*terrorist*) dinamitardo *m*, -a *f*

bomber jacket *n* bomber *m inv*

bombing *n* attentato *m* dinamitardo

bombproof *adj* a prova di bomba **bomb scare** *n* allarme-bomba *m* **bombshell** *n* (*fig*: *news*) bomba *f*; *woman* schianto *m* **bomb shelter** *n* rifugio *m* antiaereo **bomb site** *n* campo *m* di battaglia

bona fide *adj* in buona fede; ***it's a ~ offer*** è un'offerta sincera

bonanza *n fig* colpo *m* di fortuna; ***the oil ~*** il colpaccio del petrolio

bond I *n* (*tie*) legame *m*; FIN obbligazione *f*; ***government ~s*** titoli *mpl* di Stato **II** *v/i* aderire; *fig* legare; ***~ with one's baby*** legarsi al proprio bambino; ***we ~ed immediately*** abbiamo legato subito

bondage *n sexual* bondage *m*; ***~ gear*** articoli *mpl* per il bondage; *fig* ***be in ~ to sth*** *liter* essere schiavo di qc

bonded warehouse *n* deposito *m* franco

bonding *n*: ***the ~ between mother and child*** la formazione del legame madre-figlio; ***engage in some male ~*** consolidare l'amicizia tra uomini

bone I *n* osso *m*; ***I'm chilled to the ~*** il freddo mi è entrato nelle ossa; ***work one's fingers to the ~*** lavorare sodo; ***~ of contention*** pomo *m* della discordia; ***have a ~ to pick with s.o.*** *infml* avere da sistemare un problema con qn; ***I'll make no ~s about it, you're ...*** *infml* non mi faccio scrupoli a dirlo: sei... **II** *v/t meat* disossare; *fish* togliere la lisca a

◆**bone up on** *v/i + obj infml* applicarsi su

bone china *n* porcellana *f* fine **bone dry** *adj*, **bone-dry** *adj infml* a secco

bone idle *adj Br infml* pigrissimo

boner *n infml* gaffe *f*; *vulg* erezione *f*

bonfire *n* falò *m inv*

Bonfire Night *n serata del 5 novembre in cui si commemora il fallimento della Congiura delle Polveri (1605) con falò e fuochi d'artificio*

bonk *v/t & v/i Br sl* scopare *sl*

bonkers *adj infml* pazzerello

bonnet *n of car* cofano *m*

bonnie, bonny *adj esp Scot* bello; *baby* paffuto

bonus *n* (*money*) gratifica *f*; (*something extra*) vantaggio *m* in più

bony *adj* (+*er*) *fingers* ossuto; *fish* pieno di lische

boo I *int* bu; ***he wouldn't say ~ to a goose*** *infml* non farebbe male a una mosca **II** *v/t & v/i actor, speaker* fischiare

boob[1] **I** *n infml* (*mistake*) errore *m* **II** *v/i infml* (*make a mistake*) fare un errore

boob[2] *n sl* (*breast*) tetta *f sl*

boob job *n infml* ingrandimento *m* del seno

booboo *n infml* → ***boob***[1]

booby *n* babbeo *m*, -a *f*

booby prize *n premio ironico dato all'ultimo in classifica* **booby trap** *n* MIL trappola *f* esplosiva; (*trick*) tranello *m*

book I *n* libro *m*; ***be in s.o.'s good / bad ~s*** essere nelle grazie / sul libro nero di qn; ***~ of matches*** bustina *f* di fiammiferi; ***that counts as cheating in my ~*** *infml* per me quello è imbrogliare; ***go by the ~*** fare le cose secondo le regole **II** *v/t* (*reserve*) prenotare; *of policeman* multare; SPORTS ammonire; ***be ~ed for speeding*** prendere una multa per eccesso di velocità **III** *v/i* (*reserve*) prenotare

◆**book in I** *v/i* prenotare una camera; (*check in*) registrarsi; ***we booked in at*** *or* ***into the Hilton*** siamo arrivati all'Hilton **II** *v/t sep* prenotare una camera per; ***book s.o. into a hotel*** prenotare una camera d'albergo per qn; ***we're booked in at*** *or* ***into the Hilton*** ci hanno prenotato una camera all'Hilton

bookable *adj* disponibile (per la prenotazione); ***~ offence*** *Br or* ***offense*** *US* SPORTS fallo *m* punibile

bookbinding *n* rilegatura *f*

bookcase *n* scaffale *m*

booked up *adj* tutto esaurito; *person* occupatissimo

bookie *n infml* allibratore *m*

booking *n* (*reservation*) prenotazione *f*

booking clerk *n* impiegato *m* della biglietteria **booking fee** *n* (tariffa *f* di) prenotazione *f* **booking office** *n* biglietteria *f*

bookish *adj* eccessivamente studioso

bookkeeper *n* contabile *m/f*

bookkeeping *n* contabilità *f inv*

booklet *n* libretto *m*

book lover *n* amante *m/f* dei libri

bookmaker *n* allibratore *m*

bookmark I *n for book* segnalibro *m*; COMPUT bookmark *m inv* **II** *v/t* COMPUT mettere un bookmark in

books *npl* (*accounts*) libri *mpl* contabili; ***do the ~*** tenere la contabilità; ***cook the ~*** falsificare i libri contabili

bookseller *n* libraio *m*, -a *f* **bookshelf** *n* mensola *f* **bookshelves** *npl* scaffali *mpl* **bookshop** *n* libreria *f* **bookstall** *n* edicola *f* **bookstore** *n US* libreria *f*

book token *n* buono *m* libro

bookworm *n fig* topo *m* di biblioteca

boom[1] **I** *n* boom *m inv* **II** *v/i of business* andare a gonfie vele

boom[2] **I** *n* (*bang*) rimbombo *m* **II** *v/i* rimbombare

boom[3] *n* NAUT boma *m*

boomerang *n* boomerang *m*

boon *n* benedizione *f*

boor *n* zotico *m*

boorish *adj* da zotico

boost I *n* spinta *f*; ***give a ~ to s.o.'s morale*** dare un incoraggiamento morale a qn **II** *v/t production, sales* incrementare; *confidence* aumentare

booster *n* MED (*a.* **booster shot**) richiamo *m*

boot[1] *n* stivale *m*; (*climbing boot*)

scarpone *m*; *for football* scarpetta *m*; *fig* ***the ~ is on the other foot*** la situazione si è capovolta; *fig* ***give s.o. the ~*** licenziare qn; *fig* ***put the ~ into s.o./sth*** *Br infml* accanirsi contro qn/qc
boot[2] *n Br of car* bagagliaio *m*
◆**boot out** *v/t sep infml* sbattere fuori *infml*
◆**boot up** *v/t sep & v/i* COMPUT inizializzare
boot camp *n US infml* MIL campo *m* addestramento reclute
bootee *n leather* stivaletto *m*; (*sleeper*) babbuccia *f*
booth *n at market, fair* bancarella *f*; (*telephone booth*) cabina *f*
bootlace *n* stringa *f*
bootleg I *adj whisky etc* di contrabbando **II** *n* MUS bootleg *m*
bootlicker *n infml pej* leccapiedi *m/f*
bootstraps *npl*: ***pull o.s. up by one's (own) ~*** *infml* farcela da solo
booty *n* bottino *m*
booze *infml* **I** *n* alcolici *mpl* **II** *v/i* bere alcolici
boozer *n infml* (*pub*) pub *m inv*; (*person*) beone *m*, -a *f infml*
booze-up *n infml* bevuta *f*
bop I *n* (*dance*) bebop *m*; ***give s.o. a ~ on the nose*** *infml* dare un pugno sul naso a qn **II** *v/i* ⟨*pret & past part* ***-ped***⟩ (*dance*) ballare (musica pop) **III** *v/t*: ***~ s.o. on the head*** *infml* dare un pugno sulla testa a qn
border I *n between countries* confine *m*; ***on the French ~*** al confine con la Francia; (*edge*) bordo *m* **II** *v/t country* confinare con
◆**border on** *v/i country* confinare con; (*be almost*) rasentare
border dispute *n* disputa *f* di confine
border guard *n* guardia *f* di confine
borderline *adj* al limite; ***a ~ case*** un caso limite
bore[1] **I** *v/t hole* praticare **II** *v/i* penetrare (***into*** in) **III** *n* calibro *m*; ***a 12 ~ shotgun*** un fucile calibro 12
bore[2] **I** *n* (*person*) persona *f* noiosa; ***it's such a ~*** è una seccatura **II** *v/t* annoiare; ***~ s.o. stiff*** *or* ***to tears*** *infml* annoiare qn a morte
bore[3] *pret* → ***bear***[2]
bored *adj* annoiato; ***I'm ~*** mi sto annoiando; ***be ~ stiff*** *infml* annoiarsi a morte
boredom *n* noia *f*
boring *adj* noioso
born *adj*: ***be ~*** essere nato; ***where were you ~?*** dove sei nato?; ***he was ~ into a rich family*** è nato in una famiglia ricca; ***be a ~ …*** essere un … nato
born-again *adj*: ***~ Christian*** cristiano rinato
borne *past part* → ***bear***[2]
borough *n* comune *m*; *in large city* distretto *m*
borrow *v/t* prendere in prestito; ***~ sth from s.o.*** prendere in prestito qc da qn
borrower *n of capital etc* chi prende in prestito
borrowing *n*: ***government ~*** prestito *m* di stato; ***~ requirements*** fabbisogno *m* (finanziario)
borstal *n Br* carcere *m* minorile
bosh *n infml* sciocchezza *f*
Bosnia-Herzegovina *n* Bosnia-Erzegovina *f*
Bosnian I *adj* bosniaco **II** *n* bosniaco *m*, -a *f*
bosom *n of woman* seno *m*; *fig* ***in the ~ of his family*** in seno alla sua famiglia
boss *n* capo *m*; *infml* boss *m inv*; ***his wife is the ~*** comanda sua moglie; ***OK, you're the ~*** va bene, il capo sei tu
◆**boss about** *v/t sep* dare ordini a
bossy *adj* (*+er*) prepotente
botanical *adj* botanico
botanic(al) gardens *npl* orto *m* botanico
botanist *n* botanico *m*, -a *f*
botany *n* botanica *f*
botch *v/t* fare un pasticcio con
both I *adj & pron* entrambi, tutti *mpl* e due, tutte *fpl* e due, tutt'e due; ***I know ~ (of the) brothers*** conosco tutt'e due i fratelli; ***~ (of the) brothers were there*** tutt'e due i fratelli erano lì; ***~ of them*** entrambi **II** *adv*: ***~ my mother and I*** sia mia madre che io; ***he's ~ handsome and intelligent*** è bello e intelligente; ***is it business or pleasure? – ~*** per piacere o per affari? – tutt'e due
bother I *v/t* (*disturb*) disturbare; ***I'm sorry to ~ you but …*** mi dispiace disturbarti/disturbarvi, ma…; ***she***

didn't even ~ to ask non si è neanche presa la briga di chiedere; (*worry*) preoccupare **II** *v/i*: ***don't ~*** (*you needn't do it*) non preoccuparti; ***you needn't have ~ed!*** non dovevi! **III** *n* disturbo *m*; ***it's no ~*** non c'è problema; ***I didn't have any ~ getting the visa*** non ho avuto alcuna difficoltà ad ottenere il visto; ***go to a lot of ~ to do sth*** prendersi il disturbo di fare qc; ***the children were no ~ at all*** i bambini non hanno dato alcun fastidio

bottle I *n* bottiglia *f*; *for baby* biberon *m inv* **II** *v/t* imbottigliare

◆**bottle out** *v/i sl* tirarsi indietro

◆**bottle up** *v/t sep feelings* reprimere

bottle bank *n* contenitore *m* per la raccolta del vetro

bottled water *n* acqua *f* in bottiglia

bottleneck *n* ingorgo *m*

bottle-opener *n* apribottiglie *m inv*

bottom I *n* **1.** fondo *m*; ***at the ~ of the garden*** in fondo al giardino; ***get to the ~ of sth*** andare fino in fondo a qc; ***from the ~ of my heart*** con tutto il mio cuore; ***at the ~ of the screen*** in basso sullo schermo; ***at the ~ of the page/street*** in fondo alla pagina/strada; ***she started at the ~ and she's a manager now*** ha cominciato dal basso e ora è dirigente; ***the ~ dropped*** *or* ***fell out of the market*** il mercato è affondato **2.** (*buttocks*) sedere *m* **3.** ***tracksuit ~s*** pantaloni *mpl* della tuta **4.** ***~ (gear)*** AUTO prima *f*; ***in ~ (gear)*** in prima **II** *adj* più basso

◆**bottom out** *v/i* toccare il fondo

bottomless *adj fig*: ***a ~ pit*** un pozzo senza fondo

bottom line *n* (*fig: financial outcome*) risultato *m* finanziario; ***the ~*** (*the real issue*) l'essenziale *m*

bough *n* ramo *m*

bought *pret & past part* → ***buy***

bouillon *n* brodo *m* ristretto

boulder *n* macigno *m*

boulevard *n* viale *m*

bounce I *v/t ball* far rimbalzare **II** *v/i of ball* rimbalzare; *on sofa etc* saltare; *of cheque* essere protestato; ***the child ~d up and down on the bed*** i bambini saltavano sul letto

◆**bounce back I** *v/i* COMPUT *e-mail* tornare indietro; *fig infml* rimettersi in piedi **II** *v/t* COMPUT *e-mail* far tornare indietro

◆**bounce off I** *v/t always sep*: ***bounce sth off sth*** far rimbalzare qc su qc; *fig* ***bounce an idea off s.o.*** *infml* confrontare un'idea con qn **II** *v/i* rimbalzare

bouncer *n* buttafuori *m inv*

bouncy *adj* (*+er*) *ball* che rimbalza bene; *chair* molleggiato; *person* dinamico

bound[1] *adj*: ***be ~ to do sth*** (*sure to*) dover fare per forza qc; (*obliged to*) essere obbligato a fare qc; ***the train is ~ to be late*** il treno sarà senz'altro in ritardo; ***but I'm ~ to say …*** *infml* ma devo dire che…

bound[2] *adj*: ***be ~ for*** *of ship* essere diretto a; ***all passengers ~ for London will …*** tutti i passeggeri diretti a londra devono…

bound[3] **I** *n* (*jump*) balzo *m*; *usu pl* limite *m*; ***within the ~s of probability*** entro i limiti delle possibilità; ***his ambition knows no ~s*** la sua ambizione non conosce limiti; ***the bar is out of ~s*** è vietato l'ingresso al bar **II** *v/i* saltellare; ***the dog came ~ing up*** il cane arrivò saltellando

bound[4] *pret & past part* → ***bind***

boundary *n* confine *m*

boundary line *n* linea *f* di demarcazione; SPORTS linea *f* del campo

boundless *adj* illimitato

bounds *npl* limiti *mpl*; ***out of ~*** ad accesso vietato

bountiful *adj* generoso; *harvest, gifts* ampio

bounty *n* generosità *f inv*

bouquet *n* bouquet *m inv*

bourbon *n* bourbon *m inv*

bourgeois I *n* borghese *m/f* **II** *adj* borghese

bourgeoisie *n* borghesia *f*

bout *n* MED attacco *m*; ***a ~ of fever*** un attacco di febbre; *in boxing* incontro *m*; ***a drinking ~*** un breve periodo di eccesso di alcol

boutique *n* boutique *f inv*

bovine spongiform encephalopathy *n* encefalite *f* spongiforme bovina

bow[1] **I** *n as greeting* inchino *m* **II** *v/i* inchinarsi **III** *v/t head* chinare

◆**bow down** *v/i* inchinarsi; *fig* ***bow down to*** *or* ***before s.o.*** *liter* sottomettersi qn

◆**bow out** *v/i fig* ritirarsi; ***bow out of sth*** ritirarsi da qc

bow[2] *n* (*knot*) fiocco *m*; MUS archetto *m*; ***a ~ and arrow*** arco e frecce

bow[3] *n of ship* prua *f*

bowed *adj legs* piegato

bowel *n usu pl* ANAT intestino *m*; ***~ movement*** *form* evacuazione *f*; *fig* ***the ~s of the earth*** le viscere della terra

bowl[1] *n* (*container*) bacinella *f*; *for soup*, *cereal* ciotola *f*; *for cooking*, *salad* terrina *f*; *plastic* contenitore *m* di plastica

bowl[2] **I** *n ball* boccia *f* **II** *v/i in bowling* lanciare

◆**bowl over** *v/t sep* (*fig*: *astonish*) strabiliare; ***he was bowled over by the news*** rimase esterrefatto per la notizia

bow-legged *adj* con le gambe storte

bowler *n* (*hat*) bombetta *f*; *in cricket* lanciatore *m*

bowling *n* bowling *m inv*

bowling alley *n* pista *f* da bowling **bowling green** *n* campo *m* da bocce

bowls *nsg* (*game*) bocce *fpl*

bow tie *n* papillon *m*

box[1] *n container* scatola *f*; *on form* casella *f*; ***on the ~*** *Br infml* alla TV

box[2] *v/i do boxing* fare pugilato; ***he ~ed well*** ha combattuto bene

box[3] *n* BOT bosso *m*; ***a ~ hedge*** una siepe di bosso

boxer *n* pugile *m*

boxer shorts *npl* boxer *mpl*

boxing *n* pugilato *m*, boxe *f inv*

Boxing Day *n Br* Santo Stefano

boxing glove *n* guantone *m* da pugile **boxing match** *n* incontro *m* di pugilato **boxing ring** *n* quadrato *m*, ring *m inv*

box number *n at post office* casella *f*

box office *n* botteghino *m*

boy *n child* bambino *m*; *youth* ragazzo *m*; *son* figlio *m*; *fellow* tipo *m*; ***the Jones ~*** il figlio dei Jones; ***the old ~*** il vecchio; ***~s will be ~s*** *prov* gli uomini sono tutti uguali

boy band *n* MUS boy-band *f*

boycott I *n* boicottaggio *m* **II** *v/t* boicottare

boyfriend *n* ragazzo *m*; fidanzato *m*

boyish *adj* da ragazzo

boyscout *n* boy-scout *m inv*

bpi *abbr* (= **bits per inch**) COMPUT bpi

bps, BPS *abbr* (= **bits per second**) COMPUT bps (bit al secondo)

bra *n* reggiseno *m*

brace I *n on teeth* apparecchio *m* (ai denti) **II** *v/r* tenersi forte; ***~ o.s. for sth*** tenersi forte in vista di qc; ***~ yourself, I've got bad news for you*** tieniti forte, ho brutte notizie

bracelet *n* braccialetto *m*

braces *npl* bretelle *fpl*

bracken *n* felce *f*

bracket I *n for shelf* staffa *f*; *in text* parentesi *f inv*; ***in ~s*** tra parentesi **II** *v/t* (*a.* **bracket together**) *fig* raggruppare

brackish *adj* salmastro

brag *v/i* ⟨*pret & past part* ***-ged***⟩ vantarsi

braggart *n* spaccone *m*, -a *f*

braid *n* (*trimming*) passamaneria *f*; *US* (*plait*) treccia *f*

braille *n* braille *m*

brain *n* cervello *m*; ***use your ~*** usa il cervello

brain dead *adj* MED cerebralmente morto

brainless *adj infml* deficiente

brains *npl* (*intelligence*) cervello *msg*

brainstorm *n Br* attacco *m* di follia

brainstorming *n* brainstorming *m inv*

brain surgeon *n* neurochirurgo *m* **brain surgery** *n* neurochirurgia *f* **brain tumour**, *US* **brain tumor** *n* tumore *m* al cervello **brainwash** *v/t* fare il lavaggio del cervello a; ***we've been ~ed into believing that …*** ci hanno fatto il lavaggio del cervello per convincerci che … **brainwave** *n* (*brilliant idea*) lampo *m* di genio

brainy *adj* (+*er*) *infml* geniale

braise *v/t* COOK brasare

brake I *n* freno *m* **II** *v/i* frenare

brake disc *n* disco *m* del freno **brake fluid** *n* AUTO liquido *m* dei freni **brake light** *n* AUTO fanalino *m* d'arresto **brake lining** *n* guarnizione *f* del freno **brake pedal** *n* AUTO pedale *m* del freno

braking distance *n* spazio *m* di frenata

bramble *n* (*bush*) rovo *m*; (*berry*) mora *f*

bran *n* crusca *f*

branch *n of tree* ramo *m*; *of bank*,

company filiale *f*
◆**branch off** *v/i of road* diramarsi
◆**branch out** *v/i* diversificarsi
branch line *n* RAIL diramazione *f* **branch manager** *n* direttore *m*, -trice *f* di filiale **branch office** *n* filiale *f*
brand I *n* marca *f* **II** *v/t goods* mettere il marchio a; *cattle* marchiare; (*stigmatize*) stigmatizzare; ***~ed goods*** prodotti *mpl* di marca; ***be ~ed a traitor*** essere tacciato di tradimento
brand image *n* brand image *f inv*
brandish *v/t* brandire
brand leader *n* marca *f* leader di mercato **brand loyalty** *n* fedeltà *f inv* alla marca **brand name** *n* marca *f*
brand-new *adj* nuovo di zecca
brandy *n* brandy *m inv*
brash *adj* (+*er*) *person* invadente; *look* chiassoso
brass *n* (*alloy*) ottone *m*; *infml* (*effrontery*) sfacciataggine *f*; *infml* (*high rank*) pezzi *mpl* grossi; ***the ~*** MUS gli ottoni; ***top ~*** gli alti ranghi
brass band *n* fanfara *f*
brassiere *n US* reggiseno *m*
brat *n pej* marmocchio *m*
bravado *n* spavalderia *f*
brave *adj* (+*er*) coraggioso
bravely *adv* coraggiosamente
bravery *n* coraggio *m*
bravo *int* bravo
brawl I *n* rissa *f* **II** *v/i* azzuffarsi
brawn *n* forza *f*; *Br* COOK *carne della testa del maiale bollita e pressata*; ***he's all ~ and no brains*** è tutto muscoli e niente cervello
brawny *adj* (+*er*) muscoloso
bray *v/i ass* ragliare
brazen *adj* di ottone; *lie* spudorato **brazenly** *adv* spudoratamente
Brazil *n* Brasile *m*
Brazilian I *adj* brasiliano **II** *n* brasiliano *m*, -a *f*
breach *n* (*violation*) violazione *f*; *in party* rottura *f*
breach of contract *n* JUR inadempienza *f* di contratto
bread *n* pane *m*; *fig* ***he knows which side his ~ is buttered (on)*** *infml* sa curare i suoi interessi; *fig* ***writing is his ~ and butter*** si guadagna da vivere scrivendo
bread bin, bread box *n US* portapane *m inv* **breadcrumbs** *npl for cooking* pane *msg* grattato; *for bird* briciole *fpl* **bread knife** *n* coltello *m* per il pane
breadline *n fig*: ***be on the ~*** essere ridotti all'indigenza
bread roll *n* panino *m* **breadstick** *n* grissino *m*
breadth *n* larghezza *f*; ***a hundred metres*** *Br or* ***meters*** *US* ***in ~*** cento metri di larghezza
breadwinner *n*: ***be the ~*** mantenere la famiglia
break I *v/t* ⟨*pret* ***broke***, *past part* ***broken***⟩ **1.** *china*, *egg*, *bone* rompere; ***~ one's arm*** rompersi il braccio **2.** *rules*, *law* violare; *promise* non mantenere **3.** *news* comunicare; ***how can I ~ it to her?*** come faccio a darle la notizia? **4.** *record* battere **5.** (*destroy*) *person* distruggere; *strike* soffocare; *code* decifrare; ***~ s.o. (financially)*** distruggere qn finanziariamente; ***37p, well, that won't exactly ~ the bank*** 37 penny non manderanno in rovina la banca; ***~ wind*** fare un peto **II** *v/i* ⟨*pret* ***broke***, *past part* ***broken***⟩ **1.** *of china*, *egg*, *toy* rompersi **2.** *of news* diffondersi **3.** *of storm* scoppiare **4.** *of boy's voice* cambiare; ***his voice is beginning to ~*** la sua voce comincia a cambiare **III** *n* **1.** *a. fig* rottura *f* **2.** (*rest*) pausa *f*; ***take a ~*** fare una pausa; ***without a ~*** *work*, *travel* senza sosta **3.** (*opportunity*) ***give s.o. a ~*** *infml* dare un'opportunità a qn; ***she had her first big ~ in a Broadway play*** ha avuto il suo primo grande successo a Broadway; ***lucky ~*** colpo di fortuna; ***at ~ of day*** al sorgere del sole; ***they made a ~ for it*** *infml* hanno tentato la fuga; ***~ in the weather*** schiarita *f*; ***give me a ~!*** *infml* fammi il favore!
◆**break away** *v/i* scappare; *from organization*, *tradition* staccarsi
◆**break down I** *v/i of vehicle*, *machine* avere un guasto; *of talks* arenarsi; *in tears* scoppiare in lacrime; (*mentally*) avere un esaurimento **II** *v/t sep door* buttare giù; *figures* analizzare
◆**break even** *v/i* COMM coprire le spese
◆**break in** *v/i* (*interrupt*) interrompere; *of burglar* entrare con la forza
◆**break into** *v/t house* entrare (scassi-

nando); *savings* intaccare; ***break into a car / a safe*** scassinare una macchina / una cassaforte; ***break into song*** mettersi a cantare
◆**break off I** *v/t sep* staccare; *engagement* rompere; ***they've broken it off*** si sono lasciati **II** *v/i* (*stop talking*) interrompersi
◆**break out** *v/i* (*start up*) scoppiare; *of prisoners* evadere; ***he broke out in a rash*** gli è venuta l'orticaria
◆**break up I** *v/t sep* (*into component parts*) scomporre; *fight* far cessare **II** *v/i of ice* spaccarsi; *of couple* separarsi; *of band, meeting* sciogliersi; *Br* EDU chiudere; ***you're breaking up*** *on mobile phone* non ti sento più; ***when do you break up?*** *school* quando finisci la scuola?
breakable *adj* fragile
breakage *n* danni *mpl*; ***pay for ~s*** pagare i danni
breakaway *adj group* dissidente
breakdancing *n* break dance *f*
breakdown *n of vehicle, machine* guasto *m*; *of talks* rottura *f*; (*nervous breakdown*) esaurimento *m* (nervoso); *of figures* analisi *f inv*
breakdown service *n* servizio *m* di soccorso stradale
breakdown truck *n* carro *m* attrezzi
breaker *n* (*wave*) frangente *m*; (*a.* **breaker's (yard)**) ***send a vehicle to the ~'s (yard)*** portare un veicolo allo sfasciacarrozze
break-even point *n* punto *m* di rottura di pareggio
breakfast *n* colazione *f*; ***have ~*** fare colazione
breakfast cereal *n* cereali *mpl* per la prima colazione **breakfast television** *n* programmi *mpl* televisivi del mattino
break-in *n* furto *m* (con scasso); ***we've had a ~*** abbiamo avuto un furto
breaking point *n*: *fig* ***she is at*** *or* ***has reached ~*** ha raggiunto il limite (della sopportazione)
breakneck *adj*: ***at ~ speed*** *Br* a rotta di collo
breakthrough *n in plan, negotiations* passo *m* avanti; *of science, technology* scoperta *f* **breakup** *n of marriage, partnership* rottura *f*
breakwater *n* frangiflutti *m*
breast *n of woman* seno *m*
breast augmentation ingrandimento *m* del seno
breastbone *n* sterno
breast cancer *n* cancro *m* della mammella
breasted *adj*: ***a double-/ single-~ jacket*** giacca *f* ad un petto / a doppio petto
breastfeed *v/t* ⟨*pret & past part* ***breastfed***⟩ allattare **breast-pocket** *n* taschino *m* **breaststroke** *n* nuoto *m* a rana
breath *n* respiro *m*; ***there wasn't a ~ of air*** non c'era un filo d'aria; ***be out of ~*** essere senza fiato; ***get one's ~ back*** riprendere fiato; ***say sth under one's ~*** dire qc sottovoce; ***you're wasting your ~*** stai sprecando il fiato; ***take a deep ~*** fai un respiro profondo; ***bad ~*** alito *m* cattivo
breathable *adj fabric, garment* traspirante
breathalyze *v/t* sottoporre ad alcoltest
breathalyzer® *n* alcoltest *m inv*
breathe *v/t & v/i* respirare; ***~ one's last*** esalare l'ultimo respiro; ***don't ~ a word of it!*** non fiatare!; ***now I can ~ again*** ora respiro di nuovo; ***be breathing down s.o.'s neck*** stare col fiato sul collo a qn
◆**breathe in I** *v/i* inspirare **II** *v/t sep* respirare
◆**breathe out** *v/i* espirare
breather *n infml* attimo *m* per riprendersi; ***take*** *or* ***have a ~*** prendersi una pausa
breathing *n* respiro *m*
breathing space *n fig* attimo *m* di respiro
breathless *adj* senza fiato; ***~ with excitement*** sopraffatto dalla gioia
breathlessness *n* fiato *m* corto
breathtaking *adj* mozzafiato
bred *pret & past part* → ***breed***
breeches *npl* pantaloni *mpl* alla zuava; (*riding breeches*) pantaloni *mpl* alla cavallerizza
breed I *v/t* ⟨*pret & past part* ***bred***⟩ allevare; *fig* generare **II** *v/i* ⟨*pret & past part* ***bred***⟩ *of animals* riprodursi **III** *n* razza *f*
breeder *n* allevatore *m*, -trice *f*
breeding *n* allevamento *m*; *of person* educazione *f*

breeding ground *n fig* terreno *m* fertile
breeze *n* brezza *f*
breeze-block *n Br* BUILD *mattoncino leggero fatto di calcestruzzo di scorie*
breezily *adv fig* con disinvoltura
breezy *adj* (+*er*) ventoso; *fig* brioso
breviary *n* breviario *m*
brevity *n* (*concision*) concisione *f*; (*shortness*) brevità *f inv*
brew I *v/t beer* produrre; *tea* fare **II** *v/i of storm* prepararsi; ***there's trouble ~ing*** ci sono guai in vista
brewer *n* produttore *m* di birra
brewery *n* fabbrica *f* di birra
bribe I *n* bustarella *f* **II** *v/t* corrompere; ***~ s.o. to do sth*** corrompere qn perché faccia qc
bribery *n* corruzione *f*
bric-a-brac *n* bric-à-brac *m inv*
brick *n* mattone *m*; *Br* (*toy*) costruzione *f*; ***he came*** *or* ***was down on me like a ton of ~s*** *infml* si è scagliato contro di me come una furia; ***box of*** (***building***) ***~s*** scatola *f* di costruzioni; ***he's a real ~*** è un brav'uomo
bricklayer *n* muratore *m*
brick red *adj* rosso mattone **brick wall** *n fig infml*: ***it's like banging one's head against a ~*** è come sbattere la testa contro un muro
brickwork *n* muratura *f*
brickyard *n* mattonificio *m*
bridal *adj* nuziale; ***~ gown*** abito *m* da sposa
bridal suite *n* suite *f inv* nuziale
bride *n* sposa *f*
bridegroom *n* sposo *m*
bridesmaid *n* damigella *f* d'onore
bridge[1] I *n* ponte *m*; *of ship* ponte *m* di comando; ***~ of the nose*** setto *m* nasale **II** *v/t gap* colmare
bridge[2] *n* (*card game*) bridge *m inv*
bridgehead *n* testa *f* di ponte
bridging loan *n* credito *m* ponte
bridle I *n* briglia *f* **II** *v/i* inalberarsi (***at*** per)
bridle path *n* pista *f* per cavalli
brief[1] *adj* (+*er*) breve; ***to be ~, …*** per farla breve, …
brief[2] I *n* (*mission*) missione *f*; (*sl: lawyer*) avvocato *m* **II** *v/t*: ***~ s.o. on sth*** *instruct* dare istruzioni a qn su qc; *inform* mettere qn al corrente di qc
briefcase *n* valigetta *f*
briefing *n* briefing *m inv*
briefly *adv* (*for a short period of time*) brevemente; (*in a few words, to sum up*) in breve
briefs *npl* slip *m inv*
brig *n* NAUT brigantino *m*
brigade *n* MIL brigata *f*
bright *adj* (+*er*) *colour* vivace; *smile, future* radioso; (*sunny*) luminoso; (*intelligent*) intelligente; ***~ and early*** di buon mattino; ***~ red*** rosso vivo
brighten *v/i of sky* schiarirsi; *of face* illuminarsi
◆**brighten up I** *v/t sep* ravvivare **II** *v/i of weather* schiarirsi; *of face, person* rallegrarsi
brightly *adv smile* in modo radioso; *shine, lit* intensamente; *coloured* in modo sgargiante
brightness *n* luminosità *f inv*
brill[1] *n* ZOOL rombo *m* liscio
brill[2] *adj Br infml* eccellente
brilliance *n of person* genialità *f inv*; *of colour* vivacità *f inv*
brilliant *adj sunshine etc* sfolgorante; (*very good*) eccezionale; ***he is ~ with children*** ci sa fare con i bambini; (*very intelligent*) brillante; ***~!*** fantastico!
brilliantine *n* brillantina *f*
brilliantly *adv shine, lit* vividamente; (*superbly*) in modo eccellente; *perform* brillantemente; *funny, simple* estremamente; ***~ coloured*** *Br or* ***colored*** *US* dai colori brillanti
brim I *n of container* orlo *m*; *of hat* falda *f* **II** *v/i* ⟨*pret & past part* ***-med***⟩: ***~ with sth*** *tears* traboccare di qc; *enthusiasm* essere pieno di qc
◆**brim over** *v/i* traboccare (***with*** di)
brimful *adj* colmo
brindled *adj* pezzato
brine I *n* acqua *f* salmastra; *for pickling* salamoia *f* **II** *v/t* mettere in salamoia
bring *v/t* ⟨*pret & past part* ***brought***⟩ **1.** portare; ***~ it here, will you*** portalo qui, per favore; ***can I ~ a friend?*** posso portare un amico? **2.** ***~ o.s. to do sth*** costringersi a fare qc
◆**bring about** *v/t sep* causare
◆**bring along** *v/t sep* portare con sé
◆**bring around** *v/t sep from a faint* far rinvenire; (*persuade*) convincere
◆**bring back** *v/t sep* (*return*) restitui-

re; (*re-introduce*) reintrodurre; *memories* risvegliare
◆**bring down** *v/t sep tree, government, aeroplane* abbattere; *rates, inflation, price* far scendere
◆**bring forward** *v/t sep event* anticipare; ***amount brought forward*** COMM totale *m* a riporto
◆**bring in** *v/t sep interest, income* rendere; *legislation* introdurre; *verdict* emettere; (*involve*) coinvolgere
◆**bring on** *v/t sep illness* provocare
◆**bring out** *v/t sep* (*produce*: *book*) pubblicare; *new product* lanciare; (*draw out*) *person* indurre ad aprirsi; ***bring out the best in s.o.*** tirar fuori il meglio di qn
◆**bring to** *v/t always sep from a faint* far rinvenire
◆**bring up** *v/t sep child* allevare; *subject* sollevare; (*vomit*) vomitare
bring-and-buy (sale) *n Br* vendita *f* di beneficenza
brink *n a. fig* orlo *m*; ***on the ~ of*** sull'orlo di
brink(s)manship *n* politica *f* del rischio calcolato
brisk *adj* (+*er*) *person, tone* spiccio; *walk* svelto; *trade* vivace
brisket *n* COOK punta *f* di petto
bristle **I** *n* pelo *m*; setola *f* **II** *v/i* (*person*) adirarsi; ***~ with anger*** reagire con rabbia
bristling *adj*: ***be ~ with*** brulicare di
bristly *adj* (+*er*) *chin* irsuto; *hair, beard* ispido
Brit *n infml* britannico *m*, -a *f*
Britain *n* Gran Bretagna *f*
British **I** *adj* britannico **II** *n*: ***the ~*** i britannici
British Isles *npl* Isole *fpl* Britanniche
Briton *n* britannico *m*, -a *f*
brittle **I** *adj* fragile; ***~ bones*** MED osteoporosi *f* **II** *n*: ***peanut ~*** COOK croccante *m* di arachidi
broach *v/t subject* affrontare
broad **I** *adj* (+*er*) largo; (*general*) generale; ***in ~ daylight*** in pieno giorno **II** *n US pej* donna *f*
B-road *n Br* strada *f* secondaria
broadband COMPUT **I** *adj* a banda larga **II** *n* banda *f* larga
broad bean *n* fava *f*
broadcast **I** *n* trasmissione *f* **II** *v/t* ⟨*pret & past part* ***-cast***⟩ trasmettere
broadcaster *n* giornalista *m/f* radiotelevisivo, -a
broadcasting *n* diffusione *f* radiotelevisiva; ***work in ~*** lavorare nel settore radiotelevisivo
broaden **I** *v/i* allargarsi **II** *v/t* allargare
broadly *adv*: ***~ speaking*** parlando in senso lato
broadminded *adj* di larghe vedute
broadmindedness *n* larghezza *f* di vedute
broadsheet *n* giornale *m* di grande formato
broadside *n* aspra critica *f*
broad-spectrum *adj* ad ampio spettro; ***~ drug*** farmaco *m* ad ampio spettro
brocade *n* broccato *m*
broccoli *n* broccoli *mpl*
brochure *n* dépliant *m inv*, opuscolo *m*
broderie anglaise *n* ricamo *m* a punto inglese
brogue[1] *n accento dialettale tipico degli irlandesi*
brogue[2] *n scarpa da uomo da passeggio*
broil *v/t US* cuocere alla griglia
broke **I** *adj* al verde; ***go ~*** (*go bankrupt*) andare sul lastrico **II** *pret* → ***break***
broken **I** *adj* rotto; *English* stentato; *marriage* fallito; ***she's from a ~ home*** i suoi sono separati **II** *past part* → ***break***
broken-down *adj* a pezzi
broken-hearted *adj* col cuore spezzato
broker *n* mediatore *m*, -trice *f*
brokerage *n* FIN mediazione *f*
brolly *n infml* ombrello *m*
bronchitis *n* bronchite *f*
bronze *n* bronzo *m*
Bronze Age *n* età *f inv* del bronzo
bronzed *adj face, person* abbronzato
brooch *n* spilla *f*
brood **I** *v/i of person* rimuginare; ***~ on*** *or* ***over*** *or* ***about sth*** rimuginare su qc **II** *n* nidiata *f*; ***the mother hen and her ~*** la chioccia con la sua nidiata
◆**brood over** *or* **(up)on** *v/i +obj* rimuginare
brood mare *n* cavalla *f* da monta
broody *adj person* pensieroso; (*sad,*

moody) malinconico; ***be feeling ~*** *infml hum* desiderare un figlio
brook *n* ruscello *m*
broom *n* scopa *f*
broomstick *n* manico *m* di scopa; ***a witch on her ~*** una strega sulla scopa
Bros *abbr* (= **Brothers**) F.lli (fratelli)
broth *n* (*soup*) minestra *f*; (*stock*) brodo *m*
brothel *n* bordello *m*
brother *n* fratello *m*; ***they're ~s*** sono fratelli; ***~s and sisters*** fratelli e sorelle; ***the Clarke ~s*** i fratelli Clarke; ***his ~ officers*** i suoi colleghi ufficiali; ***lay ~*** REL converso *m*; ***oh ~!*** *esp US infml* caspita!
brother-in-law *n* ⟨*pl* ***brothers-in-law***⟩ cognato *m*
brotherly *adj* fraterno
brought *pret & past part* → ***bring***
brow *n* (*forehead*) fronte *f*; *of hill* cima *f*
browbeat *v/t* ⟨*pret* ***browbeat***, *past part* ***browbeaten***⟩ intimidire; ***~ s.o. into doing sth*** costringere qn a fare qc
brown I *adj* (*+er*) marrone; *eyes, hair* castano; (*tanned*) abbronzato **II** *n* marrone *m*; ***dressed in ~*** vestito di marrone **III** *v/t in cooking* rosolare **IV** *v/i in cooking* rosolarsi
◆**brown off** *v/t*: ***be browned off with s.o. / sth*** *esp Br infml* essere stufo di qn / qc
brown ale *n* birra *f* scura **brown bread** *n* pane *m* integrale
brownie *n elf* folletto *m*; COOK *torta di cioccolato con nocciole*
Brownie *n* giovane esploratrice *f*
brownie points *npl*: ***score ~ with s.o.*** guadagnare punti con qn
brown-nose *v/t infml* arruffianarsi; ***he ~d his way to power*** si è fatto strada arruffianandosi **brown paper** *n* carta *f* da pacchi **brown paper bag** *n* sacchetto *m* di carta **brown rice** *n* riso *m* integrale **brown sugar** *n* zucchero *m* non raffinato; *drug* eroina *f*
browse I *v/i in shop* curiosare; ***~ through a book*** sfogliare un libro **II** *n*: ***have a ~ through the books*** dare una scorsa ai libri
browser *n* COMPUT browser *m inv*
bruise I *n* livido *m*; *on fruit* ammaccatura *f* **II** *v/t person* fare un livido a; *fruit* ammaccare **III** *v/i of person* coprirsi di lividi; *of fruit* ammaccarsi
bruiser *n infml* omaccione *m*
bruising *adj fig* doloroso
brunch *n* brunch *m inv*
brunette *n* brunetta *f*
brunt *n*: ***bear the ... of ...*** subire il peggio di ...
brush I *n* spazzola *f*; (*paintbrush*) pennello *m*; (*toothbrush*) spazzolino *m* da denti; (*conflict*) scontro *m* **II** *v/t* spazzolare; (*touch lightly*) sfiorare; (*move away*) spostare; ***~ your teeth*** lavati i denti
◆**brush against** *v/t* sfiorare
◆**brush aside** *v/t sep* ignorare
◆**brush off** *v/t sep* spazzolare via; *criticism* ignorare
◆**brush up** *v/t sep* ripassare
brushoff *n*: ***give s.o. the ~*** *infml* rispondere picche a qn *infml*
brushwork *n* PAINT pennellata *f*
brusque *adj* brusco
Brussels *n* Bruxelles *f*
Brussels sprout *n* cavolino *m* di Bruxelles
brutal *adj* brutale
brutality *n* brutalità *f inv*
brutalize *v/t* brutalizzare
brutally *adv* brutalmente
brute *n* bruto *m*
brute force *n* forza *f* bruta
BSc *abbr* (= **Bachelor of Science**) (*degree*) *laurea in discipline scientifiche*; (*person*) *laureato in discipline scientifiche*
BSE *abbr* (= **bovine spongiform encephalopathy**) BSE
BST *abbr* (= **British Summer Time**) ora *f* legale britannica
BT *abbr* (= **British Telecom**) *società telefonica britannica*
bub *n US as a term of address* figliolo *m*
bubble I *n* bolla *f*; *fig* ***the ~ has burst*** è finita la pacchia **II** *v/i form bubbles* fare le bollicine; ***~ over with*** *excitement, enthusiasm* traboccare di
bubble bath *n* bagnoschiuma *m inv*
bubble gum *n* gomma *f* da masticare
bubble jet printer *n* COMPUT stampante *f* a getto d'inchiostro **bubble wrap** *n* involucro *m* a bolle
bubbly *n infml* (*champagne*) champagne *m inv*
buccaneer *n* bucaniere *m*

Bucharest *n* Bucarest *f*
buck[1] *n US infml* (*dollar*) dollaro *m*; ZOOL maschio *m*; ***make a ~*** fare soldi; ***make a fast*** *or* ***quick ~*** fare soldi alla svelta
buck[2] **I** *v/i of horse* sgroppare **II** *v/t*: ***you can't ~ the market*** non puoi andare contro il mercato; ***~ the trend*** opporsi alla tendenza
◆**buck up** *infml* **I** *v/i* (*hurry up*) sbrigarsi; (*cheer up*) rincuorarsi; ***buck up!*** coraggio! **II** *v/t sep* (*make cheerful*) fare coraggio a; ***buck one's ideas up*** *infml* mettere la testa a posto
buck[3] *n*: ***pass the ~*** scaricare la responsabilità
bucket **I** *n* secchio *m* **II** *v/i Br infml*: ***it's ~ing (down)!*** piove a catinelle
bucketful *n* secchiata *f*; *fig* ***by the ~*** *infml* a catinelle
bucket shop *n agenzia di viaggi che pratica forti sconti*
buckle[1] **I** *n* fibbia *f* **II** *v/t belt* allacciare
buckle[2] *v/i of wood, metal* piegarsi
◆**buckle down** *v/i* mettersi a lavorare
buckskin *n* pelle *f* di daino
buck tooth *n* ⟨*pl* ***buck teeth***⟩ dente *m* (incisivo) sporgente; *adj* **buck-toothed** con i denti sporgenti
buckwheat *n* grano *m* saraceno
bud *n* BOT bocciolo *m*; ***be in ~*** essere in boccio
Buddha *n* Budda *m*
Buddhism *n* buddismo *m*
Buddhist **I** *adj* buddista **II** *n* buddista *m/f*
budding *adj* emergente
buddy *n infml* amico *m*, -a *f*
budge **I** *v/t* smuovere; ***~ up*** *or* ***over!*** fatti più in là!; (*make reconsider*) far cambiare idea a; ***I will not ~ an inch*** non mi smuovo di un millimetro **II** *v/i* muoversi; (*change one's mind*) cambiare idea
budgerigar *n* pappagallino *m*
budget **I** *n* budget *m inv*; *of company* bilancio *m* preventivo; *of state* bilancio *m* dello Stato; ***I'm on a ~*** devo stare attento ai soldi **II** *v/i* prevedere le spese
◆**budget for** *v/t* preventivare
budget account *n* conto *m* di credito **budget deficit** *n* deficit *m inv* di budget
budgie *n infml* pappagallino *m*
buff[1] *adj* (*colour*) beige *inv*
buff[2] *n* appassionato *m*, -a *f*; ***a movie ~*** un patito di cinema
buff[3] *v/t* lucidare
buffalo *n* bufalo *m*
buffer *n* RAIL respingente *m*; COMPUT buffer *m inv*; *fig* cuscinetto *m*
buffet[1] *n* (*meal*) buffet *m inv*
buffet[2] *v/t of wind* sballottare
buffet car *n Br* carrozza *f* ristorante
bug **I** *n* (*insect*) insetto *m*; (*virus*) virus *m inv*; (*spying device*) microspia *f*; COMPUT bug *m inv*; ***there must be a ~ going about*** deve esserci un virus in giro; ***she's got the travel ~*** *infml* ha il pallino dei viaggi **II** *v/t* ⟨*pret & past part* ***-ged***⟩ *room* installare microspie in; *telephone* mettere sotto controllo; *infml* (*annoy*) seccare; ***this room is ~ged*** questa stanza è sotto controllo
bugbear *n* spauracchio *m*
bugger *Br vulg* **I** *n* stronzo *m*, -a *f*; ***you lucky ~!*** *vulg* che culo che hai! *vulg* **II** *int* merda **III** *v/t*: ***~ it!*** vaffanculo! *vulg*
◆**bugger about, bugger around** *Br infml* **I** *v/i* (*laze about etc*) perdere tempo; ***bugger about*** *or* ***around with sth*** perdere tempo con qc **II** *v/t sep* importunare
◆**bugger off** *v/i Br vulg* andarsene; ***bugger off!*** levati dai coglioni!
bugger all *n Br vulg* un bel niente
buggered *adj Br vulg* scassato; ***I'm ~!*** *vulg expressing surprise* cazzo! *vulg*
buggery *n Br* JUR rapporto *m* anale
buggy *n for baby* passeggino *m*
bugle *n* tromba *f*
build **I** *v/t* ⟨*pret & past part* ***built***⟩ costruire **II** *n of person* corporatura *f*
◆**build on** *v/t sep* (*develop*) sviluppare
◆**build up** **I** *v/t sep relationship* consolidare; *collection* mettere insieme **II** *v/i of tension, traffic* aumentare; ***build up one's strength*** rimettersi in forze
builder *n person* muratore *m*; *company* impresario *m* edile
building *n* edificio *m*, palazzo *m*; (*activity*) costruzione *f*
building blocks *npl for child* mattoncini *mpl* **building contractor** *n* imprenditore *m*, -trice *f* edile **building materials** *npl* materiali *mpl* da co-

struzione **building site** *n* cantiere *m* edile **building society** *n Br istituto di credito immobiliare* **building trade** *n* edilizia *f*

build-up *n of traffic, pressure* aumento *m*; *of arms, forces* ammassamento *m*; (*publicity*) pubblicità *f inv*

built *pret & past part* → ***build***

built-in *adj wardrobe* a muro; *flash* incorporato

built-up area *n* abitato *m*

bulb *n* BOT bulbo *m*; (*light bulb*) lampadina *f*

bulbous *adj plant* bulboso; (*bulb-shaped*) *growth* a bulbo; ***~ nose*** naso *m* a patata

bulge I *n* rigonfiamento *m* **II** *v/i* sporgere

bulging *adj stomach* prominente; *pocket* rigonfio

bulimia *n* bulimia *f*

bulimic *adj* bulimico

bulk *n* grosso *m*; ***the ~ of*** il grosso di; ***in ~*** in grande quantità; *wholesale* all'ingrosso

bulky *adj* (*+er*) voluminoso

bull *n* toro *m*; *infml* (*nonsense*) fandonie *fpl*; (*papal edict*) bolla *f*; ***like a ~ in a china shop*** come un elefante in un negozio di porcellane; ***take the ~ by the horns*** prendere il toro per le corna

bulldog *n* bulldog *m inv*

bulldoze *v/t* (*demolish*) abbattere con il bulldozer; *fig* ***~ s.o. into sth*** costringere qn a fare qc

bulldozer *n* bulldozer *m inv*

bullet *n* proiettile *m*, pallottola *f*; ***bite the ~*** *infml* ingoiare il rospo

bulletin *n* bollettino *m*

bulletin board *n* COMPUT bulletin board *m inv*; *US*: *on wall* bacheca *f*

bullet-proof *adj* antiproiettile

bullion *n*: ***gold ~*** oro *m* in lingotti

bullish *adj*: ***be ~ about sth*** essere ottimista su qc

bull market *n* FIN mercato *m* in ascesa

bullock *n* manzo *m*

bullring *n* arena *f*

bull's-eye *n* centro *m* del bersaglio; ***hit the ~*** fare centro

bullshit I *n vulg* stronzate *fpl vulg* **II** *v/i* ⟨*pret & past part* ***-ted***⟩ *vulg* dire stronzate *vulg* **III** *v/t*: ***~ s.o.*** raccontare stronzate a qn

bully I *n* prepotente *m/f* **II** *v/t* ⟨*pret & past part* ***-ied***⟩ tiranneggiare

bullying *n* prepotenze *fpl*

bulrush *n* giunco *m* di palude

bulwark *n* baluardo *m*

bum I *n infml worthless person* mezza calzetta *f infml*; (*Br: bottom*) sedere *m*; (*US: tramp*) barbone *m* **II** *adj infml* (*useless*) del piffero **III** *v/t* ⟨*pret & past part* ***-med***⟩ *infml cigarette etc* scroccare; ***could I ~ a lift into town?*** posso scroccare un passaggio in città?

◆**bum around, bum about** *v/i infml* (*travel*) vagabondare; (*be lazy*) oziare

bumbag *n US infml* marsupio *m*

bumblebee *n* bombo *m*

bumbling *adj* (*clumsy*) maldestro; ***some ~ idiot*** qualche inetto

bummer *n infml*: ***what a ~!*** che seccatura!

bump I *v/t* battere; ***~ one's car*** andare a sbattere con la macchina; ***~ one's head on the cupboard*** urtare la testa contro il mobile **II** *n* (*swelling*) gonfiore *m*; (*lump*) bernoccolo *m*; *on road* cunetta *f*; ***get a ~ on the head*** prendere un colpo in testa

◆**bump into** *v/t table* battere contro; (*meet*) incontrare

◆**bump off** *v/t sep infml* (*murder*) far fuori *infml*

◆**bump up** *v/t sep infml* (*prices*) aumentare

bumper I *n* AUTO paraurti *m inv*; ***the traffic was ~ to ~*** c'era una coda di macchine **II** *adj* (*extremely good*) eccezionale

bumph *n Br infml* scartoffie *fpl*

bumpkin *n* (*a.* **country bumpkin**) sempliciotto *m*, -a *f* (di campagna)

bump-start *v/t car* mettere in moto a spinte; (*fig: economy*) dare una spinta a

bumptious *adj* borioso

bumpy *adj* (*+er*) *road* accidentato; *flight* movimentato

bun *n hairstyle* chignon *m inv*; *for eating* panino *m* dolce; ***~s*** *pl infml* chiappe *fpl infml*

bunch *n of people* gruppo *m*; *of keys, flowers* mazzo *m*; ***a ~ of grapes*** un grappolo d'uva; ***the best of the ~*** il migliore di tutti; ***thanks a ~*** *US infml iron* grazie mille

bundle I *n of clothes* fagotto *m*; *of*

wood fascina *f*; ***a ~ of nerves*** tesissimo **II** *v/t* (*tie in a bundle*) raggruppare; ***~d software*** COMPUT software *m* in bundle

◆**bundle off** *v/t sep person* spedire difilato

◆**bundle up** *v/t sep* fare un fagotto di; (*dress warmly*) coprire bene

bun fight *n Br infml festa formale per occasioni importanti*

bung *Br* **I** *n of cask* zipolo *m* **II** *v/t infml* buttare

◆**bung up** *v/t sep infml pipe* intasare; ***I'm all bunged up*** *cold* sono tutto intasato

bungalow *n* bungalow *m inv*

bungee jumping *n* salto *m* con l'elastico

bungle *v/t* pasticciare

bunion *n* infiammazione *f* dell'alluce

bunk *n* cuccetta *f*; ***do a ~*** *Br infml* sparire

bunk beds *npl* letti *mpl* a castello

bunker *n* MIL bunker *m*

bunkum *n infml* sciocchezze *fpl*

bunny *n infml* coniglio *m*

bunting *n* bandierine *fpl*; ZOOL migliarino *m*

buoy *n* NAUT boa *f*

◆**buoy up** *v/t sep* FIN tenere alto; *s.o.'s hopes* incoraggiare

buoyant *adj ship* capace di galleggiare; *fig mood* allegro; *fig economy* sostenuto

BUPA *abbr* (= **British United Provident Association**) *associazione britannica di previdenza*

bur *n* → **burr**

burble *v/i stream* gorgogliare; *person* borbottare; ***what's he burbling*** (***on***) ***about?*** di cosa sta cianciando?

burden **I** *n a. fig* peso *m*; ***be a ~ to s.o.*** essere di peso a qn **II** *v/t*: *fig* ***~ s.o. with sth*** opprimere qn con qc

bureau *n* (*office*) ufficio *m*

bureaucracy *n* burocrazia *f*

bureaucrat *n* burocrate *m/f*

bureaucratic *adj* burocratico

bureau de change *n* agenzia *f* di cambio

burgeoning *adj industry*, *market* fiorente; *career* in ascesa; *demand* in crescita

burger *n* hamburger *m inv*

burgher *n* cittadino *m*, -a *f*

burglar *n* ladro *m*

burglar alarm *n* antifurto *m*

burglarize *v/t US* svaligiare

burglary *n* furto *m* (con scasso)

burgle *v/t* svaligiare

burial *n* sepoltura *f*

burial ground *n* cimitero *m*

burlap *n* tela *f* da imballaggio

burlesque *n* THEAT farsa *f*

burly *adj* (+*er*) robusto

Burma *n* Birmania *f*

burn **I** *v/t* ⟨*pret & past part* **burnt**⟩ bruciare; *of sun* scottare; COMPUT, *CD*, *DVD* masterizzare; ***~ one's fingers*** restare scottato; *fig* ***~ one's bridges*** *Br* bruciarsi i ponti alle spalle **II** *v/i* ⟨*pret & past part* **burnt**⟩ ardere; *of house* bruciare; *of toast* bruciarsi; (*get sunburnt*) scottarsi, bruciarsi; ***~ to death*** morire carbonizzato **III** *n* bruciatura *f*; *superficial* scottatura *f*; *very serious* ustione *f*

◆**burn down** **I** *v/t sep* dare alle fiamme **II** *v/i* essere distrutto dal fuoco

◆**burn out** *v/t sep*: ***burn o.s. out*** esaurirsi; ***a burned-out car*** un'auto bruciata

◆**burn up** *v/t sep fuel*, *energy* bruciare

burner *n* fornello *m*

burnt *pret & past part* → **burn**

burp **I** *v/i* ruttare **II** *v/t baby* far fare il ruttino a **III** *n* rutto *m*

burr *n* BOT cardo *m*; *Br* LING *pronuncia arrotata della r*; (*whirr*) ronzio *m*

burrow **I** *n* tana *f* **II** *v/i* scavare

bursary *n Br* borsa *f* di studio

burst **I** *v/t* ⟨*pret & past part* **burst**⟩ *balloon* far scoppiare; ***the river has ~ its banks*** il fiume ha rotto gli argini **II** *v/i* ⟨*pret & past part* **burst**⟩ **1.** *of balloon*, *tyre* scoppiare; *fig* ***~ out laughing*** scoppiare a ridere **2.** ***~ into flames*** incendiarsi; ***~ into tears*** scoppiare in lacrime **3.** ***~ into a room*** irrompere in una stanza **III** *n in water pipe* rottura *f*; *of gunfire* raffica *f*; ***a ~ of energy*** un'esplosione d'energia; ***a ~ of applause*** uno scroscio d'applausi **IV** *adj tyre* bucato

◆**burst out** *v/i*: ***burst out laughing*/*crying*** scoppiare a ridere / piangere

bursting *adj*: ***be ~ with*** *full of* scoppiare di; ***be ~ to*** *keen to* morire dalla voglia di

bury *v/t* ⟨*pret & past part* **-ied**⟩ seppellire; *hide* nascondere; **~ *o.s. in work*** immergersi nel lavoro; *fig* ***that's all dead and buried*** è morto e sepolto; *fig* **~ *one's head in the sand*** nascondere la testa sotto la sabbia

bus I *n* (*local*) autobus *m inv*; (*long distance*) pullman *m inv* **II** *v/t* ⟨*pret & past part* **-sed**⟩ trasportare in autobus

bus conductor *n* bigliettaio *m*, -a *f*

bus driver *n* autista *m/f* di autobus

bush *n* (*plant*) cespuglio *m*; (*land*) boscaglia *f*; *in Africa, Australia* savana *f*; ***beat around the ~*** *infml* menare il can per l'aia

bushed *adj infml* (*tired*) distrutto

bushel *n unit of capacity* bushel *m*

bushfire *n* incendio *m* boschivo

bush telegraph *n fig* voce *f*, diceria *f*

bushy *adj* (+*er*) *eyebrows* irsuto; **~ *tailed*** dalla coda folta

business *n* **1.** (*trade*) affari *mpl*; (*company*) impresa *f*; (*work*) lavoro *m*; ***in the insurance ~*** (*sector*) nel campo delle assicurazioni; ***on ~*** per affari; ***do ~*** fare affari; ***go out of ~*** ritirarsi dagli affari **2.** (*affair, matter*) faccenda *f*; ***that's none of your ~!, mind your own ~!*** fatti gli affari tuoi!; ***make it one's ~ to do sth*** assumersi il compito di fare qc; *fig* ***mean ~*** *infml* fare sul serio **3.** (*as subject of study*) economia *f* aziendale

business address *n* indirizzo *m* dell'ufficio **business associate** *n* socio *m*, -a *f* in affari **business card** *n* biglietto *m* da visita (della ditta) **business class** *n* business class *f inv* **business expenses** *npl* spese *fpl* di esercizio **business hours** *npl* orario *msg* di apertura **businesslike** *adj* efficiente **business lunch** *n* pranzo *m* d'affari **businessman** *n* uomo *m* d'affari **business meeting** *n* riunione *f* d'affari **business park** *n* centro *m* d'affari **business proposition** *n* proposta *f* commerciale **business school** *n* istituto *m* commerciale **business sector** *n* settore *m* aziendale **business sense** *n* senso *m* degli affari **business studies** *nsg* (*course*) economia *f* aziendale **business suit** *n da uomo* completo *m*; *da donna* tailleur *m inv* **business trip** *n* viaggio *m* d'affari **businesswoman** *n* donna *f* d'affari

busk *v/i* esibirsi per strada

busker *n* musicista *m/f* ambulante

bus lane *n* corsia *f* riservata (ai mezzi pubblici) **busload** *n*: ***a ~ of children*** un autobus pieno di bambini **bus pass** *n* tessera *f* dell'autobus **bus route** *n* tratta *f* dell'autobus **bus service** *n* servizio *m* di autobus **bus shelter** *n* pensilina *f* (dell'autobus) **bus station** *n* autostazione *f* **bus stop** *n* fermata *f* dell'autobus

bust[1] *n* ANAT petto *m*; **~ *measurement*** SEW circonferenza *f* del torace

bust[2] **I** *adj infml* (*broken*) scassato; ***go ~*** fallire **II** *v/t* scassare

bus ticket *n* biglietto *m* dell'autobus

bustle *n* andirivieni *m inv* (**of** di)

◆**bustle about** *v/i* affaccendarsi; ***the marketplace was bustling with activity*** il mercato era brulicante di attività

bust-up *n infml* rottura *f*; ***they had a ~*** *couple, friends* hanno rotto

busty *adj* prosperoso

busy I *adj* (+*er*) **1.** occupato; ***be ~ doing sth*** essere occupato a fare qc; ***I'm ~ talking to Gran*** sto parlando con la nonna; ***I'm ~ on Wednesday*** sono impegnato mercoledì **2.** *day* intenso **3.** *street* animato; *shop, restaurant* affollato **4.** TEL occupato **II** *v/t* ⟨*pret & past part* **-ied**⟩: **~ *o.s. with*** tenersi occupato con

busybody *n* impiccione *m*, -a *f*

busy signal *n US* segnale *m* di occupato

but *unstressed* **I** *cj* ma; **~ *then*** (***again***) d'altra parte **II** *prep*: ***all ~ him*** tutti tranne lui; ***the last ~ one*** il penultimo; ***the next ~ one*** il secondo; **~ *for you*** se non fosse per te; ***nothing ~ the best*** solo il meglio

butch *adj infml* mascolino; ***the short hair makes her look a bit ~*** con i capelli corti ha un aspetto mascolino

butcher *n* macellaio *m*, -a *f*

butcher's *n* macelleria *f*; ***at the ~*** in macelleria

butchery *n* (*slaughter*) carneficina *f*

butler *n* maggiordomo *m*

butt I *n of cigarette* mozzicone *m*; *of joke* bersaglio *m*; *US sl* (*backside*) culo *m sl*; *fig* ***she's always the ~ of his jokes*** è sempre il bersaglio dei suoi scherzi; ***get up off your ~*** *US sl* alza il culo *vulg* **II** *v/t* dare una testata a; *of goat, bull* dare una cornata a

◆**butt in** *v/i* interrompere; ***butt in on s.o. / sth*** interrompere qn / qc

butter I *n* burro *m*; ***she looks as if ~ wouldn't melt in her mouth*** fa l'ingenua **II** *v/t* imburrare; *fig* ***he knows which side his bread is ~ed on*** sa fare i propri interessi

◆**butter up** *v/t sep infml* arruffianarsi *infml*

buttercup *n* ranuncolo *m* **butter dish** *n* portaburro *m*

butterfly *n a. swimming* farfalla *f*; ***have butterflies in one's stomach*** essere molto agitato

butterfly valve *n* valvola *f* a farfalla

buttermilk *n* latticello *m*

butterscotch *adj tipo di caramella*

buttocks *npl* natiche *fpl*

button I *n* bottone *m*; *on machine* pulsante *m* **II** *v/t* abbottonare

◆**button up** *v/t sep* → ***button***

buttonhole I *n in suit* occhiello *m* **II** *v/t* attaccare un bottone a

button mushroom *n* champignon *m*

buttress *n* contrafforte *m*

butty *n Br* tramezzino *m*

buxom *adj* formoso

buy I *v/t* ⟨*pret & past part* **bought**⟩ **1.** (*purchase*) comprare; ***~ sth from s.o.*** comprare qc da qn; ***can I ~ you a drink?*** posso offrirti da bere?; ***£5 doesn't ~ much*** con 5 sterline non si compra granché **2.** (*believe*) bere; ***I don't ~ that*** non la bevo **II** *n* acquisto *m*

◆**buy in** *v/t sep Br* comprare in blocco

◆**buy off** *v/t sep* (*bribe*) comprare

◆**buy out** *v/t sep* COMM rilevare

◆**buy up** *v/t sep* accaparrarsi

buyer *n* acquirente *m/f*; *for department store, supermarket* buyer *m inv*

buyout *n* rilevamento *m*

buzz I *n* ronzio *m*; *infml* (*thrill*) emozione *f*; *infml* (*phone call*) squillo *m*; ***I get a ~ out of*** mi piace da morire; ***give s.o. a ~*** fare uno squillo a qc **II** *v/i of insect* ronzare; *with buzzer* suonare **III** *v/t with buzzer* chiamare

◆**buzz off** *v/i infml* levarsi di torno *infml*

buzzard *n* poiana *f*

buzzer *n* cicalino *m*

buzzword *n* parola *f* di moda

by I *prep* **1.** *agency* da **2.** (*near, next to*) vicino a, accanto a; ***side ~ side*** fianco a fianco **3.** (*no later than*) entro, per; ***can you do it ~ tomorrow?*** puoi farlo per domani? **4.** (*past*) davanti a; ***as we drove ~ the church*** mentre passavamo davanti alla chiesa **5.** (*mode of transport*) in; ***~ bus / train*** in autobus / treno **6.** *time*: ***~ day / night*** di giorno / notte; ***~ a couple of minutes*** per pochi minuti; ***~ this time tomorrow*** domani a quest'ora; ***be here ~ 4.30*** sii qui per le 4.30 **7.** ***~ my watch*** secondo il mio orologio **8.** *agent*: ***a book ~ ...*** un libro di ...; ***murdered ~ her husband*** assassinata dal marito; ***~ o.s.*** da solo **9.** *method, manner*: ***~ doing sth*** facendo qc; ***pay ~ cheque*** pagare con un assegno ***~ the hour / ton*** a ore / tonnellate; ***divide / multiply ~*** dividere / moltiplicare per; ***2 ~ 4*** (*measurement*) 2 per 4 **10.** ***~ and large*** nel complesso **II** *adv*: ***~ and ~*** (*soon*) tra breve

bye(-bye) *int* ciao

by-election *n elezione straordinaria di un parlamentare*

Byelorussia *n* Bielorussia *f*

bygone I *n*: ***let ~s be ~s*** metterci una pietra sopra **II** *adj*: ***in ~ days*** nei giorni andati

by-law *n* ordinanza *f* locale**by-line** *n* PRESS firma *f*

bypass I *n* (*road*) circonvallazione *f*; MED bypass *m inv* **II** *v/t* aggirare

by-product *n* sottoprodotto *m* **by-road** *n* strada *f* secondaria

bystander *n* astante *m/f*

byte *n* byte *m inv*

byway *n* strada *f* poco frequentata

byword *n*: ***be a ~ for*** essere sinonimo di

Byzantine *adj* bizantino

Byzantium *n* Bisanzio *f*

C

C, c c, C *f inv*; MUS do *m inv*; EDU (*mark*) più che sufficiente *m*; ***C sharp*** do *m inv* diesis; ***C flat*** do *m inv* bemolle
c, c. *abbr* **1.** (*a.* **C** = **century**) secolo *m* **2.** (= **circa**) circa **3.** (= **cup**) *US* COOK tazza *f*
C *abbr* **1.** (= **centigrade**) C (centigrado) **2.** (= **see**) *infml* COMPUT: ***CU*** (= ***see you***) a presto
c/a *abbr* (= **current account**) conto *m* corrente
CA *abbr* **1.** (= **chartered accountant**) commercialista *m/f* **2.** (= **Central America**) America Centrale *f*
cab *n* (*taxi*) taxi *m inv*; *of truck* cabina *f*; ***~ driver*** tassista *m/f*
cabal *n form* conventicola *f*
cabaret *n* spettacolo *m* di cabaret
cabbage *n* cavolo *m*
cabbie, cabby *n infml* tassista *m/f*
cab driver *n* tassista *m/f*
cabin *n of plane*, *ship* cabina *f*
cabin attendant *n* assistente *m/f* di volo
cabin crew *n* equipaggio *m* di volo
cabinet *n* armadietto *m*; POL consiglio *m* dei ministri; ***display ~*** vetrina *f*; ***drinks ~*** mobile *m* bar
cabinet maker *n* ebanista *m/f* **cabinet meeting** *n* riunione *f* del Consiglio dei ministri **cabinet minister** *n* membro *m* del Consiglio dei ministri **cabinet reshuffle** *n* rimpasto *m* del governo
cable *n* ELEC, *for securing* cavo *m*; **~** (***TV***) tv *f* via cavo
cable car *n* cabina *f* (di funivia) **cable channel** *n* canale *m* via cavo **cable stitch** *n* punto *m* cordoncino **cable television** *n* televisione *f* via cavo
caboodle *n infml*: ***the whole*** (***kit and***) **~** tutta la baracca
cacao *n* BOT cacao *m*
cache *n of weapons* deposito *m* segreto; COMPUT memoria *f* cache
cachet *n* prestigio *m*; ***the social ~ of living in the neighbourhood was worth the high rent*** il prestigio sociale di vivere in quel quartiere valeva l'affitto elevato
cack-handed *adj infml* maldestro
cackle **I** *n of hens* schiamazzo *m*; (*laughter*) risata *f* chioccia **II** *v/i hens* schiamazzare; (*laugh*) ridacchiare
cacophony *n* cacofonia *f*
cactus *n* cactus *m inv*
cad *n* mascalzone *m*
CAD *abbr* (= **computer-aided design**) CAD *m*
cadaver *n* cadavere *m*
cadaverous *adj* cadaverico
CAD-CAM *abbr* (= **computer assisted design-computer assisted manufacture**) CAD-CAM *m*
caddie **I** *n in golf* portamazze *m inv* **II** *v/i* portare le mazze
caddy[1] *n* → ***caddie***; (*tea caddy*) barattolo *m* per il tè; (*shopping trolley*) carrello *m*
caddy[2] *v/i* → ***caddie***
cadence *n* cadenza *f*
cadenza *n* MUS cadenza *f*
cadet *n* cadetto *m*
cadge *v/t*: ***~ sth from s.o.*** scroccare qc a qn; ***could I ~ a lift with you?*** posso scroccarti un passaggio?
cadre *n Br* gruppo *m* (scelto)
Caesarean, *US* **Cesarean** *n* parto *m* cesareo; MED (*a.* **Caesarean section**) taglio *m* cesareo; ***she had a*** (***baby by***) **~** ha partorito con il cesareo
café *n* caffè *m inv*, bar *m*
cafeteria *n* tavola *f* calda
caff *n Br infml* caffè *m*
caffeine *n* caffeina *f*
cage *n* gabbia *f*
cagey *adj* evasivo
cagoule *n Br* k-way *m inv*
cahoots *n infml*: ***be in ~ with*** essere in combutta con
cajole *v/t* convincere con le lusinghe; **~ *s.o. into doing sth*** convincere qn a fare qc con le lusinghe
cake **I** *n* dolce *m*, torta *f*; ***be a piece of ~*** *infml* essere un gioco da ragazzi; ***sell like hot ~s*** andare a ruba; ***you can't have your ~ and eat it*** *prov* non si può avere la botte piena e la moglie ubriaca **II** *v/i of mud*, *blood*

indurirsi
cakehole *n Br infml* bocca *f*
cake mix *n* preparato *m* per torte **cake shop** *n* pasticceria *f* **cake tin** *n Br for baking* tortiera *f*; *for storage* scatola *f* per torte
cakewalk *n US infml* gioco *m* da ragazzi
calamity *n* calamità *f inv*
calcium *n* calcio *m*
calculate *v/t* calcolare
calculated *adj* (*deliberate*) calcolato; ***a ~ risk*** un rischio calcolato
calculating *adj* calcolatore
calculation *n* calcolo *m*
calculator *n* calcolatrice *f*
calculus *n* MATH calcolo *m*
calendar *n* calendario *m*; ***~ of events*** calendario *m* degli eventi
calendar month *n* mese *m* civile
calf[1] ⟨*pl* ***calves***⟩ *n young cow* vitello *m*
calf[2] ⟨*pl* ***calves***⟩ *n of leg* polpaccio *m*
calfskin *n* vitello *m*
calibrate *v/t* TECH calibrare
calibre, *US* **caliber** *n of gun* calibro *m*; ***a man of his ~*** un uomo del suo calibro
call I *v/t* **1.** *on phone* chiamare **2.** (*summon*) chiamare; ***~ s.o. as a witness*** citare qn a testimoniare; ***~ a flight*** annunciare un volo **3.** (*shout*) gridare **4.** (*describe as*) definire **5.** (*name*): ***what have they ~ed the baby?*** come hanno chiamato il bambino?; ***I'm ~ed Charlotte*** mi chiamo Charlotte; ***what do you ~ this in Italian*** come si dice in italiano? **6.** ***~ s.o. names*** dare dei titoli a qn **7.** *meeting*, *election* indire, convocare **II** *v/i* **1.** *on phone* chiamare; ***who's ~ing, please?*** chi parla, scusi? **2.** (*shout*) gridare **3.** (*visit*) passare **III** *n* **1.** (*phone call*) telefonata *f*; ***give s.o. a ~*** telefonare a qn **2.** (*shout*) grido *m* **3.** (*demand*) richiesta *f* **4.** (*visit*) visita *f*; ***pay s.o. a ~*** far visita a qn **5.** ***be on ~*** *of doctor* essere di guardia
◆**call at** *v/i* (*stop at*) passare da
◆**call back I** *v/t sep a.* TEL richiamare **II** *v/i on phone* richiamare; (*make another visit*) ripassare
◆**call for** *v/t* (*collect*) passare a prendere; (*demand*) reclamare; (*require*) richiedere; ***this calls for a celebration!*** questo va festeggiato
◆**call in I** *v/t sep* (*summon*) far venire **II** *v/i on phone* chiamare; ***call in sick*** chiamare per dire di essere ammalato
◆**call off** *v/t sep strike* revocare; *wedding*, *appointment* disdire
◆**call on** *v/t* (*urge*) sollecitare; (*visit*) visitare; ***call on s.o. to*** sollecitare qn a
◆**call out I** *v/t sep* (*shout*) chiamare ad alta voce; (*summon*) chiamare **II** *v/i for help* gridare
◆**call up** *v/t sep on phone* chiamare; COMPUT aprire
call box *n* cabina *f* telefonica
call centre, *US* **call center** *n* centro *m* chiamate
caller *n on phone* persona *f* che ha chiamato; (*visitor*) visitatore *m*, -trice *f*
call girl *n* squillo *f inv*
calling *n* vocazione *f*; *form* (*profession*, *trade*) occupazione *f*
callisthenics, *US* **calisthenics** *nsg or npl* ginnastica *f* ritmica
callous *adj* freddo, insensibile
callously *adv* freddamente, insensibilmente
callousness *n* freddezza *f*, insensibilità *f inv*
callus *n* callo *m*
calm I *adj* (+*er*) calmo; ***please keep ~*** state calmi per favore **II** *n* calma *f*; ***the ~ before the storm*** la calma prima della tempesta **III** *v/t* calmare; ***~ s.o.'s fears*** placare i timori di qn
◆**calm down I** *v/t sep* calmare **II** *v/i* calmarsi
calmly *adv* con calma
calorie *n* caloria *f*
calorie-conscious *adj* attento alle calorie
calumny *n* calunnia *f*
calves → ***calf***
calypso *n* MUS calipso *m*
CAM *abbr* (= **computer-aided manufacture**) CAM *m*
camaraderie *n* cameratismo *m*
Cambodia *n* Cambogia *f*
camcorder *n* videocamera *f*
came *pret* → ***come***
camel *n* cammello *m*
cameo *n* (*role*) piccola parte *f* (*interpretata da attore famoso*); (*jewellery*) cammeo *m*

camera *n* macchina *f* fotografica; (*video camera*) videocamera *f*; (*television camera*) telecamera *f*; ***be caught on ~*** essere ripreso; ***in ~*** JUR a porte chiuse

camera crew *n* troupe *f* **cameraman** *n* cameraman *m inv* **camerawoman** *n* cineoperatrice *f* **camerawork** *n* uso *m* delle telecamere

camisole *n* camiciola *f*

camomile, chamomile *n* camomilla *f*; ***~ tea*** (infuso *m* di) camomilla

camouflage I *n* mimetizzazione *f*; *of soldiers* tuta *f* mimetica **II** *v/t* mimetizzare; *fig* mascherare

camp[1] **I** *n* campo *m*; ***make ~*** accamparsi; ***pitch ~*** piantare le tende; ***have a foot in both ~s*** tenere il piede in due staffe **II** *v/i* accamparsi

camp[2] **I** *adj* (*effeminate*) effeminato **II** *v/t*: ***~ it up*** comportarsi in modo effeminato

campaign I *n* campagna *f* **II** *v/i* militare; ***~ for/against*** fare una campagna a favore di/contro

campaigner *n* militante *m/f*

camp bed *n* brandina *f*

camper *n person* campeggiatore *m*, -trice *f*; *vehicle* camper *m inv*

campfire *n* fuoco *m* di bivacco

campground *n US* camping *m inv*, campeggio *m*

camping *n* campeggio *m*; ***go ~*** andare in campeggio

campsite *n* camping *m inv*, campeggio *m*

campus *n* campus *m inv*

can[1] *unstressed v/mod* ⟨*pret* **could**⟩ **1.** *ability* potere; ***~ you hear me?*** mi senti? ***I can't see*** non vedo; ***~ you speak French?*** sai parlare il francese?; ***~ you swim?*** sai nuotare?; ***~ he call me back?*** mi può richiamare?; ***as fast as you ~*** più veloce che puoi; ***as well as you ~*** meglio che puoi **2.** (*permission*) potere; ***~ I help you?*** posso aiutarla?; ***~ you help me?*** mi può aiutare?; ***~ I have a beer/coffee?*** posso avere una birra/un caffè? **3.** *possibility*: ***that can't be right*** non può essere giusto

can[2] **I** *n for drinks* lattina *f*; *for food* scatola *f*; *US infml* gabinetto *m*; ***carry the ~*** *Br infml* prendersi la responsabilità **II** *v/t* ⟨*pret & past part* **-ned**⟩ inscatolare; *US infml* licenziare

Canada *n* Canada *m*

Canadian I *adj* canadese **II** *n* canadese *m/f*

canal *n* (*waterway*) canale *m*

canapé *n* canapé *m*

Canaries *npl* Canarie *fpl*

canary *n* canarino *m*

Canary Isles *npl* (Isole) Canarie *fpl*

cancel *v/t* annullare

cancellation *n* annullamento *m*

cancellation fee *n* penalità *f inv* (per annullamento)

cancer *n* cancro *m*

Cancer *n* ASTROL Cancro *m*

cancerous *adj* canceroso

candelabra *n* candelabro *m*

c&f *abbr* (= **cost and freight**) costo e nolo

candid *adj* franco

candidacy *n* candidatura *f*

candidate *n* candidato *m*, -a *f*; ***stand as (a) ~*** presentarsi come candidato; ***the obese are prime ~s for heart disease*** gli obesi sono i principali candidati alle cardiopatie

candidly *adv* francamente

candied *adj* candito

candle *n* candela *f*

candlelight *n* luce *f* delle candele; ***by ~*** a lume di candela **candlelit** *adj dinner* a lume di candela **candlestick** *n* portacandele *m inv* **candlewick** *n* ciniglia *f*; ***a ~ bedspread*** un copriletto in ciniglia

candour, *US* **candor** *n* franchezza *f*

candy *n US* (*sweet*) caramella *f*; (*sweets*) dolciumi *mpl*

candyfloss *n* zucchero *m* filato

cane I *n* canna *f*; *for walking* bastone *m*; ***get the ~*** assaggiare il bastone **II** *v/t* fustigare

canine I *adj* canino **II** *n* (*tooth*) canino *m*

canister *n* barattolo *m*; *spray* bombola *f*

cannabis *n* hashish *m*

canned *adj fruit, tomatoes* in scatola; (*inebriated*) *infml* sbronzo; (*recorded*) registrato; ***~ music*** *infml* musica *f* registrata; ***~ laughter*** risate *fpl* registrate

cannibal *n* cannibale *m*

cannibalism *n* cannibalismo *m*

cannibalize *v/t* riciclare parti di

cannon *n* cannone *m*
cannonade **I** *v/t & v/i* cannoneggiare **II** *n* cannoneggiamento *m*
cannonball *n* palla *f* di cannone
cannon fodder *n* carne *f* da cannone
cannot → ***can***1
canny *adj* (+*er*) (*astute*) arguto
canoe *n* canoa *f*
canon *n* regola *f*, canone *m*; (*priest*) canonico *m*
canonize *v/t* REL canonizzare
canon law *n* REL diritto *m* canonico
can opener *n* apriscatole *m inv*
canopy *n* baldacchino *m*
cant *n* ipocrisie *fpl*
can't → ***can***1
cantaloup(e) *n* BOT cantalupo *m*
cantankerous *adj* irascibile
canteen *n in factory* mensa *f*
canter *v/i* andare al piccolo galoppo
canton *n* cantone *m*
Cantonese **I** *adj* cantonese **II** *n* abitante *m/f* di Canton; LING cantonese
canvas *n* tela *f*
canvass **I** *v/t* (*seek opinion of*) fare un sondaggio tra **II** *v/i* POL fare propaganda elettorale
canvasser *n* POL galoppino *m* elettorale; COMM piazzista *m*
canyon *n* canyon *m inv*
cap **I** *n* (*hat*) berretto *m*; *of bottle*, *jar* tappo *m*; *of pen* cappuccio *m*; *for lens* coperchio *m*; (*lid*) coperchio *m*; *of pen*, *valve* tappo *m*; (*contraceptive*) diaframma *m*; ***if the ~ fits (wear it)*** *Br prov* l'osservazione coglie nel segno; ***he has won 50 ~s for Scotland*** *Br* SPORTS ha giocato 50 volte nella nazionale scozzese **II** *v/t* ⟨*pret & past part* **-ped**⟩: ***he was ~ped four times for England*** SPORTS è stato convocato quattro volte nella nazionale inglese; ***and then to ~ it all ...*** e a completare il tutto; ***they ~ped spending at £50,000*** hanno limitato la spesa a 50.000 sterline
capability *n of person* capacità *f inv*; MIL potenziale *m*
capable *adj* (*efficient*) capace; ***be ~ of*** essere capace di
capacious *adj* capiente
capacity *n* capacità *f inv*; *of car engine* potenza *f*; *of factory* capacità *f inv* produttiva; (*role*) funzione *f*; ***in my ~ as ...*** in qualità di ...; ***seating ~ of 400*** capienza di 400 posti a sedere; ***working at full ~*** lavorare a pieno regime; ***the Stones played to ~ audiences*** i concerti degli Stones hanno registrato il tutto esaurito; ***his ~ for learning*** la sua capacità di apprendimento; ***speaking in his official ~ as mayor, he said ...*** parlando a titolo ufficiale come sindaco ha dichiarato ...
cape *n* GEOG capo *m*; *clothing* mantella *f*
Cape Horn *n* Capo *m* Horn **Cape of Good Hope** *n* Capo *m* di Buona Speranza; (*cloak*) mantella *f*
caper1 **I** *v/i* fare capriole **II** *n* (*prank*) capriola *f*
caper2 *n* BOT, COOK cappero *m*; *clothing* mantella *f*
Cape Town *n* Città del Capo *f*
capillarity *n* capillarità *f inv*
capillary *n* capillare *m*
capital **I** *n of country* capitale *f*; (*capital letter*) maiuscola *f*; *money* capitale *m*; FIN, *fig* capitale *m*; ARCH capitello *m*; *fig* ***make ~ out of sth*** fare tesoro di qc; ***the columns were surmounted with ornate ~s*** le colonne erano sormontate da capitelli decorati **II** *adj letter* maiuscolo; *offence* punibile con la pena di morte; (*excellent*) eccellente; (*serious*) fatale; ***a ~ blunder*** un errore fatale
capital expenditure *n* spese *fpl* in conto capitale **capital gains tax** *n* imposta *f* sui redditi di capitale **capital growth** *n* aumento *m* del capitale **capital investment** *n* investimento *m* di capitale
capitalism *n* capitalismo *m*
capitalist **I** *adj* capitalista **II** *n* capitalista *m/f*
◆**capitalize on** *v/t* trarre vantaggio da
capital letter *n* lettera *f* maiuscola **capital offence** *n* delitto *m* capitale **capital punishment** *n* pena *f* capitale
Capitol *n* Campidoglio *m*
capitular *adj* capitolare
capitulate *v/i* capitolare
capitulation *n* capitolazione *f*
capon *n* COOK cappone *m*
capricious *adj* capriccioso
Capricorn *n* ASTROL Capricorno *m*
capsicum *n* capsico *m*
capsize **I** *v/i* ribaltarsi **II** *v/t* far ribal-

tare
capsule *n of medicine* cachet *m inv*; (*space capsule*) capsula *f*
captain I *n* capitano *m*; ***yes, ~!*** agli ordini, capitano!; ***~ of industry*** capitano *m* d'industria **II** *v/t team* capitanare; *ship* esser il capitano di
caption *n* didascalia *f*
captious *adj* ipercritico
captivate *v/t* affascinare
captivating *adj* affascinante
captive I *n* prigioniero; ***hold s.o. ~*** tenere qn prigioniero **II** *adj*: ***~ audience*** pubblico *m* involontario
captivity *n* cattività *f inv*
captor *n*: ***his ~s treated him kindly*** i suoi carcerieri lo hanno trattato con gentilezza
capture I *v/t person*, *animal* catturare; *city*, *building* occupare; *city* prendere; *market share* conquistare; (*portray*) cogliere **II** *n of building*, *city* occupazione *f*; *of city* presa *f*; *of criminal*, *animal* cattura *f*
car *n* macchina *f*, auto *f inv*; *of train* vagone *m*; ***by ~*** in macchina
car accident *n* incidente *m* automobilistico
carafe *n* caraffa *f*
car alarm *n* allarme *m* antifurto
caramel *n sweet* caramella *f* morbida
carat *n* carato *m*; ***nine ~ gold*** oro *m* a nove carati
caravan *n* roulotte *f inv*
caravan site *n* campeggio *m* per roulotte
carbohydrate *n* carboidrato *m*
car bomb *n* autobomba *f*
carbon *n* (*element*) carbonio *m*; (*paper*) foglio *m* di carta carbone
carbonated *adj* gassato; ***~ water*** acqua *f* gassata
carbon copy *n* identica copia *f* **carbon dioxide** *n* diossido *m* di carbonio **carbon monoxide** *n* monossido *m* di carbonio **carbon paper** *n* carta *f* carbone
car-boot sale *n vendita all'aperto con esposizione delle merci nei bagagliai delle auto dei venditori*
carburettor, *US* **carburetor** *n* carburatore *m*
carcass *n* carcassa *f*
car chase *n* inseguimento *m* in auto
carcinogen *n* cancerogeno *m*
carcinogenic *adj* cancerogeno
card[1] *n to mark special occasion* biglietto *m*; (*postcard*) cartolina *f*; (*business card*) biglietto *m* (da visita); (*playing card*) carta *f*; *fig* ***put*** *or* ***lay one's ~s on the table*** mettere le carte in tavola; ***play one's ~s right*** giocare bene le proprie carte; *fig* ***have a ~ up one's sleeve*** avere un asso nella manica; COMPUT scheda *f*; *material* cartoncino *m*
card[2] **I** *n* TEX carda *f* **II** *v/t* TEX cardare
cardamom *n* cardamomo *m*
cardboard *n* cartone *m* **cardboard box** *n* scatola *f* di cartone
cardiac *adj* cardiaco
cardiac arrest *n* arresto *m* cardiaco
cardigan *n* cardigan *m inv*
cardinal *n* REL cardinale *m*
card index *n* schedario *m* **card key** *n* tessera *f* magnetica **card phone** *n* telefono *m* a scheda **card trick** *n* trucco *m* con le carte
care I *n* **1.** *of baby*, *pet* cure *fpl*; *of the elderly* assistenza *f*; ***medical ~*** cure *fpl* mediche; *of the sick* cura *f*; ***take ~ of*** (*look after*: *baby*, *dog*) prendersi cura di; *tool*, *house*, *garden* tenere bene; (*deal with*) occuparsi di **2.** (*carefulness*) ***take ~*** (*be cautious*) fare attenzione; ***take ~*** (***of yourself***)***!*** (*goodbye*) stammi bene; (***handle***) ***with ~!*** *on label* maneggiare con cura **3.** (*worry*) preoccupazione *f*; ***he hasn't a ~ in the world*** non ha una preoccupazione al mondo **II** *v/i* interessarsi; ***I don't ~!*** non mi importa; ***I couldn't ~ less*** non potrebbe importarmene di meno
◆**care about** *v/t* interessarsi a
◆**care for** *v/t* (*look after*) prendersi cura di; (*love*) voler bene a; ***I don't care for your tone*** non mi piace il tuo tono; ***would you care for a tea?*** *form* gradirebbe un tè?
career *n* (*profession*) carriera *f*; (*path through life*) vita *f*
careerism *n* carrierismo *m*
careerist *n* carrierista *m*/*f*
careers officer *n* consulente *m*/*f* professionale
carefree *adj* spensierato
careful *adj* (*cautious*) attento; (*thorough*) attento; (***be***) ***~!*** (stai) attento!; ***be ~ to*** fare attenzione a; ***be ~ with***

stare attento con
carefully *adv* con cautela
careless *adj* incurante; *driver, worker* sbadato; *work* fatto senza attenzione; *error* di disattenzione; ***you are so ~!*** sei così sbadato!
carelessly *adv* senza cura
care of → ***c/o***
carer *n* badante *m/f*
caress I *n* carezza *f* **II** *v/t* accarezzare
caretaker *n* custode *m/f*
careworn *adj* provato
car ferry *n* traghetto *m* (per le macchine)
cargo *n* carico *m*
car hire *n* autonoleggio *m* **car hire company** *n* compagnia *f* di autonoleggio
caricature *n* caricatura *f*
caring *adj* premuroso
car insurance *n* assicurazione *f* automobilistica **car jack** *n* cric *m inv*
carjacking *n furto di un'automobile mentre il proprietario è all'interno*
car keys *npl* chiave *fpl* dell'auto
carload *n* AUTO carico *m* completo
car mechanic *n* meccanico *m* per auto
carnage *n* carneficina *f*
carnal *adj* carnale; ***~ desires*** desideri *mpl* carnali
carnation *n* garofano *m*
carnival *n* carnevale *m*
carnivore *n* carnivoro *m*
carnivorous *adj* carnivoro
carob *n* BOT carruba *f*
carol *n* canzone *f* di Natale
carol singers *npl* coro *m* di canzoni natalizie
carouse I *n* bevuta *f* **II** *v/i* fare baldoria
carousel *n at airport* nastro *m* trasportatore; *for slide projector* carrello *m*
carp[1] *n* (*fish*) carpa *f*
carp[2] *v/i* lagnarsi
car park *n* parcheggio *m* **car park attendant** *n* parcheggiatore *m*, -trice *f*
carpenter *n* falegname *m*
carpentry *n* falegnameria *f*
carpet I *n* tappeto *m*; (*fitted carpet*) moquette *f inv* **II** *v/t* mettere la moquette in
carpet sweeper *n* battitappeto *m*
car phone *n* telefono *m* da automobile **carpool** *n uso m condiviso della macchina dell'uno o dell'altro tra un gruppo di persone* **car port** *n* posto *m* auto coperto **car radio** *n* autoradio *f inv* **car rental** *n US* autonoleggio *m*
carriage *n* carrozza *f*; COMM trasporto *m*
carrier *n* (*company*) compagnia *f* di trasporto; *of disease* portatore *m* sano, portatrice *f* sana
carrier bag *n* sacchetto *m* **carrier pigeon** *n* piccione *m* viaggiatore
carrion *n* carogna *f*
carrion crow *n* ZOOL cornacchia *f* nera
carrot *n* carota *f*
carry ⟨*pret & past part* ***-ied***⟩ **I** *v/t* portare; *of pregnant woman* portare in grembo; *of ship, plane, bus etc* trasportare; *proposal* approvare; ***get carried away*** farsi prendere dall'entusiasmo; ***people ~ing the AIDS virus*** MED persone che trasmettono il virus dell'AIDS; ***this coach carries 30 people*** questo pullman trasporta 30 persone; ***the current carried them along*** sono stati trascinati via dalla corrente; ***the motion was carried unanimously*** la mozione è stata approvata all'unanimità; *fig* ***this job carries a lot of responsibility*** questo lavoro comporta molte responsabilità; ***the offence carries a penalty of £50*** l'infrazione comporta una sanzione di 50 sterline **II** *v/i of sound* sentirsi
◆**carry forward** *v/t sep* riportare
◆**carry off** *v/t sep* (*succeed in*) riuscire in; (*prize*) aggiudicarsi
◆**carry on I** *v/i* (*continue*) andare avanti, continuare; (*make a fuss*) fare storie; (*have an affair*) avere una storia **II** *v/t sep* (*conduct*) portare avanti
◆**carry out** *v/t sep survey etc* effettuare; *orders etc* eseguire
◆**carry over** *v/t sep fig* portarsi dietro; *holiday* conteggiare più tardi
carrycot *n* porte-enfant *m inv*
car seat *n for child* seggiolino *m* per auto
carsick *adj*: ***be ~*** avere il mal d'auto
cart I *n* carretto *m* **II** *v/t fig infml* portare
◆**cart around** *v/t sep* scarrozzare
◆**cart away** *or* **off** *v/t sep* trascinare
carte blanche *n*: ***give s.o. ~*** lasciare carta bianca a qn
cartel *n* cartello *m*

Cartesian *adj* cartesiano
carthorse *n* cavallo *m* da tiro
cartilage *n* cartilagine *f*
cartload *n* carrettata *f*
carton *n for storage*, *transport* cartone *m*; *of cigarettes* stecca *f*
cartoon *n in newspaper*, *magazine* fumetto *m*; *on TV*, *film* cartone *m* animato
cartoonist *n for newspaper etc* vignettista *m*/*f*
cartoon strip *n esp Br* striscia *f* (di vignette)
cartridge *n for gun*, *printer* cartuccia *f*
cartridge belt *n* cartucciera *f*
cartwheel *n liter* ruota *f* di carro; SPORTS ruota *f*; ***turn** or **do ~s*** fare capriole
carve *v/t meat* tagliare; *wood* intagliare; *stone etc* scolpire; ***~d in(to) the wood*** inciso nel legno; ***~d in(to) the stone*** scolpito nella pietra
◆**carve out** *v/t*: ***carve out a career for o.s.*** farsi strada
◆**carve up** *v/t sep meat* suddividere; *fig inheritance*, *country* spartire
carving *n figure* scultura *f*
carving knife *n* trinciante *m*
car wash *n* lavaggio *m* per auto
cascade I *n* cascata *f* **II** *v/i* (*a.* **cascade down**) venire giù a cascata (***onto*** su)
case¹ *n for glasses*, *pen* astuccio *m*; *of whisky*, *wine* cassa *f*; (*suitcase*) valigia *f*; ***glass ~*** teca *f*; ***upper*/ *lower ~*** TYPO maiuscole *fpl* / minuscole *fpl*
case² *n* **1.** (*instance*, *for police*), MED caso *m*; ***in ~ ...*** in caso ...; ***in ~ of*** in caso di; ***take an umbrella in ~ it rains*** prendi un ombrello in caso piovesse; ***in any ~*** in ogni caso; ***in that ~*** in questo caso; *infml* (*person*) caso *m*; ***a hopeless ~*** un caso disperato **2.** (*argument*) argomentazione *f* **3.** JUR causa *f*; ***win one's ~*** JUR vincere la causa; ***the ~ for the defence*** la tesi della difesa; ***in the ~ Higgins v Schwarz*** nella causa Higgins contro Schwarz; ***the ~ for*/ *against capital punishment*** le ragioni a favore della / contro la pena capitale **4.** GRAM caso *m*; ***in the genitive ~*** al (caso) genitivo
case history *n* MED cartella *f* clinica
caseload *n* numero *m* di assistiti; ***my doctor's ~*** il numero dei pazienti del mio dottore
casement *n* (*window*) finestra *f* a battenti
case study *n* casistica *f*
cash I *n* contanti *mpl*; *infml* (*money*) soldi *mpl*; ***~ down*** in contanti; ***pay (in) ~*** pagare in contanti; ***be short of ~*** essere a corto di soldi; ***~ in advance*** pagamento *m* anticipato; ***~ on delivery*** → ***COD*** **II** *v/t cheque* incassare
◆**cash in on** *v/t* approfittare di
cash and carry *n* COMM cash-and-carry *m* **cash card** *n* tessera *f* Bancomat® **cash cow** *n* vacca *f* da mungere **cash desk** *n* cassa *f* **cash discount** *n* sconto *m* su pagamento in contanti **cash dispenser** *n* (sportello *m*) Bancomat® *m*
cashew *n* BOT anacardio *m*
cash flow *n* flusso *m* di cassa
cashier *n in shop etc* cassiere *m*, -a *f*
cash machine *n* (sportello *m*) Bancomat® *m*
cashmere *adj* cashemere *m inv*
cashpoint *n* (sportello *m*) Bancomat® *m* **cash register** *n* cassa *f*
casino *n* casinò *m inv*
cask *n* barile *m*
casket *n US* (*coffin*) bara *f*
casserole *n* COOK stufato *m*; *container* teglia *f*; ***lamb ~*** stufato *m* di agnello
cassette *n* cassetta *f*
cassette player *n* mangiacassette *m inv* **cassette recorder** *n* registratore *m* (a cassette)
cassock *n* tonaca *f*
cast I *v/t* ⟨*pret & past part* **cast**⟩ **1.** *doubt*, *suspicion* far sorgere (**on** su) **2.** *shadow* proiettare **3.** *metal* colare (in uno stampo) **4.** *play* assegnare le parti per; ***~ s.o. as ...*** *for play* far fare a qn il ruolo di ...; ***he was ~ as Romeo*** gli è stata assegnata la parte di Romeo **5.** *fig* ***~ a glance at s.o.*/ *sth*** gettare uno sguardo su qn / qc; ***~ a vote*** votare **II** *n of play* cast *m inv*; (*mould*) stampo *m*; ***he had his arm in a ~*** MED aveva il braccio ingessato
◆**cast about** *Br*, **cast around for** *v/t* cercare; ***he was casting about** or **around for something to say*** stava cercando qc da dire
◆**cast aside** *v/t sep* mettere da parte

◆**cast off** *v/i* NAUT sciogliere gli ormeggi; *knitting* chiudere
◆**cast on** *v/t & v/i sep knitting* mettere su le maglie
◆**cast out** *v/t sep liter demons* scacciare
castanets *npl* nacchere *fpl*
castaway *n* naufrago *m*, -a *f*
caste *n* casta *f*
caster *n on chair etc* rotella *f*
caster sugar *n* zucchero *m* raffinato
castigate *v/t* castigare
cast iron **I** *n* ghisa *f* **II** *adj* di ghisa
castle *n* castello *m*
cast-off **I** *adj* smesso **II** *n* abito *m* smesso
castor *n* → ***caster***
castrate *v/t* castrare
castration *n* castrazione *f*
casual *adj* (*chance*) casuale; (*offhand*) disinvolto; (*irresponsible*) noncurante; *remark* poco importante; *clothes* casual *inv*; (*not permanent*) occasionale; ***~ sex*** rapporti *mpl* occasionali; ***a ~ shirt*** una camicia casual; ***he was wearing ~ clothes*** era vestito casual; ***it was just a ~ remark*** era tanto per dire; ***he was very ~ about it*** era molto disinvolto in merito
casually *adv dressed* (in modo) casual; *say* con disinvoltura
casualty *n dead person* vittima *f*; *injured* ferito *m*; (*hospital department*) *Br* pronto soccorso *m*; ***be in ~*** essere al pronto soccorso
casualty ward *n* pronto soccorso *m*
casual wear *n* abbigliamento *m* casual
cat *n* gatto *m*; *wild* felino *m*; ***let the ~ out of the bag*** lasciarsi sfuggire un segreto; ***play a ~-and-mouse game with s.o.*** giocare con qn come il gatto con il topo; ***there isn't room to swing a ~*** *infml* non c'è spazio nemmeno per muoversi; ***that's put the ~ among the pigeons!*** ha provocato un gran trambusto!; ***he doesn't have a ~ in hell's chance of winning*** non ha alcuna probabilità di vincere; ***when*** *or* ***while the ~'s away the mice will play*** *prov* quando il gatto non c'è i topi ballano; ***has the ~ eaten your tongue?*** *infml* ti ha mangiato la lingua il gatto?
CAT *abbr* (= **computerized axial tomography**) MED TAC (tomografia assiale computerizzata)
cataclysm *n* cataclisma *m*
catacombs *npl* catacombe *fpl*
catalepsy *n* catalessi *f*
catalogue, *US* **catalog** **I** *n* catalogo *m*; ***a ~ of errors*** una serie di errori **II** *v/t* catalogare
catalyst *n* catalizzatore *m*
catalytic converter *n* marmitta *f* catalitica
catamaran *n* catamarano *m*
catapult **I** *v/t fig*: *to fame*, *stardom* catapultare **II** *n* catapulta *f*; *toy* fionda *f*
cataract *n* MED cataratta *f*
catarrh *n* catarro *m*
catastrophe *n* catastrofe *f*
catastrophic *adj* catastrofico
catcall *n* THEAT: ***~s*** fischi *mpl*
catch **I** *v/t* ⟨*pret & past part* ***caught***⟩ **1.** *ball*, *escaped prisoner* prendere; *bus*, *train* prendere; *fish* prendere; (*in order to speak to*) trovare; ***~ s.o.'s eye*** *of person*, *object* attirare l'attenzione di qn; ***~ sight of***, ***~ a glimpse of*** intravedere; ***~ s.o. doing sth*** sorprendere qn a fare qc; ***~ s.o. at a bad time*** sorprendere qn in un brutto momento; ***I caught him flirting with my wife*** l'ho sorpreso a flirtare con mia moglie; ***you won't ~ me signing any contract*** *infml* non mi sorprenderai a firmare un contratto; ***caught in the act*** colto sul fatto **2.** (*hear*) afferrare; ***I didn't ~ what you said*** non ho afferrato ciò che hai detto **3.** *illness* prendere; ***~ (a) cold*** prendere un raffreddore; ***you'll ~ it!*** *Br infml* guai a te! **II** *n* presa *f*; *of fish* pesca *f*; *on handbag*, *box* chiusura *f*; *on door*, *window* fermo *m*; *on brooch* fermaglio *m*; (*problem*) inghippo *m*; ***there's a ~!*** c'è un inghippo!
◆**catch on** *v/i* (*become popular*) fare presa; (*understand*) afferrare
◆**catch out** *v/t sep* cogliere in fallo
◆**catch up** *v/i* **1.** recuperare; ***catch up with s.o.*** raggiungere qn; ***catch up with sth*** *work*, *studies* mettersi in pari con qc **2.** (*tenersi al passo*) aggiornarsi
◆**catch up on** *v/t* recuperare; ***catch up on one's sleep*** recuperare il sonno; ***catch up on*** *or* ***with one's work*** mettersi in pari con il lavoro

catching *adj a. fig* contagioso
catchphrase *n* slogan *m inv*
Catch-22 *n*: ***it's a ~ situation*** è una situazione senza via d'uscita
catchword *n* slogan *m*
catchy *adj* (+*er*) *tune* orecchiabile
catechism *n* catechismo *m*
categoric *adj* categorico
categorical *adj* categorico; ***he was quite ~ about it*** è stato piuttosto categorico in merito
categorically *adv* categoricamente
categorize *v/t* classificare
category *n* categoria *f*
◆**cater for** *v/t* (*meet the needs of*) rispondere alle esigenze di; (*provide food for*) organizzare rinfreschi per
caterer *n* ristoratore *m*, -trice *f*
catering *n* rinfresco *m* (**for** per); ***who's doing the ~?*** chi si occupa del rinfresco?; ***~ trade*** ristorazione *f*
caterpillar *n* bruco *m*
catfish *n* pesce *m* gatto
cat flap *n* gattaiola *f*
cathartic *adj* LIT, PHIL catartico
cathedral *n* cattedrale *f*, duomo *m*
catherine wheel *n firework* girandola *f*
catheter *n* MED catetere *m*
cathode-ray tube *n* tubo *m* a raggi catodici
Catholic I *adj* cattolico **II** *n* cattolico *m*,-a *f*
Catholicism *n* cattolicesimo *m*
catkin *n* BOT amento *m*
cat litter *n* lettiera *f* per gatti **catnap I** *n* pisolino *m* **II** *v/i* ⟨*pret & past part* ***-ped***⟩ schiacciare un pisolino **cat's eye** *n on road* catarifrangente *m*
cattle *n* bestiame *m*
cattle-grid, *US* **cattle guard** *n griglia di barre metalliche posta su un fossato che impedisce il passaggio del bestiame ma non ostacola il passaggio dei veicoli* **cattle market** *n* mercato *m* del bestiame **cattle shed** *n* stalla *f* per bovini **cattle truck** *n* RAIL carro *m* bestiame
catty *adj* (+*er*) maligno
catwalk *n* passerella *f*
caught *pret & past part* → ***catch***
cauldron *n* calderone *m*
cauliflower *n* cavolfiore *m*
cause I *n* causa *f*; (*grounds*) motivo *m*; (*objective*) causa *f*; ***~ of death*** causa *f* del decesso; ***~ and effect*** causa *f* ed effetto *m*; ***with (good) ~*** con giusta causa; ***there's no ~ for alarm*** non c'è ragione di allarmarsi; ***you have every ~ to be worried*** hai tutti i motivi per essere preoccupato; ***work for or in a good ~*** darsi da fare per una buona causa; ***he died for the ~ of peace*** è morto per la pace; ***it's all in a good ~*** è tutto per una buona causa **II** *v/t* causare; ***what ~d you to leave so early?*** perché sei andato via così presto?***~ s.o. grief*** causare dolore a qn; ***~ s.o. to do sth*** *form* indurre qn a fare qc
causeway *n* strada *f* rialzata
caustic *adj* CHEM, *fig* caustico; ***his ~ remark left us all speechless*** la sua osservazione caustica ci ha lasciato senza parole
caution I *n* (*carefulness*) cautela *f*, prudenza *f*; ***~ is advised*** si raccomanda la prudenza **II** *v/t* (*warn*) mettere in guardia; ***~ s.o. against doing sth*** mettere in guardia qn dal fare qc
cautious *adj* cauto, prudente
cautiously *adv* con cautela; ***he is ~ optimistic*** è cautamente ottimista
cavalcade *n* corteo *m*
cavalier *adj* sprezzante
cavalry *n* cavalleria *f*
cavalry officer *n* ufficiale *m* di cavalleria
cave *n* caverna *f*, grotta *f*
◆**cave in** *v/i of roof* crollare
cavern *n* caverna *f*
cavernous *adj* cavernoso
caviar *n* caviale *m*
cavity *n* cavità *f inv*; *in tooth* carie *f inv*
CBE *abbr* (= **Commander of the Order of the British Empire**) *Br* comandante *m* dell'ordine dell'Impero britannico
CBI *abbr* (= **Confederation of British Industry**) *Br* confederazione *f* dell'industria britannica
CBS *abbr* (= **Columbia Broadcasting System**) *rete televisiva statunitense*
cc I *abbr* **1.** (= **carbon copy**) cc (copia *f* carbone) **2.** (= **cubic centimetres**) cc *m inv* (centimetri cubici); AUTO cilindrata *f* **II** *v/t memo* fare una copia di; *person* mandare una copia per co-

noscenza a
CCTV *abbr* (= **closed circuit television**) televisione *f* a circuito chiuso
CD *abbr* (= **compact disc**) CD *m inv*
CD burner *n* masterizzatore *m* CD **CD player** *n* lettore *m* CD **CD-ROM** *n* CD-ROM *m inv* **CD-ROM drive** *n* drive *m inv* per CD-ROM
CD-RW *n abbr* (= **compact disk rewritable**) COMPUT CD *m inv* riscrivibile
CDT *abbr* (= **Central Daylight Time**) *US fuso orario degli Stati Uniti*
cease *v/t & v/i* cessare
cease-fire *n* cessate il fuoco *m inv*
ceaseless *adj* incessante
ceaselessly *adv* incessantemente
cedar *n* cedro *m*; (*a.* **cedarwood**) legno *m* di cedro
cede *v/t territory* cedere (***to*** a)
Ceefax® *n servizio teletext della BBC*
ceiling *n of room* soffitto *m*; (*limit*) tetto *m*, plafond *m inv*
celebrate **I** *v/i* festeggiare **II** *v/t* celebrare, festeggiare; (*observe*) festeggiare
celebrated *adj* acclamato; ***be ~ for*** essere famoso per
celebration *n* celebrazione *f*, festeggiamento *m*
celebratory *adj meal*, *drink* celebrativo
celebrity *n* celebrità *f inv*
celeriac *n* sedano *m* rapa
celery *n* sedano *m*; ***three stalks of ~*** tre gambi di sedano
celestial *adj* ASTR celeste
celibacy *n* celibato *m*
celibate *adj man* celibe; *woman* nubile
cell *n for prisoner* cella *f*; BIOL cellula *f*; *in spreadsheet* casella *f*, cella *f*
cellar *n of house* cantina *f*; *of wine* collezione *f* di vini
cellist *n* violoncellista *m/f*
cello *n* violoncello *m*
cellophane® *n* cellofan *m inv*
cellphone *n US* telefono *m* cellulare, cellulare *m*
cellular phone *n* telefono *m* cellulare, cellulare *m*
cellulite *n* cellulite *f*
Celsius *adj*: ***10 degrees ~*** 10 gradi centigradi
cement **I** *n* cemento *m*; (*adhesive*) mastice *m* **II** *v/t* cementare; *friendship* consolidare
cement mixer *n* betoniera *f*
cemetery *n* cimitero *m*
censor *v/t* censurare
censorship *n* censura *f*
censure *form* **I** *n* censura *f*, biasimo *m* **II** *v/t* censurare, biasimare
census *n* censimento *m*
cent *n* centesimo *m*
centenary *n* centenario *m*
centennial *n esp US* centenario *m*
center *US* → ***centre***
centigrade *adj* centigrado; ***10 degrees ~*** 10 gradi centigradi
centilitre, *US* **centiliter** *n* centilitro *m*
centimetre, *US* **centimeter** *n* centimetro *m*
centipede *n* millepiedi *m inv*
central *adj location*, *flat* centrale; (*main*) principale, centrale; ***~ London/France*** il centro di Londra/della Francia; ***be ~ to sth*** essere fondamentale per qc
Central America *n* America *f* centrale **Central Europe** *n* Europa *f* centrale **Central European Time** *n* ora *f* dell'Europa centrale **central government** *n* governo *m* centrale **central heating** *n* riscaldamento *m* autonomo
centralize *v/t decision making* accentrare
central locking *n* AUTO chiusura *f* centralizzata **central processing unit** *n* unità *f inv* centrale **central reservation** *n* AUTO banchina *f* spartitraffico **Central Standard Time** *n fuso orario degli Stati Uniti*
centre, *US* **center** **I** *n* centro *m*; ***in the ~ of*** al centro di **II** *v/t* centrare
◆**centre on**, *US* **center on** *v/t* essere incentrato su
centrefold, *US* **centerfold** *n* pagina *f* centrale
centre forward, *US* **center forward** *n* SPORTS centravanti *m inv* **centre half**, *US* **center half** *n* SPORTS centro mediano *m*
centre of gravity, *US* **center of gravity** *n* centro *m* di gravità
centrepiece, *US* **centerpiece** *n fig* pezzo *m* forte
centrifugal *adj*: ***~ force*** forza *f* centrifuga

centrifuge *n* centrifuga *f*
century *n* secolo *m*
CEO *abbr* (= **Chief Executive Officer**) direttore *m* generale
ceramic *adj* ceramico
ceramics *n* (*pl*: *objects*) ceramiche *fpl*; (*sg*: *art*) ceramica *f*
cereal *n* (*grain*) cereale *m*; (*breakfast cereal*) cereali *mpl*
cerebral *adj*: ***~ palsy*** MED paralisi *f inv* cerebrale
ceremonial **I** *adj* da cerimonia **II** *n* cerimoniale *m*
ceremoniously *adv* cerimoniosamente
ceremony *n* (*event*) cerimonia *f*; (*ritual*) cerimonie *fpl*; (*formality*) formalità *fpl*; ***stand on ~*** fare cerimonie
cert *n Br infml*: ***it's a (dead) ~*** è più che certo
cert. *abbr* (= **certificate**) certificazione *f*
certain **I** *adj* (*sure*, *particular*) certo; ***it's ~ that …*** è certo che …; ***it's ~ to happen*** accadrà di sicuro; ***make ~*** accertarsi; ***know / say for ~*** sapere / dire con certezza; ***he is ~ to come*** è certo che lui verrà; ***a ~ Mr S.*** un certo Sig S.; ***to a ~ extent*** *or* ***degree*** fino a un certo punto; ***of a ~ age*** di una certa età **II** *pron* alcuni; ***~ of you*** alcuni di voi
certainly *adv* certamente; ***~ not!*** certo che no!
certainty *n* certezza *f*; ***it's a ~*** è una cosa certa; ***he's a ~ to win*** vincerà di certo
certifiable *adj infml* da manicomio
certificate *n qualification* certificazione *f*; *official paper* certificato *m*
certified mail *n US* posta *f* raccomandata
certify *v/t* ⟨*pret & past part* **-ied**⟩ dichiarare ufficialmente
certitude *n* certezza *f*
cervical cancer *n* cancro *m* cervicale **cervical smear** *n* striscio *m* cervicale
cervix *n* ANAT cervice *f*
Cesarean *n US* → ***Caesarean***
cessation *n* cessazione *f*
cesspit *n*, **cesspool** *n* pozzo *m* nero
CET *abbr* (= **Central European Time**) ora *f* dell'Europa centrale
c / f *abbr* (= **cost and freight**) costo *m* e nolo *m*
cf *abbr* (= **confer**) cfr. (confronta)
CFC *abbr* (= **chlorofluorocarbon**) CFC *m inv* (clorofluorocarburi *mpl*)
chafe **I** *v/t* irritare; ***his shirt ~d his neck*** la camicia gli irritava il collo **II** *v/i* irritarsi; *fig* infastidirsi (***at, against*** per)
chaffinch *n* fringuello *m*
chain **I** *n* catena *f*; ***~ of shops*** catena *f* di negozi; ***~ of events*** catena *f* di eventi; ***~ of command*** MIL catena *f* di comando **II** *v/t*: ***~ sth / s.o. to sth*** incatenare qc / qn a qc
chain gang *n fila di forzati incatenati* **chain letter** *n* catena *f* di sant'Antonio **chain mail** *n* corazza *f* a maglia **chain reaction** *n* reazione *f* a catena **chainsaw** *n* motosega *f* **chain smoke** *v/i* fumare una sigaretta dopo l'altra **chain smoker** *n* fumatore *m*, -trice *f* incallito **chain stitch** *n* punto *m* catenella **chain store** *n store* negozio *m* di una catena; *company* catena *f* di negozi
chair **I** *n* sedia *f*; (*arm chair*) poltrona *f*; *at university* cattedra *f*; ***the ~*** (*electric chair*) la sedia elettrica; *at meeting* presidente *m/f*; ***take the ~*** presiedere **II** *v/t meeting* presiedere
chair lift *n* seggiovia *f*
chairman *n* presidente *m*
chairmanship *n* presidenza *f*
chairperson *n* presidente *m/f* **chairwoman** *n* presidente *f*
chaise longue *n* chaise-longue *f*
chalet *n* chalet *m inv*
chalice *n* REL calice *m*
chalk *n* gesso *m*; ***not by a long ~*** *Br infml* per nulla; ***they're as different as ~ and cheese*** *Br* sono di gran lunga diversi
challenge **I** *n* sfida *f*; ***I see this task as a ~*** considero questo compito come una sfida; ***a direct ~ to his authority*** una sfida diretta alla sua autorità **II** *v/t* sfidare; (*call into question*) mettere alla prova; ***~ s.o. to do sth*** sfidare qn a fare qc; ***~ s.o. to a duel*** sfidare qn a duello
challenger *n* sfidante *m/f*
challenging *adj job*, *undertaking* stimolante
chamber *n* (*room*) sala *f*; POL camera *f*
chambermaid *n* cameriera *f* **chamber music** *n* musica *f* da camera **Cham-**

ber of Commerce *n* Camera *f* di Commercio; ***the Upper/Lower Chamber*** POL camera *f* alta/bassa **chamber orchestra** *n* orchestra *f* da camera **chamber pot** *n* vaso *m* da notte

chameleon *n* ZOOL, *fig* camaleonte *m*

chamois (leather) *n* camoscio *m*

champ *v/t & v/i* masticare rumorosamente; ***~ at the bit*** mordere il freno

champagne *n* champagne *m inv*; ***~ glass*** bicchiere *m* di champagne

champion I *n* SPORTS campione *m*, -essa *f*; *of cause* difensore *m*, -a *f* **II** *v/t* (*cause*) difendere

championship *n event* campionato *m*; *title* titolo *m* di campione; *of cause* difesa *f*

chance I *n* **1.** (*possibility*) probabilità *f inv*; (*opportunity*) opportunità *f inv*, occasione *f*; ***you don't stand a ~*** non hai nessuna possibilità **2.** (*risk*) rischio *m*; ***take a ~*** correre un rischio; ***I'm not taking any ~s*** non voglio correre nessun rischio **3.** (*luck*) caso *m* **4.** (*coincidence*): ***by ~*** per caso **II** casuale; ***~ meeting*** incontro *m* casuale **III** *v/t*: ***I'll ~ it!*** *infml* ci proverò!

◆**chance (up)on** *v/t person* incontrare per caso; *thing* imbattersi in

Chancellor *n in Germany* cancelliere *m*; ***~ (of the Exchequer)*** *in Britain* ministro *m* del tesoro

chancy *adj infml* rischioso; (*uncertain*) incerto

chandelier *n* lampadario *m*

change I *v/t* **1.** (*alter*) cambiare; ***~ planes/trains*** cambiare aereo/treno **2.** *one's clothes* cambiarsi **3.** (*exchange*) cambiare; ***she ~d the dress for one of a different colour*** ha cambiato il vestito con uno di diverso colore **4.** *Br* AUTO: ***~ gear*** cambiare (marcia) **II** *v/i* **1.** cambiare; ***you ~ at Crewe*** devi cambiare a Crewe **2.** (*put on different clothes*) cambiarsi; ***I'll ~ into something more comfortable*** mi metto qualcosa di più comodo **III** *n* **1.** cambiamento *m*; ***for a ~*** per cambiare; ***a ~ of clothes*** un ricambio di vestiti; ***a ~ for the better/worse*** un cambiamento in meglio/peggio; ***~ of address*** cambio *m* di indirizzo; ***a ~ in the weather*** un mutamento del tempo **2.** *small coins* moneta *f*; *from purchase* resto *m*; ***can you give me ~ for a pound?*** ha da scambiarmi una sterlina?

◆**change over I** *v/i* (*to sth different*) passare (***to a***); *exchange activities etc*) scambiarsi; ***we have just changed over from gas to electricity*** siamo appena passati dal gas all'elettricità **II** *v/t sep* scambiare

changeable *adj* incostante; *weather* variabile

changeling *n* idiota *m/f*

change of life *n* menopausa *f*

changeover *n* passaggio *m*; *period* fase *f* di transizione; *in relay race* passaggio *m* del testimone

changing room *n* SPORTS spogliatoio *m*; *in shop* camerino *m*

channel *n water* canale *m*; *fig*, *usu pl of bureaucracy etc* vie *fpl*; *of information etc* canale *m*; ***the (English) Channel*** la Manica; ***go through the official ~s*** passare attraverso le vie ufficiali; ***change*** *or* ***switch ~s*** cambiare canale

Channel ferry *n Br* traghetto *m* sulla Manica **channel-hopping** *n Br* TV *infml* zapping *m* **Channel Islands** *npl* Isole *fpl* della Manica **Channel Tunnel** *n* tunnel *m* della Manica

chant I *n* slogan *m inv*; REL canto *m* **II** *v/i* gridare; *of demonstrators* gridare slogan; REL cantare

chaos *n* caos *m inv*; ***complete ~*** caos completo

chaotic *adj* caotico

chap *n infml* tipo *m infml*

chapel *n* cappella *f*

chaperon(e) I *n* chaperon *m inv* **II** *v/t* accompagnare

chaplain *n* cappellano *m*

chapped *adj* screpolato; ***~ lips*** labbra *fpl* screpolate

chapter *n of book* capitolo *m*; *of organization* filiale *f*

char[1] *v/t* bruciacchiare

char[2] *n Br infml* (*a.* **charwoman**, **charlady**) domestica *f*

character *n* (*nature*) carattere *m*; (*person*) tipo *m*; *in book*, *play* personaggio *m*; *in writing* carattere *m*; ***he's a real ~*** è un tipo speciale; ***it's out of ~ for him to do that*** non è nel suo carattere farlo; ***be of good/bad ~*** avere un buon/cattivo carattere; ***she has***

no ~ non ha carattere
characteristic I *n* caratteristica *f* **II** *adj* caratteristico
characteristically *adv* in modo caratteristico; ***he was ~ rude*** era maleducato, come al solito
characterization *n in a novel etc* caratterizzazione *f*
characterize *v/t* caratterizzare
character set *n* COMPUT set *m inv* di caratteri **character space** *n* COMPUT spazio *m*
charade *n fig* farsa *f*
charcoal *n for barbecue* carbonella *f*; *for drawing* carboncino *m*
charge I *n* **1.** (*fee*) costo *m*; ***free of ~*** gratis **2.** (*responsibility*) ***be in ~*** essere responsabile; ***take ~*** assumersi l'incombenza; ***the children were placed in their aunt's ~*** i bambini sono stati affidati alla zia; ***take ~ of sth*** farsi carico di qc **3.** JUR accusa *f* **II** *v/t* **1.** *sum of money* far pagare; *person* far pagare a; (*put on account*) addebitare; ***how much do you ~ for ...?*** quanto prende per ...? **2.** JUR accusare; ***~ s.o. with sth*** imputare qn di qc **3.** *battery* caricare **III** *v/i* (*attack*) attaccare; (*rush*) precipitarsi; ***he ~d into the room*** si precipitò nella stanza
charge account *n* conto *m* (spese) **charge card** *n* carta *f* di addebito
chariot *n* cocchio *m*
charisma *n* carisma *m*
charismatic *adj* carismatico
charitable *adj institution* di beneficenza; *donation* in beneficenza; *person* caritatevole
charity *n assistance* carità *f inv*; *organization* associazione *f* di beneficenza
charlady *n Br* domestica *f*
charlatan *n* ciarlatano *m*, -a *f*
Charlie *n*: ***he behaved like a right ~*** *Br* si è comportato da perfetto cretino
charm I *n appealing quality* fascino *m*; ***turn on the ~*** fare ricorso al proprio fascino; *on bracelet etc* ciondolo *m*; ***lucky ~*** ciondolo *m* portafortuna **II** *v/t* (*delight*) conquistare
charming *adj* affascinante; *house*, *village* incantevole
charred *adj* carbonizzato
chart I *n diagram* diagramma *m*; *for ship* carta *f* nautica; *for aeroplane* carta *f* aeronautica; ***the ~s*** MUS l'hit parade *f inv* **II** *v/t progress* registrare
charter I *n* contratto *m* di noleggio; (*town charter*) statuto *m* **II** *v/t plane*, *boat* noleggiare
chartered accountant *n Br* commercialista *m/f*
charter flight *n* volo *m* charter *inv*
charwoman *n Br* → ***charlady***
chary *adj* cauto
chase¹ I *v/t* inseguire **II** *v/i*: ***~ around*** affrettarsi **III** *n* inseguimento *m*; ***a car ~*** un inseguimento in auto
◆**chase away** *v/t sep* cacciare (via)
chase² *v/t* (*emboss*) cesellare
chaser *n alcolico bevuto dopo un altro di diverso tipo*
chasm *n* baratro *m*
chassis *n of car* telaio *m*
chaste *adj* (+*er*) casto
chasten *v/t*: ***~ed by ...*** frenato da
chastise *v/t* (*verbally*) criticare aspramente
chastity *n* castità *f inv*
chat I *n* chiacchierata *f*; *useless talk* chiacchiere *fpl*; ***have a ~ with*** fare una chiacchierata con **II** *v/i* ⟨*pret & past part* ***-ted***⟩ chiacchierare
◆**chat up** *v/t sep infml* abbordare *infml*; ***he tried chatting me up*** ha cercato di abbordarmi
chat room *n* stanza *f* di chat **chat show** *n* talk show *m inv* **chat show host** *n* conduttore *m*, -trice *f* di un talk show
chatter I *v/i talk* fare chiacchiere; *of teeth* battere **II** *n* parlantina *f*
chatterbox *n* chiacchierone *m*, -a *f*
chatty *adj* (+*er*) *person* chiacchierone; *letter* familiare; ***written in a ~ style*** scritto in stile amichevole
chauffeur *n* autista *m/f*
chauffeur-driven *adj* con autista
chauvinism *n* sciovinismo *m*
chauvinist *n* sciovinista *m/f*; (*male chauvinist*) maschilista *m*
chauvinistic *adj* sciovinista
cheap I *adj* (+*er*) (*inexpensive*) economico; ***it's ~ at the price*** a buon mercato;(*nasty*) cattivo; ***feel ~*** vergognarsi; (*mean*) tirchio **II** *n*: ***buy sth on the ~*** *infml* comprare qc a basso costo; ***make sth on the ~*** *infml* fare qc in economia
cheat I *v/t* imbrogliare; ***~ s.o. out of sth*** estorcere qc a qn con l'inganno

II *v/i* imbrogliare; *in cards* barare **III** *n person* imbroglione *m*, -a *f*; *in cards* baro *m*; (*deception*) truffa *f*

◆ **cheat on** *v/t* tradire; ***cheat on one's wife*** tradire la propria moglie

check[1] **I** *adj shirt* a quadri **II** *n* quadro *m*

check[2] **I** *v/t* (*verify*) verificare; (*restrain*) controllare; (*stop*) bloccare; *with a tick* marcare **II** *v/i* verificare; ***did you ~ for signs of forced entry?*** hai guardato se c'erano segni di effrazione?; ***I was just ~ing*** stavo solo controllando **III** *n* **1.** *to verify sth* verifica *f*; ***keep in ~, hold in ~*** tenere sotto controllo; ***keep a ~ on*** tenere sotto controllo **2.** (*bill*) *US* conto *m*; ***~, please*** *US* il conto, per favore

◆ **check in I** *v/i at airport* fare il check-in; *at hotel* registrarsi; ***what time do you have to check in?*** a che ora devi fare il check-in? **II** *v/t sep at airport* fare il check-in di; *at hotel* registrare

◆ **check off** *v/t sep* segnare; ***can you check these items off the list?*** puoi spuntare queste voci dell'elenco?

◆ **check on** *v/t* controllare

◆ **check out I** *v/i of hotel* saldare il conto **II** *v/t sep* (*look into*) verificare; *club, restaurant etc* provare; ***check it out with the boss*** chiedi conferma al capo; ***let's check out the new restaurant*** proviamo il nuovo ristorante

◆ **check up on** *v/t* fare dei controlli su

◆ **check with** *v/i of person* verificare con; (*tally: of information*) combaciare con

check[3] *n US* → ***cheque***

checkbook *n US* → ***chequebook***

checked *adj material* a quadri

checkers *nsg US: game* dama *f*

check-in (counter) *n* banco *m* dell'accettazione; *at airport* check-in *m inv*; *at hotel* reception *f inv*

checking account *n US* conto *m* corrente

check-in time *n* check in *m inv* **checklist** *n* lista *f* di verifica **checkmark** *n US* segno *m* **checkmate** *n* scacco *m* matto **check-out** *n* cassa *f* **check-out time** *n from hotel* ora *f* di check-out **checkpoint** *n military, police* posto *m* di blocco **checkroom** *n US for coats* guardaroba *m inv* **checkup** *n medical* check up *m inv*; *dental* visita *f* di controllo

cheek *n* guancia *f*; (*impudence*) sfacciataggine *f*; ***turn the other ~*** porgere l'altra guancia; ***have the ~ to do sth*** avere la sfacciataggine di fare qc; ***enough of your ~!*** basta con questa sfacciataggine!

cheekbone *n* zigomo *m*

cheekily *adv* sfacciatamente

cheeky *adj* (*+er*) sfacciato; ***it's a bit ~ asking for another pay rise so soon*** è un po' sfacciato chiedere un aumento di stipendio così presto

cheer I *n* acclamazione *f*; (*comfort*) conforto *m*; ***three ~s for ...*** hip, hip, hurrà per ...; ***~s!*** (*toast*) salute!; ***~s!*** *infml* (*thanks*) grazie!; ***be of good ~!*** stai allegro! **II** *v/t* acclamare **III** *v/i* fare acclamazioni

◆ **cheer on** *v/t sep* incitare

◆ **cheer up I** *v/i* consolarsi; ***cheer up!*** su con la vita! **II** *v/t sep* tirare su

cheerful *adj* allegro

cheering *n* acclamazioni *fpl*

cheerio *int infml* ciao *infml*

cheerleader *n US* ragazza *f* pompon

cheery *adj* (*+er*) → ***cheerful***

cheese *n* formaggio *m*

cheeseburger *n* cheeseburger *m inv* **cheesecake** *n* dolce *m* al formaggio **cheesecloth** *n* stamigna *f*

cheesed off *adj Br infml* stufo

cheesy *adj infml* scadente; ***the film had a ~ sentimental ending*** il film ha un finale sentimentale e scadente

cheetah *n* ghepardo *m*

chef *n* chef *m/f inv*

chemical I *adj* chimico **II** *n* sostanza *f* chimica

chemical engineering *n* ingegneria *f* chimica **chemical toilet** *n* gabinetto *m* chimico **chemical warfare** *n* guerra *f* chimica

chemist *n in laboratory* chimico *m*, -a *f*; *Br who dispenses medicine* farmacista *m/f*

chemistry *n* chimica *f*; *fig* alchimia *f*

chemist's (shop) *n Br* farmacia *f*

chemo *n abbr* (= **chemotherapy**) chemio *f*

chemotherapy *n* chemioterapia *f*

cheque, *US* **check** *n* assegno *m*

chequebook, *US* **checkbook** *n* libretto *m* degli assegni

cheque (guarantee) card *n* carta *f* as-

segni
cherish *v/t* avere a cuore
cheroot *n* sigaro *m* spuntato
cherry **I** *n fruit* ciliegia *f*; *tree* ciliegio *m* **II** *adj* (*colour*) color ciliegia
cherub *n* cherubino *m*
chess *n* scacchi *mpl*
chessboard *n* scacchiera *f* **chessman, chesspiece** *n* pezzo *m* degli scacchi
chest *n of person* petto *m*; (*box*) cassa *f*; **~ pains** dolori *mpl* al petto; ***I'm glad I've got that off my ~*** sono contento di essermi tolto questo peso dallo stomaco
chestnut **I** *n* castagna *f*; *tree* castagno *m*; (*colour*) color *m* castano; (*horse*) baio *m* castano **II** *adj* castano
chest of drawers *n* comò *m inv*, cassettone *m*
chest pain *n* dolore *m* al petto
chew *v/t* masticare; *of dog*, *rats* rosicchiare
◆**chew on** *v/t* (*a.* **chew over**: *infml*) *problem* meditare su
chewing gum *n* gomma *f* da masticare
chic *adj* (+*er*) chic *inv*
chick *n* pulcino *m*; *infml* (*girl*) ragazza *f*
chicken **I** *n* pollo *m*; ***don't count your ~s*** (***before they're hatched***) *prov* non vendere la pelle dell'orso prima di averlo preso; *infml* fifone *m*, -a *f* *infml* **II** *adj infml* (*cowardly*) fifone; ***he's ~*** è fifone
◆**chicken out** *v/i infml* tirarsi indietro per la fifa *infml*
chickenfeed *n infml* una bazzecola **chicken-livered** *adj* pauroso **chickenpox** *n* varicella *f*
chickpea *n* cece *m*
chicory *n* indivia *f*
chief **I** *n* (*head*) principale *m/f*; *of tribe* capo *m* **II** *adj* principale
chief executive officer *n* direttore *m*, -trice *f* generale
chiefly *adv* principalmente
chiffon **I** *n* chiffon *m inv* **II** *adj* di chiffon
chilblain *n* gelone *m*
child *n* ⟨*pl* **children**⟩ *a. pej* bambino *m*, -a *f*; ***they have two children*** hanno due figli
child abuse *n* violenza *f* sui minori
child-bearing **I** *n* gravidanza *f* **II** *adj*: ***of ~ age*** in età fertile **child benefit** *n Br* assegno *m* familiare **childbirth** *n* parto *m*
childhood *n* infanzia *f*
childish *adj pej* infantile, puerile
childishly *adv pej* puerilmente
childishness *n pej* puerilità *f inv*
childless *adj* senza figli
childlike *adj* innocente
child lock *n* blocco *m* (di sicurezza) per bambini **childminder** *n* baby-sitter *m/f inv*
childproof *adj* a prova di bambino
children *pl* → ***child***
children's home *n* istituto *m* per l'infanzia
Chile *n* Cile *m*
Chilean **I** *adj* cileno **II** *n* cileno *m*, -a *f*
chili *n US* → ***chilli***
chill **I** *n in air* freddo *m*; *illness* colpo *m* di freddo; ***there's a ~ in the air*** l'aria è fredda **II** *v/t wine* mettere in fresco
◆**chill out** *v/i infml* rilassarsi
chillax *v/i infml* rilassarsi
chilli (**pepper**) *n* peperoncino *m*
chilling *adj* agghiacciante
chilly *adj* (+*er*) *weather*, *welcome* freddo; ***I'm feeling a bit ~*** ho un po' freddo; ***it's a bit ~ this morning*** sta freddino stamattina
chim(a)era *n* chimera *f*
chime **I** *v/i* suonare **II** *n* rintocco *m*
chimney *n* camino *m*
chimp *n infml* → ***chimpanzee***
chimpanzee *n* scimpanzé *m inv*
chin *n* mento *m*; ***keep your ~ up!*** su con la vita!; *fig* ***he took it on the ~*** *infml* ha subito uno smacco
china *n* porcellana *f*
China *n* Cina *f*
Chinese **I** *adj* cinese **II** *n language* cinese *m*; *person* cinese *m/f*
chink *n gap* fessura *f*; ***a ~ of light*** uno spiraglio di luce; *sound* tintinnio *m*
chinwag *n Br infml* chiacchierata *f*
chip **I** *n fragment* scheggia *f*; *damage* scheggiatura *f*; *in gambling* fiche *f inv*; COMPUT chip *m inv*; ***~s*** patate *fpl* fritte; *US* patatine *fpl*; ***this cup has a ~*** questa tazza è scheggiata; *fig* ***when the ~s are down*** quando la situazione diventa critica **II** *v/t* ⟨*pret & past part* **-ped**⟩ *damage*

scheggiare
◆**chip in** *v/i* (*interrupt*) intervenire; *with money* contribuire
chipboard *n* truciolato *m*
chipmunk *n* ZOOL tamia *m inv*, scoiattolo *m* striato
chip shop *n Br* friggitoria *f* specializzata in pesce e patatine
chiropodist *n* pedicure *m/f inv*
chiropractor *n* chiroterapeuta *m/f*
chirp *v/i* cinguettare
chisel I *n* scalpello *m* **II** *v/t* cesellare; *in wood* intagliare
chitchat *n* chiacchiere *fpl*
chivalrous *adj* cavalleresco
chivalry *n* cavalleria *f*
chives *npl* erba *f* cipollina
chivvy *v/t* ⟨*pret & past part* ***-ied***⟩ *Br* mettere fretta a qn; ***she chivvied her children off to school*** mise fretta ai figli perché uscissero per la scuola
chlorine *n* cloro *m*
chloroform *n* cloroformio *m*
chocaholic *n infml* fanatico *m*, -a *f* del cioccolato
chock-a-block *adj infml* pieno zeppo
chock-full *adj infml* strapieno
chocolate *n* cioccolato *m*; *in box* cioccolatino *m*; ***hot ~*** cioccolata *f* calda
chocolate cake *n* dolce *m* al cioccolato
choice I *n* scelta *f*; (*variety*) assortimento *m* (***of*** di); ***of ~*** preferito,-a; ***I had no ~*** non avevo scelta **II** *adj* (*top quality*) di prima scelta; ***a ~ cut of beef*** un taglio di manzo di prima scelta
choir *n* coro *m*
choirboy *n* corista *m*
choke I *n* AUTO starter *m inv* **II** *v/i* soffocare; ***he ~d on a bone*** si è strozzato con un osso **III** *v/t* soffocare
choker *n* collana *f* girocollo
cholera *n* colera *m*
cholesterol *n* colesterolo *m*
choose *v/t & v/i* ⟨*pret* ***chose***, *past part* ***chosen***⟩ scegliere; ***~ to do sth*** scegliere di fare qc; ***there are five to ~ from*** ce ne sono cinque tra cui scegliere
choosey *adj* (*+er*) *infml* selettivo
chop I *v/t* ⟨*pret & past part* ***-ped***⟩ *wood* spaccare; *meat, vegetables* tagliare a pezzi **II** *n action* colpo *m*; *meat* braciola *f*
◆**chop down** *v/t sep tree* abbattere
◆**chop off** *v/t sep* mozzare
◆**chop up** *v/t sep* → ***chop***
chopper *n tool* accetta *f*; *infml* (*helicopter*) elicottero *m*
chopping block *n* tagliere *m*; *for wood, executions etc* ceppo *m* **chopping board** *n* tagliere *m*
choppy *adj* (*+er*) *sea* increspato
chopsticks *npl* bastoncini *mpl* (cinesi)
choral *adj* corale
chord *n* MUS accordo *m*
chore *n household* faccenda *f* domestica
choreograph *v/t* coreografare
choreographer *n* coreografo *m*, -a *f*
choreography *n* coreografia *f*
chortle *v/i* ridacchiare
chorus *n singers, of song* coro *m*
chose *pret* → ***choose***
chosen *past part* → ***choose***
choux pastry *n* COOK pasta *f* choux
chowder *n* COOK *specie di zuppa di pesce*
Christ *n* Cristo *m*; ***~!*** Cristo!
christen *v/t* battezzare
christening *n* battesimo *m*
Christian I *n* cristiano *m*, -a *f* **II** *adj* cristiano; *attitude* da cristiano
Christianity *n* cristianesimo *m*
Christian name *n* nome *m* di battesimo
Christmas *n* Natale *m*; ***at ~*** a Natale; ***Merry ~!*** Buon Natale!
Christmas card *n* biglietto *m* di auguri natalizi **Christmas carol** *n* canto *m* di Natale **Christmas Day** *n* giorno *m* di Natale **Christmas Eve** *n* vigilia *f* di Natale **Christmas present** *n* regalo *m* di Natale **Christmas pudding** *n Br dolce natalizio a base di uvette e spezie* **Christmas tree** *n* albero *m* di Natale
chrome, chromium *n* cromo *m*
chromosome *n* cromosomo *m*
chronic *adj* cronico
chronicle *n* cronaca *f*
chronological *adj* cronologico; ***in ~ order*** in ordine cronologico
chrysanthemum *n* crisantemo *m*
chubby *adj* (*+er*) paffuto
chuck *v/t infml* buttare
◆**chuck in** *v/t sep Br infml job* pian-

tare; ***chuck it (all) in*** piantare tutto
◆**chuck out** *v/t sep infml object* buttare via; *person* buttare fuori
◆**chuck up** *v/t sep US infml* vomitare; ***he chucked his breakfast up all over the car*** ha vomitato la colazione per tutta la macchina
chucking-out time *n infml* ora *f* di chiusura
chuckle I *v/i* ridacchiare **II** *n* risatina *f*
chuffed *adj Br infml* felice
chug *v/i* ⟨*pret & past part* ***-ged***⟩ *train* sbuffare; *engine* scoppiettare
◆**chug along** *v/i train* avanzare sbuffando; *engine* avanzare scoppiettando; *fig infml* andare avanti
chum *n* amico *m*, -a *f*
chummy *adj* (+*er*) *infml* pappa e ciccia *infml*; ***be ~ with*** essere pappa e ciccia con
chunder *AUS infml* **I** *v/i* vomitare **II** *n* vomito *m*
chunk *n* pezzo *m*
chunky *adj* (+*er*) *sweater* spesso; *tumbler* tozzo; *person*, *build* tarchiato
Chunnel *n infml* tunnel *m* della Manica
church *n* chiesa *f*; ***go to ~*** andare in chiesa
church hall *n* sala *f* parrocchiale **Church of England** *n* Chiesa *f* Anglicana **church service** *n* funzione *f* religiosa **churchyard** *n* cimitero *m* (di una chiesa)
churlish *adj* sgarbato
chute *n* scivolo *m*; *for waste disposal* canale *m* di scarico
chutney *n salsa agrodolce a base di frutta, aceto e spezie mangiata insieme a carne o formaggio*
CIA *abbr* (= **Central Intelligence Agency**) CIA *f*
CID *abbr* (= **Criminal Investigation Department**) *Br polizia investigativa in Gran Bretagna*
cider *n* sidro *m*
CIF *abbr* (= **cost insurance freight**) costo *m* assicurazione e nolo
cigar *n* sigaro *m*
cigarette *n* sigaretta *f*
cigarette end *n* mozzicone *m* di sigaretta **cigarette lighter** *n* accendino *m* **cigarette paper** *n* carta *f* per sigarette
cilantro *n US* coriandolo *m*
cinder *n* cenere *f*
cinema *n* cinema *m*
cinnamon *n* canella *f*
cipher *n* (*code*) scrittura *f* cifrata; ***in ~*** cifrato
circle I *n* cerchio *m*; (*group*) cerchia *f*; ***go around in ~s*** tornare sempre allo stesso punto **II** *v/t* (*draw circle around*) cerchiare **III** *v/i of plane* girare in tondo; *of bird* volteggiare
circs *abbr* (= **circumstance**) *infml* circostanze *fpl*; ***under the ~*** date le circostanze
circuit *n* ELEC circuito *m*; (*lap*) giro *m*
circuit board *n* COMPUT circuito *m* stampato **circuit breaker** *n* ELEC interruttore *m* automatico **circuit training** *n* SPORTS percorso *m* ginnico
circular I *adj* circolare **II** *n giving information* circolare *f*
circulate I *v/i* circolare **II** *v/t memo* far circolare
circulation *n* BIOL circolazione *f*; *of newspaper*, *magazine* tiratura *f*
circumcision *n* circoncisione *f*
circumference *n* circonferenza *f*
circumspect *adj* circospetto
circumstances *npl* circostanze *fpl*; (*financial*) situazione *fsg* (economica); ***under no ~*** in nessuna circostanza; ***under the ~*** date le circostanze
circus *n* circo *m*
cirrhosis (of the liver) *n* cirrosi *f* (epatica)
cissy *n* → ***sissy***
cistern *n* cisterna *f*; *of WC* serbatoio *m*
cite *v/t* citare
citizen *n* cittadino *m*, -a *f*
citizenship *n* cittadinanza *f*
citrus fruit *n* agrume *m*
city *n* città *f inv*; ***the City*** *Br* la City
city centre, *US* **city center** *n* centro *m* (della città) **city hall** *n* sala *f* municipale
cityscape *n* paesaggio *m* urbano
civic *adj* civico
civil *adj* civile
civil defence, *US* **civil defense** *n in wartime* difesa *f* civile; *in peace* protezione *f* civile **civil disobedience** *n* disobbedienza *f* civile **civil engineer** *n* ingegnere *m* civile
civilian I *n* civile *m/f* **II** *adj clothes* civile
civility *n* civiltà *f inv*

civilization *n* civilizzazione *f*
civilize *v/t person* civilizzare
civil rights *npl* diritti *mpl* civili **civil servant** *n* impiegato *m*, -a *f* statale **civil service** *n* pubblica amministrazione *f* **civil war** *n* guerra *f* civile
CJD *abbr* (= **Creutzfeld-Jakob disease**) morbo *m* di Creutzfeld-Jakob
clad *adj liter* vestito; ***lightly ~*** vestito leggero
claim I *v/t* (*ask for as a right*) rivendicare; *damages* richiedere; (*assert*) affermare; *lost property* reclamare; ***they have ~ed responsibility for the attack*** hanno rivendicato l'attentato **II** *n* (*request*) richiesta *f*; (*right*) diritto *m*; (*assertion*) affermazione *f*; ***I make no ~ to be a genius*** non sostengo di essere un genio
◆**claim back** *v/t sep* farsi rimborsare; ***claim sth back*** (***as expenses***) farsi rimborsare qc per le spese
claimant *n* richiedente *m/f*
clairvoyant *n* chiaroveggente *m/f*
clam *n* vongola *f*
◆**clam up** *v/i* ⟨*pret & past part* **-med**⟩ *infml* chiudersi come un riccio
clamber *v/i* arrampicarsi
clammy *adj* (*+er*) *hands* appiccicaticcio; *weather* afoso
clamour, *US* **clamor** *n noise* clamore *m*; (*outcry*) protesta *f*
◆**clamour for** *v/t* chiedere a gran voce
clamp I *n fastener* morsa *f*; *for wheel* ceppo *m* (bloccaruote) **II** *v/t fasten* bloccare (con una morsa); *fig*: *hand etc* stringere; *car* mettere i ceppi a
◆**clamp down** *v/i* usare il pugno di ferro
◆**clamp down on** *v/t* mettere un freno a
clan *n* clan *m inv*
clandestine *adj* clandestino
clang I *n* suono *m* metallico **II** *v/i*: ***~ shut*** chiudersi con un suono metallico
clanger *n infml* gaffe *f inv*; ***drop a ~*** fare una gaffe
clap I *v/t & v/i* ⟨*pret & past part* **-ped**⟩ (*applaud*) applaudire; ***~ one's hands*** battere le mani **II** *n* (*Gonorrhoea*) *vulg* scolo *m*
clapped-out *adj*, **clapped out** *adj infml* scassato; ***a ~ old car*** una vecchia macchina scassata
clapper *n*: ***go / drive / work like the ~s*** *Br infml* andare / guidare / lavorare molto velocemente
claptrap *n infml* sproloquio *m*
claret *n wine* claret *m inv*
clarification *n* chiarimento *m*
clarify *v/t* ⟨*pret & past part* **-ied**⟩ chiarire
clarinet *n* clarinetto *m*
clarity *n* chiarezza *f*
clash I *v/i* scontrarsi; *of opinions* essere in contrasto; *of colours* stonare; *of events* coincidere **II** *n* scontro *m*
clasp I *n fastener* chiusura *f* **II** *v/t in hand* stringere
class I *n* (*lesson*) lezione *f*; (*group of people, category*) classe *f*; ***social ~*** classe *f* sociale; ***have ~*** *infml* avere stile **II** *v/t* classificare; ***~ as*** considerare
class conscious *adj* classista
classic I *adj* (*typical*) classico; (*definitive*) eccellente; ***she wrote the ~ biography of ...*** la sua biografia di ... è un classico **II** *n* classico *m*; ***~s*** *pl* UNIV studi *mpl* classici
classical *adj* classico; ***~ Greek*** greco *m* classico
classification *n* classificazione *f*
classified *adj information* riservato
classified ad(**vertisement**) *n* inserzione *f*, annuncio *m*
classify *v/t* ⟨*pret & past part* **-ied**⟩ (*categorize*) classificare
classmate *n* compagno *m*, -a *f* di classe **classroom** *n* aula *f* **class warfare** *n* lotta *f* di classe
classy *adj* (*+er*) *infml* d'alta classe
clatter I *v/i* fare baccano; ***~ down the stairs*** scendere rumorosamente le scale **II** *n* frastuono *m*
clause *n in agreement* articolo *m*; GRAM proposizione *f*
claustrophobia *n* claustrofobia *f*
clavichord *n* MUS clavicordo *m*
claw I *n* artiglio *m*; *of lobster* chela *f* **II** *v/t* (*scratch*) graffiare; ***he ~ed his way to the top*** *fig* si è fatto strada per arrivare in alto **III** *v/i*: ***~ at sth*** aggrapparsi a qc
clay *n* argilla
clay court *n tennis* campo *m* in terra battuta **clay pigeon shooting** *n* tiro *m* al piattello
clean I *adj* (*+er*) pulito; ***wipe a disk ~***

COMPUT cancellare un disco; ***make a ~ start*** ricominciare da zero; ***he has a ~ record*** ha la fedina penale pulita; ***~ driving licence*** *patente di guida che non è mai stata soggetta a sanzioni*; *fig* ***make a clean break*** darci un taglio netto; ***make a ~ breast of sth*** togliersi qc dalla coscienza **II** *v/t* pulire; *teeth* lavarsi; *car, hands, face* lavare; *clothes* lavare *or* pulire a secco; ***~ one's teeth*** lavarsi i denti; ***~ the dirt off one's face*** pulirsi il viso; ***have sth ~ed*** far pulire qc **III** *adv infml* (*completely*) completamente; ***I ~ forgot*** me ne sono completamente dimenticato; ***he got ~ away*** l'ha fatta franca; ***come ~*** *infml* confessare, vuotare il sacco

◆**clean out** *v/t sep room, cupboard* pulire a fondo; *fig* ripulire

◆**clean up I** *v/t sep a. fig* ripulire; *fig* ***the new mayor cleaned up the city*** il nuovo sindaco ha ripulito la città **II** *v/i* pulire; (*wash*) ripulirsi; *on stock market etc* fare fortuna

clean-cut *adj person* per bene, a posto; ***~ features*** lineamenti *mpl* marcati

cleaner *n male* uomo *m* delle pulizie; *female* donna *f* delle pulizie; (*dry cleaner*) lavanderia *f*, tintoria *f*

cleaning *n* pulizia *f*; ***do the ~*** fare le pulizie; ***~ fluid*** liquido *m* detergente

cleaning lady *n*, **cleaning woman** *n* donna *f* delle pulizie

cleanliness *n* pulizia *f*; ***~ is next to godliness*** *prov* la pulizia è una virtù fondamentale

clean-out *n*: ***give sth a ~*** dare una ripulita a qc

cleanse *v/t skin* detergere

cleanser *n for skin* detergente *m*

clean-shaven *adj* ben sbarbato

cleansing cream *n* latte *f* detergente

clear I *adj* (*+er*) chiaro; *weather, sky* sereno; *water, eyes* limpido; *skin* uniforme; *conscience* pulito; (*free*) libero; ***I'm not ~ about it*** non l'ho capito bene; ***I didn't make myself ~*** non mi sono spiegato bene; ***I made it ~ to him*** gliel'ho fatto capire; ***he doesn't want to: that's ~*** non vuole, è chiaro; ***a ~ profit*** un guadagno netto; ***be ~ of sth*** essere privo di qc; ***we're now ~ of debts*** abbiamo saldato i nostri debiti; ***the bottom of the door should be about 3 mm ~ of the floor*** la parte inferiore della porta deve distare circa 3 mm dal pavimento; ***Rangers are now three points ~ of Celtic*** *Br* i Rangers hanno tre punti di vantaggio sui Celtic **II** *v/t roads etc* sgomb(e)rare; (*acquit*) scagionare; (*authorize*) autorizzare; (*earn*) guadagnare al netto; *fence* scavalcare con un salto; *debt* saldare; ***~ one's throat*** schiarirsi la gola; ***~ the table*** sparecchiare (la tavola) **III** *v/i of sky* schiarirsi; *of mist* diradarsi **IV** *adv*: ***loud and ~*** forte e chiaro; ***stand ~ of*** stare lontano da; ***steer ~ of*** stare alla larga da; ***he leapt ~ of the burning car*** è saltato fuori dall'auto in fiamme

◆**clear away** *v/t sep* mettere via

◆**clear off** *v/i infml* filarsela *infml*

◆**clear out I** *v/t sep cupboard* sgomb(e)rare **II** *v/i* sparire

◆**clear up I** *v/i* (*tidy up*) mettere in ordine; *of weather* schiarirsi; *of illness, rash* sparire **II** *v/t sep* (*tidy*) mettere in ordine; *mystery, problem* risolvere

clearance *n space* spazio *m* libero; (*authorization*) autorizzazione *f*

clearance sale *n* liquidazione *f*

clear-cut *adj* così semplice **clear-headed** *adj person, decision* lucido

clearing *n in woods* radura *f*

clearing bank *n banca associata alla stanza di compensazione* **clearing house** *n* stanza *f* di compensazione

clearly *adv* chiaramente

clear-sighted *adj fig* perspicace **clear soup** *n* brodo *m*

clearway *n Br* strada *f* con divieto di sosta

cleavage *n* décolleté *m inv*

cleaver *n* mannaia *f*

clef *n* chiave *f*

cleft I *adj* (*split*) spaccato; (*partly divided*) diviso; ***a ~ chin*** mento *m* con fossetta **II** *n* (*fissure*) fessura *f*; (*split*) spaccatura *f*; *in chin* fossetta *f*

cleft lip *n* labbro *m* leporino **cleft palate** *n* MED palatoschisi *f*

clematis *n* BOT clematide *f*

clemency *n* clemenza *f*

clementine *n* BOT clementina *f*

clench *v/t* serrare

clergy *n* clero *m*

clergyman *n* ecclesiastico *m*

cleric *n* ecclesiastico *m*

clerical *adj staff* amministrativo; *work* impiegatizio
clerk *n* impiegato *m*, -a *f*; *US*: *in shop* commesso *m*, -a *f*
clever *adj* intelligente; *gadget*, *device* ingegnoso; ***don't get ~ with me*** non fare il furbo con me
clever-clever *adj infml* saputo **clever dick** *n infml* sapientone *m*, -a *f*
cleverly *adv* intelligentemente
cliché *n* frase *f* stereotipata
clichéd *adj* stereotipato
click I *v/i of camera etc* scattare; (*light switch*) far scattare; (*fingers*) far schioccare; ***suddenly it all ~ed*** (***into place***) *infml* all'improvviso mi fu tutto chiaro; ***some people you ~ with straight away*** persone con cui si va subito d'accordo **II** *n* scatto *m*, clic *m inv*; *of light switch* scatto *m*; *of fingers* schiocco *m*; COMPUT clic *m inv*
◆**click on** *v/t* COMPUT cliccare su
client *n* cliente *m/f*
clientele *n* clientela *f*
cliff *n* scogliera *f*
climactic *adj*: ***~ scene*** scena *f* culminante
climate *n* clima *m*
climate change *n* mutazione *f* climatica
climatic *adj* climatico
climatology *n* climatologia *f*
climax *n* punto *m* culminante
climb I *v/t* salire su; *clamber up* arrampicarsi su; *mountaineering* scalare **II** *v/i of plane*, *road*, *inflation* salire; *clamber* arrampicarsi **III** *n up mountain* scalata *f*, arrampicata *f*
◆**climb down** *v/i* scendere; *fig* fare marcia indietro
climbdown *n* marcia *f* indietro
climber *n person* alpinista *m/f*
climbing *n* alpinismo *m*
climbing wall *n parete f artificiale per esercitarsi nella scalata*
clinch *v/t deal* concludere; ***that ~es it*** questo risolve la questione
cling *v/i* ⟨*pret & past part* **clung**⟩ *of clothes* essere attillato
◆**cling to** *v/t of child* avvinghiarsi a; *ideas*, *tradition* aggrapparsi a
clingfilm *n* pellicola *f* trasparente
clingy *adj child*, *boyfriend* appiccicoso
clinic *n* clinica *f*
clinical *adj* clinico
clink I *v/i* tintinnare **II** *n noise* tintinnio *m*; *infml* (*jail*) galera *f*
clip[1] **I** *n fastener* fermaglio *m*; *for hair* molletta *f*; *for paper* graffetta *f* **II** *v/t* ⟨*pret & past part* **-ped**⟩: ***~ sth to sth*** attaccare qc a qc
clip[2] **I** *n from film* spezzone *m*; *wool* tosatura *f*; ***he gave him a ~ round the ear*** gli ha dato uno scappellotto **II** *v/t* ⟨*pret & past part* **-ped**⟩ *hair*, *hedge*, *grass* tagliare; *enunciation* biascicare, smozzicare; ***~ped speech*** frasi *fpl* farfugliate
clip art *n* COMPUT clip art *f* **clipboard** *n* portablocco *m inv* **clip-on** *adj tie* a clip; ***~ earrings*** orecchini *mpl* a clip, clip *mpl*; ***~ sunglasses*** *occhiali con lenti da sole sovrapposte*
clipper *n* (*boat*) clipper *m*
clippers *npl for hair* rasoio *m*; *for nails* tronchesina *f*; *for gardening* tosasiepi *fpl*
clipping *n from newspaper* ritaglio *m*
clique *n* combriccola *f*
clitoris *n* clitoride *m/f*
cloak I *n* mantello *m*; *fig* manto *m*, velo *m*; ***under the ~ of darkness*** avvolto nell'oscurità **II** *v/t fig* nascondere, mascherare
cloak-and-dagger *adj* di spionaggio **cloakroom** *n* guardaroba *m inv*; (*euph*: *toilet*) servizi *mpl*
clobber *infml* **I** *n Br* (*belongings*) roba *f*; (*clothes*) indumenti *mpl* **II** *v/t*: ***get ~ed*** essere colpito duramente; *infml* venire stracciato
clock *n* orologio *m*; (*speedometer*) contachilometri *m inv*; ***around the ~*** ventiquattr'ore su ventiquattro; ***work against the ~*** combattere contro il tempo; ***beat the ~*** rispettare i tempi; ***put the ~ back/forward*** mettere l'orologio indietro/avanti; *fig* ***turn the ~ back*** far tornare indietro il tempo; ***it's got 100,000 miles on the ~*** *infml* ha percorso 100.000 miglia
◆**clock in** *v/i* timbrare il cartellino all'entrata
◆**clock out** *v/i* timbrare il cartellino all'uscita
clock radio *n* radiosveglia *f* **clockwise** *adv* in senso orario **clockwork** *n* meccanismo *m* di orologio; ***it went like ~*** è andato liscio come l'olio

clod *n of earth* zolla *f*
clodhopper *n* (*person*) zoticone *m*, -a *f*; **~s** *pl* (*shoes*) *hum* scarpe *fpl* grosse
clog **I** *n* (*shoe*) zoccolo *m* **II** *v/t* ⟨*pret & past part* **-ged**⟩ bloccare, ostruire; **~ged with traffic** intasato dal traffico **III** *v/i pipe etc* ostruirsi, otturarsi
◆**clog up** **I** *v/i* intasarsi **II** *v/t* intasare
cloister *n* (*covered walk*) portico *m*; (*monastery*) monastero *m*
cloistered *adj fig* appartato, isolato
clone **I** *n* clone *m* **II** *v/t* clonare
close[1] **I** *adj* (+*er*) *family*, *friend* intimo; *resemblance* stretto; (*near*) vicino (**to** a); *examination* accurato; (*stuffy*) soffocante, afoso; *fight*, *result* testa a testa; **we are very ~** siamo molto uniti; **be ~ to s.o.** *emotionally* essere vicino a qn; **at ~ quarters** corpo a corpo; **is Glasgow ~ to Edinburgh?** Glasgow è vicino a Edimburgo?; **now pay ~ attention to me** prestami attenzione; **you have to pay very ~ attention to the traffic signs** è necessario prestare la massima attenzione ai cartelli stradali; **a ~(-fought) match** SPORTS un incontro serrato; **a ~ finish** SPORTS un arrivo serrato **II** *adv* (+*er*) vicino; **~ at hand** a portata di mano; **he lives ~ by** abita nelle vicinanze; **this pattern comes ~st to the sort of thing we wanted** questo modello si avvicina molto a ciò che desideriamo
close[2] **I** *v/t* chiudere **II** *v/i of door, eyes* chiudersi; *of shop* chiudere **III** *n* (*end*) termine *m*; **come to a ~** volgere al termine
◆**close down** *v/t sep & v/i* chiudere
◆**close in** *v/i* circondare; *of fog*, *night* calare
◆**close off** *v/t sep* chiudere
◆**close up** **I** *v/t sep building* chiudere **II** *v/i* (*move closer*) avvicinarsi
closed *adj* chiuso; **behind ~ doors** a porte chiuse; **"closed"** "chiuso"; **sorry, we're ~** spiacente, siamo chiusi; **~ circuit** ELEC circuito *m* chiuso
closed-circuit television *n* televisione *f* a circuito chiuso
close-knit *adj* ⟨*comp* **closer-knit**⟩ affiatato
closely *adv listen*, *watch* attentamente; *cooperate* fianco a fianco
close-set *adj* ⟨*comp* **closer-set**⟩ *eyes* ravvicinato
closet *n* **I** *US* armadio *m*; *fig* **come out of the ~** rivelare la propria omosessualità **II** *adj*: **~ queen** omosessuale *m* non dichiarato **III** *v/t* chiudere, rinchiudere
close-up *n* primo piano *m*; **in ~** in primo piano
closing date *n* termine *m* **closing-down sale** *n* COMM liquidazione *f*, svendita *f* **closing time** *n* ora *f* di chiusura
closure *n* chiusura *f*
clot **I** *n of blood* grumo *m*; *Br infml* stupido *m*, -a *f* **II** *v/i* ⟨*pret & past part* **-ted**⟩ *of blood* coagularsi; **~ted cream** COOK *panna densa caratteristica del Devon e della Cornovaglia*
cloth *n* (*fabric*) tessuto *m*; *for cleaning* straccio *m*; (*tablecloth*) tovaglia *f*; **the ~** abito *m* talare
clothe *v/t* vestire
clothes *npl* vestiti *mpl*; **his mother still washes his ~** la madre gli fa ancora il bucato; **with one's ~ on/off** vestito/svestito; **put on/take off one's ~** vestirsi/svestirsi
clothes brush *n* spazzola *f* per vestiti **clothes hanger** *n* attaccapanni *m inv* **clotheshorse** *n* stendibiancheria *m inv* **clothesline** *n* filo *m* stendibiancheria *inv* **clothes peg, clothespin** *n US* molletta *f* per i panni
clothing *n* abbigliamento *m*
cloud **I** *n* nuvola *f*; **a ~ of smoke/dust** una nuvola di fumo/polvere; **have one's head in the ~s** avere la testa tra le nuvole; **be on ~ nine** *infml* essere al settimo cielo; **every ~ has a silver lining** *prov* non tutto il male viene per nuocere **II** *v/t fig judgement* offuscare; (*make confusing*) confondere; **~ the issue** imbrogliare le carte
◆**cloud over** *v/i of sky* rannuvolarsi
cloudburst *n* temporale *m*
cloud-cuckoo-land *n*: **you're living in ~** vivi nel mondo dei sogni
cloudless *adj sky* sereno
cloudy *adj* (+*er*) nuvoloso
clout *infml* **I** *n* (*blow*) botta *f*; (*fig: influence*) influenza *f*; **he has a certain ~ with the powers that be** ha una certa influenza sul potere costituito **II** *v/t* dare una botta a
cloven-hooved *adj* dal piede caprino

clove of garlic *n* spicchio *m* d'aglio
clover *n* trifoglio *m*
clown I *n in circus* pagliaccio *m*; (*joker, a. pej*) pagliaccio *m*; ***act the ~*** fare il pagliaccio **II** *v/i* fare il pagliaccio
club I *n weapon* clava; *in golf* mazza *f*; *organization* club *m inv*; ***join the ~!*** *infml* benvenuto nel gruppo! *infml*; ***the London ~ scene*** i locali notturni londinesi; ***clubs*** *npl cards* fiori *mpl*; ***the nine of ~s*** il nove di fiori **II** *v/t* bastonare
◆**club together** *v/i* fare cassa comune
clubbing *n*: ***go ~*** andare in discoteca
clubhouse *n* sede *f* del circolo
cluck I *v/i* chiocciare **II** *n* chiocciare *m*
clue *n* indizio *m*; *in crosswords* definizione *f*; ***I haven't a ~*** *infml* non ne ho la minima idea; ***he hasn't a ~*** (*is useless*) non ci capisce niente
clued-up *adj infml* beninformato
clueless *adj infml* all'oscuro
clump *n of earth* zolla *f*; *group* gruppo *m*
clumsiness *n* goffaggine *f*
clumsy *adj* (*+er*) *person* goffo, maldestro
clung *pret & past part* → ***cling***
cluster I *n* gruppo *m* **II** *v/i of people* raggrupparsi; *of houses* essere raggruppato
clutch I *n* AUTO frizione *f* **II** *v/t* stringere
◆**clutch at** *v/t* cercare di afferrare
clutter I *n* oggetti *mpl* alla rinfusa **II** *v/t* (*a.*: ***~ up***) ingombrare
cm *abbr*(= **centimetre**) cm (centimetro)
c/o *abbr* (= **care of**) presso
Co. *abbr* (= **Company**) C.ia (compagnia)
C.O. *abbr*(= **Commanding Officer**) ufficiale *m* comandante
coach I *n* (*trainer*) allenatore *m*, -trice *f*; *of singer etc* maestro *m*, -a *f*; *on train* vagone *m*; (*Br*: *bus*) pullman *m inv* **II** *v/t* allenare; *singer, actor* dare lezioni a; ***~ s.o. for an exam*** preparare qn per un esame
coaching *n* allenamento *m*; *of singer, actor* lezioni *fpl*
coach party *n* gruppo *m* di turisti **coach station** *n* stazione *f* dei pullman **coach tour** *n* viaggio *m* turistico in pullman
coagulate *v/i of blood* coagularsi
coal *n* carbone *m*
coalesce *v/i fig* unirsi, fondersi
coalface *n Br* fronte *m* di abbattimento
coal fire *n* camino *m* a carbone **coal-fired** *adj* a carbone
coalition *n* coalizione *f*
coalmine *n* miniera *f* di carbone
coarse *adj* (*+er*) *skin, fabric* ruvido; *hair* spesso; (*vulgar*) grossolano; ***~ fishing*** *tipo di pesca in acque interne che esclude la pesca della trota e del salmone*
coarsely *adv* (*vulgarly*) grossolanamente; *ground* a grani grossi
coarsen *v/t skin* irruvidire
coarseness *n of texture* grossolanità *f inv*; *fig* (*vulgarity*) rozzezza *f*; *of joke* volgarità *f inv*; *of s.o.'s language* trivialità *f inv*
coast *n* costa *f*; ***at the ~*** sulla costa; *fig* ***the ~ is clear*** la via è libera
coastal *adj* costiero
coaster *n for glass* sottobicchiere *m*; *for bottle* sottobottiglia *m*
coastguard *n organization, person* guardia *f* costiera **coastline** *n* costa *f*, litorale *m*
coat I *n* (*overcoat*) cappotto *m*; *of animal* pelliccia *f*; *of paint etc* mano *f* **II** *v/t* (*cover*) ricoprire
coathanger *n* attaccapanni *m inv*, gruccia *f* **coat hook** *n* gancio *m* appendiabiti
coating *n* strato *m*
coat of arms *n* stemma *m* **coat of mail** *n* cotta *f* di maglia
co-author I *n* co-autore *m*, -trice *f* **II** *v/t* scrivere insieme
coax *v/t* convincere con le moine; ***~ sth out of s.o.*** ottenere qc da qn con le moine
cob *n* cob *m inv*, *cavallo di piccola statura*; ***corn on the ~*** pannocchia *f* di mais
cobalt *n* cobalto *m*
cobalt blue *adj* blu cobalto
cobble *n* **I** ciottolo *m* **II** *v/t* pavimentare con ciottoli; ***a ~d street*** strada *f* in acciottolato
cobbled *adj* lastricato (a ciottoli)
cobbler *n* (*shoe mender*) calzolaio *m*; ***~s*** *npl vulg* (*testicles*) palle *fpl*; (*nonsense*) sciocchezze *fpl*; ***a load of old ~***

un cumulo di sciocchezze
cobblestone *n* ciottolo *m*
COBOL *abbr* (= **common business oriented language**) COMPUT COBOL *m*
cobweb *n* ragnatela *f*
cocaine *n* cocaina *f*
coccyx *n* ⟨*pl* ***coccyges***⟩ ANAT coccige *m*
cochineal *n* cocciniglia *f*
cock I *n chicken* gallo *m*; *any male bird* maschio *m* (di uccelli); *vulg* (*penis*) cazzo *m vulg* **II** *v/t ears* drizzare
◆**cock up** *v/t sep Br infml* mandare a monte
cock-a-doodle-doo *n* chicchirichì *m*
cock-a-hoop *adj* compiaciuto
cockatiel *n* ZOOL calopsite *m*
cockatoo *n* ZOOL cacatua *m*
cockerel *n* galletto *m*
cockeyed *adj infml idea etc* strampalato
cockle *n* ZOOL cardio *m*
cockney I *n* (*person*) cockney *m*/*f inv*, *persona dell'East End londinese*; (*dialect*) cockney *m inv*, *parlata dell'East End londinese* **II** *adj* cockney *inv*, *dell'East End londinese*
cockpit *n of plane* cabina *f* (di pilotaggio)
cockroach *n* scarafaggio *m*
cockscomb *n* cresta *f* di gallo; *person* damerino *m*
cocktail *n* cocktail *m inv* **cocktail party** *n* cocktail party *m inv* **cocktail shaker** *n* shaker *m inv*
cock-up *n Br infml* gran casino *m*; ***it's a ~*** è un gran casino; ***make a ~ of sth*** combinare un gran casino con qc
cocky *adj* (*+er*) *infml* arrogante
cocoa *n drink* cioccolata *f* calda
coconut *n* cocco *m*
coconut palm *n* palma *f* di cocco
cocoon I *n* bozzolo *m* **II** *v/t* avvolgere in un bozzolo, *fig* proteggere
cod *n* ZOOL merluzzo *m*
COD *abbr* (= **cash on delivery**) pagamento *m* contrassegno
coddle *v/t sick person* coccolare; *pej: child* viziare; ***~d eggs*** uova *fpl* bazzotte
code I *n* codice *m*; TEL prefisso *m*; ***in ~*** in codice; ***put into ~*** cifrare; ***~ of conduct*** codice *m* di condotta; ***~ of practice*** deontologia *f*; ***post*** *or* ***zip*** *US* ***~*** codice *m* postale **II** *v/t* codificare; COMPUT creare codice
codeine *n* CHEM codeina *f*
code name *n* nome *m* in codice
coding *n* codifica *f*; COMPUT creazione *f* di codice; ***a new ~ system*** un nuovo sistema di codifica
cod-liver oil *n* olio *m* di fegato di merluzzo
codpiece *n* HIST brachetta *f*
codswallop *n* fesserie *fpl*
co-ed, coed I *n Br infml* (*school*) coeducazione *f*, istruzione *f* in classi miste **II** *adj* → ***coeducational***
coeducational *adj* misto
coerce *v/t* costringere
coercion *n* coercizione *f*
coexist *v/i* coesistere; ***~ with*** *or* ***alongside s.o. / sth*** coesistere con qn / qc
coexistence *n* coesistenza *f*
C of E *abbr* (= **Church of England**) *Br infml* Chiesa *f* Anglicana
coffee *n* caffè *m inv*
coffee bar *n* caffè *m inv* **coffee bean** *n* chicco *m* di caffè **coffee break** *n* pausa *f* per il caffè **coffee cup** *n* tazza *f* da caffè **coffee grinder** *n* macinacaffè *m inv* **coffee maker** *n* caffettiera *f* **coffee pot** *n* caffettiera *f* **coffee shop** *n* caffetteria *f* **coffee table** *n* tavolino *m* **coffee table book** *n* libro *m* in edizione di lusso
coffer *n*: *fig* ***the ~s*** fondi *mpl*
coffin *n* bara *f*
cog *n* MECH dente *m*; *fig* ***he's only a ~ in the machine*** è solo una rotella di un grande ingranaggio
cognac® *n* cognac® *m inv*
cogwheel *n* ruota *f* dentata
cohabit *v/i* convivere
coherent *adj* coerente
cohesion *n of group* coesione *f*
coil I *n of rope* rotolo *m*; *of smoke* spirale *f*; *of hair* crocchia *f*; ELEC bobina *f*; (*contraceptive*) spirale *f* **II** *v/t*: ***~*** (***up***) avvolgere
coin I *n* moneta *f*; ***they are two sides of the same ~*** sono due facce della stessa medaglia **II** *v/t phrase* coniare; *fig* ***to ~ a phrase*** tanto per dire qualcosa di originale
coinage *n* (*system*) monete *fpl*
coincide *v/i* coincidere; ***~ with*** coincidere con
coincidence *n* coincidenza *f*

coincidental *adj* casuale
coin-operated *adj* a gettoni; **~ machine** macchina *f* a gettoni
coitus *n* MED coito *m*
coke[1] *n* (*carbon*) coke *m*
coke[2] *n sl* (*cocaine*) coca *sl f*
Coke® *n* Coca® *f*
col *abbr* (= **column**) col. (colonna *f*)
Col. *abbr* (= **Colonel**) Col. (colonnello *m*)
colander *n* scolapasta *m inv*
cold I *adj* (*+er*) freddo; (*knocked out*) svenuto; ***I'm*** (***feeling***) **~** ho freddo; ***it's* ~** *of weather* fa freddo; ***in* ~ *blood*** a sangue freddo; ***get* ~ *feet*** *infml* farsi prendere dalla fifa *infml*; ***be* ~ *to s.o.*** essere freddo nei confronti di qn; ***that leaves me* ~** mi lascia indifferente; ***be out* ~** *infml* essere privo di sensi **II** *n* freddo *m*; MED raffreddore *m*; ***I have a* ~** ho il raffreddore; ***catch*** (***a***) **~** prendere il raffreddore
cold-blooded *adj a. murder* a sangue freddo; *person* spietato
cold calling *n* porta-a-porta *m*; *by phone* televendite *fpl*
cold cuts *npl* affettati *mpl*
coldly *adv* freddamente
cold meat *n* affettati *mpl*
coldness *n fig* freddezza *f*
cold room *n* cella *f* frigorifera **cold shoulder** *n infml*: ***give s.o. the* ~** trattare qn con freddezza **cold sore** *n* febbre *f* del labbro **cold storage** *n* conservazione *f* in cella frigorifera **cold turkey** *n* crisi *f* di astinenza (dalla droga); ***go* ~** andare in crisi di astinenza **cold war** *n* guerra *f* fredda
coleslaw *n insalata di cavolo, carote, cipolle tritati e maionese*
colic *n* colica *f*
colitis *n* MED colite *f*
collaborate *v/i* collaborare
collaboration *n* collaborazione *f*; *with enemy* collaborazionismo *m*
collaborator *n* collaboratore *m*, -trice *f*; *with enemy* collaborazionista *m/f*
collage *n* collage *m*
collapse I *v/i* crollare; *of person* accasciarsi **II** *n* crollo *m*; *of person* collasso *m*
collapsible *adj* pieghevole
collar *n* collo *m*, colletto *m*; *of dog, cat* collare *m*
collar-bone *n* clavicola *f*
collate *v/t* collazionare
collateral *n* FIN garanzia *f* collaterale
collateral damage *n* MIL, POL danni *mpl* collaterali
colleague *n* collega *m/f*
collect I *v/t person: go* andare a prendere; *person: come* venire a prendere; *tickets, cleaning etc* ritirare; *as hobby* collezionare; (*gather*) raccogliere **II** *v/i* (*gather together*) radunarsi; **~ *for charity*** chiedere contributi per beneficenza **III** *adv US*: ***call* ~** telefonare a carico del destinatario
collected *adj person* controllato; ***the* ~ *works of ...*** l'opera omnia di ...
collection *n* collezione *f*; *in church* colletta *f*; *of poems, stories* raccolta *f*
collective *adj* collettivo
collective bargaining *n* trattative *fpl* sindacali
collector *n* collezionista *m/f*
college *n* istituto *m* parauniversitario; *at Oxford and Cambridge* college *m inv*; ***go to* ~** andare all'università
college of education *n istituto superiore per la formazione degli insegnanti*
collide *v/i* scontrarsi; **~ *with*** scontrarsi con
collie *n* ZOOL collie *m*
collier *n* (*coal miner*) minatore *m* di carbone; (*coal-ship*) carboniera *f*
colliery *n* miniera *f* di carbone
collision *n* collisione *f*, scontro *m*
colloquial *adj* colloquiale
colloquialism *n* espressione *f* colloquiale
collude *v/i form* colludere; **~ *with s.o.*** colludere con qn
collusion *n* JUR collusione *f*; ***they're acting in* ~** agiscono in collusione
cologne *n* acqua *f* di colonia
Cologne *n* Colonia
colon *n punctuation* due punti *mpl*; ANAT colon *m inv*
colonel *n* colonnello *m*
Colonel Blimp *n anziano reazionario e pomposo*
colonial *adj* coloniale
colonialism *n* colonialismo *m*
colonization *n* colonizzazione *f*
colonize *v/t country* colonizzare
colonnade *n* colonnato *m*
colony *n* colonia *f*
color *etc US* → ***colour*** *etc*

coloratura *n* MUS coloratura *f*
colossal *adj* colossale
colostomy *n* MED colostomia *f*; **~ *bag*** sacca *f* per colostomia
colour, *US* **color I** *n* **1.** colore *m*; ***what ~ is …?*** di che colore è …?; ***in ~*** *film etc* a colori **2.** *in cheeks* colorito *m* **3. *~s*** MIL bandiera *f* **II** *v/t* colorare; *one's hair* tingere **III** *v/i* (*blush*) diventare rosso
colour-blind, *US* **color-blind** *adj* daltonico
coloured, *US* **colored** *adj person* di colore
colour fast, *US* **color fast** *adj* con colori resistenti
colourful, *US* **colorful** *adj* pieno di colori; *account* pittoresco
colouring, *US* **coloring** *n* colorito *m*
colour photograph, *US* **color photograph** *n* fotografia *f* a colori **colour scheme**, *US* **color scheme** *n* abbinamento *m* dei colori **colour supplement** *n Br* inserto *m* a colori **colour TV**, *US* **color TV** *n* tv *f inv* a colori
colt *n* puledro *m*
column *n* colonna *f*; (*newspaper feature*) rubrica *f*
columnist *n giornalista che cura una rubrica*
coma *n* coma *m inv*; ***be in a ~*** essere in coma; ***fall into a ~*** entrare in coma
comatose *adj* comatoso
comb I *n* pettine *m* **II** *v/t* pettinare; *area* rastrellare; ***~ one's hair*** pettinarsi
◆**comb through** *v/t files etc* spulciare; *shops* setacciare
combat I *n* combattimento *m* **II** *v/t* combattere
combatant *n* combattente *m*
combative *adj* (*pugnacious*) bellicoso; (*competitive*) combattivo
combat jacket *n* giacca *f* da combattimento **combat troops** *npl* truppe *fpl* da combattimento
combination *n* combinazione *f*
combine I *v/t* unire; *ingredients* mescolare; ***~ business with pleasure*** unire l'utile al dilettevole **II** *v/i of chemical elements* combinarsi
combine harvester *n* mietitrebbia *f*
combustible *adj* combustibile
combustion *n* combustione *f*
come *v/i* ⟨*pret* ***came***, *past part* ***come***⟩ venire; *of train, bus* arrivare; (*be, become*) diventare; COMM (*be available*) essere disponibile; *infml* (*have orgasm*) venire; ***coming!*** arrivo!; ***he came to see us*** è venuto a trovarci; ***how ~?*** *infml* come mai? *infml*; ***how ~ you're so late?*** come mai sei così in ritardo?; ***his dreams came true*** i suoi sogni si sono avverati; ***the handle has ~ loose*** la maniglia si è allentata; ***milk now ~s in plastic bottles*** il latte viene venduto in bottiglie di plastica; (*+inf*) ***I have ~ to believe him*** ho finito per credergli; ***(now I) ~ to think of it*** ora che ci penso; ***~ again?*** *infml* come?, che hai detto?; ***she is as vain as they ~*** *infml* è estremamente vanitosa; ***don't ~ the innocent with me*** *Br infml* non fare l'innocente con me
◆**come about** *v/i* (*happen*) succedere; ***this is why it came about*** è successo per questo motivo
◆**come across I** *v/t* (*find*) trovare; ***if you come across my watch …*** se trovi per caso il mio orologio … **II** *v/i of idea, humour* essere capito; ***she comes across as …*** dà l'impressione di essere …
◆**come along** *v/i* (*come too*) venire; (*turn up*) presentarsi; (*progress*) fare progressi; ***how is it coming along?*** come sta andando?; ***your Italian has come along a lot*** il tuo italiano è migliorato molto
◆**come apart** *v/i* smontarsi; (*break*) andare in pezzi; ***the chair is coming apart*** la sedia si sta sfasciando
◆**come away** *v/i of person, button* venire via; (*become detached*) staccarsi; ***come away with me for a few days*** vieni via con me per alcuni giorni; ***come away from there!*** vieni via di lì!
◆**come back** *v/i* ritornare; ***it came back to me*** mi è tornato in mente; ***the colour is coming back to her cheeks*** le sue guance stanno riprendendo colore
◆**come by I** *v/i* passare **II** *v/t* (*acquire*) ottenere
◆**come down** *v/i* venire giù; *in price, amount etc* scendere; *of rain, snow* cadere; ***he came down the stairs*** è sceso dalle scale
◆**come down to** *v/t* essere tutta una

questione di

◆ **come down with** *v/t* prendersi; ***he came down with measles*** si è preso il morbillo

◆ **come for** *v/t* (*attack*) assalire; (*collect*) venire a prendere

◆ **come forward** *v/i* (*present o.s.*) farsi avanti; ***come forward with help*** offrire aiuto; ***come forward with a good suggestion*** avanzare un buon suggerimento

◆ **come from** *v/t* venire da; ***where do you come from?*** di dove sei?

◆ **come in** *v/i* entrare; *of train, in race* arrivare; *of tide* salire; ***come in!*** entra!; ***a report has just come in of ...*** è appena arrivata notizia di ...; ***he came in fourth*** è arrivato quarto; ***he has £15,000 coming in every year*** ha 15.000 sterline di entrate all'anno; ***where do I come in?*** qual è il mio ruolo?; ***that will come in handy*** *infml or* ***useful*** ciò si rivelerà utile

◆ **come in for** *v/t* attirare; ***come in for criticism*** attirare delle critiche

◆ **come in on** *v/t* partecipare a; ***come in on a deal*** stare a un accordo

◆ **come into** *v/t money* ereditare; ***come into being*** nascere; ***come into one's own*** farsi valere; ***come into s.o.'s possession*** passare in possesso di qn

◆ **come off I** *v/i of handle etc* staccarsi; ***he came off well in comparison to his brother*** se l'è cavata bene rispetto a suo fratello **II** *v/t* cadere da; *drug* smettere di prendere; ***he came off his bicycle*** è caduto dalla bicicletta; ***come off it!*** *infml* ma smettila! *infml*

◆ **come on** *v/i* (*progress*) fare progressi; ***how's the work coming on?*** come sta venendo il lavoro?; ***come on!*** dai!; *in disbelief* ma dai!

◆ **come out** *v/i of person, book, sun* uscire; *of results, product* venir fuori; *of stain* venire via; *of gay* rendere nota la propria omosessualità; ***come out for / against sth*** pronunciarsi a favore / sfavore di qc; ***he came out in a rash*** gli è venuto uno sfogo; ***the photo of the hills hasn't come out very well*** PHOT la foto delle colline non è venuta bene

◆ **come out with** *v/t* venir fuori con

◆ **come over I** *v/i* (*change allegiance*) passare dall'altra parte; *infml* (*become suddenly*) sentirsi improvvisamente; ***he came over to our side*** è passato dalla nostra parte; ***I came over (all) queer*** mi sono sentito improvvisamente strano **II** *v/t feelings* impossessarsi di; ***what's come over you?*** che cosa ti prende?

◆ **come round** *v/i to s.o.'s home* passare; (*regain consciousness*) rinvenire

◆ **come through I** *v/i* arrivare; ***your papers haven't come through yet*** i tuoi documenti non sono ancora arrivati; ***his divorce has come through*** gli è arrivato il divorzio **II** *v/t illness, danger* superare

◆ **come to I** *v/t place, position* arrivare a; ***that comes to £70*** fanno 70 sterline; ***that didn't come to anything*** non ha portato a nulla; ***when it comes to mathematics ...*** se si tratta di matematica ...; ***it comes to the same thing*** il risultato è lo stesso; ***come to a decision*** giungere a una decisione; ***what is the world coming to!*** il mondo sta andando a rotoli! **II** *v/i* (*a.* **come to oneself**) (*regain consciousness*) rinvenire

◆ **come up** *v/i* salire; *of sun* sorgere; ***something has come up*** si è presentato qualcosa

◆ **come up against** *v/t* trovarsi di fronte; *opposing team* affrontare

◆ **come up to** *v/t* avvicinarsi a

◆ **come up with** *v/t new idea etc* venir fuori con

comeback *n* ritorno *m*; ***make a ~*** tornare alla ribalta

comedian *n* comico *m*, -a *f*; *pej* buffone *m*

comedienne *n* attrice *f* comica

comedown *n* passo *m* indietro

comedy *n* commedia *f*; FILM film *m* comico

come-hither *adj* seducente

comely *adj* avvenente

come-on *n infml* occhiata *f* (*or* gesto *m*) invitante; *fig* **give s.o. the ~** allettare qn

comet *n* cometa *f*

comeuppance *n infml*: ***he'll get his ~*** avrà quello che si merita

comfort I *n* comodità *f inv*; ***live in ~*** vivere nell'agiatezza; ***with all modern ~s*** con tutte le comodità moderne; (*consolation*) conforto *m*; ***take ~ from the fact that ...*** trarre conforto dal fatto che ...; ***you are a great ~ to me*** mi sei di grande conforto; ***too close for ~*** troppo vicino (per poter stare tranquilli) **II** *v/t* confortare

comfortable *adj chair, room* comodo; ***be ~*** *in chair* stare comodo; *in situation* essere a proprio agio; (*financially*) essere agiato

comfortably *adj be sitting* comodamente; ***be ~ off*** essere benestante

comforter *n US* (*quilt*) trapunta *f*; *US* (*baby's dummy*) ciucciotto *m*; *Br* (*scarf*) sciarpa *f*

comfrey *n* BOT consolida *f* maggiore

comfy *adj* (*+er*) *infml* → ***comfortable***

comic I *n to read* fumetto *m*; (*comedian*) comico *m*, -a *f* **II** *adj* comico

comical *adj* comico

comic book *n* fumetto *m* **comic opera** *n* opera *f* buffa **comic strip** *n* striscia *f* (di fumetti)

coming I *adj week* prossimo **II** *n of spring* arrivo *m*; ***~s and goings*** via-vai

comma *n* virgola *f*

command I *n* comando *m*; *fig* (*mastery*) padronanza *f*; ***be in ~*** essere al comando; ***his ~ of English is excellent*** ha un'eccellente padronanza dell'inglese; ***I am at your ~*** sono ai tuoi ordini **II** *v/t* (*order*) ordinare; *army, ship* comandare; ***~ s.o.'s respect*** imporre rispetto a qn

commandant *n* MIL comandante *m*

commandeer *v/t* appropriarsi di

commander *n* comandante *m*

commander-in-chief *n* comandante *m* in capo

commanding officer *n* ufficiale *m* comandante

commandment *n*: ***the Ten Commandments*** REL i Dieci Comandamenti

commando *n* (*soldier*) componente *m* di un commando

commemorate *v/t* commemorare

commemoration *n*: ***in ~ of*** in commemorazione di

commemorative *adj* commemorativo

commence *v/t & v/i* cominciare

commend *v/t* (*praise*) lodare; (*recommend*) raccomandare

commendable *adj* lodevole

commendation *n for bravery* riconoscimento *m*

commensurate *adj*: ***~ with*** commisurato a

comment I *n* commento *m*; ***no ~!*** no comment! **II** *v/i* fare commenti; ***~ on*** fare commenti su

commentary *n* cronaca *f*

commentate *v/i* commentare; ***~ on*** commentare

commentator *n on TV* telecronista *m/f*; *on radio* radiocronista *m/f*

commerce *n* commercio *m*

commercial I *adj* commerciale; ***of no ~ value*** privo di valore commerciale; ***it makes good ~ sense*** è commercialmente opportuno **II** *n* (*advert*) pubblicità *f inv*; ***during the ~s*** durante la pubblicità

commercial bank *n* banca *f* commerciale **commercial break** *n* interruzione *f* pubblicitaria

commercialize *v/t Christmas etc* commercializzare

commercial television *n* televisione *f* privata **commercial traveller** *n* rappresentante *m/f*

commiserate *v/i* esprimere rincrescimento (***with*** a)

commiseration *n* commiserazione *f*; ***my ~s*** mi rincresce (***on*** per)

commissary *n* delegato *m*; MIL spaccio *m*

commission I *n* (*payment, committee*) commissione *f*; (*job*) incarico *m*; (*committee*) commissione *f*; ***charge ~*** addebitare una commissione; (***EC***) ***Commission*** Commissione europea **II** *v/t for a job* incaricare; ***~ s.o. to do sth*** incaricare qn di fare qc

commissionaire *n* portiere *m*

commissioned officer *n* ufficiale *m* incaricato

Commissioner *n in European Union* Commissario *m*, -a *f*

commit *v/t* ⟨*pret & past part* ***-ted***⟩ *crime* commettere; *money* assegnare; (*involve, obligate*) impegnare (***to*** a); ***~ o.s.*** impegnarsi (***to*** per); ***~ s.o.*** (***to prison***) far incarcerare qn; ***have s.o. ~ted*** (***to an asylum***) far internare qn (in manicomio); ***~ s.o. for trial*** rinviare qn a giudizio; ***~ s.o. / sth to s.o.'s care*** affidare qn / qc alle cure di qn; ***~ resources to a project*** assegnare le risorse per un progetto; ***that doesn't ~ you to buying the book*** in questo modo non sei tenuto ad acquistare il libro; ***you have to ~ yourself totally to the cause*** devi essere completamente votato alla causa; ***the government has ~ted itself to reforms*** il governo si è impegnato ad attuare le riforme

commitment *n* impegno *m*; ***his family ~s*** i suoi impegni familiari; ***his teaching ~s*** i suoi impegni di insegnamento; ***make a ~ to do sth*** *form* prendere l'impegno di fare qc; ***he is frightened of ~*** ha paura di impegnarsi

committed *adj* (*dedicated*) impegnato; ***he is so ~ to his work that …*** è talmente devoto al suo lavoro che …; ***all his life he has been ~ to this cause*** si è dedicato a questa causa per tutta la vita

committee *n* comitato *m*

commode *n* (*chest of drawers*) comò *m*; (*night-commode*) seggetta *f*

commodious *adj* spazioso

commodity *n* prodotto *m*

commodore *n* MIL commodoro *m*

common *adj* (*+er*) comune; (*frequently seen etc*) frequente; *belief*, *custom* diffuso; ***in ~*** in comune; ***have sth in ~ with s.o.*** avere qc in comune con qn; ***~ land*** terre *fpl* di proprietà pubblica; ***it is ~ knowledge that …*** è universalmente noto che …; ***find ~ ground*** trovare un punto d'incontro; ***sth is ~ to everyone / sth*** qc è comune a tutti / qc; ***it's quite a ~ sight*** è molto comune; ***it's ~ for visitors to feel ill here*** è frequente che i visitatori qui si sentano male; ***the ~ man*** l'uomo comune; ***the ~ people*** la gente comune

Common Agricultural Policy *n* politica *f* agricola comune **common cold** *n* raffreddore *m* **common denominator** *n*: ***lowest ~*** MATH, *fig* minimo comun denominatore *m*

commoner *n* persona *f* non nobile

common law husband *n convivente al quale spettano legalmente i diritti di un marito* **common law wife** *n convivente alla quale spettano legalmente i diritti di una moglie*

commonly *adv* comunemente; ***a ~ held belief*** una convinzione diffusa; (***more***) ***~ known as …*** (più) comunemente noto come …

Common Market *n* Mercato *m* Comune **common-or-garden** *adj Br* ordinario **commonplace** *adj* comune **common room** *n* sala *f* comune

Commons *npl*: ***the ~*** la Camera dei Comuni

common sense *n* buon senso *m*

Commonwealth *n* Commonwealth *m*

commotion *n* confusione *f*; ***cause a ~*** causare scompiglio

communal *adj* comune

communally *adv* in comune; ***be ~ owned*** essere di proprietà comune

commune *n* comune *f*

communicate *v/t & v/i* comunicare; ***~ with s.o.*** comunicare con qn; ***~ sth to s.o.*** comunicare qc a qn

communication *n* comunicazione *f*; ***be in ~ with s.o.*** essere in contatto con qn

communication cord *n Br* freno *m* d'emergenza

communications *npl* comunicazioni *fpl*

communications satellite *n* satellite *m* per telecomunicazioni **communications software** *n* software *m* di comunicazione

communicative *adj person* comunicativo

communion *n* (*intercourse etc*) relazioni *fpl*

Communion *n* REL comunione *f*; ***take ~*** ricevere la comunione

communiqué *n* comunicato *m* ufficiale

Communism *n* comunismo *m*

Communist I *adj* comunista **II** *n* comunista *m/f*

community *n* comunità *f inv*; ***the ~ at large*** la collettività; ***sense of ~*** senso *m* della comunità; ***work in the ~*** operare nella comunità

community centre, *US* **community center** *n* centro *m* comunitario **community chest** *n US fondo di beneficenza della comunità* **community college** *n US istituto di istruzione post-secondaria di durata biennale* **community home** *n* istituto *m* per minori **community service** *n* servizio *m* civile (come pena per reati minori)

commute I *v/i* fare il / la pendolare;

within commuting distance all'interno della distanza pendolare **II** *v/t* JUR commutare
commuter *n* pendolare *m/f*
commuter belt *n area intorno a una metropoli da cui provengono i pendolari che si recano quotidianamente in città*
commuter traffic *n* traffico *m* dei pendolari **commuter train** *n* treno *m* dei pendolari
compact I *adj* (+*er*) compatto **II** *n for powder* portacipria *m inv* **III** *v/t snow, soil* compattare
compact disc *n* → ***CD***; **~ *player*** lettore *m* di CD
companion *n* compagno *m*, -a *f*; ***travelling ~*** compagno *m* di viaggio; ***drinking ~*** compagno *m* di bevute
companionable *adj* socievole
companionship *n* compagnia *f*
company[1] *n* COMM società *f inv*; (*ballet company, theatre company*) compagnia *f*; (*companionship, guests*) compagnia *f*; MIL compagnia *f*
company[2] *n*: ***keep s.o. ~*** fare compagnia a qn
company car *n* auto *f inv* della ditta **company director** *n* amministratore *m* di società **company law** *n* diritto *m* societario **company policy** *n* politica *f* societaria
comparable *adj* paragonabile; (*similar*) simile
comparably *adv* in modo analogo
comparative I *adj* (*relative*) relativo; ***live in ~ luxury*** vivere relativamente nel lusso; *study, method* comparato; GRAM comparativo **II** *n* GRAM comparativo *m*
comparatively *adv* relativamente
compare I *v/t* paragonare; **~ *sth with sth / s.o. with s.o.*** paragonare qc a qc / qn a qn; ***~d with ...*** rispetto a ... **II** *v/i* reggere il confronto; ***how did he ~?*** com'era rispetto gli altri?
comparison *n* paragone *m*, confronto *m*; ***in ~ with*** in confronto a; ***there's no ~*** non c'è paragone
compartment *n* scomparto *m*; RAIL scompartimento *m*
compartmentalize *v/t* dividere in compartimenti
compass *n* bussola *f*; (***pair of***) ***~es*** *for geometry* compasso *m*
compass bearing *n* rilevamento *m* alla bussola
compassion *n* compassione *f*
compassionate *adj* compassionevole
compassionate leave *n* congedo *m* per motivi familiari
compatibility *n* compatibilità *f inv*
compatible *adj a.* COMPUT compatibile; ***we're not ~*** siamo incompatibili; ***be ~ with*** essere compatibile con
compatriot *n* compatriota *m/f*
compel *v/t* ⟨*pret & past part* **-led**⟩ costringere; ***be ~led to*** essere costretto a
compelling *adj argument* convincente; *film, book* avvincente
compendium *n* compendio *m*; ***~ of games*** compendio di giochi
compensate I *v/t with money* risarcire **II** *v/i*: **~ *for*** compensare
compensation *n money* risarcimento *m*; *reward* vantaggio *m*; *comfort* consolazione *f*
compensatory *adj* compensativo
compère I *n* presentatore *m*, -trice *f* **II** *v/t*: **~ *a show*** presentare uno spettacolo
compete *v/i* competere; (*take part*) gareggiare; **~ *for*** contendersi; **~ *with / against*** competere con / contro
competence *n* competenza *f*
competent *adj* competente
competently *adv* con competenza
competition *n* (*contest*) concorso *m*; SPORTS gara *f*; (*competing, competitors*) concorrenza *f*; ***be in ~ with s.o.*** essere in competizione con qn; ***unfair ~*** concorrenza sleale
competitive *adj* competitivo; *sport* agonistico; *price, offer* concorrenziale; **~ *spirit*** spirito di competizione; ***a highly ~ market*** un mercato altamente competitivo
competitively *adv*: **~ *priced*** a prezzi concorrenziali
competitiveness *n* competitività *f inv*
competitor *n in contest* concorrente *m/f*; ***our ~s*** COMM la concorrenza
compilation *n* compilazione *f*; *of material* raccolta *f*
compile *v/t* compilare
complacency *n* autocompiacimento *m*
complacent *adj* compiaciuto; ***be ~ about sth*** compiacersi di qc

complain *v/i* lamentarsi; **(*I*) *can't ~*** *infml* non mi posso lamentare; *to shop*, *manager* reclamare; ***~ about*** lamentarsi di; ***~ of*** MED accusare

complaint *n* lamentela *f*; *to shop* reclamo *m*; MED disturbo *m*; ***make a ~*** fare reclamo; ***~s department*** COMM ufficio *m* reclami; ***a very rare ~*** un disturbo estremamente raro

complaisant *adj* cortese

complement I *n* (*addition*) aggiunta *f*; (*number*) organico *m*; ***we've got our full ~ in the office now*** l'organico dell'ufficio è ora al completo GRAM complemento *m* **II** *v/t* completare; ***they ~ each other*** si completano bene

complementary *adj* complementare

complementary angles *npl* angoli *mpl* complementari **complementary colour** *n* colore *m* complementare

complete I *adj* (*entire*) completo; (*finished*) terminato; (*absolute*) assoluto; *beginner*, *disaster* totale; *surprise* vero (e proprio); ***we were ~ strangers*** eravamo perfetti estranei; ***I made a ~ fool of myself*** mi sono comportato da perfetto idiota **II** *v/t task*, *building etc* completare; *form* compilare

completely *adv* completamente

completion *n* completamento *m*; ***payment on ~*** pagamento a conclusione lavori; ***on ~ of the course*** a corso ultimato

complex I *adj* complesso **II** *n* complesso *m*; ***industrial ~*** complesso *m* industriale; ***he has a ~ about his ears*** i suoi orecchi gli creano complessi

complexion *n facial* carnagione *f*

complexity *n* complessità *f inv*

compliance *n* conformità *f inv*

complicate *v/t* complicare

complicated *adj* complicato

complication *n* complicazione *f*; ***~s*** MED complicazioni

compliment I *n* complimento *m*; ***pay s.o. a ~*** fare un complimento a qn; **(*with the*) *~s of*** omaggio di **II** *v/t* fare i complimenti a; ***~ s.o. on sth*** complimentarsi con qn per qc

complimentary *adj* lusinghiero; (*free*) in omaggio; ***be ~ about s.o. / sth*** fare complimenti a qn / per qc; ***~ copy*** copia *f* (in) omaggio

compliments slip *n* biglietto *m* intestato della ditta

comply *v/i* ⟨*pret & past part* ***-ied***⟩ ubbidire; ***~ with*** osservare; *of products*, *equipment* essere conforme a

component *n* componente *m*

comportment *n* comportamento *m*

compose *v/t music*, *poetry* comporre; ***be ~d of*** essere composto da; ***~ o.s.*** ricomporsi; ***water is ~d of ...*** l'acqua è composta da ...; ***~ one's thoughts*** ricomporsi

composed *adj* (*calm*) calmo

composer *n* MUS compositore *m*, -trice *f*

composite I *adj* composito **II** *n* misto *m*; *US* identikit *m*

composition *n a.* MUS composizione *f*; (*essay*) tema *m*

compost I *n* concime *m* **II** *v/t plants* far diventare concime

composure *n* calma *f*

compote *n* composta *f*

compound[1] **I** *n* CHEM composto *m* **II** *adj* GRAM composto **III** *v/t* comporre; *problem* aggravare

compound[2] *n* (*enclosed area*) complesso *m*; *in zoo* recinto *m*

compound fracture *n* MED frattura *f* esposta **compound interest** *n* interesse *m* composto

comprehend *v/t* (*understand*) capire

comprehensible *adj* comprensibile

comprehension *n* comprensione *f*; EDU esercizio *m* di comprensione; ***that is beyond my ~*** è al di là della mia comprensione

comprehensive *adj* esauriente

comprehensive insurance *n* polizza *f* casco

comprehensively *adv* in modo esauriente

comprehensive school *n* scuola *f* secondaria

compress I *v/t air*, *gas* comprimere; *information* condensare **II** *n* MED impacco *m*

compressed air *n* aria *f* compressa

comprise *v/t* comprendere; (*make-up*) costituire; ***be ~d of*** essere composto da

compromise I *n* compromesso *m*; ***reach a ~*** arrivare a un compromesso **II** *v/i* arrivare a un compromesso **III** *v/t* (*jeopardize*) compromettere; ***~***

o.s. compromettersi
compulsion *n* PSYCH compulsione *f*; (*forcing*) coercizione *f*; ***you are under no ~*** non sei assolutamente costretto
compulsive *adj behaviour* patologico; *reading*, *viewing* avvincente
compulsory *adj* obbligatorio; ***~ education*** scuola *f* dell'obbligo
compunction *n* rimorso *m*; ***he appeared to have no ~ about telling her*** sembrava non provare alcun rimorso per averglielo detto
computer *n* computer *m inv*; ***have sth on ~*** avere qc sul computer
computer-aided design *n* progettazione *f* assistita dall'elaboratore **computer-aided manufacture** *n* produzione *f* computerizzata **computer-controlled** *adj* controllato dal computer **computer dating** *n*: ***~ agency*** *or* ***bureau*** agenzia *f* matrimoniale computerizzata **computer game** *n* computer game *m inv* **computer-generated** *adj* generato da computer **computer graphics** *npl* computer grafica *f*
computerization *n of information etc* informatizzazione *f*; ***the ~ of the factory*** l'informatizzazione *f* della fabbrica
computerize *v/t* informatizzare
computerized axial tomography *n* (*abbr* **CAT**) tomografia *f* assiale computerizzata (*abbr* TAC)
computer literate *adj* che ha dimestichezza con il computer **computer model** *n* modello *m* informatico **computer network** *n* rete *f* di computer **computer-operated** *adj* computerizzato **computer operator** *n* operatore *m* informatico **computer printout** *n* stampa *f* al computer **computer program** *n* programma *m* informatico **computer programmer** *n* programmatore *m* informatico **computer science** *n* informatica *f* **computer scientist** *n* informatico *m*, -a *f* **computer studies** *npl* informatica *f* **computer virus** *n* virus *m inv* informatico
computing *n* informatica *f*; ***her husband's in ~*** suo marito si occupa di informatica
comrade *n a.* POL compagno *m*, -a *f*
comradeship *n* cameratismo *m*

con[1] → ***pro***
con[2] **I** *v/t* ⟨*pret & past part* **-ned**⟩ *infml* truffare; ***~ s.o. into doing sth*** far fare qc a qn con l'inganno; ***~ s.o. out of sth*** sottrarre qc a qn con l'inganno **II** *n infml* truffa *f*
concave *adj* concavo
conceal *v/t* nascondere; ***~ sth from s.o.*** tenere nascosto qc a qn
concealment *n* occultazione *f*
concede *v/t* (*admit*) ammettere; *right* concedere; ***~ defeat*** ammettere la sconfitta; ***~ a goal*** SPORTS incassare un goal; ***~ a point*** SPORTS regalare un punto; ***I ~ that ...*** ammetto che ...
conceit *n* presunzione *f*
conceited *adj* presuntuoso
conceivable *adj* concepibile
conceive I *v/i child* concepire; (*imagine*) immaginare **II** *v/i* (*woman*) rimanere incinta
◆**conceive of** *v/t* immaginare; ***he would never conceive of doing anything like that*** non si sognerebbe mai di fare una cosa del genere
concentrate I *v/i* concentrarsi; ***~ on*** concentrarsi su **II** *v/t one's attention*, *energies* concentrare **III** *n* concentrato *m*
concentrated *adj juice etc* concentrato
concentration *n* concentrazione *f*; (*gathering*) concentramento *m*; ***powers of ~*** capacità *f inv* di concentrazione
concentration camp *n* campo *m* di concentramento
concentric *adj* concentrico
concept *n* concetto *m*; ***his ~ of marriage*** il suo concetto del matrimonio
conception *n of child* concepimento *m*; (*idea*) concezione *f*; ***he has no ~ of how difficult it is*** non ha la minima idea di quanto sia difficile
concern I *n* **1.** (*anxiety*) preoccupazione *f*; (*care*) interesse *m*; ***~ at*** *or* ***about*** *or* ***for*** preoccupazione per; ***there's no cause for ~*** non c'è motivo di preoccuparsi; ***issues of national ~*** problemi *mpl* di interesse nazionale **2.** (*business*) affare *m*; (*company*) impresa *f*; ***it's none of your ~*** non sono affari tuoi **II** *v/t* (*involve*) riguardare; (*worry*) preoccupare; ***~ o.s. with*** preoccuparsi di

concerned *adj* **1.** (*anxious*) preoccupato; (*caring*) interessato; ***be ~ at** or **about** or **for*** essere preoccupato per; ***be ~ with*** preoccuparsi di **2.** (*involved*) in questione; ***as far as I'm ~*** per quanto mi riguarda
concerning *prep* riguardo a
concert I *n* concerto *m*; ***were you at the ~?*** sei stato al concerto?; ***Madonna in ~*** Madonna in concerto **II** *v/t* concertare
concerted *adj* (*joint*) congiunto; ***they made a ~ effort to get it right*** hanno compiuto uno sforzo congiunto per ottenere il risultato desiderato
concertgoer *n* frequentatore *m*, -trice *f* di concerti
concert hall *n* sala *f* da concerto
concertina *n* MUS concertina *f*
concertmaster *n* primo violino *m*
concerto *n* concerto *m*
concession *n* (*compromise*) concessione *f*; ***make ~s to s.o.*** fare concessioni a qn
concessionaire *n* concessionario *m*
conch *n* conchiglia *f*
concierge *n* portiere *m*, -a *f*
conciliatory *adj* conciliatorio
concise *adj* conciso
conclude I *v/t* concludere; ***~ sth from sth*** concludere qc da qc; ***~ that*** concludere che **II** *v/i* concludere; ***I would like to ~ by saying ...*** vorrei concludere dicendo ...
conclusion *n* conclusione *f*; ***come to the ~ that*** giungere alla conclusione che; ***in ~*** in conclusione
conclusive *adj* conclusivo
concoct *v/t meal*, *drink* mettere insieme; *excuse*, *story* inventare
concoction *n food*, *drink* intruglio *m*
concomitance *n* concomitanza *f*
concomitant *adj* concomitante
concord *n* concordia *f*
concordance *n* concordanza *f*
concordant *adj* concordante
concourse *n* atrio *m*
concrete[1] *adj* concreto
concrete[2] *n* calcestruzzo *m*; ***~ jungle*** giungla *f* di cemento
concretion *n* concrezione *f*
concubine *n* concubina *f*
concur *v/i* ⟨*pret & past part* **-red**⟩ essere d'accordo
concurrence *n* concomitanza *f*; (*agreement*) approvazione *f*
concurrent *adj* simultaneo; ***be ~ with sth*** *form* concordare con qc
concuss *v/t* causare una commozione cerebrale; ***be ~ed*** avere una commozione cerebrale
concussion *n* commozione *f* cerebrale
condemn *v/t action* condannare; *building* dichiarare inagibile; (*doom*) condannare; ***~ s.o. to death*** condannare qn a morte
condemnation *n of action* condanna *f*
condensation *n on walls*, *windows* condensa *f*
condense I *v/t* (*make shorter*) condensare **II** *v/i of steam* condensarsi
condensed milk *n* latte *m* condensato
condescend *v/i*: ***he ~ed to speak to me*** si è degnato di rivolgermi la parola
condescending *adj* (*patronizing*) condiscendente
condescendingly *adv pej* con condiscendenza
condescension *n* condiscendenza *f* (*a. pej*)
condiment *n* condimento *m*
condition I *n* condizione *f*; MED disturbo *m*; ***~s*** (*circumstances*) condizioni; ***working ~s*** condizioni di lavoro; ***living ~s*** condizioni di vita; ***weather ~s*** condizioni atmosferiche; ***on ~ that*** a condizione che; ***in / out of ~*** in / fuori forma; ***on no ~*** a nessuna condizione; ***he made it a ~ that ...*** ha posto come condizione che; ***it is in bad ~*** è in cattive condizioni; ***he is in a critical ~*** si trova in una condizione critica; ***you're in no ~ to drive*** non sei in condizione di guidare; ***keep in / get into ~*** mantenersi / mettersi in forma; ***he has a heart ~*** MED ha un disturbo cardiaco **II** *v/t* PSYCH condizionare; *train* preparare
conditional I *adj acceptance* condizionale **II** *n* GRAM condizionale *m*
conditioner *n for hair* balsamo *m*; *for fabric* ammorbidente *m*
conditioning *n* PSYCH condizionamento *m*
condolences *npl* condoglianze *fpl*
condom *n* preservativo *m*
condominium *n US* (*house*) condominio *m*; (*apartment*) appartamento *m*

(in un condominio)
condone *v/t actions* scusare
condor *n* condor *m*
conducive *adj*: ***be ~ to*** favorire
conduct I *n* (*behaviour*) condotta *f* **II** *v/t* (*carry out*) condurre; ***he ~ed his own defence*** ha assunto la propria difesa; ELEC condurre; MUS dirigere; ***~ o.s.*** comportarsi **III** *v/i* MUS dirigere
conducted tour *n* visita *f* guidata
conductor *n* MUS direttore *m* d'orchestra; *on bus* bigliettaio *m*; PHYS conduttore *m*
conductress *n* bigliettaia *f*
cone *n* cono *m*; *of pine tree* pigna *f*; *on motorway* birillo *m*
◆**cone off** *v/t sep* chiudere al traffico
confectioner *n* pasticciere *m*, -a *f*
confectioner's sugar *n US* zucchero *m* a velo
confectionery *n* dolciumi *mpl*
confederacy *n* POL confederazione *f*
confederate I *adj* confederato **II** *n* confederato *m*, -a *f*; (*accomplice*) complice *m/f* **III** *v/t* confederare **IV** *v/i* confederarsi
confederation *n* confederazione *f*
confer ⟨*pret & past part* **-red**⟩ **I** *v/t* (*bestow*) conferire; ***~ sth on s.o.*** conferire qc a qn **II** *v/i* (*discuss*) confabulare; ***~ about*** confabulare di
conference *n* congresso *m*; ***family ~*** consiglio *m* di famiglia
conference call *n* TEL conferenza *f* telefonica **conference centre**, *US* **conference center** *n* centro *m* congressi **conference room** *n* sala *f* riunioni
confess I *v/t sin*, *crime* confessare **II** *v/i* confessare; REL confessarsi; ***~ to sth*** confessare qc; ***~ to a weakness for sth*** confessare di avere un debole per qc
confession *n* confessione *f*
confessional *n* REL confessionale *m*
confessor *n* REL confessore *m*
confetti *n* coriandoli *mpl*
confidant *n* confidente *m*
confidante *n* confidente *f*
confide *v/t* confidare
◆**confide in** *v/t* confidarsi con; ***confide in s.o. about sth*** confidarsi con qn su qc
confidence *n* (*assurance*) sicurezza *f* (di sé); (*trust*) fiducia *f*; ***have ~ in*** avere fiducia in; ***in ~*** in confidenza
confidence trick *n* truffa *f* **confidence trickster** *n* → ***con man***
confident *adj* sicuro; *person* sicuro di sé; ***be ~ of sth*** essere sicuro di qc; ***be ~ that*** essere sicuro che
confidential *adj* riservato, confidenziale; *adviser* di fiducia
confidentially *adv* in confidenza
confidently *adv* con sicurezza
configuration *n* configurazione *f*; PSYCH gestalt *f*
configure *v/t* COMPUT configurare
confine *v/t* (*imprison*) richiudere; (*restrict*) limitare; ***be ~d to one's bed*** essere costretto a letto; ***~ o.s. to sth*** limitarsi a qc
confined *adj space* ristretto
confinement *n* (*imprisonment*) reclusione *f*; MED parto *m*
confines *npl* confini *mpl*
confirm *v/t* confermare
confirmation *n* conferma *f*; REL confermazione *f*; *of Roman Catholics* cresima *f*
confirmed *adj bachelor* incallito; *atheist* convinto; *booking* confermato
confiscate *v/t* sequestrare
confiscation *n* confisca *f*
conflagration *n* conflagrazione *f*
conflate *v/t* combinare
conflict I *n* conflitto *m*; ***be in ~ with s.o.* / *sth*** essere in contrasto con qn / qc; ***~ of interests*** conflitto di interessi **II** *v/i of statements*, *accounts* essere in conflitto; *of dates* coincidere
conflicting *adj* in conflitto
confluence *n* confluenza *f*
conform *v/i* conformarsi; ***~ to*** *of products*, *acts etc* essere conforme a
conformation *n* conformazione *f*
conformist *n* conformista *m/f*
conformity *n* conformità *f inv*
confound *v/t* (*bewilder*) sconcertare; (*mix up*) confondere
confounded *adj infml* maledetto
confront *v/t* (*face*) affrontare; ***~ s.o. with sth*** mettere qn di fronte a qc; ***the problems ~ing us*** i problemi che dobbiamo affrontare
confrontation *n* scontro *m*
confuse *v/t* confondere; ***~ s.o. with s.o.*** confondere qn con qn
confused *adj* confuso
confusing *adj* che confonde
confusion *n* (*disorder*) confusione *f*;

be in ~ essere in imbarazzo; ***throw everything into ~*** gettare tutto nel caos
confutation *n* confutazione *f*
confute *v/t* confutare
congeal *v/i of blood, fat* rapprendersi
congenial *adj* (*pleasant*) simpatico
congenital *adj* MED congenito
congested *adj* congestionato
congestion *n* congestione *f*; ***traffic ~*** la congestione del traffico
conglomerate *n* conglomerato *m*
congratulate *v/t* congratularsi con; ***~ s.o. on sth*** congratularsi con qn per qc
congratulations *npl* congratulazioni *fpl*; ***~ on …*** congratulazioni per …
congratulatory *adj* di congratulazioni
congregate *v/i* (*gather*) riunirsi
congregation *n* REL fedeli *mpl*
congress *n* (*conference*) congresso *m*; (*intercourse*) rapporti *mpl*; ***Congress*** *in US* il Congresso
Congressional *adj* del Congresso
Congressman *n* membro *m* del Congresso
Congresswoman *n* membro *m* (donna) del Congresso
conifer *n* conifera *f*
conjecture *n* (*speculation*) congettura *f*
conjugal *adj* coniugale
conjugate *v/t* GRAM coniugare
conjunction *n* GRAM congiunzione *f*; ***in ~ with*** insieme a
conjunctivitis *n* congiuntivite *f*
◆**conjure up** *v/t sep* (*produce*) far apparire (come) per magia; (*evoke*) evocare
conjurer, conjuror *n* (*magician*) prestigiatore *m*, -trice *f*
conjuring tricks *npl* giochi *mpl* di prestigio
◆**conk out** *v/i infml* rompersi
conker *n Br infml* castagna *f* d'India
con man *n infml* truffatore *m*
connect *v/t* (*join, link*) collegare; *to power supply* allacciare; ***~ s.o. with s.o.*** TEL mettere in comunicazione qn con qn; ***I always ~ Paris with springtime*** associo sempre Parigi alla primavera
◆**connect up** *v/t sep* ELEC *etc* allacciare (***to, with*** a)
connected *adj*: ***be well-~*** avere conoscenze influenti; ***be ~ with …*** essere collegato con; *by marriage* essere imparentato con
connecting flight *n* coincidenza *f* (volo)
connection *n* (*link*) collegamento *m*; *when travelling* coincidenza *f*; (*personal contact*) conoscenza *f*; ***in ~ with*** a proposito di
connective tissue *n* tessuto *m* connettivo
connive *v/i* (*conspire*) cospirare
connoisseur *n* intenditore *m*, -trice *f*
connotation *n* connotazione *f*
conquer *v/t* conquistare; *fig*: *fear etc* vincere
conqueror *n* conquistatore *m*, -trice *f*
conquest *n* conquista *f*
conscience *n* coscienza *f*; ***have a guilty / clear ~*** avere la coscienza sporca / a posto; ***on one's ~*** sulla coscienza
conscientious *adj* coscienzioso
conscientiousness *n* coscienziosità *f inv*
conscientious objector *n* obiettore *m* di coscienza
conscious *adj* (*aware*) consapevole; ***environmentally ~*** rispettoso dell'ambiente; (*deliberate*) conscio; MED cosciente; ***be / become ~ of*** rendersi conto di
consciously *adv* consapevolmente
consciousness *n* (*awareness*) consapevolezza *f*; MED conoscenza *f*; ***lose / regain ~*** perdere / riprendere conoscenza
conscript[1] *v/t* arruolare
conscript[2] *n* recluta *f*
conscription *n* coscrizione *f*
consecrate *v/t* consacrare
consecration *n* consacrazione *f*
consecutive *adj* consecutivo
consensual *adj* consensuale
consensus *n* consenso *m*; ***what's the ~?*** qual è l'opinione generale?; ***the ~ is that …*** è opinione generale che …; ***there was no ~ (among them)*** non è stata raggiunta l'unanimità
consent I *n* consenso *m*; ***he is by general ~ …*** è opinione generale che lui sia … **II** *v/i* acconsentire; ***~ to sth*** acconsentire a qc; ***~ to do sth*** acconsentire a fare qc
consentient *adj* consenziente

consequence *n* (*result*) conseguenza *f*; ***as a ~*** di conseguenza; ***as a ~ of*** in conseguenza a; ***~s*** *party game* gioco *m* delle conseguenze
consequential *adj* conseguente; (*significant*) importante
consequently *adv* (*therefore*) di conseguenza
conservation *n* (*preservation*) tutela *f*
conservation area *n area soggetta a vincoli urbanistici e ambientali*
conservationist *n* ambientalista *m/f*
conservative **I** *adj* (*conventional*) conservatore; *clothes* tradizionale; *estimate* cauto; ***Conservative*** *Br* POL conservatore **II** *n Br* POL ***Conservative*** conservatore *m*, -trice *f*
conservatoire *n Br* MUS conservatorio *m*
conservatory *n Br* veranda *f*; *US* MUS conservatorio *m*
conserve **I** *n* (*jam*) marmellata *f* **II** *v/t energy*, *strength* risparmiare
consider *v/t* (*regard*) considerare; (*show regard for*) tener conto di; (*think about*) pensare a; ***~ doing sth*** prendere in considerazione la possibilità di fare qc; ***it is ~ed to be his best work*** è considerata la sua opera migliore
considerable *adj* considerevole
considerably *adv* considerevolmente
considerate *adj person*, *attitude* premuroso; ***be ~ of*** avere riguardo per
considerately *adv* premurosamente
consideration *n* **1.** (*thought*) considerazione *f*; (*thoughtfulness*, *concern*) riguardo *m*; ***show*** *or* ***have ~ for s.o.*** mostrare considerazione per qn; ***his lack of ~*** (***for others***) la sua mancanza di considerazione (per gli altri); ***take sth into ~*** prendere in considerazione qc; ***under ~*** in esame **2.** (*factor*) fattore *m*; ***money is not a ~*** il denaro non conta
considering **I** *prep* considerato **II** *cj*: ***~*** (***that***) considerato che **III** *adv* tutto considerato
consign *v/t*: ***~ s.o. / sth to sth*** relegare qn / qc a qc; ***it was ~ed to the rubbish heap*** è stato relegato nel mucchio dei rifiuti
consignment *n* COMM consegna *f*
◆**consist of** *v/t* consistere in
consistency *n* (*texture*) consistenza *f*; (*unchangingness*) coerenza *f*
consistent *adj* (*unchanging*) coerente
consistently *adv* in modo coerente; *always* costantemente
consolation *n* consolazione *f*; ***it is some ~ to know that ...*** è già una consolazione sapere che ...; ***old age has its ~s*** sono le consolazioni della vecchiaia
consolation prize *n* premio *m* di consolazione
console¹ *v/t* consolare
console² *n* console *f inv*
consolidate *v/t* consolidare
consolidation *n* (*strengthening*) consolidamento *m*
consommé *n* consommé *m*
consonant *n* GRAM consonante *f*
consort **I** *n* consorte *m/f* **II** *v/i* unirsi
consortium *n* consorzio *m*
conspicuous *adj*: ***be*** *or* ***look ~*** spiccare; ***feel ~*** sentirsi fuori posto
conspicuous consumption *n* consumo *m* vistoso
conspiracy *n* cospirazione *f*
conspirator *n* cospiratore *m*, -trice *f*
conspire *v/i* cospirare; ***~ against*** cospirare contro; ***~ to*** cospirare per; ***~*** (***together***) ***to do sth*** concorrere a fare qc
constable *n* agente *m* di polizia
constabulary *n Br* corpo *m* di polizia
constancy *n* costanza *f*
constant *adj* (*continuous*) costante
constantly *adv* costantemente
constellation *n* costellazione *f*
consternation *n* costernazione *f*
constipate *v/t* costipare
constipated *adj* stitico
constipation *n* stitichezza *f*
constituency *n Br* POL circoscrizione *f* elettorale
constituent **I** *n* (*component*) componente *m*; *Br* POL elettore *m*, -trice *f* **II** *adj*: ***~ part*** parte *f* costituente
constitute *v/t* costituire
constitution *n a.* POL costituzione *f*
constitutional **I** *adj* POL costituzionale; ***~ monarchy*** monarchia *f* costituzionale **II** *n* (*walk*) passeggiata *f* igienica
constitutive *adj* costitutivo
constrained *adj* costretto; ***feel ~ by sth*** sentirsi costretto da qc
constraint *n* (*restriction*) restrizione *f*

constrict *v/t* (*compress*) restringere; (*hamper*) inibire
constriction *n of movements* costrizione *f*
construct I *v/t building etc* costruire **II** *n* costruzione *f*
construction *n* costruzione *f*; ***under ~*** in costruzione
construction industry *n* edilizia *f* **construction site** *n* cantiere *m* edile **construction worker** *n* operaio *m* edile
constructive *adj* costruttivo; ***~ criticism*** critica *f* costruttiva
constructivism *n* costruttivismo *m*
construe *v/t* interpretare
consubstantiation *n* REL consustanziazione *f*
consul *n* console *m*
consulate *n* consolato *m*
consult *v/t* (*seek the advice of*) consultare; ***~ s.o. about*** consultare qn riguardo a
consultancy *n* (*company*) società *f inv* di consulenza; (*advice*) consulenza *f*
consultant *n* consulente *m/f*; *Br* MED primario *m*; ***~ obstetrician*** MED primario *m* di ostetricia
consultation *n* consultazione *f*
consulting hours *n* MED orario *m* di visita **consulting room** *n* MED ambulatorio *m*
consume I *v/t food, drink* consumare; ECON consumare; *fire* distruggere; *fuel* consumare; *energy* esaurire; *engrossed* assorbire; ***~d by jealousy*** essere divorato dalla gelosia **II** *v/i expended* consumarsi
consumer *n* (*purchaser*) consumatore *m*, -trice *f*
consumer borrowing *n* prestito *m* al consumo **consumer confidence** *n* fiducia *f* dei consumatori **consumer credit** *n* credito *m* al consumo **consumer demand** *n* domanda *f* dei consumatori **consumer goods** *npl* beni *mpl* di consumo **consumer group** *n* gruppo *m* dei consumatori
consumerism *n* consumismo *m*; (*protection of consumers' interests*) tutela *f* del consumatore
consumer research *n* ricerca *f* tra i consumatori **consumer society** *n* società *f inv* dei consumi
consummate *v/t form marriage* consumare
consumption *n* consumo *m*; MED consunzione *f*
consumptive *adj* MED tubercolotico
contact I *n* contatto *m*; (*person*) conoscenza *f*; ***keep in ~ with s.o.*** mantenere i contatti con qn; ***come into ~ with*** venire a contatto con **II** *v/t* mettersi in contatto con
contact lens *n* lente *f* a contatto
contact number *n numero presso cui si è reperibili*
contagion *n* contagio *m*
contagious *adj a. fig* contagioso
contain *v/t* (*hold*) contenere; *flood, disease, revolt* contenere; ***~ o.s.*** contenersi
container *n* (*recipient*) contenitore *m*; COMM container *m inv*
container ship *n* nave *f* portacontainer
contaminate *v/t* contaminare
contamination *n* contaminazione *f*
contd *abbr* (= **continued**) continua
contemplate *v/t* (*look at*) contemplare; (*think about*) considerare; ***~ doing sth*** considerare la possibilità di fare qc
contemplation *n* contemplazione *f*
contemporary I *adj* contemporaneo **II** *n* coetaneo *m*, -a *f*
contempt *n* disprezzo *m*; ***~ (of court)*** oltraggio *m* alla corte; ***be beneath ~*** essere spregevole
contemptible *adj* spregevole
contemptuous *adj* sprezzante
contend *v/i*: ***~ for sth*** contendersi qc; ***~ with s.o. / sth*** confrontarsi con qc / qn
contender *n in sport, competition* concorrente *m/f*; *against champion* sfidante *m/f*; POL candidato *m*, -a *f*
content[1] *n* contenuto *m*
content[2] **I** *adj* contento; ***be ~ with*** soddisfatto di **II** *v/t*: ***~ o.s. with*** accontentarsi di
contented *adj* contento
contention *n* (*assertion*) opinione *f*; ***be in ~ for*** essere in lizza per; *fig* ***a bone of ~*** (*argument*) pomo *m* della discordia
contentious *adj* polemico
contentment *n* soddisfazione *f*
contents *npl of house, letter, bag etc*

contentuto *m*; (***table of***) **~** sommario *m*
contest¹ *n* (*competition*) concorso *m*; (*struggle*, *for power*) lotta *f*
contest² *v/t leadership etc* essere in lizza per; *will* impugnare
contestant *n* concorrente *m/f*
context *n* contesto *m*; ***look at sth in*** **~**/ ***out of*** **~** considerare qc in / fuori contesto
contiguous *adj* contiguo
continent¹ *n* continente *m*; ***the*** **~** l'Europa continentale
continent² *adj* MED continente
continental *adj* continentale
continental breakfast *n colazione a base di caffè, pane, burro e marmellata* **continental drift** *n* deriva *f* dei continenti **continental quilt** *n Br* piumino *m* **continental shelf** *n* piattaforma *f* continentale
contingency *n* eventualità *f inv*
contingent *n* contingente *m* (*a.* MIL)
continual *adj* continuo
continually *adv* continuamente
continuation *n* seguito *m*
continue I *v/t* continuare; **~ *doing*** *or* ***to do sth*** continuare a fare qc; **~ *with sth*** continuare qc; ***please*** **~** prego, continui; ***he*** **~*s to be optimistic*** continua a essere ottimista; ***be*** **~*d*** continua … **II** *v/i* continuare
continuity *n* continuità *f inv*; *in films* ordine *m* della sceneggiatura
continuous *adj* ininterrotto
continuously *adv* ininterrottamente
continuum *n* continuo *m*
contort *v/t* contorcere; ***a face*** **~*ed with pain*** un volto stravolto dal dolore
contortion *n* contorsione *f*
contortionist *n* contorsionista *m/f*
contour *n* profilo *m*; *on map* curva *f* di livello
contour line *n* curva *f* di livello **contour map** *n* mappa *f* a curve di livello
contraband *n* merce *f* di contrabbando
contraception *n* contraccezione *f*
contraceptive I *n* anticoncezionale *m*, contraccettivo *m* **II** *adj* contraccettivo, anticoncezionale
contract¹ *n* contratto *m*
contract² I *v/i* (*shrink*) contrarsi **II** *v/t illness* contrarre
contract bridge *n* bridge *m* contratto
contraction *n* contrazione *f*
contractor *n* appaltatore *m*, -trice *f*; ***building*** **~** ditta *f* di appalti (edili)
contractual *adj* contrattuale
contradict *v/t* contraddire
contradiction *n* contraddizione *f*
contradictory *adj account* contraddittorio
contraflow system *n Br* circolazione *f* a senso unico alternato
contralto I *n* contralto *m* **II** *adj voice* contralto
contraption *n infml* aggeggio *m*
contrary¹ I *adj* contrario; **~ *to*** contrariamente a **II** *n*: ***on the*** **~** al contrario
contrary² *adj*: ***be*** **~** (*perverse*) essere un bastian contrario
contrast I *n* contrasto *m*; **~ *between*/ *with*** contrasto tra / con; ***by*** **~** invece; ***in*** **~ *to*** a differenza di **II** *v/t* confrontare **III** *v/i* contrastare; **~ *with*** contrastare con
contrasting *adj* contrastante
contravene *v/t* contravvenire a
contravention *n*: ***be in*** **~ *of …*** trasgredire a …
contretemps *n* contrattempo *m*; ***they had a little*** **~ *with the driver*** hanno avuto un piccolo contrattempo con l'autista
contribute I *v/i with money*, *material*, *time* contribuire; *to magazine*, *paper* collaborare (***to*** con); *to discussion* intervenire (***to*** in); (*help to cause*) contribuire a creare **II** *v/t money* contribuire con
contribution *n money* offerta *f*; *to political party*, *church* donazione *f*; *of time*, *effort* contributo *m*; *to debate* intervento *m*; *to magazine* collaborazione *f*
contributor *n of money* finanziatore *m*, -trice *f*; *to magazine* collaboratore *m*, -trice *f*
contributory *adj pension scheme* basato sui contributi; ***it's certainly a*** **~ *factor*/ *cause*** è certamente una causa concomitante
con trick *n infml* truffa *f*
contrive I *v/t meeting* combinare **II** *v/i*: **~ *to do*** riuscire a fare
contrived *adj* forzato
control I *n* **1.** controllo *m*; ***take*** **~ *of*** assumere il controllo di; ***lose*** **~ *of*** perdere il controllo di; ***lose*** **~ *of***

o.s. perdere il controllo; ***circumstances beyond our ~*** cause indipendenti dalla nostra volontà; ***be in ~ of sth*** tenere qc sotto controllo; ***get out of ~*** diventare incontrollabile; ***the situation is under ~*** la situazione è sotto controllo; ***bring a blaze under ~*** circoscrivere un incendio **2.** ***~s*** *of aircraft, vehicle* comandi **3.** ***~s*** (*restrictions*) restrizioni **II** *v/t* ⟨*pret & past part* ***-led***⟩ (*govern*) controllare; *traffic* dirigere; (*restrict*) contenere; (*regulate*) regolare; ***~ o.s.*** controllarsi

control centre, *US* **control center** *n* centro *m* di controllo **control freak** *n infml persona che vuole avere tutto e tutti sotto controllo*; ***most men are total ~s*** gli uomini sono per la maggior parte fissati con il controllo **control key** *n* tasto *m* Control

controlled substance *n* sostanza *f* stupefacente

controlling interest *n* FIN maggioranza *f* delle azioni

control panel *n* quadro *m* dei comandi **control tower** *n* torre *f* di controllo

controversial *adj* controverso

controversy *n* polemica *f*

conundrum *n* enigma *m*

conurbation *n* conurbazione *f*

convalesce *v/i* rimettersi (in salute)

convalescence *n* convalescenza *f*

convect *v/t propagare calore per convezione*

convection *n* convezione *f*

convection oven *n* forno *m* a convezione

convene I *v/t* convocare **II** *v/i* convenire; (*parliament, court*) riunirsi

convenience *n of having sth, location* comodità *f inv*; *Br* (*toilet*) gabinetto *m*; ***at my / your ~*** a mio / tuo comodo; ***all*** (***modern***) ***~s*** tutti i comfort

convenience food *n scatolame, cibi precotti etc* **convenience store** *n* negozio *m* alimentari

convenient *adj location, device* comodo; ***whenever it's ~*** quando ti va bene; ***be ~ for s.o.*** essere comodo per qn; ***my house is ~ for the station*** da casa mia si arriva facilmente alla stazione

conveniently *adv* comodamente

convent *n* convento *m*

convention *n* (*tradition*) convenzione; (*conference*) congresso *m*; (*agreement*) convenzione *f*

conventional *adj person, ideas* convenzionale; *method* tradizionale; ***~ medicine*** medicina *f* tradizionale

converge *v/i* (*lines*) convergere (***at*** in); MATH, PHYS convergere

convergence *n fig of views etc* convergenza *f*; ***~ criteria*** *in EU* criteri *mpl* di convergenza

conversant *adj*: ***be ~ with*** essere pratico di

conversation *n* conversazione *f*; ***have a ~*** fare una conversazione; ***get into a ~ with s.o.*** cominciare a fare conversazione con qn

conversational *adj* colloquiale

converse [1] *n* (*opposite*) contrario *m*

converse [2] *v/i* conversare; ***~ with s.o. about sth*** conversare con qn di qc

conversely *adv* per contro

conversion *n* conversione *f*; *of house* trasformazione *f*

conversion table *n* tabella *f* di conversione

convert I *n* convertito *m*, -a *f* **II** *v/t* convertire **III** *v/i* trasformarsi (***into*** in); *house, room* trasformare

convertible *n car* cabriolet *f inv*, decappottabile *f*

convex *adj* convesso

convey *v/t* (*transmit*) comunicare; (*carry*) trasportare

conveyance *n* trasporto *m*; JUR cessione *f*

conveyancing *n* JUR *preparazione dei documenti per un trasferimento di proprietà*

conveyor belt *n* nastro *m* trasportatore

convict I *n* carcerato *m*, -a *f* **II** *v/t* JUR condannare; ***~ s.o. of sth*** condannare qn per qc; ***a ~ed criminal*** un reo convinto

conviction *n* JUR condanna *f*; (*belief*) convinzione *f*; ***previous ~s*** JUR condanne precedenti; ***his speech lacked ~*** il suo discorso era privo di convinzione; ***his fundamental political ~s*** le sue convinzioni politiche fondamentali

convince *v/t* convincere; ***~ s.o. of sth*** convincere qn di qc; ***~ s.o. that*** convincere qn che

convincing *adj* convincente

convivial *adj* (*friendly*) gioviale
convocation *n* convocazione f; REL sinodo *m*
convoluted *adj* contorto
convolution *n* circonvoluzione *f*
convoy *n* convoglio *m*
convulsion *n* MED convulsione *f*
coo *v/i* tubare
cook I *v/t vegetables*, *meat* cucinare; *meal*, *dinner* preparare; ***a ~ed meal*** un pasto caldo; ***~ the books*** *infml* falsificare i registri II *v/i of person* cucinare; *of vegetables*, *meat* cuocere III *n* cuoco *m*, -a *f*; ***I'm a good ~*** cucino bene
cookbook *n* ricettario *m*
cooker *n* cucina *f*
cookery *n* cucina *f*
cookery book *n* ricettario *m*
cookie *n US* biscotto *m*; COMPUT cookie *m*
cooking *n food* cucina *f*; ***he does all the ~*** è lui che cucina
cool I *adj* (*+er*) *weather*, *breeze*, *drink* fresco; (*calm*) calmo; (*unfriendly*) freddo; (*audacious*) impudente; (*great*) fantastico; ***a ~ customer*** *infml* un tipo spavaldo; ***act ~*** restare calmo II *v/i of food* raffreddarsi; *of tempers* calmarsi; *of interest* raffreddarsi III *v/t infml*: ***~ it!*** calma! IV *n infml*: ***keep / lose one's ~*** conservare / perdere la calma
◆**cool down** I *v/i* raffreddarsi; *of weather* rinfrescare; *fig*: *of tempers* calmarsi II *v/t sep food* raffreddare; *fig* calmare
◆**cool off** *v/i* calmarsi
coolbag *n*, **coolbox** *n* borsa *f* termica
cooling-off period *n* periodo *m* di riflessione
coop *n* pollaio *m*
◆**coop up** *v/t sep* rinchiudere
co-op *n* (*shop*) cooperativa *f*
cooper *n* bottaio *m*
cooperate *v/i* cooperare; ***~ with*** cooperare con
cooperation *n* cooperazione *f*
cooperative I *n* COMM cooperativa *f* II *adj* COMM cooperativo; (*helpful*) disponibile (a collaborare)
cooperative bank *n US* banca *f* cooperativa
co-opt *v/t* cooptare; ***he was ~ed onto the committee*** è stato cooptato nel comitato
coordinate *v/t* coordinare
coordination *n of activities* coordinamento *m*; *of body* coordinazione *f*
cop I *n infml* poliziotto *m*; *Br infml* cattura *f*; ***not much ~*** non un granché II *v/t* ⟨*pret & past part* ***-ped***⟩ acchiappare; *infml* ***you're going to ~ it*** ne buscherai
◆**cop out** *v/i infml*: ***cop out of sth*** sottrarsi alla responsabilità di qc
cope *v/i* farcela; ***~ with*** farcela con
copier *n machine* fotocopiatrice *f*
copilot *n* secondo pilota *m*
copious *adj* abbondante
cop-out *n infml* scappatoia *f*; ***what a ~!*** che pretesto!
copper *n metal* rame *m*; (*colour*) (color) rame *m*; (*policeman*) sbirro *m*; ***~s*** *esp Br* (*coin*) spiccioli *mpl*
coppice I *n* bosco *m* ceduo II *v/t* tagliare periodicamente
co-produce *v/t* coprodurre
copse *n* → ***coppice*** *n*
copulate *v/i* copulare
copulation *n* copulazione *f*; GRAM copula *f*
copy I *n* copia *f*; *written material* materiale *m*; ***fair ~*** bella copia *f*; ***rough ~*** brutta copia *f*; ***make a ~ of a file*** fare una copia di un file II *v/t* ⟨*pret & past part* ***-ied***⟩ copiare
copy cat *n infml* copione *m*, -a *f infml*
copycat crime *n reato a imitazione di un altro*
copyright *n* diritti *mpl* d'autore, copyright *m inv*
copy-writer *n in advertising* copywriter *m*
coquet *v/i* civettare
coquetry *n* civetteria *f*
coquette *n* civetta *f*
coquettish *adj* civettuolo
coral *n* corallo *m*
coral reef *n* scogliera *f* corallina
cord *n* (*string*) corda *f*; (*cable*) filo *m*
cordial I *adj* cordiale II *n* (*drink*) cordiale *m*
cordless phone *n* cordless *m inv*
cordon *n* cordone *m*
◆**cordon off** *v/t sep* transennare; *put cordon around* recintare
cordon bleu *adj cook* cordon bleu; *recipe*, *dish* cordon bleu
cords *npl trousers* pantaloni *mpl* di velluto a coste
corduroy *n* velluto *m* a coste

core **I** *n of fruit* torsolo *m*; *of problem* nocciolo *m*; *of organization, party* cuore *m*; ***to the ~*** fino al midollo; *fig* ***rotten to the ~*** corrotto fino al midollo; ***shaken to the ~*** turbare nel profondo dell'anima **II** *v/t fruit* togliere il torsolo a **III** *adj issue, meaning* essenziale; ***~ activity*** COMM attività *f inv* di base; ***~ business*** COMM core business *m*

coriander *n Br* coriandolo *m*

cork *n in bottle* tappo *m* di sughero; (*material*) sughero *m*

corkscrew *n* cavatappi *m inv*

corn[1] *n grain* frumento *m*; *US* (*maize*) granturco *m*

corn[2] *n on foot* callo *m*; ***~ plaster*** cerotto *m* per calli

corned beef *n* carne *f* in scatola

corner **I** *n* **1.** *of page, room, street* angolo *m*; *of table* spigolo *m*; ***in the ~*** nell'angolo; ***on the ~*** *of street* all'angolo; ***around the ~*** dietro l'angolo **2.** *in football* calcio *m* d'angolo, corner *m inv* **II** *v/t person* bloccare; ***~ a market*** prendersi il monopolio di un mercato **III** *v/i of driver, car* affrontare una curva

corner kick *n in football* calcio *m* d'angolo **corner shop** *n* piccola drogheria *f*

cornerstone *n* pietra *f* angolare

cornet *n* MUS cornetta *f*

cornflakes *npl* fiocchi *mpl* di granturco, cornflakes *mpl* **cornflour** *n* farina *f* di granturco

cornice **I** *n* ARCH cornice *f* **II** *v/t* fornire di cornice

cornmeal *n* farina *f* gialla

cornucopia *n fig* abbondanza *f*

corny *adj* (+*er*) *infml* scontato; *sentimental* sdolcinato

corollary **I** *n* corollario *m* **II** *adj* conseguente

coronary **I** *adj* coronario **II** *n* infarto *m*

coronation *n* incoronazione *f*

coroner *n ufficiale pubblico che indaga sui casi di morte sospetta*

corporal *n* caporale *m* maggiore

corporal punishment *n* punizione *f* corporale

corporate *adj* COMM aziendale; ***~ image*** corporate image *f inv*; ***sense of ~ loyalty*** corporativismo *m*; ***~ finance*** finanza *f* societaria; ***~ identity*** identità *f inv* aziendale; ***move up the ~ ladder*** fare carriera all'interno di una società

corporate hospitality *n* ospitalità *f inv* aziendale **corporate law** *n* diritto *m* societario

corporation *n* (*business*) corporation *f inv*

corps *nsg* corpo *m*

corps de ballet *n* corpo *m* di ballo

corpse *n* cadavere *m*

corpulent *adj* corpulento

corpuscle *n* globulo *m*

corral *n* recinto *m* per il bestiame

correct **I** *adj* giusto; *behaviour* corretto; ***she's ~*** ha ragione; ***am I ~ in thinking that ...?*** ho ragione a ritenere che ...?; ***~ change only*** solo importo esatto; ***it's the ~ thing to do*** è la cosa giusta da fare; ***she was ~ to reject the offer*** ha fatto bene a rifiutare l'offerta **II** *v/t* correggere; ***~ me if I'm wrong*** correggimi se sbaglio; ***I stand ~ed*** riconosco di avere torto

correction *n* correzione *f*

correction fluid *n* correttore *m* liquido

correctly *adv* giustamente; *behave* correttamente

correctness *n of behaviour etc* correttezza *f*

correlate **I** *v/t* correlare **II** *v/i* essere in correlazione (***with*** con); ***~ with sth*** essere correlato a

correlation *n* correlazione *f*

correspond *v/i* (*match, write*) corrispondere; ***~ to*** corrispondere a; ***~ with*** corrispondere con

correspondence *n* (*agreement, letters*) corrispondenza *f*

correspondent *n* corrispondente *m/f*

corresponding *adj* (*equivalent*) corrispondente

corridor *n in building* corridoio *m*

corroborate *v/t* corroborare

corroboration *n* avvaloramento *m*; ***in ~ of*** a conferma di

corroborative *adj* corroborativo

corroboree *n AUS* corroboree *m*; danza *f* indigena

corrode *v/t & v/i* corrodere

corrosion *n* corrosione *f*

corrugated cardboard *n* cartone *m* ondulato

corrugated iron *n* lamiera *f* (di ferro) ondulata
corrupt I *adj a.* COMPUT corrotto **II** *v/t morals*, *youth* traviare; (*bribe*) corrompere
corruption *n* corruzione *f*
corsair *n* corsaro *m*
corset *n* corsetto *m*
Corsica *n* Corsica *f*
Corsican I *adj* corso **II** *n* corso *m*, -a *f*
cortège *n* (*procession*) processione *f*; (*funeral cortège*) corteo *m*
cortisone *n* PHARM cortisone *m*
cos[1] *abbr* (= **cosine**) coseno *m* (cos)
cos[2] *n* (*a.* **cos lettuce**) lattuga *f* romana
cos[3] *cj infml* → ***because***
cosignatory *n* cofirmatario *m*, -a *f*
cosily, *US* **cozily** *adv* confortevolmente
cosine *n* coseno *m*
cosiness, *US* **coziness** *n* comodità *f inv*; (*warmth*) intimità *f inv*
cosmetic *adj* cosmetico; *surgery* estetico; *fig* di facciata
cosmetics *npl* cosmetici *mpl*
cosmetic surgeon *n* chirurgo *m* estetico **cosmetic surgery** *n* chirurgia *f* estetica
cosmic *adj* cosmico
cosmic dust *n* polvere *f* cosmica **cosmic radiation** *n* radiazione *f* cosmica **cosmic year** *n* anno *m* cosmico
cosmology *n* cosmologia *f*
cosmonaut *n* cosmonauta *m/f*
cosmopolitan *adj city* cosmopolita
cosmos *n* cosmo *m*
cosset *v/t* viziare
cost I *n a. fig* costo *m*; ***~, insurance and freight*** COMM costo, assicurazione e nolo; ***at all ~s*** a ogni costo; ***I've learnt to my ~*** l'ho imparato a mie spese; ***~s*** JUR spese **II** *v/t* ⟨*pret & past part* ***cost***⟩ **1.** costare; ***how much does it ~?*** quanto costa?; ***it ~ me one pound*** mi è costato una sterlina; ***it ~ me my health*** ci ho rimesso la salute **2.** FIN: *proposal*, *project* fare il preventivo di
cost and freight *n* COMM costo e nolo
costar I *n* coprotagonista *m/f* **II** *v/i* ⟨*pret & past part* ***-red***⟩ essere coprotagonista; ***~ with*** essere coprotagonista insieme a **III** *v/t* ⟨*pret & past part* ***-red***⟩ avere come coprotagonista
cost-conscious *adj*: ***be ~*** fare attenzione ai consumi **cost-cutting I** *n* taglio *m* dei costi **II** *adj*: ***~ exercise*** esercizio *m* dei costi **cost-effective** *adj* conveniente
costly *adj mistake* costoso; ***it would be a ~ mistake*** potresti pagarla cara
cost of living *n* costo *m* della vita **cost price** *n* prezzo *m* di costo
costume *n for actor* costume *m*
costume jewellery, *US* **costume jewelry** *n* bigiotteria *f*
cosy, *US* **cozy** *adj* (+*er*) (*comfortable*) gradevole; (*intimate and friendly*) intimo; ***be nice and ~ in bed*** starsene al calduccio a letto; ***a nice ~ little job*** un lavoretto tranquillo
cot *n for child* lettino *m*
cot death *n Br* morte *f* in culla
cottage *n* cottage *m inv*
cottage cheese *n* fiocchi *mpl* di latte
cotton I *n* cotone *m* **II** *adj* di cotone
◆**cotton on** *v/i infml* afferrare *infml*
◆**cotton on to** *v/t infml* afferrare *infml*
cotton bud *n Br* bastoncino *m* di cotone **cotton candy** *n US* zucchero *m* filato **cotton wool** *n* ovatta *f*
couch *n* divano *m*
couchette *n* cuccetta *f*
couch potato *n infml* teledipendente *m/f*
cough I *n* tosse *f*; *to get attention* colpetto *m* di tosse; ***have a ~*** avere la tosse **II** *v/i* tossire; *to get attention* tossicchiare
◆**cough up I** *v/t insep blood etc* sputare; *sep infml money* cacciar fuori *infml* **II** *v/i infml* (*pay*) cacciare i soldi *infml*
cough medicine, cough syrup *n* sciroppo *m* per la tosse **cough sweet** *n Br* pastiglia *f* per la tosse
could[1] *v/mod*: ***~ I have my key?*** mi dà la chiave?; ***~ you help me?*** mi puoi dare una mano?; ***this ~ be our bus*** questo potrebbe essere il nostro autobus; ***you ~ be right*** magari hai ragione; ***I ~n't say for sure*** non potrei giurarci; ***he ~ have got lost*** può darsi che si sia smarrito; ***you ~ have warned me!*** *in indignation* avresti potuto avvisarmi!
could[2] *pret* → ***can***
council I *n* (*assembly*) consiglio *m*;

(*city council*) comune *m*; ***Council of Europe*** Consiglio d'Europa; ***Council of Ministers*** POL Consiglio dei ministri **II** *adj*: ***~ meeting*** assemblea *f* del consiglio

council estate *n Br* complesso *m* di case popolari **council house** *n* casa *f* popolare

councillor, *US* **councilor** *n* consigliere *m* (comunale)

council tax *n* imposta *f* comunale sugli immobili

counsel I *n* (*advice*) consiglio *m*; (*lawyer*) avvocato *m* **II** *v/t course of action* consigliare; *person* offrire consulenza a

counselling, *US* **counseling** *n* terapia *f*

counsellor, *US* **counselor** *n* (*adviser*) consulente *m/f*

count[1] *n aristrocrat* conte *m*

count[2] **I** *v/i* contare; ***that doesn't ~*** questo non conta **II** *v/t* contare; ***~ yourself lucky*** considerati fortunato **III** *n* conteggio *m*; ***keep / lose ~ of*** tenere / perdere il conto di; ***what's your ~?*** quanti ne hai contati?; ***keep / lose ~ of*** tenere / perdere il conto di; ***what's your ~?*** quanti ne hai contati?

◆**count against** *v/t* essere a svantaggio di

◆**count for** *v/t* contare; ***it doesn't count for much*** non conta granché

◆**count in** *v/t sep* includere

◆**count on** *v/t* contare su

◆**count out** *v/t sep* escludere

◆**count up** *v/t sep* fare il conto di

countdown *n* conto *m* alla rovescia

countenance I *v/t* approvare **II** *n* (*support*) approvazione *f*; (*face, expression*) espressione *f*

counter[1] *n in shop, café* banco *m*; *in game* segnalino *m*

counter[2] **I** *v/t* neutralizzare **II** *v/i* (*retaliate*) rispondere

counter[3] *adv*: ***run ~ to*** andare contro

counteract *v/t* neutralizzare

counterargument *n* controargomento *m* **counter-attack I** *n* contrattacco *m* **II** *v/i* contrattaccare **counterbalance I** *n* contrappeso *m* **II** *v/t* fare da contrappeso a

counterclockwise *adv US* in senso antiorario

counterespionage *n* controspionaggio *m*

counterfeit I *v/t* falsificare **II** *adj* falso

counterfoil *n* matrice *f*

counterintelligence *n* controspionaggio *m*

counterpart *n person* omologo *m*, -a *f*

counterpoint *n* MUS contrappunto *m*

counterproductive *adj* controproducente **countersign** *v/t* controfirmare

countess *n* contessa *f*

countless *adj* innumerevole

country I *n* (*nation*) paese *m*; *as opposed to town* campagna *f*; ***in the ~*** in campagna **II** *adj roads, life* di campagna

country and western *n* MUS country and western *m inv* **countryman** *n* (*fellow countryman*) connazionale *m*; (*country dweller*) campagnolo *m* **countryside** *n* campagna *f* **countrywide** *adj* esteso a tutto il paese **countrywoman** *n* (*compatriot*) connazionale *f*; (*country dweller*) campagnola *f*

county *n* contea *f*

coup *n* POL colpo *m* di stato, golpe *m inv*; *fig* colpo *m*

coup de grâce *n* colpo *m* di grazia

coup d'état *n* colpo *m* di stato

couple *n* coppia *f*; ***just a ~*** solo un paio; ***a ~ of*** un paio di

couplet *n* distico *m*

coupling *n* (*linking*) appaiamento *m*; *of carriages etc* agganciamento *m*; (*linking device*) giunto *m*

coupon *n* buono *m*

courage *n* coraggio *m*

courageous *adj* coraggioso

courgette *n Br* zucchina *f*

courier *n* (*messenger*) corriere *m*; *with tourist party* accompagnatore *m* turistico, accompagnatrice *f* turistica

course *n* **1.** *series of lessons* corso *m* **2.** *part of meal* portata *f*; ***first ~*** primo *m*; ***second ~*** secondo *m*; ***a three-~ meal*** un pasto di tre portate **3.** *of ship, plane* rotta *f* **4.** *for golf* campo *m*; *for race, skiing* pista *f* **5.** ***of ~*** (*certainly*) certo; (*naturally*) ovviamente; ***of ~ not*** certo che no **6.** ***~ of action*** linea *f* di condotta; ***~ of treatment*** cura *f*; ***in the ~ of*** nel corso di

court *n* **1.** JUR corte *f*; (*courthouse*) tribunale *m*; ***take s.o. to ~*** fare causa a qn **2.** SPORTS campo *m* **3.** *fig* ***out of ~***

in via amichevole
court case *n* caso *m* (giudiziario)
courteous *adj* cortese
courtesy *n* cortesia *f*; **(*by*) ~ *of*** per gentile concessione di
courtesy car *n* vettura *f* di cortesia
courthouse *n* tribunale *m*, palazzo *m* di giustizia **court martial I** *n* corte *f* marziale **II** *v/t* processare in corte marziale **court order** *n* ingiunzione *f* del tribunale **courtroom** *n* aula *f* del tribunale **courtyard** *n* cortile *m*
cousin *n* cugino *m*, -a *f*
couth *adj* raffinato
couture *n* alta moda *f*
couturier *n* couturier *m*
cove *n small bay* cala *f*; *Br man* tizio *m*
cover I *v/t* / coprire; *distance* percorrere; *of journalist* fare un servizio su; ***~ s.o.* / *sth with sth*** coprire qn / qc con qc; ***we're not ~ed for theft*** non siamo coperti contro i furti; ***will £30 ~ the drinks?*** 30 sterline saranno sufficienti per le bevande? **II** *n protective* fodera *f*; *of book*, *magazine* copertina *f*; (*shelter*) riparo *m*; *insurance* copertura *f*; ***~s*** *for bed* coperte *fpl*: ***take ~*** ripararsi; ***read a book from ~ to ~*** leggere un libro dalla prima all'ultima pagina; ***on the ~*** sulla copertina; ***do you have adequate ~?*** disponete di una copertura adeguata?; ***she pulled the ~s up to her chin*** si tirò su le coperte fino al mento
◆**cover for** *v/t absent person* fare le veci di
◆**cover up I** *v/t sep* coprire; *fig* insabbiare **II** *v/i*: *fig* **cover up for s.o.** coprire qn
coverage *n by media* copertura *f*; ***the trial got a lot of ~*** il processo ha avuto molta risonanza
cover charge *n* coperto *m*
covered market *n* mercato *m* coperto
cover girl *n* ragazza *f* copertina
covering letter, *US* **cover letter** *n* lettera *f* d'accompagnamento
covert *adj* segreto
cover-up *n* insabbiamento *m*; ***it looks like a ~*** sembra che qualcuno stia cercando di insabbiare le prove
covet *v/t form* agognare
cow[1] *n* mucca *f*; *pej* (*woman*) stupida *f*; *fig* ***till the ~s come home*** *infml* fino alle calende greche; ***cheeky ~!*** che sfacciataggine!
cow[2] *v/t* intimidire
coward *n* vigliacco *m*, -a *f*
cowardice *n* vigliaccheria *f*
cowardly *adj* vile
cowbell *n* campanaccio *m*
cowboy *n* cow boy *m inv*
cower *v/i* rannicchiarsi
cowgirl *n* cow-girl *f*
cowhand *n* cow-boy *m*; *on farm* vaccaio *m*
cowhide *n untanned* pelle *f* di vacca; (*whip*) *frusta di pelle non conciata*; *only sg* (*leather*) cuoio *m*
cowl *n* cappuccio *m*
cowpat *n* escremento *m* di vacca
cowshed *n* stalla *f*
cox *n* timoniere *m*
coy *adj* (+*er*) (*evasive*) evasivo; (*flirtatious*) civettuolo
coyote *n* coyote *m inv*
cozy *US* → ***cosy***
C / P *abbr* (= **carriage paid**) COMM franco di porto
CPU *abbr* (= **central processing unit**) unità *f inv* centrale di elaborazione
crab *n* granchio *m*; *pl vulg* piattoni *mpl*
crack I *v/t cup*, *glass* incrinare; *nut* schiacciare; *code* decifrare; *infml* (*solve*) risolvere; ***~ a joke*** fare una battuta **II** *v/i* incrinarsi; ***get ~ing*** *infml* darsi una mossa *infml* **III** *n* crepa *f*; (*joke*) battuta *f*; (*drug*) crack *m inv*; (*sharp noise*) schianto *m*; *of gun* scoppio *m*; *of whip* schiocco *m*; ***leave the window open a ~*** lasciare la finestra aperta di uno spiraglio; ***we heard his arm go ~*** abbiamo sentito il suo braccio che si rompeva
◆**crack down on** *v/t* prendere serie misure contro
◆**crack open** *v/t sep* stappare; ***crack open the champagne*** stappare lo champagne
◆**crack up** *v/i* (*have breakdown*) avere un esaurimento; *infml* (*laugh*) scoppiare a ridere; ***I must be cracking up*** *hum* devo essere esaurito
crackbrained *adj infml* pazzoide *f*
crackdown *n* intensificazione *f* dei controlli (***on*** su)
cracked *adj cup*, *glass* incrinato; *infml* (*crazy*) tocco *infml*

cracker *n to eat* cracker *m inv*; (***Christmas***) ~ *mortaretto natalizio contenente una sorpresa*
crackers *adj Br infml* pazzo
crackhead *n* crack-dipendente *m/f*
crackle *v/i of fire* schioppettare
crackling *n* → ***crackle***; COOK cotenna *f* croccante
crackpot *infml* **I** *n* picchiatello *m*, -a *f* **II** *adj* strambo
cradle I *n for baby* culla *f* **II** *v/t* cullare
craft[1] *n* NAUT imbarcazione *f*
craft[2] *n* (*skill*) attività *f inv* artigiana; (*trade*) mestiere *m*; (*cunning*) astuzia *f*
craftsman *n* artigiano *m*
craftsmanship *n* arte *f*
crafty *adj* (+*er*) astuto
crag *n rock* rupe *f*
cram *v/t* ⟨*pret & past part* **-med**⟩ *papers, food* infilare; *people* stipare
cramp I *n* crampo *m*; (*clamp*) morsa *f* **II** *v/t*: ~ ***s.o.'s style*** essere di impedimento a qn
cramped *adj room, flat* esiguo
cranberry *n* mirtillo *m* rosso
crane I *n machine* gru *f inv* (*a.* ZOOL); ~ ***driver*** gruista *m/f* **II** *v/t*: ~ ***one's neck*** allungare il collo **III** *v/i* (*a.* **crane forward**) protendersi
crank[1] *n strange person* tipo *m* strambo
crank[2] **I** *n* MECH manovella *f* **II** *v/t* (*a.* **crank up**) mettere in moto
crankshaft *n* albero *m* a gomiti
crap I *n vulg* (*excrement*) merda *f vulg*; (*nonsense*) stronzate *fpl vulg* **II** *v/i* ⟨*pret & past part* **-ped**⟩ *sl* cacare **III** *adj infml*: ***this show is ~!*** questo spettacolo è uno schifo!
crap game *n US gioco d'azzardo con i dadi*
crappy *adj* (+*er*) *sl* schifoso
crash I *v/i fall noisily* fracassarsi; *of thunder* rombare; *of car* schiantarsi; *of two cars* scontrarsi, schiantarsi; *of plane* precipitare; COMM *of market* crollare; COMPUT fare un crash; *infml* (*sleep*) dormire; ~ ***into s.o. / sth*** andare a sbattere contro qn / qc; ~ ***into the sea / the mountains*** schiantarsi in mare / sulle montagne; ~ ***to the ground*** schiantarsi al suolo; ***the whole roof came ~ing down*** (***on him***) il tetto gli crollò interamente addosso **II** *v/t car* avere un incidente con **III** *n noise* fragore *m*; *accident* incidente *m*; COMM crollo *m*; COMPUT crash *m inv*
◆**crash out** *v/i infml* (*fall asleep*) addormentarsi; *without meaning to* crollare *infml*
crash barrier *n* barriera *f* protettiva **crash course** *n* corso *m* intensivo **crash diet** *n* dieta *f* lampo **crash helmet** *n* casco *m* (di protezione) **crash-land** *v/i* fare un atterraggio di fortuna **crash landing** *n* atterraggio *m* di fortuna **crash test** *n* AUTO crash test *m*
crass *adj* (+*er*) greve
crate *n* (*packing case*) cassetta *f*
crater *n of volcano* cratere *m*
crave *v/t* smaniare dalla voglia di
craving *n* voglia *f*; *pej* smania *f*
crawl I *v/i on floor* andare (a) carponi; (*move slowly*) avanzare lentamente; *infml* (*suck up*) fare il leccapiedi (**to** con); ***he makes my skin ~*** mi fa accapponare la pelle; ***he went ~ing to teacher*** è andato a fare il leccapiedi con il professore **II** *n in swimming* crawl *m*, stile *m* libero; ***at a ~*** (*very slowly*) a passo d'uomo
◆**crawl with** *v/t* brulicare di; ***the street was crawling with police*** la strada brulicava di poliziotti
crayfish *n* gambero *m* d'acqua dolce
crayon *n* matita *f* colorata; *wax* pastello *m* a cera
craze *n* moda *f*
crazily *adv skid, whirl* come un matto; (*madly*) follemente
craziness *n* pazzia *f*
crazy *adj* (+*er*) pazzo; ***be ~ about s.o.*** essere pazzo di qn; ***be ~ about sth*** andare matto per qc; ***football-~*** pazzo per il calcio
crazy paving *n* pavimentazione *f* irregolare
creak I *v/i* scricchiolare **II** *n* scricchiolio *m*
creaky *adj* (+*er*) che scricchiola; *argument* traballante
cream I *n for skin* crema *f*; *for coffee, cake* panna *f*; (*colour*) color *m* panna; *fig* (*best*) crema *f*, fior fiore *m*; ***the ~ of the crop*** (*people*) i migliori del gruppo **II** *adj* color panna **III** *v/t butter* amalgamare; (*skim*) scremare; *US infml* (*vanquish*) stracciare

◆**cream off** *v/t sep fig* scremare
cream cake *n* torta *f* alla panna; (*small*) pasticcino *m* alla panna
cream cheese *n* formaggio *m* fresco da spalmare
creamer *n for coffee* panna *f* liofilizzata
creamery *n* (*place of production*) caseificio *m*; (*place of sale*) latteria *f*
creaminess *n* (*richness*) cremosità *f inv*; (*softness*) morbidezza *f*
cream of tartar *n* cremore *m* di tartaro, cremortartaro *m* **cream puff** *n* bigné *m inv* (alla panna *or* alla crema) **cream sauce** *n condimento a base di burro o panna*; *white* béchamel *f* **cream tea** *n tè servito con biscotti, pasticcini, pane, burro e marmellata*
creamy *adj* (+*er*) *with lots of cream* cremoso
crease I *n accidental* grinza *f*; *deliberate* piega *f*; SPORTS *linea che indica la posizione del battitore nel cricket* **II** *v/t accidentally* sgualcire
crease-proof *adj*, **crease-resistant** *adj make up* a prova di grinze; *fabric* ingualcibile
create *v/t the world, man* creare; *draught, noise* provocare; *impression* dare; *problems* (*person*) provocare; (*action, event*) causare; COMPUT *file* creare
creation *n* creazione *f*; ART creazione *f*; ***the Creation*** la Creazione *f*; ***the whole of ~*** tutto il Creato
creationism *n* creazionismo *m*
creative *adj* creativo; ***the ~ use of language*** l'uso creativo della lingua
creative accounting *n iron* contabilità *f inv* allegra
creatively *adv* creativamente
creative writing *n* scrittura *f* creativa
creativity *n* creatività *f inv*
creator *n* creatore *m*, -trice *f*; ***the Creator*** REL il Creatore
creature *n* creatura *f*
creature comforts *npl* comodità *fpl* materiali
crèche *n for children* asilo *m* nido; REL presepe *m*
credence *n form*: ***give ~ to*** dare credito a
credentials *npl* credenziali *fpl*
credibility *n* credibilità *f inv*
credibility gap *n* gap *m inv* di credibilità
credible *adj* credibile
credit I *n* **1.** FIN credito *m*; ***the bank will let me have £5,000 ~*** la banca mi concede un creduto di 5.000 sterline; ***his ~ is good*** ha un buon fido; ***be in ~*** avere un saldo attivo; ***on ~*** a credito; ***give ~ to sth*** dare credito a qc **2.** (*honour*) merito *m*; ***get the ~ for sth*** prendersi il merito di qc; ***be a ~ to s.o.*** *or* ***do s.o. ~*** fare onore a qn; ***her generosity does her ~*** la sua generosità le fa onore; ***come out of sth with ~*** venire fuori da qc con onore; **3.** ***the ~s*** *film* (*at beginning*) i titoli di testa; *film* (*at end*) i titoli di coda **II** *v/t* (*believe*) credere; FIN accreditare; (*attribute*) attribuire; ***~ an amount to an account*** accreditare una cifra su un conto; ***~ s.o. with sth*** dare atto a qn di qc; ***I ~ed him with more sense*** pensavo che avesse più buon senso; ***he was ~ed with having invented it*** gli è stato riconosciuto il merito di averlo inventato
creditable *adj* lodevole
creditably *adv* in modo lodevole
credit account *n* conto *m* di credito
credit balance *n* saldo *m* attivo **credit card** *n* carta *f* di credito **credit check** *n* controllo *m* del credito; ***run a ~ on s.o.*** eseguire un controllo del credito **credit limit** *n* limite *m* di credito **credit note** *n* nota *f* di accredito
creditor *n* creditore *m*, -trice *f*
credit rating *n* posizione *f* creditizia **credit risk** *n*: ***be a good / poor ~*** avere un basso / alto rischio di insolvenza **credit squeeze** *n* stretta *f* creditizia **credit status** *n* posizione *f* creditizia **credit union** *n* cooperativa *f* di credito **creditworthy** *adj* solvibile
credo *n* credo *m*
credulity *n* credulità *f inv*
credulous *adj* credulo
creed *n* credo *m inv*
creek *n* cala *f*; ***be up the ~*** *infml* essere nei pasticci
creep I *v/i* ⟨*pret & past part* **crept**⟩ *quietly* avanzare quatto quatto; *slowly* avanzare lentamente; ***the water level crept higher*** il livello dell'acqua aumentava lentamente; ***the story made my flesh ~*** la storia mi

fece rabbrividire **II** *n infml pej* tipo *m* odioso
creeper *n* BOT rampicante *m*
creeps *npl infml*: ***the house / he gives me the ~*** la casa / lui mi fa venire la pelle d'oca
creepy *adj* (*+er*) *infml* che dà i brividi; ***be ~*** *infml* far paura
creepy-crawly *n infml* insetto *m* ripugnante
cremate *v/t* cremare
cremation *n* cremazione *f*
crematorium *n* crematorio *m*
crème de la crème *n* crème de la crème *f*
Creole I *n* LING creolo *m*; *people* creolo *m*, -a *f* **II** *adj* creolo; ***he is ~*** è creolo
creosote I *n* creosoto *m* **II** *v/t* trattare con creosoto
crêpe I *n* SEW crêpe *m*, crespo *m*; COOK crêpe *f* **II** *adj* crespato; *fabric* in crespo / crêpe
crêpe paper *n* carta *f* crespata
crept *pret & past part* → ***creep***
crescendo *n* MUS crescendo *m*; *fig* apice *m*
crescent *n shape* mezzaluna *f*
cress *n* crescione *m*
crest *n of hill, bird* cresta *f*
crestfallen *adj* abbattuto
Crete *n* Creta *f*
cretin *n infml* cretino *m*, -a *f*
cretinism *n* MED cretinismo *m*
cretinous *adj infml* cretino
cretonne *n* TEX cretonne *m*
Creutzfeldt-Jakob disease *n* MED morbo *m* di Creutzfeldt-Jakob
crevasse *n* voraggine *f*
crevice *n* crepa *f*
crew *n of ship, plane* equipaggio *m*; *of workers etc* squadra *f*; (*film crew*) troupe *f inv*; (*crowd, group*) ghenga *f*
crew cut *n* taglio *m* a spazzola **crew neck** *n* girocollo *m*; (*a.* **crew-neck pullover** *or* **sweater**) maglione *m* girocollo
crib I *n Br* (*cradle*) culla *f*; *US* (*cot*) lettino *m*; *infml* EDU foglietto *m* per copiare **II** *v/t* ⟨*pret & past part* ***-bed***⟩ *infml* EDU copiare
crick *n*: ***~ in the neck*** torcicollo *m*
cricket *n insect* grillo *m*; SPORTS cricket *m inv*; *fig* ***that's not ~*** *infml* non è leale
cricket bat *n* mazza *f* da cricket
cricketer *n* giocatore *m* di cricket
cricket match *n* partita *f* di cricket **cricket pitch** *n* campo *m* di cricket
cri de coeur *n* ⟨*pl* ***cris de coeur***⟩ appello *m*
crier *n* (*bellman*) banditore *m*, -trice *f*; (*whiner*) piagnone *m*, -a *f*
crikey *int Br infml* perdinci
crime *n* (*offence*) reato *m*; (*criminality*) criminalità *f inv*; (*shameful act*) crimine *m*
crime prevention *n* prevenzione *f* del crimine **crime rate** *n* tasso *m* di criminalità **crime wave** *n* ondata *f* di criminalità
criminal I *n* delinquente *m/f* **II** *adj* JUR penale; (*shameful*) vergognoso; ***a ~ offence*** un reato
criminal charge *n*: ***she faces ~s*** affronta un'accusa penale **criminal code** *n* codice *m* penale **criminal conversation** *n* (*adultery*) adulterio *m* **criminal court** *n* tribunale *m* penale **Criminal Investigation Department** *n Br divisione investigativa della polizia britannica* **criminal lawyer** *n* (avvocato *m/f*) penalista *m/f* **criminal offence**, *US* **criminal offense** *n* crimine *m*
criminologist *n* criminologo *m*, -a *f*
criminology *n* criminologia *f*
crimp *v/t* (*pleat*) pieghettare; (*curl*) arricciare
crimson *adj* cremisi *inv*
cringe I *v/i* morire di vergogna **II** *n* atteggiamento *m* servile
crinkle I *n* grinza *f* **II** *v/t* spiegazzare **III** *v/i* raggrinzirsi
crinkly *adj* (*+er*) *paper etc* sgualcito; *edges* arricciato
crinoline *n* crinolina *f*
cripes *int Br infml* caspita
cripple I *n* (*disabled person*) invalido *m*, -a *f* **II** *v/t person* rendere invalido; *fig* paralizzare
crisis *n* ⟨*pl* ***crises***⟩ crisi *f inv*; ***reach ~ point*** raggiungere un punto critico
crisis centre *n* unità *f inv* di crisi **crisis management** *n* gestione *f* della crisi
crisp *adj* (*+er*) *weather, air, lettuce, new shirt* fresco; *bacon, toast* croccante; *bank notes* nuovo di zecca
crispbread *n pane sottile e croccante a*

base di farina di farro
crisps *npl Br* patatine *fpl*
crisscross **I** *adj pattern* a linee incrociate **II** *v/t* coprire a reticolo
criterion *n* ⟨*pl* ***criteria***⟩ criterio *m*
critic *n* critico *m*, -a *f*; ***literary ~*** critico *m* letterario; ***he's his own worst ~*** e il peggior critici di sé stesso
critical *adj* critico; ***be ~ of s.o. / sth*** criticare qn / qc
critically *adv speak etc* criticamente; ***~ ill*** gravemente malato
criticism *n* critica *f*; ***literary ~*** critica *f* letteraria; ***come in for a lot of ~*** ricevere molte critiche
criticize *v/t* criticare; ***~ s.o. for doing sth*** criticare qn per aver fatto qc; ***I ~d her for always being late*** l'ho criticata perché è sempre in ritardo
critique *n* critica *f*
critter *n US infml* → ***creature***
croak **I** *v/i of frog* gracidare; *of person* parlare con voce rauca; (*die*) *infml* crepare **II** *n of frog* gracidio *m*; *of person* rantolo *m*
Croat *n* (*person*) croato *m*, -a *f*; (*language*) croato *m*
Croatia *n* Croazia *f*
Croatian **I** *n* → ***Croat*** **II** *adj* croato; ***she is ~*** è croata
crochet **I** *n* lavoro *m* all'uncinetto **II** *v/t* lavorare all'uncinetto
crockery *n* stoviglie *fpl*
crocodile *n* coccodrillo *m*
crocodile tears *npl* lacrime *fpl* di coccodrilo; ***shed ~*** versare lacrime di coccodrillo
crocus *n* croco *m*
crony *n infml* amico *m*, -a *f*
cronyism *n* nepotismo *m*; ***political ~*** nepotismo *m* politico
crook **I** *n* truffatore *m*, -trice *f*; *of shepherd* bastone *m* **II** *v/t finger, arm* piegare **III** *adj* (*sick*) *AUS infml* malato
crooked *adj streets* tortuoso; *picture* storto; (*dishonest*) disonesto
crop **I** *n* raccolto *m*; *type of grain etc* coltura *f*; *fig* scaglione *m*; (*whip*) frustino *m*; *bird* gozzo *m* **II** *v/t* ⟨*pret & past part* ***-ped***⟩ *hair, photo* tagliare
◆**crop up** *v/i* venir fuori; ***something's cropped up*** è venuto fuori qualcosa
cropper *n* capitombolo *m*; ***come a ~*** *Br infml* (*fall*) prendere una caduta; *fig* (*fail*) andare a scatafascio
cross **I** *v/t* **1.** (*go across*) attraversare; ***it never ~ed my mind*** non mi è passato per la testa **2.** ***~ o.s.*** REL farsi il segno della croce **3.** ***~ one's legs*** accavallare le gambe; ***keep one's fingers ~ed*** fare gli scongiuri **4.** (*go against*) ***~ s.o.*** opporsi a qn **II** *v/i* (*go across*) attraversare; *of lines* intersecarsi; ***our paths have ~ed several times*** *fig* le nostre strade si sono incrociate diverse volte **III** *n* croce *f* **IV** *adj* (+*er*) (*angry*) arrabbiato; ***be ~ with s.o.*** essere arrabbiato con qn
◆**cross off** *v/t sep* depennare
◆**cross out** *v/t sep* cancellare
◆**cross over** *v/i* (*cross the road*) attraversare; (*change sides*) passare (***to*** a)
crossbar *n of goal* traversa *f*; *of bicycle* canna *f*; *in high jump* asticella *f*
crossbeam *n* trave *f* trasversale
cross-bench *n Br* POL banco *m* di deputato indipendente **cross-bencher** *n Br* POL deputato *m* indipendente
crossbow *n* balestra *f*
crossbreed **I** *n* incrocio *m* **II** *v/t* incrociare, ibridare
cross-Channel *adj* che attraversa la Manica **crosscheck** **I** *v/t* fare un controllo incrociato su **II** *n* controllo *m* incrociato **cross-country** *n* **I** *adj*; ***~ run*** corsa *f* campestre; ***~ skiing*** sci *m* di fondo **II** *adv* attraverso i campi **III** *n* (*race*) fare una corsa campestra **cross-dress** *v/i* travestirsi da uomo / donna **cross-dresser** *n* travestito *m* **cross-dressing** *n* travestitismo *m*
crossed cheque, *US* **crossed check** *n* assegno *m* sbarrato
cross-examination *n* JUR controinterrogatorio *m* **cross-examine** *v/t* JUR interrogare in contraddittorio
cross-eyed *adj* strabico
crossfire *n* MIL fuoco *m* incrociato; ***be caught in the ~*** essere raggiunto dal fuoco incrociato
crossing *n* NAUT traversata *f*; *for pedestrians* attraversamento *m* pedonale
cross-legged *adj*/*adv* a gambe incrociate
cross-purposes *npl*: ***talk at ~*** fraintendersi **cross-reference** *n* rimando *m* **crossroads** *nsg* incrocio *m*; *fig* bivio *m* **cross-section** *n of people*

campione *m* rappresentativo **cross-walk** *n US* passaggio *m* pedonale **crossways, crosswise** *adv* di traverso **crossword (puzzle)** *n* cruciverba *m inv*

crotch *n of person* inguine *m*; *of trousers* cavallo *m*

crotchet *n Br* MUS semiminima *f*; (*small hook, handknitting*) uncinetto *m*; (*stubborn notion*) capriccio *m*

crouch *v/i* accovacciarsi

crow I *n bird* corvo *m*; ***as the ~ flies*** in linea d'aria **II** *v/i cockerel* cantare; *person* vantarsi; ***~ over sth*** vantarsi di qc

crowbar *n* piede *m* di porco

crowd I *n* folla *f*; ***get lost in the ~(s)*** perdersi nella folla; ***~s of people*** una folla di gente; ***follow the ~*** seguire la massa; ***she hates to be just one of the ~*** non sopporta essere una qualsiasi **II** *v/t place* gremire

◆**crowd into** *v/t* ammassarsi in

◆**crowd out** *v/t sep* ***the pub was crowded out*** il pub si è svuotato

crowded *adj* affollato; ***be ~ with*** essere affollato di

crown I *n* corona *f*; *on tooth* capsula *f*; *of head* testa; *of hill* cima; ***be heir to the ~*** essere erede al trono **II** *v/t king* incoronare; *tooth* incapsulare

Crown Court *n* corte *f* d'assise **crown graft** *n* BOT innesto *m* a corona **crown jewels** *npl* gioielli *mpl* della corona

crow's feet *npl* zampe *fpl* di gallina **crow's nest** *n* NAUT coffa *f*

crucial *adj* essenziale

crucible *n* crogiolo *m*

crucifix *n* crocifisso *m*

crucifixion *n* crocifissione *f*

crucify *v/t* ⟨*pret & past part* **-ied**⟩ REL crocifiggere; *fig* fare a pezzi

crud *n infml* schifo *m*

crude I *adj* (+*er*) (*unprocessed*) grezzo; (*vulgar*) volgare; (*unsophisticated*) rudimentale **II** *n*: ***~ (oil)*** (petrolio *m*) greggio *m*

crudely *adv speak* volgarmente; *made* rozzamente

cruel *adj* crudele; ***be ~ to s.o.*** essere crudele con qn

cruelty *n* crudeltà *f inv*

cruet *n Br for salt* saliera *f*; *for pepper* pepiera *f*; *US for oil* ampolla *f* dell'olio; *for vinegar* ampolla *f* dell'aceto

cruise I *n* crociera *f* **II** *v/i of people* fare una crociera; *of car, plane* viaggiare a velocità di crociera **III** *v/t* (*ship*) navigare; (*car*) *streets* procedere a velocità di crociera; *area* percorrere; *infml* andare in giro

cruise liner *n* nave *f* da crociera **cruise missile** *n* missile *m* cruise

cruiser *n* MIL incrociatore *m*; *for pleasure* cabinato *m*

cruiserweight *n* SPORTS mediomassimo *m*

cruising speed *n a. fig* velocità *f inv* di crociera

crumb *n* briciola *f*

crumble I *v/t* sbriciolare **II** *v/i of bread* sbriciolarsi; *of stonework* sgretolarsi; *fig*: *of opposition etc* crollare **III** *n Br* COOK *dolce a base di frutta ricoperta da un impasto di farina, burro e zucchero*; (*topping*) briciole *fpl*; ***rhubarb ~*** crumble al rabarbaro

crumbly *adj* (+*er*) friabile

crummy *adj* (+*er*) *infml* schifoso; ***feel ~*** sentirsi una schifezza

crumpet *n* COOK *focaccina rotonda, bucherellata da un lato, consumata calda e imburrata*; *vulg* gran bella ragazza *f*

crumple I *v/t* (*crease*) sgualcire **II** *v/i* (*collapse*) accasciarsi

crunch I *n infml*: ***when it comes to the ~*** al momento cruciale **II** *v/i of snow, gravel* scricchiolare

crunchy *adj* (+*er*) croccante

crusade *n a. fig* crociata *f*

crush I *v/t* schiacciare; (*crease*) sgualcire; ***they were ~ed to death*** sono morti schiacciati **II** *v/i* (*crease*) sgualcire **III** *n crowd* ressa *f*; (*drink*) spremuta *f*; ***it'll be a bit of a ~*** ci sarà un po' di calca; ***have a ~ on*** avere una cotta per

crust *n on bread* crosta *f*; ***the earth's ~*** la crosta terreste; ***earn a ~*** *infml* guadagnarsi il pane

crusty *adj* (+*er*) *bread* croccante; (*surly*) scontroso

crutch *n for injured person* stampella *f*; (*genitals*) cavallo *m*

crux *n*: ***the ~ of the matter*** il nocciolo della questione

cry I *v/t* ⟨*pret & past part* **-ied**⟩ (*call*) gridare **II** *v/i* ⟨*pret & past part* **-ied**⟩ (*weep*) piangere; ***~ for help*** gridare

aiuto **III** *n* (*call*) grido *m*; ***have a ~*** piangere
◆**cry off** *v/i Br appointment* disdire; *promise* tirarsi indietro
◆**cry out** *v/t & v/i* gridare
◆**cry out for** *v/t* (*need*) aver fortemente bisogno di
crybaby *n infml* piagnucolone *m*, -a *f*
crying I *adj fig* ***it is a ~ shame*** è un vero peccato **II** *n* (*weeping*) pianto *m*; *of baby* vagito *m*
crypt *n* cripta *f*
cryptic *adj* sibillino
cryptogram *n* crittogramma *m*
cryptographer *n* crittografo *m*, -a *f*
cryptography *n* crittografia *f*
cryptology *n* crittologia *f*
crystal I *n mineral* cristallo *m*; *glass* cristalli *mpl* **II** *adj* di cristallo
crystal ball *n* sfera *f* di cristallo **crystal clear** *adj concept* chiarissimo; *water* cristallino
crystallize I *v/t* concretizzare; ***~d*** cristallizzato; *fruit* candito **II** *v/i of thoughts etc* concretizzarsi
cub *n* cucciolo *m*; ***Cub*** (*Cub Scout*) lupetto *m*
Cuba *n* Cuba *f*
Cuban I *adj* cubano **II** *n* cubano *m*, -a *f*
cubbyhole *n* (*intimate room*) angolo accogliente; (*small room*) stanzino
cube I *n shape* cubo *m* **II** *v/t* MATH elevare al cubo; ***four ~d*** il cubo di quattro
cubic *adj* cubico; ***~ metre*** metro *m* cubico
cubic capacity *n* TECH cilindrata *f*
cubicle *n* (*changing room*) cabina *f*
cubism *n* cubismo *m*
cubist I *n* cubista *m/f* **II** *adj* cubista
Cub Scout *n* lupetto *m*
cuckoo I *n* cuculo *m*; (*fool*) pazzo *m*, -a *f* **II** *adj* (*foolish*) stupido
cuckoo clock *n* orologio *m* a cucù
cucumber *n* cetriolo *m*
cud *n*: ***chew the ~*** *liter* ruminare
cuddle I *n* coccole *fpl*; ***give s.o. a ~*** fare le coccole a qn **II** *v/t* coccolare
cuddly *adj* (*+er*) *kitten etc* tenero; *liking cuddles* coccolone
cudgel I *n Br* randello *m* **II** *v/t* randellare
cue *n* THEAT, *fig* imbeccata *f*; FILM, TV segnale *m* di inizio; MUS attacco *m*; *billiards* stecca *f*; ***take one's ~ from s.o.*** prendere lo spunto da qn; ***she arrived right on ~*** è arrivata proprio al momento giusto
cuff I *n of shirt* polsino *m*; *US of trousers* risvolto *m*; (*blow*) schiaffo *m*; ***off the ~*** improvvisando **II** *v/t hit* dare uno schiaffo a
cuff link *n* gemello *m*
cuisine *n* cucina *f*
cul-de-sac *n* vicolo *m* cieco
culinary *adj* culinario
cull I *n killing* selezione **II** *v/t* (*kill as surplus*) selezionare
culminate *v/i* culminare; ***~ in*** culminare in
culmination *n* culmine *m*
culottes *npl* gonna *f* pantalone
culpability *n form* colpevolezza *f*
culpable *adj* colpevole
culprit *n* colpevole *m/f*
cult I *n* culto *m* **II** *adj figure, film* di culto
cultivar *n* cultivar *f*
cultivate *v/t land* coltivare; *person* coltivarsi; *fig links etc* coltivare
cultivated *adj person* colto; AGR coltivato
cultivation *n of land* coltivazione *f*; *fig of links etc* il coltivare
cultivator *n* (*machine*) coltivatore *m*
cult movie *n* film *m inv* culto, cult movie *m inv*
cultural *adj* culturale
culture *n* cultura *f*; ***a man of ~ / of no ~*** un uomo di cultura / senza cultura
cultured *adj* (*cultivated*) colto
culture shock *n* shock *m inv* culturale
culture vulture *n* intellettualoide *m/f*
cum *prep*: ***a sort of sofa-~-bed*** una specie di divano-letto
cumber *v/t* ostacolare
cumbersome *adj* ingombrante; *procedure* macchinoso
cumin *n* cumino *m*
cummerbund *n* fascia *f* (per lo smoking)
cumulative *adj* cumulativo
cumulative interest *n* FIN interesse *m* cumulativo
cumuliform *adj* METEO cumuliforme
cunnilingus *n* cunnilingio *m*
cunning I *n* astuzia *f* **II** *adj* astuto
cunt *n vulg* (*vagina*) fica *f*; (*term of abuse*) stronzo *m*, -a *f*
cup I *n* tazza *f*; (*trophy*) coppa *f*; ***a ~ of***

tea una tazza di tè; *fig* ***that's not my ~ of tea*** *infml* non fa per me; ***they're out of the Cup*** sono fuori dalla Coppa **II** *v/t* ⟨*pret & past part* ***-ped***⟩ *hands* tenere tra le mani; ***~ one's hand to one's ear*** tenere la mano dietro all'orecchio

cupboard *n* armadio *m*

cupboard love *n* amore *m* interessato

cupcake *n pasticcino confezionato in piccole formine di carta*

cup final *n* finale *f* di coppa

cupful *n* ⟨*pl* ***cupsful*** *or* ***cupfuls***⟩ tazza *f*

cupid *n* cupido *m*; ***Cupid*** Cupido *m*

cupidity *n* cupidigia *f*

cupola *n* cupola *f*

cuppa *n Br infml* tazza *f* di tè

cup tie *n* partita *f* di coppa

cur *n* bastardo *m*

curable *adj* curabile

curate *n* curato *m*

curative I *n* curativo *m* **II** *adj* curativo

curator *n* direttore *m*, -trice di museo

curb I *n on powers etc* freno *m*; *esp US* (*curbstone*) → ***kerb*** **II** *v/t* tenere a freno

curd *n* cagliata *f*

curd cheese *n formaggio fresco simile al formaggio in fiocchi*

curdle *v/i of milk* cagliare

cure I *n* MED cura *f*; ***a ~ for Aids*** una cura per l'Aids **II** *v/t* MED guarire; *by drying* essiccare; *by salting* salare; *by smoking* affumicare; *fig inflation etc* porre rimedio a; *food* stagionare; (*salt*) salare; (*smoke*) affumicare; (*dry*) essiccare; ***~ s.o. of sth*** guarire qn da qc **III** *v/i*: ***it is left to ~*** COOK viene lasciato stagionare

cure-all *n* panacea *f*

curfew *n* coprifuoco *m*

curio *n* curiosità *f inv*

curiosity *n* curiosità *f inv*

curious *adj* (*inquisitive*) curioso; (*strange*) strano

curiously *adv* (*inquisitively*) con curiosità; (*strangely*) stranamente; ***~ enough ...*** sembrerà strano ma ...

curl I *n in hair* ricciolo *m*; *of smoke* spirale *f* **II** *v/t* arricciare **III** *v/i of hair* arricciarsi; *of leaf, paper etc* accartocciarsi; SPORTS giocare a curling

◆**curl up I** *v/i* acciambellarsi; ***curl up in bed*** rannicchiarsi nel letto; ***curl up with a good book*** rannicchiarsi con un buon libro **II** *v/t sep* accartocciare; *edges* piegare; ***curl o.s. / itself up*** raggomitolarsi

curler *n* bigodino *m*

curlicue *n* ghirigoro *m*

curling *n* SPORTS curling *m*

curling tongs, *US* **curling iron** *npl* arricciacapelli *m inv*; (*electric*) arricciacapelli *m*

curly *adj* (*+er*) *hair* riccio; *tail* a ricciolo

curmudgeon *n* bisbetico *m*, -a *f*

curmudgeonly *adj* bisbetico

currant *n* (*dried fruit*) uva *f* passa; BOT uva *f* sultanina; ***~ bush*** cespuglio di uva sultanina

currency *n money* valuta *f*; ***foreign ~*** valuta estera; ***gain ~*** diffondersi

current I *n* corrente *f* **II** *adj* (*present*) attuale

current account *n* conto *m* corrente

current affairs, current events *npl* attualità *f inv* **current affairs programme**, *US* **current affairs program** *n* programma *m* di attualità **current expenses** *npl* spese *fpl* correnti

currently *adv* attualmente

curriculum *n* ⟨*pl* ***curricula***⟩ programma *m* (scolastico)

curriculum vitae *n* ⟨*pl* ***curricula vitae***⟩ curriculum *m inv* vitae

curry[1] *n dish* piatto *m* al curry; *spice* curry *m inv*

curry[2] *v/t*: ***~ favour*** (***with s.o.***) ingraziarsi qn (con qc)

curry powder *n* curry *m*

curse I *n spell* maledizione *f*; *infml* (*nuisance*) disgrazia; *Br infml* (*menstruation*) mestruazioni *fpl*; (*swearword*) imprecazione *f* **II** *v/t* maledire; (*swear at*) imprecare contro **III** *v/i* (*swear*) imprecare

cursive I *adj* corsivo **II** *n* corsivo *m*

cursor *n* COMPUT cursore *m*

cursorily *adv* rapidamente

cursory *adj* di sfuggita

curt *adj* (*+er*) brusco

curtail *v/t trip etc* accorciare

curtain *n* tenda *f*; THEAT sipario *m*

◆**curtain off** *v/t sep* separare con una tenda

curtain call *n* THEAT chiamata *f* alla ribalta; ***take a ~*** essere chiamato alla ribalta **curtain hook** *n* gancetto *m* **curtain pole** *n* bastone *m* per la tenda **curtain rail** *n* guida *f* per la tenda **curtain raiser** *n* THEAT spettacolo *m* di apertura; SPORTS partita *f* di apertura **curtain ring** *n* anello *m* per tende **curtain wall** *n* cortina *f*

curts(e)y **I** *n* riverenza *f* **II** *v/i* fare una riverenza

curvaceous *adj* formoso

curvature *n* curvatura *f*; (*misshapen*) incurvatura *f*; **~ *of the spine*** (*normal*) curvatura; (*abnormal*) incurvamento della spina dorsale

curve **I** *n* curva *f*; ***learning ~*** curva *f* di apprendimento **II** *v/i* (*bend*) fare una curva **III** *v/t bend* piegare; *hump* incurvare

cushion **I** *n for couch etc* cuscino *m* **II** *v/t blow, fall* attutire

cushy *adj* (+*er*) *infml* facile; ***a ~ job*** un lavoro non impegnativo

cusp *n*: ***on the ~ of*** *fig* a cavallo di

cuss *infml* **I** *n* bestemmia *f* **II** *v/t* bestemmiare

cussed *adj infml* maledetto

cussword *n US infml* parolaccia *f*

custard *n* crema *f* (pasticciera)

custard apple *n* BOT anona *f*

custodial *adj form*: ***~ sentence*** pena *f* detentiva

custodian *n of museum* custode *m/f*

custody *n of children* custodia *f*; ***the mother was awarded ~ of the children after the divorce*** dopo il divorzio la madre ha ricevuto l'affidamento dei figli; ***in ~*** JUR in detenzione preventiva; ***take s.o. into ~*** JUR arrestare qn

custom **I** *n* (*tradition*) usanza *f*; COMM clientela *f*; ***as was his ~*** com'era suo solito; ***take one's ~ elsewhere*** andare a servirsi altrove **II** *adj US suit* su misura; *carpenter* su ordinazione

customary *adj* consueto; ***it is ~ to ...*** è consuetudine ...

custom-built *adj* costruito su richiesta

customer *n* (*client*) cliente *m/f*; ***a strange ~*** un tipo strano

customer relations *npl* relazione *f* clienti **customer service** *n* servizio *m* assistenza clienti **customer support** *n* supporto *m* clienti

customize *v/t* modificare a seconda delle esigenze

custom-made *adj clothes* fatto su misura; *furniture, car* fatto su richiesta

customs *npl* dogana *f*; ***go through ~*** passare la dogana

Customs and Excise *n* Ufficio *m* Dazi e Dogana **customs clearance** *n* sdoganamento *m* **customs inspection** *n* controllo *m* doganale **customs officer** *n* doganiere *m*, -a *f*

cut **I** *v/t* ⟨*pret & past part* ***cut***⟩ tagliare; (*reduce*) ridurre; ***~ one's nails*** tagliarsi le unghie; ***get one's hair ~*** tagliarsi i capelli; ***I ~ my finger*** mi sono tagliato un dito; *engine* spegnere; *teeth* mettere (i denti); ***the government ~ unemployment by half in five years*** in cinque anni il governo ha ridotto la disoccupazione del 50 %; ***~ the cards / the pack*** tagliare le carte / il mazzo **II** *n with knife, of hair, clothes* taglio *m*; (*reduction*) riduzione *f*; *in public spending* taglio *m*; *of meat* taglio *m*; (*share, infml*) fetta *f*; ***my hair needs a ~*** devo tagliarmi i capelli; ***take one's ~*** prendersi la propria parte; ***power / electricity ~*** ELEC interruzione *f* di corrente

◆**cut across** *v/t*: ***if you cut across the fields*** se tagli attraverso i campi; *fig* ***this problem cuts across all ages*** questo problema riguarda tutte le età

◆**cut back** **I** *v/i in costs* limitare le spese; FILM fare un flashback **II** *v/t sep employees* ridurre

◆**cut back on** *v/t staff, expenditure, salt* ridurre

◆**cut down** **I** *v/t sep tree* abbattere **II** *v/i in smoking etc* limitarsi

◆**cut down on** *v/t cigarettes, chocolate* ridurre la quantità di; ***cut down on smoking*** fumare di meno

◆**cut in** *v/i* (*when talking*) interrompere; (*when driving*) tagliare la strada

◆**cut off** *v/t sep with knife, scissors etc* tagliare; (*isolate*) isolare; ***I've been cut off*** TEL è caduta la linea

◆**cut out** *v/t sep with scissors* ritagliare; (*eliminate*) eliminare; ***cut that out!*** *infml* smettila!; ***be cut out for sth*** essere tagliato per qc

◆**cut up** *v/t sep meat etc* sminuzzare

cut-and-dried *adj fig* definitivo; ***as far as he's concerned the whole issue is now ~*** per lui il problema è molto

semplice
cut-and-paste *adj US*: ***a ~ job*** un taglia e incolla
cutback *n in production* riduzione *f*; *in public spending* taglio *m*
cute *adj* (+*er*) (*pretty*) carino; (*smart, clever*) furbo
cut glass *n* cristallo *m* lavorato
cuticle *n* pellicina *f*
cutlery *n* posate *fpl*
cutlet *n* cotoletta *f*
cut-off *n* TECH (*device*) chiusura *f*; (*a.* **cutoff point**) limite *m*; (*deadline*) termine *m*
cut-off date *n* scadenza *f*
cut-price, *US* **cut-rate** *adj goods* a prezzo ridotto; *store* di articoli scontati **cut-throat** *adj competition* spietato
cutting I *n from newspaper etc* ritaglio *m*; *of glass, jewel* taglio *m*; *of prices, working hours* riduzione *f*; *of expenses* taglio *m*; *salary* riduzione *f*; FILM montaggio *m*; *Br* (*railway cutting*) trincea *f*; BOT talea *f*; ***take a ~*** prendere una scorciatoia **II** *adj* tagliente; *fig remark* pungente; ***be at the ~ edge of sth*** essere all'avanguardia in
cuttlefish *n* seppia *f*
cut up *adj infml*: ***he was very ~ about it*** ci è rimasto molto male
CV *abbr* (= **curriculum vitae**) CV *m inv* (curriculum *m inv* vitae)
cwt *abbr* (= **hundredweight**) cinquanta chili
cyanide *n* cianuro *m*
cybercafé *n* cybercafè *m*
cybernetics *nsg* cibernetica *f*
cyberspace *n* ciberspazio *m*
cycle I *n* (*bicycle*) bicicletta *f*; *of events* ciclo *m* **II** *v/i to work* andare in bicicletta
cycle lane *n* pista *f* ciclabile **cycle path** *n* pista *f* ciclabile **cycle track** *n* pista *f* ciclabile; *for racing* pista *f* (del velodromo)
cyclic(al) *adj a.* ECON ciclico
cycling *n* ciclismo *m*; ***he's taken up ~*** ha cominciato ad andare in bicicletta
cycling holiday *n* cicloturismo *m* **cycling shorts** *npl* SEW ciclisti *mpl*
cyclist *n* ciclista *m/f*
cyclone *n* ciclone *m*
cygnet *n* cigno *m* giovane
cylinder *n* cilindro *m*; ***a four-~ car*** una quattro cilindri; ***be firing on all ~s*** *fig* andare al massimo
cylinder head *n* AUTO testa *f* del cilindro
cylindrical *adj* cilindrico
cymbal *n* cembalo *m*; ***~s*** piatti *mpl*
cynic *n* cinico *m*, -a *f*
cynical *adj* cinico; ***he was very ~ about it*** ha reagito in modo molto cinico
cynically *adv* cinicamente
cynicism *n* cinismo *m*
cypher → ***cipher***
cypress *n* cipresso *m*
Cypriot I *adj* cipriota **II** *n* cipriota *m/f*
Cyprus *n* Cipro *m*
Cyrillic *adj* cirillico
cyst *n* cisti *f inv*
czar *n hist* zar *m inv*
Czech I *adj* ceco; ***the ~ Republic*** la Repubblica Ceca **II** *n person* ceco *m*, -a *f*; *language* ceco *m*

D

D,d *n* d, D *f inv*; MUS re *m inv*; EDU (*mark*) sufficiente *m*
DA *abbr* (= **district attorney**) *US* procuratore *m* distrettuale
dab I *n* (*small amount*) tocco *m*, pochino *m* **II** *v/t* (*remove*) ⟨*pret & past part* ***-bed***⟩ tamponare; (*apply*) applicare; ***~ a cut with ointment*** applicare una pomata sul taglio; ***~ one's eyes*** sfiorarsi gli occhi
DAB *abbr* (= **Digital Audio Broadcast**); ***~ radio*** radio *f* DAB
◆**dabble in** *v/t* dilettarsi di
dacha *n* dacia *f*
dachshund *n* bassotto *m*
dad *n* papà *m inv*

Dada, dada *n*, **Dadaism** *n* dadaismo *m*
daddy *n* papà *m inv*
daddy longlegs *n* zanzarone *m*
daffodil *n* BOT giunchiglia *f*
daft *adj* (+*er*) stupido
dagger *n* pugnale *m*
dahlia *n* dalia *f*
daily I *n* (*paper*) quotidiano *m*; (*cleaning woman*) domestica *f* **II** *adj* quotidiano **III** *adv* tutti i giorni
daily bread *n fig*: ***earn one's ~*** guadagnarsi il pane quotidiano
dainty *adj* (+*er*) aggraziato
dairy *n* (*shop*) latteria *f*; (*farm building*) *parte di una fattoria in cui si fa il formaggio*
dairy cattle *n* vacche *fpl* da latte **dairy farming** *n* produzione *f* di latticini **dairy products** *npl* latticini *mpl*
dais *n* palco *m*
daisy *n* margherita *f*
daisy chain *n* ghirlanda *f* di margherite
daisywheel *n* TYPO, COMPUT margherita *f*
daisywheel printer *n* stampante *f* a margherita
dale *n Br liter* valle *f*; ***up hill and down ~*** per monti e per valli
Dalmatian *n* (*dog*) dalmata *m*
dam[1] I *n for water* diga *f* **II** *v/t* ⟨*pret & past part* ***-med***⟩ *river* costruire una diga su
dam[2] *n female parent* madre *f*
damage I *n a. fig* danno *m*; ***~ limitation*** limitazione *f* dei danni; ***do s.o./sth a lot of ~*** causare molti danni a qn/qc; ***the ~ is done*** *fig* il danno è fatto **II** *v/t* danneggiare; *fig*: *reputation etc* compromettere; ***~ one's eyesight*** rovinare la propria vista; ***~ one's chances*** compromettere le proprie possibilità
damages *npl* JUR risarcimento *msg*
damaging *adj* nocivo
damask *n* TEX damasco *m*
dame *n* THEAT *ruolo comico femminile interpretato da un uomo*; *US infml* (*woman*) tizia *f infml*; **Dame** *Br titolo di ordine cavalleresco concesso ad una donna*; ***she's quite a ~!*** che donna!
damn I *int infml* accidenti **II** *n*: *infml* ***I don't give a ~!*** non me ne frega niente! *infml* **III** *adj infml* maledetto; ***a ~ sight better*** molto meglio; ***pretty ~ good/quick*** proprio buono/veloce **IV** *adv infml* incredibilmente; ***it's ~ cold*** fa un freddo cane; ***he ~ well ought to know!*** cavolo! dovrebbe saperlo **V** *v/t* (*condemn*) maledire; ***~ it!*** *infml* accidenti!; ***I'm ~ed if I will*** *infml* non me lo sogno nemmeno
damned I *adj soul* dannato; *infml* maledetto **II** *n* REL *liter*: ***the ~*** i dannati
damning *adj evidence* schiacciante; *report* incriminante
damp I *adj* (+*er*) umido **II** *n* umido *m*
damp course *n* strato *m* impermeabile (alla base di una parete)
dampen *v/t* inumidire; ***~ s.o.'s enthusiasm*** raffreddare l'entusiasmo di qn
damper *n stove* valvola *f* di tiraggio; *piano* smorzatore *m*; *infml* guastafeste *m*; ***put a ~ on sth*** rovinare qc
damp-proof course *n* → ***damp course***
damsel *n* damigella *f*; ***a ~ in distress*** *hum* una donzella in pericolo
damson *n* (*fruit*) susina *f* selvatica
dance I *n* ballo *m* **II** *v/i* ballare; *of ballerina* danzare; ***would you like to ~?*** ti va di ballare?; *form* posso invitarla a ballare?; ***~ with s.o.*** ballare con qn **III** *v/t* ballare
dance band *n complesso che suona musica per ballare* **dance floor** *n* pista (da ballo) **dance music** *n* musica *f* dance
dancer *n* (*performer*) ballerino *m*, -a *f*; ***be a good ~*** ballare bene
dancing *n* ballo *m*, danza *f*
dandelion *n* dente *m* di leone
dandruff *n* forfora *f*
dandruff shampoo *n* shampoo *m inv* antiforfora *inv*
Dane *n* danese *m/f*
danger *n* pericolo *m*; ***be in ~*** essere in pericolo; ***out of ~*** *of patient* fuori pericolo
danger money *n* indennità *f inv* di rischio
dangerous *adj* pericoloso; ***the Bronx can be a ~ place*** il Bronx può essere un luogo pericoloso; ***this is a ~ game we're playing*** stiamo facendo un gioco pericoloso
dangerous driving *n* guida *f* pericolosa

dangerously *adv drive* spericolatamente; **~ *ill*** gravemente malato
dangle I *v/t* dondolare **II** *v/i* pendere
Danish I *adj* danese **II** *n language* danese *m*; ***the ~*** i danesi
Danish blue (cheese) *n* COOK *formaggio danese simile al gorgonzola* **Danish (pastry)** *n dolcetto ripieno*
dank *adj* umido
dapper *adj* azzimato
dappled *adj light* screziato; *horse* pezzato
dare I *v/i* osare; ***~ to do sth*** osare fare qc; ***how ~ you!*** come osi!; ***I ~ say*** direi **II** *v/t*: ***~ s.o. to do sth*** sfidare qn a fare qc
daredevil *n* scavezzacollo *m*
daring I *adj* (*courageous*) coraggioso; (*imprudent*) temerario; (*audacious*) audace; *writer, book* audace **II** *n* audacia *f*
dark I *adj* (+*er*) *room, night* buio; *hair, eyes, colour* scuro; ***~ green / blue*** verde / blu scuro; ***the room suddenly went ~*** nella stanza all'improvviso fu buio; ***it's getting ~*** comincia a fare buio **II** *n* buio *m*, oscurità *f inv*; ***after ~*** dopo il calare della notte; ***be in the ~*** essere all'oscuro; *fig* ***keep s.o. in the ~*** tenere qn all'oscuro
Dark Ages *npl* secoli *mpl* bui; ***be living in the ~*** *pej* vivere un periodo nero
dark chocolate *n* cioccolato *m* fondente
darken I *v/t liter light* oscurare; *colour* scurire **II** *v/i of sky* oscurarsi
dark-eyed *adj* con gli occhi scuri **dark glasses** *npl* occhiali *mpl* scuri
darkly *adv* cupamente
darkness *n* oscurità *f inv*; ***in total ~*** nel buio totate; ***the house was in ~*** la casa era al buio
darkroom *n* PHOT camera *f* oscura **dark-skinned** *adj* con gli occhi scuri
darling I *n* tesoro *m*; ***be a ~ and ...*** sii carino e ... **II** *adj* caro
darn¹ I *n* (*mend*) rammendo *m* **II** *v/t* (*mend*) rammendare
darn² (*a.* **darned**) *infml* **I** *adj* maledetto; ***a ~ sight better*** molto meglio **II** *adv* maledettamente; ***we'll do as we ~ well please*** faremo come ci pare; ***~ near impossible*** maledettamente impossibile **III** *int*: ***~ it!*** maledizione!
darned *adj/adv infml* → ***darn²***
dart I *n for throwing* freccetta *f* **II** *v/i* scagliarsi
darts *nsg* (*game*) freccette *fpl*
dart(s)board *n* tabellone *m* delle freccette
dash I *n in punctuation* trattino *m*, lineetta *f*; *of whisky, milk* goccio *m*; *of salt* pizzico *m*; (AUTO: *dashboard*) cruscotto *m*; ***make a ~ for*** precipitarsi su **II** *v/i* precipitarsi; ***I must ~*** devo scappare **III** *v/t hopes* stroncare
◆**dash off I** *v/i* scappare **II** *v/t sep* (*write quickly*) buttare giù
dashboard *n* cruscotto *m*
dashing *adj person* brillante
DAT *n abbr* (= **digital audio tape**) DAT
data *n* dati *mpl*
database *n* base *f* dati **data capture** *n* inserimento *m* dati **data processing** *n* elaborazione *f* dati **data protection** *n* protezione *f* dati **data storage** *n* memorizzazione *f* dati, archiviazione *f* dati
date¹ *n* (*fruit*) dattero *m*
date² I *n* **1.** data *f*; ***what's the ~ today?*** quanti ne abbiamo oggi?; ***to ~*** *form* fino a oggi **2.** *fig* ***out of ~*** *clothes* fuori moda; *passport* scaduto; ***up to ~*** aggiornato; (*fashionable*) attuale; ***bring s.o. up to ~*** aggiornare qn; ***bring sth up to ~*** aggiornare qc **3.** (*meeting*) appuntamento *m*; ***have a ~ with s.o.*** avere un appuntamento romantico con qn **4.** *person*: ***your ~ is here*** è arrivato il tuo ragazzo, è arrivata la tua ragazza **II** *v/t letter, cheque* datare; (*go out with*) dare appuntamento a; (*regularly*) uscire con; ***that ~s you*** (*shows your age*) quanto sei vecchio
◆**date back to** *v/t* risalire a
◆**date from** *v/t* risalire a
dated *adj* superato
date rape *n stupro commesso in seguito ad un incontro galante*
dating agency *n* agenzia *f* di appuntamenti
daub *v/t*: ***~ paint on a wall*** imbrattare il muro di vernice
daughter *n* figlia *f*
daughter-in-law *n* ⟨*pl* ***daughters-in--law***⟩ nuora *f*
daunt *v/t* scoraggiare

daunting *adj* che intimorisce
dawdle *v/i* ciondolare
dawdler *n* perdigiorno *m/f*
dawn I *n* alba *f*; ***at ~*** all'alba; ***it's almost ~*** è quasi l'alba; ***from ~ to dusk*** dall'alba al tramonto; *fig*: *of new age* albori *mpl* **II** *v/i* (*day*) spuntare; ***It ~ed on me that ...*** mi sono reso conto che ...
day *n* giorno *m*; ***what ~ is it today?*** che giorno è oggi?; ***~ off*** giorno *m* di ferie; ***~ out*** gita *f*; ***by ~*** di giorno; ***~ by ~*** giorno per giorno; ***~ after ~*** giorno dopo giorno; ***the ~ after*** il giorno dopo; ***the ~ after tomorrow*** dopodomani; ***the ~ before*** il giorno prima; ***the ~ before yesterday*** l'altro ieri; ***~ in ~ out*** senza tregua; ***these ~s*** di questi tempi; ***in those ~s*** a quei tempi; ***in my ~*** ai miei tempi; ***one ~*** un giorno; ***the other ~*** (*recently*) l'altro giorno; ***let's call it a ~!*** lasciamo perdere!
day bed *n* divano letto *m* **day boy** *n* alunno *m* esterno **daybreak** *n*: ***at ~*** allo spuntare del giorno **day care** *n* asilo *m* **daydream I** *n* sogno *m* ad occhi aperti **II** *v/i* essere sovrappensiero **day dreamer** *n* sognatore *m*, -trice *f* **day girl** *n* alunna *f* esterna **day labourer**, *US* **day laborer** *n* avventizio *m*, -a *f* **daylight** *n* luce *f* (del giorno); ***~ robbery*** *Br infml* furto *m* (alla luce del sole) **daylight saving time** *n* ora *f* legale **daylong** *adj* che dura tutto il giorno **day return** *n* biglietto *m* di andata e ritorno in giornata **day shift** *n* turno *m* di giorno **daytime** *n*: ***in the ~*** durante il giorno **daytime television** *n* televisione *f* del mattino e del pomeriggio **day-to-day** *adj* quotidiano **daytrip** *n* gita *f* di un giorno **day tripper** *n* escursionista *m/f*
daze I *n* stupore *m*; ***in a ~*** sbalordito **II** *v/t* sbalordire
dazed *adj by good / bad news* sbalordito; *by a blow* stordito
dazzle *v/t of light*, *fig* abbagliare
DC *abbr* **1.** (= **direct current**) c.c. (corrente *f* continua) **2.** (= **District of Columbia**) DC
D / D *abbr* (= **direct debit**) ordine *m* di addebito automatico
D-day *n* giorno *m* dello sbarco in Normandia
deacon *n* diacono *m*
deactivate *v/t* disattivare
dead I *adj person*, *plant* morto; *battery* scarica; *phone* muto; *light bulb* bruciato; ***shoot s.o. ~*** uccidere qn (con arma da fuoco); ***be ~*** *infml of place* essere un mortorio *infml* **II** *adv infml* (*very*) da matti *infml*; ***~ beat, ~ tired*** stanco morto; ***that's ~ right*** è assolutamente vero; ***it's ~ interesting*** è interessante da matti; ***it was ~ easy*** è stato facilissimo; ***be ~ against sth*** essere contrarissimo a qc; ***be ~ set on doing sth*** essere deciso a fare qc **III** *n*: ***the ~*** (*dead people*) i morti; ***in the ~ of night*** nel cuore della notte
deadbeat I *n* fannullone *m*, -a *f* **II** *adj* stanco morto
deaden *v/t pain* attenuare; *sound* attutire
dead end *n* (*street*) vicolo *m* cieco **dead-end job** *n* lavoro *m* senza prospettive **deadhead** *v/i & v/t* eliminare i fiori secchi da **dead heat** *n* pareggio *m* **deadline** *n* scadenza *f*; *for newspaper*, *magazine* termine *m* per l'invio in stampa **deadlock** *n in talks* punto *m* morto **dead loss** *n Br infml* buono *m*, -a *f* a nulla
deadly *adj* (+*er*) (*fatal*) mortale; *infml* (*boring*) di una noia mortale *infml*
deadpan *adj face* impassibile; *style*, *humour* glaciale; ***with a ~ expression*** con un espressione impietrita **dead weight** *n* TECH peso *m* morto
deaf I *adj* (+*er*) sordo; ***be ~ to sth*** essere sordo a qc; ***as ~ as a (door)post*** sordo come una campana **II** ***the ~*** i sordi
deaf-and-dumb *adj* sordomuto
deafen *v/t* assordare
deafening *adj* assordante
deafness *n* sordità *f inv*
deal[1] **I** *n* **1.** accordo *m*; ***make a ~ with s.o.*** accordarsi con qn; ***it's a ~!*** affare fatto!; ***a good ~*** (*bargain*) un affare; (*a lot*) molto **2. *a great ~ of*** (*lots*) un bel po' di **3.** *in games*: ***it's your ~*** tocca a te **II** *v/t* ⟨*pret & past part* **dealt**⟩ *cards* distribuire; *drugs* spacciare; ***~ a blow to*** inferire un duro colpo a **III** *v/i cards* dare le carte; *in drugs* spacciare
◆**deal in** *v/t* (*trade in*) trattare; *drugs* trafficare

◆**deal out** *v/t sep cards* distribuire
◆**deal with** *v/t* (*handle*) occuparsi di; *situation* gestire; (*do business with*) trattare con
deal[2] *n wood* abete *m*
dealer *n* (*merchant*) commerciante *m/f*; (*drug dealer*) spacciatore *m*, -trice *f*
dealing *n* (*drug dealing*) spaccio *m*
dealings *npl* (*business*) rapporti *mpl*
dealt *pret & past part* → ***deal***
dean *n of college* preside *m*; UNIV rettore *m*; REL decano *m*
dear I *adj* (+*er*) caro; (*expensive*) caro; ***Dear Sir*** Egregio Signore; ***Dear Richard / Dear Margaret*** caro Richard / cara Margareth; ***hold sth. ~*** aver caro qc **II** *int*: (***oh***) ***~!, ~ me!*** povero me! **III** *n* caro *m*, -a *f*; ***old ~*** *Br pej* vecchia *f*; ***be a ~ …*** *Br infml* sii gentile … **IV** *adv* a caro prezzo; ***this will cost them ~*** gli costerà molto
dearly *adv love* teneramente; ***I would ~ love to marry*** mi piacerebbe molto sposarmi; *fig* ***he paid ~*** (***for it***) lo ha pagato a caro prezzo
death *n* morte *f*; ***beat s.o. to ~*** ammazzare qn di botte; ***scare s.o. to ~*** spaventare qn a morte; ***~ by drowning*** morte *f* per annegamento; ***be burned to ~*** essere arso vivo; ***starve to ~*** morire di fame; ***a fight to the ~*** un combattimento all'ultimo sangue; ***put s.o. to ~*** condannare a morte qn; ***drink o.s. to ~*** uccidersi a furia di bere; ***be at ~'s door*** essere in punto di morte
deathbed *n* letto *m* di morte; ***be on one's ~*** essere sul prorio letto di morte **death blow** *n* colpo *m* di grazia **death certificate** *n* certificato *m* di decesso **death duties** *npl Br* tassa *f* di successione
deathly I *adj*: ***~ hush*** *or* ***silence*** silenzio *m* mortale **II** *adv*: ***~ pale*** pallore cadaverico; ***~ quiet*** calma mortale
death mask *n* colpo *m* di grazia **death penalty** *n* pena *f* di morte **death rate** *n* tasso *m* di mortalità **death rattle** *n* rantolo *m* di morte **death row** *n* braccio *m* della morte; ***be on ~*** essere nel braccio della morte **death sentence** *n* condanna *f* a morte; ***be on ~*** essere condannato a morte **death toll** *n* numero *m* delle vittime **death trap** *n* trappola *f* mortale **death warrant** *n fig*: ***sign one's own ~*** firmare la propria condanna a morte **death wish** *n* PSYCH desiderio *m* suicida
debacle *n* sconfitta *f*
debar *v/t* ⟨*pret & past part* ***-red***⟩ impedire a; ***~ s.o. from doing sth*** impedire a qn di fare qc
debase *v/t form* svilire; ***~ o.s.*** svilirsi
debatable *adj* discutibile
debate I *n* dibattimento *m*; POL dibattito *m*; ***a ~ on*** *or* ***about*** un dibattito su; ***after much ~*** dopo molto dibattere; ***be open to ~*** restare da decidere **II** *v/i* dibattere; ***~ with o.s. whether …*** considerare se … **III** *v/t* dibattere su
debauched *adj* debosciato
debauchery *n* depravazione *f*; ***a life of ~*** una vita dissoluta
debilitate *v/t* debilitare
debilitating *adj* debilitante
debility *n* debolezza *f*; MED astenia *f*
debit I *n* addebito *m* **II** *v/t*: ***~ £150 to s.o.'s account*** addebitare £ 150 a qn; ***~ an account with £ 150*** addebitare £ 150 su un conto
debit card *n* carta *f* di debito
debrief *v/t* chiamare a rapporto
debris *n of plane* rottami *mpl*; *of building* macerie *fpl*
debt *n* debito *m*; ***be in ~*** (*financially*) avere dei debiti; ***be in s.o's ~, be in ~ to s.o.*** essere in debito con qn; ***he is in my ~*** *for money*, *help etc* mi è debitore; ***repay a ~*** saldare un debito
debtor *n* debitore *m*, -trice *f*
debt relief *n* riduzione *f* del debito
debt-ridden *adj* sommerso dai debiti
debug *v/t* ⟨*pret & past part* ***-ged***⟩ *room* togliere le microspie da; COMPUT togliere gli errori da
debunk *v/t infml* smontare
début *n* debutto *m*; ***make one's ~*** THEAT fare il proprio debutto; ***~ album*** album *m inv* di esordio
debutante *n* debuttante *f* (in società)
Dec. *abbr* (= **December**) dic. (dicembre)
decade *n* decennio *m*, decade *f*
decadence *n* decadenza *f*
decadent *adj* decadente
decaf *n infml* decaffeinato *m*
decaffeinated *adj* decaffeinato
decal *n US* adesivo *m*

decamp *v/i* levare le tende
decant *v/t* travasare
decanter *n* caraffa *f per servire alcolici*
decapitate *v/t* decapitare
decathlon *n* decathlon *m inv*
decay I *n of organic matter* decomposizione *f*, *of civilization* declino *m*; (*decayed matter*) marciume *m*; ***tooth ~*** carie *f inv* **II** *v/i of organic matter* decomporsi; *of civilization* declinare; *of teeth* cariarsi
deceased *n*: ***the ~*** il defunto *m*, la defunta *f*
deceit *n* falsità *f inv*, disonestà *f inv*
deceitful *adj* falso, disonesto
deceive *v/t* ingannare; *wife* tradire; ***~ o.s.*** illudersi
decelerate I *v/i* decelerare, rallentare **II** *v/t* rallentare
December *n* dicembre *m*
decency *n* decenza *f*; ***it's only common ~ to ...*** è una semplice norma del vivere civile…; ***he had the ~ to ...*** ha avuto la decenza di ...
decent *adj price*, *proposition* corretto; *meal*, *sleep* decente; (*adequately dressed*) presentabile; ***a ~ guy*** un uomo per bene; ***that's very ~ of you*** è molto gentile da parte tua
decentralization *n* decentramento *m*
decentralize *v/t* decentralizzare
deception *n* inganno *m*
deceptive *adj* ingannevole; ***appearances can be ~*** le apparenze ingannano
deceptively *adv*: ***it looks ~ simple*** sembra semplice solo all'apparenza
decibel *n* decibel *m inv*
decide I *v/t* (*make up one's mind*) decidere; (*conclude*, *settle*) risolvere; ***~ to do sth*** decidere di fare qc **II** *v/i* decidere; ***you ~*** decidi tu; ***~ against / in favour of s.o.*** JUR pronunciarsi contro / a favore di qn
◆**decide on** *v/t* scegliere
decided *adj* (*definite*) deciso
decidedly *adv* decisamente; ***he's ~ uncomfortable about it*** lo fa sentire chiaramente a disagio; ***~ dangerous*** duvvero pericoloso
decider *n*: ***be the ~*** *of match etc* essere decisivo
deciduous *adj* che perde le foglie in inverno; ***~ tree / forest*** albero / foresta a foglie decidue
decigram *n* decigrammo *m*
decilitre *n* decilitro *m*
decimal I *adj* decimale **II** *n* decimale
decimal point *n punto che separa i decimali*; *in Italy* virgola *f*
decimate *v/t* decimare
decipher *v/t* decifrare
decision *n* decisione *f*; (*conclusion*) risoluzione *f*, ***a ~ about*** *or* ***on*** decisione riguardo a; ***make*** *or* ***take a ~*** prendere una decisione; ***come to a ~*** prendere una decisione
decision-maker *n* responsabile *m/f*; ***be a ~*** (*be able to make decisions*) saper prendere delle decisioni **decision-making** *adj*: ***~ skills*** capacità decisionali; ***the ~ process*** il processo decisionale
decisive *adj* risoluto; (*crucial*) decisivo
deck *n of ship* ponte *m*; *of bus* piano *m*; *of cards* mazzo *m*; ***on ~*** sul ponte; ***top*** *or* ***upper ~*** ponte / piano superiore
deckchair *n* sedia *f* a sdraio, sdraio *f inv*
decking *n of ship* rivestimento *m* del ponte; (*wooden floor*) copertura *f*
declaim *v/t & v/i* declamare
declamation *n* declamazione *f*
declamatory *adj* declamatorio
declaration *n* dichiarazione *f*; ***~ of love*** dichiarazione *f* d'amore; ***~ of bankruptcy*** dichiarazione *f* di fallimento; ***~ of war*** dichiarazione *f* di guerra
declare *v/t* dichiarare
declass *v/t* declassare
decline I *n in number*, *standards* calo *m*; *in health* peggioramento *m*; ***be in ~*** *or* ***be on the ~*** essere in declino **II** *v/t invitation* declinare; GRAM declinare; ***~ to comment / accept*** esimersi dal commentare / accettare **III** *v/i* (*refuse*) declinare; (*decrease*) diminuire; *of health* peggiorare; GRAM declinarsi; ***~ in value*** svalutarsi
declutch *v/i* lasciare andare la frizione
decode *v/t* decodificare
decoder *n* decodificatore *m*, decoder *m*
décolletage *n* décolleté *m*
décolleté *adj* scollato
decolorant *n* decolorante *m*
decompose *v/i* decomporsi
decomposition *n* decomposizione *f*
decompress *v/t* decomprimere

decompression *n* decompressione *f*
decompression chamber *n* camera *f* di decompressione **decompression sickness** *n* embolia *f* gassosa
decongestant *n* decongestionante *m*
deconstruction *n a.* PHIL decostruzione *f*
décor *n* arredamento *m*
decorate *v/t with paint* imbiancare; *with paper* tappezzare; (*adorn*), MIL decorare
decoration *n paint* vernice *f*; *paper* tappezzeria *f*; (*ornament*) addobbi *mpl*; MIL decorazione *f*; ***interior ~*** decorazione *f* di interni
decorative *adj* decorativo
decorative arts *n* arte *f* ornamentale
decorator *n* (*interior decorator*) imbianchino *m*
decorum *n* decoro *m*
decoupage *n* decoupage *m*
decoy *n* esca *f*
decrease **I** *n* diminuzione *f*; ***the ~ in inflation*** il calo dell'inflazione **II** *v/t* ridurre **III** *v/i* ridursi; ***~ in value*** svalutarsi
decree **I** *n* decreto *m* **II** *v/t* decretare; ***~ that*** decretare che; ***he ~d an annual holiday on 1st April*** ha decretato che il primo aprile è festa
decree absolute *n* JUR sentenza *f* definitiva
decree nisi *n* JUR sentenza *f* provvisoria
decrepit *adj* decrepito
dedicate *v/t book etc* dedicare; ***~ o.s. to …*** consacrarsi a …; ***~ o.s.*** *or* ***one's life to s.o. / sth*** dedicarsi *or* dedicare la propria vita a qn / qc
dedicated *adj* dedito; ***a ~ nurse*** un infermiere coscienzioso; ***she's ~ to her students*** si dedica molto ai suoi studenti; ***~ graphics card*** scheda *f* grafica dedicata
dedication *n in book* dedica *f*; *to cause, work* dedizione *f*
deduce *v/t* dedurre
deduct *v/t* detrarre; ***~ sth from sth*** detrarre qc da qc
deduction *n from salary* trattenuta *f*; (*conclusion*) deduzione *f*; ***~ at source*** ritenuta *f* alla fonte; ***by a process of ~*** per deduzione
deed *n* (*act*) azione *f*; JUR atto *m*
deejay *n infml* dj *m/f inv*
deem *v/t* ritenere
deep *adj* (+*er*) *hole, water, voice, thinker* profondo; *colour* intenso; ***you're in ~ trouble*** sei davvero nei guai; ***two feet ~ in water*** sotto mezzo metro d'acqua; ***the ~ end*** *of pool* il lato profondo; ***go off*** (***at***) ***the ~ end*** *fig infml* avere uno scatto d'ira; ***jump in at the ~ end*** *fig* lanciarsi (a fare qc); ***the spectators stood ten ~*** gli spettatori erano in piedi disposti su dieci file; ***~est sympathy*** sentite condoglianze; ***~ down, she knew he was right*** dentro di sé sapeva di avere ragione; ***~ in conversation*** immerso nella conversazione
deepen **I** *v/t* rendere più profondo **II** *v/i* diventare più profondo; *of crisis* aggravarsi; *of mystery* infittirsi
deep freeze *n* congelatore *m* **deep-frozen food** *n* surgelati *mpl* **deep-fry** *v/t* ⟨*pret & past part* ***-ied***⟩ friggere (immergendo nell'olio) **deep fryer** *n* padella *f* (per friggere); *electric* friggitrice *f*
deeply *adv* profondamente
deep-pan pizza *n pizza molto alta e soffice* **deep-rooted** *adj* ⟨*comp* ***deeper-rooted***⟩ *fig* profondamente radicato **deep-sea** *adj* di alto mare **deep-seated** *adj* ⟨*comp* ***deeper-seated***⟩ profondamente radicato **deep-set** *adj* ⟨*comp* ***deeper-set***⟩ infossato **deep space** *n* spazio *m* profondo **deep vein thrombosis** *n* MED trombosi *f* profonda della vena
deer *n* ⟨*pl* ***deer***⟩ cervo *m*
deerhound *n* levriero *m* scozzese
deface *v/t* vandalizzare
de facto *adj* de facto, di fatto
defamation *n* diffamazione *f*
defamatory *adj* diffamatorio
defame *v/t* diffamare
default **I** *n* inadempienza *f*; COMPUT di default; ***~ drive*** drive predefinito; ***win by ~*** vincere per abbandono **II** *v/i* (*not perform duty*) essere inadempiente **III** *v/t*: ***he ~ed on his payments*** non ha rispettato i pagamenti
defeat **I** *n* sconfitta *f*; ***admit ~*** ammettere la sconfitta **II** *v/t* sconfiggere; ***this problem ~s me*** questo problema è troppo grande per me; ***that would be ~ing the purpose of the exercise*** questo vanificherebbe lo scopo del-

l'esercizio
defeatist *adj attitude* disfattista
defecate *v/i* defecare
defecation *n* defecazione *f*
defect[1] *n* difetto *m*
defect[2] *v/i* defezionare
defective *adj* difettoso
defence, *US* **defense** *n* difesa *f*; ***come to s.o.'s ~*** venire in aiuto a qn
defence budget, *US* **defense budget** *n* POL budget *m inv* della difesa **defence lawyer**, *US* **defense lawyer** *n* avvocato *m* difensore
defenceless, *US* **defenseless** *adj* indifeso
defence mechanism, *US* **defense mechanism** *n* PSYCH meccanismo *m* di difesa **defence minister**, *US* **defense minister** *n* ministro *m* della difesa **defence player**, *US* **defense player** *n* SPORTS difensore *m* **defence witness**, *US* **defense witness** *n* JUR testimone *m/f* della difesa
defend *v/t* difendere; ***~ s.o. / sth from / against*** difendere qn / qc da / contro
defendant *n* JUR accusato *m*, -a *f*; *in criminal case* imputato *m*, -a *f*
defender *n* SPORTS difensore *m*; (*supporter*) sostenitore *m*, -trice *f*
defense *etc US* → ***defence*** *etc*
defensive I *n*: ***on the ~*** sulla difensiva; ***go on the ~*** mettersi sulla difensiva **II** *adj weaponry* difensivo; *person* sulla difensiva
defensively *adv* sulla difensiva; ***play ~*** SPORTS ritirarsi in difesa
defer *v/t* ⟨*pret & past part* ***-red***⟩ (*postpone*) rinviare
◆ **defer to** *v/t form* rimettersi a
deference *n* deferenza *f*
deferential *adj* deferente
deferment *n* differimento *m*
deferred payment *n* pagamento *m* dilazionato; *US by instalments* pagamento *m* a rate
defiance *n* sfida *f*; ***in ~ of*** a dispetto di
defiant *adj* provocatorio
deficiency *n* (*lack*) carenza *f*
deficient *adj* carente; ***be ~ in ...*** essere carente di ...
deficit *n* deficit *m inv*
definable *adj* definibile
define *v/t* definire
definite *adj date*, *time*, *answer* preciso; *improvement* netto; (*certain*) certo; ***are you ~ about that?*** ne sei sicuro?; ***nothing ~ has been arranged*** non è stato previsto niente di preciso
definite article *n* GRAM articolo *m* determinativo
definitely *adv* senza dubbio; ***~ not*** assolutamente no; ***he ~ wanted to come*** voleva venire sicuramente; *smell*, *hear* distintamente
definition *n* definizione *f*
definitive *adj biography* più completo; *performance* migliore
deflagrate *v/t* deflagrare
deflagration *n* deflagrazione *f*
deflate *v/t baloon* sgonfiare; *argument* far crollare; *person* smontare ECON deflazionare; ***he felt a bit ~d when ...*** è stato un po' smontato quando...
deflation *n* deflazione *f*
deflect *v/t ball*, *blow* deviare; sviare; ***be ~ed from*** essere sviato da
deflection *n* deviazione *f*; PHYS *of light* deviazione *f*
deflower *v/t girl* deflorare; (*destroy*) devastare
defoliant *adj* defogliante
defoliate *v/t* defogliare
deforestation *n* disboscamento *m*
deform *v/t* deformare
deformed *adj* deforme; TECH deformato
deformity *n* deformità *f inv*
defraud *v/t* defraudare; *Inland Revenue* frodare
defrock *v/t* sospendere dall'ordine (sacerdotale)
defrost *v/t food* scongelare; *fridge* sbrinare
deft *adj* agile
defunct *adj fig institution etc* sciolto; *law* cessato
defuse *v/t bomb* disinnescare; *situation* placare
defy *v/t* ⟨*pret & past part* ***-ied***⟩ (*disobey*) disobbedire a; (*challenge*) ***~ s.o. to*** sfidare qn a
dégagé *adj* dégagé
degenerate *v/i* degenerare; ***~ into*** degenerare in; ***the protest ~d into violence*** la protesta è degenerata nella violenza
degeneration *n* degenerazione *f*
degradation *n* umiliazione *f* (*squalor*) degrado *m*; GEOL, CHEM degradazione *f*

degrade *v/t* degradare

degrading *adj position, work* degradante

degree *n* **1.** *from university* laurea *f*; ***get one's ~*** prendere la laurea; ***do a ~ in law*** fare legge (all'università) **2.** *of temperature, angle, latitude* grado *m*; ***by ~s*** per gradi **3.** (*amount*) ***a ~ of*** un po' di; ***there is a ~ of truth in that*** c'è del vero in questo **4.** (*extent*) ***to a certain ~*** fino a un certo punto

degree course *n* corso *m* di laurea

dehumanize *v/t* disumanizzare

dehumidifier *n* deumidificatore *m*

dehumidify *v/t* ⟨*pret & past part* ***-ied***⟩ deumidificare

dehydrated *adj* disidratato

de-ice *v/t* togliere il ghiaccio da

de-icer *n* (*spray*) antigelo *m inv*

deification *n* deificazione *f*

deify *v/t* ⟨*pret & past part* ***-ied***⟩ deificare

deign *v/i*: ***~ to …*** degnarsi di …

deity *n* divinità *f inv*

dejected *adj* sconfortato

dejection *n* (*depression*) depressione *f*; MED deiezione *f*

delay I *n* ritardo **II** *v/t* ritardare; ***be ~ed*** (*be late*) essere in ritardo; ***~ doing sth*** tardare a fare qc; ***sorry, I've been ~ed*** scusa, sono stato trattenuto **III** *v/i* tardare

delegate I *n* delegato *m*, -a *f* **II** *v/t task, person* delegare; ***~ s.o. to do sth*** delegare qc a qn

delegation *n of task* delega *f*; (*people*) delegazione *f*

delete *v/t* cancellare

delete key *n* COMPUT tasto *m* 'cancella'

deletion *n act* cancellazione *f*; *that deleted* cancellatura *f*; ***make a ~*** fare una cancellazione

deli *n* → ***delicatessen***

deliberate I *adj* deliberato **II** *v/i* riflettere

deliberately *adv* deliberatamente

deliberation *n* (*consideration*) riflessione *m* (**on** su); ***~s*** *npl* (*discussions*) discussione *f* (**of, on** di, su)

delicacy *n* delicatezza *f*; (*food*) prelibatezza *f*

delicate *adj* delicato; *operation, subject, situation* delicato; ***she's feeling a bit ~ after the party*** si sente un po' debole per via della festa

delicatessen *n* gastronomia *f*

delicious *adj* delizioso, ottimo

deliciously *adv tender, creamy* deliziosamente; *warm, fragrant* piacevolmente

delight *n* gioia *f*; ***to my great ~*** con mio grande piacere

delighted *adj* lieto

delightful *adj* molto piacevole

delimit *v/t* delimitare

delinquency *n* delinquenza *f* (minorile)

delinquent *n* delinquente *m/f*

delirious *adj* MED delirante; (*ecstatic*) in delirio

deliver *v/t* consegnare; *message* trasmettere; *baby* far nascere; ***~ a speech*** tenere un discorso

delivery *n of goods, mail* consegna *f*; *of baby* parto *m*

delivery charge *n*: ***there is no ~*** la consegna è gratuita **delivery date** *n* termine *m* di consegna **delivery man** *n* fattorino *m* **delivery note** *n* bolla *f*, documento *m* di trasporto **delivery room** *n* sala *f* parto **delivery service** *n* consegna *f* a domicilio **delivery van** *n* furgone *m* delle consegne

delude *v/t* ingannare; ***~ s.o. into believing sth*** far credere qc a qn; ***you're deluding yourself*** ti sbagli

deluge I *n* temporale *m*; *fig* valanga *f* **II** *v/t fig* sommergere

delusion *n* illusione *f*; *of others* inganno *m*; PSYCH delirio *m*; ***be under a ~*** avere un'illusione; ***have ~s of grandeur*** avere manie di grandezza

delusional *adj* maniacale

de luxe *adj* di lusso

◆**delve into** *v/t* addentrarsi in; *s.o.'s past* scavare in

demand I *n* rivendicazione *f*; COMM domanda *f*; ***in ~*** richiesto; ***on ~*** su richiesta; ***~ for sth*** COMM richiesta di qc; ***make ~s on s.o.*** essere molto impegnativo per qn **II** *v/t* esigere; (*require*) richiedere; ***he ~ed to know what had happened*** pretendeva di sapere cos'era successo; ***he ~ed to see my passport*** esigeva di vedere il mio passaporto

demanding *adj job* impegnativo; *person* esigente

demarcate *v/t* demarcare

demarcation *n* demarcazione *f*
demean *v/t form* sminuire; **~ *o.s.*** abbassarsi
demeaning *adj* avvilente
demeanour, *US* **demeanor** *n* contegno *m*
demented *adj* demente
dementia *n* demenza *f*
demerara (sugar) *n* zucchero *m* di canna
demerge *v/t company* scorporare
demerit *n* demerito *m*
demigod *n* semidio *m*
demilitarization *n* smilitarizzazione *f*
demilitarize *v/t* smilitarizzare; ***~d zone*** zona *f* smilitarizzata
demise *n* scomparsa *f*
demister *n* sbrinatore *m*
demo *n* (*protest*) manifestazione *f*; *of video etc* dimostrazione *f*
demob *v/t* ⟨*pret & past part* **-bed**⟩ *Br infml* smobilitare
demobilize *v/t* smobilitare
democracy *n* democrazia *f*
democrat *n* democratico *m*, -a *f*; ***Democrat*** POL democratico *m*, -a *f*
democratic *adj* democratico; ***the Social Democratic Party*** il partito socialdemocratico; ***the Christian Democratic Party*** il partito cristiano democratico
democratically *adv* democraticamente
demo disk *n* disco *m* dimostrativo
demographic *adj* demografico
demography *n* demografia *f*
demolish *v/t* demolire
demolition *n* demolizione *f*
demolition squad *n* squadra *f*di demolizione
demon *n* demone *m*
demoniac *adj* demoniaco; (*posessed*) demonico
demonic *adj* demoniaco; (*hellish*) infernale
demonstrable *adj* dimostrabile
demonstrably *adv* chiaramente
demonstrate I *v/t* (*prove*) dimostrare; *machine* fare una dimostrazione di **II** *v/i politically* manifestare
demonstration *n* dimostrazione *f*; (*protest*) manifestazione *f*
demonstrative *adj* espansivo
demonstrator *n* COMM dimostratore *m*, -trice *f*; POL (*protester*) manifestante *m/f*
demoralized *adj* demoralizzato
demoralizing *adj* demoralizzante
demote *v/t* retrocedere; MIL degradare; ***be ~d*** SPORTS essere retrocesso
demure *adj* contegnoso
den *n of lion etc* tana *f*; *of thieves* covo *m*; (*study*) studio *m*
denationalize *v/t* denazionalizzare
denial *n of rumour, accusation* negazione *f*; *of request, right* negazione *f*, rifiuto *m*; ***be in ~ about sth*** negare qc
denigrate *v/t form* denigrare
denim *n* denim *m inv*
denims *npl* (*jeans*) jeans *m inv*
Denmark *n* Danimarca *f*
denomination *n of money* banconota *f*; REL confessione *f*; ***money in small ~s*** denaro *m* in banconote di piccolo taglio
denote *v/t* denotare; *symbol* indicare; *word* significare
denouement *n* scioglimento *m* di un intreccio; (*finale*) finale *m*; *fig* rivelazione *f* finale
denounce *v/t* denunciare
dense *adj* (*+er*) fitto; (*stupid*) ottuso
densely *adv*: **~ *populated*** densamente popolato
density *n of population* densità *f inv*
dent I *n* ammaccatura *f* **II** *v/t* ammaccare
dental *adj treatment* dentario, dentale; *hospital* dentistico
dental floss *n* filo *m* interdentale **dental hygiene** *n* igiene *f* dentale **dental nurse** *n* infermiere *m*, -a *f* di un dentista **dental surgeon** *n* odontoiatra *m/f*
dented *adj* ammaccato
dentist *n* dentista *m/f*
dentistry *n* odontoiatria *f*
dentures *npl* dentiera *f*
denudation *n* denudamento *m*; GEOL denudazione *f*
denude *v/t* denudare
denunciation *n* denuncia *f*
Denver boot *n US* ceppo *m* bloccaruota
deny *v/t* ⟨*pret & past part* **-ied**⟩ negare; *rumour* smentire; ***I was denied the right to ...*** mi è stato negato il diritto di …
deodorant *n* deodorante *m*

deodorize *v/t* deodorare
depart *v/i* partire; **~ from** (*deviate from*) allontanarsi da
department *n of university* dipartimento *m*; *of government* ministero *m*; *of store*, *company* reparto *m*
departmental *adj* dipartimentale; EDU, UNIV del dipartimento; *in civil service* di reparto
departmentalize *v/t* dividere in reparti
department store *n* grande magazzino *m*
departure *n* partenza *f*; (*deviation*) allontanamento *m*; ***a new ~ for*** *government*, *organization* una svolta
departure gate *n* gate *m* **departure lounge** *n* sala *f* partenze **departure time** *n* ora *f* di partenza
depend *v/i*: ***that ~s*** dipende; ***it ~s on the weather*** dipende dal tempo; ***I am ~ing on you*** conto su di te
dependable *adj* affidabile
dependant → ***dependent***
dependence, dependency *n* dipendenza *f*; ***drug / alcohol ~*** tossicodipendenza *f* / alcolismo *m*
dependent I *adj* dipendente; ***be ~ on*** dipendere da; ***~ on insulin*** che deve assumere insulina; ***be ~ on charity / s.o.'s goodwill*** fare affidamento sulla carità / benevolenza di qn; ***~ children*** figli *mpl* a carico **II** *n* persona *f* a carico; ***a married man with ~s*** un uomo sposato con famiglia a carico
depict *v/t in painting*, *writing* raffigurare
depiction *n* pittura *f*; (*representation*) rappresentazione *f*
depilate *v/t* depilare
depilatory I *adj* depilatorio; ***~ cream*** crema *f* depilatoria **II** *n* depilatore *m*
deplete *v/t* intaccare
depletion *n* (*exhausting*) esaurimento *m*; (*reduction*) riduzione *f*
deplorable *adj* deplorevole; ***it is ~ that …*** è deplorevole che…
deplore *v/t* deplorare, lamentarsi di; (*disapprove of*) disapprovare
deploy *v/t* MIL, *fig* spiegare; (*position*) schierare; ***the number of troops ~ed in Germany*** il numero di truppe spiegate in Germania
deployment *n* MIL, *fig* spiegamento *m*; (*positioning*) schieramento *m*
depopulation *n* spopolamento *m*
deport *v/t* deportare
deportation *n* deportazione *f*
deportation order *n* ordine *m* di deportazione
depose *v/t* deporre
deposit I *n in bank* versamento *m*, deposito *m*; *of mineral* deposito *m*; *on purchase* acconto *m*; (*against loss*, *damage*) cauzione *f*; ***make a ~*** fare un versamento; ***a ~ on a new car*** un acconto per una macchina nuova **II** *v/t money* versare, depositare; (*put down*) lasciare; *silt*, *mud* depositare
deposit account *n* libretto *m* di risparmio
depositary *n* depositario *m*
depository *n* deposito *m*
depot *n* (*train station*) stazione *f* ferroviaria; (*bus station*) rimessa *f* degli autobus; *for storage* magazzino *m*
depraved *adj* depravato
depravity *n* depravazione *f*
deprecate *v/t* deprecare
deprecatory *adj* deprecativo
depreciate *v/i* FIN svalutarsi
depreciation *n* FIN svalutazione *f*
depredation *n* depredazione *f*
depress *v/t person* deprimere
depressed *adj person* depresso; *market*, *economy* depresso; ***look ~*** avere un aspetto abbattuto
depressing *adj* deprimente; ***these figures make ~ reading*** leggere queste cifre è deprimente
depressingly *adv* in modo deprimente; ***it all sounded ~ familiar*** suonava tutto familiare in modo deprimente
depression *n* depressione *f*; ***the Depression*** la Grande depressione
depressurize *v/t* depressurizzare
deprivation *n* privazione *f*; (*lack*: *of sleep*, *food*) carenza *f*
deprive *v/t*: ***~ s.o. of sth*** privare qn di qc
deprived *adj* socialmente svantaggiato
depth *n* **1.** profondità *f inv*; ***in the ~s of winter*** in pieno inverno **2.** ***in ~*** (*thoroughly*) a fondo **3.** ***be out of one's ~*** *in water* non toccare (il fondo); ***when they talk about politics I'm out of my ~*** la politica va al di là della mia comprensione

depth charge *n* carica *f* di profondità **depth of field** *n* profondità *f inv* di campo **depth of focus** *n* profondità *f* di fuoco **depth psychology** *n* psicologia *f* del profondo
deputation *n* deputazione *f*
♦ **deputize for** *v/t* fare le veci di
deputy *n* vice *m/f inv*
deputy leader *n of party* vice segretario *m*
derail *v/t*: **be ~ed** *of train* essere deragliato
deranged *adj* squilibrato
derby *n* SPORTS derby *m inv*; *US* (*hat*) bombetta *f*
deregulate *v/t* deregolamentare
deregulation *n* deregolamentazione *f*
derelict *adj* desolato
deride *v/t* deridere
derision *n* derisione *f*; ***be greeted with ~*** essere deriso
derisive *adj remarks*, *laughter* derisorio
derisively *adv* con aria derisoria
derisory *adj amount*, *salary* irrisorio
derivation *n* origine *f*; CHEM derivazione *f*
derivative *adj* (*not original*) derivato
derive *v/t* trarre; ***be ~d from*** *of word* derivare da
dermatitis *n* dermatite *f*
dermatologist *n* dermatologo *m*, -a *f*
dermatology *n* dermatologia *f*
derogatory *adj* peggiorativo
derrière *n infml* didietro *m*
dervish *n* derviscio *m*
descant *n* MUS discanto *m*
descend **I** *v/t* scendere; ***be ~ed from*** discendere da **II** *v/i* scendere; *of mood*, *darkness* calare; ***~ (up)on s.o.*** piombare su qn; ***thousands of fans are expected to ~ on the city*** si attende l'arrivo in città di migliaia di fan; ***~ into chaos*** piomabre nel caos
descendant *n* discendente *m/f*
descent *n* discesa *f*; (*ancestry*) discendenza *f*; ***of Chinese ~*** di origini cinesi; ***~ by parachute*** discesa *f* in paracadute
descramble *v/t* TEL decodificare
describe *v/t* descrivere; ***~ sth as sth*** descrivere qc come qc; ***he is ~d as being tall with short fair hair*** lo descrivono come un uomo alto con in capelli biondi e corti
description *n* descrizione *f*; (*sort*) tipo *m*; ***she gave a detailed ~ of what had happened*** ha fornito una descrizione dettagliata di quello che è successo; ***answer (to)*** *or* ***fit the ~ of ...*** corrispondere alla descrizione di...; ***do you know anyone of this ~?*** conosci nessuno che risponde a questa descrizione?; ***vehicles of every ~*** *or* ***of all ~s*** veicoli di ogni sorta
descry *v/t* scorgere
desecrate *v/t* profanare
desecration *n* profanazione *f*
desegregate *v/t* eliminare la segregazione in
desert[1] *n a. fig* deserto *m*
desert[2] **I** *v/t* (*abandon*) abbandonare **II** *v/i of soldier* disertare
deserted *adj* deserto
deserter *n* MIL disertore *m*
desertification *n* desertificazione *f*
desertion *n* (*abandoning*) abbandono *m*; MIL diserzione *f*
desert island *n* isola *f* deserta
deserts *npl*: ***get one's just ~*** avere quello che ci si merita
deserve *v/t* meritare
deserving *adj* meritevole
desiccate *v/t* seccare; *food* essiccare
desiccated *adj* secco, essiccato
design **I** *n* design *m*; (*drawing*) progetto *m*, disegno *m*; progettazione *f*; (*pattern*) motivo *m*; (*intention*) intenzione *f*; ***the machine's unique ~*** la concezione unica della macchina *technical*; ***by ~*** di proposito; ***have ~s on s.o. / sth*** avere mire su qn / qc **II** *v/t house*, *car* progettare; *clothes* disegnare; ***this machine is not ~ed for ...*** questa macchina non è stata concepita per ...; ***be ~ed to*** essere concepito per
designate *v/t person* designare; ***it has been ~d a no smoking area*** quest'area è riservata ai non fumatori
designer *n* designer *m/f inv*; *of building*, *car*, *ship* progettista *m/f*; ***costume ~*** costumista *m/f*; ***fashion ~*** stilista *m/f*; ***interior ~*** arredatore *m*, -trice *f*
designer clothes *npl* abiti *mpl* firmati
design fault *n* difetto *m* di concezione
design school *n* scuola *f* di design

desirable *adj* desiderabile; (*advisable*) preferibile
desire I *n* desiderio *m*; **~ for** desiderio di; ***I have no ~ to see him*** non ho alcuna voglia di vederlo **II** *v/t* desiderare; ***if ~d*** se preferite; ***have the ~d effect*** vere l'effetto desiderato; ***it leaves much*** *or* ***a lot to be ~d*** lascia molto a desiderare; ***it leaves something to be ~d*** lascia un po' a desiderare
desist *v/i* desistere
desk *n* scrivania *f*; *in hotel* reception *f inv*
desk clerk *n US* receptionist *m/f inv* **desk diary** *n* agenda *f* da tavolo **desk job** *n* lavoro *m* in ufficio **desktop** *n* scrivania *f*; (*computer*) computer *m inv* da tavolo; (*screen*) desktop *m inv* **desktop publishing** *n* editoria *f* elettronica
desolate *adj place* desolato
desolation *n by war* devastazione *f*; (*grief*) desolazione *f*
despair I *n* disperazione *f*; **in ~** disperato **II** *v/i* disperare; ***~ of sth / s.o.*** aver perso la fiducia in qc / qn; ***~ of doing sth*** disperare di fare qc
desperado *n* bandito *m*
desperate *adj* disperato; ***be ~ for a cigarette / drink*** morire dalla voglia di una sigaretta / bere qualcosa; ***be ~ to*** morire dalla voglia di
desperately *adj try*, *need* disperatamente; *ill* gravemente, *tired*, *sad* estremamente
desperation *n* disperazione *f*; **in ~** per la disperazione
despicable *adj* deplorevole
despicably *adv* (+*v*) in modo spregevole; ***he behaved ~*** si è comportato in modo spregevole
despise *v/t* disprezzare; ***~ o.s.*** (***for sth***) disprezzarsi (per qc)
despite *prep* malgrado, nonostante; ***~ his warnings*** nonostante i suoi avvertimenti; ***~ what she says*** malgrado quello che dice
despoil *v/t* spogliare; (*plunder*) saccheggiare
despoliation *n* spoliazione *f*; (*plunder*) saccheggio *m*
despondency *n* abbattimento *m*
despondent *adj* abbattuto
despot *n* despota *m*
despotism *n* despotismo *m*
dessert *n* dolce *m*, dessert *m inv*
dessertspoon *n* cucchiaio *m* da dessert
dessert wine *n* vino *m* da dessert
destabilization *n* destabilizzazione *f*
destabilize *v/t* destabilizzare
destination *n* destinazione *f*
destine *v/t* (*set apart*, *predestine*) destinare; ***be ~d to do sth*** essere destinato a fare qc; ***we were ~d to meet*** era destino che ci incontrassimo; ***I was ~d never to see them again*** ero destinato a non rincontrarli più
destined *adj fig* ***be ~ for*** essere destinato a; *fig* ***be ~ to*** essere destinato a
destiny *n* destino *m*; ***control one's own ~*** controllare il proprio destino
destitute *adj* indigente
destroy *v/t* distruggere
destroyer *n* NAUT cacciatorpediniere *m*
destruction *n* distruzione *f*
destructive *adj* distruttivo; *child* scalmanato
destructiveness *n* distruttività *f inv*; *of fire*, *war* forza *f* distruttrice; *of weapon* carica *f* distruttiva
desultory *adj* (*jerky*) sconnesso; (*systemless*) disordinato; (*at random*) a casaccio
detach *v/t* staccare; ***~ sth from sth*** staccare qc da qc
detachable *adj* staccabile
detached *adj* (*objective*) distaccato
detached house *n* villetta *f*
detachment *n* (*objectivity*) distacco *m*; MIL *of troops* distaccamento *m*; ***he cannot view the subject with ~*** non riesce a vedere la cosa con distacco
detail I *n* dettaglio *m*; **in ~** dettagliatamente; ***go into ~*** scendere nei particolari; ***for further ~s, contact ...*** per ulteriori informazioni contattare ... **II** *v/t* descrivere nel dettagli; MIL distaccare
detailed *adj* dettagliato
detain *v/t* (*hold back*) trattenere; *as prisoner* trattenere; ***be ~ed*** (*be arrested*) essere arrestato; (*be in detention*) essere detenuto; ***~ s.o. for questioning*** essere trattenuto per essere sottoposto a interrogatorio
detainee *n* detenuto *m*, -a *f*

detect *v/t* rilevare; *anxiety*, *irony* cogliere
detection *n of criminal*, *crime* investigazione *f*; *of smoke etc* rilevamento *m*; ***avoid** or **escape** ~* non essere scoperto
detective *n* (*policeman*) agente *m/f* investigativo
detective agency *n* agenzia *f* investigativa **detective inspector** *n ispettore incaricato delle indagini* **detective novel** *n* romanzo *m* giallo, giallo *m*
detector *n* rilevatore *m*
détente *n* POL distensione *f*
detention *n* (*imprisonment*) detenzione *f*; EDU *punizione che consiste nel rimanere a scuola dopo la fine delle lezioni*; ***get ~*** essere messi in castigo
detention centre, *US* **detention center** *n* centro *m* di detenzione
deter *v/t* ⟨*pret & past part* ***-red***⟩ dissuadere; ***~ s.o. from doing sth*** dissuadere qn dal fare qc
detergent *n* detergente *m*
deteriorate *v/i* deteriorarsi
deterioration *n* deterioramento *m*
determination *n* (*resolution*) determinazione *f*; ***he has great ~*** ha una grande determinazione
determine *v/t* (*establish*) determinare
determined *adj* determinato, deciso; ***be ~ to*** essere deciso a
deterrent *n* deterrente *m*; ***be a ~*** essere un deterrente
detest *v/t* detestare
detestable *adj* detestabile
dethrone *v/t* detronizzare
detonate I *v/t* fare detonare **II** *v/i* detonare
detonation *n* detonazione *f*
detonator *n* detonatore *m*
detour *n* deviazione *f*; *for traffic* deviazione *f*; ***make a ~*** fare una deviazione
detox *n infml* disintossicare
detoxification *n* disintossicazione *f*
◆**detract from** *v/t merit*, *value* sminuire; *enjoyment* rovinare; *room*, *décor* rovinare l'effetto di
detriment *n*: ***to the ~ of*** a scapito di
detrimental *adj* nocivo
detritus *n* detriti *mpl*
deuce *n in tennis* 40 pari *m inv*
devaluation *n of currency* svalutazione *f*
devalue *v/t currency* svalutare
devastate *v/t town*, *land* devastare; *economy* devastare; (*overwhelm*) distruggere; ***I was ~d*** ero distrutta; ***they were ~d by the news*** sono stati distrutti dalla notizia
devastating *adj* (*destructive*) devastante; *fig news* sconvolgente; *defeat*, *blow* disastroso; ***be ~ to** or **for sth*** (*or* ***have a ~ effect on sth***) avere un effetto devastante su qc; ***a ~ blow / loss*** un colpo / una perdita devastante
develop I *v/t film*, *business* sviluppare; *land*, *site* valorizzare; (*originate*) scoprire; *illness*, *cold* contrarre **II** *v/i* (*grow*) svilupparsi; ***~ into*** diventare
developer *n of property* impresario *m*, -a *f* edile; ***late ~*** bambino *m* tardivo
developing country *n* paese *m* in via di sviluppo
development *n* sviluppo *m*; *of land*, *site* valorizzazione *f*; (*origination*) scoperta *f*
development agency *n* agenzia *f* per lo sviluppo **development area** *n* area *f* di sviluppo **development grant** *n* sovvenzione *f* per lo sviluppo
deviate *v/i*: ***~ from*** (*route*) deviare da; (*subject*) discostarsi da
device *n* (*tool*) dispositivo *m*
devil *n* diavolo *m*; ***who / what the ~ ...?*** chi / che diavolo ...; ***you little ~!*** che peste!; ***go on, be a ~*** andiamo, lasciati tentare; ***I had a ~ of a job getting here*** *infml* è stato infernale arrivare là; ***be between the Devil and the deep blue sea*** tra l'incudine e il martello; ***go to the ~!*** *infml* va' al diavolo; ***speak of the ~!*** parli del diavolo (spuntano le corna)!; ***better the ~ you know*** (***than the ~ you don't***) *prov* chi lascia la via vecchia per la nuova sa quello che lascia ma non sa quello che trova
devious *adj* (*sly*) subdolo; ***by ~ means*** per vie traverse; ***have a ~ mind*** avere una mente contorta
deviously *adv* (*+v*) in modo contorto
deviousness *n* ambiguità *f inv*; *road* tortuosità *f inv*
devise *v/t* escogitare
devoid *adj*: ***be ~ of*** essere privo di
devolution *n* POL decentramento *m*
devolve *v/t right* devolvere; *autority*, *power* trasmettere (***on, upon*** a) ***a***

~d government governo *m* decentrato
devote *v/t time* dedicare; *money* destinare; ***~ sth to sth*** dedicare qc a qc; ***~ o.s. to sth*** dedicarsi a qc
devoted *adj son etc* devoto; ***be ~ to a person*** essere molto attaccato a una persona
devotee *n* appassionato *m*, -a *f*
devotion *n to a person* attaccamento *m*; *to one's job* dedizione *f*; ***~ to duty*** dedizione al dovere
devour *v/t food*, *book* divorare
devout *adj* devoto; ***a ~ Catholic*** un cattolico fervente
dew *n* rugiada *f*
dexterity *n* destrezza *f*
DfEE *abbr* (= **Department for Education and Employment**) *Br* Dipartimento per l'Educazione e l'Occupazione
diabetes *nsg* diabete *m*
diabetic **I** *n* diabetico *m*, -a *f* **II** *adj* diabetico; *foods* per diabetici
diabolical *adj sl* (*very bad*) penoso; ***diabolical weather*** tempo infernale
diagnose *v/t* diagnosticare
diagnosis *n* ⟨*pl* ***diagnoses***⟩ diagnosi *f inv*; ***make a ~*** fare una diagnosi
diagonal *adj* diagonale
diagonally *adv* diagonalmente; ***crossed the street ~*** ha attraversato la strada in diagonale; ***~ opposite s.o. / sth*** diagonalmente opposto a qn / qc
diagram *n* diagramma *m*; ***as shown in the ~*** come mostra il diagramma
dial **I** *n of clock*, *meter* quadrante *m*; TEL disco *m* combinatore **II** *v/i* ⟨*pret & past part* **-led**, *US* **-ed**⟩ TEL comporre il numero **III** *v/t* ⟨*pret & past part* **-led**, *US* **-ed**⟩ TEL *number* comporre
dialect *n* dialetto *m*; ***the country people spoke in ~*** la gente di campagna parlava in dialetto
dialectic *n* dialettica *f*
dialectics *nsg* dialettica *f*
dialling code *n* prefisso *m*
dialling tone, *US* **dial tone** *n* segnale *m* di linea libera
dialogue, *US* **dialog** *n* dialogo *m*
dialogue box *n* COMPUT riquadro *m* di dialogo
dial-up *adj* COMPUT commutato, dial-up; ***~ link*** collegamento *m* commutato *or* dial-up; ***~ modem*** modem *m inv* dial-up
dialysis *n* dialisi *f inv*
diamanté *n* strass *m inv*
diameter *n* diametro *m*
diametrically *adv*: ***~ opposed*** diametricalmente opposto
diamond *n* (*jewel*) diamante *m m*; (*shape*) losanga *f*; ***~s*** *in cards* quadri *mpl*
diamond lane *n US* corsia *f* preferenziale
diaper *n US* pannolino *m*
diaphragm *n* diaframma *m*
diarrhoea, *US* **diarrhea** *n* diarrea *f*
diary *n for thoughts* diario *m*; *for appointments* agenda *f*
dice **I** *n* dado *m* **II** *v/t* (*cut*) tagliare a dadini
dicey *adj* azzardato
dichotomy *n* dicotomia *f*
dick *n infml* (*penis*) cazzo *m*
dickhead *n pej infml* testa *f* di cazzo
dicky *adj Br infml* debole
dicky bow *n Br* (*bow tie*) cravattino *m* a farfalla
dictate **I** *v/t letter*, *novel* dettare; *course of action* imporre **II** *n* dettame *m*
◆**dictate to** *v/t* comandare; ***I won't be dictated to*** non accetto imposizioni
dictation *n* dettatura *f*
dictator *n* POL dittatore *m*
dictatorial *adj* dittatoriale
dictatorship *n* dittatura *f*
dictionary *n* dizionario *m*
dictum *n* detto *m*; JUR affermazione *f*
did *pret* → ***do***
diddle *v/t infml* fregare; ***~ s.o. out of sth*** fregare qc a qn
didn't → ***do***
die **I** *v/i* morire; ***~ of cancer / Aids*** morire di cancro / AIDS; *fig infml* ***I'm dying to know / leave*** muoio dalla voglia di sapere / andare via; ***I'm dying for a cigarette*** muoio dalla voglia di fumare; ***I'm dying of thirst*** sto morendo di sete; ***I'm dying for him to visit*** quanto vorrei che venisse a trovarmi **II** *v/t*: ***~ a hero's / a violent death*** morire da eroe / di morte violenta
◆**die away** *v/i of noise* estinguersi
◆**die down** *v/i of noise*, *fire* estinguersi; *of storm*, *excitement* placarsi

◆**die off** *v/i* morire uno dopo l'altro
◆**die out** *v/i of custom* scomparire; *of species* estinguersi
die-hard *adj* duro a morire; *pej* intransigente
diesel *n* (*fuel*) diesel *m*
diesel engine *n* motore *m* diesel **diesel oil** *n* gasolio *m*
diet I *n* dieta *f*; ***be on a ~*** essere a dieta **II** *v/i to lose weight* essere a dieta
dietitian *n* dietologo *m*, -a *f*
differ *v/i* **1.** (*be different*) differire, essere differente; ***~ from*** essere differente da **2.** (*disagree*) non essere d'accordo; ***~ about*** *or* ***on*** *or* ***over*** non essere d'accordo su
difference *n* **1.** differenza *f*; ***~ between*** differenza tra; ***~ in age*** *or* ***age ~*** differenza di età; ***it doesn't make any ~*** non fa nessuna differenza **2.** (*disagreement*) divergenza *f*; ***~ of opinion*** disaccordo *m* **3.** *between amounts* differenza *f*
different *adj* diverso, differente; ***be ~ from*** essere diverso da
differentiate *v/i* distinguere; ***~ between*** *things* distinguere tra; *people* fare distinzioni tra
differently *adv* diversamente, differentemente
difficult *adj* difficile; ***it was ~ for me to …*** mi è stato difficile; ***the ~ thing is that …*** la cosa difficile è che…; ***it was a ~ decision to make*** è stata una decisione difficile da prendere; ***it's ~ for youngsters*** *or* ***youngsters find it ~ to get a job*** per i giovani è difficile trovare un lavoro; ***he's ~ to get on with*** è difficile andare d'accordo con lui
difficulty *n* difficoltà *f inv*; ***with ~*** a fatica; ***have ~ (in) doing sth*** avere difficoltà a fare qc; ***get into difficulties*** essere in difficoltà
diffidence *n* diffidenza *f*
diffident *adj* diffidente
diffuse *v/t tension* diffondere
dig I *v/t* ⟨*pret & past part* **dug**⟩ scavare; *garden* zappare; (*poke, thrust*) conficcare (***sth into sth*** qc in qc); *infml* (*enjoy*) piacere; ***~ s.o. in the ribs*** dare una gomitata a qn nelle costole **II** *v/i* ⟨*pret & past part* **dug**⟩: ***it was ~ging into me*** mi si stava conficcando dentro **III** *n* **1.** (*insult*) frecciata *f*; ***a ~ at*** una frecciata rivolta a **2.** (*excavation*) scavi *mpl*
◆**dig around** *v/i infml* dare un'occhiata a *or* in
◆**dig in I** *v/i infml* (*eat*) buttarsi sul cibo **II** *v/t sep*: ***dig one's heels in*** *fig* impuntarsi
◆**dig out** *v/t sep* tirar fuori
◆**dig up** *v/t sep garden* scavare; *buried object* dissotterare; *tree* sradicare; *information* scovare; ***where did you dig her up?*** *infml* da dove l'hai tirata fuori?
digest *v/t a. fig* digerire
digestible *adj food* digeribile
digestion *n* digestione *f*
digestive *adj* digestivo; ***~ juices*** succhi *mpl* gastrici; ***~ system*** apparato *m* digerente
digestive biscuit *n biscotto poco dolce a base di farina integrale*
digger *n* (*machine*) scavatrice *f*
digicam *n* COMPUT fotocamera *f* digitale
digit *n* (*number*) cifra *f*; ***a 4 ~ number*** un numero di 4 cifre
digital *adj* digitale; ***~ display*** display *f* digitale; ***~ technology*** tecnologia *f* digitale
digital audio tape *n* audiocassetta *f* digitale **digital camera** *n* fotocamera *f* digitale
digitally *adv* in digitale; ***~ remastered*** rimasterizzato in digitale; ***~ recorded*** registrato in digitale
digital radio *n* radio *f* digitale **digital recording** *n* registrazione *f* digitale **digital television, digital TV** *n* televisione *f* digitale
dignified *adj* dignitoso
dignitary *n* dignitario *m*
dignity *n* dignità *f inv*; ***die with ~*** morire con dignità; ***lose one's ~*** perdere la propria dignità
digress *v/i* fare una digressione
digression *n* digressione *f*
digs *npl* camera *f* in affitto
dike *n along a river* argine *m*; *across a river* diga *f*
dilapidated *adj* rovinato; *house* cadente
dilapidation *n* (*squandering*) dilapidazione *f*; (*disrepay*) fatiscenza *f*; ***the house was in a state of complete ~*** la casa era completamente fatiscen-

te
dilate *v/i of pupils* dilatarsi
dildo *n* vibratore *m*
dilemma *n* dilemma *m*; ***be in a ~*** trovarsi in un dilemma
dilettante *n* dilettante *m/f*
diligence *n* diligenza *f*; *coach* diligenza *f*
diligent *adj* diligente
diligently *adv* diligentemente; *carefully* accuratamente
dill *n* aneto *m*
dill pickle *n* sottaceto *m* all'aneto
dilute *v/t* diluire
dim I *adj* (*+er*) *room* buio; *light* fioco; *outline* indistinto; (*stupid*) idiota; *prospects* vago; ***I have a ~ recollection of it*** ne ho un vago ricordo **II** *v/t* ⟨*pret & past part* ***-med***⟩: ***~ the headlights*** abbassare le luci **III** *v/i* ⟨*pret & past part* ***-med***⟩ *of lights* abbassarsi
dime *n moneta da dieci centesimi*
dimension *n* (*measurement*) dimensione *f*
diminish *v/t & v/i* diminuire
diminutive I *n* diminutivo *m* **II** *adj* minuscolo
dimly *adv shine* debolmente; (*vaguely*) vagamente; *see* indistintamente; ***I was only ~ aware that ...*** non mi rendevo del tutto conto del fatto che...; ***~ lit*** poco illuminato
dimmer switch *n* dimmer *m inv*
dimple *n* fossetta *f*
din *n* baccano *m*; ***an infernal ~*** un baccano infernale
dine *v/i form* cenare; ***they always ~ at 8.00*** cenano sempre alle 8 di sera; ***they ~d on caviare every night*** mangiavano ogni sera
◆**dine out** *v/i* andare a cena fuori
diner *n in a restaurant* cliente *m/f*; (*café etc*) tavola *f* calda; ***fellow ~*** commensale *m/f*
dinghy *n small yacht* dinghy *m*; *rubber boat* gommone *m*
dinginess *n* (*squalor*) squallore *m*; (*dirt*) sporcizia *f*
dingy *adj* (*+er*) *atmosphere* offuscato; (*dirty*) sporco
dining car *n* RAIL vagone *m* ristorante **dining hall** *n* sala *f* da pranzo **dining room** *n in house* sala *f* da pranzo; *in hotel* sala *f* ristorante **dining table** *n* tavolo *m* da pranzo
dinky *adj Br infml* (*cute*) carino; *US infml* (*small*) piccolo
dinner *n in the evening* cena *f*; *at midday* pranzo *m*; *formal gathering* ricevimento *m*; ***we're having people to ~*** abbiamo gente a cena; ***~'s ready*** a tavola; ***finish one's ~*** finire di mangiare; ***go out to ~*** *in restaurant* uscire fuori a cena
dinner dance *n* cena *f* danzante **dinner guest** *n* invitato *m*, -a **dinner jacket** *n* smoking *m inv* **dinner party** *n* cena *f* **dinner plate** *n* piatto *m* piano **dinner service** *n* servizio *m* (di piatti)
dinnertime *n* ora *f* di cena
dinosaur *n* dinosauro *m*
dint *n*: ***by ~ of*** grazie a
diocese *n* diocesi *f inv*
diode *n* diodo *m*
dip I *v/t* ⟨*pret & past part* ***-ped***⟩ immergere; ***~ the headlights*** abbassare le luci **II** *v/i* ⟨*pret & past part* ***-ped***⟩ *of road* scendere **III** *n* (*swim*) tuffo; *for food* COOK salsa *f*; *in road* pendenza *f*; *in prices* calo *m*; ***go for a ~*** fare un tuffo
◆**dip into** *v/t fig book* dare un'occhiata; ***dip into one's pocket*** crecare qc nella tasca; ***dip into one's savings*** attingere ai propri risparmi
Dip *abbr* (= **diploma**) dipl. (diploma)
diphtheria *n* difterite *f*
diphthong *n* dittongo *m*
diploma *n* diploma *m*
diplomacy *n* diplomazia *f*; ***use ~*** usare la diplomazia
diplomat *n* diplomatico *m*, -a *f*
diplomatic *adj* diplomatico
diplomatically *adv* con diplomazia
diplomatic bag *n Br* valigia *f* diplomatica **diplomatic immunity** *n* immunità *f* diplomatica **diplomatic pouch** *n US* valigia *f* diplomatica **Diplomatic Service** *n servizio diplomatico britannico*
dipper *n* ASTR: ***the Big*** *or* ***Great / Little Dipper*** l'Orsa Maggiore / Minore
dippy *adj infml* pazzo
dipstick *n* AUTO asta *f* dell'olio
dip switch *n* AUTO commutatore dei fari
DIP switch *n* COMPUT DIP switch *m*
dire *adj* tremendo

direct I *adj* diretto; ***be a ~ descendant of s.o.*** essere un discendente diretto di qn; ***pay by ~ debit*** *Br or* ***deposit*** *US* pagare con addebito diretto; ***avoid ~ sunlight*** evitare la luce diretta del sole; ***take a ~ hit*** fare centro **II** *v/t play* mettere in scena; *film* curare la regia di; *attention* dirigere; ***could you please ~ me to …?*** mi può per favore indicare la strada per …?; ***~ sth at*** rivolgere qc a; ***the violence was ~ed against the police*** la violenza era rivolta contro la polizia **III** *adv*: ***fly ~*** non fare scalo

direct access *n* COMPUT accesso *m* diretto **direct action** *n* azione *f* diretta; ***take ~*** prendere un'azione diretta **direct current** *n* ELEC corrente *f* continua **direct debit** *n* FIN ordine *m* di addebito automatico

direction *n* direzione *f*; *of film*, *play* regia *f*; ***in the ~ of*** in direzione di; ***from / in all ~s*** da / in tutte le direzioni; ***~s*** (*instructions*), *to a place* indicazioni *fpl*; *for use* istruzioni *fpl*

direction indicator *n* AUTO freccia *f*

directive *n of EU etc* direttiva *f*

directly I *adv* (*straight*, *bluntly*) direttamente; (*soon*, *immediately*) immediatamente **II** *cj* (non) appena; ***I'll do it ~ I've finished this*** lo faccio (non) appena ho finito questo

direct object *n* GRAM oggetto *m* diretto

director *n of company* direttore *m*, -trice *f*; *of play*, *film* regista *m/f*

director's chair *n* FILM sedia *f* del regista **director's cut** *n* FILM director's cut *m*, *montaggio eseguito secondo le direttive del regista*

directory *n* elenco *m*; TEL guida *f* telefonica

directory enquiries *nsg Br* informazioni *fpl* elenco abbonati

dirt *n* sporco *m*, sporcizia *f*

dirt cheap *adj infml* a un prezzo stracciato **dirt track** *n* strada *f* sterrata; SPORTS pista *f* in terra battuta

dirty I *adj* (*+er*) sporco; (*pornographic*) sconcio; ***don't get your trousers ~!*** non sporcarti i pantaloni!; ***a ~ mind*** una mente perversa; ***~ old man*** *pej* vecchio sporcaccione *m*; ***give s.o. a ~ look*** *infml* lanciare un'occhiataccia a qn **II** *v/t* ⟨*pret & past part* ***-ied***⟩ sporcare

dirty bomb *n* MIL bomba *f* sporca **dirty trick** *n* tiro *m* mancino **dirty weekend** *n hum weekend trascorso con l'amante* **dirty work** *n fig*: ***do s.o.'s ~*** fare il lavoro sporco (al posto di qn)

disability *n* handicap *m inv*, invalidità *f inv*

disabled I *n* handicappato *m*, -a *f*; ***the ~*** i disabili **II** *adj* handicappato; ***severely / partially ~*** gravemente / parzialmente disabile; ***physically ~*** fisicamente disabile; ***mentally ~*** minorato mentale; ***~ toilet*** toilet per disabili

disadvantage *n* (*drawback*) svantaggio *m*; ***be at a ~*** essere svantaggiato

disadvantaged *adj* penalizzato

disadvantageous *adj* svantaggioso

disaffected *adj* disamorato; ***become ~*** diventare ostile

disagree *v/i of person* non essere d'accordo; (*quarrel*) litigare

◆**disagree with** *v/t of person* non essere d'accordo con; *of food* fare male a; ***garlic disagrees with me*** io e l'aglio non andiamo d'accordo

disagreeable *adj* sgradevole

disagreement *n* disaccordo *m*; (*argument*) discussione *f*

disallow *v/t goal* annullare

disappear *v/i* sparire, scomparire

disappearance *n* sparizione *f*, scomparsa *f*

disappoint *v/t* deludere

disappointed *adj* deluso; ***be ~ with*** essere deluso di; ***she was ~ to learn that …*** era delusa di sapere che…

disappointing *adj* deludente; ***how ~!*** che delusione!

disappointment *n* delusione *f*

disapproval *n* disapprovazione *f*; ***~ of*** disapprovazione per

disapprove *v/i* disapprovare; ***~ of*** disapprovare

disapproving *adj look* di disapprovazione

disapprovingly *adv* con disapprovazione

disarm I *v/t* disarmare **II** *v/i* disarmarsi

disarmament *n* disarmo *m*

disarming *adj* disarmante

disarray *n* confusione *f*; ***be in ~*** (*thoughts*, *organization*) essere nel caos

disassemble *v/t* smontare
disassociate *v/t* → ***dissociate***
disaster *n* disastro *m*
disaster area *n* area *f* disastrata; (*fig: person*) disastro *m*
disastrous *adj* disastroso
disastrously *adv* in modo disastroso; ***it all went ~ wrong*** è andato tutto in modo disastroso
disband I *v/t* sciogliere **II** *v/i* sciogliersi
disbelief *n* incredulità *f*; ***in ~*** con incredulità
disc *n* disco *m*
discard *v/t* sbarazzarsi di
disc brakes *npl* AUTO freni *mpl* a disco
discern *v/t improvement*, *intentions* percepire; *outline* distinguere
discernible *adj improvement* percepibile; *outline* distinguibile
discerning *adj person* perspicace; ***the car for the ~ driver*** la macchina per i guidatori che sanno fare la differenza
discharge I *n from hospital* dimissione *f*; *from army* congedo *m*; ELEC scarica *f*; *of gas*, *liquid* scarico *m*; *of pus* escrezione *f* **II** *v/t from hospital* dimettere; *from army* congedare; *from job* licenziare; JUR prosciogliere
disciple *n* discepolo *m*, -a *f*
disciplinary *adj* disciplinare; ***~ proceedings*** *or* ***procedures*** procedure disciplinari
discipline I *n* disciplina *f* **II** *v/t child*, *dog* imporre disciplina a; *employee* applicare provvedimenti disciplinari a
disciplined *adj* disciplinato
disc jockey *n* disc jockey *m/f inv*
disclaim *v/t* negare; *responsibility* declinare
disclose *v/t* svelare, rivelare
disclosure *n* rivelazione *f*
disco *n* discoteca *f*
discoloration *n* scolorimento *m*
discolour, *US* **discolor** *v/i* scolorire
discomfit *v/t* sconcertare
discomfort *n* disagio *m*; (*pain*) fastidio *m*
disconcert *v/t* sconcertare
disconcerted *adj* sconcertato
disconnect *v/t* (*detach*) sconnettere; *supply*, *telephones* staccare; ***they'll ~ you if you don't pay your phone bill*** ti staccheranno il telefono se non paghi la bolletta; ***I was ~ed*** TEL è caduta la linea
disconsolate *adj* sconsolato
discontent *n* malcontento *m*
discontented *adj* scontento
discontinue *v/t* interrompere; ***be a ~d line*** essere fuori produzione
discord *n* MUS dissonanza *f*; *in relations* contrasto *m*
discotheque *n* discoteca *f*
discount I *n* sconto *m*; ***a 10 % ~*** uno sconto del 10 %; ***a ~ on sth*** uno sconto su qc **II** *v/t goods* scontare; *theory* trascurare
discount rate *n* FIN tasso *m* di sconto
discount store *n* discount *m*
discourage *v/t* (*dissuade*) scoraggiare; ***~ s.o. from doing sth*** scoraggiare qn dal fare qc
discouragement *n being disheartened* scoraggiamento *m*; ***meet with ~*** non avere incoraggiamento
discouraging *adj* scoraggiante
discouragingly *adv* in modo scoraggiante
discover *v/t* scoprire
discoverer *n* scopritore *m*, -trice *f*
discovery *n* scoperta *f*
discredit *v/t* screditare
discreet *adj* discreto
discreetly *adv* discretamente
discrepancy *n* incongruenza *f*
discretion *n* discrezione *f*; ***at your ~*** a tua discrezione
discriminate *v/i*: ***~ against*** discriminare; ***~ between*** (*distinguish between*) distinguere tra
discriminating *adj* esigente
discrimination *n sexual*, *racial etc* discriminazione *f*
discus *n* SPORTS: *object* disco *m*; SPORTS: *event* lancio *m* del disco
discuss *v/t* discutere; *of article* trattare di; ***the article ~es whether …*** l'articolo esamina se …
discussion *n* discussione *f*; ***have a ~ about*** discutere di qc; ***be under ~*** essere all'esame; ***open to ~*** da discutere; ***a subject for ~*** un argomento di discussione; ***come up for ~*** essere affontato
discus thrower *n* lanciatore *m*, -trice *f* di disco
disdain *n* sdegno *m*
disdainful *adj* sprezzante

disdainfully *adv* con disdegno; *look* in modo sprezzante
disease *n* malattia *f*
disembark *v/i* sbarcare
disenchanted *adj* disincantato; **~ with** disilluso di
disenfranchise *v/t person privare qualcuno dei diritti, specialmente elettorali*
disengage *v/t* svincolare
disentangle *v/t* districare
disfavour, *US* **disfavor** *n* disapprovazione *f*; **fall into ~ (with)** cadere in disgrazia (presso)
disfigure *v/t* sfigurare; *fig* deturpare
disgrace I *n* vergogna *f*; **it's a ~** è una vergogna; **in ~** in disgrazia **II** *v/t* disonorare
disgraceful *adj behaviour*, *situation* vergognoso
disgruntled *adj* scontento
disguise I *n* travestimento *m*; **be in ~** essere travestito **II** *v/t one's voice*, *handwriting* camuffare; *fear*, *anxiety* dissimulare; **~ o.s. as** travestirsi da; **he was ~d as a woman** era travestito da donna
disgust I *n* disgusto *m*; **~ at** *or* **with** disgusto per; **in ~** disgustato **II** *v/t* disgustare
disgusting *adj* disgustoso
dish *n part of meal* piatto *m*; *for serving* piatto *m*; *for cooking* recipiente *m*; **the ~es** i piatti; **wash** *or* **do the ~es** lavare i piatti
◆**dish out** *v/t sep* (*serve*) mettere in tavola; *infml* (*distribute*) distribuire
◆**dish up** *v/t sep* mettere in tavola
dishcloth *n* strofinaccio *m*
disheartened *adj* demoralizzato
disheartening *adj* demoralizzante
dishevelled, *US* **disheveled** *adj person*, *appearance* arruffato; *after effort* scompigliato
dishonest *adj* disonesto
dishonesty *n* disonestà *f*
dishonor *etc US* → **dishonour** *etc*
dishonour, *US* **dishonor** *n* disonore *m*; **bring ~ on** coprire di disonore
dishonourable, *US* **dishonorable** *adj* disdicevole
dishtowel *n US*, *Scot* strofinaccio *m* (per asciugare le stoviglie)
dishwasher *n machine* lavastoviglie *f inv*; *person* lavapiatti *m/f inv*
dishwashing liquid *n US* detersivo *m* per i piatti
dishwater *n* acqua *f* dei piatti
dishy *adj* (*+er*) *infml woman*, *man* attraente
disillusion *v/t* disilludere
disillusionment *n* disillusione *f*
disincentive *n* disincentivo *m*
disinclination *n* riluttanza *f*
disinclined *adj* restio (**to** a)
disinfect *v/t* disinfettare
disinfectant *n* disinfettante *m*
disinfest *v/t* disinfestare
disinformation *n* (*false information*) disinformazione *f*
disinherit *v/t* diseredare
disintegrate *v/i* disintegrarsi; *of marriage*, *building* andare in pezzi
disintegration *n* disintegrazione *f*; *of group* disgregazione *f*; *of marriage*, *society* disintegrazione *f*
disinterest *n* disinteresse *m* (**in** per)
disinterested *adj* (*unbiased*) disinteressato
disjointed *adj* sconnesso
disk *n* disco *m*; (*diskette*) dischetto *m*; **on ~** su dischetto *m*
disk drive *n* COMPUT lettore *m or* drive *m inv* di dischetti
diskette *n* dischetto *m*
disk operating system *n* disco *m* del sistema operativo **disk space** *n* spazio *m* su disco
dislike I *v/t*: **I ~ cats** non mi piacciono i gatti; **I ~ watching TV** non mi piace guardare la TV **II** *n* antipatia *f*; **take a ~ to s.o.** prendere qn in antipatia
dislocate *v/t shoulder* lussare
dislodge *v/t* rimuovere
disloyal *adj* sleale
disloyalty *n* slealtà *f*
dismal *adj weather*, *news* deprimente; *person* (*sad*), *failure* triste; *person* (*negative*) ombroso
dismantle *v/t* smontare; *organization* demolire
dismay I *n* costernazione *f* **II** *v/t* costernare
dismember *v/t* smembrare
dismiss *v/t employee* licenziare; *suggestion*, *possibility* scartare; *idea*, *thought* accantonare; *speculation*, *claims* rigettare; JUR *appeal* respingere; **~ sth from one's mind** scacciare dalla mente qc

dismissal *n of employee* licenziamento *m*
dismissive *adj* che ha scarsa considerazione; *remark* sdegnoso; *gesture* sbrigativo
dismount *v/i* smontare
disobedience *n* disobbidienza *f*
disobedient *adj* disobbidiente
disobey *v/t* disobbedire a
disorder *n* (*untidiness*) disordine *m*; (*unrest*) disordini *mpl*; MED disturbo *m*; ***in ~*** in disordine
disorderly *adj room*, *desk* in disordine; *mob* turbolento
disorganized *adj* disorganizzato; ***he is completely ~*** è completamente disorganizzato
disorient *v/t*, **disorientate** *v/t* disorientare
disoriented *adj*, **disorientated** *adj* disorientato
disown *v/t* disconoscere
disparagement *n* disistima *f*
disparaging *adj* dispregiativo
disparate *adj* disparato
disparity *n* disparità *f inv*
dispassionate *adj* (*objective*) spassionato
dispatch **I** *v/t* (*send*) spedire **II** *n* (*report*) dispaccio *m*
dispatch note *n with goods* bollettino *m* di spedizione **dispatch rider** *n* corriere *m*
dispel *v/t* ⟨*pret & past part* **-led**⟩ *doubt*, *fear* dissipare; *myth* sfatare
dispensable *adj* superfluo
dispensary *n in pharmacy* dispensario *m*
dispensation *n* dispensa *f*
dispense *v/t justice* amministrare
◆**dispense with** *v/t* fare a meno di
dispensing chemist *n Br* farmacia *f*
dispersal *n* dispersione *f*
disperse **I** *v/t* dissipare **II** *v/i of crowd* disperdersi; *of mist* dissiparsi
dispersion *n* dispersione *f*
dispersive *adj* dispersivo
dispirited *adj* abbattuto
displace *v/t* (*supplant*) rimpiazzare
displaced person *n* profugo *m*, -a *f*
displacement *n* spostamento *m*; *of people* trasferimento *m*; (*replacement*) sostituzione *f*
display **I** *n* esposizione *f*, mostra *f*; *in shop window* articoli *mpl* in esposizione; COMPUT visualizzazione *f*; ***be on ~*** *at exhibition* essere in esposizione *or* mostra; (*be for sale*) essere esposto in vendita **II** *v/t emotion* manifestare; *at exhibition* esporre; (*for sale*) esporre in vendita; COMPUT visualizzare
display cabinet *n in museum* teca *f*; *in shop* vetrinetta *f* **display case** *n* vetrina *f* **display unit** *n* COMPUT unità *f* di visualizzazione
displease *v/t* contrariare; ***they were ~d with her*** erano contrariati con lei
displeasure *n* disappunto *m*
disport *v/t & v/i* divertirsi
disposable *adj* usa e getta *inv*; ***~ razor*** rasoio usa e getta; ***~ nappy*** *Br* pannolino usa e getta; ***~ needle*** ago usa e getta; ***~ contact lenses*** lenti a contatto usa e getta
disposable income *n* reddito *m* disponibile
disposal *n* (*getting rid of*) eliminazione *f*; *of pollutants*, *nuclear waste* smaltimento *m*; ***I am at your ~*** sono a tua disposizione; ***put sth at s.o.'s ~*** mettere qc a disposizione di qn
◆**dispose of** *v/t* (*get rid of*) sbarazzarsi di
disposed *adj*: ***be ~ to do sth*** (*willing*) essere disposto a fare qc; ***be well ~ towards*** essere ben disposto verso
disposition *n* (*nature*) indole *f*
dispossess *v/t* espropriare
dispossession *n* espropriazione *f*
disproportionate *adj* sproporzionato
disproportionately *adv* (+*agg*) sproporzionatamente; ***~ large numbers of …*** numeri sproporzionatamente elevati di …
disprove *v/t* smentire
disputable *adj* discutibile
disputation *n* disputa *f*
dispute **I** *n* controversia *f*; ***there is some ~ about which horse won*** è oggetto di controversia quale cavallo abbia vinto; (*industrial*) contestazione *f*; ***be in ~*** essere controverso **II** *v/t* contestare; (*fight over*) contendersi; ***the issue was hotly ~d*** la questione era estremamente controversa
disqualification *n* squalifica *f*; ***it's a ~*** è penalizzante
disqualify *v/t* ⟨*pret & past part* **-ied**⟩ squalificare

disquiet I *v/t* turbare **II** *n* inquietudine *f*
disquieting *adj* inquietante
disquisition *n* disquisizione *f*
disregard I *n* mancanza *f* di considerazione; **~ *for*** mancanza di considerazione per **II** *v/t* ignorare
disrepair *n*: ***in a state of ~*** in cattivo stato
disreputable *adj* depravato; *area* malfamato
disrepute *n* discredito *m*; ***bring sth into ~*** screditare
disrespect *n* mancanza *f* di rispetto
disrespectful *adj* irriverente
disrupt *v/t train service* creare disagi a; *meeting*, *class* disturbare; (*intentionally*) creare scompiglio in
disruption *n of train service* disagio *m*; *of meeting*, *class* disturbo *m*; (*intentional*) scompiglio *m*
disruptive *adj influence* deleterio; ***he's very ~ in class*** è un elemento di disturbo nella classe
dissatisfaction *n* insoddisfazione *f*
dissatisfied *adj* insoddisfatto; **~ *with*** insoddisfatto di
dissect *v/t* MED sezionare; *subject* approfondire nei minimi dettagli
dissection *n* MED dissezione *f*
dissemblance *n* dissimulazione *f*
dissemble *v/t & v/i* dissimulare, celare
disseminate *v/t & v/i* diffondere
dissemination *n* diffusione *f*
dissension *n* dissenso *m*
dissent I *n* dissenso *m* **II** *v/i*: **~ *from*** dissentire da
dissenter *n* dissenziente *m/f*
dissertation *n* tesi *f inv* di laurea
disservice *n*: ***do s.o. a ~*** non rendere un buon servizio a
dissidence *n* dissidenza *f*
dissident *n* dissidente *m/f*
dissimilar *adj* dissimile
dissimulate *v/t & v/i* dissimulare
dissimulation *n* dissimulazione *f*
dissipate I *v/i mist*, *heat*, *energy* disperdersi **II** *v/t heat*, *energy* disperdere; *money* dissipare
dissipated *adj* dissipato
dissipation *n* dissipazione *f*
dissociate *v/t*: **~ *o.s. from*** dissociarsi da
dissociation *n* dissociazione *f*
dissolute *adj* dissoluto
dissolution *n* POL scioglimento *m*
dissolve I *v/t substance* sciogliere **II** *v/i of substance* sciogliersi
dissonance *n* dissonanza *f*
dissonant *adj* dissonante
dissuade *v/t* dissuadere; **~ *s.o. from doing sth*** dissuadere qn dal fare qc
dissuasion *n* dissuasione *f*
distance I *n* distanza *f*; ***in the ~*** in lontananza; ***at a ~*** a distanza; ***from a ~*** da lontano; ***keep one's ~*** tenere le distanze; ***what's the ~ between London and Glasgow?*** qual è la distanza tra Londra e Glasgow?; ***gaze into the ~*** fissare in lontananza; ***the race is over a ~ of 3 miles*** la gara copre una distanza di 3 miglia; *fig* ***he admired her from a ~*** la ammirava a distanza; ***it's within walking ~*** è raggiungibile a piedi **II** *v/t*: **~ *o.s. from*** prendere le distanze da
distant *adj* lontano
distaste *n* avversione *f*
distasteful *adj* spiacevole
distil, *US* **distill** *v/t* CHEM distillare (*a. whisky etc*)
distillate *n* distillato *m*
distillery *n* distilleria *f*
distinct *adj* (*clear*) netto; ***have ~ memories of s.o. / sth*** ricordare chiaramente qn / qc; ***get the ~ idea*** *or* ***impression that …*** avere la netta idea / impressione che …; (*different*) distinto; ***as ~ from*** contrariamente a
distinction *n* (*differentiation*) distinzione *f*; ***draw*** *or* ***make a ~*** fare una distinzione; ***hotel / product of ~*** hotel *m* / prodotto *m* d'eccezione; EDU, UNIV lode *f*; ***he got a ~ in French*** ha preso la lode in francese
distinctive *adj* caratteristico; **~ *features*** *of person* tratti *mpl* distintivi
distinctly *adv* distintamente; (*decidedly*) decisamente
distinguish I *v/t* (*see*) distinguere; **~ *s.o. / sth from s.o. / sth*** distinguere qn / qc da qn / qc **II** *v/i*: **~ *between X and Y*** distinguere tra X e Y
distinguishable *adj* distinguibile; ***be*** (***barely***) **~ *from sth*** essere a malapena distinguibile da qc; ***be ~ by sth*** essere distinguibile per
distinguished *adj* (*famous*) insigne; (*dignified*) distinto

distinguishing mark *n* segno *m* particolare
distort *v/t* distorcere
distortion *n* distorsione *f*
distract *v/t person* distrarre; *attention* distogliere; ***~ s.o. from sth*** distrarre qn da qc
distracted *adj* assente
distraction *n of attention* distrazione *f*; ***drive s.o. to ~*** fare impazzire qn
distrait *adj* disattento
distraught *adj* affranto
distress I *n* sofferenza *f*; ***in ~*** *of ship, aircraft* in difficoltà; ***~ call*** S.O.S. *m* **II** *v/t* (*upset*) angosciare; ***don't ~ yourself*** non ti angosciare
distressful *adj* angoscioso
distressing *adj* sconvolgente
distress signal *n* segnale *m* di pericolo
distribute *v/t* distribuire
distribution *n* distribuzione *f*; ***~ network*** rete *f* di distribuzione; ***~ system*** sistema *m* di distribuzione
distributor *n* COMM distributore *m*
district *n* quartiere *m*; ***shopping/business ~*** zona *f* commerciale
district attorney *n US* procuratore *m* distrettuale **district council** *n Br* consiglio *m* distrettuale **district court** *n US* JUR corte *f* distrettuale federale; **district nurse** *n Br* assistente *f* sanitaria di zona
distrust I *n* diffidenza *f* **II** *v/t* non fidarsi di
distrustful *adj* diffidente (***of*** verso)
disturb *v/t* disturbare; ***do not ~*** non disturbare; ***sorry to ~ you*** mi spiace disturbarti; ***~ the peace*** turbare la pace
disturbance *n* (*interruption*) fastidio *m*; ***~s*** (*civil unrest*) disordini *mpl*; ***cause*** *or* ***create a ~*** causare / creare disturbo
disturbed *adj* (*concerned, worried*) turbato; *psychologically* malato di mente
disturbing *adj* inquietante
disunite *v/t & v/i* dividere
disunity *n* disunione *f*
disuse *n* disuso *m*; ***fall into ~*** cadere in disuso
disused *adj* inutilizzato
ditch I *n* fosso *m* **II** *v/t infml boyfriend* scaricare *infml*; *infml car* sbarazzarsi di
dither *v/i* titubare
ditto *adv* idem
ditty *n* canzonetta *f*
diuretic I *n* diuretico *m* **II** *adj* diuretico
diva *n* MUS diva *f*
divan *n* (*bed*) divano *m*
dive I *v/i* ⟨*pret* ***dived***, *US* ***dove***⟩ tuffarsi; (*underwater*) fare immersione; *of submarine* immergersi; *of plane* scendere in picchiata; ***the goalie ~d for the ball*** il portiere si è tuffato per prendere la palla; *infml* ***he ~d under the table*** si è gettato sotto il tavolo; ***~ for cover*** gettarsi a terra in cerca di riparo; ***he ~d into a taxi*** si è lanciato in un taxi **II** *n* tuffo *m*; (*underwater*) immersione *f*; *of plane* picchiata *f*; *infml* (*bar etc*) bettola *f infml*; ***take a ~*** *infml of sterling etc* crollare
diver *n off board* tuffatore *m*, -trice *f*; (*underwater*) sub *m/f inv*, sommozzatore *m*, -trice *f*
diverge *v/i* divergere; ***~ from*** divergere da
diverse *adj* svariato
diversification *n* COMM diversificazione *f*
diversify *v/i* ⟨*pret & past part* ***-ied***⟩ COMM diversificare
diversion *n for traffic* deviazione *f*; *to distract attention* diversivo *m*
diversity *n* varietà *f inv*
divert *v/t traffic* deviare; *attention* sviare, distogliere
divertissement *n* THEAT intermezzo *m*
divest *v/t*: ***~ s.o. of sth*** privare qn di qc
divide I *v/t* dividere; ***the river ~s the city into two*** il fiume divide in due la città; ***~ 6 into 36*** *or* ***~ 36 by 6*** dividere 36 per 6 **II** *v/i* dividersi; ***~ into groups*** dividersi in gruppi **III** *n*: ***the cultural ~*** la divisione culturale
◆**divide off** *v/t sep* tenere divisi
◆**divide out** *v/t sep* distribuire (***among*** tra)
◆**divide up** *v/t* → ***divide***
dividend *n* FIN dividendo *m*; *fig* ***pay ~s*** dare i suoi frutti
dividing line *n* linea *f* di demarcazione
divine *adj* REL, *infml* divino
diving *n from board* tuffi *mpl*; (*scuba diving*) immersione *f*
diving board *n* trampolino *m* **diving**

suit *n* scafandro *m*
divining rod *n* bacchetta *f* da rabdomante
divinity *n* (*quality, god*) divinità *f inv*; (*theology*) teologia *f*
divisible *adj* divisibile
division *n* divisione *f*; *of company* sezione *f*
divisive *adj*: ***be ~*** causare discordia
divorce **I** *n* divorzio *m*; ***get a ~*** divorziare **II** *v/t* divorziare da; ***get ~d*** divorziare **III** *v/i* divorziare
divorced *adj* divorziato
divorcee *n* divorziato *m*, -a *f*
divot *n* SPORTS divot *m*
divulge *v/t* divulgare
DIY *abbr* (= **do it yourself**) fai da te *m inv*, bricolage *m*; ***she was doing some ~*** si stava dedicando al bricolage
DIY store *n* negozio *m* di bricolage; *smaller shop* ferramenta *f*
dizziness *n* giramento *m* di testa, vertigini *fpl*
dizzy *adj* (*+er*) stordito; ***I feel ~*** mi gira la testa
DJ *abbr* **1.** (= **disc jockey**) dj *m/f inv* **2.** (= **dinner jacket**) smoking *m inv*
DNA *abbr* (= **deoxyribonucleic acid**) DNA *m inv* (acido *m* deossiribonucleico)
DNA profiling *n* determinazione *f* del profilo del DNA **DNA test** *n* test *m inv* del DNA
do ⟨*pret* **did**, *past part* **done**⟩ **I** *v/t* **1.** fare; *one's hair* sistemare; ***~ one's teeth*** *Br* lavarsi i denti; ***~ the ironing / cooking*** stirare / cucinare; ***what are you ~ing tonight?*** cosa fai stasera?; ***I don't know what to ~*** non so cosa fare; ***no, I'll ~ it*** no, lo faccio; *stress on I* no, lo faccio io; ***~ it right now!*** fallo subito!; ***have you done this before?*** lo hai già fatto?; ***have one's hair done*** farsi fare i capelli; ***sorry, we don't ~ lunches*** siamo spiacenti, non serviamo il pranzo; ***we ~ a wide range of herbal teas*** prepariamo un vasto assortimento di tè alle erbe; ***who did the food for your reception?*** chi ha preparato il cibo per il ricevimento? **2.** *100mph etc* andare a **3.** *only pret and past part* finire; ***the work's done now*** il lavoro è completato; ***I haven't done*** *Br or* ***I'm not done telling you what I think of you*** non ho ancora finito di dirti quello che penso di te; ***done!*** d'accordo!; ***are you done?*** *infml* hai finito?; ***it's all over and done with*** è tutto finito **4.** (*study*) fare; ***I've never done any Italian*** non ho mai fatto italiano **II** *v/i* (*be suitable, enough*) andare bene; ***that will ~!*** basta così!; ***~ well*** (*do a good job*) essere bravo; (*be in good health*) stare bene; *of business* andare bene; ***well done!*** (*congratulations!*) bravo!; ***how ~ you ~?*** molto piacere **III** *v/aux* **1.** *in questions*: ***~ you know him?*** lo conosci?; ***~n't you believe me?*** non mi credi? **2.** *in negatives*: ***I ~n't know*** non (lo) so **3.** *for emphasis*: ***~ be quick*** sii veloce **4.** *in answers*: ***~ you like London? – yes I ~*** ti piace Londra? – sì (mi piace) **5.** *in question tags*: ***he works hard, doesn't he?*** lavora sodo, no?; ***you ~ believe me, ~n't you?*** mi credi, non è vero?; ***you ~n't know the answer, ~ you? – no I ~n't*** non sai la risposta, vero? – no, non la so **IV** *n Br* (*event*) fatto *m*; (*party*) festa *f*
◆**do away with** *v/t* (*abolish*) abolire
◆**do for** *v/t infml person* distruggere; ***if we get caught, we're done for*** *infml* se ci prendono siamo fritti *infml*
◆**do in** *v/t sep infml* (*exhaust*) stravolgere *infml*; ***I'm done in*** sono stravolto
◆**do out of** *v/t*: ***do s.o. out of sth*** *infml* fregare qc a qn *infml*
◆**do up** *v/t sep* (*renovate*) restaurare; (*fasten*) allacciare; ***do up your buttons*** abbottonati; ***do up your shoe-laces*** allacciati le scarpe
◆**do with** *v/t*: ***I could do with ...*** mi ci vorrebbe ...; ***he won't have anything to do with it*** (*won't get involved*) non vuole averci niente a che fare; ***it has nothing to do with you*** (*doesn't concern*) tu non c'entri niente
◆**do without** **I** *v/i* farne a meno **II** *v/t* fare a meno di; ***I can do without your advice*** non posso fare a meno dei tuoi consigli; ***I could have done without that!*** avrei potuto farne a meno!
docile *adj* docile
dock[1] **I** *n* NAUT bacino *m*; ***~s*** zona *f* portuale **II** *v/i of ship* entrare in por-

to; *of spaceship* agganciarsi
dock[2] *n* JUR banco *m* degli imputati; ***stand in the ~*** essere al banco degli imputati
dock[3] *v/t wages* detrarre; *points* decurtare; ***~ £ 100 off s.o.'s wages*** detrarre 100 sterline dalla paga di qn
dock[4] *n* BOT romice *f*
docker *n* portuale *m*
docket *n* COMM etichetta *f*
dockhand *n* scaricatore *m* di porto **dockland** *n* bacini *mpl* portuali **dockyard** *n* cantiere *m* navale
doctor I *n* MED dottore *m*, -essa *f*; ***go to*** *or* ***see the ~*** andare dal dottore **II** *v/t* adulterare
doctorate *n* dottorato *m*
doctrinaire *adj* dogmatico
doctrine *n* dottrina *f*
docudrama *n* ricostruzione *f* filmata
document *n* documento *m*
documentary *n programme* documentario *m*
documentation *n* documentazione *f*
dodder *v/i* barcollare
doddering *adj* vacillante
doddle *n Br infml* ***it was a ~*** è stata una bazzecola
dodecaphonic *adj* MUS dodecafonico
dodge *v/t blow* schivare; *person*, *issue* evitare; *question* aggirare
dodgems *npl* autoscontro *m*
dodger *n* imbroglione *m*, -a *f*
dodgy *adj Br infml deal*, *character* losco
dodo *n* ZOOL dodo *m*; ***as dead as a ~*** morto e sepolto
doe *n di cervo* cerva *f*; *di coniglio* coniglia *f*
does → ***do***
doesn't → ***does not***
dog I *n* cane *m*; *fig* ***it's ~ eat ~*** mors tua vita mea; ***work like a ~*** *infml* lavorare come un cane **II** *v/t* ⟨*pret & past part* ***-ged***⟩ *of bad luck* perseguitare; ***~ged by controversy / injury*** perseguitato dalle polemiche / dagli infortuni
dog catcher *n* accalappiacani *m inv* **dog collar** *n for dog* collare *m* da cane; *for priest*, *minister* collare *m* da prete
dog-eared *adj book* con le orecchie
dogged *adj* accanito
doggedly *adv* caparbiamente
doggerel *n* burlesco
doggie *n in children's language* cagnolino *m*
doggy bag *n pacchetto con gli avanzi di una cena al ristorante per l'asporto*
doghouse *n*: ***be in the ~*** *infml* essere nei casini *infml*
dogma *n* dogma *m*
dogmatic *adj* dogmatico
do-gooder *n pej* impiccione *m*, -a *f*
dogsbody *n infml* bestia *f* da soma, galoppino *m*, -a *f*
dog show *n* mostra *f* canina **dog-tired** *adj infml* stravolto
doing *n*: ***it was your ~*** è opera tua; ***that takes some ~*** non è una cosa facile; ***~s*** imprese *fpl*
do-it-yourself *n* fai da te *m inv*; → ***DIY***
doldrums *npl*: ***be in the ~*** *of economy* essere in stallo; *of person* essere giù di corda
dole *n Br infml* assegno *m* di disoccupazione; ***be on the ~*** ricevere l'assegno di disoccupazione
◆**dole out** *v/t sep* distribuire
dole money *n Br infml* indennità *f* di disoccupazione
doll *n toy*, *infml woman* bambola *f*
◆**doll up** *v/t sep*: ***get dolled up*** mettersi in ghingheri
dollar *n* dollaro *m*
dollop *n infml* cucchiaiata *f*
doll's house, *US* **doll house** *n* casa *f* delle bambole
dolly *n* bambola *f*; TECH carrello *m*
dolomite *n* dolomite *f*; ***the Dolomites*** le Dolomiti
dolphin *n* delfino *m*
domain *n* (*area of activity*) settore *m*; (*land*) dominio *m*; COMPUT dominio *m*
domain name *n* COMPUT nome *m* di dominio
dome *n of building* cupola *f*
domestic *adj* domestico; *news*, *policy* interno; ***~ trade*** commercio *m* interno
domestic animal *n* animale *m* domestico **domestic appliance** *n* elettrodomestico *m*
domesticate *v/t animal* addomesticare; ***be ~d*** *of person* essere incline a fare i lavori di casa
domestic flight *n* volo *m* nazionale **domestic market** *n* POL, COMM mercato *m* interno **domestic servant** *n* do-

mestico *m*, -a *f* **domestic violence** *n* violenza *f* domestica
domicile *n* domicilio *m*
dominant *adj* dominante; *member* principale; ***be ~*** *or* ***the ~ force in sth*** trovarsi in posizione dominante rispetto a qc
dominate *v/t* dominare
domination *n* dominio *m*
domineering *adj* autoritario
Dominican Republic *n* Repubblica Dominicana *f*
dominion *n* sovranità *f* (***over*** su); (*territory*) dominio *m*
domino *n* domino *m*; ***play ~s*** giocare a domino
don[1] *n Br* UNIV docente *m/f*; *infml* (*mafia boss*) padrino *m*
don[2] *v/t* indossare
donate *v/t* donare
donation *n* donazione *f*
done I *past part* → ***do*** **II** *int* fatto
donee *n* JUR donatario *m*, -a *f*; MED *persona che riceve una trasfusione di sangue o un trapianto d'organo*
donkey *n* asino *m*
donkey jacket *n giaccone di stoffa impermeabile, usato soprattutto da addetti stradali ecc.*
donor *n* donatore *m*, -trice *f*
don't → ***do not***
donut *n US* → ***doughnut***
doodah, *US* **doodad** *n infml* coso *m*
doodle I *v/i* scarabocchiare **II** *n* scarabocchio *m*
doom *n* (*fate*) destino *m*; (*ruin*) rovina *f*
doomed *adj project* condannato al fallimento; ***we are ~*** siamo condannati; ***the ~ ship*** la nave destinata ad affondare; ***the ~ plane*** l'aereo destinato a cadere; ***be ~ to failure*** *or* ***to fail*** essere destinato a fallire
doomsday *n* giorno *m* del giudizio
door *n* porta *f*; *of car* portiera *f*; ***there's someone at the ~*** stanno suonando alla porta; ***answer the ~*** andare ad aprire la porta; ***see s.o. to the ~*** accompagnare qn alla porta; (*phrases*) ***by*** *or* ***through the back ~*** dalla porta posteriore; ***have a foot*** *or* ***toe in the ~*** riuscire a infilarsi; ***be at death's ~*** avere un piede nella fossa
doorbell *n* campanello *m*
doorjamb *n* stipite *m*
doorknob *n* pomello *m* della porta
doorman *n* usciere *m* **doormat** *n* zerbino *m* **doorstep** *n* gradino *m* della porta; ***the bus stop is just on my ~*** la fermata dell'autobus è proprio davanti alla mia porta **door-to-door** *adj*: ***~ salesman*** venditore *m* porta a porta; *delivery* a domicilio; ***police are carrying out ~ inquiries*** la polizia sta facendo indagini porta a porta
doorway *n* vano *m* della porta
dope I *n* (*drugs*) droga *f* leggera; *in sport* doping *m inv*; *infml* (*idiot*) cretino *m*, -a *f*; *infml* (*information*) soffiata *f* **II** *v/t* dopare
dope-fiend *n* tossicodipendente *m/f*
dop(e)y *adj* (*+er*) *infml* (*stupid*) ebete *infml*; (*dazed*) intontito
dorm *abbr* (= **dormitory**) *infml* dormitorio *m*
dormant *adj*: ***~ volcano*** vulcano *m* inattivo; ***lie ~*** *ofplant* rimanere latente
dormer (window) *n* abbaino *m*
dormitory *n* dormitorio *m*
dormouse *n* ZOOL ghiro *m*
DOS *abbr* (= **disk operating system**) COMPUT DOS
dosage *n* dosaggio *m*
dose I *n* dose *f*; ***he needs a ~ of his own medicine*** *fig* deve essere ripagato con la sua stessa moneta; ***in small/large ~s*** *fig* in piccole dosi/in dosi elevate; ***she's all right in small ~s*** lei è sopportabile in piccole dosi **II** *v/t person* curare
doss *Br infml* **I** *n* branda *f* **II** *v/i* (*a.* **doss down**) dormire
dossier *n* dossier *m*
dot I *n* puntino *m*; *in email address* punto *m*; ***on the ~*** (*exactly*) in punto **II** *v/t*: ***~ted line*** linea *f* tratteggiata; ***tear along the ~ted line*** strappare lungo la linea tratteggiata; ***sign on the ~ted line*** *fig* sottoscrivere; (*sprinkle*) cospargere; ***pictures ~ted around the room*** quadri sparsi in tutta la stanza
dotage *n* rimbambimento *m*
dot.com *n* azienda *f* che opera tramite Internet
◆**dote on** *v/t* stravedere per
doting *adj* adorante
dot matrix (printer) *n* stampante *f* a

matrice di punti
dotted line *n* linea *f* tratteggiata
dotty *adj* (+*er*) *infml* svitato
double I *adj* doppio; ***in ~ figures*** a due cifre **II** *n* (*amount*) doppio; (*person*) sosia *m inv*; *of film star* controfigura *f*; (*room with two beds*) doppio; (*room with double bed*) matrimoniale; ***at the ~*** *a.* MIL a passo di corsa; *fig* di corsa **III** *v/t* raddoppiare **IV** *v/i* raddoppiare **V** *adv*: ***~ the amount*** il doppio della quantità; ***it costs ~ what it did last time*** costa il doppio dell'ultima volta; ***see ~*** vederci doppio
◆**double back** *v/i* (*go back*) fare dietrofront
◆**double up** *v/i in pain* piegarsi in due; (*share a room*) dividere la stanza
double act *n esp* THEAT duo *m* **double agent** *n* agente *m* doppiogiochista; *Br* **double-barrelled name** *n* cognome *m* doppio **double-barrelled**, *US* **double-barreled** *adj shotgun* a due canne **double-bass** *n* contrabbasso *m* **double bed** *n* letto *m* matrimoniale **double-breasted** *adj* a doppio petto **doublecheck** *v/t & v/i* ricontrollare **double chin** *n* doppio mento *m* **doubleclick** *v/i* fare doppio click; ***~ on*** fare doppio click su **doublecross** *v/t* fare il doppio gioco con **double dealing I** *n* doppiezza *f* **II** *adj* falso **double decker bus** *n* autobus *m inv* a due piani **double density** *adj* COMPUT a doppia densità **double door** *n* porta *f* a due battenti **double-Dutch** *n esp Br* arabo *m*, linguaggio *m* incomprensibile; ***it was ~ to me*** per me era arabo **double-edged** *adj* a doppio taglio **double entendre** *n esp Br* doppio senso *m* **double-entry** *n* (*accounting*) partita *f* doppia **double faced** *adj* a due facce **double fault** *n* (*tennis*) doppio fallo *m* **double figures** *npl* numeri *mpl* a due cifre **double glazing** *n* doppi vetri *mpl* **double knot** *n* doppio nodo *m* **double life** *n* doppia vita *f* **double meaning** *n*: ***it has a ~*** ha un doppio senso **doublepark** *v/i* parcheggiare in doppia fila **double-quick** *adj*: ***in ~ time*** in un batter d'occhio **double room** *n with two beds* camera *f* doppia; *with double bed* camera *f* matrimoniale
doubles *npl in tennis* doppio *msg*
double-sided *adj* COMPUT a doppia faccia **double-space** *v/t* TYPO spazio *m* doppio **double spacing** *n* interlinea *f* doppia **double take** *n*: ***he did a ~*** ha reagito a scoppio ritardato **double vision** *n* MED: ***he suffered from ~*** vedeva doppio **double whammy** *n* doppia sfortuna *f* **double yellow lines** *npl* doppia linea *f* gialla
doubly *adv* doppiamente; ***make ~ sure (that …)*** essere doppiamente sicuro che …
doubt I *n* dubbio *m*; ***be in ~*** essere in dubbio; ***cast ~ on*** mettere in dubbio qc; ***without ~*** indubbiamente; ***no ~*** (*probably*) senz'altro; ***no ~ he will come tomorrow*** verrà senz'altro domani; ***without (a) ~*** senza dubbio **II** *v/t*: ***~ s.o./sth*** dubitare di qn/qc; ***~ that …*** dubitare che …; ***I don't ~ it*** non ne dubito; ***I ~ whether he will come*** dubito che verrà
doubtful *adj remark, look* dubbio; ***be ~*** *of person* essere dubbioso; ***it is ~ whether …*** è in dubbio se …; ***I was ~ whether I could manage it*** dubito che potrò riuscirci; ***it is ~ that…*** è improbabile che…
doubtfully *adv* con aria dubbiosa
doubtless *adj* senza dubbio
dough *n* impasto *m*; *infml* (*money*) quattrini *mpl*
doughnut, *US* **donut** *n* bombolone *m*, krapfen *m inv*
doughty *adj* prode
dour *adj* austero
douse *v/t fire* spegnere
dove[1] *n* colomba *f*; *fig* pacifista *m/f*
dove[2] *US* → ***dive***
dovecote *n*, **dovecot** *n* colombaia *f*
dovetail I *n* incastro *m* a coda di rondine **II** *v/t* far combaciare **III** *v/i* combaciare
dowager *n vedova che ha ereditato dal marito un possedimento o un titolo*
dowdy *adj* (+*er*) scialbo
dowel *n* cavicchio *m*
down[1] **I** *adv* (*downwards*) giù; ***~ there*** laggiù; ***fall ~*** cadere giù; ***die ~*** calmarsi; ***£200 ~*** (*as deposit*) un acconto di £200; ***~ south*** a sud; ***I'll be ~ in a minute*** scenderò tra un minuto; ***I've been ~ with flu*** sono stato a letto con l'influenza; ***be ~*** *of price, rate* es-

sere diminuito; (*not working*) non funzionare; *infml* (*depressed*) essere giù; **~ *with ...!*** abbasso ...! **II** *prep* giù da; (*along*) lungo; ***I looked ~ the list*** ho scorso la lista; ***the third door ~ this corridor*** la terza porta lungo questo corridoio; ***walk ~ a street*** percorrere una strada; ***he's already halfway ~ the hill*** è già a metà strada giù dalla collina **III** *v/t* (*swallow*) buttare giù; (*destroy*) abbattere; **~ *tools*** incrociare le braccia **IV** *adj infml* ***he was*** (***feeling***) ***a bit ~*** era un po' giù; ***be ~*** *computer* essere inattivo

down² *n* (*feathers*) piuma *f*, piumino *m*

down³ *n* (*grassland*) collina *f*

down-and-out *n* senza tetto *m/f inv*

downcast *adj* (*dejected*) abbattuto

downfall *n* rovina *f*; *of politician, government* caduta *f* **downgrade** *v/t* ridimensionare; *employee* retrocedere di livello

downhearted *adj* abbattuto

downhill *adv* in discesa; *fig* ***go ~*** peggiorare **downhill skiing** *n* discesa *f* libera

Downing Street *n Br* Downing Street; (*the government*) governo *m* britannico

download *v/t* COMPUT scaricare

downmarket *adj* di fascia medio-bassa

down payment *n* deposito *m*, acconto *m*

downplay *v/t* minimizzare

downpour *n* acquazzone *m*

downright I *adj*: ***it's a ~ lie*** è una bugia bella e buona; ***he's a ~ idiot*** è un perfetto idiota **II** *adv dangerous, stupid etc* assolutamente

downside *n* (*disadvantage*) contropartita *f*

downsize I *v/t*: *company* ridimensionare; ***the ~d version*** *of car* la versione ridotta **II** *v/i of company* ridimensionarsi

Down's syndrome MED **I** *n* sindrome *f* di Down **II *a ~ baby*** un bambino Down

downstairs *adj/adv* al piano di sotto

downstream *adv* verso valle

down-to-earth *adj approach* pratico; ***she's very ~ about it*** ha i piedi molto per terra al riguardo

down-town *adj/adv* in centro

downtrodden *adj* oppresso

downturn *n in economy* flessione *f*; ***his fortunes took a ~*** le sue fortune hanno subito una flessione

down under *infml* **I** *n* antipodi *mpl* **II** *adv be, live, go* agli antipodi

downward *adj* in discesa;

downwards *adj/adv* verso il basso

downwind *adj* sottovento

downy *adj* coperto di peluria

dowry *n* dote *f*

dowse *v/t* → ***douse***

doyen *n* decano *m*

doyenne *n* decana *f*

doze I *v/i* fare un sonnellino **II** *n* sonnellino *m*

◆**doze off** *v/i* assopirsi

dozen *n* dozzina *f*; ***~s of ...*** *infml* un sacco di ... *infml*; ***baker's ~*** tredici

dozy *adj* (*sleepy*) intontito; *Br infml* (*stupid*) cretino *infml*

dpi *abbr* (= **dots per inch**) COMPUT dpi

dpt *abbr* (= **department**) *of university* dipartimento *m*; *of government* ministero *m*; *of store, company* reparto *m*

Dr *abbr* (= **doctor**) Dott. (dottore *m*)

drab *adj* (*+er*) scialbo

Draconian *adj* draconiano

draft I *n of document* bozza *f*; *US* MIL leva *f*; *US* → ***draught*** **II** *v/t document* fare una bozza di; *US* MIL arruolare

draft dodger *n US* MIL renitente *m* alla leva

draftsman *n US* → ***draughtsman*** *n* disegnatore *m*

drafty *adj US* → ***draughty***

drag I *v/t* ⟨*pret & past part* **-ged**⟩ (*pull*) trascinare; COMPUT *text, window* trascinare; (*search*) dragare **II** *v/i* ⟨*pret & past part* **-ged**⟩ *of time* non passare mai; *of show, film* trascinarsi; ***~ s.o. into sth*** (*involve*) tirare in ballo qn in qc; ***~ sth out of s.o.*** (*get information from*) tirare fuori qc da qn **III** *n*: ***it's a ~ having to ...*** *infml* è una rottura dover ... *infml*; ***he's a ~*** *infml* è una pizza *infml*; ***the main ~*** *sl* il corso principale; ***in ~*** vestito da donna; ***a man in ~*** un travestito

◆**drag along** *v/t sep* trascinare

◆**drag away** *v/t sep*: ***drag o.s. away from the TV*** staccarsi dalla TV

◆**drag in** *v/t sep into conversation* tirare fuori

◆**drag on** *v/i* (*last long time*) trascinarsi
◆**drag out** *v/t sep* (*prolong*) tirare per le lunghe; (*extract*) ***eventually I had to drag it out of him*** alla fine ho dovuto strapparglielo fuori
◆**drag up** *v/t sep infml* (*mention*) rivangare
drag and drop *n* COMPUT trascinamento *m* della selezione
dragon *n* drago *m*; *fig* strega *f*
dragonfly *n* libellula *f*
drag queen *n infml* travestito *m*
drain **I** *n* (*pipe*) tubo *m* di scarico; *under street* tombino *m*; ***a ~ on resources*** un salasso per le risorse **II** *v/t water* fare colare; *oil* fare uscire; *vegetables* scolare; *land* drenare; *glass*, *tank* svuotare; (*exhaust*: *person*) svuotare **III** *v/i of dishes* scolare
◆**drain away** *v/i of liquid* defluire
◆**drain off** *v/t sep water* fare defluire
drainage *n* (*drains*) fognatura *f*; *of water from soil* drenaggio *m*
draining board, *US* **drain board** *n kitchen* scolatoio *m*
drainpipe *n* tubo *m* di scarico
dram *n Br* (*small drink*) sorso *m*
drama *n* (*art form*) arte *f* drammatica; (*acting*) recitazione *f*; (*excitement*) dramma *m*; (*play*: *on* TV) sceneggiato *m*; ***~ classes*** corso *m* di recitazione
dramatic *adj* drammatico; (*exciting*) sorprendente; *gesture* teatrale
dramatically *adv say* drammaticamente; *decline*, *rise*, *change etc* drasticamente
dramatist *n* drammaturgo *m*, -a *f*
dramatization *n* (*play*) adattamento *m* teatrale
dramatize *v/t story* adattare; *fig* drammatizzare
drank *pret* → ***drink***
drape **I** *v/t cloth*, *coat* appoggiare; ***~d in*** (*covered with*) avvolto in **II** *n* **drapes** *npl US* drappeggi *mpl*
drapery *n* drappeggio *m*
drapes *npl US* tende *fpl*
drastic *adj* drastico
draught, *US* **draft** *n of air* corrente *f* (d'aria); ***there's a terrible ~ in here*** qui c'è una corrente terribile; ***~ (beer), beer on ~*** birra *f* alla spina
draughtboard *n Br* scacchiera
draughts *nsg game* dama *f*
draughtsman, *US* **draftsman** *n* disegnatore *m* industriale; *of plan* disegnatore *m*, -trice *f*
draughty, *US* **drafty** *adj* (*+er*) pieno di correnti d'aria
draw **I** *v/t* ⟨*pret* ***drew***, *past part* ***drawn***⟩ *picture*, *map* disegnare; *cart*, *curtain*, tirare; *in lottery*, *gun*, *knife* estrarre; (*attract*) attirare; (*lead*) tirare; *from bank account* ritirare; *conclusion*, *comparison* ricavare; (*choose*) sorteggiare; (*take*) trarre; ***he drew his chair nearer the fire*** avvicinò la sedia al fuoco; ***~ inspiration from s.o./sth*** trarre ispirazione da qn/qc; ***~ strength from sth*** trarre forza da qc; ***~ comfort from sth*** trarre conforto da qc; ***~ one's pension*** ritirare la pensione; ***~ a distinction*** fare una distinzione; ***~ a match*** SPORTS pareggiare **II** *v/i* ⟨*pret* ***drew***, *past part* ***drawn***⟩ disegnare; *in match*, *competition* pareggiare; ***~ near*** avvicinarsi **III** *n in match*, *competition* pareggio *m*; *in lottery* estrazione *f*, sorteggio *m*; (*attraction*) attrazione *f*
◆**draw apart** *v/i* (*move away*) allontanarsi
◆**draw aside** *v/t sep person* prendere da parte
◆**draw away** *v/i* (*car etc*) allontanarsi; (*runner etc*) staccarsi (***from s.o.*** da qn); (*move away*: *person*) scostarsi; ***she drew away from him when he put his arm around her*** si scostò da lui quando la cinse con il braccio
◆**draw back** **I** *v/i* (*recoil*) tirarsi indietro **II** *v/t sep hand* ritirare; *curtains* aprire
◆**draw in** *v/i* (*arrive*) arrivare
◆**draw off** *v/i* (*car*) andarsene
◆**draw on** **I** *v/i* (*approach*) avvicinarsi **II** *v/t* (*make use of*) attingere a
◆**draw out** *v/t sep wallet etc* estrarre; *money from bank* ritirare
◆**draw up** **I** *v/t sep document* redigere; *chair* accostare **II** *v/i of vehicle* fermarsi; ***draw up alongside s.o.*** accostarsi a qn
drawback *n* inconveniente *m*
drawbridge *n* ponte *m* levatoio
drawer[1] *n of desk etc* cassetto *m*
drawer[2] *n* (*person*) disegnatore *m*, -trice *f*; ***she's a good ~*** disegna bene
drawing *n* disegno *m*

drawing board *n* tecnigrafo *m*; *fig* ***go back to the ~*** ricominciare da capo
drawing pin *n* puntina *f*
drawing room *n* soggiorno *m*
drawl *n* pronuncia *f* strascicata
drawn *past part* → ***draw***
drawstring *n* cordone *m* di chiusura
dread I *v/t* aver il terrore di; ***I ~ him finding it out*** ho il terrore che lo scopra; ***I'm ~ing Christmas this year*** quest'anno ho terrore del Natale; ***I ~ to think what may happen*** il solo pensiero di ciò che potrebbe accadere mi spaventa **II** *n* terrore *m*; ***the thought filled me with ~*** quel pensiero mi riempiva di terrore; ***live in ~ of being found out*** vivere nel terrore di essere scoperto
dreadful *adj* terribile
dreadfully *adv infml* (*extremely*) terribilmente; *behave* malissimo
dreadlocks *npl* treccine *fpl* da rasta
dream I *n* sogno *m*; ***have a bad ~*** fare un brutto sogno; ***the whole business was like a bad ~*** l'intera faccenda è stata come un brutto sogno; ***sweet ~s!*** sogni d'oro!; ***have a ~ about s.o. / sth*** sognare qn / qc; ***it worked like a ~*** *infml* funzionava a meraviglia; ***she goes round in a ~*** si aggira con la testa tra le nuvole; ***the woman of his ~s*** la donna dei suoi sogni; ***never in my wildest ~s did I think I'd win*** neanche nei miei sogni più arditi avrei pensato di vincere **II** *adj infml house etc* dei sogni **III** *v/t* ⟨*pret & past part* ***-ed*** *or* ***dreamt***⟩ sognare **IV** *v/i* ⟨*pret & past part* ***-ed*** *or* ***dreamt***⟩ sognare; ***I ~t about you*** ti ho sognato; ***~ of doing sth*** sognare di fare qc; ***I wouldn't ~ of telling him*** non mi sognerei di dirglielo
◆**dream up** *v/t sep* sognare; ***where did you dream that up?*** come hai immaginato una cosa del genere?
dreamboat *n* uomo *m*, donna *f* dei sogni
dreamer *n* (*daydreamer*) sognatore *m*, -trice *f*
dreamscape *n* paesaggio *m* di sogno
dreamy *adj* (+*er*) *voice*, *look* sognante
dreary *adj* (+*er*) deprimente; (*boring*) noioso
dredge *v/t harbour*, *canal* dragare
◆**dredge up** *v/t sep fig* scovare
dregs *npl of coffee* fondi *mpl*; ***the ~ of society*** la feccia della società
drench *v/t* inzuppare; ***get ~ed*** inzupparsi; ***I'm ~ed*** sono fradicio
dress I *n for woman* vestito *m*; (*clothing*) abbigliamento *m* **II** *v/t person* vestire; *wound* medicare; *salad* condire; ***get ~ed*** vestirsi **III** *v/i* vestirsi; ***~ in red*** vestirsi di rosso
◆**dress down I** *v/t sep*: ***dress s.o. down*** rimproverare qn **II** *v/i* vestirsi alla buona
◆**dress up** *v/i* vestirsi elegante; (*wear a disguise*) travestirsi; ***dress up as a ghost*** travestirsi da fantasma
dress circle *n* prima galleria *f*
dresser *n in kitchen* credenza *f*
dressing *n for salad* condimento *m*; *for wound* medicazione *f*
dressing down *n* sgridata *f* **dressing gown** *n* vestaglia *f* **dressing room** *n in theatre* spogliatoio *m* **dressing table** *n* toilette *f inv*
dressmaker *n* sarto *m*, -a *f* **dress rehearsal** *n* prova *f* generale **dress sense** *n*: ***her ~ is appalling*** il suo gusto nel vestire è spaventoso
dressy *adj infml* sull'elegante *infml*
drew *pret* → ***draw***
dribble I *v/i of person* sbavare; *of water* gocciolare; SPORTS dribblare **II** *v/t*: ***he ~d milk down his chin*** si è sbavato il latte sul mento; ***~ the ball*** SPORTS dribblare **III** *n of water* goccia *f*; *of saliva* bava *f*
dribs and drabs *n*: ***in ~*** a gruppetti
dried *adj fruit etc* essicato
drier *n* → ***dryer***
drift I *v/i of snow* accumularsi; *of ship* andare alla deriva; (*go off course*) uscire dalla rotta; *of person* vagabondare **II** *n of snow* cumulo *m*; (*meaning*) significato *m* generale; ***I caught the ~ of what he said*** ho colto il significato generale di ciò che hai detto; ***if you get my ~*** se capisci dove voglio arrivare
◆**drift apart** *v/i of couple* allontanarsi (l'uno dall'altro)
◆**drift off** *v/i*: ***drift off*** (***to sleep***) appisolarsi
drifter *n* vagabondo *m*, -a *f*; ***he's a bit of a ~*** è un po' incostante
driftnet *n* rete *f* a deriva
driftwood *n* legname *m* galleggiante

drill I *n* (*tool*) trapano *m*; (*exercise*), MIL esercitazione *f* II *v/t tunnel* scavare; *~ a hole* fare un foro col trapano; *teeth* trapanare III *v/i for oil* trivellare; MIL addestrarsi

drilling rig *n* (*platform*) sonda *f*

drily *adv remark* ironicamente

drink I *v/t & v/i* ⟨*pret* **drank**, *past part* **drunk**⟩ bere; *I don't ~* non bevo II *n* bevanda *f*; (*alcohol*) drink *m*; *non-alcoholic ~* bibita *f* (analcolica); *a ~ of ...* un bicchiere di ...; *go for a ~* andare a bere qualcosa; *the ~s are on me* le bevande le offro io; *he has a ~ problem* beve troppo; *be the worse for ~* sentirsi male per aver bevuto troppo; *the ~ infml* il mare, l'oceano

◆**drink up** I *v/i* (*finish drink*) finire il bicchiere II *v/t sep* (*drink completely*) finire di bere

drinkable *adj* potabile

drink-driver *n Br* automobilista *m/f* in stato di ebbrezza **drink driving** *n* guida *f* in stato di ebbrezza

drinker *n* bevitore *m*, -trice *f*

drinking *n of alcohol* consumo *m* di alcolici; *he has a ~ problem* beve troppi alcolici; *underage ~ consumo di alcolici al di sotto dell'età consentita*

drinking chocolate *n* bevanda *f* al cioccolato **drinking fountain** *n* fontanella *f* **drinking problem** *n* problema *m* di alcol **drinking water** *n* acqua *f* potabile

drinks machine *n* distributore *m* di bevande

drip I *n action* gocciolamento *m*; *amount* goccia *f*; *infml* (*person*) persona *f* insulsa; MED flebo *f inv*; *be on a ~* avere la flebo II *v/i* ⟨*pret & past part* **-ped**⟩ gocciolare; *be ~ping with sweat* grondare sudore; *be ~ping with blood* sanguinare

drip-dry *adj* non-stiro **drip irrigation** *n* irrigazione *f* a goccia **drip pan** *n* COOK leccarda *f*

dripping I *adv*: *~ wet* fradicio II *n* sugo *m* d'arrosto

drippy *adj infml* sdolcinato

drive I *v/t* ⟨*pret* **drove**, *past part* **driven**⟩ 1. *vehicle* guidare; (*take in car*) portare (in macchina) 2. TECH azionare 3. *that noise / this man is driving me mad* questo rumore / quest'uomo mi fa diventare matto II *v/i* ⟨*pret* **drove**, *past part* **driven**⟩ guidare; *I ~ to work* vado al lavoro in macchina III *n* 1. percorso *m* in macchina; (*outing*) giro *m* in macchina; *two hours' ~* due ore di macchina; *it's a short ~ from the station* in macchina è poco distante dalla stazione 2. (*driveway*) viale *m* 3. (*energy*) grinta *f* 4. COMPUT lettore *m* 5. (*campaign*) campagna *f* 6. *left- / right-hand ~* AUTO guida *f* a sinistra / destra 7. SPORTS drive *m*

◆**drive at** *v/t*: *what are you driving at?* dove vuoi andare a parare?

◆**drive away** I *v/t sep* portare via (in macchina); (*chase off*) cacciare II *v/i* andare via (in macchina)

◆**drive in** *v/t sep nail* piantare

◆**drive off** → *drive away*

◆**drive out** *v/t sep person* cacciare

◆**drive up** I *v/i* accostarsi II *v/t prices* far aumentare

drive-in I *adj*: *~ cinema esp Br* drive-in *m inv*; *~ restaurant* ristorante *m* drive-in II *n* ristorante *m* drive-in

drivel *n* sciocchezze *fpl*

driven I *past part* → **drive** II *adj motivated* motivato

driver *n* guidatore *m*, -trice *f*, conducente *m/f*; *of train* macchinista *m/f*; COMPUT driver *m inv*

driver's license *n US* patente *f* (di guida) **driver's seat** *n* posto *m* del guidatore

drive-through, *esp US* **drive-thru** *n ristorante, banca ecc. dotato di una finestra attraverso la quale i clienti possono essere serviti senza scendere dall'auto*

driveway *n* viale *m*

driving I *n* guida *f*; *I don't like ~* non mi piace guidare II *adj* violento; *~ rain* pioggia *f* battente; *the ~ force behind sth* la forza trainante di qc

driving instructor *n* istruttore *m*, -trice *f* di guida **driving lesson** *n* lezione *f* di guida **driving licence** *n* patente *f* (di guida) **driving school** *n* scuola *f* guida **driving test** *n* esame *m* di guida

drizzle I *n* pioggerella *f* II *v/i* piovigginare

droll *adj* buffo

drone[1] I *n* (*noise*) ronzio *m* II *v/i bee, engine* ronzare

◆**drone on** *v/i* fare discorsi noiosi
drone² *n* (*bee*) ronzio *m*
drool *v/i*: ~ **over** sbavare dietro
droop I *v/i* abbassarsi; *of plant* afflosciarsi **II** *n* abbassamento *m*; **brewer's** ~ *vulg assenza di erezione dovuta ad abuso di alcol*
droopy *adj tail, eyelids* cadente; *moustache* spiovente
drop I *v/t* ⟨*pret & past part* **-ped**⟩ far cadere; *from plane* sganciare; *person from car* lasciare; *person from team* scartare; (*stop seeing*) smettere di frequentare; *charges, demand etc* abbandonare; (*give up*) lasciare perdere; ~ **a line to** scrivere due righe a; ~ **everything** mollare tutto; ~ **it!** *subject* lascia perdere! **II** *v/i* ⟨*pret & past part* **-ped**⟩ cadere; (*decline*) calare; ~ **dead!** crepa! **III** *n of rain* goccia *f*; **a** ~ **in the ocean** una goccia nell'oceano; (*small amount*) goccio *m*; **a** ~ **of wine?** un goccio di vino?; *in price, temperature* calo *m*; *in number* calo *m*; (*distance downwards*) salto *m*; **it's a** ~ **of ten metres** c'è un salto di 10 metri
◆**drop back** *v/i* ritirarsi
◆**drop behind** *v/i* rimanere indietro; **drop behind s.o.** rimanere indietro rispetto a qn
◆**drop by** *v/i infml* (*visit*) passare
◆**drop down** *v/i* buttarsi giù; **drop down dead** cadere a terra morto; **he has dropped down to eighth** è sceso all'ottavo posto
◆**drop in** *v/i* (*visit*) passare; **I've just dropped in for a minute** sono passato solo per un minuto
◆**drop off I** *v/t sep person, goods* lasciare **II** *v/i* (*fall asleep*) addormentarsi; (*decline*) calare
◆**drop out** *v/i from competition, school* ritirarsi; **he dropped out of the course** si è ritirato dal corso; **drop out of society** emarginarsi; **drop out of school** abbandonare la scuola
drop-down menu *n* COMPUT menu *m inv* a discesa **drop-in centre** *n centro di ritrovo e assistenza* **dropkick** *n* SPORTS calcio *m* di rimbalzo **drop leaf** *n* piano *m* ribaltabile
droplet *n* gocciolina *f*
drop-off *n* crollo *m* **dropout** *n* (*from school*) *persona che ha abbandonato gli studi*; (*from society*) emarginato *m*, -a *f*
droppings *npl* escrementi *mpl*
drops *npl for eyes* collirio *m*
drop scone *n focaccia cotta sulla piastra del forno* **drop shot** *n* SPORTS tiro *m* corto
dropsy *n* MED idropisia *f*
dross *n* ciarpame *m*
drought *n* siccità *f*
drove¹ *n* branco *m*; **they came in** ~**s** sono arrivati in branchi
drove² *pret* → **drive**
drown I *v/i* annegare **II** *v/t person* annegare; *sound* coprire; **be** ~**ed** annegare
◆**drown out** *v/t noise, voice* coprire
drowsiness *n* sonnolenza *f*; **cause** ~ causare sonnolenza
drowsy *adj* (+*er*) sonnolento
drudgery *n* lavoro *m* ingrato
drug I *n* MED, PHARM droga *f*; **be on** ~**s** drogarsi; **take** *or* **do** ~**s** drogarsi **II** *v/t* ⟨*pret & past part* **-ged**⟩ drogare
drug abuse *n* abuso *m* di stupefacenti **drug addict** *n* tossicodipendente *m/f* **drug addiction** *n* tossicodipendenza *f* **drug dealer** *n* spacciatore *m*, -trice *f* (di droga)
druggist *n US* farmacista *m/f*
drug pusher *n* spacciatore *m*, -trice *f* (di droga)
drugstore *n esp US negozio-bar che vende articoli vari, inclusi medicinali*
drug trafficking *n* traffico *m* di droga
drum I *n* MUS tamburo *m*; (*container*) bidone *m*; ~**s** *in pop music* batteria *f* **II** *v/i* MUS suonare il tamburo; *fig* tamburellare **III** *v/t*: ~ **one's fingers on the table** tamburellare con le dita sul tavolo
◆**drum into** *v/t always sep* ⟨*pret & past part* **-med**⟩ **drum sth into s.o.** inculcare qc in qn
◆**drum up** *v/t sep* **drum up support** cercare supporto
drumbeat *n* colpo *m* di tamburo
drum break *n* MECH freno *m* a tamburo
drumfire *n* MIL fuoco *m* tambureggiante
drummer *n* batterista *m/f*; *in brass band* percussionista *m/f*
drum-roll *n* rullo *m* di tamburi

drumstick *n* MUS bacchetta *f*; *of poultry* coscia *f*

drunk **I** *n* ubriacone *m*, -a *f* **II** *adj* (+*er*) ubriaco; ***be as ~ as a lord*** *or* ***skunk*** *infml* essere ubriaco fradicio; ***get ~*** ubriacarsi **III** *past part* → ***drink***

drunkard *n* ubriacone *m*, -a *f*

drunk driver *n esp US* automobilista *m/f* in stato di ebbrezza **drunk driving** *n* guida *f* in stato di ebbrezza

drunken *adj voices, laughter* da ubriaco; ***~ party*** festa *f* in cui si beve molto; ***in a ~ rage*** *in stato di ubriachezza violenta*; ***in a ~ stupor*** stordito dall'alcol

drunkenness *n* ubriachezza *f*

drunkometer *n US* → ***Breathalyzer***®

dry **I** *adj* secco; ***run ~*** (*river*) prosciugarsi; ***~ spell*** periodo *m* di tempo asciutto; ***the ~ season*** la stagione secca; ***~ bread*** pane *m* asciutto; ***~ wine*** vino *m* secco; (*ironic*) ironico; ***~ humour*** umorismo *m* pungente; *clothes* asciutto; ***rub o.s. ~*** asciugarsi strofinandosi; (*where alcohol is banned*) *dove la vendita e il consumo di alcolici sono illegali*; ***this is a ~ county*** in questa contea la vendita e il consumo di alcolici sono illegali **II** *v/t & v/i* ⟨*pret & past part* ***-ied***⟩ asciugare; ***~ o.s.*** asciugarsi; ***~ one's hands*** asciugarsi le mani

◆ **dry out** *v/i* asciugare; *of alcoholic* disintossicarsi

◆ **dry up** **I** *v/i of river* prosciugarsi; *infml* (*be quiet*) stare zitto **II** *v/t sep dishes* asciugare; *river bed* prosciugare

dryclean *v/t* pulire *or* lavare a secco **dry cleaner** *n* tintoria *f* **drycleaning** *n* (*clothes*) abiti *mpl* portati in tintoria **dry dock** *n* bacino *m* di carenaggio

dryer *n* (*machine*) asciugatrice *f*

dry ice *n* ghiaccio *m* secco

drying-up *n*: ***do the ~*** asciugare le stoviglie

dryness *n* aridità *f*

dry-roasted *adj* tostato a secco **dry rot** *n* carie *f* del legno **dry run** *n* prova *f* generale **dry-salt** *v/t* mettere sotto sale **dry-stone wall** *n* muro *m* a secco

DSL *abbr* (= **digital subscriber line**) TECH DSL

DST *abbr* (= **daylight saving time**) *esp US* ora *f* legale

DTI *abbr* (= **Department of Trade and Industry**) *Br* dipartimento *m* del commercio e dell'industria

DTP *abbr* (= **desk-top publishing**) desk-top publishing *m*, impaginazione *f* elettronica

DT's *abbr* (= **delirium tremens**) *infml* delirium tremens *m*

dual *adj* doppio

dual carriageway *n Br* carreggiata *f* a due corsie

dualism *n* PHIL dualismo *m*

dual nationality *n* doppia cittadinanza *f* **dual-purpose** *adj* a doppio uso

dub *v/t* ⟨*pret & past part* ***-bed***⟩ *film* doppiare

dubious *adj* equivoco; (*having doubts*) dubbioso; ***be ~ about*** nutrire dubbi su

dubitable *adj* dubitabile

duchess *n* duchessa *f*

duchy *n* ducato *m*

duck[1] *n* anatra *f*; ***take to sth like a ~ to water*** mettersi a fare qc con estrema naturalezza; ***it's (like) water off a ~'s back to him*** non gli fa né caldo né freddo; *Br infml* tesoro; *cricket* zero *m*

duck[2] **I** *n person* tipo *m* **II** *v/i* piegarsi; ***he ~ed out of the room*** è sparito dalla stanza **III** *v/t one's head* piegare; *question* aggirare

duck[3] *n* TEX tela *f* olona

duckboard *n* passerella *f* di legno

duck-egg blue *n colore azzurro verdastro chiaro*

duckling *n* anatroccolo *m*

ducks and drakes *n* rimbalzello *m*

ducky **I** *n Br infml* tesoro *m* **II** *adj Br infml* carino

duct *n* ANAT canale *m*, dotto *m*; *for liquid, gas* conduttura *f*; ELEC canaletta *f*

dud **I** *adj infml* inutile; (*counterfeit*) falso; ***~ batteries*** batterie *fpl* scariche **II** *n infml* (*false note*) falso *m*; (*bomb*) bomba *f* inesplosa; (*person*) buono *m*, -a *f* a nulla; ***this battery is a ~*** questa batteria è scarica

dude *n US infml* tizio *m*

due **I** *adj* (*owed, proper*) dovuto; ***with all ~ respect*** con tutto il rispetto; ***be ~*** *of train, baby etc* essere previsto; ***I'm ~ to meet him*** dovrei incontrarlo; ***~ to*** (*because of*) a causa di; ***be ~ to*** (*be

caused by) essere dovuto a; ***be ~ back*** *library book* dover essere restituito; ***in ~ course*** a tempo debito **II** *n*: ***to give him his ~***, … a onor del vero, … **III** *adv*: ***~ north*** esattamente a nord; ***~ east of the village*** direttamente a est del villaggio
duel *n* duello *m*
dues *npl* quota *fsg*
duet *n* MUS duetto *m*
duffel bag *n* sacca *f* da viaggio **duffel coat** *n* montgomery *m*
duffer *n infml* persona *f* incapace
dug *pret & past part* → ***dig***
dugout *n* MIL trincea
duh *int US* ma guarda! *iron*
duke *n* duca *m*
dukedom *n territory, title* ducato *m*
dull I *adj* (*+er*) *weather* grigio; *sound, pain* sordo; (*boring*) noioso; ***there's never a ~ moment*** non c'è un attimo di noia; *sound, ache* sordo **II** *v/t pain* attutire; *senses* appannare; *sound* smorzare
duly *adv* (*as expected*) come previsto; (*properly*) debitamente; ***be ~ impressed*** sono debitamente impressionato
dumb *adj* (*+er*) (*mute*) muto; *infml* (*stupid*) stupido; ***play ~*** fare il finto tonto; ***she was struck ~ with fear*** è ammutolita dallo spavento; ***it was just ~ luck*** è stata solo fortuna
◆**dumb down** *v/t sep* semplificare
dumbbell *n* SPORTS manubrio *m*
dumbfound *v/t* far ammutolire
dumbfounded *adj* ammutolito
dumb waiter *n* montavivande *m*
dummy I *n for clothes* manichino *m*; *for baby* succhiotto *m*; (*fool*) stupido *m*, -a *f* **II** *adj* finto; ***a ~ bomb*** una bomba a salve
dump I *n for rubbish* discarica *f*; (*unpleasant place*) postaccio *m* **II** *v/t* (*deposit*) lasciare; (*dispose of*) scaricare; *toxic waste etc* sbarazzarsi di; ***he ~ed his girlfriend*** ha mollato la ragazza
◆**dump on** *v/i +obj infml*: ***dump on sth on s.o.*** scaricare qc a qn
dumper *n* (*dump truck*) autocarro *m* con cassone ribaltabile
dumping *n of load, rubbish* scarico *m*; ***"no ~"*** *Br* "divieto di discarica"
dumping ground *n fig* discarica *f*
dumpling *n* COOK *fagotto di pasta ripieno, sia dolce che salato*
dumps *npl*: ***he was down in the ~*** era giù di corda
Dumpster® *n US contenitore standard per rifiuti*
dump truck *n US* autocarro *m* con cassone ribaltabile
dumpy *adj* tozzo
dun *adj* grigio spento
dunce *n* tonto *m*, -a *f*
dunderhead *n* testone *m*, -a *f*
dune *n* duna *f*
dung *n* sterco *m*
dungarees *npl* salopette *f inv*
dungeon *n* prigione *f* sotterranea
dunk *v/t in coffee etc* inzuppare
dunno → ***(I) don't know***
dunny *n AUS infml* gabinetto *m*
duo *n* MUS duo *m inv*
dupe I *v/t* abbindolare; ***he was ~d into believing it*** è stato abbindolato fino a crederci **II** *n* gonzo *m*, -a *f*
duplex *n esp US* → ***duplex apartment / house*** *n* appartamento *m* su due piani / casa *f* bifamiliare
duplicate I *n* duplicato *m*; ***in ~*** in duplicato **II** *v/t* (*copy*) duplicare; (*repeat*) rifare **III** *adj* duplice; ***a ~ copy*** una doppia copia; ***a ~ key*** una chiave gemella
duplication *n of documents* duplicazione *f*; *of efforts, work* raddoppiamento *m*
duplicity *n* doppiezza *f*
durability *n* durevolezza *f* (*a. fig*)
durable *adj material* resistente; *relationship* durevole
durable goods *n* beni *mpl* durevoli
duration *n* durata *f*; ***for the ~ of*** per tutta la durata di
duress *n*: ***under ~*** sotto costrizione
Durex® *n* preservativo *m*
during *prep* durante
durum *n* grano *m* duro
dusk *n* crepuscolo *m*
dusky *adj* (*+er*) *liter skin, colour* scuro; *person* bruno; ***~ pink*** rosa scuro
dust I *n* polvere *f*; ***covered in ~*** coperto di polvere **II** *v/t* spolverare; ***~ sth with sth*** (*sprinkle*) spolverare qc con qc
◆**dust down** *v/t sep* spolverare; ***dust o.s. down*** risistemarsi
◆**dust off** *v/t sep dirt* spolverare; ***dust o.s. off*** rispolverarsi

dust-bath *n* bagno *m* di polvere **dustbin** *n* bidone *m* della spazzatura **dustbin man** *n* spazzino *m* **dust bowl** *n* Dust Bowl *m*, *territorio degli Stati Uniti colpito da tempeste di sabbia*

dustcart *n Br* autocarro *m* della nettezza urbana

dust cover *n for book* sopraccoperta *f*

duster *n* (*cloth*) straccio *m* (per spolverare)

dusting *n* spolverata *f*; ***do the ~*** spolverare; ***a ~ of snow*** una spolverata di neve

dust jacket *n of book* sopraccoperta *f*

dustman *n* spazzino *m* **dustpan** *n* paletta *f*

dustsheet *n* copertura *f* contro la polvere

dusty *adj* (*+er*) *table* impolverato; *road* polveroso

Dutch I *adj* olandese **II** *n language* olandese *m*; ***the ~*** gli Olandesi **III** *adj*: ***go ~*** *infml* fare alla romana *infml*

Dutch cap *n* (*diaphragm*) diaframma *m* **Dutch courage** *n infml*: ***give o.s. ~*** farsi coraggio bevendo (***from*** st)

Dutchman *n* olandese *m*

Dutchwoman *n* olandese *f*

duteous *adj* obbediente

dutiful *adj* rispettoso

duty *n* dovere *m*; ***do one's ~*** (***by s.o.***) fare il proprio dovere verso qn; ***report for ~*** presentarsi in servizio; ***who's on ~ tomorrow?*** chi è di servizio domani?; ***he went on ~ at 9*** è entrato in servizio alle 9; *on goods* tassa *f* doganale, dazio *m*; ***pay ~ on sth*** pagare il dazio doganale su qc; ***be on ~*** essere di servizio; ***be off ~*** essere fuori servizio

duty-bound *adj* vincolato **duty-free I** *adj* duty free *inv* **II** *n* acquisto *m* fatto in un duty free **duty-free allowance** *n* limite *m* di acquisto in un duty free **duty-free shop** *n* duty free *m inv* **duty officer** *n* ufficiale *m* di servizio

duvet *n* piumino *m*

DVD *abbr* (= **digital versatile disc**) DVD *m inv*

DVD player *n* lettore *m* DVD

DVT *abbr* (= **deep vein thrombosis**) MED trombosi *f inv* venosa profonda (TVP)

dwarf I *n* ⟨*pl* ***dwarves***⟩ nano *m*, -a *f* **II** *v/t* fare scomparire **III** *adj*: ***~ shrubs*** arbusti *mpl* nani

dwarfism *n* nanismo *m*

dwell *v/i* ⟨*pret & past part* ***dwelt***⟩ *form* abitare

◆**dwell (up)on** *v/t* rimuginare; ***dwell (up)on the past*** rimuginare sul passato; ***let's not dwell (up)on it*** non rimuginiamoci

dwelling *n form* dimora; ***~ house*** casa *f* d'abitazione

dwindle *v/i* diminuire

dye I *n* tintura *f*; ***hair ~*** tintura *f* per capelli; *for food* colorante *m* **II** *v/t* colorare, tingere; ***~d blonde hair*** capelli *mpl* biondi tinti

dyed-in-the-wool *adj fig* dalla testa ai piedi

dyestuff *n* sostanza *f* colorante

dying I *adj person* morente; *industry, tradition* in via di disparizione; ***his ~ day*** il giorno della sua morte **II** *n*: ***the ~*** i morenti

dyke, *US* **dike** *n* argine *m*; *infml* (*lesbian*) lesbica *f*

dynamic I *adj person* dinamico **II** *n* forza *f* motrice

dynamics *nsg or npl* dinamica *f*

dynamism *n* dinamismo *m*

dynamite *n* dinamite *f*

dynamo *n* TECH dinamo *f inv*

dynasty *n* dinastia *f*

dysentery *n* dissenteria *f*

dysfunction *n* disfunzione *f*

dysfunctional *adj* disfunzionale

dyslexia *n* dislessia *f*

dyslexic I *adj* dislessico; ***she is ~*** è dislessica **II** *n* dislessico *m*, -a *f*

dyspepsia *n* MED dispepsia *f*

dystrophy *n* MED distrofia *f*

E

e- *pref* (= **electronic**) e-
E *abbr* (= **east**) est (E)
E, e *n* e, E *f inv*; MUS mi *m inv*; EDU (*mark*) insufficiente *m*; ***E flat*** mi *m inv* bemolle; ***E sharp*** mi *m inv* diesis
each I *adj* ogni **II** *adv* ciascuno; ***they're £ 1.50 ~*** costano £ 1,50 ciascuno **III** *pron* ciascuno *m*, -a *f*, ognuno *m*, -a *f*; ***~ of them*** ciascuno di loro; ***~ other*** l'un l'altro *m*, l'una l'altra *f*; ***we know ~ other*** ci conosciamo; ***they haven't seen ~ other for a long time*** non si vedono da tempo; ***we drive ~ other's car*** guidiamo l'uno la macchina dell'altro
eager *adj* entusiasta; ***be ~ to do sth*** essere ansioso di fare qc; ***be ~ for*** essere desideroso di
eager beaver *n infml* fanatico *m*, -a *f infml*
eagerly *adv* ansiosamente; ***~ awaited*** atteso con ansia
eagerness *n* smania *f*
eagle *n* aquila *f*
eagle-eyed *adj*: ***be ~*** avere l'occhio di falco
ear¹ *n of person*, *animal* orecchio *m*; *fig* ***play it by ~*** decidere volta per volta; ***be all ~s*** essere tutt'orecchi; ***it goes in one ~ and out the other*** entra da un orecchio ed esce dall'altro; ***be up to one's ~s in work*** essere oberato di lavoro; ***he's got money** etc* ***coming out of his ~s*** *infml* gli escono i soldi dalle orecchie; ***have a good ~ for music*** avere orecchio per la musica
ear² *n of corn* spiga *f*
earache *n* mal *m* d'orecchi **eardrum** *n* timpano *m*
earful *n infml*: ***get an ~*** ricevere una sgridata; ***give s.o. an ~*** sgridare qn
earl *n* conte *m*
earlier I *adj comp* → **early**; ***at an ~ date*** in una data più vicina **II** *adv*: ~ (***on***) precedentemente; ***I cannot do it ~ than Thursday*** non posso farlo prima di giovedì
earliest I *adj sup* → **early II** *n*: ***at the ~*** non prima (di); ***work will begin in April at the very ~*** il lavoro non inizierà prima di aprile
earlobe *n* lobo *m* dell'orecchio
early I *adj* (+*er*) **1.** (*not late*) primo; ***in the ~ hours*** nelle prime ore; ***in the ~ stages*** nelle fasi iniziali; ***in ~ spring*** all'inizio della primavera; ***~ October*** inizio ottobre; ***at an ~ age*** in giovane età; ***I'm an ~ riser*** mi alzo sempre presto; ***let's have an ~ supper*** ceniamo presto; ***I look forward to an ~ reply*** resto in attesa di una sollecita risposta **2.** *arrival* anticipato **3.** (*farther back in time*) antico; ***an ~ Picasso*** un Picasso primo periodo; ***the ~ Romans*** gli antichi Romani **4.** ***~ music*** musica *f* antica **II** *adv* **1.** (*not late*) presto; ***~ in the morning*** la mattina presto; ***it's too ~*** è troppo presto **2.** (*ahead of time*) in anticipo; ***you're a bit ~*** sei un po' in anticipo
early bird *n* persona *f* mattiniera; *planning ahead* persona *f* previdente
early closing *n*: ***it's ~ today*** oggi è giorno di chiusura anticipata **early retirement** *n* prepensionamento *m*; ***take ~*** andare in pensione anticipata
early riser *n* persona *f* mattiniera
early warning *adj*:***~ system*** *n* radar *m inv* d'avvistamento
earmark *v/t* riservare; ***~ sth for sth*** riservare qc a qc
earmuff *n* paraorecchie *m inv*
earn *v/t* guadagnare; *of interest* fruttare; *holiday*, *drink etc* guadagnarsi; ***~ one's living*** guadagnarsi da vivere; ***his honesty ~ed him everybody's respect*** la sua onestà gli è valsa il rispetto di tutti
earnest *adj* serio; ***in ~*** sul serio
earnings *npl* guadagno *m*
earphones *npl* cuffie *fpl* (d'ascolto) **earpiece** *n* auricolare *m* **ear-piercing** *adj* perforante **earplug** *n* tappino *m* per le orecchie **earring** *n* orecchino *m* **earshot** *n*: ***within ~*** a portata d'orecchio; ***out of ~*** fuori dalla portata d'orecchio **ear-splitting** *adj* assordante
earth I *n* (*soil*, *planet*) terra *f*; ***cost the***

~ costare un patrimonio; ***where on ~ have you been?*** *infml* dove cavolo sei stato? *infml*; ***to the ends of the ~*** in capo al mondo; ***nothing on ~ will stop me now*** per niente al mondo mi fermerò; ***there's no reason on ~ why …*** non esiste una ragione al mondo per cui …; *fig* ***come back down to ~*** scendere dalle nuvole; *fig* ***bring s.o. down to ~*** (***with a bump***) riportare qn con i piedi per terra **II** *v/t* ELEC collegare a terra

earthbound *adj* terrestre; *fig* terreno

earthenware *n* terracotta *f*

earthling *n* terrestre *m/f*

earthly *adj* terreno; ***it's no ~ use …*** *infml* è perfettamente inutile …

earth mother *n* madre *f* terra

earthquake *n* terremoto *m*

earth-shattering *adj* sconvolgente

earthwork *n* terrapieno *m*

earthworm *n* lombrico *m*

earthy *adj smell* di terra; *humour*, *language* grossolano

ease I *n* facilità *f*; ***with ~*** con facilità; ***be at*** (***one's***) ***~***, ***feel at ~*** essere *or* sentirsi a proprio agio; ***be*** *or* ***feel ill at ~*** essere *or* sentirsi a disagio; ***I am never at ~ in his company*** non mi sento mai a mio agio in sua compagnia **II** *v/t* (*relieve*) alleviare; ***it will ~ my mind*** mi darà sollievo **III** *v/i of pain* alleviarsi

◆**ease off I** *v/t* (*remove*) togliere con cautela **II** *v/i of pain*, *rain* diminuire

easel *n* cavalletto *m*

easily *adv* (*with ease*) facilmente; (*by far*) di gran lunga

easiness *n* disinvoltura *f*

east I *n* est *m*; ***in the ~ of*** nella parte orientale di; ***to the ~ of*** a est di; ***the East*** l'Oriente **II** *adj* orientale **III** *adv travel* a est; ***~ of*** a est di

Easter *n* Pasqua *f*

Easter Bunny *n* coniglio *m* pasquale **Easter Day** *n* il giorno *or* la domenica di Pasqua **Easter egg** *n* uovo *m* di Pasqua **Easter Island** *n* Isola *f* di Pasqua

easterly *adj*: ***~ wind*** vento *m* dell'est; ***in an ~ direction*** verso est

Easter Monday *n* lunedì *m inv* di Pasqua, Pasquetta *f*

eastern *adj* orientale

Easter Sunday *n* domenica *f* di Pasqua

eastward(**s**) *adv* verso est

easy I *adj* (*+er*) facile; ***he was an ~ winner*** è stata una vittoria facile per lui; ***~ prey*** preda *f* facile; ***as ~ as pie*** facile come bere un bicchier d'acqua; (*relaxed*) tranquillo; ***be ~ on the eye*** / ***ear*** piacevole da guardare / ascoltare; ***at an ~ pace*** con passo tranquillo; ***I don't feel ~ about it*** non mi sento tranquillo; ***I've had it ~*** ho avuto una vita facile **II** *adv*: ***take things ~*** (*slow down*) prendersela con calma; ***take it ~!*** (*calm down*) calma!; ***~ does it*** stai attento

easy chair *n* poltrona *f*

easy-going *adj*: ***he's very ~*** gli va bene quasi tutto

easy money *n* soldi *mpl* facili; ***you can make ~*** puoi fare soldi facilmente **easy touch** *n*: ***be an ~*** *infml* essere facile da convincere

eat *v/t & v/i* ⟨*pret* ***ate***, *past part* ***eaten***⟩ mangiare; ***~ one's lunch*** / ***dinner*** pranzare / cenare; ***he was forced to ~ his words*** è stato costretto a rimangiarsi la parola; ***I won't ~ you*** *infml* non ti mangio mica; ***what's ~ing you?*** *infml* che ti prende?

◆**eat into** *v/t metal* corrodere; *capital* intaccare; *time* portare via

◆**eat out** *v/i* mangiare fuori

◆**eat up** *v/t sep finish* finire di mangiare; *fig* mangiare; *with jealousy* consumare; ***eat up your beans*** *eat them all* mangia tutti i fagioli

eatable *adj* commestibile; *lunch*, *dish* mangiabile

eaten *past part* → ***eat***

eating disorder *n* disturbo *m* alimentare

eau de Cologne *n* acqua *f* di Colonia

eaves *npl* cornicione *m*

eavesdrop *v/i* ⟨*pret & past part* ***-ped***⟩ origliare; ***~ on s.o.*** / ***sth*** origliare qn / qc

ebb I *n* riflusso *m*; *fig* ***~ and flow*** il flusso e riflusso; *fig* ***at a low ~*** in cattive condizioni **II** *v/i of tide* rifluire

◆**ebb away** *v/i fig*: *of courage*, *strength* venire meno

ebb tide *n* bassa marea *f*

ebony *n wood*, *colour* ebano *m*

e-book *n* e-book *m inv*

ebullient *adj person* pieno di vita;

spirits, *mood* esuberante
e-business *n* e-business *m inv*
EC *abbr* (= **European Community**) Comunità *f* europea
e-cash *n* e-cash *m inv*
ECB *abbr* (= **European Central Bank**) BCE *f* (Banca Centrale Europea)
eccentric I *adj* eccentrico **II** *n* eccentrico *m*, -a *f*
eccentricity *n* eccentricità *f inv*
ecclesiastical *adj* ecclesiastico
ECG *abbr* (= **electrocardiogram**) elettrocardiogramma *m* (ECG)
echo I *n* eco *f* **II** *v/i* risuonare **III** *v/t* *words* ripetere; *views* condividere
éclair *n* bignè *m*
éclat *n* sfarzo *m*
eclectic *adj* eclettico
eclecticism *n* eclettismo *m*
eclipse I *n* eclissi *f inv* **II** *v/t fig* eclissare
eco- *pref* eco-
ecofriendly *adj Br* che rispetta l'ambiente
ecological *adj* ecologico; ***~ balance*** equilibrio *m* ecologico
ecologically *adv* ecologicamente
ecologically friendly *adj* ecologico
ecologist *n* ecologista *m/f*
ecology *n* ecologia *f*
e-commerce *n* e-commerce *m inv*
economic *adj* economico; ***~ growth*** crescita *f* economica; (*cost-effective*) *price*, *rent* conveniente
economical *adj* (*cheap*) economico; (*thrifty*) parsimonioso; ***they were ~ with the truth*** non hanno detto tutta la verità; ***an ~ style*** LIT uno stile conciso
economically *adv* (*in terms of economics*) economicamente; ***after the war, the country suffered ~*** nel dopoguerra il paese ha sofferto problemi economici; (*thriftily*) con parsimonia; ***use sth ~*** utilizzare con parsimonia
economics *n* (*sg:*) *science* economia *f*; (*pl:*) *financial aspects* aspetti *mpl* economici
economist *n* economista *m/f*
economize *v/i* risparmiare, fare economia
◆**economize on** *v/t* risparmiare su
economy *n of a country* economia *f*; (*saving*) risparmio *m*, economia *f*
economy class *n* classe *f* economica
economy drive *n* regime *m* di risparmio **economy size** *n* confezione *f* famiglia
ecosphere *n* ecosfera *f*
ecosystem *n* ecosistema *m*
ecotourism *n* agriturismo *m*
ecotype *n* ecotipo *m*
ecstasy *n* estasi *f*; ***be in ~*** essere in estasi; (*drug*) ecstasy *f*
ecstatic *adj* in estasi
ecumenical *adj form* ecumenico
eczema *n* eczema *m*
ed *abbr* **1.** (= **editor**) redattore *m*, -trice *f* **2.** (= **edition**) edizione *f* (ed.)
ED *abbr* (= **Emergency Department**) pronto soccorso *m*
eddy I *n* vortice *m* **II** *v/i* turbinare
edge I *n of knife* filo *m*; *of table*, *seat*, *lawn* bordo *m*; ***the film had us on the ~ of our seats*** il film ci ha tenuti con il fiato sospeso; *of road* ciglio *m*; *of cliff* orlo *m*; *in voice* sfumatura *f* tagliente; ***there's an ~ of cynicism in his voice*** c'è una punta di cinismo nella sua voce; ***on ~*** → ***edgy***; *advantage* ***have the ~ on s.o. / sth*** essere in vantaggio rispetto a qn / qc; ***it gives her / it that extra ~*** le / gli garantisce un vantaggio aggiuntivo **II** *v/t* profilare; ***~d in black*** profilato in nero **III** *v/i* (*move slowly*) muoversi con cautela; ***he ~d past me*** mi superò con cautela
edgeways *adv*, **edgewise** *adv*: ***I couldn't get a word in ~*** non sono riuscito a piazzare una parola
edgy *adj* (*+er*) teso
EDI *abbr* (= **electronic data interchange**) EDI
edible *adj* commestibile
edict *n* editto *m*
edification *n* edificazione *f*
edifice *n* edificio *m*
Edinburgh *n* Edimburgo *f*
edit *v/t text* rivedere; *prepare for publication* curare; *newspaper* dirigere; *TV program*, *film* montare; COMPUT modificare
◆**edit out** *v/t sep* eliminare; *from film*, *tape* tagliare
edition *n* edizione *f*
editor *n of text* revisore *m*; *of publication* curatore *m*, -trice *f*; *of newspaper* direttore *m*, -trice; *of TV program* re-

sponsabile *m/f* del montaggio; *of film* tecnico *m* del montaggio; ***sports ~*** redattore *m*, -trice sportivo, -a; *in charge* caporedattore *m*, -trice *f* sportivo, -a

editorial I *adj* editoriale; ***the ~ staff*** la redazione **II** *n* editoriale *m*, articolo *m* di fondo

EDP *abbr* (= **electronic data processing**) EDP (elaborazione *f* elettronica dei dati)

educate *v/t child* istruire; *consumers* educare; ***he was ~d at Cambridge*** ha studiato a Cambridge

educated *adj person* istruito; ***make an ~ guess*** fare una supposizione ben fondata

education *n* istruzione *f*; ***the ~ system*** la pubblica istruzione

educational *adj* didattico; (*informative*) istruttivo; ***~ level*** *or* ***standard*** livello *m* d'istruzione; ***~ system*** (*institutions*) sistema *m* d'istruzione; (*structure*) struttura *f* didattica; ***~ film*** film *m inv* istruttivo; ***~ toy*** gioco *m* educativo

educator *n* insegnante *m/f*

edutainment *n* edutainment *m*

Edwardian *adj* edoardiano; ***~ England*** Inghilterra *f* edoardiana

EEC *n abbr* (= **European Economic Community**) *hist* CEE *f* (Comunità Economica Europea)

EEG *abbr* (= **electroencephalogram**) elettroencefalogramma *m* (EEG)

eel *n* anguilla *f*

eerie *adj* (*+er*) inquietante

effect I *n* effetto *m*; ***the ~ of this is that …*** ciò ha come effetto che …; ***have an ~ on s.o. / sth*** avere un effetto su qn / qc; ***only for ~*** solo per far colpo; ***we received a letter to the ~ that …*** abbiamo ricevuto una lettera in base alla quale …; ***have an ~ on*** influenzare; ***take ~*** *of medicine, drug* fare effetto; ***come into ~*** *of law* entrare in vigore; ***with ~ from 3 March*** a partire dal 3 marzo; ***sound ~s*** effetti audio **II** *v/t* produrre

effective *adj* (*efficient*) efficace; ***be ~ against sth*** (*drug*) essere efficace contro qc; (*striking*) d'effetto; ***~ May 1*** con decorrenza dal 1 maggio; ***a very ~ combination*** un abbinamento di grande effetto

effectively *adv* (*succesfully*) efficacemente; (*in fact*) effettivamente

effectiveness *n* efficacia *f*

effeminate *adj* effeminato

effervescent *adj a. fig* effervescente

efficacious *adj* efficace

efficacy *n* efficacia *f*

efficiency *n* efficienza *f*; *of machine* rendimento *m*

efficient *adj* efficiente; *machine* ad alto rendimento; ***be ~ at (doing) sth*** essere efficiente nel fare qc

efficiently *adv* con efficienza; ***work more ~*** lavorare con più efficienza

effigy *n* effige *f*

effluent *n* scarichi *mpl*

effort *n* sforzo *m*; ***make an ~ to do sth*** fare uno sforzo per fare qc; ***come on, make an ~*** andiamo, fai uno sforzo; ***it was well worth the ~*** ne è valsa la pena

effortless *adj* facile

effrontery *n* sfrontatezza *f*, sfacciataggine *f*

effusion *n* effusione *f*

effusive *adj thanks, welcome* caloroso

E-fit *n* identikit *m inv* elettronico

EFL *abbr* (= **English as a Foreign Language**) *insegnamento dell'inglese come lingua straniera*

e.g. *abbr* ad *or* per esempio

EGA *abbr* (= **enhanced graphics adapter**) COMPUT scheda *f* video EGA

egalitarian *adj* egualitario

egg *n* uovo *m*; *of woman* ovulo *m*; ***put all one's ~s in one basket*** *prov* puntare tutto su una sola carta

◆**egg on** *v/t sep* istigare

eggcup *n* portauovo *m inv*

egghead *n infml* intellettualoide *m/f*

eggnog *n bevanda calda a base di latte (o birra) e uova*

eggplant *n US* melanzana *f*

eggshell *n* guscio *m* d'uovo

egg timer *n timer per misurare il tempo di cottura delle uova* **egg whisk** *n* frullino *m* per le uova **egg white** *n* albume *m* **egg yolk** *n* tuorlo *m*

ego *n* ego *m*; ***his ~ won't allow him to admit he is wrong*** il suo ego non gli consentirà di ammettere di aver sbagliato

egocentric *adj* egocentrico

egoism *n* egoismo *m*
egoist *n* egoista *m/f*
egomania *n* egomania *f*
egotistic *adj* egocentrico
ego trip *n infml* delirio *m* di egocentrismo
Egypt *n* Egitto *m*
Egyptian I *adj* egiziano **II** *n* egiziano *m*, -a *f*
Egyptian cotton *n* cotone *m* egiziano
Egyptology *n* egittologia *f*
EIB *abbr* (= **European Investment Bank**) banca *f* europea per gli investimenti
eiderdown *n* (*quilt*) piumino *m*
eight *num* otto
eighteen *num* diciotto
eighteenth *n/adj* diciottesimo, -a
eighth *n/adj* ottavo, -a
eightieth *n/adj* ottantesimo, -a
eighty *num* ottanta
either I *adj* l'uno o l'altro; (*both*) entrambi *pl*; ***at ~ side of the street*** da entrambi i lati della strada; ***~ day would suit me*** mi andrebbero bene entrambi i giorni **II** *pron* l'uno o l'altro *m*, l'una o l'altra *f* **III** *adv* nemmeno, neppure; ***she inherited some money and not an insignificant amount ~*** ha ereditato del denaro e nemmeno in misura irrilevante; ***I won't go ~*** non vado nemmeno *or* neppure io **IV** *cj*: ***~ my mother or my sister*** mia madre o mia sorella; ***he doesn't like ~ wine or beer*** non gli piacciono né il vino, né la birra; ***~ you write or phone*** o scrivi, o telefoni
ejaculate *v/i* eiaculare
ejaculation *n* eiaculazione *f*
eject I *v/t* espellere **II** *v/i from plane* eiettarsi
ejector seat, *US* **ejection seat** *n* AVIAT sedile *m* eiettabile
◆**eke out** *v/t sep* usare con parsimonia; *grant etc* arrotondare; ***eke out a living*** sbarcare il lunario
EKG *n US* → ***ECG***
elaborate I *adj* elaborato **II** *v/i* fornire particolari; ***~ on*** fornire particolari riguardo a; ***would you care to*** *or* ***could you ~ on that?*** ti dispiacerebbe / potresti fornirmi particolari al riguardo?
elaborately *adv* in modo elaborato; ***an ~ staged press conference*** una conferenza stampa organizzata in modo elaborato
élan *n* slancio *m*
elapse *v/i* trascorrere
elastic I *adj* elastico **II** *n* elastico *m*
elasticated *adj* elasticizzato
elastic band *n* elastico *m*
elasticity *n* elasticità *f*
Elastoplast® *n* cerotto *m*
elated *adj* esultante
elation *n* esultanza *f*
elbow I *n* gomito *m* **II** *v/t*: ***~ out of the way*** allontanare a spintoni; ***he ~ed his way through the crowd*** si è fatto largo a gomitate tra la folla; ***~ s.o. aside*** scostare qn a gomitate; ***he ~ed me in the stomach*** mi ha dato una gomitata nello stomaco
elbow grease *n infml* olio *m* di gomito
elbowroom *n infml* spazio *m* per muoversi liberamente
elder[1] **I** *adj* maggiore; ***she's two years my ~*** è più vecchia di me di due anni **II** *n* maggiore *m/f*; *of tribe*, *Church* anziano *m*; ***Pliny the ~*** Plinio il Vecchio; ***respect your ~s*** rispetta chi è più vecchio di te
elder[2] *n* BOT sambuco *m*
elderberry *n* bacca *f* di sambuco; ***~ wine*** vino *m* di sambuco
elderflower *n* fiore *m* di sambuco
elderly *adj* anziano; ***the ~*** gli anziani
eldest I *adj* maggiore **II** *n* maggiore *m/f*; ***the ~*** il / la maggiore
elect I *v/t* eleggere; ***~ s.o.*** (***as***) ***president*** eleggere qn presidente; ***~ to ...*** decidere di ... **II** *adj*: ***the president ~*** il futuro presidente
election *n* elezione *f*
election campaign *n* campagna *f* elettorale **election day** *n* giorno *m* delle elezioni
electioneering *n* (*campaign*) campagna *f* elettorale; (*propaganda*) propaganda *f* elettorale
elective *adj* facoltativo
elector *n* elettore *m*, -trice *f*
electoral college *n US* assemblea *f* dei grandi elettori **electoral register**, **electoral roll** *n* lista *f* elettorale **electoral system***n* sistema *m* elettorale
electorate *n* elettorato *m*
electric *adj a. fig* elettrico; ***car / ve-***

hicle auto *f* elettrica / veicolo *m* elettrico; ~ ***kettle*** bollitore *m* elettrico

electrical *adj* elettrico; ~ ***appliance*** elettrodomestico *m*

electrical engineer *n* ingegnere *m* elettrico **electrical engineering** *n* ingegneria *f* elettrica

electric bill *n infml* bolletta *f* della luce **electric blanket** *n* coperta *f* elettrica **electric chair** *n* sedia *f* elettrica **electric cooker** *n* cucina *f* elettrica **electric fence** *n* recinzione *f* elettrica **electric fire** *n* camino *m* elettrico **electric guitar** *n* chitarra *f* elettrica **electric heater** *n* stufa *f* elettrica

electrician *n* elettricista *m*/*f*

electricity *n* elettricità *f*

electricity meter *n* contatore *m* dell'elettricità

electric light *n* luce *f* elettrica **electric organ** *n* MUS organo *m* elettrico **electric razor** *n* rasoio *m* elettrico

electrics *npl* sistema *m* elettrico; AUTO circuito *m* elettrico

electric shock *n* scossa *f* elettrica **electric toothbrush** *n* spazzolino *m* da denti elettrico

electrify *v/t* ⟨*pret & past part* ***-ied***⟩ elettrificare; *fig* elettrizzare

electrocardiogram *n* elettrocardiogramma *m*

electrocute *v/t* fulminare

electrode *n* elettrodo *m*

electrolysis *n* elettrolisi *f*

electrolyte *n* elettrolita *m*

electromagnetic *adj* elettromagnetico

electromagnetic field *n* campo *m* elettromagnetico **electromagnetic radiation** *n* radiazione *f* elettromagnetica **electromagnetic spectrum** *n* spettro *m* elettromagnetico

electron *n* elettrone *m*

electronic *adj* elettronico

electronic banking *n* e-banking *m* **electronic data interchange** *n* COMPUT scambio *m* elettronico di dati, EDI **electronic data processing** *n* elaborazione *f* elettronica dei dati **electronic mail** *n* posta *f* elettronica

electronics *nsg* elettronica *f*

electronic tagging *n monitoraggio mediante applicazione di un dispositivo elettronico*

electroplated *adj* placcato tramite galvanostegia

electroshock therapy *n* terapia *f* con elettrochoc

electrostatic *adj* elettrostatico

elegance *n* eleganza *f*

elegant *adj* elegante

elegantly *adv* elegantemente

elegy *n* elegia *f*

element *n* elemento *m*; ***one of the key ~s of the peace plan*** uno degli elementi chiave del piano di pace; ***an ~ of danger*** un elemento di pericolo; ***an ~ of truth*** un elemento di verità; ***a criminal ~*** un elemento criminale; ***be in one's ~*** essere nel proprio elemento; METEO ***the ~s*** gli elementi

elemental *adj liter* elementare; ~ ***force*** forza *f* degli elementi

elementary *adj* (*rudimentary*) elementare; EDU *level* elementare; ~ ***mistake*** errore *m* elementare; ~ ***skills / knowledge*** competenze / conoscenze *fpl* elementari; ~ ***maths*** matematica *f* elementare

elementary particle *n* particella *f* elementare **elementary school** *n US* scuola *f* elementare **elementary teacher** *n* maestro *m*, -a *f* elementare

elephant *n* elefante *m*

elephantine *adj* elefantesco

elevate *v/t* elevare; *blood pressure etc* aumentare; *fig mind* elevare; ~ ***s.o. to the peerage*** elevare qn al titolo di pari

elevated *adj status, style, language* elevato; (*raised*) sopraelevato; ~ ***railway*** *Br or* ***railroad*** *US* ferrovia *f* sopraelevata; ***the ~ section of the M4*** *Br* il tratto sopraelevato dell'autostrada M4

elevation *n* (*altitude*) altitudine *f*

elevator *n US* ascensore *m*

eleven *num* undici; ***the second ~*** *football* la seconda squadra

elevenses *nsg or npl Br* spuntino *m* (a metà mattinata)

eleventh *n*/*adj* undicesimo, -a; ***at the ~ hour*** all'ultima ora, all'ultimo momento

elf *n* ⟨*pl* ***elves***⟩ elfo *m*

elfin *adj* minuto

elfish *adj* di elfo

elicit *v/t form* ottenere; ~ ***sth from s.o.*** ottenere qc da qn

elide *v/t* elidere

eligibility *n* idoneità *f*
eligible *adj*: ***be ~ to do sth*** avere il diritto di fare qc; ***be ~ for sth*** avere diritto a qc
eligible bachelor *n* buon partito *m*
eliminate *v/t* eliminare; ***be ~d*** *from competition* essere eliminato
elimination *n* eliminazione *f*; ***by (a) process of ~*** procedendo per eliminazione
elision *n* elisione *f*
elite **I** *n* elite *f inv* **II** *adj* elitario
elitism *n* elitarismo *m*
elitist *n/adj* elitista *m/f*
elixir *n* elisir *m*
Elizabethan **I** *adj* elisabettiano **II** *n* elisabettiano *m*, -a *f*
elk *n* alce *m*
ellipse *n* ellisse *f*
ellipsis *n* GRAM ellissi *f*
elliptic, elliptical *adj* MATH *etc* ellittico
elm *n* olmo *m*
elocution *n* dizione *f*; ***~ lessons*** lezioni *fpl* di dizione
elongate *v/t* allungare; (*stretch out*) stendersi
elongated *adj shape* allungato; (*stretched*) steso
elope *v/i* scappare (per sposarsi)
eloquence *n* eloquenza *f*
eloquent *adj* eloquente
eloquently *adv* con eloquenza
else *adv*: ***anything ~*** qualcos'altro; ***anything ~?*** *in shop* (desidera) altro?; ***nothing ~*** nient'altro; ***if you've got nothing ~ to do*** se non hai altro da fare; ***if nothing ~, you'll enjoy it*** se non altro, ti piacerà; ***nobody ~*** nessun altro; ***everyone ~ is going*** tutti gli altri vanno; ***who ~ was there?*** chi altro c'era?; ***what ~ can we do?*** cos'altro possiamo fare?; ***someone ~*** qualcun altro; ***something ~*** qualcos'altro; ***that car is something ~*** *infml* quell'auto è fantastica; ***if all ~ fails*** se tutto il resto va male; ***above all ~*** al di sopra di tutto; ***how ~ can I do it?*** come posso fare altrimenti?; ***what ~ could I have done?*** che altro avrei potuto fare?; ***let's go somewhere ~*** andiamo da qualche altra parte; ***or ~*** altrimenti
elsewhere *adv* altrove
ELT *abbr* (= **English Language Teaching**) *Br insegnamento della lingua inglese*
elucidate *v/t text* delucidare; *situation* spiegare
elude *v/t* (*escape from*) sfuggire a; (*avoid*) sfuggire a; ***~ capture*** sfuggire alla cattura; ***sleep ~d her*** non riusciva a prendere sonno; ***the name ~s me*** il nome mi sfugge
elusive *adj person* difficile da trovare; ***financial success proved ~*** il successo finanziario si è dimostrato irraggiungibile; *quality* raro; *criminal* inafferrabile
elves → ***elf***
emaciated *adj* emaciato
e-mail **I** *n* e-mail *m inv* **II** *v/t person* mandare un e-mail a; *text* mandare per e-mail
e-mail address *n* indirizzo *m* e-mail
emanate *v/i* provenire (***from*** da); (*odour*) emanare (***from*** da)
emancipated *adj woman* emancipato
emancipation *n* emancipazione *f*
emasculate *v/t* (*weaken*) indebolire
emasculation *n* indebolimento *m*
embalm *v/t* imbalsamare
embankment *n of river* argine *m*; RAIL massicciata *f*
embargo *n* embargo *m inv*; ***trade ~*** embargo *m* commerciale; ***place / lift an ~ on sth*** mettere / togliere l'embargo su qc
embark *v/i* imbarcarsi
◆**embark on** *v/t* imbarcarsi in
embarkation *n* imbarco *m*
embarkation papers *npl* documenti *mpl* di imbarco
embarrass *v/t* imbarazzare; ***she was ~ed by the question*** la domanda la imbarazzò
embarrassed *adj* imbarazzato; ***I am / feel so ~ (about it)*** mi sento così imbarazzato (per questo); ***she was ~ to be seen with him*** *or* ***about being seen with him*** la imbarazzava essere vista con lui
embarrassing *adj* imbarazzante
embarrassingly *adv* in modo imbarazzante
embarrassment *n* imbarazzo *m*; ***be an ~ to s.o.*** essere motivo d'imbarazzo per qn
embassy *n* ambasciata *f*
embattled *adj fig government* assediato

embed *v/t* ⟨*pret & past part* ***-ded***⟩: ***~ sth in sth*** conficcare qc in qc
embellish *v/t* ornare; *story* ricamare su
embellishment *n* abbellimento *m*
embers *npl* brace *fsg*
embezzle *v/t* appropriarsi indebitamente di
embezzlement *n* appropriazione *f* indebita
embezzler *n* malversatore *m*, -trice *f*
embitter *v/t* amareggiare
emblazon *v/t*: ***the name "Jones" was ~ed on the cover*** il nome "Jones" spiccava in copertina
emblem *n* emblema *f*
emblematic *adj* emblematico (***of*** di)
embodiment *n* incarnazione *f*; ***be the ~ of evil*** essere l'incarnazione del male
embody *v/t* ⟨*pret & past part* ***-ied***⟩ incarnare
embolism *n* embolia *f*
emboss *v/t metal* lavorare a sbalzo; *paper, fabric* stampare in rilievo
embossed *adj* goffrato; *design* in rilievo
embrace **I** *n* abbraccio *m* **II** *v/t* (*hug, include*) abbracciare **III** *v/i of two people* abbracciarsi
embrocate *v/t* frizionare con un linimento
embrocation *n* linimento *m*
embroider *v/t* ricamare; *fig* ricamare su
embroidery *n* ricamo *m*
embroil *v/t*: ***become ~ed in a dispute*** venire coinvolto in una controversia
embryo *n* embrione *m*
embryonic *adj fig* embrionale
emerald *n precious stone* smeraldo *m*; *colour* verde *m* smeraldo
emerge *v/i* (*appear*) emergere; ***it has ~d that …*** è emerso che …; ***one arm ~d from beneath the blanket*** un braccio emerse da sotto la coperta; ***he ~d from the house*** emerse dalla casa; ***he ~d (as) the winner*** ne uscì vincitore
emergency *n* emergenza *f*; ***in an ~*** in caso di emergenza
emergency brake *n US* freno *m* a mano **emergency cord** *n* RAIL corda *f* di emergenza **emergency exit** *n* uscita *f* di sicurezza **emergency landing** *n* atterraggio *m* di fortuna **emergency number** *n* numero *m* per le emergenze **emergency room** *n US* pronto *m* soccorso **emergency services** *npl* servizi *mpl* di soccorso **emergency stop** *n* frenata *f* di emergenza
emergent *adj form nation etc* emergente
emeritus *adj* emerito; ***~ professor*** *or* ***professor ~*** professore *m* emerito
emery board *n* limetta *f* (da unghie)
emery paper *n* carta *f* smerigliata **emery wheel** *n* mola *f* a smeriglio
emigrant *n* emigrante *m/f*
emigrate *v/i* emigrare
emigration *n* emigrazione *f*
émigré *n* emigrato *m* politico
eminence *n* (*distinction*) eccellenza *f*
Eminence *n*: REL ***His ~*** Sua Eminenza
eminence grise *n* eminenza *f* grigia
eminent *adj* eminente
eminently *adv* decisamente; ***~ suitable*** perfettamente idoneo; ***be ~ capable of sth*** essere decisamente in grado di
emir *n* emiro *m*
emirate *n* emirato *m*
emissary *n* emissario *m*
emission *n of gases* emanazione *f*
emit *v/t* ⟨*pret & past part* ***-ted***⟩ *heat, gases* emanare; *light, smoke* emettere; *smell* esalare
emollient **I** *n* emolliente *m* **II** *adj* emolliente
emotion *n* emozione *f*
emotional *adj problems, development* emozionale; (*causing emotion*) commovente; (*showing emotion*) commosso; ***get ~ about*** commuoversi per; ***~ outburst*** scoppio *m* emotivo; ***~ state*** stato *m* emotivo
emotional blackmail *n* ricatto *m* emotivo
emotionally *adv* (*psychologically*) emozionalmente; (*in emotional manner*) emotivamente; ***I don't want to get ~ involved*** non voglio essere emotivamente coinvolto; ***~ disturbed*** con turbe emotive; ***~ charged*** intenso
emotive *adj issue* scottante; *word* toccante
empathize *v/i* immedesimarsi; ***~ with s.o.*** immedesimarsi con qn; ***~ with sth*** capire qc

empathy *n* empatia *f*
emperor *n* imperatore *m*
emphasis *n* enfasi *f*; *on word* rilievo *m*; ***place** or **put ~ on*** dare importanza a; ***say sth with ~*** dire qc con enfasi; ***there is too much ~ on research*** viene dato troppo risalto alla ricerca
emphasize *v/t* enfatizzare; *word* dare rilievo a
emphatic *adj* enfatico; ***be ~ that ...*** sostenere con enfasi che ...; ***be ~ about sth*** porre l'enfasi su qc
empire *n* impero *m*; ***the Holy Roman Empire*** il Sacro Romano Impero; ***the British Empire*** l'Impero britannico; *esp* COMM impero *m*; ***his business ~*** il suo impero commerciale
empirical *adj* empirico
empiricism *n* PHIL empirismo *m*
employ *v/t* **1.** dare lavoro a; ***she's ~ed as a secretary*** lavora come segretaria; ***he hasn't been ~ed for six months*** non lavora da sei mesi **2.** (*take on*) assumere **3.** (*use*) impiegare
employee *n* dipendente *m/f*
employer *n* datore *m*, -trice *f* di lavoro
employment *n* occupazione *f*; (*work*) impiego *m*; ***be seeking ~*** essere in cerca di occupazione
employment agency *n* agenzia *f* di collocamento
emporium *n* emporio *m*
empower *v/t* dare più potere a; ***~ s.o. to do sth*** mettere in grado qn di fare qc
empress *n* imperatrice *f*
emptiness *n* vuoto *m*
empty I *adj* (*+er*) vuoto; *fig* ***feel ~*** sentirsi vuoto; ***there were no ~ seats*** non c'erano posti vuoti; ***on an ~ stomach*** a stomaco vuoto **II** *v/t* ⟨*pret & past part* ***-ied***⟩ vuotare **III** *v/i* ⟨*pret & past part* ***-ied***⟩ *of room*, *street* svuotarsi **IV** *n usu pl* ***empties*** vuoti *mpl*
◆**empty out** *v/t sep* vuotare
empty-handed *adv* a mani vuote
empty-headed *adj infml* scervellato
EMS *abbr* (= **European Monetary System**) SME *m* (Sistema Monetario Europeo)
EMU *abbr* (= **European Monetary Union**) UME *f* (Unione Monetaria Europea)
emulate *v/t* emulare
emulsion *n paint* emulsione *f*
enable *v/t person* permettere a; *thing* permettere; ***~ s.o. to do sth*** permettere a qn di fare qc
enact *v/t law* emanare; THEAT rappresentare
enamel I *n* smalto *m* **II** *adj* smaltato; ***~ paint*** pittura *f* a smalto **III** *v/t* smaltare
enamoured, *US* **enamored** *adj form* entusiasta; ***be ~ of sth*** essere entusiasta di qc; ***she was not exactly ~ of the idea*** non era esattamente entusiasta dell'idea
enc *abbr* (= **enclosure(s)**) all. (allegato *m*)
encapsulate *v/t fig* sintetizzare
encase *v/t* incassare (***in*** in); *wires* rivestire (***in*** con)
encaustic I *n* encausto *m* **II** *adj* a encausto
enchant *v/t* (*delight*) incantare
enchanting *adj smile*, *village*, *person* incantevole
encircle *v/t* circondare
encl *abbr* (= **enclosure(s)**) all. (allegato *m*)
enclave *n* enclave *f*
enclose *v/t in letter* allegare; ***please find ~d ...*** in allegato, ...; *area* recintare
enclosure *n with letter* allegato *m*; (*ground enclosed*) terreno *m* recintato; *for animals* recinto *m*
encode *v/t a.* COMPUT codificare
encomium *n* encomio *m*
encompass *v/t* comprendere
encore *n* bis *m inv*
encounter I *n* incontro *m*; ***sexual ~*** incontro *m* sessuale **II** *v/t* incontrare
encourage *v/t* incoraggiare; ***~ s.o. to*** incoraggiare qn a; ***be ~d by sth*** essere incoraggiato da qc
encouragement *n* incoraggiamento *m*
encouraging *adj* incoraggiante; ***I found him very ~*** l'ho trovato molto incoraggiante
◆**encroach on** *v/t land*, *time* invadere; *rights* violare
encroachment *n on land* invasione *f*; *on rights* violazione *f*
encrust *v/t*: ***~ed with earth*** incrostato di terra; ***a jewel-~ed brooch*** una spilla tempestata di pietre preziose
encrypt *v/t* criptare

encryption *n* criptazione *f*
encumber *v/t* ostacolare
encumbrance *n* JUR impedimento *m*
encyclopedia *n* enciclopedia *f*
encyclopedic *n* enciclopedico
end **I** *n* **1.** (*extremity*) estremità *f inv*; ***at the other ~ of town*** all'estremo opposto della città; ***in the ~*** alla fine; ***for hours on ~*** senza sosta; ***stand sth on ~*** mettere qc verticale; ***at the ~ of July*** alla fine di luglio; ***come to an ~*** finire; ***put an ~ to*** mettere fine a; ***we met no ~ of famous people*** *esp Br* abbiamo incontrato moltissime persone famose; ***it pleased her no ~*** *esp Br* le ha fatto molto piacere **2.** (*conclusion*) fine *f* **3.** (*purpose*) fine *m* **II** *v/t* terminare **III** *v/i* finire **IV** *adj* in fondo; ***the ~ house*** la casa in fondo
◆**end in** *v/t* finire con
◆**end up** *v/i* finire; ***I'll end up doing it myself*** finirò per farlo io stesso
endanger *v/t* mettere in pericolo
endangered species *n* specie *f* in via d'estinzione
endear *v/t* far affezionare (***to*** a); ***~ o.s. to s.o.*** farsi benvolere da qn
endearing *adj* accattivante
endearment *n*: ***term of ~*** vezzeggiativo *m*
endeavour, *US* **endeavor** **I** *n* tentativo *m*; ***in an ~ to please her*** nel tentativo di compiacerla **II** *v/t* tentare; ***~ to do sth*** tentare di fare qc
endemic *adj* endemico
endgame *n* finale *m*
ending *n* finale *m*; GRAM desinenza *f*
endive *n* indivia *f*
endless *adj* interminabile; (*countless*) infinito; ***the list is ~*** l'elenco è interminabile; ***the possibilities are ~*** le possibilità sono infinite
endorse *v/t cheque* girare; *candidacy* appoggiare; *product* fare pubblicità a; ***I had my licence ~d*** *Br* JUR ho ricevuto un'annotazione sulla patente
endorsement *n of cheque* girata *f*; *of candidacy* appoggio *m*; *of product* pubblicità *f*
endow *v/t school, hospital* fare una donazione a; ***be ~ed with*** (*possess*) essere dotato di
endowment *n* donazione *f*
end product *n* prodotto *m* finale **end result** *n* risultato *m* finale
endurance *n* resistenza *f*
endurance test *n* prova *f* di resistenza
endure **I** *v/t* sopportare; ***she can't ~ being laughed at*** non può sopportare che si rida di lei **II** *v/i* (*last*) resistere
enduring *adj* durevole
end-user *n* utilizzatore *m* finale
enema *n* clistere *m*
enemy **I** *n* nemico *m*, -a *f*; ***make an ~ of*** inimicarsi; ***he is his own worst ~*** è il peggior nemico di se stesso **II** *adj* nemico
energetic *adj* energico; ***be very ~*** essere pieno di energie
energetically *adv* con energia
energize *v/t fig person* stimolare
energy *n* energia *f*
energy conservation *n* conservazione *f* dell'energia **energy-efficient** *adj* con consumo efficiente di energia
energy-saving *adj device* per risparmiare energia
energy supply *n* rifornimento *m* di energia elettrica
enforce *v/t* far rispettare; ***the police ~ the law*** la polizia fa rispettare la legge
enforcement *n* applicazione *f*
Eng. *abbr* **1.** (= **England**) Inghilterra *f* **2.** (= **English**) inglese
engage **I** *v/t* (*hire*) ingaggiare; ***~ the services of s.o.*** avvalersi dei servizi di qn; *of lawyer* assumere; *attention* assorbire; ***~ s.o. in conversation*** attaccare discorso con qn; AUTO ***~ the clutch*** innestare la frizione **II** *v/i* TECH ingranare; ***~ with the enemy*** MIL attaccare il nemico
◆**engage in** *v/t* occuparsi di; *conversation* coinvolgere in
engaged *adj to be married* fidanzato; ***get ~*** fidanzarsi; ***be ~ to s.o.*** essere fidanzato con qn; ***be ~ in doing sth*** (*occupied*) essere impegnato in qc
engaged tone *n Br* TEL segnale *m* d'occupato
engagement *n* (*appointment*) impegno *m*; *to be married* fidanzamento *m*; MIL scontro *m*; ***terms of ~*** *form* (*employment*) condizioni *fpl* d'impiego
engagement ring *n* anello *m* di fidanzamento

engaging *adj smile, person* accattivante
engender *v/t fig* causare
engine *n* motore *m*
-engined *adj suf* a motore; ***twin-engined*** bimotore
engine driver *n* macchinista *m*
engineer I *n* ingegnere *m*; *for sound, software* tecnico *m*; NAUT macchinista *m* **II** *v/t fig*: *meeting etc* macchinare, architettare
engineering *n* ingegneria *f*
England *n* Inghilterra *f*
English I *adj* inglese **II** *n language* inglese *m*; ***in ~*** in inglese; ***the ~*** gli inglesi
English Channel *n* Manica *f*
Englishman *n* inglese *m*
Englishwoman *n* inglese *f*
engrave *v/t* incidere; ***~ sth on / in sth*** incidere qc su / in qc
engraving *n* (*drawing*) stampa *f*; (*design*) incisione *f*
engrossed *adj*: ***~ in*** assorto in; ***become ~ in one's work*** essere assorbito dal proprio lavoro; ***be ~ in conversation*** essere preso dalla conversazione
engrossing *adj* avvincente
engulf *v/t fig* sommergere; ***be ~ed by bad luck*** sprofondare nella sfortuna
enhance *v/t* accrescere; *performance, reputation* migliorare
enigma *n* enigma *m*
enigmatic *adj* enigmatico
enjoin *v/t* ingiungere
enjoy *v/t*: ***did you ~ the film?*** ti è piaciuto il film?; ***I ~ reading*** mi piace leggere; ***~ your meal!*** buon appetito!; ***~ o.s.*** divertirsi
enjoyable *adj* piacevole
enjoyment *n* piacere *m*, divertimento *m*; ***she gets a lot of ~ from reading*** trae molto piacere dalla lettura
enlace *v/t* intrecciare
enlarge *v/t* ingrandire
enlargement *n* ingrandimento *m*
enlighten *v/t* illuminare
enlightening *adj* istruttivo
enlightenment *n* chiarimento *m*; ***the Enlightenment*** l'Illuminismo
enlist I *v/i* MIL arruolarsi **II** *v/t*: ***~ the help of ...*** ottenere l'appoggio di ...
enliven *v/t* animare
en masse *adv* in massa
enmesh *v/t* irretire
enmity *n* inimicizia *f*
enormity *n* enormità *f inv*
enormous *adj* enorme; ***he has ~ talent*** ha un talento enorme; ***~ amounts of money*** enormi quantità di denaro, ***an ~ amount of work*** un'enorme quantità di lavoro
enormously *adv* enormemente
enough I *adj* sufficiente, abbastanza *inv*; ***is there ~ sugar?*** c'è abbastanza zucchero? **II** *pron* abbastanza; ***will £50 be ~?*** saranno sufficienti £50?; ***I've had ~!*** ne ho abbastanza!; ***thanks, I've had ~*** *food, drinks* grazie, basta così; ***that's ~, calm down!*** adesso basta, calmati! **III** *adv* abbastanza; ***are you warm ~?*** hai mica freddo?; ***would you be good ~ to ...?*** *form* mi farebbe la cortesia di ...; ***strangely ~*** per quanto strano; ***he knows well ~ what I said*** sa molto bene ciò che ho detto; ***be happy ~ to do sth*** essere piuttosto felice di fare qc; ***she sounded sincere ~*** sembrava abbastanza sincera; ***it is easy ~ to make them yourself*** è sufficientemente facile perché tu possa occupartene da solo
enquire *v/i* chiedere informazioni, informarsi; ***~ about sth*** chiedere informazioni su qc; ***~ into sth*** fare delle ricerche su qc
enquiring *adj*: ***have an ~ mind*** avere una mente curiosa
enquiry *n* richiesta *f* di informazioni; (*public enquiry*) indagine *f*; ***make enquiries about*** chiedere informazioni su
enrage *v/t* far infuriare
enraged *adj* arrabbiato
enrapture *v/t* incantato
enrich *v/t* arricchire
enrichment *n* arricchimento *m*
enrobe *v/t* abbigliare
enrol, *US* **enroll** *v/i* iscriversi
enrolment, *US* **enrollment** *n* iscrizione *f*
en route *adv* lungo la strada; ***~ to / for / from*** in viaggio verso / per / da
ensemble *n* SEW completo *m*; (*collection*) insieme *m*
enshrine *v/t fig* custodire gelosamente
ensign *n* (*flag*) insegna *f*; *US* NAUT guardiamarina *m*

enslave *v/t* assoggettare
ensnare *v/t liter* intrappolare; *fig* accalappiare
ensue *v/i* seguire
en suite (bathroom) *n* bagno *m* in camera
ensure *v/t* assicurare; ***~ that*** assicurarsi che; ***will you ~ that I get a seat?*** ti assicurerai che io ottenga un posto?
ENT *abbr* (= **ear, nose and throat**) otorinolaringoiatria *f*
entail *v/t* comportare; ***what is ~ed in buying a house?*** che cosa comporta l'acquisto di una casa?; ***this will ~ (my) buying a new car*** ciò comporterà l'acquisto di una nuova auto
entangle *v/t in rope* impigliare; ***become ~d in*** impigliarsi in; *in love affair* invischiarsi in
enter **I** *v/t room, house* entrare in; *competition* iscriversi a; *person, horse in race* iscrivere; (*write down*) registrare; COMPUT inserire; ***~ the Church*** farsi prete; ***it never ~ed my head*** *or* ***mind*** non mi è mai passato per la testa **II** *v/i* entrare; THEAT entrare in scena; *in competition* iscriversi **III** *n* COMPUT invio *m*
◆**enter into** *v/t correspondence, negotiations* entrare in; *agreement* stipulare; (*figure in*) entrarci
enter key *n* COMPUT invio *m*
enterprise *n* (*initiative*) intraprendenza *f*; (*venture*) impresa *f*; ***private ~*** impresa privata
enterprising *adj* intraprendente
entertain **I** *v/t* (*amuse*) intrattenere; (*consider: idea*) considerare **II** *v/i* (*have guests*) ricevere
entertainer *n* artista *m/f*
entertaining **I** *adj* divertente **II** *n*: ***she does a lot of ~*** dà molti ricevimenti
entertainment *adj* divertimento *m*
entertainment industry *n* industria *f* dello spettacolo
enthral *v/t* affascinare
enthralling *adj* affascinante
enthuse *v/i* entusiasmarsi (***over*** per)
enthusiasm *n* entusiasmo *m*; ***~ for*** passione per; ***she showed little ~ for the scheme*** ha mostrato scarso entusiasmo per il progetto; ***I can't work up any ~ for the idea*** non riesco a provare entusiasmo per questa idea
enthusiast *n* appassionato *m*, -a *f*
enthusiastic *adj* entusiasta; ***be ~ about*** *or* ***over*** essere entusiasta di
enthusiastically *adv* con entusiasmo
entice *v/t* attirare; ***~ s.o. (away) from sth*** persuadere qn a lasciare qc; ***~ s.o. into sth*** attirare qn in qc
enticing *adj* allettante
entire *adj* intero
entirely *adv* interamente; ***it's ~ up to you*** assolutamente come preferisci tu; ***I'm not ~ happy with their plans*** non sono completamente d'accordo con i loro progetti
entirety *n* totalità *f*; ***in its ~*** per intero
entitle *v/t* dare il diritto a; ***be ~d to do sth*** avere il diritto di fare qc
entitled *adj book* intitolato
entitlement *n* diritto *m* (***to*** a); ***what is your holiday ~?*** *Br* a quante ferie hai diritto?
entity *n* entità *f*
entourage *n* entourage *m*
entrails *npl liter* interiora *fpl*
entrance[1] *n* entrata *f*, ingresso *m*; THEAT entrata *f* in scena; (*admission*) ammissione *f*
entrance[2] *v/t* incantare
entranced *adj* incantato; ***be ~ by/ with sth*** essere incantato da qc
entrance exam(ination) *n* esame *m* di ammissione
entrance fee *n* quota *f* di ingresso **entrance hall** *n* atrio *m*
entrant *n* concorrente *m/f*
entreat *v/t* supplicare; ***~ s.o. to do sth*** supplicare qn di fare qc
entreaty *n* supplica *f*
entrée *n Br* (*starter*) entrée *f*; *esp US* (*main course*) piatto *m* principale
entrenched *adj attitudes* radicato
entrepreneur *n* imprenditore *m*, -trice *f*
entrepreneurial *adj* imprenditoriale
entropy *n* entropia *f*
entrust *v/t* affidare; ***~ s.o. with sth, ~ sth to s.o.*** affidare qc a qn
entry *n* **1.** (*way in*) entrata *f*; (*admission*) ingresso *m*; ***gain*** *or* ***obtain ~ to*** entrare in; ***no ~!*** *to room, building* vietato l'ingresso; *to road* divieto d'accesso **2.** *in diary* annotazione *f*; *in accounts, dictionary* voce *f* **3.** ***the winning ~*** partecipazione *f* vincente
entry form *n* modulo *m* d'iscrizione

entry permit *n* permesso *m* d'ingresso
Entryphone® *n* citofono *m*
entry visa *n* visto *m* d'ingresso
entryway *n US* ingresso *m* (*a. for vehicles*)
entwine *v/t* intrecciare
enucleate *v/t* enucleare
E number *n lettera E seguita da un codice numerico che indica gli additivi alimentari contenuti nel prodotto*
enumerate *v/t* enumerare
enunciate *v/t* pronunciare
envelop *v/t* avviluppare; ***flames ~ed the house*** le fiamme hanno avviluppato la casa
envelope *n* busta *f*
enviable *adj* invidiabile
envious *adj* invidioso; ***be ~ of s.o.*** essere invidioso di qn
environment *n* ambiente *m*
environmental *adj* ambientale; ***~ disaster*** disastro *m* ambientale; ***~ impact*** impatto *m* ambientale; ***~ group*** associazione *f* ambientalista
environmentalist *n* ambientalista *m/f*
environmentally *adv*: ***~ correct*** corretto per l'ambiente; ***~ conscious*** *or* ***aware*** attento all'ambiente; ***~ friendly/unfriendly*** che rispetta/non rispetta l'ambiente
environmental pollution *n* inquinamento *m* ambientale **environmental protection** *n* tutela *f* dell'ambiente **Environmental Protection Agency** *n* agenzia *f* per la protezione ambientale
environs *npl* dintorni *mpl*
envisage *v/t* prevedere
envoy *n* inviato *m*, -a *f*
envy I *n* invidia *f*; ***be the ~ of*** essere invidiato da **II** *v/t* ⟨*pret & past part* ***-ied***⟩: ***~ s.o. sth*** invidiare qc a qn
enzyme *n* enzima *m*
ephemeral *adj* effimero
epic I *n* epopea *f* **II** *adj journey* mitico; ***a task of ~ proportions*** un'impresa titanica
epicentre, *US* **epicenter** *n* epicentro *m*
epicure *n* buongustaio *m*, -a *f*
Epicurean *adj* epicureo
epidemic *n* epidemia *f*
epidemiology *n* epidemiologia *f*
epidural *n* anestesia *f* epidurale
epilepsy *n* epilessia *f*
epileptic *n* epilettico *m*, -a *f*
epileptic fit *n* attacco *m* epilettico
epilogue, *US* **epilog** *n* epilogo *m*
Epiphany *n* Epifania *f*
episcopal *adj* episcopale
episode *n* episodio *m*
episodic *adj* episodico
epistle *n* epistola *f* (*a. hum*)
epistolary *adj* epistolare
epitaph *n* epitaffio *m*
epithet *n* epiteto *m*
epitome *n* esempio *m* supremo
epoch *n* epoca *f*
epoch-making *adj* che fa epoca
equable *adj* tranquillo
equal I *adj* uguale, pari *inv*; ***be ~ in size*** *or* ***of ~ size*** avere le stesse dimensioni; ***~ rights for women*** parità di diritti per le donne; ***be on ~ terms (with)*** essere alla pari (di); ***be ~ to*** *task* essere all'altezza di **II** *n*: ***be the ~ of*** essere equivalente a; ***treat s.o. as his ~*** trattare qualcuno alla pari **III** *v/t* ⟨*pret & past part* ***-led***, *US* ***-ed***⟩ **1.** (*be as good as*) uguagliare **2.** MATH ***4 times 12 ~s 48*** 4 per 12 fa 48
equality *n* uguaglianza *f*, parità *f*
equalize I *v/t* uniformare **II** *v/i Br* SPORTS pareggiare
equalizer *n Br* SPORTS goal *m inv* del pareggio; ***score/get the ~*** segnare/prendere il goal del pareggio
equally *adv* ugualmente; ***~, ...*** allo stesso modo, …
equal opportunities *npl* pari opportunità *fpl* **equal rights** *npl* parità *f* di diritti
equals sign *n* segno *m* uguale
equate *v/t* equiparare; ***~ sth with sth*** equiparare qc e qc
equation *n* MATH equazione *f*
equator *n* equatore *m*
equatorial *adj* equatoriale
equestrian *adj* ippico; ***~ events*** eventi *mpl* ippici
equidistant *adj* equidistante (***from*** da)
equilateral *adj* equilatero
equilibrium *n* equilibrio *m*
equinox *n* equinozio *m*
equip *v/t* ⟨*pret & past part* ***-ped***⟩ equipaggiare; ***~ s.o./sth with sth*** equipaggiare qn/qc di qc; ***~ s.o. for sth***

preparare qn a qc; *fig* ***he's not ~ped to handle it*** non ha la capacità di gestirlo

equipment *n* equipaggiamento *m*; *electrical*, *electronic* apparecchiature *fpl*; ***a piece of ~*** un apparecchio

equitable *adj* equo

equitably *adv* equamente

equitation *n* equitazione *f*

equity *n* FIN capitale *m* azionario

equity of redemption *n* JUR diritto *m* di redenzione **equity stock** *n* FIN capitale *m* azionario

equivalence *n* equivalenza *f*

equivalent **I** *adj* equivalente; ***be ~ to*** essere equivalente a **II** *n* equivalente *m*

equivocal *adj* equivoco

equivocate *v/i* giocare sull'equivoco

ER *abbr* (= **emergency room**) *US* pronto soccorso *m*

era *n* era *f*; ***the Christian ~*** l'era cristiana

ERA *abbr* (= **Equal Rights Amendment**) *US* emendamento *m* sui pari diritti

eradicate *v/t* sradicare

eradication *n* sradicamento *m*

erase *v/t* cancellare

eraser *n* gomma *f* (da cancellare)

ere **I** *prep liter* prima di **II** *cj liter* prima che

erect **I** *adj* eretto; ***stand ~*** stare dritto; ***walk ~*** camminare in posizione eretta; ANAT *penis*, *nipples* eretto **II** *v/t* erigere; *scaffolding* montare; *tent* montare; *fig barrier* erigere

erectile *adj* erettile

erection *n* erezione *f*; *of statue*, *memorial*, *barrier* costruzione *f*

ergo *cj* ergo

ergonomic *adj furniture* ergonomico

ergonomically *adj designed* ergonomicamente

ergonomics *nsg* ergonomia *f*

ERM *n abbr* (= **exchange rate mechanism**) *meccanismo europeo di cambio*

ermine *n* ermellino *m*

erode *v/t* erodere; *of acid* corrodere; *fig*: *rights*, *power* eliminare

erogenous *adj* erogeno

erosion *n* erosione *f*; *of acid* corrosione *f*; *fig* eliminazione *f*

erotic *adj* erotico

erotica *npl* ART, LIT *insieme di opere a carattere erotico*

eroticism *n* erotismo *m*

err *v/i* errare; ***~ in one's judgement*** esprimere un giudizio sbagliato; ***it is better to ~ on the side of caution*** è meglio peccare per eccesso di prudenza

errand *n* commissione *f*; ***run ~s*** fare commissioni

errant *adj ways* errante; *husband etc* che erra

erratic *adj* irregolare; ***be*** (***very***) ***~*** (*figures*) essere (molto) stravagante; ***~ mood swings*** imprevedibili cambiamenti di umore; ***his ~ driving*** il suo modo di guida inaffidabile

erroneous *adj* erroneo; *assumption*, *belief* sbagliato

erroneously *adv* erroneamente

error *n* errore *m*; ***do sth in ~*** fare qc per errore; ***see the ~ of one's ways*** rendersi conto dei propri errori

error message *n* COMPUT messaggio *m* di errore

ersatz **I** *adj* surrogato **II** *n* surrogato *m*

erstwhile *adj* di una volta

erudite *adj* erudito

erudition *n* erudizione *f*

erupt *v/i of volcano* eruttare; *of violence* esplodere; *of person* dare in escandescenze

eruption *n of volcano* eruzione *f*; *of violence* esplosione *f*

escalate *v/i of costs* aumentare; *of war* intensificarsi

escalation *n* escalation *f inv*

escalator *n* scala *f* mobile

escalope *n Br* scaloppina *f*

escapade *n* avventura *f*

escape **I** *v/i of prisoner*, *animal* scappare, fuggire; *of gas* fuoriuscire; ***~ from*** fuggire da; ***he ~d from the fire*** è sfuggito all'incendio; ***~ from poverty*** sfuggire dalla povertà **II** *v/t*: ***the word ~s me*** la parola mi sfugge; ***no department will ~ these cuts*** nessun dipartimento eviterà questi tagli; ***he narrowly ~d injury*** non si è fatto male per un pelo; ***he narrowly ~d being run over*** per poco non è stato investito; ***but you can't ~ the fact that ...*** ma non puoi ignorare il fatto che... **III** *n of prisoner*, *animal*, *gas* fuga *f*; ***have a narrow ~*** scamparla

per un pelo; COMPUT ***hit ~*** premere il tasto escape
escape chute *n* AVIAT scivolo *m* **escape clause** *n* JUR clausola *f* di recesso
escapee *n* evaso *m*, -a *f*
escape key *n* COMPUT tasto *m* escape
escape route *n* via *f* di fuga
escapism *n* escapismo *m*
escarpment *n* scarpata *f*
eschatology *n* PHIL escatologia *f*
eschew *v/t* evitare; (*abstain from*) astenersi da
escort I *n* accompagnatore *m*, -trice *f*; (*guard*) scorta *f*; ***under ~*** sotto scorta; ***armed ~*** scorta *f* armata **II** *v/t socially* accompagnare; *act as guard to* scortare
escort agency *n* agenzia *f* di accompagnatrici e accompagnatori
Eskimo *pej* **I** *adj* eschimese **II** *n* eschimese
ESL *abbr* (= **English as a Second Language**) inglese come seconda lingua
esophagus *n esp US* → ***oesophagus***
esoteric *adj* esoterico
esp. *abbr* (= **especially**) specialmente
espalier I *v/t* far crescere alberi/piante a spalliera **II** *n* spalleria *f*; (*trellis*) traliccio *m*
especial *adj* → ***special***
especially *adv* specialmente; ***not ~*** non particolarmente; ***~ in summer*** soprattutto d'estate; ***why Jim ~?*** perché proprio Jim?; (*specifically*) appositamente; ***I came ~ to see you*** sono venuto apposta per vedere te
espionage *n* spionaggio *m*
esplanade *n* passeggiata *f* (lungo il mare)
espouse *v/t* sposare; ***~ a cause*** abbracciare una causa
espresso (coffee) *n* espresso *m*
esprit de corps *n* spirito *m* di corpo
espy *v/t* ⟨*pret & past part* **-ied**⟩ scorgere
Esq. *abbr* (= **esquire**): ***James Jones, Esq.*** *Br* Egr. sig. James Jones; *US* Avv. James Jones
ESRO *abbr* (= **European Space Research Organisation**) Organizzazione europea di ricerche spaziali
essay I *n* saggio *m*; *in school* tema *m*; LIT prova *f* **II** *v/t* tentare
essayist *n* LIT saggista *m/f*
essence *n* essenza *f*; ***in ~*** in sostanza; ***time is of the ~*** il tempo è di estrema importanza; ***the novel captures the ~ of life in the city*** il romanzo cattura l'essenza della vita nella città; CHEM, COOK essenza *f*
essential *adj* essenziale; ***be ~ to*** essere indispensabile a; ***it is ~ to act quickly*** bisogna agire rapidamente; ***it is ~ that you understand this*** è indispensabile che tu capisca questo; ***~ for good health*** essenziale per la salute; (*basic*) essenziale; *question*, *role* fondamentale; ***I don't doubt his ~ goodness*** non metto in dubbio la sua bontà di fondo
essentially *adv* essenzialmente
essential oil *n* olio *m* essenziale
essentials *npl* rudimenti *mpl*; ***just bring the ~*** porta solo le cose essenziali; ***with only the bare ~*** con il minimo indispensabile; ***the ~ of German grammar*** i rudimenti della grammatica tedesca
est. *abbr* **1.** (= **established**) fondato **2.** (= **estimated**) stimato
establish *v/t company* fondare; (*create*, *determine*) stabilire; ***~ o.s. as*** imporsi come; ***he has now firmly ~ed himself in the company*** oramai si è affermato all'interno dell'azienda; ***it's an ~ed practice*** *or* ***custom*** è una pratica *or* usanza riconosciuta; ***well ~ed as sth*** (*recognized*) riconosciuto come qc; ***it's an ~ed fact that …*** è un fatto consolidato che…
establishment *n firm* azienda *f*; *hotel*, *restaurant* struttura *f*; ***the Establishment*** la classe dirigente
estate *n* (*area of land*) tenuta *f*; (*possessions of dead person*) patrimonio *m*; *Br* (*houses*) complesso *m* di case popolari; JUR (*possessions of deceased*) patrimonio; ***leave one's ~ to s.o.*** lasciare i propri beni a qn
estate agency *n* agenzia *f* immobiliare **estate agent** *n* agente *m/f* immobiliare **estate car** *n* station wagon *f*
esteem I *v/t person* stimare *f* **II** *n* stima; ***hold s.o./sth in (high) ~*** avere (molta) stima di qn/qc; ***be held in great ~*** essere molto apprezzato; ***he went down in my ~*** la mia stima nei suoi confronti è diminuita

esthetic *etc US* → ***aesthetic*** *etc*
estimable *adj* stimabile
estimate I *n* stima *f*, valutazione *f*; COMM preventivo *m* **II** *v/t* stimare
estimation *n* stima *f*; ***he has gone up / down in my ~*** è salito / sceso nella mia stima; ***in my ~*** (*opinion*) a mio giudizio
Estonia *n* Estonia *f*
Estonian I *adj* estone **II** *n* estone *m/f*; *language* estone *m*
estranged *adj wife, husband* separato; ***his ~ wife*** la sua ex moglie
estrogen *n US* → ***oestrogen***
estuary *n* estuario *m*
ET *abbr* (= **Eastern Time**) *US* orario della costa orientale degli USA
ETA *abbr* (= **estimated time of arrival**) ora *f* d'arrivo prevista
etc *abbr* (= **et cetera**) ecc. (eccetera)
etcetera *adv* eccetera
etching *n* acquaforte *f*
eternal *adj* eterno
eternally *adv* eternamente; *optimistic* per sempre; ***be ~ grateful*** (***to s.o. / for sth***) eternamente riconoscente (a qn / per qc)
eternity *n* eternità *f*
ether *n* CHEM, *liter* etere *m*
ethereal *adj* etereo
ethic *n* etica *f*
ethical *adj* etico; ***it is not ~ to ...*** non è eticamente corretto...
ethically *adv* eticamente; (*with correct ethics*) in modo etico
ethics *nsg* etica *f*
Ethiopia *n* Etiopia *f*
ethnic *adj* etnico; ***~ violence*** violenza *f* etnica; ***~ music*** musica *f* etnica
ethnic cleansing *n* pulizia *f* etnica
ethnic group *n* gruppo *m* etnico, etnia *f*
ethnicity *n* etnicità *f*
ethnic minority *n* minoranza *f* etnica
ethnographic *adj* etnografico
ethnography *n* etnografia *f*
ethnology *n* etnologia *f*
ethnomusicology *n* etnomusicologia *f*
ethology *n* etologia *f*
ethos *n* ethos *m*
e-ticket *n* biglietto *m* elettronico
etiolate *v/t* BOT far scolorire; *fig* far intristire
etiquette *n* etichetta *f*
etymological *adj* etimologico
etymologically *adv* etimologicamente
etymology *n* etimologia *f*
EU *abbr* (= **European Union**) UE *f* (Unione *f* europea)
eucalyptus *n* eucalipto *m*
Eucharist *n* REL Eucarestia *f*; ***the ~*** l'Eucarestia
eulogise, *US* **eulogize** *v/t* elogiare
eulogy *n* elogio *m*
eunuch *n* eunuco *m*
euphemism *n* eufemismo *m*
euphemistic *adj* eufemistico
euphemistically *adv* in maniera eufemistica; ***be ~ described / known as ...*** essere descritto / conosciuto eufemisticamente come...
euphoria *n* euforia *f*
euphoric *adj* euforico
Eurasian I *adj* eurasiatico **II** *n* eurasiatico *m*, -a *f*
euro *n* euro *m inv*
eurocentric *adj* eurocentrico
Eurocrat *n* funzionario *m*, -a *f* della Commissione europea
Euro MP *n* eurodeputato *m*, -a *f*, europarlamentare *m/f*
Europe *n* Europa *f*
European I *adj* europeo **II** *n* europeo *m*, -a *f*
European Commission *n* Commissione *f* europea **European Commissioner** *n* Commissario *m* europeo **European Community** *n* Comunità Europea *f* **European Court of Justice** *n* Corte Europea di Giustizia *f* **European Economic Community** *n* Comunità Economica Europea *f* **European Investment Bank** *n* Banca Europea di Investimento *f* **European Monetary System** *n* Sistema Monetario Europeo *m* **European Monetary Union** *n* Unione Monetaria Europea *f* **European Parliament** *n* Parlamento *m* Europeo **European Union** *n* Unione *f* Europea
Euro-sceptic *n* euroscettico *m*, -a *f*
euro zone *n* zona *f* euro, Eurolaudia *f*, eurozona *f*
euthanasia *n* eutanasia *f*
evacuate *v/t* evacuare; MIL sgombrare
evacuation *n* evacuazione *f*
evacuee *n* evacuato *m* -a *f*
evade *v/t* eludere; *taxes* evadere
evaluate *v/t* valutare

evaluation *n* valutazione *f*
evanescent *adj* evanescente
evangelical *adj* evangelico
evangelism *n* evangelismo *m*
evangelist *n* evangelizzatore *m*, -trice *f*
evaporate *v/i of water* evaporare; *of confidence* svanire
evaporated milk *n* latte *m* condensato
evaporation *n of water* evaporazione *f*
evasion *n* elusione *f*; *of taxes* evasione *f*
evasive *adj* evasivo; ***they were ~ about it*** sono stati evasivi sull'argomento; ***take ~ action*** disimpegnarsi
eve *n* vigilia *f*
even I *adv* persino; ***the car ~ has a CD player*** la macchina ha persino un lettore CD; ***~ bigger*** ancora più grande; ***~ better / worse*** ancora meglio / peggio; ***not ~*** nemmeno, neppure; ***it's not ~ ten o'clock yet*** non sono nemmeno le dieci; ***~ so*** nonostante questo; ***~ if*** *or* ***~ though*** anche se **II** *adj* **1.** (*regular*) omogeneo; *breathing* regolare; *surface* piano; *hem* diritto **2.** (*number*) pari *inv* **3.** *players*, *game* alla pari; ***now we're ~*** ora siamo pari; ***get ~ with ...*** farla pagare a ... **III** *v/t*: ***~ the score*** pareggiare
◆**even out I** *v/i* (*prices*) livellare **II** *v/t sep*: ***that should even things out a bit*** questo dovrebbe livellare le cose
◆**even up** *v/t sep*: ***that will even things up*** questo metterà a posto le cose
even-handed *adj* imparziale
even-handedly *adv* in modo imparziale
evening *n* sera *f*; ***in the ~*** di sera; ***this ~*** stasera; ***yesterday ~*** ieri sera; ***good ~*** buona sera
evening class *n* corso *m* serale **evening dress** *n for woman* vestito *m* da sera; *for man* abito *m* scuro **evening paper** *n* giornale *m* della sera
evenly *adv* (*regularly*) in modo omogeneo; *breathe* regolarmente; ***the contestants were ~ matched*** i partecipanti erano ad armi pari; ***public opinion seems to be ~ divided*** l'opinione pubblica sembra equamente divisa
evensong *n Catholic* vespro *m*; *Anglican* preghiera *f* della sera
event *n* evento *m*, avvenimento *m*; *social* manifestazione *f*; SPORTS prova *f*; ***at all ~s, in any ~*** ad ogni modo; ***in the ~*** in realtà; ***in the ~ of*** in caso di; ***in the ~ that it happens*** in caso succeda
even-tempered *adj* calmo
eventful *adj* movimentato
eventide *n* LIT sera *f*
eventual *adj* finale; ***he predicted the ~ fall of the government*** ha predetto la futura caduta del governo; ***the ~ success of the project is not in doubt*** il successo finale del progetto è fuori dubbio; ***he lost to the ~ winner*** ha perso contro il vincitore finale
eventuality *n* eventualità *f inv*; ***be ready for any ~*** essere pronto ad ogni eventualità
eventually *adv* finalmente, alla fine
ever *adv* mai; ***have you ~ been to ...?*** sei mai stato in ...?; ***nothing ~ happens*** non succede mai niente; ***it hardly ~ snows here*** qui non nevica quasi mai; ***seldom, if ~*** quasi mai; ***he's a rascal if ~ there was one*** è un furfante, se mai ne esiste uno; ***for ~*** per sempre; ***as ~*** come sempre; ***~ more*** sempre di più; ***~ since he left I have been worried*** da quando è partito sono preoccupato; ***~ since his sister's death*** dalla morte di sua sorella; ***he's been depressed ~ since*** è depresso da allora; ***she's the best grandmother ~*** è la migliore nonna del mondo; ***what ~ shall we do?*** cosa dovremo mai fare?; ***why ~ not?*** perché no?; *infml* ***~ so / such*** così tanto
Everest *n*: (***Mount***) ***~*** l'Everest *m*
evergreen *n* sempreverde *m*
everlasting *adj* eterno; ***to his ~ shame*** con suo grande disonore
every *adj* ogni; ***one in ~ ten houses*** una casa su dieci; ***~ other day*** un giorno sì, uno no; ***~ now and then*** ogni tanto; ***~ man for himself*** si salvi chi può; ***in ~ way*** (*in all respects*) sotto tutti gli aspetti; ***he is ~ bit as clever as his brother*** è proprio intelligente come suo fratello; ***his ~ word*** ogni sua singola parola; ***I have ~ confidence in him*** ho totale fiducia in lui; ***I have / there is ~ hope that ...*** ho / ci sono tutte le speranze che...;

there was ~ prospect of success c'erano tutte le speranze di successo
everybody *pron* ognuno, ciascuno, tutti; ***~ has finished*** hanno finito tutti; ***it's not ~ who can afford a big house*** non tutti possono permettersi una casa grande
everyday *adj* di tutti i giorni; ***~ clothes*** i vestiti di tutti i giorni; ***be an ~ occurrence*** essere una cosa di tutti i giorni; ***for ~ use*** per uso quotidiano; ***~ life*** la vita di ogni giorno
Everyman *n* l'uomo qualunque
everyone *pron* → ***everybody***
everything *pron* tutto; ***money isn't ~*** i soldi non sono tutto; ***my son means ~ to me*** mio figlio per me è tutto; ***~ possible*** tutto il possibile; ***~ you have*** tutto ciò che hai; ***is ~ all right?*** va tutto bene?
everywhere *adv* dovunque, dappertutto; (*wherever*) dovunque; ***from ~*** da tutte le parti; ***~ you look there's a mistake*** ovunque guardi c'è un errore
evict *v/t* sfrattare; ***they were ~ed*** sono stati sfrattati
eviction *n* sfratto *m*
eviction order *n* ordine *m* di sfratto
evidence *n* prova *f*; ***there is no ~ that ...*** non ci sono prove che...; ***give ~*** JUR testimoniare; ***for lack of ~*** per insufficienza di prove; ***all the ~ was against him*** tutte le prove erano contro di lui; ***be in ~*** essere in evidenza
evident *adj* evidente
evidently *adv* evidentemente
evil I *adj* cattivo; ***~ deed*** un'azione malvagia; ***with ~ intent*** con cattive intenzioni **II** *n* male *m*; ***the lesser / greater of two ~s*** il minore / peggiore dei mali
evildoer *n* malfattore *m*, -trice *f*
evil eye *n* malocchio *m* **evil-minded** *adj* malvagio
evocation *n* evocazione *f*
evocative *adj* evocativo
evoke *v/t image* evocare
evolution *n* evoluzione *f*
evolutionary *adj* evolutivo; ***~ theory*** teoria *f* evolutiva
evolutionism *n* evoluzionismo *m*
evolve I *v/t* sviluppare **II** *v/i* evolvere
ewe *n* pecora *f* femmina
ewer *n* brocca *f*
ex *n infml* (*former wife*) ex *f inv infml*; (*former husband*) ex *m inv infml*
ex- *pref* ex-
exacerbate *v/t* aggravare
exact I *adj* esatto; ***be ~ about sth*** essere precisi su qc; ***do you have the ~ amount?*** hai l'importo preciso?; ***until this ~ moment*** fino a questo preciso istante; ***the ~ same thing*** esattamente la stessa cosa; ***he's 47 to be ~*** per la precisione, ha 47 anni **II** *v/t*: ***~ sth from s.o.*** ottenere qc da qn
exacting *adj task* impegnativo; *employer* esigente; *standards* rigido
exactly *adv* esattamente; ***~!*** esatto!, esattamente!; ***I wanted to know ~ where my mother was buried*** volevo sapere dove esattamente è stata sepolta mia madre; ***that's ~ what I was thinking*** è esattamente quello che stavo pensando; ***at ~ five o'clock*** alle cinque precise; ***who ~ will be in charge?*** chi esattamente sarà incaricato?; ***you mean we are stuck? — ~*** vuoi dire che siamo bloccati? – proprio così; ***not ~*** non esattamente
exaggerate *v/t & v/i* esagerare; ***he ~d what really happened*** ha esagerato quello che è successo in realtà
exaggeration *n* esagerazione *f*
exalt *v/t* esaltare
exaltation *n* (*feeling*) esaltazione *f*
exalted *adj position* altolocato; *style* elevato
exam *n* esame *m*; ***sit an ~*** dare *or* sostenere un esame; ***pass an ~*** passare *or* superare un esame; ***fail an ~*** essere bocciato a un esame
examination *n* esame *m*; *of patient* visita *f*
examine *v/t* esaminare; *patient* visitare
examiner *n* EDU esaminatore *m*, -trice *f*
example *n* esempio *m*; ***for ~*** ad *or* per esempio; ***set a good / bad ~*** dare il buon / cattivo esempio; ***take sth as an ~*** prendere qc come esempio; ***make an ~ of s.o.*** fare un esempio di qc
exasperate *v/t* esasperare; ***become*** *or* ***get ~d*** esasperarsi (***with*** per colpa di)
exasperated *adj* esasperato
exasperating *adj* esasperante
exasperation *n* esasperazione *f*
excavate *v/t* (*dig*) scavare; *of archae-*

ologist riportare alla luce
excavation *n* scavo *m*
excavator *n* escavatrice *f*
exceed *v/t* (*be more than*) eccedere, superare; (*go beyond*) oltrepassare, superare; **~ *5 kilos in weight*** supera il peso di cinque chili; ***a fine not ~ing £500*** una multa non superiore a 500 sterline
exceedingly *adj* estremamente
excel ⟨*pret & past part* **-led**⟩ **I** *v/i* eccellere; **~ *at*** eccellere in **II** *v/t*: **~ *o.s.*** superare se stesso
excellence *n* eccellenza *f*
Excellency *n*: ***Your / His ~*** Vostra / Sua Eccellenza *f*
excellent *adj* eccellente
except I *prep* eccetto; ***what can they do ~ wait?*** cosa possono fare se non aspettare; **~ *for*** fatta eccezione per; **~ *that …*** eccetto che …; **~ *when*** tranne quando **II** *cj* (*only*) salvo che **III** *v/t* escludere; **~ *s.o. from sth*** escludere qn da qc
excepting *prep* eccetto; ***not ~ X*** senza escludere X
exception *n* eccezione *f*; ***the ~ to the rule*** l'eccezione che conferma la regola; ***with the ~ of*** con l'eccezione di; ***take ~ to*** avere da ridire su; (*be offended by*) risentirsi per
exceptional *adj* eccezionale; ***of ~ quality*** di qualità eccezionale; **~ *case*** caso eccezionale; ***in ~ cases*** (*or* ***in*** *or* ***under ~ circumstances*** in casi eccezionali)
exceptionally *adv* (*extremely*) eccezionalmente
excerpt *n* estratto *m*
excess I *n* eccesso *m*; ***eat / drink to ~*** mangiare / bere all'eccesso; ***be in ~ of*** eccedere **II** *adj* in eccesso
excess baggage *n* eccedenza *f* di bagaglio **excess fare** *n* supplemento *m* tariffa
excessive *adj* eccessivo
excessively *adv* eccessivamente
excess weight *n* peso *m* eccedente
exchange I *n of views, information* scambio *m*; *between schools* scambio *m* culturale; FIN cambio *m*; ***in ~ (for)*** in cambio (di); ***in ~ for lending me your car*** in cambio del prestito della tua macchina; (***telephone***) **~** centralino *m* **II** *v/t* cambiare; **~ *sth for sth*** cambiare qc con qc; **~ *words*** scambiare una parola; **~ *letters*** scambiarsi lettere; **~ *greetings*** scambiarsi i saluti; **~ *insults*** scambiarsi insulti; **~ *one thing for another*** scambiare una cosa per un'altra
exchange rate *n* FIN tasso *m* di cambio **exchange rate mechanism** *n* FIN meccanismo *m* europeo di cambio
exchange student *n studente che studia all'estero grazie ad un programma di scambio culturale*
Exchequer *n* Scacchiere *m*
excise duties *npl Br*, **excise tax** *n US* accisa *f*
excitable *adj* eccitabile
excite *v/t* (*make enthusiastic*) eccitare; ***the whole village was ~d by the news*** tutto il paese era in subbuglio per la notizia
excited *adj* eccitato; ***get ~*** eccitarsi; ***get ~ about sth*** eccitarsi per qc
excitement *n* eccitazione *f*; ***there was great ~ when …*** ci fu una grande eccitazione quando…; ***what's all the ~ about?*** perché tanta agitazione?; ***his novel has caused great ~*** il suo romanzo ha suscitato grandi emozioni
exciting *adj* eccitante, emozionante
excl *abbr* **1.** (= **excluding**) escluso **2.** (= **exclusive**) esclusivo
exclaim I *v/i*: ***he ~ed in surprise when he saw it*** è rimasto a bocca aperta per la sopresa quando l'ha visto **II** *v/t* esclamare
exclamation *n* esclamazione *f*
exclamation mark, *US* **exclamation point** *n* punto *m* esclamativo
exclude *v/t* escludere; **~ *s.o. from sth*** escludere qn da qc; **~ *s.o. from the team / an occupation*** escludere qualcuno dalla squadra / da un'occupazione; **~ *a child from school*** espellere un alunno da scuola
excluding *prep* ad esclusione di; ***£200 excluding VAT*** *Br* 200 sterline IVA esclusa; ***everything excluding the house*** tutto ad esclusione della casa
exclusive I *adj* esclusivo; ***a highly ~ resort*** un luogo di vacanza molto esclusivo; ***be ~ of sth*** non includere qc; **~ *interview*** intervista esclusiva; **~ *offer*** offerta esclusiva; **~ *rights to sth*** esclusiva su qc; PRESS esclusivo; ***they are mutually ~*** sono incompati-

bili **II** *n story, interview* esclusiva *f*
excommunicate *v/t* REL scomunicare
excrement *n* escrementi *mpl*
excrescence *n* escrescenza *f*
excreta *npl* escrementi *mpl*
excrete *v/t* espellere; BIOL secernere
excruciating *adj pain* lancinante, atroce
excursion *n* escursione *f*, gita *f*; ***go on an ~*** andare in gita
excursus *n* excursus *m*
excusable *adj* scusabile
excuse I *v/t* scusare; ***~ s.o. from sth*** dispensare qn da qc; ***~ me*** *to get attention, interrupting* scusami, mi scusi *form*; *to get past* permesso **II** *n* scusa *f*
ex-directory *adj Br* ***be ~*** non comparire sull'elenco telefonico
exeat *n Br permesso di assentarsi nei college di Oxford e Cambridge*; ***they had their mid term ~ in May*** hanno avuto il permesso di metà semestre a maggio
execrable *adj* esecrabile
execrate *v/t* esecrare
execration *n* esecrazione *f*
execute *v/t criminal* giustiziare; *plan* attuare
execution *n of criminal* esecuzione *f*; *of plan* attuazione *f*; ***in the ~ of his duties*** nell'esercizio delle sue funzioni
executioner *n* carnefice *m*
executive I *n* dirigente *m/f*; COMM, POL esecutivo *m*; ***senior ~*** dirigente *m/f* superiore; ***be on the ~*** essere nell'esecutivo **II** *adj* esecutivo; (*luxury*) di lusso; ***~ power*** potere *m* esecutivo; ***~ decision*** decisione *f* esecutiva
executive board *n* consiglio *m* direttivo **executive briefcase** *n* ventiquattrore *f inv* **executive committee** *n* comitato *m* esecutivo **executive officer** *n* alto dirigente *m*; funzionario *m* **executive toy** *n* giocattolo *m* da scrivania **executive washroom** *n* bagno *m* della direzione
executor *n* esecutore *m* testamentario
exemplary *adj* esemplare
exemplify *v/t* ⟨*pret & past part* ***-ied***⟩ esemplificare
exempt I *adj*: ***be ~ from*** essere esente da **II** *v/t* esentare; ***~ s.o. / sth from sth*** esentare qn / qc da qc
exemption *n* esenzione *f*; ***~ from taxes*** esenzione fiscale
exercise I *n* (*physical*), EDU esercizio *m*; ***do one's ~s in the morning*** fare la ginnastica di mattina; ***physical ~*** esercizio *m* fisico; ***take ~*** fare esercizio; MIL esercitazione *f*; ***it was a pointless ~*** è stato un tentativo inutile; ***it was a useful ~ in public relations*** è stato uno sforzo utile per le pubbliche relazioni **II** *v/t muscle* fare esercizio con; *dog* far fare esercizio a; *caution, restraint* adoperare **III** *v/i* fare esercizio; ***you don't ~ enough*** non fai abbastanza esercizio
exercise bike *n* cyclette *f inv* **exercise book** *n* EDU quaderno *m* di esercizi **exercise class** *n* esercitazione *f*
exert *v/t authority* esercitare; ***~ o.s.*** sforzarsi
exertion *n* sforzo *m*; ***rugby requires strenuous physical ~*** il rugby richiede un enorme sforzo fisico; ***after the day's ~s*** dopo le fatiche della giornata
exfoliate I *v/t* esfoliare **II** *v/i* esfoliarsi
exhalation *n* esalazione *f*; (*expiration*) espirazione *f*
exhale *v/t* esalare
exhaust I *n fumes* gas *mpl* di scarico; *pipe* tubo *m* di scappamento **II** *v/t* (*tire*) estenuare; (*use up*) esaurire; ***we have ~ed the subject*** abbiamo esaurito l'argomento
exhausted *adj* (*tired*) esausto; *savings* esaurito; ***she was ~ from digging the garden*** era sfinita per aver zappato il giardino; ***his patience was ~*** aveva esaurito la pazienza
exhaust fumes *npl* gas *mpl* di scarico
exhausting *adj* estenuante
exhaustion *n* spossatezza *f*
exhaustive *adj* esauriente
exhaust pipe *n* tubo *m* di scappamento
exhibit I *n in exhibition* oggetto *m* esposto; JUR prova *f* **II** *v/t of gallery, artist* esporre; (*give evidence of*) manifestare
exhibition *n* esposizione *f*; *of bad behaviour* manifestazione *f*; *of skill* dimostrazione *f*; ***make an ~ of o.s.*** dare spettacolo
exhibition centre, *US* **exhibition center** *n* centro *m* espositivo; (*for trade fair*) centro *m* fieristico

exhibitionist *n* esibizionista *m/f*
exhibitor *n* espositore *m*, -trice *f*; FILM gestore *m*
exhilarate *v/t* entusiasmare
exhilarated *adj* euforico
exhilarating *adj* emozionante
exhilaration *n* euforia *f*
exhort *v/t* esortare
exhortation *n* esortazione *f*
exhume *v/t* esumare
exile I *n* esilio *m*; *person* esiliato *m*, -a *f*; ***go into ~*** andare in esilio; ***in ~*** in esilio **II** *v/t* esiliare
exist *v/i* esistere; ***doubts still ~*** persistono ancora dei dubbi; ***the understanding which ~s between the two countries*** l'intesa che esiste tra i due paesi; ***the possibility ~s that ...*** esiste la possibilità che…; ***~ on*** vivere di
existence *n* esistenza *f*;(*life*) vita *f*; ***she had a wretched ~*** ha avuto un'esistenza infelice; ***means of ~*** mezzi di sopravvivenza; ***in ~*** esistente; ***come into ~*** nascere
existential *adj* esistenziale
existentialism *n* PHIL esistenzialismo *m*
existing *adj* attuale
exit I *n* uscita *f*; ***make an/one's ~*** (*from stage*) uscire di scena; (*from room*) uscire **II** *v/i* COMPUT uscire **III** *v/t* COMPUT chiudere
exit poll *n* exit poll *mpl* **exit strategy** *n* strategia *f* di uscita **exit visa** *n* visto *m* d'uscita
exodus *n* esodo *m*; ***general ~*** esodo *m* generale
exonerate *v/t* scagionare
exorbitant *adj* esorbitante
exorbitantly *adv*: ***~ priced*** *or* ***expensive*** costoso in modo esorbitante
exorcise, *US* **exorcize** *v/t* exit poll *m inv*
exorcism *n* esorcismo *m*
exotic *adj* esotico; ***~ holidays*** *esp Br or* ***vacation*** *US* vacanza *f* esotica
exotica *npl* oggetti *mpl* esotici
expand I *v/t* espandere; ***~ one's muscles*** gonfiare i propri muscoli; ***he ~ed his business*** ha aumentato i suoi affari; ***studying ~s your mind*** lo studio ti allarga la mente **II** *v/i* espandersi; *of metal* dilatarsi; ***we want to ~*** vogliamo espanderci; ***the market is ~ing*** il mercato si sta espandendo
◆**expand on** *v/t* dilungarsi su
expanse *n* distesa *f*
expansion *n* espansione *f*; *of metal* dilatazione *f*
expansion board *n* COMPUT scheda *f* di espansione **expansion card** *n* COMPUT scheda *f* di espansione **expansion slot** *n* COMPUT slot *m inv* di espansione
expansive *adj person* espansivo; ***~ definition*** definizione *f* dettagliata
expat → ***expatriate***
expatriate I *adj* residente all'estero; ***~ community*** comunità *f* di stranieri **II** *n* residente *m/f* all'estero **III** *v/t* espatriare; (*exile*) esiliare **IV** *v/i* espatriare; (*go into exile*) andare in esilio
expect I *v/t* aspettare; (*suppose*, *demand*) aspettarsi; ***that was to be ~ed*** c'era da aspettarselo; ***I know what to ~*** so quello che c'è da aspettarsi; ***I ~ed as much*** me l'aspettavo; ***he failed as (we had) ~ed*** ha sbagliato come (avevamo) previsto; ***are we ~ed to tip the waiter?*** normalmente si lascia la mancia al cameriere?; ***I will be ~ing you tomorrow*** ti aspetto domani; ***we'll ~ you when we see you*** *infml* quando arrivi arrivi; (*suppose*) supporre; ***I ~ you're tired*** immagino che tu sia stanco; ***yes, I ~ so*** immagino di sì; ***~ s.o. to do sth*** aspettarsi che qn faccia qc **II** *v/i*: ***be ~ing*** aspettare un bambino
expectant *adj* pieno di aspettativa
expectant mother *n* donna *f* in stato interessante
expectation *n* aspettativa *f*; ***~s*** (*demands*) aspettative *fpl*; ***against all*** *or* ***contrary to all ~s*** contro ogni aspettativa
expedient *n* espediente *m*
expedite *v/t* accelerare; (*facilitate*) facilitare
expedition *n* spedizione *f*; ***go on a shopping/sightseeing ~*** andare a fare spese/in giro a visitare
expel *v/t* ⟨*pret & past part* **-led**⟩ espellere; (*from school*) espellere; ***~ s.o. from sth*** espellere qn da qc
expend *v/t energy* spendere
expendable *adj person* sacrificabile
expenditure *n* spesa *f*

expense *n* spesa *f*; ***at the company's ~*** a spese della società; ***a joke at my ~*** uno scherzo a mie spese; ***at the ~ of his health*** a spese della sua salute
expense account *n* nota *f* spese
expenses *npl* spese *fpl*
expensive *adj* caro
experience I *n* esperienza *f*; ***I know from ~ that ...*** so per esperienza che ...; ***he has no ~ of living in the country*** non ha esperienza di vita in campagna; ***I gained a lot of useful ~*** ho acquisito molta esperienza utile; ***have you had any ~ of driving a bus?*** hai mai guidato un autobus?; ***~ in a job / in business*** esperienza *f* nel lavoro / negli affari; ***have a lot of teaching ~*** avere molta esperienza d'insegnamento; ***he is working in a factory to gain ~*** lavora in una fabbrica per acquisire esperienza; ***I had a nasty ~*** ho avuto una brutta esperienza; ***it was a new ~ for me*** è stata un'esperienza nuova per me **II** *v/t pain, pleasure* provare; *problem, difficulty* incontrare
experienced *adj* con esperienza; ***he's ~ in teaching*** ha esperienza nell'insegnamento
experiment I *n* sperimento *m*; ***conduct*** *or* ***perform ~s*** fare esperimenti **II** *v/i* fare esperimenti; ***~ on*** *animals* sperimentare su; ***~ with*** (*try out*) sperimentare
experimental *adj* sperimentale
experimentation *n* sperimentazione *f*
expert I *adj* esperto; ***be ~ at*** *or* ***in sth*** essere esperto di *or* in qc **II** *n* esperto *m*, -a *f*
expert advice *n* parere *m* di un esperto
expertise *n* competenza *f*
expiate *v/t & v/i* espiare
expiation *n* espiazione *f*
expiration *n US* scadenza *f*
expiration date *n US* data *f* di scadenza
expire *v/i* scadere
expiry *n* scadenza *f*
expiry date *n* data *f* di scadenza
explain I *v/t* spiegare; ***~ sth to s.o.*** spiegare qc a qn; ***that is easy to ~*** (*or* ***that is easily ~ed***) è facile da spiegare; ***he wanted to see me but wouldn't ~ why*** voleva vedermi ma non me ne diceva il motivo **II** *v/i* spiegarsi **III** *v/r* spiegarsi; ***~ yourself!*** spiegati!
explanation *n* spiegazione *f*; ***it needs some ~*** ha bisogno di spiegazioni
explanatory *adj* esplicativo
explant I *v/t* espiantare **II** *n* espianto *m*; ***tissue ~*** espianto *m* di tessuto
expletive *n* imprecazione *f*
explicable *adj* spiegabile
explicit *adj instructions* esplicito; (*sexually*) *details* esplicito; ***sexually ~*** che mostra scene di sesso
explicitly *adv state, forbid* esplicitamente
explode I *v/i of bomb* esplodere; ***~ with anger*** esplodere di rabbia **II** *v/t bomb* fare esplodere
exploit[1] *n* exploit *m inv*
exploit[2] *v/t person, resources* sfruttare
exploitation *n* sfruttamento *m*
exploration *n* esplorazione *f*
exploratory *adj surgery* esplorativo; ***an ~ operation*** MED un'operazione esplorativa; ***~ talks*** colloqui esplorativi; ***~ trip / expedition*** viaggio / spedizione esplorativa
explore I *v/t country, possibility etc* esplorare **II** *v/i*: ***he went off into the village to ~*** è andato in paese in esplorazione
explorer *n* esploratore *m*, -trice *f*
explosion *n* esplosione *f*; ***a population ~*** un'esplosione demografica
explosive I *n* esplosivo *m* **II** *adj* esplosivo; *temper* collerico; ***~ device*** ordigno; ***~ charge*** carica esplosiva
expo *n infml* esposizione *f*
exponent *n of theory, art* esponente *m/f*; MATH esponente *m*
exponential *adj* esponenziale
exponential growth *n* crescita *f* esponenziale **exponential series** *n* MATH serie *f* esponenziale
export I *n action* esportazione *f*; *item* prodotto *m* di esportazione **II** *v/t goods*, COMPUT esportare
export campaign *n* campagna *f* per l'esportazione **export duty** *n* dazio *m* di esportazione
exporter *n* esportatore *m*, -trice *f*
export licence, *US* **export license** *n* licenza *f* di esportazione
expose *v/t* (*uncover*) scoprire; *scandal, person* denunciare; ***~ sth to sth***

esporre qc a qc; *one's ignorance* mostrare; ~ ***o.s.*** (*indecently*) esibirsi; *abuse* scoprire i genitali; *scandal*, *plot* rivelare; *person* mostrare; PHOT esporre
exposé *n* rivelazione *f*
exposure *n* esposizione *f*; *to cold weather* esposizione *f* prolungata al freddo; *of dishonest behaviour* denuncia *f*; PHOT (*frame*) scatto *m*; ***die of*** ~ MED morire per assideramento
expound *v/t theory* esporre
express I *v/t* (*speak of*, *voice*) esprimere; ***if I may*** ~ ***my opinion*** se posso espireme la mia opinione…; ~ ***o.s. well / clearly*** esprimersi bene / chiaramente; ~ ***o.s.*** (*emotionally*) esprimersi **II** *adj* (*fast*, *explicit*) espresso **III** *n* (*train*) espresso *m* **IV** *adv*: ***send a letter*** ~ mandare una lettera per espresso
express delivery *n* consegna *f* per espresso
expression *n* espressione *f*; ***as an*** ~ ***of our gratitude*** a dimostrazione della nostra gratitudine; (*expressiveness*) espressività *f*; ***give*** ~ ***to sth*** dare voce a qc
expressionism *n* ART espressionismo *m*
expressionist I *n* ART espressionista *m/f* **II** *adj* ART espressionista
expressionless *adj* privo di espressione; (*inexpressive*) inespressivo
expressive *adj* espressivo
expressly *adv* espressamente; ***he did it*** ~ ***to annoy me*** l'ha fatto a posta per infastidirmi
express train *n* treno *m* espresso
expressway *n* autostrada *f*
expropriate *v/t* espropriare
expulsion *n* espulsione *f*; (*from school*) espulsione *f*
expunge *v/t* espungere
expurgate *v/t* espurgare
exquisite *adj* (*beautiful*) squisito
exquisitely *adv dress* in modo squisito; *crafted* squisitamente
ex-serviceman *n* ⟨*pl* ***-men***⟩ ex militare *m*
ex-servicewoman *n* ⟨*pl* ***-women***⟩ ex militare *m*
ext *abbr* (= **extension**) TEL interno *m*
extant *adj* esistente
extend I *v/t* estendere; *house*, *powers*, *repertoire* ampliare; ~ ***one's lead*** aumentare il proprio vantaggio; *runway*, *path* prolungare; *contract*, *visa* prorogare; *thanks*, *congratulations* porgere; ~ ***a welcome to s.o.*** dare il benvenuto a qn **II** *v/i of garden etc* estendersi
extended family *n* famiglia *f* allargata
extended memory *n* COMPUT memoria *f* estesa
extension *n to house* annesso *m*; *of contract*, *visa* proroga *f*; TEL interno *m*
extension cable *n* prolunga *f* **extension lead** *n* prolunga *f*
extensive *adj* ampio; *research*, *experience* completo; *collection*, *network* vasto; *repairs* su larga scala; *knowledge* ampio; *burns* esteso; *damage* grave; ***the facilities available are very*** ~ le attrezzature a disposizione sono notevoli; ***we had fairly*** ~ ***discussions*** abbiamo avuto delle discussioni piuttosto lunge
extensively *adv travel* molto; *use*, *write* ampiamente; *research*, *report*, *discuss* in modo esauriente; *alter* notevolmente; ***the clubhouse was*** ~ ***damaged*** il locale è stato gravemente danneggiato; ***this edition has been*** ~ ***revised*** questa edizione è stata riveduta e corretta in modo approfondito
extent *n* ampiezza *f*, portata *f*; ***to such an*** ~ ***that*** a un punto tale che; ***to a certain*** ~ fino a un certo punto; ***to a large*** ~ in gran parte
extenuate *v/t* attenuare
extenuating *adj* attenuante; ~ ***circumstances*** circostanze attenuanti
exterior I *adj* esterno; ~ ***wall*** muri esterni; ~ ***decoration / paintwork*** decorazione *f* / verniciatura *f* esterna **II** *n of building* esterno *m*; *of person* aspetto *m* esteriore; ***on the*** ~ dall'esterno
exterminate *v/t* sterminare
extermination *n people* sterminio *m*; (*pest control*) disinfestazione *f*; *animals* eliminazione *f*
extermination camp *n* campo *m* di sterminio
external *adj* (*outside*) esterno; *dimensions* esterno; ***the*** ~ ***walls of the house*** i muri esterni della casa; ~ ***ap-***

pearance aspetto *m* esteriore; ***for ~ use*** PHARM per uso esterno; ***~ call*** TEL chiamata *f* esterna; *affairs*, *policy* estero; *examiner* esterno
external borders *npl of country* confini *mpl* esterni **external combustion engine** *n* MECH motore *m* a combustione esterna **external ear** *n* orecchio *m* esterno
externalise, *US* **externalize** *v/t* esternare
extinct *adj species* estinto; *volcano* estinto; *fig way of life* scomparire; ***become ~*** estinguersi
extinction *n of species* estinzione *f*; ***this animal was hunted to ~*** la caccia di questo animale ne ha provocato l'estinzione
extinguish *v/t* spegnere
extinguisher *n* estintore *m*
extol *v/t* ⟨*pret & past part* **-led**⟩ *form* decantare
extort *v/t* estorcere; ***~ money from ...*** estorcere denaro da ...
extortion *n* estorsione *f*; ***this is sheer ~!*** *infml* è un furto!
extortionate *adj prices* esorbitante; ***that's ~!*** è un furto!
extra I *adj* in più; ***we need an ~ chair*** ci serve un'altra sedia; ***work ~ hours*** fare gli straordinari; ***make an ~ effort*** fare uno sforzo in più; ***~ troops were called in*** sono state chiamate truppe supplementari; ***take ~ care!*** fate molta attenzione!; ***an ~ £30 a week*** altre 30 sterline a settimana; ***send 75p ~ for postage and packing*** mandare altri 75; ***there is no ~ charge for breakfast*** non si paga un supplemento per la colazione; ***available at no ~ cost*** disponibile senza spese aggiuntive **II** *adv* **1.** (*especially*) particolarmente; ***an ~ special day*** un giorno particolarmente speciale **2.** (*more*) di più; ***breakfast costs ~*** la colazione ha un costo aggiuntivo; ***post and packing ~*** supplemento spedizione e confezione; ***charge ~ for sth*** far pagare un supplemento per qc **III** *n* extra *m inv*; THEAT comparsa *f*
extra- *pref* extra; ***~large*** extra-large
extra charge *n* costo *m* aggiuntivo
extract[1] *n* estratto *m*
extract[2] *v/t* estrarre; *information* estorcere; ***~ sth from sth*** estrarre qc da qc
extraction *n* estrazione *f*; (*oil*, *DNA*) estrazione *f*; (*dentistry*) ***he had to have an ~*** ha dovuto farsi estrarre un dente; (*descent*) estrazione *f*
extractor fan *n* aspiratore *m*
extracurricular *adj* extracurricolare; ***~ activity*** *hum* attività extracurricolari
extradite *v/t* estradare
extradition *n* estradizione *f*
extradition treaty *n* accordo *m* di estradizione
extramarital *adj* extraconiugale
extramural *adj* esterno; *Br* ***~ courses*** *corsi universitari per studenti part-time*
extraneous *adj form* estraneo; (*external*) esterno
extraordinarily *adv* eccezionalmente
extraordinary *adj* straordinario; ***it's ~ to think that ...*** è straordinario se si pensa che...; ***what an ~ thing to say!*** che cosa incredibile da dire!; ***it's ~ how much he resembles his brother*** è straordinario quanto assomiglia a suo fratello; *Br form measure* straordinario; ***~ meeting*** riunione *f* straordinaria
extrapolate *v/t & v/i* estrapolare (***from*** da)
extras *npl* (*extra expenses*) extra *mpl*
extrasensory *adj* extrasensoriale; ***~ perception*** percezione *f* extrasensoriale
extraterrestrial I *adj* extraterrestre **II** *n* extraterrestre *m/f*
extraterritorial *adj* extraterritoriale
extra time *n* SPORTS tempi *mpl* supplementari; ***we had to play ~*** siamo andati ai tempi supplementari
extrauterine *adj* extrauterino
extravagance *n* stravaganza *f*; (*wastefulness*) sperpero *m*; ***if you can't forgive her little ~s*** se non puoi perdonarle i suoi piccoli lussi
extravagant *adj with money* stravagante; ***your ~ spending habits*** le tue abitudini da spendaccione; *gift* stravagante; *lifestyle* dispendioso; *behaviour*, *praise*, *claim* stravagante
extravaganza *n* grande evento *m*
extreme I *n* estremo *m*; ***go to ~s*** spingere all'estremo; ***go from one ~ to the other*** andare da un estremo all'altro; ***take*** *or* ***carry sth to ~s*** portare

qc agli estremi **II** *adj* estremo; ***of ~ importance*** di estrema importanza; ***~ case*** caso *m* estremo; ***fascists of the ~ right*** fascisti di estrema destra; ***at the ~ left of the picture*** all'estrema sinistra dell'immagine; ***~ sport*** sport *m inv* estremi
extremely *adv* estremamente
extremist *n* estremista *m/f*
extremity *n* estremità *f inv*
extricate *v/t* districare; ***~ o.s. from sth*** districarsi da qc
extrinsic *adj* estrinseco
extrovert *n/adj* estroverso *m*, -a *f*
exuberance *n* esuberanza *f*
exuberant *adj* esuberante
exult *v/i* esultare
exultant *adj expression*, *cry* di esultanza; ***he was ~*** era esultante; ***have an ~ mood*** sentirsi esultante
eye I *n* **1.** occhio *m*; ***keep an ~ on*** tenere d'occhio; ***in my ~s*** ai miei occhi; ***I don't have ~s in the back of my head*** non ho cento occhi; ***keep one's ~s open*** *or* ***peeled*** *infml* tenere gli occhi aperti; ***see ~ to ~ with s.o.*** vedere le cose allo stesso modo di qn; ***make ~s at s.o.*** fare gli occhi dolci a qn; ***catch s.o.'s ~*** attirare l'attenzione di qn; ***in the ~s of the law*** agli occhi della legge; ***with a critical ~*** con un occhio critico; ***with an ~ to the future*** con un occhio rivolto al futuro; ***with an ~ to buying sth*** con l'occhio rivolto all'acquisto di qc; ***he has a good ~ for colour*** ha un buon occhio per il colore; ***an ~ for detail*** un occhio per i dettagli; ***be up to one's ~s in work*** *Br infml* averne fin sopra ai capelli del proprio lavoro; **2.** *of needle* cruna *f* **II** *v/t* scrutare
eyeball I *n* bulbo *m* oculare; ***drugged up to the ~s*** *esp Br infml* imbottito di droga / medicine **II** *v/t infml* fissure
eyebath *n* lavaggio *m* oculare **eyebrow** *n* sopracciglio *m*; ***that will raise a few ~s*** *or* ***there will be a few raised ~s*** (***at that***) questo susciterà la sorpresa / il disappunto di diverse persone
eyebrow pencil *n* matita *f* per gli occhi **eyecatching** *adj* appariscente **eye contact** *n*: ***make / avoid ~ with s.o.*** cercare / evitare lo sguardo di qn
-eyed *adj suf* dagli occhi…; ***green-eyed*** con gli occhi verdi
eyedrops *npl* collirio *m*
eyeful *n*: ***get an ~ of sth*** *infml* vedere qc; ***I opened the door and got quite an ~*** ho aperto la porta e ho assistito ad un bello spettacolo; ***an ~*** *infml* (*woman*) una gioia per gli occhi; ***he got an ~ of sand*** gli è andata la sabbia negli occhi
eyeglasses *npl US* occhiali *mpl* **eyelash** *n* ciglio *m* **eyelet** *n* occhiello *m*
eyelevel *adj grill* all'altezza degli occhi **eyelid** *n* palpebra *f* **eyeliner** *n* eyeliner *m inv* **eye-opener** *n*: ***that was a real ~ to me*** mi ha veramente aperto gli occhi **eye patch** *n* benda *f* (per occhi) **eyepiece** *n* oculare *m* **eyeshadow** *n* ombretto *m* **eyesight** *n* vista *f* **eyesore** *n* pugno *m* in un occhio **eye strain** *n* affaticamento *m* della vista **eye test** *n* esame *m* della vista **eyewash** *n fig infml* fandonie *fpl*; (*deception*) fumo *m* negli occhi **eyewitness** *n* testimone *m/f* oculare
e-zine *n* COMPUT rivista *f* elettronica

F

F, f *n* f, F *f inv*; MUS fa *m inv*; EDU (*mark*) gravemente insufficiente *m*; ***F sharp*** fa *m inv* diesis; ***F flat*** fa *m inv* bemolle
f *abbr* (= **feminine**) f (femminile)
F *abbr* (= **Fahrenheit**) F (Fahrenheit)
FA *abbr* (= **Football Association**) *associazione calcistica britannica*
fab *abbr* (= **fabulous**) *infml* fantastico
fable *n* favola *f*
fabled *adj* leggendario
fabric *n* (*material*) tessuto *m*; *of society etc* tessuto *m*; *of building* struttura *f*

fabrication *n* (*lie*) invenzione *f*; ***it's (a) pure ~*** è una pura invenzione;(*production*) fabbricazione *f*
fabulous *adj* fantastico
fabulously *adv* incredibilmente
façade *n of building, person* facciata *f*
face I *n* viso *m*, faccia *f*; *of clock* quadrante *m*; ***~ to ~*** faccia a faccia; ***lose ~*** perdere la faccia; ***in the ~ of*** nonostante; ***on the ~ of it*** a prima vista; ***the changing ~ of politics*** il volto mutevole della politica; ***he/it vanished off the ~ of the earth*** *infml* è scomparso dalla faccia della terra; ***make*** *or* ***pull a ~*** fare una smorfia; ***make*** *or* ***pull ~s/a funny ~*** fare le boccacce (***at s.o.*** a qn); ***put a brave ~ on it*** affrontare la cosa con coraggio **II** *v/t* **1.** *person, the sea etc* essere di fronte a **2.** *facts, truth* affrontare; ***be ~d with*** avere di fronte; ***let's ~ it*** parliamoci chiaro; ***~ the music*** accettare le conseguenze
◆**face up to** *v/t* affrontare
facecloth *n* guanto *m* di spugna **face cream** *n* crema *f* per il viso
faceless *adj fig* senza volto
facelift *n* lifting *m inv* del viso **face pack** *n* maschera *f* di bellezza **face powder** *n* cipria **face-saving** *adj*: ***a ~ measure*** una soluzione per salvare la faccia
facet *n* aspetto *m*
facetious *adj* spiritoso
face value *n* valore *m* nominale; ***take sth at ~*** giudicare qc dalle apparenze
facial I *n* pulizia *f* del viso **II** *adj* facciale; ***~ expression*** espressione del volto
facile *adj pej solution* troppo facile; *remark* superficiale
facilitate *v/t* facilitare
facilities *npl* strutture *fpl*; (*equipment*) attrezzature *fpl*; *transportation* mezzi *mpl*; SPORTS impianto *m*; ***we have no ~ for disposing of toxic waste*** non siamo attrezzati per lo smaltimento dei rifiuti tossici; ***~ for the disabled*** attrezzature *fpl* per i disabili; ***cooking ~*** attrezzatura *f* da cucina; ***toilet ~*** servizi *mpl*; ***credit ~*** agevolazione *f* creditizia
facing I *n* SEW fodera *f*; *building* rivestimento *m* **II** *adj*: ***on the ~ page*** sulla pagina a fronte
facsimile *n* facsimile *m*
fact *n* fatto *m*; ***hard ~s*** verità *f*; ***~s and figures*** fatti e cifre; ***~ and fiction*** realtà e finzione; ***in ~, as a matter of ~*** in realtà; ***be based on ~*** essere basato su eventi reali; ***know sth for a ~*** sapere qc per certo
fact-finding *adj*: ***~ board*** commissione *f* d'inchiesta
faction *n* fazione *f*
factious *adj* fazioso
factitious *adj* fittizio
fact of life *n*: ***that's just a ~*** è la realtà della vita; ***tell s.o. the facts of life*** raccontare a qn come si nascono i bambini; ***know the facts of life*** conoscere le cose della vita (*con riferimento al sesso*)
factor I *n* fattore *m*; ***be a ~ in determining sth*** essere un fattore determinante per qc; ***by a ~ of three*** *etc* per il fattore tre **II** *v/t & v/i* fattorizzare
◆**factor in** *v/t* tenere conto di
factory *n* fabbrica *f*
factory farming *n* allevamento *m* industriale **factory floor** *n* (*workshop*) officina *f*; (*workers*) operai *mpl*
factsheet *n* scheda *f* informativa
factual *adj* basato su fatti; ***~ information*** informazioni fattuali; ***~ error*** errore di fatto; ***the book is largely ~*** il libro si basa fondamentalmente sui fatti
faculty *n* facoltà *f inv*; ***mental faculties*** facoltà *fpl* mentali; ***~ of hearing/sight*** facoltà *f* dell'udito/della vista; ***be in (full) possession of (all) one's faculties*** essere in (pieno) possesso delle proprie facoltà; ***the medical ~*** *or* ***the ~ of medicine*** la facoltà di medicina
fad *n* mania *f* passeggera
fade *v/i of colours* sbiadire; *of light* smorzarsi; *of memories* svanire; (*flower, beauty*) avvizzire; (*sight*) abbassarsi; (*feeling*) scemare; (*hopes*) svanire; (*sound*) affievolirsi; (*radio signal*) attenuarsi; ***hopes are fading of finding any more survivors*** diminuisce la speranza di trovare altri superstiti; ***~ into the background*** (*person*) confondersi sullo sfondo; ***~ to another scene*** RADIO, TV, FILM passare (in dissolvenza) ad un'altra scena
◆**fade away** *v/i* (*sound*) affievolirsi

◆**fade in** *v/t sep* RADIO, TV, FILM aprire in dissolvenza

◆**fade out** *v/t sep* RADIO, TV, FILM chiudere in dissolvenza

faded *adj colour*, sbiadito; *jeans* scolorito; *flowers*, *beauty* appassito

faeces, *US* **feces** *npl form* feci *fpl*

fag *n Br infml* (*cigarette*) sigaretta *f*; *esp US sl* (*homosexual*) frocio *m*

fag end *n Br infml* (*cigarette end*) mozzicone *m* di sigaretta

faggot *n* (*twigs*) fascina *f*; (*meat*) *polpette di carne e interiora*; *esp US sl* (*homosexual*) frocio *m*

Fahrenheit *adj* Fahrenheit

fail **I** *v/i* fallire; (*health*) peggiorare; (*eyesight*) abbassarsi; (*engine*, *brakes*) guastarsi; (*battery*) fermarsi; (*heart*) arrestarsi; **~ *in one's duty*** venire meno al proprio dovere; ***if all else* ~*s*** se tutto il resto non funzionasse; ***the crops* ~*ed*** il raccolto è andato perso; ***he* ~*ed to arrive in time*** non è riuscito ad arrivare in tempo; ***he never* ~*s to write*** non manca mai di scrivere; ***I* ~ *to see why*** non riesco a capire perché **II** *v/t test*, *exam* essere bocciato a; (*let down*) abbandonare; **~ *s.o.*** EDU bocciare qn; ***words* ~ *me*** mi mancano le parole **III** *n*: ***without* ~** con certezza

failing **I** *n* difetto *m* **II** *prep*: **~ *this*/*that*** altrimenti; **~ *which*** se no

failure *n* fallimento *m*; *of generator* interruzione *f*; *of brakes* guasto *m*; ***I feel such a* ~** sono un gran fallito; ***because of his* ~ *to act*** a causa della sua incapacità di agire; ***liver* ~** insufficienza *f* epatica

faint **I** *adj* (*+er*) vago; ***I haven't the* ~*est idea*** non ne ho la più pallida idea; ***I have a* ~ *memory of that day*** ho un vago ricordo di quel giorno; ***your voice is very* ~** *on telephone* ti sento lontano; ***be or feel* ~** MED svenire **II** *v/i* svenire **III** *n* MED ***she fell to the ground in a* ~** è caduta a terra svenuta

faint-hearted *adj* debole di cuore; ***it's not for the* ~** non è per i deboli di cuore

faintly *adv* vagamente; ***the words are just* ~ *visible*** le parole sono poco visibili; ***I could hear the siren* ~** riuscivo appena a sentire la sirena

fair¹ *n* (*fun fair*) luna park *m inv*; COMM fiera *f*

fair² **I** *adj* (*+er*) **1.** *hair* biondo; *complexion* chiaro **2.** (*just*) giusto; ***it's not* ~** non è giusto; ***all's* ~ *in love and war*** in amore e in guerra tutto è permesso **3.** (*considerable*) discreto; ***a* ~ *amount of*** un bel po' di **4.** *assessment*, *idea* ragionevole; ***I've a* ~ *idea that he's going to resign*** ho ragione di credere che darà le dimissioni **5.** *weather* sereno **II** *adv*: ***play* ~** comportarsi correttamente; **~ *enough*** e va bene; ***they beat us* ~ *and square*** ci hanno battuto lealmente

fair copy *n* bella copia *f*; ***write out a* ~ *of sth*** scrivere qc in bella **fair game** *n fig* bersaglio *m* facile

fairground *n* piazzale *m* del luna park

fair-haired *adj* ⟨*comp* **fairer-haired**⟩ biondo

fairly *adv treat* giustamente; (*quite*) piuttosto; ***he speaks Italian* ~ *well*** parla abbastanza bene l'italiano

fair-minded *adj* imparziale

fairness *n of treatment* giustizia *f*; ***in all* ~** in tutta onestà

fair play *n* SPORTS, *fig* fair play *m* **fair trade** *n* commercio *m* equo e solidale; *US* correttezza *f* commerciale

fairway *n golf* fairway *m*

fair-weather friend *n amico che scompare nel momento del bisogno*

fairy *n* fata *f*; *infml pej* checca *f*

fairy godmother *n* fata *f* buona

fairyland *n* regno *m* delle fate

fairy lights *npl* decorazioni *fpl* luminose **fairy story, fairy tale** *n* fiaba *f*, favola *f*

fait accompli *n* fatto *m* compiuto

faith *n* fede *f*; ***have* ~ *in*** aver fiducia in; ***act in good*/*bad* ~** agire in mala/buona fede; (*religion*) fede; ***keep* ~ *with s.o.*** tenere fede a qc

faithful *adj* fedele; *copy* fedele; ***be* ~ *to one's partner*** essere fedele al proprio compagno

faithfully *adv* fedelmente; ***Yours* ~** distinti saluti

faith healer *n* guaritore *m*, -trice *f*

faithless *adj* infedele

fake **I** *n* falso *m*; ***the painting was a* ~** il dipinto era un falso **II** *adj* falso; *banknote*, *painting* falso; **~ *fur*** pelliccia *f* sintetica; ***a* ~ *suntan*** un'abbron-

zatura finta **III** *v/t* (*forge*) falsificare; (*feign*) simulare
falcon *n* falcone *m*
falconer *n* falconiere *m*
falconry *n* falconeria *f*
Falkland Islands *npl*, **Falklands** *npl* Isole Falkland
fall[1] *n US* autunno *m*
fall[2] **I** *v/i* ⟨*pret* **fell**, *past part* **fallen**⟩ **1.** *of person*, *government*, *night* cadere; *of prices*, *temperature* calare **2.** *date etc*: ***it ~s on a Tuesday*** cade di martedì **3.** (*become*) ***~ ill*** ammalarsi; ***~ asleep*** addormentarsi; ***~ in love*** innamorarsi; ***~ into bad habits*** prendere cattive abitudini **4.** (*die*) cadere **II** *n of person*, *government* caduta *f*; ***~ of rain*** rovescio *m* di pioggia; ***there was another heavy ~*** (***of snow***) c'è stata un'altra pesante precipitazione (di neve); (*waterfall*: *a.* **falls**) cascata *f*; ***Niagara Falls*** Cascate del Niagara; *in price*, *temperature* calo *m*
◆**fall about** (*a.* **fall about laughing**) *v/i Br infml* sbellicarsi
◆**fall apart** *v/i object* cadere a pezzi; *organization* andare in sfacelo; *person* crollare; ***I fell apart when he left me*** quando mi ha lasciato sono crollata
◆**fall away** *v/i* (*ground*) digradare; *paint* staccarsi; *feeling* svanire; *Br* (*fall*) diminuire, calare
◆**fall back** *v/i* (*retreat*) arretrare
◆**fall back on** *v/t* ricorrere a
◆**fall behind** *v/i with work*, *studies* rimanere indietro
◆**fall down** *v/i* cadere
◆**fall for** *v/t* (*fall in love with*) innamorarsi di; (*be deceived by*) abboccare a
◆**fall in** *v/i* (*roof*) cedere; (*soldiers*) allinearsi
◆**fall in with** *v/t* (*meet*) incontrare; *bad company* frequentare
◆**fall off** *v/i +obj* staccarsi; *amount* calare, diminuire; ***I nearly fell off my chair*** sono rimasto a bocca aperta
◆**fall on** *v/i +obj* (*trip on*) inciampare; *duty*, *decision*, *task* toccare a; (*blame*) cadere su; (*attack*) assalire; (*food*) avventarsi su; ***the responsibility falls on your shoulders*** le responsabilità ricadono sulle tue spalle
◆**fall out** *v/i of hair* cadere; (*argue*) litigare; ***fall out with s.o.*** litigare con qn
◆**fall over I** *v/i* cadere **II** *v/t* (*trip over*) inciampare; ***they were falling over each other to get the book*** facevano a pugni per prendere il libro; ***fall over o.s. to do sth*** farsi in quattro per fare qc
◆**fall through** *v/i of plans* andare a monte
◆**fall to** *v/i* (*be responsibility of*) spettare; ***fall to doing sth*** cominciare a fare qc
fallacious *adj* fallace
fallacy *n* (*wrong belief*) errata convinzione *f*; (*mistake in argument*) fallacia *f*
fallen *past part* → ***fall***[2]
fall guy *n esp US* (*scapegoat*) capro *m* espiatorio
fallibility *n* fallibilità *f*
fallible *adj* fallibile
falling *adj* diminuito; *membership* in calo
falling-off *n* → ***fall-off*** **falling-out** *n* (*quarrel*) litigio *m* **falling star** *n* stella cadente
fall-off *n* diminuzione *f* **fallout** *n* precipitazione *f*
fallow *adj* a maggese; ***lie ~*** essere a maggese
falls *npl* cascate *fpl*
false *adj* (*+er*) falso; *eyelashes* finto; *papers* falso; ***that's a ~ economy*** è un finto risparmio; ***~ imprisonment*** arresto *m* illegale; ***under*** *or* ***by ~ pretences*** *Br or* ***pretenses*** *US* con false dichiarazioni; ***ring ~*** sembrare falso
false alarm *n* falso allarme *m* **false friend** *n* LING falso amico *m*
falsehood *n* falso *m*; (*lie*) bugia *f*
falsely *adv*: ***be ~ accused of sth*** essere ingiustamente accusato di qc
false move *n fig* mossa *f* falsa **false start** *n in race* falsa partenza *f* **false teeth** *npl* dentiera *f*
falsification *n* falsificazione *f*
falsify *v/t* ⟨*pret & past part* **-ied**⟩ falsificare
falter *v/i* (*lose effectiveness*) dare segni di crisi; (*lose confidence*, *determination*) vacillare
fame *n* fama *f*; ***~ and fortune*** gloria e ricchezza
famed *adj* famoso
familial *adj* familiare

familiar *adj* (*intimate*) intimo; *form of address*, (*well-known*) familiare; ***be ~ with sth*** conoscere bene qc; ***that looks / sounds ~*** ha un'aria familiare; ***his face is ~*** ha un volto familiare; ***are you ~ with these modern techniques?*** hai familiarità con queste tecniche moderne?; ***be on ~ terms with s.o.*** essere in confidenza con qn
familiarise, familiarize *v/t* familiarizzare; ***~ o.s. with …*** familiarizzarsi con …
familiarity *n with subject etc* buona conoscenza *f*
family I *n* famiglia *f*; ***start a ~*** mettere su famiglia; ***has he any ~?*** ha figli?; ***it runs in the ~*** è una caratteristica della famiglia; ***he's one of the ~*** è uno di famiglia **II** *adj* di famiglia; ***~ business*** azienda di famiglia; ***a ~ friend*** un amico di famiglia
family allowance *n* assegno *m* familiare **family business** *n* azienda *f* familiare **family doctor** *n* medico *m* di famiglia **family name** *n* cognome *m* **family planning** *n* pianificazione *f* familiare **family planning clinic** *n* consultorio *m* per la pianificazione familiare **family room** *n esp US in house* soggiorno *m*; *Br sala del pub dove sono ammessi i bambini* **family-size** *adj* in formato famiglia; *packet* confezione *f* famiglia **family tree** *n* albero *m* genealogico **family values** *npl* i valori della famiglia
famine *n* fame *f*
famished *adj infml* affamato
famous *adj* famoso; ***be ~ for …*** essere noto per …
famously *adv* (*notoriously*) notoriamente
fan[1] *n* (*supporter*) fan *m/f*; SPORTS tifoso *m*, -a *f*; ***I'm quite a ~ of yours*** sono un vostro grande tifoso
fan[2] **I** *n for cooling*: *electric* ventilatore *m*; *handheld* ventaglio *m* **II** *v/t* ⟨*pret & past part* **-ned**⟩: ***~ o.s.*** farsi aria; ***~ the flames*** *fig* soffiare sul fuoco
◆ **fan out** *v/i* (*scarchers etc*) disporsi a ventaglio
fanatic *n* fanatico *m*, -a *f*
fanatical *adj* fanatico; ***he is ~ about it*** ne va matto; ***I'm ~ about fitness*** sono un fanatico del fitness
fanaticism *n* fanatismo *m*
fan belt *n* AUTO cinghia *f* della ventola
fanciful *adj idea*, *suggestion* strampalato; ***I think you're being somewhat ~*** credo che ti stia comportando in modo un po' capriccioso
fan club *n* fan club *m inv*
fancy I *v/t* ⟨*pret & past part* **-ied**⟩ *infml* avere voglia di; ***do you ~ a beer / a walk?*** ti va di fare una passeggiata? / ti va una birra?; (*like*) ***I'm sure he fancies you*** sono sicuro che gli piaci ***I ~ that car*** mi piace quella macchina; ***he fancies a house on Crete*** vorrebbe una casa a Creta; ***I didn't ~ that job*** non mi piaceva quel lavoro; *surprise* ***~ seeing you here!*** che combinazione vederti qua!; ***~ that!*** *infml* pensa un po'; ***~ him winning!*** chi avrebbe pensato che vinceva lui; (*flatter oneself*) ***he fancies himself as an expert*** si crede un esperto **II** *n*: ***as the ~ takes you*** quanto ti va; ***take a ~ to s.o.*** prendere a benvolere qn **III** *adj* (*+er*) *design* stravagante; *infml clothes* costoso; *hairdo* ricercato; *food* elaborato; ***nothing ~*** niente di speciale
fancy dress *n* costume *m* **fancy-dress party** *n* festa *f* in maschera **fancy-free** *adj* senza legami **fancy goods** *npl* articoli *mpl* vari **fancy man** *n pej* amante *m* **fancy woman** *n pej* amante *f*
fanfare *n* fanfara *f*; *fig* clamore *m*
fang *n* dente *m* aguzzo
fan heater *n* termoventilatore *m*
fanlight *n* ARCH lunetta *f* a ventaglio
fan mail *n* lettere *fpl* dei fans
fanny *n esp US infml* culo *m vulg*; *Br sl* fica *f vulg*
fanny pack *n US* SEW marsupio *m*
fantasize *v/i* fantasticare; ***~ about*** fantasticare su
fantastic *adj* (*very good*) fantastico; (*very big*) enorme; ***a ~ amount of*** *or* ***~ amounts of*** una montagna di *or* montagne di
fantastically *adv* (*extremely*) incredibilmente
fantasy *n* fantasia *f*
fanzine *n* fanzine *f*
FAO *abbr* (= **Food and Agriculture Organisation**) FAO *f*
FAQ *n abbr* (= **frequently asked questions**) COMPUT FAQ (*domande poste più frequentemente*)

far ⟨*comp* ***further, farther***, *sup* ***furthest, farthest***⟩ **I** *adv* **1.** lontano; ***~ away*** lontano; ***how ~ is it to …?*** quanto dista …?; ***~ from*** lontano da ***as ~ as the corner/hotel*** fino all'angolo/hotel; ***~ and wide*** in lungo e in largo; ***as ~ as I can see*** per quanto posso vedere; ***as ~ as I know*** per quanto ne so; ***by ~, ~ and away*** di gran lunga; ***you've gone too ~*** *in behaviour* sei andato troppo oltre; ***how ~ has he got with the project?*** a che punto è col progetto?; ***so ~ so good*** fin qui tutto bene; ***~ from satisfactory*** lungi dall'essere soddisfacente; ***~ from liking him I find him quite unpleasant*** lungi dal piacermi, lo trovo molto piacevole; ***~ from it!*** tutt'altro!; ***~ be it from me to …*** lungi da me…; ***so ~*** (*up to now*) finora; (*up to this point*) fino a questo punto; ***so ~ so good*** fin qui tutto bene; ***go ~*** (*supplies etc*) bastare; (*person succeed*) spingersi; ***I would go so ~ as to say …*** non arrivere a dire altro che…; ***not ~ off*** *in space* non distante; *in guess, aim* non lontano; ***the weekend isn't ~ off now*** non manca molto al weekend **2.** (*much*) molto; ***~ bigger/faster*** molto più grande/veloce; ***you're ~ too young*** sei decisamente troppo giovane **II** *adj*: ***at the ~ end of*** all'altro capo di; ***the ~ door*** la porta più lontana; ***on the ~ side of*** sull'altro lato del; ***in the ~ distance*** in lontananza; ***it's a ~ cry from …*** *fig* è molto lontano da…

faraway, far-away *adj place* remoto; *country* lontano; *sound* distante; *look* assente

farce *n* farsa *f*

farcical *adj fig* farsesco

fare I *n for travel* tariffa *f*; (*food*) cibo *m*; ***traditional Christmas ~*** cibo *m* tradizionale di Natale **II** *v/i*: ***he ~d well*** se l'è passata bene; ***the dollar ~d well on the stock exchange*** il dollaro è andato bene in borsa

Far East *n* Estremo Oriente *m*

farewell *n* addio *m*

farewell party *n* festa *f* d'addio

far-fetched *adj* inverosimile

far-flung *adj* (*distant*) molto lontano; (*spread out*) diffuso

farm I *n* fattoria *f*; (*bigger*) tenuta *f*; ***chicken ~*** allevamento *m* di polli **II** *adj* agricolo; ***~ labourer*** *Br or* ***laborer*** *US* lavoratore *m* agricolo; ***~ animals*** animali di allevamento **III** *v/t land* coltivare; *livestock* allevare **IV** *v/i* fare l'agricoltore

◆**farm out** *v/t sep work* dare in appalto (***on, to*** a); (*child*) affidare

farmer *n* agricoltore *m*, -trice *f*

farmers' market *n* mercato *m* agricolo

farmhand *n* bracciante *m/f* agricolo,-a

farmhouse *n* casa *f* colonica

farming *n* agricoltura *f*

farmland *n* terreno *m* coltivato **farmstead** *n* fattoria *f* **farmworker** *n* bracciante *m/f* **farmyard** *n* aia *f*

far-off *adj* lontano

far-reaching *adj* di ampia portata

farsighted *adj* previdente; *US* presbite

fart I *n infml* scoreggia *f infml*, peto *m*; ***he's a boring old ~*** *infml* è un pezzo di cretino **II** *v/i infml* scoreggiare *infml*, petare

farther *comp* → ***far*** **I** *adv* → ***further*** **II** *adj* più lontano; ***at the ~ end*** all'altro capo

farthest *adj/adv sup* → ***far***; ***the ~ point of the island*** il punto più lontano dell'isola

farthing *n Br antica moneta del valore di un quarto di penny*; ***not worth a ~*** non vale una lira

fascinate *v/t* affascinare; ***I always was ~d by the idea of …*** mi ha sempre affascinato l'idea di …

fascinating *adj* affascinante

fascination *n with subject* fascino *m*; ***watch in ~*** guardare affascinato; ***his ~ with the cinema*** la sua passione per il cinema

fascism *n* fascismo *m*

fascist I *n* fascista *m/f* **II** *adj* fascista

fashion I *n* moda *f*; (*manner*) maniera *f*, modo *m*; ***in the usual ~*** al solito modo; ***in ~*** alla moda; ***out of ~*** fuori moda; ***it's all the ~*** è molto di moda; ***she always wears the latest ~s*** si veste sempre all'ultima moda; ***after a ~*** più o meno **II** *v/t* forgiare; (*make*) fare

fashionable *adj* alla moda

fashionably *adv dressed* alla moda

fashion-conscious *adj* fanatico della moda **fashion designer** *n* stilista *m/f*

fashion magazine *n* rivista *f* di moda
fashion parade *n* sfilata *f* di moda
fashion show *n* sfilata *f* di moda
fashion victim *n pej infml* schiavo *m*, -a *f* della moda
fast[1] **I** *adj* (+*er*) veloce, rapido; *dye* che non stinge; ***she's a ~ runner*** corre veloce; ***pull a ~ one (on s.o.)*** *infml* giocare un brutto tiro (a qn); ***be ~*** *of clock* essere avanti **II** *adv* velocemente; ***stuck ~*** fissato saldamente; ***~ asleep*** profondamente addormentato
fast[2] **I** *v/i* (*not eat*) digiunare **II** *n not eating* digiuno *m*
fast-breeder reactor *n* reattore *m* autofertilizzante veloce
fast buck *n infml* soldi *mpl* facili; ***make a ~*** fare soldi velocemente
fasten I *v/t* chiudere; *dress, seat-belt* allacciare; ***~ sth onto sth*** attaccare qc a qc; *brooch* appuntare qc su qc **II** *v/i of dress etc* allacciarsi
◆**fasten on** *v/t sep* tenersi stretto (***to*** a)
◆**fasten up** *v/t sep dress etc* abbottonare; *strings* allacciare
fastener *n* chiusura *f*
fast food *n* fast food *m inv* **fastfood restaurant** *n* fast food *m inv* **fast forward I** *n on video etc* riavvolgimento *m* rapido **II** *v/i* riavvolgere rapidamente
fastidious *adj* pignolo
fast lane *n on road* corsia *f* di sorpasso; *fig* ***in the ~*** *of life* a cento all'ora **fast talk** *n infml* raggiro *m*; ***his ~ left me cold*** i suoi discorsi da ciarlatano non mi hanno fatto né caldo né freddo **fast-track** *adj process, procedure* preferenziale **fast train** *n* rapido *m*
fat I *adj* (+*er*) grasso; ***get*** *or* ***become ~*** ingrassare; ***that's a ~ lot of good*** *infml iron* questo sì che ci serve; ***~ lot of help she was*** c'è stata di grande aiuto; ***~ chance!*** impossibile! **II** *n* grasso *m*; ***reduce the ~ in your diet*** riduci i grassi nella tua dita; ***chew the ~*** *infml* fare quattro chiacchiere
fatal *adj* fatale; ***he had a ~ accident*** ha avuto un incidente fatale; ***be prove ~ to*** *or* ***for s.o. / sth*** rivelarsi fatale per qn / qc; ***it would be ~ to do that*** farlo sarebbe un errore fatale
fatalism *n* fatalismo
fatalistic *adj* fatalistico
fatality *n* fatalità *f inv*
fatally *adv*: ***~ injured*** ferito a morte
fat cat *n infml* pezzo *m* grosso
fate *n* fato *m*
fated *adj*: ***be ~ to do sth*** essere destinato a fare qc; ***they were ~ never to meet again*** erano destinati a non incontrarsi mai più
fateful *adj* fatidico
fatfree *adj* privo di grassi
fathead *n infml* zuccone *m*, -a *f*
father I *n* padre *m*; ***like ~ like son*** tale padre, tale figlio; ***Father Martin*** REL padre Martin; ***~s*** (*ancestors*) i padri **II** *v/t child etc* generare
Father Christmas *n* Babbo *m* Natale
father figure *n* figura *f* paterna
fatherhood *n* paternità *f*
father-in-law *n* ⟨*pl* ***fathers-in-law***⟩ suocero *m*
fatherland *n* patria *f*
fatherly *adj* paterno
fathom *n* NAUT fathom *m inv*
◆**fathom out** *v/t fig* spiegarsi; ***I just can't fathom you out*** proprio non ti capisco
fatigue *n* stanchezza *f*; TECH (*metal fatigue*) fatica *f*; ***~s*** *pl* MIL uniforme *f*
fatso *n infml* ciccione *m*, -a *f infml*
fat stock *n* bestiame *m* da macello
fatten *v/t animal* ingrassare
fattening *adj* ingrassante; ***chocolate is ~*** la cioccolata da ingrassare
fatty I *adj* (+*er*) grasso **II** *n infml person* ciccione *m*, -a *f infml*
fatuous *adj form* sciocco
faucet *n US* rubinetto *m*
fault I *n* (*defect*) difetto *m*; ***it's your / my ~*** è colpa tua / mia; ***find ~ with*** criticare; ***be at ~*** avere torto; GEOL faglia *f* **II** *v/t*: ***I can't ~ him*** non posso biasimarlo
fault-finding I *adj* che critica tutto **II** *n* rilevazione *f* dei guasti
faultless *adj person, performance* impeccabile
fault line *n* GEOL linea *f* di faglia
faulty *adj* (+*er*) *goods* difettoso
fauna *n form* fauna *f*
faux pas *n* passo *m* falso
fava bean *n US* fava *f*
favor *etc US* → ***favour*** *etc*
favour, *US* **favor I** *n* **1.** favore *m*; ***do s.o. a ~*** fare un favore a qn; ***do me***

a ~! (*don't be stupid*) fammi il piacere!; ***ask s.o. a ~, ask a ~ of s.o.*** chiedere un favore a qn **2.** *fig* ***in ~ of …*** a favore di …; ***be in ~ of …*** essere a favore di …; ***a point in his ~*** un punto a suo favore; ***the judge ruled in his ~*** il giudice ha espresso una sentenza a suo favore; ***all those in ~ raise their hands*** tutti quelli a favore alzino la mano; ***he rejected socialism in ~ of the market economy*** ha rinnegato il socialismo a favore dell'economia di mercato **II** *v/t* (*prefer*) preferire, prediligere

favourable, *US* **favorable** *adj reply etc* favorevole; ***her request met with a ~ response*** la sua richiesta ha avuto una risposta favorevole; (*beneficial*) propizio (***to*** per); *comparison* vantaggioso; ***show sth in a ~ light*** mostrare qc sotto una luce favorevole; ***on ~ terms*** in termini vantaggiosi; ***conditions are ~ for development*** le condizioni sono propizie per lo sviluppo

favourably, *US* **favorably** *adv respond* favorevolmente; *receive, think* di buon occhio; (*advantageously*) vantaggiosamente; ***he was ~ impressed by it*** ne è stato favorevolmente colpito; ***be ~ disposed*** *or* ***inclined to(wards) s.o./sth*** vedere qn/qc di buon occhio; ***compare ~*** reggere il paragone

-favoured *adj* favorito; ***well ~*** privilegiato; ***ill~*** sfavorito

favourite, *US* **favorite I** *n* prediletto *m*, -a *f*; (*food*) piatto *m* preferito; *in race, competition* favorito *m*, -a *f* **II** *adj* preferito

favouritism, *US* **favoritism** *n* favoritismo *m*

fawn[1] **I** *n* (*animal*) cerbiatto *m* **II** *adj* (*brown*) fulvo chiaro

fawn[2] *v/i fig* adulare; *dog* fare le feste

◆**fawn on** *v/t* comportarsi in modo servile con

fax I *n* fax *m inv*; ***send sth by ~*** inviare qc per fax **II** *v/t* inviare per fax; ***~ sth to s.o.*** inviare qc per fax a qc

fax machine *n* → ***fax***

fax number *n* numero *m* di fax

faze *v/t infml* lasciare di stucco; ***the question didn't ~ me at all*** la domanda non mi ha affatto impressionato

FBI *abbr* (= **Federal Bureau of Investigation**) FBI *f*

FC *abbr* (= **football club**) *Br* AC (Associazione Calcistica)

FDA *abbr* (= **Food and Drug Administration**) FDA *f*

fear I *n* paura *f*; ***~ of failure/flying*** paura di sbagliare/volare; ***there are ~s that …*** si teme che…; ***be in ~ of s.o./sth*** avere timore di qn/qc; ***she talked quietly for ~ of waking the baby*** parlava a bassa voce per paura di svegliare il bambino; ***no ~!*** *infml* non c'è pericolo; ***there's no ~ of that happening again*** non c'è pericolo che succeda di nuovo **II** *v/t* avere paura di; ***he's a man to be ~ed*** è un uomo di cui avere paura; ***many women ~ to go out at night*** molte donne hanno paura di uscire di sera **III** *v/i*: ***~ for*** avere paura per; ***never ~!*** niente paura!

fearful *adj* (*afraid*) timoroso; (*awful*) tremendo; *liter* (*terrifying*) spaventoso; ***be ~ of s.o./sth*** temere qn/qc; ***be ~ that*** temere che

fearless *adj* intrepido

fearlessly *adv* intrepidamente

fearsome *adj* pauroso

feasibility study *n* studio *m* di fattibilità

feasible *adj* fattibile; (*plausible*) plausibile

feast I *n* banchetto *m*; ***a ~ for the eyes*** un piacere per gli occhi; REL festa *f*; ***~ day*** giorno *m* di festa **II** *v/i* banchettare **III** *v/t*: ***~ one's eyes on s.o./sth*** rifarsi gli occhi con qn/qc

◆**feast on** *v/t* banchettare con

feat *n* prodezza *f*

feather I *n* piuma *f*; ***as light as a ~*** leggero come una piuma; ***they are birds of a ~*** Dio li fa e poi li accoppia **II** *v/t* ornare di piume; NAUT spalare; *fig* ***he ~ed his nest when they were in power*** quando erano al potere si sono arricchiti in modo disonesto

feature I *n on face* tratto *m*; *of city, building, plan, style* caratteristica *f*; *in paper* servizio *m*; (*film*) lungometraggio *m*; ***make a ~ of …*** mettere l'accento su … **II** *v/t of film* avere come protagonista; ***the album ~s their latest hit single*** l'album contiene il loro ultimo singolo **III** *v/i* (*occur*) presentarsi; ***the story ~d on all today's front pages*** la storia che appare sulle prime pagine di tutti i giornali

feature film *n* lungometraggio *m* **feature-length** *adj*: ***~ film*** lungometraggio *m*

featureless *adj* scialbo

Feb. *abbr* (= **February**) feb. (febbraio)

February *n* febbraio *m*

feces *US* → ***faeces***

feckless *adj* inetto

fecund *adj* fecondo

fecundate *v/t* fecondare

fecundity *n* fecondità *f*

fed *pret & past part* → ***feed***

Fed *n US* (agente) federale *m/f*

federal *adj* federale

Federal Bureau of Investigation *n* Ufficio *m* investigativo federale, FBI *f*

federalism *n* federalismo *m*

federation *n* federazione *f*

fed up *adj infml* stufo *infml*; ***be ~ with ...*** essere stufo di ...

fee *n* tariffa *f*; *of lawyer, doctor etc* onorario *m*; (***school***) ***~s*** tasse scolastiche

feeble *adj* (*+er*) debole

feeble-minded *adj* (*stupid*) stupido; (*retarded*) ritardato

feeble-mindedness *n* (*stupidity*) stupidità *f*; (*being retarded*) ritardo *m* mentale

feebly *adv* fiaccamente; *smile* debolmente; *say* in modo poco convincente

feed I *n* (*meal*) pasto *m*; *of baby* poppata *f*; *of animals* mangime *m*; TECH, COMPUT alimentazione *f*; ***when is the baby's next ~?*** a che ora è la prossima poppata del bambino? **II** *v/t* ⟨*pret & past part* **fed**⟩ nutrire; *family* mantenere; *baby* dare da mangiare a **III** *v/i* (*animal*) mangiare; (*baby*) prendere il latte

◆**feed in** *v/t sep wire etc* introdurre; *information* inserire

◆**feed on** *v/t* nutrirsi di

feedback *n* riscontro *m*, feedback *m inv*

feeding-bottle *n* biberon *m inv* **feeding time** *n for animal* ora *f* del pasto; *for baby* ora *f* della poppata

feel ⟨*pret & past part* **felt**⟩ **I** *v/t* **1.** (*touch*) toccare **2.** (*sense*) sentire; *pain, pleasure, sensation* sentire **3.** (*think*) pensare; ***~ that*** pensare che **II** *v/i* **1.** *person* sentirsi; ***I ~ hungry*** ho fame; ***I ~ tired*** sono stanco; ***how are you ~ing today?*** come ti senti oggi?; ***I ~ ill*** mi sento male **2.** *material, things*: ***it ~s like silk/cotton*** sembra seta/cotone al tatto; ***your hand ~s hot/cold*** la tua mano è calda/fredda; ***how does it ~ to be rich?*** che sensazione fa essere ricchi? **3.** (*think*) ***how do you ~ about it?*** cosa ne pensi? **4.** ***do you ~ like a drink/meal?*** hai voglia di bere/mangiare qualcosa?; ***I ~ like going/staying*** ho voglia di andare/rimanere; ***I don't ~ like it*** non ne ho voglia **III** *n*: ***let me have a ~!*** fammi toccare!; ***it has a papery ~*** ti dà la sensazione della carta; ***the room has a cosy ~*** la camera ha un'atmosfera intima; *fig* ***get a ~ for sth*** prendere la mano con qc

◆**feel for** *v/t* (*sympathize with*) provare compassione; (*search for*) cercare a tastoni; *in pocket etc* palpare; ***I feel for you*** ti compatisco

◆**feel up to** *v/t* sentirsi in grado di

feeler *n of insect* antenna *f*

feelgood factor *n* fattore *m* tranquillizzante

feeling *n* sentimento *m*;(*emotion*) sensazione *f*; (*sensation*) sensibilità *f*; ***what are your ~s about it?*** quali sono le tue impressioni in proposito?; ***have ~s for s.o.*** provare qualcosa per qn; ***it's a great ~ when ...*** è una grande emozione ...; ***no hard ~s?*** senza rancore?; ***I have mixed ~s about him*** ho sensazioni contrastanti nei suoi riguardi; ***I have this ~ that ...*** ho la sensazione che ...; ***~s were running high*** l'atmosfera si stava surriscaldando; ***I know the ~*** so cosa stai provando

fee-paying *adj school* a pagamento; *student, patient* pagante

feet *pl* → ***foot***

feign *v/t form* fingere; ***~ illness*** fingersi ammalato

feigned *adj* simulato

feisty *adj* (*+er*) aggressivo

felicitate *v/t* felicitarsi con

felicitation *n* felicitazione *f*

felicitous *adj* felice
felicity *n* (*happiness*) felicità *f*; (*suitability*) appropriatezza *f*
feline *adj* felino
fell[1] *pret* → ***fall***[2]
fell[2] *v/t tree* abbattere; *person* atterrare
fella, feller *n infml* tizio *m*
fellatio *n* fellatio *f*
fellow I *n* (*man*) tipo *m*; *US* UNIV assegnista *m/f* di ricerca; *Br of a society* membro *m*; ***poor ~!*** poveretto!; ***this journalist ~*** questo tale che fa il giornalista **II** *adj*: ***our ~ bankers/doctors*** i nostri colleghi banchieri/dottori; ***~ student*** compagno *m* di corso; ***~ member*** *in club* consocio *m*; ***~ sufferer*** compagno *m* di sofferenza; ***~ worker*** collega *m* di lavoro; ***he is a ~ lexicographer*** è un collega lessicografo; ***my ~ Americans...*** i miei concittadini americani…
fellow citizen *n* concittadino *m*, -a *f* **fellow countryman** *n* compatriota *m/f* **fellow man** *n* prossimo *m*
fellowship *n* (*friendship*) cameratismo *m*; (*group*) compagnia *f*; (*academic position*) *carica universitaria di alto livello*; (*academic grant*) borsa *f* di ricerca
fellow traveller, *US* **fellow traveler** *n liter* compagno *m*, -a *f* di viaggio
felon *n* criminale *m/f*
felony *n US* delitto *m*
felt[1] *n* feltro *m*
felt[2] *pret & past part* → ***feel***
felt tip, felt-tip(ped) pen *n* pennarello *m*
female I *adj* femmina; *typical of women* femminile; ***a ~ doctor*** una dottoressa; ***a ~ companion*** una compagna; ***a ~ football team*** una squadra di calcio femminile **II** *n* femmina *f*; *infml* (*woman*) donna *f*
feminine I *adj* femminile **II** *n* GRAM femminile *m*
feminine hygiene *n* igiene *f* (intima) femminile; ***~ products*** prodotti per l'igiene intima femminile
femininity *n* femminilità *f*
feminism *n* femminismo *m*
feminist I *n* femminista *f* **II** *adj* femminista; ***the ~ movement*** il movimento femminista
femur *n* femore *m*
fence I *n round garden etc* recinto *m*; SPORTS ostacolo *m*; *infml criminal* ricettatore *m*, -trice *f*; ***sit on the ~*** non prendere partito **II** *v/i* SPORTS tirare di scherma
◆**fence in** *v/t sep land* recintare
◆**fence off** *v/t sep* recintare
fenced community *n* quartiere *m* recintato
fencing *n* SPORTS scherma *f*
fend *v/i*: ***~ for o.s.*** badare a se stesso
◆**fend off** *v/t sep attacker, criticism* respingere; *questions* eludere
fender *n in front of fire* parafuoco *m*; *US on vehicle* parafango *m*
fennel *n* BOT finocchio *m*
ferment[1] *v/i of liquid* fermentare
ferment[2] *n* (*unrest*) fermento *m*
fermentation *n* fermentazione *f*
fern *n* felce *f*
ferocious *adj* feroce
ferociously *adv fight, argue* ferocemente
ferocity *n of animal* ferocia *f*; (*cruelty*) crudeltà *f*
ferret *n* furetto *m*
◆**ferret around, ferret about** *v/i* frugare
◆**ferret out** *v/t sep Br infml* scovare
Ferris wheel *n* ruota *f* panoramica
ferrous *adj* ferroso
ferrule *n* TECH ghiera *f*
ferry I *n* traghetto *m* **II** *v/t* (*a.* **ferry across** *or* **over**) (*by boat*) traghettare; (*by car etc*) portare; ***~ s.o. across a river*** traghettare qn dall'altro lato del fiume; ***~ s.o./sth back and forth*** portare qn avanti e indietro
fertile *adj* fertile; ***this is ~ ground for racists/ethnic hatred*** questo è terreno fertile per l'odio razzista/etnico
fertilise, fertilize *v/t ovum* fecondare
fertiliser, fertilizer *n for soil* fertilizzante *m*
fertility *n* fertilità *f*
fertility drug *n* cura *f* per sviluppare la fertilità **fertility rate** *n* tasso *m* di fertilità
fervent *adj admirer* fervente
fervently *adv* ardentemente
fervid *adj* fervido
fervour, *US* **fervor** *n* fervore *m*
fester *v/i of wound* fare infezione
festival *n* festival *m inv*
festive *adj* festivo; ***the ~ season*** le festività

festivities *npl* festeggiamenti *mpl*
festivity *n* (*celebration*) celebrazione *f*
festoon *v/t*: ***~ sth with sth*** decorare qc con festoni fatti di qc; ***be ~ed with sth*** essere decorato con qc
fetal *adj US* → ***foetal***
fetch **I** *v/t* (*go and fetch*) andare a prendere; (*come and fetch*) venire a prendere; *thing* prendere; *price* rendere **II** *v/i*: ***~ and carry for s.o.*** fare lavoretti per qn
fetching *adj* seducente
fête **I** *n* festa *f* **II** *v/t* festeggiare; ***he was ~d for his accomplishment*** è stato festeggiato per i suoi risultati
fetid, foetid *adj* fetido
fetish *n* feticismo *m*; ***have a ~ for leather / cleanliness*** avere una mania per la pelle / pulizia
fetter **I** *n* catena *f*; ***~s*** *pl* i ferri **II** *v/t* incatenare
fettle *n* condizione *f*; ***be in fine ~*** essere in buona forma
fetus *n US* → ***foetus***
feud **I** *n* faida *f* **II** *v/i* litigare
feudal *adj* feudale; ***~ system*** sistema *m* feudale
feudalism *n* feudalesimo *m*
fever *n* febbre *f*; ***election ~*** febbre da elezioni; ***a ~ of excitement*** un eccitamento febbrile
feverish *adj a. fig* febbrile; ***I'm feeling ~*** mi sento la febbre
feverishly *adv work*, *try* febbrilmente
fever pitch *n*: ***reach ~*** raggiungere il colmo dell'eccitazione
few **I** *adj* (+*er*) (*not many*) pochi; ***~ people come to see him*** in pochi sono venuti a vederlo; ***~ and far between*** rarissimi; ***as ~ as ten cigarettes a day*** solo dieci sigarette al giorno; ***there were 3 too ~*** ne mancavano tre; ***he is one of the ~ people who ...*** è una delle poche persone che…; ***a ~ ...*** alcuni …; ***a ~ people*** alcune persone, qualche persona; ***a ~ books*** alcuni libri, qualche libro; ***every ~ days*** ogni due o tre giorni; ***quite a ~, a good ~*** (*a lot*) parecchi **II** *pron* (*not many*) pochi; ***a ~*** (*some*) alcuni; ***quite a ~, a good ~*** (*a lot*) parecchi
fewer *adj* meno; ***~ than ...*** meno di …
fiancé *n* fidanzato *m*
fiancée *n* fidanzata *f*
fiasco *n* fiasco *m*
fib **I** *n* frottola *f*; ***don't tell ~s*** non raccontare balle **II** *v/i* ⟨*pret & past part* ***-bed***⟩ raccontare frottole
fiber *US* → ***fibre***
fibre, *US* **fiber** *n* fibra *f*
fibreglass, *US* **fiberglass** *n* fibra *f* di vetro **fibre optic**, *US* **fiber optic** *adj* fibra *f* ottica **fibre optics**, *US* **fiber optics** *n* tecnologia *f* delle fibre ottiche
fibroid *n* MED fibroide *m*
fibrous *adj* fibroso
fibula *n* MED perone *m*
fickle *adj* incostante
fiction *n* (*novels*) LIT narrativa *f*; (*made-up story*) storia *f*; ***that's pure ~*** è pura invenzione
fictional *adj* immaginario
fictitious *adj* fittizio
fictive *adj US* fittizio
fiddle **I** *n infml* (*violin*) violino *m*; ***it's a ~*** *infml* (*cheat*) è una fregatura *infml* **II** *v/i*: ***~ with ...*** giocherellare con …; ***~ around with ...*** trafficare con … **III** *v/t accounts*, *results* truccare; ***he ~d it so that ...*** l'ha truccato in modo che…
◆**fiddle about** *Br or* **around** *v/i*: ***fiddle about*** *or* ***around with sth*** perdere tempo con qc; (*fidget with*) giocherellare nervosamente
fiddle-de-dee *int* sciocchezze **fiddle-faddle** **I** *int* schiocchezze **II** *n* dire sciocchezze
fiddler *n* MUS *infml* violinista *m/f*
fiddlesticks *int* sciocchezze
fiddling *adj* insignificante
fiddly *adj* (+*er*) *infml* complicato
fidelity *n* fedeltà *f*
fidget *v/i* agitarsi
fidgety *adj* in agitazione; ***get ~*** mettersi in agitazione
field **I** *n* campo *m*; ***potato ~*** campo *m* di patate; ***in the ~s*** nei campi; ***~ of battle*** campo *m* di battaglia; ***~ of vision*** campo *m* visivo; ***sports*** *or* ***games ~*** campo sportivo *or* di gioco; (*competitors in race*) formazione *f*; ***that's not my ~*** non è il mio campo; ***work in the ~*** lavorare nel campo; COMPUT campo **II** *v/t ball* prendere e rilanciare; *fig question etc* parare; ***he had to ~ calls from customers*** ha dovuto parare le chiamate dei

clienti; *team* mettere in campo; POL *candidate* presentare **III** *v/i baseball etc* giocare in ricezione

field day *n fig* ***have a ~*** andare a nozze

fielder *n in cricket* esterno *m*

field events *npl* atletica *f* leggera (escluse le specialità su pista) **field glasses** *npl* binocolo *m* da campagna **field study** *n* ricerca *f* sul campo **field trip** *n* gita *f* didattica

fiend *n form* (*evil being*) mostro *m*; *infml* (*enthusiast*) fanatico *m*, -a *f*; ***tennis ~*** fanatico del tennis

fiendish *adj plan, grin* diabolico; *question, exam* difficile; ***he took a ~ delight in doing it*** ha provato un piacere perverso nel farlo

fiendishly *adv infml difficult* diabolicamente

fierce *adj* (+*er*) *animal* feroce; *wind, storm* violento; ***he has a ~ temper*** ha un carattere focoso

fiercely *adv* ferocemente; ***say sth ~*** dire qc in tono aggressivo; ***the fire was burning ~*** il fuoco bruciava ardentemente

fiery *adj* (+*er*) *personality, temper* focoso

FIFA *abbr* (= **Federation of International Football Associations**) FIFA *f* (federazione calcistica internazionale)

fifteen *num* quindici

fifteenth *n/adj* quindicesimo, -a

fifth I *n/adj* quinto, -a **II** *n* (*part, fraction*) quinto *m*; MUS quinta *f*

fifthly *adv* al quinto posto

fiftieth *n/adj* cinquantesimo, -a

fifty *num* cinquanta

fifty-fifty *adv* metà e metà; ***go ~ with s.o.*** fare a metà con qn

fig *n* fico *m*

fig. *abbr* (= **figure(s)**) fig. (figura, -e)

fight I *v/t* ⟨*pret & past part* ***fought***⟩ (*brawl*) azzuffare; *in war* combattere; *in boxing* battersi contro; *disease, injustice* combattere; ***~ a duel*** combattere un duello; ***~ one's way through the crowd*** farsi largo tra la folla **II** *v/i* ⟨*pret & past part* ***fought***⟩ *in war* combattere; *of drunks, schoolkids* azzuffarsi; (*argue*) litigare; ***~ over*** *or* ***about*** litigare per; ***~ against disease*** lottare contro una mallatia; ***~ for s.o. / sth*** lottare per qn / qc; ***~ for breath*** respirare a fatica **III** *n* lotta *f*; *in war* combattimento *m*; (*argument*) litigio *m*; *in boxing* incontro *m*; ***the ~ for survival*** la lotta per la sopravvivenza; ***there was no ~ left in him*** non aveva più voglia di lottare

◆**fight against** *v/t enemy, opponent* combattere contro; *injustice, racism* lottare contro

◆**fight back I** *v/i* (*retaliate*) contrattaccare; (*defend o.s.*) difendersi **II** *v/t sep tears* trattenere

◆**fight for** *v/t one's rights, a cause* lottare per

◆**fight off** *v/t sep attacker* respingere; *illness* lottare contro

◆**fight out** *v/t sep* ***fight it out*** vedersela

fighter *n* combattente *m/f*; *aeroplane* caccia *m inv*; (*boxer*) pugile *m*; ***she's a ~*** è combattiva

fighter pilot *n* pilota *m/f* da caccia

fighting *n* risse *fpl*; ***he's always in trouble for ~*** è sempre nei guai perché scatena risse

fighting chance *n*: ***he's in with a ~*** ha una possibilità di essere ammesso **fighting fit** *adj Br infml* in gran forma **fighting spirit** *n* spirito *m* combattivo

fig leaf *n* foglia *f* di fico

figment *n*: ***a ~ of his imagination*** frutto della sua immaginazione

figurative *adj use of word* figurato; ART figurativo

figuratively *adv* in senso figurato

figure I *n* (*digit*) cifra *f*; *of person* linea *f*; ***lose one's ~*** perdere la linea; (*form, shape*) figura *f*; ***~*** (***of***) ***eight*** otto; nodo *m* sabaudo; ***she's a fine ~ of a woman*** ha una figura perfetta; (*human form*) figura *f*; (*personality*) personaggio *m*; ***the great ~s of history*** le grandi figure della storia; ***a key public ~*** un personaggio pubblico importante; ***~ of fun*** un tipo ridicolo; LIT ***~ of speech*** figura retorica; ***it's just a ~ of speech*** è solo un modo di dire **II** *v/t esp US* (*think*) pensare; *US* (*figure out*) immaginare **III** *v/i* (*appear*) figurare; ***he ~d prominently in my plans*** aveva un posto preminente nei miei progetti; *infml* ***that ~s*** (la cosa) quadra

◆**figure out** *v/t sep* (*understand*) capire; *calculation* calcolare

figurehead *n* prestanome *m*
figure of speech *n* figura *f* retorica
figure skater *n* pattinatore *m*, -trice *f* artistico, -a **figure skating** *n* pattinaggio *m* artistico
figurine *n* statuetta *f*
filament *n* ELEC filamento *m*
filch *v/t* rubacchiare
file[1] **I** *n for papers* raccoglitore *m*; *contents* dossier *m inv*, pratica *f*; COMPUT file *m inv*; ***on ~*** in archivio; ***it's in the ~s somewhere*** è da qualche parte negli schedari; ***have we got that on ~?*** ce l'abbiamo in archivio?; ***open** or **start a ~ on s.o. / sth*** aprire un dossier su qn / qc; ***keep s.o. / sth on ~*** tenere un dossier su qn / qc **II** *v/t documents* schedare; PRESS *report* inviare; JUR *complaint* presentare (un reclamo); (*law*)*suit* intentare (una causa) **III** *v/i*: ***~ for divorce*** presentare istanza di divorzio; ***~ for bankruptcy*** presentare istanza di fallimento
◆**file away** *v/t sep documents* archiviare
file[2] **I** *n for wood*, *fingernails* lima *f* **II** *v/t* limare; ***~ one's nails*** limarsi le unghie
file[3] **I** *n* (*row*) fila *f*; ***in single ~*** in fila indiana **II** *v/i*: ***~ in*** entrare in fila; ***they ~d out of the classroom*** uscirono dalla classe in fila; ***the troops ~d past the general*** le truppe passarono in fila davanti al generale
file manager *n* COMPUT file manager *m inv* **file name** *n* COMPUT nome *m* del documento
filet *n US* → ***fillet***
filial *adj* filiale
filing cabinet *n* schedario *m*
filings *npl* limatura *f*
filing system *n* sistema *m* di archiviazione **filing tray** *n* vaschetta *f* per l'archiviazione
fill I *v/t* riempire; *tooth* otturare; ***~ sth with sth*** riempire qc di qc; ***~ed with admiration*** pieno di ammirazione; ***~ed with emotion*** colmo di emozione; ***I had three teeth ~ed*** ho avuto un'otturazione a tre denti **II** *n*: ***eat one's ~*** mangiare a sazietà; ***I've had my ~ of him*** *infml* ne ho avuto abbastanza da lui
◆**fill in** *v/t sep form* compilare; *hole* riempire; ***fill s.o. in*** mettere al corrente qn
◆**fill in for** *v/t* sostituire temporaneamente
◆**fill out I** *v/t sep form* compilare **II** *v/i* (*get fatter*) arrotondarsi
◆**fill up I** *v/t sep* riempire; ***fill it up, please*** il pieno, per favore; ***that pie has really filled me up*** quella torta mi ha veramente saziato **II** *v/i of stadium*, *theatre* riempirsi
fillet I *n* COOK filetto *m* **II** *v/t* COOK tagliare a filetti
fillet steak *n* filetto *m*
filling I *n in sandwich* ripieno *m*; *in tooth* otturazione *f*; ***I had to have three ~s*** ho dovuto farmi fare tre otturazioni **II** *adj food* pesante
filling station *n* stazione *f* di rifornimento
filly *n* puledra *f*
film I *n for camera* pellicola *f*; *at cinema* film *m inv*; ***make** or **shoot a ~*** fare *or* girare un film; ***make a ~*** (*actor*) fare un film; ***go to (see) a ~*** andare a vedere un film **II** *v/t person*, *event* riprendere, filmare; *scene* girare **III** *v/i* filmare; ***we start ~ing** or **~ing starts tomorrow*** le riprese cominciano domani
film clip *n* spezzone *m* di un film **film festival** *n* festival *m* cinematografico **film industry** *n* industria *f* cinematografica **film-maker** *n* regista *m/f* **film script** *n* copione *m* del film **film star** *n* stella *f* del cinema **film studio** *n* studio *m* cinematografico
filmy *adj* (*transparent*) trasparente; (*light*) leggero
Filofax® *n* organizer *m inv*
filter I *n* filtro *m* **II** *v/t coffee*, *liquid* filtrare **III** *v/i* (*light*, *liquid*, *sound*) filtrare (in)
◆**filter in** *v/i* (*people*) entrare lentamente
◆**filter out I** *v/i* (*people*) uscire lentamente **II** *v/t sep liter* eliminare filtrando
◆**filter through** *v/i of news*, *reports* diffondersi
filter coffee *n* caffè *m inv* lungo **filter paper** *n* carta *f* filtrante **filter tip** *n* (*cigarette*) filtro *m*
filth *n* sporcizia *f*; (*obscenities*) sconcezze *fpl*
filthy *adj* (+*er*) sporco; *language etc*

volgare; ***live in ~ conditions*** vivere in condizioni indecenti; ***you've got a ~ mind!*** hai una mente perversa!
fin *n of fish* pinna *f*; AVIAT deriva *f*
fin. *abbr* (= **finance, financial**) finanza *f*, finanziario
final I *adj* finale; ***~ round*** ultimo turno *m*; *in a tournament* ultimo round *m inv*; ***~ score*** risultato *m* finale **II** *n* SPORTS finale *f*; ***the ~s*** le finali; ***~s*** *pl Br* UNIV esami *mpl* finali
finale *n* finale *m*
finalise, finalize *v/t plans, design* mettere a punto
finalist *n* finalista *m/f*
finality *n of decision* l'essere definitivo
finally *adv* infine; (*at last*) finalmente
finals *npl* EDU esami *mpl* finali
final whistle *n football* il fischio della fine; ***blow the ~*** fischiare la fine
finance I *n* finanza *f*; ***it's a question of ~*** è una questione di mezzi finanziari; ***~s*** finanze *fpl* **II** *v/t* finanziare
finance director *n* direttore, *m* -trice *f* finanziario, -a
finances *npl* finanze *fpl*
financial *adj* finanziario; ***~ resources*** risorse *fpl* finanziarie; ***on the ~ markets*** sui mercati finanziari; ***~ investment*** investimenti *mpl* finanziari
financial adviser, financial consultant *n* consulente *m/f* finanziario **financial director** *n* COMM direttore *m*, -trice *f* finanziario, -a
financially *adv* finanziariamente; ***the company is ~ sound*** l'azienda è finanziariamente solida; ***~ viable*** fattibile dal punto di vista finanziario
financial services *npl* servizi *mpl* finanziari **financial year** *n* esercizio *m* (finanziario)
financier *n* finanziatore *m*, -trice *f*
finch *n* fringuello *m*
find I *v/t* ⟨*pret & past part* ***found***⟩ trovare; ***if you ~ it too hot / cold*** se lo trovi troppo caldo / freddo; ***~ a person innocent / guilty*** JUR giudicare una persona innocente / colpevole; ***you'll ~ that …*** vedrà che …; ***he was found dead in bed*** è stato trovato morto nel letto; ***where am I going to ~ the time?*** dove troverò il tempo?; ***I don't ~ it easy to tell you this*** non trovo semplice dirti questo; ***he always found learning languages easy*** ha sempre trovato facile imparare le lingue; ***I ~ it impossible to understand him*** o trovo impossibile da comprendere; ***I found myself smiling*** mi sono ritrovato a sorridere; ***this flower is found all over England*** questo fiore si trova in tutta l'Inghilterra; ***we'll have to ~ him a desk*** dovremo trovargli una scrivania; ***we found the car wouldn't start*** abbiamo scoperto che l'auto non si accendeva **II** *v/i* JUR ***~ for / against the accused*** pronunciarsi a favore / contro qn **III** *n* ritrovamento *m*
◆**find out I** *v/t sep & v/i* scoprire; (*discover misdeeds of*) smascherare; (*come to know about*) scoprire; ***you've been found out*** sei stato scoperto **II** *v/i* scoprire (per caso); ***find out about s.o. / sth*** (*discover existence of*) scoprire l'esistenza di qn / qc; ***help children find out about other countries*** aiutare i bambini a informarsi sul proprio paese
finder *n* chi trova; ***~s keepers*** (***losers weepers***) *prov* chi trova tiene (chi perde piange)
findings *npl of report* conclusioni *fpl*
fine[1] *adj* (*+er*) **1.** *day, weather, city* bello; *wine, performance* buono; ***these apples are ~ for cooking*** queste mele vanno bene per cucinare; ***the ~st ingredients*** gli ingredienti migliori; ***a ~ rain*** una pioggia sottile; ***your idea sounds ~*** la tua idea mi sembra ottima; ***you're doing a ~ job*** stai facendo un buon lavoro; ***she's a ~ woman*** è una donna perbene; ***how's that? – that's ~*** com'è? – va benissimo; ***that's ~ by me*** a me sta bene; ***how are you? – ~*** come stai? – bene **2.** *distinction, line* sottile; ***read the ~ print*** leggere i dettagli (scritti in piccolo); ***not to put too ~ a point on it*** per dirla tutta
fine[2] **I** *n penalty* multa *f* **II** *v/t* multare; ***he was ~d £100*** gli hanno fatto una multa di 100 sterline; ***he was ~d for speeding*** ha preso una multa per eccesso di velocità
finery *n* eleganza *f*; ***wedding guests in all their ~*** gli ospiti del matrimonio in tutto il loro splendore
finesse *n* finezza *f*
fine-tooth comb *n*: ***go through sth***

with a ~ passare qc al setaccio
fine-tune *v/t liter, fig* mettere a punto
fine-tuning *n* finezza *f*; *playing cards* impasse *m*
finger I *n* dito *m*; ***she can twist him round her little ~*** può farne quelle che vuole; ***I didn't lay a ~ on her*** non l'ho sfiorata neanche con un dito; ***he wouldn't lift a ~ to help me*** non ha alzato un dito per aiutarmi; ***pull your ~ out!*** *Br infml* datti una mossa!; ***give s.o. the ~*** *esp US infml* mandare qn a farsi fottere; ***I can't quite put my ~ on it*** non riesco a capire esattamente cosa; ***have a ~ in the pie*** *infml* avere le mani in pasta **II** *v/t* passare le dita su
finger food *n cibo che può essere mangiato con le mani (tartine, pizzette, ecc.)* **fingernail** *n* unghia *f* **fingerprint I** *n* impronta *f* digitale **II** *v/t* prendere le impronte digitali di **fingertip** *n* punta *f* del dito; ***have sth at one's ~s*** *knowledge* sapere qc a menadito
finicky *adj person* pignolo; *design, pattern* complicato
finish I *v/t* finire; ***~ doing sth*** finire di fare qc **II** *v/i* finire; ***~ first / second*** *in race* arrivare primo / secondo **III** *n of product* finitura *f*; *finishing line* traguardo *m*
◆**finish off** *v/t sep* finire
◆**finish up** *v/t sep food* finire; ***he finished up liking London*** Londra ha finito per piacergli
◆**finish with** *v/t boyfriend etc* lasciare
finished *adj* finito; (*used up*) rovinato; (*treated*) raffinato; (*fed up*) stufo; ***I'm nearly ~*** ho quasi finito; ***be ~ doing sth*** *US* aver finito di fare qc; ***be ~ with s.o. / sth*** farla finita con qn / qc; ***I'm ~ with politics*** ne ho abbastanza della politica; ***~ goods*** prodotti *mpl* finiti; ***the ~ article*** l'articolo finito; (*piece of writing, work of art*) l'opera completa; ***the wine is ~*** il vino è finito; ***be ~*** *infml* (*politician etc*) essere finito (***as*** come); ***we're ~*** *or* ***it's ~ between us*** tra di noi è finita
finishing line *n* traguardo *m*
finishing school *n scuola di buone maniere per ragazze* **finishing touch** *n* tocco *m* finale
finite *adj* limitato; ***a ~ number*** un numero finito; MATH finito; ***coal and oil are ~ resources*** il carbone e il petrolio sono risorse limitate
Finland *n* Finlandia *f*
Finn *n* finlandese *m/f*
Finnish I *adj* finlandese, finnico **II** *n language* finlandese *m*
fir *n* abete *m*
fir cone *n* pigna *f* (di abete)
fire I *n* fuoco *m*; (*blaze*) incendio *m*; (*bonfire, campfire etc*) falò *m inv*; ***be on ~*** essere in fiamme; ***catch ~*** prendere fuoco; ***set sth on ~, set ~ to sth*** dare fuoco a qc **II** *v/i* (*shoot*) sparare; (*engine*) accendersi; ***~ at*** *or* ***on*** sparare contro; ***~!*** fuoco! **III** *v/t infml* (*dismiss*) licenziare; *pottery* cuocere; *arrow* tirare; *shot* sparare; *rocket* lanciare; *fig imagination* accendere; ***~ a gun at s.o.*** sparare contro; *fig* ***~ s.o. with enthusiasm*** accendere l'entusiasmo di qn; *fig* ***~ questions at s.o.*** bombardare qn di domande
fire alarm *n* allarme *m* antincendio **fire-and-brimstone** *adj* apocalittico
firearm *n* arma *f* da fuoco
fireball *n explosion* palla *f* di fuoco; *fig* persona *f* energica
fire brigade *n* vigili *mpl* del fuoco
firecracker *n* petardo *m*
fire department *n US* vigili *mpl* del fuoco **fire door** *n* porta *f* taglia-fuoco **fire drill** *n* esercitazione *f* antincendio **fire-eater** *n* mangiatore *m* di fuoco **fire engine** *n* autopompa *f* **fire escape** *n* scala *f* antincendio **fire exit** *n* uscita *f* di sicurezza **fire extinguisher** *n* estintore *m* **fire fighter** *n* pompiere *m*
firefly *n* lucciola *f*
fireguard *n* parafuoco *m inv*
fire hazard *n*: **be a ~** essere in grado di provocare un incendio
firehouse *n US* caserma dei pompieri
fire hydrant *n* idrante *m* antincendio **fire insurance** *n* assicurazione contro gli incendi
firelight *n* luce *f* del fuoco
firelighter *n* esca *f* per il fuoco
fireman *n* pompiere *m*
fireplace *n* camino *m*;
fire prevention *n* prevenzione antincendio
fireproof *adj* resistente al fuoco
fire-raising *n esp Br* incendio *m* dolo-

so **fire regulations** *npl* norme *fpl* antincendio **fire retardant** *adj* ignifugo;
fireside *n*: ***by the ~*** vicino al caminetto
fire station *n* caserma *f* dei pompieri
firestorm *n* tempesta *f* di fuoco
firetrap *n luogo privo di uscite antincendio*
fire truck *n US* autopompa *f*
firewall *n* muro *m* tagliafuoco; COMPUT firewall *m*
firewater *n* superalcolico *m*
firewoman *n* vigile *f* del fuoco (donna)
firewood *n* legna *f* da ardere
fireworks *npl* fuochi *mpl* d'artificio
firing line *n* MIL, *fig* linea *f* di tiro; ***be in the ~*** essere in prima linea
firing squad *n* plotone *m* d'esecuzione
firm[1] *adj* (+*er*) *grip*, *handshake* energico; *flesh*, *muscles* sodo; *voice*, *parents* deciso; *decision* risoluto; *date*, *offer* definitivo; *control* rigido; *foundations* solido; *believer* convinto; ***a ~ deal*** un accordo definito
firm[2] *n* COMM azienda *f*; ***~ of lawyers*** studio *m* legale associato
first I *adj* primo; ***who's ~ please?*** chi è il primo, per favore?; ***his ~ novel*** il suo primo romanzo; ***he was ~ in the queue*** *Br or* ***in line*** *US* era il primo della fila; ***he was ~ in Latin*** era il più bravo in latino; ***why didn't you say so in the ~ place?*** perché non l'hai detto subito? **II** *n* primo *m*, -a *f* **III** *adv arrive*, *finish* per primo; (*beforehand*) prima; (*before all else*) prima di tutto; *in listing* primo; (*for the first time*) per la prima volta; ***~ of all*** (*for one reason*) per prima cosa; ***at ~*** in un primo tempo, al principio; ***~ come ~ served*** *prov* chi primo arriva meglio alloggia; *sistema di assegnazione in base all'ordine di arrivo*; ***you*** (***go***) ***~*** tu vai per primo; ***he says ~ one thing then another*** dice prima una cosa e poi un'altra; ***he always puts his job ~*** mette sempre il lavoro davanti a tutto; ***~ and foremost*** innanzitutto; ***when this model was ~ introduced*** quando questo modello è stato introdotto per la prima volta; ***I must finish this ~*** prima devo finire questo; ***I'd die ~!*** meglio morire!
first aid *n* pronto soccorso *m* **first-aid box, first-aid kit** *n* cassetta *f* del pronto soccorso **firstborn** *adj* primogenito
first class I *n* prima classe *f*; ***that's absolutely ~!*** è una cosa di prim'ordine! **II** *adv travel* in prima classe
first-class *adj* (*excellent*) di prima classe; ***he's a ~ cook*** è un cuoco di prima classe; ***~ compartment*** compartimento *m* di prima classe; ***~ stamp*** francobollo *m* di posta prioritaria; ***~ letter*** lettera *f* spedita con posta prioritaria; ***~*** (***honours***) ***degree*** *Br* UNIV *laurea con lode*; ***he graduated with ~ honours*** si è laureato con il massimo dei voti **first-degree** *adj*: ***~ burn*** ustione *f* di primo grado **first edition** *n* prima edizione *f* **first floor** *n* primo piano *m*; *US* pianoterra *m* **first form** *n* EDU prima *f* **first-former** *n* EDU studente *m*, -essa *f* di prima **first-generation** *adj* prima generazione *f* **firsthand I** *adj* diretto; ***have ~ knowledge of sth*** avere conoscenza di prima mano su qc; ***they have ~ experience of charitable organizations*** hanno esperienza diretta nelle organizzazioni di beneficenza **II** *adv hear*, *experience* da fonte diretta **First Lady** *n of US* First Lady *f inv* **first language** *n* prima lingua *f*
firstly *adv* in primo luogo
first mate *n* primo ufficiale *m* **First Minister** *n* POL Primo Ministro *m/f* **first name** *n* nome *m* di battesimo **first night** *n* prima serata *f* **first offender** *n* delinquente *m/f* non pregiudicato, -a **first-rate** *adj* di prima qualità **first refusal** *n* diritto *m* di prelazione **first-time buyer** *n* chi acquista la prima casa **First World War** *n*: ***the ~*** la prima guerra mondiale
fir tree *n* abete *m*
fiscal *adj* fiscale; ***~ policy*** politica *f* fiscale
fiscal drag *n* fiscal drag *m*; drenaggio *m* fiscale
fish I *n* ⟨*pl* **fish**⟩ pesce *m*; ***drink like a ~*** *infml* bere come una spugna *infml*; ***feel like a ~ out of water*** sentirsi come un pesce fuor d'acqua **II** *v/i* pescare; *fig compliments* andare alla ricerca; ***they were fishing for information*** erano a caccia di informazioni
fish and chips *npl pesce e patate fritte*
fishbone *n* lisca *f* **fishcake** *n sformato*

di pesce e patate
fisherman *n* pescatore *m*
fishery *n industry* pesca *f*; (*fish farm*) vivaio *m*
fish farm *n* vivaio *m* **fish finger** *n* bastoncino *m* di pesce **fish-hook** *n* amo *m*
fishing *n* pesca *f*; ***go ~*** andare a pesca; *as industry* pesca *f*
fishing boat *n* peschereccio *m* **fishing line** *n* lenza *f* **fishing net** *n* rete *f* da pesca **fishing rod** *n* canna *f* da pesca **fishing tackle** *n* (*for sport*) articoli *mpl* per la pesca **fishing village** *n* villaggio *m* di pescatori
fishmonger *n* pescivendolo *m*
fishnet **I** *n* rete *f* **II** *adj* a rete; ***~ tights*** calze *fpl* a rete
fish pond *n natural* vasca *f* per i pesci; *in fish farm* stagno *m* dei pesci **fish stick** *n US* bastoncino *m* di pesce **fish tank** *n* acquario *m*
fishwife *n* pescivendola *f*; ***she swears like a ~*** bestemmia come una turca
fishy *adj* (+*er*) ***~ smell*** puzza *f* di pesce; *infml* (*suspicious*) sospetto
fission *n* fissione *f*; ***nuclear ~*** fissione *f* nucleare
fissure *n* fessura *f*; (*deep*) crepa *f*
fist *n* pugno *m*
fistful *n* manciata *f*; ***a ~ of pound coins*** una manciata di monete da una sterlina
fisticuffs *n* scazzottata *f*
fistula *n* fistola *f*
fit¹ *n* MED attacco *m*; ***a ~ of rage / jealousy*** un accesso di rabbia / gelosia
fit² *adj* (+*er*) *physically* in forma; *morally* adatto; ***she's not ~ to be a mother*** non è adatta ad essere una madre; ***keep ~*** tenersi in forma; (*suitable*) ***be ~ for*** essere adatto a *or* per; ***~ to eat*** commestibile; ***~ to drink*** potabile; ***be ~ to*** essere in grado di
fit³ **I** *v/t* ⟨*pret & past part* ***-ted***⟩ *of clothes* andare bene a; (*attach*) installare; ***"one size ~s all"*** taglia unica; ***that part won't ~ this machine*** quel pezzo non va bene per questa macchina; ***she was ~ted for her wedding dress*** le hanno preso le misure per l'abito da sposa **II** *v/i* ⟨*pret & past part* ***-ted***⟩ *of clothes* andare bene; *of piece of furniture etc* starci; ***the facts don't ~*** i fatti non corrispondono; ***it all ~s*** tutto quadra **III** *n*: ***it is a good ~*** *of piece of furniture etc* ci sta perfettamente; *of clothes* calza a pennello; ***it's a tight ~*** *of piece of furniture etc* ci sta appena; *of clothes* va giusto giusto
◆**fit in** **I** *v/i of person in group* integrarsi; ***it fits in with our plans*** si concilia con i nostri programmi **II** *v/t sep*: ***fit s.o. in*** *into schedule* fissare un appuntamento a qn
◆**fit on** **I** *v/i* (*be right size, shape*) andare bene; (*be fixed*) andare su **II** *v/t sep* (*put in place, fix on*) mettere
◆**fit out** *v/t sep ship* equipaggiare; *person* (*with clothes etc*) mettere (vestiti, ecc.); ***they've fitted one room out as an office*** da una stanza hanno ricavato un ufficio
◆**fit up** *v/t sep* ***fit s.o. / sth up with sth*** attrezzare qn / qc con qc
fitful *adj sleep* a tratti
fitfully *adv sleep* a tratti; *work* in modo discontinuo
fitment *n* attrezzatura *f*; ***bathroom ~*** i sanitari *mpl*
fitness *n physical* forma *f*; *suitability* idoneità *f*
fitness centre, *US* **fitness center** *n* palestra *f*
fitted *adj*: ***be ~ with*** essere corredato di
fitted carpet *n* moquette *f inv* **fitted kitchen** *n* cucina *f* componibile **fitted sheet** *n* lenzuolo *m* con gli angoli
fitter *n* assemblatore *m*, -trice *f*
fitting *adj* appropriato
fittingly *adv* in modo appropriato
fitting room *n* sala *f* di prova; (*cubicle*) camerino *m* di prova
fittings *npl* equipaggiamento *msg*
five *num* cinque
fiver *n infml* banconota *f* da cinque sterline
fives *npl* SPORTS pallamuro *f*
fix **I** *n* (*solution*) soluzione *f*; ***be in a ~*** *infml* essere nei casini *infml*; ***give o.s. a ~*** *infml* farsi una pera *sl* **II** *v/t* (*attach*) fissare; (*repair*) aggiustare; (*arrange*: *meeting etc*) fissare; *lunch* preparare; *dishonestly*: *match etc* manipolare; ***~ sth onto sth*** attaccare qc a qc; ***I'll ~ you a drink*** ti preparo da bere

◆**fix on** *v/t sep* attaccare; (*fit on*) fissare
◆**fix together** *v/t sep* fissare insieme
◆**fix up** *v/t sep meeting* fissare; ***it's all fixed up*** è tutto stabilito
fixate I *v/t* fissare **II** *v/i* fissarsi
fixation *n* PSYCH fissazione *f*; ***she has a ~ about*** *or* ***on cleanliness*** ha la fissazione per la pulizia
fixative *n* ART fissativo *m*; PHOT fissatore *m*
fixed *adj in one position* fisso; *timescale, exchange rate* stabilito; *smile, grin* immobile; *election, game* truccato; ***there's no ~ agenda*** non è stata stabilita nessuna agenda; ***of no ~ abode*** *or* ***address*** *Br* JUR senza fissa dimora; ***~ price*** prezzo *m* fisso; ***~ rate*** FIN tasso *m* fisso; ***~ penalty*** pena *f* irremovibile; ***the whole thing was ~*** era già tutto stabilito; ***how are we ~ for Saturday?*** *infml arrangement* come siamo rimasti per sabato?; ***how are you ~ for money?*** *infml* come stai a soldi?
fixed assets *npl* COMM attività *fpl* fisse
fixed-interest *adj*: ***~ loan*** prestito *m* a tasso fisso
fixedly *adv* fissamente
fixed-rate *adj* a tasso fisso; ***~ mortgage*** mutuo *m* a tasso fisso
fixed-term contract *n* contratto *m* a tempo indeterminato
fixer *n infml* corruttore *m*, -trice *f*
fixer-upper *n infml* (*house*) *casa da ristrutturare*
fixings *npl* COOK guarnizioni *fpl*
fixity *n* fissità *f*
fixtures *npl in room* installazioni *fpl* fisse; SPORTS incontro *m*
fizz I *v/i of liquid* fare le bollicine **II** *n infml* champagne *m*
fizzle *v/i* frizzare
◆**fizzle out** *v/i infml* sfumare *infml*
fizzy *adj* (+*er*) *drink* gassato
fjord *n* fiordo *m*
F key *n* COMPUT tasto *m* funzione
fl. *abbr* (= **floor**) piano *m*
flab *n on body* ciccia *f*
flabbergast *v/t infml* ***be ~ed*** cadere dalle nuvole
flabby *adj* (+*er*) *muscles, stomach* flaccido; ***he's getting ~*** sta diventando fiacco
flaccid *adj liter* flaccido; *prose* debole
flag[1] *n* bandiera *f*; ***fly the ~*** (***for***) *fig* portare alta la bandiera (di)
flag[2] *v/i* ⟨*pret & past part* **-ged**⟩ (*tire*) soccombere
◆**flag down** *v/t sep cab* fermare
flag day *n Br giorno in cui si vendono bandierine per beneficenza*; **Flag Day** *US 14 luglio, commemorazione dell'adozione della bandiera americana*
flagellant *n* flagellante *m/f*
flagellate *v/t* flagellare
flagon *n* (*bottle*) fiasco *m*; (*jug*) caraffa *f*
flagpole *n* asta *f*
flagrant *adj* flagrante
flagship I *n fig* cavallo *m* di battaglia **II** *adj* principale; ***~ store*** negozio più importante **flagstaff** *n* asta *f* **flagstone** *n* lastra *f* di pietra **flag-waving** *n* sbandieramento *m*; *fig* patriottismo *m* eccessivo
flail I *v/t*: ***he ~ed his arms about*** *or* ***around wildly*** dimenava concitatamente le braccia **II** *v/i*: ***~*** (***about***) agitarsi convulsamente
flair *n* (*talent*) talento *m*; (*style*) stile *m*
flak *n fig* ***he's been getting a lot of ~*** (***for it***) ha ricevuto un mucchio di critiche (per quello)
flake I *n of snow* fiocco *m*; *of paint, plaster* scaglia *f* **II** *v/i* (*stone etc*) scheggiarsi; (*paint*) sfaldarsi
◆**flake off** *v/i* squamarsi
◆**flake out** *v/i* (*become exhausted*) crollare; (*fall asleep*) addormentarsi
flak jacket *n* giubotto *m* antiproiettile
flaky *adj* (+*er*) squamato; *paint* che si sfalda; *crust* che si sgretola; *esp US infml* suonato
flaky pastry *n* pasta *f* sfoglia
flamboyance *n* l'essere sgargiante
flamboyant *adj personality* esuberante
flamboyantly *adv dressed* in modo vistoso
flame I *n* fiamma *f*; ***go up in ~s*** incendiarsi **II** *v/i* COMPUT *mandare un messaggio offensivo via e-mail o Internet*
flame retardant *adj* ignifugo
flaming *adj* fiammante; *Br* (*bloody*) maledetto; ***~ red hair*** capelli *mpl* rosso fuoco; ***have a ~ row*** (***with s.o.***) avere una violenta lite (con qn); ***it's a ~ nuisance*** *Br infml* è una dannata seccatura

flamingo *n* ⟨*pl* ***flamingo(e)s***⟩ fenicottero *m*
flammable *adj* infiammabile
flan *n* sformato *m*
flank I *n* fianco *m* **II** *v/t*: ***be ~ed by*** essere affiancato da
flannel *n* TEX flanella *f*; *for washing* guanto *m* di spugna
flap I *n of envelope, pocket* falda *f*; *of table* ribalta; AVIAT aletta *f*; ***be in a ~*** *infml* essere in fibrillazione *infml* **II** *v/t* ⟨*pret & past part* ***-ped***⟩ *wings* sbattere **III** *v/i* ⟨*pret & past part* ***-ped***⟩ *of flag etc* sventolare; *infml* (*panic*) andare in fibrillazione *infml*; ***don't ~!*** non ti agitare!
flapjack *n Br* (*biscuit*) biscotto *m* di avena; *US* (*pancake*) crêpe *f inv*
flare I *n* (*distress signal*) razzo *m*; *in dress* svasatura *f*; ***~s*** *trousers* pantaloni *mpl* a zampa di elefante **II** *v/t fig* (*trouble*) divampare; ***tempers ~d*** gli animi si scaldavano; *nostrils* allargare
◆**flare up** *v/i of violence, illness, temper* esplodere; *of fire* divampare
flash I *n of light* lampo *m*; PHOT flash *m inv*; ***in a ~*** *infml* in un istante; ***have a ~ of inspiration*** avere un lampo di genio; ***~ of lightning*** lampo *m*; ***a ~ in the pan*** un fuoco di paglia **II** *v/i of light* lampeggiare; *holidays* passare in un baleno; *infml* (*expose o.s.*) mostrare i propri organi sessuali; ***~ past*** *or* ***by*** sfrecciare vicino; ***it ~ed through my mind that …*** mi balenò l'idea che … **III** *v/t* (*show*) mostrare (per un momento);: ***~ one's headlights*** AUTO lampeggiare; ***she ~ed him a look of contempt*** gli lanciò uno sguardo di disprezzo; ***don't ~ all that money around*** non sfoggiare tutti quei soldi **IV** *adj* (*showy*) vistoso; (*smart*) alla moda
flashback *n* FILM flashback *m inv*
flashcard *n* EDU flashcard *f*, *cartoncino colorato per insegnare le parole*
flasher *n* AUTO freccia *f*; *infml person* esibizionista *m*
flash flood *n* piena *f* improvvisa **flashlight** *n US* pila *f*; PHOT flash *m inv*
flashy *adj* (+*er*) *pej* appariscente
flask *n* (*vacuum flask*) termos *m inv*
flat[1] **I** *adj* (+*er*) **1.** *surface, land, tone* piatto **2.** *beer* sgassato **3.** *battery, tyre* a terra **4.** *shoes* basso **5.** ***A/B ~*** MUS la/si bemolle **6.** ***and that's ~*** *infml* punto e basta *infml* **7.** COMM inattivo; ***~ rate*** tasso *m* fisso **II** *adv* MUS sotto tonalità; ***fall ~ on one's face*** cadere a faccia in giù; ***lie ~*** giacere disteso; ***fall ~*** (*joke*) fallire; ***~ broke*** *infml* totalmente al verde; ***~ out*** *work, run, drive* a tutto gas **III** *n of hand* palmo *m*; *of blade* piatto *m*; MUS bemolle *m*; AUTO gomma *f* a terra
flat[2] *n Br* (*apartment*) appartamento *m*
flat-chested *adj* piatto
flat-footed *adj* con i piedi piatti
flatlet *n Br* appartamentino *m*
flatly *adv refuse, deny* risolutamente; ***be ~ opposed to sth*** opporsi nettamente a qc
flatmate *n persona con cui si divide la casa*
flatness *n of surface* piattezza *f*
flat-pack *adj*: ***~ furniture*** moblio *m* da montare **flat racing** *n* corsa *f* piana **flat rate** *n* tariffa *f* forfettaria **flat screen** *n* COMPUT schermo *m* piatto **flat spin** *n* AVIAT vite *f* piatta; *infml* ***in a ~*** in agitazione
flatten *v/t land, road* livellare; *by bombing, demolition* radere al suolo
flatter *v/t* adulare
flatterer *n* adulatore *m*, -trice *f*
flattering *adj comments* lusinghiero; ***Jane's dress is very ~*** il vestito di Jane le dona molto
flattery *n* adulazione *f*
flatulence *n* flatulenza *f*
flatware *n US* stoviglie *fpl*
flaunt *v/t* ostentare
flautist *n* flautista *m/f*
flavor *etc US* → ***flavour*** *etc*
flavour, *US* **flavor I** *n* gusto *m*; (*flavouring*) aroma *m*; *fig* atmosfera *f*; ***strawberry-~ ice cream*** gelato al gusto di fragola; ***he is ~ of the month*** *infml* è l'idolo del momento **II** *v/t food* insaporire
flavouring, *US* **flavoring** *n* aroma *m*
flavourless, *US* **flavorless** *adj* insipido
flaw I *n* difetto *m* **II** *v/t* rovinare; ***his logic was ~ed*** la sua logica non tornava **III** *v/i* rovinarsi
flawless *adj* perfetto; *performance* impeccabile; *complexion* perfetto; ***~ English*** inglese impeccabile
flax *n* BOT lino *m*

flaxen *adj* biondo
flaxseed *n* seme *m* di lino
flay *v/t* (*skin*) scorticare; (*critisize*) stroncare
flea *n* pulce *f*
fleabag *n pej* sacco *m* di pulci
fleabite *n* morso *m* di pulce
flea-bitten *adj* morso dalle pulci; *infml* lurido **flea market** *n* mercatino *m* delle pulci
fleapit *n Br infml* topaia *f*
fleck **I** *n* puntino *m*; *of mud, paint* chiazza *f*; (*speckle*) macchiolina *f*; *of dust* granello *m* **II** *v/t*: ***~ed wool*** lana *f* mélange; ***blue ~ed with white*** blu screziato di bianco
fled *pret & past part* → ***flee***
fledg(e)ling **I** *n* ZOOL uccellino *m* **II** *adj democracy* giovane
flee *v/i* ⟨*pret & past part* ***fled***⟩ scappare
fleece **I** *n* vello *m*; (*garment*) pile *m inv* **II** *v/t infml* fregare *infml*
fleecy *adj* lanoso
fleet *n* NAUT flotta *f*; *of taxis, trucks* parco *m* macchine
fleeting *adj visit etc* di sfuggita; ***catch a ~ glimpse of*** vedere di sfuggita
Flemish **I** *adj* fiammingo **II** *n* LING fiammingo *m*
flesh *n* carne *f*; *of fruit* polpa *f*; ***meet / see a person in the ~*** incontrare / vedere una persona in carne e ossa; ***my own ~ and blood*** sangue del mio sangue
◆**flesh out** *v/t sep* rimpolpare; *details* arricchire
flesh-coloured, *US* **flesh-colored** *adj* color carne **flesh wound** *n* ferita *f* superficiale
fleshy *adj* (*+er*) carnoso
flew *pret* → ***fly³***
flex **I** *v/t muscles* flettere **II** *n* ELEC cavo *m*
flexibility *n* flessibilità *f*
flexible *adj* flessibile; ***I'm quite ~*** *about arrangements, timing* sono abbastanza flessibile
flex(i)time *n* orario *m* flessibile
flibbertigibet *n* pettegolo *m*, -a *f*
flick **I** *n* (*with finger*) schiocco *m*; ***with a ~ of the whip*** con uno schiocco di frusta; ***a ~ of the wrist*** con un movimento veloce del polso **II** *v/t tail* agitare; ***he ~ed a fly off his hand*** ha cacciato via una mosca dalla mano; ***she ~ed her hair out of her eyes*** si è tolta i capelli dagli occhi con un gesto
◆**flick through** *v/t book, magazine* sfogliare
flicker *v/i of light* tremolare
flick-knife *n* coltello *m* a scatto
flicks *npl infml* cinema *m*; ***at the ~*** al cinema
flier *n* (*circular*) volantino *m*; ***be a frequent ~*** prendere spesso l'aereo
flies *npl on trousers* patta *f*
flight *n* volo *m*; (*fleeing*) fuga *f*; ***~*** (***of stairs***) rampa *f* (di scale); ***~ of fancy*** volo *m* della fantasia; *fig* ***be in the top ~*** essere a livelli di eccellenza
flight attendant *n* assistente *m/f* di volo **flight crew** *n* equipaggio *m* di volo **flight deck** *n in aeroplane* cabina *f* di pilotaggio; *of aircraft carrier* ponte *m* di decollo **flight number** *n* numero *m* di volo **flight path** *n* rotta *f* (di volo) **flight recorder** *n* registratore *m* di volo **flight simulator** *n* simulatore *m* di volo **flight time** *n departure* orario *m* di volo; *duration* durata *f* di volo
flighty *adj* (*+er*) volubile
flimsy *adj* (*+er*) *structure, furniture* leggero; *dress, material* sottile; *excuse* debole
flinch *v/i* sobbalzare; ***without ~ing*** senza esitazione; *fig* ***~ from sth*** sottrarsi a qc
fling **I** *v/t* ⟨*pret & past part* ***flung***⟩ scagliare; ***~ o.s. into a chair*** buttarsi su una sedia; ***~ the window open*** spalancare la finestra; ***the door was flung open*** la porta era spalancata; ***~ one's arms round s.o.'s neck*** gettare le braccia al collo di qn **II** *n infml* (*affair*) avventura *f*; *fig* ***have a final ~*** *infml* godersela per l'ultima volta
◆**fling off** *v/t sep liter coat* sbarazzarsi
◆**fling out** *v/t sep object* gettare; *person* mettere alla porta
◆**fling up** *v/t sep*: ***fling one's arms up in horror*** alzare le braccia al cielo per l'orrore
flint *n* (*stone*) selce *f*; *in lighter* pietrina *f*
flip **I** *n*: ***by the ~ of a coin*** facendo testa o croce **II** *v/t* ⟨*pret & past part* ***-ped***⟩ lanciare; *switch* girare; ***~ a coin*** lanciare una moneta **III** *v/i infml* andare fuori di testa

◆**flip out** *v/t* andare fuori di testa
◆**flip over** **I** *v/t sep* girare **II** *v/i* (*plane*) capovolgersi
◆**flip through** *v/t book, magazine* sfogliare
flip-flop *n* infradito *f inv*
flippant *adj* impertinente
flipper *n for swimming* pinna *f*
flip phone *n* TEL telefono *m* a scrigno
flip side *n fig* rovescio *m* della medaglia; *record* lato *m* B
flirt **I** *v/i* flirtare; **~ *with*** flirtare con **II** *n* flirt *m inv*
flirtatious *adj* civettuolo
float **I** *n on fishing line* galleggiante *m*; (*vehicle*) carro *m di una sfilata* **II** *v/i* galleggiare; FIN fluttuare **III** *v/t* COMM, FIN *company* lanciare; *fig ideas* proporre
floating voter *n elettore che cambia spesso opinione*
flock **I** *n of sheep* gregge *m* **II** *v/i* accorrere in massa
flog *v/t* ⟨*pret & past part* **-ged**⟩ (*whip*) fustigare; *infml* (*sell*) vendere; ***you're ~ging a dead horse*** *Br infml* stai sprecando fiato
flogging *n* fustigazione *f*; JUR punizione corporale
flood **I** *n* inondazione *f*; ***she was in ~s of tears*** era in un mare di lacrime **II** *v/t of river* inondare; **~ *its banks*** *of river* straripare; **~ *the engine*** ingolfare il motore; ***~ed with complaints*** sommerso di reclami; ***~ed with light*** inondato di luce **III** *v/i river* straripare; *bath etc* allagare; *land* inondare; *people* riversarsi
◆**flood in** *v/i* affluire
floodgate *n* chiusa *f*; *fig* ***open the ~s*** dare libero sfogo
flooding *n* inondazione *f*
floodlight *n* riflettore *m*
floodlit *adj match* illuminato da riflettori
flood plain *n pianura soggetta a inondazioni periodiche* **flood tide** *n* flusso *m* della marea **flood victim** *n* vittima *f* dell'alluvione
floodwaters *npl* acque *fpl* di inondazione
floor **I** *n* pavimento *m*; (*dance floor*) pista (da ballo); ***ocean ~*** fondo *m* dell'oceano; ***stone / tiled ~*** pavimento in pietra / in mattonelle; ***take to the ~*** (*dance*) scendere in pista; ***hold** or **have the ~*** (*speaker*) prendere la parola;(*storey*) piano *m* **II** *v/t* (*knock down*) mettere al tappeto; (*bewilder*) sbalordire
floor area *n* superficie *f* calpestabile
floorboard *n* asse *f* del pavimento
floor cloth *n* straccio *m* per lavare per terra
flooring *n* (*floor*) pavimento *m*; (*material*) materiale *m* per pavimentazione
floorlamp *n US* lampada *f* a stelo **floor plan** *n* pianta *f* **floor polish** *n* cera *f* per pavimenti **floor space** *n* superficie *f* utile; ***if you've got a sleeping bag we have plenty of ~*** se porti un sacco a pelo puoi sistemarti dove vuoi
flop **I** *v/i* ⟨*pret & past part* **-ped**⟩ crollare; *infml* (*fail*) fare fiasco **II** *n infml* (*failure*) fiasco *m*
floppy *adj* (+*er*) *not stiff* floscio; (*weak*) moscio
floppy (disk) *n* floppy *m inv*, floppy disk *m inv*
flora *n form* flora *f*
Florence *n* Firenze
Florentine **I** *adj* fiorentino **II** *n* fiorentino *m*, -a *f*
florist *n* fiorista *m/f*
floss **I** *n for teeth* filo *m* interdentale **II** *v/t*: **~ *one's teeth*** passare il filo interdentale
flotation *n* COMM *of firm* lancio *m*; FIN emissione *f*
flotilla *n* flottiglia *f*
flotsam *n*: **~ *and jetsam*** (*floating*) relitti *mpl* galleggianti; (*washed ashore*) relitti *mpl*
flounce **I** *v/i* agitarsi; **~ *out*** precipitarsi fuori **II** *n* scatto *m*
flounder **I** *v/i* annaspare **II** *n* (*fish*) passera *f* nera
flour *n* farina *f*
flourish **I** *v/i* fiorire; *of business, civilization* prosperare **II** *v/t stick etc* brandire **III** *n* (*decoration*) svolazzo *m*
flourishing *adj business, trade* prospero
floury *adj* coperto di farina; *texture* farinoso
flout *v/t* sfidare
flow **I** *v/i of river, traffic, current* scor-

rere; *of work* procedere **II** *n of river, ideas* flusso *m*; ***the ~ of traffic*** la circolazione del traffico; *fig* ***go with the ~*** seguire la corrente; *fig* ***go against the ~*** andare contro corrente; ***he was in full ~*** era nel bel mezzo del discorso

flowchart *n* diagramma *m* (di flusso)

flower I *n* fiore *m* **II** *v/i* fiorire

flowerbed *n* aiuola *f* **flowerpot** *n* vaso *m* per fiori **flower show** *n* esposizione *f* floreale

flowery *adj pattern* a fiori; *style of writing* fiorito

flown *past part* → ***fly³***

fl. oz. *abbr* (= **fluid ounce(s)**) oncia *f* fluida, once *fpl* fluide (*misura*)

flu *n* influenza *f*; ***get*** *or* ***catch/have (the) ~*** prendere/avere l'influenza

fluctuate *v/i* oscillare

fluctuation *n* oscillazione *f*

flue *n* canna *f* fumaria

fluency *n in a language* scioltezza *f*

fluent *adj* fluente; ***he speaks ~ Spanish*** parla correntemente lo spagnolo

fluently *adv speak, write* correntemente

fluff I *n material* lanugine *f*; ***a bit of ~*** *Br vulg* un po' di pelo *vulg* **II** *v/t pillow* sprimaccare; (*make a mistake*) prendere una cantonata

◆**fluff up** *v/t sep pillow etc* sprimacciare

fluffy *adj* (+*er*) *material, hair* lanuginoso; *clouds* soffice; ***~ toy*** peluche *m inv*

fluid *n* fluido *m*

fluke *n infml* colpo *m* fortuna; ***it was a (pure) ~*** è stato un (puro) colpo di fortuna

flummox *v/t infml* sconcertare; ***be ~ed by sth*** essere messo in imparazzo da qc

flung *pret & past part* → ***fling***

flunk *v/t US infml* essere bocciato a; ***~ German/an exam*** essere bocciato ad un esame/di tedesco

fluorescent *adj light* fluorescente

fluorescent lighting *n* illuminazione *f* a fluorescenza

fluoride *n* fluoruro *m*

flurry *n of snow* raffica *f*; *fig* ***a ~ of activity*** un vortice di attività; ***a ~ of excitement*** un'ondata di entusiasmo

flush I *v/t toilet* tirare l'acqua di; ***~ sth down the toilet*** buttare qc giù dal water **II** *v/i* (*go red in the face*) diventare rosso; ***the toilet won't ~*** lo sciacquone del bagno non funziona **III** *adj* (*level*) a filo; ***be ~ with …*** a filo con …

◆**flush away** *v/t sep down toilet* buttare giù dal water

◆**flush out** *v/t sep rebels etc* scovare

fluster *v/t* mettere in agitazione; ***get ~ed*** mettersi in agitazione

flute *n* MUS flauto *m* traverso; *glass* flute *m inv*

flutist *n US* flautista *m/f*

flutter I *v/i of bird* sbattere le ali; *of wings* sbattere; *of flag* sventolare; *of heart* battere forte **II** *n infml* (*bet*) piccola scommessa *f*; ***all of a ~*** tutto agitato

flux *n* flusso *m*; ***in a state of ~*** in continuo mutamento

fly¹ *n insect* mosca *f*; ***he wouldn't hurt a ~*** non farebbe del male a una mosca; ***that's the only ~ in the ointment*** *infml* quello è l'unico piccolo difetto che rovina tutto

fly² *n on trousers* patta *f*

fly³ ⟨*pret* **flew**, *past part* **flown**⟩ **I** *v/i* volare; *of flag* sventolare; (*rush*) precipitarsi; ***~ into a rage*** perdere le staffe; ***time flies!*** il tempo vola; ***the door flew open*** la porta di spalancò; ***~ at s.o.*** *infml* avventarsi contro qn; ***he really let ~*** si è davvero infuriato; ***send s.o./sth ~ing*** mandare qn a gambe all'aria; ***go ~ing*** (*person*) fare un volo; ***~ in the face of authority/tradition*** sfidare l'autorità/la tradizione **II** *v/t aeroplane* pilotare; *airline* volare con; (*transport by air*) spedire per via aerea

◆**fly away** *v/i of bird, plane* volare via

◆**fly back** *v/i* (*travel back*) ritornare (in aereo)

◆**fly in I** *v/i of plane, passengers* arrivare **II** *v/t sep supplies etc* mandare per via aerea

◆**fly off** *v/i of hat etc* volare via

◆**fly out** *v/i* partire in aereo

◆**fly past** *v/i in formation* volare in formazione; *of time* volare

fly-by-night *adj* FIN, COMM *operation* sospetto **fly-fishing** *n* pesca *f* con la mosca

flying *n* volare *m*; ***he's afraid of ~*** ha

paura di volare
flying boat *n* idrovolante *m* a scafo **flying buttress** *n* ARCH arco *m* rampante **flying colours**, *US* **flying colors** *npl*: ***pass with ~*** superare un esame a pieni voti **flying leap** *n*: ***take a ~*** saltare con la rincorsa **flying saucer** *n* disco *m* volante **flying start** *n*: ***get off to a ~*** SPORTS fare una partenza lanciata; *fig* partire in quarta **flying visit** *n* visita *f* lampo
fly leaf *n* risguardo *m*
flyover *n* AUTO cavalcavia *m inv*
flypaper *n* carta *f* moschicida
flypast *n Br* parata *f* aerea
flysheet *n* telo *m* esterno (di una tenda)
fly spray *n* spray *m* moschicida **fly swat(ter)** *n* acchiappamosche *m* **fly-tipping** *n gettare rifiuti in una scarica abusiva*
flywheel *n* volano *m*
FM *abbr* (= **frequency modulation**) FM (modulazione *f* di frequenza)
foal I *n* puledro *m* **II** *v/i* partorire
foam I *n on liquid* schiuma *f* **II** *v/i of liquid* fare schiuma; ***~ at the mouth*** avere la schiuma alla bocca
foam rubber *n* gommapiuma® *f*
foamy *adj* (+*er*) spumeggiante
FOB *abbr* (= **free on board**) FOB (franco a bordo)
◆**fob off** *v/t*: ***fob s.o. off with sth*** liquidare qn con qc; ***fob sth off on s.o.*** rifilare qc a qn
focal point *n* punto *m* principale
focus I *n of attention* centro *m*; PHOT fuoco *m*; ***be in ~ / be out of ~*** PHOT essere a fuoco / non essere a fuoco **II** *v/t*: ***~ one's attention on*** focalizzare l'attenzione su **III** *v/i* mettere a fuoco
◆**focus on** *v/t problem, issue* focalizzare l'attenzione su; PHOT mettere a fuoco
fodder *n* foraggio *m*
foe *n form* nemico *m*, -a *f*
foetal *adj* fetale
foetus feto *m*
fog *n* nebbia *f*
◆**fog up** *v/i* ⟨*pret & past part* **-ged**⟩ appannarsi
fogbound *adj* bloccato dalla nebbia
foggy *adj* (+*er*) nebbioso; ***I haven't the foggiest*** (***idea***) non ne ho la più pallida idea
foghorn *n* sirena *f* da nebbia
fog lamp, fog light *n* AUTO fendinebbia *m*
foible *n* fisima *f*
foil[1] *n* carta *f* stagnola
foil[2] *v/t* (*thwart*) sventare
foist *v/t*: ***~ sth*** (***off***) ***on s.o.*** *goods* rifilare qc a qn; *task* imporre
fold[1] **I** *v/t paper etc* piegare; ***~ one's arms*** incrociare le braccia **II** *v/i of business* chiudere i battenti **III** *n in cloth etc* piega *f*
◆**fold away** *v/i* (*table*) piegarsi
◆**fold back** *v/t sep bedclothes* rimboccare
◆**fold down** *v/t sep corner* piegare
◆**fold up I** *v/t sep chairs etc* chiudere; *clothes* piegare **II** *v/i of chair, table* chiudere
fold[2] *n for sheep etc* ovile *m*
folder *n for documents* cartellina *f*; COMPUT cartella *f*
folding *adj* pieghevole; ***~ chair*** sedia *f* pieghevole
foliage *n* fogliame *m*
folk *n* (*people*) gente *f*; ***my ~*** (*family*) i miei parenti; ***come in, ~s*** *infml* entrate, gente *infml*
folk dance *n* danza *f* popolare **folklore** *n* folclore *m* **folk music** *n* musica *f* folk **folk singer** *n* cantante *m/f* folk **folk song** *n* canzone *f* popolare
folksy *adj US manner* alla buona
folk tale *n* leggenda *f* popolare
follicle *n* follicolo *m*
follow I *v/t* (*a. understand*) seguire **II** *v/i* seguire; *logically* quadrare; ***it ~s from this that …*** ne consegue che …; ***as ~s*** quanto segue
◆**follow on** *v/i* derivare
◆**follow through** *v/i*: ***follow through with sth*** (*with plan*) portare a termine; (*with threat*) mettere in atto
◆**follow up** *v/t sep letter, inquiry* dare seguito a
follower *n of politician etc* seguace *m/f*; *of football team* tifoso *m*, -a *f*; ***are you a ~ of …?*** *of TV programme* segui …?
following I *adj* seguente **II** *n people* seguito *m*; ***the man has quite a ~*** quell'uomo ha parecchi sostenitori; ***the ~*** quanto segue
follow-up meeting *n* riunione *f* ulteriore **follow-up visit** *n to doctor etc*

visita *f* successive

folly *n* (*madness*) follia *f*; ***it is sheer ~*** è pura follia

foment *v/t* fomentare

fond *adj* (+*er*) (*loving*) affezionato; *memory* caro; ***he is ~ of travel*** gli piace viaggiare; ***have ~ memories of sth*** avere cari ricordi di qc; (*foolish*, *vain*) ***in the ~ hope / belief that …*** nella vana speranza / illusione che…

fondant *n* fondente

fondle *v/t* accarezzare

fondness *n for person* affetto *m*; *for wine*, *food* gusto *m*

font *n for printing* carattere *m*; *in church* fonte *f* battesimale

food *n* cibo *m*; ***I like Italian ~*** mi piace la cucina italiana; ***there's no ~ in the house*** non c'è niente da mangiare in casa; ***~ for thought*** oggetto di riflessione

food additives *npl* additivi *mpl* per alimenti **food chain** *n* catena *f* alimentare

foodie *n infml* buongustaio *m*, -a *f*

food mixer *n* mixer *m inv* **food poisoning** *n* intossicazione *f* alimentare **food processor** *n* robot *m inv* da cucina

foodstuff *n form* generi *mpl* alimentari

fool[1] **I** *n* pazzo *m*, -a *f*; ***make a ~ of o.s.*** rendersi ridicolo **II** *v/t* ingannare; ***~ s.o. into believing that …*** far credere a qn che …

◆**fool about, fool around** *v/i* fare lo sciocco; *sexually* avere l'amante

◆**fool around with** *v/t knife*, *drill etc* trastullarsi con; *s.o.'s wife* avere una relazione con

fool[2] *n Br* COOK *dolce di frutta cotta e panna*

foolhardy *adj* temerario

foolish *adj* sciocco; ***don't do anything ~*** non fare niente di sciocco; ***what a ~ thing to do*** che cosa stupida da fare; ***it made him look ~*** gli ha fatto fare la figura dello stupido

foolishly *adv* scioccamente

foolproof *adj* a prova di idiota

foot I *n* ⟨*pl* **feet**⟩ *a. measurement* piede *m*; ***on ~*** a piedi; ***I've been on my feet all day*** sono stato in piedi tutto il giorno; ***be back on one's feet*** essere di nuovo in piedi; ***at the ~ of the page*** a piè di pagina; ***at the ~ of the hill*** ai piedi della collina; ***put one's ~ in it*** *infml* fare una gaffe; ***put one's ~ down*** (*act with authority*) puntare i piedi; AUTO schiacciare l'acceleratore; ***find one's feet*** cavarsela da solo; ***get / be under s.o.'s feet*** stare tra i piedi a qn; ***get off on the wrong ~*** partire con il piede sbagliato; ***stand on one's own two feet*** stare in piedi da solo; ***a nice area, my ~!*** *infml* bella zona, un corno! **II** *v/t bill* pagare

footage *n* pellicola *f* cinematografica

football *n* (*soccer*) calcio *m*; *American style* football *m* americano; (*ball*) pallone *m* da calcio; *for American football* pallone *m* da football americano

footballer *n* calciatore *m*, -trice *f*

football hooligan *n* teppista *m* del calcio **football pitch** *n* campo *m* da calcio **football player** *n soccer* calciatore *m*, -trice *f*; *American style* giocatore *m* di football americano **football pools** *npl Br* totocalcio *m*

footbridge *n* passerella *f*

-footed *adj suf* a piedi; ***four-footed*** quadrupede

footer *n* COMPUT piè *m inv* di pagina

foothills *npl* colline *fpl* pedemontane

foothold *n in climbing* punto *m* d'appoggio; *fig* ***gain a ~*** conquistarsi uno spazio

footing *n* (*basis*) presupposti *mpl*; ***lose one's ~*** perdere il punto d'appoggio; ***be on the same ~ / a different ~*** essere sullo stesso piano / su un piano diverso; ***be on a friendly ~ with …*** avere rapporti amichevoli con …

footlights *npl* luci *fpl* della ribalt

footman *n* lacchè *m*

footmark *n* impronta *f* di piede **footnote** *n* nota *f* a piè di pagina **footpath** *n* sentiero *m* **footprint** *n* impronta *f* di piede **footstep** *n* passo *m*; ***follow in s.o.'s ~s*** seguire i passi di qn **footstool** *n* sgabello *m* per i piedi **footwear** *n* calzatura *f* **footwork** *n* SPORTS gioco *m* di gambe

for *prep* **1.** *purpose*, *destination etc* per; ***a train ~ …*** un treno per …; ***clothes ~ children*** abbigliamento *m* per bambini; ***it's too big / small ~ you*** è troppo grande / piccolo per te; ***here's a***

letter ~ you c'è una lettera per te; ***this is ~ you*** questo è per te; ***what is there ~ lunch?*** cosa c'è per pranzo?; ***the steak is ~ me*** la bistecca è per me; ***what is this ~?*** a cosa serve?; ***what ~?*** a che scopo?, perché?; ***please get it done ~ Monday*** per favore, fallo per lunedì **2.** *time* per; ***~ three days / two hours*** per tre giorni / due ore; ***I have been waiting ~ an hour*** ho aspettato (per) un'ora **3.** *distance* per; ***I walked ~ a mile*** ho camminato per un miglio; ***it stretches ~ 100 miles*** si estende per 100 miglia **4.** (*in favour of*) per; ***campaign ~*** fare una campagna per; ***I am ~ the idea*** sono a favore dell'idea **5.** (*instead of, on behalf of*) per; ***let me do that ~ you*** lascia che te lo faccia io, lascia che faccia questo per te; ***we are agents ~ ...*** siamo rappresentanti di ... **6.** (*in exchange for*) per; ***I bought it ~ £25*** l'ho comprato per 25 sterline; ***how much did you sell it ~?*** a quanto l'hai venduto?

forage I *v/i* foraggio *m* **II** *n* (*rummage*) l'andare alla ricerca (**for** di)

foray I *n* incursione *m*; *fig* tentativo di sfondare (*into* in) **II** *v/i & v/t* fare un'incursione

forbade *pret* → ***forbid***

forbear *v/i & v/t* astenersi

forbid *v/t* ⟨*pret* ***forbade***, *past part* ***forbidden***⟩ vietare, proibire; ***~ s.o. to do sth*** vietare *or* proibire a qn di fare qc

forbidden I *adj* vietato, proibito; ***smoking ~*** vietato fumare; ***parking ~*** divieto di sosta **II** *past part* → ***forbid***

forbidding *adj* ostile

force I *n* (*violence*) forza *f*; ***by ~*** per forza; ***come into ~*** *of law etc* entrare in vigore; ***the ~s*** MIL le forze armate **II** *v/t door, lock* forzare; ***~ s.o. to do sth*** forzare *or* costringere qn a fare qc; ***~ sth open*** aprire qc con la forza

◆**force back** *v/t sep tears etc* trattenere

◆**force down** *v/t sep food* mandare giù

◆**force off** *v/t sep lid* togliere

forced *adj laugh, smile* forzato

forced landing *n* atterraggio *m* d'emergenza

force-feed *v/t* ⟨*pret & past part* ***force-fed***⟩ alimentare artificialmente

forceful *adj argument, speaker* convincente; *character* energico

forcefully *adv* in modo energico

forcefulness *n* forza *f*; (*energy*) energia *f*; (*conviction*) efficacia *f*

forceps *npl* MED forcipe *f*

forcible *adj entry* forzato; *argument* convincente

forcibly *adv restrain* con la forza

ford *n* **I** *n* guado *m* **II** *v/t* guadare

fore *n*: ***come to the ~*** salire alla ribalta

forearm *n* avambraccio *m*

forebears *npl* antenati *mpl*

foreboding *n* presentimento *m*

forecast I *n* previsione *f* **II** *v/t* ⟨*pret & past part* ***forecast***⟩ prevedere

forecourt *n of garage* area *f* di rifornimento

forefathers *npl* antenati *mpl*

forefinger *n* indice *m*

forefront *n*: ***be in the ~ of*** essere all'avanguardia in

foregone *adj*: ***that's a ~ conclusion*** è una conclusione scontata

foreground *n* primo piano *m*; ***in the ~*** in primo piano

forehand *n in tennis* diritto *m*

forehead *n* fronte *f*

foreign *adj* straniero; *trade, policy* estero

foreign affairs *npl* affari *mpl* esteri

foreign aid *n* aiuti *mpl* ad altri paesi

foreign body *n* corpo *m* estraneo

foreign currency *n* valuta *f* estera

foreigner *n* straniero *m*, -a *f*

foreign exchange *n* cambio *m* valutario

foreign language *n* lingua *f* straniera

foreign minister *n* ministro *m* degli esteri

Foreign Office *n in UK* Ministero *m* degli esteri

foreign policy *n* politica *f* estera

Foreign Secretary *n in UK* ministro *m* degli esteri

foreign trade *n* commercio *m* estero

foreman *n* caposquadra *m*

foremost I *adv* (*uppermost*) soprattutto **II** *adj* (*leading*) principale

forensic medicine *n* medicina *f* legale

forensic scientist *n* medico *m* legale

foreplay *n sexual* preliminari *mpl*

forerunner *n* precursore *m*

foresaw *pret* → ***foresee***

foresee *v/t* ⟨*pret* ***foresaw***, *past part* ***foreseen***⟩ prevedere

foreseeable *adj* prevedibile; ***in the ~ future*** per quanto si possa prevedere

in futuro
foreseen *past part* → ***foresee***
foreshadow *v/t* preannunciare **foresight** *n* lungimiranza *f* **foreskin** *n* prepuzio *m*
forest *n* foresta *f*
forestall *v/t* prevenire
forester *n* guardaboschi *m/f*
forest ranger *n US* guardia *f* forestale
forestry *n* scienze *fpl* forestali
foretaste *n* anteprima *m*, assaggio *m*
foretell *v/t* ⟨*pret & past part* ***foretold***⟩ predire
foretold *pret & past part* → ***foretell***
forever *adv* per sempre; ***it is ~ raining here*** piova continuamente qui; ***Scotland ~!*** viva la Scozia!; ***it takes ~*** *infml* non finisce più; ***these slate roofs last ~*** *infml* questi tetti di ardesia durano una vita; *change* definitivamente; ***the old social order was gone ~*** il vecchio ordine sociale era finito per sempre
forewarn *v/t* preavvisare
foreword *n* prefazione *f*
forfeit I *v/t right, privilege etc* perdere **II** *n esp* JUR multa *f*; *fig* pegno *m*; *in game* penitenza *f*
forgave *pret* → ***forgive***
forge I *n* forgia *f* **II** *v/t* (*counterfeit*) contraffare; *signature* falsificare
◆**forge ahead** *v/i* prendere il sopravvento
forger *n* falsario *m*, -a *f*
forgery *n* (*banknote*) falsificazione *f*; (*document*) falso *m*; ***the signature was a ~*** la firma era falsificata
forget *v/t & v/i* ⟨*pret* **forgot**, *past part* **forgotten**⟩ dimenticare; ***~ about*** dimenticarsi di; ***~ to do sth*** dimenticare di fare qc; ***~ him, he's a waste of time*** lascialo perdere, ti fa solo perdere tempo
forgetful *adj* smemorato
forget-me-not *n* non-ti-scordar-di-me *m inv*
forgettable *adj*: ***it was an instantly ~ game*** è stata una partita molto poco memorabile
forgive *v/t & v/i* ⟨*pret* **forgave**, *past part* **forgiven**⟩ perdonare
forgiven *past part* → ***forgive***
forgiveness *n* perdono *m*
forgo *v/t* ⟨*pret* **forwent**, *past part* **forgone**⟩ rinunciare a; *lunch* saltare
forgot *pret* → ***forget***
forgotten *past part* → ***forget***
fork I *n for eating* forchetta *f*; *for gardening* forca *f*; *in road* biforcazione *f* **II** *v/i* (*road, branch*) biforcarsi; ***~ (to the) right*** (*road*) svoltare a destra
◆**fork out** *v/t sep & v/i infml* (*pay*) sborsare *infml*
forked *adj* biforcuto
forklift truck *n* muletto *m*
forlorn *adj* (*desolate*) desolato; (*miserable*) misero; *attempt* vano; ***in the ~ hope of finding a better life*** nella vana speranza di trovare una vita migliore
forlornly *adv stand, wait* tristemente; *hope, try* disperatamente; (*vainly*) in vano
form I *n* (*shape*) forma *f*; (*document*) modulo *m*; *in school* classe *f*; ***be on/off ~*** essere in/fuori forma; ***in the ~ of*** sotto forma di; ***be in the ~ of*** avere la forma di; ***fill in a ~*** compilare un modulo **II** *v/t in clay etc* modellare; *friendship* creare; *opinion* formarsi; *past tense etc* formare; (*constitute*) costituire; ***~ a queue*** *Br or* ***line*** *US* mettersi in fila **III** *v/i* (*take shape, develop*) formarsi
formal *adj* formale; ***make a ~ apology*** presentare una scusa formale; ***~ dress*** abito da cerimonia
formalise, formalize *v/t rules* formalizzare; *agreement* rendere formale
formality *n* formalità *f inv*; ***it's just a ~*** è solo una formalità; ***the formalities*** le formalità
formally *adv* formalmente
format I *v/t* ⟨*pret & past part* ***-ted***⟩ COMPUT formattare; *document* impaginare **II** *n* (*size*: *of magazine etc*) formato *m*; (*makeup*: *of programme*) formula *f*
formation *n* formazione *f*; ***battle ~*** in formazione da battaglia
formative *adj* formativo; ***in his ~ years*** nei suoi anni formativi
former *adj wife*, *president* ex *inv*; *statement, arrangement* precedente; ***in ~ times*** in passato; ***the ~*** quest'ultimo
-former *n suf* EDU ***fifth-former*** studente del quinto anno
formerly *adv* precedentemente
formidable *adj* imponente
formula *n* formula *f*; (*a.* **formula milk**)

latte *m* in polvere; ***there's no sure ~ for success*** non esiste una formula per il successo
Formula One *n* Formula Uno *f*
formulate *v/t* (*express*) formulare
formulation *n* formulazione *f*
fornicate *v/i form* fornicare
fornication *n form* fornicazione *f*
forsake *v/t* 〈*pret* ***forsook***, *past part* ***forsaken***〉 *form* abbandonare
forswear *v/t* 〈*pret* ***forswore***, *past part* ***forsworn***〉 rinunciare a
fort *n* MIL forte *m*
forte *n* (*strong point*) il forte *m*; ***her ~ is cooking*** la cucina è il suo forte
forth *adv*: ***back and ~*** avanti e indietro; ***and so ~*** eccetera; ***from that day ~*** da quel giorno in poi
forthcoming *adj* (*future*) prossimo; *personality* comunicativo; ***be ~*** (*money*) essere disponibile
forthright *adj* schietto
fortieth *n/adj* quarantesimo, -a
fortification *npl* MIL fortificazione *f*
fortified wine *n* vino *m* liquoroso
fortify *v/t* 〈*pret & past part* ***-ied***〉 MIL *town* fortificare; *person* rinvigorire
fortitude *n* forza *f* d'animo
fortnight *n* due settimane
fortnightly *esp Br* **I** *adj* quindicinale; ***~ visits*** visite quindicinali **II** *adv* due volte al mese
fortress *n* MIL fortezza *f*
fortuitous *adj* fortuito
fortuitously *adv* casualmente
fortuity *n* casualità *f*
fortunate *adj* fortunato; ***it is ~ that*** è una fortuna che
fortunately *adv* fortunatamente; ***~ for me, my friend noticed it*** fortunatamente per me, i miei amici l'hanno notato
fortune *n* sorte *f*; (*lot of money*) fortuna *f*; ***ill ~*** malasorte *f*; ***personal ~*** patrimonio *m* personale; ***be worth a ~*** valere una fortuna; ***have the good ~ to*** avere la fortuna di; ***make a ~*** fare fortuna; ***tell s.o.'s ~*** predire il futuro a qn
fortune-teller *n* chiromante *m/f*
forty *num* quaranta; ***have ~ winks*** *infml* fare un pisolino *infml*
forum *n fig* foro *m*
Forum *n Roman* foro *m*
forward I *adv* avanti; ***take two steps ~*** fare due passi avanti; ***rush ~*** precipitarsi davanti; ***go straight ~*** andare dritto; ***he drove backward(s) and ~(s) between the station and the house*** ha guidato avanti e indietro tra la stazione e la casa, (*in time*) ***from this time ~*** (*from then*) da allora in poi; (*from now*) d'ora in poi; ***come ~*** avanzare; ***bring ~ new evidence*** produrre nuove prove **II** *adj* in avanti; *planning* in anticipo; *pej person* diretto; ***this seat is too far ~*** questo seggiolino è troppo avanti **III** *n* SPORTS attaccante *m* **IV** *v/t letter* inoltrare
forwarding address *n* recapito *m* **forwarding agent** *n* COMM spedizioniere *m*
forward-looking *adj* progressista
forwards *adv* → ***forward***
forward slash *n* barra *f* in avanti
forwent *pret* → ***forgo***
fossil *n* fossile *m*
fossil fuel *n* combustibile *m* fossile
fossilized *adj* fossilizzato
foster I *adj* JUR in affidamento; ***their children are in ~ care*** i loro bambini sono in affidamento **II** *v/t child* avere in affidamento; *attitude*, *belief* incoraggiare
foster child *n* figlio *m*, -a *f* in affidamento **foster family** *n* famiglia *f* di accoglienza **foster home** *n* famiglia *f* di accoglienza **foster parents** *npl* genitori *mpl* con affidamento
fought *pret & past part* → ***fight***
foul I *n* SPORTS fallo *m* **II** *adj smell*, *taste* pessimo; *weather* orribile; ***~ language*** linguaggio *m* scurrile; ***fall ~ of the law*** incorrere nei rigori della legge; ***fall ~ of s.o.*** entrare in conflitto con qn **III** *v/t air* inquinare; *pavement* sporcare; SPORTS fare un fallo contro
foul-mouthed *adj* sboccato **foul play** *n* SPORTS gioco *m* irregolare; *fig* ***the police do not suspect ~*** la polizia non sospetta alcun crimine
found[1] *v/t school etc* fondare
found[2] *pret & past part* → ***find***
foundation *n of theory etc* fondamenta *fpl*; (*organization*) fondazione *f*; *make-up* fondotinta *m*
foundation *n of building* fondamenta *fpl*
foundation stone *n* prima pietra *f*
founder[1] *n* fondatore *m*, -trice *f*

founder[2] *v/i ship* affondare; *fig project* colare a picco
founder member *n* membro *m* fondatore
founding *n* fondazione *f*
Founding Fathers *npl US* Padri *mpl* Fondatori
foundling *n* trovatello *m*, -a *f*
foundry *n* fonderia *f*
fount *n* (*source*) fonte *f*; TYPO font *m*
fountain *n* fontana *f*
fountain pen *n* penna *f* stilografica
four I *num* quattro **II** *n*: ***on all ~s*** a quattro zampe
four-door *adj* a quattro porte **four-figure** *adj* a quattro cifre **fourfold I** *adj* quadruplo **II** *adv* per quattro volte **four-leaf clover** *n* quadrifoglio *m* **four-legged** *adj* a quattro zampe **four-letter word** *n* parolaccia *f* **four-poster (bed)** *n* letto *m* a baldacchino **four-seater I** *adj* a quattro posti **II** *n* auto *f* a quattro posti **foursome** *n* quartetto *m* **four-star** *adj hotel etc* a quattro stelle **four-star (petrol)** *n* super *f*
fourteen *num* quattordici
fourteenth *n/adj* quattordicesimo, -a
fourth *n/adj* quarto, -a; ***in ~*** AUTO in quarta
fourthly *adv* in quarto luogo
four-wheel drive *n* AUTO trazione *f* integrale
fowl *n* pollame *m*
fox I *n* volpe *f* **II** *v/t* (*puzzle*) mettere in difficoltà; (*deceive*) imbrogliare
foxglove *n* BOT digitale *m*
fox-hunting *n* caccia *f* alla volpe; ***go ~*** andare a fare la caccia alla volpe
foyer *n* atrio *m*
fracas *n* baruffa *f*
fraction *n* frazione *f*; *fig* pochino; ***move it just a ~*** spostalo solo un pochino; ***for a ~ of a second*** per una frazione di secondo
fractionally *adv* lievemente
fractious *adj* intrattabile; *child* stizzoso
fracture I *n* frattura *f* **II** *v/t* fratturare; ***he ~d his shoulder*** si è fratturato la spalla; ***~d skull*** cranio *m* fratturato
fragile *adj* fragile; ***"fragile (handle) with care"*** "fragile, maneggiare con cura"; ***feel ~*** *infml* sentirsi debole
fragility *n* fragilità *f*; *of health* delicatezza *f*
fragment I *n* frammento *m* **II** *v/i & v/t* (*society*) frammentare
fragmentary *adj* frammentario
fragmentation *n of society* frammentazione *f*
fragmentation bomb *n* MIL bomba *f* a frammentazione
fragrance *n* fragranza *f*
fragrant *adj* profumato
frail *adj* (+*er*) gracile; ***look ~*** avere un aspetto gracile
frailty *n of person* gracilità *f*
frame I *n* FILM, PHOT fotogramma *m*; *of picture*, *window* cornice *f*; *of glasses* montatura *f*; *of bicycle* telaio *m*; ***~ of mind*** stato *m* d'animo **II** *v/t picture* incorniciare; *infml person* incastrare *infml*; *infml* ***he said he had been ~d*** sostiene di essere stato incastrato
frame-up *n infml* montatura *f* **framework** *n* struttura *f*; ***within the ~ of ...*** nell'ambito di ...
France *n* Francia *f*
franchise I *n* COMM concessione *f*; POL diritto *m* di voto **II** *v/t* concedere il diritto di voto a
Franco- *pref* franco-
frank[1] *adj* (+*er*) franco; ***be (perfectly) ~ (with s.o.)*** essere (molto) franco con qn
frank[2] *v/t letter* spedire in franchigia; (*postmark*) affrancare
frankfurter *n* wurstel *m inv*
frankincense *n* incenso *m*
franking machine *n* affrancatrice *f*
frankly *adv* francamente; ***quite ~, I don't care*** francamente, me ne infischio
frankness *n* franchezza *f*
frantic *adj search*, *attempt* frenetico; ***~ activity*** (*generally*) frenesia *f*; (*particular instance*) attività *f* frenetica; (*worried*) agitatissimo; ***I was ~*** ero agitatissimo; ***drive s.o. ~*** far impazzire qn
frantically *adv* freneticamente
fraternal *adj* fraterno
fraternity *n* (*friendship*) fratellanza *f*; (*group*) comunità *f*; *US of male students* confraternita *f* studentesca; ***the medical / legal ~*** la comunità medica / forense; ***the criminal ~*** la consorteria criminale
fraternize, fraternise *v/i* fraternizzare

(***with*** con)
fraud *n* frode *f*; *person* impostore *m*, -trice *f*
fraudulent *adj* fraudolento
fraudulently *adv* in modo fraudolento
fraught *adj* teso; ***~ with difficulty*** denso di difficoltà; ***~ with danger*** pieno di pericoli
fray¹ *n*: *fig* ***enter the ~*** entrare in lite
fray² *v/i* (*cloth*) logorarsi; (*rope*) sfilacciarsi; ***tempers began to ~*** cominciavano a logorarsi i nervi
frayed *adj cuffs* liso; ***have ~ nerves*** avere i nervi a fior di pelle
freak I *n unusual event* fenomeno *m* anomalo; *two-headed person, animal etc* scherzo *m* di natura; *infml strange person* tipo *m*, -a *f* strambo, -a; ***movie / jazz ~*** *infml* (*fanatic*) fanatico *m*, -a *f* del cinema / del jazz **II** *adj wind, storm etc* violento
◆**freak out** *v/i* (*get angry*) andare in bestia; (*get upset*) mettersi in agitazione
freakish *adj weather* anomalo
freckle *n* lentiggine *f*
free I *adj* (*+er*) **1.** (*at liberty, not occupied*) libero; ***are you ~ this afternoon?*** sei libero oggi pomeriggio?; ***is this seat ~?*** è libero questo posto?; ***~ from*** *or* ***of sth*** libero da qc; ***he's ~ to go*** è libero di andarsene; ***feel ~ to ask*** chiedi pure; ***~ and easy*** spensierato **2.** (*no cost*) gratuito; ***for ~*** *travel, get sth* gratis; ***admission ~*** entrata *f* libera; ***~ delivery*** consegna *f* gratuita; ***be ~ with one's money*** essere spendaccione; ***be ~ with one's advice*** essere prodigo di consigli **3.** (*unconfined*) ***~ jazz*** free jazz *m*; ***~ fall*** caduta *f* libera **4.** (*without*) ***fat ~*** senza grassi; ***duty ~*** esente da dazio **II** *v/t prisoners* liberare
◆**free up** *v/t person, time* liberare; *money* rendere disponibile
free agent *n* persona *f* indipendente
free-and-easy *adj*, **free and easy** *adj* senza cerimonie; (*morally*) disinvolto
freebie, freebee *n infml* omaggio *m*
free copy *n* copia *f* omaggio
freedom *n* libertà *f*; ***~ from sth*** libertà da qc
freedom fighter *n* combattente *m/f* per la libertà **freedom of speech** *n* libertà *f* di parola **freedom of the press** *n* libertà *f* di stampa
free enterprise *n* liberalismo *m* economico
Freefone® *n* numero *m* verde
free-for-all *n* (*fight*) mischia *f* generale
freehand *adv* a mano libera
freehold I *n* allodio *m* **II** *adj*: ***~ property*** proprietà *f* allodiale
free house *n Br birreria che serve diverse marche di birra* **free kick** *n in soccer* calcio *m* di punizione **freelance I** *adj* free lance *inv* **II** *adv work* free lance *inv* **freelancer** *n* free lance *m/f inv* **freeloader** *n infml* scroccone *m*, -a *f*
freely *adv admit* apertamente; ***I ~ admit that …*** ammetto apertamente che …; (*liberally*) generosamente; ***use sth ~*** usare qc liberamente; *move, talk,* facilmente; *flow* liberamente; ***be ~ available*** trovarsi facilmente
free market economy *n* economia *f* del libero mercato **Freemason** *n* massone *m* **free-range chicken** *n* pollo *m* ruspante **free-range eggs** *npl* uova *fpl* di galline ruspanti **free sample** *n* campione *m* gratuito **free speech** *n* libertà *f* di espressione **freestanding** *adj* non fissato al muro **freestyle** *n* stile *m* libero **free time** *n* tempo *m* libero **free-to-air** *adj Br* TV *programme, channel* in chiaro **free trade** *n* libero scambio *m* **freeware** *n* COMPUT freeware *m* **freeway** *n US* autostrada *f* **freewheel** *v/i on bicycle* andare a ruota libera **free will** *n* libero arbitrio *m*; ***he did it of his own ~*** l'ha fatto di sua spontanea volontà
freeze ⟨*pret* ***froze***, *past part* ***frozen***⟩ **I** *v/t food, wages, account* congelare; *video* bloccare **II** *v/i river* ghiacciare; *food, machine* congelarsi; *weather* gelare; (*keep still*) restare immobile; ***~ to death*** morire assiderato; ***~!*** fermi!; *fig* ***I felt my blood ~*** mi si è gelato il sangue **III** *n* COMM blocco *m*; METEO gelata *f*; ***~ on wages*** blocco *m* dei salari
◆**freeze over** *v/i of river* gelare
freeze up *v/i* ghiacciare
freeze-dried *adj* liofilizzato
freezer *n* freezer *m inv*, congelatore *m*
freezing I *adj* gelato; ***it's ~ out here*** si gela qui fuori; ***it's ~*** (***cold***) *of weather*

si gela; *of water* è gelata; ***I'm ~*** (*cold*) sono congelato **II** *n*: ***10 below ~*** 10 gradi sotto zero; COOK congelamento *m*

freezing compartment *n* freezer *m inv* **freezing point** *n* punto *m* di congelamento

free zone *n* porto *m* franco

freight I *n* carico *m*; *costs* trasporto *m* **II** *v/t* trasportare

freightage *n* spese *fpl* di trasporto

freight depot *n US* deposito *m* merci

freighter *n ship* nave *f* da carico; *aeroplane* aereo *m* da carico

freightliner® *n* portacontainer *m*

freight train *n* treno *m* merci

French I *adj* francese **II** *n language* francese *m*; ***the ~*** i francesi

French beans *npl* fagiolini *mpl* **French bread** *n* baguette *fpl* **French doors** *npl* portafinestra *f* **French dressing** *n* vinaigrette *f inv* **French fries** *npl* patate *fpl* fritte **French horn** *n* MUS corno *m* da caccia **French kiss** *n* bacio *m* in bocca **French leave** *n* fuga *f* all'inglese; ***take ~*** svignarsela all'inglese **French letter** *n* preservativo *m* **French loaf** *n* baguette *f* **Frenchman** *n* francese *m* **French polish I** *n* gommalacca *f* **II** *v/t* verniciare con gommalacca **French seam** *n* cucitura *f* inglese **French stick** *n* baguette *f inv* **French windows** *npl* portafinestra *f* **Frenchwoman** *n* francese *f*

frenetic *adj* frenetico

frenetically *adv* freneticamente; *dance* forsennatamente

frenzied *adj attack*, *activity* frenetico; *mob* impazzito

frenzy *n* frenesia *f*; ***in a ~*** freneticamente; ***he worked himself up into a ~*** si fece prendere dalla frenesia; ***~ of activity*** attività *f* frenetica; ***~ of excitement*** eccitazione *f* frenetica

frequency *n* frequenza *f*; ***high / low ~*** alta / bassa frequenza *f*

frequency band *n* banda *f* di frequenza **frequency curve** *n* curva *f* di frequenza **frequency distribution** *n* distribuzione *f* di frequenza **frequency modulation** *n* RADIO modulazione *f* di frequenza

frequent[1] *adj* frequente; ***there are ~ trains*** passano molti treni; ***violent clashes were a ~ occurrence*** erano frequenti scontri violenti

frequent[2] *v/t bar etc* frequentare

frequently *adv* frequentemente

fresco *n* affresco *m*

fresh I *adj fruit*, *meat etc*, (*cold*) fresco; (*new*: *start*) nuovo; ***~ supplies*** provviste *fpl* fresche; ***make a ~ start*** ricominciare da capo; ***as ~ as a daisy*** fresco come una rosa;(*impertinent*) ***don't get ~ with me!*** non prenderti delle libertà con me! **II** *adv* (*straight*) ***young men ~ out of university*** giovani *mpl* appena usciti dall'università; ***cakes ~ from the oven*** torte *fpl* appena sfornate; *infml* ***we're ~ out of cheese*** abbiamo appena terminato il formaggio; ***they are ~ out of ideas*** hanno esaurito le idee

fresh air *n* aria *f* fresca

freshen *v/i of wind* rinfrescare

◆**freshen up I** *v/i* rinfrescarsi **II** *v/t sep room*, *paintwork* rinfrescare

fresher *n* matricola *f*

freshly *adv* appena; ***a ~ baked cake*** una torta appena fatta

freshman *n US* matricola *f*

freshness *n of fruit*, *meat*, *climate* freschezza *f*; *of style*, *approach* novità *f*

fresh orange *n* spremuta *f* d'arancia

freshwater *adj* d'acqua dolce; ***~ fish*** pesce *m* d'acqua dolce

fret[1] *v/i* ⟨*pret & past part* **-ted**⟩ agitarsi; ***don't ~*** non agitarti

fret[2] *n on guitar* stanghetta *f* trasversale

fretful *adj child* stizzoso; *adult* irritabile

fretsaw *n* sega *f* da traforo

fretwork *n* lavoro *m* di traforo

Freudian *adj* freudiano

Freudian slip *n* (*spoken*) lapsus *m inv* freudiano

Fri. *abbr* (= **Friday**) venerdì *m inv*

friable *adj* friabile

friar *n* frate *m*; ***Friar John*** fra Giovanni

fricassee I *n* COOK fricassea *f* **II** *v/t* cucinare in fricassea

friction *n* PHYS frizione *f*; *between people* attrito *m*

Friday *n* venerdì *m inv*; ***on ~*** venerdì; ***on ~s*** tutti i venerdì

fridge *n* frigo *m*

fridge-freezer *n frigorifero con repar-*

to surgelati
fried egg *n* uovo *m* fritto **fried potatoes** *npl* patate *fpl* saltate
friend *n* amico *m*, -a *f*; ***make ~s*** fare amicizia; ***make ~s with s.o.*** fare amicizia con qn; ***be ~s with s.o.*** essere amico di qn
friendliness *n* amichevolezza *f*
friendly I *adj* (+*er*) **1.** amichevole; ***be ~ with s.o.*** (*be friends*) essere in rapporti d'amicizia con qn; ***they're very ~** with each other* sono molto in confidenza; ***~ relations*** rapporti *mpl* d'amicizia; ***be on ~ terms with s.o.*** essere in buoni rapporti con qn; ***he started getting too ~*** ha cominciato a prendersi troppa confidenza **2.** (*easy to use*) facile da usare **II** *n* SPORTS amichevole *f*
friendship *n* amicizia *f*
fries *npl* patate *fpl* fritte
Friesian *adj* (*cow*) frisone
frieze *n* (*picture*) fregio *m*; (*thin band*) fascia *f* ornamentale
frigate *n* NAUT fregata *f*
fright *n* paura *f*; ***get a ~*** prendersi uno spavento; ***give s.o. a ~*** far paura a qn
frighten *v/t* spaventare; ***be ~ed*** (***of***) aver paura (di); ***don't be ~ed*** non aver paura; ***you're ~ing me*** mi fai paura
◆**frighten away** *v/t sep* far scappare
frightening *adj* spaventoso; ***look ~*** avere un aspetto spaventoso; ***it is ~ to think what could happen*** è spaventoso pensare a ciò che sarebbe potuto succedere
frightful *adj infml* orribile
frigid *adj* (*sexually*) frigido; *form* (*cold*) rigido
frill *n on dress etc* volant *m inv*; ***~s*** (*fancy extras*) fronzoli *mpl*; *fig* ***with all the ~s*** con tutti i fronzoli; ***a simple meal without ~s*** un pasto semplice senza fronzoli; ***no ~s flights to the USA*** voli no frills per gli Stati Uniti
frilly *adj* (+*er*) pieno di volant
fringe I *n* frangia *f*; (*edge*) margini *mpl*; ***on the ~ of the forest*** al margine della foresta **II** *v/t* contornare
fringe benefits *npl* benefici *mpl* accessori
fringed *adj skirt, shawl* con frange
fringe group *n* frangia *f* **fringe theatre**, *US* **fringe theater** *n* teatro *m* sperimentale
Frisbee® *n* frisbee® *m*
frisk *v/t infml* frugare *infml*; (*move briskly*) saltellare
frisky *adj* (+*er*) *puppy etc* vivace; (*sexually aroused*) *infml* **feel ~** sentirsi eccitato
fritter[1] *v/t Br* frantumare
◆**fritter away** *v/t time, fortune* sprecare
fritter[2] *n* COOK frittella *f*
frivolity *n* frivolezza *f*
frivolous *adj person, pleasures* frivolo
frizzy *adj* (+*er*) *hair* crespo
fro *adv* → ***to***; → ***to-ing and fro-ing***
frock *n* vestito *m*
frog *n* rana *f*
frogman *n* sommozzatore *m*, -trice *f*
frogmarch *v/t Br* trascinare di peso
frogspawn *n* uova *fpl* di rana
frolic *v/i* ⟨*pret & past part* ***frolicked***⟩ (*a.* **frolic about** *or* **around**) divertirsi
from *prep* **1.** *in time* da; ***~ 9 to 5*** (***o'clock***) dalle 9 alle 5; ***~ the 18th century*** dal XVIII secolo; ***~ today on*** da oggi in poi; ***~ next Tuesday*** da martedì della prossima settimana; ***~ now on*** d'ora in poi; ***~ then on*** da allora in poi; ***~ time to time*** di quando in quando; ***as ~ the 6th May*** a partire dal 6 maggio; ***5 years ~ now*** fra 5 anni **2.** *in space* da; ***~ here to there*** da qui a lì; ***we drove here ~ Paris*** siamo venuti qui in macchina da Parigi; ***the train ~ Bristol*** il treno da Bristol **3.** *origin* di; ***a letter ~ Jo*** una lettera di Jo; ***a gift ~ the management*** un regalo della direzione; ***it doesn't say who it's ~*** non c'è scritto di chi è; ***I am ~ Liverpool*** sono di Liverpool; ***made ~ bananas*** fatto di banane; ***where did you get that ~?*** dove l'hai preso?; ***I got it ~ the supermarket / Kathy*** l'ho preso al supermercato / da Kathy; ***quotation ~ "Hamlet" / the Bible / Shakespeare*** citazione da "Amleto" / dalla Bibbia / da Shakespeare; ***translated ~ the English*** tradotto dall'inglese **4.** (*because of*) di; ***tired ~ the journey*** stanco del viaggio; ***it's ~ overeating*** è a causa del troppo mangiare **5.** (*indicating change*) ***things went ~ bad to worse*** le cose sono andate di male in peggio; ***he went ~ office boy to director***

è passato da fattorino a direttore; ***a price increase ~ £1 to £1.50*** un aumento di prezzo da 1 a 1,50 sterline **6.** (*indicating difference*) ***he is quite different ~ the others*** è completamente diverso dagli altri; ***tell black ~ white*** distinguere il bianco dal nero **7.** MATH ***3 ~ 8 leaves 5*** 8 meno 3 fa 5; ***take 12 ~ 18*** sottrarre 12 da 18; ***£10 will be deducted ~ your account*** verranno detratte 10 sterline dal tuo conto

fromage frais *n Br* formaggio *m* bianco, *crema di formaggio simile allo yogurt*

frond *n of fern* fronda *f*; *of palm* foglia *f*

front I *n* **1.** *of building* lato *m* principale; *of car, statue* davanti *m inv*; ***she spilled tea down the ~ of her dress*** si è versata il tè sul davanti del vestito; *of book* copertina *f* **2.** (*cover organization*) facciata *f* **3.** MIL, POL, METEO fronte *m* **4.** ***in ~*** davanti; ***in ~ of*** davanti a; ***at the ~*** davanti; ***at the ~ of*** *of bus etc* nella parte anteriore di **II** *adj wheel, seat* anteriore; ***~ tooth / wheel / room*** dente / ruota / stanza anteriore **III** *v/t TV programme* presentare; *organization* essere a capo di; ***her property ~s on the main road*** la sua proprietà fronteggia la strada principale **IV** *adv*: ***up ~*** in anticipo; ***50 % up ~*** il 50 % in anticipo

frontal I *adj*: ***~ attack*** attacco *m* frontale **II** *n* ARCH facciata *f*

front bench *n* POL *principali esponenti del governo e dell'opposizione nel Parlamento* **front cover** *n* copertina *f* **front door** *n* porta *f* principale **front entrance** *n* entrata *f* principale **front garden** *n* giardino *m* sul davanti della casa

frontier *n a. fig* frontiera *f*

frontispiece *n* TYPO frontespizio *m*; ARCH frontone *m*

front line *n* MIL fronte *m* **front man** *n pej* uomo *m* di paglia **front of house** *n Br* THEAT foyer *m inv*; *hotel* hall *f inv* **front page** *n of newspaper* prima pagina *f* **front page news** *nsg* notizia *f* di prima pagina **front row** *n* prima fila *f*

front-runner *n fig* candidato *m*, -a *f* favorito,-a

front seat passenger *n in car* passeggero *m* davanti

frontwards *adv* in avanti

front-wheel drive *n* trazione *f* anteriore

frost I *n* brina *f* **II** *v/t* coprire di ghiaccio; *esp US cake* glassare

frostbite *n* congelamento *m* **frostbitten** *adj* congelato

frosted *adj esp US* (*iced*) glassato

frosted glass *n* vetro *m* smerigliato

frosting *n US* glassa *f*

frosty *adj* (+*er*) *a. fig* gelido

froth I *n* spuma *f* **II** *v/i* schiumare; ***the dog was ~ing at the mouth*** il cane aveva la bava alla bocca; ***he was ~ing at the mouth*** (***with rage***) stava schiumando di rabbia

frothy *adj* (+*er*) *cream etc* spumoso

frown I *v/i* aggrottare le sopracciglia **II** *n* cipiglio *m*

◆**frown on** *v/t* non vedere di buon occhio; ***this practice is frowned*** (***up***)***on*** questa pratica non è vista di buon occhio

frowzy, frowsy *adj* trasandato

froze *pret* → ***freeze***

frozen I *adj* gelato; *wastes* gelido; *food* surgelato; ***I'm ~*** *infml* sono congelato *infml* **II** *past part* → ***freeze***

frozen food *n* cibi *mpl* surgelati

FRS *abbr* (= **Fellow of the Royal Society**) *membro della Royal Society, accademia scientifica britannica*

fructose *n* fruttosio *m*

frugal *adj person* parsimonioso; *meal* frugale

fruit I *n* frutto *m*; *collective* frutta *f*; *results* frutto *m*; ***the ~s of her labours*** i frutti delle sue fatiche; *Br infml* ***old ~*** vecchio mio **II** *v/t & v/i* fruttare

fruit cake *n dolce con frutta candita*; *Br infml* svitato *m*, -a *f* **fruit cocktail** *n* macedonia *f*

fruitful *adj discussions etc* fruttuoso

fruit juice *n* succo *m* di frutta **fruit knife** *n* coltello *m* da frutta **fruitless** *adj attempt* vano; *argument* inutile **fruit machine** *n* slot machine *f inv* **fruit salad** *n* macedonia *f* **fruit tree** *n* albero *m* da frutto

fruity *adj* (+*er*) *taste* fruttato; *voice* morbido

frump *n pej* sciattona *f*

frumpy *adj* sciatto

frustrate *v/t person* frustrare; *plans* scombussolare; ***he was ~d in his efforts*** i suoi sforzi sono stati frustrati

frustrated *adj look, sigh* frustrato; ***I get ~ when …*** resto deluso quando …; ***he's a ~ poet*** è un poeta mancato

frustrating *adj* frustrante

frustratingly *adv slow, hard* in modo frustrante

frustration *n* frustrazione *f*; ***sexual ~*** insoddisfazione *f* sessuale; ***the ~s of modern life*** le frustrazioni della vita moderna

fry I *v/t* ⟨*pret & past part* ***-ied***⟩ friggere; ***~ an egg*** friggere un uovo **II** *v/i* friggere **III** *n* (*small fish*) pesciolini *mpl*; *US* bambini *mpl*

frying pan *n* padella *f*; ***out of the ~ into the fire*** *prov* dalla padella nella brace

fry-up *n* frittura *f* mista

ft *abbr* (= **foot, feet**) piede *m* (*misura*)

FT *abbr* (= **full-time**) a tempo pieno

fuchsia *n* BOT fucsia *f*

fuck I *v/t vulg* scopare *vulg*; ***~ you!*** vaffanculo!; ***~ him!*** che vada a farsi fottere! **II** *int vulg* ***~!*** cazzo! *vulg* **III** *n vulg* scopata *f vulg*; ***I don't give a ~*** *vulg* non me ne frega un cazzo *vulg*; ***who the ~ is that?*** *vulg* chi cazzo è? *vulg*

◆**fuck off** *v/i vulg* andare affanculo *vulg*; ***fuck off!*** vaffanculo!

◆**fuck up** *vulg* **I** *v/t sep* mandare a puttane; *piece of work* incasinare; ***she is really fucked up*** è davvero nei casini; ***heroin will really fuck you up*** l'eroina finirà davvero per rovinarti **II** *v/i* fare casini

fuck-all *n vulg* cazzo *m*; ***he knows ~ about it*** non ne sa un cazzo; ***I've done ~ all day*** non ho fatto un cazzo tutto il giorno

fucker *n vulg pej* cazzone *m*, -a *f*

fucking I *adj vulg* del cazzo *vulg*; ***this ~ machine*** questa macchina del cazzo **II** *adv vulg*; ***I'm ~ late!*** *vulg* sono in ritardo, cazzo!; ***I'm ~ tired*** cazzo, come sono stanco; ***a ~ awful film*** un film dannatamente brutto

fuddy-duddy *n infml*: ***an old ~*** vecchio parruccone *m*, - a *f*

fudge I *n dolciume simile alla caramella mou* **II** *v/t issue* eludere **III** *int* sciocchezze

fuel I *n* carburante *m*; ***add ~ to the flames*** *or* ***fire*** *fig* versare benzina sul fuoco **II** *v/t* ⟨*pret & past part* ***-led***, *US* ***-ed***⟩ *fig* alimentare; *fig conflict* fomentare; *speculation* favorire; ***power stations fuelled*** *Br or* ***fueled*** *US* ***by oil*** centrali *fpl* elettriche alimentate a petrolio

fuel gauge *n* indicatore *m* del livello di carburante

fueling station *n US* stazione *f* di rifornimento

fuel-injected *adj*: ***~ engine*** motore *m* a iniezione **fuel injection** *n* iniezione *f* (di carburante) **fuel pump** *n* pompa *f* del carburante **fuel tank** *n* serbatoio *m* del carburante

fug *n* aria *f* viziata

fugacious *adj* fugace

fuggy *adj air* viziato

fugitive *n* fuggiasco *m*, -a *f*

fugue *n* MUS fuga *f*

fulfil, *US* **fulfill** *v/t* ⟨*pret & past part* ***-led***⟩ *dreams* realizzare; *needs, expectations* soddisfare; *contract* eseguire; *requirements* corrispondere a; ***feel ~led*** *in job, life* sentirsi soddisfatto

fulfilling *adj*: ***a ~ job*** un lavoro appagante

fulfilment, *US* **fulfillment** *n of contract* esecuzione *f*; *of dreams* realizzazione *f*; *moral, spiritual* soddisfazione *f*

full I *adj* (*+er*) pieno (**of** di); *account, report* esauriente; *figure, skirt* abbondante; *life* intenso; ***I have a ~ day ahead of me*** ho davanti a me una giornata intensa; ***I am ~*** (***up***) *infml* sono sazio; ***we are ~ up for July*** per luglio siamo al completo; ***at ~ speed*** a tutta velocità; ***make ~ use of sth*** fare pieno uso di qc; ***that's a ~ day's work*** è un'intera giornata di lavoro; ***I waited two ~ hours*** ho aspettato due ore piene; ***the ~ details*** tutti i dettagli; ***be ~ of o.s.*** essere pieno di sé; ***she was ~ of it*** ne era completamente assorbita; ***~ up*** *hotel, with food* pieno **II** *adv*: ***know ~ well that*** sapere perfettamente che **III** *n*: ***in ~*** per esteso; ***write one's name in ~*** scrivere il proprio nome per esteso; ***pay in ~*** saldare il conto; ***in ~*** *write* per intero

fullback *n* SPORTS terzino *m*

full-blooded *adj* (*vigorous*) energico; ***he's a ~ Scot*** è uno scozzese purosangue **full-blown** *adj Aids* conclamato **full board** *n* pensione *f* completa **full-bodied** *adj wine* corposo **full-cream** *adj*: ***~ milk*** latte *m* intero **full employment** *n* piena occupazione *f* **full-face** *adj portrait* di fronte; ***~ photograph*** fotografia *f* frontale **full-fledged** *adj US* → ***fully-fledged*** **full-grown** *adj* adulto; ***~ adult*** *person* adulto in età matura; *animal* adulto completamente sviluppato **full house** *n* THEAT tutto esaurito; *cards* full *m*; ***they played to a ~*** il loro spettacolo ha registrato il tutto esaurito **full-length** *adj dress* lungo; ***~ film*** lungometraggio *m* **full moon** *n* luna *f* piena **full name** *n* nome e cognome *m* **full-page** *adj* a tutta pagina **full professor** *n* UNIV ordinario *m* **full-scale** *adj* vero e proprio **full stop** *n* punto *m* fermo **full-time** *adj/adv worker, job* a tempo pieno

fully *adv booked, recovered* completamente; *understand, explain* perfettamente; *describe* ampiamente

fully-fledged, *US* **full-fledged** *adj* più che qualificato **fully qualified** *adj* pienamente qualificato

fulsome *adj* smaccato

fumble *v/t catch* farsi sfuggire

◆**fumble about, around** *v/i in bags, pockets* frugare; *move in the dark* andare a tastoni; *search in the dark* cercare a tastoni

fume *v/i*: ***be fuming*** *infml* (*be very angry*) essere nero *infml*

fumes *npl* esalazioni *fpl*

fumigate *v/t* disinfestare tramite irrorazione

fun I *n* divertimento *m*; ***it's no ~ living on your own*** non è divertente vivere da soli; ***he is great ~*** è uno spasso; ***the party was good ~*** la festa è stata molto divertente; ***that sounds like ~*** sembra divertente; ***it was great ~*** era molto divertente; ***he's good ~*** con lui ci si diverte; ***bye, have ~!*** ciao, divertiti!; ***for ~*** per divertirsi; (*joking*) per scherzo; ***in ~*** per scherzo; ***make ~ of*** prendere in giro **II** *adj infml* divertente; ***squash is a ~ game*** lo squash è un gioco divertente; ***he's a real ~ person*** è una persona davvero divertente

function I *n* (*purpose*) funzione *f*; (*reception etc*) cerimonia *f* **II** *v/i* funzionare; ***~ as*** servire da

functional *adj* (*utilitarian*) funzionale; (*able to operate*) funzionante

functionary *n* funzionario *m*, -a *f*

function key *n* COMPUT tasto *m* funzione

fund I *n* fondo *m*; ***public ~s*** fondi *mpl* pubblici; ***be short of ~s*** essere a corto di denaro **II** *v/t project etc* finanziare

fundamental I *adj* fondamentale; ***~ to*** fondamentale per; ***of ~ importance*** di fondamentale importanza; ***~ structure*** struttura *f* fondamentale **II** *npl*: ***~s*** *of subject* fondamenti *mpl*

fundamentalism *n* fondamentalismo *m*

fundamentalist *n* fondamentalista *m/f*

fundamentally *adv* fondamentalmente; ***the treaty is ~ flawed*** il trattato presenta un vizio fondamentale

funding *n money* fondi *mpl*

fundraiser *n* responsabile *m/f* della raccolta fondi

fundraising *n* raccolta *f* di fondi; ***~ campaign*** campagna *f* di raccolta fondi; (*for donations*) colletta *f*

funeral *n* funerale *m*

funeral director *n* impresario *m* delle pompe funebri **funeral parlour**, *US* **funeral home** *n* obitorio *m*; **funeral service** *n* servizio *m* funebre

funfair *n* luna park *m inv*

fungal *adj* fungino; ***~ infection*** infezione *f* fungina

fungi → ***fungus***

fungicide *n* fungicida *m*

fungus *n* fungo *m*

funicular (railway) *n* funicolare *f*

funk I *n* MUS funk *m*; *Br infml* fifa *f* **II** *v/t & v/i Br infml* avere fifa

funky *adj* MUS funky; (*fashionable*) alla moda; ***~ clothes*** vestiti *mpl* alla moda

funnel I *n* (*for pouring*) imbuto *m*; NAUT, RAIL fumaiolo *m* **II** *v/t fig* incanalare

funnily *adv* (*oddly*) stranamente; (*comically*) in modo divertente; ***~ enough*** per quanto strano

funny I *adj* (+*er*) (*comical*) divertente;

(*odd*) strano; ***wickedly ~*** estremamente divertente; ***go ~*** *Br infml* diventare matto; ***it's not ~*** non c'è niente da ridere; ***I'm not being ~*** *Br infml* non sto scherzando; ***I feel a bit ~*** mi sento poco bene **II** *npl*: ***the funnies*** *US infml* PRESS fumetti *mpl*
funny bone *n* osso *m* del gomito **funny business** *n infml* affare *m* poco pulito
fur I *n* pelliccia *f*; *on animal* pelo *m*; incrostazione *f*; ***~ coat*** pelliccia *f*;***~ collar*** collo *m* di pelliccia **II** *v/t*: ***eating unripe fruit ~s the tongue*** la frutta acerba allappa
◆**fur up** *v/i* (*kettle*) incrostarsi
furious *adj* (*angry*) furioso; (*intense*) spaventoso; ***at a ~ pace*** a tutta velocità
furiously *adv* furiosamente
furl *v/t sail*, *flag* ammainare; *umbrella* chiudere
furlong *n* furlong *m*
furnace *n* forno *m*; *for metal* fornace *f*
furnish *v/t room* arredare; (*supply*) fornire; ***~ s.o. with sth*** fornire qc a qn
furnishings *npl* mobili *mpl*
furniture *n* mobili *mpl*; ***a piece of ~*** un mobile
furore, *US* **furor** *n* scalpore *m*; ***cause a ~*** fare scalpore
furred *adj tongue* impastata
furrier *n* pellicciaio *m*, -a *f*
furrow I *n* AGR solco *m*; *on brow* ruga *f* profonda **II** *v/t brow* corrugare
furry *adj* (+*er*) *animal* coperto di pelliccia
further I *adj* (*additional*) ulteriore; (*more distant*) più lontano; ***~ details*** ulteriori dettagli *mpl*; ***until ~ notice*** fino a nuovo avviso; ***have you anything ~ to say?*** ha qualcosa da aggiungere? **II** *adv walk*, *drive* oltre; ***~, I want to say …*** inoltre, volevo dire …; ***nothing could be ~ from the truth*** niente potrebbe essere più lontano dal vero; ***he has decided not to take the matter any ~*** ha deciso di non portare più avanti la questione; ***in order to make the soup go ~*** per allungare la minestra; ***two miles ~ (on)*** due miglia più avanti **III** *v/t cause etc* favorire; ***~ one's career*** favorire la propria carriera
further education *n Br istruzione para-universitaria*
furthermore *adv* inoltre
furthermost *adj* il più lontano
furthest I *adj* più lontano **II** *adv*; ***this is the ~ north*** è il punto più a nord; ***the ~ man has travelled in space*** il punto più lontano che si è raggiunto nello spazio; ***this is the ~ north you can go*** è il punto più a nord che è possibile raggiungere; ***it was the ~ the Irish team had ever got*** è stato il traguardo più lontano raggiunto dalla squadra irlandese
furtive *adj glance* furtivo
furtively *adv* furtivamente
fury *n* (*anger*) furore *m*; ***in a ~*** su tutte le furie
fuse I *n* ELEC fusibile *m* **II** *v/i* ELEC bruciarsi; ***the lights ~d*** sono saltati i fusibili **III** *v/t* (*metals*) fondere; (*bones*) saldare; ELEC bruciare
fusebox *n* scatola *f* dei fusibili
fuselage *n* fusoliera *f*
fuse wire *n* filo *m* per fusibili
fusillade *n* raffica *f*
fusion *n* fusione *f*
fuss I *n* agitazione *f*; *about film*, *event* scalpore *m*; ***I don't know what all the ~ is about*** non capisco a cosa sia dovuto tanto scompiglio; ***without (any) ~*** senza (tanto) chiasso; ***cause a ~*** causare scompiglio; ***make a ~*** *complain* fare storie; *behave in exaggerated way* agitarsi; ***make a ~ of*** *be very attentive to* colmare qn di attenzioni **II** *v/i* agitarsi; ***don't ~, mother!*** mamma, non ti agitare!
◆**fuss over** *v/t details* preoccuparsi di; *guests* darsi da fare per
fussed *adj Br infml* ***I'm not ~ (about it)*** non mi importa
fusspot *n Br infml* pignolo *m*, -a *f*
fussy *adj* (+*er*) *person* difficile; *design etc* complicato; ***be a ~ eater*** essere schizzinoso nel mangiare; ***be ~ about one's appearance*** essere esigente riguardo al proprio aspetto
fusty *adj* (+*er*) stantio
futile *adj* futile
futility *n* futilità *f inv*
futon *n* futon *m*
future I *n* futuro *m*; ***in ~*** in futuro; ***in the foreseeable ~*** nell'immediato futuro; ***what plans do you have for the ~?*** che piani hai per il futuro?; ***the ~***

GRAM il futuro **II** *adj* futuro; ***at a*** *or* ***some ~ date*** in data futura; ***his ~ plans*** i suoi piani futuri; ***in ~ years*** negli anni futuri; ***you can keep it for ~ reference*** lo puoi tenere per futura consultazione; ***the ~ tense*** GRAM il futuro
futures *npl* FIN titoli *mpl* a termine
futures market *n* FIN mercato *m* dei titoli a termine
future tense *n* futuro *m*
futuristic *adj design* futuristico
futurology *n* futurologia *f*
fuze *US* → ***fuse***
fuzz *n* lanugine *f*; *infml* ***the ~*** piedipiatti *mpl*
fuzzy *adj* (+*er*) *hair* crespo; (*out of focus*) sfuocato
fuzzy logic *n* ELEC logica *f* fuzzy
fwd *abbr* (= **forward**) avanti
f-word *n infml euph* (= **fuck**): ***I try not to use the ~ in front of the children*** cerco di non dire c... davanti ai bambini
FYI *abbr* (= **for your information**) per vostra informazione

G

G, g *n* g, G *f inv*; MUS sol *m inv*; ***G sharp*** sol *m inv* diesis; ***G flat*** sol *m inv* bemolle
g *abbr* (= **gram(s)**, **gramme(s)**) g (grammo)
G *abbr* (= **general audience**) *US* FILM *film adatto a tutti*
gab I *n*: ***have the gift of the ~*** *infml* avere la parlantina *infml* **II** *v/i* ⟨*pret & past part* ***-bed***⟩ cianciare
gabble I *v/i* parlare troppo in fretta **II** *v/t prayer* borbottare; *excuse* farfugliare **III** *n* borbottio *m*
gaberdine, gabardine *n* TEX gabardine *f*
gable *n* ARCH timpano *m*
gabled *adj* ARCH ***~ house/roof*** casa/tetto a due spioventi
◆**gad about** *v/i* ⟨*pret & past part* ***-ded***⟩ andarsene in giro
gadget *n* congegno *m*; ***the latest electronic ~*** gli ultimi congegni elettronici
gadgetry *n* congegni *mpl*
Gaelic *n language* gaelico *m*
gaffe *n* gaffe *f inv*
gaffer *n* FILM capo elettricista *m*
gag I *n* bavaglio *m*; (*joke*) battuta *f* **II** *v/t* ⟨*pret & past part* ***-ged***⟩ *person* imbavagliare; *the press* azzittire **III** *v/i* (*retch*) avere conati di vomito (***on*** a)
gaga *adj Br infml* fanatico; *old person* rimbambito
gage *US* → ***gauge***
gaggle *n of geese* schiamazzo *m*
gaiety *n* allegria *f*
gaily *adv* (*blythely*) allegramente
gain¹ *v/t* (*acquire*) acquisire, acquistare; (*watch*) andare avanti; (*profit*) guadagnarci (***by*** da); ***~ speed*** acquistare velocità; ***~ 10 pounds*** aumentare di 10 libbre; ***what does he hope to ~ by it?*** cosa spera di guadagnarci?; ***~ independence*** ottenere l'indipendenza; ***~ s.o.'s confidence*** guadagnare la fiducia di qn; ***~ experience*** acquisire esperienza; ***~ ground*** guadagnare terreno; ***~ time*** guadagnare tempo; ***he ~ed a reputation as ...*** si è guadagnato la reputazione di; ***~ popularity*** guadagnare popolarità; ***~ in confidence*** acquisire sicurezza
gain² *n* (*advantage*) vantaggio *m*; (*profit*) guadagno *m*; (*increase*) aumento *m*; ***~s*** *pl* (*winnings*) vincite *fpl*; (*profits*) profitti *mpl*; ***his loss is our ~*** mors tua vita mea; ***~ in weight*** *or* ***weight ~*** aumento *m* di peso
gainful *adj* remunerativo; ***be in ~ employment*** avere un impiego remunerativo
gainfully *adv*: ***~ employed*** con un impiego remunerativo
gait *n* andatura *f* (*a. of horse*)
gala *n concert etc* serata *f* di gala; ***swimming/sports ~*** gara *f* di nuoto/sportiva

galaxy *n* ASTR galassia *f*
gale *n* bufera *f*; **~ force 8** vento *m* forza 8; *fig* **~s of laughter** scoppi *mpl* di risa
gall I *n infml*: **have the ~ to do sth** avere la sfacciataggine di fare qc II *v/t fig* irritare
gallant *adj* galante; (*courageous*) valoroso **gallantly** *adv* galantemente; (*courageously*) valorosamente
gallantry *n* (*attentiveness to women*) galanteria *f*; (*bravery*) valore *m*
gall bladder *n* cistifellea *f*
galleon *n* galeone *m*
gallery *n* galleria *f*; THEAT loggione *m*
galley *n* cambusa *f*
galley proof *n* TYPO bozza *f* in colonna **galley slave** *n* galeotto *m*
Gallic *adj* gallico
galling *adj* irritante
◆**gallivant around** *v/i* andarsene a spasso
gallon *n* gallone *m*; **~s of tea** *infml* litri *mpl* di tè
gallop I *v/i* galoppare II *n* galoppo *m*; **at a ~** al galoppo
gallows *npl* forca *fsg*; **send / bring s.o. to the ~** mandare / portare qn sulla forca
gallstone *n* calcolo *m* biliare
galore *adj*: **apples / novels ~** mele / romanzi a iosa
galvanize *v/t* TECH galvanizzare; *fig* stimolare; **~ s.o. into doing** *or* **to do sth** spronare qn a fare qc
gambit *n* mossa *f*; *chess* gambetto *m*
gamble I *v/i* giocare (d'azzardo); **~ on** scommettere su II *v/t money* scommettere; **~ sth on sth** scommettere qc su qc III *n* rischio *m*; **it was a ~, but it paid off** è stato rischioso ma ha reso bene
◆**gamble away** *v/t sep* perdere al gioco
gambler *n* giocatore *m*, -trice *f* (d'azzardo)
gambling *n* gioco *m* (d'azzardo)
gambol I *v/i* sgambettare; (*lambs*) saltellare II *n* saltello *m*
game[1] *n* gioco *m*; (*match, in tennis*) partita *f*; **do you fancy a quick ~ of tennis / chess?** ti va una partita veloce a tennis / scacchi?; **I never liked card ~s** non mi è mai piaciuto giocare a carte; **~ of chance** gioco *m* d'azzardo; **play ~s with s.o.** *fig* prendersi gioco di qn; **the ~ is up** la partita è persa; **two can play at that ~** chi la fa l'aspetti; **beat s.o. at his own ~** battere qn con le sue stesse armi; **give the ~ away** tradirsi; **I wonder what his ~ is?** mi chiedo a che gioco stia giocando; *fig* **be / keep ahead of the ~** essere / restare in vantaggio; **games** *npl* (*sports event*) giochi *mpl*; *nsg* EDU educazione *f* fisica
game[2] *adj* (*brave*) coraggioso; **be ~** (*willing*) essere disposto; **be ~ for anything** essere pronto a tutto; **be ~ for a laugh** essere pronto alla risata
game[3] *n* (*hunting*) selvaggina *f*
game bird *n* selvaggina *f* da penna **gamekeeper** *n* guardacaccia *m/f inv* **game reserve** *n* riserva *f* di caccia
game show *n* TV gioco *m* televisivo
gamesmanship *n capacità di un giocatore di vincere sfruttando a proprio vantaggio le regole del gioco*
games software *n* software *m* per giochi **games theory** *n* MATH teoria *f* dei giochi
game warden *n* guardacaccia *m*
gaming *n* → **gambling**
gammon *n* coscia *f* di maiale affumicata; **~ steak** bistecca *f* di prosciutto
gammy *adj Br infml* zoppo
gamut *n fig* gamma *f*
gander *n* oca *f* maschio
gang *n* banda *f*
◆**gang up on** *v/t* mettersi contro
gangbang *vulg* I *n* stupro *m* collettivo II *v/t* stuprare in massa
gangland *adj* malavitoso
gangling *adj* allampanato
ganglion *n* ANAT ganglio *m*
gangplank *n* passerella *f*
gang rape I *n* stupro *m* collettivo II *v/t* stuprare in massa
gangrene *n* MED cancrena *f*
gangster *n* malvivente *m*, gangster *m inv*
gang warfare *n* guerra *f* tra bande
gangway *n* passaggio *m*; *for ship* passerella *f*
gaol → **jail**
gap *n in wall, for parking* buco *m*; *in conversation, life* vuoto *m*; *in time* intervallo *m*; *between two people's characters* scarto *m*; *in story, education* lacuna *f*; **a four-year ~** un inter-

vallo di quattro anni; ***a ~ in one's knowledge*** una lacuna nelle proprie conoscenze; ***close the ~*** *in race* avvicinarsi
gape *v/i of person* rimanere a bocca aperta; *of hole* spalancarsi
◆**gape at** *v/t* guardare a bocca aperta
gaping *adj hole* spalancato
gap year *n anno tra la fine del liceo e l'inizio dell'università dedicato ad altre attività*
garage *n for parking* garage *m inv*; *for petrol* stazione *f* di servizio; *for repairs* officina *f*
garage sale *n vendita di oggetti usati che avviene nel garage di un'abitazione privata*
garb I *n* abito *m* **II** *v/t* abbigliare
garbage *n* rifiuti *mpl*; (*fig*: *nonsense*) idiozie *fpl*; COMPUT informazioni *fpl* inutili
garbage can *n US* pattumiera *f*; (*outside*) bidone *m* dei rifiuti **garbage collector** *n US* spazzino *m* **garbage disposal** *n esp US* tritarifiuti *m inv* **garbage man** *n US* → ***garbage collector***
garbled *adj message* ingarbugliato
garden I *n* giardino *m*; *for vegetables* orto *m*; ***the Garden of Eden*** il giardino dell'Eden **II** *v/i* praticare il giardinaggio
garden apartment *n US appartamento* (*a piano terra o nel seminterrato*) *con accesso al giardino* **garden centre**, *US* **garden center** *n* centro *m* per il giardinaggio
gardener *n* giardiniere *m*, -a *f*
garden flat *n Br appartamento* (*a piano terra o nel seminterrato*) *con accesso al giardino*
gardening *n* giardinaggio *m*; ***she loves ~*** lei adora il giardinaggio; ***~ tools*** utensili *mpl* da giardinaggio
garden party *n* ricevimento *m* all'aperto **garden path** *n*: *fig* ***lead s.o. up*** *esp Br or* ***down*** *esp US* ***the ~*** raggirare
gargantuan *adj* gigantesco
gargle *v/i* fare i gargarismi
gargoyle *n* ARCH gargouille *f inv*
garish *adj* sgargiante
garland *n* ghirlanda *f*
garlic *n* aglio *m*
garlic bread *n* pane *m* all'aglio
garment *n* capo *m* d'abbigliamento
garnish *v/t* guarnire
garret *n* soffitta *f*
garrison *n* guarnigione *f*
garrulous *adj* garrulo
garter *n* giarrettiera *f*
gas I *n* gas *m inv*; ***cook with ~*** cucinare a gas;(*US gasoline*) benzina *f*; ***step on the ~*** accelerare **II** *v/t* ⟨*pret & past part* ***-sed***⟩ gassare; ***~ o.s.*** suicidarsi con il gas
gasbag *n infml* chiacchierone *m*, -a *f*
gas bill *n* bolletta *f* del gas
gas chamber *n* camera *f* a gas
gas cooker *n* cucina *f* a gas
gaseous *adj* gassoso
gas fire *n* fornello *m* a gas
gash I *n* taglio *m* **II** *v/t* tagliare; ***he fell and ~ed his knee*** è caduto e si è tagliato un ginocchio
gas heater *n* stufa *f* a gas **gas jet** *n* bruciatore *m* a gas
gasket *n* TECH guarnizione *f*; *fig* ***he blew a ~*** perse le staffe
gas main *n* conduttura *f* del gas **gas man** *n* impiegato *m* del gas **gas mask** *n* maschera *f* antigas **gas meter** *n* contatore *m* del gas
gasoline *n US* benzina *f*
gas oven *n* forno *m* a gas
gasp I *v/i* rimanere senza fiato; ***~ for breath*** essere senza fiato; ***he collapsed ~ing for breath*** si è accasciato senza fiato; ***he ~ed with astonishment*** restare a bocca aperta dallo stupore; ***I'm ~ing for a cup of tea*** *infml* muoio dalla voglia di una tazza di tè **II** *n* sussulto *m*
gas pedal *n US* acceleratore *m* **gas pipeline** *n* gasdotto *m* **gas pump** *n US* pompa *f* della benzina **gas station** *n US* stazione *f* di rifornimento **gas stove** *n* cucina *f* a gas **gas tank** *n US* serbatoio *m* della benzina **gas tap** *n* rubinetto *m* del gas
gastric *adj* MED gastrico
gastric flu *n* MED influenza *f* intestinale **gastric juices** *npl* succhi *mpl* gastrici **gastric ulcer** *n* MED ulcera *f* gastrica
gastroenteritis *n* gastroenterite *f*
gastronomic *adj* gastronomico
gastronomy *n* gastronomia *f*
gasworks *n* stabilimento *m* del gas
gate *n* cancello *m*; *of city*, *castle*, *at air-*

port porta *f*
gateau *n* torta *f*
gatecrash *v/t infml* intrufolarsi in; **~ *a party*** intrufolarsi a una festa **gatecrasher** *n infml* ospite *m* non invitato
gatehouse *n at park, estate* portineria *f*;
gated community *n* quartiere *m* recintato
gate money *n* SPORTS incasso *m* **gatepost** *n* pilastro *m* del cancello **gateway** *n* ingresso *m*; *fig* via *f* d'accesso
gather I *v/t facts, information* raccogliere; SEW increspare; ***~ one's strength*** raccogliere le forze; ***~ one's thoughts*** raccogliere le idee; ***it just sat there ~ing dust*** stava lì a prendere polvere; ***~ speed*** acquistare velocità; ***am I to ~ that ...?*** devo dedurre che ...?; ***from what*** *or* ***as far as I can ~*** da quanto riesco a dedurre; ***I ~ she won't be coming*** ne deduco che non verrà; ***as you might have ~ed ...*** come avrai capito ... **II** *v/i* (*understand*) dedurre; (*people*) radunarsi; (*objects, dust etc*) ammassarsi; (*clouds*) addensarsi
◆**gather (a)round** *v/i* avvicinarsi; ***come on, children, gather (a)round!*** venite, bambini, avvicinatevi!
◆**gather together** *v/t sep* raccogliere; *people* radunare
◆**gather up** *v/t sep possessions* radunare
gathering I *n* (*group of people*) raduno *m*; ***family ~*** riunione *f* familiare; ***social ~*** riunione *f* sociale **II** *adj storm* in intensificazione
GATT *abbr* (= **General Agreement on Tariffs and Trade**) *hist* accordo *m* generale sulle tariffe e il commercio (GATT)
gauche *adj* (*socially*) goffo
gaudily *adv* in modo pacchiano
gaudy *adj* (+*er*) pacchiano
gauge I *n* indicatore *m* **II** *v/t pressure* misurare; *opinion* valutare; ***I tried to ~ whether she was pleased or not*** ho cercato di valutare se le facesse piacere o meno
gaunt *adj* smunto
gauntlet[1] *n fig*: ***throw down the ~*** gettare il guanto
gauntlet[2] *n*: (***have to***) ***run the ~ of sth*** esporsi al fuoco incrociato di qc
gauze *n* garza *f*
gave *pret* → ***give***
gawk *v/i infml* → ***gawp***
gawky *adj* impacciato
gawp *v/i infml* fissare come un ebete *infml*, **~ *at sth*** fissare qc con aria inebetita
gay I *n* (*homosexual*) omosessuale *m/f* **II** *adj* (+*er*) *infml* omosessuale; *club* gay *inv*; ***~ bar*** locale *m* per gay; ***the ~ community*** la comunità gay
gay pride *n* gay pride *m*, orgoglio gay *m*
gaze I *v/i* fissare **II** *n* sguardo *m*
◆**gaze at** *v/t* fissare
GB *abbr* **1.** (= **Great Britain**) GB (Gran Bretagna *f*) **2.** (= **gigabyte**) GB (gigabyte *m inv*)
GCSE *abbr* (= **General Certificate of Secondary Education**) *esame in una scelta di materie sostenuto nelle scuole superiori inglesi e gallesi verso i 15 anni*
GDP *abbr* (= **gross domestic product**) PIL *m* (prodotto *m* interno lordo)
GDR *abbr* (= **German Democratic Republic**) *hist* RDT (Repubblica *f* Democratica Tedesca)
gear I *n* (*equipment*) equipaggiamento *m*; *in vehicles* marcia *f*; ***a bicycle with three ~s*** una bicicletta a tre marce; ***the car is in ~*** l'auto ha la marcia ingranata; ***the car is / you're not in ~*** sei / la macchina è in folle; ***change*** *esp Br or* ***shift*** *US* **~** cambiare marcia **II** *v/t fig*: ***be ~ed to(wards) s.o. / sth*** essere mirato a qn / qc; (*be suitable*) essere tagliato per qn / qc
◆**gear up** *v/t sep*: ***gear o.s. up for sth*** *fig* prepararsi per qc
gearbox *n* AUTO scatola *f* del cambio
gear lever, gear shift *n* AUTO leva *f* del cambio
gee *int esp US infml* hop; ***~ up!*** hop, hop!
geek *n esp US infml* sfigato *m*, -a *f*; ***computer ~*** geek *m/f*, *persona brillante in ambito informatico ma goffa nella vita quotidiana*
geese *pl* → ***goose***
gel *n for hair, shower* gel *m inv*
gelatine *n* gelatina *f*
geld *v/t* castrare
gelding *n* cavallo *m* castrato

gelignite *n* gelignite *f*
gem *n* gemma *f*; *fig book etc* capolavoro *m*; *person* perla *f* rara; ***thanks Pat, you're a ~*** grazie, Patrizia, sei una perla rara
Gemini *n* ASTROL Gemelli *mpl*
gemstone *n* pietra *f* preziosa
gen *n Br infml* informazioni *fpl*
◆**gen up** *v/i Br infml* ***gen up on sth*** informarsi su qc
gender *n* genere *m*; ***what ~ is this word?*** di che genere è questa parola?; ***the feminine / masculine / neuter ~*** il genere femminile / maschile / neutro
gender bender *n infml persona che si comporta o si veste in maniera tipica del sesso opposto* **gender studies** *npl* studi *mpl* di genere
gene *n* gene *m*; ***it's in his ~s*** è una sua caratteristica innata
genealogy *n* genealogia *f*
genera → ***genus***
general I *n* MIL generale *m*; ***in ~*** in generale **II** *adj* generale; ***be ~*** (*wording*) essere generico; (*vague*) vago; ***his ~ appearance*** il suo aspetto generale; ***there was ~ agreement among the two groups*** esisteva un accordo generale tra i due gruppi; ***I've got the ~ idea*** mi sono fatto un'idea generale; ***in ~ terms*** in generale; ***in the ~ direction of the village*** più o meno in direzione del villaggio; ***as a ~ rule*** come regola generale
general anaesthetic, *US* **general anesthetic** *n* anestetico *m* generale **General Assembly** *n* assemblea *f* generale **general confession** *n* REL confessione *f* generale **general dealer** *n US* → ***general store*** **general delivery** *adv US* (*Can*) fermoposta *m* **general election** *n* elezioni *fpl* politiche
generality *n*: ***talk in generalities*** fare osservazioni generali
generalization *n* generalizzazione *f*
generalize *v/i* generalizzare
general knowledge *n* conoscenza *f* generale
generally *adv* generalmente; ***~ speaking*** in generale
general manager *n* direttore *m*, -trice *f* generale **general meeting** *n* assemblea *f* generale **general practitioner** *n* medico *m* generico **general public** *n* pubblico *m* **general-purpose** *adj* multiuso; ***~ cleaner*** detersivo *m* multiuso **General Secretary** *n* segretario *m* generale **general store** *n* negozio *m* di generi diversi **general strike** *n* sciopero *m* generale
generate *v/t* generare; *in linguistics* formare; *income* produrre; *excitement* provocare
generation *n* generazione *f*
generation gap *n* scarto *m* generazionale
generator *n* ELEC generatore *m*
generic *adj* generico; ***~ name*** *or* ***term*** nome / termine *m* generico; ***~ brand*** *US* marchio *m* generico
generic drug *n* MED farmaco *m* generico
generosity *n* generosità *f*
generous *adj* generoso; ***be ~ in one's praise*** essere prodigo di lodi; ***with the ~ support of …*** con il generoso supporto di; (*magnanimous*) magnanimo
generously *adv give* generosamente; *reward* abbondantemente; ***please give ~ (to …)*** siate generosi (con …)
genesis *n* ⟨*pl* ***geneses***⟩ genesi *f*
genetic *adj* genetico
genetically *adv* geneticamente; ***~ modified*** transgenico; ***~ engineered*** ottenuto con manipolazione genetica
genetic code *n* codice *m* genetico **genetic engineering** *n* ingegneria *f* genetica **genetic fingerprint** *n* esame *m* del DNA
geneticist *n* genetista *m/f*
genetics *nsg* genetica *f*
Geneva *n* Ginevra *f*; ***Lake ~*** lago *m* di Ginevra
genial *adj person, company* gioviale
genie *n* genio *m*
genii → ***genius***
genital *adj* genitale; ***~ organs*** organi *mpl* genitali
genital herpes *n* herpes *m* genitale
genitalia *npl* genitali *mpl*
genitals *npl* genitali *mpl*
genitival *adj* GRAM genitivo
genitive I *n* GRAM genitivo *m*; ***in the ~*** al genitivo **II** *adj* genitivo; ***~ case*** caso *m* genitivo
genius *n* ⟨*pl* ***genies*** *or* ***genii***⟩ genio *m*; ***a man of ~*** un uomo di genio;

have a ~ for sth/doing sth (*talent*) essere tagliato per qc/fare qc
Genoa *n* Genova *f*
genocide *n* genocidio *m*
genome *n* genoma *m*
genre *n* genere *m*
gent *n abbr* (= **gentleman**) *infml* signore *m*; ***where is the ~s?*** (*lavatory*) dov'è il bagno degli uomini?
genteel *adj* distinto
Gentile *n* REL gentile *m/f*
gentility *n* distinzione *f*
gentle *adj* (+*er*) delicato; *breeze*, *slope* dolce
gentleman *n* signore *m*; ***he's a real ~*** è un vero gentleman
gentleman farmer *n proprietario terriero che si dedica alla gestione della tenuta per passione, piuttosto che per profitto*
gentlemanly *adj* signorile; ***that is hardly ~ conduct*** non è da gentiluomini
gentleman's agreement *n* accordo *m* verbale
gentleness *n* delicatezza *f*; *of breeze*, *slope* dolcezza *f*
gently *adv* delicatamente; *blow*, *slope* dolcemente; ***she needs to be handled ~*** deve essere trattata con delicatezza; ***~ does it!*** piano!
gentry *npl* persone *fpl* di buona famiglia
gents *n toilet* bagno *m* degli uomini
genuflect *v/i* genuflettersi
genuflection *n* genuflessione *f*
genuine *adj* autentico; (*sincere*) sincero; (*not affected*) genuino; ***~ leather*** vero cuoio *m*; ***the ~ article*** *infml* l'esempio tipico
genuinely *adv* sinceramente; ***they are ~ concerned*** sono sinceramente preoccupati
genuineness *n*; (*authenticity*) autenticità *f*; (*honesty*, *sincerity*) genuinità *f*
genus *n* ⟨*pl* ***genera***⟩ BIOL genere *m*
geographical *adj* geografico
geography *n* geografia *f*
geological *adj* geologico
geologist *n* geologo *m*, -a *f*
geology *n* geologia *f*
geometric, geometrical *adj* geometrico
geometry *n* geometria *f*
Georgian *adj Br* georgiano
geranium *n* geranio *m*
gerbil *n* ZOOL gerbillo *m*
geriatric I *adj* geriatrico **II** *n* anziano *m*, -a *f*
geriatric care *n* assistenza *f* geriatrica
geriatrics *nsg* geriatria *f*
germ *n a. fig* germe *m*
German I *adj* tedesco **II** *n person* tedesco *m*, -a *f*; *language* tedesco *m*
Germanic *adj* HIST, LING germanico
German measles *nsg* rosolia *f* **German shepherd** *n* pastore *m* Tedesco
Germany *n* Germania *f*
germ-free *adj* asettico
germinate *v/i of seed* germogliare
germination *n liter* sviluppo *m*
germ warfare *n* guerra *f* batteriologica
gesticulate *v/i* gesticolare
gesture *n a. fig* gesto *m*
get I *v/t* ⟨*pret & past part* ***got***, *US past part* ***gotten***⟩ **1.** (*obtain*) prendere; (*fetch*) andare a prendere; (*receive*: *letter*) ricevere; (*receive*: *knowledge*, *respect etc*) ottenere; (*catch*: *bus*, *train*, *flu*) prendere; ***~ sth for s.o.***, ***~ s.o. sth*** prendere qc a qn; ***have got*** avere; ***I'll ~ you some breakfast*** ti preparerò qc per colazione; ***we could ~ a taxi*** potremmo prendere un taxi; ***could you ~ me a taxi?*** puoi chiamarmi un taxi?; ***~ s.o. from the station*** prendere qn alla stazione; ***can I ~ you a drink?*** posso prenderti qc da bere?; ***I got him a drink*** gli ho preso da bere; ***he got the idea for his book while he was abroad*** l'idea per il suo libro gli è venuta mentre si trovava all'estero; ***I got quite a surprise*** sono rimasto piuttosto sorpreso; ***I ~ the feeling that …*** ho la sensazione che; ***what do you ~ from it?*** che cosa ne ottieni? **2.** (*understand*) afferrare; ***I don't ~ it*** *infml* non afferro; ***I don't ~ you*** non ti capisco; ***~ it?*** *infml* capito? **3.** (*causative*) ***~ sth done*** farsi fare qc; ***~ one's hair cut*** tagliarsi i capelli; ***~ sth ready*** preparare qc; ***has she got the baby dressed yet?*** è riuscita a vestire il bambino?; ***~ the washing done*** fare il bucato; ***~ sth made for s.o./o.s.*** farsi fare qc/far fare qc per qn; ***I'll ~ the house painted soon*** (*by s.o. else*) presto farò dipingere la casa; ***did you ~ your expenses paid?***

hai ottenuto il pagamento delle spese?; ~ ***s.o.* / *sth ready*** preparare qn / qc; ~ ***sth clean* / *open*** pulire / aprire qc; ~ ***s.o. drunk*** far ubriacare qn; ~ ***one's hands dirty*** *liter*, *fig* sporcarsi le mani; ***he can't ~ the lid to stay open*** non riesce a tenere aperto il coperchio; ***can you ~ these two pieces to fit together?*** riesci a unire questi due pezzi?; ~ ***sth going*** *machine* far partire; *party* dare inizio a; ~ ***s.o. talking*** far parlare qn **4.** ~ ***s.o. to do sth*** far fare qc a qn; ***I'll ~ him to do it*** glielo faccio fare; ***I'll ~ him to phone you back*** ti farò richiamare; ***you'll never ~ him to understand*** non glielo farai mai capire; ***you'll ~ yourself thrown out*** ti farai buttare fuori **5.** ~ ***to do sth*** *have opportunity* avere occasione di fare qc; ~ ***to know*** venire a sapere; ~ ***to know s.o.* / *sth*** fare la conoscenza di qn / venire a conoscenza di qc; ***how did you ~ to know about that?*** come ne siete venuti a conoscenza?; ~ ***to like s.o.*** arrivare ad apprezzare qn; ~ ***to like sth*** arrivare ad apprezzare qc **6.** (*convey oneself*) recarsi; (*come*) arrivare; ***I had to ~ myself to the hospital*** mi sono dovuto recare in ospedale; ~ ***o.s. pregnant*** restare incinta; ~ ***o.s. washed*** lavarsi; ***you'll ~ yourself killed if you go on driving like that*** finirai per ammazzarti se continui a guidare in quel modo **7.** ***I have got to study* / *see him*** devo studiare / vederlo; ***I don't want to, but I've got to*** non voglio, ma devo **II** *v/i* **1.** (*arrive*) arrivare; ~ ***home*** arrivare a casa; ~ ***here*** arrivare fin qui; ***can you ~ to work by bus?*** puoi andare a lavorare in autobus?; ***I've got as far as page 16*** sono arrivato a pagina 16; ~ ***there*** (*succeed*) farcela; ***how's the work going? — we're ~ting there!-*** come sta andando il lavoro? — ce la stiamo facendo!; ***you won't ~ far on £ 10*** non andrai lontano con 10 sterline; ~ ***going*** (*leave*) andare via **2.** (*become*) diventare; ***I'm ~ting cold*** sto prendendo freddo; ~ ***dressed*** *etc* vestirsi; ~ ***married*** sposarsi; ***I'm ~ting bored*** mi sto annoiando; ***how stupid can you ~?*** quanto si può essere stupidi?; ~ ***started*** iniziare; ~ ***to work*** mettersi al lavoro; ~ ***working*** *etc* cominciare a lavorare; ***I got talking to him*** ho cominciato a parlargli; ***have got to do sth*** dover fare qc; ***I've got to*** devo

◆**get about** *v/i* (*travel*) andare in giro; (*be mobile*) muoversi

◆**get across I** *v/i meaning* essere recepito (***to*** da) **II** *v/t always sep one's ideas* trasmettere (***to s.o.*** a qn)

◆**get ahead** *v/i* fare progressi (***in*** in); ***get ahead of s.o.*** (*overtake*) superare qn

◆**get along** *v/i* (*progress*) procedere; ***how is he getting along at school?*** come se la cava a scuola?; *come to party etc* venire; *with s.o.* andare d'accordo

◆**get around I** *v/t problem* aggirare; ***there's no getting around it*** non se ne scampa **II** *v/i story*, *news* spargersi; ***get around to doing sth*** avere modo di fare qc

◆**get at** *v/t* (*criticize*) prendersela con; (*imply*, *mean*) volere arrivare a; ***I don't understand what you're getting at*** non capisco dove vuoi arrivare; ***get at the truth*** *find out* arrivare alla verità; (*reach*) ***don't let him get at the whisky*** non lasciare che arrivi all'whisky

◆**get away I** *v/i* (*leave*) andare via; ***I'd like to get away early today*** oggi vorrei andarmene presto **II** *v/t always sep* ***get sth away from s.o.*** togliere qc a qn; ***get him* / *that dog away from me*** allontanalo da me / allontanami quel cane

◆**get away with** *v/t* cavarsela per; ***he'll (etc) never get away with that*** non se la caverà mai; ***he got away with it*** l'ha fatta franca

◆**get back I** *v/i* (*return*) ritornare; (*move back*) indietreggiare; ***get back!*** indietro!; ***I'll get back to you on that*** ti faccio sapere **II** *v/t sep* (*obtain again*) recuperare

◆**get back at** *v/t infml* vendicarsi di; ***get back at s.o. for sth*** vendicarsi di qn per qc

◆**get by** *v/i* (*pass*) passare; *financially* tirare avanti

◆**get down I** *v/i from ladder etc* scendere; (*duck etc*) abbassarsi **II** *v/t sep* (*depress*) buttare giù

◆**get down to** *v/t* (*start*: *work*) mettersi a; (*reach*: *real facts*) arrivare a; ***let's get down to business*** parliamo d'affari

◆**get in I** *v/i* (*arrive*: *of train*, *plane*) arrivare; (*come home*) arrivare a casa; *to car* salire; ***how did they get in?*** *of thieves*, *mice etc* come sono entrati? **II** *v/t sep to suitcase etc* far entrare

◆**get into I** *v/i +obj debt*, *trouble etc* cacciarsi; *fight* entrare; *put on* indossare; (*fit into*) entrare; ***get into bed*** infilarsi a letto; ***what's got into him?*** *infml* che cosa gli è saltato in mente? ***I can't get into my red dress*** non riesco a entrare nel vestito rosso **II** *v/t always sep debt etc* cacciare; ***get o.s. into trouble*** cacciarsi nei guai

◆**get in with** *v/t* (*associate with*) fare amicizia con; (*ingratiate oneself with*) farsi amico; ***he could easily get in with the wrong sort of people*** è facile che faccia amicizia con le persone sbagliate

◆**get off I** *v/i from bus etc* scendere; (*finish work*) finire; (*not be punished*) cavarsela; ***get off to a good/ bad start*** cominciare bene / male **II** *v/t always sep* (*remove*) togliere; *clothes*, *hat*, *footgear* togliersi; ***get off the grass!*** togliti dal prato!; ***get off your ass!*** *US vulg* muovi il culo! *vulg*

◆**get off with** *v/t infml sexually* rimorchiare *infml*; ***get off with a small fine*** cavarsela con una piccola multa

◆**get on I** *v/i* **1.** *to bike*, *bus*, *train* salire **2.** (*be friendly*) andare d'accordo; ***I don't get on with him*** non vado d'accordo con lui **3.** (*advance*: *of time*) farsi tardi; ***it's getting on*** *getting late* si sta facendo tardi **4.** (*become old*) invecchiare; ***he's getting on*** *getting old* sta invecchiando; ***he's getting on for 50*** va per i 50 anni **5.** (*make progress*) procedere; ***he's getting on well at school*** se la sta cavando bene a scuola **II** *v/t sep* ***get on the bus/one's bike*** salire sull'autobus / sulla bici; ***get one's hat on*** mettersi il cappello; ***I can't get these trousers on*** non riesco a mettermi questi pantaloni

◆**get on to** *v/i +obj infml* (*contact*) rivolgersi a; ***I'll get on to him about it*** mi rivolgerò a lui

◆**get on with** *v/i +obj* (*continue*) procedere; (*manage to get on with*) andare avanti; ***get on with it!*** vai avanti!; ***let s.o. get on with sth*** lasciare che qn vada avanti con qc; ***this will do to be getting on with*** questo ci consentirà di andare avanti

◆**get out I** *v/i of car etc* scendere; *of prison* uscire; ***get out!*** fuori!; ***let's get out of here*** usciamo da qui; ***I don't get out much these days*** non esco molto in questi giorni **II** *v/t sep* (*extract*: *nail*, *something jammed*) tirare fuori; (*remove*: *stain*) mandare via; (*pull out*: *gun*, *pen*) tirare fuori; ***get the best / most out of s.o. / sth*** tirare fuori il meglio / massimo da qn / qc

◆**get over** *v/t sep fence*, *disappointment etc* superare; *lover etc* dimenticare

◆**get over with** *v/t always sep* togliersi; ***let's get it over with*** togliamocelo

◆**get round** *esp Br* **I** *v/i news*, *information* diffondersi, *infml* fare il giro **II** *v/t always sep difficulty* eludere; ***I still can't get my head round it*** *infml* non riesco ancora a capirlo

◆**get round to** *v/t esp Br infml* ***get round to sth*** trovare il tempo per qc; ***get rpund to doing sth*** trovare il tempo di fare qc

◆**get through** *v/i* **1.** *on telephone* prendere la linea; ***I called you all day but I didn't manage to get through*** ti ho chiamato tutto il giorno, ma era sempre occupato **2.** farsi capire; ***get through to s.o.*** farsi capire da qn

◆**get to** *v/t* (*annoy*, *upset*) dare sui nervi

◆**get together** *v/i* ritrovarsi

◆**get up I** *v/i of person*, *wind* alzarsi **II** *v/t always sep* (*climb*: *hill*) salire su

◆**get up to** *v/t sep infml* combinare

getaway I *n from robbery* fuga *f*, ***make one's ~*** darsi alla fuga **II** *adj*: ***~ car*** auto *f* per la fuga **get-together** *n* ritrovo *m* **getup** *n infml* tenuta *f* **get-up-and-go** *n infml* energia *f* **get-well card** *n biglietto di auguri di pronta guarigione*

gewgaw *n* ninnolo *m*

geyser *n* GEOL geyser *m*

ghastly *adj* (+*er*) *colour, experience, person etc* orrendo; ***you look ~*** hai un aspetto orribile
gherkin *n* cetriolino *m* sotto aceto
ghetto *n* ghetto *m*
ghetto blaster *n infml* (grosso) stereo *m* portatile
ghost *n* fantasma *m*, spettro *m*; *fig* ***I don't have*** *or* ***stand the ~ of a chance*** non ho la minima probabilità; ***give up the ~*** *infml* esalare l'ultimo respiro
ghostly *adj* (+*er*) spettrale
ghost story *n* storia *f* di fantasmi **ghost town** *n* città *f inv* fantasma **ghost train** *n Br* (*funfair*) tunnel *m* degli orrori
ghostwrite *v/t & v/i* scrivere per conto di altri
ghost writer *n* scrittore *m*, -trice *f* fantasma
ghoul *n* persona *f* morbosa
ghoulish *adj* macabro
GHQ *abbr* (= **General Headquarters**) quartieri *mpl* generali
GHz *abbr* (= **gigahertz**) GHz *m*
GI *n abbr* (= **government issue**) *US rifornimenti all'esercito emessi dal governo*
giant I *n* gigante *m*; ***a ~ of a man*** un gigante d'uomo; ***publishing ~*** gigante *m* dell'editoria **II** *adj* gigante; ***~ panda*** *n* panda *m* gigante
gibber *v/i* farfugliare; ***a ~ing idiot*** un perfetto idiota
gibberish *n infml* bestialità *fpl infml*
gibe *n* frecciatina *f*
giblets *npl* frattaglie *fpl* (di volatili)
Gibraltar *n* Gibilterra *f*
giddiness *n* giramenti *mpl* di testa
giddy *adj* (+*er*): ***I feel ~*** mi gira la testa
gift *n* regalo *m*; ***have a ~ for sth*** essere portato per qc; ***she has a ~ for teaching*** è portata per l'insegnamento
gift certificate *n US* buono *m* premio
gifted *adj* dotato
gift token, gift voucher *n* buono *m* d'acquisto **giftwrap I** *n* carta *f* da regalo **II** *v/t* ⟨*pret & past part* **-ped**⟩ impacchettare; ***would you like it ~ped?*** le faccio un pacco regalo?
gig *n infml* concerto *m*; ***do a ~*** dare un concerto
gigabyte *n* COMPUT gigabyte *m inv*
gigantic *adj* gigante
giggle I *v/i* ridacchiare **II** *n* risatina *f*; ***get the ~s*** essere preso dalla ridarella
giggly *adj* (+*er*) ridacchiante
gild *v/t* dorare; *liter* indorare; ***~ the lily*** strafare
gill *n of fish* branchia *f*
gilt I *n* doratura *f* **II** *adj* dorato; ***~s*** FIN titoli *mpl* obbligazionari
gimmick *n* trovata *f*
gimmicky *adj* appariscente
gin *n* gin *m inv*; ***~ and tonic*** gin and tonic *m inv*
ginger I *n spice* zenzero *m* **II** *adj hair* rosso carota; *cat* rosso
ginger ale *n*, **ginger beer** *n* bibita *f* allo zenzero **gingerbread** *n* pan *m* di zenzero
gingerly *adv* con cautela
gingham *n* TEX percalle *m*
gipsy *n* zingaro *m*, -a *f*
giraffe *n* giraffa *f*
gird *v/t*: ***~ o.s. for sth*** prepararsi a qc; ***~*** (***up***) ***one's loins*** *hum* rimboccarsi le maniche
girder *n* trave *f*
girdle *n* panciera *f*
girl *n* ragazza *f*; ***my little ~*** la bambina
girlfriend *n of boy* ragazza *f*; *of girl* amica *f*
girl guide *n* guida *f* scout
girlhood *n* giovinezza *f*; ***in her ~*** in giovinezza
girlie *adj infml* da femminuccia *infml*
girlie magazine *n pornographic* rivista *f* per soli uomini
girlish *adj* tipicamente femminile
girl scout *n US* guida *f* scout
giro *n* bonifico *m*
girth *n* circonferenza *f*
gismo *n infml* → ***gizmo***
gist *n* sostanza *f*; ***I got the ~ of it*** ho colto il nocciolo della questione
git *n Br pej* essere *m* spregevole
give I *v/t* ⟨*pret* **gave**, *past part* **given**⟩ dare; *present* fare; (*supply*: *electricity etc*) fornire; *talk*, *groan* fare; *party* dare; *pain*, *appetite* far venire; ***the teacher gave us three exercises*** l'insegnante ci ha dato tre esercizi; ***~ s.o. one's cold*** *infml* attaccare il raffreddore a qn; ***~ sth for sth*** (*pay*) pagare qc per qc; (*exchange*) dare in cambio; ***what will you ~ me for it?*** che cosa mi darai in cambio?; ***how much did you ~ for it?*** quanto

hai pagato per questo?; ***six foot, ~ or take a few inches*** due metri, centimetro più centimetro meno; ***it was ~n to me by my uncle*** mi è stato affidato da mio zio; ***it ~s me great pleasure to …*** è un grande piacere per me …; ***~ s.o. a shock*** dare una violenta emozione a qn; ***he gave the child a smack*** dette uno schiaffo al bambino; ***~ s.o. five years*** dare cinque anni a qn; ***~ yourself time to recover*** darsi il tempo di riprendersi; ***~ a cry*** emettere un grido; ***~ her my love*** salutala da parte mia; ***the child gave a little jump of excitement*** il bambino fece un piccolo salto per l'eccitazione; ***he gave a shrug*** fece spallucce **II** *v/i* (*collapse, yield*) cedere; *give money etc* donare; ***you have to be prepared to ~ and take*** *fig* devi essere pronto a un compromesso **III** *n* elasticità *f*

◆ **give away** *v/t sep as present* regalare; (*betray*) tradire; ***give o.s. away*** tradirsi; ***give the game away*** *infml* tradire un segreto

◆ **give back** *v/t sep* restituire

◆ **give in I** *v/i surrender* arrendersi; ***give in to temptation*** cedere alla tentazione **II** *v/t* (*hand in*) consegnare

◆ **give off** *v/t insep smell, fumes* emettere

◆ **give onto** *v/t* (*open onto*) dare su

◆ **give out I** *v/t sep leaflets etc* distribuire **II** *v/i of supplies, strength* esaurirsi; ***my voice gave out*** ho esaurito la voce

◆ **give over I** *v/t sep* (*hand over*) consegnare (***to*** a) **II** *v/i* (*stop*) cessare **III** *v/i +obj* smettere; ***give over tickling me!*** smetti di farmi il solletico!

◆ **give up I** *v/t sep smoking etc* rinunciare a; ***he gave up smoking*** ha smesso di fumare; ***give o.s. up to the police*** consegnarsi alla polizia; ***give s.o. up for lost*** dare qn per disperso **II** *v/i* (*cease habit*) smettere; (*stop making effort*) lasciar perdere

◆ **give way** *v/i of bridge etc* cedere; ***the ladder gave way*** la scala cedette; ***after five minutes she gave way to hysteria*** dopo cinque minuti cedette all'isteria; AUTO dare la precedenza

give-and-take *n* concessioni *fpl* reciproche

giveaway *n*: ***it was a real ~ when he said …*** fu una vera rivelazione quando disse …

given I *past part* → ***give*** **II** *adj* dato; ***in a ~ period*** in un dato periodo; ***within the ~ period*** entro il periodo stabilito; ***~ name*** *esp US* nome *m* di battesimo; ***be ~ to sth*** essere propenso a qc **III** *cj*: ***~ that he …*** dato che lui …; ***~ time, we can do it*** avendone il tempo, possiamo farlo; ***~ the chance, I would …*** avendone l'opportunità, potrei …

given name *n* nome *m* di battesimo

gizmo *n infml* aggeggio *m*

glacé I *adj* glassato **II** *v/t* glassare

glacial *adj* glaciale

glacier *n* ghiacciaio *m*

glad *adj* (*+er*) contento; ***~ about*** contento di; ***~ that*** contento che; ***I'm ~ to be leaving*** sono contento di andare via; ***I'd be ~ of your opinion on this*** sarei lieto di conoscere la tua opinione; ***I'm ~ you like it*** sono contento che ti piaccia

gladden *v/t liter* rallegrare

glade *n* radura *f*

glad eye *n infml* occhi *mpl* dolci; ***he certainly gave you the ~*** ti ha indubbiamente fatto gli occhi dolci

gladiator *n* gladiatore *m*

gladly *adv* volentieri

glad rags *npl infml* vestito *m* della festa

glamor *US* → ***glamour***

glamorize *v/t* esaltare

glamorous *adj* affascinante

glamour, *US* **glamor** *n* fascino *m*

glance I *n* sguardo *m*; ***at first ~*** a prima vista; ***cast a sidelong ~*** guardare con la coda dell'occhio; ***we exchanged ~s*** ci siamo scambiati uno sguardo **II** *v/i* dare un'occhiata *or* uno sguardo

◆ **glance at** *v/t* dare un'occhiata *or* uno sguardo a

◆ **glance off** *v/i bullet* essere deviato da

gland *n* ghiandola *f*

glandular fever *n* mononucleosi *f*

glare I *n of sun, headlights* luce *f* abbagliante **II** *v/i of sun, headlights* splendere di luce abbagliante

◆ **glare at** *v/t* guardare di storto

glaring *adj mistake* lampante

glaringly *adv*: ***be ~ obvious*** essere più che ovvio
glass *n material* vetro *m*; *for drink* bicchiere *m*; ***wine ~*** bicchiere *m* da vino; ***a ~ of wine*** un bicchiere di vino
glass case *n* teca *f* **glass ceiling** *n fig* soffitto *m* di cristallo; *fig* ***shatter the ~*** sfondare il soffitto di cristallo
glasses *npl* occhiali *mpl*; ***a pair of ~*** un paio di occhiali
glass fibre, *US* **glass fiber** *n* fibra *f* di vetro
glassful *n* bicchiere *m*
glasshouse *n* serra *f* **glass wool** *n* lana *f* di vetro **glassworks** *n* vetreria *f*
glassy *adj* (+*er*) *surface*, *sea etc* cristallino; ***~-eyed*** *look* vitreo
glaze I *n* smalto *m* trasparente **II** *v/t window* invetriare; *pottery* smaltare; *cake* glassare **III** *v/i* appannarsi; ***she had a ~d look in her eyes*** aveva lo sguardo appannato
◆**glaze over** *v/i of eyes* appannarsi
glazed *adj expression* assente
glazier *n* vetraio *m*
glazing *n* vetri *mpl*
gleam I *v/i* luccicare **II** *n* luccichio *m*; ***a ~ of light*** un bagliore di luce; ***he had a ~ in his eye*** aveva un barlume nello sguardo
glean *v/t fig* racimolare; ***~ sth from s.o.* / *sth*** racimolare qc da qn / qc
glee *n* allegria *f*; ***he shouted with ~*** gridò di gioia
gleeful *adj* allegro
glen *n valle stretta e lunga*
glib *adj* (+*er*) poco convincente
glibly *adv* in modo poco convincente
glide *v/i of skier*, *boat* scivolare; *of bird*, *plane* planare
glider *n* aliante *m*
gliding *n* planata *f*
glimmer I *n of light* barlume *m*; ***~ of hope*** barlume *m* di speranza **II** *v/i* emettere un barlume
glimpse I *n* occhiata *f*; ***catch a ~ of*** intravedere **II** *v/t* intravedere
glint I *v/i of light*, *eyes* luccicare **II** *n* luccichio *m*; ***a ~ of light*** un bagliore di luce; ***he has a wicked ~ in his eyes*** ha un luccichio maligno nello sguardo
glisten *v/i* scintillare
glitch *n* COMPUT problema *m*; ***a technical ~*** un problema tecnico
glitter I *n* scintillio *m*; ***the ~ of show-business*** lo scintillio del mondo dello spettacolo; (*for decoration*) lustrini *mpl* **II** *v/i* brillare
glitterati *npl*: ***the ~*** il bel mondo
gloaming *n liter* crepuscolo *m*
gloat *v/i* gongolare; ***~ over*** *or* ***about sth.*** covare qc. con gli occhi
◆**gloat over** *v/t* compiacersi di
glob *n infml* goccia *f*; ***he had a ~ of peanut butter on his chin*** aveva una goccia di burro di arachidi sul mento
global *adj* (*worldwide*) mondiale; *recession* globale; ***~ peace*** pace *f* globale; *without exceptions* globale
global economy *n* economia *f* mondiale
globalization *n* globalizzazione *f*
globally *adv* (*worldwide*) a livello mondiale; (*universally*) globalmente
global market *n* mercato *m* mondiale **global trade** *n* commercio *m* globale **global village** *n* villaggio *m* globale **global warming** *n* effetto *m* serra
globe *n* globo *m*; *model of earth* mappamondo *m*; ***all over the ~*** in ogni parte del globo
globe artichoke *n Br* carciofo *m*
globetrotter *n* giramondo *m/f*, globe-trotter *m/f*
globe-trotting I *n* il viaggiare per il mondo **II** *adj* che viaggia per il mondo
globule *n* globulo *m*; *of oil*, *water* goccia *f*
gloom *n* (*darkness*) penombra *f*; *mood* tristezza *f*
gloomily *adv* tristemente
gloomy *adj* (+*er*) *room* buio; *mood*, *person* triste; *day* grigio; ***he is very ~ about his chances of success*** è molto pessimista riguardo alle sue probabilità di successo
gloop *n*, *US* **glop** *n infml* massa *f* gelatinosa, *infml* pappa *f*
gloopy *adj*, *US* **gloppy** *adj infml* gelatinoso, *infml* papposo
glorification *n* glorificazione *f*
glorify *v/t* ⟨*pret & past part* **-ied**⟩ glorificare; ***I'm just a glorified secretary*** *infml* sono poco più di una segretaria
glorious *adj weather*, *day* splendido; *victory* glorioso

gloriously *adv* magnificamente; ***~ happy*** meravigliosamente felice
glory I *n* gloria *f*; (*beauty*) splendore *m*; ***moment of ~*** momento *m* di gloria; (*magnificence*) splendore *m*; ***they restored the car to its former ~*** hanno riportato la macchina all'antico splendore **II** *v/i*: ***~ in one's success*** gloriarsi del proprio successo
gloss[1] **I** *n* (*shine*) lucido *m*; ***~ finish*** PHOT *on paper* finitura *f* lucida **II** *v/i & v/t* lucidare
gloss[2] **I** *n* (*explanation*) chiosa; ***put a ~ on sth*** inserire una chiosa su qc **II** *v/i & v/t* chiosare
◆**gloss over** *v/t sep* sorvolare su
glossary *n* glossario *m*
gloss paint *n* vernice *f* lucida
glossy I *adj* (*+er*) *paper* patinato **II** *n magazine* rivista *f* femminile
glove *n* guanto *m*; ***it fits like a ~*** calza come un guanto
glove box, glove compartment *n in car* cruscotto *m* **glove puppet** *n* burattino *m*
glow I *n of light*, *fire* bagliore *m*; *in cheeks* colorito *m* vivo; *of candle* luce *f* fioca **II** *v/i of light* brillare; ***her cheeks ~ed*** è diventata rossa
glower *v/i*: ***~ at s.o.*** guardare qn in cagnesco
glowing *adj description* entusiastico
glow-worm *n* lucciola *f*
glucose *n* glucosio *m*
glue I *n* colla *f* **II** *v/t*: ***~ sth to sth*** incollare qc a qc; ***be ~d to the TV*** *infml* essere incollato alla TV *infml*; ***we were ~d to our seats*** eravamo incollati ai nostri posti; ***keep one's eyes ~d to s.o. / sth*** tenere gli occhi incollati su qn / qc
glue-sniffing *n* lo sniffare colla
glum *adj* (*+er*) triste
glumly *adv* tristemente
glut *n* eccesso *m*
gluten *n* glutine *m*
glutinous *adj* colloso
glutton *n* ghiottone *m*, -a *f*; ***she's a ~ for punishment*** è una vera masochista
gluttony *n* ghiottoneria *f*
glycerin(e) *n* glicerina *f*
gm *abbr* (= **gram(s)**, **gramme(s)**) g (grammo)
GM *abbr* (= **genetically modified**) GM (transgenico)
GM food *n* alimenti *mpl* GM
GMT *abbr* (= **Greenwich Mean Time**) ora *f* di Greenwich
gnarled *adj branch, hands* nodoso
gnash *v/t*: ***~ one's teeth*** digrignare i denti
gnat *n* moscerino *m*
gnaw I *v/t bone* rosicchiare **II** *v/i* rosicchiare; ***~ at*** *or* ***on sth*** rosicchiare qc; ***~ at s.o.*** *fig* tormentare qn
gnawing *adj doubt*, *pain* lancinante; *fear* attanagliante
gnome *n* gnomo *m*; ***garden ~*** nano *m* da giardino
GNP *abbr* (= **gross national product**) PNL *m* (prodotto *m* nazionale lordo)
go I *v/i* ⟨*pret* **went**, *past part* **gone**⟩ **1.** andare; ***~ shopping / ~ jogging*** andare a fare spese / andare a correre; ***~ for a walk*** andare a fare una passeggiata; ***~ to bed*** andare a letto; ***~ to school*** andare a scuola; ***let's ~!*** andiamo!; ***I've gone 15 miles*** ho fatto 15 miglia; ***there are two days to ~ before ...*** mancano due giorni a ...; ***~ to evening classes*** frequentare corsi serali; ***~ to work*** andare a lavorare; ***~ to s.o. for sth*** rivolgersi a qn per qc; ***the doll ~es everywhere with her*** si porta sempre dietro la bambola; ***you ~ first*** prima tu; *fig* ***where do we ~ from here?*** e adesso che facciamo?; ***to ~*** *US food* da asporto **2.** (*leave*: *of train*, *plane*) partire; (*leave*: *of people*) andare via; ***~ on holiday*** *Br or* ***vacation*** *US* andare in vacanza; ***I must be ~ing*** devo andare; ***be all gone*** (*finished*) essere finito **3.** (*work*, *function*) funzionare; ***how's the work ~ing?*** come va il lavoro?; ***get sth ~ing*** mettere in moto qc; ***keep ~ing*** (*person*) tenere duro; (*machine etc*) continuare a funzionare; (*car*) continuare ad andare; ***keep the fire ~ing*** tenere acceso il fuoco; ***this prospect kept her ~ing*** questa prospettiva la spinse ad andare avanti; ***here's £50 to keep you ~ing*** ecco 50 sterline per andare avanti **4.** (*become*) diventare; ***he's ~ing crazy*** sta impazzendo **5.** (*come out*: *of stain etc*) andare via; (*cease*: *of pain etc*) sparire **6.** (*match*: *of colours etc*) stare bene insieme **7.** ***they're***

~ing for £50 (*being sold at*) li vendono a £50; (*be sold*) ***the hats aren't ~ing very well*** i cappelli non hanno molto successo; ***~ing, ~ing, gone!*** *auction* ... e uno, ... e due, ... e tre, aggiudicato! **8.** ***the story ~es that ...*** la storia dice che ...; ***we'll see how things ~*** *infml* vedremo come vanno le cose; ***the way things are ~ing I'll ...*** da come vanno le cose, io...; ***she has a lot ~ing for her*** ha un sacco di qualità; ***how's it ~ing?*** *infml* come va?; ***how did it ~?*** com'è andata?; ***how's the essay ~ing?*** come procede il saggio?; ***everything is ~ing well*** sta andando tutto bene; ***if everything ~es well*** se tutto va bene **9.** *future* ***I'm ~ing to meet him tomorrow*** lo incontrerò domani; ***it's ~ing to snow*** sta per nevicare **10.** (*fail*) cedere; (*strength, eyesight etc*) venire meno; ***his mind is ~ing*** la sua mente viene meno **II** *n* (*try*) tentativo *m*; ***it's my ~*** tocca a me, è il mio turno; ***have a ~ at sth*** (*try*) fare un tentativo in qc; (*complain about*) lamentarsi di qc; ***have a ~ at s.o.*** (*criticize*) fare una parte a qn; ***be on the ~*** essere indaffarato; ***in one ~*** *drink, write etc* tutto in una volta

◆**go about I** *v/i Br* andare in giro; *flu* circolare; ***go about with s.o.*** andare in giro con qn **II** *v/t task* affrontare; *work* occuparsi di; ***how does one go about finding a job?*** come si affronta la ricerca di un lavoro?; ***go about one's business*** occuparsi dei propri affari

◆**go across I** *v/i +obj* attraversare **II** *v/i* attraversare

◆**go after** *v/t* (*follow*) rincorrere; *in vehicle* inseguire; (*try to obtain*) fare di tutto per avere; ***the police went after the escaped criminal*** la polizia inseguì l'evaso

◆**go against** *v/t luck* essere sfavorevole a; (*be contrary to*) andare contro a; (*oppose*) essere contrario a; ***the verdict went against her*** il verdetto le era sfavorevole; ***the vote went against her*** il voto le fu sfavorevole

◆**go ahead** *v/i and do sth* andare avanti; ***go ahead!*** (*on you go*) fai pure!

◆**go ahead with** *v/t plans etc* andare avanti con

◆**go along with** *v/t suggestion* concordare con

◆**go at** *v/t* (*attack*) scagliarsi contro

◆**go away** *v/i of person, pain* andare via; *of rain* smettere

◆**go back** *v/i* (*return*) ritornare; (*date back*) rimontare; ***we go back a long way*** ci conosciamo da una vita; ***go back to sleep*** tornare a dormire

◆**go back on** *v/t promise* rimangiarsi

◆**go by** *v/i of car, people, time* passare

◆**go down** *v/i* scendere; *of sun, ship* tramontare; *of ship* affondare; *of swelling* diminuire; ***will it go down well with them?*** la prenderanno bene?

◆**go for** *v/t* (*attack*) attaccare; ***I don't much go for gin*** non vado matto per il gin; ***she really goes for him*** le piace davvero

◆**go in** *v/i to room, house* entrare; *of sun* andare via; (*fit: of part etc*) andare

◆**go in for** *v/t competition, race* iscriversi a; (*like, take part in*) dedicarsi a

◆**go into** *v/t politics* entrare in; *teaching* darsi a

◆**go off I** *v/i* (*leave*) andarsene; *of bomb* esplodere; *of gun* sparare; *of alarm* scattare; *of light* spegnersi; *of milk etc* andare a male **II** *v/t* (*stop liking*) stufarsi di

◆**go on** *v/i* (*continue*) andare avanti; (*happen*) succedere; (*time*) passare; ***go on with sth.*** continuare qc; ***go on doing sth*** continuare a fare qc; ***go on about s.o./sth*** continuare a parlare di qc; ***go on, do it!*** *encouraging* dai, fallo!; ***as time goes on*** col passare del tempo; ***don't go on (about it)*** smettila; ***have you got enough money to be going on with?*** hai abbastanza soldi per tirare avanti?; ***I'm going on for 40*** *age* vado per i quaranta; ***the way he/she's going on ...*** se continua così ...; ***this has been going on for a long time*** questa storia va avanti da tempo; ***we've got nothing to go on*** non abbiamo niente su cui basarci; ***what's going on?*** cosa sta succedendo?

◆**go on at** *v/t* (*nag*) sgridare

◆**go on for** *v/i +obj*: ***be going on for*** *age* essere vicino a; *time* essere quasi

◆**go out** *v/i of person* uscire; *of light, fire* spegnersi; ***go out for a meal*** andare a mangiare fuori; ***go out to work*** andare al lavoro; ***go out on strike*** entrare in sciopero; (*tide*) calare; ***my heart went out to him*** gli sono vicino con tutto il cuore; ***the fun had gone out of it*** non c'era più divertimento

◆**go out with** *v/t romantically* uscire con

◆**go over** *v/t* (*check*) esaminare; (*do again*) rifare

◆**go round** *v/i esp Br* (*spin*) girare; (*make a detour*) fare una deviazione; *tour, round museum* visitare; (*be sufficient*) bastare; (*visit*) andare in visita (***to*** da); ***go round sth*** fare un giro intorno a qc; ***go round the long way*** fare il giro più lungo; ***there's enough food to go round*** c'è abbastanza cibo per tutti

◆**go through** *v/t illness, hard times* passare; (*check*) controllare; (*read through*) leggere

◆**go through with** *v/t* andare avanti con

◆**go together** *v/i* (*harmonize*) intonarsi

◆**go under** *v/i* (*sink*) affondare; *of company* fallire

◆**go up** *v/i* salire

◆**go without** **I** *v/t food etc* fare a meno di; ***go without food*** fare a meno del cibo; ***go without breakfast*** fare a meno della colazione; ***have to go without sth*** dover rinunciare a qc **II** *v/i* farne a meno

goad **I** *v/t* spronare **II** *n* pungolo *m*

go-ahead **I** *n* via libera *m*; ***get the ~*** avere il via libera **II** *adj* (*enterprising, dynamic*) intraprendente

goal *n* (*sport*: *target*) rete *f*; ***score a ~*** segnare un gol; (*sport*: *points*) gol *m inv*; (*objective*) obiettivo *m*; ***set*** (***o.s.***) ***a ~*** porsi un obiettivo

goalie *n infml* portiere *m*

goalkeeper *n* portiere *m* **goal kick** *n* rimessa *f* **goalmouth** *n* area *f* di porta **goalpost** *n* palo *m*; *fig* ***move the ~s*** *Br infml* cambiare le carte in tavola

goat *n* capra *f*; ***he really gets my ~*** mi fa davvero perdere le staffe

goatee (**beard**) *n* pizzo *m*

goatherd *n* capraio *m*, -a *f*

goat's cheese *n* formaggio *m* di capra

gob[1] *v/i Br infml* sputare; ***~ at s.o.*** sputare a qn

gob[2] *n Br* (*mouth*) bocca *f*; ***shut your ~!*** chiudi la bocca!

gobble *v/t* trangugiare

◆**gobble up** *v/t sep* trangugiare

gobbledygook *n infml* linguaggio *m* incomprensibile

go-between *n* mediatore *m*, -trice *f*

goblet *n* calice *m*

goblin *n* spirito *m* maligno

gobsmacked *adj sl* sbigottito

god *n* dio *m*; ***thank God!*** grazie a Dio!; ***oh God!*** Dio mio!; ***God willing*** se Dio vuole; ***God*** (***only***) ***knows*** *infml* Dio solo lo sa; ***for God's sake!*** *infml* per amor di Dio!; ***where in God's name have you been?*** ma dove (diavolo) sei stato?

god-awful *adj infml* spaventoso **godchild** *n* figlioccio *m*, -a *f*

goddamn, goddam *adj esp US infml* maledetto; ***it's no ~ use!*** è maledettamente inutile!

goddamned *adj/adv* → ***goddamn***

goddaughter *n* figliaccia *f*

goddess *n* dea *f*

godfather *n a. in mafia* padrino *m* **godforsaken** *adj place, town* dimenticato da Dio

godless *adj* blasfemo; ***~ person*** senzadio *m/f*

godly *adj* devoto

godmother *n* madrina *f* **godparent** *n man* padrino *m*; *woman* madrina *f* **godsend** *n* benedizione *f* **godson** *n* figlioccio *m*

-goer *n suf*: ***cinemagoer*** frequentatore *m*, -trice *f* di cinema

goes → ***go***

gofer *n infml* galoppino *m*, -a *f infml*

go-getter *n infml* persona *f* intraprendente

goggle *v/i* guardare attonito; ***~ at s.o./sth*** guardare attonito qn / qc

gogglebox *n* tivù *f inv*

goggle-eyed *adj* dagli occhi sporgenti

goggles *npl* occhialini *mpl*

going **I** *n* (*departure*) partenza *f*; ***it's slow ~*** si procede lentamente; ***that's good ~*** è una bella andatura; ***it's heavy ~ talking to him*** è pesante parlare con lui; ***while the ~ is good*** prima che sia troppo tardi **II** *adj price*

etc corrente; ***the best thing ~*** la cosa migliore; ***~ concern*** azienda *f* florida
goings-on *npl* vicende *fpl*
goitre, *US* **goiter** *n* gozzo *m*
go-kart *n* go-kart *m*
gold I *n* oro *m* **II** *adj* d'oro; ***~ jewellery*** *Br or* ***jewelry*** *US* gioielli *mpl* d'oro; ***~ coin*** moneta *f* d'oro
gold disc *n* disco *m* d'oro **gold dust** *n fig*: ***be (like) ~*** essere una rarità
golden *adj sky, hair* dorato; ***fry until ~*** COOK dorare; ***a ~ opportunity*** un'opportunità d'oro
golden age *n fig* età *f* dell'oro **golden eagle** *n* aquila *f* reale **golden goal** *n football* golden goal *m* **golden handshake** *n* buonuscita *f* **golden jubilee** *n* cinquantesimo anniversario *m* **golden mean** *n* aurea mediocrità *f* **golden rule** *n* regola *f* aurea; ***my ~ is never to …*** la mia regola aurea è: mai … **golden syrup** *n Br* melassa *f* **golden wedding (anniversary)** *n* nozze *fpl* d'oro
goldfinch *n* ZOOL cardellino *m* **goldfish** *n* pesce *m* rosso **goldfish bowl** *n* boccia *f* per pesci rossi **gold leaf** *n* lamina *f* d'oro **gold medal** *n* medaglia *f* d'oro **gold mine** *n fig* miniera *f* d'oro **gold plate** *n* vasellame *m* d'oro **gold-plated** *adj* placcato in oro **gold reserve** *n* riserva *f* aurea **gold rush** *n* corsa *f* all'oro **goldsmith** *n* orefice *m/f*
golf *n* golf *m*
golf bag *n* sacca *f* da golf **golf ball** *n* palla *f* da golf **golf club** *n organization* club *m inv* di golf; *stick* mazza *f* da golf **golf course** *n* campo *m* di golf
golfer *n* giocatore *m*, -trice di golf
golf links *npl* campo *m* di golf
gondola *n* gondola *f*
gondolier *n* gondoliere *m*
gone I *prep*: ***it's ~ six (o'clock)*** sono le sei passate **II** *past part* → ***go***
goner *n infml* caso *m* disperato
gong *n* gong *m inv*
good ⟨*comp* ***better***, *sup* ***best***⟩ **I** *adj* buono; *weather, film* bello; *actor, child* bravo; ***be ~!*** fai il bravo!; ***a ~ many*** un bel po' (di); ***be ~ at*** essere bravo in; ***be ~ for s.o.*** fare bene a qn; ***be ~ for sth*** andare bene per qc; ***~!*** bene!; ***it's ~ to see you*** è bello vederti; ***that's a ~ one!*** *iron* questa sì che è bella!; ***you've done a ~ day's work*** hai sbrigato il lavoro di un'intera giornata; ***a ~ meal*** un buon pasto; ***be ~ with people*** saperci fare con le persone; ***it's too ~ to be true*** troppo bello per essere vero; ***be ~ for s.o.*** fare bene a qn; ***it's a ~ thing*** *or* ***job I was there*** meno male che ero là; ***~ nature*** buon carattere *m*; ***take a ~ look at sth*** osservare bene qc; ***it's a ~ 8 km*** sono 8 km buoni; ***a ~ many people*** parecchie persone; ***~ morning*** buon giorno **II** *n* bene *m*; ***it did him no ~*** non gli ha fatto bene; ***it did him a lot of ~*** gli ha fatto molto bene; ***it's no ~*** non serve a nulla; ***it's for your own ~*** è per il tuo bene; ***what ~ is that to me?*** a che cosa mi serve?; ***for ~*** per sempre; ***he'll come to no ~*** andrà a finire male; ***what's the ~ of hurrying?*** a che serve affrettarsi?; ***if that is any ~ to you*** se ti è utile; ***the ~*** il buono; *people* i buoni **III** *adv* bene; ***how are you? — ~!*** come stai? bene!
goodbye *int* arrivederci; ***say ~ to s.o., wish s.o. ~*** salutare qn
good-for-nothing *n* buono *m*, -a *f* a nulla **Good Friday** *n* venerdì *m inv* santo **good-humoured**, *US* **good-humored** *adj* di buon umore **good-looking** *adj* attraente **good-natured** *adj* di buon cuore
goodness *n* bontà *f*; ***thank ~!*** grazie al cielo; ***for ~ sake*** per l'amor del cielo; ***out of the ~ of his/her heart*** per bontà d'animo; ***~ knows*** lo sa il cielo; ***(my) ~!*** santo cielo!
goodnight *adj*: ***~ kiss*** bacio *m* della buonanotte
good offices *npl* buoni uffici *mpl*
goods *npl* COMM merce *fsg*; ***leather ~*** oggetti *mpl* di pelle; ***stolen ~*** refurtiva *f*; ***if we don't come up with the ~ on time*** *infml* se non manteniamo puntualmente i nostri impegni
good-sized *adj* ampio
goods train *n* treno *m* merci
good-tempered *adj person* di buon carattere; *animal* mansueto **good turn** *n* favore *m*
goodwill *n* buona volontà *f*; ***a gesture of ~*** un gesto di buona volontà
goody-goody *n infml* santarellino *m*,

-a *f infml*
gooey *adj* (+*er*) appiccicoso
goof *v/i infml* fare una gaffe
goofy *adj* (+*er*) *infml* sciocco
goolies *npl vulg* palle *fpl vulg*
goose I *n* ⟨*pl* ***geese***⟩ oca *f* **II** *v/t vulg* dare una pacca sul sedere a
gooseberry *n* uva *f* spina
goose bumps *npl US* pelle *f* d'oca
goose pimples *npl* pelle *f* d'oca
goosestep I *n* passo *m* dell'oca **II** *v/i* ⟨*pret & past part* ***-ped***⟩ marciare col passo dell'oca
gopher *n* ZOOL geomide *m*
gore I *n* sangue *m* rappreso **II** *v/t* incornare
gorge I *n* gola *f* **II** *v/t*: ***~ o.s. on sth*** strafogarsi di qc
gorgeous *adj* stupendo; *smell* ottimo
gorilla *n* gorilla *m*
gormless *adj Br infml* stupido
gory *adj* esplicito; ***I want all the ~ details*** voglio tutti i particolari
gosh *int* caspita
go-slow *n* sciopero *m* bianco
gospel *n in Bible* vangelo *m*
gospel truth *n* sacrosanta verità *f inv*
gossip I *n* pettegolezzo *m*; ***have a ~ with s.o.*** spettegolare con qn; *person* pettegolo *m*, -a *f* **II** *v/i* spettegolare; ***~ about*** spettegolare su
gossip column *n* cronaca *f* rosa **gossip columnist** *n* giornalista *m/f* di cronaca rosa
gossipmonger *n* pettegolo *m*, -a *f*
gossipy *adj letter* pieno di chiacchiere
got *pret & past part* → ***get***
Gothic *adj* gotico
gotten *past part US* → ***get***
gouge *v/t* scavare; ***the river ~d a channel in the mountainside*** il fiume ha scavato un canale nel fianco della montagna
◆**gouge out** *v/t sep* cavare; ***gouge s.o.'s eyes out*** cavare gli occhi a qn
goulash *n* gulasch *m inv*
gourd *n* zucca *f*; (*dried*) *recipiente ricavato da una zucca*
gourmet *n* buongustaio *m*, -a *f*
gout *n* MED gotta *f*
gouty *adj* gottoso
Gov *abbr* (= **governor**) governatore *m*
govern *v/t country* governare
governess *n* governante *f*
governing body *n* consiglio *m* d'amministrazione
government *n* governo *m*; ***~ official*** funzionario *m* pubblico; ***~ backing*** sostegno *m* governativo; ***~ intervention*** intervento *m* del governo
government department *n* dipartimento *m* governativo **government-funded** *adj* finanziato dal governo **government spending** *n* spesa *f* pubblica
governor *n* governatore *m*; *of school* membro *m* del consiglio d'istituto; ***the*** (***board of***) ***~s*** il consiglio d'amministrazione
govt *abbr* (= **government**) governo *m*
gown *n* (*long dress*) abito *m* lungo; (*wedding dress*) abito *m* da sposa; *of academic*, *judge* toga *f*; *of surgeon* camice *m*
GP *abbr* (= **General Practitioner**) medico *m* generico
GPS *n abbr* (= **global positioning system**) GPS *m*
grab I *v/t* ⟨*pret & past part* ***-bed***⟩ afferrare; ***~ a bite to eat*** fare uno spuntino rapido; ***~ some sleep*** farsi una dormita **II** *n*: ***make a ~ at*** *or* ***for sth*** tentare di afferrare qc; ***sth is up for ~s*** *infml job*, *price* qualcosa è a disposizione di chi vuole prenderlo **III** *v/i*: ***~ at*** tentare di afferrare; ***he ~bed at the chance of promotion*** tentò di afferrare l'opportunità di una promozione
grace I *n of dancer etc* grazia *f*; *before meals* preghiera *f* (prima di un pasto); ***say ~*** dire la preghiera(*respite*) dilazione *f*; ***give s.o. a few days' ~*** dare a qn una dilazione di alcuni giorni; ***fall from ~*** cadere in disgrazia **II** *v/t* (*honour*) fare onore a (***with*** con); *event etc* onorare
graceful *adj* aggraziato
gracefully *adv move* con grazia; ***grow old ~*** invecchiare con eleganza
graceless *adj* inelegante
grace note *n* MUS fioritura *f*
gracious *adj person* cortese; *style* elegante; *living* agiato; ***good ~!*** santo cielo!
gradation *n* gradazione *f*
grade I *n* (*quality*) qualità *f inv*; EDU voto *m* **II** *v/t* classificare
grade crossing *n US* passaggio *m* a livello **grade school** *n US* scuola *f* elementare

gradient *n* pendenza *f*; ***a ~ of 1 in 10*** una pendenza del 10 %
gradual *adj* graduale
gradually *adv* gradualmente
graduate I *n* laureato *m*, -a *f*; ***high-school ~*** *US* diplomato *m*, -a *f* di scuola secondaria **II** *v/i from university* laurearsi; ***~ in English*** laurearsi in inglese; ***she ~d to television from radio*** è passata dalla radio alla televisione
graduate school *n US* corso *m* di perfezionamento post-laurea
graduate student *n US studente che segue un corso di perfezionamento post-laurea*
graduation *n* laurea *f*; *ceremony* cerimonia *f* di laurea
graffiti *n* graffiti *mpl*
graffiti artist *n* graffitista *m/f*
graft I *n* BOT innesto *m*; MED trapianto *m*; *infml* (*hard work*) duro lavoro *m*; *infml* (*corruption*) appropriazione *f* indebita **II** *v/t* BOT innestare; MED trapiantare
grail *n* Graal *m*
grain *n* cereali *mpl*; *seed* granello *m*; *of rice*, *wheat* chicco *m*; *in wood* venatura *f*; ***go against the ~*** essere contro natura
grainy *adj* (+*er*) *photograph* a grana grossa
gram *n* grammo *m*
grammar *n* grammatica *f*; ***that is bad ~*** è grammaticalmente scorretto
grammar school *n* liceo *m*
grammatical *adj* grammaticale; ***~ error*** errore *m* grammaticale; ***his English is not ~*** il suo inglese è grammaticalmente scorretto
grammatically *adv* grammaticalmente
gramme *n* → ***gram***
gramophone *n Br* grammofono *m*; ***~ record*** disco *m* grammofonico
gran *n infml* nonna *f*
granary *n* granaio *m*
grand I *adj* (+*er*) grandioso; *infml* (*very good*) eccezionale; ***on a ~ scale*** su vasta scala; ***~ occasion*** grande evento *m*; ***~ opening*** inaugurazione *f* **II** *n infml* (*£1000*) mille sterline *fpl*; ***ten ~*** diecimila sterline
grandad *n* nonno *m* **grandchild** *n* nipote *m/f* **granddaughter** *n* nipote *f* **grand duchy** *n* granducato *m*
grandee *n* grande *m* di Spagna
grandeur *n* grandiosità *f*
grandfather *n* nonno *m* **grandfather clock** *n* pendolo *m* **grand finale** *n* gran finale *m*
grandiloquent *adj* magniloquente
grandiose *adj* grandioso
grandiosity *n* grandiosità *f*
grand jury *n* JUR giuria *f* dell'udienza preliminare
grandly *adv* (*impressively*) grandiosamente; (*pompously*) pomposamente
grandma *n infml* nonna *f*
grandmaster *n* (*chess*) grande maestro *m*
grandmother *n* nonna *f*
grandpa *n infml* nonno *m*
grandparents *npl* nonni *mpl*
grand piano *n* pianoforte *m* a coda **grand slam** *n* SPORTS grande slam *m inv*
grandson *n* nipote *m*
grandstand *n* tribuna *f*
grand total *n* importo *m* totale; ***a ~ of £50*** un importo totale di 50 sterline **grand tour** *n* viaggio *m* attraverso il continente europeo
grange *n* residenza *f* di campagna
granite *n* granito *m*
granny *n infml* nonna *f*
granny flat *n* appartamento *m* annesso
grant I *n money* sussidio *m*; *for university* borsa *f* di studio **II** *v/t visa* assegnare; *permission* concedere; *request*, *wish* esaudire; ***take sth for ~ed*** dare qc per scontato; ***he takes his wife for ~ed*** considera quello che fa sua moglie come dovuto
granulated sugar *n* zucchero *m* granulato
granule *n* granello *m*
grape *n* acino *m* d'uva; ***~s*** uva *fsg*; ***a bunch of ~s*** un grappolo d'uva
grapefruit *n* pompelmo *m* **grapefruit juice** *n* succo *m* di pompelmo **grapevine** *n* vite *f*; ***I heard over the ~ that ...*** ho sentito dire che ...
graph *n* grafico *m*
graphic I *adj* grafico; (*vivid*) vivido; ***describe sth in ~ detail*** descrivere qc con vividi dettagli **II** *n* COMPUT grafico *m*, -a *f*; ***~s*** grafica *f*
graphically *adv describe* in modo vivi-

do
graphic artist *n* artista *m/f* grafico, -a
graphic designer *n* grafico *m*, -a *f*
graphic equalizer *n* equalizzatore *m* grafico
graphics **I** *npl* (*drawings*) grafica *f*; COMPUT elementi *mpl* grafici **II** *adj* COMPUT grafico
graphics card *n* COMPUT scheda grafica
graphite *n* grafite *f*
graph paper *n* carta *f* millimetrata
grapple *v/i liter* lottare corpo a corpo
◆**grapple with** *v/t attacker* lottare con; *problem etc* essere alle prese con
grasp **I** *n physical* presa *f*; *mental* comprensione *f*; ***have a good ~ of sth*** avere buone conoscenze di qc **II** *v/t physically*, *mentally* afferrare; ***he ~ed the bundle in his arms*** afferrò il fagotto tra le braccia
grasping *adj fig* avido
grass *n* erba *f*
grasshopper *n* cavalletta *f* **grassland** *n* prato *m* **grass roots** **I** *npl people* massa *f* popolare **II** *adj* della base; ***at ~ level*** al livello della base; ***a ~ movement*** un movimento popolare **grass snake** *n* biscia *f* **grass widow** *n donna il cui marito è spesso assente* **grass widower** *n uomo la cui moglie è spesso assente*
grassy *adj* (+*er*) erboso
grate¹ *n metal* grata *f*; *in fire* griglia *f*
grate² **I** *v/t in cooking* grattugiare **II** *v/i of sounds* stridere
grateful *adj* grato; ***be ~ to s.o.*** essere grato a qn; ***I'm ~ to you for buying the tickets*** ti sono grato per aver comprato i biglietti
gratefully *adv* con gratitudine
grater *n* grattugia *f*
gratification *n* soddisfazione *f*
gratify *v/t* ⟨*pret & past part* **-ied**⟩ soddisfare
gratifying *adj* piacevole; ***it is ~ to learn that …*** fa piacere sapere che …
grating **I** *n* grata *f* **II** *adj sound*, *voice* stridente
gratis **I** *adj* gratuito **II** *adv* gratis; ***free, ~ and for nothing*** *hum* completamente gratuito
gratitude *n* gratitudine *f*; ***in ~ for*** come ringraziamento per
gratuitous *adj* gratuito
gratuity *n* (*tip*) mancia *f*
grave¹ *n* tomba *f*
grave² *adj* (+*er*) (*serious*) grave
gravedigger *n* becchino *m*, -a *f*
gravel *n* ghiaia *f*
gravely *adj say*, *nod* con fare grave; ***~ ill*** gravemente malato
graven image *n* immagine *f* scolpita
gravestone *n* lapide *f* **graveyard** *n* cimitero *m*
gravitas *n* solennità *f*
gravitate *v/i liter* gravitare
◆**gravitate towards** *v/t* gravitare intorno a
gravity *n* PHYS forza *f* di gravità; *of person*, *situation* solennità *f*; ***the ~ of the news*** la gravità delle notizie
gravy *n* sugo *m* della carne
gravy boat *n* salsiera *f* **gravy train** *n fig* miniera *f* d'oro
gray *US* → ***grey***
graze¹ *v/i of cow*, *horse* brucare
graze² **I** *v/t arm etc* graffiare; ***~ one's knees*** graffiarsi le ginocchia **II** *n* graffio *m*
grease *n* grasso *m*
greasepaint *n* THEAT cerone *m*
greaseproof paper *n* carta *f* oleata
greasy *adj* (+*er*) *food*, *hair*, *skin* grasso; *hands*, *plate* unto
greasy spoon *n infml* bettola *f*
great **I** *adj* (+*er*) grande; *infml* (*very good*) fantastico; ***a ~ deal of*** un sacco di; ***a ~ many*** *or* ***a ~ number of*** moltissimi; ***his ~est work*** la sua opera principale; ***in ~ detail*** nei minimi dettagli; ***of no ~ importance*** di importanza limitata; ***to a ~ extent*** considerevolmente; ***be ~ at football*** essere bravissimo a calcio; ***be a ~ believer in sth*** essere un acceso sostenitore di qc; ***~ to see you!*** sono contento di vederti!; ***take a ~ interest in sth*** interessarsi molto a qc; ***it gives me a ~ pleasure to …*** è con immenso piacere che …; ***it's ~ to be home*** è bello essere a casa; ***it's a ~ pity that …*** è davvero un peccato che …; ***it was ~ fun*** è stato molto divertente; ***the weather is ~*** il tempo è bellissimo **II** *int infml* bene; ***oh ~*** *iron* perfetto! **III** *adv*: ***she's doing ~*** *in job* le cose le vanno bene; *healthwise* sta benissimo; ***everything's going ~*** sta andato tutto benissimo; ***~ big*** *infml* grandis-

simo **IV** *n usu pl* (*person*) grandi *mpl*
great-aunt *n* prozia *f* **Great Britain** *n* Gran Bretagna *f* **Great Dane** *n* ZOOL danese *m*
Greater London *n* area *f* metropolitana di Londra
great-grandchild *n* pronipote *m/f* **great-granddaughter** *n* pronipote *f* **great-grandfather** *n* bisnonno *m* **great-grandmother** *n* bisnonna *f* **great-grandparents** *npl* bisnonni *mpl* **great-grandson** *n* pronipote *m*
Great Lakes *npl*: ***the ~*** i grandi laghi
greatly *adv* molto; ***he was not ~ surprised*** non era molto sorpreso
great-nephew *n* pronipote *m*
greatness *n* grandezza *f*
great-niece *n* pronipote *f* **great-uncle** *n* prozio *m*
Great War *n* HIST Grande Guerra *f*
Greece *n* Grecia *f*
greed *n* avidità *f*; ***~ for money / power*** avidità *f* di denaro / potere; *for food* ingordigia *f*
greedily *adv* con avidità; *eat* con ingordigia
greediness *n* avidità *f*; (*gluttony*) ingordigia *f*
greedy *adj* (+*er*) avido; *for food* ingordo
Greek I *n* greco *m*, -a *f*; *language* greco *m*; ***Ancient ~*** greco *m* antico; ***it's all ~ to me*** *infml* questo è arabo per me **II** *adj* greco
Greek cross *n* croce *f* greca
green I *adj* (+*er*) verde; *environmentally* ecologico; ***be ~ with envy*** essere verde d'invidia **II** *n* verde *m*; ***dressed in ~*** vestito di verde; ***the lights are at ~*** il semaforo è verde; (***village***) ***~*** *area verde pubblica nel centro di un paese*; ***the Greens*** POL i verdi
greenback *n US infml* banconota *f*
green beans *npl* fagiolini *mpl* **green belt** *n zona verde tutt'intorno ad una città* **green card** *n driving insurance* carta *f* verde
greenery *n* serra *f*; (*foliage*) fogliame *m*
greenfield *adj*: ***~ site*** terreno *m* non costruito
green fingers *npl*: ***have ~*** avere il pollice verde
greenfly *n* afide *m*
greengrocer *n* fruttivendolo *m*, -a *f*; ***at the ~'s*** (***shop***) dal fruttivendolo
greenhorn *n infml* pivello *m*, -a *f infml*
greenhouse *n* serra *f*
greenhouse effect *n* effetto *m* serra **greenhouse gas** *n* gas *m inv* serra
greenish *adj* verdastro
Greenland *n* Groenlandia *f*
green light *n* segnale *m* di via libera; ***give s.o. / sth the ~*** dare il via libera a qn / qc **green man** *n* (*at street crossing*) *segnale di via libera per i pedoni* **green onion** *n US* cipolla *f* verde **green pepper** *n vegetable* peperone *m*
greens *npl* verdura *f*
green thumb *n US*: ***have a ~*** avere il pollice verde
greet *v/t* salutare
greeting *n* saluto *m*
greetings card *n* biglietto *m* d'auguri
gregarious *adj person* socievole
grenade *n* granata *f*
grew *pret* → ***grow***
grey, *US* **gray I** *adj* (+*er*) grigio; *hair* bianco; ***be going ~*** cominciare ad avere i capelli bianchi **II** *n* grigio *m*; ***dressed in ~*** vestito di grigio
grey area *n fig* zona *f* grigia
grey-haired, *US* **gray-haired** *adj* con i capelli bianchi
greyhound *n* levriero *m*
greyish, *US* **grayish** *adj* grigiastro
grey matter *n* MED *infml* materia *f* grigia **grey squirrel** *n* scoiattolo *m* grigio
grid *n* grata *f*; *on map* reticolato *m*
griddle *n* COOK piastra *f*
gridiron *n* COOK gratella *f*; *US football* campo *m* di football
gridlock *n in traffic* ingorgo *m* **grid reference** *n* reticolo *m* di riferimento
grief *n* dolore *m*
grief-stricken *adj* addolorato
grievance *n* rimostranza *f*
grieve *v/i* essere addolorato; ***~ for s.o.*** essere addolorato per qn
grievous *adj form* doloroso; *error* deplorevole; ***~ bodily harm*** JUR grave danno *m* fisico
grill I *n for cooking* grill *m inv*; *metal frame* griglia *f*; *dish* grigliata *f*; *on window* grata *f* **II** *v/t food* fare alla griglia; (*interrogate*) mettere sotto

torchio
grille *n* grata *f*
grilling *n* COOK grigliata *f*; (*interrogation*) terzo grado *m*
grill pan *n Br* gratella *f*
grim *adj* (+*er*) cupo; *determination* accanito
grimace I *n* smorfia *f* **II** *v/i* fare smorfie
grime *n* sporcizia *f*
grimly *adv* con aria grave
Grim Reaper *n liter*: ***the ~*** la morte, *liter* la falciatrice
grimy *adj* sudicio
grin I *v/i* ⟨*pret & past part* **-ned**⟩ sorridere; ***~ at s.o.*** sorridere a qn; ***~ and bear it*** fare buon viso a cattivo gioco **II** *n* sorriso *m*
grind I *v/t* ⟨*pret & past part* **ground**⟩ *coffee*, *meat* macinare; ***~ one's teeth*** digrignare i denti **II** *v/i*: ***~ to a halt*** *or* ***standstill*** *liter* fermarsi gradualmente *a. fig* **III** *n fig infml* (*drudgery*) sfacchinata *f*; *US* (*swot*) secchione *m*, -a *f*; ***the daily ~*** il tran tran quotidiano; ***it's a real ~*** è una bella sfacchinata
◆**grind up** *v/t sep* macinare
grindstone *n*: ***keep one's nose to the ~*** lavorare sodo; ***back to the ~*** di nuovo al lavoro
grip I *n on rope etc* presa *f*; ***he's losing his ~*** *losing skills* sta perdendo dei colpi; ***get to ~s with sth*** affrontare qc; ***get a ~ on the rope*** stringere la presa sulla corda; ***these shoes / tyres*** *Br or* ***tires*** *US* ***have got a good ~*** queste scarpe / gomme hanno una buona presa; ***the country is in the ~ of a general strike*** il paese è in preda a uno sciopero generale **II** *v/t* ⟨*pret & past part* **-ped**⟩ afferrare; *of brakes* fare presa su; ***be ~ped by sth*** *by panic* essere preso da qc
gripe I *n* lamentela *f* **II** *v/i* lamentarsi
gripping *adj* avvincente
grisly *adj* (+*er*) orrendo
grist *n*: ***it's all ~ to his / the mill*** (per lui) tutto fa brodo
gristle *n* cartilagine *f*
grit I *n* (*dirt*) granelli *mpl*; *for roads* sabbia *f* **II** *v/t* ⟨*pret & past part* **-ted**⟩ ***~ one's teeth*** stringere i denti
gritty *adj* (+*er*) *infml book*, *film etc* realistico
grizzly *n* (*a.* **grizzly bear**) grizzly *m*
groan I *v/i* gemere; ***the table ~ed under the weight*** il tavolo gemette per il peso **II** *n* gemito *m*; ***let out*** *or* ***give a ~*** emettere un gemito
grocer *n* droghiere *m*; ***at the ~'s*** (***shop***) dal droghiere
groceries *npl* generi *mpl* alimentari
grocery store *n* drogheria *f*
groggy *adj* (+*er*) *infml* intontito
groin *n* ANAT inguine *m*; ***kick s.o. in the ~*** dare un calcio all'inguine a qn
groom I *n for bride* sposo *m*; *for horse* stalliere *m* **II** *v/t horse* strigliare; (*train*, *prepare*) preparare; ***well ~ed*** *in appearance* ben curato
groove I *n* scanalatura *f* **II** *v/t* scanalare **III** *v/i infml* divertirsi
groovy *adj* (+*er*) *infml* all'ultima moda
grope I *v/i in the dark* brancolare **II** *v/t sexually* palpeggiare
◆**grope for** *v/t door handle* cercare a tastoni; *the right word* cercare di trovare
gross I *adj* (+*er*) (*coarse*, *vulgar*) volgare; *exaggeration* madornale; (*disgusting*) disgustoso; FIN lordo; ***~ amount*** importo *m* lordo; ***~ income*** reddito *m* lordo **II** *v/t* avere un introito lordo di
gross domestic product *n* prodotto *m* interno lordo
grossly *adj exaggerated*, *overweight*, *unfair* estremamente
gross national product *n* prodotto *m* nazionale lordo
grotesque *adj* grottesco
grotesquely *adv* grottescamente
grotto *n* grotta *f*
grotty *adj* (+*er*) *infml street*, *flat* squallido; ***I feel ~*** sto da schifo *infml*
grouch *n* (*complaint*) rimostranza *f*; (*person*) brontolone *m*, -a *f*; ***have a ~*** avercela (***about*** per)
grouchy *adj* (+*er*) di cattivo umore
ground[1] **I** *n* **1.** suolo *m*; (*area*, *for sport*) terreno *m*; ***on the ~*** per terra; ***above ~*** in superficie; ***below ~*** sottoterra; ***gain ~*** guadagnare terreno; *fig* ***hold*** *or* ***stand one's ~*** tenere duro **2.** (*reason*) motivo *m*, ragione *f*; ***have ~(s) for sth*** avere motivi per qc; ***~s for dismissal*** motivi *mpl* di licenziamento; ***on the ~s that …*** per il fatto

che; ***on health ~s*** per motivi di salute; ***on the ~s of*** a causa di **3.** ELEC terra *f* **4.** (*pitch*) campo *m* **5. grounds** *npl* (*premises*) sede *f*; (*gardens*) terreni *mpl* **6. grounds** *npl* (*sediment*) deposito *m* **II** *v/t* AVIAT *plane* tenere a terra; *child* proibire di uscire a; ELEC mettere a terra; ***be ~ed by bad weather*** AVIAT restare a terra a causa del maltempo; ***she was ~ed for a week*** le è stato proibito di uscire per una settimana

ground² *pret & past part* → ***grind***

ground beef *n US* macinato *m* di manzo **ground-breaking** *adj* innovativo **ground control** *n* controllo *m* da terra **ground crew** *n* personale *m* di terra **ground floor** *n* pianoterra *m inv* **ground frost** *n* gelo *m*

grounding *n in subject* basi *fpl*; ***have a good ~ in*** avere delle buoni basi di

groundkeeper *n US* → ***groundsman***

groundless *adj* infondato

ground level *n* livello *m* del suolo; ***below ~*** sotto il livello del suolo

groundnut *n* arachide *f*

ground plan *n* pianta *f* del piano terra **ground rules** *npl* regole *fpl* di base

groundsheet *n telone impermeabile usato dai campeggiatori*

groundsman *n* 〈*pl* ***groundsmen***〉 *esp Br* addetto *m*, -a *f* al campo

ground staff *n* SPORTS *personale addetto alla manutenzione dei campi sportivi*; *at airport* personale *m* di terra **groundwater** *n* acqua *f* freatica **groundwork** *n* lavoro *m* di preparazione

group I *n* gruppo *m* **II** *v/t* raggruppare

group booking *n* prenotazione *f* di gruppo

groupie *n infml ragazza che segue un gruppo o cantante rock in tutti i concerti*

group therapy *n* terapia *f* di gruppo

grouse¹ *n* 〈*pl* ***grouse***〉 *bird* gallo *m* cedrone

grouse² I *n infml* lamentela *f* **II** *v/i infml* brontolare

grove *n* frutteto *m*

grovel *v/i* 〈*pret & past part* ***-led***, *US* ***-ed***〉 *fig* umiliarsi

grow 〈*pret* ***grew***, *past part* ***grown***〉 **I** *v/i of child, animal, plant* crescere; *of number, amount* aumentare; ***pressure is ~ing for him to resign*** crescono le pressioni perché lui si dimetta; *of business* svilupparsi; ***the economy is ~ing by 2 % a year*** l'economia ha una crescita del 2 % annuo; ***let one's hair ~*** farsi crescere i capelli; ***~ old / tired*** invecchiare / stancarsi;(*become*) diventare; ***~ to be sth*** finire per essere qc; ***~ to hate s.o.*** finire per odiare qn; ***I've ~n to like him*** ha cominciato a piacermi; ***~ into sth*** diventare qc **II** *v/t flowers* coltivare; ***~ a beard*** farsi crescere la barba

◆**grow apart** *v/i fig* allontanarsi

◆**grow from** *v/i +obj* (*arise from*) nascere da

◆**grow into** *v/t job* abituarsi a; *clothes* diventare abbastanza grande per; (*become*) diventare; ***grow into a man / woman*** diventare un uomo / una donna

◆**grow on** *v/t*: ***it'll grow on you*** ti piacerà sempre di più

◆**grow out** *v/i perm, colour* eliminare con la ricrescita

◆**grow out of** *v/t clothes* non entrare più in; ***grow out of one's temper tantrums*** non fare più i capricci

◆**grow up** *v/i of person* crescere; *of city* svilupparsi; ***grow up!*** comportati da adulto!; ***what are you going to do when you grow up?*** cosa farai da grande?; ***when are you going to grow up?*** quando ti comporterai da adulto?

grower *n* coltivatore *m*, -trice *f*

growing *adj* crescente; *child* in fase di crescita; *importance, number etc* sempre maggiore

growing pains *n* dolori *mpl* della crescita **growing season** *n* stagione *f* di coltivazione

growl I *v/i* ringhiare; ***~ at s.o.*** ringhiare a qc **II** *n* grugnito *m*

grown *past part* → ***grow***

grown-up I *n* adulto *m*, -a *f* **II** *adj* adulto

growth *n of person* crescita *f*; *of company* sviluppo *m*; (*increase*) aumento *m*; MED tumore *m*

grub¹ *n of insect* larva *f*

grub² *n infml* (*food*) mangiare *m*

grubby *adj* (*+er*) sporco

grudge I *n* rancore *m*; ***bear s.o. a ~*** portare rancore a qn **II** *v/t* dare a ma-

lincuore; **~ s.o. sth** invidiare qc a qn
grudging *adj* riluttante
grudgingly *adv* a malincuore
gruel *n farina di orzo o avena cotta nell'acqua o nel latte*
gruelling, *US* **grueling** *adj climb, task* estenuante
gruesome *adj* raccapricciante
gruff *adj* burbero
grumble *v/i* brontolare; **~ about** lamentarsi di
grumbler *n* brontolone *m*, -a *f*
grump *n* (*fit of temper*) malumore *m*; (*person*) brontolone *m*, -a *f*; ***he was a terrible old ~*** era un vecchio brontolone
grumpy *adj* (+*er*) scontroso
grunge *n* grunge *m*
grungy *adj infml* sporco
grunt I *v/i* grugnire **II** *n* grugnito *m*
G-string *n* perizoma *m*; MUS corda *f* del sol
guarantee I *n* garanzia *f*; ***the watch is still under ~*** l'orologio è ancora in garanzia; ***~ period*** periodo *m* di garanzia; ***that's no ~ that ...*** ciò non garantisce che ... **II** *v/t* garantire; ***I can't ~ (that) he will be any good*** non posso garantire che sarà utile
guarantor *n* garante *m*
guard I *n* guardia *m*; ***change ~*** cambiare guardia; ***be under ~*** essere sotto scorta; ***be on one's ~ against*** stare in guardia contro; ***drop*** *or* ***lower one's ~*** *liter* abbassare la guardia *a. fig*; ***the invitation caught me off ~*** l'invito mi ha colto alla sprovvista **II** *v/t* fare la guardia a; ***a closely ~ed secret*** un segreto custodito gelosamente
◆ **guard against** *v/t* guardarsi da; ***you must guard against catching cold*** devi fare attenzione a non prendere il raffreddore
guard dog *n* cane *m* da guardia **guard duty** *n*: ***be on ~*** essere in servizio di guardia
guarded *adj reply* cauto
guardian *n* JUR tutore *m*, -trice *f*
guardian angel *n* angelo *m* custode
guardrail *n* guardrail *m*
guardsman *n* ⟨*pl* **guardsmen**⟩ *Br* membro *m* delle guardie reali; *US* membro *m* della guardia nazionale
guard's van *n* RAIL carrozza *f* del capotreno
guerrilla *n* guerrigliero *m*, -a *f*
guerrilla warfare *n* guerriglia *f*
guess I *v/t the answer* indovinare; ***I ~ so*** suppongo di sì; ***I ~ not*** suppongo di no **II** *v/i correctly* indovinare; ***I was just ~ing*** ho tirato a indovinare; ***~ at sth*** avanzare ipotesi su qc **III** *n* supposizione *f*; ***I give you three ~es*** ti do tre possibilità di indovinare; ***at a ~*** a occhio e croce
guesstimate *n* stima *f* a occhio e croce
guesswork *n* congettura *f*
guest *n* ospite *m/f*; ***be my ~*** fai pure
guesthouse *n* pensione *f* **guest list** *n* elenco *m* degli invitati **guestroom** *n* camera *f* degli ospiti **guest speaker** *n* oratore *m* ospite
guffaw I *n* sghignazzata *f* **II** *v/i* sghignazzare
GUI *abbr* (= **graphical user interface**) interfaccia *f* grafica
guidance *n* consigli *mpl*
guide I *n person*, *book* guida *f*; ***~ to sth*** guida a *or* di qc; ***as a rough ~*** a titolo indicativo **II** *v/t* guidare
guidebook *n* guida *f* turistica
guided missile *n* missile *m* guidato
guide dog *n* cane *m* per ciechi
guided tour *n* visita *f* guidata
guideline *n* direttiva *f*; ***safety ~s*** direttive *fpl* di sicurezza; ***I gave her a few ~s on looking after a kitten*** le ho dato alcune direttive su come prendersi cura di un gattino
guild *n* HIST corporazione *f*; (*association*) associazione *f*
guile *n form* scaltrezza *f*
guileless *adj* schietto
guillotine I *n for executing people* ghigliottina *f*; *for cutting paper* taglierina *f* **II** *v/t* ghigliottinare
guilt *n* colpa *f*; JUR colpevolezza *f*
guilty *adj* (+*er*) *a.* JUR colpevole; ***be ~ of sth*** essere colpevole di qc; ***feel ~ about sth*** sentirsi in colpa per qc; ***have a ~ conscience*** avere la coscienza sporca; ***~ conscience*** coscienza *f* sporca; ***~ feelings*** sensi *mpl* di colpa; ***feel ~ (about doing sth)*** sentirsi in colpa (per aver fatto qc); ***make s.o. feel ~*** far sentire in colpa qn; ***the ~ person*** il colpevole; ***the ~ party*** il colpevole; ***plead (not) ~ to a crime*** dichiararsi (non)

colpevole di un crimine; ***a ~ verdict*** *or* ***a verdict of ~*** un verdetto di colpevolezza; ***their parents are ~ of gross neglect*** i genitori sono colpevoli di grave negligenza; ***we're all ~ of neglecting the problem*** siamo tutti colpevoli di aver trascurato il problema

guinea pig *n* porcellino *m* d'india; *for experiments*, *fig* cavia *f*

guise *n* abito *m*; (*pretence*) apparenza *f*; ***in the ~ of a clown*** in abito da pagliaccio; ***under the ~ of*** dietro la maschera di

guitar *n* chitarra *f*

guitar case *n* custodia *f* della chitarra

guitarist *n* chitarrista *m*/*f*

guitar player *n* chitarrista *m*/*f*

gulf *n* golfo *m*; *fig* divario *m*; ***the Gulf*** il Golfo

gull *n bird* gabbiano *m*

gullet *n* ANAT esofago *m*

gullible *adj* credulone

gully *n* (*ravine*) gola *f*; (*narrow channel*) cunetta *f*

gulp I *n of water* sorso *m*; *of air* boccata *f* **II** *v/i in surprise* deglutire

◆**gulp down** *v/t drink* ingoiare; *food* trangugiare

gum[1] *n in mouth* gengiva *f*

gum[2] *n* (*glue*) colla *f*; (*chewing gum*) gomma *f*

gummy *adj* (+*er*) appiccicoso; *glue* colloso; ***~ smile*** sorriso *m* sdentato

gumption *n infml* sale *m* in zucca *infml*

gun I *n pistol*, *revolver*, *rifle* arma *f* da fuoco; (*cannon*) cannone *m*; ***carry a ~*** portare una pistola; ***draw a ~ on s.o.*** estrarre una pistola contro qn; *fig* ***big ~*** *infml* persona *f* importante (***in*** in); ***stick to one's ~s*** mantenere le proprie posizioni; *fig* ***jump the ~*** essere precipitoso; ***be going great ~s*** *Br infml* (*team*, *person*) fare scintille; (*car*) funzionare perfettamente; (*business*) andare forte **II** *v/t person* sparare a **III** *v/i infml* ***be ~ning for s.o.*** *fig* mirare a qn

◆**gun down** *v/t* ⟨*pret & past part* ***-ned***⟩ sparare a morte a

gunboat *n* cannoniera *f* **gunfight** *n* scontro *m* a fuoco **gunfire** *n* spari *mpl*

gunge *n Br infml* sostanza *f* appiccicosa

gunk *n esp US infml* → ***gunge***

gunman *n* uomo *m* armato; *robber* rapinatore *m* **gunpoint** *n*: ***at ~*** con un'arma puntata addosso **gunpowder** *n* polvere *f* da sparo **gunrunner** *n* contrabbandiere *m*, -a *f* d'armi **gunrunning** *n* contrabbando *m* d'armi **gunshot** *n* sparo *m* **gunshot wound** *n* ferita *f* da arma da fuoco

gurgle *v/i of baby*, *drain* gorgogliare

gurney *n US* barella *f*

guru *n fig* guru *m inv*

gush I *n of liquid* fiotto *m*; *of words* ondata *f*; *of emotion* impeto *m* **II** *v/i* uscire a fiotti; *infml* (*talk*) prorompere; *of liquid* sgorgare

gushy *adj infml* (*enthusiastic*) iper--entusiastico

gusset *n* SEW gherone *m*

gust *n* raffica *f*; ***a ~ of wind*** una raffica di vento

gusto *n*: ***with ~*** con slancio

gusty *adj* (+*er*) *of weather* ventoso; ***~ wind*** vento a raffiche

gut I *n* intestino *m*; *infml* (*stomach*) pancia *f*; ***slog*** *or* ***work one's ~s out*** *infml* lavorare sodo; ***~ reaction*** reazione *f* istintiva; ***my ~ feeling is that ...*** in base al mio istinto ...; **guts** *npl* (*courage*) fegato *m*; ***have the ~ to do sth*** avere il fegato di fare qc; ***hate s.o.'s ~*** odiare qn a morte **II** *v/t* ⟨*pret & past part* ***-ted***⟩ (*fire*) sventrare; *animal* sbudellare (*remove contents*) distruggere (lasciando le strutture); ***it was completely ~ted by the fire*** è stato completamente distrutto dalle fiamme

gutless *adj fig infml* codardo

gutsy *adj infml person* che ha fegato; *infml thing to do* che richiede fegato

gutter *n on pavement* canaletto *m* di scolo; *on roof* grondaia *f*

guttering *n* grondaie *fpl*

gutterpress *n pej* stampa *f* scandalistica

guttural *adj* gutturale

guv *n infml* capo *m*, -a *f infml*

guy *n infml* tipo *m infml*; ***hey, you ~s*** ei, gente

Guy Fawkes' Night *n serata del 5 novembre in cui si brucia il fantoccio di Guy Fawkes, capo della sventata Congiura delle Polveri* (*1605*)

guzzle *v/t* ingozzarsi di
gym *n* palestra *f*; (*activity*) ginnastica *f*
gym class *n* educazione *f* fisica
gymnasium *n* palestra *f*
gymnast *n* ginnasta *m/f*
gymnastics *nsg* ginnastica *f*
gym shoes *npl* scarpe *fpl* da ginnastica **gym teacher** *n* insegnante *m/f* di educazione fisica
gynaecologist, *US* **gynecologist** *n* ginecologo *m*, -a *f*
gynaecology, *US* **gynecology** *n* ginecologia *f*
gypsy *n* zingaro *m*, -a *f*
gyrate *v/i* volteggiare
gyroscope *n* giroscopio *m*

H

H, h *n* h, H *f inv*
habit *n* abitudine *f*; ***get into the ~ of doing sth*** prendere l'abitudine di fare qc
habitable *adj* abitabile
habitat *n* habitat *m inv*
habitation *n*: ***unfit for human ~*** non idoneo all'abitazione
habitual *adj* solito; *smoker*, *drinker* incallito; ***~ criminal*** criminale *m* incallito
habitué *n* habitué *m/f*
hack[1] *n* (*poor writer*) scribacchino *m*
hack[2] *v/t*: ***~ s.o. / sth to pieces*** fare a pezzi qn / qc
◆ **hack into** *v/t* COMPUT inserirsi illecitamente in
hacker *n* COMPUT hacker *m/f inv*
hacking I *adj*: ***~ cough*** tosse *f* secca **II** *n* COMPUT intrusione *f*
hackles *npl*: ***get s.o.'s ~ up*** far arrabbiare qn
hackneyed *adj* trito
hacksaw *n* sega *f* per metalli
had *pret & past part* → ***have***
haddock *n* haddock *m inv*
hadn't → ***have***
haemoglobin, *US* **hemoglobin** *n* emoglobina *f*
haemophilia, *US* **hemophilia** *n* emofilia *f*
haemophiliac, *US* **hemophiliac** *n* emofiliaco *m*, -a *f*
haemorrhage, *US* **hemorrhage I** *n* emorragia *f* **II** *v/i* avere un'emorragia
haemorrhoids, *US* **hemorrhoids** *npl* emorroidi *fpl*
hag *n* megera *f*
haggard *adj* tirato
haggis *n* COOK *piatto a base di interiora di pecora cotte nello stomaco dell'animale*
haggle *v/i* contrattare; ***~ about*** *or* ***over*** contrattare per *or* su
hagiography *n* agiografia *f*
hail[1] **I** *n* grandine *f*; ***a ~ of bullets*** una pioggia di proiettili **II** *v/i* grandinare
hail[2] **I** *v/t* *taxi* fermare; ***~ s.o. / sth as sth*** salutare qn / qc come qc; ***within ~ing distance*** a distanza di chiamata **II** *v/i*: ***they ~ from …*** vengono da…
hailstone *n* chicco *m* di grandine **hailstorm** *n* grandinata *f*
hair *n* capelli *mpl*; *single* capello *m*; *on body*, *of animal* pelo *m*; ***do one's ~*** farsi i capelli; ***let one's ~ down*** *fig* rilassarsi; ***keep your ~ on!*** *Br infml* sta' calmo!; ***I'm allergic to cat ~*** sono allergico ai peli del gatto
hairband *n* cerchietto *m* **hairbrush** *n* spazzola *f* per capelli **hair clip** *n* molletta *f* **haircut** *n* taglio *m* di capelli **hairdo** *n infml* pettinatura *f* **hairdresser** *n* parrucchiere *m*, -a *f*; ***at the ~'s*** dal parrucchiere **hairdrier, hairdryer** *n* fon *m inv* **hair gel** *n* gel *m inv* per capelli **hair grip** *n* molletta *f* per capelli
hairless *adj* glabro
hairline *n* attaccatura *f* dei capelli **hairline crack** *n* sottile incrinatura *f* **hairline fracture** *n* sottile frattura *f* **hairnet** *n* retina *f* per capelli **hairpiece** *n* toupet *m* **hairpin** *n* forcina *f* **hairpin bend** *n* tornante *m* **hair-raising** *adj* terrificante **hair remover** *n* crema *f* depilatoria
hair's breadth *n fig*: ***by a ~*** per un pe-

lo

hair slide *n* fermacapelli *m inv* **hair-splitting** *n* pedanteria *f* **hair spray** *n* lacca *f* per capelli **hairstyle** *n* acconciatura *f* **hairstylist** *n* parrucchiere *m*, -a *f*

hairy *adj* (+*er*) *arm*, *animal* peloso; *infml* (*frightening*) preoccupante

hake *n* merluzzo *m*

half **I** *n* ⟨*pl* ***halves***⟩ metà *f inv*, mezzo *m*; ***in ~*** a metà; ***~ past ten***, *US* ***~ after ten*** le dieci e mezza; ***~ an hour*** mezz'ora *f*; ***~ a dozen*** mezza dozzina *f*; ***~ a pound*** mezza libbra *f*; ***go halves with s.o. on sth*** fare a metà di qc con qn; ***he's not ~ the man he used to be*** non è neanche l'ombra dell'uomo di un tempo; ***he's two and a ~*** ha due anni e mezzo; ***he doesn't do things by halves*** non lascia le cose a metà; ***~ and ~*** metà e metà; ***my better*** *hum or* ***other ~*** la mia dolce metà **II** *adj* mezzo **III** *adv* a metà; ***~ dead*** mezzo morto

half-baked *adj infml idea* che non si regge in piedi **half-blooded** *adj* mezzosangue **half board** *n* mezza pensione *f* **half brother** *n* fratellastro *m* **half-circle** *n* semicerchio *m* **half-day** *n* (*holiday*) mezza giornata *f*; ***we've got a ~*** abbiamo preso mezza giornata **half-dozen** *n* mezza dozzina *f* **half-dressed** *adj* mezzo vestito **half-empty** *adj* mezzo vuoto **half-fare** *n* metà prezzo *m* **half-full** *adj* mezzo pieno **half-hearted** *adj* poco convinto; ***he was rather ~ about accepting*** era poco convinto di accettare **half-mast** *n*: ***at ~*** a mezz'asta **half moon** *n* mezzaluna *f* **half pint** *n* birra *f* piccola **half-price** *adj* a metà prezzo **half-sister** *n* sorellastra *f* **half term** *n vacanza a metà trimestre* **half-timbered** *adj* in legno e muratura **half-time** **I** *n* SPORTS intervallo *m* **II** *adj*: ***~ job*** lavoro a metà giornata; ***~ score*** risultato alla fine del primo tempo **halfway** **I** *adj stage*, *point* intermedio **II** *adv a. fig* a metà strada; ***~ finished*** fatto a metà **halfway house** *n fig* via *f* di mezzo **halfwit** *n fig* imbecille *m*/*f* **half-yearly** *adv* ogni sei mesi

halibut *n* halibut *m*

halitosis *n* alitosi *f*

hall *n large room* sala *f*; *hallway in house* ingresso *m*

hallelujah **I** *int* alleluia **II** *n* alleluia *m*

hallmark *n* marchio *m*

hallo *int* → ***hello***

hall of residence *n* casa *f* dello studente

Hallowe'en *n* vigilia *f* d'Ognissanti

hallucinate *v/i* avere le allucinazioni

hallucination *n* allucinazione *f*

hallucinatory *adj drug* allucinogeno; *state*, *effect* allucinatorio

hallway *n* corridoio *m*

halo *n* aureola *f*

halt **I** *v/i* fermarsi **II** *v/t* fermare **III** *n*: ***come to a ~*** arrestarsi; ***the government called for a ~ to the fighting*** il governo ordinò di arrestare il combattimento

halter *n* (*horse's*) cavezza *f*

halterneck *adj con collo all'americana che lascia la schiena scoperta*

halting *adj voice* esitante; *speech* incerto; *foreign language* zoppicante

halt sign *n* AUTO segnale *m* di stop

halve *v/t* dimezzare

halves → ***half***

ham *n* prosciutto *m*; ***~s*** *infml* cosce e natiche *fpl*; (*actor*) attore *m*, -trice *f* da strapazzo

◆**ham up** *v/t sep infml* ***ham it up*** gigioneggiare

hamburger *n* hamburger *m inv*

hamlet *n* borgo *m*

hammer **I** *n* martello *m*; ***go at it ~ and tongs*** *infml* battersi con impeto **II** *v/i* martellare; ***~ at the door*** picchiare alla porta

◆**hammer home** *v/t sep* inculcare; ***he tried to hammer it home to the pupils that …*** cercava di inculcare agli alunni che…

◆**hammer out** *v/t sep fig agreement* giungere a

hammock *n* amaca *f*

hamper[1] *n for food* cestino *m*

hamper[2] *v/t* (*obstruct*) ostacolare; ***be ~ed*** (***by sth***) essere ostacolato da qc; ***the police were ~ed in their search by the shortage of clues*** la polizia era ostacolata nelle ricerche dalla carenza di indizi

hamster *n* criceto *m*

hand **I** *n* **1.** mano *f*; ***~s off!*** giù le mani!; ***~s up!*** mani in alto!; ***on*** (***one's***) ***~s and knees*** a quattro zampe; ***take***

s.o. by the ~ prendere qn per mano; ~ ***in*** ~ mano nella mano; ***go ~ in ~ with sth*** essere correlato a qc; ***live*** (***from***) ~ ***to mouth*** vivere alla giornata; *fig* ***with a heavy/ firm*** ~ con mano pesante / ferma; ***get one's ~s dirty*** *fig* sporcarsi le mani; ***wait on s.o.*** ~ ***and foot*** servire qn in tutti i modi; ***have a ~ in sth*** avere parte in qc; ***change ~s*** cambiare di mano; ***give s.o. a*** ~ dare una mano a qn **2.** *fig* ***at ~, to*** ~ a portata di mano; ***at first*** ~ di prima mano; ***by*** ~ a mano; ***in*** ~ (*being done*) in corso; ***he has five children on his ~s*** ha cinque bambini da gestire; ***everything she could get her ~s on*** tutto ciò su cui poteva mettere le mani; ***ask for a lady's*** ~ (***in marriage***) chiedere la mano di una donna; ***win ~s down*** vincere a mani basse; ***have the upper*** ~ avere la meglio; ***there were no experts on*** ~ non c'erano esperti a disposizione; ***things got out of*** ~ le cose ci sono sfuggite di mano; ***I dismissed the idea out of*** ~ ho accantonato subito l'idea; **3.** (*side, direction*) ***on the one ~ ..., on the other ~ ...*** da un lato ..., dall'altro ...; ***on your right*** ~ sulla tua destra **4.** *of clock* lancetta *f* **5.** (*worker*) operaio *m* **II** *v/t*: ~ ***sth to s.o.*** passare qc a qn; *fig* ***you've got to ~ it to him*** *infml* devi riconoscergli i suoi meriti

◆**hand (a)round** *v/t sep* passare di mano in mano; (*distribute*) distribuire

◆**hand back** *v/t sep* restituire

◆**hand down** *v/t sep* passare; ***the farm's been handed down from generation to generation*** la tenuta è stata tramandata di generazione in generazione

◆**hand in** *v/t sep* consegnare

◆**hand on** *v/t sep* passare

◆**hand out** *v/t sep* distribuire

◆**hand over** *v/t sep* consegnare; *child to parent etc* dare

◆**hand up** *v/t sep* trasmettere l'atto d'accusa

handbag *n* borsetta *f* **hand baggage** *n* bagaglio *m* a mano **handball** *n* (*game*) palla *f* a muro; (*foul*) fallo *m* di mano **hand basin** *n* lavabo *m* **handbill** *n* volantino *m* **handbook** *n* manuale *m* **handbrake** *n* freno *m* a mano **hand cream** *n* crema *f* per le mani **handcuff** *v/t* ammanettare **handcuffs** *npl* manette *fpl*

handful *n* pugno *m*; ***a ~ of ...*** *sand, coins* un pugno di ...; *people* un gruppetto di ...; *fig* ***those children are a*** ~ quei bambini sono difficili da trattare

hand grenade *n* bomba *f* a mano

handicap *n* handicap *m inv*

handicapped *adj a. fig* handicappato

handicraft *n* artigianato *m*

handiwork *n* opera *f*

handkerchief *n* fazzoletto *m*

handle I *v/t goods* maneggiare; *case, deal* trattare; *difficult person* prendere; ***let me ~ this*** lascia fare a me; ***be able to ~ s.o.*** saperci fare con qn; ***glass - ~ with care!*** vetro - maneggiare con cura!; ***how would you ~ the situation?*** come gestiresti la situazione?; ***I can't ~ pressure*** non posso reggere la pressione; ***you keep quiet, I'll ~ this*** stai calmo, me ne occupo io **II** *n* maniglia *f*; ***fly off the*** ~ *infml* perdere le staffe; ***have/ get a ~ on sth*** *infml* riuscire a capire qc

handlebars *npl* manubrio *msg*

handler *n* (*dog-handler*) addestratore *m*, -trice *f*; ***baggage*** ~ addetto *m*, -a *f* ai bagagli

handling *n* trattamento *m* (***of*** di); *of matter, problem* gestione *f* (***of*** di); (*official handling of matters*) direzione *f*; ***her adroit ~ of the economy*** la sua abile direzione dell'economia; ***his ~ of the matter*** la sua gestione della questione; ***his successful ~ of the crisis*** la sua gestione vincente della crisi **handling charge** *n* spesa *f* di trasporto; *in banking* spesa *f* di movimentazione

hand lotion *n* sapone *m* liquido **hand luggage** *n* bagaglio *m* a mano **handmade** *adj* fatto a mano **hand mirror** *n* specchietto *m* **hand-operated** *adj* azionato a mano **handout** *n* (*aid*) donazione *f*; (*piece of paper*) prospetto *m* **handover** *n* POL trasferimento *m*; ~ ***of power*** trasferimento *m* di potere **hand-picked** *adj fig* scelto con cura **hand puppet** *n US* burattino *m* **handrail** *n* corrimano *m inv* **handset** *n* TEL microtelefono *m* **handshake** *n* stretta *f* di mano

hands-off *adj approach* teorico; ***he has a ~ style of management*** non partecipa direttamente agli aspetti pratici della gestione

handsome *adj* bello; ***he is ~*** lui è bello; *profit* considerevole; *reward* generoso

handsomely *adv pay* profumatamente; *reward* generosamente; *win* lautamente

hands-on *adj experience* pratico; ***he has a ~ style of management*** partecipa direttamente agli aspetti pratici della gestione

handstand *n* SPORTS verticale *f* **hand-to-hand** *adj*: ***~ fighting*** combattimento *m* corpo a corpo **hand-to-mouth** *adj* alla giornata **hand towel** *n* asciugamano *m* **handwriting** *n* calligrafia *f* **handwritten** *adj* scritto a mano

handy *adj* (+*er*) *tool, device* pratico; ***it's ~ for the shops*** è comodo per i negozi; ***it might come in ~*** potrebbe tornare utile; ***be ~ with a tool*** essere abile con uno strumento; ***keep*** *or* ***have sth ~*** tenere *or* avere qc a portata di mano

handyman *n* tuttofare *m inv*

hang I *v/t* ⟨*pret & past part* **hung**⟩ *picture* appendere; *person* impiccare; ***~ o.s.*** impiccarsi **II** *v/i* ⟨*pret & past part* **hung**⟩ *of dress, hair* cadere; ***his coat was ~ing behind the door*** il suo cappotto era appeso dietro la porta **III** *n*: ***get the ~ of sth*** *infml* capire qc

◆**hang about, hang around** *v/i on streets* gironzolare; ***hang about a minute!*** *infml* un attimo!

◆**hang on** *v/i* (*wait*) aspettare; (*hold*) tenersi; ***hang on tight!*** tenetevi forte!

◆**hang on to** *v/t* (*keep*) tenere

◆**hang out** *v/i infml*: ***hang out in a place*** bazzicare un posto

◆**hang up** *v/i* TEL riattaccare

hangar *n* hangar *m inv*

hanger *n for clothes* gruccia *f*

hanger-on *n* ⟨*pl* **hangers-on**⟩ tirapiedi *m/f*

hang glider *n* deltaplano *m*

hang gliding *n* deltaplano *m*

hanging *n of criminal* impiccagione *f*; ***~s*** *pl* (*tapestry*) tendaggi *mpl*

hanging basket *n cestino o vaso di piante decorative che viene appeso*

hangman *n* boia *m*; (*game*) impiccato *m*

hangout *n infml* ritrovo *m* abituale

hangover *n* postumi *mpl* della sbornia

hangup *n infml* mania *f*, fissazione *f*

hanker *v/i* bramare

◆**hanker after** *v/t* desiderare

hankie, hanky *n infml* fazzoletto *m*

hanky-panky *n infml, esp Br* porcherie *fpl*

haphazard *adj* a casaccio

happen *v/i* succedere; ***if you ~ to see him*** se ti capita di vederlo; ***as it ~s I don't like that kind of thing*** guarda caso, non mi piace quel genere di cose; ***what has ~ed to you?*** cosa ti è successo?; ***don't let it ~ again*** non lasciare che capiti di nuovo; ***if anything should ~ to me*** se dovesse capitarmi qualcosa…; ***it all ~ed so quickly*** è successo così in fretta; ***I picked up the nearest paper, which ~ed to be the Daily Mail*** ho scelto il giornale più vicino, che per caso era il Daily Mail

◆**happen across** *v/t* trovare per caso

happening *n* avvenimento *m*

happily *adv* allegramente; (*gladly*) volentieri; (*luckily*) per fortuna; ***~ married*** felicemente sposato; ***it all ended ~*** tutto si è concluso felicemente; ***they lived ~ ever after*** *in fairy tales* e vissero felici e contenti; ***I would ~ have lent her the money*** le avrei prestato i soldi volentieri

happiness *n* felicità *f inv*

happy *adj* (+*er*) felice; ***~ with*** contento di; ***~ at*** *or* ***about*** contento di; ***be ~ to do sth*** essere felice di fare qc

happy camper *n infml* persona *f* spensierata; ***I'm not a ~*** non sono dell'umore giusto **happy-go-lucky** *adj* spensierato **happy hour** *n orario in cui le consumazioni costano meno*

harangue I *v/t* arringare **II** *n* arringa *f*

harass *v/t* tormentare; *sexually* molestare

harassed *adj* stressato

harassment *n* persecuzione *f*; ***sexual ~*** molestie *fpl* sessuali

harbour, *US* **harbor I** *n* porto *m* **II** *v/t criminal* dar rifugio a; *grudge* covare

hard I *adj* (+*er*) **1.** duro **2.** (*difficult*) difficile; ***it's ~ to believe that …*** è difficile credere che … **3.** *facts, evidence* concreto **4.** *drug* pesante **5.** *fig* ***be ~ on s.o.*** essere duro con qn; ***no ~ feel-***

ings? nessun risentimento?; ***be as ~ as nails*** essere duro di cuore; ***~ of hearing*** duro d'orecchio; ***~ left*** POL estrema sinistra *f* **II** *adv* **1.** *work* duro **2.** *hit* forte **3.** ***try ~ to*** sforzarsi di; ***think ~*** riflettere bene; ***I've been ~ at work since this morning*** lavoro sodo da stamani; ***she works ~ at keeping herself fit*** si impegna molto per tenersi in forma; ***be ~ pushed*** *or* ***put to do sth*** trovarsi in difficoltà a fare qc; ***be ~ done by*** essere trattato male da; ***they are ~ hit by the cuts*** hanno ricevuto un duro colpo dai tagli

hard-and-fast *adj* categorico **hardback** *n* libro *m* con copertina rigida **hard-boiled** *adj egg* sodo **hard cash** *n* contante *m* **hard copy** *n* copia *f* stampata **hard core** *n* (*pornography*) pornografia *f* hard-core **hard currency** *n* valuta *f* forte **hard disk** *n* hard disk *m inv* **hard disk drive** *n* unità *f* disco rigido **hard drugs** *n* droghe *fpl* pesanti **hard-earned** *adj cash* guadagnato a caro prezzo; *victory* ottenuto a caro prezzo **hard-edged** *adj fig* critico

harden I *v/t* indurire **II** *v/i of glue* indurirsi; *of attitude* irrigidirsi

hardened *adj steel* temprato; *troops* agguerrito; *arteries* indurito; ***~ criminal*** criminale *m* incallito; ***you become ~ to it after a while*** dopo un po' ci si assuefa

hard hat *n* casco *m*; (*construction worker*) muratore *m* **hardheaded** *adj* pratico **hardhearted** *adj* dal cuore duro **hard-hitting** *adj report* incisivo **hard labour**, *US* **hard labor** *n* lavori *mpl* forzati **hard line** *n* linea *f* dura **hardliner** *n* sostenitore *m*, -trice *f* della linea dura

hardly *adv* a malapena; ***~ ever*** quasi mai; ***you can ~ expect him to ...*** non puoi certo aspettarti che lui ...; ***~!*** ci mancherebbe!

hardness *n* durezza *f*; (*difficulty*) difficoltà *f inv*

hard-nosed *adj infml person* caparbio; *attitude* duro **hard-on** *n sl* erezione *f*; ***have a ~*** avere un'erezione **hard-pressed** *adj* sotto pressione; ***be ~ to do sth*** avere difficoltà a fare qc **hard right** *n* POL ***the ~*** l'estrema destra

hardsell *n* tecnica *f* aggressiva di vendita

hardship *n* difficoltà *fpl* economiche

hard shoulder *n* corsia *f* di emergenza

hard up *adj* al verde

hardware *n* ferramenta *fpl*; COMPUT hardware *m inv*

hardware store *n* negozio *m* di ferramenta

hard-won *adj* combattuto

hardwood *n* legno *m* duro

hard-working *adj* che lavora duro

hardy *adj* (*+er*) resistente

hare *n* lepre *f*

harebrained *adj* pazzo

harelip *n* labbro *m* leporino

harem *n* harem *m*

haricot *n*: **~ (*bean*)** fagiolo *m* bianco

harlequin *n* arlecchino *m*

harlot *n* prostituta *f*

harm I *n* danno *m*; ***the children had come to no ~*** ai bambini non era successo niente; ***do s.o. ~*** fare del male a qn; ***you could do somebody / yourself ~ with that knife*** con quel coltello potresti farti del male / fare del male a qn; ***it will do more ~ than good*** farà più male che bene; ***no ~ done*** poco male; ***there's no ~ in doing sth*** non c'è niente di male a fare qn; ***it wouldn't do any ~ to ...*** non sarebbe una cattiva idea ... **II** *v/t* danneggiare

harmful *adj* dannoso; ***be ~ to one's health*** nuocere alla salute di qn

harmless *adj* innocuo; ***he seemed ~ enough*** sembrava sufficientemente innocuo

harmonic *adj* armonico

harmonica *n* armonica *f*

harmonic progression *n* MATH progressione *f* armonica **harmonic series** *n* MATH serie *f* armonica

harmonious *adj* armonioso

harmonize *v/i* armonizzare

harmony *n* armonia *f*

harness I *n on horse* bardatura *f*; *on person* imbracatura *f* **II** *v/t power* sfruttare; *horse* bardare

harp *n* arpa *f*

◆**harp on about** *v/t infml* menarsela su *infml*; ***harp on about sth*** *infml* continuare a battere su qc; ***he's always harping on about ...*** continua

sempre a battere su...
harpist *n* arpista *m/f*
harpoon *n* arpione *m*
harpsichord *n* arpicordo *m*
Harpy *n* MYTH arpia *f*
harridan *n pej* strega *f*
harrow I *n* AGR erpice *m* **II** *v/t* AGR erpicare
harrowing *adj story* straziante; *experience* atroce
harsh *adj* (+*er*) (*criticism, words*) duro; (*colour, light*) troppo forte; (*climate*) rigido; ***don't be too ~ with him*** non essere troppo duro con lui; ***they have very ~ winters*** hanno inverni molto rigidi
harshly *adv* duramente
harvest I *n* raccolto *m*; ***a bumper potato ~*** un raccolto di patate eccezionale **II** *v/t* (*reap*) mietere
harvest festival *n Br* festa *f* del raccolto
has → ***have***
has-been *n* ex famoso *m*, -a *f*
hash I *n* TEL cancelletto *m*; (*hashish*) hashish *m inv*; ***make a ~ of*** *infml* fare un pasticcio di **II** *v/t* combinare un pasticcio
hashish *n* hashish *m inv*
hash mark *n* cancelletto *m*
hasn't → ***has not***
hassle I *n* scocciatura *f*; ***it was a real ~*** è stata proprio scocciatura; ***give s.o. ~*** scocciare qn; ***getting there is such a ~*** è una tale scocciatura arrivare là **II** *v/t* scocciare; ***stop hassling me*** smettila di scocciare; ***I'm feeling a bit ~d*** sono un po' scocciato
haste *n* fretta *f*
hasten *form* **I** *v/i*: ***~ to do sth*** affrettarsi a fare qc **II** *v/t* affrettare
hastily *adv* in fretta
hasty *adj* (+*er*) frettoloso
hat *n* cappello *m*; ***put on one's ~*** mettersi il cappello; ***take one's ~ off*** togliersi il cappello; *fig* ***I'll eat my ~ if ...*** scommetto la testa che ...; ***I take my ~ off to him*** gli faccio tanto di cappello; ***keep sth under one's ~*** *infml* mantenere il segreto su qc; ***at the drop of a ~*** senza esitazioni; ***that's old ~*** *infml* è una vecchia storia
hatch[1] I *v/t* (*a.* **hatch out**) schiudersi **II** *v/i* (*a.* **hatch out**: *bird*) nascere; ***when will the eggs ~?*** quando si schiuderanno le uova?
◆**hatch out** *v/i of eggs* schiudersi
hatch[2] *n for serving food* passavivande *m inv*; *on ship* boccaporto *m*; AVIAT portello *m*; ***down the ~!*** *infml* cin cin!
hatchback *n* auto *f inv* a tre *or* cinque porte
hatchet *n* ascia *f*; ***bury the ~*** seppellire l'ascia di guerra
hate I *v/t* odiare; ***~ doing sth*** odiare fare qc; ***I ~ to say this, but ...*** mi dispiace dirlo, ma ...; ***I ~ to admit it but ...*** odio ammetterlo, ma ...; ***she ~s me having any fun*** detesta che io mi diverta; ***I'd ~ to think I'd never see him again*** mi dispiacerebbe pensare di non rivederlo più **II** *n* odio *m*; ***one of his pet ~s is plastic cutlery/having to wait*** una delle sue bestie nere sono le posate di plastica/è dover aspettare
hate campaign *n* campagna *f* d'odio
hate mail *n* lettere *fpl* minatorie
hatpin *n* spillone *m* per cappelli
hatred *n* odio *m*; ***racial ~*** odio *m* razziale
hat stand, *US* **hat tree** *n* attaccapanni *m inv* a stelo **hat-trick** *n* tripletta *f*
haughty *adj* (+*er*) altezzoso
haul I *n of fish* pescata *f*; (*booty*) bottino *m*; *of cocaine etc* partita *f*; *fig* ***it's a long ~*** la strada è lunga; ***short/long/medium ~ aircraft*** aereo per brevi/lunghe/medie distanze; ***over the long ~*** *esp US* a lungo termine **II** *v/t* (*pull*) trascinare; (*transport*) trasportare: ***he ~ed himself to his feet*** tirarsi su in piedi
haulage *n* autotrasporto *m*
haulage company *n* impresa *f* di autotrasporto
haulier *n* autotrasportatore *m*
haunch *n* anca *f*; ***squat on one's ~es*** accovacciarsi
haunt I *v/t*: ***this place is ~ed*** questo posto è infestato dai fantasmi **II** *n* ritrovo *m*
haunting *adj tune* indimenticabile
have ⟨*pret & past part* ***had***⟩ **I** *v/t* **1.** avere; ***can I ~ ...?*** posso avere ...?; ***I don't ~ a TV*** non ho la TV; ***do you ~ ...?*** ha ...?; ***~ a nice weekend!*** buon fine settimana; ***I just had a letter from ...*** ho appena ricevuto una lettera da ...; ***thanks for having me***

grazie dell'invito; ***he has diabetes*** ha il diabete; ***~ a heart attack*** avere un infarto; ***I've*** (***got*** *esp Br*) ***a headache*** ho mal di testa; ***~ a pleasant evening*** passare una serata piacevole **2.** *breakfast, shower* fare; ***I must ~ something to eat*** devo mangiare qc; ***I'll ~ a coffee*** prendo un caffè; ***~ lunch / dinner*** pranzare / cenare; ***~ a walk*** fare una passeggiata **3.** *must*: ***~*** (***got***) ***to*** dovere; ***I ~*** (***got***) ***to go*** devo andare **4.** *causative*: ***~ sth done*** far fare qc; ***I had the printer fixed*** ho fatto riparare la stampante; ***I had my hair cut*** mi sono tagliata i capelli; ***he had his car stolen*** gli hanno rubato la macchina **5.** (*accept*) ***I won't ~ this sort of rudeness!*** non accetterò una tale scortesia!; ***I won't ~ him insulted*** non accetterò che lo insultino **6.** (*finished, in trouble*) ***that coat has had it*** *infml* quel cappotto ha fatto il suo tempo; ***if I miss the bus, I've had it*** *infml* se perdo l'autobus, sono rovinato **II** *v/aux* avere; *with verbs of motion* essere; ***~ you seen her?*** l'hai vista?; ***I ~ come*** sono venuto; ***you've met her, haven't you?*** la conosci, no?

◆**have against** *v/t always sep*: ***have sth against s.o.*** avercela con qn; ***have sth against sth*** essere contrario a qc; ***have nothing against s.o.*** non avere niente contro qn

◆**have back** *v/t sep*: ***when can I have it back?*** quando posso riaverlo?

◆**have in** *v/t always sep in the house* avere; ***have it in for s.o.*** *infml* avercela con qn; ***I didn't know he had it in him*** non sapevo che ne fosse capace

◆**have on** *v/t always sep* (*wear*) portare, indossare; ***do you have anything on tonight?*** (*have planned*) hai programmi per stasera?; ***he's having you on*** *infml* (*kidding you*) ti sta prendendo in giro

◆**have out** *v/t always sep* (*have taken out*) farsi togliere; ***he had his tonsils out*** si è fatto togliere le tonsille; ***I'll have it out with him*** mi farò dare una spiegazione (da lui)

◆**have over** *or esp Br* **round** *v/t always sep* invitare

haven *n fig* oasi *f inv*

haven't → ***have not***

havoc *n* caos *m inv*; ***play ~ with*** scombussolare

hawk[1] *n a. fig* falco *m*; ***watch s.o. like a ~*** osservare qn con molta attenzione

hawk[2] *v/t* vendere di casa in casa; *in street* vendere per strada

hawker *n* venditore *m* ambulante

hawk-eyed *adj* dagli occhi di falco

hawthorn *n* (*a.* **hawthorn bush / tree**) biancospino *m*

hay *n* fieno *m*; ***make ~ while the sun shines*** *prov* battere il ferro mentre è caldo

hay fever *n* raffreddore *m* da fieno

haystack *n*, **hayrick** *n* pagliaio *m*

haywire *adj infml* ***go ~*** andare in tilt

hazard I *n* rischio *m*; ***it's a fire ~*** è a rischio d'incendio; ***pose a ~*** (***to s.o. / sth***) mettere a rischio qn / qc; **hazards** *npl* AUTO: *a.* **hazard (warning) lights** luci *fpl* di emergenza **II** *v/t* azzardare; ***if I might ~ a suggestion*** se posso azzardare un suggerimento; ***~ a guess*** azzardare un'ipotesi

hazard lights *npl* AUTO luci *fpl* di emergenza

hazardous *adj* rischioso

haze *n* foschia *f*

hazel *n* (*tree*) nocciolo *m*

hazelnut *n* nocciola *f*

hazy *adj* (*+er*) *view, image* indistinto; *memories* vago; ***I'm a bit ~ about it*** non ne sono certo

H-bomb *n* bomba *f* H

hdqrs *abbr* (= **headquarters**) MIL quartieri *mpl* generali

he *pron* lui; ***~'s French*** è francese; ***you're funny, ~'s not*** tu sei spiritoso, lui no; ***there ~ is*** eccolo

head I *n* **1.** testa *f*; ***£15 a ~*** 15 sterline a testa; ***~s or tails?*** testa o croce?; ***~ over heels*** *fall* a capofitto; ***~ over heels in love*** pazzamente innamorato; ***lose one's ~*** (*go crazy*) perdere la testa; ***we put our ~s together*** ci siamo consultati; ***the joke went over his ~*** la barzelletta era troppo difficile per lui; ***he has a good ~ for figures*** è abile con i numeri; ***you need a good ~ for heights*** è necessario non soffrire di vertigini; ***come to a ~*** maturare; ***bring matters to a ~***

far precipitare le cose **2.** (*boss, leader*) capo *m*; *of primary school* direttore *m*, -trice *f*; *of secondary school* preside *m/f*; ***~ of department*** UNIV preside *m/f* di facoltà; ***~ of state*** capo *m* dello stato **3.** *on beer* schiuma *f*; ***~ of steam*** pressione *f* di vapore **4.** *of nail* capocchia *f* **5.** *of queue, line* inizio *m*; ***at the ~ of the list*** in cima alla lista; ***at the ~ of the page / stairs*** in cima alla pagina / alle scale; ***at the ~ of the table*** a capotavola **6.** ***twenty ~ of cattle*** venti capi di bestiame **7.** *of tape recorder* testina *f* **II** *v/t* (*lead*) essere a capo di; *ball* colpire di testa

◆**head back** *v/i* tornare indietro; ***it's time we were heading back now*** è ora di tornare indietro

◆**head for** *v/t place* dirigersi a; ***she's heading for trouble*** è in cerca di guai; ***head for victory / defeat*** andare incontro alla vittoria / sconfitta

◆**head off I** *v/t sep* (*divert*) deviare; *war, strike* prevenire **II** *v/i* (*set off*) partire

headache *n* mal *m* di testa **headband** *n* fascia *f* per i capelli **headboard** *n* testiera *f* **head boy** *n* EDU rappresentante *m* degli studenti **headbutt** *v/t* dare una testata a **head cold** *n* raffreddore *m* di testa **head count** *n*: ***have*** *or* ***take a ~*** contare i presenti **headdress** *n* acconciatura *f*

headed notepaper *n* carta *f* da lettere intestata

header *n in soccer* colpo *m* di testa; *in document* intestazione *f*

headfirst *adv* a capofitto **headgear** *n* copricapo *m* **head girl** *n* EDU rappresentante *f* degli studenti **headhunt** *v/t* COMM: ***be ~ed*** essere selezionato da un cacciatore di teste **headhunter** *n* COMM cacciatore *m* di teste

heading *n in list* titolo *m*

headlamp *n* fanale *m* **headland** *n* promontorio *m* **headlight** *n* faro *m* **headline** *n in newspaper* titolo; ***make the ~s*** fare titolo **headlong** *adv fall* a testa in giù **headmaster** *n in primary school* direttore *m*; *in secondary school* preside *m* **headmistress** *n in primary school* direttrice *f*; *in secondary school* preside *f* **head office** *n of company* sede *f* centrale **head-on I** *adv crash* frontalmente **II** *adj crash* frontale **headphones** *npl* cuffie *fpl* **headquarters** *npl* sede *fsg*; MIL quartier *msg* generale **headrest** *n* poggiatesta *m inv* **headroom** *n for vehicle under bridge* altezza *f* utile; *in car* altezza *f* dell'abitacolo **headscarf** *n* foulard *m inv* **head start** *n* vantaggio *m*; ***have a ~ on s.o.*** trovarsi in vantaggio rispetto a qn; ***give s.o. a ~*** avvantaggiare qn **headstrong** *adj* testardo **head teacher** *n in primary school* direttore *m*, -trice *f*; *in secondary school* preside *m/f* **head waiter** *n* capocameriere *m* **headwind** *n* vento *m* di prua

heady *adj* (+*er*) *drink, wine etc* inebriante; ***~ prose style*** prosa *f* esaltante

heal *v/t & v/i* guarire

◆**heal up** *v/i* cicatrizzarsi

health *n* salute *f*; (*public health*) sanità *f inv*; ***your ~!*** (alla) salute!; ***suffer from poor*** *or* ***bad ~*** soffrire di cattiva salute; ***~ and safety regulations*** norme *fpl* sanitarie e di sicurezza

health care *n* assistenza *f* sanitaria **health centre**, *US* **health center** *n* poliambulatorio *m* **health club** *n* centro *m* fitness **health farm** *n* beauty farm *f inv* **health food** *n* alimenti *mpl* macrobiotici **health food store** *n* negozio *m* di macrobiotica **health insurance** *n* assicurazione *f* contro le malattie **health resort** *n* stazione *f* termale **health service** *n* servizio *m* sanitario **health warning** *n on cigarette packet* avviso *m* per la salute

healthy *adj* (+*er*) *a. fig* sano; ***earn a ~ profit*** guadagnare bene

heap I *n* mucchio *m*; ***he fell in a ~ on the floor*** si è afflosciato sul pavimento; *fig* ***at the bottom / top of the ~*** in cima / fondo al mucchio; ***~s of*** *infml* un mucchio di; ***~s of times*** spessissimo; ***~s of enthusiasm*** un sacco di entusiasmo **II** *v/t* accumulare; ***~ praise on s.o. / sth*** coprire qn / qc di lodi; ***a ~ed spoonful*** un cucchiaio colmo

◆**heap up** *v/t sep* ammucchiare

hear *v/t & v/i* ⟨*pret & past part* **heard**⟩ sentire; JUR dare udienza; ***I ~d him say that …*** gli ho sentito dire che …; ***there wasn't a sound to be ~d*** non volava una mosca; ***make o.s.***

~d farsi sentire; ***you're not going, do you ~ me!*** senti, tu non ci andrai!; ***I ~ you play chess*** ho sentito dire che giochi a scacchi; ***I've ~d it all before*** l'ho già sentita; ***I must be ~ing things*** avrò le allucinazioni; **~ *a case*** JUR esaminare un caso; **~ *evidence*** JUR esaminare le prove; ***he cannot ~ very well*** non ci sente molto bene; ***~, ~!*** bravo!; ***he's left his wife — yes, so I ~*** ha lasciato sua moglie - sì, l'ho sentito dire

◆**hear about** *v/t* sapere di

◆**hear from** *v/t* (*have news from*) avere notizie di

◆**hear of** *v/t* (*find out about*) sapere di; ***have you heard of …?*** sai niente su …?

heard *pret & past part* → ***hear***

hearing *n* udito *m*; JUR udienza *f*; ***be within / out of ~*** essere / non essere a portata di voce; ***have a keen sense of ~*** avere l'orecchio fine; ***disciplinary ~*** udienza *f* disciplinare

hearing aid *n* apparecchio *m* acustico

hearsay *n* diceria *f*; ***by ~*** per sentito dire

hearse *n* carro *m* funebre

heart *n* cuore *m*; *of problem etc* nocciolo *m*; ***know sth by ~*** sapere qc a memoria; ***break s.o.'s ~*** spezzare il cuore a qn; ***from the bottom of one's ~*** dal profondo del cuore; ***put (one's) ~ and soul into sth*** dedicarsi a qc anima e corpo; ***take sth to ~*** prendere a cuore qc; ***we (only) have your interests at ~*** abbiamo a cuore soltanto i tuoi interessi; ***set one's ~ on sth*** tenere molto a qc; ***to one's ~'s content*** a proprio piacimento; ***most men are boys at ~*** in fondo all'animo quasi tutti gli uomini sono dei bambini; ***his ~ isn't in it*** non riesce ad appassionarcisi; ***give s.o. ~*** fare coraggio a qn; ***lose ~*** avvilirsi; ***take ~*** farsi animo; ***her ~ is in the right place*** *infml* è di buon cuore; ***queen of ~s*** regina di cuori

heartache *n* angoscia *f* **heart attack** *n* infarto *m* **heartbeat** *n* battito *m* cardiaco **heartbreaking** *adj* straziante **heartbroken** *adj* affranto **heartburn** *n* bruciore *m* di stomaco **heart condition** *n* disturbo *m* cardiaco; ***he has a ~*** ha un disturbo cardiaco **heart disease** *n* cardiopatia *f*

hearten *v/t* incoraggiare

heartening *adj* incoraggiante

heart failure *n* infarto *m*; ***he suffered ~*** ha avuto un infarto **heartfelt** *adj sympathy* sentito; *apology*, *tribute*, *appeal* sincero

hearth *n* focolare *m*

heartily *adv laugh*, *say* di cuore; *eat* di gusto; *recommend* calorosamente; *agree* entusiasticamente; *welcome* cordialmente; ***be ~ sick of sth*** essere proprio stufo di qc

heartless *adj* spietato

heartrending *adj plea*, *sight* straziante

hearts *npl in cards* cuori *mpl*

heartstrings *npl*: ***pull*** *or* ***tug at s.o.'s ~*** fare appello ai sentimenti di qn

heart throb *n infml* idolo *m* **heart-to-heart I** *adj* franco; ***have a ~ talk with s.o.*** parlare a qn col cuore in mano **II** *n* discorso fatto col cuore in mano; ***it's time we had a ~*** è il momento di parlare col cuore in mano **heart transplant** *n* trapianto *m* cardiaco **heart-warming** *adj* confortante

hearty *adj* (*+er*) *appetite* robusto; *meal* sostanzioso; *person* gioviale; ***a ~ eater*** un gran mangiatore; ***a ~ welcome*** un cordiale benvenuto

heat I *n* calore *m*; (*hot weather*) caldo *m*; ***on*** *or* ***over (a) low ~*** a fuoco lento; ***in the ~ of the moment*** nell'eccitazione del momento **II** *v/t* scaldare; *room*, *house*, *pool* riscaldare **III** *v/i* scaldarsi

◆**heat up** *v/t sep* riscaldare

heated *adj swimming pool* riscaldato; *discussion* animato

heater *n radiator* termosifone *m*; *electric*, *gas* stufa *f*; *in car* riscaldamento *m*

heath *n* brughiera *f*

heathen I *adj* pagano **II** *n* pagano *m*, -a *f*

heather *n* erica *f*

heating *n* riscaldamento *m*

heating engineer *n* caldaista *m/f*

heatproof, heat-resistant *adj* termoresistente **heat rash** *n* MED infiammazione *f* cutanea **heatstroke** *n* colpo *m* di calore **heatwave** *n* ondata *f* di caldo

heave I *v/t* (*lift*) sollevare; (*drag*) trascinare; (*throw*) gettare; *sigh* tirare

II *v/i* (*pull*) tirare; *waves, bosom* sollevarsi; *infml* vomitare

heaven *n* paradiso *m*; ***good ~s!*** santo cielo!; ***for ~'s sake!*** per l'amor del cielo!; ***the ~s*** *liter* il cielo *m*; ***in ~*** in paradiso; ***go to ~*** salire al cielo; ***he is in (seventh) ~*** è al settimo cielo; ***it was ~*** era il paradiso; ***~ knows what ...*** Dio solo lo sa ...; ***~ forbid!*** il cielo non voglia!; ***what in ~'s name ...?*** in nome del cielo, che cosa ...?

heavenly *adj infml* divino

heavily *adv rain* forte; *smoke* molto; ***~ guarded*** sotto stretta sorveglianza; ***~ disguised*** pesantemente mascherato; ***be ~ involved in*** *or* ***with sth*** essere seriamente coinvolto in qc; ***be ~ into sth*** *infml* essere un patito di qc; ***be ~ outnumbered*** essere in netta inferiorità numerica; ***be ~ defeated*** essere pesantemente sconfitti; ***~ laden*** sovraccarico; ***~ built*** massiccio

heavy *adj* (*+er*) pesante; *cold, rain, accent* forte; *traffic* intenso; *food* pesante; *smoker* accanito; *drinker* forte; *financial loss, casualties* ingente; ***be a ~ sleeper*** avere il sonno pesante

heavy-duty *adj* resistente **heavy goods vehicle** *n* veicolo *m* per merci pesanti **heavy-handed** *adj* autoritario **heavy industry** *n* industria *f* pesante **heavy metal** *n* MUS heavy metal *m* **heavyweight** *adj* SPORTS di pesi massimi

Hebrew I *adj* ebraico **II** *n* ebreo *m*, -a *f*; *language* ebraico *m*

Hebrides *npl* Ebridi *fpl*

heck *int* cavolo; ***who/what the ~ ...?*** chi/cosa cavolo ...?; ***a ~ of a lot*** un casino

heckle *v/t* interrompere di continuo

hectare *n* ettaro *m*

hectic *adj* frenetico

he'd = ***he had***; ***he would***

hedge I *n* siepe *f* **II** *v/i* tergiversare **III** *v/t*: ***~ one's bets*** scommettere pro e contro

hedge fund *n* FIN fondo *m* di copertura

hedgehog *n* riccio *m*

hedgerow *n* siepe *f*

hedge trimmer *n* potasiepi *f*

hedonism *n* edonismo *m*

heed I *n*: ***pay ~ to ...*** ascoltare ... **II** *v/t* tenere conto di; ***he never ~s my advice*** non tiene mai conto dei miei consigli

heedful *adj* vigile

heedless *adj*: ***be ~ of sth*** essere incurante di qc

heel *n of foot* tallone *m*, calcagno *m*; *of shoe* tacco *m*; ***be right on s.o.'s ~s*** tallonare qn; ***the police were hot on our ~s*** la polizia ci era alle calcagna; ***be down at ~*** essere scalcagnato; ***take to one's ~s*** darsela a gambe; ***~!*** (*to dog*) al piede!; ***bring s.o. to ~*** riportare qn all'ordine

heel bar *n* calzoleria *f* istantanea

hefty *adj* (*+er*) massiccio

heifer *n* giovenca *f*

height *n* altezza *f*; *of aeroplane* altitudine *f*; ***ten feet in ~*** alto circa 3 metri; ***what ~ are you?*** quanto sei alto?; ***at the ~ of summer*** nel pieno dell'estate; ***at shoulder ~*** all'altezza della spalla; ***at the ~ of his power*** al culmine del suo potere; ***the ~ of luxury*** l'apice del lusso; ***during the war emigration was at its ~*** durante la guerra l'emigrazione era al culmine; ***be the ~ of fashion*** essere all'ultima moda

heighten I *v/t effect, tension* aumentare; ***~ed awareness*** maggiore consapevolezza *f* **II** *v/i fig* intensificarsi

heinous *adj* atroce; ***a ~ crime*** un crimine atroce

heir *n* erede *m*; ***~ to the throne*** erede al trono

heiress *n* ereditiera *f*

heirloom *n* cimelio *m* di famiglia

heist *n esp US infml* rapina *f* a mano armata

held *pret & past part* → ***hold***

helicopter *n* elicottero *m*

helipad *n* piattaforma *f* (di atterraggio) per elicotteri

heliport *n* eliporto *m*

helium *n* elio *m*

hell *n* inferno *m*; ***what the ~ are you doing/do you want?*** *infml* che diavolo fai/vuoi? *infml*; ***go to ~!*** *infml* va' all'inferno! *infml*; ***a ~ of a lot*** *infml* un casino *infml*; ***one ~ of a nice guy*** *infml* un tipo in gambissima; ***all ~ broke loose*** si è scatenato l'interno; ***it's ~ working there*** lavorare là è un inferno; ***a living ~*** un inferno vivente; ***go through ~*** soffrire le pene dell'inferno; ***she made his life ~*** ha reso la sua vita un inferno; ***give s.o. ~*** (*tell off*) fare una sfuriata a qn; ***there'll be ~ to pay when he finds out*** scoppierà un casino quando lo scoprirà; ***the mother-in-law from ~*** la suocera insopportabile; ***the holiday from ~*** la vacanza infernale; ***a ~ of a noise*** *infml* un fracasso infernale; ***run like ~*** correre come un pazzo; ***it hurts like ~*** fa un male del diavolo; ***a ~ of a lot*** moltissimo; ***she's a*** *or* ***one ~ of a girl*** è una ragazza straordinaria; ***you scared the ~ out of me*** mi hai spaventato a morte

he'll = ***he will***

hellbent *adj* accanito (**on** in)

Hellenic *adj* ellenico

Hellenism *n* ellenismo *m*

Hellenistic *adj* ellenistico

hellfire I *n* fiamme *fpl* dell'inferno **II** *adj*: ***~ preacher*** *predicatore che descrive le pene dell'inferno*

hell-for-leather *adv infml* a più non posso

hellhole *n* luogo *m* squallido

hellish *adj fig infml* infernale; *traffic, cold* terribile; ***it's ~*** è terribile

hellishly *adv infml hot* in modo infernale

hello *int informal* ciao; *more formal* buongiorno; buona sera; TEL pronto; ***say ~ to s.o.*** salutare qn

hell-raiser *n infml* casinista *m/f*

Hell's Angel *n motociclista appartenente a una banda di ispirazione neonazista*

helluva *adj infml* straordinario

helm *n* NAUT timone *m*

helmet *n of motorcyclist* casco *m*; *of soldier* elmetto *m*

help I *v/t* aiutare; ***~ o.s.*** *to food* servirsi; ***I can't ~ it*** non ci posso far niente; ***I couldn't ~ laughing*** non ho potuto fare a meno di ridere; ***~ s.o. with the cooking / his bags*** aiutare qn in cucina / con i sacchetti; ***~!*** aiuto!; ***can I ~ you?*** posso esserti d'aiuto?; ***that won't ~ you*** non ti sarà d'aiuto; ***not if I can ~ it*** non se posso evitarlo; ***it can't be ~ed*** non se ne può fare a meno **II** *v/i* aiutare; ***and your attitude didn't ~ either*** e il tuo atteggiamento certo non aiuta **III** *n* aiuto *m*; ***with his brother's ~*** con l'aiuto di suo fratello; ***his ~ with the project*** il suo aiuto nel progetto; ***ask s.o. for ~*** chiedere aiuto a qn; ***be of ~ to s.o.*** essere di aiuto a qn; ***he isn't much ~ to me*** non mi è di grande aiuto

◆**help out** *v/t sep & v/i* aiutare

help desk *n* servizio *m* d'assistenza, help desk *m*

helper *n* aiutante *m/f*

helpful *adj person* di aiuto; *advice* utile; ***he was very ~*** mi è stato di grande aiuto

helping I *n of food* porzione *f*; ***take a second ~ of sth*** prendere una seconda porzione di qc **II** *adj*: ***give*** *or* ***lend a ~ hand to s.o.*** dare una mano a qn

helpless *adj* (*unable to cope*) indifeso; (*powerless*) impotente; ***he was ~ to prevent it*** non è riuscito a impedirlo; ***she was ~ with laughter*** non riusciva a smettere di ridere

helplessly *adv*: ***we watched ~*** guardavamo impotenti

helplessness *n* impotenza *f*

help line *n* assistenza *f* telefonica **help menu** *n* COMPUT menu *m inv* della guida in linea **help screen** *n* COMPUT schermata *f* della guida in linea

helter-skelter *adv* precipitosamente

hem I *n of dress etc* orlo *m* **II** *v/t* bordare

he-man *n* ⟨*pl* ***he-men***⟩ *infml* fusto *m*

hemisphere *n* emisfero *m*

hemline *n* orlo *m*

hemo- *pref US* → ***haemo-***

hemorrhage *US* → ***haemorrhage***

hemorrhoids *US* → ***haemorrhoids***

hemp *n* BOT canapa *f*

hen *n* gallina *f*

hence *adv* (*for this reason*) quindi; ***~ the name*** da cui il nome; ***two years ~*** di qui a due anni

henceforth *adv* d'ora in avanti

henchman *n pej* scagnozzo *m*

henna I *n* henné *m inv* **II** *v/t* dare l'henné a

hen night *n*, **hen party** *n equivalente al femminile della festa d'addio al celibato*

henpecked *adj*: ***~ husband*** marito *m* succube della moglie

hepatitis *n* epatite *f*

her I *adj* il suo *m*, la sua *f*, i suoi *mpl*, le sue *fpl*; ***~ ticket*** il suo biglietto; ***~***

brother/sister suo fratello/sua sorella **II** *pron direct object* la; *indirect object* le; *after prep* lei; ***I know ~*** la conosco; ***I gave ~ the keys*** le ho dato le chiavi; ***this is for ~*** questo è per lei; ***he is younger than ~*** lui è più giovane di lei; ***she looked behind ~*** guardò dietro di sé; ***who? – ~*** chi? – lei; ***it's ~*** è lei

herald I *n fig* messaggero *m* **II** *v/t* annunciare; ***tonight's game is being ~ed as the match of the season*** la partita di stasera è stata annunciata come l'incontro della stagione

heraldry *n* araldica *f*

herb *n for medicines* erba *f* medicinale; *for flavouring* erba *f* aromatica

herbaceous *adj* erbaceo

herbaceous border *n* aiuola *f* di piante perenni

herbal *adj* a base di erbe; ***~ tea*** tisana

herbalist *n* erborista *m/f*

herb garden *n* orto *m* di erbe aromatiche

herbicide *n* diserbante *m*

herbivore *n* erbivoro *m*

herbivorous *adj form* erbivoro

herd I *n* mandria *f* **II** *v/t* radunare

herd instinct *n* PSYCH gregarismo *m*

herdsman *n* pastore *m*

here *adv* qui, qua; ***~ and there*** qui e lì; ***~'s to you!*** *as toast* salute!; ***~ you are*** *giving sth* ecco qui; ***~!*** *in roll-call* presente!; ***~ I am*** eccomi; ***~'s the taxi*** ecco il taxi; ***I won't be ~ for lunch*** non ci sarò per pranzo; ***~ we go again, another crisis*** eccoci di nuovo, un'altra crisi; ***~ goes!*** cominciamo!; ***~, let me do that*** su, lascia fare a me; ***it's neither ~ nor there*** non ha nessuna importanza

hereabouts *adv* nei dintorni

hereafter *adv* d'ora in poi

hereby *adv form* con ciò

hereditary *adj disease* ereditario

heredity *n* ereditarietà *f inv*

heresy *n* eresia *f*

heretic *n* eretico *m*, -a *f*

heretical *adj* eretico

herewith *adv form* con la presente

heritage *n* patrimonio *m*

hermaphrodite *n* ermafrodito *m*

hermetically *adv*: ***~ sealed*** sigillato ermeticamente

hermit *n* eremita *m/f*

hermitage *n* eremo *m*

hernia *n* MED ernia *f*

hero *n* eroe *m*

heroic I *adj* eroico; ***~ action*** *or* ***deed*** atto *m* eroico; ***~ attempt*** eroico tentativo *m* **II** *n*: **heroics** atteggiamenti *mpl* melodrammatici

heroically *adv* eroicamente

heroic couplet *n* LIT distico *m* eroico

heroic verse *n* LIT verso *m* eroico

heroin *n* eroina *f*

heroin addict *n* eroinomane *m/f*

heroine *n* eroina *f*

heroism *n* eroismo *m*

heron *n* airone *m*

hero worship *n* culto *m* degli eroi

herpes *n* MED herpes *m*

herring *n* aringa *f*

herringbone *adj*: ***~ pattern*** SEW spina *f* di pesce

hers *pron* il suo *m*, la sua *f*, i suoi *mpl*, le sue *fpl*; ***~ are red*** i suoi sono rossi; ***a friend of ~*** un suo amico

herself *pron reflexive* si; *emphatic* se stessa; *after prep* sé, se stessa; ***she must be proud of ~*** dev'essere fiera di sé *or* se stessa; ***she hurt ~*** si è fatta male; ***she bought ~ a car*** si è comprata la macchina; ***she told me so ~*** me l'ha detto lei stessa; ***by ~*** da sola

he's = ***he is***; ***he has***

hesitant *adj* esitante

hesitantly *adv* con esitazione

hesitate *v/i* esitare; ***not ~ to do sth*** non esitare a fare qc; ***I am still hesitating about what I should do*** sono ancora incerto su ciò che dovrei fare

hesitation *n* esitazione *f*; ***after some/a moment's ~*** dopo qualche attimo di esitazione

heterogeneity *n* eterogeneità *f*

heterogeneous *adj* eterogeneo

heterosexual *adj* eterosessuale

heterosexuality *n* eterosessualità *f*

het up *adj Br infml* arrabbiato; ***get ~ about/over sth*** andare in collera per qc

hew *v/t* ⟨*pret* **hewed**, *past part* **hewn** *or* **hewed**⟩ fendere

hex I *n* malocchio *m* **II** *v/t* stregare

hexagon *n* esagono *m*

hexagonal *adj* esagonale

heyday *n* tempi *mpl* d'oro

hf *abbr* (= **high frequency**) alta frequenza *f*

HGV *abbr* (= **heavy goods vehicle**) *Br* veicolo *m* per merci pesanti
H.H. *abbr* (= **His / Her Highness**; **His Holiness**) Sua Altezza (S.A.)
hi *int* ciao
hiatus *n* iato *m*
hiatus hernia *n* MED ernia *f* iatale
hibernate *v/i* andare in letargo
hibernation *n liter*, *fig* letargo *m*
hiccup I *n* singhiozzo *m*; (*minor problem*) intoppo *m*; ***have the ~s*** avere il singhiozzo; ***without any ~s*** senza intoppi **II** *v/i* ⟨*pret & past part* ***-ped***⟩ avere il singhiozzo; ***he has been ~ing all morning*** ha avuto il singhiozzo per tutta la mattina
hick *n US infml* campagnolo *m*, -a *f*
hid *pret* → ***hide***[1]
hidden I *adj* nascosto **II** *past part* → ***hide***[1]
hidden agenda *n fig* secondo fine *m*
hide[1] ⟨*pret* ***hid***, *past part* ***hidden***⟩ **I** *v/t* nascondere; ***hidden from view*** nascosto alla vista **II** *v/i* nascondersi; ***he was hiding in the cupboard*** si nascondeva nell'armadio
◆**hide away I** *v/i* nascondersi **II** *v/t sep* nascondere
◆**hide out** *v/i* darsi alla macchia
hide[2] *n of animal* pelle *f*
hide-and-seek *n* nascondino *m* **hideaway** *n* rifugio *m*
hideous *adj face*, *weather* orrendo; *crime* atroce
hideout *n* nascondiglio *m*
hiding[1] *n* (*beating*) batosta *f*; ***give s.o. a good ~*** dare a qn una bella batosta; *infml* ***the team got a real ~*** la squadra ha preso una bella batosta
hiding[2] *n*: ***be in ~*** tenersi nascosto; ***go into ~*** darsi alla macchia
hiding place *n* nascondiglio *m*
hierarchy *n* gerarchia *f*
hieroglyphic *n* geroglifico *m*
hi-fi *n* hi-fi *m inv*
higgledy-piggledy *adj*/*adv* alla rinfusa
high I *adj* (+*er*) **1.** *building*, *price*, *mountain*, *note*, *temperature*, *salary* alto; ***~ in the sky*** in alto nel cielo; ***on the ~est authority*** presso persone molto in alto; ***be ~ and mighty*** essere arrogante; ***casualties were ~*** ci sono state molte vittime; MIL ci furono molti caduti; ***the temperature was in the ~ twenties*** la temperatura era prossima a trenta gradi; ***pay a ~ price for sth*** pagare un prezzo elevato per qc; ***the ~est degree*** il massimo grado; ***in ~ spirits*** di buonumore; ***~ in fat*** con un elevato contenuto di grassi **2.** *wind*, *speed* forte **3.** *quality*, *hopes* buono; ***have a very ~ opinion of ...*** stimare molto ... **4.** *on drugs* fatto *infml*; ***get ~ on cocaine*** sballare con la cocaina **5.** ***it is ~ time he left*** sarebbe ora che se ne andasse **6.** ***~ ground*** altopiano *m*; *fig* ***claim the moral ~ ground*** ritenersi moralmente migliore **II** *n in statistics* livello *m* record; ***the pound has reached a new ~*** la sterlina ha raggiunto un nuovo record; ***sales have reached an all-time ~*** le vendite hanno raggiunto un record storico; ***the ~s and lows of my career*** gli alti e i bassi della mia carriera **III** *adv* (+*er*) in alto; ***~er up the hill was a small farm*** più in alto sulla collina c'era una piccola fattoria; ***~ up in the organization*** a un livello elevato dell'organizzazione; ***one floor ~er*** un piano più in alto; ***go as ~ as £200*** arrivare a 200 sterline; ***feelings ran ~*** si infiammarono gli animi; ***search ~ and low*** cercare in lungo e in largo
high altar *n* altare *m* maggiore **high and mighty** *adj* arrogante **high beams** *npl* AUTO abbaglianti *mpl*
highbrow *adj* intellettuale
highchair *n* seggiolone *m*
high-class *adj* di (prima) classe
High Court *n* Corte *f* Suprema
high-density *adj* COMPUT *disk* ad alta densità **high diving** *n* tuffo *m* **high-energy** *adj* ad alta energia
higher education *n* istruzione *f* universitaria
Higher National Certificate *n Br diploma universitario di livello inferiore in una materia economica o tecnica* **Higher National Diploma** *n Br diploma universitario di livello superiore in una materia economica o tecnica*
highfalutin *adj* ampolloso
high-fibre, *US* **high-fiber** *adj* ricco di fibre **high-flier, high flyer** *n infml* ambizioso *m*, -a *f* **high-frequency** *adj* ad alta frequenza **high-grade** *adj* di buona qualità **high-handed**

adj autoritario **high-heeled** *adj* col tacco alto **high-interest** *adj* FIN ad interesse elevato **high jinks** *npl infml* baldoria *f* **high jump** *n* salto *m* in alto

Highlands *npl* Highland *fpl, regione montuosa nella Scozia settentrionale*

high-level *adj* ad alto livello **high life** *n* bella vita *f*

highlight I *n* (*main event*) clou *m inv*; *in hair* colpo *m* di sole **II** *v/t with pen* evidenziare; COMPUT selezionare

highlighter *n pen* evidenziatore *m*

highly *adv desirable, likely* molto; ***be ~ paid*** essere pagato profumatamente; ***think ~ of s.o.*** stimare molto qn

highly strung *adj* nervoso

high-minded *adj ideals* nobile

Highness *n*: ***Her*** (***Royal***) **~** Sua Altezza (Reale)

high performance *adj drill, battery* ad alto rendimento **high-pitched** *adj* acuto **high point** *n* clou *m inv* **high-powered** *adj engine* potente; *intellectual* di prestigio **high pressure I** *n weather* alta pressione *f* **II** *adj* TECH ad alta pressione; *salesman* aggressivo **high priest** *n* gran sacerdote *m* **high priestess** *n* gran sacerdotessa *f* **high-profile** *adj* di primo piano **high-quality** *adj* di alta qualità **high-ranking** *adj* di rango elevato **high-resolution** *adj* ad alta risoluzione **high-rise** *n* palazzone *m*; ***~ building*** edificio *m* a molti piani; ***~ office*** (***block***) palazzo *m* di uffici; ***~ flats*** *Br* casermone *m infml* **high-risk** *adj* ad alto rischio; ***~ group*** gruppo ad alto rischio **high school** *n* scuola *f* superiore **high seas** *npl*: ***the ~*** le acque *fpl* internazionali; ***on the ~*** in acque internazionali **high season** *n* alta stagione *f* **high-security** *adj*: ***~ prison*** carcere *m* di massima sicurezza **high society** *n* alta società *f inv* **high--speed train** *n* treno *m* ad alta velocità **high spirits** *npl* buonumore *m*; ***youthful ~*** euforia *f* giovanile **high street** *n* via *f* principale **high tea** *n pasto consumato nel tardo pomeriggio* **high tech I** *n* high-tech *m inv* **II** *adj* high tech **high tide** *n* alta marea *f* **high treason** *n* alto tradimento *m* **high-up** *adj person* alto papavero *m* **high-voltage** *n* alta tensione *f* **high water** *n* alta marea *f*

highway *n US* strada *f* statale

Highway Code *n* Codice *m* stradale

high wire *n* corda *f* tesa

hijack I *v/t* dirottare **II** *n* dirottamento *m*

hijacker *n* dirottatore *m*, -trice *f*

hike[1] **I** *n* camminata *f* **II** *v/i* fare camminate

hike[2] *n in prices* aumento *m*

hiker *n* escursionista *m/f*

hiking *n* escursionismo *m*

hiking boots *npl* scarponcini *mpl* da camminata

hilarious *adj* divertentissimo

hilariously *adv* allegramente

hilarity *n* ilarità *f*; (*gaiety*) allegria *f*

hill *n* collina *f*; (*slope*) altura *f*; *fig* ***be over the ~*** *infml* aver superato la crisi

hillbilly *n US infml* montanaro *m*, -a *f*

hillock *n* collinetta *f*

hillside *n* pendio *m*

hilltop *n* cima *f* della collina

hill-walker *n Br* escursionista *m/f*, *camminatore amante delle colline*

hilly *adj* (+*er*) collinoso

hilt *n* impugnatura *f*; *fig* (***up***) ***to the ~*** fino in fondo

him *pron direct object* lo; *indirect object* gli; *after prep* lui; ***I know ~*** lo conosco; ***I gave ~ the keys*** gli ho dato le chiavi; ***this is for ~*** questo è per lui; ***she's younger than ~*** lei è più giovane di lui; ***he looked about ~*** si guardò intorno; ***who? – ~*** chi? – lui; ***it's ~*** è lui

himself *pron* se stesso; *after prep* sé, se stesso; ***he must be proud of ~*** dev'essere fiero di sé *or* se stesso; ***he hurt ~*** si è fatto male; ***he told me so ~*** me l'ha detto lui stesso; ***by ~*** da solo

hind[1] *n* ZOOL cervo *m* femmina

hind[1] *adj* posteriore; ***~ legs*** zampe *fpl* posteriori

hinder *v/t* intralciare

Hindi *n* hindi *m*

hindquarters *npl* posteriore *m*; *of horse* quarti *mpl* posteriori

hindrance *n* intralcio *m*

hindsight *n*: ***with ~*** con il senno di poi; ***it was, in ~, a mistaken judgement*** con il senno di poi, è stato un errore di giudizio

Hindu I *adj* indù **II** *n* induista *m/f*

Hinduism *n* induismo *m*

hinge *n* cardine *m*

◆**hinge on** *v/t* dipendere da

hint I *n* (*clue*) accenno *m*; (*piece of advice*) consiglio *m*; (*implied suggestion*) allusione *f*; ***give a / no ~ of sth*** (non) far capire qc; ***drop s.o. a ~*** lanciare un'allusione a qn; ***OK, I can take a ~*** OK, ho capito; *of red, sadness etc* punta *f*; ***a ~ of garlic*** un pizzico di aglio; ***a ~ of irony*** un pizzico di ironia; ***with just a ~ of sadness in his smile*** con una punta di tristezza nel suo sorriso; ***at the first ~ of trouble*** al primo accenno di problemi **II** *v/i* fare allusioni; ***~ at*** fare allusioni a; ***he hinted at my involvement in the affair*** fece allusione al mio coinvolgimento nella vicenda **III** *v/t*: ***~ (that)*** alludere che

hinterland *n* hinterland *m*

hip[1] *n* fianco *m*; ***with one's hands on one's ~s*** con una mano sui fianchi

hip[2] *int*: ***~! ~!, hurrah!*** hip, hip, hurrà!

hip[3] *adj infml* moderno

hipbone *n* ANAT ileo *m*

hip flask *n* fiaschetta *f* da tasca

hippie *n* hippy *m/f*

hippo *n infml* ippopotamo *m*

hip pocket *n* tasca *f* posteriore

hippopotamus *n* ippopotamo *m*

hip replacement *n* sostituzione *f* della testa del femore

hipsters *npl* pantaloni *mpl* a vita bassa

hire I *v/t room, hall* affittare; *workers, staff* assumere; *conjuror etc* ingaggiare **II** *n of room* affitto *m*; *of car* noleggio *m*; ***for ~*** a noleggio

hire purchase *n* acquisto *m* rateale; ***on ~*** a rate; ***~ agreement*** contratto *m* di acquisto rateale

his I *adj* il suo *m*, la sua *f*, i suoi *mpl*, le sue *fpl*; ***~ bag*** la sua valigia; ***~ brother / sister*** suo fratello / sua sorella **II** *pron* il suo *m*, la sua *f*, i suoi *mpl*, le sue *fpl*; ***~ are red*** i suoi sono rossi; ***a friend of ~*** un suo amico

Hispanic I *adj* ispanico **II** *n* ispanico *m*, -a *f*

hiss *v/i* sibilare

historian *n* storico *m*, -a *f*

historic *adj* storico

historical *adj* storico

history *n* storia *f*; *fig* ***that's all ~ now*** è acqua passata; ***he has a ~ of violence*** ha un passato di violenze; ***he has a ~ of heart disease*** ha precedenti di cardiopatie

hit I *v/t* ⟨*pret & past part* ***hit***⟩ **1.** colpire; (*collide with*) sbattere contro; ***I ~ my knee*** ho battuto il ginocchio; ***he was ~ by a bullet*** è stato colpito da un proiottile; ***it suddenly ~ me*** (*I realized*) improvvisamente ho realizzato; ***the car ~ a tree*** la macchina ha sbattuto contro un albero; ***the tree was ~ by lightning*** l'albero è stato colpito da un fulmine; ***you won't know what has ~ you*** *infml* resterai frastornato **2.** ***~ town*** (*arrive*) arrivare (in città); ***be hard ~ by sth*** essere duramente colpito da qc; ***~ a problem*** incontrare un problema; *fig* ***~ the bottle*** *infml* darsi all'alcol; ***~ the roof*** andare su tutte le furie; ***~ the road*** mettersi in viaggio **II** *n* (*blow*) colpo *m*; (*success*) successo *m*; (*visit to website*) accesso *m*; ***be a ~ with s.o.*** far colpo su qn

◆**hit back** *v/i* reagire

◆**hit off** *v/t sep* ***hit it off with s.o.*** *infml* fare subito amicizia con qn

◆**hit on** *v/t idea* trovare

◆**hit out at** *v/t* (*criticize*) attaccare

hit-and-run *adj*: ***~ accident*** *incidente con omissione di soccorso*

hitch I *n* (*problem*) contrattempo *m*; ***without a ~*** senza contrattempi; ***a technical ~*** un contrattempo tecnico **II** *v/t*: ***~ sth to sth*** legare qc a qc; *with hook* agganciare qc a qc; ***~ a lift*** chiedere un passaggio; ***she ~ed a lift*** *or* ***ride with a truck driver*** chiese un passaggio a un camionista **III** *v/i* (*hitchhike*) fare l'autostop

◆**hitch up** *v/t sep wagon, trailer* attaccare; *skirt* tirare su

hitchhike *v/i* fare l'autostop **hitchhiker** *n* autostoppista *m/f* **hitchhiking** *n* autostop *m inv*

hi-tech I *n* high-tech *m inv* **II** *adj* high tech

hither *adv*: ***~ and thither*** *liter* qua e là

hitherto *adv* finora

hitlist *n* libro *m* nero **hitman** *n* sicario *m* **hit-or-miss** *adj*: ***on a ~ basis*** affidandosi al caso **hit squad** *n* commando *m*

HIV *abbr* (= **human immunodeficiency virus**) HIV *m*

hive *n for bees* alveare *m*; *fig* ***the of-***

fice was a ~ of activity l'ufficio ferveva di attività

◆**hive off** *v/t sep* (COMM: *separate off*) separare

HIV-positive *adj* sieropositivo

HM *abbr* (= **His / Her Majesty**) Sua Maestà *f*

HMS *abbr* (= **His / Her Majesty's Ship**) *Br* nave *f* di Sua Maestà

HNC *abbr* (= **Higher National Certificate**) *Br diploma universitario di livello inferiore in una materia economica o tecnica*

HND *abbr* (= **Higher National Diploma**) *Br diploma universitario di livello superiore in una materia economica o tecnica*

hoard I *n* provvista *f*; ***~ of money*** gruzzolo *m* **II** *v/t* accumulare

hoarder *n persona che non butta mai niente*

hoarse *adj* (+*er*) rauco

hoary *adj* canuto

hoax *n* scherzo *m*; *malicious* falso allarme *m*

hob *n on cooker* piano *m* di cottura

hobble *v/i* zoppicare

hobby *n* hobby *m inv*

hobnob *v/i* ⟨*pret & past part* **-bed**⟩: ***she's been seen ~bing with the chairman*** è stata vista intrattenersi amichevolmente con il presidente

hobo *n US* (*tramp*) vagabondo *m*, -a *f*

Hobson's choice *n*: ***it's ~*** scelta *f* forzata

hockey *n* hockey *m* (su prato)

hockey player *n* giocatore *m*, -trice *f* di hockey **hockey stick** *n* bastone *m* da hockey

hodgepodge *n US* → ***hotchpotch***

hoe I *n* zappa *f* **II** *v/t & v/i* zappare

hog I *n* porco *m*; (*pig*) maiale *m* **II** *v/t* ⟨*pret & past part* **-ged**⟩ *infml* monopolizzare; ***a lot of drivers ~ the middle of the road*** molti guidatori monopolizzano il centro della strada; ***~ the limelight*** monopolizzare la ribalta

Hogmanay *n Scot* veglione *m* di capodanno

hogwash *n* (*nonsense*) sciocchezze *fpl*

hoist I *n* montacarichi *m inv* **II** *v/t* (*lift*) sollevare; *flag* issare

hoity-toity *adj* presuntuoso

hold I *v/t* ⟨*pret & past part* **held**⟩ **1.** *in hand* tenere; ***~ hands*** tenersi per mano; tenere; ***this car ~s the road well*** questa macchina tiene bene la strada; ***~ sth in place*** tenere qc a posto **2.** (*support, keep in place*) reggere; ***he can ~ his drink*** regge bene l'alcol **3.** *passport, licence* avere **4.** *prisoner, suspect* trattenere; ***~ s.o. hostage*** tenere qn in ostaggio; ***there's no ~ing him*** non lo tiene nessuno **5.** (*contain*) contenere; ***this room ~s twenty people*** questa stanza contiene venti persone; ***what does the future ~?*** cosa ci riserva il futuro? **6.** *job, post* occupare; ***~ office*** rivestire una carica; ***~ one's own*** tenere duro; ***~ s.o.'s attention*** tenere desta l'attenzione di qn **7.** *course* tenere **8.** ***~ one's breath*** trattenere il fiato; ***~ it!*** un attimo! **9.** (*consider*) ***~ s.o. responsible*** ritenere qn responsabile; ***~ that ...*** (*believe, maintain*) sostenere che ...; ***I have always held that ...*** ho sempre sostenuto che ...; ***~ the view*** *or* ***opinion that ...*** ritenere che ... **10.** ***~ the line*** TEL resti in linea **II** *n in ship, plane* stiva *f*; ***take ~ of sth*** prendere qc; ***catch ~ of sth*** afferrare qc; ***lose one's ~ on sth*** *on rope etc* perdere la presa su qc; ***get ~ of s.o.*** (*contact*) rintracciare qn

◆**hold against** *v/t always sep* ***hold sth against s.o.*** volerne a qn per qc

◆**hold back I** *v/t sep crowds* contenere; *facts, information* nascondere **II** *v/i* (*hesitate*) esitare; ***he's holding back*** *not telling all* non sta dicendo tutta la verità

◆**hold on** *v/i* (*wait*) attendere; TEL restare in linea; ***now hold on a minute!*** aspetta un attimo!; ***hold on tight!*** tieniti forte!

◆**hold on to** *v/t* (*keep*) tenere; *belief* aggrapparsi a

◆**hold out I** *v/t sep hand* tendere; *prospect* offrire **II** *v/i of supplies* durare; *of trapped miners etc* resistere

◆**hold up** *v/t sep hand* alzare; *bank etc* rapinare; (*make late*) trattenere; ***hold sth up as an example*** portare qc ad esempio

◆**hold with** *v/t* (*approve of*) essere d'accordo con; ***I don't hold with that*** non sono d'accordo

holdall *n* borsone *m*

holder *n* (*container*) contenitore *m*; *of passport* titolare *m*; *of ticket* possessore *m*; *of record* detentore *m*, -trice *f*

holding *n* FIN *of shares* pacchetto *m* azionario (**In** in); *of land* tenuta *f*

holding company *n* holding *f inv*

holdup *n* (*robbery*) rapina *f*; (*delay*) ritardo *m*; ***what's the ~?*** qual è l'intoppo?

hole *n* buco *m*; (*awkward situation*) ***be in a ~*** essere in un pasticcio; ***get s.o. out of a ~*** tirare fuori qn dai pasticci

◆**hole up** *v/i infml* rintanarsi

hole-in-the-wall *n Br infml* sportello *m* bancomat

holiday I *n* vacanza *f*; *public* giorno *m* festivo; (*day off*) giorno *m* di ferie; ***be on ~*** (*abroad, from school*) essere in vacanza; (*off work*) essere in ferie; ***go on ~*** andare in vacanza; ***the Christmas ~s*** le vacanze di Natale; ***take a month's ~*** prendersi un mese di vacanza **II** *v/i esp Br* trascorrere le vacanze

holiday camp *n* villaggio *m* turistico **holiday entitlement** *n* diritto *m* alle ferie **holiday home** *n* seconda casa *f* **holidaymaker** *n* vacanziere *m*, -a *f* **holiday resort** *n* luogo *m* di villeggiatura **holiday season** *n* stagione *f* delle vacanze

holier-than-thou *adj* bigotto

holiness *n* santità *f*; ***His / Your Holiness*** REL Sua Santità *f*

holistic *adj* olistico

Holland *n* Olanda *f*

holler *v/t & v/i infml*: *a.* **holler out** urlare

hollow I *adj object* cavo, vuoto; *cheeks* infossato; ***a ~ victory*** una vittoria vana **II** *n* (*cavity*) cavità *f*; (*depression*) avvallamento *m*; (*valley*) valletta *f* **III** *v/t* scavare

holly *n* agrifoglio *m*

holocaust *n hist* olocausto *m*

hologram *n* ologramma *m*

hols *abbr* (= **holidays**) *Br infml* vacanze *fpl*

holster *n* fondina *f*

holy *adj* santo

Holy Bible *n*: ***the ~*** la Sacra Bibbia **Holy Communion** *n* santa comunione *f* **Holy Father** *n*: ***the ~*** (*the Pope*) il Santo Padre **Holy Ghost, Holy Spirit** *n* Spirito *m* Santo **Holy Land** *n*: ***the ~*** la Terra Santa **holy water** *n* acqua *f* benedetta **Holy Week** *n* settimana *f* santa

home I *n* **1.** casa *f*; ***at ~*** a casa; ***make yourself at ~*** fai come a casa tua; ***be away from ~*** essere via da casa; ***work from ~*** lavorare da casa **2.** (*native country*) patria *f*; ***at ~ and abroad*** in patria e all'estero; ***the city is ~ to some 1,500 students*** la città accoglie circa 1.500 studenti **3.** *for old people* casa *f* di riposo; *for children* istituto *m* **4.** ***at ~*** SPORTS in casa **II** *adv* a casa; ***go ~*** andare a casa; ***is she ~ yet?*** è tornata?; ***I have to get ~ before ten*** devo rincasare prima delle dieci; ***return ~ from abroad*** rientrare in patria dall'estero; ***bring sth ~ to s.o.*** far comprendere qc a qn

◆**home in** *v/i* (*missiles*) puntare (***on sth*** su qc); ***home in on a target*** puntare su un obiettivo; ***he homed in on the essential point*** puntò alla questione essenziale

home address *n* indirizzo *m* di casa **home-baked** *adj* fatto in casa **home banking** *n* home-banking *m inv* **homecoming** *n* ritorno *m* **home computer** *n* computer *m inv* (per casa) **home cooking** *n* cucina *f* casereccia **Home Counties** *npl* contee *fpl* intorno a Londra **home economics** *nsg* economia *f* domestica **home entertainment system** *n* home entertainment *m inv* **home game** *n* SPORTS partita *f* in casa **home ground** *n* SPORTS campo *m* di casa; *fig* ***be on ~*** giocare in casa **home-grown** *adj vegetables* nostrano **home help** *n* assistenza *f* domestica **home key** *n* COMPUT tasto *m* HOME

homeland *n* patria *f*

homeless *adj* senza tetto; ***the ~*** i senzacasa

homelessness *n* l'essere senza tetto

home life *n* vita *f* domestica **homeloving** *adj* casalingo

homely *adj* (-*er*) *US* semplice; *Br* (*welcoming*) accogliente

homemade *adj* fatto in casa, casalingo

homemaker *n US* casalinga *f* **home match** *n* incontro *m* casalingo **home movie** *n* filmino *m* (casalingo) **Home Office** *n* Ministero *m* degli Interni

homeopathy *n* omeopatia *f*
homeowner *n* proprietario *m*, -a *f* di una casa
home page *n* home page *f* **Home Secretary** *n* Ministro *m* degli Interni
homesick *adj*: ***be ~*** avere nostalgia di casa
homestead *n* casa *f* con terreno circostante; *US* terreno *m* concesso dallo stato
home team *n* SPORTS squadra *f* di casa **home town** *n* città *f inv* natale **home truth** *n Br* verità *f* lampante; ***tell s.o. a few ~s*** illustrare a qn alcune verità lampanti **home video** *n* home video *m*
homeward *adv* verso casa; ***~ journey*** viaggio *m* verso casa; ***we are ~ bound*** siamo diretti verso casa
homework *n* EDU compiti *mpl* a casa **homeworking** *n* COMM telelavoro *m inv*
homey *adj* (+*er*) *US infml* confortevole
homicidal *adj* omicida; ***that man is a ~ maniac*** quell'uomo è un maniaco omicida
homicide *n crime* omicidio *m*; *US*: *police department* (squadra *f*) omicidi *f*
homily *n* predica *f*
homing pigeon *n* piccione *m* viaggiatore
homogeneous *adj* omogeneo
homogenize *v/t* omogeneizzare
homogenous *adj* omogeneo
homograph *n* omografo *m*
homonym *n* omonimo *m*
homonymous *adj* omonimo
homophobia *n* omofobia *f*
homophobic *adj* omofobo
homosexual **I** *adj* omosessuale **II** *n* omosessuale *m/f*
homosexuality *n* omosessualità *f*
Hon *abbr* **1.** (= **Honourable**) onorevole **2.** (= **honorary**) onorario
hone *v/t blade* affilare; *fig skills* perfezionare
honest *adj* onesto; ***to be ~ with you ...*** onestamente ...; ***the ~ truth*** la pura verità; (*law-abiding, decent*) *person* onesto; ***make an ~ living*** guadagnarsi da vivere onestamente
honestly *adv* onestamente; ***~!*** ma insomma!
honest-to-goodness *adj* genuino
honesty *n* onestà *f inv*
honey *n* miele *m*; *infml* (*darling*) tesoro *m*
honeybee *n* ape *f* domestica
honeycomb *n* favo *m*
honeydew melon *n varietà di melone dalla polpa verdastra molto dolce*
honey fungus *n* BOT chiodino *m*
honeymoon **I** *n* luna *f* di miele; ***be on one's ~*** essere in luna di miele **II** *v/i* trascorrere la luna di miele; ***they are ~ing in Spain*** stanno trascorrendo la luna di miele in Spagna
honeysuckle *n* caprifoglio *m*
honk **I** *v/i* (*car*) colpo *m* di clacson; (*geese*) grido *m* (dell'oca selvatica) **II** *v/t horn* suonare
honor *etc US* → ***honour*** *etc*
honorary *adj* onorario
honorary degree *n* laurea *f* ad honorem
honour, *US* **honor** **I** *n* onore *m*; ***in ~ of*** in onore di; ***sense of ~*** senso dell'onore; ***man of ~*** uomo d'onore; ***if you would do me the ~ of accepting*** *form* se vuole farmi l'onore di accettare; ***Your Honour, His Honour*** Vostro Onore; ***do the ~s*** *infml* fare gli onori di casa; ***get First Class Honours*** conseguire una laurea specialistica di primo livello **II** *v/t person* onorare; *promise* mantenere; *agreement* rispettare; ***I would be ~ed*** ne sarei onorato
honourable, *US* **honorable** *adj* onorevole, d'onore
honourable mention *n* menzione *f* d'onore
honourably, *US* **honorably** *adv* con onore; *behave* onorevolmente
honours degree *n Br* laurea *f* specialistica
hooch *n esp US infml* liquore *m*
hood *n over head* cappuccio *m*; *over cooker* cappa *f*; AUTO: *on convertible* capote *f inv*; *n esp US* cofano *m*
hoodlum *n* gangster *m inv*
hoodwink *v/t infml* imbrogliare; ***~ s.o. into doing sth*** indurre qn a fare qc con l'imbroglio
hoof *n* ⟨*pl* **hoofs** *or* **hooves**⟩ zoccolo *m*
hook **I** *n* gancio *m*; *for fishing* amo *m*; ***off the ~*** TEL staccato; ***he fell for it ~, line and sinker*** ci è cascato in pieno;

by ~ or by crook in ogni modo; ***that lets me off the ~*** *infml* questo mi scagiona; ***the phone was ringing off the ~*** *US infml* il telefono suonava insistentemente **II** *v/t*: ***~ a trailer to a car*** agganciare un rimorchio a una macchina; ***~ one's arm around sth*** passare il braccio intorno a qc; ***be/get ~ed on sth*** *infml on drugs* assuefarsi a qc; *on film, place etc* essere attratti da; ***he's ~ed on the idea*** è attratto dall'idea

◆**hook up I** *v/i*: ***hook up with s.o.*** *US infml* mettersi insieme a qn *infml* **II** *v/t sep dress etc* allacciare; *trailer* agganciare; *computer etc* collegare (***to*** a); RADIO, TV collegare (***with a***)

hookah *n* narghilè *m*

hook and eye *n* gancetto *m*

hooked *adj* ***~ nose*** naso *m* adunco; ***be ~ on s.o./sth*** essere fanatico di qn/qc; ***be ~ on sth*** *on drugs* essere assuefatto a qc

hooker *n infml* prostituta *f*; *in rugby* tallonatore *m*

hooky *n US infml*: ***play ~*** marinare la scuola

hooligan *n* teppista *m/f*

hooliganism *n* teppismo *m*

hoop *n* cerchio *m*

hoopla *n* strombazzamento *m*

hoot I *n of owl* grido *m*; AUTO colpo *m* di clacson; ***~s of laughter*** risate *fpl*; ***I don't care*** *or* ***give a ~*** *or* ***two ~s*** *infml* non me ne importa un fico *or* non me ne importa niente; ***be a ~*** *infml* essere uno spasso **II** *v/t horn* suonare **III** *v/i of car* suonare il clacson; *of owl* gufare

hoover®I *n* aspirapolvere *m* **II** *v/t carpets, room* pulire con l'aspirapolvere

hoovering *n*: ***do the ~*** passare l'aspirapolvere

hop[1] *n plant* luppolo *m*

hop[2] **I** *v/i* ⟨*pret & past part* ***-ped***⟩ saltare **II** *n* salto *m*; *fig* ***catch s.o. on the ~*** *infml* cogliere qn alla sprovvista; AVIAT *infml* ***a short ~*** un salto **III** *v/t*: ***~ it!*** *Br infml* sloggia!

hope I *n* speranza *f*; ***there's no ~ of that*** non farci conto; ***beyond ~*** senza speranza; ***in the ~ of doing sth*** nella speranza di poter fare qc; ***have*** (***high*** *or* ***great***) ***~s of doing sth*** sperare di poter fare qc; ***don't get your ~s up*** non crearti speranze; ***some ~!*** *infml* magari!; ***she hasn't got a ~ in hell of passing her exams*** *infml* non ha nessuna speranza di passare gli esami **II** *v/i* sperare; ***~ for sth*** augurarsi qc; ***I ~ so*** spero di sì; ***I ~ not*** spero di no **III** *v/t*: ***I ~ you like it*** spero che ti piaccia; ***~ against ~ that …*** sperare fino all'ultimo che …

hopeful *adj person* ottimista; (*promising*) promettente

hopefully *adv say, wait* con ottimismo; (*I/we hope*) si spera

hopeless *adj position, prospect* senza speranza; (*useless*: *person*) negato *infml*

hopelessly *adv*: ***~ confused*** estremamente confuso; ***I feel ~ inadequate*** mi sento completamente inadeguato; ***he got ~ lost*** si è completamente perso

hopelessness *n of situation* l'essere senza speranza

hopping mad *adj infml* furioso

hopscotch *n* (*children's game*) campana *f*

horde *n infml* orda *f*; *of children* frotta *f*

horizon *n* orizzonte *m*; ***on the ~*** all'orizzonte (*a. fig*); ***below the ~*** sotto l'orizzonte

horizontal *adj* orizzontale

hormone *n* ormone *m*

hormone replacement therapy *n* terapia *f* ormonale sostitutiva

horn *n of animal* corno *m*; AUTO clacson *m inv*

hornet *n* calabrone *m*

horn-rimmed spectacles *npl* occhiali *mpl* con montatura di tartaruga

horny *adj* (*+er*) *infml sexually* arrapato *sl*

horoscope *n* oroscopo *m*

horrendous *adj* spaventoso; *crime, attack* orrendo; *infml conditions* terribile; *loss, price* spaventoso; ***children's shoes are a ~ price*** le scarpe per bambini hanno prezzi spaventosi

horrendously *adv infml expensive* spaventosamente

horrible *adj* orribile

horribly *adv* orrendamente; *infml drunk, expensive* terribilmente; ***they died ~*** sono morti in maniera orribile

horrid *adj* molto sgradevole

horrific *adj* orripilante
horrify *v/t* ⟨*pret & past part* **-ied**⟩ inorridire; ***I was horrified*** ero scioccato
horrifying *adj experience* terrificante; *idea*, *prices* allucinante
horror *n* orrore *m*; ***the ~s of war*** le atrocità della guerra; ***have a ~ of sth*** provare ribrezzo per qc; ***they watched in ~*** assistettero con orrore; *infml* ***you little ~!*** piccola peste!
horror movie *n* film *m inv* dell'orrore
horror-stricken *adj*, **horror-struck** *adj* inorridito
hors d'oeuvre *n* antipasto *m*
horse *n* cavallo *m*; ***eat like a ~*** mangiare come un lupo; ***I could eat a ~*** ho una fame da lupo; ***straight from the ~'s mouth*** da fonte sicura
◆**horse about** *Br or* **around** *v/i infml* giocare in modo scatenato
horseback *n*: ***on ~*** a cavallo **horsebox** *n* AUTO van *m* **horse chestnut** *n* ippocastano *m* **horse-drawn** *adj*: ***~ cart*** carro *m* a cavalli; ***~ carriage*** carrozza *f* a cavalli **horseman** *n* cavallerizzo *m* **horsemanship** *n* equitazione *f* **horseplay** *n* gioco *m* scatenato **horsepower** *n* cavallo-vapore *m*; ***a 200 ~ engine*** un motore da 200 cavalli **horse racing** *n* ippica *f* **horseradish** *n* barbaforte *m* **horse riding** *n* equitazione *f* **horseshoe** *n* ferro *m* di cavallo **horse-trading** *n fig* traffico *m* losco **horsewoman** *n* cavallerizza *f*
horticultural *adj* orticolo; ***~ show*** mostra *f* orticola
horticulture *n* orticoltura *f*
hose I *n* (*stockings*) calze *fpl*; tubo *m* di gomma **II** *v/t* (*a.* **hose down**) annaffiare
hosepipe *n esp Br* tubo *m* di gomma
hosiery *n* maglieria *f*
hospice *n* ospedale *m* per i malati terminali
hospitable *adj* ospitale; ***be ~ to s.o.*** essere ospitale con qn
hospital *n* ospedale *m*; ***go into ~***, *US* ***go into the ~*** essere ricoverato (in ospedale)
hospital corner *n letto rifatto come in ospedale*
hospitalise, hospitalize *v/t Br* ricoverare in ospedale
hospitality *n* ospitalità *f inv*
hospitality industry *n* industria *f* dell'ospitalità
host[1] **I** *n at party*, *reception* padrone *m* di casa; *of TV programme* presentatore *m*, -trice *f*; ***be or play ~ to s.o.*** ricevere qn **II** *v/t TV programme* presentare; (*country*, *city*) *event* ospitare
host[2] *n* moltitudine *f*, miriade *f*; ***he has a ~ of friends*** ha una miriade di amici
host[3] *n* REL ostia *f*
hostage *n* ostaggio *m*; ***be taken ~*** essere preso in ostaggio
hostage-taker *n* sequestratore *m*, -trice *f*
hostel *n for students* pensionato *m*; (*youth hostel*) ostello *m* (della gioventù)
hostess *n at party*, *reception* padrona *f* di casa; *on aeroplane* hostess *f inv*; *in nightclub* entraineuse *f*
hostile *adj* ostile; ***~ to*** ostile a *or* verso
hostility *n* ostilità *f inv*; ***he feels no ~ toward(s) anybody*** non prova ostilità nei confronti di nessuno; ***~ to foreigners*** ostilità per gli stranieri; **hostilities** *npl* ostilità *fpl*
hot I *adj* (+*er*) *weather*, *water* caldo; (*spicy*) piccante; *infml* (*good*) bravo (***at sth*** in qc); ***it's ~*** fa caldo; ***I'm ~*** ho caldo; ***~ food*** pasti *mpl* caldi; ***~ news*** notizie *fpl* fresche; ***~ tip*** soffiata *f*; ***~ off the press*** fresco di stampa; ***be (a) ~ favourite*** *Br or* ***favorite*** *US* essere il gran favorito; ***get (all) ~ and bothered*** *infml* agitarsi (***about*** per); ***get ~ under the collar about sth*** adirarsi per qc; ***get into ~ water*** finire nei pasticci; ***the water's very ~*** l'acqua è bollente **II** *adv* (+*er*) ***he keeps blowing ~ and cold*** è una banderuola al vento **III** *n*: ***have the ~s for s.o.*** *infml* eccitarsi per qn
hot air *n fig* aria *f* fritta; ***he talks a load of ~*** fa un sacco di discorsi campati in aria **hot-air balloon** *n* mongolfiera *f* **hotbed** *n fig* focolaio *m* (***of*** di) **hot-blooded** *adj* focoso
hotchpotch *n Br* pot-pourri *m*
hot dog *n* hot dog *m inv*
hotel *n* albergo *m*
hotelier *n* albergatore *m*, -trice *f*
hotel manager *n* direttore *m*, -trice *f* d'albergo **hotel room** *n* camera *f* d'albergo
hot flush *n* MED caldana *f* **hotfoot I** *v/i*

precipitarsi **II** *adv* in fretta e furia **hot-gospeller** *n* revivalista *m/f* **hot-head** *n* testa *f* calda **hot-headed** *adj* impulsivo **hothouse** *n* serra *f* **hot key** *n* COMPUT tasto *m* di scelta rapida **hot line** *n for emergency* linea *f* diretta di assistenza; POL telefono *m* rosso

hotly *adv debate*, *deny* con veemenza; *contest*, *dispute* violentemente; ***he was ~ pursued by two policemen*** due poliziotti lo inseguivano da vicino

hotplate *n* piastra *f* riscaldante **hot potato** *n fig infml* patata *f* bollente **hot property** *n infml persona molto attraente* **hot rod** *n* macchina *f* truccata **hot seat** *n*: ***be in the ~*** essere in una posizione difficile **hotshot** *infml n* pezzo *m* grosso **hot spot** *n military*, *political* zona *f* calda **hot spring** *n* sorgente *f* termale **hot stuff** *n infml*: ***this is ~*** (*very good*) è eccezionale; (*provocative*) sexy; ***she's / he's ~*** (*very good*) è una persona eccezionale; (*very sexy*) è molto sexy **hot-tempered** *adj* irascibile

hottie *n infml* figo *m*, figa *f infml*

hot water *n fig infml* pasticci *mpl*; ***he got into ~ over that*** si è messo nei pasticci per questo **hot-water bottle** *n* borsa *f* per l'acqua calda

hound I *n* segugio *m* **II** *v/t* perseguitare; ***be ~ed by the press*** essere perseguitato dai giornalisti

◆**hound out** *v/t sep* cacciare

hour *n* ora *f*; ***~s*** *pl of shops*, *pubs etc* orario *m*; ***half an ~*** *or* ***a half ~*** mezzora *f*; ***three-quarters of an ~*** tre quarti d'ora; ***a quarter of an ~*** un quarto d'ora; ***an ~ and a half*** un'ora e mezzo; ***for ~s*** (***and ~s***) per ore (ed ore); ***it's two ~s' walk*** sono due ore di cammino; ***at fifteen hundred ~s*** *infml* alle 15; ***on the ~*** ogni ora esatta; ***20 minutes past the ~*** 20 minuti dopo l'ora esatta; ***at all ~s*** (***of the day and night***) a tutte le ore (del giorno e della notte); ***what! at this ~ of the night!*** ma come! a quest'ora della notte!; ***drive at 50 kilometres an ~*** andare a 50 chilometri all'ora; ***be paid by the ~*** essere pagato all'ora; ***he took ~s to do it*** gli ci sono volute ore per farlo; ***the man / hero of the ~*** l'uomo / l'eroe del momento; ***out of / after ~s*** *in pubs*, *in office etc* fuori orario; ***work long ~s*** avere un lungo orario lavorativo

hourglass *n* clessidra *f*

hour hand *n* lancetta *f* delle ore

hourly I *adj pay*, *rate* orario, a ora; ***at ~ intervals*** ad ogni ora; ***an ~ bus service*** un servizio di autobus ogni ora; ***at ~ intervals*** a intervalli orari; ***~ wage*** *or* ***pay*** salario *m* orario; ***~ rate*** tariffa *f* oraria; ***on an ~ basis*** all'ora **II** *adv* ogni ora; *pay* all'ora

house I *n* casa *f*; POL camera *f*; THEAT sala *f*; *in boarding school* convitto *m*; ***at your ~*** a casa tua, da te; ***this one is on the ~*** questo lo offre la casa; ***keep ~*** (***for s.o.***) badare alla casa (di qn); ***they set up ~ together*** hanno messo su casa insieme; *fig* ***put*** *or* ***set one's ~ in order*** sistemare i propri affari; ***they get on like a ~ on fire*** *infml* andare d'amore e d'accordo; ***as safe as ~s*** *Br* sicuro come una fortezza; ***the upper / lower ~*** POL la camera alta / bassa; ***House of Commons / Lords*** *Br* Camera *f* dei comuni / dei lord; ***House of Representatives*** *US* Camera *f* dei Rappresentanti; ***the Houses of Parliament*** le camere del parlamento; ***bring the ~ down*** *infml* far crollare il teatro dagli applausi **II** *v/t* alloggiare; ***this building ~s ten families*** in questo edificio alloggiano dieci famiglie

house arrest *n* arresti *mpl* domiciliari

houseboat *n* house boat *f inv*

housebound *adj* costretto in casa

housebreaking *n* furto *m* con scasso

house-broken *adj US* abituato a vivere in casa

housecoat *n* vestaglia *f*

houseguest *n* ospite *m/f*

household *n* famiglia *f*

household name *n* nome *m* conosciuto

house husband *n* casalingo *m*

housekeeper *n* governante *f*

housekeeping *n activity* governo *m* della casa; *money* soldi *mpl* per le spese di casa

housemate *n Br* coinquilino *m*, -a *f*

house music *n* house music *f*

houseplant *n* pianta *f* da appartamento

house-proud *adj*: ***she is ~*** è orgogliosa della propria casa **house rules** *npl* regole *fpl* della casa **house-to-house** *adj* porta a porta **house-trained** *adj Br animal* abituato a vivere in casa
housewarming (party) *n festa per inaugurare la nuova casa*
housewife *n* casalinga *f*
house wine *n* vino *m* della casa
housework *n* lavori *mpl* domestici
housing *n* alloggi *mpl*; TECH alloggiamento *m*
housing association *n* cooperativa *f* edilizia **housing benefit** *n Br denaro concesso da un'autorità locale a persone a basso reddito per pagare l'affitto* **housing development, housing estate** *n* complesso *m* di case popolari
hovel *n* tugurio *m*
hover *v/i* librarsi; ***he was ~ing between life and death*** era sospeso tra la vita e la morte; ***the exchange rate is ~ing around 110 yen to the dollar*** il tasso di cambio si aggira intorno a 110 yen per dollaro; ***don't ~ over me*** non ronzarmi intorno
◆**hover about** *Br or* **around** *v/i* gironzolare; ***he was hovering around, waiting to speak to us*** gironzolava in attesa di parlare con noi
hovercraft *n* hovercraft *m inv*
how *adv* **1.** come; ***~ are you?*** come stai?; ***~ do you do?*** *form* piacere!; ***~ are things?*** *infml* come vanno le cose?; ***~ come?*** *infml* come mai?; ***~ do you mean?*** *infml* cosa intendi?; ***~ is it that we*** *or* ***~ come*** *infml* ***we earn less?*** come mai guadagniamo meno?; ***I'd like to learn ~ to swim*** mi piacerebbe imparare a nuotare; ***~ nice!*** che carino!; ***~ about going for a walk?*** che ne dici di una passeggiata?; ***I've had enough, ~ about you?*** ne ho avuto abbastanza, e tu?; ***and ~!*** eccome!; ***~ do you know?*** come fai a saperlo?; ***~ much?*** quanto?; ***~ much is it?*** *of cost* quant'è?; ***~ many?*** quanti?; ***~ often?*** ogni quanto?; ***I know ~ to do it*** so come si fa **2.** *in exclamations*: ***~ odd / lovely!*** che strano / bello!***~ he's grown!*** come è cresciuto!
however I *adv* comunque; ***~ big / rich they are*** per quanto grandi / ricchi siano; ***wait 30 minutes or ~ long it takes*** aspetta 30 minuti o per il tempo comunque necessario **II** *cj* in qualunque modo; ***~ you do it*** in qualunque modo tu lo faccia
howl I *n* urlo *m*; *of animal, wind* ululato *m*; ***~s of laughter*** risata *f* fragorosa; ***~s (of protest)*** grida *fpl* (di protesta) **II** *v/i of dog* ululare; *of person in pain* urlare; ***~ with laughter*** sbellicarsi dalle risate
howler *n mistake* strafalcione *m*; ***he made a real ~*** ha fatto un vero strafalcione
hp *abbr* (= **horse-power**) cv (cavallo *m* vapore)
HP *abbr* (= **hire purchase**) acquisto *m* rateale; ***buy sth on ~*** comprare qc a rate
HQ *abbr* (= **headquarters**) QG (quartier *m* generale)
hr *abbr* (= **hour**) h (ora)
HRH *abbr* (= **His / Her Royal Highness**) Sua Altezza Reale (S.A.R.)
HRT *abbr* (= **hormone replacement therapy**) trattamento *m* ormonale sostitutivo
HST *abbr* (= **Hawaiian Standard Time**) *US* ora *f* solare delle Hawaii
ht *abbr* (= **height**) altezza *f*
HTML *abbr* (= **hypertext mark-up language**) COMPUT HTML *m*
hub *n of wheel* mozzo *m*
hubbub *n* baraonda *f*; ***a ~ of voices*** una baraonda di voci
hubby *n infml* marito *m*
hubcap *n* coprimozzo *m*
hubris *n* arroganza *f*
huddle I *n* mucchio *m*; *of people* calca *f*; ***in a ~*** in mucchio **II** *v/i* (*a.* **to be huddled**) accalcarsi; ***they ~d under the umbrella*** si accalcarono sotto l'ombrello; ***we ~d around the fire*** ci siamo accalcati intorno al fuoco
◆**huddle together** *v/i* stringersi l'un l'altro
hue *n* tinta *f*
huff *n*: ***be in a ~*** essere imbronciato
huffy *adj* (*+er*) *infml* (*in a huff*) imbronciato; (*touchy*) permaloso; ***get / be ~ about sth*** imbronciarsi per qc *or* essere imbronciato per qc
hug I *v/t* ⟨*pret & past part* **-ged**⟩ abbracciare **II** *n* abbraccio *m*; ***give s.o. a ~*** abbracciare qn

huge *adj* (+*er*) enorme; ***a ~ job*** un compito enorme; ***~ numbers of these children*** enormi quantità di bambini
hugely *adv* immensamente; ***the whole thing is ~ enjoyable*** tutto ciò è immensamente divertente
hugger-mugger **I** *n* segretezza *f* **II** *adj* segreto; ***~ political deeds*** segrete azioni *fpl* politiche
hulk *n* NAUT carcassa *f*; *infml* (*person*) omaccione *m*
hulking *adj*: ***~ great*** *or* ***great ~*** enorme
hull[1] *n* NAUT scafo *m*
hull[2] **I** *n* guscio *m* **II** *v/t* sgusciare
hullabaloo *n* baccano *m*
hullo → ***hello***
hum ⟨*pret & past part* ***-med***⟩ **I** *v/t song*, *tune* canticchiare **II** *v/i of person* canticchiare; *of machine* ronzare; *fig infml* fervere; ***the headquarters was ~ming with activity*** il quartier generale ferveva di attività; ***~ and haw*** *infml* esitare nel parlare (***over, about*** di) **III** *n* ronzio *m*; *of voices* brusio *m*
human **I** *n* essere *m* umano **II** *adj* umano; ***~ error*** errore *m* umano; ***~ shield*** scudo *m* umano; ***I'm only ~*** sono un essere umano
human being *n* essere *m* umano
humane *adj* umano
humanely *adv treat* con umanità; *kill* umanamente
human interest *n in newspaper story etc* interesse *m* umano; ***a ~ story*** una storia di interesse umano
humanism *n* umanesimo *m*
humanitarian *adj* umanitario
humanity *n* umanità *f inv*; ***humanities*** *pl* studi *mpl* umanistici
humankind *n* genere *m* umano
humanly *adv* umanamente; ***as far as ~ possible*** per quanto umanamente possibile; ***do all that is ~ possible*** fare tutto ciò che è umanamente possibile
human nature *n* natura *f* umana; ***it's ~ to do that*** è nella natura umana farlo
human race *n* genere *m* umano
human resources *npl* risorse *fpl* umane
human rights *npl* diritti *mpl* dell'uomo
humble **I** *adj* (+*er*) *origins*, *person* umile; *house* modesto; ***my ~ apologies!*** chiedo umilmente scusa! **II** *v/t* umiliare; ***be / feel ~d*** venire / sentirsi umiliato
humble pie *n*: ***eat ~*** umiliarsi
humbug *n Br* (*sweet*) caramella *f* alla menta; *infml* (*talk*) ipocrisia *f*
humdinger *n infml* cannonata *f*; ***that meal was a real ~*** quel pasto è stato una vera cannonata
humdrum *adj* monotono
humid *adj* umido
humidifier *n* umidificatore *m*
humidity *n* umidità *f inv*
humiliate *v/t* umiliare
humiliating *adj* umiliante
humiliation *n* umiliazione *f*
humility *n* umiltà *f inv*
hummingbird *n* colibrì *m*
humor *US* → ***humour***
humorous *adj person* spiritoso; *story* umoristico
humour, *US* **humor** *n* umorismo *m*; (*mood*) umore *m*; ***sense of ~*** senso dell'umorismo
hump **I** *n of camel*, *person* gobba *f*; *on road* dosso *m*; *Br infml* ***he's got the ~*** ha la gobba **II** *v/t infml* (*carry*) portare; *vulg* fottere
humpbacked *adj bridge* curvo
hunch **I** *n* (*idea*) impressione *f*; *of detective* intuizione *f*; ***act on a ~*** agire in base a un'intuizione; ***your ~ paid off*** la tua intuizione ha dato buoni risultati **II** *v/t* (*a.* **hunch up**) ***~ one's shoulders*** piegare le spalle in avanti; ***he was ~ed over his desk*** era chinato sulla sua scrivania
hunchback *n* gibbosità *f*
hunchbacked *adj* gibboso
hundred *num* cento *m*; ***a ~ ...*** cento ...; ***~s of times*** centinaia di volte; ***~s and ~s*** centinaia e centinaia; ***~s of*** *or* ***and thousands*** confettini *mpl*; ***he earns nine ~ a month*** guadagna novecento sterline al mese; ***live to be a ~*** vivere fino a cent'anni; ***they came in their ~s*** *or* ***by the ~*** vennero a centinaia
hundredth *n/adj* centesimo, -a
hundredweight *n* cinquanta chili (*circa*)
hung *pret & past part* → ***hang***
Hungarian **I** *adj* ungherese **II** *n person* ungherese *m/f*; *language* ungherese *m*

Hungary *n* Ungheria *f*
hunger *n* fame *f*
◆**hunger after** *or* **for** *v/i +obj liter* agognare
hunger march *n* marcia *f* della fame
hunger strike *n* sciopero *m* della fame; ***be on*** (***a***) **~** fare lo sciopero della fame; ***go on*** (***a***) **~** iniziare lo sciopero della fame
hung-over *adj*: ***feel*** **~** avere i postumi della sbornia
hung parliament *n parlamento in cui nessuna parte riesce a raggiungere la maggioranza*; ***the election resulted in a*** **~** dalle elezioni è risultato un parlamento in cui nessuna parte riesce a raggiungere la maggioranza
hungrily *adv liter, fig* avidamente
hungry *adj* (*+er*) affamato; ***I'm*** **~** ho fame
hung-up *adj infml* infatuato; ***be / get*** **~** ***about sth*** essere infatuato / infatuarsi di qc; ***he's*** **~** ***on her*** *infml* è infatuato di lei
hunk *n* tocco *m*; *infml* (*man*) fusto *m infml*
hunky-dory *adj infml*: ***everything's*** **~** tutto va a meraviglia
hunt I *n for animals* caccia *f*; *for job, house, missing child* ricerca *f*; ***the*** **~** ***is on*** è aperta la caccia; ***have a*** **~** ***for sth*** cercare qc **II** *v/t animal* cacciare **III** *v/i* cacciare; ***go*** **~*ing*** andare a caccia; (*search*) cercare (***for, after*** qc); ***he is*** **~*ing for a job*** sta cercando lavoro
◆**hunt down** *v/t sep* perseguitare; (*capture*) dare la caccia a
◆**hunt out** *v/t sep* scovare
hunter *n* cacciatore *m*, -trice *f*
hunting *n* caccia *f*
hurdle *n a. fig* ostacolo *m*; *fig* ***fall at the first*** **~** cadere al primo ostacolo
hurdler *n* SPORTS ostacolista *m/f*
hurdles *npl* SPORTS: ***100 metres*** **~** i cento metri a ostacoli
hurl *v/t* scagliare; **~** ***insults at s.o.*** scagliare insulti contro qn
hurly-burly *n* trambusto *m*; ***the*** **~** ***of politics*** il trambusto della politica
hurrah *int*, **hurray** *int* urrà!
hurricane *n* uragano *m*
hurricane lamp *n* lanterna *f* controvento
hurried *adj* frettoloso
hurry I *n* fretta *f*; ***be in a*** **~** avere fretta; ***do sth in a*** **~** fare qc in fretta **II** *v/i* ⟨*pret & past part* **-ied**⟩ sbrigarsi **III** *v/t person* fare fretta a; *work etc* fare in fretta; (*do too quickly*) affrettare; ***don't*** **~** ***me*** non farmi fretta
◆**hurry along I** *v/i* affrettarsi; ***hurry along there, please!*** affrettati, per piacere! **II** *v/t sep person* sollecitare; *things, work etc* accelerare
◆**hurry up I** *v/i* sbrigarsi; ***hurry up!*** sbrigati! **II** *v/t sep* fare fretta a
hurt ⟨*pret & past part* **hurt**⟩ **I** *v/i* far male; ***does it*** **~*?*** ti fa male? **II** *v/t physically* far male a; *emotionally* ferire; **~** ***o.s.*** ferirsi; **~** ***one's knee*** farsi male al ginocchio **III** *n* dolore *m*; (*to feelings*) ferita (***to a***) **IV** *adj limb, feelings* ferito; *look* offeso
hurtful *adj* ingiurioso
hurtle *v/i* precipitarsi; ***the car was hurtling along*** la macchina divorava la strada; ***he came hurtling round the corner*** si precipitò dietro l'angolo; ***the river hurtles over the waterfall*** il fiume si precipita sulla cascata
husband I *n* marito *m*; ***my*** **~** mio marito; ***they are*** **~** ***and wife*** sono marito e moglie **II** *v/t resources* risparmiare
husbandry *n* (*farming*) agricoltura *f*
hush I *v/t person* far tacere **II** *v/i* tacere **III** *n* silenzio *m*; ***a*** **~** ***fell over the crowd*** scese il silenzio sulla folla **IV** *int*: **~*!*** silenzio!
◆**hush up** *v/t sep scandal etc* mettere a tacere
hushed *adj voices* sommesso; *crowd* tranquillo; *courtroom* silenzioso; ***in*** **~** ***tones*** in toni sommessi
hush-hush *adj infml* segretissimo
hush money *n infml* prezzo *m* del silenzio
husk *n* pula *f*
husky[1] *adj* (*+er*) *voice* roco
husky[2] *n* (*dog*) husky *m*
hussy *n* (*pert girl*) ragazza *f* sfacciata; (*whorish woman*) sgualdrina *f*
hustings *npl Br* campagna *f* elettorale
hustle I *n*: **~** ***and bustle*** trambusto *m* **II** *v/t person* spingere; **~** ***s.o. out of a building*** spingere qn fuori da un edificio
hut *n* capanno *m*
hutch *n* conigliera *f*
hyacinth *n* giacinto *m*
hybrid I *n plant, animal* ibrido *m* **II** *adj*

BOT, ZOOL ibrido; ~ ***vehicle*** veicolo *m* ibrido
hydrangea *n* BOT ortensia *f*
hydrant *n* idrante *m*
hydrate *v/t* idratare
hydraulic *adj* idraulico
hydraulics *nsg* idraulica *f*
hydrocarbon *n* idrocarburo *m*
hydrochloric acid *n* acido *m* cloridrico
hydroelectric *adj* idroelettrico
hydroelectric power station *n* centrale *f* idroelettrica
hydrofoil *n boat* aliscafo *m*
hydrogen *n* idrogeno *m*
hydrogen bomb *n* bomba *f* H
hyena *n* ZOOL iena *f*
hygiene *n* igiene *f*; ***personal*** ~ igiene *f* personale
hygienic *adj* igienico
hymen *n* ANAT imene *m*
hymn *n* inno *m* (sacro)
hymnal *n* innario *m*
hymn book *n* innario *m*
hype I *n infml* pubblicità *f inv*; ***media*** ~ pubblicità *f* dei media; ***all this ~ about …*** tutta questa pubblicità su … **II** *v/t* (*a.* **hype up**) *infml* pubblicizzare; ***the film was ~d up too much*** il film è stato eccessivamente pubblicizzato
hyperactive *adj* iperattivo
hyperbole *n* iperbole *f*
hyperbolic *adj* iperbolico
hypercritical *adj* ipercritico
hyperlink COMPUT **I** *n* collegamento *m* ipertestuale **II** *v/t* inserire un collegamento ipertestuale a
hypermarket *n* ipermercato *m*
hypersensitive *adj* ipersensibile
hypertension *n* ipertensione *f*
hypertext *n* COMPUT ipertesto *m*
hyperventilate *v/i* iperventilare
hyphen *n* trattino *m*
hyphenate *v/t* unire con un trattino; ***~d word*** parola *f* con trattino
hypnosis *n* ipnosi *f*; ***under ~*** sotto ipnosi
hypnotherapy *n* ipnoterapia *f*
hypnotic *adj trance* ipnotico; ~ ***state*** stato *m* ipnotico
hypnotise, hypnotize *v/t* ipnotizzare; ***be ~d by s.o. / sth*** restare ipnotizzato da qn / qc
hypnotism *n* ipnotismo *m*
hypo- *pref* ipo-; ***hypoallergenic*** ipoallergenico
hypochondria *n* ipocondria *f*
hypochondriac *n* ipocondriaco *m*, -a *f*
hypocrisy *n* ipocrisia *f*
hypocrite *n* ipocrita *m/f*
hypocritical *adj* ipocrita
hypothermia *n* ipotermia *f*
hypothesis *n* ⟨*pl* ***hypotheses***⟩ ipotesi *f inv*
hypothetical *adj* ipotetico
hysterectomy *n* isterectomia *f*
hysteria *n* isteria *f*
hysterical *adj person*, *laugh* isterico; *infml* (*very funny*) buffissimo; ***become ~*** avere una crisi isterica **hysterically** *adv* istericamente; ~ ***funny*** *infml* estremamente buffo
hysterics *npl laughter* attacco *m* di risa; ***have ~*** ridere come un matto; MED crisi *f inv* isterica
Hz *abbr* (= **hertz**) Hz (hertz)

I

I, i *n* i, I *f inv*; ***dot the i's and cross the t's*** *infml* mettere i puntini sulle i
I *pron* io; ~ ***am English*** sono inglese; ***you're crazy, ~'m not*** tu sei pazzo, io no; ***I'm not late, am I?*** non sono in ritardo, vero?
IAEA *abbr* (= **International Atomic Energy Agency**) agenzia *f* internazionale per l'energia atomica (IAEA)
IAS *abbr* (= **indicated air speed**) AVIAT velocità *f* indicata
IATA *abbr* (= **International Air Transport Association**) AVIAT associazione internazionale dei trasporti aerei (IATA)

I-beam *n* trave *f* a doppia T
ibid *abbr* (= **ibidem**) ibid. (ibidem)
IC *abbr* (= **integrated circuit**) circuito *m* integrato
ICA *abbr* **1.** (= **Institute of Contemporary Arts**) istituto *m* di arte contemporanea **2.** (= **International Cooperation Administration**) Alleanza Cooperativa Internazionale *f*
ice *n* ghiaccio *m*; *Br* (*ice cream*) ghiacciolo *m*; (*drug*) metanfetamine *fpl*; ***my hands are like ~*** ho le mani ghiacciate; *fig* ***break the ~*** rompere il ghiaccio; *fig* ***skating on thin ~*** camminare sul filo del rasoio; ***that cuts no ~ with me*** *infml* non mi fa nessun effetto
◆ **ice up** *v/i of engine*, *wings* ghiacciarsi
Ice Age *n* era *f* glaciale **ice axe**, *US* **ice ax** *n* piccozza *f*
iceberg *n* iceberg *m inv*; ***the tip of the ~*** la punta dell'iceberg
iceberg lettuce *n* insalata *f* iceberg
icebound *adj port*, *lake* ostruito dal ghiaccio; *ship*, *place* imprigionato dal ghiaccio **icebox** *n US* frigo *m* **icebreaker** *n ship* rompighiaccio *m inv* **ice bucket** *n* secchiello *m* del ghiaccio **ice cap** *n* (*polar*) calotta *f* di ghiaccio **ice-cold** *adj* freddissimo **ice-cool** *adj fig person* gelido **ice cream** *n* gelato *m* **ice cream parlour**, *US* **ice cream parlor** *n* gelateria *f* **ice cube** *n* cubetto *m* di ghiaccio
iced *adj drink* ghiacciato; *cake* glassato
iced coffee *n* caffè *m inv* freddo **iced tea** *n* tè *m inv* freddo
ice floe *n* ghiaccio *m* galleggiante **ice hockey** *n* hockey *m inv* sul ghiaccio
Iceland *n* Islanda *f*
Icelandic I *adj* islandese **II** *n language* islandese *m*
ice lolly *n* ghiacciolo *m* **ice pack** *n on head* impacco *m* di ghiaccio **ice pick** *n* rompighiaccio *m* **ice rink** *n* pista *f* di pattinaggio **ice skate** *v/i* pattinare (sul ghiaccio) **ice skating** *n* pattinaggio *m* (sul ghiaccio)
icicle *n* ghiacciolo *m*
icily *adv fig* gelidamente; *smile* freddamente
iciness *n* freddezza *f*
icing *n* COOK glassa *f*; ***this is the ~ on the cake*** *fig* è la ciliegina sulla torta
icing sugar *n* zucchero *m* a velo
icon *n* ART, REL icona *f*; *cultural* mito *m*; COMPUT icona *f*
iconic *adj*: ***an ~ figure*** un'icona
iconography *n* ART iconografia *f*
iconology *n* ART iconologia *f*
ICU *abbr* (= **intensive care unit**) reparto *m* di terapia intensiva
icy *adj* (*+er*) *road*, *surface* ghiacciato; *welcome* glaciale
I'd = ***I had***; ***I would***
ID *abbr* (= **identity**): ***have you got any ~ on you?*** ha un documento d'identità?
ID card *n* carta *f* d'identità
idea *n* idea *f*; ***good ~!*** ottima idea!; ***I have no ~*** non ne ho la minima idea; ***it's not a good ~ to …*** non è una buona idea …; ***hit upon the ~ of doing sth*** avere l'idea di fare qc; ***that gives me an ~, we could …*** questo mi fa venire un'idea, potremmo …; ***he got the ~ for his novel while having a bath*** l'idea per il suo romanzo gli è venuta mentre faceva il bagno; ***he's got the ~ into his head that …*** ha in mente l'idea che …; ***where did you get the ~ that I was ill?*** come ti è venuta l'idea che fossi malato?; ***don't you go getting ~s about promotion*** non farti venire delle idee su una promozione; ***that's the ~*** questo è il succo; ***you're getting the ~*** stai afferrando il concetto; ***if that's your ~ of fun*** se questo lo chiami divertimento; ***this isn't my ~ of a holiday*** non è la mia idea di vacanza; ***to give you an ~ of how difficult it is*** per darti un'idea di quanto sia difficile
ideal *adj* (*perfect*) ideale; ***it's not ~ but we'll take it*** non è l'ideale ma lo prendiamo lo stesso; ***in an ~ world*** in un mondo ideale
idealism *n* idealismo *m*
idealist *n* idealista *m/f*
idealistic *adj person* idealista; *views* idealistico
ideally *adv*: ***the hotel is ~ situated*** l'albergo si trova in una posizione ideale; ***~, we would do it like this*** l'ideale sarebbe farlo così
idée fixe *n* idea *f* fissa
identical *adj* identico; ***~ twins*** gemelli

mpl monozigotici; ***we have ~ views*** abbiamo opinioni identiche
identifiable *adj* riconoscibile; ***he is ~ by his red hair*** è riconoscibile dai capelli rossi
identification *n* identificazione *f*, riconoscimento *m*; *papers etc* documento *m* di riconoscimento *or* d'identità
identification parade *n* confronto *m* all'americana
identify ⟨*pret & past part* **-ied**⟩ **I** *v/t* (*recognize*) identificare, riconoscere; (*point out*) individuare **II** *v/i* (*with film hero etc*) identificarsi
Identikit® *n*: ~ (***picture***) identikit *m*
identity *n* identità *f inv*; ***~ card*** carta *f* d'identità; ***a case of mistaken ~*** uno scambio di persona
identity card *n* carta *f* d'identità **identity crisis** *n* crisi *f inv* d'identità **identity papers** *npl* documenti *mpl* di identità **identity parade** *n* confronto *m* all'americana
ideological *adj* ideologico
ideology *n* ideologia *f*
idiom *n* (*saying*) locuzione *f* idiomatica; (*language*) idioma *m*
idiomatic *adj* naturale; ***speak ~ Italian*** parlare in italiano corrente; ***an ~ expression*** una frase idiomatica
idiosyncrasy *n* piccola mania *f*
idiosyncratic *adj* peculiare
idiot *n* idiota *m/f*; ***what an ~ I am / was!*** che idiota che sono / sono stato!; ***feel like an ~*** sentirsi un idiota
idiotic *adj* idiota
idle I *adj person* disoccupato; *threat* vuoto; *machinery* inattivo; ***in an ~ moment*** in un momento libero; ***~ curiosity*** curiosità *f* oziosa **II** *v/i of engine* girare al minimo
◆ **idle away** *v/t sep the time etc* trascorrere oziando
idleness *n* (*state of not working*) inattività *f*; (*pleasurable*) ozio *m*; (*laziness*) pigrizia *f*
idler *n* fannullone *m*, -a *f*
idly *adv* (*without working*) pigramente; (*pleasurably*) oziosamente; ***stand ~ by*** starsene in ozio
idol *n* idolo *m*
idolatry *n liter* idolatria *f*; *fig* ammirazione *f* sconfinata
idolize *v/t* idolatrare
I'd've → ***I would have***
idyll *n* idillio *m*
idyllic *adj* idilli(a)co
i. e. *abbr* (= **id est**) ad es. (ad esempio)
if I *cj* se; ***~ I were you*** se fossi in te; ***~ so*** in qual caso; ***he asked ~ you could help*** ha chiesto se potevi aiutare; ***~ only you had told me*** se (solo) me l'avessi detto; ***even if they are poor, at least they are happy*** anche se sono poveri, sono almeno felici; ***it's not as if I meant to hurt her*** non è che io le abbia fatto del male; ***if necessary*** se necessario; ***if I know Pete, he'll ...*** per quanto lo conosco, Pete ...; ***well, if it isn't old Jim!*** *infml* guarda, il vecchio John **II** *n*: ***ifs and buts*** i se e i ma
iffy *adj infml* dubbio
igloo *n* igloo *m*
ignite *v/t* dar fuoco a
ignition *n in car* accensione *f*; ***~ key*** chiave *f* dell'accensione
ignoble *adj* ignobile
ignominious *adj* vergognoso
ignoramus *n* ignorante *m/f*
ignorance *n* ignoranza *f*; ***keep s.o. in ~ of sth*** tenere qn all'oscuro di qc
ignorant *adj* (*rude*) cafone; ***be ~ of sth*** ignorare qc
ignore *v/t* ignorare
ikon *n* → ***icon***
ilk *n*: ***people of that ~*** le persone di quello stampo
ill I *adj* ammalato; ***fall ~, be taken ~*** ammalarsi; ***feel ~*** sentirsi male; ***look ~*** avere una brutta cera; ***feel ~ at ease*** sentirsi a disagio; ***I don't bear them any ~ will*** non gli porto alcun rancore; ***due to ~ health*** per problemi di salute **II** *n*: ***ills*** *pl* mali *mpl* **III** *adv* male; ***bode ~*** *form* essere di cattivo augurio; ***speak ~ of s.o.*** *form* parlar male di qn
I'll = ***I will***; ***I shall***
ill-advised *adj* imprudente; ***you would be ~ to trust her*** saresti imprudente a fidarti di lei **ill-at-ease** *adj* a disagio **ill-conceived** *adj plan* mal concepito **ill-disposed** *adj*: ***be ~ to(wards) s.o.*** essere maldisposto verso qn
illegal *adj* illegale
illegality *n* illegalità *f*
illegally *adv* (*against the law*) illegalmente; ***~ imported*** importato illegal-

mente; ***they were convicted of ~ possessing a handgun*** sono stati condannati per possesso illegale di armi

illegible *adj* illeggibile

illegitimacy *n of child* illegittimità *f*

illegitimate *adj child* illegittimo

ill-fated *adj* sfortunato **ill-favoured** *adj* brutto **ill feeling** *n* risentimento *m* **ill-fitting** *adj clothes* che veste male; *dentures* inadatto; *shoes* che calza male **ill-gotten gains** *npl* guadagni *mpl* disonesti

illiberal *adj* illiberale

illicit *adj copy, imports* illegale; *pleasure, relationship* illecito

illiterate I *adj* analfabeta; ***many people are computer-~*** molti non conoscono il computer **II** *n* analfabeta *m/f*

ill-judged *adj* sconsiderato **ill-mannered** *adj* maleducato **ill-matched** *adj* mal assortito; ***they're ~*** sono mal assortiti **ill-natured** *adj* d'indole cattiva

illness *n* malattia *f*

illogical *adj* illogico

ill-tempered *adj* irascibile **ill-timed** *adj* inopportuno **ill-treat** *v/t* maltrattare

illuminate *v/t building etc* illuminare; *fig subject* illustrare; *manuscript* chiarire

illuminating *adj remarks etc* chiarificatore

illumination *n* illuminazione *f*

illuminations *npl* luci *fpl*

illusion *n* illusione *f*; ***have no ~s*** non farsi illusioni; ***be under the ~ that ...*** illudersi che ...; ***it gives the ~ of space*** dà l'illusione dello spazio

illusory *adj* illusorio

illustrate *v/t* illustrare; ***his lecture was ~d by coloured slides*** la sua lezione era illustrata da diapositive a colori; ***~d (magazine)*** rivista *f* illustrata

illustration *n* (*picture*) illustrazione *f*; *with examples* esemplificazione *f*

illustrative *adj* chiarificatore; ***~ of*** che illustra...

illustrator *n* illustratore *m*, -trice *f*

illustrious *adj* illustre; *person* insigne

ill will *n* rancore *m*

I'm = ***I am***

image *n* immagine *f*; (*exact likeness*) ritratto *m*; ***he is the ~ of his father*** è il ritratto di suo padre; ***brand ~*** immagine *f* di marca

image-conscious *adj* attento all'immagine **image converter** *n* convertitore *m* di immagini **image intensifier** *n* amplificatore *m* di immagini **image maker** *n* creatore *m*, -trice *f* di immagine

imagery *n* immagini *fpl*; ***visual ~*** immagini *fpl* visive

imaginable *adj* immaginabile; ***the biggest / smallest size ~*** la misura più grande / piccola che si possa immaginare

imaginary *adj* immaginario; ***~ world*** mondo *m* immaginario

imagination *n* immaginazione *f*, fantasia *f*; ***it's all in your ~*** è tutto frutto della tua immaginazione

imaginative *adj* fantasioso

imagine I *v/t* immaginare; ***I can just ~ it*** me l'immagino; ***I can't ~ living there*** non posso immaginare di vivere là; ***you're imagining things*** è frutto della tua immaginazione **II** *v/i* immaginare; ***I ~ so*** immagino di sì; ***just ~!*** pensa!

imbalance *n* squilibrio *m*

imbecile *n* ebete *m/f*

imbibe *v/t* assorbire

imbue *v/t fig* impregnare

IMF *abbr* (= **International Monetary Fund**) FMI *m* (Fondo *m* Monetario Internazionale)

imitate *v/t* imitare

imitation I *n* imitazione *f*; ***learn by ~*** imparare copiando **II** *adj* finto; ***~ leather*** finta pelle *f*; ***~ jewellery*** bigiotteria *f*

immaculate *adj* immacolato

immaterial *adj* (*not relevant*) irrilevante; ***that's (quite) ~*** è (del tutto) irrilevante

immature *adj* immaturo

immaturity *n* immaturità *f*

immediacy *n* immediatezza *f*; (*urgency*) prontezza *f*

immediate *adj* immediato; ***the ~ family*** i familiari più stretti; ***the ~ problem*** il problema più immediato; ***in the ~ neighbourhood*** nelle immediate vicinanze; ***my ~ concern was for the children*** il mio primo pensiero sono stati i bambini

immediately I *adv* immediatamente; **~ after the bank / church** subito dopo la banca / chiesa II *cj* non appena; **~ you said that** non appena l'hai detto
immemorial *adj* immemorabile; **from time ~** da tempo immemorabile
immense *adj* immenso
immerse *v/t* immergere; **~ o.s. in** immergersi in; **~ sth in water** immergere qc in acqua; *fig* **~ o.s. in one's work** immergersi nel lavoro
immersion heater *n* scaldabagno *m* elettrico
immigrant I *n* immigrato *m*, -a *f* II **the ~ community** la comunità degli immigrati
immigrate *v/i* immigrare
immigration *n act* immigrazione *f*; **Immigration** *government department* ufficio *m* stranieri
imminent *adj* imminente
immobile *adj* immobile; (*not able to move*) fisso
immobilism *n* immobilismo *m*
immobilize *v/t factory, person, car* immobilizzare; **be ~d by fear / pain** restare immobilizzato dalla paura / dal dolore
immobilizer *n on car* immobilizzatore *m*
immoderate *adj* smodato
immodest *adj* immodesto (*indecent*) indecoroso
immoral *adj* immorale
immorality *n* immoralità *f inv*
immortal I *adj* immortale II *n* essere *m* immortale
immortalise, immortalize *v/t* rendere immortale
immortality *n* immortalità *f inv*
immovable *adj liter* immobile; *fig obstacle* irremovibile
immune *adj to illness, infection* immune; *from ruling, requirement* esente; **~ from prosecution** non perseguibile
immune system *n* MED sistema *m* immunitario
immunity *n to infection* immunità *f inv*; *from ruling* esenzione *f*; **diplomatic ~** immunità *f inv* diplomatica; **~ from prosecution** immunità *f* legale
immunology *n* MED immunologia *f*
immunosuppressive *adj* antirigetto
imp *n* folletto *m*; *infml* (*child*) monello *m*, -a *f*
impact *n of meteorite, vehicle* urto *m*; *of new manager etc* impatto *m*; (*effect*) effetto *m*; **make an ~ on** avere un impatto su
impair *v/t* danneggiare
impaired *adj* danneggiato
impairment *n* menomazione *f*; **visual ~** menomazione *f* visiva
impale *v/t* trafiggere (**on** con)
impalpable *adj* impalpabile
impart *v/t form* conferire; *information* comunicare; *knowledge* trasmettere
impartial *adj* imparziale
impartiality *n* imparziale
impartially *adv act* imparzialmente; *judge* in modo equanime
impassable *adj road* impraticabile
impasse *n in negotations etc* impasse *m inv*
impassible *adj* imperturbabile
impassioned *adj speech, plea* appassionato
impassive *adj* impassibile
impatience *n* impazienza *f*
impatient *adj* impaziente; **be ~ to do sth** essere impaziente di fare qc
impatiently *adv* con impazienza
impeach *v/t President* mettere in stato d'accusa
impeachment *n* JUR incriminazione *f*; *US of president* impeachment *m*
impeccable *adj* impeccabile
impeccably *adv* impeccabilmente
impecunious *adj* squattrinato
impede *v/t* ostacolare
impediment *n in speech* difetto *m*
impel *v/t*: **~ s.o. to do sth** spingere qn a fare qc; **I felt ~led to speak my mind** mi sentivo obbligato a dire la mia opinione
impending *adj* imminente; **a sense of ~ doom** un tragico presentimento
impenetrable *adj* impenetrabile
impenitent *adj* impenitente
imperative I *adj* essenziale II *n* GRAM imperativo *m*; **in the ~** all'imperativo
imperceptible *adj* impercettibile
imperceptibly *adv* impercettibilmente
imperfect I *adj* imperfetto II *n* GRAM imperfetto *m*
imperfection *n* imperfezione *f*
imperial *adj* imperiale
imperialism *n* imperialismo *m*

imperial system *n* sistema *m* imperiale
imperil *v/t* mettere in pericolo
imperious *adj* autoritario; ***his manner is horribly ~*** i suoi modi sono terribilmente autoritari
imperishable *adj* indistruttibile
impermanent *adj* transitorio
impermeable *adj* impermeabile
impersonal *adj* impersonale
impersonate *v/t as a joke* imitare; *illegally* fingersi
impersonation *n* imitazione *f*; ***he does ~s of politicians*** fa imitazioni dei politici; ***his Elvis ~*** la sua imitazione di Elvis
impersonator *n* imitatore *m*, -trice *f*
impertinence *n* impertinenza *f*
impertinent *adj* impertinente
imperturbable *adj* imperturbabile; ***he is completely ~*** è assolutamente imperturbabile
impervious *adj*: ***~ to*** indifferente a; ***~ to water*** impenetrabile dall'acqua
impetuous *adj* impetuoso
impetus *n of campaign etc* impeto *m*
impiety *n* empietà *f*
impinge *v/i* influire (***on*** su); *on s.o.'s rights* ledere (***on*** qc)
impious *adj* empio
impish *adj* birichino
implacable *adj* inesorabile
implacably *adv* inesorabilmente
implant **I** *v/t* MED impiantare; *fig* inculcare (***in s.o.*** in qn) **II** *n* impianto *m*
implausible *adj* non plausibile
implement **I** *n* utensile *m* **II** *v/t* implementare; *measures* attuare, implementare
implementation *n of law* attuazione *f*; *of plan* implementazione *f*
implicate *v/t* implicare; ***~ s.o. in sth*** implicare qn in qc
implication *n* conseguenza *f* possibile; ***by ~*** implicitamente
implicit *adj* implicito; *trust* assoluto; *threat* tacito; ***be ~ in sth*** essere implicito in qc
implicitly *adv* implicitamente; ***trust s.o. ~*** fidarsi di qn senza riserve
implode *v/i* implodere
implore *v/t* implorare
imply *v/i* ⟨*pret & past part* ***-ied***⟩ implicare; ***are you ~ing I was lying?*** stai insinuando che ho mentito?
impolite *adj* maleducato
import **I** *n* importazione *f*; *item* articolo *m* d'importazione **II** *v/t* importare
importance *n* importanza *f*; ***be of great ~*** essere di estrema importanza; ***attach the greatest ~ to sth*** attribuire la massima importanza a qc
important *adj* importante; ***the most ~ thing is that ...*** la cosa più importante è che ...; ***this is very ~ to me*** questo per me è molto importante
importantly *adv usu pej* (*self-importantly*) con importanza; ***... and, more ~, ...*** e, ancora più importante, ...
importation *n* importazione *f*
import duty *n* dazio *m* d'importazione
importer *n* importatore *m*, -trice *f*
importunate *adj* importuno
importune *v/t* importunare
impose *v/t tax* imporre; ***~ o.s. on s.o.*** disturbare qn
imposing *adj* imponente
imposition *n* imposizione *f*; ***I'd love to stay if it's not too much of an ~ (on you)*** mi piacerebbe restare, se non è chiedere troppo
impossibility *n* impossibilità *f inv*
impossible **I** *adj* impossibile; ***it is ~ for me to come*** mi è impossibile venire; ***this cooker is ~ to clean*** questo fornello è impossibile da pulire; ***make it ~ for s.o. to do sth*** mettere qn nell'impossibilità di fare qc; *situation* impossibile; ***an ~ choice*** una scelta impossibile; ***you put me in an ~ position*** mi metti in una posizione impossibile; *infml person* impossibile **II** *n* impossibile *m*; ***do the ~*** fare l'impossibile
impostor *n* impostore *m*, -a *f*
impotence *n* impotenza *f*
impotent *adj* impotente
impoverish *v/t* impoverire
impoverished *adj* impoverito
impracticable *adj* inattuabile
impractical *adj person* senza senso pratico; *suggestion* poco pratico
imprecate *v/t* imprecare contro
imprecation *n* imprecazione *f*
imprecise *adj* impreciso
impregnable *adj* MIL *fortress* inespugnabile; *fig position* inattaccabile
impregnate *v/t* BIOL fecondare
impress *v/t* fare colpo su; ***be ~ed by s.o./sth*** essere colpito da qn/qc;

$ 500 an hour? – I'm ~ed 500 dollari all'ora? – però; ***terrible work, I'm not ~ed*** pessimo lavoro, vergogna
impression *n* **1.** impressione *f*; ***make a good / bad ~ on s.o.*** fare buona / cattiva impressione su qn; ***I get the ~ that …*** ho l'impressione che …; ***be under the ~ that …*** avere l'impressione che …; ***I don't want to give you the wrong ~*** non vorrei ti facessi un'idea sbagliata **2.** (*impersonation*) imitazione *f*; ***do an ~ of s.o.*** fare l'imitazione di qn
impressionable *adj* impressionabile; ***at an ~ age*** a un'età impressionabile
impressionism *n* impressionismo *m*
impressionist *n* impressionista *m/f*; (*impersonator*) imitatore *m*, -trice *f*
impressive *adj* notevole
imprint I *n of credit card* impressione *f* **II** *v/t fig* imprimere (***on s.o.*** in qn); ***be ~ed on s.o.'s mind*** essere impresso nella mente di qn
imprison *v/t* incarcerare
imprisonment *n* carcerazione *f*; ***15 years' ~*** 15 anni di carcere *or* reclusione
improbable *adj* improbabile
impromptu *adj* improvvisato
improper *adj behaviour* sconveniente; *use* improprio
impropriety *n* sconvenienza *f*; ***financial ~*** irregolarità *f* finanziaria
improve *v/t & v/i* migliorare; *knowledge* perfezionare; *appearance* migliorare; *production* aumentare; ***~ one's mind*** sviluppare la mente; ***the invalid is improving*** le condizioni dell'invalido stanno migliorando; ***things are improving*** le cose stanno migliorando
improvement *n* miglioramento *m*; ***a slight ~ in the weather*** un lieve miglioramento del tempo
improvident *adj* incauto
improvisation *n* improvvisazione *f*
improvise *v/i* improvvisare
imprudent *adj* incauto
imprudently *adv* incautamente
impudence *n* impudenza *f*
impudent *adj* impudente
impulse *n* impulso *m*; ***do sth on an ~*** fare qc d'impulso
impulse buy *n* acquisto *m* d'impulso
impulsive *adj* impulsivo
impunity *n*: ***with ~*** impunemente
impure *adj* impuro
impurity *n* impurità *f*
in I *prep* **1.** *place, position*: ***~ Birmingham / Milan*** a Birmingham / Milano; ***~ the street*** per strada; ***~ the box*** nella scatola; ***put it ~ your pocket*** mettitelo in tasca; ***wounded ~ the leg / arm*** ferito alla gamba / al braccio; ***~ his first novel*** nel suo primo romanzo **2.** *time*: ***~ 2006*** nel 2006; ***~ two hours*** *from now* tra due ore; *over period of* in due ore; ***~ the morning*** la mattina; ***~ the summer*** d'estate; ***~ September*** a *or* in settembre; ***~ the daytime*** di giorno; ***~ those days*** a quel tempo; ***she is ~ her thirties*** ha tra i trenta e i quarant'anni; ***~ old age*** nella vecchiaia; ***~ my childhood*** da bambino; ***she did it ~ three hours*** ha finito in tre ore; ***~ a week('s time)*** in una settimana; ***I haven't seen him ~ years*** non lo vedo da anni **3.** *manner*: ***~ English / Italian*** in inglese / italiano; ***~ a loud voice*** a voce alta; ***~ his style*** nel suo stile; ***~ yellow*** di giallo; ***pay ~ dollars*** pagare in dollari; ***~ this way*** in questo modo; ***she squealed ~ delight*** gridò di gioia; ***live ~ luxury*** vivere nel lusso; ***~ his shirt*** in camicia; ***dressed ~ white*** vestito di bianco; ***write ~ ink*** scrivere con l'inchiostro; ***a rise ~ prices*** un aumento dei prezzi; ***ten feet ~ height*** dieci piedi (tre metri) di altezza; ***the latest thing ~ hats*** l'ultima moda in fatto di cappelli **4.** ***~ crossing the road*** (*while*) mentre attraversava la strada; ***~ agreeing to this*** (*by virtue of*) accettando questo **5.** ***~ Dante*** in Dante **6.** ***three ~ all*** tre in tutto **7.** *ratio*: ***one ~ ten*** uno su dieci; ***one book ~ ten*** un libro su dieci; ***one ~ five children*** un bambino su cinque; ***a tax of twenty pence ~ the pound*** una tassa del 20 % **8.** (*occupation*) ***he is ~ the army*** è nell'esercito; ***he is ~ banking*** lavora nel settore bancario **II** *adv*: ***be ~*** *at home* essere a casa; *in the building etc* esserci; *arrived*: *of train* essere arrivato; *in its position* essere dentro; ***is she ~?*** c'è?; ***~ here / there*** qui / lì (dentro); ***there is nobody ~*** non c'è nessuno; ***the tide is ~*** si è alzata la marea; ***he's ~ for a surprise*** avrà una sorpre-

sa; ***we are ~ for rain*** andiamo incontro alla pioggia; ***have it ~ for s.o.*** *infml* avercela con qn; ***be ~ on sth*** essere coinvolto in qc **III** *adj* (*fashionable*, *popular*) in, di moda; ***long skirts are ~*** le gonne lunghe sono di moda; ***the ~ thing is to ...*** è di moda... **IV** *n*: ***the ~s and outs*** i retroscena; ***know the ~s and outs of sth*** conoscere i retroscena di qc

inability *n* incapacità *f inv*; ***~ to pay*** impossibilità *f* di pagare

inaccessible *adj* inaccessibile *fig music*, *novel* incomprensibile; ***be ~ by land / sea*** essere inaccessibile dal mare / da terra

inaccuracy *n* imprecisione *f*; (*incorrectness*) inesattezza *f*

inaccurate *adj* inaccurato

inaction *n* inattività *f*

inactive *adj* inattivo

inadequacy *n* inadeguatezza *f*; *of measures* insufficienza *f*

inadequate *adj* inadeguato; ***she makes him feel ~*** lo fa sentire inadeguato

inadmissible *adj* inammissibile

inadvertent *adj* involontario

inadvertently *adv* involontariamente

inadvisable *adj* sconsigliabile

inane *adj* idiota

inanimate *adj* inanimato

inanity *n* sciocchezza *f*

inappropriate *adj* inappropriato; ***you have come at a most ~ time*** sei arrivato nel momento più inappropriato

inarticulate *adj* che si esprime male

inasmuch *adv*: ***~ as*** visto che; (*to the extent that*) nella misura in cui

inattention *n* disattenzione *f*; ***~ to detail*** disattenzione per i dettagli

inattentive *adj* disattento

inaudible *adj* impercettibile

inaugural *adj speech* inaugurale

inaugurate *v/t* inaugurare

inauguration *n of president etc* insediamento *m* in carica; *of building* inaugurazione *f*

inauspicious *adj* infausto; ***get off to an ~ start*** (*campaign*) avere un inizio sfortunato

in-between *adj infml* intermedio; ***it is sort of ~*** è una specie di via di mezzo; ***~ stage*** fase *f* intermedia

inborn *adj* innato

inbound *adj flight* diretto verso l'interno

inbox *n e-mail* posta *f* in arrivo

inbred *adj* innato (***in s.o.*** in qn)

inbreeding *n* unioni *fpl* tra consanguinei

inbuilt *adj safety features etc* strutturale; *dislike* radicato

inc. *abbr* (= **incorporated**) *US* S.p.a (società *f* per azioni)

incalculable *adj damage* incalcolabile

incandescent *adj liter* incandescente

incantation *n* incantesimo *m*

incapability *n* incapacità *f*

incapable *adj* incapace; ***be ~ of doing sth*** essere incapace di fare qc; ***she is physically ~ of lifting it*** è fisicamente incapace di sollevarlo; ***~ of working*** incapace di lavorare

incapacitate *v/t* rendere incapace (***from doing sth*** di fare qc)

incapacitated *adj* inabile; ***~ by his broken ankle*** impedito dalla caviglia rotta

incapacity *n* inabilità *f* (**for** a)

incapacity benefit *n Br* indennità *f* di inabilità

incarcerate *v/t* incarcerare

incarceration *n* (*act*) incarcerazione *f*; (*period*) detenzione *f*

incarnate *adj*: ***he's the devil ~*** è il diavolo in persona

incautious *adj* incauto

incautiously *adv* incautamente

incendiary *adj* incendiario

incendiary device *n* ordigno *m* incendiario

incense[1] *n* incenso *m*

incense[2] *v/t* fare infuriare

incentive *n* incentivo *m*; ***~ scheme*** schema *m* di incentivi

inception *n* inizio *m*

incessant *adj* incessante

incessantly *adv* incessantemente

incest *n* incesto *m*

incestuous *adj* incestuoso

inch I *n* pollice *m*; ***5 ~ disk*** disco *m* da 3,5 pollici; ***he came within an ~ of being killed*** fu a un passo dal restare ucciso; ***they beat him (to) within an ~ of his life*** l'hanno picchiato fin quasi ad ucciderlo; ***the lorry missed me by ~es*** il camion mi ha mancato per un pelo; ***he knows every ~ of the area***

conosce la zona centimetro per centimetro; ***he is every ~ a soldier*** è un soldato da capo a piedi; ***they searched every ~ of the room*** hanno perquisito la stanza centimetro per centimetro **II** *v/i*: ***~ forward*** avanzare lentamente **III** *v/t* spostare lentamente; ***he ~ed his way through*** avanzò lentamente attraverso
incidence *n* incidenza *f*; ***a high ~ of crime*** l'alta incidenza di crimini
incident *n* incidente *m*
incidental *adj* casuale; ***~ expenses*** spese accessorie
incidentally *adv* (*by the way*) a proposito
incidental music *n* THEAT musica *f* di scena; FILM colonna *f* sonora
incinerate *v/t* incenerire
incineration *n* incenerimento *m*
incinerator *n* inceneritore *m*
incision *n* incisione *f*
incisive *adj mind*, *analysis* acuto
incite *v/t* incitare; ***~ s.o. to do sth*** istigare qn a fare qc
incl *abbr* (= **inclusive(ly)**, **including**) incluso
inclement *adj weather* inclemente
inclination *n tendency*, *liking* inclinazione *f*; ***my (natural) ~ is to carry on*** il mio impulso è quello di continuare; ***I have no ~ to see him again*** non ho nessuna voglia di rivederlo; ***he showed no ~ to leave*** non mostrò alcuna voglia di andarsene
incline I *v/t*: ***be ~d to believe sth*** essere propenso a credere qc; ***be ~d to do sth*** avere la tendenza di fare qc; ***if you're that way ~d*** se sei così poco propenso; ***artistically ~d*** incline all'arte **II** *v/i slope*, *ground* pendere; (*tend towards*) propendere verso **III** *n* inclinazione *f*; *of hill* pendenza *f*
inclose, inclosure → ***enclose***, ***enclosure***
include *v/t* includere, comprendere; ***all ~d*** tutto compreso; ***your name is not ~d on the list*** il tuo nome non è incluso nell'elenco; ***service not ~d*** servizio escluso; ***does that ~ me?*** riguarda anche me?
including *prep* compreso, incluso
inclusion *n* inclusione *f*
inclusive I *adj price* tutto compreso **II** *prep*: ***~ of VAT*** IVA compresa **III** *adv*: ***from Monday to Thursday ~*** dal lunedì al giovedì compreso
incognito *adv* in incognito
incoherent *adj* incoerente
income *n* reddito *m*; ***low-~ families*** famiglie *fpl* a basso reddito
income bracket *n* fascia *f* di reddito
income support *n Br sussidio governativo britannico paragonabile al reddito di ultima istanza* **income tax** *n* imposta *f* sul reddito
incoming *adj flight*, *phonecall*, *mail* in arrivo; *tide* montante; *president* entrante
incommunicado *adj* segregato
incomparable *adj* incomparabile
incompatibility *n* incompatibilità *f inv*; ***divorce on grounds of ~*** divorzio *m* per incompatibilità
incompatible *adj* incompatibile
incompetence *n* incompetenza *f*
incompetent *adj* incompetente
incomplete *adj* incompleto
incomprehensible *adj* incomprensibile
inconceivable *adj* inconcepibile; ***it is ~ to me that*** per me è inconcepibile che
inconclusive *adj* inconcludente
incongruity *n of remark*, *presence* incongruenza *f*; *of situation* inopportunità *f*; *of behaviour* incoerenza *f*
incongruous *adj* fuori luogo
inconsequential *adj* irrilevante
inconsiderable *adj* insignificante
inconsiderate *adj* poco gentile
inconsistency *n* incoerenza *f*; (*contradiction*) contraddizione *f*
inconsistent *adj* incoerente
inconsolable *adj* inconsolabile
inconspicuous *adj* poco visibile; ***make o.s. ~*** passare inosservato
inconstancy *n* incostanza *f*
inconstant *adj* incostante
incontinence *n* MED incontinenza *f*
incontinent *adj* incontinente
incontrovertible *adj* incontrovertibile; *evidence* inconfutabile
inconvenience I *n* inconveniente *m*; ***put s.o. to ~, be an ~ to s.o.*** disturbare qn; ***it was something of an ~ not having a car*** è stato un inconveniente non avere una macchina; ***I don't want to cause you any ~*** non voglio causarti inconvenienti **II**

v/t disturbare; ***I don't want to ~ you in any way*** non voglio assolutamente disturbarti; ***don't ~ yourself*** non ti disturbare
inconvenient *adj* scomodo; *time* poco opportuno
inconveniently *adv* in modo poco opportuno
inconvertible *adj* immutabile
incorporate *v/t* includere
incorporated *adj US*: ***ABC ~*** ABC S.p. a.
incorrect *adj answer* errato; *behaviour* scorretto; ***am I ~ in thinking …?*** sbaglio a pensare che …?
incorrectly *adv* in modo errato
incorrigible *adj* incorreggibile
incorruptible *adj person* integerrimo; (*not bribable*) incorruttibile; (*not subject to decay*) inalterabile
increase I *v/t & v/i* aumentare; ***~ in price*** aumentare di prezzo; ***industrial output ~d by 2% last year*** l'anno scorso la produzione industriale è aumentata del 2%; ***he ~d his efforts*** ha incrementato i suoi sforzi; ***they ~d her salary by £2,000*** le hanno aumentato lo stipendio di 2.000 sterline **II** *n* aumento *m*; ***on the ~*** in aumento; ***get an ~ of £5 per week*** ottenere un aumento di 5 sterline alla settimana; ***~ in value*** aumento *m* di valore; ***rent ~*** aumento *m* dell'affitto
increasing *adj* crescente
increasingly *adv* sempre più
incredible *adj* (*amazing, very good*) incredibile
incredibly *adv* incredibilmente; ***~, he wasn't there*** incredibilmente, non c'era; ***it was an ~ stupid thing to do*** è stata una cosa incredibilmente stupida da fare
incredulity *n* incredulità *f*
incredulous *adj* incredulo
increment *n* incremento *m*
incremental *adj Br* incrementale; ***~ costs*** costi *mpl* incrementali
incriminate *v/t* compromettere; ***~ o.s.*** compromettersi
incriminating *adj* incriminante
in-crowd *n infml* élite *f*
incubate I *v/t egg* covare; *bacteria* mantenere in incubazione **II** *v/i* essere in incubazione
incubation *n of egg* cova *f*; *of bacteria* incubazione *f*
incubator *n* incubatrice *f*
inculcate *v/t* inculcare
inculpable *adj* privo di colpa
incumbency *n* permanenza *f* in carica
incumbent *form* **I** *adj*: ***be ~ upon s.o.*** toccare a qn **II** *n* titolare *m/f* (di una carica)
incur *v/t* ⟨*pret & past part* ***-red***⟩ *costs* affrontare; *debts* contrarre; *s.o.'s anger* esporsi a; *expenses* andare incontro a; ***~ the wrath of s.o.*** attirare la collera d qn
incurable *adj* incurabile
incursion *n* incursione *f* (*into* in)
indebted *adj*: ***be ~ to s.o.*** essere (molto) obbligato a qn
indebtedness *n fig* l'essere in debito (***to*** con); FIN debiti *mpl*
indecency *n* indecenza *f*
indecent *adj* indecente; *joke* osceno; *amount* esagerato; ***with ~ haste*** con fretta esagerata
indecent assault *n* molestie *fpl* sessuali **indecent exposure** *n* esibizionismo *m*
indecently *adv* in modo indecente; ***behave ~*** comportarsi in modo indecente
indecipherable *adj* indecifrabile
indecisive *adj* indeciso
indecisiveness *n* indecisione *f*
indecorous *adj* disdicevole
indecorum *n* condotta *f* indecorosa
indeed *adv* (*in fact*) in effetti; ***I feel, ~ I know he is right*** sento, anzi so, che ha ragione; (*yes, agreeing*) esatto; ***isn't that strange? — ~ (it is)*** non è strano? in effetti (lo è); ***are you coming? — ~ I am!*** vieni? davvero!; ***are you pleased? — yes, ~!*** sei contento? sì!; ***if ~ …*** se davvero; ***very much ~*** moltissimo; ***thank you very much ~*** grazie mille
indefatigable *adj* instancabile
indefatigably *adv* instancabilmente
indefensible *adj behaviour etc* imperdonabile; *policy* indifendibile; ***morally ~*** moralmente imperdonabile
indefinable *adj* indefinibile
indefinite *adj* indeterminato; ***~ article*** GRAM articolo *m* indeterminativo
indefinitely *adv* a tempo indeterminato; ***we can't go on like this ~*** non possiamo andare avanti così a tempo

indeterminato

indelible *adj* incancellabile; *fig impression* indelebile

indelicate *adj* indelicato

indent I *n in text* rientro *m* a margine II *v/t line* rientrare il margine di

indentation *n in edge* dentellatura *f*; TYPO capoverso *m*

independence *n* indipendenza *f*; ***gain*** *or* ***achieve / declare ~*** ottenere *or* raggiungere / dichiarare l'indipendenza

Independence Day *n 4 luglio, anniversario dell'indipendenza americana*

independent *adj* indipendente

independently *adv* indipendentemente; ***~ of*** indipendentemente da; ***they each came ~ to the same conclusion*** sono giunti alla stessa conclusione indipendentemente l'uno dall'altro

in-depth *adj* approfondito

indescribable *adj* indescrivibile

indescribably *adv*: ***~ beautiful*** di una bellezza indescrivibile; ***~ bad*** pessimo

indestructible *adj* indistruttibile

indeterminate *adj* indeterminato

index I *n* ⟨*pl* ***indexes*** *or* ***indices***⟩ indice *m*; ***cost-of-living ~*** indice *m* del costo della vita II *v/t* indicizzare

index card *n* scheda *f* **index finger** *n* indice *m* **index-linked** *adj* indicizzato

India *n* India *f*

Indian I *adj* indiano II *n person* indiano *m*, -a *f*; *American* indiano *m*, -a *f* d'America

Indian Ocean *n* Oceano *m* Indiano **Indian summer** *n* estate *f* di San Martino

indicate I *v/t* indicare; ***opinion polls ~ that …*** i sondaggi d'opinione indicano che… II *v/i when driving* segnalare (il cambiamento di direzione)

indication *n* indicazione *f*; ***he gave no ~ that he was ready*** non ha dato alcuna indicazione di essere pronto; ***that is some ~ of what we can expect*** è una qualche indicazione di ciò che possiamo aspettarci

indicative I *adj* indicativo (***of*** di); ***~ mood*** GRAM modo *m* indicativo II *n* GRAM indicativo *m*; ***in the ~*** all'indicativo

indicator *n on car* indicatore *m* di direzione, freccia *f infml*; ***altitude / pressure ~*** indicatore *m* di altitudine / pressione; ***this is an ~ of economic recovery*** è un indice di ripresa economica

indicator board *n* tabellone *m*

indices → ***index***

indict *v/t* incriminare

indictment *n* prova *f* d'accusa; ***be an ~ of sth*** *fig* essere una prova di qc

indifference *n* indifferenza *f*; ***it's a matter of complete ~ to me*** mi è completamente indifferente

indifferent *adj* indifferente; (*mediocre*) mediocre; ***~ to*** indifferente a

indigence *n* indigenza *f*

indigenous *adj* indigeno; ***plants ~ to Canada*** piante indigene del Canada

indigent *adj form* indigente

indigestible *adj* indigesto

indigestion *n* indigestione *f*

indignant *adj* indignato; ***~ at*** *or* ***about sth*** indignato per qc

indignation *n* indignazione *f*

indignity *n* trattamento *m* indegno

indigo *adj* indaco

indirect *adj* indiretto; ***by an ~ route*** per un percorso indiretto; ***make an ~ reference to s.o. / sth*** fare indirettamente riferimento a qn / qc

indirect lighting *n* illuminazione *f* indiretta

indirectly *adv* indirettamente

indirect object *n* GRAM oggetto *m* indiretto **indirect question** *n* domanda *f* indiretta **indirect speech** *n* GRAM discorso *m* indiretto

indiscernible *adj* indistinguibile; *noise* impercettibile

indiscipline *n* indisciplina *f*

indiscreet *adj* indiscreto; ***be ~ about sth*** essere indiscreto in merito a qc

indiscreetly *adv* sconsideratamente; (*tactlessly*) indiscretamente

indiscretion *n* indiscrezione *f*; *sexual* scappatella *f*

indiscriminate *adj* indiscriminato

indiscriminately *adv* indiscriminatamente; *choose* a casaccio

indispensable *adj* indispensabile

indisposed *adj* (*not well*) indisposto; (*disinclined*) non disposto

indisposition *n* indisposizione *f*

indisputable *adj* indiscutibile

indisputably *adv* indiscutibilmente

indissoluble *adj* indissolubile; ***they actually signed an ~ contract*** hanno firmato un contratto indissolubile
indistinct *adj* indistinto
indistinguishable *adj* indistinguibile; ***the twins are ~*** (***from one another***) i gemelli sono indistinguibili
individual I *n* individuo *m* II *adj* (*separate*) singolo; (*personal*) individuale
individualist *adj* individualista
individually *adv* individualmente
indivisible *adj* indivisibile
Indo- *pref* indo-
indoctrinate *v/t* indottrinare
indoctrination *n* indottrinamento *m*
indolence *n* indolenza *f*
indolent *adj* indolente
indomitable *adj* indomabile
Indonesia *n* Indonesia *f*
Indonesian I *adj* indonesiano II *n person* indonesiano *m*, -a *f*
indoor *adj activities*, *games* al coperto; *arena*, *swimming pool* coperto
indoors *adv in building* all'interno; *at home* in casa; ***go ~*** andare dentro
indorse *etc* → ***endorse***
indubitable *adj* indubitabile
indubitably *adv* indubitabilmente
induce *v/t labour* indurre; ***~ s.o. to do sth*** persuadere qn a fare qc
inducement *n* incentivo *m*
induction course *n* corso *m* d'avviamento
indulge I *v/t o.s.*, *one's tastes* soddisfare; (*overindulge*) *children* viziare; ***he ~s her every whim*** soddisfa ogni suo capriccio; ***she ~d herself with a glass of wine*** si è concessa un bicchiere di vino II *v/i*: ***~ in sth*** lasciarsi andare a qc; *in joke* permettersi qc; ***dessert came, but I didn't ~*** *infml* è arrivato il dessert, ma non mi sono lasciata andare
indulgence *n of tastes*, *appetite etc* soddisfazione *f*; (*laxity*) indulgenza *f*
indulgent *adj* (*not strict enough*) indulgente
industrial *adj* industriale; ***~ nation*** nazione *f* industrializzata
industrial action *n* agitazione *f* sindacale **industrial archaeology** *n* archeologia *f* industriale **industrial design** *n* industrial design *m* **industrial dispute** *n* vertenza *f* sindacale **industrial estate** *n* zona *f* industriale
industrialist *n* industriale *m*/*f*
industrialization *n* industrializzazione *f*
industrialize I *v/t* industrializzare II *v/i* industrializzarsi; ***~d nation*** nazione *f* industrializzata
industrial park *n US* zona *f* industriale **industrial relations** *npl* relazioni *fpl* industriali **industrial revolution** *n* rivoluzione *f* industriale **industrial site** *n* sito *m* industriale **industrial tribunal** *n* tribunale *m* del lavoro **industrial waste** *n* scorie *fpl* industriali
industrious *adj* diligente
industry *n* industria *f*; ***heavy ~*** industria *f* pesante
inebriate *v/t* inebriare
inebriated *adj form* ebbro
inedible *adj* non commestibile; (*unpleasant*) immangiabile
ineducable *adj* ineducabile
ineffable *adj form* ineffabile
ineffective *adj* inefficace; ***be ~ against sth*** essere inefficace contro qc
ineffectual *adj person* inetto
inefficacious *adj* inefficace
inefficacy *n* inefficacia *f*
inefficiency *n* inefficienza *f*; *of machine* inutilità *f*
inefficient *adj* inefficiente
inelegant *adj* inelegante
inelegantly *adv* in modo inelegante
ineligible *adj*: ***be ~ for sth*** non avere diritto a qc; ***~ for military service*** non idoneo al servizio militare; ***be ~ for a pension*** non avere diritto alla pensione
ineloquent *adj* privo di eloquenza
ineluctable *adj* ineluttabile
inept *adj* inetto
ineptitude *n* inettitudine *f*
inequality *n* disuguaglianza *f*
inequitable *adj* iniquo
inert *adj* inerte
inert gas *n* CHEM gas *m inv* inerte
inertia *n* inerzia *f*
inertia selling *n Br* vendita *f* per inerzia, *prestazione di servizi senza l'accordo del cliente*
inescapable *adj* inevitabile
inessential *adj* secondario
inestimable *adj* inestimabile
inevitable *adj* inevitabile; ***the ~ bottle of ...*** l'immancabile bottiglia di ...;

defeat seemed ~ la sconfitta sembrava inevitabile
inevitably *adv* inevitabilmente; ***one question ~ leads to another*** una domanda ne attira inevitabilmente un'altra; **~, *he got drunk*** si è immancabilmente ubriacato; ***as ~ happens on these occasions*** come succede immancabilmente in queste occasioni
inexact *adj* inesatto
inexcusable *adj* imperdonabile
inexhaustible *adj supply* inesauribile
inexorable *adj* inesorabile
inexpensive *adj* poco costoso, economico
inexperience *n* inesperienza *f*
inexperienced *adj* inesperto
inexpert *adj* inesperto
inexpertly *adv* da inesperto
inexplicable *adj* inspiegabile
inexpressible *adj* inesprimibile
inextricable *adj* inestricabile
inextricably *adv entangled* inestricabilmente; *linked* indissolubilmente
infallible *adj* infallibile
infamous *adj* famigerato
infamy *n* infamia *f*
infancy *n of person* infanzia *f*; ***in early ~*** nella prima infanzia; *of state*, *institution* stadio *m* iniziale; ***be still in its ~*** essere agli inizi
infant *n* bambino *m* piccolo, bambina *f* piccola; ***she teaches ~s*** insegna ai bambini piccoli; **~ *class*** *Br* classe di bambini piccoli
infanticide *n* infanticidio *m*
infantile *adj pej* infantile
infantry *n* fanteria *f*
infantry soldier *n* fante *m*
infant school *n* scuola *f* elementare
infatuated *adj*: ***be ~ with s.o.*** essere infatuato di qn
infatuation *n* infatuazione *f* (***with*** per)
infect *v/t of person* contagiare; *food*, *water* contaminare; ***become ~ed*** *of wound* infettarsi; *of person* contagiarsi
infection *n* infezione *f*
infectious *adj disease* infettivo, contagioso; *fig*: *laughter* contagioso
infer *v/t* ⟨*pret & past part* ***-red***⟩: ***~ sth from sth*** dedurre qc da qc
inference *n* deduzione *f*
inferior I *adj quality*, *workmanship* inferiore; *in rank* subalterno; ***be ~ to*** essere inferiore a; ***he feels ~*** si sente inferiore **II** *n*: ***one's ~s*** *in rank* i subalterni
inferiority *n in quality* inferiorità *f inv*
inferiority complex *n* complesso *m* d'inferiorità
infernal *adj infml nuisance* terribile; *noise* infernale
infertile *adj* sterile
infertility *n* sterilità *f inv*
infibulate *v/t* infibulare
infibulation *n* infibulazione *f*
infidel *n* HIST, REL infedele *m/f*
infidelity *n* infedeltà *f inv*
in-fighting *n fig* rivalità *f* interna
infiltrate *v/t* infiltrare
infiltration *n* POL infiltrazione *f*
infiltrator *n* POL infiltrato *m*, -a *f*
infinite *adj* infinito
infinitely *adv* infinitamente; *better* immensamente
infinitesimal *adj* infinitesimale
infinitesimal calculus *n* MATH calcolo *m* infinitesimale
infinitive *n* GRAM infinito *m*
infinitude *n* infinità *f*
infinity *n* infinito *m*
infirm *adj* infermo
infirmary *n* infermeria *f*
infirmity *n* infermità *f inv*; ***the infirmities of (old) age*** gli acciacchi della vecchiaia
in flagrante delicto *adv* JUR in flagrante
inflame *v/t passions* accendere; MED infiammare; ***become ~d*** infiammarsi
inflammable *adj* infiammabile
inflammation *n* MED infiammazione *f*
inflatable *adj dinghy* gonfiabile
inflate *v/t tyre*, *dinghy* gonfiare; *economy* inflazionare
inflation *n* inflazione *f*
inflationary *adj* inflazionistico; ***~ pressures / politics*** pressioni *fpl* inflazionistiche / politica *f* inflazionistica
inflected *adj* GRAM *form*, *ending* flesso; *language* flessivo
inflection *n of voice* intonazione *f*
inflexible *adj attitude*, *person* inflessibile
inflict *v/t*: ***~ sth on s.o.*** *punishment* infliggere qc a qn; *wound*, *suffering* procurare qc a qn

infliction *n of suffering* l'infliggere
in-flight *adj*: ~ ***entertainment*** intrattenimento a bordo
inflow *n of water, air* afflusso *m*; *fig* affluenza *f*; ~ ***pipe*** tubo *m* di afflusso
influence I *n* influenza *f*; ***be a good / bad ~ on s.o.*** avere una buona / cattiva influenza su qn; ***people who have ~*** persone influenti; ***a man of ~*** un uomo influente; ***who were your main ~s?*** chi si è ispirato principalmente?; ***under the ~*** (*drunk*) in stato di ebbrezza **II** *v/t s.o.'s thinking* esercitare un'influenza su; *decision* influenzare
influential *adj writer, philosopher, film-maker* autorevole; ***she knows ~ people*** conosce gente influente
influenza *n* influenza *f*
influx *n of capital, goods* afflusso *m*; *of people* affluenza *f*
info *n infml* → ***information***
inform I *v/t* informare; ~ ***s.o. about sth*** informare qn di qc; ***please keep me ~ed*** tienimi informato; (*imbue*) permeare **II** *v/i* denunciare; ~ ***on s.o.*** denunciare qn
informal *adj* informale
informality *n* informalità *f inv*
informant *n* informatore *m*, -trice *f*
information *n* informazione *f*; ***a bit of ~*** un'informazione; ***for your ~*** per tua informazione; ***for further ~ please contact this number …*** per ulteriori informazioni, contattare questo numero …; COMM a titolo informativo
information desk *n* ufficio *m* informazioni **information pack** *n* materiale *m* informativo **information science** *n* informatica *f* **information scientist** *n* informatico *m*, -a *f* **information superhighway** *n* autostrada *f* informatica **information technology** *n* informatica *f*
informative *adj article etc* istruttivo; ***he wasn't very ~*** non è stato di grande aiuto
informed *adj observer* informato; *guess* fondato
informer *n* informatore *m*, -trice *f*; ***police ~*** informatore *m* della polizia
infotainment *n* TV infotainment *m*
infraction *n* infrazione *f*
infra dig *adj infml* disdicevole
infrangible *adj* infrangibile
infra-red *adj* infrarosso
infrastructure *n* infrastruttura *f*
infrequency *n* rarità *f*
infrequent *adj* raro; ***at ~ intervals*** a rari intervalli
infringe I *v/t* infrangere, violare **II** *v/i*: ~ ***(up)on s.o.'s rights*** usurpare i diritti di qn
infringement *n* violazione *f*
infuriate *v/t* far infuriare
infuriating *adj* esasperante; ***an ~ person*** una persona esasperante
infuse *v/i*: ***let the tea ~*** lasciare in infusione il tè
infusion *n* (*herb tea*) infuso *m*
ingenious *adj* ingegnoso
ingénue *n* LIT ingenua *f*
ingenuity *n* ingegnosità *f inv*
ingenuous *adj* senza malizia; (*naïve*) ingenuo
ingest *v/t* ingerire; ***she ~ed a huge quantity of icecream, then said she felt sick*** ha ingerito un'enorme quantità di gelato e poi ha dichiarato di sentirsi male
inglenook *n* cantuccio *m* del focolare
inglorious *adj* inglorioso
ingoing I *adj* in entrata **II** *n* entrata *f*
ingot *n* lingotto *m*
ingrained *adj fig habit, prejudice* radicato; *dirt* incrostato
ingratiate *v/t*: ~ ***o.s. with s.o.*** ingraziarsi qn
ingratitude *n* ingratitudine *f*
ingredient *n for cooking* ingrediente *m*; *fig*: *for success* elemento *m*
ingrowing *adj*: ~ ***toenail*** unghia *f* incarnita (del piede)
ingrown *adj*: ~ ***toenail*** unghia *f* incarnita (del piede); ~ ***habit*** abitudine *f* innata
inhabit *v/t* abitare
inhabitable *adj* abitabile
inhabitant *n* abitante *m/f*
inhale I *v/t* inalare **II** *v/i when smoking* aspirare
inhaler *n* inalatore *m*
inherent *adj* intrinseco
inherently *adv* per natura
inherit *v/t* ereditare; ***the problems which we ~ed from the last government*** i problemi che abbiamo ereditato dall'ultimo governo
inheritance *n* eredità *f inv*
inheritance tax *n* JUR tassa *f* di succes-

sione
inhibit *v/t growth, conversation etc* inibire
inhibited *adj* inibito
inhibition *n* inibizione *f*
inhibitor, inhibiter *n* inibitore *m*, -trice *f*; PHARM inibitore *m*
inhospitable *adj* inospitale
in-house I *adj* aziendale II *adv work* all'interno dell'azienda
inhuman *adj* disumano
inhumane *adj* disumano
initial I *adj* iniziale; ***my ~ reaction*** la mia reazione iniziale; ***in the ~ stages*** nelle fasi iniziali II *n* iniziale *f* III *v/t* ⟨*pret & past part* **-led**, *US* **-ed**⟩ (*write initials on*) siglare (con le iniziali)
initially *adv* inizialmente
initiate *v/t* avviare; *into club* iniziare; ***~ s.o. into sth*** iniziare qn a qc
initiation *n* avviamento *m*
initiation ceremony *n* cerimonia *f* di iniziazione
initiative *n* iniziativa *f*; ***do sth on one's own ~*** fare qc di propria iniziativa; ***take the ~*** prendere l'iniziativa
initiator *n* iniziatore *m*, -trice *f*
inject *v/t medicine, drug, fuel* iniettare; *capital* investire
injection *n* MED, *of fuel* iniezione *f*; *of capital* investimento *m*; ***give s.o. an ~*** fare un'iniezione a qn
injection moulding *n* formatura *f* per iniezione
in-joke *n*: ***it's an ~*** è una battuta tra di noi / loro
injudicious *adj* sventato
injudiciously *adv* sventatamente
injunction *n* ingiunzione *f*; ***take out an ~ against*** ottenere un'ingiunzione contro
injure *v/t* ferire; ***~ o.s.*** farsi male; ***~ one's leg*** farsi male alla gamba
injured I *adj leg* ferito; ***the ~ party*** JUR la parte lesa; *feelings* offeso II *npl* feriti *mpl*
injurious *adj* dannoso
injury *n* ferita *f*; ***do s.o. / o.s. an ~*** fare del male a qn / farsi del male
injury time *n* SPORTS minuti *mpl* di recupero
injustice *n* ingiustizia *f*; ***do s.o. an ~*** essere ingiusto con qn
ink *n* inchiostro *m*
ink drawing *n* disegno *m* a inchiostro
inkjet (printer) *n* stampante *f* a getto d'inchiostro
inkling *n*: ***have no ~ of sth*** non avere idea di qc
inkstain *n* macchia *f* di inchiostro
inkwell *n* calamaio *m*
inland *adj areas* dell'interno; *mail* nazionale; *sea* interno
inland lake *n* lago *m* interno **Inland Revenue** *n* fisco *m* **inland sea** *n* mare *m* interno
in-law *n* parente *m* acquisito; ***~s*** *npl famiglia della moglie / del marito*; (*wife's / husband's parents*) suoceri *mpl*
inlay *n* intarsio *m*
inlet *n of sea* insenatura *f*; *in machine* presa *f*
inmate *n of prison* detenuto *m*, -a *f*; *of mental hospital* ricoverato *m*, -a *f*
inmost *adj* → ***innermost***
inn *n* locanda *f*
innards *npl* viscere *fpl*
innate *adj* innato
inner *adj* interno
inner city *n centro in degrado di una zona urbana*; ***~ decay*** degrado del centro urbano **innermost** *adj thoughts etc* più intimo **inner tube** *n* camera *f* d'aria
innings *nsg in cricket* turno *m* di battuta; ***he has had a good ~*** ha avuto un'esistenza lunga e felice
innkeeper *n* locandiere *m*, -a *f*
innocence *n* innocenza *f*
innocent I *adj* innocente; ***~ of sth*** innocente di qc; ***she is ~ of the crime*** è innocente di quel crimine II *n* innocente *m/f*
innocently *adv* in modo innocente; ***the quarrel began ~ enough*** il litigio iniziò in modo innocente
innocuous *adj* innocuo
innovate *v/i* fare innovazioni
innovation *n* innovazione *f*
innovative *adj* innovativo
innovator *n* innovatore *m*, -trice *f*
innuendo *n* allusioni *fpl*
innumerable *adj* innumerevole
inoculate *v/t* vaccinare
inoculation *n* vaccinazione *f*
inoffensive *adj* inoffensivo
inoperable *adj* inoperabile
inoperative *adj law* non in vigore; ***be ~*** *machine* non essere in funzione

inopportune *adj* inopportuno
inordinate *adj* smodato; *sum*, *demand* eccessivo
inordinately *adv* smodatamente; *large* eccessivamente
inorganic *adj* inorganico
in-patient *n* degente *m/f*
input I *n* contributo *m*; COMPUT input *m inv* **II** *v/t* ⟨*pret & past part* **-ted** *or* **input**⟩ *into project* contribuire con; COMPUT inserire
inquest *n* inchiesta *f* giudiziaria
inquire *v/i* domandare; **~ into sth** svolgere indagini su qc; **~ about** fare domande su
inquiry *n* richiesta *f* di informazioni; (*public inquiry*) indagine *f*; (*investigation*) inchiesta *f*; ***he is helping the police with their inquiries*** *Br euph* la polizia lo sta interrogando; ***hold an ~ into the cause of the accident*** condurre un'inchiesta sulle cause dell'incidente
inquisitive *adj* curioso
inroads *npl*: ***make ~ into sth*** intaccare qc
insalubrious *adj* malsano
insane I *adj* pazzo; ***drive s.o. ~*** *infml* far impazzire qn **II** *npl*: ***the ~*** i pazzi
insanely *adv* follemente; ***she is ~ jealous*** è follemente gelosa
insanitary *adj* antigienico
insanity *n* infermità *f* mentale
insatiable *adj* insaziabile
inscribe *v/t* incidere (***sth on sth*** qc su qc); *book* dedicare; ***a watch, ~d ...*** un orologio con l'incisione ...
inscription *n* iscrizione *f*
inscrutable *adj* imperscrutabile
insect *n* insetto *m*
insect bite *n* puntura *f* di insetto
insecticide *n* insetticida *m*
insect repellent *n* insettifugo *m*
insecure *adj* insicuro; ***they feel ~ in their jobs*** non si sentono sicuri del proprio posto di lavoro
insecurity *n* insicurezza *f*
inseminate *v/t* fecondare; *cattle* inseminare
insemination *n* fecondazione *f*; *of cattle* inseminazione *f*
insensitive *adj* insensibile; (*unappreciative*) indifferente; ***~ to pain*** insensibile al dolore; ***be ~ to*** *or* ***about s.o.'s feelings*** essere insensibile verso i sentimenti di qn
insensitivity *n* insensibilità *f inv*
inseparable *adj two issues* inscindibile; *two people* inseparabile
insert I *n in magazine etc* inserto *m* **II** *v/t* inserire; ***~ sth into sth*** inserire qc in qc
insertion *n* (*act*) inserimento *m*
in-service *adj*: ***~ training*** *formazione professionale che avviene all'interno dell'azienda*
inset *n in the corner of a page* riquadro *m*
inshore I *adj* costiero **II** *adv* verso la costa
inside I *n* **1.** *of house*, *box* interno *m* **2.** *of road* destra *f*; sinistra *f* **3.** ***someone on the ~ at Lloyds*** qualcuno che lavora ai Lloyds **4.** ***~ out*** a rovescio; ***turn sth ~ out*** rivoltare qc; ***know sth ~ out*** sapere qc a menadito **II** *prep* **1.** *place* dentro; ***go ~ the house*** entrare in casa **2.** *time*: ***~ of 2 hours*** in meno di due ore **III** *adv stay*, *remain*, *go*, *carry* dentro; ***I've never been ~*** non sono mai entrato **IV** *adj* interno; ***~ information*** informazioni riservate; ***~ lane*** SPORTS corsia *f* interna; *on road* corsia *f* di marcia; ***~ pocket*** tasca *f* interna
insider *n*: ***an ~ from the Department ...*** un impiegato del Ministero ...
insider dealing *n* FIN insider trading *m inv*
insides *npl* pancia *fsg*; *intestines* budella *fpl*
insidious *adj* insidioso
insight *n*: ***it offers an ~ into ...*** permette di capire ...; ***full of ~*** molto intuitivo
insignia *npl* insegne *fpl*
insignificance *n* irrilevanza *f*
insignificant *adj* insignificante
insincere *adj* falso
insincerity *n* falsità *f inv*
insinuate *v/t* (*imply*) insinuare
insinuation *n* insinuazione *f* (***about*** su); ***he objected strongly to any ~ that ...*** obiettò fermamente a qualsiasi insinuazione che ...
insipid *adj* insipido; *colour* insulso
insist *v/i* insistere; ***please keep it, I ~*** tienilo, ci tengo!
◆**insist on** *v/t* esigere; ***insist on doing sth*** insistere per fare qc

insistent *adj* insistente
in situ *adv* in loco
insofar *adv*: **~ as** per quanto
insole *n* soletta *f*
insolent *adj* insolente
insoluble *adj problem* insolvibile; *substance* insolubile
insolvent *adj* insolvente
insomnia *n* insonnia *f*
insomniac *n* persona *f* che soffre di insonnia
insomuch *adv* → ***inasmuch***
inspect *v/t work*, *tickets*, *baggage* controllare; *building*, *factory*, *school* ispezionare
inspection *n of work*, *tickets*, *baggage* controllo *m*; *of building*, *factory*, *school* ispezione *f*
inspector *n in factory* ispettore *m*, -trice *f*; *on buses* controllore *m*; *of police* ispettore *m*
inspiration *n* ispirazione *f*; (*very good idea*) lampo *m* di genio; ***be an ~ to s.o.*** essere di ispirazione a qn; ***get one's ~ from sth.*** prendere ispirazione da qc
inspirational *adj* ispiratore
inspire *v/t respect etc* suscitare; ***be ~d by s.o. / sth*** essere ispirato da qn / qc
inspired *adj* ispirato; ***it was an ~ choice*** è stata una scelta felice
inspiring *adj* ispiratore
instability *n of character*, *economy* instabilità *f inv*
install *v/t computer*, *telephones*, *software* installare
installation *n of new equipment*, *software* installazione *f*; ***military ~*** struttura *f* militare
instalment, *US* **installment** *n of story*, *TV drama etc* puntata *f*; (*payment*) rata *f*; ***in ~s*** a rate
instance *n* (*example*) esempio *m*; ***for ~*** per esempio; ***in the first ~*** in primo luogo
instant I *adj* immediato; COOK istantaneo; ***~ mashed potatoes*** purè *m inv* istantaneo **II** *n* istante *m*; ***in an ~*** in un attimo; ***he left the ~ he heard the news*** se ne è andato nel momento stesso in cui ha saputo la notizia
instantaneous *adj* immediato; ***death was ~*** la morte è stata immediata
instant coffee *n* caffè *m inv* istantaneo *or* solubile
instantly *adv* istantaneamente
instant messaging *n* COMPUT messaggistica *f* immediata **instant replay** *n* TV replay *m* immediato
instead *adv* invece; ***~ of*** invece di; ***~ of going to school*** invece di andare a scuola; ***~ of that*** invece; ***his brother came ~ of him*** è venuto suo fratello al posto suo; ***if he doesn't want to go, I'll go ~*** se non vuole andare, andrò io al posto suo
instep *n* ANAT collo *m* del piede
instigate *v/t form reform* promuovere; *attack* istigare
instigation *n*: ***at s.o.'s ~*** su istigazione di qn
instil, *US* **instill** *v/t*: ***~ sth into s.o.*** instillare qc in qn
instinct *n* istinto *m*; ***the survival ~*** l'istinto di sopravvivenza; ***by*** *or* ***from ~*** per istinto; ***follow one's ~s*** seguire l'istinto
instinctive *adj* istintivo
institute I *n* istituto *m* **II** *v/t new law* introdurre; *enquiry* avviare
institution *n governmental* istituto *m*; *sth traditional* istituzione *f*; (*setting up*) avviamento *m*
institutional *adj* istituzionale
institutionalized *adj* istituzionalizzato
in-store *adj all'interno di un negozio più grande*; ***~ bakery*** *piccola panetteria all'interno di un supermercato o di un centro commerciale*
instruct *v/t* (*order*) dare istruzioni a; (*teach*) istruire; ***~ s.o. to do sth*** (*order*) dare istruzioni a qn di fare qc
instruction *n* istruzione *f*; ***what were your ~s?*** quali istruzioni avevi?; ***~s for use*** istruzioni per l'uso
instruction manual *n* libretto *m* d'istruzioni
instructive *adj* istruttivo
instructor *n* istruttore *m*, -trice *f*
instrument *n* strumento *m*
instrumental *adj* strumentale; ***be ~ in sth*** contribuire fattivamente a qc; MUS strumentale; ***~ music / version*** musica / versione *f* strumentale
instrumentalist *n* strumentista *m/f*
instrumentation *n* strumentazione *f*
instrument panel *n* quadro *m* degli strumenti
insubordinate *adj* insubordinato

insubordination *n* insubordinazione *f*
insubstantial *adj* inconsistente; *accusation* infondato; *amount* misero; *meal* poco sostanzioso
insufferable *adj* intollerabile
insufferably *adv* intollerabilmente
insufficient *adj* insufficiente
insular *adj* insulare; (*narrow-minded*) provinciale
insulate *v/t* ELEC isolare; *against cold* isolare termicamente
insulating tape *n* nastro *m* isolante
insulation *n* ELEC isolamento *m*; *against cold* isolamento *m* termico
insulin *n* insulina *f*
insult **I** *n* insulto *m*; ***an ~ to my intelligence*** un insulto alla mia intelligenza; ***add ~ to injury*** aggiungere la beffa al danno **II** *v/t* insultare
insuperable *adj* insuperabile
insurance *n* assicurazione *f*; ***take out ~ against sth*** assicurarsi contro qc
insurance broker *n* broker *m inv* di assicurazioni **insurance company** *n* compagnia *f* di assicurazioni **insurance policy** *n* polizza *f* di assicurazione **insurance premium** *n* premio *m* assicurativo
insure *v/t* assicurare
insured **I** *adj* assicurato; ***be ~*** essere assicurato **II** *n*: ***the ~*** l'assicurato
insurgency *n form* insurrezione *f*
insurgent *form* **I** *adj* insorto **II** *n* insorto *m*, -a *f*
insurmountable *adj* insormontabile
insurrection *n* insurrezione *f*
insusceptible *adj* insensibile
intact *adj* (*not damaged*) intatto
intake *n of college etc* (numero *m* di) iscrizioni *fpl*; ***food ~*** assunzione *f* di cibo; ***(sharp) ~ of breath*** (forte) inspirazione *f*
intangible *adj* intangibile
integer *n* numero *m* intero
integral *adj part, feature* integrante; ***be ~ to sth*** essere parte integrante di qc
integrate *v/t* integrare
integrated circuit *adj* circuito *m* integrato
integration *n* integrazione *f* (*into* in); ***(racial) ~*** integrazione *f* razziale
integrity *n* integrità *f inv*
intellect *n* intelletto *m*
intellectual **I** *adj* intellettuale **II** *n* intellettuale *m/f*
intelligence *n* intelligenza *f*; (*information*) informazioni *fpl*
intelligence officer *n* agente *m/f* dei servizi segreti **intelligence service** *n* servizi *mpl* segreti
intelligent *adj* intelligente
intelligentsia *n* intellighenzia *f*
intelligible *adj* intelligibile
intemperance *n* intemperanza *f*
intemperate *adj* intemperante
intend *v/i*: ***~ to do sth*** (*do on purpose*) volere fare qc; (*plan to do*) avere intenzione di fare qc; ***that's not what I ~ed*** non è quello che intendevo
intense *adj pleasure, heat, pressure* intenso; *concentration* profondo; ***he's too ~*** è troppo serio
intensely *adv* (*extremely*) profondamente; ***I dislike it ~*** lo detesto profondamente; *stare, study* intensamente
intensify ⟨*pret & past part* **-ied**⟩ **I** *v/t effect, pressure* intensificare **II** *v/i of pain* acuirsi; *of fighting* intensificarsi
intensity *n* intensità *f inv*
intensive *adj* intensivo
intensive care (unit) *n* MED (reparto *m* di) terapia *f* intensiva **intensive course** *n* corso *m* intensivo
intent *adj*: ***be ~ on doing sth*** (*determined to do*) essere deciso a fare qc; (*concentrating on*) essere intento a fare qc
intention *n* intenzione *f*; ***I have no ~ of ...*** (*refuse to*) non ho intenzione di ...; ***what was your ~ in publishing the article?*** che intenzioni avevi pubblicando l'articolo?; ***it is my ~ to punish you severely*** è mia intenzione punirti severamente; ***I have every ~ of doing it*** ho tutte le intenzioni di farlo; ***with the best of ~s*** con le migliori intenzioni
intentional *adj* intenzionale
intentionally *adv* intenzionalmente
inter *v/t form* sotterrare
inter- *pref* inter-; ***interpersonal*** interpersonale
interact *v/i* interagire *a.* PSYCH
interaction *n* interazione *f*
interactive *adj* interattivo
interbreed *v/i* ⟨*pret & past part* **-bred**⟩ (*inbreed*) ibridare; (*crossbreed*) incrociare
intercede *v/i* intercedere

intercept *v/t* intercettare; ***they ~ed the enemy*** intercettarono il nemico
intercession *n* intercessione *f*; *in argument* mediazione *f*
interchange *n US* AUTO interscambio *m*
interchangeable *adj* interscambiabile
intercom *n* citofono *m*
interconnect I *v/t*: ***~ed events*** eventi *mpl* interconnessi **II** *v/i* collegarsi
intercourse *n* rapporto *m*; *sexual* rapporto *m* sessuale
interdenominational *adj* interconfessionale
interdepartmental *adj relations* tra dipartimenti; *committee* interdipartimentale
interdependent *adj* interdipendente
interest I *n* interesse *m*; FIN: *rate* interesse *m*; *money paid / received* interessi *mpl*; ***take an ~ in sth*** interessarsi di qc **II** *v/t* interessare; ***does that offer ~ you?*** t'interessa l'offerta?
interested *adj* interessato; ***be ~ in sth*** interessarsi di qc; ***thanks, but I'm not ~*** grazie, non mi interessa
interest-free loan *n* prestito *m* senza interessi **interest group** *n* gruppo *m* di interesse
interesting *adj* interessante
interest rate *n* FIN tasso *m* d'interesse
interface I *n* interfaccia *f* **II** *v/i* interfacciarsi
interfere *v/i* interferire
◆**interfere with** *v/t* manomettere; *plans* intralciare
interference *n* interferenza *f*; *on radio* interferenze *fpl*
interfering *adj person* che si intromette
intergovernmental *adj* intergovernativo
interim I *adj government*, *measure* provvisorio **II** *n*: ***in the ~*** nel frattempo
interior I *adj* interno **II** *n of house* interno *m*; *of country* entroterra *m*
interior decorator *n* arredatore *m*, -trice *f* **interior design** *n* architettura *f* d'interni **interior designer** *n* architetto *m* d'interni
interject *v/t* interrompere con
interjection *n* (*exclamation*) interiezione *f*; (*remark*) interruzione *f*
interlink *v/i* collegarsi; *fig theories etc* essere interconnesso
interlock *v/i* intrecciarsi
interlocutor *n* interlocutore *m*, -trice *f*
interloper *n* intruso *m*, -a *f*
interlude *n at theatre*, *concert* intervallo *m*, (*period*) parentesi *f*
intermarry *v/i* ⟨*pret & past part* ***-ied***⟩ fare matrimoni misti
intermediary *n* intermediario *m*, -a *f*
intermediate *adj* intermedio; ***~ stage*** fase intermedia; ***the ~ stations*** le stazioni intermedie; ***an ~ student*** uno studente di livello intermedio
interminable *adj* interminabile
intermingle *v/i* mescolarsi (***with*** con)
intermission *n in theatre*, *cinema* intervallo *m*
intermittent *adj* intermittente
intern¹ *v/t* internare
intern² *n US* (*junior doctor*) medico *m* tirocinante; (*trainee*) tirocinante *m/f*
internal *adj* interno; ***~ call*** chiamata *f* interna; ***~ flight*** volo *m* interno
internal affairs *npl* affari *mpl* interni
internal combustion engine *n* motore *m* a scoppio
internalize *v/t* interiorizzare
internally *adv*: ***he's bleeding ~*** ha un'emorragia interna; ***not to be taken ~*** per uso esterno
Internal Revenue Service *n US* fisco *m*
international I *adj* internazionale; ***~ code*** TEL prefisso *m* internazionale; ***~ money order*** assegno *m* circolare internazionale **II** *n match* partita *f* internazionale; *player* giocatore *m*, -trice *f* della nazionale
International Court of Justice *n* Corte *f* Internazionale di Giustizia **International Date Line** *n* linea *f* internazionale del cambio di data
internationally *adv* a livello internazionale
International Monetary Fund *n* Fondo *m* Monetario Internazionale **International Phonetic Alphabet** *n* alfabeto *m* fonetico internazionale
internee *n* internato *m*, -a *f*
Internet *n* Internet *m inv*; ***on the ~*** su Internet; ***~ service provider***; ***surf the ~*** navigare in Internet
Internet banking *n* Internet banking *m* **Internet café** *n* Internet café *m* **Internet connection** *n* connessione *f*

Internet
internment *n* internamento *m*
internship *n US* MED tirocinio *m* medico; *as trainee* tirocinio *m*
interplay *n* interazione *f*
interpose *v/t object* interporre; *remark* intervenire con; ~ ***o.s. between*** interporsi tra
interpret I *v/t linguistically* tradurre; *piece of music, comment etc* interpretare; ***how would you ~ what he said?*** come interpreteresti ciò che ha detto? **II** *v/i* fare da interprete
interpretation *n linguistic* traduzione *f*; *of piece of music, meaning* interpretazione *f*
interpreter *n* interprete *m/f*
interrelate *v/i* essere in correlazione
interrelated *adj* correlato
interrogate *v/t* interrogare
interrogation *n* interrogatorio *m*
interrogative I *adj* GRAM interrogativo; ***~ pronoun / clause*** pronome *m* interrogativo / proposizione *f* interrogativa **II** *n* GRAM forma *f* interrogativa
interrogator *n* interrogante *m/f*
interrupt *v/t & v/i* interrompere
interruption *n* interruzione *f*
intersect I *v/t* intersecare **II** *v/i* intersecarsi
intersection *n* (*crossroads*) incrocio *m*
intersperse *v/t* cospargere; ***~d with sth*** cosparso di qc; ***a speech ~d with quotations*** un discorso inframezzato da citazioni; ***periods of sunshine ~d with showers*** periodi di bel tempo alternati a rovesci
interstate *n US* autostrada *f* interstatale
intertwine *v/i* intrecciare
interval *n* intervallo *m*; ***at regular ~s*** a intervalli regolari; ***sunny ~s*** METEO schiarite *fpl*
intervene *v/i of person, police etc* intervenire; *of time* trascorrere
intervening *adj* intermedio; ***in the ~ period*** nel periodo intermedio
intervention *n* intervento *m*
interview I *n on TV, in paper* intervista *f*; *for job* intervista *f* d'assunzione, colloquio *m* di lavoro; ***give s.o. an ~*** fare un colloquio a qn **II** *v/t on TV, for paper* intervistare; *for job* sottoporre a intervista
interviewee *n on TV* intervistato *m*, -a *f*; *for job* candidato *m*, -a *f*
interviewer *n on TV, for paper* intervistatore *m*, -trice *f*; (*for job*) *persona che conduce un'intervista d'assunzione*
interwar *adj* tra le due guerre
interweave ⟨*pret* ***-wove***, *past part* ***-woven***⟩ **I** *v/t* mescolare **II** *v/i* mescolarsi
intestate *adj* JUR ***die ~*** morire intestato
intestinal *adj* intestinale
intestine *n* intestino *m*
intimacy *n* intimità *f inv*
intimate[1] *adj friend, thoughts* intimo; ***be ~ with s.o.*** *sexually* avere rapporti intimi con qn; ***be on ~ terms with s.o.*** essere intimo di qn; ***be / become ~ with s.o.*** essere / entrare in intimità con qn; ***have an ~ knowledge of sth*** avere una profonda conoscenza di qc
intimate[2] *v/t* lasciare intendere; ***he ~d to them that they should stop*** lasciò loro intendere che dovevano smettere
intimately *adv acquainted* intimamente; *related* strettamente; *know* profondamente
intimidate *v/t* intimidire; ***they ~d him into not telling the police*** lo costrinsero con le minacce a non raccontarlo alla polizia
intimidation *n* intimidazione *f*
intl. *abbr* (= **international**) internazionale
into *prep* in; ***he put it ~ his suitcase*** l'ha messo in valigia; ***translate ~ English*** tradurre in inglese; ***be ~ sth*** *infml* (*like*) amare qc; (*be involved with*) interessarsi di qc; ***be ~ drugs*** fare uso di droga; ***when you're ~ the job*** quando sei pratico del lavoro; ***change euros ~ pounds*** cambiare euro in sterline; ***divide 3 ~ 9*** dividere 9 per 3; ***3 ~ 9 goes 3*** il 3 nel 9 ci sta 3 volte; ***he's well ~ his sixties*** ha sessant'anni suonati; ***research ~ cancer*** ricerca *f* sul cancro
intolerable *adj* intollerabile
intolerance *n* intolleranza *f* (***of*** verso)
intolerant *adj* intollerante
intonation *n* intonazione *f*
intone *v/t* intonare
intoxicate *v/t* ubriacare
intoxicated *adj* ubriaco

intoxication *n* ebbrezza *f*; ***in a state of ~*** *form* in stato di ebbrezza
intractable *adj problem* intrattabile
intranet *n* COMPUT Intranet *f*
intransigence *n* intransigenza *f*
intransigent *adj* intransigente
intransitive *adj* intransitivo
intrastate *adj US* all'interno di uno stato
intrauterine device *n* dispositivo *m* intrauterino
intravenous *adj* endovenoso; ***~ drug user*** consumatore *m*, -trice *f* di droghe per via endovenosa
in-tray *n* vassoio *m* per pratiche da evadere
intrepid *adj* intrepido
intricacy *n* complessità *f*
intricate *adj* complicato
intrigue I *n* intrigo *m* **II** *v/t* intrigare; ***I would be ~d to know …*** m'interesserebbe molto sapere … **III** *v/i* ordire intrighi
intriguing *adj* intrigante
intrinsic *adj form* intrinseco
intro *n abbr* (= **introduction**) *infml* introduzione *f*
introduce *v/t person* presentare; *new technique etc* introdurre; ***~ sth onto the market*** introdurre qc sul mercato; ***may I ~ …?*** permette che le presenti …?; ***~ s.o. to sth*** far conoscere qc a qn
introduction *n to person* presentazione *f*; *to a new food*, *sport etc* approccio *m*; *in book*, *of new technique* introduzione *f*; ***letter of ~*** lettera *f* di presentazione; ***an ~ to French*** (*elementary course*) un'introduzione al francese
introductory *adj course* introduttivo; *remarks* preliminare
introit *n* REL introito *m*
introspection *n* introspezione *f*
introspective *adj* introspettivo
introvert *n* introverso *m*, -a *f*
introverted *adj* introverso
intrude *v/i* importunare; ***~ on s.o.*** importunare qn; ***~ on s.o.'s privacy*** violare la privacy di qn
intruder *n* intruso *m*, -a *f*
intrusion *n* intrusione *f*; ***forgive the ~, I just wanted to ask …*** mi perdoni l'intrusione, volevo solo chiedere …
intrusive *adj person* invadente; *presence* importuno
intuit *v/t & v/i* intuire
intuition *n* intuito *m*
intuitive *adj* intuitivo
inundate *v/t* inondare; ***~ s.o. / sth with sth*** inondare qn / qc di qc; ***have you a lot of work on? — I'm ~d*** hai molto lavoro? — sono sommerso
inure to *v/t*: ***get inured to*** abituarsi a
invade *v/t* invadere
invalid[1] *adj* non valido; ***declare sth ~*** dichiarare non valido qc
invalid[2] **I** *adj* infermo; (*disabled*) invalido **II** *n* MED invalido *m*, -a *f*
invalidate *v/t claim*, *theory* invalidare
invaluable *adj help*, *contributor* prezioso
invariably *adv* (*always*) invariabilmente
invasion *n* invasione *f*; ***the German ~ of Poland*** l'invasione tedesca della Polonia
invasive *adj* MED invasivo
invective *n* invettiva *f* (***against*** contro)
inveigh *v/i* inveire; ***he spent the whole evening ~ing against the government*** passò l'intera serata ad inveire contro il governo
invent *v/t* inventare
invention *n* invenzione *f*
inventive *adj* fantasioso
inventor *n* inventore *m*, -trice *f*
inventory *n* inventario *m*; ***make*** *or* ***take an ~ of sth*** fare un inventario di qc
inverse I *adj order* inverso **II** *n* inverso *m*
invert *v/t* invertire
invertebrate *n* invertebrato *m*
inverted commas *npl* virgolette *fpl*
inverted snobbery *n* snobismo *m* al contrario
invest *v/t & v/i* investire; ***~ s.o. with sth*** *form* investire qn di qc; *fig* ***~ sth with sth*** avvolgere qc di qc; ***~ in*** investire in
investigate *v/t* indagare su
investigation *n* indagine *f*
investigative journalism *n* giornalismo *m* investigativo
investigator *n* investigatore *m*
investiture *n* investitura *f*
investment *n* investimento *m*; ***we need more ~ in industry*** abbiamo bi-

sogno di maggiori investimenti nell'industria; ***foreign ~*** investimento *m* straniero; ***this company is a good ~*** questa società è un buon investimento; ***a portable TV is a good ~*** un televisore portatile è un buon investimento
investment grant *n* ECON sovvenzione *f* agli investimenti **investment trust** *n* fondo *m* comune di investimento
investor *n* investitore *m*, -trice
inveterate *adj hatred* inveterato; *liar* incallito; ***~ criminal*** criminale *m* incallito
invidious *adj* antipatico
invigilate *v/i Br examination* essere di sorveglianza
invigorate *v/t* tonificare
invigorating *adj climate* tonificante
invincible *adj* invincibile
inviolable *adj* inviolabile
inviolate *adj* inviolato
invisible *adj* invisibile; ***~ to the naked eye*** invisibile a occhio nudo
invitation *n* invito *m*; ***by ~*** (***only***) solo su invito; ***at s.o.'s ~*** dietro invito di qn; ***~ to tender*** invito *m* d'asta
invite I *v/t* invitare; *suggestions* incoraggiare; *ridicule* essere causa di; ***can I ~ you for a meal?*** posso invitarti a pranzo?; ***~ s.o. to a party*** invitare qn a una festa; ***~ s.o. to do sth*** invitare qn a fare qc **II** *n infml* invito *m*
◆**invite (a)round** *v/t sep* invitare (a casa)
◆**invite in** *v/t sep* invitare a entrare; ***could I invite you in for (a) coffee?*** posso invitarti a entrare per un caffè?
◆**invite out** *v/t sep* invitare a uscire; ***I invited her out*** l'ha invitata a uscire con lui; ***invite s.o. out for a meal*** invitare qn a pranzo fuori
inviting *adj* invitante; *prospect, meal* allettante
in vitro *adj* BIOL ***~ fertilization*** fecondazione *f* in vitro
invoice I *n* fattura *f* **II** *v/t customer* fatturare
invoke *v/t*; *God, the law* invocare; *treaty etc* appellarsi a
involuntarily *adv* involontariamente; (*automatically*) automaticamente
involuntary *adj* involontario
involve *v/t* **1.** *hard work, expense* comportare; ***what does it ~?*** che cosa comporta? **2.** (*concern*) riguardare; ***the book doesn't ~ the reader*** il libro non coinvolge il lettore; ***it wouldn't ~ you at all*** non ti riguarderebbe affatto **3.** (*entangle*) ***get ~d in an accident*** rimanere coinvolto in un incidente; ***get ~d with sth*** entrare a far parte di qc; ***get ~d with s.o.*** *emotionally, romantically* legarsi a qn
involved *adj* (*complex*) complesso
involvement *n in a project etc* partecipazione *f*; *in a crime, accident* coinvolgimento *m*; ***she denied any ~ in*** *or* ***with drugs*** ha negato qualsiasi coinvolgimento con la droga
invulnerable *adj* invulnerabile
inward I *adj direction* verso l'interno; *feeling, thoughts* intimo **II** *adv* verso l'interno
inward-looking *adj* dalle vedute ristrette
inwardly *adv* dentro di sé
in-your-face, in-yer-face *adj infml attitude etc* aggressivo
IOC *abbr* (= **International Olympic Committee**) CIO *m* (Comitato Olimpico Internazionale)
iodine *n* iodio *m*
ion *n* ione *m*
iota *n*: ***not one ~*** non un briciolo
IOU *abbr* (= **I owe you**) pagherò *m*
IQ *abbr* (= **intelligence quotient**) quoziente *m* d'intelligenza
IRA *abbr* (= **Irish Republican Army**) IRA *f*
Iran *n* Iran *m*
Iranian I *adj* iraniano **II** *n person* iraniano *m*, -a *f*
Iraq *n* Iraq *m*
Iraqi I *adj* iracheno **II** *n person* iracheno *m*, -a *f*
irascible *adj* irascibile
irate *adj* furioso
Ireland *n* Irlanda *f*; ***Northern ~*** Irlanda *f* del Nord; ***Republic of ~*** Repubblica *f* d'Irlanda
iris *n of eye* iride *f*; *flower* iris *m inv*
Irish I *adj* irlandese **II** *n language* irlandese; ***the ~*** gli irlandesi
Irishman *n* irlandese *m* **Irishwoman** *n* irlandese *f*
irk *v/t* seccare; ***it really ~s me that he's never punctual*** mi secca che non sia mai puntuale
irksome *adj* seccante

iron I *n substance* ferro *m*; *for clothes* ferro *m* da stiro; ***pump ~*** *infml* fare sollevamento pesi; ***he has too many ~s in the fire*** ha troppa carne al fuoco; ***strike while the ~ is hot*** *prov* battere il ferro finché è caldo **II** *v/t shirts etc* stirare
◆ **iron out** *v/t sep* appianare
Iron Age *n* età *f* del ferro **Iron Curtain** *n* cortina *f* di ferro **iron hand** *n fig* pugno *m* di ferro
ironic(al) *adj* ironico
ironically *adv* ironicamente; ***and then, ~, it was he himself who had to do it*** e poi, per ironia, è stato lui stesso a doverlo fare
ironing *n*: ***do the ~*** stirare
ironing board *n* asse *m* da stiro
ironmonger *n Br* commerciante *m/f* di ferramenta **ironworks** *n* stabilimento *m* siderurgico
irony *n* ironia *f*; ***the ~ of it is that ...*** l'ironia è che ...
irradiate *v/t & v/i* irradiare
irrational *adj* irrazionale
irreconcilable *adj* inconciliabile
irrecoverable *adj* irrecuperabile
irredeemable *adj* irrimediabile, *loss* irreparabile
irredeemably *adv* irrimediabilmente, *lost* irreparabilmente; ***democracy was ~ damaged*** la democrazia è stata irrimediabilmente danneggiata
irrefutable *adj* irrefutabile
irregular *adj* irregolare; *US infml* stitico; ***well, it's a bit ~, but I'll ...*** non è molto regolare, ma lo farò ...
irrelevance *n* irrilevanza *f*; ***it's become something of an ~*** è diventato irrilevante
irrelevant *adj* non pertinente; ***these issues are ~ to the younger generation*** questi problemi sono irrilevanti per la nuova generazione
irreparable *adj* irreparabile
irreparably *adv* irreparabilmente; ***his reputation was ~ damaged*** la sua reputazione ne è stata irreparabilmente danneggiata
irreplaceable *adj object*, *person* insostituibile
irrepressible *adj sense of humour* incontenibile; *person* che non si lascia abbattere
irreproachable *adj* irreprensibile
irresistible *adj* irresistibile
irrespective *adj*: ***~ of*** a prescindere da
irresponsible *adj* irresponsabile
irretrievable *adj* irrecuperabile; ***the information is ~*** le informazioni sono irrecuperabili
irreverent *adj* irriverente
irreversible *adj decision* irrevocabile; *damage* irreversibile
irreversibly *adv* irreversibilmente; ***the peace process has been ~ damaged*** il processo di pace ha subito un danno irreversibile
irrevocable *adj* irrevocabile
irrigate *v/t* irrigare
irrigation *n* irrigazione *f*
irrigation canal *n* canale *m* d'irrigazione
irritability *n* irritabilità *f*
irritable *adj* irritabile
irritate *v/t* irritare; ***I get ~d with him*** mi irrito con lui; ***he ~s me*** mi irrita
irritating *adj* irritante; ***I find his jokes ~*** trovo irritanti le sue battute; ***the ~ thing is that ...*** la cosa irritante è che ...
irritation *n* irritazione *f*
IRS *abbr* (= **Internal Revenue Service**) *US* fisco *m*
is → ***be***
ISA *n abbr* (= **Individual Savings Account**) FIN conto *m* di risparmio individuale
ISDN *abbr* (= **Integrated Services Digital Network**) ISDN
Islam *n* Islam *m*
Islamic *adj* islamico
island *n* isola *f*; (***traffic***) ***~*** isola *f* spartitraffico
islander *n* isolano *m*, -a *f*
isle *n*: ***the Isle of Man / Wight*** l'isola di Man / Wight
isn't = ***is not***
ISO *abbr* (= **International Stardards Organisation**) ISO *f*
isolate *v/t* isolare
isolated *adj house*, *occurrence* isolato
isolation *n of a region* isolamento *m*; ***in ~*** *taken etc* da solo
isolation ward *n* reparto *m* d'isolamento
ISP *abbr* (= **Internet service provider**) provider *m inv* di servizi Internet
Israel *n* Israele *m*
Israeli I *adj* israeliano **II** *n person* isra-

eliano *m*, -a *f*

issue I *n* **1.** (*matter*) questione *f*; (*result*) risultato *m*; ***the point at ~*** il punto in discussione; ***take ~ with s.o./sth*** prendere posizione contro qn/qc; ***she raised the ~ of human rights*** ha sollevato la questione dei diritti umani; ***the whole future of the country is at ~*** è in discussione tutto il futuro del paese; ***this matter/question is not at ~*** la questione non è in discussione; ***make an ~ of sth*** fare un caso di qc; ***avoid the ~*** evitare la questione **2.** *of magazine* numero *m* **3.** (*children*) **~** prole *f* **4.** *of banknotes* emissione *f* **II** *v/t passports, visa* rilasciare; *supplies* distribuire; *coins* emettere; *warning* dare; ***~ sth to s.o./s.o. with sth*** dare qc in dotazione a qn; ***all troops are ~d with ...*** tutte le truppe ricevono in dotazione ... **III** *v/i liquid, gas* scaturire (***from*** da)

isthmus *n* istmo *m*

it *pron* **1.** *as subject*: ***what colour is ~? – ~ is red*** di che colore è? – è rosso; ***~'s raining*** piove; ***who is ~?*** chi è?; ***~'s me/him*** sono io/è lui; ***~'s Charlie here*** TEL sono Charlie; ***is ~ a boy or a girl?*** è un maschio o una femmina?; ***that's ~!*** (*that's right*) proprio così!; (*finished*) finito!; ***this is ~, he thought, as he heard the mast crack*** ci siamo, pensò sentendo scricchiolare l'albero; ***you're ~!*** *infml in games* tocca a te!; ***he thinks he's ~*** *infml* si crede qualcuno **2.** *as object* lo *m*, la *f*; ***I broke ~*** l'ho rotto, -a; ***I can't eat ~ all*** non posso mangiarla tutta; ***he'd had ~; he resigned the next day*** aveva esaurito la pazienza, si dimise il giorno successivo

IT *abbr* (= **information technology**) IT *f* (informatica *f*)

Italian **I** *adj* italiano **II** *n person* italiano *m*, -a *f*; *language* italiano *m*

italic *adj* in corsivo

italics *npl* corsivo *msg*; ***in ~*** in corsivo

Italy *n* Italia *f*

itch **I** *n* prurito *m*; ***I have an ~*** avere il prurito; ***I have the ~ to do sth*** muoio dalla voglia di fare qc **II** *v/i* prudere; ***my back is ~ing*** mi prude la schiena; *fig* ***he is ~ing to ...*** *infml* morire dalla voglia di ...

itchy *adj* (+*er*) (*itching*) che prude; *cloth* che dà prurito; ***my back is ~*** mi prude la schiena; ***I've got an ~ leg*** mi prude una gamba; ***I've got ~ feet*** *infml* non riesco a restare a lungo nello stesso luogo

item *n on agenda* punto *m* (all'ordine del giorno); *on shopping list* articolo *m*; *in accounts* voce *f*; ***news ~*** notizia *f*; ***~ of clothing*** capo *m* di vestiario; *infml* ***Lynn and Craig are an ~*** Lynn e Craig stanno insieme

itemize *v/t invoice* dettagliare

itinerant *adj* nomade, itinerante; ***an ~ lifestyle*** uno stile di vita nomade; ***~ worker*** lavoratore *m*, -trice *f* itinerante

itinerary *n* itinerario *m*

it'll = ***it will***

its *adj* il suo *m*, la sua *f*, i suoi *mpl*, le sue *fpl*; ***where is ~ box?*** dov'è la scatola di questo?; ***the dog has hurt ~ leg*** il cane si è fatto male alla zampa

it's = ***it is***; ***it has***

itself *pron reflexive* si; *emphatic* di per sé; ***the dog hurt ~*** il cane si è fatto male; ***the hotel ~ was unimpressive*** l'hotel di per sé non era niente di speciale; ***the frame ~ is worth £1,000*** la sola cornice vale 1.000 sterline; ***she has been kindness ~*** è stata la gentilezza in persona; ***in ~, the amount is not important*** di per sé, la somma non è importante; ***by ~*** (*alone*) da solo; (*automatically*) da sé

itsy-bitsy *adj infml* piccolissimo

ITV *abbr* (= **Independent Television**) *Br rete televisiva privata*

IUD *abbr* (= **intrauterine device**) dispositivo *m* intrauterino, IUD *m*

I've = ***I have***

IVF *abbr* (= **in vitro fertilization**) fecondazione *f* in vitro

ivory *n* avorio *m*

ivy *n* edera *f*

Ivy League *n gruppo di prestigiose università americane*

J

J, j *n* j, J *f inv*
jab I *v/t* ⟨*pret & past part* **-bed**⟩ conficcare; ***he ~bed his finger at the map*** tamburellava con il dito sulla mappa **II** *v/i* SPORTS tirare un jab (***at s.o.*** a qn) **III** *n with elbow* colpetto *m*; *Br infml* puntura *f*
jabber I *v/i* parlare fitto fitto; ***he ~ed away, but no one was really listening*** cianciava, ma nessuno lo stava davvero ascoltando **II** *n* borbottio *m*
jack *n* AUTO cric *m inv*; *in cards* fante *m*; ***a ~ of all trades*** un factotum
◆**jack up** *v/t sep* AUTO sollevare con il cric; (*raise*) ***they jacked up the prices when the Euro came in*** hanno rialzato i prezzi con l'avvento dell'euro
jackdaw *n* ZOOL taccola *f*
jacket *n* giacca *f*; *of book* copertina *f*; *US of record* copertina *f*
jacket potato *n* patata *f* al forno con la buccia
jack-in-the-box *n* scatola *f* a sorpresa
jack-knife I *n* coltello *m* a serramanico **II** *v/i*: ***the lorry ~d*** il rimorchio dell'articolato si è messo di traverso
jack-of-all-trades *n*: ***be*** (***a***) ~ *prov* fare da jolly **jack-o'-lantern** *n lanterna fatta con una zucca vuota* **jackpot** *n* primo premio *m*; ***hit the ~*** vincere il primo premio; *fig* fare un terno al lotto **jack rabbit** *n lepre diffusa nel Nord America*
jacks *n* gioco *m* dei sassolini
Jacobean *adj* HIST dell'epoca di Giacomo I
Jacobin *n* HIST giacobino *m*, -a *f*
Jacquard *n* TEX jacquard *m*
jade *n* giada *f*
jaded *adj* spossato; *from overindulgence etc* sazio
jagged *adj* frastagliato
jaguar *n* ZOOL giaguaro *m*
jail I *n* prigione *f*; ***in ~*** in prigione; ***go to ~*** andare in prigione **II** *v/t* incarcerare
jailbird *n* avanzo *m* di galera
jailbreak *n* evasione *f*
jailer *n Br* secondino *m*, -a *f*
jailhouse *n US* prigione *f*
jam[1] *n for bread* marmellata *f*
jam[2] **I** *n* AUTO ingorgo *m*; ***be in a ~*** *infml* (*difficulty*) essere in difficoltà; ***get s.o. / o.s. out of a ~*** tirare qn / tirarsi fuori dai guai **II** *v/t* ⟨*pret & past part* **-med**⟩ (*ram*) ficcare;; (*cause to stick*) bloccare; *broadcast* disturbare; ***~ one's foot on the accelerator*** premere il piede sull'acceleratore; ***~ the switchboard*** TEL intasare il centralino; ***be ~med*** *of roads* essere congestionato; *of door, window* essere bloccato **III** *v/i* ⟨*pret & past part* **-med**⟩ (*stick*) bloccarsi; (*squeeze*) stiparsi
◆**jam on** *v/t sep*: ***jam on the brakes*** inchiodare
Jamaica *n* Giamaica *f*
jamb *n of door, window* stipite *m*
jamboree *n* raduno *m*
jam jar *n Br* vasetto *m* di marmellata
jammy *adj* (+*er*) *Br infml* (*very lucky*) fortunato; (*very easy*) facilissimo; ***a ~ shot*** un colpo fortunato
jam-packed *adj infml* pieno zeppo
jam session *n* MUS jam session *f*
Jan *abbr* (= **January**) gennaio *m*
jangle I *v/i bells* tintinnare **II** *v/t money, keys* far tintinnare
janitor *n* custode *m*
January *n* gennaio *m*
japan I *n* lacca *f* (del Giappone) **II** *adj* laccato **III** *v/t* laccare
Japan *n* Giappone *m*
Japanese I *adj* giapponese **II** *n person* giapponese *m/f*; *language* giapponese *m*; ***the ~*** i giapponesi
jar[1] *n container* barattolo *m*
jar[2] **I** *v/i* ⟨*pret & past part* **-red**⟩ *of noise* stridere; ***~ on*** dar fastidio a **II** *n* (*jolt*) scossone *m*
jargon *n* gergo *m*
jasmin(e) *n* BOT gelsomino *m*
jasper *n* diaspro *m*
jaundice *n* itterizia *f*
jaundiced *adj fig* cinico
jaunt *n* gita *f*; ***go for a ~*** fare una gita
jauntily *adv* in modo sbarazzino; ***with his hat perched ~ over one ear*** con il cappello appollaiato in modo sbaraz-

zino su un orecchio
jaunty *adj* (+*er*) sbarazzino
javelin *n* (*spear*) giavellotto *m*; *event* lancio *m* del giavellotto
jaw *n* mascella *m*; ***the lion opened its ~s*** il leone spalancò le fauci; ***his ~ dropped*** rimase a bocca aperta
jawbone *n* osso *m* mascellare
jay *n* ZOOL ghiandaia *f*
jaywalker *n* pedone *m* indisciplinato
jazz *n* jazz *m inv*
◆**jazz up** *v/t sep infml* ravvivare
jazzy *adj* (+*er*) *colour, dress, tie* vistoso; *pattern* vivace; *music* jazzistico
JCB® *n* escavatore *m* JCB®
jealous *adj* geloso; ***be ~ of …*** essere geloso di …
jealously *adv* gelosamente
jealousy *n* gelosia *f*
jeans *npl* jeans *mpl*
jeep® *n* jeep® *f inv*
jeer I *n* scherno *m* **II** *v/i* schernire; ***~ at*** schernire
Jello® *n US* gelatina *f*
jelly *n* gelatina *f*
jelly baby *n* bonbon *m inv* di gelatina **jelly bean** *n* bonbon *m inv* di gelatina **jellyfish** *n* medusa *f*
jeopardize *v/t* mettere in pericolo
jeopardy *n*: ***be in ~*** essere in pericolo
jerk[1] **I** *n* scossone *m*; ***the train stopped with a ~*** il treno si fermò con uno scossone **II** *v/t* dare uno strattone; ***he ~ed his head back*** tirò la testa indietro con uno strattone **III** *v/i*: ***the car ~ed forward*** la macchina avanzava a scatti; ***the car ~ed to a stop*** la macchina si fermò con uno scossone
jerk[2] *n infml* idiota *m/f*
◆**jerk off** *v/i sl* masturbarsi
jerky[1] *adj* (+*er*) *movement* a scatti
jerky[2] *n* COOK carne *f* essiccata
jeroboam *n* bottiglione *m* di vino
jerry-built *adj* costruito con materiale scadente **jerry can** *n* bidone *m* per benzina
jersey *n* (*sweater*) maglia *f*; *fabric* jersey *m inv*
Jersey *n* isola *f* di Jersey; (*cow*) mucca *f* di razza Jersey
Jerusalem *n* Gerusalemme *f*
Jerusalem artichoke *n* topinambur *m*
jest I *n* scherzo *m*; ***in ~*** per scherzo **II** *v/i* scherzare
jester *n* HIST giullare *m*
Jesus *n* Gesù *m*
jet I *n of water* zampillo *m*; (*nozzle*) becco *m*; *airplane* jet *m inv* **II** *v/i* ⟨*pret & past part* **-ted**⟩ *travel* volare
jet-black *adj* (nero) corvino **jet engine** *n* motore *m* a reazione **jetlag** *n* jet-lag *m inv*; ***he's suffering from ~*** soffre di jet-lag **jet-propelled** *adj* a reazione **jet set** *n* jet-set *m inv*
jettison *v/t* gettare; *fig* abbandonare
jetty *n* molo *m*
Jew *n* ebreo *m*, -a *f*
jewel *n* gioiello *m*; *fig*: *person* perla *f*
jeweller, *US* **jeweler** *n* gioielliere *m*
jewellery, *US* **jewelry** *n* gioielli *mpl*; ***a piece of ~*** un gioiello
Jewish *adj* ebraico; *people* ebreo
jiffy *n infml*: ***in a ~*** in un batter d'occhio, in un attimo
Jiffy bag® *n Br* busta *f* imbottita
jig I *n* giga *f* **II** *v/i* ⟨*pret & past part* **-ged**⟩ *fig a.* **jig about** saltellare; ***~ up and down*** saltare su e giù
jiggle I *v/t* dondolare **II** *v/i* (*a.* **jiggle about**) dondolare
jigsaw (puzzle) *n* puzzle *m inv*
jihad *n* jihad *f*, guerra *f* santa
jilt *v/t* piantare *infml*
jingle I *n song* jingle *m inv* **II** *v/i of keys, coins* tintinnare
jinx *n person* iettatore *m*, -trice *f*; (*bad luck*) ***there's a ~ on this project*** questo progetto è iellato
jitters *npl infml*: ***get the ~*** avere fifa *infml*
jittery *adj infml* nervoso
jive *v/t US infml* prendere in giro
Jnr *abbr* (= **junior**) jr (junior)
job *n* (*employment*) lavoro *m*; (*task*) compito *m*; ***out of a ~*** senza lavoro; ***it's a good ~ you …*** meno male che tu …; ***make a good/bad ~ of sth*** fare un buon/pessimo lavoro con qc; ***you'll have a ~*** (*it'll be difficult*) sarà un'impresa; (*duty*) dovere *m*; ***that's not my ~*** non spetta a me; ***it's not my ~ to tell him*** non spetta a me dirglielo; ***I had the ~ of breaking the news to her*** avevo il dovere di comunicarle la notizia; ***he's not doing his ~*** non sta facendo il suo dovere; ***I'm only doing my ~*** sto solo facendo il mio dovere; ***that's a***

good ~! meno male!; ***it's a good ~ I brought my cheque book*** meno male che ho portato il libretto degli assegni; ***give s.o. / sth up as a bad ~*** mollare qn / qc; ***make the best of a bad ~*** fare buon viso a cattivo gioco; ***that should do the ~*** dovrebbe funzionare; ***this is just the ~*** è proprio quello che ci vuole; *infml* (*operation*) intervento *m*; ***have a nose ~*** farsi rifare il naso; ***on the ~*** sul lavoro; *Br infml* durante il rapporto sessuale
job application *n* domanda *f* di lavoro
jobber *n* FIN jobber *m/f*
job centre *n Br* ufficio *m* di collocamento **job description** *n* elenco *m* delle mansioni **jobhunt** *v/i*: ***be ~ing*** cercare lavoro
jobless *adj* disoccupato
job loss *n*: ***there were 1,000 ~es*** 1.000 persone hanno perso il posto di lavoro **job lot** *n* COMM lotto *m* **job satisfaction** *n* soddisfazione *f* nel lavoro
Job's comforter *n* cattivo consolatore *m*
job security *n* sicurezza *f* del posto di lavoro **job seeker** *n* persona *f* alla ricerca di un lavoro; ***~'s allowance*** *Br* indennità *f* per chi è alla ricerca di un lavoro **job-sharing** *n* job sharing *m*
jock *n US studente molto sportivo e poco intelligente*; *Br pej* scozzese *m/f*; (*disc jockey*) disc jockey *m/f*
jockey *n* fantino *m*
jockstrap *n* sospensorio *m*
jocular *adj* scherzoso
jocund *adj* giocondo
jodhpurs *npl* calzoni *mpl* alla cavallerizza
jog **I** *n* corsa *f*; ***go for a ~*** andare a fare footing **II** *v/i* ⟨*pret & past part* ***-ged***⟩ *as exercise* fare footing **III** *v/t* ⟨*pret & past part* ***-ged***⟩ *elbow etc* urtare; ***~ s.o.'s memory*** rinfrescare la memoria a qn
◆**jog along** *v/i infml* procedere
jogger *n person* persona *f* che fa footing; *US shoe* scarpa *f* da ginnastica
jogging *n* footing *m inv*; ***go ~*** fare footing
jogging suit *n* tuta *f* da ginnastica
john *n US infml* (*toilet*) cesso *m infml*
John Bull *n* Inghilterra *f*, inglese *m* tipico **John Doe** *n US* N.N. **John Hancock** *n infml* (*signature*) firma *f* autografa
joie de vivre *n* gioia *f* di vivere
join **I** *v/i of roads*, *rivers* unirsi; (*become a member*) iscriversi **II** *v/t* (*connect*) unire; *person* unirsi a; *club* iscriversi a; (*go to work for*) entrare in; *of road* congiungersi a; ***can I ~ you?*** va bene se mi unisco a voi?; ***~ hands*** tenersi per mano; ***~ the queue*** mettersi in coda **III** *n* giuntura *f*
◆**join in** *v/i* partecipare; ***he didn't want to join in the fun*** non volle andare a divertirsi con gli altri
◆**join up** *v/i* MIL arruolarsi
joiner *n* falegname *m*
joint **I** *n* ANAT articolazione *f*; *in woodwork* giunto *m*; *of meat* arrosto *m*; *infml place* locale *m*; *of cannabis* spinello *m* **II** *adj* (*shared*) comune; ***he finished ~ second*** *or* ***in ~ second place*** *Br* arrivò al secondo posto ex aequo; ***it was a ~ effort*** fu uno sforzo congiunto
joint account *n* conto *m* comune
jointed *adj* snodabile
jointly *adv* congiuntamente; ***be ~ owned by …*** essere comproprietà di …
joint owner *n* comproprietario *m*, -a *f* **joint ownership** *n* comproprietà *f* **joint stock** *n* capitale *m* azionario **joint-stock company** *n* società *f* per azioni **joint venture** *n* joint venture *f inv*
joist *n* travetto *m*
joke **I** *n story* barzelletta *f*; (*practical joke*) scherzo *m*; ***play a ~ on*** fare uno scherzo a; ***he can't take a ~*** non sa stare allo scherzo; ***it's no ~*** non è uno scherzo **II** *v/i* (*pretend*) scherzare; ***he was only joking*** stava solo scherzando; ***you must be joking!*** stai scherzando!
joker *n in cards* jolly *m inv*; *infml* burlone *m*, -a *f*
joking: ***~ apart*** *or* ***aside*** scherzi a parte
jokingly *adv* scherzosamente
jollification *n* baldoria *f*
jollify **I** *v/i* fare baldoria **II** *v/t* rallegrare
jollity *n* allegria *f*
jolly **I** *adj* (+*er*) allegro **II** *adv Br infml* ***~ good*** benissimo; ***I should ~ well hope so!*** lo spero bene!
jolt **I** *n* (*jerk*) scossone *m* **II** *v/t* (*push*)

urtare
jostle *v/t* spintonare
jot *n*: ***it won't do a ~ of good*** non sarà affatto utile; ***this won't affect my decision one ~*** ciò non influirà minimamente sulla mia decisione
◆**jot down** *v/t sep* ⟨*pret & past part* **-ted**⟩ annotare
jotter *n Br* taccuino *m*
journal *n magazine* rivista *f*; *diary* diario *m*; ***keep a ~*** tenere un diario
journalism *n* giornalismo *m*
journalist *n* giornalista *m/f*
journey **I** *n* viaggio *m*; ***go on a ~*** fare un viaggio; ***the ~ home*** il viaggio verso casa; ***he has quite a ~ to get to work*** per andare al lavoro deve fare un bel viaggio; ***a ~ of discovery*** un viaggio di scoperta **II** *v/i* viaggiare
jovial *adj* gioviale
jowl *n spesso pl* guancia *f*
joy *n* gioia *f*; ***to my great ~*** con mia grande gioia; ***this car is a ~ to drive*** è una gioia guidare questa macchina; *Br infml* (*success*) successo *m*; ***any ~?*** hai avuto successo?; ***you won't get any ~ out of him*** da lui non otterrai grandi soddisfazioni
joyful *adj* gioioso
joyless *adj* triste
joyous *adj liter* gioioso
joyrider *n autore di scorribande su un'auto rubata* **joyriding** *n il fare scorribande su un'auto rubata* **joystick** *n* COMPUT joystick *m inv*
JPEG *n abbr* (= **Joint Photographic Experts Group**) JPEG
Jr *abbr* (= **junior**) jr (junior)
jubilant *adj* esultante
jubilation *n* giubilo *m*
jubilee *n* anniversario *m*
Judaism *n* giudaismo *m*
Judas *n* giuda *m*
Judas tree *n* BOT albero *m* di Giuda
judder *v/i Br* vibrare; (*car etc*) sussultare; ***the train ~ed to a halt*** il treno si fermò sussultando
judge **I** *n* giudice *m*; ***be a good ~ of character*** essere bravo a giudicare il carattere (di una persona); ***I'll be the ~ of that*** sarò io a giudicare **II** *v/t* giudicare; *competition* fare da giudice a; ***you shouldn't ~ people by appearances*** non dovresti giudicare le persone dalle apparenze; ***you can ~ for yourself*** puoi giudicare da solo; ***how would you ~ him?*** come lo giudicheresti? **III** *v/i* giudicare; ***judging by ...*** a giudicare da ...; ***he let me ~ for myself*** lasciò che giudicassi da solo
judg(e)ment *n* giudizio *m*; ***I agreed, against my better ~*** ho accettato, pur pensando che fosse sbagliato; ***an error of ~*** un errore di valutazione
judg(e)mental *adj* sentenzioso
Judg(e)ment Day *n* il giorno *m* del giudizio
judicial *adj* giudiziario
judiciary *n* magistratura *f*
judicious *adj* giudizioso
judo *n* judo *m inv*
jug **I** *n* brocca *f*; *infml* prigione *f* **II** *v/t* ⟨*pret & past part* **-ged**⟩ COOK cuocere in salmì; ***~ged hare was her speciality*** la lepre in salmì era la sua specialità
juggernaut *n Br* bisonte *m* della strada *infml*
juggle *v/t* fare giochi di destrezza con; *fig*: *conflicting demands* destreggiarsi fra; *figures* manipolare
juggler *n* giocoliere *m*
jugular *n*: **~ (*vein*)** vena *f* giugulare
juice *n* succo *m*
juicer *n* spremiagrumi *m*
juicy *adj* (*+er*) succoso; *news*, *gossip* piccante
jukebox *n* juke-box *m inv*
Jul *abbr* (= **July**) luglio *m*
julienne *adj* julienne; ***~ potatoes*** patate *fpl* julienne
July *n* luglio *m*
jumble **I** *v/t* mettere alla rinfusa; *fig facts* confondere; ***a ~d mass of wires*** una massa di fili alla rinfusa; ***his clothes are ~d together on the bed*** i suoi vestiti erano alla rinfusa sul letto **II** *n* mucchio *m*; *of words* guazzabuglio *m*; *for jumble sale* cianfrusaglie *fpl*
◆**jumble up** *v/t* mescolare
jumble sale *n* vendita *f* di beneficenza
jumbo (jet) *n* jumbo *m* (jet)
jumbo-sized *adj* gigante
jump **I** *v/i* saltare; (*increase*) aumentare rapidamente, avere un'impennata; *in surprise* sobbalzare; ***~ to one's feet*** balzare in piedi; ***~ to conclusions*** arrivare a conclusioni affrettate **II** *v/t*

fence etc saltare; *infml* (*attack*) aggredire; *~ the queue* non rispettare la fila; *~ the lights* passare col rosso **III** *n* salto *m*; (*increase*) impennata *f*; ***give a ~** of surprise* sobbalzare

◆**jump at** *v/t opportunity* prendere al balzo, cogliere al volo

◆**jump down** *v/i* saltare giù (***from*** da); ***jump down s.o.'s throat*** saltare al collo a qn

◆**jump in** *v/i* saltare dentro; ***jump in!*** *to car* sali!

◆**jump off** *v/i* cominciare; *from train, bus* saltare giù

◆**jump on** *v/i liter onto vehicle*: montare (***to*** in); ***jump on*** (***to***) ***s.o.*** / ***sth*** criticare qc / qn

◆**jump out** *v/i* saltare fuori (***of*** da); ***jump out of the window*** saltare dalla finestra

◆**jump up** *v/i* (*stand up quickly*) alzarsi di scatto

jumper[1] *n* maglione *m inv*; *US* scamiciato *m*

jumper[2] *n* SPORTS saltatore *m*, -trice *f*

jumper cables *n US* AUTO → ***jump leads***

jump leads *npl* AUTO cavi *mpl* di avviamento **jump rope** *n US* corda *f* per saltare

jumpsuit *n* SEW tuta *f* intera

jumpy *adj* (*+er*) nervoso

Jun *abbr* (= **June**) giugno *m*

junction *n of roads* incrocio *m*

junction box *n* ELEC scatola *f* di giunzione **junction transistor** *n* transistor *m inv* a giunzione

juncture *n form*: ***at this ~*** in questo frangente

June *n* giugno *m*

jungle *n* giungla *f*

junior I *adj* (*subordinate*) subalterno; (*younger*) giovane; ***Hiram Schwarz, ~*** Hiram Schwarz junior **II** *n in rank* subalterno *m*, -a *f*; ***she is ten years my ~*** ha dieci anni meno di me

junior high school *n US* scuola *f* media **junior partner** *n* socio *m* minoritario **junior school** *n* scuola *f* elementare

junk *n* (*rubbish*) robaccia *f*

junket *n US infml* visita *f* ufficiale (a spese del governo)

junk food *n* alimenti *mpl* poco sani

junkie *n infml* tossico *m*, -a *f infml*

junk mail *n* posta *f* spazzatura **junk shop** *n* negozio *m* di chincaglierie

junkyard *n* deposito *m* di robivecchi

Juno *n* MYTH Giunone *f*

Junoesque *adj* giunonico

junta *n* giunta *f* (militare)

Jupiter *n* Giove *m*

Jurassic *adj* GEOL giurassico

jurisdiction *n* JUR giurisdizione *f*

jurisprudence *n* JUR giurisprudenza *f*

juror *n* giurato *m*, -a *f*

jury *n* giuria *f*; ***sit** or **be on the ~*** fare parte della giuria

jury box *n* banco *m* della giuria **jury service** *n*: ***do ~*** essere membro di una giuria

just I *adv* **1.** (*barely*) appena; ***I've ~ seen her*** l'ho appena vista; ***it's ~ past Hope Street*** è appena dopo Hope Street; ***I arrived ~ in time*** sono arrivato appena in tempo **2.** (*only*) solo; ***~ the three of us*** solo noi tre **3.** ***~ about*** (*almost*) quasi; ***I was ~ about to leave when …*** stavo proprio per andarmene quando … **4.** (*exactly*) proprio; ***a house ~ like that*** una casa proprio così; ***~ now*** (*a few moments ago*) proprio ora; (*at the moment*) al momento; ***~ as rich*** altrettanto ricco **5.** (*simply*) ***he left her ~ like that*** l'ha lasciata così, senza spiegazioni; ***he agreed ~ like that*** ha accettato così, senza pensarci due volte **6.** (*absolutely*) proprio; ***it's ~ terrible*** è proprio terribile **7.** ***~ as*** esattamente, così come; ***the blue hat is ~ as nice as the red one*** il cappello blu è bello esattamente come quello rosso; ***it's ~ as well …*** tanto meglio; ***~ as I thought!*** proprio come pensavo!; ***~ about*** quasi; ***I am ~ about ready*** sono quasi pronto; ***did he make it in time? — ~ about*** ha fatto in tempo? — quasi **8.** ***~ wait!*** aspetta un po'!; ***~ be quiet!*** fai silenzio! **II** *adj* (*+er*) giusto; ***I had ~ cause to be alarmed*** avevo un giusto motivo per allarmarmi

justice *n* giustizia *f*; (*judge*) giudice *m/f*; ***bring s.o. to ~*** assicurare qn alla giustizia; ***do him ~*** rendergli giustizia; ***this photograph doesn't do her ~*** la tua fotografia non le rende giustizia; ***you didn't do yourself ~ in the exams*** non ti sei fatto onore agli esami; ***ministry of ~*** *Br* ***Department of Jus-***

tice *US* ministero / dipartimento *m* della giustizia; ***Justice of the Peace*** giudice *m/f* di pace

justifiable *adj* giustificabile

justifiably *adv* a ragione

justification *n* giustificazione *f*; ***as (a) ~ for his action*** a titolo di giustificazione per la sua azione

justify *v/t* ⟨*pret & past part* ***-ied***⟩ *a. text* giustificare; ***he was justified in doing that*** la sua azione era giustificata

justly *adv* giustamente

◆**jut out** *v/i* ⟨*pret & past part* ***-ted***⟩ sporgere; ***the peninsula juts out into the sea*** la penisola si protende nel mare; ***jut out over the street*** sporgersi sulla strada

jute *n* TEX iuta *f*

juvenile **I** *adj* minorile; *pej* puerile **II** *n form* minore *m/f*

juvenile delinquency *n* delinquenza *f* minorile **juvenile delinquent** *n* delinquente *m/f* minorile

juxtapose *v/t* giustapporre

juxtaposition *n* giustapposizione *f*

K

K, k *n* k, K *f inv*

k *abbr* **1.** (= **kilobyte**) k (kilobyte *m inv*) **2.** (= **thousand**) mille; ***earn 25K*** guadagnare 25 mila sterline

kabob *n US* → ***kebab***

kale *n* cavolo *m* comune

kaleidoscope *n* caleidoscopio *m*

kaleidoscopic *adj* caleidoscopico

kamikaze *adj* kamikaze

kangaroo *n* canguro *m*

kaput *adj infml* kaputt *inv infml*

karaoke *n* karaoke *m inv*

karate *n* karate *m inv*

karate chop *n* colpo *m* di karate

kayak *n* kayak *m inv*

KB *abbr* (= **kilobyte**) kB (kilobyte *m inv*)

kcal *abbr* (= **kilocalorie**) kcal (chilocaloria *f*)

kebab *n* spiedino *m* di carne

keel *n* NAUT chiglia *f*

◆**keel over** *v/i of boat* capovolgersi; *of structure* crollare; *of person* cascare per terra; *faint* svenire

keen *adj* (+*er*) *person* entusiasta; *interest*, *competition* vivo; *blade* affilato; *wind* pungente; ***be ~ on sth*** essere appassionato di qc; ***I'm not ~ on the idea*** l'idea non mi va tanto; ***he's ~ on her*** lei gli piace molto; ***be ~ to do sth*** aver molta voglia di fare qc

keenly *adv feel* intensamente; *interested* vivamente; (*enthusiastically*) ardentemente; ***~ awaited*** atteso ardentemente

keenness *n* (*enthusiasm*) entusiasmo *m*; *of applicant*, *learner* vivo interesse *m*

keep **I** *v/t* ⟨*pret & past part* ***kept***⟩ **1.** tenere; (*not lose*) mantenere; ***~ sth to o.s.*** (*not tell*) tenere qc per sé **2.** (*detain*) trattenere; ***what kept you?*** cosa ti ha trattenuto?; ***~ sth from s.o.*** nascondere qc a qn; ***~ s.o. from doing sth*** impedire a qn di fare qc **3.** *family* mantenere; ***I earn enough to ~ myself*** guadagno abbastanza da mantenermi; ***I have six children to ~*** ho sei figli da mantenere **4.** *animals* allevare **5.** ***~ a promise*** mantenere una promessa; ***can you ~ a secret?*** sai tenere un segreto? **6.** ***~ s.o. company*** tenere compagnia a qn **7.** (*maintain in a certain state or condition*) ***~ s.o. waiting*** far aspettare qn **II** *v/i* ⟨*pret & past part* ***kept***⟩ **1.** (*remain*) rimanere; ***~ left*** tenere la sinistra; ***~ straight on*** vai sempre dritto; ***~ still*** stare fermo; ***~ calm!*** calma!; ***~ quiet!*** fate silenzio! **2.** (*continue*) ***~ trying!*** continua a provare!; ***don't ~ interrupting!*** non interrompere in continuazione! **3.** *of food*, *milk* conservarsi **III** *n* (*maintenance*) vitto e alloggio *m*; (*stronghold*) maschio *m*; ***for ~s*** *infml* per sempre

◆**keep at** *v/t* persistere; ***keep at it*** tenere duro; ***keep s.o. (hard) at it*** far continuare a lavorare (duramente) qn

◆**keep away I** *v/i* stare alla larga; ***keep away from ...*** stai alla larga da ... **II** *v/t always sep* tenere lontano; ***keep s.o. away from sth*** tenere qn lontano da qc

◆**keep back** *v/t sep* (*hold in check*) trattenere; *information* nascondere

◆**keep down** *v/t sep voice* abbassare; *costs*, *inflation etc* contenere; *food* trattenere; ***keep the noise down, will you?*** fate meno rumore!; ***keep one's weight down*** tenere il proprio peso sotto controllo

◆**keep from** *v/t* impedire; ***I couldn't keep him from doing it*** non sono riuscito a impedirglielo; ***the bells keep me from sleeping*** le campane mi hanno impedito di dormire; ***keep them from getting wet*** impedisci che si bagnino; ***keep s.o. from harm*** impedire a qn di farsi male; ***keep sth from s.o.*** nascondere qc a qn

◆**keep in** *v/t sep in hospital* trattenere; ***keep a pupil in*** *punire uno studente trattenendolo oltre l'orario scolastico*

◆**keep in with** *v/t* restare in buoni rapporti con; ***he's just trying to keep in with her*** sta appunto cercando di restare in buoni rapporti con lei

◆**keep off I** *v/t sep* (*avoid*) evitare; ***keep off the grass*** non calpestare l'erba **II** *v/i*: ***if the rain keeps off*** se non piove

◆**keep on I** *v/i* continuare; ***keep on doing sth*** continuare a fare qc **II** *v/t sep employee*, *coat* tenere

◆**keep on at** *v/t* (*nag*) assillare

◆**keep out I** *v/t sep the cold* proteggere da; *person* escludere **II** *v/i of room* non entrare (***of*** in); *of argument etc* non immischiarsi (***of*** in); ***keep out*** *as sign* vietato l'ingresso; ***you keep out of this!*** non immischiarti!

◆**keep to** *v/t path*, *rules* seguire; ***keep to the left / right*** tenere la sinistra / destra; ***keep to the point*** non divagare; ***keep s.o. to his word / promise*** far rispettare una promessa / la parola data a qn; ***keep your hands to yourself!*** tieni a posto le mani!; ***keep sth to a minimum*** mantenere qc al minimo

◆**keep together** *v/t sep* tenere insieme; (*unite*) *things*, *people* tenere uniti

◆**keep up I** *v/i when walking*, *running etc* tener dietro; ***keep up with the news*** tenersi al corrente **II** *v/t sep pace*, *payments* stare dietro a; *bridge*, *pants* reggere; ***keep up the good work!*** continui a lavorare così!; ***I try to keep up my Spanish*** cerco di esercitarmi in spagnolo; ***keep one's morale up*** non perdersi d'animo; ***that child kept me up all night*** il bambino mi ha tenuto sveglio tutta la notte

◆**keep up with** *v/t* stare al passo con; (*stay in touch with*) mantenere i rapporti con

keeper *n in zoo* guardiano *m*, - a *f*; *Br* (*goalkeeper*) portiere *m*

keep-fit *n* ginnastica *f*

keeping *n*: ***be in ~ with*** essere in armonia con; ***be in safe ~*** essere in buone mani

keepsake *n* ricordo *m*

keg *n* barilotto *m*

keg beer *n* birra *f* alla spina

kelp *n* BOT macrocistide *f*

ken *n* comprensione *f*; ***it's beyond my ~*** è al di là della mia comprensione

kennel *n* canile *m*

kennels *npl* canile *m*

Kenya *n* Kenia *m*

kept *pret & past part* → **keep**

kerb *n* orlo *m* del marciapiede

kerb crawler *n autista che abborda prostitute guidando lentamente lungo il marciapiede*

kernel *n* nocciolo *m*

kerosene *n* cherosene *m*

kestrel *n* ZOOL gheppio *m*

ketchup *n* ketchup *m inv*

kettle *n* bollitore *m*; ***I'll put the ~ on*** metterò su l'acqua (per il tè); ***the ~'s boiling*** l'acqua bolle

kettledrum *n* MUS timpano *m*

key I *n to door*, *drawer*, MUS chiave *f*; *on keyboard* tasto *m*; ***the ~ to success*** la chiave del successo **II** *adj* (*vital*) chiave **III** *v/t* COMPUT battere

◆**key in** *v/t sep data* immettere

keyboard *n* COMPUT, MUS tastiera *f*

keyboarder *n* COMPUT, MUS tastierista *m/f*

keycard *n* tessera *f* magnetica

keyed-up *adj* agitato

keyhole *n* buco *m* della serratura

keynote speech *n* discorso *m* programmatico

keypad *n* tastierino *m* nume-

rico **keyring** *n* portachiavi *m inv* **keyword** *n* COMPUT parola *f* chiave
kg *abbr* (= **kilogramme(s)**, **kilogram(s)**) kg (chilogrammo *m*)
khaki *adj colour* cachi *inv*
kick I *n* calcio *m*; *infml* (*thrill*) gusto *m*; (***just***) ***for ~s*** *infml* (solo) per il gusto di farlo; ***he gets a ~ out of it*** lo trova eccitante **II** *v/t* dare un calcio a; ***~ s.o. in the stomach*** dare un calcio nello stomaco a qn; ***~ the bucket*** *infml* tirare le cuoia; ***I could have ~ed myself*** *infml* mi sarei preso a schiaffi da solo; *infml* ***~ the habit*** liberarsi da **III** *v/i* dare calci; SPORTS calciare; *of horse* scalciare
◆**kick around** *v/t sep* (*treat harshly*) maltrattare; *infml* (*discuss*) discutere di; ***kick a ball around*** giocare a pallone
◆**kick in I** *v/t sep door* sfondare a calci; ***kick s.o.'s teeth in*** spaccare i denti a calci a qn **II** *v/i* (*drug etc*) *sl* entrare in funzione
◆**kick off I** *v/i infml* (*start*) iniziare; *of player* dare il calcio d'inizio **II** *v/t sep* iniziare; *shoes* liberarsi con un calcio di; ***they kicked him off the committee*** *infml* lo esclusero dal comitato
◆**kick out** *v/t sep* buttar fuori; ***be kicked out of the company/army*** essere buttato fuori dalla ditta/dall'esercito
◆**kick up** *v/t sep*: ***kick up a fuss*** fare una scenata
kickback *n infml* (*bribe*) tangente *f*
kickboxing *n* kick boxing *m*
kickoff *n* SPORTS calcio *m* d'inizio
kickstand *n bicycle*, *motorcycle* cavalletto *m*
kick-start *v/t* mettere in moto
kid I *n infml* (*child*) bambino *m*, -a *f*; *infml* (*young person*) ragazzo *m*, -a *f*; (*young goat*) capretto *m* **II** *adj*: ***~ gloves*** guanti *mpl* di capretto; ***~ brother/sister*** fratello *m*/sorella *f* minore **III** *v/t* ⟨*pret & past part* **-ded**⟩ *infml* prendere in giro; ***are you ~ding me?*** mi stai prendendo in giro? **IV** *v/i* ⟨*pret & past part* **-ded**⟩ *infml* scherzare; ***I was only ~ding*** stavo solo scherzando
◆**kid around** *v/i* fare il buffone
kidder *n infml* burlone *m*, -a *f*
kid gloves *npl*: ***handle s.o. with ~*** trattare qn coi guanti
kidnap *v/t* ⟨*pret & past part* **-ped**⟩ rapire, sequestrare
kidnapper *n* rapitore *m*, -trice *f*, sequestratore *m*, -trice *f*
kidnapping *n* rapimento *m*, sequestro *m* (di persona)
kidney *n* ANAT rene *m*; *in cooking* rognone *m*
kidney bean *n* fagiolo *m* comune
kidney machine *n* MED rene *m* artificiale **kidney stone** *n* MED calcolo *m* renale
kill I *v/t* uccidere; *plant*, *time* ammazzare; TECH *engine etc* spegnere; ***be ~ed in an accident*** morire in un incidente; ***~ o.s.*** suicidarsi; ***~ o.s. laughing*** *infml* morire dalle risate; ***my feet are ~ing me*** *infml* i piedi mi fanno un male da morire; ***I'll do it*** (***even***) ***if it ~s me*** *infml* lo farò anche se dovessi rimetterci le penne **II** *v/i* uccidere; ***cigarettes can ~*** le sigarette possono uccidere **III** *n fig*: ***move in for the ~*** avvicinarsi alla preda
◆**kill off** *v/t sep* sterminare; *fig* distruggere
killer *n* (*murderer*) assassino *m*, -a *f*; (*hired killer*) killer *m/f inv*; ***flu can be a ~*** si può morire d'influenza
killer whale *n* ZOOL orca *f* assassina
killing *n* omicidio *m*; ***make a ~*** *infml* (*lots of money*) fare un pacco di soldi *infml*
killingly *adv infml*: ***~ funny*** divertentissimo
killjoy *n* guastafeste *m/f*
kiln *n* fornace *f*
kilo *n* chilo *m*
kilobyte *n* COMPUT kilobyte *m inv*
kilogramme, *US* **kilogram** *n* chilogrammo *m*
kilometre, *US* **kilometer** *n* chilometro *m*
kilowatt *n* kilowatt *m inv*
kilt *n* kilt *m inv*
kin *n* parenti *mpl*; ***next of ~*** parenti *mpl* stretti
kind[1] *adj* (*+er*) gentile; ***~ to*** gentile con; ***that's very ~ of you*** è molto gentile da parte tua
kind[2] *n* **1.** (*sort*) tipo *m*; ***all ~s of people*** gente di tutti i tipi; ***the only one of its ~*** l'unico del suo genere; ***a fun-***

ny ~ of name un nome piuttosto buffo; ***he's not that ~ of person*** non è quel tipo di persona; ***nothing of the ~!*** niente affatto!; ***did you have a nice time? – yeah, ~ of*** sei stato bene? – sì, abbastanza; ***~ of sad/ strange*** *infml* un po' triste / strano **2.** (*make, brand*) marca *f* **3.** ***payment in ~*** pagamento *m* in natura
kindergarten *n* asilo *m*
kind-hearted *adj* di buon cuore
kindle *v/t* accendere
kindling *n* legna *f* minuta
kindly I *adj* (*+er*) gentile; ***her ~ demeanour made us feel better*** il suo comportamento gentile ci fece sentire meglio **II** *adv* gentilmente; (*please*) per cortesia; ***I don't take ~ to not being asked*** non accetto di buon grado che non mi venga chiesto; ***~ shut the door*** chiudi la porta, per cortesia
kindness *n* gentilezza *f*; ***out of the ~ of one's heart*** per pura gentilezza
kindred I *n* parenti *mpl* **II** *adj* imparentato; ***~ spirit*** spirito *m* affine
kinetic *adj* cinetico
king *n* re *m inv*; ***live like a ~*** vivere come un pascià
kingdom *n* regno *m*; REL ***~ of heaven*** regno *m* dei cieli; ***blow sth to ~ come*** *infml* distruggere completamente qc; ***you can go on doing that till ~ come*** *infml* puoi continuare in eterno; ***the animal ~*** il regno animale
kingpin *n fig* (*person*) perno *m*
king post *n* monaco *m* (di capriata) **king prawn** *n* gamberone *m* **king-size(d)** *adj bed* matrimoniale grande; *cigarettes* lungo
kink *n in hose etc* attorcigliamento *m*; *in hair* riccio *m*
kinky *adj* (*+er*) *infml* particolare *infml*; ***he loved leather gear and ~ underwear*** amava gli abiti in pelle e la biancheria stravagante
kinship *n* parentela *f*
kiosk *n* edicola *f*
kip I *n sl* pisolino *m*; ***I've got to get some ~*** devo schiacciare un pisolino **II** *v/i* ⟨*pret & past part* **-ped**⟩ (*a.* **kip down**) andare a letto
kipper *n* aringa *f* affumicata
kirk *n Scot* chiesa *f*
kiss I *n* bacio *m* **II** *v/t* baciare **III** *v/i* baciarsi
kiss of life *n* respirazione *f* bocca a bocca
kit *n* kit *m inv*; (*equipment*) attrezzatura *f*; ***gym ~*** tenuta *f* da ginnastica; ***get your ~ off!*** *infml* spogliati!; *for assembly* kit *m inv* di montaggio
♦**kit out** *or* **up** *v/t sep Br* attrezzare; (*clothe*) equipaggiare
kitbag *n* sacca *f* da viaggio
kitchen *n* cucina *f*
kitchenette *n* cucinino *m*
kitchen foil *n* carta *f* stagnola **kitchen garden** *n* orto *m* **kitchen knife** *n* coltello *m* da cucina **kitchen roll** *n* carta *f* da cucina **kitchen scales** *npl* bilancia *f* da cucina **kitchen sink** *n*: ***she packs everything but the ~*** *infml* si porta dietro tutta la casa **kitchen unit** *n* modulo *m* di cucina componibile
kite *n* aquilone *m*; ZOOL nibbio *m*; *fig* ***fly a ~*** sondare l'opinione pubblica
kitten *n* gattino *m*
kitty *n money* cassa *f* comune
kiwi *n* ZOOL kiwi *m inv*; *infml* neozelandese *m/f*
kiwi fruit *n* kiwi *m inv*
Kleenex® *n* Kleenex® *m*
km *abbr* (= **kilometre(s)**) km (chilometro *m*)
km/h, kmph *abbr* (= **kilometres per hour**) km/h (chilometri *mpl* all'ora)
kn *abbr* (= **knot(s)** *nautical*) nodo *m*
knack *n* capacità *f inv*; ***there's a ~ to it*** bisogna saperlo fare; ***have a ~ of doing sth*** avere un vero talento per fare qc; ***you'll soon get the ~ of it*** ci prenderai presto la mano
knackered *adj Br sl* distrutto *infml*
knapsack *n* zaino *m*
knead *v/t dough* lavorare
knee I *n* ginocchio *m*; ***be on one's ~s*** essere in ginocchio; ***go*** (***down***) ***on one's ~s*** *liter* cadere in ginocchio **II** *v/t*: ***~ s.o. in the groin*** dare una ginocchiata all'inguine a qn
kneecap *n* rotula *f* **knee-deep** *adj* fino al ginocchio **knee-high** *adj* (alto) fino alle ginocchia **knee jerk** *n* riflesso *m* patellare **knee-jerk** *adj infml* istintivo; ***a ~ reaction*** una reazione istintiva
kneel *v/i* ⟨*pret & past part* **knelt**⟩ inginocchiarsi

◆**kneel down** *v/i* inginocchiarsi

knee-length *adj* al ginocchio **kneepad** *n* ginocchiera *f*

knelt *pret & past part* → ***kneel***

knew *pret* → ***know***

knickers *npl* mutandine *fpl*; ***get one's ~ in a twist*** *sl* agitarsi

knick-knacks *npl infml* ninnoli *mpl*

knife **I** *n* ⟨*pl* ***knives***⟩ coltello *m* **II** *v/t* accoltellare

knife-edge *n fig*: ***be balanced on a ~*** essere sul filo del rasoio **knifepoint** *n*: ***hold s.o. at ~*** tenere qn sotto la minaccia di un coltello

knight **I** *n hist* cavaliere *m*; *chess* cavallo *m* **II** *v/t* fare cavaliere

knighthood *n* titolo *m* di cavaliere; ***receive a ~*** ricevere il titolo di cavaliere

knit ⟨*pret & past part* ***-ted***⟩ **I** *v/t* fare a maglia; ***~ three, purl two*** tre maglie a diritto, due a rovescio **II** *v/i* lavorare a maglia

◆**knit together** *v/i of broken bone* saldarsi

knitting *n sth being knitted* lavoro *m* a maglia; *activity* il lavorare *m* a maglia

knitting machine *n* macchina *f* per maglieria **knitting needle** *n* ferro *m* (da calza)

knitwear *n* maglieria *f*

knives → ***knife***

knob *n on door* pomello *m*; *of butter* noce *f*; *vulg* (*penis*) cazzo *m*

knock **I** *v/t* (*hit*) colpire; *head*, *knee* battere; *infml* (*criticize*) criticare; ***~ s.o. to the ground*** far cadere a terra qn; ***~ s.o. unconscious*** far perdere i sensi a qn; ***~ two rooms into one*** unire due stanze in una **II** *v/i at the door* bussare (***at*** a); ***~ on doors*** andare di porta in porta; ***his knees were ~ing*** gli tremavano le ginocchia **III** *n on door* colpo *m*; *blow* botta *f*; ***there was a ~ at the door*** sentirono un colpo alla porta; ***I got a ~ on the head*** ho preso una botta in testa; ***he took a few ~s*** *infml* ha avuto delle belle botte *infml*

◆**knock around** **I** *v/t sep infml* (*beat*) picchiare **II** *v/i infml* (*travel*) vagabondare

◆**knock back** *v/t sep infml* ***he knocked back his whisky*** si scolò il suo whisky

◆**knock down** *v/t sep of car* investire; ***she was knocked down and killed*** fu investita e uccisa; *object*, *building etc* buttar giù; *infml* (*reduce the price of*) scontare

◆**knock off** **I** *v/t sep sl* (*steal*) fregare *sl* **II** *v/i infml* (*stop work for the day*) smontare *infml*

◆**knock out** *v/t sep tooth* far saltare via; (*make unconscious*) mettere K.O. *infml*; *power lines etc* mettere fuori uso; (*eliminate*) eliminare

◆**knock over** *v/t sep* far cadere; *of car* investire

◆**knock up** *v/t sep meal* preparare in fretta; *shelter* improvvisare; *tennis* palleggiare; *Br infml* svegliare (bussando alla porta)

knockdown *adj*: ***a ~ price*** un prezzo stracciato

knocker *n on door* battente *m*

knockers *npl Br infml* tette *fpl*

knock-kneed *adj* con le gambe storte

knock-on effect *n Br* effetto *m* a catena (***on*** su) **knockout** *n in boxing* K.O. *m inv* **knock-up** *n tennis* palleggio *m*

knot **I** *n* nodo *m*; ***tie/untie a ~*** fare/sciogliere un nodo; *fig* ***tie the ~*** sposarsi; *in wood* nodo *m* **II** *v/t* ⟨*pret & past part* ***-ted***⟩ annodare

knotty *adj problem* spinoso

know **I** *v/t* ⟨*pret* ***knew***, *past part* ***known***⟩ **1.** sapere; ***he might even be dead for all I ~*** per quel che ne so potrebbe anche essere morto; ***that's worth ~ing*** vale la pena di saperlo; ***before you ~ where you are*** prima che tu sappia dove ti trovi; *person*, *place* conoscere; ***if I ~ John, he'll already be there*** se conosco John, sarà già lì; ***she wishes to be ~n as Mrs White*** desidera essere conosciuta come signora White; (*experience*) sperimentare; ***I've never ~n it to rain so heavily*** non ho mai sperimentato una pioggia così intensa; ***~ about*** sapere di *or* su; ***~ how to waltz*** saper ballare il valzer **2.** (*recognize*) riconoscere; ***~ s.o. by his voice*** riconoscere qn dalla voce; ***the welfare system as we ~ it*** il sistema assistenziale così come lo conosciamo; ***do you ~ the difference between…?*** riconosci la differenza tra …? **II** *v/i* ⟨*pret* ***knew***, *past* *part* **known**⟩ sapere; ***I don't ~*** non so; ***yes, I ~*** sì, lo so; ***as far as I ~*** a quanto so; ***who ~s?*** chissà?; ***you never ~*** non si sa mai **III** *n*: ***be in the ~*** *infml* essere beninformato

◆**know about** **I** *v/t history* conoscere; (*have been told about*) essere al corrente di; ***I know about that*** ne sono al corrente; ***did you know about Maggie?*** lo sai di Maggie?; ***I don't know about that*** non lo so; (*don't agree*) non ne sarei così sicuro; ***I don't know about you, but I'm hungry*** non so cosa ne pensi, ma io ho fame **II** *v/t sep*: ***know a lot about sth*** conoscere bene qc; ***I know all about that*** lo conosco molto bene; (*I'm aware of that*) ne sono consapevole; (*I've been told about it*) ne sono stato informato

◆**know of** *v/t* sentire di; ***not that I know of*** non che io sappia

know-all *n infml* sapientone *m*, -a *f*

knowhow *n infml* know-how *m inv*

knowing *adj* d'intesa

knowingly *adv* (*wittingly*) deliberatamente; *smile etc* con aria d'intesa

know-it-all *n US infml* → ***know-all***

knowledge *n* conoscenza *f*; ***to the best of my ~*** per quanto ne sappia; ***have a good ~ of …*** avere una buona conoscenza di …; ***without my ~*** a mia insaputa; (***secure***) ***in the ~ that …*** sapendo che …; ***be common ~*** essere di dominio pubblico; ***have no ~ of sth.*** non sapere niente di qc; ***deny all ~ of sth.*** dichiarare di non sapere niente di qc

knowledgeable *adj* ferrato

known *past part* → ***know***

knuckle *n* nocca *f*

◆**knuckle down** *v/i infml* impegnarsi

◆**knuckle under** *v/i infml* cedere

KO *n* (*knockout*) K.O. *m inv*

Koran *n* Corano *m*

Korea *n* Corea *f*

Korean **I** *adj* coreano **II** *n* coreano *m*, -a *f*; *language* coreano *m*

kosher *adj* REL kasher; *infml* a posto

kowtow *v/i infml* prostrarsi

kph *abbr* (= **kilometres per hour**) km/h (chilometri *mpl* all'ora)

kraut *n pej* tedesco *m*, -a *f*

Kremlin *n*: ***the ~*** il Cremlino

kudos *n* gloria *f*

kumquat *n* BOT kumquat *m*

kw *abbr* (= **kilowatt(s)**) kW (chilowatt *m*)

L

L, l *n* l, L *f inv*

l *abbr* **1.** (= **litre(s)**) l (litro *m*) **2.** (= **left**) sinistra *f* (sin.)

L *abbr* **1.** (= **Learner**) *Br* AUTO P (= principiante) **2.** (= **large**) *on clothes* L *f*

LA *abbr* (= **Los Angeles**) Los Angeles *f*

lab *n* laboratorio *m*

Lab *abbr* (= **Labour**) partito *m* laburista

label **I** *n* etichetta *f* **II** *v/t* ⟨*pret & past part* **-led**, *US* **-ed**⟩ *baggage* mettere l'etichetta su; ***~ s.o.*** (***as***) ***a criminal*** considerare qn un delinquente

labor *etc US* → ***labour*** *etc*

laboratory *n* laboratorio *m*

laboratory technician *n* tecnico *m* di laboratorio

Labor Day *n US* festa *f* del lavoro (*il primo lunedì di settembre*)

laborious *adj* laborioso

labor union *n US* sindacato *m*

labour, *US* **labor** **I** *n* (*work*) lavoro *m*; *in pregnancy* travaglio *m*; ***be in ~*** avere le doglie; ***withdraw one's ~*** incrociare le braccia, scioperare; ***she went into ~*** le sono venute le doglie **II** *v/i* lavorare duro; ***~ to do sth*** faticare a fare qc; ***~ up a hill*** salire a fatica una collina

labour camp *n* campo *m* di lavoro **Labour Day** *n* festa *f* del lavoro

laboured, *US* **labored** *adj style*, *speech* pesante; *breathing* affannoso

labourer, *US* **laborer** *n* manovale *m*

labour force *n* forza *f* lavoro **labour-intensive** *adj* con un alto impiego di manodopera **labour market** *n* mercato *m* del lavoro **labour pains** *npl* travaglio *m* **Labour Party** *n* partito *m* laburista **labour-saving** *adj* che fa risparmiare lavoro **labour ward**, *US* **labor ward** *n* MED sala *f* travaglio
labrador *n* labrador *m inv*
labyrinth *n* labirinto *m*
lace I *n material* pizzo *m*; *for shoe* laccio *m* **II** *v/t shoe* allacciare; **~ a drink with drugs / poison** drogare / avvelenare una bevanda; **~d with brandy** corretto al brandy
◆ **lace up** *v/t sep shoes* allacciare
lacerate *v/t* lacerare
laceration *n* lacerazione *f*; (*tear*) strappo *m*
lace-up (shoe) *n* scarpa *f* allacciata
lack I *n* mancanza *f*; **there was no ~ of applicants** non mancavano candidati; **~ of time** mancanza di tempo **II** *v/t* mancare di **III** *v/i*: **be ~ing** mancare; **he is ~ing in courage** manca di coraggio
lackadaisical *adj* indolente
lackey *n liter*, *fig* lacchè *m*
lacking *adj*: **be found ~** rivelarsi carente
lacklustre, *US* **lackluster** *adj* scialbo
laconic *adj* laconico
lacquer I *n for hair* lacca *f* **II** *v/t* laccare; *hair* spruzzare la lacca su
lactose *n* lattosio *m*
lacy *adj* (+*er*) di pizzo; **~ underwear** biancheria *f* di pizzo
lad *n* ragazzo *m*; **young ~** ragazzo *m* giovane; **he's a bit of a ~** *infml* è un birbantello; **he likes a night out with the ~s** *Br infml* gli piace passare una serata fuori con gli amici
ladder I *n* scala *f* (a pioli); *Br*: *in tights* sfilatura *f* **II** *v/t Br* **I've ~ed my tights** mi sono smagliata i collant **III** *v/i Br* (*stocking*) smagliarsi
ladderproof *adj Br* indemagliabile
laden *adj* carico
ladies (room) *n* bagno *m* per donne
ladle I *n* mestolo *m* **II** *v/t* versare con un mestolo
◆ **ladle out** *v/t sep* prodigare
lady *n* signora *f*; **ladies and gentlemen!** signore e signori!; **ladies' bicycle** bicicletta *f* da donna; (*noble*) dama *f*; **Lady** (*as a title*) lady *f*
ladybird, *US* **ladybug** *n* coccinella *f*
lady-in-waiting *n* dama *f* di compagnia **lady-killer** *n infml* rubacuori *m inv* **ladylike** *adj* da signora; **she's not very ~** non è certo una signora
lag I *n* (*time-lag*) ritardo *m* **II** *v/i* ⟨*pret & past part* **-ged**⟩ *in pace* restare indietro **III** *v/t pipes* isolare
◆ **lag behind** *v/i* essere indietro; **the government is lagging behind in the polls** nei sondaggi il governo è indietro
lager *n* birra *f* (bionda); **a glass of ~** un bicchiere di birra
lager lout *n Br* giovane ubriacone *m*
lagging *n Br* (materiale) isolante *m*
lagoon *n* laguna *f*
laid *pret & past part* → **lay**[2]
laidback *adj* rilassato
lain *past part* → **lie**[2]
lair *n* tana *f*; (*den*) covo *m*
laissez-faire *n* laissez-faire *m*
laity *n* laici *mpl*
lake[1] *n* lago *m*
lake[2] *n* (*colour*) pigmento *m* rosso
lamb *n animal*, *meat* agnello *m*; (*meat*) agnello *m*; **you poor ~!** povero tesoro!; **like a ~ to the slaughter** come una bestia condotta al macello
lambaste, lambast *v/t* criticare aspramente
lamb chop *n* costoletta *f* d'agnello
lambskin *n* pelle *f* d'agnello
lamb's-lettuce *n* valerianella *f*
lambswool *n* lana *f* d'agnello
lame *adj* (+*er*) *person* zoppo; *excuse* zoppicante
lamé *n* TEX lamé *m*
lame duck *n infml* persona *f* inerme
lament I *n* lamento; LIT, MUS lamento *m m* **II** *v/t* piangere; **~ the fact that …** lamentarsi del fatto che …
lamentable *adj* deplorevole
lamented *adj*: **the late ~** il compianto
laminated *adj surface* laminato; *paper* plastificato
laminated glass *n* vetro *m* laminato
lamp *n* lampada *f*
lamplight *n*: **in the ~** alla luce artificiale
lampoon *v/t* satireggiare
lamppost *n* lampione *m* **lampshade** *n* paralume *m*
LAN *abbr* (= **local area network**)

COMPUT rete *f* locale, LAN *f*

lance I *n* lancia *f* **II** *v/t* MED incidere

lance corporal *n* appuntato *m*

land I *n* terreno *m*; (*shore*) terra *f*; (*country*) paese *m*; ***by ~*** per via di terra; ***on ~*** sulla terraferma; ***work on the ~*** *as farmer* lavorare la terra **II** *v/t aeroplane* far atterrare; *job* accaparrarsi; ***~ o.s. in trouble*** *infml* cacciarsi nei guai; ***he got ~ed with the problem*** *infml* gli è stato rifilato il problema; *Br infml* ***he ~ed him one*** *or* ***he ~ed him a punch on the jaw*** gli assestò un pugno sulla mascella **III** *v/i of aeroplane* atterrare; *of ball, sth thrown* cadere, finire; ***the bomb ~ed on the building*** la bomba cadde sull'edificio; ***~ on one's feet*** *fig* cadere in piedi

◆**land up** *v/i infml* finire; ***land up in prison*** finire in carcere

landing *n of aeroplane* atterraggio *m*; *top of staircase* pianerottolo *m*

landing field *n* terreno *m* d'atterraggio **landing gear** *n* carrello *m* d'atterraggio **landing strip** *n* pista *f* d'atterraggio

landlady *n of bar* proprietaria *f*; *of rented room* padrona *f* di casa **land line** *n* TEL linea *f* telegrafica **landlocked** *adj* senza sbocco sul mare **landlord** *n of bar* proprietario *m*; *of rented room* padrone *m* di casa **landmark** *n* punto *m* di riferimento; *fig* pietra *f* miliare **land owner** *n* proprietario *m*, -a *f* terriero, -a **land registry** *n Br* catasto *m*

landscape I *n* paesaggio *m* **II** *adv print* landscape, orizzontale **III** *v/t* abbellire

landscape gardening *n* architettura *f* di giardini

landslide *n* frana *f* **landslide victory** *n* vittoria *f* schiacciante

lane *n in country* viottolo *m*; (*alley*) vicolo *m*; AUTO corsia *f*; *shipping lane* rotta *f*; *fig* ***in the fast ~*** in corsia di sorpasso; ***change ~s*** cambiare corsia; ***get in ~*** immettersi in corsia

language *n* lingua *f*; (*speech, style*) linguaggio *m*; ***your ~ is appalling*** il tuo linguaggio è esecrabile; ***bad ~*** *or* ***strong ~*** linguaggio *m* volgare

language barrier *n* barriera *f* linguistica **language course** *n* corso *m* di lingue **language lab(oratory)** *n* laboratorio *m* linguistico **language school** *n* scuola *f* di lingue

lank *adj pej*: *hair* diritto

lanky *adj* (+*er*) *person* allampanato

lantern *n* lanterna *f*

lap¹ *n of track* giro *m* (di pista)

lap² *n of person* grembo *m*; ***in or on her ~*** in grembo; ***live in the ~ of luxury*** vivere nel lusso

lap³ *n of water* sciabordio *m*

◆**lap up** *v/t sep* ⟨*pret & past part* **-ped**⟩ *drink, milk* leccare; *flattery* compiacersi di

lap dancer *n* ballerina *f* di lap dance **lap dancing** *n* lap dance *f* **lap dog** *n* cagnolino *m* da grembo

lapel *n* bavero *m*

lapse I *n* (*mistake, slip*) mancanza *f*; *of time* intervallo *m*; ***~ of memory*** vuoto *m* di memoria; ***~ of taste*** caduta *f* di tono **II** *v/i* scadere; ***~ into*** cadere in; ***he ~d into silence*** cadde in silenzio; ***he ~d into a coma*** cadde in coma

lapsed *adj Catholic* apostata

laptop *n* COMPUT laptop *m inv*, portatile *m*

larceny *n* furto *m*

larch *n* (*a.* **larch tree**) BOT larice *m*

lard *n* lardo *m*

larder *n* dispensa *f*

large *adj* (+*er*) grande; ***in ~ print*** a grandi caratteri; ***as ~ as life*** in carne ed ossa; ***the world at ~*** il mondo in generale; ***he spoke at ~ on the housing problem*** parlò diffusamente del problema degli alloggi; ***there is a dangerous man at ~*** c'è un uomo pericoloso a piede libero

largely *adv* (*mainly*) in gran parte

large-print *adj book* a grandi caratteri **large-scale** *adj* in grande; *changes* su vasta scala

largesse *n* generosità *f*

lark¹ *n* ZOOL allodola *f*

lark² *n infml, esp Br* (*fun*) divertimento *m*; ***do sth for a ~*** fare qc per divertimento

◆**lark about** *or* **around** *v/i Br infml* spassarsela

larva *n* larva *f*

laryngitis *n* laringite *f*

larynx *n* laringe *f*

lasagne, *US* **lasagna** *n* lasagne *fpl*

lascivious *adj* lascivo

laser *n* laser *m inv*

laser beam *n* raggio *m* laser **laser disk** *n* disco *m* laser **laser pointer** *n* puntatore *m* laser **laser printer** *n* stampante *f* laser

lash¹ I *n* (*as punishment*) frustata *f* II *v/t with whip* frustare; (*rain*) sferzare; (*tie*) legare (**to** a); **~ sth together** legare qc III *v/i*: **~ against** battere violentemente contro

◆**lash down** *v/t sep with rope* assicurare

◆**lash out** *v/i with fists* menar colpi; *words* inveire; **lash out at s.o.** scagliarsi contro qn

lash² *n* (*eyelash*) ciglio *m*

lashing *n*: **peaches with ~s of cream** pesche con una montagna di panna

lass *n* ragazza *f*

lasso I *n* lazo *m inv* II *v/t* prendere al lazo

last¹ I *adj in series* ultimo; (*preceding*) precedente; **~ but one** penultimo; **~ night** ieri sera; **~ Friday** venerdì scorso; **~ year** l'anno scorso II *adv*: **he finished ~** ha finito per ultimo; *in race* è arrivato ultimo; **when I ~ saw him** l'ultima volta che l'ho visto; **~ but not least** per finire; **at ~** finalmente III *n* ultimo *m*, -a *f*; **he was the ~ to leave** è stato l'ultimo ad andarsene; **I'm always the ~ to know** sono sempre l'ultimo a sapere; **the ~ of his money** il resto dei suoi soldi; **the ~ of the cake** il resto della torta; **that was the ~ we saw of him** fu l'ultima volta che lo vedemmo; **the ~ I heard, they were getting married** l'ultima che ho sentito è che stavano per sposarsi; **we shall never hear the ~ of it** non finirà mai

last² *v/i* durare I *v/t*: **I only have $30 to ~ me the rest of the month** ho solo 30 dollari per arrivare alla fine del mese

last³ *n* (*shoe*) forma *f*

last-ditch *adj attempt* estremo

lasting *adj* duraturo; **to my ~ shame** a mia perenne vergogna

last judgment *n*: **the ~** REL il giudizio universale

lastly *adv* per finire

last-minute *adj changes* dell'ultimo minuto

last-minute deal *n* COMM offerta *f* last minute

last name *n US* cognome *m*

last rites *npl*: **the ~** REL l'unzione degli infermi

latch *n* chiavistello *m*

◆**latch on** *v/i Br infml* capire

◆**latch onto** *v/t* attaccarsi a

late I *adj* (+*er*) **1.** (*behind time*) in ritardo **2.** *in day* tardi; **~ summer** estate *f* avanzata; **~ 19th century** il tardo XIX secolo; **have a ~ breakfast** fare colazione tardi **3. of ~** recentemente **4.** (*deceased*) defunto; **your ~ wife** la sua defunta moglie II *adv* tardi; **it's getting ~** si sta facendo tardi; **I'll be home ~ today** oggi tornerò a casa tardi; **the train was running ~** il treno era in ritardo; **the baby was born two weeks ~** il bambino è nato con due settimane di ritardo; **better ~ than never** meglio tardi che mai; **stay up ~** restare alzato fino a tardi

latecomer *n* ritardatario *m*, -a *f*

lately *adv* recentemente

late-night *adj*: **~ movie** ultimo film *m inv*; **~ shopping** apertura *f* serale dei negozi

latent *adj* latente

later *adv* più tardi; **see you ~!** a più tardi; **~ on** più tardi; **at a ~ time** in un secondo momento; **the weather cleared up ~ (on) in the day** il tempo migliorò poi nel corso della giornata; **~ (on) in the play** più avanti nello spettacolo; **I'll tell you ~ (on)** te lo dirò più tardi; **no ~ than Monday** non più tardi di lunedì

lateral *adj* laterale

laterally *adv* lateralmente

lateral thinking *n* pensiero *m* laterale

latest I *adj* ultimo, più recente; **the ~ news** le ultime notizie; **the ~ fashion** l'ultima moda II *n*: **at the ~** al più tardi; **wait till you hear the ~!** aspetta di sentire le ultime notizie!

lathe *n* tornio *m*

lather *n from soap* schiuma *f*; **the horse is in a ~** il cavallo è sudato; **work o.s. up into a ~ (about sth)** *infml* agitarsi eccessivamente (per qc)

Latin I *adj* latino II *n* latino *m*

Latin America *n* America *f* Latina

Latin American I *n* latino-americano *m*, -a *f* II *adj* latino-americano

Latino, **Latina** **I** *n* latino-americano *m*, -a *f* **II** *adj* latino-americano
latitude *n geographical* latitudine *f*; (*freedom to act*) libertà *f inv* d'azione
latrine *n* latrina *f*
latter **I** *adj* (*second*) secondo, ***the ~ part of the book / story is better*** la seconda parte del libro / della storia è migliore; ***the ~ half of the week*** la seconda metà della settimana **II** *n* ***the ~*** quest'ultimo
latter-day *adj* dei giorni nostri
latterly *adv* (*recently*) recentemente
lattice *n* grata *f*
Latvia *n* Lettonia *f*
laudable *adj* lodevole
laugh **I** *v/i* ridere; ***you'll be ~ing on the other side of your face*** *Br or* ***mouth*** *US* ***soon*** piangerai presto; ***~ out loud*** scoppiare a ridere; ***~ in s.o.'s face*** fare una risata in faccia a qn; ***don't make me ~!*** *iron infml* non farmi ridere! **II** *n* risata *f*; ***it was a ~*** *infml* ci siamo divertiti; ***with a ~*** con una risata; ***she gave a loud ~*** scoppiò in una sonora risata; ***have a good ~ about sth*** farsi una bella risata su qc; ***it'll give us a ~*** *infml* ci sarà da divertirsi; ***have the last ~*** ridere per ultimo; ***get a ~*** fare ridere
◆ **laugh at** *v/t* ridere di
◆ **laugh off** *v/t always sep* prendere sul ridere; ***he laughed off their accusations*** prese sul ridere le loro accuse; ***laugh one's head off*** sganasciarsi dalle risate
laughable *adj* ridicolo
laughing **I** *adj*: ***it's no ~ matter*** c'è poco da ridere **II** *n* riso *m*
laughing stock *n* zimbello *m*; ***become a ~*** rendersi ridicolo
laugh lines *npl US* → ***laughter lines***
laughter *n* risata *f*; ***sounds of ~*** delle risate
laughter lines *npl Br* zampe *fpl* di gallina
launch **I** *n boat* lancia *f*; *of rocket, product* lancio *m*; *of ship* varo *m* **II** *v/t rocket, product* lanciare; *ship* varare; ***the attack was ~ed at 15.00 hours*** l'attacco fu sferrato alle 15.00; ***~ a takeover bid*** COMM lanciare un'offerta pubblica di acquisto
◆ **launch into** *v/t* lanciarsi in; ***he launched into a description of his house*** si lanciò in una descrizione della sua casa
launch ceremony *n* cerimonia *f* di lancio
launch(ing) pad *n* rampa *f* di lancio
launder *v/t clothes* lavare e stirare; ***~ money*** riciclare denaro sporco
launderette *n* lavanderia *f* automatica
Laundromat® *n US* lavanderia *f* automatica
laundry *n place* lavanderia *f*; *clothes* bucato *m*; ***do the ~*** fare il bucato
laundry basket *n* cesto *m* del bucato
laurel *n* alloro *m*; ***rest on one's ~s*** riposare sugli allori
lava *n* lava *f*
lavatory *n* gabinetto *m*
lavatory attendant *n* addetto *m*, -a *f* ai gabinetti **lavatory paper** *n* carta *f* igienica **lavatory seat** *n* sedile *m* del gabinetto
lavender *n* lavanda *f*
lavish **I** *adj meal* lauto; *reception*, *lifestyle* sontuoso; ***be ~ with sth*** essere prodigo di qc **II** *v/t*: ***~ sth on s.o.*** colmare qn di qc
lavishly *adv equipped* sontuosamente; *praise* a profusione; *entertain* con grande generosità; ***~ furnished*** arredato sontuosamente
law *n* legge *f*; ***criminal / civil ~*** diritto *m* penale / civile; ***study ~*** studiare legge; ***~ and order*** ordine *m* pubblico; ***break the ~*** infrangere la legge; ***against the ~*** contro la legge; ***forbidden by ~*** vietato dalla legge; ***the ~*** la polizia; ***the ~ of averages*** il calcolo delle probabilità; ***be a ~ unto himself / herself*** fare razza per conto proprio; ***be above the ~*** essere al di sopra della legge; ***go to ~*** adire vie legali; ***take the ~ into one's own hands*** farsi giustizia da sé
law-abiding *adj* che rispetta la legge
law court *n* tribunale *m*
lawful *adj* legale
lawfully *adv* legalmente; ***he is ~ entitled to compensation*** ha legalmente diritto a un risarcimento
lawless *adj* senza legge
lawlessness *n* illegalità *f*
lawn *n* prato *m* all'inglese; ***play on the ~*** giocare sul prato
lawn mower *n* tagliaerba *m inv* **lawn tennis** *n* tennis *m* su prato

lawsuit *n* azione *f* legale; ***bring a ~ against s.o.*** fare causa a qn
lawyer *n* avvocato *m*
lax *adj* (*+er*) permissivo; ***be ~ about sth*** essere permissivo riguardo a qc
laxative **I** *adj* lassativo **II** *n* lassativo *m*
lay[1] *pret* → ***lie***[2]
lay[2] **I** *v/t* ⟨*pret & past part* ***laid***⟩ (*put down*) posare; *eggs* deporre; *vulg* (*sexually*) scopare *vulg*; ***~ the table*** apparecchiare (la tavola); ***~ (one's) hands on*** (*get hold of*) mettere le mani su; ***~ the blame for sth on s.o. / sth*** incolpare qn / qc di qc; ***~ waste*** devastare; ***~ bets on sth*** scommettere su qc **II** *v/i* (*hen*) deporre le uova
◆**lay aside** *v/t sep newspaper, differences, money* mettere da parte; *knitting* mettere via
◆**lay down** *v/t sep book etc* posare; *rules* imporre; ***he laid his bag down on the table*** posò la borsa sul tavolo; ***lay down one's arms*** deporre le armi; ***lay down one's life*** sacrificare la vita; ***lay down the law*** *infml* dettare legge (***to s.o.*** a qn)
◆**lay into** *v/t* (*attack*) aggredire
◆**lay off** *v/t sep workers* licenziare; *temporarily* mettere in cassa integrazione; ***lay off him, will you!*** *infml* lascialo stare!; ***be laid off*** essere messo in cassa integrazione; (*permanently*) essere licenziato
◆**lay on** *v/t sep* (*provide*) offrire
◆**lay out** *v/t sep objects* disporre; *page* impaginare
◆**lay up** *v/t sep*: ***be laid up (in bed)*** essere costretto a letto
lay[3] *adj* laico; ***the ~ clergy*** il clero laico
layabout *n infml* scansafatiche *m/f inv*
lay-by *n on road* piazzola *f* di sosta
layer **I** *n* strato *m*; ***arrange sth in ~s*** disporre qc in strati; ***several ~s of clothing*** diversi strati di abbigliamento **II** *v/t hair* scalare; *vegetables etc* disporre a strati
layette *n* corredino *m* per neonato
layman *n* laico *m*
lay-off *n* licenziamento *m*; ***there have been 50 ~s*** *temporary* 50 operai sono stati messi in cassa integrazione
layout *n of building* pianta *f*; *of garden* disposizione *f*; *of keyboard* impostazione *f*; *of letter* impaginazione *f*; ***page ~*** impaginazione *f*
layover *n US* sosta *f*
layperson *n* laico *m*, -a *f*
◆**laze around** *v/i* oziare
lazily *adv* oziosamente; (*languidly*) pigramente
laziness *n* pigrizia *f*
lazy *adj* (*+er*) *person* pigro; *day* passato a oziare
lazybones *n* pigrone *m*, -a *f*
lb *abbr* (= **pound**) libbra *f*
lbw *abbr* (= **leg before wicket**) *nel cricket, fallo del battitore che ferma con il corpo una palla diretta sul wicket*
LCD *abbr* (= **liquid crystal display**) display *m inv* a cristalli liquidi
lead[1] **I** *v/t* ⟨*pret & past part* ***led***⟩ **1.** *procession, race* essere in testa a; *company, team* essere a capo di; ***~ the way*** essere all'avanguardia **2.** (*guide, take*) condurre; ***~ a life of luxury*** vivere nel lusso **3.** ***this ~s me to believe that ...*** ciò mi fa pensare che ... **II** *v/i* ⟨*pret & past part* ***led***⟩ **1.** *in race, competition* essere in testa; (*provide leadership*) dirigere **2.** ***a street ~ing off the square*** una strada che parte dalla piazza; ***a street ~ing into the square*** una strada che sbocca nella piazza; ***this street ~s to the station*** questa strada porta alla stazione **3.** ***where is this ~ing?*** dove vuoi andare a parare?; ***remarks like that could ~ to trouble*** osservazioni del genere possono causare guai **III** *n in race* posizione *f* di testa; ***be in the ~*** essere in testa; ***take the ~*** passare in testa **IV** *adj singer, story* principale; *guitarist* primo
◆**lead away** *v/t sep prisoner* portare via
◆**lead off** *v/i* cominciare
◆**lead on** **I** *v/i* (*go in front*) guidare **II** *v/t sep* (*deceive*) ingannare; ***she's just leading him on*** lo sta prendendo in giro
◆**lead up** *v/t sep* portare (***to*** a); *fig* ***lead s.o. up the garden path*** menare qn per il naso
◆**lead up to** *v/i* preludere; ***the events that led up to the war*** gli eventi che hanno portato alla guerra; ***what are you leading up to?*** dove vuoi arrivare?; ***what's all this leading up to?*** a

cosa porterà tutto questo?
lead[2] *n for dog* guinzaglio *m*
lead[3] *n substance* piombo *m*; *in pencil* mina *f*
leaded *adj petrol* con piombo
leader *n person* capo *m*; *in race*, *on market* leader *m/f inv*; *in newspaper* editoriale *m*
leadership *n of party etc* direzione *f*, leadership *f inv*; ***under his ~*** sotto la sua direzione; ***~ skills*** capacità *f* di comando; ***~ contest*** lotta *f* per la direzione
lead-free *adj petrol* senza piombo
leading *adj runner* in testa; *company*, *product* leader *inv*
leading-edge *adj company*, *technology* all'avanguardia **leading lady** *n* attrice *f* protagonista **leading light** *n* fanale *m* di direzione **leading man** *n* attore *m* protagonista **leading question** *n* domanda *f* tendenziosa
lead poisoning *n* MED avvelenamento *m* da piombo
leaf *n* ⟨*pl* ***leaves***⟩ foglia *f*; *of paper* foglio *m*; *of table* ribalta *f*; ***he swept the leaves into a pile*** spazzare le foglie in un mucchio; *fig* ***take a ~ out of*** *or* ***from s.o.'s book*** seguire l'esempio di qn; ***turn over a new ~*** voltare pagina
◆**leaf through** *v/t* sfogliare
leaflet *n* dépliant *m inv*
leaf mould *n* pacciame *m*
leafy *adj tree* frondoso; *lane* ricco di verde
league *n* lega *f*; SPORTS campionato *m*; ***League of Nations*** Lega *f* delle Nazioni; ***be in ~ with s.o.*** essere in combutta con qn; *fig* ***he was not in the same ~*** non era allo stesso livello; ***this is way out of your ~!*** è al di sopra delle tue capacità; ***the club is top of the ~*** il club è in testa al campionato
leak I *n of water* perdita *f*; *of gas* fuga *f*; ***that tank is ~ing acid*** il serbatoio perde acido; ***there's been a ~*** *of information* c'è stata una fuga di notizie **II** *v/i of pipe* perdere; *of boat* far acqua; ***water is ~ing (in) through the roof*** c'è una perdita d'acqua dal tetto
◆**leak out** *v/i of air*, *gas* fuoriuscire; *of news* trapelare
leakage *n* (*act*) fuoriuscita *f*
leaky *adj* (+*er*) *pipe* che perde; *boat* che fa acqua
lean[1] ⟨*pret & past part* ***-ed*** *or* ***leant***⟩ **I** *v/i be at an angle* pendere; (*rest*) appoggiarsi; ***~ against sth*** appoggiarsi a qc; ***~ back/forward*** tendersi indietro/in avanti; ***he ~ed across the counter*** si appoggiò sul banco; ***she ~ed on my arm*** si appoggiò al mio braccio; ***~ toward(s) socialism*** propendere per il socialismo **II** *v/t* appoggiare; ***~ sth against sth*** appoggiare qc a qc
◆**lean back** *v/i* appoggiarsi indietro
◆**lean forward** *v/i* sporgersi in avanti
◆**lean on** *v/i*: ***lean on s.o.*** contare su qn; *infml* (*put pressure on*) fare pressioni su
◆**lean out** *v/i* sporgersi (***of*** da)
◆**lean over backwards** *v/i* fare di tutto; *fig* ***she leant over backwards to help him*** fece di tutto per aiutarlo
lean[2] *adj* (+*er*) *meat* magro; *style*, *prose* asciutto; ***go through a ~ patch*** attraversare un periodo di magra
lean-to *n piccola costruzione addossata a un edificio più grande*
leap I *n* salto *m*; ***a great ~ forward*** un grande balzo in avanti; *fig* ***a ~ into the unknown*** *or* ***a ~ in the dark*** un salto nel buio; *fig* ***by ~s and bounds*** a passi da gigante **II** *v/i* ⟨*pret & past part* ***-ed*** *or* ***leapt***⟩ saltare; ***~ to one's feet*** balzare in piedi
◆**leap at** *v/i opportunity* scattare davanti a
◆**leap out** *v/i* balzare fuori (***of*** da); ***he leapt out of the car*** balzò fuori dalla macchina
◆**leap up** *v/i* (*prices*) aumentare improvvisamente
leapfrog *n* cavallina *f*; ***play ~*** giocare alla cavallina
leap year *n* anno *m* bisestile
learn ⟨*pret & past part* ***-ed*** *or* ***learnt***⟩ **I** *v/t* imparare; (*hear*) apprendere; ***~ (how) to do sth*** imparare a fare qc; ***I ~ed (how) to swim*** ho imparato a nuotare **II** *v/i* imparare; ***~ from experience*** apprendere dall'esperienza; ***~ about*** *or* ***of*** venire a sapere di; ***you just never ~, do you!*** ma quando imparerai?; ***you live and ~*** non si finisce mai d'imparare
learned *adj* colto; ***a ~ man*** un uomo

colto

learner *n* principiante *m/f*

learner driver *n* principiante *m/f* (alla guida)

learning *n* (*knowledge*) sapere *m*; ***a man of ~*** un uomo di cultura; (*act*) apprendimento *m*

learning curve *n* processo *m* di apprendimento; ***be constantly on the ~*** non finire mai di imparare

learnt *pret & past part* → ***learn***

lease I *n* (contratto *m* di) affitto *m*; ***a new ~ of life*** nuove prospettive *fpl* (di vita) **II** *v/t flat, equipment* affittare; ***~ sth from s.o.*** affittare qc da qn; ***~ sth to s.o.*** affittare qc a qn

◆ **lease out** *v/t flat, equipment* dare in affitto

leaseback *n* FIN leaseback *m*

leasehold I *n* immobile *f* in locazione **II** *adj/adv* in locazione

leaseholder *n* affittuario *m*, -a *f*

lease purchase *n* acquisto *m* in leasing

leash *n for dog* guinzaglio *m*

leasing *n* leasing *m*

least I *adj* (*slightest*) minimo; ***I've the ~ debt*** io ho il debito minore **II** *adv* meno **III** *n* minimo *m*; ***not in the ~ suprised/disappointed*** per niente sorpreso/deluso; ***at ~*** almeno; ***to say the ~*** a dir poco; ***that's the ~ of my worries*** è l'ultima delle mie preoccupazioni

leather I *n* pelle *f*, cuoio *m* **II** *adj* di pelle, di cuoio

leathery *adj skin* coriaceo

leave I *v/t* ⟨*pret & past part* ***left***⟩ **1.** lasciare; *room, house, office* uscire da; *station, airport* partire da; ***~ school*** finire gli studi; ***let's ~ things as they are*** lasciamo le cose come stanno; ***how did you ~ things with him?*** come sei rimasto d'accordo con lui?; ***she left him for another man*** lo ha lasciato per un altro; ***~ home*** andare via di casa; ***~ the country*** abbandonare il paese; ***~ the road*** uscire di strada; ***~ s.o. dead*** causare la morte di qn; ***~ s.o. standing*** *infml* superare qn; ***~ for good*** abbandonare per sempre; ***~ s.o. doing sth*** lasciar fare qc a qn; ***~ the children with s.o.*** lasciare i bambini da qn; ***~ sth lying about*** lasciare in giro qc; ***~ the light on*** lasciare la luce accesa; ***~ a lot to be desired*** lasciare (molto) a desiderare; ***I'll ~ you to it*** ti lascio fare; ***let's ~ it at that*** chiudiamo qui **2.** ***~ s.o./sth alone*** lasciare stare qn/qc **3.** ***be left*** rimanere; ***there is nothing left*** non è rimasto niente **4.** (*forget*) dimenticare **II** *v/i* ⟨*pret & past part* ***left***⟩ *of person, plane, bus* partire; ***he's just left*** è appena uscito **III** *n* (*holiday*) congedo *m*; MIL licenza *f*; ***on ~*** in congedo, in licenza; ***ask s.o.'s ~ to do sth*** chiedere a qn il permesso di fare qc; ***I've got ~ to attend the conference*** ho il permesso di partecipare alla conferenza; ***~ of absence*** permesso *m*; ***take ~ of one's senses*** perdere il ben dell'intelletto

◆ **leave behind** *v/t sep intentionally* lasciare; ***we've left all that behind us*** ci siamo lasciati tutto alle spalle; ***he left all his fellow students behind*** si è lasciato alle spalle i suoi compagni di studi; (*forget*) dimenticare

◆ **leave off I** *v/t sep lid* non mettere; *lights* lasciare spento; ***you left her name off the list*** hai lasciato il suo nome fuori dall'elenco **II** *v/t & v/i infml* smettere; ***leave off!*** smettila!; ***he picked up where he left off*** ha ripreso da dove aveva smesso

◆ **leave on** *v/t sep hat, coat* non togliersi; *TV, computer* lasciare acceso

◆ **leave out** *v/t sep word, figure* omettere; (*not put away*) lasciare in giro; ***leave me out of this*** non mi immischiare in questa faccenda; ***he got left out of things*** restò escluso dalla faccenda

◆ **leave over** *v/t sep*: ***be left over*** avanzare; ***the meat is left over from yesterday*** la carne è avanzata da ieri

leaven I *v/t form* vivacizzare **II** *n* lievito *m*

leaves *pl* → ***leaf***

leave-taking *n* commiato *m*

leaving party *n* festa *f* d'addio

lech *v/i*: ***~ after/over s.o.*** *Br infml* sbavare per qn

lecher *n* sporcaccione *m*

lecherous *adj* lussurioso

lectern *n* leggio *m*

lecture I *n* conferenza *f*; UNIV lezione *f*; (*scolding*) paternale *f* **II** *v/i at uni-*

versity insegnare; ***he ~s in English*** insegna inglese; ***he ~s at Princeton*** insegna a Princeton **III** *v/t*: ***~ s.o. on sth*** fare lezione a qn su qc; *fig* fare una paternale a qn su qc; ***he ~s us in French*** ci fa lezione di francese
lecture hall *n* aula *f* magna
lecturer *n* docente *m/f* universitario, -a; ***assistant ~*** *Br docente universitario, paragonabile all'assistente*; ***senior ~*** *Br docente universitario di grado superiore, corrispondente al ricercatore*
led *pret & past part* → ***lead***[1]
LED *abbr* (= **light-emitting diode**) LED *m inv*
ledge *n of window* davanzale *m*; *on rock face* sporgenza *f*
ledger *n* COMM libro *m* mastro
leech *n* sanguisuga *f*
leek *n* porro *m*
leer I *n sexual* sguardo *m* libidinoso; *evil* sguardo *m* malvagio **II** *v/i*: ***he ~ed at the girl*** lanciava sguardi maliziosi alla ragazza
leeway *n fig* spazio *m* di manovra; *in a decision* libertà *f* di movimento; ***he has given them too much ~*** ha lasciato loro troppa libertà di movimento
left[1] **I** *adj* sinistro; POL di sinistra **II** *n* sinistra *f*; ***the ~*** POL la sinistra; ***on the ~*** a sinistra; ***on the ~ of sth*** a sinistra di qc; ***to the ~*** *turn*, *look* a sinistra **III** *adv turn*, *look* a sinistra
left[2] *pret & past part* → ***leave***
left back *n* SPORTS difensore *m* sinistro
left-click COMPUT **I** *v/i* fare clic con il pulsante sinistro del mouse **II** *v/t* fare clic con il pulsante sinistro del mouse su **left-hand** *adj* sinistro; ***~ side*** lato *m* sinistro; ***he stood on the ~ side of the king*** stava a sinistra del re; ***take the ~ turn*** svoltare a sinistra **left-hand drive** *n* guida *f* a sinistra **left-handed I** *adj* mancino; ***~ compliment*** *US* falso complimento *m* **II** *adv* con la sinistra **left-hander** *n* mancino *m*, -a *f*
leftist *adj* POL di sinistra
left luggage (office) *n* deposito *m* bagagli **left-overs** *npl food* avanzi *mpl* **left-wing** *adj* POL di sinistra
leg *n of person* gamba *f*; *of animal* zampa *f*; *of turkey*, *chicken* coscia *f*; *of lamb* cosciotto *m*; *of journey* tappa *f*; *of competition* girone *m*; ***pull s.o.'s ~*** prendere in giro qn; ***be on one's last ~s*** essere ridotto al lumicino; ***he hasn't (got) a ~ to stand on*** (*no excuse*) non ha una scusa che tenga; (*no proof*) non ha un motivo convincente
legacy *n* eredità *f inv*
legal *adj* legale; ***make sth ~*** rendere legale qc; ***it is not ~ to sell drink to children*** non è legale vendere da bere ai bambini; ***~ limit*** limite *m* legale; ***women had no ~ status*** le donne erano prive di status legale; ***for ~ reasons*** per motivi legali; ***~ charges*** *or* ***fees*** *or* ***costs*** spese *fpl* legali; ***the British ~ system*** il sistema giudiziario britannico; ***the ~ profession*** la professione legale
legal action *n* azione *f* legale; ***take ~ against s.o.*** procedere per via legale contro qn **legal adviser** *n* consulente *m/f* legale **legal aid** *n* patrocinio *m* gratuito
legality *n* legalità *f inv*
legalize *v/t* legalizzare
legally *adv* legalmente; ***~ responsible*** legalmente responsabile; ***be ~ entitled to sth*** avere legalmente diritto a qc; ***~ binding*** legalmente vincolante
legal tender *n* moneta *f* a corso legale
legate *n* legato *m*
legation *n* legazione *f*
legend *n* leggenda *f*; ***become a ~ in one's lifetime*** diventare una leggenda vivente
legendary *adj* leggendario
-legged *adj suf* dalle gambe …, a gambe …; ***bare-legged*** a gambe nude
leggings *npl* fuseau *m*
legible *adj* leggibile
legion I *n* legione *f* **II** *adj* numerosissimo
legislate *v/i* legiferare
legislation *n* legislazione *f*
legislative *adj* legislativo
legislature *n* POL legislatura *f*
legitimacy *n* legittimità *f*
legitimate I *adj* legittimo **II** *v/t* legittimare
legless *adj Br infml* ubriaco
leg-pull *n infml* presa *f* in giro **leg room** *n* spazio *m* per le gambe

legume *n* legume *m*
leguminous *adj* delle leguminose
leg-up *n*: ***give s.o. a ~*** dare una spinta a qn
legwork *n*: ***do the ~*** fare il galoppino
leisure *n* svago *m*; ***at your ~*** con comodo
leisure centre, *US* **leisure center** *n* centro *m* sportivo e ricreativo
leisurely *adj pace, lifestyle* tranquillo; senza fretta; ***go at a ~ pace*** (*person*) camminare senza fretta; ***have a ~ breakfast*** fare colazione senza fretta
leisure time *n* tempo *m* libero
leisurewear *n* abbigliamento *m* per il tempo libero
lemma ⟨*pl* ***lemmas*** *or* ***lemmata***⟩ *n* LING lemma *m*
lemon *n* limone *m*; (*defective*) bidone *m*
lemonade *n fizzy* gazzosa *f*; *made from lemon juice* limonata *f*
lemon balm *n* BOT melissa *f* **lemon curd** *n* COOK crema *f* al limone **lemon grass** *n* BOT, COOK citronella *f* **lemon juice** *n* succo *m* di limone **lemon sole** *n* ZOOL limanda *f* **lemon squeezer** *n* spremilimoni *m inv* **lemon tea** *n* tè *m inv* al limone
lend *v/t* ⟨*pret & past part* ***lent***⟩ prestare; ***~ s.o. sth*** prestare qc a qn; *fig* (*give*) dare (***to*** a); ***~ (one's) support to s.o. / sth*** dare sostegno a qn; ***~ a hand*** dare una mano
lending library *n* biblioteca *f* (per prestito)
length *n* **1.** lunghezza *f*; ***what ~ is it?*** quanto è lungo?; ***two metres in ~*** lungo due metri; *fig* ***go to great ~s to do sth*** fare ogni sforzo per fare qc **2.** *piece*: *of material* taglio *m* **3.** ***at ~*** *describe, explain* a lungo; (*eventually*) alla fine
lengthen *v/t* allungare
lengthways, **lengthwise** **I** *adj* messo per (il) lungo **II** *adv* per (il) lungo
lengthy *adj* (*+er*) *speech, stay* lungo
lenience *n*, **leniency** *n* indulgenza *f* (***towards*** verso); *of judge, sentence* clemenza *f*
lenient *adj* indulgente; ***be ~ with s.o.*** essere indulgente con qn
lens *n of camera* obiettivo *m*; *of spectacles* lente *f*; *of eye* cristallino *m*
lens cap *n* copriobiettivo *m* **lens cover** *n of camera* copriobiettivo *m*
lent *pret & past part* → ***lend***
Lent *n* REL Quaresima *f*
lentil *n* lenticchia *f*
lentil soup *n* minestra *f* di lenticchie
Leo *n* ASTROL Leone *m*
leopard *n* leopardo *m*
leotard *n* body *m inv*
leper *n* lebbroso *m*, - a *f*
leprosy *n* lebbra *f*
lesbian **I** *n* lesbica *f* **II** *adj* di / per lesbiche; ***~ and gay rights / issues*** problemi / diritti di gay e lesbiche
lesion *n* lesione *f*
less **I** *adv* (di) meno; ***eat / talk ~*** parlare / mangiare (di) meno; ***~ interesting / serious*** meno interessante / serio; ***it costs ~*** costa (di) meno; ***~ than £200*** meno di £200 **II** *adj* meno; ***in ~ time*** in meno tempo; ***~ and ~*** sempre meno; ***none the ~*** ciò nonostante
lessen *v/t & v/i* diminuire
lesser *adj* minore; ***to a ~ extent*** in misura minore; ***a ~ amount*** un importo minore
lesson *n* lezione *f*
let *v/t* ⟨*pret & past part* ***let***⟩ **1.** (*allow*) lasciare; ***~ s.o. do sth*** lasciar fare qc a qn; ***~ me think*** *or* ***see, where did I put it?*** lasciami pensare, dove l'ho messo?; ***~ me go!*** lasciami andare!; ***~ him come in!*** fallo entrare!; ***~'s go / stay*** andiamo / restiamo; ***~'s not argue*** non litighiamo; ***~ alone*** tanto meno; ***~ go of sth*** *of rope, handle* mollare qc **2.** (*rent*) affittare; ***room to ~*** affittasi camera; ***we can't find a house to ~*** non riusciamo a trovare una casa da affittare
◆**let down** *v/t sep hair* sciogliersi; *blinds* abbassare; (*disappoint*) deludere; *dress, trousers* allungare; ***the weather let us down*** il tempo ci ha delusi; ***feel let down*** sentirsi deluso; ***let a tyre*** *Br or* ***tire*** *US* ***down*** sgonfiare una gomma; *fig* ***at the party she really let her hair down*** alla festa si è davvero rilassata
◆**let in** *v/t sep to house* far entrare; ***he let himself in (with his key)*** è entrato (con la chiave); ***let o.s. in for sth*** cacciarsi in qc; ***let s.o. in on sth*** mettere qn al corrente di qc
◆**let off** *v/t always sep not punish* perdonare; *from car* far scendere; ***let off***

steam sfogarsi; ***let s.o. off*** lasciare andare; (*allow not to do*) esonerare; ***I'll let you off this time*** stavolta ti lascio andare; ***let s.o. off with a warning*** lasciare andare qn con un ammonimento

◆**let on I** *v/t*: ***don't let on that ...*** non dire che ... **II** *v/i*: ***he knew but he never let on*** lo sapeva ma non lo ha rivelato

◆**let out** *v/t sep of room, building* far uscire; *jacket etc* allargare; *groan, yell* emettere; ***I'll let myself out*** esco

◆**let up** *v/i* (*stop*) smettere

letdown *n* delusione *f*

lethal *adj* mortale; ~ ***injection*** iniezione *f* letale

lethal dose *n* dose *f* letale **lethal gene** *n* gene *f* letale

lethargic *adj* fiacco

lethargy *n* fiacchezza *f*

letter *n* lettera *f*; ***to the*** ~ alla lettera; ***by*** ~ per lettera; ***write a*** ~ ***of complaint / apology*** scrivere una lettera di reclamo / scuse; ~ ***of recommendation*** *US* lettera *f* di raccomandazione; ~***s*** LIT lettere *fpl*

letter bomb *n* lettera-bomba *f*

letterbox *n on street* buca *f* delle lettere; *in door* cassetta *f* della posta

letterhead *n heading* intestazione *f*; (*headed paper*) carta *f* intestata

lettering *n* lettere *fpl*

letter of credit *n* COMM lettera *f* di credito

letters page *n* PRESS pagina *f* delle lettere al direttore

lettuce *n* lattuga *f*

letup *n*: ***without a*** ~ senza sosta

leukaemia, *US* **leukemia** *n* leucemia *f*

levee *n* argine *m*

level I *adj field, surface* piano; *in competition, scores* pari; ~ ***with*** allo stesso livello di; ***it should lie*** ~ ***with*** dovrebbe essere allo stesso livello di ...; ***draw*** ~ ***with s.o.*** *in match* pareggiare; ***he drew*** ~ ***with the leading car*** ha raggiunto l'auto in testa **II** *n* livello *m*; (*amount*) tasso *m*; (*height*) altezza *f*; (*storey*) piano *m*; TECH livella *f*; ***on the*** ~ *infml* (*honest*) onesto; ~ ***of inflation*** tasso *m* di inflazione; ***a high*** ~ ***of interest*** un alto tasso d'interesse; ***the*** ~ ***of alcohol in the blood*** il tasso alcolico; ***at eye*** ~ all'altezza degli occhi; ***on a*** ~ ***playing field*** allo stesso livello **III** *v/t ground* livellare; *town* radere al suolo; *weapon* spianare (***at*** contro); *accusation* lanciare (***at*** contro); ~ ***the match*** SPORTS pareggiare la partita; ~ ***the score*** pareggiare

◆**level out** *v/i* (*ground*) diventare piano; *fig* stabilizzarsi

level crossing *n Br* passaggio *m* a livello

level-headed *adj* posato

lever I *n* leva *f* **II** *v/t*: ~ ***sth up / off*** sollevare / togliere qc con una leva; ~ ***sth open*** aprire qc facendo leva; ***he*** ~***ed the machine-part into place*** mise il pezzo nella posizione corretta con l'aiuto di una leva

leverage *n* forza *f*; (*influence*) influenza *f*; *fig* ***use sth as*** ~ fare leva su qc

levy I *n* (*act*) esazione *f*; (*tax*) imposta *f* **II** *v/t* ⟨*pret & past part* **-ied**⟩ *taxes* imporre

lewd *adj* (+*er*) osceno

lexicography *n* lessicografia *f*

lexicon *n* lessico *m*

liability *n* (*responsibility*) responsabilità *f inv*; ***we accept no*** ~ ***for ...*** non ci assumiamo alcuna responsabilità per ...; *infml person* peso *m* morto; *infml thing* peso *m*; FIN ***liabilities*** passivo *m*

liable *adj* (*answerable*) responsabile; ***be*** ~ ***for sth*** essere responsabile di qc; ***it's*** ~ ***to break*** (*likely*) è probabile che si rompa; ***be*** ~ ***for tax*** essere soggetto a tassazione; ***be*** ~ ***to prosecution*** essere perseguibile; ***we are*** ~ ***to get shot here*** qui rischiamo di restare colpiti; ***if you don't write it down I'm*** ~ ***to forget it*** se non lo scrivi è probabile che me ne dimentichi

◆**liaise with** *v/t* tenere i contatti con

liaison *n* (*contacts*) contatti *mpl*; (*affair*) relazione *f*

liar *n* bugiardo *m*, -a *f*

lib *n abbr* (= **liberation**) liberazione *f*

libation *n form* libagione *f*

Lib Dem *n abbr* (= **Liberal Democrat**) *Br* POL liberal-democratico *m*, -a *f*

libel I *n* diffamazione *f* **II** *v/t* ⟨*pret & past part* **-led**, *US* **-ed**⟩ diffamare

libellous, *US* **libelous** *adj* diffamatorio

liberal *adj* (*broad-minded*), POL liberale; *portion etc* abbondante; ***be*** ~ ***with one's praise / comments*** essere prodigo di lodi / complimenti; POL liberale

liberate *v/t* liberare

liberated *adj woman* emancipato

liberation *n* liberazione *f*

liberty *n* libertà *f inv*; ***at ~*** *of prisoner etc* in libertà; ***be at ~ to do sth*** poter fare qc; ***I have taken the ~ of giving your name*** mi sono preso la libertà di fare il tuo nome

libidinous *adj* libidinoso

libido *n* libido *f*

Libra *n* ASTROL Bilancia *f*

librarian *n* bibliotecario *m*, -a *f*

library *n* biblioteca *f*

library book *n* libro *m* della biblioteca

library ticket *n* tessera *f* della biblioteca

librettist *n* librettista *m/f*

libretto *n* MUS libretto *m*

Libya *n* Libia *f*

Libyan I *adj* libico **II** *n person* libico *m*, -a *f*

lice *pl* → ***louse***

licence, *US* **license** *n* (*driving licence*) patente *f*; (*road tax licence*) bollo *m* (auto); *for TV* canone *m* (televisivo); *for gun* porto *m* d'armi; *for imports / exports* licenza *f*; *for dog* tassa *f*; ***poetic ~*** licenza *f* poetica

license I *v/t issue license* rilasciare la licenza a; ***be ~d*** *to sell alcohol* essere autorizzato alla vendita di alcolici; ***the car isn't ~d*** la macchina non ha il bollo **II** *n US* → ***licence***

license plate *n US* targa *f*

licentious *adj* licenzioso

lichen *n* BOT lichene *m*

lick I *v/t* leccare; (*flames*) lambire; *infml* (*defeat*) battere; ***~ one's lips*** leccarsi i baffi; *fig* ***~ s.o.'s boots*** leccare i piedi a qn; ***I think we've got it ~ed*** penso che abbiamo risolto il problema **II** *n* leccata *f*; ***a ~ of paint*** una passata di vernice

lickety-split *adv US infml* di gran carriera

licking *n infml* (*defeat*): ***get a ~*** prendere una batosta

lickspittle *n* leccapiedi *m/f*

licorice *n* → ***liquorice***

lid *n* coperchio *m*

lie[1] **I** *n* bugia *f*; ***tell ~s*** dire bugie; ***I tell a ~, it's tomorrow*** non è vero, è domani **II** *v/i* mentire; ***~ to s.o.*** mentire a qn

lie[2] **I** *n* (*position*) disposizione *f*; ***the ~ of the land*** la configurazione del terreno **II** *v/i* ⟨*pret* ***lay***, *past part* ***lain***⟩ *of person* sdraiarsi; *of object* stare; (*be situated*) trovarsi; ***our road lay along the river*** la nostra strada costeggiava il fiume; ***~ dying*** essere in fin di vita; ***~ low*** non farsi vedere; ***that responsibility ~s with your department*** è di responsabilità del vostro reparto

◆**lie about, lie around** *v/i* essere in giro; ***leave sth lying about*** lasciare qc in giro

◆**lie down** *v/i* sdraiarsi

◆**lie in** *v/i* restare a letto fino a tardi

lie detector *n* macchina *f* della verità

lie-down *n infml*: ***have a ~*** fare un sonnellino

lie-in *n*: ***have a ~*** restare a letto fino a tardi

lieu *n*: ***in ~ of*** invece di

lieutenant *n* tenente *m*

life *n* ⟨*pl* ***lives***⟩ vita *f*; *of machine* durata *f*; *of battery* autonomia *f*; ***all her ~*** tutta la vita; ***that's ~!*** così è la vita!; ***plant ~*** vita *f* vegetale; ***this is a matter of ~ and death*** è questione di vita o di morte; ***bring s.o. back to ~*** riportare in vita qn; ***his book brings history to ~*** il suo libro fa rivivere la storia; *fig* ***come to ~*** animarsi; ***at my time of ~*** alla mia età; ***a job for ~*** un lavoro per la vita; ***he's doing ~*** (***for murder***) *infml* sta scontando l'ergastolo (per omicidio); ***he got ~*** *infml* è stato condannato all'ergastolo; ***take one's own ~*** togliersi la vita; ***save s.o.'s ~*** salvare la vita a qn; ***I couldn't do it to save my ~*** non ne sarei assolutamente capace; ***the church is my ~*** la chiesa è la mia vita; ***early in ~*** *or* ***in early ~*** da giovane; ***run for your lives!*** si salvi chi può!; ***I can't for the ~ of me ...*** *infml* non riesco assolutamente a ...; ***never in my ~ have I heard such nonsense*** non ho mai sentito sciocchezze simili in vita mia; ***not on your ~!*** *infml* neanche per sogno!; ***get a ~!*** *infml* lasciami vivere!; ***he is the ~ and soul*** *Br or* ***~*** *US* ***of every party*** è l'anima di ogni festa; ***village ~*** vita *f* di paese; ***this is the ~!*** questa sì che è vita!; ***the good ~*** la bella vita

life assurance *n Br* assicurazione *f* sulla vita **life belt** *n* salvagente *m inv* **lifeblood** *n* linfa *f* vitale **lifeboat** *n* lancia *f* di salvataggio **life buoy** *n* ciambella *f* di salvataggio **life cycle** *n* ciclo *m* vitale **life expectancy** *n* aspettativa *f* di vita **lifeguard** *n* bagnino *m*, -a *f* **life history** *n* ciclo *m* vitale **life imprisonment** *n* ergastolo *m* **life insurance** *n* assicurazione *f* sulla vita **life jacket** *n* giubbotto *m* di salvataggio

lifeless *adj* senza vita

lifelike *adj* fedele

lifeline *n fig* ancora *f* di salvezza **lifelong** *adj* di vecchia data **lifesaver** *n*: ***it was a ~*** mi ha salvato la vita **life-saving** *adj medical equipment*, *drug* salvavita **life sentence** *n* ergastolo *m* **lifesized** *adj* a grandezza naturale **lifestyle** *n* stile *m* di vita **life-threatening** *adj* mortale **lifetime** *n*: ***in my ~*** in vita mia; ***once in a ~*** una volta nella vita; ***during** or **in my ~*** nell'arco della mia vita; ***the chance of a ~*** l'occasione di una vita

lift I *v/t* sollevare; *restrictions* togliere; *infml* (*steal*) grattare; (*plagiarize*) copiare **II** *v/i of fog* diradarsi; *of sadness* scomparire **III** *n Br*: *in building* ascensore *m*; *in car* passaggio *m*; ***give s.o. a ~*** dare un passaggio a qn

◆**lift off** *v/i of rocket* decollare

lift-off *n of rocket* decollo *m*

ligament *n* legamento *m*

light[1] **I** *n* luce *f*; (*lamp*) lampada *f*; ***in the ~ of*** alla luce di; ***have you got a ~?*** hai da accendere?; ***by the ~ of a candle*** a lume di candela; ***at first ~*** all'alba; ***shed ~ on sth*** *fig* fare luce su qc; ***see s.o. / sth in a different ~*** vedere qn / qc sotto una diversa luce; ***in the ~ of*** alla luce di; ***bring sth to ~*** mettere in luce qc; ***finally I saw the ~*** *infml* alla fine ho capito; ***put out the ~s*** spegnere le luci; ***the ~s*** AUTO i fanali; ***~s out!*** spegnere le luci!; ***set ~ to sth*** dare fuoco a qc; ***the ~s*** il semaforo **II** *v/t* ⟨*pret & past part* **lit**⟩ *fire*, *cigarette* accendere; (*illuminate*) illuminare **III** *adj* (+*er*) *not dark* chiaro

◆**light up I** *v/t sep* (*illuminate*) illuminare; ***a smile lit up his face*** un sorriso gli illuminò il volto; ***Piccadilly Circus was all lit up*** Piccadilly Circus era tutta illuminata; ***flames lit up the night sky*** le fiamme illuminavano il cielo notturno **II** *v/i* (*start to smoke*) accendersi una sigaretta; ***the men took out their pipes and lit up*** gli uomini tirarono fuori le pipe e le accesero

◆**light (up)on** *v/t infml* posarsi

light[2] **I** *adj* (+*er*) *not heavy* leggero; *pale* chiaro; ***~ blue*** celeste; ***~ industry*** industria *f* leggera; ***~ opera*** operetta *f*; ***~ reading*** lettura *f* leggera; ***with a ~ heart*** a cuor leggero; ***as ~ as a feather*** leggero come una piuma; ***make ~ of one's difficulties*** non dar peso alle difficoltà; ***you shouldn't make ~ of her problems*** non dovresti prendere alla leggera i suoi problemi; ***make ~ work of sth*** fare qc senza difficoltà **II** *adv*: ***travel ~*** viaggiare leggero

light bulb *n* lampadina *f* **light-coloured**, *US* **light-colored** *adj* ⟨*comp* ***lighter-colo(u)red***, *sup* ***lightest-colo(u)red***⟩ chiaro

lighten[1] *v/t colour* schiarire

lighten[2] *v/t load* alleggerire; ***~ s.o.'s workload*** alleggerire il carico di lavoro di qn

◆**lighten up** *v/i of person* rilassarsi

lighter *n for cigarettes* accendino *m*

lighter fuel *n* gas *m* per accendino

light-fingered *adj* ⟨*comp* ***lighter-fingered***, *sup* ***lightest-fingered***⟩ lesto di mano

light fitting, light fixture *n* (*lightbulb holder*) portalampada *m*; (*bracket*) lampadario *m*

light-headed *adj* ⟨*comp* ***lighter-headed***, *sup* ***lightest-headed***⟩ (*dizzy*) stordito **light-hearted** *adj film* leggero

lighthouse *n* faro *m*

lighting *n* illuminazione *f*; AVIAT luce *f*

lightly *adv touch* leggermente; ***get off ~*** cavarsela con poco; ***sleep ~*** avere il sonno leggero; ***touch ~ on a subject*** sfiorare un argomento; ***speak ~ of s.o. / sth*** parlare alla leggera di qn / qc; ***treat sth too ~*** trattare qc con troppa leggerezza; ***a responsibility not to be ~ undertaken*** una responsabilità da non prendere alla leggera

lightness *n* leggerezza *f*

lightning **I** *n* fulmine *m*; ***a flash of ~*** un fulmine; ***be struck by ~*** essere colpito da un fulmine; ***like (greased) ~*** come un lampo **II** *adj* lampo; ***~ strike*** sciopero *m* lampo; ***with ~ speed*** a velocità lampo; ***~ visit*** visita *f* lampo

lightning conductor *n* parafulmine *m*

light pen *n* penna *f* luminosa **light show** *n* gioco *m* di luci **light switch** *n* interruttore *m* della luce

lightweight *n in boxing* peso *m* leggero; *fig* mezzacalzetta *f*

light year *n* anno *m* luce

like[1] **I** *prep* come; ***~ this / that*** così; ***what is she ~?*** *in looks, character* com'è?; ***it's not ~ him*** *not his character* non è da lui; ***look ~ s.o.*** assomigliare a qn; ***what's he ~?*** com'è?; ***he's bought a car - what is it ~?*** ha comprato una macchina - com'è?; ***she was ~ a sister to me*** era come una sorella per me; ***that's just ~ him!*** è da lui!; ***I never saw anything ~ it*** non ho mai visto niente di simile; ***that's more ~ it!*** così va meglio!; ***it will cost something ~ £10*** costerà circa 10 sterline; ***that sounds ~ a good idea*** sembra una buona idea; ***~ mad*** *or* ***~ anything*** *infml* come un pazzo *infml* **II** *adj*: ***on this and ~ occasions*** in questa e altre occasioni simili **III** *cj infml* (*as*) come; ***~ I said*** come ho già detto **IV** *n*: ***smoking, drinking and the ~*** fumare, bere e cose del genere; ***we shall not see his ~ again*** non rivedremo persone come lui; ***the ~s of me*** quelli come me

like[2] **I** *v/t*: ***I ~ it / her*** mi piace; ***I would ~ …*** vorrei …; ***I would ~ to …*** vorrei …; ***would you ~ …?*** ti va …?; ***would you ~ to …?*** ti va di …?; ***he ~s swimming*** gli piace nuotare; ***if you ~*** se vuoi **II** *n*: ***~s and dislikes*** ciò che piace e ciò che non piace

-like *adj suf* simile a …

likeable *adj* simpatico

likelihood *n* probabilità *f inv*; ***in all ~*** molto probabilmente; ***the ~ is that …*** è probabile che …; ***is there any ~ of him coming?*** esiste qualche probabilità che venga?

likely *adj* (*+er*) (*probable*) probabile; ***not ~!*** difficile!; ***a ~ story!*** a chi la racconti?; ***they are ~ to accept / refuse*** è probabile che accettino / rifiutino; ***he is a ~ person for the job*** è un probabile candidato al posto; ***~ candidates*** probabili candidati *mpl*

like-minded *adj* della stessa idea; ***~ people*** persone della stessa idea

liken *v/t* paragonare (***to*** a)

likeness *n* (*resemblance*) somiglianza *f*

likewise *adv* altrettanto

liking *n* predilezione *f*; ***is it to your ~?*** *form* è di tuo gradimento?; ***take a ~ to s.o.*** prendere qn in simpatia; ***she took a ~ to him*** lo ha preso in simpatia

lilac **I** *n flower* lillà *m inv*; *colour* lilla *m inv* **II** *adj* (color) lilla

lilliputian *adj* lillipuziano

Lilo® *n* materassino *m* gonfiabile

lilt *n* ritmo *m*

lilting *adj accent* cadenzato; *tune* ritmato

lily *n* giglio *m*

lily-livered *adj* codardo **lily of the valley** *n* mughetto *m*

limb *n* arto *m*; ***be out on a ~*** ritrovarsi solo

◆**limber up** *v/i of person* fare riscaldamento

limbo *n fig* limbo *m*; ***our plans are in ~*** i nostri piani sono nel limbo; ***I'm in a sort of ~*** mi trovo in una specie di limbo

lime[1] *n* BOT (*citrus fruit*) limetta *f*

lime[2] *n* BOT (*linden, a.* **lime tree**) tiglio *m*

lime[3] *n* GEOL calce *f*

limegreen *adj* verde *m* acido

limelight *n*: ***be in the ~*** essere in vista

limerick *n* limerick *m inv*

limestone *n* calcare *m*

limit **I** *n* limite *m*; ***within ~s*** entro certi limiti; ***off ~s*** off-limits; ***that's the ~!*** *infml* è il colmo!; ***the city ~s*** i limiti della città; ***a 40-mile ~*** un raggio di 40 miglia; ***the 50 km / h ~*** il limite di 50 km / h; ***is there any ~ on the size?*** esistono limiti di dimensioni?; ***you shouldn't drive, you're over the ~*** non dovresti guidare, hai bevuto troppo; ***that child is the ~!*** quel bambino è insopportabile! **II** *v/t* limitare; ***~ s.o. / sth to sth*** limitare qn / qc a qc

limitation *n* limite *m*; ***know one's ~s***

conoscere i propri limiti
limited *adj* limitato; *esp Br* COMM a responsabilità limitata; ***this offer is for a ~ period only*** questa offerta è valida solo per un periodo limitato; ***this is only true to a ~ extent*** è vero solo in misura limitata; ***ABC Travel Limited*** ABC Viaggi s.r.l.
limited company *n* società *f inv* a responsabilità limitata
limo *n infml* limousine *f inv*
limousine *n* limousine *f inv*
limp[1] *adj* (+*er*) floscio
limp[2] **I** *v/i* zoppicare **II** *n*: ***walk with a ~*** zoppicare; ***he has a ~*** zoppica
limpet *n* patella *f*; ***stick to s.o. like a ~*** stare appiccicato a qn
linchpin *n fig* perno *m*
linden *n* (*a.* **linden tree**) tiglio *m*
line[1] *n* **1.** *on paper, road* linea *f*; *of text* riga *f*; ***draw the ~ at sth*** non tollerare qc; ***in ~ with …*** (*conforming with*) in linea con …; ***drop s.o. a ~*** mandare due righe a qn; ***learn one's ~s*** THEAT imparare le battute; ***read between the ~s*** leggere tra le righe; ***the*** (***fine*** *or* ***thin***) ***~ between right and wrong*** la linea sottile tra il bene e il male; ***behind enemy ~s*** oltre le linee nemiche **2.** *of people, trees* fila *f*; ***stand in ~*** *US* fare la fila; ***he was descended from a long ~ of farmers*** discendeva da una lunga stirpe di agricoltori; ***it's the latest in a long ~ of tragedies*** è l'ultima di una lunga serie di tragedie; ***be next in ~*** essere il successivo nella fila **3.** (*cord*) filo *m*; *fig* ***toe the ~*** rigare dritto **4.** *of business* settore *m*; ***it's all in the ~ of duty*** rientra nell'adempimento del dovere **5.** TEL linea *f*; ***the ~ is busy*** è occupato; ***hold the ~*** rimanga in linea **6.** *fig*: ***~ of inquiry*** pista *f*; ***~ of reasoning*** filo *m* del ragionamento; ***~ of credit*** castelletto *m*
line[2] *v/t* foderare; ***~ the box with paper*** foderare di carta la scatola; ***the membranes which ~ the stomach*** le membrane che rivestono internamente lo stomaco; ***~ one's pockets*** riempirsi le tasche
◆**line up I** *v/i* mettersi in fila **II** *v/t sep prisoners* mettere in fila; *books* allineare; *entertainment* organizzare; ***what have you got lined up for me today?*** cos'hai organizzato oggi per me?; ***I've lined up a meeting with the directors*** ho organizzato una riunione con i direttori
lineage *n* lignaggio *m*
linear *adj* lineare
linebacker *n* SPORTS line-backer *m inv*
lined *adj face* rugoso; *paper* rigato
line dancing *n danza popolare in cui i ballerini si muovono allineati* **line drawing** *n* disegno *m* a tratteggio
line manager *n* dirigente *m/f* di linea
linen I *n material* lino *m*; *sheets etc* biancheria *f*; ***wash one's dirty ~ in public*** lavare i panni sporchi in pubblico **II** *adj* di lino
linen basket *n esp Br* cesto *m* del bucato **linen closet, linen cupboard** *n* armadio *m* della biancheria
liner *n ship* transatlantico *m*
linesman *n* SPORTS guardalinee *m inv*
line-up *n* SPORTS formazione *f*; *for a show* ospiti *mpl*; (*identity parade*) confronto *m* all'americana
linger *v/i of person* attardarsi; ***many of the guests ~ed in the hall*** molti ospiti si attardarono in sala; ***~ over a meal*** attardarsi a tavola; *of smell, pain* persistere
lingerie *n* lingerie *f inv*
lingo *n infml* lingua *f*
linguist *n professional* linguista *m/f*; *person good at languages* poliglotta *m/f*
linguistic *adj* linguistico
linguistics *nsg* linguistica *f*
lining *n of clothes* fodera *f*; *of brakes* guarnizione *f*; ***the ~ of the stomach*** la parete dello stomaco
link I *n* (*connection*) legame *m*; ***a rail ~*** un collegamento ferroviario; ***cultural ~s*** legami *mpl* culturali; ***the strong ~s between Britain and Australia*** gli stretti legami tra Gran Bretagna e Australia; COMPUT collegamento *m*; *in chain* anello *m* **II** *v/t* collegare; ***~ arms*** prendere sottobraccio (***with*** qn); ***do you think these murders are ~ed?*** pensi che questi omicidi siano collegati?; ***his name has been ~ed with several famous women*** il suo nome è stato legato a diverse donne famose; COMPUT collegare
◆**link up** *v/i* riunirsi; TV collegarsi
link road *n Br* bretella *f* (di raccordo)
link-up *n* collegamento *m*

lino *n esp Br*, **linoleum** *n* linoleum *m*
linseed *n* semi *mpl* di lino
linseed oil *n* olio *m* di lino
lint *n* garza *f*
lintel *n* ARCH architrave *f*
lion *n* leone *m*; **~ cub** leoncino; ***take the ~'s share*** prendere la fetta più grossa
lioness *n* leonessa *f*
lip *n* ANAT labbro *m*; **~s** labbra; *infml* (*cheek*) insolenza *f*; *of cup* orlo *m*; ***keep a stiff upper ~*** tenere duro; *fig* ***lick one's ~s*** leccarsi i baffi; ***the question on everyone's ~s*** la questione è sulla bocca di tutti; ***none of your ~!*** *infml* basta con le tue solite insolenze!
lip gloss *n* lucidalabbra *m inv*
liposuction *n* liposuzione *f*
lipread *v/i* ⟨*pret & past part* **-read**⟩ leggere le labbra **lipring** *n* piercing *m inv* al labbro **lip salve** *n* burro *m* di cacao **lip service** *n*: ***pay ~ to*** appoggiare soltanto a parole **lipstick** *n* rossetto *m*
liquefy **I** *v/t* liquefare **II** *v/i* liquefarsi
liqueur *n* liquore *m*
liquid **I** *n* liquido *m* **II** *adj* liquido
liquid assets *n* valori *mpl* liquidi
liquidate *v/t* liquidare
liquidation *n* liquidazione *f*; ***go into ~*** andare in liquidazione
liquid-crystal *adj*: **~ *display*** display *m* a cristalli liquidi
liquidity *n* FIN liquidità *f inv*
liquidize *v/t* frullare
liquidizer *n* frullatore *m*
liquor *n* superalcolici *mpl*
liquorice *n* liquirizia *f*
Lisbon *n* Lisbona *f*
lisp **I** *n* lisca *f* **II** *v/i* parlare con la lisca
list[1] **I** *n* elenco *m*, lista *f*; ***it's not on the ~*** non è in elenco; **~ *of names*** elenco di nomi **II** *v/t* elencare; ***it is not ~ed*** non è incluso nell'elenco
list[2] *n* NAUT inclinazione *f*
listed building *n edificio di interesse storico o artistico*
listen *v/i* ascoltare; **~ *to the radio*** ascoltare la radio; ***if you ~ hard, you can hear the sea*** se ascolti con attenzione, puoi sentire il mare; ***she ~ed carefully to everything he said*** ascoltò attentamente tutto ciò che lui disse; **~ *for sth*** aspettare di sentire qc; (*heed*) dare retta; **~ *to me!*** dammi retta!; **~, *I know what we'll do*** ascolta, so ciò che faremo
◆**listen in** *v/i* ascoltare (di nascosto); ***I'd like to listen in on*** *or* ***to your discussion*** mi piacerebbe ascoltare di nascosto la vostra discussione
◆**listen to** *v/t radio*, *person* ascoltare
listener *n to radio* ascoltatore *m*, -trice *f*; ***he's a good ~*** sa ascoltare
listeria *n* listeria *f*
listings magazine *n* guida *f* dei programmi radio / TV
listless *adj* apatico
list price *n* prezzo *m* di listino
lit *pret & past part* → ***light***[1]
litany *n* litania *f*; ***a ~ of complaints*** una litania di lamentele
liter *US* → ***litre***
literacy *n* alfabetismo *m*; **~ *test*** test *m inv* di lettura e scrittura
literal *adj* letterale; ***in the ~ sense*** (***of the word***) nel senso letterale (del termine); ***that is the ~ truth*** è la pura verità
literally *adv* letteralmente; ***take s.o.*** / ***sth ~*** prendere qn / qc alla lettera; (*really*) letteralmente; ***I was ~ shaking with fear*** tremavo letteralmente dalla paura
literary *adj* letterario; **~ *man*** letterato *m*
literary critic *n* critico *m*, -a *f* letterario **literary criticism** *n* critica *f* letteraria
literate *adj*: ***be ~*** saper leggere e scrivere
literature *n* letteratura *f*; *infml* (*leaflets*) opuscoli *mpl*
lithe *adj* (+*er*) agile
lithograph *n* litografia *f*
Lithuania *n* Lituania *f*
litigation *n* JUR contestazione *f* giudiziaria
litigious *adj* JUR sempre pronto a fare causa
litmus paper *n* cartina *f* di tornasole **litmus test** *n fig* cartina *f* di tornasole
litre, *US* **liter** *n* litro *m*
litter **I** *n* rifiuti *mpl*; *of animals* cucciolata *f*; *for cat's tray* lettiera *f*; ***the park was strewn with ~*** il parco era disseminato di rifiuti **II** *v/t*: ***be ~ed with*** essere cosparso di; ***glass ~ed the streets*** le strade erano cosparse di

vetri

litter basket *n* cestino *m* dei rifiuti **litter bin** *n* bidone *m* dei rifiuti **litter lout** *n infml persona che getta i rifiuti per strada* **litter tray** *n* cassetta *f* (*per gatti*)

little I *adj* piccolo; ***the ~ ones*** i piccoli; ***a ~ house*** una casetta; ***a ~ while ago*** poco fa **II** *n*: ***the ~ I know*** il poco che so; ***a ~*** un po'; ***a ~ bread / wine*** un po' di pane / vino; ***a ~ is better than nothing*** meglio poco che niente **III** *adv*: ***~ by ~*** (a) poco a poco; ***a ~ better / bigger*** un po' meglio / più grande; ***~ did I think that …*** non pensavo affatto che …; ***~ does he know that …*** non sa affatto che …; ***there was ~ we could do*** potevamo fare ben poco; ***a ~ before 6*** un po' prima delle 6

live[1] **I** *v/t life* vivere; ***~ one's own life*** vivere la propria vita **II** *v/i* (*reside*) abitare; ***he ~s with his parents*** abita con i genitori; ***a house not fit to ~ in*** una casa non adatta come abitazione; (*be alive*) vivere; ***his music will ~ for ever*** la sua musica vivrà in eterno; ***he ~d through two wars*** è sopravvissuto a due guerre; ***~ through an experience*** passare attraverso un'esperienza; ***you'll ~ to regret it*** te ne pentirai

◆**live down** *v/t sep* scordare; ***he'll never live it down*** non gli verrà mai perdonato

◆**live off** *v/t*: ***he lives off his parents*** si fa mantenere dai genitori

◆**live on I** *v/t rice*, *bread* vivere di; ***live on eggs*** nutrirsi solo di uova; ***earn enough to live on*** guadagnare abbastanza da viverci; **II** *v/i continue living* sopravvivere

◆**live together** *v/i* convivere

◆**live up** *v/t always sep*: ***live it up*** fare la bella vita

◆**live up to** *v/t* essere all'altezza di; ***live up to expectations*** essere all'altezza delle aspettative; ***live up to one's reputation*** essere all'altezza della propria reputazione; ***he's got a lot to live up to*** deve soddisfare aspettative elevate

◆**live with** *v/t* vivere con

live[2] **I** *adj broadcast* dal vivo; ***a ~ programme*** *Br or* ***program*** *US* un programma in diretta; ***a real ~ movie star*** una stella del cinema in carne ed ossa **II** *adv broadcast* in diretta; *record* dal vivo; *ammunition* carico

live-in *adj* che abita nella casa in cui lavora; ***they have a ~ cook*** hanno un cuoco che abita con loro

livelihood *n* mezzi *mpl* di sostentamento; ***earn one's ~*** guadagnarsi da vivere; ***fishing is their ~*** vivono di pesca

liveliness *n* vivacità *f inv*

lively *adj* (*+er*) vivace; ***things are getting ~*** la situazione si sta animando; ***look ~!*** muoviti!

◆**liven up I** *v/t sep* ravvivare **II** *v/i person* ravvivarsi

liver *n* fegato *m*

liverish *adj Br*: ***feel ~*** non sentirsi bene

livery *n* livrea *f*

livestock *n* bestiame *m*

live wire *n* filo *m* sotto tensione; *fig* persona *f* dinamica

livid *adj* (*angry*) furibondo

living I *adj* in vita; ***~ conditions*** condizioni *fpl* di vita; ***in ~ memory*** a memoria d'uomo; ***the greatest ~ playwright*** il più grande commediografo vivente; ***I have no ~ relatives*** non ho parenti in vita **II** *n*: ***earn one's ~*** guadagnarsi da vivere; ***what do you do for a ~?*** che lavoro fai?; ***standard of ~*** tenore *m* di vita; ***cost of ~*** costo *m* della vita

living room *n* salotto *m*, soggiorno *m* **living will** *n* testamento *m* biologico

lizard *n* lucertola *f*

llama *n* lama *m inv*

load I *n* carico *m*; ***~s of*** *infml* un sacco di; ***we have ~s*** ne abbiamo un sacco; ***I put a ~ in the washing machine*** ho caricato la lavatrice; ***that's a ~ off my mind!*** mi togli un peso dal cuore; ***we're knocking down a ~-bearing wall*** stiamo buttando giù un muro portante; ***it's a ~ of old rubbish*** *Br* sono un sacco di sciocchezze; ***get a ~ of this!*** (*listen*) senti un po'! **II** *v/t* caricare; ***~ sth onto sth*** caricare qc su qc; ***the ship was ~ed with bananas*** la nave era carica di banane; ***~ a camera*** caricare una macchina fotografica

◆**load up I** *v/i* caricare (*a.* COMPUT) **II** *v/t sep* caricare (**with** di)

loaded *adj infml* (*very rich*) ricco sfondato; *dice* truccato; *gun* carico; *software* caricato; ***a ~ question*** una domanda capziosa

loader *n* caricatore *m*, -trice *f*; ***their washing machine is a top ~*** hanno una lavatrice con carica dall'alto

load factor *n* fattore *m* di carico

loading bay *n* piattaforma *f* di carico

loading program *n* COMPUT programma *m* di caricamento

loaf *n* ⟨*pl* ***loaves***⟩: ***a ~ of bread*** una pagnotta; ***a small white ~*** una pagnottina di pane bianco

◆**loaf about** *v/i infml* oziare

loafer *n* fannullone *m*, - a *f*; *shoe* mocassino *m*

loam *n* terriccio *m*

loan I *n* prestito *m*; ***on ~*** in prestito; ***he let me have the money as a ~*** mi ha concesso il denaro in prestito; ***he gave me the ~ of his bicycle*** mi ha prestato la sua bicicletta **II** *v/t*: ***~ s.o. sth*** prestare qc a qn

loan shark *n infml* strozzino *m*, -a *f*

loan translation *n* LING calco *m*

loath *adj*: ***be ~ to do sth*** essere riluttante a fare qc

loathe *v/t* detestare; ***I ~ doing it*** detesto farlo; ***he ~s spinach*** detesto gli spinaci

loathing *n* disgusto *m*

loathsome *adj* disgustoso

lob SPORTS **I** *v/t* ⟨*pret & past part* ***-bed***⟩ rinviare con un lob; ***he ~bed the grenade over the wall*** lanciò la granata oltre il muro **II** *n* lob *m inv*

lobby I *n in hotel*, *theatre* atrio *m*; POL lobby *f inv* **II** *v/t*: ***~ s.o. for sth*** fare pressione su qn per ottenere qc **III** *v/i*: ***the farmers are ~ing for higher subsidies*** i contadini stanno facendo pressione per ottenere sussidi più elevati

lobbyist *n* lobbista *m/f*

lobe *n* ANAT lobo *m*

lobotomy *n* lobotomia *f*

lobster *n* aragosta *f*

local I *adj people*, *bar* del posto; *council*, *services* locale; ***~ radio station*** stazione *f* radio locale; ***~ newspaper*** giornale *m* locale; ***the ~ residents*** i residenti del posto; ***~ community*** comunità *f* locale; ***at ~ level*** a livello locale; ***~ train*** treno *m* locale; ***~ time*** ora *f* locale; ***go into your ~ branch*** recatevi presso la filiale locale; ***I'm not ~*** non sono del posto **II** *n* persona *f* del posto; ***are you a ~?*** sei del posto?; *Br infml* (*pub*) ***the ~*** il locale della zona

local anaesthetic *n* MED anestesia *f* locale **local area network** *n* COMPUT rete *f* in area locale **local authority** *n* autorità *f* locale **local call** *n* TEL telefonata *f* urbana **local elections** *npl* elezioni *fpl* amministrative **local government** *n* amministrazione *f* locale

localise, localize *v/t*: ***this custom is very ~d*** questa usanza è molto circoscritta

locality *n* località *f inv*

locally *adv live*, *work* nella zona

local produce *n* prodotti *mpl* locali

local time *n* ora *f* locale

locate *v/t new factory etc* situare; *identify position of* localizzare; ***be ~d*** essere situato

location *n* (*siting*) ubicazione *f*; ***this would be an ideal ~ for the airport*** sarebbe un'ubicazione ideale per l'aeroporto; (*positioning*, *siting*) ***they discussed the ~ of the proposed airport*** hanno discusso dell'ubicazione dell'aeroporto oggetto della proposta; *identifying position of* localizzazione *f*; ***on ~*** *film* in esterni; ***the film was shot on ~ in …*** gli esterni del film sono stati girati in …

loch *n Scot* lago *m*

lock¹ *n of hair* ciocca *f*

lock² I *n on door* serratura *f*; (*canal lock*) chiusa *f*; ***put sth under ~ and key*** mettere qc sotto chiave **II** *v/t door* chiudere a chiave; ***~ sth in position*** bloccare qc; ***~ s.o. in a room*** chiudere a chiave qn in una stanza; ***~ed in combat*** impegnato nella lotta; ***they were ~ed in each other's arms*** si stringevano tra le braccia; ***this bar ~s the wheel in position*** questa sbarra blocca la ruota **III** *v/i* chiudersi (a chiave); (*wheel*) bloccarsi

◆**lock away** *v/t sep* mettere sottochiave

◆**lock in** *v/t sep person* chiudere dentro

◆**lock out** *v/t sep of house* chiudere fuori; ***I've locked myself out*** mi sono chiuso fuori

◆**lock up** *v/t sep in prison* mettere dentro
locker *n* armadietto *m*
locker room *n* spogliatoio *m*
locket *n* medaglione *m*
lockout *n* serrata *f*
locksmith *n* fabbro *m* ferraio
locomotive *n* locomotiva *f*; *adj* locomotore
locum *n* supplente *m*
locust *n* locusta *f*
lode *n* filone *m*
lodestar *n* stella *f* polare
lodge **I** *v/t complaint* presentare **II** *v/i of bullet* conficcarsi **III** *n in grounds* casetta *f*; (*shooting lodge etc*) capanno *m*
lodger *n* pensionante *m/f*; ***take in ~s*** affittare camere
lodgings *npl* camera *f* in affitto
loft *n* soffitta *f*
loft conversion *n ristrutturazione di una soffitta per renderla abitabile*
lofty *adj* (+*er*) *peak* alto; *ideals* nobile
log¹ *n wood* ceppo *m*; ***sleep like a ~*** dormire come un ciocco
log² **I** *n written record* giornale *m*; NAUT giornale *m* di bordo; ***keep a ~ of sth*** tenere una registrazione di qc **II** *v/t* registrare; ***details are ~ged in the computer*** nel computer sono registrate informazioni dettagliate
◆**log off** *v/i* ⟨*pret & past part* **-ged**⟩ disconnettersi (***from*** da)
◆**log on** *v/i* connettersi
◆**log on to** *v/t* connettersi a
◆**log out** *v/i* COMPUT disconnettersi
logarithm *n* logaritmo *m*
logbook *n* giornale *m* di bordo
log cabin *n* casetta *f* di legno
loggerheads *npl*: ***be at ~*** essere ai ferri corti
logic *n* logica *f*; ***there's no ~ in that*** non c'è nessuna logica
logical *adj* logico
logically *adv* a rigor di logica; *arrange* in modo logico
logistics *npl* logistica *f*
logo *n* logo *m inv*
logorrhoea *n* logorrea *f*
logroll *v/t & v/i US infml* scambiarsi favori per far passare una legge
loin *n* lombata *f*; ***~s*** regione *f* lombare; *fig* ***gird up (one's) ~s*** rimboccarsi le maniche
loincloth *n* perizoma *m*
loiter *v/i* gironzolare; ***~ with intent*** aggirarsi con atteggiamento sospetto
loll *v/i head* ciondolare
◆**loll about** *v/i person* spaparanzarsi
lollipop *n* lecca lecca *m inv*
lollipop man *n Br uomo che aiuta i bambini ad attraversare la strada* **lollipop woman** *n Br donna che aiuta i bambini ad attraversare la strada*
lolly *n* (*ice lolly*) ghiacciolo *m*; *infml* (*money*) grana *f infml*
London *n* Londra *f*
lone *adj* solo; ***a ~ gunman*** un singolo tiratore
loneliness *n* solitudine *f*
lonely *adj* (+*er*) *person* solo; ***~ hearts column*** rubrica *f* per cuori solitari; ***~ hearts club*** club *m inv* per cuori solitari; *place* isolato
loner *n* persona *f* solitaria
lonesome *adj esp US* solo
long¹ **I** *adj* (+*er*) lungo; ***it's a ~ way*** è lontano; ***it is 6 feet ~*** è lungo sei piedi; ***pull a ~ face*** fare il muso; ***a ~ memory*** una memoria lunga; ***it's a ~ time since I saw her*** è da tanto tempo che non la vedo; ***she was abroad for a ~ time*** è stata all'estero per molto tempo; ***take a ~ look at sth*** dare un lungo sguardo a qc; ***how ~ is the film?*** quanto dura il film?; ***he's getting a bit ~ in the tooth*** sta diventando troppo vecchio **II** *adv* **1.** ***don't be ~*** torna presto; ***5 weeks is too ~*** 5 settimane è troppo; ***will it take ~?*** ci vorrà tanto?; ***that was ~ ago*** è stato tanto tempo fa; ***~ before then*** molto prima di allora; ***before ~*** poco tempo dopo; ***we can't wait any ~er*** non possiamo attendere oltre; ***he no ~er works here*** non lavora più qui **2.** ***so ~ as*** (*provided*) sempre che **3.** ***so ~!*** arrivederci! **III** *n*: ***before ~*** tra non molto; ***are you going for ~?*** sarai assente a lungo?; ***it won't take ~*** non ci vorrà molto; ***the ~ and the short of it is that…*** il succo del discorso è che…
long² *v/i*: ***~ for sth*** desiderare ardentemente qc; ***be ~ing to do sth*** desiderare ardentemente fare qc; ***he ~ed for his wife to return*** desiderava ardentemente che sua moglie tornasse; ***he is ~ing for me to make a mistake*** de-

sidera ardentemente che io commetta un errore; ***I am ~ing to go abroad*** desidero ardentemente andare all'estero; ***I'm ~ing to see that film*** desidero ardentemente vedere quel film

long-distance *adj phonecall* interurbano; *race* di fondo; *flight* intercontinentale; ***~ lorry driver*** *Br* camionista *m/f* **long-drawn-out** *adj* che va per le lunghe **long drink** *n* long drink *m*

longevity *n* longevità *f inv*

long-haired *adj* coi capelli lunghi

longhand *n* scrittura *f* a mano

long-haul *adj*: ***~ truck driver*** camionista *m/f*

longing *n* desiderio *m*

longitude *n* longitudine *f*

long johns *npl infml* mutandoni *mpl* **long jump** *n* salto *m* in lungo **long jumper** *n* atleta *m* di salto in lungo **long-life milk** *n* latte *m* a lunga conservazione **long-lost** *adj person* che non si vede da molto tempo **long-playing record** *n* long-playing *m inv*, LP *m inv* **long-range** *adj missile* a lunga gittata; *forecast* a lungo termine **long-running** *adj series* che dura da molto tempo **longshoreman** *n US* scaricatore *m* di porto **long shot** *n*: ***it's a ~*** le probabilità sono minime; ***not by a ~*** niente affatto **long-sighted** *adj* presbite **long-sleeved** *adj* a maniche lunghe **long-standing** *adj* di vecchia data **long-stay** *adj Br car park* a lunga permanenza **long-suffering** *adj* paziente **long-term** *adj plans, investment* a lunga scadenza; *relationship* stabile; *memory* a lungo termine; ***in the ~*** a lungo termine **long vacation** *n* EDU vacanze *fpl* estive **long wave** *n* RADIO onde *fpl* lunghe **long-ways** *adj* nel senso della lunghezza

longwinded *adj* prolisso

loo *n infml* gabinetto *m*; ***go to the ~*** andare al gabinetto; ***in the ~*** al gabinetto

look I *n* **1.** (*appearance*) aspetto *m*; ***I don't like the ~ of him*** il suo aspetto non mi piace; ***by the ~ of him*** a giudicare dal suo aspetto **2.** (*glance*) sguardo *m*; ***give s.o./sth a ~*** dare uno sguardo a qn/qc; ***she gave me a dirty ~*** mi ha lanciato un'occhiataccia; ***she gave me a ~ of disbelief*** mi ha dato un'occhiata scettica; ***have a ~ at sth*** *examine* dare un'occhiata a qc; ***can I have a ~ around?*** *in shop etc* posso dare un'occhiata? **3.** ***~s*** (*beauty*) bellezza *f* **II** *v/i* **1.** guardare; ***~, there's a better solution*** guarda, c'è una soluzione migliore; ***~ before you leap*** *prov* rifletti prima di agire **2.** (*search*) cercare **3.** (*seem*) sembrare; ***it ~s like rain*** sembra voglia piovere; ***you ~ tired/different*** sembri stanco/diverso; ***it ~s all right to me*** mi sembra tutto a posto; ***how does it ~ to you?*** che te ne pare?; ***the car ~s about 10 years old*** la macchina sembra vecchia di 10 anni; ***the picture doesn't ~ like him*** in quella foto non sembra lui; ***it ~s as if we'll be late*** sembra che saremo in ritardo **III** *v/t*: ***he ~s his age*** dimostra gli anni che ha; ***he's not ~ing himself these days*** in questi giorni non sembra lui; ***I want to ~ my best tonight*** stasera voglio stare benissimo; ***~ what you've done!*** guarda che cosa hai fatto!; ***~ where you're going!*** guarda dove vai!; ***~ who's here!*** guarda chi c'è!

◆**look after** *v/t* badare a

◆**look ahead** *v/i fig* pensare al futuro

◆**look around** *v/i in shop etc* dare un'occhiata in giro; (*look back*) guardarsi indietro

◆**look at** *v/t* guardare; (*consider*) considerare; ***look at him!*** guarda lui!; ***look at the time*** guardare l'ora; ***he looked at his watch*** guardò l'orologio

◆**look away** *v/i* distogliere lo sguardo

◆**look back** *v/i* guardare indietro; ***he's never looked back*** *fig infml* non si è mai guardato indietro

◆**look down on** *v/t* disprezzare

◆**look for** *v/t* cercare; ***he's looking for trouble*** sta cercando guai

◆**look forward to** *v/t*: ***look forward to doing sth*** non veder l'ora di fare qc; ***I'm looking forward to the holidays*** non vedo l'ora che arrivino le vacanze; ***I'm not looking forward to it*** non ne ho proprio voglia

◆**look in on** *v/t* (*visit*) passare a trovare

◆**look into** *v/t* (*investigate*) esaminare; ***look into s.o.'s face*** guardare in faccia qn; ***look into the future*** guardare al futuro

◆**look on** **I** *v/i* (*watch*) rimanere a guardare **II** *v/t*: ***I look on you as a friend*** (*consider*) ti considero un amico

◆**look onto** *v/t garden*, *street* dare su

◆**look out** *v/i of window etc* guardare fuori; (*pay attention*) fare attenzione; ***look out!*** attento!

◆**look out for** *v/t* cercare; (*be on guard against*) fare attenzione a; ***look out for pickpockets*** fare attenzione ai borseggiatori

◆**look out of** *v/t window* guardare da

◆**look over** *v/t sep house*, *translation* esaminare

◆**look round** *v/t museum*, *city* visitare

◆**look through** *v/t sep magazine*, *notes* scorrere

◆**look to** *v/t* (*rely on*) contare su; ***they looked to him to solve the problem*** contavano su di lui per risolvere il problema; ***we look to you for support*** contavamo sul tuo supporto

◆**look up** **I** *v/i from paper etc* sollevare lo sguardo; (*improve*) migliorare; ***things are looking up*** le cose stanno migliorando **II** *v/t sep word*, *phone number* cercare; (*visit*) andare a trovare

◆**look up to** *v/t* (*respect*) avere rispetto per

lookalike *n* sosia *m/f inv*; ***a Rupert Murdoch ~*** un sosia di Rupert Murdoch

look-in *n* visitina *f*; ***I didn't get a ~*** è stato come se non ci fossi

lookout *n person* sentinella *f*; *place* posto *m* di guardia; ***~ tower*** torre *f* di vedetta; ***be on the ~*** stare all'erta; ***be on the ~ for*** *accommodation etc* cercare di trovare; *new staff etc* essere alla ricerca di

loom[1] *n* telaio *m*

loom[2] *v/i* delinearsi; ***~ large*** incombere

◆**loom up** *v/i* apparire; ***the ship loomed up out of the mist*** la nave apparve dalla nebbia

loony **I** *n infml* matto *m*, -a *f* **II** *adj* (*+er*) *infml* matto

loony bin *n infml* manicomio *m*

loop **I** *n* cappio *m* **II** *v/t*: ***~ sth around sth*** avvolgere qc intorno a qc

loophole *n in law etc* scappatoia *f*

loopy *adj* (*+er*) *mad* pazzo

loose **I** *adj* (*+er*) *wire*, *button* allentato; *clothes* ampio; *tooth* che tentenna; *morals* dissoluto; *wording* vago; ***~ change*** spiccioli *mpl*; ***~ ends*** *of problem*, *discussion* aspetti *mpl* da esaminare; ***come ~*** allentarsi; ***be at a ~ end*** non sapere cosa fare; ***~ talk*** discorso *m* incauto; ***break*** *or* ***get ~*** *person*, *animal* liberarsi (***from*** da); (*break out*) evadere; ***turn ~*** liberare; ***he's a ~ cannon*** è inaffidabile **II** *n*: ***be on the ~*** essere scappato

loose change *n* spiccioli *mpl* **loose-fitting** *adj* ampio

loose-leaf binder *n* raccoglitore *m*

loosely *adv tied* senza stringere; *worded* vagamente; ***~ based on Shakespeare*** liberamente tratto da Shakespeare

loosen **I** *v/t collar*, *knot* allentare; ***~ one's grip on sth*** allentare la presa su qc **II** *v/i* allentarsi

◆**loosen up** **I** *v/t sep muscles* sciogliere **II** *v/i before game* sciogliere i muscoli; (*relax*) rilassarsi

loot **I** *n* bottino *m* **II** *v/t & v/i* saccheggiare

looter *n* saccheggiatore *m*, -trice *f*

◆**lop off** *v/t* ⟨*pret & past part* ***-ped***⟩ tagliar via

lop-sided *adj* sbilenco

loquacious *adj* loquace

lord **I** *n Br* (*nobleman*) lord *m inv* **II** *v/t*: ***~ it over s.o.*** spadroneggiare su qn

Lord *n* (*God*) Signore *m*; ***the*** (***House of***) ***~s*** la camera dei Lord; ***the ~*** (***our***) ***God*** il Signore nostro Dio; (***good***) ***~!*** *infml* Dio mio!; ***~ knows*** *infml* Dio solo lo sa

Lord Chancellor *n Br* lord *m inv* cancelliere **Lord Mayor** *n Br sindaco di Londra o di una delle grandi città inglesi*

Lordship *n*: ***His*** / ***Your ~*** Sua / Vostra Signoria *f*

Lord's Prayer *n* il Padrenostro *m*

lore *n* tradizione *f* orale

lorry *n Br* camion *m inv*

lose ⟨*pret & past part* **lost**⟩ **I** *v/t object* perdere; ***~ weight*** dimagrire; ***I've lost ten pounds*** sono dimagrito di circa quattro chili e mezzo; ***~ one's job***

perdere il lavoro; ***many men ~ their hair*** molti uomini perdono i capelli; ***~ no time in doing sth*** perdere tempo a fare qc; ***my watch lost three hours*** il mio orologio è rimasto indietro di tre ore **II** *v/i* SPORTS perdere; *of clock* andare indietro

◆**lose out** *v/i* rimetterci

loser *n in contest* perdente *m/f*; *infml in life* sfigato *m*, -a *f infml*; ***what a ~!*** *infml* che schiappa!; ***be a bad ~*** non saper perdere

losing *adj team* perdente; ***be fighting a ~ battle*** combattere una battaglia persa; ***be on the ~ side*** essere dalla parte degli sconfitti

loss *n* perdita *f*; ***make a ~*** subire una perdita; ***be at a ~*** essere perplesso; ***we are at a ~ for what to do*** non sappiamo cosa fare; ***be at a ~ to explain sth*** non riuscire a spiegare qc; ***be at a ~ for words*** non riuscire a trovare le parole; ***hair ~*** caduta *f* dei capelli; ***weight ~*** perdita *f* di peso; ***memory ~*** perdita *f* della memoria; ***the factory closed with the ~ of 300 jobs*** la fabbrica ha chiuso con la perdita di 300 posti di lavoro; ***he felt his wife's ~ very deeply*** soffriva profondamente per la perdita della moglie; ***there was a heavy ~ of life*** ci sono state molte vittime; ***sell sth at a ~*** vendere qc in perdita; ***it's your ~*** sarai tu a perderci; ***be a dead ~*** *Br infml* non valere niente; (*person*) essere un caso disperato; ***cut one's ~es*** *fig* limitare i danni

lost I *adj* perso; ***he was soon lost in the crowd*** si perse subito nella folla; ***lost at sea*** disperso in mare; ***all is (not) lost!*** (non) tutto è perduto!; ***the joke was lost on her*** non ha colto la battuta; ***he was lost for words*** era senza parole; ***lost in thought*** immerso nei propri pensieri; ***I'm lost*** mi sono perso; ***get lost!*** *infml* sparisci! **II** *pret & past part* → ***lose***

lost and found *n US* ufficio *m* oggetti smarriti **lost cause** *n* causa *f* persa **lost property office** *n Br* ufficio *m* oggetti smarriti **lost wax process** *n* processo *m* a cera persa

lot[1] *n*: ***the ~*** tutto; ***a ~, ~s*** molto; ***a ~ of ice cream*** *or* ***~s of ice cream*** molto gelato; ***a ~ of ice creams*** *or* ***~s of ice creams*** molti gelati; ***a ~ better/easier*** molto meglio / più facile; ***I feel ~s*** *or* ***a ~ better*** mi sento molto meglio; ***such a ~ of books*** così tanti libri; ***~s and ~s of mistakes*** un sacco di errori; ***we see a ~ of John*** vediamo spesso John; ***things have changed a ~*** le cose sono cambiate molto; ***I like him a ~*** mi piace molto

lot[2] *n in auction* lotto *m*; (*destiny*) sorte *f*; *esp Br infml* (*people*) combriccola *f*; (*things*) roba *f*; ***draw ~s*** tirare a sorte; ***they drew ~s to see who would begin*** hanno tirato a sorte per decidere chi avrebbe iniziato; ***throw in one's ~ with s.o.*** unire la propria sorte a quella di qn; ***improve one's ~*** migliorare la propria sorte; ***building ~*** lotto *m* edificabile; ***parking ~*** *US* parcheggio *m*; ***where shall I put this ~?*** *esp Br* dove devo mettere questa roba?; ***divide the books up into three ~s*** dividere i libri in tre gruppi; ***he is a bad ~*** *infml* è un tipaccio; ***the ~*** *Br infml* tutto; ***that's the ~*** questo è tutto

lotion *n* lozione *f*

lottery *n* lotteria *f*; ***~ ticket*** biglietto *m* della lotteria; ***the National Lottery*** la lotteria nazionale

lotus *n* loto *m*

lotus position *n* posizione *f* del loto

louche *adj* losco

loud I *adj* (*+er*) *music*, *voice*, *noise* forte; *colour* sgargiante **II** *adv* forte; ***~ and clear*** forte e chiaro; ***say sth out ~*** dire qc ad alta voce

loud-hailer *n* megafono *m*

loudly *adv* forte; *criticize* con veemenza

loudmouth *n* blaterone *m*, -a *f*

loudspeaker *n* altoparlante *m*; *for stereo* cassa *f* dello stereo

lounge I *n in house* soggiorno *m*; *in hotel* salone *m*; *at airport* sala *f* partenze **II** *v/i* poltrire; ***~ against a wall*** poltrire contro un muro

◆**lounge about** *v/i* poltrire

lounge bar *n in pub* sala *f* interna **lounge chair** *n* poltrona *f* **lounge lizard** *n* frequentatore *m* di salotti **lounge suit** *n* completo *m* da uomo

louse *n* ⟨*pl* ***lice***⟩ pidocchio *m*

lousy *adj infml* schifoso *infml*; ***I feel ~*** mi sento uno schifo; ***I'm ~ at arith-***

metic faccio schifo in aritmetica; ***he is a ~ golfer*** come golfista fa schifo; ***a ~ £3*** 3 pidocchiose sterline
lout *n* teppista *m/f*
loutish *adj* zotico
louvre, *US* **louver** *n* persiana *f*
lovable *adj* adorabile
love I *n* **1.** amore *m*, ***be in ~*** essere innamorato; ***fall in ~*** innamorarsi; ***make ~*** fare l'amore; ***make ~ to*** fare l'amore con; ***yes, my ~*** sì, tesoro; ***~ from*** *end of letter* baci; ***give him my ~*** portagli i miei affettuosi saluti; ***he sends his ~*** ti manda i suoi saluti **2.** *in tennis* zero *m* **II** *v/t person, country, wine* amare; ***~ doing sth*** amare fare qc; ***they ~ each other*** si amano; ***I'd ~ a cup of tea*** mi farebbe piacere una tazza di tè; ***I ~ the way she smiles*** amo il modo in cui sorride
love affair *n* relazione *f*
lovebirds *n hum* passerottini *mpl*
love bite *n* succhiotto *m* **love child** *n* figlio *m* dell'amore **love-hate relationship** *n* relazione *f* d'amore-odio **love knot** *n jewelry* nodo *m* celtico
loveless *adj marriage* senza amore
love letter *n* lettera *f* d'amore **lovelife** *n* vita *f* sentimentale
lovelorn *adj liter* che si strugge per un amore infelice
lovely *adj (+er) face, colour, holiday* bello; *meal, smell* buono; ***we had a ~ time*** siamo stati benissimo; ***that dress looks ~ on you*** quel vestito ti sta benissimo; ***it's ~ and warm*** è bello caldo; ***it's been ~ to see you*** è stato bello vederti
lovemaking *n* rapporto *m* sessuale
lover *n sexual partner* amante *m/f*; ***she had a string of ~s*** aveva una sfilza di amanti; *enthusiast* appassionato *m*, -a *f*; ***an art ~*** un appassionato d'arte
lovesick *adj* malato d'amore; ***he was so ~ he couldn't eat*** soffriva talmente tanto per amore da non riuscire a mangiare
love song *n* canzone *f* d'amore **love story** *n* storia *f* d'amore
lovey-dovey *adj infml* sdolcinato
loving *adj* affettuoso; ***your ~ son ...*** il tuo affezionato figlio ...
lovingly *adv* amorosamente
low I *adj (+er) bridge, price, voice* basso; *quality* scarso; ***the sun was ~ in the sky*** il sole era basso sull'orizzonte; ***the river is ~*** il fiume è poco profondo; ***a ridge of ~ pressure*** un fronte di bassa pressione; ***speak in a ~ voice*** parlare a bassa voce; ***be feeling ~*** sentirsi giù; ***be ~ on petrol*** avere poca benzina **II** *n in weather* depressione *f*; *in sales, statistics* minimo *m*; ***they hit an all time ~*** hanno toccato il livello più basso
lowbrow *adj* di scarso spessore culturale
low-calorie *adj* ipocalorico **low-cost** *adj* economico **Low Countries** *npl*: ***the ~*** i Paesi Bassi **low-cut** *adj dress* scollato
lowdown *n* informazioni *fpl*; ***get the ~*** ricevere tutte le informazioni; ***give s.o. the ~*** dare a qn tutte le informazioni; ***what's the ~ on Kowalski?*** quali informazioni abbiamo su Kowalski?; ***he gave me the ~ on it*** mi ha dato tutte le informazioni in merito
low-emission *adj car* a bassa emissione
lower I *adj in height* più basso; *part, limb, note* inferiore; GEOG basso; ***the Lower Rhine*** il Basso Reno; ***~ leg*** gamba *f* (tra ginocchio e caviglia; ***the ~ of the two holes*** il foro più basso tra i due; ***the ~ deck*** *of bus* il piano inferiore; *of ship* il ponte inferiore; ***the ~ classes*** le classi inferiori; ***a ~ middle-class family*** una famiglia di classe medio-bassa; ***the ~ school*** la scuola inferiore **II** *adv* più in basso; ***~ down the mountain*** più in basso (nella montagna); ***~ down the list*** più in basso nell'elenco **III** *v/t boat, sth to the ground* calare; *flag, hemline* ammainare; *pressure, price* abbassare
lower case I *n* lettere *fpl* minuscole **II** *adj* minuscolo **Lower Chamber** *n* camera *f* bassa
low-fat *adj* magro **low frequency** *n* bassa frequenza *f* **low-income** *adj families* a basso reddito **lowkey** *adj* discreto **lowlands** *npl* bassopiano *m* **low-level** *adj radiation* debole **low life** *n* persona *f* dei bassifondi
lowly *adj (+er)* umile
low-necked *adj* scollato **low-pitched** *adj sound, roof* basso **low-pressure area** *n* area *f* di bassa pressione

low-profile *adj* di basso profilo **low-rise** *adj building* basso **low season** *n* bassa stagione *f* **low-tar** *adj* a basso contenuto di catrame **low-tech** *adj* tecnologicamente poco avanzato; ***it's pretty ~*** è tecnologicamente poco avanzato **low-tension** *adj* a bassa tensione **low tide** *n* bassa marea *f* **low-wage** *adj* a salario basso

loyal *adj* (+*er*) leale; ***he was very ~ to his friends*** era molto leale con gli amici; ***he remained ~ to his wife/the king*** è rimasto fedele alla moglie/al re

loyalist I *n* lealista *m/f* **II** *adj* lealista

loyally *adv* lealmente

loyalty *n* lealtà *f inv*

loyalty card *n Br* COMM carta *f* fedeltà

lozenge *n shape* rombo *m*; *tablet* pastiglia *f*

LP *abbr* (= **long-playing record**) LP *m inv* (long-playing *m inv*)

LPG *abbr* (= **liquefied petroleum gas**) GPL *m* (gas *m inv* di petrolio liquefatto)

L-plate *n cartello per conducenti con foglio rosa*

LSD *m* LSD *m inv*

L.S.E. *abbr* (= **London School of Economics**) *facoltà di economia dell'università di Londra*

Lt. *abbr* (= **lieutenant**) tenente *m* (Ten.)

LT *abbr* (= **low tension**) bassa tensione *f* (BT)

Lt. Col. *abbr* (= **lieutenant-colonel**) tenente colonnello *m* (Ten. Col.)

Ltd *abbr* (= **limited**) s.r.l. (società *f inv* a responsabilità limitata)

Lt. Gen. *abbr* (= **lieutenant-general**) tenente generale *m*

Lt. Gov. *abbr* (= **lieutenant-governor**) vicegovernatore *m*

lubricant *n* lubrificante *m*

lubricate *v/t* lubrificare

lubrication *n* lubrificazione *f*

lucid *adj* (+*er*) (*clear*) chiaro; (*sane*) lucido; ***he was ~ for a few minutes*** rimase lucido per alcuni minuti

luck *n* fortuna *f*; ***bad ~*** sfortuna; ***hard ~!*** che sfortuna!; ***good ~*** fortuna *f*; ***good ~!*** buona fortuna!; ***be in ~*** avere fortuna; ***no such ~!*** no, purtroppo!; ***just my ~!*** la mia solita (s)fortuna!; ***with any ~*** con un po' di fortuna; ***he was a bit down on his ~*** era in un periodo sfortunato

luckily *adv* fortunatamente; ***~ for me*** per mia fortuna

lucky *adj* (+*er*) fortunato; ***you were ~*** hai avuto fortuna; ***he's ~ to be alive*** è vivo per miracolo; ***that's ~!*** che fortuna!; ***~ charm*** portafortuna; ***you'll be ~ to make it in time*** ti andrà bene se riuscirai a fare in tempo; ***it must be my ~ day*** deve essere il mio giorno fortunato

lucky dip *n* pesca *f* a sorpresa

lucrative *adj* redditizio

lucre *n* lucro *m*; ***filthy ~*** *hum* vile denaro *m*

Luddite *n hum* luddista *m/f*

ludicrous *adj* ridicolo

ludicrously *adv* ridicolmente; ***~ expensive*** estremamente caro

lug *v/t* ⟨*pret & past part* **-ged**⟩ *infml* trascinare

luggage *n* bagagli *mpl*

luggage locker *n* armadietto *m* per bagagli **luggage rack** *n in train* portabagagli *m inv* **luggage trolley** *n* carrello *m* portabagagli **luggage van** *n Br* RAIL (vagone) bagagliaio *m*

lukewarm *adj* tiepido; ***he's ~ about*** *or* ***on the idea/about her*** dimostra scarso entusiasmo per l'idea/per lei

lull I *n in fighting* momento *m* di calma; *in conversation* pausa *f* **II** *v/t*: ***~ o.s. into a false sense of security*** illudersi che tutto vada bene

lullaby *n* ninnananna *f*

lumbago *n* lombaggine *f*

lumber I *n* (*timber*) legname *m* **II** *v/t*: ***I got ~ed with it all*** *infml* è stato appioppato tutto a me

lumberjack *n* taglialegna *m inv*

lumberyard *n US* deposito *m* di legname

luminary *n fig* luminare *m*

luminous *adj* luminoso

lump I *n of sugar* zolletta *f*; (*swelling*) nodulo *m*; ***with a ~ in one's throat*** *fig* con un nodo in gola; ***it brings a ~ to my throat*** mi fa venire un nodo in gola **II** *v/t esp Br infml* ***if he doesn't like it he can ~ it*** se non gli piace dovrà ingoiare il rospo

◆ **lump together** *v/t sep* mettere insieme

lump sum *n* pagamento *m* unico

lumpy *adj* (+*er*) *sauce* grumoso; *mattress* pieno di buchi; ***go ~*** (*sauce, rice*) fare i grumi
lunacy *n* pazzia *f*
lunar *adj* lunare
lunatic **I** *n* pazzo *m*, -a *f* **II** *adj* pazzo
lunatic asylum *n* manicomio *m*
lunch **I** *n* pranzo *m*; ***have ~*** pranzare; ***how long do you get for ~?*** quanto dura la pausa pranzo?; ***he's at ~*** è andato a pranzo; ***she's completely out to ~*** *infml* è completamente fuori di testa **II** *v/i* pranzare; ***let's do ~*** *infml* pranziamo insieme
lunch box *n* cestino *m* del pranzo
lunch break *n* pausa *f* pranzo
luncheon *n form* pranzo *m*
luncheon meat *n* carne *f* in scatola
luncheon voucher *n* buono *m* pasto
lunch hour *n* pausa *f* pranzo **lunchtime** *n* ora *f* di pranzo; ***they arrived at ~*** sono arrivati all'ora di pranzo
lunette *n* ARCH lunetta *f*
lung *n* polmone *m*
lung cancer *n* cancro *m* al polmone
lunge **I** *n* scatto *m* in avanti **II** *v/i* scagliarsi
◆**lunge at** *v/t* scagliarsi contro
lurch[1] *n*: ***leave s.o. in the ~*** lasciare qn nei pasticci
lurch[2] **I** *n*: ***give a ~*** sbandare **II** *v/i* barcollare; ***the train ~ed to a standstill*** il treno si fermò sbandando
lure **I** *n* attrattiva *f* **II** *v/t* attirare; ***~ s.o. away from sth*** distogliere qn da qc; ***~ s.o. into a trap*** far cadere qn in trappola
lurex® *n* TEX Lurex® *m*; ***she was wearing a hideous gold ~ dress*** indossava un orrendo vestito di lurex dorato
lurid *adj colour* sgargiante; *details* scandaloso
lurk *v/i of person* appostarsi; *of doubt* persistere
luscious *adj* sensuale
lush **I** *adj vegetation* lussureggiante; ***they had ~ carpets fitted wall to wall*** avevano lussuosi tappeti da parete a parete; ***the season for really ~ melons is late summer*** la stagione in cui si trovano meloni veramente rigogliosi è la tarda estate **II** *n infml* liquore *m*
lust *n* libidine *f*; (*greed*) brama *f* (***for*** di); ***~ for power*** brama *f* di potere
◆**lust after** *v/t person* desiderare ardentemente
lustful *adj* lussurioso
lustre, *US* **luster** *n* lucentezza *f*; *fig* lustro *m*
lustrous *adj* lucente
lusty *adj* vigoroso
lute *n* MUS liuto *m*
lutenist *n* liutista *m*/*f*
Luxembourg *n* Lussemburgo *m*
luxuriant *adj* rigoglioso
luxuriate *v/i*: ***~ in sth*** (*people*) crogiolarsi in qc
luxurious *adj* lussuoso
luxuriously *adv* lussuosamente
luxury **I** *n* lusso *m* **II** *adj* di lusso
LV *abbr* (= **luncheon voucher**) buono *m* pasto
lychee *n* litchi *m inv*
Lycra® *n* lycra® *f inv*
lymph *n* linfa *f*
lymph gland *n* ANAT ghiandola *f* linfatica
lynch *v/t* linciare
lynch mob *n* linciatori *mpl*
lynx *n* lince *f*
lyre *n* MUS lira *f*
lyrical *adj* lirico; ***wax ~ about sth*** parlare entusiasticamente di qc
lyricism *n* lirismo *m*
lyricist *n* paroliere *m*
lyrics *npl* parole *fpl*, testi *mpl*

M

M, m *n* m, M *f inv*
m *abbr* **1.** (= **million(s)**) milione *m* **2.** (= **metre(s)**) metro *m* (m) **3.** (= **mile(s)**) miglio *m* **4.** (= **masculine**) maschile *m* (m)
M *abbr* **1.** (= **medium**) M (medio) **2.** (=

motorway) A (autostrada)
MA *abbr* (= **Master of Arts**) master *m inv*
ma'am *n US* signora *f*
mac *n infml* (*mackintosh*) impermeabile *m*
macabre *adj* macabro
macaroni *n* maccheroni *fpl*
macaronic *adj* maccheronico
macaroon *n* amaretto *m*
mace *n* (*mayor's*) mazza *f*; (*spice*) macis *m/f*
Macedonia *n* Macedonia *f*
machete *n* macete *m*
machination *n usu pl* macchinazioni *fpl*
machine I *n* macchina *f* **II** *v/t with sewing machine* cucire a macchina; TECH lavorare a macchina
machine gun *n* mitragliatrice *f* **machine-readable** *adj* leggibile dalla macchina
machinery *n* (*machines*) macchinario *m*; ***the ~ of government*** l'apparato del governo
machine tool *n* macchina *f* utensile **machine translation** *n* traduzione *f* fatta dal computer
machismo *n* machismo *m*
macho *adj* macho *m*
mackerel *n* sgombro *m*
mackintosh *n* impermeabile *m*
macramé *n* macramè *m*
macro *n* COMPUT macro *f*
macro- *pref* macro-
macrobiotic *adj* macrobiotico
macrocosm *n* macrocosmo *m*
macroeconomics *nsg* macroeconomia *f*
mad *adj* (+*er*) (*insane*) pazzo *m*; ***you must be ~!*** devi essere pazzo!; *infml* (*angry*) furioso; ***be ~ about*** *infml* andar matto per; ***drive s.o. ~*** far impazzire qn; ***go ~*** impazzire; ***like ~*** *infml run, work* come un matto; ***why the ~ rush?*** perchè questa fretta pazzesca?; ***he was ~ at her for telling them*** era infuriato con lei per averlo detto
madam *n* signora *f*; ***can I help you, ~?*** posso esserle d'aiuto, signora?; ***Dear Madam*** *esp Br* Gentile signora
madcap I *n* testa *f* matta **II** *adj idea* avventato
mad cow disease *n infml* morbo *m* della mucca pazza
madden *v/t* (*infuriate*) esasperare
maddening *adj* esasperante
maddeningly *adv* in modo esasperante; ***the train ride was ~ slow*** il viaggio in treno fu di una lentezza esasperante
made *pret & past part* → ***make***
made-to-measure *adj* su misura
made-up *adj* (*invented*) inventato; (*wearing make-up*) truccato
madhouse *n fig* manicomio *m*
madly *adv* come un matto; ***~ in love*** pazzamente innamorato
madman *n* pazzo *m*
madness *n* pazzia *f*
Madonna *n* Madonna *f*
madwoman *n* pazza *f*
Mafia *n* Mafia *f*
mag *n infml* rivista *f*; ***porn ~*** rivista *f* pornografica
magazine *n printed* rivista *f*; (*store*) deposito *m*; *arms* arsenale *m*
maggot *n* verme *m*
Magi *n* REL Re Magi *mpl*
magic I *n* magia *f*; *tricks* giochi *mpl* di prestigio; ***he made the spoon disappear by ~*** fece sparire il cucchiaio per magia; ***as if by ~*** come per magia; (*charm*) fascino *m*; *infml* ***like ~*** come per magia **II** *adj* magico; ***he hasn't lost his ~ touch*** non ha perso il suo tocco magico
magical *adj powers, moment* magico
magic carpet *n* tappeto *m* volante
magician *n performer* mago *m*, -a *f*
magic lantern *n* lanterna *f* magica **magic mushroom** *n* fungo *m* magico **magic spell** *n* incantesimo *m*; ***cast a ~ on s.o.*** stregare qn **magic trick** *n* gioco *m* di prestigio **magic wand** *n* bacchetta *f* magica; ***wave a ~*** agitare una bacchetta magica
magisterial *adj* magistrale; ***his conference was ~*** la sua conferenza fu magistrale
magistrate *n* magistrato *m*
Magistrate's court *n Br tribunale di primo grado in Inghilterra e Galles*
magnanimity *n* magnanimità *f*
magnanimous *adj* magnanimo
magnate *n* magnate *m*
magnesium *n* magnesio *m*
magnet *n* calamita *f*, magnete *m*
magnetic *adj* calamitato; *fig* magnetico; ***he has a ~ personality*** ha una

personalità magnetica
magnetic disk *n* COMPUT disco *m* magnetico **magnetic field** *n* campo *m* magnetico **magnetic media** *npl* media *mpl* magnetici **magnetic north** *n* nord *m* magnetico **magnetic pole** *n* polo *m* magnetico **magnetic stripe** *n* striscia *f* magnetizzata
magnetism *n of person* magnetismo *m*
magnetize, magnetise *v/t* magnetizzare
magnification *n* ingrandimento *m*; ***high / low ~*** alto / basso ingrandimento *m*
magnificence *n* magnificenza *f*
magnificent *adj* magnifico; ***he has done a ~ job*** ha svolto un lavoro magnifico
magnify *v/t* ⟨*pret & past part* **-ied**⟩ ingrandire; *difficulties* ingigantire
magnifying glass *n* lente *f* d'ingrandimento
magnitude *n of problem* portata *f*; ASTR magnitudine *f*; ***order of ~*** ordine *m* di grandezza
magnolia *n* magnolia *f*
magpie *n* gazza *f*; *infml* collezionista *m/f*
mahogany *n* mogano *m*
maid *n servant* domestica *f*; *in hotel* cameriera *f*
maiden **I** *n liter* fanciulla *f* **II** *adj* inaugurale
maiden name *n* nome *m* da ragazza **maiden speech** *n* discorso *m* inaugurale **maiden voyage** *n* viaggio *m* inaugurale
maid of honour, *US* **maid of honor** *n* damigella *f* d'onore
maidservant *n* domestica *f*
mail[1] **I** *n* posta *f*; ***is there any ~ for me?*** c'è posta per me?; ***put sth in the ~*** spedire qc **II** *v/t letter* spedire; *person* spedire a
mail[2] *n* (*armour*) maglia *f*; ***coat of ~*** cotta *f* di maglia
mailbag *n* sacco *m* postale **mailbox** *n US* buca *f* delle lettere; *US*: *of house* cassetta *f* delle lettere; COMPUT casella *f* postale **mail coach** *n* vagone *m* postale
mailing address *n US* indirizzo *m* postale **mailing list** *n* mailing list *m inv*
mailman *n US* postino *m* **mail merge** *n* COMPUT stampa *f* unione **mail-order catalogue**, *US* **mail-order catalog** *n* catalogo *m* di vendita per corrispondenza **mail-order firm** *n* ditta *f* di vendita per corrispondenza **mailroom** *n esp US* ufficio *m* spedizioni **mailshot** *n* mailing *m inv*
maim *v/t* mutilare
main[1] *adj* principale
main[2] *n* conduttura *f*; ***a water ~*** una conduttura dell'acqua; ***the ~s*** le condutture principali
main chance *n* proprio *m* interesse; ***have an eye for the ~*** badare solo al proprio interesse **main clause** *n* proposizione *f* principale **main course** *n* piatto *m* principale **main entrance** *n* entrata *f* principale
mainframe *n* COMPUT mainframe *m inv*
mainland *n* terraferma *f*, continente *m*; ***on the ~*** sul continente
mainline *v/t* & *v/i* (*drugs*) *infml* farsi una pera (di)
main line *n* RAIL linea *f* principale
mainly *adv* principalmente
main road *n* strada *f* principale
mains-operated, **mains-powered** *adj* con alimentazione di rete
mainspring *n* molla *f* principale; ***he was the ~ of the reform*** è stato la molla principale della riforma
mainstay *n* sostegno *m* principale
mainstream **I** *n* corrente *f* principale **II** *adj* convenzionale; ***~ society*** società *f* tradizionale; ***~ cinema*** cinema *m* commerciale
main street *n* corso *m*
maintain *v/t pace*, *speed*, *relationship*, *machine*, *house*, *family* mantenere; ***~ sth at a constant temperature*** mantenere qc a una temperatura costante; ***products which help to ~ healthy skin*** prodotti che consentono di mantenere una pelle sana; *innocence*, *guilt* sostenere; ***he still ~ed his innocence*** continuava a sostenere la propria innocenza; ***~ that*** sostenere che
maintenance *n of machine*, *house* manutenzione *f*; *money* alimenti *mpl*; ***he has to pay ~*** deve pagare gli alimenti; *of law and order* mantenimento *m*
maintenance costs *npl* spese *fpl* di manutenzione **maintenance staff** *n*

addetti *mpl* alla manutenzione

maize *n* mais *m inv*

majestic *adj* maestoso

majesty *n* (*grandeur*) maestà *f inv*; ***Her Majesty*** Sua Maestà

major I *adj* (*significant*) importante, principale; ***a ~ road*** una strada principale; ***a ~ operation*** un'operazione importante; MUS ***~ key*** chiave *f* maggiore; ***in C ~*** MUS in Do maggiore **II** *n* MIL maggiore *m*; *US* (*subject*) specializzazione *f*; ***he's a psychology ~*** è uno specializzando in psicologia **III** *v/i US* ***I hope to ~ in French*** spero di specializzarmi in francese

majorette *n* majorette *f*

majority *n a.* POL maggioranza *f*; ***~ vote*** voto *m* di maggioranza; ***be in the ~*** essere in maggioranza

majority rule *n* POL regola *f* della maggioranza

make I *v/t* ⟨*pret & past part* ***made***⟩ **1.** fare; *decision* prendere; MATH fare; ***~ s.o. do sth*** (*force to*) far fare qc a qn; (*cause to*) spingere qn a fare qc; ***you can't ~ me do it!*** non puoi costringermi a farlo!; ***~ s.o. happy/angry*** far felice/arrabbiare qn; ***~ s.o. happy/sad*** rendere felice/triste qn; ***~ a decision*** prendere una decisione; ***~ a telephone call*** fare una telefonata; ***made in Japan*** made in Japan; ***~ a guess*** tirare a indovinare; ***it's made of gold*** è d'oro; ***show what one is made of*** mostrare di che pasta si è fatti; ***the job is made for him*** quel lavoro è fatto per lui; ***they're made for each other*** sono fatti l'uno per l'altra; ***~ s.o. happy*** fare felice qn; ***he was made a judge*** è stato nominato giudice; ***we decided to ~ a day/night of it*** decidemmo di trascorrere così l'intera giornata/notte; ***you've made my day*** mi hai reso molto felice; ***~ o.s. heard*** farsi sentire; ***~ o.s. understood*** farsi capire; ***~ do with*** arrangiarsi con; ***~ the meeting*** *infml* partecipare al meeting **2.** ***~ it*** *catch bus, train, come, succeed, survive* farcela; ***sorry I couldn't ~ your party*** mi spiace non essere riuscito a venire alla tua festa; ***we'll never ~ the airport in time*** non arriveremo mai all'aeroporto in tempo **3.** (*estimate, think*) ***what time do you ~ it?*** che ore fai?; ***what do you ~ of it?*** cosa ne pensi? **4.** ***~ believe*** far finta **5.** (*earn*) guadagnare; ***she made herself a lot of money on the deal*** ha guadagnato un bel po' di soldi dall'affare; ***he's just made himself look ridiculous*** ha ottenuto soltanto di rendersi ridicolo **II** *n brand* marca *f*; ***be on the ~*** *infml* essere in cerca di fortuna

◆**make for** *v/t* (*go towards*) dirigersi verso; ***we are making for London*** ci dirigiamo verso Londra

◆**make of** *v/t* pensare; ***don't make too much of it*** non farne una questione di stato

◆**make off** *v/i* svignarsela

◆**make off with** *v/t* (*steal*) svignarsela con; ***she made off with the money*** se la svignò con i soldi; ***he made off with his best friend's wife*** se l'è svignata con la moglie del suo migliore amico

◆**make out** *v/t sep list* fare; *cheque* compilare; ***who shall I make the cheque out to?*** a chi devo intestare l'assegno?; (*see*) distinguere; (*imply*) far capire; ***I can't make out what he wants*** non capisco cosa voglia; ***he made out that he was hurt*** fece capire di essere ferito; ***make s.o. out to be clever/a genius*** far passare qn per intelligente/un genio

◆**make over** *v/t sep*: ***make sth over to s.o.*** cedere qc a qn

◆**make up I** *v/i of woman, actor* truccarsi; *after quarrel* fare la pace **II** *v/t sep story, excuse* inventare; *face* truccare; (*constitute*) costituire; ***you're making that up!*** te lo stai inventando!; ***make s.o./o.s. up*** truccare qn/truccarsi; ***be made up of*** essere composto da; ***make up one's mind*** decidersi; ***make it up*** *after quarrel* fare la pace

◆**make up for** *v/t* compensare; ***I'll make up for forgetting your birthday*** mi farò perdonare di essermi scordato del tuo compleanno; ***make up for lost time*** recuperare il tempo perduto; ***that still doesn't make up for the fact that you were very rude*** ciò non compensa il fatto che sei stato molto sgarbato

make-believe *n* finzione *f* **make-or-break** *adj infml* senza via di mezzo

makeover *n* trasformazione *f*; ***give s.o. a ~*** trasformare l'immagine di qn
maker *n manufacturer* fabbricante *m/f*
makeshift *adj* improvvisato; ***~ accommodation*** sistemazione *f* improvvisata
make-up *n* (*cosmetics*) trucco *m*; *of team* composizione *f*; (*character*) carattere *m*; ***she spends hours on her ~*** dedica ore al trucco
make-up bag *n* trousse *f inv* da trucco
make-up remover *n* struccante *m*
making *n* preparazione *f*; ***in the ~*** in via di formazione; ***the film was three months in the ~*** FILM il film ha richiesto tre mesi di lavorazione; ***star in the ~*** FILM stellina *f*; ***it's a disaster in the ~*** si sta preparando una catastrofe; ***her problems are of her own ~*** sono problemi che si è creata da sola; ***it was the ~ of him*** ha segnato una svolta per lui; ***have the ~s of*** *person* avere la stoffa di; ***the situation has all the ~s of a strike*** la situazione presenta tutte le caratteristiche di uno sciopero
maladjusted *adj* disadattato
malady *n* male *m*
malaise *n fig* malessere *m*
malapropism *n* LIT malapropismo *m*, *scambio di parole aventi suono simile*
malaria *n* malaria *f*
malcontent *n* scontento *m*, -a *f*
male I *adj* (*masculine*) maschile; *animal, bird, fish* maschio **II** *n man* uomo *m*; *animal, bird, fish* maschio *m*
male chauvinism *n* maschilismo *m*
male chauvinist pig *n* maschilista *m*
male nurse *n* infermiere *m*
malevolence *n* malevolenza *f*
malevolent *adj* malevolo
malfeasance *n* JUR illecito *m*
malformation *n* malformazione *f*
malformed *adj* deforme
malfunction I *n* cattivo *m* funzionamento **II** *v/i* funzionare male
malice *n* cattiveria *f*, malvagità *f*
malicious *adj* cattivo, malvagio
malign I *adj liter influence* malefico **II** *v/t* calunniare; (*run down*) parlare male di
malignancy *n* malignità *f*; (*tumour*) tumore *m* maligno
malignant *adj tumour* maligno
malingerer *n chi si dà malato*
mall *n* (*shopping mall*) centro *m* commerciale
mallard *n* anatra *f* selvatica
malleable *adj* malleabile
mallet *n* mazzuolo *m*
malnourished *adj form* denutrito
malnutrition *n* denutrizione *f*
malpractice *n* negligenza *f*
malt I *n* malto *m*; ***~ whisky*** whisky *m inv* di malto **II** *v/t* trasformare in malto
maltreat *v/t* maltrattare
maltreatment *n* maltrattamento *m*
malversation *n* malversazione *f*
mam(m)a *n infml* mamma *f*
mammal *n* mammifero *m*
mammary *adj* mammario; ***~ gland*** ghiandola *f* mammaria
mammogram *n* MED mammogramma *m*
mammography *n* MED mammografia *f*
mammoth I *n* mammut *m inv* **II** *adj* (*enormous*) colossale
man I *n* ⟨*pl* **men**⟩ *person, human being* uomo *m*; *humanity* umanità *f inv*; *in draughts* pedina *f*; ***make a ~ out of s.o.*** fare di qn un uomo; ***he took it like a ~*** si è comportato da uomo; ***~ and wife*** marito e moglie; ***the ~ in the street*** l'uomo della strada; ***~ of God*** uomo *m* di Dio; ***~ of letters*** (*writer*) uomo *m* di lettere; ***~ of property*** possidente *m*; ***a ~ of the world*** un uomo di mondo; ***be ~ enough*** essere abbastanza uomo; ***~'s bicycle*** bicicletta *f* da uomo; ***the right ~*** l'uomo giusto; ***you've come to the right ~*** ti sei rivolto all'uomo giusto; ***he's not the ~ for the job*** non è l'uomo giusto per quel lavoro; ***he's a family ~*** è un uomo di famiglia; ***it's got to be a local ~*** deve essere qualcuno del posto; ***follow me, men!*** seguitemi!; ***they are communists to a ~*** sono tutti quanti comunisti; **II** *v/t* ⟨*pret & past part* **-ned**⟩ *telephones, front desk* essere di servizio a; ***it was ~ned by a crew of three*** aveva un equipaggio di tre uomini
man-about-town *n* uomo *m* di mondo
manacle *n usu pl* manetta *f*
manage I *v/t business, money* gestire; ***he managed the company badly*** ha gestito male la società; ***can you ~ the***

suitcase? ce la fai a portare la valigia?; ***two hours is the most I can ~*** posso liberarmi per due ore al massimo; ***she can't ~ the stairs*** non riesce a fare le scale; ***can you ~ two more in the car?*** hai posto in macchina per altre due persone?; ***can you ~ 8 o'clock?*** ce la fai a liberarti per le 8?; ***can you ~ another cup?*** ne bevi un'altra tazza?; ***I could ~ another piece of cake*** potrei mangiare un altro pezzo di torta; ***she ~d a weak smile*** riuscì a fare un debole sorriso; ***~ to ...*** riuscire a ... **II** *v/i cope, financially* tirare avanti; (*financially*); ***can you ~?*** ce la fai?; ***I can ~ by myself*** posso farcela da solo; ***how do you ~ on £100 a week?*** ce la fai a tirare avanti con 100 sterline a settimana?

manageable *adj suitcase etc* maneggevole; *hair* docile; *able to be done* fattibile; ***the situation is ~*** la situazione è gestibile; ***pieces of a more ~ size*** pezzi di dimensioni più gestibili

management *n* (*managing*) gestione *f*; (*managers*) direzione *f*; ***under his ~*** durante la sua gestione; ***time ~*** gestione *f* del tempo; ***"under new ~"*** "nuova gestione"

management buyout *n acquisizione di un'impresa da parte dei suoi dirigenti* **management consultant** *n* consulente *m/f* di gestione aziendale **management studies** *n* corso *m* di formazione manageriale **management team** *n* team *m inv* manageriale

manager *n* manager *m/f inv*, direttore *m*, -trice *f*

managerial *adj* manageriale

managing director *n* direttore *m* generale

mandarin *n* (*fruit*, *official*) mandarino *m*; ***Mandarin*** (*language*) mandarino *m*

mandarin orange *n* mandarino *m*

mandate *n* (*authority*, *task*) mandato *m*

mandatory *adj* obbligatorio; JUR *sentence etc* vincolante

mandolin(e) *n* MUS mandolino *m*

mane *n of horse* criniera *f*

man-eating *adj* che si nutre di carne umana

maneuver *US* → ***manoeuvre***

manfully *adv* virilmente

manger *n* mangiatoia *f*

mangetout *n* pisello *m* mangiatutto

mangle **I** *v/t* (*crush*) stritolare **II** *n* mangano *m*

mango *n* mango *m*

mangy *adj* (+*er*) *dog* rognoso

manhandle *v/t person* malmenare; *object* caricare; ***he was ~d into the back of the van*** è stato fatto entrare a forza nel retro del furgone

manhole *n* botola *f*

manhood *n maturity* età *f inv* adulta; (*virility*) virilità *f inv*

man-hour *n* ora *f* lavorativa **manhunt** *n* caccia *f* all'uomo

mania *n* (*craze*) mania *f*; ***he has a ~ for collecting things*** ha la mania di raccogliere oggetti

maniac *n infml* pazzo *m*, -a *f*; ***sports ~s*** fanatici *mpl* dello sport; ***you ~!*** ma sei fissato!; ***sex ~*** maniaco *m* sessuale

manic *adj activity* frenetico; *person* ossessivo; PSYCH maniaco

manic-depressive **I** *adj* maniaco-depressivo **II** *n* soggetto *m* maniaco-depressivo

manicure *n* manicure *f inv*

manicured *adj nails*, *lawn* curato

manifest **I** *adj* palese **II** *v/t* manifestare; ***~ itself*** manifestarsi

manifestation *n* manifestazione *f*

manifesto *n* manifesto *m*, programma *m*

manifold *adj* molteplice

manila, manilla *n* cartoncino *m* manilla

manipulate *v/t person*, *bones* manipolare; ***~ s.o. into doing sth*** indurre qn a fare qc; *equipment* maneggiare

manipulation *n of person*, *bones* manipolazione *f*

manipulative *adj* manipolatore; ***he was very ~*** era un grande manipolatore

mankind *n* umanità *f inv*

manly *adj* (+*er*) virile

man-made *adj* sintetico; ***~ fibres*** *Br or* ***fibers*** *US* fibre *fpl* sintetiche; *disaster* causato dall'uomo

manner *n of doing sth* maniera *f*, modo *m*; (*attitude*) modo *m* di fare; ***in this ~*** in questo modo; ***in the Spanish ~*** alla spagnola; ***in such a ~ that ...*** in modo tale che...; ***in a ~ of***

speaking per così dire; ***all ~ of birds*** ogni genere di uccelli
mannerism *n* modi *mpl*
mannerist *n* ART manierista *m/f*
manners *npl*: ***good / bad ~*** buone / cattive maniere *fpl*; ***have no ~*** essere maleducato
mannish *adj* maschile
manoeuvre, *US* **maneuver I** *n* manovra *f* **II** *v/t* manovrare
man-of-letters *n* letterato *m*
manor *n* maniero *m*
manor house *n* casa *f* padronale
manpower *n* manodopera *f*, personale *m*
manservant *n* ⟨*pl* ***menservants***⟩ servitore *m*
mansion *n* villa *f*
manslaughter *n* omicidio *m* colposo
mantelpiece *n* mensola *f* del caminetto
man-to-man *adj/adv* da uomo a uomo
manual I *adj* manuale; ***~ labourer*** *Br or* ***laborer*** *US* lavoratore *m* manuale; ***~ worker*** operaio *m* **II** *n* manuale *m*
manually *adv* manualmente; ***~ operated*** azionato manualmente
manual transmission *n* trasmissione *f* manuale
manufacture I *n* manifattura *f* **II** *v/t* fabbricare; ***~d goods*** manufatti *mpl*
manufacturer *n* fabbricante *m/f*
manufacturing *adj industry* manifatturiero
manure *n* letame *m*
manuscript *n* manoscritto *m*; *typed* dattiloscritto *m*
many I *adj* molti; ***~ times*** molte volte; ***not ~ people / taxis*** poche persone / pochi taxi; ***too ~ problems / beers*** troppi problemi / troppe birre **II** *pron* molti *m*, molte *f*; ***a great ~, a good ~*** moltissimi; ***how ~ do you need?*** quanti te ne servono?; ***as ~ as 200*** ben 200; ***there's one too ~*** ce n'è uno di troppo; ***he's had one too ~*** *infml* ne ha bevuto uno di troppo
many-coloured, *US* **many-colored** *adj* multicolore
man-year *n* anno / uomo *m*
many-sided *adj* multiforme
map I *n* cartina *f*; (*street map*) pianta *f*, piantina *f*; *fig* ***this will put the place on the ~*** questo renderà famoso il posto **II** *v/t* ⟨*pret & past part* ***-ped***⟩ fare una mappa di
◆**map out** *v/t sep* ⟨*pret & past part* ***-ped***⟩ pianificare
maple *n* acero *m*
maple syrup *n* sciroppo *m* d'acero
mar *v/t* ⟨*pret & past part* ***-red***⟩ guastare
Mar *abbr* (= **March**) marzo *m*
marathon *n race* maratona *f*
marauder *n* predone *m*
marble I *n material* marmo *m*; (*glass ball*) biglia *f*; ***he's lost his ~s*** *infml* è uscito di senno **II** *adj* marmoreo
marbled *adj* marmorizzato; ***~ effect*** effetto *m* marmorizzato
march I *n* MIL, MUS marcia *f*; (*demonstration*) dimostrazione *f*, manifestazione *f* **II** *v/i* marciare; *in protest* dimostrare, manifestare; ***~ from A to B*** *in protest* sfilare in corteo da A a B; ***~ s.o. off*** costringere qn ad andare; ***forward ~!*** *or* ***quick ~!*** avanti, marc'!; ***she ~ed straight up to him*** è andata dritta da lui
March *n* marzo *m*
marcher *n* dimostrante *m/f*, manifestante *m/f*
marching orders *npl Br* ***the new manager got his ~*** il nuovo dirigente è stato licenziato; ***she gave him his ~*** gli ha dato il benservito
marchioness *n* marchesa *f*
Mardi Gras *n* martedì *m inv* grasso
mare *n* cavalla *f*, giumenta *f*
margarine *n* margarina *f*
margin *n of page* margine *m*; ***a note (written) in the ~*** una nota scritta a margine; (COMM: *profit margin*) margine *m* di guadagno; ***by a narrow ~*** di stretta misura; ***allow for a ~ of error*** tenere conto di un margine di errore
marginal *adj* marginale
marginalize *v/t* marginalizzare
marginally *adv* (*slightly*) leggermente
marihuana, marijuana *n* marijuana *f*
marina *n* porticciolo *m*
marinade *n* marinata *f*
marinate *v/t* marinare
marine I *adj* marino **II** *n* MIL marina *f* militare
mariner *n* marinaio *m*
marionette *n* marionetta *f*
marital *adj* coniugale
marital status *n* stato *m* civile

maritime *adj* marittimo
marjoram *n* maggiorana *f*
mark I *n* **1.** (*stain*) macchia *f* **2.** (*sign, token*) segno *m*; ***leave one's ~*** lasciare un segno **3.** EDU voto *m*; ***high or good ~s*** voti *mpl* alti / buoni voti *mpl*; *fig* ***he gets full ~s for punctuality*** è di una puntualità lodevole **4.** ***on your ~s*** *at start of race* ai posti di partenza; *fig* ***be slow off the ~*** essere lento a reagire **II** *v/t* **1.** (*stain*) macchiare **2.** EDU correggere; ***your essays will be ~ed out of ten*** ai temi sarà assegnata una votazione da 1 a 10 **3.** (*indicate*) indicare; ***the bottle was ~ed "poison"*** la bottiglia portava l'indicazione "veleno"; ***~ where you have stopped in your reading*** prendi nota del punto in cui hai interrotto la lettura; ***~ sth with an asterisk*** contrassegnare qc con un asterisco; ***it's not ~ed on the map*** non è segnato sulla mappa; ***it's ~ed with a blue dot*** è indicato con un puntino blu **4.** (*characterize*) caratterizzare; ***a decade ~ed by violence*** un decennio caratterizzato dalla violenza; ***~ a change of policy*** segnalare un cambiamento di politica; ***it ~ed the end of an era*** ha contrassegnato la fine di un'epoca **5.** (*commemorate*) celebrare **III** *v/i* *of fabric* macchiarsi
◆**mark down** *v/t sep goods* ribassare
◆**mark out** *v/t sep with a line etc* delimitare; ***he's been marked out for promotion*** è stato designato per una promozione; (*fig: set apart*) distinguere
◆**mark up** *v/t sep price* aumentare; *goods* aumentare il prezzo di
marked *adj* (*definite*) spiccato; ***in ~ contrast (to s.o. / sth)*** in netto contrasto (con qn / qc); ***he's a ~ man*** il suo destino è segnato
marker *n* (*highlighter*) evidenziatore *m*
market I *n* mercato *m*; *for particular commodity*; (*stock market*) mercato *m* azionario; ***on the ~*** sul mercato; (*house*) ***put on the ~*** mettere in vendita **II** *v/t* vendere
marketable *adj* commercializzabile
market day *n* giorno *m* di mercato **market economy** *n* economia *f* di mercato **market forces** *npl* forze *fpl* di mercato **market garden** *n* azienda *f* ortofrutticola
marketing *n* marketing *m inv*
marketing campaign *n* campagna *f* di marketing **marketing department** *n* reparto *m* marketing **marketing mix** *n* marketing mix *m inv* **marketing strategy** *n* strategia *f* di marketing
market leader *n* leader *m inv* del mercato **market-place** *n in town* piazza *f* del mercato; *for commodities* piazza *f*, mercato *m* **market research** *n* ricerca *f* di mercato **market share** *n* quota *f* di mercato **market town** *n* città *f* sede di mercato **market trader** *n Br* venditore *m*, -trice *f* ambulante **market value** *n* valore *m* di mercato
marking *n on road*, *wall* segni *mpl*; *on animal* macchia *f*; *correcting* valutazione *f*; (*grading*) voti *mpl*
marksman *n* ⟨*pl* ***marksmen***⟩ buon tiratore *m*; *police etc* tiratore *m* scelto
mark-up *n* ricarico *m*
marmalade *n* marmellata *f* d'arance
maroon[1] **I** *adj* bordeaux *inv* **II** *n* bordeaux *m*
maroon[2] *v/t*: ***~ed*** abbandonato; ***~ed by floods*** isolato dall'alluvione
marquee *n* padiglione *f*
marquetry *n* intarsio *m*
marriage *n* matrimonio *m*; *event* nozze *fpl*; ***~ of convenience*** matrimonio *m* di convenienza; ***be related by ~*** essere imparentati per matrimonio; ***an offer of ~*** un'offerta di matrimonio
marriage certificate *n* certificato *m* di matrimonio **marriage guidance counsellor** *n* consulente *m/f* matrimoniale; **marriage licence**, *US* **marriage license** *n* licenza *f* matrimoniale
married *adj* sposato; ***be ~ to …*** essere sposato con …; ***just*** *or* ***newly ~*** appena sposato; ***~ couple*** coppia *f* di sposi; ***~ couple's allowance*** *detrazione fiscale per le coppie sposate*; ***~ life*** vita *f* matrimoniale; ***he is a ~ man*** è un uomo sposato
married life *n* vita *f* coniugale
marrow *n vegetable* zucca *f*; ANAT midollo *m*; ***frozen to the ~*** gelato fino al midollo
marry I *v/t* ⟨*pret & past part* ***-ied***⟩ sposare; *of priest* unire in matrimonio; ***will you ~ me?*** vuoi sposarmi? **II**

v/i (*a.* **get married**) sposarsi; ***~ into a rich family*** sposare una persona ricca
Mars *n* Marte *m*
marsh *n* palude *f*
marshal I *n* maresciallo *m*; *official* membro *m* del servizio d'ordine II *v/t* (*lead*) condurre
marshland *n* regione *f* paludosa
marshmallow *n caramella soffice e gommosa*
marshy *adj* (+*er*) paludoso
marsupial *n* marsupiale *m*
martial arts *npl* arti *fpl* marziali
martial law *n* legge *f* marziale
Martian *n* marziano *m*
martyr I *n* martire *m/f* II *v/t*: ***thousands of Christians were ~ed*** migliaia di cristiani hanno subito il martirio
martyrdom *n* martirio *m*
martyred *adj fig* da martire
marvel *n* I meraviglia *f*; ***it's a ~ to me how he does it*** *infml* mi stupisce come riesca a farlo II *v/i* meravigliarsi
◆**marvel at** *v/t* meravigliarsi di
marvellous, *US* **marvelous** *adj* meraviglioso; ***isn't it ~?*** non è meraviglioso?; ***they've done a ~ job*** hanno fatto uno splendido lavoro
Marxism *n* marxismo *m*
Marxist I *adj* marxista II *n* marxista *m/f*
marzipan *n* marzapane *m*
mascara *n* mascara *m inv*
mascot *n* mascotte *f inv*
masculine I *adj* maschile; GRAM maschile II *n* GRAM maschile *m*
masculinity *n* (*virility*) virilità *f inv*
mash I *n* pastone *m*; (*potatoes*) purè *m inv* II *v/t* passare, schiacciare
mashed potatoes *npl* purè *m inv* di patate
masher *n* (*for potatoes*) schiacciapatate *m*
mask I *n* maschera *f*; ***surgeon's ~*** mascherina *f* da chirurgo II *v/t feelings* mascherare
masked ball *n* ballo *m* in maschera
masking tape *n nastro adesivo di carta*
masochism *n* masochismo *m*
masochist *n* masochista *m/f*
mason *n* scalpellino *m*; (*freemason*) massone *m*
masonic *adj* massonico
masonry *n* muratura *f*
masque *n* LIT masque *m*
masquerade I *n fig* messinscena *f* II *v/i*: ***~ as*** farsi passare per
mass[1] I *n great amount* massa *f*; ***a ~ of rubble*** un cumulo di macerie; ***I've got ~es to do*** ho molto da fare; ***the ~es*** le masse; ***~es of*** *infml* un sacco di *infml* II *v/i* radunarsi; ***they're ~ing for an attack*** si stanno radunando per un attacco
mass[2] *n* REL messa *f*
massacre I *n a. fig* massacro *m* II *v/t a. fig* massacrare
massage I *n* massaggio *m* II *v/t* massaggiare; *figures* manipolare
massage parlour, *US* **massage parlor** *n euph* casa *f* d'appuntamenti
mass destruction *n*: ***weapons of ~*** armi *fpl* di distruzione di massa
masseur *n* massaggiatore *m*
masseuse *n* massaggiatrice *f*
mass grave *n* fossa *f* comune **mass hysteria** *n* isteria *f* di massa
massive *adj* enorme; *heart attack* grave; ***on a ~ scale*** su vasta scala
mass media *npl* mass media *mpl* **mass murderer** *n* autore *m*, -trice *f* di una strage **mass-produce** *v/t* produrre in serie **mass production** *n* produzione *f* in serie **mass tourism** *n* turismo *m* di massa **mass unemployment** *n* disoccupazione *f* di massa
mast *n* NAUT albero *m*; RADIO *etc* palo *m* dell'antenna
mastectomy *n* mastectomia *f*
master I *n of dog* padrone *m*; *of ship* capitano *m*; ***be a ~ of*** essere un maestro di II *v/t skill*, *language* avere completa padronanza di; *situation* dominare III *adj* principale; (*skilled*) professionista; ***~ switch*** interruttore *m* principale; ***he was a ~ thief*** era un ladro professionista
master bedroom *n* camera *f* da letto principale **master class** *n* MUS master class *f*, *lezione speciale tenuta da un musicista famoso* **master craftsman** *n* maestro *m*, -a *f* **master disk** *n* COMPUT master *m* **master file** *n* COMPUT file *m* master
masterful *adj* imperioso
master key *n* passe-partout *m inv*
masterly *adj* magistrale

mastermind **I** *n fig* cervello *m* **II** *v/t* ideare; ***who ~ed the robbery?*** chi ha ideato la rapina? **Master of Arts** *n* master *m inv* **master of ceremonies** *n* maestro *m* di cerimonie **masterpiece** *n* capolavoro *m* **master plan** *n* piano *m* generale **master's (degree)** *n* master *m inv* **masterstroke** *n* colpo *m* maestro **master tape** *n* master *m inv*; COMPUT nastro *m* master **masterwork** *n* capolavoro *m*

mastery *n* padronanza *f*

masturbate *v/i* masturbarsi

masturbation *n* masturbazione *f*

mat *n for floor* tappetino *m*; SPORTS tappeto *m*; *for table* tovaglietta *f* all'americana

match[1] *n for cigarette* fiammifero *m*; *wax* cerino *m*

match[2] **I** *n* (*competition*) partita *f*; *boxing*, *tennis* incontro *m*; ***be no ~ for s.o.*** non poter competere con qn; ***meet one's ~*** trovare pane per i propri denti; ***I want a ~ for this yellow paint*** cerco un colore corrispondente a questa vernice gialla; ***she made a good ~*** ha sposato un buon partito; ***athletics ~*** incontro *m* di atletica; ***we must have another ~ some time*** dobbiamo giocare un'altra partita prima o poi **II** *v/t* (*be the same as*) abbinare; ***~ textures and fabrics so that ...*** abbinare trame e tessuti in modo che...; (*equal*) uguagliare; ***a quality that has never been ~ed since*** una qualità ineguagliata da...; ***be ~ed against s.o.*** competere con qn **III** *v/i of colours, patterns* intonarsi; ***with a skirt to ~*** con gonna coordinata

◆**match up** **I** *v/i* corrispondere **II** *v/t sep colours* abbinare; ***I matched the lampshade up with the wallpaper*** ho abbinato il paralume alla carta da parati

matchbook *n esp US* bustina *f* di fiammiferi

matchbox *n* scatola *f* di fiammiferi

matching *adj* abbinato; ***they form a ~ pair*** formano una coppia coordinata; ***a ~ set of wine glasses*** un insieme coordinato di bicchieri da vino

matchless *adj* ineguagliabile

matchmaker *n* sensale *m/f*

match point *n tennis* match point *m*

matchstick *n* fiammifero *m*

mate **I** *n of animal* compagno *m*, -a *f*; NAUT secondo *m*; *infml friend* amico *m*, -a *f*; ***listen, ~*** ascolta, vecchio mio **II** *v/i* accoppiarsi

material **I** *n fabric* stoffa *f*, tessuto *m*; *substance* materia *f*; ***raw ~s*** materie *fpl* prime; ***~s*** occorrente *m*; ***writing ~s*** occorrente *m* per scrivere **II** *adj* materiale; ***~ damage*** danno *m* materiale

materialise, materialize *v/i* materializzarsi; ***the meeting never ~d*** la riunione non è mai stata attuata; ***the money never ~d*** i soldi non si sono mai materializzati

materialism *n* materialismo *m*

materialist *n* materialista *m/f*

materialistic *adj* materialistico

maternal *adj* materno; ***~ grandfather*** nonno *m* materno; ***~ affection** or **love*** affetto *m or* amore *m* materno

maternity *n* maternità *f inv*

maternity dress *n* vestito *m* prémaman **maternity leave** *n* congedo *m* per maternità **maternity pay** *n Br* sussidio *m* di maternità **maternity rights** *npl* diritti *mpl* di maternità **maternity ward** *n* reparto *m* maternità

matey *adj Br infml*: ***be ~ with s.o.*** essere in confidenza con qn

math *n US* → ***maths***

mathematical *adj* matematico

mathematician *n* matematico *m*, -a *f*

mathematics *nsg* matematica *f*

maths *nsg*, *US* **math** *n* matematica *f*

matinée *n* matinée *f inv*

mating call *n* ZOOL richiamo *m* **mating season** *n* ZOOL stagione *f* degli amori

matins *n* REL mattutino *m*

matriarch *n* matriarca *f*

matriarchal *adj* matriarcale

matriarchy *n* matriarcato *m*

matriculate *v/i* iscriversi all'università

matriculation *n* iscrizione *f*

matrimonial *adj* matrimoniale

matrimony *n* matrimonio *m*

matrix *n* ⟨*pl* ***matrices***⟩ matrice *f*

matron *n* matrona *f*; (*nursing*) caposala *f inv*

matronly *adj* matronale

matt *adj* opaco; ***a paint with a ~ finish*** una vernice opaca

matted *adj* arruffato; ***hair ~ with blood / mud*** capelli *mpl* pieni di sangue / fango
matter **I** *n* **1.** (*affair*) questione *f*, faccenda *f*; ***as a ~ of course*** per abitudine, ***as a ~ of fact*** a dir la verità; ***what's the ~?*** cosa c'è?; ***no ~ what she says*** qualsiasi cosa dica; ***a ~ of great urgency*** una questione molto urgente; ***that's quite another ~*** è tutta un'altra faccenda; ***it will be no easy ~ (to) ...*** non sarà una cosa facile; ***the ~ is closed*** è una faccenda chiusa; ***for that ~*** (in) quanto a ciò; ***it's a ~ of time / opinion*** è questione di tempo / opinioni; ***it's a ~ of life and death*** è questione di vita o di morte; ***it will be a ~ of a few weeks*** sarà una questione di poche settimane; ***~s*** *pl* situazione *f*; ***to make ~s worse*** a peggiorare la situazione **2.** PHYS materia *f*; ***vegetable ~*** sostanza *f* vegetale **II** *v/i* importare; ***it doesn't ~*** non importa; ***it doesn't ~ to me what you do*** non mi importa cosa fai; ***the things which ~ in life*** le cose che contano nella vita
matter-of-fact *adj* distaccato; ***he was very ~ about it*** era molto distaccato in merito
mattress *n* materasso *m*
mature **I** *adj* (*+er*) maturo **II** *v/i of person, insurance policy etc* maturare; *of wine* invecchiare
mature student *n studente che riprende gli studi a un'età successiva a quella regolare*
maturity *n* maturità *f inv*; JUR, COMM scadenza *f*
maudlin *adj* lacrimoso
maul *v/t a. fig* sbranare
mausoleum *n* mausoleo *m*
mauve **I** *adj* malva *inv* **II** *n* malva *f*
maverick *n* nonconformista *m/f*
mawkish *adj* sdolcinato
max *n abbr* (= **maximum**) *infml* massimo *m*
maxim *n* massima *f*
maximize *v/t* massimizzare
maximum **I** *adj* massimo; ***~ penalty*** pena *f* massima; ***~ fine*** ammenda *f* massima; ***for ~ effect*** per ottenere il massimo dell'effetto; ***he scored ~ points*** ha segnato il punteggio massimo; ***~ security prison*** prigione *f* di massima sicurezza **II** *n* massimo *m*; ***up to a ~ of £8*** fino a un massimo di 8 sterline; ***temperatures reached a ~ of 34°*** le temperature hanno raggiunto un massimo di 34°
may *v/mod* **1.** (*possibility*): ***it ~ rain*** potrebbe piovere, può darsi che piova; ***you ~ be right*** potresti aver ragione, può darsi che abbia ragione; ***it ~ not happen*** magari non succederà, può darsi che non succeda; ***he ~ not be hungry*** può darsi che non abbia fame; ***they ~ be brothers*** potrebbero essere fratelli; ***that's as ~ be*** (*not might*) può darsi che sia così; ***you ~ well ask*** puoi chiedere **2.** (*permission*): ***~ I help / smoke?*** posso aiutare / fumare?; ***you ~ if you like*** puoi farlo se vuoi; ***~ you be very happy together*** possiate essere molto felici insieme; ***~ the Lord have mercy on your soul*** possa Dio avere misericordia della tua anima
May *n* maggio *m*
maybe *adv* forse; ***~, ~ not*** forse no
May Day *n* il primo maggio
mayhem *n* pandemonio *m*
mayo *n US infml* maionese *f*
mayonnaise *n* maionese *f*
mayor *n* sindaco *m*
mayoress *n* moglie *f* del sindaco; (*lady mayor*) sindaca *f*
maze *n a. fig* dedalo *m*, labirinto *m*
MB *abbr* **1.** (= **megabyte**) MB *m* (megabyte *m inv*) **2.** (= **Bachelor of Medicine**) (*degree*) *laurea in medicina*; (*person*) *laureato in medicina*
MBA *abbr* (= **master of business administration**) master *m inv* in amministrazione aziendale; ***he's doing an ~*** sta facendo un master in amministrazione aziendale
MBE *abbr* (= **Member of the Order of the British Empire**) membro *m* dell'ordine dell'impero britannico
MBO *abbr* (= **management buyout**) *acquisizione di un'impresa da parte dei suoi dirigenti*
MC *abbr* (= **master of ceremonies**) maestro *m* di cerimonie
MD *abbr* (= **Doctor of Medicine**) dottore *m* in medicina
me *pron direct & indirect object* mi; *after prep, stressed* me; ***he's older than me*** è più vecchio di me; ***she knows ~***

mi conosce; ***she spoke to ~*** mi ha parlato; ***she spoke to ~ but not to him*** ha parlato a me ma non a lui; ***without ~*** senza di me; ***it's ~*** sono io; ***who? ~?*** chi? io?

mead *n* idromele *m*

meadow *n* prato *m*

meagre, *US* **meager** *adj* scarso; ***he earns a ~ £500 a month*** ha un misero guadagno di 500 sterline al mese

meal[1] *n* farina *f*

meal[2] *n* pasto *m*; (*lunch*) pranzo *m*; (*supper*) cena *f*; ***come round for a ~*** venire a pranzo / cena; ***go for a ~*** andare a pranzo / cena; ***have a (good) ~*** mangiare bene; ***make a ~ of sth*** *infml* fare un dramma di qc; ***enjoy your ~!*** buon appetito!

meals-on-wheels *n* pasti *mpl* a domicilio

meal ticket *n* buono *m* pasto; *fig* mezzo *m* di sostentamento

mealtime *n* ora *f* di pranzo

mealy-mouthed *adj* insincero

mean[1] *adj* (+*er*) *with money* avaro; (*nasty*) cattivo; (*wretched*) squallido; ***that's no ~ feat*** non è cosa da poco; (*skilful*) formidabile; ***he plays a ~ game of poker*** gioca a poker in modo formidabile

mean[2] ⟨*pret & past part* ***meant***⟩ **I** *v/t* (*signify*) significare, voler dire; ***do you ~ it?*** (*intend*) dici sul serio?; ***~ to do sth*** avere l'intenzione di fare qc; ***I was ~t to do that*** ero destinato a farlo; ***I thought it was ~t to be hot in the south*** pensavo dovesse essere caldo a sud; ***he ~s well / no harm*** ha buone intenzioni; ***be ~t for*** essere destinato a; *of remark* essere diretto a; ***doesn't it ~ anything to you?*** (*doesn't it matter?*) non conta niente per te? **II** *v/i*: ***~ well*** avere buone intenzioni

mean[3] *n* MATH media *f*

meander *v/i river* serpeggiare; *person* girovagare; *conversation* divagare

meaning I *n of word* significato *m*; ***what's the ~ of (the word) "hick"?*** che cosa significa (la parola) "sempliciotto"?; ***I'm sorry, I don't get your ~*** mi spiace, non capisco cosa vuoi dire **II** *adj* eloquente; ***she gave him a ~ look*** gli lanciò uno sguardo eloquente

meaningful *adj* (*comprehensible*) comprensibile; (*constructive*) costruttivo; *glance* eloquente

meaningless *adj sentence etc* senza senso; *gesture* vuoto; ***my life is ~*** la mia vita è priva di senso

meanness *n esp Br* (*miserliness*) avarizia *f*; (*unkindness*) scortesia *f*; (*viciousness*) cattiveria *f*

means *npl financial* mezzi *mpl*; (*nsg*: *way*) modo *m*; ***a man of ~*** un uomo facoltoso; ***live beyond one's ~*** vivere al di sopra dei propri mezzi; ***a ~ of escape*** una via di fuga; ***a ~ to an end*** un mezzo per raggiungere uno scopo; ***there is no ~ of doing it*** non è possibile farlo in alcun modo; ***~ of transport*** mezzo *m* di trasporto; ***by all ~*** (*certainly*) certamente; ***by no ~ rich / poor*** lungi dall'essere ricco / povero; ***by ~ of*** per mezzo di

means test *n* accertamento *m* patrimoniale

meant *pret & past part* → ***mean***[2]

meantime I *adv* intanto **II** *n*: ***in the ~*** nel frattempo

meanwhile I *adv* intanto **II** *n*: ***in the ~*** nel frattempo

measles *nsg* morbillo *m*

measure I *n* (*step*) misura *f*, provvedimento *m*; ***a ~ of success*** *certain amount* un certo successo; ***have sth made to ~*** farsi fare qc su misura; ***beyond ~*** oltre misura; ***in large ~*** in larga misura; ***for good ~*** in più; ***get the ~ of sth*** prendere confidenza con qc; *fig* ***get the ~ of s.o.*** *Br* prendere le misure a qn **II** *v/t* prendere le misure di **III** *v/i* misurare; ***what does it ~?*** quanto misura?

◆**measure out** *v/t sep amount* dosare; *area* misurare

◆**measure up to** *v/t* dimostrarsi all'altezza di; ***he didn't measure up to expectations*** non si è dimostrato all'altezza delle aspettative

measured *adj tone* misurato; *response* controllato; ***at a ~ pace*** a passo cadenzato

measurement *n action* misurazione *f*; (*dimension*) misura *f*; ***take s.o.'s ~s*** prendere le misure a qn; ***system of ~*** sistema *m* di misura

measuring jug *n* misurino *m*

measuring tape *n* metro *m* a nastro

meat *n* carne *f*; ***crab ~*** polpa *f* di granchio; *fig* ***easy ~*** bersaglio *m* facile
meatball *n* polpetta *f* **meatloaf** *n* polpettone *m*
meaty *adj* (+*er*) polposo; *hands* paffuto; *fig role* importante
Mecca *n* Mecca *f*
mechanic *n* meccanico *m*
mechanical *adj a. fig* meccanico; ***a ~ device*** un dispositivo meccanico
mechanical engineer *n* ingegnere *m* meccanico **mechanical engineering** *n* ingegneria *f* meccanica
mechanically *adv a. fig* meccanicamente
mechanics *nsg* meccanica *f*; *fig of writing* tecnica *f*
mechanisation *n* meccanizzazione *f*
mechanise, mechanize *v/t* meccanizzare
mechanism *n* meccanismo *m*
medal *n* medaglia *f*
medallion *n* medaglione *m*
medallist, *US* **medalist** *n* vincitore *m*, -trice *f* di una medaglia
meddle *v/i* (*interfere*) immischiarsi; ***~ with*** (*tinker*) mettere le mani in
meddlesome *adj*, **meddling** *adj*: ***she's a ~ old busybody*** è una vecchia ficcanaso intrigante
media *npl*: ***the ~*** i mass media *mpl*; ***he works in the ~*** lavora nel settore dei media
media coverage *n*: ***it was given a lot of ~*** gli è stato dato molto spazio in tv e sui giornali; ***an event that got a lot of ~*** un avvenimento di grande risonanza
mediaeval → ***medieval***
media event *n* spettacolo *m* sensazionale **media hype** *n* montatura *f* della stampa
median *adj* medio
median strip *n US* spartitraffico *m inv*
media studies *npl* scienze *fpl* delle comunicazioni
mediate *v/i* fare da mediatore *m*, -trice *f*
mediation *n* mediazione *f*
mediator *n* mediatore *m*, -trice *f*
Medicaid *n negli Stati Uniti, assistenza sanitaria statale per le persone più povere*
medical I *adj* medico; *treatment, staff* medico; ***the ~ profession*** la professione medica; ***~ condition*** condizione *f* medica **II** *n* visita *f* medica
medical certificate *n* certificato *m* medico **medical examination** *n* visita *f* medica **medical history** *n* anamnesi *f inv* **medical insurance** *n* assicurazione *f* sanitaria **medical officer** *n* MIL medico *m* militare; (*official*) ufficiale *m* sanitario **medical practice** *n* (*business*) esercizio *m* della professione medica **medical profession** *n* professione *f* medica; corpo *m* medico **medical record** *n* cartella *f* clinica **medical school** *n* facoltà *f* di medicina **medical science** *n* scienza *f* medica **medical student** *n* studente *m* di medicina
Medicare *n negli Stati Uniti, assistenza sanitaria statale per le persone oltre i 65 anni*
medicated *adj* medicato
medication *n* medicina *f*
medicinal *adj* medicinale; ***for ~ purposes*** a fini terapeutici; ***the ~ properties of various herbs*** le proprietà medicinali di diverse erbe
medicine *n* medicina *f*; *fig* ***take one's ~*** ingoiare la pillola; *fig* ***give s.o. a taste of his own ~*** ripagare qn della stessa moneta; (*science*) medicina *f*; ***practise*** *Br or* ***practice*** *US* ***~*** esercitare la professione medica
medicine cabinet *n* armadietto *m* dei medicinali
medieval *adj* medievale; ***in ~ times*** in era medievale
mediocre *adj* mediocre
mediocrity *n* mediocrità *f inv*
meditate *v/i* meditare
meditation *n* meditazione *f*
Mediterranean I *adj* mediterraneo; ***the ~ diet*** la dieta mediterranea **II** *n*: ***the ~*** il Mar Mediterraneo; *area* i paesi mediterranei
medium I *adj* (*average*) medio; *steak* cotto al punto giusto **II** *n in size* media *f*; (*vehicle*) strumento *m*; (*spiritualist*) medium *m/f inv*; ***advertising ~*** veicolo *m* pubblicitario; ***strike a happy ~*** trovare il giusto mezzo
medium-dry *adj* semisecco **medium-range** *adj*: ***~ ballistic missile*** missile *m* balistico a media portata **medium-rare** *adj* poco cotto **medium-sized** *adj* di grandezza media **medi-**

um term *n*: ***in the ~*** a medio termine
medium wave *n* RADIO onde *fpl* medie
medley *n* (*assortment*) misto *m*
meek *adj* (*+er*) mite
meet I *v/t* ⟨*pret & past part* **met**⟩ incontrare; ***arrange to ~ s.o.*** combinare un incontro con qn; (*get to know*) conoscere; (*collect*) andare *or* venire a prendere; *in competition* affrontare; *of eyes* incrociare; (*satisfy*) soddisfare; ***I'll ~ you there*** ci vediamo lì; ***there's more to it than ~s the eye*** c'è sotto qc; ***~ halfway*** arrivare a un compromesso **II** *v/i* ⟨*pret & past part* **met**⟩ incontrarsi; *in competition* affrontarsi; *of eyes* incrociarsi; *of committee etc* riunirsi; ***have you two met?*** (*do you know each other?*) vi conoscete?; ***haven't we met before?*** non ci siamo già incontrati? **III** *n US* SPORTS raduno *m* sportivo
◆**meet up** *v/i* incontrarsi
◆**meet with** *v/t person* avere un incontro con; *opposition, approval etc* incontrare; ***it met with success / failure*** ha avuto successo / è fallito; ***I was met with a blank stare*** fui accolto da uno sguardo assente
meeting *n* incontro *m*; *of committee, in business* riunione *f*; appuntamento *m*; ***he's in a ~*** è in riunione; ***the minister had a ~ with the ambassador*** il ministro ebbe una riunione con l'ambasciatore; ***the committee has three ~s a year*** il comitato si riunisce tre volte l'anno
meeting-house *n* REL luogo *m* di riunione (*dei quaccheri*) **meeting place** *n* luogo *m* d'incontro
megabyte *n* COMPUT megabyte *m inv*; ***a 40-~ memory*** una memoria di 40 megabyte
megahertz *n* megahertz *m*
megalith *n* megalite *m*
megalomania *n* megalomania *f*
megalomaniac *n* megalomane
megaphone *n* megafono *m*
megastar *n infml* superstar *f*
megastore *n* megastore *m*
melancholy I *adj* malinconico **II** *n* malinconia *f*
melanoma *n* melanoma *m*
mellifluous *adj* soave
mellow I *adj* (*+er*) maturo; *wine, flavour* pastoso; *colour, light* caldo; *person* calmo **II** *v/i of person* addolcirsi
melodious *adj* melodioso
melodrama *n* melodramma *m*
melodramatic *adj* melodrammatico
melody *n* melodia *f*
melon *n* melone *m*
melt I *v/i* sciogliersi **II** *v/t* sciogliere
◆**melt away** *v/i fig* svanire
◆**melt down** *v/t sep metal* fondere
meltdown *n* meltdown *m inv*
melting pot *n fig* crogiolo *m* di culture
member *n of family* componente *m/f*; *of club* socio *m*; *of organization* membro *m*; (*penis*) membro *m*; ***if any ~ of the audience …*** se uno qualsiasi degli spettatori…; ***the ~ states*** gli stati membri
Member of Parliament *n* deputato *m*
membership *n* iscrizione *f*; *number of members* numero *m* dei soci
membership card *n* tessera *f* d'iscrizione
membrane *n* membrana *f*
memento *n* souvenir *m inv*
memo *n* circolare *f*
memoir *n form* memoriale *m*
memoirs *npl* memorie *fpl*; ***she's writing her ~*** sta scrivendo le sue memorie
memo pad *n* blocco *m* notes
memorabilia *npl* memorabilia *mpl*
memorable *adj* memorabile
memorandum *n* ⟨*pl* **memoranda**⟩ promemoria *m*
memorial I *adj* commemorativo **II** *n a. fig* memorial *m inv*
memorial service *n* commemorazione *f*
memorise, memorize *v/t* memorizzare
memory *n* (*recollection*) ricordo *m*; ***I have no ~ of it*** non ricordo niente; ***he had happy memories of his father*** aveva ricordi felici di suo padre; *power of recollection* memoria *f*; ***from ~*** a memoria; ***lose one's ~*** perdere la memoria; ***commit sth to ~*** imparare qc a memoria; ***have a ~ for faces*** essere fisionomista; ***if my ~ serves me right*** se la memoria non m'inganna; COMPUT memoria *f*; ***in ~ of*** in memoria di
memory bank *n* COMPUT banco *m* di memoria **memory expansion card**

n COMPUT scheda *f* di espansione della memoria **memory span** *n* estensione *f* della memoria
men *pl* → ***man***
menace I *n* (*threat*) minaccia *f*; *person* pericolo *m* pubblico; ***she's a ~ on the roads*** è un pericolo pubblico in strada; (*nuisance*) peste *f* **II** *v/t* minacciare
menacing *adj* minaccioso; ***look ~*** apparire minaccioso
mend I *v/t* riparare; *clothes* aggiustare **II** *v/i* (*bone*) guarire **III** *n*: ***be on the ~*** *after illness* essere in via di guarigione; ***the ~ on his cuff was very visible*** il rammendo sul polsino era ben visibile
mendacious *adj* falso
mending *n* rammendo *m*; ***she comes in to do the ~*** viene a fare dei rammendi
menial *adj* umile
meningitis *n* meningite *f*
menopause *n* menopausa *f*
men's room *n US* bagno *m* (degli uomini)
menstrual period *n* ciclo *m* mestruale
menstruate *v/i* avere le mestruazioni
menstruation *n* mestruazione *f*
menswear *n* abbigliamento *m* maschile
mental *adj* mentale; ***make a ~ note of sth*** prendere mentalmente nota di qc; ***~ process*** processo *m* mentale; *infml* (*crazy*) pazzo
mental arithmetic *n* calcolo *m* mentale **mental block** *n*: ***have a ~*** avere un blocco mentale **mental breakdown** *n* crollo *m* mentale **mental cruelty** *n* crudeltà *f inv* mentale **mental health** *n* salute *f* mentale **mental hospital** *n* ospedale *m* psichiatrico **mental illness** *n* malattia *f* mentale
mentality *n* mentalità *f inv*
mentally *adv inwardly* mentalmente; *calculate etc* a mente
mentally handicapped *adj* handicappato mentale
mentally ill *adj* malato di mente
mention I *v/t* accennare a; ***she ~ed that ...*** ha accennato al fatto che ...; ***France and Spain, not to ~ Holland*** Francia e Spagna, per non parlare dell'Olanda; ***don't ~ it*** (*you're welcome*) non c'è di che **II** *n* cenno *m*; ***get*** *or* ***receive a ~*** essere citato; ***his contribution deserves special ~*** il suo contributo merita una menzione speciale; ***he made no ~ of it*** non ne ha fatto cenno
mentor *n* guida *f* spirituale
menu *n a.* COMPUT menu *m inv*; ***may we see the ~?*** possiamo vedere il menu?
menu bar *n* COMPUT barra *f* dei menu **menu-driven** *adj* COMPUT basato su menu
MEP *abbr* (= **Member of the European Parliament**) eurodeputato *m*
mercenary I *adj* mercenario; (*greedy*) venale; ***don't be so ~*** non essere così venale **II** *n* MIL mercenario *m*
merchandise *n* merce *f*
merchant *n* commerciante *m/f*; ***corn ~*** commerciante *m/f* di grano
merchant bank *n* banca *f* d'affari **merchant banker** *n* banchiere *m* d'affari **merchant marine** *n US* marina *f* mercantile **merchant navy** *n Br* marina *f* mercantile
merciful *adj* misericordioso
mercifully *adv* (*thankfully*) per fortuna
merciless *adj* spietato
mercury *n* mercurio *m*
Mercury *n* Mercurio *m*
mercy *n* misericordia *f*; ***be at s.o.'s ~*** essere alla mercé di qn; ***beg for ~*** implorare pietà; ***show s.o. ~ / no ~*** avere / non avere pietà di qn; *infml* (*blessing*) benedizione *f*
mere *adj* semplice; ***he's a ~ child*** è solo un bambino; ***he's a ~ clerk*** è un semplice impiegato; ***a ~ 3% / two hours*** soltanto il 3% / due ore; ***the ~ thought of food made me hungry*** il solo pensiero del cibo mi fece venire fame
merely *adv* soltanto
merge I *v/i of two lines etc* unirsi; *of companies* fondersi; ***~ with sth*** fondersi con qc; ***~ (in) with / into the crowd*** confondersi nella folla; ***~ into sth*** unirsi a qc **II** *v/t* unire (*a.* COMPUT); COMM fondere
merger *n* COMM fusione *f*
meringue *n* meringa *f*
merit I *n* (*worth*) merito *m*; (*advantage*) vantaggio *m*; ***a work of great literary ~*** un'opera di grande pregio let-

terario; ***all students are selected on ~*** gli studenti vengono selezionati in base al merito; ***judge a case on its ~s*** giudicare un caso per quel che vale; ***pass an exam with ~*** passare un esame con merito **II** *v/t* meritare
meritocracy *n* meritocrazia *f*
meritorious *adj form* meritevole
mermaid *n* sirena *f*
merriment *n* ilarità *f inv*
merry *adj* (+*er*) allegro; ***Merry Christmas!*** Buon Natale!
merry-go-round *n* giostra *f*
mesh I *n in net* maglia *f* **II** *v/i* MECH ingranare (***with*** con); *fig views* accordarsi
mesmerize *v/t* ammaliare; ***the audience sat ~d*** il pubblico era ammaliato
mess[1] **I** *n* (*untidiness*) disordine *m*; (*trouble*) pasticcio *m*; *fig* guai *mpl*; *euph* (*excreta*) cacca *f*; ***be a ~*** *of room, desk, hair* essere in disordine; *of situation, s.o.'s life* essere un pasticcio; ***make a ~*** fare disordine; (*be dirty*) sporcare; ***make a ~ of (doing) sth*** fare un casino *infml*; (*bundle*) non saperci fare; ***you've really made a ~ of things*** hai combinato un vero casino; ***what a ~!*** che casino!; ***the cat has made a ~ on the carpet*** il gatto ha fatto la cacca sul tappeto **II** *v/i*: ***don't try ~ing with me*** non provare ad intrometterti
◆**mess about, mess around I** *v/i* (*waste time*) trastullarsi **II** *v/t sep person* menare per il naso
◆**mess around with** *v/t* (*play with*) giocare con; (*interfere with*) armeggiare con; *s.o.'s wife* avere una relazione con
◆**mess up** *v/t sep room, papers* mettere sottosopra; *task, plans, marriage* rovinare; ***that's really messed things up*** questo ha mandato tutto all'aria
mess[2] *n* MIL mensa *f*; NAUT quadrato *m*
message *n a. fig* messaggio *m*; ***would you give John a ~ (for me)?*** riferiresti un messaggio a John da parte mia?; ***send s.o. a ~*** inviare un messaggio a qn; ***leave a ~ for s.o.*** lasciare un messaggio per qn; ***can I take a ~ (for him)?*** TEL vuole lasciare un messaggio?; ***get one's ~ across to s.o.*** far recepire il proprio messaggio a qn; *fig* ***get the ~*** *infml* capire l'antifona
message board *n* COMPUT bacheca *f*
messenger *n* (*courier*) fattorino *m*, -a *f*
Messiah *n* Messia *m*
mess kit *n US* corredo *m* per la mensa
messy *adj* (+*er*) *room* in disordine; *person* disordinato; ***he's a ~ eater*** quando mangia si sporca sempre; *job* sporco; *divorce, situation* antipatico
met *pret & past part* → ***meet***
metabolic *adj* metabolico
metabolism *n* metabolismo *m*
metal I *adj* in *or* di metallo **II** *n* metallo *m*
metal detector *n* metal detector *m*
metallic *adj* metallico; ***~ paint*** vernice *f* metallizzata; ***a ~ blue car*** una macchina di colore blu metallizzato; ***a ~ voice*** una voce metallica
metallurgy *n* metallurgia *f*
metalwork *n* lavorazione *f* del metallo; ***we did ~ at school*** a scuola abbiamo seguito corsi di lavorazione del metallo
metamorphosis *n* ⟨*pl* ***metamorphoses***⟩ metamorfosi *f inv*
metaphor *n* metafora *f*
metaphorical *adj* metaforico
metaphorically *adv* metaforicamente; ***~ speaking*** in senso metaforico
metaphysical *adj* metafisico
mete *v/t*: ***~ out punishment to s.o.*** infliggere una punizione a qn
meteor *n* meteora *f*
meteoric *adj fig* fulmineo
meteorite *n* meteorite *m or f*
meteorological *adj* meteorologico
meteorologist *n* meteorologo *m*, -a *f*
meteorology *n* meteorologia *f*
meter I *n for gas etc* contatore *m*; (*parking meter*) parchimetro *m*; *US*: *length* metro *m* **II** *v/t* misurare (con un contatore)
meter maid *n Br infml* ausiliaria *f* del traffico **meter reading** *n* lettura *f* del contatore
methadone *n* metadone *m*
methane *n* metano *m*
method *n* metodo *m*; ***~ of payment*** metodo *m* di pagamento
methodical *adj* metodico

methodically *adv* metodicamente
meticulous *adj* meticoloso
meticulously *adv* meticolosamente
met office *n Br* ufficio *m* meteorologico
metre, *US* **meter** *n* metro *m*
metric *adj* metrico
metric system *n* sistema *m* metrico
metronome *n* metronomo *m*
metropolis *n* metropoli *f inv*
metropolitan *adj* metropolitano
mettle *n* coraggio *m*
mew *n & v/i* → ***miaow***
mews *n vicolo o cortile dove un tempo erano tenuti i cavalli*
Mexican I *adj* messicano **II** *n* messicano *m*, -a *f*
Mexico *n* Messico *m*
mezzanine (floor) *n* mezzanino *m*
MF *abbr* (= **medium frequency**) MF (media frequenza *f*)
mg *abbr* (= **milligram(s)**, **milligramme(s)**) mg (milligrammo *m*)
MHz *abbr* (= **megahertz**) MHz (megahertz *m*)
MI5 *abbr* (= **Military Intelligence, section 5**) *Br servizio segreto militare, sezione 5*
MI6 *abbr* (= **Military Intelligence, section 6**) *Br servizio segreto militare, sezione 6*
miaow I *n* miao *m* **II** *v/i* miagolare
mice *pl* → ***mouse***
mickey *n*: ***take the ~*** (***out of s.o.***) *infml* prendere in giro (qn)
mickey mouse *adj sl course*, *qualification* del piffero *infml*
micro- *pref* micro-
microbe *n* microbo *m*
microbiology *n* microbiologia *f* **microchip** *n* microchip *m inv* **microclimate** *n* microclima *m* **microcosm** *n* microcosmo *m* **microelectronics** *nsg* microelettronica *f* **microfiche** *n* microfiche *f* **microfilm** *n* microfilm *m inv* **microlight** *n* ultraleggero *m* **microorganism** *n* microrganismo *m* **microphone** *n* microfono *m* **microprocessor** *n* microprocessore *m* **microscope** *n* microscopio *m* **microscopic** *adj* microscopico **microsurgery** *n* microchirurgia *f* **microwave** *n oven* forno *m* a microonde
mid *adj*: ***in ~ June*** a metà giugno; ***in the ~ 1950s*** a metà degli anni Cinquanta; ***be in one's ~ forties*** essere sui quarantacinque anni; ***in ~ morning/afternoon*** a metà mattina/pomeriggio; ***a ~-morning snack*** uno spuntino di metà mattina
midair *n*: ***in ~*** a mezz'aria
midday *n* mezzogiorno *m*
middle I *adj* di mezzo **II** *n* mezzo *m*; ***in the ~ of*** *of floor*, *room* nel centro di, in mezzo a; *of period of time* a metà di; ***be in the ~ of doing sth*** stare facendo qc
middle age *n* mezza età *f* **middle-aged** *adj* di mezz'età **Middle Ages** *npl* Medioevo *m* **Middle America** *n ceto medio americano di tendenze conservatrici* **middle class** *adj* borghese; ***the ~(es)*** *npl* la borghesia *f* **Middle East** *n* Medio Oriente *m* **Middle England** *n fig* (*middle classes*) *ceto medio inglese di tendenze conservatrici* **middle finger** *n* dito *m* medio **middle-income** *adj family* di reddito medio **middleman** *n* intermediario *m* **middle management** *n* quadri *mpl* intermedi **middle name** *n* secondo nome *m*; *fig* ***modesty is my ~*** modestia è il mio secondo nome
middle-of-the-road *adj* moderato; (*conventional*) banale
middle school *n Br* scuola *f* media **middleweight** *n boxer* peso *m* medio
middling *adj* medio; ***how are you? — ~*** come stai? così così
midfield *n* SPORTS centrocampo *m*; ***~ player/position*** giocatore *m*/posizione *f* di centrocampo
midfielder *n* SPORTS centrocampista *m*
midge *n* moscerino *m*
midget I *n* nanerottolo *m*, -a *f* **II** *adj* di dimensioni ridotte
Midlands *npl regione nell'Inghilterra centrale*
midnight I *n* mezzanotte *f*; ***at ~*** a mezzanotte **II** *adj* di mezzanotte; ***~ mass*** messa *f* di mezzanotte; ***the ~ hour*** la mezzanotte **midpoint** *n* metà *f* **midriff** *n* parte *f* bassa del torace
midst *n* mezzo *m*; ***in the ~ of*** in mezzo a; ***in our ~*** in mezzo a noi
midstream *n*: ***in ~*** a metà (strada, discorso ecc.) **midsummer** *n* piena estate *f* **midterm** *adj*: ***~ elections*** POL elezioni *fpl* di medio termine
midway *adv* a metà strada; ***Siena***

is ~ between Arezzo and the coast Siena è a metà strada tra Arezzo e la costa; ***~ through*** a metà di **midweek** *adj/adv* a metà settimana; ***he booked a ~ flight*** ha prenotato un volo infrasettimanale **Midwest** *n regione medio-occidentale degli USA* **midwife** *n* ostetrica *f* **midwinter** *n* pieno inverno *m*

miff *v/t infml* ***be ~ed about sth*** essere seccato per qc

might[1] *v/mod*: ***I ~ be late*** potrei far tardi; ***it ~ rain*** magari piove; ***it ~ never happen*** potrebbe non succedere mai; ***I ~ have lost it*** *perhaps I did* forse l'ho perso; *it would have been possible* avrei potuto perderlo; ***he ~ have left*** forse se n'è andato; ***you ~ as well spend the night here*** tanto vale che passi la notte qui; ***you ~ have told me!*** potevi dirmelo!

might[2] *n* (*power*) forze *fpl*; ***with all one's ~*** con le proprie forze

mighty I *adj* potente **II** *adv infml* (*extremely*) molto

migraine *n* emicrania *f*

migrant worker *n* emigrante *m/f*

migrate *v/i* emigrare; *of birds* migrare

migration *n* emigrazione *f*; *of birds* migrazione *f*

mike *n infml* microfono *m*

Milan *n* Milano *f*

mild I *adj* (+*er*) *weather, climate* mite; *cheese, person, voice* dolce; *curry* poco piccante; *punishment, symptoms, sedative* leggero **II** *n Br* birra *f* scura leggera

mildew *n* muffa *f*

mildly *adv* gentilmente; (*slightly*) moderatamente; ***to put it ~*** a dir poco

mildness *n of weather* mitezza *f*; *of person, voice* dolcezza *f*

mile *n* miglio *m*; ***a fifty-~ journey*** un tragitto di cinquanta miglia; ***~s*** (***and ~s***) *infml* lontanissimo; ***they live ~s away*** vivono molto lontano; ***sorry, I was ~s away*** *infml* scusa, avevo la testa altrove; ***it stands out a ~*** si vede lontano un miglio; ***~s better/easier*** *infml* molto meglio/più facile

mileage *n* chilometraggio *m*; *fig* ***he gets a lot of ~ out of that story*** sfrutta molto quella storia

mileometer *n* contamiglia *m inv*

milestone *n a. fig* pietra *f* miliare

militant I *adj* militante **II** *n* militante *m/f*

military I *adj* militare; ***~ personnel*** personale *m* militare **II** *n*: ***the ~*** l'esercito *m*, le forze *fpl* armate; ***it's run by the ~*** è in mano ai militari

military academy *n* accademia *f* militare **military police** *n* polizia *f* militare **military service** *n* servizio *m* militare; ***he's doing his ~*** sta facendo il servizio militare

militia *n* milizia *f*

milk I *n* latte *m* **II** *v/t* mungere; ***he ~ed the system from day one*** ha sfruttato il sistema fin dal primo giorno

milk bottle *n* bottiglia *f* del latte **milk chocolate** *n* cioccolato *m* al latte **milk float** *n* furgone *m* del lattaio **milk jug** *n* bricco *m* del latte **milkman** *n* lattaio *m* **milk of magnesia** *n* latte *m* di magnesia **milkshake** *n* frappé *m inv*

milky *adj* (+*er*) con tanto latte

Milky Way *n* Via *f* Lattea

mill *n for grain* mulino *m*; *for textiles* fabbrica *f*; ***go through the ~*** passarsela male; ***in training you're really put through the ~*** *infml* l'addestramento ti mette davvero a dura prova

◆**mill about, mill around** *v/i* brulicare

millennium *n* millennio *m*

miller *n* mugnaio *m*, -a *f*

millet *n* BOT miglio *m*

milli- *pref* milli-; ***millisecond*** millisecondo *m* **milligram** *n* milligrammo *m* **millimetre**, *US* **millimeter** *n* millimetro *m*

million *n* milione *m*; ***4 ~ people*** 4 milioni di persone; ***for ~s and ~s of years*** per milioni e milioni di anni; ***she's one in a ~*** *infml* è più unica che rara

millionaire *n* miliardario *m*, -a *f*

millionairess *n* miliardaria *f*

millionth I *adj* milionesimo **II** *n* milionesimo *m*

millipede *n* millepiedi *m*

millpond *n* gora *f*

millstone *n* macina *f*; ***she's a ~ around his neck*** lei è per lui una palla al piede

mime I *n* mimica *f*; THEAT pantomima *f* **II** *v/i* fare il mimo **III** *v/t* mimare

mime artist *n* mimo *m*, -a *f*
mimic I *n* imitatore *m*, -trice *f*; ***he's a very good ~*** è un ottimo imitatore **II** *v/t* ⟨*pret & past part* ***-ked***⟩ imitare
mince I *n esp Br* (*minced meat*) macinato *m* **II** *v/t esp Br* tritare; ***he doesn't ~ his words*** non ha peli sulla lingua **III** *v/i Br* (*walk*) camminare a passettini
mincemeat *n frutta secca tritata*
mince pie *n pasticcino ripieno di frutta secca tritata*
mincer *n* tritatutto *m inv*
mind I *n* mente *f*, cervello *m*; ***it's all in your ~*** è solo la tua immaginazione; ***be out of one's ~*** essere matto; ***keep sth in ~*** tenere presente qc; ***I've a good ~ to ...*** ho proprio voglia di ...; ***change one's ~*** cambiare idea; ***it didn't enter my ~*** non mi è passato per la testa; ***give s.o. a piece of one's ~*** cantarne quattro a qn; ***make up one's ~*** decidersi; ***have sth on one's ~*** essere preoccupato per qc; ***keep one's ~ on sth*** concentrarsi su qc; ***she couldn't get the song out of her ~*** non riusciva a togliersi la canzone dalla testa; ***the idea never entered my ~*** l'idea non mi ha mai sfiorato; ***nothing was further from my ~*** non ci pensavo neanche; ***in my ~'s eye*** con l'occhio della mente; ***bring sth to ~*** fare venire in mente qc; ***I'm bored out of my ~*** sono annoiato a morte; ***it's a case of ~ over matter*** è questione di controllare razionalmente i propri impulsi **II** *v/t* **1.** (*look after*) tenere d'occhio; *children* badare a; (*heed*) fare attenzione a **2.** (*object to*, *care*) ***I don't ~ tea if that's all you've got*** il tè va bene se non hai altro; ***I don't ~ what we do*** non importa cosa facciamo; ***do you ~ if I smoke?, do you ~ my smoking?*** le dispiace se fumo?; ***would you ~ opening the window?*** le dispiace aprire la finestra?; ***do you ~ coming with me?*** ti dispiace venire con me?; ***I wouldn't ~ a cup of tea*** non mi dispiacerebbe una tazza di tè; ***never ~ that now*** non preoccupartene adesso **3.** (*pay attention*) ***~ the step!*** attento al gradino!; ***~ your own business!*** fatti gli affari tuoi! **III** *v/i* **1.** ***~!*** (*be careful*) attenzione! **2.** ***I don't ~*** è uguale *or* indifferente; ***never ~!*** non farci caso!; ***oh, never ~, I'll do it myself*** oh, non preoccuparti, lo farò da solo **3.** ***~ you get that done*** bada di farlo; ***~ you*** intendiamoci; ***~ you, he did try*** intendiamoci, ci ha provato; ***he's quite good, ~ you*** è piuttosto bravo, intendiamoci; ***I'm not going to finish school, never ~ go to university*** non ho intenzione di finire la scuola, figuriamoci andare all'università
◆**mind out** *v/i Br* fare attenzione (***for*** a)
mind-blowing *adj infml* allucinante
mind-boggling *adj* incredibile
-minded *adj suf*: ***she's very politically-minded*** è molto portata per la politica
minder *n of child* bambinaia *f*; (*bodyguard*) gorilla *m inv*
mindful *adj* consapevole
mindless *adj violence* insensato
mindset *n* atteggiamento *m* mentale
mine[1] *pron* il mio *m*, la mia *f*, i miei *mpl*, le mie *fpl*; ***a cousin of ~*** un mio cugino; ***this car is ~*** questa macchina è mia; ***his friends and ~*** i suoi amici e i miei; ***a favourite*** *Br or* ***favorite*** *US* ***expression of ~*** una delle mie espressioni preferite
mine[2] **I** *n for coal etc* miniera *f*; ***work down the ~s*** lavorare in miniera; *fig* ***he is a ~ of information*** è una miniera di informazioni **II** *v/i* ***~ for*** estrarre **III** *v/t coal* estrarre
mine[3] **I** *n explosive* mina *f* **II** *v/t* minare
minefield *n a. fig* campo *m* minato
miner *n* minatore *m*
mineral I *n* minerale *m* **II** *adj* minerali; ***~ deposits*** depositi *mpl* minerali
mineral water *n* acqua *f* minerale
minesweeper *n* NAUT dragamine *m inv*
mingle *v/i of sounds*, *smells* mischiarsi; *at party* mescolarsi
mini- *pref* mini-
miniature I *n* ART miniatura *f*; (*bottle*) miniatura *f*; ***in ~*** in miniatura **II** *adj* in miniatura
miniature golf *n* minigolf *m*
minibar *n* minibar *m inv* **mini-break** *n tennis* mini break *m inv* **minibus** *n* minibus *m inv* **minicab** *n* radiotaxi

m inv **minicam** *n* minitelecamera *f*
Mini Disc® *n* MUS Minidisc® *m*; **~ *player*** lettore di Minidisc
minim *n Br* MUS minima *f*
minimal *adj* minimo; ***at ~ cost*** a costo minimo; ***with ~ effort*** con sforzo minimo
minimalism *n* minimalismo *m*
minimize *v/t* minimizzare
minimum I *adj* minimo; **~ *age*** età *f* minima; **~ *temperature*** temperatura *f* minima **II** *n* minimo *m*; ***what is the ~ you will accept?*** qual è il minimo che sei disposto ad accettare?; ***a ~ of 2 hours / 10 people*** un minimo di 2 ore / 10 persone; ***keep / reduce sth to a ~*** mantenere / ridurre qc al minimo
minimum wage *n* salario *m* minimo garantito
mining *n* industria *f* mineraria
mining town *n* città *f* mineraria
minion *n fig* tirapiedi *m/f*
miniseries *n* TV miniserie *f inv* **miniskirt** *n* minigonna *f*
minister I *n* POL ministro *m*; REL pastore *m* **II** *v/i*: **~ *to s.o.*** assistere qn; **~ *to s.o.'s needs*** provvedere ai bisogni di qn
ministerial *adj* ministeriale; **~ *post*** carica *f* di ministro; ***his ~ duties*** i suoi doveri ministeriali
ministry *n* POL ministero *m*; **~ *of education*** ministero *m* dell'istruzione; ***go into the ~*** REL diventare sacerdote
minivan *n US* furgoncino *m*
mink I *adj fur* di visone **II** *n coat* visone *m*
minor I *adj* piccolo; ***in D ~*** MUS in Re minore **II** *n* JUR minorenne *m/f*
minority I *n* minoranza *f*; ***be in the ~*** essere in minoranza **II** *adj* di minoranza; **~ *group*** gruppo *m* di minoranza; (***ethnic***) **~ *students*** studenti *mpl* di minoranze etniche
minority government *n* governo *m* di minoranza
minster *n* cattedrale *f*
minstrel *n* menestrello *m*
mint I *n herb* menta *f*; *chocolate* cioccolato *m* alla menta; *sweet* mentina *f*; ***the Royal ~*** *for coins* la Zecca; ***make a ~*** *infml* fare una fortuna **II** *adj*: ***in ~ condition*** come nuovo **III** *v/t coins* coniare
minus I *n* (*minus sign*) meno *m* **II** *prep* meno; **~ *10 degrees*** 10 gradi sotto zero; ***£ 100 ~ taxes*** 100 sterline meno le imposte **III** *adj Br* in meno; **~ *point*** aspetto *m* negativo; ***A ~*** EDU (*mark*) *voto tra buono e ottimo*
minuscule *adj* minuscolo
minus sign *n* segno *m* meno
minute[1] *n of time* minuto *m*; ***in a ~*** (*soon*) in un attimo; ***just a ~*** un attimo; ***it's 23 ~s past 3*** sono le 3 e 23 minuti; ***tell me the ~ he comes*** avvisami nel momento in cui arriva; ***have you got a ~?*** hai un minuto?; ***I don't believe for a*** *or* ***one ~ that …*** non credo neanche per un minuto che…; ***at the last ~*** all'ultimo minuto
minute[2] *adj* (*tiny*) piccolissimo; (*detailed*) minuzioso; ***in ~ detail*** minuziosamente
minute hand *n* lancetta *f* dei minuti
minutely *adv* (*in detail*) minuziosamente; (*very slightly*) appena
minutes *npl of meeting* verbale *m*
minutiae *npl* minuzie *fpl*
minx *n* sfacciata *f*
miracle *n* miracolo *m*; ***work*** *or* ***perform ~s*** *liter* fare miracoli; ***I can't work ~s*** non posso fare miracoli; *fig* ***by some ~*** per qualche miracolo; ***it'll take a ~ for us*** *or* ***we'll need a ~ to be finished on time*** ci vorrà un miracolo per finire in tempo
miracle drug *n* medicina *f* miracolosa
miracle play *n* THEAT miracolo *m*, sacra rappresentazione *f*
miraculous *adj* miracoloso; ***that is nothing / little short of ~*** è davvero miracoloso
miraculously *adv* miracolosamente; **~ *the baby was unhurt*** il bambino era miracolosamente illeso
mirage *n* miraggio *m*
mire *n liter* pantano *m*
mirror I *n* specchio *m*; AUTO specchietto *m* **II** *v/t* riflettere; ***be ~ed in sth*** *in water etc* specchiarsi in qc; *fig* rispecchiarsi in qc
mirth *n* ilarità *f inv*
mis- *pref* (*badly*) mis-, mal-; (*opposite*) dis-
misadventure *n* disavventura *f*; ***death by ~*** JUR morte *f* accidentale
misanthropist *n* misantropo *m*
misapply *v/t* ⟨*pret & past part* **-ied**⟩

applicare male
misapprehension *n*: ***be under a ~*** sbagliarsi
misbehave *v/i* comportarsi male
misbehaviour, *US* **misbehavior** *n* comportamento *m* scorretto
miscalculate *v/t* & *v/i* calcolare male
miscalculation *n* errore *m* di calcolo
miscarriage *n* MED aborto *m* spontaneo; ***~ of justice*** errore *m* giudiziario
miscarry *v/i* ⟨*pret & past part* ***-ied***⟩ *of plan* fallire
miscellaneous *adj* eterogeneo; ***~ expenses / income*** spese / entrate *fpl* varie
mischief *n* (*naughtiness*) birichinate *fpl*; JUR danno *m*; ***he's always getting into ~*** combina sempre dei guai; ***keep out of ~*** tenersi lontano dai guai; ***make ~*** seminare zizzania; ***do s.o. / o.s. a ~*** *infml* fare del male a qn / farsi del male
mischievous *adj* (*naughty*) birichino; (*malicious*) perfido
misconceived *adj* sbagliato
misconception *n* idea *f* sbagliata
misconduct *n* reato *m* professionale
misconstrue *v/t* interpretare male; ***you have ~d my meaning*** hai interpretato male ciò che intendevo
miscount *v/t* & *v/i* contare male
misdemeanour, *US* **misdemeanor** *n* infrazione *f*
misdiagnose *v/t* MED *illness* diagnosticare erroneamente
misdirect *v/t* *letter* sbagliare l'indirizzo di; *person* dare indicazioni sbagliate a
miser *n* avaro *m*, -a *f*
miserable *adj* (*unhappy*) infelice; ***make life ~ for s.o.*** *or* ***to make s.o.'s life ~*** rendere la vita intollerabile a qn; *weather, performance* deprimente; ***be a ~ failure*** essere un penoso fallimento
miserly *adj person* avaro; *amount* misero; ***a ~ £8*** 8 misere sterline; ***be ~ with sth*** essere avaro di qc
misery *n* (*unhappiness*) tristezza *f*; (*wretchedness*) miseria *f*; ***make s.o.'s life a ~*** rendere la vita impossibile a qn; ***put an animal out of its ~*** dare il colpo di grazia a un animale; *fig* ***put s.o. out of his ~*** porre fine alle sofferenze di qn
misfire *v/i* *of joke, scheme* far cilecca; *of engine* perdere colpi
misfit *n in society* disadattato *m*, -a *f*
misfortune *n* sfortuna *f*; ***it was my ~*** *or* ***I had the ~ to ...*** ho avuto la sfortuna di ...
misgivings *npl* dubbi *mpl*; ***I had ~ about the scheme*** avevo dubbi in merito al progetto
misguided *adj attempts, theory* sbagliato; ***he was ~ in maintaining that ...*** sbagliava a sostenere che ...
mishandle *v/t situation* gestire male
mishap *n* incidente *m*; ***he's had a slight ~*** ha avuto un piccolo incidente
mishear *v/t* & *v/i* ⟨*pret & past part* ***misheard***⟩ fraintendere
mishmash *n* miscuglio *m*
misinform *v/t* informare male; ***you've been ~ed*** sei stato informato male
misinformation *n* informazione *f* sbagliata
misinterpret *v/t* interpretare male; ***he ~ed her silence as agreement*** ha male interpretato il suo silenzio come un consenso
misinterpretation *n* interpretazione *f* errata
misjudge *v/t person, situation* giudicare male
mislay *v/t* ⟨*pret & past part* ***-laid***⟩ smarrire
mislead *v/t* ⟨*pret & past part* ***-led***⟩ trarre in inganno; ***you have been misled*** sei stato tratto in inganno
misleading *adj* fuorviante
misled *pret & past part* → ***mislead***
mismanage *v/t* gestire male
mismanagement *n* cattiva gestione *f*
mismatch **I** *v/t* assortire male **II** *n* discordanza *f*
misname *v/t* chiamare col nome sbagliato
misnomer *n* denominazione *f* impropria
misogynist *n* misogino *m*
misplace *v/t* non riuscire a trovare
misplaced *adj loyalty, enthusiasm* malriposto
misprint *n* refuso *m*
mispronounce *v/t* pronunciare male
mispronunciation *n* errore *m* di pronuncia
misquote *v/t* citare erroneamente
misread *v/t* ⟨*pret & past part* ***-read***⟩

word, *figures* leggere male; *situation* interpretare male
misrepresent *v/t facts*, *truth* travisare; ***I've been ~ed*** hanno travisato quello che ho detto
miss[1] *n*: ***Miss Smith*** signorina Smith; ***~!*** signorina!
miss[2] **I** *v/t* **1.** (*not hit*) mancare; *bus*, *train*, *plane* perdere; ***you've just ~ed him*** *he's just gone* è appena uscito; ***we must have ~ed the turnoff*** ci dev'essere sfuggito lo svincolo; ***he doesn't ~ much*** *infml* non gli sfugge niente **2.** *emotionally* sentire la mancanza di; ***I ~ you*** mi manchi **3.** (*not be present at*) mancare a; ***~ breakfast*** saltare la colazione; ***he ~ed school for a week*** ha saltato la scuola per una settimana **II** *v/i* fallire **III** *n*: ***give the meeting / party a ~*** non andare alla riunione / festa; ***we had a near ~ with that car*** abbiamo mancato di poco quella macchina
◆ **miss out I** *v/t sep* omettere; *last line etc* tralasciare **II** *v/i infml* perdersi il divertimento; ***miss out on sth*** lasciarsi sfuggire qc
missal *n* messale *m*
misshapen *adj* deforme
missile *n* (*rocket*) missile *m*
missing *adj* scomparso; ***be ~*** *of person*, *plane* essere disperso; ***there's a piece ~*** manca un pezzo; ***go ~*** (*person*) scomparire; (*object*) andare perduto; ***~ in action*** disperso in azione; ***~ link*** anello *m* mancante; ***~ person*** persona *f* scomparsa
mission *n* (*task*, *people*) missione *f*; ***~ control*** sala *f* di controllo di missione spaziale
missionary *n* REL missionario *m*, -a *f*
missionary position *n* posizione *f* del missionario
misspell *v/t* scrivere male
misspelling *n* errore *m* di ortografia
mist *n* foschia *f*
◆ **mist over** *v/i of eyes* velarsi di lacrime
◆ **mist up** *v/i of mirror*, *window* appannarsi
mistake I *n* errore *m*, sbaglio *m*; ***make a ~*** fare un errore, sbagliarsi; ***by ~*** per errore **II** *v/t* ⟨*pret* ***mistook***, *past part* ***mistaken***⟩ sbagliare; ***~ sth for sth*** scambiare qc per qc
mistaken I *adj* sbagliato; ***be ~*** sbagliarsi **II** *past part* → ***mistake***
mister → ***Mr***
mistime *v/t* scegliere un momento poco opportuno per
mistletoe *n* vischio *m*
mistreat *v/t* maltrattare
mistreatment *n* maltrattamento *m*
mistress *n lover* amante *f*; *of servant*, *of dog* padrona *f*
mistrust I *n* diffidenza *f* **II** *v/t* diffidare di
mistrustful *adj* diffidente; ***be ~ of s.o. / sth*** diffidare di qn / qc
misty *adj* (+*er*) *weather* nebbioso; *eyes* velato
misunderstand *v/t* ⟨*pret & past part* ***-stood***⟩ fraintendere; ***don't ~ me ...*** non fraintendermi...
misunderstanding *n mistake* malinteso *m*, equivoco *m*; ***there must be some ~*** deve esserci un malinteso; *argument* dissapore *m*
misuse I *n* uso *m* improprio; ***~ of power / authority*** abuso *m* di potere / autorità **II** *v/t* usare impropriamente
mite[1] *n* ZOOL acaro *m*
mite[2] *adv infml*: ***a ~ surprised*** un tantino sorpreso
mitigate *v/t* mitigare; ***mitigating circumstances*** circostanze *fpl* attenuanti
mitt *n baseball* guanto *m*; → ***mitten***
mitten *n* muffola *f*
mix I *n* (*mixture*) mescolanza *f*; ***a real ~ of people*** un'autentica mescolanza di persone; ***a broad racial ~*** un vasto miscuglio di razze; *in cooking* miscuglio *m*; *in cooking*: *ready to use* preparato *m* **II** *v/t* mescolare; ***you shouldn't ~ your drinks*** non dovresti mescolare le bevande; ***~ sth into sth*** incorporare qc a qc; ***I never ~ business with*** *or* ***and pleasure*** non mescolo mai affari e piacere **III** *v/i socially* socializzare; ***he finds it hard to ~*** trova difficoltà a socializzare
◆ **mix up** *v/t sep* confondere; ***mix sth up with sth*** scambiare qc per qc; ***be mixed up*** *emotionally* avere disturbi emotivi; *of figures*, *papers* essere in disordine; ***be mixed up in*** essere coinvolto in; ***get mixed up with*** avere a che fare con; ***he's got himself mixed up with that gang*** ha avuto a che fare

con quella banda
◆**mix with** *v/t* (*associate with*) frequentare
mixed *adj* misto; *reactions*, *reviews* contrastante; ~ ***nuts/biscuits*** noccioline *fpl* miste/biscotti *mpl* misti; ***of ~ parentage*** di genitori misti; ***I've got ~ feelings*** sono combattuto; ***a ~ bag*** un miscuglio; ***be a ~ blessing*** avere i suoi vantaggi e i suoi svantaggi
mixed ability *adj*: ~ ***class*** EDU classe *f* eterogenea **mixed doubles** *npl* SPORTS doppio *m* misto **mixed grill** *n* grigliata *f* mista **mixed marriage** *n* matrimonio *m* misto **mixed-race** *adj* meticcio **mixed up, mixed-up** *adj* coinvolto; (*muddled*) *person*, *ideas* confuso; ***I'm all ~*** sono confuso; ***he got all ~*** è rimasto turbato
mixer *n for food* mixer *m inv*; (*drink*) *bibita da mischiare a un superalcolico*; ***she's a good ~*** è molto socievole
mixture *n* miscuglio *m*; COOK miscela *f*; (*cake mixture*) impasto *m*; ***fold the eggs into the cheese ~*** unire le uova alla miscela di formaggio; *medicine* sciroppo *m*
mix-up *n* confusione *f*
ml *abbr* **1.** (= **millilitre**) ml (millilitro *m*) **2.** (= **mile**) mi (miglio *m*)
MLD *abbr* (= **Minimum lethal dose**) dose *f* minima letale
mm *abbr* (= **millimetre(s)**) mm (millimetro *m*)
Mme *abbr* (= **Madame**) sig.ra (signora *f*)
MMR *abbr* (= **Measles, Mumps and Rubella**) *vaccinazione contro morbillo, orecchioni e rosolia*
mo *n abbr* (= **moment**) *infml*: ***wait a ~!*** (aspetta) un attimo!
moan I *n of pain* lamento *m*, gemito *m*; (*complaint*) lamentela *f*; ***have a ~ about sth*** avere una lamentela in merito a qc **II** *v/i in pain* lamentarsi, gemere; (*complain*) lamentarsi
moat *n* fossato *m*
mob I *n* folla *f* **II** *v/t* ⟨*pret & past part* ***-bed***⟩ prendere d'assalto
mobile I *adj that can be moved* mobile; ***she's less ~ now*** non si può muovere tanto, ora **II** *n for decoration* mobile *m inv*; *phone* telefonino *m*
mobile home *n* casamobile *f* **mobile phone** *n* telefono *m* cellulare
mobility *n* mobilità *f inv*
mobilize I *v/t* mobilitare **II** *v/i* mobilitarsi
mobster *n* gangster *m inv*
moccasin *n* mocassino *m*
mocha *n* moka *m inv*
mock I *adj* finto; *exam*, *election* simulato; ~ ***leather*** similpelle *f*; ***a ~-Tudor house*** una casa in stile Tudor **II** *v/t* deridere **III** *v/i*: ***don't ~*** non prendere in giro **IV** *n* **mocks** *Br* EDU *infml* simulazione *f* d'esame
mockery *n* (*derision*) scherno *m*; (*travesty*) farsa *f*; ***make a ~ of sth*** mettere in ridicolo qc
mock-up *n* (*model*) modello *m*
MOD *abbr* (= **Ministry of Defence**) *Br* ministero *m* della difesa
modal *n* GRAM verbo *m* modale
modal verb *n* GRAM verbo *m* modale
mod cons *npl abbr* (= **modern conveniences**) *Br infml*: ***with all ~*** con tutti i comfort
mode *n form* mezzo *m*; COMPUT modalità *f inv*
model I *n* (*miniature*) modellino *m*; (*pattern*) modello *m*; (*fashion model*) indossatrice *f*; ***male ~*** indossatore *m*; ***hold s.o. up as a ~*** prendere qn a modello **II** *adj employee*, *husband* modello; ~ ***pupil*** alunno *m* modello; *boat*, *plane* in miniatura; ~ ***railway*** *Br or* ***railroad*** *US* modellino *m* ferroviario **III** *v/t* indossare; ***be ~led*** *Br or* ***~ed*** *US* ***on sth*** essere modellato su qc; ~ ***o.s. on s.o.*** prendere qn a modello **IV** *v/i for designer* fare l'indossatore, l'indossatrice; *for artist*, *photographer* posare
modem *n* modem *m inv*
moderate I *adj* moderato; ***a ~ amount*** una quantità moderata **II** *n* POL moderato *m*, -a *f* **III** *v/t* moderare **IV** *v/i* calmarsi
moderately *adv* abbastanza; ***a ~ priced suit*** un abito dal prezzo abbordabile
moderation *n* (*restraint*) moderazione *f*; ***in ~*** con moderazione
moderator *n* moderatore *m*
modern *adj* moderno
modern-day *adj* dei giorni nostri; ~ ***America*** l'America dei giorni nostri
modernisation, modernization *n*

modernizzazione *f*
modernise, modernize I *v/t* modernizzare **II** *v/i of business, country* modernizzarsi
modernism *n* modernismo *m*
modernist I *adj* modernista **II** *n* modernista *m/f*
modern languages *npl* lingue *fpl* moderne
modest *adj* modesto; ***be ~ about one's successes*** non vantarsi dei propri successi; ***on a ~ scale*** su modesta scala
modesty *n* modestia *f*
modicum *n*: ***a ~ (of)*** un po' di
modification *n* modifica *f*; ***make ~s to sth*** apportare modifiche a qc
modify *v/t* ⟨*pret & past part* **-ied**⟩ modificare
modular *adj furniture* modulare
module *n* modulo *m*; (*space module*) modulo *m* spaziale
mohair *n* mohair *m inv*
mohican *n hair style* cresta *f* (punk)
moist *adj* (+*er*) umido
moisten *v/t* inumidire
moisture *n* umidità *f inv*
moisturizer *n for skin* idratante *m*
molar *n* molare *m*
molasses *n* melassa *f*
mold *etc US* → ***mould*** *etc*
mole *n on skin* neo *m*; ZOOL, *spy* talpa *f*
molecular *adj* molecolare
molecule *n* molecola *f*
molehill *n cumulo di terra sopra la tana di una talpa*; *fig* ***make mountains out of ~s*** fare di una mosca un elefante
molest *v/t child, woman* molestare
moll *n* amante *f* di un gangster
mollify *v/t* ⟨*pret & past part* **-ied**⟩ rabbonire
mollusc *n* mollusco *m*
mollycoddle *v/t infml* coccolare
Molotov cocktail *n* bomba *f* molotov
molt *n, v/t & v/i US* → ***moult***
molten *adj* fuso
mom *n US infml* → ***mum²***
moment *n* attimo *m*, istante *m*; ***at the ~*** al momento; ***for the ~*** per il momento; ***just a ~!*** *or* ***wait a ~!*** (aspetta) un attimo!; ***I shan't be a ~*** ci metterò un attimo; ***I have just this ~ heard about it*** l'ho sentito proprio in questo momento; ***we haven't a ~ to lose*** non ho un momento da perdere; ***not a ~'s peace*** non un attimo di pace; ***one ~ she was laughing, the next she was crying*** un attimo rideva, un attimo dopo stava piangendo; ***the ~ I saw him I knew ...*** nel momento in cui l'ho visto ho saputo...; ***tell me the ~ he comes*** avvisami nel momento in cui arriva; ***the ~ of truth*** il momento della verità; ***the film has its ~s*** il film ha momenti buoni
momentarily *adv* (*for a moment*) per un momento; (*US*: *in a moment*) da un momento all'altro
momentary *adj* momentaneo; ***there was a ~ silence*** ci fu un momentaneo silenzio
momentous *adj* importante
momentum *n* impeto *m*; ***gather*** *or* ***gain ~*** *liter* acquistare velocità; *fig* prendere slancio; ***lose ~*** rallentare
Mon *abbr* (= **Monday**) lunedì *m inv*
monarch *n* monarca *m*
monarchist *n* monarchico *m*, -a *f*
monarchy *n* monarchia *f*
monastery *n* monastero *m*
monastic *adj* monastico; ***~ order*** ordine *m* monastico
Monday *n* lunedì *m inv*
monetarism *n* monetarismo *m*
monetary *adj* monetario; ***~ policy*** politica *f* monetaria; ***~ union*** unione *f* monetaria
money *n* denaro *m*, soldi *mpl*; ***make ~*** fare i soldi; ***be in the ~*** *infml* essere pieno di soldi; ***what's the ~ like in this job?*** quanto si guadagna con questo lavoro?; ***earn good ~*** guadagnare bene; ***get one's ~'s worth*** spendere bene il proprio denaro; ***put one's ~ where one's mouth is*** *infml* essere coerente con ciò che si dice
money belt *n* marsupio *m*
moneybox *n* salvadanaio *m*
money laundering *n* riciclaggio *m* di denaro
moneylender *n* prestasoldi *m/f*
money market *n* mercato *m* monetario **money order** *n* vaglia *m* **money-spinner** *n infml* miniera *f* d'oro **money supply** *n* massa *f* monetaria
-monger *n suf* -vendolo *m*, -a *f*; ***fishmonger*** pescivendolo *m*, -a *f*

mongrel *n* cane *m* bastardo
monitor **I** *n* COMPUT monitor *m inv* **II** *v/t* osservare
monk *n* frate *m*, monaco *m*
monkey *n* scimmia *f*; *infml* (*child*) diavoletto *m*; ***I don't give a ~'s*** *Br infml* non me ne frega niente
◆**monkey about with** *v/t infml* armeggiare con
monkey business *n infml*: ***no ~!*** niente intrighi! **monkey wrench** *n* chiave *f* a rullino
mono[1] *n infml US* MED mononucleosi *f*; *infml* (*recording*) registrazione *f* mono
mono[2] *adj* mono
monochrome *adj* monocromatico
monocle *n* monocolo *m*
monogamous *adj* monogamo
monogamy *n* monogamia *f*
monogram *n* monogramma *m*
monogrammed *adj* con il monogramma
monolingual *adj* monolingue
monolith *n fig* struttura *f* monolitica
monolithic *adj fig* monolitico
monologue, *US* **monolog** *n* monologo *m*
monopolise, monopolize *v/t a. fig* monopolizzare
monopoly *n* monopolio *m*
monorail *n* monorotaia *f*
monosodium glutamate *n* glutammato *m* di sodio
monotone *n* tono *m* monotono
monotonous *adj* monotono
monotony *n* monotonia *f*
monoxide *n* monossido *m*
monsoon *n* monsone *m*
monster **I** *n* mostro *m* **II** *adj infml* (*enormous*) colossale
monstrosity *n* obbrobrio *m*
monstrous *adj* mostruoso
montage *n* montaggio *m*
month *n* mese *m*; ***it went on for ~s*** è andata avanti per mesi; ***one ~'s salary*** stipendio *m* di un mese; ***by the ~*** mensilmente
monthly **I** *adj* mensile; ***pay on a ~ basis*** pagare mensilmente; ***twice ~*** due volte al mese **II** *adv* mensilmente **III** *n magazine* mensile *m*
monument *n* monumento *m*
monumental *adj fig* monumentale
moo *v/i* muggire
mooch *v/i infml* bighellonare; ***I spent all day just ~ing about*** *Br or* ***around the house*** ho trascorso tutto il giorno bighellonando per casa
mood[1] *n* (*frame of mind*) umore *m*; (*bad mood*) malumore *m*; *of meeting, country* clima *m*; ***be in a good / bad ~*** essere di cattivo / buon umore; ***he's in a ~*** gli girano; ***be in the ~ for*** aver voglia di; ***I'm in no ~ for laughing*** non ho nessuna voglia di ridere
mood[2] *n* GRAM modo *m*; ***indicative ~*** modo *m* indicativo
moodily *adv* con aria cupa
moody *adj* (+*er*) lunatico; (*bad-tempered*) di cattivo umore
moon *n* luna *f*; ***be over the ~*** essere al settimo cielo; ***when the ~ is full*** con la luna piena; ***promise s.o. the ~*** promettere la luna a qn
◆**moon about** *v/i infml* ciondolare
moonbeam *n* raggio *m* di luna **moonlight** **I** *n* chiaro *m* di luna **II** *v/i infml* lavorare in nero **moonlit** *adj night* illuminato dalla luna **moonshine** *n* (*moonlight*) chiaro *m* di luna; (*talk*) *infml* sciocchezze *fpl*; (*alcohol*) *infml* distillato *m* clandestino
moor[1] *n* brughiera *f*
moor[2] *v/t boat* ormeggiare
moorings *npl* ormeggio *m*
moose *n* alce *m*
moot *adj*: ***a ~ point*** un punto discutibile
mop **I** *n for floor* mocio® *m*; *for dishes* spazzolino *m* per i piatti; *of hair* massa *f* **II** *v/t* ⟨*pret & past part* **-ped**⟩ *floor* lavare; *eyes*, *face* asciugare
◆**mop up** *v/t sep* raccogliere; ***she mopped up the sauce with a piece of bread*** raccolse la salsa con un pezzo di pane; MIL eliminare
mope *v/i* essere depresso
moped *n* motorino *m*
moral **I** *adj* morale; *person* di saldi principi morali; ***~ values*** valori *mpl* morali; ***give s.o. ~ support*** prestare supporto morale a qn **II** *n of story* morale *f*; ***~s*** principi *mpl* morali
morale *n* morale *m*; ***boost s.o.'s ~*** tirare su di morale qn
moralistic *adj* moralistico
morality *n* moralità *f inv*
morally *adv* dal punto di vista morale
morass *n*: ***a ~ of problems*** un grovi-

glio di problemi
moratorium *n* moratoria *f*
morbid *adj* morboso; ***don't be so ~!*** non essere così morboso!
mordacious *adj* pungente, caustico
mordant *adj* pungente, caustico
more I *adj* più, altro; ***some ~ tea?*** dell'altro tè?; ***a few ~ sandwiches*** qualche altro tramezzino; ***for ~ information*** per maggiori informazioni; ***two ~ miles*** altre due miglia; ***~ and ~ students/time*** sempre più studenti/tempo; ***there's no ~ …*** non c'è più … **II** *adv* più; *with verbs* di più; ***~ important*** più importante; ***~ often*** più spesso; ***~ and ~*** sempre di più; ***~ or less*** più o meno; ***once ~*** ancora una volta; ***~ than 100*** oltre 100; ***~ than happy*** più che contento; ***I don't live there any ~*** non abito più lì; ***it will ~ than meet the demand*** sarà superiore alla domanda **III** *pron*: ***do you want some ~?*** ne vuoi ancora?, ne vuoi dell'altro?; ***a little ~*** un altro po'
moreish *adj infml* invitante
moreover *adv* inoltre
morganatic *adj* morganatico
morgue *n* obitorio *m*
moribund *adj* agonizzante
Mormon I *adj* mormone; ***~ church*** chiesa *f* mormonica **II** *n* mormone *m/f*
morning I *n* mattino *m*, mattina *f*; ***in the ~*** di mattina; (*tomorrow*) domattina; ***early in the ~*** la mattina presto; ***this ~*** stamattina; ***tomorrow ~*** domani mattina; ***good ~*** buongiorno **II** *adj* mattutino; (*regular*) del mattino; ***~ flight*** volo *m* del mattino
morning-after pill *n* pillola *f* del giorno dopo **morning sickness** *n* nausee *fpl* mattutine
moron *n infml* idiota *m/f*
morose *adj* imbronciato
morph *v/i* trasformarsi
morpheme *n* morfema *m*
morphine *n* morfina *f*
morphology *n* morfologia *f*
morse *n* (*a.* **Morse code**) alfabeto *m* Morse
morsel *n* pezzetto *m*
mortal I *adj* mortale; ***deal* (*s.o./sth*) *a ~ blow*** dare un colpo fatale (a qn/qc); ***~ enemy*** nemico *m* mortale **II** *n* mortale *m/f*
mortality *n* mortalità *f inv*; ***~ rate*** tasso *m* di mortalità
mortar[1] *n* MIL mortaio *m*; ***pestle and ~*** pestello e mortaio
mortar[2] *n cement* malta *f*
mortgage I *n* mutuo *m* ipotecario; ***take out a ~*** fare un mutuo **II** *v/t* ipotecare; ***he ~d the house to buy a Ferrari*** ha ipotecato la casa per comprarsi una Ferrari
mortgage rate *n* tasso *m* di interesse ipotecario
mortician *n US* impresario *m*, -a *f* di pompe funebri
mortify *v/t* 〈*pret & past part* **-ied**〉 mortificare; ***he was mortified*** era mortificato
mortuary *n* camera *f* mortuaria
mosaic *n* mosaico *m*
Moscow *n* Mosca *f*
Moslem I *adj* islamico **II** *n* musulmano *m*, -a *f*
mosque *n* moschea *f*
mosquito *n* zanzara *f*
mosquito net *n* zanzariera *f*
moss *n* muschio *m*
mossy *adj* (+*er*) coperto di muschio; ***~ teeth*** denti *mpl* neri
most I *adj* la maggior parte di; ***~ Saturdays*** quasi tutti i sabati; ***for the ~ part*** prevalentemente **II** *adv* (*very*) estremamente; ***the ~ beautiful/interesting*** il più bello/interessante; ***that's the one I like ~*** è quello che mi piace di più; ***~ of all*** soprattutto; ***what ~ displeased him …*** *or* ***what displeased him ~ …*** la cosa che più gli dispiaceva…; ***~ likely*** quasi certamente **III** *n* la maggior parte (***of*** di); ***~ of her novels/friends*** la maggior parte dei suoi romanzi/amici; ***at* (*the*) *~*** al massimo; ***make the ~ of*** approfittare (al massimo) di
mostly *adv* per lo più
MOT *abbr Br revisione annuale obbligatoria dei veicoli*; ***it failed its ~*** non ha superato la revisione
M.O.T. *abbr* (= **Ministry of Transport**) ministero *m* dei trasporti
motel *n* motel *m inv*
motet *n* MUS mottetto *m*
moth *n* falena *f*; (*clothes moth*) tarma *f*
mothball *n* naftalina *f* **moth-eaten** *adj* roso dalle tarme; *fig* logoro
mother I *n* madre *f*; ***she's a ~ of three***

ha tre figli; ***necessity is the ~ of invention*** il bisogno aguzza l'ingegno; (*nun*) ***Mother Superior*** madre *f* superiora **II** *v/t* fare da mamma a **III** *adj* madre; ***~ duck*** anatra *f* madre; ***the ~ church*** la madre chiesa

motherboard *n* COMPUT scheda *f* madre **mother hen** *n* chioccia *f* **motherhood** *n* maternità *f inv*

Mothering Sunday → ***Mother's Day***

mother-in-law *n* ⟨*pl* ***mothers-in-law***⟩ suocera *f*

motherly *adj* materno

mother-of-pearl *n* madreperla *f* **Mothers Day** *n* Festa *f* della mamma **mother-to-be** *n* ⟨*pl* ***mothers-to-be***⟩ futura mamma *f* **mother tongue** *n* madrelingua *f* **mother wit** *n* buon senso *m*

motif *n* ART, MUS motivo *m*

motion I *n* (*movement*) moto *m*; (*proposal*) mozione *f*; ***set things in ~*** metter in moto le cose; ***go through the ~s*** fare qc meccanicamente; (*evacuation*) defecazione *f* **II** *v/t*: ***he ~ed me forward*** mi ha fatto cenno di avvicinarmi

motionless *adj* immobile; ***stand ~*** stare immobile

motion picture *n esp US* film *m inv* **motion sickness** *n* MED chinetosi *f*; *in the air* mal *m* d'aria; *in car* mal *m* d'auto

motivate *v/t person* motivare

motivation *n* motivazione *f*

motive *n* motivo *m*

motley *adj* eterogeneo

motocross *n* motocross *m*

motor *n* motore *m*; *Br infml car* macchina *f*

motorbike *n* moto *f* **motorboat** *n* motoscafo *m* **motorcade** *n* corteo *m* di auto **motorcycle** *n* motocicletta *f* **motorcyclist** *n* motociclista *m/f* **motor home** *n* casamobile *f* **motor industry** *n* industria *f* automobilistica

motorist *n* automobilista *m/f*

motor mechanic *n* meccanico *m* **motor neurone disease** *n* malattia *f* dei neuroni motori **motor racing** *n* automobilismo *m* **motorscooter** *n* scooter *m inv* **motor show** *n* salone *m* dell'automobile **motor vehicle** *n* autoveicolo *m* **motorway** *n Br* autostrada *f*

mottled *adj* a chiazze

motto *n* motto *m*

mould¹, *US* **mold** *n on food* muffa *f*

mould², *US* **mold I** *n* stampo *m*; *fig* ***be cast in*** *or* ***from the same / a different ~*** (*people*) essere dello stesso stampo / di un diverso stampo; *fig* ***break the ~*** rinnovare **II** *v/t a. fig* plasmare

moulding, *US* **molding** *n* ARCH modanatura *f*

mouldy, *US* **moldy** *adj* (+*er*) *food* ammuffito; ***get*** *or* ***go ~*** ammuffire

moult *v/i bird* perdere le penne; *dog* perdere il pelo

mound *n* (*hillock*) collinetta *f*; *in baseball* pedana *f* del lanciatore; (*pile*) mucchio *m*

mount¹ *n*: ***on Mount Sinai*** sul monte Sinai; ***Mount McKinley*** il Monte McKinley

mount² I *n* (*horse*) cavalcatura *f* **II** *v/t steps* salire; *horse* montare a; *bicycle* montare in; *campaign* organizzare; *jewel* montare; *photo*, *painting* incorniciare **III** *v/i* (*increase*) aumentare; ***the death toll has ~ed to 800*** le vittime sono salite a 800; ***pressure is ~ing on him to resign*** aumentano le pressioni perché lui si dimetta

◆**mount up** *v/i* accumularsi

mountain *n* montagna *f*; ***in the ~s*** in montagna; ***make a ~ out of a molehill*** fare d'una mosca un elefante

mountain bike *n* mountain bike *f inv* **mountain chain** *n* catena *f* montuosa

mountaineer *n* alpinista *m/f*

mountaineering *n* alpinismo *m*

mountainous *adj* montuoso

mountain rescue service *n* soccorso *m* alpino

mounted police *n* polizia *f* a cavallo

mourn I *v/t* piangere **II** *v/i*: ***~ for*** piangere la morte di

mourner *n persona che partecipa a un corteo funebre*

mournful *adj* triste

mourning *n* lutto *m*; ***be in ~*** essere in lutto; ***wear ~*** portare il lutto; ***next Tuesday has been declared a day of national ~*** per il prossimo martedì è stata proclamata una giornata di lutto nazionale

mouse *n* ⟨*pl* ***mice***⟩ topo *m*; COMPUT mouse *m inv*

mouse mat, mouse pad *n* COMPUT

tappetino *m* del mouse **mouse potato** *n* COMPUT *infml persona che passa tutto il tempo al computer*
mousetrap *n* trappola *f* per topi
mousse *n* mousse *f inv*
moustache, *US* **mustache** *n* baffi *mpl*
mousy *adj* (+*er*) *hair* grigio topo; *person* anonimo
mouth[1] *n of person* bocca *f*; *of river* foce *f*; ***keep one's*** (***big***) ***~ shut*** (***about sth***) *infml* tenere la bocca chiusa (su qc); ***me and my big ~!*** *infml* tutta colpa della mia boccaccia!; ***he has three ~s to feed*** ha tre bocche da sfamare; ***shoot o's ~ off*** spararle grosse; *infml* ***down in the ~*** giù di morale
mouth[2] *v/t soundlessly* esprimere col semplice movimento delle labbra
mouthful *n of food* boccone *m*; *of drink* sorsata *f*
mouthorgan *n* armonica *f* a bocca **mouthpiece** *n of instrument* bocchino *m*; (*spokesperson*) portavoce *m/f* **mouth-to-mouth resuscitation** *n* respirazione *f* bocca a bocca **mouthwash** *n* colluttorio *m* **mouthwatering** *adj* che fa venire l'acquolina
movable, moveable *adj* mobile
movable feast *n Br* REL festa *f* mobile; ***be a ~*** *Br infml* non essere mai alla stessa ora
move I *v/t* **1.** *object* spostare, muovere; (*transfer*) trasferire; ***you'll have to ~ these books*** dovrai spostare questi libri; ***his parents ~d him to another school*** i suoi genitori lo hanno trasferito in un'altra scuola; ***we've been ~d to a new office*** è stato trasferito in un nuovo ufficio; ***~ house*** traslocare **2.** *emotionally* commuovere; ***be ~d to tears*** essere commosso fino alle lacrime **II** *v/i* muoversi, spostarsi; (*transfer*) trasferirsi; ***the wheel began to ~*** la ruota cominciò a muoversi; ***nothing ~d*** non si mosse niente; ***don't ~!*** non muoverti!; ***keep s.o. / sth moving*** mantenere qn / qc in movimento; ***~ away from sth*** allontanarsi da qc; ***things are moving at last*** le cose si stanno finalmente muovendo; ***~ with the times*** stare al passo coi tempi; ***~ in royal circles*** frequentare l'ambiente reale; ***we ~d to London / to a bigger house*** ci siamo trasferiti a Londra / in una casa più grande; ***he has ~d to room 52*** si è trasferito nella stanza 52; ***this car can really ~!*** *infml* questa macchina viaggia davvero!; ***we'll have to ~ quickly*** dovremo muoverci velocemente **III** *n* **1.** (*step, action*) mossa *f*; ***get a ~ on!*** *infml* spicciati!; ***don't make a ~!*** non ti muovere!; ***it's your ~*** *in game* tocca a te muovere; ***make the first ~*** fare il primo passo; ***be on the ~*** essere indaffarato **2.** *change of house* trasloco *m*
◆**move along I** *v/t sep* far andare avanti; ***they are trying to move things along*** stanno cercando di far andare avanti le cose **II** *v/i along seat etc* fare posto; *along pavement* andare avanti
◆**move around, move about** *v/i in room* muoversi; *from place to place* spostarsi; ***we moved around a lot*** ci spostavamo spesso
◆**move away I** *v/t sep* allontanare; ***move s.o. away from s.o. / sth*** allontanare qn da qn / qc **II** *v/i* allontanarsi; *move house* traslocare
◆**move back I** *v/t sep to former place* rimettere a posto; *into old house* ritrasferire; *to the rear things* riportare indietro **II** *v/i to former place* tornare a posto; *into house* tornare a vivere (*into* in); *to the rear* arretrare; ***move back, please!*** indietro, prego!
◆**move down** *v/i* scendere; ***he had to move down a year*** EDU fu spostato in una classe inferiore
◆**move forward I** *v/t sep person, car* far avanzare; *chair* spostare in avanti; *fig event* promuovere **II** *v/i person, car* avanzare
◆**move in** *v/i* trasferirsi; (*come closer*) farsi avanti (**on** verso); *police, troops* attaccare
◆**move in with** *v/t* andare a vivere con
◆**move off** *v/i Br* partire
◆**move on I** *v/t sep*: ***the policeman moved them on*** il poliziotto li fece sloggiare **II** *v/i* ripartire; *in discussion* andare avanti; ***move on to sth*** passare a qc; *fig* ***it's about time I was moving on*** *to new job etc* è tempo di passare oltre; ***time is moving on*** *Br infml* il tempo passa

◆**move out I** *v/t sep of room* sgombrare; *troops* ritirare; ***they moved everybody out of the danger zone*** fecero sgombrare tutti dalla zona di pericolo **II** *v/i of house* andare via; *of troops* ritirarsi

◆**move over I** *v/t sep* spostare; ***he moved the car over to the side*** spostò la macchina da parte **II** *v/i* farsi da parte; ***move over!*** spostati!; ***move over to a new system*** cedere il posto a un nuovo sistema

◆**move up I** *v/t sep* mettere più in alto; (*promote*) promuovere; *pupil* spostare in una classe superiore; ***they moved him up two places*** è stato promosso di due livelli **II** *v/i in league* avanzare; (*make room*) spostarsi

movement *n* movimento *m*; *fig* (*trend*) tendenza *f* ***towards*** a; ***the ~ of traffic*** la corrente del traffico; MUS movimento *m*

mover *n* (*walker, dancer etc*) ***he is a good / poor ~*** si muove bene / male; ***be a fast ~*** *infml* muoversi velocemente; ***he's a real ~ and shaker*** *infml* è molto influente

movie *n* film *m inv*; ***go to a ~ / the ~s*** andare al cinema

moviegoer *n* frequentatore *m*, -trice *f* di cinema

movie star *n* stella *f* del cinema **movie theater** *n US* cinema *m inv*

moving *adj which can move* mobile; *emotionally* commovente

moving company *n US* società *f* di traslochi

mow *v/t & v/i* ⟨*pret* ***mowed***, *past part* ***mown*** *or* ***mowed***⟩ *grass* tagliare, falciare

◆**mow down** *v/t sep* falciare

mower *n* tosaerba *m inv*

mown *past part* → ***mow***

MP *abbr* **1.** (= **Member of Parliament**) deputato *m* **2.** (= **Military Policeman**) polizia *f* militare

mpg *abbr* (= **miles per gallon**) miglia *fpl* per gallone

mph *abbr* (= **miles per hour**) miglia *fpl* orarie

MP3 *abbr* MP3 *m inv*

MP3 player *n* lettore *m* MP3

MPV *abbr* (= **Multi-Purpose Vehicle**) MPV *m inv*

Mr *abbr* signor

MRI *n abbr* (= **magnetic resonance imaging**) MED risonanza *f* magnetica per immagini

Mrs *abbr* signora

MRSA *abbr* (= **methicillin-resistant Staphylococcus aureus**) MRSA (Staphylococcus aureus meticillino--resistente)

Ms *abbr* signora *appellativo usato sia per donne sposate che nubili*

MS *n abbr* (= **multiple sclerosis**) sclerosi *f* multipla

MSc *abbr* (= **Master of Science**) *master in una materia scientifica*

MSG *abbr* (= **monosodium glutamate**) glutammato *m* di sodio

mss, MSS *abbr* (= **manuscripts**) manoscritti

Mt *abbr* (= **Mount**) M. (monte *m*)

much I *adj* molto; ***so ~ money*** tanti soldi; ***how ~ sugar?*** quanto zucchero?; ***as ~ … as …*** tanto … quanto …; ***we don't see ~ of each other*** non ci frequentiamo molto; ***it's not up to ~*** *infml* non è un granché; ***I'm not ~ of a cook*** non sono granché come cuoco; ***that wasn't ~ of a party*** non era un granché come festa; ***I find that a bit (too) ~ after all I've done for him*** trovo che sia troppo dopo tutto quello che ho fatto per lui; ***I thought as ~*** me l'aspettavo; ***it's not so ~ a problem of modernization as …*** non è tanto un problema di modernizzazione, quanto…; ***I couldn't make ~ of that chapter*** non ho capito bene quel capitolo **II** *adv* molto; ***very ~*** moltissimo; ***too ~*** troppo; ***as ~ as …*** tanto quanto …; ***as ~ as a million dollars*** addirittura un milione di dollari; ***I thought as ~*** me l'aspettavo; ***he's ~ more intelligent than …*** è molto più intelligente di …; ***he's ~ too old*** è decisamente troppo vecchio; ***a ~-admired woman*** una donna molto ammirata; ***I like it very ~*** mi piace molto; ***I don't like him ~*** lui non mi piace; ***thank you very ~*** grazie mille; ***I don't ~ care*** *or* ***care ~*** non mi importa granché; ***however ~ he tries*** per quanto ci provi; ***~ as I like him*** per quanto mi piaccia; ***I would ~ rather stay*** preferirei di gran lunga restare; (*almost*) ***they are produced in ~ the same way*** sono fatti più o meno allo

stesso modo **III** *pron* molto; ***nothing ~*** niente di particolare; ***there's not ~ left*** non ne è rimasto, -a molto, -a
muchness *n*: ***much of a ~*** più o meno uguale
muck *n* (*dirt*) sporco *m*
◆**muck about, muck around** *v/i* gingillarsi
◆**muck in** *v/i Br infml* dare una mano
◆**muck out** *v/t & v/i sep Br* pulire
◆**muck up** *v/t sep plan* rovinare; *exam* non far bene
muckamuck *n Can* cibo *m*
muckrake I *v/i* divulgare scandali **II** *n* divulgazione *f* di scandali
mucky *adj* (+*er*) sporco; ***you ~ pup!*** *Br infml* cucciolo, sei tutto sporco!
mucus *n* muco *m*
mud *n* fango *m*; *fig* ***his name is ~*** *infml* non lo voglio nemmeno sentir nominare
mudbath *n* fanghi *mpl*
muddle I *n* disordine *m*; ***I'm in a ~*** sono confuso **II** *v/t* confondere
◆**muddle along** *v/i* tirare avanti
◆**muddle through** *v/i* cavarsela alla meno peggio
◆**muddle up** *v/t sep* (*mess up*) mettere in disordine; (*confuse*) confondere
muddle-headed *adj Br* tonto
muddy I *adj* (+*er*) fangoso; *hands, boots* sporco di fango; ***I'm all ~*** sono tutto sporco di fango **II** *v/t* confondere; ***that's ~ing the issue*** ciò confonde la questione
mudflat *n* distesa *f* fangosa
mudguard *n Br* parafango *m*
mudpack *n* maschera *f* di fango
mudslinging *n infml* diffamazione *f*
muesli *n* muesli *m inv*
muff[1] *n* manicotto *m*
muff[2] *v/t infml shot* sbagliare
muffin *n Br* (*bread roll*) *panino tondo e schiacciato da mangiare caldo col burro*; (*cake*) *dolcetto spesso contenente uvette*
muffle *v/t sound* attutire; *voice* camuffare
◆**muffle up** *v/i* coprirsi bene
muffler *n US* AUTO marmitta *f*
mug[1] *n for tea, coffee* tazzone *m*; *infml* (*face*) faccia *f*; *infml* (*fool*) sempliciotto *m*
mug[2] *v/t* ⟨*pret & past part* ***-ged***⟩ *attack* aggredire
◆**mug up** *v/t sep Br infml*: *a.* **mug up on**: ***mug sth/one's French up*** *or* ***mug up on sth/one's French*** mettersi a studiare di brutto qc/il francese
mugger *n* aggressore *m*
mugging *n* aggressione *f*
muggy *adj* (+*er*) afoso
mugshot *n* foto *f* segnaletica
mulch BOT **I** *n* pacciame *m* **II** *v/t* ricoprire di pacciame
mule *n animal* mulo *m*; ***(as) stubborn as a ~*** testardo come un mulo; (*slipper*) mule *f inv*
◆**mull over** *v/t sep* riflettere su
mulled wine *n* vin *m* brûlé
mullion *n* ARCH montante *m*
multicoloured, *US* **multicolored** *adj* multicolore
multicultural *adj* multiculturale
multifocals *npl* lenti *fpl* multifocali
multilateral *adj* POL multilaterale
multilingual *adj* multilingue *inv*
multimedia I *adj* multimediale **II** *n* multimedialità *f inv*
multimillionaire *n* plurimiliardario *m*, -a *f*
multinational I *adj* multinazionale **II** *n* COMM multinazionale *f*
multiple *adj* multiplo
multiple choice question *n* esercizio *m* a scelta multipla
multiple sclerosis *n* sclerosi *f* multipla
multiplex (cinema) *n* cinema *m inv* multisale
multiplication *n* moltiplicazione *f*
multiplication table *n* MATH tavola *f* pitagorica; ***he knows his ~s*** sa le tabelline
multiplicity *n* molteplicità *f*
multiply ⟨*pret & past part* ***-ied***⟩ **I** *v/t* moltiplicare; ***4 multiplied by 6 is 24*** 4 moltiplicato per 6 fa 24 **II** *v/i* moltiplicarsi
multipurpose *adj* multiuso
multi-storey (car park) *n* parcheggio *m* a più piani
multi-tasking *n* multiprogrammazione *f*
multitude *n* moltitudine *f*; ***a ~ of*** una moltitudine di
multivitamin I *n* preparato *m* polivitaminico **II** *adj* polivitaminico
mum[1] *adj* zitto; *infml* ***keep ~*** non fare

parola
mum[2] *n* mamma *f*
mumble **I** *n* borbottio *m* **II** *v/t & v/i* borbottare
mumbo jumbo *n* (*empty ritual, superstition*) cerimoniale *m* astruso; (*gibberish*) gergo *m* incomprensibile
mummy[1] *n* (*corpse*) mummia *f*
mummy[2] *n Br* mamma *f*
mummy's boy *n Br infml* cocco *m* di mamma
mumps *nsg* orecchioni *mpl*
munch *v/t & v/i* sgranocchiare
mundane *adj fig* ordinario
Munich *n* Monaco *f* (di Baviera)
municipal *adj* municipale; **~ *elections*** elezioni *fpl* municipali
municipality *n* amministrazione *f* comunale
munificence munificenza *f*
munition *n usu pl* munizioni *fpl*
mural **I** *n* murale *m* **II** *adj* murale; ***it was decorated with ~ paintings and mosaics*** era decorato con mosaici e dipinti murali
murder **I** *n* omicidio *m*; ***get away with ~*** farla franca; *fig infml* ***it was ~*** è stato un inferno **II** *v/t person* uccidere; *song* rovinare
murderer *n* omicida *m/f*
murderous *adj rage, look* omicida; **~ *attack*** attacco *m* omicida
murky *adj* (*+er*) *a. fig* torbido
murmur **I** *n* mormorio *m*; ***there was a ~ of approval / discontent*** ci fu un mormorio di approvazione / scontento; ***without a ~*** senza fiatare **II** *v/t* mormorare
muscle *n* muscolo *m*; ***he never moved a ~*** non ha mai mosso un muscolo
◆**muscle in** *v/i infml* immischiarsi
muscular *adj pain, strain* muscolare; **~ *cramp*** *or* ***spasm*** crampo *m or* spasmo *m* muscolare; *person* muscoloso
muscular dystrophy *n* distrofia *f* muscolare
muse *v/i* riflettere
Muse *n* MYTH musa *f*
museum *n* museo *m*
mush *n* poltiglia *f*
mushroom **I** *n* fungo *m* **II** *v/i* crescere rapidamente; ***unemployment has ~ed*** la disoccupazione è cresciuta rapidamente
mushy *adj* (*+er*) (*soft*) molle; (*sentimental*) sdolcinato
music *n* musica *f*; *in written form* spartito *m*; ***set*** *or* ***put sth to ~*** mettere in musica qc; ***it was (like) ~ to my ears*** era musica per le mie orecchie; ***face the ~*** accettare le conseguenze delle proprie azioni
musical **I** *adj* musicale; *person* portato per la musica; *voice* melodioso; (*tuneful*) armonioso **II** *n* musical *m inv*
music(al) box *n* carillon *m inv* **musical chairs** *nsg* gioco *m* delle sedie
musical instrument *n* strumento *m* musicale
musician *n* musicista *m/f*
musicianship *n* abilità *f* di musicista
music stand *n* leggio *m* **music therapy** *n* musicoterapia *f*
musk *n* muschio *m*
musket *n* moschetto *m*
musketeer *n* moschettiere *m*
musky *adj* (*+er*): **~ *smell*** *or* ***scent*** odore *m or* profumo *m* muschiato
Muslim → ***Moslem***
muslin *n* mussola *f*
muss *v/t US infml* (*a.* **muss up**) scompigliare
mussel *n* cozza *f*
must[1] **I** *v/mod* **1.** *necessity* ***I ~ be on time*** devo arrivare in orario; ***I ~*** devo; ***I ~n't be late*** non devo far tardi **2.** *probability* ***it ~ be about 6 o'clock*** devono essere circa le sei; ***they ~ have arrived by now*** ormai devono essere arrivati; ***I ~ have been dreaming*** devo aver sognato; ***you ~ be crazy!*** devi essere pazzo! **II** *n infml*: ***it's a ~*** è un must
must[2] *n grapes* mosto *m*
mustache *US* → ***moustache***
mustard *n* senape *f*
mustard gas *n* iprite *f*
muster **I** *v/t* (*gather*) chiamare a raccolta; *fig*: *a.* **muster up** *courage* raccogliere coraggio **II** *n* adunata *f*; ***pass ~*** essere passabile
musty *adj* (*+er*) *smell* di stantio; *room* che sa di stantio
mutant *n* mutante *m*
mutation *n* mutamento *m*; BIOL mutazione *f*
mute **I** *adj* muto **II** *n* muto *m*, -a *f*; MUS sordina *f* **III** *v/t* (*muffle*) smorzare il

suono di
muted *adj* tenue
mutilate *v/t* mutilare
mutilation *n* mutilazione *f*
mutinous *adj* NAUT ammutinato; *fig* ribelle
mutiny I *n* ammutinamento *m* **II** *v/i* ⟨*pret & past part* **-ied**⟩ ammutinarsi
mutism *n* mutismo *m*
mutt *n* cane *m* bastardo
mutter I *n* mormorio *m* **II** *v/t & v/i* farfugliare
mutton *n* montone *m*
muttonhead *n infml* stupido *m*, -a *f*
mutual *adj admiration* reciproco; ***the feeling is ~*** il sentimento è reciproco; *friend* in comune
mutual fund *n* fondo *m* comune di investimento
mutually *adv* per entrambi
Muzak® *n programma registrato di musica leggera, trasmesso in treno, aereo, sale d'aspetto ecc.*
muzzle I *n of animal* muso *m*; *for dog* museruola *f* **II** *v/t*: ***~ the press*** imbavagliare la stampa
MW *abbr* **1.** (= **medium wave**) onde *fpl* medie **2.** (= **megawatt**) megawatt *m*
my *adj* il mio *m*, la mia *f*, i miei *mpl*, le mie *fpl*; ***~ bag*** *said by man / woman* la mia valigia; ***~ sister / brother*** mia sorella / mio fratello; ***I've hurt my leg*** mi sono fatto male alla gamba
myopic *adj* miope
myriad I *n*: ***a ~ of*** una miriade di **II** *adj* innumerevole
myrrh *n* mirra *f*
myrtle *n* BOT mirto *m*
myself *pron reflexive* mi; *emphatic* io stesso; *after prep* me stesso; ***I've hurt ~*** mi sono fatto male; ***I said to ~*** allora mi sono detto; ***singing to ~*** canticchiando tra me e me; ***~, I'd prefer ...*** quanto a me, preferirei ...; ***by ~*** da solo; (*one's normal self*) ***I'm not*** (***feeling***) ***~ today*** oggi non sono in me; ***I just tried to be ~*** ho solo cercato di essere me stesso
mysterious *adj* misterioso
mysteriously *adv* misteriosamente
mystery *n* mistero *m*; ***be shrouded*** *or* ***surrounded in ~*** essere avvolto nel *or* circondato dal mistero
mystery play *n* THEAT mistero *m* **mystery tour** *n* gita *f* con destinazione a sorpresa
mystic *adj* mistico
mystical *adj* mistico
mysticism *n* misticismo *m*
mystified *adj* sconcertato; ***I am ~ as to how this could happen*** sono sconcertato da come sia potuto accadere
mystify *v/t* ⟨*pret & past part* **-ied**⟩ lasciare perplesso
mystique *n* fascino *m* misterioso
myth *n a. fig* mito *m*
mythical *adj* mitico; ***the ~ figure / character of Arthur*** la figura mitica di Artù
mythological *adj* mitologico
mythology *n* mitologia *f*

N

N, n *n* n, N *f inv*; MATH n (numero intero generico)
N *abbr* (= **north**) nord *m* (N)
n / a *abbr* (= **not applicable**) non pertinente
nab *v/t* ⟨*pret & past part* **-bed**⟩ *infml take for o.s.* prendere
nadir *n* ASTR nadir *m*; *fig* punto *m* più basso
naff *adj Br infml* (*stupid*) ridicolo; *design*, *car* fuori moda
nag[1] ⟨*pret & past part* **-ged**⟩ **I** *v/i of person* brontolare di continuo; ***stop ~ging*** smetti di brontolare di continuo **II** *v/t* assillare; ***~ s.o. to do sth*** assillare qn perché faccia qc; ***don't ~ me*** non assillarmi **III** *n* brontolone *m*, -a *f*; (*pestering*) piaga *f infml*
nag[2] *n* ronzino *m*
nagging *adj person* brontolone; *doubt*, *pain* assillante
nail I *n on finger*, *toe* unghia *f*; *for*

wood chiodo *m*; ***as hard as ~s*** essere duro di cuore; ***hit the ~ on the head*** *fig* colpire nel segno; ***be a ~ in s.o.'s coffin*** *fig* essere un brutto colpo per qn **II** *v/t* inchiodare (*a. fig*); ***~ sth to the floor*** inchiodare qc al pavimento
nailbiting *adj finish* da cardiopalma
nailbrush *n* spazzolino *m* per le unghie
nail clippers *npl* tagliaunghie *m inv*
nail file *n* limetta *f* per unghie **nail polish** *n* smalto *m* per unghie **nail polish remover** *n* solvente *m* per unghie **nail scissors** *npl* forbicine *fpl* per unghie **nail varnish** *n* smalto *m* per unghie
naive *adj* (*+er*) ingenuo
naivety *n*, **naiveté** *n* ingenuità *f*
naked *adj* nudo; ***to the ~ eye*** a occhio nudo
namby-pamby *adj* svenevole
name I *n* nome *m*; ***what's your ~?*** come ti chiami?; ***call s.o. ~s*** insultare qn; ***make a ~ for o.s.*** farsi un nome; ***a man by the ~ of Gunn*** un uomo di nome Gunn; ***know s.o. by ~*** conoscere qn per nome; ***in the ~ of*** nel nome di; ***put o.s'~ down*** iscriversi; ***not to have a penny/cent to one's ~*** non avere un centesimo; ***have a good/bad ~*** avere una buona/cattiva reputazione; ***give s.o. a bad ~*** rovinare la reputazione di qn **II** *v/t* chiamare; ***I ~ this child/ship X*** ho chiamato il bambino/la nave X; ***the child is ~d Peter*** il bambino si chiama Peter; ***they refused to ~ the victim*** rifiutarono di rivelare l'identità della vittima; ***~ ~s*** fare nomi; ***~ three US states*** dimmi il nome di tre stati degli Stati Uniti; ***you ~ it, he's done it*** qualsiasi cosa tu dica, lui l'ha già fatto; ***~ s.o. as leader*** eleggere qn a leader; ***they ~d her as the winner of the award*** l'hanno nominata vincitrice del premio
◆**name after** *v/t*: ***they named him after his grandfather*** gli hanno messo il nome del nonno
◆**name for** *US* → ***name after***
name-drop *v/i infml* fare sfoggio di conoscenze importanti
nameless *adj* senza nome
namely *adv* cioè
nameplate *n* targhetta *f* **namesake** *n* omonimo *m*, -a *f* **nametag** *n on clothing etc* targhetta *f* col nome
nan bread *n* naan *m*
nancy *n infml* finocchio *m infml*
nan(na) *n Br* nonna *f*
nanny *n* bambinaia *f*
nanny goat *n* capra *f* (femmina)
nanotechnology *n* nanotecnologia *f*
nap¹ I *n* sonnellino *m*; ***have a ~*** schiacciare un pisolino **II** *v/i* fare un sonnellino; ***catch s.o. ~ping*** *fig* essere preso alla sprovvista
nap² *n* TEX pelo *m*
napalm *n* napalm *m*
nape *n*: ***~ of the neck*** nuca *f*
napkin *n* (*table napkin*) tovagliolo *m*; *US* (*sanitary napkin*) assorbente *m*
Naples *n* Napoli *f*
nappy *n Br* pannolino *m*
nappy rash *n Br infml baby* culetto arrossato *infml*
narcissism *n* narcisismo *m*
narcissistic *adj* narcisista
narcotic *n* narcotico *m*
nark *n Br infml* informatore *m* (della polizia)
narrate *v/t* raccontare, narrare
narration *n telling* narrazione *f*
narrative I *n story* racconto **II** *adj poem, style* narrativo
narrator *n* narratore *m*, -trice *f*; ***first-person ~*** narratore *m* in prima persona
narrow I *adj* (*+er*) *street, bed etc* stretto; *views, mind* ristretto; *victory* di stretta misura; ***that was a ~ escape*** c'è mancato un pelo **II** *v/i road* restringersi; *eyes* socchiudersi; *gap* ridursi **III** *v/t eyes* socchiudere; *gap* ridurre; ***they decided to ~ the focus of their investigation*** decisero di restringere il campo dell'indagine
◆**narrow down** *v/t sep choice* limitare
narrow gauge *n* scartamento *m* ridotto
narrowly *adv win* di stretta misura; ***~ escape sth*** scampare a qc per un pelo *infml*
narrow-minded *adj* di idee ristrette
NASA *abbr* (= **National Aeronautics and Space Administration**) NASA *f*
nasal *adj voice* nasale
nasal spray *n* spray *m* nasale
nascent *adj* nascente

nasty *adj* (+*er*) *person*, *thing to say*, *smell*, *weather* cattivo; *cut*, *wound*, *illness* brutto; ***that's a ~-looking cut*** è un brutto taglio; ***turn ~*** *person* incattivirsi; ***he has a ~ temper*** ha un brutto carattere; ***be ~ to s.o.*** essere cattivo con qn; ***that was a ~ thing to say/do*** era una cattiveria; ***what a ~ man*** che uomo cattivo

nation *n* nazione *f*; ***address the ~*** rivolgersi alla nazione; ***the whole ~ watched him do it*** l'intera nazione lo ha visto farlo

national I *adj* nazionale **II** *n* cittadino *m*, -a *f*

national anthem *n* inno *m* nazionale

national debt *n* debito *m* pubblico

National Front *n Br partito nazionalista inglese* **National Guard** *n esp US* Guardia *f* nazionale **National Health Service** *n* servizio *m* sanitario nazionale britannico **National Insurance** *n* previdenza *f* sociale

nationalism *n* nazionalismo *m*

nationalist I *adj* nazionalista **II** *n* nazionalista *m*/*f*

nationality *n* nazionalità *f inv*; ***what ~ is he?*** di quale nazionalità è?; ***she is of German ~*** è di nazionalità tedesca

nationalize *v*/*t industry etc* nazionalizzare

National Lottery *n Br* lotteria *f* nazionale

national park *n* parco *m* nazionale **national security** *n* sicurezza *f* nazionale **national service** *n* servizio *m* militare

National Trust *n Br ente per la salvaguardia di luoghi di interesse storico o naturalistico*

nationwide I *adj* su scala nazionale **II** *adv* in tutto il paese

native I *adj* indigeno; ***~ language*** madrelingua *f* **II** *n* (*tribesman*) indigeno *m*, -a *f*; ***she's a ~ of New York*** è originaria di New York; ***she speaks Chinese like a ~*** parla cinese come una madrelingua

Native American I *n* indiano *m*, -a *f* d'America **II** *adj* degli indiani d'America

native country *n* patria *f* **native speaker** *n*: ***English ~*** persona *f* di madrelingua inglese

nativity *n*: ***the Nativity*** la natività; ***~ play*** natività *f*

NATO *abbr* (= **North Atlantic Treaty Organization**) NATO *f*

natter *Br infml* **I** *v*/*i* chiacchierare **II** *n*: ***have a ~*** fare una chiacchierata

natty *adj* (+*er*) *infml* elegante

natural I *adj* naturale; ***~ resources*** risorse *fpl* naturali; ***it is (only) ~ for him to think ...*** è del tutto normale per lui pensare...; ***the ~ world*** il mondo della natura; ***die of ~ causes*** morire per cause naturali; ***~ remedy*** rimedio *m* naturale; ***she is a ~ blonde*** è una bionda naturale; *ability* innato; ***a ~ talent*** un talento innato; ***he is a ~ comedian*** è un attore nato; *parents* naturale **II** *n* MUS bequadro *m*; ***D ~*** re *m* naturale; ***be a ~*** *infml person* avere doti innate

natural childbirth *n* parto *m* naturale

natural gas *n* gas *m inv* naturale

naturalist *n* naturalista *m*/*f*

naturalization *n* naturalizzazione *f*; ***~ papers*** documenti *mpl* di naturalizzazione

naturalize *v*/*t*: ***become ~d*** naturalizzarsi

naturally *adv* (*of course*) naturalmente; *behave*, *speak* con naturalezza; (*by nature*) per natura; ***~, he wasn't that keen to pay*** naturalmente, non era così entusiasta di pagare; ***it comes ~ to him*** gli viene naturale

natural science *n* scienze *fpl* naturali

natural scientist *n* studioso *m*, -a *f* di scienze naturali

nature *n* natura *f*; ***Nature*** natura *f*; ***laws of ~*** leggi *fpl* di natura; ***it is not in my ~ to say that*** non è nella mia natura dirlo; ***it is in the ~ of young people to want to travel*** è nella natura dei giovani voler viaggiare; ***the ~ of the case is such ...*** la natura del caso è tale che...; ***things of this ~*** cose *fpl* di questa natura; ***... or something of that ~*** ... o qualcosa di tale natura

nature reserve *n* riserva *f* naturale

nature study *n* studio *m* della natura

nature trail *n percorso naturalistico con segnalazione dei vari tipi di piante, animali ecc.*

naturism *n* naturismo *m*

naturist I *n* naturista *m*/*f* **II** *adj* naturista; ***~ beach*** spiaggia *f* naturista

naughty *adj* (+*er*) cattivo; *photograph, word etc* spinto; *child, dog* disubbidiente; ***it was ~ of him to break it*** è stato un birbante a romperlo
nausea *n* nausea *f*
nauseate *v/t* (*fig: disgust*) disgustare
nauseating *adj smell, taste* nauseante; *person* disgustoso
nauseous *adj*: ***feel ~*** avere la nausea
nautical *adj* nautico
nautical mile *n* miglio *m* nautico
naval *adj* navale; *officer, uniform* della marina
naval base *n* base *f* navale **naval battle** *n* battaglia *f* navale **naval officer** *n* ufficiale *m* di marina
nave *n of church* navata *f* centrale
navel *n* ombelico *m*
navel orange *n* arancia *f* navel
navigable *adj river* navigabile
navigate I *v/i in ship, in aeroplane* navigare; *in car* fare da navigatore/-trice; COMPUT navigare; ***~ by the stars*** orientarsi guardando le stelle **II** *v/t aircraft, ship* governare; *ocean* attraversare
navigation *n* navigazione *f*
navigator *n on ship, in aeroplane* ufficiale *m* di rotta; *in car* navigatore *m*, -trice *f*
navvy *n Br infml* sterratore *m*, -trice *f*
navy *n* marina *f* militare
navy blue I *n* blu *m inv* scuro **II** *adj* blu scuro
NB *abbr* (= **nota bene**) *Br* NB
NBC *abbr* **1.** (= **National Broadcasting Company**) *US una delle maggiori emittenti televisive americane* **2.** (= **nuclear, biological and chemical**) MIL nucleare, biologico e chimico (*abbr* NBC)
NE *abbr* (= **north-east**) nordest *m* (NE)
near I *adv* vicino; ***come ~er*** vieni più vicino; ***he lives quite ~*** abita piuttosto vicino; ***be ~ at hand*** essere a portata di mano; *shops* essere vicino; ***as ~ as I can tell*** per quanto ne so; (***that's***) ***~ enough*** è abbastanza; (*almost*) ***he very ~ succeeded*** ci è quasi riuscito; *negative* ***it's nowhere ~ enough*** non è per niente sufficiente; ***he is nowhere*** *or* ***not anywhere ~ as clever as you*** non è neanche lontanamente intelligente quanto te **II** *prep* vicino a; ***~ the bank*** vicino alla banca; ***do you go ~ the bank?*** va dalle parti della banca?; ***don't come ~ me*** non avvicinarti; ***be ~*** (***to***) ***tears*** essere sul punto di piangere; ***~ the end of the play*** verso la fine della rappresentazione **III** *adj* (+*er*) vicino; ***the ~est stop*** la fermata più vicina; ***in the ~ future*** nel prossimo futuro; ***a ~ disaster*** quasi un disastro; ***his ~est rival*** il suo rivale più prossimo; ***round up a figure to the ~est pound*** arrotondare un numero per eccesso; ***my ~est and dearest*** i miei cari **IV** *v/t* avvicinare; *fig* ***be ~ing sth*** avvicinarsi a qc; ***she was ~ing fifty*** si stava avvicinando ai cinquanta; ***~ completion*** essere prossimo al completamento **V** *v/i* avvicinarsi
nearby *adv live* vicino
Near East *n* Medio Oriente *m*; ***in the ~*** in Medio Oriente
nearly *adv* quasi; ***I ~ laughed*** a momenti ridevo; ***we are ~ there*** *at a place* ci siamo quasi; ***he very ~ drowned*** c'è mancato proprio poco che annegasse; ***not ~*** affatto
nearly-new *adj*: ***~ shop*** negozio *m* di articoli usati d'occasione
near-sighted *adj* miope
near thing *n*: ***that was a ~*** c'è mancato poco
neat *adj* (+*er*) *room, desk, person* ordinato; *handwriting* preciso; *whisky* liscio; *solution* efficace; *US infml* (*terrific*) fantastico
neatness *n* ordine *m*
nebulous *adj* nebuloso
necessarily *adv* necessariamente; ***not ~*** non necessariamente
necessary I *adj* necessario; ***it is ~ to ...*** è necessario ..., bisogna ...; ***if ~*** se necessario; ***all the ~ qualifications*** tutte le qualifiche necessarie; ***that won't be ~*** non sarà necessario; ***make the ~ arrangements*** prendere gli accordi necessari; ***do everything ~*** fare tutto il necessario **II** *n usu pl*: ***the ~*** *or* ***necessaries*** necessario *m*
necessitate *v/t* rendere necessario
necessity *n* necessità *f inv*; ***of ~*** necessariamente
neck I *n* collo *m*; ***be ~ and ~*** essere testa a testa; ***break one's ~*** rompersi il collo; ***risk one's ~*** rischiare il collo;

save one's ~ salvare il collo; ***be up to one's ~ in work*** essere sommerso dal lavoro fino al collo; ***stick one's ~ out*** esporsi alle critiche; ***in this ~ of the woods*** *infml* da queste parti; *of dress etc* collo *m*; ***it has a high ~*** è a collo alto **II** *v/i infml* pomiciare

necklace *n* collana *f*

neckline *n of dress* scollo *m*

necktie *n esp US* cravatta *f*

necro- *pref* necro-

necrology *n* necrologio *m*

necropolis *n* necropoli *f*

necrosis *n* necrosi *f*

nectar *n* nettare *m*

nectarine *n* pesca *f* noce

née *adj*: ***Lisa Higgins, ~ Smart*** Lisa Higgins nata Smart

need I *v/t* avere bisogno di; ***you'll ~ to buy one*** dovrai comprarne uno; ***you don't ~ to wait*** non c'è bisogno che aspetti; ***I ~ to talk to you*** ti devo parlare; ***~ I say more?*** devo aggiungere altro?; ***you ~n't have come*** non c'era bisogno tu venissi; ***much ~ed*** estremamente necessario; ***just what I ~ed*** proprio ciò di cui avevo bisogno; ***this incident ~s some explanation*** deve essere fornita una spiegazione dell'incidente; ***it ~s a coat of paint*** ha bisogno di una mano di vernice; ***you shouldn't ~ to be told*** non dovrebbe essere necessario dirtelo; ***~ he go?*** deve andare?; ***you only ~ed to ask*** dovevi solo chiedere; ***we ~n't have gone*** non era necessario che andassimo **II** *n* bisogno *m*; ***if ~ be*** se necessario; ***be in ~*** (*be needy*) essere bisognoso; ***be in ~ of sth*** aver bisogno di qc; ***there's no ~ to be rude / upset*** non c'è bisogno di essere maleducato / triste; ***in ~ of repair*** bisognoso di riparazioni; ***in time(s) of ~*** nel momento del bisogno; ***those in ~*** i bisognosi; ***your ~ is greater than mine*** le tue esigenze sono superiori alle mie

needle I *n for sewing, on dial* ago *m*; *on record player* puntina *f*; *for knitting* uncinetto; ***it's like looking for a ~ in a haystack*** è come cercare un ago in un pagliaio **II** *v/t infml* punzecchiare *m*

needlecord *n* TEX velluto *m* millerighe

needlepoint *n* TEX ricamo *m* ad ago

needless *adj* inutile; ***~ to say*** inutile dirlo

needlessly *adv* inutilmente; ***you are worrying quite ~*** ti stai preoccupando inutilmente

needlewoman *n* cucitrice *f*

needlework *n* cucito *m*

needy I *adj* (+*er*) bisognoso **II** *n*: ***the ~*** i bisognosi

negate *v/t* negare

negative I *adj* negativo; GRAM negativo **II** *n* ELEC polo *m* negativo; PHOT negativa *f*; ***answer in the ~*** rispondere negativamente

negative feedback *n* controreazione *f*

neglect I *v/t garden, one's health* trascurare; ***~ to do sth*** trascurare di fare qc **II** *n* trascuratezza *f*; ***the garden was in a state of ~*** il giardino era trascurato

neglected *adj gardens, author* trascurato; ***feel ~*** sentirsi trascurato

negligence *n* negligenza *f*

negligent *adj* negligente

negligible *adj quantity, amount* trascurabile

negotiable *adj salary, contract* negoziabile; ***the price is ~*** il prezzo è negoziabile

negotiate I *v/i* trattare **II** *v/t deal, settlement* negoziare; *obstacles* superare; *bend in road* affrontare

negotiation *n* negoziato *m*, trattativa *f*; ***the matter is still under ~*** la questione è ancora oggetto di trattative

negotiator *n* negoziatore *m*, -trice *f*

Negro *pej* **I** *adj* negro **II** *n* negro *m*, -a *f*

neigh *v/i* nitrire

neighbor *etc US* → ***neighbour*** *etc*

neighbour, *US* **neighbor** *n* vicino *m*, -a *f*

neighbourhood, *US* **neighborhood** *n in town* quartiere *m*; *fig* ***in the ~ of*** intorno a

neighbouring, *US* **neighboring** *adj house, state* confinante

neighbourly, *US* **neighborly** *adj* amichevole

neither I *adj*: ***~ player*** nessuno dei due giocatori; ***~ one of them*** nessuno di loro due **II** *pron* nessuno *m* dei due, nessuna *f* delle due, né l'uno né l'altro, né l'una né l'altra **III** *adv*: ***~ ... nor ...*** né … né …; ***he ~ knows nor cares*** non lo sa né se ne interessa **IV** *cj* neanche; ***~ do I*** neanch'io; ***he didn't do it*** (***and***) ***~ did his sister*** lui non se n'è occupato e neanche sua sorella

nelly *n Br infml*: ***not on your ~*** neanche per sogno

nemesis *n* nemesi *f*

neo- *pref* neo-

neoclassical *adj* neoclassico

Neolithic *adj* neolitico

neologism *n* neologismo *m*

neon light *n* luce *f* al neon

nephew *n* nipote *m* (di zii)

nepotism *n* nepotismo *m*

Neptune *n* SPACE, MYTH Nettuno *m*

nerd *n sl* fesso *m*, -a *f sl*; *in style* tamarro *m sl*

nerve *n* **1.** nervo *m*; ***lose one's ~*** farsi prendere dal panico: ***it's bad for my ~s*** mi mette in agitazione; ***get on s.o.'s ~s*** dare sui nervi a qn **2.** (*courage*) coraggio *m* **3.** (*impudence*) faccia *f* tosta

nerve cell *n* cellula *f* nervosa **nerve centre**, *US* **nerve center** *n fig* centro *m* vitale **nerve gas** *n* gas *m* nervino

nerve-racking *adj* snervante

nervous *adj* nervoso; ***~ tension***; ***be ~ about doing sth*** essere ansioso all'idea di fare qc; ***be*** *or* ***feel ~*** essere nervoso; ***I was rather ~ about giving him the job*** ero piuttosto nervoso all'idea di affidargli il lavoro

nervous breakdown *n* esaurimento *m* nervosa **nervous energy** *n*: ***be full of ~*** essere sovraeccitato

nervously *adv* nervosamente

nervousness *n* nervosismo *m*

nervous wreck *n*: ***be a ~*** avere i nervi a pezzi

nervy *adj* agitato

nest I *n* nido *m* **II** *v/i* fare il nido

nest egg *n* gruzzoletto *m*

nestle *v/i* rannicchiarsi; ***~ against s.o.*** accoccolarsi vicino a qn; ***the village nestling in the hills*** il villaggio era annidato nelle colline

net[1] **I** *n for fishing* retino *m*; *for tennis* rete *f*; *fig* ***slip through the ~*** liberarsi dalla trappola **II** *v/t fish* prendere con la rete

net[2] *adj* COMM netto; ***~ disposable income*** reddito *m* netto disponibile; ***~ result*** risultato *m* netto

Net *n* COMPUT Internet *m*; ***surf the ~*** navigare in Internet

netball *n Br gioco simile alla pallacanestro, prevalentemente femminile*

net curtain *n* tenda *f* di tulle

nether *adj liter*, *hum* inferiore; ***~ parts*** parti *fpl* basse

netiquette *n* COMPUT netiquette *f inv*

net profit *n* guadagno *m or* utile *m* netto

netspeak *n* COMPUT *infml* gergo *m* di Internet

netting *n* rete *f*; *wire netting* rete *f* metallica; *for curtains etc* tulle *m*

nettle *n* BOT ortica *f*; *fig* ***grasp the ~*** prendere il toro per le corna

nettle rash *n Br* orticaria *f*

net weight *n* peso *m* netto

network *n of contacts*, *cells* rete *f*; COMPUT network *m inv*

networking *n with contacts* creazione *f* di una rete di contatti

neural *adj* neurale

neuralgia *n* nevralgia *f*

neurologist *n* neurologo *m*, -a *f*

neurosis *n* nevrosi *f inv*

neurosurgeon *n* neurochirurgo *m*

neurotic I *adj* nevrotico; ***be ~ about sth*** avere la fissa di qc **II** *n* nevrotico *m*, -a *f*

neurotransmitter *n* neurotrasmettitore *m*

neuter I *adj* GRAM neutro **II** *v/t animal* sterilizzare

neutral I *adj country* neutrale; *colour* neutro **II** *n gear* folle *m*; ***in ~*** in folle

neutrality *n* neutralità *f inv*

neutralize *v/t* neutralizzare

neutron *n* neutrone *m*

never *adv* mai; ***~!*** *in disbelief* ma va'!; ***you're ~ going to believe this*** non ci crederesti mai; ***you ~ promised, did you?*** non l'avrai promesso, spero!; ***Spurs were beaten — ~!*** *infml* gli Spurs sono stati battuti - non è possibile!; ***well I ~*** (***did***)***!*** *infml* questa poi!; ***~ fear*** niente paura

never-ending *adj* senza fine **never-never** *n infml*: ***he bought it on the ~*** l'ha comprato a rate

nevertheless *adv* comunque, tuttavia

new *adj* (+*er*) nuovo; ***what's ~?*** *infml* che c'è di nuovo?; ***this system is still ~ to me*** non sono ancora abituato al sistema; ***I'm ~ to the job*** sono nuovo del mestiere; ***that's nothing ~*** non è

una novità
New Age traveller *n Br seguace della New Age con stile di vita nomade*
new blood *n fig* nuovo impulso *m*
newborn *adj* neonato
newcomer *n* nuovo arrivato *m*, nuova arrivata *f*; ***they are ~s to this town*** sono arrivati da poco in città
newfangled *adj pej* moderno
new-found *adj happiness* recente; *confidence* nuovo
newly *adv* (*recently*) recentemente; ***~ made*** appena fatto; *bread, cake etc* appena sfornato; ***~ arrived*** appena arrivato; ***~ married*** appena sposato
newly weds *npl* sposini *mpl*
new moon *n* luna *f* nuova; ***there's a ~ tonight*** stanotte c'è la luna nuova
news *nsg* notizia *f*; *on TV, radio* notiziario *m*; novità *f inv*; ***any ~?*** ci sono novità?; ***that's ~ to me*** mi giunge nuovo; ***a piece of ~*** una notizia; ***I have no ~ of him*** non ho sue notizie; ***have you heard the ~?*** hai sentito la novità?; ***tell us your ~*** raccontaci le novità; ***I have ~ for you*** *iron* ho una notizia per te; ***who will break the ~ to him?*** chi gli darà la cattiva notizia?
news agency *n* agenzia *f* di stampa **newsagent** *n* giornalaio *m* **news bulletin** *n* notiziario *m* **newscast** *n* telegiornale *m* **newscaster** *n* giornalista *m/f* televisivo, -a **news flash** *n* notizia *f* flash **newsgroup** *n* COMPUT newsgroup *m* **newsletter** *n* bollettino *m* **newspaper** *n* giornale *m* **newsreader** *n* giornalista *m/f* radiotelevisivo, -a **news report** *n* notiziario *m* **newsroom** *n* sala *f* stampa **newsstand** *n* edicola *f* **newsvendor** *n* edicolante *m/f*
newsworthy *adj*: ***be ~*** fare notizia
newsy *adj* ricco di notizie
newt *n* ZOOL tritone *m*
new technology *n* nuova tecnologia *f* **New Testament** *n*: ***the ~*** il Nuovo Testamento **new wave I** *n* new wave *f* **II** *adj* new wave **New World** *n*: ***the ~*** il nuovo mondo **new year** *n* anno *m* nuovo; ***Happy New Year!*** buon anno! **New Year's Day** *n* capodanno *m* **New Year's Eve** *n* San Silvestro *m* **New Zealand** *n* Nuova Zelanda *f* **New Zealander** *n* neozelandese *m/f*
next I *adj in time* prossimo; *in space* vicino; ***the ~ week/ month he came back again*** la settimana / il mese dopo ritornò; ***who's ~?*** a chi tocca?; ***this time ~ week*** tra una settimana; ***the year after ~*** tra due anni; ***the ~ day but one*** dopo due giorni; ***my name is ~ on the list*** nell'elenco, il mio nome viene subito dopo; ***the ~ size up/ down*** la taglia più grande / piccola **II** *adv* dopo; ***~ to*** (*beside*) accanto a; (*in comparison with*) a paragone di; ***what shall we do ~?*** che facciamo adesso?; ***whatever ~?*** *in surprise* cos'altro ancora?; ***~ to impossible*** quasi impossibile; ***this is the ~ best thing*** l'alternativa migliore
next door I *adj*: ***~ neighbour*** vicino *m*, -a *f* di casa **II** *adv live* nella casa accanto **next of kin** *n* parente *m/f* prossimo
NFL *abbr* (= **National Football League**) *US lega professionistica di football americano*
NGO *abbr* (= **non-governmental organization**) ONG *f* (organizzazione *f* non governativa)
NHS *abbr* (= **National Health Service**) servizio *m* sanitario nazionale britannico
nibble I *v/t* mordicchiare **II** *v/i* sbocconcellare (***at*** qc) **III** *n*: ***~s*** *Br* snack *mpl*
nice *adj* (+er) *person* carino, gentile; *day, weather, party* bello; ***have a ~ day!*** *esp US* buona giornata!; ***the ~ thing about Venice*** l'aspetto piacevole di Venezia; ***it's been ~ meeting you*** mi ha fatto piacere incontrarti; ***I had a ~ rest*** ho fatto un bel riposino; ***~ one!*** bravo!; *meal, food* buono; ***be ~ to your sister!*** sii carino con tua sorella!; ***that's very ~ of you*** molto gentile da parte tua!; ***a ~ long bath*** un bagno piacevolmente lungo; ***~ and warm*** piacevolmente caldo; ***take it ~ and easy*** prenditela con calma; ***you're in a ~ mess*** *iron* sei in un bel pasticcio; ***that's a ~ way to talk to your mother*** bel modo di parlare a tua madre
nicely *adv written, presented* bene; ***say thank you ~!*** ringrazia gentilmente!; ***that will do ~*** quello andrà bene; ***he's doing very ~ for himself*** sta avendo

successo; ***be ~ spoken*** essere detto educatamente
niceties *npl*: ***social ~*** convenevoli *mpl*
niche *n in market* nicchia *f* (di mercato); *special position* nicchia *f*; ***Brunello is a ~ product*** il brunello è un prodotto di nicchia
nick[1] **I** *n cut* taglietto *m*; ***in the ~ of time*** appena in tempo; *Br infml* ***in good / bad ~*** in buone / cattive condizioni **II** *v/t*: ***~ o.s.*** *infml* farsi un taglietto
nick[2] *Br* **I** *v/t infml* (*arrest*) pizzicare; (*steal*) grattare **II** *n infml* (*prison*) galera *f*
nickel *n material* nichel *m inv*; (*US*: *coin*) *moneta da 5 centesimi di dollaro*
nickname I *n* soprannome *m* **II** *v/t*: ***they ~d him Baldy*** l'hanno soprannominato Kojak
nicotine *n* nicotina *f*
nicotine patch *n* cerotto *m* alla nicotina
niece *n* nipote *f* (di zii)
nifty *adj* (+*er*) *infml* abile; *gadget* carino; ***a ~ little car*** una macchina piccola e carina
niggardly *adj amount* misero; *person* tirchio
niggle I *v/i* (*complain*) menarla ***about*** con **II** *v/t* (*worry*) infastidire
niggling *adj doubt*, *pain* assillante
nigh I *adj liter* vicino **II** *adv*: ***~ on*** quasi
night *n* notte *f*; (*evening*) sera *f*; ***at ~*** di notte / di sera; ***last ~*** ieri notte / ieri sera; ***travel by ~*** viaggiare di notte; ***during the ~*** durante la notte; ***stay the ~*** rimanere a dormire; ***a room for 2 ~s*** una stanza per due notti; ***work ~s*** fare il turno di notte; ***good ~*** buona notte; ***in the middle of the ~*** a notte fonda; ***have an early ~*** andare a letto presto
nightcap *n* (*drink*) *bicchierino bevuto prima di andare a letto* **nightclub** *n* night(-club) *m inv* **nightdress** *n* camicia *f* da notte **nightfall** *n*: ***at ~*** al calar della notte **night flight** *n* volo *m* notturno **nightgown** *n* camicia *f* da notte
nightie *n infml* camicia *f* da notte
nightingale *n* usignolo *m*
nightlife *n* vita *f* notturna; **nightlight** *n for child etc* lumino *m* da notte
nightly *adj/adv* ogni sera; *late at night* ogni notte
nightmare *n a. fig* incubo *m*; ***that was a ~ of a journey*** quel viaggio è stato un incubo; **night owl** *n infml* nottambulo *m*, -a *f* **night porter** *n* portiere *m* notturno **night safe** *n* cassa *f* continua **night school** *n* scuola *f* serale **night shift** *n* turno *m* di notte **nightshirt** *n* camicia *f* da notte *da uomo* **nightspot** *n* locale *m* notturno **nighttime I** *n*: ***at ~, in the ~*** di notte, la notte **II** *adj* notturno; ***~ temperature*** temperatura *f* notturna **night watchman** *n* guardia *f* notturna
nil *n* SPORTS zero *m*
Nile *n* Nilo *m*
nimble *adj* (+*er*) agile
nine I *num* nove; ***~ times out of ten*** nove volte su dieci **II** *n* nove *m*; ***dressed (up) to the ~s*** in ghingheri
9 / 11, nine-eleven *n* 11 settembre *m*
nineteen I *num* diciannove **II** *n* diciannove *m*; ***she talks ~ to the dozen*** *Br infml* parla incessantemente
nineteenth *n/adj* diciannovesimo, -a
ninetieth *n/adj* novantesimo, -a
nine-to-five I *adj*: ***a ~ job*** un lavoro con orario regolare **II** *adv*: ***work ~*** avere un orario lavorativo regolare
ninety *num* novanta
ninth *n/adj* nono
nip[1] **I** *n* (*pinch*) pizzico *m*; (*bite*) morso *m*; ***there's a ~ in the air*** c'è un freddo pungente **II** *v/t* (*pinch*) pizzicare; (*bite*) mordicchiare; ***~ in / out*** *infml* entrare / uscire un attimo; ***the dog ~ped his ankle*** il cane gli diede un morso alla caviglia; ***~ sth in the bud*** *fig* stroncare qc sul nascere **III** *v/i Br infml* fare un salto; ***~ up(stairs)*** fare un salto di sopra; ***I'll just ~ down to the shops*** farò solo un salto nei negozi di sotto
nip[2] *n infml* (*drink*) sorso *m*; ***a ~ of brandy*** un sorso di brandy
nipper *n* (*claw*) chela *f*; *Br infml* moccioso *m*
nipple *n* capezzolo *m*
nippy *adj* (+*er*) *infml* (*cold*) freddo; (*fast*) veloce
nit *n* ZOOL pidocchio *m*; *Br infml* zuccone *m*, -a *f*
nit-pick *v/i infml* cercare il pelo nell'uovo

nitrate *n* nitrato *m*
nitric acid *n* acido *m* nitrico
nitrogen *n* azoto *m*
nitty-gritty *n infml* ***get down to the ~*** venire al dunque
nitwit *n infml* zuccone *m*, -a *f*
nix *US* **I** *adv* no **II** *v/t infml* opporsi a
no I *adv* no **II** *adj* nessuno; ***there's ~ coffee / tea left*** non c'è più caffè / tè; ***I have ~ family / money*** non ho famiglia / soldi; ***I'm ~ linguist / expert*** non sono un linguista / esperto; ***this is ~ place for children*** non è un luogo adatto ai bambini; ***in no time*** in un batter d'occhio; ***at ~ little expense*** a caro prezzo; ***there is ~ such thing*** non esiste una cosa del genere; ***~ parking*** sosta vietata; ***~ smoking*** vietato fumare
No, no *abbr* (= **number**) n. (numero)
nob *n Br infml* persona *f* altolocata
nobility *n* nobiltà *f inv*
noble *adj* (+*er*) nobile; ***of ~ birth*** di nobili natali
nobleman *n* nobile *m*
noble rot *n wine* muffa *f* nobile
noblesse *n* nobiltà *f*
noblesse oblige *n* noblesse oblige
noblewoman *n* nobile *f*
nobly *adv* (*finely*) nobilmente; (*bravely*) valorosamente; *infml* (*selflessly*) generosamente
nobody I *pron* nessuno; ***~ knows*** nessuno lo sa; ***there was ~ at home*** non c'era nessuno in casa; ***~ else offered to give them money*** nessun altro si offrì di dar loro del denaro; ***like ~'s business*** come un pazzo **II** *n* nullità *f*; ***he was a complete ~*** era una totale nullità
no-claim(s) bonus *n* riduzione *f* bonus malus
nocturnal *adj* notturno; ***~ animal*** animale *m* notturno
nod I *v/i* ⟨*pret & past part* **-ded**⟩ fare un cenno col capo; ***~ in agreement*** annuire **II** *v/t*: ***~ one's head*** annuire col capo **III** *n* cenno *m* del capo; ***give a ~*** fare un cenno del capo
◆**nod off** *v/i* (*fall asleep*) appisolarsi
nodal *adj* nodale
node *n* nodo *m* (*a.* COMPUT)
nodule *n* nodulo *m*
Noel *n* Natale *m*
no-fault *adj* JUR *divorce* consensuale
no-frills *adj flight* no frills; *style* senza fronzoli **no-go area** *n quartiere particolarmente pericoloso in cui neanche la polizia osa avventurarsi* **no-good** *adj* inetto **no-holds-barred** *adj* senza regole
no-hoper *n infml* buono *m*, -a *f* a nulla
noise *n* (*sound*) rumore *m*; *loud*, *unpleasant* chiasso *m*; ***~s off*** THEAT rumori *mpl* fuori scena; ***whistling ~*** fischio *m*; ***make a ~*** fare rumore
noisy *adj* (+*er*) rumoroso; *children*, *party* chiassoso; ***don't be so ~*** non fate tanto rumore
nomad *n* nomade *m/f*
nomadic *adj tribe* nomade; *life* da nomade
no-man's-land *n* terra *f* di nessuno
nominal *adj amount* simbolico
nominal value *n* valore *m* nominale
nominate *v/t* (*appoint*) designare; ***~ s.o. for a post*** proporre qn come candidato per una posizione; ***he was ~d chairman*** è stato designato presidente; ***he was ~d for the presidency*** è stato candidato per la presidenza
nomination *n* (*appointing*) nomina *f*; (*proposal*) candidatura *f*; *person proposed* candidato *m*, -a *f*
nominative GRAM **I** *n* nominativo *m* **II** *adj*: ***~ case*** caso *m* nominativo
nominee *n* candidato *m*, -a *f*
non ... *pref* non ...
nonagenarian *n* nonagenario *m*, -a *f*
non-aggression *n*: ***~ treaty*** trattato *m* di non aggressione
non-alcoholic *adj* analcolico
non-aligned *adj* non allineato
non-attendance *n* assenza *f* (***at*** a)
nonchalant *adj* noncurante
non-commissioned officer *n* sottufficiale *m*
non-committal *adj person*, *response* evasivo; ***be ~ about whether ...*** essere evasivo sul fatto se...
nonconformist I *n* anticonformista *m/f* **II** *adj* anticonformista
nondescript *adj* ordinario
none I *pron* nessuno *m*, -a *f*; ***~ of the students*** nessuno degli studenti; ***there are ~ left*** non ne sono rimasti; ***there is ~ left*** non ne è rimasto, non è rimasto niente; ***their guest was ~ other than ...*** il loro ospite non era

altri che…; ***he would have ~ of it*** non ne voleva sentir parlare **II** *adv*: ***she looks ~ the worse for her ordeal*** sembra uscita incolume dalle sue traversie; ***he was ~ too happy about it*** non ne sembrava affatto felice; ***I was ~ the wiser*** ne sapevo quanto prima

nonentity *n* nullità *f inv*; ***he was a bit of a ~*** era una nullità

non-essential **I** *adj* non indispensabile **II** *npl*: ***~s*** dettagli *mpl* non essenziali

nonetheless *adv* nondimeno

non-event *n infml* evento *m* deludente

non-executive director *n* direttore *m*, -trice *f* non esecutivo,-a

nonexistent *adj* inesistente; ***discipline is ~ here*** la disciplina qui è inesistente

non-fat *adj* privo di grassi

non-fattening *adj* che non fa ingrassare; ***fruit is ~*** la frutta non fa ingrassare

non-fiction **I** *n* opere *fpl* non di narrativa **II** *adj*: ***~ book*** libro *m* non di narrativa

non(in)flammable *adj* non infiammabile

noninterference, nonintervention *n* non intervento *m*

non-iron *adj shirt* che non si stira, non stiro

non-member *n*: ***open to ~s*** aperto ai non iscritti

non-negotiable *adj*: ***the price is ~*** il prezzo non è negoziabile

no-no *n*: ***that's a ~*** *infml* non si fa

no-nonsense *adj approach* pragmatico

non-payment *n* mancato pagamento *m*

nonplus *v/t*: ***completely ~sed*** assolutamente perplesso

nonpolitical *adj* apolitico

nonpolluting *adj* non inquinante

non-profitmaking, *US* **non-profit** *adj* no profit *inv*

non-redeemable *adj* FIN non riscattabile

non-renewable *adj* non rinnovabile

non-resident *n in country* non residente *m/f*; *in hotel persona chi non è cliente di un albergo*; ***open to ~s*** aperto ai non residenti

nonreturnable *adj* a fondo perduto; ***~ bottle*** bottiglia *f* a perdere; ***~ deposit*** deposito *m* non rimborsabile

nonsense *n* sciocchezze *fpl*; ***don't talk ~*** non dire sciocchezze; ***~, it's easy!*** sciocchezze, è facile!; ***he will stand no ~ from anybody*** non ammetterà sciocchezze da nessuno

nonsense verse *n* LIT nonsense *m*

non sequitur *n* non sequitur *m*, *conclusione che non deriva dalle premesse*

nonskid *adj tyres* antisdrucciolevole

non-slip *adj surface* antiscivolo *inv*

non-smoker *n person* non fumatore *m*, -trice *f*

non-standard *adj* fuori standard, non di serie; *use of a word* che fa eccezione

nonstarter *n fig idea che non ha possibilità di successo*

non-stick *adj pans* antiaderente

nonstop **I** *adj flight*, *train* diretto; *chatter* continuo **II** *adv fly*, *travel* senza scalo; *chatter*, *argue* di continuo

nonswimmer *n persona che non sa nuotare*

non-union *adj* non appartenente al sindacato

nonverbal *adj* non verbale

non-violence *n* non violenza *f*

non-violent *adj* non violento

noodle[1] *npl* COOK pasta *f*

noodle[2] *n infml* sciocco *m*, -a *f*

nook *n* angolino *m*

nookie, nooky *n infml*: ***have a bit of ~*** fare sesso

noon *n* mezzogiorno *m*; ***at ~*** a mezzogiorno

no one, no-one → ***nobody***

noontime *esp US* **I** *n* mezzogiorno *m*; ***at ~*** a mezzogiorno **II** *adj* di mezzogiorno

noose *n* cappio *m*

nope *adv infml* no

no place *adv esp US infml* → ***nowhere***

nor *adv & cj* né; ***~ do I*** neanch'io, neanche a me; ***I shan't go, ~ will you*** io non andrò e nemmeno tu

Nordic *adj* nordico

norm *n* norma *f*

normal **I** *adj* normale; ***it's ~ practice*** è la normale procedura; ***he is not his ~ self*** non è se stesso; ***a higher than ~ risk of infection*** un rischio di infezione superiore alla norma **II** *n*: ***her temperature is below / above ~*** la sua temperatura è inferiore / superiore alla norma; ***when things are back to*** *or* ***return to ~*** quando le cose torneranno alla normalità; ***carry on as ~*** continuare come al solito

normality *n* normalità *f inv*; ***return to ~*** tornare alla normalità

normalize *v/t relationships* normalizzare

normally *adv* (*usually*) di solito; *in a normal way* normalmente

Norman I *adj* normanno; ***the ~ Conquest*** la conquista normanna **II** *n* normanno *m*, -a *f*

Normandy *n* Normandia *f*

Norse *adj* LING norreno

north I *n* nord *m*; ***to the ~ of*** a nord di; ***the wind is in the ~*** il vento viene da nord; ***face ~*** essere rivolto a nord; ***the North of Scotland*** il nord della Scozia **II** *adj* settentrionale, nord *inv* **III** *adv travel* verso nord; ***~ of*** a nord di

North America *n* America *f* del Nord **North American I** *n* nordamericano *m*, -a *f* **II** *adj* nordamericano

northbound *adj* diretto a nord

northeast I *n* nord-est; ***in the ~*** a nordest; ***from the ~*** da nordest **II** *adj* nordorientale; ***~ England*** Inghilterra nordorientale **III** *adv* a nordest; ***~ of*** a nordest di **northeasterly** *adj* di nordest

northerly *adj wind* settentrionale; *direction* nord *inv*

northern *adj* settentrionale; ***~ Italy*** Italia *f* settentrionale; ***Northern Irish*** *adj* nordirlandese

northerner *n* settentrionale *m/f*; ***he is a ~*** è settentrionale

Northern Ireland *n* Irlanda *f* del Nord

northernmost *adj* più settentrionale

North Korea *n* Corea *f* del Nord **North Korean I** *adj* nordcoreano **II** *n* nordcoreano *m*, -a *f* **North Pole** *n* polo *m* nord

northwards *adv travel* verso nord

northwest I *n* nordovest *m* **II** *adj* nordoccidentale; ***~ England*** Inghilterra nordoccidentale **III** *adv* a nordovest; ***~ of*** a nordovest di

northwesterly *adj* di nordovest

Norway *n* Norvegia *f*

Norwegian I *adj* norvegese **II** *n person* norvegese *m/f*; *language* norvegese *m*

Nos., nos. *abbr* (= **numbers**) numeri *mpl*

nose I *n* naso *m*; AVIAT muso *m*; ***right under my ~!*** proprio sotto il naso!; ***hold one's ~*** turarsi il naso; ***my ~ is bleeding*** mi sanguina il naso; ***follow your ~*** vai sempre a diritto; ***she always has her ~ in a book*** ha sempre il naso dentro ai libri; ***do sth under s.o.'s ~*** fare qc sotto il naso di qn; ***he can't see beyond*** *or* ***further than the end of his ~*** non riesce a vedere oltre il proprio naso; *fig* ***get up s.o.'s ~*** *infml* irritare qn; ***poke one's ~ into sth*** *fig* ficcare il naso in qc; ***you keep your ~ out of this*** *infml* non ficcare il naso; ***cut off one's ~ to spite one's face*** *prov* darsi la zappa sui piedi; ***look down one's ~ at s.o. / sth*** guardare qn / qc dall'alto in basso; ***pay through the ~*** *infml* pagare profumatamente; ***~ to tail*** *Br cars* in coda uno dietro l'altro **II** *v/t*: ***the car ~d its way into the stream of traffic*** la macchina si fece strada nel (flusso del) traffico

◆**nose about** *v/i infml* curiosare

nosebag *n Br horse* musetta *f*

noseband *n* museruola *f*

nosebleed *n* emorragia *f* nasale; ***he has a ~*** gli esce sangue dal naso

nosedive I *n* AVIAT picchiata *f*; ***the company's profits took a ~*** i profitti della società sono scesi in picchiata **II** *v/i* scendere in picchiata

nosedrops *npl* gocce *fpl* per il naso

nosegay *n* mazzolino *m* di fiori

nose ring *n* ZOOL nasiera *f*

nosey *adj* → ***nosy***

nosh I *n Br infml* (*food*) cibo **II** *v/i* mangiare

nosh-up *n* mangiata *f*

nostalgia *n* nostalgia *f*; ***overcome by feelings of ~*** sopraffatto dalla nostalgia

nostalgic *adj* nostalgico; ***feel ~ for sth*** avere nostalgia di qc

nostril *n* narice *f*

nosy *adj* (*+er*) *infml* curioso

nosy parker *n Br infml* ficcanaso *m/f*

not *adv* non; ***~ this one, that one*** non questo, quello; ***~ a lot*** non molto; ***I hope ~*** spero di no; ***I am ~ American*** non sono americano; ***he didn't help***

non ha aiutato; ***I don't know*** non so; ***he told me ~ to do that*** mi disse di non farlo; ***~ a word*** nemmeno una parola; ***~ a bit*** assolutamente no; ***~ one of them*** nessuno di loro; ***~ yet*** non ancora; ***~ me*** io no; ***~ at all*** di niente

notable *adj* notevole; ***with a few ~ exceptions*** con poche notevoli eccezioni

notary *n* notaio *m*

notation *n* notazione *f*; ***musical ~*** notazione *f* musicale

notch *n* tacca *f*

◆**notch up** *v/t sep* ottenere

note **I** *n short letter* biglietto *m*; MUS nota *f*; *memo to self* appunto *m*; *comment on text* nota *f*; *fig* ***hit / strike the right / wrong ~*** toccare il tasto giusto / sbagliato; ***on a personal ~*** con un tocco personale; ***there was a ~ of warning in his voice*** nella sua voce c'era una nota di allarme; ***take ~s*** prendere appunti; ***speak without ~s*** fare un discorso a braccio; ***take ~ of sth*** prendere nota di qc; *Br* FIN banconota *f*; ***a £5 ~*** *or* ***a five-pound ~*** una banconota da cinque sterline **II** *v/t* (*notice*) notare; (*pay attention to*) fare attenzione a; → ***note down***

◆**note down** *v/t sep* annotare

notebook *n* taccuino *m*; COMPUT notebook *m inv*

noted *adj* noto

notelet *n Br* biglietto *m* illustrato

notepad *n* bloc-notes *m inv* **notepaper** *n* carta *f* da lettere; **noteworthy** *adj* degno di nota

nothing *n* niente; ***~ but*** nient'altro che; ***~ much*** niente di speciale; ***for ~*** (*for free*) gratis; (*for no reason*) per un nonnulla; ***I'd like ~ better*** non chiedo di meglio; ***it's ~ to do with you*** non c'entri niente; ***there's ~ like ...*** non c'è niente di meglio che ...; ***£500 is ~ to her*** 500 sterline non sono niente per lei; ***it came to ~*** non ha portato a niente; ***I'd like ~ more than that*** non chiedo di meglio

nothingness *n* nulla *m*

notice **I** *n* **1.** *on notice board, in street* avviso *m*; ***at short ~*** con un breve preavviso; ***until further ~*** fino a nuovo avviso **2.** (*advance warning*) preavviso *m* **3.** *in newspaper* annuncio *m* **4.** (*leave house*) disdetta *f*; (*dismissal from job*) ***give s.o. his / her ~*** licenziare qn; ***hand in one's ~*** *to employer* presentare le dimissioni; ***four weeks' ~*** quattro settimane di preavviso **5.** (*attention*) ***take ~ of sth*** fare caso a qc; ***take no ~ of s.o. / sth*** non fare caso a qn / qc **II** *v/t* notare; ***I ~d her hesitating*** ho notato che esitava; ***get o.s. ~d*** farsi notare; ***without my noticing it*** senza che io lo notassi

noticeable *adj* sensibile; ***the stain is very ~*** la macchia è molto evidente; ***it is ~ that ...*** è evidente che...

noticeably *adv* nettamente

notice board *n* bacheca *f*

notification *n* notifica *f*

notify *v/t* ⟨*pret & past part* **-ied**⟩ informare

notion *n* idea *f*; ***I have no ~ of time*** non ho idea dell'ora; ***he got the ~ (into his head) that she wouldn't help him*** si è messo in mente che lei non l'avrebbe aiutato

notoriety *n* cattiva fama *f*

notorious *adj* famigerato; ***a ~ gambler*** un famigerato giocatore d'azzardo

notwithstanding **I** *prep* malgrado; ***she left ~ her mother's tears*** partì malgrado le lacrime della madre **II** *adv*: ***she set out, ~*** malgrado ciò, se ne è andata

nougat *n* torrone *m*

nought *n* zero *m*; *liter* niente *m*; ***come to ~*** non portare a niente

noughts and crosses *n Br* (*game*) tris *m*, filetto *m*

noun *n* nome *m*, sostantivo *m*

nourish *v/t liter* nutrire

nourishing *adj* nutriente

nourishment *n* nutrimento *m*

nous *n* PHIL intelletto *m*; *Br infml* buonsenso *m*

nouveau riche *adj* arricchito *m*, -a *f*

nouvelle cuisine *n* nouvelle cuisine *f*

nouvelle vague *n* nouvelle vague *f*

novel[1] *n* romanzo *m*

novel[2] *adj* originale

novelist *n* romanziere *m*, -a *f*

novella *n* romanzo *m* breve

novelty *n* novità *f inv*

November *n* novembre *m*

novice *n* principiante *m/f*; REL novizio *m*, -a *f*

now I *adv* ora, adesso; ***~ and again, ~ and then*** ogni tanto; ***by ~*** ormai; ***from ~ on*** d'ora in poi; ***for ~*** per il momento; ***even ~*** anche adesso; ***any day ~*** da un giorno all'altro; ***right ~*** subito; ***just ~*** (proprio) adesso; ***~, ~!*** su, su!; ***~, where did I put it?*** allora, dove l'ho messo? **II** *cj*: ***~ (that) you've seen him*** ora che lo hai visto **III** *n*: ***~ is the time to enjoy life*** è ora il momento di godersi la vita

nowadays *adv* oggigiorno

no way *adv infml*: ***would you go there? ~!*** ci andresti? niente affatto!

nowhere *adv* da nessuna parte; ***there's ~ to sit*** non c'è posto; ***it's ~ near finished*** è ben lontano dall'essere terminato; ***appear out of ~*** apparire dal nulla; ***we're getting ~*** non andremo da nessuna parte; ***rudeness will get you ~*** la maleducazione non ti porterà da nessuna parte

noxious *adj* (*harmful*) dannoso; (*toxic*) nocivo

nozzle *n* bocchetta *f*

nr *abbr* (= **near**) vicino

N.S.P.C.C *abbr* (= **National Society for the Prevention of Cruelty to Children**) *associazione per la tutela dell'infanzia*

N.S.W. *abbr* (= **New South Wales**) Nuovo Galles del Sud

NT *abbr* (= **National Trust**; **New Testament**) *ente per la salvaguardia di luoghi di interesse storico o naturalistico*; Nuovo Testamento *m*

nuance *n* sfumatura *f*

nubile *adj* attraente

nuclear *adj* nucleare

nuclear bomb *n* bomba *f* atomica **nuclear energy** *n* energia *f* nucleare **nuclear family** *n* nucleo *m* familiare **nuclear fission** *n* fissione *f* nucleare **nuclear-free** *adj* denuclearizzato **nuclear physics** *nsg* fisica *f* nucleare **nuclear power** *n* energia *f* nucleare; POL potenza *f* nucleare **nuclear powered** *adj* a energia nucleare **nuclear power station** *n* centrale *f* nucleare **nuclear reactor** *n* reattore *m* nucleare **nuclear waste** *n* scorie *fpl* radioattive **nuclear weapon** *n* arma *f* nucleare

nucleus *n* ⟨*pl* ***nuclei***⟩ nucleo *m*

nude I *adj* nudo; ***~ figure*** figura *f* nuda **II** *n* ART nudo *m*; ***in the ~*** nudo

nudge I *n* gomitata *f* **II** *v/t* dare un colpetto di gomito a

nudist *n* nudista *m/f*

nudist beach *n* spiaggia *f* nudisti

nudity *n* nudità *f inv*

nugget *n* pepita *f*; *fig of information* informazioni *fpl* preziose

nuisance *n* seccatura *f*; ***make a ~ of o.s.*** dare fastidio; ***what a ~!*** che seccatura!; *thing* ***be a ~*** dare fastidio

nuisance call *n* TEL molestia *f* telefonica

nuke I *v/t infml* distruggere con armi atomiche **II** *n infml* arma *f* atomica

null *adj* JUR nullo

null and void *adj* nullo

nullify *v/t* ⟨*pret & past part* ***-ied***⟩ rendere nullo

numb I *adj* (+*er*) intirizzito; *emotionally* impietrito; ***hands ~ with cold*** mani intirizzite dal freddo **II** *v/t* (*cold*) intirizzire; (*injection, fig*) intorpidire

number I *n* (*figure*) numero *m*, cifra *f*; (*quantity*) quantità *f inv*; ***a ~ of problems*** un certo numero di problemi; ***large ~s of people*** molte persone; ***on a ~ of occasions*** in un certo numero di occasioni; ***found in large ~s*** presente in grandi quantità; ***any ~ can play*** è ammesso qualsiasi numero di giocatori; ***boys and girls in equal ~s*** ragazzi e ragazze in numero uguale; ***in a small ~ of cases*** in un numero ridotto di casi; *of hotel room, house, phone number etc* numero *m*; ***ten in ~*** dieci di numero; ***at ~ 4*** al numero 4; ***the ~ 47 bus*** l'autobus numero 47; ***I've got the wrong ~*** ho il numero sbagliato; (*group*) ***one of their/our ~*** uno dei loro/nostri **II** *v/t put a number on* contare; ***the group ~ed 50*** il gruppo ammontava a 50; ***his days are ~ed*** ha i giorni contati

number one *n infml* cosa *f* più importante; ***all you think of is ~*** pensi solo a te stesso **number plate** *n* AUTO targa *f*

numeracy *n* capacità *f* di calcolo

numeral *n* numero *m*

numerate *adj*: ***be ~*** avere buone basi in matematica; *of children* saper contare

numerical *adj* numerico

numerous *adj* numeroso; ***on ~ occasions*** in numerose occasioni
numismatics *nsg* numismatica *f*
nun *n* suora *f*
nunnery *n* convento *m*
nurse I *n* infermiere *m*, -a *f* **II** *v/t patient* assistere; ***~ s.o. back to health*** rimettere in salute qn; ***he stood there nursing his bruised arm*** rimase lì a curarsi il braccio ferito; *desire* nutrire; (*breastfeed*) allattare; (*bear*) provare; ***she ~s a terrible grudge against him*** prova un tremendo rancore verso di lui
nursery *n school* asilo *m*; *in house* stanza *f* dei bambini; *for plants* vivaio *m*
nurseryman *n* arboricoltore *m*
nursery rhyme *n* filastrocca *f* **nursery school** *n* scuola *f* materna **nursery school teacher** *n* insegnante *m/f* di scuola materna
nursing *n* professione *f* d'infermiere; ***she went into ~*** è diventata infermiera
nursing home *n for old people* casa *f* di riposo
nurture *v/t talent* coltivare; *idea* nutrire
nut *n* noce *f*; *fig* ***a tough ~ to crack*** un osso duro; *for bolt* dado *m*; *person infml* svitato *m*, -a *f*; ***~s*** *infml* (*testicles*) palle *fpl*
nutcase *n infml* matto *m*, -a *f*
nutcrackers *npl* schiaccianoci *m inv*
nuthouse *n infml* manicomio *m*
nutmeg *n* noce *f* moscata
nutrient *n* sostanza *f* nutritiva
nutrition *n* alimentazione *f*
nutritional *adj informations* nutrizionale; *value* nutritivo
nutritionist *n* nutrizionista *m/f*
nutritious *adj* nutriente
nuts *adj infml* (*crazy*) svitato; ***be ~ about s.o.*** essere pazzo di qn
nutshell *n*: ***in a ~*** in poche parole
nutter *n Br infml* svitato *m*, -a *f*; *dangerous* pazzo *m*, -a *f*; ***he's a ~*** è un pazzo
nutty *adj* (+*er*) *taste* di noce; *infml* (*crazy*) pazzo
nuzzle I *v/t* strofinare il muso contro **II** *v/i*: ***~ (up) against s.o.*** *person*, *animal* rannicchiarsi contro qn
NW *abbr* (= **north-west**) nord-ovest *m* (NO)
NY *abbr* (= **New York**) New York *f*
nylon® I *n* nylon® *m inv* **II** *adj* di nylon
nymph *n* MYTH ninfa *f*
nymphomaniac *n* ninfomane *f*
NZ *abbr* (= **New Zealand**) Nuova Zelanda *f*

O

O, o *n* o, O *f inv*; *infml* TEL zero *m*; MED zero
oaf *n* bietolone *m*, -a *f*
oak *n tree* quercia *f*; *wood* rovere *m*
oak apple *n* galla *f* di quercia
oaken *adj* di quercia
OAP *abbr* (= **old age pensioner**) pensionato *m*, -a *f*
oar *n* remo *m*
oasis *n* ⟨*pl* ***oases***⟩ *a. fig* oasi *f inv*
oatcake *n* COOK focaccia *f* di farina d'avena
oath *n* JUR giuramento *m*; (*swearword*) imprecazione *f*; ***on ~*** sotto giuramento; ***he took an ~ of loyalty to the government*** giurò fedeltà al governo; ***be under ~*** JUR essere sotto giuramento; ***take** or **swear an ~*** giurare
oatmeal *n* farina *f* d'avena
oats *npl* avena *f*
obdurate *adj* caparbio
OBE *abbr* (= **Officer of the Order of the British Empire**) *ufficiale dell'ordine dell'impero britannico*
obedience *n* ubbidienza *f*
obedient *adj* ubbidiente
obediently *adv* docilmente
obeisance *n* riverenza *f*
obelisk *n* ARCH obelisco *m*
obese *adj* obeso
obesity *n* obesità *f inv*
obey I *v/t parents* ubbidire a; *law* os-

servare; ***I expect to be ~ed*** mi aspetto di essere ubbidito **II** *v/i* ubbidire
obfuscate *v/t* disorientare
obituary *n* necrologio *m*
object[1] *n* (*thing*) oggetto *m*; (*aim*) scopo *m*; GRAM complemento *m*; ***he was an ~ of scorn*** era oggetto di disprezzo; ***the ~ of the exercise*** lo scopo dell'esercizio; ***that defeats the ~*** ciò vanifica lo scopo; ***money is no ~*** i soldi non sono un ostacolo
object[2] **I** *v/i* avere da obiettare; ***I don't ~ to that*** non ho niente da obiettare; ***he ~s to my drinking*** è contrario al fatto che io beva; ***I ~ to people smoking in my house*** mi dà fastidio che si fumi in casa mia; ***I ~ to him bossing me around*** mi dà fastidio che mi comandi a bacchetta **II** *v/t* obiettare
objection *n* obiezione *f*; ***I have no ~*** non ho niente in contrario; ***make an ~*** (***to sth***) fare obiezione (a qc); ***are there any ~s?*** nessuna obiezione?
objectionable *adj* (*unpleasant*) antipatico; ***he's a most ~ person*** è una persona estremamente antipatica
objective **I** *adj* obiettivo **II** *n* obiettivo *m*
objectively *adv* obiettivamente
objectivity *n* obiettività *f inv*
objector *n* oppositore *m*, -trice *f*; ***he was a conscientious ~*** era obiettore di coscienza
objet d'art *n* ART object d'art *m*
objet trouvé *n* ART objet trouvé *m*
obligation *n* obbligo *m*; ***be under an ~ to s.o.*** essere in debito con qn
obligatory *adj* obbligatorio; ***attendance is ~*** la frequenza è obbligatoria; ***identity cards were made ~*** le carte d'identità sono state rese obbligatorie
oblige *v/t*: ***much ~d!*** grazie mille!; ***you are not ~d to answer this question*** non sei obbligato a rispondere a questa domanda; ***could you ~ me by opening the window?*** potrebbe essere così gentile da aprire la finestra?
obliging *adj* servizievole
oblique **I** *adj reference* indiretto **II** *n in punctuation* barra *f*
obliterate *v/t city* annientare; *memory* cancellare
oblivion *n* oblio *m*; ***fall into ~*** cadere in oblio
oblivious *adj*: ***be ~ of sth*** essere ignaro di qc; ***he was quite ~ of his surroundings*** sembrava non rendersi conto dell'ambiente circostante
oblong **I** *adj* rettangolare **II** *n* rettangolo *m*
obnoxious *adj* offensivo; ***an ~ person*** una persona offensiva; *smell* sgradevole
oboe *n* oboe *m*
obscene *adj* osceno; *salary*, *poverty* vergognoso
obscenity *n* oscenità *f inv*; ***he used an ~*** ha detto un'oscenità
obscure **I** *adj* (+*er*) oscuro; (*unknown*) sconosciuto; ***for some ~ reason*** per qualche oscuro motivo **II** *v/t view* oscurare; *truth* nascondere
obscurity *n* oscurità *f inv*
obsequious *adj* ossequioso
observable *adj* visibile
observance *n* osservanza *f*
observant *adj* osservante; ***that's very ~ of you*** sei un ottimo osservatore
observation *n* osservazione *f*; ***be under ~*** *patient* essere in osservazione; *suspect* essere sotto sorveglianza; ***he's in hospital for ~*** è in ospedale per osservazioni
observatory *n* osservatorio *m*
observe *v/t* osservare; ***~ a minute's silence*** osservare un minuto di silenzio
observer *n* osservatore *m*, -trice *f*
obsess *v/t*: ***be ~ed by/with*** essere fissato con
obsession *n* fissazione *f*; ***this ~ with order*** questa fissazione per l'ordine
obsessive *adj person*, *behaviour* ossessivo; ***be ~ about sth*** essere maniaco di qc; ***become ~*** diventare ossessivo
obsolescent *adj*: ***be ~*** diventare obsoleto; *machine* obsolescente
obsolete *adj model* obsoleto; *word* disusato, antiquato
obstacle *n a. fig* ostacolo *m*; ***be an ~ to s.o./sth*** essere di ostacolo a qn/qc
obstacle race *n* corsa *f* a ostacoli
obstetrician *n* ostetrico *m*, -a *f*
obstetrics *nsg* ostetricia *f*
obstinacy *n* ostinazione *f*
obstinate *adj* ostinato
obstinately *adv* ostinatamente

obstreperous *adj* turbolento
obstruct *v/t road, passage* ostruire; ***you're ~ing my view*** mi stai ostruendo la vista; *investigation, police* ostacolare
obstruction *n on road etc* ostruzione *f*; ***cause an ~*** ostruire; (*obstacle*) ostacolo; ***there is an ~ in the pipe*** il tubo è ostruito
obstructive *adj behaviour, tactics* ostruzionista
obtain *v/t* ottenere; ***~ sth through hard work*** ottenere qc con il duro lavoro; *possession* ottenere; ***they ~ed the release of the hostages*** hanno ottenuto il rilascio degli ostaggi
obtainable *adj products* reperibile
obtrusive *adj music* invadente; *colour* stonato
obtuse *adj fig* ottuso
obverse *n* fronte *m*
obversely frontalmente
obviate *v/t* ovviare a
obvious *adj* ovvio, evidente; ***that's the ~ solution*** è la soluzione ovvia; ***for ~ reasons*** per ovvi motivi; ***it was ~ he didn't want to come*** era evidente che non voleva venire; ***I would have thought that was perfectly ~*** avrei pensato che fosse evidente; ***with the ~ exception of …*** con l'evidente eccezione di…
obviously *adv* ovviamente, evidentemente; ***~!*** ovviamente!
occasion I *n* occasione *f*; ***on that ~*** in tale occasione; ***rise to the ~*** essere all'altezza della situazione; ***on the ~ of his birthday*** in occasione del suo compleanno; ***should the ~ arise*** se dovesse presentarsi l'occasione **II** *v/t* causare
occasional *adj* sporadico; ***I like the ~ whisky*** bevo un whisky ogni tanto; ***she made ~ visits to England*** visita sporadicamente l'Inghilterra
occasionally *adv* ogni tanto
occult I *adj* occulto **II** *n*: ***the ~*** l'occulto *m*
occupancy *n* occupazione *f*
occupant *n of vehicle* occupante *m/f*; *of building, flat* abitante *m/f*
occupation *n* (*job*) professione *f*; ***what is his ~?*** qual è la sua occupazione?; *of country* occupazione *f*; ***army of ~*** esercito *m* di occupazione
occupational hazard *n* rischio *m* professionale **occupational therapist** *n* ergoterapeuta *m/f* **occupational therapy** *n* ergoterapia *f*
occupied *adj* occupato; ***a room ~ by four people*** una stanza occupata da quattro persone; ***keep s.o. ~*** tenere qn occupato; ***he kept his mind ~*** si tiene la mente occupata
occupier *n of house* occupante *m*
occupy *v/t* ⟨*pret & past part* **-ied**⟩ occupare; ***is this seat occupied?*** è occupato questo posto?; ***~ o.s. with sth*** tenersi occupato con qc
occur *v/i* ⟨*pret & past part* **-red**⟩ accadere; ***it ~red to me that …*** mi è venuto in mente che …; ***that doesn't ~ very often*** non accade molto spesso; ***it didn't even ~ to him to ask*** non gli è nemmeno venuto in mente di chiedere
occurrence *n* evento *m*; ***further ~s of this nature must be avoided*** ulteriori eventi di questo genere devono essere evitati; ***it's a relatively rare ~*** è un evento relativamente raro
ocean *n* oceano *m*
Oceania *n* Oceania *f*
ocean liner *n* transatlantico *m*
oceanographer *n* oceanografo *m*, -a *f*
oceanography *n* oceanografia *f*
ochre, *US* **ocher** *n* ocra *f*
ocker I *adj AUS infml* australiano **II** *n AUS infml* australiano *m*
o'clock *adv*: ***at five / six ~*** alle cinque / sei; ***it's one ~*** è l'una; ***it's three ~*** sono le tre
OCR *abbr* (= **Optical Character Recognition**) OCR *f* (lettura ottica dei caratteri)
Oct *abbr* (= **October**) ottobre *m* (ott.)
octagon *n* ottagono *m*
octagonal *adj* ottagonale
octane *n* ottano *m*
octave *n* MUS ottava *f*
October *n* ottobre *m*
octopus *n* polpo *m*
OD *v/i*: *infml* ***~ on*** *drug* fare un'overdose di
odd I *adj* (+*er*) (*strange*) strano; ***how ~*** che strano; ***the ~ thing about it is that …*** la cosa strana è che …; ***it seemed ~ to me*** mi sembrava strano; (*not even*) dispari; ***the ~ one out*** l'eccezione *f*; ***50 ~*** 50 e rotti; ***~ socks*** cal-

zini spaiati; ***at ~ times*** occasionalmente; ***he likes the ~ drink*** gli piace bere di tanto in tanto; ***he does all the ~ jobs*** si occupa di tutti i lavoretti occasionali **II** *adv infml* ***he was acting a bit ~*** si comportava in modo un po' strano

oddball *n infml* persona *f* stramba; ***he's an ~*** è un tipo strambo

oddity *n* (*odd thing*) stranezza *f*

odd-jobman *n* uomo *m* tuttofare

oddly *adv* stranamente; ***an ~ shaped room*** una stanza dalla forma strana; ***~ enough*** per quanto strano

odds *npl*: ***be at ~ with*** essere in disaccordo con; ***the ~ are 10 to one*** le probabilità sono 10 contro una; ***the ~ are that …*** è probabile che …; ***against all the ~*** contro ogni aspettativa; ***be at ~ with s.o. over sth*** trovarsi in disaccordo con qn su qc

odds and ends *npl objects* cianfrusaglie *fpl*; *things to do* cose *fpl* **odds-on** *adj*: ***the ~ favourite*** il favorito; ***it's ~ that …*** è praticamente scontato che …

ode *n* ode *f* (***to, on*** a)

odious *adj* odioso

odometer *n* odometro *m*

odorous *n* odoroso

odour, *US* **odor** *n* odore *m*

odyssey *n* odissea *f*

OECD *abbr* (= **Organization for Economic Cooperation and Development**) OCSE *f* (organizzazione *f* per la cooperazione e lo sviluppo economico)

OED *abbr* (= **Oxford English Dictionary**) *dizionario Oxford della lingua inglese*

oesophagus, *US* **esophagus** *n* esofago *m*

oestrogen *n Br* estrogeno *m*

oeuvre *n* opera *f*

of *prep* di; ***the works ~ Dickens*** le opere di Dickens; ***a friend ~ mine*** un mio amico; ***the wife of the doctor*** la moglie del dottore; ***fear of God*** timor di Dio; ***his love of his father*** il suo affetto per il padre; ***it's made ~ steel*** è di acciaio; ***die ~ cancer*** morire di cancro; ***it tastes of garlic*** sa di aglio; ***very nice ~ him*** molto gentile da parte sua; ***~ the three this is …*** dei tre questo è …; ***he asked the six of us to lunch*** invitò noi sei a pranzo; ***you of all people*** tu, fra tutti; ***he warned us of the danger*** ci avvisò del pericolo; ***what of it?*** che importa?; ***a man of courage*** un uomo coraggioso; ***a girl of ten*** una bambina di dieci anni; ***that idiot of a waiter*** quell'idiota di un cameriere; ***of late*** ultimamente; ***of an evening*** *infml* di sera

off I *prep* **1.** *distance*: ***a lane ~ the main road*** *not far from* un sentiero poco lontano dalla strada principale; *leading off* un sentiero che parte dalla strada principale **2.** *price*: ***£20 ~ the price*** 20 sterline di sconto **3.** ***he's ~ his food*** ha perso l'appetito; ***he jumped ~ the roof*** saltò dal tetto; ***I got it ~ my friend*** *infml* l'ho avuto dal mio amico; ***we live ~ cheese on toast*** viviamo di toast al formaggio; ***he got £2 ~ the shirt*** ha tirato fuori dalla camicia 2 sterline **II** *adv* **1. be ~** *of light, TV etc* essere spento; *of gas, tap* essere chiuso; (*cancelled*) essere annullato; *of food* essere finito **2.** (*not at work*) ***she was ~ today*** oggi non era al lavoro; ***take a day ~*** prendere un giorno libero **3.** (*removed*) ***you've left the lid ~*** non hai messo il coperchio; ***with his trousers / hat ~*** senza pantaloni / cappello **4.** (*away*) ***we're ~ tomorrow*** *leaving* partiamo domani; ***I'm ~ to New York*** vado a New York; ***I must be ~*** devo andare; ***it's 3 miles ~*** dista 3 miglia; ***it's a long way ~*** è molto lontano; ***August isn't very far ~*** non manca molto ad agosto; ***drive ~*** partire (in macchina); ***walk ~*** allontanarsi **5.** ***~ and on*** ogni tanto **III** *adj food* andato a male; ***the fish smells a bit off*** dall'odore il pesce sembra andato a male; ***~ switch*** interruttore *m* di spegnimento

off-air *adv* TV, RADIO non in onda; ***go ~*** cessare le trasmissioni

offal *n* frattaglie *fpl*

off-balance *adj* sbilanciato

offbeat *adj* non convenzionale

off-centre, *US* **off-center** *adj/adv* fuori centro **off-chance** *n*: ***I just did it on the ~ that*** l'ho fatto nella remota possibilità che…; ***I came on the ~ of seeing her*** sono venuto per la remota possibilità di vederla **off-colour**,

US **off-color** *adj esp Br* (*unwell*) fuori fase; ***feel / be ~*** sentirsi / essere fuori fase **off-cut** *n* materiale *m* di scarto **off-duty** *adj* non in servizio
offence, *US* **offense** *n* JUR reato *m*; ***commit an ~*** commettere un reato; ***it is an ~ to …*** non è un reato…; ***take ~ at sth*** offendersi per qc; ***cause ~ to s.o.*** offendere qn; ***no ~ to the Germans, of course!*** senza offesa per i tedeschi, naturalmente!; ***no ~ (meant)*** senza offesa
offend *v/t* (*insult*) offendere
offender *n* JUR delinquente *m/f*; ***~s will be prosecuted*** i trasgressori saranno perseguiti a norma di legge; ***sex ~*** criminale *m* sessuale
offense *US* → ***offence***
offensive **I** *adj behaviour*, *remark*, offensivo; ***he was ~ to her*** è stato offensivo nei suoi confronti; *smell* sgradevole **II** *n* (MIL: *attack*) offensiva *f*; ***go onto the ~*** passare all'offensiva
offer **I** *n* offerta *f*; ***did you have many ~s of help?*** hai molte offerte di aiuto?; ***he made me an ~ (of £50)*** mi ha fatto un'offerta (di 50 sterline); ***on ~*** *available* disponibile; *at a reduced price* in offerta; ***our house is under ~*** ci hanno fatto un'offerta d'acquisto per la casa **II** *v/t* offrire; ***~ s.o. sth*** offrire qc a qn; ***~ to do sth*** offrirsi di fare qc; ***~ an opinion*** dare un'opinione
offhand **I** *adj attitude* disinvolto; ***be ~ with s.o.*** essere brusco con qn **II** *adv* su due piedi; ***I couldn't tell you ~*** non saprei dirti, così su due piedi
office *n* ufficio *m*; (*position*) carica *f*; ***be in ~*** essere in carica
office block *n* complesso *m* di uffici **office hours** *npl* orario *m* d'ufficio; ***work ~*** lavorare in orario d'ufficio **office job** *n* lavoro *m* d'ufficio **office manager(ess)** *n* capufficio *m/f* **office party** *n* festa *f* aziendale
officer *n* MIL ufficiale *m*; *in police* agente *m/f*; ***excuse me, ~*** scusi, agente
office supplies *npl* forniture *fpl* d'ufficio **office worker** *n* impiegato *m*, -a *f*
official **I** *adj* ufficiale; ***~ language*** lingua *f* ufficiale; ***is that ~?*** è ufficiale? **II** *n* funzionario *m*, -a *f*
officialdom *n pej* burocrazia *f*
officialese *n* burocratese *m*
officially *adv* ufficialmente
officiate *v/i* officiare
officious *adj* invadente
offing *n*: ***be in the ~*** essere in vista
off-key *adj* MUS fuori tono **off-licence** *n Br negozio di alcolici*
offline *adj/adv* off-line
off-peak *adj rates* ridotto; ***~ electricity*** elettricità *f* a tariffa ridotta **off-putting** *adj* poco allettante **off-road** *adj driving* fuoristrada; ***~ vehicle*** (veicolo) fuoristrada *m* **off-screen** *adj/adv* FILM, TV nella vita privata **off-season** **I** *adj rates* di bassa stagione **II** *n* bassa stagione *f*
offset *v/t* ⟨*pret & past part* **-set**⟩ *losses*, *disadvantage* compensare
offshoot *n fig of organization* diramazione *f*
offshore *adj drilling rig*, *investment* off-shore *inv* **offside** **I** *adj on vehicle* lato guidatore **II** *adv* SPORTS in fuorigioco
offspring *n* figli *mpl*; *of animal* piccoli *mpl*
offstage **I** *adj* dietro le quinte; *voice* fuori scena **II** *adv* dietro le quinte
off-the-cuff *adj* istintivo
off-the-peg *adj clothes* confezionato
off-the-record *adj* ufficioso **off-the-wall** *adj infml* bizzarro **off-white** *adj* bianco sporco
oft *adv liter* spesso
OFT *abbr* (= **Office of Fair Trading**) *ente che vigila sulla correttezza commerciale*
often *adv* spesso; ***how ~ did it happen?*** ogni quanto succedeva?; ***as ~ as not*** la maggior parte delle volte; ***every so ~*** ogni tanto; ***more ~ than not*** il più delle volte
ogle *v/t* lanciare occhiate ammiccanti a
ogre *n fig* orco *m*
oh *int* oh; *surprised*, *disappointed* ah; ***oh, good!*** bene!; ***oh, well!*** non farci caso!; ***oh dear!*** oh, santo cielo!
OHP *abbr* (= **overhead projector**) lavagna *f* luminosa
oik *n Br infml pej* idiota *m/f*
oil **I** *n* olio *m*; ART ***to paint in ~s*** dipingere a olio; *petroleum* petrolio *m*; ***strike ~*** trovare il petrolio; *for central*

heating nafta *f* **II** *v/t hinges, bearings* oliare; *fig* ***if you ~ the wheels you can get things done faster*** ungendo le ruote puoi ottenere risultati più velocemente

oilcan *n* oliatore *m* **oil change** *n* cambio *m* dell'olio **oilcloth** *n* tela *f* cerata **oil company** *n* compagnia *f* petrolifera **oilfield** *n* giacimento *m* petrolifero **oil-fired** *adj central heating* a gasolio **oil painting** *n* quadro *m* a olio **oil-producing country** *n* paese *m* produttore di petrolio **oil refinery** *n* raffineria *f* di petrolio **oil rig** *n* piattaforma *f* petrolifera **oilskins** *npl* abiti *mpl* di tela cerata **oil slick** *n* chiazza *f* di petrolio **oil spill** *n* fuoriuscita *f* di petrolio **oil tanker** *n* (*ship*) petroliera *f* **oil well** *n* pozzo *m* petrolifero

oily *adj* (+*er*) unto; *person* untuoso

ointment *n* pomata *f*

OK, ok, okay I *adj/adv infml*: ***is it ~ with you if …?*** ti va bene se …?; ***does that look ~?*** ti sembra che vada bene?; ***that's ~ by me*** per me va bene; ***are you ~?*** stai bene?; ***are you ~ for Friday?*** ti va bene venerdì?; ***he's ~*** (*is a good guy*) è in gamba; ***how's your mother? — she's ~*** come sta tua madre? – bene **II** *v/t plan* approvare; ***you have to ~ it with the boss*** devi ottenere l'approvazione del capo

old I *adj* (+*er*) **1.** vecchio; ***he's getting ~*** sta invecchiando; ***an ~ friend of mine/his*** un mio/suo vecchio amico **2.** ***how ~ are you/is he?*** quanti anni hai/ha?; ***a ten-year-~ boy*** un ragazzino di dieci anni **3.** (*previous*) precedente; ***my ~ school*** la mia vecchia scuola **4.** *infml* ***she dresses any ~ how*** si veste a casaccio; ***good ~ Tim*** *infml* il caro vecchio Tim; ***always the same ~ excuse*** sempre la stessa vecchia scusa **II** *n* (*old people*) ***the ~*** i vecchi

old age *n* vecchiaia *f* **old age pension** *n* pensione *f* di anzianità **old-age pensioner** *n* pensionato *m*, -a *f* **old bird** *n Br infml person* vecchia volpe *f infml* **old boy** *n Br* EDU ex-alunno *m* **old boy network** *n Br* associazione *f* di ex-alunni

olden *adj liter*: ***in ~ times*** *or* ***days*** un tempo

old-fashioned *adj* antiquato; **old girl** *n Br* EDU ex-alunna *f* **Old Glory** *n US* (*flag*) bandiera *f* degli Stati Uniti **old hand** *n* veterano *m*, -a *f* (***at sth*** di qc) **old hat** *adj infml* sorpassato **old lady** *n infml*: ***my ~*** mia moglie **old maid** *n* (vecchia) zitella *f* **old man** *n infml*: ***my ~*** mio marito **old master** *n* ART grande maestro *m* del passato **old people's home** *n* casa *f* di riposo (per anziani) **old-style** *adj* vecchio stile **Old Testament** *n* Antico Testamento *m* **old-timer** *n* veterano *m*, -a *f* **old wives' tale** *n* superstizione *f* da donnette

olfactory *adj* olfattivo

oligarchy *n* oligarchia *f*

olive I *n* oliva *f* **II** *adj* (*a.* **olive-coloured**) verde oliva

olive oil *n* olio *m* d'oliva **olive tree** *n* olivo *m*

Olympian *adj* MYTH olimpico; (*stately*) maestoso

Olympic I *adj* olimpico; ***~ medallist*** *Br or* ***medalist*** *US* vincitore *m*, -trice *f* di una medaglia olimpica **II** *n*: ***the ~s*** le olimpiadi

Olympic Games *npl* Olimpiadi *fpl*, giochi *mpl* olimpici

ombudsman *n* ⟨*pl* **-men**⟩ difensore *m* civico

omelette, *US* **omelet** *n* frittata *f*

omen *n* presagio *m*

ominous *adj* sinistro; *fig* ***that sounds/looks ~*** suona/ha un aspetto sinistro

ominously *adv* in modo inquietante

omission *n* omissione *f*; *on purpose* esclusione *f*

omit *v/t* ⟨*pret & past part* **-ted**⟩ omettere; *on purpose* escludere; ***~ to do sth*** tralasciare di fare qc

omnibus (*a.* **omnibus edition**) *n* (*book*) omnibus *m*

omnipotence *n* onnipotenza *f*

omnipotent *adj* onnipotente

omniscient *adj* onnisciente

omnivore *n* onnivoro *m*, -a *f*

omnivorous *adj* onnivoro

on I *prep* **1.** *place, position*: su; ***~ the table/wall*** sul tavolo/muro; ***~ the bus/train*** in autobus/treno; ***get ~ the bus/train*** salire sull'autobus/sul treno; ***have you any money ~ you?*** hai dei soldi con te?; ***he put the book on the table*** mise il libro sul tavolo; ***he hung it on the wall*** lo appese al muro; ***on the coast*** sulla costa; ***with a smile on her face*** con un sorriso sul volto; ***a ring on his finger*** un anello al dito **2.** *time*: **~ *Sunday*** domenica; **~ *Sundays*** di domenica; **~ *the 1st of June*** il primo di giugno; **~ *his arrival / departure*** al suo arrivo / alla sua partenza; **~ *hearing this*** al sentire queste parole **3.** **~ *TV / the radio*** alla tv / radio ***I'm ~ antibiotics*** sto prendendo antibiotici; ***be ~ holiday / sale / offer*** essere in vacanza / vendita / offerta **4.** ***this is ~ me*** (*I'm paying*) offro io **5.** (*concerning*) ***a talk ~ Brecht*** una conferenza su Brecht **6.** (*by means of*) ***we went on the train / bus*** andammo in treno / autobus; ***on a bicycle*** in bicicletta; ***run on oil*** andare a petrolio **7.** (*as a result of*) ***on receiving my letter*** al ricevimento della mia lettera **II** *adv* **1.** ***be ~*** *of light, TV etc* essere acceso; *of gas, tap* essere aperto; *of machine* essere in funzione; *of handbrake* essere inserito; ***it's ~ after the news*** *of programme* è dopo il notiziario; ***the meeting is ~*** *scheduled to happen* la riunione si fa **2.** ***put the lid ~*** metti il coperchio; ***with his jacket / hat ~*** con la giacca / il cappello **3.** (*happening*) ***what's ~ tonight?*** *on TV etc* cosa c'è stasera?; ***I've got something ~ tonight*** *planned* stasera ho un impegno **4.** ***you're ~*** (*I accept your offer*) *etc* d'accordo **5.** ***that's not ~*** (*not allowed, not fair*) non è giusto **6.** ***from that day on*** da quel giorno in poi; ***she went on and on*** continuò a lungo; ***he's always on at me to get my hair cut*** continua a insistere perché mi tagli i capelli **7.** *continuing* **~ *you go*** (*go ahead*) fai pure; ***walk / talk ~*** continuare a parlare / camminare; ***and so ~*** e così via; **~ *and ~*** *talk etc* senza sosta **III** *adj*: ***the ~ switch*** l'interruttore *m* d'accensione; ***leave the engine on*** lasciare il motore acceso; ***tell me when Madonna is on*** dimmi quando è in onda Madonna

once I *adv* **1.** (*one time*) una volta; **~ *again,* ~ *more*** ancora una volta; **~ *in a while*** ogni tanto; **~ *and for all*** una volta per tutte; ***for ~*** per una volta **2.** (*formerly*) un tempo; **~ *upon a time there was ...*** c'era una volta ... **3.** ***at ~*** (*immediately*) subito; ***all at ~*** (*suddenly*) improvvisamente; **(*all*) *at ~*** (*together*) contemporaneamente **II** *cj* non appena; **~ *you have finished*** non appena hai finito

once-over *n infml* rapida occhiata *f*; ***we gave him the ~*** gli abbiamo dato una rapida occhiata

oncology *n* MED oncologia *f*

oncoming *adj traffic* proveniente dalla direzione opposta

one I *n number* uno *m*; *infml* ***you are a ~!*** sei un bel tipo! **II** *adj* uno, -a; **~ *day*** un giorno; **~ *person too many*** una persona di troppo; **~ *girl was pretty, the other was ugly*** una ragazza era carina, l'altra era brutta; ***the baby is ~*** (***year old***) il bambino ha un anno; ***it is ~*** (***o'clock***) è l'una; **~ *hundred pounds*** cento sterline **III** *pron* uno *m*, -a *f*; ***which ~?*** quale?; ***that ~*** quello *m*, -a *f*; ***this ~*** questo *m*, -a *f*; **~ *by ~*** *enter, deal with* uno alla volta; **~ *another*** l'un l'altro, a vicenda; ***what can ~ say / do?*** cosa si può dire / fare?; **~ *would have thought that ...*** si sarebbe pensato che ...; ***the more ~ thinks about it ...*** più ci si pensa ...; ***the little ~s*** i piccoli; ***I for ~*** per quanto mi riguarda; ***break ~'s leg*** rompersi una gamba; ***take ~ or the other*** scegli l'uno o l'altro; ***he is ~ of us*** è uno di noi; **~ *must learn*** si deve imparare; ***help ~ another*** aiutarsi a vicenda

one-armed bandit *n* slot-machine *f inv* **one-dimensional** *adj pej* superficiale; **one-horse** *adj* mediocre; ***a ~ town*** una piccola città **one-liner** *n infml* battuta *f* di spirito **one-man band** *n suonatore ambulante che suona contemporaneamente più strumenti*; *fig infml* persona *f* che fa tutto da sè **one-man show** *n* one man show *m*, *spettacolo in cui si esibisce una sola persona* **one-night stand** *n* avventura *f* di una notte **one-off I** *n* fatto *m* eccezionale; ***that mistake*** *etc* ***was just a ~*** quell'errore fu un fatto eccezionale; *person* persona *f* eccezionale **II** *adj* unico **one-parent family** *n* famiglia *f* monogenitore **one-party** *adj* POL: **~ *state*** stato *m* monopartitico **one-piece I** *adj* intero **II** *n* (*bathing costume*) costume *m* intero **one-**

room, one-roomed *adj*: *~ **flat** Br or **apartment*** monolocale *m*
onerous *adj* oneroso
oneself *pron reflexive* si; *after prep* se stesso *m*, -a *f*, sé; ***cut ~*** tagliarsi; ***do sth ~*** fare qc da sé; ***do sth by ~*** fare qc da solo
one-sided *adj* unilaterale **one-time** *adj* ex **one-to-one** *adj discussion* a quattr'occhi; *tuition* individuale **one-track mind** *n hum*: ***have a ~*** essere fissato col sesso **one-way street** *n* strada *f* a senso unico **one-way ticket** *n* biglietto *m* di sola andata
ongoing *adj* in corso; ***~ crisis*** crisi *f inv* in corso; ***this is an ~ situation*** è una situazione in corso
onion *n* cipolla *f*
online *adj/adv* on-line *inv*; COMPUT ***~ service*** *n* servizio *m* on-line; ***~ banking*** servizio *m* bancario on-line
onlooker *n* astante *m*
only I *adv* solo; ***not ~ X but also Y*** non solo X ma anche Y; ***~ just*** a malapena; ***I ~ hope he gets here in time*** spero solo che arrivi in tempo; ***you ~ have to ask*** devi solo chiedere; ***"members ~"*** "riservato ai soci"; ***if ~ that hadn't happened*** se solo non fosse successo **II** *adj* unico; ***~ son*** unico figlio maschio; ***the ~ thing I have against it is that ...*** l'unica cosa che ho in contrario è che...; ***the ~ thing*** *or* ***problem is ...*** l'unica cosa / l'unico problema è...; ***my ~ wish*** il mio unico desiderio **III** *cj* solo (che); ***I would do it myself, ~ I don't have the time*** lo farei io stesso, solo che non ho tempo
o.n.o. *abbr* (= **or near(est) offer**) *Br in advertisements* trattabili
on-off switch *n* interruttore *m* di accensione e spegnimento
onrush *n of people* assalto *m*
on-screen *adj/adv* COMPUT video; TV, FILM sullo schermo
onset *n* inizio *m*
onshore I *adj* a riva; ***~ wind*** vento *m* dal largo **II** *adv* (*a.* **on shore**) a riva
onside *adv* SPORTS non in fuorigioco
on-site *adj* sul posto
onslaught *n* assalto *m* furibondo
on-the-job training *n* training *m inv* sul lavoro **on-the-spot** *adj fine* sul posto; *decision* immediato; *reporting* dal luogo dei fatti
onto *prep*: ***put sth ~ sth*** mettere qc sopra qc; ***get ~ the committee*** *Br* riferire al comitato; ***come ~ the market*** arrivare sul mercato; ***get ~ the next chapter*** passare al capitolo successivo; ***be ~*** *or* ***on to s.o.*** scoprire il gioco di qn; *police* essere alle costole di qn; ***I think we're ~ something*** penso che stiamo scoprendo qc
onus *n* responsabilità *f*; (*burden*) onere *m*; ***the ~ is on him*** l'onere spetta a lui
onwards *adv* in avanti; ***from ... ~*** da ... in poi
oomph *n infml* (*energy*) vitalità *f*
ooze I *v/i of liquid*, *mud* colare **II** *v/t*: ***he ~s charm*** è di una gentilezza esagerata
◆**ooze out** *v/i* filtrare; *water etc* colare
op *n infml* → ***operation***
opacity *n* opacità *f*
opal *n* opale *m/f*
opalescent *adj* opalescente
opaque *adj glass* opaco
op art *n* op art *f*
OPEC *abbr* (= **Organization of Petroleum Exporting Countries**) OPEC *f*
open I *adj* aperto; *flower* sbocciato; (*honest*, *frank*) aperto, franco; ***in the ~ air*** all'aria aperta; ***the baker is ~*** il panettiere è aperto; ***~ to the public*** aperto al pubblico; ***she gave us an ~ invitation to visit*** ci ha invitato ad andare da lei quando vogliamo; ***be ~ to suggestions*** essere aperto ai suggerimenti; ***keep one's options ~*** riservarsi di decidere; ***keep an ~ mind*** mantenere una mentalità aperta **II** *v/t* aprire; *officially exhibition* inaugurare; ***~ fire*** MIL aprire il fuoco (***on*** su) **III** *v/i of door*, *shop* aprirsi; *of flower* sbocciare; ***I couldn't get the box / bottle to ~*** non sono riuscito a fare in modo che la scatola / la bottiglia si aprisse; ***the play ~s next week*** la prima dello spettacolo sarà la prossima settimana **IV** *n*: ***in the ~*** all'aperto; ***bring sth out into the ~*** portare qc alla luce del sole
◆**open on to** *v/i +obj door* aprirsi su
◆**open out** *v/i of street* allargarsi; *of person* diventare più aperto

◆**open up** **I** *v/i of person* aprirsi **II** *v/t sep mine, new horizons* aprire; *house etc* aprire; (*start*) *shop* aprire
open-air *adj meeting, concert* all'aperto; *pool* scoperto **open day** *n giornata di apertura al pubblico* **open-ended** *adj contract etc* aperto
opener *n for tins* apriscatole *m inv*; *for bottles* apribottiglie *m inv*
opening *n in wall etc* apertura *f*; *of film, novel etc* inizio *m*; (*job going*) posto *m* vacante
opening ceremony *n* cerimonia *f* d'apertura **opening hours** *npl* orario *m* d'apertura **opening night** *n* prima *f* **opening time** *n* ora *f* d'apertura; ***what are the bank's ~s?*** qual è l'ora di apertura delle banche?
openly *adv* (*honestly, frankly*) apertamente
open-minded *adj* aperto **open-necked** *adj shirt* con il collo aperto
openness *n* franchezza *f*
open plan office *n* open space *m inv* **open ticket** *n* biglietto *m* aperto **Open University** *n* università *f* a distanza
openwork *n* lavoro *m* a traforo
opera *n* lirica *f*, opera *f*
operable *adj* MED operabile
opera glasses *npl* binocolo *m* da teatro **opera house** *n* teatro *m* dell'opera **opera singer** *n* cantante lirico *m*, -a *f*
operate **I** *v/i of company* operare; ***I don't like the way he ~s*** non mi piace come opera; *of airline, bus service* essere in servizio; *of machine* funzionare; ***~ at maximum capacity*** funzionare alla massima capacità; MED operare, intervenire **II** *v/t machine* far funzionare
◆**operate on** *v/t* MED operare
operatic *adj* lirico
operating instructions *npl* istruzioni *fpl* per l'uso **operating system** *n* COMPUT sistema *m* operativo **operating theatre**, *US* **operating room** *n* MED sala *f* operatoria
operation *n* operazione *f*; MED intervento *m* (chirurgico), operazione *f*; *of machine* funzionamento *m*; ***~s*** *of company* operazioni *fpl*; ***have an ~*** MED subire un intervento (chirurgico)
operational *adj* (*ready for use*) operativo; (*in use*) in funzione; TECH, COMM d'esercizio
operative **I** *adj* (*working*) operativo **II** *n* (*worker*) operaio *m*, -a *f*
operator *n* TEL centralinista *m/f*; *of machine* operatore *m*, -trice *f*; (*tour operator*) operatore *m* turistico
ophthalmic *adj* oftalmico
ophthalmologist *n* oftalmologo *m*, -a *f*
opiate *n* oppiato *m*
opinion *n* opinione *f*, parere *m*; ***in my ~*** a mio parere; ***it is a matter of ~*** è questione di opinioni; ***have a good*** *or* ***high / low*** *or* ***poor ~ of s.o. / sth*** avere una buona *or* alta / bassa *or* cattiva opinione di qn / qc; ***it is the ~ of the court that ...*** è opinione della corte che...; ***seek*** *or* ***get a second ~*** *esp* MED cercare un secondo parere
opinionated *adj* intransigente
opinion poll *n* sondaggio *m* d'opinione
opium *n* oppio *m*
opponent *n* avversario *m*, -a *f*
opportune *adj form* opportuno; ***at an ~ moment*** al momento opportuno
opportunist *n* opportunista *m/f*
opportunistic *adj* opportunistico
opportunity *n* opportunità *f inv*; ***take the ~ to do sth*** cogliere l'occasione per fare qc; ***as soon as I get the ~*** non appena ne avrò l'opportunità; ***equality of ~*** pari opportunità *fpl*
oppose *v/t* opporsi a; ***be ~d to ...*** essere contrario a ...; ***as ~d to ...*** piuttosto che ...
opposite **I** *adj direction* opposto; *meaning, views* contrario; *house* di fronte; ***the ~ side of the road*** l'altro lato della strada; ***the ~ sex*** l'altro sesso **II** *prep* di fronte a; ***~ the station*** di fronte alla stazione **III** *n* contrario *m*
opposite number *n* omologo *m*
opposition *n* opposizione *f*; ***the Opposition*** *esp Br* POL l'opposizione; SPORTS avversario *m*
oppress *v/t the people* opprimere
oppression *n* oppressione *f*
oppressive *adj rule, dictator* oppressivo; *weather* opprimente
opt *v/t*: ***~ to do sth*** optare per fare qc
◆**opt out** *v/i* decidere di non partecipare
optical character reader *n* COMPUT

lettore *m* ottico di caratteri **optical disk** *n* disco *m* ottico **optical fibre**, *US* **optical fiber** *n material*, *cable* fibra *f* ottica **optical illusion** *n* illusione *f* ottica
optician *n dispensing* ottico *m*, -a *f*; *ophthalmic* optometrista *m/f*
optic nerve *n* nervo *m* ottico
optics *nsg* ottica *f*
optimal *adj* ottimale
optimism *n* ottimismo *m*
optimist *n* ottimista *m/f*
optimistic *adj attitude*, *view* ottimistico; *person* ottimista
optimistically *adv* ottimisticamente
optimize *v/t* ottimizzare
optimum I *adj* ottimale II *n* optimum *m inv*
option *n* possibilità *f inv*, opzione *f*; ***he had no other ~*** non ha avuto scelta; ***you have the ~ of leaving or staying*** hai la possibilità di andartene o restare; ***keep one's ~s open*** riservarsi di decidere
optional *adj* facoltativo
optional extras *npl* optional *m inv*
optometrist *n US* (*optician*) optometrista *m/f*
opulent *adj* opulento
or *cj* o; (*otherwise*) altrimenti; ***he can't hear ~ see*** non può né sentire né vedere; ***you'd better go or*** (***else***) ***you'll be late*** sarà meglio che tu vada, altrimenti farai tardi; ***~ else!*** o guai a te!
oracle *n* oracolo *m*
oral I *adj* orale II *n exam* orale *m*
oral history *n* storia *f* orale
oral sex *n* sesso *m* orale
orange I *adj colour* arancione II *n fruit* arancia *f*; *colour* arancione *m*
orangeade *n* aranciata *f*
orange juice *n* succo *m* d'arancia **orange squash** *n* spremuta *f* d'arancia
orator *n* oratore *m*, -trice *f*
oratory *n speech* oratoria *f*; *place* oratorio *m*
orb *n liter* globo *m*, orbe *m*
orbit I *n of earth* orbita *f*; ***send sth into ~*** lanciare in orbita qc II *v/t the earth* orbitare intorno a
orchard *n* frutteto *m*
orchestra *n* orchestra *f*
orchestra pit *n* THEAT golfo *m* mistico
orchestrate *v/t* MUS orchestrare; *arrange* orchestrare
orchid *n* orchidea *f*
ordain *v/t priest* ordinare
ordeal *n* esperienza *f* traumatizzante
order I *n* **1.** ordine *m*; ***restore ~*** *to town*, *classroom* ristabilire l'ordine **2.** *for goods*, *in restaurant* ordinazione *f* **3.** ***in ~ to do sth*** così da fare qc; ***he stood down in ~ that she could get the job*** si è ritirato, così che lei potesse avere il lavoro **4.** ***out of ~*** *not functioning* guasto, fuori servizio; *not in sequence* fuori posto; ***he's out of ~*** *not doing the proper thing* si sta comportando in modo scorretto **5.** *as it should be* ***his passport was in ~*** il suo passaporto era in ordine **6.** (*commands*) ***I don't take ~s from anyone*** non accetto ordini da nessuno; ***be under ~s to do sth*** avere l'ordine di fare qc **7.** *fig* (*class*, *degree*) ordine *m*; ***something in the ~ of ten per cent*** all'incirca nell'ordine del 10 %; ***something in the ~ of one in ten applicants*** all'incirca nell'ordine di un candidato su dieci **8.** REL (*of monks etc*) ordine *m* **9.** **orders** *npl*: (**holy**) **~s** REL ordini *mpl*; **take** (**holy**) **~s** prendere gli ordini II *v/t* ordinare; ***~ s.o. to do sth*** ordinare a qn di fare qc; ***he ~ed his gun to be brought*** (***to him***) ordinò che gli venisse portata la pistola III *v/i* ordinare
◆**order around** *or* **about** *v/t sep person* dare ordini a
order form *n* modulo *m* d'ordine
orderly I *adj room*, *mind* ordinato; *crowd* disciplinato; ***in an ~ manner*** in modo ordinato II *n in hospital* inserviente *m/f*
ordinal number *n* numero *m* ordinale
ordinarily *adv* (*as a rule*) normalmente
ordinary I *adj* normale; ***the ~ Englishman*** l'inglese comune; *pej* ordinario; ***nothing out of the ~*** niente di straordinario II *n*: ***out of the ~*** straordinario
ore *n* minerale *m* grezzo
organ *n* ANAT, MUS organo *m*
organ donor *n* donatore *m*, -trice *f* di organi
organic *adj food*, *fertilizer* biologico
organically *adv grown* biologicamente
organism *n* organismo *m*
organist *n* organista *m/f*

organization *n* organizzazione *f*
organization chart *n* organigramma *m*
organize *v/t* organizzare; **~ things so that ...** organizzare le cose in modo che...; **they ~d (it) for me to go to London** hanno organizzato le cose in modo che andassi a Londra
organized crime *n* criminalità *f inv* organizzata
organizer *n person* organizzatore *m*, -trice *f*
orgasm *n* orgasmo *m*; **have an ~** provare l'orgasmo
orgy *n* orgia *f*
Orient I *n* Oriente *m* **II** *v/t* → **orientate**
Oriental I *adj* orientale **II** *n* orientale *m/f*
orientate *v/t* (*direct*) orientare; **~ o.s.** (*get bearings*) orientarsi; **money-~d** interessato al denaro; **family-~d** dedito alla famiglia
orientation *n* (*direction*) orientamento *m*; **political ~** orientamento *m* politico; **sexual ~** tendenze *fpl* sessuali
origin *n* origine *f*; **of Chinese ~** di origine cinese; **have its ~ in sth** avere origine in qc; **country of ~** paese di origine; **nobody knew the ~ of that story** nessuno conosceva l'origine di quella storia
original I *adj* originale; **~ inhabitants** abitanti *mpl* originali; **~ version** *of book* versione *f* originale **II** *n painting etc* originale *m*
originality *n* originalità *f inv*
originally *adv* (*at first*) in origine; **~ he comes from France** è di origini francesi
original sin *n* peccato *m* originale
originate I *v/t scheme, idea* dare origine a **II** *v/i of idea, belief* avere origine
originator *n of scheme etc* ideatore *m*, -trice *f*
ornament I *n* soprammobile *m* **II** *v/t* adornare
ornamental *adj* ornamentale; **be purely ~** essere puramente ornamentale; **~ garden / pond** giardino / laghetto *m* ornamentale
ornamentation *n* ornamento *m*
ornate *adj style, architecture* ornato
orphan I *n* orfano *m*, -a *f* **II** *v/t*: **he was ~ed at the age of ten** è rimasto orfano all'età di dieci anni
orphanage *n* orfanotrofio *m*
orthodontist *n* ortodontista *m/f*
orthodox *adj a. fig* ortodosso
orthopaedic *adj* ortopedico; **~ surgeon** chirurgo *m* ortopedico
oscillate *v/i* oscillare
ostensibly *adv* apparentemente
ostentation *n* ostentazione *f*
ostentatious *adj* ostentato
ostentatiously *adv* con ostentazione
osteopath *n* osteopata *m/f*
ostracize *v/t* ostracizzare
ostrich *n* struzzo *m*
other I *adj* altro; **the ~ day** l'altro giorno; **every ~ day** a giorni alterni; **every ~ person** una persona su due; **any ~ questions?** altre domande?; **some writer or ~** uno scrittore o l'altro **II** *n* l'altro *m*, -a *f*; **the ~s** gli altri; **can you tell one from the ~?** puoi distinguerli l'uno dall'altro? **III** *pron*: **it was none ~ than my father** non era altri che mio padre
otherwise *adv* altrimenti; (*differently*) diversamente; **I am ~ engaged** *form* ho altri impegni; **Richard I, ~ known as the Lionheart** Riccardo I, altrimenti noto come Cuor di Leone; **you seem to think ~** sembri pensarla diversamente
otherworldly *adj* spirituale
OTT *abbr* (= **over the top**) *infml* esagerato
otter *n* lontra *f*
ouch *int* ahi
ought *v/mod*: **I / you ~ to know** dovrei / dovresti saperlo; **you ~ to have done it** avresti dovuto farlo; **you ~ to see that film** dovresti vedere quel film; **he ~ to win the race** dovresti vincere la gara; **he ~ to have left by now** dovrebbe essersene andato ormai; **... and I ~ to know!** ... e dovrei saperlo!
ounce *n* oncia *f*
our *adj* il nostro *m*, la nostra *f*, i nostri *mpl*, le nostre *fpl*; **~ brother / sister** nostro fratello / nostra sorella
ours *pron* il nostro *m*, la nostra *f*, i nostri *mpl*, le nostre *fpl*
ourselves *pron reflexive* ci; *emphatic* noi stessi / noi stesse; *after prep* noi; **we did it ~** l'abbiamo fatto noi (stessi / stesse); **we talked about ~** abbiamo parlato di noi; **by ~** da soli
oust *v/t from office* esautorare; **~ s.o.**

from power estromettere qn dal potere

out I *adv* **1.** ***be ~*** *of light, fire* essere spento; *of flower* essere sbocciato; *of sun* splendere; ***the tide is ~*** la marea si è ritirata; *not at home, not in building* essere fuori; *of calculations* essere sbagliato; ***you're not far ~*** non sei lontano; *be published* essere uscito; *of secret* essere svelato; *no longer in competition* essere eliminato; *of workers* essere in sciopero; (*no longer in fashion*) essere out **2.** ***~ here in Dallas*** qui a Dallas **3.** *outside, not in* ***he's ~ in the garden*** è in giardino; (***get***) ***~!*** fuori!; (***get***) ***~ of my room!*** fuori dalla mia stanza! **4.** ***that's ~!*** (*out of the question*) è fuori discussione! **5.** ***he's ~ to win*** *fully intends to* è deciso a vincere **6.** ***when he was ~ in Persia*** quando era in Persia; ***go ~ to China*** andare in Cina **7.** (*lacking*) ***we're ~ of coffee*** siamo senza caffè **II** *prep* fuori (da); ***go ~ the door*** uscire dalla porta; → ***out of*** **III** *v/t homosexual* rivelare l'omosessualità di

outback *n in Australia* outback *m inv*

outboard motor *n* motore *m* fuoribordo

outbound *adj*: ***~ flight*** volo *m* all'estero

outbox *n e-mail* posta *f* in uscita

outbreak *n of war, disease* scoppio *m*

outbuilding *n* annesso *m*

outburst *n emotional* reazione *f* violenta; ***~ of anger*** esplosione *f* di rabbia

outcast *n* emarginato *m*, -a *f*

outclass *v/t* surclassare

outcome *n* risultato *m*

outcrop *n* GEOL: ***an ~*** (***of rock***) un affioramento (di roccia)

outcry *n* protesta *f*

outdated *adj* sorpassato

outdistance *v/t* staccare

outdo *v/t* ⟨*pret* ***-did***, *past part* ***-done***⟩ superare; ***but Jimmy was not to be ~ne*** Jimmy non si fece superare

outdoor *adj toilet, activities, life* all'aperto; *swimming pool* scoperto

outdoors *adv* all'aperto

outer *adj wall etc* esterno

outer space *n* spazio *m* intergalattico

outfit I *n* (*clothes*) completo *m*; (*company, organization*) organizzazione *f* **II** *v/t* equipaggiare

outgoing *adj flight, mail* in partenza; *personality* estroverso

outgoings *npl* FIN spese *fpl*

outgrow *v/t* ⟨*pret* ***-grew***, *past part* ***-grown***⟩ *bad habits, interests* perdere

outing *n* (*trip*) gita *f*

outlast *v/t* durare più di

outlaw I *n* fuorilegge *m/f inv* **II** *v/t activity* dichiarare illegale

outlay *n* FIN spesa *f*

outlet *n of pipe* scarico *m*; *for sales* punto *m* di vendita

outline I *n of person, building etc* profilo *m*; ***he drew the ~ of a head*** disegnò il profilo di una testa; *of plan, novel* abbozzo *m*; ***just give*** (***me***) ***the broad ~s*** dammi soltanto lo schema generale **II** *v/t plans etc* abbozzare

outlive *v/t* sopravvivere a

outlook *n* (*prospects*) prospettiva *f*

outlying *adj areas* periferico

outnumber *v/t* superare numericamente; ***we were ~ed*** (***by them***) eravamo in inferiorità numerica

out of *prep* **1.** *motion* fuori; ***fall ~ the window*** cadere fuori dalla finestra **2.** *position* da; ***20 miles ~ Newcastle*** 20 miglia da Newcastle **3.** *cause* per; ***~ jealousy / curiosity*** per gelosia / curiosità **4.** *without* senza; ***we're ~ petrol / beer*** siamo senza benzina / birra **5.** *from a group* su; ***5 ~ 10*** 5 su 10

out-of-date *adj passport* scaduto; *values* superato **out-of-place** *adj*, **out of place** *adj remark etc* fuori luogo **out-of-pocket** *adj*, **out of pocket** *adj Br*: ***be out of pocket*** averci rimesso; ***I was £5 out of pocket*** ci avevo rimesso 5 sterline **out-of-the-way** *adj* fuori mano

outpatient *n* paziente *m/f* esterno, -a

outpatients' (clinic) *n* ambulatorio *m*

outperform *v/t of machine, investment* rendere meglio di; *of company, economy* andare meglio di

outpost *n* avamposto *m*

output I *n of factory* produzione *f*; COMPUT output *m inv* **II** *v/t* ⟨*pret & past part* ***-ted*** *or* ***output***⟩ (*produce*) produrre; COMPUT: *signal* emettere

outrage I *n feeling* sdegno *m*; *act* atrocità *f inv* **II** *v/t* indignare

outrageous *adj acts* scioccante; *prices*

scandaloso; ***it's absolutely ~ that …*** è assolutamente scandaloso che…
outré *adj* eccentrico
outreach **I** *v/t* eccedere **II** *n* raggio *m* d'azione
outrider *n on motorcycle* motociclista *m/f* di scorta
outright **I** *adj winner* assoluto **II** *adv win* nettamente; *kill* sul colpo
outrun *v/t* ⟨*pret* ***-ran***, *past part* ***-run***⟩ *u. fig* superare; *run faster than* correre più veloce di
outset *n*: ***at / from the ~*** all' / dall'inizio
outshine *v/t* ⟨*pret & past part* ***-shone***⟩ eclissare
outside **I** *adj surface*, *wall*, *lane* esterno; ***the ~ of the car is green*** l'esterno della macchina è verde; ***open the door from the ~*** aprire la porta dall'esterno; *unlikely*: ***~ chance*** remota possibilità *f* **II** *adv sit*, *go* fuori **III** *prep* fuori da; ***~ California*** fuori dalla California; (*apart from*) al di fuori di **IV** *n of building*, *case etc* esterno *m*; ***at the ~*** al massimo
outside broadcast *n* trasmissione *f* in esterni
outsider *n* estraneo *m*, -a *f*; *in election*, *race* outsider *m inv*
outsize *adj clothing* di taglia forte
outskirts *npl* periferia *f*
outsmart *v/t* → ***outwit***
outsource *v/t work* appaltare ad aziende esterne
outspoken *adj* franco
outstanding *adj success*, *writer* eccezionale; FIN: *invoice*, *sums* da saldare
outstay *v/t*: ***I don't want to ~ my welcome*** non voglio trattenermi più del necessario
outstretched *adj hands* teso
out tray *n* vaschetta *f* della corrispondenza in partenza
outvote *v/t* mettere in minoranza
outward *adj appearance* esteriore; ***he put on an ~ show of confidence*** faceva esteriormente mostra di sicurezza; ***~ journey*** viaggio *m* d'andata
outwardly *adv* esteriormente
outweigh *v/t* contare più di
outwit *v/t* ⟨*pret & past part* ***-ted***⟩ riuscire a gabbare
outworker *n* lavoratore *m*, -trice *f* a domicilio
oval *adj* ovale
ovary *n* ovaia *f*
ovation *n* ovazione *f*; ***she was given a standing ~*** il pubblico s'è alzato in piedi per applaudirla
oven *n in kitchen* forno *m*; *in factory* fornace *f*; ***cook in a hot / moderate / slow ~*** cuocere in forno a temperatura elevata / moderata / bassa; ***it's like an ~ in here*** qui è un forno
oven glove, oven mitt *n* guanto *m* da forno **ovenproof** *adj* pirofilo **oven-ready** *adj* pronto da mettere al forno
over **I** *prep* **1.** (*above*) sopra, su **2.** (*across*) dall'altra parte; ***hit s.o. ~ the head*** colpire qn sulla testa; ***look ~ the wall*** guardare oltre il muro **3.** (*more than*) oltre **4.** (*during*) nel corso di; ***let's talk ~ a meal*** parliamone a pranzo; ***~ Christmas*** nel periodo di Natale; ***the visits were spread ~ several months*** le visite furono distribuite nel corso di sei mesi **5.** ***~ the phone*** al telefono **6.** (*everywhere*) ***travel all ~ Brazil*** girare tutto il Brasile; ***you find them all ~ Brazil*** si trovano dappertutto in Brasile **7.** ***we're ~ the worst*** il peggio è passato **8.** ***~ and above*** oltre a; ***~ and above that*** oltre a ciò; ***well ~ a year ago*** ben oltre un anno fa; ***~ the summer*** nel corso dell'estate; ***~ the years*** nel corso degli anni **II** *adv* **1.** ***be ~*** (*finished*) essere finito; (*left*) essere rimasto **2.** ***~ to you*** (*your turn*) tocca a te; ***and now ~ to Paris where …*** passiamo ora a Parigi, dove… **3.** *place*: ***~ in Japan*** in Giappone; ***~ here / there*** qui / lì **4.** (*everywhere*) ***it hurts all ~*** mi fa male dappertutto; ***painted white all ~*** tutto dipinto di bianco **5.** (*ended*) ***it's all ~*** è finito **6.** (*repeated*) ***I've told you ~ and ~ again*** te l'ho detto mille volte; ***do sth ~ again*** rifare qc
overabundance *n* sovrabbondanza *f*
overact *v/i* recitare con troppa enfasi
overage *adj* troppo vecchio
overall **I** *adj length* totale **II** *adv measure* complessivamente; (*in general*) nell'insieme
overalls *npl* tuta *f* da lavoro
overawe *v/t* intimidire; ***be ~d by s.o. / sth*** essere intimidito da qn / qc
overbalance *v/i* perdere l'equilibrio
overbearing *adj* autoritario
overblown *adv* spampanato

overboard *adv*: ***man ~!*** uomo in mare!; ***go ~ for s.o. / sth*** entusiasmarsi per qn / qc
overbook *v/t flight* prenotare in overbooking
overcast *adj day, sky* nuvoloso
overcharge *v/t customer* far pagare più del dovuto a; ***they ~d me by £2*** mi hanno fatto pagare 2 sterline in più
overcoat *n* cappotto *m*
overcome *v/t* ⟨*pret* **-came**, *past part* **-come**⟩ *difficulties, shyness* superare; ***be ~ by emotion*** essere sopraffatto dall'emozione; ***he was ~ by the fumes*** fu sopraffatto dalle esalazioni
overcrowded *adj* sovraffollato
overdo *v/t* ⟨*pret* **-did**, *past part* **-done**⟩ (*exaggerate*) esagerare; *in cooking* stracuocere; ***you're ~ing things*** *taking on too much* ti stai strapazzando; ***I'm afraid you've rather overdone it with the garlic*** temo tu abbia un po' esagerato con l'aglio
overdone *adj meat* stracotto
overdose **I** *n* overdose *f inv* **II** *v/i* prendere una dose eccessiva di; ***~ on heroin*** farsi un'overdose di eroina
overdraft *n* scoperto *m* (di conto); ***have an ~*** avere il conto scoperto; ***~ facility*** facilitazione *f* di scoperto
overdraw *v/t* ⟨*pret* **-drew**, *past part* **-drawn**⟩: ***~ one's account*** andare allo scoperto; ***be £800 ~n*** essere (allo) scoperto di 800 sterline
overdressed *adj* troppo elegante; ***I felt distinctly ~ for the occasion*** mi sentivo decisamente troppo elegante per l'occasione
overdrive *n* AUTO overdrive *m inv*
overdue *adj bill, rent* arretrato; *train, baby* in ritardo
overeat *v/i* ⟨*pret* **-ate**, *past part* **-eaten**⟩ esagerare nel mangiare
overestimate *v/t abilities, value* sovrastimare
overexcited *adj* sovreccitato
overexpose *v/t photograph* sovraesporre
overflow[1] *n pipe* troppopieno *m inv*
overflow[2] **I** *v/i of water* traboccare; *of river* straripare **II** *v/t*: ***the river has ~ed its banks*** il fiume è straripato; ***the crowd ~ed into the street*** la folla si riversò in strada
overgrown *adj garden* coperto d'erbacce; ***he's an ~ baby*** è un bambinone
overhang *v/t* ⟨*pret & past part* **-hung**⟩ sporgere sopra
overhaul *v/t engine* revisionare; *plans* rivedere
overhead[1] *adj lights, cables* in alto, aereo; *railway* soprelevato
overhead[2] *nsg US* FIN costi *mpl* di gestione; ***travel ~*** spese *fpl* di viaggio
overhead kick *n in football* rovesciata *f* **overhead projector** *n* lavagna *f* luminosa
overheads *npl* FIN costi *mpl* di gestione; ***travel ~*** spese *fpl* di viaggio
overhear *v/t* ⟨*pret & past part* **-heard**⟩ sentire per caso; ***we don't want him to ~ us*** non vogliamo che per caso ci senta; ***I ~d them plotting*** li ho sentiti per caso complottare
overheated *adj room, engine* surriscaldato
overjoyed *adj* felicissimo
overkill *n*: ***that's ~*** è un'esagerazione
overland *adj/adv* via terra
overlap *v/i* ⟨*pret & past part* **-ped**⟩ (*partly cover*) sovrapporsi; (*partly coincide*) coincidere
overleaf *adv*: ***see ~*** a tergo
overload *v/t* sovraccaricare
overlook *v/t of tall building etc* dominare, dare su; *deliberately* chiudere un occhio su; ***I am prepared to ~ it this time*** sono disposto a chiudere un occhio stavolta; *accidentally* non notare; ***the room ~s the garden*** la stanza dà sul giardino
overly *adv* troppo; ***not ~ ...*** non particolarmente ...
overnight **I** *adv travel* di notte; *stay* per la notte **II** *adj stop* notturno; ***~ stay*** pernottamento *m*
overnight bag *n* piccola borsa *f* da viaggio
overpaid *adj* strapagato
overpopulated *adj* sovrappopolato
overpower *v/t physically* sopraffare
overpowering *adj smell* asfissiante; *sense of guilt* opprimente; ***I felt an ~ desire ...*** sentivo il desiderio irresistibile...
overpriced *adj* troppo caro
overrated *adj* sopravvalutato
overreact *v/i* reagire in modo eccessi-

vo

override *v/t* ⟨*pret* ***-rode****, past part* ***-ridden***⟩ annullare; *person* annullare la decisione di; (*be more important than*) prevalere su

overriding *adj concern* principale

overripe *adj* troppo maturo

overrule *v/t decision* annullare

overrun **I** *v/t* ⟨*pret* ***-ran****, past part* ***-run***⟩ *country* invadere; *time* sforare; ***be ~ with*** essere invaso da **II** *v/i in time* sforare; ***his speech overran by ten minutes*** il suo discorso sforò di dieci minuti

overseas *adj, adv* all'estero; ***~ student*** studente *m* straniero; ***from ~*** dall'estero

oversee *v/t* ⟨*pret* ***-saw****, past part* ***-seen***⟩ sorvegliare

overshadow *v/t fig* eclissare

overshoot *v/t* ⟨*pret & past part* ***-shot***⟩ superare

oversight *n* svista *f*; ***through an ~*** per una svista

oversimplification *n* semplificazione *f* eccessiva

oversimplify *v/t* ⟨*pret & past part* ***-ied***⟩ semplificare troppo

oversleep *v/i* ⟨*pret & past part* ***-slept***⟩ non svegliarsi in tempo

overspend *v/i* ⟨*pret & past part* ***overspent***⟩ spendere troppo; ***we've overspent by £10*** abbiamo speso 10 sterline in più

overstaffed *adj* con esubero di personale

overstate *v/t* esagerare

overstatement *n* esagerazione *f*

overstep *v/t* ⟨*pret & past part* ***-ped***⟩: *fig* ***~ the mark*** passare il segno

oversubscribed *adj*: ***the zoo outing was ~*** per la gita allo zoo c'è stato un numero eccessivo di adesioni

overtake *v/t* ⟨*pret* ***-took****, past part* ***-taken***⟩ *in work, development* superare; AUTO sorpassare

over-the-counter *adj* da banco

overthrow[1] *v/t* ⟨*pret* ***-threw****, past part* ***-thrown***⟩ *government* rovesciare

overthrow[2] *n of government* rovesciamento *m*

overtime *Br* **I** *n* straordinario *m*; ***I am doing ~*** sto facendo gli straordinari **II** *adv*: ***work ~*** fare lo straordinario

overtones *npl* sfumatura *f*

overture *n* MUS ouverture *f inv*; ***make ~s to*** fare approcci a

overturn **I** *v/t vehicle, object* ribaltare; *government* rovesciare **II** *v/i of vehicle* ribaltarsi

overview *n* visione *f* d'insieme

overweight *adj* sovrappeso

overwhelm *v/t with work* oberare; *with emotion* sopraffare; ***be ~ed by*** *by response* essere colpito da; ***he was ~ed when they gave him the present*** rimase colpito quando gli consegnarono il regalo

overwhelming *adj feeling* profondo; *majority* schiacciante

overwork **I** *n* lavoro *m* eccessivo **II** *v/i* lavorare troppo **III** *v/t* far lavorare troppo

ovulate *v/i woman* ovulare

owe *v/t* dovere; ***~ s.o. £500*** dovere £500 a qn; ***I still ~ him for the meal*** gli devo ancora dei soldi per il pasto; ***~ s.o. an apology*** dovere delle scuse a qn; ***how much do I ~ you?*** quanto le devo?

owing to *prep* a causa di

owl *n* gufo *m*

own[1] *v/t* possedere; ***who ~s that?*** chi è il proprietario?; ***he looks as if he ~s the place*** *infml* si comporta come se fosse il padrone

own[2] **I** *adj* proprio; ***my ~ car*** la mia macchina; ***my very ~ mother*** proprio mia madre **II** *pron*: ***a car of my ~*** un'auto tutta mia; ***on my / his ~*** da solo; ***it has a beauty all its ~*** *or* ***of its ~*** ha una bellezza tutta sua; ***get one's ~ back on s.o.*** *esp Br* prendersi la rivincita su qn

◆**own up** *v/i* ammettere; ***own up to sth / to doing sth*** ammettere qc / di aver fatto qc; ***he owned up to stealing the money*** ammise di aver rubato il denaro

owner *n* proprietario *m*, -a *f*

ownership *n* proprietà *f inv*; ***under new ~*** nuova gestione

own goal *n in football* autogoal *m inv*; ***score an ~*** fare autogoal

ox *n* ⟨*pl* ***oxen***⟩ bue *m*

oxblood red *n* rosso *m* sangue di bue

Oxbridge *n le università di Oxford e Cambridge*

oxide *n* ossido *m*

oxidize *v/t* ossidare

oxtail soup *n* zuppa *f* di coda di bue
oxygen *n* ossigeno *m*; *~ mask* maschera *f* a ossigeno; *~ tent* tenda *f* a ossigeno
oyster *n* ostrica *f*; ***the world's his ~*** il mondo è tuo
oz *abbr* (= **ounce(s)**) oncia *f*
Oz *abbr* (= **Australia**) *infml* Australia *f*
ozone *n* ozono *m*
ozone-friendly *adj* non dannoso all'ozono **ozone layer** *n* fascia *f or* strato *m* d'ozono; ***a hole in the ~*** un buco nell'ozono

P

P, p *n* p, P *f inv*
p *abbr* (**= penny; pence**) penny *m inv*
pa *n infml* papà *m*
p. a. *abbr* (= **per annum**) all'anno
Pa. *abbr* (= **Pennsylvania**) Pennsylvania *f*
PA *abbr* (= **personal assistant**) assistente *m/f* personale
P / A *abbr* (= **power of attorney**) procura *f*
pace I *n* (*step*) passo *m*; ***put s.o. through his ~s*** *fig* mettere qn alla prova; ***quicken one's ~*** affrettare il passo; (*working*) ritmo; (*speed*) ritmo *m*; ***at a good ~*** ad una buona andatura; ***at a slow ~*** lentamente; ***at one's own ~*** al proprio ritmo; ***keep ~ with sth*** andare al passo con qs; ***set the ~*** dare il passo; ***I'm getting old, I can't stand the ~ any more*** *infml* sto diventanto vecchio, non riesco più a stare al passo **II** *v/i*: ***~ up and down*** camminare su e giù
pacemaker *n* MED pacemaker *m inv*; SPORTS battistrada *m inv*
Pacific *n*: ***the ~*** (***Ocean***) il Pacifico
pacification *n* pacificazione *f*
pacifier *n US for baby* ciuccio *m*
pacifism *n* pacifismo *m*
pacifist *n* pacifista *m/f*
pacify *v/t* ⟨*pret & past part* **-ied**⟩ placare
pack I *v/t bag* fare; *item of clothing etc* mettere in valigia; *goods* imballare; *groceries* imbustare; *crate etc* riempire; *meat in tin etc* mettere in scatola; ***the snow on the path was ~ed hard*** la neve sul vialetto era diventata molto compatta; ***the film ~s a real punch*** *fig* quel film è un pugno nello stomaco **II** *v/i* fare la valigia / le valigie; ***the crowds ~ed into the stadium*** la folla si è ammassata nello stadio; ***we all ~ed into one car*** ci siamo stipati tutti in un'auto; *infml* ***send s.o. ~ing*** togliersi qn dai piedi **III** *n* (*backpack*) zaino *m*; *of cereal*, *food* confezione *f*; *of cigarettes* pacchetto *m*; *of peas etc* confezione *f*; *of cards* mazzo *m*; *on animal* soma *f*; *of wolves* branco *m*; ***a ~ of lies*** un mucchio di bugie; ***a ~ of thieves*** una banda di ladri
◆**pack away** *v/t sep* mettere via; ***I've packed all your books away in the attic*** ho riposto tutti i tuoi libri in soffitta
◆**pack in** *v/t sep infml job*, *boyfriend* mollare
◆**pack off** *v/t sep* ***she packed them off to bed*** li ha spediti tutti a letto
◆**pack out** *v/t sep usu pass*: ***be packed out*** essere gremito di gente
◆**pack up I** *v/t sep* mettere in valigia **II** *v/i* fare i bagagli; *Br infml* (*engine*) piantarsi; (*person*) piantarla; ***he just packed up and left*** ha fatto i bagagli ed è partito
package I *n* (*parcel*) pacco *m*; *of offers etc* pacchetto *m*; ***software ~*** pacchetto di software **II** *v/t* confezionare
package deal *n for holiday* offerta *f* tutto compreso **package holiday** *n* viaggio *m* organizzato
packager *n* TYPO, FILM packager *m/f inv*
packaging *n a. fig* confezione *f*
packed *adj* (*crowded*) affollato
packed lunch *n* cestino *m* pranzo
packet *n* confezione *f*; *of cigarettes*, *crisps* pacchetto *m*; ***cost a ~*** costare

una barca di soldi

pack horse *n* cavallo *m* da soma; **pack ice** *n* banchisa *f*

packing *n*: ***do one's ~*** fare le valigie

packing case *n* cassa *f* da imballaggio

pact *n* patto *m*; ***make a ~ with s.o.*** fare un patto con qn

pad[1] **I** *n piece of cloth etc* tampone *m*; *for writing* blocchetto *m*; (*brake pad etc*) pastiglia *f*; *of paw* cuscinetto *m* carnoso; *infml* (*home*) casa **II** *v/t* 〈*pret & past part* **-ded**〉 *with material* imbottire; *speech*, *report* farcire

◆ **pad out** *v/t sep essay* infarcire

pad[2] *v/i* (*move quietly*) camminare a passi felpati

◆ **pad about, around** *v/i* camminare con passo felpato

padded *adj jacket*, *shoulders* imbottito

padding *n material* imbottitura *f*; *in speech etc* riempitivo *m*

paddle I *n for canoe* pagaia *f* **II** *v/i in canoe* pagaiare; *in water* sguazzare **III** *v/t boat* muovere una canoa con remi o pagoie n n

paddle boat *n* barca *f* a pale; **paddle steamer** *n* piroscafo *m* a ruota

paddling pool *n* piscinetta *f* per bambini

paddock *n* paddock *m inv*

paddy *n* (*a.* **paddy field**) risaia *f*

padlock I *n* lucchetto *m* **II** *v/t gate* chiudere col lucchetto; ***~ X to Y*** fissare col lucchetto X a Y

paediatric, *US* **pediatric** *adj* pediatrico

paediatrician, *US* **pediatrician** *n* pediatra *m/f*

paediatrics, *US* **pediatrics** *nsg* pediatria *f*

paedophile, *US* **pedophile** *n* pedofilo *m*, -a *f*

pagan *n/adj* pagano *m*, -a *f*

page[1] *n of book etc* pagina *f*

page[2] **I** *n* (*a.* **pageboy**) paggio *m* **II** *v/t* (*call*) chiamare con l'altoparlante; *with pager* chiamare col cercapersone; ***paging Mr Cousin*** il signor Cousin al telefono

pageant *n* (*show*) ricostruzione *f* storica; (*procession*) corteo *m* storico

pageantry *n* pompa *f*

pageboy *n* paggio *m*; *Br at wedding*: paggetto *m*

page break *n* COMPUT interruzione *f* di pagina

pager *n* cercapersone *m inv*

paginate *v/t document* numerare le pagine di

pagination *n* paginatura *f*

pagoda *n* pagoda *f*

paid I *pret & past part* → **pay II** *adj work* retribuito; *esp Br* ***put ~ to sth*** mettere fine a qc; ***that's put ~ to my weekend*** quello ha messo fine al mio weekend

paid employment *n* occupazione *f* rimunerata

pail *n* secchio *m*

pain I *n* dolore *m*; ***be in ~*** soffrire; ***take ~s to …*** fare il possibile per …; ***she takes great ~s with her appearance*** si dà molta pena per il suo aspetto; ***a ~ in the neck*** *or* ***arse*** *Br infml* una rottura *f* di scatole / palle *infml* **II** *v/t* (*mentally*) addolorare; ***it ~s me to see their ignorance*** mi addolora vedere la loro ignoranza

pain barrier *n* soglia *f* del dolore

pained *adj expression* afflitto

painful *adj* (*distressing*) doloroso; (*laborious*) difficile; ***my leg is still ~*** la gamba mi fa ancora male; ***it is my ~ duty to inform you …*** siamo addolorati di comunicarle …

painfully *adv* (*extremely*, *acutely*) estremamente; ***it was ~ obvious*** era fin troppo ovvio

painkiller *n* analgesico *m*

painless *adj* indolore; ***don't worry, it's quite ~*** *infml* non preoccuparti, non fa male

painstaking *adj* accurato

painstakingly *adv* meticolosamente

paint I *n for wall*, *car* vernice *f*; *for artist* colore *m*; ***wet ~*** pittura *f* fresca **II** *v/t wall etc* pitturare; *picture* dipingere; ***~ one's face*** (*with make-up*) imbellettarsi; ***~ the town red*** *infml* fare baldoria; ***he ~ed a very convincing picture of life on the moon*** ha dipinto un'immagine molto convincente della vita sulla musica **III** *v/i as art form* dipingere

paintbox *n* scatola *f* dei colori

paintbrush *n* pennello *m*

painter *n decorator* imbianchino *m*; *artist* pittore *m*, -trice *f*

painting *n activity* pittura *f*; (*picture*) quadro *m*

paint stripper *n* sverniciatore *m*
paintwork *n* vernice *f*
pair I *n* paio *m*; ***buy a ~ of socks*** comprare un paio di calzini; ***I've only got one ~ of hands*** ho solo un paio di mani; *of objects* paio *m*; *of animals, people* coppia *f*; ***a ~ of shoes*** un paio di scarpe; ***a ~ of scissors*** un paio di forbici **II** *v/t*: ***I was ~ed with Bob for the next round*** sono stato messo in coppia con Bob per il prossimo round
◆**pair off** *v/i people* mettersi insieme
pajamas *US* → ***pyjamas***
Paki *pej infml* **I** *n* (*person*) pachistano *m*, -a *f* **II** *adj* pachistano
Pakistan *n* Pakistan *m*
Pakistani I *n* pakistano *m*, -a *f* **II** *adj* pakistano
pal *n infml* (*friend*) amico *m*, -a *f*
PAL *abbr* (= **Phase alternation line**) TV PAL *m*
palace *n* palazzo *m* signorile
palatable *adj* gradevole
palate *n* palato *m*
palatial *adj* sfarzoso
palaver *n infml* preoccupazione *f* inutile
pale[1] **I** *adj* (*+er*) *person* pallido; ***~ pink / blue*** rosa / celeste pallido; ***go*** *or* ***turn ~*** impallidire **II** *v/i* (*person*) impallidire; *fig* ***~ into insignificance*** impallidire
pale[2] *n* (*stake*) recintare con uno steccato
Palestine *n* Palestina *f*
Palestinian I *n* palestinese *m/f* **II** *adj* palestinese
palette *n* tavolozza *f*
palette knife *n* mestichino *m*
paling *n* (*fence*) paletto *m*
palisade *n* palizzata *f*
pallbearer *n persona che porta la bara a un funerale*
pallet *n* pallet *m inv*
pallid *adj person* pallido
pallor *n* pallore *m*
palm[1] *n tree* palma *f*
palm[2] *n of hand* palma *f*; ***he had the audience in the ~ of his hand*** aveva il pubblico in pugno; ***read s.o.'s ~*** leggere la mano a qn
◆**palm off** *v/t sep infml rubbish* rifilare (***on***(***to***) ***s.o.*** a qn); *person* affibbiare; ***they palmed him off on me*** l'hanno affibbiato a me
palmcorder *n telecamera digitale di dimensioni molto ridotte*
palmistry *n* chiromanzia *f*
palm oil *n* olio *m* di palma **Palm Sunday** *n* domenica *f* delle Palme
palmtop *n* (*computer*) palmare *m*
palpable *adj* palpabile
palpitate *v/i* (*heart*) palpitare
palpitations *npl* MED palpitazioni *fpl*
palsy *n* paralisi *f*
paltry *adj* irrisorio; ***he gave some ~ excuse*** ha dato delle scuse meschine
pamper *v/t* viziare
pamphlet *n* volantino *m*
pan I *n for cooking* pentola *f*; *for frying* padella *f* **II** *v/t* ⟨*pret & past part* **-ned**⟩ *infml* (*criticize*) stroncare *infml*
◆**pan out** *v/i* (*develop*) sviluppare; ***it didn't pan out*** non è andata a finere bene
Pan-American *adj* panamericano
pancake *n* crêpe *f inv*; ***Pancake Day*** martedì *m inv* grasso
pancreas *n* pancreas *m inv*
panda *n* panda *m inv*
Panda car *n Br auto della polizia bianca e nera*
pandemic I *n* pandemia *f* **II** *adj* pandemico
pandemonium *n* pandemonio *m*
◆**pander to** *v/t* assecondare; ***pander to s.o.'s whims*** assecondare i capricci di qn
pane *n*: ~ (***of glass***) vetro *m*
panegyric *n* panegirico *m*
panel *n* pannello *m*; ***instrument ~*** quadro *m* degli strumenti; *of experts* gruppo *m*; *of judges* giuria *f*; ***a ~ of judges*** commissione *f* di giudici
panel beater *n* carrozziere *m* **panel discussion** *n* tavola *f* rotonda **panel game** *n* gioco *m* televisivo *or* radiofonico a quiz
panelling *n* rivestimento *m* a pannelli
panellist, *US* **panelist** *n chi partecipa ad una tavola rotonda*
pang *n of remorse* fitta *f*; ***~s of hunger*** morsi *mpl* della fame
panic I *n* panico *m*; ***in a*** (***blind***) ***~*** in preda al panico (totale); ***flee in ~*** fuggire in preda al panico; ***the country was thrown into a*** (***state of***) ***~*** il paese è stato gettato nel panico **II** *v/i* ⟨*pret & past part* **-ked**⟩: ***don't ~*** non

farti prendere dal panico
panic attack *n* PSYCH attacco *m* di panico; ***have a ~*** avere un attacco di panico **panic buying** *n* FIN *acquisto motivato dal panico*
panicky *adj* preso dal panico
panic selling *n* FIN *vendita motivata dal panico* **panic-stricken** *adj* in preda al panico
pannier *n* paniere *m*; *on bike* borsa *f* per bicicletta; *on motor-cycle* bauletto *m*
panorama *n* panorama *m*
panoramic *adj view* panoramico
pansy *n* BOT viola *f* del pensiero; *Br pej* (*homosexual*) checca *f*
pant *v/i* ansimare; (*dog*) ansimare; ***~ for breath*** avere il fiatone
pantheism *n* PHIL panteismo *m*
pantheon *n* pantheon *m*
panther *n* pantera *f*
panties *npl* mutandine *fpl*; ***a pair of ~*** un paio di mutandine
panto *n Br infml* pantomima *f*
pantomime *n spettacolo teatrale per bambini ispirato a una favola, tipico del periodo natalizio*
pantry *n* dispensa *f*
pants *npl* (*underpants*) mutande *fpl*; *US* (*trousers*) pantaloni *mpl*; ***a pair of ~*** *Br* un paio di mutande; *US* un paio di pantaloni; ***charm the ~ off s.o.*** *infml* incantare qualcuno
pantyhose *n US* collant *mpl*
panty liner *n* salvaslip *m inv*
papal *adj* pontificio
Papal States *n* HIST Stato Pontificio *m*
paper I *n material* carta *f*; ***get*** *or* ***put sth down on ~*** mettere qc su carta *or* per iscritto; (*newspaper*) giornale *m*; ***in the ~s*** sui giornali; (*wallpaper*) carta *f* da parati; *academic* relazione *f*; (*examination paper*) esame *m*; ***~s*** (*identity papers*, *documents*) documenti *mpl*; ***a piece of ~*** un pezzo di carta; ***on ~*** *written down* per iscritto; *in theory* sulla carta **II** *adj* di carta **III** *v/t room*, *walls* tappezzare
paperback *n* tascabile *m* **paper bag** *n* sacchetto *m* di carta **paper boy** *n ragazzo che recapita i giornali a domicilio* **paper chain** *n* festone *m* **paper clip** *n* graffetta *f* **paper cup** *n* bicchiere *m* di carta **paper feed** *n* COMPUT alimentatore di fogli **paper money** *n* moneta *f* cartacea **paper plate** *n* piatto *m* di carta **paper round** *n Br*: ***do a ~*** consegnare i giornali a domicilio **paper route** *n US* → ***paper round*** **paper shop** *n Br* giornalaio *m* **paper-thin** *adj* sottilissimo **paper tray** *n* COMPUT vassoio *m* per fogli **paperweight** *n* fermacarte *m inv* **paperwork** *n disbrigo delle pratiche*
paprika *n* paprica *f*
par I *n in golf* par *m inv*; ***be on a ~ with*** essere allo stesso livello di; ***feel below ~*** non sentirsi bene **II** *adj*; ***that's ~ for the course for him*** *fig infml* per lui questo è nella norma
par. *abbr* **1.** (= **paragraph**) paragrafo *m* **2.** (= **parallel**) parallelo *m* **3.** (= **parenthesis**) parentesi *f inv* **4.** (= **parish**) parrocchia *f*
parable *n* parabola *f*
paracetamol *n* paracetamolo *m*
parachute I *n* paracadute *m inv* **II** *v/i* paracadutarsi **III** *v/t troops*, *supplies* paracadutare
parachutist *n* paracadutista *m/f*
parade I *n* (*procession*) sfilata *f*; ***be on ~*** MIL essere in parata **II** *v/i* sfilare **III** *v/t knowledge*, *new car* fare sfoggio di; ***~ up and down*** (*show off*) fare la sfilata
paradigm *n* paradigma *m*
paradise *n* paradiso *m*; ***a shopper's ~*** un paradiso degli amanti dello shopping; ***an architect's ~*** un paradiso per gli architetti
paradox *n* paradosso *m*
paradoxical *adj* paradossale
paradoxically *adv* paradossalmente
paraffin *n* cherosene *m*
paragliding *n* parapendio *m*
paragraph *n* paragrafo *m*
paralegal *n esp US* paralegale *m*
parallel I *n in geometry* parallela *f*; GEOG, *fig* parallelo *m*; ***do two things in ~*** fare due cose in parallelo; ***without ~*** senza paragone; ***draw a ~ between X and Y*** stabilire un parallelo tra X e Y **II** *adj a. fig* parallelo; ***~ interface*** COMPUT interfaccia *f* parallela; ***the two systems developed along ~ lines*** i due sistemi si sono sviluppati lungo linee parallele **III** *v/t* (*match*) uguagliare; ***a case ~ed only by ...*** un caso paragonabile solo a…

paralyse *v/t a. fig* paralizzare; ***he was left ~d*** è rimasto paralizzato; ***~d from the waist down*** paralizzato dalla vita in giù; *fig* ***be ~d with fear*** essere paralizzato dalla paura
paralysis *n a. fig* paralisi *f inv*
paralytic *adj* paralitico; *Br infml* (*very drunk*) ubriaco fradicio
paramedic *n* paramedico *m*, -a *f*
parameter *n* parametro *m*
paramilitary **I** *adj* paramilitare **II** *n appartenente ad un'organizzazione paramilitare*
paramount *adj* vitale; ***be ~*** essere di vitale importanza
paramour *n liter* amante *m/f*
paranoia *n* paranoia *f*
paranoid *adj* paranoico; ***or am I just being ~?*** o sono solo paranoico?
paranormal **I** *adj* paranormale **II** *n*: ***the ~*** il paranormale
parapet *n* parapetto *m*
paraphernalia *n* armamentario *m*
paraphrase *v/t* parafrasare
paraplegic *n* paraplegico *m*, -a *f*
parasite *n a. fig* parassita *m*
parasol *n* parasole *m*
paratrooper *n* MIL paracadutista *m*
paratroops *npl* reparto *m* di paracadutisti
parboil *v/t* sbollentare
parcel *n* pacco *m*
◆**parcel out** *v/t sep* distribuire
◆**parcel up** *v/t sep* impacchettare
parch *v/t* riardere; ***be ~ed*** *infml of person* essere assetato
parchment *n* pergamena *f*
pardon **I** *n* JUR grazia *f*; ***grant s.o. a ~*** concedere la grazia a qn; ***I beg your ~?*** (*what did you say*) prego?; ***I beg your ~*** (*I'm sorry*) scusi **II** *v/t* scusare; JUR graziare
pare *v/t* (*peel*) pelare
◆**pare down** *v/t sep fig expenses* ridurre
parent *n* genitore *m*
parental *adj* dei genitori
parent company *n* società *f inv* madre
parenthesis *n* ⟨*pl* ***parentheses***⟩ parentesi *f inv*
parenthood *n* genitorialità *f*; (*fatherhood*) paternità *f*; (*motherhood*) maternità *f*
parenting *n* educazione *f* dei figli
parents evening *n* EDU riunione *f* dei genitori
parents-in-law *npl* suoceri *mpl*
parent-teacher association *n organizzazione composta da genitori e insegnanti*
parish *n* parrocchia *f*
parish church *n* chiesa *f* parrocchiale **parish council** *n* consiglio *m* parrocchiale
parishioner *n* parrocchiano *m*
parish priest *n* parroco *m*
parity *n* parità *f*
park[1] *n* parco *m*; ***national ~*** parco *m* nazionale
park[2] *v/t & v/i* AUTO parcheggiare; ***a ~ed car*** un'auto parcheggiata; ***he ~ed himself right in front of the fire*** si era piazzato proprio davanti al fuoco; ***there was nowhere to ~*** non si trovava dove parcheggiare; ***find a place to ~*** trovare un posto per parcheggiare
parka *n* parka *m inv*
parking *n* AUTO parcheggio *m*; ***no ~*** sosta *f* vietata
parking attendant *n* custode *m/f* di parcheggio **parking bay** *n* posto *m* (di un parcheggio) **parking brake** *n US* freno *m* a mano **parking disc** *n* disco *m* orario **parking fine** *n* multa *f* per divieto di sosta **parking garage** *n US* parcheggio *m* **parking lot** *n US* parcheggio *m* **parking meter** *n* parchimetro *m* **parking place** *n* parcheggio *m* **parking ticket** *n* multa *f* per sosta vietata
park keeper *n* custode *m/f* del parco
parkland *n* parco *m*
park ranger, park warden *n in national park* guardaparco *m/f*
parkway *n US* viale *m* alberato
parky *adj Br infml* fresco
parliament *n* parlamento *m*
parliamentary *adj* parlamentare; ***~ seat*** seggio *m* parlamentare
parlour, *US* **parlor** *n* (*beauty parlour etc*) salone *m*; ***ice-cream ~*** gelateria *f*
parlour game *n Br* gioco *m* di società
parody **I** *n* parodia *f* **II** *v/t* fare la parodia di
parole **I** *n* libertà *f inv* vigilata; ***be out on ~*** essere rimesso in libertà vigilata **II** *v/t* concedere la libertà vigilata a
parquet *n* parquet *m inv*

parrot **I** *n* pappagallo *m*; ***he felt as sick as a ~*** *Br infml* rimanerci male **II** *v/t* ripetere a pappagallo

parry *v/t & v/i* ⟨*pret & past part* ***-ied***⟩ *fig* schivare (*a. boxing*)

parse *v/t & v/i* GRAM fare l'analisi grammaticale *or* logica

parsimony *n* parsimonia *f*

parsley *n* prezzemolo *m*

parsnip *n* pastinaca *f*

parson *n* parroco *m*

parsonage *n* canonica *f*

parson's nose *n* boccone *m* del prete

part **I** *n* parte *f*; *of machine* pezzo *m*; *US* (*in hair*) riga *f*; TV puntata *f*; THEAT ruolo *m*; ***take ~ in sth*** prendere parte in; ***the best ~*** la parte migliore; ***in ~*** in parte; ***a ~ of the country / city I don't know*** una parte del paese / della città che non conosco; ***for the most ~*** per la maggior parte; ***in the latter ~ of the year*** nell'ultima parte dell'anno; ***it's all ~ of growing up*** è tipico della crescita; ***it is ~ and parcel of the job*** è parte integrante del lavoro; ***spare ~*** pezzo *m* di ricambio; ***end of ~ one*** TV fine della prima parte; *fig* ***play one's ~*** recitare la propria parte; ***he looks the ~*** è perfetto per la parte; ***play no ~ in sth*** non avere niente a che fare con qc; ***we want no ~ of it*** non vogliamo saperne niente; ***from all ~s*** da tutte le parti; ***in*** *or* ***around these ~s*** da queste parti; ***in foreign ~s*** in zone straniere; ***he's not from these ~s*** non è di queste parti; ***take s.o.'s ~*** prendere le parti di qn; ***for my ~*** da parte mia; ***on my ~*** da parte mia; ***on the ~ of*** da parte di **II** *adv* (*partly*) in parte; ***~ iron and ~ copper*** in parte ferro e in parte rame **III** *v/i* separarsi; ***her lips ~ed in a smile*** le sue labbra si aprirono in un sorriso; ***we ~ed friends*** ci siamo lasciati da amici **IV** *v/t*: ***~ one's hair*** farsi la riga; ***~ s.o. from s.o. / sth*** separare qn da qn / qc; ***till death us do ~*** finché morte non ci separi; ***~ company with s.o. / sth*** porre fine ad un'amicizia con qn / prepararsi da qc

◆**part with** *v/t* separarsi da; ***part with money*** disfarsi del denaro

partake *v/i* ⟨*pret* ***-took***, *past part* ***-taken***⟩ prendere parte; ***he didn't ~ in the festivities*** non ha participato ai festeggiamenti; *liter* ***together they partook of food before leaving*** insieme presero una porzione di cibo prima di partire

parterre *n garden* parterre *m inv*

part exchange *n* permuta *f*; ***take sth in ~ exchange*** prendere qc in permuta

partial *adj* (*incomplete*) parziale; ***a ~ success*** un successo parziale; ***make a ~ recovery*** guarire parzialmente; ***be ~ to*** avere un debole per; ***she's very ~ to chocolate*** ha un debole per il cioccolato

partiality *n* parzialità *f*

partially *adv* parzialmente; ***partially sighted*** ipovedente

participant *n* partecipante *m/f*

participate *v/i* partecipare; ***~ in sth*** partecipare a qc

participation *n* partecipazione *f*

participle *n* GRAM participio *m*

particle *n* PHYS particella *f*; *small amount* briciolo *m*

particular **I** *adj* (*specific*) particolare; ***this ~ house*** questa casa in particolare; ***in this ~ instance*** in questo caso particolare; ***at that ~ time*** in quel preciso momento; ***be of ~ concern to s.o.*** essere di particolare interesse per qn; (*fussy*) pignolo; ***he is very ~ about cleanliness*** è molto esigente sulla pulizia; ***he's ~ about his car*** è molto scrupoloso con la sua auto; ***in ~*** in particolare; ***the wine in ~ was excellent*** in particolare il vino era eccellente; ***did you want to speak to anyone in ~?*** voleva parlare con qualcuno in particolare? **II** ***particulars*** *npl* dati *mpl* personali; ***for further ~s apply to ...*** per ulteriori dettagli rivolgersi a…

particularly *adv* particolarmente; ***do you want it ~ for tomorrow?*** lo volevi in particolare per domani; ***not ~*** non particolarmente; ***it's important, ~ since ...*** è importante, specialmente perché…

parting **I** *n of people* separazione *f*; *in hair* riga *f* **II** *adj* d'addio; ***his ~ words*** le sue parole d'addio

partisan *n* MIL partigiano *m*, -a *f*

partition **I** *n* (*screen*) tramezzo *m*; *of country* suddivisione *f* **II** *v/t country* suddividere

◆**partition off** *v/t sep* tramezzare
partly *adv* in parte
partner *n* COMM socio *m*, -a *f*; *in relationship* partner *m/f inv*; *in particular activity* compagno *m*, -a *f*
partnership *n* COMM società *f inv*; ***enter into a ~*** entrare in società con qn; ***go into ~ with s.o.*** associarsi con qn; *in particular activity* sodalizio *m*; ***do sth in ~ with s.o.*** fare qc in società con qn
part of speech *n* GRAM parte *f* del discorso **part owner** *n* comproprietario *m*, -a *f* **part payment** *n* pagamento *m* parziale
partridge *n* pernice *f*
part-time *adj/adv* part-time; ***I'm just ~*** lavoro part-time; ***on a ~ basis*** part-time; ***she only teaches ~*** insegna ad orario ridotto
part-timer *n* lavoratore *m*, -trice *f* part-time
party I *n* (*celebration*) festa *f*; POL partito *m*; (*group*) gruppo *m*; ***a ~ of tourists*** una comitiva di turisti; ***a third ~*** una terza parte; ***be a ~ to*** essere coinvolto in **II** *v/i* ⟨*pret & past part* **-ied**⟩ *infml* far baldoria
partygoer *n* festaiolo *m*, -a *f*
party line *n*: ***follow the ~*** seguire la linea di partito **party political broadcast** *n* tribuna *f* politica; **party pooper** *n infml* guastafeste *m/f inv*
pass I *v/t* **1.** (*hand*) passare; ***~ (me) the salt, please*** passami il sale, per favore **2.** (*go past*) passare davanti a; ***he ~ed me without even saying hello*** è passato davanti a me senza neanche salutarmi **3.** (*overtake*) sorpassare **4.** (*go beyond*) superare **5.** (*approve*) approvare **6.** SPORTS passare **7.** ***~ an exam*** superare un esame **8.** ***~ sentence*** JUR emanare la sentenza **9.** ***~ the time*** passare il tempo **II** *v/i* passare; *in exam* essere promosso; ***the street was too narrow for the cars to ~*** la strada era troppo stretta perché le macchine potessero passare; ***we ~ed in the corridor*** siamo passati per il corridoio; ***the procession ~ed down the street*** la processione era passata per la strada; ***the virus ~es easily from one person to another*** il virus si trasmette facilmente da una persona all'altra; ***the land has now ~ed into private hands*** il terreno ora è passato nelle meni dei privati; ***let it ~!*** non ci fare caso!; ***this little room has to ~ for an office*** questa stanzetta deve passare per un ufficio; ***she could ~ for 25*** potrebbe passare per una venticinquenne **III** *n* **1.** *for getting into a place* lasciapassare *m inv*; ***make a ~ at*** fare avances a **2.** SPORTS passaggio *m* **3.** *in mountains* passo *m* **4.** ***get a ~*** *in exam* prendere la sufficienza **5.** ***things had come to such a ~ that ...*** le cose avevano raggiunto il punto per cui…
◆**pass around** *v/t* far circolare
◆**pass away** *v/i euph* spegnersi *euph*
◆**pass by I** *v/t sep* (*go past*) passare davanti a; ***life has passed her by*** la vita le era passata davanti **II** *v/i* (*go past*) passare
◆**pass down** *v/t sep traditions* tramandare (***to*** a); *characteristics* trasmettere (***to*** a)
◆**pass off I** *v/i* (*take place*) svolgersi; (*be taken as*) spacciarsi (***as*** per) **II** *v/t sep* ***pass s.o. / sth off as sth*** spacciare qn / qc per qc
◆**pass on I** *v/t sep information*, *book*, *savings* passare (***to*** a); ***take a leaflet and pass them on*** prendi un volantino e fallo girare **II** *v/i* (*euph*: *die*) mancare *euph*
◆**pass out** *v/i* (*faint*) svenire
◆**pass over** *v/t sep* trasmettere; (*hand in*) tramandare
◆**pass round** *v/t sep* fare circolare; ***pass the biscuits round, would you?*** ti dispiacerebbe offrire i biscotti?
◆**pass through** *v/t town* passare per
◆**pass up** *v/t sep opportunity* lasciarsi sfuggire
passable *adj road* transitabile; (*acceptable*) passabile
passage *n* (*corridor*) passaggio *m*; ***secret ~*** passaggio *m* segreto; *from poem*, *book* passo *m*; ***a ~ from Shakespeare*** un passo da Shakespeare; ***the ~ of time*** il passare del tempo; (*transit*) viaggio *m*; ***they booked their ~ on the slow boat*** hanno prenotato il viaggio sulla nave lenta; (*duct*) condotto; ***the nasal ~s*** il condotto nasale
passageway *n* corridoio *m*
passbook *n* libretto *m* di risparmio

passé *adj* superato
passenger *n* passeggero *m*, -a *f*
passenger seat *n* sedile *m* del passeggero
passe-partout *n* passe-partout *m inv*
passer-by *n* ⟨*pl* **passers-by**⟩ passante *m/f*
passing I *n* passaggio *m* (*a.* SPORTS); (*overtaking*) sorpasso *m*; *euph* (*death*) dipartita *f*; ***mention sth in ~*** nominare qc en passant **II** *adj* (*fleeting*) passeggero; ***with each ~ day*** con il passare dei giorni; ***make (a) ~ reference to sth*** fare un riferimento casuale a qc; ***bear a ~ resemblance to s.o./sth*** avere una vaga somiglianza con qn/qc
passion *n* passione *f*
passionate *adj* appassionato; ***be ~ about sth*** essere appassionato di qc
passionflower *n* passiflora *f*
passion fruit *n* frutto *m* della passione **passion play** *n* THEAT passione *f*, *rappresentazione della Passione di Cristo* **Passion Sunday** *n* domenica *f* di Passione
Passiontide *n* periodo *m* della Passione
Passion Week *n* settimana *f* santa
passive I *adj* passivo **II** *n* GRAM passivo *m*; ***in the ~*** al passivo
passive resistance *n* resistenza *f* passiva **passive smoking** *n* fumo *m* passivo
passkey *n* passe-partout *m inv*
pass mark *n* EDU voto *m* sufficiente
Passover *n* REL Pasqua *f* ebraica
passport *n* passaporto *m*
passport control *n* controllo *m* passaporti
password *n* parola *f* d'ordine; COMPUT password *f inv*
past I *adj* (*former*) precedente; ***in the ~ few days*** nei giorni scorsi; ***that's all ~ now*** è acqua passata ormai; GRAM ***~ tense*** tempo *m* passato **II** *n* passato *m*; ***in the ~*** nel passato; ***that's all in the ~ now*** ora appartiene al passato; GRAM ***the verb is in the ~*** il verbo è al passato **III** *prep in position* oltre; ***it's half ~ two*** sono le due e mezza; ***it's ~ seven o'clock*** sono le sette passate; ***I wouldn't put it ~ him*** ne sarebbe pure capace; ***it's (well) ~ your bedtime*** l'ora di andare a letto è passata da un pezzo; (*beyond*) oltre; ***~ forty*** oltre quaranta; ***the patient is ~ saving*** il paziente non può essere più salvato; ***we're ~ caring*** non c'importa più niente **IV** *adv*: ***run ~*** passare di corsa
pasta *n* pasta *f*
paste I *n* (*adhesive*) colla *f* **II** *v/t* incollare
pastel I *n* pastello *m* **II** *adj* pastello; ***~ colour*** *Br or* ***color*** *US* colore *m* pastello; ***~ drawing*** disegno a pastello
pasteurize *v/t* pastorizzare
pastime *n* passatempo *m*
pastor *n* pastore *m*
pastoral *adj care* spirituale
past participle *n* GRAM participio *m* passato **past perfect** *n* GRAM trapassato *m* prossimo
pastrami *n affettato di carne di manzo speziata*
pastry *n for pie* pasta *f* (sfoglia); (*small cake*) pasticcino *m*
past tense *n* GRAM passato *m*
pasture *n* (*field*) pascolo *m*; (*a.* **pasture land**) terreno *m* da pascolo; *fig* ***move on to ~s new*** partire verso nuovi lidi
pasty[1] *adj complexion* smorto
pasty[2] *n esp Br pasticcio di carne*
pasty-faced *adj* pallido come un morto
pat[1] *n of butter* panetto *m*; ***cow ~*** sterco *m*
pat[2] *adv*: ***know sth off ~*** conoscere qc a memoria; ***learn sth off ~*** imparare qc a memoria
pat[3] **I** *n* colpetto *m*; *affectionate* buffetto *m*; ***he gave his nephew a ~ on the head*** ha dato uno buffetto sulla testa di suo nipote; ***give one's horse a ~*** accarezzare il proprio cavallo; *fig* ***give s.o. a ~ on the back*** dare una pacca sulla spalla a qn **II** *v/t* ⟨*pret & past part* **-ted**⟩ dare un colpetto a; *affectionately* dare un buffetto a; *fig* ***~ s.o. on the back*** fare i complimenti a qn; *fig* ***~ o.s. on the back*** essere fiero di se stesso
◆ **pat down** *v/t sep* comprimere
patch I *n* **1.** *on clothing* pezza *f* **2.** (*period of time*) periodo *m*; ***go through a bad ~*** attraversare un brutto periodo **3.** (*area*) zona *f*; ***~es of fog*** banchi *mpl* di nebbia; ***a ~ of blue sky*** uno squarcio di cielo blu **4.** *fig* ***be not a***

~ on non essere niente a paragone di **II** *v/t clothing* rattoppare

◆**patch up** *v/t sep* (*repair temporarily*) riparare alla meglio; *quarrel* risolvere; ***I want to patch things up between us*** voglio aggiustare le cose tra di noi

patch test *n* test *m inv* cutaneo

patchwork I *n* patchwork *m inv* **II** *adj quilt* patchwork *inv*

patchy *adj* (+*er*) *quality* irregolare; *work, performance* discontinuo, disuguale

pâté *n* pâté *m inv*

patent I *adj* palese **II** *n for invention* brevetto *m* **III** *v/t invention* brevettare

patent leather *n* vernice *f*

patently *adv* (*clearly*) palesemente; ***it was ~ obvious he was lying*** era palese che stava mentendo

paternal *adj* paterno; ***my ~ grandmother*** *etc* la mia nonna paterna

paternalism *n* paternalismo *m*

paternalistic *adj* paternalistico

paternity *n* paternità *f inv*; ***be on ~ leave*** essere in congedo di paternità

path *n* sentiero *m*; *fig* strada *f*; COMPUT percorso *m*

pathetic *adj invoking pity* patetico; ***a ~ sight*** una visione commovente; *infml* (*very bad*) penoso; ***honestly you're ~*** sinceramente sei patetico

path name *n* COMPUT path name *m inv*

pathological *adj* patologico

pathologist *n* patologo *m*, -a *f*

pathology *n* patologia *f*

pathos *n* pathos *m inv*

pathway *n* sentiero *m*

patience *n* pazienza *f*; *Br*: *card game* solitario *m*

patient I *n* paziente *m/f* **II** *adj* paziente; ***just be ~!*** abbi pazienza!

patiently *adv* pazientemente

patina *n* patina *f*

patio *n* terrazza *f*

patois *n* patois *m inv*

patriarch *n* patriarca *m*

patriarchal *adj* patriarcale

patriarchate *n* patriarcato *m*

patriarchy *n* società *f* partiarcale

patrician *n* patrizio *m*, -a *f*

patricide *n* parricidio *m*

patrimony *n* patrimonio *m*

patriot *n* patriota *m/f*

patriotic *adj* patriottico

patriotism *n* patriottismo *m*

patrol I *n* pattuglia *f*; ***be on ~*** essere di pattuglia; ***the navy carry out*** *or* ***make weekly ~s of the area*** la marina effettua ricognizioni settimanali dell'area **II** *v/t* ⟨*pret & past part* **-led**⟩ *streets, border* pattugliare

patrol car *n* autopattuglia *f*

patrolman *n* agente *m/f* di pattuglia

patron *n of artist* mecenate *m/f*; ***~ of the arts*** protettore *m*, -trice *f* delle arti; *of charity* patrono *m*, -essa *f*; *of shop, cinema* cliente *m/f*

patronage *n of artist* patronato *m*; *of charity* patrocinio *m*

patronize *v/t shop* essere cliente di; *person* trattare con condiscendenza

patronizing *adj* condiscendente; ***he was horribly ~ in his treatment of her*** il suo atteggiamento nei suoi confronti era tremendamente paternalistico

patron saint *n* patrono *m*, -a *f*

patter I *n of rain etc* picchiettio *m*; *of salesman etc.* imbonimento *m* **II** *v/i* picchiettare; (*glib talk*) parlare in fretta

pattern I *n on wallpaper, fabric* motivo *m*, disegno *m*; *for knitting, sewing* (carta) modello *m*; *in behaviour, events* schema *m*; ***there's a distinct ~ / no ~ to these crimes*** c'è uno schema preciso / non c'è uno schema preciso in questi crimini; ***the ~ of events*** la serie degli avvenimenti; ***eating ~s*** modelli di alimentazione; ***follow the usual / same ~*** seguire il solito / lo stesso schema **II** *v/t esp US* (*model*) modellare (**on** su); ***be ~ed on sth*** essere modellato su qc

patterned *adj* fantasia *inv*

paunch *n* pancia *f*

pauper *n* indigente *m/f*

pause I *n* pausa *f*; ***a pregnant ~*** una pausa densa di significato; ***there was a ~ while ...*** c'è stata un'interruzione mentre; *hesitation* ***his words gave me ~*** le sue parole mi hanno fatto esitare; MUS pausa *f* **II** *v/i* fermarsi; ***he ~d for breath*** si è fermato per riprendere fiato; ***~ for thought*** fare una pausa di riflessione; ***he spoke for thirty minutes without once pausing*** ha parlato per trenta minuti senza posa; ***it made him ~*** lo ha interrotto **III** *v/t tape* fermare

pave *v/t* pavimentare; *fig* ***~ the way for*** aprire la strada a

pavé *n* pavé *m inv*

pavement *n Br* marciapiede *m*

pavilion *n* padiglione *m*; *Br* SPORTS *edificio accanto ad un campo da cricket per il ristoro di giocatori e spettatori*

paving stone *n* lastra *f* di pavimentazione

paw I *n of animal, infml* (*hand*) zampa *f* **II** *v/t infml* palpare

pawn[1] *n in chess* pedone *m*; *fig* pedina *f*

pawn[2] *v/t* impegnare; ***she had to ~ her jewellery to pay the rent*** ha dovuto dare in pegno i propri gioielli per pagare l'affitto

pawnbroker *n* prestatore *m*, -trice *f* su pegno **pawnshop** *n* monte *m* di pietà

pay I *v/t* ⟨*pret & past part* ***paid***⟩ pagare; ***how much is there still to ~?*** quanto c'è ancora da pagare?; ***~ the price for sth*** pagare il prezzo di qc; ***~ attention*** fare attenzione; ***~ s.o. a compliment*** fare un complimento a qn; ***~*** (***s.o.*** / ***a place***) ***a visit*** *or* ***~ a visit to s.o.*** / ***a place*** fare visita (a qn / ad un luogo); ***~ a visit to the doctor*** andare a fare una visita dal dottore **II** *v/i* ⟨*pret & past part* ***paid***⟩ pagare; (*be profitable*) rendere; ***it doesn't ~ to ...*** non conviene ...; ***~ for*** *purchase* pagare; ***they ~ well for this sort of work*** hanno pagato bene per questo tipo di lavoro; ***they paid for her to go to America*** hanno pagato tutto per farla andare in America; ***crime doesn't ~*** *prov* il crimine non paga; *fig* ***you'll ~ for this!*** la pagherai! **III** *n* paga *f*; ***in the ~ of*** al soldo di; ***three months' ~*** lo stipendio di tre mesi; ***what's the ~ like?*** com'è la paga qui?; ***it comes out of my ~*** viene detratto dal mio stipendio

◆**pay back** *v/t sep person* restituire i soldi a; ***I'll pay the money back as soon as I get home*** restituirò i soldi appena tornerò a casa; *loan* restituire; (*get revenge on*) farla pagare a; ***he'll pay you back for that insult, so watch out!*** te la farà pagare per quell'insulto, quindi sta' attento!

◆**pay in** *v/t sep to bank* versare

◆**pay off I** *v/t sep debt* estinguere; ***I'll pay off my mortgage next year*** estinguerò il mio mutuo l'anno prossimo; *workers* liquidare; *corrupt official* comprare **II** *v/i* (*be profitable*) dare frutti; ***being unscrupulous doesn't always pay off*** essere spregiudicati non dà sempre buoni risultati

◆**pay up** *v/i* pagare

payable *adj* pagabile; ***make a cheque*** *Br or* ***check*** *US* ***~ to s.o.*** emettere un assegno pagabile a qn

pay-and-display *adj Br*: ***~ parking space*** *parcheggio con pagamento di ticket da esporre all'interno dell'auto*

pay-as-you-go *adj*: ***~ mobile phone*** cellulare *m* ricaricabile

payback *n fig* (*revenge*) vendetta *f*; ***it's ~ time*** è periodo di rimborso

paycheque, *US* **paycheck** *n* assegno *m* paga

payday *n* giorno *m* di paga

PAYE *abbr* (= **pay as you earn**) *pagamento con ritenuta delle imposte alla fonte*; ***~ tax system*** *sistema di tassazione con ritenute in busta paga*

payee *n* beneficiario *m*, -a *f*

payer *n* pagatore *m*, -trice *f*

paying-in slip *n Br* distinta *f* di versamento

payment *n* pagamento *m*; ***three monthly ~s*** tre rate mensili; ***in ~ of a debt*** a pagamento di un debito; ***on ~ of*** come pagamento per

payoff *n* (*final payment*) saldo *m*; *infml* (*bribe*) tangente *f*

payout *n* (*from insurance*) indennizzo *m*

pay packet *n* busta *f* paga **pay-per-view TV** *n* pay TV *f inv* **pay phone** *n* telefono *m* pubblico; **pay rise** *n* aumento *m* di stipendio **payroll** *n money* stipendi *mpl*; *employees* personale *m*; ***be on the ~*** essere sul libro paga **payslip** *n* busta *f* paga **pay television, pay TV** *n* pay TV *f inv*

PC *abbr* **1.** (= **personal computer**) PC *m inv* **2.** (= **politically correct**) politicamente corretto **3.** (= **police constable**) agente *m* di polizia

pcm *abbr* (= **per calendar month**) al mese

PDA *abbr* (= **personal digital assist-**

ant) PDA *m*
PDF *n abbr* (= **portable document format**) COMPUT PDF *m inv*
PDQ *abbr* (= **pretty damned quick**) *infml* immediatamente
PDSA *abbr* (= **People's Dispensary for Sick Animals**) *Br organizzazione veterinaria britannica di beneficenza*
PE *abbr* (= **physical education**) educazione *f* fisica
pea *n* pisello *m*
peace *n* pace *f*; ***the two countries are at ~*** i due paesi sono in pace; ***make (one's) ~ (with s.o.)*** fare la pace (con qn); ***make ~ between ...*** stabilire la pace tra...; ***keep the ~*** (*citizen*) mantenere la pace; ***~ and quiet*** calma e tranquillità; ***give s.o. some ~*** lasciare qn in pace; ***~ of mind*** tranquillità *f*
peaceable *adj person* pacifico
peaceful *adj* tranquillo; *demonstration* pacifico
peacefully *adv* tranquillamente; *demonstrate* pacificamente
peacekeeping I *n* mantenimento *m* della pace **II** *adj*: ***~ force*** forze *mpl* di pace; ***UN troops have a purely ~ role*** il ruolo delle truppe ONU è esclusivamente quello di stabilire la pace; ***a ~ operation*** un'operazione di pace
peace-loving *adj* amante della pace
peacemaker *n* mediatore *m*, -trice *f* di pace
peace offering *n* REL sacrificio *m* propiziatorio; *fig* dono *m* di riconciliazione
peacetime *n* tempo *m* di pace
peach[1] *n* pesca *f*; *tree* pesco *m*
peach[2] *v/i infml* fare una soffiata; ***the police found out because she ~ed on him*** la polizia l'ha scoperto perché lei ha fatto una soffiata su di lui
peachy *adj* vellutato (come una pesca); *fig* eccezionale
peacock *n* pavone *m*
pea green *n* verde *m* pisello
peak I *n* vetta *f*; *fig* apice *m*; *of hat* visiera *f* **II** *adj* massimo; ***in ~ condition*** al meglio della forma; ***at ~ time*** TV, RADIO all'ora di punta **III** *v/i* raggiungere il livello massimo; ***inflation ~ed at 9 %*** l'inflazione ha raggiunto il picco del 9 %
peak consumption *n* periodo *m* di massimo consumo
peaked *adj cap* con visiera
peak hours *npl* ore *fpl* di punta **peak rate** *n* TEL tariffa *f* intera **peak-time** *adj Br*: ***~ traffic*** il traffico dell'ora di punta **peak viewing hours** *npl* prima serata *f*
peaky *adj* (+*er*) *Br infml complexion* pallidino; *look*, *child* malaticcio
peal *n of bells* scampanio *m*; ***~s of laughter*** scoppi di risate
peanut *n* arachide *f*; ***get paid ~s*** *infml* essere pagati una miseria *infml*; ***that's ~s to him*** sono briciole per lui
peanut butter *n* burro *m* d'arachidi
peapod *n* baccello *m* di pisello
pear *n* pera *f*; *tree* pero *m*
pearl I *n* perla *f*; ***~ of wisdom*** perla *f* di saggezza **II** *adj*: ***~ necklace*** collana *f* di perle
pearly *adj* perlato
pear-shaped *adj* a forma di pera; *fig* ***go ~*** *Br infml* andare a monte
peasant *n* contadino *m*, -a *f*; ***~ farmer*** agricoltore *m*, -trice *f*
peasantry *n* classe *f* contadina
peasouper *n Br fig infml* nebbia *f* fitta
peat *n* torba *f*
pebble *n* ciottolo *m*
pecan *n* noce *m* pecan
peck I *n* (*bite*) beccata *f*; (*kiss*) bacetto *m* **II** *v/t* (*bite*) beccare; (*kiss*) dare un bacetto a
pecking order *n* ordine *m* gerarchico
peckish *adj Br infml* ***I'm (feeling) a bit ~*** sento un certo languorino
pecs *npl abbr* (= **pectorals**) *infml* pettorali *mpl*; ***big ~*** pettorali *mpl* grandi
pectin *n* pectina *f*
pectoral *adj* pettorale
pectorals *npl* pettorali *mpl*
peculate I *v/t* appropriarsi indebitamente di **II** *v/i* commettere peculato
peculiar *adj* (*strange*) strano; ***~ to*** (*special*) caratteristico di; ***his own ~ style*** uno stile tutto suo
peculiarity *n* (*strangeness*) stranezza *f*; (*special feature*) caratteristica *f*
peculiarly *adv* (*strangely*) stranamente
pecuniary *adj* pecuniario
pedagogical *adj form* pedagocico
pedagogy *n* pedagogia *f*

pedal I *n of bike* pedale *m* II *v/i turn pedals* pedalare; ***he ~led for all he was worth*** ha pedalato mettendocela tutta; (*cycle*) andare in bicicletta
pedal bin *n Br* pattumiera *f* con pedale **pedal boat** *n* pattino *m* **pedal car** *n* automobilina *f* a pedali
pedant *n* persona *f* pedante
pedantic *adj* pedante
peddle *v/t* fare il venditore ambulante di; ***he ~d goods from door to door*** vendeva merce porta a porta; *drugs* spacciare
pederast *n* pederasta *m*
pederasty *n* pederastia *f*
pedestal *n for statue* piedistallo *m*
pedestrian I *n* pedone *m* II *adj* pedonale; ***his prose was ~*** la sua prosa era pedestre
pedestrian crossing *n* passaggio *m* pedonale
pedestrianize *v/t street* pedonalizzare
pedestrian precinct *n* zona *f* pedonale
pediatric *etc US* → ***paediatric*** *etc*
pediatrician *n* pediatra *m/f*
pediatrics *nsg US* pediatria *f*
pedicure *n* pedicure *f inv*
pedigree I *n* pedigree *m inv* II *adj* di razza pura
pedophile *etc US* → ***paedophile*** *etc*
pee I *v/i infml* fare pipì *infml* II *n infml* pipì *f inv*; ***have a ~*** fare pipì; ***need a ~*** devo fare pipì
peek I *n* sbirciata *infml*; ***take*** *or* ***have a ~*** dare una sbirciatina (***at*** a) II *v/i* sbirciare *infml*
peel I *n* buccia *f*; *of citrus fruit* scorza *f* II *v/t fruit*, *vegetables* sbucciare III *v/i of nose*, *shoulders* spellarsi; *of paint* scrostarsi
◆ **peel off** I *v/t sep wrapper etc* togliere II *v/i of wrapper* venir via
peeler *n* sbucciatore *m*
peep I *n* (*look*) occhiata *f*; (*furtive*) sbirciata *f*; ***get a ~ at sth*** dare un'occhiata a qc; ***take a ~*** (***at sth***) sbirciare (qc) II *v/i* dare un'occhiata (***at*** a); ***~ from behind sth*** sbirciare da dietro a qc; ***no ~ing!*** *or* ***don't ~!*** senza sbirciare!
◆ **peep out** *v/i* spuntare; ***the sun peeped out from behind the clouds*** il sole faceva capolino da dietro le nuvole
peephole *n* spioncino *m*
Peeping Tom *n* guardone *m*
peepshow *n* spettacolo *m* di spogliarello
peer[1] *n* (*equal*) pari *m/f inv*; (*noble*) nobile *m/f*; ***he was well-liked by his ~s*** era molto apprezzato dai suoi colleghi
peer[2] *v/i* guardare attentamente; ***~ through the mist*** guardare attraverso la foschia; ***~ at*** scrutare; ***~ into the darkness*** scrutare nel buio
peerage *n* (*peers*) paria *f*; *in GB* nobiltà *f*; (*rank*) titolo *m* di pari; ***get a ~*** ricevere il titolo di pari
peer group *n* pari *mpl*
peerless *adj* senza pari
peer pressure *n pressione esercitata dal gruppo di coetanei*
peeved *adj infml* seccato
peevish *adj* irascibile
peg I *n for coat* attaccapanni *m inv*; *for tent* picchetto *m*; ***off the ~*** prêt-à-porter; ***take*** *or* ***bring s.o. down a ~ or two*** *infml* ridimensionare qc; ***a square ~ in a round hole*** un pesce fuor d'acqua II *v/t* ⟨*pret & past part* ***-ged***⟩ *with stake* fissare; *with clothes peg* appendere al filo
◆ **peg out** *v/i* (*clothes*) stendere il bucato; (*land*) picchettare; *fig* crepare
pejorative *adj* peggiorativo
pekin(g)ese *n* (*person*) pechinese *m/f*; (*dog*) pechinese *m*
pelican *n* pellicano *m*
pelican crossing *n Br attraversamento pedonale con semaforo azionato dai pedoni*
pellet *n* pallina *f*; (*bullet*) pallino *m*
pell-mell *adv* alla rinfusa
pelmet *n* mantovana *f*
pelt[1] I *v/t*: ***~ s.o with sth*** tirare qc a qn II *v/i*: ***they ~ed along the road*** *infml* sono sfrecciati per strada; ***it's ~ing down*** *infml* piove a dirotto III *n infml* ***at full ~*** a rotta di collo
pelt[2] *n* (*skin*) pelle *f*
pelvic *adj* pelvico
pelvis *n* pelvi *f inv*
pen[1] I *n* penna *f*; ***put ~ to paper*** mettersi a scrivere II *v/t* scrivere; ***I penned him a brief explanatory letter*** gli ho scritto una breve lettera di chiarimento
pen[2] *n* (*enclosure*) recinto *m*

penal *adj*: **~ *reform*** riforma *f* penale
penal code *n* codice *m* penale **penal colony** *n* colonia *f* penale
penalize *v/t* penalizzare
penalty *n* ammenda *f*; ***the ~* (*for this*) *is death*** (per questo delitto) è prevista la pena di morte; ***"penalty £50"*** multa di 50 sterline; ***carry the death ~*** *country* perpetrare la pena di morte; *crime* punibile con la pena di morte ***pay the ~*** pagare lo scotto; *in soccer* rigore *m*; *in rugby* punizione *f*; ***take the ~*** battere il rigore / la punizione
penalty area *n* SPORTS area *f* di rigore **penalty clause** *n* JUR penale *f* **penalty kick** *n in soccer* calcio *m* di rigore; *in rugby* calcio *m* di punizione **penalty shoot-out** *n* rigori *mpl* **penalty spot** *n* dischetto *m* di rigore
penance *n* REL penitenza *f*; *fig* penitenza *f*; ***do ~*** fare penitenza; *fig* fare penitenza
pence *npl* penny *m inv*
penchant *n* propensione *f*; ***he had a ~ sports cars*** aveva la predilezione per le auto sportive
pencil *n* matita *f*
◆**pencil in** *v/t sep date, meeting* fissare provvisoriamente; ***can I pencil you in for Tuesday?*** posso segnarti a matita per martedì?
pencil case *n* portamatite *m inv* **pencil sharpener** *n* temperamatite *m inv*
pendant *n necklace* pendaglio *m*
pending **I** *prep* in attesa di **II** *adj*: ***be ~*** essere in sospeso
pendulous *adj* penzolante
pendulum *n* pendolo *m*
penetrate *v/t* penetrare in
penetrating *adj stare, scream* penetrante; *analysis* perspicace
penetration *n* penetrazione *f*
pen friend *n* amico *m*, -a *f* di penna
penguin *n* pinguino *m*
penicillin *n* penicillina *f*
peninsula *n* penisola *f*
penis *n* pene *m*
penitence *n* penitenza *f*
penitent *adj* pentito
penitentiary *n esp US* penitenziario *m*
penknife *n* temperino *m*
pen name *n* pseudonimo *m*
pennant *n* gagliardetto *m*
penniless *adj* al verde
penny *n* penny *m inv*; ***spend a ~*** *Br infml* andare al gabinetto; ***the ~ dropped*** *infml* finalmente hai capito; ***two*** o ***ten a ~*** *infml* a bizzeffe
penny-wise *adj* oculato (nelle spese)
pen pal *n* amico *m*, -a *f* di penna
pension[1] *n* pensione *f*; ***company ~*** pensione *f* aziendale; ***get a ~*** percepire una pensione
◆**pension off** *v/t sep* mandare in pensione
pension[2] *n* (*boarding house*) pensione *f*
pensioner *n* pensionato *m*, -a *f*
pension fund *n* fondo *m* pensioni **pension scheme** *n* schema *m* pensionistico
pensive *adj* pensieroso
Pentagon *n*: ***the ~*** il Pentagono
pentathlon *n* pentathlon *m inv*
Pentecost *n* Pentecoste *f*
penthouse *n* attico *m*
pent-up *adj* represso
penultimate *adj* penultimo
penury *n* penuria *f*
people *npl* gente *f*, persone *fpl*; (*nsg*: *race, tribe*) popolazione *f*; ***the ~*** (*the citizens*) il popolo; ***the American ~*** gli americani; ***~ say ...*** si dice che ...; ***all ~ with red hair*** tutti quelli con i capelli rossi; ***some ~ don't like it*** ad alcuni non piace; ***why me of all ~?*** perché proprio io?; ***what do you ~ think?*** voi cosa ne pensate?; ***country ~*** gente di campagna; ***some ~ have all the luck*** ad alcune persone capitano tutte le fortune; ***~ say that ...*** la gente dice che; ***People's Republic*** *etc* Repubblica Popolare
people carrier *n* monovolume *f inv*
pep *n* energia *f*
◆**pep up** *v/t sep person, occasion* dare vigore a
pepper *n spice* pepe *m*; *vegetable* peperone *m*
peppercorn *n* grano *m* di pepe nero
peppercorn rent *n* affitto *m* nominale
pepper mill *n* macinino *m* per il pepe
peppermint *n sweet* mentina *f*; *flavouring* menta *f*
peppery *adj hot* pepato
pep pill *n* pillola *f* eccitante
pep talk *n* discorso *m* d'incoraggiamento
per *prep* a; ***100 km ~ hour*** 100 km

all'ora; ***£50 ~ night*** 50 sterline a notte; ***~ annum*** all'anno
percale *n* TEX percalle *m*
per capita *adj/adv* pro capita
perceive *v/t with senses* percepire; (*view, interpret*) interpretare
percent *n* per cento; ***a 10 ~ discount*** uno sconto del 10 per cento; ***I'm 99 ~ certain that ...*** sono sicuro al 99 per cento che…
percentage *n* percentuale *f*
perceptible *adj* percettibile
perceptibly *adv* percettibilmente
perception *n through senses* percezione *f*; (*insight*) sensibilità *f inv*; ***his powers of ~*** i suoi poteri di percezione
perceptive *adj person, remark* perspicace
perch **I** *n for bird* posatoio *m* **II** *v/i of bird* posarsi; *of person* appollaiarsi; ***a village ~ on a hillside*** un paese appollaiato sul fianco di una collina; ***with his glasses ~ on the end of his nose*** con gli occhiali posati sulla punta del naso
percolate *v/i of coffee* filtrare
percolator *n* caffettiera *f* a filtro
percussion *n* percussioni *fpl*
percussion instrument *n* strumento *m* a percussione
percussionist *n* percussionista *m/f*
peremptory *adj* perentorio
perennial **I** *n* BOT pianta *f* perenne **II** *adj* (*perpetual*) perenne
perfect **I** *n* GRAM passato *m* prossimo **II** *adj* perfetto; ***be ~ for doing sth*** essere perfetto per fare qc; ***the ~ moment*** il momento perfetto; ***in a ~ world*** in un mondo perfetto; (*absolute*) perfetto; ***a ~ stranger*** un perfetto sconosciuto **III** *v/t* perfezionare
perfection *n* perfezione *f*; ***to ~*** alla perfezione
perfectionist *n* perfezionista *m/f*
perfectly *adv* perfettamente; ***the climate suited us ~*** ci siamo adattati perfettamente al clina; ***I understand you ~*** ti capisco perfettamente; (*absolutely*) assolutamente; ***we're ~ happy about it*** ne siamo veramente felici; ***you know ~ well that ...*** sai perfettamente che…; ***to be ~ honest, ...*** ad essere totalmente onesti, …; ***a Lada is a ~ good car*** la Lada è un'ottima auto
perforated *adj line* perforato
perforations *npl* linea *fsg* perforata
perform **I** *v/t* (*carry out*) eseguire; *of actors* rappresentare; *of musician* eseguire **II** *v/i of actor, musician, dancer* esibirsi; *of actor* recitare; ***the car ~s well*** la macchina dà ottime prestazioni
performance *n by actor* rappresentazione *f*; *by musician* esecuzione *f*; ***he gave a splendid ~*** ha eseguito una splendida interpretazione; ***we are going to hear a ~ of Beethoven's 5th*** ascolteremo un'esecuzione della 5° sinfonia di Beethoven; (*show*) spettacolo *m*; *of employee, company etc* rendimento *m*; *of machine* prestazioni *fpl*; *of candidate* risultato *m*; ***he put up a good ~*** si è difeso bene; *infml* (*palaver*) impresa *f*
performance car *n* auto *f inv* di alte prestazioni
performer *n* artista *m/f*
performing *adj animal* ammaestrato; ***the ~ arts*** le arti dello spettacolo
perfume **I** *n* profumo *m* **II** *v/t* profumare
perfunctory *adj* superficiale
perhaps *adv* forse; ***~ the greatest exponent of the art*** forse i maggiori esponenti dell'arte; ***~ so*** forse sì; ***~ not*** forse no; ***~ I might keep it for a day or two?*** potrei tenerlo per un paio di giorni?
peril *n* pericolo *m*; ***he is in great ~*** è in grande pericolo
perilous *adj* pericoloso
perimeter *n* perimetro *m*
perimeter fence *n* recinzione *f*
period *n time* periodo *m*; ***for a ~ of eight weeks*** per un periodo di otto settimane; ***for a three-month ~*** per un periodo di tre mesi; ***at that ~*** in quel periodo; ***a ~ of cold weather*** un periodo di tempo freddo; (*menstruation*) mestruazioni *fpl*; ***she*** EDU ora *f* (di lezione); ***missed a ~*** perdere una lezione; ***double ~*** lezione di due ore; ***I don't want to, ~!*** *US* non voglio, punto e basta!
periodic *adj* periodico
periodical *n* periodico *m*
periodically *adv* periodicamente
peripheral **I** *adj not crucial* marginale

II *n* COMPUT periferica *f*
periphery *n* periferia *f*
periscope *n* periscopio *m*
perish *v/i of rubber* deteriorarsi; *of person* perire
perishable *adj food* deteriorabile
perishing *adj infml*: ***it's ~*** fa un freddo da cane *infml*
peristalsis *n* ANAT peristalsi *f*
peristyle *n* ARCH peristilio *m*
peritonitis *n* MED peritonite *f*
periwig *n* parrucca *f*
periwinkle *n* BOT pervinca *f*; *colour* pervinca *m*
perjure *v/r*: ***~ o.s.*** spergiurare
perjury *n* falso giuramento *m*
perk *n of job* vantaggio *m*
◆**perk up I** *v/t sep infml* tirare su di morale **II** *v/i infml* animarsi
perky *adj* (*+er*) *infml* (*cheerful*) allegro
perm I *n* permanente *f* **II** *v/t* fare la permanente a
permafrost *n* permafrost *m*
permanence, **permanency** *n* posto *m* (di lavoro) fisso
permanent *adj* permanente; *job*, *address* fisso
permanently *adv* permanentemente; ***~ employed*** assunto a tempo indeterminato; ***are you living ~ in Brighton?*** ti sei stabilito a Brighton?
permeable *adj* permeabile
permeate *v/t* permeare
permissible *adj* permesso, ammissibile
permission *n* permesso *m*; ***get s.o.'s ~*** ricevere il permesso di qn; ***give s.o. ~*** (***to do sth***) dare il permesso a qn (di fare qc); ***ask s.o.'s ~*** chiedere il permesso a qn
permissive *adj* permissivo
permissive society *n* società *f inv* permissiva
permit I *v/t* ⟨*pret & past part* ***-ted***⟩ permettere; ***~ s.o. to do sth*** permettere a qn di fare qc **II** *v/i*: ***weather ~ting*** tempo permettendo **III** *n* permesso *m*; ***~ holder*** chi possiede un permesso; ***work ~*** permesso *m* di lavoro
pernickety *adj infml* pignolo
peroxide *n* CHEM perossido *m*; *infml* acqua ossigenata
peroxide blonde *n* biondo *m*, -a *f* ossigenato, a
perpendicular *adj* perpendicolare
perpetrate *v/t* perpetrare
perpetrator *n* perpetratore *m*, -trice *f*; ***the ~ of this crime*** il perpetratore di questo crimine
perpetual *adj* perenne
perpetually *adv* perennemente
perpetuate *v/t* perpetuare
perpetuity *n* eternità *f*; ***in ~*** JUR in perpetuo
perplex *v/t* lasciare perplesso
perplexed *adj* perplesso
perplexity *n* perplessità *f inv*
perry *n* sidro *m* di pere
persecute *v/t* perseguitare
persecution *n* persecuzione *f*
persecutor *n* persecutore *m*, -trice *f*
perseverance *n* perseveranza *f*
persevere *v/i* perseverare; ***~ in one's attempts to do sth*** perseverare nel tentativo di fare qc
Persia *n* Persia *f*
Persian *adj* persiano; ***the ~ Gulf*** il Golfo Persico
Persian carpet *n* tappeto *m* persiano
persiflage *n* canzonatura *f*
persimmon *n* BOT cachi *m inv*
persist *v/i* persistere; ***~ in*** persistere in; ***we shall ~ in*** *or* ***with our efforts*** dobbiamo insistere con i nostri tentativi
persistence *n* (*perseverance*) perseveranza *f*; (*continuation*) persistere *m*
persistent *adj person*, *questions* insistente; *rain*, *unemployment etc* continuo; ***~ offender*** recidivo *m*, -a *f*
persistently *adv* (*continually*) continuamente
person *n* persona *f*; ***I like him as a ~*** mi piace come tipo; ***I know no such ~*** non conosco persone simili; ***per ~*** a persona; ***I'm more of a cat ~*** sono più un tipo da gatti; GRAM persona *f*; ***first ~ singular/plural*** prima persona singolare/plurale; ***in ~*** di persona
personable *adj* di bell'aspetto
persona grata *n* persona *f* grata
personal *adj* personale; ***don't make ~ remarks*** non fare commenti personali
personal assistant *n* assistente *m/f* personale **personal column** *n* annunci *mpl* personali **personal computer** *n* personal computer *m inv* **personal**

hygiene *n* igiene *f* personale
personality *n* personalità *f inv*
personally *adv* personalmente; ***don't take it ~*** non offenderti; ***~, I think that ...*** Personalmente, penso che...; ***hold s.o. ~ responsible*** ritenere qn personalmente responsabile
personal organizer *n* agenda *f* elettronica **personal pronoun** *n* pronome *m* personale **personal stereo** *n* Walkman® *m inv* **personal trainer** *n* allenatore *m*, -trice *f* personale
personification *n* personificazione *f*; ***he is the ~ of good taste*** è il buon gusto fatto persona
personify *v/t* ⟨*pret & past part* **-ied**⟩ *of person* personificare; ***he personifies evil*** è il diavolo personificato
personnel *n employees* personale *m*; *department* ufficio *m* del personale
personnel manager *n* direttore *m*, -trice *f* del personale
perspective *n* PAINT prospettiva *f*; ***get sth into ~*** vedere qc nella giusta prospettiva
Perspex® *n Br* perspex® *m inv*
perspicacious *adj* perspicace
perspiration *n* traspirazione *f*
perspire *v/i* sudare
persuade *v/t* persuadere, convincere; ***~ s.o. to do sth*** persuadere *or* convincere qn a fare qc; ***she is easily ~d*** si persuade facilmente
persuasion *n* persuasione *f*; ***powers of ~*** forza *f* di persuasione; ***it took a great deal of ~ to get her to accept*** c'è voluto molto lavoro di persuasione per convincerla ad accettare
persuasive *adj* persuasivo
pert *adj* (+*er*) impertinente
pertain *v/i* (*belong*) appartenere; essere di pertinenza a; ***the house and the large garden ~ing to it*** la casa e il giardino grande che gli appartengono
pertinent *adj form* pertinente
perturb *v/t* inquietare
perturbing *adj* inquietante
peruse *v/t form* leggere
pervade *v/t* pervadere
pervasive *adj influence*, *ideas* diffuso
perverse *adj* ostinato, irragionevole; *sexually* pervertito; ***be ~*** (*awkward*) essere un bastian contrario; ***take a ~ delight in doing sth*** provare un piacere perverso a fare qc
perversion *n sexual* perversione *f*; *of truth etc* distorsione *f*
perversity *n* cattiveria *f*
pervert I *n sexual* pervertito *m*, -a *f* **II** *v/t*: ***~ the course of justice*** ostacolare il corso della giustizia
pesky *adj* (+*er*) *esp US infml* fastidioso
pessary *n* (*contraceptive*) pessario *m*
pessimism *n* pessimismo *m*
pessimist *n* pessimista *m/f*
pessimistic *adj attitude*, *view* pessimistico; *person* pessimista
pest *n* animale / insetto *m* nocivo; ***~ control*** *insects* disinfestazione; *rats* derattizzazione; *infml person* peste *f*
pester *v/t* assillare; ***~ s.o. to do sth*** assillare qn perché faccia qc; ***she ~ed me for the book*** mi ha tormentato per via del libro
pesticide *n* pesticida *m*
pet I *n animal* animale *m* domestico; (*favourite*) favorito *m*, -a *f*; ***teacher's ~*** il cocco del professore **II** *adj* preferito; *for animals* per animali domestici; ***~ food*** cibo *m* per animali domestici; ***her ~ dogs*** il suo cagnolino; ***~ theory*** teoria *f* preferita; ***a ~ name*** vezzeggiativo *m* **III** *v/t* ⟨*pret & past part* **-ted**⟩ *animal* accarezzare **IV** *v/i* ⟨*pret & past part* **-ted**⟩ *of couple* pomiciare *infml*
petal *n* petalo *m*
◆ **peter out** *v/i of rebellion*, *rain* cessare; *of path* finire
petit bourgeois *adj* piccolo borghese
petite *adj* minuta
petition I *n* petizione *f*; ***get up a ~*** fare una petizione **II** *v/t* (*hand petition to*) presentare una petizione a **III** *v/i* fare una petizione
pet name *n* nomignolo *m*
petrified *adj* terrorizzato; ***she is ~ of spiders*** è terrorizzata dai ragni
petrify *v/t* ⟨*pret & past part* **-ied**⟩ terrorizzare; ***he really petrifies me*** mi fa davvero impietrire; ***a ~ing experience*** un'esperienza terrorizzante
petrochemical *adj* petrolchimico
petrol *n* benzina *f*
petroleum *n* petrolio *m*
petrol gauge *n* spia *f* della benzina **petrol pump** *n* pompa *f* della benzina **petrol station** *n* stazione *f* di servizio
petticoat *n* sottoveste *f*

pettiness *n* (*small-mindedness*) piccolezza *f*
petting *n* petting *m inv*
pettish *adj* permaloso
petty *adj* (+*er*) *person*, *behaviour* meschino; *details*, *problem* insignificante
petty cash *n* piccola cassa *f* **petty crime** *n* reato *m* minore **petty theft** *n* piccolo furto *m*
petulant *adj* petulante
pew *n* banco *m* (di chiesa); (*chair*) posto a sedere; ***take a ~!*** accomodatevi!
pewter *n* peltro *m*
PG *abbr* (= **parental guidance**) *Br sigla che contrassegna film non adatti ai bambini*
phallic *adj* fallico; ***~ symbol*** simbolo *m* fallico
phallus *n* ⟨*pl* ***phalluses*** *or* ***phalli***⟩ fallo *m*
phantom *n*/*adj* fantasma *m*
pharmaceutical *adj* farmaceutico
pharmaceuticals *npl* farmaceutici *mpl*
pharmacist *n* farmacista *m*/*f*
pharmacology *n* farmacologia *f*
pharmacy *n* farmacia *f*
phase I *n* fase *f*; ***a passing ~*** una fase di passaggio; ***he's just going through a ~*** sta solo attraversando una fase **II** *v*/*t*: ***a ~d withdrawal*** un ritiro graduale
◆**phase in** *v*/*t sep* introdurre gradualmente
◆**phase out** *v*/*t sep* eliminare gradualmente
PhD *abbr* (= **Doctor of Philosophy**) *dottorato di ricerca*
pheasant *n* fagiano *m*
phenix *n US* → ***phoenix***
phenomenal *adj* fenomenale; ***at a ~ rate*** ad un tasso fenomenale
phenomenally *adv* straordinariamente
phenomenon *n* ⟨*pl* ***phenomena***⟩ fenomeno *m*
phew *int relief* fiu; *nuisance* uff
phial *n* flacone *m*; (*for serum*) fiala *f*
philander *v*/*i* fare il cascamorto
philanthropic *adj* filantropico
philanthropist *n* filantropo *m*, -a *f*
philanthropy *n* filantropia *f*
-phile *n suf* -filo *m*, -a *f*
philharmonic I *adj* filarmonico **II** *n*: ***Philharmonic*** Filarmonica *f*
Philippines *npl*: ***the ~*** le Filippine *fpl*
philistine *n* filisteo *m*, -a *f*
philology *n* filologia *f*
philosopher *n* filosofo *m*, -a *f*
philosophical *adj* filosofico; ***be philosophical about sth*** prendere qc con filosofia
philosophize *v*/*i* filosofare
philosophy *n* filosofia *f*
phlegm *n* muco *m*
phlegmatic *adj* flemmatico
-phobe *n suf* - fobo *m*, -a *f*
phobia *n* fobia *f*; ***she has a ~ about rats*** ha la fobia dei topi
phoenix, *US* **phenix** *n* fenice *f*; ***like a ~ from the ashes*** come una fenice dalle proprie ceneri
phone I *n* telefono *m*; ***be on the ~*** *have one* avere il telefono; *be talking* essere al telefono; ***I'll give you a ~*** *infml* ti faccio un colpo di telefono **II** *v*/*t* telefonare a **III** *v*/*i* telefonare
◆**phone back** *v*/*i* & *v*/*t sep* richiamare
◆**phone in I** *v*/*i a radio* / *TV show* chiamare; ***phone in sick*** chiamare il posto di lavoro per comunicare una malattia **II** *v*/*t sep order* ordinare
◆**phone up I** *v*/*i* dare un colpo di telefono **II** *v*/*t sep* telefonare a
phone bill *n* bolletta del telefono **phone book** *n* guida *f* telefonica, elenco telefonico *m* **phone booth** *n* cabina *f* telefonica **phone box** *n* cabina *f* telefonica **phone call** *n* telefonata *f* **phone card** *n* scheda *f* telefonica **phone-in** *n on radio programma con gli interventi degli ascoltatori* **phone number** *n* numero *m* di telefono
phonetic *adj*, fonetico
phonetically *adv* foneticamente
phonetic alphabet *n* alfabeto *m* fonetico
phonetics *nsg* fonetica *f*
phon(e)y *adj infml* falso; ***a ~ company*** un'azienda fasulla; ***a ~ war*** una guerra dichiarata ma non combattuta; (*insincere*) *person* impostore
phosphate *n* CHEM fosfato *m*
phosphorescent *adj* fosforescente
photo *n* foto *f*
photo album *n* album *m inv* fotografico **photo booth** *n* macchinetta *f* automatica per le fotografie **photocop-**

ier *n* fotocopiatrice *f* **photocopy I** *n* fotocopia *f* **II** *v/t* ⟨*pret & past part* ***-ied***⟩ fotocopiare **photo finish** *n* fotofinish *m inv* **Photofit®** *n* (*a.* **Photofit picture**) fotofit *m*
photogenic *adj* fotogenico
photograph I *n* fotografia *f*; ***take a ~*** fare una fotografia **II** *v/t* fotografare
photographer *n* fotografo *m*, -a *f*
photography *n* fotografia *f*
photojournalism *n* fotogiornalismo *m*
photomontage *n* fotomontaggio *m*
photon *n* fotone *m*
photo opportunity *n opportunità per un personaggio famoso di venire ripreso dai fotografi*
photosynthesis *n* fotosintesi *f inv*
photovoltaic *adj* ELEC fotovoltaico
phrasal verb *n* verbo *m* frasale
phrase I *n* frase *f* **II** *v/t* esprimere
phrasebook *n* vocabolarietto *m* di frasi utili
phraseology *n* fraseologia *f*
phrasing *n* formulazione *f*; *spoken* enunciazione *f*; MUS fraseggio *m*
pH-value *n* valore *m* del PH
physical I *adj* fisico **II** *n* MED visita *f* medica
physical education *n* educazione *f* fisica **physical handicap** *n* handicap *m inv* fisico
physically *adv* fisicamente; ***be ~ sick*** essere fisicamente malato; ***~ impossible*** materialmente impossibile; ***they removed him ~ from the meeting*** lo hanno fisicamente portato via dalla riunione; ***as long as is ~ possible*** finché è materialmente possibile
physically handicapped *adj*: ***be ~*** essere portatore *m*, -trice *f* di handicap fisico
physical sciences *npl* scienze *fpl* fisiche
physician *n* medico *m*
physicist *n* fisico *m*, -a *f*
physics *nsg* fisica *f*
physio *n esp Br infml* fisioterapista *m/f*
physiological *adj* fisiologico
physiology *n* fisiologia *f*
physiotherapist *n* fisioterapeuta *m/f*
physiotherapy *n* fisioterapia *f*
physique *n* fisico *m*
pianist *n* pianista *m/f*
piano *n* piano *m*
piano accordion *n* fisarmonica *f* **piano player** *n* pianista *m/f*
picaresque *adj* picaresco
piccalilli *n* COOK *giardiniera con senape e spezie*
piccolo *n* MUS ottavino *m*
pick¹ *n tool* piccone *m*; (*choice*) scelta *f*; (*best choice*) il meglio *m*
pick² I *v/t* (*choose*) scegliere; *flowers, fruit* raccogliere; ***~ one's nose*** mettersi le dita nel naso; ***~ a lock*** forzare una serratura; ***~ a team*** formare una squadra; ***~ s.o. to do sth*** scegliere qn per fare qc; ***~ sides*** schierarsi; ***~ one's way through sth*** camminare con cautela in mezzo a qc; *scab* grattarsi una crosta; *hole* fare il buco; *fig* ***she's always ~ing holes in things*** trova sempre i punti deboli delle cose **II** *v/i*: ***~ and choose*** fare i difficili **III** *n*: ***take your ~*** scegli quello che vuoi; (*choice*) ***she could have her ~ of any man in the room*** potrebbe avere qualsiasi uomo in questa stanza; ***have first ~*** avere la prima scelta; (*best*) il meglio; ***our puppy was the ~ of the litter*** il nostro cucciolo era il migliore della cucciolata
◆**pick at** *v/t*: ***pick at one's food*** mangiucchiare poco
◆**pick on** *v/t treat unfairly* prendersela con; (*select*) scegliere
◆**pick out** *v/t sep* (*identify*) riconoscere; ***pick out a tune*** MUS strimpellare un motivo
◆**pick up I** *v/t sep* prendere; *phone* sollevare; *baby* prendere in braccio; *from ground* raccogliere; (*collect*) andare / venire a prendere; *information* raccogliere; *in car* far salire; *man, woman* rimorchiare *infml*; *language, skill* imparare; *habit, illness* prendere; (*buy*) trovare; *criminal* arrestare; *idea* sviluppare; ***you just have to pick up the phone*** devi solo sollevare la cornetta; ***pick up the pieces*** raccogliere i pezzi; ***you'll soon pick it up*** lo imparerai presto; ***where did you pick up that idea?*** dove hai trovato quell'idea?; ***pick sth up at a sale*** fare un affare ai saldi; ***pick up a story*** continuare una storia; ***pick up the tab*** *infml* pagare (il con-

to); ***pick up speed*** prendere velocità **II** *v/i* (*improve*) migliorare; ***pick up where one left off*** riprendere da dove si era rimasti
pickaxe, *US* **pickax** *n* piccone *m*
picket I *n of strikers* picchetto *m* **II** *v/t* picchettare
picket line *n* cordone *m* degli scioperanti
pickle I *n* sottaceto *m*; ***he was in a bit of a ~*** *infml* era nei pasticci; ***get* (*o.s.*) *into a ~*** mettersi nei pasticci **II** *v/t* conservare sott'aceto
pickled *adj* sott'aceto; *infml* sbronzo
pick-me-up *n infml* cordiale *m* **pickpocket** *n* borseggiatore *m*, -trice *f*
pick-up *n truck* furgoncino *m* a sponde basse; ***~ point*** *goods* punto di carico; *people* punto di raccolta
picky *adj* (*+er*) *infml* difficile (da accontentare)
picnic I *n* picnic *m inv*; ***have a ~*** fare un picnic; ***go for*** *or* ***on a ~*** fare un picnic **II** *v/i* ⟨*pret & past part* ***-ked***⟩ fare un picnic
picnic basket, picnic hamper *n* cestino *m* da picnic
pictograph *n* pittogramma *m*
pictorial *adj* (*with images*) illustrato; *style* pittorico; (*lively*) vivace
picture I *n* (*photo*) foto *f*; (*painting*) quadro *m*; ***(as) pretty as a ~*** bello come un dipinto; (*illustration*) figura *f*; *film* film *m inv*; ***put / keep s.o. in the ~*** mettere / tenere al corrente qn; ***OK, I get the ~*** ok, ho capito; (*image*) ***this will give you a ~ of what life is like here*** questo ti darà un'idea di com'è la vita qui; ***she was the ~ of health*** era il ritratto della salute **II** *v/t* immaginare
picture book *n* libro *m* illustrato **picture frame** *n* cornice *f* **picture gallery** *n* pinacoteca *f* **picture postcard** *n* cartolina *f* illustrata
pictures *npl* cinema *m*; *Br* ***go to the ~*** andare al cinema
picturesque *adj* pittoresco
piddle *v/i infml* fare pipì
piddling *adj pej infml* insignificante
pidgin *n* pidgin *m*
pidgin English *n* pidgin English *m*
pie *n sweet* torta *f*; *savoury* pasticcio *m*; ***that's all ~ in the sky*** *infml* tutto questo è pura utopia; ***as easy as ~*** *infml* un gioco da ragazzi; *fig* ***she's got a finger in every ~*** *infml* ha le mani in pasta
piebald *adj* pezzato
piece *n* pezzo *m*; ***a ~ of pie / bread*** una fetta di torta / pane; ***a ~ of furniture*** un mobile; ***a ~ of advice*** un consiglio; ***a 10p ~*** una moneta da 10 penny; *fig infml* ***it's a ~ of cake*** è un gioco da ragazzi; ***go to ~s*** crollare; ***take to ~s*** smontare; ***he tore the letter (in)to ~s*** ha strappato la lettera in mille pezzi; ***he tore me to ~s during the debate*** durante il dibattito mi ha fatto a pezzi; ***all in one ~*** tutto intero; ***are you still in one ~ after your trip?*** sei ancora tutto intero dopo il viaggio?; ***give s.o. a ~ of one's mind*** dire a qn il fatto suo
◆**piece together** *v/t sep broken plate* rimettere insieme; *facts*, *evidence* ricostruire
piecemeal *adv* poco alla volta
piecework *n* lavoro *m* a cottimo
pie chart *n* diagramma *m* a torta
pied *adj* variopinto; *horse* pezzato
Pied Piper *n* Pifferaio Magico
pie-eyed *adj Br infml* sbronzo
pier *n at seaside* pontile *m*
pierce *v/t* (*penetrate*) trapassare; *ears* farsi i buchi in
piercing I *adj noise* lacerante; *eyes* penetrante; *wind* pungente **II** *n in body* piercing *m inv*
pig I *n a. fig* maiale *m*; ***make a ~ of o.s.*** mangiare come un maiale; ***~s might fly*** *Br prov* e gli asini volano **II** *v/t* ⟨*pret & past part* ***-ged***⟩ ingozzarsi; ***they were ~ging it over at John's flat*** vivevano come porci nell'appartamento di John
◆**pig out** *v/i infml* abbuffarsi
pigeon *n* piccione *m*
pigeonhole I *n* casella *f* **II** *v/t person* etichettare; *proposal* archiviare
piggy *adj* (*+er*) ***~ eyes*** occhi porcini
piggyback *n*: ***give s.o. a ~*** portare qn a cavalluccio
piggybank *n* salvadanaio *m*
pigheaded *adj* testardo
piglet *n* maialino *m*
pigment *n* pigmento *m*
pigmy *n* → ***pygmy***
pigpen *n US* → ***pigsty***
pigskin *n* (*leather*) pelle *f* di maiale

pigsty *n a. fig* porcile *m* **pigtail** *n* codino *m*; *plaited* treccina *f*
pile[1] **I** *n* mucchio *m*; TEX pelo *m*; *beam* palo *m*; ***put things in a ~*** mettere cose una sull'altra; *fig* ***at the bottom/top of the ~*** in fondo / cima alla scala; ***a ~ of work*** *infml* un sacco di lavoro *infml* **II** *v/t* ammucchiare; ***a table ~d high with books*** un tavolo coperto di libri; ***the sideboard was ~d high with presents*** la credenza era piena di regali
◆**pile on I** *v/i infml*: ***pile it on*** esagerare, *infml* gonfiare **II** *v/t sep liter* accumulare; ***she piled rice on(to) my plate*** ha messo una montagna di riso nel mio piatto; ***they are really piling on the pressure*** si stanno facendo sentire
◆**pile up I** *v/i of work, bills* accumularsi **II** *v/t sep* ammucchiare
piles *npl* MED emorroidi *fpl*
pile-up *n* AUTO tamponamento *m* a catena
pilfer *v/t* rubacchiare
pilfering *n* piccoli furti *mpl*
pilgrim *n* pellegrino *m*, -a *f*; ***the Pilgrim Fathers*** i Padri Pellegrini
pilgrimage *n* pellegrinaggio *m*; ***go on a ~*** andare in pellegrinaggio
pill *n* pastiglia *f*; ***the ~*** la pillola; ***be on the ~*** prendere la pillola
pillage I *n* saccheggio *m* **II** *v/t & v/i* saccheggiare
pillar *n* colonna *f*; *of bridge* pilastro *m*; ***a ~ of society*** una colonna della società
pillar box *n* buca *f* delle lettere (a colonnina)
pillbox *n* portapillole *m*; *hat piccolo cappello tondo da donna con calotta piatta e tesa rigida*; *bunker* casamatta *f*
pillion *n of motor bike* sellino *m* posteriore; ***ride ~*** viaggiare nel sellino posteriore
pillow *n* guanciale *m*
pillowcase, pillowslip *n* federa *f*; **pillow talk** *n* conversazioni *fpl* intime (a letto)
pilot I *n of aeroplane* pilota *m/f*; *of TV show* programma *m* pilota **II** *v/t aeroplane* pilotare
pilot light *n* fiamma *f* pilota **pilot plant** *n* stabilimento *m* pilota **pilot scheme** *n* progetto *m* pilota **pilot study** *n* studio *m* pilota
pimp *n* magnaccia *m*
pimple *n* brufolo *m*
pin I *n for sewing* spillo *m*; *in bowling* birillo *m*; (*badge*) spilla *f*; ELEC spinotto *m*; ***I've got ~s and needles in my foot*** ho un formicolio nel piede; ***you could have heard a ~ drop*** non si sentiva volare una mosca; ***a two-~ plug*** una presa a due spine **II** *v/t* ⟨*pret & past part* **-ned**⟩ (*hold down*) immobilizzare; (*attach*) attaccare; *on lapel* appuntare; *fig* ***~ s.o. to the ground*** tenere qn inchiodato; ***~ s.o.'s arm behind his back*** immobilizzare il braccio di qn dietro la schiena; ***~ one's hopes on s.o./sth*** riporre le proprie speranze in qn/qc; ***~ the blame (for sth) on s.o.*** *infml* addossare la colpa (di qc) su qn; ***~ one's hair back*** fissare i capelli con uno spillo
◆**pin down** *v/t sep*: ***pin s.o. down to a date*** far fissare una data a qn
◆**pin up** *v/t sep notice* appuntare
PIN *abbr* (= **personal identification number**) numero *m* di codice segreto, PIN
pinafore *n* grembiule *m*
pinball *n* flipper *m inv*
pincers *npl tool* tenaglie *fpl*; ***a pair of ~*** un paio di pinze; *of crab* chele *fpl*
pinch I *n* pizzico *m*; ***at a ~*** al massimo **II** *v/t* pizzicare; *infml steal* fregare; ***~ s.o.'s bottom*** dare un pizzicotto a qn sul sedere; ***~ o.s.*** darsi un pizzico; *Br* (*steal*) fregare ***don't let anyone ~ my seat*** non lasciare che mi freghino il posto; (*catch stealing*) *infml* pizzicare; **III** *v/i of shoes* stringere
pincushion *n* puntaspilli *m*
pine[1] *n* pino *m*; ***~ furniture*** mobili *mpl* di pino
pine[2] *v/i*: ***~ for*** soffrire per la mancanza di
◆**pine away** *v/i* languire
pineapple *n* ananas *m inv*; ***~ juice*** succo *m* di ananas
pine cone *n* pigna *f* **pine needle** *n* ago *m* di pino **pine tree** *n* pino *m*
pinewood *n* (*material*) (legno *m* di) pino *m*
ping I *n* suono *m* metallico **II** *v/i* fare un suono metallico

ping-pong *n* ping-pong *m inv*
pinhead *n* capocchia *f* di spillo; *infml* testa *f* di rapa
pink I *n* (*colour*) rosa *m*; ***that horse is in the ~ of condition*** quel cavallo è in forma smagliante **II** *adj* rosa *inv*; ***go*** *or* ***turn ~*** arrossire
pinkeye *n* MED congiuntivite *f* batterica
pinkie *n US* mignolo *m*
pinking shears *n* forbici *fpl* seghettate
pin money *n* spiccioli *mpl*
pinnacle *n* pinnacolo *m*; *fig* apice *m*
pinny *n infml* grembiulino *m*
pinpoint I *n* punta di spillo; ***a ~ of light*** un puntino luminoso **II** *v/t* indicare con esattezza; (*highlight*) mettere in evidenza
pinprick *n* puntura *f* di spillo; (*annoyance*) seccatura *f*
pins and needles *npl* formicolio *m*
pinstripe *adj* gessato
pint *n* pinta *f*; ***go*** (***out***) ***for a ~*** andare a prendere una birra
pint-sized *adj* piccolo; *pej* insignificante
pin-up (**girl**) *n* pin-up *f inv*
pioneer I *n fig* pioniere *m*, -a *f* **II** *v/t* essere il/la pioniere di; ***~ the use of sth*** essere uno dei primi a usare qc
pioneering *adj work* pionieristico; ***~ spirit*** spirito *m* pionieristico
pious *adj* pio
pip I *n of fruit* seme *m* **II** *v/t* ⟨*pret & past part* ***-ged***⟩: ***~ s.o. at the post*** battere qn sul traguardo
pipe I *n for smoking* pipa *f*; *for water, gas, sewage* tubo *m*; MUS ***~s*** (*bagpipes*) cornamusa *f* **II** *v/t* trasportare con condutture; ***the chair was ~d in a contrasting fabric*** la poltrona era profilata con un tessuto a colori contrastanti
◆**pipe down** *v/i infml* far silenzio; ***he asked them to pipe down or go out of the room*** chiese loro di abbassare la voce o di uscire dall'aula
◆**pipe up** *v/i infml* alzare la voce; ***suddenly a little voice piped up*** improvvisamente si levò una vocina
pipe cleaner *n* scovolino *m*
piped music *n* musica *f* di sottofondo
pipe dream *n* sogno *m* irrealizzabile; ***that's just a ~*** è solo una fantasticheria
pipeline *n* conduttura *f*; *fig* ***in the ~*** in arrivo
piper *n* suonatore *m* di cornamusa
piping *n* (*pipework*) tubatura *f*
piping hot *adj* caldissimo
pipsqueak *n pej* mezzacalzetta *f*
piquant *adj* piccante
pique *n* ripicca *f*; ***he resigned in a fit of ~*** si è dimesso per ripicca
piracy *n of software* pirateria *f*
pirate I *n at sea* pirata *m* **II** *adj*: ***~ copy*** copia *f* pirata **III** *v/t software* piratare
Pisces *nsg* ASTROL Pesci *m/f inv*
piss I *v/i sl* (*urinate*) pisciare *sl* **II** *n* (*urine*) piscia *f sl*; ***take the ~ out of s.o.*** *sl* prendere qn per il culo *sl*
◆**piss off** *v/i sl* sparire; ***piss off!*** levati dalle palle! *sl*
piss artist *n Br infml vulg* (*drunk*) ubriacone *m*; (*boaster*) fanfarone *m*
pissed *adj sl* (*drunk*) sbronzo *infml*; *US* (*annoyed*) seccato
pissed off *adj sl* (*annoyed*) incavolato *infml*
piss-up *n Br vulg* sbevazzata *f*
pistachio *n* pistacchio *m*
pistol *n* pistola *f*
piston *n* pistone *m*
pit[1] *n* (*hole*) buca *f*; (*coal mine*) miniera *f*; THEAT (*orchestra pit*) golfo *m* mistico; ***have a sinking feeling in the ~ of one's stomach*** avere un senso di vuoto alla bocca dello stomaco; ***he works down the ~***(***s***) lavora giù in miniera; SPORTS ***make a ~ stop*** fare una sosta ai box/un pit stop; ***the ~s*** *infml* la schifezza
pit[2] **I** *n* (*kernel*) nocciolo *m* **II** *v/t* snocciolare; ***we spent the evening ~ting the olives*** abbiamo passato la serata a snocciolare le olive
pitch[1] *n* MUS intonazione *f*; *Br* (*field*) campo *m*; ***cricket ~*** campo *m* da cricket; ***she had the gift of perfect ~*** aveva l'orecchio assoluto
pitch[2] **I** *v/t tent* piantare; *ball* lanciare; *note* intonare; ***he ~ed the ball short*** ha fatto un lancio corto; ***she ~ed her voice higher*** ha impostato la voce più in alto **II** *v/i* (*fall*) cadere; NAUT beccheggiare; AVIAT impennarsi; *baseball* servire; ***~ forward*** cadere in avanti
pitch[3] *n* (*tar*) pece *f*

pitch black *adj* buio pesto
pitched roof *n* tetto *m* spiovente
pitcher[1] *n container* brocca *f*
pitcher[2] *n baseball* lanciatore *m*, -trice *f*
pitchfork *n* forcone *m*
piteous *adj* pietoso
pitfall *n* tranello *m*
pith *n of citrus fruit* parte *f* bianca della scorza
pithy *adj* conciso
pitiful *adj sight* pietoso; *excuse*, *attempt* penoso
pitiless *adj* spietato
pits *npl* → ***pit***[1]
pit stop *n in motor racing* sosta *f* ai box
pitta bread *n* pane *m* pitta
pittance *n* miseria *f*
pity **I** *n* pietà *f inv*; ***it's a ~ that*** è un peccato che; ***what a ~!*** che peccato!; ***take ~ on*** avere pietà di **II** *v/t* ⟨*pret & past part* **-ied**⟩ *person* avere pietà di
pivot *v/i* ruotare
pixel *n* COMPUT pixel *m inv*
pizza *n* pizza *f*
placard *n* cartello *m*
placate *v/t* placare
place **I** *n* **1.** posto *m*; ***we found a good ~ to watch the procession from*** abbiamo trovato un buon posto dal quale guardare la processione; ***this is no ~ for you*** non c'è posto per te; ***it was the last ~ I expected to find him*** era l'ultimo posto nel quale mi aspettavo di trovarlo; ***this isn't the ~ to discuss politics*** non è la sede adatta per discutere di politica; ***I can't be in two ~s at once!*** non posso essere in due posti allo stesso tempo!; ***feel out of ~*** sentirsi fuori posto; ***people in high ~s*** persone delle alte sfere; ***know one's ~*** saper stare al proprio posto; ***it's not my ~ to comment*** non spetta a me fare commenti; ***keep*** *or* ***put s.o. in his ~*** tenere *or* mettere qualcuno al proprio posto; *fig* ***in the first ~*** (*firstly*) in primo luogo; ***she shouldn't have been there in the first ~*** prima di tutto non avrebbe dovuto trovarsi là **2.** *flat*, *house* casa *f*; ***at my / his ~*** a casa mia / sua **3.** ***I've lost my ~*** *in book* ho perso il segno **4.** ***in ~ of*** invece di **5.** ***take ~*** aver luogo **II** *v/t* (*put*) piazzare; ***I can't quite ~ you*** non mi ricordo dove ci siamo conosciuti; ***~ an order*** fare un'ordinazione; ***she slowly ~d one foot in front of the other*** metteva lentamente un piede davanti all'altro; ***she ~d a finger on her lips*** appoggiò un dito sulle labbra; ***~ a strain on sth*** sottoporre qc a sforzo; ***~ confidence in s.o. / sth*** riporre fiducia in qn / qc; ***how are you ~d for time?*** come ti sei classificato con il tuo tempo?; ***we are well ~d for the shops*** siamo in buona posizione rispetto ai negozi; ***Liverpool are well ~d in the league*** il Liverpool ha un buon piazzamento nella serie; (*rank*) classificare; ***that should be ~d first*** dovrebbe essere al primo posto; ***the German runner was ~d third*** il corridore tedesco si è piazzato al terzo posto
placebo *n* placebo *m inv*
place mat *n* tovaglietta *f* all'americana
placement *n for work* stage *m inv*; ***I'm here on a six-month ~*** (*for in-service training etc*) sono qui per un tirocinio di sei mesi
placenta *n* placenta *f*
placid *adj* placido
plagiarism *n* plagio *m*
plagiarize *v/t* plagiare
plague **I** *n* peste *f*; ***avoid s.o. / sth like the ~*** evitare qualcuno come la peste **II** *v/t* (*bother*) tormentare; ***be ~d by doubts*** essere tormentato dai dubbi; ***~ s.o. with questions*** tartassare qn di domande
plaice *n fish* platessa *f*
plaid *n* tartan *m inv*
plain[1] *n* pianura *f*
plain[2] **I** *adj* (*+er*) (*clear*, *obvious*) chiaro; ***it is ~ to see that …*** si capisce chiaramente che…; ***make sth ~ to s.o.*** chiarire qc a qn; ***the reason is ~ to see*** il motivo si vede chiaramente; ***I'd like to make it quite ~ that …*** vorrei chiarire che…; *not fancy* semplice; *not pretty* scialbo; *not patterned* in tinta unita; (*blunt*) franco; *knitting* dritto; ***~ chocolate*** cioccolato *m* fondente **II** *adv* semplicemente; ***it's ~ crazy*** è semplicemente matto; ***I can't put it ~er than that*** non riesco a dirlo più chiaramente di così
plain clothes *npl*: ***in ~*** in borghese
plain flour *n* farina *f* normale

plainly *adv* (*clearly*) chiaramente; **~, *these new techniques are impractical*** ovviamente queste nuove tecniche non sono utilizzabili; (*bluntly*) francamente; (*simply*) semplicemente

plain-spoken *adj* franco

plaintiff *n* JUR attore *m*, -trice *f*

plaintive *adj* lamentoso

plait I *n in hair* treccia *f* II *v/t hair* intrecciare

plan I *n* (*project, intention*) piano *m*; ***~ of action*** piano *m* di azione; ***the ~ is to meet at six*** il piano è di incontrarci alle sei; ***make ~s (for sth)*** fare progetti (per qc); ***have you any ~s for tonight?*** hai programmi per stasera?; ***according to ~*** come previsto; (*drawing*) progetto *m* II *v/t* ⟨*pret & past part* **-ned**⟩ (*prepare*) organizzare; (*design*) progettare; ***~ to do, ~ on doing*** avere in programma di III *v/i* ⟨*pret & past part* **-ned**⟩ pianificare; ***~ ahead*** programmare in anticipo

◆**plan on** *v/t*: ***plan on doing sth*** avere in programma di fare qc

◆**plan out** *v/t sep* pianificare dettagliatamente

plane[1] *n* (*aeroplane*) aereo *m*

plane[2] *n tool* pialla *f*

planet *n* pianeta *m*

planetarium *n* planetario *m*

plank *n of wood* asse *f*; *fig*: *of policy* punto *m*

plankton *n* plancton *m inv*

planner *n person* progettista *m*/*f*; *chart* calendario *m*

planning *n* pianificazione *f*; ***at the ~ stage*** allo stadio di progettazione; ***~ permission*** licenza *f* edilizia

plant[1] I *n* pianta *f*; ***rare/tropical ~s*** piante rare/tropicali II *v/t* piantare

plant[2] *n* (*factory*) stabilimento *m*; (*equipment*) impianto *m*

plantation *n* piantagione *f*

planter *n* (*pot*) vaso *m*; (*person*) piantatore *m*, -trice *f*

plaque *n* lapide *f*; *teeth* placca *f*

plasma *n in blood* plasma *m inv*

plasma screen *n on TV* schermo *m* al plasma

plaster I *n on wall, ceiling* intonaco *m*; ART, MED (*a.* **plaster of Paris**) gesso *m* da presa; ***have one's leg in ~*** avere una gamba ingessata; *Br* (*sticking plaster*) cerotto *m* II *v/t wall, ceiling* intonacare; ***be ~ed with*** essere ricoperto di; ***~ one's face with make-up*** *infml* truccarsi

plasterboard *n* cartongesso *m*

plaster cast *n* ingessatura *f*

plastered *adj infml* (*drunk*) sbronzo *infml*

plastic I *n* plastica *f*; *infml* (*money*) carte *fpl* di credito II *adj made of plastic* di plastica

plastic bag *n* sacchetto *m* di plastica **plastic explosive** *n* esplosivo *m* al plastico **plastic money** *n* carte *fpl* di credito **plastic surgeon** *n* chirurgo *m* plastico **plastic surgery** *n* chirurgia *f* plastica **plastic wrap** *n US* pellicola *f* adesiva

plate *n for food* piatto *m*; TECH, PHOT lastra *f*; (*name plate*) targa *f*; ***have sth handed to one on a ~*** *Br fig infml* ricevere qc su un piatto d'argento; *fig* ***have a lot on one's ~*** *infml* avere molto da fare

plateau *n* altopiano *m*

plateful *n* piatto *m*

plate glass *n* vetro *m* piano

platelet *n* MED piastrina *f*

platform *n* (*stage*) palco *m*; *of railway station* binario *m*; *fig*: *political* piattaforma *f*; COMPUT piattaforma *f*

platform shoe *n* scarpa *f* con la zeppa

platinum I *n* platino *m* II *adj* di platino

platinum blonde *n* biondo *m*, -a *f* platinato, -a

platitude *n* banalità *f inv*

platonic *adj relationship* platonico

platoon *n of soldiers* plotone *m*

platter *n for meat, fish* vassoio *m*; *fig* ***have sth handed to one on a (silver) ~*** ricevere qc su un piatto d'argento

plausible *adj* plausibile

play I *v/i of children*, SPORTS giocare; ***can Johnny come out to ~?*** Johnny può uscire a giocare?; ***~ at cowboys and Indians*** giochiamo ai cowboy e agli indiani; ***~ in defence*** SPORTS giocare in difesa; ***~ in goal*** segnare un goal; ***what are you ~ing at?*** *infml* che gioco stai giocando?; ***~ for money*** giocare a soldi; ***~ for time*** *fig* cercare di guadagnare tempo; ***~ into s.o.'s hands*** *fig* fare il gioco di qn; *of musician* suonare II *v/t* MUS suonare; ~ ***the piano*** suonare il pianoforte; *game* giocare a; *opponent* giocare contro; (*perform*: *Macbeth etc*) rappresentare; *particular role* interpretare; ~ ***a joke on*** fare uno scherzo a; ~ ***the fool*** fare lo stupido **III** *n in theatre, on TV* rappresentazione *f*; ***the ~s of Shakespeare*** le opere teatrali di Shakespeare; *of children*, TECH, SPORTS gioco *m*; ***abandon ~*** SPORTS interrompere il gioco; ***come into ~*** entrare in gioco; ~ ***on words*** gioco *m* di parole

◆**play along** *v/i*: ***play along with s.o.*** stare al gioco di qn; ***play along with a suggestion*** mostrare di accettare una proposta

◆**play around** *v/i infml* (*be unfaithful*): ***his wife's been playing around*** sua moglie lo ha tradito; ***her husband was playing around with his secretary*** suo marito aveva una relazione con la segretaria

◆**play back** *v/t sep recording* rivedere; *answering machine* riascoltare

◆**play down** *v/t sep* minimizzare

◆**play off** *v/t sep* ***play X off against Y*** mettere X contro Y

◆**play on I** *v/i* continuare a suonare **II** *v/t* (*a.* **play upon**) *s.o.'s fears* speculare; ***the hours of waiting played on my nerves*** le ore di attesa mi hanno logorato i nervi

◆**play up** *v/i of machine* dare noie; *of child* fare i capricci; *of tooth, bad back etc* fare male

◆**play with** *v/t*: ***we don't have much time to play with*** non abbiamo molto tempo da sprecare; ***play with o.s.*** toccarsi

playact *v/i* (*pretend*) fare la commedia

playback *n* playback *m inv*

playboy *n* playboy *m inv*

player *n* SPORTS giocatore *m*, -trice *f*; *musician* musicista *m/f*; *actor* attore *m*, -trice *f*

playful *adj punch, mood* scherzoso; *puppy* giocherellone

playground *n in school* cortile *m* per la ricreazione; *in park* parco *m* giochi

playgroup *n* asilo *m* **playhouse** *n* teatro *m*

playing card *n* carta *f* da gioco

playing field *n* campo *m* sportivo

playmate *n* compagno *m*, -a *f* di gioco

playoff *n match* spareggio *m* **playpen** *n* box *m inv* **playtime** *n* ricreazione *f*

playwright *n* commediografo *m*, -a *f*

plaza *n* piazza *f*; *US* (*shopping complex*) centro *m* commerciale

plc *abbr* (= **public limited company**) società *f inv* a responsabilità limitata quotata in borsa

plea *n* appello *m*

plead *v/i*: ~ ***for*** supplicare; ~ ***for mercy*** supplicare perdono; ~ ***guilty / not guilty*** dichiararsi colpevole / innocente; ~ ***with*** supplicare

pleasant *adj* piacevole

pleasantry *n* facezia *f*

please I *int* per favore; ~ ***pass the salt, pass the salt,*** ~ passami il sale, per favore; ***more tea? – yes,*** ~ ancora tè? – sì, grazie; ~ ***do*** fai pure, prego **II** *v/i*: (***just***) ***as you*** ~ come preferisci; ***do as one ~s*** fare come si vuole; (*cause satisfaction*) soddisfare; ***be eager to*** ~ fare di tutto per piacere **III** *v/t* far piacere a; ***the idea ~d him*** l'idea gli piaceva; ***just to ~ you*** solo per farti piacere; ***it ~s me to see him so happy*** mi fa piacere vederlo così felice; ***you can't ~ everybody*** non puoi contentare tutti; ***there's no pleasing him*** non c'è niente che gli faccia piacere; ***he is easily ~d*** si accontenta facilmente; ~ ***yourself*** fai come ti pare

pleased *adj* contento; ~ ***to meet you*** piacere!

pleasing *adj* piacevole

pleasurable *adj* piacevole

pleasure *n* (*happiness, satisfaction*) contentezza *f*; (*as opposed to work*) piacere *m*; ***business or ~?*** lavoro o piacere?; (*delight*) gioia *f*; ***have the ~ of doing sth*** avere il piacere di fare qc; ***do sth for ~*** fare qc per piacere; ***get ~ out of doing sth*** provare piacere a fare qc; ***he takes ~ in annoying me*** gli piace darmi fastidio; (*US usement*) divertimento *m*; ***it's a ~ to meet you*** è un piacere conoscerti; ***he's a ~ to teach*** è un piacere fargli da insegnante; ***it's a ~*** (*you're welcome*) è un piacere; ***with ~*** con vero piacere

pleat *n in skirt* piega *f*

pleated skirt *n* gonna *f* a pieghe

pleb *n pej* plebeo *m*, -a *f*

plebiscite *n* plebiscito *m*
plectrum *n* plettro *m*
pledge I *n* (*promise*) promessa *f*; ***as a ~ of*** come pegno per; ***election ~s*** promesse fatte durante le elezioni **II** *v/t* (*promise*) promettere; ***~ support for s.o. / sth*** impegnarsi a sostenere qn / qc; ***~ (one's) allegiance to s.o. / sth*** giurare fedeltà a qn / qc
plenary session *n* sessione *f* plenaria
plenipotentiary *adj* plenipotenziario; *n* plenipotenziario *m*, -a *f*
plenteous *adj* copioso
plentiful *adj* abbondante
plenty *n* (*abundance*) abbondanza *f*; ***~ of*** molto; ***that's ~*** basta così; ***there's ~ for everyone*** ce n'è per tutti; ***... in ~*** in abbondanza; ***three kilos will be ~*** tre chili basteranno; ***there's ~ more where that came from*** ce n'è in quantità; ***there are still ~ left*** ce ne sono ancora molti; ***a country with ~ of natural resources*** un paese con abbondanti risorse naturali; ***he had been given ~ of warning*** aveva ricevuto molti avvertimenti; ***there's ~ of time*** c'è ancora molto tempo
pleurisy *n* MED pleurite *f*
pliable *adj* flessibile
pliers *npl* pinze *fpl*; ***a pair of ~*** un paio di pinze
plight *n* situazione *f* critica; ***the country's economic ~*** la difficile situazione economica del paese
plimsoll *n* scarpa *f* da tennis
plinth *n* base *f*
plod *v/i* ⟨*pret & past part* **-ded**⟩ *walk* trascinarsi; ***~ up a hill*** trascinarsi in cima a una collina
◆**plod on** *v/i with a job* sgobbare
plodder *n at work, school* sgobbone *m*, -a *f*
plonk[1] *v/i*: ***~ sth down*** *infml* mollare qc *infml*
plonk[2] *n Br infml* (*wine*) vino *m* di scarsa qualità
plot[1] *n land* appezzamento *m*
plot[2] **I** *n* (*conspiracy*) complotto *m*; *of novel* trama *f*; *fig* ***lose the ~*** *infml* perdere il senno **II** *v/t & v/i* ⟨*pret & past part* **-ted**⟩ complottare; *course* tracciare; *on map* rilevare; ***they ~ted to kill him*** complottavano per ucciderlo
plotter *n* cospiratore *m*, -trice *f*; COMPUT plotter *m inv*
plough, *US* **plow I** *n* aratro *m*; ***the Plough*** ASTR il Grande Carro **II** *v/t & v/i* arare
◆**plough back** *v/t sep profits* reinvestire
◆**plough through** *v/t book, work* faticare per finire; ***we ploughed through the snow*** avanzammo a fatica nella neve; ***plough through a novel*** *infml* leggere a fatica un romanzo
ploughman, *US* **plowman** *n* contadino *m*
ploughman's lunch *n Br piatto a base di pane, formaggio, insalata e sottaceti*
plow *etc US* → ***plough*** *etc*
ploy *n trick* stratagemma *m*
pluck *v/t eyebrows* pinzare; *chicken* spennare; ***~ (at) s.o.'s sleeve*** tirare qn per la manica; ***she was ~ed from obscurity to become a film star*** è uscita dall'anonimato per diventare una star del cinema; ***he was ~ed to safety*** è stato tirato in salvo; ***~ a name out of the air*** dire un nome a casaccio
◆**pluck up** *v/t*: ***pluck up courage*** trovare il coraggio
plucky *adj* (*+er*) coraggioso
plug I *n for sink, bath* tappo *m*; *electrical* spina *f*; (*spark plug*) candela *f*; *for new book etc* pubblicità *f inv* **II** *v/t* ⟨*pret & past part* **-ged**⟩ *hole* tappare; *new book etc* fare pubblicità a
◆**plug away** *v/i infml* sgobbare
◆**plug in** *v/t sep* attaccare (alla presa)
◆**plug up** *v/t sep hole* tappare
plug-and-play *adj* COMPUT *peripheral* che funziona senza installazione
plughole *n* scarico *m*; *fig* ***go down the ~*** *infml* andare perso
plum I *n* susina *f* **II** *adj*: ***~ job*** *infml* un lavoro favoloso
plumage *n* piumaggio *m*
plumb I *adj* a piombo **II** *adv* proprio; ***~ in the middle*** proprio nel mezzo **III** *v/t*: ***~ the depths of despair*** toccare il fondo della disperazione
◆**plumb in** *v/t sep washing machine* collegare all'impianto idraulico
plumber *n* idraulico *m*
plumbing *n pipes* impianto *m* idraulico

plumb line *n* filo *m* a piombo
plume *n* piuma *f*; **~ *of smoke*** pennacchio *m* di fumo
plummet *v/i of aeroplane* precipitare; *of share prices* crollare
plummy *adj* color prugna; ***she spoke in a ~ voice*** parlava con una voce affettata
plump I *adj (+er) person, chicken* in carne; *hands, feet, face* paffuto **II** *v/t*: **~ *sth down*** lasciare cadere qc; ***she ~ed herself down in the armchair*** sprofondò nella poltrona
◆ **plump for** *v/t* scegliere
◆ **plump up** *v/t sep cushions* sprimacciare
plum pudding *n dolce natalizio fatto con farina e frutta secca* **plum tomato** *n* pomodoro *m* oblungo
plunder I *n* saccheggio *m* **II** *v/t* saccheggiare
plunge I *v/i* precipitare; *of prices* crollare; **~ *to one's death*** morire precipitando; ***he ~d into the crowd*** si tuff nella folla **II** *v/t knife* conficcare; *tomatoes* immergere; ***the city was ~d into darkness*** la città fu immersa nel buio; ***the news ~d him into despair*** la notizia lo gettò nella disperazione **III** *n* caduta *f*; *in prices* crollo *m*; ***shares took a ~*** i titoli hanno avuto un crollo; ***take the ~*** fare il gran passo
plunger *n for sinks* sturalavandini *m inv*
plunging *adj neckline* profondo
pluperfect *n* GRAM piuccheperfetto *m*
plural I *n* GRAM plurale *m*; ***in the ~*** al plurale **II** *adj* plurale; **~ *ending*** finale multiplo
pluralism *n* pluralismo *m*
plus I *prep* più **II** *adj*: ***£500 ~*** oltre 500 sterline **III** *n symbol* più *m inv*; (*advantage*) vantaggio *m*; ***a ~ figure*** una cifra positiva; ***on the ~ side*** il lato positivo; **~ *10 degrees*** più 10 gradi; ***he got B ~*** ha avuto B + **IV** *cj* (*moreover, in addition*) per di più
plus fours *n* pantaloni *mpl* alla zuava
plush *adj* (+*er*) di lusso; ***a ~ hotel*** un hotel di lusso
plus sign *n* segno *m* più
Pluto *n* ASTR Plutone *m*
plutocracy *n* plutocrazia *f*
plutonium *n* plutonio *m*
ply I *v/t*: **~ *s.o. with drink*** offrire continuamente da bere a qn **II** *v/i*: **~ *back and forth*** fare avanti e indietro
plywood *n* compensato *m*
p.m. *abbr* (= **post meridiem**): ***at 2 ~*** alle 2 del pomeriggio; ***at 10.30 ~*** alle 10.30 di sera
PM *abbr* (= **Prime Minister**) primo ministro *m*
PMS *n abbr* (= **pre-menstrual syndrome**) sindrome *f* premestruale
PMT *n abbr* (= **pre-menstrual tension**) *Br* sindrome *f* premestruale
pneumatic *adj* pneumatico
pneumatic drill *n* martello *m* pneumatico
pneumonia *n* polmonite *f*
poach[1] *v/t cook* bollire; *egg* fare in camicia
poach[2] **I** *v/i for game* cacciare di frodo; *for fish* pescare di frodo **II** *v/t* cacciare / pescare di frodo
poached egg *n* uovo *m* in camicia
poacher *n of salmon, game* cacciatore / pescatore *m* di frodo; *Br for cooking* pentolino *m* (per le uova in camicia)
P.O. Box *n* casella *f* postale
pocket I *n* tasca *f*; ***line one's ~s*** arricchirsi; ***be out of ~*** averci rimesso; ***pay for sth out of one's own ~*** pagare qc di tasca propria; (*area*) tasca; **~ *of resistance*** sacca *f* di resistenza **II** *adj* (*miniature*) in miniatura **III** *v/t* intascare
pocket book *n US* (*wallet*) portafoglio *m*; (*handbag*) borsetta *f* **pocket calculator** *n* calcolatrice *f* tascabile **pocket money** *n* paghetta *f*
pockmarked *adj* butterato
pod *n of peas, beans* baccello *m*; *of spaceship* modulo *m*
podium *n* podio *m*
poem *n* poesia *f*
poet *n* poeta *m*, -essa *f*
poetic *adj person, description* poetico
poetic justice *n* giustizia *f* divina **poetic licence** *n* licenza *f* poetica
poet laureate *n* poeta *m* laureato; *poeta di corte scelto dai reali d'Inghilterra*
poetry *n* poesia *f*
pogrom *n* pogrom *m*
poignancy *n* intensità *f*
poignant *adj* commovente

poinsettia *n* poinsettia *f*

point I *n* **1.** *of pencil, knife* punta *f* **2.** *in competition, exam* punto *m*; ***win on ~s*** vincere ai punti; **3.** (*purpose*) senso *m*; ***there's no ~ in staying*** non ha senso rimanere; ***I don't see the ~ of carrying on*** non capisco a cosa serva continuare; ***what's the ~?*** a che scopo?; ***the ~ is that ...*** il fatto è che ...; ***that's the whole ~*** il punto è tutto qui; ***miss the ~*** non capire **4.** (*moment*) punto *m*; ***be on the ~ of*** stare sul punto di; ***severe to the ~ of cruelty*** severo ai limiti della crideltà; ***the ~ of no return*** *fig* il punto di non ritorno **5.** *in argument, discussion* punto *m*; ***that's beside the ~*** non c'entra; ***get to the ~*** venire al dunque; ***stick to the ~*** non divagare; ***make a ~ of doing sth*** non mancare di fare qc; ***that's a ~*** questo, in effetti, è vero; ***you've got a ~ there*** su questo, hai ragione; ***I take your ~*** su questo, ti do ragione; ***there's no ~ in waiting/trying*** non ha senso aspettare/tentare; ***what's the ~?*** a che scopo? **6.** *in decimals* virgola *f*; (***nought***) ***~ seven*** (***0.7***) zero virgola sette **II** *v/i* indicare; ***it's rude to ~*** (***at strangers***) non è cortese indicare gli sconosciuti col dito; ***he ~ed toward(s) the house*** ha indicato in direzione di quella casa; ***everything ~s that way*** tutto sembra indicare quella direzione; ***all the signs ~ to success*** tutti i segnali fanno pensare al successo **III** *v/t gun* puntare (***at*** contro); ***~ the way*** indicare la direzione

◆**point at** *v/t with finger* indicare col dito

◆**point out** *v/t sep sights, advantages* indicare

◆**point to** *v/t with finger* additare; (*fig: indicate*) far presupporre

point-blank I *adj refusal, denial* categorico; ***at ~ range*** a bruciapelo **II** *adv refuse, deny* categoricamente

pointed *adj remark, question* mirato; ***that was rather ~*** era piuttosto pungente

pointer *n for teacher* bacchetta *f*; (*hint*) consiglio *m*; (*sign, indication*) indizio *m*

pointing *n grout* stuccatura dei giunti in vista con malta

pointless *adj* inutile; ***it's ~ trying*** è inutile tentare; ***a ~ exercise*** un esercizio inutile

point of honour *n* questione *f* d'onore **point of no return** *n* punto *m* di non ritorno **point of reference** *n* punto di riferimento **point-of-sale** *n* punto *m* vendita **point of view** *n* punto *m* di vista

poise I *n* padronanza *f* di sé; *of head, body* portamento *m*; (*grace*) compostezza *f* **II** *v/t* bilanciare; ***the tiger was ~d ready to spring*** la tigre si teneva pronta a saltare; ***we sat ~d on the edge of our chairs*** eravamo seduti in equilibrio sul bordo della sedia

poised *adj person* posato

poison I *n* veleno *m*; ***they put down rat ~*** hanno sparso il veleno per topi; ***her criticism was pure ~*** la sua critica era veleno puro **II** *v/t* avvelenare; ***~ s.o.'s mind against s.o.*** mettere qn contro qn

poisoning *n* avvelenamento *m*

poisonous *adj* velenoso

poison-pen letter *n* lettera *f* diffamatoria

poke I *n* colpetto *m* **II** *v/t* (*prod*) dare un colpetto a; *stick* ficcare; *vulg* (*have sex with*) scopare; ***~ fun at*** prendere in giro; ***~ one's nose into*** ficcare il naso in; ***~ the fire*** attizzare il fuoco; ***he accidentally ~d me in the eye*** mi ha dato una botta nell'occhio per sbaglio; ***he ~d his head round the door*** ha sporto la testa dalla porta **III** *v/i*: ***~ at sth*** giocherellare con qc; ***she ~d at her food with a fork*** giocherellava con il cibo con la forchetta

◆**poke around, about** *v/i infml* curiosare

◆**poke out I** *v/i* spuntare fuori **II** *v/t sep* (*extend*) tirare fuori; ***he poked the dirt out with his fingers*** tirò fuori la sporcizia con le dita; ***poke s.o.'s eye out*** cavare un occhio a qn

poker *n card game* poker *m inv*; *for fire* attizzatoio *m*

poker-faced *adj* con il volto impassibile

poky *adj* (*+er*) *infml* (*cramped*) angusto; ***she lived in a ~ little flat*** viveva in un appartamento angusto

Poland *n* Polonia *f*
polar *adj* polare
polar axis *n* asse *m* polare **polar bear** *n* orso *m* polare **polar circle** *n* circolo *m* polare
polarise, *US* **polarize** *v/t* polarizzare
polarity *n* polarità *f*
pole[1] *n* *of wood, metal* paletto *m*
pole[2] *n* GEOG, SPACE, ELEC polo *m*; ***be ~s apart*** essere agli antipodi
Pole *n* polacco *m*, -a *f*
polecat *n* puzzola *f*
polemical *adj* polemico
pole position *n* SPORTS pole position *f inv*; ***be*** *or* ***start in ~*** essere *or* partire in pole position **pole star** *n* stella *f* polare **polevault** *n* salto *m* con l'asta **pole-vaulter** *n* saltatore *m*, -trice *f* con l'asta
police I *n* polizia *f*; ***join the ~*** entrare in polizia; ***he is in the ~*** fa parte della polizia **II** *n* poliziotti *mpl*; ***hundreds of ~*** centinaia di poliziotti **III** *v/t* mantenere l'ordine in *or* su
police car *n* auto *f* della polizia **police dog** *n* cane *m* poliziotto **police force** *n* corpo *m* di polizia **police headquarters** *nsg or npl* centrale *f* di polizia **policeman** *n* poliziotto *m* **police officer** *n* agente *m/f* di polizia **police record** *n* fedina *f* penale **police state** *n* stato *m* di polizia **police station** *n* commissariato *m* di polizia **policewoman** *n* donna *f* poliziotto
policy[1] *n* politica *f*; ***our ~ on recruitment*** la nostra politica delle assunzioni; ***a ~ of restricting immigration*** una politica per restringere l'immigrazione; ***a matter of ~*** una questione di politica; ***your ~ should always be to give people a second chance*** la tua regola dovrebbe essere quella di dare alle persona una seconda possibilità; ***my ~ is to wait and see*** la mia tattica è aspettare e vedere; ***it was good/bad ~*** è stata una buona/cattiva politica
policy[2] *n* (*insurance policy*) polizza *f*; ***take out a ~*** sottoscrivere una polizza
polio *n* polio *f*
polish I *n* *product* lucido *m*; (*nail polish*) smalto *m*; (*elegance*) ***he was a man of real ~*** era un uomo di grande raffinatezza **II** *v/t* lucidare; *speech* rifinire; ***she spent ages ~ing her piano technique*** ha passato anni a perfezionare la sua tecnica al pianoforte; ***~ o's manners*** affinare i propri modi
◆**polish off** *v/t sep food* spazzolare *infml*; ***they polished off the remains of yesterday's lunch*** hanno ripulito gli avanzi del pranzo di ieri
◆**polish up** *v/t sep skill* perfezionare; ***I need to polish up on my French*** ho bisogno di migliorare il francese
Polish I *adj* polacco **II** *n* polacco *m*
polished *adj performance* impeccabile
polite *adj* (+*er*) cortese; ***be ~ to s.o.*** essere gentile con qn
politely *adv* cortesemente
politeness *n* cortesia *f*
politic *adj* saggio
political *adj* politico
political asylum *n* asilo *m* politico; ***he was granted ~*** gli è stato concesso l'asilo politico
politically correct *adj* politicamente corretto
political party *n* partito *m* politico **political prisoner** *n* prigionero *m*, -a *f* politico, a
politician *n* uomo *m* politico, donna *f* politica
politics *nsg* politica *f*; ***what are his ~?*** di che tendenze politiche è?; ***go into ~*** entrare in politica; ***office ~*** intrighi *mpl*
polka *n* polka
polka dot I *n* pois *m inv* **II** *adj* a pois
poll I *n* (*survey*) sondaggio *m*; ***a ~ was taken among the villagers*** è stata fatta una votazione tra gli abitanti del paese; ***the ~s*** (*election*) le elezioni *fpl*; ***go to the ~s*** (*vote*) andare alle urne **II** *v/t people* fare un sondaggio tra; *votes* guadagnare
pollen *n* polline *m*
pollen count *n* concentrazione *f* di polline
pollinate *v/t* impollinare
pollination *n* impollinazione *f*
polling booth *n* cabina *f* elettorale **polling day** *n* giorno *m* delle elezioni **polling station** *n* seggio *m* elettorale
pollster *n* esperto *m*, -a *f* di sondaggi
poll tax *n* imposta *f* pro capite
pollutant *n* sostanza *f* inquinante
pollute *v/t* inquinare
pollution *n* inquinamento *m*

polo *n* SPORTS polo *m*

polo-neck *adj sweater* a collo alto **polo shirt** *n* polo *f inv*

poltergeist *n* poltergeist *m inv*

polychromatic *adj* policromatico

polyester *n* poliestere *m*

polygamy *n* poligamia *f*

polyglot *n* poliglotta

polymer *n* polimero *m*

polyp *n* polipo *m*

polyphony *n* MUS polifonia *f*

polystyrene *n* polistirolo *m*

polysyllabic *adj* polisillabico

polytechnic *n Br istituto di studi superiori con indirizzo tecnico-scientifico*; (*degree-awarding*) politecnico *m*

polythene *n* polietilene *m*

polythene bag *n* sacchetto *m* di plastica

polyunsaturated *adj* polinsaturo

pomegranate *n* melagrana *f*

pomp *n* pompa *f*

pompom *n* pompon *m inv*

pompous *adj* pomposo

ponce I *n Br infml* magnaccia *m* **II** *v/i* fare il magnaccia

poncy *adj* (+*er*) *Br infml walk, actor* da finocchio

pond *n* stagno *m*

ponder *v/i* riflettere

ponderous *adj* pesante; *movement* lento

pong I *n* puzzo *m*; ***there's a bit of a ~ in here*** c'è un certo tanfo qui dentro **II** *n infml* puzza *f*

pontiff *n* pontefice *m*

pony *n* pony *m inv*

ponytail *n* coda *f* (di cavallo); ***she was wearing her hair in a ~*** portava i capelli legati a coda di cavallo

poo I *n infml* popò *f*; ***do a ~*** fare la popò **II** *v/i infml* fare la popò

poodle *n* barboncino *m*

poof(ter) *n Br infml pej* finocchio *m*

pooh *int* bleah

pool[1] *n* (*swimming pool*) piscina *f*; *of water, blood* pozza *f*

pool[2] *n game* biliardo *m*

pool[3] **I** *n common fund* cassa *f* comune; ***car ~*** *gruppo di persone che per recarsi in un certo luogo fa uso di un'unica macchina* **II** *v/t resources* mettere insieme

pool hall *n* sala *f* da biliardo

pools *npl* totocalcio *m*; ***do the ~*** giocare al totocalcio

pool table *n* tavolo *m* da biliardo

poop I *n US infml* (*excrement*) cacca **II** *v/t & v/i* fare la cacca

pooped *adj infml* stanco morto

pooper scooper *n infml* paletta *f* (per gli escrementi del cane)

poor I *adj* (+*er*) *not wealthy, unfortunate* povero; *not good* misero; ***be in ~ health*** essere in cattiva salute; ***~ old Tony!*** povero Tony! **II** *n*: ***the ~*** i poveri

poorly I *adv* male **II** *adj* (*unwell*) indisposto

pop[1] **I** *v/i* ⟨*pret & past part* ***-ped***⟩ *of balloon etc* scoppiare **II** *v/t* ⟨*pret & past part* ***-ped***⟩ *cork* stappare; *balloon* far scoppiare **III** *n noise* schiocco *m*

pop[2] **I** *n* MUS pop *m inv* **II** *adj* pop *inv*

pop[3] *v/t* ⟨*pret & past part* ***-ped***⟩ *infml* (*put*) ficcare *infml*; ***~ one's head around the door*** sbucare con la testa dalla porta; ***~ the question*** (*propose*) fare una proposta di matrimonio; ***~ a letter into the postbox*** *Br or* ***mailbox*** *US* infilare una lettera nella buca delle lettere; ***~ a jacket on*** infilarsi una giacca

◆**pop in** *v/i infml* (*make a brief visit*) entrare un attimo

◆**pop out** *v/i infml* (*go out for a short time*) fare un salto fuori

◆**pop up** *v/i infml* (*appear suddenly*) saltare fuori

pop concert *n* concerto *m* pop

popcorn *n* popcorn *m inv*

pope *n* papa *m*

pop group *n* gruppo *m* pop

poplar *n* pioppo *m*

pop music *n* musica *f* pop

poppet *n Br* tesoro *m*

poppy *n* papavero *m*

poppycock *n* sciocchezze *fpl*

Poppy Day *n Br giorno di commemorazione per i caduti delle guerre mondiali*

poppyseed *n* seme *m* di papavero

Popsicle® *n US* ghiacciolo *m*

pop singer *n* cantante *m/f* pop **pop song** *n* canzone *m* pop

popular *adj* popolare; ***he was very ~ with the girls*** aveva molto successo con le ragazze; (*for general public*) popolare; *music* leggera; ***~ appeal*** successo con il pubblico; ***~ science***

scienza di divulgazione; *belief, support* diffuso; ***contrary to ~ opinion*** contrariamente a quanto tutti credono; ***fruit teas are becoming increasingly ~*** gli infusi alla frutta sono sempre più apprezzati; ***~ uprising*** sollevamento *m* popolare; ***by ~ request*** a grande richiesta

popularity *n* popolarità *f inv*; ***he'd do anything to win ~*** farebbe qualsiasi cosa per guadagnare popolarità; ***the sport is growing in ~*** lo sporto sta acquisendo maggiore popolarità

popularize *v/t* diffondere

popularly *adv*: ***it is ~ believed that*** è opinione comune che; ***he is ~ believed to be rich*** tutti credono che sia ricco; ***be ~ known as s.o. / sth*** essere generalmente conosciuto come qn / qc

populate *v/t* popolare

population *n* popolazione *f*; ***the growing black ~ of London*** la crescente popolazione di colore di Londra

populism *n* populismo *m*

populous *adj country* popoloso; *town* densamente popolato

pop-up **I** *n* pop-up *m inv* **II** *adj*: ***~ menu / window*** menu / finestra pop-up

porcelain **I** *n* porcellana *f* **II** *adj* di porcellana

porch *n* portico *m*; *US* veranda *f*

porcupine *n* porcospino *m*

pore *n of skin* poro *m*

◆ **pore over** *v/t* studiare attentamente; ***pore over one's books*** sgobbare sui libri

pork *n* maiale *m*

porker *n infml* maiale *m* da ingrasso

pork pie *n Br* pasticcio *m* di maiale

porky *infml* **I** *adj* (*+er*) (*fat*) grasso (come un maiale) **II** *n* frottola *f*

porn *n infml* porno *m infml*

porn(o) *adj infml* porno *inv infml*

pornographic *adj* pornografico

pornography *n* pornografia *f*

porous *adj* poroso

porpoise *n* focena *f*

porridge *n* porridge *m inv*

port[1] *n* (*harbour*) porto *m*; ***~ of call*** porto *m* di scalo; ***any ~ in a storm*** *prov* in tempi di tempesta ogni buco è un porto

port[2] *adj* (*left-hand*) babordo; ***on the ~ side*** a babordo

port[3] *n wine* porto

portable **I** *adj* portatile **II** *n* portatile *m*

portal *n* COMPUT portale *m*

portcullis *n* saracinesca *f*

portend *v/t* presagire

portent *n* presagio *m*

porter *n* portiere *m*

portfolio *n of drawings, work* portfolio *m*; FIN *of shares* portafoglio *m*

porthole *n* NAUT oblò *m inv*

portion *n* parte *f*; *of food* porzione *f*

portmanteau *n Br* baule *m*

portrait **I** *n* ritratto *m* **II** *adv print* verticale

portray *v/t of artist, photographer* ritrarre; *of actor* interpretare; *of author* descrivere

portrayal *n by actor* rappresentazione *f*; *by author* descrizione *f*

Portugal *n* Portogallo *m*

Portuguese **I** *adj* portoghese **II** *n person* portoghese *m/f*; *language* portoghese *m*

pose **I** *v/i for artist, photographer* posare; ***~ (in the) nude*** posare nudo; ***~ as*** farsi passare per **II** *v/t*: ***~ a problem / a threat*** creare un problema / una minaccia **III** *n* (*pretence*) posa *f*

poseur *n persona affettata cui piace farsi notare*

posh *adj* (*+er*) *infml* elegante; *pej* snob

position **I** *n* posizione *f*; ***what would you do in my ~?*** cosa faresti al mio posto?; ***be in a ~ to do sth*** essere nella posizione per fare qc; ***what is the government's ~ on …?*** qual è la posizione del governo su…? **II** *v/t* sistemare, piazzare; ***he ~ed himself where he could see her*** si piazzò dove poteva vederla

positive **I** *adj* positivo; ***be ~*** (*sure*) essere certo; ***he is a very ~ person*** è una persona molto ottimista; ***take ~ action*** prendere un'azione concreta; ***this is a ~ disgrace*** questa è una vera disgrazia; ***a ~ genius*** un autentico genio **II** *adv*: ***test ~*** MED risultare positivo al test; ***think ~*** pensare positivo

positive discrimination *n* discriminazione *f* positiva **positive feedback** *n* reazione *f* positiva; ***get ~ (about s.o. /***

sth) ricevere commenti positivi (su qn / qc)
positively *adv* (*downright*) decisamente; (*definitely*) assolutamente; *think* in modo positivo
possess *v/t* possedere
possession *n* (*ownership*) possesso *m*; *thing owned* bene *m*; ***~s*** averi *mpl*; ***take ~ of*** prendere possesso di; ***be in ~ of sth*** essere in possesso di qc; ***all his ~s*** tutti i suoi possedimenti
possessive *adj a.* GRAM possessivo
possessor *n* possessore *m*, ditrice *f*
possibility *n* possibilità *f inv*; ***the house has possibilities*** la casa ha del potenziale; ***there's not much ~ of success*** non c'è molto possibilità di successo; ***the ~ of doing sth*** la possibilità di fare qc; ***it's a distinct ~ that …*** c'è la netta possibilità che…
possible *adj* possibile; ***the shortest / quickest ~ …*** la … più breve / veloce possibile; ***the best ~ …*** la miglior … possibile
possibly *adv* (*perhaps*) forse; ***that can't ~ be right*** non è possibile che sia giusto; ***could you ~ tell me …?*** potrebbe per caso dirmi …?; ***they're doing everything they ~ can*** fanno assolutamente tutto il possibile
post[1] **I** *n of wood, metal* palo *m*; ***a wooden ~*** un palo *m* di legno; ***finishing ~*** traguardo *m* **II** *v/t notice* affiggere; *profits* annunciare; ***keep s.o. ~ed*** tenere informato qn
post[2] **I** *n* (*place of duty*) posto *m* **II** *v/t soldier, employee* assegnare; *guards* piazzare
post[3] **I** *n* (*mail*) posta *f*; ***by ~*** per posta **II** *v/t letter* spedire (per posta); (*put in the mail*) imbucare
postage *n* affrancatura *f*
postage stamp *n form* francobollo *m*
postal *adj* postale
postal order *n* vaglia *m* postale **postal vote** *n* voto *m* per posta
postbox *n* buca *f* delle lettere **postcard** *n* cartolina *f* **postcode** *n* codice *m* di avviamento postale **postdate** *v/t* postdatare
poster *n* manifesto *m*; *for decoration* poster *m inv*
poste restante *n Br* fermo posta *m inv*
posterior *n* (*hum: buttocks*) posteriore *m*
posterity *n* posteri *mpl*
postgraduate I *n studente di un corso post-universitario* **II** *adj* post-universitario
posthumous *adj* postumo
posthumously *adv* dopo la sua morte; ***it was published ~*** è stato pubblicato postumo
posting *n* (*assignment*) incarico *m*
postman *n* postino *m*
postmark I *n* timbro *m* postale **II** *v/t* timbrare; ***the letter is ~ed "Birmingham"*** la lettera ha il timbro di Birmingham
postmodern *adj* postmoderno
postmortem *n* autopsia *f*
postnatal *adj* post-parto
post office *n* ufficio *m* postale
postoperative *adj* postoperatorio
postpone *v/t* rinviare; ***it has been ~d till Tuesday*** è stato rinviato a martedì
postponement *n* rinvio *m*
postscript *n* poscritto *m*
postulate *v/t* postulare
posture *n* posizione *f*
postwar *adj* del dopoguerra
postwoman *n esp Br* postina *f*
posy *n* mazzolino *m* di fiori
pot[1] **I** *n for cooking* pentola *f*; *for coffee* caffettiera *f*; *for tea* teiera *f*; *for plant* vaso *m*; ***go to ~*** *infml* (*person, business*) lasciarsi andare; ***have ~s of money*** *infml* avere un sacco di soldi **II** *v/t plant* piantare in vaso; *billiards*: *ball* mandare in buca
pot[2] *n infml* (*marijuana*) erba *f infml*
potassium *n* potassio *m*
potato *n* patata *f*
potato chips *npl US* patatine *fpl* **potato crisps** *npl Br* patatine *fpl*
potbelly *n* pancetta *infml*
potboiler *n infml* opera *f* commerciale; (*film*) film di cassetta
potbound *adj* piantato in un vaso troppo piccolo
potency *n of drug* potenza *f*; *of image* forza *f*
potent *adj* potente
potentate *n* potentato *m*
potential I *adj* potenziale **II** *n* potenziale *m*; ***~ for growth*** potenziale di crescita; ***have ~*** avere un potenziale; ***he shows quite a bit of ~*** dimostra di

avere un certo potenziale; ***achieve** or **fulfil** or **realize one's*** ~ raggiungere *or* mettere a frutto *or* realizzare il proprio potenziale; ***she has management*** ~ ha un potenziale come dirigente
potentially *adv* potenzialmente
potentiate *v/t* potenziare
pothead *n infml* spinellato *m*, -a *f*
pothole *n in road* buca *f*
potholing *n* speleologia *f*
potion *n* pozione *f*
pot luck *n pasto al quale ognuno porta una pietanza*; ***we took ~ and went to the nearest pub*** abbiamo tentato la sorte e siamo andati al pub più vicino
potpourri *n liter* pot-pourri *m inv*
pot roast *n* brasato *m* **pot shot** *n*: ***take a ~ at s.o. / sth*** tirare a caso su qn / qc
pottage *n* COOK zuppa *f* densa
potted *adj meat* in scatola; (*shortened*) ridotto; ***~ plant*** pianta *f* in vaso
potter *n* vasaio *m*, -a *f*
◆**potter about** *v/i* lavoricchiare
pottery *n activity* ceramica *f*; *items* vasellame *m*; *place* laboratorio *m* di ceramica
potty[1] *n for baby* vasino *m*
potty[2] *adj* (+*er*) *Br infml* (*mad*) matto; ***drive s.o. ~*** fare impazzire qn; ***he's ~ about her*** è pazzo di lei
pouch *n* (*bag*) borsa *f*
poultry *n birds* volatili *mpl*; *meat* pollame *m*
pounce *v/i of animal* balzare; *fig* piombare
pound[1] *n weight* libbra *f*; ***two ~s of apples*** due libbre di mele; ***by the ~*** alla libbra; FIN sterlina *f*
pound[2] *n for strays* canile *m* municipale; *for cars* deposito *m* auto
pound[3] *v/i of heart* battere forte; ***~ on*** (*hammer on*) picchiare su
pound cake *n* COOK *pesante torta fatta con circa una libbra di ogni ingrediente*
pounding *n* battito *m*; ***take a ~*** prendere una bella batosta
pound sterling *n* sterlina *f*
pour I *v/t liquid* versare; ***~ money into a project*** investire denaro in un progetto **II** *v/i*: ***it's ~ing (with rain)*** sta diluviando; ***the sweat ~ed off his face*** il sudore gli scorreva sul viso; ***this jug doesn't ~ well*** questa brocca non versa bene
◆**pour out** *v/t sep liquid* versare; *troubles* sfogarsi raccontando; ***pour out one's heart (to s.o.)*** sfogarsi (con qn)
pout *v/i* fare il broncio
poverty *n* povertà *f inv*
poverty line *n* soglia *f* della povertà
poverty-stricken *adj* poverissimo
POW *abbr* (= **prisoner of war**) prigioniero *m*, -a *f* di guerra
powder I *n* polvere *f*; *for face* cipria *f* **II** *v/t*: ***~ one's face*** mettersi la cipria
powder room *n infml* toilette *f inv* per signore
power I *n* **1.** (*strength*) forza *f*; *of engine* potenza *f*; (*energy*) energia *f*; ***the ~ of love*** la forza dell'amore; ***purchasing / spending ~*** potere *m* d'acquisto / di spesa **2.** (*authority*) potere *m*; ***he did everything in his ~*** ha fatto tutto quanto era in suo potere; ***a naval ~*** una potenza navale; ***in ~*** POL al potere; ***~ of attorney*** JUR procura *f*; ***be the ~ behind the throne*** essere l'eminenza grigia; ***the ~s that be*** *infml* il potere costituito; ***the ~s of evil*** le forze del male; ***fall from ~*** POL perdere il potere; ***on full ~*** con pieni poteri **3.** (*electricity*) elettricità *f inv*; ***they cut off the ~*** (*electricity*) hanno staccato la corrente; *of machine* hanno staccato il filo **4.** MATH potenza *f*; ***to the ~ (of) 2*** alla potenza di **5.** *infml* ***that did me a ~ of good*** è stato un toccasana per me **II** *v/t*: ***~ed by atomic energy*** a propulsione atomica
power-assisted steering *n* servosterzo *m* **power cut** *n* interruzione *f* di corrente **power failure** *n* guasto *m* alla linea elettrica
powerful *adj* potente
powerless *adj* impotente; ***be ~ to ...*** non poter far niente per ...
power line *n* linea *f* elettrica **power point** *n* (*socket*) presa *f* di corrente **power-sharing** *n* POL condivisione *f* del potere **power station** *n* centrale *f* elettrica **power steering** *n* servosterzo *m* **power tool** *n* attrezzo *m* elettrico **power unit** *n* alimentatore *m*
powwow *n infml* riunione *f*
PR *abbr* (= **public relations**) relazioni *fpl* pubbliche

practicable *adj* attuabile
practical *adj* pratico
practical joke *n* scherzo *m*
practically *adv behave, think* in modo pratico; (*almost*) praticamente; ***~ speaking*** parlando in termini pratici
practice I *n* pratica *f*; (*training*) esercizio *m*: ***be out of ~*** essere fuori allenamento; ***~ makes perfect*** *prov* vale più la pratica che la grammatica; (*rehearsal*) prove *fpl*; ***this piece of music needs a lot of ~*** questo brano musicale ha bisogno di molto esercizio; ***do 10 minutes' ~*** fare 10 minuti di esercizio; ***in ~*** (*in reality*) in pratica; (*custom*) consuetudine *f*; ***this is normal business ~*** questa è una comune prassi aziendale; ***that's common ~*** è una procedura comune; ***that won't work in ~*** non funzionerà in pratica; ***put sth into ~*** mettere in pratica qc **II** *v/t & v/i US* → ***practise***
practise, *US* **practice I** *v/t* esercitarsi in; ***~ the violin*** esercitarsi al violino; ***~ doing sth*** esercitarsi a fare qc; ***I'm practising my English on him*** sto facendo pratica di inglese con lui; *profession* praticare; *religion* osservare; *law, medicine* esercitare **II** *v/i* esercitarsi
practised, *US* **practiced** *adj*: ***~ at*** *or* ***in*** esperto in
pragmatic *adj* pragmatico
pragmatism *n* pragmatismo *m*
pragmatist *n* pragmatico *m*, -a *f*
Prague *n* Praga *f*
prairie *n* prateria *f*
praise I *n* lode *f*; ***a hymn of ~*** un inno di elogio; ***he made a speech in ~ of their efforts*** ha fatto un discorso in lode ai loro sforzi; ***win ~*** (*person*) ricevere elogi; ***I have nothing but ~ for him*** non ho che lodi per lui **II** *v/t* lodare; ***he ~d her for her bravery*** la elogiò per il suo coraggio
praiseworthy *adj* lodevole
pram *n* carrozzina *f*
prance *v/i* impennarsi; (*jump around*) saltellare
prank *n* birichinata *f*
prankster *n* birichino *m*, -a *f*
prat *n Br infml* cretino *m*, -a *f*
prattle *v/i* cianciare
prawn *n* gamberetto *m*
pray *v/i* pregare; ***~ for s.o. / sth*** pregare per qn / qc
prayer *n* preghiera *f*; ***say one's ~s*** recitare le proprie preghiere
prayer beads *n* rosario *m* **prayer book** *n* libro *m* di preghiere **prayer mat** *n* tappetino *m* per la preghiera **prayer meeting** *n* riunione *f* di preghiera
praying mantis *n* mantide *f* religiosa
preach I *v/i* predicare; *fig* ***~ to the converted*** sfondare una porta aperta **II** *v/t sermon* predicare; ***~ the gospel*** predicare il Vangelo
preacher *n* predicatore *m*, -trice *f*
preamble *n* preambolo *m*
prearrange *v/t* predisporre
precarious *adj* precario
precariously *adv* precariamente; ***~ perched on the edge of the table*** appollaiato precariamente sul bordo del tavolo
precaution *n* precauzione *f*; ***security ~s*** precauzioni *fpl* di sicurezza; ***take ~s against sth*** prendere precauzioni contro qc; ***do you take ~s?*** *euph* (*use contraception*) hai preso precauzioni?
precautionary *adj measure* di precauzione, precauzionale
precede *v/t* precedere
precedence *n* precedenza *f*; ***take ~ over …*** avere la precedenza su …
precedent *n* precedente *m*; ***without ~*** senza precedenti; ***establish*** *or* ***create*** *or* ***set a ~*** stabilire *or* creare un precedente
preceding *adj* precedente
precept *n* precetto *m*
precinct *n* (*US: district*) distretto *m*; *Br* (*pedestrian precinct*) zona *f* pedonale; (*shopping precinct*) zona *f* commerciale
precious I *adj* prezioso **II** *adv infml*: ***~ little / few*** ben poco; ***~ little else*** poc'altro
precipice *n* precipizio *m*
precipitate *v/t* CHEM precipitare; *crisis* accelerare
precipitation *n*; METEO precipitazione *f*; *form* precipitazione *f*
precipitous *adj* ripido
précis *n* riassunto *m*
precise *adj* preciso; ***at that ~ moment*** in quel preciso momento; ***please be more ~*** sii più preciso, per favore; ***18, to be ~*** 18, ad essere precisi

precisely *adv* precisamente; ***at ~ 7 o'clock*** *or* ***at 7 o'clock ~*** alle 7 precise; ***that is ~ why I don't want it*** è esattamente il motivo per cui non voglio
precision *n* precisione *f*
preclude *v/t* impedire
precocious *adj child* precoce
preconceived *adj idea* preconcetto
precondition *n* condizione *f* indispensabile
precook *v/t* cuocere prima
precooked *adj* precotto
precursor *n* precursore *m*, -corritrice *f*; (*herald*) messaggero *m*, -a *f*
predate *v/t* (*precede*) precedere; *cheque* retrodatare
predator *n animal* predatore *m*, -trice *f*
predatory *adj* rapace
predecessor *n* predecessore *m*
predestination *n* predestinazione *f*
predestined *adj*: ***be ~ to*** essere predestinato a
predetermine *v/t* decidere in anticipo
predicament *n* situazione *f* difficile
predicate **I** *v/t* sostenere **II** *n* GRAM predicato *m*
predict *v/t* predire
predictable *adj* prevedibile; ***you're so ~*** sei così prevedibile
prediction *n* predizione *f*
predispose *v/t* predisporre; ***~ s.o. toward(s) s.o. / sth*** predisporre qn verso qn / qc
predisposition *n* predisposizione *f* (***to*** a)
predominance *n* preponderanza *f*; ***the ~ of women in the office*** la preponderanza delle donne in ufficio
predominant *adj* predominante
predominantly *adv* prevalentemente
predominate *v/i* predominare
pre-eminent *adj* superiore
pre-empt *v/t* anticipare
preemptive *adj* preventivo
preen *v/t*: ***~ o.s.*** *fig* farsi bello
pre-existent *adj* preesistente
prefabricated *adj* prefabbricato
preface **I** *n* prefazione *f* **II** *v/t* introdurre
prefect *n* EDU *studente dell'ultimo anno di liceo con responsabilità disciplinari*
prefer *v/t* ⟨*pret & past part* ***-red***⟩ preferire; ***~ X to Y*** preferire X a Y; ***~ to do*** preferire fare; ***I ~ it that way*** preferisco così; ***which (of them) do you ~?*** quale preferisci?; ***I ~ not to say*** preferisco non dirlo; ***would you ~ me to drive?*** preferiresti che guidassi io?
preferable *adj* preferibile; ***anything would be ~ to sharing a flat with Sophie*** qualsiasi cosa sarebbe preferibile rispetto a dividere un appartamento con Sophie; ***it would be ~ to do it that way*** sarebbe preferibile fare così; ***infinitely ~*** infinitamente preferibile
preferably *adv* preferibilmente; ***tea or coffee? — coffee, ~*** tè o caffè? - preferibilmente caffè; ***but ~ not Tuesday*** ma preferibilmente non martedì
preference *n* preferenza *f*; ***give ~ to*** dare *or* accordare la preferenza a
preferential *adj* preferenziale; ***give s.o. ~ treatment*** riservare a qn un trattamento preferenziale
preferment *n* promozione *f*
prefix *n* GRAM prefisso *m*
pregnancy *n* gravidanza *f*
pregnant *adj* incinta; ***get ~*** restare incinta; ***get*** *or* ***make s.o. ~*** mettere incinta qn; ***3 months ~*** incinta di tre mesi; ***Gill was ~ by her new boyfriend*** Gill era incinta del suo nuovo ragazzo; *fig pause* denso di significato
preheat *v/t oven* far riscaldare
prehensile *adj* prensile
prehistoric *adj* preistorico
prehistory *n* preistoria *f*
prejudge *v/t* giudicare a priori
prejudice **I** *n* pregiudizio *m*; ***his ~ against …*** il suo pregiudizio verso…; ***racial ~*** pregiudizio *m* razziale **II** *v/t person* influenzare; *chances* pregiudicare; ***smoking can ~ your health*** il fumo può compromettere la tua salute
prejudiced *adj* prevenuto
prejudicial *adj*: ***be ~ to*** essere pregiudizievole a
prelate *n* prelato *m*
preliminary *adj* preliminare
preliminary hearing *n* JUR udienza *f* preliminare
prelims *n* TYPO pagine *fpl* titolari
prelude *n* preludio *m*

premarital *adj* prematrimoniale
premature *adj* prematuro; ***the baby was three weeks ~*** il bambino era prematuro di tre settimane; ***~ baby*** bambino *m* prematuro; ***~ ejaculation*** eiaculazione *f* precoce
premeditated *adj* premeditato
premenstrual syndrome, premenstrual tension *n esp Br* sindrome *or* tensione *f* premestruale
premier *n* (*Prime Minister*) premier *m inv*
première *n* premiere *f inv*, prima *f*
premise *n* premessa *f*
premises *npl* locali *mpl*; ***that's not allowed on these ~*** non è consentito in questi locali
premium I *n* (*bonus*) premio *m*; *in insurance* premio *m*; ***be at a ~*** valere oro **II** *adj* (*top-quality*) ottimo; ***~ petrol*** *Br or* ***gas*** *US* benzina *f* super; ***~ price*** prezzo *m* superiore a quello di mercato; ***callers are charged a ~ rate of £1.50 a minute*** al chiamante viene addebitata una tariffa superiore pari a 1,50 sterline al minuto
premonition *n* premonizione *f*
prenatal *adj* prenatale
prenuptial agreement *n* contratto *m* prematrimoniale
preoccupation *n*: ***her ~ with making money was such that ...*** la sua preoccupazione per i soldi era tale che ...; ***that was his main ~*** era la sua principale preoccupazione
preoccupied *adj* preoccupato; ***be ~ with sth*** essere preoccupato per qc; ***he has been looking rather ~ recently*** recentemente sembrava piuttosto preoccupato
preoccupy *v/t* ⟨*pret & past part* ***-ied***⟩ preoccupare
preowned *adj DVD*, *video game* usato
prep I *n* (*homework*) compito *m* a casa **II** *v/t* ⟨*pret & past part* ***-ped***⟩ preparare
preparation *n* preparazione *f*; ***in ~ for*** in vista di; ***~s*** preparativi *mpl*
preparatory *adj* preliminare
preparatory school *n Br scuola di preparazione alla scuola superiore*; *US scuola di preparazione al college*
prepare I *v/t* preparare; ***be ~d to do sth*** (*willing*) essere preparato a fare qc; ***be ~d for sth*** (*be expecting*) essere preparato per qc; ***~ yourself for a shock!*** preparati a uno choc! **II** *v/i* prepararsi; ***the country is preparing for war*** il paese si sta preparando alla guerra
preparedness *n* preparazione *f*
prepay *v/t* ⟨*pret & past part* ***prepaid***⟩ pagare in anticipo; ***they sent him a prepaid ticket*** gli mandarono un biglietto prepagato
preponderance *n* preponderanza *f*
preposition *n* GRAM preposizione *f*
prepossessing *adj* attraente
preposterous *adj* ridicolo
preprogram *v/t* ⟨*pret & past part* ***-med***⟩ *machine*, *device* programmare (in anticipo)
prep school *n scuola privata di preparazione alla scuola superiore*
prerequisite *n* condizione *f* indispensabile
prerogative *n* prerogativa *f*
Presbyterian I *adj* presbiteriano **II** *n* presbiteriano *m*, -a *f*
preschool I *adj children* di età prescolare; *education* prescolare **II** *n US* (*nursery*) scuola *f* materna
prescribe *v/t of doctor* prescrivere; (*order*) stabilire
prescription *n* MED ricetta *f* medica; ***on ~*** dietro presentazione di ricetta medica
prescription charge *n* ticket *m inv* sui farmaci **prescription drugs** *npl* farmaci *mpl* venduti dietro presentazione di ricetta medica
presence *n* presenza *f*; ***in the ~ of*** in presenza di
presence of mind *n* presenza *f* di spirito
present[1] **I** *adj* (*current*) attuale; ***be ~*** essere presente; ***all those ~*** tutti i presenti; ***at the ~ moment*** al momento attuale; ***the ~ day*** (*nowadays*) oggi; ***in the ~ circumstances*** nelle attuali circostanze **II** *n*: ***the ~*** *a.* GRAM il presente; ***~ continuous*** presente *m* progressivo; ***at ~*** al momento; ***there's no time like the ~*** *prov* se non ora, quando?; ***that will be all for the ~*** per ora è tutto
present[2] *n* (*gift*) regalo *m*
present[3] *v/t award* consegnare; *bouquet* offrire; *programme* presentare; ***~ s.o. with sth, ~ sth to s.o.*** offrire

qc a qn
presentable *adj* (*quite smart*) distinto
presentation *n* presentazione *f*
present-day *adj* di oggi
presenter *n* presentatore *m*, -trice *f*
presently *adv* (*at the moment*) attualmente; (*soon*) tra breve
present tense *n* presente *m*
preservation *n of food* conservazione *f*; *of standards*, *peace etc* mantenimento *m*; ***be in a good state of ~*** essere in buono stato di conservazione
preservative *n for wood*; *in food* conservante *m*
preserve I *v/t standards*, *peace etc* mantenere; *wood etc* proteggere; *food* conservare **II** *n* (*domain*) dominio *m*; *for hunting* riserva *f*; ***this was once the ~ of the wealthy*** una volta questo era riservato solo ai ricchi
preserves *npl* conserve *fpl*; ***peach ~*** conserva *f* di pesche
preset *v/t* ⟨*pret & past part* ***preset***⟩ programmare
preside *v/i at meeting* presiedere; ***~ over*** *meeting* presiedere a
presidency *n* presidenza *f*
president *n* presidente *m*; *esp US of company* presidente *m*
president-elect *n presidente eletto ma non ancora insediato*
presidential *adj* presidenziale
press I *n* stampa *f*; (*push*) pressione *f*; *grapes* spremitura *f*; ***get a bad ~*** avere cattiva stampa; ***go to ~*** andare in stampa **II** *v/t button* premere; (*urge*) far pressione su; (*squeeze*) stringere; *clothes* stirare; *grapes*, *olives* spremere; ***be ~ed for time*** avere fretta **III** *v/i*: ***~ for*** fare pressioni per ottenere
◆ **press on** *v/i* (*continue*) continuare
press agency *n* agenzia *f* di stampa **press agent** *n* addetto *m* stampa **press box** *n* tribuna *f* stampa **press conference** *n* conferenza *f* stampa **press cutting** *n esp Br from newspaper* ritaglio *m* di giornale **press-gang I** *n hist gruppo di uomini incaricati di eseguire l'arruolamento forzato* **II** *v/t esp Br infml*: ***~ s.o. into (doing) sth*** forzare qn a fare qc
pressing *adj* urgente
press office *n* ufficio *m* stampa **press officer** *n* addetto *m*, -a *f* stampa **press release** *n* comunicato *m* stampa
press-stud *n* (bottone *m*) automatico
press-up *n* flessione *f* sulle braccia
pressure I *n* pressione *f*; ***be under ~ (to do)*** essere sotto pressione (per fare); ***at high / full ~*** ad alta pressione; ***parental ~*** pressione *f* dei genitori; ***put ~ on s.o.*** fare pressione su qn; ***the ~s of modern life*** lo stress della vita moderna **II** *v/t* fare delle pressioni su
pressure cooker *n* pentola *f* a pressione **pressure gauge** *n* manometro *m* **pressure group** *n* gruppo *m* di pressione **pressure point** *n* punto *m* di pressione
pressurize *v/t person* fare delle pressioni su
prestige *n* prestigio *m*
prestigious *adj* prestigioso
presumable *adj* presumibile
presumably *adv* presumibilmente
presume *v/i* presumere; ***~ to do*** *form* permettersi di fare; ***be ~d innocent*** essere presunto innocente; ***he's ~d dead*** si presume che sia morto
presumption *n of innocence*, *guilt* presunzione *f*
presumptuous *adj* impertinente; ***it would be ~ of me to ...*** sarebbe impertinente da parte mia…
presuppose *v/t* presupporre
pre-tax *adj* al lordo d'imposta; ***~ profit*** profitto *m* al lordo d'imposta
pretence, *US* **pretense** *n* finta *f*; ***under false ~s*** con l'inganno; ***under the ~ of doing sth*** facendo finta di fare qc; ***make a ~ of doing sth*** fare finta di fare qc
pretend I *v/t* fingere; ***~ to be interested*** fingere di essere interessato **II** *v/i* fare finta; ***he is only ~ing*** fa solo finta; ***let's stop ~ing*** smettiamo di fingere **III** *adj infml* ***~ money*** soldi *mpl* finti
pretense *US* → ***pretence***
pretension *n* (*claim*) pretesa *f*
pretentious *adj* pretenzioso
pretentiousness *n* pretenziosità *f*
preterite I *adj* GRAM: ***the ~ tense*** il tempo preterito **II** *n* preterito *m*
preternatural *adj* preternaturale
pretext *n* pretesto *m*
prettify *v/t* ⟨*pret & past part* ***-ied***⟩ abbellire

prettiness *n* grazia *f*; *of place* amenità *f*

pretty I *adj* (+*er*) carino; ***she's not just a ~ face!*** *infml* non è soltanto carina!; ***it wasn't a ~ sight*** non era un bel vedere; ***it'll cost a ~ penny*** costerà una bella somma **II** *adv* (*quite*) piuttosto; ***~ well finished*** quasi finito; ***how's the patient? — ~ much the same*** come sta il paziente? - più o meno come prima

pretty-pretty *adj* lezioso

prevail *v/i* (*triumph*) prevalere

prevailing *adj* prevalente

prevalence *n* prevalenza *f*; *of disease* diffusione *f*

prevalent *adj* molto diffuso

prevaricate *v/i* tergiversare

prevent *v/t* prevenire; ***~ s.o. (from) doing sth*** impedire a qn di fare qc; ***the gate is there to ~ them from falling down the stairs*** il cancelletto serve ad impedire che cadano dalle scale

prevention *n* prevenzione *f*

preventive *adj* preventivo

preview I *n of film, exhibition* anteprima *f*; ***print ~*** anteprima *f* di stampa **II** *v/t* (*view beforehand*) vedere in anteprima; *show beforehand* mostrare in anteprima

previous *adj* precedente; ***the / a ~ holder of the title*** il / un precedente detentore del titolo; ***in ~ years*** negli anni precedenti; ***he's already been the target of two ~ attacks*** è già stato l'obiettivo di due precedenti attacchi; ***on a ~ occasion*** in una precedente occasione; ***I have a ~ engagement*** sono già impegnato; ***no ~ experience necessary*** non è richiesta esperienza nel settore; ***~ to*** prima di

previously *adv* precedentemente

pre-war *adj* dell'anteguerra

prey *n* preda *f*; ***bird of ~*** uccello *m* da preda; ***fall ~ to s.o. / sth*** *fig* cadere preda di qn / qc

◆**prey on** *v/t* far preda di; *fig*: *of con-man etc* approfittarsi di; ***prey on s.o.'s mind*** preoccupare qn

price I *n* prezzo *m*; ***at a ~*** a caro prezzo; ***the ~ of coffee*** il prezzo del caffè; ***go up*** *or* ***rise / go down*** *or* ***fall in ~*** aumentare / diminuire di prezzo; ***they range in ~ from £ 10 to £ 30*** hanno un prezzo compreso tra 10 e 30 sterline; ***what is the ~ of that?*** quanto costa?; ***the ~ of victory*** il prezzo della vittoria; ***not at any ~*** per nessun prezzo **II** *v/t* COMM fissare il prezzo di; ***it was ~d at £ 5*** il prezzo è stato fissato in 5 sterline; ***reasonably ~d*** a prezzo ragionevole

price bracket *n* → ***price range***

price cut *n* riduzione *f* del prezzo **price freeze** *n* blocco *m* dei prezzi

priceless *adj* (*valuable*) di valore inestimabile

price list *n* listino *m* prezzi **price range** *n* fascia *f* dei prezzi **price tag** *n* cartellino *m* del prezzo **price war** *n* guerra *f* dei prezzi

pricey *adj infml* caro

prick[1] **I** *n pain* puntura *f*; ***~ of conscience*** rimorso *m* di coscienza **II** *v/t* (*jab*) pungere; ***~ one's finger (on sth)*** pungersi un dito (con qc); ***she ~ed his conscience*** gli fece venire rimorsi di coscienza

◆**prick up** *v/t sep*: ***prick up one's ears*** *a. fig* drizzare le orecchie

prick[2] *n vulg* (*penis*) cazzo *m vulg*; *person* testa *f* di cazzo *vulg*

prickle I *n on plant* spina *f* **II** *v/i* (*beard*) pungere

prickly *adj* (+*er*) *plant* spinoso; *beard* ispido; (*irritable*) permaloso

prickly heat *n* MED eruzione *f* di calore **prickly pear** *n* BOT fico *m* d'India

pride I *n in person, achievement* orgoglio *m*; (*self-respect*) amor *m* proprio; ***take ~ in*** essere orgoglioso di; ***it's her ~ and joy*** è il suo orgoglio **II** *v/t*: ***~ o.s. on*** vantarsi di

priest *n* prete *m*

priestess *n* sacerdotessa *f*

priesthood *n* sacerdozio *m*

prim *adj* (+*er*) compito; ***~ and proper*** compassato

primaeval *adj* → ***primeval***

primarily *adv* principalmente

primary I *adj* principale; ***our ~ concern*** la nostra preoccupazione primaria; ***of ~ importance*** di primaria importanza **II** *n esp Br* (*primary school*) scuola *f* elementare; *US* (*election*) primarie *fpl*

primary colour, *US* **primary color** *n* colore *m* fondamentale, **primary education** *n* istruzione *f* elementare **primary election** *n US* elezioni *mpl* primarie **primary school** *n* scuola *f* elementare

primate *n* primate *m*

prime I *n*: ***be in one's ~*** essere nel fiore degli anni **II** *adj example, reason* principale; (*very good*) ottimo; ***of ~ importance*** della massima importanza; ***~ suspect*** principale sospettato *m*; ***my ~ concern*** la mia principale preoccupazione **III** *v/t* preparare; ***the artist ~d the canvas*** l'artista preparò la tela; ***they were ~d for war*** erano pronti per la guerra

Prime Minister *n* Primo Ministro *m*

prime number *n* MATH numero *m* primo **prime time TV** *n* TV programmi *mpl* tv di prima serata

primeval *adj* primordiale

primitive *adj a. fig* primitivo

primrose *n* BOT primula *f*

primula *n* BOT primula *f*

prince *n* principe *m*

princess *n* principessa *f*

principal I *adj* principale; ***my ~ concern*** la mia principale preoccupazione **II** *n of school* preside *m/f*

principality *n* principato *m*

principally *adv* principalmente

principle *n* principio *m*; ***on ~*** per principio; ***in ~*** in linea di principio; ***a man of ~(s)*** un uomo di sani principi; ***it's a matter of ~*** *or* ***it's the ~ of the thing*** è una questione di principio

principled *adj* di principio; *person* di sani principi

print I *n in book, newspaper etc* caratteri *mpl*; *photograph* stampa *f*; *mark* impronta *f*; ***in large ~*** a grandi caratteri; ***thumb ~*** impronta *f* digitale; ***out of ~*** esaurito **II** *v/t* stampare; (*use block capitals*) scrivere in stampatello **III** *v/i* stampare; (*write clearly*) scrivere in stampatello

◆**print out** *v/t sep* stampare

printed circuit *n* circuito *m* stampato

printed matter *n* stampe *fpl*

printer *n person* tipografo *m*; *machine* stampante *f*

printhead *n* COMPUT testina *f* di stampa

printing press *n* pressa *f* tipografica

printmaking *n* arte *f* grafica

printout *n* stampato *m* **print run** *n* tiratura *f*

prior[1] **I** *adj* precedente; ***a ~ engagement*** un impegno precedente **II** *prep*: ***~ to*** prima di; ***~ to going out*** prima di uscire

prior[2] *n monk* priore *m*

prioress *n nun* priora *f*

prioritize *v/t* (*put in order of priority*) classificare in ordine d'importanza; (*give priority to*) dare precedenza a

priority *n* priorità *f inv*; ***have ~*** avere la precedenza; ***a top ~*** una priorità principale; ***in order of ~*** in ordine di priorità; ***get one's priorities right*** definire correttamente le proprie priorità; ***high / low on the list of priorities*** *or* ***the ~ list*** in cima / in fondo all'elenco delle priorità

priory *n* monastero *m* (retto da un priore / una priora)

prise, *US* **prize** *v/t*: ***~ sth open*** aprire qc (facendo leva); ***~ the lid off*** togliere il coperchio (facendo leva)

prism *n* prisma *m*

prismatic *adj* prismatico

prison *n* prigione *f*; ***be in ~*** essere in prigione; ***go to ~ for 5 years*** andare in prigione per 5 anni; ***send s.o. to ~*** mandare qn in prigione

prisoner *n* prigioniero *m*, -a *f*; ***take s.o. ~*** fare prigioniero qn

prisoner of war *n* prigioniero *m* di guerra

prissy *adj* perbenino

pristine *adj* immacolato

privacy *n* privacy *f inv*; ***in the ~ of one's own home*** nell'intimità della propria casa; ***in the strictest ~*** con la massima riservatezza

private I *adj* privato; ***~ and confidential*** privato e confidenziale; ***keep sth ~*** mantenere il riserbo su qc; ***his ~ life*** la sua vita privata; ***~ address*** indirizzo *m* privato; ***~ education*** istruzione *f* privata **II** *n* MIL soldato *m* semplice; ***in ~*** in privato; *infml* ***~s*** parti *fpl* intime

private detective *n* detective *m/f* privato **private enterprise** *n* iniziativa *f* privata **private investigator** *n* investigatore *m*, -trice *f* privato

privately *adv* (*in private*) in privato; (*inwardly*) dentro di sé; ***~ funded*** finanziato da privati; ***~ owned*** privato; ***the meeting was held ~*** la riunione è stata tenuta in privato

private parts *npl* parti *fpl* intime **pri-**

vate practice *n Br* esercizio *m* privato della professione; ***he is in ~*** esercita privatamente **private property** *n* proprietà *f* privata **private school** *n* scuola *f* privata **private secretary** *n* segretario *m*, -a *f* personale **private sector** *n* settore *m* privato
privation *n* privazione *f*
privatization *n* privatizzazione *f*
privatize *v/t* privatizzare
privilege *n special treatment* privilegio *m*; (*honour*) onore *m*
privileged *adj* privilegiato; ***for a ~ few*** per pochi privilegiati; (*honoured*) onorato; ***be ~ to do sth*** avere il privilegio di fare qc; ***I was ~ to meet him*** ho avuto il privilegio di incontrarlo
privy I *adj* informato, al corrente; ***I wasn't ~ to his intentions*** non ero al corrente delle sue intenzioni **II** *n* (*toilet*) latrina *f*; ***there was an old ~ in the garden*** nel giardino c'era una vecchia latrina
Privy Council *n* consiglio *m* della corona
prize I *n* premio *m* **II** *v/t* dare molto valore a
◆**prize off, prize open** *v/t* togliere / aprire facendo leva
prizewinner *n* vincitore *m*, -trice *f*
prizewinning *adj* vincente
pro[1] *n*: ***the ~s and cons*** i pro e i contro
pro[2] → ***professional***
pro[3] *prep*: ***be ~ …*** (*in favour of*) essere a favore di …; ***~-European*** favorevole all'Europa
proactive *adj* proattivo
probability *n* probabilità *f inv*; ***in all ~*** molto probabilmente; ***what's the ~ of that happening?*** quante probabilità ci sono che accada?
probability theory *n* MATH teoria *f* delle probabilità
probable *adj* probabile
probably *adv* probabilmente; ***most ~*** più probabilmente; ***~ not*** probabilmente no
probate *n* JUR omologazione *f*
probation *n in job* periodo *m* di prova; JUR libertà *f inv* vigilata; ***on ~*** *in job* in prova
probation officer *n funzionario che sorveglia i vigilati* **probation period** *n in job* periodo *m* di prova
probe I *n* (*investigation*) indagine *f*; *scientific* sonda *f* **II** *v/t* esplorare; (*investigate*) investigare; ***~ into s.o.'s private life*** indagare nella vita privata di qn
probing *adj question* inquisitorio
probity *n* probità *f*
problem *n* problema *m*; ***no ~*** non c'è problema; ***what's the ~?*** qual è il problema; ***he's got a drink(ing) ~*** ha problemi con l'alcol
problematic(al) *adj* problematico
problem-solving *n* risoluzione *f* dei problemi
proboscis *n* proboscide *f*
procedure *n* procedura *f*; ***what would be the correct ~ in such a case?*** quale sarebbe la procedura corretta in un caso del genere?
proceed I *v/i of people* proseguire; *of work etc* procedere; ***please ~ to gate 3*** *form* proseguite fino all'uscita 3; ***can we now ~ to the next item on the agenda?*** possiamo passare alla prossima voce dell'ordine del giorno?; ***everything is ~ing smoothly*** tutto procede senza difficoltà; ***negotiations are ~ing well*** le trattative stanno procedendo bene **II** *v/t*: ***~ to do sth*** cominciare a fare qc
proceedings *npl* (*events*) avvenimenti *mpl*; ***take ~ against s.o.*** JUR intraprendere un procedimento contro qn
proceeds *npl* ricavato *m*
process I *n* processo *m*; ***in the ~*** *while doing it* nel far ciò; ***in the ~ of learning*** durante l'apprendimento; ***be in ~*** (*be happening now*) essere in corso **II** *v/t food, raw materials* trattare; *data* elaborare; *application etc* sbrigare; ***~ed cheese*** formaggio *m* fuso
processing *n of data* elaborazione *f*; *of waste* trattamento *m*; *of food* trasformazione *f*; *of application* esame *m*; *of film* sviluppo *m*
processing language *n* COMPUT linguaggio *m* di elaborazione **processing plant** *n* impianto *m* di trasformazione **processing speed** *n* COMPUT velocità *f* di elaborazione
procession *n* processione *f*; (*line*) corteo *m*; ***carnival ~*** sfilata *f* di carnevale
processor *n* COMPUT processore *m*;

(***food***) ~ robot *m inv* da cucina
proclaim *v/t* proclamare; ***the day had been ~ed a holiday*** quel giorno è stato proclamato giorno festivo
proclamation *n* proclamazione *f*
procrastinate *v/i* rimandare; ***he always ~s*** rimanda sempre
procrastination *n* dilazione *f*
procreate *v/i* riprodursi
procreation *n* procreazione *f*
procurator *n* JUR procuratore *m*
procure *v/t form* procurare
prod I *n* colpetto *m*; *fig* ***give s.o. a ~*** spronare qn **II** *v/t* ⟨*pret & past part* ***-ded***⟩ dare un colpetto a; ***he ~ded the hay with his stick*** dette un colpetto al fieno con il bastone; ***..., he said, ~ding the map with his finger*** disse, toccando la mappa con il dito
prodigal *adj* prodigo
prodigality *n* prodigalità *f*
prodigious *adj* straordinario
prodigy *n*: (***infant***) ~ bambino *m*, -a *f* prodigio
produce[1] *n* prodotti *mpl*; AGR prodotti *mpl* agricoli; ~ ***of Italy*** prodotto italiano
produce[2] *v/t* produrre; (*bring about*) dare origine a; (*bring out*) tirar fuori; *play*, *play* mettere in scena
producer *n* produttore *m*, -trice *f*; *of play* regista *m/f*
product *n* prodotto *m*; ***food ~s*** prodotti *mpl* alimentari; ~ ***range*** COMM gamma *f* di prodotti; (*result*) risultato *m*
production *n* produzione *f*; *of play* regia *f*; ***a new ~ of ...*** una nuova messa in scena di ...; ***go into ~*** essere prodotto
production capacity *n* capacità *f inv* produttiva **production costs** *npl* costi *mpl* di produzione **production line** *n* catena *f* di montaggio
productive *adj* produttivo; ***lead a ~ life*** condurre una vita produttiva
productivity *n* produttività *f inv*
product liability *n* responsabilità *f* sui prodotti
Prof. *abbr* (= **Professor**) Prof. (Professore)
profanation *n* profanazione *f*
profane *adj* (*secular*) profano; *language* sacrilego
profanity *n* (*swearword*) imprecazione *f*
profess *v/t* dichiarare
profession *n* professione *f*; ***the teaching ~*** l'insegnamento; ***by ~*** di professione; ~ ***of faith*** professione *f* di fede
professional I *adj not amateur* professionale; ~ ***army*** esercito *m* professionista; *advice, help* di un esperto; ***seek/take ~ advice*** chiedere il consiglio di un esperto; *piece of work* da professionista; ***turn ~*** passare al professionismo; ***he's now doing it on a ~ basis*** se ne sta occupando a titolo professionale; ***in his ~ capacity as ...*** nella sua qualità professionale di...; ***be a ~ singer*** *etc* essere un cantante professionista; ***our relationship is purely ~*** i nostri rapporti sono esclusivamente professionali **II** *n* professionista *m/f*
professionalism *n* professionalità *f*
professionally *adv play sport* a livello professionistico; (*well, skilfully*) in modo professionale
professor *n* professore *m* (universitario)
proffer *v/t* porgere
proficiency *n* competenza *f*; ***her ~ as a secretary*** la sua competenza come segretaria; ***his ~ in English*** le sue conoscenze di inglese; ***her ~ in translating*** la sua competenza nella traduzione
proficient *adj* competente; ***he is ~ in English*** è bravo in inglese
profile I *n* profilo *m*; ***in ~*** di profilo; ***keep a low ~*** mantenere un basso profilo **II** *v/t* tracciare il profilo di
profit I *n* profitto *m*; ~ ***and loss account*** *Br or* ***statement*** *US* conto *m* profitti e perdite; ***show*** *or* ***yield a ~*** dare un profitto; ***sell sth at a ~*** vendere qc con profitto; ***the business is now running at a ~*** l'azienda lavora ora in utile; *fig*; ***you might well learn something to your ~*** potresti anche imparare qc a tuo vantaggio **II** *v/i*: ~ ***by***, ~ ***from*** trarre profitto da
profitability *n* redditività *f inv*
profitable *adj* redditizio
profit centre, *US* **profit center** *n* centro *m* di profitto
profiteering *n* accumulo *m* di grossi profitti (*tramite speculazioni riprovevoli in periodi di guerra o di bisogno*)

profiterole *n* COOK profiterole *m*
profit margin *n* margine *m* di profitto
profit sharing *n* compartecipazione *f* agli utili
profligate I *n* scialacquatore *m*, -trice *f* **II** *adj* scialacquatore
pro forma *adj/adv* pro forma
profound *adj* profondo
profoundly *adv* profondamente
profundity *n* profondità *f*
profuse *adj* abbondante
profusely *adv thank* con grande effusione; ***he apologized ~*** si scusò profusamente; *bleed* copiosamente
profusion *n* profusione *f*
progeny *n* progenie *f*
prognosis *n* prognosi *f inv*
program I *n* COMPUT programma *m* **II** *v/t* ⟨*pret & past part* **-med**⟩ COMPUT programmare
programme, *US* **program I** *n* programma *m*; ***what's the ~ for tomorrow?*** qual è il programma per domani? **II** *v/t* programmare
programmer *n* COMPUT programmatore *m*, -trice *f*
programming *n* programmazione *f*; **~ *language*** linguaggio *m* di programmazione
progress I *n* progresso *m*; ***make ~*** fare progressi; ***we made slow ~ through the mud*** avanzammo lentamente nel fango; ***each week he wrote a ~ report*** ogni settimana scriveva un rapporto sull'andamento del lavoro; ***in ~*** in corso **II** *v/i* (*advance in time*) procedere; (*move on*) avanzare; (*make progress*) fare progressi, progredire; ***how is the work ~ing?*** come procede il lavoro?; ***how far have you ~ed?*** quanto sei andato avanti?; **~ *through the ranks*** fare carriera
progression *n* avanzamento *m*; (*development*) progresso *m*; ***his ~ from a junior clerk to managing director*** il suo avanzamento da impiegato subalterno a direttore generale
progressive *adj* (*enlightened*) progressista; *which progresses* progressivo
progressively *adv* progressivamente
prohibit *v/t* proibire; **~ *s.o. from doing sth*** proibire a qn di fare qc; ***"smoking ~ed"*** "vietato fumare"
prohibition *n* proibizione *f*; ***Prohibition*** il Proibizionismo
prohibitive *adj prices* proibitivo; ***the costs of producing this model have become ~*** i costi di produzione di questo modello sono diventati proibitivi
project[1] *n* (*plan*) piano *m*; (*undertaking*) progetto *m*; EDU ricerca *f*
project[2] **I** *v/t figures*, *sales* fare una proiezione di; *film* proiettare; **~ *one's voice*** parlare forte e chiaro **II** *v/i* (*stick out*) sporgere in fuori
projectile *n* proiettile *m*
projection *n* (*forecast*) proiezione *f*
projectionist *n* proiezionista *m/f*
projector *n for slides* proiettore *m*
prolapse I *v/i* MED abbassarsi **II** *n* MED prolasso *m*
prole *n infml pej* proletario *m*, -a *f*
proletarian *n/adj* POL proletario *m*, -a *f*
proletariat *n* POL proletariato *m*
pro-life *adj* per la vita
proliferate *v/i* (*number*) proliferare
proliferation *n* proliferazione *f*
prolific *adj writer, artist* prolifico
prologue, *US* **prolog** *n* prologo *m*
prolong *v/t* prolungare
prom *n Br on seafront* lungomare *m inv*; *student dance* ballo *m* di fine anno
promenade I *n esp Br* (*esplanade*) passeggiata *f*; *US* (*ball*) ballo *m* studentesco; **~ *concert*** *Br concerto a cui il pubblico può assistere in piedi* **II** *v/i* passeggiare
prominence *n of ideas* rilievo *m*; *of politician* importanza *f*; ***rise to ~*** assumere rilievo
prominent *adj nose, chin* sporgente; (*significant*) prominente
promiscuity *n* promiscuità *f inv*
promiscuous *adj* promiscuo; **~ *behaviour*** comportamento *m* promiscuo
promise I *v/t* promettere; **~ *to …*** promettere di …; **~ *sth to s.o.*** promettere qc a qn; ***I've ~d myself never to do it again*** mi sono ripromesso di non farlo mai più **II** *v/i* promettere; ***I ~*** lo prometto; ***I'll try, but I'm not promising*** proverò, ma non prometto niente **III** *n* promessa *f*; ***their ~ of help*** la loro promessa di aiuto; ***is that a ~?*** è una promessa; ***I'm not making any ~s*** non faccio promesse; ***~s, ~s!*** sono solo promesse!; ***show ~*** promet-

tere bene
Promised Land *n* terra *f* promessa
promising *adj* promettente
promissory *adj* promissorio
promissory note *n* pagherò *m*
promo *n infml* promo *m*
promontory *n* promontorio *m*
promote *v/t* promuovere; ***our team was ~d*** SPORTS la nostra squadra è stata promossa
promoter *n of sports event* promoter *m/f inv*
promotion *n* promozione *f*; ***get ~*** essere promosso
prompt I *adj* (+*er*) (*on time*) puntuale; (*speedy*) tempestivo **II** *adv*: ***at two o'clock ~*** alle due in punto **III** *v/t* (*cause*) causare; *actor* dare l'imbeccata a **IV** *n* COMPUT prompt *m inv*
prompter *n* suggeritore *m*
promptly *adv* (*on time*) puntualmente; (*immediately*) prontamente
prone *adj* ***be or lie ~*** stare bocconi; ***in a ~ position*** a faccia in giù; ***be ~ to*** essere soggetto a
prong *n* dente *m*
pronoun *n* GRAM pronome *m*
pronounce *v/t word* pronunciare; ***Russian is hard to ~*** il russo è difficile da pronunciare; (*declare*) dichiarare; ***the doctors ~d him unfit for work*** i dottori lo hanno dichiarato non idoneo al lavoro; ***~ o.s. in favour of / against sth*** pronunciarsi in favore di / contro qc
pronounced *adj accent* spiccato; ***he has a ~ limp*** zoppica in modo pronunciato; *views* preciso
pronouncement *n* dichiarazione *f*; ***make a ~*** fare una dichiarazione
pronto *adv infml* immediatamente
pronunciation *n* pronuncia *f*
proof *n* prova *f*; ***~ of purchase*** prova *f* d'acquisto; *of book* bozza *f*; *alcohol* ***be 8% ~*** avere 8 gradi
proofreader *n* correttore *m*, -trice *f* di bozze
prop I *v/t* ⟨*pret & past part* **-ped**⟩ appoggiare; ***~ the door open*** tenere la porta aperta **II** *n* THEAT materiale *m* di scena
◆**prop up** *v/t sep a. fig* sostenere; ***prop o.s. / sth up against sth*** appoggiarsi / appoggiare qc a qc
propaganda *n* propaganda *f*
propagate *v/t* propagare
propagation *n* propagazione *f*
propane *n* propano *m*
propel *v/t* ⟨*pret & past part* **-led**⟩ spingere; *of engine, fuel* azionare
propellant *n in aerosol* propellente *m*
propeller *n* elica *f*
proper *adj* (*real*) vero e proprio; ***a ~ job*** un lavoro vero e proprio; (*correct*) giusto; ***in the ~ way*** nel modo giusto; ***it's only right and ~*** è sacrosanto che…; ***do the ~ thing*** fare la cosa giusta; ***the ~ thing to do would be to apologize*** la cosa giusta da fare sarebbe scusarsi; (*seemly*) decoroso; ***prim and ~*** compassato; (*fitting*) appropriato
properly *adv* (*correctly*) correttamente; (*fittingly*) in modo appropriato
proper noun *n* GRAM nome *m* proprio
property *n* proprietà *f inv*; ***common ~*** *liter* proprietà *f* comune; ***~ in London is dearer*** le proprietà immobiliari a Londra sono più care; ***healing properties*** proprietà *fpl* curative
property developer *n* impresario *m* edile
prophecy *n* profezia *f*
prophesy *v/t* ⟨*pret & past part* **-ied**⟩ profetizzare
prophet *n* profeta *m*
prophetic *adj* profetico
proponent *n* fautore *m*, -trice *f*
proportion *n* proporzione *f*; *fig* ***he has let it all get out of ~*** ha esagerato; ***a certain ~ of the population*** una certa parte della popolazione; ***the ~ of drinkers in our society is rising constantly*** il numero di bevitori nella nostra società è in costante crescita; ***be out of ~*** (*painting*) essere sproporzionato; (*reaction*) essere esagerato
proportional *adj* proporzionale
proportional representation *n* POL rappresentanza *f* proporzionale
proportionate *adj* proporzionato
proposal *n* proposta *f*; (*proposal of marriage*) proposta *f*; ***make s.o. a ~*** fare una proposta a qn
propose I *v/t* (*suggest*) proporre; ***~ to do sth*** (*plan*) proporsi di fare qc; ***how do you ~ to pay for it?*** quanto intendi pagare per questo? **II** *v/i make offer of marriage* fare una pro-

posta di matrimonio
proposition I *n* proposta *f* **II** *v/t woman* fare proposte sessuali a; ***he ~ed me*** mi ha fatto delle avance
proprietor *n* proprietario *m*, -a *f*
proprietress *n* proprietaria *f*
propriety *n* decenza *f*
propulsion *n* propulsione *f*
pro rata *adj/adv* pro rata; ***on a ~ basis*** su base proporzionale
prosaic *adj* banale
proscribe *v/t* (*forbid*) proscrivere
prose *n* prosa *f*
prosecute *v/t* JUR intentare azione legale contro; ***"trespassers will be ~d"*** "i trasgressori saranno perseguiti"; *of lawyer* sostenere l'accusa contro
prosecution *n* JUR azione *f* giudiziaria; (*lawyers*) accusa *f*; ***(the) counsel for the ~*** pubblico ministero *m*; ***witness for the ~*** testimone *f* d'accusa
prosecutor *n* JUR pubblico ministero *m*
proselyte *n* proselito *m*, -a *f*
prose poem *n* LIT poema *m* in prosa
prospect I *n* (*chance, likelihood*) probabilità *f inv*; *thought of something in the future* prospettiva *f*; ***~s*** *for company, in job* prospettive *fpl*; ***a job with no ~s*** un lavoro senza prospettive **II** *v/i*: ***~ for*** *gold* cercare
prospective *adj* potenziale; *MP* aspirante
prospectus *n* prospetto *m*
prosper *v/i* prosperare
prosperity *n* prosperità *f inv*
prosperous *adj* prospero
prostate (gland) *n* prostata *f*
prostitute I *n* prostituta *f*; ***male ~*** prostituto *m* **II** *v/t* prostituire
prostitution *n* prostituzione *f*
prostrate I *adj*: ***be ~ with grief*** essere abbattuto dal dolore **II** *v/t* prostrare; ***he ~d himself before the authorities*** si prostrò di fronte alle autorità
protagonist *n esp* LIT protagonista *m/f*
protect *v/t* proteggere; ***don't try to ~ the culprit*** non provare a proteggere il colpevole
protection *n* protezione *f*; ***be under s.o.'s ~*** essere sotto la protezione di qn
protection money *n* pizzo *m infml*
protective *adj* protettivo
protective clothing *n* indumenti *mpl* protettivi
protective custody *n* JUR *provvedimento in base al quale la polizia tiene in custodia una persona per proteggerla*
protector *n* protettore *m*, -trice *f*
protectorate *n* protettorato *m*
protégé, protégée *n* protetto *m*, -a *f*
protein *n* proteina *f*
protest I *n* protesta *f*; ***~ march*** marcia *f* di protesta **II** *v/t* protestare **III** *v/i* protestare; POL manifestare, protestare
Protestant I *n* protestante *m/f* **II** *adj* protestante
protestation *n* (*protest*) protesta *f*
protester *n* dimostrante *m/f*, manifestante *m/f*
protest march *n* marcia *f* di protesta
protocol I *n* protocollo *m* **II** *v/t* protocollare
proton *n* protone *m*
prototype *n* prototipo *m*
protracted *adj* prolungato
protractor *n* goniometro *m* rapportatore
protrude *v/i* sporgere
protruding *adj* sporgente
protuberance *n* protuberanza *f*
proud I *adj* orgoglioso, fiero; ***it made his parents feel very ~*** ha reso i suoi genitori molto orgogliosi; ***be ~ of*** essere fiero di **II** *adv* ***you've done us ~*** ci hai fatto onore; ***the shelf fitted just ~ of the wall*** la mensola sporgeva appena dalla parete
proudly *adv* con orgoglio
prove *v/t* dimostrare
proven I *past part* → ***prove*** **II** *adj* comprovato
provenance *n* provenienza *f*
proverb *n* proverbio *m*
proverbial *adj liter, fig* proverbiale
provide *v/t money, food* fornire; ***~ s.o. with sth*** fornire qn di qc; ***X ~d the money and Y (~d) the expertise*** X fornì il denaro e Y (fornì) la competenza; ***candidates must ~ their own pens*** i candidati devono portarsi le penne; *opportunity* offrire
◆**provide for** *v/t family* provvedere a; *of law etc* contemplare
provided *cj*: ***~ (that)*** (*on condition that*) a condizione che
providence *n* provvidenza *f*
provident *adj* previdente

providential *adj* provvidenziale
provider *n* fornitore *m*
providing *cj*: ~ (*that*) (*on condition that*) a condizione che
province *n* provincia *f*; **provinces** *npl*: ***the ~s*** la provincia
provincial *adj a. pej* provinciale
provincialism *n* provincialismo *m*
provision *n* (*supply*) fornitura *f*; *of law, contract* disposizione *f*; ***with the ~ that …*** a condizione che …; ***make ~ for s.o.*** provvedere a qn
provisional *adj* provvisorio; ***~ driving licence*** *Br* patente *f* di guida provvisoria
provisions *npl* (*supplies*) provviste *fpl*
proviso *n* condizione *f*; ***with the ~ that …*** a patto che …
provocation *n* provocazione *f*; ***he acted under ~*** agì dietro provocazione; ***he hit me without any ~*** mi colpì senza essere stato provocato
provocative *adj* provocatorio; *sexually* provocante
provoke *v/t* (*cause*) causare; ***~ an argument*** (*person*) provocò una discussione; (*annoy*) provocare; ***~ s.o. into doing sth*** spingere qn a fare qc
prow *n* NAUT prua *f*
prowess *n* abilità *f inv*
prowl *v/i* aggirarsi
prowler *n* tipo *m* sospetto
proximity *n* prossimità *f inv*
proxy *n* (*authority*) procura *f*; *person* procuratore *m*, -trice *f*, mandatario *m*, -a *f*; ***by ~*** per procura
prude *n*: ***be a ~*** scandalizzarsi facilmente
prudence *n* prudenza *f*
prudent *adj* prudente
prudish *adj* che si scandalizza facilmente
prune[1] *n* prugna *f*; *Br infml* imbecille *m/f*
prune[2] *v/t plant* potare; *fig* ridurre
prurient *adj* lascivo
Prussia *n* HIST Prussia *f*
Prussian blue *n* blu *m inv* di Prussia
pry *v/i* ⟨*pret & past part* **-ied**⟩ essere indiscreto
◆**pry into** *v/t* ficcare il naso in
PS *abbr* (= **postscript**) P.S. (post scriptum *m inv*)
psalm *n* inno *m*; *Bible* salmo *m*
pseud *n Br infml* pallone *m* gonfiato
pseudo *adj Br infml* finto
pseudonym *n* pseudonimo *m*
PST *abbr US* (= **Pacific Standard Time**) ora *f* solare del Pacifico
psych *v/t infml*: ~ ***s.o.*** (***out***) intimidire qn; ***she ~ed out her opponents with her stare*** intimidì i suoi avversari con il suo sguardo fisso
◆**psych up** *v/t sep infml* preparare psicologicamente; ***psych o.s. up*** prepararsi psicologicamente
psyche *n* psiche *f*
psychedelic *adj* psichedelico
psychiatric *adj* psichiatrico
psychiatrist *n* psichiatra *m/f*
psychiatry *n* psichiatria *f*
psychic I *adj* psichico; ***I'm not ~!*** non sono un indovino! **II** *n* medium *m/f*
psycho *n infml* psicopatico *m*, -a *f*
psychoanalyse *v/t* psicanalizzare
psychoanalysis *n* psicanalisi *f*
psychoanalyst *n* psicanalista *m/f*
psychobabble *n hum* linguaggio *m* psicologico
psychological *adj* psicologico; ***he's not really ill, it's all ~*** non è realmente malato, è tutta una questione psicologica
psychologically *adv* psicologicamente
psychologist *n* psicologo *m*, -a *f*
psychology *n* psicologia *f*
psychopath *n* psicopatico *m*, -a *f*
psychosomatic *adj* psicosomatico
psychotherapy *n* psicoterapia *f*
psychotic *adj* psicotico
pt *abbr* **1.** (= **part**) parte *f* **2.** (= **pint**) pinta *f* **3.** (= **point**) punto *m*
PT *abbr* (= **physical training**) educazione *f* fisica
PTA *abbr* (= **parent-teacher association**) *organizzazione composta da genitori e insegnanti*
PTO *abbr* (= **please turn over**) vedi retro
pub *n* pub *m inv*
pub-crawl *n*: ***go on a ~*** fare il giro dei pub
puberty *n* pubertà *f inv*; ***reach ~*** raggiungere la pubertà
pubes *npl infml* pelo *m* pubico
pubescent *adj* pubere
pubic hair *n* peli *mpl* del pube
publ. *abbr* (= **published**) pubblicato
public I *adj* pubblico; ***make sth ~*** ren-

dere pubblico qc; ***be ~ knowledge*** essere pubblicamente noto; ***become ~*** diventare pubblico; ***at ~ expense*** a spese dei contribuenti; ***~ pressure*** pressione *f* pubblica; ***a ~ figure*** una figura *f* pubblica; ***in the ~ eye*** sotto i riflettori dell'opinione pubblica; ***in the ~ interest*** nel pubblico interesse **II** *n*: ***the ~*** il pubblico; ***in ~*** in pubblico; ***the viewing ~*** i telespettatori
public access channel *n* TV canale *m* ad accesso pubblico **public address system** *n* sistema *m* di altoparlanti
publican *n Br* gestore *m*, -trice *f* di pub
publication *n* pubblicazione *f*
public company *n* società *f* per azioni **public convenience** *n* gabinetti *mpl* pubblici **public defender** *n US* difensore *m* d'ufficio **public domain** *n* dominio *m* pubblico **public enemy** *n* pericolo *m* pubblico **public gallery** *n* galleria *f* per il pubblico **public health** *n* sanità *f* pubblica **public holiday** *n* giorno *m* festivo **public housing** *n US* case *fpl* popolari **public inquiry** *n* inchiesta *f* pubblica
publicist *n* pubblicitario *m*, -a *f*
publicity *n* pubblicità *f inv*; ***~ campaign*** campagna *f* pubblicitaria
publicize *v/t make known* far sapere in giro; COMM reclamizzare
public law *n* diritto *m* pubblico **public library** *n* biblioteca *f* pubblica **public life** *n* vita *f* pubblica **public limited company** *n* società *f inv* a responsabilità limitata quotata in borsa
publicly *adv* pubblicamente
public nuisance disturbo *m* della quiete pubblica **public opinion** *n* opinione *f* pubblica **public ownership** *n* nazionalizzazione *f*; ***under*** *or* ***in ~*** nazionalizzato **public property** *n* proprietà *f* pubblica **public prosecutor** *n* pubblico ministero *m* **public relations** *npl* relazioni *fpl* pubbliche **public school** *n Br* scuola *f* privata **public sector** *n* settore *m* pubblico **public servant** *n* pubblico funzionario *m* **public service** *n* (*Civil Service*) servizio *m* pubblico **public speaking** *n* arte *f* di parlare in pubblico; ***I'm no good at ~*** non sono bravo a parlare in pubblico **public spending** *n* spesa *f* pubblica **public television** *n US* televisione *f* pubblica **public transport** *n* mezzi *mpl* pubblici **public utility** *n* servizio *m* di pubblica utilità
publish *v/t* pubblicare; ***~ed by Collins*** pubblicato da Collins
publisher *n* editore *m*
publishing *n* editoria *f*
publishing company *n* casa *f* editrice
puce I *n* color *m* pulce **II** *adj* color pulce
pucker I *v/t* increspare; *forehead* corrugare; ***she ~ed her lips as she thought about it*** increspò le labbra mentre ci pensava **II** *v/i* incresparsi **III** *n* piega *f*; ***the ~s in the cloth were part of its decorative appeal*** le pieghe nel tessuto fanno parte dell'aspetto decorativo
pud *n Br infml* → ***pudding***
pudding *n dish* budino *m*; *part of meal* dolce *m*
puddle *n* pozzanghera *f*
pudgy *adj* (*+er*) cicciottello
puerile *adj* puerile
puff I *v/i* (*pant*) ansimare; ***~ on a cigarette*** tirare boccate da una sigaretta **II** *n of wind*, *smoke* soffio *m*; ***out of ~*** *infml* senza fiato
◆**puff out** *v/t sep chest*, *cheeks* gonfiare; (*emit*) sbuffare
◆**puff up I** *v/t sep feathers* arruffare **II** *v/i* (*face etc*) gonfiarsi
puffball *n* vescia *f*
puffin *n* ZOOL pulcinella *f* di mare
puff pastry *n* pasta *f* sfoglia
puffy *adj* (*+er*) *eyes*, *face* gonfio
pug *n dog* carlino *m*
pugnacious *adj* bellicoso
pug nose *n* naso *m* rincagnato
puke I *v/i infml* vomitare; ***he makes me ~*** mi fa vomitare **II** *n* vomito *m*
◆**puke up** *v/i infml* vomitare
pukka *adj Br infml* fichissimo
pull I *v/t* (*drag*) tirare; (*tug*) dare uno strappo a; *beer* spillare; *crowd* attirare; *tooth* togliere; ***~ a door shut*** chiudere la porta (tirando); ***~ a gun on s.o.*** puntare un'arma su qn; ***~ a muscle*** farsi uno strappo muscolare; *fig* ***~ to pieces*** (*criticize*) fare a pezzi; *fig* ***~ s.o.'s leg*** *infml* prendere in giro qn; ***~ s.o.'s licence*** *infml* ritirare la patente a qn; *fig* ***~ strings*** usare la propria influenza; ***she was the one ~ing the***

strings era lei a tirare i fili; **~ *the other one*** (***it's got bells on***) *Br infml* chi credi di prendere in giro? **II** *v/i* tirare; *Br infml sexually* attrarre; **~ *to the left*** *car* spostarsi vestro sinistra; ***he ~ed across to the left-hand lane*** si spostò nella corsia di sinistra; ***he ~ed into the side of the road*** si spostò a lato della strada; **~ *alongside*** avanzare; **~ *on one's cigarette*** dare un tiro alla sigaretta **III** *n on rope* tirata *f*; ***I felt a ~ at my sleeve*** mi sentii tirare la manica; *infml* (*appeal*) attrattiva *f*; *infml* (*influence*) influenza *f*

◆**pull ahead** *v/i in race*, *competition* portarsi in testa

◆**pull apart** *v/t sep* (*separate*) separare; ***they pulled the two dogs apart*** separarono i due cani

◆**pull away** *v/t sep* spostare; ***she pulled it away from him*** lo allontanò da lui; ***the car pulled away from the others*** la macchina staccò le altre

◆**pull down** *v/t sep* (*lower*) tirar giù; (*demolish*) demolire

◆**pull in I** *v/i of bus*, *train* arrivare; ***the train pulled in at night*** il treno arrivò di notte **II** *v/t*: ***the orator pulled in quite a crowd*** l'oratore attirò una discreta folla

◆**pull off** *v/t sep* togliere; *infml deal etc* portare a termine; ***pull off the road*** lasciare la strada; ***they pulled off the bank robbery of the century*** riuscirono a fare la rapina in banca del secolo

◆**pull out I** *v/t sep* tirar fuori; *troops* (far) ritirare; *fig* ***pull the rug out from under s.o.*** ritirare il proprio appoggio per qn; ***the car pulled out from behind the lorry*** la macchina si spostò per superare da dietro il camion **II** *v/i of agreement*, *competition*, MIL ritirarsi; ***it's high time the troops pulled out*** è ormai tempo che le truppe si ritirino; *of ship* partire

◆**pull over I** *v/i of driver* accostarsi **II** *v/t sep*: ***the police pulled me over and checked my papers*** la polizia mi ha fatto accostare e mi ha controllato i documenti

◆**pull through** *v/i from an illness* farcela *infml*; ***things didn't look good, but she pulled through*** le cose non si presentavano bene, ma ce la fece

◆**pull together I** *v/i* (*cooperate*) cooperare **II** *v/t sep*: ***pull o.s. together*** darsi una mossa *infml*

◆**pull up I** *v/t sep* (*raise*) tirar su; *plant*, *weeds* strappare; ***pull up a chair and join in!*** avvicina una sedia e unisciti a noi! **II** *v/i of car etc* fermarsi

pull-down *adj bed* ribaltabile; **~ *menu*** COMPUT menu *m inv* a discesa

pulley *n* puleggia *f*

pull-out *adj table* estraibile; *supplement* inserto *m*

pullover *n* pullover *m inv*

pull tab *n US* linguetta *f*

pulp I *n soft mass* poltiglia *f*; *of fruit* polpa *f*; *for paper-making* pasta *f*; ***beat s.o. to a ~*** *infml* ridurre qn in poltiglia **II** *v/t fruit etc* ridurre in poltiglia; *paper* mandare al macero

pulp fiction *n* romanzetti *mpl* da poco (*infarciti di vicende truculente e scene di sesso*)

pulpit *n* pulpito *m*

pulsate *v/i of heart*, *blood* pulsare; *of rhythm* vibrare

pulse[1] **I** *n* ANAT polso *m*; PHYS impulso *m*; ***feel s.o.'s ~*** tastare il polso a qn; ***he still has*** *or* ***keeps his finger on the ~ of economic affairs*** ha ancora il polso della situazione economica **II** *v/i* pulsare

pulse[2] *n seed* legume *m*

pulverise, *US* **pulverize** *v/t* polverizzare

puma *n* puma *m inv*

pumice *n* (pietra) pomice *f*

pummel *v/t* prendere a pugni

pump I *n* pompa *f* **II** *v/t* pompare; **~ *water out of sth*** pompare acqua da qc; **~ *s.o.*** (***for information***) spremere informazioni da qn; **~ *iron*** *infml* fare sollevamento pesi; **~ *s.o. full of drugs*** *infml* imbottire qn di droga **III** *v/i* pompare; (*water*, *blood*) sgorgare; ***the piston ~ed up and down*** il pistone andava su e giù

◆**pump into** *v/t sep*: ***pump money into sth*** investire denaro in qc

◆**pump out** *v/t sep* svuotare

◆**pump up** *v/t sep* gonfiare

pumpkin *n* zucca *f*

pun I *n* gioco *m* di parole **II** *v/i* fare un gioco di parole

punch[1] **I** *n blow* pugno *m*; *implement* punzonatrice *f* **II** *v/t with fist* dare un pugno a; ***I wanted to ~ him in the face*** volevo dargli un pugno in faccia; *hole* perforare; *ticket* forare
◆**punch in** *v/t sep* COMPUT *data* introdurre
punch[2] *n* (*drink*) punch *m*, ponce *m*
Punch *n Br* ***~ and Judy show*** spettacolo *m* di burattini; ***be*** (***as***) ***pleased as ~*** *infml* essere contento come una pasqua
punchbag *n boxing* sacco *m*
punchbowl *n* coppa *f* da ponce
punch-drunk *adj* stordito
punch line *n* finale *m*
punch-up *n* (*fight*) scazzottata *f*
punchy *adj* vibrante
punctual *adj* puntuale
punctuality *n* puntualità *f inv*
punctually *adv* puntualmente
punctuate *v/t* mettere la punteggiatura in; (*intersperse*) costellare
punctuation *n* punteggiatura *f*
punctuation mark *n* segno *m* d'interpunzione
puncture I *n* foratura *f* **II** *v/t* forare
pundit *n* esperto *m*, -a *f*
pungent *adj* acre; *taste* aspro
punish *v/t person* punire; ***he was ~ed by a fine*** è stato punito con una multa; ***the other team ~ed us for that mistake*** l'altra squadra ci ha fatto pagare quell'errore
punishable *adj offence* punibile
punishing *adj pace, schedule* estenuante; ***he worked ~ hours*** ha lavorato per ore in modo estenuante
punishment *n* punizione *f*
punk (rock) I *n* MUS punk *m inv*; *US infml* (*hoodlum*) vandalo *m*, -a *f* **II** *adj* punk
punk rocker *n* MUS artista *m/f* punk
punnet *n* cestello *m*
punt I *n* barchino *m*; (*gamble*) scommessa *f* **II** *v/t* trasportare su un barchino **III** *v/i* andare su un barchino
punter *n* (*gambler*) scommettitore *m*, -trice *f*; *infml* (*customer*) cliente *m/f*
puny *adj* (*+er*) *person* gracile
pup *n* cucciolo *m*
pupil[1] *n* ANAT pupilla *f*
pupil[2] *n* (*student*) allievo *m*, -a *f*
puppet *n* burattino *m*; *with strings* marionetta *f*
puppeteer *n* burattinaio *m*, -a *f*
puppet government *n* governo *m* fantoccio
puppetry *n* burattini *mpl*
puppy *n* cucciolo *m*
puppy fat *n infml* pinguedine *f* infantile **puppy love** *n* amore *m* acerbo
purchase[1] **I** *n* acquisto *m*; ***make a ~*** fare un acquisto **II** *v/t* acquistare
purchase[2] *n* (*grip*) presa *f*
purchase order *n* ordine *m* d'acquisto **purchase price** *n* prezzo *m* d'acquisto
purchaser *n* acquirente *m/f*
pure *adj* (*+er*) puro; ***~ new wool*** pura lana *f* vergine; ***in ~ disbelief*** con assoluta incredulità; ***by ~ chance*** per puro caso; ***malice ~ and simple*** pura e semplice malizia *f*
purebred *adj* di razza pura
purée *n* purè *m inv*; ***apple ~*** purè *m inv* di mele
purely *adv* puramente
purgatory *n* purgatorio *m*
purge I *n* purga *f*; *of political party* epurazione *f* **II** *v/t* purgare; epurare
purify *v/t* ⟨*pret & past part* ***-ied***⟩ *water* purificare
purist *n* purista *m/f*
puritan *n* puritano *m*, -a *f*
puritanical *adj* puritano
purity *n* purezza *f*
purple *adj* viola *inv*
purport *v/t* dare a intendere
purpose *n* (*aim, object*) scopo *m*; ***on ~*** di proposito
purposeful *adj* risoluto
purposely *adv* di proposito
purr *v/i of cat* far le fusa
purse *n for money* borsellino *m*; *US* (*handbag*) borsetta *f*
pursue *v/t person* inseguire; *career* intraprendere; *course of action* proseguire
pursuer *n* inseguitore *m*, -trice *f*
pursuit *n* (*chase*) inseguimento *m*; *of happiness etc* ricerca *f*; *activity* occupazione *f*; ***those in ~*** gli inseguitori; ***he set off in ~*** partì all'inseguimento; ***in hot ~ of s.o.*** alle calcagna di qn; ***in*** (***the***) ***~ of his goal*** nel perseguimento del suo scopo; (*occupation*) ricerca; ***gardening is his favourite weekend ~*** il giardinaggio è il suo passatempo preferito nel fine settimana

pus *n* pus *m inv*

push I *v/t* (*shove*) spingere; *button* premere; (*pressurize*) fare pressioni su; *infml drugs* spacciare; ***be ~ed for*** *infml* essere a corto di; ***be ~ing 40*** *infml* essere sulla quarantina; ***he ~ed his way through the crowd*** si aprì un varco attraverso la folla; ***he ~ed the thought to the back of his mind*** respinse quel pensiero; ***don't ~ your luck*** non sfidare la sorte; ***they ~ed him to the limits*** lo spinsero al limite; ***that's ~ing it a bit*** *infml* è un po' azzardato **II** *v/i* spingere **III** *n* (*shove*) spinta *f*; ***at the ~ of a button*** premendo un pulsante; ***get the ~*** *infml* (*lose one's job*) essere licenziato; ***at a ~*** *infml* (*if essential*) se proprio necessario; ***if / when ~ comes to shove*** *infml* quando arriva il momento critico

◆**push ahead** *v/i* andare avanti; ***push ahead with one's plans*** andare avanti con i propri piani

◆**push around** *v/t sep liter* tiranneggiare; *fig infml* (*bully*) *child* fare il prepotente con; *adult* comandare a bacchetta; ***dont push me around*** non comandarmi a bacchetta

◆**push along** *v/t sep cart etc* spingere; ***he was pushing his bike along the pavement*** stava spingendo la sua bicicletta lungo il marciapiede

◆**push aside** *v/t sep* spingere da parte; *quickly* scostare; *fig* accantonare

◆**push away** *v/t sep* respingere

◆**push back** *v/t sep people* respingere; *with one push* spingere indietro; *cover*, *hair* spingere indietro

◆**push forward** *v/i* → ***push ahead***

◆**push in I** *v/t sep button* far premere con forza **II** *v/i in queue* passare avanti

◆**push off I** *v/t sep lid* spingere via **II** *v/i infml* (*leave*) andarsene; ***push off!*** sparisci! *infml*

◆**push on** *v/i* (*continue*) continuare; ***they pushed on, regardless of the rain*** continuarono senza badare alla pioggia

◆**push to** *v/t always sep door* chiudere con una spinta; ***please would you push the door to?*** potresti chiudere la porta, per favore?

◆**push up** *v/t sep prices* far salire

push-bike *n Br infml* bicicletta *f* **push-button** *adj* a tastiera **push-chair** *n* passeggino *m*

pusher *n infml of drugs* spacciatore *m*, -trice *f*

pushover *n infml* pollo *m*, -a *f infml*; ***it was a ~*** è stata una passeggiata *infml*

push-up *n* flessione *f* sulle braccia

pushy *adj* (*+er*) *infml* troppo intraprendente

puss, pussy (cat) *n infml* micio *m*, -a *f*

pussy *n infml vulg* (*female genitals*) fica *f*

◆**pussyfoot about** *v/i infml* tentennare

put *v/t* ⟨*pret & past part* **put**⟩ mettere; *question* porre; ***~ the cost at …*** stimare il costo intorno a …; ***they ~ a plank across the stream*** misero un'asse attraverso il ruscello; ***~ sth in a drawer*** mettere qc in un cassetto; ***he ~ his hand in his pocket*** si mise la mano in tasca; ***~ the dog in the kitchen*** mettere il cane in cucina; ***~ sugar in one's coffee*** mettere lo zucchero nel caffè; ***~ s.o. in a good mood*** mettere qn di buonumore; ***~ a lot of effort into sth*** mettere molto impegno in qc; ***~ money into sth*** investire soldi in qc; ***~ the lid on the box*** mettere il coperchio sulla scatola; ***he ~ his head on my shoulder*** mise la testa sulla mia spalla; ***her aunt ~ her on the train*** sua zia la mise sul treno; ***~ money on a horse*** puntare denaro su un cavallo; ***~ one's hand over one's mouth*** portare la mano alla bocca; ***he ~ his head (a)round the door*** sporse la testa dalla porta; ***~ a glass to one's lips*** portare un bicchiere alle labbra; ***she ~ the shell to her ear*** si portò la conchiglia all'orecchio; ***~ s.o. to bed*** mettere a letto qn; ***~ s.o. to great expense*** far sostenere forti spese a qn; ***we'll each ~ £5 toward(s) it*** ci metteremo 5 sterline ciascuno; ***they ~ her to work on the new project*** la misero a lavorare sul nuovo progetto; ***stay ~*** resta lì; ***~ a cross / tick against s.o.'s name*** mettere una croce / un segno di spunta sul nome di qn; *question, proposal* esporre; ***I ~ it to you that …***

ti faccio presente che ...; ***that's one way of ~ting it*** puoi anche metterla così; ***how shall I ~ it?*** come dovrei metterla?; ***~ it bluntly*** sii franco; ***he ~s money before his family's happiness*** dà più importanza al denaro che alla felicità della sua famiglia

◆**put across** *v/t sep ideas etc* trasmettere

◆**put aside** *v/t sep* mettere da parte

◆**put away** *v/t sep in cupboard etc* mettere via; *in institution* rinchiudere; (*consume*) far fuori; *money* mettere da parte; ***put the car away*** mettere a posto la macchina

◆**put back** *v/t sep* (*replace*) rimettere a posto; (*postpone*) rimandare

◆**put by** *v/t sep money* mettere da parte

◆**put down** *v/t sep* mettere giù; ***put it down on the floor*** mettilo giù sul pavimento; ***I couldn't put that book down*** non riesco a posare quel libro; ***put down the phone*** mettere giù il telefono; *deposit* versare; *rebellion* reprimere; *animal* abbattere; ***I had the dog put down when he went blind*** feci abbattere il cane quando diventò cieco; (*belittle*) sminuire; ***you shouldn't keep putting him down like that*** non dovresti continuare a sminuirlo in quel modo; *in writing* scrivere; ***put one's foot down*** *in car* accelerare; (*be firm*) farsi valere; ***put X down to Y*** (*attribute*) attribuire X a Y; ***you can put me down for £ 10*** puoi segnarmi per 10 sterline; ***put it down under sundries*** segnalo sotto articoli vari

◆**put forward** *v/t sep idea etc* avanzare

◆**put in** *v/t sep* inserire; *overtime* fare; *time*, *effort* dedicare; ***put in a few hours' work at the weekend*** dedicaci alcune ore di lavoro nel fine settimana; *request*, *claim* presentare

◆**put in for** *v/t* (*apply for*) fare domanda per; ***I put in for that job too*** ho fatto domanda anche per quel lavoro

◆**put off** *v/t sep light*, *radio*, *TV* spegnere; (*postpone*) rimandare; ***put sth off for 10 days / until January*** rimandare qc per 10 giorni / fino a gennaio; (*deter*) scoraggiare; ***don't let his rudeness put you off*** non lasciarti scoraggiare dalla sua maleducazione; (*repel*) disgustare; ***the accident put me off driving*** l'incidente mi ha fatto passare la voglia di guidare; (*distract*) distrarre; ***I'd like to watch you if it won't put you off*** mi piacerebbe guardarti, se non ti distrae

◆**put on** *v/t sep light*, *radio*, *TV* accendere; *tape*, *music* mettere su; *jacket*, *shoes*, *glasses* mettersi; *makeup* mettere; (*perform*) mettere in scena; (*assume*) affettare; ***she's just putting it on*** sta solo fingendo; ***put on the brakes*** frenare; ***put on weight*** ingrassare; *on telephone* ***put s.o. on to s.o.*** mettere qn in comunicazione con qn; ***would you put him on?*** può passarmelo?

◆**put out** *v/t sep hand* allungare; *fire*, *light* spegnere; ***put the washing out (to dry)*** stendere il bucato; ***that goal put them out of the competition*** quel gol li estromise dalla gara; ***she could not put him out of her mind*** non riusciva a toglierselo dalla mente; ***put one's head out of the window*** mettere la testa fuori dal finestrino; ***be put out (by sth)*** essere contrariato (per qc); ***put s.o. out*** disturbare qn; ***put o.s. out (for s.o.)*** scomodarsi (per qn); ***I don't want to put you out*** non ti voglio disturbare

◆**put through** *v/t sep*: ***I'll put you through (to him)*** glielo passo; ***I'll put you through to sales*** le passo l'ufficio vendite; ***he has put his family through a lot (of suffering)*** ne ha fatte passare tante alla sua famiglia

◆**put together** *v/t sep* (*assemble*) montare; (*organize*) organizzare; ***he's better than all the others put together*** è meglio di tutti gli altri messi insieme

◆**put up** *v/t sep hand* alzare; *person* ospitare; (*erect*) costruire; *prices* aumentare; *poster*, *notice* affiggere; *money* fornire; ***put up for sale*** mettere in vendita; ***put one's child up for adoption*** dare un bambino in adozione; ***put up resistance*** opporre resistenza

◆**put up to** *v/t* (*incite*) spingere; ***put s.o. up to doing sth*** spingere qn a fare qc

◆**put up with** *v/i* (*tolerate*) sopportare; ***I won't put up with that*** non lo tolle-

rerò
put-down *n* commento *m* umiliante
put-on *adj US infml* affettato; ***her accent sounded very ~*** il suo accento suonava molto affettato
put-put *n infml* scoppiettio *m*; ***a little ~ engine*** un motorino scoppiettante
putrefaction *n* putrefazione *f*
putrefy *v/i* ⟨*pret & past part* **-ied**⟩ imputridire
putrid *adj* putrido
putt I *n golf* putt *m inv* **II** *v/t & v/i golf* colpire con un putt
putting green *n area erbosa pianeggiante intorno alla buca da golf*
putty *n* mastice *m*
put-up job *n* imbroglio *m*
puzzle I *n* (*mystery*) mistero *m*; *game* rebus *m inv*; *jigsaw* puzzle *m inv*; *crossword* cruciverba *m inv* **II** *v/t* lasciar perplesso **III** *v/i*: ***~ over sth*** scervellarsi su qc
puzzlement *n* perplessità *f*
puzzling *adj* inspiegabile
PVC *abbr* (= **polyvinyl chloride**) PVC *m inv* (polivinilcloruro *m*)
pygmy, pigmy I *n*: ***Pygmy*** pigmeo *m*, -a *f* **II** *adj*: ***Pygmy*** pigmeo
pyjamas, *US* **pajamas** *npl* pigiama *m*
pylon *n* pilone *m*
pyramid *n* piramide *f*
pyramid selling *n* sistema *m* di vendita piramidale
pyre *n* pira *f*
Pyrenean *adj* dei Pirenei
Pyrenees *npl* Pirenei *mpl*
Pyrex® *n* Pyrex® *m inv*
pyromania *n* piromania *f*
python *n* pitone *m*

Q

Q, q *n* q, Q *f inv*
QC *abbr* (= **Queen's Counsel**) *Br* JUR patrocinante *m/f* per la corona
quack[1] I *n of duck* qua qua *m inv* **II** *v/i* fare qua qua
quack[2] *n infml* (*bad doctor*) ciarlatano *m*, -a *f*; ***I'm going to see the ~*** vado dal dottore
quad bike *n Br* quad *m inv*
quadrangle *n figure* quadrilatero *m*; *courtyard* cortile *m*
quadruped *n* quadrupede *m*
quadruple *v/i* quadruplicare
quadruplets *npl* quattro gemelli *mpl*
quads *npl infml* quattro gemelli *mpl*
quagmire *n fig* ginepraio *m*
quail[1] *v/i* perdersi d'animo
quail[2] *n* ZOOL quaglia *f*
quaint *adj* (+*er*) *pretty* pittoresco; *slightly eccentric*: *ideas etc* curioso
quake I *n* (*earthquake*) terremoto *m* **II** *v/i a. fig* tremare
qualification *n from university etc* titolo *m* di studio; *of remark etc* riserva *f*; ***have the right ~s for a job*** *skills* avere tutti i requisiti per un lavoro
qualified *adj doctor*, *engineer etc* abilitato; (*restricted*) con riserva; ***I am not ~ to judge*** non sono in grado di valutare; ***~ engineer*** ingegnere *m* abilitato; ***highly ~*** altamente qualificato; ***he is / is not ~ to teach*** è / non è abilitato all'insegnamento; ***he was not ~ for the job*** non aveva i requisiti per quel lavoro; ***he is fully ~*** ha tutti i titoli richiesti
qualify ⟨*pret & past part* **-ied**⟩ **I** *v/t of degree*, *course etc* abilitare; *remark etc* precisare **II** *v/i* (*get certificate etc*) ottenere la qualifica (**as** di); *in competition* qualificarsi; ***our team has qualified for the semi-final*** la nostra squadra è entrata in semifinale; ***that doesn't ~ as …*** non può essere considerato …; ***does he ~ for admission to the club?*** ha i requisiti necessari per l'ammissione al circolo?; ***let me ~ that by saying…*** lasciami precisare che …
quality I *n* qualità *f inv* **II** *adj*: ***~ goods*** articoli *mpl* di qualità; *newspaper* di qualità
quality control *n* controllo *m* (di) qualità **quality of life** *n* qualità *f* della

vita **quality time** *n* tempo *m* di qualità

qualm *n*: ***have no ~s about …*** non aver scrupoli a …; ***without a ~*** senza scrupoli

quandary *n* dilemma *m*; ***be in a ~*** avere un dilemma; ***he was in a ~ about what to do*** aveva un dilemma su cosa fare

quango *n abbr* (= **quasi-autonomous nongovernmental organization**) *Br ente parastatale finanziato dallo stato*

quantifier *n* MATH, LING quantificatore *m*

quantify *v/t* ⟨*pret & past part* **-ied**⟩ quantificare

quantity *n* quantità *f inv*

quantum leap *n fig* grande progresso *m*

quantum mechanics *nsg* meccanica *f* quantistica **quantum physics** *nsg* teoria *f* fisica dei quanti

quarantine I *n* quarantena *f*; ***put s.o. in ~*** mettere qn in quarantena **II** *v/t* mettere in quarantena

quarrel I *n* litigio *m* **II** *v/i* ⟨*pret & past part* **-led**, *US* **-ed**⟩ litigare

quarrelsome *adj* litigioso

quarry[1] *n in hunt* preda *f*

quarry[2] **I** *n for mining* cava *f* **II** *v/t* estrarre

quart *n* quarto *m* di gallone

quarter I *n* **1.** quarto *m*; ***for a ~ (of) the price*** per un quarto del prezzo; ***a mile and a ~*** un miglio e un quarto; ***a ~ of an hour*** un quarto d'ora; ***a ~ past six*** *or* ***a ~ after six*** *US* le sei e un quarto; **(*a*) *~ to 5*** le cinque meno un quarto; **(*a*) *~ past 5*** le cinque e un quarto **2.** *part of town* quartiere *m* **3.** ***from all ~s*** da ogni parte; ***in these ~s*** in questi ambienti; ***he won't get help from that ~*** non avrà alcun aiuto da quella parte; ***in various ~s*** in diversi ambienti; ***at close ~s*** da vicino; **quarters** *npl* (*lodgings*) alloggio (*a.* MIL); (*mercy in battle*) clemenza *f*; ***he gave no ~*** non dette quartiere **II** *v/t* dividere in quattro parti

quarterback *n* SPORTS quarterback *m inv*

quarter-final *n* partita *f* dei quarti *mpl* di finale

quarter-finalist *n* concorrente *m/f* dei quarti di finale

quarterly I *adj* trimestrale **II** *adv* trimestralmente

quarter note *n US* MUS semiminima *f*

quarters *npl* MIL quartieri *mpl*

quartet *n* MUS quartetto *m*

quartz *n* quarzo *m*

quash *v/t rebellion* reprimere; *court decision* annullare

quaver I *n in voice* tremolio *m*; MUS croma *f* **II** *v/i of voice* tremolare

quay *n* banchina *f*

quayside *n* banchina *f*

queasy *adj* (+*er*) nauseato; ***I feel ~*** ho la nausea

queen *n* regina *f*; *cards*, *chess* regina *f*; ***~ of spades*** regina *f* di picche; *infml* checca *f*; ***drag ~*** drag queen *f*

queen bee *n* ape *f* regina

queenly *adj* regale

Queen's Counsel *n Br* JUR patrocinante *m/f* per la corona

Queen's English *n* inglese *m* corretto

queer I *adj* (+*er*) (*peculiar*) strano; *pej infml* (*homosexual*) da frocio *sl*; ***he's a bit ~ in the head*** *infml* è un po' strambo; ***there's something ~ about it*** c'è qualcosa di strano **II** *n pej infml* (*homosexual*) frocio *m*

queerly *adv* stranamente

quell *v/t* soffocare

quench *v/t a. fig* spegnere

query I *n* interrogativo *m* **II** *v/t* ⟨*pret & past part* **-ied**⟩ *express doubt about* contestare; ***~ sth with s.o.*** contestare qc a qn; *check* controllare

quest *n* ricerca *f*; ***in ~ of*** in cerca di

question I *n* **1.** domanda *f* **2.** (*matter*) questione *f*; ***in ~*** *being talked about* in questione; ***it's a ~ of money/time*** è questione di soldi/tempo; ***that's out of the ~*** è fuori discussione **3.** (*doubt*) ***in ~*** in dubbio; ***call sth into ~*** mettere in questione qc **II** *v/t person* interrogare; (*doubt*) dubitare di; ***that's not being ~ed*** nessuno lo mette in dubbio

questionable *adj* discutibile; (*dubious*) dubbio

questioner *n* interrogatore *m*, -trice *f*

questioning I *adj look*, *tone* interrogativo **II** *n* interrogatorio *m*

question mark *n* punto *m* interrogativo **question master** *n* presentatore *m*, -trice *f* di quiz

questionnaire *n* questionario *m*

queue I *n* coda *f*, fila *f*; ***jump the ~*** non rispettare la fila; ***stand in a ~*** stare in fila **II** *v/i* fare la fila *or* la coda; ***they were queuing for the bus*** stavano facendo la coda per l'autobus
queue-jumper *n* persona *f* che non rispetta la coda
quibble *v/i* cavillare; ***~ over details*** cavillare sui dettagli
quiche *n* COOK quiche *f*
quick I *adj* (+*er*) *person* svelto; *reply*, *change* veloce; ***be ~!*** fai presto!, fai in fretta!; ***let's have a ~ drink*** beviamo qualcosina?; ***can I have a ~ look?*** posso dare un'occhiatina?; ***that was ~!*** già fatto? **II** *n*: ***cut s.o. to the ~*** pungere qn sul vivo
quick-acting *adj drug* a effetto rapido
quicken I *v/t* (*a.* **quicken up**) accelerare **II** *v/i* (*a.* **quicken up**) accelerare
quick fix *n* soluzione *f* rapida
quickie *n infml*: ***have a ~*** *quick drink* bere qualcosina
quickly *adv* rapidamente, in fretta
quicksand *n* sabbie *fpl* mobili **quicksilver** *n* mercurio *m* **quick-tempered** *adj* impulsivo **quick-witted** *adj* sveglio
quid *n infml* sterlina *f*; ***50 ~*** 50 sterline
quiet I *adj* (+*er*) *voice*, *music* basso; *engine* silenzioso; *street*, *life*, *town* tranquillo; ***keep ~ about sth*** tenere segreto qc; ***~!*** silenzio!, stai zitto!; ***she was as ~ as a mouse*** fu silenziosissima; ***that book should keep him ~*** quel libro dovrebbe farlo tacere **II** *n* silenzio *m*; ***in the ~ of the night*** nel silenzio della notte; ***on the ~*** di nascosto **III** *v/t* → ***quieten down***
◆**quieten down I** *v/t sep* calmare **II** *v/i* calmarsi; ***things have quietened down a lot*** le cose si sono decisamente calmate
quietly *adv not loudly* silenziosamente, senza far rumore; (*without fuss*) semplicemente; (*peacefully*) tranquillamente
quietness *n of night*, *street* tranquillità *f*, calma *f*; *of voice* dolcezza *f*
quilt *n on bed* piumino *m*
quilted *adj* trapuntato
quinine *n* chinino *m*
quintet *n* MUS quintetto *m*
quip I *n* battuta *f* (di spirito) **II** *v/i* ⟨*pret & past part* **-ped**⟩ scherzare
quirk *n* bizzarria *f*
quirky *adj* (+*er*) bizzarro
quit ⟨*pret & past part* **quit**⟩ **I** *v/t job* mollare *infml*; ***~ doing sth*** smettere di fare qc **II** *v/i* (*leave job*) licenziarsi; COMPUT uscire; ***get one's notice to ~*** *from landlord* ricevere la disdetta
quite *adv* **1.** (*fairly*) abbastanza, piuttosto; ***I ~ like this painting*** questo dipinto mi piace abbastanza; ***~ a lot*** *drink*, *change* parecchio; ***~ a lot better*** molto meglio; ***~ a few*** un bel po'; ***it was ~ a surprise / change*** è stata una bella sorpresa / un bel cambiamento **2.** (*completely*) completamente; ***not ~ ready*** non ancora pronto; ***I didn't ~ understand*** non ho capito bene; ***is that right? – not ~*** giusto? – non esattamente; ***~!*** esatto!; ***I am ~ happy where I am*** sono del tutto felice dove mi trovo; ***it's ~ impossible to do that*** è del tutto impossibile farlo
quits *adj*: ***be ~ with s.o.*** essere pari con qn; ***let's call it ~*** così siamo pari
quitter *n infml* rinunciatario *m*, -a *f*; ***he's no ~*** non si dà per vinto facilmente
quiver I *v/i* tremare **II** *n* (*tremble*) tremito *m*; *for arrows* faretra *f*
quiz I *n* quiz *m inv* **II** *v/t* ⟨*pret & past part* **-zed**⟩ interrogare (*a. US infml* EDU); *look* scrutare
quiz master *n* conduttore *m*, -trice *f* (di gioco a quiz) **quiz show** *n* gioco *m* a quiz
quizzical *adj* interrogativo
quota *n* quota *f*
quotation *n from author* citazione *f*; *price* preventivo *m*; ***give s.o. a ~ for sth*** fare un preventivo a qn per qc
quotation marks *npl* virgolette *fpl*
quote I *n from author* citazione *f*; *price* preventivo *m*; (*quotation mark*) virgoletta *f*; ***in ~s*** tra virgolette **II** *v/t text* citare; *price* stimare; ***~d on the Stock Exchange*** quotato in Borsa **III** *v/i*: ***~ from an author*** citare un autore; ***~ … unquote*** aperte virgolette … chiuse virgolette
quotient *n* quoziente *m*

R

R, r *n* r, R *f inv*; *US film* vietato ai minori di 17 anni
R *abbr* (= **river**) fiume *m*
rabbi *n* rabbino *m*
rabbit *n* coniglio *m*
◆**rabbit on** *v/i sl* blaterare
rabble *n* marmaglia *f*
rabble-rouser *n* agitatore *m*, -trice *f*
rabble-rousing *n* sobillazione *f*
rabid *adj dog* idrofobo
rabies *nsg* rabbia *f*, idrofobia *f*
RAC *abbr* (= **Royal Automobile Club**) *club automobilistico inglese*
rac(c)oon *n* procione *m*
race[1] *n of people* razza *f*; ***of mixed ~*** di razza mista
race[2] **I** *n* SPORTS gara *f*; ***the ~s*** (*horse races*) le corse **II** *v/i* (*run fast*) correre; ***he ~d against the world champion*** ha gareggiato contro il campione del mondo; ***he ~d through his work*** fece velocemente il suo lavoro; (*pulse, heart*) battere forte; (*mind*) lavorare freneticamente **III** *v/t*: ***I'll ~ you*** facciamo una gara; ***they ~d him to hospital*** lo portarono di corsa all'ospedale
racecourse *n* ippodromo *m*
racehorse *n* cavallo *m* da corsa
race meeting *n* concorso *m* ippico **race relations** *npl* rapporti *mpl* interrazziali **race riot** *n* scontri *mpl* razziali
racetrack *n* pista *f*; *for horses* ippodromo *m*
racial *adj* razziale; ***~ equality*** parità *f inv* razziale
racing *n* corse *fpl*
racing bike *n* bicicletta *f* da corsa **racing car** *n* auto *f inv* da corsa **racing driver** *n* pilota *m* automobilistico
racism *n* razzismo *m*
racist I *n* razzista *m/f* **II** *adj* razzista
rack[1] **I** *n for parking bikes* rastrelliera *f*; *for bags on train* portabagagli *m inv*; *for CDs* porta-CD *m inv*; ***~ of lamb*** costata *f* d'agnello; ***go to ~ and ruin*** (*country*) andare in rovina **II** *v/t*: ***~ one's brains*** scervellarsi
rack[2] *v/t wine*
racket[1] *n* SPORTS racchetta *f*
racket[2] *n* (*noise*) baccano *m*; *criminal activity* racket *m inv*
racketeering *n criminal activity* racket *m*
rackets *n* SPORTS *sport simile allo squash giocato con una pallina dura*
raconteur *n* narratore *m*, -trice *f* di aneddoti
racoon *n* ZOOL procione *m*
racquetball *n* SPORTS squash *m*
racy *adj* (+*er*) *style* vivido; *story, novel* esplicito
RADA *abbr* (= **Royal Academy of Dramatic Art**) *accademia reale di arte drammatica*
radar *n* radar *m inv*
radar screen *n* schermo *m* radar **radar trap** *n* autovelox® *m*
radial tyre, *US* **radial tire** *n* pneumatico *m* radiale
radiance *n* splendore *m*
radiant *adj smile* splendente; *appearance* raggiante; ***be ~ with joy*** essere raggiante di gioia
radiate *v/i of heat, light* diffondersi
radiation *n* PHYS radiazione *f*; ***contaminated by*** *or* ***with ~*** contaminato da radiazioni
radiation sickness *n* malattia *f* da radiazioni
radiator *n in room* termosifone *m*; *in car* radiatore *m*
radical I *adj* radicale **II** *n* radicale *m/f*
radical chic *n* radical chic *m/f inv* **radical expression** *n* MATH espressione *f* radicale
radicalism *n* POL radicalismo *m*
radically *adv* radicalmente
radio I *n* radio *f inv*; ***on the ~*** alla radio; ***by ~*** via radio **II** *v/i* comunicare via radio; ***~ for help*** chiedere aiuto via radio
radioactive *adj* radioattivo
radioactive waste *n* scorie *fpl* radioattive
radioactivity *n* radioattività *f inv*
radio alarm *n* radiosveglia *f* **radio cab** *n* radiotaxi *m inv* **radio-cassette recorder** *n Br* radioregistratore *m* a

cassette **radio frequency** *n* radiofrequenza *f*
radiography *n* radiografia *f*
radio ham *n* radioamatore *m*, -trice *f*
radiologist *n* radiologo *m*, -a *f*
radiology *n* radiologia *f*
radio station *n* stazione *f* radiofonica, radio *f inv* **radio taxi** *n* radiotaxi *m inv* **radio telephone** *n* radiotelefono *m* **radiotherapy** *n* radioterapia *f* **radio wave** *n* radioonda *f*
radish *n* ravanello *m*
radius *n* ⟨*pl* ***radii***⟩ raggio *m*; ANAT radio *m*; ***within a 6 km ~*** entro un raggio di 6 km
RAF *abbr* (= **Royal Air Force**) *aviazione militare britannica*
raffle I *n* lotteria *f* **II** *v/t* mettere in palio in una lotteria
raft *n* zattera *f*; ***a whole ~ of*** *proposals etc* tutta una serie di
rafter *n* travicello *m*
rag[1] *n for cleaning etc* straccio *m*; ***dressed in ~s*** vestito di stracci; ***go from ~s to riches*** (*by luck*) passare dalla miseria alla ricchezza; *pej infml* (*newspaper*) giornalaccio *m*
rag[2] **I** *n Br prank* burla *f* **II** *v/t* (*taunt*) prendere in giro
ragbag *n* accozzaglia *f*
rag doll *n* bambola *f* di pezza
rage I *n* rabbia *f*, collera *f*; ***be in a ~*** essere furioso; ***be all the ~*** *infml* essere di moda **II** *v/i of person* infierire; *of storm* infuriare
ragged *adj* stracciato
raglan I *adj* raglan **II** *n* raglan *m*
ragtime *n* ragtime *m*
rag trade *n infml* industria *f* dell'abbigliamento
raid I *n* raid *m inv* **II** *v/t of police, robbers* fare un raid in; *fridge, orchard* fare razzia in
raider *n on bank etc* rapinatore *m*, -trice *f*
rail[1] *n on track* rotaia *f*; (*handrail*) corrimano *m*; (*barrier*) parapetto *m*; ***curtain ~*** bastone *m* per tende; ***towel ~*** portasciugamano *m inv*; ***by ~*** in treno; ***go off the ~s*** uscire dai binari
rail[2] *v/i*: ***~ at s.o./sth*** inveire contro qn/qc; ***she's always ~ing against her mother-in-law*** inveisce sempre contro sua suocera
railcard *n Br* RAIL tessera *f* ferroviaria
railings *npl around park etc* inferriata *f*
railroad *etc US* → ***railway*** *etc*
railway, *US* **railroad** *n* ferrovia *f*
railway engine *n* locomotiva *f* **railway line**, *US* **railroad line** *n* linea *f* ferroviaria **railway network** *n* rete *f* ferroviaria **railway station**, *US* **railroad station** *n* stazione *f* ferroviaria
rain I *n* pioggia *f*; ***in the ~*** sotto la pioggia **II** *v/i* piovere; ***it's ~ing*** sta piovendo; ***it never ~s but it pours*** *Br prov or* ***when it ~s, it pours*** *US prov* piove sempre sul bagnato **III** *v/t*: ***it's ~ing cats and dogs*** *infml* piove a catinelle
◆**rain off** *v/t sep*: ***be rained off*** *match* essere rimandato a causa della pioggia
rainbow *n* arcobaleno *m* **raincheck** *n*: ***can I take a ~ on that?*** va bene se facciamo un'altra volta? **raincoat** *n* impermeabile *m* **raindrop** *n* goccia *f* di pioggia **rainfall** *n* piovosità *f inv* **rain forest** *n* foresta *f* pluviale **rainproof** *adj fabric* impermeabile **rainstorm** *n* temporale *m* **rainwater** *n* acqua *f* piovana
rainy *adj* (+*er*) *day* di pioggia; *weather* piovoso; ***it's ~*** piove molto; ***~ season*** stagione *f* delle piogge; ***save sth for a ~ day*** *fig* risparmiare qc per i tempi difficili
raise I *n US*: *in salary* aumento *m* **II** *v/t shelf, question* sollevare; *offer* aumentare; *children* allevare; *money* raccogliere; ***~ a laugh*** fare ridere; ***~ one's glass to s.o.*** brindare a qn; ***~ s.o. from the dead*** risuscitare qn; ***~ one's voice*** alzare la voce; ***~ s.o.'s hopes*** alimentare le speranze di qn; ***~ a family*** tirare su una famiglia; *objection* sollevare
◆**raise up** *v/t sep* alzare; ***he raised himself up on his elbow*** si alzò su un gomito
raisin *n* uva *f* passa
rake *n for garden* rastrello *m*
◆**rake in** *v/t sep money* fare un sacco di
◆**rake up** *v/t sep leaves* rastrellare; *fig* rivangare; *fig* ***rake up the past*** rivangare il passato
rally *n meeting* raduno *m*; ***electoral ~*** raduno *m* elettorale; ***peace ~*** manifestazione *f* per la pace; AUTO rally *m*

inv; *in tennis* scambio *m*

◆ **rally round** 〈*pret & past part* **-ied**〉 **I** *v/i* offrire aiuto **II** *v/t*: ***rally round s.o.*** aiutare qn

ram I *n* montone *m* **II** *v/t* 〈*pret & past part* **-med**〉 *ship*, *car* sbattere contro

◆ **ram down** *v/t sep* conficcare

RAM *abbr* (= **random access memory**) COMPUT RAM *f inv*; ***128 megabytes of ~*** 128 megabyte di RAM

ramble I *n walk* escursione *f* **II** *v/i walk* fare passeggiate; *in speaking* divagare; *talk incoherently* vaneggiare

rambler *n walker* escursionista *m/f*

rambling I *adj speech* sconnesso; ***~ club*** *esp Br* club *m inv* di escursionisti **II** *n esp Br* (*hiking*) escursione *f*; ***go ~*** fare escursioni

ramification *n form* implicazione *f*

ramify I *v/t* suddividere **II** *v/i* diramarsi

ramp *n* rampa *f*; *for raising vehicle* ponte *m* idraulico

rampage I *v/i* scatenarsi **II** *n*: ***go on the ~*** scatenarsi

rampant *adj inflation* dilagante

rampart *n* bastione *m*

ramrod *n for cleaning guns* scovolino *m*; ***stiff as a ~*** rigido come un manico di scopa

ramshackle *adj* sgangherato

ran *pret* → ***run***

ranch *n* ranch *m inv*

rancher *n* ranchero *m*

ranch house *n US* terra-tetto *m*

rancid *adj* rancido

rancour *n* rancore *m*

R&D *abbr* (= **research and development**) ricerca *f* e sviluppo *m*

random I *adj* casuale; ***~ sample*** campione *m* casuale; ***take a ~ sample*** prendere un campione a caso **II** *n*: ***at ~*** a caso

random access *n* COMPUT accesso *m* casuale **random access memory** *n* COMPUT memoria *f* ad accesso casuale

randomize *v/t* scegliere a caso

randy *adj* (+*er*) *Br infml* arrapato *infml*

rang *pret* → ***ring***[2]

range I *n of products* gamma *f*; ***we have the whole ~ of models*** abbiamo l'intera gamma di modelli; ***in this price ~*** in questa gamma di prezzo; *of missile*, *gun* gittata *f*; ***at close ~*** a corta gittata; ***be out of ~*** essere fuori portata; *of salary* scala *f*; *of voice* estensione *f*; *of mountains* catena *f*; (*shooting range*) poligono *m* (di tiro); ***at close ~*** a distanza ravvicinata **II** *v/i*: ***~ from X to Y*** variare da X a Y

ranger *n in park*, *forest* guardia *f* forestale

rank[1] **I** *n* MIL grado *m*; *in society* rango *m*; ***a person of ~*** una persona di alto rango; ***the ~s*** MIL la truppa; ***break ~(s)*** rompere le righe; ***pull ~ on s.o.*** far valere la propria autorità su qn; ***rise from the ~s*** venire dalla truppa; *fig* venire dalla gavetta **II** *v/t* classificare; ***~ s.o. among the best*** considerare qn tra i migliori; ***where would you ~ Napoleon?*** come reputeresti Napoleone? **III** *v/i*: ***~ among*** collocarsi tra; ***~ high among the world's statesmen*** collocarsi tra i più importanti statisti del mondo

rank[2] *adj* (+*er*) *smell* puzzolente; *injustice* bell'e buono; *outsider* vero e proprio; ***be ~*** puzzare

rank and file *n* base *f*

ranking *n in list etc* posizione *f*

rankle *v/i* bruciare

ransack *v/t* saccheggiare

ransom *n* riscatto *m*; ***hold s.o. to ~*** tenere in ostaggio qn

ransom money *n* (soldi *mpl* del) riscatto *m*

rant I *v/i*: ***~ and rave*** inveire; ***what's he ~ing (on) about?*** contro cosa sta inveendo? **II** *n* invettiva *f*; ***she went on the usual ~*** si lanciò nella consueta invettiva

rap I *n at door etc* colpo *m*; MUS rap *m inv*; ***take the ~ for sth*** prendersi la colpa di qc; ***he got a ~ on the knuckles for that*** si prese una lavata di capo per quel motivo **II** *v/t* 〈*pret & past part* **-ped**〉 *table etc* battere

◆ **rap at** *v/t window etc* bussare a

rape[1] **I** *n* stupro *m* **II** *v/t* violentare

rape[2] *n* BOT colza *f*

rapeseed oil *n* olio *m* di semi di colza

rape victim *n* vittima *f* stupro

rapid *adj* rapido

rapidity *n* rapidità *f inv*

rapidly *adv* rapidamente

rapids *npl* rapide *fpl*

rapist *n* violentatore *m*

rapper *n* MUS rapper *m/f inv*

rapport *n* rapporto *m*
rapt *adj* rapito; ***with ~ attention*** completamente rapito; ***~ in thought*** assorto nei propri pensieri
rapture *n*: ***go into ~s over*** andare in estasi per
rapturous *adj* entusiastico
rare *adj* (+*er*) raro; ***with very ~ exceptions*** con rarissime eccezioni; ***it's ~ for her to come*** è raro che venga; *steak* al sangue
rarefied *adj atmosphere* rarefatto
rarely *adv* raramente
raring *adj*: ***be ~ to go*** essere impazienté di andare
rarity *n* rarità *f inv*
rascal *n* birbante *m/f*
rash[1] *n* MED orticaria *f*; ***come out in a ~*** avere uno sfogo
rash[2] *adj* (+*er*) *action*, *behaviour* avventato
rasher *n* fettina *f*
rashly *adv* avventatamente
rasp I *n* (*tool*) raspa *f*; (*noise*) stridore *m* **II** *v/i* stridere
raspberry *n* lampone *m*; ***blow a ~*** (***at sth***) *infml* fare una pernacchia a qc
Rasta *n* rasta
Rastafarian *n* rasta *m/f inv*
rat *n* ratto *m*; ***smell a ~*** (*suspect something*) sentire puzza di bruciato
rate I *n* **1.** *of exchange* tasso *m*; ***~ of interest*** FIN tasso *m* d'interesse; ***the failure ~ for small businesses*** il tasso di fallimento per le piccole imprese; ***at a ~ of 100 litres*** *Br or* ***liters*** *US* ***an hour*** a un ritmo di 100 litri all'ora **2.** *of pay*, *pricing* tariffa *f*; ***there is a reduced ~ for children*** per i bambini c'è una tariffa ridotta; ***pay s.o. at the ~ of £ 10 per hour*** pagare qn con una tariffa di 10 sterline all'ora; *fig* ***at any ~*** in ogni modo **3.** (*speed*) ritmo *m*; ***at this ~*** (*at this speed*) di questo passo **II** *v/t* **1.** (*consider*, *rank*) reputare; ***~ s.o./sth highly*** avere una grande considerazione per qn/qc; ***be ~d*** (***as the best***) essere considerato (il migliore) **2.** (*deserve*) meritare **3.** *infml* (*think highly of*) ammirare; ***I really/don't really ~ him*** lo ammiro/non lo ammiro molto **III** *v/i*: ***~ as ...*** essere considerato ...; ***~ among ...*** essere considerato tra ...
rather *adv* piuttosto; ***I would ~ stay here*** preferirei stare qui; ***or would you ~ ...?*** o preferiresti ...?; ***I would ~ be happy than rich*** preferirei essere felice piuttosto che ricco; ***it would be better to phone ~ than*** (***to***) ***write*** sarebbe meglio telefonare piuttosto che scrivere; ***he is, or ~ was, a soldier*** è, o meglio era, un soldato
ratification *n* ratifica *f*
ratify *v/t* ⟨*pret & past part* **-ied**⟩ ratificare
ratings *npl* indice *m* d'ascolto
ratio *n* proporzione *f*, rapporto *m*; ***the ~ of men to women*** la proporzione tra uomini e donne; ***in a ~ of 100 to 1*** in un rapporto di 100 a 1
ration I *n* razione *f* **II** *v/t supplies* razionare; ***he ~ed himself to five cigarettes a day*** si è razionato le sigarette a cinque al giorno
rational *adj* razionale
rationale *n* spiegazione *f* logica
rationalisation, *US* **rationalization** *n* razionalizzazione *f*
rationalise, *US* **rationalize** *v/t & v/i* razionalizzare
rationality *n* razionalità *f inv*
rationally *adv* razionalmente
rat race *n* corsa *f* al successo **rat run** *n* *strada secondaria usata nelle ore di punta per aggirare il traffico delle strade principali*
rattle I *n noise* rumore *m*; *toy* sonaglio *m* **II** *v/t* scuotere; *infml* (*fluster*) innervosire **III** *v/i* far rumore
◆ **rattle off** *v/t sep poem*, *list of names* snocciolare
◆ **rattle on** *v/i infml* parlare di continuo (***about*** di)
◆ **rattle through** *v/t* fare di gran carriera
rattled *adj* (*shaken*) scosso
rattlesnake *n* serpente *m* a sonagli
ratty *adj* (+*er*) (*bad-tempered*) irritabile
raucous *adj* sguaiato
raunchy *adj* (+*er*) *infml person* volgare; *film*, *novel* piccante
ravage I *n*: ***the ~s of time*** le ingiurie del tempo **II** *v/t*: ***~d by war*** devastato dalla guerra
rave I *v/i* delirare; ***~ about sth*** *be very enthusiastic* entusiasmarsi per qc **II** *n party* rave *m inv*
raven *n* corvo *m*

ravenous *adj* famelico; ***I'm ~*** ho una fame da lupi
ravenously *adv* voracemente; ***be ~ hungry*** avere una fame da lupi
rave review *n* recensione *f* entusiastica
rave up *n Br* festa *f* scatenata
ravine *n* burrone *m*
raving I *adv*: ***~ mad*** matto da legare **II** *adj*: ***a ~ lunatic*** *infml* un pazzo furioso
ravioli *nsg* ravioli *mpl*
ravishing *adj* incantevole
raw I *adj* (+*er*) *meat, vegetable* crudo; *sugar, iron* grezzo; ***~ data*** COMPUT dati *mpl* non elaborati; *sewage* non trattato; ***get a ~ deal*** essere trattato ingiustamente **II** ***in the ~*** *infml* nudo
raw material *n* materia *f* prima
ray *n* raggio *m*; ***a ~ of hope*** un raggio di speranza; ***a ~ of sunshine*** *fig* un raggio di sole
raze *v/t*: ***~ to the ground*** radere al suolo
razor *n* rasoio *m*
razor blade *n* lametta *f* da barba **razor-sharp** *adj knife* affilato come un rasoio; *fig mind* acuto
razzmatazz *n* strombazzamento *m*
RC *abbr* (= **Roman Catholic**) cattolico (romano)
Rd *abbr* (= **Road**) strada *f*, via *f* (v.)
re *prep* COMM con riferimento a
RE *abbr* **1.** (= **religious education**) *Br* EDU religione *f* **2.** (= **Right Excellent**) *grado della gerarchia massonica* **3.** (= **Royal Engineers**) *arma del genio britannico* **4.** (= **Royal Exchange**) *sede della borsa*
reach I *v/t city etc* arrivare a; *decision, agreement, conclusion* raggiungere; ***to ~ the terrace you have to cross the garden*** per raggiungere la terrazza devi attraversare il giardino; ***this advertisement is geared to ~ a younger audience*** questa pubblicità è mirata a raggiungere un pubblico più giovane; ***you can ~ me at my hotel*** puoi raggiungermi al mio albergo; ***can you ~ it?*** ci arrivi? **II** *n*: ***within ~*** vicino (***of*** a); *within arm's reach* a portata (di mano); ***out of ~*** non a portata (***of*** di); ***within easy ~ of the sea*** a poca distanza dal mare; ***keep out of ~ of children*** tenere lontano dalla portata dei bambini
◆**reach down** *v/i curtains* arrivare (***to*** fino a); *person* abbassarsi (***for*** per prendere qc)
◆**reach out** *v/i* allungare la mano
◆**reach up** *v/i level* spingersi in alto (***to*** fino a); *person* allungarsi verso l'alto (***for*** per prendere qc)
react *v/i* reagire
reaction *n* reazione *f*
reactionary I *n* POL reazionario *m*, -a *f* **II** *adj* POL reazionario
reactivate *v/t* riattivare
reactive *adj substance* reattivo
reactor *n nuclear* reattore *m*
read ⟨*pret & past part* ***read***⟩ **I** *v/i* leggere; ***~ to s.o.*** leggere a qn; ***~ aloud*** *or* ***out loud*** leggere a voce alta; ***this paragraph ~s well*** questo paragrafo scorre bene; ***the letter ~s as follows*** nella lettera c'è scritto quanto segue **II** *v/t* leggere; (*study*) studiare; ***~ my lips!*** *infml* leggi le mie labbra!; ***~ s.o.'s mind*** leggere nel pensiero di qn; ***don't ~ too much into his words*** non prendere troppo sul serio le sue parole **III** *n*: ***a good ~*** una buona lettura
◆**read back** *v/t sep* (*to s.o.*) rileggere (*a qn*)
◆**read off** *v/t sep* leggere; *without pause* leggere a voce alta (da un elenco)
◆**read out** *v/t sep aloud* leggere a voce alta
◆**read up on** *v/t* documentarsi su
readable *adj handwriting* leggibile; *book* di piacevole lettura
reader *n person* lettore *m*, -trice *f*
readership *n number of readers* lettori *mpl*
readily *adv* (*willingly*) volentieri; (*easily*) facilmente; ***~ available*** facilmente disponibile
readiness *n for action* disponibilità *f inv*; *to agree* prontezza *f*
reading *n a. from meter* lettura *f*; ***the Senate gave the bill its first ~*** il senato eseguì la prima lettura del disegno di legge; (*interpretation*) interpretazione *f*
reading matter *n* roba *f* da leggere
readjust I *v/t equipment, controls* regolare **II** *v/i to conditions* riadattarsi
readjustment *n of instrument* rimessa

f a punto; (*correction*) riadattamento *m*; *of prices* ritocco *m*

read-only file *n* COMPUT file *m inv* di sola lettura **read-only memory** *n* COMPUT memoria *f* di sola lettura **read-out** *n* COMPUT presentazione *f* dei dati **read-write head** *n* COMPUT testina *f* di lettura / scrittura **read-write memory** *n* COMPUT memoria *f* di lettura / scrittura

ready I *adj* pronto; ***be ~ to do sth*** essere pronto a fare qc; ***he was ~ to cry*** era sul punto di piangere; ***~ to leave*** pronto ad andarsene; ***~ for anything*** pronto a tutto; ***dinner's ~*** la cena è pronta; ***get (o.s.) ~*** prepararsi; ***get sth ~*** preparare qc; ***~ and waiting*** pronto ad agire **II** *n*: *fig* ***at the ~*** a immediata disposizione; ***with his pen at the ~*** pronto a scrivere

ready cash *n* contanti *mpl* **ready-cooked** *adj meal* pronto **ready-made** *adj stew etc* pronto; *solution* bell'e pronto **ready-to-wear** *adj* confezionato

real I *adj* vero; ***in ~ life*** nella realtà; ***the danger was very ~*** il pericolo era estremamente reale; ***it's the ~ thing or McCoy, this whisky!*** questo whisky è l'originale!; ***it's a ~ shame*** è un vero peccato; ***he doesn't know what ~ contentment is*** non sa cosa significhi essere realmente soddisfatti; ***that's what I call a ~ car*** è quello che io chiamo una vera macchina; ***in ~ trouble*** in guai seri; ***in ~ terms*** in realtà **II** *adv esp US infml* molto; ***~ soon*** molto presto **III** *n*: ***for ~*** davvero

real estate *n* proprietà *fpl* immobiliari

realisation, realization *n* realizzazione *f*

realise, realize *v/t* rendersi conto di, realizzare; FIN realizzare; ***I ~ now that ...*** ora capisco che ...

realism *n* realismo *m*

realist *n* realista *m/f*

realistic *adj* realistico

realistically *adv* realisticamente

reality *n* realtà *f inv*

reality check *n infml*: ***give s.o. a ~*** aprire gli occhi a qn; ***he needs a ~*** deve guardare in faccia la realtà **reality show** *n* TV reality show *m inv*

real-life *adj event* della vita reale; *person* reale; *story* di vita reale

really *adv* veramente; ***~?*** davvero?; ***not ~*** (*not much*) non proprio; ***I ~ don't know*** non so proprio; ***I don't ~ think so*** non lo penso davvero; ***well yes, I ~ think we should*** beh, sì, penso proprio che dovremmo; ***before he ~ understood*** prima che capisse davvero; ***~ and truly*** veramente; ***I ~ must say ...*** devo proprio dire ...; ***~!*** *in indignation* insomma!

realm *n* regno *m*; ***be within the ~s of possibility*** essere possibile

real time *n* COMPUT tempo *m* reale **real-time** *adj* COMPUT in tempo reale

realtor *n US* agente *m* immobiliare

reap *v/t* mietere; ***~ the benefits of sth*** trarre beneficio da qc

reaper *n* mietitore *m*, -trice *f*; ***the grim ~*** (*death*) la falciatrice

reappear *v/i* riapparire

reappearance *n* ricomparsa *f*

reappraisal *n* riesame *m*

reappraise *v/t* riesaminare

rear[1] I *n of building* retro *m*; *of train* coda *f*; ***to(wards) the ~ of the plane*** verso la coda dell'aereo; ***bring up the ~*** chiudere la fila **II** *adj* posteriore

rear[2] I *v/t esp Br animals*, *family* allevare; ***racism ~ed its ugly head*** si riaffaccia lo spettro del razzismo **II** *v/i* (*horse*: *a.* **rear up**) impennarsi

rear end *n infml of person* posteriore *m* **rear-end** *v/t*: ***be ~ed*** *infml* essere tamponato

rearguard I *n* retroguardia *f* **II** *adj* di retroguardia

rear light *n of car* fanalino *m* posteriore

rearm I *v/t* riarmare **II** *v/i* riarmarsi

rearmost *adj* ultimo

rearrange *v/t furniture* spostare; *schedule*, *meetings* cambiare

rear-view mirror *n* specchietto *m* retrovisore **rear-wheel drive** *n* AUTO trazione *f* posteriore

reason I *n faculty* ragione *f*; (*cause*) motivo *m*; ***we'll do anything within ~ to ...*** entro limiti ragionevoli faremo qualsiasi cosa per ...; ***~ for living*** ragione *f* di vita; ***my ~ for going*** il motivo per cui me ne sono andato; ***what's the ~ for this celebration?*** qual è il motivo di questo festeggiamento?; ***I want to know the ~ why***

voglio conoscerne il motivo; ***for no ~ at all*** per nessun motivo al mondo; ***why did you do that? — no particular ~*** perché lo hai fatto? - per nessun motivo in particolare; ***for ~s best known to himself / myself*** per motivi che solo lui conosce / io conosco davvero; ***all the more ~ for doing it*** ragione di più per farlo; ***see / listen to ~*** ascoltare ragione; ***it stands to ~*** è ovvio **II** *v/i*: ***~ with s.o.*** far ragionare con qn **III** *v/t* (*a.* **reason out**) elaborare

reasonable *adj person, price* ragionevole; ***beyond (all) ~ doubt*** al di là di ogni ragionevole dubbio; ***it would be ~ to assume that …*** sarebbe ragionevole supporre che …; *weather, health* discreto; ***a ~ number of people*** un discreto numero di persone

reasonably *adv act, behave* ragionevolmente; (*quite*) abbastanza

reasoning *n* ragionamento *m*

reassure *v/t* rassicurare

reassuring *adj* rassicurante

rebate *n money back* rimborso *m*

rebel I *n* ribelle *m/f*; ***~ forces*** forze *fpl* ribelli **II** *v/i* ⟨*pret & past part* **-led**⟩ ribellarsi

rebellion *n* ribellione *f*

rebellious *adj* ribelle

rebelliously *adv* con atteggiamento ribelle

rebelliousness *n* spirito *m* di ribellione

rebirth *n* rinascita *f*

reboot *v/i & v/t* COMPUT riavviare

rebound I *v/i of ball etc* rimbalzare **II** *n of ball* rimbalzo *m*; ***he married her on the ~*** l'ha sposata per ripicca

rebuff I *n* secco rifiuto *m* **II** *v/t*: ***~ s.o. / s.o.'s advances*** respingere in modo secco qn / le proposte di qn

rebuild *v/t* ⟨*pret & past part* **-built**⟩ ricostruire

rebuke *v/t* rimproverare

recalcitrant *adj* recalcitrante

recall I *v/t* richiamare; (*remember*) ricordare; COMPUT *file* richiamare **II** *n* (*summoning back*) richiamare

recant *v/t & v/i* ritrattare

recap *infml* **I** *n* ricapitolazione *f* **II** *v/i* ⟨*pret & past part* **-ped**⟩ *infml* ricapitolare

recapitulate *v/t & v/i* ricapitolare

recapitulation *n* ricapitolazione *f*

recapture *v/t criminal* ricatturare; *town* riconquistare

recede *v/i* ritirarsi; *of flood waters* abbassarsi

receding *adj forehead, chin* sfuggente; ***have a ~ hairline*** essere stempiato

receipt *n for purchase* ricevuta *f*, scontrino *m*; ***acknowledge ~ of sth*** accusare ricevuta di qc; ***~s*** FIN introiti *mpl*; ***pay on ~ (of the goods)*** pagare al ricevimento delle merci

receive *v/t* ricevere; ***he ~d his guests in the hall*** ha ricevuto i suoi ospiti nell'atrio; ***~ a warm welcome*** ricevere un caldo benvenuto; TEL, RADIO, TV ricevere; ***are you receiving me?*** mi ricevi?

receiver *n of letter* destinatario *m*, -a *f*; TEL ricevitore *m*; *for radio* apparecchio *m* ricevente; FIN curatore *m*, -trice *f* fallimentare

receivership *n*: ***be in ~*** essere in amministrazione controllata

recent *adj* recente; ***a ~ decision*** una decisione recente; ***a ~ publication*** una pubblicazione recente; ***her ~ trip*** il suo recente viaggio; ***he is a ~ arrival*** è un nuovo arrivo; ***in ~ years*** negli ultimi anni

recently *adv* recentemente

receptacle *n* contenitore *m*

reception *n in hotel, company* reception *f inv*; *formal party* ricevimento *m*; (*welcome*) accoglienza *f*; *on radio, mobile phone* ricezione *f*

reception desk *n* banco *m* della reception

receptionist *n* receptionist *m/f inv*

receptive *adj*: ***be ~ to sth*** essere ricettivo verso qc

recess *n in wall etc* rientranza *f*; *of parliament* vacanza *f*; *US* EDU intervallo *m*

recession *n economic* recessione *f*

recharge *v/t battery* ricaricare; ***~ one's batteries*** *fig* ricaricare le batterie

rechargeable *adj battery* ricaricabile

recipe *n* ricetta *f*; ***that's a ~ for disaster*** è una strada che conduce al disastro

recipe book *n* ricettario *m*

recipient *n* destinatario *m*, -a *f*

reciprocal *adj* reciproco

reciprocate *v/i* ricambiare

recital *n* MUS recital *m inv*
recite *v/t poem* recitare; *details, facts* enumerare
reckless *adj* spericolato
recklessly *adv behave, drive* in modo spericolato; *spend* avventatamente
reckon *v/i* (*think, consider*) pensare; ***what do you ~?*** che cosa ne pensi?; (*estimate*) calcolare; ***ho ~ed the cost to be £ 40.51*** ho calcolato che il costo sarà 40,51 sterline; ***I ~ he must be about forty*** in base ai miei calcoli deve avere circa quarant'anni
◆**reckon on** *v/t* contare su; ***I was reckoning on doing that tomorrow*** contavo di farlo domani
◆**reckon up** *v/t sep* (*add*) fare la somma di
◆**reckon with** *v/t*: ***have s.o. / sth to reckon with*** dover fare i conti con qn / qc
reckoning *n* calcoli *mpl*; ***by my ~*** secondo i miei calcoli
reclaim **I** *v/t land* bonificare; *lost item* recuperare; *tax* chiedere la restituzione di **II** *n*: ***baggage*** *or* ***luggage ~*** ritiro *m* bagagli
recline *v/i* sdraiarsi; ***she was reclining on the sofa*** era sdraiata sul divano
recliner *n chair* poltrona *f* reclinabile
recluse *n* eremita *m/f*; ***he's a bit of a ~*** è un po' un eremita
reclusive *adj* solitario
recognition *n of state, s.o.'s achievements* riconoscimento *m*; ***in ~ of*** come riconoscimento per; ***he achieved widespread ~*** ha ottenuto un vasto riconoscimento; ***have changed beyond ~*** essere irriconoscibile
recognizable *adj* riconoscibile
recognize *v/t* riconoscere; ***it can be ~d by …*** si riconosce da …
recoil *v/i* indietreggiare
recollect *v/t* rammentare
recollection *n* ricordo *m*
recommend *v/t* consigliare; ***~ doing sth*** consigliare di fare qc; ***what do you ~ for a cough?*** cosa mi consiglia per la tosse?; ***this book has little to ~ it*** questo libro non è particolarmente raccomandabile
recommendation *n* consiglio *m*
recompense *form* **I** *n* ricompensa *f*; JUR risarcimento *m* **II** *v/t* ricompensare
reconcile *v/t people, differences* riconciliare; *facts* conciliare; ***~ o.s. to …*** rassegnarsi a …; ***they are now ~d*** si sono riconciliati
reconciliation *n of people, differences* riconciliazione *f*; *of facts* conciliazione *f*
recondite *adj* recondito; ***~ scholarship*** sapere *m* astruso
recondition *v/t* ricondizionare
reconnaissance *n* MIL ricognizione *f*; ***~ mission*** missione *f* di ricognizione
reconnoitre, *US* **reconnoiter** *v/i* fare ricognizione
reconsider **I** *v/t offer, one's position* riconsiderare **II** *v/i* ripensare
reconstitute *v/t* ricostituire
reconstruct *v/t city, crime, life* ricostruire
reconstruction *n of a crime etc* ricostruzione *f*
record[1] **I** *n* **1.** MUS disco *m* **2.** SPORTS *etc* record *m inv*, primato *m* **3.** *written document etc* nota *f*; ***keep a ~ of*** prendere nota di; ***say sth off the ~*** dire qc ufficiosamente; ***it is on ~ that …*** è noto che … **4.** *in database* record *m inv* **5.** ***~s*** archivio *m* **6.** ***have a criminal ~*** avere precedenti penali; ***he has a good ~ for punctuality / reliability*** è sempre stato puntuale / affidabile; ***have a good safety ~*** vantare buoni precedenti in materia di sicurezza **II** *adj time* da record
record[2] *v/t electronically* registrare; ***~ed message*** messaggio *m* registrato; *in writing* annotare; ***by ~ed delivery*** per raccomandata
record-breaking *adj* da record
recorder *n* MUS flauto *m* dolce; ***cassette ~*** registratore *m* a cassette; ***tape ~*** registratore *m* a nastro
record holder *n* primatista *m/f*
recording *n* registrazione *f*
recording studio *n* sala *f* di registrazione
record player *n* giradischi *m inv*
recount *v/t* (*tell*) raccontare
re-count **I** *n of votes* nuovo conteggio *m* **II** *v/t* (*count again*) ricontare
recoup *v/t financial losses* rifarsi di
recourse *n* ricorso *m*
recover **I** *v/t stolen goods* recuperare; COMPUT *file* recuperare; ***~ conscious-***

ness riprendere conoscenza **II** *v/i from illness* rimettersi

recovery *n of stolen goods* recupero *m*; *from illness* guarigione *f*; ***he has made a speedy ~*** è guarito in fretta; ***be on the road to ~*** essere in via di guarigione

recovery vehicle *n* veicolo *m* di soccorso

recreation *n* ricreazione *f*

recreational *adj done for pleasure* ricreativo; ***~ drug*** droga *f* ricreativa

recrimination *n* recriminazione *f*

recruit I *n* MIL recluta *f*; *to company* neoassunto *m*, -a *f* **II** *v/t new staff* assumere; *members* arruolare

recruiter *n* recruiter *m/f*, *consulente ingaggiato dalle aziende per trovare impiegati*

recruitment *n* assunzione *f*; MIL, POL reclutamento *m*

recruitment drive *n* campagna *f* di arruolamento

rectangle *n* rettangolo *m*

rectangular *adj* rettangolare

rectify *v/t* ⟨*pret & past part* ***-ied***⟩ (*put right*) rettificare

rector *n* (*minister*) pastore *m*; *head of some universities* rettore *m*; *of some schools* preside *m*

rectory *n* (*vicarage*) presbiterio *m*

rectum *n* ⟨*pl* ***rectums*** *or* ***recta***⟩ ANAT retto *m*

recumbent *adj* disteso

recuperate I *v/i* recuperare **II** *v/t losses* rifarsi di

recur ⟨*pret & past part* ***-red***⟩ *v/i of error, event* ripetersi; *of symptoms* ripresentarsi

recurrent *adj* ricorrente

recyclable *adj* riciclabile

recycle *v/t* riciclare; ***made from ~d paper*** di carta riciclata

recycling *n* riciclo *m*

recycling bin *n* cestino *m* dei rifiuti (riciclabili)

red *adj* rosso; ***go ~*** diventare rosso; ***in the ~*** FIN in rosso; ***~ as a beetroot*** rosso come un peperone; *fig* ***see ~*** vedere rosso

red alert *n* allarme *m* rosso; ***be on ~*** essere in stato di allarme rosso **red cabbage** *n* cavolo *m* rosso **red card** *n in football* cartellino *m* rosso **red carpet treatment** *n*: ***give s.o. the ~*** trattare qn coi guanti **Red Cross** *n* Croce *f* Rossa

redcurrant *n Br* ribes *m*

red deer *n* cervo *m* nobile

redden *v/i* (*blush*) arrossire

redecorate *v/t* ritinteggiare; *change wallpaper* ritapezzare

redeem *v/t debt* estinguere; *sinners* redimere

redeeming *adj*: ***~ feature*** aspetto *m* positivo

redemption *n* REL redenzione *f*

redeploy *v/t troops, staff* reimpiegare

redeployment *n of troops, staff* reimpiego *m*

redevelop *v/t part of town* risanare

redevelopment area *n* area *f* di valorizzazione

red-eye *n infml flight* volo *m* notturno **red fox** *n* volpe *f* **red-handed** *adj*: ***catch s.o. ~*** cogliere qn in flagrante **redhead** *n* rosso *m*, -a *f* **red herring** *n false clue* pista *f* falsa **red-hot** *adj* rovente; ***~ favourite*** favorito *m*

redial I *v/t* rifare **II** *v/i on phone* rifare il numero **III** *n*: ***automatic ~*** ricomposizione *f* automatica

redirect *v/t letter* rispedire a un nuovo indirizzo; (*forward*) reindirizzare; *traffic* deviare

rediscover *v/t* riscoprire

red-letter day *n* giorno *m* memorabile **red light** *n at traffic lights* rosso *m* **red light district** *n* quartiere *m* a luci rosse **red meat** *n* carni *fpl* rosse

redneck *n pej persona rozza e ignorante appartenente ai ceti bassi del Sud degli Stati Uniti*

redouble *v/t*: ***~ one's efforts*** intensificare gli sforzi

redoubtable *adj* temibile

red pepper *n* peperone *m* rosso

redress *v/t grievance* riparare; *balance* ristabilire

Red Sea *n* Mar *m* Rosso

red tape *n infml* burocrazia *f*

reduce *v/t* ridurre; ***~ speed*** ridurre la velocità; ***it has been ~d to nothing*** non ne restò niente; ***~ s.o. to tears*** far piangere qn

reduced *adj* ridotto; ***in ~ circumstances*** in ristrettezze; ***at a ~ price*** a prezzo ridotto

reduction *n* riduzione *f*

redundancy *n Br at work* licenziamento *m*

redundancy notice *n Br* avviso *m* di licenziamento **redundancy payment** *n Br* indennità *f inv* di licenziamento

redundant *adj* (*unnecessary*) superfluo; *Br* ***be made ~*** *at work* essere licenziato; *Br* ***make s.o. ~*** licenziare qn

reed *n* BOT canna *f*

re-educate *v/t* rieducare

reef *n in sea* scogliera *f*

reef knot *n* nodo *m* piano

reek *v/i* puzzare; ***~ of …*** puzzare di…

reel I *n of film* rullino *m*; *of thread* rocchetto *m*; *of tape* bobina *f*; *of fishing line* mulinello *m* **II** *v/i*: ***my head's ~ing*** mi gira la testa; ***the blow sent him ~ing*** il colpo lo fece vacillare; ***the whole country is still ~ing from the shock*** l'intero paese non si è ancora ripreso dallo choc

◆**reel off** *v/t sep* snocciolare

re-elect *v/t* rieleggere

re-election *n* rielezione *f*

re-enact *v/t event, crime* ricostruire

re-enactment *n of event, crime* ricostruzione *f*

re-enter *v/t atmosphere* rientrare in

re-entry *n of spacecraft* rientro *m*

re-examine *v/t* riesaminare

ref *n infml* arbitro *m*

reface *v/t building* rinnovare la facciata di; *garment* rifoderare

refectory *n* refettorio *m*

refer I *v/t* ⟨*pret & past part* ***-red***⟩: ***~ a decision/problem to s.o.*** rinviare una decisione/un problema a qn; ***~ s.o. to a specialist*** mandare qn da uno specialista **II** *v/i*: ***~ to …*** (*allude to*) riferirsi a …; ***I am not ~ring to you*** non mi riferisco a te; *dictionary etc* consultare …

referee *n* SPORTS arbitro *m*; *for job* referenza *f*

reference *n* (*allusion*) allusione *f*; *for job* referenza *f*; (*reference number*) (numero *m* di) riferimento *m*; ***with ~ to*** con riferimento a

reference book *n* opera *f* di consultazione **reference library** *n* biblioteca *f* di consultazione **reference number** *n* numero *m* di riferimento

referendum *n* referendum *m inv*

refill I *v/t glass* riempire **II** *n for pen* cartuccia *f*; ***would you like a ~?*** *infml* vuoi ancora da bere?

refine *v/t* raffinare

refined *adj manners, language* raffinato

refinement *n to process, machine* miglioramento *m*

refinery *n* raffineria *f*

reflation *n* reflazione *f*

reflect I *v/t light* riflettere; ***be ~ed in …*** riflettersi in … **II** *v/i* (*think*) riflettere

reflection *n in water, glass etc* riflesso *m*; (*consideration*) riflessione *f*; ***on ~*** dopo averci riflettuto; ***on further ~*** riflettendoci meglio; ***this is no ~ on your ability*** questo non va a demerito delle tue capacità

reflective *adj surface* riflettente; *person, mood* riflessivo

reflex *n in body* riflesso *m*

reflex angle *n* angolo *m* di riflessione **reflex arc** *n* arco *m* riflesso **reflex camera** *n* PHOT reflex *f*

reflexive *adj verb, pronoun* riflessivo

reflex reaction *n* riflesso *m*

reform I *n* riforma *f* **II** *v/t* riformare

reformat *v/t* ⟨*pret & past part* ***-ted***⟩ COMPUT *disk, computer* riformattare

Reformation *n*: ***the ~*** la Riforma

reformed *adj* riformato; ***he's a ~ character*** ha messo la testa a posto

reformer *n* riformatore *m*, -trice *f*

refract *v/t* rifrangere

refraction *n* rifrazione *f*

refractory *adj* refrattario; (*obstinate*) ostinato

refrain[1] *v/i form*: ***please ~ from smoking*** si prega di non fumare

refrain[2] *n in song* ritornello *m*

refresh *v/t person* ristorare; ***feel ~ed*** sentirsi ristorato; ***~ one's memory*** rinfrescarsi la memoria

refresher course *n* corso *m* di aggiornamento

refreshing *adj drink* rinfrescante; *experience* piacevole

refreshingly *adv honest* piacevolmente

refreshments *npl* rinfreschi *mpl*

refrigerate *v/t*: ***keep ~d*** conservare in frigo

refrigerator *n* frigorifero *m*

refuel I *v/t aeroplane* rifornire di carburante **II** *v/i of aeroplane, car* fare rifornimento

refuge *n* rifugio *m*; ***take ~*** *from storm etc* ripararsi; ***a ~ for battered women*** un rifugio per le donne maltrattate
refugee *n* rifugiato *m*, -a *f*, profugo *m*, -a *f*
refugee camp *n* campo *m* profughi
refund I *n* rimborso *m* **II** *v/t* rimborsare
refurbish *v/t* rinnovare
refusal *n* rifiuto *m*; ***get a ~*** ricevere un rifiuto; ***he offered me first ~*** mi ha offerto il diritto d'opzione
refuse[1] *v/t & v/i* rifiutare; ***~ to do sth*** rifiutare di fare qc
refuse[2] *n* (*garbage*) rifiuti *mpl*
refuse collection *n* raccolta *f* dei rifiuti **refuse dump** *n* discarica *f* (dei rifiuti)
refute *v/t* confutare
reg. *abbr* **1.** (= **registered**) registrato **2.** (= **regiment**) reggimento *m*
regain *v/t control, lost territory, the lead* riconquistare
regal *adj* regale
regale *v/t* intrattenere; ***he ~d us with amusing anecdotes*** ci ha intrattenuto con aneddoti divertenti
regalia *npl* insegne *fpl*
regard I *n*: ***have great ~ for s.o.*** avere molta stima di qn; ***hold s.o. in high ~*** avere molta stima di qn; ***in this ~*** a questo riguardo; ***with ~ to*** riguardo a; (***kind***) ***~s*** cordiali saluti; ***give my ~s to Paola*** saluti a Paola; ***with no ~ for …*** senza alcun riguardo per … **II** *v/t*: ***~ s.o. / sth as sth*** considerare qn / qc come qc; ***as ~s …*** riguardo a …
regarding *prep* riguardo a
regardless *adv* lo stesso; ***~ of*** senza tener conto di
regenerate *v/t area* rimettere a nuovo
regeneration *n* rigenerazione *f*
regent *n* reggente *m/f*
reggae *n* MUS reggae *m*
regime *n* (*government*) regime *m*
regimen *n* MED regime *m*
regiment *n* reggimento *m*
region *n* regione *f*; ***in the ~ of*** intorno a
regional *adj* regionale
regionalism *n* regionalismo *m*
register I *n* registro *m* **II** *v/t birth, death: by individual* denunciare; *by authorities* registrare; *vehicle* iscrivere; *letter* assicurare; *emotion* mostrare; ***send a letter ~ed*** spedire una lettera assicurata **III** *v/i at university* iscriversi; ***I'm ~ed with Dr Lee*** il mio medico è il dottor Lee; ***it didn't ~*** non me ne ero reso conto
registered letter *n* (lettera *f*) assicurata *f* **registered trademark** *n* marchio *m* registrato
registrar *n of births etc* ufficiale *m* di stato civile
registration *n Br* (*vehicle number*) numero *m* di targa; *at university* iscrizione *f*
registration number *n Br* AUTO numero *m* di targa
registry office *n* ufficio *m* di stato civile
regress I *v/i* regredire **II** *n* regresso *m*
regret I *v/t* ⟨*pret & past part* **-ted**⟩ rammaricarsi di; *missed opportunity* rimpiangere; ***we ~ to inform you that …*** siamo spiacenti di informarla che … **II** *n* rammarico *m*; ***have no ~s*** non avere rimpianti
regretful *adj* di rammarico
regretfully *adv* con rammarico
regrettable *adj* deplorevole
regrettably *adv* purtroppo
regular I *adj* regolare; ***at ~ intervals*** a intervalli regolari; ***on a ~ basis*** regolarmente; ***be in ~ contact*** essere regolarmente in contatto; ***eat ~ meals*** fare pasti regolari; (*US*: *ordinary*) normale; ***he's just a ~ guy*** è un tipo normale; ***~ customer*** cliente *m/f* abituale; ***his ~ pub*** *Br* il suo pub abituale **II** *n at bar etc* cliente *m/f* abituale
regularity *n* regolarità *f inv*
regularly *adv* regolarmente
regulate *v/t* regolare
regulation *n* (*rule*) regolamento *m*; ***be contrary to ~s*** essere contrario al regolamento; *control* controllo *m*
rehab *n infml* riabilitazione *f*; ***she went into ~ to try to kick her habit*** è andata in riabilitazione per provare a perdere il vizio
rehabilitate *v/t ex-criminal* riabilitare
rehearsal *n* prova *f*
rehearse *v/t & v/i* THEAT, MUS provare; ***~ what one is going to say*** fare le prove di ciò che si intende dire
reign I *n* regno *m* **II** *v/i* regnare
reimburse *v/t* rimborsare

rein *n* redine *f*; ***give free ~ to one's imagination*** dare libero sfogo alla fantasia

◆**rein in** *v/t* tenere a freno

reincarnation *n* reincarnazione *f*

reindeer *n* renna *f*

reinforce *v/t* rinforzare; ***~ the message*** rafforzare il messaggio

reinforced concrete *n* cemento *m* armato

reinforcements *npl* MIL rinforzi *mpl*

reinstate *v/t* reintegrare

reintegrate *v/t* reintegrare (*into* in)

reintegration *n* reintegrazione *f*

reintroduce *v/t measure* reintrodurre

reinvent *v/t*: ***~ the wheel*** scoprire l'acqua calda; ***~ o.s.*** reinventarsi

reissue I *v/t book* ristampare; *stamps* riemettere; *recording* ridistribuire **II** *n of book* ristampa *f*; *of stamps* riemissione *f*; *of recording* ridistribuzione *f*

reiterate *v/t form* ripetere

reject *v/t* respingere

rejection *n* rifiuto *m*

rejoice *v/i* gioire

rejoin *v/t & v/i* (*attach*) riunire; (*answer*) replicare

rejoinder *n* replica *f*

rejuvenate *v/t* ringiovanire

rekindle *v/t fig passions* riaccendere; *interest* ravvivare

relapse *n* MED ricaduta *f*; ***have a ~*** avere una ricaduta

relapsed *adj*; ***he's a ~ alcoholic*** è un alcolista recidivo

relate I *v/t story* raccontare; ***~ sth to sth*** collegare qc a qc **II** *v/i*: ***~ to …*** *be connected with* riferirsi a …; ***he doesn't ~ to people*** non sa stabilire un rapporto con gli altri

related *adj by family* imparentato; *events, ideas etc* collegato; ***two closely ~ questions*** due domande strettamente collegate; ***health-~ problems*** problemi *mpl* relativi alla salute

relation *n in family* parente *m/f*; (*connection*) rapporto *m*; ***business / diplomatic ~s*** rapporti d'affari / diplomatici; ***with ~ to*** in relazione a; ***bear no ~ to*** non avere nulla a che vedere con

relationship *n* rapporto *m*; ***what is your ~ (to him)?*** in che rapporti sei con lui?; ***have a (sexual) ~ with s.o.*** avere una relazione (sessuale) con qn; ***have a good ~ with s.o.*** avere un bel rapporto con qn

relative I *n* parente *m/f* **II** *adj* relativo; ***X is ~ to Y*** X è legato a Y; GRAM ***~ clause*** proposizione *f* relativa

relatively *adv* relativamente

relativism *n* PHIL relativismo *m*

relativity *n* relatività *f inv*

relaunch *v/t product, campaign* rilanciare

relax I *v/i* rilassarsi; ***~!, don't get angry*** rilassati! non te la prendere **II** *v/t* rilassare

relaxation *n* relax *m inv*; *of rules etc* rilassamento *m*

relaxed *adj* rilassato

relaxing *adj* rilassante

relay I *v/t* trasmettere **II** *n*: ***~ (race)*** (corsa *f* a) staffetta *f*; *team, crew* squadra *f*

relay station *n* ripetitore *m*

release I *n* **1.** *from prison* rilascio *m* **2.** *of CD etc* uscita *f*; *of software* versione *f*; ***this film is a new ~*** è un film appena uscito; ***on general ~*** in tutte le sale **3.** *deliverance* liberazione *f* **4.** JUR cessione *f* **II** *v/t prisoner* rilasciare; *handbrake* togliere; *film, record* far uscire; *information* rendere noto

relegate *v/t* relegare; ***be ~d*** SPORTS essere retrocesso

relegation *n* SPORTS retrocessione *f*

relent *v/i* cedere

relentless *adj* incessante, implacabile

relentlessly *adv* incessantemente

relevance *n* pertinenza *f*

relevant *adj* pertinente

reliability *n* affidabilità *f inv*

reliable *adj* affidabile

reliably *adv*: ***I am ~ informed that …*** so da fonte certa che …

reliance *n* dipendenza *f*; ***~ on s.o. / sth*** dipendenza da qn / qc

reliant *adj*: ***be ~ on*** dipendere da

relic *n* reliquia *f*

relief *n* sollievo *m*; ***that's a ~*** che sollievo; ***tax ~*** sgravio *m* fiscale; ***in ~*** *in art* in rilievo

relief map *n* carta *f* orografica **relief model** *n* plastico *m* **relief road** *n* circonvallazione *f* **relief supplies** *npl* soccorsi *mpl* **relief workers** *npl* cooperanti *mpl*; *in disaster* soccorritori *mpl*

relieve *v/t pressure, pain* alleviare; (*take over from*) dare il cambio a; ***~ s.o. of sth*** alleggerire qn di qc; ***be ~d*** *at news etc* essere sollevato; ***~ o.s.*** *euph* fare i propri bisogni
religion *n* religione *f*
religiosity *n* religiosità *f*; *pej* bigotteria *f*
religious *adj* religioso
religiously *adv* (*conscientiously*) religiosamente
relinquish *v/t* rinunciare a
relish I *n sauce* salsa *f*; (*enjoyment*) gusto *m* **II** *v/t idea, prospect* gradire; ***I don't ~ the thought of getting up at 5 a. m.*** non mi entusiasma il pensiero di alzarmi alle 5 di mattina
relive *v/t* rivivere
reload *v/t gun, camera* ricaricare
relocate *v/i of business, employee* trasferirsi
relocation *n of business, employee* trasferimento *m*
reluctance *n* riluttanza *f*; ***do sth with ~*** fare qc con riluttanza
reluctant *adj* riluttante; ***be ~ to do sth*** essere restio a fare qc
reluctantly *adv* a malincuore
◆**rely on** *v/t* ⟨*pret & past part* ***-ied***⟩ contare su; ***rely on s.o. to do sth*** contare su qn perché faccia qc
REM *abbr* (= **rapid eye movement**) REM (movimento *m* oculare rapido)
remain *v/i* rimanere
remainder I *n a.* MATH resto *m* **II** *v/t* svendere
remaining *adj* restante
remains *npl of meal* avanzi *mpl*; *of ancient buildings* rovine *fpl*; *of body* resti *mpl*
remake I *n of film* remake *m inv* **II** *v/t* ⟨*pret & past part* ***-made***⟩ rifare; ***~ a film*** fare il remake di un film
remand I *v/t*: ***~ s.o. in custody*** ordinare la custodia cautelare di qn **II** *n*: ***be on ~*** essere in attesa di giudizio
remark I *n* commento *m* **II** *v/t* osservare; ***nobody ~ed on it*** nessuno fece commenti
remarkable *adj* notevole
remarkably *adv* notevolmente; ***~ little*** notevolmente piccolo
remarry *v/i* ⟨*pret & past part* ***-ied***⟩ risposarsi
remediable *adj* sanabile
remedial *adj class* di recupero; *exercises* correttivo
remedy I *n* rimedio *m* **II** *v/t fig problem* rimediare a; *situation* porre rimedio a
remember I *v/t* ricordare; ***~ to lock the door*** ricordati di chiudere la porta a chiave; ***~ doing sth*** ricordarsi di fare qc; ***do you ~ when ...?*** (*reminiscing*) ti ricordi di quando ...?; ***~ me to her*** dalle i miei saluti **II** *v/i* ricordare, ricordarsi; ***not as far as I ~*** non per quel che mi ricordo
remembrance *n* ricordo *m*; ***in ~ of*** in ricordo di
Remembrance Day *n 11 novembre, commemorazione dei caduti in guerra*
remind *v/t*: ***~ s.o. of s.o. / sth*** ricordare qn / qc a qn; ***~ s.o. to do sth*** ricordare a qn di fare qc
reminder *n* promemoria *m*; COMM: *for payment* sollecito *m*
reminisce *v/i* rievocare il passato
reminiscent *adj*: ***be ~ of sth*** far venire in mente qc
remiss *adj form* negligente
remission *n* remissione *f*; *Br* JUR condono *m*; ***be in ~*** MED essere in remissione
remit I *v/t* rimettere **II** *n Br* competenze *fpl*
remittance *n* rimessa *f*
remittance advice *n* avviso *m* di rimessa
remnant *n* resto *m*; *of fabric* scampolo *m*
remodel *v/t* rimodellare
remonstrate *v/i* protestare
remonstration *n* rimostranza *f*
remorse *n* rimorso *m*; ***feel ~*** provare rimorso; ***without ~*** *merciless* senza pietà
remorseless *adj* spietato
remote *adj* (+*er*) *village* isolato; *possibility, connection* remoto; (*aloof*) distante; *ancestor* lontano
remote access *n* COMPUT accesso *m* remoto **remote control** *n* telecomando *m* **remote controlled** *adj* telecomandato
remotely *adv related, connected* lontanamente; ***just ~ possible*** vagamente possibile
remoteness *n* isolamento *m*
removable *adj* staccabile

removal *n* rimozione *f*; *from home* trasloco
removal firm *n* ditta *f* di traslochi **removal van** *n* furgone *m* dei traslochi
remove *v/t top, lid* togliere; MED asportare; *doubt, suspicion* eliminare
remunerate *v/t* rimunerare; (*reward*) ricompensare
remuneration *n* rimunerazione *f*
remunerative *adj* rimunerativo
Renaissance *n hist* Rinascimento *m*
rename *v/t* ribattezzare; *file* rinominare
render *v/t service* rendere; ***~ s.o. helpless*** rendere infermo qn; (*plaster*) rinzaffare; (*portray*) rendere
rendering *n of piece of music* interpretazione *f*; (*plastering*) rinzaffo *m*
rendez-vous *n* (*meeting*) incontro *m*
rendition *n* interpretazione *f*
renegade I *n* rinnegato *m*, -a *f* **II** *adj* rinnegato
renege *v/i* tirarsi indietro; ***he ~d on his contract*** è receduto dal contratto
renew *v/t contract, licence* rinnovare; ***feel ~ed*** sentirsi rinato; ***~ed efforts*** nuovi sforzi *mpl*; ***~ed strength*** rinnovata energia *f*
renewable *adj resources, contract etc* rinnovabile
renewal *n of contract etc* rinnovo *m*
rennet *n* caglio *m*
renounce *v/t title, rights* rinunciare a
renovate *v/t* ristrutturare
renovation *n* ristrutturazione *f*
renown *n* fama *f*; ***of great ~*** di grande notorietà
renowned *adj* famoso; ***be ~ for sth*** essere famoso per qc
rent I *v/t flat* affittare; *car equipment*, noleggiare; (*rent out*) affittare **II** *n* affitto *m*; ***for ~*** affittasi
rental *n for flat* affitto *m*; *for car* noleggio *m*; *for TV, phone* canone *m*
rental agreement *n* contratto *m* di noleggio
rent boy *n Br infml* marchetta *f* (uomo)
rent-free *adv* gratis
renunciation *n of right, violence* rinuncia *f* (***of*** a); *of terrorism* ripudio *m*
reopen *v/t & v/i* riaprire
reorder *v/t & v/i* fare una nuova ordinazione (di)
reorganisation, reorganization *n* riorganizzazione *f*
reorganise, reorganize *v/t* riorganizzare
re-orientate *v/t* riorientare
rep[1] *n abbr* (= **representative**) COMM rappresentante *m/f*; ***holiday** or **travel ~*** assistente *m/f* turistico
rep[2] *n abbr* (= **repertory company**) THEAT compagnia *f* di repertorio
Rep. *abbr US* **1.** (= **Representative**) deputato *m* **2.** (= **Republican Party**) repubblicano
repaint *v/t* ridipingere
repair I *v/t* riparare **II** *n*: ***in a good / bad state of ~*** in buono / cattivo stato; ***beyond ~*** irreparabile; ***~s*** riparazioni *fpl*
repairable *adj*, **reparable** *adj* riparabile
repairman *n* tecnico *m* **repair shop** *n* officina *f* di riparazioni
reparation *n* (*for damage*) risarcimento *m*; *usu pl* (*after war*) riparazioni *fpl* di guerra
reparatory *adj* riparatore
repartee *n* scambio *m* di battute
repartition *n* ripartizione *f*
repast *n* pasto *m*
repatriate *v/t* rimpatriare
repatriation *n* rimpatrio *m*
repay *v/t* ⟨*pret & past part* **-paid**⟩ *money* restituire; *person* ripagare; *kindness* ricambiare
repayable *adj* pagabile
repayment *n* pagamento *m*
repeal *v/t law* abrogare
repeat I *v/t* ripetere; ***am I ~ing myself?*** l'ho già detto? **II** *n programme* replica *f*
repeat business *n* COMM ulteriori ordini *mpl*
repeated *adj* ripetuto
repeatedly *adv* ripetutamente
repeat function *n* COMPUT funzione *f* di ripetizione **repeat order** *n* COMM ulteriore ordine *m* **repeat performance** *n* bis *m* (*a. fig*) **repeat prescription** *n* MED ricetta *f* ripetibile
repel *v/t* ⟨*pret & past part* **-led**⟩ *invaders, attack* respingere; (*disgust*) ripugnare
repellent I *n* (*insect repellent*) insettifugo *m* **II** *adj* ripugnante
repent *v/i* pentirsi
repentance *n* pentimento *m*

repentant *adj* pentito
repercussion *n* ripercussione *f*; ***that is bound to have ~s*** è destinato ad avere ripercussioni
repertoire *n* repertorio *m*
repertory *n* (*repertory theatre*) teatro *m* di repertorio; → ***repertoire***
repetition *n* ripetizione *f*
repetitious *adj* ripetitivo
repetitive *adj* ripetitivo
replace *v/t* (*put back*) mettere a posto *v/t* (*take the place of*) sostituire
replacement *n person* sostituto *m*, -a *f*; *act* sostituzione *f*; ***this is the ~ for the old model*** questo è il modello che sostituisce il vecchio
replacement part *n* pezzo *m* di ricambio
replant *v/t plant* ripiantare; *garden* cambiare le piante di
replay **I** *n recording* replay *m inv*; *match* spareggio *m* **II** *v/t match* rigiocare
replenish *v/t container* riempire; *supplies* rifornire
replete *adj* pieno (***with*** di)
replica *n* copia *f*
replicate *v/t* replicare
reply **I** *n* risposta *f* **II** *v/t & v/i* ⟨*pret & past part* ***-ied***⟩ rispondere
reply card *n* cartolina *f* di risposta
report **I** *n* (*account*) resoconto *m*; *by journalist* servizio *m*; EDU pagella *f* **II** *v/t facts* fare un servizio su; *to authorities* denunciare; ***~ one's findings to s.o.*** riferire sulle proprie conclusioni a qn; ***~ a person to the police*** denunciare qualcuno alla polizia; ***he is ~ed to be in London*** si dice che sia a Londra **III** *v/i of journalist* fare un reportage; (*present o.s.*) presentarsi; ***~ for duty*** prendere servizio; ***~ sick*** darsi malato
◆ **report to** *v/t in business* rendere conto a
report card *n* EDU pagella *f*
reported speech *n* GRAM discorso *m* indiretto
reporter *n* giornalista *m/f*
repose **I** *n* riposo *m* **II** *v/t* posare **III** *v/i* riposare
repository *n* deposito *m*
repossess *v/t* COMM riprendersi
reprehend *v/t* biasimare
reprehensible *adj* riprovevole
represent *v/t* rappresentare
representation *n* (*depiction*) rappresentazione *f*; POL rappresentanza *f*
representative **I** *n* rappresentante *m/f* **II** *adj* (*typical*) rappresentativo
repress *v/t* reprimere
repression *n* POL repressione *f*
repressive *adj* POL repressivo
reprieve **I** *n* JUR sospensione *f* della pena capitale; *fig* proroga *f* **II** *v/t* JUR sospendere l'esecuzione di; ***he was ~d*** la sua esecuzione è stata sospesa
reprimand **I** *n* rimprovero *m*; (*official*) ammonimento *m* **II** *v/t* ammonire
reprint **I** *n* ristampa *f* **II** *v/t* ristampare
reprisal *n* rappresaglia *f*; ***take ~s*** fare delle rappresaglie; ***in ~ for*** per rappresaglia contro
repro **I** *n infml* riproduzione *f* **II** *adj*: ***~ furniture*** mobili *mpl* riprodotti
reproach **I** *n* rimprovero *m*; ***be beyond ~*** essere irreprensibile **II** *v/t* rimproverare
reproachful *adj* di rimprovero
reproachfully *adv* con aria di rimprovero
reprobate **I** *n* canaglia *f* **II** *adj* reprobo
reprocess *v/t* riprocessare, ritrattare
reprocessing plant *n* impianto *m* di riprocessamento
reproduce **I** *v/t* riprodurre **II** *v/i* riprodursi
reproduction *n* riproduzione *f*
reproductive *adj* riproduttivo
reptile *n* rettile *m*
republic *n* repubblica *f*
republican **I** *n* repubblicano *m*, -a *f* **II** *adj* repubblicano
repudiate *v/t* (*deny*) respingere
repudiation *n* rifiuto *m*
repugnance *n* ripugnanza *f* (***towards, for*** per)
repugnant *adj* ripugnante
repulse *v/t* MIL respingere; *fig* ***be ~d by sth*** essere disgustato da qc
repulsion *n* disgusto *m* (***for*** per)
repulsive *adj* ripugnante
reputable *adj* rispettabile
reputation *n* reputazione *f*; ***have a good / bad ~*** avere una buona / cattiva reputazione
repute **I** *n*: ***of ~*** rinomato **II** *v/t*: ***he is ~d to be ...*** è rinomato per essere; ***he is ~d to be the best*** è rinomato per

essere il migliore
reputed *adj*: ***be ~ to be*** avere la fama di essere
reputedly *adv* a quanto si dice
request **I** *n* richiesta *f*; ***at s.o.'s ~*** su richiesta di qn; ***on ~*** su richiesta **II** *v/t* richiedere; ***~ sth of*** *or* ***from s.o.*** richiedere qc a qn
request stop *n Br* fermata *f* a richiesta
requiem *n* MUS requiem *m inv*
require *v/t* (*need*) aver bisogno di; ***it ~s great care*** richiede molta cura; ***as ~d by law*** come prescritto dalla legge; ***guests are ~d to ...*** i signori clienti sono pregati di ...
required *adj* (*necessary*) necessario; ***the ~ amount*** la somma necessaria
requirement *n* (*need*) esigenza *f*; (*condition*) requisito *m*; ***meet the ~s*** soddisfare le esigenze
requisite **I** *adj* (*necessary*) richiesto **II** *n* (*requirement*) requisito *m*
requisition *v/t* requisire
reran *pret* → ***rerun***
reread *v/t* ⟨*pret & past part* ***reread***⟩ rileggere
reroute *v/t aeroplane etc* deviare
rerun **I** *n of programme* replica *f* **II** *v/t* ⟨*pret* ***-ran***, *past part* ***-run***⟩ *programme* replicare
resale *n* rivendita *f*; ***~ value*** valore *m* di rivendita
resat *pret & past part* → ***resit***
reschedule *v/t* stabilire di nuovo
rescue **I** *n* salvataggio *m*; ***come to s.o.'s ~*** andare in aiuto a qn **II** *v/t* salvare
rescue party *n* squadra *f* di soccorso
research **I** *n* ricerca *f*; ***~ into sth*** ricerca su qc; ***do ~*** fare ricerche; ***carry out ~ into the effects of sth*** svolgere ricerche sugli effetti di qc **II** *v/i* indagare; ***~ into sth*** indagare su qc **III** *v/t* fare ricerche su
research and development *n* ricerca *f* e sviluppo *m* **research assistant** *n* assistente ricercatore *m*, -trice *f*
researcher *n* ricercatore *m*, -trice *f*
research project *n* ricerca *f*
resemblance *n* somiglianza *f*
resemble *v/t* (as)somigliare a; ***bear a strong ~ to s.o./sth*** (as)somigliare molto a qn/qc
resent *v/t* risentirsi per; ***he ~ed her for the rest of his life*** ce l'ha avuta con lei per il resto dei suoi giorni; ***he ~ed the fact that ...*** ha mal tollerato il fatto che ...
resentful *adj* pieno di risentimento; ***feel ~ toward(s) s.o. for doing sth*** essere risentito con qn per qc
resentfully *adv* con risentimento
resentment *n* risentimento *m*
reservation *n of room, table* prenotazione *f*; *mental, special area* riserva *f*; ***I have a ~*** *in hotel, restaurant* ho prenotato; ***with ~s*** *with doubts* con delle riserve
reserve **I** *n* (*store*) riserva *f*; (*aloofness*) riserbo *m*; SPORTS riserva *f*; ***~s*** FIN riserve *fpl*; ***keep sth in ~*** tenere qc di riserva **II** *v/t seat, table* prenotare; *judgment* riservarsi
reserved *adj person, manner* riservato; *table, seat* prenotato
reserve price *n* prezzo *m* minimo
reservoir *n for water* bacino *m* idrico
reset *v/t* ⟨*pret* ***-set***, *past part* ***-set***⟩ reimpostare; MED *bone* rimettere a posto
reshape *v/t clay etc* rimodellare
reshuffle **I** *n* POL rimpasto *m* **II** *v/t* POL rimpastare
reside *v/i form* risiedere
residence *n form: house etc* residenza *f*; (*stay*) permanenza *f*; ***country of ~*** paese *m* di residenza
residence permit *n* permesso *m* di residenza
resident **I** *n* residente *m/f* **II** *adj living in a building* residente sul posto; ***the ~ population*** la popolazione locale
residential *adj district* residenziale
residential home *n* casa *f* protetta
residual *adj* residuo
residue *n* residuo *m*
resign **I** *v/t position* dimettersi da; ***~ o.s. to*** rassegnarsi a **II** *v/i from job* dimettersi; ***~ from office*** dimettersi dall'incarico
resignation *n from job* dimissioni *fpl*; *mental* rassegnazione *f*; ***hand in one's ~*** rassegnare le dimissioni
resigned *adj* rassegnato; ***we have become ~ to the fact that ...*** ci siamo rassegnati al fatto che ...
resilience *n of material* resilienza *f*; *fig of person* capacità *f* di recupero
resilient *adj personality* che ha molte

risorse; *material* resistente
resin *n* resina *f*
resist I *v/t* resistere a **II** *v/i* resistere
resistance *n* resistenza *f*; ***meet with ~*** incontrare resistenza; ***offer no ~*** (***to s.o.*** / ***sth***) (*to attacker, advances etc*) non opporsi a qn / qc
resistant *adj material* resistente; ***~ to heat*** / ***rust*** resistente al calore / alla ruggine
resit *v/t* ⟨*pret & past part* ***-sat***⟩ *exam* ridare
resolute *adj* risoluto
resolution *n* (*decision*) risoluzione *f*; *made at New Year etc* proposito *m*; (*determination*) risolutezza *f*; *of problem* soluzione *f*; *of image* risoluzione *f*
resolve *v/t problem, mystery* risolvere; ***~ to do sth*** decidere di fare qc
resonance *n* risonanza *f*
resonate *v/i* risuonare
resort *n place* località *f inv*; ***holiday ~*** luogo *m* di villeggiatura; ***seaside ~*** stazione *f* balneare; ***ski ~*** stazione *f* sciistica; ***as a last ~*** come ultima risorsa
◆**resort to** *v/t violence, threats* far ricorso a
◆**resound with** *v/t* risuonare di
resounding *adj success, victory* clamoroso; ***the response was a ~ "no"*** la risposta fu un clamoroso rifiuto
resource *n* risorsa *f*; ***financial ~s*** mezzi *mpl* economici; ***mineral ~s*** risorse *fpl* minerali; ***natural ~s*** risorse *fpl* naturali; ***human ~s*** risorse *fpl* umane; ***leave s.o. to his own ~s*** lasciare qn in balia di se stesso
resourceful *adj* pieno di risorse
respect I *n* rispetto *m*; ***show ~ to*** avere rispetto per; ***treat with ~*** *person* trattare con rispetto; ***with*** (***due***) ***~, I still think that …*** con il dovuto rispetto, ritengo comunque che …; ***with ~ to*** riguardo a; ***in this*** / ***that ~*** quanto a questo; ***in many ~s*** sotto molti aspetti; ***pay one's last ~s to s.o.*** rendere omaggio a qn **II** *v/t* rispettare
respectability *n* rispettabilità *f inv*
respectable *adj* rispettabile
respectably *adv* rispettabilmente
respectful *adj* rispettoso
respectfully *adv* con rispetto
respective *adj* rispettivo; ***they each have their ~ merits*** ciascuno di loro ha i rispettivi meriti
respectively *adv* rispettivamente; ***Mr and Mrs Jones, 35 and 33 years old ~*** il signore e la signora Jones, rispettivamente di 35 e 33 anni
respiration *n* respirazione *f*
respirator *n* MED respiratore *m*
respiratory *adj system, failure* respiratorio
respite *n* tregua *f*; ***without ~*** senza tregua
resplendent *adj* splendido
respond *v/i* rispondere; ***~ to a question*** rispondere a una domanda; ***the patient ~ed to treatment*** il paziente ha risposto al trattamento
response *n* risposta *f*; ***in ~ to your letter*** in risposta alla sua lettera
responsibility *n* responsabilità *f inv*; ***accept ~ for*** assumersi la responsabilità di; ***a job with more ~*** un lavoro con più responsabilità; ***that's his ~*** la responsabilità è sua
responsible *adj* responsabile (***for*** di); *job, position* di responsabilità; ***hold s.o. ~*** ritenere qn responsabile; ***what's ~ for the hold-up?*** che cosa ha causato il ritardo?; ***who is ~ for breaking the window?*** chi è il responsabile della rottura della finestra?
responsive *adj audience* caloroso; ***be ~*** *of brakes* rispondere bene
rest¹ I *n* riposo *m*; ***have a ~*** riposarsi; ***set s.o.'s mind at ~*** tranquillizzare qn; ***give it a ~!*** *infml* piantala!; ***lay to ~*** *euph* seppellire; ***come to ~*** (*ball etc*) fermarsi **II** *v/i* riposare; ***~ on …*** (*be based on*) basarsi su …; (*lean against*) poggiare su …; ***it all ~s with him*** dipende tutto da lui; ***she will not ~ until …*** non avrà pace finché …; ***let the matter ~!*** lascia perdere!; ***may he ~ in peace*** riposi in pace; (***you may***) ***~ assured that …*** puoi stare certo che …; ***her elbows were ~ing on the table*** teneva i gomiti poggiati sul tavolo **III** *v/t* (*lean, balance*) appoggiare; ***~ one's hand on s.o.'s shoulder*** appoggiare la mano sulla spalla di qn
rest² *n*: ***the ~*** il resto *m*
restart *v/t car, engine* riaccendere; *ne-*

gotiations riprendere
restaurant *n* ristorante *m*
restaurant car *n* RAIL vagone *m* ristorante
rest cure *n* cura *f* del riposo
restful *adj* riposante
rest home *n* casa *f* di riposo
restitution *n* restituzione *f*
restive *adj* insofferente
restless *adj* irrequieto; ***have a ~ night*** passare una notte agitata
restlessly *adv* nervosamente
restlessness *n* irrequietezza *f*
restock *v/t shelves* rifornire
restoration *n* restauro *m*
restorative **I** *n* ricostituente *m* **II** *adj* corroborante
restore *v/t building etc* restaurare; (*bring back*) restituire; ***~d to health*** ristabilito; ***~ to power*** riportare al potere
restrain *v/t dog*, *troops* frenare; *emotions* reprimere; ***~ o.s.*** trattenersi
restrained *adj person* pacato; *manner* compassato
restraint *n* (*self-control*) autocontrollo *m*; ***without ~*** liberamente; (*moderation*) moderazione *f*; ***show a lack of ~*** dimostrare scarsa moderazione; ***wage ~*** controllo *m* dei salari
restrict *v/t* limitare; ***I'll ~ myself to …*** mi limiterò a …
restricted *adj view* limitato
restricted area *n* MIL zona *f* militare
restriction *n* restrizione *f*; ***place ~s on sth*** imporre restrizioni su qc
restrictive *adj rules*, *parents* rigido
rest room *n US* gabinetto *m*
restructure *v/t* COMM riorganizzare
rest stop *n* AUTO area *f* di sosta
result *n* risultato *m*; ***as a ~ of this*** in conseguenza a ciò; ***get ~s*** avere successo
◆**result from** *v/t* risultare da, derivare da
◆**result in** *v/t* dare luogo a; ***this resulted in him feeling even worse*** questo ha fatto sì che stesse ancora peggio
resume *v/t & v/i* riprendere
résumé *n US* curriculum vitae *m inv*
resumption *n* ripresa *f*
resurface **I** *v/t roads* asfaltare **II** *v/i* (*reappear*) riaffiorare
resurgence *n* ripresa *f*
resurrection *n* resurrezione *f*
Resurrection *n* REL resurrezione *f*
resuscitate *v/t* rianimare
resuscitation *n* rianimazione *f*
retail **I** *adv* al dettaglio **II** *v/i*: ***~ at …*** essere in vendita a … **III** *n* dettaglio *m*
retailer *n* dettagliante *m/f*
retail outlet *n* punto *m* (di) vendita **retail park** *n Br area commerciale con negozi di grandi dimensioni e ampio parcheggio* **retail price** *n* prezzo *m* al dettaglio **retail therapy** *n hum* shopping-terapia *f* **retail trade** *n* commercio *m* al dettaglio
retain *v/t* conservare
retainer *n* FIN onorario *m*; (*attendant*) servitore *m*, -trice *f*
retake *v/t* ⟨*pret* ***-took***, *past part* ***-taken***⟩ *exam* ripetere; *city* riconquistare
retaliate *v/i* vendicarsi; ***then she ~d by calling him a pig*** e allora lei si vendicò chiamandolo porco
retaliation *n* rappresaglia *f*; ***in ~ for*** per rappresaglia contro
retard **I** *v/t & v/i* ritardare **II** *n sl pej* ritardato *m*, -a *f*
retarded *adj mentally* ritardato
retch *v/i* avere conati di vomito
retd *abbr* (= **retired**) in pensione
rethink **I** *v/t* ⟨*pret & past part* ***-thought***⟩ riconsiderare **II** *n infml* ripensamento *m*; ***we'll have to have a ~*** dovremo riconsiderare la cosa
reticence *n* riservatezza *f*
reticent *adj* riservato
retina *n* ⟨*pl* ***retinae*** *or* ***retinas***⟩ retina *f*
retinue *n* seguito *m*
retire *v/i from work* andare in pensione; ***~ from business*** ritirarsi dagli affari; SPORTS ritirarsi; (*jury*) ritirarsi; ***~ from public life*** ritirarsi dalla vita pubblica
retired *adj* in pensione
retirement *n* pensione *f*; *act* pensionamento *m*; ***~ at 65*** pensionamento *m* a 65 anni
retirement age *n* età *f inv* pensionabile **retirement home** *n* casa *f* di riposo **retirement pension** *n* pensione *f* d'anzianità
retiring *adj* riservato
retort **I** *n* replica *f* **II** *v/t* replicare
retortion, retorsion *n* ritorsione *f*
retrace *v/t*: ***~ one's footsteps*** ritorna-

re sui propri passi
retract *v/t claws* ritrarre; *undercarriage* far rientrare; *statement* ritrattare
re-train *v/i* riqualificarsi
retread **I** *v/t* replicare **II** *n tyre* pneumatico *m* ricostruito
retreat **I** *v/i* ritirarsi **II** *n* MIL ritirata *f*; *place* rifugio *m*; *fig* ***beat a*** (***hasty***) ***~*** battere velocemente in ritirata
retrench *v/t & v/i* tagliare le spese
retrenchment *n* taglio *m* (delle spese)
retrial *n* nuovo processo *m*
retribution *n* castigo *m*
retrievable *adj* COMPUT *data* recuperabile; *after a crash* riparabile
retrieval *n* recupero *m*; COMPUT *of information* recupero *m*
retrieve *v/t* recuperare
retriever *n dog* cane *m* da riporto
retro- *pref* retro-
retroactive *adj law etc* retroattivo
retroactively *adv* retroattivamente
retrograde *adj move, decision* retrogrado
retrospect *n*: ***in ~*** ripensandoci
retrospective *n* retrospettiva *f*
retrovirus *n* MED retrovirus *m inv*
retry *v/t* JUR *case* ridiscutere; *person* sottoporre a nuovo processo
return **I** *v/t* ⟨*pret & past part* ***-ied***⟩ (*give back*) restituire; ***~ s.o.'s*** (***phone***) ***call*** richiamare qn; (*put back*) rimettere; ***~ a book to the shelf / box*** rimettere a posto un libro sul ripiano / nella scatola; *favour, invitation* ricambiare***~ fire*** MIL rispondere al fuoco; ***~ a verdict of guilty*** (***on s.o.***) JUR emettere un verdetto di colpevolezza (per qn) **II** *v/i* (*go back, come back*) ritornare; *of symptoms, doubts etc* ricomparire; ***~ to school*** ritornare a scuola; ***~ to*** (***one's***) ***work*** (*after pause*) tornare al lavoro; ***~ to a subject*** riprendere un argomento **III** *n* **1.** ritorno *m*; ***by ~*** (***of post***) a stretto giro di posta; ***many happy ~s*** (***of the day***) cento di questi giorni **2.** (*giving back*) restituzione *f*; ***in ~ for*** in cambio di **3.** COMPUT (tasto *m*) invio *m* **4.** *in tennis* risposta *f* al servizio **5.** ***tax ~*** dichiarazione *f* dei redditi **6.** ***~s*** (*profit*) rendimento *m*
returnable *adj bottle* a rendere
return flight *n* volo *m* di ritorno **return journey** *n* viaggio *m* di ritorno **return match** *n* partita *f* (del girone) di ritorno **return ticket** *n* biglietto *m* (di) andata e ritorno
reunification *n* riunificazione *f*
reunify *v/t* ⟨*pret & past part* ***-ied***⟩ riunificare
reunion *n* riunione *f*
reunite **I** *v/t* riunire; ***they were ~d at last*** si sono infine ricongiunti **II** *v/i* (*countries etc*) riunificarsi
reusable *adj* riutilizzabile
reuse *v/t* riutilizzare
rev *n*: ***~s per minute*** giri al minuto
◆ **rev up** *v/t sep* ⟨*pret & past part* ***-ved***⟩ *engine* far andare su di giri
Rev, Revd *abbr* (= **Reverend**) Reverendo
revaluation *n* rivalutazione *f*
revamp *v/t* (*modernize*) *infml* modernizzare
reveal *v/t* (*make visible*) mostrare; (*make known*) rivelare
revealing *adj remark* rivelatore; *dress* scollato
revel **I** *v/i*: ***they ~led***, *US* ***~ed all night*** hanno fatto baldoria tutta la notte **II** *n* **revels** *npl* baldoria *f*
◆ **revel in** *v/t* ⟨*pret & past part* ***-led***, *US* ***-ed***⟩ godere di
revelation *n* rivelazione *f*
revelationist *n persona che crede nella rivelazione divina*
revenge **I** *v/t* vendicare **II** *n* vendetta *f*; ***take one's ~*** vendicarsi; ***in ~ for*** per vendicarsi di
revenue *n* reddito *m*
reverberate *v/i of sound* rimbombare
revere *v/t* riverire
reverence *n* rispetto *m*
Reverend *n* REL reverendo *m*
reverent *adj* riverente
reverie *n* fantasticheria *f*
reversal *n* inversione *f*; *of policy, decision* capovolgimento *m*; *of fortune* rovescio *m*
reverse **I** *adj sequence* opposto; ***in ~ order*** in ordine inverso **II** *n* (*opposite*) contrario *m*; (*back*) rovescio *m*; AUTO retromarcia *f* **III** *v/t sequence* invertire; ***~ the car*** fare marcia indietro; ***~ the charges*** TEL telefonare a carico del destinatario **IV** *v/i* AUTO fare marcia indietro
◆ **reverse out** *v/i car, driver* fare retromarcia

reverse-charge call *n Br* telefonata *f* a carico del destinatario **reverse gear** *n* AUTO retromarcia *f*
reversible *adj coat etc* double-face *inv*
reversing light *n* luce *f* di retromarcia
revert *v/i*: ***~ to*** ritornare a
review I *n of book*, *film* recensione *f*; *of troops* rivista *f*; *of situation etc* revisione *f*; ***be under ~*** essere riesaminato; ***his salary is due for ~ in January*** il suo stipendio verrà rivisto in gennaio **II** *v/t book*, *film* recensire; *troops* passare in rivista; *situation etc* riesaminare
reviewer *n of book*, *film* critico *m*, -a *f*
revise I *v/t opinion*, *text* rivedere; EDU ripassare **II** *v/i* EDU ripassare
revision *n of opinion*, *text* revisione *f*; *for exam* ripasso *m*
revisit *v/t* rivisitare
revitalize *v/t* rivitalizzare
revival *n of custom*, *old style etc* revival *m inv*; *of patient* ripresa *f*
revive I *v/t custom*, *old style etc* riportare alla moda; *patient* rianimare **II** *v/i of business etc* riprendersi
revocation *n* revoca *f*
revoke *v/t licence* revocare
revolt I *n* rivolta *f* **II** *v/i* ribellarsi
revolting *adj* (*disgusting*) schifoso
revolution *n* rivoluzione *f*
revolutionary I *n* POL rivoluzionario *m*, -a *f* **II** *adj* rivoluzionario
revolutionize *v/t* rivoluzionare
revolve *v/i & v/t* ruotare
revolver *n* revolver *m inv*
revolving door *n* porta *f* girevole
revue *n* THEAT rivista *f*
revulsion *n* ribrezzo *m*
reward I *n financial* ricompensa *f*; *benefit derived* vantaggio *m*; ***the ~s of this job*** i vantaggi del suo lavoro **II** *v/t financially* ricompensare
rewarding *adj experience* gratificante; ***bringing up a child is ~*** tirare su un bambino è gratificante
rewind *v/t* ⟨*pret & past part* ***-wound***⟩ *film*, *tape* riavvolgere; ***~ button*** pulsante *m* di riavvolgimento
rewire *v/t building* rifare l'impianto elettrico di
reword *v/t letter* riformulare
rewrite *v/t* ⟨*pret* ***-wrote***, *past part* ***-written***⟩ riscrivere; ***~ the record books*** segnare nuovi record

RF *abbr* (= **radio frequency**) RADIO radiofrequenza *f*
RH *abbr* (= **Royal Highness**) Altezza *f* Reale
rhapsody *n* MUS rapsodia *f*; *fig* espressione *f* entusiastica
rhetoric *n* retorica *f*
rhetorical question *n* domanda *f* retorica
rheumatic *adj* reumatico
rheumatism *n* reumatismo *m*
rheumatoid *adj* reumatoide
rheumatoid arthritis *n* artrite *f* reumatoide
rhinestone *n* strass *m*
rhinoceros *n* rinoceronte *m*
rhododendron *n* rododendro *m*
rhomboid I *n* romboide *m* **II** *adj* romboidale
rhombus *n* rombo *m*
rhubarb *n* rabarbaro *m*
rhyme I *n* rima *f* **II** *v/i* rimare; ***~ with*** fare rima con
rhythm *n* ritmo *m*
rhythmic *adj* ritmato
rib I *n* ANAT costola *f*; ***poke s.o. in the ~s*** dare una gomitata nelle costole a qn **II** *v/t* ⟨*pret & past part* ***-bed***⟩ munire di nervature; *infml* (*tease*) prendere in giro
ribald *adj* scurrile
ribaldry *n* scurrilità *f*
ribbing *n* nervatura *f*; *knitting* bordo *m* a coste; *infml* (*tease*) presa *f* in giro
ribbon *n* nastro *m*; ***tear sth to ~s*** ridurre qc a brandelli
ribbon development *n sviluppo edilizio lungo le principali strade in uscita da una città*
rib cage *n* cassa *f* toracica
rice *n* riso *m*
rice pudding *n* budino *m* di riso
rich I *adj* (*+er*) (*wealthy*) ricco; *food* pesante; ***~ in vitamin C*** ricco di vitamina C; *soil* fertile; *smell* intenso; ***that's ~!*** *iron* questa è bella! **II** *n*: ***the ~*** i ricchi *mpl*; **riches** *npl* ricchezze *fpl*
richly *adv deserved* pienamente
richness *n* ricchezza *f* (***in*** di); *of style* sontuosità *f*; *of soil* fertilità *f*; ***the ~ of his voice*** la pienezza della sua voce
rickety *adj* traballante
ricochet *v/i* rimbalzare
rictus *n* MED rictus *m inv*

rid I *v/t*: ⟨*pret & past part* ***-rid***⟩ ***~ of*** liberare da; ***~ o.s. of s.o. / sth*** liberarsi di qn / qc II *adj*: ***get ~ of*** sbarazzarsi di

riddance *n infml*: ***good ~!*** che liberazione!

ridden *past part* → ***ride***

riddle[1] *v/t*: ***be ~d with*** essere crivellato di; ***~d with holes*** pieno di fori; ***~d with woodworm*** pieno di tarli; ***~d with corruption*** infestato dalla corruzione; ***~d with mistakes*** pieno di errori

riddle[2] *n* indovinello *m*; ***speak in ~s*** parlare per enigmi

ride I *v/t* ⟨*pret* ***rode***, *past part* ***ridden***⟩: ***~ a horse*** andare a cavallo; ***~ a bike*** andare in bicicletta II *v/i* ⟨*pret* ***rode***, *past part* ***ridden***⟩ *on horse* andare a cavallo; *on bike* andare; *in vehicle* viaggiare; ***he rode home*** è andato a casa in bicicletta; *fig* ***let sth ~*** lasciar perdere qc III *n on horse* cavalcata *f*; *in vehicle* giro *m*; (*journey*) viaggio *m*; ***do you want a ~ into town?*** *US* vuoi uno strappo in città?; *fig* ***take s.o. for a ~*** *infml* prendere in giro qn

rider *n on horse* cavallerizzo *m*, -a *f*; *on bike* ciclista *m/f*

ridge *n raised strip* sporgenza *f*; *of mountain* cresta *f*; *of roof* punta *f*; ***a ~ of high pressure*** METEO un fronte di alta pressione

ridicule I *n* ridicolo *m* II *v/t* ridicolizzare

ridiculous *adj* ridicolo; ***don't be ~*** non essere ridicolo; ***make o.s. (look) ~*** rendersi ridicolo

ridiculously *adv* incredibilmente

riding *n on horseback* equitazione *f*; ***I enjoy ~*** mi piace l'equitazione

rife *adj* diffuso; ***be ~*** dilagare; ***~ with*** pieno di

riff *n* MUS riff *m inv*

riffraff *n* marmaglia *f*

rifle *n* fucile *m*

◆**rifle through** *v/t drawer* rovistare in; *papers* rovistare tra

rift *n in earth* crepa *f*; *in party etc* spaccatura *f*

rig I *n* (*oil rig*) piattaforma *f* petrolifera II *v/t* ⟨*pret & past part* ***-ged***⟩ *elections* manipolare

◆**rig up** *v/t sep* (*build*) montare

right I *adj* **1.** (*correct*) esatto; (*proper, just*) giusto; (*suitable*) adatto; ***be ~*** *of answer* essere esatto; *of person* avere ragione; *of clock* essere giusto; ***put things ~*** sistemare le cose; → ***alright***; ***it's only ~ (and proper)*** è sacrosanto; ***you were ~ to refuse*** hai avuto ragione a rifiutare; ***put ~*** *error* correggere; *situation* sistemare; ***Mr / Miss Right*** *infml* l'uomo giusto / la donna giusta; ***we will do what is ~ for the country*** faremo ciò che è giusto per il paese; ***the medicine soon put him ~*** la medicina lo ha subito rimesso in sesto; ***he's not ~ in the head*** *infml* è fuori di testa; ***~ enough!*** senza dubbio! **2.** *not left* destro II *adv* **1.** (*directly*) proprio; (*correctly*) bene; (*completely*) completamente; ***~ in front of you*** proprio davanti a te; ***~ away*** immediatamente; ***~ here*** proprio qui; ***~ now*** (*immediately*) subito; (*at the moment*) adesso; ***~ in the middle*** proprio nel mezzo **2.** *not left* a destra III *n* **1.** *civil, legal etc* diritto *m*; ***be in the ~*** avere ragione; ***know ~ from wrong*** saper distinguere il bene dal male **2.** *not left* destra *f*; ***the ~*** POL la destra; ***on the ~*** a destra; ***turn to the ~, take a ~*** girare a destra

right-angle *n* angolo *m* retto; ***at ~s to ...*** ad angolo retto con ... **right-angled** *adj triangle* rettangolo

◆**right-click on** *v/t* COMPUT *icon* cliccare col pulsante destro (del mouse) su

righteous *adj* virtuoso; *anger* legittimo

rightful *adj heir, owner etc* legittimo

righthand *adj* destro; ***on the ~ side*** a destra **righthand drive** *n* AUTO guida *f* a destra; *car* auto *f inv* con guida a destra **righthanded** *adj*: ***be ~*** usare la (mano) destra **righthand man** *n* braccio *m* destro

rightly *adv correctly* correttamente; *justifiably* giustamente; ***they are ~ regarded as ...*** sono giustamente considerati ...; ***if I remember ~*** se ricordo bene; ***and ~ so*** ed è giusto che sia così

right-minded *adj* retto **right of way** *n in traffic* (diritto *m* di) precedenza *f*; *across land* diritto *m* di accesso **right wing** *n* POL destra *f*; SPORTS esterno *m* destro **right-wing** *adj* POL di destra

right winger *n* POL persona *f* di destra
right-wing extremism *n* POL estremismo *m* di destra
rigid *adj material, principles* rigido; *attitude* inflessibile; ***~ with fear*** irrigidito dalla paura; ***be bored ~*** essere annoiato a morte
rigmarole *n* trafila *f*
rigor *US* → ***rigour***
rigorous *adj* rigoroso
rigorously *adv check, examine* rigorosamente
rigour, *US* **rigor** *n of discipline* rigore *m*; ***the ~s of the winter*** i rigori dell'inverno
rile *v/t infml* irritare
rim I *n of wheel* cerchione *m*; *of cup* orlo *m*; *of spectacles* montatura *f* **II** *v/t* orlare
rind *n of lemon* scorza *f*; *of bacon* cotenna *f*; *of cheese* crosta *f*
ring[1] *n* (*circle*) cerchio *m*; *on finger* anello *m*; *in boxing* ring *m inv*, quadrato *m*; *at circus* pista *f*
ring[2] **I** *n of bell* trillo *m*; *of voice* suono *m*; ***give s.o. a ~*** TEL dare un colpo di telefono a qn **II** *v/t* ⟨*pret* ***rang***, *past part* ***rung***⟩ *bell* suonare; TEL chiamare **III** *v/i* ⟨*pret* ***rang***, *past part* ***rung***⟩ *of bell* suonare; TEL chiamare; ***please ~ for attention*** suonare il campanello
◆**ring back** *v/t sep & v/i* TEL richiamare
◆**ring off** *v/i* TEL riagganciare
◆**ring out** *v/i* (*bell*) suonare; (*shot*) rimbombare
◆**ring up** *v/t sep* TEL telefonare a; (*cashier*) battere
ringbinder *n* quaderno *m* con gli anelli **ring finger** *n* anulare *m* **ringleader** *n* capobanda *m inv* **ring-pull** *n* linguetta *f* **ring road** *n* circonvallazione *f* **ring tone** *n* TEL segnale *m* di libero
ringworm *n* tigna *f*
rink *n* pista *f* di pattinaggio su ghiaccio
rinse I *n for hair colour* cachet *m inv* **II** *v/t* sciacquare
riot I *n* sommossa *f*; ***run ~*** scatenarsi **II** *v/i* causare disordini
rioter *n* dimostrante *m/f*
riotous *adj person* chiassoso; *behaviour* dissoluto
riot police *n* reparti *mpl* (di polizia) antisommossa
rip I *n in cloth etc* strappo *m* **II** *v/t* ⟨*pret & past part* ***-ped***⟩ *cloth etc* strappare; ***~ sth open*** aprire qc strappandolo
◆**rip off** *v/t sep clothing* strappare; *infml customers* fregare *infml*
◆**rip up** *v/t sep letter, sheet* strappare
RIP *abbr* (= **rest in peace**) riposi in pace
ripe *adj* (+*er*) *fruit, cheese* maturo; *infml* puzzolente; ***live to a ~ old age*** vivere fino a tarda età; ***be ~ for the picking*** essere maturo per la raccolta
ripen *v/i of fruit* maturare
ripeness *n of fruit* maturazione *f*
rip-off *n infml* fregatura *f infml*
ripple I *n on water* increspatura *f*; ***a ~ of laughter*** una leggera risata **II** *v/i* (*water*) incresparsi **III** *v/t water* increspare; *muscles* far guizzare
rise I *v/i* ⟨*pret* ***rose***, *past part* ***risen***⟩ *from chair etc* alzarsi; *of sun* sorgere; *of price, temperature* aumentare; *of water level* salire; ***~ to a crescendo*** salire in un crescendo; ***~ to fame*** diventare famoso; ***he rose to be President*** diventò presidente; *ground* salire **II** *n* aumento *m*; ***~ to power*** salita *f* al potere; ***give ~ to*** dare origine a; ***there has been a ~ in the number of participants*** c'è stato un aumento nel numero di partecipanti
◆**rise above** *v/t level* superare; *insults etc* mostrarsi superiore a
◆**rise up** *v/i mountain etc* innalzarsi; (*rebel*) ribellarsi
risen *past part* → ***rise***
riser *n*: ***be an early / be a late ~*** essere mattiniero / alzarsi sempre tardi; *stair step* alzata *f*
rising *adj sun* che sorge, nascente; *prices* in aumento; *ground* in pendio; *star* nascente
risk I *n* rischio *m*; ***take a ~*** correre un rischio; ***health ~*** rischio *m* per la salute; ***run the ~ of doing sth*** correre il rischio di fare qc; ***at ~*** a rischio **II** *v/t* rischiare; ***let's ~ it*** proviamo
risky *adj* (+*er*) rischioso
risotto *n* risotto *m*
risqué *adj* osé
rissole *n* COOK polpetta *f*
rite *n* rito *m*; ***perform the last ~s over s.o.*** dare l'estrema unzione a qn
rite of passage *n* rito *m* di passaggio
ritual I *n* rituale *m* **II** *adj* rituale

ritzy *adj infml* chic
rival **I** *n in sport, love* rivale *m/f*; *in business* concorrente *m/f* **II** *v/t* competere con; ***I can't ~ that*** non posso competere con quello
rivalry *n* rivalità *f inv*
river *n* fiume *m*
riverbank *n* sponda *f* del fiume **riverbed** *n* letto *m* del fiume **riverside** **I** *adj* sul fiume **II** *n* riva *f* del fiume
rivet **I** *n* ribattino *m* **II** *v/t* rivettare
riveting *adj* avvincente
Riviera *n*: ***the Italian ~*** la riviera (ligure)
roach[1] *n fish* triotto *m*
roach[2] *n insect* blatta *f*
road *n* strada *f*; ***it's just down the ~*** è qui vicino; ***be on the ~*** *band* essere in tournée; ***be off the ~*** *car* essere fuori uso; ***take to the ~*** mettersi in viaggio; ***have one for the ~*** *infml* bere il bicchiere della staffa; *fig* ***you're on the right ~*** sei sulla buona strada; *fig* ***on the ~ to ruin*** sulla strada della rovina; *fig* ***on the ~ to recovery*** essere sulla via della guarigione
roadblock *n* posto *m* di blocco **road hog** *n* pirata *m* della strada **road holding** *n of vehicle* tenuta *f* di strada **road map** *n* carta *f* automobilistica **road rage** *n* aggressività *f* degli automobilisti **road safety** *n* sicurezza *f* sulle strade **roadside** *n*: ***at the ~*** sul ciglio della strada **roadsign** *n* cartello *m* stradale **roadway** *n* carreggiata *f* **road works** *npl* lavori *mpl* stradali **roadworthy** *adj* in buono stato di marcia
roam *v/i* vagabondare
roaming *n* TEL roaming *m inv*
roar **I** *v/i of engine* rombare; *of lion* ruggire; *of person* gridare; ***~ with laughter*** ridere fragorosamente **II** *n of engine* rombo *m*; *of lion* ruggito *m*; *of traffic* fragore *m*
roaring *adj fire* scoppiettante; ***do a ~ trade*** fare affari d'oro
roast **I** *n beef etc* arrosto *m* **II** *v/t chicken, potatoes* arrostire; *coffee beans, peanuts* tostare **III** *v/i of food* arrostire; *in hot room, climate* scoppiare di caldo
roast beef *n* arrosto *m* di manzo
roasting tin *n* teglia *f* per arrosti
roast pork *n* arrosto *m* di maiale
rob *v/t* ⟨*pret & past part* ***-bed***⟩ *person, bank* rapinare; ***I've been ~bed*** mi hanno rapinato
robber *n* rapinatore *m*, -trice *f*
robbery *n* rapina *f*; ***armed ~*** rapina *f* a mano armata; ***bank ~*** rapina *f* in banca
robe *n of judge* toga *f*; *of priest* tonaca *f*; *US (dressing gown)* vestaglia *f*
robin *n* pettirosso *m*
robot *n* robot *m inv*
robust *adj* robusto
rock[1] *n* roccia *f*; ***as solid as a ~*** *structure* solido come una roccia; ***on the ~s*** *drink* con ghiaccio; *marriage* in crisi
rock[2] *n* **I** MUS rock *m inv* **II** *v/t baby* cullare; *cradle* far dondolare; *(surprise)* sconvolgere; *fig* ***~ the boat*** *infml* provocare guai **III** *v/i on chair* dondolarsi; *of boat* dondolare
rock band *n* gruppo *m* rock **rock bottom** *n*: ***reach ~*** toccare il fondo **rock-bottom** *adj prices* bassissimo **rock climber** *n* rocciatore *m*, -trice *f* **rock climbing** *n* roccia *f*
rocker *n US* sedia *f* a dondolo; MUS rocker *m/f inv*; ***he's off his ~*** *infml* è matto
rockery *n* giardino *m* di pietre
rocket[1] **I** *n* razzo *m*; ***give s.o. a ~*** *infml* fare una parte a qn **II** *v/i of prices etc* salire alle stelle
rocket[2] *n* BOT, COOK ruchetta *f*
rocket science *n*: ***it's not ~*** *infml* non c'è bisogno di un genio
rocking chair *n* sedia *f* a dondolo
rocking horse *n* cavallo *m* a dondolo
rock music *n* rock *m inv*
rock 'n' roll *n* rock and roll *m inv*
rock star *n* rockstar *f inv*
rocky *adj* (+*er*) *shore* roccioso; *(shaky)* instabile
rod *n* sbarra *f*; *for fishing* canna *f*; *for punishment* verga *f*
rode *pret* → ***ride***
rodent *n* roditore *m*
rodeo *n* rodeo *m*
roe *n* uova *fpl* di pesce
roger *v/t & v/i Br vulg* fottere *vulg*
rogue *n* briccone *m*, -a *f*
roguish *adj* furbo
role *n* ruolo *m*
role model *n* modello *m* di comportamento **role play** *n* EDU gioco *m* di ruolo; PSYCH psicodramma *m inv*
roll **I** *n of bread* panino *m*; *of film* rul-

lino *m*; *of thunder* rombo *m*; (*list, register*) lista *f*; **~ of honour** *Br* ruolo *m* d'onore; ***be on a ~*** *infml* avere successo **II** *v/i of ball etc* rotolare; *of boat* dondolare; *camera* entrare in azione; ***he's ~ing in it*** *infml* nuotare nell'oro **III** *v/t*: ***~ sth into a ball*** appallottolare qc; ***~ sth along the ground*** far rotolare qc; ***~ a cigarette*** arrotolare una sigaretta; ***~ one's eyes*** roteare gli occhi; ***kitchen and dining room ~ed into one*** cucina e sala da pranzo sono mescolati in un tutt'uno

◆**roll out** *v/t sep pastry* spianare

◆**roll over I** *v/i* rigirarsi **II** *v/t sep person, object* girare; *loan, agreement* rinnovare

◆**roll up I** *v/t sep sleeves* arrotolare **II** *v/i infml* (*arrive*) arrivare

roll call *n* appello *m*

roller *n for hair* bigodino *m*; ***put one's hair in ~s*** mettersi i bigodini

roller blade® *n* roller blade® *m inv* **roller blind** *n* tenda *f* a rullo **roller coaster** *n* montagne *fpl* russe **roller skate** *n* pattino *m* a rotelle **roller skating** *n* pattinaggio *m* a rotelle

rolling *adj hills, landscape* ondulato; *programme* graduale

rolling pin *n* matterello *m*

rollneck *adj* a collo alto

roll-on *n* deodorante *m* roll-on

rollover *n Br in National Lottery*: ***~ week*** *settimana con montepremi cumulativo per mancata vincita nella settimana precedente*; ***~ jackpot*** jackpot *m inv* accumulato

roly-poly *adj infml* cicciotto

ROM *n abbr* (= **read only memory**) COMPUT ROM *f* (memoria *f* di sola lettura)

Roman I *adj* romano **II** *n* romano *m*, -a *f*

Roman Catholic I *n* REL cattolico *m*, -a *f* **II** *adj* cattolico

romance I *n* (*affair*) storia *f* d'amore; *novel* romanzo *m* rosa; *film* film *m inv* d'amore **II** *adj*: ***Romance** language etc* romanzo

Romanesque *adj* romanico

Romania *n* Romania *f*

Romanian I *adj* rumeno **II** *n* rumeno *m*, -a *f*; (*language*) rumeno *m*

roman numeral *n* numero *m* romano

romantic *adj* romantico

romantically *adv* romanticamente; ***~ involved with s.o.*** legato sentimentalmente a qn

romanticise, romanticize *v/t* romanzare

romanticism *n* romanticismo *m*

Romany I *n* zingaro *m*, -a *f*; (*language*) lingua *f* rom **II** *adj culture* gitano

Rome *n* Roma *f*

romp I *n storia o commedia brillante* **II** *v/i* scatenarsi; ***~ home*** (*win*) vincere con facilità

◆**romp about, romp around** *v/t & v/i* giocare rumorosamente (in)

◆**romp through** *v/t infml* (*do quickly*) finire agevolmente

rompers *npl* SEW pagliaccetto *m*

roof *n* tetto *m*; ***have a ~ over one's head*** avere un tetto sulla testa; ***live under the same ~ as s.o.*** vivere sotto lo stesso tetto con qn; ***go through the ~*** *infml person* andare su tutte le furie; *prices etc* salire alle stelle; ***~ of the mouth*** palato *m* duro

roof rack *n* AUTO portabagagli *m inv*

rooftop *n* tetto *m*; ***shout** or **scream sth from the ~s*** gridare qc ai quattro venti

rook I *n bird* corvo *m*; *chess piece* torre *f* **II** *v/t infml* raggirare

room *n* stanza *f*; (*bedroom*) camera *f* (da letto); (*space*) posto *m*; ***there's no ~ for …*** non c'è posto per …; ***make ~ for s.o./sth*** fare spazio per qn/qc; ***there is ~ for improvement*** esiste un margine di miglioramento; ***~ for manoeuvre*** *Br or* ***maneuver*** *US* margine *m* di manovra

room mate *n* compagno *m*, -a *f* di stanza **room service** *n* servizio *m* in camera **room temperature** *n* temperatura *f* ambiente

roomy *adj* (*+er*) *house, car etc* spazioso; *clothes* ampio

roost I *n* (*pole*) posatoio *m*; *fig* ***come home to ~*** ritorcersi **II** *v/i* appollaiarsi

rooster *n* gallo *m*

root I *n* radice *f*; ***~s*** *of person* radici *fpl* **II** *v/i* mettere radici; (*dig with snout*) grufolare; *AUS vulg* scopare

◆**root for** *v/t infml* fare il tifo per

◆**root out** *v/t sep* (*get rid of*) eradicare; (*find*) scovare

root beer *n US bevanda frizzante estratta da radici*

rooted *adj*: ***be ~ in sth*** essere radicato

in qc; ***be ~ to the spot*** rimanere inchiodato lì
rootstock *n* tubero *m*
root vegetable *n* verdura *f* a radice
rope *n* corda *f*, fune *f*; ***skipping ~, jump ~*** *US* corda *f* per saltare; ***show s.o. the ~s*** *infml* insegnare il mestiere a qn; ***know the ~s*** *infml* essere pratico del mestiere; ***on the ~s*** alle corde
◆**rope in** *v/t sep esp Br fig* coinvolgere; ***how did you get roped into that?*** come ti sei fatto coinvolgere?
◆**rope off** *v/t sep* transennare
rope ladder *n* scala *f* di corda
ropy *adj* filamentoso; *Br* scadente
rosary *n* REL rosario *m*
rose[1] **I** *n* BOT rosa *f*; ***everything's coming up ~s*** *infml* tutto sta andando a meraviglia; ***that will put the ~s back in your cheeks*** *infml* questo ti farà riprendere colore **II** *adj* rosa; ***see the world through ~-tinted spectacles*** *infml* vedere (il mondo) tutto rosa
rose[2] *pret* → ***rise***
rosé I *adj* rosé **II** *n* rosé *m inv*
rosebud *n* bocciolo *m* di rosa
rosehip *n* BOT cinorrodo *m*
rosemary *n* rosmarino *m*
rosette *n* coccarda *f*
rosewater *n* acqua *f* di rose
rose window *n* ARCH rosone *m*
roster *n* lista *f* dei turni
rostrum *n* podio *m*
rosy *adj* (*+er*) roseo
rot I *n* marciume *m*; (*rubbish*) stupidaggini *fpl*; ***stop the ~*** *Br* arrestare il declino; *fig* ***then the ~ set in*** poi le cose cominciarono a guastarsi **II** *v/i* ⟨*pret & past part* ***-ted***⟩ marcire; ***~ in jail*** marcire in prigione **III** *v/t* far marcire
rota *n* turni *mpl*; *actual document* tabella *f* dei turni; ***on a ~ basis*** a turno
rotate I *v/i of blades, earth* ruotare **II** *v/t* girare; *crops* avvicendare
rotation *n around the sun etc* rotazione *f*; ***in ~*** a turno
rote *n*: ***by ~*** *learn* a memoria
rotgut *n infml* liquore *m* scadente
rotor *n* rotore *m*
rotten *adj food, wood etc* marcio; *infml* (*very bad*) schifoso *infml*; ***what ~ luck!*** che scalogna!; ***what a ~ thing to do!*** che carognata!; ***feel ~ about doing sth*** sentirsi in colpa per qc; ***spoil s.o. ~*** viziare troppo qn
roué *n* depravato *m*; ***he was a bit of an old ~*** era un vecchio depravato
rough I *adj* (*+er*) *hands, skin, surface* ruvido; *ground* accidentato; (*coarse*) rozzo; (*violent*) violento; *crossing* movimentato; *seas* grosso; (*approximate*) approssimativo; ***~ draft*** abbozzo *m*; ***~ sketch*** schizzo *m* sommario; ***at a ~ guess*** a occhio e croce; ***have a ~ idea*** avere un'idea approssimativa; ***face a ~ ride*** andare incontro ad un periodo difficile; ***when the going gets ~ …*** quando il gioco si fa duro … **II** *adv*: ***sleep ~*** dormire all'addiaccio **III** *v/t*: ***~ it*** *infml* vivere senza confort **IV** *n in golf* erba *f* alta
◆**rough up** *v/t sep infml* malmenare
roughage *n in food* fibre *fpl*
rough-and-ready *adj method* spiccio; *person* sbrigativo **rough-and-tumble** *n* (*play*) baruffa *f*; (*fighting*) lotta *f*
roughcast I *n* intonaco *m* rustico **II** *v/t* intonacare (con intonaco rustico)
rough copy *n* brutta copia *f*
roughly *adv* (*approximately*) circa; (*harshly*) bruscamente; ***~ speaking*** grosso modo
roughneck *n* operaio *m* su piattaforma petrolifera
roughshod *adv*: *fig* ***ride ~ over s.o. / sth*** *US* mettere sotto i piedi qn / qc
roulette *n* roulette *f inv*
round I *adj* (*+er*) rotondo; ***in ~ figures*** in cifra tonda **II** *n of postman, doctor* giro *m*; *of toast* fetta *f*; *of drinks* giro *m*; *of competition* girone *m*; *in boxing match* round *m inv* **III** *v/t the corner* girare **IV** *adv / prep* → ***around***; *esp Br* ***there was a wall right ~*** *or* ***all ~*** c'era un muro tutt'intorno; ***~ and ~*** in cerchio
◆**round down** *v/t sep figure* arrotondare per difetto
◆**round off** *v/t sep edges* smussare; *meeting, night out* chiudere
◆**round up** *v/t sep figure* arrotondare; *suspects, criminals* radunare
roundabout I *adj route, way of saying sth* indiretto **II** *n on road* rotatoria *f*; (*merry-go-round*) giostra *f*
rounded *adj* arrotondato; *person* paffuto

round-the-clock *adj/adv* ventiquattr'ore su ventiquattro **round--the-world** *adj* intorno al mondo **round trip ticket** *n US* biglietto *m* (di) andata e ritorno **round-up** *n of cattle* raduno *m*; *of suspects, criminals* retata *f*; *of news* riepilogo *m*

rouse *v/t from sleep* svegliare; *interest, emotions* risvegliare

rousing *adj speech, finale* entusiasmante

rout **I** *n* disfatta *f* **II** *v/t* sconfiggere

route *n of car* itinerario *m*; *of plane, ship* rotta *f*; *of bus* percorso *m*

routine **I** *adj* abituale **II** *n* routine *f*; ***as a matter of ~*** d'abitudine

rove *v/i & v/t* vagare (per); ***he has a roving eye*** *hum* essere un farfallone

row[1] *n* (*line*) fila *f*; ***5 days in a ~*** 5 giorni di fila

row[2] *v/t & v/i boat* remare

row[3] **I** *n* (*quarrel*) litigio *m*; (*noise*) baccano *m*; ***make a ~*** fare chiasso; ***have a ~ with s.o.*** litigare con qn **II** *v/i* litigare

rowboat *n US* barca *f* a remi

rowdy *adj* (*+er*) turbolento

row house *n US* villetta *f* a schiera

rowing boat *n* barca *f* a remi

royal **I** *adj* reale; *Br* ***the ~ family*** la famiglia reale **II** *n Br infml* membro *m* della famiglia reale

royal blue *adj* blu scuro

Royal Highness *n*: ***Your ~*** Vostra Altezza Reale

royalty *n* (*royal persons*) reali *mpl*; *on book, recording* royalty *f inv*

RP *abbr* (= **received pronunciation**) *pronuncia dell'inglese considerata standard*

rpm *abbr* (= **revolutions per minute**) giri *mpl* al minuto (giri / min.)

RSI *abbr* MED (= **repetitive strain injury**) lesioni *fpl* da stiramento ripetuto

RSVP *abbr* (= **répondez s'il vous plaît**) RSVP (si prega rispondere)

Rt Hon *abbr Br* (= **Right Honourable**): ***the ~ John Williams MP*** l'onorevole deputato John Williams

rub **I** *n* strofinata *f*; ***give sth a ~*** dare una strofinata a qc; ***there's the ~*** qui sta il guaio **II** *v/t* ⟨*pret & past part* **-bed**⟩ sfregare, strofinare; ***~ lotion into sth*** frizionare la lozione su qc; ***~ one's hands*** (***together***) strofinarsi le mani; *fig* ***~ s.o.'s nose in sth*** rinfacciare qc a qn; *fig* ***~ shoulders*** *Br or* ***elbows*** *US* ***with all sorts of people*** frequentare persone di tutti i tipi; ***~ s.o.*** (***up***) ***the wrong way*** *US infml* prendere qn per il verso sbagliato **III** *v/i* strusciare (***against*** contro); ***the cat ~bed against my legs / the tree*** il gatto si è strusciato contro le mie gambe / contro l'albero

◆**rub down** *v/t sep to clean* levigare

◆**rub in** *v/t sep cream, ointment* far penetrare; *fig* ***don't rub it in!*** non rivoltare il coltello nella piaga!

◆**rub off** **I** *v/t sep dirt* levare (strofinando) **II** *v/i*: ***it rubs off on you*** ti si comunica

◆**rub out** *v/t sep with eraser* cancellare

rubber **I** *n* gomma *f* **II** *adj* di gomma

rubber band *n* elastico *m* **rubber gloves** *npl* guanti *mpl* di gomma

rubberneck *v/i infml* guardare

rubbery *adj* che sembra di gomma

rubbish **I** *n* spazzatura *f*, immondizia *f*; (*poor quality*) porcheria *f*; (*nonsense*) sciocchezza *f*; ***household ~*** rifiuti *mpl* domestici; ***don't talk ~!*** non dire sciocchezze! **II** *v/t* fare a pezzi; ***the reviewer really ~ed her book*** il critico ha davvero fatto a pezzi il suo libro

rubbish bin *n* pattumiera *f* **rubbish dump** *n* discarica *f*

rubble *n* macerie *fpl*

ruby **I** *n jewel* rubino *m* **II** *adj* (rosso) rubino

rucksack *n* zaino *m*

ruckus *n infml* tafferuglio *m*

rudder *n* timone *m*

ruddy *adj* (*+er*) *complexion* rubicondo; *infml* dannato

rude *adj* (*+er*) *person, behaviour* maleducato; *language* volgare; ***don't be so ~!*** non essere maleducato; ***a ~ word*** una parolaccia; ***it's ~ to ...*** è maleducazione ...

rudely *adv* (*impolitely*) scortesemente

rudeness *n* maleducazione *f*

rudimentary *adj* rudimentale

rudiments *npl* rudimenti *mpl*

rueful *adj* rassegnato

ruefully *adv* con aria rassegnata

ruffian *n* delinquente *m/f*

ruffle **I** *n on dress* gala *f* **II** *v/t hair* scompigliare; *person* turbare; ***get ~d*** agitarsi; ~ ***s.o.'s feathers*** turbare qn

rug *n* tappeto *m*; ***pull the ~ from under s.o.*** *fig* far mancare il terreno sotto i piedi a qn; (*blanket*) coperta *f* (da viaggio)

rugby *n* SPORTS rugby *m inv*

rugby league *n* rugby *m inv* a tredici **rugby match** *n* partita *f* di rugby **rugby player** *n* giocatore *m* di rugby **rugby union** *n* rugby *m inv* a quindici

rugged *adj coastline* frastagliato; *face, features* marcato

ruin I *n* rovina *f*; ***~s*** rovine; ***in ~s*** *city, building* in rovina; ***in ~s*** *plans, career* rovinato; ***be the ~ of s.o.*** essere la rovina di qn **II** *v/t* rovinare; ***be ~ed*** *financially* essere rovinato

rule I *n of club, game* regola *f*; (*authority*) dominio *m*; *for measuring* metro *m* (a stecche); ***as a ~*** generalmente; ***as a ~ of thumb*** come regola pratica **II** *v/t country* governare; ***the judge ~d that …*** il giudice ha stabilito che; ***~ the roost*** *fig* spadroneggiare; ***be ~d by emotions*** lasciarsi guidare dalle emozioni; ***he let his heart ~ his head*** ha lasciato che l'istinto prevalesse sulla ragione; *line* tirare; ***~d paper*** foglio *m* a righe **III** *v/i of monarch* regnare

◆**rule out** *v/t sep* escludere

ruler *n for measuring* righello *m*; *of state* capo *m*

ruling I *n* decisione *f* **II** *adj party* di governo

rum *n drink* rum *m inv*

rumble *v/i of stomach* brontolare; *of thunder* rimbombare

ruminate *v/i fig* rimuginare (***over, about, on*** su)

rummage I *n*: ***have a good ~ in sth*** rovistare in qc **II** *v/i* rovistare (***among*** tra, ***in*** in, ***for*** alla ricerca di)

◆**rummage around** *v/i* frugare

rummage sale *n US* vendita *f* di beneficenza

rumour, *US* **rumor I** *n* voce *f*; ***~ has it that …*** corre voce che; ***there are ~s of war*** circolano voci di guerra **II** *v/t*: ***it is ~ed that …*** corre voce che …

rump *n of animal* groppa *f*

rumple *v/t clothes, paper* spiegazzare

rumpsteak *n* bistecca *f* di girello

rumpus *n infml* baccano *m*; ***make a ~*** fare baccano

rumpus room *n US* sala *f* dei giochi

run I *v/i* ⟨*pret* **ran**, *past part* **run**⟩ **1.** *of person, animal* correre; ***~ for President*** *in election* candidarsi alla presidenza; ***it ~s in the family*** è un tratto di famiglia **2.** *of river* scorrere; *of paint, makeup* sbavare; *of nose* colare; ***don't leave the tap ~ning*** non lasciare il rubinetto aperto **3.** *of trains, buses* viaggiare **4.** *of play* tenere il cartellone **5.** *of software* girare **6.** *of engine, machine* funzionare **7.** ***supplies are ~ning low*** le provviste si stanno esaurendo **II** *v/t* ⟨*pret* **ran**, *past part* **run**⟩ **1.** (*move fast*) correre **2.** (*take part in: race*) partecipare a **3.** *business, hotel, project etc* gestire **4.** *software* lanciare **5.** *car* usare **6.** *risk* correre **7.** ***can I ~ you to the station?*** ti porto alla stazione? **8.** ***he ran his eye down the page*** diede uno sguardo alla pagina **III** *n* **1.** *on foot* corsa *f*; ***go for a ~*** andare a correre; ***go for a ~ in the car*** andare a fare un giro in macchina; ***make a ~ for it*** scappare; ***a criminal on the ~*** un evaso, un'evasa **2.** *distance* tragitto *m* **3.** *in tights* sfilatura *f* **4.** ***in the short ~ / in the long ~*** sulle prime / alla lunga **5.** (*series*) ***a ~ of bad luck*** una sventura dietro l'altra; ***it's had a three year ~*** *of play* ha tenuto cartellone per tre anni **6.** (*rush*) ***a ~ on the dollar*** una forte richiesta di dollari **7.** ***have the ~ of the place*** avere il posto a propria disposizione **8.** ***ski ~*** pista *f* da sci

◆**run across** *v/t* imbattersi in

◆**run away** *v/i* scappare

◆**run down I** *v/t sep* (*knock down*) investire; (*criticize*) parlare male di; *stocks* ridurre **II** *v/i of battery* scaricarsi

◆**run into** *v/t* (*meet*) imbattersi in; *difficulties* trovare

◆**run off I** *v/i* scappare **II** *v/t sep* (*print off*) stampare

◆**run out** *v/i of contract, time* scadere; *of supplies* esaurirsi

◆**run out of** *v/t patience* perdere; *supplies* rimanere senza; ***I ran out of petrol*** ho finito la benzina; ***we are running out of time*** il tempo sta per scadere

◆**run over I** *v/t* (*knock down*) investire; ***can we run over the details again?*** possiamo rivedere i particolari? **II** *v/i of water etc* traboccare

◆**run through** *v/t rehearse*, *go over* rivedere

◆**run up** *v/t sep debts*, *large bill* accumulare; *clothes* mettere insieme

runabout *n infml* utilitaria *f*

runaround *n*: ***give s.o. the ~*** *infml* inventare a qn un sacco di scuse

runaway *n* ragazzo *m*, -a *f* scappato di casa

run-down *adj person* debilitato; *part of town*, *building* fatiscente

rung[1] *n of ladder* piolo *m*

rung[2] *past part* → ***ring²***

run-in *n infml* battibecco *m*

runner *n athlete* velocista *m/f*

runner beans *npl* fagiolini *mpl*

runner-up *n* secondo *m*, -a *f* classificato, -a

running I *n* SPORTS corsa *f*; *of business* gestione *f*; ***be out of the ~*** essere fuori gara **II** *adj*: ***for two days ~*** per due giorni di seguito

running battle *n* lotta *f* continua **running costs** *npl* FIN costi *mpl* di gestione **running water** *n* acqua *f* corrente

runny *adj* (+*er*) *substance* liquido; *nose* che cola

run-of-the-mill *adj* banale **run-through** *n*: ***let's have a final ~*** facciamo una prova finale **run-up** *n* SPORTS rincorsa *f*; ***in the ~ to*** nel periodo che precede … **runway** *n* pista *f*

rupture I *n* rottura *f*; MED lacerazione *f*; (*hernia*) ernia *f* **II** *v/i of pipe etc* scoppiare

rural *adj* rurale

ruse *n* stratagemma *m*

rush[1] *n* BOT giunco *m*

rush[2] **I** *v/t person* mettere fretta *or* premura a; *meal* mangiare in fretta; ***~ s.o. to hospital / the airport*** portare qn di corsa all'ospedale / aeroporto **II** *v/i* affrettarsi **III** *n* corsa *f*; ***do sth in a ~*** fare qc di corsa; ***be in a ~*** andare di fretta; ***what's the big ~?*** che fretta c'è?; FILM ***~s*** prima stampa *f*

◆**rush into** *v/t* (*be too hasty*) buttarsi in

rush hour *n* ora *f* di punta; ***rush-hour traffic*** traffico *m* dell'ora di punta

rusk *n* fetta *f* biscottata

russet *n colour* color *m* ruggine; *apple* mela *f* ruggine

Russia *n* Russia *f*

Russian I *adj* russo **II** *n* russo *m*, -a *f*; *language* russo *m*

rust I *n* ruggine *f* **II** *v/i* arrugginirsi

rustic I *adj* rustico **II** *n liter* contadino *m*, -a *f*

rustle I *n of silk*, *leaves* fruscio *m* **II** *v/i of silk*, *leaves* frusciare

◆**rustle up** *v/t sep meal* improvvisare

rust-proof *adj* a prova di ruggine

rust remover *n* smacchiatore *m* per la ruggine

rusty *adj* (+*er*) *a. fig* arrugginito; ***I'm a little ~*** sono un po' arrugginito

rut *n in road* solco *m*; ZOOL calore *m*; *fig* ***be in a ~*** essersi fossilizzato

rutabaga *n US* rutabaga *f*

ruthless *adj* spietato

ruthlessly *adv* spietatamente

ruthlessness *n* spietatezza *f*

RV *abbr* (= **recreational vehicle**) camper *m inv*

Rwanda *n* Ruanda *m*

rye *n* segale *f*

rye bread *n* pane *m* di segale

S

S, s *n* s, S *f inv*

's I *abbr* (= **is / has** *infml* **does / us**): ***he's → he is / has***; ***what's → what is / has / does?***; ***let's → let us*** **II** *suf*: ***John's book*** il libro di John; ***my brother's car*** la macchina di mio fratello; ***at the butcher's*** dal macellaio

SA *abbr* (= **Salvation Army**) esercito *m* della salvezza

Sabbath *n* giorno *m* del Signore

sabbatical *n of academic* anno *m* sabbatico

SABC *abbr* (= **South African Broad-

casting Corporation) *emittente radiotelevisiva sudafricana*

sable I *n* zibellino *m* II *adj* di zibellino

sabotage I *n* sabotaggio *m* II *v/t* sabotare

saboteur *n* sabotatore *m*, -trice *f*

sabre, *US* **saber** *n* sciabola *f*

saccharin *n* saccarina *f*

sachet *n of shampoo, cream etc* bustina *f*

sack[1] I *n bag* sacco *m*; ***get the ~*** *infml* essere licenziato; ***2 ~s of coal*** 2 sacchi di carbone; *infml* ***hit the ~*** andarsene a letto; ***get s.o. in the ~*** *infml* portarsi a letto qn II *v/t infml* licenziare

sack[2] I *n* (*pillage*) saccheggio *m* II *v/t* saccheggiare

sackful *n quantity* sacco *m*; ***two ~s of potatoes*** due sacchi di patate

sacking *n* (*dismissal*) licenziamento *m*; *cloth* tela *f* da sacco

sacrament *n* sacramento *m*

sacred *adj* sacro

sacrifice I *n* sacrificio *m*; *fig* ***make ~s*** fare sacrifici II *v/t* sacrificare

sacrilege *n* sacrilegio *m*

sad *adj* (+*er*) triste; *state of affairs* deplorevole; (*pathetic*) penoso

SAD *abbr* (= **seasonal affective disorder**) MED disturbo *m* dell'umore ad andamento stagionale

sadden *v/t* rattristare

saddle I *n* sella *f* II *v/t horse* sellare; *fig* ***~ s.o. with sth*** affibbiare qc a qn; ***how did I get ~d with him?*** come ho fatto ad accollarmelo?

saddlebag *n* bisaccia *f*

sadism *n* sadismo *m*

sadist *n* sadico *m*, -a *f*

sadistic *adj* sadistico

sadly *adv* tristemente; (*regrettably*) purtroppo

sadness *n* tristezza *f*

SAE *abbr* (= **stamped addressed envelope**) busta *f* affrancata e con l'indirizzo per la risposta

safari *n* safari *m inv*; ***go on ~*** andare in safari

safari park *n* zoosafari *m inv*

safe I *adj* (+*er*) *not dangerous* sicuro; *not in danger* al sicuro; *driver* prudente; ***is it ~ to walk here?*** non è pericoloso camminare qui?; ***to be on the ~ side*** per sicurezza; ***~ and sound*** sano e salvo; ***better ~ than sorry*** meglio prevenire che curare II *n* cassaforte *f*

safe conduct *n* salvacondotto *m* **safe-deposit box** *n* cassetta *f* di sicurezza

safeguard I *n* protezione *f*, salvaguardia *f*; ***as a ~ against*** per proteggersi contro II *v/t* proteggere **safe house** *n* covo *m* **safe keeping** *n*: ***give sth to s.o. for ~*** dare qc in custodia a qn

safely *adv arrive, complete first test etc* senza problemi; *drive* prudentemente; *assume* tranquillamente; ***I think I can ~ say …*** penso di poter tranquillamente dire …; ***once the children are ~ tucked up in bed*** una volta che i bambini saranno al sicuro sotto le coperte

safe sex *n* sesso *m* sicuro

safety *n* sicurezza *f*

safety belt *n* cintura *f* di sicurezza **safety-conscious** *adj* attento ai problemi di sicurezza **safety first** *n* prudenza *f* **safety helmet** *n* casco *m* di protezione **safety match** *n* fiammifero *m* di sicurezza (*or* svedese) **safety net** *n* rete *f* di sicurezza **safety pin** *n* spilla *f* di sicurezza **safety razor** *n* rasoio *m* di sicurezza **safety valve** *n* valvola *f* di sicurezza

sag I *n in ceiling* incurvatura *f* II *v/i* ⟨*pret & past part* **-ged**⟩ *of ceiling* incurvarsi; *of rope* allentarsi; *in the middle* infossarsi; *shoulders* incurvarsi; *spirit* cedere

saga *n* saga *f*

sagacious *adj* sagace

sagacity *n* sagacia *f*

sage[1] I *adj* (*wise*) saggio II *n* saggio *m*

sage[2] *n* BOT salvia *f*

saggy *adj* (+*er*) *mattress* che si incurva; *bottom* floscio

Sagittarius *n* ASTROL Sagittario *m*

said *pret & past part* → ***say***

sail I *n of boat* vela *f*; *trip* veleggiata *f*; ***go for a ~*** fare un giro in barca (a vela); ***set ~*** (*depart*) salpare II *v/t yacht* pilotare III *v/i* fare vela; (*depart*) salpare; *fig* ***he ~s close to the wind*** si trova sul filo del rasoio; ***she ~ed past / out of the room*** passò davanti con grazia / uscì con grazia dalla stanza; ***she ~ed through all her exams*** passò facilmente tutti i suoi esami

◆**sail through** *v/t exam* passare senza

problemi
sailboard I *n* windsurf *m inv* **II** *v/i* fare windsurf **sailboarding** *n* windsurf *m inv* **sailboat** *n US* barca *f* a vela **sailcloth** *n* TEX tela *f* per vele
sailing *n* SPORTS vela *f*
sailing boat *n* barca *f* a vela **sailing ship** *n* veliero *m*
sailor *n* marinaio *m*; ***be a bad / good ~*** soffrire / non soffrire il mal di mare
saint *n* santo *m*, -a *f*; ***St John*** San Giovanni; ***St Mark's*** (***Church***) San Marco (Chiesa di)
saintly *adj* (*+er*) da santo; *fig pej* da santarello
sake *n*: ***for my / your ~*** per il mio / il tuo bene; ***for the ~ of*** per; ***for the ~ of peace*** per amor di pace
salad *n* insalata *f*
salad bar *n* buffet *m inv* delle insalate **salad bowl** *n* insalatiera *f* **salad cream** *n salsa per condire l'insalata* **salad days** *n* anni *mpl* verdi **salad dressing** *n* condimento *m* per l'insalata
salary *n* stipendio *m*
salary scale *n* scala *f* salariale
sale *n* vendita *f*; *at reduced prices* svendita *f*, saldi *mpl*; **for ~** *sign* in vendita; **be on ~** essere in vendita
sales *npl department* reparto *m* vendite
sales assistant, sales clerk *n US in shop* commesso *m*, -a *f* **sales figures** *npl* fatturato *m* **salesman** *n* venditore *m* **sales manager** *n* direttore *m*, -trice *f* delle vendite **sales meeting** *n* riunione *f* marketing e vendite **sales pitch** *n* discorso *m* da imbonitore **sales rep** *n infml*, **sales representative** *n* agente *f* di commercio **sales tax** *n US* tassa *f* sulle vendite **sales woman** *n* venditrice *f*
salient *adj* saliente
saline I *n* soluzione *f* salina **II** *adj* salino
saliva *n* saliva *f*
salivate *v/i* salivare
sallow *adj colour* giallastro
salmon *n* ⟨*pl* **salmon**⟩ salmone *m*
salmonella *n* salmonella *f*
salon *n* salone *m*
saloon *n* AUTO berlina *f*; *US*: *bar* bar *m inv*
salsa *n* (*dip*) salsina *f* piccante; (*dance*) salsa *f*
salt I *n* sale *m*; *fig* ***take sth with a pinch of ~*** prendere qc con qualche riserva; *fig* ***rub ~ into the wound*** mettere il dito nella piaga **II** *v/t food* salare
saltcellar *n* saliera *f* **salt water** *n* acqua *f* salata **salt-water fish** *n* pesce *m* di mare
salty *adj* (*+er*) salato
salutary *adj experience* salutare
salute I *n* MIL saluto *m*; ***take the ~*** ricevere i saluti **II** *v/t & v/i* salutare
salvage *v/t from wreck* ricuperare
salvation *n* salvezza *f*
Salvation Army *n* Esercito *m* della Salvezza
salve *n* balsamo *m*
SAM *abbr* (= **surface-to-air missile**) missile *m* terra-aria
Samaritan *n* samaritano *m*, -a *f*; ***the Good ~*** il buon Samaritano
same I *adj* stesso **II** *pron* stesso; ***the ~*** lo stesso, la stessa; ***Happy New Year – the ~ to you*** Buon anno! – Grazie e altrettanto!; ***he's not the ~ any more*** non è più lo stesso; ***all the ~*** (*even so*) eppure; ***men are all the ~*** gli uomini sono tutti uguali; ***it's all the ~ to me*** per me è uguale **III** *adv*: ***the ~*** allo stesso modo; ***I still feel the ~ about that*** la penso sempre allo stesso modo
same-day *adj delivery* in giornata
same-sex *adj marriage*, *relationship* tra persone dello stesso sesso
sample I *n of cloth*, *food*, *etc* campione *m* **II** *v/t food*, *product* provare
sanatorium *n* casa *f* di cura
sanctify *v/t* ⟨*pret & past part* ***-ied***⟩ santificare
sanctimonious *adj* moraleggiante
sanction I *n* (*approval*) approvazione *f*; (*penalty*) sanzione *f* **II** *v/t* (*approve*) sancire
sanctity *n* santità *f*
sanctuary *n* REL santuario *m*; *for wild animals* riserva *f*
sand I *n* sabbia *f* **II** *v/t with sandpaper* smerigliare
sandal *n* sandalo *m*
sandbag *n* sacchetto *m* di sabbia **sandbank** *n* banco *m* di sabbia **sandblast** *v/t* sabbiare **sandbox** *n US grande vasca piena di sabbia per far*

giocare i bambini **sandcastle** *n* castello *m* di sabbia **sand dune** *n* duna *f*
sander *n tool* smerigliatrice *f*
sandpaper I *n* carta *f* smerigliata **II** *v/t* smerigliare **sandpit** *n Br grande vasca piena di sabbia per far giocare i bambini* **sandstone** *n* arenaria *f*
sandwich I *n* tramezzino *m* **II** *v/t*: ***be ~ed between two ...*** essere incastrato tra due ...
sandy *adj* (+*er*) *beach* sabbioso; *full of sand* pieno di sabbia; *hair* rossiccio
sane *adj* (+*er*) sano di mente
sang *pret* → ***sing***
sanguine *adj* ottimista
sanitary *adj conditions* igienico; *installations* sanitario
sanitary towel *n* assorbente *m* (igienico)
sanitation *n* (*sanitary installations*) impianti *mpl* igienici; (*removal of waste*) fognature *fpl*
sanity *n* sanità *f inv* mentale
sank *pret* → ***sink***
Santa Claus *n* Babbo *m* Natale
sap I *n in tree* linfa *f* **II** *v/t* ⟨*pret & past part* **-ped**⟩ *s.o.'s energy* indebolire
sapling *n* albero *m* giovane
sapphire *n jewel* zaffiro *m*
sappy *n US infml* (*sentimental*) melenso
sarcasm *n* sarcasmo *m*
sarcastic *adj* sarcastico
sarcastically *adv* sarcasticamente
sardine *n* sardina *f*; ***packed* (*in*) *like ~s*** pigiati come sardine in scatola
Sardinia *n* Sardegna *f*
Sardinian I *adj* sardo **II** *n* sardo *m*, -a *f*
sardonic *adj* sardonico
sardonically *adv* sardonicamente
sari *n* SEW sari *m*
sarnie *n Br infml* sandwich *m*
sarong *n* SEW sarong *m*
SARS *abbr* (= **severe acute respiratory syndrome**) MED SARS (sindrome respiratoria acuta grave)
SASE *n abbr* (= **self-addressed stamped envelope**) *US* busta preindirizzata e affrancata
sash *n on dress* fusciacca *f*; *on uniform* fascia *f*; *on window* vetro *m* scorrevole (di finestra a ghigliottina)
sashay *v/i US infml* camminare con disinvoltura
sash window *n* finestra *f* a ghigliottina
sass *n US infml* sfacciataggine *f*
sassy *adj US infml* sfacciato
sat *pret & past part* → ***sit***
Sat *abbr* (= **Saturday**) sabato
Satan *n* Satana *m*
satanic *adj* satanico
satchel *n for schoolchild* cartella *f*
satellite *n* satellite *m*
satellite dish *n* antenna *f* parabolica **satellite town** *n* città *f* satellite **satellite TV** *n* TV *f inv* satellitare
satiate *v/t appetite etc* soddisfare; *person* saziare
satin *adj* satin *m inv*
satire *n* satira *f*
satirical *adj* satirico
satirise, satirize *v/t* satireggiare
satirist *n* satirista *m*
satisfaction *n* soddisfazione *f*; ***I get ~ out of my job*** il lavoro mi dà molte soddisfazioni; ***is that to your ~?*** è di suo gradimento?; ***she would not give him the ~ of seeing how annoyed she was*** non gli dava la soddisfazione di mostrargli quanto le dava fastidio; COMM ***customer ~*** soddisfazione del cliente
satisfactory *adj* soddisfacente; *just good enough* sufficiente; ***this is not ~*** non è sufficiente
satisfy *v/t* ⟨*pret & past part* **-ied**⟩ *customers, needs, curiosity* soddisfare; *requirement* rispondere a; ***~ s.o.'s hunger*** sfamare qn; ***I am satisfied*** *had enough to eat* sono sazio; ***I am satisfied that ...*** (*convinced*) sono convinto che ...; ***I hope you're satisfied!*** sei contento?
saturate *v/t* (*drench*) impregnare; *market* saturare; ***be ~d with*** essere impregnato di
saturation *n* saturazione *f*; ***reach ~ point*** giungere al punto di saturazione
Saturday *n* sabato *m*
Saturn *n* SPACE, MYTH Saturno *m*
saturnine *adj* saturnino
sauce *n* salsa *f*, sugo *m*
sauce boat *n* salsiera *f*
saucebox *n infml* impertinente *m/f*
saucepan *n* pentolino *m*
saucer *n* piattino *m*
saucy *adj* (+*er*) *person, dress* provo-

cante; (*cheeky*) sfacciato
Saudi Arabia *n* Arabia *f* Saudita
Saudi Arabian I *adj* saudita **II** *n person* saudita *m/f*
sauna *n* sauna *f*
saunter *v/i* passeggiare; ***he ~ed in at 10.30*** è arrivato tranquillamente alle 10.30
sausage *n* salsiccia *f*; ***not a ~*** *Br infml* un bel niente
sausage dog *n Br infml* bassotto *m*
sausage meat *n* carne *f* tritata per salsicce **sausage roll** *n* pasta *f* salata farcita di wurstel
savage I *adj animal* selvaggio; *attack, criticism* feroce **II** *n* selvaggio *m*, -a *f*
savagery *n* ferocia *f*
save I *v/t* (*rescue*) salvare; *money, time, effort* risparmiare; (*collect*) raccogliere; COMPUT salvare; *goal* parare; ***~ the day*** salvare la situazione; ***~ one's neck*** *infml* salvare la pelle; ***he ~d me from falling*** mi ha impedito di cadere; ***you could ~ yourself a lot of effort*** potresti risparmiarti parecchi sforzi; ***~ as*** COMPUT salva con nome **II** *v/i* (*put money aside*) risparmiare; SPORTS parare **III** *n* SPORTS parata *f*; ***what a ~!*** che parata!
◆**save up for** *v/t* risparmiare per
saver *n person* risparmiatore *m*, -trice *f*
saving *n* risparmio *m*
savings *npl* risparmi *mpl*
savings account *n* libretto *m* di risparmio **savings and loan** *n US* → ***building society*** **savings bank** *n* cassa *f* di risparmio
saviour, *US* **savior** *n* REL salvatore *m*
savor *etc US* → ***savour*** *etc*
savour, *US* **savor I** *n* sapore *m* **II** *v/t* assaporare
savoury, *US* **savory** *adj not sweet* salato (*non dolce*)
saw¹ I *n tool* sega *f* **II** *v/t* segare
◆**saw off** *v/t sep* segare via
saw² *pret* → ***see***
sawdust *n* segatura *f* **sawmill** *n* segheria *f*
Saxon I *n* sassone *m/f*; HIST sassone *m/f* **II** *adj* sassone; HIST sassone
Saxony *n* Sassonia *f*
saxophone *n* sassofono *m*
say I *v/t* ⟨*pret & past part* **said**⟩ dire; ***can I ~ something?*** posso dire una cosa?; ***that is to ~*** sarebbe a dire; ***what do you ~ to that?*** cosa ne dici?; ***what does the note ~?*** cosa dice il biglietto?; ***that ~s a lot about his state of mind*** la dice lunga sul suo stato d'animo; ***that's not ~ing much*** non dice granché; ***there's no ~ing what might happen*** non si può sapere cosa succederà; ***~ a prayer*** pregare; ***if I save, ~, £20 a month*** se metto da parte, diciamo, 20 sterline al mese; ***you don't ~*** *used sarcastically*: non mi dire; ***~, what a great idea!*** *esp US* ehi, ma è un'idea grandiose!; ***I should ~ so!*** direi proprio di sì!; ***you said it!*** l'hai detto!; ***you can ~ that again!*** puoi dirlo forte!; ***~ no more!*** non aggiungere altro; ***~s you!*** *infml* lo dici tu!; ***~s who?*** *infml* e chi lo dice? **II** *n*: ***have one's ~*** dire la propria; ***have a ~ in sth*** avere voce in capitolo in qc
saying *n* detto *m*; ***as the ~ goes*** come dice il proverbio
scab *n on skin* crosta *f*
scaffold *n on building* impalcatura *f*; *for execution* forca *f*
scaffolding *n on building* impalcature *fpl*
scalawag *n US* → ***scallywag***
scald *v/t* scottare; ***~ o.s.*** scottarsi
scale¹ *n on fish* scaglia *f*
scale² I *n of map*, MUS scala *f*; *on thermometer* scala *f* graduata; *of project* portata *f*; ***drawn to ~*** disegnato in scala; ***on a large ~*** su vasta scala; ***on a small ~*** su scala ridotta **II** *v/t cliffs etc* scalare
◆**scale down** *v/t sep* ridurre
scale drawing *n* disegno *m* in scala
scales *npl for weighing* bilancia *fsg*
scallion *n US* → ***spring onion***
scallop *n* capasanta *f*
scallywag *n Br infml* birbante *m/f*
scalp I *v/t* togliere lo scalpo; *US infml* fare bagarinaggio di **II** *n* cuoio *m* capelluto
scalpel *n* bisturi *m*
scaly *adj* (*+er*) squamoso
scam *n infml* truffa *f*
scamp *n infml* birbante *m/f*
scamper *v/i* sgambettare
scampi *npl gamberoni in pastella fritti*
scan I *v/t* ⟨*pret & past part* **-ned**⟩ *horizon* scrutare; *page* scorrere; *foetus*

fare l'ecografia di; *brain* fare la TAC di; COMPUT scannerizzare **II** *n* (*brain scan*) TAC *f inv*; *of foetus* ecografia *f*
◆ **scan in** *v/t sep* COMPUT scannerizzare
scandal *n* scandalo *m*
scandalize *v/t* scandalizzare
scandalous *adj* scandaloso
Scandinavia *n* Scandinavia *f*
scanner *n* scanner *m inv*
scant *adj* (+*er*) scarso; ***pay ~ attention to sth*** fare poca attenzione a qc
scantily *adv*: ***~ clad*** succintamente vestito
scanty *adj* (+*er*) *clothes* succinto
scapegoat *n* capro *m* espiatorio
scar I *n* cicatrice *f* **II** *v/t* ⟨*pret & past part* ***-red***⟩ *face* lasciare cicatrici su; *fig* segnare; ***he was ~red for life*** *liter* gli è rimasta una cicatrice permanente; *fig* è stato segnato per tutta la vita
scarce *adj* (+*er*) *in short supply* scarso; ***make o.s. ~*** squagliarsela *infml*
scarcely *adv* appena; ***there was ~ anything left*** non rimaneva quasi più niente; ***I ~ know what to say*** so a malapena cosa dire
scarcity *n* scarsità *f inv*
scare I *v/t* spaventare; ***be ~d of*** avere paura di; ***be ~d stiff*** essere morto di paura **II** *n* (*panic*, *alarm*) panico *m*; ***give s.o. a ~*** mettere paura a qn; ***a bomb ~*** un allarme bomba
◆ **scare away** *v/t sep* far scappare
scarecrow *n* spaventapasseri *m inv*
scaremonger *n* allarmista *m*/*f*
scarf *n* ⟨*pl* ***scarves***⟩ *around neck* sciarpa *f*; *over head* foulard *m inv*
scarlet *adj* scarlatto; ***go ~*** diventare rosso come un peperone
scarlet fever *n* scarlattina *f*
scar tissue *n* tessuto *m* cicatriziale
scary *adj* (+*er*) che fa paura; *film* dell'orrore; ***it was pretty ~*** faceva abbastanza paura; ***that's a ~ thought*** è un pensiero terribile
scathing *adj* caustico
scatter I *v/t leaflets*, *seeds* spargere; *crowd* disperdere **II** *v/i of people* disperdersi
scatterbrained *adj* sventato
scattered *adj family*, *villages* sparpagliato; ***~ showers*** precipitazioni sparse
scatty *adj* sventato
scavenge *v/i* frugare tra i rifiuti
scavenger *n animal* animale *m* necrofago; (*person*) *persona che fruga tra i rifiuti*
scenario *n* scenario *m*
scene *n* **1.** scena *f*; ***be on the ~*** essere sul posto; ***the ~ of the crime*** la scena del delitto; ***set the ~*** creare la scena; ***a change of ~ will do you good*** cambiare aria ti farà bene **2.** (*argument*) scenata *f*; ***make a ~*** fare una scenata **3.** ***~s*** THEAT scenografia *f*; ***behind the ~s*** dietro le quinte **4.** ***jazz/rock ~*** il mondo del jazz/rock; ***the drug ~*** il mondo della droga; ***that's not my ~*** non è il mio genere
scenery *n* paesaggio *m*; THEAT scenario *m*
scenic *adj* panoramico
scent *n of roses* profumo *m*; *of animal* odore *m*
sceptic, *US* **skeptic** *n* scettico *m*, -a *f*
sceptical, *US* **skeptical** *adj* scettico
sceptically, *US* **skeptically** *adv* scetticamente
scepticism, *US* **skepticism** *n* scetticismo *m*
sceptre, *US* **scepter** *n* scettro *m*
schedule I *n of events*, *work* programma *m*; *for trains* orario *m*; ***be on ~*** *of work*, *of train etc* essere in orario; ***be behind ~*** *of work*, *of train etc* essere in ritardo; ***be three months ahead of ~*** essere in anticipo di tre mesi sul programma **II** *v/t put on schedule* programmare; ***it's ~d for completion next month*** il completamento dei lavori è previsto per il mese prossimo
scheduled flight *n* volo *m* di linea
schematic *adj* schematico
schematically *adv* schematicamente
scheme I *n* (*plan*) piano *m*; (*plot*) complotto *m* **II** *v/i* (*plot*) complottare, tramare
scheming *adj* intrigante
schizophrenia *n* schizofrenia *f*
schizophrenic I *n* schizofrenico *m*, -a *f* **II** *adj* schizofrenico
schmaltzy *adj infml* (*overly sentimental*) sdolcinato
scholar *n* studioso *m*, -a *f*
scholarly *adj* dotto
scholarship *n* (*scholarly work*) erudizione *f*; (*financial award*) borsa *f* di studio
school[1] **I** *n* scuola *f*; *US* UNIV diparti-

mento *m*; *US of medicine*, *law* facoltà *f*; ***at ~*** a scuola; ***go to ~*** andare a scuola **II** *v/t horse* addestrare
school[2] *n of fish* branco *m*
school age *n* età *f inv* scolare; ***be of ~*** essere in età scolare **school bag** *n* (*satchel*) cartella *f* **schoolboy** *n* scolaro *m* **school bus** *n* pulmino *m* della scuola **schoolchildren** *npl* scolari *mpl* **school days** *npl* tempi *mpl* della scuola **schoolgirl** *n* scolara *f* **school-leaver** *n* neodiplomato *m*, -a *f* **schoolmaster** *n* maestro *m* **schoolmate** *n* compagno *m*, -a *f* di scuola **schoolmistress** *n* maestra *f* **schoolteacher** *n* insegnante *m/f* **school uniform** *n* uniforme *f* scolastica **schoolwork** *n at home* compiti *mpl* a casa; *in class* lavoro *m* scolastico
sciatica *n* sciatica *f*
science *n* scienza *f*
science fiction *n* fantascienza *f*
scientific *adj* scientifico
scientist *n* scienziato *m*, -a *f*
sci-fi *n infml* fantascienza *f*
scintillating *adj fig performance* strepitoso; *person*, *speech* brillante
scion *n* rampollo *m*
scissors *npl* forbici *fpl*
scoff[1] *v/t food* sbafare
scoff[2] *v/i* (*mock*) canzonare
◆**scoff at** *v/t* deridere
scold *v/t* sgridare
scolding *n* rimprovero *m*; (*act*) sgridata *f*; ***he gave the boy a good ~*** fece una bella sgridata al ragazzo
scone *n focaccina o dolcetto da mangiare con il tè*
scoop I *n for grain*, *flour* paletta *f*; *for ice cream* cucchiaio *m* dosatore; *of ice cream* pallina *f*; (*story*) scoop *m inv* **II** *v/t* (*pick up*) raccogliere
◆**scoop out** *v/t sep*: ***scoop out the flesh of sth*** togliere la polpa di qc; ***scoop out an avocado*** scavare un avocado
◆**scoop up** *v/t sep* sollevare tra le braccia
scooter *n with motor* scooter *m inv*; *child's* monopattino *m*
scope *n* portata *f*; (*opportunity*) possibilità *f inv*; ***~ for*** possibilità di; ***there is ~ for further growth in the tourist industry*** esiste l'opportunità di una crescita ulteriore nel settore del turismo; ***be within / beyond the ~ of*** rientrare / non rientrare nell'ambito di
scorch *v/t* bruciare
scorched earth policy *n* MIL tattica *f* della terra bruciata
scorcher *n infml* inferno *m infml*
scorching hot *adj* torrido
score I *n* **1.** SPORTS punteggio *m*; ***what's the ~?*** SPORTS a quanto sono / siamo?; ***keep (the) ~*** tenere il punteggio; *fig* ***have a ~ to settle with s.o.*** avere un conto in sospeso con qn; *fig* ***know the ~*** sapere come funziona **2.** (*written music*) spartito *m* **3.** *of film etc* colonna *f* sonora **4.** (*reason*) ***on that ~*** in merito **5.** ***~s of*** moltissimi **II** *v/t* **1.** *goal*, *point* segnare **2.** (*cut*) incidere **3.** MUS spartito *m* **III** *v/i* **1.** segnare; (*keep the score*) tenere il punteggio **2.** *infml drugs* ottenere una dose **3.** *infml* (*seduce*) fare colpo
scoreboard *n* segnapunti *m inv* **scorecard** *n* (scheda *f*) segnapunti *m*
scorer *n of goal*, *point* marcatore *m*, -trice *f*; (*score-keeper*) segnapunti *m/f inv*
scorn I *n* disprezzo *m*; ***pour ~ on sth*** deridere qc **II** *v/t idea*, *suggestion* disprezzare
scornful *adj* sprezzante
scornfully *adv* sprezzantemente
Scorpio *n* ASTROL Scorpione *m*
scorpion *n* scorpione *m*
Scot *n* scozzese *m/f*
Scotch *n* (*whisky*) scotch *m inv*
Scotch egg *n* COOK *uovo sodo ricoperto da un carne trita e pane e fritto* **Scotch tape®** *n US* scotch® *m*
scot-free *adv*: ***get off ~*** farla franca
Scotland *n* Scozia *f*
Scotsman *n* scozzese *m*
Scotswoman *n* scozzese *f*
Scottish *adj* scozzese
scoundrel *n* birbante *m/f*
scour[1] *v/t* (*search*) setacciare
scour[2] *v/t pans* sfregare
scourer *n* paglietta *f* metallica
scourge *n* frusta *f*
Scouse I *adj* di Liverpool **II** *n* (*person*) abitante *m/f* di Liverpool; (*dialect*) dialetto *m* di Liverpool
scout I *n* (*boy scout*) boy-scout *m inv*; (*talent scout*) talent scout *m/f inv*; ***have a ~ (a)round for sth*** andare in ricognizione in cerca di qc **II** *v/i*

andare in perlustrazione; **~ for sth** essere alla ricerca di qc **III** *v/t area, country* perlustrare
◆**scout around for** *v/t* cercare
scowl I *n* sguardo *m* torvo **II** *v/i* guardare storto
scrabble *v/i* (*a.* **scrabble about** *Br or* **around**) rovistare; **~ for a hold** cercare un appiglio
scraggly *adj* (+*er*) *beard, hair* incolto
scraggy *adj* (+*er*) (*scrawny*) smunto
scram *v/i* ⟨*pret & past part* **-med**⟩ *infml* filare *infml*
scramble I *n* (*rush*) corsa *f* **II** *v/t message* rendere indecifrabile **III** *v/i climb* inerpicarsi; **he ~d to his feet** si rialzò in fretta
scrambled eggs *npl* uova *fpl* strapazzate
scrap I *n metal* rottame *m*; (*fight*) zuffa *f*; (*little bit*) briciolo *m*; **there isn't a ~ of food** non c'è una briciola di cibo; **a few ~s of information** qualche informazione frammetaria; **not a ~ of evidence** neanche uno straccio di prova **II** *v/t* ⟨*pret & past part* **-ped**⟩ *car* demolire; *plan, project* abbandonare
scrapbook *n* album *m inv*
scrape I *n on paintwork* graffio *m*; *predicament* guai *mpl*; **they got into some terrible ~s at school** si sono messi in brutti guai a scuola **II** *v/t paintwork, one's arm etc* graffiare; *vegetables* raschiare; **~ a living** sbarcare il lunario
◆**scrape by** *v/i with little money* tirare avanti
◆**scrape off** *v/t sep* scrostare
◆**scrape through** *v/i in exam* passare per il rotto della cuffia
◆**scrape together** *v/t sep money* raggranellare
scrap heap *n* cumulo *m* di rottami; **good for the ~** da buttare via **scrap metal** *n* rottami *mpl* **scrap paper** *n* carta *f* già usata
scrappy *adj* (+*er*) *work, writing* senza capo né coda
scrapyard *n* deposito *m* di rottami
scratch I *n mark* graffio *m*; **have a ~** *to stop itching* grattarsi; **start from ~** ricominciare da zero; **not up to ~** non all'altezza **II** *v/t* (*mark*) graffiare; *because of itch* grattare; **~ the surface of sth** *fig* sfiorare appena qc **III** *v/i of cat, nails* graffiare
scratchcard *n* gratta e vinci *m inv*
scratchpad *n* COMPUT foglio *m* per appunti
scratch paper *n US* carta *f* per appunti
scratchy *adj* (+*er*) ruvido
scrawl I *n* scarabocchio *m* **II** *v/t* scarabocchiare
scrawny *adj* (+*er*) scheletrico
scream I *n* urlo *m*; **~s of laughter** risate *fpl* fragorose; **be a ~** *infml* essere uno spasso *infml* **II** *v/i* urlare **III** *v/t* urlare; **~ sth at s.o.** gridare qc a qn; **~ one's head off** *infml* urlare a squarciagola
screech I *v/i of tyres* stridere; (*scream*) strillare **II** *n of tyres* stridio *m*; (*scream*) strillo *m*; **~ with laughter** ridere fragorosamente; **~ with delight** gridare per la gioia **III** *v/t* gridare; *high notes* dire con voce stridula
screech owl *n* ZOOL barbagianni *m*
screed *n writing* composizione *f* lunga e noiosa; *in building* guida *f* per l'intonaco
screen I *n in room, hospital* paravento *m*; *of smoke* cortina *f*; *cinema*, COMPUT, *of television* schermo *m*; **on the ~** *in film* sullo schermo; **on (the) ~** COMPUT su schermo **II** *v/t* (*protect, hide*) riparare; *film* proiettare; *for security reasons* vagliare; *for an illness* sottoporre a test diagnostici
screenplay *n* sceneggiatura *f* **screen printing** *n* serigrafia *f* **screen saver** *n* COMPUT salvaschermo *m inv* **screen test** *n for film* provino *m* **screenwriter** *n* sceneggiatore *m*, -trice *f*
screw I *n* vite *f* (metallica); **he's got a ~ loose** *infml* è un po' svitato; **put** *or* **turn** *or* **tighten the ~s on s.o.** *infml* aumentare la pressione su qn; *prison infml* guardia *f* carceraria; *vulg* (*sex*) scopata *f vulg* **II** *v/t*: **~ sth to sth** avvitare qc a qc; **she ~ed her handkerchief into a ball** ha appallottolato il suo fazzoletto; *vulg* scopare *vulg*; **~ you!** *sl* vaffanculo!; *infml* (*cheat*) fregare *infml*
◆**screw down** *v/t sep* avvitare
◆**screw in I** *v/t sep* avvitare (**to** a) **II** *v/i* avvitarsi (**to** a)
◆**screw off I** *v/t sep* svitare **II** *v/i* svi-

tarsi

◆**screw on I** *v/t sep* avvitare; ***screw sth on(to) sth*** avvitare qc su qc; *lid, top* serrare **II** *v/i* avvitarsi

◆**screw together I** *v/t sep* avvitare insieme; ***he screwed them together*** li ha fissati con delle viti **II** *v/i* avvitarsi

◆**screw up I** *v/t sep eyes* strizzare; *piece of paper* appallottolare; *infml* (*make a mess of*) mandare all'aria **II** *v/i infml* (*make a bad mistake*) fare un casino *infml*

screwdriver *n* cacciavite *m*

screwed up *adj infml psychologically* complessato

screw top *n on bottle* tappo *m* a vite

screwy *adj infml* svitato

scribble I *n* scarabocchio *m* **II** *v/t & v/i* (*write quickly*) scarabocchiare

scrimp *v/i*: ***~ and scrape*** risparmiare fino all'ultimo soldo

script *n for film, play* copione *m*; (*form of writing*) scrittura *f*

scripture *n* testo *m* sacro; ***the (Holy) Scriptures*** le Sacre Scritture *fpl*

scriptwriter *n* sceneggiatore *m*, -trice *f*

scroll *n* rotolo *m* di pergamena

◆**scroll down** *v/i* COMPUT far scorrere il testo in avanti

◆**scroll up** *v/i* COMPUT far scorrere il testo indietro

scroll bar *n* COMPUT barra *f* di scorrimento

Scrooge *n* spilorcio *m*, -a *f*

scrotum *n* scroto *m*

scrounge *v/t* scroccare

scrounger *n* scroccone *m*, -a *f*

scrub[1] *n* (*scrubland*) sterpaglia *f*

scrub[2] *v/t* ⟨*pret & past part* **-bed**⟩ *floors, hands* sfregare (con spazzola)

scrubbing brush *n for floor* spazzolone *m*

scruff[1] *n*: ***by the ~ of the neck*** per la collottola

scruff[2] *n infml* (*scruffy person*) persona *f* trasandata

scruffy *adj* (*+er*) trasandato

scrum *n of reporters etc, in rugby* mischia *f*

scrumptious *adj* delizioso

◆**scrunch up** *v/t plastic cup etc* accartocciare

scruples *npl* scrupoli *mpl*; ***have no ~ about doing sth*** non avere scrupoli a fare qc

scrupulous *adj* scrupoloso; ***he is not too ~ in his business dealings*** non è molto scrupoloso nei suoi affari

scrupulously *adv* (*meticulously*) scrupolosamente

scrutinise, scrutinize *v/t text* esaminare attentamente; *face* scrutare

scrutiny *n* attento esame *m*; ***come under ~*** essere sottoposto ad attento esame

scuba diving *n* immersione *f* subacquea

scuffle *n* tafferuglio *m*

sculpt *v/t* scolpire

sculptor *n* scultore *m*, -trice *f*

sculpture *n* scultura *f*

scum *n on liquid* schiuma *f*; (*pej: people*) feccia *f*; ***the ~ of the earth*** la feccia della società

scumbag *n infml* stronzo *m*

scupper I *v/t Br* (*ruin*) mandare a picco **II** *n* NAUT ombrinale *m*

scurf *n on the head* forfora *f*; *on the skin* squama *f*

scurrilous *adj* scurrile

scurry *v/i* ⟨*pret & past part* **-ied**⟩ (*move quickly*) schizzare

scurvy I *n* MED scorbuto *m* **II** *adj* spregevole

scuttle[1] *v/i* (*hurry*) correre

scuttle[2] *v/t* NAUT oblò *m*

scythe *n* falce *f*

SDP *abbr* (= **Social Democratic Party**) POL partito *m* socialdemocratico

SE *abbr* (= **southeast, southeastern**) sud-est (SE)

sea *n* mare *m*; ***by the ~*** al mare; ***by ~*** per mare; *fig* ***be all at ~*** essere in alto mare (***with*** con); *infml confused* sentirsi confuso

sea anemone *n* anemone *f* di mare **seabed** *n* fondale *m* marino **seabird** *n* uccello *m* marino **seaboard** *n US* litorale *m* **sea change** *n* inversione *f* di rotta **sea dog** *n* lupo *m* di mare **seafaring** *adj nation* marinaro **seafood** *n* frutti *mpl* di mare **seafront** *n* lungomare *m inv* **seagoing** *adj vessel* d'alto mare **seagull** *n* gabbiano *m* **seahorse** *n* cavalluccio *m* marino

seal[1] *n animal* foca *f*

seal[2] **I** *n on document* sigillo *m*; TECH chiusura *f* ermetica **II** *v/t container* chiudere ermeticamente; *envelope* sigillare; ***my lips are ~ed*** sarò una tomba

◆**seal off** *v/t sep area* bloccare l'accesso a

sea level *n*: ***above / below ~*** sopra / sotto il livello del mare **sea lion** *n* leone *m* marino

seam *n on garment* cucitura *f*; ***come apart at the ~s*** scucirsi; *fig* andare in frantumi; ***be bursting at the ~s*** essere pieno zeppo; *of ore* filone *m*

seaman *n* marinaio *m*

seamstress *n* sarta *f*

seamy *adj* (+*er*) *club*, *past* squallido; *person* sgradevole; *area*, malfamato

séance *n* seduta *f* spiritica

seaport *n* porto *m* marittimo **sea power** *n nation* potenza *f* marittima

sear *v/t & v/i* appassire; *fig* inaridire

search I *n for s.o. / sth* ricerca *f*; *of person*, *building* perquisizione *f*; ***in ~ of*** alla ricerca di **II** *v/t person*, *building*, *baggage* perquisire; *area* perlustrare

◆**search for** *v/t* cercare

search engine *n* COMPUT motore *m* di ricerca

searching *adj look* penetrante

searchlight *n* riflettore *m* **search party** *n* squadra *f* di ricerca **search warrant** *n* mandato *m* di perquisizione

seashell *n* conchiglia *f* **seashore** *n* riva *f* (del mare) **seasick** *adj* con il mal di mare; ***be ~*** avere il mal di mare; ***get ~*** soffrire il mal di mare **seaside** *n*: ***at the ~*** al mare; ***go to the ~*** andare al mare; ***~ resort*** località *f* balneare

season I *n* stagione *f*; ***in / out of ~*** in / fuori stagione; ***rainy ~*** stagione *f* delle pioggie; ***hunting ~*** stagione della caccia; ***their bitch is in ~*** la loro cagna è in calore; ***the ~ of good will*** il Natale *m*; ***"Season's greetings"*** buone feste *fpl*; ***a ~ of Dustin Hoffman films*** una rassegna di film con Dustin Hoffman **II** *v/t food* condire

seasonal *adj* stagionale; ***~ fruit*** frutta *f* di stagione

seasoned *adj wood* stagionato; *food* condito; *traveller*, *campaigner etc* esperto

seasoning *n* COOK condimento *m*

season ticket *n* RAIL, THEAT abbonamento *m*

seat I *n* posto *m*; *of trousers* fondo *m*; POL seggio *m*; AUTO sedile *m*; ***~ of learning ~*** sede di studi; ***of the government*** sede de governo; ***please take a ~*** si accomodi; ***will you keep my ~ for me?*** mi tieni il posto? **II** *v/t* (*have seating for*) avere posti a sedere per; ***the table / sofa ~s 4*** il tavolo / divano è per 4; ***please remain ~ed*** state seduti, per favore

seat belt *n* cintura *f* di sicurezza; ***fasten one's ~*** allacciare la cintura di sicurezza

sea urchin *n* riccio *m* di mare **seaweed** *n* alga *f* **seaworthy** *adj* in condizioni di navigare

sec *abbr* (= **second**) secondo *m*; ***wait a ~*** *infml* aspetta un attimo

secede *v/t form*: ***~ from*** separarsi da

secluded *adj* appartato

seclusion *n* isolamento *m*

second[1] **I** *n of time* secondo *m*; ***just a ~*** un attimo; AUTO ***~ (gear)*** seconda *f* (marcia) **II** *adj* secondo; ***in ~ place*** SPORTS *etc* al secondo posto; ***be ~ in command*** MIL essere il secondo al comando; ***~ time around*** secondo tentativo; ***you won't get a ~ chance*** non avrai una seconda possibilità **III** *adv come in* secondo **IV** *v/t motion* appoggiare

second[2] *v/t*: ***be ~ed to*** essere assegnato a

secondary *adj* secondario

secondary education *n* istruzione *f* secondaria

second best *adj* secondo (dopo il migliore) **second biggest** *adj* secondo in ordine di grandezza **second class** *adj ticket* di seconda classe **second floor** *n* secondo piano *m*; *US* primo piano *m* **second gear** *n* AUTO seconda *f* (marcia) **second-guess** *v/t*: ***~ s.o.*** anticipare le mosse di qn; *US* rivalutare qn **second hand** *n on clock* lancetta *f* dei secondi **second-hand** *adj/adv* di seconda mano; ***a ~ bookshop*** un negozio di libri usati

secondly *adv* in secondo luogo

second-rate *adj* di second'ordine **second thoughts** *npl*: ***I've had ~*** ci ho ripensato

secrecy *n* segretezza *f*

secret I *n* segreto *m*; ***do sth in ~*** fare qc in segreto; ***tell s.o. a ~*** raccontare un segreto a qn; ***can you keep a ~?*** sai mantenere un segreto? **II** *adj* se-

greto; ***keep sth ~*** tenere segreto qc
secret agent *n* agente *m* segreto
secretaire *n* secretaire *m inv*
secretarial *adj tasks*, *job* di segretaria
secretariat *n* segretariato *m*
secretary *n* segretario *m*, -a *f*; POL ministro *m*
secretary general *n* ⟨*pl* ***secretaries-general, secretary-generals***⟩ segretario *m* generale
Secretary of State *n in USA* Segretario *m* di Stato
secrete *v/t* (*give off*) secernere; (*hide away*) nascondere
secretion *n* secrezione *f*
secretive *adj* riservato
secretly *adv* segretamente
secret police *n* polizia *f* segreta **secret service** *n* servizio *m* segreto
sect *n* setta *f*
sectarian **I** *adj* settario **II** *n* settario *m*, -a *f*
section **I** *n* sezione *f*; ***the string ~*** la sezione degli archi; MIL plotone *m* **II** *v/t* sezionare
◆**section off** *v/t sep* separare
sector *n* settore *m*
secular *adj* laico
secularise, secularize *v/t* secolarizzare
secularism *n* laicismo *m*
secure **I** *adj* (+*er*) *shelf etc* saldo *feeling* sicuro; ***~ in the knowledge that ...*** avere la certezza che…; ***financially ~*** finanziariamente tranquillo; *job* stabile **II** *v/t shelf etc* fissare; *s.o.'s help*, *finances* ottenere; ***~ sth for s.o.*** assicurare qc per qn
securities market *n* FIN mercato *m* dei titoli
security *n* **1.** *in job* sicurezza *f*; *in relationship* stabilità *f inv*; *for investment* garanzia *f* **2.** *at airport etc* sicurezza *f*; ***will you call ~?*** chiami le guardie di sicurezza; ***go through ~*** passare i controlli di sicurezza
security alert *n* stato *m* di allarme **security camera** *n* telecamera *f* di sicurezza **security check** *n* controllo *m* di sicurezza **security clearance** *n* superamento *m* del controllo di sicurezza **security-conscious** *adj* attento alla sicurezza **Security Council** *n* Consiglio *m* di Sicurezza **security firm** *n* agenzia *f* di sorveglianza **security forces** *npl police* forze *fpl* dell'ordine, forze *fpl* di sicurezza **security guard** *n* guardia *f* giurata **security risk** *n* minaccia *f* per la sicurezza
sedan *n US car* berlina *f*; (*a.* **sedan chair**) portantina *f*
sedate **I** *v/t* somministrare sedativi a **II** *adj* (+*er*) tranquillo
sedation *n*: ***be under ~*** essere sotto l'effetto di sedativi
sedative *n* sedativo *m*
sedentary *adj job* sedentario
sediment *n* sedimento *m*
seditious *adj* sedizioso
seduce *v/t* sedurre
seduction *n* seduzione *f*
seductive *adj smile*, *look* seducente; *offer* allettante
see *v/t* ⟨*pret* ***saw***, *past part* ***seen***⟩ **1.** vedere; ***~ you!*** *infml* ciao! *infml* **2.** (*understand*) capire; ***I ~*** capisco **3.** *romantically* uscire con **4.** (*meet*, *talk to*) ***can I ~ the manager?*** vorrei vedere il direttore; ***you should ~ a doctor*** dovresti andare dal medico **5.** (*accompany*) ***~ s.o. home*** accompagnare a casa qn; ***I'll ~ you to the door*** t'accompagno alla porta **6.** (*make sure*) ***~ that it is done by tomorrow*** fai in modo che sia pronto per domani **7.** (*experience*) conoscere; ***it's ~n a lot of hard wear*** ha sopportato il lavoro duro **8.** (*check*) vedere
◆**see about** *v/t* (*look into*) provvedere a; ***I'll see about it*** ci penso io; ***he came to see about the rent*** è venuto per occuparsi dell'affitto
◆**see off** *v/t sep at airport etc* salutare; (*chase away*) scacciare
◆**see out** **I** *v/i* vedere; ***I can't see out of the window*** non riesco a vedere fuori dalla finestra **II** *v/t sep*: ***see s.o. out*** accompagnare qn alla porta; ***I'll see myself out*** trovo l'uscita da solo
◆**see through** *v/t*: ***I could see through him*** sapevo a che gioco giocava; ***see sth through*** *to the end* seguire qc fino in fondo; (*help through difficult time*) essere d'aiuto; ***he had £100 to see him through the term*** aveva 100 sterline che gli sarebbero bastate fino alla fine del semestre
◆**see to** *v/t*: ***see to sth*** occuparsi di qc; ***see to it that sth gets done*** assi-

curarsi che qc venga fatto
◆**see up** *v/i +obj* (*look up*) vedere in alto; ***I could see up her skirt*** riuscivo a vedere sotto la sua gonna
seed I *n single* seme *m*; *collective* semi *mpl*; *in tennis* testa *f* di serie; ***go to ~*** *of person, district* ridursi male; ***the number one ~*** SPORTS la testa di serie **II** *v/t plant* seminare; *in tennis*: ***be ~ed number three*** essere testa di serie numero tre
seed bank *n* banca *f* del seme
seed cake *n torta aromatizzata al cumino*
seedling *n* semenzale *m*
seed pearl *n* perlina *f*
seedy *adj* (*+er*) *bar, district* squallido
seeing (that) *cj* visto che
seek *v/t & v/i* ⟨*pret & past part* ***sought***⟩ cercare
seem *v/i* sembrare; ***it seems that …*** sembra che …; ***he ~s younger than he is*** sembra più giovane di quanto non lo sia; ***things aren't what they ~*** le cose non sono come sembrano; ***I ~ to have heard that before*** mi sembra di averlo già sentito prima; ***what ~s to be the trouble?*** quale sarebbe il problema?
seemingly *adv* apparentemente
seemly *adj* decoroso
seen *past part* → ***see***
seep *v/i of liquid* filtrare
◆**seep out** *v/i of liquid* filtrare
seepage *n* infiltrazione *f*
seer *n* veggente
seersucker *n* TEX *tessuto di cotone a strisce di cosistenza diversa*
seesaw *n* altalena *f* (a bilico)
seethe *v/i fig* fremere di rabbia
see-through *adj dress, material* trasparente
segment *n* segmento *m*; *of orange* spicchio *m*
segmented *adj* frazionato
segregate *v/t* separare
segregation *n* segregazione *f*
seismic *adj* sismico; *fig changes, events* di grande rilievo
seismology *n* sismologia *f*
seize *v/t s.o., s.o.'s arm* afferrare; *power* prendere; *opportunity* cogliere; *of Customs, police etc* sequestrare
◆**seize up** *v/i of engine* grippare
seizure *n* MED attacco *m*; *of drugs etc* sequestro *m*
seldom *adv* raramente
select I *v/t* selezionare **II** *adj* (*exclusive*) scelto
selection *n* scelta *f*; *that / those chosen* selezione *f*
selection process *n* procedimento *m* di selezione
selective *adj* selettivo
self *n* ⟨*pl* ***selves***⟩ io *m*; ***he showed his true ~*** ha mostrato la sua vera natura; ***he's quite his old ~ again*** *or* ***he's back to his usual ~*** è di nuovo quello di un tempo
self-abnegation *n* abnegazione *f* **self-absorbed** *adj* che pensa solo a sé stesso **self-abuse** *n pej* masturbazione *f* **self-addressed envelope** *n* busta *f* col proprio nome e indirizzo **self-adhesive** *adj label* autoadesivo **self-appointed** *adj* autonominatosi **self-assertive** *adj* che si fa valere **self-assurance** *n* sicurezza *f* di sé **self-assured** *adj* sicuro di sé **self-awareness** *n* autocoscienza *f* **self-belief** *n* fiducia in sé stesso **self-catering apartment** *n* appartamento *m* indipendente con cucina **self-centred**, *US* **self-centered** *adj* egocentrico **self-cleaning** *adj oven* autopulente **self-confessed** *adj* dichiarato **self-confidence** *n* fiducia *f* in se stessi **self-confident** *adj* sicuro di sé **self-conscious** *adj* insicuro; *smile* imbarazzato; ***feel ~*** sentirsi a disagio **self-consciousness** *n* disagio *m* **self-contained** *adj flat* indipendente **self control** *n* autocontrollo *m* **self-defence**, *US* **self-defense** *n personal* legittima difesa *f*; *of state* autodifesa *f* **self-denial** *n* abnegazione *f* **self-deprecating** *adj person* che disapprova sé stesso; *remark* autodenigratorio; ***be ~*** essere troppo modesto **self-destruction** *n* autodistruzione *f* **self-destructive** *adj* autodistruttivo **self-determination** *n* autodeterminazione *f* (*a.* POL) **self-discipline** *n* autodisciplina *f* **self-discovery** *n* scoperta *f* di sé **self-doubt** *n* dubbi *mpl* personali **self-effacing** *adj* che si tiene in disparte **self-employed** *adj* autonomo **self-esteem** *n* autostima *f* **self-evident** *adj* evidente **self-explanatory** *adj* ovvio **self-expression** *n* espres-

sione *f* di sé **self-government** *n* autogoverno *m* **self-harm I** *n* autolesionismo *m* **II** *v/i* autolesionarsi **self-help** *n* self-help *m inv*; **~ group** gruppo *m* di self-help **self-image** *n* immagine di sé **self-importance** *n* presunzione *f* **self-imposed** *adj* autoimposto **self-improvement** *n* miglioramento *m* personale **self-indulgence** *n* indulgenza *f* verso sé stesso; *in eating* concessione *f* a sé stesso **self-indulgent** *adj* indulgente con sé stesso; *in eating* che concede a sé stesso **self-inflicted** *adj wounds* inflitto a sé stesso **self-interest** *n* interesse *m* personale

selfish *adj* egoista

self-justification *n* autogiustificazione *f* **self-knowledge** *n* conoscenza *f* di sé **selfless** *adj person* altruista; *attitude*, *dedication* altruistico **self-made man** *n* self-made man *m inv* **self-pity** *n* autocommiserazione *f* **self-portrait** *n* autoritratto *m* **self-possessed** *adj* padrone di sé **self-possession** *n* padronanza *f* di sé **self-preservation** *n* autoconservazione *f* **self-raising**, *US* **self-rising** *adj*: **~ flour** farina *f* con lievito **self-regard** *n* considerazione di sé **self-reliant** *adj* indipendente **self-reproach** *n* rimorso *m* **self-respect** *n* dignità *f inv* **self-restraint** *n* autocontrollo *m* **self-righteous** *adj pej* presuntuoso **self-sacrifice** *n* sacrificio *m* di sé **self-satisfied** *adj pej* soddisfatto di sé **self-service** *adj* self-service **self-service restaurant** *n* self-service *m inv* **self-serving** *adj* che fa i propri interessi **self-styled** *adj* sedicente **self-sufficient** *adj* autosufficiente **self-taught** *adj* autodidatta

sell ⟨*pret & past part* **sold**⟩ **I** *v/t* vendere; ***you have to ~ yourself*** devi saperti vendere **II** *v/i of products* vendere

◆**sell off** *v/t sep* svendere

◆**sell out I** *v/t* esaurire; ***we are sold out of candles*** abbiamo esaurito le candele **II** *v/i* vendere fino a esaurimento; ***we sold out in two days*** abbiamo venduto tutto in due giorni; ***he sold out to the enemy*** *infml* si è venduto al nemico

◆**sell up** *v/i* vendere

sell-by date *n* data *f* di scadenza; ***be past its ~*** essere scaduto

seller *n* venditore *m*, -trice *f*; ***it's a good ~*** *product* si vende bene

selling *n* COMM vendita *f*

selling point *n* COMM punto *m* forte (che fa vendere il prodotto)

Sellotape® *n* scotch® *m*

sellout *n*: ***be a ~*** fare il tutto esaurito; *fig* (*person*) essere una delusione

semantic *adj* semantico

semantics *nsg* semantica *f*

semaphore *n* semaforo *m*

semblance *n* parvenza *f* (***of*** di)

semen *n* sperma *m*

semester *n US* semestre *m*

semi *n* → ***semidetached house***

semicircle *n* semicerchio *m*

semicircular *adj* semicircolare

semi-colon *n* punto e virgola *m*

semiconductor *n* ELEC semiconduttore *m*

semidetached (**house**) *n* villa *f* bifamiliare

semifinal *n* semifinale *f*

semifinalist *n* semifinalista *m/f*

seminar *n* seminario *m*

seminary *n* seminario *m*

semiprecious *adj*: **~ *stone*** pietra *f* dura

semiquaver *n esp Br* semicroma *f*

semiskilled *adj* parzialmente qualificato

semi-skimmed milk *n* latte *m* parzialmente scremato

sen *abbr* (= **senior**) senior

Sen. *abbr* (= **Senator**) *US* senatore *m*, -trice *f*

senate *n* senato *m*

senator *n* senatore *m*, -trice *f*

send *v/t* ⟨*pret & past part* **sent**⟩ mandare; **~ *sth to s.o.*** mandare qc a qn; **~ *s.o. to s.o.*** mandare qn da qn; **~ *her my best wishes*** mandale i miei saluti; ***it ~s the wrong signal*** *or* ***message*** *fig* mandare un segnale *or* messaggio sbagliato; ***this sent him into a fury*** lo ho mandato su tutte le furie

◆**send away for** *v/t by mail order* ordinare per posta

◆**send back** *v/t sep* mandare indietro

◆**send for** *v/t doctor*, *help* (mandare a) chiamare

◆**send in** *v/t sep troops* inviare; *next interviewee* far entrare; *application form* spedire

◆**send off** *v/t sep letter, fax etc* spedire; *footballer* espellere
◆**send on** *v/t sep letter* inoltrare; *luggage etc* spedire; *substitute* mandare avanti
◆**send out** *v/t sep of room* mandare fuori (***of*** da); *signals* inviare; *light* diffondere; *invitations* spedire; ***she sent me out to buy a paper*** mi ha mandato a prendere il giornale
◆**send up** *v/t sep* (*mock*) prendere in giro
sender *n of letter* mittente *m/f*
send-off *n*: ***give s.o. a good ~*** dare calorosamente l'addio a qn
senile *adj pej* rimbambito
senility *n pej* rimbambimento *m*
senior **I** *adj* (*older*) più anziano; *in rank* di grado superiore; ***be ~ to s.o.*** *in rank* essere di grado superiore rispetto a qn; ***J. B. Schwartz, Senior*** J. B. Schwarz senior; *hum* ***Excuse me, I'm having a ~ moment*** scusate, ho un vuoto di memoria **II** *n* EDU *studente dai 12 ai 16 anni*; *US* UNIV studente dell'ultimo anno; ***he is two years my ~*** è di due anni più vecchio di me
senior citizen *n* anziano *m*, -a *f*
seniority *n in job* anzianità *f inv*
senior partner *n* socio *m* principale
senior school *n* scuola *f* media; **senior high school** *n US* scuola *f* media superiore
sensation *n* (*feeling*) sensazione *f*; ***a ~ of falling*** la sensazione di cadere; (*surprise event*) scalpore *m*; ***be a ~*** essere sensazionale
sensational *adj* sensazionale
sensationalism *n* sensazionalismo *m*
sense **I** *n* **1.** (*meaning*) significato *m*; (*purpose, point*) senso *m*; ***in a ~*** in un certo senso; ***it doesn't make ~*** non ha senso; ***there's no ~ in trying/waiting*** non ha senso provare/aspettare **2.** (*common sense*) buonsenso *m*; ***talk ~, man!*** ragiona!; ***come to one's ~s*** tornare in sé; ***have the ~ to do sth*** avere il buonsenso di fare qc **3.** (*sight, smell etc*) senso *m*; (*feeling*) sensazione *f*; ***~ of direction*** senso dell'orientamento; ***~ of humour*** senso dell'umorismo **II** *v/t* sentire; ***I could ~ that something was wrong*** avevo l'impressione che c'era qualcosa che non andava
senseless *adj* (*pointless*) assurdo
sensibility *n* sensibilità *f*; ***sensibilities*** suscettibilità *f*
sensible *adj person, decision* assennato; *advice* sensato; *clothes, shoes* pratico
sensibly *adv* assennatamente
sensitise, sensitize *v/t & v/i* sensibilizzare
sensitive *adj* sensibile; ***be ~ to sth*** *pain, light, heat* essere sensibile a qc; ***he has access to some highly ~ information*** ha accesso a informazioni riservate
sensitivity *n* sensibilità *f inv*
sensor *n* sensore *m*
sensory *adj* sensoriale
sensual *adj* sensuale
sensuality *n* sensualità *f inv*
sensuous *adj* sensuale
sent *pret & past part* → **send**
sentence **I** *n* GRAM frase *m*; JUR condanna *f* **II** *v/t* JUR condannare
sentiment *n* (*sentimentality*) sentimentalismo *m*; (*opinion*) opinione *f*
sentimental *adj* sentimentale
sentimentalise, sentimentalize **I** *v/i* fare il sentimentale **II** *v/t* rendere sentimentale
sentimentalism *n* sentimentalismo *m*
sentimentality *n* sentimentalismo *m*
sentry *n* sentinella *f*; ***be on ~ duty*** fare la sentinella
SEO *abbr* (= **Senior Executive Officer**) alto dirigente *m*
Sep *abbr* (= **September**) settembre
separable *adj* separabile
separate **I** *adj* separato; ***a ~ issue*** un problema diverso; ***on two ~ occasions*** in due distinte occasioni; ***they live ~ lives*** vivono vite separate **II** *v/t* separare; ***~ sth from sth*** separare qc da qc **III** *v/i of couple* separarsi **IV** *n* **separates** *npl* coordinati *mpl*
separated *adj couple* separato
separately *adv* separatamente
separation *n* separazione *f*
separatism *n* separatismo *m*
sepia **I** *n* seppia *f*; *drawing* seppia *m* **II** *adj* seppia
September *n* settembre *m*
septet *n* MUS settetto *m*; (*piece of music*) settimino *m*
septic *adj* infetto; ***go ~*** *of wound* infet-

tarsi
septic tank *n* fossa *f* settica
sepulchre, *US* **sepulcher** *n* sepolcro *m*; *fig* ***a whited ~*** un sepolcro imbiancato
sequel *n* seguito *m*
sequence *n* sequenza *f*; ***in ~*** di seguito; ***out of ~*** fuori tempo; ***the ~ of events*** l'ordine dei fatti
sequin *n* lustrino *m*
Serb *n* serbo *m*, -a *f*
Serbia *n* Serbia *f*
Serbian I *adj* serbo **II** *n* serbo *m*, -a *f*; (*language*) serbo *m*
Serbo-Croat *n* (*language*) serbocroato *m*
serenade I *n* serenata *f* **II** *v/t* fare una serenata a
serendipity *n* serendipità *f*
serene *adj* sereno
serenity *n* serenità *f*
serf *n* servo *m*, -a *f*
serge *n* TEX serge *f*
sergeant *n* sergente *m*
sergeant major *n* MIL *US* maresciallo *m*; *Br grado più alto tra i sottufficiali*
serial *n* serial *m inv*
serialise, serialize *v/t novel on TV* trasmettere a puntate
serial killer *n* serial killer *m/f inv* **serial number** *n of product* numero *m* di serie **serial port** *n* COMPUT porta *f* seriale
series *nsg* serie *f inv*
serigraph *n* (stampa *f* in) serigrafia *f*
serious *adj illness*, *situation*, *damage* grave; *person*, *company* serio; ***I'm ~*** dico sul serio; ***listen, this is ~*** ascolta, è una cosa seria; ***we'd better take a ~ look at it*** dovremo considerarlo seriamente; ***he is ~ about her*** fa sul serio con lei; ***earn ~ money*** *infml* guadagnare un sacco di soldi
seriously *adv injured* gravemente; (*extremely*) estremamente; ***~ though, …*** scherzi a parte, …; ***~?*** davvero?; ***take s.o. ~*** prendere sul serio qn
seriousness *n of person* serietà *f inv*; *of situation*, *illness etc* gravità *f inv*
sermon *n* predica *f*
sermonise, sermonize *v/i* sermoneggiare
serotonin *n* MED, BIOL serotonina *f*
serrated *adj* dentellato; ***~ knife*** coltello *m* seghettato
serried *adj* serrato
servant *n* domestico *m*, -a *f*
serve I *v/t food*, *customer*, *one's country*, servire; ***his knowledge of history ~d him well*** la sua conoscenza della storia gli è stata utile; ***it ~s you / him right*** ti / gli sta bene; ***are you being ~d?*** la stanno servendo? **II** *v/i give out food*, *in tennis* servire; ***dinner is ~d*** la cena è servita; *as politician etc* prestare servizio; ***~ on a committee*** far parte di una commissione **III** *n in tennis* servizio *m*
◆**serve out** *v/t sep time* finire; *apprenticeship* portare a termine; *term* completare
◆**serve up** *v/t sep meal* servire
server *n* COMPUT server *m inv*
service I *n* **1.** *to customers*, *community* servizio *m* **2.** *for vehicle*, *machine* manutenzione *f*; *for vehicle* revisione *f*; ***put one's car in for a ~*** portare l'auto a revisionare **3.** *in tennis* servizio *m* **4.** ***~s*** servizi **5.** ***the ~s*** MIL le forze armate **6.** ***be out of ~*** essere guasto **II** *v/t vehicle* revisionare; *machine* fare la manutenzione di
service area *n* area *f* di servizio **service charge** *n in restaurant*, *club* servizio *m* **service contract** *n on appliance* contratto *m* di assistenza **service industry** *n* settore *m* terziario **serviceman** *n* MIL militare *m* **service provider** *n* COMPUT fornitore *m* di servizi **service road** *n* via *f* d'accesso *m* **service sector** *n* settore *m* terziario **service station** *n* stazione *f* di servizio **servicewoman** *n* militare *m* (donna)
serviette *n* tovagliolino *m*
servile *adj pej* servile
serving *n of food* porzione *f*
serving dish *n* piatto *m* di portata **serving spoon** *n* cucchiaio *m* di portata
sesame *n* sesamo *m*
session *n of parliament* sessione *f*; *with psychiatrist*, *consultant etc* seduta *f*; ***be in ~*** essere in seduta
set I *v/t* ⟨*pret & past part* **set**⟩ **1.** (*place*) mettere; ***~ sth in motion*** mettere qc in moto; ***~ sth to music*** mettere qc in musica; ***~ a dog / the police on s.o.*** mettere un cane / la polizia sulle tracce di qn **2.** *film*, *novel etc* ambientare **3.**

date, time, limit fissare; ***~ a value/ price on sth*** fissare un valore/prezzo su qc; ***~ a task for s.o.*** assegnare un compito a qn; ***~ a good example*** dare il buon esempio; ***~ sth/ things right*** sistemare qc/le cose; ***~ s.o. right*** (***about sth***) chiarire qc a qn; ***~ s.o. straight*** spiegare a qn come stanno le cose **4.** *mechanism* regolare; *alarm clock* mettere; *jewel* montare; (*typeset*) comporre **5.** *broken limb* ingessare **6.** ***~ the table*** apparecchiare (la tavola) **7.** ***~ s.o. free*** liberare qn **II** *v/i* ⟨*pret & past part* ***set***⟩ *of sun* tramontare; *of glue* indurirsi **III** *n of tools* set *m inv*; *of dishes, knives* servizio *m*; *of books* raccolta *f*; *group of people* cerchia *f*; MATH insieme *m*; (THEAT: *scenery*) scenografia *f*; *where a film is made* set *m inv*; *in tennis* set *m inv*; ***television ~*** televisore *m* **IV** *adj* **1.** *views, ideas* rigido; ***be very ~ in one's ways*** essere abitudinario; ***~ book/ reading*** *in course* libro/lettura in programma; ***~ meal*** menù *m inv* fisso **2.** (*ready*) pronto; ***be all ~*** essere tutto pronto **3.** ***be dead ~ on*** (***doing***) ***sth*** essere deciso a fare qc

◆**set about** *v/t*: ***set about doing sth*** cominciare a fare qc; (*attack*) attaccare

◆**set apart** *v/t sep*: ***set sth apart from sth*** distinguere qc da qc

◆**set aside** *v/t sep for future use* mettere da parte

◆**set back** *v/t sep in plans etc* ritardare; ***it set me back £400*** *infml* mi è costato 400 sterline; ***be set back from the road*** essere distante dalla strada

◆**set down** *v/t sep suitcase* mettere giù

◆**set in** *v/i winter, rain, recession* arrivare

◆**set off I** *v/i on journey* partire **II** *v/t sep explosion* causare; *chain reaction, alarm* far scattare

◆**set out I** *v/i on journey* partire **II** *v/t sep ideas, proposal, goods* esporre; ***set out to do sth*** (*intend*) proporsi di fare qc

◆**set to** *v/i start on a task* mettersi all'opera

◆**set up I** *v/t sep new company* fondare; *system* mettere in opera; *equipment, machine* piazzare; *infml* (*frame*) incastrare *infml* **II** *v/i in business* mettersi in affari

setback *n* contrattempo *m* **set piece** *n* pezzo *m* forte; SPORTS mossa *f* **set-square** *n* squadra *f* da disegno

settee *n* (*couch, sofa*) divano *m*

setter *n* setter *m*

set theory *n* MATH teoria *f* degli insiemi

setting *n of novel etc* ambientazione *f*; *of house* posizione *f*

settle I *v/i of bird, dust, beer* posarsi; *of building* assestarsi; *to live* stabilirsi **II** *v/t dispute* comporre; ***~ a case out of court*** raggiungere un accordo amichevole; *issue, uncertainty* risolvere; *s.o.'s debts, the bill* saldare; *nerves, stomach* calmare; ***~ o.s. comfortably in an armchair*** mettersi comodo su una poltrona; ***that ~s it!*** è deciso!

◆**settle back** *v/i* mettersi comodo

◆**settle down** *v/i* (*stop being noisy*) calmarsi; (*stop wild living*) mettere la testa a posto; ***it's time he settled down*** era ora che si sistemasse; ***marry and settle down*** trova moglie e sistemati; *in an area* stabilirsi

◆**settle for** *v/t* (*take, accept*) accontentarsi di

◆**settle in** *v/i in house, town* stabilirsi; *in job, school* ambientarsi; ***how are you settling in?*** ti stai ambientando?

◆**settle up** *v/i* (*pay*) regolare i conti; *in hotel etc* pagare il conto

settled *adj weather* stabile

settlement *n of dispute* composizione *f*; (*payment*) pagamento *m*

settler *n in new country* colonizzatore *m*, -trice *f*

set-top box *n for digital television* decodificatore *m inv* **set-up** *n* (*structure*) organizzazione *f*; (*relationship*) relazione *f*; *infml* (*frameup*) montatura *f*

seven *num* sette

seventeen *num* diciassette

seventeenth *n/adj* diciassettesimo, -a

seventh *n/adj* settimo, -a

seventieth *n/adj* settantesimo, -a

seventy *num* settanta; ***he's in his seventies*** ha oltre settant'anni

sever *v/t arm, cable etc* recidere; *relations* troncare

several I *adj* parecchi **II** *pron* parecchi *m*, -ie *f*

severance pay *n* indennità *f inv* di fine rapporto
severe *adj* (+*er*) *illness* grave; *penalty, teacher, face* severo; *winter, weather* rigido
severely *adv punish* severamente; *speak, stare* duramente; *injured, disrupted* gravemente
severity *n of illness* gravità *f inv*; *of look etc* durezza *f*; *of penalty* severità *f inv*; *of winter* rigidità *f inv*
sew *v/t & v/i* ⟨*pret* **-ed**, *past part* **sewn**⟩ cucire
◆**sew on** *v/t button* attaccare
◆**sew up** *v/t sep liter* ricucire; *fig* monopolizzare; ***we've got the game all sewn up*** ci siamo accaparrati la partita
sewage *n* acque *fpl* di scolo
sewage plant *n* impianto *m* per il riciclaggio delle acque di scolo **sewage works** *nsg or npl azienda agricola che sfrutta la fertilizzazione con i liquami*
sewer *n* fogna *f*
sewerage *n* acque *fpl* di scolo
sewing *n* cucito *m*
sewing machine *n* macchina *f* da cucire
sewn *past part* → ***sew***
sex *n* sesso *m*; ***have ~ with*** avere rapporti sessuali con
sex appeal *n* sex appeal *m* **sex change** *n* cambiamento *m* di sesso **sex discrimination** *n* discriminazione *f* sessuale **sex drive** *n* impulso *m* sessuale **sex education** *n* educazione *f* sessuale
sexism *n* sessismo *m*
sexist I *adj* sessista **II** *n* sessista *m/f*
sex offender *n* criminale *m/f* sessuale
sexpot *n infml* bomba *f* sexy
sex shop *n* sexy shop *m inv* **sex symbol** *n* sex symbol *m inv*
sextet(te) *n* sestetto *m*
sextuplet *n uno di sei gemelli*
sexual *adj* sessuale
sexual assault *n* violenza *f* sessuale **sexual harassment** *n* molestie *fpl* sessuali **sexual intercourse** *n* rapporti *mpl* sessuali
sexuality *n* sessualità *f inv*
sexually *adv* sessualmente; ***be ~ attracted to s.o.*** essere sessualmente attratti da qn
sexually transmitted disease *n* malattia *f* venerea
sexy *adj* (+*er*) sexy *inv*
SF *abbr* (= **science fiction**) fantascienza *f*
Sgt *abbr* (= **sergeant**) sergente *m*
sh *int* sssh
shabbily *adv dressed* in modo trasandato; *treat* in modo meschino
shabbiness *n of coat etc* trasandatezza *f*
shabby *adj* (+*er*) *coat etc* trasandato; *treatment* meschino
shack *n* baracca *f*
◆**shack up with** *v/i infml* convivere
shackle I *n usu pl* catena *f* **II** *v/t* incatenare
shade I *n for lamp* paralume *m*; *of colour* tonalità *f inv*; ***in the ~*** all'ombra **II** *v/t from sun, light* riparare; ***he ~d his eyes with his hand*** si riparò gli occhi con la mano; ***~ sth in*** ombreggiare
shading *n* ART ombreggiatura *f*
shadow I *n* ombra *f* **II** *v/t* (*follow*) pedinare
shadow box *v/i boxe* combattere contro l'ombra (in allenamento) **Shadow Cabinet** *n* gabinetto *m* ombra
shadowy *adj* ombroso; *fig* ***a ~ figure*** un personaggio enigmatico
shady *adj* (+*er*) *spot* all'ombra; *character, dealings* losco
shaft *n of axle* albero *m*; *of mine* pozzo *m*; *of light* raggio *m*; *of lift* tromba *f*
shag I *s Br vulg* scopata *f vulg*; (*tobacco*) trinciato *m*; ***have a ~*** *vulg* farsi una scopata *vulg* **II** *v/t & v/i* ⟨*pret & past part* **-ged**⟩ *vulg* scopare *vulg*
shaggy *adj* (+*er*) *hair* arruffato; *dog* dal pelo arruffato
shaggy-dog story *n lunga barzelletta con finale paradossale*
shake I *v/t* ⟨*pret* **shook**, *past part* **shaken**⟩ scuotere; *emotionally* sconvolgere; ***~ hands*** stringersiela la mano; ***~ hands with s.o.*** stringere la mano a qn **II** *v/i of hands, voice, building* tremare; ***~ like a leaf*** tremare come una foglia; ***he was shaking all over*** tremava tutto; ***~ in one's shoes*** *infml* farsela addosso dalla paura; ***~ (on it)!*** *infml* qua la mano! **III** *n*: ***give sth a good ~*** dare una scrollata a qc; ***in***

two ~s (*in a moment*) in un battibaleno
◆**shake off** *v/t sep cold* guarire da
◆**shake out** *v/t sep liter* scuotere fuori; *tablecloth* scrollare
◆**shake up** *v/t sep bottle*, *liquid* agitare; (*upset*) turbare; *system* dare uno scossone; *country*, *industry* stimolare; ***he was badly shaken up by the accident*** l'incidente gli ha dato una brutta scossa; ***she's still a bit shaken up*** è ancora un po' turbata; ***shake things up*** darsi una mossa
shaken I *adj emotionally* scosso **II** *past part* → ***shake***
shake-up *n* rimpasto *m*
shaky *adj* (*+er*) *table etc* traballante; *after illness*, *shock* debole; *grasp of sth*, *grammar etc* incerto; *voice*, *hand* tremante
shall *v/mod* **1.** *future*: ***I ~ do my best*** farò del mio meglio; ***I shan't see them*** non li vedrò **2.** *suggesting*: ***~ we go now?*** andiamo?
shallot *n* scalogno *m*
shallow *adj water* poco profondo; *person* superficiale
shallowness *n of water* scarsa profondità *f*; *also*, *person* superficialità *f*; *novel* mancanza *f* di profondità; *of soil* bassezza *f*
sham *n* farsa *f*
shamble *v/i* camminare con andatura dinoccolata
shambles *nsg* casino *m infml*; ***the room was a ~*** la camera era un macello
shambolic *adj* sottosopra
shame I *n* vergogna *f*; ***bring ~ on …*** disonorare …; ***what a ~!*** che peccato!; ***~ on you!*** vergognati! **II** *v/t*: ***~ s.o. into doing sth*** indurre qn a fare qc per vergogna
shamefaced *adj* vergognoso; *embarrassed* imbarazzato
shameful *adj* vergognoso
shamefully *adv* vergognosamente
shameless *adj* svergognato
shampoo I *n* shampoo *m inv*; ***a ~ and set*** shampoo e messa in piega **II** *v/t* fare lo shampoo a
shamrock *n* trifoglio *m*; *simbolo della Repubblica d'Irlanda*
shandy *n birra mescolata a gazzosa*
shank *n* ANAT gamba *f*; *meat* stinco *m*; *of tool* gambo *m*
shan't → ***shall not***
shantytown *n* baraccopoli *f inv*
shape I *n* forma *f*; ***it's rectangular*** *etc* ***in ~*** ha una forma rettangolare; ***take ~*** prendere forma; ***of all ~s and sizes*** di tutte le forme e le misure; ***I don't accept gifts in any ~ or form*** non accetto regali di nessun tipo; ***be in good / bad ~*** essere in buono / cattivo stato **II** *v/t clay* dar forma a; *person's life*, *character* forgiare; *the future* determinare
◆**shape up** *v/i* (*improve*) migliorare
shapeless *adj dress etc* informe
shapely *adj* (*+er*) *figure* ben fatto
shard *n* frammento *m*
share I *v/t* dividere; *s.o.'s feelings*, *opinions* condividere **II** *v/i* dividere; ***do you mind sharing with Patrick?*** ti dispiace dividere con Patrick?; ***~ and ~ alike*** dividere in parti uguali **III** *n* parte *f*; FIN azione *f*; ***do one's ~ of the work*** fare la propria parte del lavoro; ***I want my fair ~*** voglio la parte che mi spetta
◆**share out** *v/t sep* spartire
share capital *n* capitale *m* azionario **share certificate** *n* certificato *m* azionario **share cropper** *n* AGR mezzadro *m*, -a *f* **shareholder** *n* azionista *m/f* **share index** *n* indice *m* di borsa **shareware** *n* COMPUT shareware *m inv*
shark *n fish* squalo *m*; (*swindler*) squalo *m*; ***loan ~*** usuraio *m*, -a *f*
sharp I *adj* (*+er*) *knife* affilato; *mind*, *pain* acuto; *taste* aspro **II** *adv* (*+er*) MUS in diesis; ***at 3 o'clock ~*** alle 3 precise **III** *n* MUS diesis *m*
sharpen *v/t knife* affilare; *skills* raffinare
sharpener *n for knife* affilatoio *m*; *for pencil* temperino *m*
sharp-eyed *adj* vigile
sharp practice *n* pratiche *fpl* poco oneste **sharp-tongued** *adj* dalla lingua tagliente **sharp-witted** *adj* acuto
shat *pret & past part* → ***shit***
shatter I *v/t glass* frantumare; *illusions* distruggere **II** *v/i of glass* frantumarsi
shattered *adj infml* (*exhausted*) esausto; (*very upset*) sconvolto
shattering *adj news*, *experience* sconvolgente; *effect* tremendo
shatterproof *adj* infrangibile

shave **I** *v/t* radere **II** *v/i* farsi la barba **III** *n*: ***have a ~*** farsi la barba; ***that was a close ~*** ce l'abbiamo fatta per un pelo
◆**shave off** *v/t sep beard* tagliarsi; *from piece of wood* piallare
shaven *adj head* rasato
shaver *n electric* rasoio *m*
shaving brush *n* pennello *m* da barba
shaving foam *n* schiuma *f* da barba
shaving soap *n* sapone *m* da barba
shawl *n* scialle *m*
she *pron* lei; ***~ has three children*** ha tre figli; ***you're funny, ~'s not*** tu sei spiritoso, lei no; ***there ~ is*** eccola
sheaf *n* ⟨*pl* ***sheaves***⟩ covone *m*
shear *v/t* ⟨*pret* ***sheared***, *past part* ***sheared*** *or* ***shorn***⟩ *sheep* tosare
shears *npl for gardening* cesoie *fpl*; *for sewing* forbici *fpl*
sheath *n for knife* guaina *f*; *contraceptive* preservativo *m*
sheath knife *n* coltello *m* a lama fissa
shed[1] *v/t* ⟨*pret & past part* ***shed***⟩ *blood* spargere; *tears* versare; *leaves* perdere; ***~ skin*** mutare pelle; ***~ a few pounds*** perdere un paio di chili; *fig* ***~ light on*** fare luce su
shed[2] *n* rimessa *f*
she'd → ***she would***, ***she had***
she-devil *n* diavolessa *f*
sheen *n* lucentezza *f*
sheep *n* ⟨*pl* ***sheep***⟩ pecora *f*
sheepdog *n* cane *m* pastore
sheepish *adj* imbarazzato
sheepskin *adj lining* di montone
sheer[1] *adj* (+*er*) *madness*, *luxury* puro; ***by ~ chance*** per pura coincidenza; ***by ~ hard work*** grazie al duro lavoro; ***a ~ hell*** un vero inferno; *drop*, *cliffs* ripido; (*transparent*) trasparente
sheer[2] *v/i* virare; ***the car ~ed away to the right*** l'auto fece una virata a destra
sheet[1] *n for bed* lenzuolo *m*; *of paper* foglio *m*; *of metal*, *glass* lastra *f*
sheet[2] *n* NAUT (*rope*) scotta *f*
sheet ice *n* lastra *f* di ghiaccio
sheeting *n*: ***plastic ~*** rivestimento *m* in plastica
sheet metal *n* lamiera *f* **sheet music** *n* spartiti *mpl*
sheik(h) *n* sceicco *m*
shelf *n* ⟨*pl* ***shelves***⟩ mensola *f*; ***shelves*** scaffale *msg*, ripiani *mpl*
shelflife *n of product* durata *f* di conservazione
shell **I** *n of mussel etc* conchiglia *f*; *of egg* guscio *m*; *of tortoise* corazza *f*; MIL granata *f*, *fig* ***come out of one's ~*** uscire dal guscio **II** *v/t peas* sbucciare; MIL bombardare
◆**shell out** *v/t sep infml money* sborsare
she'll → ***she will***, ***she shall***
shellfire *n* bombardamento *m*; ***come under ~*** essere bombardato
shellfish *n* crostacei *mpl*
shell-shocked *adj*: ***be ~*** *liter* aver subito un trauma causato da un bombardamento; *fig* essere sotto choc
shell suit *n* tuta *f* impermeabile
shelter **I** *n* (*refuge*) riparo *m*; *construction* rifugio *m* **II** *v/i from rain*, *bombing etc* ripararsi **III** *v/t* (*protect*) proteggere
sheltered *adj place* riparato; ***lead a ~ life*** vivere nella bambagia
sheltered housing *n sistemazione e assistenza per persone bisognose*
shelve *v/t fig* accantonare
shelving *n* scaffalatura *f*
shepherd *n* pastore *m*
shepherd's pie *n pasticcio di carne tritata e verdure ricoperto di puré di patate*
sherbet *n* (*powder*) magnesia *f*; (*water ice*) sorbetto *m*
sheriff *n* sceriffo *m*; *Scot* giudice *m* di contea
sherry *n* sherry *m inv*
she's → ***she is***, ***she has***
shield **I** *n* scudo *m*; *sports trophy* scudetto *m*; TECH schermo *m* di protezione *f* **II** *v/t* (*protect*) proteggere
shift **I** *v/t* (*move*) spostare; ***~ the blame onto somebody else*** scarica la colpa a qualcun altro; ***~ the table over to the wall*** sposta il tavolo vicino al tavolo; *stains etc* togliere **II** *v/i* (*move*) spostarsi; *of wind* cambiare direzione; ***that's ~ing!*** *infml* è un bolide! **III** *n* (*change*) cambiamento *m*; ***a ~ in public opinion*** un cambiamento dell'opinione pubblica; *period of work* turno *m*; (*gear shift*) cambio *m*; (*dress*) chemisier *m inv*; (*under garment*) sottoveste *f*
shift key *n* COMPUT tasto *m* shift **shift work** *n* turni *mpl* **shift worker** *n* tur-

nista *m/f*
shifty *adj* (+*er*) *pej* losco
shifty-looking *adj pej* dall'aria losca
shilly-shally *v/i* 〈*pret & past part* **-ied**〉 *infml* tentennare
shimmer *v/i* luccicare
shin *n* stinco *m*
◆**shin up** *v/t tree, pipe* arrampicarsi su
shinbone *n* tibia *f*
shindig, shindy *n infml* casino *m*
shine I *v/i* 〈*pret & past part* **shone**〉 *of sun, shoes, metal* splendere; *fig*: *of student etc* brillare; **~ at** *or* **in sth** brillare in qc **II** *v/t* 〈*pret & past part* **shone**〉 *torch etc* puntare **III** *n on shoes etc* lucentezza *f*; ***take a ~ to s.o.*** *infml* prendersi una cotta per qn
shingle *n on beach* ciottoli *mpl*
shingles *nsg* MED fuoco *m* di Sant'-Antonio
shin pad *n* parastinchi *m inv*
shiny *adj* (+*er*) *surface* lucido
ship I *n* nave *f* **II** *v/t* 〈*pret & past part* **-ped**〉 (*send*) spedire; (*send by sea*) spedire via mare
shipbuilding *n* costruzione *f* navale
shipmate *n* compagno *m*, -a *f* di bordo
shipment *n* (*consignment*) carico *m*
shipowner *n* armatore *m*
shipping *n* (*sea traffic*) navigazione *f*; (*sending*) trasporto *m* (via mare)
shipping company *n* compagnia *f* di navigazione **shipping lane** *n* corridoio *m* di navigazione
shipshape *adj* in perfetto ordine **shipwreck I** *n* naufragio *m* **II** *v/t*: ***be ~ed*** naufragare **shipyard** *n* cantiere *m* navale
shirk *v/t* scansare
shirker *n* scansafatiche *m/f inv*
shirt *n* camicia *f*; ***in his ~ sleeves*** in maniche di camicia
shit I *n sl* merda *f sl*; ***have the ~s*** avere la cacarella; *bad quality goods, work* stronzata *f sl*; ***be in the ~*** essere nella merda; ***I don't give a ~*** non me ne fotte un cazzo; ***tough ~!*** che cazzo di sfiga!*business*; ***she's really got her ~ together*** è davvero ben organizzata **II** *v/i* 〈*pret & past part* **shat**〉 cagare *sl*; ***be ~ting themselves*** cagarsi sotto **III** *int* merda *sl* **IV** *adv*:***~ scared*** spaventato da cagarsi sotto
shitfaced *adj* (*drunk*) *infml vulg* ubriaco fradicio
shithead *n vulg* pezzo *m* di merda *vulg*
shit-hot *adj Br infml vulg* favoloso
shitless *adj infml*: ***be scared ~*** cacarsi sotto dalla paura
shitty *adj* (+*er*) *infml* di merda *sl*
shiver I *v/i* rabbrividire **II** *n* brivido *m*
shoal *n of fish* banco *m*
shock I *n* shock *m inv*; ELEC scossa *f*; ***it comes as a ~ to hear that …*** è uno shock sentire che…; ***get the ~ of one's life*** avere un colpo terribile; ***he is in for a ~!*** *infml* sta per avere un bel colpo!; ***be in ~*** MED essere in stato di shock **II** *v/t* scioccare; ***be ~ed by*** essere scioccato da
shock absorber *n* AUTO ammortizzatore *m*
shocker *n event* evento *m* sconvolgente; *story* racconto *m* sconvolgente; *infml* racconto *m* scandalistico
shockheaded *adj* con la zazzera
shocking *adj behaviour, poverty* scandaloso; *infml very bad* allucinante *infml*
shockingly *adv behave* scandalosamente; *bad, late, expensive* terribilmente
shockproof *adj* antiurto
shock wave *n*: ***send ~s through*** scioccare
shoddy *adj* (+*er*) *goods* scadente; *behaviour* meschino
shoe I *n* scarpa *f*; ***I wouldn't like to be in his ~s*** non vorrei essere nei suoi panni **II** *v/t* 〈*pret & past part* **shod**〉 *horse* ferro *m*
shoehorn *n* calzascarpe *m inv* **shoe-lace** *n* laccio *m* di scarpa **shoemaker, shoe mender** *n* calzolaio *m* **shoe polish** *n* lucido *m* da scarpe **shoe-shop** *n* negozio *m* di scarpe **shoestring** *n*: ***do sth on a ~*** fare qc con pochi soldi **shoetree** *n* forma *f* per scarpe
shone *pret & past part* → ***shine***
◆**shoo away** *v/t children, chicken* scacciare
shook *pret* → ***shake***
shoot I *v/t* 〈*pret & past part* **shot**〉 sparare; *film* girare; ***~ s.o. in the leg*** colpire qn alla gamba; ***~ s.o. for desertion*** fucilare qn per diserzione **II** *v/i* 〈*pret & past part* **shot**〉: ***~ at*** *person* sparare a *or* contro; *goal* tirare in

III *n* (*photo shoot*) servizio *m* fotografico; (*hunt*) partita *f* di caccia; BOT germoglio *m*
◆**shoot down** *v/t sep aeroplane* abbattere
◆**shoot off** *v/i* (*rush off*) precipitarsi
◆**shoot up** *v/i of prices* salire alle stelle; *of children* crescere molto; *of new suburbs, buildings etc* spuntare; *infml of drug addict* farsi *infml*
shooting star *n* stella *f* cadente
shoot-out *n with guns* sparatoria *f*; ***penalty ~*** rigori *mpl* a fine partita
shop I *n* negozio *m*; ***talk ~*** parlare di lavoro **II** *v/i* ⟨*pret & past part* ***-ped***⟩ fare acquisti; ***go ~ping*** andare a fare spese
◆**shop around** *v/i* vedere cosa c'è sul mercato; ***shop around for sth*** vedere cosa c'è sul mercato quanto a qc
shop assistant *n* commesso *m*, -a *f* **shopkeeper** *n* negoziante *m/f* **shoplifter** *n* taccheggiatore *m*, -trice *f* **shoplifting** *n* taccheggio *m*
shopper *n person* acquirente *m/f*
shopping *n activity* fare spese; *items* spesa *f*; ***do one's ~*** fare la spesa
shopping bag *n* borsa *f* per la spesa **shopping cart** *n US* → ***shopping trolley*** **shopping centre**, *US* **shopping center** *n* centro *m* commerciale **shopping list** *n* lista *f* della spesa **shopping mall** *n* centro *m* commerciale **shopping spree** *n* spese *fpl* folli **shopping trolley** *n Br* carrello *m* della spesa
shopsoiled *adj Br* sciupato
shop steward *n* rappresentante *m/f* sindacale **shop window** *n* vetrina *f*
shore[1] *n* riva *f*; ***a house on the ~s of the lake*** una casa sulla riva del lago; ***on ~*** *not at sea* a terra
shore[2] *v/t a.* **shore up** puntellare; *fig* sostenere
short I *adj* (*+er*) *in length, distance* corto; *in height* basso; *in time* breve; ***be ~ of*** essere a corto di; ***be ~ for*** essere l'abbreviazione di **II** *adv.* ***cut a vacation/meeting ~*** interrompere una vacanza/riunione; ***stop a person ~*** interrompere una persona; ***go ~ of*** fare a meno di; ***in ~*** in breve **III** *n* (*short drink*) cicchetto *m*; FILM cortometraggio *v/t & v/i* ELEC corto *m* (circuito)
shortage *n* mancanza *f*
shortbread *n* frollino *m* **shortcake** *n torta di pasta frolla* **short-change** *v/t* dare meno del resto dovuto, *fig* truffare **short circuit** *n* corto *m* circuito **shortcoming** *n* difetto *m* **shortcrust pastry** *n* pasta *f* brisée **short cut** *n* scorciatoia *f*
shorten I *v/t* accorciare **II** *v/i* accorciarsi
shortening *n* COOK *grasso usato in pasticceria*
shortfall *n* deficit *m inv*; *in hours etc* mancanza *f* **shorthand** *n* stenografia *f* **short-handed** *adj*: ***be ~*** essere a corto di personale **shorthaul** *adj* a breve raggio **shortlist I** *n of candidates* rosa *f* dei candidati **II** *v/t candidates* selezionare
short-lived *adj* di breve durata
shortly *adv* (*soon*) tra breve; ***~ before/after*** poco prima/dopo
shortness *n of visit* brevità *f inv*; *in height* bassa statura *f*; ***~ of breath*** mancanza *f* di fiato
short-range *adj* a breve termine; AVIAT a corto raggio; ***~ missile*** missile *m* a corta gittata
shorts *npl* calzoncini *mpl*
shortsighted *adj a. fig* miope **short-sleeved** *adj* a maniche corte **short-staffed** *adj* a corto di personale **short story** *n* racconto *m* **short-tempered** *adj* irascibile **short-term** *adj* a breve termine **short time** *n*: ***be on ~*** *of workers* lavorare a orario ridotto **short wave** *n* RADIO onde *fpl* corte
shot[1] **I** *n from gun* sparo *m*; (*photograph*) foto *f*; (*injection*) puntura *f*; ***be a good/poor ~*** essere un buon/pessimo tiratore; ***like a ~*** *accept, run off* come un razzo; ***have a ~ at doing sth*** *try* provare a fare qc; PHOT foto *f*; FILM ***out of ~*** fuori campo **II** *pret & past part* → ***shoot***
shot[2] *adj* (*iridescent*) cangiante; (*worn*) distrutto
shotgun *n* fucile *m* da caccia **shot put** *n* SPORTS lancio *m* del peso **shot putter** *n* SPORTS lanciatore *m*, -trice *f* del peso
should *v/mod*: ***what ~ I do?*** cosa devo fare?; ***you ~n't do that*** non dovresti farlo; ***that ~ be long enough*** dovrebbe essere lungo abbastanza; ***you ~***

have heard him! avresti dovuto sentirlo!; ***he's coming to apologize — I ~ think so*** sta vedendo a scusarsi - spero proprio di sì; ***he ~ be there by now*** dovrebbe essere già arrivatp; ***I ~ think there were about 40*** credo che fossero in 40; ***~ I open the window?*** vuoi che apra la finestra?; ***who ~ I see but Anne!*** e chi vado a incontrare? Anne!

shoulder I *n* ANAT spalla *f*; ***shrug one's ~s*** scrollare le spalle; ***a ~ to cry on*** una spalla su cui piangere; ***~ to ~*** spalla a spalla; ***she gave him the cold ~*** lo ha trattato con freddezza **II** *v/t fig responsibilities* caricarsi di

shoulder bag *n* borsa *f* a tracolla **shoulder blade** *n* scapola *f* **shoulder-length** *adj hair* che arriva fino alle spalle **shoulder pad** *n* spallina *f* **shoulder strap** *n* spallina *f*

shouldn't → ***should not***

shout I *v/t & v/i* gridare, urlare; *AUS infml buy drinks* pagare un giro di drink **II** *n* grido *m*, urlo *m*; *AUS infml* ***it's my ~*** offro io

◆**shout at** *v/t* urlare a

◆**shout down** *v/t sep person* zittire qn (a forza di gridare)

◆**shout out** *v/t sep* dire gridando

shouting *n* urla *fpl*

shove I *v/t & v/i* spingere; ***he ~d a book into my hand*** mi ha piazzato un libro in mano **II** *n* spinta *f*; ***give sth a ~*** dare una spinta a qc; ***when push comes to ~*** nella peggiore delle ipotesi

◆**shove in** *v/i* passare davanti; ***he shoved in in front of me*** mi è passato davanti

◆**shove off** *v/i infml* (*go away*) levarsi di torno

shovel I *n* pala *f* **II** *v/t* spalare; ***she ~led cake into her mouth*** si è ingozzata con il dolce

show I *v/t* ⟨*pret* **-ed**, *past part* **shown**⟩ *passport*, *ticket* mostrare; *interest*, *emotion* dimostrare; *at exhibition* esporre; *film* proiettare; ***~ s.o. sth, ~ sth to s.o.*** mostrare qc a qn; ***~ s.o. how to do sth*** mostrare a qn come fare qc; ***~ s.o. to the door*** accompagnare qn alla porta; ***they were ~n (a)round the factory*** li hanno portati in giro per mostrare loro la fabbrica **II** *v/i* ⟨*pret* **-ed**, *past part* **shown**⟩ (*be visible*) vedersi; ***does it ~?*** si vede?; ***the dirt doesn't ~*** lo sporco non si vede; ***it just goes to ~!*** come volevasi dimostrare!; ***what's ~ing at the cinema?*** cosa danno al cinema? **III** *n* THEAT, TV spettacolo *m*; (*display*) manifestazione *f*; ***on ~*** *at exhibition* esposto; ***it's all done for ~*** *pej* è tutta una scena***~ of force*** dimostrazione *f* di forza; ***~ of hands*** alzata *f* di mano; ***put up a good / poor ~*** *esp Br infml* fare una bella / brutta figura; *infml* ***he runs the ~*** è lui che comanda

◆**show around** *v/t* far visitare

◆**show in** *v/t* far entrare

◆**show off I** *v/t sep skills* mettere in risalto **II** *v/i pej* mettersi in mostra

◆**show up I** *v/t sep s.o.'s shortcomings etc* far risaltare; ***don't show me up in public*** non farmi fare brutta figura **II** *v/i infml* (*arrive, turn up*) farsi vedere *infml*; (*be visible*) notarsi; ***he showed up three hours late*** si è presentato con tre ore di ritardo

show biz *n infml* → ***show business***

show business *n* il mondo dello spettacolo **showcase** *n* vetrinetta *f*; *fig* vetrina *f* **showdown** *n* regolamento *m* di conti

shower I *n of rain* acquazzone *m*; *to wash* doccia *f*; ***take a ~*** fare una doccia **II** *v/i* fare la doccia **III** *v/t*: ***~ s.o. with praise*** coprire qn di lodi

shower cap *n* cuffia *f* da doccia **shower cubicle** *n* cabina *f* doccia **shower curtain** *n* tenda *f* della doccia **shower gel** *n* gel *m inv* doccia **showerproof** *adj* impermeabile

showery *adj* piovoso

showjumper *n* cavaliere *m*, cavallerizza *f* di concorso ippico

showjumping *n* concorso *m* ippico

showmanship *n* arte *f* dello showman

shown *past part* → ***show***

show-off *n pej* esibizionista *m/f* **showpiece** *n* pezzo *m* in mostra **showroom** *n* show-room *m inv*; ***in ~ condition*** mai usato **show stopper** *n infml pezzo che scatena l'applauso*

showy *adj* (+*er*) appariscente

shrank *pret* → ***shrink***[1]

shrapnel *n* shrapnel *f*

shred I *n of paper* strisciolina *f*; *of cloth* brandello *m*; *of evidence*, *etc* briciolo *m*; ***not a ~ of evidence*** neanche uno straccio di prova; ***his reputation was in ~s*** la sua reputazione era a pezzi; ***tear sth to ~s*** ridurre a brandelli; *fig* fare a pezzi **II** *v/t* ⟨*pret & past part* ***-ded***⟩ *paper* stracciare; *in cooking* sminuzzare

shredder *n for documents* distruttore *m* di documenti

shrew *n* toporagno *m*; *fig* bisbetica *f*

shrewd *adj* (*+er*) *person*, *businessman* scaltro; *investment* oculato

shrewdly *adv* oculatamente

shrewdness *n* oculatezza *f*

shriek I *v/i* strillare **II** *n* strillo *m*; ***a ~ of laughter*** una risata stridula

shrill *adj* (*+er*) stridulo

shrimp *n* gamberetto *m*

shrine *n* santuario *m*

shrink[1] *v/i* ⟨*pret* ***shrank***, *past part* ***shrunk***⟩ *of material* restringersi; *level of support etc* diminuire

shrink[2] *n infml* (*psychiatrist*) strizzacervelli *m/f inv*

shrinkage *n of material* restringimento *m*; COMM calo *m*

shrink-wrap *v/t* cellofanare **shrink-wrapping** *n process* cellofanatura *f*; *material* cellophane® *m inv*

shrivel *v/i* avvizzire

shroud I *n for body* lenzuolo *m* funebre **II** *v/t*: ***be ~ed in mist / mystery*** essere avvolto nella nebbia / nel mistero

Shrove Tuesday *n* martedì *m inv* grasso

shrub *n* arbusto *m*

shrubbery *n* arboreto *m*

shrug I *v/i* ⟨*pret & past part* ***-ged***⟩ alzare le spalle **II** *v/t* ⟨*pret & past part* ***-ged***⟩: ***~ one's shoulders*** alzare le spalle **III** *n* alzata *f* di spalle

◆**shrug off** *v/t sep criticism*, *problem* non dare importanza a

shrunk *past part* → ***shrink***[1]

shudder I *v/i with fear*, *disgust* rabbrividire; *of earth*, *building* tremare; ***the train ~ed to a halt*** il treno ebbe uno scossone e poi si fermò; ***I ~ to think*** non oso immaginare **II** *n of fear*, *disgust* brivido *m*; *of earth etc* tremore *m*

shuffle I *v/t cards* mescolare; ***he ~d the papers on his desk*** mescolò le carte sulla sua scrivania **II** *v/i in walking* strascicare i piedi; ***he ~d into the bathroom*** è andato in bagno strascicando i piedi **III** *n* strascicamento *m*; (*change round*) rimpasto *m*

shun *v/t* ⟨*pret & past part* ***-ned***⟩ evitare

shut ⟨*pret & past part* ***shut***⟩ **I** *v/t* chiudere **II** *v/i of door*, *box* chiudersi; *of shop*, *bank* chiudere **III** ***they were ~*** era chiuso; ***sorry sir, we're ~*** mi dispiace, signore, siamo chiusi; ***the door swung ~*** la porta si è chiusa sbattendo

◆**shut away** *v/t sep* (*put away*) mettere via; *in sth* rinchiudere (***in*** in); ***shut o.s. away*** ritirarsi

◆**shut down I** *v/t sep business* chiudere; *computer* spegnere **II** *v/i of business* chiudere i battenti; *of computer* spegnersi

◆**shut in** *v/t sep* rinchiudere

◆**shut off** *v/t sep* chiudere

◆**shut out** *v/t sep person*, *cat* chiudere fuori; *light*, *noise* eliminare; ***she closed the door to shut out the noise*** chiuse la porta per non far entrare il rumore

◆**shut up I** *v/t sep house* chiudere; (*imprison*) rinchiudere; (*silence*) zittire; ***that'll soon shut him up*** questo lo farà stare zitto **II** *v/i infml* (*be quiet*) star zitto; ***shut up!*** zitto!

shutter *n on window* battente *m*; PHOT otturatore *m*

shutter speed *n* PHOT tempo *m* di apertura

shuttle I *v/i* fare la spola **II** *n of loom* navetta *f*; *space shuttle* shuttle *m inv*

shuttlebus *n at airport* bus *m inv* navetta **shuttlecock** *n* SPORTS volano *m*

shuttle service *n* servizio *m* navetta

shy I *adj* (*+er*) timido; ***don't be ~*** non essere timido; ***feel ~*** intimidirsi **II** *v/i* (*horse*) fare uno scarto (***at*** a)

◆**shy away from** *v/t* (*avoid*) evitare

shyness *n* timidezza *f*

shyster *n US infml* imbroglione *m*, -a *f*

Siamese twins *npl* gemelli *mpl* siamesi

sibling *n brother* fratello *m*; *sister* sorella *f*

Sicilian I *adj* siciliano **II** *n* siciliano *m*, -a *f*

Sicily *n* Sicilia *f*

sick I *adj* (*+er*) malato; *sense of hu-*

mour crudele; ***I feel ~ about to vomit*** ho la nausea; ***I'm going to be ~ vomit*** ho voglia di vomitare; ***be ~ of*** (*fed up with*) essere stufo di; ***it makes you ~ the way he's always right*** *infml* fa stare male per il modo in cui riesce ad avere sempre ragione; ***I am worried ~*** sono preoccupato da morire; ***I'm ~ and tired of her*** sono arcistufo di lei **II** *n* (*vomit*) vomito *m*

sickbag *n* sacchetto *m* per il vomito

sickbay *n* infermeria *f*

sickbed *n* capezzale *m*

sicken I *v/t* (*disgust*) disgustare **II** *v/i*: ***be ~ing for sth*** covare qc

sickening *adj* disgustoso

sickle *n* falcetto *m*

sick leave *n*: ***be on ~*** essere in (congedo per) malattia; ***employees are allowed six weeks' ~ per year*** i dipendenti hanno diritto a sei settimane di malattia

sickly *adj* (+*er*) *person* delicato; *smell* stomachevole

sickness *n* malattia *f*; (*vomiting*) nausea *f*

sickness benefit *n Br* indennità *f inv* di malattia

sick pay *n* indennità *f* per malattia

side I *n* **1.** *of box, house* lato *m*; *of person, mountain* fianco *m*; *of page, record* facciata *f*; ***~ by ~*** fianco a fianco; ***at the ~ of the road*** sul ciglio della strada; ***the path goes down the ~ of the house*** il vialetto va lungo il lato della casa; ***the enemy attacked them on*** *or* ***from all ~s*** il nemico li attaccò su / da tutti i fronti; ***I'll put that issue on*** *or* ***to one ~*** metterò la questione da parte; ***the other ~ of Christmas*** l'altra faccia del Natale; ***I'm on your ~*** sono dalla tua (parte); ***on the ~*** *as a sideline* come attività collaterale **2.** SPORTS squadra *f* **3.** *fig* ***take ~s*** (*favour one side*) prendere posizione; ***take ~s with*** parteggiare per; ***on the big / small ~*** piuttosto grande / piccolo; ***your ~ of the story*** la tua versione della storia; ***we'll take £ 50 just to be on the safe ~*** prenderemo 50 sterline per stare sul sicuro; ***look on the bright ~*** (*be optimistic*) guarda sempre il lato positivo **II** *adj door* laterale; *issue* secondario; ***~ road*** strada laterale

◆**side against** *v/t* schierarsi contro

◆**side with** *v/t* prendere le parti di

sideboard *n* credenza *f*

sideboards, *US* **sideburns** *npl* basette *fpl*

sidecar *n* sidecar *m inv*

-sided *adj suf* ***one-sided*** unilaterale

side dish *n* contorno *m* **side effect** *n* effetto *m* collaterale **sidekick** *n infml* amico *m*, -a *f* intimo, a **sidelight** *n* AUTO luce *f* di posizione **sideline I** *n* attività *f inv* collaterale; ***on the ~s*** in disparte **II** *v/t*: ***feel ~d*** sentirsi sminuito **sidelong** *adj glance* furtivo **side-saddle** *n* sella *f* dell'amazzone **side-splitting** *adj* che fa morire dal ridere **sidestep** *v/t* ⟨*pret & past part* ***-ped***⟩ scansare; *fig* schivare **side street** *n* via *f* laterale **sidetrack** *v/t* distrarre; ***get ~ed by*** essere distratto da **sidewalk** *n US* marciapiede *m* **sideways** *adv* di lato

sidle *v/i*: ***~ up to s.o.*** avvicinarsi furtivamente a qn

SIDS *n abbr* (= **sudden infant death syndrome**) MED (sindrome *f* della) morte *f* in culla

siege *n* assedio *m*; ***lay ~ to*** assediare

sieve I *n* colino *m* **II** *v/t* → ***sift***

sift *v/t* setacciare

◆**sift through** *v/t details, data* passare al vaglio

sigh I *v/i* sospirare **II** *n* sospiro *m*; ***heave a ~ of relief*** tirare un respiro di sollievo

sight I *n* vista *f*; ***~s*** *of city* luoghi *mpl* da visitare; ***catch ~ of*** intravedere; ***know by ~*** conoscere di vista; ***be within ~ of*** essere visibile da; ***out of ~*** non visibile; ***out of ~ of*** fuori dalla vista di; ***what a ~ you are!*** come sei conciato!; ***lose ~ of*** *main objective etc* perdere di vista; ***at first ~*** a prima vista; ***set one's ~s on sth*** mettere gli occhi su qc; ***what a horrible ~!*** che orribile spettacolo!; ***it was a ~ for sore eyes*** ci si rifaceva gli occhi a guardarlo; ***out of ~, out of mind*** *prov* lontano dagli occhi, lontano dal cuore; *on telescope, gun* mirino *m*; *fig* ***set one's ~s too high*** puntare troppo in alto **II** *v/t* avvistare

sightless *adj person* non vedente

sightly *adj* attraente

sight-read *v/t & v/i* suonare / cantare a

prima vista

sightseeing *n* visita *f* turistica; ***I enjoy ~*** mi piace visitare i posti; ***go ~*** fare un giro turistico

sightseeing tour *n* giro *m* turistico

sightseer *n* turista *m/f*

sign I *n* (*indication*) segno *m*; (*road sign*) segnale *m*; *outside shop* insegna *f*; ***it's a ~ of the times*** è tipico dei nostri giorni; ***~ of the zodiac*** segno *m* zodiacale; ***there was no ~ of him*** di lui non c'era traccia; ***there was no ~ of life in the village*** non c'era segno di vita in paese II *v/t & v/i document* firmare

◆**sign for** *v/t parcel* firmare per la consegna di

◆**sign in** *v/i* firmare il registro (all'arrivo)

◆**sign off** *v/i* RADIO, TV chiudere la trasmissione; *in letter* concludere una lettere con la firma

◆**sign on** *v/i for unemployment benefit infml* essere iscritto alle liste di collocamento

◆**sign out** I *v/i* firmare all'uscita II *v/t sep* registrare l'uscita di

◆**sign up** *v/i* (*join the army*) arruolarsi

signal I *n* segnale *m*; ***warning ~*** segnale *m* di avvertimento; *fig* ***be sending out the right / wrong ~s*** lanciare il messaggio giusto / sbagliato II *v/i of driver* segnalare; ***he signalled*** *Br or* ***signaled*** *US* ***to the waiter*** ha fatto segno al cameriere III *v/t* (*indicate*) indicare; *arrival etc* annunciare; ***~ s.o. to do sth*** fare segno a qn di fare qc

signal box *n* cabina *f* di manovra

signalman *n* RAIL segnalatore *m*

signatory *n* firmatario *m*, -a *f*

signature *n* firma *f*

signature tune *n* sigla *f* musicale

signet ring *n* anello *m* con sigillo

significance *n* importanza *f*; (*meaning*) significato *m*; ***what is the ~ of this?*** che significato ha questo?; ***of no ~*** di nessuna importanza

significant *adj event etc* significativo; (*quite large*) notevole

significantly *adv larger, more expensive* notevolmente; ***it is not ~ different*** non è sostanzialmente diverso

signify *v/t* ⟨*pret & past part* **-ied**⟩ significare

sign language *n* linguaggio *m* dei segni **signpost** *n* cartello *m* stradale

silence I *n* silenzio *m*; ***in ~*** *work, march* in silenzio; ***there was a short ~*** ci fu un breve silenzio; ***break the ~*** rompere il silenzio; ***~!*** silenzio! II *v/t* mettere a tacere

silencer *n on gun* silenziatore *m*; *on car* marmitta *f*

silent *adj* silenzioso; *film* muto; ***stay ~*** *not comment* tacere

silent partner *n US* COMM socio *m* non operante

silhouette I *n* sagoma *f* II *v/t*: ***be ~d against*** stagliarsi contro

silicon *n* silicio *m*

silicon chip *n* chip *m inv* al silicio

silicone *n* silicone *m*

silicone implant *n* protesi *f* al silicone

silk I *n* seta *f* II *adj shirt etc* di seta

silky *adj* (*+er*) *hair, texture* setoso

sill *n* davanzale *m*

silliness *n* stupidità *f inv*

silly *adj* (*+er*) stupido; ***don't be ~*** non dire sciocchezze; ***it was a ~ thing to say*** era una cosa stupida da dire; ***I hope he doesn't do anything ~*** spero che non faccia nessuna stupidaggine; ***he was ~ to resign*** è stato sciocco da parte sua dimettersi; ***I feel ~ in this hat*** con questo cappello mi sento ridicolo; ***make s.o. look ~*** far sembrare ridicolo qn

silo *n* silo *m*

silver I *n metal* argento *m*; *silver objects* argenteria *f* II *adj ring* d'argento; *colour* argentato

silver jubilee *n* venticinquesimo *m* anniversario **silver-plated** *adj* placcato d'argento **silverware** *n* argenteria *f* **silver wedding** *n* nozze *fpl* d'argento

Sim card *n for mobile phone* Sim card *f inv*

similar *adj* simile; ***they are very ~ in character*** hanno caratteri molto simili

similarity *n* rassomiglianza *f*

similarly *adv* allo stesso modo

simile *n* similitudine *f*

simmer *v/i in cooking* sobbollire; *with rage* ribollire

◆**simmer down** *v/i* calmarsi

simple *adj* (*+er*) *method, life, dress* semplice; *person* sempliciotto; ***it's as ~ as ABC*** è semplice come

l'ABC; ***the ~ fact is ...*** è semplicemente che...
simple-minded *adj pej* sempliciotto
simple tense *n* GRAM tempo *m* semplice
simplicity *n* semplicità *f inv*
simplify *v/t* ⟨*pret & past part* ***-ied***⟩ semplificare
simplistic *adj* semplicistico
simply *adv* (*absolutely*) assolutamente; *in a simple way* semplicemente; ***it is ~ the best*** è assolutamente il migliore; ***I was ~ trying to help*** stavo semplicemente cercando di aiutare
simulate *v/t* simulare
simulation *n* simulazione *f*
simultaneous *adj* simultaneo
simultaneously *adv* simultaneamente
sin I *n* peccato *m*; ***live in ~*** *infml* vivere nel peccato **II** *v/i* ⟨*pret & past part* ***-ned***⟩ peccare
since I *prep* da; ***~ last week*** dalla scorsa settimana **II** *adv* da allora; ***I haven't seen him ~*** non lo vedo da allora **III** *cj* **1.** *in expressions of time* da quando; ***~ you left*** da quando sei andato via; ***ever ~ I have known her*** da quando la conosco **2.** (*seeing that*) visto che; ***~ you don't like it*** visto che non ti piace
sincere *adj* sincero
sincerely *adv* con sincerità; *hope* sinceramente; ***Yours ~*** Distinti saluti
sincerity *n* sincerità *f inv*
sinecure *n* sinecura *f*
sinew *n* tendine *m*
sinful *adj* peccaminoso
sing *v/t & v/i* ⟨*pret* **sang**, *past part* **sung**⟩ cantare; ***~ the praises of s.o. / sth*** cantare le lodi di qn / qc
singe *v/t* bruciacchiare
singer *n* cantante *m/f*
singer-songwriter *n* cantautore *m*, -trice *f*
single I *adj* **1.** (*sole*) solo; ***there wasn't a ~ ...*** non c'era nemmeno un ...; ***every ~ day*** tutti i santi giorni **2.** (*not double*) singolo; *bed, sheet* a una piazza; ***in ~ file*** in fila indiana; ***in ~ figures*** inferiore a 10 **3.** (*not married*) single **4.** *with reference to Europe* unico **II** *n* MUS singolo *m*; (*single room*) (camera *f*) singola *f*; *ticket* biglietto *m* di sola andata; ***two ~s to Ayr*** *Br* due biglietti di andata per Ayr; *person* single *m/f inv*; ***~s*** *in tennis* singolo
◆**single out** *v/t sep* (*choose*) prescegliere; (*distinguish*) distinguere
single bed *n* letto *m* a una piazza **single-breasted** *adj* a un petto **single combat** *n* corpo a corpo *m* **single cream** *n Br* panna *f* liquida **single currency** *n* moneta *f* unica **single-density** *adj* COMPUT *disk* a densità singola **single entry** *n* partita *f* semplice **single European market** *n* mercato *m* unico europeo **single file** *n*: ***in ~*** in fila indiana **single-handed** *adj/adv* da solo **single malt** *n* (*whiskey*) single malt *m* **Single Market** *n* mercato *m* unico **single-minded** *adj* determinato; ***be ~ about doing sth*** essere deciso nel fare qc **single mother** *n* ragazza *f* madre **single parent** *n* genitore *m* single **single parent family** *n* famiglia *f* monoparentale **single room** *n* (camera *f*) singola *f*
singles *nsg or npl* SPORTS singolare *m*
single-sex *adj*: ***a ~ school*** una scuola non mista **single-sided** *adj* COMPUT *disk* a singola faccia **single-storey**, *US* **single-story** *adj* a un piano
singly *adv* (*individually*) singolarmente; (*alone*) da solo
singsong *n*: ***we often have a ~*** ci troviamo spesso a cantare insieme
singular I *adj* GRAM singolare; (*outstanding*) singolare **II** *n* GRAM singolare *m*; ***in the ~*** al singolare
sinister *adj* sinistro
sink I *v/i* ⟨*pret* **sank**, *past part* **sunk**⟩ *of ship* affondare; *of object* andare a fondo; *of sun* calare; *of interest rates, pressure etc* scendere; ***he sank onto the bed*** crollò sul letto; ***he sank up to his knees in the mud*** è affondato nel fango fino alle ginocchia; ***the sun sank beneath the horizon*** il sole calò oltre l'orizzonte **II** *v/t* ⟨*pret* **sank**, *past part* **sunk**⟩ *ship* (far) affondare; *funds* investire; ***~ one's teeth into a juicy steak*** affondare i denti in una succosa bistecca **III** *n* lavandino *m*; (*cesspool*) pozzo *m* nero
◆**sink in** *v/i of liquid* penetrare; ***it still hasn't really sunk in*** *of realization* ancora non mi rendo conto
sinking feeling *n* sensazione *f* ango-

sciante

sinner *n* peccatore *m*, -trice *f*

Sinology *n* sinologia *f*

sinuous *adj* sinuoso

sinus *n* seno *m* paranasale; ***my ~es are blocked*** ho il naso bloccato

sinusitis *n* MED sinusite *f*

sip I *v/t* ⟨*pret & past part* ***-ped***⟩ sorseggiare **II** *n* sorso *m*

siphon *n* sifone *m*

◆**siphon off** *v/t sep liquid* travasare (con un un sifone); *money* stornare

sir *n* signore *m*; ***Sir Charles*** Sir Charles; ***Dear Sir*** (***or Madam***), ... Egregio signore (*or* signora)

siren *n* sirena *f*

sirloin *n* controfiletto *m*

sirup *n US* → ***syrup***

sis *n infml* sorella *f*

sissy *n infml* femminuccia *f*

sister *n* sorella *f*; *in hospital* (infermiera *f*) caposala *f*

sisterhood *n* sorellanza *f*; REL congregazione *f* religiosa femminile

sister-in-law *n* ⟨*pl* ***sisters-in-law***⟩ cognata *f*

sit ⟨*pret & past part* ***sat***⟩ **I** *v/i* sedere; ***don't just ~ there, do something!*** non startene seduto, fai qualcosa!; (*sit down*) sedersi; *for a portrait* posare; *of objects* stare; *of committee, assembly etc* riunirsi; ***~ on a committee*** fare parte di una commissione **II** *v/t exam* dare; ***~ a child on one's knee*** mettere un bambino a sedere sul proprio ginocchio

◆**sit about** *Br or* **around** *v/i* starsene seduto

◆**sit back** *v/i* appoggiarsi all'indietro con la schiena; (*do nothing*) starsene seduto

◆**sit down** *v/i* sedersi

◆**sit in** *v/i* (*attend*) assistere (***on sth*** a qc)

◆**sit on** *v/t committee* fare parte di

◆**sit out** *v/t sep meeting* restare fino alla fine di; *storm* aspettare la fine di; *dance* non ballare

◆**sit through** *v/t* restare fino alla fine di

◆**sit up** *v/i in bed* mettersi a sedere; *straighten back* star seduto bene; *wait up at night* rimanere alzato

sitcom *n* sitcom *f inv*

site I *n* luogo *m* **II** *v/t new offices etc* situare

sit-in *n* sit-in *m inv*

sitter *n* (*babysitter*) babysitter *m/f inv*

sitting I *n of committee, court* sessione *f*; *for artist* seduta *f*; *for meals* turno *m*; ***they have two ~s for lunch*** hanno due turni per il pranzo **II** *adj* seduto; ***be in a ~ position*** essere seduto

sitting duck *n fig* bersaglio *m* facile

sitting room *n* salotto *m*

situate *v/t* situare

situated *adj* situato; ***be ~*** trovarsi

situation *n* situazione *f*; *of building etc* posizione *f*; (*job*) lavoro *m*; ***situations vacant*** *Br* offerte *fpl* di lavoro; ***situations wanted*** *Br* domande *fpl* di lavoro

situation comedy *n* situation comedy *f*

sit-up *n exercise* addominale *m*

six *n* sei; ***she is ~*** (***years old***) ha sei anni; ***at*** (***the age of***) ***~*** a (l'età di) sei anni; ***it's ~*** (***o'clock***) sono le sei; ***there are ~ of us*** siamo in sei; ***knock s.o. for ~*** *Br infml* lasciare qn di stucco; *infml* ***he's all at sixes and sevens*** è totalmente confuso; *infml* ***~ of one and half a dozen of the other*** se non è zuppa è pan bagnato

sixfold I *adj* sestuplo **II** *adv* per sei volte

six-footer *n* persona alta sei piedi **six-pack** *n muscles infml* addominali *mpl*; *beer* pacco *m* da sei lattine

sixpence *n moneta da sei penny*

sixteen *num* sedici

sixteenth *n/adj* sedicesimo, -a

sixth I *adj* sesto; ***a ~ part*** una sesta parte; ***he was*** *or* ***came ~*** è arrivato seso; ***he was ~ from the left*** era il sesto da sinistra **II** *n* sesto *m*; MUS sesta *f*; ***Charles the Sixth*** Carlo VI; ***the ~ of September*** *or* ***September the ~*** il sei settembre

sixth form *n Br ultimi due anni di scuola superiore propedeutici per gli esami degli A Levels* **sixth form college** *n Br scuola in cui si insegna solo il "sixth form"* **sixth grade** *n* EDU *US classe che si frequenta tra i 10 e gli 11 anni* **sixth sense** *n* sesto senso *m*

sixtieth *n/adj* sessantesimo, -a

sixty *num* sessanta; ***he's in his sixties*** ha oltre sessant'anni; ***during the Sixties*** negli anni sessanta

size *n* dimensioni *fpl*; *of clothes* taglia *f*, misura *f*; ***dress ~*** taglia *f* del vestito; ***he's about your ~*** è della tua taglia; ***what ~ is it?*** di che misura è?; (*clothes etc*) di che misura è?; ***it's two ~s too big*** è di due taglie in più; *of shoes* numero *m*
◆**size up** *v/t sep* valutare
sizeable *adj* considerevole
sizzle *v/i* sfrigolare
skate[1] *n* (*fish*) razza *f*
skate[2] **I** *n* pattino *m*; ***get your ~s on*** *fig infml* pedala **II** *v/i* pattinare
skateboard *n* skateboard *m inv*
skateboarder *n* skateboarder *m/f inv*
skateboarding *n* skateboard *m inv*
skatepark *n* parco *m* skateboard
skater *n* pattinatore *m*, -trice *f*
skating *n* pattinaggio *m*
skating rink *n* pista *f* di pattinaggio
skein *n* matassa *f*; *geese* stormo *m*
skeletal *adj person* scheletrico
skeleton *n* scheletro *m*
skeleton key *n* passe-partout *m inv*
skeptic *etc US* → ***sceptic*** *etc*
sketch I *n* abbozzo *m*; THEAT sketch *m inv* **II** *v/t* abbozzare
sketchbook *n* album *m inv* da disegno
sketchpad *n* album *m inv* da disegno
sketchy *adj* (+*er*) *knowledge etc* lacunoso
skew I *v/t & v/i* (*make crooked*) mettere di sghembo; (*distort*) distorcere **II** *adj* sbilenco
skewer *n* spiedino *m*
skewwhiff *adj Br infml* storto
ski I *n* sci *m inv* **II** *v/i* sciare
ski boots *npl* scarponi *mpl* da sci
skid I *n* sbandata *f* **II** *v/i* ⟨*pret & past part* ***-ded***⟩ sbandare
skidmark *n* segno *m* di uno slittamento
skid row *n US infml* quartiere *m* malfamato
skier *n* sciatore *m*, -trice *f*
skiing *n* sci *m inv*; ***go ~*** andare a sciare
ski instructor *n* maestro *m*, -a *f* di sci
ski jump *n* salto *m* dal trampolino
skilful, *US* **skillful** *adj* abile
skilfully, *US* **skillfully** *adv* abilmente
ski lift *n* impianto *m* di risalita
skill *n* (*ability*) abilità *f inv*; ***what ~s do you have?*** quali capacità possiede?
skilled *adj* abile
skilled worker *n* operaio *m*, -a *f* specializzato, -a
skillet *n* padella *f*
skillful *etc US* → ***skilful*** *etc*
skim *v/t* ⟨*pret & past part* ***-med***⟩ *surface* sfiorare; *read quickly* scorrere; *milk* scremare
◆**skim off** *v/t sep the best* selezionare
◆**skim through** *v/t text* scorrere
skimmed milk *n* latte *m* scremato
skimp *v/i* lesinare
◆**skimp on** *v/t* lesinare su
skimpy *adj* (+*er*) *account etc* scarso; *dress* succinto
skin I *n of person, animal* pelle *f*; ***be soaked to the ~*** essere bagnato fino alle ossa; ***that's no ~ off my nose*** *esp Br infml* non sono affari che mi riguardano; ***save one's own ~*** salvarsi la pelle; ***jump out of one's ~*** *infml* saltare per la paura; ***get under s.o.'s ~*** (*irritate*) infastidire qn; *fig* ***have a thick / thin ~*** avere la pelle dura / essere delicato; ***by the ~ of one's teeth*** *infml* per il rotto della cuffia; *of fruit* buccia *f* **II** *v/t* ⟨*pret & past part* ***-ned***⟩ scoiare
skin diving *n* immersioni *fpl* subacquee
skinflint *n infml* spilorcio *m infml*
skin graft *n* innesto *m* epidermico
skinhead *n infml* skinhead *m inv*
skinny *adj* (+*er*) magro
skinny-dipping *v/i infml* bagno *m* senza costume
skint *adj Br infml* al verde
skin-tight *adj* aderente
skip[1] **I** *v/i* ⟨*pret & past part* ***-ped***⟩ saltellare; *with skipping rope* saltare **II** *v/t* ⟨*pret & past part* ***-ped***⟩ (*omit*) saltare **III** *n little jump* salto *m*
◆**skip through** *v/i +obj book* sfogliare
skip[2] *n* BUILD cassone *m* per materiale di scarto
ski pole *n* racchetta *f* da sci
skipper I *n* NAUT skipper *m inv*; *of team* capitano *m* **II** *v/t* essere il capitano di
skipping *n* il saltare *m*
skipping rope *n* corda *f* (per saltare)
ski resort *n* stazione *f* sciistica
skirmish *n* MIL scaramuccia *f*; (*scrap, fig*) rissa *f*
skirt I *n* gonna *f*; *infml pej* donna *f*; ***a bit of ~*** una bella ragazza **II** *v/t* cir-

condare; ***the road ~ed the town*** la strada circondava la città; (*elude*) girare attorno a
◆**skirt around** *v/t problem* girare attorno a
skirting board *n* battiscopa *m inv*
ski run *n* pista *f* da sci **ski stick** *n* racchetta *f* da sci **ski tow** *n* sciovia *f*
skitter *v/i* correre rapidamente
skittish *adj* capriccioso; (*nervous*) nervoso
skittle *n* birillo *m*
skittles *nsg* (*game*) birilli *mpl*
skive *v/i infml* fare lo scansafatiche *infml*
◆**skive off** *v/i Br infml* squagliarsela
skiver *n Br infml* scansafatiche
skivvy I *n Br infml pej* sguattera *f* **II** *v/i Br infml* fare la sguattera
skulk *v/i* (*move*) muoversi furtivamente; (*lurk*) appostarsi
skull *n* cranio *m*
skunk *n* moffetta *f*
sky *n* cielo *m*
sky-blue *adj* celeste **skydiving** *n* skydiving *m* **sky-high I** *adj prices* alle stelle; *confidence* alto **II** *adv* fino al cielo; ***blow a bridge ~*** *infml* far saltare in aria un ponte; ***blow a theory ~*** *infml* mandare all'aria una teoria **skyjack** *v/t* dirottare **skylight** *n* lucernario *m* **skyline** *n* profilo *m* (contro il cielo) **sky pilot** *n infml* prete *m* **skyrocket I** *n* razzo *m* **II** *v/i* salire alle stelle **skyscraper** *n* grattacielo *m* **skyward** *adj* che va verso il cielo **skywards** *adv* verso il cielo
slab *n of stone* lastra *f*; *of cake etc* fetta *f*
slack I *adj* (+*er*) *rope* allentato; *person*, *work* negligente; *period* lento; ***business is ~*** gli affari sono in stasi **II** *n of rope* allentato; *fig* ***cut s.o. some ~*** *infml* risparmiare le critiche a qn **III** *v/i* impigrirsi
slacken *v/t rope* allentare; *pace* rallentare
◆**slacken off** *v/i* rallentare
slacker *n* fannullone *m*, -a *f*
slacks *npl* pantaloni *mpl*
slag *n* scorie *fpl*; *Br sl* (*woman*) donnaccia *f*
◆**slag off** *v/t sep sl* parlare male di
slag heap *n* cumulo *m* di scorie
slain *past part* → ***slay***
slake *v/t & v/i* estinguere; ***~ one's thirst*** placare la sete
slam *v/t & v/i* ⟨*pret & past part* **-med**⟩ *door* sbattere
◆**slam down** *v/t sep* sbattere
slander I *n* diffamazione *f* **II** *v/t* diffamare
slanderous *adj* diffamatorio
slang *n* slang *m inv*; *of a specific group* gergo *m*
slant I *v/i* pendere **II** *v/t* inclinare **III** *n* pendenza *f*; *given to a story* angolazione *f*
slanting *adj roof* spiovente
slap I *v/t* ⟨*pret & past part* **-ped**⟩ schiaffeggiare **II** *n blow* schiaffo *m*; ***a ~ in the face*** *fig* uno schiaffo morale; ***give s.o. a ~ on the back*** dare una pacca sulla spalla; *fig* congratularsi; ***give s.o. a ~ on the wrist*** *fig infml* dare una tirata d'orecchi a qn
◆**slap down** *v/t sep infml* dare una bella lezione a
◆**slap on** *v/t sep infml* (*apply carelessly*) mettere senza attenzione; *fig tax*, *money* aumentare
slap bang *adv esp Br infml*: ***it was ~ in the middle*** si trovava nel bel mezzo; ***run ~ into s.o. / sth*** andare a sbattere contro qn / qc **slapdash** *adj work* frettoloso; *person* pressapochista **slapstick** *n* comica *f*
slapper *n Br infml* vacca *f*
slap-up meal *n infml* pranzo *m* coi fiocchi
slash I *v/t skin*, *painting* squarciare; *prices*, *costs* abbattere; ***~ one's wrists*** tagliarsi le vene **II** *n cut* taglio *m*; *in punctuation* barra *f*
slat *n* stecca *f*
slate[1] *n* ardesia *f*; ***wipe the ~ clean*** metterci una pietra sopra
slate[2] *v/t Br* (*criticize*) stroncare; *person* rimproverare
slaughter I *n of animals* macellazione *f*; *of people*, *troops* massacro *m* **II** *v/t animals* macellare; *people*, *troops* massacrare
slaughterhouse *n for animals* macello *m*
Slav *adj* slavo
slave *n* schiavo *m*, -a *f*
◆**slave away** *v/i* sgobbare; ***slave away at sth*** sgobbare su qc
slave-driver *n infml* negriero *m*, -a *f*

infml **slave labour** *n* lavoro *m* degli schiavi
slaver *v/i* sbavare; **~ *over s.o. / sth*** sbavare per qn / qc
slavery *n* schiavitù *f inv*
slavish *adj* servile; ***a ~ imitazione of the original*** un'imitazione pedissequa copia dell'originale
slay *v/t* 〈*pret* ***slew***, *past part* ***slain***〉 ammazzare
sleaze *n* POL corruzione *f*
sleazy *adj* (*+er*) *bar, characters* sordido
sled(ge) *n* slitta *f*
sledge hammer *n* mazza *f*
sleek *adj* (*+er*) *fur* lucente; *figure* di linea slanciata; (*elegant*) elegante
sleep I *v/i* 〈*pret & past part* ***slept***〉 dormire **II** *v/t*: ***this tent ~s four*** in questa tenda possono dormire quattro persone **III** *n* sonno *m*; ***go to ~*** addormentarsi; ***I need a good ~*** ho bisogno di una bella dormita; ***I couldn't get to ~*** non sono riuscito a dormire; ***talk in one's ~*** parlare nel sonno; ***put to ~*** *animal* (farlo) abbattere
◆**sleep around** *v/i* (*have sex with different people*) andare a letto con varia gente
◆**sleep in** *v/i* (*have a long lie*) dormire fino a tardi
◆**sleep off** *v/t sep alcohol* smaltire dormendo gli effetti di; ***sleep it off*** smaltire la sbornia con una bella dormita
◆**sleep on** *v/t proposal, decision* dormire su; ***sleep on it*** dormirci su
◆**sleep with** *v/t* (*have sex with*) andare a letto con
sleeper *n* RAIL: *on track* traversina *f*; (*sleeping car*) vagone *m* letto; *train* treno *m* notturno; ***be a light / heavy ~*** avere il sonno leggero / pesante
sleepily *adv* con aria assonnata
sleeping bag *n* sacco *m* a pelo **sleeping car** *n* RAIL vagone *m* letto **sleeping partner** *n Br* COMM socio *m* inattivo **sleeping pill** *n* sonnifero *m*
sleepless *adj night* in bianco
sleepover *n pernottamento di uno o più bambini a casa di un amichetto*
sleepwalker *n* sonnambulo *m*, -a *f*
sleepwalking *n* sonnambulismo *m*
sleepy *adj* (*+er*) *child* assonnato; *town* addormentato; ***I'm ~*** ho sonno
sleepyhead *n infml* dormiglione *m*, -a *f*
sleet I *n* nevischio *m* **II** *v/i*: ***it was ~ing*** sta cadendo il nevischio
sleeve *n of jacket etc* manica *f*; *fig* ***roll one's ~s up*** rimboccarsi le maniche; *fig* ***have sth up one's ~*** *infml* tenere qc di riserva
sleeveless *adj* senza maniche
sleigh *n* slitta *f*
sleight of hand *n* gioco *m* di prestigio
slender *adj figure, arms* snello; *chance, income, margin* piccolo
slept *pret & past part* → ***sleep***
sleuth *n infml* segugio *m*
slew *pret* → ***slay***
slice I *n a. fig* fetta *f* **II** *v/t loaf etc* affettare
◆**slice off** *v/t sep* tagliare via
sliced bread *n* pane *m* a cassetta; ***the greatest thing since ~*** *infml* il non plus ultra
slick I *adj* (*+er*) *performance* brillante; (*pej: cunning*) scaltro **II** *n of oil* chiazza *f* di petrolio **III** *v/t* lucidare
◆**slick back** *v/t sep* ***slick one's hair back*** lisciarsi i capelli all'indietro
slid *pret & past part* → ***slide***
slide I *n for kids* scivolo *m*; PHOT diapositiva *f*; *in hair* fermacapelli *m inv* **II** *v/i* 〈*pret & past part* ***slid***〉 scivolare; *of exchange rate etc* calare; *fig* ***let things ~*** lasciar correre **III** *v/t* 〈*pret & past part* ***slid***〉 far scivolare
slide projector *n* proiettore *m* per diapositive **slide show** *n* proiezione *f* di diapositive
sliding door *n* porta *f* scorrevole
sliding scale *n* ECON scala *f* mobile
slight I *adj* (*+er*) *person, figure* gracile; (*small*) leggero; ***no, not in the ~est*** no, per nulla; ***the wall's at a ~ angle*** la parete ha una leggera inclinazione; ***have a ~ cold*** ho un leggero raffreddore; ***just the ~est bit short*** appena appena troppo corto; ***he is upset by at the ~est thing*** se la prende per la minima cosa **II** *n* (*insult*) offesa *f* **III** *v/t* (*offend*) offendere
slighted *adj* (*offended*) offeso
slightly *adv* leggermente; ***~ injured*** lievemente ferito; ***he hesitated ever so ~*** ha esitato veramente poco; ***~ built*** *person* esile
slim I *adj* (*+er*) slanciato; *chance* scar-

so **II** *v/i* ⟨*pret & past part* ***-med***⟩ dimagrire; ***I'm ~ming*** sono a dieta
◆**slim down I** *v/t sep fig business etc* ridimensionare **II** *v/i person* dimagrire
slime *n* melma *f*
slimebag *n infml* verme *m*
slimeball *n infml* verme *m*
slimy *adj* (+*er*) *liquid* melmoso; *person* viscido
sling I *n for arm* fascia *f* a tracolla; *drink bevanda alcolica con gin, zucchero, acqua e limone* **II** *v/t* ⟨*pret & past part* ***slung***⟩ (*throw*) lanciare; ***he slung the box onto his back*** si mise la scatola sulla schiena
slingback *n scarpa da donna con cinturino al calcagno*
slink *v/i* ⟨*pret & past part* ***slunk***⟩ sgattaiolare; ***~ off*** svignarsela
slinky *adj dress* sexy
slip I *v/i* ⟨*pret & past part* ***-ped***⟩ **1.** *on ice etc* scivolare **2.** *of quality etc* peggiorare **3.** *quickly*: ***he ~ped out of the room*** è sgattaiolato fuori dalla stanza **4.** ***let sth ~*** (*reveal*) farsi scappare qc **II** *v/t* ⟨*pret & past part* ***-ped***⟩ (*put*) far scivolare; ***it ~ped my mind*** mi è passato di mente; ***he ~ped it into his briefcase*** l'ha fatto scivolare nella valigetta; ***she ~ped the dress over her head*** si infilò il vestito; ***~ a disc*** MED avere un ernia discale **III** *n* **1.** *on ice etc* scivolata *f* **2.** (*mistake*) errore *m*; ***a ~ of the tongue*** un lapsus **3.** ***a ~ of paper*** un foglietto **4.** *fig* ***give s.o. the ~*** seminare qn **5.** *clothing* sottoveste *f*
◆**slip away** *v/i of time* passare; *of opportunity* andare sprecato; (*die quietly*) spirare
◆**slip back** *v/i* andare dietro; (*quickly*) ritornare furtivamente
◆**slip behind** *v/i* arretrare
◆**slip by** *v/i* (*person*) scorrere accanto; (*years*) scorrere via
◆**slip down** *v/i* (*fall*) scivolare per terra; (*go down*) scendere
◆**slip in I** *v/i* intrufolarsi **II** *v/t sep mention* scappare; ***slip sth into s.o.'s pocket*** infilare qc dentro la tasca di qn
◆**slip off** *v/t sep jacket etc* togliersi
◆**slip on** *v/t sep jacket etc* infilarsi
◆**slip out** *v/i* (*go out*) sgattaiolare
◆**slip up** *v/i make mistake* sbagliarsi
slipknot *n* cappio *m*
slip-ons *npl* scarpe *fpl* non allacciate
slipped disc *n* ernia *f* del disco
slipper *n* pantofola *f*
slippery *adj* scivoloso; ***he's on the ~ slope*** *fig* è su una brutta china; *pej infml person* disonesto; ***a ~ customer*** un tipo infido
slippy *adj* scivoloso
slip road *n* rampa *f* di accesso
slipshod *adj* trascurato
slip-up *n* (*mistake*) errore *m*
slipway *n* scalo *m* di alaggio
slit I *n* (*tear*) strappo *m*; (*hole*) fessura *f*; *in skirt* spacco *m* **II** *v/t* ⟨*pret & past part* ***slit***⟩ *envelope*, *packet* aprire (tagliando); *throat* tagliare
slither *v/i* strisciare
sliver *n* scheggia *f*
slob *n pej* sudicione *m*, -a *f*
slobber I *n* bava *f* **II** *v/i* sbavare
slog *n* faticata *f*
◆**slog away at** *v/t infml* (*work hard*) sgobbare su
slogan *n* slogan *m inv*
slop I *n* brodaglia *f* **II** *v/t* ⟨*pret & past part* ***-ped***⟩ rovesciare, versare **III** *v/i*: ***~ over*** (***into sth***) rovesciarsi (in qc)
slope I *n* pendenza *f*; *of mountain* pendio *m*; ***built on a ~*** costruito in pendio **II** *v/i* essere inclinato; ***the road ~s down to the sea*** la strada scende fino al mare
sloppy *adj* (+*er*) *work*, *editing* trascurato; *in dressing* sciatto; (*too sentimental*) sdolcinato
slosh *infml* **I** *v/t* (*splash*) versare **II** *v/i*: ***~*** (***around***) sciabordare; ***~ through mud / water*** sguazzare nel fango / nell'acqua
sloshed *adj infml* (*drunk*) sbronzo *infml*
slot *n* fessura *f*; *in schedule* spazio *m*
◆**slot in** ⟨*pret & past part* ***-ted***⟩ **I** *v/t sep* infilare; ***I can slot you in at 2 pm*** posso piazzarti alle due **II** *v/i* infilarsi; ***suddenly everything slotted into place*** improvvisamente tutto si sistemò
◆**slot together I** *v/i* (*parts*) incastrarsi **II** *v/t sep* incastrare
sloth *n* bradipo *m*
slothful *adj* accidioso
slot machine *n for vending* distribu-

tore *m* automatico; *for gambling* slot--machine *f inv*

slouch **I** *n* (*posture*) andatura *f* dinoccolata **II** *v/i*: ***don't ~!*** su con la schiena!; ***he was ~ed over his desk*** era seduto al banco in modo scomposto

slovenly *adj* sciatto

slow *adj* (+*er*) **1.** lento; ***be ~*** *of clock* essere indietro; ***he's a ~ learner*** impara lentamente; ***it was ~ going*** procedeva lentamente; ***get off to a ~ start*** (*race*) partire con un inizio lento; ***be ~ to do sth*** essere lento a fare qc; ***business is ~*** gli affari vanno piano **2.** (*not clever*) lento

◆**slow down** *v/t sep & v/i* rallentare

slowcoach *n Br infml* lumaca *f infml* **slowdown** *n in production* rallentamento *m* **slow lane** *n* AUTO corsia *f* per i veicoli lenti

slowly *adv* lentamente

slow motion *n*: ***in ~*** al rallentatore

slowness *n* lentezza *f*

slowpoke *n US infml* lumaca *f infml* **slow-witted** *adj* duro di comprendonio

sludge *n* melma *f*

slug[1] *n* ZOOL lumaca *f*

slug[2] *n infml* ***a ~ of whisky*** un sorso di whisky

slug[3] **I** *v/t* tracannare; ***he ~ged the man on the jaw*** ha colpito l'uomo sulla mascella **II** *n* botta *f*

sluggish *adj* lento

sluice *n* (*sluice gate*) chiusa *f*

slum **I** *n* quartiere *m* degradato; ***~s*** bassifondi *mpl* **II** *v/t & v/i infml*: *a.* **slum it** vivere arrangiandosi

slump **I** *n in trade* crollo *m* **II** *v/i economically* crollare; (*collapse*: *of person*) accasciarsi

slung *pret & past part* → ***sling***

slunk *pret & past part* → ***slink***

slur **I** *n* calunnia *f* **II** *v/t* ⟨*pret & past part* **-red**⟩ *words* biascicare

slurp *v/t* bere rumorosamente

slurred *adj speech* impappinato

slush *n* fanghiglia *f*; (*pej*: *sentimental stuff*) smancerie *fpl*

slush fund *n* fondi *mpl* neri

slushy *adj* (+*er*) *snow* ridotto in fanghiglia; *film, novel* sdolcinato

slut *n pej* sgualdrina *f*

sly *adj* (+*er*) scaltro; ***on the ~*** di nascosto

smack **I** *v/t child* picchiare; *bottom* sculacciare **II** *n on the bottom* sculacciata *f*; *in the face* schiaffo *m*; *infml* eroina *f* **III** *adv infml* in pieno; ***be ~ in the middle of sth*** essere nel bel mezzo di qc

◆**smack of** *v/t* (*be a sign of*) sapere di; ***it smacks of intrigue*** puzza di intrigo

small **I** *adj* (+*er*) piccolo; ***feel ~*** (*feel ashamed*) sentirsi umiliato **II** *n*: ***the ~ of the back*** le reni; *Br* ***~s*** biancheria *f* intima

small ad *n* piccolo annuncio *m* **small beer** *n* (*person*) persona *f* insignificante; (*thing*) cosa *f* da poco **small change** *n* spiccioli *mpl* **small fry** *npl fig* pesci *mpl* piccoli **smallholder** *n* piccolo proprietario *m* terrieri **small hours** *npl*: ***the ~*** le ore *fpl* piccole **small-minded** *adj* gretto **smallpox** *n* vaiolo *m* **small print** *n* parte *f* scritta in caratteri minuti **small--scale** *adj model* in scala ridotta; *industry* piccolo **small screen** *n*: TV ***on the ~*** sul piccolo schermo **small--sized** *adj* di piccole dimensioni **small talk** *n* conversazione *f* di circostanza **small-time** *adj infml crook* di poca importanza **small-town** *adj* di provincia

smarmy *adj* (+*er*) *infml* untuoso

smart **I** *adj* (+*er*) (*elegant*) elegante; ***the ~ set*** il bel mondo; (*intelligent*) intelligente; ***that wasn't very ~ (of you)*** non è stato molto furbo da parte tua; *pace* svelto; ***get ~ with*** fare il furbo con *infml* **II** *v/i* (*hurt*) bruciare

smart alec(k) *n infml* sapientone *m infml* **smart arse**, *US* **smart ass** *n sl* sapientone *m* **smart bomb** *n* bomba *f* intelligente **smart card** *n* smart card *f inv*

◆**smarten up** *v/t & v/i* sistemare; ***smarten o.s. up*** mettersi in ghingheri; ***you'd better smarten up your ideas*** *infml* farai meglio a riordinare le idee

smartly *adv dressed* elegantemente

smart money *n* FIN investitori esperti; ***the ~ is on him winning*** gli scommettitori esperti lo danno per vincitore

smartphone *n* TEL smartphone *m*

smash **I** *v/t break* spaccare; *hit hard* sbattere; ***~ sth to pieces*** mandare in frantumi qc **II** *v/i break* frantumar-

si; ***the driver ~ed into …*** l'automobilista si è schiantato contro … **III** *n noise* fracasso *m*; (*car crash*) scontro *m*; *in tennis* schiacciata *f*
◆**smash up** *v/t sep place* distruggere
smash-and-grab *adj furto di merce esposta in vetrina*
smasher *n Br infml* schianto *m*
smash hit *n infml* successone *m*
smashing *adj infml* fantastico
smattering *n of a language* infarinatura *f*
SME *abbr* (= **small and medium-sized enterprises**) piccola e media impresa *f*
smear I *n of ink etc* macchia *f*; MED striscio *m*; *on character* calunnia *f* **II** *v/t*; *character* calunniare; ***~ mud over the wall*** imbrattare il muro di fango
smear campaign *n* campagna *f* diffamatoria **smear test** *n* MED striscio *m* vaginale
smell I *n* odore *m*; ***it has no ~*** non ha odore; ***sense of ~*** olfatto *m*, odorato *m* **II** *v/t* sentire odore di; *test by smelling* sentire; *fig danger* sentire puzza di; ***~ trouble*** sentire puzza di guai; ***I ~ a rat*** *infml* gatta ci cova **III** *v/i unpleasantly* puzzare; (*sniff*) odorare; ***what does it ~ of?*** che odore ha?; ***his breath ~s*** gli puzza l'alito; ***you ~ of beer*** puzzi di birra; ***it ~s good*** ha un buon profumino
smelling salts *n* sali *mpl* ammoniacali
smelly *adj* (+*er*) puzzolente; ***it's so ~ in here*** qui dentro c'è puzza
smelt[1] *esp Br pret & past part* → ***smell***
smelt[2] *v/t ore* fondere; (*refine*) affinare
smile I *v/i* sorridere **II** *n* sorriso *m*; ***be all ~s*** essere tutto contento
◆**smile at** *v/t* sorridere a
smirk I *v/i* sorridere con compiacimento **II** *n* sorriso *m* compiaciuto
smithereens *npl*: ***smash sth to ~*** mandare qc in frantumi
smithy *n* fucina *f*
smitten *adj*: ***he's really ~ with her*** *infml* è follemente innamorato di lei
smock *n* grembiule *m*; (*shirt*) camicione *m*
smog *n* smog *m inv*
smoke I *n* fumo *m*; ***have a ~*** fumare **II** *v/t cigarettes etc* fumare; *bacon* affumicare **III** *v/i* fumare; ***I don't ~*** non fumo
smoke alarm *n* allarme *m* antincendio
smoked *adj bacon*, *cheese* affumicato; *glass* fumé
smoker *n person* fumatore *m*, -trice *f*
smoking *n* fumo *m*; ***no ~*** vietato fumare
smoking compartment *n* RAIL carrozza *f* fumatori
smoky *adj* (+*er*) *room*, *air* pieno di fumo
smolder *US* → ***smoulder***
smooth I *adj* (+*er*) *surface*, *skin*, *sea* liscio; *sea* calmo; *transition* senza problemi; *pej*: *person* mellifluo **II** *v/t hair* lisciare
◆**smooth down** *v/t sep with sandpaper etc* levigare
◆**smooth out** *v/t sep paper*, *cloth* lisciare
◆**smooth over** *v/t sep*: ***smooth things over*** appianare le cose
smoothie *n drink* frullato *m*
smoothly *adv without any problems* senza problemi
smother *v/t flames*, *person* soffocare; ***~ s.o. with kisses*** coprire qn di baci
smoulder, *US* **smolder** *v/i of fire* covare sotto la cenere; *fig*: *with anger*, *desire* consumarsi (***with*** di)
SMS *abbr* (= **short message system**) SMS *m inv*
smudge I *n* sbavatura *f* **II** *v/t* sbavare
smug *adj* (+*er*) compiaciuto
smuggle *v/t* contrabbandare
smuggler *n* contrabbandiere *m*, -a *f*
smuggling *n* contrabbando *m*
smugly *adv* con compiacimento
smutty *adj* (+*er*) *joke*, *sense of humour* sconcio
snack *n* spuntino *m*
snack bar *n* snack bar *m inv*
snag *n* (*problem*) problema *m*
snail *n* chiocciola *f*, *in cooking* lumaca *f*
snail mail *n* COMPUT *infml* posta-lumaca *f*
snake *n* serpente *m*
snap I *v/t* ⟨*pret & past part* ***-ped***⟩ *break* spezzare; (*say sharply*) dire bruscamente **II** *v/i* ⟨*pret & past part* ***-ped***⟩ *break* spezzarsi; ***~ at s.o.*** (*speak sharply*) rispondere male a qn **III** *n sound* botto *m*; PHOT foto *f* **IV** *adj decision*, *judgement* immedia-

to

◆**snap up** *v/t sep bargains* accaparrarsi

snappy *adj* (*+er*) *person, mood* irritabile; *infml* (*quick*) rapido; (*elegant*) elegante

snapshot *n* istantanea *f*

snare *n* (*trap*) trappola *f*

snarl **I** *v/i* ringhiare **II** *n of dog* ringhio *m*

snatch **I** *v/t* afferrare; (*steal*) scippare; (*kidnap*) rapire **II** *v/i* strappare di mano

◆**snatch at** *v/t object* cercare di afferrare; *opportunity* cercare di cogliere

snazzy *adj infml* chic

sneak **I** *v/t* (*remove, steal*) rubare; ***~ a glance at*** dare una sbirciatina a **II** *v/i* (*tell tales*) fare la spia; ***~ out of ...*** sgattaiolare fuori da ... **III** *n* (*telltale*) spione *m*, -a *f*

◆**sneak up on** *v/t person* avvicinarsi di soppiatto a

sneakers *npl US* scarpe *fpl* da ginnastica

sneaking *adj*: ***have a ~ suspicion that ...*** avere il vago sospetto che ...

sneaky *adj* (*+er*) *infml* (*crafty*) scaltro

sneer **I** *v/i* sogghignare; ***~ at*** deridere **II** *n* sogghigno *m*

sneeze **I** *v/i* starnutire **II** *n* starnuto *m*

sniff **I** *v/i to clear nose* tirare su col naso; *of dog* fiutare **II** *v/t smell* annusare

snigger **I** *v/i* ridacchiare **II** *n* risolino *m*

snip *n infml* (*bargain*) affare *m*

sniper *n* cecchino *m*

snippet *n* (*bit*) frammento *m*

snivel *v/i pej* frignare

snob *n* snob *m/f inv*

snobbery *n* snobismo *m*

snobbish *adj* snob *inv*

snog ⟨*pret & past part* ***-ged***⟩ *infml* **I** *v/t* sbaciucchiare **II** *v/i* sbaciucchiarsi

snooker *n* biliardo *m*

snoop *n* ficcanaso *m/f inv*

◆**snoop around** *v/i* ficcanasare

snooty *adj* (*+er*) snob *inv*

snooze **I** *n* sonnellino *m*; ***have a ~*** fare un sonnellino **II** *v/i* sonnecchiare

snore *v/i* russare

snoring *n* russare *m*

snorkel *n* boccaglio *m*

snort *v/i* sbuffare

snot *n infml* moccio *m infml*

snotty *adj* (*+er*) *infml nose* moccioso *infml*

snout *n of pig* grugno *m*; *of dog* muso *m*

snow **I** *n* neve *f* **II** *v/i* nevicare

◆**snow in** *v/t sep*: ***be snowed in*** essere bloccati per la neve

◆**snow under** *v/t sep*: ***be snowed under with ...*** essere sommerso di ...

snowball *n* palla *f* di neve **snowboard** *v/i* fare snowboard **snowboarding** *n* snowboard *m inv* **snowbound** *adj* isolato dalla neve **snow chains** *npl* AUTO catene *fpl* da neve **snowdrift** *n* cumulo *m* di neve **snowdrop** *n* bucaneve *m inv* **snowflake** *n* fiocco *m* di neve **snowman** *n* pupazzo *m* di neve **snowplough**, *US* **snowplow** *n* spazzaneve *m inv* **snowstorm** *n* tormenta *f*

snowy *adj* (*+er*) *weather* nevoso; *roofs, hills* innevato

snub **I** *n* affronto *m* **II** *v/t* ⟨*pret & past part* ***-bed***⟩ snobbare

snub-nosed *adj* col naso all'insù

snug *adj* (*+er*) al calduccio; (*tight-fitting*) attillato

◆**snuggle down** *v/i* accoccolarsi

◆**snuggle up to** *v/t* rannicchiarsi accanto a

so **I** *adv* **1.** così; ***~ hot / cold*** così caldo / freddo; ***not ~ much*** non così tanto; ***~ much better / easier*** molto meglio / più facile; ***you shouldn't eat / drink ~ much*** non dovresti mangiare / bere così tanto; ***I miss you ~*** mi manchi tanto; ***and ~ on*** e così via **2.** (*also*) ***~ am / do I*** anch'io; ***~ is she / does she*** anche lei **II** *pron*: ***I hope / think ~*** spero / penso di sì; ***I don't think ~*** non credo, credo di no; ***you didn't tell me – I did ~*** non me l'hai detto – e invece sì; ***50 or ~*** circa 50 **III** *cj* **1.** (*for that reason*) così; ***and ~ I missed the train*** e così ho perso il treno **2.** (*in order that*) così che; ***~ (that) I could come too*** così che potessi venire anch'io **3.** ***~ what?*** *infml* e allora?

soak *v/t* (*steep*) mettere a bagno; *of water, rain* inzuppare

◆**soak up** *v/t sep liquid* assorbire; ***soak up the sun*** crogiolarsi al sole

soaked *adj* fradicio; ***be ~ to the skin***

essere bagnato fradicio
soaking (wet) *adj* bagnato fradicio
so-and-so *n infml unknown person* tal dei tali *m/f inv*; (*euph: annoying person*) impiastro *m*
soap *n for washing* sapone *m*
soap (opera) *n* soap (opera) *f inv*, telenovela *f*
soapy *adj* (+*er*) *water* saponato
soar *v/i of rocket etc* innalzarsi; *of prices* aumentare vertiginosamente
sob I *v/i* ⟨*pret & past part* ***-bed***⟩ singhiozzare **II** *n* singhiozzo *m*
sober *adj* (*not drunk*) sobrio; (*serious*) serio
◆ **sober up** *v/i* smaltire la sbornia
sob story *n infml* storia *f* strappalacrime
so-called *adj* cosiddetto
soccer *n* calcio *m*
soccer hooligan *n* hooligan *m/f inv*
sociable *adj* socievole
social *adj* sociale
social democrat *n* socialdemocratico *m*, -a *f*
socialism *n* socialismo *m*
socialist I *adj* socialista **II** *n* socialista *m/f*
socialize *v/i* socializzare; ***I don't ~ much*** non vedo molta gente
social life *n* vita *f* sociale **social science** *n* scienza *f* sociale **social security** *n Br* sussidio *m* della previdenza sociale **social services** *npl Br* servizi *mpl* sociali **social work** *n* assistenza *f* sociale **social worker** *n* assistente *m/f* sociale
society *n* società *f inv*; (*organization*) associazione *f*
sociologist *n* sociologo *m*, -a *f*
sociology *n* sociologia *f*
sock[1] *n* calzino *m*; ***pull one's ~s up*** (*try harder*) fare di meglio
sock[2] **I** *n infml* (*punch*) pugno *m* **II** *v/t infml* (*punch*) dare un pugno a
socket *n for light bulb* portalampada *m inv*; *in wall* presa *f* (di corrente); *of eye* orbita *f*
soda *n* (*soda water*) seltz *m inv*
sodden *adj* zuppo
sodium *n* sodio *m*
sofa *n* divano *m*
sofa-bed *n* divano *m* letto
soft *adj* (+*er*) *pillow* soffice; *chair, skin* morbido; *light, colour* tenue; *music* soft; *voice* sommesso; (*lenient*) indulgente; ***have a ~ spot for*** avere un debole per
soft-boiled *adj*: **~ *egg*** uovo alla coque
soft drink *n* bibita *f* analcolica **soft drug** *n* droga *f* leggera
soften I *v/t butter etc* ammorbidire; *position* attenuare; *impact, blow* attutire **II** *v/i of butter, ice-cream* ammorbidirsi
soft-hearted *adj* dal cuore tenero
softly *adv speak* sommessamente
soft toy *n* giocattolo *m* di pezza
software *n* software *m inv*
soggy *adj* (+*er*) molle e pesante
soil I *n* (*earth*) terra *f* **II** *v/t* sporcare
soiled *adj dirty* sporco; (*goods*) deteriorato
solace *n* conforto *m*
solar *adj* solare; **~ *power*** energia *f* solare
solar eclipse *n* eclissi *f inv* di sole **solar energy** *n* energia *f* solare
solarium *n* ⟨*pl* ***solaria***⟩ solarium *m*
solar panel *n* pannello *m* solare **solar system** *n* sistema *m* solare
sold *pret & past part* → ***sell***
solder I *n* lega *f* per saldature **II** *v/t* saldare
soldier *n* soldato *m*
◆ **soldier on** *v/i* perseverare
sole[1] *n of foot* pianta *f* (del piede); *of shoe* suola *f*
sole[2] *adj* unico; (*exclusive*) esclusivo
sole[3] *n* (*fish*) sogliola *f*
solely *adv* solamente; ***be ~ responsible*** essere il solo / la sola responsabile
solemn *adj* solenne
solemnity *n* solennità *f inv*
solemnly *adv* solennemente
solicit I *v/t* sollecitare **II** *v/i of prostitute* adescare
solicitor *n* avvocato *m*
solid I *adj* (*hard*) solido; (*without holes*) compatto; *gold, silver* massiccio; (*sturdy*) robusto; *evidence* concreto; *support* forte; ***a ~ hour*** un'ora intera; ***be frozen ~*** essere completamente ghiacciato; ***the square was packed ~ with cars*** la piazza era piena zeppa di auto; ***they worked for two ~ days*** hanno lavorato per due giorni pieni **II** *n* solido *m*; **solids** *npl* cibi *mpl* solidi
solidarity *n* solidarietà *f inv*

solidify *v/i* ⟨*pret & past part* **-ied**⟩ solidificarsi
solidity *n of substance* solidità *f*; *of support* stabilità *f*
solidly *adv built* solidamente; *in favour of sth* all'unanimità
soliloquy *n on stage* monologo *m*
solipsism *n* PHIL solipsismo *m*
solitaire *n US*: *card game* solitario *m*
solitary *adj life*, *activity* solitario; (*single*) solo
solitary confinement *n* isolamento *m*
solitude *n* solitudine *f*
solo **I** *n* MUS assolo *m* **II** *adj performance* solista; *flight* in solitario **III** *adv* MUS ***go ~*** fare un assolo
soloist *n* solista *m/f*
so long *int US* arrivederci
solstice *n* solstizio *m*
soluble *adj substance* solubile; *problem* risolvibile
solution *n* soluzione *f*
solve *v/t* risolvere
solvent **I** *adj financially* solvibile **II** *n* solvente *m*
sombre, *US* **somber** *adj* (*dark*) scuro; (*serious*) tetro
some **I** *adj* (*unspecified amount*) un po' di, del; (*unspecified number*) qualche, dei *m*, delle *f*; ***would you like ~ water?*** vuoi un po' d'acqua *or* dell'acqua?; ***would you like ~ biscuits?*** vuoi dei biscotti *or* qualche biscotto?; ***~ people say that …*** alcuni dicono che …; ***~ 30 people*** una trentina di persone; (*certain*) certo; ***~ people say …*** certe persone dicono…; ***~ people just don't care*** ad alcune persone non interessa niente; (*indeterminate*) ***~ book or other*** un libro o un altro; ***~ woman, whose name I forget …*** una donna, il cui nome ho dimenticato; ***or ~ such name*** o un nome del genere; ***~ day next week*** un giorno della settimana prossima; (*intensifier*); ***it took ~ courage*** c'è voluto del coraggio; (***that was***) ***~ party!*** che festa (che è stata)!; ***~ people!*** che gente! **II** *pron* (*unspecified amount*) un po'; (*unspecified number*) alcuni *m*, -e *f*; ***would you like ~?*** ne vuoi un po'?; ***give me ~*** dammene un po'; ***~ of the students*** alcuni studenti; ***have you got money? — no, but he has ~*** hai dei soldi? – no, ma lui ne ha un po'; ***~ of the finest poetry in the English language*** tra i migliori esempi di poesia in lingua inglese
somebody *pron* qualcuno; ***~ else*** qualcun altro; ***~ or other*** una persona o un'altra; ***~ knocked at the door*** qualcuno ha bussato alla porta; ***we need ~ German*** abbiamo bisogno di un tedesco; ***you must have seen ~*** devi aver visto qualcuno; ***he really thinks he's ~*** si crede veramente qualcuno **someday** *adv* un giorno
somehow *adv* (*by one means or another*) in qualche modo; (*for some unknown reason*) per qualche motivo
someone *pron* → ***somebody*** **someplace** *pron US* → ***somewhere***
somersault **I** *n* capriola *f* **II** *v/i* fare una capriola
something **I** *pron* qualcosa; ***would you like ~ to drink / eat?*** vuoi (qualcosa) da mangiare / bere?; ***is ~ wrong?*** c'è qualcosa che non va?; ***a little ~*** qualcosina; ***he's ~ of a hero*** è un po' un eroe; ***she's called Rachel ~*** si chiama Rachel Vattelapesca; ***three hundred and ~*** trecento e qualcosa; ***are you drunk or ~?*** *infml* sei ubriaco o cosa?; (*something special*) ***it was ~ else*** *esp US or* ***quite ~*** era una cosa speciale **II** *n*: ***a little ~*** una cosetta; ***a certain ~*** un certo non so che **III** *adv*: ***she looks ~ like me*** ha un aspetto simile al mio
sometime *adv* (*one of these days*) uno di questi giorni; ***~ last year*** l'anno scorso; ***write to me ~ soon*** scrivimi appena puoi; ***~ before tomorrow*** entro domani **sometimes** *adv* a volte
somewhat *adv* piuttosto; ***the system is ~ less than perfect*** a volte il sistema non è esattamente perfetto
somewhere **I** *adv* da qualche parte; ***take one's business ~ else*** portare i propri affari da qualche altra parte; ***I know ~ where …*** conosco un posto in cui…; ***I needed ~ to live in London*** avevo bisogno di un posto in cui vivere a Londra; ***we just wanted ~ to go after school*** volevamo solo un posto dove andare dopo la scuola; ***~ nice*** un posto carino; ***the ideal place to go is ~ like New York*** il luogo ideale dove andare è un posto co-

me New York; ***don't I know you from ~?*** non ti ho già visto da qualche parte; *fig* **~ *about 40° C*** sui 40° centigradi; **~ *about £ 50*** sulle 50 sterline; ***now we're getting ~*** ora sì che ci siamo **II** *pron* un posto; ***let's go ~ quiet*** andiamo in un posto tranquillo
somniferous *adj* soporifero
somnolence *n* sonnolenza *f*
somnolent *adj* sonnolento
son *n* figlio *m*; ***he's his father's ~*** è proprio figlio di suo padre; **~ *of a bitch*** *esp US infml* figlio di puttana
sonata *n* MUS sonata *f*
song *n* canzone *f*; *of birds* canto *m*; ***burst into ~*** mettersi a cantare; *Br fig infml* ***make a ~ and dance about sth*** scatenare un putiferio su qc; ***be on ~*** *Br* essere in sintonia; ***it was going for a ~*** lo davano via per due lire
songbird *n* uccello *m* canoro **songwriter** *n* compositore *m*, -trice *f*
sonic *adj* sonoro
son-in-law *n* ⟨*pl* ***sons-in-law***⟩ genero *m*
sonnet *n* sonetto *m*
sonny *n US infml* figliolo *m*
soon *adv* presto; ***as ~ as*** non appena; ***as ~ as possible*** prima possibile; ***~er or later*** presto o tardi; ***the ~er the better*** prima è, meglio è; ***how ~ can you be ready?*** fra quanto sei pronto?; ***I would*** (***just***) ***as ~ you didn't tell him*** avrei preferito che non glielo dicessi; ***I would ~er … than …*** (*I'd prefer*) preferirei … piuttosto che …
soot *n* fuliggine *f*
soothe *v/t* calmare; *pain* lenire
sop I *v/t* ⟨*pret & past part* ***-ped***⟩ inzuppare **II** *n* contentino *m*; (*food*) pezzo *m* (di cibo) inzuppato
SOP *abbr* (= **standard operating procedure**) procedura *f* operativa standard
sophism *n* sofisma *m*
sophisticate I *v/t* (*refine*) rendere sofisticato; (*alter*) sofisticare **II** *n person* persona *f* sofisticata
sophisticated *adj* sofisticato; ***she thinks she looks more ~ with a cigarette*** ha un aspetto molto più sofisticato con una sigaretta; (*complex*) complesso; *method* complesso; *device* sofisticato; (*subtle*) sottile; *system*, *approach* sofisticato
sophistication *n of person* raffinatezza *f*; *of machine* complessità *f inv*
sophistry *n* sofistica *f*
sophomore *n US studente del secondo anno di università*
soporific *adj* soporifero
sopping *adj* u. **sopping wet** bagnato fradicio
soppy *adj infml* sdolcinato
soprano *n* soprano *m/f*
sorbet *n* sorbetto *m*
sorcerer *n* stregone *m*
sorcery *n* stregoneria *f*
sordid *adj affair*, *business* sordido; ***spare me the ~ details*** risparmiami i dettagli squallidi
sore I *adj* (*+er*) (*painful*) dolorante; ***is it ~?*** fa male?; **~ *point*** punto *m* dolente; ***have a ~ throat*** avere il mal di gola; ***my eyes are ~*** mi fanno male gli occhi; ***have ~ muscles*** avere i muscoli indolenziti; ***be in ~ need of sth*** avere il bisogno disperato di qc; *esp US infml* (*angry*) arrabbiato (***about sth*** per qc, ***at s.o.*** con qn) **II** *n* piaga *f*
sorehead *n US* persona *f* irritabile
sorely *adv*: ***he'll be ~ missed*** si sentirà estremamente la sua mancanza
sorghum *n* BOT sorgo *m*; saggina *f*
sorority *n* UNIV associazione *f* universitaria femminile
sorrel *n* BOT acetosella *f*; *colour* rosso *m* scuro
sorrow *n* dispiacere *m*, dolore *m*; ***drown one's ~s*** affogare i propri dispiaceri
sorrowful *adj* addolorato
sorrowfully *adv* tristemente
sorry *adj* (*+er*) *day*, *sight* triste; (***I'm***) **~!** *apologizing* scusa!; *polite form* scusi!; ***I'm ~*** *regretting* mi dispiace; ***I won't be ~ to leave here*** non vedo l'ora di andarmene da qui; ***I feel ~ for her*** mi dispiace per lei
sort I *n* **1.** tipo *m*; ***all ~s of things*** un po' di tutto; ***make a curtain of ~s*** realizzare una specie di tenda; ***he's a good ~*** è una brava persona; ***he's not my ~*** non è il mio tipo; ***I don't trust his ~*** non mi fido di tipi come lui; ***be out of ~s*** *Br* sentirsi fuori fase **2.** **~ *of …*** *infml* un po' …; ***is it finished? – ~ of*** *infml* è terminato? –

quasi **II** *v/t* separare; COMPUT ordinare
◆**sort out** *v/t sep papers* mettere in ordine; *problem* risolvere; ***sort things out*** sistemare le cose
sort code *n* FIN codice *m* bancario
sorting office *n Br* ufficio *m* di smistamento
SOS *n* SOS *m inv*
so-so *adv infml* così così
soufflé *n* soufflé *m inv*
sought *pret & past part* → ***seek***
sought-after *adj* (*desirable*) ricercato
soul *n* anima *f*; ***the poor ~*** il poverino, la poverina; ***All Souls' Day*** il giorno *m* dei morti; ***God rest his ~!*** che Dio l'abbia in gloria!; ***not a ~*** neanche un'anima; ***he loved her with all his ~*** l'amava con tutta l'anima
soul-destroying *adj* che sfinisce
soulful *adj* profondo
soulless *adj person* senza anima; *place* anonimo
soul mate *n* anima *f* gemella **soul music** *n* MUS musica *f* soul **soul-searching** *n* esame *m* di coscienza
sound[1] **I** *adj* (+*er*) (*sensible*) valido; (*healthy*) sano; *sleep* profondo; *structure, walls* solido **II** *adv* (+*er*): ***be ~ asleep*** dormire profondamente
sound[2] **I** *n* suono *m*; (*verbal*, FILM *etc*) suono *m*; ***I don't like the ~ of it*** non mi ispira per niente; (*noise*) rumore *m* **II** *v/t* (*pronounce*) pronunciare; MED auscultare; ***~ one's horn*** suonare il clacson **III** *v/i*: ***that ~s interesting*** sembra interessante; ***that ~s like a good idea*** mi sembra un'ottima idea; ***she ~ed unhappy*** dalla voce sembrava infelice
◆**sound out** *v/t sep infml* sondare l'opinione di
sound barrier *n* muro *m* del suono **soundbite** *n* slogan *m inv* **soundcard** *n* COMPUT scheda *f* audio **sound effects** *npl* effetti *mpl* sonori **sound engineer** *n* tecnico *m* del suono
sounding board *n fig* cassa *f* di risonanza; ***he used the committee as a ~ for his ideas*** usava la commissione come cassa di risonanza per le sue idee
soundly *adv sleep* profondamente; *beaten* duramente
soundproof *adj* insonorizzato **soundproofing** *n* insonorizzazione *f* **soundtrack** *n* colonna *f* sonora
soup *n* minestra *f*
soup bowl *n* scodella *f*
souped-up *adj infml* truccato *infml*
soup kitchen *n* mensa *f* per i poveri **soup plate** *n* piatto *m* fondo **soup spoon** *n* cucchiaio *m* da minestra
soupy *adj* mieloso; (*foggy*) denso
sour I *adj* (+*er*) *apple, orange* aspro; *milk, expression, comment* acido; ***turn ~*** *milk* inacidire; *situation* guastarsi; *fig* ***it's just ~ grapes*** fai come la volpe con l'uva **II** *v/i fig relationship* guastarsi
source I *n* fonte *f*; *of river* sorgente *f*; ***he is a ~ of embarrassment to us*** per noi è causa di imbarazzo; ***I have it from a good ~ that ...*** ho sentito da fonti sicure che... **II** *v/t* COMM rintracciare la fonte di
source code *n* COMPUT codice *m* di sorgente
sour cream *n* panna *f* acida
sourdough *n* COOK lievito *m* naturale
sour grapes *n ciò che si disprezza perché non si può ottenere*
sourpuss *n infml* brontolone *m*
souse I *v/t* (*marinade*) marinare; (*soak*) immergere **II** *v/i* tuffarsi
south I *adj* meridionale, del sud **II** *n* sud *m*; ***to the ~ of*** a sud di; ***the wind is in the ~*** il vento è a sud; ***the South of France*** il sud della Francia; ***down ~*** giù al sud **III** *adv* verso sud; ***be further ~*** essere ancora più a sud; ***~ of*** a sud di
South Africa *n* Repubblica *f* Sudafricana **South African I** *adj* sudafricano **II** *n* sudafricano *m*, -a *f* **South America** *n* Sudamerica *m* **South American I** *adj* sudamericano **II** *n* sudamericano *m*, -a *f*
southbound *adj train* in direzione sud **southeast I** *n* sud-est *m* **II** *adj* sud-orientale **III** *adv* verso sud-est; ***it's ~ of ...*** è a sud-est di ... **southeastern** *adj* sud-orientale
southerly *adj* meridionale
southern *adj* del sud
southerner *n* abitante *m/f* del sud
southernmost *adj* più a sud
South Korea *n* Corea *f* del Sud **South Korean I** *adj* sudcoreano **II** *n* sudcoreano *m*, -a *f* **South Pacific** *n* Pacifico *m* meridionale **South Pole** *n* polo *m*

sud **South Seas** *npl* i mari del Sud
southwards *adv* verso sud
southwest I *n* sud-ovest *m* **II** *adj* sud-occidentale **III** *adv* verso sud-ovest; ***it's ~ of …*** è a sud-ovest di … **south-western** *adj* sud-occidentale
souvenir *n* souvenir *m inv*
sovereign I *n* (*monarch*) sovrano *m*, -a *f* **II** *adj state* sovrano
sovereignty *n of state* sovranità *f inv*
Soviet *adj hist* sovietico
Soviet Union *n hist* Unione *f* Sovietica
sow¹ *n* (*female pig*) scrofa *f*
sow² *v/t* ⟨*pret* ***sowed***, *past part* ***sown, sowed***⟩ *seeds* seminare; ***this field has been ~n with barley*** questo campo è stato seminato a orzo; ***~ (the seeds of) hatred / discord*** seminare i semi dell'odio / della discordia
sown *past part* → ***sow²***
soya bean *n* seme *m* di soia **soya milk** *n* latte *m* di soia **soy(a) sauce** *n* salsa *f* di soia
spa *n* località *f inv* termale
space *n* spazio *m*; ***stare into ~*** fissare il vuoto; *in car park* posto *m*; (*room*) posto; ***take up a lot of ~*** prendere un sacco di spazio; ***clear / leave some ~ for s.o. / sth*** liberare / lasciare dello spazio per qn / qc; ***in a short ~ of time*** in un breve periodo di tempo; ***in the ~ of …*** nello spazio di
◆ **space out** *v/t* distanziare
space-age *adj technology* all'avanguardia **space-bar** *n* COMPUT barra *f* spaziatrice **space capsule** *n* capsula spaziale **spacecraft** *n* veicolo *m* spaziale
spaced out *adj* (*confused*) confuso; *on drugs* fatto
space flight *n* volo *m* spaziale **space heater** *n esp US* stufetta *f* elettrica **spacelab** *n* laboratorio *m* spaziale **spaceman** *n* astronauta *m* **space rocket** *n* missile *m* spaziale **space-saving** *adj* salvaspazio **spaceship** *n* astronave *f* **space shuttle** *n* shuttle *m inv* **space station** *n* stazione *f* spaziale **spacesuit** *n* tuta *f* spaziale **space walk** *n* passeggiata *f* spaziale **space-woman** *n* astronauta *f* (donna)
spacing *n in typing* spaziatura *f*
spacious *adj* spazioso
spade *n for digging* vanga *f*; ***~s*** *in card game* picche
spadework *n fig* preparativi *mpl*
spaghetti *nsg* spaghetti *mpl*
Spain *n* Spagna *f*
spam *n* COMPUT spam *m inv*
span¹ I *n of hand* spanna *f*; *of bridge etc* campata *f*; (*time span*) arco *m* di tempo; (*range*) distanza *f* **II** *v/t* ⟨*pret & past part* ***-ned***⟩ coprire; *of bridge* attraversare
span² *pret* → ***spin***
Spaniard *n* spagnolo *m*, -a *f*
Spanish I *adj* spagnolo **II** *n language* spagnolo *m*
spank *v/t* sculacciare
spanking *n* sculaccione *m*
spanner *n Br* chiave *f* inglese; ***throw a ~ in the works*** *fig* mettere i bastoni tra le ruote
spare I *v/t* (*do without*) fare a meno di; ***~ s.o. sth*** risparmiare qc a qn; ***can you ~ £50?*** mi puoi prestare 50 sterline?; ***can you ~ the time?*** hai tempo?; ***have money / time to ~*** avere soldi / tempo d'avanzo; ***there were 5 to ~*** (*left over, in excess*) ce n'erano 5 d'avanzo **II** *adj* in più; ***~ bed*** letto in più; ***have you any ~ string?*** hai dei lacci in più?; ***when you have a few minutes ~*** quando hai due minuti liberi; *infml* ***~ tyre*** ruota di scorta; *infml* ***I've lost the paper and the boss is going ~*** ho perso i documenti e il capo è su tutte le furie **III** *n* ricambio *m*
spare part *n* pezzo *m* di ricambio **spare ribs** *npl* costine *fpl* di maiale **spare room** *n* stanza *f* degli ospiti **spare time** *n* tempo *m* libero **spare tyre**, *US* **spare tire** *n* AUTO ruota *f* di scorta
sparing *adj*: ***be ~ with*** andarci piano con *infml*
sparingly *adv* con moderazione
spark *n* scintilla *f*; ***a bright ~*** *iron* un intelligentone
sparking plug *n* AUTO candela *f*
sparkle I *n star* scintillio; *eyes* luccichio; *snow* splendore *m* **II** *v/i* brillare; ***her eyes ~d with excitement*** gli occhi le brillavano per l'emozione
sparkler *n* stella *f* filante
sparkling *adj* frizzante; ***~ (mineral) water*** acqua (minerale) frizzante; ***~ wine*** spumante *m*; ***in ~ form*** in splendida forma

spark plug *n* AUTO candela *f*
sparring partner *n* sparring partner *m inv*; *fig persona con cui si discute spesso e amichevolmente*
sparrow *n* passero *m*
sparse *adj vegetation* rado
sparsely *adv*: ***~ populated*** scarsamente popolato
spartan *adj* spartano
spasm *n* MED spasmo *m*
spasmodic *adj* MED spasmodico; *fig* irregolare
spastic I *adj* spasitco **II** *n* spastico *m*, -a *f*
spat[1] *pret & past part* → ***spit***[2]
spat[2] *n* (*quarrel*) battibecco *m*
spate *n fig* ondata *f*
spatial *adj* spaziale
spatter I *v/t mud, paint* schizzare; ***~ s.o. with water*** schizzare qn con l'acqua **II** *v/i*: ***it ~ed all over the room*** ha schizzato in tutta la stanza **III** *n*: ***a ~ of rain*** due gocce di pioggia
spatula *n* spatola *f*
spawn I *n of frog* uova *fpl* **II** *v/i* deporre le uova **III** *v/t fig* produrre
spay *v/t dog* sterilizzare
speak ⟨*pret* ***spoke***, *past part* ***spoken***⟩ **I** *v/i* parlare; ***we're not ~ing*** (***to each other***) (*we've quarrelled*) non ci rivolgiamo la parola; ***~ing*** TEL sono io; ***so to ~*** per così dire **II** *v/t foreign language* parlare; *the truth* dire; ***~ one's mind*** dire quello che si pensa **III** *n suf* ***Euro-~*** linguaggio dell'Euro
◆**speak for** *v/t* parlare a nome di; ***it speaks for itself*** (*it's obvious*) parla da sé; ***be spoken for*** essere fidanzato
◆**speak out** *v/i* prendere posizione; *say what you think* farsi sentire
◆**speak up** *v/i* (*speak louder*) parlare ad alta voce; *fig* ***speak up for s.o. / sth*** dichiararsi a favore di qn / qc; ***what's wrong? speak up!*** cosa c'è che non va? fatti sentire!
speaker *n* oratore *m*, -trice *f*; ***all German ~s*** tutti le persone di lingua tedesca; *of sound system* cassa *f*
speaking terms *npl*: ***be on ~ with s.o.*** rivolgersi la parola
spear *n* lancia *f*
spearmint *n* menta *f*
spec *n infml*: ***on ~*** per speculare
special I *adj* speciale; (*particular*) particolare; ***nothing ~*** niente di speciale; ***he's very ~ to her*** è molto speciale per lei; ***what's so ~ about that?*** che cos'ha di così speciale; ***~ discount*** sconto speciale **II** *n* TV, RADIO special *m*; COOK piatto *m* del giorno; ***chef's ~*** la specialità dello chef
special agent *n* agente *m* speciale
special delivery *n* consegna *f* rapida; ***by ~*** per espresso **special effects** *npl* effetti *mpl* speciali
specialisation, specialization *n* specializzazione *f* (***in*** in)
specialise, specialize *v/i* specializzarsi; ***~ in ...*** specializzarsi in; ***we ~ in ...*** siamo specializzati in ...
specialist *n* specialista *m/f*
speciality *n* specialità *f inv*
specially *adv* → ***especially***
special needs *npl Br*: ***~ children*** bambini *mpl* con difficoltà di apprendimento **special school** *n scuola per bambini con difficoltà di apprendimento*
specialty *n US* specialità *f inv*
species *nsg* specie *f inv*
specific *adj* specifico; ***can you be a bit more ~?*** puoi essere un po' più specifico?; ***he was quite ~ on that point*** è stato molto preciso sul quel punto
specifically *adv* specificamente
specification *n* (*stipulation*) specificazione *f*; ***~s*** specifiche *fpl*; *of machine etc* caratteristiche *fpl* tecniche, specifiche *fpl*
specify *v/t* ⟨*pret & past part* ***-ied***⟩ specificare
specimen *n* campione *m*; *of plant, animal* esemplare *m*; ***a beautiful*** *or* ***rare ~*** un esemplare bellissimo o raro
speck *n of dust, soot* granello *m*
speckled *adj* screziato
specs *npl infml* (*spectacles*) occhiali *mpl*
spectacle *n* (*impressive sight*) spettacolo *m*; (***a pair of***) ***~s*** (un paio di) occhiali *mpl*; ***make a ~ of o.s.*** rendersi ridicolo
spectacular *adj* spettacolare
spectator *n* spettatore *m*, -trice *f*
spectator sport *n* sport *m inv* spettacolo
spectre, *US* **specter** *n* spettro *m*
spectrum *n fig* gamma *f*
speculate *v/i* fare congetture (***on*** su);

FIN speculare
speculation *n* congetture *fpl*; FIN speculazione *f*
speculative *adj* speculativo
speculator *n* FIN speculatore *m*, -trice *f*
sped *pret & past part* → **speed**
speech *n* (*address*) discorso *m*; ***give*** *or* ***make a ~*** fare un discorso; GRAM ***direct / indirect*** *or* ***reported ~*** discorso *m* diretto / indiretto; *in play* monologo *m*; (*ability to speak*) parola *f*; (*way of speaking*) linguaggio *m*; ***faculty / power of ~*** facoltà / uso della parola; ***her ~ was slurred*** biascicava le parole; ***freedom of ~*** libertà di parola
speech defect *n* difetto *m* del linguaggio
speechless *adj with shock, surprise* senza parole; ***his remark left me ~*** il suo commento mi ha lasciato senza parole
speech recognition *n* COMPUT riconoscimento *m* vocale; ***~ software*** programma di riconoscimento vocale
speech therapist *n* logopedista *m/f*
speech therapy *n* logopedia *f*
speech writer *n* ghost writer *m inv*
speed **I** *n* velocità *f inv*; (*quickness*) rapidità *f inv*; ***at a ~ of 150 mph*** a una velocità di 150 miglia orarie; ***reduce your ~*** rallentare; ***at full ~*** a tutta velocità; *infml drug* speed *m* **II** *v/i* ⟨*pret & past part* **sped**⟩ (*go quickly*) andare a tutta velocità; ***the years sped by*** gli anni sono volati; (*drive too quickly*) superare il limite di velocità
◆ **speed by** *v/i* sfrecciare; *of days* volare
◆ **speed off** *v/i* ⟨*pret & past part* ***speeded*** *or* ***sped off***⟩ prendere il largo
◆ **speed up** **I** *v/i* andare più veloce **II** *v/t* accelerare
speedboat *n* motoscafo *m* **speed bump** *n* dosso *m* di rallentamento **speed camera** *n* (*police*) autovelox *m* **speed dial(ing)** *n esp US* TEL memorizzazione *f* dei numeri
speedily *adv* rapidamente
speeding *n when driving* eccesso *m* di velocità
speeding fine *n* multa *f* per eccesso di velocità
speed limit *n on roads* limite *m* di velocità
speedometer *n* tachimetro *m*
speed skating *n* pattinaggio *m* di velocità **speed trap** *n sistema con cui la polizia individua chi supera il limite di velocità*
speedway *n* SPORTS speedway *m*; (*expressway*) pista *f* per speedway
speedy *adj* (+*er*) rapido; ***we wish Joan a ~ recovery*** auguriamo a Joan una pronta guarigione
spell[1] **I** *v/t*: ***how do you ~ …?*** come si scrive …?; ***could you ~ that please?*** me lo può dettare lettera per lettera? **II** *v/i* sapere come si scrivono le parole
◆ **spell out** *v/t sep*: ***spell sth out*** (*explain in detail*) spiegare chiaramente
spell[2] *n* (*period of time*) periodo *m*; (*turn*) turno *m*; ***a cold ~*** un'ondata di freddo
spell[3] *n* magia *f*; (*incantation*) incantesimo *m*; ***be under a ~*** *liter* essere sotto un incantesimo; *fig* essere stregato; ***put a ~ on s.o.*** *liter* fare un incantesimo a qn; *fig* stregare qn; ***break the ~*** rompere l'incantesimo
spellbinding *adj* incantevole **spellbound** *adj* incantato **spellcheck** *n* COMPUT controllo *m* ortografico; ***do a ~ on …*** fare il controllo ortografico di … **spellchecker** *n* COMPUT correttore *m* ortografico
spelling *n* ortografia *f*
spelling bee *n* gara *f* di ortografia
spelt[1] *esp Br pret & past part* → **spell**[1]
spelt[2] *n* BOT farro *m*
spend *v/t* ⟨*pret & past part* **spent**⟩ *money* spendere; *time* passare; ***~ the night*** trascorrere la notte; ***he ~s his time reading*** passa il tempo a leggere
spending *n* spesa *f*; ***~ cuts*** tagli *mpl* alle spese
spending money *n* denaro per piccole spese; *child* paghetta *f* **spending power** *n* potere *m* d'acquisto **spending spree** *n* spese *fpl* folli; ***go on a ~*** fare spese folli
spendthrift *n pej* spendaccione *m*, -a *f*
spent **I** *pret & past part* → **spend** **II** *adj cartridge* esaurito; *person* esausto
sperm *n* spermatozoo *m*; (*semen*) sperma *m*

sperm bank *n* banca *f* dello sperma **sperm count** *n* numero *m* degli spermatozoi
spermicide *n* spermicida *m*
spew *v/t smoke* emettere; *oil* riversare; *infml* (*vomit*) vomitare
◆**spew out** *v/t* buttare fuori
◆**spew up** *v/t* sgorgare
sphere *n a. fig* sfera *f*; **~ of influence** sfera d'influenza
spherical *adj* sferico
sphincter *n* ANAT sfintere *m*
spice *n* (*seasoning*) spezia *f*; *fig* gusto *m*
◆**spice up** *v/t fig* dare gusto
spiced *adj* COOK speziato; **~ wine** vino *m* aromatizzato; **highly ~** molto gustoso
spick-and-span *adj* lindo e lucente
spicy *adj* (+*er*) *food* piccante
spider *n* ragno *m*
spider's web *n* ragnatela *f*
spidery *adj writing* sottile
spigot *n* tappo *m*; *US* rubinetto *m*
spike I *n on railings* spunzone *m*; *on plant* spina *f*; *on animal* aculeo *m*; *on running shoes* chiodo *m*; **~s** scarpette *fpl* da corsa **II** *v/t drink* correggere con alcol
spiky *adj* (+*er*) irto
spill I *v/t* versare; **~ the beans about sth** vuotare il sacco su qc **II** *v/i* versarsi **III** *n of oil etc* fuoriuscita *f*
◆**spill out** *v/i* (**of** da) (*liquid*) rovesciarsi; (*money*) versarsi; *fig* (*people*) riversarsi
◆**spill over** *v/i unrest* estendersi
spillage *n* fuoriuscita *fpl*
spin I *n* giro *m*; *on ball* effetto *m*; *on washing machine* centrifuga *f*; **put a different ~ on sth** dare una diversa interpretazione a qc **II** *v/t* ⟨*pret & past part* **spun**⟩ far girare; *ball* imprimere l'effetto a **III** *v/i* ⟨*pret & past part* **spun**⟩ *of wheel* girare; **my head is ~ning** mi gira la testa
◆**spin around** *v/i of person, car* girarsi
◆**spin out** *v/t sep infml* far durare
spinach *n* spinaci *mpl*
spinal *adj* spinale
spinal column *n* colonna *f* vertebrale, spina *f* dorsale **spinal cord** *n* midollo *m* spinale
spindle *n* fuso *m*
spindly *adj* (+*er*) affusolato
spin doctor *n infml persona incaricata di far apparire un personaggio politico nella luce migliore* **spin-dry** *v/t* centrifugare **spin-dryer** *n* centrifuga *f*
spine *n of person, animal* spina *f* dorsale; *of book* dorso *m*; *on plant, hedgehog* spina *f*
spine-chilling *adj* (*terrifying*) da brivido
spineless *adj* (*cowardly*) smidollato
spinning wheel *n* filatoio *m* a mano
spin-off *n* applicazione *f* secondaria
spinster *n* zitella *f*
spiny *adj* (+*er*) spinoso
spiral I *n* spirale *f* **II** *v/i* (*rise quickly*) salire vertiginosamente
spiral staircase *n* scala *f* a chiocciola
spire *n* spira *f*, guglia *f*
spirit I *n* spirito *m*; **we did it in a ~ of cooperation** abbiamo agito per spirito di collaborazione; **I'll be with you in ~** sarò con te nello spirito; **enter into the ~ of sth** entrare nello spirito di qc; **that's the ~!** *infml* questo è lo spirito giusto!; **be in high ~s** essere di ottimo umore; **spirits** *npl* (*alcohol*) superalcolici *mpl* **II** *v/t*: **~ s.o. / sth away** far scomparire qn / qc
spirited *adj debate* animato; *defence* energico; *performance* brioso
spirit level *n* livella *f* a bolla d'aria
spiritual *adj* spirituale
spiritualism *n* spiritismo *m*
spiritualist *n* spiritista *m/f*
spit[1] *n* COOK spiedo *m*; *of land* promontorio *m*
spit[2] **I** *v/i* ⟨*pret & past part* **spat**⟩ *of person* sputare; **it's ~ting with rain** pioviggina **II** *n* (*saliva*) sputo *m*
◆**spit out** *v/t sep food, liquid* sputare; **spit it out!** *infml* (*speak!*) sputa il rospo! *infml*
spite *n* dispetto *m*; **she acted out of ~** ha agito per pura cattiveria; **in ~ of** malgrado; **it was a success in ~ of his absense** è stato un successo nonostante la sua assenza
spiteful *adj* dispettoso
spitefully *adv* dispettosamente
spitting image *n*: **be the ~ of s.o.** essere il ritratto sputato di qn
spittle *n* saliva *f*
splash I *v/t person* schizzare; *water,*

mud spruzzare **II** *v/i* schizzare; *of waves* infrangersi **III** *n* (*noise*) tonfo *m*; (*small amount of liquid*) schizzo *m*; *of colour* macchia *f*; *fig* ***make a ~*** fare colpo; (*news*) avere un grande effetto
◆**splash down** *v/i of spacecraft* ammarare
◆**splash out** *v/i Br infml in spending* spendere un sacco di soldi (***on*** per); ***she splashed out on a new coat*** ha fatto una pazzia e si è comprata un cappotto nuovo
splashdown *n* ammaraggio *m*
splatter *v/t with mud, paint etc* cospargere di
splay I *v/t fingers* allargare; *legs* divaricare **II** *v/i*: ***he was ~ed out on the ground*** stava con le gambe divaricate sul pavimento
spleen *n* ANAT milza *f*; *fig* spleen *m*
splendid *adj* magnifico
splendour, *US* **splendor** *n* magnificenza *f*
splice I *v/t* giuntare; ***get ~d*** *infml* sposarsi **II** *n* giuntura *f*
splint *n* MED stecca *f*
splinter I *n* scheggia *f* **II** *v/i* scheggiarsi
splinter group *n* gruppo *m* scissionista
split I *v/t* ⟨*pret & past part* ***split***⟩ *leather* strappare; *wood, logs* spaccare; (*cause disagreement in*) spaccare; (*divide*) dividere **II** *v/i* ⟨*pret & past part* ***split***⟩ *of leather* strapparsi; *of wood* spaccarsi; (*disagree*) spaccarsi **III** *n in leather* strappo *m*; *in wood* crepa *f*; (*disagreement*) spaccatura *f*; (*division, share*) divisione *f*; ***do the ~s*** fare la spaccata
◆**split up** *v/i of couple* separarsi
split ends *npl* doppie punte *fpl* **split infinitive** *n* GRAM *forma di infinito il cui il "to" è seguito da un avverbio*
split-level *adj flat, room, oven* su due livelli
split personality *n* PSYCH sdoppiamento *m* della personalità **split screen** *n* COMPUT schermo *m* suddiviso **split second** *n*: ***in a ~*** in una frazione di secondo **split-second** *adj*: ***~ timing*** tempismo *m* perfetto
splitting *adj*: ***~ headache*** feroce mal *m inv* di testa
splodge, *US* **splotch** *n* macchia *f*; *of cream* chiazza *f*
splurge (out) on I *v/i +obj infml* scialacquare **II** *n infml* spesa *f* folle
splutter *v/i* farfugliare
spoil I *v/t child* viziare; *surprise, party* rovinare **II** *v/i food* guastarsi; ***be ~ing for a fight*** avere voglia di fare a botte **III** *n usu pl* guadagni *mpl*
spoiler *n for TV programme*: *recenzione o trailer di serie televisiva che rivelando gli sviluppi della trama sciupa tutta la sorpresa*; AUTO spoiler *m*
spoilsport *n infml* guastafeste *m/f*
spoilt *adj child* viziato; ***be ~ for choice*** avere (solo) l'imbarazzo della scelta
spoke[1] *n of wheel* raggio *m*
spoke[2] *pret* → ***speak***
spoken *past part* → ***speak***
spokesman *n* portavoce *m*
spokesperson *n* portavoce *m/f*
spokeswoman *n* portavoce *f*
sponge *n* spugna *f*; COOK **sponge cake** pan *m* di Spagna
◆**sponge down** *v/t sep* lavare con la spugna
◆**sponge off, sponge on** *v/t infml* vivere alle spalle di
sponge bag *n Br* trousse *f* **sponge bath** *n* spugnatura *f* **sponge cake** *n* pan *m inv* di Spagna
sponger *n infml* scroccone *m*, -a *f*
spongy *adj* (*+er*) spugnoso
sponsor I *n for immigration* garante *m/f inv*; *for membership* socio *m*, -a *f* garante; *of TV programme, sports event, for fundraising* sponsor *m inv* **II** *v/t for immigration, membership* garantire per; *TV programme, sports event* sponsorizzare
sponsorship *n* sponsorizzazione *f*
spontaneity *n* spontaneità *f*
spontaneous *adj* spontaneo
spontaneously *adv* spontaneamente
spoof *n infml* caricatura *f* (***of*** di)
spook *infml* **I** *n* fantasma *m* **II** *v/t esp US* spaventare
spooky *adj* (*+er*) *infml* sinistro
spool *n* bobina *f*
spoon I *n* cucchiaio *m* **II** *v/t* prendere con il cucchiaio
◆**spoon out** *v/t sep* servire qc con il cucchiaio
spoonerism *n gioco di parole per scambio di iniziali delle parole*

spoonfeed *v/t* ⟨*pret & past part* **-fed**⟩ *fig* scodellare la pappa a
spoonful *n* cucchiaio *m*
sporadic *adj* sporadico
spore *n* BOT spora *f*
sporran *n borsa tipica scozzese di pelo*
sport *n* sport *m inv*; **sports** *npl* (*a.* **sports meeting**) incontri sportivi; ***be a good ~*** saper essere sportivo
sporting *adj* sportivo; ***a ~ gesture*** un gesto sportivo
sporting chance *n* buone probabilità *fpl*
sports bra *n* reggiseno *m* sportivo **sports car** *n* auto *f inv* sportiva **sports centre**, *US* **sports center** *n indoor* palazzetto *m* dello sport **sports jacket** *n* giacca *f* sportiva **sportsman** *n* sportivo *m* **sportsmanship** *n* sportività *f inv* **sports medicine** *n* medicina *f* dello sport **sports news** *nsg* notizie *fpl* sportive **sports page** *n* pagina *f* dello sport **sportswear** *n* abbigliamento *m* sportivo **sportswoman** *n* sportiva *f*
sporty *adj* (+*er*) sportivo
spot[1] *n* (*pimple*) brufolo *m*; *caused by measles etc* foruncolo *m*; *part of pattern* pois *m inv*; ***a ~ of ...*** *Br infml* (*a little*) un po' di ...; ***we had a ~ of rain*** / ***a few ~s of rain*** ha fatto un po' di pioggia / due gocce di pioggia; ***a ~ of bother*** un bel grattacapo
spot[2] *n* (*place*) posticino *m*; ***on the ~*** (*in the place in question*) sul posto; (*immediately*) immediatamente; ***put s.o. on the ~*** mettere in difficoltà qn; ***be in a ~*** (*in difficulties*) essere nei pasticci
spot[3] *v/t* ⟨*pret & past part* **-ted**⟩ (*notice*) notare; (*identify*) trovare
spot check *n* controllo *m* casuale
spotless *adj* pulitissimo
spotlight *n* faretto *m*
spotted *adj fabric* a pois; ***~ with blood*** con macchie di sangue
spotty *adj* (+*er*) *with pimples* brufoloso
spouse *n form* coniuge *m/f*
spout **I** *n* beccuccio *m*; ***up the ~*** *Br infml* (*plans etc*) rovinato **II** *v/i of liquid* sgorgare **III** *v/t infml*: ***~ nonsense*** ciarlare
sprain **I** *n* slogatura *f* **II** *v/t* slogarsi; ***~ one's ankle*** slogarsi la caviglia
sprang *pret* → ***spring***[2]
sprawl *v/i* stravaccarsi; *of city* estendersi; ***urban ~*** espansione urbana; ***send s.o. ~ing*** *of punch* mandare qn a gambe all'aria
sprawling *adj city, suburbs* tentacolare
spray[1] *n* (*bouquet*) fascio *m*
spray[2] **I** *n of sea water, from fountain* spruzzi *mpl*; *for hair* lacca *f*; (*container*) spray *m inv* **II** *v/t* spruzzare; ***~ s.o.*** / ***sth with sth*** spruzzare qn / qc di qc
spraygun *n* pistola *f* a spruzzo **spray-on** *adj* spray
spread **I** *v/t* ⟨*pret & past part* ***spread***⟩ (*lay*) stendere; *butter, jam* spalmare; *news, rumour, disease* diffondere; *arms, legs* allargare **II** *v/i* ⟨*pret & past part* ***spread***⟩ diffondersi; *of butter* spalmarsi **III** *n of disease, religion etc* diffusione *f*; *infml big meal* banchetto *m*; *of wings* apertura *f*; *of interests* allargamento *m*; ***middle-age ~*** pancetta *f* della mezza età; ***cheese ~*** COOK formaggio *m* spalmabile; ***a full-page*** / ***double ~*** PRESS, TYPO un articolo a tutta pagina / su due pagine; (*advertisement*) una pubblicità a tutta pagina / su due pagine
◆ **spread out** *v/i countryside* estendersi; *runners* sparpagliarsi
spread-eagle *v/t*: ***lie ~d*** stendersi a braccia e gambe divaricate
spreadsheet *n* COMPUT spreadsheet *m inv*
spree *n infml*: ***go*** (***out***) ***on a ~*** *having fun* andare a far baldoria; ***go on a shopping ~*** andare a fare spese folli
sprig *n* rametto *m*
sprightly *adj* (+*er*) arzillo
spring[1] *n season* primavera *f*; *device* molla *f*; (*stream*) sorgente *f*; (*jump*) balzo *m*; ***with a ~ in one's step*** con un andatura *f* scattante
spring[2] *v/i* ⟨*pret* ***sprang***, *past part* ***sprung***⟩ scattare; ***~ from*** derivare da
spring binder *n* raccoglitore a molla
springboard *n* trampolino *m*
spring chicken *n hum*: ***she's no ~*** non è più una ragazzina **spring-cleaning** *n* pulizie *fpl* di primavera **spring-form mould** *n* tortiera *f* a cerniera **spring-loaded** *adj* caricato a molla **spring onion** *n* cipollotto *m*

spring roll *n* involtino *m* primavera
springtime *n* primavera *f*
springy *adj* (+*er*) *mattress, walk* molleggiato; *ground* morbido; *material* elastico
sprinkle I *v/t* spruzzare; *~ **sth with*** cospargere qc di **II** *n* spolverata *f*; *of salt* pizzico *m*
sprinkler *n for garden* irrigatore *m*; *in ceiling* sprinkler *m inv*
sprint I *n* scatto *m*; ***the 100 metres ~*** i cento metri piani **II** *v/i* fare uno scatto
sprinter *n* SPORTS velocista *m/f*
sprite *n fairy* folletto *m*
spritzer *n vino bianco con acqua gassata*
sprog *n Br infml* marmocchio *m*
sprout I *v/i of seed* spuntare **II** *v/t leaves* spuntare; *horns etc* spuntare; *infml beard* uscire **III** *n* germoglio *m*; (**Brussels**) ***~s*** cavolini *mpl* di Bruxelles
spruce[1] *n* (*a.* **spruce fir**) abete *m*
spruce[2] *adj* (+*er*) curato
◆ **spruce up** *v/t sep* (*smarten*) agghindare
sprung *past part* → ***spring***[2]
spry *adj* arzillo
spud *n infml* patata *f*
spun *pret & past part* → ***spin***
spur *n* sperone *m*; *fig* sprone *m*; ***on the ~ of the moment*** su due piedi
◆ **spur on** *v/t* ⟨*pret & past part* ***-red***⟩ (*encourage*) spronare
spurious *adj claim, claimant* falso; *account* falso; *interest* fittizio; *document* spurio
spurn *v/t* rifiutare con sdegno
spur-of-the-moment *adj decision* impulsiva
spurt I *n*: ***put on a ~*** *in race* fare uno scatto; *in work* accelerare il ritmo **II** *v/i of liquid* sprizzare **III** *v/t*: ***the wound ~ed blood*** il sangue usciva a fiotti dalla ferita
sputter *v/i of engine* scoppiettare
spy I *n* spia *f* **II** *v/i* ⟨*pret & past part* ***-ied***⟩ fare la spia **III** *v/t* ⟨*pret & past part* ***-ied***⟩ *infml* scorgere
◆ **spy on** *v/t* spiare
◆ **spy out** *v/t sep* indagare su; *fig* ***spy out the land*** tastare il terreno
spyhole *n* spioncino *m*
sq *abbr* (= **square**); ***sq m*** metro *m* quadrato
Sq *abbr* (= **Square**) piazza *f*
squabble I *v/i* bisticciare **II** *n* bisticcio *m*
squad *n* squadra *f*; MIL drappello *m*; (*special unit*) squadra *f*; (*police squad*) pattuglia *f*; SPORTS squadra *f*
squadron *n of planes* squadriglia *f*
squalid *adj* squallido
squalor *n* squallore *m*
squander *v/t money* dilapidare
square I *adj* (+*er*) *in shape* quadrato; ***~ mile*** miglio *m* quadrato; ***we're all ~*** siamo pari; ***be a ~ peg in a round hole*** essere come un pesce fuor d'acqua; (*conventional*) inquadrato **II** *n shape* quadrato *m*; *in town* piazza *f*; *in board game* casella *f*; MATH quadrato *m*; ***we're back to ~ one*** siamo punto e a capo;(*conventional person*) persona *f* inquadrata **III** *v/t* MATH *number* elevare al quadrato
◆ **square up** *v/i* (*settle up*) fare i conti
square bashing *n Br* MIL esercitazione *f* militare **square bracket** *n* parentesi *f* quadra **square dance** *n* quadriglia *f*
squarely *adv directly* diretto; *honestly* apertamente; ***hit s.o. ~ in the stomach*** colpire qualcuno in pieno stomaco; ***place the blame for sth ~ on s.o.*** dare tutta la colpa per qc a qn
square meal *n* pasto *m* complete **square rig** *n* NAUT vela *f* quadra **square root** *n* MATH radice *f* quadrata
squash[1] *n* BOT zucca *f*
squash[2] *n* SPORTS squash *m inv*
squash[3] **I** *v/t* (*crush*) schiacciare **II** *v/i*: ***could you ~ up?*** potete stringervi un po'?; ***~ up against*** schiacciarsi contro **III** *n* ***it's a bit of a ~*** si sta un po' stretti; ***orange / lemon ~*** sciroppo *m* di arancia / limone
squat I *adj* (+*er*) *in shape* tozzo **II** *v/i* ⟨*pret & past part* ***-ted***⟩ (*sit*) accovacciarsi; *illegally* occupare abusivamente
squatter *n* squatter *m inv*, occupante *m/f* abusivo, -a
squawk I *n* (*raucous cry*) gracchio *m*; ***he let out a ~*** gli è uscito un lamento **II** *v/i* sbraitare
squeak I *v/i of mouse* squittire; *of hinge* cigolare; *of shoes* scricchiolare **II** *n of mouse* squittio *m*; *of hinge* ci-

golio *m*
squeaky *adj* (+*er*) *hinge* cigolante; *shoes* scricchiolante; *voice* stridulo
squeaky clean *adj infml* pulito
squeal I *v/i* strillare; *of brakes* stridere **II** *n of pain, laughter* strillo *m*; *of brakes* stridore *m*
squeamish *adj*: ***be ~*** fare lo schizzinoso
squeeze I *v/t hand* stringere; *orange, lemon* spremere; *sponge* strizzare; ***I'll see if we can ~ you in the list*** vedrò se possiamo inserirla nella lista **II** *n of hand, shoulder* stretta *f*; ***a ~ of lemon*** una spruzzata di limone; ***it was a tight ~*** ci siamo entrati per un pelo **III** *v/i*: ***you should be able to ~ through*** dovresti riuscire a passarci attraverso; ***~ past*** riuscire a infilarsi; ***~ onto the bus*** infilarsi sull'autobus; ***~ up a bit*** stringersi un po'
◆**squeeze in I** *v/i to a car etc* infilarsi **II** *v/t* infilare
◆**squeeze up** *v/i to make space* stringersi
squelch *v/i mud* fare cic ciac
squid *n* calamaro *m*
squiggle *n* ghirigoro *m*
squiggly *adj* (+*er*) pieno di ghirigori
squint I *v/i* (*half-close eyes*) strizzare gli occhi **II** *n* MED strabismo *m*; ***have a ~*** essere strabico **III** *adj* (*crooked*) storto
squire *n* (*country gentleman*) signorotto *m*; (*henchman*) scudiero *m*
squirm *v/i* (*wriggle*) contorcersi; ***~*** (***with embarrassment***) morire di vergogna
squirrel *n* scoiattolo *m*
squirt I *v/t* spruzzare **II** *n infml pej* microbo *m infml*
squishy *adj* (+*er*) *infml* appiccicaticcio
squit *n Br infml* ometto *m* insignificante
Sr *abbr* (= **senior**) senior
Sri Lanka *n* Sri Lanka *m*
St *abbr* **1.** (= **saint**) S. (santo *m*, santa *f*) **2.** (= **street**) v. (via *f*)
stab I *n* coltellata *f*; ***~ wound*** ferita *f* da taglio; ***~ of pain*** fitta *f* di dolore; *fig* ***she felt a ~ of jealousy*** sentì una fitta di gelosia; *fig* ***a ~ in the back*** una pugnalata alla schiena; ***have a ~ at doing sth*** *infml* provare a fare qc **II** *v/t* ⟨*pret & past part* **-bed**⟩ *person* accoltellare; ***he was ~bed through the arm / heart*** è stato accoltellato al braccio / al cuore
stabbing I *n* accoltellamento *m* **II** *adj pain* lancinante
stabilise, stabilize I *v/t prices, boat* stabilizzare **II** *v/i of prices etc* stabilizzarsi
stability *n* stabilità *f inv*
stabilizer *n* stabilizzatore *m*
stable[1] **I** *n building* stalla *f*; *establishment* scuderia *f*; ***riding ~s*** scuderia **II** *v/t* mettere un cavallo in scuderia
stable[2] *adj* (+*er*) stabile
stablelad *n Br*, **stableman** *n US* stalliere *m*
stack I *n* (*pile*) pila *f*; (*smokestack*) ciminiera *f*; ***~s of*** *infml* un sacco di *infml* **II** *v/t* mettere in pila; ***the cards*** *or* ***odds are ~ed against us*** *fig* le carte *or* le probabilità sono a nostro svantaggio
stadium *n* stadio *m*
staff[1] **I** *n* (*employees*) personale *msg*; (*teachers*) corpo *m* insegnante; ***we don't have enough ~ to complete the project*** non abbiamo personale sufficiente per finire il progetto; ***a member of ~*** un membro del personale; EDU membro *m* del corpo insegnante; ***be on the ~*** far parte dello staff **II** *v/t* fornire di personale; ***the kitchens are ~ed by foreigners*** il personale delle cucine è tutto straniero
staff[2] *n* (*rod*) bastone *m*
staffroom *n in school* sala *f* professori
stag *n* cervo *m*
stage[1] *n in life, project etc* fase *f*; *of journey* tappa *f*
stage[2] **I** *n* THEAT palcoscenico *m*; ***go on the ~*** *become actor* fare teatro **II** *v/t play* mettere in scena; *demonstration* organizzare
stagecoach *n* diligenza *f*
stage door *n* ingresso *m* degli artisti
staged reading *n* THEAT lettura *f* drammatica
stage fright *n* attacco *m* di panico
stage hand *n* macchinista *m/f*
stage-manage *v/t* mettere in scena
stage manager *n* direttore *m*, -trice *f* di scena
stage set *n* scenario *m*
stagestruck *adj* amante del teatro

stage whisper *n* a parte; *fig* sussurro *m* volutamente udibile
stagflation *n* ECON stagflazione *f*
stagger I *v/i* barcollare **II** *v/t* (*amaze*) sbalordire; *holidays*, *breaks etc* scaglionare
staggering *adj* sbalorditivo
stagnant *adj a. fig* stagnante
stagnate *v/i of person*, *mind* vegetare
stagnation *n* ristagno *m*
stag party *n* (festa *f* di) addio *m* al celibato
stain I *n* (*dirty mark*) macchia *f*; *for wood* mordente *m* **II** *v/t* (*dirty*) macchiare; *wood* dare il mordente a **III** *v/i of wine etc* macchiare; *of fabric* macchiarsi
stained-glass window *n* vetrata *f* colorata
stainless steel I *n* acciaio *m* inossidabile **II** *adj* d'acciaio inossidabile
stain remover *n* smacchiatore *m*
stair *n* scalino *m*; ***the ~s*** le scale
staircase *n* scala *f* **stairway** *n* scala *f*
stake I *n of wood* paletto *m*; *when gambling* puntata *f*; (*investment*) partecipazione *f*; ***be at ~*** essere in gioco; ***raise the ~s*** alzare la posta **II** *v/t tree* puntellare; *money* puntare; ***~ one's reputation on sth*** rischiare la propria reputazione per qc; ***~ one's claim to sth*** avanzare diritti su qc
stakeholder *n* chi tiene le poste (delle scommesse)
stalactite *n* stalattite *f*
stalagmite *n* stalagmite *f*
stale *adj* (*+er*) *bread* raffermo; *air* viziato; *fig*: *news* vecchio
stalemate *n in chess* stallo *m*; *fig* punto *m* morto
stalk[1] *n of fruit* picciolo *m*; *of plant* gambo *m*
stalk[2] *v/t animal* seguire; *person* perseguitare (con telefonate, lettere *etc*)
stalker *n persona che perseguita qualcun altro con telefonate, lettere etc*
stall[1] *n at market* bancarella *f*; *for cow*, *horse* box *m inv*; AVIAT stallo *m*
stall[2] **I** *v/i of engine* spegnersi; *of vehicle* fermarsi; (*play for time*) temporeggiare **II** *v/t engine* far spegnere; *people* trattenere
stallion *n* stallone *m*
stalls *npl* platea *f*
stalwart *adj support*, *supporter* fedele
stamen *n* BOT stame *m*
stamina *n* resistenza *f*
stammer I *v/i* balbettare **II** *n* balbuzie *f*; ***have a ~*** essere balbuziente
stamp[1] **I** *n for letter* francobollo *m*; (*date stamp etc*) timbro *m* **II** *v/t letter* affrancare; *document*, *passport* timbrare; ***~ed addressed envelope*** busta *f* affrancata per la risposta
stamp[2] *v/t* ***~ one's feet*** pestare i piedi
◆**stamp out** *v/t sep* (*eradicate*) eliminare
stamp album *n* album *m inv* di francobolli **stamp collecting** *n* filatelia *f* **stamp collection** *n* collezione *f* di francobolli **stamp collector** *n* collezionista *m/f* di francobolli
stampede I *n of cattle etc* fuga *f* precipitosa; *of people* fuggi-fuggi *m inv* **II** *v/i of cattle etc* fuggire precipitosamente; *of people* precipitarsi
stamping ground *n infml* luogo *m* di ritrovo
stance *n* (*position*) presa *f* di posizione
stand I *v/i* ⟨*pret & past part* ***stood***⟩ **1.** (*be situated*: *of person*) stare; *of object*, *building* trovarsi; ***where do you ~ on the issue?*** qual è la tua posizione sulla questione? **2.** *as opposed to sit* stare in piedi; (*rise*) alzarsi in piedi; ***~ still*** stare fermo; ***don't just ~ there!*** non startene lì impalato!; ***~ as a candidate*** presentarsi come candidato; *fig* ***we ~ to gain a lot*** abbiamo la possibilità di guadagnare molto; ***as things ~*** per come stanno le cose; ***~ firm*** tenere duro; ***nothing now ~s between us*** ora non c'è niente che ci separi **II** *v/t* ⟨*pret & past part* ***stood***⟩ **1.** (*tolerate*) sopportare; ***I can't ~ him*** non lo sopporto; ***I can't ~ being kept waiting*** non sopporto quando mi fanno aspettare **2.** ***~ trial*** subire un processo **3.** (*put*) mettere **4.** ***you don't ~ a chance*** non hai alcuna probabilità; ***~ one's ground*** non mollare, tenere duro **5.** ***~ s.o. a drink*** offrire da bere a qn **III** *n* **1.** *at exhibition* stand *m inv*; (*witness stand*) banco *m* dei testimoni; ***take the ~*** JUR testimoniare **2.** (*support*, *base*) base *f*; (*music stand etc*) leggio *m*
◆**stand apart** *v/i liter* essere distante; *fig* stare in disparte

◆ **stand aside** *v/i liter* farsi da parte
◆ **stand back** *v/i* farsi indietro
◆ **stand by I** *v/i* (*not take action*) stare a guardare; ***stand by and do nothing*** stare a guardare senza fare niente; (*be ready*) tenersi pronto **II** *v/t person* stare al fianco di; *decision* mantenere
◆ **stand down** *v/i* (*withdraw*) ritirarsi
◆ **stand for** *v/t* (*tolerate*) tollerare; (*mean*) significare; *freedom etc* rappresentare; ***stand for election*** candidarsi alle elezioni
◆ **stand in for** *v/t* sostituire
◆ **stand out** *v/i* spiccare; *of person, building* distinguersi
◆ **stand over** *v/t* (*supervise*) supervisionare
◆ **stand up I** *v/i* alzarsi in piedi; ***stand up straight!*** stai dritto! **II** *v/t sep infml on date* dare buca a *infml*
◆ **stand up for** *v/t* difendere
◆ **stand up to** *v/t* far fronte a

standard[1] **I** *n level* livello *m*; *expectation* aspettativa *f*; TECH standard *m inv*; ***moral ~s*** principi *mpl*; ***be / not be up to ~*** essere / non essere di buona qualità; ***set high ~s*** stabilire standard alti **II** *adj* (*usual*) comune; *model, size* standard *inv*; ***be ~ practice*** essere normale procedura; ***~ English*** l'inglese standard

standard[2] *n* (*flag*) stendardo *m*

standard-bearer *n* portabandiera *f*

standardisation *n* standardizzazione *f*

standardise, standardize *v/t* standardizzare

standard lamp *n Br* lampada *f* a stelo **standard of living** *n* tenore *m* di vita

standby *n ticket* biglietto *m* stand-by; *for emergency* riserva *f*; ***on ~*** *at airport* in lista d'attesa; ***on ~*** *of troops etc* pronto **standby passenger** *n* passeggero *m*, -a *f* in lista d'attesa **stand-in** *n replacement* rimpiazzo *m*

standing I *n in society etc* posizione *f*; (*repute*) reputazione *f*; ***a musician of some ~*** un musicista di una certa importanza; ***a friendship of long ~*** un'amicizia di lunga durata; ***her husband of five years' ~*** il marito che dura da cinque anni **II** *adj* (*permanent*) fisso; *army* permanente; ***it's a ~ joke*** è una barzelletta

standing army *n* MIL esercito *m* permanente **standing order** *n* FIN ordine *m* permanente **standing room** *n* posto *m* in piedi

standoffish *adj* scostante **standpoint** *n* punto *m* di vista **standstill** *n*: ***be at a ~*** essere fermo; ***bring to a ~*** fermare

stand-up *n comedy* cabaret *m inv*

stank *pret* → ***stink***

stanza *n of poem* stanza *f*

staple[1] *n* (*foodstuff*) alimento *m* base

staple[2] **I** *n* (*fastener*) graffa *f* **II** *v/t* pinzare

staple diet *n* alimentazione *f* base **staple gun** *n* pistola *f* sparachiodi

stapler *n* pinzatrice *f*

star I *n in sky* stella *f*; *fig* star *f inv*; ***the Stars and Stripes*** la Stelle e Strisce; ***you can thank your lucky ~s that …*** devi rigraziare la tua buona stella se… **II** *adj* stellare; ***~ player*** giocatore di punta **III** *v/t* ⟨*pret & past part* **-red**⟩: ***a film ~ring Julia Roberts*** un film interpretato da Julia Roberts **IV** *v/i* ⟨*pret & past part* **-red**⟩: ***he ~red in Psycho*** è il protagonista di Psycho

starboard *adj* a tribordo

starch *n in foodstuff* amido *m*

starchy *adj* ricco di amido; *fig* affettato

stardom *n* celebrità *f inv*

stare I *v/i* fissare; ***~ at*** fissare **II** *v/t*: ***the answer was staring us in the face*** la risposta era sotto in nostri occhi; ***~ defeat in the face*** essere sull'orlo della sconfitta **III** *n* sguardo *m* fisso

starfish *n* stella *f* di mare **stargaze** *v/i* osservare le stelle; *fig* sognare ad occhi aperti **stargazer** *n infml* (*astronomer*) astronomo *m*, -a *f*; (*astrologer*) astrologo *m*, -a *f*; *fig* sognatore *m*, -trice *f*

stark I *adj* (+*er*) *landscape* desolato; *colour scheme* austero; *reminder, contrast etc* brusco **II** *adv*: ***~ naked*** completamente nudo

starling *n* storno *m*

starlit *adj night* illuminato dalle stelle

starry *adj* (+*er*) *night* stellato

starry-eyed *adj person* idealista

Stars and Stripes *nsg* bandiera *f* degli Stati Uniti

star-studded *adj fig*: ***~ cast*** cast pieno di grandi attori

start[1] **I** *v/i* iniziare, cominciare; *of engine, car* partire; ***~ing from tomor-***

row a partire da domani; ***to ~ with*** per cominciare **II** *v/t* cominciare; *engine*, *car* mettere in moto; *business* mettere su; ***~ to do sth, ~ doing sth*** cominciare a fare qc **III** *n* (*beginning*) inizio *m*; ***make a ~ on sth*** iniziare qc; ***get off to a good / bad ~*** *in marriage*, *career* cominciare bene / male; ***from the ~*** dall'inizio; ***well, it's a ~!*** è pur sempre un inizio!

◆ **start back** *v/i* cominciare il viaggio di ritorno; (*jump back*) fare un salto indietro

◆ **start off I** *v/i* (*begin*) cominciare; (*set out*) muoversi **II** *v/t sep* ***the thunder started the dog off*** (**barking**) il tuono fece iniziare il cane ad abbaiare; ***start s.o. off on sth*** avviare qn a qc

◆ **start out** *v/i* (*begin*) cominciare; *on journey* partire (**for** per)

◆ **start up** *v/t sep business* mettere su; *engine* avviare

start[2] *n* (*jump*) sussulto *m*

starter *n part of meal* antipasto *m*; *of car* motorino *m* d'avviamento; *in race* starter *m inv*

starting gun *n* pistola *f* dello starter **starting point** *n* punto *m* di partenza **starting salary** *n* stipendio *m* iniziale

startle *v/t* far trasalire

startling *adj* sorprendente

start-up *n* nuova azienda; ***~ costs*** costi *mpl* di avviamento

starvation *n* fame *f*

starve *v/i* soffrire la fame; ***~ to death*** morire di fame; ***I'm starving*** *infml* sto morendo di fame

stash I *n infml* nascondiglio *m* **II** *v/t infml* nascondere

◆ **stash away** *v/t* mettere via; *money* nascondere

state[1] **I** *n of car*, *house etc* stato *m*, condizione *f*; ***~ of mind*** stato *m* d'animo; ***the present ~ of the economy*** lo stato attuale dell'economia; ***he's in no*** (***fit***) ***~ to do that*** non è in condizioni di farlo; ***what a ~ of affairs!*** che strana situazione!; ***look at the ~ of your hands!*** guarda in che stato sono le tue mani!; ***the room was in a terrible ~*** la camera era in uno stato terribile; (*country*) stato *m*; ***the States*** gli Stati Uniti; ***be in a ~*** essere agitato **II** *adj* di stato; *school* statale; *banquet etc* ufficiale

state[2] *v/t* dichiarare; ***~ one's case*** esporre le proprie ragioni; ***as ~d in my letter I ...*** come è indicato nella mia lettera, io…

statecraft *n* arte *f* di governare

State Department *n in USA* Ministero *m* degli Esteri

state education *n* istruzione *f* pubblica

Statehouse *n US Campidoglio di ciascuno degli stati degli USA*

stateless *adj* apolide

stately *adj* (*+er*) *person* maestoso; ***~ home*** palazzo *m* monumentale

statement *n to police* deposizione *f*; (*announcement*) dichiarazione *f*; (*bank statement*) estratto *m* conto

state of emergency *n* stato *m* d'emergenza **state-of-the-art** *adj* modernissimo; ***~ technology*** tecnologia *f* all'avanguardia **state-owned** *adj* di proprietà dello stato, statale **state school** *n Br* scuola *f* pubblica **state secret** *n* segreto *m* di stato

stateside *adj US infml* degli Stati Uniti

statesman *n* statista *m*

statesmanship *n* arte *f* di governare

stateswoman *n* ⟨*pl* ***stateswomen***⟩ statista *f* (donna)

state visit *n* visita *f* ufficiale

static *adj* (*unchanging*) immutabile

static (**electricity**) *n* elettricità *f inv* statica

station I *n* stazione *f* **II** *v/t guard etc* disporre; ***be ~ed at*** *of soldier* essere di stanza in / a

stationary *adj* fermo

stationer's *n* cartoleria *f*

stationery *n* articoli *mpl* di cancelleria

station manager *n* dirigente *m* della stazione ferroviaria **station wagon** *n US* giardiniera *f*

statistical *adj* statistico

statistically *adv* statisticamente

statistician *n* esperto *m*, -a *f* di statistica

statistics *nsg science* statistica *f*; *npl figures* statistiche *fpl*

statue *n* statua *f*

statuesque *adj* statuario

statuette *n* statuetta *f*

stature *n* statura *f*

status *n* posizione *f*; ***marital ~*** stato *m* civile; ***equal ~*** medesimo statuto *m*

status bar *n* COMPUT barra *f* di stato
status quo *n* status quo *m*
status symbol *n* status symbol *m inv*
statute *n* statuto *m*
statute book *n esp Br* raccolta *f* di leggi **statute of limitations** *n* JUR legge *f* sulla prescrizione
statutory *adj* ufficiale
statutory rape *n US* JUR corruzione *f* di minorenne
staunch *adj* (+*er*) leale
stay I *v/i in a place* stare; ***I ~ed in Italy for a few weeks*** sono rimasto in Italia per qualche settimana; ***my brother came to ~*** mio fratello viene a stare per un po'; *in a condition* restare; ***~ in a hotel*** stare in albergo; ***~ right there!*** non ti muovere!; ***~ put*** non muoversi **II** *v/t*: ***~ the night*** dormire (da qn) **III** *n* soggiorno *m*
◆**stay away** *v/i* stare alla larga
◆**stay away from** *v/t* stare alla larga da
◆**stay behind** *v/i* rimanere
◆**stay in** *v/i at home* restare a casa; *in position* starci
◆**stay off** *v/i +obj*: ***stay off school*** non andare a scuola
◆**stay on** *v/i in post* rimanere; *at school* proseguire gli studi
◆**stay out** *v/i* restare fuori; (*not come home*) non tornare a casa; ***stay out of sth*** non estrare in qc; ***he never managed to stay out of trouble*** non è mai riuscito a stare fuori dai guai
◆**stay up** *v/i* (*not go to bed*) rimanere alzato; ***his trousers won't stay up*** i suoi pantaloni non restano su
stay-at-home *n* pantofolaio *m*, -a *f*
staying power *n* resistenza *f*
std *abbr* (= **standard**) standard
STD *abbr* (= **sexually transmitted disease**) MST *f inv* (malattia *f* sessualmente trasmessa)
stead *n*: ***stand s.o. in good ~*** tornare utile a qn
steadfast *adj friend* fedele
steadily *adv improve etc* costantemente; *look* fisso
steady I *adj* (+*er*) *voice*, *hands* fermo; *job*, *boyfriend* fisso; *beat* regolare; *improvement*, *decline*, *progress* costante **II** *adv*: ***be going ~*** fare coppia fissa; ***~ on!*** calma! **III** *v/t* ⟨*pret & past part* ***-ied***⟩ *bookcase etc* rendere saldo; ***~ o.s.*** ritrovare l'equilibrio
steak *n* bistecca *f*, carne *f* (di manzo)
steal ⟨*pret* ***stole***, *past part* ***stolen***⟩ **I** *v/t money etc* rubare; ***~ sth from s.o.*** rubare qc da qn; ***~ the show*** rubare la scena; ***~ a glance at s.o.*** rubare uno sguardo a qn **II** *v/i* (*be a thief*) rubare; ***~ in/out*** (*move quietly*) entrare/uscire furtivamente; ***~ away*** *or* ***off*** sgattaiolare; ***~ up on s.o.*** avvicinarsi di soppiatto a qn
stealth *n* furtività *f*; ***by ~*** furtivamente
stealthy *adj* (+*er*) furtivo
steam I *n* vapore *m*; ***full ~ ahead*** NAUT a tutto vapore; *fig* ***get*** *or* ***pick up ~*** acquistare velocità; ***let off ~*** sfogarsi; *fig* ***run out of ~*** esaurire l'energia **II** *v/t food* cuocere al vapore
◆**steam up I** *v/i of window* appannarsi **II** *v/t sep*: ***be steamed up*** *infml angry* essere furibondo
steam engine *n* motore *m* a vapore
steamer *n for cooking* vaporiera *f*
steam iron *n* ferro *m* a vapore
steamroller *n* rullo *m* compressore
steamship *n* nave *f* a vapore
steamy *adj* (+*er*) pieno di vapore; *fig affair* erotico
steel I *n* acciaio *m* **II** *adj* d'acciaio **III** *v/r*: ***~ o.s. for sth*** farsi forza per qc
steel band *n* MUS steel band *f inv* **steel wool** *n* lana *f* di acciaio **steelworker** *n* operaio *m* di acciaieria **steelworks** *n* acciaieria *f*
steep[1] *adj* (+*er*) *hill etc* ripido; *infml prices* alto; ***it's a ~ climb*** è una salita molto ripida; ***that's a bit ~*** *expensive* è un po' caro
steep[2] *v/t* (*soak*) lasciare a bagno; ***~ed in history*** immerso nella storia
steepen *v/i* (*slope*) diventare ripido; (*cost*) aumentare
steeple *n* campanile *m*
steeplechase *n in athletics* corsa *f* ad ostacoli
steeply *adv*: ***climb ~*** *of path* salire ripidamente; *of prices* salire vertiginosamente
steer[1] *n animal* manzo *m*
steer[2] *v/t car*, *boat* manovrare; *person* guidare; *conversation* spostare
steerage *n* ponte *m* di terza classe
steering *n of motor vehicle* sterzo *m*
steering committee *n* comitato *m* direttivo **steering wheel** *n* volante *m*

stellar *adj* stellare
stem[1] *n of plant, glass* stelo *m*; *of word* radice *f*
◆**stem from** *v/t* derivare da
stem[2] *v/t* 〈*pret & past part* ***-med***〉 (*block*) arginare
stem cell *n* BIOL, MED cellula *f* staminale
stench *n* puzzo *m*
stencil I *n* stencil *m inv* **II** *v/t* 〈*pret & past part* ***-led***, *US* ***-ed***〉 *pattern* disegnare con lo stencil
step I *n* (*pace*) passo *m*; (*stair*) gradino *m*; (*measure*) provvedimento *m*; ***~ by ~*** poco a poco; ***~s*** *npl Br* (*stepladder*) scaletta *f*; ***be in ~*** andare al passo; *fig* essere in sintonia; ***be out of ~*** non essere al passo; *fig* ***be one ~ ahead of s.o.*** essere un passo avanti rispetto a qn; ***watch one's ~*** guardare dove si mettono i piedi; ***mind the ~*** attenzione allo scalino **II** *v/i* 〈*pret & past part* ***-ped***〉 mettere il piede; ***~ into / out of*** salire in / scendere da
◆**step aside** *v/i* farsi da parte
◆**step back** *v/i liter* fare un passo indietro; *fig* prendere le distanze
◆**step down** *v/i from post etc* dimettersi
◆**step forward** *v/i a. fig* farsi avanti
◆**step in** *v/i* (*intervene*) intervenire
◆**step up** *v/t sep infml* (*increase*) aumentare
stepbrother *n* fratellastro *m* **stepdaughter** *n* figliastra *f* **stepfather** *n* patrigno *m* **stepladder** *n* scala *f* a libretto **stepmother** *n* matrigna *f*
stepping stone *n* pietra *f* di un guado; *fig* trampolino *m* di lancio
stepsister *n* sorellastra *f* **stepson** *n* figliastro *m*
stereo *n* (*sound system*) stereo *m inv*; ***in ~*** in stereo
stereotype *n* stereotipo *m*
sterile *adj* sterile
sterility *n* sterilità *f inv*
sterilize *v/t* sterilizzare
sterling I *adj* eccellente *f*; *fig* genuino **II** *n* FIN sterlina *f*; ***in ~*** in sterline
stern[1] *adj* (+*er*) severo
stern[2] *n* NAUT poppa *f*
sternly *adv* severamente
steroids *npl* anabolizzanti *mpl*
stethoscope *n* fonendoscopio *m*
stew I *n* spezzatino *m*; ***be in a ~*** *infml* essere nei guai **II** *v/t meat* stufare *m*; *fruit* cuocere **III** *v/i*: ***~ in one's own juice*** *Br infml* arrovellarsi
steward *n on plane, ship* steward *m inv*; *at demonstration, meeting* membro *m* del servizio d'ordine
stewardess *n on plane, ship* hostess *f inv*
stewed *adj apples, plums* cotto
stick[1] *n wood* rametto *m*; (*walking stick*) bastone *m*; ***out in the ~s*** *infml* a casa del diavolo *infml*; ***give s.o. / sth some / a lot of ~*** *Br infml* criticare qn / qc leggermente / violentemente; *fig* ***get the wrong end of the ~*** *infml* capire fischi per fiachi; *fig* ***he's a dry old ~*** *infml* è un vecchio barboso
stick[2] 〈*pret & past part* ***stuck***〉 **I** *v/t with adhesive* attaccare; *needle, knife* conficcare; *infml* (*put*) mettere; ***~ it on the shelf*** ficcalo sulla mensola; ***he stuck his head round the corner*** cacciò la testa da dietro l'angolo; *Br infml* (*abide*) sopportare; ***I just can't ~ him*** non lo sopporto più **II** *v/i* (*jam*) bloccarsi; (*adhere*) attaccarsi; ***the name seems to have stuck*** il nome è rimasto impresso in mente
◆**stick around** *v/i infml* restare
◆**stick at** *v/t infml*: ***stick at sth*** (*persevere*) insistere con qc
◆**stick by** *v/t infml*: ***stick by s.o.*** rimanere al fianco di qn
◆**stick out** *v/i* (*protrude*) sporgere; (*be noticeable*) spiccare; ***it sticks out like a sore thumb*** è un pugno in un occhio
◆**stick to** *v/t infml* (*keep to*) attenersi a; *infml* (*follow*) seguire
◆**stick together** *v/i infml* restare uniti
◆**stick up I** *v/t sep poster, leaflet* affiggere; ***stick 'em up!*** *infml* mani in alto!; ***three pupils stuck up their hands*** tre alunni hanno alzato le mani **II** *v/i* (*nail etc*) attaccare; (*hair*) rizzarsi
◆**stick up for** *v/t infml* difendere
◆**stick with** *v/t* restare con; (*keep*) mantenere
sticker *n* adesivo *m*
sticking plaster *n* cerotto *m*
stickler *n*: ***be a ~ for sth*** essere un accanito sostenitore di qc
stick-in-the-mud *n infml* abitudinario *m*, -a *f*

stick-up *n in bank* rapina *f* a mano armata
sticky *adj* (+*er*) *hands*, *surface* appiccicoso; *label* adesivo; *fig infml situation* difficile; ***go through a ~ patch*** attraversare un momento difficile; ***come to a ~ end*** fare una brutta fine
stickybeak **I** *n AUS* ficcanaso **II** *v/i* ficcanasare
stiff **I** *adj* (+*er*) *brush*, *cardboard*, *leather* rigido; *muscle*, *body* anchilosato; *mixture*, *paste* sodo; *in manner* freddo; *drink*, *competition* forte; *fine* salato; ***have a ~ neck*** avere il torcicollo; ***be*** (***as***) ***~ as a board*** *or* ***poker*** essere rigido come un manico di scopa **II** *adv*: ***be scared ~*** *infml* essere spaventato a morte *infml*; ***be bored ~*** *infml* essere annoiato a morte *infml* **III** *n infml* (*corpse*) cadavere *m*; (*prig*) persona rigida e fredda
stiffen *v/i* irrigidirsi
◆**stiffen up** *v/i of muscle* anchilosarsi
stiffly *adv* rigidamente; *fig* freddamente
stiffness *n of muscles* indolenzimento *m*; *of material* rigidità *f*; *fig*: *of manner* freddezza *f*
stifle *v/t a. fig* soffocare
stifling *adj* soffocante
stigma *n* vergogna *f*
stigmatise, stigmatize *v/t*: ***~ s.o. as sth*** bollare qn come qc
stiletto *npl* (*shoes*) scarpe *fpl* con tacco a spillo
still[1] **I** *adj* (+*er*) (*motionless*) immobile; *without wind* senza vento; *drink* non gas(s)ato; ***it was very ~ outside*** tutto era calmo fuori **II** *adv*: ***keep/stand ~!*** stai fermo!; ***time stood ~*** il tempo rimase immobile **III** *n* FILM fotogramma *m*; *distillation* distillato *m*
still[2] *adv* **1.** (*yet*) ancora; ***she ~ hasn't finished*** non ha ancora finito; ***~ more*** (*even more*) ancora più; ***do you mean you ~ don't believe me?*** vuoi dire che ancora non mi credi?; ***It ~ hasn't come*** non è ancora venuto; ***there are ten weeks ~ to go*** devono passare ancora dieci settimane; ***worse ~, ...*** ancora peggio: ... **2.** (*nevertheless*) comunque; ***they are ~ my parents*** sono pur sempre i miei genitori; ***is he ~ coming?*** verrà comunque?***~, it was worth it*** in fondo ne valeva la pena
stillborn *adj* nato morto
still life *n* natura *f* morta
stilted *adj* poco naturale
stilts *npl* trampoli *mpl*
stimulant *n* stimolante *m*
stimulate *v/t* stimolare
stimulating *adj* stimolante
stimulation *n* stimolazione *f*
stimulus *n* (*incentive*) stimolo *m*
sting **I** *n from bee* puntura *f*; *actual organ* pungiglione *m*; *from jellyfish* pizzico *m*; ***take the ~ out of sth*** rendere qc meno spiacevole; ***have a ~ in its tail*** (*story*, *film*) avere un epilogo spiacevole **II** *v/t* ⟨*pret & past part* ***stung***⟩ *of bee* pungere; *of jellyfish* pizzicare; ***she was stung by the nettles*** si è irritata con le ortiche; ***~ s.o. into action*** spronare qn **III** *v/i* ⟨*pret & past part* ***stung***⟩ *of eyes*, *scratch* bruciare
stinging *adj remark*, *criticism* pungente
stingy *adj* (+*er*) *infml* tirchio *infml*
stink **I** *v/i* ⟨*pret* ***stank***, *past part* ***stunk***⟩ (*smell bad*) puzzare; *infml* (*be very bad*) fare schifo *infml* **II** *n* (*bad smell*) puzza *f*; *infml* (*fuss*) putiferio *m infml*; ***kick up a ~*** *infml* fare un casino *infml*
stinking *adj*: ***~ rich*** *infml* ricco sfondato
stint **I** *n* periodo *m*; ***do a ~ in the army*** arruolarsi nell'esercito per un periodo; ***do you want to do a ~ now?*** vuoi darmi il cambio? **II** *v/t*: ***he ~ed the rations to make them last*** ha ristretto le razioni per farle durare di più
◆**stint on** *v/t infml* lesinare su
stipend *n esp Br for official*: stipendio *m*; REL congrua *f*
stipulate *v/t & v/i* stabilire
stipulation *n* condizione *f*
stir **I** *n*: ***give the soup a ~*** mescolare la minestra; ***cause a ~*** fare scalpore **II** *v/t* ⟨*pret & past part* ***-red***⟩ mescolare **III** *v/i* ⟨*pret & past part* ***-red***⟩ *of sleeping person* muoversi
◆**stir up** *v/t sep* fomentare; ***stir up trouble*** provocare problemi
stir-fry *v/t* ⟨*pret & past part* ***-ied***⟩ saltare (in padella)
stirring *adj music*, *speech* commovente

stirrup *n* staffa *f*
stirrup cup *n* bicchiere *m* della staffa **stirrup leather** *n* staffile *m* **stirrup pump** *n* piccolo estintore *m* portatile
stitch I *n in sewing* punto *m*; *in knitting* maglia *f*; ***~es*** MED punti *mpl* (di sutura); ***be in ~es*** *laughing* ridere a crepapelle; ***have a ~*** avere una fitta al fianco **II** *v/t sew* cucire
◆**stitch up** *v/t sep wound* suturare; *seam* rammendare; ***I've been stitched up*** *Br infml* sono stato incastrato
stitching *n* (*stitches*) cucitura *f*
stock I *n* (*reserves*) provvista *f*; COMM: *of store* stock *m inv*; *animals* bestiame *m*; FIN titoli *mpl*; *for soup etc* brodo *m*; ***in ~ / out of ~*** disponibile / esaurito; ***take ~*** fare il punto **II** *v/t* COMM *goods* vendere; *cupboard* provvista *f*; *shop* scorta *f*
◆**stock up on** *v/t* fare provvista di; ***I must stock up on rice, I've almost run out*** devo fare scorta di riso, è quasi finito
stockade I *n* palizzata *f* **II** *v/t* cingere con una palizzata
stockbreeding *n* allevamento *m* di bestiame **stockbroker** *n* agente *m/f* di cambio **stock cube** *n* dado *m* (da brodo) **stock exchange** *n* borsa *f* valori **stockfish** *n* COOK stoccafisso *m* **stockholder** *n US* azionista *m/f*
stockily *adv*: ***~ built*** tozzo
stocking *n* calza *f* (da donna)
stocking filler *n Br* regalo da mettere nella calza per Natale
stock-in-trade *n* ferri *mpl* del mestiere
stockist *n* rivenditore *m*
stock market *n* mercato *m* azionario **stock market crash** *n* crollo *m* del mercato azionario **stockpile I** *n of food, weapons* scorta *f* **II** *v/t* fare scorta di **stockroom** *n* magazzino *m* **stock-still** *adv*: ***stand ~*** stare immobile **stocktaking** *n* inventario *m*
stocky *adj* (+*er*) tarchiato
stockyard *n* recinto *m* per il bestiame
stodge *n food, book* mattone *m*; *person* persona *f* pesante
stodgy *adj* (+*er*) *food* pesante
stoical *adj* stoico
stoicism *n* stoicismo *m*
stoke *v/t fire* attizzare
stole[1] *n* (*shawl*) stola *f*
stole[2] *pret* → ***steal***
stolen *past part* → ***steal***
stolid *adj* compassato
stomach I *n* stomaco *m*; (*abdomen*) pancia *f* **II** *v/t* (*tolerate*) sopportare
stomachache *n* mal *m* di stomaco **stomach upset** *n* stomaco *m* in disordine
stomp I *n* passo *m* pesante; (*dance*) ballo *m* sincopato **II** *v/i* camminare con il passo pesante
stone I *n material* pietra *f*; (*pebble*) sasso *m*; (*precious stone*) pietra *f* preziosa; *in fruit* nocciolo *m* **II** *v/t*: ***~ s.o. to death*** lapidare qn a morte
Stone Age *n* età *f* della pietra **stone-broke** *adj US infml* spiantato
stone-cold *adj* gelido; ***~ sober*** perfettamente sobrio
stoned *adj infml on drugs* fatto *infml*
stone-deaf *adj* sordo (come una campana)
stonemason *n* scalpellino *m*
stone's throw *n* tiro *m* di schioppo; ***they lived within a ~ of the bridge*** abitavano ad un tiro di schioppo dal ponte
stonewall *v/i infml* menare il can per l'aia **stoneware** *n* articoli *mpl* in gres **stonework** *n* lavorazione della pietra; BUILD (lavoro *m* in) muratura *f*
stony *adj* (+*er*) *ground, path* sassoso
stony-broke *adj infml* in bolletta **stony-faced** *adj* impassibile
stood *pret & past part* → ***stand***
stool *n seat* sgabello *m*; ***fall between two ~s*** fare come l'asino di Buridano; (*faeces*) feci *fpl*
stool pigeon *n* piccione *m* da richiamo; (*informer*) informatore *m*
stoop I *n*: ***walk with a ~*** camminare con la schiena curva **II** *v/i* (*bend down*) chinarsi; (*have bent back*) essere curvo; ***~ to doing sth*** abbassarsi a fare qc
stop I *v/t* ⟨*pret & past part* **-ped**⟩ (*put an end to*) mettere fine a; (*prevent*) fermare; (*cease*) smettere; *person, car, bus* fermare; ***it has ~ped raining*** ha smesso di piovere; ***I ~ped her from leaving*** le ho impedito di andar via; ***I'm trying to ~ smoking*** sto cercando di smettere di fumare; ***~ it!*** smettila!; ***there's no ~ping him*** *infml*

non c'è niente che lo possa fermare; ~ ***a cheque*** bloccare un assegno **II** *v/i* ⟨*pret & past part* **-ped**⟩ (*come to a halt*) fermarsi; ***we ~ped for a drink at the pub*** ci siamo fermati al pub a bere qualcosa; ~ ***at nothing*** (***to do sth***) *fig* non fermarsi davanti a nulla (per fare qc); ~ ***dead*** *or* ***in one's tracks*** fermarsi di colpo; *of rain, noise* smettere **III** *n for train, bus* fermata *f*; ***come to a ~*** fermarsi; ***put a ~ to*** mettere fine a

◆**stop by** *v/i* (*visit*) passare

◆**stop off** *v/i* fermarsi, fare sosta; *at post office* passare a

◆**stop over** *v/i* fare sosta

◆**stop up** *v/t sep sink* intasare

stopcock *n* rubinetto *m* di arresto **stopgap** *n person* tappabuchi *m/f inv*; *thing* soluzione *f* temporanea **stoplight** *n US* (*traffic lights*) semaforo *m*; (*red light*) semaforo *m* rosso; (*brake light*) stop *m inv* **stopover** *n* sosta *f*; *in air travel* scalo *m* intermedio

stoppage *n* (*strike*) astensione *f* dal lavoro

stoppage time *n* SPORTS tempi *mpl* di recupero

stopper *n* tappo *m*

stop press *n Br* ultimissime *fpl* **stop sign** *n* (segnale *m* di) stop *m inv* **stopwatch** *n* cronometro *m*

storage *n*: ***put sth in ~*** mettere qc in magazzino; ***not much space for ~*** poco spazio per riporre la roba

storage capacity *n* COMPUT capacità *f* di memoria **storage device** *n* COMPUT dispositivo *m* di memoria **storage heater** *n* calorifero *m* ad accumulazione di calore **storage space** *n* spazio *m* per riporre la roba

store I *n large shop* negozio *m*; (*stock*) riserva *f*; (*storehouse*) deposito *m*; ***what has the future in ~ for us?*** che cosa ci riserva il futuro? **II** *v/t* tenere; COMPUT memorizzare; ~ ***sth away*** mettere via qc; ~ ***sth up*** fare scorta di qc

storecard *n carta di credito rilasciata da un grande magazzino* **store detective** *n* sorvegliante *m/f* in un grande magazzino **storefront** *n* vetrina *f* **storekeeper** *n US* negoziante *m/f* **storeroom** *n* magazzino *m*

storey, *US* **story** *n* piano *m*

stork *n* cicogna *f*

storm I *n* tempesta *f*; ***take sth / s.o. by ~*** prendere qc / qn d'assalto **II** *v/i*: ~ ***in / out*** entrare / uscire come una furia **III** *v/i* (*talk angrily*) sbraitare (***at*** contro); ~ ***out of a room*** uscire da una stanza su tutte le furie

storm cloud *n a. fig* nube *f* minacciosa **storm troopers** *npl* soldato *m* dei reparti d'assalto **storm warning** *n* avviso *m* di tempesta

stormy *adj* (+*er*) *a. fig* tempestoso

story[1] *n* (*tale*) racconto *m*; (*account*) storia *f*; (*newspaper article*) articolo *m*; *infml* (*lie*) bugia *f*

story[2] *US* → ***storey***

storybook *n* libro *m* di fiabe

storyline *n* (*narrative*) trama *f*

storyteller *n* cantastorie *m/f inv*; (*novelist*) narratore *m*, -trice *f*

stout I *adj* (+*er*) *person* robusto; *defender* tenace **II** *n Br birra forte e scura*

stout-hearted *adj* coraggioso

stove *n for cooking* cucina *f*; *for heating* stufa *f*

stow *v/t* riporre

◆**stow away** *v/i* imbarcarsi clandestinamente

stowaway *n* passeggero *m*, -a *f* clandestino, -a

straddle *v/t* stare a cavalcioni di

straggle *v/i houses, trees* sparpagliarsi; *plant* crescere in modo disordinato; ~ ***behind*** attardarsi

straggler *n* persona *f* che rimane indietro

straggly *adj hair* arruffato

straight I *adv* **1.** (*in a straight line*) dritto; ***stand up ~!*** stai dritto!; ***look s.o. ~ in the eye*** guardare qn dritto negli occhi; ***carry ~ on*** proseguire dritto; ***go ~*** *infml of criminal* rigare dritto; ~ ***ahead*** avanti dritto **2.** (*directly, immediately*) dritto, direttamente; ***give it to me ~*** *infml* dimmi francamente; ~ ***away,*** ~ ***off*** immediatamente; ~ ***out*** *say sth* chiaro e tondo **3.** (*clearly: think*) con chiarezza; ***set s.o. ~*** chiarire le idee a qn **II** *adj* (+*er*) **1.** *line* retto; *hair, whisky* liscio; *back, knees* dritto **2.** (*honest, direct*) onesto **3.** (*tidy*) in ordine **4.** (*conservative*) convenzionale **5.** (*not homosexual*) etero

6. ***keep a ~ face*** non ridere **7.** ***win / lose in ~ sets*** vincere / perdere in set consecutivi
straight and narrow *n* retta via *f*
straighten *v/t* raddrizzare
◆**straighten out I** *v/t sep situation* sistemare; *infml person* mettere in riga *infml* **II** *v/i of road* tornare diritto
◆**straighten up** *v/i* raddrizzarsi
straightfaced *n* con un'espressione seria **straightforward** *adj* (*honest*, *direct*) franco; (*simple*) semplice
strain[1] **I** *n physical* sforzo *m*; *mental* tensione *f*; *poetry*, *music* melodia *f*; *breed* razza *f*; *of virus* ceppo *m* **II** *v/t* (*injure*) affaticare; *fig*: *finances*, *budget* gravare su; *ears*, *eyes* aguzzare
strain[2] *v/t vegetables* scolare; *oil*, *fat etc* filtrare
strained *adj* teso
strainer *n for vegetables etc* colino *m*
strait *n* GEOG stretto *m*; *fig* ***be in dire ~s*** essere in serie difficoltà
straitjacket *n* camicia *f* di forza
straitlaced *adj* puritano
strand[1] *n of wool*, *thread* filo *m*; *of hair* ciocca *f*
strand[2] **I** *n shore* spiaggia *f* **II** *v/t* piantare in asso *infml*; ***be ~ed*** essere bloccato
strange *adj* (+*er*) (*odd*, *curious*) strano; ***I felt rather ~ at first*** mi sono sentito strano all'inizio; (*unknown*, *foreign*) sconosciuto; ***don't talk to ~ men*** non parlare agli sconosciuti
strangely *adv* (*oddly*) stranamente; ***~ enough*** strano ma vero
stranger *n person you don't know* sconosciuto *m*, -a *f*; ***I'm a ~ here myself*** non sono di queste parti
strangle *v/t person* strangolare
stranglehold *n* controllo *m*; ***have a ~ on sth*** avere il controllo di qc
strangulation *n* strangolamento *m*; MED strozzamento *m*
strap *n of bag* tracolla *f*; *of bra*, *dress* bretellina *f*, spallina *f*; *of watch* cinturino *m*; *of shoe* listino *m*
◆**strap in** *v/t* ⟨*pret & past part* **-ped**⟩ *with seatbelt* allacciare la cintura di sicurezza a
◆**strap on** *v/t* allacciare
strapless *adj* senza spalline
strapped *adj*: ***~ for cash*** essere a corto di soldi
strapping *adj infml* robusto
strappy *adj*: ***~ sandals*** sandali *mpl* con cinturino; ***~ top*** top *m* con le spalline; ***~ dress*** vestito *m* con le spalline
strategic *adj* strategico
strategist *n* stratega *m/f*
strategy *n* strategia *f*
stratification *n* stratificazione *f*
stratosphere *n* stratosfera *f*
straw[1] *n* paglia *f*; ***that's the last ~!*** questa è la goccia che fa traboccare il vaso!; ***clutch at ~s*** aggrapparsi a qualsiasi cosa; ***draw the short ~*** non avere la sorte dalla propria parte
straw[2] *n for drink* cannuccia *f*
strawberry *n* fragola *f*
strawberry blonde I *adj* biondo ramato **II** *n* donna *f* dai capelli biondo ramato
straw poll, straw vote *n* sondaggio *m* d'opinione pubblica; *in election* sondaggio *m* preelettorale
stray I *adj animal* randagio; *bullet* vagante **II** *n dog*, *cat* randagio *m* **III** *v/i of animal* smarrirsi; *of child* allontanarsi; *fig*: *of eyes*, *thoughts* vagare
streak I *n of dirt*, *paint* stria *f*; *fig*: *of nastiness etc* vena *f*; ***be on a winning / losing ~*** attraversare un periodo fortunato / sfortunato **II** *v/i move quickly* sfrecciare **III** *v/t*: ***be ~ed with*** essere striato di
streaker *n persona che per protesta si esibisce completamente nuda in una corsetta in pubblico*
streaky *adj* (+*er*) striato
stream I *n* ruscello *m*; *fig*: *of people*, *complaints* fiume *m*; ***come on ~*** *of plant* entrare in attività; *of oil* arrivare **II** *v/i* riversarsi; ***tears were ~ing down her face*** le lacrime le scorrevano sul viso; ***~ing in the wind*** ondeggiante al vento
◆**stream down** *v/i* (*liquid*) colare giù; (+*ogg*) ***tears streamed down her face*** le lacrime le scendevano sul viso
◆**stream in** *v/i* riversarsi dentro
◆**stream out** *v/i* riversarsi fuori (***of*** da); (*liquid*) uscire a fiotti (***of*** da)
streamer *n* stella *f* filante
streaming *adj windows* grondante; *eyes* lucido; ***I have a ~ cold*** *Br* ho il naso che mi cola per il raffreddore
streamline *v/t fig* snellire **streamlined**

adj car, plane aerodinamico; *fig*: *organization* snellito **stream of consciousness** *n* LIT flusso *m* di coscienza

street *n* strada *f*; *in address* via *f*; ***be right up s.o.'s ~*** (*be suitable*) essere proprio quello che fa per qn

streetcar *n US* tram *m inv* **street cred** *n infml* popolarità *f* tra i coetanei **streetlight** *n* lampione *m* **streetlighting** *n* illuminazione *f* stradale **street map** *n* stradario *m* **street people** *npl* gente *f* di strada **street value** *n of drugs* valore *m* di mercato **streetwalker** *n infml* passeggiatrice *f* **streetwise** *adj* scafato *infml*

strength *n of person, wind, emotion, currency* forza *f*; (*strong point*) punto *m* forte; ***on the ~ of sth***; ***save one's ~*** risparmiare le proprie forze; ***go from ~ to ~*** andare di bene in meglio; ***be at full ~*** essere al completo

strengthen I *v/t* rinforzare **II** *v/i* consolidarsi

strenuous *adj* faticoso

strenuously *adv deny* recisamente

stress I *n* (*emphasis*) accento *m*; (*tension*) stress *m inv*; ***be under ~*** essere sotto pressione **II** *v/t syllable* accentare; *importance etc* sottolineare

stressed out *adj* stressato

stress-free *adj* senza stress

stressful *adj* stressante

stretch I *v/t* **1.** *material* tendere **2.** *small income* far bastare; ***~ the rules*** *infml* fare uno strappo (alla regola) ***~ one's legs*** sgranchirsi le gambe **3.** ***a job that ~es me*** un lavoro che mi impegna **II** *v/i to relax muscles* stirarsi; *to reach sth* allungarsi; (*spread*) estendersi; *of fabric*: *give* cedere; *of fabric*: *sag* allargarsi; ***~ from X to Y*** (*extend*) estendersi da X a Y **III** *n of land, water* tratto *m*; ***at a ~*** (*non-stop*) di fila; ***for 8 hours at a ~*** per otto ore di fila; ***by no ~ of the imagination*** neanche per sogno; ***not by a long ~*** neanche per sogno **IV** *adj fabric* elasticizzato; ***~ trousers*** pantaloni *mpl* elasticizzati

◆**stretch out I** *v/t sep arm, leg* stendere; ***he stretched out his hand*** allungò la mano **II** *v/i* (*lie down*) stendersi

stretcher *n* barella *f*

stretch limo *n* limousine *f inv* extralunga

stretch marks *n* smagliatura *f*

stretchy *adj* (*+er*) elastico

stricken *adj*: ***be ~ with sth*** *illness, remorse* essere colpito da qc; ***grief-stricken*** afflitto dal dolore

strict *adj* (*+er*) *person* severo; *instructions, rules* tassativo

strictly *adv*: ***be brought up ~*** ricevere un'educazione rigida; ***it is ~ forbidden*** è severamente proibito; ***~ personal*** strettamente personale; ***~ speaking*** in senso stretto; ***not ~ true*** non del tutto vero; ***~ between ourselves*** che resti tra noi; ***unless ~ necessary*** se non strettamente necessario; ***the car park is ~ for the use of residents*** l'uso del parcheggio è riservato ai residenti

strictness *n* severità *f inv*

stricture *n* restrizione *f*; (*criticism*) critica *f*

stridden *past part* → ***stride***

stride I *n* falcata *f*; ***take sth in one's ~*** affrontare qc senza drammi; *fig* ***make great ~s*** far passi da gigante; *AUS* ***~s*** pantaloni *mpl* **II** *v/i* ⟨*pret* ***strode***, *past part* ***stridden***⟩ procedere a grandi passi; ***he strode up to me*** avanzò verso di me

strident *adj* stridulo; *fig*: *demands* veemente

strike I *v/i* ⟨*pret & past part* ***struck***⟩ *of workers* scioperare; (*attack*) aggredire; *of disaster* colpire; ***be struck by lightning*** essere colpito da un fulmine; *of clock* suonare **II** *v/t* ⟨*pret & past part* ***struck***⟩ **1.** (*hit*) colpire; ***~ the hour*** battere l'ora; ***~ one's head against sth*** battere la testa contro qc **2.** *match* accendere (sfregando) **3.** *of idea, thought* venire in mente a **4.** *oil* trovare **5.** (*impress*) ***she struck me as being …*** mi ha dato l'impressione di essere … **III** *n* **1.** *of workers* sciopero *m*; ***be on ~*** essere in sciopero; ***go on ~*** entrare in sciopero **2.** *of oil* scoperta *f*

◆**strike back** *v/i* (*retaliate*) rispondere

◆**strike down** *v/t sep* abbattere

◆**strike off** *v/t sep*: ***be struck off*** *doctor* essere radiato dall'albo

◆**strike out I** *v/t sep* depennare **II** *v/i*: ***strike out on one's own*** intraprendere qc da soli

◆**strike up** *v/t insep conversation,*

friendship avviare
strike ballot *n votazione per decidere se scioperare o meno* **strikebreaker** *n* crumiro *m*, -a *f*
striker *n person on strike* scioperante *m/f*; *in football* attaccante *m inv*, cannoniere *m*, punta *f*
striking *adj* (*marked*) marcato; (*eye-catching*) impressionante; (*attractive*) attraente; *colour* forte
striking distance *n*: ***be within ~*** *of missile* essere a tiro
string *n* (*cord*) spago *m*; *of violin, tennis racket* corda *f*; ***the ~s*** MUS gli archi; ***pull ~s*** esercitare la propria influenza; ***a ~ of*** (*series*) una serie di
◆**string along** ⟨*pret & past part* ***strung***⟩ **I** *v/i infml*: ***do you mind if I string along?*** posso venire anch'io? **II** *v/t sep infml*: ***string s.o. along*** menare qn per il naso
◆**string out** *v/t sep* prolungare
◆**string together** *v/t sep* mettere insieme
◆**string up** *v/t sep infml* impiccare
string bean *n* fagiolino *m*
stringed instrument *n* strumento *m* ad arco
stringent *adj* rigoroso
stringer *n journalist* giornalista *m/f* freelance
string player *n* suonatore *m*, -trice *f* di strumento ad arco **string quartet** *n* quartetto *m* d'archi **string vest** *n* canottiera *f* a maglie larghe
stringy *adj* (+*er*) *meat* tiglioso
strip I *v/t* ⟨*pret & past part* ***-ped***⟩ (*remove*) staccare; *bed* disfare; (*undress*) spogliare; ***~ s.o. of sth*** spogliare qn di qc **II** *v/i* ⟨*pret & past part* ***-ped***⟩ (*undress*) spogliarsi; *of stripper* fare lo spogliarello; ***~ naked*** spogliarsi completamente **III** *n* striscia *f*; (*comic strip*) fumetto *m*; *of soccer player* divisa *f*
◆**strip down I** *v/t sep engine* smontare **II** *v/i*: ***strip down to one's underwear*** spogliarsi fino alle mutande
◆**strip off I** *v/t sep clothes, wallpaper* togliere **II** *v/i* spogliarsi; (*at doctor's*) svestirsi
strip cartoon *n Br* fumetto *m*
strip club *n* locale *m* di spogliarelli
stripe *n* striscia *f*; *indicating rank* gallone *m*
striped *adj* a strisce
strip joint *n infml* → ***strip club***
strip lighting *n* luce *f* al neon **strip mining** *n* coltivazione *f* a cielo aperto
stripper *n* spogliarellista *f*; ***male ~*** spogliarellista *m*
strip poker *n* strip poker *m* **strip show** *n* spogliarello *m* **striptease** *n* spogliarello *m*
strive *v/i* ⟨*pret* ***strove***, *past part* ***striven***⟩: ***~ to do sth*** sforzarsi di fare qc; ***~ for sth*** lottare per (ottenere) qc
striven *past part* → ***strive***
strobe (light) *n* luce *f* stroboscopica
strode *pret* → ***stride***
stroke I *n* **1.** MED ictus *m inv* **2.** *when painting* pennellata *f* **3.** *in swimming* bracciata *f*; *style of swimming* stile *m* di nuoto **4.** *fig*: ***~ of luck*** colpo di fortuna; ***she never does a ~ (of work)*** non fa mai un bel niente; ***at a ~*** in un colpo solo; ***on the ~ of twelve*** allo scoccare delle dodici **II** *v/t* accarezzare
stroll I *n* passeggiata *f*; ***go for a ~*** fare una passeggiata **II** *v/i* fare due passi; ***she ~ed back to the office*** tornò in ufficio in tutta calma
stroller *n US* (*pushchair*) passeggino *m*
strong *adj* (+*er*) *person, wind, drink, currency* forte; *structure* resistente; *candidate* valido; *taste, smell* intenso; *views, beliefs* fermo; *arguments* convincente; *objections* energico; ***~ support*** largo consenso; ***an 8,000-~ community*** una comunità di 8.000 persone
strong-arm *adj* forte; ***~ tactics*** maniere *fpl* forti **strongbox** *n* cassaforte *f*
stronghold *n fig* roccaforte *f*
strongly *adv believe, object* fermamente; *built* solidamente; ***feel ~ about sth*** avere molto a cuore qc
strong meat *n* roba *f* forte **strong-minded** *adj* risoluto **strong point** *n* (punto *m*) forte *m* **strongroom** *n* camera *f* blindata **strong-willed** *adj* deciso
stroppy *adj* (+*er*) *Br infml* irascibile; *answer, children* indisponente
strove *pret* → ***strive***
struck *pret & past part* → ***strike***
structural *adj* strutturale
structurally *adv* strutturalmente; ***~***

sound dalla struttura solida
structure **I** *n something built* costruzione *f*; *of novel, society etc* struttura *f* **II** *v/t* strutturare
struggle **I** *n* (*fight*) colluttazione *f*; *fig* lotta *f*; (*hard time*) fatica *f*; ***put up a ~*** opporre resistenza; ***it was a ~*** è stata dura **II** *v/i with a person* lottare; (*have a hard time*) faticare; ***~ to do sth*** faticare a fare qc; ***are you struggling?*** stai facendo fatica?; ***~ to one's feet*** alzarsi con difficoltà; ***~ on*** *liter* continuare a stento
strum *v/t* ⟨*pret & past part* ***-med***⟩ strimpellare
strumpet *n liter* sgualdrina *f*
strung *pret & past part* → ***string***
strung-out *adj infml* completamente fatto
strut[1] *v/i* ⟨*pret & past part* ***-ted***⟩ camminare impettito
strut[2] *n* (*horizontal*) puntone *m*; (*vertical*) montante *m*
stub **I** *n of cigarette* mozzicone *m*; *of cheque, ticket* matrice *f* **II** *v/t* ⟨*pret & past part* ***-bed***⟩: ***~ one's toe*** urtare il dito del piede
◆**stub out** *v/t* spegnere; ***stub out a cigarette*** spegnere una sigaretta
stubble *n on man's face* barba *f* ispida
stubborn *adj person* testardo; *defence, refusal, denial* ostinato
stubbornness *n* caparbietà *f*, testardaggine *f*
stubby *adj* (*+er*) tozzo
stuck **I** *pret & past part* → ***stick***[2] **II** *adj* (*unable to move*) bloccato; (*in difficulties*) in difficoltà; *infml* ***be ~ on s.o.*** essere cotto di qn *infml*; ***be ~ with s.o.*** / ***sth*** non riuscire a liberarsi di qn / qc; *Br infml* ***get ~ into sth*** mettersi a fare qc con grinta
stuck-up *adj infml* presuntuoso
stud *n on jacket* borchia *f*; *on football boot* tacchetto *m*; (*group of horses: for breeding*) cavalli *mpl* da monta; *attractive man infml* stallone *m infml*
studded *adj*: ***be ~ with*** cosparso di
student *n* studente *m*, -essa *f*
student nurse *n* infermiere *m*, -a *f* tirocinante **student teacher** *n* insegnante *m/f* tirocinante
stud farm *n* stazione *f* di monta
studio *n* studio *m*; (*recording studio*) sala *f* di registrazione
studio flat, studio apartment *n* monolocale *m*
studious *adj* studioso
study **I** *n* studio *m*; (*research*) ricerca *f*; *of evidence* esame *m*; ***African studies*** UNIV africanistica *f* **II** *v/t & v/i* ⟨*pret & past part* ***-ied***⟩ studiare
stuff **I** *n* roba *f*; ***there is some good ~ in that book*** c'è qualcosa di buono in quel libro; ***and ~ like that*** e cose del genere; ***all that ~ about how he wanted to help us*** tutta il discorso su come voleva aiutarci; ***~ and nonsense*** sciocchezze; ***do one's ~*** fare ciò che si deve; ***know one's ~*** sapere il fatto proprio **II** *v/t turkey* farcire; ***~ sth into sth*** ficcare qc in qc; ***~ one's face*** *infml* abbuffarsi; ***be ~ed up*** avere il naso tappato; ***a ~ed toy*** un pupazzo *m*; *Br infml* ***get ~ed!*** va a farti fottere!; ***~ it*** al diavolo
stuffing *n for turkey* farcia *f*; *in chair, teddy bear* imbottitura *f*
stuffy *adj* (*+er*) *room* mal ventilato; *person* inquadrato
stumble *v/i* inciampare
◆**stumble across** *v/t* trovare per caso
◆**stumble over** *v/t* inciampare in; *words* incespicare in
stumbling-block *n fig* scoglio *m*; *fig* ***be a ~ to sth*** essere di ostacolo a qc
stump **I** *n of tree* ceppo *m* **II** *v/t of question, questioner* sconcertare; *fig infml* ***you've got me ~ed*** mi hai lasciato senza parole
◆**stump up** *v/t insep infml* sganciare *infml*
stumpy *adj* (*+er*) *person* tarchiato; *legs* tozzo
stun *v/t* ⟨*pret & past part* ***-ned***⟩ *of blow* stordire; *of news* sbalordire
stung *pret & past part* → ***sting***
stunk *past part* → ***stink***
stunner *n infml* schianto *m*
stunning *adj* (*amazing*) sbalorditivo; (*very beautiful*) splendido
stunt **I** *n for publicity* trovata *f* pubblicitaria; *in film* acrobazia *f* **II** *v/t growth, development* impedire
stuntman *n in film* cascatore *m*
stupefy *v/t* ⟨*pret & past part* ***-ied***⟩ sbalordire
stupendous *adj* (*marvellous*) fantastico; *mistake* enorme
stupid *adj* stupido; ***don't be ~*** non es-

sere stupido; ***that was a ~ thing to do*** è stata una mossa stupida; ***make s.o. look ~*** far fare la figura dello stupido a qn; ***bore s.o. ~*** instupidire qn

stupidity *n* stupidità *f inv*

stupor *n* stordimento *m*; ***in a drunken ~*** stordito dall'alcool

sturdy *adj* (*+er*) robusto

stutter I *n* balbuzie *f*; ***he has a ~*** balbetta **II** *v/t & v/i* balbettare

sty *n for pig* porcile *m*

sty(e) *n* MED orzaiolo *m*

style I *n* stile *m*; (*fashion*) moda *f*; (*fashionable elegance*) classe *f*; (*hairstyle*) pettinatura *f*; ***go out of ~*** passare di moda; ***~ of management*** stile *m* gestionale; ***that house is not my ~*** quella casa non è nel mio stile; ***the man has ~*** quell'uomo ha stile **II** *v/t hair* acconciare

stylish *adj* elegante

stylist *n* (*hair stylist*) parrucchiere *m*, -a *f*

stylistic *adj* stilistico

stylized *adj* stilizzato

suave *adj* mellifluo

subcommittee *n* sottocommissione *f*

subconscious *adj* subconscio; ***the ~ (mind)*** il subconscio

subconsciously *adv* inconsciamente

subcontinent *n* subcontinente *m*

subcontract *v/t* subappaltare

subcontractor *n* subappaltatore *m*, -trice *f*

subculture *n* sottocultura *f*

subdivide *v/t* suddividere

subdue *v/t* sottomettere

subdued *adj person*, *voice* pacato; *light*, *colour* soffuso

subheading *n* sottotitolo *m*

subhuman *adj* subumano

subject I *n of monarch* suddito *m*, -a *f*; (*topic*) argomento *m*; EDU materia *f*; GRAM soggetto *m*; ***change the ~*** cambiare argomento **II** *adj*: ***be ~ to*** essere soggetto a; ***~ to availability*** nei limiti della disponibilità; ***all trains are ~ to delay*** tutti i treni possono subire dei ritardi; ***~ to flooding*** soggetto a inondazioni **III** *v/t* sottoporre; ***be ~ed to criticism*** essere criticato

subjective *adj* soggettivo; GRAM ***~ case*** caso *m* nominativo

subject matter *n* argomento *m*

subjugate *v/t* soggiogare

subjunctive *n* GRAM congiuntivo *m*

sublet *v/t* 〈*pret & past part* ***-let***〉 subaffittare

sublimate *v/t* sublimare

sublime *adj* sublime

subliminal *adj* subliminale

submachine gun *n* mitra *m*

submarine *n* sottomarino *m*, sommergibile *m*

submenu *n* COMPUT sottomenu

submerge I *v/t* sommergere **II** *v/i of submarine* immergersi

submission *n* (*surrender*) sottomissione *f*; *request to committee etc* richiesta *f*; ***force s.o. into ~*** costringere qn a sottomettersi

submissive *adj* sottomesso

submit 〈*pret & past part* ***-ted***〉 **I** *v/t plan*, *proposal* presentare **II** *v/i* sottomettersi

subnormal *adj temperature* inferiore alla norma; *person* subnormale

subordinate I *adj employee*, *position* subalterno; ***~ clause*** GRAM subordinata *f* **II** *n* subalterno *m*, -a *f*

subplot *n* trama *f* secondaria

subpoena I *n* citazione *f* **II** *v/t person* citare in giudizio

◆**subscribe to** *v/t magazine etc* abbonarsi a; *theory* condividere

subscriber *n to magazine* abbonato *m*, -a *f*

subscription *n* abbonamento *m*

subsection *n a.* JUR sottosezione

subsequent *adj* successivo

subsequently *adv* successivamente

subservient *adj pej* subordinato (***to*** a)

subside *v/i of waters*, *winds* calare; *of building* sprofondare; *of fears*, *panic* calmarsi

subsidence *n* subsidenza *f*

subsidiary I *n* filiale *f* **II** *adj*: ***~ role*** ruolo *m* secondario; ***~ subject*** materia *f* complementare; ***~ company*** società *f* consociata

subsidise, subsidize *v/t* sovvenzionare

subsidy *n* sovvenzione *f*

◆**subsist on** *v/t* vivere di

subsistence farming *n* agricoltura *f* di sussistenza **subsistence level** *n* livello *m* minimo di vita

subsoil *n* sottosuolo *m*

substance *n* (*matter*) sostanza *f*; ***a man of ~*** un uomo benestante

substance abuse *n* abuso *m* di sostante stupefacenti
substandard *adj* scadente
substantial *adj* considerevole; *meal* sostanzioso
substantially *adv* (*considerably*) considerevolmente; (*in essence*) sostanzialmente
substantiate *v/t* comprovare
substantive *adj* sostanziale
substitute I *n for person* sostituto *m*, -a *f*; *for commodity* alternativa *f*; SPORTS riserva *f* **II** *v/t*: **~ *X for Y*** sostituire Y con X **III** *v/i*: **~ *for s.o.*** sostituire qn
substitution *n* (*act*) sostituzione *f*; ***make a ~*** SPORTS fare una sostituzione
subterfuge *n* sotterfugio *m*
subterranean *adj* sotterraneo
subtitle *n* sottotitolo *m*
subtle *adj hint*, *difference* sottile; *flavour* delicato
subtlety *n* finezza *f*
subtotal *n* subtotale *m*
subtract *v/t number* sottrarre
subtraction *n* sottrazione *f*
subtropical *adj* subtropicale
suburb *n* sobborgo *m*; ***the ~s*** la periferia
suburban *adj* di periferia
suburbia *n* periferia *f*
subversive I *adj* sovversivo **II** *n* sovversivo *m*, -a *f*
subway *n Br* (*passageway*) sottopassaggio *m*; *US* metropolitana *f*
subzero *adj*: **~ *temperatures*** temperature sottozero
succeed I *v/i* (*be successful*) avere successo; *to throne* succedere; **~ *in doing sth*** riuscire a fare qc **II** *v/t* (*come after*) succedere a
succeeding *adj* successivo
success *n* successo *m*; ***be a ~*** avere successo
successful *adj person* affermato; *marriage*, *party* riuscito; ***be ~*** riuscire; ***he's very ~*** è arrivato
successfully *adv* con successo; ***we ~ completed …*** siamo riusciti a portare a termine …
succession *n* (*sequence*) sfilza *f*; *to the throne* successione *f*; ***in ~*** di seguito
successive *adj* successivo; ***three ~ days*** tre giorni di seguito
successor *n* successore *m*
succinct *adj* succinto
succulent *adj* succulento
succumb *v/i* (*give in*) cedere; **~ *to temptation*** cedere alla tentazione
such I *adj* (*of that kind*) del genere; **~ *a*** (*so much of a*) un / una tale; **~ *as*** come; **~ *people*** gente del genere; ***he made ~ a fuss*** ha fatto una tale scenata; ***there is no ~ word as …*** la parola … non esiste **II** *adv* così; **~ *nice people*** gente così simpatica; ***as ~*** (*in that capacity*) in quanto tale; ***as ~*** (*in itself*) di per sé; **~ *is life*** è la vita
suchlike *infml* **I** *adj* così **II** *pron* simili
suck I *v/t lollipop etc* succhiare; **~ *one's thumb*** succhiarsi il dito **II** *v/i*: ***it ~s*** *sl* (*is awful*) fa schifo *sl*
◆**suck up** *v/t sep* assorbire; *dust* aspirare
◆**suck up to** *v/t infml* leccare i piedi a *infml*
sucker *n infml person* pollo *infml*; ***be a ~ for sth*** farsi incantare da qc
suckle *v/t baby* allattare
suction *n* aspirazione *f*
sudden *adj* improvviso; ***all of a ~*** all'improvviso
suddenly *adv* improvvisamente
suds *npl* (*soap suds*) schiuma *fsg*
sue I *v/t* fare causa a **II** *v/i* fare causa; **~ *for*** fare causa per
suede *n* pelle *f* scamosciata
suet *n* sugna *f*
Suez Canal *n* canale *m* di Suez
suffer I *v/i* (*be in great pain*) soffrire; (*deteriorate*) risentirne; ***be ~ing from*** avere; **~ *from*** soffrire di **II** *v/t loss*, *setback* subire
sufferance *n* sopportazione *f*; ***on ~*** tollerato con riluttanza
suffering *n* sofferenza *f*
suffice *form* **I** *v/i* bastare **II** *v/t*: **~ *it to say …*** basti dire che…
sufficiency *n* (*adequacy*) quantità *f* sufficiente
sufficient *adj* sufficiente
sufficiently *adv* abbastanza
suffix *n* LING suffisso *m*
suffocate *v/t & v/i* soffocare
suffocation *n* soffocamento *m*
suffrage *n* diritto *m* di voto
sugar I *n* zucchero *m*; *US endearment* dolcezza *f* **II** *v/t* zuccherare; **~ *the pill*** indorare la pillola

sugar beet *n* BOT barbabietola *f* da zucchero **sugar bowl** *n* zuccheriera *f* **sugarcane** *n* canna *f* da zucchero **sugar daddy** *n infml vecchio ricco che mantiene l'amante giovane* **sugar soap** *n* negozio *m* di caramelle
sugary *adj taste* zuccherino; *fig* sdolcinato
suggest *v/t* proporre, suggerire; ***I ~ that we stop now*** propongo di fermarci ora
suggestion *n* proposta *f*, suggerimento *m*
suggestive *adj* allusivo; (*lewd*) provocante
suicidal *adj person* con tendenze suicide; *tendencies* suicida
suicide *n* suicidio *m*; ***commit ~*** suicidarsi
suicide bomber *n* kamikaze *m/f inv* **suicide pact** *n* patto *m* suicida
suit I *n for man* vestito *m*, completo *m*; *for woman* tailleur *m inv*; ***~ of armour*** armatura *f*; *in cards* seme *m*; *fig* ***follow ~*** seguire l'esempio; *in law* azione *f* legale **II** *v/t of clothes, colour* stare bene a; ***~ yourself!*** *infml* fai come ti pare!; ***be ~ed for sth*** essere fatto per qc; ***does the climate ~ you?*** il clima vi giova?
suitable *adj* adatto
suitably *adv* adeguatamente
suitcase *n* valigia *f*
suite *n of rooms* suite *f inv*; ***bathroom en ~*** bagno in camera; *of furniture* divano *m* e poltrone *fpl* coordinati; ***3-piece ~*** salotto di un divano e due poltrone; MUS suite *f inv*
sulfur *etc US* → ***sulphur*** *etc*
sulk *v/i* fare il broncio
sulky *adj* (*+er*) imbronciato
sullen *adj* crucciato
sully *v/t* 〈*pret & past part* ***-ied***〉 macchiare
sulphate, *US* **sulfate** *n* solfato *m*
sulphur, *US* **sulfur** *n* zolfo *m*
sulphuric acid, *US* **sulfuric acid** *n* acido *m* solforico
sultan *n* sultano *m*
sultana *n Br* (*fruit*) uva *f* sultanina
sultanate *n* sultanato *m*
sultry *adj climate* afoso; *sexually* sensuale
sum *n* somma *f*; *in arithmetic* addizione *f*; ***a large ~ of money*** una forte somma di denaro; ***that's the ~ total of his efforts*** quello è tutto quello che ha fatto
◆**sum up** 〈*pret & past part* ***-med***〉 **I** *v/t sep* (*summarize*) riassumere; (*assess*) valutare **II** *v/i* JUR riepilogare
summarise, summarize *v/t* riassumere
summary *n* riassunto *m*
summer I *n* estate *f* **II** *adj* estivo **III** *v/i* trascorrere l'estate
summer camp *n* campeggio *m* estivo
summerhouse *n* gazebo *m*
summer pudding *n* COOK *dolce di pan di Spagna e frutti di bosco* **summer school** *n* corso *m* estivo **summer solstice** *n* ASTR solstizio *m* d'estate
summertime *n* estate *f*
summery *adj* estivo
summing-up *n* JUR ricapitolazione *f*
summit *n of mountain* vetta *f*; POL summit *m inv*
summit meeting *n* → ***summit***
summon *v/t meeting* convocare; JUR citare; *fire brigade etc* radunare; *help* chiamare
◆**summon up** *v/t sep strength* raccogliere
summons *nsg* JUR citazione *f*
sump *n for oil* coppa *f* dell'olio; *drainage* pozzo *m* di drenaggio
sumptuous *adj* sontuoso
sun I *n* sole *m*; ***in the ~*** al sole; ***out of the ~*** all'ombra; ***he has had too much ~*** ha preso troppo sole; ***you've caught the ~*** hai preso il sole; ***he's tried everything under the ~*** ha provato di tutto **II** *v/r*: ***~ o.s.*** prendere il sole
sunbathe *v/i* prendere il sole **sunbeam** *n* raggio di sole **sunbed** *n* lettino *m* solare **sunblock** *n* protezione *f* solare totale **sunburn** *n* scottatura *f* **sunburnt** *adj* scottato
sundae *n coppa gelato con frutta e granella di nocciole*
Sunday *n* domenica *f*
Sunday best *n* vestito della domenica; ***all dressed up in his ~*** tutto vestito a festa **Sunday school** *n* scuola *f* domenicale (di catechismo)
sundeck *n* ponte *m* scoperto **sundial** *n* meridiana *f* **sundown** *n Br* tramonto *m*; ***at / before ~*** al / prima del tramonto **sundress** *n* prendisole *m*

sun-dried *adj* seccato al sole
sundries *npl* varie *fpl*
sundry *adj* vario
sunflower *n* BOT girasole *m*
sung *past part* → ***sing***
sunglasses *npl* occhiali *mpl* da sole
sunk *past part* → ***sink***
sunken *adj cheeks* incavato
sunlamp *n* lampada *f* abbronzante
sunlight *n* luce *f* del sole
sunny *adj* (+*er*) *day* di sole; ***it's ~*** c'è il sole; *spot* soleggiato; *disposition* allegro; ***look on the ~ side (of things)*** guardare le cose dal lato positivo
sunny-side up *adj US eggs* all'occhio di bue
sunrise *n* alba *f* **sunroof** *n* tettuccio *m* apribile **sunscreen** *n* crema *f* solare **sunset** *n* tramonto *m* **sunshade** *n* ombrellone *m* **sunshine** *n* (luce *f* del) sole *m* **sunspot** *n* macchia solare; *place* luogo *m* del sole **sunstroke** *n* colpo *m* di sole **suntan** *n* abbronzatura *f*; ***get a ~*** abbronzarsi
super *adj infml* fantastico
superannuate *v/t* mandare in pensione
superannuated *adj* in pensione
superb *adj* magnifico
superbug *n in hospitals* batterio *m* resistente agli antibiotici
supercilious *adj* altezzoso
superciliously *adv* altezzosamente
superficial *adj* superficiale
superfluity *n* superfluità *f*
superfluous *adj* superfluo
superglue *n* attaccatutto *m*
supergrass *n infml* importante informatore della polizia
superhero *n* supereroe *m*
superhighway *n US* autostrada *f*; ***the information ~*** Internet *m*
superhuman *adj efforts* sovrumano
superimpose *v/t*: ***~ sth on sth*** sovrapporre qc a qc; PHOT mettere in sovrimpressione
superintend *v/t* sovraintendere
superintendent *n of police* commissario *m*
superior I *adj* (*better*) superiore; ***he thinks he's so ~*** pensa di essere tanto superiore **II** *n in organization, society* superiore *m*
superiority *n* superiorità *f*
superiority complex *n* complesso *m* di superiorità
superlative I *adj* (*superb*) eccellente **II** *n* GRAM superlativo *m*
supermarket *n* supermarket *m inv*, supermercato *m*
supernatural I *adj powers* soprannaturale **II** *n*: ***the ~*** il soprannaturale
supernumerary I *adj* soprannumerario **II** *n actor* comparsa *f*
superpower *n* POL superpotenza *f*
superscript *adj* TYPO soprascritto
supersede *v/t* (*replace*) sostituire
supersonic *adj flight, aircraft* supersonico
superstar *n* superstar *f inv*; divo *m*, -a *f*
superstition *n* superstizione *f*
superstitious *adj person* superstizioso
superstore *n* ipermercato *m*; (*large shop*) grande negozio *m*
superstructure *n* sovrastruttura *f*
supertanker *n* superpetroliera *f*
supervise *v/t* supervisionare
supervision *n* supervisione *f*
supervisor *n at work* supervisore *m*
supervisory board *n* consiglio *m* direttivo
super yacht *n* super yacht *m inv*
supper *n* cena *f*
supple *adj* (+*er*) *person, limbs* snodato; *material* flessibile
supplement *n* supplemento *m*
supplementary *n* supplementario
supplier *n* COMM fornitore *m*, -trice *f*
supply I *n* fornitura *f*; ***electricity ~*** erogazione *f* di elettricità; ***a month's ~*** la scorta di un mese; ***be in short ~*** essere in scarsa quantità; ***~ and demand*** domanda e offerta; ***supplies*** rifornimenti **II** *v/t* ⟨*pret & past part* ***-ied***⟩ *goods* fornire; ***~ s.o. with sth*** fornire qc a qn; ***be supplied with*** *fitted with etc* essere dotato di; ***pens and paper are supplied by the firm*** carta e penne sono forniti dalla ditta
supply teacher *n* supplente *m/f*
support I *n for structure* supporto *m*; (*backing*) sostegno *m* **II** *v/t building, structure* sostenere; *financially* mantenere; (*back*) sostenere; *football team* fare il tifo per; (*endure*) sopportare
supportable *adj* (*bearable*) sopportabile; (*tenable*) sostenibile

supporter *n* sostenitore *m*, -trice *f*; *of football team etc* tifoso *m*, -a *f*
supporting *adj role* secondario; *actor* non protagonista
supportive *adj*: ***be ~ towards s.o.*** dare il proprio appoggio a qn
suppose *v/t* (*imagine*) pensare; (*assume*) supporre; ***let us ~ we are living in the 8th century*** supponiamo di vivere nell'ottavo secolo; ***so you see, it can't be true — I ~ not*** vedi, non può essere vero – penso di no; ***I ~ so*** suppongo di sì; ***I ~ I must have fallen asleep*** credo di essermi addormentato; ***it is ~d to...***; ***~ you have a wash?*** e se ti lavassi?; (*is meant to*) dovrebbe …; (*is said to*) dicono che …; ***you are not ~d to …*** (*not allowed to*) non dovresti …
supposedly *adv* presumibilmente
supposing *cj* e se; ***~ he can't do it?*** e se non potesse farlo?
supposition *n* supposizione *f*
suppository *n* MED supposta *f*
suppress *v/t rebellion etc* reprimere
suppression *n* repressione *f*
supremacy *n* supremazia *f*
supreme *adj* supremo
supremo *n* ⟨*pl* ***supremos***⟩ *Br infml* capo *m* supremo
surcharge *n for travel* sovrapprezzo *m*; *for mail* soprattassa *f*
sure I *adj* (+*er*) sicuro; ***I'm ~*** sono sicuro; ***be ~ about sth*** essere sicuro di qc; ***make ~ that …*** assicurarsi che …; ***it's ~ to rain*** pioverà sicuramente; ***be ~ to turn the gas off*** assicurarsi di spegnere il gas; ***I've made ~ that there's enough coffee*** mi sono accertato che ci sia abbastanza caffè; ***I'll find out for ~*** me ne accerterò; ***do you want to see that film? — I'm not ~*** vuoi vedere il film? – non lo so; ***be ~ of o.s.*** essere sicuro di sé **II** *adv* certamente; ***will you go there? — ~!*** *infml* ci andrai? – certo!; ***~ enough*** infatti; ***~!*** *infml* certo!
sure-fire *adj infml* garantito; ***a ~ plan*** un piano infallibile **sure-footed** *adj* che non fa passi falsi
surely *adv* certamente; (*gladly*) volentieri; ***~ that's not right!*** non può essere!; ***oh, ~ you've heard of him*** non puoi non conoscerlo; ***~ somebody knows the answer*** sicuramente qualcuno lo sa
surety *n for loan* cauzione *f*
surf I *n on sea* spuma *f* **II** *v/i* fare surf **III** *v/t the Net* navigare
surface I *n of table, object, water* superficie *f*; *fig* ***on the ~*** superficialmente, in apparenza **II** *v/i of swimmer, submarine* risalire in superficie, riemergere, (*appear*) farsi vivo
surface mail *n* posta *f* ordinaria
surfboard *n* tavola *f* da surf
surfer *n on sea* surfista *m/f*
surfing *n* surf *m inv*; ***go ~*** fare surf
surge I *n in electric current* sovratensione *f* transitoria; *in demand* impennata *f*; *of interest, financial growth etc* aumento *m*; *of water* ondata *f*; ***he felt a sudden ~ of rage*** avvertì un improvviso impeto di rabbia **II** *v/i* (*river*) gonfiarsi; ***the crowd ~d into the square*** la folla si riversava nella piazza; ***~ ahead*** partire rapidamente
◆**surge forward** *v/i of crowd* buttarsi avanti
surgeon *n* chirurgo *m*
surgery *n* intervento *m* chirurgico; *Br: place of work* ambulatorio *m*; ***undergo ~*** sottoporsi a un intervento chirurgico; ***~ hours*** orario *m* d'ambulatorio
surgical *adj* chirurgico
surgically *adv* chirurgicamente
surgical mask *n* maschera *f* chirurgica
surly *adj* (+*er*) scontroso
surmise *v/t* congetturare
surmount *v/t difficulties* sormontare
surname *n* cognome *m*
surpass *v/t* superare
surplice *n* REL cotta *f*
surplus I *n* surplus *m inv* **II** *adj* eccedente
surprise I *n* sorpresa *f*; ***it'll come as no ~ to hear that …*** non ti sorprenderà sapere che …; ***take s.o. by ~*** cogliere qn di sorpresa **II** *v/t* sorprendere; ***be ~d*** essere sorpreso; ***look ~d*** avere l'aria sorpresa
surprising *adj* sorprendente
surprisingly *adv* sorprendentemente; ***not ~, …*** non c'è da meravigliarsi che …
surreal *adj* surreale
surrealism *n* surrealismo *m*
surrender I *v/i of army* arrendersi **II**

v/t weapons etc consegnare **III** *n* resa *f*

surreptitious *adj* furtivo; JUR surrettizio

surrogate *n* sostituto *m*, -a *f*

surrogate mother *n* madre *f* biologica

surround I *v/t* circondare; ***be ~ed by …*** essere circondato da … **II** *n of picture etc* bordo *m*

surrounding *adj* circostante

surroundings *npl of village etc* dintorni *mpl*; *fig* ambiente *m*

surround-sound *adj speakers* suono *m* surround

surtitles *npl* sopratitoli *mpl*

surveillance *n* sorveglianza *f*; ***keep s.o. under ~*** tenere qn sotto sorveglianza

survey I *n of modern literature etc* quadro *m* generale; *of building* perizia *f*; *poll* indagine *f* **II** *v/t* (*look at*) osservare; *building* periziare

surveyor *n* perito *m*

survival *n* sopravvivenza *f*

survival kit *n* kit *m inv* di sopravvivenza

survive I *v/i* sopravvivere; ***how are you? – I'm surviving*** come stai? – si tira avanti; ***his two surviving daughters*** le due figlie ancora in vita **II** *v/t* sopravvivere a

survivor *n* superstite *m/f*; *fig* ***he's a ~*** se la cava sempre

susceptible *adj emotionally* impressionabile; ***be ~ to the cold / heat*** soffrire il freddo / caldo

sushi *n* sushi *m inv*

suspect I *v/t person* sospettare; (*suppose*) supporre; ***I ~ her of having stolen it*** sospetto che sia stata lei a rubarlo; ***does he ~ anything?*** sospetta qualcosa?; ***I ~ed as much*** lo sospettavo **II** *n* indiziato *m*, -a *f* **III** *adj* (*suspicious*) sospetto; ***a ~ package*** un pacco sospetto

suspected *adj murderer* presunto; *cause, heart attack etc* sospetto

suspend *v/t* (*hang*) sospendere; *from office, duties* sospendere

suspenders *npl* giarrettiere *fpl*; *US* (*braces*) bretelle *fpl*

suspense *n* suspense *f inv*

suspension *n* sospensione *f*

suspension bridge *n* ponte *m* sospeso

suspicion *n* sospetto *m*

suspicious *adj causing suspicion* sospetto; *feeling suspicion* sospettoso; ***be ~ of*** sospettare di

suspiciously *adv watch, act* sospettosamente

suss *v/t Br infml* ***~ s.o. out*** sgamare qn; ***I can't ~ him out*** non riesco a scoprirlo; ***I've got him ~ed (out)*** l'ho sgamato

sustain *v/t* sostenere

sustainable *adj* sostenibile

sustenance *n* sostentamento *m*; (*nourishment*) sostanza *f* nutritiva

SW *abbr* **1.** (= **south-west**) SO (sud-ovest) **2.** (= **short wave**) OC (onda corta)

swab *n* tampone *m*

swag *n infml* malloppo *m*

swagger *n* andatura *f* spavalda

swallow[1] **I** *v/t liquid, food* inghiottire **II** *v/i* inghiottire

◆**swallow down** *v/t sep* ingurgitare

◆**swallow up** *v/t sep fig* inghiottire

swallow[2] *n bird* rondine *f*

swam *pret* → ***swim***

swamp I *n* palude *f* **II** *v/t*: ***be ~ed with*** essere sommerso da

swampy *adj ground* paludoso

swan I *n* cigno *m* **II** *v/i Br infml* ***~ off*** tagliare la corda; ***~ around (the house)*** gironzolare (intorno alla casa)

swanky *adj restaurant, hotel* sciccoso

swan song *n* canto *m* del cigno

swap ⟨*pret & past part* **-ped**⟩ **I** *v/t*: ***~ sth for sth*** scambiare qc con qc; ***~ places*** cambiare di posto **II** *v/i* fare scambio **III** *n* scambio *m*; ***do a ~*** fare a scambio

swarm I *n of bees* sciame *m* **II** *v/i*: ***the town was ~ing with …*** la città brulicava di …

swarthy *adj* (+*er*) *face, complexion* scuro

swastika *n* svastica *f*

swat *v/t* ⟨*pret & past part* **-ted**⟩ *insect, fly* schiacciare

sway I *n* (*influence, power*) influenza *f* **II** *v/i* barcollare

swear ⟨*pret* **swore**, *past part* **sworn**⟩ **I** *v/i* (*use swearword*) imprecare; ***~ at s.o.*** imprecare contro qn **II** *v/t* (*promise*) giurare; JUR, *on oath* giurare; ***~ s.o. to secrecy*** far giurare a qn

di mantenere il segreto
◆**swear by** *v/t infml* credere ciecamente in
◆**swear in** *v/t sep*: ***the witness was sworn in*** il testimone ha prestato giuramento
swearword *n* parolaccia *f*
sweat I *n* sudore *m*; ***covered in ~*** tutto sudato; *fig* ***what a ~!*** che sudata! **II** *v/i* sudare; ***~ like a pig*** *infml* sudare come un porco
◆**sweat out** *v/t sep*: ***sweat it out*** tener duro
sweat band *n* fascia *f* asciugasudore
sweater *n* maglione *m*
sweatshirt *n* felpa *f*
sweaty *adj* (+*er*) *hands* sudato; *smell* di sudore
swede *n esp Br* navone *m*
Swede *n* svedese *m*/*f*
Sweden *n* Svezia *f*
Swedish I *adj* svedese **II** *n* svedese *m*
sweep I *v/t* ⟨*pret & past part* **swept**⟩ *floor*, *leaves* spazzare; ***~ s.o. off their feet*** far perdere la testa a qn **II** *v/i with broom* scopare; ***she swept out the room*** ha spazzato la camera da cima a fondo; ***he swept into power one year ago*** è salito al potere un anno fa; (*majestically*) entrare maestosamente; (*river*) estendersi; ***the disease swept through Europe*** la malattia si è propagata in tutta Europa **III** *n* ***give sth a ~*** dare una spazzata a qc; *fig* ***make a clean ~*** fare piazza pulita; (*movement*) movimento *m*; (*tour*) giro *m*; ***a long ~ of lawn*** una lunga distesa di prato
◆**sweep aside** *v/t sep* ingorare
◆**sweep up** *v/t sep mess*, *crumbs* spazzare via
sweeping *adj changes* radicale; ***a ~ statement*** una generalizzazione
sweepstake *n scommessa abbinata alle corse di cavalli*
sweet I *adj* (+*er*) *taste*, *tea* dolce; *infml* (*kind*) gentile; *infml* (*cute*) carino **II** *n* caramella *f*; (*dessert*) dolce *m*
sweet and sour *adj* agrodolce **sweetbread** *n* COOK animella *f* **sweetcorn** *n* mais *m inv*
sweeten *v/t drink*, *food* zuccherare; ***~ the pill*** indorare la pillola
sweetener *n for drink* dolcificante *m*
sweetheart *n* innamorato *m*, -a *f*
sweetie *n infml* (*sweet*, *candy*) caramella *f*; *endearment* tesoro *m*
sweetie pie *n Br infml* tesoro *m*
sweetmeat *n* dolce *m*
sweet potato *n* patata *f* dolce **sweet shop** *n Br* negozio *m* di caramelle **sweet-talk** *v/t infml*: ***~ s.o. into doing sth*** convincere qn a fare qc con lusinghe **sweet-tempered** *adj character* dolce **sweet tooth** *n* goloso *m*, -a *f* (di dolci)
swell I *v/i* ⟨*pret* **swelled**, *past part* **swollen** *or* **swelled**⟩ *of wound*, *limb* gonfiarsi **II** *v/t sail* gonfiare; *numbers* ingrossare **III** *n of the sea* mare *m* lungo **IV** *adj esp US* (*excellent*) formidabile
swelling *n* MED gonfiore *m*
swelter *v/i* soffocare per il caldo
sweltering *adj heat*, *day* afoso, soffocante
swept *pret & past part* → ***sweep***
swerve I *n* deviazione *f* **II** *v/i of driver*, *car* sterzare (bruscamente); ***the road ~s*** (***round***) ***to the right*** la strada devia verso destra; ***the car ~d in and out of the traffic*** l'auto sbandava in mezzo al traffico **III** *v/t car etc* far deviare
swift *adj* (+*er*) rapido
swig *infml* **I** *n* sorsata *f*; ***have*** *or* ***take a ~ of beer*** prendere un bel sorso di birra **II** *v/t* ⟨*pret & past part* **-ged**⟩ (*a.* **swig down**) tracannare
swill I *n* (*animal food*) broda *f*; ***give sth a ~*** (***out***) tracannarsi qc **II** *v/t esp Br a.* **swill out** lavare a fondo; *cup* sciacquare bene; *infml beer etc* sbevazzare
swim I *v/i* ⟨*pret* **swam**, *past part* **swum**⟩ nuotare; ***go ~ming*** andare a nuotare; ***my head is ~ming*** mi gira la testa **II** *n* nuotata *f*; ***go for a ~*** andare a nuotare
swimmer *n* nuotatore *m*, -trice *f*
swimming *n* nuoto *m*
swimming baths *npl* piscina *f* pubblica **swimming cap** *n* cuffia *f* (da bagno) **swimming costume** *n* costume *m* da bagno
swimmingly *adv* a meraviglia
swimming pool *n* piscina *f* **swimming trunks** *npl* calzoncini *mpl* da bagno
swim noodle *n* SPORTS cilindro *m* flessibile

swimsuit *n* costume *m* intero
swindle I *v/t* truffare; *~ **s.o. out of sth*** estorcere qc a qn (con l'inganno) **II** *n* truffa *f*
swine *n infml person* mascalzone *m*
swing I *v/t* ⟨*pret & past part* ***swung***⟩ far dondolare; *~ **one's hips*** ancheggiare; ***his speech swung the decision in our favour*** il suo discorso fece cambiare la decisione a nostro favore **II** *v/i* ⟨*pret & past part* ***swung***⟩ dondolare; (*turn*) girare; *of public opinion etc* indirizzarsi **III** *n of pendulum etc* oscillazione *f*; *for child* altalena *f*; ***a ~ to the left*** una svolta verso la sinistra; ***be in full ~*** *of party etc* essere in pieno svolgimento
◆**swing (a)round I** *v/i* (*person*) girarsi bruscamente; (*car, plane*) virare bruscamente **II** *v/t sep* girare
◆**swing back** *v/i* voltarsi all'indietro
◆**swing to** *v/i* (*door*) chiudersi
swing-door *n* porta *f* a vento
swipe I *v/t plastic card* strisciare; *infml* (*steal*) fregare **II** *v/i*: *~ **at*** cercare di colpire **III** *n* (*blow*) botta *f*; ***take a ~ at s.o. / sth*** cercare di colpire qn / qc
swipe card *n* carta *f* magnetica
swirl *v/i water, smoke* turbinare
swish I *n* fruscio *m*; *of whip, sword* sibilo *m* **II** *v/t cane* far frusciare; *whip* far sibilare **III** *v/i* frusciare; *ship, sword* sibilare **IV** *adj infml* (*elegant*) alla moda
Swiss I *adj* svizzero **II** *n person* svizzero *m*, -a *f*; ***the ~*** gli svizzeri
switch I *v/t* (*change*) cambiare; *~ **sides*** scambiare i lati; *~ **channels*** cambiare canale **II** *v/i* (*change*) cambiare; *~ **to*** passare a **III** *n* ELEC interruttore *m*; (*change*) cambiamento *m*
◆**switch (a)round** *v/t sep* (*swap round*) spostare; (*rearrange*) ridisporre
◆**switch back I** *v/i* TV tornare (***to*** su) **II** *v/t sep* ***switch the light back on*** accendere di nuovo la luce
◆**switch off** *v/t sep* spegnere
◆**switch on** *v/t sep* accendere
◆**switch over** *v/i*: ***switch over to*** *method* passare a; TV *channel* mettere
switchboard *n* centralino *m*
Switch card® *n Br* carta *f* di debito
switchover *n to new system* passaggio *m*
Switzerland *n* Svizzera *f*
swivel *v/i* ⟨*pret & past part* ***-led****, US* ***-ed***⟩ *of chair, monitor* girarsi
swollen *adj* gonfio
swoon *v/i fig* andare in estasi (***over s.o. / sth*** per qn / qc)
swoop *v/i of bird* scendere in picchiata
◆**swoop down on** *v/t prey* scendere in picchiata su
◆**swoop on** *v/t of police etc* piombare su
swop *n, v/t & v/i* → ***swap***
sword *n* spada *f*
swordfish *n* pesce *m* spada
swore *pret* → ***swear***
sworn *past part* → ***swear***
swot *infml* **I** *n person* secchione *m*, -a *f* **II** *v/i for exam* sgobbare; *~ **up** (**on**) **one's maths*** sgobbare per l'esame di matematica
swum *past part* → ***swim***
swung *pret & past part* → ***swing***
sycamore *n* sicomoro *m*
sycophant *n* sicofante *m/f*; (*bootlicker*) leccapiedi *m*
syllable *n* sillaba *f*
syllabus *n* programma *m*
sylph *n* silfide *f*
symbiosis *n* simbiosi *f inv*
symbol *n* simbolo *m*
symbolic *adj* simbolico
symbolise, symbolize *v/t* simboleggiare
symbolism *n* simbolismo *m*
symbolist *n* simbolista *m/f*
symmetric(al) *adj* simmetrico
symmetry *n* simmetria *f*
sympathetic *adj* (*showing pity*) compassionevole; (*understanding*) comprensivo; ***be ~ towards an idea*** simpatizzare per un'idea
◆**sympathize with** *v/t person, views* capire
sympathizer *n* POL simpatizzante *m/f*
sympathy *n* (*pity*) compassione *f*; (*understanding*) comprensione *f*; ***don't expect any ~ from me!*** non venire a lamentarti da me!; ***be in ~ with s.o. / sth*** essere solidale con qn / qc
symphony *n* sinfonia *f*
symphony orchestra *n* orchestra *f* sinfonica
symposium *n* simposio *m*
symptom *n a. fig* sintomo *m*

symptomatic *adj*: *fig* ***be ~ of*** essere sintomatico di
synagogue *n* sinagoga *f*
synchronise, synchronize *v/t* sincronizzare
syncopate *v/t* GRAM, MUS sincopare
syncopation *n* GRAM, MUS sincope *f*
syncope *n* GRAM, MED sincope *f*
syndicate I *n* associazione *f*; (*consortium*) consorzio *m*; PRESS agenzia *f* di stampa; (*crime syndicate*) associazione *f* a delinquere **II** *v/t & v/i* unire in sindacato; PRESS pubblicare
syndrome *n* sindrome *f*
synecdoche *n* GRAM sineddoche *f*
synergetic *adj* sinergico
synergism *n* sinergismo *m*
synergy *n* sinergia *f*
synod *n* sinodo *m*
synonym *n* sinonimo *m*
synonymous *adj* sinonimo; *fig* ***be ~ with*** essere sinonimo di
synopsis *n* ⟨*pl* ***synopses***⟩ sinossi *f*
syntax *n* GRAM sintassi *f inv*
synthesis *n* sintesi *f inv*
synthesizer *n* MUS sintetizzatore *m*
synthetic *adj* sintetico
syphilis *n* sifilide *f*
syphon *n* → ***siphon***
Syria *n* Siria *f*
Syrian I *adj* siriano **II** *n* siriano *m*, -a *f*
syringe *n* siringa *f*
syrup *n* sciroppo *m*
system *n* (*method*) metodo *m*, sistema *m*; (*orderliness*) ordine *m*; (*computer*) sistema *m*; ***the braking ~*** il sistema di frenata; ***the digestive ~*** l'apparato digerente
systematic *adj approach, person* sistematico
systematically *adv* sistematicamente
systemic *adj* sistematico; LING sistemico
systems analyst *n* COMPUT analista *m/f* di sistemi **systems disk** *n* COMPUT disco *m* di sistema **systems engineering** *n* ingegneria *f* dei sistemi **systems software** *n* software *m* di sistema

T

T, t *n* t, T *f inv*; ***to a T*** *infml* a pennello
ta *int Br infml* grazie
TA *abbr Br* HIST (= **Territorial Army**) comando *m* militare territoriale
tab *n for pulling* linguetta *f*; *in text* tabulazione *f*; ***pick up the ~*** pagare; ***keep ~s on s.o. / sth*** *infml* tenere d'occhio qn / qc
tabby *n* (*a.* **tabby cat**) gatto *m* tigrato
tab key *n* tasto *m* tab; *on typewriter* tabulatore *m*
table I *n* tavolo *m*; *of figures* tabella *f*, tavola *f*; ***sit at the ~*** sedersi a tavola; ***turn the ~s (on s.o.)*** girare le carte in tavola (a danno di qn) **II** *v/t motion etc* presentare; (*postpone*) *bill* rinviare
tablecloth *n* tovaglia *f* **table lamp** *n* lampada *f* da tavolo **tableland** *n* GEOG tavolato *m* **table manners** *npl* buone maniere *fpl* a tavola **tablemat** *n* tovaglietta *f* (all'americana) **table of contents** *n* indice *m* **tablespoon** *n* cucchiaio *m* da tavola
tablet *n* PHARM compressa *f*; *of soap* saponetta *f*
table tennis *n* ping pong *m* **tableware** *n* stoviglie *fpl*
tabloid *n newspaper* quotidiano *m* formato tabloid; *pej* quotidiano *m* scandalistico
taboo *adj* tabù *m inv*
tachometer *n* contagiri *m inv*
tacit *adj* tacito
taciturn *adj* taciturno
tack I *n* (*nail*) chiodino *m*; NAUT (*course*) bordata *f*; *for horse* bardatura *f*; *fig* ***try another ~*** provare un approccio diverso **II** *v/t* (*sew*) imbastire **III** *v/i of yacht* virare di bordo
tackle I *n* (*equipment*) attrezzatura *f*; SPORTS: *in rugby* placcaggio *m*; *in football, hockey* contrasto *m* **II** *v/t in rugby* placcare; *in football, hockey*

contrastare; *problem*, *intruder* affrontare

tacky *adj* (↑er) *paint* fresco; *glue* appiccicoso; *infml* (*cheap*, *poor quality*) di cattivo gusto

tact *n* tatto *m*

tactful *adj* pieno di tatto

tactfully *adv* con grande tatto

tactical *adj* tattico

tactics *npl* tattica *f*

tactless *adj* privo di tatto

tadpole *n* girino *m*

tag **I** *n* (*label*) etichetta *f*; (*game*) acchiapparello *m* **II** *v/t* ⟨*pret & past part* ***-ged***⟩ contrassegnare

◆**tag along** *v/i* accodarsi; ***why don't you tag along?*** *infml* perché non ti aggreghi?

◆**tag on** *v/t sep* (*add*) aggiungere

tail **I** *n* coda *f*; ***turn ~*** darsela a gambe; ***he was right on my ~*** mi stava alle calcagna; ***~s*** *npl on coin* croce *f*; **tails** *npl* (*jacket*) frac *m inv* **II** *v/t* pedinare

◆**tail back** *v/i Br* incolonnarsi

◆**tail off** *v/i* (*dwindle*) calare

tailback *n* coda *f* **tail coat** *n* frac *m inv* **tail end** *n* fine *f* **tail light** *n* luce *f* posteriore

tailor **I** *n* sarto *m*, -a *f* **II** *v/t dress etc* confezionare; *fig holiday*, *policy* fare su misura (***to*** per); *products* personalizzare (***to*** per)

tailor-made *adj suit*, *solution* (fatto) su misura

tailpipe *n US* tubo *m* di scappamento **tailspin** *n* avvitamento *m* **tailwind** *n* vento *m* in coda

taint **I** *n* (*blemish*) macchia *f* **II** *v/t fig reputation* macchiare

tainted *adj* contaminato

Taiwan *n* Taiwan *f*

Taiwanese **I** *adj* taiwanese **II** *n* taiwanese *m/f*; *dialect* taiwanese *m*

take **I** *v/t* ⟨*pret* ***took***, *past part* ***taken***⟩ **1.** prendere; (*accept*: *money*, *gift*) accettare; ***I'll ~ it*** *when shopping* lo prendo **2.** (*transport*) prendere; ***he ~s the train every morning*** prende il treno ogni mattina **3.** (*accompany*) accompagnare; ***I'll ~ you to the station*** ti accompagno alla stazione; ***this bus will ~ you into town*** questo autobus ti porta al centro; ***this road will ~ you to Paris*** questa strada ti porta fino a Parigi **4.** *maths*, *French*, *photograph*, *exam*, *shower*, *stroll* fare **5.** (*endure*) sopportare; ***I just can't ~ it any more*** non lo sopporto proprio più **6.** (*require*) richiedere; ***how long does it ~?*** quanto ci vuole?; ***he's got what it ~s*** ha tutto quel che serve; *clothes size* portare; ***it took ten men to complete it*** ci sono voluti dieci uomini per completarlo; ***it took a lot of courage*** c'è voluto molto coraggio; ***it ~s time*** ci vuole tempo **7.** (*consider*, *assume*) ***I ~ it you agree?*** allora sei d'accordo?; ***I would ~ that to mean ...*** suppongo che significhi che...; ***~ s.o./sth for*** *or* ***to be ...*** prendere qn/qc per... **8.** (*occupy*, *possess*) prendere; ***~ a seat!*** accomodatevi!; ***this seat is ~n*** questo posto è occupato **9.** *news* prendere; ***she took his death badly*** ha preso male la notizia della sua morte **10.** GRAM reggere; (*preposition*) essere seguito da; ***verbs that ~ "avere"*** i verbi che prendono "avere" **11.** ***be ~n ill*** ammalarsi **II** *n* FILM ripresa *f*; ***what's their ~ on the question?*** che opinione hanno sulla questione?; *infml* ***clearly he was in on the ~*** è chiaro che si è fatto corrompere

◆**take aback** *v/t sep* prendere alla sprovvista; ***I was taken aback by his comments*** sono stato preso alla sprovvista dai suoi commenti

◆**take after** *v/t* aver preso da

◆**take apart** *v/t sep* (*dismantle*) smontare; *infml* (*criticize*, *beat*) fare a pezzi *infml*

◆**take (a)round** *v/t sep* (*show around*) portare in giro

◆**take away** *v/t sep pain* far sparire; (*remove*: *object*) togliere; MATH sottrarre; ***take sth away from s.o.*** togliere qc a qn; ***take away*** *food* da asporto

◆**take back** *v/t sep* **1.** (*return*: *object*) riportare **2.** (*receive back*) riprendere; (*accept back*: *husband etc*) rimettersi insieme a; ***I take back what I said*** ritiro quello che ho detto **3.** *person* riaccompagnare **4.** ***that takes me back*** *of music*, *thought etc* mi riporta al passato

◆**take down** *v/t sep from shelf* tirare giù; *scaffolding* smontare; *trousers* allungare; (*write down*) annotare

◆**take for** *v/t someone else* prendere per; ***what do you take me for?*** per chi mi prendi?
◆**take in** *v/t sep* (*take indoors*) portare dentro; (*give accommodation*) ospitare; (*make narrower*) stringere; (*deceive*) imbrogliare; (*include*) includere; *dress* stringere; *surroundings* comprendere; (*understand*) capire; ***be taken in*** farsi imbrogliare
◆**take off I** *v/t sep clothes, 10 %* togliere; (*mimic*) imitare; ***he took his clothes off*** si è tolto i vestiti; ***take s.o.'s mind off sth*** togliere qc dalla mente di qn; ***can you take a bit off here?*** *to barber* può spuntare un po' qui?; ***take a day/week off*** prendere un giorno/una settimana di ferie **II** *v/i of aeroplane* decollare; (*become popular*) far presa
◆**take on** *v/t sep job* intraprendere; *staff* assumere; ***when he married her he took on more than he bargained for*** quando l'ha sposata si è caricato di molto più di quanto si pensasse; ***she took him on at tennis and won*** lo ha sfidato a tennis e ha vinto
◆**take out** *v/t sep from bag, pocket* tirare fuori; *stain, appendix, tooth, word* togliere; *money from bank* prelevare; *to dinner etc* portar fuori; *insurance policy* stipulare, fare; ***take it out on s.o.*** prendersela con qn; ***take s.o. out of himself*** aiutare qn a distrarsi; ***take time out from doing sth*** fare una breve pausa (durante un'attività)
◆**take over I** *v/t sep company etc* assumere il controllo di; ***tourists take over the town*** i turisti invadono la città **II** *v/i of new management etc* assumere il controllo; (*do sth in s.o.'s place*) dare il cambio; ***he's ill so I have to take over*** è malato quindi devo dargli il cambio
◆**take to** *v/t* (*like*) prendere in simpatia; (*form habit of*) prendere l'abitudine di; ***take to drink*** darsi all'alcol; ***he immediately took to the idea*** la nuova idea gli è piaciuta subito; ***take to one's bed*** rimanere a letto
◆**take up** *v/t sep carpet etc* togliere; (*carry up*) portare sopra; (*shorten: dress etc*) accorciare; *judo, Spanish, new job* incominciare; *offer* accettare; *space, time* occupare; ***I'll take you up on your offer*** accetto la tua offerta; ***I'll take you up on that*** su questo ho qualcosa da ridire; (*busy*) ***be taken up with s.o./sth*** essere assorbito da qn/qc
◆**take upon** *v/t*: ***he took it upon himself to answer for me*** si è preso il compito di rispondere al posto mio
takeaway *n meal* piatto *m* da asporto; (*restaurant*) *ristorante che prepara piatti da asporto* **take-home pay** *n* stipendio *m* in busta
taken *past part* → ***take***
take-off *n of aeroplane* decollo *m*; (*impersonation*) imitazione *f* **takeover** *n* COMM rilevamento *m* **takeover bid** *n* offerta *f* pubblica di acquisto, OPA *f*
taking *n*: ***it's yours for the ~*** non devi fare altro che prenderlo
takings *npl* incassi *mpl*
talcum powder *n* talco *m*
tale *n* storia *f*
talent *n* talento *m*
talented *adj* pieno di talento; ***he's not very ~*** non ha molto talento
talent scout *n* talent scout *m/f inv*
talisman *n* talismano *m*
talk I *v/i* parlare; ***can I ~ to …?*** posso parlare con …?; ***I'll ~ to him about it*** gliene parlo **II** *v/t* **1.** *English etc* parlare **2.** *business, politics* parlare di **3.** ***~ s.o. into doing sth*** convincere qn a fare qc; ***~ s.o. out of doing sth*** dissuadere qn dal fare qc **III** *n* **1.** (*conversation*) conversazione *f*; (*lecture*) conferenza *f*; ***give a ~*** tenere una conferenza; ***there is some ~ of his returning*** corre voce di un suo ritorno; ***he's all ~*** *pej* è tutto chiacchiere; ***be the ~ of the town*** essere sulla bocca di tutti **2.** ***~s*** (*negotiations*) trattative *fpl*, negoziati *mpl*
◆**talk back** *v/i* ribattere
◆**talk down to** *v/t* trattare dall'alto in basso
◆**talk into** *v/t*: ***talk s.o. into doing sth*** convincere qn a fare qc
◆**talk out of** *v/t*: ***talk s.o. out of doing sth*** dissuadere qn da fare qc
◆**talk over** *v/t sep* discutere di
◆**talk through** *v/t sep*: ***talk s.o. through sth*** spiegare qc a qn passo per passo

talkative *adj* loquace
talking head *n infml* TV mezzobusto *m* **talking picture** *n* FILM film *m inv* sonoro **talking point** *n* argomento *m* di discussione
talking-to *n* sgridata *f*
talk show *n* talk show *m inv*
tall *adj* (+*er*) alto
tall order *n* bella impresa *f* **tall story** *n* baggianata *f*
tally I *n* conto *m* **II** *v/i* ⟨*pret & past part* **-ied**⟩ quadrare
◆**tally with** *v/t* quadrare con
talon *n* artiglio *m*
tambourine *n* tamburello *m*
tame I *adj* (+*er*) *animal* addomesticato; *joke etc* blando **II** *v/t animal* addomesticare
◆**tamper with** *v/t* manomettere
tampon *n* tampone *m*
tan I *n from sun* abbronzatura *f*; *colour* marrone *m* rossiccio **II** *v/i* ⟨*pret & past part* **-ned**⟩ *in sun* abbronzarsi **III** *v/t* ⟨*pret & past part* **-ned**⟩ *leather* conciare
tandem *n bike* tandem *m inv*
tang *n taste* gusto *m* intenso
tangent *n* MATH tangente *f*; ***go off at a ~*** (*digress*) partire per la tangente
tangerine *n* tangerino *m*
tangible *adj* tangibile
tangle I *n* nodo *m*; *fig* groviglio *m*; ***get into a ~*** mettersi nei pasticci **II** *v/t*: ***the cat ~d the wools together*** il gatto ha aggrovigliato i fili di lana
◆**tangle up** *v/t sep*: ***get tangled up*** *of string etc* aggrovigliarsi
tango *n* tango *m*
tank *n* recipiente *m*; AUTO serbatoio *m*; MIL carro *m* armato; *for skin diver* bombola *f* (d'ossigeno)
tankard *n mug* boccale *m*
tanker *n ship* nave *f* cisterna; *truck* autocisterna *f*
tankini *n* tankini *m*, *costume da bagno composto da canottiera e slip*
tank top *n Br* canottiera *f* di lana; *US* canottiera *f* di cotone
tanned *adj* abbronzato
tannin *n* tannino *m*
Tannoy® *n* altoparlante *m*
tantalise, tantalize *v/t* tenere sulla corda
tantalising *adj* allettante; *smell* stuzzicante
tantamount *adj*: ***be ~ to*** essere equivalente a
tantrum *n* capricci *mpl*; ***throw a ~*** fare (i) capricci
tap I *n* rubinetto *m*; ***have sth on ~*** avere qc alla spina **II** *v/t* ⟨*pret & past part* **-ped**⟩ (*hit*) dare un colpetto a; ***~ at the door*** bussare piano alla porta; *phone* mettere sotto controllo; ***he was ~ping his fingers on the table*** tamburellava con le dita sul tavolo; ***~ s.o. on the shoulder*** dare a qn un colpetto sulla spalla
◆**tap into** *v/t resources* attingere a
tap dance *n* tip tap *m*
tape I *n magnetic* nastro *m* magnetico; *recorded* cassetta *f*; (*sticky*) nastro *m* adesivo; ***on ~*** registrato **II** *v/t conversation etc* registrare; ***~ sth to sth*** attaccare qc a qc col nastro adesivo
◆**tape down** *v/t sep* fermare con nastro adesivo
◆**tape over** *v/t sep*: ***tape A over B*** registrare A su B
◆**tape up** *v/t sep parcel* impacchettare con nastro adesivo
tape deck *n* registratore *m* **tape drive** *n* COMPUT unità *f inv* di backup a nastro **tape measure** *n* metro *m* a nastro
taper I *n candle* cero *m* **II** *v/i* assottigliarsi
◆**taper off** *v/i of production* calare gradualmente; *of figures* decrescere
tape recorder *n* registratore *m* a cassette **tape recording** *n* registrazione *f* su cassetta
tapestry *n* arazzo *m*
tapeworm *n* verme *m* solitario
tapioca *n* tapioca *f*
tap water *n* acqua *f* del rubinetto
tar I *n* catrame *m* **II** *v/t* asfaltare
tardy *adj* (+*er*) *form* tardo; (*person*) in ritardo
target I *n in shooting* bersaglio *m*; *for sales*, *production* obiettivo *m* **II** *v/t market* rivolgersi a
target audience *n* target *m inv* di pubblico **target date** *n* data *f* fissata **target figure** *n* target *m inv* **target group** *n* COMM gruppo *m* target **target language** *n* lingua *f* d'arrivo **target market** *n* mercato *m* target
tariff *n* (*price*) tariffa *f*; (*tax*) tassa *f*
tarmac *n at airport* pista *f*

tarnish *v/t metal* ossidare; *reputation* macchiare
tarot card *n* tarocco *m*
tarpaulin *n* tela *f* cerata
tarragon *n* dragoncello *m*
tart[1] *n* torta *f*, crostata *f*
tart[2] *n infml* (*prostitute*) sgualdrina *f*; *pej*: *woman* stronza *f*
◆**tart up** *v/t sep esp Br infml* risistemare in modo più pacchiano; *oneself* agghindare in modo pacchiano
tartan *n* tartan *m*
tartar *n* CHEM, MED tartaro *m*; ***beware, he's a bit of a ~*** *Br infml* attento, è un tipo un po' irascibile
tartar(e) sauce *n* COOK salsa *f* tartara
tartlet *n* COOK pasticcino *m*
tarty *adj* da sgualdrina
task *n* compito *m*
task force *n* task force *f inv*
taskmaster *n*: ***he's a hard ~*** è un vero negriero
tassel *n* nappa *f*
taste I *n* gusto *m*; ***I don't like the ~*** non mi piace il sapore; ***it's an acquired ~*** è un gusto acquisito; ***my ~ in music*** i miei gusti musicali; ***in good ~*** con buon gusto; ***he has no ~*** non ha nessun gusto; ***a ~ of things to come*** un assaggio di ciò che seguirà **II** *v/t food* assaggiare; (*experience*: *freedom etc*) provare; ***I can't ~ anything*** non sento nessun sapore **III** *v/i*: ***it ~s like …*** ha sapore di …; ***it ~s very nice*** è molto buono
taste bud *n* papilla *f* gustativa
tasteful *adj* di gusto
tastefully *adv* con gusto
tasteless *adj food* insapore; *remark*, *person* privo di gusto
tasting *n of wine* degustazione *f*
tasty *adj* (+*er*) gustoso
tat *n Br infml* robaccia *f*; ***tit for ~*** occhio per occhio
ta-ta *int Br infml* ciao ciao
tattered *adj clothes*, *book* malridotto
tatters *npl*: ***in ~*** *of clothes* a brandelli; *of reputation*, *career* a pezzi
tattle I *n* pettegolezzi *mpl* **II** *v/i* spettegolare
tattoo I *n* tatuaggio *m* **II** *v/t* tatuare
tatty *adj* (+*er*) malandato
taught *pret & past part* → ***teach***
taunt I *v/t* schernire **II** *n* scherno *m*
Taurus *n* ASTROL Toro *m*
taut *adj* (+*er*) teso
tauten I *v/t rope* tirare; *muscle* tendere **II** *v/i* irrigidirsi
tavern *n liter* taverna *f*
tawdry *adj* (+*er*) pacchiano
tax I *n* tassa *f*; ***before / after ~*** al lordo / al netto di imposte **II** *v/t* tassare
taxable income *n* reddito *m* imponibile
taxation *n* tassazione *f*
tax avoidance *n* elusione *f* fiscale **tax bracket** *n* fascia *f* di reddito **tax code** *n* codice *m* fiscale **tax consultant** *n* consulente *m/f* fiscale **tax deductible** *adj* deducibile dalle imposte **tax disc** *n for car* bollo *m* (di circolazione) **tax evasion** *n* evasione *f* fiscale **tax-exempt** *adj US income* esentasse **tax exile** *n* esule *m/f* per motivi fiscali **tax free** *adj* esentasse *inv*
taxi I *n* taxi *m inv* **II** *v/i of plane* rullare
taxi driver *n* tassista *m/f*
taxing *adj* estenuante
tax inspector *n* ispettore *m*, -trice *f* fiscale
taxi rank, taxi stand *n* stazione *f* dei taxi
taxman *n* fisco *m* **tax payer** *n* contribuente *m/f* **tax relief** *n* sgravio *m* fiscale **tax return** *n form* dichiarazione *f* dei redditi **tax year** *n* anno *m* fiscale
TB *abbr* (= **tuberculosis**) tbc *f* (tubercolosi *f*)
T-bar lift *n* ski lift *m inv* ad ancora
T-bone steak *n* bistecca *f* con osso
tbs., tbsp. *abbr* (= **tablespoon**; **tablespoonful**) cucchiaio *m*
tea *n drink* tè *m inv*; *Br* (*afternoon tea*) tè *m inv*; *meal* cena *f*
teabag *n* bustina *f* di tè
tea break *n esp Br* pausa *f* per il tè **tea caddy** *n esp Br* barattolo per il tè
teacake *n Br* pasticcino *m*
teach ⟨*pret & past part* **taught**⟩ **I** *v/t subject* insegnare; *person* insegnare a; ***~ s.o. to do sth*** insegnare a qn a fare qc; ***that'll ~ him!*** così impara! **II** *v/i* insegnare
teacher *n* insegnante *m/f*
teacher training *n* tirocinio *m* per insegnanti
tea chest *n* cassa *f* da tè
teaching *n profession* insegnamento *m*
teaching aid *n* sussidio *m* didattico

teaching hospital *n* clinica *f* universitaria

tea cloth *n* strofinaccio *m* da cucina

tea cosy *n* copriteiera *f inv* **teacup** *n* tazza *f* da tè **tea drinker** *n* bevitore *m*, -trice *f* di tè **tea garden** *n* posto *m* di ristoro all'aperto **teahouse** *n* (*tearoom*) sala *f* da té; (*tea shop*) negozio *m* di té

teak *n* tek *m*

teal *n bird* alzavola *f*; *colour* verde-blu *m*

tea leaf *n* foglia *f* di tè

team I *n in sport* squadra *f*; *at work* équipe *f inv* **II** *v/t & v/i* (*match*) abbinare; (*unite*) unire

◆**team up** *v/i with someone* collaborare

team mate *n* compagno *m*, -a *f* di squadra **team spirit** *n* spirito *m* d'équipe **teamwork** *n* lavoro *m* d'équipe

teapot *n* teiera *f*

tear[1] **I** *v/t* ⟨*pret* **tore**, *past part* **torn**⟩ *paper, cloth* strappare; **~ *sth in two*** strappare qc in due; **~ *sth to pieces*** fare a pezzi qc; **~ *sth open*** aprire qc on uno strappo; **~ *one's hair* (*out*)** strapparsi i capelli; ***be torn between two alternatives*** essere combattuto tra due alternative **II** *v/i* ⟨*pret* **tore**, *past part* **torn**⟩ (*run fast, drive fast*) sfrecciare; **~ *along the dotted line*** strappare lungo la linea tratteggiata **III** *n in cloth etc* strappo *m*

◆**tear along** *v/i* andare a tutta velocità

◆**tear apart** *v/t sep place* mettere sottosopra; *country* dilaniare; ***it tore me apart to leave you*** lasciarti mi ha fatto a pezzi

◆**tear at** *v/t* tirare con forza

◆**tear away** *v/t sep* ***if you can, tear yourself away from that place*** se ci riesci, staccati da quel posto

◆**tear down** *v/t sep poster* strappare; *building* buttar giù

◆**tear into** *v/t* criticare aspramente

◆**tear off I** *v/i* (*rush off*) scappare di fretta; *cheque* staccare strappando **II** *v/t sep wrapping, clothes* strappare

◆**tear out** *v/t sep* strappare

◆**tear up** *v/t sep paper* distruggere; *agreement* rompere

tear[2] *n in eye* lacrima *f*; ***burst into ~s*** scoppiare a piangere; ***be in ~s*** essere in lacrime; ***the ~s were running down her cheeks*** le lacrime le correvano giù sul viso

tearaway *n* scavezzacollo *m/f inv*

teardrop *n* lacrima *f*

tear duct *n* ANAT condotto *m* lacrimale

tearful *adj person* in lacrime; *look, voice* piangente

tear gas *n* gas *m inv* lacrimogeno

tear jerker *n* film *m inv or* libro *m* strappalacrime

tearoom *n* sala *f* da tè

tease I *v/t person* prendere in giro; *animal* stuzzicare; (*raise nap*) TEX caardare; *US* (*backcomb*) pettinare **II** *v/i* scherzare **III** *n person* provocatore *m*, -trice *f*

tea service, tea set *n* servizio *m* da tè **teaspoon** *n* cucchiaino *m* da caffè **tea strainer** *n* colino *m* da tè

teat *n* capezzolo *m*; *made of rubber* tettarella *f*

tea towel *n* strofinaccio *m* da cucina

technical *adj* tecnico

technical drawing *n* disegno *m* tecnico

technicality *n* (*technical nature*) tecnicismo *m*; JUR vizio *m* di procedura; ***that's just a ~*** è solo un dettaglio

technically *adv* tecnicamente

technical support *n* COMPUT supporto *m* tecnico

technician *n* tecnico *m*

technicolour *adj* in technicolour

technicolour yawn *n AUS infml* vomito *m*

technique *n* tecnica *f*

techno *n* MUS musica *f* techno

technocracy *n* tecnocrazia *f*

technological *adj* tecnologico

technology *n* tecnologia *f*

technophobia *n* tecnofobia *f*

tectonic *adj* tettonico

teddy bear *n* orsacchiotto *m*

tedious *adj* noioso

tedium *n* tedio *m*

tee *n in golf* tee *m inv*

teem *v/i* pullulare; ***be ~ing with rain*** piovere a dirotto; ***be ~ing with tourists/ants*** pullulare di turisti/formiche

teen *adj esp US movie* per i teen-ager

teenage *adj problems* degli adolescenti; *gangs* di ragazzi; **~ *boy/girl*** ragazzo *m*/ragazza *f* adolescente; **~ *fash-***

ions moda *f* giovane
teenager *n* adolescente *m/f*
teens *npl* adolescenza *f*; ***be in one's ~*** essere adolescente; ***reach one's ~*** entrare nell'adolescenza
teeny *adj infml* piccolissimo
teeny-weeny *adj infml* minuscolo
tee-shirt *n* maglietta *f*
teeter *v/i* barcollare; ***~ on the brink*** *or* ***edge of sth*** *liter fig* essere sull'orlo di qc
teeter-totter *n US* altalena *f*
teeth *pl* → ***tooth***
teethe *v/i* mettere i denti
teething problems *npl* difficoltà *fpl* iniziali
teetotal *adj person* astemio; *party* senza alcolici
teetotaller *n* astemio *m*, -a *f*
TEFL *abbr* (= **Teaching of English as a Foreign Language**) *Br* insegnamento *m* dell'inglese come lingua straniera
tel *abbr* (= **telephone** (**number**) telefono (tel)
telebanking *n* telephone banking *m*
telecommunications *n* telecomunicazioni *fpl*
telecommuting *n* telelavoro *m*
telegram *n* telegramma *m*
telegraph *n* telegrafo *m*
telegraphic *adj* telegrafico
telegraph pole *n* palo *m* del telegrafo
telepathic *adj* telepatico; ***you must be ~!*** devi avere poteri telepatici!
telepathy *n* telepatia *f*
telephone I *n* telefono *m*; ***be on the ~*** *be speaking* essere al telefono; *possess a phone* avere il telefono **II** *v/t person* telefonare a **III** *v/i* telefonare
telephone banking *n* servizi *mpl* bancari telefonici **telephone bill** *n* bolletta *f* del telefono **telephone book** *n* guida *f* telefonica **telephone booth** *n* cabina *f* telefonica **telephone box** *n* cabina *f* telefonica **telephone call** *n* telefonata *f* **telephone conversation** *n* conversazione *f* telefonica **telephone directory** *n* elenco *m* telefonico **telephone exchange** *n* centralino *m* telefonico **telephone message** *n* messaggio *m* telefonico **telephone number** *n* numero *m* telefonico
telephoto lens *n* teleobiettivo *m*
telesales *n* vendita *f* telefonica
telescope *n* telescopio *m*
telescopic lens *n* lente *f* telescopica
teleshopping *n* acquisti *mpl* per telefono *or* Internet
teletext *n* teletext *m inv*
telethon *n* telethon *m inv*
televise *v/t* trasmettere in televisione
television *n* televisione *f*; *set* televisione *f*, televisore *m*; ***on ~*** alla televisione; ***watch ~*** guardare la televisione
television audience *n* pubblico *m* televisivo **television licence** *n* canone *m* (televisivo) **television programme** *n* programma *m* televisivo **television set** *n* televisore *m* **television studio** *n* studio *m* televisivo
tell ⟨*pret & past part* ***told***⟩ **I** *v/t* dire; *story* raccontare; ***~ s.o. sth*** dire qc a qn; ***don't ~ Mum*** non dirlo alla mamma; ***~ s.o. to do sth*** dire a qn di fare qc; ***I've been told that …*** mi hanno detto che …; ***it's hard to ~*** è difficile a dirsi; ***you never can ~*** non si può mai dire; ***~ X from Y*** distinguere X da Y; ***I can't ~ the difference between …*** non vedo nessuna differenza tra …; ***you're ~ing me!*** *infml* a chi lo dici! *infml* **II** *v/i* (*have effect*) farsi sentire; ***the heat is ~ing on him*** il caldo si fa sentire su di lui; ***time will ~*** il tempo lo dirà
◆**tell apart** *v/t* (*distinguish*) distinguere
◆**tell off** *v/t sep* rimproverare
◆**tell on** *v/i +obj* (*inform on*) denunciare; (*affect*) avere un effetto su
teller *n in bank* cassiere *m*, -a *f*
telling *adj argument* efficace; ***a ~ sign*** un segnale chiaro
telling off *n* rimprovero *m*; ***give s.o. a ~*** rimproverare qn
telltale I *adj signs* rivelatore **II** *n* spione *m*, spiona *f*
telly *n infml* tele *f*; ***on ~*** alla tele; ***watch ~*** guardare la tele
temerity *n* temerarietà *f*
temp I *n employee* impiegato *m*, -a interinale **II** *v/i* fare lavori interinali
temper I *n* (*bad temper*): ***have a terrible ~*** essere irascibile; ***be in a ~*** essere arrabbiato; ***keep one's ~*** mantenere la calma; ***lose one's ~*** perdere le staffe **II** *v/t* (*modify*) temperare; ***he ~ed severity with kindness*** ha moderato la severità con la gentilezza; (*forge*)

forgiare; ***the smith ~ed the iron over a flame*** il fabbro forgiava il ferro sulla fiamma
temperament *n* temperamento *m*
temperamental *adj* (*moody*) lunatico; *machine* imprevedibile
temperance *n* temperanza *f*
temperate *adj* temperato
temperature *n* temperatura *f*; (*fever*) febbre *f*; ***have a ~*** avere la febbre; ***take s.o.'s ~*** prendere la temperatura a qn
tempest *n* tempesta *f*
tempestuous *adj fig* tempestoso
temping agency *n* agenzia *f* di lavoro temporaneo
template *n* (*pattern*) sagoma *f*
temple[1] *n* REL tempio *m*
temple[2] *n* ANAT tempia *f*
tempo *n* ritmo *m*; MUS tempo *m*
temporal *adj* temporale
temporal lobe *n* ANAT lobo *m* temporale
temporarily *adv* temporaneamente
temporary *adj* temporaneo, provvisorio
tempt *v/t* tentare
temptation *n* tentazione *f*
tempting *adj* allettante; *meal* appetitoso
ten *num* dieci
tenacious *adj* tenace
tenacity *n* tenacità *f*
tenancy *n*: ***conditions of ~*** termini *mpl* del contratto di affitto
tenant *n* inquilino *m*, -a *f*, locatario *m*, -a *f form*; *in office* affittuario *m*, -a *f*
tenant farmer *n* fittavolo *m*, -a *f*
tend[1] *v/t* (*look after*) prendersi cura di
tend[2] *v/i*: ***~ to do sth*** tendere a fare qc, avere la tendenza a fare qc; ***~ towards sth*** avere una tendenza verso qc
tendency *n* tendenza *f*: ***have a ~ to do sth*** avere la tendenza a fare qc
tendentious, tendencious *adj* tendenzioso
tender[1] *adj* (*sore*) sensibile; (*affectionate*) tenero; *steak* tenero
tender[2] *n* COMM offerta *f* ufficiale
tenderhearted *adj* dal cuore tenero
tenderloin *n* COOK filetto *m*
tenderness *n* (*soreness*) sensibilità *f*; *of kiss*, *steak* tenerezza *f*
tendon *n* tendine *m*
tendril *n* BOT viticcio *m*; ***a ~ of hair framed her forehead*** una ciocca di riccioli le incorniciava il viso
tenement *n* casa *f* popolare
tenet *n* dogma *f*; (*principle*) principio *m*
tenfold I *adj* decuplo **II** *adv* dieci volte tanto; ***increase ~*** decuplicare
tenner *n infml* (*ten-pound note*) biglietto *m* da dieci sterline
tennis *n* tennis *m*
tennis ball *n* palla *f* da tennis **tennis court** *n* campo *m* da tennis **tennis elbow** *n* MED gomito *m* del tennista **tennis player** *n* tennista *m*/*f* **tennis racket** *n* racchetta *f* da tennis
tenor *n* MUS tenore *m*
tenpin bowling *n* bowling *m inv* (con dieci birilli)
tense[1] *n* GRAM tempo *m*; ***present ~*** tempo *m* presente
tense[2] **I** *adj* (+*er*) *voice*, *person* teso; *moment*, *atmosphere* carico di tensione **II** *v/t* tendere **III** *v/i* irrigidirsi
◆**tense up** *v/i of muscles* contrarre; *of person* irrigidirsi
tension *n* tensione *f*
tent *n* tenda *f*
tentacle *n* tentacolo *m*
tentative *adj* (*not definite*) provvisorio;(*hesitant*) *conclusion*, *suggestion* esitante; ***we've a ~ arrangement to play tennis tonight*** abbiamo un mezzo appuntamento per una partita di tennis stasera
tenterhooks *npl*: ***be on ~*** essere sulle spine
tenth *n*/*adj* decimo, -a
tenuous *adj fig connection etc* fragile; *position* precario; ***have a ~ grasp of sth*** avere una scarsa conoscenza di qc
tenure *n* (*holding of office*) permanenza *f* (in carica); (*period of office*) mandato *m*; ***during her ~ of the farm*** durante il suo periodo di proprietà della fattoria
tepid *adj water*, *reaction* tiepido
term *n* **1.** periodo *m*; *of office* durata *f* in carica; ***~ of imprisonment*** periodo *m* di detenzione; ***elected for a three-year ~*** eletto per un periodo di tre anni; EDU: *of three months* trimestre *m*; *of two months* bimestre *m*; ***in the long / short ~*** a lungo / breve termine

2. (*word*) termine *m*; ***in simple ~s*** in parole semplici **3.** (*conditions*, *relations*) termine *m*; ***~s of surrender / payment*** condizioni *fpl* di resa / termini *mpl* di pagamento; ***be on good / bad ~s with s.o.*** essere in buoni / cattivi rapporti con qn; ***come to ~s with sth*** venire a patti con qc **4.** ***in ~s of*** dal punto di vista di
terminal **I** *n at airport*, *for containers*, COMPUT terminale *m*; *for buses* capolinea *m inv*; ELEC morsetto *m* **II** *adj illness* in fase terminale
terminally *adv*: ***~ ill*** malato (in fase) terminale
terminate **I** *v/t contract*, *pregnancy* interrompere **II** *v/i* terminare
termination *n of contract*, *pregnancy* interruzione *f*
terminology *n* terminologia *f*
terminus *n for buses* capolinea *m inv*; *for trains* stazione *f* di testa
termite *n* termite *f*
terrace **I** *n of houses* fila *f* di case a schiera; *on hillside*, *at hotel* terrazza *f* **II** *v/t* terrazzare; ***a ~d hillside*** una collina terrazzata
terraced house *n* casa *f* a schiera
terra cotta *adj* di terracotta
terrain *n* terreno *m*
terrestrial **I** *n* terrestre *m/f* **II** *adj television* di terra
terrible *adj* terribile
terribly *adv play* malissimo; ***they behaved ~*** si sono comportati in modo terribile; (*very*) molto; ***I'm not ~ good with money*** non sono estremamente bravo con i soldi
terrific *adj* eccezionale; ***~!*** bene!
terrifically *adv* (*very*) eccezionalmente
terrify *v/t* ⟨*pret & past part* ***-ied***⟩ terrorizzare; ***be terrified*** essere terrorizzato; ***I am terrified of spiders*** sono terrorizzato dai ragni
terrifying *adj* terrificante
terrine *n container* terrina *f*; COOK patè *m inv*
territorial *adj* territoriale
Territorial Army *n Br esercito territoriale volontario*
territorial waters *npl* acque *fpl* territoriali
territory *n a. fig* territorio *m*
terror *n* terrore *m*
terrorism *n* terrorismo *m*
terrorist *n* terrorista *m/f*
terrorist attack *n* attentato *m* terroristico **terrorist organization** *n* organizzazione *f* terroristica
terrorize *v/t* terrorizzare
terse *adj* (*+er*) brusco
tertiary *adj* terziario; ***~ level exam*** esame *m* di livello superiore; ***~ burns*** ustioni *fpl* di terzo grado
TESL *abbr* (= **Teaching of English as a Second Language**) insegnamento *m* dell'inglese come seconda lingua
TESOL *abbr* (= **Teaching of English as a Second or Other Language**) *US* insegnamento *m* dell'inglese come lingua straniera
test **I** *n* prova *f*, test *m inv*; ***he gave them a vocabulary ~*** li abbiamo sottoposti ad una verifica di vocabolario; ***put s.o. / sth to the ~*** mettere qn / qc alla prova; *for driving*, *medical* esame *m*; ***blood ~*** analisi *f inv* del sangue **II** *v/t soup*, *bathwater* provare; *machine*, *theory* testare; *person*, *friendship* mettere alla prova; *fig* ***~ the water*** tastare il terreno
testament *n* testimonianza *f* (***to*** di); ***Old / New Testament*** REL Vecchio / Nuovo Testamento
test case *n caso giuridico che costituisce un precedente* **test-drive** **I** *n*: ***go for a ~*** fare un giro di prova **II** *v/t car* fare un giro di prova su
tester *n* (*sample*) campione *m*
testicle *n* testicolo *m*
testify *v/i* ⟨*pret & past part* ***-ied***⟩ JUR testimoniare
testimonial *n* referenze *fpl* scritte
testimony *n* JUR testimonianza *f*
testosterone *n* ANAT, CHEM testosterone *m*
test tube *n* provetta *f* **test tube baby** *n* bambino *m*, -a *f* (concepito, -a) in provetta
testy *adj* (*+er*) suscettibile
tetanus *n* tetano *m*
tetchy *adj* irascibile
tether **I** *v/t horse* legare **II** *n*: ***be at the end of one's ~*** essere allo stremo
text **I** *n* testo *m*; (*text message*) sms *m inv*, messaggino *m* **II** *v/t* (*send text message*) mandare un sms a
textbook *n* libro *m* di testo
textile *n* tessuto *m*

text message *n* sms *m inv*, messaggino *m*
textual *adj* testuale
texture *n* consistenza *f*
Thai I *adj* tailandese **II** *n person* tailandese *m/f*; *language* tailandese *m*
Thailand *n* Tailandia *f*
Thames *n* Tamigi *m*
than I *cj* di; che; ***I'd rather do anything ~ that*** farei qualsiasi cosa piuttosto che quello; ***no sooner had I sat down ~ he began to talk*** non appena mi ero seduto ha cominciato a parlare; ***who better to help us ~ he?*** chi meglio di lui può aiutarci? **II** *prep*: ***older/faster ~ me*** più vecchio/veloce di me; ***she's more French ~ Italian*** è più francese che italiana
thank *v/t* ringraziare; ***~ you*** grazie; ***no, ~ you*** no, grazie; ***he has his brother/he only has himself to ~ for this*** deve ringraziare suo fratello/solo se stesso per questo; ***~ goodness*** *or* ***heavens*** *or* ***God*** *infml* grazie al cielo *or* a Dio
thankful *adj* riconoscente
thankfully *adv* con riconoscenza; (*luckily*) fortunatamente
thankless *adj* ingrato
thanks *npl* ringraziamenti *mpl*; ***~!*** grazie!; ***~ to*** grazie a; ***accept sth with ~*** accettare qc con gratitudine; ***and that's all the ~ I get*** e questo è il ringraziamento che ricevo; ***~ for nothing!*** *iron* grazie tante!
Thanksgiving *n* festa *f* del Ringraziamento
that I *adj* quel; *with masculine nouns before s+consonant, gn, ps and z* quello; ***~ one*** quello; ***what was ~ noise?*** che cos'è quel rumore; ***~ dog!*** quel cane! **II** *pron* quello *m*, -a *f*; ***what is ~?*** cos'è?; ***who is ~?*** chi è?; ***~'s mine*** è mio; ***~'s tea*** quello è tè; ***~'s very kind*** è molto gentile; ***and ~'s ~*** punto e basta; ***if she's as stupid as (all) ~*** se è così stupida; ***... and all ~*** e così via; ***like ~*** così; ***~ is (to say)*** cioè **III** *relative pron* che; ***the person/car ~ you saw*** la persona/macchina che hai visto; ***the day ~ he was born*** il giorno in cui è nato **IV** *adv* (*so*) così; ***~ big/expensive*** così grande/caro; ***it's not ~ good*** non è così buono **V** *cj* che; ***I think ~ ...*** credo che ...
thatched *adj cottage* col tetto di paglia
thaw I *v/t snow* sciogliere; *frozen food* scongelare **II** *v/i* sgelare; (*snow*) sciogliersi **III** *n* disgelo *m*
◆**thaw out I** *v/i* sgelarsi **II** *v/t sep liter* scongelare
the[1] *art* il *m*, la *f*; i *mpl*, le *fpl*; *with masculine nouns before s+consonant, gn, ps and z* lo *m*, gli *mpl*; *before vowel* l' *m/f*, gli *mpl*; ***to ~ bathroom*** al bagno; ***in ~ room*** nella stanza; ***play ~ piano*** suonare il pianoforte; ***all ~ windows*** tutte le finestre; ***have you invited ~ Browns?*** hai invitato i Brown?; ***Henry ~ Eighth*** Enrico VIII; ***by ~ hour*** all'ora
the[2] *adv*: ***~ sooner ~ better*** prima è, meglio è; ***~ more he has ~ more he wants*** più ne ha, più e vuole
theater *US* → ***theatre***
theatre, *US* **theater** *n* teatro *m*
theatre critic, *US* **theater critic** *n* critico *m* teatrale
theatregoer, *US* **theatergoer** *n* frequentatore *m*, -trice *f* di teatro
theatrical *adj a. fig* teatrale
theft *n* furto *m*
their *adj* il loro *m*, la loro *f*; i loro *mpl*, le loro *fpl*; (*his or her*) il suo *m*, la sua *f*, i suoi *mpl*, le sue *fpl*; ***~ daughter/son*** la loro figlia/il loro figlio
theirs *pron* il loro *m*, la loro *f*; i loro *mpl*, le loro *fpl*; ***it's ~*** è loro; ***it was an idea of ~*** è stata una loro idea
them *pron direct object* li *m*, le *f*; *referring to things* essi *m*, esse *f*; *indirect object* loro, gli; *after preposition* loro; *referring to things* essi *m*, esse *f*; (*him or her*) lo *m*, la *f*; ***I know ~*** li/le conosco; ***I sold it to ~*** gliel'ho venduto, l'ho venduto a loro; ***I gave ~ the keys*** ho dato loro le chiavi; ***both of ~*** entrambi; ***none of ~*** nessuno di loro; ***it's ~*** sono loro
thematic *adj* tematico
theme *n* tema *m*
theme music *n* FILM tema *m* musicale; TV sigla *f* **theme park** *n* parco *m* a tema **theme song** *n* canzone *f* principale
themselves *pron reflexive* si; *emphatic* loro stessi *mpl*, loro stesse *fpl*; *after prep* se stessi/se stesse; ***they ~*** loro stessi/stesse; ***they enjoyed ~*** si sono

divertiti; ***they only think about ~*** pensano solo a se stessi / stesse; ***by ~*** (*alone*) da soli *mpl*, da sole *fpl*

then *adv* (*at that time*) allora; (*after that*) poi; (*deducing*) allora; ***by ~*** allora; ***from ~ on*** da allora in poi; ***and ~ what happened?*** e poi cos'è successo?; ***I don't want that — ~ what DO you want?*** non voglio quello - allora cos'è che vuoi?; ***but ~ that means that ...*** ma allora significa che...; ***all right ~*** allora va bene; ***(so) I was right ~*** allora avevo ragione; ***but ~ ...*** ma poi...; ***but ~ again he is my friend*** ma del resto è un mio amico; ***now ~, what's the matter?*** allora, che problema c'è?; ***come on ~*** allora andiamo

theocracy *n* teocrazia *f*

theologian *n* teologo *m*, -a *f*

theological *adj* teologico

theology *n* teologia *f*

theoretical *adj* teorico

theoretically *adv* teoricamente

theorise, theorize *v/i* teorizzare

theorist *n* teorico *m*, -a *f*

theory *n* teoria *f*; ***in ~*** in teoria

theosophy *n* PHIL, REL teosofia *f*

therapeutic *adj* terapeutico

therapist *n* terapista *m/f*, terapeuta *m/f*

therapy *n* terapia *f*; ***be in ~*** essere in terapia

there I *adv* lì, là; ***over ~*** là; ***down ~*** laggiù; ***~ is ...*** c'è; ***~ are ...*** ci sono; ***is ~ ...?*** c'è ...?; ***are ~ ...?*** ci sono ...?; ***isn't ~?*** non c'è ...?; ***aren't ~?*** non ci sono ...?; ***~ you are*** *giving sth* ecco qui; *finding sth* ecco; *completing sth* ecco fatto; ***~ and back*** andata e ritorno; ***~ and then*** lì per lì; ***~ he is!*** eccolo!; ***~, ~!*** *comforting* su, dai! **II** *pron*: ***~ were three of us*** eravamo in tre; ***~ is a mouse in the room*** c'è un topo nella stanza **III** *int*: ***~! ~!*** dai!; ***stop crying now, ~'s a good boy*** ora smettila di piangere, da bravo; ***now ~'s a good boy, don't tease your sister*** da bravo, non dare fastidio a tua sorella; ***hey, you ~!*** *infml* ehi, tu!

thereabouts *adv* giù di lì

thereafter *adv form* in seguito

thereby *adv* così

therefore *adv* quindi, pertanto; ***the rumour was false and ~ I was wrong*** le voci erano false, dunque mi ero sbagliato

thereupon *adv* (*then*) quindi

thermal *adj energy, clothing* termico; *springs* termale

thermals *npl infml underwear* biancheria *f* termica

thermal spring *n* sorgente *f* termale

thermometer *n* termometro *m*

thermos flask *n* termos *m inv*

thermostat *n* termostato *m*

thesaurus *n* thesaurus *m*

these I *adj* questi **II** *pron* questi *m*, -e *f*

thesis *n* ⟨*pl* ***theses***⟩ tesi *f inv*

thespian *liter, hum* **I** *adj* drammatico **II** *n* attore *m*, -trice *f* drammatico, -a

they *pron* **1.** loro; ***~'re going to the theatre*** vanno a teatro; ***~'re going to the theatre, we're not*** loro vanno a teatro, noi no; ***there ~ are*** eccoli *mpl*, eccole *fpl* **2.** ***if anyone looks at this, ~ will see that ...*** se qualcuno lo guarda, vedrà che ...; ***~ say that ...*** si dice che ...; ***~ are going to change the law*** cambieranno la legge

thick I *adj* (*+er*) spesso; ***a wall three feet ~*** una parete spessa tre piedi; *hair* folto; *fog, forest* fitto; *accent* forte; *liquid* denso; *infml* (*stupid*) ottuso; ***he's a bit ~*** *Br infml* è un po' stupido; ***get sth into*** *or* ***through s.o.'s ~ head*** far entrare qc nella testa dura di qn **II** *n*: ***in the ~ of*** nel bel mezzo di

thicken *v/t sauce* ispessire; *fig* (*mystery*) infittire; ***aha, the plot ~s!*** ah, la trama si ingarbuglia!

thickening *n* ispessimento *m*; COOK addensante *m*

thicket *n* boschetto *m*

thickhead *n* testa *f* dura

thickheaded *adj* duro

thickness *n* spessore *m*

thickset *adj* tarchiato

thickskinned *adj fig* insensibile

thick-witted *adj* stupido

thief *n* ⟨*pl* ***thieves***⟩ ladro *m*, -a *f*

thieve I *v/t* rubare **II** *v/i* fare il ladro

thigh *n* coscia *f*

thimble *n* ditale *m*

thin I *adj* (*+er*) sottile; *person* magro; *hair* rado; *liquid* fluido; ***he's a bit ~ on top*** sta diventando pelato; *fig* ***be ~ on the ground*** essere raro; ***vanish into ~ air*** *fig* volatilizzarsi **II** *v/i* ⟨*pret & past part* ***-ned***⟩ *hair* diradarsi

◆**thin down** *v/i person* dimagrire
◆**thin out I** *v/i* (*crowd*) ridursi; (*trees*) sfoltirsi **II** *v/t sep* ridurre; *forest* diradare
thing *n* cosa *f*; **~s** (*belongings*) cose *fpl*; ***how are ~s?*** come vanno le cose?; ***it's a good ~ you told me*** è un bene che tu me l'abbia detto; ***what a ~ to do/say!*** che razza di cosa da fare/dire!; ***there's no such ~ as ...*** non esiste/esistono ...; ***I don't have a ~ to wear*** non ho niente da mettere; ***poor little ~*** poverino; ***you lucky ~!*** che fortunato!; ***have you got your swimming ~s?*** hai le tue cose per il nuoto?; ***it's a good ~ I came*** ho fatto bene a venire; ***he's on to** or **onto a good ~*** *infml* ha qualcosa di buono per le mani; ***I must be hearing ~s!*** credo di sentire le voci!; ***yes, but the ~ is ...*** sì, ma il fatto è...
thingamabob, thingumabob *n infml* coso *m*
thingumajig *n infml* coso *m*, cosa *f infml*
think I *v/i* ⟨*pret & past part* **thought**⟩ pensare; ***I ~ so*** penso *or* credo di sì; ***I don't ~ so*** non credo; ***I ~ so too*** lo penso anch'io; ***what do you ~?*** cosa ne pensi?; ***what do you ~ of it?*** cosa ne pensi?; ***I can't ~ of anything more*** non mi viene in mente nient'altro; ***~ hard!*** pensaci bene!; ***I'm ~ing about emigrating*** sto pensando di emigrare **II** *n*: ***have a ~ about sth*** avere un debole per qc
◆**think about** *v/i +obj* pensare (di fare qc); (*reflect on*) pensarci (su), riflettere; ***I'll think about it*** ci penserò; ***what are you thinking about?*** a che pensi?; ***think twice about sth*** pensarci due volte; ***that'll give him something to think about*** ora ha qualcosa su cui riflettere; → ***think of***
◆**think ahead** *v/i* pensare in anticipo
◆**think back** *v/i* ripensare (***to*** a)
◆**think of** *v/t* pensare (a); *solution, idea* escogitare; (*have opinion of*) avere un'opinione di, pensare di; ***he thinks of nobody but himself*** non pensa che a se stesso; ***what was I thinking of!*** *infml* a cosa ero andato a pensare!; ***come to think of it*** ora che ci penso; ***I can't think of her name*** non riesco a ricordare il suo nome; ***who thought of that idea?*** a chi è venuta quell'idea?; ***think highly of s.o./sth*** avere molta stima di qn/qc; ***think little** or **not to think much of s.o./sth*** non avere un'ottima opinione di qn/qc; ***I told him what I thought of him*** gli ho detto cosa pensavo di lui
◆**think over** *v/t sep* riflettere su
◆**think through** *v/t sep* analizzare a fondo
◆**think up** *v/t sep plan* escogitare; ***who thought up that idea?*** chi ha avuto quell'idea
thinkable *adj* pensabile; ***in the ~ future*** nel futuro immaginabile
thinking *n* opinione *f*
think tank *n* comitato *m* di esperti
thinly *adv* sottilmente; *fig disguised* a malapena
thinner *n* diluente *m*
thin-skinned *adj fig* sensibile
third *n/adj* terzo, -a
third-class *adj/adv* di terza classe; ***~ degree*** UNIV *diploma con il minimo dei voti* **third-degree** *adj*: ***~ burn*** MED ustione *f* di terzo grado
thirdly *adv* in terzo luogo
third-party *n* terzi *mpl* **third-party insurance** *n* assicurazione *f* sulla responsabilità civile **third person** *n* GRAM terza persona *f* **third-rate** *adj* scadente **Third World** *n* Terzo Mondo *m*
thirst *n* sete *f*; ***die of ~*** morire di sete; ***~ for knowledge*** sete *f* di sapere
thirsty *adj* (*+er*) assetato; ***be ~*** avere sete; ***gardening is ~ work*** il giardinaggio è un'attività che fa venir sete
thirteen *num* tredici
thirteenth *n/adj* tredicesimo, -a
thirtieth *n/adj* trentesimo, -a
thirty *num* trenta; ***be in one's thirties*** avere oltre trent'anni
this I *adj* questo; ***~ one*** questo (qui); ***~ time last week*** esattamente una settimana fa; ***~ time*** questa volta; ***these days*** in questi giorni **II** *pron* questo *m*, -a *f*; ***~ is easy*** è facile; ***~ is ...*** *introducing s.o.* questo/questa è ...; TEL sono ...; ***~ is John*** ti presento John; ***these are my children*** questi sono i miei bambini; ***~ is where I live*** è chi que abito **III** *adv*: ***~ big/high*** grande/alto così

thistle *n* cardo *m*
thistledown *n* lanugine *m* del cardo
thither *adv*: ***hither and ~*** qua e là
tho, tho' *abbr* (= **though**) anche se
thong *n underwear* perizoma *m inv*
thorax *n* ANAT torace *m*
thorn *n* spina *f*
thorny *adj* (+*er*) *a. fig* spinoso
thorough *adj search, knowledge* approfondito; *person* scrupoloso; ***she's a ~ nuisance*** è assolutamente insopportabile
thoroughbred *n horse* purosangue *inv*
thoroughfare *n* strada *f*; ***no ~*** divieto *m* di transito
thoroughly *adv clean, search for* accuratamente; *know, understand* perfettamente; *agree, spoil* completamente; ***~ stupid*** stupidissimo; ***I ~ enjoyed it*** mi è piaciuto davvero
those I *adj* quelli; *with masculine nouns before s+consonant, gn, ps and z* quegli **II** *pron* quelli *m*, -e *f*; *with masculine nouns before s+consonant, gn, ps and z* quegli
though I *cj* (*although*) benché; ***~ it might fail*** benché possa non riuscire; ***say it as ~ you meant it*** dillo come se lo sentissi davvero; ***it looks as ~ ...*** sembra che ...; ***even ~*** anche se; ***~ I say it*** *or* ***so myself*** anche se non dovrei essere io a dirlo **II** *adv* però; ***it's not finished ~*** non è finito, però
thought I *n* pensiero *m*; ***be lost in ~*** essere assorto nei propri pensieri; ***that's a ~!*** ottima idea!; ***it's the ~ that counts, not how much you spend*** è il pensiero che conta, non quanto spendi; ***give some ~ to sth*** fare un pensiero su qc; ***I never gave it a moment's ~*** non me ne sono mai preoccupato **II** *pret & past part* → ***think***
thoughtful *adj* pensieroso; *reply* meditato; (*considerate*) gentile
thoughtfully *adv* (*pensively*) con aria pensierosa; (*considerately*) gentilmente
thoughtless *adj* sconsiderato
thoughtlessly *adv* in modo sconsiderato
thought-provoking *adj* che fa pensare
thousand *num* mille; ***a ~ pounds*** mille sterline; ***~s of*** migliaia di
thousandth *n/adj* millesimo, -a
thrall *n* schiavo *m*, -a *f*; ***she was completely in his ~*** era completamente alla sua mercè
thrash *v/t* picchiare; SPORTS battere
◆**thrash about** *v/i with arms etc* sferrare colpi in aria
◆**thrash out** *v/t sep solution* mettere a punto
thrashing *n* botte *fpl*; SPORTS batosta *f*; ***give s.o. a good ~*** darle di santa ragione a qn
thread I *n* filo *m*; COMPUT thread *m*; *of screw* filettatura *f*; *fig* ***hang by a ~*** appendere a un filo; ***he lost the ~ of what he was saying*** ha perso il filo di quello che stava dicendo **II** *v/t needle* infilare il filo in; *beads* infilare; ***~ one's way through the crowd*** infilarsi fra la folla
threadbare *adj* liso
threat *n* minaccia *f*; ***make a ~*** fare una minaccia; ***under ~ of sth*** con la minaccia di qc
threaten *v/t* minacciare; ***~ to do sth*** minacciare di fare qc
threatening *adj* minaccioso; ***~ letter*** lettera *f* minatoria
three *num* tre
three-D I *n*: ***be in ~*** essere in 3 D **II** *adj* in 3 D
three-dimensional *adj* tridimensionale
threefold I *adj* triplo **II** *adv* tre volte tanto
three-piece suite *n esp Br salotto composto da due poltrone e un divano* **three quarters** *npl* tre quarti *mpl*
thresh *v/t corn* trebbiare
threshold *n of house, new era* soglia *f*; ***on the ~ of*** sulla soglia di
threw *pret* → ***throw***
thrice *adv* tre volte
thrift *n* parsimonia *f*
thrifty *adj* (+*er*) parsimonioso
thrill I *n* emozione *f*; *physical feeling* brivido *m* **II** *v/t*: ***be ~ed*** essere emozionato
thriller *n* giallo *m*
thrilling *adj* emozionante
thrive *v/i of plant* crescere rigoglioso; *of business, economy* prosperare; ***he ~s on stress*** nelle situazioni stressanti trova una marcia in più
thro, thro' *abbr* → ***through***
throat *n* gola *f*; ***have a sore ~*** avere

mal di gola
throat lozenge *n* pastiglia *f* per la gola
throb *v/i* ⟨*pret & past part* **-bed**⟩ pulsare; *of heart* battere; *of music* rimbombare
throbbing *n* pulsazione *f*; *of heart* battito *m*; *of music* rimbombo *m*
throes *npl*: ***be in the ~ of sth*** essere nel bel mezzo di qc
thrombosis *n* trombosi *f inv*
throne *n* trono *m*
throng *n* calca *f*
throttle I *n on motorbike* manetta *f* di accelerazione; *on boat* leva *f* di accelerazione II *v/t* (*strangle*) strozzare
◆**throttle back** *v/i* decelerare
through I *prep* **1.** (*across*) attraverso; ***go ~ the city*** attraversare la città **2.** (*during*) durante; *US* (*up to*) da … a; ***~ the winter/summer*** per tutto l'inverno/tutta l'estate; ***Monday ~ Friday*** *US* da lunedì a venerdì **3.** (*by means of*) tramite; ***arranged ~ him*** organizzato tramite lui II *adv*: ***wet ~*** completamente bagnato; ***watch a film ~*** guardare un film fino alla fine; ***a democrat ~ and ~*** un democratico verace; ***he's ~ in the other office*** è in linea dall'altro ufficio III *adj*: ***be ~*** *of couple* essersi lasciati; *have arrived*: *of news etc* essere arrivato; ***you're ~*** TEL è in linea; ***I'm ~ with …*** (*finished with*) ho finito con …; ***I'm ~ with him*** ho chiuso con lui
through flight *n* volo *m* diretto
throughout I *prep*: ***~ the night*** per tutta la notte II *adv* (*in all parts*) completamente
through traffic *n* traffico *m* in transito
through train *n* treno *m* diretto
throw I *v/t* ⟨*pret* ***threw***, *past part* ***thrown***⟩ lanciare; *into bin etc* gettare; *of horse* disarcionare; (*disconcert*) sconcertare; *party* dare II *n* lancio *m*
◆**throw about** *Br or* **around** *v/t always sep* (*scatter*) sparpagliare; *fig money* sperperare; (*toss*) lanciare
◆**throw away** *v/t sep* buttare via, gettare
◆**throw down** *v/t sep* buttare giù; ***it's throwing it down*** (*raining*) sta iovendo a diritto
◆**throw in** *v/t sep* aggiungere; ***get sth thrown in*** *as a gift* avere qc in omaggio
◆**throw into** *v/r*: ***throw o.s. into sth*** *with gusto* buttarsi in qc
◆**throw off** *v/t sep jacket etc* togliersi in fretta; *cold etc* liberarsi di
◆**throw on** *v/t sep clothes* mettersi in fretta
◆**throw open** *v/t sep door* spalancare
◆**throw out** *v/t sep old things* buttare via; *from bar, house etc* buttare fuori; *plan* scartare
◆**throw together** *v/t sep meal* mettere insieme; *people* far incontrare
◆**throw up** I *v/t sep ball* lanciare; ***throw up one's hands*** alzare le mani al cielo II *v/i* (*vomit*) vomitare
throw-away *adj remark* buttato lì; (*disposable*) usa e getta *inv*
throwback *n* (*return*) ritorno *m* (***to*** a)
thrower *n* lanciatore *m*, -trice *f*
throw-in *n* SPORTS rimessa *f*
thrown *past part* → ***throw***
thrush *n bird* tordo *m*
thrust I *n* spinta *f*; *of knife* coltellata *f* II *v/t* ⟨*pret & past part* ***thrust***⟩ (*push hard*) spingere; *knife* conficcare; ***~ sth into s.o.'s hands*** ficcare qc in mano a qn; *fig* ***I had the job ~ upon me*** il lavoro mi era stato imposto; ***~ one's way through the crowd*** farsi largo tra la folla
thruway *n US road* superstrada *f*
thud *n* tonfo *m*
thug *n hooligan* teppista *m*; *tough guy* bullo *m*
thumb I *n* pollice *m*; ***she has him under her ~*** lo tiene sotto controllo II *v/t*: ***~ a lift*** fare l'autostop
thumb index *n* indice *m* a tacche
thumbnail sketch *n* abbozzo *m*
thumbscrew *n*: ***put the ~s on s.o.*** costringere qn con la forza
thumbs down *n* pollice *m* verso; ***they gave the plan the ~*** hanno bocciato il piano **thumbs up** *n* approvazione *f*
thumbtack *n US drawing pin* puntina *f* da disegno
thump I *v/t person* dare un pugno a; ***~ one's fist on the table*** dare un pugno sul tavolo II *v/i of heart* palpitare; ***~ on the door*** battere alla porta III *n blow* pugno *m*; *noise* colpo *m*
thumping *adj* (*large*) enorme
thunder *n* tuono *m*
thunderbolt *n* fulmine *m* **thunderclap** *n* tuono *m* **thundercloud** *n* nuvolone

m **thunderhead** *n* incudine *f*
thunderous *adj applause* fragoroso
thunderstorm *n* temporale *m*
thunderstruck *adj* allibito
thundery *adj weather* temporalesco
Thursday *n* giovedì *m inv*
thus *adv* (*in this way*) così; (*consequently*) di conseguenza; ***~ far*** finora
thwack I *n* (*blow*) botta *f*; (*noise*) colpo *m* **II** *v/t* battere
thwart *v/t person, plans* ostacolare
thyme *n* timo *m*
thyroid gland *n* tiroide *f*
Tiber *n* Tevere *m*
tic *n* MED tic *m*
tick I *n of clock* ticchettio *m*; *in text* segno *m*; ZOOL zecca *f*; ***in a ~*** (*soon*) tra un attimo; ***on ~*** *infml* (*on credit*) a credito **II** *v/i of clock* ticchettare; *infml* ***what makes him ~?*** cosa lo spinge a comportarsi così? **III** *v/t with a tick* segnare
◆**tick off** *v/t sep* rimproverare; *item in a list* segnare
◆**tick over** *v/i* (*engine*) essere in moto; *fig* tirare avanti; *pej* andare a rilento
ticket *n* biglietto *m*; *in cloakroom* scontrino *m*; *for parking, speeding* multa *f*
ticket collector *n* bigliettaio *m*, -a *f* **ticket inspector** *n* controllore *m* **ticket machine** *n* distributore *m* di biglietti **ticket office** *n* biglietteria *f*
tickety-boo *adj Br infml* a posto
ticking *n* TEX fodera *f*; *of clock* tic tac *m inv*
ticking-off *n Br infml* sgridata *f*
tickle I *v/t person* fare il solletico a **II** *v/i of material* dare prurito; *of person* fare il solletico **III** *n* solletico *m*; ***have a ~ in one's throat*** avere un pizzicore alla gola
ticklish *adj*: ***be ~*** soffrire il solletico; *problem* delicato; ***it was a ~ problem*** era un problema delicato
tidal wave *n* onda *f* di marea
tidbit *n US* → ***titbit***
tiddlywinks *n* gioco *m* delle pulci
tide *n* marea *f*; ***high ~*** alta marea; ***low ~*** bassa marea; ***the ~ is in / out*** c'è l'alta / la bassa marea; *fig* ***the ~ of public opinion*** la corrente dell'opinione pubblica; ***the ~ has turned*** la marea è cambiata
◆**tide over** *v/t always sep* togliere d'impiccio; ***is that enough money to tide you over?*** questo denaro basta a toglierti d'impiccio?
tidiness *n* ordine *m*
tidy I *adj* (+*er*) ordinato; (*considerable*) discreto; ***a ~ sum of money*** una discreta somma di denaro **II** *v/t* sistemare; *drawer, desk* mettere in ordine
◆**tidy away** *v/t sep* ⟨*pret & past part* ***-ied***⟩ mettere a posto
◆**tidy up I** *v/t sep room, shelves* mettere in ordine; ***tidy o.s. up*** darsi una sistemata **II** *v/i* mettere in ordine
tie I *v/t knot, hands* legare; ***~ a knot*** fare un nodo; ***~ two ropes together*** annodare due corde **II** *v/i* SPORTS pareggiare **III** *n* (*necktie*) cravatta *f*; (SPORTS: *even result*) pareggio *m*; ***there was a ~ for second place*** sono arrivati pari al secondo posto; ***he doesn't have any ~s*** non ha legami
◆**tie down** *v/t sep with rope* legare; (*restrict*) vincolare
◆**tie in with** *v/t* combaciare con
◆**tie up** *v/t sep person, laces, hair* legare; *boat* ormeggiare; ***I'm tied up tomorrow*** sono impegnato domani; *parcel* chiudere con lo spago; FIN *capital* vincolare
tie beam *n* BUILD tirante *m*
tie-break(er) *n in tennis* tiebreak *m inv*; *in quiz* domanda *f* di spareggio
tier *n of hierarchy* livello *m*; *in stadium* anello *m*
tiff *n infml* battibecco *m*
tiger *n* tigre *f*
tight I *adj* (+*er*) *clothes* stretto; *security* rigido; *rope* teso; *hard to move* bloccato; *not leaving much time* giusto; *schedule* serrato; *infml* (*drunk*) sbronzo *infml*; *situation* difficile; *fig* ***in a ~ spot*** in una situazione difficile **II** *adv* (+*er*): ***hold s.o. / sth ~*** tenere qn / qc stretto; ***shut sth ~*** chiudere bene qc; ***sleep ~!*** dormi bene!
tighten *v/t screw* serrare; *belt* stringere; *rope* tendere; *control, security* intensificare
◆**tighten up** *v/i in discipline, security* intensificare il controllo
tight-fisted *adj* taccagno
tightknit *adj community* unito
tight-lipped *adj* (*silent*) con la bocca cucita; (*angry*) *person* con le labbra

serrate; *smile* a denti stretti
tightly *adv* → ***tight*** *adv*
tightrope *n* fune *f* (per funamboli)
tights *npl* collant *mpl*
tightwad *n US infml* tirchio *m*, -a *f*
tigress *n* tigre *f* femmina
tile I *n on floor* mattonella *f*; *on wall* piastrella *f*; *on roof* tegola *f* **II** *v/t roof* tegola *f*; *floor, wall* piastrella *f*, mattonella *f*
till[1] *prep / conj* → ***until***
till[2] *n* (*cash register*) cassa *f*
till[3] *v/t soil* arare
tiller *n on boat* barra *f* (del timone)
tilt I *v/t* inclinare **II** *v/i* inclinarsi **III** *n*: ***at a ~*** inclinato; ***at full ~*** a tutta velocità
◆**tilt back I** *v/i* inclinarsi indietro **II** *v/t sep* inclinare indietro
◆**tilt forward I** *v/i* inclinarsi avanti **II** *v/t sep* inclinare avanti
◆**tilt up I** *v/i* rovesciarsi **II** *v/t sep bottle* rovesciare
timber *n* legname *m*
timber-framing *n* struttura *f* in legno
timbre *n* LING, MUS timbro *m*
time I *n* **1.** tempo *m*; ***~ is up*** il tempo è scaduto; ***for the ~ being*** al momento; ***have a good ~*** divertirsi; ***have a good ~!*** divertiti!; ***~ and again*** ripetutamente; ***all the ~*** per tutto il tempo; ***I've been here for some ~*** sono qui da un po'; ***take your ~*** fai con calma; ***for a ~*** per un po' (di tempo); ***in ~*** in tempo; (*eventually*) col tempo; ***in no ~*** in un attimo; ***be in good ~*** essere in largo anticipo; ***for the ~ being*** (*provisionally*) per il momento **2.** *by the clock* ora *f*; ***what's the ~?, what ~ is it?*** che ora è?, che ore sono?; ***at any ~*** in qualsiasi momento; ***at the same ~*** *speak, reply etc* contemporaneamente; (*however*) nel contempo; ***by the ~ you finish*** quando avrai finito; ***on ~*** in orario; (***and***) ***about ~!*** era ora! **3.** (*occasion*) volta *f*; ***the first ~*** la prima volta; ***four ~s*** quattro volte; ***how many ~s?*** quante volte?; ***two / three at a ~*** due / tre alla volta **4.** MATH ***3 ~s 5 equals 15*** 3 x 5 fa 15 **5.** (*period*) ***in Victorian ~s*** nell'epoca vittoriana; ***~s are hard*** i tempi sono difficili; ***be behind the ~s*** essere antiquato **6.** *rhythm* tempo *m*; ***keep ~*** tenere il tempo **7.** *prison* ***do ~*** stare al fresco **II** *v/t* (*measure time*) cronometrare; (*choose time*) programmare
time bomb *n* bomba *f* a orologeria **time card** *n in factory* cartellino *m* **time clock** *n in factory* bollatrice *f* **time-consuming** *adj* lungo **time difference** *n* fuso *m* orario **time frame** *n* periodo *m* di tempo **time fuse** *n* spoletta *f* a tempo **time-honoured**, *US* **time-honored** *adj* antico **time immemorial** *n* tempo *m* immemorabile **timekeeper** *n* cronometrista *m/f* **time-lag** *n* scarto *m* di tempo **time-lapse** *adj*: ***~ photography*** fotografia *f* al rallentatore **timeless** *adj* senza tempo **time limit** *n* limite *m* temporale
timely *adj* tempestivo
timeout *n* periodo *m* di pausa; *football* time-out *m inv*
timer *n* cronometro *m*; *person* cronometrista *m/f*; *on oven* timer *m inv*
timesaving *n* risparmio *m* di tempo **timescale** *n of project* cronologia *f* **time share** *n Br* (*house, apartment*) multiproprietà *f inv* **time span** *n* periodo *m* **time switch** *n* interruttore *m* a tempo **timetable** *n* orario *m* **timewarp** *n* trasposizione *f* temporale **timeworn** *adj* logoro **time zone** *n* zona *f* di fuso orario
timid *adj* timido
timidly *adv* timidamente
timing *n* (*choosing a time*) tempismo *m*; ***that's good ~!*** che tempismo!
timorous *adj* timoroso
tin *n metal* stagno *m*; *container* barattolo *m*; *Br infml* lattina *f*
tin can *n* lattina *f*
tincture *n* PHARM tintura *f*; *Br infml* tocco *m*
tinder *n* esca *f* (per il fuoco)
tinfoil *n* carta *f* stagnola
tinge I *n of colour, sadness* sfumatura *f* **II** *v/t*: ***be ~d with*** essere sfumato di
tingle I *v/i* pizzicare **II** *n* formicolio *m*
tingly *adj* che formicolano; ***my arm feels*** (***all***) ***~*** mi formicola tutto il braccio
tinker I *n* stagnino *m*; *Br pej* ***you little ~!*** *infml* pasticcione! **II** *v/i* armeggiare; *unskilfully* cercare di riparare
◆**tinker with** *v/t* armeggiare con
tinkle I *v/i* (*bells etc*) tintinnare; *Br infml* (*urinate*) fare pipì **II** *n of bell*,

glass tintinnio *m*; *Br infml* (*urination*) pipì *f inv*; *Br infml phone* squillo *m*; ***give me a ~ in the afternoon*** fammi uno squillo nel pomeriggio
tinned *adj* in scatola
tinnitus *n* MED acufene *m*
tinny *adj* che ha un suono metallico
tin opener *n* apriscatole *m inv*
tinsel *n* fili *mpl* d'argento
tint **I** *n of colour* sfumatura *f*; *in hair* riflessante *m* **II** *v/t hair* fare dei riflessi a
tinted *adj glasses* fumé *inv*
tiny *adj* (*+er*) piccolissimo
tip[1] **I** *n of stick*, *finger* punta *f*; *of cigarette* filtro *m*; ***it's on the ~ of my tongue*** ce l'ho sulla punta della lingua; ***on the ~s of one's toes*** in punta di piedi; ***the ~ of the iceberg*** *fig* la punta dell'iceberg **II** *v/t*: ***steel-~ped*** con la punta in acciaio
tip[2] **I** *n* (*piece of advice*) consiglio *m*; *money* mancia *f* **II** *v/t* 〈*pret & past part* ***-ped***〉 *waiter etc* dare la mancia a
tip[3] **I** *v/t* (*tilt*) inclinare; (*pour*, *empty*) versare; (*overturn*) rovesciare; ***~ sth backwards / forwards*** inclinare qc in avanti / indietro; ***~ the balance*** *fig* spostare l'equilibrio **II** *v/i* (*incline*) inclinarsi **III** *n Br for rubbish* discarica *f*; (*untidy place*) immondezzaio *m*
◆**tip off** *v/t* fare una soffiata a
◆**tip over** *v/t sep jug*, *liquid* rovesciare; ***he tipped water all over me*** mi ha rovesciato dell'acqua addosso
tip-off *n* soffiata *f*
tipped *adj cigarettes* col filtro
Tipp-Ex® *n* bianchetto *m*
tipple **I** *v/t & v/i drink* bere **II** *n* cicchetto *m*
tipster *n* informatore *m*, -trice *f*
tipsy *adj* (*+er*) alticcio
tiptoe **I** *n*: ***on ~*** in punta di piedi **II** *v/i* camminare in punta di piedi
tiptop **I** *n* apice *m* **II** *adj* eccellente
tip-up truck *n* autocarro a cassone ribaltabile
tirade *n* tirata *f*
tire[1] **I** *v/t* stancare **II** *v/i* stancarsi; ***he never ~s of it*** non se ne stanca mai
tire[2] *US n* → ***tyre***
tired *adj* stanco; ***be ~ of s.o. / sth*** essere stanco di qn / qc; ***~ out*** sfinito
tiredness *n* stanchezza *f*
tireless *adj* instancabile
tiresome *adj* (*annoying*) fastidioso
tiring *adj* stancante
Tirol → ***Tyrol***
tissue *n* ANAT tessuto *m*; (*handkerchief*) fazzolettino *m* (di carta)
tissue paper *n* carta *f* velina
tit[1] *n bird* cincia *f*
tit[2] *n*: ***~ for tat*** pan per focaccia
tit[3] *n vulg* (*breast*) tetta *f vulg*
titanic *adj* titanico
titanium *n* titanio *m*
titbit, *US* **tidbit** *n* leccornia *f*; (*information*) notizia *f* ghiotta
titillate *v/t person*, *senses* titillare; *interest* solleticare
titivate *v/t* agghindare
title *n* titolo *m*; JUR diritto *m*
titleholder *n* SPORTS detentore *m*, -trice *f* del titolo **title role** *n in play*, *film* ruolo *m* principale
titter **I** *v/i* ridacchiare **II** *n* risolino *m*
T-junction *n Br* incrocio *m* a T
TLC *abbr* (= **tender loving care**) *infml* affetto *m*
TM *abbr* (= **trademark**) marchio *m* registrato
to, *unstressed* **I** *prep* **1.** *direction* a; ***~ Italy*** in Italia; ***~ Rome*** a Roma; ***let's go ~ my place*** andiamo a casa mia; ***walk ~ the station*** andare a piedi alla stazione; ***~ the north / south of …*** a nord / sud di … **2.** ***give sth ~ s.o.*** dare qc a qn; ***invite s.o. ~ dinner*** invitare qn a cena **3.** (*until*) ***from Monday ~ Wednesday*** da lunedì a mercoledì; ***from 10 ~ 15 people*** tra 10 e 15 persone; ***count ~ 20*** contare fino a venti **4.** *time*: ***it's 5 ~ 11*** sono le undici meno cinque **II** **1.** *in infinitives*: ***~ speak, ~ see*** parlare, vedere **2.** ***learn ~ drive*** imparare a guidare; ***nice ~ eat*** buono da mangiare; ***too heavy ~ carry*** troppo pesante da trasportare **3.** *used as preposition*: ***~ be honest …*** per essere franco … **4.** (*in order to*) ***~ learn Italian*** per imparare l'italiano **III** *adv*: ***~ and fro*** avanti e indietro
toad *n* rospo *m*
toadstool *n* fungo *m* velenoso
toady **I** *n* leccapiedi *m/f inv* **II** *v/t & v/i* fare il leccapiedi
to and fro *adv* avanti e indietro
toast **I** *n* pane *m* tostato; (*drinking*) brindisi *m inv*; ***propose a ~ to s.o.*** fare un brindisi in onore di qn; ***she***

was the ~ of the town era la reginetta della città **II** *v/t bread* tostare; *drinking* fare un brindisi a
toaster *n* tostapane *m*
toastmaster *n* chi propone il brindisi
tobacco *n* tabacco *m*
tobacconist *n* tabaccaio *m*
to-be *adj*: ***the bride-~*** la futura sposa; ***the mother-~*** la futura mamma
toboggan I *n* toboga *m inv* **II** *v/i* discendere in toboga
today *n/adv* oggi; ***here ~ and gone tomorrow*** *fig* oggi qui, domani chi lo sa; (*these days*) oggigiorno; ***the youth of ~*** il giovani d'oggi; ***a week ~** or **~ week*** fra una settimana a partire da oggi; ***a week ago ~*** una settimana oggi
toddle *v/i of child* gattonare
toddler *n* bambino *m*, -a *f* ai primi passi
to-do *n infml* casino *m infml*
toe I *n* dito *m* del piede; *of shoes, socks* punta *f*; ***big ~*** alluce *m* **II** *v/t*: ***~ the line*** attenersi alle direttive
TOEFL *abbr* (= **Test of English as a Foreign Language**) TOEFL (esame di inglese come lingua straniera)
toehold *n* appoggio *m*; *fig* ***gain a ~ in*** fare ingresso in
toenail *n* unghia *f* del piede
toff *n Br infml* aristocratico *m*, -a *f*
toffee *n* caramella *f* al mou
tofu *n* tofu *m*
together *adv* insieme
toggle I *n* olivetta *f* **II** *v/i* COMPUT attivare / disattivare
toggle key *n* COMPUT chiave di attivazione / disattivazione **toggle switch** *n* interruttore *m* a levetta
togs *npl infml* vestiti *mpl*
◆**toggle between** *v/t* COMPUT *programs* commutare tra
toil *n* duro lavoro *m*
toilet *n* gabinetto *m*; *place* bagno *m*, gabinetto *m*; ***go to the ~*** andare in bagno
toilet bag *n* nécessaire *m inv* **toilet paper** *n* carta *f* igienica
toiletries *npl* prodotti *mpl* da toilette
toilet roll *n* rotolo *m* di carta igienica **toilet seat** *n* sedile *m* del gabinetto **toilet tissue** *n* carta *f* igienica **toilet water** *n* acqua *f* del gabinetto
to-ing and fro-ing *n esp Br* andirivieni *m inv*
token I *n* (*sign*) pegno *m*; *for gambling* gettone *m*; (*gift token*) buono *m*; ***by the same ~*** per la stessa ragione **II** *adj* simbolico; ***~ gesture*** gesto simbolico
told *pret & past part* → ***tell***
tolerable *adj pain etc* tollerabile; (*quite good*) accettabile
tolerance *n* tolleranza *f*
tolerant *adj* tollerante
tolerate *v/t noise, person* tollerare; ***I won't ~ it!*** non intendo tollerarlo!
toleration *n* tolleranza *f*
toll[1] *v/i of bell* suonare
toll[2] *n* (*deaths*) bilancio *m* delle vittime
toll[3] *n for bridge, road* pedaggio *m*
toll booth *n* casello *m* **toll-free** *adj/adv US call* gratuito; *number* verde **toll road** *n* strada *f* a pedaggio
tomato *n* pomodoro *m*
tomato ketchup *n* ketchup *m inv* **tomato sauce** *n for pasta etc* salsa *f or* sugo *m* di pomodoro; (*ketchup*) ketchup *m inv*
tomb *n* tomba *f*
tomboy *n* maschiaccio *m*
tombstone *n* lapide *f*
tomcat *n* gatto *m* (maschio)
tome *n* tomo *m*
tomorrow *n/adv* domani; ***the day after ~*** dopodomani; ***~ morning*** domattina, domani mattina; ***a week ~** or **~ week*** fra una settimana a partire da domani
ton *n* tonnellata *f*; **~s** (**of**) (*a lot*) *infml* montagne (di) *infml*
tonal *adj* tonale
tonality *n* MUS tonalità *f inv*
tone *n of colour, musical instrument* tonalità *f inv*; *of conversation etc* tono *m*; *of neighbourhood* livello *m* sociale; ***~ of voice*** tono di voce
◆**tone down** *v/t sep demands, criticism* moderare il tono di
◆**tone up** *v/t sep muscles* tonificare
tone-deaf *adj* che non ha orecchio musicale
toner *n* toner *m inv*
tongs *npl* pinze *fpl*; *for hair* ferro *m* arricciacapelli
tongue *n* lingua *f*; ***hold one's ~*** (*say nothing*) tenere a freno la lingua
tongue twister *n* scioglilingua *m inv*
tonic *n* MED ricostituente *m*

tonic (water) *n* acqua *f* tonica
tonight *n* stanotte; (*this evening*) stasera
tonsil *n* tonsilla *f*
tonsillitis *n* tonsillite *f*
too *adv* **1.** (*also*) anche; ***me ~*** anch'io **2.** (*excessively*) troppo; ***~ big / hot*** troppo grande / caldo; ***~ much rice*** troppo riso; ***~ many mistakes*** troppi errori; ***eat ~ much*** mangiare troppo
took *pret* → ***take***
tool *n* attrezzo *m*; *fig* strumento *m*
toolbar *n* COMPUT barra *f* degli strumenti
toolbox *n* cassetta *f* degli attrezzi
tooling *n* decorazione *f*; (*tools*) utensili *mpl*
tool kit *n* kit *m inv* degli attrezzi **tool shed** *n* capanno *m* degli attrezzi
toot I *v/t infml* suonare **II** *n* suono *m* del clacson
tooth *n* ⟨*pl* ***teeth***⟩ dente *m*
toothache *n* mal *m* di denti **toothbrush** *n* spazzolino *m* da denti
toothless *adj* sdentato
toothpaste *n* dentifricio *m* **toothpick** *n* stuzzicadenti *m inv*
top I *n* **1.** *of mountain*, *tree* cima *f*; *of wall*, *screen* parte *f* alta; *of page*, *list*, *street* inizio *m*; (*lid*: *of bottle etc*, *pen*) tappo *m*; *of the class*, *league* testa *f*; ***on ~ of*** in cima a; ***at the ~ of*** *list*, *tree*, *mountain* in cima a; *league* in testa a; *page*, *street* all'inizio di; ***at the ~ of one's voice*** (*loudly*) a squarciagola; ***get to the ~*** *of company etc* arrivare in cima; ***get to the ~*** *of mountain* arrivare alla vetta; ***are things getting on ~ of him?*** la situazione lo sta sopraffacendo?; ***be over the ~*** (*exaggerated*) essere esagerato **2.** (*clothing*) maglia *f* **3.** (AUTO: *gear*) marcia *f* più alta **II** *adj branches* più alto; *floor* ultimo; *management* di alto livello; *official* di alto rango; *player* migliore; *speed*, *note* massimo; ***at ~ speed*** a tutta velocità **III** *v/t* ⟨*pret & past part* ***-ped***⟩: ***~ped with cream*** ricoperto di crema
◆**top up** *v/t sep glass* riempire; ***top up the tank*** fare il pieno
top hat *n* cilindro *m*
topic *n* argomento *m*
topical *adj* attuale
topless *adj* topless *inv*
topmost *adj branches*, *floor* più alto
topping *n on pizza* guarnizione *f*
topple I *v/i* crollare **II** *v/t government* far cadere
◆**topple over** *v/i* (*fall*) rovesciarsi
top secret *adj* top secret *inv*
topsy-turvy *adj* sottosopra *inv*
top-up card *n* TEL ricarica *f*
torch *n Br* pila *f*; *with flame* torcia *f*
tore *pret* → ***tear***
torment I *n* tormento *m* **II** *v/t person*, *animal* tormentare; ***~ed by doubt*** tormentato dal dubbio
torn *past part* → ***tear***[1]
tornado *n* tornado *m*
torpedo I *n* siluro *m* **II** *v/t* silurare; *fig* far saltare
torpid *adj* torpido
torpor *n* (*lethargy*) torpore *m*; (*apathy*) apatia *f*
torrent *n* torrente *m*; *of lava* fiume *m*; *of abuse*, *words* valanga *f*
torrential *adj rain* torrenziale
torrid *adj heat* torrido; ***she was having a ~ affair*** aveva un'ardente relazione amorosa
torso *n* torso *m*
tort *n* JUR illecito *m*
tortoise *n* tartaruga *f*
tortoiseshell *n* tartaruga *f*
tortuous *adj liter path* tortuoso; *fig* contorto
torture I *n* tortura *f* **II** *v/t* torturare
Tory I *n* POL conservatore *m*, -trice *f* **II** *adj* POL conservatore
toss I *v/t ball* lanciare; *rider* disarcionare; *salad* mescolare; ***~ a coin*** fare testa o croce **II** *v/i*: ***~ and turn*** rigirarsi; ***~ for sth*** fare testa o croce per qc **III** *n*: ***win the ~*** vincere a testa o croce
◆**toss about** *Br or* **around** *v/t sep* (*move*) sballottolare; *ball* fare dei lanci con; *fig ideas* lanciare
◆**toss away** *v/t sep* gettare
◆**toss off** *v/t* buttare giù; ***he tossed off a few jokes*** ha buttato giù un paio di barzellette; *Br vulg* (*masturbate*) masturbare
◆**toss out** *v/t sep rubbish* buttare via; *person* cacciare
◆**toss up** *v/t sep* fare testa o croce
toss-up *n*: ***it was a ~ whether …*** *infml* si doveva scegliere tra…
tot *n* (*child*) bimbo *m*, -a *f*; *esp Br of alcohol* goccio *m*

◆**tot up** *v/t sep* ⟨*pret & past part* ***-ted***⟩ *bill* calcolare; *figures, votes* farc il conto di
total I *n* totale *m*; ***in ~*** in totale **II** *adj amount, disaster* totale; *eclipse* totale; ***be in ~ ignorance*** (***of sth***) essere completamente ignorante (riguardo a qc); *stranger* perfetto **III** *v/t* (*amount to*) ammontare a
totalisator *n betting* totalizzatore *m*
totalitarian *adj* totalitario
totally *adv* totalmente, completamente
tote[1] *abbr* → ***totalisator***
tote[2] **I** *v/t infml* (*haul*) portare **II** *n* trasporto *m*
tote bag *n borsa di stoffa con due manici*
tother, t'other *n* (= **the other**) *sl* l'altro
totter I *v/i of person* barcollare **II** *n* barcollamento *m*
touch I *v/t* toccare; *emotionally* commuovere; ***~ wood*** toccare ferro **II** *v/i* toccare; *of two lines etc* toccarsi **III** *n* **1.** tocco *m*; ***he felt a ~ on his shoulder*** si è sentito toccare sulla spalla; ***at the ~ of a button*** premendo semplicemente un bottone **2.** *sense* tatto *m*; ***be cold to the ~*** essere freddo al tatto **3.** (*small quantity*) tocco *m*; ***a ~ of*** *little bit* un po' di …; ***a ~ of flu*** una leggera influenza **4.** *in rugby* touche *f*; ***kick the ball into ~*** calciare la palla fuoricampo **5.** (*contact*) ***lose ~ with s.o.*** perdere i contatti con qn; ***keep in ~ with s.o.*** rimanere in contatto con qn; ***we kept in ~*** siamo rimasti in contatto; ***be out of ~*** *with news* non essere al corrente; *with people* non avere contatti **6.** ***a personal ~*** un tocco personale; ***a nice ~*** un bel gesto; ***put the finishing ~es to sth*** dare il tocco finale a qc **7.** ***lose one's ~*** perdere la mano
◆**touch down** *v/i of aeroplane* atterrare; SPORTS fare meta
◆**touch on** *v/t* (*mention*) accennare a; ***he barely touched on the question*** non ha neanche sfiorato la questione
◆**touch up** *v/t sep photo* ritoccare; *sexually* palpeggiare
touch-and-go *adj*: ***it was ~*** la situazione era critica
touchdown *n of aeroplane* atterraggio *m*
touché *int* SPORTS touché
touched *adj* (*crazy*) toccato
touching *adj* commovente
touchline *n* SPORTS linea *f* laterale
touch screen *n* schermo *m* tattile
touch-sensitive *adj*: ***~ screen*** touch screen *m inv*
touchstone *n fig* pietra *f* di paragone
touch-type *v/i* battere (a macchina) senza guardare la tastiera **touch-up** *n* ritocco *m*
touchy *adj person* suscettibile
tough I *adj* (+*er*) *person* forte; *question, exam, meat, punishment* duro; (***as***) ***~ as old boots*** *Br hum or* ***shoe leather*** *US hum* duro come una suola di scarpa; ***he'll get over it, he's ~*** lo supererà, è forte; ***get ~*** (***with s.o.***) *fig* usare le maniere forti (con qn); ***it was ~ going*** è stata dura; ***I had a ~ time controlling my anger*** è stato difficile controllare la mia rabbia; ***she's a ~ customer*** è una tipa difficile; ***it was ~ on the others*** *infml* è stato un brutto colpo per gli altri; ***~*** (***luck***)***!*** *infml* che sfortuna!; *material* resistente **II** *n infml* duro *m*, -a *f*
◆**toughen up** *v/t sep person* rendere più forte
tough guy *n infml* duro *m infml*
tough-minded *adj* deciso
toupee *n* toupet *m inv*
tour I *n* visita *f*; ***be on ~*** essere in tournée **II** *v/t area* fare il giro di; ***~ the world*** girare il mondo; THEAT essere in tournée in **III** *v/i on holiday* viaggiare; THEAT essere in tournée; ***we're ~ing*** (***around***) stiamo viaggiando
tour de force *n* tour de force *m inv*
tour guide *n* guida *f* turistica
tourism *n* turismo *m*
tourist *n* turista *m/f*
tourist attraction *n* attrazione *f* turistica **tourist class** *n* classe *f* turistica **tourist industry** *n* industria *f* del turismo **tourist (information) office** *n* azienda *f* (autonoma) di soggiorno **tourist season** *n* stagione *f* turistica **tourist trap** *n* trappola *f* per turisti
touristy *adj infml pej* troppo turistico
tournament *n* torneo *m*
tourniquet *n* laccio *m* emostatico
tour operator *n* operatore *m* turistico
tousled *adj hair* scompigliato

tout *n* bagarino *m*
tow **I** *v/t car, boat* rimorchiare **II** *n*: ***give s.o. a ~*** rimorchiare qn
◆**tow away** *v/t sep car* portare via col carro attrezzi
toward(s) *prep* (*with motion*) verso; ***sail ~ China*** navigare verso la Cina; ***it's further north, ~ Milan*** è più a nord, verso Milano; ***he turned ~ her*** si è girato verso di lei; (*in relation to*) nei confronti di; ***what are your feelings ~ him?*** quali sono i tuoi sentimenti nei suoi confronti; ***rude ~*** maleducato nei confronti di; ***work ~ (achieving) sth*** lavorare per (raggiungere) qc; ***a contribution ~ sth*** un contributo a qc
towbar *n* barra *f* di rimorchio
towel *n* asciugamano *m*
◆**towel down** *v/t sep* asciugare
towelling *n* (tessuto *m* di) spugna *f*
tower *n* torre *f*
◆**tower over** *v/t* sovrastare
tower block *n* condominio *m* a torre
towering *adj fig achievement* straordinario
tower of strength *n*: ***his brother was a ~ for him*** suo fratello è stato per lui un grande sostegno
town *n* città *f inv*; *opposed to city* cittadina *f*; ***he's out of ~*** è fuori città; ***go to ~ on sth*** *fig infml* spassarsela facendo qc; ***be out on the ~*** fare baldoria
town centre *n Br* centro *m* **town council** *n* consiglio *m* comunale **town councillor** *n* consigliere *m*, -a *f* comunale **town hall** *n* municipio *m* **town house** *n* casa *f* di città; (*type of house*) villetta *f* a schiera **town planner** *n* urbanista *m/f* **town planning** *n* urbanistica *f*
townsfolk *npl* cittadini *mpl*
township *n US* municipalità *f*; *in Sudafrica quartiere abitato da gente di colore*
townspeople *npl* cittadini *mpl*
towpath *n* alzaia *f* **towrope** *n* cavo *m* da rimorchio
toxic *adj* tossico
toxic waste *n* scorie *fpl* tossiche
toxin *n* BIOL tossina *f*
toy *n* giocattolo *m*
◆**toy with** *v/t object* giocherellare con; *idea* accarezzare
toy boy *n infml amante giovane di una donna più matura* **toy shop** *n* negozio *m* di giocattoli
tr. *abbr* **1.** (= **transitive**) GRAM transitivo **2.** (= **translated**) tradotto **3.** (= **treasurer**) tesoriere **4.** (= **trustee**) JUR fiduciario
trace **I** *n of substance* traccia *f*; ***without (a) ~*** senza lasciare traccia **II** *v/t* (*find*) rintracciare; ***I can't ~ your file*** non riesco a trovare il tuo documento; (*follow*: *footsteps*) seguire; (*draw*) tracciare; (*with tracing paper*) ricalcare; ***~ a call*** rintracciare una chiamata
◆**trace back** *v/t sep descent* far risalire a; *problem etc* ricondurre (***to*** a)
trace element *n* elemento *m* in traccia
tracery *n* ARCH traforo *m*
tracing *n* ricalco *m*
tracing paper *n* carta *f* da ricalco
track **I** *n* (*path*) sentiero *m*; *on race course* pista *f*; (*race course*) circuito *m*; RAIL binario *m*; *on record*, *CD* brano *m*; ***I can't keep ~ of your girlfriends*** è difficile tenersi aggiornato sulle tue fidanzate; ***lose ~ of s.o. / sth*** (*lose contact with*) perdere traccia di qn / qc; ***keep ~ of sth*** tenersi al passo con qc; *keep record of* registrare; ***be on the wrong ~*** essere fuori strada; ***get sth back on ~*** rimettere qc sulla strada giusta **II** *v/t animal* seguire le orme di
◆**track down** *v/t sep* rintracciare
track and field *n* SPORTS atletica *f* leggera
trackball *n* COMPUT trackball *f inv*
tracker dog *n* cane *m* poliziotto
track event *n* SPORTS gara *f* (di atletica leggera) su pista **track record** *n fig*: ***have a good ~*** avere dei buoni precedenti **track rod** *n* AUTO barra *f* di accoppiamento **track shoe** *n* SPORTS scarpetta *f* (da corsa) chiodata **tracksuit** *n* tuta *f* (da ginnastica)
tract[1] *n* zona *f*
tract[2] *n* (*pamphlet*) trattatello *m*
traction *n* MECH trazione *f*
tractor *n* trattore *m*
trade **I** *n* (*commerce*) commercio *m*; ***how's ~?*** come vanno gli affari?; ***do a good ~*** fare buoni affari; (*profession*, *craft*) mestiere *m*; ***he's a bricklayer by ~*** è un muratore di pro-

fessione **II** *v/i* (*do business*) essere in attività; **~ *in sth*** commerciare in qc **III** *v/t* (*exchange*) scambiare; **~ *sth for sth*** scambiare qc con qc

◆**trade in** *v/t sep when buying* dare in permuta

trade fair *n* fiera *f* campionaria **trademark** *n* marchio *m* registrato **trade name** *n* nome *m* commerciale **trade-off** *n*: ***there's always a ~*** c'è sempre una via di mezzo

trader *n* commerciante *m/f*

trade secret *n* segreto *m* industriale

tradesman *n plumber etc* operaio *m*; *milkman etc* fornitore *m*

tradespeople *npl* commercianti *mpl*; (*craftsmen*) artigiani *mpl*

trade(s) union *n* sindacato *m*

trade unionist *n* sindacalista *m/f*

trading *n* (*trade*) commercio *m*; *stock exchange* trading *m*

trading estate *n* zona *f* industriale

tradition *n* tradizione *f*

traditional *adj* tradizionale

traditionally *adv* tradizionalmente

traffic I *n on roads, in drugs* traffico *m*; *at airport* traffico *m* aereo **II** *v/i usu pej* trafficare

traffic circle *n US* rotonda *f* **traffic cone** *n* cono *m* spartitraffico **traffic cop** *n infml* vigile *m* (urbano) **traffic island** *n* isola *f* salvagente **traffic jam** *n* ingorgo *m*

trafficker *n usu pej etc* trafficante *m/f*

traffic lights *npl* semaforo *m* **traffic police** *npl* polizia *f* stradale **traffic sign** *n* segnale *m* stradale **traffic warden** *n* ausiliario *m* (del traffico)

tragedy *n* tragedia *f*

tragic *adj* tragico

tragically *adv* tragicamente

tragicomedy *n* tragicommedia *f*

trail I *n* (*path*) sentiero *m*; *of person, animal* tracce *fpl*; *of blood* scia *f*; ***be hot on s.o.'s ~*** stare sul punto di scovare qn **II** *v/t* (*follow*) seguire; (*drag*) trascinare; *caravan etc* trainare **III** *v/i* (*lag behind*) trascinarsi; ***they're ~ing 3-1*** stanno perdendo 3 a 1

◆**trail away** *or* **off** *v/i* (*voice*) affievolirsi

◆**trail behind** *v/i* rimanere indietro; *in competition* arrancare

trailblazer *n* (*innovator*) innovatore *m*, -trice *f*; (*pioneer*) pioniere *m*

trailer *n pulled by vehicle* rimorchio *m*; FILM, TV trailer *m inv*; *US* (*caravan*) roulotte *f inv*

train[1] *n* treno *m*; ***go by ~*** andare in treno; **~ *of thought*** filo *m* di pensieri

train[2] **I** *v/t team, athlete* allenare; *employee* formare; *dog* addestrare; ***this dog has been ~ed to kill*** questo cane è stato addestrato per uccidere; (*aim*) *gun, telescope* puntare (**on** su); *plant* far crescere **II** *v/i of team, athlete* allenarsi; ***he ~ed as a teacher*** ha fatto un tirocinio da insegnante

train driver *n* macchinista *m/f*

trainee *n* praticante *m/f*

trainer *n* SPORTS allenatore *m*, -trice *f*; *of dog* addestratore *m*, -trice *f*

trainers *npl shoes* scarpe *fpl* da ginnastica

training *n of new staff* formazione *f*; SPORTS allenamento *m*; ***be in ~*** SPORTS allenarsi; ***be out of ~*** SPORTS essere fuori allenamento

training course *n* corso *m* di formazione **training ground** *n* campo *m* di allenamento **training scheme** *n* programma *m* di formazione

trainspotting *n* trainspotting *m inv*, *passatempo che consiste nell'osservazione del passaggio dei treni* **train station** *n* stazione *f* ferroviaria

traipse *v/i infml* trascinarsi

trait *n* tratto *m*

traitor *n* traditore *m*, -trice *f*

trajectory *n* traiettoria *f*

tram *n* tram *m inv*

tramline *n* rotaia *f* del tram; *tennis* corridoio *m*

tramp I *n* (*vagabond*) barbone *m*, -a *f* **II** *v/i* camminare con passo pesante

trample *v/t*: ***be ~d to death*** morire travolto; ***be ~d underfoot*** essere calpestato

◆**trample on** *v/t person, object* calpestare

trampoline *n* trampolino *m*

tramway *n Br* linea *f* tranviaria

trance *n* trance *f inv*; ***go into a ~*** cadere in trance

tranquil *adj* tranquillo

tranquillise, tranquillize *v/t* sedare

tranquilliser, tranquillizer *n* tranquillante *m*

tranquillity *n* tranquillità *f*

transact *v/t deal, business* trattare

transaction *n* transazione *f*
transatlantic *adj* transatlantico
transcend *v/t* trascendere
transcendental *adj* trascendentale
transcribe *v/t* trascrivere
transcript *n* trascrizione *f*
transfer I *v/t* ⟨*pret & past part* **-red**⟩ trasferire; JUR cedere **II** *v/i* ⟨*pret & past part* **-red**⟩ cambiare **III** *n* trasferimento *m*; JUR cessione *f*; *of money* bonifico *m* bancario; *of prisoner* trasferimento *m*
transferable *adj ticket* trasferibile
transfer fee *n for football player* prezzo *m* d'acquisto
transfiguration *n* trasfigurazione *f*
transfix *v/t* impietrire
transform *v/t* trasformare
transformation *n* trasformazione *f*
transformer *n* ELEC trasformatore *m*
transfusion *n* trasfusione *f*
transgression *n of law* violazione *f*; (*sin*) peccato *m*
transient *adj* passeggero
transistor *n* transistor *m inv*; *radio* radiolina *f*
transit *n*: ***in ~*** *of goods*, *passengers* in transito
transit camp *n* campo *m* di smistamento
transition *n* transizione *f*
transitional *adj* di transizione
transitive *adj* GRAM transitivo
transit lounge *n at airport* sala *f* passeggeri in transito
transitory *adj* transitorio; ***the ~ nature of sth*** la natura transitoria di qc
transit passenger *n* passeggero *m*, -a *f* in transito
translate *v/t* tradurre
translation *n* traduzione *f*
translator *n* traduttore *m*, -trice *f*
translucent *adj glass etc* traslucido; *skin* luminoso
transmission *n* trasmissione *f*
transmit *v/t* ⟨*pret & past part* **-ted**⟩ *news*, *programme*, *disease* trasmettere
transmitter *n for radio*, *TV* trasmettitore *m*
transparency *n* PHOT diapositiva *f*
transparent *adj* trasparente
transpire *v/i* (*happen*) accadere
transplant I *v/t* MED trapiantare **II** *n* MED trapianto *m*
transport I *v/t goods*, *people* trasportare **II** *n of goods*, *people* trasporto *m*; *means of transport* mezzo *m* di trasporto; ***have you got your own ~?*** hai un tuo mezzo di trasporto?; ***public ~*** i trasporti pubblici; (*rapture*) trsaporto *m*
transportation *n of goods*, *people* trasporto *m*; ***means of ~*** mezzo *m* di trasporto
transport café *n Br* autogrill®
transporter *n for cars* bisarca *f*
transpose *v/t* spostare; MUS trasporre; MATH traspostare
transsexual *n* transessuale *m/f*
transverse *adj* trasversale
transvestite *n* travestito *m*
trap I *n* trappola *f*; *question* tranello *m*; ***set a ~ for s.o.*** tendere una trappola a qn; *infml* ***shut your ~!*** chiudi il becco! **II** *v/t* ⟨*pret & past part* **-ped**⟩ *animal* intrappolare; *person* incastrare; ***be ~ped*** *by enemy*, *flames*, *landslide etc* essere intrappolato
trapdoor *n* botola *f*
trapeze *n* trapezio *m*
trapper *n persona che tende trappole per animali da pelliccia*
trappings *npl of power* segni *mpl* esteriori
trash I *n* (*garbage*) spazzatura *f*; *poor product* robaccia *f*; *despicable person* fetente *m/f* **II** *v/t* (*discard*) scartare; *infml place* devastare
trash can *n US* bidone *m* della spazzatura
trashy *adj* (*+er*) *goods*, *novel* scadente
trauma *n* trauma *m*
traumatic *adj* traumatico
traumatise, traumatize *v/t* traumatizzare
travel I *n* viaggiare *m*; ***~s*** viaggi *mpl* **II** *v/i* ⟨*pret & past part* **-led**, *US* **-ed**⟩ viaggiare; ***I ~ to work by train*** vado a lavorare in treno **III** *v/t* ⟨*pret & past part* **-led**, *US* **-ed**⟩ *miles* percorrere
travel agency *n* agenzia *f* di viaggio **travel agent** *n* agente *m/f* di viaggio **travel bag** *n* borsa *f* da viaggio **travel expenses** *npl* spese *fpl* di viaggio **travel insurance** *n* assicurazione *f* di viaggio
traveller, *US* **traveler** *n* viaggiatore *m*, -trice *f*; *Br salesman* rappresentante *m/f* di commercio; *Br gypsy* nomade

m/f

traveller's cheque, *US* **traveler's check** *n* traveller's cheque *m inv*

travelling expenses *npl* spese *fpl* di viaggio; *on business* indennità *f* di trasferta **travelling salesman** *n* commesso *m* viaggiatore

travel programme, *US* **travel program** *n on TV etc* programma *m* di viaggi **travelsick** *adj*: ***be ~*** soffrire il mal d'auto / mal d'aria / mal di mare **travelsickness** *n* chinetosi *f inv*

trawl I *v/i*: ***~*** (***for fish***) pescare con la rete a strascico; *US* pescare alla traina **II** *v/t esp Br Internet etc* setacciare

trawler *n* peschereccio *m*

tray *n for food, photocopier* vassoio *m*; *to go in oven* teglia *f*

treacherous *adj* traditore, infido

treachery *n* tradimento *m*

treacle *n* melassa *f*

tread I *n* passo *m*; *of staircase* gradino *m*; *of tyre* battistrada *m inv* **II** *v/i* ⟨*pret* ***trod***, *past part* ***trodden***⟩ camminare; ***~ carefully*** *fig* andarci con i piedi di piombo **III** *v/t path* (*make*) tracciare; (*follow*) seguire; ***~ a fine line between …*** tracciare una linea sottile tra…; ***it got trodden underfoot*** è stato calpestato; ***~ water*** stare a galla in posizione verticale; *fig* restare a galla

◆**tread on** *v/t s.o.'s foot* pestare

treadmill *n* ruota *f* di mulino; *in gym* tapis roulant *m inv*; *fig* tran tran *m inv*

treason *n* tradimento *m*

treasure I *n a. person* tesoro *m* **II** *v/t gift etc* custodire gelosamente; ***I shall ~ this memory*** custodirò questo ricordo

treasure hunt *n* caccia *f* al tesoro

treasurer *n* tesoriere *m*, -a *f*

treasure trove *n* tesoro *m*

Treasury *n* POL Ministero *m* del Tesoro

treat I *v/t* trattare; ***~ sth seriously*** trattare qc seriamente; *illness* curare; ***the doctor is ~ing him for nervous exhaustion*** il medico lo sta curando da un esaurimento nervoso; ***~ s.o. to sth*** offrire qc a qn; ***~ o.s. to sth*** regalarsi qc **II** *n* trattamento *m* speciale; ***it was a real ~*** è stato magnifico; ***I thought I'd give myself a ~*** ho pensato di farmi un regalo; ***I have a ~ for you*** ho una sorpresa per te; ***it's my ~*** (*I'm paying*) offro io

treatise *n* trattato *m*

treatment *n* trattamento *m*; *of illness* cura *f*

treaty *n* trattato *m*; ***the Treaty of Rome*** il trattato di Roma

treble[1] *n* MUS: *boy's voice* voce *f* bianca; *register* alti *mpl*

treble[2] **I** *adv*: ***~ the price*** il triplo del prezzo **II** *v/i* triplicarsi

tree *n* albero *m*; ***an oak ~*** una quercia; ***bark up the wrong ~*** essere fuori strada; ***money doesn't grow on ~s*** il denaro non cresce sugli alberi

treehouse *n* casa *f* sull'albero

tree structure *n* COMPUT struttura *f* ad albero

treetop *n* cima *f* di un albero

tree trunk *n* tronco *m* d'albero

trek *n* escursione *f* faticosa

trellis I *n* traliccio *m* **II** far crescere su tralicci

trelliswork *n* graticcio *m*

tremble *v/i* tremare

tremendous *adj* (*very good*) fantastico; ***a ~ success*** un successo eccezionale; ***she has done a ~ job*** ha fatto uno splendido lavoro; (*enormous*) enorme

tremendously *adv* (*very*) incredibilmente; (*a lot*) moltissimo

tremor *n* tremore *m*; (*trembling*) tremolio *m*; *of earth* scossa *f*

trench *n* trincea *f*

trenchant *adj* incisivo; ***~ judgement*** giudizio *m* acuto

trench coat *n* trench *m inv*

trench warfare *n* guerra *f* di trincea

trend *n* (*tendency*) tendenza *f*; ***upward ~*** tendenza al rialzo; ***set a ~*** lanciare una moda; (*fashion*) ***the latest ~*** l'ultima moda

trendsetter *n* trend-setter *m/f inv*

trendy *adj* (*+er*) alla moda

trepidation *n* trepidazione *f*

trespass *v/i* invadere una proprietà privata; ***no ~ing*** divieto d'accesso

◆**trespass on** *v/t s.o.'s land, privacy* invadere; *s.o.'s rights, time* abusare di

trespasser *n* intruso *m*, -a *f*; ***~s will be prosecuted*** i trasgressori verranno puniti ai termini di legge

tress *n* treccia *f*; ***she wore her hair in long ~es*** portava i capelli legati in lunghe trecce

trestle *n* cavalletto *m*
trestle table *n* tavolo sostenuto da cavalletti
triad *n* triade *f* (*a.* MUS)
trial *n* JUR processo *m*; *of equipment* prova *f*; ***on ~*** JUR sotto processo; ***stand ~ for sth*** essere processato per qc; ***~ by jury*** processo *m* con giuria; ***have sth on ~*** *equipment* avere qc in prova; ***by ~ and error*** per tentativi
trial court *n* JUR tribunale *m* di primo grado **trial marriage** *n* matrimonio *m* di prova **trial period** *n* periodo *m* di prova **trial run** *n* prova *f*; *of machine* collaudo *m*
triangle *n* triangolo *m*
triangular *adj* triangolare
triathlon *n* SPORTS triathlon *m*
tribal *adj* tribale
tribe *n* tribù *f inv*
tribesman *n* membro *m* di una tribù
tribeswoman *n* membro *m* (donna) di una tribù
tribunal *n* tribunale *m*
tribune *n* (*platform*) tribuna *f*
tributary *n of river* affluente *m*
tribute *n* tributo *m*; ***pay ~ to s.o./sth*** rendere omaggio a qn/qc; ***be a ~ to s.o.*** fare onore a qn
trick I *n to deceive* stratagemma *m*; (*knack*) trucco *m*; ***a ~ of the light*** un effetto di luce; ***play a ~ on s.o.*** fare uno scherzo a qn; ***that should do the ~*** *infml* questo dovrebbe andare bene; ***have a ~ of doing sth*** avere l'abitudine di fare qc **II** *v/t* ingannare; ***~ s.o. into doing sth*** convincere qn con l'inganno a fare qc
trickery *n* truffa *f*
trickle I *n* filo *m*; ***a ~ of replies*** poche risposte sporadiche **II** *v/i* gocciolare; ***tears ~d down her cheeks*** le lacrime le colavano sulle guance
trick or treat *n* dolcetto o scherzetto, *frase pronunciata dai bambini che bussano alle porte dei vicini per ricevere dolciumi nel giorno di Halloween* **trick question** *n* domanda *f* a trabocchetto
trickster *n* truffatore *m*, -trice *f*
tricky *adj* (+*er*) (*difficult*) complicato; *situation, problem* difficile; ***~ customer*** cliente *m* difficile
tricycle *n* triciclo *m*
tried-and-tested, tried and tested *adj* ben sperimentato
trifle *n* (*triviality*) inezia *f*; ***a ~ hot*** *etc* leggermente caldo; *Br* COOK zuppa *f* inglese
◆**trifle with** *v/t affections* scherzare con; ***he is not a person to be trifled with*** non è una persona con la quale si più scherzare
trifling *adj* insignificante
trigger *n on gun* grilletto *m*; *on camcorder* pulsante *m* (di accensione); *fig* ***be the ~ for sth*** scatenare qc
◆**trigger off** *v/t* scatenare
trilogy *n* trilogia *f*
trim I *v/t* ⟨*pret & past part* **-med**⟩ *hair, hedge* spuntare; *budget, costs* tagliare; (*decorate*: *dress*) ornare **II** *adj* (+*er*) (*neat*) ordinato; *figure* snello **III** *n* (*light cut*) spuntata *f*; ***in good ~*** in buone condizioni
◆**trim back** *v/t sep hedge, roses* potare; *costs* ridurre; *staff* tagliare
◆**trim down** *v/t sep essay* tagliare
◆**trim off** *v/t sep* eliminare
trimming *n on clothes* ornamento *m*; ***with all the ~s*** con tutti gli annessi e connessi; ***roast beef with all the ~*** roast beef con contorni vari
Trinity *n* trinità *f*
trinket *n* ninnolo *m*
trio *n* MUS trio *m*
trip I *n* (*journey*) viaggio *m*, gita *f*; *infml on drugs* trip *m inv*; ***he is away on a ~*** è partito per un viaggio; ***take a ~*** (***to***) fare una gita a; *fig* ***she was on a major power ~*** *infml* era partita, dava ordini a tutti; ***he'd dropped a ~ and wasn't there for us*** si era fatto un trip e non potevamo contare su di lui **II** *v/i* ⟨*pret & past part* **-ped**⟩ (*stumble*) inciampare (***over*** in); ***a phrase which ~s off the tongue*** una frase facile da pronunciare **III** *v/t* ⟨*pret & past part* **-ped**⟩ (*make fall*) fare inciampare
◆**trip over** *v/i* inciampare
◆**trip up I** *v/t sep* (*make fall*) fare inciampare; *cause to make a mistake* confondere **II** *v/i* (*stumble*) inciampare; (*make a mistake*) sbagliarsi
tripe *n* trippa *f*; *fig infml* sciocchezza; ***they were talking complete ~*** stavano dicendo un sacco di cretinate
triple → ***treble***[2]
triple jump *n* salto *m* triplo

triplets *npl* tre gemelli *mpl*
triplicate *n*: ***in ~*** in triplice copia
tripod *n* PHOT treppiedi *m inv*
trip switch *n* ELEC interruttore *m* di sicurezza
tripwire *n* filo *m* d'innesco
trite *adj* trito
triumph **I** *n* trionfo *m* **II** *v/i* trionfare
triumphant *adj* trionfante
trivia *npl* banalità *f inv*
trivial *adj* banale
triviality *n* banalità *f inv*
trod *pret* → ***tread***
trodden *past part* → ***tread***
trolley *n in supermarket*, *at airport* carrello *m*
trolleybus *n* filobus *m inv*
trolley car *n US* tram *m inv*
trombone *n* trombone *m*
troop *v/i*: ***~ out*** uscire in gruppo; ***~ past sth*** passare in gruppo davanti a qc
trooper *n US* agente *f* di polizia
troops *npl* MIL truppe *fpl*
trophy *n* trofeo *m*
tropic *n* tropico *m*
tropical *adj* tropicale
tropics *npl* tropici *mpl*
trot ⟨*pret & past part* ***-ted***⟩ **I** *n* trotto *m*; ***for five days on the ~*** *infml* non fermarsi un attimo per cinque giorni; ***he won three games on the ~*** ha vinto cinque partite di fila **II** *v/i* trottare
trouble **I** *n* (*difficulties*) problemi *mpl*; (*inconvenience*) fastidio *m*; (*disturbance*) disordini *mpl*; ***go to a lot of ~ to do sth*** darsi molto da fare per fare qc; ***no ~!*** nessun problema!; ***the ~ with you is …*** il tuo problema è …; ***get into ~*** mettersi nei guai; ***make ~*** creare problemi; ***money ~s*** problemi *mpl* di soldi; ***be in a ~*** *marriage* essere in crisi; ***look for ~*** *or* ***go around looking for ~*** andare in cerca di guai; ***there'll be ~ if he finds out*** se lo scopre sono guai; ***he's been no ~ at all*** *child* non ha dato alcun fastidio **II** *v/t* (*worry*) preoccupare; (*bother*, *disturb*) disturbare; *of back*, *liver etc* dare dei fastidi a; ***I'm sorry to ~ you, but …*** mi dispiace disturbarti, ma …
troubled *adj* preoccupato; (*grieved*) afflitto; *relationship* tormentato
trouble-free *adj* senza problemi **troublemaker** *n* attaccabrighe *m/f inv* **troubleshooter** *n* (*mediator*) mediatore *m*, -trice *f* **troubleshooting** *n* mediazione *f*; *in software manual* ricerca *f* problemi e soluzioni
troublesome *adj* fastidioso
trouble spot *n* punto *m* caldo
trough *n for animals* abbeveratoio *m*; (*low point*) minimo *m*
trounce *v/t* SPORTS sconfiggere
troupe *n* THEAT troupe *f inv*
trousers *npl* pantaloni *mpl*; ***a pair of ~*** un paio di pantaloni
trouser suit *n* tailleur *m inv* pantalone
trout *n* ⟨*pl* ***trout***⟩ trota *f*
trowel *n* cazzuola *f*
truancy *n* il marinare la scuola
truant *n*: ***play ~*** marinare la scuola
truce *n* tregua *f*
truck **I** *n* (*lorry*) camion *m inv*; ***have no ~ with*** (*have nothing to do with*) non avere niente a che vedere con **II** *v/t* trasportare in camion
truck driver *n* autotrasportatore *m*, -trice *f*
trucker *n* (*truck driver*) autotrasportatore *m*, -trice *f*
truck farm *n US* azienda *f* ortofrutticola
truckload *n* carico *m* (di un camion)
truck stop *n US* ristorante *m* per camionisti
trudge **I** *v/i* arrancare; ***~ around the shops*** trascinarsi per i negozi **II** *n* camminata *f* stancante
true **I** *adj* vero; ***come ~*** *of hopes*, *dream* realizzarsi; ***the frog is not a ~ reptile*** la rana non è un vero rettile; ***spoken like a ~ football fan*** detto da un vero amante del calcio; ***~ love*** vero amore; *wall* dritto; MUS *note* intonato **II** *n alignment* ***out of ~*** fuori allineamento
true-life *adj* basato su fatti realmente accaduti
truffle *n* tartufo *m*
trug *n Br gardening* canestro *m*
truly *adv* davvero; ***Yours ~*** distinti saluti
trump *n in cards* briscola *f*
trumpet *n* tromba *f*
trumpeter *n* trombettiere *f*
truncate *v/t* troncare
truncheon *n* manganello *m*

trunk *n of tree*, *body* tronco *m*; *of elephant* proboscide *f*; (*large case*) baule *m*; *US* AUTO bagagliaio *m inv*
trunks *npl for swimming* calzoncini *mpl* da bagno
truss *n* MED cinto *m* erniario; ARCH capriata *f*; *engineering* travatura *f* reticolare
trust I *n* fiducia *f*; FIN fondo *m* fiduciario; COMM trust *m inv* **II** *v/t* fidarsi di; ***I ~ you*** mi fido di te; ***~ s.o. to do sth*** confidare che qn faccia qc; ***~ him!*** *hum* vatti a fidare!
trusted *adj* fidato
trustee *n* amministratore *m*, -trice *f* fiduciario, -a
trustful, trusting *adj* fiducioso
trustworthy *adj* affidabile
truth *n* verità *f inv*
truthful *adj account* veritiero; *person* sincero
try I *v/t* ⟨*pret & past part* **-ied**⟩ provare; JUR processare; ***~ to do sth*** provare a fare qc, cercare di fare qc **II** *v/i* ⟨*pret & past part* **-ied**⟩ provare, tentare; ***you must ~ harder*** devi provare con più impegno; ***~ and work harder*** cerca di fare meglio **III** *n* tentativo *m*; *in rugby* meta *f*; ***can I have a ~?*** *of food* posso assaggiare?; *at doing sth* posso fare un tentativo?
◆**try for** *v/t* cercare di ottenere
◆**try on** *v/t sep clothes* provare
◆**try out I** *v/t sep new machine*, *method* provare **II** *v/i for a team etc* tentare di entrare
trying *adj* (*annoying*) difficile
T-shirt *n* maglietta *f*
tub *n* (*bath*) vasca *f* da bagno; *of liquid* tinozza *f*; *for yoghurt*, *icecream* barattolo *m*
tubby *adj* (+*er*) tozzo
tube *n* (*pipe*) tubo *m*; (*underground railway*) metropolitana *f*; *of toothpaste*, *ointment* tubetto *m*; ANAT tuba *f*; ***by ~*** / ***on the ~*** con la / sulla metropolitana; ***~ station*** stazione *f* di metropolitana
tubeless *adj tyre* senza camera d'aria
tuberculosis *n* tubercolosi *f*
TUC *abbr* (= **Trades Union Congress**) *Br* congresso dei sindacati britannici
tuck I *n in dress* pince *f inv*; *Br* dolciumi *mpl* **II** *v/t*: ***~ sth into sth*** infilare qc in qc
◆**tuck away** *v/t sep* (*put away*) mettere via; (*eat quickly*) sbafare; ***be tucked away*** *of house*, *village* essere nascosto
◆**tuck in I** *v/t sep children* rimboccare le coperte a; *sheets* rimboccare; *shirt* infilare nei pantaloni **II** *v/i* (*eat*) mangiare; (*start eating*) incominciare a mangiare
◆**tuck up** *v/t sep sleeves etc* rimboccarsi; ***tuck s.o. up in bed*** rimboccare le coperte a qn
Tuesday *n* martedì *m inv*
tuft *n* ciuffo *m*; ***a ~ of hair*** un ciuffo di capelli
tug I *n* (*pull*) tirata *f*; NAUT rimorchiatore *m*; ***I felt a ~ at my sleeve*** mi sono sentito tirare la manica **II** *v/t* ⟨*pret & past part* **-ged**⟩ (*pull*) tirare
tug-of-war *n* SPORTS tiro *m* alla fune
tuition *n* lezioni *fpl*
tulip *n* tulipano *m*
tumble I *n* (*fall*) cadere **II** *v/i* ruzzolare; *of wall*, *prices* crollare
◆**tumble down** *v/i* (*person*) ruzzolare giù; (*object*) cadere a pezzi; ***tumble down the stairs*** rotolare giù per le scale
◆**tumble over** *v/i* cadere da
tumbledown *adj* in rovina, fatiscente
tumble-dryer *n* asciugatrice *f*
tumbler *n for drinker* bicchiere *m* (senza stelo); *in circus* acrobata *m/f*
tummy *n infml* pancia *f*
tummy ache *n* mal *m* di pancia
tumour *n* tumore *m*
tumult *n* tumulto *m*; ***his mind was in a ~*** la sua mente era in subbuglio
tumultuous *adj* tumultuoso
tuna *n* tonno *m*; ***~ salad*** insalata *f* di tonno
tundra *n* tundra *f*
tune I *n* motivo *m*; ***in ~*** *instrument* accordato; *person* intonato; ***out of ~*** *instrument* scordato; *person* stonato; *fig* ***change one's ~*** cambiare musica; *fig* ***call the ~*** avere il controllo; ***to the ~ of £500*** a suon di 500 sterline **II** *v/t instrument* accordare; *engine* mettere a punto
◆**tune in** *v/i of radio*, *TV* sintonizzarsi
◆**tune in to** *v/t radio*, *TV* sintonizzarsi su
◆**tune out** *v/i of radio TV* non ascol-

tare; *fig* staccare la spina

◆**tune up** I *v/i of orchestra, players* accordare gli strumenti II *v/t sep engine* mettere a punto

tuneful *adj* melodioso

tuner *n* (*hi-fi*) sintonizzatore *m*, tuner *m inv*

tune-up *n of engine* messa *f* a punto

tunic *n* tunica *f*; (*shirt*) casacca *f*; *of uniform* giacca *f*

Tunisia *n* Tunisia *f*

tunnel I *n* galleria *f*, tunnel *m inv*; *fig* ***at last we can see the light at the end of the ~*** finalmente riusciamo a vedere la luce in fondo al tunnel II *v/i* scavare una galleria

◆**tunnel through** *v/t mountain etc* traforare

tunnel vision *n* MED visione *f* tubolare; *fig* miopia *f*

tuppence *n Br* due soldi; ***I don't give a ~*** non me ne importa un fico secco

turban *n* turbante *m*

turbine *n* turbina *f*

turbot *n* ⟨*pl* ***turbot***⟩ rombo *m* chiodato

turbulence *n in air travel* turbolenza *f*

turbulent *adj* turbolento

turd *n sl* stronzo *m*

tureen *n* zuppiera *f*

turf *n* tappeto *m* erboso; (*piece*) zolla *f*; ***the ~*** il mondo dell'ippica

◆**turf out** *v/t sep Br infml* buttare fuori

turgid *adj fig* ampolloso

Turin *n* Torino *f*

Turk *n* turco *m*, -a *f*

turkey *n* tacchino *m*; *US fig* fiasco *m*

Turkey *n* Turchia *f*

Turkish I *adj* turco II *n language* turco *m*

turmeric *n* curcuma *f*

turmoil *n* agitazione *f*

turn I *v/t wheel, corner* girare; ***~ one's back on s.o.*** girare le spalle a qn; ***as soon as his back is ~ed*** non appena volta le spalle; ***the sight of all that food quite ~ed my stomach*** la vista di tutto quel cibo mi ha dato il voltastomaco; ***he can ~ his hand to anything*** è capace di imparare a fare qualsiasi cosa II *v/i* **1.** *of driver, car, wheel* girare; ***~ right/left here*** gira a destra/sinistra qui **2.** (*become*) diventare; ***it has ~ed sour/cold*** è diventato acido/freddo; ***he has ~ed 40*** ha compiuto 40 anni; ***~ professional*** diventare professionista III *n* **1.** (*rotation*) giro *m* **2.** *in road* curva *f* **3.** *in variety show* numero *m* **4.** *in games, series*: ***in ~*** a turno; ***take ~s in doing sth*** fare a turno a fare qc; ***it's my ~*** è il mio turno, tocca a me; ***it's not your ~ yet*** non è ancora il tuo turno; ***take a ~ at the wheel*** prendere il volante per un po' **5.** (*service*) ***do s.o. a good ~*** fare un favore a qn **6.** (*change*) ***at the ~ of the century*** al volgere del secolo; ***take a ~ for the worse/better*** subire un peggioramento/miglioramento **7.** ***~ of phrase*** giro *m* di frase **8.** (*occasion*) ***he was thwarted at every ~*** veniva contrastato ad ogni occasione

◆**turn against** I *v/t* rivoltarsi contro II *v/t sep*: ***turn s.o. against s.o.*** far ribellare qn contro qn

◆**turn around** I *v/t sep object* girare; *company* dare una svolta positiva a; (COMM: *deal with*) eseguire; *order* evadere II *v/i of person* girarsi; *of driver* girare

◆**turn away** I *v/t sep* (*send away*) mandare via II *v/i* (*walk away*) andare via; (*look away*) girarsi dall'altra parte

◆**turn back** I *v/t sep edges, sheets* ripiegare; ***turn back the clock*** tornare indietro II *v/i of walkers etc* tornare indietro; *in course of action* tirarsi indietro

◆**turn down** *v/t sep offer, invitation* rifiutare; *volume, TV, heating* abbassare; *edge, collar* ripiegare

◆**turn in** I *v/i* (*go to bed*) andare a letto II *v/t to police* denunciare

◆**turn into** *v/t* (*become*) diventare

◆**turn off** I *v/t sep radio, TV, heater, engine* spegnere; *tap* chiudere; *infml sexually* far passare la voglia a II *v/i of car, driver* svoltare

◆**turn on** I *v/t sep radio, TV, heater, engine* accendere; *tap* aprire; *infml sexually* eccitare; ***whatever turns you on*** *infml* qualsiasi cosa ti stimoli II *v/i of machine* accendersi

◆**turn out** I *v/t sep lights* spegnere II *v/i*: ***as it turned out*** come è emerso; ***it turned out well*** è andata bene

◆**turn over** I *v/i in bed* girarsi; *of vehicle* capottare; ***please turn over***

page vedi retro **II** *v/t sep object, page* girare; FIN fatturare
◆**turn up I** *v/t sep collar, volume, heating* alzare **II** *v/i* (*arrive*) arrivare
turncoat *n* voltagabbana *m inv*
turning *n* svolta *f*
turning point *n* svolta *f* decisiva
turnip *n* rapa *f*
turn-off *n from road* traversa *f*; *unpleasant thing*: **be a ~** *infml* far passare la voglia **turn-on** *n sexually exciting thing*: **be a ~** *infml* essere eccitante **turnout** *n of people* affluenza *f* **turnover** *n* FIN fatturato *m*; *of staff* ricambio *m* **turnpike** *n US* (*toll road*) autostrada *f* **turnstile** *n* cancelletto *m* girevole **turntable** *n of record player* piatto *m* **turn-up** *n on trousers* risvolto *m*
turpentine *n* trementina *f*
turquoise *adj* turchese
turret *n of castle, tank* torretta *f*
turtle *n* tartaruga *f* marina
turtleneck sweater *n US* maglione *m* a collo alto
Tuscany *n* Toscana *f*
tusk *n* zanna *f*
tussle I *n* zuffa *f* **II** *v/i* azzuffarsi (***with s.o. for sth*** con qn per qc)
tutor I *n* EDU *insegnante universitario che segue un piccolo gruppo di studenti*; (**private**) **~** insegnante *m/f* privato, -a **II** *v/t* seguire attentamente; (*teach*) dare lezioni private a
tutorial *n at university* incontro *m* con il tutor
tutu *n* tutù *m inv*
tux *n infml*, **tuxedo** *n esp US* smoking *m inv*
tuxedo *n US* smoking *m inv*
TV *n* tv *f inv*; **on ~** alla tv
TV dinner *n* piatto *m* pronto **TV guide** *n* guida *f* dei programmi tv **TV programme** *n* programma *m* televisivo
twang I *n in voice* suono *m* nasale **II** *v/t guitar string* vibrare
tweak I *v/t* (*pull gently*) tirare **II** *n* (*gentle pull*) ***give sth a ~*** dare un pizzicotto a qc
twee *adj* (+*er*) *Br infml* stucchevole
tweed I *n* (*cloth*) tweed *m inv* **II** *adj* di tweed
tweet I *n of birds* cinguettio *m* **II** *v/i* cinguettare
tweezers *npl* pinzette *fpl*
twelfth *n/adj* dodicesimo, -a
Twelfth Night *n* notte *m* dell'Epifania
twelve *num* dodici
twentieth *n/adj* ventesimo, -a
twenty *num* venti; ***be in one's twenties*** avere oltre vent'anni
twenty-four seven, 24/7 I *n negozio aperto 24 ore al giorno, 7 giorni su 7* **II** *adj* sempre aperto; **~ *service*** servizio 24 ore su 24
twerp *n infml* fesso *m*, -a *f*
twice *adv* due volte; **~ *as much*** il doppio; **~ *as fast*** veloce due volte tanto
twiddle *v/t* girare; **~ *one's thumbs*** girarsi i pollici
twig I *n* ramoscello *m* **II** *v/t* 〈*pret & past part* ***-ged***〉 *Br infml* capire
twilight *n* crepuscolo *m*
twilight zone *n* zona *f* crepuscolare; ***she was in the ~*** era un po' confusa
twin I *n* gemello *m* **II** *v/t towns* gemellare
twin beds *npl* due lettini *mpl*
twine I *n string* spago *m* **II** *v/t twist* attorcigliare
twinge *n of pain* fitta *f*
twinkle I *v/i of stars, eyes* scintillare **II** *n* luccichio *m*; ***with a ~ in his/her eye*** con un luccichio negli occhi
twin room *n* camera *f* a due letti
twinset *n* twin set *m inv*
twin town *n* città *f inv* gemellata
twirl I *v/t* fare roteare **II** *n of cream etc* ricciolo *m*
twist I *v/t* attorcigliare; **~ *one's ankle*** prendere una storta **II** *v/i of road* snodarsi; *of river* serpeggiare **III** *n in rope* attorcigliata *f*; *in road* curva *f*; *in plot, story* svolta *f*
◆**twist off I** *v/i*: ***the top twists off*** la parte superiore è svitabile **II** *v/t sep* svitare
twisted *adj rope* attorcigliato; (*bent*) torto; (*tangled, fig warped*) contorto; *ankle* storto; ***bitter and ~*** inacidito
twister *n US infml* (*tornado*) tornado *m inv*
twisty *adj road* contorto
twit *n infml* scemo *m*, -a *f*
twitch I *n nervous* spasmo *m* **II** *v/i* (*jerk*) contrarsi
twitter I *v/i* cinguettare **II** *n of birds* cinguettio *m*
two *num* due; ***the ~ of them*** loro due; ***in ~s*** due a due; ***break/cut sth in ~***

spaccare / tagliare qc in due; ***put ~ and ~ together*** fare due più due
two-faced *adj* falso **two-piece** *n* (*woman's suit*) tailleur *m inv* **two--seater** *adj car, settee* a due posti **two-stroke** *adj engine* a due tempi **two-time** *v/t boyfriend, girlfriend* tradire **two-way traffic** *n* traffico *m* nei due sensi di marcia
tycoon *n* magnate *m*
tymbal *n* MUS timpano *m*
type I *n* (*sort*) tipo *m*; ***what ~ of …?*** che tipo di …?; ***they're totally different ~s of person*** sono tipi di persona totalmente diversi; ***that ~ of behaviour*** *Br or* **behavior** *US* quel tipo di comportamento; ***it's not my ~ of film*** non è il mio tipo di film; ***he's not my ~*** non è il mio tipo **II** *v/t & v/i* (*use a keyboard*) battere (a macchina)
typecast *v/t* ⟨*pret & past part* **typecast**⟩ *actor*: ***be ~ as*** fare sempre la parte di
typeface *n* TYPO occhio *m*
typescript *n* dattiloscritto *m*
typewriter *n* macchina *f* da scrivere
typewritten *adj* dattiloscritto
typhoid *n* febbre *f* tifoide
typhoon *n* tifone *m*
typhus *n* tifo *m*
typical *adj* tipico; ***that's ~ of you / him!*** tipico!
typically *adv*: ***~ American*** tipicamente americano; ***he would ~ arrive late*** arriva sempre tardi
typist *n* dattilografo *m*, -a *f*
tyrannical *adj* tirannico
tyrannise, tyrannize *v/t* tiranneggiare
tyranny *n* tirannia *f*
tyrant *n* tiranno *m*, -a *f*
tyre *n* gomma *f*, pneumatico *m*
Tyrol *n* Tirolo *m*
Tyrolean *adj* tirolese
Tyrrhenian Sea *n* mar *m* Tirreno

U

U, u *n* u, U *f inv*; *Br film* per tutti; *Br* EDU (*mark*) non classificabile *m*
ubiquitous *adj* ubiquitario; (*omnipresent*) onnipresente
ubiquity *n* ubiquità *f*
udder *n* mammella *f*
UFO *abbr* (= **unidentified flying object**) UFO *m inv* (oggetto *m* volante non identificato)
ugly *adj* (+*er*) brutto
UHF *abbr* (= **ultra-high frequency**) UHF
UHT *abbr* (= **ultra heat treated**) UHT; ***~ milk*** latte UHT
UK *abbr* (= **United Kingdom**) Regno *m* Unito
Ukraine *n* Ucraina *f*
ulcer *n* ulcera *f*
ulcerate *n* v/i ulcerarsi
ulterior *adj purpose* nascosto; ***~ motive*** secondo fine *m*
ultimate I *adj* (*best, definitive*) definitivo; (*final*) ultimo; (*basic*) fondamentale; ***~ goal*** il traguardo finale; ***what is your ~ ambition in life?*** qual è la tua ambizione fondamentale nella vita? **II** *n* massimo *m*; ***that is the ~ in comfort*** è il non plus ultra del confort
ultimately *adv* (*in the end*) in definitiva
ultimatum *n* ultimatum *m inv*
ultrasonic *adj* ultrasonico
ultrasound *n* MED ecografia *f*
ultraviolet *adj* ultravioletto
umbilical cord *n* cordone *m* ombelicale
umbrella *n* ombrello *m*
umbrella organisation *n* organizzazione *f* ombrello
umpire I *n* arbitro *m* **II** *v/t & v/i cricket match* arbitrare
umpteen *adj infml* ennesimo
umpteenth *adj*: ***for the ~ time*** *infml* per l'ennesima volta
UN *abbr* (= **United Nations**) ONU *f inv* (Organizzazione *f* delle Nazioni Unite)
unabated *adj* invariato; ***the storm continued ~*** il temporale continuò

implacabile

unable *adj*: ***be ~ to do sth*** *not know how to* non saper fare qc; *not be in a position to* non poter fare qc

unabridged *adj* non abbreviato; ***~ edition*** edizione *f* integrale

unacceptable *adj* inaccettabile; ***it is ~ that …*** è inaccettabile che …

unaccompanied *adj person* non accompagnato

unaccountable *adj* inspiegabile

unaccounted *adj*: ***be ~ for*** *missing person* essere ancora disperso

unaccustomed *adj*: ***be ~ to sth*** non essere abituato a qc

unadulterated *adj* (*fig*: *absolute*) puro

unaffected *adj* semplice; ***be ~ by*** non essere toccato da

unalloyed *adj* puro

un-American *adj activities* anti-americano

unanimous *adj verdict* unanime; ***be ~ on*** essere unanimi su

unanimously *adv vote*, *decide* all'unanimità

unapologetic *adj* che non esprime scuse; ***he was so ~ about his words*** non si è affatto scusato di quello che ha detto

unappealing *adj* poco interessante; *prospect* poco attraente

unappetising *adj* poco appetitoso

unappreciated *adj* non apprezzato; ***she felt she was ~ by him*** non si sentiva apprezzata da lui

unappreciative *adj* irriconoscente; *audience* indifferente

unapproachable *adj person* inavvicinabile

unarmed *adj person* disarmato; ***~ combat*** combattimento senz'armi

unashamed *adj* senza vergogna

unashamedly *adv* apertamente; *say*, *admit* spudoratamente

unasked *adj* senza invito

unassisted *adj* da solo

unassuming *adj* senza pretese

unattached *adj without a partner* libero

unattended *adj* incustodito; ***leave sth ~*** lasciare qc incustodito

unattested *adj* non attestato

unattractive *adj* poco attraente

unauthorized *adj* non autorizzato

unavoidable *adj* inevitabile

unavoidably *adv* inevitabilmente; ***be ~ detained*** essere trattenuto per cause di forza maggiore

unaware *adj*: ***be ~ of*** non rendersi conto di

unawares *adv*: ***catch s.o. ~*** prendere qn alla sprovvista

unbalanced *adj* non equilibrato; PSYCH squilibrato

unbearable *adj* insopportabile

unbeatable *adj team*, *quality* imbattibile

unbeaten *adj team* imbattuto

unbecoming *adj behaviour*, *language etc* sconveniente; *clothes* ch non dona

unbeknown, **unbeknownst** *adv* all'insaputa; ***~ to me, they had already left*** a mia insaputa erano già partiti

unbelief *n liter* incredulità *f*

unbelievable *adj* incredibile

unbending *adj* (*stiff*) rigido

unbias(s)ed *adj* imparziale

unblemished *adj* senza macchia

unblock *v/t pipe* sbloccare

unbolt *v/t* togliere il chiavistello; ***he left the door ~ed*** ha lasciato la porta aperta

unborn *adj* non ancora nato

unbounded *adj* immenso; ***~ enthusiasm*** smisurato entusiasmo *m*

unbreakable *adj plates* infrangibile; *world record* imbattibile

unbridled *adj passion* sfrenato

unbroken *adj* (*intact*) intatto; (*continuous*) ininterrotto; *record* imbattuto

unbuckle *v/t* slacciare

unburden *v/t*: **~ o.s. to s.o.** sfogarsi con qn

unbutton *v/t* sbottonare

uncalled-for *adj* ingiustificato

uncanny *adj resemblance*, *skill* sorprendente; (*worrying*: *feeling*) inquietante

uncap *v/t* ⟨*pret & past part* **-ped**⟩ togliere il cappuccio a

uncaring *adj* indifferente; *parents* non attento

unceasing *adj* incessante

uncensored *adj* non censurato

unceremoniously *adv* (*abruptly*) senza cerimonie

uncertain *adj future*, *weather* incerto; *origins* dubbio; ***what will happen? – it's ~*** cosa succederà? – non si sa; ***be ~ about sth*** non essere certo su qc

uncertainty *n of the future* incertezza *f*; ***there is still ~ about …*** ci sono ancora dubbi su …
unchallenged *adj* incontestato
unchanged *adj* immutato
unchanging *adj* immutabile
uncharacteristic *adj* non caratteristico (***of*** di)
uncharitable *adj remark* crudele *view, person* spietato; *attitude* non caritatevole
uncharted *adj*: ***enter ~ territory*** *fig* entrare in un territorio inesplorato
unchecked *adj*: ***let sth go ~*** non controllare qc
uncivil *adj* incivile
uncivilised *adj* non civilizzato; (*inhumane*) disumano
unclaimed *adj prize* non riscosso
unclassified *adj* (*not arranged*) non ordinato; (*not secret*) non riservato
uncle *n* zio *m*
unclean *adj* sporco
unclear *adj* non chiaro; ***be ~ about sth*** essere poco chiaro su qc
unclog *v/t* ⟨*pret & past part* ***-ged***⟩ sbloccare
uncollected *adj rubbish* non raccolto; *tax* non riscosso
uncombed *adj* spettinato
uncomfortable *adj* scomodo; ***feel ~ about sth*** sentirsi a disagio per qc; ***I feel ~ with him*** mi sento a disagio con lui
uncommon *adj* raro; ***it's not ~*** non è raro
uncommonly *adv* insolitamente
uncommunicative *adj* riservato
uncomplaining *adj* rassegnato
uncomplicated *adj* semplice
uncomplimentary *adj* poco complimentoso
uncompromising *adj* fermo; *in a negative way* intransigente
unconcerned *adj* indifferente; ***be ~ about s.o./sth*** non darsi pensiero di qn/qc
unconditional *adj* incondizionato
unconscionable *adj* eccessivo
unconscious *adj* MED svenuto; PSYCH inconscio; ***knock s.o. ~*** stordire qn con un colpo; ***be ~ of sth*** (*not aware*) non rendersi conto di qc
unconstitutional *adj* incostituzionale
uncontaminated *adj a. fig* incontaminato
uncontrollable *adj anger, desire, children* incontrollabile
unconventional *adj* poco convenzionale
uncooperative *adj* poco cooperativo
uncork *v/t bottle* stappare
uncorroborated *adj* non corroborato; *evidence* non avvalorato
uncountable *adj* GRAM *noun* non numerabile
uncouple *v/t* sganciare
uncouth *adj* (*rough*) rozzo
uncover *v/t* scoprire
uncritical *adj* non critico (***of, about*** su)
uncritically *adv* senza criticare
uncross *v/t*: ***he ~ed his legs*** ha disteso le gambe (che erano accavallate); ***she ~ed her arms*** ha sciolto le braccia (che erano incrociate)
uncrowded *adj* non affollato
uncrowned *adj liter* non incoronato; *fig* ***the ~ queen of soul music*** la regina del soul
unctuous *adj* untuoso
uncultivated *adj* incolto
uncut *adj* non tagliato; (*unabridged*) integrale; ***~ diamond*** diamante *m* grezzo
undamaged *adj* intatto
undaunted *adj*: ***carry on ~*** continuare imperterrito
undecided *adj question* irrisolto; ***be ~ about sth*** essere indeciso su qc
undemonstrative *adj* non espansivo
undeniable *adj* innegabile
undeniably *adv* innegabilmente
under **I** *prep* (*beneath*) sotto; (*less than*) meno di; ***it is ~ review/investigation*** viene rivisto/indagato; ***it is ~ construction*** è in costruzione **II** *adv* (*anaesthetized*) sotto anestesia
underachieve *v/i student* non fare quanto si potrebbe
underage *adj*: ***~ drinking*** alcolismo *m* minorile
underappreciation sottovalutazione *f*
underarm *adv throw* sottinsù
underbelly *n* bassoventre *m*
underbid *v/i & v/t* fare un'offerta troppo bassa
undercarriage *n* carrello *m* d'atterraggio
undercharge *v/t customer* far pagare

meno del dovuto a
underclothes *npl* biancheria *f* intima
undercoat *n* (*paint*) prima mano *f*; *on animals* (*hair*) peluria *f*; (*down*) piumino *m*
undercook *v/t* cuocere troppo poco
undercover **I** *adj* segreto; **~ agent** agente segreto **II** *adv*: **work ~** lavorare clandestinamente
undercut *v/t* ⟨*pret & past part* **-cut**⟩ COMM vendere a minor prezzo di
underdeveloped *adj* sottosviluppato
underdog *n*: **they were the ~s** dovevano perdere
underdone *adj meat* al sangue; *not cooked enough* non cotto abbastanza
underdressed *adj* mal vestito, *vestito in modo inadeguato alla situazione*
underestimate *v/t person*, *skills*, *task* sottovalutare
underexposed *adj* PHOT sottoesposto
underfed *adj* malnutrito
underfloor *adj* sotto il pavimento; **~ heating** riscaldamento *m* a terra
underfoot *adv* sotto i piedi; **it is wet ~** è bagnato sotto i piedi; **trample s.o. / sth ~** calpestare qn / qc
undergo *v/t* ⟨*pret* **-went**, *past part* **-gone**⟩ *surgery*, *treatment* sottoporsi a; *experiences* vivere; **~ refurbishment** venire ristrutturato
undergraduate *n* studente *m*, -essa *f* universitario, -a
underground **I** *adj passages etc* sotterraneo; POL: *resistance*, *newspaper etc* clandestino **II** *adv work* sottoterra; **go ~** POL entrare in clandestinità **III** *n* RAIL metropolitana *f*
undergrowth *n* sottobosco *m*
underhand *adj* (*devious*) subdolo
underlie *v/t* ⟨*pret* **-lay**, *past part* **-lain**⟩ (*form basis of*) essere alla base di
underline *v/t text* sottolineare
underlying *adj causes*, *problems* di fondo
undermine *v/t s.o.'s position* minare
underneath **I** *prep* sotto **II** *adv* sotto
undernourished *adj* malnutrito
underpaid *adj* malpagato
underpants *npl* mutande *fpl* (da uomo)
underpass *n for pedestrians* sottopassaggio *m*
underprivileged *adj* svantaggiato
underqualified *adj* che non ha le qualifiche necessarie
underquote *v/t* offrire a un prezzo inferiore
underrate *v/t* sottovalutare
undersell *v/t* ⟨*pret & past part* **-sold**⟩ vendere a un prezzo inferiore
undershirt *n US* canottiera *f*
undersigned *adj*: **we, the ~** noi sottoscritti
undersized *adj* troppo piccolo
underskirt *n* sottogonna *f*
understaffed *adj* a corto di personale
understand ⟨*pret & past part* **-stood**⟩ **I** *v/t* capire; **I ~ that you …** mi risulta che tu …; **they are understood to be in Canada** pare che siano in Canada **II** *v/i* capire
understandable *adj* comprensibile
understandably *adv* comprensibilmente
understanding **I** *adj person* comprensivo **II** *n of problem*, *situation* comprensione *f*; (*agreement*) intesa *f*; **on the ~ that we agree a price** a patto che ci troviamo d'accordo sul prezzo
understate *v/t* minimizzare
understatement *n* understatement *m inv*
understudy **I** *n* THEAT sostituto *m*, -a *f* **II** *v/t & v/i* ripiegare
undertake *v/t* ⟨*pret* **-took**, *past part* **-taken**⟩ *task* intraprendere; **~ to do sth** impegnarsi a fare qc
undertaker *n* impresario *m* di pompe funebri
undertaking *n* (*enterprise*) impresa *f*; (*promise*) promessa *f*
under-the-counter *adj*: → **counter**
under-the-table *adj* venduto sottobanco
undertone *n*: **in an ~** a voce bassa; *fig* **an ~ of racism** un sottofondo di razzismo
undertow *n* risacca *f*
undervalue *v/t* sottovalutare
underwater **I** *adj* subacqueo **II** *adv* sott'acqua
underwear *n* biancheria *f* intima
underweight *adj* sottopeso
underwent *pret* → **undergo**
underworld *n criminal* malavita *f inv*; *in mythology* inferi *mpl*
underwrite *v/t* ⟨*pret* **-wrote**, *past part* **-written**⟩ FIN sottoscrivere

undeserved *adj* immeritato
undesirable *adj features, changes* indesiderato; *person* poco raccomandabile; **~ element** *person* persona indesiderabile
undetected *adj* non visto; **go ~** passare inosservato
undeterred *adj* non scoraggiato; **the teams were ~ by the weather** le squadre non sono state scoraggiate dal tempo
undeveloped *adj* non sviluppato; *land* non edificato
undid *pret* → **undo**
undies *npl infml* biancheria *f* intima
undignified *adj* (*inelegant*) indecoroso
undiluted *adj* non diluito; *fig truth* puro
undiminished *adj* non sminuito
undiplomatic *adj* che manca di tatto
undiplomatically *adv* senza tatto
undisciplined *adj person* indisciplinato
undisclosed *adj* non rivelato
undisputed *adj champion, leader* indiscusso
undisturbed *adj papers, village* tranquillo; *sleep* indisturbato
undivided *adj attention* assoluto; *support* unanime; *loyalty* assoluto
undo *v/t* ⟨*pret* **-did**, *past part* **-done**⟩ *parcel, wrapping* disfare; *shirt* sbottonare; *shoes, shoelaces* slacciare; *s.o. else's work* annullare, sciupare
undone *adj* slacciato; **come ~** slacciarsi
undoubtedly *adv* indubbiamente
undreamt-of *adj riches* impensato
undress I *v/t* spogliare; **get ~ed** spogliarsi **II** *v/i* spogliarsi
undue *adj* (*excessive*) eccessivo
undulate *v/t & v/i* ondulare
unduly *adv punished, blamed* ingiustamente; (*excessively*) eccessivamente
undying *adj love* eterno
unearth *v/t ancient remains* portare alla luce; (*fig: find*) scovare
unearthly *adv*: **at this ~ hour** a quest'ora (impossibile)
uneasy *adj relationship, peace* precario; **feel ~ about** non sentirsela di
uneatable *adj* immangiabile
uneconomic *adj* poco redditizio
uneducated *adj* senza istruzione
unemployed *adj* disoccupato; **the ~** i disoccupati
unemployment *n* disoccupazione *f*; **~ benefit** sussidio *m* di disoccupazione
unending *adj* interminabile
unequal *adj* disuguale; **be ~ to the task** non essere all'altezza del compito
unerring *adj judgement, instinct* infallibile
UNESCO *abbr* (= **United Nations Educational, Scientific, and Cultural Organisation**) UNESCO (Organizzazione delle Nazioni Unite per l'istruzione, la scienza e la cultura)
unethical *adj* immorale
uneven *adj quality* irregolare; *ground* accidentato
unevenly *adv distributed, applied* in modo irregolare; **~ matched** *of two contestants* mal assortiti
uneventful *adj day, journey* tranquillo
unexceptional *adj* non eccezionale
unexciting *adj* non eccitante; (*boring*) noioso
unexpected *adj* inatteso
unexpectedly *adv* inaspettatamente
unfair *adj* ingiusto
unfaithful *adj husband, wife* infedele; **be ~ to s.o.** essere infedele a qn
unfamiliar *adj* sconosciuto; **be ~ with sth** non conoscere qc
unfasten *v/t belt* slacciare
unfavourable, *US* **unfavorable** *adj report, review* negativo; *weather conditions* sfavorevole
unfeeling *adj person* insensibile
unfinished *adj job, letter, building* non terminato; *business* in sospeso; **leave sth ~** non terminare qc
unfit *adj physically* fuori forma; **be ~ to ...** *morally* non essere degno di ...; **he is ~ to be a lawyer** non è adatto a fare l'avvocato; **~ to eat / drink** non commestibile / non potabile
unflagging *adj* indefesso
unflappable *adj infml* calmo, imperturbabile
unflattering *adj* che non dona
unflinching *adj* fisso; *support* instancabile
unfocus(s)ed *adj eyes* vago; *debate* non focalizzato
unfold I *v/t sheets, letter* spiegare; *one's arms* aprire **II** *v/i of story etc*

svolgersi; *of view* spiegarsi
unforeseen *adj* imprevisto
unforgettable *adj* indimenticabile
unforgivable *adj* imperdonabile; ***that was ~ (of you)*** è una mancanza imperdonabile
unformatted *adj* COMPUT non formattato
unforthcoming *adj* riservato; ***be ~ about sth*** essere riservato su qc
unfortunate *adj people* sfortunato; *event, choice of words* infelice; ***that's ~ for you*** è spiacevole per lei
unfortunately *adv* sfortunatamente
unfounded *adj* infondato
unfriendly *adj* poco amichevole; *software* di non facile uso
unfulfilled *adj* non esaudito; *person, life* non realizzato
unfurl I *v/t* spiegare **II** *v/i* spiegarsi
unfurnished *adj* non ammobiliato
ungainly *adj* sgraziato
ungenerous *adj* poco generoso
ungodly *adj*: ***at this ~ hour*** ad un'ora impossibile
ungraceful *adj* sgraziato
ungracious *adj grunt, refusal* scortese; *answer* sgarbato
ungrammatical *adj* sgrammaticato
ungrammatically *adv* in modo sgrammaticato
ungrateful *adj* ingrato
ungrudging *adj* incondizionato
unguarded *adj* (*undefended*) senza sorveglianza; (*careless*) sconsiderato; ***in an ~ moment he …*** in un momento di debolezza…
unguent *n* unguento *m*
unhampered *adj* non ostacolato
unhappiness *n* infelicità *f inv*
unhappy *adj* (*+er*) infelice; *customers etc* non soddisfatto; ***be ~ with the service / an explanation*** non essere soddisfatto del servizio / della giustificazione
unharmed *adj* illeso
unhealthy *adj person* malaticcio; *conditions* malsano; *food, atmosphere* poco sano; *economy* traballante; *balance sheet* in passivo
unheard-of *adj* inaudito
unheeded *adj* inosservato; ***go ~*** passare inosservato
unhelpful *adj person* di nessun aiuto; *advice* inutile; ***you are being very ~*** non mi stai aiutando per niente
unhindered *adj* (*by luggage etc*) senza l'ingombro di; (*by regulations*) non vincolato
unhinged *adj* scardinato; *infml* confuso
unholy *adj* (*+er*) REL *alliance* scellerato; *mess* spaventoso; ***he called at an ~ hour*** ha chiamato ad un'ora assurda
unhook I *v/t latch* slacciare; *dress* sbottonare **II** *v/i* slacciarsi
unhoped-for *adj* insperato
unhurried *adj pace, person* calmo
unhurt *adj* illeso
unhygienic *adj* non igienico
unicorn *n* unicorno *m*
unidentified *adj* non identificato
unification *n* unificazione *f*
uniform I *n of school pupil, air hostess* divisa *f*; *of soldier* divisa *f*, uniforme *f* **II** *adj* uniforme
uniformity *n* uniformità
unify *v/t* ⟨*pret & past part* ***-ied***⟩ unificare
unilateral *adj* unilaterale
unimaginable *adj* inimmaginabile
unimaginative *adj* senza fantasia
unimpaired *adj* intatto
unimpeachable *adj reputation, character* irreprensibile; *proof, honesty* incontestabile
unimpeded *adj* senza impedimenti
unimportant *adj* senza importanza
uninhabitable *adj* inabitabile
uninhabited *adj building* disabitato; *region* deserto
uninhibited *adj person* disinibito
uninitiated I *adj* non iniziato **II** *n*: ***the ~*** i profani
uninjured *adj* incolume
uninspired *adj performance* piatto
uninspiring *adj* noioso; *idea* che non dà ispirazione
uninstall *v/t* COMPUT disinstallare
unintelligible *adj* incomprensibile
unintentional *adj* involontario
unintentionally *adv* involontariamente
uninterested *adj* disinteressato
uninteresting *adj* poco interessante
uninterrupted *adj sleep, work* ininterrotto
union *n* POL unione *f*; (*trade union*) sindacato *m*
unionise, unionize *v/t* sindacalizzare

unique *adj* (*a. very good*) unico; ***with his own ~ humour / style*** con quel senso dell'umorismo / quello stile tutto suo
unisex *adj* unisex
unison *n*: ***in ~*** all'unisono
unit *n of measurement* unità *f inv*; (*section*: *of machine*, *structure*) elemento *m*; (*part with separate function*) unità *f inv*; (*department*) reparto *m*; MIL unità *f inv*; ***we must work together as a ~*** dobbiamo lavorare insieme come squadra
unit cost *n* COMM costo *m* unitario
unite I *v/t* unire **II** *v/i* unirsi
united *adj* unito
United Kingdom *n* Regno *m* Unito
United Nations *n* Nazioni *fpl* Unite
United States (of America) *npl* Stati *mpl* Uniti (d'America)
unity *n* unità *f inv*
universal *adj* universale
universally *adv* universalmente
universe *n* universo *m*
university I *n* università *f inv*; ***he is at ~*** fa l'università **II** *adj* universitario
unjust *adj* ingiusto
unjustifiable *adj* ingiustificabile
unkempt *adj hair* scarmigliato; *appearance* trasandato
unkind *adj* (*+er*) cattivo
unknowingly *adv* senza saperlo
unknown I *adj* sconosciuto **II** *n*: ***a journey into the ~*** un viaggio nell'ignoto
unlawful *adj* illegale
unleaded *adj* senza piombo
unleash *v/t fig* dare libero sfogo a; *dog* squinzagliare; (*provoke*) provocare
unleavened *adj* non lievitato
unless *cj* a meno che; ***~ he pays us tomorrow*** a meno che non ci paghi domani; ***~ I am mistaken*** se non mi sbaglio
unlicensed *adj premises* non autorizzato
unlike *prep* diverso da; ***it's ~ him to drink so much*** non è da lui bere così tanto; ***the photograph was completely ~ her*** la foto non le somigliava per niente; ***~ Tom, I ...*** a differenza di Tom, io ...
unlikeable *adj* sgradevole
unlikely *adj* (*+er*) improbabile; ***he is ~ to win*** è improbabile che vinca; ***it is ~ that ...*** è improbabile che ...
unlimited *adj* illimitato
unlisted *adj number* non in elenco
unload *v/t lorry*, *goods* scaricare
unlock *v/t* aprire (con la chiave)
unloved *adj* impopolare
unluckily *adv* sfortunatamente
unlucky *adj* (*+er*) *day*, *choice*, *person* sfortunato; ***that was so ~ for you!*** che sfortuna hai avuto!
unmade *adj bed* disfatto
unmade-up *adj face* acqua e sapone
unmanageable *adj size*, *number* fuori dalla norma; *person* intrattabile; *hair* ribelle; *situation* incontrollabile
unmanly *adj* codardo
unmanned *adj spacecraft* senza equipaggio
unmarked *adj grave* privo di lapide
unmarried *adj* non sposato
unmask *v/t plot*, *con man* smascherare
unmatched *adj* senza pari; ***~ record*** record *m inv* ineguagliato
unmentionable *adj* inenarrabile
unmistakable *adj* inconfondibile
unmitigated *adj infml disaster* completo; *success* assoluto
unmoved *adj*: ***be ~*** *emotionally* non essere commosso
unmusical *adj person* non portato per la musica; *sounds* disarmonico
unnamed *adj* (*anonymous*) anonimo
unnatural *adj* non normale; ***it's not ~ to be annoyed*** è naturale essere seccati
unnecessary *adj* non necessario; *comment*, *violence* gratuito
unnerve *v/t* snervare; (*gradually*) indebolire; (*discourage*) spaventare; ***~d by their reaction*** spaventati dalla loro reazione
unnerving *adj* inquietante
unnoticed *adj* inosservato; ***it went ~*** passare inosservato
U.N.O. *abbr* (= **United Nations Organisation**) ONU (Organizzazione delle Nazioni Unite)
unobtainable *adj goods* introvabile; TEL non ottenibile
unobtrusive *adj* discreto
unoccupied *adj building*, *house* vuoto; *post* vacante; *room* libero; ***he doesn't like being ~*** *person* non gli piace stare senza far niente
unofficial *adj world record*, *leader* non

ufficiale; *announcement* ufficioso
unofficially *adv* non ufficialmente
unopened *adj* non aperto
unorganized *adj* non organizzato; *person* non organizzato in sindacato
unoriginal *adj* non originale
unorthodox *adj* non ortodosso
unpack I *v/t* disfare **II** *v/i* disfare le valige
unpaid *adj work* non retribuito
unparalleled *adj success* inuguagliato
unpatriotic *adj* non patriottico
unpaved *adj* non pavimentato
unperfumed *adj* inodore
unperturbed *adj* imperturbabile
unpleasant *adj person*, *thing to say* antipatico; *smell*, *taste* sgradevole; ***he was very ~ to her*** si è comportato malissimo con lei
unplug *v/t* ⟨*pret & past part* **-ged**⟩ *TV*, *computer* staccare (la spina di)
unpolluted *adj* non inquinato
unpopular *adj person* mal visto; *decision* impopolare; ***an ~ teacher with the students*** un insegnante che non ha la simpatia degli studenti
unprecedented *adj* senza precedenti; ***it was ~ for a woman to be …*** è senza precedenti che una donna sia …
unpredictable *adj person*, *weather* imprevedibile
unprepared *adj* impreparato
unprepossessing *adj* non attraente
unpretentious *adj person*, *style*, *hotel* senza pretese
unprincipled *adj* senza scrupoli
unproductive *adj meeting*, *discussion* sterile; *soil* improduttivo
unprofessional *adj person*, *workmanship* poco professionale; ***it is ~ not to …*** è mancanza di professionalità non …; ***~ behaviour*** *of doctor etc* scorrettezza *f* professionale
unprofitable *adj* non redditizio
unpronounceable *adj* impronunciabile
unprotected *adj borders* indifeso; *machine* non riparato; ***~ sex*** sesso non protetto
unprovoked *adj attack* non provocato
unpunished *adj* impunito; ***go ~*** rimanere impunito
unputdownable *adj*: ***an ~ book*** un libro che non si riesce a smettere di leggere
unqualified *adj worker*, *instructor* non qualificato; *doctor*, *teacher* non abilitato
unquestionably *adv* (*without doubt*) indiscutibilmente
unquestioning *adj attitude*, *loyalty* assoluto
unravel *v/t* ⟨*pret & past part* **-led**, *US* **-ed**⟩ *string* dipanare; *knitting* disfare; *mystery*, *complexities* risolvere
unreadable *adj book* illeggibile
unready *adj* impreparato; (*non ready*) non pronto
unreal *adj creature* irreale; *impression* inverosimile; ***this is ~!*** *infml* incredibile!
unrealistic *adj person* poco realista; *expectations* poco realistico
unreasonable *adj person* irragionevole; *demand*, *expectation* eccessivo
unrelated *adj issues* senza (alcuna) attinenza; *people* non imparentato
unrelenting *adj* incessante
unreliable *adj* poco affidabile
unremarkable *adj* ordinario
unremitting *adj efforts* incessante
unrepeatable *adj words* irripetibile
unrepentant *adj* impenitente
unreported *adj events* non riportato; *crime* non denunciato
unrequited *adj love* non corrisposto
unreserved *adj apology*, *support* senza riserve
unresponsive *adj* che non reagisce
unrest *n* agitazione *f*
unrestrained *adj emotions* incontrollato, sfrenato
unrighteous *adj* empio
unripe *adj* acerbo
unrivalled *adj* senza pari
unroadworthy *adj* non sicuro
unroll *v/t carpet*, *scroll* srotolare
unruffled *adj* imperturbato
unruly *adj* (*+er*) indisciplinato
unsaddle *v/t horse* dissellare; *person* disarcionare
unsafe *adj bridge*, *vehicle*, *wiring*, *district* pericoloso; ***~ to drink / eat*** non potabile / non commestibile, ***it is ~ to …*** è rischioso …
unsaid *adj*: ***be left ~*** essere taciuto
unsanitary *adj conditions*, *drains* antigienico
unsatisfactory *adj* poco soddisfacente

unsaturated *adj* CHEM insaturo
unsavoury *adj person*, *reputation*, poco raccomandabile; *district* brutto
unscathed *adj* (*not injured*) incolume; (*not damaged*) intatto
unscrew *v/t* svitare
unscrupulous *adj* senza scrupoli
unsealed *adj* non sigillato
unseasonable *adj* fuori stagione
unseasonably *adv* in modo insolito per la stagione
unseat *v/t rider* disarcionare
unseeing *adj gaze* perso nel vuoto
unseemly *adj* sconveniente
unseen *adj* invisibile; (*unobserved*) inosservato
unselfconscious *adj* naturale; (*spontaneaous*) spontaneo
unselfconsciously *adv* con naturalezza
unselfish *adj person* altruista; *act*, *gesture*, *behaviour* altruistico
unsettled *adj issue* irrisolto; *weather*, *stock market* instabile; *lifestyle* irrequieto; *bills* non pagato
unshaven *adj* non rasato
unsightly *adj* brutto
unskilled *adj* non specializzato
unsociable *adj* poco socievole
unsocial *adj hours* poco pratico
unsold *adj* non venduto; ***be left ~*** rimanere invenduto
unsolicited *adj* non richiesto
unsolved *adj problem etc* insoluto; *crime* irrisolto
unsophisticated *adj person*, *beliefs* semplice; *equipment* rudimentale
unsound *adj structurally* malsicuro; ***be of ~ mind*** essere incapace
unsparing *adj* (*lavish*) generoso; (*unmerciful*) *criticism* spietato; ***be ~ in one's efforts*** non risparmiarsi nel fare qc; ***the report was ~ in its criticism*** la relazione aveva delle critiche spietate
unspeakable *adj* (*horrible*) terribile
unspecified *adj time*, *amount* non precisato; *location* imprecisato
unspectacular *adj* non spettacolare
unspoiled *adj countryside* incontaminato
unspoken *adj thoughts* inespresso; *agreement* tacito
unsporting *adj* non sportivo
unsportsmanlike *adj* sleale
unstable *adj person* squilibrato; *structure*, *area*, *economy* instabile
unsteady *adj ladder* malsicuro; ***be ~ on one's feet*** non reggersi bene sulle gambe
unstinting *adj support* incondizionato; *generosity* illimitato; *praise* senza riserve; ***be ~ in one's efforts*** prodigarsi negli sforzi
unstressed *adj word*, *syllable* atono
unstuck *adj*: ***come ~*** *of notice etc* staccarsi; *infml of plan etc* fallire
unsubtle *adj* che manca di sottigliezza
unsuccessful *adj writer etc* di scarso successo; *candidate*, *party* sconfitto; *attempt* fallito; ***he tried but was ~*** ha provato ma non ha avuto fortuna
unsuccessfully *adv try*, *apply* senza successo
unsuitable *adj partner*, *clothing* inadatto; *thing to say*, *language* inappropriato; ***be ~ for*** non essere adatto per; ***they're ~ for each other*** non sono fatti l'uno per l'altra
unsure *adj* (*uncertain*) incerto; ***be ~ of*** *or* ***about sth*** non essere sicuro di qc; ***be ~ of o.s.*** essere insicuro
unsurpassed *adj* senza pari
unsurprising *adj* prevedibile
unsurprisingly *adv* in modo prevedibile
unsuspecting *adj* ignaro
unsweetened *adj* non zuccherato
unswerving *adj loyalty*, *devotion* incrollabile
untangle *v/t hair*, *threads* districare
unthinkable *adj* impensabile
untidy *adj* (+*er*) *room*, *desk*, *hair* in disordine
untie *v/t knot* disfare; *laces* slacciare; *prisoner* slegare
until **I** *prep* fino a; ***I can wait ~ tomorrow*** posso aspettare fino a domani; ***from Monday ~ Friday*** da lunedì a venerdì; ***not ~ Friday*** non prima di venerdì; ***it won't be finished ~ July*** non sarà finito prima di luglio **II** *cj* finché (non); ***can you wait ~ I'm ready?*** puoi aspettare che sia pronta?; ***they won't do anything ~ you say so*** non faranno niente finché non glielo dici tu
untimely *adj death* prematuro
untiring *adj efforts* instancabile
untold *adj riches* incalcolabile; *suffer-*

ing indescrivibile; *story* inedito
untouchable *adj* intoccabile
untouched *adj* non toccato; *bottle etc* intatto; (*unharmed*) indenne
untrained *adj person* non specializzato; *voice*, *mind* non esercitato; ***to the ~ eye*** all'occhio inesperto
untranslatable *adj* intraducibile
untreated *adj medical condition* non curato; *wood* non trattato
untried *adj person* inesperto; *method* non sperimentato
untroubled *adj*: ***be ~ by the news*** non essere turbato dalla notizia; ***he seemed ~ by the heat*** sembrava non essere disturbato dal caldo
untrue *adj* falso
untrustworthy *adj* inaffidabile
untruthful *adj statement* falso; *person* bugiardo
untypical *adj* non tipico (**of** di)
unusable *adj* inutilizzabile
unused[1] *adj goods* mai usato
unused[2] *adj*: ***be ~ to sth*** non essere abituato a qc; ***be ~ to doing sth*** non essere abituato a fare qc
unusual *adj* insolito; ***it's ~ for them not to write*** non è da loro non scrivere
unusually *adv* insolitamente
unvarnished *adj wood* non trattato; ***the ~ truth*** la verità nuda e cruda
unveil *v/t memorial*, *statue etc* scoprire
unwanted *adj child* non voluto; *pregnancy* indesiderato
unwarranted *adj* ingiustificato
unwell *adj*: ***be/feel ~*** stare/sentirsi male
unwieldy *adj suitcase* ingombrante; *system* complicato
unwilling *adj*: ***be ~ to do sth*** non essere disposto a fare qc
unwillingly *adv* malvolentieri
unwind ⟨*pret & past part* ***-wound***⟩ **I** *v/t tape* svolgere **II** *v/i of tape* svolgersi; *of story* dipanarsi; *infml* (*relax*) rilassarsi
unwise *adj* avventato, imprudente
unwitting *adj* (*unaware*) inconsapevole
unwittingly *adv* involontariamente
unworkable *adj* inattuabile
unworldly *adj person* non attaccato alle cose; (*naive*) ingenuo; (*unusual*) non di questo mondo
unworried *adj* indisturbato
unworthy *adj* (*undeserving*) indegno (**of** di); (*discreditable*) disdicevole
unwound *pret & past part* → **unwind**
unwrap *v/t* ⟨*pret & past part* ***-ped***⟩ *gift* aprire, scartare
unwritten *adj law*, *rule* tacito
unyielding *adj* inflessibile
unzip *v/t* ⟨*pret & past part* ***-ped***⟩ *dress etc* aprire (la chiusura lampo di); COMPUT espandere
up I *adv* **1.** *position*, *direction*: ***~ in the sky/~ on the roof*** in alto nel cielo/sul tetto; ***~ here/there*** quassù/lassù; ***he came ~ to me*** mi si è avvicinato; ***be ~ and about*** *after illness* essersi ristabilito **2. *be ~*** (*out of bed*) essere in piedi; *of sun* essere sorto; (*be built*) essere costruito; *of shelves* essere montato; *of prices*, *temperature* essere aumentato; (*have expired*) essere scaduto **3. *the road is ~*** ci sono lavori in corso **4.** (*as far as*) ***~ to the year 2007*** fino al 2007 **5. *what's ~?*** *infml* che c'è? **6.** (*doing*) ***what are you ~ to these days?*** cosa fai di bello?; ***what are those kids ~ to?*** cosa stanno combinando i bambini?; ***be ~ to something*** (***bad***) stare architettando qualcosa **7.** (*good enough for*) ***I don't feel ~ to it*** non me la sento **8.** *duty*: ***it's ~ to you*** dipende da te; ***it is ~ to them to solve it*** *their duty* sta a loro risolverlo **9.** *infml* (*keen*) ***I'm ~ for it*** io ci sto **II** *prep*: ***further ~ the mountain*** più in alto sulla montagna; ***he climbed ~ the tree*** si è arrampicato sull'albero; ***they ran ~ the street*** corsero per strada; ***the water goes ~ this pipe*** l'acqua sale su per questo tubo; ***we travelled ~ to Milan*** siamo arrivati fino a Milano **III** *n*: ***~s and downs*** alti e bassi *mpl* **IV** *v/i* ⟨*pret & past part* ***-ped***⟩: ***he ~ped and left her*** prese e la lasciò
up-and-coming *adj young politician*, *area* promettente
up-and-down *adj movement* su e giù; *fig career etc* con molti alti e bassi
up arrow *n* COMPUT freccia *f* verso l'alto
upbeat *adj infml* (*cheerful*) allegro; (*optimistic*) ottimista; ***be ~ about sth*** essere positivo su qc
upbringing *n* educazione *f*

upcoming *adj* (*forthcoming*) prossimo
update I *v/t file*, *records* aggiornare; **~ *s.o. on sth*** mettere qn al corrente di qc **II** *n*: (**update**) *of files*, *records* aggiornamento *m*; *software version* upgrade *m inv*; ***can you give me an ~ on the situation?*** può darmi gli ultimi aggiornamenti sulla situazione?
upend *v/t* (*turn upside down*) capovolgere
upfront I *adj infml* (*honest*) schietto; *costs* pagato in anticipo **II** *adv pay* in anticipo
upgrade I *n* COMPUT aggiornamento *m*; *US* salita *f* **II** *v/t computers*, *equipment etc* aggiornare; *memory* potenziare, aumentare; (*replace with new versions*); *passenger* promuovere a una classe superiore; *product* migliorare; ***I ~d the monitor*** ho comprato un monitor migliore; ***we could ~ you to a bigger room*** possiamo offrirle una camera più grande
upheaval *n emotional* sconvolgimento *m*; *physical* scombussolamento *m*; *political*, *social* sconvolgimento *m*
uphill I *adv*: ***go** or **walk ~*** salire **II** *adj climb* in salita; *struggle* arduo
uphold *v/t* ⟨*pret & past part* **-held**⟩ *traditions*, *rights* sostenere; (*vindicate*) confermare
upholstery *n coverings of chairs* tappezzeria *f*; *padding of chairs* imbottitura *f*
upkeep *n of old buildings*, *parks etc* manutenzione *f*
upload *v/t* COMPUT caricare
upmarket *adj restaurant*, *hotel* elegante; *product* di qualità
upon *prep* → **on**
upper I *adj part of sth* superiore; *deck*, *rooms* di sopra; ***the earth's ~ atmosphere*** la parte più alta dell'atmosfera terrestre; ***the ~ Thames*** l'alto Tamigi **II** *n* **uppers** *npl of shoe* tomaia *f*; *fig* ***he was on his ~s*** era al verde
upper-case *adj letter* maiuscolo
upper class *adj accent* aristocratico; *family* dell'alta borghesia
upper classes *npl* alta borghesia *f*
upper crust *n infml*: ***the ~*** la crema
upper hand *n* sopravvento *m*
uppermost I *adj* più alto; ***be ~ in s.o.'s thoughts*** essere il pensiero principale di qn **II** *adv* verso l'alto
upright I *adj citizen* onesto **II** *adv sit* (bcn) dritto
upright (piano) *n* pianoforte *m* verticale
uprising *n* insurrezione *f*
uproar *n loud noise* trambusto *m*; (*protest*) protesta *f*
uproot *v/t plant* sradicare; ***he ~ed his whole family and moved them to New York*** ha sradicato la sua famiglia facendola trasferire a New York
upset I *v/t* ⟨*pret & past part* **-set**⟩ *drink*, *glass* rovesciare; (*make sad*) fare stare male; (*distress*) sconvolgere; (*annoy*) seccare; ***the fish has ~ my stomach*** il pesce mi ha fatto male **II** *adj* (*sad*) triste; (*distressed*) sconvolto; (*annoyed*) seccato; ***be/get ~*** prendersela (***about*** per); ***get ~ about sth*** prendersela per qc; ***have an ~ stomach*** avere l'intestino in disordine
upsetting *adj*: ***it's so ~*** (***for me***) mi fa stare male, mi turba
upshot *n* (*result*, *outcome*) risultato *m*
upside *n* vantaggio *m*
upside down *adv* capovolto; ***turn sth ~*** capovolgere qc
upstage I *adj* che si trova in fondo al palco **II** *v/t*: **~ *s.o.*** *fig* oscurare
upstairs I *adv* di sopra **II** *adj room* al piano di sopra
upstanding *adj* (*honest*) onesto; (*upright*) eretto
upstart *n novellino che si comporta in modo arrogante*
upstream *adv* a monte; ***follow the river ~*** risalire la corrente
upsurge *n of fighting* aumento *m*; *of feelings* impeto *m*
upswing *n* (*increase*) aumento *m*; (*improvement*) ripresa *f*
uptake *n*: ***be quick on the ~*** capire le cose al volo; ***be slow on the ~*** essere lento nel capire
uptight *adj infml* (*nervous*) nervoso; (*inhibited*) inibito
up-to-date *adj information* aggiornato; *fashions* più attuale
up-to-the-minute *adj information* aggiornatissimo; *style* attualissimo
uptown I *adj US house* nei quartieri alti; *train* per i quartieri alti **II** *adv US live* nei quartieri alti; *drive* verso i quartieri alti

upturn *n in economy* ripresa *f*
upwards *adv fly, move* in su; **~ of 10,000** oltre 10.000
upwind *adj/adv* sopravvento; **be ~ of s.o.** essere sopravvento rispetto a qn
uranium *n* uranio *m*
Uranus *n* ASTR Urano *m*
urban *adj areas, population* urbano; *redevelopment* urbanistico
urbane *adj* raffinato
urbanisation, urbanization *n* urbanizzazione *f*
urbanite *n* cittadino *m*, -a *f*
urban sprawl *n* espansione *f* urbana incontrollata
urchin *n* monello *m*, -a *f*
urge I *n* (forte) desiderio *m*; **feel an ~ to do sth** essere preso dall'impulso di fare qc **II** *v/t*: **~ s.o. to do sth** raccomandare (caldamente) a qn di fare qc; **~ caution** raccomandare di avere cautela
◆**urge on** *v/t sep* (*encourage*) incitare
urgency *n* urgenza *f*; **the ~ of the situation** la gravità della situazione
urgent *adj job, letter* urgente; **be in ~ need of sth** avere bisogno urgente di qc; **is it ~?** è urgente?
urinal *n* (*room*) orinatoio *m*; (*vessel*) orinale *m*
urinate *v/i* orinare
urine *n* urina *f*
urn *n* urna *f*
us *pron direct & indirect object* ci; *when two pronouns are used* ce; *after prep* noi; **they know ~** ci conoscono; **don't leave ~** non ci lasciare, non lasciarci; **she gave ~ the keys** ci ha dato le chiavi; **she gave them to ~** ce le ha date; **both of ~** entrambi; **that's for ~** quello è per noi; **who's that? – it's ~** chi è? – siamo noi
US *abbr* (= **United States**) USA *mpl*, Stati *mpl* Uniti
USA *abbr* (= **United States of America**) USA *mpl*, Stati *mpl* Uniti d'America
usable *adj* utilizzabile
usage *n linguistic* uso *m*
USB *n abbr* (= **universal serial bus**) COMPUT USB; **~ interface** interfaccia *f* USB
use I *v/t tool, skills, knowledge* usare, utilizzare; *word, s.o.'s car* usare; *a lot of petrol* consumare; *pej: person* usare; **I could ~ a drink** *infml* berrei volentieri qualcosa **II** *n* uso *m*; **be of great ~ to s.o.** essere di grande aiuto a qn; **be of no ~ to s.o.** non essere d'aiuto a qn; **is that of any ~?** ti è d'aiuto?; **it's no ~** non c'è verso, **it's no ~ trying / waiting** non serve a niente provare / aspettare
◆**use up** *v/t sep* finire
used[1] *adj car etc* usato
used[2] *adj*: **be ~ to s.o. / sth** essere abituato a qn / qc; **get ~ to s.o. / sth** abituarsi a qn / qc; **be ~ to doing sth** essere abituato a fare qc; **get ~ to doing sth** abituarsi a fare qc
used[3] *v/mod* (*only in past*): **I ~ to know him** lo conoscevo; **I ~ to like him** un tempo mi piaceva; **I don't work there now, but I ~ to** ora non più, ma una volta lavoravo lì
useful *adj information, gadget* utile; *person* di grande aiuto
usefulness *n* utilità *f inv*
useless *adj information, advice* inutile; *infml person* incapace; *machine, computer* inservibile; **feel ~** sentirsi inutile; **it's ~ trying** *there isn't any point* non serve a niente provare
user *n of product* utente *m/f*
userfriendly *adj software, device* di facile uso
usher *n* (*at wedding*) *persona che accompagna gli invitati ai loro posti*; *in a cinema* maschera *f*
◆**usher in** *v/t sep new era* inaugurare
usherette *n* maschera *f*
usual I *adj* solito; **it's not ~ for this to happen** non succede quasi mai; **as ~** come al solito **II** *n infml* **what sort of mood was he in? — the ~** di che umore era? - il solito
usually *adv* di solito
usurp *v/t* usurpare
usurper *n* usurpatore *m*, -trice *f*
usury *n* usura *f*
utensil *n* utensile *m*
uterus *n* utero *m*
utilisation, utilization *n* utilizzo *m*; utilizzazione *f*; *of resources* sfruttamento *m*
utilise, utilize *v/t* utilizzare
utilitarian I *adj* (*functional*) utilitario; *principle* utilitaristico **II** *n* utilitarista *m/f*
utility *n* (*usefulness*) utilità *f inv*; **pub-**

lic utilities servizi pubblici

utility company *n* società *f* di servizi pubblici **utility program** *n* COMPUT programma *m* di utilità **utility room** *n* ripostiglio *m*

utmost I *adj* massimo **II** *n*: ***do one's ~*** fare (tutto) il possibile

Utopia *n* utopia *f*

utter I *adj* totale **II** *v/t sound* emettere; *word* proferire

utterance *n* LING enunciato *m*; (*statement*) dichiarazione *f*; (*word*) parola *f*; (*pronunciation*) pronuncia *f*

utterly *adv* totalmente

U-turn *n* inversione *f* a U; *fig*: *in policy* dietro-front *m inv*

UV *abbr* (= **Ultraviolet**) UV (ultravioletto)

V

V, v *n* v, V *f inv*

v *abbr* (= **versus**) JUR contro; ***Italy v Germany*** SPORTS Italia-Germania

vacancy *n at work* posto *m* vacante; *in hotel* camera *f* libera; ***~ for a driver*** *as advert* autista cercasi; ***do you have any vacancies?*** avete bisogno di personale?; ***"no vacancies"*** "completo"

vacant *adj building* vuoto; *room* libero; *position* vacante; *look*, *expression* assente

vacantly *adv* con sguardo assente

vacate *v/t room* lasciar libero

vacation *n US* vacanza *f*; ***be on ~*** essere in vacanza

vacationer *n US* vacanziere *m*, -a *f*

vaccinate *v/t* vaccinare; ***be ~d against …*** essere vaccinato contro …

vaccination *n* vaccinazione *f*

vaccine *n* vaccino *m*

vacillate *v/i liter*, *fig* vacillare

vacuity *n* vacuità *f*

vacuum I *n a. fig* vuoto *m* **II** *v/t floors* passare l'aspirapolvere su

vacuum cleaner *n* aspirapolvere *m inv* **vacuum flask** *n* termos *m inv* **vacuum-packed** *adj* sottovuoto

vagabond I *n* vagabondo *m*, -a *f* **II** *v/i* vagabondare **III** *adj* vagabondo

vagina *n* vagina *f*

vaginal *adj* vaginale

vagrant *n* vagabondo *m*, -a *f*

vague *adj* (+*er*) vago; (*absent-minded*) distratto; ***I'm still ~ about it*** non ho ancora le idee chiare al riguardo; ***there's a ~ resemblance*** c'è una vaga somiglianza

vaguely *adv* vagamente

vain I *adj* (+*er*) *person* vanitoso; *hope* vano **II** *n*: ***in ~*** invano; ***their efforts were in ~*** i loro sforzi sono stati inutili

valedictory I *adj form* di commiato **II** *n* EDU discorso *m* di commiato (alla cerimonia di consegna delle lauree)

valency *n* CHEM valenza *f*

valentine *n* (*card*) *biglietto per San Valentino*; ***Valentine's Day*** San Valentino

valet I *n person* cameriere *m* personale **II** *v/t*: ***have one's car ~ed*** far lavare la macchina dentro e fuori

valet service *n for clothes* servizio *m* di lavanderia; *for cars* servizio *m* completo di lavaggio

valiant *adj* valoroso

valiantly *adv* valorosamente

valid *adj* valido

validate *v/t with official stamp* convalidare; *s.o.'s alibi* confermare

validity *n of reason*, *argument* validità *f inv*

valley *n* valle *f*

valour, *US* **valor** *n liter* valore *m*

valuable I *adj* prezioso **II** *n*: ***~s*** oggetti *mpl* di valore

valuation *n* valutazione *f*; ***at his ~*** secondo la sua valutazione

value I *n* valore *m*; ***be good ~*** essere conveniente; ***get ~ for money*** fare un affare; ***rise / fall in ~*** aumentare / perdere di valore **II** *v/t s.o.'s friendship*, *one's freedom* tenere a; ***I ~ your advice*** ci tengo alla tua opinione; ***have an object ~d*** far valutare un og-

getto
value-added tax *n* imposta *f* sul valore aggiunto
valve *n* valvola *f*
vamp *n infml* vamp *f inv*
vampire *n* vampiro *m*
van *n* furgone *m*
vandal *n* vandalo *m*
vandalise, vandalize *v/t* vandalizzare
vandalism *n* vandalismo *m*
vanguard *n* avanguardia *f*; ***be in the ~ of*** essere all'avanguardia di
vanilla I *n* vaniglia *f* **II** *adj ice cream* alla vaniglia; *flavour* di vaniglia
vanish *v/i* sparire
vanity *n of person* vanità *f inv*
vanity case *n* beauty-case *m inv*
vantage point *n on hill etc* punto *m* d'osservazione
vapid *adj* scialbo
vapor *US* → ***vapour***
vaporise, vaporize *v/t* vaporizzare
vapour, *US* **vapor** *n* vapore *m*
vapour trail, *US* **vapor trail** *n of aeroplane* scia *f*
variable I *adj* variabile **II** *n* MATH, COMPUT variabile *f*
variance *n*: ***be at ~ with*** essere inconciliabile con
variant *n* variante *f*
variation *n* variazione *f*
varicose vein *n* vena *f* varicosa
varied *adj range, diet* vario; *life* movimentato
variegated *adj* variegato; *colour* screziato
variety *n* varietà *f inv*; (*type*) tipo *m*; THEAT varietà *f inv*; ***a ~ of things to do*** varie cose da fare
varifocals *npl glasses* multifocali
various *adj* (*several*) vario; (*different*) diverso
varnish I *n for wood* vernice *f*; (*nail varnish*) smalto *m* **II** *v/t wood* verniciare; *nails* smaltare
vary *v/t & v/i* ⟨*pret & past part* ***-ied***⟩ variare
vase *n* vaso *m*
vasectomy *n* vasectomia *f*
vast *adj* (+*er*) *desert, knowledge* vasto; *improvement* immenso
vastly *adv* immensamente
vat *n* tino *m*; (*without lid*) vasca *f*
VAT *abbr* (= **value added tax**) IVA *f* (imposta *f* sul valore aggiunto)
Vatican *n*: ***the ~*** il Vaticano
vaudeville *n US* varietà *f inv*
vault[1] *n in roof* volta *f*; *cellar* cantina *f*; ***~s*** *of bank* caveau *m inv*
vault[2] **I** *n* SPORTS volteggio *m* **II** *v/t* saltare
vaunt I *n* vanto *m* **II** *v/t* vantare
vCJD *abbr* (= **new variant Creutzfeldt-Jakob disease**) vCJD *f* (nuova variante *f* del morbo di Creutzfeldt-Jakob)
VCR *abbr* (= **video cassette recorder**) videoregistratore *m*
VD *abbr* (= **venereal disease**) malattia venerea
VDU *abbr* (= **visual display unit**) VDU *f* (unità *f* di display video), monitor *m inv*
veal *n* (carne *f* di) vitello *m*
veer *v/i of car* sterzare; *of wind, party* cambiare direzione; ***~ to the left / right*** sterzare a sinistra / destra
veg *n infml* verdure *fpl*
vegan I *n* vegetaliano *m*, -a *f* **II** *adj* vegetaliano
vegetable *n* verdura *f*
vegetarian I *n* vegetariano *m*, -a *f* **II** *adj* vegetariano
vegetarianism *n* vegetarianismo *m*
vegetate *v/i of person* vegetare
vegetation *n* vegetazione *f*
vehemence *n* veemenza *f*
vehement *adj* veemente
vehemently *adv* veementemente
vehicle *n* veicolo *m*; *for information etc* mezzo *m*
veil I *n* velo *m*; ***draw*** *or* ***throw a ~ over sth*** stendere un velo pietoso su qc; ***under a ~ of secrecy*** sotto un velo di segretezza **II** *v/t* velare; *fig* ***the town was ~ed by mist*** la città era coperta dalla foschia
vein *n* ANAT vena *f*; *fig* ***in this ~*** su questo tono
Velcro® *n* velcro® *m*
velocity *n* velocità *f inv*
velour *n* TEX velours *m inv*
velvet *n* TEX velluto *m*
velveteen *n* TEX velluto *m* di cotone
velvety *adj* vellutato
venal *adj* venale
vendetta *n* vendetta *f*
vending machine *n* distributore *m* automatico
vendor *n* JUR venditore *m*, -trice *f*

veneer *n on wood* impiallacciatura *f*; *of politeness etc* parvenza *f*
venerable *adj* venerabile
venerate *v/t* venerare
veneration *n* venerazione *f*
venereal disease *n* malattia *f* venerea
Venetian I *adj* veneziano **II** *n* veneziano *m*, -a *f*
venetian blind *n* veneziana *f*
Venezuela *n* Venezuela *m*
vengeance *n* vendetta *f*; ***with a ~*** a più non posso
Venice *n* Venezia *f*
venison *n* (carne *f* di) cervo *m*
venom *n a. fig* veleno *m*
venomous *adj a. fig* velenoso
vent I *n for air* presa *f* d'aria; ***give ~ to*** *feelings, emotions* dare sfogo a **II** *v/t feelings* sfogare (***on*** su); ***~ one's spleen*** sfogare la propria collera
ventilate *v/t room, building* ventilare
ventilation *n* ventilazione *f*
ventilation shaft *n* condotto *m* di aerazione
ventilator *n* ventilatore *m*; MED respiratore *m*
ventricle *n* ANAT ventricolo *m*
ventriloquist *n* ventriloquo *m*, -a *f*
venture I *n* impresa *f*; ***mountain-climbing is his latest ~*** l'utlima avventura che ha intrapreso è l'alpinismo; ***the astronauts on their ~ into the unknown*** gli astronauti nel loro viaggio verso l'ignoto **II** *v/i* avventurarsi; ***~ to do sth*** avventurarsi a fare qc **III** *v/t life, money* scommettere (***on*** su); *guess, opinion* azzardare; ***I would ~ to say that …*** mi permetto di dire che…
venture capital *n* FIN capitale *m* di rischio
venue *n for meeting, concert etc* luogo *m*
veranda *n* veranda *f*
verb *n* verbo *m*
verbal *adj* verbale; ***~ abuse*** insulti *mpl*; ***~ attack*** attacco *m* verbale
verbalise, verbalize *v/t* esprimere a parole
verbally *adv* verbalmente; ***~ abuse s.o.*** insultare qn
verbal noun *n* GRAM sostantivo *m* verbale
verbatim *adv* parola per parola
verbose *adj* verboso
verdant *adj liter* verdeggiante
verdict *n* JUR verdetto *m*; (*opinion, judgment*) giudizio *m*; ***a ~ of guilty / not guilty*** un verdetto di colpevolezza / non colpevolezza; ***what's the ~?*** qual è il tuo parere?; ***what's your ~ on this wine?*** che ne pensi di questo vino?
verge *n of road* bordo *m*; ***be on the ~ of …*** *ruin, collapse* essere sull'orlo di …; ***on the ~ of tears*** sul punto di piangere
◆**verge on** *v/t* rasentare
verification *n* verifica *f*
verify *v/t* ⟨*pret & past part* **-ied**⟩ verificare
veritable *adj* vero
vermicelli *nsg* vermicelli *mpl*
vermin *n* animali *mpl* nocivi
vermouth *n* vermut *m inv*
vernacular *n* vernacolo *m*
versatile *adj* versatile
versatility *n* versatilità *f inv*
verse *n poetry* poesia *f*; *part of poem, song* strofa *f*
versed *adj*: ***be well ~ in a subject*** essere versato in una materia
version *n* versione *f*
versus *prep* SPORTS, JUR contro
vertebra *n* ⟨*pl* **vertebrae**⟩ vertebra *f*
vertebrate *n* vertebrato *m*
vertical *adj* verticale; ***~ cliffs*** scogliere a picco; ***~ stripes*** strisce *fpl* verticali; *wine* ***~ tasting*** degustazione *f* verticale
vertigo *n* vertigini *fpl*
verve *n* brio *m*
very I *adv* molto; ***was it cold? – not ~*** faceva freddo? – non molto; ***~ fast / easy*** molto veloce / semplice, velocissimo / semplicissimo; ***the ~ best*** il meglio; ***I ~ much hope that …*** spero tanto che …; ***that's not ~ funny*** non è molto divertente; ***I'm not ~ good at maths*** non sono molto bravo in matematica; ***~ little*** molto poco; ***~ much*** molto **II** *adj*: ***at that ~ moment*** in quel preciso momento; ***that's the ~ thing I need*** è proprio quello che mi serve; ***the ~ thought*** il solo pensiero; ***right at the ~ top / bottom*** proprio in cima / in fondo
vessel *n* NAUT natante *m*; (*receptacle*) recipiente *m*; ANAT vaso *m*
vest[1] *n* canottiera *f*; *US* (*waistcoat*) gi-

lè *m inv*
vest[2] *v/t form*: ***have a ~ed interest in sth*** avere un interesse personale in qc
vestibule *n* vestibolo *m*
vestige *n* vestigio *m* (*pl* vestigia *f*); ***not a ~ of truth*** neanche un'ombra di verità
vestigial *adj* residuo; BIOL vestigiale
vestment *n of priest* paramento *m*, (*ceremonial robe*) abito *m*
vestry *n* sagrestia *f*
vet[1] *n* (*veterinary surgeon*) veterinario *m*, -a *f*; *infml* (*veteran*) reduce *m*
vet[2] *v/t* ⟨*pret & past part* **-ted**⟩ *applicants etc* passare al vaglio; ***they ~ all candidates for the job*** hanno esaminato tutti i candidati per il lavoro
veteran I *n* veterano *m*, -a *f*; MIL reduce *m/f* **II** *adj* veterano
veterinarian *n US* veterinario *m*, -a *f*
veterinary surgeon *n* veterinario *m*, -a *f*
veto I *n* veto *m*; ***power of ~*** diritto di veto **II** *v/t* mettere il veto a
vex *v/t* (*concern, worry*) preoccupare; (*annoy*) irritare
vexation *n* (*annoyance*) fastidio *m*; (*concern*) preoccupazione *f*
vexatious *adj* (*annoying*) fastidioso; (*worrisome*) preoccupante
vexed *adj* (*worried*) preoccupato; (*annoyed*) irritato; ***the ~ question of ...*** la questione controversa di ...
VHF *abbr* (= **very high frequency**) VHF *f* (altissima frequenza *f*)
via *prep* attraverso
viability *n of plan, project* fattibilità *f*; *of firm* vitalità *f*
viable *adj life form, company* in grado di sopravvivere; ***the company is not economically ~*** l'azienda non è economicamente vitare; *alternative, plan* fattibile; ***a ~ form of government*** una forma di governo realizzabile
viaduct *n* viadotto *m*
vibes *npl infml* vibrazioni *fpl*
vibrant *adj* vivace
vibrate *v/i* vibrare
vibration *n* vibrazione *f*
vibrator *n* vibratore *m*
vicar *n* parroco *m* anglicano
vicarage *n* casa *f* del parroco
vice[1], *US* **vise** *n for holding* morsa *f*
vice[2] *n* vizio *m*
vice-chairman *n* vicepresidente *m*
vice-chairwoman *n* vicepresidente *f*
vice-chancellor *n Br* UNIV vicerettore *m*, -trice *f* **vice consul** *n* viceconsole *m* **vice president** *n* vice-presidente *m* **viceroy** *n* viceré *m inv*
vice squad *n* buoncostume *f*
vice versa *adv* viceversa
vicinity *n*: ***in the ~ of ...*** *the church etc* nelle vicinanze di ...; *£500 etc* approssimativamente ...; ***do you live in the ~?*** abiti dei dintorni?
vicious *adj dog* feroce; *attack, criticism* brutale
vicious circle *n* circolo *m* vizioso
viciously *adv* brutalmente
vicissitude *n* vicissitudine *f*
victim *n* vittima *f*; ***fall ~ to sth*** cadere vittima di qc
victimise, victimize *v/t* perseguitare
victor *n* vincitore *m*, -trice *f*
Victorian I *n* vittoriano *m*, -a *f* **II** *adj* vittoriano
victorious *adj army* vittorioso; *team* vincente; ***be ~ over s.o. / sth*** uscire vittorioso su qc / qn
victory *n* vittoria *f*; ***win a ~ over ...*** riportare una vittoria su ...
video I *n* video *m inv*; *tape* videocassetta *f*; (*VCR*) videoregistratore *m*: ***on ~*** in videocassetta **II** *v/t* registrare
video camera *n* videocamera *f* **video cassette** *n* videocassetta *f* **video clip** *n* videoclip *m inv* **video conference** *n* TEL videoconferenza *f* **video game** *n* videogame *m inv* **video library** *n* videoteca *f* **video nasty** *n Br video contenente immagini violente e offensive* **videophone** *n* videotelefono *m* **video recorder** *n* videoregistratore *m* **video recording** *n* videoregistrazione *f* **video rental** *n* videonoleggio *m*; ***~ shop*** *esp Br or* ***store*** videonoleggio *m* **video shop** *n* videonoleggio *m* **videotape** *n* videocassetta *f*
vie *v/i* competere; ***~ with s.o. for sth*** gareggiare con qn per qc
Vietnam *n* Vietnam *m*
Vietnamese I *adj* vietnamita *m/f* **II** *n* vietnamita *m/f*; *language* vietnamita *m*
view I *n* veduta *f*; ***keep sth in ~*** non perdere di vista; ***the house is within ~ of the sea*** dalla casa si vede il mare; ***hidden from ~*** nascosto dalla vista; *of situation* parere *m*; ***in ~ of*** con-

siderato; ***be on ~*** *of paintings* essere esposto; ***come into ~*** apparire, ***with a ~ to*** con l'intenzione di; ***I have no ~s on that*** non ho opinioni a riguardo; ***take the ~ that …*** pensare che…; ***an overall ~ of a problem*** una visione generale del problema; ***in full ~ of*** davanti a **II** *v/t events*, *situation* vedere; *TV programme* guardare; *house for sale* vedere **III** *v/i* (*watch TV*) guardare la TV

viewer *n TV* telespettatore *m*, -trice *f*

viewfinder *n* PHOT mirino *m* **viewpoint** *n* punto *m* di vista; ***from the ~ of economic growth*** dal punto di vista della crescita economica; ***see sth from s.o.'s ~*** vedere qc dal punto di vista di qn

vigil *n* veglia *f*; ***keep ~*** vegliare

vigilance *n* vigilanza *f*

vigilant *adj* vigile

vigilante *n* vigilante *m/f*

vigor *US* → ***vigour***

vigorous *adj* vigoroso

vigorously *adv* vigorosamente

vigour, *US* **vigor** *n* vigore *m*

Viking I *n* vichingo *m*, -a *f* **II** *adj* vichingo

vile *adj* disgustoso

vilify *v/t* ⟨*pret & past part* ***-ied***⟩ diffamare

villa *n* villa *f*

village *n* paese *m*

villager *n* abitante *m/f* (del paese)

villain *n* cattivo *m*, -a *f*; *infml criminal* delinquente *m/f*

villainous *adj* malvagio

villainy *n* infamia *f*

vim *n infml* forza *f*

vinaigrette *n* vinaigrette *f inv*

vindicate *v/t show to be correct* confermare; *show to be innocent* scagionare; ***I feel ~d by the report*** il resoconto mi dà ragione

vindication *n of opinion*, *action*, *decision* difesa *f*; (*exoneration*) discolpa *f*

vindictive *adj* vendicativo

vindictively *adv* vendicativamente

vine *n* (*grapevine*) vite *f*; *climber* rampicante *m*

vinedresser *n* vignaiolo *m*, -a *f*

vinegar *n* aceto *m*

vinegary *adj* agro; ***he was a ~ old man*** era un vecchio acido

vineyard *n* vigneto *m*

vintage I *n of wine* annata *f* **II** *adj* (*classic*) d'annata

vintage car *n* auto *f* d'epoca **vintage wine** *n* vino *m* d'annata **vintage year** *n*: ***a ~ for wine*** una buona annata per il vino

vinyl *n* vinile *m*

viola *n* MUS viola *f*

violate *v/t* violare

violation *n* violazione *f*; *of holy place* profanazione *f*; ***a ~ of a treaty*** una violazione del trattato; ***traffic ~*** violazione *f* del codice stradale

violence *n* violenza *f*; ***outbreaks of ~*** episodi *mpl* di violenza; ***act of ~*** atto *m* di violenza; ***was there any ~?*** c'è stato uso della forza?

violent *adj* violento; ***have a ~ temper*** avere un carattere violento; ***turn ~*** diventare violento

violently *adv* violentemente; ***fall ~ in love*** innamorarsi follemente; ***be ~ against sth*** *or* ***opposed to sth*** opporsi violentemente a qc; ***be ~ ill*** *or* ***sick*** avere violenti attacchi di vomito; ***cough ~*** tossire violentemente

violet *n colour* viola *m*; *plant* viola *f*

violin *n* violino *m*

violinist *n* violinista *m/f*

VIP *abbr* (= **very important person**) VIP *m/f* (persona *f* molto importante); ***he got / we gave him ~ treatment*** lo abbiamo trattato da signore

viper *n snake* vipera *f*

viperous *adj* viperino

virago *n* virago *f*

viral *adj infection* virale

virgin I *n* vergine *m/f*; ***the Virgin Mary*** la Vergine Maria; ***he's still a ~*** è ancora vergine **II** *adj fig forest etc* vergine; ***~ olive oil*** olio d'oliva extravergine

virginal I *adj* verginale **II** *n* MUS virginale

virginity *n* verginità *f inv*; ***lose one's ~*** perdere la verginità

Virgo *n* ASTROL Vergine *f*

virile *adj* virile

virility *n* virilità *f inv*

virology *n* MED virologia *f*

virtual *adj* effettivo; ***she was a ~ prisoner*** era praticamente un prigionero; ***it was a ~ admission of guilt*** è stata di fatto un'ammissione di colpa; COMPUT virtuale

virtually *adv* (*almost*) praticamente; ***be ~ certain*** essere praticamente sicuro
virtual reality *n* realtà *f* virtuale
virtue *n* virtù *f inv*; ***in ~ of*** in virtù di
virtuoso *n* MUS virtuoso *m*, -a *f*
virtuous *adj* virtuoso
virulent *adj disease* virulento; *fig: attack, hatred* feroce
virus *n* MED, COMPUT virus *m inv*; ***polio ~*** virus della polio; ***she's got a ~*** *infml* ha un virus
virus scanner *n* COMPUT antivirus *m inv*
visa *n* visto *m*
visage *n liter* volto *m*
vis-à-vis *prep* vis-à-vis
viscera *npl* viscere *fpl*
visceral *adj* viscerale; (*instinctive*) istintivo
viscose *n* viscosa *f*
viscount *n* visconte *m*
viscountess *n* viscontessa *f*
viscous *adj* viscoso
vise *US* → ***vice***[1]
visibility *n* visibilità *f inv*; METEO visibilità *f*; ***poor ~*** scarsa visibilità
visible *adj object, difference* visibile; *anger* evidente; ***not ~ to the naked eye*** invisible ad occhio nudo
visibly *adv different* visibilmente; ***he was ~ moved*** era visibilmente emozionato
vision *n* (*eyesight*) vista *f*; REL *etc* visione *f*; (*foresight*) lungimiranza *f*; *in dream* immagine *f*; ***within ~*** in vista
visionary *n* lungimirante *m/f*
visit I *v/t person* andare a trovare; ***come and ~ some time*** vieni a trovarmi qualche volta; *place, country, city* visitare; ***I'm only ~ing*** sono venuto solo a farti un saluto; *doctor, dentist* andare da **II** *n* visita *f*; ***pay a ~ to the doctor / dentist*** andare dal medico / dentista; ***pay s.o. a ~*** fare una visita a qn
◆ **visit with** *v/t US* fare due chiacchiere con
visitation *n* visita *f*; (*punishment*) castigo *m* divino; REL visitazione *f*
visiting card *n* biglietto *m* da visita
visiting hours *npl at hospital* orario *m* delle visite **visiting professor** *n* visiting professor *m/f inv* **visiting time** *n* orario *m* delle visite
visitor *n* (*guest*) ospite *m*; *to museum etc* visitatore *m*, -trice *f*; (*tourist*) turista *m/f*
visor *n* visiera *f*
vista *n* vista *f*
visual *adj organs, memory* visivo, *arts* figurativo
visual aid *n* sussidio *m* visivo **visual arts** *n*: ***the ~*** le arti figurative **visual display unit** *n* videoterminale *m*
visualise, visualize *v/t* immaginare; (*foresee*) prevedere
visually impaired *adj* videoleso
vital *adj* (*essential*) essenziale; ***it is ~ that …*** è essenziale che …; ***of ~ importance*** di vitale importanza; ***how ~ is this?*** quanto è indispensabile questo?
vitality *n of person, city etc* vitalità *f inv*
vitally *adv*: ***~ important*** di vitale importanza
vital organs *npl* organi *mpl* vitali **vital signs** *npl* MED segni *mpl* di vita **vital statistics** *npl of woman* misure *fpl*
vitamin *n* vitamina *f*
vitamin pill *n* (confetto *m* di) vitamina *f*
vitiate *v/t* viziare
viticulture *n* viticoltura *f*
vitreous *adj* vitreo
vitrification *n* vetrificazione *f*
vitrify I *v/t* vetrificare **II** *v/i* vetrificarsi
vitriolic *adj* caustico
vitro *adj/adv* → ***in vitro***
vituperate *v/t* vituperare
vituperation *n* ingiurie *fpl*
vituperative *adj* ingiurioso
vivacious *adj* vivace
vivacity *n* vivacità *f inv*
viva voce *n Br* esame *m* orale
vivid *adj* vivido; ***in ~ detail*** con abbondanza di dettagli; ***the memory of that day is still quite ~*** il ricordo di quel giorno è ancora piuttosto nitido
vividly *adv* in modo vivido; ***the red stands out ~ against its background*** il rosso risalta vivacemente sul fondo
vivisection *n* vivisezione *f*
vivisectionist *n* vivisettore *m*, -trice *f*
vixen *n* volpe *f* femmina
V-neck *n* maglione *m* con scollo a V
V-necked *adj* con scollo a V
vocabulary *n* vocabolario *m*; *list of*

words glossario *m*
vocal I *adj to do with the voice* vocale; *expressing opinions* eloquente; ***become ~*** cominciare a farsi sentire **II** *n*: ***~s: Van Morrison*** voce: Van Morrison; ***featuring Madonna on ~s*** con Madonna alla voce; ***backing ~s*** accompagnamento vocale
vocal cords *npl* corde *fpl* vocali **vocal group** *n* MUS gruppo *m* vocale
vocalist *n* MUS cantante *m/f*
vocal score *n* MUS partitura *f* vocale
vocation *n* (*calling*) vocazione *f* (***for*** a); (*profession*) professione *f*
vocational *adj guidance* professionale; ***~ training*** formazione *f* professionale
vocational school *n US* scuola *f* (per l'avviamento) professionale
vociferate *v/t & v/i* vociferare
vociferous *adj* che si fa sentire
vodka *n* vodka *f inv*
vogue *n* moda *f*; ***be in ~*** essere in voga
voice I *n* voce *f*; ***I've lost my ~*** ho perso la voce; ***in a deep ~*** con voce profonda; ***his ~ has broken*** la sua voce è cambiata; ***give ~ to sth*** dare voce a qc; GRAM voce *f*; ***the passive ~*** la forma passiva **II** *v/t opinions* esprimere
voice-activated *adj* COMPUT con attivazione vocale **voice box** *n* laringe *f* **voice mail** *n* segreteria *f* telefonica **voice-operated** *adj* a comando vocale **voice-over** *n* voce *f* fuori campo **voice recognition** *n* riconoscimento *m* vocale
void I *n* vuoto *m* **II** *adj*: ***~ of*** privo di; ***~ of any sense of decency*** privo di ogni senso della decenza **III** *v/t* annullare
voile *n* TEX voile *m inv*
vol *abbr* (= **volume**) volume
volatile *adj personality, moods* volubile; CHEM volatile
vol-au-vent *n* vol-au-vent *m inv*
volcanic *adj liter* vulcanico
volcano *n* vulcano *m*
volcanology *n* vulcanologia *f*
vole *n cards* cappotto *m*; (*common vole*) topo *m* campagnolo
volition *n* volizione *f*; ***of one's own ~*** di propria sponte
volley I *n of shots* raffica *f*; *in tennis* volée *f inv* **II** *v/t*: ***~ a ball*** (*tennis*) prendere la palla di volée **III** *v/i* (*tennis*) fare una volée
volleyball *n* pallavolo *f*
volt *n* ELEC volt *m inv*
voltage *n* ELEC voltaggio *m*; ***high ~*** alta tensione *f*
voltaic *adj* ELEC voltaico
voltaic battery *n* ELEC batteria *f* voltaica **voltaic cell** *n* ELEC cellula *f* galvanica
voluble *adj* (*talkative*) loquace
volume *n* volume *m*; ***a six-~ dictionary*** un dizionario in sei volumi; ***that speaks ~s*** *fig* la dice lunga (***for*** su); (*USount*) volume *m* (***of*** di); ***the ~ of traffic*** il volume di traffico; (*sound*) volume *m*; ***turn the ~ up / down*** alzare / abbassare il volume
volume control *n* volume *m*
voluminous *adj skirts etc* ampio
voluntarily *adv* spontaneamente
voluntary *adj helper* volontario; ***~ work*** volontariato; ***a ~ organization for social work*** un'organizzazione volontaria per l'assistenza sociale
voluntary redundancy *n* dimissioni *fpl* volontarie; ***take ~*** presentare le dimissioni
volunteer I *n* volontario *m*, -a *f* **II** *v/i* offrirsi volontario; ***~ to do sth*** offrirsi di fare qc; ***who will ~ to clean the windows?*** chi si offre volontario per pulire le finestre?; MIL arruolarsi come volontario
voluptuous *adj woman, figure* giunonico
volute *n* ARCH voluta *f*
vomit I *v/i* vomitare **II** *n* vomito *m*
◆**vomit up** *v/t sep* vomitare
voracious *adj appetite* vorace
voraciously *adv eat* voracemente; *fig: read* avidamente
vote I *v/i* POL votare; ***~ for / against s.o. / sth*** votare a favore di / contro qn / qc **II** *v/t*: ***they ~d him President*** l'hanno eletto presidente; ***I ~ we stay behind*** propongo di rimanere **III** *n* voto *m*; *right to vote* diritto *m* di voto; ***take a ~ on sth*** votare per qc; ***get the ~*** ottenere il diritto di voto; ***put sth to the ~*** mettere qc al voto; ***he won by 22 ~s*** ha vinto per 22 voti; ***the Labour ~*** il voto laburista
◆**vote in** *v/t sep new member* eleggere
◆**vote on** *v/t issue* mettere ai voti
◆**vote out** *v/t sep of office* respingere

voter *n* POL elettore *m*, -trice *f*
voting *n* POL votazione *f*; ***a system of ~*** sistema *f* di votazione; ***~ was heavy*** si sono presentati molti votanti
voting booth *n* cabina *f* elettorale
votive *adj* votivo
◆**vouch for** *v/t truth of sth* garantire; *person* garantire per
voucher *n* buono *m*
vouchsafe *v/t liter* concedere
vow I *n* voto *m*; REL voto *m*; ***make a ~ to do sth*** fare voto per fare qc; ***take one's ~s*** prendere i voti **II** *v/t*: ***~ to do sth*** giurare di fare qc
vowel *n* vocale *f*; ***~ sound*** suono *m* vocalico
voyage I *n by sea, in space* viaggio *m*; ***go on a ~*** intraprendere un viaggio **II** *v/t* viaggiare **III** *v/i* percorrere
voyeur *n* voyeur *m inv*
vs *abbr* (= **versus**)
V-sign *n for victory* segno *m* di vittoria; ***give s.o. the ~*** *mandare qn a quel paese*
VSO *abbr* **1.** (= **very superior old**) *cognac* stravecchio superiore **2.** (= **Voluntary Service Overseas**) servizio volontario oltremare
VSOP *abbr* (= **very special** *or* **superior old pale**) *cognac* stravecchio superiore paglierino
VTOL *abbr* (= **vertical takeoff and landing**) VTOL (decollo e atterraggio verticale)
vulgar *adj person, language* volgare
vulgarity *n* volgarità *f*
vulgate *n* vulgata *f*
vulnerable *adj* vulnerabile
vulture *n* avvoltoio *m*; ***culture ~*** persona *f* avida di cultura
vulva *n* ANAT vulva *f*

W

W, w *n* w, W *f inv*
W *abbr* (= **west**) ovest (O)
wacky *adj* (*+er*) *infml* (*crazy*) eccentrico
wad *n of cotton wool* batuffolo *m*; *of paper* fascio *m*; *of banknotes* mazzetta *f*
wadding *n* (*for packing*) imbottitura *f*
waddle *v/i* camminare ondeggiando
wade *v/i* guadare
◆**wade in** *v/i liter* gettarsi nella mischia; *fig infml* mettersi di buona lena
◆**wade into** *v/i +obj fig infml* (*attack*) ***wade into s.o.*** scagliarsi contro qn; ***wade into sth*** buttarsi a capofitto su qc
◆**wade through** *v/t*: ***I've still got this lot to wade through*** devo ancora leggermi tutto questo
wader *n bird* trampoliere *m*
waders *npl* stivaloni *mpl* (da pesca)
WAF *abbr US* (= **Women in the Air Force**) *corpo femminile delle forze aeree*
wafer *n biscuit* cialda *f*; REL ostia *f*
wafer-thin *adj* sottilissimo
waffle[1] *n* COOK *tipo di cialda*
waffle[2] **I** *v/i* parlare a vuoto **II** *n* sproloquio *m*
waft I *n* soffio *m* **II** *v/i of smell, noise* diffondersi; ***a delicious smell ~ed up from the kitchen*** un odore delizioso si diffondeva dalla cucina
wag[1] ⟨*pret & past part* **-ged**⟩ **I** *v/t finger* scuotere; ***the dog ~ged its tail*** il cane scodinzolò **II** *v/i*: ***the dog's tail was ~ging*** il cane scodinzolava
wag[2] *n* (*wit, clown*) burlone *m*
wage[1] *v/t*: ***~ war against*** *a. fig* fare la guerra a
wage[2] *n* paga *f*; ***~s*** paga *f*
wage claim *n* rivendicazione *f* salariale **wage earner** *n* salariato *m*, -a *f* **wage freeze** *n* blocco *m* dei salari **wage negotiations** *npl* rivendicazioni *fpl* salariali **wage packet** *n fig* busta *f* paga
wager I *v/t* (*bet*) scommettere **II** *n* (*bet*) scommessa *f*; ***make a ~*** scommettere
waggle *v/t ears, loose screw, tooth etc* far

muovere; **~ one's hips** ancheggiare
wagon, *US* **waggon** *n* RAIL carro *m* merci; **be on the ~** *infml* non bere alcolici
wail I *v/i of person* gemere; *of baby* vagire; *of siren* ululare **II** *n of person* gemito *m*; *of baby* vagito *m*; *of siren* ululato *m*
waist *n* vita *f*; **she has a slim ~** ha una vita sottile
waistband *n* cintura *f* **waistcoat** *n* gilè *m inv* **waist-deep** *adj* che arriva in vita; **we stood ~ in the snow** la neve ci arrivava in vita **waistline** *n* vita *f*
wait I *v/i* aspettare; **we'll ~ until he's ready** aspetteremo che sia pronto; **I can't ~ to ...** non vedo l'ora di ...; **~ and see!** aspetta e vedrai! **II** *v/t meal* ritardare; **~ tables** *US* servire ai tavoli **III** *n* attesa *f*; **have a long ~** dover aspettare a lungo; **lie in ~ for s.o.** aspettare qn al varco
◆**wait about** *Br or* **around** *v/i* restare ad aspettare
◆**wait for** *v/t* aspettare; **wait for me!** aspettami!; **wait for s.o. to do sth** aspettare che qn faccia qc
◆**wait on** *v/t* (*serve*) servire
◆**wait up** *v/i* restare alzato ad aspettare
waiter *n* cameriere *m*; **~!** cameriere!
waiting *n* attesa *f*; **no ~ sign** divieto *m* di sosta; **all this ~ (around)** tutta questa attesa; **~ is hard work** l'attesa è un lavoro duro
waiting list *n* lista *f* d'attesa **waiting room** *n* sala *f* d'attesa
waitress *n* cameriera *f*
waive *v/t* (*renoune*) rinunciare a; (*dispense with*) fare al meno di, lasciar perdere
waiver *n* JUR rinuncia *f* (**of** di); (*document*) deroga *f*
wake[1] ⟨*pret* **woke**, *past part* **woken**⟩ **I** *v/i*: **~ (up)** svegliarsi; **he woke to find himself in prison** si svegliò e si ritrovò in prigione **II** *v/t* svegliare
wake[2] *n of ship* scia *f*; *fig* **in the ~ of** a seguito di; **follow in the ~ of** seguire le tracce di
wakeful *adj* sveglio
waken *form* **I** *v/t* svegliare **II** *v/i* svegliarsi
wake-up call *n* sveglia *f* (telefonica)
Wales *n* Galles *m*
walk I *v/i* camminare; *as opposed to taking the car, bus etc* andare a piedi; (*hike*) passeggiare; **learn to ~** imparare a camminare; **we ~ed for hours** abbiamo camminato per ore; **she ~ed over to the window** andò alla finestra **II** *v/t dog* portare fuori; **I'll ~ you home** ti accompagno a casa; **~ the streets** (*walk around*) girare in lungo e in largo; *prostitute* passeggiare **III** *n* camminata *f*; **it's a long ~ to the office** è una bella camminata fino all'ufficio; **it's a short ~ to the office** l'ufficio è a due passi; **go for a ~** fare due passi; **from all ~s of life** di ogni ceto
◆**walk about** *Br or* **around** *v/i* andare in giro
◆**walk away** *v/i* andare via; **walk away with a prize** portarsi a casa un premio
◆**walk in on** *v/t* scoprire
◆**walk into** *v/t room* entrare in; *wall* sbattere contro; **walk into a trap** cadere in una trappola; **he just walked into the first job he applied for** ha avuto il primo lavoro per il quale aveva fatto domanda; **walk right into sth** *liter* cascarci in pieno
◆**walk off I** *v/t sep* **walk off one's lunch** *etc* camminare per digerire il pranzo **II** *v/i* andarsene
◆**walk off with** *v/t infml* (*take*) (*unintentionally*) andarsene con; (*intentionally*) portare via; *prize* portare a casa
◆**walk on I** *v/t grass etc* camminare su **II** *v/i* (*continue walking*) continuare a camminare
◆**walk out** *v/i of husband etc*, *from theatre* andarsene; (*go on strike*) scendere in sciopero
◆**walk out on** *v/t spouse*, *family* abbandonare
walkabout *n* bagno *m* di folla; **go (on) ~** *infml of monarch, politician* fare un bagno di folla
walker *n* (*hiker*) escursionista *m/f*; *for baby* girello *m*; *for old person* deambulatore *m*; **be a slow / fast ~** avere il passo lento / spedito
walkie-talkie *n* walkie-talkie *m inv*
walk-in *adj*: **~ closet** cabina armadio *f*
walking I *n as opposed to driving* camminare *m*; (*hiking*) escursionismo *m*;

we did a lot of ~ while we were in Wales abbiamo fatto molte camminate quando eravamo in Galles **II** *adj encyclopaedia etc* ambulante; ***at (a) ~ pace*** a passo d'uomo; ***the ~ wounded*** feriti in grado di camminare, ***it's within ~ distance*** ci si arriva a piedi

walking boots *npl* scarponi *mpl* da escursione **walking frame** *n* deambulatore *m* **walking shoes** *npl* scarpe *fpl* da passeggio **walking stick** *n* bastone *m* da passeggio **walking tour** *n* escursionismo *m*

Walkman® *n* walkman® *m inv* **walk-on part** *n in film, play* ruolo *m* di comparsa **walkout** *n strike* sciopero *m* selvaggio **walkover** *n (easy win)* vittoria *f* facile

wall *n external* muro *m*; ***the Great Wall of China*** la grande muraglia cinese; *internal* parete *f*; *fig*: *of silence etc* muro *m*; ***go to the ~*** *of company* andare in rovina; ***~s*** *of a city* mura *fpl*; ***drive s.o. up the ~*** *infml* far diventare matto qn

◆**wall off** *v/t sep* separare con un muro

wall bars *npl* spalliera *f* (svedese)

wallchart *n* cartellone *m*

wall clock *n* orologio *m* da muro

wallet *n* portafoglio *m*

walleye *n* MED *(glaucoma)* glaucoma *f* della cornea; *(strabismus)* strabismo *m* divergente

wallflower *n flower* violacciocca *f* gialla; ***be a ~*** *infml* fare tappezzeria

wallop I *v/t infml* colpire; *opponent* stracciare *infml* **II** *n infml blow* colpo *m*

wallow *v/i* rotolarsi; ***~ in mud*** rotolarsi nel fango; *fig*: ***~ in self-pity*** *etc* autocommiserarsi

wallpaper I *n* tappezzeria *f*, carta *f* da parati **II** *v/t* tappezzare **wall-to-wall** *adj*: ***~ carpet*** moquette *f*

wally *n Br infml* stupido *m*, -a *f*

walnut *n* noce *f*

walrus *n* tricheco *m*

waltz I *n* valzer *m inv* **II** *v/i* ballare il valzer

◆**waltz in** *v/i infml* ***come waltzing in*** entrare in modo disinvolto

◆**waltz off** *v/i infml* uscire in modo disinvolto

◆**waltz off with** *v/t infml prizes* vincere senza difficoltà

wan *adj face* pallido

wand *n* bacchetta *f* magica

wander I *n* passeggiata *f*; ***go for a ~ (a)round the shops*** fare un giro per negozi **II** *v/t*: ***~ the streets*** andare in giro per le strade **III** *v/i (roam)* gironzolare; *(more aimlessly)* vagabondare (***through, about*** per); *(leisurely)* girovagare; ***he ~ed in a dream state*** farneticava come se fosse in un sogno; ***he ~ed over to me*** si è avvicinato tranquillamente verso di me; *(stray)* allontanarsi; ***the children had ~ed out onto the street*** il bambini erano usciti in strada; ***my attention began to ~*** mi sono distratto

◆**wander about** *Br or* **around** *v/i* girovagare

◆**wander around** *v/i* girare

◆**wander in** *v/i* arrivare tranquillamente

◆**wander off** *v/i* allontanarsi; ***he must have wandered off somewhere*** sarà andato a nascondersi da qualche parte

wane I *n*: *fig* ***be on the ~*** essere in declino **II** *v/i moon* essere calante; *of interest, enthusiasm* calare

wangle *v/t infml* rimediare *infml*; ***~ sth out of s.o.*** strappare qc a qn

wank *v/i Br vulg (a.* **wank off**) farsi una sega

wanker *n Br vulg* segaiolo *m*

wanna → ***want to***; ***I ~ go*** voglio andare

wannabe *n infml* aspirante *m/f*

want I *v/t* **1.** volere; ***~ to do sth*** volere fare qc; ***I ~ to stay here*** voglio stare qui; ***do you ~ to come too? – no, I don't ~ to*** vuoi venire anche tu? – no, grazie; ***you can have whatever you ~*** puoi avere tutto ciò che vuoi; ***it's not what I ~ed*** non è quello che volevo; ***she ~s you to go back*** vuole che torni indietro **2.** *(need)* avere bisogno di; ***he ~s a haircut*** dovrebbe tagliarsi i capelli **II** *v/i*: ***~ for nothing*** non mancare di niente **III** *n*: ***for ~ of*** per mancanza di; ***it wasn't for ~ of trying*** non perché non ci avevamo provato

want ad *n* annuncio *m* economico

wanted *adj by police* ricercato

wanting *adj*: ***be ~ in*** mancare di; ***it's***

good, but there is something ~ è buono ma ci manca qualcosa; ***his courage was found ~*** il suo coraggio non è stato ritenuto all'altezza
wanton *adj cruelty, neglect* gratuito; (*lewd*) licenzioso
WAP *abbr* (= **wireless application protocol**) WAP *m*
war *n* guerra *f*; *fig* lotta *f*; ***be at ~*** essere in guerra; ***this is ~!*** *fig* ora te la faccio vedere io; ***the ~ against disease*** la lorra contro la malattia; ***~ of words*** conflitto verbale; ***declare ~*** dichiarare guerra (***on*** a); ***I hear you've been in the ~s recently*** *infml* ho sentito che recentemente sei conciato male
warble I *n* gorgheggio *m* **II** *v/i of bird* gorgheggiare
warbler *n bird* uccello *m* canoro; *singer* gorgheggiatore *m*, trice *f*
war bride *n* sposa *f* di guerra **war crime** *n* crimine *m* di guerra **war cry** *n* grido *m* di guerra
ward *n in hospital* corsia *f*; JUR *child* minore *m* sotto tutela; ***~ of court*** minore *m/f* (sotto tutela)
◆**ward off** *v/t sep blow* parare; *attacker* respingere; *cold* combattere
warden *n* (*traffic warden*) vigile *m* urbano; *of hostel* direttore *m*, -trice *f*; *of nature reserve* guardiano *m*, -a *f*; *US*: *of prison* agente *m/f* di custodia
warder *n* agente *m/f* di custodia
wardrobe *n for clothes* armadio *m*; *clothes* guardaroba *m*
ware *n* articoli *mpl*; ***they sell their ~s on the streets*** vendono la loro merce per strada
warehouse *n* magazzino *m*
warfare *n* guerra *f*; ***chemical ~*** guerra *f* chimica **warhead** *n* testata *f* **war hero** *n* eroe *m* di guerra
warhorse *n liter*, *fig* cavallo *m* di battaglia
warily *adv* con aria guardinga
warlord *n in China*, *Japan* signore *m* della guerra; *fig* dittatore *m*, trice *f*
warm I *adj* (*+er*) caldo; *welcome*, *smile* caloroso; ***it's ~*** *of weather* fa caldo; ***it's ~ in here*** qui c'è caldo; ***are you ~ enough?*** ti fa freddo? **II** *n*: ***get into the ~*** mettersi al caldo; ***give sth a ~*** riscaldare qc **III** *v/t* riscaldare; ***your smile ~s my heart*** il tuo sorriso mi scalda il cuore **IV** *v/i*: ***the milk was ~ing on the stove*** il latte si stava scaldando sul fuoco; ***I ~ed to him*** l'ho preso in simpatia
◆**warm up I** *v/t sep* scaldare **II** *v/i* scaldarsi; *of athlete etc* fare riscaldamento
warm-blooded *adj* passionale
warmhearted *adj* cordiale
warmly *adv dressed* con abiti pesanti; *welcome*, *smile* calorosamente
warmonger *n* guerrafondaio *m*, -a *f*
warmth *n* calore *m*; *of welcome*, *smile* calorosità *f inv*
warm-up *n* SPORTS riscaldamento *m*; ***the teams had a ~ before the game*** le squadre hanno fatto riscaldamento prima della partita
warn *v/t* avvertire; ***~ s.o. not to do sth*** avvertire qn di non fare qc; ***you have been ~ed!*** sei stato avvisato!; ***you might have ~ed us that you were coming*** ci avresti potuto avvisare del fatto che stavi arrivando
◆**warn off** *v/t sep person* sconsigliare
warning *n* avvertimento *m*; ***without ~*** senza preavviso
warning light *n* spia *f* luminosa
warp I *v/t wood* deformare; *character* segnare **II** *v/i of wood* deformarsi
war paint *n tribe* pittura *f* di guerra; *fig hum* trucco *m*
warpath *n*: ***be on the ~*** essere sul piede di guerra
warped *adj fig* contorto; *fig sense of humour* perverso; *judgement* distorto
warplane *n* aereo *m* militare
warrant I *n* mandato *m*; ***a ~ of arrest*** mandato *m* d'arresto **II** *v/t* (*deserve*, *call for*) giustificare
warranty *n* (*guarantee*) garanzia *f*; ***be under ~*** essere in garanzia
warrior *n* guerriero *m*, -a *f*
warship *n* nave *f* da guerra
wart *n* verruca *f*
wartime *n* tempo *m* di guerra
wary *adj* (*+er*) guardingo; ***be ~ of*** diffidare di
war zone *n* zona *f* di guerra
was *pret* → ***be***
wash I *v/t* lavare; ***~ one's hands / hair*** lavarsi le mani / i capelli **II** *v/i* lavarsi; ***he always ~es for dinner*** si lava sempre prima di andare a cena; ***a material that ~es well*** un materiale che si

lava bene; (*sea etc*) lambire; ***the sea ~ed over the promenade*** il mare spazzava il lungomare; *Br infml* ***your excuse doesn't ~ with me*** la tua scusa con me non attacca **III** *n*: ***have a ~*** darsi una lavata; ***that skirt needs a ~*** quella gonna va lavata; ***be in the ~*** (*waiting to be washed*) essere con la biancheria da lavare; (*being washed*) essere a lavare
◆**wash away** *v/t sep liter* lavare via
◆**wash down** *v/t sep walls* lavare con l'acqua; *food* aiutare a mandare giù
◆**wash off** **I** *v/i* andare via (con il lavaggio) **II** *v/t sep* rimuovere (con il lavaggio); ***wash that grease off your hands*** lava via quel grasso dalle mani
◆**wash out** **I** *v/i* andare via (con il lavaggio) **II** *v/t sep* (*clean*) lavare; *mouth* sciacquare; *game etc* far annullare
◆**wash over** *v/t*: ***he lets everything just wash over him*** tutto lo lascia totalmente indifferente
◆**wash up** *v/i Br* (*wash the dishes*) lavare i piatti
washable *adj* lavabile
washbag *n* nécessaire *m inv* da toeletta **washbasin, washbowl** *n* lavandino *m* **washcloth** *n US* asciugamano *m* per il viso
washed out *adj* sfinito
washer *n for tap etc* guarnizione *f*; → ***washing machine***
washing *n washed clothes* bucato *m*; *clothes to be washed* biancheria *f* da lavare; ***do the ~*** fare il bucato
washing machine *n* lavatrice *f* **washing powder** *n* detersivo *m* per bucato **washing-up** *n*: ***do the ~*** lavare i piatti **washing-up liquid** *n* detersivo *m* per i piatti
washout *n infml failure* fiasco *m*
washroom *n US toilet* toilette *f inv*
washstand *n* lavabo *m*
washy *adj* acquoso
wasn't → ***was not***
wasp *n* vespa *f*
waspish *adj* stizzoso
wastage *n* spreco *m*
waste **I** *n* spreco *m*; *from industrial process* rifiuti *mpl*; ***it's a ~ of time / money*** è tempo sprecato / sono soldi sprecati; ***go to ~*** (*food*) andare a male; (*energy*) andare sprecato; (*land*) rinselvatichire **II** *adj material* di scarto **III** *v/t* sprecare; ***don't ~ my time*** non farmi sprecare tempo; ***you didn't ~ much time getting here!*** *infml* non hai perso un minuto per venire qua!; ***all our efforts were ~d*** tutti i nostri sforzi sono andati sprecati; ***I wouldn't ~ my breath talking to him*** non sprecherei il mio fiato per parlare con lui; ***Beethoven is ~d on him*** non sa apprezzare Beethoven
◆**waste away** *v/i* deperire
wastebasket *n*, **wastebin** *n esp US* cestino *m* per la carta
wasted *adj* (*emaciated*) emaciato; ***I've had a ~ journey*** ho fatto un viaggio a vuoto
waste disposal (unit) *n* tritarifiuti *m inv*
wasteful *adj person* sprecone; *methods, processes* dispendioso
wasteland *n* distesa *f* desolata **wastepaper** *n* cartaccia *f* **wastepaper basket** *n* cestino *m* della cartaccia **waste pipe** *n* tubo *m* di scarico **waste product** *n* scorie *fpl* industriali
waster *n* sprecone *m*, a *f*
wastrel *n* sprecone *m*, a *f*
watch **I** *v/t film, TV* guardare; (*spy on*) sorvegliare; (*look after*) tenere d'occhio; ***~ it!*** occhio! **II** *v/i* guardare **III** *n timepiece* orologio *m*; MIL guardia *f*; ***keep ~*** stare all'erta
◆**watch for** *v/t* aspettare
◆**watch out** *v/i* fare attenzione; ***watch out!*** attento!
◆**watch out for** *v/t* fare attenzione a
◆**watch over** *v/t* proteggere
watchdog *n* comitato *m* di controllo
watchful *adj* vigile; ***keep a ~ eye on s.o. / sth*** tenere d'occhio qn / qc
watchmaker *n* orologiaio *m*, -a *f* **watchman** *n* guardiano *m* **watchstrap** *n* cinturino *m* dell'orologio **watchtower** *n* torre *f* di guardia **watchword** *n* motto *m*; (*password*) parola *f* d'ordine
water **I** *n* acqua *f*; ***~s*** NAUT acque (territoriali); ***be under ~*** essere sott'acqua; ***take in ~*** (*ship*) imbarcare acqua; ***not to hold ~*** fare acqua; ***~s*** acque *fpl*; ***pass ~*** fare acqua; *fig* (*phrases*) ***keep one's head above ~*** stare a galla; ***pour cold ~ on s.o.'s idea*** raffreddare gli entusiasmi di qn; ***get (o.s.)***

into deep ~(s) mettersi nei guai; ***a lot of ~ has flowed under the bridge since then*** ne è passata di acqua sotto i ponti da allora; ***get into hot ~*** *infml* mettersi nei pasticci **II** *v/t plant* annaffiare **III** *v/i of eyes* lacrimare; ***my mouth is ~ing*** ho l'acquolina in bocca

◆**water down** *v/t sep drink* diluire

water bed *n* letto *m* con materasso ad acqua **waterborne** *adj*: ***a ~ disease*** una malattia trasmessa attraverso l'acqua **water bottle** *n* borraccia *f* **water butt** *n* cisterna per la raccolta dell'acqua **water cannon** *n* idrante *m* **watercolour**, *US* **watercolor** *n* acquerello *m* **water cooler** *n* distributore *m* d'acqua fresca **watercourse** *n* (*stream*) corso *m* d'acqua; (*artificial*) canale; (*bed*) letto *m* del fiume **watercress** *n* crescione *m*

watered down *adj fig* edulcorato

waterfall *n* cascata *f* **waterfowl** *npl* uccello *m* acquatico **waterfront** *n* lungomare *m inv*, lungofiume *m inv* **water gun** *n esp US* = ***water pistol*** **water heater** *n* scaldaacqua *m*

watering can *n* annaffiatoio *m* **watering hole** *n hum* bar *m inv*

water level *n* livello *m* delle acque **water lily** *n* ninfea *f* **water line** *n* linea *f* di galleggiamento

waterlogged *adj* allagato

water main *n* conduttura *f* dell'acqua **water mark** *n* filigrana *f* **water melon** *n* anguria *f*, cocomero *m* **water meter** *n* contatore *m* dell'acqua **water mill** *n* mulino *m* ad acqua **water noodle** *n* SPORTS cilindro *m* flessibile **water pistol** *n* pistola *f* ad acqua **water pollution** *n* inquinamento *m* dell'acqua **water polo** *n* pallanuoto *f* **waterproof** *adj* impermeabile **water-repellent** *adj* idrorepellente **water-resistant** *adj* impermeabile; *sunscreen* resistente all'acqua **watershed** *n fig* svolta *f*; TV *ora dopo la quale sono ammessi programmi per un pubblico adulto* **waterside** *n*: ***at the ~*** sulla riva **waterskiing** *n* sci *m inv* nautico **watertight** *adj compartment* stagno; *fig* inattaccabile **waterway** *n* corso *m* d'acqua navigabile **waterwings** *npl* braccioli *mpl* **waterworks** *nsg or npl*: ***turn on the ~*** *infml* piangere

watery *adj* acquoso; *eye* che lacrima; *sun* pallido

watt *n* watt *m inv*

wave[1] *n in sea* onda *f*; ***a ~ of strikes*** un'ondata di scioperi; ***make ~s*** *fig infml* creare problemi

wave[2] **I** *n of hand* saluto *m* (con la mano) **II** *v/i with hand* salutare (con la mano); ***~ to s.o.*** salutare qn (con la mano); ***~ goodbye to*** salutare con la mano **III** *v/t flag etc* sventolare; ***he ~d his hat*** sventolava il cappello; ***he ~d me over*** mi fece segno di avvicinarmi

◆**wave aside** *v/t sep fig suggestions etc* scartare

◆**wave on** *v/t sep* ***the policeman waved us on*** il poliziotto ci fece segno di proseguire

wavelength *n* RADIO lunghezza *f* d'onda; *fig* ***be on the same ~*** essere sulla stessa lunghezza d'onda

waver *v/i* vacillare

wavy *adj* (*+er*) *hair*, *line* ondulato

wax I *n for floor*, *furniture* cera *f*; *in ear* cerume *m* **II** *v/t floor*, *furniture* lucidare*car* dare la cera a; *legs* fare la ceretta a

waxen *adj* di cera; (*pale*) cereo

waxworks *nsg museum* museo *m* delle cere

way I *n* **1.** (*method*, *manner*) modo *m*; (*manner*) maniera *f*; ***this ~*** (*like this*) così; ***OK, we'll do it your ~*** OK, faremo come dici tu; ***in a ~*** (*in certain respects*) in un certo senso; ***that's his ~ of saying thank you*** questo è il suo modo di ringraziare; ***the French ~ of doing it*** la maniera francese di farlo; ***learn the hard ~*** imparare a proprie spese; ***~ of thinking*** modo di pensare; ***what a ~ to live!*** (*unpleasant*) che maniera di vivere!; ***get one's (own) ~*** fare di testa propria; ***have it your own ~!*** fai come vuoi!; ***one ~ or another/the other*** in un modo o nell'altro; ***it does not matter (to me) one ~ or the other*** in un modo o in un altro non importa; ***either ~*** in ogni caso; ***no ~!*** *infml* non esiste proprio! **2.** (*route*) strada *f*; ***this ~*** (*in this direction*) da questa parte; ***across*** *or* ***over the ~*** dall'altra parte della strada; ***ask the ~*** chiedere la via; ***along the ~*** *learn skill etc* strada facendo;

go the wrong ~ andare nella direzione sbagliata; *in car* sbagliare strada; ***go down the wrong ~*** (*food*) andare di traverso; ***there's no ~ out*** *fig* non c'è via di uscita; ***find a ~ in*** trovare l'entrata; ***the ~ up*** la salita; ***get under ~*** mettersi in cammino; ***be well under ~*** essere a buon punto; ***I know my ~ around the town*** so orientarmi bene in città; ***can you find your ~ home?*** riesci a trovare la strada di casa?; ***give ~*** AUTO dare la precedenza; (*collapse*) crollare; ***X has given ~ to Y*** (*been replaced by*) Y ha preso il posto di X; ***lead the ~*** *a. fig* fare strada; ***lose one's ~*** smarrirsi; ***be in the ~*** (*be an obstruction*) essere d'intralcio; ***it's on the ~ to the station*** è sulla strada della stazione; ***I was on my ~ to the station*** stavo andando alla stazione; ***go out of one's ~*** (***to do sth***) farsi in quattro (per fare qc) **3.** *fig* ***by the ~*** (*incidentally*) a proposito; ***by ~ of*** (*via*) passando per; (*in the form of*) come; ***be under ~*** essere in corso; ***have one's*** (***own***) ***~*** averla vinta; ***no ~!*** neanche per sogno!; ***there's no ~ he can do it*** è impossibile che ce la faccia **II** *adv infml* (*much*); ***it's ~ too soon to decide*** è veramente troppo presto per decidere; ***they are ~ behind with their work*** sono molto indietro con il lavoro

way in *n* entrata *f*

waylay *v/t* ⟨*pret & past part* **-laid**⟩ fermare

way of life *n* stile *m* di vita **way out** *n* uscita *f*; *fig*: *from situation* via *f* d'uscita

wayside *n* margine *m*, ciglio *m*; *fig* ***fall by the ~*** (*fail*) fare fiasco; (*fall through*) andare in fumo

wayward *adj* difficile

WC *abbr* (= **water closet**) *esp Br* WC

we *pron* noi; ***~'re the best*** siamo i migliori; ***they're going, but ~'re not*** loro vanno, noi no

weak *adj* (*+er*) *physically, morally* debole, *tea, coffee* leggero; ***~ moment*** momento *m* di debolezza; ***go ~ at the knees*** avere le gambe tremanti; ***what are his ~ spots?*** quali sono i suoi punti deboli?

weaken I *v/t* indebolire **II** *v/i* indebolirsi

weak-kneed *adj* debole

weakling *n morally* smidollato *m*, -a *f*; *physically* mingherlino *m*, -a *f*

weakness *n* debolezza *f*; ***have a ~ for sth*** (*liking*) avere un debole per qc

weak-willed *adj* con poca forza di volontà

weal *n mark on skin* piaga *f*

wealth *n* ricchezza *f*; ***a ~ of*** una grande abbondanza di

wealthy *adj* (*+er*) ricco

wean *v/t baby* svezzare; ***~ s.o. off sth*** far perdere a qn il vizio di qc

weapon *n* arma *f*

wear I *v/t* ⟨*pret* **wore**, *past part* **worn**⟩ (*have on*) indossare; (*damage*) logorare; ***~ a hole in sth*** fare un buco in qc **II** *v/i* ⟨*pret* **wore**, *past part* **worn**⟩ (*wear out*) logorarsi; (*last*) durare **III** *n*: ***~*** (***and tear***) usura *f*; ***clothes for everyday ~*** vestiti per tutti i giorni; ***clothes for evening ~*** abiti da sera

◆**wear away I** *v/i* consumarsi **II** *v/t sep* consumare

◆**wear down** *v/t sep resistance* fiaccare

◆**wear off** *v/i of effect, feeling* svanire; ***don't worry, it'll wear off!*** non preoccuparti, passerà!

◆**wear on** *v/i* passare lentamente; (*year*) trascorrere; ***as the evening wore on*** col trascorrere della serata

◆**wear out I** *v/t sep* (*tire*) estenuare; ***wear o.s. out*** logorarsi; *shoes* consumare **II** *v/i of shoes, carpet* consumarsi

◆**wear through** *v/i* bucarsi; (*shoes*) sfondarsi

wearily *adv* stancamente

wearing *adj* (*tiring*) stancante

weary *adj* (*+er*) stanco

weasel I *n* donnola *f* **II** *v/i US infml* svicolare; ***he ~ed out as soon as things got sticky*** se l'è svignata appena le cose si sono complicate

weather I *n* tempo *m*; ***be feeling under the ~*** sentirsi poco bene **II** *v/t crisis* superare; ***~ the storm*** superare la crisi **III** *v/i* (*rock etc*) erodersi

weather-beaten *adj* segnato **weather chart** *n* carta *f* meteorologica **weathercock** *n* banderuola *f* **weather conditions** *npl* condizioni *fpl* meteorologiche **weathered** *adj* segnato dalle intemperie **weather forecast** *n* previsioni *fpl* del tempo **weatherman** *n* meteorologo *m***weather map** *n* carta del tempo **weatherproof** *adj* impermeabile **weather report** *n* bollettino del tempo **weather station** *n* stazione *f* meteorologica **weather vane** *n* banderuola *f* **weatherworn** *n* consumato dalle intemperie

weave **I** *v/t* ⟨*pret* ***wove***, *past part* ***woven***⟩ *cloth* tessere; *basket* intrecciare; ***~ one's way through sth*** insinuearsi in qc **II** *v/i* (*move*) zigzagare

weaver *n* tessitore *m*, trice *f*

web *n of spider* ragnatela *f*; ***the Web*** COMPUT il web *m inv*, la Rete *f inv*

webbed feet *npl* piedi *mpl* palmati

webbing *n* tessuto *m* robusto

web browser *n* COMPUT browser *m inv*

webcam *n* COMPUT webcam *f inv*

webcast *n* COMPUT *programma trasmesso via internet*

web designer *n* COMPUT disegnatore *m*, trice *f* di siti web

webmaster *n* COMPUT webmaster *m inv*

web page *n* pagina *f* web **web site** *n* sito *m* web

wed *v/i* ⟨*pret & past part* ***wed*** *or* ***wedded***⟩ sposarsi

we'd → ***we would***, ***we had***

Wed *abbr* (= **Wednesday**) mercoledì

wedding *n* matrimonio *m*; ***have a registry office*** *Br* / ***church ~*** celebrare il matrimonio in comune / chiesa; ***go to a ~*** andare ad un matrimonio

wedding anniversary *n* anniversario *m* di matrimonio **wedding cake** *n* torta *f* nuziale **wedding day** *n* giorno *m* del matrimonio **wedding dress** *n* abito *m or* vestito *m* da sposa **wedding reception** *n* rinfresco di nozze **wedding ring** *n* fede *f* **wedding vows** *npl* promesse *fpl* matrimoniali

wedge **I** *n to hold sth in place* zeppa *f*; *of cheese etc* fetta *f* **II** *v/t*: ***~ open*** tenere aperto; ***be ~d between two people*** essere incastrato tra due persone

wedlock *n* matrimonio *m*; ***be born out of ~*** essere un figlio illegittimo

Wednesday *n* mercoledì *m inv*

wee[1] *adj* (+*er*) *infml* piccolo; *Scot* ***a ~ bit*** un pochino

wee[2] *Br infml* **I** *n* ***have*** *or* ***do a ~*** fare la pipì **II** *v/i* fare la pipì *infml*

weed **I** *n* erbaccia *f*; *US infml* (*marijuana*) erba *f*; *infml* (*person*) rammollito *m*, a *f* **II** *v/t & v/i* diserbare

◆**weed out** *v/t sep* (*remove*) eliminare

weeding *n*: ***do some ~*** togliere le erbacce

weed-killer *n* diserbante *m*

weedy *adj* (+*er*) *infml* mingherlino

week *n* settimana *f*; ***a ~ tomorrow*** una settimana a domani; ***~ in, ~ out*** tutte le settimane; ***twice a ~*** due volte alla settimana; ***a ~'s holiday*** *Br or* ***vacation*** *US* una settimana di vacanza; ***a 40-hour ~*** una settimana (lavorativa) di 40 ore

weekday *n* giorno *m* feriale **weekend** *n* fine *m* settimana, weekend *m inv*; ***at*** *or US* ***on the ~*** durante il fine settimana; ***take a long ~*** prendersi un weekend lungo

weekly **I** *adj* settimanale **II** *n magazine* settimanale *m* **III** *adv* settimanalmente

weep *v/i* ⟨*pret & past part* ***wept***⟩ piangere

weeping willow *n* salice *m* piangente

weepy *adj* (+*er*): ***be ~*** essere piagnucoloso

wee-wee **I** *n infml* pipì *f inv infml*; ***do a ~*** fare la pipì **II** *v/i infml* fare la pipì

weft *n* TEX trama *f*

weigh *v/t & v/i* pesare; ***~ anchor*** levare l'ancora

◆**weigh down** *v/t sep*: ***be weighed down with*** *with bags* curvarsi sotto il peso di; *with worries* essere oppresso da

◆**weigh on** *v/t* preoccupare

◆**weigh out** *v/t sep* (*measure*) pesare

◆**weigh up** *v/t sep* (*assess*) valutare

weight *n of person*, *object* peso *m*; ***3 kilos in ~*** tre chili di peso; ***the branches broke under the ~ of the snow*** i rami si sono spezzati per il peso della neve; ***it's worth its ~ in gold*** vale tanto oro quanto pesa; ***lift ~s*** sollevare pesi; ***that's a ~ off my mind*** mi sono tolto un peso dalle spalle; ***add ~ to sth*** dare peso a qc; ***pull one's ~*** fare la propria parte; ***throw*** *or* ***chuck*** *infml* ***one's ~ about*** *Br or* ***around*** farla da padrone; ***put on*** / ***lose ~*** ingrassare / dimagrire

◆**weight down** *v/t sep* fermare con pesi

weightless *adj environment* privo di gravità; *condition* di assenza di gravità; ***be ~*** *person* non essere soggetti alla gravità
weightlessness *n* assenza *f* di peso
weightlifter *n* pesista *m/f* **weightlifting** *n* sollevamento *m* pesi
weighty *adj* (*+er*) *fig*: *important* importante
weir *n* chiusa *f*
weird *adj* (*+er*) strano
weirdly *adv* stranamente
weirdo *n infml* pazzoide *m/f*
welcome I *v/t guests etc* accogliere; ***they ~d him home with a big party*** l'hanno accolto in casa con una grande festa; *fig*: *decision etc* rallegrarsi di; ***she ~s a challenge*** apprezza le sfide **II** *adj* **1.** benvenuto; ***make s.o. ~*** accogliere bene qn; ***it makes a ~ change*** è un gradito cambiamento; ***~ home!*** bentornato a casa! **2.** ***you're ~!*** prego!; ***you're ~ to try some*** serviti pure **III** *n a. fig* accoglienza *f*; *fig*: *to news*, *proposal* accoglienza *f*
weld *v/t* saldare
welder *n* saldatore *m*, -trice *f*
welfare *n* bene *m inv*; ***be on ~*** *US* ricevere sussidi
welfare benefits *npl US* sussidio *m* **welfare services** *npl* servizi *mpl* sociali **welfare state** *n* stato *m* sociale **welfare work** *n* assistenza *f* sociale **welfare worker** *n* assistente *m/f* sociale
well¹ I *n for water*, *oil* pozzo *m* **II** *v/i* scaturire; ***tears ~ed in her eyes*** le vennero le lacrime agli occhi
◆**well up** *v/i* sgorgare; *fig* crescere
well² ⟨*comp* ***better***, *sup* ***best***⟩ **I** *adv* **1.** bene; ***do ~*** (*be successful*) andare bene; ***~ done!*** bravo!; ***very ~*** *acknowledging an order* benissimo; *when you don't agree with sth but are doing it anyway* va bene; ***~, ~!*** *surprise* bene, bene!; ***~ …*** *uncertainty*, *thinking* beh …; ***I couldn't very ~ say no*** mi è stato impossibile dire di no; ***it's just as ~ you told me*** hai fatto bene a dirmelo **2.** ***as ~*** (*too*) anche; ***as ~ as*** *in addition to* oltre a **II** *adj*: ***be ~*** stare bene; ***feel ~*** sentirsi bene; ***get ~ soon!*** guarisci presto! **III** *int* bene; (*doubtfully*) beh; ***~, ~!*** guarda, guarda! ***~, I never!*** chi l'avrebbe mai detto!; ***very ~ then!*** d'accordo!; (*indignantly*) staremo a vedere!
well-adjusted *adj*, **well adjusted** *adj* PSYCH ben inserito **well-advised** *adj*, **well advised** *adj*: ***he would be well advised to …*** farebbe bene a… **well-appointed** *adj* ben arredato **well-balanced** *adj person*, *meal* equilibrato; *meal*, *diet* equilibrato **well-behaved** *adj* educato **well-being** *n* benessere *m* **well-born** *adj* ben nato **well-bred** *adj*, **well bred** *adj person* beneducato; *horse* di razza **well-built** *adj* ben fatto; *euph* (*fat*) robusto **well-chosen** *adj* ben scelto **well-connected** *adj* ben introdotto **well-disposed** *adj*, **well disposed** *adj*: ***be ~ toward(s) s.o. / sth*** essere ben disposto verso qn / qc **well-done** *adj meat* ben cotto **well-dressed** *adj* ben vestito **well-earned** *adj* meritato **well-educated** *adj*, **well educated** *adj* colto **well-equipped** *adj*, **well equipped** *adj office*, *studio* ben attrezzato; *army* ben equipaggiato **well-established** *adj*, **well established** *adj practice* affermato; *company* solido **well-fed** *adj*, **well fed** *adj* ben nutrito **well-heeled** *adj infml* danaroso **well-hung** *adj infml vulg* ben dotato
wellies *npl infml* → ***wellingtons***
well-informed *adj* ben informato
wellingtons *npl* stivali *mpl* di gomma
well-kept *adj garden* ben tenuto; *secret* ben custodito **well-known** *adj* famoso **well-made** *adj* ben fatto **well-mannered** *adj* ben educato **well-meaning** *adj* spinto da buone intenzioni **well-off** *adj* benestante **well-paid** *adj* ben pagato **well-read** *adj* colto **well-stocked** *adj*, **well stocked** *adj* ben fornito **well thought of** *adj* stimato da tutti **well-timed** *adj* tempestivo **well-to-do** *adj* abbiente **well-tried** *adj* sperimentato **well-wisher** *n* sostenitore *m*, -trice *f* **well-worn** *adj* liso
Welsh I *adj* gallese **II** *n language* gallese *m*; ***the ~*** i gallesi
Welshman *n* gallese *m*
Welsh rabbit, Welsh rarebit *n* COOK *formaggio fuso servito su pane tostato*
Welshwoman *n* gallese *f*
welt *n on shoe* tramezza *f*; *on fabric* orlo *m*

wend *v/t*: **~ *one's way home*** prendere la strada di casa
went *pret* → **go**
wept *pret & past part* → **weep**
were *pret pl* → **be**
we're → ***we are***
weren't → ***were not***
werewolf *n* ⟨*pl* **werewolves**⟩ lupo *m* mannaro
west **I** *n* ovest *m*, occidente *m*; ***the West*** POL l'Occidente; *western part of a country* parte *f* occidentale del paese **II** *adj* occidentale **III** *adv* verso ovest; **~ *of*** a ovest di; ***it faces ~*** è esposto a ovest
westbound *adj train* in direzione ovest
westerly *adj* occidentale; ***in a ~ direction*** verso ovest
western **I** *adj* occidentale; ***Western*** occidentale **II** *n* (*film*) western *m inv*
Westerner *n* occidentale *m/f*
westernised, westernized *adj* occidentalizzato
West Indies *npl* Indie *fpl* occidentali
westward *adv* verso ovest
wet **I** *adj* (+*er*) bagnato; (*rainy*) piovoso; **~ *paint*** *as sign* vernice fresca; ***be ~ through*** essere fradicio; ***be ~ behind the ears*** *infml* puzza ancora di latte; *Br infml* (*weak*) essere un novellino **II** *v/t* ⟨*pret & past part* **wet**⟩ bagnare; **~ *the bed*** *infml* fare la pipì a letto *infml* **III** *n* (*moisture*) il bagnato *m*; (*rain*) pioggia *f*; *Br infml* (*weak person*) pappamolle *m/f*
wet blanket *n infml* guastafeste *m/f inv* **wet suit** *n for diving* muta *f*
whack **I** *n infml* (*blow*) colpo *m*; *infml* (*share*) parte *f* **II** *v/t infml* colpire
whacked *adj infml* stanco morto
whacking *adj infml* enorme
whale *n* balena *f*; *infml* ***have a ~ of a time*** divertirsi da matti
whaling *n* caccia *f* alla balena
wharf *n* ⟨*pl* **wharves**⟩ banchina *f*
what **I** *pron* (che) cosa; **~ *is that?*** (che) cos'è?; **~ *is it?*** (*what do you want*) (che) cosa c'è?; **~*?*** cosa?; *astonishment* (che) cosa?; ***it's not ~ I meant*** non è ciò che volevo dire; **~ *about some dinner?*** e se mangiassimo qualcosa?; **~ *about heading home?*** e se ce ne andassimo a casa?; **~ *is the date today?*** quanti ne abbiamo oggi?; **~ *for?*** (*why*) perché?; ***so ~?*** e allora?; **~ *if ...?*** e se ...?; **~ *is the book about?*** di cosa parla il libro? **II** *adj* che *inv*, quale; **~ *colour is the car?*** di che colore è la macchina?; **~ *university are you at?*** in quale università studi?; ***I gave him ~ money I had*** gli ho dato i soldi che avevo **III** *adv*: **~ *a brilliant idea!*** che bella idea! **IV** *int* cosa; ***is he good-looking, or ~?*** allora, è bello?
whatever **I** *pron*; ***I'll do ~ you want*** farò (tutto) quello che vuoi; **~ *I do, it'll be a problem*** qualsiasi cosa faccia, ci saranno problemi; **~ *the season*** *regardless of* in qualunque stagione; **~ *people say*** qualunque cosa dica la gente; **~ *gave you that idea?*** cosa mai te lo ha fatto pensare? **II** *adj* qualunque; ***you have no reason ~ to worry*** non hai nessun motivo di preoccuparti; **~ *book you choose*** qualsiasi libro scegli; **~ *else you do*** qualunque cosa tu faccia
whatsit *n* coso *m*
whatsoever *adv*: ***I had no help ~*** non ho avuto aiuto alcuno
wheat *n* grano *m*, frumento *m*
wheat germ *n* germe *m* di grano
wheedle *v/t infml*: **~ *sth out of s.o.*** ottenere qc da qn con lusinghe
wheel **I** *n* ruota *f*; (*steering wheel*) volante *m*; ***at the ~*** al volante **II** *v/t bicycle* spingere **III** *v/i of birds* roteare
◆**wheel around** *v/i* voltarsi
wheelbarrow *n* carriola *f* **wheelchair** *n* sedia *f* a rotelle **wheel clamp** *n* ceppo *m* bloccaruote
wheelie *n infml on bike* impennata *f*
wheelie bin *n Br for rubbish* bidone *m* della spazzatura (con rotelle)
wheeze **I** *v/i* ansimare **II** *n* sibilo *m*; *infml* ***a clever ~*** un'idea geniale
when **I** *adv* quando; ***say ~!*** *when pouring drink* dimmi quando basta! **II** *cj* quando; **~ *I was a child*** quand'ero bambino
whenever *adv* (*each time*) ogni volta che; *regardless of when* in qualunque momento
where **I** *adv* dove **II** *cj* dove; ***this is ~ I used to live*** io abitavo qui
whereabouts **I** *adv* dove **II** *npl*: ***know s.o.'s ~*** sapere dove si trova qn
whereas *cj* mentre

whereby *adv* (*by which*) per cui
wherever I *cj* dovunque; ***~ you go*** dovunque tu vada **II** *adv* dove; ***~ can he be?*** dove sarà mai?
whet *v/t* ⟨*pret & past part* ***-ted***⟩ *appetite* stuzzicare
whether *pron* se
whey *n* siero *m*
which I *adj* quale; ***~ one is yours?*** qual è il tuo? **II** *pron interrogative* quale; *relative* che; ***on/in ~*** su/in cui; ***take one, it doesn't matter ~*** prendine uno, non importa quale
whichever I *adj* qualunque **II** *pron* quello che *m*, quella che *f*; ***~ of the methods*** qualunque metodo
whiff *n unpleasant* zaffata *f*; ***catch a ~ of*** sentire
while I *cj* mentre; (*although*) benché **II** *n*: ***a long ~ ago*** molto tempo fa; ***wait a long ~*** aspettare molto *or* lungo; ***for a ~*** per un po'; ***in a ~*** fra poco; ***I'll wait a ~ longer*** aspetto un altro po'; ***once in a ~*** una volta tanto
◆**while away** *v/t sep* passare
whilst *cj* mentre
whim *n* capriccio *m*; ***do sth on a ~*** fare qc per capriccio
whimper I *v/i of person, baby* gemere; *of animal* mugolare **II** *n of person, baby* gemito *m*; *of animal* mugolio *m*
whine *v/i of dog* guaire; *infml* (*complain*) piagnucolare
whinge I *v/i Br infml* lagnarsi **II** *n* lagna *f*
whining I *n of do*) guaito *m* **II** *adj voice* lamentoso; *sound* che sibila; *dog* che guaisce
whinny *v/i* ⟨*pret & past part* ***-ied***⟩ *of horse* nitrire
whip I *v/t* ⟨*pret & past part* ***-ped***⟩ (*beat*) sbattere; *cream* montare; *infml* (*defeat*) stracciare *infml* **II** *n* frusta *f*
◆**whip off** *v/t sep clothes* togliere velocemente; *tablecloth* sfilare
◆**whip out** *v/t sep infml* tirar fuori (fulmineamente)
◆**whip up** *v/t sep* (*arouse*) sobillare; *infml meal* improvvisare
whiplash *n neck injury* colpo *m* di frusta
whipped cream *n* panna *f* montata
whipping *n* (*beating*) bastonata *f*; *infml* (*defeat*) batosta *f*
whipping boy *n* capro *m* espiatorio
whipping cream *n* panna *f* da montare
whipround *n infml* colletta *f*; ***have a ~*** fare una colletta
whirl I *v/i of blades etc* roteare; *of leaves* volteggiare; *of person* girarsi; ***~ (a)round*** girare velocemente; ***my head is ~ing*** mi gira la testa **II** *n*: ***my mind is in a ~*** ho una gran confusione in testa; *fig* ***give sth a ~*** *infml* (*try out*) provare qc
whirlpool *n in river* mulinello *m*; *for relaxation* vasca *f* per idromassaggio
whirlwind *n* tromba *f* d'aria
whirr *v/i* ronzare
whisk I *n* frusta *f*; *mechanical* frullino *m* **II** *v/t eggs* frullare
◆**whisk away** *v/t sep* togliere in fretta; ***he whisked her away to the Bahamas*** l'ha portata su due piedi alle Bahamas
whiskers *npl of man* basette *fpl*; *of animal* baffi *mpl*
whiskey *n Irish, American* whisky *m inv*
whisky *n* whisky *m inv*
whisper I *v/t & v/i* bisbigliare **II** *n* bisbiglio *m*; (*rumour*) voce *f*; ***say sth in a ~*** bisbigliare qc
whist *n* whist *m inv*
whistle I *v/i* fischiare **II** *v/t* fischiettare **III** *n sound* fischio *m*; *device* fischietto *m*
whistle-blower *n infml persona che denuncia irregolarità all'interno della propria azienda*
whistle-stop *adj*: ***~ tour*** *giro di politici o diplomatici con soste brevi in piccoli centri*
white I *n colour* bianco *m*; *of egg* albume *m*, bianco *m infml*; *person* bianco *m*, -a *f* **II** *adj* (*+er*) bianco; *person* bianco; ***go ~*** sbiancare (in viso); ***as ~ as a sheet*** bianco come un cencio
whitebait *n* bianchetto *m*
whitecap *n* onda *f* increspata
white cell *n* globulo *m* bianco **white Christmas** *n* Natale *m* con la neve **white coffee** *n Br* caffè *m inv* con latte *or* panna **white-collar crime** *n frode o furto interni* **white-collar worker** *n* impiegato *m*, -a *f*
whited sepulchre sepolcro *m* imbiancato

white goods *npl* COMM elettrodomestici *mpl* bianchi **white-haired** *adj* dai capelli bianchi
Whitehall *n il governo britannico*
white-hot *adj* incandescente **White House** *n* Casa *f* Bianca **white lie** *n* bugia *f* innocente **white meat** *n* carne *f* bianca
whiten *v/t & v/i* (far) diventare bianco
whiteness *n* biancore *m*; *of skin* pallore *m*
white out *n* tempesta *f* di neve
White-Out® *n US* bianchetto *m*
White Paper *n* POL libro *m* bianco (**on** su) **white sauce** *n* besciamella *f* **white spirit** *n Br* acquaragia *f* minerale **white stick** *n* bastone *m* per non vedenti **white-tie** *n*: ***a ~ occasion*** un'occasione formale **white trash** *n US pej* bianchi *mpl* **whitewash I** *n* calce *f*; *fig* copertura *f* **II** *v/t* imbiancare (con calce) **white wine** *n* vino *m* bianco
Whitsun *n* Pentecoste *f*
Whit Sunday *n* domenica *f* di Pentecoste
whittle *v/t wood* intagliare
◆**whittle away** *v/t sep* ridurre; *rights* limitare
◆**whittle down** *v/t sep* ridurre
whiz(z) *n*: ***be a ~ at*** *infml* essere un genio in; ***a computer ~*** un mago del computer
◆**whizz by, whizz past** *v/i of time, car* sfrecciare
whizzkid *n infml* mago *m*, -a *f infml*; ***a computer ~*** un mago dei computer
who *pron interrogative* chi; *relative* che; ***the man ~ I was talking to*** l'uomo con cui parlavo; ***I don't know ~ to believe*** non so a chi credere; ***~ do you think you are?*** chi credi di essere?; ***~ did you stay with?*** con chi sei stato?
W.H.O. *abbr* (= **World Health Organisation**) OMS (organizzazione mondiale della sanità)
whodun(n)it *n* giallo *m*
whoever *pron* chiunque; (*interrogative*) chi mai; ***~ can that be?*** chi sarà mai?
whole I *adj*: ***the ~ town*** tutta la città; ***two ~ hours/days*** ben due ore/giorni; ***a ~ chicken*** un pollo intero; ***he drank/ate the ~ lot*** ha bevuto/mangiato tutto; ***it's a ~ lot easier/better*** è molto più facile/meglio **II** *n* tutto *m*; ***the ~ of the United States*** tutti gli Stati Uniti; ***on the ~*** nel complesso
wholefood *n* alimenti *mpl* integrali **whole-hearted** *adj* senza riserve **whole-heartedly** *adv* senza riserve **wholemeal bread** *n* pane *m* integrale **wholesale I** *adj* all'ingrosso; *fig* in massa; ***the ~ slaughter of cattle*** l'abbattimento in massa dei bovini **II** *adv* all'ingrosso **wholesaler** *n* grossista *m/f* **wholesome** *adj* sano **wholewheat** *adj* integrale
wholly *adv* completamente
wholly owned subsidiary *n* consociata *f* interamente controllata
whom *pron form* chi; ***to*** *or* ***for ~*** a cui; ***..., all of ~ were drunk*** i quali erano tutti ubriachi
whoop *v/i shout* gridare
whooping cough *n* pertosse *f*
whoops *int* accidenti
whoosh I *n of water* fruscio *m*; *of air* sibilo *m* **II** *v/i* sfrecciare; *air* sibilare
whopper *n infml* balla *f*
whopping *adj infml* enorme
whore *n* puttana *f*
whorehouse *n* bordello *m*
whorl *n* spirale *f*; *of shell* voluta *f*
who's → ***who has***, ***who is***
whose I *pron interrogative* di chi; *relative* il/la cui; ***~ is this?*** di chi è questo?; ***a man ~ wife ...*** un uomo la cui moglie ...; ***a country ~ economy is booming*** un paese dall'economia fiorente **II** *adj* di chi; ***~ bike is that?*** di chi è quella bici?; ***~ car are we taking?*** che macchina prendiamo?
why *adv* perché; ***that's ~*** ecco perché; ***~ not?*** perché no?; ***the reason ~ he left*** il motivo per cui se ne è andato
wick *n* stoppino *m*
wicked *adj* (*evil*) malvagio; (*mischievous*) malizioso
wicker *adj* di vimini
wicker chair *n* poltrona *f* di vimini
wickerwork *n* oggetti *mpl* di vimini
wicket *n* porta *f*
wide *adj* (+*er*) largo; *experience* vasto; *range* ampio; ***be 12 metres ~*** essere largo 12 metri
wide-angle lens *n* grandangolo *m* **wide awake** *adj* sveglio **wide-eyed**

adj con gli occhi sgranati
widely *adv used, known* largamente; ***it is ~ believed that ...*** è una credenza diffusa che ...
widen I *v/t* allargare **II** *v/i* allargarsi
wide-open *adj* spalancato **wide-ranging** *adj* di largo respiro **widescreen** *adj television* widescreen *inv* **widespread** *adj* diffuso
widget *n infml* coso *m*
widow I *n* vedova *f* **II** *v/t* rimanere vedovo; ***she was twice ~ed*** è rimasta vedova due volte
widower *n* vedovo *m*
widow's peak *n* attaccatura *f* dei capelli a V
width *n* larghezza *f*; *of fabric* altezza *f*
wield *v/t weapon* brandire; *power* esercitare
wieldy *adj* maneggevole
wife *n* ⟨*pl* **wives**⟩ moglie *f*
wig *n* parrucca *f*
wigging *n Br infml* sgridata *f*; ***he gave the boy a real ~*** ha fatto al ragazzo una bella lavata di capo
wiggle I *v/t*: ***~ one's hips*** ancheggiare; *loose screw etc* muovere **II** *n* movimento *m* rapido
wiggly *adj* sinuoso; ***~ line*** linea *f* serpeggiante
wigwam *n* wigwam *m inv*
wild I *adj* (+*er*) *animal, flowers* selvatico; *teenager, party* scatenato; (*crazy: scheme*) folle; *applause* fragoroso; ***be ~ about ...*** (*keen on*) andare pazzo per ...; ***go ~*** impazzire; (*become angry*) andare su tutte le furie; ***run ~*** *of children* scatenarsi; *of plants* crescere senza controllo **II** *n*: ***the ~s*** le zone sperdute
wild boar *n* cinghiale *m*
wildcat *n* gatto *m* selvatico
wildcat strike *n* sciopero *m* selvaggio
wilderness *n empty place* deserto *m*; *fig: garden etc* giungla *f*
wild-eyed *adj* con gli occhi spiritati
wildfire *n*: ***spread like ~*** allargarsi a macchia d'olio **wildgoose chase** *n* ricerca *f* inutile **wildlife** *n* fauna *f*; ***~ programme*** programma *m* sulla natura
wildly *adv infml* terribilmente
wild oats *n* avena *f* matta; *fig* cavallina *f* **wild rice** *n riso che cresce in Nord America*
wilful, *US* **willful** *adj person* ostinato; *action* intenzionale; *action*
will[1] *n* JUR testamento *m*
will[2] **I** *n* (*willpower*) volontà *f inv*; ***have a ~ of one's own*** avere una volontà di ferro; ***the ~ to live*** il desiderio di vivere; ***against one's ~*** contro la propria volontà; ***at ~*** a piacimento; ***of one's own free ~*** di propria spontanea volontà; ***with the best ~ in the world*** con tutta la buona volontà; *prov* ***where there's a ~ there's a way*** volere è potere **II** *v/t* volere; ***~ s.o. to do sth*** invogliare qn a fare qc
will[3] *v/mod*: (*future*) ***I ~ let you know tomorrow*** ti farò sapere entro domani; ***~ you be there?*** ci sarai?; ***I won't be back*** non tornerò; ***you ~ call me, won't you?*** mi chiamerai, vero?; (*expressing willingness, capability*) ***I'll pay for this – no you won't*** questo lo pago io – no, lascia stare; ***the car won't start*** la macchina non parte; ***~ you tell her that ...?*** dille che ...; ***~ you have some more tea?*** vuoi dell'altro tè?; ***~ you stop that!*** smettila!; ***shut the window, ~ you?*** chiudi la finestra, ti dispiace?
willful *US* → ***wilful***
willies *npl infml* ***it / he gives me the ~*** mi fa venire il nervoso
willing *adj* disponibile; ***are you ~ to pay more?*** sei disposto a pagare di più?; ***he was not ~ to accept*** no ha voluto accettare
willingly *adv* volentieri
willingness *n* disponibilità *f inv*
willow *n* salice *m*
willowy *adj* slanciato
willpower *n* forza *f* di volontà
willy *n Br* (*penis*) pisellino *m*
willy-nilly *adv* (*at random*) a casaccio
wilt *v/i of plant* appassire
wily *adj* (+*er*) astuto
wimp *n infml* pappamolle *m/f*
win I *v/t & v/i* ⟨*pret & past part* **won**⟩ vincere **II** *n* vittoria *f*
◆**win back** *v/t sep* riconquistare
wince I *n* sussulto *m* **II** *v/i* fare una smorfia
winch I *n* argano *m* **II** *v/t* tirare su con l'argano
wind[1] **I** *n* vento *m*; (*flatulence*) aria *f*; ***break ~*** fare un peto; ***get ~ of ...*** venire a sapere ... **II** *v/t*: ***~ s.o.*** togliere

il fiato a qn; ***he was ~ed by the run*** era rimasto senza fiato per la corsa

wind[2] ⟨*pret & past part* ***wound***⟩ **I** *v/i of path, stream* snodarsi; *of plant* avvolgersi **II** *v/t* avvolgere

◆**wind around I** *v/t sep* avvolgere; ***wind it twice around the post*** avvolgilo due volte intorno al palo; ***wind itself around sth*** inerpicarsi intorno a qc **II** *v/i* (*road*) snodarsi **III** *v/t* (*road*) snodarsi tra

◆**wind back** *v/t sep tape* riavvolgere

◆**wind down I** *v/i*: ***the party began to wind down*** la gente cominciò ad andar via dalla festa **II** *v/t sep car window* abbassare; *business* chiudere gradualmente

◆**wind forward** *or* **on** *v/t sep film* far scorrere

◆**wind round** *v/t & v/i sep esp Br* → ***wind around***

◆**wind up I** *v/t sep clock* caricare; *car window* tirar su; *speech, presentation* concludere; *business, affairs, company* chiudere **II** *v/i*: ***wind up in hospital*** finire in ospedale

wind-bag *n infml* trombone *m*

windbreak *n* frangivento *m inv*

wind-cheater, *US* **wind breaker** *n* giacca *f* a vento

wind chill *n* METEO raffreddamento *m* da vento

windfall *n fig* colpo *m* di fortuna **wind gauge** *n* anemometro *m*

winding *adj* tortuoso

wind instrument *n* strumento *m* a fiato **windmill** *n* mulino *m*

window *n of house* finestra *f*; *of shop* vetrina *f*; *of car, train* finestrino *m*; COMPUT finestra *f*; ***in the ~*** *of shop* in vetrina

window box *n* fioriera *f* **window cleaner** *n* lavavetri *m/f inv* **window display** *n* esposizione *f* in vetrina **window-dressing** *n* allestimento *m* di vetrine; *fig* specchietto per le allodole; ***that's just ~*** è solo uno specchietto per le allodole **window ledge** *n* → ***windowsill*** **windowpane** *n* vetro *m* (della finestra) **window seat** *n on plane, train* posto *m* di finestrino **window-shop** *v/i* ⟨*pret & past part* ***-ped***⟩: ***go ~ping*** guardare le vetrine **windowsill** *n* davanzale *m*

windpipe *n* ANAT trachea *f* **windscreen** *n* parabrezza *m inv* **windscreen wiper** *n* tergicristallo *m* **windshield** *n US* parabrezza *m inv* **windsock** *n* manica *f* a vento **windsurfer** *n person* windsurfista *m/f*; *board* windsurf *m inv* **windsurfing** *n* windsurf *m inv* **wind tunnel** *n* galleria *f* del vento **wind turbine** *n* aeroturbina *f*

windy *adj* (+*er*) *weather, day* ventoso; ***it's getting ~*** si sta alzando il vento

wine I *n* vino *m*; ***cheese and ~ party*** *rinfresco informale a base di vino e formaggio* **II** *v/t*: ***they ~d and dined us in great style*** ci hanno offerto una cena in grande stile

wine bar *n* enoteca *f*, bar *m inv* **wine cellar** *n* cantina *f* **wine glass** *n* bicchiere *m* da vino **wine grower** *n* viticoltore *m*, trice *f* **wine growing** *adj* viticoltura *f*; ***~ region*** regione *f* vinicola **wine list** *n* lista *f* dei vini **wine maker** *n* viticoltore *m*, -trice *f* **wine merchant** *n company* azienda *f* vinicola; *individual* vinaio *m*, -a *f* **wine press** *n* pigiatrice *f*

winery *n* industria *f* vinicola

wine tasting *n* degustazione *f* di vini

wing I *n* ala *f*; AUTO parafango *m*; *fig* ***take s.o. under one's ~*** prendere qn sotto le proprie ali; *fig* ***spread one's ~s*** spiccare il volo; ***play on the*** (***left / right***) ***~*** SPORTS giocare sull'ala (destra / sinistra); **wings** *npl* THEAT quinte *fpl*; ***wait in the ~s*** attendere nell'ombra **II** *v/t*: ***~ one's way*** volare verso **III** *v/i* volare

winger *n* SPORTS ala *f*

wing nut *n* galletto *m* **wingspan** *n* apertura *f* alare

wink I *n* occhiolino *m*; ***I didn't sleep a ~*** *infml* non ho chiuso occhio **II** *v/t* strizzare (l'occhio) **III** *v/i of person* strizzare gli occhi; ***~ at s.o.*** fare l'occhiolino a qn

winner *n* vincitore *m*, -trice *f*; ***be onto a ~*** *infml* puntare sul (cavallo) vincente

winning *adj* vincente

winning post *n* traguardo *m*

winnings *npl* vincita *fsg*

wino *n infml* ubriacone *m*, a *f*

winsome *adj* seducente

winter I *n* inverno **II** *adj* invernale **III** *v/i* svernare; ***they generally ~ed in St Moritz*** normalmente passano l'inver-

no a St. Moritz
Winter Olympics *npl* olimpiadi *fpl* invernali
winter sports *npl* sport *m inv* invernali
wintertime *n* inverno *m*
wintry *adj* invernale
wipe I *n* pulita *f*; ***give sth a ~*** dare una pulita a qc **II** *v/t* (*dry*) asciugare; (*clean*) pulire; *tape* cancellare; ***~ one's nose*** pulirsi il naso; ***~ one's feet*** pulirsi i piedi; *fig* ***~ the floor with s.o.*** *infml* dare una brutta lezione a qn
◆**wipe away** *v/t sep* asciugare strofinando
◆**wipe off** *v/t sep* cancellare; ***wipe that smile off your face*** *infml* togliti quel sorriso dalla faccia; ***be wiped off the map*** *or* ***the face of the earth*** essere eliminati dalla faccia della terra
◆**wipe out** *v/t sep* (*kill*, *destroy*) distruggere; *debt* estinguere; *sth on blackboard* cancellare; *disease*, *race* sterminare
◆**wipe up I** *v/t sep* asciugare **II** *v/i* asciugare i piatti
wiper *n* → ***windscreen wiper***
wire I *adj* metallico **II** *n* fil *m* di ferro; ELEC filo *m* elettrico **III** *v/t plug* collegare; *house* installare l'impianto elettrico; TEL mandare un telegramma a; (*fix with wire*) fissare con un filo metallico
◆**wire up** *v/t sep lights* collegare a
wireless *n* radio *f inv*
Wireless Application Protocol *n* COMPUT wap *m inv*
wire netting *n* rete *f* metallica
wiretap *n* TEL intercettazione *f* telefonica
wire wool *n* lana *f* di acciaio
wiring *n* ELEC impianto *m* elettrico
wiry *adj* (*+er*) *person* dal fisico asciutto
wisdom *n* saggezza *f*
wisdom tooth *n* dente *m* del giudizio
wise *adj* (*+er*) saggio
wisecrack *n infml* spiritosaggine *f*
wise guy *n pej* spiritoso *m*
wisely *adv act* saggiamente
wish I *v/t* volere; ***I ~ that he'd stop*** vorrei che la smettesse; ***~ s.o. well*** fare tanti auguri a qn; ***I ~ed him good luck*** gli ho augurato buona fortuna **II** *v/i*: ***wish for*** desiderare **III** *n* desiderio *m*; ***make a ~*** esprimere un desiderio; ***against his family's ~es*** contro il volere della famiglia; ***best ~es*** *for birthday etc* tanti auguri; *as greetings* cordiali saluti
wishbone *n* forcella *f* (di pollo)
wishful thinking *n* illusione *f*
wishy-washy *adj person* insulso; *colour* slavato
wisp *n of hair* ciocca *f*; *of smoke* filo *m*
wistful *adj* malinconico
wistfully *adv* malinconicamente
wit *n* (*humour*) spirito *m*; *person* persona *f* di spirito; ***be at one's ~s' end*** non sapere più che fare; ***keep one's ~s about one*** non perdere la testa; ***be scared out of one's ~s*** essere spaventato a morte
witch *n* strega *f*
witchcraft *n* stregoneria *f* **witch-doctor** *n* stregone *m* **witch-hazel** *n* amamelide *f* **witchhunt** *n fig* caccia *f* alle streghe
with *prep* **1.** *possession*, *proximity*, *agency etc* con; ***a girl ~ blue eyes*** una ragazza dagli *or* con gli occhi azzurri; ***~ a smile / a wave*** con un sorriso / un gesto della mano; ***~ no money*** senza soldi **2.** ***are you ~ me?*** (*do you understand*) mi segui? **3.** *cause* di; ***shiver ~ fear*** tremare di paura
withdraw 〈*pret* ***-drew***, *past part* ***-drawn***〉 **I** *v/t complaint*, *application*, *troops* ritirare; *money from bank* prelevare; *troops* ritirare **II** *v/i* ritirarsi
withdrawal *n of complaint*, *application*, *troops* ritiro *m*; *of money* prelievo *m*; *of troops* ritiro *m*; *from drugs* crisi *f inv* di astinenza
withdrawal symptoms *npl* sindrome *f* da astinenza
withdrawn *adj person* chiuso
wither *v/i* seccare
withering *adj heat* che inaridisce; *look* fulminante
withhold *v/t* 〈*pret & past part* ***-held***〉 *information* nascondere; *consent* rifiutare; *payment* trattenere
withholding tax *n US* ritenuta *f* alla fonte
within *prep* **1.** (*inside*) dentro **2.** *in expressions of time* nel giro di, entro **3.** *in expressions of distance etc* a meno di; ***is it ~ walking distance?*** ci si ar-

riva a piedi?; ***we kept ~ the budget*** abbiamo rispettato il budget; ***it is not ~ my power*** non rientra nelle mie competenze; ***~ reach*** a portata di mano
without *prep* senza; ***~ you/him*** senza (di) te/lui; ***~ looking/asking*** senza guardare/chiedere; ***~ his seeing*** senza che lo vedesse
withstand *v/t* ⟨*pret & past part* ***-stood***⟩ resistere a
witless *adj*: ***be scared ~*** essere spaventato a morte
witness I *n* testimone *m/f*; ***~ for the defence*** *Br or* ***defense*** *US* teste *m* a discarico; ***bear ~ to sth*** deporre per qc **II** *v/t accident, crime* essere testimone di; *signature* attestare l'autenticità di
witness box *n* banco *m* dei testimoni
witticism *n* arguzia *f*
witty *adj* (*+er*) arguto
wives → ***wife***
wizard *n* mago *m*
wizardry *n* magia *f*
wizen *v/t & v/i* appassire
wizened *adj* avvizzito
wk *abbr* (= **week**) settimana
WMD *abbr* (= **weapons of mass destruction**) ADM (armi di distruzione di massa)
wobble *v/i of person* vacillare; *of object* traballare
wobbly *adj* (*+er*) *person* vacillante; *object* traballante; *voice, hand* tremante
wodge *n Br infml* mucchio *m*
woe *n* pena *f*; *liter, hum* (*sorrow*) sventura *f*; ***~ (is me)!*** me misero!; ***~ betide him who ...!*** guai a chi...!
woebegone *adj* afflitto
woeful *adj* afflitto; *lack* deprecabile
wok *n* wok *m inv*
woke *pret* → ***wake***[1]
woken *past part* → ***wake***[1]
wolf I *n* ⟨*pl* ***wolves***⟩ *animal* lupo *m*; (*fig: womanizer*) donnaiolo *m* **II** *v/t*: ***~ (down)*** divorare
wolf whistle *n* fischio *m* **wolf-whistle** *v/i*: ***~ at s.o.*** fischiare dietro a qn
woman I *n* ⟨*pl* ***women***⟩ donna *f* **II** *adj*: ***~ doctor*** dottoressa; ***~ driver*** autista
womanhood *n*: ***reach ~*** diventare donna
womanise, womanize *v/i* andare a donne
womaniser, womanizer *n* donnaiolo *m*
womankind *n* sesso *m* femminile
womanly *adj* da donna
woman priest *n* donna *f* sacerdote
womb *n* utero *m*
women *pl* → ***woman***
women's lib *n* movimento *m* di liberazione della donna
women's libber *n* femminista *f*
won *pret & past part* → ***win***
wonder I *n* (*amazement*) stupore *m*, meraviglia *f*; *of science etc* meraviglia *f*; ***no ~!*** non mi stupisce!; ***it's a ~ that ...*** è incredibile che ... **II** *v/i* pensare **III** *v/t* domandarsi; ***I ~ if you could help*** mi chiedevo se potessi aiutarmi
wonderful *adj* stupendo
wonderfully *adv* (*extremely*) estremamente
wonderland *n* paese *m* delle meraviglie
wonderment *n* meraviglia *f*
wondrous *adj liter* meraviglioso
wonky *adj* (*+er*) *Br infml chair, marriage, grammar* traballante; *machine* che non funziona bene; ***your collar's all ~*** il tuo colletto è tutto storto
won't = ***will not***
woo *v/t* corteggiare
wood *n* legno *m*; *for fire* legna *f*; (*forest*) bosco *m*; ***touch ~!*** *esp Br or* ***knock on ~!*** *esp US* tocca ferro!; ***we're not out of the ~s yet*** *fig* non siamo ancora fuori pericolo; ***he can't see the ~ for the trees*** *Br prov* si perde nei dettagli
wooded *adj* boscoso
wooden *adj made of wood* di legno
woodland *n* boschi *mpl* **woodpecker** *n* picchio *m* **woodpile** *n* catasta *f* di legna **woodwind** *n* MUS fiati *mpl* **woodwork** *n parts made of wood* strutture *fpl* in legno; *activity* lavorazione *f* del legno; *fig* ***come out of the ~*** uscire allo scoperto **woodworm** *n* tarlo *m*
woody *adj* (*+er*) *in texture* legnoso
woof[1] *n* TEX trama *f*
woof[2] **I** *n of dog* latrato *m* **II** *v/i* abbaiare
woofter *n Br infml pej* frocio *m*
wool *n* lana *f*; ***pull the ~ over s.o.'s***

eyes *infml* gettare fumo negli occhi a qn
woollen, *US* **woolen I** *adj* di lana **II** *n* indumento *m* di lana
woolly, *US* **wooly** *adj* (+*er*) (*woollen*) di lana; *thinking* confuso
woozy *adj* (+*er*) *infml* stordito
word I *n* **1.** parola *f*; ***have ~s*** (*argue*) litigare; ***have a ~ with s.o.*** parlare con qn; ***~ for ~*** parola per parola **2.** (*news*) notizie *fpl*; ***is there any ~ from …?*** ci sono notizie da …? **3.** (*promise*) parola *f*; ***you have my ~*** hai la mia parola **II** *v/t article*, *letter* formulare
wording *n* formulazione *f*
word-perfect *adj*: ***be ~*** recitare perfettamente
wordplay *n* gioco *m* di parole
word processing *n* trattamento *m* testi **word processor** *n software* word processor *m inv*
wordy *adj* (+*er*) prolisso
wore *pret* → ***wear***
work I *v/i* **1.** *of person* lavorare; *study* studiare; ***I used to ~ with him*** lavoravamo insieme **2.** *of machine*, (*succeed*) funzionare; ***how does it ~?*** *of device* come funziona? **II** *v/t employee* far lavorare; *machine* far funzionare **III** *n* lavoro *m*; ***out of ~*** disoccupato; ***be at ~*** essere al lavoro; ***I go to ~ by bus*** vado a lavorare in autobus; ***he doesn't like ~*** non gli piace lavorare; ***that's a good piece of ~*** è un bel lavoro; ***is this all your own ~?*** è tutta opera tua?; ***a ~ of art*** un'opera d'arte; ***a fine piece of ~*** un oggetto raffinato; **works** *nsg or npl Br* (*factory*) fabbrica *f*; ***steel ~s*** acciaieria *f*
◆**work off** *v/t sep bad mood*, *anger* sfogare; *flab* smaltire
◆**work out I** *v/t sep problem* capire; *solution* trovare **II** *v/i at gym* fare ginnastica; *of relationship etc* funzionare
◆**work out to** *v/t* (*add up to*) ammontare a
◆**work up** *v/t sep*: ***work up enthusiasm*** entusiasmarsi; ***I worked up an appetite*** mi è venuto appetito; ***get worked up*** (*get angry*) infuriarsi; (*get nervous*) agitarsi
workable *adj solution* realizzabile
workaholic *n infml* stacanovista *m/f*
workbench *n* banco *m* da lavoro
workbook *n* libro *m* degli esercizi
workday *n hours of work* giornata *f* lavorativa; *not a holiday* giorno *m* feriale
worker *n* lavoratore *m*, -trice *f*; ***she's a good ~*** lavora bene
workforce *n* forza *f* lavoro
working *adj day*, *week* lavorativo; *clothes* da lavoro; *lunch* di lavoro; ***in ~ order*** funzionante
working class *n* classe *f* operaia **working-class** *adj* operaio **working conditions** *npl* condizioni *fpl* di lavoro **working day** → ***workday*** **working hours** *npl* orario *m* di lavoro **working knowledge** *n* conoscenza *f* di base **working lunch** *n* pranzo *m* di lavoro **working mother** *n* madre *f* che lavora
workload *n* carico *m* di lavoro **workman** *n* operaio *m* **workmanlike** *adj* professionale **workmanship** *n* fattura *f* **workmate** *n* collega *m/f* **work of art** *n* opera *f* d'arte **workout** *n* allenamento *m* **work permit** *n* permesso *m* di lavoro **workplace** *n* posto *m* di lavoro **workshop** *n* laboratorio *m*; *for mechanic* officina *f*; (*seminar*) workshop *m inv* **work station** *n* work station *f inv* **worktop** *n* piano *m* di lavoro **work-to-rule** *n* sciopero *m* bianco
world *n* mondo *m*; ***the ~ of computers / the theatre*** il mondo dei computer / del teatro; ***out of this ~*** *infml* fantastico; ***what in the ~ …?*** *infml* cosa diavolo …? *infml*
world-class *adj* di livello internazionale
World Cup *n* mondiali *mpl* (di calcio)
world-famous *adj* di fama mondiale
worldly *adj* (+*er*) *goods* materiale; *not spiritual* terreno; *power* temporale; *person* mondano
world power *n* potenza *f* mondiale **world record** *n* record *m inv* mondiale **world war** *n* guerra *f* mondiale **world-weary** *adj* stanco della vita **worldwide I** *adj* mondiale **II** *adv* a livello mondiale
worm I *n* verme *m*; COMPUT virus *m inv*; ***~s*** MED vermi *mpl*; ***a can of ~s*** il marciume *m* **II** *v/t*: ***~ one's way through sth*** farsi strada attraverso

qc; **~ *one's way into a group*** infiltrarsi in un gruppo

worn *past part* → ***wear***

worn-out *adj shoes, carpet, part* logoro; *person* esausto, sfinito

worried *adj* preoccupato; ***be ~ about*** essere preoccupato per

worriedly *adv* con aria preoccupata

worrisome *adj* preoccupante

worry I *v/t* ⟨*pret & past part* ***-ied***⟩ preoccupare; ***~ o.s. sick*** *or* ***silly*** (***about*** *or* ***over sth***) *infml* preoccuparsi da morire (per qc) *infml*; ***~ s.o. with sth*** allarmare qc con qc; (*upset*) turbare **II** *v/i* ⟨*pret & past part* ***-ied***⟩ proccuparsi; ***it will be alright, don't ~!*** andrà tutto bene, non preoccuparti! **III** *n* preoccupazione *f*; ***no worries!*** *infml* nessun problema!

worry beads *n rosario pallini da sgranare per rilassarsi*

worrying *adj* preoccupante

worse I *adj* peggiore; ***things will get ~*** le cose peggioreranno; ***to make matters ~*** a peggiorare le cose **II** *adv* peggio

worsen *v/i* peggiorare

worship I *n* culto *m* **II** *v/t* ⟨*pret & past part* ***-ped***⟩ venerare; *fig* adorare

worst I *adj* peggiore **II** *adv* peggio **III** *n*: ***the ~*** il peggio; ***if the ~ comes to the ~*** nel peggiore dei casi

worst-case scenario *n*: ***the ~*** la peggiore delle ipotesi

worth I *adj*: ***be ~*** valere; ***it's ~ reading / seeing*** vale la pena leggerlo / vederlo; ***be ~ it*** valerne la pena; ***it's ~ a try*** vale la pena tentare; ***will you do this for me? — what's it ~ to you?*** faresti questa cosa per me? – che importanza ha per te?; ***he's ~ all his brothers put together*** vale tutti i suoi fratelli messi insieme; ***for all one is ~*** facendo del proprio meglio; ***you need to exploit the idea for all it's ~*** devi sfruttare l'idea per quel che vale; ***for what it's ~, I personally don't think …*** per quel che vale la mia opionione, personalmente non credo…; ***it's not ~ the trouble*** non vale la pena **II** *n* valore *m*; ***£20 ~ of petrol*** 20 sterline di benzina

worthless *adj object* senza valore; *person* inetto

worthwhile *adj cause* lodevole; ***be ~*** (*beneficial, useful*) essere utile; (*worth the effort, worth doing*) valere la pena

worthy *adj* (+*er*) degno; *cause* lodevole; ***be ~ of*** (*deserve*) meritare

would *v/mod*: ***I ~ help if I could*** ti aiuterei se potessi; ***I said that I ~ go*** ho detto che sarei andato; ***I told him I ~ not leave unless …*** gli ho detto che non me ne sarei andato se non …; ***~ you like to go to the cinema?*** vuoi andare al cinema?; ***~ you mind if I smoked?*** la disturba se fumo?; ***~ you tell her that …?*** le dica che …; ***~ you close the door?*** le dispiace chiudere la porta?; ***I ~ have told you but …*** te l'avrei detto ma …; ***I ~ not have been so angry if …*** non mi sarei arrabbiato tanto se …

would-be *adj writer, actor* aspirante

wound[1] **I** *n* ferita *f* **II** *v/t* ferire

wound[2] *pret & past part* → ***wind***[2]

wove *pret* → ***weave***

woven *past part* → ***weave***

wow *int* wow

WPC *n abbr* (= **Woman Police Constable**) *Br* poliziotta *f*

wrangle *v/i* litigare; ***~ with s.o.*** (***over sth***) litigare con qn (per qc)

wrap I *v/t* ⟨*pret & past part* ***-ped***⟩ *parcel, gift* incartare; (*wind, cover*) avvolgere **II** *n* (*stole*) scialle *m*; *sandwich piadina ripiena e arrotolata*

◆**wrap up** *v/i against the cold* coprirsi bene

wrapper *n* incarto *m*

wrapping *n* involucro *m*

wrapping paper *n* carta *f* da regalo

wrath *n* ira *f*

wreak *v/t revenge* compiere

wreath *n* corona *f*; *for funeral* corona *f* funebre

wreathe *v/t* intrecciare; (*mist*) avviluppare

wreck I *n of ship* relitto *m*; *of car* carcassa *f*; ***be a nervous ~*** sentirsi un rottame **II** *v/t ship* far naufragare; *car* demolire; *plans, career, marriage* distruggere

wreckage *n of car, plane* rottami *mpl*; *of marriage, career* brandelli *mpl*

wren *n* scricciolo *m*

wrench I *n tool* chiave *f* inglese; *injury* slogatura *f* **II** *v/t injure* slogarsi; (*pull*) strappare

wrest *v/t*: **~ *sth from s.o.*** strappare qc a qn
wrestle *v/i* fare la lotta
◆**wrestle with** *v/t problems* lottare con
wrestler *n* lottatore *m*, -trice *f*
wrestling *n* lotta *f* libera
wrestling match *n* incontro *m* di lotta libera
wretch *n* disgraziato *m*, -a *f*
wretched *adj* disgraziato
wriggle *v/i* (*squirm*) dimenarsi; *along the ground* strisciare
◆**wriggle out of** *v/t* sottrarsi a
◆**wring out** *v/t* ⟨*pret & past part* ***wrung***⟩ *cloth* strizzare
wrinkle I *n in skin* ruga *f*; *in clothes* grinza *f* **II** *v/t clothes* stropicciare **III** *v/i of clothes* stropicciarsi
wrist *n* polso *m*
wrist watch *n* orologio *m* da polso
write ⟨*pret* ***wrote***, *past part* ***written***⟩ **I** *v/t* scrivere; *cheque* fare **II** *v/i* scrivere; *of author* scrivere; (*send a letter*) scrivere
◆**write down** *v/t sep* annotare, scrivere
◆**write off** *v/t sep debt* cancellare; *car* distruggere
write-off *n infml crashed car* rottame *m*
writer *n* autore *m*, -trice *f*; *professional* scrittore *m*, -trice *f*
write-up *n infml* recensione *f*
writhe *v/i* contorcersi
writing *n as career* scrivere *m*; (*hand-writing*) scrittura *f*; (*words*) scritta *f*; (*script*) scritto *m*; ***in ~*** per iscritto
writing paper *n* carta *f* da lettere
written *past part* → ***write***
wrong I *adj* sbagliato; ***be ~*** *of person* sbagliare; *of answer* essere errato; *morally* essere ingiusto; ***it's ~ to steal*** non si deve rubare; ***what's ~?*** cosa c'è?; ***there is something ~ with the car*** la macchina ha qualcosa che non va **II** *adv* in modo sbagliato; ***go ~*** *of person* sbagliare; *of marriage, plan etc* andar male; *of printer etc* non funzionare bene **III** *n immoral action* torto *m*; *immorality* male *m*; ***be in the ~*** avere torto
wrongdoer *n* malfattore *m*, -trice *f*
wrong-foot *v/t* prendere in contropiede
wrongful *adj* illegale
wrongly *adv* erroneamente
wrong number *n* numero *m* sbagliato
wrote *pret* → ***write***
wrought iron *n* ferro *m* battuto
wrung *pret & past part* → ***wring***
wry *adj* beffardo
W.W.I. *abbr* (= **World War I**) prima guerra mondiale
W.W.II. *abbr* (= **World War II**) seconda guerra mondiale
WWW *abbr* (= **World Wide Web**) COMPUT WWW, Web *m inv*
WYSIWYG *abbr* (= **what you see is what you get**) COMPUT WYSIWYG *m inv* (quello che vedi è quello che ottieni)

X

X, x *n* X, X *f inv*; MATH X *f inv*; EDU *segno di errore*
xenophobia *n* xenofobia *f*
Xmas *n infml* Natale *m*
X-ray I *n* raggio *m* X; *picture* radiografia *f*; ***have an ~*** farsi fare una radiografia **II** *v/t* radiografare
xylophone *n* xilofono *m*

Y

Y, y *n* y, Y *f inv*
yacht *n for pleasure* yacht *m inv*; *for racing* imbarcazione *f* da diporto
yachting *n* navigazione *f* da diporto
yachtsman *n* diportista *m*
yank *v/t* dare uno strattone a
Yank *n infml* yankee *m inv*
yap *v/i* ⟨*pret & past part* **-ped**⟩ *of small dog* abbaiare; *infml talk a lot* chiacchierare
yard[1] *n of prison, institution etc* cortile *m*; *for storage* deposito *m* all'aperto
yard[2] *n measurement* iarda *f*
yardstick *n fig* metro *m*
yarn *n* (*thread*) filato *m*; *infml story* racconto *m*
yawn I *v/i* sbadigliare **II** *n* sbadiglio *m*
yeah *int infml* sì
year *n* anno *m*; ***I've known her for ~s*** la conosco da (tanti) anni; ***it will last for ~s*** durerà anni; ***we were in the same ~*** *at school* frequentavamo lo stesso anno; ***be six ~s old*** avere sei anni; ***~ in, ~ out*** anno dopo anno
yearly I *adj* annuale **II** *adv* annualmente; ***twice ~*** due volte (al)l'anno
yearn *v/i*: ***~ to do sth*** struggersi dal desiderio di fare qc
◆**yearn for** *v/t* desiderare ardentemente
yearning *n* desiderio *m* struggente
yeast *n* lievito *m*
yell I *v/t & v/i* urlare **II** *n* urlo *m*
yellow I *adj* (+*er*) giallo **II** *n* giallo *m*
yellow card *n* cartellino *m* giallo; ***show s.o. the ~*** mostrare il cartellino giallo a qn **yellow pages®** *npl* pagine *fpl* gialle
yelp I *v/i* guaire **II** *n* guaito *m*
yen *n* FIN yen *m inv*
yes *int* sì; ***say ~*** dire di sì
yesman *n pej* yes man *m inv*
yesterday I *adv* ieri; ***the day before ~*** l'altro ieri **II** *n* ieri *m inv*
yet I *adv* finora; ***the fastest ~*** il più veloce finora; ***as ~*** *up to now* per ora; ***it is as ~ undecided*** rimane ancora da decidere; ***have you finished ~?*** (non) hai (ancora) finito?; ***he hasn't arrived ~*** non è ancora arrivato; ***is he here yet? – not ~*** è arrivato? – non ancora; ***~ bigger/longer*** ancora più grande/lungo **II** *cj* eppure; ***~ I'm not sure*** eppure non sono sicuro
yew *n* tasso *m*
Y-fronts *npl mutande da uomo con cucitura a Y rovesciata sul davanti*
yield I *v/t fruit, harvest* dare, produrre; *interest* fruttare **II** *v/i* (*give way*) cedere **III** *n from fields etc* raccolto *m*; *from investment* rendita *f*
yob *n sl* teppista *m/f*
Y.O.B. *abbr* (= **year of birth**) anno *m* di nascita
yoga *n* yoga *m*
yoghurt *n* yogurt *m inv*
yoke *n* giogo *m*
yokel *n pej* bifolco *m*
yolk *n* tuorlo *m*
you *pron* **1.** *subject*: *familiar singular* tu; *familiar polite plural* voi; *polite singular* lei; ***do ~ know him?*** lo conosci/conosce/conoscete?; ***~ go, I'll stay*** tu vai/lei vada/voi andate, io resto **2.** *direct object*: *familiar singular* ti; *familiar polite plural* vi; *polite singular* la; ***he knows ~*** ti/vi/la conosce **3.** *indirect object*: *familiar singular* ti; *when two pronouns are used* te; *familiar polite plural* vi; *when two pronouns are used* ve; *polite singular* le; ***did he talk to ~?*** ti/vi/le ha parlato?; ***I need to talk to ~*** devo parlarti/parlarvi/parlarle; ***I told ~*** te/ve l'ho detto, glielo ho detto **4.** *after prep familiar singular* te; *familiar polite plural* voi; *polite singular* lei; ***this is for ~*** questo è per te/voi/lei **5.** *impersonal*; ***~ never know*** non si sa mai; ***~ have to pay*** si deve pagare; ***fruit is good for ~*** la frutta fa bene
young *adj* (+*er*) giovane
youngster *n* ragazzo *m*, -a *f*
your *adj familiar singular* il tuo *m*, la tua *f*, i tuoi *mpl*, le tue *fpl*; *polite singular* il suo *m*, la sua *f*, i suoi *mpl*, le sue *fpl*; *familiar & polite plural* il vostro *m*, la vostra *f*, i vostri *mpl*, le vostre *fpl*; ***~ brother*** tuo/suo/vostro fratello

yours *pron familiar singular* il tuo *m*, la tua *f*, i tuoi *mpl*, le tue *fpl*; *polite singular* il suo *m*, la sua *f*, i suoi *mpl*, le sue *fpl*; *familiar & polite plural* il vostro *m*, la vostra *f*, i vostri *mpl*, le vostre *fpl*; ***a friend of ~*** un tuo / suo / vostro amico; ***Yours …*** *at end of letter* saluti …; ***Yours sincerely*** distinti saluti
yourself *pron reflexive* ti; *reflexive polite* si; *emphatic* tu stesso *m*, tu stessa *f*; *emphatic polite* lei stesso *m*, lei stessa *f*; ***did you hurt ~?*** ti sei / si è fatto male?; ***you said so ~*** l'hai detto tu stesso / l'ha detto lei stessa; ***keep it for ~*** tienilo per te / lo tenga per sé; ***by ~*** da solo
yourselves *pron reflexive* vi; *emphatic* voi stessi *mpl*, voi stesse *fpl*; ***did you hurt ~?*** vi siete fatti male?; ***can you do it ~?*** potete farlo da voi?; ***by ~*** da soli *mpl*, da sole *fpl*
youth *n age* gioventù *f inv*; (*young man*) ragazzo *m*; (*young people*) giovani *mpl*
youth club *n* circolo *m* giovanile
youthful *adj* giovanile; *ideas* giovane; *idealism* di gioventù
youth hostel *n* ostello *m* della gioventù
Yugoslavian *hist* **I** *adj* jugoslavo **II** *n* jugoslavo *m*, -a *f*
yummy *adj* (*+er*) *cake*, *chocolate infml* buonissimo
yuppie *n infml* yuppie *m/f inv*

Z

Z, z *n* z, Z *f inv*; ***catch*** *or* ***get some Z's*** *US infml* dormire
zap *v/t* ⟨*pret & past part* ***-ped***⟩ *infml* COMPUT (*delete*) cancellare; (*kill*) annientare; (*hit*) colpire; (*send*) mandare; ***~ channels*** TV fare zapping
◆**zap along** *v/i infml move fast* sfrecciare
zapped *adj infml* (*exhausted*) stanchissimo
zapper *n for changing TV channels* telecomando *m*
zappy *adj infml car*, *pace* veloce; (*lively*, *energetic*) brioso
zeal *n* zelo *m*
zealous *adj* appassionato
zebra *n* zebra *f*
zebra crossing *n Br* strisce *fpl* pedonali
zero *num* zero *m*; ***10 below ~*** 10 (gradi) sotto zero
◆**zero in on** *v/t* (*identify*) identificare
zero growth *n* crescita *f* zero **zero tolerance** *n* tolleranza *f* zero
zest *n* (*enthusiasm*) gusto *m*; (*peel*) scorza *f*
zigzag I *n* zigzag *m inv* **II** *v/i* ⟨*pret & past part* ***-ged***⟩ zigzagare
zilch *n infml* un bel niente
zinc *n* zinco *m*
zip *n* (cerniera *f*) lampo *f*
◆**zip up** *v/t sep* ⟨*pret & past part* ***-ped***⟩ *dress*, *jacket* allacciare; COMPUT zippare, comprimere
zip code *n US* codice *m* di avviamento postale **zip file** *n* COMPUT file *m inv* zippato
zipper *n US* cerniera *f* lampo
zit *n US infml* brufolo *m*
zodiac *n* ASTROL zodiaco *m*; ***signs of the ~*** segni *mpl* zodiacali
zombie *n infml* (*idiot*) cretino *m*, -a *f*; ***feel like a ~*** *exhausted* sentirsi uno zombie
zone *n* zona *f*
zonked *adj sl* (*exhausted*) stanco morto
zoo *n* zoo *m inv*
zoological *adj* zoologico
zoologist *n* zoologo *m*, -a *f*
zoology *n* zoologia *f*
zoom *v/i infml move fast* sfrecciare
◆**zoom in on** *v/t* PHOT zumare su
zoom lens *n* zoom *m inv*
zucchini *n US* zucchino *m*
Zurich *n* Zurigo *f*

Appendix

Italian verb conjugations

You can find the conjugation pattern of an Italian verb by looking up the infinitive form in the dictionary.
The numbers and letters given there after the infinitive refer to the conjugation patterns listed below.
The tables (**1a**, **2a**, **3a**, **4a**) show the full conjugations. The verb stem is given in ordinary type and the endings in *italics*. Compound tenses are given at **1a**. The three main conjugations (-are, -ere, -ire) are divided into four sets so as to illustrate the two different stress patterns of the second conjugation. Variations in form, stress pattern and vowel length are then shown for each of these four sets. An underscore shows the stressed vowel in each conjugated form.

The following abbreviations have been used:

pres congiunt = *presente del congiuntivo*
pres ind = *presente dell'indicativo*

First conjugation

1a mandare. The stem remains the same with regard to both spelling and pronunciation.

I. Simple tenses

Indicativo				Condizionale
presente	*imperfetto*	*passato remoto*	*futuro*	
mand*o*	mand*avo*	mand*ai*	mander*ò*	mander*ei*
mand*i*	mand*avi*	mand*asti*	mander*ai*	mander*esti*
mand*a*	mand*ava*	mand*ò*	mander*à*	mander*ebbe*
mand*iamo*	mand*avamo*	mand*ammo*	mander*emo*	mander*emmo*
mand*ate*	mand*avate*	mand*aste*	mander*ete*	mander*este*
mand*ano*	mand*avano*	mand*arono*	mander*anno*	mander*ebbero*

Congiuntivo		Imperativo
presente	*imperfetto*	
mand*i*	mand*assi*	–
mand*i*	mand*assi*	mand*a*
mand*i*	mand*asse*	mand*i*
mand*iamo*	mand*assimo*	mand*iamo*
mand*iate*	mand*aste*	mand*ate*
mand*ino*	mand*assero*	mand*ino*

Participio presente: mand*ante*
Participio passato: mand*ato*
Gerundio presente: mand*ando*

II. Compound tenses

1. Active voice

(Formed by placing *avere* before the verb form *participio passato*)

Infinito
passato: *aver* mandato

Gerundio
passato: *avendo* mandato

Indicativo
passato prossimo: *ho* mandato
trapassato prossimo: *avevo* mandato
futuro anteriore: *avrò* mandato

Condizionale
passato: *avrei* mandato

Congiuntivo
passato: *abbia* mandato
trapassato: *avessi* mandato

2. Passive voice

(formed by placing *essere* before the verb form *participio passato*)

Infinito
presente: *essere* mandato, *-a*, *-i*, *-e*
passato: *essere stato* (*stata*, *stati*, *state*) mandato, *-a*, *-i*, *-e*

Gerundio
presente: *essendo* mandato, *-a*, *-i*, *-e*
passato: *essendo stato* (*stata*, *stati*, *state*) mandato, *-a*, *-i*, *-e*

Indicativo
presente: *sono* mandato, *-a*
imperfetto: *ero* mandato, -a
passato remoto: *fui* mandato, *-a*
passato prossimo: *sono stato* (*stata*) mandato, *-a*
trapassato prossimo: *ero stato* (*stata*) mandato, *-a*
fut semplice: *sarò* mandato, *-a*
fut anteriore: *sarò* stato (stata) mandato, *-a*

Condizionale
presente: *sarei* mandato, *-a*
passato: *sarei stato* (*stata*) mandato, *-a*

Congiuntivo
presente: *sia* mandato, *-a*
imperf: *fossi* mandato, *-a*
passato: *sia stato* (*stata*) mandato, *-a*
trapassato: *fossi stato* (*stata*) mandato, *-a*

Imperativo
sii mandato, *-a*

This pattern applies to the compound tenses of all verbs.

pres ind	*passato remoto*	*futuro*	*pres congiunt*	*imperfetto*

1b celare. The stressed, closed *-e* in the stem becomes an open *e*.

celo	celai	celerò	celi	–
celiamo	celammo	celeremo	celiamo	celiamo
celano	celarono	celeranno	celino	celino

participio passato: celato

1c lodare. The stressed, closed *-o* in the stem becomes an open *o*.

lodo	lodai	loderò	lodi	–
lodiamo	lodammo	loderemo	lodiamo	lodiamo
lodano	lodarono	loderanno	lodino	lodino

participio passato: lodato

1d cercare. The final consonant in the verb stem, *-c*, becomes *ch* before *i* and *e*.

cerco	cercai	cercherò	cerchi	–
cerchiamo	cercammo	cercheremo	cerchiamo	cerchiamo
cercano	cercarono	cercheranno	cerchino	cerchino

participio passato: cercato

pres ind	*passato remoto*	*futuro*	*pres congiunt*	*imperfetto*

1e pagare. The final consonant in the verb stem, *-g*, becomes *gh* before *i* and *e*.

pago	pagai	pagherò	paghi	–
paghiamo	pagammo	pagheremo	paghiamo	paghiamo
pagano	pagarono	pagheranno	paghino	paghino

participio passato: pagato

1f baciare. The *i* is dropped if it is followed immediately by a second *i* or an *e*.

bacio	baciai	bacerò	baci	–
baciamo	baciammo	baceremo	baciamo	baciamo
baciano	baciarono	baceranno	bacino	bacino

participio passato: baciato

1g pigliare. The *i* is dropped if it is followed immediately by a second *i*.

piglio	pigliai	piglierò	pigli	–
pigliamo	piagliammo	piglieremo	pigliamo	pigliamo
pigliano	pigliarono	piglieranno	piglino	piglino

participio passato: pigliato

1h inviare. Verb forms in which the *i* is stressed retain the *i* even if it is followed by another *i*.

invio	inviai	invierò	invii	–
inviamo	inviammo	invieremo	inviamo	inviamo
inviano	inviarono	invieranno	inviino	inviino

participio passato: inviato

1i annoiare. Verbs ending in *-iare* with an unstressed *i* and a preceding vowel drop the *i* which would be added.

annoio	annoiai	annoierò	annoi	–
annoiamo	annoiammo	annoieremo	annoiamo	annoiamo
annoiano	annoiarono	annoieranno	annoino	annoino

participio passato: annoiato

1k studiare. Verbs ending in *-iare* with an unstressed *i* and a preceding consonant usually drop the *i* which would be added, even when the *i* in the verb stem is stressed: i.e. *tu studi.*Verbs ending in *-liare* always have *-lii*, e.g. *esiliare*, *esilii*.

studio	studiai	studierò	studi	–
studiamo	studiammo	studieremo	studiamo	studiamo
studiano	studiarono	studieranno	studino	studino

participio passato: studiato

1l abitare. In the verb forms in which the stem is stressed, the stress comes on the first syllable.

abito	abitai	abiterò	abiti	–
abitiamo	abitammo	abiteremo	abitiamo	abitiamo
abitano	abitarono	abiteranno	abitino	abitino

participio passato: abitato

1m collaborare. In the verb forms in which the stem is stressed, the stress comes on the second syllable.

collaboro	collaborai	collaborerò	collabori	–
collaboriamo	collaborammo	collaboreremo	collaboriamo	collaboriamo
collaborano	collaborarono	collaboreranno	collaborino	collaborino

participio passato: collaborato

pres ind	*passato remoto*	*futuro*	*pres congiunt*	*imperfetto*

1n aggomitolare. In the verb forms in which the stem is stressed, the stress comes on the third or fourth syllable.

aggomitolo	~mitolai	~mitolerò	~mitoli	–
~mitoliamo	~mitolammo	~mitoleremo	~mitoliamo	~mitoliamo
~mitolano	~mitolarono	~mitoleranno	~mitolino	~mitolino

participio passato: aggomitolato

1o giocare. The stressed *-o* in the stem can be extended to *-uo*, but this is rarer.

gi(u)oco	giocai	giocherò	gi(u)ochi	–
giochiamo	giocammo	giocheremo	giochiamo	giochiamo
gi(u)ocano	giocarono	giocheranno	gi(u)ochino	gi(u)ochino

participio passato: giocato

1p andare. Two stems: *and-* and *vad-*. In *futuro* and *condizionale* the *e* at the start of the ending is dropped.

vado	andai	andrò	vada	–
vai	andasti	andrai	vada	va, va', vai,
va	andò	andrà	vada	vada
andiamo	andammo	andremo	andiamo	andiamo
andate	andaste	andrete	andiate	andate
vanno	andarono	andranno	vadano	vadano

participio passato: andato

1q stare. Verb stem *sta*; *passato remoto* (*stetti* etc); *imperfetto del congiuntivo* (*stessi* etc) as in the 2nd conjugation; in *futuro* and *condizionale e* becomes *a*.

sto	stetti	starò	stia	–
stai	stesti	starai	stia	sta', stai
sta	stette	starà	stia	stia
stiamo	stemmo	staremo	stiamo	stiamo
state	steste	starete	stiate	state
stanno	stettero	staranno	stiano	stiano

participio passato: stato

1r dare. Verb stem *da*; *imperfetto del congiuntivo dessi* etc; in the *passato remoto* alternative forms *detti*, *dette*, *dettero*.

do	diedi, detti	darò	dia	–
dai	desti	darai	dia	da', dai
dà	diede, dette	darà	dia	dia
diamo	demmo	daremo	diamo	diamo
date	deste	darete	diate	date
danno	diedero, dettero	daranno	diano	diano

participio passato: dato

Second conjugation – First pattern

2a temere. The stem remains the same with regard to both spelling and pronunciation.

I. Simple tenses

Indicativo				Condizionale
presente	*imperfetto*	*passato remoto*	*futuro*	
temo	temevo	temei, temetti	temerò	temerei
temi	temevi	temesti	temerai	temeresti
teme	temeva	temette	temerà	temerebbe
temiamo	temevamo	tememmo	temeremo	temeremmo
temete	temevate	temeste	temerete	temereste
temono	temevano	temettero, temerono	temeranno	temerebbero

Congiuntivo		Imperativo
presente	*imperfetto*	
tema	temessi	–
tema	temessi	temi
tema	temesse	tema
temiamo	temessimo	temiamo
temiate	temeste	temete
temano	temessero	temano

Participio presente: temente
Participio passato: temuto
Gerundio presente: temendo

II. Compound tenses

Auxiliary verb *essere* or *avere*, followed by *participio passato* (see **1a**).

pres ind	*passato remoto*	*futuro*	*pres congiunt*	*imperfetto*
2b avere. In *futuro* and *condizionale* the final *e* in the ending is omitted.				
ho	ebbi	avrò	abbia	–
hai	avesti	avrai	abbia	abbi
ha	ebbe	avrà	abbia	abbia
abbiamo	avemmo	avremo	abbiamo	abbiamo
avete	aveste	avrete	abbiate	abbiate
hanno	ebbero	avranno	abbiano	abbiano
participio passato: avuto				
2c cadere. In *futuro* and *condizionale* the final *e* in the ending is omitted.				
cado	caddi	cadrò	cada	–
cadiamo	cademmo	cadremo	cadiamo	cadiamo
cadono	caddero	cadranno	cadano	cadano
participio passato: caduto				

2d calere. Used almost exclusively in 3rd person singular; now obsolete.

pres ind	*passato remoto*	*futuro*	*pres congiunt*	*imperfetto*
cale	calse	–	caglia	–

participio passato: caluto

2e dolere. In *presente*, *g* is added between the verb stem and the ending *o* or *a*. In *futuro* and *condizionale l* becomes *r* and the final *e* of the ending is dropped.

pres ind	*passato remoto*	*futuro*	*pres congiunt*	*imperfetto*
dolgo	dolsi	dorrò	dolga	–
duole	dolse	dorrà	dolga	dolga
dogliamo	dolemmo	dorremo	dogliamo	dogliamo
dolgono	dolsero	dorranno	dolgano	dolgano

participio passato: doluto

2f dovere. In the forms with the emphasis on the stem vowel, *o* becomes *e*. Omission of *e* in *futuro* and *condizionale.*

pres ind	*passato remoto*	*futuro*	*pres congiunt*	*imperfetto*
devo	dovetti	dovrò	debba, deva	–
devi	dovesti	dovrai	debba, deva	devi
deve	dovette	dovrà	debba, deva	debba, deva
dobbiamo	dovemmo	dovremo	dobbiamo	dobbiamo
dovete	doveste	dovrete	dobbiate	dovete
devono	dovettero	dovranno	debbano, devano	debbano, devano

participio passato: dovuto

2g lucere. Used only in 3rd person singular and plural of *presente dell'indicativo* (luce, lucono), *imperfetto* (luceva, lucevano), *futuro* (lucerà, luceranno), *presente del congiuntivo* (luca, lucano), and *imperfetto del congiuntivo* (lucesse, lucessero). Also *participio presente* lucente, *gerundio* lucendo.

2h parere. In *futuro* and *condizionale* the final *e* in the ending is omitted.

pres ind	*passato remoto*	*futuro*	*pres congiunt*	*imperfetto*
paio	parvi	parrò	paia	–
pa(r)iamo	paremmo	parremo	pa(r)iamo	–
paiono	parvero	parranno	paiano	–

participio passato: parso

2i persuadere.

pres ind	*passato remoto*	*futuro*	*pres congiunt*	*imperfetto*
persuado	persuasi	persuaderò	persuada	–
persuadiamo	persuademmo	persuaderemo	persuadiamo	persuadiamo
persuadono	persuasero	persuaderanno	persuadano	persuadano

participio passato: persuaso

2k piacere.

pres ind	*passato remoto*	*futuro*	*pres congiunt*	*imperfetto*
piaccio	piacqui	piacerò	piaccia	–
piacciamo	piacemmo	piaceremo	piacciamo	piacciamo
piacciono	piacquero	piaceranno	piacciano	piacciano

participio passato: piaciuto

2l potere. In *futuro* and *condizionale* the final *e* in the ending is omitted.

pres ind	*passato remoto*	*futuro*	*pres congiunt*	*imperfetto*
posso	potei	potrò	possa	–
puoi	potesti	potrai	possa	–
può	poté	potrà	possa	–
possiamo	potemmo	potremo	possiamo	–
potete	poteste	potrete	possiate	–
possono	poterono	potranno	possano	–

participio passato: potuto

pres ind	*passato remoto*	*futuro*	*pres congiunt*	*imperfetto*

2m rimanere. In *presente g* is added between stem and ending *o* or *a*; *passato remoto* ending in *-si* and *participio passato* ending in *-sto* drop the *-n* from the stem; in *futuro* and *condizionale n* becomes *r*.

rimango	rimasi	rimarrò	rimanga	–
rimaniamo	rimanemmo	rimarremo	rimaniamo	rimaniamo
rimangono	rimasero	rimarranno	rimangano	rimangano

participio passato: rimasto

2n sapere. In *futuro* and *condizionale* the *e* is dropped; 2nd person plural of *imperfetto* formed from *congiuntivo*.

so	seppi	saprò	sappia	–
sai	sapesti	saprai	sappia	sappi
sa	seppe	saprà	sappia	sappia
sappiamo	sapemmo	sapremo	sappiamo	sappiamo
sapete	sapeste	saprete	sappiate	sappiate
sanno	seppero	sapranno	sappiano	sappiano

participio presente: sapiente
participio passato: saputo

2o sedere. The *e* in the stem becomes *ie* in forms with the emphasis on the stem vowel; in *presente* alternative forms with *segg…*

siedo, seggo	sedei	sederò	sieda, segga	–
sediamo	sedemmo	sederemo	sediamo	sediamo
siedono, seggono	sederono	sederanno	siedano, seggano	siedano, seggano

participio passato: seduto

2p solere. Only used in *presente*, *passato remoto*, *gerundio* and *participio passato*. In *presente dell'indicativo* (except 2nd person singular: *suoli*) and *congiuntivo* it follows the pattern of *volere*.

soglio	solei	–	soglia	–
sogliamo	–	–	sogliamo	–
sogliono	–	–	sogliano	–

gerundio: solendo
participio passato: solito

2q tenere. Addition of *g* between stem and ending *o* or *a*. In *futuro* and *condizionale n* becomes *r*.

tengo	tenni	terrò	tenga	–
tieni	tenesti	terrai	tenga	tieni
teniamo	tenemmo	terremo	teniamo	teniamo
tengono	tennero	terranno	tengano	tengano

participio passato: tenuto

2r valere. Addition of *g* between stem and ending *o* or *a*. In *futuro* and *condizionale n* becomes *r*.

valgo	valsi	varrò	valga	–
valiamo	valemmo	varremo	valiamo	valiamo
valgono	valsero	varranno	valgano	valgano

participio passato: valso

pres ind	*passato remoto*	*futuro*	*pres congiunt*	*imperfetto*

2s vedere. In *futuro* and *condizionale* the final *e* in the ending is omitted.

vedo	vidi	vedrò	veda	–
vediamo	vedemmo	vedremo	vediamo	vediamo
vedono	videro	vedranno	vedano	vedano

participio passato: visto

2t volere. In *futuro* and *condizionale l* becomes *r* and the final *e* of the ending is omitted; 2nd person plural of *imperativo* from the *congiuntivo*.

voglio	volli	vorrò	voglia	–
vuoi	volesti	vorrai	voglia	vogli
vuole	volle	vorrà	voglia	voglia
vogliamo	volemmo	vorremo	vogliamo	vogliamo
volete	voleste	vorrete	vogliate	vogliate
vogliono	vollero	vorranno	vogliano	vogliano

participio passato: voluto

Second conjugation – Second pattern

3a vendere. The stem remains the same with regard to both spelling and pronunciation.

I. Simple tenses

Indicativo				**Condizionale**
presente	*imperfetto*	*passato remoto*	*futuro*	
vend*o*	vend*evo*	vend*etti*, vend*ei*	vend*erò*	vend*erei*
vend*i*	vend*evi*	vend*esti*	vend*erai*	vend*eresti*
vend*e*	vend*eva*	vend*ette*	vend*erà*	vend*erebbe*
vend*iamo*	vend*evamo*	vend*emmo*	vend*eremo*	vend*eremmo*
vend*ete*	vend*evate*	vend*este*	vend*erete*	vend*ereste*
vend*ono*	vend*evano*	vend*ettero*, vend*erono*	vend*eranno*	vend*erebbero*

Congiuntivo		**Imperativo**
presente	*imperfetto*	
vend*a*	vend*essi*	–
vend*a*	vend*essi*	vend*i*
vend*a*	vend*esse*	vend*a*
vend*iamo*	vend*essimo*	vend*iamo*
vend*iate*	vend*este*	vend*ete*
vend*ano*	vend*essero*	vend*ano*

Participio presente: vend*ente*
Participio passato: vend*uto**
Gerundio presente: vend*endo*

**Participio passato* of *spandere* is *spanto*.

II. Compound tenses

Auxiliary verb *essere* or *avere*, followed by *participio passato* (see **1a**).

pres ind	*passato remoto*	*futuro*	*pres congiunt*	*imperfetto*
3b chiudere.				
chiudo	chiusi	chiuderò	chiuda	–
chiudiamo	chiudemmo	chiuderemo	chiudiamo	chiudiamo
chiudono	chiusero	chiuderanno	chiudano	chiudano
participio passato: chiuso				
3c prendere.				
prendo	presi	prenderò	prenda	–
prendiamo	prendemmo	prenderemo	prendiamo	prendiamo
prendono	presero	prenderanno	prendano	prendano
participio passato: preso				
3d fingere. The *participio passato* of *stringere* is *stretto.*				
fingo	finsi	fingerò	finga	–
fingiamo	fingemmo	fingeremo	fingiamo	fingiamo
fingono	finsero	fingeranno	fingano	fingano
participio passato: finto				
3e addurre. Shorter form of *adducere.*				
adduco	addussi	addurrò	adduca	–
adduci	adducesti	addurrai	adduca	adduci
adduce	addusse	addurrà	adduca	adduca
adduciamo	adducemmo	addurremo	adduciamo	adduciamo
adducete	adduceste	addurrete	adduciate	adduciate
adducono	addussero	addurranno	adducano	adducano
participio passato: addotto				
3f assistere. In *passato remoto* alternative forms end in *-etti.*				
assisto	assistei	assisterò	assista	–
assistiamo	assistemmo	assisteremo	assistiamo	assistiamo
assistono	assisterono	assisteranno	assistano	assistano
participio passato: assistito				
3g assolvere.				
assolvo	assolsi, ~vetti	assolverò	assolva	–
assolviamo	assolvemmo	assolveremo	assolviamo	assolviamo
assolvono	assolsero, assolvettero	assolveranno	assolvano	assolvano
participio passato: assolto				
3h assumere.				
assumo	assunsi	assumerò	assuma	–
assumiamo	assumemmo	assumeremo	assumiamo	assumiamo
assumono	assunsero	assumeranno	assumano	assumano
participio passato: assunto				

3i bere. Conjugated according to the pattern of *bevere*. In *futuro* and *condizionale* *v* becomes *r* and the *e* of the ending is dropped.

pres ind	*passato remoto*	*futuro*	*pres congiunt*	*imperfetto*
bevo	bevvi, bevetti	berrò	beva	–
bevi	bevesti	berrai	beva	bevi
beve	bevve, bevette	berrà	beva	beva
beviamo	bevemmo	berremo	beviamo	beviamo
bevete	beveste	berrete	beviate	bevete
bevono	bevvero, bevettero	berranno	bevano	bevano

participio passato: bevuto

3k chiedere.

pres ind	*passato remoto*	*futuro*	*pres congiunt*	*imperfetto*
chiedo	chiesi	chiederò	chieda	–
chiediamo	chiedemmo	chiederemo	chiediamo	chiediamo
chiedono	chiesero	chiederanno	chiedano	chiedano

participio passato: chiesto

3l concedere.

pres ind	*passato remoto*	*futuro*	*pres congiunt*	*imperfetto*
concedo	concessi, concedetti	concederò	conceda	–
concediamo	concedemmo	concederemo	concediamo	concediamo
concedono	concessero, concedettero	concederanno	concedano	concedano

participio passato: concesso

3m connettere.

pres ind	*passato remoto*	*futuro*	*pres congiunt*	*imperfetto*
connetto	connessi, connettei	connetterò	connetta	–
connettiamo	connettemmo	connetteremo	connettiamo	connettiamo
connettono	connessero, connetterono	connetteranno	connettano	connettano

participio passato: connesso

3n conoscere.

pres ind	*passato remoto*	*futuro*	*pres congiunt*	*imperfetto*
conosco	conobbi	conoscerò	conosca	–
conosciamo	conoscemmo	conosceremo	conosciamo	conosciamo
conoscono	conobbero	conosceranno	conoscano	conoscano

participio passato: conosciuto

3o correre.

pres ind	*passato remoto*	*futuro*	*pres congiunt*	*imperfetto*
corro	corsi	correrò	corra	–
corriamo	corremmo	correremo	corriamo	corriamo
corrono	corsero	correranno	corrano	corrano

participio passato: corso

3p cuocere. In unstressed syllables *uo* becomes *o*. *Imperfetto cocevo* or *cocessi.*

pres ind	*passato remoto*	*futuro*	*pres congiunt*	*imperfetto*
cuocio	cossi	cuocerò	cuocia	–
cociamo	cocemmo	cuoceremo	cociamo	cociamo
cuociono	cossero	cuoceranno	cuociano	cuociano

participio passato: cotto

pres ind	*passato remoto*	*futuro*	*pres congiunt*	*imperfetto*
3q decidere.				
decido	decisi	deciderò	decida	–
decidiamo	decidemmo	decideremo	decidiamo	decidiamo
decidono	decisero	decideranno	decidano	decidano
participio passato: deciso				
3r deprimere.				
deprimo	depressi	deprimerò	deprima	–
deprimiamo	deprimemmo	deprimeremo	deprimiamo	deprimiamo
deprimono	depressero	deprimeranno	deprimano	deprimano
participio passato: depresso				
3s devolvere.				
devolvo	devolvei, devolvetti	devolverò	devolva	–
devolviamo	devolvemmo	devolveremo	devolviamo	devolviamo
devolvono	devolverono, devolvettero	devolveranno	devolvano	devolvano
participio passato: devoluto, devolto				
3t dire.				
dico	dissi	dirò	dica	–
dici	dicesti	dirai	dica	
dice	disse	dirà	dica	
diciamo	dicemmo	diremo	diciamo	diciamo
dite	diceste	direte	diciate	dite
dicono	dissero	diranno	dicano	dicano
participio passato: detto				
3u dirigere.				
dirigo	diressi	dirigerò	diriga	–
dirigiamo	dirigemmo	dirigeremo	dirigiamo	dirigiamo
dirigono	diressero	dirigeranno	dirigano	dirigano
participio passato: diretto				
3v discutere.				
discuto	discussi	discuterò	discuta	–
discutiamo	discutemmo	discuteremo	discutiamo	discutiamo
discutono	discussero	discuteranno	discutano	discutano
participio passato: discusso				
3w esigere.				
esigo	esigei, esigetti	esigerò	esiga	–
esigiamo	esigemmo	esigeremo	esigiamo	esigiamo
esigono	esigerono, esigettero	esigeranno	esigano	esigano
participio passato: esatto				

3x esimere. Has no *participio passato*, and the *passato remoto esimei* is rarely used. Instead the corresponding forms of *esentare* are used. Otherwise regular, following the pattern of *vendere* **3a**.

3y espellere.

pres ind	*passato remoto*	*futuro*	*pres congiunt*	*imperfetto*
espello	espulsi	espellerò	espella	–
espelliamo	espellemmo	espelleremo	espelliamo	espelliamo
espellono	espulsero	espelleranno	espellano	espellano

participio passato: espulso

3z essere. Completely irregular. *Imperfetto dell'indicativo*: ero, eri, era, eravamo, eravate, erano; *imperfetto del congiuntivo*: fossi, fossi, fosse, fossimo, foste, fossero.

pres ind	*passato remoto*	*futuro*	*pres congiunt*	*imperfetto*
sono	fui	sarò	sia	–
sei	fosti	sarai	sia	sii
è	fu	sarà	sia	sia
siamo	fummo	saremo	siamo	siamo
siete	foste	sarete	siate	siate
sono	furono	saranno	siano	siano

participio passato: stato

3aa fare. Shorter form of *facere*. *Imperfetto* regular, following the pattern of *facere*: *facevo* etc

pres ind	*passato remoto*	*futuro*	*pres congiunt*	*imperfetto*
faccio	feci	farò	faccia	–
fai	facesti	farai	faccia	fa', fai
fa	fece	farà	faccia	faccia
facciamo	facemmo	faremo	facciamo	facciamo
fate	faceste	farete	facciate	fate
fanno	fecero	faranno	facciano	facciano

participio passato: fatto

3bb fondere.

pres ind	*passato remoto*	*futuro*	*pres congiunt*	*imperfetto*
fondo	fusi	fonderò	fonda	–
fondiamo	fondemmo	fonderemo	fondiamo	fondiamo
fondono	fusero	fonderanno	fondano	fondano

participio passato: fuso

3cc leggere.

pres ind	*passato remoto*	*futuro*	*pres congiunt*	*imperfetto*
leggo	lessi	leggerò	legga	–
leggiamo	leggemmo	leggeremo	leggiamo	leggiamo
leggono	lessero	leggeranno	leggano	leggano

participio passato: letto

3dd mescere.

pres ind	*passato remoto*	*futuro*	*pres congiunt*	*imperfetto*
mesco	mescei	mescerò	mesca	–
mesciamo	mescemmo	mesceremo	mesciamo	mesciamo
mescono	mescerono	mesceranno	mescano	mescano

participio passato: mesciuto

3ee mettere.

pres ind	*passato remoto*	*futuro*	*pres congiunt*	*imperfetto*
metto	misi	metterò	metta	–
mettiamo	mettemmo	metteremo	mettiamo	mettiamo
mettono	misero	metteranno	mettano	mettano

participio passato: messo

3ff muovere. In unstressed syllables *uo* becomes *o*.

pres ind	*passato remoto*	*futuro*	*pres congiunt*	*imperfetto*
muovo	mossi	muoverò	muova	–
muoviamo	movemmo	muoveremo	muoviamo	muoviamo
muovono	mossero	muoveranno	muovano	muovano

participio passato: mosso

3gg nascere.

pres ind	*passato remoto*	*futuro*	*pres congiunt*	*imperfetto*
nasco	nacqui	nascerò	nasca	–
nasciamo	nascemmo	nasceremo	nasciamo	nasciamo
nascono	nacquero	nasceranno	nascano	nascano

participio passato: nato

3hh nascondere.

pres ind	*passato remoto*	*futuro*	*pres congiunt*	*imperfetto*
nascondo	nascosi	nasconderò	nasca	–
nascondiamo	nascondemmo	nasconderemo	nascondiamo	nascondiamo
nascondono	nascosero	nasconderanno	nascondano	nascondano

participio passato: nascosto

3ii nuocere. In unstressed syllables *uo* becomes *o*.

pres ind	*passato remoto*	*futuro*	*pres congiunt*	*imperfetto*
nuoccio	nocqui	nuocerò	nuoccia	–
nociamo	nocemmo	nuoceremo	nociamo	nuociamo
nuocciono	nocquero	nuoceranno	nuocciano	nuocciano

participio passato: nociuto

3kk piovere. Used only in the 3rd person singular and plural, in the two participial forms and in the *gerundio*; *presente dell'indicativo* piove, piovono; *passato remoto* piovve, piovvero; *futuro* pioverà, pioveranno; *presente del congiuntivo* piova, piovano; *participio passato* piovuto.

3ll porre. When followed by an *r* in *futuro* and *condizionale n* becomes *r*.

pres ind	*passato remoto*	*futuro*	*pres congiunt*	*imperfetto*
pongo	posi	porrò	ponga	–
poni	ponesti	porrai	ponga	poni
pone	pose	porrà	ponga	ponga
poniamo	ponemmo	porremo	poniamo	poniamo
ponete	poneste	porrete	poniate	ponete
pongono	posero	porranno	pongano	pongano

participio passato: posto

3mm prefiggere.

pres ind	*passato remoto*	*futuro*	*pres congiunt*	*imperfetto*
prefiggo	prefissi	prefiggerò	prefigga	–
prefiggiamo	prefiggemmo	prefiggeremo	prefiggiamo	prefiggiamo
prefiggono	prefissero	prefiggeranno	prefiggano	prefiggano

participio passato: prefisso

3nn recere. Addition of *i* between stem and endings *o*, *a*, *u*.

pres ind	*passato remoto*	*futuro*	*pres congiunt*	*imperfetto*
recio	recetti	recerò	recia	–
reciamo	recemmo	receremo	reciamo	reciamo
reciono	recettero	receranno	reciano	reciano

participio passato: reciuto

3oo redigere.

pres ind	*passato remoto*	*futuro*	*pres congiunt*	*imperfetto*
redigo	redassi	redigerò	rediga	–
redigiamo	redigemmo	redigeremo	redigiamo	redigiamo
redigono	redassero	redigeranno	redigano	redigano

participio passato: redatto

3pp redimere.

pres ind	*passato remoto*	*futuro*	*pres congiunt*	*imperfetto*
redimo	redensi	redimerò	redima	–
redimiamo	redimemmo	redimeremo	redimiamo	redimiamo
redimono	redensero	redimeranno	redimano	redimano

participio passato: redento

3qq riflettere. In *passato remoto* and in *participio passato* in the sense of 'think about' forms usually end in *-ei* and *-uto*; in the sense of 'reflect back' usually *-ssi*, *-sso*.

pres ind	*passato remoto*	*futuro*	*pres congiunt*	*imperfetto*
rifletto	riflettei, riflessi	rifletterò	rifletta	–
riflettiamo	riflettemmo	rifletteremo	riflettiamo	riflettiamo
riflettono	rifletterono, riflessero	rifletteranno	riflettano	riflettano

participio passato: riflettuto, riflesso

3rr rompere.

pres ind	*passato remoto*	*futuro*	*pres congiunt*	*imperfetto*
rompo	ruppi	romperò	rompa	–
rompiamo	rompemmo	romperemo	rompiamo	rompiamo
rompono	ruppero	romperanno	rompano	rompano

participio passato: rotto

3ss scegliere. The stem ending *gli* becomes *lg* before endings *o* and *a*.

pres ind	*passato remoto*	*futuro*	*pres congiunt*	*imperfetto*
scelgo	scelsi	sceglierò	scelga	–
scegli	scegliesti	sceglierai	scelga	scegli
sceglie	scelse	sceglierà	scelga	scelga
scegliamo	scegliemmo	sceglieremo	scegliamo	scegliamo
scegliete	sceglieste	sceglierete	scegliate	scegliete
scelgono	scelsero	sceglieranno	scelgano	scelgano

participio passato: scelto

3tt scrivere.

pres ind	*passato remoto*	*futuro*	*pres congiunt*	*imperfetto*
scrivo	scrissi	scriverò	scriva	–
scriviamo	scrivemmo	scriveremo	scriviamo	scriviamo
scrivono	scrissero	scriveranno	scrivano	scrivano

participio passato: scritto

3uu spargere.

pres ind	*passato remoto*	*futuro*	*pres congiunt*	*imperfetto*
spargo	sparsi	spargerò	sparga	–
spargiamo	spargemmo	spargeremo	spargiamo	spargiamo
spargono	sparsero	spargeranno	spargano	spargano

participio passato: sparso

3vv spegnere. The stem sound *gn* becomes *ng* before the endings *o* and *a*.

pres ind	*passato remoto*	*futuro*	*pres congiunt*	*imperfetto*
spengo	spensi	spegnerò	spenga	–
spegni	spegnesti	spegnerai	spenga	spegni
spegne	spense	spegnerà	spenga	spenga
spegniamo	spegnemmo	spegneremo	spegniamo	spegniamo
spegnete	spegneste	spegnerete	spegniate	spegnete
spengono	spensero	spegneranno	spengano	spengano

participio passato: spento

pres ind	*passato remoto*	*futuro*	*pres congiunt*	*imperfetto*
3ww svellere.				
svello	svelsi	svellerò	svella	–
svelliamo	svellemmo	svelleremo	svelliamo	svelliamo
svellono	svelsero	svelleranno	svellano	svellano
participio passato: svelto				
3xx trarre.				
traggo	trassi	trarrò	tragga	–
trai	traesti	trarrai	tragga	trai
trae	trasse	trarrà	tragga	tragga
traiamo	traemmo	trarremo	traiamo	traiamo
traete	traeste	trarrete	traiate	traete
traggono	trassero	trarranno	traggano	traggano
participio passato: tratto				

3yy vigere. Common only in the following forms: 3rd person singular and plural of *indicativo presente*, *imperfetto* and *futuro*; *condizionale*; *congiuntivo imperfetto* and *participio presente*
Indicativo presente: vige, vigono; *imperfetto*: vigeva, vigevano; *futuro*: vigerà, vigeranno. *Congiuntivo imperfetto*: vigesse, vigessero. *Condizionale*: vigerebbe, vigerebbero. *Participio presente*: vigente.

3zz vivere.				
vivo	vissi	vivrò	viva	–
viviamo	vivemmo	vivremo	viviamo	viviamo
vivono	vissero	vivranno	vivano	vivano
participio passato: vissuto				

Third conjugation

4a partire. The stem remains the same with regard to both spelling and pronunciation.

I. Simple tenses

Indicativo				Condizionale
presente	*imperfetto*	*passato remoto*	*futuro*	
parto*	partivo	partii	partirò	partirei
parti	partivi	partisti	partirai	partiresti
parte	partiva	partì	partirà	partirebbe
partiamo	partivamo	partimmo	partiremo	partiremmo
partite	partivate	partiste	partirete	partireste
partono*	partivano	partirono	partiranno	partirebbero

Congiuntivo		Imperativo
presente	*imperfetto*	
parta*	partissi	–
parta*	partissi	parti
parta*	partisse	parta*
partiamo	partissimo	partiamo
partiate	partiste	partite
partano*	partissero	partano*

Participio presente: partente
Participio passato: partito
Gerundio presente: partendo

* In *cucire* and *sdrucire* an *i* is added before *a* and *o*: *cucio*, *sdruciono* etc.

II. Compound tenses

Auxiliary verb *essere* or *avere*, followed by *participio passato* (see **1a**).

pres ind	*passato remoto*	*futuro*	*pres congiunt*	*imperfetto*
4b sentire. The stressed, closed *-e* of stem ending becomes an open *-e*.				
sento	sentii	sentirò	senta	–
sentiamo	sentimmo	sentiremo	sentiamo	sentiamo
sentono	sentirono	sentiranno	sentano	sentano
participio passato: sentito				
4c dormire. The stressed, closed *-o* of stem ending becomes an open *-o*.				
dormo	dormii	dormirò	dorma	–
dormiamo	dormimmo	dormiremo	dormiamo	dormiamo
dormono	dormirono	dormiranno	dormano	dormano
participio passato: dormito				
4d finire. In the 1st, 2nd and 3rd person singular and 3rd person plural of *presente* (*indicativo* and *congiuntivo*) and *imperativo*, *isc* is added between stem and ending.				
finisco	finii	finirò	finisca	–
finisci	finisti	finirai	finisca	finisci
finisce	finì	finirà	finisca	finisca
finiamo	finimmo	finiremo	finiamo	finiamo
finite	finiste	finirete	finiate	finite
finiscono	finirono	finiranno	finiscano	finiscano
participio passato: finito				
4e apparire.				
appaio, apparisco	apparvi, apparsi, apparii	apparirò	appaia apparisca	
appariamo	apparimmo	appariremo	appariamo	appariamo
appaiono, appariscono	apparvero, apparsero, apparirono	appariranno	appaiano, appariscano	appaiano, appariscano
participio passato: apparso				

pres ind	*passato remoto*	*futuro*	*pres congiunt*	*imperfetto*

4f aprire.

apro	apersi, aprii	aprirò	apra	–
apriamo	aprimmo	apriremo	apriamo	apriamo
aprono	apersero, aprirono	apriranno	aprano	aprano

participio passato: aperto

4g compire. In most forms of the *presente dell'indicativo*, *presente del congiuntivo* and *imperfetto*, *compire* is conjugated according to the pattern of *compiere*. An *i* is therefore added between the stem and the ending except in forms whose ending begins with an *i*.

compio	compii	compirò	compia	–
compiamo	compimmo	compiremo	compiamo	compiamo
compiono	compirono	compiranno	compiano	compiano

participio passato: compito, compiuto
participio presente: compiente
gerundio: compiendo

4h gire. Defective verb. Apart from the forms listed below, is used only in the *imperfetto* (*indicativo* and *congiuntivo*) and in the *condizionale*. This verb is now obsolete.

–	–	girò	–	–
–	gisti	girai	–	–
–	gì	girà	–	–
–	gimmo	giremo	–	–
gite	giste	girete	–	gite
–	girono	giranno	–	–

participio passato: gito

4i ire. Defective verb. This verb is now obsolete. It was used only in *imperfetto dell'indicativo* (*ivo* etc) and in the following forms and persons:

–	2nd *pers sg* isti	–	–	–
–	–	1st *pers pl* iremo	–	–
2nd *pers pl* ite	–	2nd *pers pl* irete	–	2nd *pers pl* ite
–	3rd *pers sg* irono	3rd *pers pl* iranno	–	–

participio passato: ito

4k morire.

muoio	morii	mor(i)rò	muoia	–
moriamo	morimmo	mor(i)remo	moriamo	moriamo
muoiono	morirono	mor(i)ranno	muoiano	muoiano

participio passato: morto

4l olire. Defective verb. Used only in *imperfetto dell'indicativo* 3rd person singular (*oliva*) and 3rd person plural (*olivano*) and in *participio presente* (*olente*). This verb is now obsolete.

4m salire. *Presente* as **4a**, adding a *g* before *o* and *a*.

salgo	salii	salirò	salga	–
saliamo	salimmo	saliremo	saliamo	saliamo
salgono	salirono	saliranno	salgano	salgano

participio passato: salito

pres ind	*passato remoto*	*futuro*	*pres congiunt*	*imperfetto*

4n udire. *Presente* as **4a**, with *u* becoming *o* in the forms in which the stem is stressed.

odo	udii	ud(i)rò	oda	–
udiamo	udimmo	ud(i)remo	udiamo	udiamo
odono	udirono	ud(i)ranno	odano	odano

participio passato: udito

4o uscire.

esco	uscii	uscirò	esca	–
esci	uscisti	uscirai	esca	esci
esce	uscì	uscirà	esca	esca
usciamo	uscimmo	usciremo	usciamo	usciamo
uscite	usciste	uscirete	usciate	uscite
escono	uscirono	usciranno	escano	escano

participio passato: uscito

4p venire.

vengo	venni	verrò	venga	–
vieni	venisti	verrai	venga	vieni
viene	venne	verrà	venga	venga
veniamo	venimmo	verremo	veniamo	veniamo
venite	veniste	verrete	veniate	venite
vengono	vennero	verranno	vengano	vengano

participio passato: venuto

Numbers – Numerali

Cardinal numbers – I numeri cardinali

0	*zero* zero
1	*one* uno
2	*two* due
3	*three* tre
4	*four* quattro
5	*five* cinque
6	*six* sei
7	*seven* sette
8	*eight* otto
9	*nine* nove
10	*ten* dieci
11	*eleven* undici
12	*twelve* dodici
13	*thirteen* tredici
14	*fourteen* quattordici
15	*fifteen* quindici
16	*sixteen* sedici
17	*seventeen* diciassette
18	*eighteen* diciotto
19	*nineteen* diciannove
20	*twenty* venti
21	*twenty-one* ventuno
22	*twenty-two* ventidue
23	*twenty-three* ventitrè
28	*twenty-eight* ventotto
29	*twenty-nine* ventinove
30	*thirty* trenta
40	*forty* quaranta
50	*fifty* cinquanta
60	*sixty* sessanta
70	*seventy* settanta
80	*eighty* ottanta
90	*ninety* novanta
100	*one / a hundred* cento
101	*one / a hundred and one* centouno
102	*one / a hundred and two* centodue
200	*two hundred* duecento
201	*two hundred and one* duecento uno
300	*three hundred* trecento
400	*four hundred* quattrocento
500	*five hundred* cinquecento
600	*six hundred* seicento
700	*seven hundred* settecento
800	*eight hundred* ottocento
900	*nine hundred* novecento
1,000	*one / a thousand* mille
1,001	*one / a thousand and one* milleuno / mille e uno
2,000	*two thousand* duemila
3,000	*three thousand* tremila
4,000	*four thousand* quattromila
5,000	*five thousand* cinquemila
7,000	*seven thousand* settemila
10,000	*ten thousand* diecimila
100,000	*one / a hundred thousand* centomila
1,000,000	*one / a million* un milione
2,000,000	*two million* due milioni
1,000,000,000	*one / a billion* un miliardo

Notes:

i) In Italian numbers a comma is used for decimals:
1,25 **one point two five** uno virgola venticinque

ii) A full stop is used where, in English, we would use a comma:
1.000.000 = 1,000,000
Italian can also write numbers like this using a space instead of a comma:
1 000 000 = 1,000,000

Ordinal numbers – I numeri ordinali

1st	*first*	**1°**	il primo, la prima
2nd	*second*	**2°**	secondo
3rd	*third*	**3°**	terzo
4th	*fourth*	**4°**	quarto
5th	*fifth*	**5°**	quinto
6th	*sixth*	**6°**	sesto
7th	*seventh*	**7°**	settimo
8th	*eighth*	**8°**	ottavo
9th	*ninth*	**9°**	nono
10th	*tenth*	**10°**	decimo
11th	*eleventh*	**11°**	undicesimo
12th	*twelfth*	**12°**	dodicesimo
13th	*thirteenth*	**13°**	tredicesimo
14th	*fourteenth*	**14°**	quattordicesimo
15th	*fifteenth*	**15°**	quindicesimo
16th	*sixteenth*	**16°**	sedicesimo
17th	*seventeenth*	**17°**	diciassettesimo
18th	*eighteenth*	**18°**	diciottesimo
19th	*nineteenth*	**19°**	diciannovesimo
20th	*twentieth*	**20°**	ventesimo
21st	*twenty-first*	**21°**	ventunesimo
22nd	*twenty-second*	**22°**	ventiduesimo
30th	*thirtieth*	**30°**	trentesimo
40th	*fortieth*	**40°**	quarantesimo
50th	*fiftieth*	**50°**	cinquantesimo
60th	*sixtieth*	**60°**	sessantesimo
70th	*seventieth*	**70°**	settantesimo
80th	*eightieth*	**80°**	ottantesimo
90th	*ninetieth*	**90°**	novantesimo
100th	*hundredth*	**100°**	centesimo
101st	*hundred and first*	**101°**	centunesimo
103rd	*hundred and third*	**103°**	centotreesimo
200th	*two hundredth*	**200°**	duecentesimo
1,000th	*thousandth*	**1.000°**	millesimo
1,001st	*thousand and first*	**1.001°**	millesimo primo
2,000th	*two thousandth*	**2.000°**	duemillesimo
1,000,000th	*millionth*	**1.000.000°**	milionesimo

Note:
Italian ordinal numbers are ordinary adjectives and consequently must agree:

her 13th granddaughter la sua tredicesima nipote

Fractions – Frazioni

$^1/_2$	*one half, a half*	un mezzo
$^1/_3$	*one third, a third*	un terzo
$^2/_3$	*two thirds*	due terzi
$^1/_4$	*one quarter, a quarter*	un quarto
$^3/_4$	*three quarters*	tre quarti
$^1/_5$	*one fifth, a fifth*	un quinto
$^1/_{10}$	*one tenth, a tenth*	un decimo
$1^1/_2$	*one and a half*	uno e mezzo
$2^3/_4$	*two and three quarters*	due e tre quarti
$^1/_{100}$	*one hundredth, a hundredth*	un centesimo
$^1/_{1000}$	*one thousandth, a thousandth*	un millesimo

Approximate numbers – Valori approssimativi

a couple	un paio
about ten	una decina
about twenty	una ventina
about eighty	un'ottantina
about a hundred	un centinaio
hundreds (of people)	centinaia (di persone)
about a thousand	un migliaio
thousands	migliaia

Dates – Date

nineteen ninety-six	**1996**	millenovecentonovantasei
two thousand and eight	**2008**	duemilaotto
the 10th / 11th of November *US* November 10 / 11 (ten / eleven)	**10. / 11.11.**	il dieci / l'undici novembre
the first of March *US* March 1 (first)	**01.03.**	il primo marzo

Time – L'ora

What's the time?		**Che ore sono?** **Che ora è?**
It's midday./It's lunchtime.	**12:00**	È mezzogiorno.
It's midnight.	**0.00**	È mezzanotte.
It's one o'clock.	**1:00 a.m./p.m.**	È l'una.
It's three o'clock.	**3:00 a.m./p.m.**	Sono le tre.
It's nearly four o'clock.		Sono quasi le quattro.
It's just after 10 o'clock.		Sono le dieci passate.
It's exactly six o'clock.		Sono le sei in punto.
It's about five o'clock.		Sono più o meno le cinque.

It's ...		**Sono ...**
five past two.	**2:05 a.m./p.m.**	le due e cinque.
ten past three.	**3:10 a.m./p.m.**	le tre e dieci.
(a) quarter past four.	**4:15 a.m./p.m.**	le quattro e un quarto.
half past five.	**5:30 a.m./p.m.**	le cinque e mezzo/mezza.
twenty to seven.	**6:40 a.m./p.m.**	le sette meno venti.
five to eight.	**7:55 a.m./p.m.**	le otto meno cinque.
(a) quarter to nine.	**8:45 a.m./p.m.**	le nove meno un quarto.
twenty-five to ten.	**9:35 a.m./p.m.**	le nove e trentacinque.

(At) what time?		**A che ora?**
at one o'clock	**1:00 a.m./p.m.**	all'una
at three o'clock	**3:00 a.m./p.m.**	alle tre
at six o'clock	**6:00 a.m./p.m.**	alle sei
at about nine o'clock		verso le nove
at midday, at lunchtime		a mezzogiorno
at midnight		a mezzanotte

When?	**Quando?**
now	adesso
later	più tardi
not before six o'clock	non prima delle sei
until ten o'clock	prima delle dieci
in half an hour	fra mezz'ora
between eight and nine	fra le otto e le nove
before midday, before noon	di mattina
tomorrow	domani
the day after tomorrow	dopodomani
in the afternoon	di pomeriggio
in the evening	di sera
in the morning	di mattina

Weights and measures – Pesi e misure

Metric system

Length

1 mm	**millimetro**	millimetre	= 0.039 inches
1 cm	**centimetro**	centimetre	= 0.39 inches
1 dm	**decimetro**	decimetre	= 3.94 inches
1 m	**metro**	metre	= 1.094 yards
			= 3.28 feet
			= 39.37 inches
1 km	**chilometro**	kilometre	= 1,093.637 yards
			= 0.621 British *or* Statute Miles
1 mn	**miglio navale**	nautical mile	= 1,852 metres

Square measures

1 mm²	**millimetro quadrato**	square millimetre	= 0.015 square inches
1 cm²	**centimetro quadrato**	square centimetre	= 0.155 square inches
1 m²	**metro quadrato**	square metre	= 1.195 square yards
			= 10.76 square feet
1 km²	**chilometro quadrato**	square kilometre	= 247.11 acres
			= 0.386 square miles
1 a	**ara**		= 100 square metres
1 ha	**ettaro**	hectare	= 11,959.90 square yards
			= 2.47 acres

Cubic measures

1 cm³	**centimetro cubo**	cubic centimetre	= 0.061 cubic inches
1 dm³	**decimetro cubo**	cubic decimetre	= 61.025 cubic inches
1 m³	**metro cubo**	cubic metre	= 1.307 cubic yards
			= 35.31 cubic feet
1 TSL	**tonnellata di stazza lorda**	gross register ton	= 100 cubic feet

Volume capacity

1 ml	**millilitro**	millilitre	= 1/1000 litre
1 cl	**centilitro**	centilitre	= 1/100 litre
1 dl	**decilitro**	decilitre	= 1/10 litre
1 l	**litro**	litre	= *Br* 1.76 pints
			= *Br* 0.88 quarts
			= *Br* 0.22 gallons
			= *US* 2.11 pints
			= *US* 1.06 quarts
			= *US* 0.26 gallons
1 hl	**ettolitro**	hectolitre	= *Br* 22.009 gallons
			= *US* 26.42 gallons

Weights

1mg	**milligrammo**	milligramme	= 1/1000 gramme
1 g	**grammo**	gramme	= 1/1000 kilogramme
1 dag	**decagrammo**	decagramme	= 10 gramme
1kg	**chilogrammo**	kilogramme	= 2.204 pounds (avdp.*)
			= 2.68 pounds (troy)
1 t	**tonnellata**	ton	= 0.984 British tons
			= 1.102 US tons
			= 1.000 metric tons

* avdp. = avoirdupois

British and American weights and measures

Length

1 inch	= 2.54 cm
1 foot	= 12 inches
	= 30.48 cm
1 yard	= 3 feet
	= 91.44 cm
1 (statute) mile	= 1760 yards
	= 1.609 km

Square measures

1 square inch	= 6.452 cm²
1 square foot	= 144 square inches
	= 929.029 cm²
1 square yard	= 9 square feet
	= 8361.26 cm²
1 acre	= 4840 square yards
	= 4046.8 m²
1 square mile	= 640 acres
	= 259 ha
	= 2.59 km²

Cubic measures

1 cubic inch	= 16.387 cm³
1 cubic foot	= 1728 cubic inches
	= 0.02832 m³
1 cubic yard	= 27 cubic feet
	= 0.7646 m³

Volume capacity (Great Britain)

1 pint	= 0.568 l
1 quart	= 2 pints = 1.136 l
1 gallon	= 4 quarts
	= 4.5459 l

Volume capacity (United States)

1 pint	= 0.4732 l
1 quart	= 2 pints = 0.9464 l
1 gallon	= 4 quarts
	= 3.7853 l
1 barrel	= 42 gallons
petroleum	= 158.97 l

Weights

1 ounce	= 28.35 g
1 pound	= 16 ounces
	= 453.59 g
1 stone	= 14 pounds
	= 6.35 kg
1 hundred-	= 1 quintal
weight	= *Br* 112 pounds
	= 50.802 kg
	= *US* 100 pounds
	= 45.359 kg
1 long ton	= *Br* 20 hundred-weights
	= 1016.05 kg
1 short ton	= *US* 20 hundred-weights
	= 907.185 kg
1 metric ton	= 1000 kg

Temperature conversion

Celsius – Fahrenheit

	°C	°F	°F	°C
	220	428	**430**	221
	200	392	**390**	199
	180	356	**360**	182
boiling point	**100**	212	**200**	93
	60	140	**140**	60
	40	104	**100**	38
	30	86	**80**	27
	20	68	**60**	16
	10	50	**50**	10
freezing point	**0**	32	**32**	0
	–10	14	**0**	–18
	–15	5	**–4**	–20
	–20	–4	**–15**	–26

To convert Celsius into Fahrenheit multiply by 9, divide by 5 and add 32.
To convert Fahrenheit into Celsius subtract 32, multiply by 5 and divide by 9.

Spelling alphabets – Alfabeti telefonici

	Italy	Great Britain	USA
A	Ancona	Andrew	able
B	Bologna	Benjamin	baker
C	Catania	Charlie	Charlie
D	Domodossola	David	dog
E	Empoli	Edward	easy
F	Firenze	Fred	fox
G	Genova	George	George
H	acca (*o* hotel)	Harry	how
I	Imola	Isaac	item
J	i lunga	Jack	Juliett
K	cappa	king	king
L	Livorno	Lucy	love
M	Milano	Mary	Mike
N	Napoli	Nellie	nan
O	Otranto	Oliver	oboe
P	Palermo	Peter	Peter
Q	Quarto	queen	queen
R	Roma	Robert	Roger
S	Savona	sugar	sugar
T	Torino	Tommy	tare
U	Udine	uncle	uncle
V	Verona (*o* Venezia)	Victor	Victor
W	vu doppia	William	William
X	ics	x-ray	x-ray
Y	ipsilon (*o* i greca)	yellow	yankee
Z	Zara	zebra	zebra

Want to take your Italian further?

Try one of these language courses and join the millions of people worldwide who have learned a language with Berlitz

Compatible with iPod and MP3 devices

Go online for additional learning material

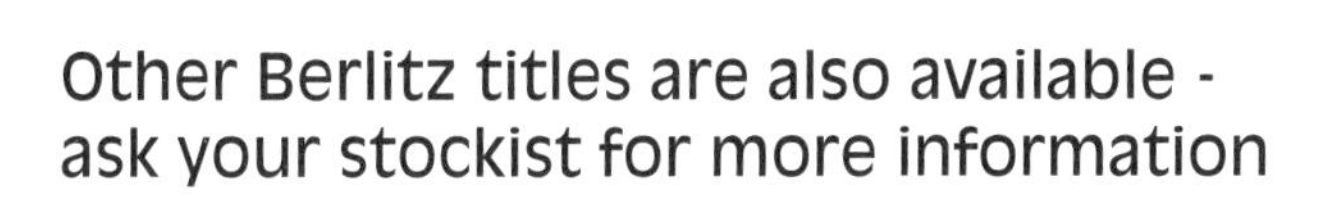

corrugated iron

corrugated iron *n* lamiera *f* (di ferro) ondulata

corrupt I *adj a.* COMPUT corrotto **II** *v/t morals, youth* traviare; (*bribe*) corrompere

corruption *n* corruzione *f*

corsair *n* corsaro *m*

corset *n* corsetto *m*

Corsica *n* Corsica *f*

Corsican I *adj* corso **II** *n* corso *m*, -a *f*

cortège *n* (*procession*) processione *f*; (*funeral cortège*) corteo *m*

cortisone *n* PHARM cortisone *m*

cos[1] *abbr* (= **cosine**) coseno *m* (cos)

cos[2] *n* (*a.* **cos lettuce**) lattuga *f* romana

cos[3] *cj infml* → ***because***

cosignatory *n* cofirmatario *m*, -a *f*

cosily, *US* **cozily** *adv* confortevolmente

cosine *n* coseno *m*

cosiness, *US* **coziness** *n* comodità *f inv*; (*warmth*) intimità *f inv*

cosmetic *adj* cosmetico; *surgery* estetico; *fig* di facciata

cosmetics *npl* cosmetici *mpl*

cosmetic surgeon *n* chirurgo *m* estetico **cosmetic surgery** *n* chirurgia *f* estetica

cosmic *adj* cosmico

cosmic dust *n* polvere *f* cosmica **cosmic radiation** *n* radiazione *f* cosmica **cosmic year** *n* anno *m* cosmico

cosmology *n* cosmologia *f*

cosmonaut *n* cosmonauta *m/f*

cosmopolitan *adj city* cosmopolita

cosmos *n* cosmo *m*

cosset *v/t* viziare

cost I *n a. fig* costo *m*; ~, ***insurance and freight*** COMM costo, assicurazione e nolo; ***at all ~s*** a ogni costo; ***I've learnt to my ~*** l'ho imparato a mie spese; **~s** JUR spese **II** *v/t* ⟨*pret & past part* ***cost***⟩ **1.** costare; ***how much does it ~?*** quanto costa?; ***it ~ me one pound*** mi è costato una sterlina; ***it ~ me my health*** ci ho rimesso la salute **2.** FIN: *proposal, project* fare il preventivo di

cost and freight *n* COMM costo e nolo

costar I *n* coprotagonista *m/f* **II** *v/i* ⟨*pret & past part* ***-red***⟩ essere coprotagonista; ***~ with*** essere coprotagonista insieme a **III** *v/t* ⟨*pret & past part* ***-red***⟩ avere come coprotagonista

First or last headword on page

Translations appear in normal type

Homonyms differentiated by superscript numbers

The feminine form of nouns is always indicated

American orthographic variants

Part of speech and gender labels given in *italics*

Field labels appear in SMALL CAPITALS

Arabic numerals used to differentiate senses

Irregular English verb forms